OTTAVIANO PETRUCCI

OTTAVIANO PETRUCCI

Catalogue Raisonne

Stanley Boorman

OXFORD
UNIVERSITY PRESS

2006

OXFORD
UNIVERSITY PRESS

Oxford University Press, Inc., publishes works that further
Oxford University's objective of excellence
in research, scholarship, and education.

Oxford   New York
Auckland   Cape Town   Dar es Salaam   Hong Kong   Karachi
Kuala Lumpur   Madrid   Melbourne   Mexico City   Nairobi
New Delhi   Shanghai   Taipei   Toronto

With offices in
Argentina   Austria   Brazil   Chile   Czech Republic   France   Greece
Guatemala   Hungary   Italy   Japan   Poland   Portugal   Singapore
South Korea   Switzerland   Thailand   Turkey   Ukraine   Vietnam

Library of Congress Cataloging-in-Publication Data
Boorman, Stanley, 1939–
Ottaviano Petrucci : catalogue raisonne / Stanley Boorman.
p. cm.
Includes bibliographical references.
ISBN-13 978-0-19-514207-5
ISBN 0-19-514207-1
1. Petrucci, Ottaviano.   2. Music publishing—Italy—History—16th century.
3. Music printing—Italy—History—16th century.   4. Music publishers—Italy.   I. Title.
ML112.B75 2004
070.5'794'094031—dc22   2003017505

1 3 5 7 9 8 6 4 2

Printed in the United States of America
on acid-free paper

ACKNOWLEDGMENTS

It is a great pleasure to be able to record with gratitude the generous assistance offered by many people, colleagues and friends, during my lengthy study of books published by Petrucci and his contemporaries. First must come those institutions that have generously funded my research at various times, the University of London (through its support of graduate students and scholars), the University of Cambridge (through sabbatical support), the National Endowment for the Humanities (for a research Fellowship at Villa I Tatti in Florence, and for a summer research grant), and the John Simon Guggenheim Foundation; and I acknowledge the support of a grant from the New York University Research Challenge Fund Emergency Support Program. Each of these allowed me to spend extended periods of time with copies of Petrucci's editions.

I owe an equal debt to those many libraries that allowed me access to their very rare copies in the flesh, as it were, and supplied microfilms of these copies. Without them, much of the following argument would have been impossible. Other libraries provided important secondary material, or acted as necessary centers for research in the many other fields that must be studied before this sort of work can be considered adequately supported by background knowledge. I wish to record here the kindness of library staff at the following institutions: Assisi, Biblioteca di San Francesco; Barcelona, Biblioteca Central de Catalunya; Bergamo, Biblioteca Civica A. Mai; Berlin, Staatsbibliothek zu Berlin—Preussischer Kulturbesitz, Musikabteilung; Bologna, Civico Museo Bibliografico Musicale (where the heads and their staff have been unfailingly helpful); Brussels, Bibliothèque royale Albert Ier; Brussels, Bibliothèque du Conservatoire (and the assistance of M. Paul Raspea); Budapest, Szechenyi Könyvtár (where Robert Muràny was kindness itself); Cambridge, Cambridge University Library; Cambridge, Sidney Sussex College; Cambridge, MA, the Houghton Library of Harvard University; Chatsworth, the private library of the Duke of Devonshire (whose courtesy in allowing me access to his collection, as well as the assistance of the curator, I am happy to acknowledge); Chicago, The Newberry Library; Evanston, IL, Northwestern University Library; Florence, Biblioteca Marucelliana; Florence, Biblioteca Nazionale Centrale; Fossombrone, Biblioteca Passionei (where Dom. Giuseppe Ceccarelli was exceptionally kind in devoting much time to my needs); Güssing, Franziskanerkloster (where Father Leopold left his sickbed to be of assistance); Koper, Arhiv stolne zupnije (with the kind assistance of Metoda Kokole of Ljubljana); Krakow, Biblioteka Jagiellonska (whose head of music, Agnieszka Mertelska-Cieperska, and library staff were continually and exceptionally helpful); Leipzig, Musikbibliothek der Stadt; Lisbon, Biblioteca Nacional (and Juan Pedro Alvarenga, who made my brief visit much more productive than it might otherwise have been); London, British Library (where I started my work on Petrucci, and whose staff have been unfailingly helpful during many years of research); Madrid, Biblioteca Nacional; Madrid, the private collection of Don Bartolomé March de Severa (to whom and to his librarian I wish to express my thanks for their courtesy); Madrid, a further private collection; Milano, Biblioteca del Conservatorio G. Verdi (especially Dr. Massimo Gentili Tedeschi and Dottoressa Agostina Zecca Laterza); Milan, Biblioteca nazionale Braidense; Munich, Bayerische Staatsbibliothek; Munich, Universitätsbibliothek; New Haven, Yale University Library; New York, Columbia University Library; New York, Library of the Union Theological Seminary; New York, the New York Public Library at Lincoln Center; New York, the Pierpont Morgan Library; Oxford, Bodleian Library; Padua, Biblioteca Antoniana, Basilica del Santo; Paris, Bibliothèque nationale and the collections of the Bibliothèque du Conservatoire National de Musique (with the generous assistance of M. François Lesure); Paris, Bibliothèque Sainte-Geneviève; Perugia, Biblioteca Comunale Augusta; Pesaro, Archivio di Stato; Regensburg, Bischöfliche Zentralbibliothek; Rochester, N.Y., the Sibley Music Library at the Eastman School of Music; Rome, Bibliotheca nazionale centrale Vittorio Emanuele III; Rome, Conservatorio di Musica S. Cecilia; Seville, Biblioteca Capitular Colombina; Santo Domingo de Silos, Archivo Musical de la Abadía; Szombathely, Püspöki Könyvtár (where Mme. Maria Dobri was very helpful); Toledo, OH, the Toledo Museum of Art; Treviso, Biblioteca Capitolare; Vatican City, the Biblioteca Apostolica Vaticana; Vendrogno, San Lorenzo di Muggiasca, Archivio (with the kind assistance of Padre Eugenio Vergottini and Signora Mariangela Rigazzoni, and the intervention of Massimo Gentili Tedeschi); Venice, Archivio di Stato; Venice, Biblioteca nazionale Marciana; Venice, Fondazione Olga e Ugo Levi; Verona, Accademia Filarmonica; Vienna, Österreichisches Nationalbibliothek; Washington, the Library of Congress (who were particularly kind in arranging photography for me); Wolfenbüttel, Herzog-August-Bibliothek; Zurich, Zentralbibliothek.

Other institutions and their staffs have at various stages been of the greatest help in allowing me to continue research, and in supplying my diverse needs: preeminent among these are the libraries of the Universities of London and Cambridge, the Harvard University Center for Renaissance Studies at Villa I Tatti in Florence, the Fondazione Giorgio Cini in Venice, and the New York Public Library at Lincoln Center. Even while this book was in press, two new copies surfaced, and I am grateful to Simon Maguire and Sotheby's auction house for allowing me to consult those copies.

There is an equally lengthy list of scholars and librarians to whom I am indebted. The debts to many of these may not even be recognized by them, for the dissemination of ideas, like that of airborne seeds, is always nebulous in its actual geography, and the fruits of such exchange are often borne long after. But many scholars have supplied me with information discovered in the course of their own researches, or have facilitated my access to copies of editions; others have heard me talk of Petrucci and his work, of the bibliographical aspects or problems of the repertoire, and have stimulated and guided my thoughts at various times. Among these, I would like to acknowledge in particular Richard Agee, Bianca Maria Antolini, Allan Atlas, Frances Barulich, Ian Bent, Jaap van Benthem, Bonnie Blackburn, Kathryn Bosi, the late Fredson Bowers, the late Howard Mayer Brown, David Bryant, Giulio Cattin, Giuseppe Ceccarelli, Roger Davidoff, Sarah Davies, Cliff Eisen, Calvin Elliker, Dinko Fabris, David Fallows, Maurice Feld, Ludwig Finscher, Massimo Gentili Tedeschi, Teresa Gialdroni, Jonathan Glixon, Anne Gross, James Haar, David and Anne Hiley, Erwin Jacobi, Talía Jiménez Ramírez, John Kmetz, Metoda Kokole, Donald Krummel, Jeffrey Kurtzman, Jan LaRue, Mary Lewis, Honey Meconi, Giovanni Morelli, O. W. Neighbour, Jeremy Noble, Thomas Noblitt, Giulio Ongaro, Jessie Ann Owens, Robert Pascall, Leeman Perkins, Giorgio Pestelli, Martin Picker, the late Samuel Pogue, Harold Powers, Susan Rankin, Joshua Rifkin, Don Roberts, Richard Sherr, Colin Slim, Martin Staehelin, Brian Trowell, Lorenz Welker, Richard Wistreich, and Agostino Ziino.

There is another group of people, research students at New York University, who (thanks to the generosity of the Graduate School of Arts and Sciences) have assisted me considerably in many aspects of the later stages of this work: they are Jeanie Im, Edward Jarvis, Karl Kügle, Beth Miller, Carol Muller, and Wojciech Typrowicz.

One or two other people stand out and seem to me even more important for their contribution to my work. The first was the late Thurston Dart, who accepted me as a so-called mature student and encouraged my work even when it went in directions he would not have followed. Others are the writers on bibliographical method and research who (though I have never discussed my work with them) have unfailingly stimulated my thought, Charlton Hinman and Thomas Tanselle. Last, and most important, is my wife, Anne, who has accepted the rigours and sacrifices of being married to a scholar and, perhaps worse, to a scholar who writes—and writes slowly.

CONTENTS

PREFACE

Certain conventions are followed throughout the following study:

Unless otherwise specifically stated, all references to folios and pages of Petrucci's (and other early) editions are by signature. This allows the bibliographical aspects of evidence and argument to be more evident. The few erroneous signatures in Petrucci's output are referred to by the corrected reading. Signatures using multiple letters (e.g., AA or bBb) are referred to in the prose simply as A or B, since for the musical books different forms of each letter are not used in the same title.

The music books are all printed in landscape format, quarto-in-eights, and therefore use two whole sheets of paper for most gatherings. When it is necessary to refer to a complete sheet of paper, rather than individual folios, the two sheets in a gathering are numbered I and II. Thus folios 1,2,7,8 comprise sheet I, and folios 3-6 make up sheet II. In those cases where a gathering uses 3 sheets, the procedure is extended accordingly.

The two formes of each sheet are indicated by lower case letters "o" and "i", for outer and inner respectively: thus, in a normal 8-folio gathering A, AIo refers to folios 1r,2v,7r,8v, and AIIi to 3v,4r,5v,6r.

These conventions are followed particularly in tables and in the bibliographies, when necessary.

Pitches are indicated according to the Helmholtz system, by which middle c is c', the octave above is c", etc. The octave indications change at c, not a. Rhythmic durations are abbreviated often (and always in the bibliographies) according to the list of abbreviations, below.

The positions of clefs are indicated with subscript numerals: thus F_4 is an F clef in the normal position, and the standard treble clef is G_2.

All libraries are regularly referred to by the sigla adopted for *RISM*.

All bibliographical citations are given in short form, using the first distinctive significant word.

A few standard abbreviations are followed:

A	Altus (part-book)
ANF	Fossombrone, Archivio Notarile, now in the Archivio di Stato in Pesaro
ASP	Pesaro, Archivio di Stato
ASV	Venice, Archivio di Stato
b	breve
B	Bassus (part-book)
BMC	*Catalogue of Books printed in the XVth century now in the British Museum* (London: Trustees of the British Museum, 1908–1971)
CC	*Census-Catalogue of manuscript sources of polyphonic music, 1400-1550*, edited by Charles Hamm and Herbert Kellman. Renaissance Manuscript Studies, i–v (s.l.: American Institute of Musicology; Neuhausen-Stuttgart: Häunssler, 1979–1988)
c.o.p.	(ligature) *cum opposite proprietate*
CT	Contratenor
d	with a duration: dotted
f	*fusa*
f., ff.	folio, folios
fn.	footnote
GW	*Gesamtkatalog der Wiegendrucke*
l	*longa*
m	minim
mm.	millimetres
ms	manuscript
m.s.	mensuration sign
p., pp.	page, pages
p.d.	*punctus divisionis*
r	with a folio number: *recto*; when describing musical changes: rest
RISM	*Répertoire international des sources musicales*
S	Superius (part-book)
sf	semifusa
sb	semibreve
sm	semiminim
T	Tenor (part-book)
Tav:	*Tavola*, or other list of contents found in the sources
v	*verso*

OTTAVIANO PETRUCCI

INTRODUCTION

t seems hardly necessary to justify a bibliographical study of Ottaviano Petrucci. For well over a century he has been seen as a
key figure in the history of music, and a producer of music to
the highest professional and artistic standards. Indeed, scholars
sometimes seem to suggest that he ushered in, single-handedly, a
revolution in the availability of music and in the level and spread of musical
literacy, a revolution almost as significant for music as Gutenberg's was for other
texts.[1] This was the view of Catelani in 1856, as of Sartori in 1948:

> Siccome la prodigiosa diffusione dei lumi è dello scibile umano è dovuta in
> gran parte al sommo alemanno Guttemberg [sic], quella in particolare della
> musica, che per ciò stesso si fece bentosto popolare ed universale, è dovuta
> all'inventore dei tipi mobili musicali Ottaviano Petrucci da Fossombrone.[2]

> L'Apparire sul mercato librario dell'*Harmonice Musices Odhecaton* nel 1501
> è il segno della grande rivoluzione, il segnale del trapasso dall'arte
> dell'amanuense all'arte del tipografo. . . . vogliamo solo ricordare che con
> questo mezzo la musica spezza i legami del ristretto ambiente privilegiato nel
> quale la difficoltà della diffusione l'ha finora rinchiusa, per spaziare in sempre
> più largo campo umano.[3]

And yet just as our view of Gutenberg's role is more sophisticated than these
statements would suggest, so must be our view of Petrucci's. While certainly an
innovator, a disseminator, and in some measure the initiator of the great explosion
in musical literacy to which Sartori refers, Petrucci was less significant in the
history of music than these statements would imply. He was necessarily responsive
to the techniques and markets of other printers and publishers, as much as to the

musical needs of his purchasers, and he was, as will appear, somewhat peripheral to the real lines of development of music and musical taste. Therefore, while he was undoubtedly significant as the first to attempt the bulk dissemination of music through print, his achievement in these areas needs to be assessed.

The first two biographers of Petrucci and his work placed him squarely in the position he has continued to occupy in the popular view of music history. To Anton Schmid, Petrucci was "erste Erfinder des Musiknotendrucks mit beweglichen Metalltypen"; to Augusto Vernarecci, he was "inventore dei tipi mobili metallici fusi della musica".[4] For over 150 years, as a result of a simplification of the titles of these studies, Petrucci has held his place in the minds of music historians and musicologists as the originator of the vast dissemination of printed music that until recently threatened to swamp us as thoroughly as does every other printed genre.[5] He has, accordingly, fired the imagination of, stimulated the thinking of, and brought to press studies from many of the major scholars of music of the mid-Renaissance. At one time, Petrucci and his output overshadowed our thinking about the music of Josquin's and Mouton's generations, to the point that Albert Smijers used Petrucci's versions wherever possible in his editions of Josquin's works, and Edward Lowinsky (among others) felt compelled to warn against a blanket acceptance of Smijers's readings.[6]

The swelling tide of detailed studies of Renaissance musical manuscripts, their provenance, destination and function, reaching flood proportions late in the last century, necessarily turned interest toward the manuscript readings of much of this repertoire. It showed what we should have known all along, that many manuscripts stand closer to the composers involved than do Petrucci's editions. As an important concomitant, it engendered among musicologists a growing interest in stemmatics and in textual criticism (rather than the mere listing of variants in a critical commentary) and therefore encouraged a reassessment of the place of the printed edition.[7] Much preliminary research has been done in the last few decades and has provided the data that will allow us to place printed sources alongside the manuscripts. Mary Lewis's work on Gardano or Donna Cardamone Jackson's on the villanesca[8] are important recent examples that happen to concern Petrucci's sphere of activity, Italy of the first half of the sixteenth century. But while Antico, Gardano and Scotto, Dorico and Marcolini, Barrè and Blado[9] have been the subject of studies and lists of publications, it is still Petrucci's name and historical position that attract; it is still his figure and his output that are seen as launching music printing and allowing music finally to take its place among printed repertoires.

In fact, music, or rather polyphony, was one of the last genres of written material to be printed from type. It is true that there had been early attempts at printing polyphonic pieces from woodblocks—most notably one play-song (in four parts) in Silber's 1493 edition of Conradus Verardus's *Historia Baetica*. But the problems of creating typefaces for other equally difficult repertoires and alphabets had already been explored. For example, Aldus Manutius's first Greek letter was mentioned in a privilege of 1496—and this referred to a font that, with its provision for breathings, was considerably more complicated than Petrucci's music fonts. Greek volumes soon came from his press and were successful enough to stimulate a rival application for a privilege from Gabriele da Brasichella, in 1498.[10]

Other relatively obscure areas of the printed repertoire had done well, and even maps had been or were about to be printed. While none of the Eastern languages were yet available, Hebrew had already appeared in print and would be represented by a major printer, Soncino, working in the Marche (as was Petrucci).[11] A generally diverse and adventurous market seems to have been presumed by the state of the craft.

This market cannot have existed only in Venice. There must also have been a widespread and flexible distribution system through individual contacts and contracts, through book dealers and traveling book salesmen. Without it, a printer such as Soncino could not have printed Hebrew texts successfully in a number of cities of the Marche. Equally significantly, few of the printers who worked in towns such as Ancona, Forlì, Pesaro, or Urbino, or (in the second decade of Petrucci's productive life) Fossombrone spent their time on books aimed solely at the local market.

Given the existence of these implications for trade, the fact of so late an appearance of printed polyphony needs examining to determine whether technical problems or issues of the size and accessibility of a specialised market were the real delaying factors. In fact, as I shall argue in chapter 9, the market for printed polyphony must have seemed to be the real problem, for it was narrowly enough circumscribed and professionally introspective, so that any printer would had to have worked hard at breaking into the field. Indeed, the slow emergence of bulk production of music, which was to take virtually forty more years, suggests that this particular market was also easily saturated during the first decades of the century.[12]

It is evident, however, from the wording of Petrucci's supplication for a privilege, as well as those that followed in the next decades, that the need for a solution to the technical problems also bulked large in the reasons for the late appearance of printed music. It is clear that Petrucci believed, or wanted the Venetian Signoria to believe, that he had solved a difficult problem. It is less clear exactly what that problem was, for both printed chant and two-colour (i.e., double-impression) printing had existed for some time. Modern scholars seem to have accepted that the discovery was no more than the recognition that polyphony could be printed, like chant, by separating the staves from the notes: and yet I have found it hard to believe that the Signoria, although increasingly casual about the granting of printers' privileges, awarded one to Petrucci solely on these grounds.

Once Petrucci had developed a viable method for music printing,[13] others soon followed. Antico in Rome, Öglin in Augsburg and Schöffer in Mainz were but the first of what would soon become an avalanche of new names, especially once the solution to single-impression music printing had been discovered.[14] Some of these first successors to Petrucci used woodblocks (as did Antico, Sambonettus in Siena, or the northern printer of de Opitiis's settings in the *Maximilaansboek,* both in 1515), while others, of the 1520s and later, were unable to find better solutions than Petrucci's multiple-impression technique.

It is perhaps, then, somewhat unfair to suggest, as I have done, that Petrucci achieved little that was technically innovative or significant.[15] We, as modern scholars, may find it hard to see what was truly new, but his contemporaries did not see things in that light. Only some fifteen years after the traditionally perceived end to Petrucci's career, Marcolini was able to say in his privilege application that the method had been lost, and that many sought for it.[16] We must not forget, either, that other contemporaries were at least as much concerned with the repertoire and its market, or with possible profits, as they were with the actual details of a novel technique.

So should we be. We cannot deny that Petrucci, for the first time, made polyphonic music available in multiple copies, that he began the process that made it accessible to the growing musical tastes of the middle classes, even perhaps that he helped to swell the numbers of such dilettantes that wanted to own, or to be seen to care about, art music.[17] In this respect, at least, Petrucci does in truth stand at the head, the front of a line stretching through all subsequent musical history. He leads the army of printers and publishers who brought music of the highest social classes and the most important religious institutions out of its limited circles of use, presenting it to any who could afford it, reflecting in this activity a growing interest in gentlemanly pursuits and a cultural awareness that is evident from the publication of works such as Castiglione's *Il Cortegiano* (in its many editions) or Elyot's *The Schoolmaster*. We have to accept that Petrucci's action is important in that it changed the nature of musical dissemination, and therefore musical taste, not at once, but within decades, and continually thereafter.

What can we say about the tastes and abilities of these groups of purchasers of printed music, as they existed during Petrucci's lifetime? Little enough, of course, although there is some evidence in the printed material itself. The actual choices of repertoire, the types of readings preserved, the notational changes made, or the care taken with details of such elements as accidentals and underlay, each presents a strand of evidence for the printer's view of the musical tastes and literacy of his audience. And yet, each has to be handled with care, and only after thorough bibliographical analysis. On one hand, the musical bibliographer can rarely say, with the reasonable confidence shown by Mary Lewis, that the presence of ligatures was a result of pressure exerted on the printer by the composer.[18] Even when we think we can make this kind of assertion, there remains the chance that we are seeing the solution to a technical problem, or a decision made by the printer on financial grounds, rather than a musical or artistic decision. Here only detailed bibliographical study can help: indeed, study of normal practices, and of special situations, helps surprisingly often to explain a musical anomaly or detail.

On the other hand, I am doubtful that we can say at all, as did Gallico,[19] that "L'edizione certifica e approva valori individuali, distingue e aggrega indirizzi stilistici, afferma tendenze, asserisce generi", or that "In Petrucci è esemplare la ratifica della musica italiana profana". For the present-day historian, each of these statements is true: he certainly does give, for us, the final validation of the frottola and related repertoires as musically important; he does confirm the growing importance of Italian over French secular genres; he does indicate the stylistic tendencies that mark the transition from early Josquin to Mouton and even Willaert. But I am most doubtful that Petrucci did any of those things for his contemporaries. The evidence of the provenance of the surviving copies, of the readings and their origins, or of the potential sources for Petrucci's texts—all these argue that his role was, at best, marginal. His "invention" was not copied for several years, and then only in a desultory manner (in Italy) before the 1540s, while Aldus's adoption of pocketbooks and an italic text-font was copied within the year by the Giunta, and his preparation of a series of Greek fonts (perhaps more precisely paralleling Petrucci's activities) within two years. It seems to me more and more possible that the claim—made in 1514 when Petrucci applied to the Signoria for an extension to his privilege—that he and his backers had not yet recouped their expenditures was after all a just one. Further, when one looks closely at the repertorial and bibliographical aspects of his work, Petrucci has to be seen as a peripheral figure, printing what his friends and patrons supplied, or perhaps what came to hand, and having little impact on musical taste or performance elsewhere.

Each of the issues I have touched on in the last few paragraphs will be addressed in greater detail in the following chapters. In a historical study, we need to assess the first figure to do anything significant, as we must accept Petrucci did, not only for how he arrived at his achievement but also for what followed, for whether that achievement is really worth recording. In the case of Petrucci, many of the questions about what followed are musical or social ones—many, but not all. We need also to examine briefly the bibliographical aspects of those strange years after he stopped work and before Gardano began the second stage of the revolution in Italy. Gardano is Lenin to Petrucci's Marx, or (perhaps more felicitously) Webern to Petrucci's Schoenberg.

These analogies are not as far-fetched as they might seem at first sight. In all three cases, the real changes followed from the work of the later figure: he it was who made a success, a *modus operandi*, a school, or a business proposition out of the work of the earlier. In each case, too, the older man developed a system that lay within the bounds of his own experience, but that was to be drastically modified by the younger, while it remains one worthy of examination as a system.

Petrucci showed that he had this kind of system. It allowed the music printer or publisher to do business almost exclusively in the musical field and still survive. That system lay not merely in the creation of a multiple-impression type font for music; it also subsisted in the whole apparatus of organizing the printing shop and the details of the appearance of the printed book, what we would call "house practice", so that the end result would be acceptable to his purchasers. These purchasers, we need to remember, were to be reckoned among the most demanding users of printed material, people who had to be able to work from the printed page almost at sight, who had no time for deciphering a difficult reading, and who would often not be able to detect and correct printer's errors without a critical breakdown in performance.[20] If the printed book, the end product, was acceptable to these demanding users—and we have to assume from the length of Petrucci's career that it was—then it was because he had been able to structure the technical aspects so that they were at the service of the textual, that is, the musical readings. The only way in which we can reconstruct how he did this is by means of a detailed analysis of the technical aspects.

When I presented my dissertation on Petrucci to London University nearly thirty years ago, I prefaced it with a quotation from one of the most influential books of bibliographical analysis to have appeared in the last half-century—Charlton

Hinman's *The Printing and Proof-reading of the First Folio of Shakespeare*. With one minor change, that quotation could hardly be bettered as a preface to the present volume: "Bibliographical analysis can establish many facts about the printing-house history of a book. It can make clear the essential nature of various textual phenomena which without its aid would not be understandable, and it can accordingly suggest what methods of attack on certain problems are most likely to be productive. . . . It can frequently demonstrate exactly how a given corruption in the text came about".[21]

The "essential nature of textual phenomena" in Renaissance music is much more complex than that for literary texts. There are problems of the function of the notation, of improvisation, of ornamentation and embellishment in performance, of scribal (or compositorial) initiatives in copying, of the levels of responsibility and flexibility felt by all concerned in the dissemination and performance of a work, of levels of acceptable ambiguity, and, not least, of what contemporaries thought the essence of a composition to be. For all those reasons, which have influenced strongly my own study of filiation in music, I would want to change the word "corruption" in Hinman's text to the word "variant". But, that change apart, my view of the function of a bibliographical study coincides largely with that of Hinman. As my dissertation shows, we truly cannot trust the printed text until we understand *how* it came to be in its present form.[22] A similar view was expressed, two years later, by Kristine Forney: "The identification of corrected musical readings, attributions and text underlay greatly decreases the need for modern editorial decisions that are often made on arbitrary grounds".[23]

For these reasons, the present study will seem to be heavily bibliographical in its orientation. Only after this kind of study is completed can we begin to say anything about the contents of the books—anything more than with the most vague generalisations. It is also for this reason that so much space is devoted below to descriptions of Petrucci's house practice, and in more detail than has so far been accorded the work of any early music publisher.

In this respect, the following volume is much more like the *catalogue raisonné* of any major artist of the Renaissance. It seeks to define Petrucci's output, to discuss his methods, to highlight (and sometimes to explain) the exceptional situation, and, through this, to help place his production more clearly in the context of the music and musical dissemination of the time.

The present volume therefore comprises three elements, not all of which are given equal weight. The central, the base on which all else must rest, is a detailed bibliographical study of the surviving printed books. The amount of detail that has been deemed necessary to unravel the complexities of early musical printing practice, or of the relationships between surviving copies, is enormous—and a great deal of it is the result of examination of these copies on the most minute level. In practice, much of this detail does not appear in the following pages: there is little benefit to the average reader in including, for example, lists of how line ends are treated in every volume, or of how many varieties of *custos* appear in any book. Work of that level has been undertaken and has been essential in reaching a number of conclusions at various points. In many cases, however, the actual data are not given in full here. But enough has to be presented to serve two functions: the first, to allow any reader to determine the date and status of any new copy that may surface; the second, to bolster the arguments that follow, covering those issues of concern to students and readers, whether their prime interests are musicological or bibliographical.

The second element of this study (which appears first) concerns printing and publishing technique. Much has been discovered about, for example, the probable text of Shakespeare's works from a study of his printers' habits, and the same can be considered true for early printed music. Our views of the details of house practice, of press work, and of editorial restraint or freedom must also affect our understanding of a printer's perception of the quality and choice of music, as well as of the merit of the readings facing him. We can show that certain procedures available when copying music by hand were impossible in the preparation of printed music, and, as a result, we can begin to say something about the nature of the music presented to the printer, and about the priorities that allowed him to ignore those procedures.

The third element therefore becomes an analysis of the music as printed, its readings and status, the taste it represents, and the market forces that may have shaped its character as a repertoire. In the present endeavour, this could easily have amounted to a full-scale study of the musical style and output of the period, supported by detailed discussions of individual composers and sources, to the point at which many compositions would be fitted into specific niches in Petrucci's (and his contemporary scribes') output. Clearly, that is not possible; it would require another volume of at least this size. Instead, I offer a series of rather diverse observations on the provenance of a repertoire, the stylistic limitations in a volume, or the types of musical changes made in the printing house—little more than an introduction to some of the relevant issues. I believe this is not an unjust procedure. For one thing, my purpose in this volume is to present the bibliographical evidence and its immediate applications, not to follow them through their myriad ramifications. (That would be the work of another lifetime, and— if this volume has been successful—will be best done by many scholars.) For another, the effect of printing music (and of the related change in the musical market) was slow to develop, and its impact on composers even slower; many aspects of style were not affected by the printer's or publisher's perception of his market's taste until some years later. A composer such as Josquin or Cara need not have cared about music printing and its circulation. However, there *are* issues in the extant repertoire that can be shown to have been directly influenced by the requirements of printing: each instance of these justifies the present undertaking.

The intention of this volume, then, is to provide a solid basis for an understanding of the role of printed music in its early years—an understanding that will be advanced only by the sort of detailed analysis offered here. The present study will have served its purpose if the reader gains an insight into how the earliest printers of music worked, and, more important, how they and their purchasers thought about music and used musical sources; and, further if it provides a similar solid basis for further bibliographical and musical study of the printed music prepared by Petrucci and other craftsmen.

The place of Petrucci in the history of music printing was already recognised during the last years of his life. In 1536 Marcolini, in his petition to the Venetian Signoria (already mentioned), referred to "Fossombrone" as the creator of the means of printing lute tabulature. Later in the century, Cimello made a point of having met Petrucci at Sora,[24] while Zacconi, Bottrigari, and Bartoli mentioned him or his output in some way.[25] For all of these men, he seems to have been a figure of some distinction. The later ones, at least, indicated that he held a special place in the history of the music of their century.

Although interest in Petrucci's volumes seems to have waned in the following century, the eighteenth saw a growing interest in him as printer and in his books, as antiquarian pursuits blossomed in general. Adami da Bolsena mentions him as the inventor of music printing, while Burney knew of him, wrote of his place in the history of music, and seems to have used some of his editions for his own examples.[26] Not surprisingly, Hawkins followed suit, and other historians of music made reference to his various editions. But the musician of the period who was most interested, and to whom (not coincidentally) we owe an enormous debt of gratitude (here as elsewhere) for his collecting instincts, was Padre Martini. This scholar's correspondence shows clearly that he knew of the significance of Petrucci and his "inventione della stampa musicale".[27] It also shows Martini noting when he owned a different edition from that described by his correspondent and soliciting new volumes for his collection, still the largest group of Petrucci's editions extant.

With the nineteenth century, we enter the era of musical and bibliographical scholarship, especially north of the Alps. It is not surprising that the work of Petrucci should interest so many scholars or librarians, or that they should begin to try to catalogue his output. While Fétis included references to a number of Petrucci's titles, more symptomatic of the growth of interest was the second *Beilage* to the first volume of Carl von Winterfeld's *Johannes Gabrieli und sein Zeitalter*, published in 1834.[28] This brief note concerns "Notendruck und Musikhandel zu Venedig im sechzehnten und siebzehnten Jahrhunderte". Winterfeld mentions a number of titles: he seems to have known firsthand only the volumes of masses by Josquin (1502), Obrecht, Brumel, Ghiselin, and La Rue (1503), and Agricola (1504), and the first book of *Motetti de la Corona* of 1514. In common with other writers of the period, he apparently knew no editions before that of Josquin, printed in 1502.

Perhaps the most important of these scholars was the Austrian musicologist and librarian Anton Schmid, a central member of the founding group of the Österreichisches Nationalbibliothek, and credited with establishing much of the organisation of the present *Musiksammlung*.[29] He was interested not only in Petrucci but in other music printers and in the act of music printing, and published accordingly. In order to facilitate his work on Petrucci, he had the Venetian copies of Petrucci's books sent to Vienna, where they were deposited in the Nationalbibliothek and indeed assigned call numbers and rebound in the library's bindings. (They were only returned to Venice after World War I, on 12 February 1919.[30]) Schmid's 1845 study of Petrucci and his technique laid much of the groundwork for the next century, and was the basis for some of Vernarecci's assertions on technical and biographical matters.[31]

The Italians were hardly later than northerners in their growing interest in music printing, and particularly in Petrucci. Baini refers to his work in 1828,[32] discussing keyboard tabulatures. A synopsis of Schmid's book, the work of one B. Malfatti, appeared in the *Gazzetta Musicale di Milano* in 1850. More significant for our purposes is the study by Catelani, appearing in the same journal in 1856, and also published by Ricordi as a separate item.[33] Catelani reported the discoveries of Gaspari in the Bologna collection and for the first time announced that editions of Petrucci had appeared before the known ones of 1502. He referred to *Canti B* and *Odhecaton A*, accepting at face value the date of February 1501 recorded in the colophon of the former; as a result, he underwent several contortions of logic in trying to explain how the *Odhecaton A* could be, as it clearly should be, the earlier book, while yet dated later. Catelani pointed out that Petrucci used two impressions, and he tried to identify the elements involved with each. He also asserted, on quite plausible grounds, that Petrucci continued printing until the year 1523, a date that has continued to be accepted until quite recently. Catelani's report that Petrucci had printed music before 1502 was not always known to later scholars. Thus Francesco Florimo, in his *Scuola musicale di Napoli e i suoi Conservatorii* of 1881–83, reports of Petrucci the following: "il quale inventò i tipi metallici, e fu il primo a trovare la maniera d'imprimere la musica con caratteri mobili. Stabilì a Venezia, verso il 1502, una stamperia".[34]

Haberl, writing in 1873, reported in German the discoveries recorded earlier by Catelani, as supplements to Schmid's study, and discussed the first editions of *Odhecaton A*, *Canti B*, *Motetti A*, and *Motetti B*.[35] As well as making brief reference to other Bolognese copies, Haberl pointed out that the dating of *Canti B* should take account of the Venetian New Year. From this point, a roll-call of the musical scholars who turned their attention at one time or another to Petrucci would comprise a list of many of the significant names, Ambros, Eitner, Gaspari, and Vogel among them. Sartori[36] has given a list of writers of the last century who added descriptions of new copies or titles.

Bibliographers, of course, also knew of Petrucci. Not only did they come across him when talking with their musical colleagues, they also were well aware of the remarkably beautiful edition of a book by the Bishop of Fossombrone, Paulus de Middelburgh, his *Paulina, de recta Paschae*, which Petrucci had printed in 1513. This edition was freely cited in catalogues and by bibliomanes across Europe. It was known to Brunet[37] and to Essling[38] as an example of fine printing, and it can still be called one of the major productions of the period.[39]

To a number of bibliographers, indeed, the non-musical publications were the only ones known, or at least worthy of mention. While the *Paulina* is in some ways more elegant than many of Petrucci's musical volumes (given the level of decoration of several pages, as well as the more expansive folio format and the impagination), much of the reason for this state of affairs probably lies in the common practice, in many libraries, of shelving, cataloguing, and making available musical volumes under a completely different part of the operation, one not regularly consulted by other bibliographers.

Thus many bibliographers, among them Michael Maittaire (in 1722) and Georg Panzer (in 1799), knew of the *Paulina*, cited it, and occasionally mentioned copies,[40] though they seemed not to know of any other works from Petrucci's press. Since the other extant non-musical works are slight and survive in very few copies, this state of affairs is not as surprising as it might at first seem. This is again the sole work mentioned by Blandinus (1791) and by Renouard in his study of Aldus (1834).[41]

There were some bibliographers who knew of early music printing and cited Petrucci's work. The fundamental work of Graesse, his *Lehrbuch* (1852), may cite the edition of 1513,[42] but later, in a section on music printing, he expands on the musical aspects—"Die Erfindung von metallenen beweglichen Druckzeichen für Figurale= und Choralnoten etc. abergebührt den Ottaviano de' Petrucci"—and discusses the initial privilege from the Venetian Signoria.[43] The first edition he is aware of, the first so far discovered ("deren erstes bisher bekannt") is the "Motetti XXXIII Venetiis die 9 Madij Salutis anno 1502". Again, a list of those early specialists who cited Petrucci's work is full of names well known to modern bibliographers: Horatio Brown, Brunet, Davari, the Prince d'Essling, Manzoni (writing on Soncino), and Ongania.

Perhaps preeminent among those nineteenth-century bibliographers interested in the musical aspects of their subject, and aware of the achievements of Petrucci, was the Venetian Carlo Castellani, who served as Prefect of the library of San Marco. This scholar was one of the first, in 1888, to document the early history of printing in Venice, and one of the earliest to study the role of the privilege.[44] Petrucci interested him. One of the five chapters in his historical study is devoted to the printer, and he kept abreast of research from abroad. He also clarified the situation regarding the date of the earliest editions, previously announced by Catelani.[45]

In the last sixty years, interest in the bibliographical aspects of music has grown beyond all measure.[46] By mid-century, there was a regular stream of articles on bibliographical matters for most periods of music printing. Indeed, when Åke Davidsson published his bibliography, he was able to cite nearly 600 items, although he did include a number of entries in *MGG*.[47] Among his citations were studies of sixteenth-century production written by early leaders in the field such as Davidsson himself, Knud Jeppesen, Dragan Plamenac, Claudio Sartori, and Albert Smijers. New information on Petrucci and his books came from several of these scholars, particularly Jeppesen in the first volume of his study of the frottola, and Plamenac in his work in the Biblioteca Colombina.[48]

At the same time, Petrucci's home city of Fossombrone has shown an active interest in its native son; the local historian August Vernarecci had much to do with this. The first edition of his book on Petrucci appeared in 1881, by which time the town's theatre had already been named after the publisher. In the same year, at a commemoration ceremony, various statues in his memory were unveiled, and a street and a piazza were renamed after him.[49] The late city archivist and librarian of the Biblioteca Passionei, Don Giuseppe Ceccarelli, fostered this local enthusiasm, working on the archives, publishing information on Petrucci's life, and (incidentally) welcoming and assisting me in the most courteous and kindly manner.[50]

But the central work, the one on which all subsequent studies have necessarily been based, was that of the late Claudio Sartori. Appearing in 1948, when access to many collections was still hampered by the effects of World War II, his catalogue of Petrucci's output[51] was a triumphant achievement. It is true that within a short time Sartori, with the help of Jeppesen, was able to publish a series of *Nuove conclusive aggiunte* to the bibliography, but that was no more than a reflection of the troubled postwar years, and of his own determination to find out all that could be known at that stage about Petrucci's output. The present volume owes a great deal to the work of Sartori, in his book on Petrucci, in his other studies of music printing, and in personal contact.

Since then, a number of important studies have opened up new aspects of research. The earliest of these include Catherine Weeks Chapman's work on Antico, while her studies of Colón's collection did much to provide a solid basis for analysing the bibliographical problems of the first decades of the century; Helen Hewitt's edition of *Odhecaton A* (actually appearing before Sartori's book) and her later edition of *Canti B*, which made us aware of the importance of much of the music contained in those volumes; and Jeppesen's study of the frottola books, which established many details of bibliographical as well as musical moment. Other names could easily be added to this short list.[52]

At the same time that increasing attention was being paid to the bibliographical aspects of Petrucci's work, so was the roll-call of his editions and copies being enlarged. For Schmid, there were twenty-four editions; for Sartori, just over a hundred years later, there were forty-nine. That number continues to increase: for Gallico in 1982,[53] there were already forty-three, with surviving copies, printed before Petrucci left Venice, while the present volume lists sixty-nine formal titles—though in practice there were at least eighty editions, not counting the many partial printings of titles. For Sartori, too, there were 204 copies of these editions,[54] whereas the following bibliography records 281 of the musical editions alone.[55] For as long as no copies have yet been located for several known editions, we may still hope for more discoveries in the next fifty years.

We have been perhaps more fortunate when considering Petrucci's biography. The recent discoveries of Franco Mariani in Sora, of Paolo Peretti, and of Teresa Maria Gialdroni and Agostino Ziino in Pesaro[56] have radically increased our knowledge of Petrucci's later life. In so doing, they must also cause us to reconsider his standing throughout his career, and to look again at the strange manner in which music printing and publishing evolved during the 1520s and 1530s.

Most of the work for this study, and much of the underlying argument, was completed by the mid-1980s. Since then, I have been able to see a few more copies and read the increasingly broad range of literature in the field. However, the basic structure of the bibliographical analyses and much of the often straightforward commentary that makes up chapters 3–6 have not been changed much. These chapters use the arguments that have dribbled out in various articles and are followed by most other musical bibliographers. At the same time, my bibliographical interests moved on, to asking again why we should do this form of research. Certainly the bibliographical detail is essential for any thoughtful student of the music printed in the books, as has been shown time and time again. But, beyond that, we need to ask what we can learn about musical taste, performance practice, the growth and character of amateur markets, and the acceptance both of new repertoires and so-called authoritative editions—indeed all the musical aspects of what has been called "print culture".[57]

During the last decade, study of music printing has begun to catch up with the advances made in more general bibliographical work, even as these advances also open up new perspectives to us. A greater awareness of the need for detailed observation of the various elements of the (musical and verbal) text and of the book, for scrupulous analysis, and for knowledge of and experience in non-musical bibliography—all have reformed our consciousness of music printing. It is perhaps no longer possible to accept the Renaissance printed word—or note—as being responsible and reliable, but it is equally no longer possible to reject it out of hand. This is the result of the work of many distinguished bibliographers, among whom I would cite Curt Bühler, Lotte Hellinga, Charlton Hinman, Armando Petrucci, Amadeo Quondam, Dennis Rhodes, and Allan Stevenson—as well as a number of critics of texts and students of the theories of textual transmission—among them Franca Brambilla Ageno, Vinton Dearing, Conor Fahy, Thomas Tanselle, James Thorpe, Sebastiano Timpanaro, and Martin West.[58]

A list of the musicologists who have been influential in changing the manner in which we look at musical editions would begin with those who have invoked the technical work of our non-musical colleagues: even in the field of early music printing, there have been many, among whom early leaders include Hilda Andrews and Peter Clulow (working on the editions of Byrd), Ernst-Ludwig Berz (for his work on Frankfurt printing), and Horst Heussner (for Nürnberg). More recent studies have illuminated ways in which non-musical approaches could be used by musicologists: Mary Kay Duggan (whose work on the typefaces of incunabula is exemplary), Don Krummel (for his thought-provoking studies of the visual appearance of musical books and of type, and for his work on methodology), Mary Lewis (on relationships between printer and composer), and Maria Przywecka-Samecka (for her work on incunables).[59] Among more specialised studies of Italian editions, I would mention those of Jane Bernstein (on the "Salamander" books), Donna Cardamone Jackson (who used type to great effect), Tim Carter (examining the Florentine archives), and James Haar (on Festa's first book).[60] Then, too, there are musicological bibliographers working in other periods, among them Cecil Hopkinson, David Hunter, and Alan Tyson.[61] Few of these people have looked at Petrucci's books, or even at his direct contemporaries, but all have, in one way or another, used the evidence before them in ways that earn the respect of their colleagues working on non-musical volumes.

At the same time, a renewed interest in musical aspects of Petrucci's volumes can be discerned in recent publications on music of his period. Many of these studies will be cited at various points throughout the following chapters. Here it is enough to mention Claudio Gallico, who raised many issues of the relation between function and format, and between the press and its market, which will be covered in detail below; Howard Mayer Brown's paper discussing the early motet volumes; Jonathan Glixon's on the Laude of Dammonis; Bonnie Blackburn's on Petrus Castellanus; Franco Mariani's on Petrucci and his paper mills; most recently Teresa Maria Gialdroni and Agostino Ziino's paper detailing the most important discoveries;[62] or a number of the papers from the celebratory conferences of 2001, held in Basel and in Venice.[63]

This evidently expanding interest in Petrucci could be paralleled with lists of studies of the work of other music printers and publishers, from Nigrinus in Prague west to the New World. The result is that we now have a corpus of studies of printed musical sources that can bear comparison with the wealth of similar studies of musical manuscripts. The new student of music printing, therefore, and even more evidently the writer of a volume such as this, has a background discipline to draw on, and a series of approaches to problems to use as guidelines.

Despite all these books and articles, two factors have finally impelled me to finish this study. One was the recent quincentenary of the first date known for Petrucci's publications, the dedication for the *Odhecaton A* on 15 May 1501. The other is the recent appearance of several books that have radically broadened the scope of our thinking about early printing. Turning from the purely bibliographical, these new studies have asked thoughtful (and essential) questions about what a book achieved or, more particularly, did not achieve; about what books represented and how they were used; about how an author and a reader gradually ceased to distrust, and then came to rely on, the printed artefact; and about the relationship of books to authors and patrons, and to patrons and readers.[64] If the titles and contents of some of these essays seem, at a casual reading, to parallel the thinking of the "New Musicologists", they are in fact firmly built on the evidence, in most cases on great amounts of diverse evidence, and on a rigorously pursued thought process. In their insistence on the mutability of the text—as printed and as perceived by its early readers (rather than in terms of contemporary literary criticism)—and on the ways readers used and trusted their texts, these writers have, usually unwittingly, drawn close parallels with the situation that I believed prevailed in the special case of music. The transition that the writers see happening, often as late as well into the seventeenth century, can, I believe, be seen in music by the mid-1530s. Petrucci played an important part in effecting that transition. While this aspect of his work is only marginally discussed here, in chapter 8, it informs many of the points I wish to make. In that sense, this book can now be finished, for it reflects my development of thought since the more purely analytical work of the 1970s and leads toward more fruitful fields.

As far as possible, I have followed the standard bibliographical procedures laid down by previous scholars of early printing. I recognise that music printing is a somewhat special case, and that the terminologies developed by Bowers, for example, need modification in a number of respects.[65] I have tended to follow his principles, however, modifying them where necessary, either in the light of work by Thomas Tanselle or Don Krummel, or according to my own views. Any rationale for a sequence of descriptions of parts of an edition is complex and depends on how one chooses, for example, to define an "ideal copy",[66] to place a cancel in the hierarchy of issues and states, or to organise in the bibliography different editions carrying the same date. Here, I have arranged that cancels should be described separately, for they represent printings subsequent to the original, while in-house manuscript changes belong with that printing. On the other hand, I have listed both these cancels and subsequent printings (editions) under the same general entry in the bibliography, when they carry the same date as an earlier printing. I have further tended to restrict the use of the term "state" to single formes, sheets or half-sheets, rather than employing it to characterise whole copies—for then every copy would represent a different state.[67]

My purpose in doing this has been to facilitate the use of the bibliography by musicologists. Bibliographers will be able to find their way around; they will be able to perceive the relationships between the various editions, impressions, and states. Musicologists will be directed to all the known copies of a single title, in the simplest manner possible. My detailed procedures and uses of terminology are explained in detail in chapter 14, where it will be seen that there are few divergences from norms followed in other fields.[68]

Notes

1. It is at least amusing that one popular software program for entering and editing music in computers, *Finale*, has used the name of Petrucci as that of its music font—a font, incidentally, which uses modern note-shapes.

2. "In that the marvellous spread of enlightened wisdom and of human knowledge is due in large part to the excellent German Gutenberg, in particular that of music, which by itself was immediately made both popular and universal, is due to the inventor of movable type for music, Ottaviano Petrucci da Fossombrone". Catelani, "Bibliografia", p. 22 of the separate edition. It is notable that Petrucci already had this reputation in 1519, for one of the documents in which the city of Sora invited him to reside there and to open a paper mill calls him "Octavio de Fossambruna imprexore de libri de canto figurato et aliter et . . . l'inventory di tal stampare de canto figurato". This is cited in Mariani, *Ottaviano*, pp. 21–22, and will be discussed in chapter 1. Not much later, in 1536, Marcolini repeated this view, in *RISM* 1536,[11] where he refers to "Fossombrone" as "inventore de lo stampare le intabolature".

3. "The appearance in the book-trade of the *Harmonice Musices Odhecaton* of 1501 is the indication of the great revolution, the sign of the passage from the art of the scribe to the art of the printer. . . . We wish only to remark that by this means music broke the bonds of the limited and privileged environment within which it had been enclosed by the difficulty of transmission, and ranged freely across an ever larger field of humanity". Sartori, *Bibliografia delle opere musicali stampate da Ottaviano Petrucci* (hereafter cited simply as Sartori, *Petrucci*), p. 7. By 1968 Sartori had both qualified and expanded his position. In *Commemorazione*, p. 9, he stated: "Ma resta il fatto indiscutibile che Ottaviano Petrucci fu il primo stampatore, tipografo ed editore, di un intero e bel volume di musica". While therefore admitting that others had printed some music before Petrucci began work, Sartori expands the printer's role to that of publisher as well.

4. "First inventor of music printing with movable type in metal": Schmid, *Petrucci*; and "inventor of movable type for music made from cast metal": Vernarecci, *Petrucci*: in each case, the cited phrase comes from the full title of the work. Both authors did have Petrucci's own claim to support their wording; in his 1514 application to the Venetian Signoria for additional privilege, he called himself the first discoverer of how to print books of polyphony—"primo Inventor de stampar libri de canto figurato".

5. There are exceptions, of course. See, for example, the references to German printers of music (in particular, liturgical music) in Riemann, "Notenschrift". In practice, it has largely been, not music historians, but bibliographers of music who have recognized that Petrucci was not strictly first. Early examples would include Molitor, *Deutsche*, and Springer, "Musiktypographie". More recently, in 1956, Castelain, "Histoire" (p. 22), quoted Goovaerts as saying that one could no longer attribute to Petrucci the invention of musical printing—"il n'est plus possible aujourd'hui d'attribuer à Ottaviano dei Petrucci l'invention de la typographie musicale". He qualifies his position, making a distinction between printer and publisher, in saying (p. 24), that Petrucci is the first music publisher in the modern manner—"Petrucci est la premier éditeur de musique au sens moderne du mot". In the same year, however, Bautier-Regnier, "L'édition" is still asserting that Petrucci is significant "surtout parce qu'il est l'inventeur des caractères musicaux mobiles" (p. 29).

6. See the lists of sources in the various volumes of Josquin, *Werken*. Lowinsky, *Medici*, iii, p. 182: "The awesome reputation of the great Petrucci, whom Smijers often . . . followed, may well be in need of a critical reappraisal in which each print, and perhaps each work, should be considered individually, while generalizations about the reliability of the Petrucci readings should be carefully avoided".

7. References to studies for the majority of the manuscripts containing music also printed by Petrucci should be sought in entries in the *Census-Catalogue*. Only selected, primarily more recent references are given here, in Part III. Significant among recent discoveries have been those instances of possible composer intervention in surviving manuscripts. Relevant to the present study, for instance, is Sherr, "Notes".

Much of the recent interest in the application of stemmatics to music was fostered by the trail-blazing study, Atlas, *Giulia*. For a review of the situation two decades ago, see Boorman, "Limitations". More recently, the papers of a conference on the subject were published as Borghi and Zappalà, *Edizione*, and a detailed and extensive bibliography (derived from secondary listings) has appeared in Caraci Vela, *Critica*.

8. Lewis, "Composer"; Lewis, *Gardano*; Lewis, "Zarlino"; Cardamone, *Canzone*; Cardamone, "Debut"; Cardamone, "Madrigali".

9. For Antico, the best essay is still that in Chapman, *Antico*, with a revised list of published volumes in Miller, "Antico", although a few detailed studies will be mentioned below. For other printers, see Agee, *Gardano*; Bernstein, *Music Printing*; Buja, *Barré*; Cusick, *Dorico*; Edwards, *Merulo*; Lewis, *Gardano*; Nielsen, *Rampazetto*; and Steele, "Barré". A number of Italian printers of the same period who included music among a more general output have been studied on that basis: see Barberi, "Dorico"; Fumagalli and Belli, *Blado*; Quondam, "Giardino". Although these authors have generally provided hand lists, lists of contents of musical volumes, and a basic level of bibliographical description, they have rarely undertaken any detailed bibliographical analysis. A few more detailed studies, covering the sixteenth and seventeenth centuries in Italy, are cited in Boorman and Miller, "Stampa". It is only fair to add that there have been several important studies of Renaissance music printers from countries other than Italy. Among them are Berz, *Frankfurter*; Forney, *Susato*; Gustavson, *Hans Ott*; Heartz, *Attaingnant*; Lesure and Thibault, "Du Chemin"; Lesure and Thibault, *Le Roy*; Meissner, *Susato*; Pogue, *Moderne*; Vanhulst, *Catalogue* (Phalèse and Bellère, accompanied by a magnificent series of supporting articles); and Weaver, *Waelrant and Laet*, with Weaver, *Catalogue*.

10. For the pattern of printing various repertoires during the Renaissance, see Eisenstein, *Printing*. For Italy, see Hirsch, *Printing*, and, for Venice in particular, Gerulaitis, *Printing*, which last needs to be read with care. Studies of the history of Greek printing in Venice include Layton, "Notes"; and Scholderer, *Greek*. For the relevant privileges, see Fulin, "Documenti", Nos.41 and 74; and Renouard, *Alde*, pp. 504–508. See also the discussion of privileges as they bear on Petrucci's activities, in chapter 2.

11. Manzoni, *Soncino*. Amram, *Makers*, fanciful in its prose, yet carries many details of interest.

12. The number of subsequent editions and impressions for many of Petrucci's and Antico's titles argues that these men were fully sensitive to this point and chose not to print too many copies too soon. I have said elsewhere (Boorman, "Working"; Boorman, "Bibliography") that I believe the obvious transition to a much more large-scale production at the end of the 1530s reflects a slightly earlier growth in the amateur market for printed music.

13. Perhaps unfairly, I propose to use the simple phrase "music printing" to refer specifically to the printing of the repertoire of polyphony and lute or keyboard music, thereby excluding the equally important, and more widespread, printing of chant.

14. A discussion of single-impression music printing clearly lies outside the scope of the present study. For studies of the first printers to succeed with true single-impression fonts, see King, "Significance"; Heartz, *Attaingnant*; Heartz, "New". The best description of the process involved is in Lewis, *Gardano*, i, chapter 4. A discussion of an earlier appearance of single-impression type is in Boorman, "Salzburg".

15. This is the line that I took in my dissertation (Boorman, *Petrucci*), and there will be echoes of this attitude in various places in the present study.

16. For Marcolini, see Casali, *Annali*; and Quondam, "Giardino". The privilege application is printed in Agee, *Privilege*, p. 207, and translated ibid., pp. 69–70. Other transcriptions of the original document can be found in Castellani, *Privilegi*, pp. 83–84; Schmid, *Petrucci*, pp. 121–22; and at the end of the present volume.

17. I have problems with the circular nature of the argument that reads as follows: the available market encouraged printers to publish a genre, which encouraged more people to buy, which encouraged more printers, etc. My difficulty is not with this sequence, but with trying to determine a starting point. It seems to me just as possible to start this formulation at the midpoint. On the other hand, it is evident there was an increasing market for frottole and, not much later, for madrigals; that institutions such as the later Accademia Filarmonica of Verona did buy music almost rapaciously; and that increasing numbers of religious institutions were establishing polyphonic choirs and expecting them to start singing at once. The *existence* (rather than the first appearance) of printed music seems to imply a growth in the music-reading public, that group of people who could pick up a printed partbook and hold their own part at sight, or at least after a minimum of rehearsal. The purchase of a printed music book, after all, allowed for none of the processes of selection of pieces that played so large a part in the compilation of a personal manuscript, where it was possible for the bulk of the anthology to be made up of pieces known to, or chosen by, the compiler. I have pursued this argument a little in Boorman, "Bibliography", partly in response to ideas presented in chapter 1 of Lewis, *Gardano*, volume 1.

18. Lewis, "Composer".

19. "The edition affirms and validates specific qualities, distinguishes and associates stylistic changes, confirms tendencies, affirms [new] genres"; and "the recognition of [the status of] Italian secular music is exemplified by [the editions of] Petrucci": Gallico, "Laboratorio", p. 200, where he adds the second sentence as a footnote to the first. James Haar has recently adopted a similar position, in Haar, "Petrucci". He suggests that the frottola editions were seen as a way of stressing Italian culture after the "French century".

20. I have discussed these particular issues, as they relate to early music printing, in a number of other places, and will make further reference to them below. At this stage, it seems enough to pass over them and to cite the following references: Boorman, "Specialized"; Boorman, "Bibliography".

21. Hinman, *Printing*, p. vii. The impact of this study on bibliographical research into the printing of many repertoires, not merely Shakespeare, can be seen by reading the contents lists of any of the major bibliographical journals for the last thirty years. On the other hand, McKenzie, "Printers", published a mere six years after Hinman's book, argued clearly for scepticism in the interpretation of this sort of research. His article has been at least as influential, especially on more recent studies.

22. Blayney, *Texts*, i, p. 8, makes much the same point when he says that "the Quarto [of Shakespeare's *King Lear*] can be investigated both textually and bibliographically, and while it is not always easy to distinguish between the two approaches it is my contention that the distinction must not be forgotten". He goes on with a most attractive example in which the textually plausible correction of a reading might be shown, on bibliographical grounds, to be improbable.

23. Forney, *Susato*, p. 189.

24. Haar, "Lessons", p. 57, asserted that the encounter fell during the 1530s, though recent discoveries suggest it might have been a little earlier.

25. These references are discussed later in this volume.

26. See Burney, *History* (1782 edition), ii, pp. 447–48, where he refers to the British Museum copies of the *Motetti de la Corona*, and of masses, and also pp. 503–506 and 535–38, where transcriptions are taken from these volumes. Adami da Bolsena, *Osservazione*, p. 160, speaks of Petrucci as a very gifted man who was the first discoverer of how to print music—"uomo di grand'ingenio il quale fu il primo inventore di stampare la musica".

27. Letters to and from Chiti in 1746, which discuss Petrucci's role, and in which Martini lists the volumes he already owns, are given in Martini, *Carteggi*, 177–205. According to Martini, he already had thirteen volumes, which will be indicated below. For further details, and citations

of many other letters in which Martini mentions Petrucci's books, see Schnoebelen, *Martini*, passim. For Girolamo Chiti, see Raeli, "Collezione".

28. Winterfeld, *Gabrieli*, i, pp. 220–22.

29. For a brief discussion of Schmid's role, see Haas, "Musiksammlung", pp. 51–52. Haas there cites his article in the *Sudetendeutsches Jahrbuch* for 1928, which I have not seen.

30. Alberati, "Musica", p. 186; Coggiola, "Ricupero". A number of my descriptions of Venetian copies mention that they still have the Viennese bindings.

31. Schmid, "Petrucci" still remains of value.

32. Baini, *Memorie*, pp. 144–45. He says that "Ottavio Petrucci rinvenne il mezzo di dare alle stampe cotal metodo d'intavolatura", and in the related footnote (n.234), that he "inventò la maniera d'imprimere il canto figurato".

33. Catelani, "Due stampe".

34. Florimo, *Scuola*, p. 26. Florimo's work is discussed in Parisini, "Studioso", and this citation appears on p. 116, fn.25. In the same year as Florimo's book, Gianandrea, "Ottaviano", pp. 124–26, did know about the earlier editions, although he still thought of the first edition of *Canti B* as dating from 1501.

As to the assertion that Petrucci printed a further edition in 1523, see, for example, the dates entered in Borsa, *Clavis*, i, p. 255. As will be shown, there are no grounds for believing that Petrucci printed in that year, and good reasons for believing that he printed nothing at all between 1520 and the mid-1530s.

35. Haberl, "Drucke".

36. Sartori, *Petrucci*, p. 8.

37. Brunet, *Manuel*, iv, pp. 451–52.

38. Essling, *Livres*, pt.2, i, 1776.

39. See, for example, the 1974 citation in Mortimer, *Italian*, ii, 744, where she compares it for execution and ornamentation with the edition of Vigerius's *Decachordum cristianum* put out by Soncino in 1507, rightly regarded as his finest book.

40. See Maittaire, *Annales*, p. 242, which cites then-known copies; Panzer, *Annales*, vii, pp. 50–51.

41. See Renouard, *Annales*, p. 394.

42. Graesse, *Lehrbuch*, iii/1 ("Das sechszehnte Jahrhundert"), p. 218, apparently referring to Petrucci's edition of Paulus de Middelburgh.

43. Ibid., p. 305. The section on music printing begins on the previous page and discusses books by Hugo von Reutlingen and Keinspeck, followed by Burzio and Gafori. The reference to Petrucci follows and leads on to editions printed by Marcolini and Gardano.

44. Castellani, *Stampa*; Castellani, *Privilegi*.

45. Castellani, "Petrucci", referring to Catelani, "Due stampe".

46. Perhaps the clearest elucidation of the growth of bibliographical interest in music is the brief article by Krummel, "Citing". Although it is largely written from the point of view of the librarian and indeed contains a reference to "Descriptive bibliography" in its title, its author is well aware of the growth of interest in analytical bibliography of musical sources and makes a number of trenchant observations both on its past and on its then (1987) parlous state (which seems to be changing only slowly). In particular, he gives well-deserved credit to the neglected bibliographical aspects of Gaspari's work in the collections derived from Padre Martini and housed in Bologna. Since then, the flood of articles continues unabated, spreading to new parts of the world, and to new printed repertoires. The separate volume devoted to music printing and publishing in the Grove series, Krummel and Sadie, *Music Printing*, documents much of this expansion in research.

47. Davidsson, *Bibliographie* (1965).

48. Jeppesen, *Frottola*, vol.1; Plamenac, "Excerpta".

49. The details of this event, which probably followed close on the publication of the first edition of Vernarecci, *Petrucci*, are recorded with what may well be self-congratulatory exuberance in the second edition, on pp. 275–79. This edition is cited throughout the present work.

50. See Ceccarelli, *Notizie*; and Ceccarelli and Spaccazocchi, *Tre Carte*.

51. It is true that this is basically a descriptive bibliography and that the analytical components are relatively few. (This has incidentally to be said about most studies of individual music printers and publishers.) Sartori, however, was labouring under great difficulty, given the political situation of the time, and yet he produced a remarkably reliable and still useful volume.

52. Chapman, *Antico*; Chapman, "Printed"; Hewitt, *Odhecaton*; Hewitt, *Canti B*; Jeppesen, *Frottola* (especially vol.1). The bibliography at the end of the present study does not set out to be comprehensive of all writings on Petrucci, but its extent does give some idea of the number of scholars who have materially contributed to the advance of research.

53. Gallico, "Laboratorio", pp. 190–93.

54. Sartori, *Petrucci*, p. 38. The number is expanded to 206 in Sartori, "Nuove".

55. Even since this introduction was written, I have heard of, and incorporated, seven more copies.

56. See Mariani, *Ottaviano*; Gialdroni and Ziino, "New Light"; and Gialdroni and Ziino, "Ancora". Dinko Fabris and Robert Kendrick kindly notified me of Peretti's discovery recorded in an exhibition held at the Santa Casa in Loreto.

57. I have attempted to address some of these issues in a number of articles. See, for example, Boorman "Music Publisher's View"; Boorman, review of Weaver; Boorman "Two aspects"; Boorman, "Bibliography"; Boorman, "Musical Text". The term "print culture" was adopted by Eisenstein and formed a central plank of her argument. See Eisenstein, *Printing*, pp. 43–159. For a serious and thoughtful analysis of Eisenstein's position, see Johns, *Nature*, in particular pp. 10–20.

58. Not all of these authors are cited with any frequency in the present study. Some, particularly those in the first list, have produced a number of studies to which reference will be made on different occasions. Others, mostly from the second list, have covered topics and concepts without which this book could not have been written, but which do not directly impinge on the matter discussed at any given point. I would like to acknowledge my debt of gratitude to them (as to the many other scholars whose contributions have also been influential on my thinking but do not receive mention here).

59. Berz, *Notendruck*; Duggan, *Incunabula*; Krummel, *Early*; Krummel, *English*; Krummel, "Oblong"; Lewis, "Composer"; Przywecka-Samecki, *Poczatki*.

60. Bernstein, "Burning"; Cardamone, "Madrigali"; Carter, "Printing"; Haar, "Festa".

61. An exhaustive list of these writers would take up much space. I apologize to any I have unwittingly omitted.

62. Blackburn, "Petrucci"; Brown, "Mirror"; Gallico, "Laboratorio"; Gialdroni and Ziino, "New"; Glixon, "Polyphonic"; Haar, "Petrucci"; Mariani, *Petrucci*.

63. These papers have yet to appear in print.

64. I include here Richardson, *Print culture* (1994); C. Brown, *Poets* (1995); Petrucci, *Scribes* (collected and translated in 1995); and Johns, *Nature* (1998). All of these seem to me to have been influential and important in the way they have taken the evidence and asked (and answered) important new questions. Many of these books actually take their starting point from the work in Eisenstein, *Printing* (from 1979), in Febvre and Martin, *Coming* (from 1958, but only translated into English in 1984), or in Chartier, *Cultural* (of 1987).

65. Nonetheless, Bowers, *Principles* remains a manual of practice with, in many situations, the authority of the Ten Commandments.

66. For one view of this term, see Tanselle, "Concept"; and Fahy, "Concetto". See also my comments in "Glossary", and in chapter 14.

67. A trenchant series of comments on this issue has recently appeared in Milsom, "Tallis". For a discussion of issue and state as concepts, see Tanselle, "Bibliographical Concepts". See also chapter 14.

68. Some of the reasoning behind these changes and detailed patterns of description can be found in Boorman, "Glossary", especially the entry "Edition".

PART A: ANALYSIS

Chapter One

BIOGRAPHY

n recent years, significant discoveries have altered our picture of
the biography of Ottaviano Petrucci, filling in a number (though
not all) of the gaps left in the work of Augusto Vernarecci over
a century ago.[1] Vernarecci, who was a resident of Fossombrone
and a dedicated historian of the city, produced a voluminous history of his home town,[2] as well as the first detailed biography of its most famous
citizen. Until recently, only a few archival documents had surfaced outside the
city, mostly indirectly and as a result of research into some other subject.[3] Recent
discoveries by Franco Mariani, and by Teresa Maria Gialdroni and Agostino Ziino,
however, have significantly helped to delineate what had been blank periods in
Petrucci's life.[4] As a result, much more is now known. This knowledge gives us
the main outline of his life, while still tantalizing us when we look for the many
commercial and social dilemmas that Petrucci must have faced, and the professional desires that must have motivated him, both of which would clothe the
skeleton of this biography. We have leads pointing in a number of directions, but
usually no conclusive evidence. In particular, many details argue strongly that,
during his Venetian years, Petrucci was never a practicing printer, but acted rather
as a publisher who seems to have had the idea of how to print polyphonic music,
perhaps without the funds to achieve that end.

Petrucci was born into a family that had been in Fossombrone for at least a
half-century, although its earlier history is not clear. Anton Schmid sought to
make it a branch of the more famous Petruccis of Siena.[5] Coincidentally, that
family did play a leading part in the political intrigues of Italy during the printer's
lifetime. Pandolfo Petrucci, with his brother Giacoppo, was a member of the
minor nobility of Siena, and, after a series of turbulent episodes between nobility
and commoners, he was able to seize control of his city by a *coup de main* char-

23

acteristic of *condottieri* of the period. He was effective ruler of Siena from the late-1490s until not long before his death in 1512. Typical of many leaders of the period, he was notable for the manner in which he played different enemies off against each other. By this means, he was able to maintain Siena's independence from Florence, through temporary pacts with the French, the Borgia, or the pope. Pandolfo's patronage of Vannoccio Biringuccio, the engineer, has been compared with the greater Lodovico Sforza's support of the greater Leonardo da Vinci. Alfonso, a son of Pandolfo, was Bishop of Massa Marittima and was made a cardinal in 1511. He supported the election of Leo X, but was later thought to have taken part in a plot to kill the pope. In 1517 he was arrested for his alleged part in that plot and died the same year.[6] It is very unlikely that Ottaviano Petrucci was descended from a branch of that family, and his relations with papal circles seem not to have been affected by its disgrace.

Nor does it seem likely that Petrucci was at all related to the family Petrucci that would produce printers in Perugia later in the sixteenth century. This family was certainly in Perugia by the time our Ottaviano Petrucci was working, although the first family member recorded as a printer was also the most important. He was Pietro Giacomo Petrucci, active from 1575 and the only member of the family to print polyphony.[7] He had apparently been a stationer before beginning the printing establishment that lasted for at least three generations. In his first year Pietro Giacomo published in conjunction with a certain Michele Porto, otherwise not known, but by 1576 he was working alone. He continued to print until his death in 1603, when his son Alessandro took over the business. The latter printed alone and also, as the Tipografia Augusta, with Marco Naccarini. Although two of Alessandro's brothers were stationers, he was succeeded on his death in 1612 by his son Pietro, who printed for at least six more years.[8]

It is much more probable that the Petruccis of Fossombrone were originally members of the Fano family, which had been active in the political history of the Marche for at least two centuries. Pietro Amiani, the historian of Fano, relates the important role the family had taken in the story of that city.[9] In 1231 one Uguccione de Petruccio had gone on crusade; in 1232 continuing troubles with the Emperor Frederick led many Fanesi to desert the city and return to their castles, which, for the Petrucci, meant the Castello della Tomba. In 1311 "Alberto dalla Tomba della Famiglia nobilissima de'Petrucci" was leader of an unsuccessful Ghibelline *coup d'état* while the leaders of the city were away assisting Perugia in a war against Todi. In 1313 the same Alberto was accepted as leader of Fano, after the citizens had driven out Pandolfo Malatesta; but Alberto seems to have behaved too autocratically, was himself driven out, and died in exile. In 1370 Federico de'Petrucci was present at the conclave following the death of Pope Urban V, but in 1387 the Petrucci, having been assisted by the English *condottiere* Hawkwood, were nevertheless defeated by the Malatesta, who had decided (with some reason) that they were mortal enemies and proceeded to sack their castles. One hundred years later, as we might expect, alignments had changed, and in 1475 Alberto de'Petrucci of Fano was knighted at the wedding of Roberto Malatesta and Isabella Montefeltro. The family is recorded as having produced many men distinguished in letters and in arms and among the best regarded in Italy. Amiani, at one point, suggested of these Petrucci that "Vantava la sua Famiglia origine dalla Casa d'Aragona, di cui l'Arma ancora portava",[10] without offering any proof thereof.[11]

Vernarecci showed that Petruccis are cited in the Fossombrone archives from the year 1423, and produced a probable family tree for Ottaviano.[12] Unfortunately, many of the relevant documents no longer exist, either in the town archives or in the Archivio di Stato in Pesaro.[13] As a result, one primary source for the earlier parts of Petrucci's life remains the material printed in Vernarecci's book and much of what follows is therefore necessarily taken from that secondary source.

Petrucci was born in Fossombrone on 18 June 1466. His father was Giovanni Lodovico Baldi Petrucci, who died sometime after 1493.[14] Ottaviano is called at one point "Ottavius quondam Ludovici de Petrutiis de Forosempronio".[15] The same Ludovico apparently made leasehold payments to the Cathedral until 1489; the property had previously (from 1439 to 1484) been paid for by a Baldo Petrucci, and prior to that by a Biagio Petrucci (from 1432).[16] Vernarecci also points out that Ludovico had three other sons and uses this as a basis for suggesting that the family was probably not financially well-to-do.[17]

The reader will already have noticed that some references to members of the family use a formulation such as "de' Petrucci". There is no evidence to suggest that this was a formal patronymic, or that it implied any noble standing on the part of this branch of the family. It appears to be used rather haphazardly, as is apparent from the documents drawn even from the Fossombrone city archives and transcribed at the end of this study. The publisher is often cited in modern literature as either Ottavio Petrucci or Ottavio dei Petrucci. His name as it appears in supplications for privileges in Venice and in documents in the Roman archive includes a formula translating as "of the Petrucci". However, he himself always presented his name in his own colophons as "Octavianus Petrutius". For that reason, I have chosen also to use the more abbreviated style, adopting the word Petrucci as a modern family name.

In the same manner, Petrucci's first name sometimes appears as "Octavius" and at other times as "Octavianus". The latter form is always found in the colophons to his editions and also in his applications for privileges. In 1498 he calls himself "Octavian de i petruci da fosonbron", and he uses the same formulation when seeking to renew the privilege, in 1514; it is also found in the privilege from Leo X, as printed in Petrucci's editions. In his letter to Girolamo Donato, printed in his first edition, he is "Octavianus Petrutius"; when he applies to be a member of the guild of Cestieri, in 1504, he is again "octaviani Petrutij de fossimbruno". He uses the same form in Rome in 1518, when laying a complaint against Manente Leontini. According to Vernarecci, he is sometimes described as Ottaviano in Fossombrone records, for example, in 1501 when leasing out his house, and in 1514 as a member of the city council. Finally, he is "Octaviano Petrutio Semproniensi" in the privilege accorded to Andrea Antico by Leo X, dated 27 December 1517 and printed in Antico's edition of Frottole intabulate (RISM 1517³).

However, the normal form in Fossombrone documents appears to be "Octavius". A number of the records described by Vernarecci use that form,[18] and it is always present in the newly discovered documents from Fossombrone discussed by Gialdroni and Ziino,[19] though they point out that the surviving documents from Sora use the longer form. It seems therefore that "Ottavio" was his given name, used in official documents in his home town, but that he preferred "Octaviano" and used it whenever outside the city, in documents for Venice, Rome, and Sora. I have chosen to follow him in this regard and use "Ottaviano" in the present study.

Petrucci's family was evidently not poor, for they owned property near the city, and he was able to lease land at various times. Further, he was a leading citizen holding office throughout his life and was selected as a representative of the city more than once. His family evidently were regarded as among the more significant members of the community. However, in 1493 he sold land, and in 1499 he needed to name a legal proxy to act for him.

However, the idea that Petrucci was supported in his youth by Guidobaldo I, Duke of Urbino, seems to have no evidence in its favour and to have been created by Schmid, who was then followed by Vernarecci and Sartori.[20] The traditionally advanced reasons for this patronage lie in Petrucci's birth in a cultural backwater, in his knowledge of music, and in the artistic quality of his work. While it is possible that Petrucci was aided and encouraged by the duke,[21] there are several problems with the proposed reasons. One is that Fossombrone was not a backwater of culture in the late fifteenth and sixteenth centuries. It was the native town of a number of writers and humanists, who, though not in the class of Bembo or Castiglione, were nevertheless well known and respected. Among them were Prospero de'Borgarucci da Cantiano, whom Vernarecci describes as a noted doctor and writer on anatomy and the plague;[22] Bartolomeo Egnazio, a friend of Aretino and later a colleague of Petrucci; Ptolomeo Egnatio (surely the same person as Bartolomeo), who had an active role in Rome as a chancery scribe and cut the blocks for Calvo's plans of Rome (published in 1527); Cristoforo Gigante (or Gigas), who wrote epigrams in three of Petrucci's editions, as well as other poems;[23] Girolamo Gigante, a noted lawyer in Venice in the 1520s; a Pré Marsilio da Fossombrone, whose edition of Petrarch in 1513 will be cited below; Hieronymus Posthumus, apparently a humanist (and Petrucci's corrector at least once), who trained others;[24] Francesco Spinacino, the lutenist; and Marsilio Umbro, a philologist living in Venice and a friend of Bembo. Later in the century, several noted scholars came from Fossombrone, among them Tommaso Azzi, Vincenzo Castellani, and Panfilo Florimbene, translator of Plato's *Republic*. It is clear, as a result, that Petrucci could have received at least enough learning to cope with the literary texts he had to print. As to whether he could have learned enough music, it is difficult to say. The earliest reference to music now extant in the city archives seems to be the agreement by the city council, reached on 18 June 1514, to pay a certain Benedictus to play the cathedral organ at specified feasts.[25]

But a more cogent reason for doubting the duke's patronage is the difficulty in understanding why Petrucci should then have decided to print, or (more specifically) to print music. Printing was certainly known in the area of Urbino, and printers had been active in the Marche before Petrucci was even of an age to be a craftsman. The first local books were printed in Cagli in 1475, and there was a press in Urbino in 1480.[26] Neither of these presses was long lasting, however, and both seem to fit the picture of printing in many provincial centers during the

fifteenth century, in which presses were often either short-lived or mobile, moving from city to city to meet short-term demands, often for civic laws and documents. The press of Neumeister at Foligno, for instance, probably lasted less than
two years.[27] It seems unlikely, therefore, that Petrucci could live in Urbino and
study the craft thoroughly, that is, well enough to be accepted as a colleague by
professional printers by 1498.

The famous, and much repeated, story of the duke's father, Federigo, not
wanting to have a printed book alongside the manuscripts in his library suggests
that he would not have encouraged a printer.[28] But the picture was almost certainly slightly different from the popular conception engendered by this story. The
evidence suggests that the printed book of the fifteenth century was not considered to be in competition with the manuscripts of such a patron, but rather was
intended to supply cheaper and more rapidly produced copies of essential texts.
Bono Accursio, writing in 1475, says that "it is not easy for everyone to acquire
manuscript books because of the price and pecuniary difficulties. . . . But the
printing art is not to be despised, both for its subtlety and because when the
impression and as it were the formation of such books is correct from the beginning, it runs through all the copies always in the same order, with scarcely the
possibility of error".[29] While my study, among many others, shows that copies do
not all present the same facade to the reader, yet it is clear that Accursio was
praising both the facility of making many copies and the possibility of reliable
texts in all those copies. It is likely, therefore, that the duke's view of a printer
would be as a proficient artisan, rather than as an educated gentleman. There is
little reason to think, as a result, that someone whom the duke had educated
would have turned to the craft of printing and publishing, or that someone who
came from the normal strata of society involved in the craft would have been
educated at the duke's expense.

Finally, there are reasons to think that Petrucci might already have settled in
Venice. These reasons are not strong; they really hinge on the extent to which
Petrucci was apparently a familiar of several members of the printing and publishing trades, as well as knowledgeable enough in the craft of printing to invent
a new procedure. It may be a coincidence that there had been an earlier press
established in Venice by a compatriot. Bartolomeo da Fossombrone opened a
printing shop with Antonio [della Paglia] da Alessandria and Marchesino di Sa-
vioni, in 1480, though the association was short-lived, lasted for perhaps less than
two years, and produced few books.[30]

At this point we must consider whether Petrucci was himself a printer, and,
if so, what the course of his life might have been between 1480 and 1498. The
year 1480 would have been an ideal time for Petrucci, at fourteen years old, to
start to learn the craft of printing.

To be an active printer petitioning for a privilege in 1498, Petrucci would
almost certainly have had to be in Venice by, at the latest, ca.1490; the laws that
laid out the provisions whereby foreigners could practice a trade in the city and
with the benefits of citizenship were very strict. Although most of these laws had
been promulgated many years earlier, they were still in effect and enforced, for
the opening folios of a sixteenth-century file from the Cinque Savi alla Mercanzia
give transcripts of these earlier documents, in a clear hand and in a manner sug-

gesting they were collected together for easy reference.[31] A law of 1304, cited on f.1v of this collection, required thirty years' residence in Venice before a foreigner could become a citizen "by privilege", and fifteen before he could engage in trade. The thirty-year provision seems soon to have become one of twenty-five years, for a law of 1382 allowed foreigners, who had for fifteen years fulfilled their obligations as if citizens, to become citizens *de intus et extra* "of twenty-five years", with eight years' residence admitting them as citizens *de intus*. Another law, of 1407, extended the privileges of a citizen *de intus* to those who had married a Venetian and borne the citizen's responsibilities for eight years. Finally, in 1508, it was decreed that a foreigner could not set up as a master in a trade, without first having been employed in Venice for ten years, including an apprenticeship. Thus, if this law represents a codification of practices of the preceding decades, it seems probable that any printer would have had to be in Venice ten years before setting up shop, and perhaps ten years before his application for a privilege. For Petrucci, this would point to 1491, or perhaps 1488. The eight-year modification of the right to practice in trade as a citizen could also be seen as pointing to 1490, eight years before Petrucci's application. If he actually printed his books, Petrucci was therefore probably in Venice by late 1490 and could fulfill eight years' residence before engaging in trade—that is, applying for his privilege—and ten years before setting up as a master in his own printing shop.[32]

In practice, any foreigner could practice a trade or act as a merchant in Venice from the moment he arrived, although he could not be a master in a craft (indeed he might not be admitted to the craft guild or mystery), nor could he trade abroad. Many managed to evade some of the more difficult provisions by adopting "sleeping partners" who were Venetian.[33] However, the benefits of citizenship included lower taxation; those of being a citizen *de intus et extra* also provided many privileges and full protection as a Venetian when trading abroad, outside the Veneto. These privileges were much sought after: the later music printer Vincenzo Valgrisi sought full citizenship in 1567 and declared thirty-six years' residence in Venice and marriage to a Venetian wife.[34] Petrucci, as a printer of a marginal subject, would have benefited considerably from both advantages offered by citizenship.

It should be added that there were two ways that Petrucci might have avoided these temporal restrictions on citizenship and craft membership. There was provision for citizenship to be granted in special cases, in particular to men with essential skills; the requirements, however, were stringent, including large majorities at voting in three major governing bodies, and there is no trace in their records that Petrucci applied for this honour.[35] Alternatively, a foreigner who took a Venetian wife could be admitted to a guild if he wished, and the guild was not allowed to refuse entry.[36] Just how far this was applied we cannot tell, though an interesting piece of evidence will be discussed below.

Almost no documents for Petrucci have surfaced, in either Fossombrone or Venice, for the years before his privilege application of 1498. He was in Fossombrone on 4 November 1493, at which point he sold property there. He was surely already in Venice by July 1499, when a proxy was appointed for him in Fossombrone.[37] But an earlier period of residence in Venice, leading up to the privilege application, has generally been assumed. In that case, it would be quite likely that

Petrucci, like most expatriates, made contact with other citizens of his home town—even if he had not come to work for one of them, the Bartolomeo who had a printing establishment in 1480. More significantly, he apparently made other important contacts, for he was able to summon the good offices of Amadeo Scotto and Niccolò di Raphael early in his career. Even though neither man is named in Petrucci's first application, it is evident from the later application that he had been in partnership with both of them, which suggests that Petrucci had been in Venice long enough to make contact with and earn the trust and support of two of the richer *librai* of the city.

Depending on one's point of view, this may have been fairly easy, or rather difficult. Venice was a bustling center for all commerce, and printing (including speciality printing) was thriving. Norton lists thirty-nine printers active in Venice in 1501,[38] and many of these were among the most important printers of the time—from their contemporaries' point of view as much as ours. For us, Aldus Manutius may be far and away the most famous, but many others were at least as prolific and served a much wider market. Indeed, one view of Aldus's activities, both as printer and as center of a learned circle, would see him carving out a special niche for himself and his own particular philological interests in a profession full of successful rivals. Among these were men who similarly created their own fields: those, such as Emmerich, Hamman, and Liechtenstein, who specialised in liturgical books (although the last also printed many scientific texts), or others who had already begun to concentrate on legal texts (de Tortis), editions of the classics (Tacuino), books in Greek (Callierges), theological tracts (de Soardis), or popular devotional literature (de Luere). There were also specialised publishers, probably often primarily booksellers, who commissioned books from various printers. Sessa and the Giunta of Venice were among other publishers who worked with several printers, and it is evident that many of the scientific and theological books signed by the Scotto house were printed by Locatelli. The virtues of this procedure were not only that each printer had an area peculiarly his own, and to some extent safe from his rivals, but also that the printer or publisher could develop and maintain his own network of like-minded booksellers and partners in other cities.

If Petrucci had trained as a printer, he would have drawn from this pattern some clear conclusions. On one hand, he could enter the market for popular books—either "popular" in the modern sense of "intended for the largest possible market", or books with a guaranteed market, such as liturgical books for specific dioceses. On the other, he could find a specific limited repertoire and try to make an effective monopoly for himself. He would not have been alone in following the second course, although polyphony represented a much smaller niche than many of those adopted by his contemporaries. However, he would not have had the experience or the contacts to ensure that his books, once printed, would reach their potential purchasers. In this respect, it would have been hard for an unknown printer to gain the support of rich patrons or contractual colleagues. If he were to follow the more popular route, he would not be able to show the "track record" that would recommend him to any astute business man; if he took the more difficult, he needed partners who already had experience in that field. Presumably Niccolò da Raphael and Amadeo Scotto were two such men.

The last few paragraphs have introduced the situation facing Petrucci, and the implications for his biography, if we assume that he was, by 1498, a qualified printer, intending to specialise in music. For a number of reasons, however, this assumption has to be questioned. First, Petrucci held office in Fossombrone during the decade of the 1490s, suggesting that he was not actively learning a craft at the time, but was free to come and go. Second, in his privilege application of 1498, he neither calls himself a printer nor claims Venetian citizenship: he is "Octavian de i petruci da fosonbron habitator in questa inclyta Cita". Given the formalistic nature of these applications, this is an important point and will be discussed further in the next chapter. Third, in claiming the invention of a method for printing music, Petrucci does not name his printing colleagues, those who were to share the costs with him; he claims the invention and then apparently sets out to finance its use. Finally, as often noted, his first book is of an outstanding technical and artistic quality, unlike the earliest productions of a newly trained printer; the few problems, discussed in chapter 4, are the result of using the new landscape (or oblong) format. Other reasons for doubting Petrucci's involvement in any technical aspects of the printing process will emerge later. For now it is enough to remark that he was probably not a printer at all, at least while in Venice.

Given this circumstance, he need not have lived consistently in Venice during the years preceding his application for a privilege. Having resolved the problems of printing music and discovered the solution (as his books reveal to us), he would need only to find suitable backers and oversee the setting up and ongoing work of a press. This approach accords well with his continuing activities in Fossombrone and makes any conjecture about the length of his stay in Venice valueless. It also explains the need for Venetian "sleeping partners". Given this need, Niccolò da Raphael and Amadeo Scotto loom larger in the plans for a music printing shop. Whether Niccolò had specific printing experience is not known. Apart from the facts that he was a *libraio*, and that he was old in 1514, when Petrucci applied for the extension to his privilege, Niccolò seems to have disappeared.[39]

Amadeo Scotto is a different person altogether. He was nephew to Ottaviano Scotto I, the founder of the famous publishing and printing firm. After Ottaviano's death in 1498, Amadeo continued the firm and eventually adopted the title *Haerede Ottaviani Scotti*. A liaison with a member of this family would have been an almost ideal solution for Petrucci. The Scottos had a wide experience of liturgical publishing, as well as practical knowledge of how to disseminate many other specialised books; they published for, and traded with, many parts of Italy and Transalpine Europe; and they had already worked as publishers with a number of other printers.[40] The remarkable element has to be why Amadeo Scotto should have been willing to underwrite a new venture, developing a novel repertoire, when he already had regular contacts with a number of reputable printers producing a large number of titles.[41] The stimulus to publish music must have come from Petrucci: if it had come from the Scotto family, they would more probably have used Locatelli or another of their printers.

There may be a reason for the connection, especially if the original contact were not with Amadeo but with his uncle Ottaviano. Ottaviano died at the end of 1498, after Petrucci had received his privilege. We have no knowledge of where

Petrucci learned enough about printing to make his discovery, but, while several Venetian printers produced liturgical books, two were specialists, and they were associated with different publishers. Emerich printed many of his liturgical books for Luc'Antonio Giunta, and Hamman, like Locatelli, worked for Ottaviano Scotto (among others).[42] Scotto used many printers and seems to have had freer connections with them than did Giunta. If Petrucci had established contacts with liturgical printers and publishers, as he must have done, Scotto might have seemed the better prospect, as one who would leave Petrucci freer to make his own decisions. Without proof, this can be no more than speculation, but it is attractive and does explain the presence of Scotto's son Amadeo as a backer for Petrucci.

Whatever his early history, Petrucci emerges from the shadows in 1498 as a petitioner for a privilege to print music, the details of which will be examined in the next chapter.[43] Here it is enough to repeat that the supplication seems, with one exception, to be absolutely typical in its details, both of Petrucci's approach and of the privileges and punishments sought.

If he was in fact a printer, Petrucci would have spent the couple of years between the grant of a privilege and the appearance of his first book in the arduous tasks of financing and establishing a printing house—men and materials.[44] The average shop employed men in a number of different categories, apart from those of foreman or owner. At the press itself, there were normally two men employed. One was responsible for running the press, a strenuous task, while the other had to undertake the cleaning and inking of the galley. (If both were master craftsmen, they would switch positions after set periods of time.) The other aspect of the work concerned the preparation of the text: this involved some sort of house editing, the act of composition (typesetting) and reading the text over after a few copies had been pulled. One man to each press seems to have been required for the typesetting, and another would sometimes be employed as "corrector", i.e., reader. Thus, even in a house containing only one press, at least four men would normally have been required, and they would have been active on the two different sides of the printing craft—dealing with the text and with the press.

Petrucci may have filled one of these positions himself, at least initially, but he would have needed skilled craftsmen for the others. The standard of the work in his early editions, the care taken with composing the text, the quality of inking and presswork—all argue that there were few apprentices or journeymen in his shop during the first years. Petrucci and his backers would have had to guarantee wages for craftsmen, from the beginning.

I am doubtful that Petrucci had any of these skills. He does say, in the prefatory letter to his Odhecaton A, that he "came to Venice with the idea of perfecting his invention of printing polyphony".[45] Indeed, to undertake such a repertoire, he surely had to be able to read the notation and perhaps know enough to make sense of the musical texts. Petrus Castellanus, editor of the Odhecaton A, was probably also his "proof"-reader. But it is hard to see how Petrucci could have persuaded backers to support him, if he were a pressman and had to look elsewhere for the house's musical expertise. It is much more likely that he was able to demonstrate a musical expertise to his backers, had already made contact with Castellanus, and was perhaps also able to forecast the probable sales pattern for his planned volumes. (This seems to imply, incidentally, that Petrucci moved in a circle including musicians, as well as in one comprising his professional col-leagues.)[46]

If a printer, Petrucci would also spend much energy and time in acquiring the necessary equipment for his shop. This included the press, the fonts of type, and the various ranges of apparatus that go with typesetting (cases, galleys, formes, furniture, and so on). Among these were elements peculiar to music printing, a music font as well as formes for the landscape format.

We might believe that he had to prepare sample sheets of printed music, in order to impress potential backers. That means he would have already commis-sioned a part of the music font and the staves, and must have had access to a press. I am not convinced that this procedure was essential, for reasons to be discussed in more detail later. Here it is enough to say that Petrucci's type was apparently not dissimilar in its technical features to fonts used by Aldus and others, while his process had much in common with the way in which chant was printed.

But whether or not he had already prepared some of his printing materials, the demands of setting up his printing shop also included finding the necessary premises, strong enough to support the presswork, well lit to allow for typesetting in winter as well as summer, spacious enough for storage of paper stock and printed copies, and airy for drying the printed sheets.[47] Finally, Petrucci had to make arrangements with his suppliers for type, ink and paper, and similar arrange-ments with outlets for the finished books. While Niccolò di Raphael and Amadeo Scotto probably took care of this last item, Petrucci must have developed his own contacts for the others.

However, the evidence does argue that he was not himself a printer. While he would still have needed to oversee the design and making of music type, and other special equipment required by his landscape format, he would have looked around for an established printer who could meet these other needs. Nonetheless we should not be surprised that it took two years for him to raise the capital and spend it, and for him to have the special music sorts and technical material pre-pared to his satisfaction.[48]

At this stage, Petrucci must have resided (for much of the time, at least) in Venice, and in 1499 he appointed two proxies to act for him in Fossombrone.[49] All Petrucci's problems and organisational details were apparently resolved by, at the latest, March 1501, if the date of publication for the first edition, the famous *Harmonice Musices Odhecaton A*, was anywhere close to that of the dedicatory letter, 15 May. The edition, as it survives in incomplete form in Bologna, shows all the evidence of having been the first in this format and the first to use most of the typographical material. The latter is clean and gives excellent sharp impressions, whereas some sorts and initials already show damage by the time of the next edition, the *Canti B* of February 1502. The presswork is careful, and the need for accurate alignment of the three impressions seems to have given neither press-man nor compositor any problems. However, there are details of layout, and even of typesetting, which suggest a lack of experience in music and in landscape format on the part of the compositor: these details, to be discussed later, are resolved by the time of later printings of the *Odhecaton A*, and even in time for the first edition of *Canti B*.

This first venture on the part of Petrucci and his partners probably involved a fairly small print-run, for the book was to go through three complete editions, with additional printings of various sheets, within a period of nearly three years. This makes sense. Although the question of the normal size of print-runs is complex at this period, and there is no evidence for several years as to the size of musical editions, yet it is hard to believe that even a member of the Scotto firm would have been able to guess at the potential sale of printed polyphony. It is even more unlikely that he could foretell the prospect for future volumes until after this one had gone on sale.

And yet it seems likely that this volume was planned as the first of a series, given the use of the letter *A* at the end of its title. However obscurely the title was constructed—in its mixture of Greek and Latin—the letter was large, dominating the page. Petrucci had had this letter cut, in a form and style that was not convenient for use anywhere other than on a title page,[50] and had even had letters *B* and *C* cut in the same style. He, at least, was looking forward to the possibility of future volumes.

Neither Petrucci nor his financial backers seem to have been content to let this new venture slide into the pool of printed material, as merely one more competently printed book, neither too expensive nor too obtrusive. The format, which would have been unusual on any bookseller's display; the erudite nature of the inscription and the quality of the decorative initial of the title page; the conscious elegance of the rest of the typographical material; the significance of the dual dedicatory letters to a high Venetian noble; the care taken over readings and corrections of the text, so that there was apparently no need for stamped-in or manuscript corrections: all suggest that the three partners were willing to spend money to achieve a splendid appearance and to spend time to match that with the quality of the contents.

It appears, too, that Petrus Castellanus was an active partner in preparing the material for the press. Bonnie Blackburn and Elena Quaranta have recently uncovered material on the life of this previously rather obscure friar.[51] He was a Dominican, probably from an area near Ancona, resident at SS. Giovanni e Paolo in Venice, certainly by 1486, a singer by 1502, and *Maestro di cappella* by 1505. He was old and living outside the house by 1514, and died on 16 May 1516. During 1505, he was out of the convent, for he was at S. Domenico in Castello, before being sent out of Venice to Recanati during May: this journey was apparently of short duration, for Castellanus had returned to SS. Giovanni e Paolo by August.[52]

A number of Petrucci's versions show an editorial hand (when compared with those in other, manuscript, sources) which is consistent in its character throughout the edition. While Petrus had perhaps possessed copies of these pieces for some time, even years in certain cases,[53] and had possibly edited them over a longish period (for his own and his friends' convenience), the consistency of editorial style suggests that he also took pains over the preparation of the edition. We cannot know whether he was paid for this work, or whether he was one of the instigators of the whole business in offering his music to Petrucci. But this active role of the editor is another indication of the care with which the professional partners had thought out as many aspects of the venture as possible, and perhaps also of their willingness to invest heavily in Petrucci.

Whatever the form of the financial conditions under which he worked, Petrucci apparently discovered quickly that his plan did not represent a financial disaster. If this first title was indeed published sometime around 15 May 1501, he and his backers seem to have been satisfied enough to launch a second title only nine months later. However, the picture suggests that, while they believed that a loss could be avoided, they were not yet convinced that the business was worth prosecuting actively. During the whole of 1502, things moved rather slowly for Petrucci. One volume in February, one in May, and one in September[54] would not have kept him or a printing shop fully occupied, even allowing for the new sheets printed to supplement the first edition of the *Odhecaton A*.[55] This seems to confirm that he had not established a full-time printing house with himself as sole employer and overseer. By comparison, 1503 looks like a fairly busy year. There were seven full new editions, with dates much closer together. It may be, therefore, that 1502 does not really mark the beginning of the press as a going concern. The first two volumes of 1502 are perhaps more correctly to be seen as extensions of the *Odhecaton A*, in that they too were experiments, testing the market and trying to demonstrate to Petrucci's backers that there was a viable future for music printing. If so, then *Canti B* and even *Motetti A* were aiming at the same sort of market, one of semi-private performance, whether among amateurs or with amateur and professional musicians in an atmosphere of affluent and cultured patronage.[56]

Petrucci's first book of masses, works by Josquin, published in September 1502 represents a deliberate exploration of a different circle of purchasers. With its new layout in partbooks, and its content of longer movements both composed and presented in a manner much less practicable for amateur or small-scale performances, this volume has to have been aimed at professional singers, at professional performing ensembles in chapels or churches, and at the patrons and their administrators who would be responsible for supplying such music. As I shall argue in chapter 9, it also represents a different supplier (or at least stimulus) for the edition.

The productive year 1503 shows the results of the exploratory years 1501 and 1502. The seven "public" editions of 1503 begin with a second edition of the *Odhecaton A* and were to include a second of *Canti B*, but the other five editions, appearing in print for the first time, are of sacred music, all but one of mass settings—by Obrecht, Brumel, Ghiselin, and La Rue—the exception being a second volume of motets. Evidently, there was a market for the chanson volumes, but it would appear that Petrucci and his backers had decided that a lucrative part of the market lay among institutional purchasers. Much of the discussion of the sources for Petrucci's music (in chapter 9) will hinge on these decisions made by the printing house and its partners, or by specific patrons. For now, it is enough to say that experience showed that they were right, for there is a similar pattern of output for much of 1504 and 1505: more mass settings (Agricola—probably to be seen as the last of the run of 1503—De Orto and Josquin's second collection), a further edition of *Odhecaton A* with the addition of a third volume in the series, *Canti C*, and a third and fourth volume of motets (with the newly discovered second edition of *Motetti A*). The first major change in this pattern is the appearance of three volumes of frottole in close succession at the end of 1504. In four years, therefore, Petrucci had established a consistent pattern of repertoires, and (to judge from the number of new titles and reeditions) also had established patterns of presentation, of house editing, and of distribution of the finished books that guaranteed him and his partners a satisfactory return on their investment.

Once Petrucci begins work on his first volume of music, he becomes a marginally less shadowy figure. In part, of course, that is because in our view he exists principally through his books; it is also, in part, because those same books do give slight hints about the professional circles within which he moved. For example, the books show what has always been assumed, that he had good contacts within the printing profession in Venice, although these books do not identify those contacts. We cannot presume a close contact with Aldus Manutius, with Torresanus or Giunta, or even with any of the leading liturgical printers from whom he might have learned the skills of two-colour printing. It is tempting, though mere speculation, to assume some contact with Manutius through his craftsman typecutter Francesco Griffo da Bologna, if only because Petrucci used Aldus's Greek fonts, and because in later years Petrucci was able to draw Francesco to Fossombrone to work for him.[57] But, as I have already said, we do not even know from whom Petrucci learned the craft. All we can know is that he did maintain his high standards for some years, and he presumably was able to work well with colleagues and craftsmen and to meet his obligations, financial and otherwise, for he used paper and ink of good quality.

The books he printed might be thought also to indicate something of Petrucci's contacts with the musical world of his time. Unfortunately, we know as little here as elsewhere: the presence of Petrus Castellanus as editor of his first volume tends, if anything, to remove Petrucci from professional musical circles, at San Marco or one of the courts of northern Italy. Petrus was apparently the direct conduit for the music printed in the *Odhecaton A*, for the phrases of Budrio's letter can surely be taken literally. Petrus has to be assumed as the conduit too for *Canti B* and *Canti C*, and for the music in *Motetti A* and *Motetti B*, drawing them from a large devotional repertoire, no doubt easily available to him.[58] If that is so, then the first volume to which we might look for information about Petrucci's other musical contacts would be that of Josquin's masses, published later in 1502. And yet, as I suggest (and will argue more fully), it is likely that the change in repertoire is more a reflection of political possibilities than of the available music.

In practice, few of Petrucci's books indicate their provenance in any clearcut manner, and it appears that many were drawn largely from music supplied on a businesslike basis, while others (among them the volumes of Bossinensis's arrangements) were acquired through personal contacts or planned as specific demonstrations of patronage. But the presumed source for a number of Petrucci's earliest editions remains the Dominican, Petrus Castellanus. Given what is known of his biography, he remains the most likely conduit for Petrucci's music from Ferrara or Rome, and there are good reasons for believing that some volumes were directly inspired by the wishes of the Ferrarese court. If Petrus was also the means of supplying these to Petrucci, it is reasonable to suppose that, for the first years at least, Petrucci would continue to turn to someone who had proven himself a reliable source. It is only in late 1504 (with the first book of frottole) or perhaps even in 1506 (with the books of Lamentations) that we need to look for other suppliers of Petrucci's music. That being so, there is little reason to believe that Petrucci himself was an active member of any specific musical group in Venice.

The few fragments of actual evidence we have concerning the circles in which Petrucci moved, therefore, are reduced to the surviving dedications and letters presented in Petrucci's editions, together with one document recently discovered. The two dedicatory letters introducing the *Odhecaton A*, signed by Petrucci and by Bartolomeo Budrio, are addressed to Girolamo Donato, nobleman of Venice. Donato was a remarkable man, typical of our view of the "Renaissance man" and, more pertinently, of the Venetian view of a patrician. His career followed the normal path for a Venetian noble, although he was in any case a skilled politician. He was ambassador to various courts, including that of the Emperor, to Milan in 1499, to Ferrara in 1499–1500, and to Rome more than once—for the last time from 1509 to 1511, when he died there.[59] He was well enough thought of and senior enough to be cited in Sanudo's diaries; he is thought to have been portrayed in the Bellini painting for the Great Council Hall of the Ducal Palace, a painting that was destroyed in the fire of 1577.[60] At the same time, he was recognised as an expert Hellenist and as a courtier; he is given a complimentary series of references in Cortese's *De cardinalatu*,[61] and Castiglione, in his *Il Cortegiano*, cites him with an example of erudite wit, adapting Ovid *ex tempore*.[62] Then, too, he was highly regarded as a literary scholar, more fluent in Greek than in Latin,[63] one of the leading humanists in northern Italy and much admired by Poliziano. The latter included Donato in a *quadrivium litterarii*, with Pico della Mirandola, Ermolao Barbaro, and himself.[64] Donato was, therefore, an ideal man for a dedication seeking to establish the enterprise, for his acceptance would convey accolades in many quarters of cultured Venice. Further, according to Petrucci's letter, Donato was knowledgeable in music; indeed his correspondence with other members of Poliziano's group included discussions of music theory. He was also known as a connoisseur of practical music; in 1491 he was apparently the recipient of a "large volume" of music by Isaac, given to him by Lorenzo de'Medici.[65] Whether Petrucci had any contact with him, or whether the contact was only through Bartolomeo Budrio or Castellanus, it is now impossible to tell, although I suspect, from the terms of Petrucci's letter, that he himself did not actually know the recipient.[66]

Probably more significant is the choice of Budrio as author of the second letter to Donato. Budrio was apparently from Capo d'Istria, for he calls himself "Iustinopolita" in his letter and thus initiates a series of connections with the eastern coast of the Adriatic, which remained an important part of Petrucci's business life throughout the rest of the decade and impinged on him later in diverse ways with the rise of Antico as a rival.

There are only two other dedications extant from Petrucci's Venetian years. One is to be found in Dammonis's *Laude libro* primo, extant in the edition of 7 July 1508. Jonathan Glixon has suggested that Dammonis, who identified himself as a member of the Canons Regular of San Salvatore, was a certain Innocentius Natalis de Venetiis.[67] The recipient of the dedication was Pater Seraphinus Venetus, who was prior of the church of San Salvatore in Venice during some of the critical years and had recently been Prior General of the Order. Clearly, in this case, the dedication has nothing to do with Petrucci. Whatever the motive for producing the volume, it seems probable that it should be looked for inside the house or the order of which both composer and dedicatee were members, as Francesco Luisi suggests.[68]

The other dedication is found in the first volume of Bossinensis's arrangements of frottole for voice and lute of 1509. The book is dedicated to Geronimo Barbadico, or Barbarigo. Barbarigo was another leading citizen, a member of the only family to have had two doges in succession, a noble of the *case nuove*, a relative of the Pietro Francesco Barbarigo who was a partner of Aldus Manutius. Geronimo had taken orders and was, according to the dedication, at the time Apostolic Protonotary in Venice and Primicerio of S. Marco. While the tone of the dedication is as sycophantic as one might expect, assuring Barbarigo that Bossinensis knew that he delighted in all the liberal arts, and especially in music— "cognosco in ogni liberal arte delectarsi: & maxime in musica", it does not suggest that Bossinensis was in any way close to his proposed patron. Saying of his compositions that they stood in the shade and protection of Barbarigo's good will, knowing that with his great understanding no composition would appear obscure or incompetent—"sotto umbra & protectione sua voglio stiano: cognoscendo per la grandezza del ingegno suo a niuna compositione esserli ocult o inexperta", the composer appears unable to refer to past benefits from his dedicatee. If Bossinensis had chosen his dedicatee for himself, then the sole reasons must have been related to Barbarigo's eminence, and the composer's hopes for future benefits. It is more likely that Petrucci recommended the choice of Barbarigo, for the nobleman had apparently favoured a petition from Petrucci in 1504. However, he did not sign the dedication, suggesting that the connection was not a close one. It is possible, though unlikely, that the selection was made by Castellanus; if, as seems possible, he knew Girolamo Donato, perhaps he also knew Geronimo Barbarigo, who would have moved in similar circles. In that case, Castellanus maintained professional contact with Petrucci for longer than I would otherwise have expected.[69]

Petrucci did in fact sign one other letter, to the reader, in the first book of Spinacino's editions. This letter tells us nothing about the circles in which he or the arranger moved and hardly hints at any aspect of the printer's personality. It is possible to read into the letter a sense of defensiveness on the part of Petrucci after the grant of a privilege to Marco dall'Aquila, yet this interpretation is probably no more than wishful thinking.[70]

In different ways, therefore, none of the letters to dedicatees or to the reader gives us much help in trying to discover anything of Petrucci beyond his skill at his craft. There is more nebulous evidence, from which it is possible to make a few speculations about Petrucci's contacts, musical and social. There is a notable change of repertoire during 1505. In the earlier years, to February 1505, out of a total of fifteen different titles (that is, excluding reprinted volumes), three are of chansons, three of motets, and six of masses; only the last three comprise frottole, appearing together between November 1504 and February 1505. The orientation of this group toward the repertoire found in Ferrara is fairly apparent and will be discussed further in chapter 9. However, from December 1505 to the end of

Petrucci's stay in Venice (a productive period), the overall pattern seems very different: three volumes of masses (one an anthology), two of lamentations, one of old-fashioned five-voiced motets, and single books of hymns and of Magnificats represent the liturgical repertoire. Alongside these are two books of laude. If these last point less toward an interest in the grand institutional markets and more to the needs of individuals and small-scale or secular institutions, then that suggestion is bolstered by the rest of the output. Five books of frottole (with reprints of earlier volumes) can be coupled with the first edition of Bossinensis's arrangements and four books of lute tabulature, all of which provide the resources for private or even domestic music making. The edition of frottole for voice and lute made by Bossinensis was of a technical simplicity (regularly abandoning the altus part) ideally suited to the amateur gentleman or courtier who wished to display his courtly skills.

This change in repertoire has to be related to two other facts. As Boer noted in 1938, Castellanus was absent from Venice during part of 1505, in the house at Recanati.[71] During that time, Petrucci continued to print and to plan for new titles. At the same time Petrucci was subjected to a potential attack on his monopoly, in the form of the successful petition to print lute music, made by Marco dall'Aquila. This petition (to be discussed further in chapter 2) was agreed to by the usual four members of the council, among whom on this occasion was Francesco Barbarigo, a relative of the Gerolamo Barbarigo who was to be the dedicatee of Bossinensis's first publication, and who acted as Petrucci's guarantor in another matter during 1504. It is generally assumed that Marco did not avail himself of his privilege.[72] Instead, as has often been remarked, Petrucci launched into printing tabulature in early 1507, with two books from his compatriot Francesco Spinacino. It seems likely that Petrucci decided to print lute music soon after the success of Marco's supplication, on 11 March 1505.[73]

While the basic technique of printing tabulature would have been easily seen as exactly parallel to printing polyphony—superimposing the numerals used in Italian tabulature on the lines representing the courses of the lute—both the type and "staves" needed would be new. The numerals would have to be on small bodies, similar to those used for the musical notation, rather than on bodies like those used for text fonts, and would have to be of the exact size needed to match the blocks of lute-notation staves. There is no reason therefore to marvel that it took Petrucci two years to publish the first volume (appearing in February 1507). It had taken him almost exactly three years to prepare for the first volume of all.

More interesting is the point that the music for this first volume came from Spinacino. Spinacino's lute technique was probably somewhat old-fashioned already, to judge from Arthur Ness's codification of styles and techniques found in Italy from the late fifteenth and early sixteenth centuries.[74] The majority of the music seems less interesting and certainly less difficult than that of Marco dall'Aquila (as that survives in manuscript). It may be that, while Petrucci was able to publish simpler material, Marco did not make use of his privilege because his music was still too difficult to guarantee a large market. We will probably never know. But it can hardly be a coincidence that Spinacino seems also to have come from Fossombrone.

These two circumstances—Castellanus's absence from Venice and the need to respond to Marco dall'Aquila's petition—highlight the timing of the change in repertoire that took place sometime during 1505. They suggest that Petrus had continued to have some sort of active role with Petrucci's shop until his departure. That role, I believe, included acting as a conduit for the contents of a number of the editions, as well as serving as in-house editor. Many years ago, I tried to suggest ways in which Castellanus edited the contents of Petrucci's first title,[75] and I assume that this function continued. As editor, Castellanus was probably also responsible for reading the "proof"-copy, the early pull of each sheet that was read for possible errors to be remedied by stop-press corrections. He may also have acted as corrector at the press, although there is no obvious alteration in correcting style during his absence from Venice. Barring any other evidence from within Venice, it seems probable that he continued in the role of principal supplier and editor for Petrucci until his departure in 1505.

There is more evidence that might point to a change of supplier for Petrucci's editions. In his first lute book, the first by Spinacino, appearing in 1507, Petrucci makes slightly defensive remarks about the pattern of attributions in his music. The remarks suggest that he had been attacked in some quarters for providing incorrect attributions. Petrucci says quite strongly that he has made and will continue to make every endeavour to assign the correct names to pieces. It may be that the new suppliers of music were not as careful as Castellanus had been; the sixth book of frottole, in particular, contains a large number of compositions not ascribed to anyone at all, and bibliographical evidence in other books, including *Canti C*, suggests that the typesetters omitted attributions on occasions when Petrucci had them to hand.

It has to be emphasised that this change in repertoire does not represent a loss of any part of Petrucci's market, but rather led to an expansion of the types of purchasers, made evident by the need for the continuing series of reprintings that appeared between 1506 and 1509. Instead, the change is in the supplier of the music. Petrucci, or his new editor, was looking in different circles, which were probably more diffuse than the ones that had been plundered by Petrus Castellanus. The new sources could supply him with a volume of Martini's hymns, but also with one of old-fashioned *cantus firmus* motets (the *Motetti a cinque I* of 1508), with a group of Lamentation settings, some of which must have been too old-fashioned for a large modern choral institution, with laude apparently drawn from Venetian confraternities, with tabulatures from a compatriot (and possible friend) and other non-Venetians, and with a new range of frottola settings. While the first three books in this list point toward a conservative and perhaps small-scale musical institution (and perhaps again to Castellanus), I can see no obvious single supplier for such a wide range of music. Pending the discovery of new documents, we have to assume that Petrucci's new musical contacts are best represented by the contents of these volumes.

It is very likely that Petrucci belonged to a confraternity in Venice. These *Scuole* served vital functions for many men in craftsman or merchant positions in the city, giving them insurance, medical attention, a social milieu, and contact with members of the Venetian nobility.[76] As a member of such a group, Petrucci would come into contact with music of a very specific type, laude for regular use, and occasionally more ambitious music (including, at the simpler end, hymn settings), perhaps performed by imported musicians. Perhaps Petrucci had direct contact with Dammonis through a confraternity associated with San Salvatore, or (and I think more probably) the music for the second volume of laude came from one or more different groups, with the idea being provoked by the first edition of the Dammonis volume. The publication in the books of Lamentations of a two-voiced setting by de Quadris may also be relevant here. As Giulio Cattin and Margaret Bent have shown, that set was old and based on even older material,[77] and its use was surely restricted to less affluent institutions (on stylistic grounds as much as because of the reduced scoring), when put alongside the sets by Agricola or Tromboncino, found in the same books.

On the other hand, even though a source within a *Scuola* might provide access to settings of Martini's hymns, it can hardly have offered large-scale *cantus firmus* settings by Isaac, Obrecht, or Regis, or the intabulations by Dalza. Some professional musicians might well have been members of any *Scuola* that included Petrucci and thus the publisher's supplier, but they would then have been acting in the manner I have suggested, as collector of music from various sources, and provider of diverse repertoires for Petrucci's last four years in Venice.

The new document I have mentioned does not help us draw an outline of Petrucci's circles, though it is valuable in other ways; it was drawn to my attention by Giulio Ongaro.[78] It is dated 18 October 1504 and takes the form of a decision by the Collegio on a petition by Petrucci to be allowed special entry to the guild of Cestieri, or box-makers. According to the decision, Petrucci had claimed to have discovered, with skill and hard work, how to make mixed colours (whether inks or paints, he does not say) for decorating fine caskets and boxes—"Qui cum Ingenio, & Industria sua Invenerit quandam tincturam: compositam ex mixtura quam ponit supra Cistellas finas": he had sought entry to the guild—"quesierit Ingredj scolam cistariorum"—which was refused because he did not meet the entrance requirements, and he had requested that the Collegio order that the entrance requirements to the guild be waived in his case. He had not been an apprentice in the guild, as was required—"nemo possit erigere appothecam nisi ab scolaribus scole non fuerit prius aprobatus Quod scriverit laborare misterium ipsum". In his supplication, Petrucci cited the approval of the Provveditori di Commune, and in particular Hieronymo (Geronimo) Barbarigo, who would later be the dedicatee of Bossinensis's first book.[79] The Collegio approved his petition, requiring the guild to admit him.

This petition throws a strange light on Petrucci's career: there can be no doubt that the music publisher is the man who made the petition, for he is called "octaviani Petrutij de fossimbruno", and there is no evidence of a son with the same name. The implication almost seems to be that he was dubious of the success of his publishing venture and was trying to ensure a second career, should it become necessary. The evidence does not support that conclusion, however. As I have remarked, Petrucci was following a fairly successful pattern of output, developed in 1503, and at the time of this petition he must have been exploring the possibility of expanding into frottole. Indeed the date of the decision on his case falls midway between the editions of *Motetti C* and of *Frottole libro primo*. It seems more likely, therefore, that Petrucci, whether or not he had truly made a new invention, had merely developed for himself skill in the technique practiced by the Mystery and Craft of Cestiere, or had actually hired a skilled man for his own ends, perhaps as decorator of his own books.[80] The reluctance of the guild to admit him seems not to have been unusual.[81]

From 1505 until early in 1509, therefore, Petrucci was presumably not only an active music publisher but also a member of the Guild of Cestieri. I know of no remains of any work he may have undertaken as a result, no actual painting or decoration signed with his initials, and no contracts such as survive for a number of painters of the period. In any case, he seems to have been fairly busy during those years with his principal occupation. With the exception of an apparent lull in 1506, he continued to turn out at least one new title (or newly dated second edition) every other month. As the record of cancels and partial reprintings will show, he maintained an even higher rate of work much of the time. He apparently saw himself, and was seen by those who offered him music to publish, as a successful producer of music, one who could oversee an elegant result, ensure the sale of his books, and (perhaps in some cases) as a result further the career of the composer. I am thinking here again of Bossinensis, of course, but also of Alemannus and Dalza, of Dammonis, and certainly of Petrucci's compatriot Spinacino. The juxtaposition of Spinacino and Cristoforo Gigas (or Gigante, another Fossombrone citizen) in a single book by the publisher from Fossombrone suggests that Petrucci kept in touch with other members of his own city, and provides the strongest evidence we have for his circle of professional or personal acquaintance.

Indeed, Petrucci had not severed his ties with his home city of Fossombrone during these years. It is true that on 10 April 1501 he had rented his house there to Francisco Gianetti.[82] However, he probably retained a residence in the city, for on 15 April 1504 Duke Guidobaldo Montefeltro II appointed him to the Fossombrone city council. Vernarecci cites an early-sixteenth-century document indicating the requirements for eligibility to hold city office: they comprised citizenship of Fossombrone (which I take to mean birth in the city), ownership of a house worth at least 100 florins, and residence for a continuous period of at least twenty years.[83] Petrucci can hardly have fulfilled the last of these requirements, at least in the preceding years, for 1504 had been an active time in Venice. The date of this appointment falls in a period between the edition of Agricola's masses on 23 March and the third edition of *Odhecaton A* on 25 May. It is possible that Petrucci was able to return to Fossombrone during this time: a third edition of any title would probably require less supervision than a new work and would (in any case) not have taken two months to complete. He may even have stayed in Fossombrone for another month or two, for the next extant edition, that of *Motetti C*, is dated in mid-September. There is no reason to believe that the duke made an exception for him, or that his colleagues on the council (who were also ducal appointments) resented his many absences. He seems instead to have been held in esteem as a member of a leading family of the city. When filling the senior positions in the city, members of the council elected from within their own body. In 1505 Petrucci was chosen Apodimatore, and later in the same year one of two Revisori delle Vie. He cannot have fulfilled either of these positions full time, for 1505 again required his presence in Venice. Even more significantly, in 1507 he was elected Primo degli Anziani, the senior of the four Fossombrone magistrates, two of whom served together at a time, and the senior of whom had to be resident in the city palace during the two-month spell of service.[84] Although, as Vernarecci remarks, each of these office-holders could supply a substitute during absence from the city, it appears that Petrucci was not thought of as being entirely resident in Venice, but was able to come and go and serve his native city sufficiently in its senior offices. In the absence of the original documents, we have to assume that Petrucci served for July and August, or else that he was able to be away from Venice while editions were completed and published.

In practice, if the constitution of Fossombrone was anything like that of other north Italian cities of the time, it is probable that it did not require full-time attendance for the whole period of the appointment. Finer remarks that in some Italian city-states pairs of office-holders were alternately on duty, for a month (or a similar period) at a time.[85]

There is, however, no trace of specific periods of residence in his home city, beyond this evidence of the offices he held, before the middle of 1508. In April of that year, the duke died, while on a visit to Fossombrone. Petrucci returned to the city soon after and was one of the speakers in council on 14 May of that year.[86] We do not know how long he stayed,[87] though again there is a slight gap in his Venetian output, from mid-March (*Missarum diversorum auctorum I*) to mid-June (the lost third book of tabulature). However, Petrucci must certainly have been in Venice at the end of the year, for there is a flurry of activity around the new year—Dalza's book of tabulature (the fourth in the series), *Frottole IX*, and the first of Bossinensis's two books, appearing within a period of under thirteen weeks. Evidently, the business was doing well.

After that last volume, however, Petrucci suddenly stopped work; apart from any cancels and reprints additional to those discussed below, his press was silent for just over two years, until it reappeared in Fossombrone. During that time, Petrucci removed from the city in which he had had all his commercial success, and which was recognised as the best place in all Italy for a printer or publisher. He set up his shop in a small city in the Papal States, one without a recognised trading pattern beyond its own area and without any of the contacts that he needed, perhaps even without any of the necessary skilled craftsmen.

Just when or why Petrucci decided to return permanently to Fossombrone cannot easily be determined. The bibliographical evidence suggests that Petrucci had left Venice by the middle of 1509. The previous years, 1507 and 1508, had been busy, with nine books (and one possible other, perhaps only a ghost) in 1507, and seven (with another probable ghost) in 1508.[88] The year 1509 started with the promise of a similar yield, with two books completed within the first three months. The evidence of the various copies of the *Fragmenta Missarum* (originally of late 1505) implies that some re-impressing of parts of earlier volumes continued as well, and this suggests that Petrucci was trying to maintain his stock at commercial levels. Thus, there is no sign that he was thinking of winding up his Venetian business during these months and preparing to leave. Finally, he probably had begun to prepare Bossinensis's second book, though it may not have been ready to go to press in Venice—and there is a radical change in the paper in mid-volume.[89] It is likely that Petrucci would have printed this book next, making a pair of volumes; if he took away a partly prepared volume, to be finished and issued later, we would have reason to believe that he may have left in something of a hurry.

The two most obvious reasons for Petrucci to leave Venice at this time were the recurrent attacks of the plague and the after effects of the League of Cambrai.[90] The plague, probably bubonic, was afflicting Venice ever more seriously in these years. Recorded major outbreaks occurred in 1502, 1507, 1510, and 1511 and apparently represented a climax in the increasingly virulent attacks of the late fifteenth century.[91] Although, evidently, this affected trade severely at times, it certainly should have affected the book trade less than many others, for that depended heavily on sales outside Venice and on a wide circulation of the product and so was less vulnerable to the presence of plague in one or another specific locality outside the city.[92] Thus, if these attacks of plague were indeed the reasons for Petrucci's departure, it need not necessarily have been an urgent matter. We would have to look for evidence of some more personal impact, for example, the death of a wife or close relative, evidence for which has not been, and may never be, found.

Perhaps, though, the effects of the League of Cambrai supply the motivation, for they would in some ways have been felt more directly. The League was, after all, a direct attack on the growing power of Venice on the *terra firma*. From the time of the lost naval battle at Zonchio in 1499, and the subsequent abandoning of many ports in Greece to the Turks, Venetian eyes had again turned more frequently to the extremes of the city's mainland territories. Venice had gradually over long years acquired possessions that reached from Bergamo, Brescia, and Cremona in the west to Trieste and Udine in the east, from the edges of the Hapsburg empire in the north to the borders of Ferrara and Mantua in the south, with ports along the Apulian coast: but she was apparently not yet satisfied. During 1503, after Cesare Borgia had seized the Duchy of Urbino, the rightful heir, Francesco Maria della Rovere, was appointed to head a papal army intended to recover not only the duchy but also much of the Romagna for the pope. Venice saw the ensuing war as a chance to expand further across the plain of the Po. During the war, parts of the Romagna voluntarily ceded themselves to the pope, while others were captured by Venetians. These included cities such as Faenza, Forlì, and Imola. Venice did not return its captured lands to the pope: coupled with its earlier conquests, these lands now stretched across the main trade routes and military passes north into the Empire;[93] they blocked many of the easiest passages toward France from central Italy; they encroached on what had traditionally been papal territory; and they indicated clearly what had become very generally feared throughout Europe, that Venice intended to be one of the principal powers, not only of Italy, but of the Western world.[94]

For reasons of self-interest, therefore, both Emperor Maximilian and King Louis XII of France were willing to be persuaded by Pope Julius II to sign a pact in which the formal wording was a specific attack on Venice. The treaty, signed on 10 December 1508 in Cambrai, was joined by Spain in March 1509, and by Julius himself on 5 April. These dates bring us significantly close to Petrucci's last dated work in Venice.

The impact of this gathering of forces against Venice was, not surprisingly, terrifying to Venetians, who had come to rely less on mercantile trade, and more on their territories on the *terra firma*, the very lands under threat. The effect was heightened by a disastrous explosion at the Arsenale, on 14 March 1509, which destroyed a significant part of the Republic's war resources;[95] and the impact was made more drastic yet by the issuance, on 27 April, of a papal bull that excommunicated Venice, included an interdict against her, and allowed any other state to attack the city, her citizens, and her trading goods (wherever found). Venice tried to reject the terms of the interdict, to appeal them in Rome, and to act as if they had not been imposed.[96] However, the interdict had its effect—Sanudo records that the Piazza of San Marco was bereft of the usual crowds of foreigners on Ascension Day of 1509, which fell on 17 May.[97] Here the book trade was perhaps *more* vulnerable than others—for the very need to disseminate books widely, which worked to Venetian printers' advantage where the plague was concerned, was itself more strongly threatened by the papal bull.

Venice had, of course, always tried to pursue a position somewhat independent of the Vatican and so might have survived again, despite the impressive power of a full interdict. But other aspects of the effect of the League, in particular the military situation, bade worse for Venice. The French had invaded Venetian territory in mid-April, and on 14 May they inflicted a remarkable defeat on the Venetian forces at Agnadello. Compared with the papal bull, this battle was seen by Venetians as the real disaster. It was evident that Venice was about to lose all her mainland territories and was without resources with which to recover them.[98]

This defeat, coupled with the loss of trade through the interdict,[99] came at just the time when we must assume that Petrucci was probably working toward a new book, the second volume of Bossinensis's arrangements. By mid-May, having printed two complete volumes and some sheets of the *Fragmenta Missarum*, he could be well into the new volume. The timing of the break in work on this title, after five gatherings, seems to be more than coincidental. It is likely that the cumulative effect on the book trade of the papal juncture to the League of Cambrai (5 April) and the papal bull (27 April), already serious enough for trade, must have been heavily augmented by the defeat of Agnadello only a few weeks later. These events certainly had an effect on other printers. Lowry has suggested that "there are even some signs that Aldus [Manutius] intended to abandon printing entirely" at this time and points out that the printer had left for Ferrara by 1 June.[100]

That Petrucci would choose to return to the Marche, and to his home town, is hardly surprising. We have seen that he had maintained ties and retained property there, which he had leased, and he had in recent years served the town in leading roles. It is evident that he still regarded himself as a citizen of the city of Fossombrone, and that he was welcome there.

This suggestion that Petrucci set out for Fossombrone in May 1509 can be supported by some circumstantial evidence, and also thrown into doubt by other evidence.[101] Petrucci had, as I have stated, retained his citizenship of Fossombrone, and hence of the Papal States. As a publisher, he would have been particularly subject to the effects of the papal bull and might well have felt safer out of Venice. Although Lord Norwich states that, in the success of the book trade, "the tribulations suffered by the Republic in the years leading up to and immediately following the formation of the League of Cambrai caused scarcely any interruption",[102] we have already seen that Aldus Manutius thought of suspending operations. Scotto seems to have cut back markedly, too, and indeed one of his principal printers, Bernardo Locatelli, virtually disappears from the record for several years. Horatio Brown has pointed out that the number of petitions for copyright (by which he meant any sort of privilege) declined radically at just this time, citing as causes, "the wars of the League of Cambrai, the unsettled state of the country, the closing of the passes, and the disturbance of trade generally".[103] The movement of several successful non-Venetian printers out of Venice and back to the Papal States is also of significance. In 1509 (or perhaps late 1508), Brentà went to Pesaro (and later to Rimini), followed by Petrucci to Fossombrone, and in later years Zanchis went to Mantova, Bernardo Vercellensis to Ancona, and, after 1509, but by 1515 at the latest, Callierges to Rome.[104] It is not difficult to see Petrucci's abrupt departure as part of a pattern, stimulated as much by the terms of the papal bull as by the commercially dangerous implications of the battle of Agnadello—the one making distribution (not only within the Papal States) easier for anyone not residing in Venice, and the other threatening actual property in Venice.[105]

We need not be surprised that Petrucci seems to have taken the sheets of a half-printed book with him. He probably took more, perhaps his entire unsold stock. Among the collections of the Biblioteca Passionei in Fossombrone is a book from the wool merchants' guild of the city, acquired from a local *libraio*, Achille Ciurlo, in 1573, with, as part of the binding, part of a sheet from Petrucci's *Misse Petri de la Rue* of 1503. There is no more likely explanation of the presence of this sheet in a local binding than that Petrucci brought it to Fossombrone, and that it was still unsold at his death.

If the cumulative effect of all this evidence is that Petrucci had left Venice in May or June 1509, there is other evidence that might appear, indeed that has been taken,[106] to suggest that he was not resident in Fossombrone until 1511. In 1510 he was again elected *Revisore delle vie* of his home town, but a substitute was acting "in absentia tamen Domini Octavi Petrutii" during the month of March.[107] Further, it is not until 16 April 1511 that Petrucci is recorded as leasing a house in Fossombrone.[108] Taken together, these items seem to imply that Petrucci was not in Fossombrone in 1510—perhaps had not even left Venice. It is hard, however, to see reasons for him to leave Venice in 1511 (especially with an incomplete book), when the political and commercial situation, though far from stable, was easier than it had been two years earlier.[109] On the other hand, a temporary absence from Fossombrone early in 1510 is easier to explain, in the light of other missions undertaken for the city, or simply from a need to clear up matters in Venice. Further, the house leased in 1511, with its supply of running water, was almost certainly needed for his printing shop, not for his residence. Indeed, the completed second volume of Bossinensis's arrangements is dated less than a month later. It is difficult to see Petrucci arriving in Fossombrone in April 1511, leasing a house, setting up a printing shop, and printing and publishing a book, all within a month. If he had already been resident in the city for some time, then he could have been ready to print as soon as he leased the house.

These two years, from mid-1509 to mid-1511, remain largely a blank in

Petrucci's life. But it is hard to see him staying silent and inactive in Venice for that time, with work on Bossinensis's book wasted, and material lying idle in his shop. It is easier to see him, having stopped work in Venice in the middle of a book, making a hasty exit, and spending two years in Fossombrone while he found craftsmen, shop, and supplies. He was not to know that Fossombrone itself would hardly be a safer place for the next decade, as the ambitious plans of Pope Leo X for creating a patrimony for his family led to conflict and tension throughout the Duchy of Urbino.

Established in Fossombrone, Petrucci moved even more slowly than he had done in Venice. In the next two years, he finished the second book of Bossinensis's intabulations and then published one other book, a tenth book of frottole, sometime during 1512. The place of this book in Petrucci's output is not clear, in part because no copies survive and we are dependent on citations by Bottrigari and Colón for our knowledge even of its existence. The more complete reference is that by Bottrigari; as transcribed by Gaspari, his notes read:[110]

> [No.] 12. Lib.10°. 1512. Philippus Mantuan[us]. Organ. Jo. Hesdi= | mitis, Jo. Scrivano, Franciscus J., G.B. de Ferro | Dionis dit Papin da Mantua, Pietro da Lodi.

Of these composers, both Hesdin and Scrivano appear as frottolists in Antico's 1510 book of *Canzoni nove,* but not as far as is known in Petrucci's editions. The same is true for a "Franciscus F" and an "S.B. de Ferro" (who may be the man named by Bottrigari):[111] it may be that Dionis is the Diniset who is responsible for one composition in the 1508 *Motetti a cinque I* (although it seems rather unlikely); Pietro da Lodi is found in Petrucci's books 7 and 11, and in the 1511 second book of Bossinensis. Unfortunately, Philippus Mantuanus (and perhaps Dionis/Papin, also of Mantua) seems to be new to the repertoire. This slight evidence does not yield enough for us to be able to place the book clearly in Petrucci's output. The additional details offered by Colón's catalogue tend, if anything, to muddy the water. He reports that the book was indeed printed in Fossombrone, that it contained seventy-five pieces (presumably according to the Tavola), and that the first piece was apparently a lauda: "Exaudi preces meas o mater gloriosa del tuo".

My belief is that this tenth book of frottole, like the second book of Bossinensis's work, contained music brought with Petrucci from Venice. He would have finished the Bossinensis first, for that book, perhaps already half-printed, represented for Petrucci a substantial commitment of capital. After he had discovered that it could be distributed and sold from Fossombrone, he went on to publish the other volume for which he already had copy—that of frottole. At that point, there is little indication that Petrucci intended to continue printing music. He had completed the two volumes that, I suggest, he had decided on before he left Venice. He would have had to look around for new music, making new contacts, perhaps discovering new repertoires and new markets. He would also have had to have some financial incentive. That incentive was available, though apparently not for music, in the person of the bishop, Paulus Adrian de

Middelburgh. The evidence, to be presented shortly, suggests that the bishop had approached Petrucci during 1511, and that he was already planning to have Petrucci publish books for him.

Both Schmid and Vernarecci assert that Petrucci acquired the patronage of not only the bishop, but also Agostino Chigi.[112] Regarding the latter, I have discovered no evidence to support the claim and find it rather improbable. Chigi himself established a press in Rome in 1515, which printed editions of Pindar in that year and Theocritus, among others, in 1516.[113] Second, there is no evidence in Petrucci's output to suggest a connection with the particular Roman circles patronised by Chigi at any time before 1518 (unless one assumes Chigi to have been the conduit for the music contained in the first book of *Motetti de la Corona*). Nor do the 1519 editions help much, for Chigi died in the following year. Before that, Petrucci's contacts with Rome had not always been of the happiest.

Paulus de Middelburgh, however, was influential on Petrucci's future career.[114] The most relevant features of Paulus's biography and scientific career are that he was physician and astrologer to Duke Federigo of Urbino from 1481, and that he came to the See of Fossombrone in 1494, translated from nearby Urbania. As an active student of astronomy, he took a particular interest in Calendar Reform, and calculating the date of Easter. Since these were among the topics taken up by the Lateran Council under the papacy of Leo X, Paulus made sure that his work was well known to the pope. He had already published a first *Parabola Christi* in 1511 (probably with Silber in Rome), and in 1513 he sought a papal privilege for his *Paulina de recta paschae*. This, his major work, was intended to be the most comprehensive statement of his research into needed reforms of the calendar, to earn him a place in the deliberations of the Lateran Council, and to be his passport to recognition by the pope and the council. He was evidently determined that it should also be an elegant and well-produced piece of work. As I shall argue, he apparently commissioned Francesco Griffo to come to Fossombrone in late 1511, specifically to design a new typeface for the book. How Paulus came to know of Griffo's work and the possible reasons why Griffo might have accepted the commission will be discussed in chapter 7.

Even without these details, however, it must seem highly likely that Paulus de Middelburgh had already decided to publish his *Paulina* as early as autumn 1511. It is hard to see why Petrucci would have acquired the new fonts or the initials and borders cut for him unless he were to publish scholarly or humanistic texts, and the borders and the series of large initials were rather too spacious for his musical volumes. But there is no other evidence (apart from the influence of Paulus) to suggest that Petrucci was interested in non-musical volumes at this time. Petrucci's pattern of work, as far as we can discern it, shows no inclination to print large amounts of non-musical material, and there is no evidence of any unsigned or non-musical books from Fossombrone before Paulus's volume.[115] Paulus thus becomes a significant patron of the printer, and through him of Francesco Griffo. While Petrucci completed his edition of Bossinensis's second book of intabulations and prepared a tenth book of frottole, Francesco was perhaps already at work preparing for an edition of Paulus's *magnum opus*.

It is not surprising that Paulus would want this volume to be as attractive and correct as possible. In addition to the new typeface and the elegantly designed and cut blocks, Petrucci apparently bought a special stock of paper for the book and prepared red ink as well as black. Early pulls were also read against copy and a number of corrections made: these include a cancel leaf in some copies, and a stamped-in addition of the omitted part of a word. In addition, there is a list of errata at the end of the volume: here, we learn that the corrector, Hieronymus Posthumus, read the text, and also that he intended to accept no blame for any errors that were missed, preferring to lay it at the door of an "ethiop youth", Johannes Baptista.

Paulus and Petrucci apparently succeeded with the book. The bishop was invited to the council and took a leading role in the debate. Petrucci, too, benefited, though not immediately. But he did decide at once to produce another book, for it appeared exactly three weeks later. This was a brief pamphlet printing the letter of Castiglione to King Henry VIII of England, in which the author described the court of Urbino.

Petrucci claimed to have published this *Epistola*—it having come to hand and being (in his opinion) worthy of the prince it praises, i.e., Guidobaldo di Montefeltro—on his own initiative. Petrucci added that he printed the book as a means of expressing his admiration for the late duke, and the tone of the text is one of admiration for the culture of the Urbino court. The text can clearly be seen, with hindsight, as a preliminary study for *Il Cortegiano*, which was already occupying Castiglione when Petrucci's edition came out.[116] It may also have been the first in a series of fragments of evidence linking Petrucci's editions to Urbino.

These two non-musical books seem to have stimulated Petrucci to become active again in music printing. The stimulus must have been a strong one, for he also had to do battle with two new apparent rivals for the field of printed polyphony, in which he had so far been virtually safe from even the threat of competition. These two were Giacomo Ungaro in Venice and (much more seriously) Andrea Antico in Rome. Thus, and by chance, the two realms in which Petrucci had his base and his home were placed at risk as commercial monopolies.

Late in 1513 Petrucci applied to the pope for a privilege for music printing in the Papal States, perhaps in response to the very recent privilege granted to Antico. The immediate formal grounds for Petrucci's supplication were described in the eventual privilege as being the invention of a method of printing organ music—"modum imprimendi organorum intabulaturas". In addition, however, he sought similar protection for other books, not necessarily of music—"necnon alios libros alterius Facultatis". In the beginning of the grant, dated 22 October 1513, the pope recognised Petrucci's original invention of a "modum imprimendi libros cantus figurati" and also the fact that the "dux et Consiliarii Civitatis Venetiarum" had given Petrucci a privilege for twenty years. The pope then awarded a privilege for fifteen years from the date of printing. This wording, with its papal acknowledgment of the Venetian grant, would protect Petrucci from any future tension between the papacy and Venice and allow him to trade freely throughout the area. It also was no doubt designed to protect him from specific intrusions by Andrea Antico into the field of music printing. The protection, however, seems to have been as much for the items printed as for the technique. In this way, the field was left open for Antico to print his own music: indeed, Antico later persuaded the pope to remove the special privilege for intabulations, insofar as Petrucci had not availed himself of its opportunities.[117]

Less than a month before the grant of the papal privilege, a Venetian rival for Petrucci's position had appeared. On 26 September 1513, Giacomo Ungaro received a privilege for all printed music—"canto figurato"—for fifteen years. There was nothing unusual about the supplication, though the grant was a little less usual. It included the clause that the award should not damage previous awards of any sort—"Quod fiat ut petitur ne preiudicitur Concessionibus di que sorte facte fuissens ante hac".[118] However, there may have been reasons for Ungaro's petition that had little or nothing to do with any intention to print music himself, as will appear in chapter 2.

Nine months later, Petrucci petitioned the Venetian Council for an extension of his own privilege (granted on 26 June 1514). He pleaded the great costs of setting up the shop, which he said had not been recouped, as a result of the war and consequent troubles; he also said that Niccolò di Raphael was now old, partly blind, and unable to pursue his business. Petrucci sought and gained five more years for his own privilege. Such extensions were not unknown in Venice: indeed Petrucci appears to have followed the model of an application from the nephews of Democrito Terracino, approved in 1513.[119] Although his motives for acting at this time were perhaps two-fold—reinforcing his position in the increasingly lax Venetian world of printing privileges, and supporting (or denying) Ungaro's grant[120]—he was not specifically insisting on rebuilding an active business. The wording (with its borrowing from Terracino's nephews) merely implies that he and his colleagues still had copies they wished to sell. The suggestion, in the Venetian petition at least, is clear: because of the war and present troubles, they were unable to ship the stated printed works, which remained a burden on their shoulders: "ma per rispetto de le guerre et turbulentie sono al presente, non hano possuto dar expeditione a le ditte opere stampate" and "perche nel poco tempo che resta de ditta gratia, e Impossibile dare idonea expeditione a ditti librj, ma lj restariano a le spale cum grandissimo detrimento de ditto Octaviano, & compagni". Both these statements suggest that the primary concern was with selling the books remaining in stock.[121]

Yet, Petrucci had to have an additional motive for seeking these grants; to say that he had not been able to sell his stock would merely condemn him as an example of incompetence, or his privilege as not worth the fuss. Therefore, in the Venetian privilege, he draws upon the illness of one of his partners as the reason for the problems before him; in the Roman, on the other hand, he advances the fact of a completely new discovery, that of how to print keyboard music. Neither reason is implausible, neither need be a figment or even an exaggeration: it was merely Petrucci's wisdom that made him choose different points for the applications, given their different circumstances. But these two points, as much as the first, could imply that Petrucci was not planning to expand his business again, at least, not beyond the third book of Josquin's masses, and perhaps another of frottole.

However we interpret their function in Petrucci's mind (and they will be discussed in the next chapter), the privileges were in fact followed by a new period of activity on his part. In 1514 he printed three new titles, in 1515 three more with one acknowledged new edition of a Venetian title, and in 1516 another re-edition. This apparent burst of activity—actually somewhat busier than it appears once hidden reprintings are taken into account—never reached the levels of his Venetian productivity; nor does it seem to indicate a new and active program of publishing, in the way that the transition of repertoires in 1505 seemed to do. The first title, a third book of masses by Josquin, built on the clear success of the previous two (both of which were about to be reprinted); the third, yet another book of frottole, followed the same principle.

In this connection, I do not think one can argue that either *Frottole XI* or *Misse Josquin III* represents music that Petrucci brought with him from Venice in 1509. The repertoires are, by definition, similar to those printed in earlier volumes; however, in neither case does the pattern of pieces look as if it were part of the repertoire acquired in Venice. The frottola volume does, it is true, contain pieces by Lulinus (called *Venetus*) and Antonius Patavus, which may well have Veneto provenances, although too little is known of the lives of these men. But the rest of the book is a real mixture, pieces by the Eustachius composers, suggesting a Roman provenance, and by Pietro da Lodi alongside works by the main Ferrarese composers. Whatever the provenance of the whole (or its parts), it does not seem to be the same as that of the Venetian books. The masses by Josquin seem also to be somewhat of a rag-bag. They include three clearly early works (the *Misse Di Dadi, Faysans regres,* and *Mater patris*) with one certainly later (the *Missa de beata virgine*) and the two fugal works (the *Missa ad fugam* and one *sine nomine*), the second of which may also be a late work. While the second volume, in particular, of Josquin's masses does not present an integrated view of one period of his life, either, this third volume suggests that Petrucci or his supplier was picking up any works by Josquin that he could find. There is therefore no reason to believe that either this or the frottola volume had been planned, or even thought of, before Petrucci left Venice: they were wholly new, contained available pieces, and built on the success of the earlier volumes in each series.

It is much more evident that a new repertoire, and therefore a new series of contacts, was represented by the book of *Motetti de la Corona*. The repertoire is new: a younger generation of composers emerges, including Mouton and Fèvin, de Silva and Therache, Longueval and Jacotin. The names themselves signal another change. The composers were well known among Italians, and the music of Mouton and others was popular at Ferrara, as Lockwood has shown.[122] However, the most active center in which these names were recognised and their music welcomed was the new papal court of Leo X. Given the situation in the Duchy of Urbino, where the duke was dependent on the fragile and erratic approval of the pope, it is tempting to see the choice of this repertoire as in part a political gesture.

Here, however, Petrucci played cautiously. He apparently had no intention of following the book with a second volume, for the addition of the *Libro primo* appellation appears only on later editions of this title. (It will be remembered that the first publication of chansons, of motets, and of frottole was in each case given a title implying that launched it a series of editions.) But, as had happened in Venice, he found that his books were selling, and that the two sacred books of 1514 had reached a good market. As a result, the edition of Mouton's masses, which appeared in mid-1515, was called *Liber primus* from the beginning. No evidence of a second volume of Mouton's masses has surfaced, and it seems likely for a number of reasons, political before all else, that it was never printed. Petrucci did follow this first volume with another, of masses by Fèvin. He also felt confident enough to label the second edition of the *Motetti de la Corona* as a *Libro Primo*.

This group of five new volumes (three in 1514 and two in 1515) directs attention to new sources on which Petrucci could draw for his music. While, again, there are traces of the repertoire that was familiar in courts of northeastern Italy—Ferrara, Mantua, Urbino (perhaps)—at first sight the ties with Rome seem much firmer. Leo X's taste for music composed by French composers was paralleled by that for the musicians themselves, actively recruited for the papal chapel. His desire to have the most up-to-date of both is indicated by the presence of youngish or lesser-known northerners at his court: the presence of Longueval is indicative. There is not yet enough evidence to show whether Roman sources stand closer to Petrucci's readings in these volumes: too few sources indicate, for example, what the Roman taste in Italian vernacular music was during the second decade of the century—while the burgeoning interest in the madrigal (which may have been stronger in Rome than has been thought)[123] suggests that the frottola repertoire may not have been in strong favour there. There may be ample Roman sources for the sacred repertoire, but there are too few from the cities that are alternative candidates—Ferrara, Urbino, Rimini, for example—for detailed study of the readings.

It is tempting, nonetheless, to look to Urbino and the duchy as the source. I have already suggested that Petrucci may have been indicating, or reflecting, ties to the Urbino court in his publication of Castiglione's letter to Henry VIII in 1513. I have also hinted that the first book of the *Motetti de la Corona* might have been commissioned by the Duke of Urbino, and I shall discuss that possibility in chapter 9. Further, we know that Petrucci had to make several visits to the city during the decade, including one of three days late in 1515.[124] Whereas these visits were principally political or administrative in function, it would make sense that a famed publisher of music would have contact with musicians at the court of Urbino and might be sought out by a possible promoter of an edition. Nonetheless, there is no concrete evidence, and that for other cities is little better.

Two strands of evidence in favour of Rome can be detected: one is the proposal to Petrucci, made some years later, that he publish Calvo's translation of Hippocrates; the second, still later, is the actual publishing of music by Pisano and the history of Petrucci's typographical material after 1520. Unfortunately, both strands date from several years later, at a time when the changed political climate in the Marche might have changed many other things too. More significant and revealing, I believe, are the title and woodblock accorded the *Motetti de la Corona*. At the moment, it is not possible to say whence Petrucci received music for these editions of 1514 and 1515.

But the editions apparently continued to sell well enough to satisfy Petrucci, for he reprinted the first two volumes of Josquin's masses, as I have said. He also had to reprint all or part of the other volumes several times, and even the books of mass music by Fèvin and Mouton went into second editions. Almost certainly this was because the print-runs were shorter, for Petrucci would not have wanted to tie up too much capital in printed copies, when the political climate was beginning to look dangerous once again.

This changed political climate also affected how Petrucci dated his editions. Many of the Venetian editions widely identified carried their own true dates. Thus, there are three editions of the *Odhecaton A*, each with its own date, and two of its successor, as well as of a number of the frottola and other volumes. In every case, these carry a date that seems to conform to the bibliographical evidence. The same is evidently true for the first Fossombrone editions of the first two books of Josquin's masses (dated 29 May 1516 and 11 April 1515, respectively); indeed, it is also true for the new titles printed there. However, whenever a Fossombrone title needed reprinting, it was treated differently, reissued with the original, now untrue, date.[125] The number of such concealed editions has only recently become apparent and is markedly increased in the bibliographical section of this study. Petrucci seems to have been fairly busy during these three years. Indeed, his output looks as though he was beginning to build towards a full-time musical press again, perhaps one that would eventually have matched his productivity in Venice.

This would be even more true if we could admit the *Messa Corale* and the *Missarum decem à clarissimis Musicis compositarum* to the canon. The first of these was reported by Vernarecci as existing "nell'archivio della Cappella Pontificia in Roma",[126] but it seems very unlikely to be from Petrucci's press, if even a printed book. Petrucci would have had to acquire a font for chant notation, and I believe he would then have used it more than once. The second title was cited by Gesner,[127] but also seems to me to be somewhat implausible, although it raises interesting questions. I shall discuss the problems surrounding this citation and its potential connection to an edition of 1522 in chapter 14, on Ghost editions.[128]

Two other titles need to be removed from the canon of Petrucci's works at Fossombrone, although they have been mentioned in the literature since the time of Schmid. Even *RISM* cites editions of Josquin's first book of masses in 1514 and of his third in 1516.[129] Either Schmid or an earlier owner exchanged the colophon folios of the Viennese copies of the Fossombrone editions of these titles (of 1516 and 1514 respectively) so that the books would appear to have been printed in numeral sequence—Book 1 in 1514, Book 2 in 1515, and Book 3 in 1516. Curiously, the same phenomenon can be seen in copies of these titles held at the Sibley Music Library in Rochester. As Jeremy Noble first pointed out, brief study of the contents, however, shows these copies were printed as parts of one of the editions known to us with the dates of 1516 (for Book 1) and 1514 (for Book 3).[130] Even without these four ghosts, there is a significant body of work suggesting that Petrucci was again intending to build a strong list of titles in the field of polyphonic music.

However, Petrucci appears suddenly to have stopped printing music once again. The latest date in this sequence of musical books is 29 May 1516, after which there is nothing for just over three years. True, there is one non-musical exception, and that is another small monograph from Paulus de Middelburgh, his *Parabola Christi* of November 1516. In addition, at the other end of this fallow period, there is the apparently abortive plan (to be discussed below) to print a translation of Hippocrates in 1518 or 1519. But each of these items was in its own way distinctive. The first was a follow-up to the previous work for Paulus and so a natural activity for Petrucci to accept. In addition, he had never been working at full stretch in Fossombrone, so that in practice, allowing for the hidden reprints of titles, he may have seen the book by Paulus as merely next on his list. In other words, there truly was a stop in publicly admitted musical editions (that is, books carrying new dates), occurring sometime after May 1516, and of all newly dated editions after the end of the year. This fallow period was possibly a response to the privileges granted to Andrea Antico on 27 January and 27 December 1516. Petrucci is mentioned in these privileges, his opportunities are curtailed, and the terms of his own privilege reduced. It even appears that he had protested Antico's earlier privilege or current application, for Antico was given protection against any disturbance that Petrucci might cause, and the terms allow Petrucci some leeway in what he might print.

But Petrucci apparently did not stop selling his books, equally covered by Antico's privileges, and even did not stop printing new editions, though they were of earlier titles and were given the old dates. It seems that Antico's privileges were, typically, for the benefit of the recipient rather than intended to be effective against Petrucci. While Petrucci was certainly aware of Antico, whose activities may have persuaded him to go to the trouble and expense of getting his own Roman privilege in 1513, he does not seem to have worried about him overmuch. I believe one has to look elsewhere for the hiatus in announced editions of music.

Another possible reason could be that Petrucci had recently acquired the lease of land at Aqua Santa. This land, the property of the Bishop of Fossombrone, and adjacent to a plot owned by Petrucci himself, included a paper mill, and Petrucci retained the mill until 1523, when he sold half to an Urbino resident.[131] Petrucci may have added paper-making to his activities, though (as will appear) this is no reason for him to have stopped printing.

However, the most plausible reason for Petrucci's apparent inactivity is political. The Duchy of Urbino had been in a somewhat ambiguous position for several years. It had had a highly regarded duke in Guidobaldo, although his successor, his nephew Francesco Maria della Rovere, was still a young man of eighteen at his accession in 1508. The duchy lay within the Papal States, and it guarded one of the main routes north and south, one that avoided Florence and Perugia. To any pope, therefore, it was a prong into the fertile and easily traversed (or fought over) plain of the Po, as well as a protection for Rome against a flank attack from the north. It was also, as a result of all these features, a worthy award for a papal relative who might otherwise have languished land- and title-less. Thus, even before Francesco Maria acceded to the title, Cesare Borgia had seized it (from Guidobaldo) during the pontificate of his uncle Alexander VI, although he failed to keep lands or title.

Francesco Maria was a nephew of the previous Duke (through his mother), and also (through his father) of Pope Julius II, who reigned until 1513. His prospects must have looked secure, particularly when he was made captain-general of the papal armies. During 1511, however, he fell foul of the ambitions of the Cardinal of Pavia and as a result was accused of being a traitor and later of killing the cardinal.[132] In 1512 the pope remitted all his sins and reinstated him as captain-general, and during 1513 he attempted to make his nephew's position secure after his own death. Julius bought Siena from the Emperor, expressly for Francesco Maria and besought the College of Cardinals to give Pesaro to the duke as vicar of the next pope.

Unfortunately, this successor was Leo X, whose dynastic ambitions for his own family were as strong as those of Julius. He planned to place Giuliano de'Medici (his brother) on the throne of Naples and, though this did not transpire, did marry him to Filiberta of Savoy, the aunt of the new King François I of France. Leo apparently was not interested in the welfare of Francesco Maria and is supposed only to have been prevented from moving against him sooner by the influence of Giuliano de'Medici. However, Giuliano died on 17 March 1516. Immediately, Leo moved against Francesco Maria: he had him accused again of the death of the Cardinal of Pavia. Within six weeks, the duke was excommunicated and then stripped of all titles and ranks. These were immediately assigned to Lorenzo de'Medici, who was formally invested with his titles and offices on 18 August 1516.[133]

Perhaps foreseeing this fate, Francesco Maria had already fortified many cities of the duchy. During June 1516, Lorenzo gathered together an army, partly papal and partly Florentine in composition, and began to attack the Urbino duchy. The ousted duke advised his cities to capitulate rather than be laid waste; Pesaro and Sinigaglia, among others, did so: Fossombrone did not. Early in 1517, the rightful Duke attempted to reclaim his lands. He captured Urbino on 5 February and waged an ongoing guerilla war against Lorenzo. Fossombrone became a vital point in this war, for it had a crucial bridge across the Meltro (or Metauro), the main access between the northern and southern parts of the duchy. In May Francesco Maria, then based near Fossombrone, made a foray toward the Tuscan border; behind his back "certain bands of footmen was removed with the rest of [Lorenzo's] army to *Fossombrono*, which city being battered with the artillery, the third day was taken and sacked".[134] Francesco Maria continued to harry Lorenzo, who was unable to clinch a victory. However, Lorenzo secured the duchy by default, when Francesco Maria's mercenaries refused to continue fighting for him.

In March 1518, Lorenzo went to France, following his late brother in marrying a member of the French royal family, in his case Madeleine de la Tour d'Auvergne. Neither lived long, for, when he died on 4 May 1519, she had already been dead for six days, but not before giving birth to the future Catherine de'Medici. Although there was no male heir, the pope did not return the duchy to its former owner, but annexed it to the Papal States. Upon Leo's own death on 1 December 1521, Francesco Maria marched to reclaim his duchy and was back in possession before the end of the year (even though he was not formally invested with the title until March 1523).

During this time, Petrucci remained an active member of the leading circles of his city and held a number of significant positions. In 1512 he was Captain of the Castles, in March and April of 1513 one of the Anziani, in December 1513 and in June 1514 one of the two Revisores Viarum, and he was again Primo degli Anziani in September and October of 1515. This record continues for the next few years. In late 1515, he with two others was commanded to Urbino, apparently to discuss the political situation with Francesco Maria. On 7 September

1516, he was the principal of three members of the city despatched to bring congratulations to Lorenzo on his accession to the duchy; according to Vernarecci, Petrucci was chosen because he was already known to Pope Leo X.[135] In 1518 he was again Primo degli Anziani; in 1519 he was one of the elected rectors of the city following the death of Lorenzo de'Medici. This leading role was to continue, for in 1520 he was sent to Rome with the notary Cristoforo Cartari to seek the reform of some clauses in the new constitution administered by, and compensation for damage caused by, the papal legate, Cardinal Bibbiena.[136] At the same time, he seems to have been financially secure: he leased some of the Bishop's land in 1515, at Aqua Santa, because it was adjacent to his own property; and in 1516 he acted as guarantor for a fellow citizen. As Gialdroni and Ziino remark, these acts "lascia supporre una sua solida posizione economica e finanziaria".[137]

One or two dates in this narrative assume a special significance when we examine the dates acknowledged on Petrucci's output at the time. His last musical book before 1519 was dated 29 May 1516; Francesco Maria had been excommunicated less than five weeks earlier, and Lorenzo was about to attack. Petrucci's next musical book appeared on 17 June 1519; Lorenzo had died on 4 May, although it is not clear how soon the news could have reached Fossombrone.

In fact, Petrucci did not stop printing music when Lorenzo moved to take over. Among the series of hidden editions and cancel leaves, at least two fall between the last musical item and the *Parabola Christi* of Paulus de Middelburgh (printed on 20 November 1516), and another three (at least) printed after that pamphlet and before the first new musical edition of 17 June 1519. Each of these editions is a reprinting of one published earlier in Fossombrone, and each carries the date of the first edition from which it is reprinted. It seems that these editions were meant to be hidden, buried in earlier editions, from a time when Francesco Maria was securely on the ducal throne.

Of course, when Fossombrone was sacked in early 1517, Petrucci's printing shop, as the property of a leading citizen, was likely to have been among the destroyed premises. In that event, Petrucci must have spent some time in reestablishing his press, and perhaps even in replacing injured or dead employees. But this need not have taken the best part of two years. The possibility of a Roman-sponsored edition of Hippocrates would have encouraged him to set up shop again, and he was probably ready for work by mid-1518. Further, the presence and the false dates of the surviving musical editions also argue that Petrucci was trying to hide his resumed musical printing.

This background argues for a political interpretation of these editions and (perhaps) their contents, one that might have been known to his contemporaries.[138] Such a coin has two faces, of course. On one, the repertoire was associated too closely with the losing side, with Duke Francesco Maria, and Petrucci may have felt it unwise to be seen to be printing it; on the other, the repertoire was too closely associated with the pope or with Lorenzo, and Petrucci could have been accused of being a collaborator if he continued to issue it. There is no strong reason for choosing one over the other. The fact that Petrucci could continue printing in a small city, where everyone would have known he was doing so, tends to suggest that the repertoire was seen as favourable to the ousted Duke. So does the form of his colophons, which in the dated 1519 editions omits any of the references to the ruling duke that had been used under Francesco Maria; much of the duchy was secretly and strongly committed to him and his return, and abetted his guerilla warfare. Possible musical reasons for believing this to be the correct political interpretation will be discussed in chapter 9.

There is an interesting point to adjoin to this matter, one for which there is no extant evidence. Whichever reason for suppressing the dates is chosen, Petrucci's ability to print these hidden editions suggests that he may have had other work at the time. If he were in the process of printing other editions (now lost), then his press would be working at a more satisfactory level, his workmen still be paid, and he himself financially more safe. No such books survive. However, with the special arrangements announced by the losing Duke, with the change of rule, and with the new constitution administered by Cardinal Bibbiena, there must have been many promulgations and new laws that needed to be printed and circulated. While none survive (and few survive from any Renaissance cities for the period), I would be surprised if Petrucci did not receive orders to print some of these. He was certainly known to Roman authorities and patrons as a printer, and not only as a printer of music (as the privileges granted to Antico might imply). There are two pieces of evidence for this assertion.

The first lies in the colophon of Paulus's pamphlet, the *Parabola Christi*. It is unusual in that it does not cite the name of the city where it was printed; instead it reads "Impressum per Octavianum petrutium habita licentia a deputatis iuxta decretum lateranensis concilii. Die vigesima Novembris, M.D.XVI". Petrucci was able to claim the special privilege of the Lateran for printing this book, and that must have been politically convenient.[139] More significant is a project I have mentioned earlier, but which does not seem to have come to fruition—the plan to print Marco Fabio Calvo's translation of the works of Hippocrates. Had it been published, it would have been a fourth non-musical volume from Petrucci's press and would have opened up a possible career as a printer of major literary and humanistic texts.

The manuscript text of Calvo's translation[140] implies that the book was, or would be, published by Petrucci on 1 January 1519 and would be financed by Manente Leontini, physician to Lorenzo de'Medici. Leontini's role in the business is a little obscure, for he was making (or had made) his own translation of the same texts. At the same time, he apparently reneged on the agreement to publish Calvo's version, for Petrucci was in Rome in August 1518, to lodge a complaint against Leontini. In this he said that Leontini had failed in his obligations.

Why Petrucci should even have been approached to print the work is not clear. Certainly, Lorenzo was currently Duke of Urbino, but he had access to leading printers in Rome, and there is no indication that he was involved in plans for the edition. Perhaps Petrucci's edition of Paulus's *Paulina* had made an impression on not only Leo X but also humanistic circles in Rome; perhaps Leontini was already planning to make his own translation (as it appears) and encouraged Calvo to look away from Rome, hoping that the edition, if not the project, would be lost to sight; perhaps the printer was suggested to Calvo by Bartolomeo Egnatio, citizen of Fossombrone, scribe in the papal chancery, and later collaborator with Petrucci himself.

Any evidence of Petrucci's reputation in Rome during this period, aside from the complaint about Leontini, has to be drawn by inference from the documents in Fossombrone. Petrucci made visits to Rome on either side of this period, in 1516 and 1520, and was "già commendato dal Pontefice Leone X".[141] In addition, of course, some members of the papal administration, as well as Antico, would have known enough of him to ensure that he was specifically mentioned in Antico's privileges.[142] Even if his later musical repertoire did not come directly from Rome, he had demonstrated with his edition of *Paulina* that he could print elegantly. Therefore, Petrucci was known in Roman circles as at least owning a printing house and probably also as a delegate from, and representative of, a city in the newly conquered territories of the Duke of Urbino.

The proposal to print Calvo's translation would have required Petrucci to have a professional printing staff available in Fossombrone: this establishment need not have been large—few Roman printing shops were—and would comprise the men who had been producing his hidden editions after the 1516 edition of Josquin's first book. This staff would have been expecting to work on the translation and apparently had been left with no other work in hand. More significantly, the proposal argues that Petrucci was now active as a printer, that is, he was technically proficient. This is supported by the wording of his Roman privileges and applications, and perhaps by the manner in which he was invited to Sora in 1519 (for which see below).

Whether as a result of the presence of a full complement of employees, or because of the removal of Antico from the Papal States to Venice, or because of the death of Lorenzo, we can no longer say, but Petrucci immediately began to think of printing music again. Lorenzo had been dead just over six weeks when Petrucci produced a second volume of *Motetti de la Corona*, the first of three such volumes that appeared in a period of less than twenty weeks. This might suggest one supplier of music, if we consider it unlikely that Petrucci could have made diverse contacts so suddenly. The repertoire of the three is not entirely consistent, however, and it seems more likely that the one supplier had access to a large repertoire and was able to pick out subsequent anthologies for Books 3 and 4, after Book 2 had begun to go on sale. The alternative hypothesis, that Petrucci himself had been collecting material during the previous years, seems unlikely, if only because of the political situation in Fossombrone.

These three books mark the end of the long run of standardised and orthodox publications of music bearing Petrucci's name. There are subsequent editions and partial reprintings, of some of these editions and of earlier Fossombronese ones. None of them has a new date, and none is more than a supplement to earlier stock, which was presumably still selling well. All of them look like Petrucci's earlier editions, using the same formes and the same types—giving the same general appearance on the page, although with a general deterioration of standards. The papers are of poor and variable quality, the ink is less well made, and both often result in poorer impressions. In addition, the presswork is much more sloppy: there are parts of a page that are hardly inked, and other parts where the register is less careful.[143] Finally, the initial letters Petrucci had bought to supplement the damaged ones from earlier years are also markedly inferior, in both design and cutting: they are smaller and often have a very cursory level of decoration.

All these features suggest that Petrucci was reaching the end of his publishing career at Fossombrone—in his own mind, at least. He may well have had problems in finding competent help, both among craftsmen for his shop and among skilled designers and cutters of initials. But there is other, stronger evidence.

By the time Petrucci had printed the first of the three *Corona* editions of 1519, he was apparently considering a move away from Fossombrone, to Sora. That city lies well south of Rome and east of Frosinone, was one of the principal fiefdoms of the Dukes of Urbino, and is so cited in Petrucci's Fossombrone colophons: "Franciscomaria Feltrio de Ruere: Vrbini Soraeque Duce: Pisauri &c Domino".[144]

As Franco Mariani has recently discovered,[145] Petrucci signed a contract with an Evangelista Carrara on 14 July 1519, by which Petrucci acquired land at Carnello, near Sora, on which to build a paper-mill. A subsequent document, signed only two weeks later, presents a slightly different picture: in it, Petrucci is named as "imprexore de libri de canto figurato et aliter" and "l'inventore di tal stampare de canto figurato", and finally as "homo experimentato". Sora had sought to persuade him to come there, to the great honour of the city as well as useful— "ad causare grandissimo honore e utile ad questa città", but they had failed for lack of a paper-mill. Now, various citizens were willing to cede to Petrucci some land at Carnello, where there was "aque che super habundano". Petrucci presumably moved to Sora sometime in the following months, although perhaps not before the production of the fourth book of *Motteti de la Corona,* at the end of October. In any case, a document of 1538 describing the sale of the paper mill reports that he was "primus concessionarius et fundator ipsius carterie" and had built the premises.

It is significant, therefore, that all the editions and partial editions that can be assigned to Petrucci's shop after this last book of the *Corona* series are different in some manner. As I say, the copies of his Fossombrone titles that represent later printings are on inferior paper, with new initials and much inferior craftsmanship. They still use his typefaces and other material, and they also follow the patterns of layout and organisation that mark the earlier editions of each title. But they seem to have abandoned the level of presentation he felt necessary.

Visually different in both format and appearance, however, is the one dated edition, of the *Musica of Bernardo Pisano* of 23 May 1520: the page sizes, lengths of staves, and text fonts are different. Certain elements are the same—the music font and some of the initial letters. However, the colophon attributing the work to Petrucci is worded in an unusual manner, and without the Roman privilege that had become almost inevitable in the earlier Fossombrone editions.[146]

Given this pattern of evidence, it seems clear that there was a general change in the administration of the printing shop after the fourth book of the *Corona* series was finished. Standards had changed, even when reprinting earlier titles. The edition of Pisano's music stresses this transition. I believe that (while it was printed in Fossombrone and in his shop) Petrucci himself had nothing to do with the actual production of the book. He probably did negotiate its publication— his contacts in Rome would have allowed for that—but the work was undertaken by a craftsman in his shop. Petrucci became, in effect, absentee owner, supplying the music for the Pisano edition, and perhaps also agreeing to specific reprintings of other titles. The actual printer of the book may have been planning to enter the Roman market, as a printer and publisher in his own right. It would be attractive to suggest that Petrucci was handing over control to a son; but, although we know of his wife Ippolita and a daughter Franceschina (as well as an uncle Luigi Ricci), there is no reference to a son; nor do we know if his wife took any role in the business. It is tempting to believe that the craftsman involved was either Bartolomeo Egnatio, as suggested by Ziino and Gialdroni,[147] or Giovanni Giacomo Pasoti, for reasons I shall advance later.

There is no reason to believe that Petrucci intended to print again in Fossombrone. The patterns of material and printing practice in these last books suggest, as I say, that control of the press had moved away from Petrucci to another, presumably younger, man: the appearance of some of the same type material elsewhere argues that the shop soon closed and that this same man left Fossombrone.

However, two other titles, both possibly printed during the early 1520s, have at various times been ascribed to the Petrucci press. The first was another text by Paulus de Middelburgh, a *Prognosticon* for 1523. The text of this short book ends "Valeat sanctitas tua quam Deus aducta conservet Ex foro sempronii Calendis Decembris .M.D.xxiii". It is evident that this conclusion was written by the writer and is by no means an addition on the part of the printer. Indeed, there is no evidence that Petrucci ever printed this text. Details of the editions of this title known to me appear in chapter 14, on "Ghosts". None of them looks plausibly like the work of Petrucci.

The second reference is yet more vague: a M. Castacane reported that he had "veduto in Olanda un Virgilio impressa superbamente in Fossombrone". The reference to this book is no stronger than this: Vernarecci is sceptical of the value of the citation, which he says Schmid had gained from Toricelli's *Antologia*.[148] If the book were indeed printed in Fossombrone, then no date can be attached to it, although Petrucci remains the only likely printer. If, further, he had printed it, we can be sure (on the evidence of Paulus de Middelburgh's *Paulina*) that it would indeed have been superbly printed.

It appears that Petrucci had made other plans for an income for the rest of his life. He certainly took up the invitation to move to Sora, and was active there for well over a decade. In addition, documents survive that place him in Fossombrone in 1523, 1527, and 1534, even still holding office there.[149] In 1523 he was an Anziano, in 1527 Primo degli Anziani: in 1534, 1535, and 1536 he was still taking these roles, and in 1535 he was Consigliere for the Catasto.[150] At some point in this period he met the theorist Cimello: the latter reports the meeting in his treatise on the mensural system.[151] "Ottaviano Petrucci of Fossombrone, the famous printer, whom I have known and spoken with, I cannot say when or on what occasion, but it was in Sora".[152] James Haar is surely correct in suggesting that this meeting took place in the 1530s.

There is no extant evidence to suggest that Petrucci printed in Sora, nor do other editions from the 1520s look as though they were printed by or for him— though some do use parts of his typographical material. True, this does not mean that Petrucci had loaned, sold, or rented out all his material—presses, punches, and matrices, and the rest of the paraphernalia essential to running a press. The punches or the matrices would have been enough for anyone to replicate a font of his music type, and Petrucci would not have been the only printer of the period to allow others to buy type from his matrices. This seems to me the most likely solution; apart from the musical type itself, which is exactly represented in some Roman editions of Pasoti and Dorico, many other elements are either new or close copies of Petrucci's material. This is particularly evident in the earliest books. Petrucci seems, therefore, not to have intended to continue printing music. Indeed, at some (presumably later) time he had allowed the matrices to be used by others; in early 1538 he sought to have them returned to him,[153] and his widow was still trying to reclaim some from Gabriele Ceccolino in 1541.[154]

Further, Petrucci's Venetian privilege had expired. The actual date of its ending depends on how the extension should be counted. The original privilege expired after twenty years, that is in 1518. The supplication for an extension was lodged in 1514. It seems probable to me that its years were counted from the date of granting the extension, and that it had expired in 1519. Even if it could be thought to extend until 1523, there is no evidence that Petrucci or his colleagues sought to use its provisions after 1520. On the other hand, there is evidence that Andrea Antico, at least, thought that Petrucci's privilege had lapsed. He published many books on the same day in 1520—too many to have been prepared in a short time: Antico seems to have saved them and then launched them all together. Petrucci, however, seems not to have been interested; nor is there any evident interest in the remaining years of his Roman privilege. His books were still on sale, for Colón was able to buy titles published by Petrucci, in Venice in 1521, in Perugia in 1530, and in Milan in 1531.[155]

Thus, the evidence shows that Petrucci had decided to abandon printing, certainly by 1520, and perhaps already by mid-1519. He had lived through several attacks of the plague and more recently a war with an effective occupation of his city and some political and diplomatic activity during a turbulent time in the Papal States. The invitation from Sora may well have come at the ideal moment, offering him a more peaceful time as well as better access to the city of Rome, where his recent contacts could be found.

In fact, Petrucci did not stay in Sora for the rest of his life, but returned to Fossombrone sometime during the 1530s, surely by 1535. Gialdroni and Ziino may be correct in questioning whether he lived in Sora more or less continuously until at least early 1535, when he sold the paper mill there,[156] and it is noticeable that he had been active in Fossombrone administration during the late-1520s and 1530s. Perhaps it is significant that he also sold his interest in the Fossombrone paper mill in 1533. Finally, I suspect that the fragment I have called "*Musica XII*", found in Fossombrone, was probably printed before (or very soon after) Antico and Scotto's edition of the Verdelot madrigal, published in 1534. These two factors taken together would suggest that Petrucci was firmly settled in Fossombrone a little earlier, probably in 1533.

However that may be, he seems to have resided in Fossombrone for the rest of his life. He was in the city in October 1537, for one of the new documents required his presence there when he named a procurator to take care of his affairs, which may mean that he was expecting to be out of the city in the near future. Gialdroni and Ziino suggest[157] that he was not well, that "Evidentemente il suo stato di salute non gli permetteva . . . di seguire direttamente i propri affari". However, he was apparently well enough, in the following year, to publish with Egnatio the newly discovered edition of *Motteti dal Fiore*. Presumably he was in the city at that time.

Vernarecci, avowedly following Schmid, asserts that in 1536 the Venetian Senate had required Petrucci to return to Venice, and that he acceded and worked there on editions of Latin and Italian classics.[158] I have always found this story hard to believe, and the recently developed biography of his later years seems to make it even less likely. It is, of course, possible that a member of the Senate might have approached Petrucci, and that Schmid interpreted this as an action on behalf of the city as a whole. But it seems inconceivable that Petrucci would have been sought after for philological editions. Despite his contacts of nearly twenty years earlier with Bembo and Calvo, he had published no editions of the classical authors of Rome or Italy[159] and had displayed no editorial prowess of the sort claimed by Aldus Manutius and others. Indeed, Petrucci had published only a handful of non-musical works, none of them requiring of him any humanistic scholarship. In other words, if Petrucci did return to Venice, there has to have been another reason.

As it happens, there are two provocative pieces of evidence, neither of which refers in any specific way to Petrucci, but both of which might imply his presence in Venice. The first is the appearance of music books from the press of Francesco Marcolini da Forlì. Marcolini seems to have printed in Venice only from 1535 and concentrated largely on humanist literature and editions of Italian classics.[160] It is possible that his family and the Petrucci family may have known one another in earlier years. Amiani[161] reports that, in 1472, Antonio Petrucci with Baldassare Marcolini and two other Fanese acted together as ambassadors to the papal court to try to resolve a dispute between Pope Sixtus IV and Fano. Both families were then among the leading citizens of Fano, and the Petruccis of that city were still closely related to the new branch at Fossombrone.

When, in May 1536, Francesco Marcolini published a volume of lute music by Francesco da Milano,[162] he remarked in the preface how lutenists were indebted to Petrucci for inventing a manner of printing tabulature. He went on to say that the manner used by Petrucci had been lost, and that others had not been able to "find the way used by him. The numbers and notes of the sound were carved [by these others] in copper and in wood with great loss of time and much expense".[163]

Editions of lute music cut in woodblocks exist from the years before Marcolini's statement. The earliest extant is Antico's edition of *Frottole di Misser Bortolomio Tromboncino et de Misser marcheto Cara*.[164] German editions include two by Judenkünig (in 1515–19 and in 1523) and the lost *Cythare germanice* tabulature of 1525 or perhaps 1532.[165] For typographical reasons, I believe that the edition of Adriano's intabulations of Verdelot madrigals prepared by Antico and published by Scotto in 1536 has to be dated at the end of the year, some months after Marcolini's preface.[166]

Copper engravings of music dated from 1536 or earlier are, of course, virtually unknown, at least as performing editions. However, the only example is also most significant, for it is of Francesco da Milano's music.[167] Arthur Ness believes this edition to have been prepared by (or for) Marcolini, and to predate his published, signed, and dated typeset edition.[168] If so, Marcolini may have been writing with a wry awareness of his own experience when he mentions "great loss of time and much expense". Ness is certainly correct when he points out that Marcolini had problems of register in his double-impression typeset edition. However, as is well known, Marcolini did advertise the intention of publishing several more musical volumes, including a second book of tabulature, and three volumes of music by Willaert, of masses, of motets, and of madrigals (of which only the first survives).

It seems at least possible, therefore, that, if Petrucci were indeed asked to return to Venice, it should be on behalf of Marcolini, who needed him to help with preparing the announced editions, after the single experience of copper engraving. Certainly, Petrucci would have helped with the double-impression process used by Marcolini, acting as "technical adviser". If that were the reason, he cannot have stayed there long, for he was back in Fossombrone before his own edition of 1538. No more music seems to have appeared from Marcolini's press after the Willaert volumes of 1536, although he published a treatise by Lusitano in 1558,[169] and continued to print up-to-date works and classics of Italian literature. Nonetheless no other printer could have drawn Petrucci back to the Serene Republic as easily. Antico, who might seem to have the same use for Petrucci, had done his best to remove him from competition in the 1510s.

The second provocative piece of evidence comes from Rome. On 5 September 1536, Costanzo Festa wrote to Filippo Strozzi, asking if one of his agents could find a music printer in Venice for his hymns and Magnificats.[170] The wording of the letter does seem to suggest that Festa meant someone capable, and also known as a music printer: "Some one who prints music (although I have been asked, I do not know the name)". This person may have been Marcolini, for his first book had been out for three or four months, although the extant Willaert mass volume was not yet off the press. It may actually have been Petrucci, for Festa would certainly have known of his editions (which included one work by the composer) and may well not have remembered the name.

But Festa's reference, I think, is unlikely to be to Antico. For one thing, Festa should have known his name well: they were both in Rome in 1517, Antico had contacts with Leo X's circle,[171] and Antico was the one person who had been freely preparing editions during the preceding years. Indeed, works by Festa had recently appeared in one of these editions.[172] It is hard to believe that Festa would have forgotten the name of Antico. Even if the editions were not associated with Antico himself, but with the name of Scotto, we still are faced with a name that should have been known to Festa.

Secondly, Antico was evidently one who reacted to other people's successes. I have discussed elsewhere some reasons why his personality does not come across well during the 1510s,[173] and I think the same features are evident during the later 1530s. His volume of *Intavolature de li Madrigali di Verdelotto* made by Adriano, as I say above, should probably be dated after Marcolini's tabulature and indeed may represent an attempt at cornering Willaert before Marcolini had gone too far.

Antico's second book of Arcadelt's madrigals[174] is evidently a direct response to the success of the first book, published by Gardano. Antico had shown absolutely no interest in Arcadelt before this; instead he produced editions and re-editions of Verdelot's madrigals and of chansons. In the same way, the second volume of Willaert's motets[175] published by the Scottos in 1539 seems to be the product of Antico's seeing and seizing a commercial opportunity. The colophon reads, curiously, that the book was published "ad instantiam Andree Antiqui". This phrase normally would imply that Antico himself underwrote the cost, though it may mean no more in this case than that he persuaded the Scottos to publish his blocks, once he had had the labour of cutting them.[176]

In these circumstances, I find it unlikely that, if Strozzi's agent had approached Antico, he would have been sent away. Here, after all, was the chance to publish for a known and prestigious market. Thus, the fact that no-one appears to have taken up Festa's offer also tends to argue against Antico's being the name Festa "did not know". This is also an argument against the name being that of Scotto. Festa must surely have known the name of the Scotto dynasty, in connection with liturgical books, if not with the wider repertoire coming from the house. But he apparently did not associate the name with music.

It therefore seems likely that the name Festa "did not know", but which would have occurred to Strozzi's agent in Venice, would be that of Marcolini or that of the now aged Petrucci. In fact, any enquiry among members of the Venetian printing community would almost certainly have elicited Marcolini's name. (That of Antico might have arisen as a cutter of music blocks, but we have no evidence of him being seen as either printer or publisher.) Even if Festa had made enquiry among Roman printers, he should also have heard of Marcolini, though not necessarily of his music printing, even though he had been in business for little over a year. But, if the name of Petrucci was still known in Rome, especially with the loss of almost all of the older generation of printers during or following the Sack of Rome in 1527, it would have been as a maker of paper or a music printer in the Papal States (at Sora or Fossombrone). Thus Marcolini's name fulfills the implications of Festa's letter better than does that of Petrucci, attractive though the possibility seems.[177]

However, neither of these strands of evidence and argument does more than hint at a remote possibility that Petrucci was actually in Venice in 1536: on analysis, both tend rather to suggest that the idea that he was "summoned" there is no more than a fanciful wish to show that the Venetians recognised his importance.

Petrucci's edition of 1538 was undertaken in collaboration with Bartolomeo Egnatio, a papal chancery scribe in the 1520s. The nature of the relationship between the two men has been explored recently by Gialdroni and Ziino,[178] who believe that it may have begun in Fossombrone before Petrucci first ceased publishing there, in 1520. I think that unlikely and will explore a different suggestion in chapter 11. But the new documents do show that Egnatio was in Fossombrone from the middle of 1533, and perhaps traveled there with Petrucci himself. If so, then the Fossombrone fragments of "*Musica XII*" and the fragments of *Motteti dal Fiore* of 1538 probably are the only remnants so far discovered of a more active printing career.[179]

However that may be, we know nothing else of his life after the document of early 1538, which sought the return of his matrices, presumably used for the new edition. According to all authorities, he died on 7 May 1539, although, as so often during his life, no contemporary record is extant.[180] He was certainly dead by 15 December 1539, when his widow Ippolita leased parts of his typographical material to Nicola di Piernicola Buzzi da Cortona, living in Urbino.[181] But, as Gialdroni and Ziino point out, a document cited by Mariani[182] and dated 1 December 1538 already refers to "Octaviani de Petrutiis de Forosempronio civis" as "quondam dominus Octavianus". It seems likely, therefore, that Petrucci died sometime in the six weeks following the publication of his last book on 15 October 1538. It is perhaps appropriate that the best evidence for many important aspects of his life continues to lie in books whose printing he oversaw, the glories of his greatest achievements.

Notes

1. Vernarecci, *Petrucci*.

2. Vernarecci, *Fossombrone*. The city of Fossombrone is justly proud of its famous son and has done much to foster interest among Italians and natives of the Marche in the life of Petrucci.

3. Among them are documents, discussed below, that have been kindly communicated to me by Bonnie Blackburn, James Haar, and Giulio Ongaro. It will become apparent that I do not agree with Blackburn, "Petrucci", p. 16, that there is any reason to believe there were two Ottaviano Petruccis at this time, one in Venice and one in Fossombrone.

4. See Gialdroni and Ziino, "New Light"; Mariani, *Ottaviano*. These scholars are continuing research in the various archives and will publish fuller accounts of their discoveries. Here, I shall merely outline the new evidence and discuss its implications, leaving the details to them. I am particularly grateful to Maria Teresa Gialdroni and Agostino Ziino for repeatedly sharing their discoveries with me in advance of publication.

5. Schmid, *Petrucci*.

6. A number of details of the lives of and roles played by Pandolfo and Alfonso Petrucci can be found in Guicciardini, *Istoria* and Machiavelli, *Istorie*. Machiavelli also mentions Pandolfo Petrucci several times in his *Discorsi* on Livy and in *Il Principe*, apparently with no great feeling of respect.

7. The basic facts about Pietro Giacomo Petrucci are collected in Cecchini, "Mostra". The four musical titles are listed in Sartori, *Dizionario*; and Guidobaldi, "Music". Guidobaldi discusses the musical volumes and their place in Perugia's musical life. A discussion of the Arcadelt volume can be found in Bridges, *Publishing*, especially pp. 248–52. I have found no confirmation of Guidobaldi's statement (probably taken from Ascarelli, *Tipografia*) that Petrucci began printing in 1567, and no titles seem to exist from before his partnership with Porto in 1575. Her list of his non-musical titles, on p. 7, fn. is very incomplete, as a quick examination of the indices of any of the more important library catalogues shows. The list remains small but varied: it includes the *Lettioni recitate nell'Accademia de gli Insensati* (1588) written by Filippo Massini under the name of *Descrittione della pompa fatta in Roma per la traslatione del corpo di S. Gregorio Nazianzeno* [1580] written by G. B. Rastelli, a few Latin works, some medical texts, and various publications for his native city of Perugia and its church, including a manual on dress, published in 1595. The most beautiful of his books is probably the edition of Valadeas's *Rhetorica christiana*, published in 1579. For this book, see Palomera, "Valadeas", and illustrations in Mortimer, *Italian*, No.510.

8. Pietro Giacomo Petrucci's heirs seem to have printed no polyphony, although Vernarecci (*Petrucci*, p. 284, fn) reports having seen a chant book prepared for the Frati Minori Conventuali at Assisi, printed by Alessandro in 1607, which (he claimed) had music, printed at a single impression.

9. Amiani, *Memorie*, i, pp. 95, 243–45, 293–94, 310–11, and ii, p. 38.

10. Ibid., p. 245. There was in fact an active Petrucci family in Naples. Antonello Petrucci,

a cultured scholar, educated by Valla and Pontano, had been confidant to Alfonso I and Ferrante of Naples. He eventually conspired against his king, was discovered, and killed in 1487. Another Neapolitan, Giannantonio de Petrucciis, was one of the better poets of the late fifteenth century. Atlas, *Music*, p. 144, places him on the level of Galeotto.

11. There is a possible connection: One Petruccio di Calabria was castellan for Taddeo Manfredi, ruler of Imola, in 1451, according to Larner, "Order", p. 54, fn.38.

12. Vernarecci, *Petrucci*, p. 22. There is little difficulty in positing a move from Fano to Fossombrone: both towns were under the rule of the Malatesta of Rimini throughout much of this period. In the late fourteenth century, Fossombrone passed to the rule of the Malatesta branch in Pesaro, who retained both cities until 1445, when they were sold. Fossombrone then passed to the Duchy of Urbino.

13. Monsignor Ceccarelli, the most helpful head of the Biblioteca Passionei in Fossombrone for many years, told me (in January 1991) that all the city's documents dating from before 1513 were given to the Red Cross in 1952, for sale as bulk scrap and to raise money. In fact, a number of notarial documents from that period do survive and are kept in the Archivio di Stato at Pesaro.

14. In 1493 Petrucci was called "dominus Octavius Johannis Lodovici Baldi Petrutii", and in 1499 he is "dominus Octavius quondam Johannis Lodovici Baldi Petrutii". These documents are cited in Vernarecci, *Fossombrone* pp. 197–98, and quoted in Gialdroni and Ziino, forthcoming.

15. Vernarecci, *Petrucci*, p. 22, fn., cites a document dated 1511, among those not now extant. In another document of 1501, our Petrucci is called "Domini Octaviani Ludovici" (Vernarecci, p. 125, fn.).

16. Vernarecci (ibid.) remarks that the name Ludovico Petrucci seems to have been held only by one man, and that he is therefore likely to have been the father of Ottaviano.

17. In his application for an extension of his Venetian privilege, granted on 26 June 1514, Petrucci calls himself poor. He uses this as the reason for having taken on two colleagues: "Et perche nel stampar de dicte opere era bisogno di gran capitale et non si trovando Il ditto Octaviano il modo, ne commodita per esser pover homo, tolse per compagni Ser Amadio Scoto mercadante de libri, & Ser Nicolo de Raphael". Apart from the question of whether this was merely a justification for some of the details later in the supplication (for which see chapter 2), the costs of establishing a publishing programme using a new series of fonts would indeed be very heavy, and even a moderately wealthy landowner would have looked to take on investors to share the burden with him.

18. These documents appear in chapter 20. Some, apparently no longer extant, are taken from Vernarecci, *Petrucci*.

19. See Gialdroni and Ziino, forthcoming. It may be that all the Fossombrone documents use the shorter form of Petrucci's name. The two examples cited by Vernarecci come from documents that have not been rediscovered by Gialdroni and Ziino; therefore, we cannot be sure that Vernarecci was not merely adopting the form that he used throughout his study.

20. See Vernarecci, *Petrucci*, pp. 27–29; Sartori, *Petrucci*, p. 14. It is notable that Petrucci is not included among the members of Duke Guidobaldo's "family", or that of his wife, given in GB-Lbl Add.Ms.22027, 131r–36r, an eighteenth-century copy of a "Catalogo fedelmente copiato da una manuscritto dell'Abbate Baldi". From the references to Paulus de Middelburgh, the list dates from between 1481 and 1494. The list does include references to musicians: 133r includes "Cantori della Cappella", 133v includes two "Maestri da Ballare", and 134v includes "Trombetti sei", "Tamburini", and two "Sonatori da Organo".

21. Unfortunately, it is unlikely that we will ever be able to find evidence for such an assertion. As pointed out by Clough, in "Sources" and in "Towards", many of the relevant documents were destroyed early in the 19th century. Of course, the duke's interest in music and his patronage of musicians are not in doubt; his support of Pietrobono is recorded in a contemporary memorial and cited in Mamini, "Documenti", p. 119, while Pietrobono's later reference to him is quoted in Bertolotti, *Musici*, pp. 12–13. Musical members of the household are listed in the manuscript cited in fn.20. Mamini's study also transcribes the payments for musicians at the wedding of Roberto Malatesta and Elisabetta Montefeltro, in Rimini in 1475. Alongside references to Pietrobono, musicians are listed from Florence, Ferrara, Mantua, Milan, and Pe-

rugia. In addition many cities under the dominion of the two families also sent performers; it is unfortunate that Fossombrone is not mentioned.

22. Vernarecci, *Petrucci*, p. 155. Other names are provided in Vernarecci's study of the history of Fossombrone.

23. This is surely the man named by Petrucci as a procurator of his property in 1499. His own letters and songs are collected in I-PApal Pal.555, ff.415–505, with another poem in I-VEcap CCLVII, 270r–v, dedicated to Domitius Calderinus (Kristeller, *Iter Italicum*, ii, pp. 36 and 296). It is tempting to suggest that he may have been related to the "Antonio da Gigari Fossombrone alle frate di S. Franco di Fossombrone" who gave a copy of *RISM* G 2980–1551² (Gombert's first book of motets à4) to the brothers of S. Francesco in Fossombrone. This copy is now in I-Vnm, Mus.284-87: see Lewis, *Gardano*, ii, p. 199.

24. He is recorded as the teacher of the poet Laurus Gorgerius Vadensis, in the latter's collection of verses, in I-Rvat, Chigi J.V.186. See Kristeller, *Iter Italicum*, ii, p. 483.

25. ANF, Atti de'Consigli Municipali, 1513–1520, f.36v. We will probably not be able to discover when Fossombrone first acquired an organ, due to the loss of the earlier documents, described above in fn.13.

26. For details of these, see Fumagalli, *Lexicon*. For Urbino in particular, see Furbetta, "L'arte".

27. *BMC*, vi, p. ix.

28. This story has been a little misunderstood, for the original assertion by Vespasiano da Bisticci does not imply that Duke Federigo was opposed to printed books. In his *Vite d'uomini illustri*, the Florentine bookseller Vespasiano states that a printed book would be embarrassed to be seen in the company of the elegant books (that is, manuscripts) found in the Urbino library. Eisenstein, *Printing*, p. 48, suggests that the truth of the matter lies in Vespasiano's own prejudices. I think rather it may lie in the statement of Bono Accursio, discussed below. See Clough, "Library", for a discussion of this library. See also the reference in Scholderer, "Printing", p. 91, suggesting that the prejudice *was* held by Ercole d'Este.

29. This opinion appears in the prefatory letter to an edition of Ovid's *Metamorphoses*, published in Milan in 1475, and is here taken from the translation in Scholderer, "Printers", p. 210, fn.2.

30. Three titles printed by this press are held by the British Library: see *BMC*, v, 297. All are addressed to the literary market, rather than being trade, legal, or theological texts. Only one is signed by the printers: in it, Bartolomeo is called *Bartolomeo da Fossombrono de la Marcha*. The British Library catalogue reports that some copies include a Giovanni Salvazo among the printers or publishers. This same title was offered for sale in Giorcelli, "Documenti", on pp. 33–34, where a slightly different reading of the colophon is given. The same catalogue lists a later book printed by Antonio de Alessandria, dated 1485.

Vernarecci believed (*Petrucci*, p. 32) that Petrucci probably had been an apprentice with Bartolomeo. Castellani (*Stampa*, p. 61, fn.2) doubted that Petrucci would have been in Venice so early and points out that no later editions from Bartolomeo's press are known. There is no real trace of any members of the company for the years after ca.1480. It is unlikely that Antonio da Alessandria is the *Allessandro de pedemonte stampadore* cited, with Hellisabeth de Riuiera and people called Zuchato in the Venetian archives in 1492. See ASV, Capi dei Consiglio de'Dieci, Notatorio, Reg.2, 25[48]r–v. Rhodes, "Facere", cites a Joannes Bartholomaeus, who appears to have been a typesetter in Venice in 1507, but there is no good reason to associate him with Bartolomeo, either. Nor is it more than an attractive hypothesis to link either of these men with the Bartolomeo Egnatio who is later associated with Petrucci (as suggested by Gialdroni and Ziino, in "New Light", p. 505).

31. ASV, Cinque Savi alla Mercanzia, Busta 25 [Capitolare 2]. Most of the documents are in the first five folios of this manuscript, although the law enacted in 1508, and cited below, is recopied on folio 67r. A similar collection of earlier laws on citizenship is collected in ASV, Provveditori di Comun, Busta 1 (Capitoli), and this series seems to have been copied even later. For a discussion of these laws and their effect, see Ellis, *Citizenship*, and, more briefly, Tucci, "Psychology".

32. There is one apparent exception to these rules: In ASV, Provveditori di Comun, Busta

1 (Capitoli), f.86*v*, an act of the Council of Ten is recorded, which allowed a foreigner with a Venetian wife to enter a guild, apparently without a waiting period. The act, transcribed here with the other documents, is dated 7 February 1460/1461 and seems part of an increasingly active move to admit skilled foreigners if they had married a Venetian. However, the relevance of this still fairly recent law to Petrucci's case is probably fairly small, for he would have needed to trade not only *de intus* but also *de extra*, and therefore to have been a full citizen of Venice, following the laws outlined above.

33. This does not seem to be a likely reason for Petrucci to have reached a contractual arrangement with Niccolò di Raphael and Scotto, as will appear.

34. Cited by Tucci, "Psychology", p. 363.

35. The documents for this provision are collected together in ASV, Provveditori di Comun, Busta 1 (Capitoli), folio 43*v*, citing a law passed in 1403.

36. This provision is in the same document, citing a law passed in the Consiglio de' Dieci on 7 February, 1460/1461. Petrucci evidently did not adopt this second course. His wife Ippolita was the daughter of one Luigi di Tommaso Ricci from Mondavio, a small town about ten miles east of Fossombrone. Luigi himself was resident in Fossombrone, for at various times he acted on Petrucci's behalf. For details, see Gialdroni and Ziino, forthcoming.

37. Vernarecci, *Fossombrone*, pp. 197 and 198; see also Gialdroni and Ziino, forthcoming.

38. Norton, *Italian*, pp. 125–26.

39. He seems to have signed no books, as publisher or printer. Nor does he appear in the list of Venetian printers, publishers, and booksellers compiled in Pastorello, "Tipografi". The will of the Maria who calls herself widow of Nicolo di Raphael, written in 1533, exists but gives no clues to the career of her erstwhile husband. It can be found in ASV, Notarile Testamento, 63 (Atti Bartoli), number 87.

40. It is notable that, when publishing under these other arrangements, the Scottos also signed the books; this was not Amadeo's practice with Petrucci. It may be therefore that Scotto was responsible only for distribution.

41. In 1498 (the year of Petrucci's application), for example, the firm employed principally B. Locatelli (for Aristotle, Boethius, Galen, Bernardus de Gordonio, Guido de Cauliaco, Hippocrates, G. M. Savonarola, M. Silvaticus, Thomas Aquinas [three titles], and Trombeta) but also Bartolomeo de Zanis (for Aristotle). In 1497 they had employed Capsaca, Gusago, and Hamman (the last already well known for liturgical books), and in 1499 de Pensis printed for them.

It may be that the Scottos were adventurous: the evidence of the contacts with Petrucci may be supplemented by the association between Ottaviano Scotto the younger, Antonio Giunta, and Andrea Antico, for printing the *Liber Quindecim Missarum* of 1516, and their support for Antico's activities in the 1530s. See Chapman, *Antico*, p. 448; Cusick, *Dorico*, p. 13; Bernstein, *Venetian*.

42. See many details entered in *GW*. More useful, because of the arrangement of the volume, is the *BMC*, in which the entries for Venetian incunable printers are found in Part V (1924, rpt. 1963). Emerich appears on pp. 536–42, Hamman on pp. 422–29, and Locatelli on pp. 435–53. For liturgical volumes printed in Venice that also contain printed music, see Meyer-Baer, *Liturgical* and, more important, Duggan, *Italian*.

43. The petition is transcribed in full in chapter 20.

44. Gialdroni and Ziino, forthcoming, argue plausibly that the documents from 1493 and 1499 suggest that Petrucci was liquidating some of his Fossombronese assets, in order to finance the establishment of his enterprise.

45. This is Blackburn's translation, in "Petrucci", p. 17.

46. The implausible alternative is that Castellanus, having this knowledge, happened to meet Petrucci, having the technical invention in hand.

47. Rummonds, *Printing*, pp. 7–8, talks about the ideal premises for a hand-press shop. He mentions the weight of the equipment and recommends northern light. He also stresses the need to keep a constantly moist atmosphere, which would hardly have been a problem in Venice. (It is true that Rummonds is writing about the later hand-press, made of iron rather than wood, but many of the details he discusses would have been equally important for earlier printers.)

Petrucci may not have established a full shop at first. Since the first two years moved slowly, no doubt while the viability of the whole exercise was tested, he may have relied on an already established printing house to do at least part of the work—such as the presswork—for him. However, the pristine condition of all the typographical material found in the *Odhecaton A* argues that none had previously been used by an earlier established press.

48. It is possible, as Gialdroni and Ziino suggest, that the decision to sell some land in 1493 may have been to generate the necessary funds to establish the press, but, in that case, I find it difficult to understand why Petrucci would have waited until 1498 to apply for a privilege, or until 1501 to publish his first book.

Richard Agee implies that it took Alessandro Gardano, with all of his experience and professional contacts, almost two years to establish himself as a printer in Rome. See Agee, *Gardano*, pp. 63–64. For Petrucci, there was the additional complication that 1499 was a very bad year in the Venetian economy. Lane, "Venetian", pp. 78–79 and 85, stresses the financial problems of 1499, and Hirsch, *Printing*, pp. 32–33, points out the high cost of equipment; he remarks that when Wenssler (of Basle) sold his equipment in 1491, for 253 guilders, the sum was roughly equivalent to fifty-five tons of wheat, eight small houses, and half an "excellent" house. It may be, therefore, that part of the delay between the granting of Petrucci's privilege and the appearance of the first book was due to a difficulty in gaining the support of business partners. Significantly, although Petrucci was to retain contacts with his home town and to visit frequently, he leased his house in Fossombrone to a Francisco Giannetti less than a month before the first edition appeared. See Vernarecci, *Petrucci*, p. 105.

49. This document is cited in Vernarecci, *Petrucci*, p. 105. Gialdroni and Ziino, "Ancora", report that the relevant notarial volume is now lost.

50. This is clear from the manner in which the letters *A* and *B* dominate the opening pages of music in Spinacino's two lute volumes.

51. Blackburn, "Petrucci", and Quaranta, *Oltre*. I am very grateful to Professor Blackburn for sending me a copy of her paper in advance of its publication. Fuller details on Petrus's life are given there. It seems to me unlikely that he was the Petro Nicolo Castellanus whose translations of Aristotle were published in Faenza by Simoneti in 1524–25.

52. Boer, *Chansonvormen*, p. 51. Quaranta, *Oltre*, pp. 341–43, transcribes the relevant documents. The Recanati connection might well repay further attention; a certain Bartolomeus de Rechanato had been singing as "discantus" in the convent chapel before 2 March 1501, when he was retired with a benefice (Quaranta, *Oltre*, pp. 71 and 340); he also was active outside the convent during 1505 (see Blackburn, "Petrucci", p. 42). Later the choir of the Santa Casa at Loreto was furnished with copies of Petrucci's books, bought at Recanati during 1515, probably at the fair (Grimaldi, *Cappella*).

53. Blackburn, "Petrucci", advances the attractive theory that Castellanus, who was known as a collector of music (see her references), would have been able to ask other Dominicans to collect music for him, and that, for example, he might have had copies of works sung in the Vatican as early as 1487.

54. These were the first edition of *Canti B* on 5 February 1501/2; the first edition of *Motetti A* on 9 May; and the first edition of the first book of *Misse Josquin* on 27 September. Once Petrucci was working at full steam, he seems to have been able to produce at least two full gatherings of music—four sheets perfected, or eight separate formes—every week. These figures are examined and some conclusions drawn from them in chapter 5.

55. A study of editions signed by the Scotto family during 1502 might yield some evidence of the use of Petrucci's typefaces or other material: this would help to explain the apparently unprofitable rate of work adopted by Petrucci during 1502. Of course, the possibility exists that other musical editions were printed during the year—although the bibliographical evidence argues against it.

56. In one sense, the motet volume was already an attempt at exploring a different realm of music making, one much more devotional than that of the chanson books; however, as Brown, "Mirror", argues, it was probably aimed at the same range of purchasers.

57. Duggan, *Italian*, makes a strong case, which I shall discuss in later chapters, for Jacomo Ungaro having been the actual typefounder for Petrucci, which would tend to associate Griffo

with him as well. If, as seems reasonable, Ungaro's and Griffo's activities for printers other than Aldus occasioned serious problems with the latter (as discussed in Lowry, *Aldus*, and touched on below), then it would seem less probable that Petrucci was on good terms with Aldus. This would add another reason why Petrucci should have sought Scotto as a business partner, rather than Aldus himself. On the other hand, there was no other Greek font available in Venice, and Petrucci would have had to turn to Aldus when he wished to print a couple of lines in Greek, in the opening pages of his *Odhecaton A*. Further, Mardersteig, "Aldo", p. 119, argues that Petrucci used one of the Roman fonts that Griffo had designed for Aldus, in the same book.

58. These issues will be discussed in detail in chapter 9; for now it is enough to draw attention to Blackburn's work, in "Petrucci". Aspects of the special nature of the repertoire of these volumes has been discussed in Brown, "Mirror". Something of the extent to which they may have circulated among the same musicians who were interested in the chansons of the *Odhecaton* series, and even in the same sources, may be gleaned from the pattern of concordances for these volumes. While that pattern includes a number of manuscripts prepared for religious choral institutions, among them the Milanese choirbooks, I-Fn II.I.232 or I-Rvat Sist.15, there are also to be found I-Bc Q18, ZA-Csa Grey 3.b.12, I-Fr 2794 and the later, and significant, I-Fn Panc.27.

59. An outline of Donato's career can be found in King, *Venetian*, pp. 366–67. Some of this material has recently been presented in Blackburn, "Lorenzo".

60. The earliest reference to this is in Sansovino's *Venetia città nobilissima e singolare* (Venice, 1581), p. 132.

61. See, in the 1510 edition, ff.161*v*, 221*v*, and 226*v*.

62. Castiglione, *Cortegiano*. In the translation by George Bull, p. 168.

63. A list of his writings, citing modern editions where available, is in King, *Venetian*, p. 460. A much more detailed study appears in Rigo, "Catalogo".

64. Poliziano and Pico are well-known figures. For Ermolao Barbaro, see Branca, "Ermolao"; Branca, "Umanesino"; and for his circle, see Marcon and Zorzi, *Aldo*, pp. 19–23.

65. Blackburn, "Lorenzo".

66. The letter is printed alongside that from Budrio, most recently, in Blackburn, "Lorenzo", pp. 43–44, with a translation on pp. 33–35. Lockwood, *Ferrara*, p. 206, fn.29, suggests that Donato might have been the direct contact between Ferrara and Petrucci: I suspect rather that he was the contact between Ferrara and Petrus Castellanus. James Haar has recently drawn attention to a mention of Petrucci during 1508, one which helps to draw a picture of his social circle. The mathematician Luca Pacioli (whose treatise on proportions includes music) published in 1509 a translation of part of Euclid's *Elements* (Venice: de Paganinis). In the preface to this edition, he gives a list of 96 guests who heard him read part of his work during 1508, a list which includes both the instrument maker Lorenzo da Pavia and "Ottavius Forosemproniensis."

67. Glixon, "Polyphonic", p. 22. See pp. 20–22, for his discussion of the evidence for and against that attribution and the alternative solution offered in Luisi, *Laudario*, i, pp. 441–45. Quaranta, *Oltre*, p. 349, identifies another musician named Natalis, this time at S. Giovanni e Paolo: he died in 1536.

68. Luisi, *Laudario*, i, p. 443.

69. This raises the spectre invoked by Blackburn, in her paper "Petrucci", that Castellanus was still supplying Petrucci with music in 1514. She bases this on the relationship of Castellanus to Giordano Passetto of Padua, who had been his pupil in Venice. Blackburn believes that the close relationship in the readings between Padua A17 and the *Motetti de la Corona* suggests that both had received their music from Castellanus. This is an attractive possibility; however, it raises problems over the choice of title for the printed book, and over the patterns of ascriptions in the two sources, which I shall address in chapter 9.

70. The letter will be touched on in chapter 8.

71. Boer, *Chansonvormen*, p. 51, fn., quoting from the *Monumenta Ordinis Praedicatorum Historia*, ix, p. 48.

72. See Ness, *Herwart*, p. 327, and the discussion in chapter 2 of the present volume.

73. The presence, as much as the wording, of Petrucci's letter to the reader in the first book of Spinacino's intabulations suggests a need to defend himself and his invention.

74. See Ness, *Herwarth*, pp. 355 et seq. Slim, "Musicians" quotes Oriola da Bassano's poem *Monte Parnaso*, which praises Spinacino, alongside other lutenists from the end of the previous century. Slim himself, in the entry on Spinacino in *The New Grove*, regards the lutenist as a skilled and idiomatic player.

75. Boorman, "First", pp. 198–207.

76. The modern literature on the *Scuole* is vast and need not be summarized here. The best discussion of their role in charitable activities is that in Pullan, *Rich*. A recent study of the many cycles of paintings commissioned by the *Scuole*, among others, is Brown, *Venetian*, which raises a number of interesting issues about the Venetian view of its own past and of the function of narrative and truth in reinforcing that past. The best discussion of the musical activities of the *Scuole grandi* is in Glixon, *Music*, with the abbreviated version in Glixon, *Music* (1981). Alongside that, reference should be made to Luisi, *Laudario*, for musical and biographical evidence.

77. Cattin, *de Quadris*; Cattin, "Sconosciuto": though see here Bent, "Pietro", which argues convincingly that de Quadris's music was composed rather later.

78. I wish to thank Professor Ongaro for giving me details of this discovery, and for assistance with its interpretation. The document is transcribed in the appendix.

79. As I pointed out above, qualified foreigners could not be barred from entry to a Venetian guild; indeed, if they were married to Venetians, an enactment of the Council of Ten from 1461 (n.s.) specifically covered the case. The point at issue in Petrucci's case, therefore, cannot have been his nationality, but rather his skill or standing in this craft. Petrucci's action in appealing to the Provveditori di Comun seems to have been standard; the detailed procedures would be outlined in 1519: see ASV, Provveditori di Comun, Busta 1 (Capitoli), 236r.

80. No copies of Petrucci's books survive with any decoration that can plausibly be Venetian in origin. That does not mean that he may not have employed a craftsman with that skill. It still seems reasonable that Petrucci must have had some second string to his bow during 1502, and perhaps also in 1504 and 1506, when relatively few editions were apparently printed, even allowing for "hidden" printings.

81. Giulio Ongaro has suggested to me that Petrucci was merely petitioning to be allowed to make his own ink. Unfortunately, neither the record of actual decisions made by the Provveditori di Comun, nor a Mariegola for the Cestieri seems to have survived from this period. Therefore, we do not know whether makers of printers' ink, often members of the printing house, were expected to be members of the guild.

82. The document, one of those now dispersed, is cited in Vernarecci, *Petrucci*, p. 125, fn. Vernarecci's suggestion that the house was perhaps sold before 1511 seems to hinge on Petrucci's acquisition of another property in that year. The argument is invalid.

83. The document apparently read "nisi sit et esse reperiatur civis originarius eiusdem civitatis, possideat bona stabilia in dicta civitate forisempronii et ejus districtu valoris centum florenorum adminus et habitaverit in dicta civitate ad minus per viginti annos continuos". Vernarecci, *Petrucci*, pp. 116–17.

84. Vernarecci, *Petrucci*, p. 151, citing the same lost documents I have mentioned above. In giving the details, Vernarecci adds that the post of Prior Antianorum, Primo degli Anziani, was given either to a "conte di feudo, o ad uomo della nobilità".

85. Finer, *History of Government*.

86. Vernarecci, *Petrucci*, p. 115; Vernarecci, *Fossombrone*, p. 206. The same statement appears in Gianandrea, "Ottaviano", p. 180.

87. Vernarecci, *Petrucci*, says that he stayed two months.

88. The copy of *Frottole libro sexto* recorded at St. Anna in Augsburg was dated 1507 (see Schaal, *Inventar*, p. 30). I doubt that this edition existed. The edition of Mouton masses reported by Vernarecci as of 1508 also seems unlikely. See "Ghosts", chapter 14.

89. Details of this evidence will be presented in the relevant entries in the bibliographical part of this study; further evidence is also discussed in the section on "Paper", in chapter 3, as illustrative of Petrucci's normal and abnormal work patterns.

90. I see no reason to accept the theory, advanced by Fumagalli (in *Lexicon*, pp. 162–64)

and Barblan ("Aspetti", p. 62) among others, that Petrucci returned to Fossombrone at the request of the bishop.

91. Pullan, *Rich*, p. 219.

92. On the other hand, Agee, *Gardano*, p. 17 is able to draw a much bleaker picture of the impact of the plague of 1575–77 on the Gardano firm. He points to a probable serious shortage of paper in the city, and the quarantine that certain other areas, in particular Milan, placed on goods from Venice.

93. Finlay, *Politics*, 164, quotes Machiavelli's assertion that the Venetian capture of Gorizia and Trieste from Maximilian in early 1508 led the Emperor to join the League of Cambrai. The Florentine reaction to all this can be seen in Landucci, *Diario*. I have consulted the English translation, here cited as Landucci, *Florentine*: references to the capture of these cities are on pp. 209–12.

94. Rubinstein, "Italian", p. 197, quotes from correspondence between the Florentine Council of Ten and Machiavelli as early as November 1503. The council wrote that "the Venetians carry on with a campaign which is leading them to the monarchy of Italy": Machiavelli, in Rome, replied that "one finds here a universal hatred of them . . . and to sum up, one draws the conclusion that the campaign of the Venetians against Faenza will either throw open to them the whole of Italy, or lead to their ruin" (quoted from Rubinstein). Guicciardini, writing after the Treaty of Cambrai in his *Historie* (p. 405), said that "there followed throughout all *Italie*, and against Thitalians themselves, a miserable trayne of many calamities and cruell accidents, infinite murders, sackings, destruction and spoyles of cities, . . . they may be seene to take their beginning of the too rashe and insolent manner of proceeding of the Venetians".

95. Norwich, *Venice*, p. 396, describes the impact of this explosion on the Venetian public consciousness. Of course, it would be a drastic financial disaster, as well. Braudel, *Capitalism*, p. 292, shows that, later in the century, the value of the gunpowder alone in the Arsenale was more than the total annual income of the city itself.

96. Venice had successfully survived a papal interdict in 1483 and seen it lifted within two years. This time, however, the pope was of a different temperament, and the forces marshalled against Venice were, if anything, more powerful.

97. Sanudo, *Diarii*, entry for this date. In a similar case, Agee, *Gardano*, p. 22, draws attention to the slump in production from Gardano's press during 1606 and suggests that the interdict by Pope Paul V of that year was a possible reason.

98. For a valuable discussion of the mood of Venice at this time, see Gilbert, "Venice". As Gilbert shows, the Venetian feeling was that the troubles were a divine punishment for corruption among the rulers, and other writers naturally had a similar viewpoint: Guicciardini's view is given above (fn.94), and Landucci, apostrophizing Venice, wrote: "Did you not understand that you were acting unconscientiously [*sic*] to attack those who had never injured you, and to take away cities from the Holy Father"; and that "this is the consequence of sin, and of acting against one's conscience, and of not fearing God" (Landucci, *Florentine*, pp. 231–32).

99. Gilbert, "Venice", points out the great decline in economic activity. He remarks that the Venetian government was reduced to offering special tax exemptions to anyone who was willing to rent a shop, at the same time that shop rents were being set lower (p. 283); and he draws attention to the new law whereby all foreigners (among whom Petrucci would have been numbered) were required to pay a new tax equivalent to 50 percent of the rent of all their properties (p. 284). Finlay, *Politics*, pp. 165–81, gives a detailed picture of the financial straits to which Venice was reduced; he points out (p. 167) that the *Fondaco dei Tedeschi* was closed in 1509.

100. Lowry, *World*, pp. 110 and 159.

101. The suggestion has been made at least once before, though it has never previously been discussed in any detail. See Vernarecci, *Fossombrone*, p. 207.

102. Norwich, *Venice*, p. 412.

103. Brown, *Venetian*, p. 97.

104. Campana, "Brentà"; Rhodes, "Zanchi"; Norton, *Italian*, pp. 158–59; and the data supplied in Isaac, *Italy* and in Johnson and Scholderer, *Short-Title Catalogue*. Zanchis was in

Mantua by 1512 and perhaps sooner, and Vercelli was publishing in the Marche, at Ancona, by late 1513. In addition, Bernardus de Vitalibus was in Rome from 1508. At the same time, printers and publishers who remained in Venice were much less active in the years following the end of 1508. Bindoni, de Bonelli, Paganino de Paganinis, Pencio, Rusconi, and the heirs of Ottaviano Scotto seem to have done little, and both Hamman and Locatelli apparently stopped work for good in 1509.

Despite the famed liberality of Venice to foreigners and Jews, it is notable that as important and Hebrew-oriented a printer as Soncino preferred to pursue his successful career in the Papal States (cf. Manzoni, "Annali"), even though the political and religious atmosphere in the Duchy of Urbino and surrounding areas was certainly less free than that in the Serene Republic.

105. Perhaps significantly in this context, the interdict was lifted and Venice absolved, on 24 February 1510, so that this motive, at least, would not have applied as a reason for Petrucci to move later, during 1511, as has been suggested.

The after-effects of the Interdict and the war do not appear to have been long lasting. While many printers did continue to print throughout this period, some with a lessened output, others began work again, or picked up their level of production within a few years: Francfordia and de Soardis in 1511, Aldus Manutius, Arrivabene, and Rusconi in 1512 (the year the Armenian press published a few books), and Alexander de Paganinis and the heirs of Ottaviano Scotto in 1513.

106. Both Vernarecci, *Petrucci*, p. 125, and Sartori, *Petrucci*, p. 17 state that Petrucci returned to Fossombrone in the first half of 1511.

107. ANF, Rogito di Giovan Paolo Mascioli, Teca V, Prot.xvii, p. 7, transcribed in the appendix.

108. See ANF, Atti di Cristoforo Cartari, Teca II, Prot.xiii, f.547.

109. As I say, the papal interdict against Venice had been lifted in February 1510.

110. I-Bc, (I). P.59, bifolio [1].

111. The same observations are made in Jeppesen, *Frottola*, i, p. 32.

112. Vernarecci, *Petrucci*, pp. 119–21, citing Schmid. The idea is also repeated in Sartori, *Petrucci*, p. 17, and Barblan, "Aspetti", p. 62.

113. This was the press of Callierges, transferred from Venice. See Norton, *Italian*, p. 96.

114. Documentation for what follows here will be found in chapter 7.

115. To suggest that Petrucci had any experience of such work while in Venice changes the patterns of his work completely, turning him into a jobbing printer who also published music under his own name. It also increases the size of his shop (the number of his employees and presses), without revealing any considerable body of editions that could be assigned to him rather than to other known printers. It is true that a history of experience with printing scholarly or classical texts in Venice before his return to Fossombrone might justify the tradition that he was recalled to Venice in 1536, specifically to assist in the preparation of classical editions. However, the further such a line of argument is taken, the more important it is that a body of editions from the first decade of the century be found and attributed to his press. Such a corpus does not seem to exist, nor, in my view, was he the man to print it.

116. See Clough, "Castiglione"; La Rocca, "Storia". It is quite probable that Petrucci decided to print this book because he already had a supply of paper in hand, left over from his printing of the *Paulina*.

117. Antico had certainly printed one book (the *Canzoni nove* of 1510) before the grant of Petrucci's privilege, and perhaps one other: it seems likely that the first edition of the second book of Canzoni appeared before October 1513, for the third book carries a copy of Antico's own privilege of 3 October. The standard work on Antico remains Chapman, *Antico*, which needs to be supplemented by a number of short articles and reviews, in particular, Miller, "Antico"; Picker, "Anthologies (1977)"; Picker *Motet*; with my review of the last. For comments on Petrucci's relationship to Antico, see Picker, "Anthologies (1981)", and Luisi, *Secondo*.

Sherr, "Relationship", suggests that Petrucci made a visit to Rome in 1513, in connection with his application for this privilege. This is highly probable; however, the assumption, implied by Sherr, and hinted at in Sherr, *Corona I*, pp. xiv–xv, that this stimulated Petrucci to print the first book of the *Motetti de la Corona*, seems to me difficult to sustain. The privilege is likely to have been sought because Petrucci had already decided to print more music. He might have planned to look for the music, while in Rome, or he might have been responding in part to the enthusiasm for the music newly heard by Paulus de Middelburgh at the council. However, the title itself demands a different conclusion, which will be addressed later.

118. The petition is recorded in ASV, Collegio, Notatorio, Registro XVII (1512–1514/5), f.78(80)r, and is transcribed in chapter 20. Sorbelli, "Mago", p. 119, maintained that Ungaro was employed in Aldo Manuzio's typefoundry, alongside Griffo.

119. These documents can be found in the ASV, Collegio, Notatorio, Reg.XVII, ff.49v (where the original grant is copied out anew) and 50r (the extension).

120. Duggan, *Italian*, p. 135, suggests that Ungaro may have been dead by the time of Petrucci's petition in 1514. This, coupled with Duggan's argument that Ungaro was closely connected with Petrucci's typeface from the beginning, provides the best explanation for the timing of Petrucci's later privilege application.

121. This concern can hardly have extended to the first two books of Josquin's masses, both of which would be reprinted during the next two years, and then again later; nor, probably, did it apply to the volume of Ghiselin's works, which also saw an edition in Fossombrone.

122. See Lockwood, "Jean Mouton", and the amplifications in Lockwood, "Ferrara", passim.

123. It seems clear that Fenlon and Haar, in *Italian*, underestimate the strength of Roman interest in the new poetic and musical forms. There are elements in some of the earliest sources suggesting that they were actually written in Rome, or represent a Roman interest in the music. At the same time, the easiest explanation of the existence of the strange printed editions of the 1520s is that they were products of a local interest in various genres, among which the madrigal is certainly to be found.

124. On 2 November 1515, Petrucci and others were reimbursed for the expenses for this last visit to Urbino, as representatives of the city. See Vernarecci, *Fossombrone*, p. 159.

125. Although there are a few Venetian titles that seem to comprise two editions carrying the same date, they represent a different phenomenon. The distinct copies of such titles are usually made up of a mix of sheets from the different printings: if the final sheet (the sheet carrying the colophon, and therefore the date) of the Bassus partbook of the various copies comes from the same printing, it will naturally have the same date. Thus it may seem that two printings carry the same date, and that one of them is erroneously or deceitfully dated, when in fact there is no evidence of what date might have been entered in the later printing.

126. Vernarecci, *Petrucci*, p. 140.

127. Gesner, *Pandectae*, VII, under the rubric *Titulus IIII. De cantionibus ecclesiasticis*. See Bernstein, "Gesner", No.130.

128. See Lockwood, "A View".

129. *RISM* numbers J667 and J674, respectively.

130. Noble, "Petrucci". Even Vernarecci doubted Schmid's testimony: see Vernarecci, *Petrucci*, p. 149, fn.

131. The evidence is outlined in Gialdroni and Ziino, "New Light", p. 509, drawing on the research of Franco Mariani.

132. Landucci, *Florentine*, p. 245, has a most circumstantial account of the event.

133. It does not appear that Leo sought the duchy for its income and wealth. Under Clement VII, a planned budget for the papal exchequer for 1525 (by which time Urbino was a vicariate of the church) showed that the former duchy was expected to produce only 1,300 ducats, out of a projected income of 432,000 ducats, while Perugia was required to yield 5,300 ducats. See Partner, "Budget", p. 275.

134. Guicciardini, *Historie*, p. 748. The original reads "la qual città [Fossombrone] battuta dalle artiglierie, fu il terzo giorno aspugnata e saccheggiata" (Guicciardini, *Istoria*, bk.13, vol.3).

135. Vernarecci, *Petrucci*, p. 160.

136. While the details of this mission and Petrucci's reimbursement are given in Vernarecci, *Petrucci*, pp. 164–65, all that survives in the Fossombrone archives held in the Biblioteca Passionei are two references in the book of Atti del Consiglio Municipale, 1520, on folio 4r. The ap-

pointment of "Dominum octavium petrutium et xprofanus canturin" as "oratores ad pontificum" was made at a council meeting of 17 January 1520. On 3 October of the same year, the appointment of Petrucci was extended, with that of a Baptista Sodimeri.

137. See Mariani, *Ottaviano*, pp. 1–9. Gialdroni and Ziino, forthcoming. These writers suggest that Petrucci leased the land at Aqua Santa primarily because it was adjacent to his own property, and not because it had a paper mill. The evidence they advance, however, argues that a mill was active in the early sixteenth century, although not that Petrucci actually operated it. But it is probably more than coincidence that Petrucci was invited to Sora in 1519 specifically to construct a paper mill. I also note that the papers used in his books changed during 1515, and that they deteriorate rapidly after 1519 (when he had moved to Sora). The invitation argues that he was at least known to be interested in papermaking, while the change in papers during the decade suggests that some may have come from a local mill, perhaps that at Aqua Santa. Given these details, it seems to me more than plausible that Petrucci did eventually take a part in the operation of the paper mill at Aqua Santa.

138. If it had been merely that Petrucci stopped printing in early 1517, after the hidden editions, one might be able to argue that the only reason for his inactivity was the sack of Fossombrone and the consequent damage to his property. However, we still have to explain the coincidence of the date that he next *does* assign to a new book, namely the date in 1519 that follows Lorenzo's death. And we also have to enquire why Petrucci should have decided not to put the correct dates on his new printings, in distinction to his practice in Venice. Finally, there is the curious form, which I am about to discuss, of the colophon for the *Parabola Christi* of Paulus. For these reasons, I am convinced that a motive for the change, occurring in mid-1516, has to be found outside the purely coincidental timing of the destruction of his city.

139. There is the possible implication that Petrucci had temporarily moved his press out of Fossombrone, installing it in a city (or even village) that was less liable to be attacked. This could be taken to explain not only this colophon but also the absence of true dates on other titles. However, the press probably *was* in Fossombrone when the city was sacked, for there is a real gap after the hidden reprints and before the 1519 editions—a gap that might be necessary if a new press had to be set up.

140. The manuscript survives in the Vatican Library, as Vat.lat.4416. Full details of the whole affair are given in chapter 7.

141. Vernarecci, *Petrucci*, p. 160. See also Sherr, "Relationship".

142. Jeppesen made the observation, in *Italienische*, that the title page of Antico's *Frottole intabulate* of 1517 probably represents a deliberate insult to Petrucci. The monkey squatting on a harpsichord and playing a lute represents Petrucci, here accompanied by a lady singer; this image refers to the fact that Petrucci's only editions of instrumental music were for lute (with or without voice), despite his privilege, whereas Antico, seated at the harpsichord that bears the Medici device, had published for keyboard. The same point has been made more recently in Minamino, "Monkey". I have used this and other evidence to draw a picture of Antico's personality, in a number of references elsewhere.

143. This created problems for the facsimile produced by Vivarelli & Gulla, cited here as Petrucci, *Missarum*. Many pages have been touched up, involving redrawing stave lines and notes, and occasionally producing new readings.

144. "Francisco Maria Feltrio della Rovere, Duke of Urbino and Sora, Lord of Pesaro, etc." The title of Sora was inherited, not from the former Dukes of Urbino, the Montefeltro, but from the duke's father, Giovanni della Rovere, who had been Prefect of Rome and Lord of Sinigaglia, as well as brother to Pope Julius II.

145. Mariani, "Petrucci", pp. 12 and 20–21. The following details are taken from this article; Gialdroni and Ziino, "New Light"; and Gialdroni and Ziino, forthcoming. These authors see some contradiction between the two documents, for the earlier one regards Petrucci as an expert able to build a papermaker's premises, "construere edificium carterie", and only invited to the city for that purpose.

146. The other edition I have previously dated in 1520 survives in fragmentary state in the Fossombrone Biblioteca Passionei. I believed it to have been printed this early, on the basis of typographical evidence, both in the surviving fragment and in other books. See "Some New".

A new dating in the 1530s is very satisfactory from a musical point of view, though it raises bibliographical issues that are not fully resolved, particularly when it is compared with Petrucci's other extant work from that decade.

147. Gialdroni and Ziino, "New Light". This article gives further details of Bartolomeo Egnatio's life, and it is notable that there is ample evidence of his presence in Fossombrone from 1533, though none for earlier years, despite the presence of his brother Girolamo. This is one of two reasons for suggesting that he was not the colleague who took Petrucci's materials to Rome. The other reason will be discussed later.

148. Vernarecci, *Petrucci*, p. 217.

149. These are cited in Vernarecci, *Petrucci*, and in Gialdroni and Ziino. This latter article ("New Light") places a more balanced interpretation on the documents, for it is able to take account of the new discoveries concerning both Fossombrone and Sora.

150. These positions are announced in Vernarecci, *Petrucci*, p. 217.

151. This treatise is now preserved at I-Bc, B 57. It has been discussed most recently and most comprehensively in Haar, "Lessons".

152. Translation from Haar, "Lessons", p. 57. Also see Gialdroni and Ziino, "New Light", p. 509.

153. The document in which he authorizes Pietrantonio detto Mazone to recover the "matrices licterarum" from various people, in particular "domino Petro Ambrosii librarii" of Naples, is discussed in Gialdroni and Ziino, "New Light"; and in Gialdroni and Ziino, forthcoming. Ascarelli and Menato, *Tipografia*, p. 317, suggest that the printer Pietro Matteo Tesori, who was active at Orvieto from 1538 to 1542, came from Petrucci's Officina. They point out, however, that he was already a *libraio* in Orvieto in 1533, so that a connection with Petrucci's later printing career seems unlikely.

154. This is discussed in Vernarecci, *Petrucci*, pp. 162–63; a better interpretation, resulting from the discovery of other documents, is in Gialdroni and Ziino, forthcoming.

155. The books are the lost volume of Magnificats, *Laude II* and *Frottole XI*, and the books of Obrecht's masses, respectively. For details, see Chapman, "Columbus", and the relevant entries in the following bibliography.

156. See Gialdroni and Ziino, forthcoming, basing their arguments on documents presented in Mariani *Petrucci*. In particular, they cite a sale of property in Sora on 5 January 1535, although there are other later similar sales.

157. Gialdroni and Ziino, forthcoming.

158. Vernarecci, *Petrucci*, p. 218. This claim is still repeated in the literature, for example, in Alberati, "Musica"; Ascarelli and Menato, *Tipografia*, p. 347; and Gallico, "Laboratorio", p. 194.

159. We have always to allow for the possibility that Petrucci did actually publish the edition of Calvo's translation of Hippocrates, and the dubious edition of Virgil, discussed above.

160. Casali, *Annali*; Quondam, "Giardino".

161. Amiani, *Memorie*, ii, p. 25.

162. *RISM* 1536[11], Brown, *Instrumental*, 1536[3], Casali, *Annali*, No.3.

163. This translation is from Ness, *Herwart*, p. 347. Alberati, "Musica", p. 181, assumes that Marcolini sought his privilege "probabilmente con l'assenso dello stesso Petrucci di cui appare il diretto successore".

164. *RISM* [ca.1520][7].

165. There is no reason to believe that Italian lutenists did not at least know of the existence of the German editions. Italian interest in German lutenists and lute technique is well documented for the early years of the sixteenth century. See, for example, Lockwood, *Ferrara*; Ness, *Herwart*; and Lockwood, "Pietrobono". On the other hand, it would appear that Marcolini, at least, did not know of Attaingnant's editions of lute music, for he makes no mention of the possibility of typeset tabulature.

166. *RISM* V1224=1104, printed in 1536. The volume was reissued in 1540 (*RISM* V1225=1105). Willaert, *Intavolatura* is a facsimile of the first edition. See Boorman, "Some Nonconflicting". Joshua Rifkin has suggested to me that it is unlikely that the "Messer Adriano" of the title of this edition could be Willaert, for the intabulations are simple and mechanical. Yet,

I think it entirely in keeping with the character of Antico that he should manage to have the name of a leading musician displayed prominently on his title page.

167. The only extant copy is at A-Wn, S A 76.D.54. The music is edited in Francesco da Milano, *Lute Music*, and Francesco da Milano, *Opere*. An inventory appears in Brown, *Instrumental*, at 1536₃. The other relevant volume is that published by Casteliono in Milan in 1536.

168. Francesco da Milano, *Lute Music*, p. 12. The copy is at A-Wn, S A 78.C.28.

169. Quondam, "Giardino", p. 87, believes that Marcolini published more musical volumes than those listed here, even with the now-lost *Musicain canto figurato*. This last, cited in Quondam's list as number 26, may have been a treatise.

170. Agee, "Filippo", which cites earlier literature.

171. Boorman, "Raphael".

172. Three madrigals that can be attributed to Festa appeared in *RISM* 153416~1220, the second book of four-voiced madrigals attributed to Verdelot. For details on the attribution of one of these works, see Boorman, "Non-conflicting".

173. See my review of Picker, "Motet".

174. *RISM* [ca.1537]⁶=A1368, dated 1539. For details of this edition and of the problems surrounding it and Gardano's editions, see Bridges, *Publishing*; and Lewis, *Gardano*, p. 209.

175. *RISM* W1108, dated 1539. Bernstein, *Music*, p. 41, sees the possible relationship between Antico and Ottaviano Scotto either as an equal partnership, or as Antico being hired by Ottaviano to prepare specific volumes. I doubt both of these suggestions: not only did Antico appear to be seizing opportunities in exactly the manner he had followed in the 1510s, he also had his name entered on the publications in a specific manner.

176. It is notable that the page size, and therefore the size of the woodblocks, in this volume is quite different from that of earlier books prepared by Antico. It seems that he tried consciously to model the layout and appearance on the recently successful books by Gardano, paralleling the reason for the choice of repertoire.

177. Whomever Festa had in mind, or Strozzi's agent proposed, the printer appears to have rejected the offer. Festa seems to have started publishing in Rome in 1538 (see Haar, "Libro"). He also took out a privilege in Venice, to protect him "ch'el possi far stampar le sue opere di musica", which might confirm that he had not found a printer who would do the work for him. Marcolini had abandoned music, and Antico was still turning out new editions with Scotto in 1538, but Festa was apparently not able to print his music in Venice. It may be more likely that the critical clause in the privilege is the one that forbade anyone else selling editions of his music, so that his own edition could be imported into the Veneto. See Agee, *Privilege*, pp. 76–78 and 208–209 (transcription of the document); Lewis, *Gardano*, p. 26.

178. Gialdroni and Ziino, "New Light", pp. 505–506. To the biography there, we can add that Egnatio was in Rome during 1532; he is mentioned in the colophon of Calvo's *Antiquae urbis Romae cum regionibus Simulacrum*, published in Rome in 1532. See chapter 7.

179. I think we have to take issue with the assertion by Gialdroni and Ziino ("New Light", p. 514) that "what we do know is that the planned collection of the *Motteti dal fiore* and the one with madrigals and villottas were never completed and put on the market". Apart from the implausibility of two incomplete editions, especially given the different typographical materials of the two (and the consequent probability that some time elapsed between them), we are not justified in asserting that the fragmentary survival of any book implies that the edition was not completed or put on sale. I accept, rather, that the print-run may have been a small one, and that the much more powerful activities of Scotto and Gardano (especially in distributing their editions) would have made Petrucci's editions less attractive to middlemen, distributors, or bookshops.

180. This date is given in, for example, Ascarelli and Menato, *Tipografia*, p. 204.

181. Once again, I am grateful to Maria Teresa Gialdroni and Agostino Ziino for sending me notice of this document, to be published in their forthcoming study.

182. The document, in Mariani, *Ottaviano*, pp. 24–25, is discussed in the forthcoming study by Gialdroni and Ziino.

Chapter Two

PETRUCCI'S PRIVILEGES

etrucci applied to the Venetian Signoria in 1498 for a privilege to protect his right to print music. The responsible members of the council approved the petition on 25 May of that year.[1] In his application (transcribed in chapter 20), Petrucci began by praising the city of Venice for the manner in which it supported new inventions, to the greater glory of the city, and thereby encouraged people to explore new ideas. He then pointed out that his own invention had cost him much labour and time ("Cum molte sue spexe, et vigilantissima cura"), and at least attempted to imply what is explicitly stated in the next clauses, that he had discovered what many others had sought long and unsuccessfully: "ha trovado quello, che molti non solo in Italia, ma etiam diode fuora de Italia za longamente indarno hanno investigato". The discovery was of a convenient way to print polyphony: "stampar commodissamente Canto figurado".

This announcement was followed by what must be seen as a piece of deliberate campaigning: Petrucci stated that the invention of this method would also make it much easier to print chant, an excellent thing for the Christian religion, and very necessary: "Et per consequens molto piu facilmente Canto fermo: cossa precipue a la Religione Christiana de grande ornamento et maxime necessaria". This seems a little ingenuous, for there had been over fifteen years of successful liturgical music printing in Venice, and Petrucci's method was comparable with that employed by the printers involved.[2] Perhaps, not being able to point to any direct benefits for the Venetian state or economy, he felt it necessary to produce some other form of advantage, and chose one, the benefit to the Christian religion, that might be expected to appeal to the moral sense of the city's rulers.

Indeed, this approach was not unusual. When Democrito Terracina petitioned on 15 July 1498 (less than eight weeks after Petrucci's successful petition) for a privilege for twenty years "da far stampar alcune opere in lingua arabica, morescha, suriana, Armenicha, Indiana et barbarescha",[3] he added a similar series of clauses: useful for the Christian community for elevating the faith, increasing knowledge of science and also of medicine, to preserve the health of mind and body of the many faithful Christians who use those languages: "in utilita de la republica christiana: et exaltation de la fede et augumento de la scientia naturale et ancor de la medicina per conseruation de la salute de le anime et corpe de molti et infiniti fidel christiani che usono le soprascripte lengue". The references to natural sciences and medicine are of course a reflection of the known strength of Arabic writings in those fields; in that sense, they correspond to Petrucci's reference to chant.

It is notable, that Petrucci gave no details of the nature of his invention; there is no evidence that it was anything more than an idea, one potentially of interest but as yet unproven. I believe that Petrucci probably had not made any sort of test, for the time lag between the grant of the privilege and the appearance of the first volume is a rather long one. It was, however, normal for the privilege itself to give no details when a discovery or invention was to be protected. I shall discuss this further below.

To some extent, all the preceding material had been preamble. An invention had been mentioned, it is true, but that is all. Petrucci then turned to the core of the application, the specific details of his request. Again he began with a short phrase of flattery: "supplicando . . . per solita sua clementia et benignita se degni concederli de gratia". This phrase was clearly deemed sufficient to remind the members of the college of their duties as supporters of innovation and trade within the republic.

Petrucci then requested the following protections:

1. that no one else within the Venetian empire should be able to print polyphony or tabulature for organ or lute, for a period of twenty years;
2. that no one should be able to import or sell these repertoires (or act as an agent for such activity) for the same period.

Petrucci followed these requests by offering suggestions for the penalties for infractions:

1. that the offending books should be confiscated;
2. that the culprit should pay a fine of ten ducats for each work.

Often it is not clear whether the word "work"—"opera" in the original—refers to a single copy or a single title.[4] However the penalties may have been intended to be assessed, the destinations for the fines collected are as usual specified. In this case, one-half was to go to the Ospedale di Sant'Antonio, and the other to the Monte Nuovo. The choice of these two institutions was typical, in that most seekers after privileges arranged for any fines to go to one or more of the charitable foundations—often Ospedali—administered or overseen by the Venetian state. The choice may have been more acute in that both destinations were relatively new on the Venetian scene, and both needed funds rather desperately.

The Monte Nuovo, founded in 1482 as a loan fund for the Venetian government, seemed to have had difficulty in paying its dividends.[5] The Ospedale di Sant'Antonio was also a new institution. Although founded in 1476, it was apparently still in construction in 1497, according to the Milanese ambassador. It was to be dedicated to ageing mariners or servants of the republic, rather than acting as a general almshouse.[6] Petrucci's choice of these two institutions, while not outside the general pattern, suggests an additional attempt at ensuring a favourable reception for his petition.[7] However that may be, Petrucci's application was approved, over the names of four members of the Collegio.

There are three aspects of this application and grant that need to be considered in some detail: two, to which I shall turn a little later, concern the extent to which the supplication was or was not out of the ordinary, in the light of other applications made to the Venetian Senate at the time; and the manner in which Petrucci identifies himself. The other point is the extent to which there may actually have been something new in the methods discovered by Petrucci. While much of the technique of his operation will be discussed in chapter 3, some aspects can be addressed here.

It is hard to see where there might have been any true invention in what Petrucci was announcing. He claimed to have found a way whereby music printing could be undertaken "commodissamente" (without excessive difficulty) and implied that there were aspects of printing polyphony that would have been specifically new and difficult of resolution. The most obvious place to look for this difficulty lies in the (evident) necessity for more than one impression, engendered by the manner in which music and staves overlapped. There are two factors here, neither of which should have been seen as a problem for Venetian printers of the time: one is the need to print in more than one impression—selecting the items to be printed at each run, and setting up the type so that the elements fit together; the other is the need for exact alignment, or register, when printing the second and third runs. In fact, there was a great deal of two-impression printing in Venice; the city, with its publishers of liturgical music books, was one of the most important centres for the practice. In such books, two colours were the norm, following scribal patterns of rubrication. In addition, when the books contained music, the notes and the staves were again printed at different impressions, often in different colours, and had to be aligned fairly precisely. Venice must, as a result, have contained a number of typesetters competent in setting type for two impressions, and pressmen capable of registering them accurately.[8]

The rest of the technique followed by Petrucci also seems to have been normal. I shall argue in the next chapter that there were special features, in the skeleton formes, for example: but none of these was likely to have been unknown to Petrucci's contemporaries. Thus, I do not believe that Petrucci had discovered a new technique in the craft of printing.

That leaves only two areas available for investigation: one concerns the actual materials used, in particular, the type; and the other involves the division of labour between the various impressions. The type seems the more obvious prospect. There was apparently nothing unusual about the press, while the patterns of paper and ink use (described in chapter 3) seem orthodox. Petrucci's music type had specific characteristics, most found elsewhere in printing, but rare in sorts cast for chant. First is the fact, to be discussed in detail, that many of the music sorts were kerned. There was rarely any reason for music sorts used in chant volumes to be kerned: the whole of the character could almost always lie on the body of the sort.[9] But Petrucci's type achieves much of its elegant effect because it can be spaced closer to the text and placed precisely. This is directly a product of the kerning, as much as it is of the strongly vertical character of the font. Kerning, however, was not a new phenomenon; other sorts, outside music, were kerned. Indeed, this seems to have been the specific characteristic that marked off Aldus's principal Greek font.[10] Petrucci and his type designer adapted the idea to musical characters and (as a result) were able to make more elegant sorts.

This elegance is also a product of the second most obvious feature of the font, the slim note-tails and the fine cutting of many features, in clefs, for instance. This fine work was akin to the new, finer serifs that were appearing on many roman fonts, or to the finely detailed elements in Aldus's Greek font. Morison has made the point that Venetian fonts of roman type-faces had previously been solid, with horizontal, unbracketed, and often blunt-ended serifs,[11] and this weighty appearance is also characteristic of earlier chant fonts. It is thought that the newly emerging fine and tapered serifs and thinner lines were made possible as a direct result of the addition of antimony to the typemetal. This would have made both the punches and the type itself harder and allowed for more delicate cutting without any loss of durability. Francesco Griffo was perhaps the first to explore the possibility, for it is in his faces designed for Aldus (and perhaps cast by Jacomo Ungaro) that the new fine work first appears. If that is so, then Petrucci, or his craftsmen, were taking advantage of a possibility that had not previously been available. This implies the presence of a highly skilled typecaster, just as the design of the sorts implies a designer of the first quality.[12]

The second area of investigation mentioned above—the division of labour between impressions—may also be relevant. Liturgical music was printed in two colours; the division of the material required that the staves (printed in red) were run off at a different impression from the notes. For most liturgical books, the notes could be printed with the text at the same (black) impression.[13] Perhaps this was seen as difficult for polyphony: the tails of standard note shapes at the end of the fifteenth century, especially while northern Italians were retaining a more Gothic shape, might well have encroached on the area of the text. As a result, a mind-set derived from liturgical printing, in which all the "real" content—notes and text—could be printed at one pull, might well have seen polyphony as raising technical difficulties.

Petrucci's "invention" may therefore consist of nothing more than realizing that the contents of different impressions were not fixed, but could be re-ordered, so that different elements were combined together. The move to separate text and notes, placing them in different impressions, might have been the result of a single idea, rather than any logical process. This suggestion has support from two small features: the initial letters, often printed with the staves in liturgical books, were now to be printed with the music; and when Petrucci does turn from three to two impressions, the text is usually printed with the staves, and not with the music. The latter seems to us necessary. There are many places where the tail of a *minima* or smaller value encroaches on the space allotted to the text, or even collides with a letter. Petrucci's "invention" may have lain in seeing how to avoid that problem, without drastically shortening the tails and losing the elegance of his typeface.

Whichever of these hypotheses is true—and to some extent they interlock, for the adoption of the changed hierarchy of impressions becomes necessary once the new type-metal allows long and elegant note tails to be retained from manuscript styles—it is difficult to regard either as a real discovery or invention. Petrucci seems to have done much as some other petitioners had done: take a marginally new idea, and by seeking protection for that, gain protection for something larger—in his case, a whole repertoire. In this respect, Petrucci's application may not have been very unusual. But it is necessary to examine other aspects of the pattern of privileges, to ensure that no other element was out of the ordinary and therefore might throw light on the beginnings of music printing.

The patterns by which printers, including music printers, acquired privileges during much of the sixteenth century have been discussed in detail by Richard Agee,[14] and many of the relevant documents published by him or elsewhere.[15] During the period when Petrucci was printing, however, the situation appears to have been somewhat different.[16] For one thing, there is no trace of any legislation on the part of the Venetian authorities, attempting to control the press or the issue of privileges, before the year 1517. The new legislation of that year ruled that only the Senate could issue privileges for printing. In earlier years, several bodies within the Venetian government had been able to issue privileges, and a majority of the surviving grants are to be found in the acts of the Collegio, apparently having been awarded by the ducal councillors: the grant of Petrucci's privilege of 1498 is an example. Occasional references to printing can be found elsewhere, for example, in the registers of the Consilio de'Dieci. As the years pass, and especially after the legislation of 1517, such privileges appear in the acts of the Senato (Terra).

The earlier privileges, especially those from the years 1490–1500, when Petrucci was preparing to start printing music, are of several principal types: those for specific texts, those for ranges of texts or for books in specific languages, and those for technical improvements or processes. Although Petrucci's application is overtly for a specific repertoire, each of these three groups of privileges throws light on the manner in which his was intended to be useful to him.[17]

There is a wealth of privilege grants to printers and authors for the years 1490–94, perhaps six or seven awards each year. However, in 1495 there is a marked decline in the number of grants; this decline might seem fortuitous, the result of a random pattern, were it not for the presence of two applications in early 1496 that make special cases for being given a privilege—problems of poverty.[18] Both suggest that the administration had become reluctant to grant privileges, and indeed immediately after they are approved the tempo increases again. The next four years see some fifty applications recorded in the registers.

Many of these privileges were granted for specific texts. Indeed, such applications had also constituted the majority of the earlier requests, those from before 1495. But the pattern continued in the following years, and the applications included privileges for named classical texts, for texts with specific commentaries, for legal, medical, philosophical, and similar works. On 23 July 1500, Aldus Manutius acquired a privilege for the works of St. Catherine of Siena, being "circa cinquanta quaterni".[19] Most of the others offer no such detail:[20] they cite the work concerned and seek an exclusive right, usually for a period of ten years. In 1499, for example, Marco Firmano and Zuanpiero Valla were given a privilege for Saraceno's commentary on Plautus, while Andrea Torresano gained one for "Egidio Romano in philosophia".[21] Other petitioners mention a group of works in a single application; they are presumably doing no more than saving themselves the burden, and no doubt the costs, of making several applications.

Not all such applications were for simple verbal texts. Later, in an application dated 20 April 1514, "Zuan da Brexa depentor", who had "fatto uno desegno et quello fatto intagliar in legno"—made a picture and cut it in wood—sought a privilege for the work, which is the story of the Emperor Trajan: "ditta sua opera laquel é, la historia de Traiano Imperator". The artist sought and gained a privilege for ten years, for the design itself, and for the act of printing it.[22] This privilege is found two folios before the second of Petrucci, also made in 1514. These applications are followed, on 9 February 1514/1515, by a petition from Bernardino Benalio, for a number of texts, coupled with historical pictures: "molte Belle ijstorie denote çioe la submersione de pharaone[,] la hijstoria di susanna, la hijstoria del sacrifitio de abraham et altre hijstorie noue che non sono mai piu sta stampate", for which he also received a privilege for ten years.[23]

Similar privileges were occasionally sought by authors, translators, or commentators. The exact purpose of this kind of application is not clear, but it would seem that the writer was trying to protect his investment and negotiate a better publishing contract for himself. For example, on 28 November 1492, Raphael Regius gained a ten-year privilege for his commentary on Quintilian, which was printed by Locatellus and published by Scotto.[24] (Despite this, another commentary, the work of Lorenzo Valla and others, appeared from the press of Pasquali in 1494. But Regius's commentary was reprinted in 1506, so he seems not to have suffered from this violation of his rights.) Similarly, in late 1495, Francesco Cataneo was awarded a privilege for his book on architecture, and, in 1496, Bernardin de Landriano for his on law.[25] The latter admitted his short residence of five years in Venice, as Lecturer in Law: "havendo lui gia per il tempo de'anni cinque passati in questa vostra inclita Citade Venexia invigilato"; but he added that he had suffered much fatigue in glossing and adding notes to many readings in civil and canon law, for general use: "sostenuto gran fatiche in apostillare & far additione a molte lecture Civile e Canonice, si per la publica utilitade". He gained the normal ten years' protection. In 1496/7, "Andrea mario bressan professor de studij de gramatica in Venetia" gained a similar privilege for his works.[26]

A second category of applications comprises those made by printers seeking to cover complete repertoires or classes of texts; there were several for printing in Greek. The first, and perhaps the best known of all these petitions, was that of Aldus in 1495/6, but it was soon followed by others, beginning with "Gabriele da brasichella et compagni" in 1498.[27] However, there are other similar supplications: for example, the one (already mentioned) by Democrito Terracina for printing in eastern languages. Some liturgical examples are listed below.

This range of examples indicates that printers could gain privileges if they were handling some peculiarly esoteric or difficult repertoire or group of languages. In this respect, the Venetian authorities seem to have recognised that Venice was the best place to print such texts, and, no doubt also, that they could expect steady taxes from a monopoly. It is this first basis on which we need to regard the grant of a privilege to Petrucci, rather than any special regard for music on the part of the Collegio or Senato of the city.

For good practical reasons, these applications made claim to technical innovations, and, in the case of Aldus's petition for protection for his Greek font, this appears to have been true: Aldus, or his type designer (Griffo), seems to have prepared a font in which the breathings of Greek texts could be mounted on kerned sorts. Whether this was also the basis of his new cursive sorts or not, he offered similar grounds for his application for protection for his cursive and *cancellaresca* fonts.[28]

These privileges are matched by some not related to printing, but reflecting a similar technical concern: exactly two weeks before Aldus's privilege of March 1501, a group of Germans received a similar one for their work in amber and gold, although here protection was given for twenty years.[29] Similarly, in 1536, Jo. Francesco Negro sought a privilege for a method of operating machinery using water mills. Unusually, this was granted for the life of the petitioner and his heirs, up to twenty-five years, with the condition that they were not to damage the city's canals.[30]

Such privileges confirm what the printers' petitions indicate, and what we have long known from the wording of many of the preambles to petitions, that the Venetian authorities were more than willing to grant privileges to protect technical innovation (or to give other benefits to those who discovered such), thereby making whatever provision they could to keep excellent craftsmen in the city.[31] This is the second basis on which we need to assess Petrucci's application.

Finally, as a third basis for measuring the implications of Petrucci's petition, we need to be aware of the normal form of such applications. Many begin as does Petrucci's, with a reference to the wisdom or magnanimity of the republic and its Senate, alongside a comment that the supplicant is a loyal member of the state, or at least a tax-paying contributor to its finances: "Serenissimo principii et excellentissimo Dominio Venetiarum humiliter supplica el fidel suo servitor et Citadin suo"; or "Serenissimo Principe et excelso Concilio volendo l'humile servidor di vostra sublimita"; or "Serenissimo Principe et Illustrissima Signoria. Sempre Vostra sublimita e stata et e larghissima donatrice delle gratie sue alli fidelissimi soi che con sincerita quella dimandano". Sentiments like these are not always present. Some petitions start straight in with the request, or with a statement of the position of the petitioner. Thus Torresano, in 1536, had a long record of achievement and could preface his request merely with the following clause: "I, Francesco d'Asola, with my father, have printed over many years an infinite number of books in this most excellent city" (Havendo Io francesco d'Asola gia molti anni con nostro padre fatto stampar infiniti libri in questa excellentissima Citta), although there is even here the adjectival compliment to Venice itself.

At the end of these sentences, or immediately (when they are not present), the business in hand is introduced. Petrucci turned to his "invention"; Torresano to the loss of books imported from France; Marcolini to the thirty years that had elapsed since Petrucci had printed music in Venice. It is here that the petitioner makes a token gesture (for it is seldom more) in the direction of the merits or utilities of the work or process in question. No doubt, in some instances the case was easier to make than in others; for new editions of liturgical books (the Psalter of St. Bernard in 1496, and see below), of editions or translations of the classics (Seneca in 1497, Ovid in 1498, Aristotle among others in 1499), or of books on medicine, philosophy, and law, the merits were probably immediately apparent to the Consilio or Senate. These officers would also have known that such books were normally large and expensive to produce, yet with a guaranteed market. A statement of the labour involved, the costs of printing, or the many years of "research", frequently found here, would resonate well.

The next point is usually the description of penalties for infractions, which again follows standard forms, involving confiscation of the offending copies, and a monetary penalty. The penalty is assessed either per book or per infraction, sometimes with a combination of the two. The proceeds were then to be divided between two or three recipients. One would often be the individual who had denounced the offender; another the official of the state who had made the confiscation of copies. One or more would be parts of the Venetian charitable system, Ospedale or Monte, for example. A final clause, not always present, merely repeats the wish of the petitioner that the republic allow the petition.

It should be evident from the above analysis that Petrucci's privilege is normal in almost every respect, corresponding to the general patterns of demands made of the Venetian authorities. First, it claimed a special ability to deal with an unique and difficult repertoire, using its own typographical symbols—music here being seen as no different from Greek, or "arabica, morescha . . ." or "barbarescha". Second, it claimed to involve some technical innovation, which should bring glory to the city, as much as it would bring deserved returns to its inventor. Third, the supplication conformed to the pattern of ordering the content, to be found in others, regardless of their subject.

There is no reason, as a result, to believe that Petrucci was seen in a special light, or that the Venetian government had any particular interest in music or its printing. Indeed, the opposite might be true: Petrucci's application was so routine, and its acceptance couched in such traditional terms, that it seems more likely that the Senate and other authorities did not contain any members especially interested in the subject.

There is one unusual and significant feature of the petition—the manner in which Petrucci identified himself. In the petition of 1498, he called himself "Octavian dei petruci da fosonbron habitator in questa inclyta Cita"; in 1514 he would be "Octaviano di petruci da fossombron presente supplicante Como a primo Inventor de stampar librj de canto figurato", taking the same position.[32] In each case, he avoided adherence to any profession and declared himself not to be a citizen. Both points are worthy of remark: printers were careful to identify their professional standing and their consequent qualification for a privilege: two and a half months before Petrucci's application, there is one from "Baptista et Silvestro di torti frateli stampadori de libri", and two weeks later Soardi calls himself "impressor diligentissimo de libri".[33] Later in the year, there is a petition from "Antonio Moreto da Bressa mercadante de libri".[34] For printers and *librai,* these descriptions were normal, and one or the other was almost always observed. In 1500 Amadeo Scotto called himself a "mercadente de libri", and in 1536 Michiel Tramezino was a "venditor de libri", thus making a clear distinction between themselves and the printers.[35]

Similarly, authors applying for protection for their own works claimed authorship, or declared their status as indicating their abilities. I have mentioned "Andrea mario bressan professor de studij de gramatica"; six months earlier, "Alexander de benedeti physico da Verona" had sought protection for his book.[36] In the same manner, in 1500 "Pre Marco Berto Marchian: al presente mansionario In sancto Zuane de Rialto" petitioned for his translation of "tuti li misterij de la santa messa".[37]

Those who were not citizens declared the fact: "Mathis de code da parma impressore de libri", "Philippus de pincijs mantuane stampator",[38] or the Antonio Moreto from Brescia mentioned above. In announcing his citizenship of Fossombrone, Petrucci was clearly following the normal procedure. In the matter of his right to claim privilege, though, he was more unusual. The lack of any statement of a profession implies that Petrucci was neither a printer nor a bookseller, that he had no standing in the printing and publishing trade at all. Since he adopted the same line in 1514, he apparently took no steps to gain professional standing as a printer, in Venice at least.

Not surprisingly, Petrucci made no mention of his musical business when he applied for admission to the guild of Cestieri; he called himself merely "octaviani Petrutij de fossimbruno".

How far these privileges were really respected by other printers we can hardly tell today. It is significant that certain texts for which privileges were sought and awarded did appear from other presses within the time limit, and also that some of the technical processes or repertorial fields that were to be protected were also adopted elsewhere before the privileges protecting them had lapsed.

In addition, there is fragmentary evidence in the documents of the Capi of the Consiglio de' Dieci: for example, on 31 March 1497 Guglielmo Fasolo sought an injunction against Lazar de Lazaro and Bernardino Benalio to prevent their printing texts they should not.[39] Then there is a similar petition, made in 1499, requesting that previous privileges be observed by other printers. The petition and the response appear twice in the same register, on 15 March and 3 April 1499, the second time with the addition of the supplicant's name, the same "antonij moreto de brixia" who apparently did not print on his own account.[40] (Several extant books are described as printed "per" Moreto, though none seem to correspond to one which was cited in a privilege. Presumably some other text, for which he had sponsored an edition, was also being printed elsewhere, thereby threatening his investment.)[41] The petition, the act of copying the response out a second time with the petitioner's name, its granting in very general terms, reminding all printers ("omnibus impressoribus librorum") that they are required to observe earlier privileges, and not break them, under pain of the specified penalties ("observare debeant antescriptam concessionem . . . et non andeant contrafacere sub pena specificata")—all these features suggest that there were many contraventions of the letter of the law, and that the Council (or perhaps merely some members who were influenced by the petitioner) wished to remedy the situation.

In fact, the market appears to have been fairly competitive. The pattern of many minor names entering the field and abandoning it after very few titles would suggest that printing (or at least publishing) was thought to present a lucrative opportunity, and that Venetian craftsmen were willing to set up shop. Which of these short-lived careers were of printers, men who had undertaken the investment of a full printing shop, and which were of publishers using other men to print for them is not always clear. In some cases, the evidence shows that the man was probably acting as a publisher, for the typefaces and initials of books signed by him can be traced to other presses.[42] In certain fields, however, there was room for competition, and an ambitious printer could be successful, as is clear merely from the number of printers active in Venice during the period from 1490 to 1510.

It seems probable that such printers or publishers would seek to include among their earliest volumes titles that could be expected to be successful.[43] This practical necessity might well have encouraged the use of the privilege system, even while it would also encourage actively breaking an existing privilege.

There were other privileges concerned with music printing. Although noted chant-books had been printed for years before Petrucci's first book, there were still some petitions for privileges that concern the printing of noted liturgy. These are of marginal interest in the present context, for the techniques involved in printing chant are scarcely different from those followed by Petrucci, and he himself referred to chant.[44] As I have suggested, almost all these applications fail to indicate on what technical or musical basis a privilege should be awarded, but stress the benefits to religion and the strengthening of the faith.

On 31 January 1496/7, Stagnino was awarded a privilege for ten years for "l'Antifonario e Graduale di canto".[45] On 5 March 1496/7, a privilege was given to "Thomasinus venetibus", to print "Graduale, Antiphonarium et psalmistum á choro" for ten years.[46] (Agee suggests that these may well have been the volumes edited by Franciscus de Brugis and published by Giunta in 1499–1500.)[47] A privilege was granted, on 21 January 1498/9, to Andrea Corbo, for his large letters for choirbooks.[48]

Some liturgical petitions probably did not involve music, among them that of Brittanico (6 December 1497) for a Gradual and an antiphoner.[49] On 4 March 1500, Bernardino Stagnino gained a privilege for several titles, the list of which ended with "et Mesal, et Breviarii d'ogni sorte", which was unusually to last for fifteen years;[50] and on 18 June 1512, Gregori de Gregorii applied for and received a privilege, claiming that he had found a way "stampar messali et breviarii".[51]

It has often been pointed out that there are many applications, including those for liturgical books, which do not seem to correspond to any surviving editions. While there is always the possibility that relevant editions have been lost over the years, there was another factor in the bid to have rights (and opportunity) for printing liturgical books. As Grendler points out,[52] these volumes "paid the bills"; they were the mainstay of many businesses and the foundations of fortunes for others and "could mean the difference between survival and failure". While

I doubt this was the reason why Petrucci included liturgical books in his application, there is no reason to believe that all the other similar petitions represent true advances in printing methods, or firm intentions to print the specified volumes. The privileges would allow the printers to have such books available to them should the opportunity arise, or, perhaps more plausibly, to advertise to church dignitaries that they were ready to print them.

More important are those applications that did involve polyphony, although, of course, all are later than Petrucci's 1498 petition. First among these is the grant to Marco dall'Aquila, dated 11 March 1505.[53] In this, Marco claims to have discovered how to print tabulature and a manner of putting any composition into tabulature. He seeks to ban any other printing of lute tabulature "de alcuna sorte", as well as its importation into the republic, for a period of ten years. These clauses are standard in intent, matching those in the Petrucci privilege. Similar, too, are the penalties. In this case, Marco seeks 10 ducats "per cadauno de quelli stampati",[54] to be divided into three parts, between the accuser, the confiscating officer, and Marco himself. His request was granted. No books seem to have been printed as a result of Marco's privilege.

Several possible explanations have been suggested. Chapman[55] proposed that Marco did not intend to print tabulature *per se*, but rather a treatise on intabulation. She cites the phrase in the petition, "rasone de metter ogni canto in liuto", and suggests that the invention might have been a new method of writing lute notation. There is no evidence for this, as she says, for Marco apparently printed nothing. Further, this phrase is preceded by the words "far stampar la tabulatura", suggesting that editions of music were also contemplated.

Agee[56] suggests that Marco may have been Petrucci's editor for his first lute tabulature book of 1507. In that case, Petrucci and Marco must have come together, resolved the issue, and decided to work as partners. I find this unlikely: none of the extant works of Marco dall'Aquila were printed by Petrucci. A number of his surviving works are sophisticated, difficult compositions, show-casing a lutenist of the highest caliber. Ness[57] argues that Marco was more advanced than the Petrucci lutenists (Spinacino and Dalza), and that he represents a more sophisticated development of their adoption of the new techniques derived from Germany. In any case, it seems to me that the patterns of correction and transmission found in the Spinacino editions argue that the lutenist-composer himself was responsible for editing and overseeing the edition.

Most interestingly (and I think very plausibly), Ness[58] argues that the surviving copies of Marco's music in D-Mbs Mus.266, ff. 19r–62v, represent copies made either from printed editions or (at worst) from a manuscript arranged according to the pattern of an Italian lute edition. While two layers, the first and last of Ness's reconstructed Munich fascicle, are too late for Petrucci, containing arrangements of works by Sermisy and his generation, the middle layer does indeed look like the repertoire one would expect from the first decade of the century. It contains a series of ricercars, followed by various dances and titled pieces—*Il Cara cossa* and *Marchesa de San Luzo* are typical examples. It is possible, therefore, that Marco did indeed plan to print an edition of his music and sought the privilege for the obvious reason. Whether he actually printed it or not, we cannot tell; it certainly does not seem to have survived, except perhaps in the evidence of the Munich manuscript.

Petrucci may have thought that Marco intended to print tabulature and perceived it as a threat to his own work. No lute music had come from Petrucci's press before 1507, though that is no obstacle to such an view. First, despite Chapman's observations to the contrary, Petrucci would have had to cast a fair amount of type before he could print tabulature, as I shall demonstrate in the next chapter. His first lute volume appeared early in 1507. It is possible, therefore, that Marco could have planned to establish the type and materials for his edition and go to press sometime in late 1505 or early 1506, and that Petrucci immediately moved to protect his interests. It would have taken him some time to prepare both type and music; in any case, the first half of 1506 was committed to the sixth book of frottole (the completion of a second group of three), and two volumes of Lamentations, the first of which appeared just before Easter.

Second, Petrucci made an addition to the colophon of some of his lute books: the fourth book, of works by Dalza, and the first of Bossinensis's "lute songs" carry the additional clauses "Cum privilegio invictissimi dominii Venetiarum: quod nullus possit intabulaturam Lauti imprimere: sub penis in ipso privilegio contentis". These words look very much as though Petrucci was trying to remind someone, probably Marco dall'Aquila, that he had already secured a privilege for this repertoire. For these reasons, if none other (and I would add the argument advanced by Ness), it looks very much as though Marco did indeed intend to print lute music and sought a privilege for that specific purpose.

It is probable that the petition for a privilege made by Jacomo Ungaro on 26 September 1513 represents a quite different situation. It is true that the petition[59] did seek "che niuno altro possa stampar o far stampare dicto Canto figurato in questa Citade, ne In lochi sotoposti a quella per anni xv. proximi: ne alcune stampati portandi a vender in questa Citade, o in lochi de quella". This sounds very much as though Ungaro were seeking to prevent others from printing music, perhaps to have a monopoly on printed music in the city; he may have sought just that.[60] It does not follow, however, that he intended to print and publish on his own behalf. Indeed, the grant of the privilege includes the most unusual clause that it be awarded on the condition that it did not prejudice earlier concessions of any sort: "ne preiudicetur Concessionibus di que sorte facte fuissens ante hac".

Ungaro had lived in the city for many years, and in his petition calls himself a typecutter—"intagliatore de lettere". He had worked for Aldus Manutius as his typecaster,[61] and was mentioned in Aldus's first will of 1506, which left bequests to Ungaro's daughters.[62] Ungaro had presumably worked alongside Griffo when the latter was preparing the path-breaking Greek and italic fonts that played a major part in Aldus's success. It seems likely that Ungaro had considerable experience in typecasting, and probably therefore in the very problems faced by Petrucci. If, as is plausible, he was not strictly an employee of Aldus, but rather was commissioned as needed, we can speculate that he may have had something to do with Petrucci's own music font, and that this led to Ungaro's petition.

Indeed, Duggan goes further and suggests that Ungaro, in his application, was actually laying claim to the invention that had been the basis for Petrucci's own privilege.[63] In her view, Ungaro had invented the font, had cast it, and had worked with Petrucci: in making his own application, he was merely protecting the circulation of music in Venice and the Veneto, once Petrucci had returned to Fossombrone.[64]

The evidence is not watertight. It consist of a few circumstantial strands:

1. Ungaro petitioned in 1513 to protect his invention of music type;
2. the petition claimed he had invented a way to print music;
3. the petition was awarded without prejudice to previous petitions;
4. Ungaro had worked for Aldus, perhaps alongside Francesco Griffo;
5. Francesco Griffo did have some sort of contact with Petrucci.

These strands do tend to point in one direction, especially when, as I have argued, the music type involved two techniques that required a master craftsman to cast good sorts. In addition, they help to solve one strange issue: whence Petrucci could have gained the requisite technical skill to design and cast a sophisticated and subtle font of type. If Griffo were responsible for the design, and Ungaro for the casting, then Petrucci need not have possessed the technical skills, but indeed could have come up with little more than the idea of how to arrange the various levels of content on the different impressions. But this solution hinges closely on a presumed relationship between Petrucci and Ungaro, and upon some pattern that stimulated Ungaro to seek a privilege in 1513. The implication is that there was a sudden occurrence in that year that alarmed Ungaro, that suggested that someone else might try to print music, and that encouraged him to seek a privilege to protect his invention, and thus Petrucci's production. Indeed, there is wording in the petition to suggest this: "fearing that others, as does happen, might take the fruit of his labours" (temendo da Altri, come accade, toglia el fructo de le sue fatiche).

Martin Lowry throws light on the relationship between Aldus and Griffo, which makes this suggestion relevant.[65] Lowry points out that, although Aldus intended his various petitions for typefaces to prevent other printers from copying the designs, they also had the effect of preventing Griffo from selling his work to any other printer or type-founder. Thus, perhaps indirectly, Aldus removed from Griffo his main source of income and tied him permanently to the printing house. Lowry believes this is the cause of the rift between the two men, and of the accusations against Aldus made in Soncino's later editions. Soncino accused Aldus of stealing from Griffo the credit for the designs, although Aldus may have thought that he was merely protecting his own investment.

Whatever the details, the evidence does throw plausible light on the petition by Ungaro, a typefounder. He claimed to have discovered "el modo de stampare Canto figurato". If he had watched Aldus stifle the career of Griffo, driving him from Venice, and setting the two men against each other, he may have wondered about the safety of his own invention. Lowry even suggests that Ungaro "protected his inventions with a privilege that declared his own special status and perhaps did something to protect him from the fate of Francesco Griffo".[66] While plausible, that argument would not explain why Ungaro should have waited until 1513 (unless, as is too often assumed, he had invented a truly *new* method).

Rather, I think, some recent stimulus drove him to protect his invention. It may be a coincidence that Griffo had recently been in Fossombrone with Petrucci and probably designing types for him. Discussions between Petrucci and Griffo might have led one of them to warn Ungaro against attacks on his invention, encouraging him to seek a privilege. This hypothesis does depend on Ungaro having helped Petrucci in his earliest stages and cannot be supported by any known facts. Equally possible, of course, is that Ungaro had heard of Andrea Antico, perhaps indeed, that Antico's music was surfacing in Venice (which is almost certain), and that Ungaro was protecting himself from attack in that quarter. Finally, it may be that Giunta seemed ready to move beyond liturgical printing, and invest in polyphonic typefaces. We will probably never know.

What does seem likely is that Ungaro had no intention of printing or publishing music on his own behalf. He was, after all, a typefounder and probably had neither the financial resources nor the expertise to launch into publishing of any sort, let alone of music. This privilege, therefore, seems less of a threat to Petrucci than a protection for Ungaro himself. This probability also has to affect our view of the timing of Petrucci's petition to extend his own privilege, made the following year.

The application was approved by the Collegio on 26 June 1514.[67] Unlike the previous application, this one begins immediately with the reminder that Petrucci, as first inventor of printed music books, had already received a privilege, to the ornament of Christianity and the benefit of all interested in music. It rehearses the terms of the privilege, although without specifying the period or the penalties for an infraction, and then turns to the present purpose.

Because printing these books required a great deal of capital, and because Petrucci, being poor, could not provide the capital, he had taken "Ser Amadio Scoto mercadante de libri & Ser Nicolo de Raphael" as partners. They had printed many volumes at great expense, with the greatest care, labour, and attentiveness, hoping that the books would be useful. But, because of the war and troubles, they had not been able to ship all the books; as a result, they had not been able to recover their capital. Therefore, knowing the republic did not desert those who continued to exploit new inventions to the glory of the city, the present application was made for the privilege to be extended for another five years, under the same terms as the original petition. In particular, it would allow some reward for the labours of Nicolò de Raphael, who was now half-blind and unable to continue his normal employment or sustain his family. In addition, it would be possible to print many more new titles, already collected from various places at great expense and labour, and even to work out new inventions.

This petition has aroused some interest. Its timing has been seen as a response to Ungaro's request, which had been approved nine months earlier, or as a way of forestalling a possible petition from another printer or publisher (such as Antico).[68] Either is possible, although I find both unlikely. My drawing of the circumstances surrounding Ungaro's petition would argue that he and Petrucci were not opposed, indeed that they were rather on the same side of the issue. Thus, the stimulus for Petrucci's petition would have to come from elsewhere. For the same reason, there would be little need to seek protection from any other preparer of music, including Antico: neither the original grant nor the renewal made any reference to the technique used to print music. Both merely referred to printing music and would therefore include the woodblock process adopted by Antico. In addition, there is no reason to believe that Antico was contemplating moving to Venice this early in the decade. It is, of course, quite possible that the privilege sought to prevent the import of Antico's editions into Venice, but Antico had been cutting blocks and publishing music since 1510—his third book of *Canzone* had appeared late in 1513—so that this would, at best, have been something of a belated response.

In any case, there were apparently few such preemptive moves in Venice. At least, none have survived. The only extant action on infractions of a privilege during Petrucci's active lifetime was the specific warning from the Consiglio de'Dieci, at the instigation of Antonio Moreto, discussed above.

Rather more significant might be the fact that Petrucci himself had just begun to print music again. His first volume in some time (the third of Josquin's masses) had appeared in March 1514, nearly four months earlier, and he was already preparing the second (the first book of *Motetti de la Corona*). It looks as though, in starting up his business again, Petrucci felt the need to renew his protection. However, the original privilege still had almost four years to run, and there can have been no specific benefit, within the terms of the privilege, in renewing it at so early a date. At first sight, it would have made more sense for Petrucci to wait until 1518 to renew his privilege.

Yet there exists one very close parallel to Petrucci's procedure, indeed a parallel that, I suspect, was the actual stimulus for his action in 1514. I have already mentioned the petition of Democrito Terracina for a privilege for "alcune opere in lingua arabica, moresca, soriana, Armenicha, Indiana et barbarescha". It was awarded on 15 August 1498, with a period of twenty-five years. Terracina had died by May 1513, when his heirs, the nephews Lelio and Paulo di Maximi, petitioned for an extension of the privilege. Their claim was that Terracina had left no estate other than the benefit of the privilege: Terracina "sia defuncto: et passado de questa presente vita senza dar' principio alcuno: ma solamente habia facte de grande et quasi intollerabel spexe sença alcuna utilita". Therefore, although the original privilege still had almost ten years to run, they sought that it be reconfirmed for the next twenty-five years.[69]

There is no evidence that either Terracina or his heirs ever printed or published in Venice. The only Armenian books published there during this period, for example, came from one unidentified press (with a device of D.I.Z.A.) during the years 1512 and 1513. It is more probable that they were involved with manuscripts, preparing them or importing them from other cities.[70] The implication in the 1513 petition is clear: the extension should be granted because the heirs had received no financial gain from the bequest. A new announcement of the privilege and a statement of support from the Collegio were expected to help; the extension would allow the heirs to plan for a longer business operation and, hopefully, begin to make a profit.

The petition, when explained in these terms, sounds very similar to that of Petrucci. Niccolo di Raphael was still alive, though quite unable to support his family.[71] There were no returns from the original privilege. An extension would allow the partners to gain some reward: "azoche possino. . . . Dar qualche bon fine per poter fruire qualche beneficio de le sue fatiche"; and to plan to print more books, from material already collected: "azoche ditti supplicanti possino piu promptamente far stampare molte altre opere noue de ditte faculta da loro racolte in diversi loci cum grandissima spesa, & fatica"; and even to improve their methods: "excogitar altre nove invention".

I believe, therefore, that Petrucci's application for a renewal, apparently made not by his partners but by himself (and therefore involving a journey from Fossombrone) was a reaction to the precedent established in the Terracina case. It was therefore specifically phrased as if to help Niccolò di Raphael. The other two partners could scarcely claim poverty; the Scotto publishing enterprise had begun renewed activity the preceding year, after having been put on hold (it is believed following the death of their printer Bonetus Locatellus). Petrucci, too, was working again and apparently relying to a great extent on contacts in the Papal States. Only Niccolò seems not to have had other prospects. In addition, Niccolò's role must have been similar to that of Terracina, acting as bookseller, as agent and distributor, rather than as printer or publisher.

Petrucci, therefore, was not reacting to the dangers of Ungaro as competitor (especially if the latter had been a partner in the original "invention", and was protecting Petrucci's interests), or to the fear of an invasion from Antico. Instead, he was following the unusual precedent of the Terracina renewal and pleading hardship.[72]

In 1517 the Senate decided to reform the privilege process, believing that it had begun to be disadvantageous to trade. All previous privileges were revoked unless they had been granted by the Senate itself—and this meant the great majority. Future privileges were only to be approved by the Senate, and with a two-thirds majority.[73] Agee has suggested that Petrucci might not have been affected by this, since his privilege concerned a "process" or a whole repertoire, rather than a specific title. Even before the reforming law, however, the Collegio had declared that, with the expiry of Aldus's privileges, there would be no privilege for books in Greek. This tends to suggest that block privileges were equally to be canceled. So does the behaviour of Andrea Antico.

There were no other printers of "canto figurado" in Venice before 1517; soon after, however, Antico appeared on the scene. His first Venetian books are in fact dated in 1520, but to me it seems likely that he had been in Venice for some time. The last Roman editions taken from his blocks, beginning in 1518, do not mention his name; they are signed by the printer, living in Rome.[74] In addition, the new Venetian editions of 1520 must have been in preparation during the previous years. If it took Antico three years to cut the blocks for his *Liber quindecim missarum* (as he claimed), it must have taken virtually two to prepare all the books issued late in 1520. That being so, it seems probable that he was already in Venice, working at these new books, at the time that Roman printers were using his blocks to reprint earlier editions.[75] Indeed, the new law of 1517 may have been the stimulus to bring Antico to Venice.

It is not likely, given the pattern of Antico's behaviour in Rome, that he was reluctant to challenge Petrucci's privilege. I am inclined to believe, therefore, that

Petrucci's privilege had been canceled, under the new law, and that Antico felt he had a free field in Venice.

Later Venetian privileges for music are of only marginal relevance to Petrucci's career. Most interesting, though for other reasons entirely, is the one awarded to Tromboncino in 1521.[76] Richard Agee suggests that Tromboncino sought this privilege after Antico had printed a volume of voice and lute intabulations, containing music by Tromboncino and Cara,[77] and that Tromboncino might have been trying to prevent another edition of the music. Whether or not this is the reason, the privilege is interesting as the first example of a composer seeking protection for his own works. Authors had been doing the same for over thirty years, often citing the labour involved in preparing their texts. In most cases, they were referring to commentaries, school texts, or legal or medical treatises. In other words, their greatest fear was that the content would be pirated by other authors.[78]

If Tromboncino reflected a similar pattern, it would make sense that such a composer would be the first to petition for protection. The composers of church polyphony or chansons, northerners and others, would have seen little benefit in this kind of protection. Their music was already disseminated freely, was a mosaic of several interlocking voice parts, and required a relatively higher level of skill for the reader/performer; in addition, each performance would reflect a similarly higher level of performing skills and could therefore produce different readings without damaging the work. Yet the frottola, especially in an intabulated form, would be another matter: its dissemination would allow amateurs to take up performances, but the details of its presentation would limit their already weaker ability to perform and to embellish and ornament. Indeed, the publication of such pieces in the form of voice and lute would fix them permanently, even more than publication in choirbook format.

Perhaps some tentative support for this view of Tromboncino's reasoning flows from the fact that the second such privilege was sought by MarcAntonio Cavazzoni, protecting a repertoire similarly circumscribed by its presentation.[79] Although Cavazzoni did publish his music, there is no evidence that Tromboncino tried so to do.

Later grants of privilege for music have been listed, and many discussed, by Richard Agee.[80] Few are significant in the present context, although there are one or two that discuss or promote new techniques of printing. For us, the most unsatisfactory of these is the concession of 15 April 1542 to Antonio Gardane "per il novo modo trovato per lui di stampar musica".[81] Since this is the complete reference in a group of concessions listed in one document, we cannot know what the "new method" comprised, but it is tempting to suggest that it refers to what Mary Lewis has called "vertical composition", a technique that must have speeded up the production of books of secular music considerably.[82]

More interesting is the grant of 31 October 1545, to Roccho Bonicello, who sought a privilege for improvements he had made to the press: it is unusual, in that both the petition and the grant survive.[83] The petition does not go into enough detail to reveal what Bonicello was claiming, but one point seems clear: he believed that he had discovered a way to print in two colours, and twice as fast as before: "cioe quante risme de carta stampano quatro homeni in quatro giorni maxime di libri che vanno stampati rossi et negri et libri de canto, tante io ge ne volio far stampar cum quelli medemi homeni in doij giorni soli", and of the same quality. Since Bonicello couples the printing of red and black with the printing of "canto", it is reasonable to assume that he is still thinking of printing at two impressions. It may be that, by speeding his process, he was attempting to compete with the new single-impression processes. An alternative interpretation, that he was actually protecting the single-impression process seems implausible, although two phrases in the petition might support it. Bonicello does not at any point try to claim a privilege for music in general, but only to ensure that others could not print "cum tal novo modo et arte da mi primo ritrovato"; and he seeks to punish those "che havesseno cum tal novo modo stampati". It is clear, therefore, that he is not challenging the books put out by Gardano or Scotto; on the other hand, it is interesting to note that Scotto virtually stopped signing his own books during the period 1545–47.[84] Perhaps Bonicello had given Scotto his "secret" and was now trying to gain some financial reward.

Even more significant are two applications of 1536, from Francesco Marcolini[85] and Francesco d'Asola (Torresano). These followed a few years in which Antico had again been producing musical volumes, mainly with the assistance of the same leading Venetian family that had helped Petrucci, the Scotti. I have discussed Marcolini's standing in music printing and possible connections with Petrucci and Festa in chapter 1. Marcolini's references to Petrucci, both in the edition discussed there and in his privilege application, clearly draw a distinction between his work and that of Antico. In the preamble to the application, he refers to "uno Ottaviano de Fossanbrono, che stampava musica nel modo, che se imprimono le lettere"—one Ottaviano of Fossombrone, who printed music with the technique by which one prints letters—and later to his own technique as being able "stampare musica, et intabolature con charatteri di stagno over di altra mestura"—to print music and tabulature with characters of lead or other mixture [of metals]. By contrast, he allows "ogn'uno stampar in legno, come alpresente sij costuma, pur che non ristampino le opre stampate per me"—anyone may print with wood, as is at present the custom, provided that they do not reprint the works printed by me. He seems clearly to see the use of type as a better technique, and much the same may be true of the letter from Festa of the same year.[86] Festa's later, and famous, application of 1538[87] has other ramifications as well. It presents evidence that Festa believed in the existence of a market for his music; it is important in this regard because, while Scotto had produced a number of volumes, there had been no growth in the publication of religious music. Festa is, in other words, already seeing signs of the much larger market that stimulated and was stimulated by the activities of Gardano and Scotto. The application is also, when taken with the slightly earlier actions of Carpentras in France[88] and the editions of lute music being promoted by the player-composers themselves, a sign that composers of complex polyphony were following the pattern initiated by Tromboncino and Cavazzoni.

Then, also in 1536, there was an application from Torresano for a petition to reprint Parisian books, including a volume of chansons, which he had been importing, but which had been lost en route.[89] This indicates not merely that Torresano wanted to print these books, but also that, in importing them and presumably selling them through his shop in Venice, he was competing with the editions prepared by Antico.

Behind all these applications is the belief that music printing, or more specifically music publishing, had become a financially viable activity in Venice. The same may have been felt to be true elsewhere, for Petrucci himself put out two editions during the 1530s. The situation seems to have changed since the 1510s, when Petrucci could still make the plea of not having recouped the initial investment, if we assume his 1514 application represents anything approaching the truth.

Other petitioners, however, seem to have thought there was room for someone to make money at publishing music. This must be at least partly true even in the case of Jacomo Ungaro: he must have thought that others would see the chance for a profit, if they encroached on his invention. Then, too, the arrival of Antico on the Venetian scene before 1520 and his immediate series of publications would have confirmed potential publishers in their opinion. The presence, in the next few years, of three different privileges for music or music theory[90] is enough support for that view. Each suggests that one specific repertoire or specific set of works was potentially viable. By the time of the applications of the 1530s, the pattern is already larger: all three petitions carry the implication that more than one printer could produce (or import) music at the same time and still reap financial rewards. The evidence of the privileges points that way, as, much more dramatically, does the appearance of Gardano in 1538 with the simultaneous presence of both Gardano and Scotto for the ensuing decades.

Not surprisingly, given the pre-eminent status of Venice as a printing center, there is much less evidence from elsewhere in Italy. Thus, in Rome, we know of only three people who made musical applications for privilege during the first twenty years of the century, and one of those is Petrucci himself; there was only one musical privilege during these years in Florence, and none at all from Milan or Naples.

Indeed, outside Venice, privileges seem to be generally rare, regardless of subject. Norton gives a survey of the privileges known to him,[91] from which it appears that, while they were accorded for books in the Duchy of Milan and the Kingdom of Naples with some irregular frequency, few were issued elsewhere. He cites some at Cuneo within the Savoy, and at Siena, but can only record one at Florence—for a translation of Caesar, and not the one known to musicologists.

Both Milan and Naples did award privileges for musical volumes, though not before 1536, as far as we know. In Naples, the two editions of lute music entitled "de la Fortuna" both carried the same statement of privilege, merely recording that the offending books should be seized and that the penalty laid down in the privilege should be inflicted. In Milan, another edition of music for lute, the *Intavolatura de leuto de diversi autori* published by Castiglione (*RISM* 1536[10]), is even more succinct: it states that the book may not be printed in the following ten years, "sotto pena de scutti cento: aplicati ala imperiale camera: come ne capitoli si contene". Two later books from the same press, Ruffo's first book of five-voiced motets (1542) and the first book of *Mutetarum divinitatis* give much more detail. The first demands ten scudi "pro uno quoque volumine" to be divided equally between the state treasury, the supplicant, and the accuser. The second seeks a penalty of "duorum aureorum pro singulis exemplaribus".[92]

The paucity of privileges in general (and in particular for music) limits what we can learn from them. General printing in Milan, in particular, and also in Bologna, Florence, Naples, and Rome was by no means an inconsiderable activity, and the number of other cities where printing was a small though flourishing activity is surprisingly large. In Brescia, for example, five or six printers had been active before the city was sacked by the French in 1512. In Ferrara, there were two significant printers, one of whom, Giovanni Mazocchi, printed the first edition of the *Orlando Furioso* in 1516;[93] Agee makes the point that Ferrarese printers held a ducal privilege, effectively a monopoly of all printing in the city, and that this would have covered the work of Francesco Rossi, who was active from the 1520s, printed music with Buglhat, Campis, and Hucher, and became *stampatore ducale*.[94] Pavia had a flourishing sequence of printers, who seem to have specialised in law books; other cities could be named as easily. Few of these printers seem to have needed or sought to protect their work with a privilege, despite the dominance of the Venetian press.

The Florentine privilege for music printing (dated 1515) has been discussed elsewhere, and the point made that no books seem to have been printed as a result of its grant.[95] As a result, it is difficult to draw any conclusions from this document. It seems to me more than likely that it was sought to resolve some personal problem, rather than to protect an edition from piracy. Even if a book printed under the terms of the privilege should surface, we would be hard pressed to decide why Florentines should fear that any other printer within the Tuscan state would suddenly start printing music.

In fact, another person did, and in the second city of the territory: Sambonettus produced his volume of *Canzone Sonetti Strambotti et frottole libro primo* (*RISM* 1515²) at Siena only a few months later. This volume, tied to Siena by both the colophon and the identifications of some of the composers, can hardly have been planned to fall under the Florentine privilege. The printer, it is true, was not local, calling himself a Neapolitan, and so might have worked anywhere in Tuscany. He is not known for any other books, and biographical data have not surfaced.[96] The book is competently printed, with woodblocks for the music, and it shows evidence that it was checked for errors, in that one signature (on folio D2r of the sole surviving copy) appears to have been stamped in later. Though much of the music is local to Siena,[97] the volume need not have circulated only there and nearby. However, given the pattern of other printing in Siena, there is no reason to believe that this repertoire would have been sent elsewhere, or that Florence, for instance, would have seen it as providing competition.[98]

Indeed, outside Venice (and Rome), there was little printing of polyphony or of intabulations before the mid-1530s: most of the books that were produced are well known and discussed in the modern literature, even while the motivations and careers of their printers and publishers remain most obscure. While no printer or publisher would want to take a loss (and the figures for the cost of books presented in the Colón catalogues are instructive), it is probable that the initial stimulus to publish music books came only occasionally from the printer's or publisher's commercial search for gain,[99] but more usually from some external promoter. This seems very likely for the Sienese frottola volume of 1515, as well as the first books from Naples and other centers.

Most important of these other centers, of course, was Rome. Privileges here were awarded by papal authorities, and the possession of a papal privilege was a matter of considerable importance. Until recently, little research on the Roman privilege was possible,[100] and the surviving evidence has been largely drawn from privileges in printed books.[101]

Petrucci's first privilege from the papal court was not in fact issued to him, but was granted, on 29 April 1513, to Paulus de Middelburgh for his text of the *Paulina*.[102] The form, following other papal privileges of the period, is quite different from that found in the Venetian documents—different principally because it is written as a papal breve, formally presented as if from the pope, rather than surviving as an approved request from the petitioner, as in Venetian examples. In addition, papal privileges bore the pope's greetings and his message, and then were signed by his secretary, in this case Pietro Bembo. Paulus's grant begins, as would any such letter, with praise of the recipient and of his particular gifts, praise that is perhaps a little more extended insofar as it is used to justify the gift of a privilege. It leads directly to praise of Paulus's work, which is defined precisely: "libros de paschae observatione, passionisque, dominicae die". This work is to be protected, so that no one else may print or publish it, nor sell copies: "ne quis imprimere possit, imprimue facere aut impressos vendere". The privilege is given without term, but the penalty is excommunication: "sub excommunicationis latae sententiae".[103] The document is signed under the papal seal, "sub Anulo Piscatoris", and given the conventional papal double date, of the calendar and of the year of the pope's rule.

It is clear that the papal privilege was a most powerful gift. Apart from the traditional power of the papal authority wherever it was encountered, the privilege regularly carried the penalty of excommunication, in addition to the normal confiscation and fines. It could be granted not only to printers working in Rome and the Papal States, but also to those in other parts of Italy, and even further afield.[104] These privileges applied widely, preventing the appearance or sale of other editions elsewhere in the whole of Italy or (on occasion) of Christendom, whereas the fines and penalties of confiscation themselves applied only within the Papal States. Yet the power was felt very generally. Norton cites a case in which an unwitting infringement in Milan led to a summons from the pope, a contrite apology and a final letter of absolution, and Grendler discusses the delicate negotiations that followed when later Venetian printers tried to bring out pirated editions of the new Tridentine liturgical books.[105] Later in the century, the Venetian authorities were sufficiently aware of the power of the papal privilege to forbid Venetian printers seeking privileges from the Curia.[106]

Therefore, when Antico received a papal privilege for music, on 3 October 1513, this was a serious matter for Petrucci. Antico's action was perhaps a response to the privilege for Paulus's book, as he may have feared that Petrucci would be more active in music. So far, Petrucci had printed only two music books in Fossombrone, the second book of Bossinensis's intabulations, and the tenth of frottole (both of which, as I have suggested, he may have brought with him from Venice). Antico had already published at least the first two books of Canzone without any privilege: the first is dated 1510, and the second must have appeared before the end of 1513, for a third book can be dated in that year.[107] Thus, the need for a privilege can reasonably be put down to some external factor—most likely knowledge that Petrucci was about to petition for a music privilege, the one awarded later in 1513.

Antico's grant is quite specific.[108] It praises the quality of his workmanship: "cum suis notis & caracteribus tua arte tuisque manibus accuratissime elaboratis": it referred to his anthologies of frottole: "cantilenas quasdam odas & varia carminum genera hetrusca lingua a Diversis auctoribus eleganter composita"; and also mentions some other unspecified books: "certa alia volumina exquisita nunquam antehac impressa". The privilege is worded as if Antico had yet to publish any books of music—the books "quos nunc in manibus habes et prope diem editurus es qui deinceps per te in eo genere imprimentur imprimerent et imprimi facerent".[109] Although this evidently gave Antico a free hand to include other things than "cantilenas" in Italian, it is notable that, as he expanded his range in Rome, to the *Liber quindecim missarum* and to the book of organ intabulations, he sought an additional privilege at each stage.

The rest of the grant is standard: it includes the penalty of excommunication for offenders, and the loss of all copies for those who were subject to the Church. The privilege was to run for ten years from the beginning of printing.

Petrucci gained his own privilege less than three weeks later, on 22 October 1513.[110] It may have been the result of a quick response to Antico's award, or it may be, as I suggest, that Petrucci's application was already in hand when Antico received his grant.

The privilege again begins with a compliment to the recipient as founder of music printing: "tua industria et solertia primus invenisses modum imprimendi libros cantus figurati". After this, it immediately notes that Petrucci had received a twenty-year privilege from the "dux et Consiliarii Civitatis Venetiarum" for the invention of printing "Cantus figuratus". Any Roman privilege for polyphony would compete directly with Antico's recent grant, and so the actual terms of Petrucci's grant avoid this problem by naming specific repertoires that had not been given to Antico. The key phrases state that Petrucci had, after the usual great labour and expense, discovered a way to print organ tabulature: "primus modum imprimendi organorum intabulaturas . . . inveneris"; and that he wanted to print a number of books on diverse subjects: "necnon alios libros alterius Facultatis, alias nunquam impressos". In theory, Petrucci should have kept to these areas distinct from Antico's field of production. Yet the privilege goes on to allow Petrucci some leeway, allowing him to print not only "aliquas organorum intabulaturas", but also "alios libros alterius facultatis per te impressos et imprimendos per alios tamen antea non impressos". Petrucci was given protection not only for tabulature, and any other book he had already printed, but also for anything he might plan to print, provided only that it had not already been printed elsewhere.

Petrucci's petition for this privilege survives and is couched in almost exactly the terms of the privilege itself.[111] Both this and Antico's privileges were, of course, drawn up and written by papal chancery scribes, and there are some phrases in common. Antico's privilege requires him to sell the books "at a reasonable price"[112] (convenienti pretio vendere cupias); Petrucci's similarly says, "provided you sell [the books] at a reasonable price" (dummodo libro justo pretio vendantur). However, the two significant differences between the two privileges—the term of the award, and the penalties to be imposed—are instructive and suggest that Petrucci had a considerable hand in the terms of his award. Although Antico had earned merely ten years' protection, Petrucci asked for and was given a privilege for fifteen. The penalties awarded to Antico comprised excommunication and the confiscation of all copies (when printed within the papal states). Petrucci included both of these, but added a significant third component. For each book, there was to be a fine of four ducats,[113] which would be divided up in a typically Venetian manner—equal thirds going to the informer, the executor of the punishment, and the papal treasury. No doubt the substitution of a papal fund for the charitable foundation of the Venetian grant is a reflection of Vatican necessity.

Petrucci's new grant seems to have had the desired effect. While he was able to print freely for the next two to three years—producing his last book of frottole, the first of the *Motetti de la Corona,* and five volumes of masses (of which two were new editions of the Venetian first two books devoted to Josquin), Antico may have produced nothing at all. The support for this is, of course, partly negative: no new editions survive from his press, and none are cited in the catalogues of Colón, for the years 1514 and 1515. However, Antico himself nearly admits as much when he does finally print a new book. In the dedicatory letter of his *Liber quindecim missarum* (dated 9 May 1516), he says that he had spent nearly three years preparing the woodblocks for the edition.[114]

Antico's privilege of 27 January 1516 applied to this book and was printed at the back:[115] it referred to "libros Cantus figurati in dicto magno volumine ac regalis Chartis"—books of polyphony in large volumes of royal folio size. The privilege has two unusual provisions that bear on Petrucci's career. The first gives protection, not against infractions of the terms of the privilege, but against civil disturbance. The crucial clauses read (in Chapman's translation): "Wherefore we commission and direct the Venerable Brother Jerome, bishop of Ascoli, and our beloved son Amadeus, the Prior of the Augustines, and the present auditors of the papal treasury and the governors of the said city [of Rome] and their lieutenants to assist you as far as is necessary for the protection of these privileges, allowing you to enjoy in peace the concessions, not allowing the above-named Octavianus or any other printer or persons of whatever authority to molest, harrass or disturb you in any manner whatsoever".[116]

It would seem from this that Petrucci had been protesting Antico's earlier privilege, perhaps even causing trouble; at the least, Antico must have claimed to fear some hazard for his work, his books, or even his person. Perhaps Petrucci, or his partners in Venice, had seized some of Antico's copies when they entered the Veneto and argued that they fell foul of Petrucci's own Venetian privilege. Perhaps Petrucci had protested Antico's earlier Roman privilege and sought some sort of restriction on the blockcutter's activities. Just possibly, printers and their staffs, notorious as disturbers of the peace, had caused some riot or turmoil in Rome. We shall probably never know; however, there is an equal possibility that Antico invented the whole thing, in order to strengthen his own position. It is significant that, during the 1510s, he was unable to retain the services of any one printer for any length of time, having to move from one to the next for virtually every volume,[117] and that he seems to have been opportunistic in his musical decisions—reprinting much from Petrucci in his first book of 1510, only turning to tabulature after Petrucci had sought a privilege for the repertoire, and going to Venice when he thought that Petrucci's privilege was about to expire. It may be, then, that Antico had created the need for these provisions in his privilege.

Apparently, the papal authorities did not intend to deprive Petrucci of his opportunities, for the second unusual feature works in his favour. Near the end of the document, a proviso is included to the effect that Petrucci's earlier privilege, of "xxii Octobris Pontificatus nostri Anno Primo" (1513) should be allowed to stand, and that he be allowed to continue printing books of polyphony, provided that he may not interfere with Antico, "tibi super hoc propterea aliquod preiudicium afferat". Although Petrucci's earlier privilege concerned tabulature only, papal authorities would certainly have known by this time that he was also printing polyphony, and they were effectively acknowledging his activities in that area, in requiring him not to compete with Antico. This may explain why, in subsequent years, Petrucci printed no new titles of either masses or frottole, perhaps feeling the force of a papal privilege and injunction.[118]

Antico seems to have had more influence with the papal authorities, given the manner in which his final Roman privilege[119] refers to Petrucci. It was issued exactly eleven months after his earlier one and specifically refers to organ tabulatures. It says: "tu primus formis tuis excussas prope diem editurus sis organis intabulaturas"—you have with your own method for the first time executed and will soon publish organ tabulatures. It is notable that Antico had already cut the blocks for tabulature, apparently in advance of the grant, and potentially in conflict with part of Petrucci's privilege of 1513. Antico therefore needed to gain his own privilege, and to justify his application (rather than as an attack on Petrucci) the privilege makes a point of saying that Petrucci had done nothing about tabulature in three (actually four) years.

Evidently, Antico and Petrucci were engaged in some sort of (probably gentle) dispute over the rules for printing music. Whereas Petrucci seems to have been content to work under the terms of his only Roman privilege, of 1513, perhaps with the support of the Venetian document of 1514, Antico steadily eroded the areas within which Petrucci could work. From the initial privilege naming the Italian genres that appeared in his frottole volumes, Antico expanded his reach through large choirbooks—and therefore music for religious choral institutions—to keyboard music. He evidently had enough influence at the Curia to have each of these expansions of his realm documented with a grant of privilege, and to have Petrucci specifically cited in each one. Petrucci, on the other hand, did have some standing, for not only was he named, but he was also allowed a certain amount of freedom, in the January 1513 privilege. Perhaps his contacts were in a different part of the papal circle, one that knew the work of Paulus de Middelburgh, and that later recommended him for the abortive attempt at publishing Calvo's translation of Hippocrates.

It is a coincidence (and probably nothing more) that Petrucci stopped printing polyphony in 1516, after Antico's first privilege of that year, and that he began again in 1519, by which time Antico was certainly in Venice. Since none of Antico's privileges actively stopped Petrucci from printing motets (such as those that appeared in 1519), and since Antico was careful to select his repertoires and then delineate them in his own privileges, those documents could not have been seen by Petrucci as preventing either publications of motets, or re-editions of his earlier volumes with the later, correct dates. Instead, the reason for the apparent hiatus in Petrucci's work, and for the false dates on editions printed between 1516 and 1519, must lie (as I suggested in chapter 1) in the political situation within the Duchy of Urbino and the turbulent history of Fossombrone.

Italian applications for privilege sought to do a number of different things, as has often been pointed out. Petrucci's musical privileges fall into the category of protecting repertoires, rather than the individual pieces preserved in his editions. This is reasonable: he was the first to explore these repertoires and needed such protection as the privileges afforded him. In any case, the compositions were not like many other works cited in specific privileges—complete, extended works and translations—but were relatively short, contained in anthologies, and easily replaced by other works. Once Antico arrived on the scene, the problem was again not the individual composition, but the repertoire. Antico's decision to print organ music probably seemed an astute move, putting pressure on Petrucci at one of his weakest points: the repertoire was (and remained for many years) difficult of execution with movable type. Similarly, the petition for a privilege for the *Liber quindecim missarum* attacked an area where Petrucci was not equipped to work, for he had none of the necessary typographical materials for folio editions of music, even though (on the strength of the *Paulina*) he evidently did have technicians capable of presenting a superlative result.

For Petrucci, therefore, the privilege was a means of protecting his base: an ability to print polyphonic or lute music from movable type at a number of impressions. The privilege protected his materials and techniques and it is to these that we must now turn.

Notes

1. The privilege is preserved in the Archivio di Stato of Venice (hereafter abbreviated to ASV), at Collegio, Notatorio, Registro XIV (1489–1499), on f.159r (now newly numbered 174r). It has been printed many times: see, for example, Schmid, *Petrucci*, pp. 10–11; Vernarecci, *Petrucci*, pp. 36–37 (with an Italian translation); Castellani, *Stampa*, p. 73; Fulin, "Documenti", No.81; Sartori, *Petrucci*, pp. 14–15; Duggan, *Italian*, p. 487. English translations are available in Reese, "First", p. 40; and Gehrenbeck, *Corona*, pp. 35–36. See also Blackburn, "Petrucci".

Throughout this chapter, and elsewhere, I have chosen to use the word "privilege" indiscriminately to refer to all the approved applications. I am aware that the various supplications were for different types of grant. Chapman, *Antico*, p. 13, makes distinctions between different types of privileges and suggests that there was a difference between monopolies and copyright privileges. I believe that Agee, *Privilege*, p. 50, is right in suggesting that the inconsistency of wording implies that any such distinctions are modern and were not perceived during the Renaissance.

2. An excellent introduction to a number of technical aspects of Venetian liturgical printing in the fifteenth century can be found in Duggan, *Italian*.

3. ASV, Collegio, Notatorio, Registro XVII, f.49v (new 51v): cited in Fulin, as document No.82. This privilege is additionally interesting in the present context: in 1513 (just over a year

before Petrucci attempted to renew his privilege), Lelio and Paolo de Maximi sought a renewal of that by Terracina, on the death of the original recipient. The two supplications will therefore be discussed below. The existence of the later request tends to discount the suggestion by Barker (in *Aldus*, p. 93, n.9) that Terracina never existed and "that the document is a parody, the product of some lawyer or notary's leisure".

4. It seems likely that it refers to a single copy, even though the figure is rather high. The professor of law, Landriano, sought a penalty of 10 ducats per volume in 1496, again using the word "opera" (ASV, Collegio, Notatoio, Registro XIV [1489–1499], f.144*v* [new 148*v*]). Later musical and other privilege applications are clearer. In 1513 Ungaro sought a fine of 100 ducats for each time the privilege is broken: "per cadauna volta dal se Contrafaçia".; and in 1536 Marcolini gained a privilege that he reported in his edition of Willaert's *Liber Quinque Missarum* (*RISM* W1103), stating the penalty in the following terms: "Sotto pena di perder tutte le opere & artificij si trouassero per far tal opere; & pagar ducati doi per volume, da esser divisi come in esso privilegio appare". (Under pain of losing all the works and the equipment that one can find, that was used to make these books; and to pay two ducats per book, to be divided as is stated in the privilege.) (Both these documents are transcribed below.) Here it seems as though the proposed fine does not relate primarily to the value that the printer, publisher, or author put on the volume itself, but rather on the financial need to protect the privilege. In the same year (1536), Torresanus, seeking a privilege to print titles he had previously tried to import from France, asked for a fine of 1 ducat per book or engraving (i.e., per copy), and 300 ducats in addition. (This penalty was in fact reduced, in the granting statement, to one ducat per volume and 100 in addition. ASV, Senato, Terra, Reg.XXIX, f.53*r–v* [new 74*r–v*]. See also the references to this document below.) Terracina, in the petition for a privilege for Arabic and similar languages mentioned above, sought a penalty of 200 gold ducats per infraction, no doubt reflecting the expense of building up all the specialised fonts and employing competent craftsmen.

5. For the origins of the Monte Nuovo, see Luzzatto, *Storia*, pp. 207–11, and for evidence that it was in financial difficulty in 1519, see Pullan, *Rich*, p. 495. The Monte Nuovo was liquidated during the 1540s.

6. For the date of its founding, see Pullan, *Rich*, p. 213. The letter of the Milanese Ambassador is cited there, on p. 211.

7. Certainly, the Senate or the Collegio took note of the proposed penalties and their destination. The change in the penalty sought by Torresanus has been mentioned in fn.4, above. In addition, the distribution of the penalty monies was changed. Torresanus had proposed giving one-third to the Pietà, one-third to the accuser, and one-third to the executing officer; the Senate instead offered one-half to the accuser and one-half to the Arsenale. In the immediately preceding supplication, the author Alberto Bruno had made no provision for a penalty, merely saying "sotto pena de confiscatione de libri, et altre solite et consuete". The senate instituted a specific fine, again giving half to the accuser and half to the Arsenale. It is not surprising that the Venetian government should have wished to fund the Arsenale in any way possible, given the onset of the Franco-Imperial War over the succession in Milan. But the Arsenal had featured in earlier awards of privilege; in 1523 the privilege recorded in Aron's *Thoscanello de la Musica* awarded one-third to the accuser, one-third to the Arsenal, and one-third to the author.

8. This point is evident throughout the discussions of Venetian printers in Duggan, *Italian*.

9. However, Duggan (writing in *Italian*) and I independently discovered evidence that some printers, including printers working in Venice, did use kerned sorts for chant.

10. See Fulin, "Documenti", item 127, and the references in chapter 1.

11. Morison, *Tally*, p. 44. The following comments about antimony are found on p. 45 of the same book.

12. I have argued in chapter 1 that Francesco Griffo was probably the designer of the type. For a discussion of the suggestion that Jacomo Ungaro was the typecaster, see below, and for the evidence of kerned sorts, see chapter 3.

13. I am assuming for the purpose of this discussion that the text did not include rubrics. The presence of these text phrases, intended to appear in red, does not affect the argument, for they were printed at the same time as the staves.

14. Agee, *Privilege*, in particular, chapter 1.

15. Despite a great many detailed and thoughtful studies in recent decades, the most important source in English for the history of printing in Renaissance and later Venice remains Horatio Brown, *Venetian*. The majority of the documents for the early Renaissance have been printed in Fulin, "Documenti" and Fulin, "Nuovi documenti". Insofar as these documents are relevant to the present study, they have been re-examined in the original, and selected transcriptions are presented in chapter 20.

16. As Agee says (p. 12), "The earliest printing legislation, from 1517, finally standardised the process".

17. The data that follow are taken from ASV, Collegio, Notatorio, Registri XIV (1489–1499), XV (1499–1507) and XVII (1512/1513–1514/1515), or Senato, Terra, Registro XIII (1497–1499) to Registro XXIX (1536–1537). Some of the documents to which I refer are transcribed in chapter 20.

18. ASV, Consilio, Notatorio, Registro XIV, f.133(137)*r* for "Bernadin Rasma marchadante de libri de stampa", and f.138(142)*r* for "benedetto fontana marchadante de libri da stampa" (Fulin, "Documenti", Nos.44 and 47). These are matched by a further plea from Fontana at the end of 1496 (f.145[149]*r–v*), repeating that he was an orphan, had three young sisters, and so on (Fulin, "Documenti", No.56).

19. ASV, Collegio, Notatorio, Registro XV, f.23(25)*v*: an extract is transcribed in Fulin, "Documenti", no.104.

20. Bernardino Stagnino does, however, mention the format of a book in his application of 17 September 1497 (ASV, Collegio, Notatorio, XIV, f.162[166]*r*: transcribed, in part, in Fulin, "Documenti", No.71, and cited as Agee, "Privilege", No.1).

21. ASV, Collegio, Notatorio, Registro XV, ff.I(3)*v* and 13(15)*v*: transcribed in Fulin, "Documenti", Nos.91 and 96.

22. ASV, Collegio, Notatorio, Registro XVII, ff.87(89)*v*–88(90)*r*. Fulin, "Documenti", No.192.

23. "Many beautiful pictures, that is the drowning of Pharoah, the story of Susannah, the story of Abraham's sacrifice, and other new [pictorial] stories which have not yet been printed": ASV, Collegio, Notatorio, Registro XVII, f.103(105)*r*. Fulin, "Documenti", No.196.

24. ASV, Collegio, Notatorio, Registro XIV, f.73(77)*v*: Fulin, "Documenti", No.11.

25. ASV, Collegio, Notatorio, Registro XIV, ff.130(134)*r* and 144(148)*v*: Fulin, "Documenti", Nos.39 and 51.

26. ASV, Collegio, Notatorio, Registro XIV, f.148(152)*r*. Fulin, "Documenti", No.63.

27. ASV, Collegio, Notatorio, Registro XIV, f.133(137)*v* for Aldus; and ff.167(171)*r* and 173(177)*r* for Brasichella: see Fulin, "Documenti", Nos.41 and 76. The Aldine petition is transcribed in Castellani, *Stampa*, p. 72, and his further petition of 1498 (in part), ibid., p. 74. The first is translated in Barker, *Aldus*, p. 92: Barker's point, there, that Aldus is attempting to protect his techniques, as well as the repertoire, as defense against rivals in Venice, seems to argue further for the view I have tacitly adopted elsewhere in this study—that Aldus was aggressive in the protection of his presumed rights. (Barker himself says, p. 94, that Aldus's partner "Andrea Torresani was notoriously tight-fisted".)

There is a growing literature on Greek printing in Venice. See the short bibliography at the end of Davies, *Aldus*; the studies listed in Beck, Manoussacas, and Pertusi, "Venetia"; Layton, "Notes"; and the catalogue from Athens, Manoussakas and Staikos, *Greek*. The lawsuit between Brasichella and Aldus is discussed in Barker, *Aldus*, pp. 94–96. It is possible that this suit and Aldus's second privilege had some effect on the wording of Petrucci's application.

28. ASV, Collegio, Notatorio, Registro XV, f.33(35)*v*. Horatio Brown, *Venetian*, p. 54, remarks that such privileges, concerning fonts for specific purposes, often carried the effect of a monopoly. He cites the Aldine privileges for Greek in 1495 and for a cursive font in 1501, and that of Bomberger for Hebrew type in 1515, as well as Petrucci's privilege.

29. ASV, Collegio, Notatorio, Registro XV (1499–1507), f.33(35)*v*.

30. ASV, Senato, Terra, XXIX, f.51(72)*r*.

31. For example, the records of the Capi del Consiglio de'Dieci indicate that a number of *ex gratia* payments were made to members of the Zecha (or Mint) for technical innovations. Daniel de freschi and Zuanjacomo di stefani, having found a way to stamp better, ask the Council

of Ten to take note of the fact, and to "remember them". ASV, Capi de Consilio de'Dieci, Notatorio, II, f.115(138)r, dated 22 February 1496/97.

32. Both of these documents are transcribed in chapter 20.

33. ASV, Collegio, Notatorio, Registro XIV (1489–1499), ff.169(173)r and 172(176)r.

34. Ibid., ff.182(186)r.

35. ASV, Collegio, Notatorio, Registro XV (1499–1507), f.28(30)r; and ASV, Senato, Terra, XXIX (March 1536–Feb. 1537/38), f.2(23)r.

36. Ibid., f.141(145)r.

37. ASV, Collegio, Notatorio, Registro XV (1499–1507), f.17(19)v.

38. ASV, Collegio, Notatorio, Registro XIV (1498–1499), ff.111(115)r and 116(120)r.

39. ASV, Capi del Consiglio de'Dieci, Notatorio, Registro 2 (1491–1500), f.116(139)v). This petition is not entirely clear, for it does not appear that Fasolo was a printer: his name is not listed in *BMC*, in Johnson and Scholder, *Short-Title Catalogue*, or in Norton, *Italian*. Indeed, at a later point in the same Register (141[165]v) he is called "servitore consilij" and as such may merely have been an informant, seeking rewards for himself.

40. Both versions are transcribed below, with the other documents.

41. Antonius Moretus was the fifth partner whose name was added to the well-known contract between the de Tortis brothers, Arrivabene, LucAntonio Giunta, and Amadeo Scotto, signed in 1507, and printed in Fulin, "Documenti", pp. 401–05.

42. The conclusion does not always follow: the *BMC* cites a number of cases where the type seems to have been owned by a printer for a short while and then passed on to another, and Dennis Rhodes, in "Di alcuni", has demonstrated that both type and ornamental material were loaned to, and directly copied by, other printers. However, Rhodes's recent book, *Silent Printers*, presents conclusions largely based on identification of type and initial letters.

43. This practice is true for music printers and publishers through much of the sixteenth century. The role of Arcadelt's first book of madrigals, as an early edition for a number of printers, can be seen in studying the lists in *RISM*. It is one of the four put out by Pietrasanta in 1557; in 1572 it is one of the first two books put out by Angelieri; and it is one of the first few from Guglielmi, in 1575. Outside the international center of Venice, the picture is different, for printers tended to concentrate more on the local repertoire. However, the Arcadelt book is the only non-Florentine book printed by Marescotti, in 1585, and the first non-Roman put out by the Roman printer Paolo Masotti, in 1627 and 1630. Similarly, in Naples Giovanni Antonio de Franceschi printed the Arcadelt book in 1592, and Gioseffo Ricci did likewise in 1654 (in a group of only three extant titles).

For later printers, Palestrina, Agazzari, or Millioni sometimes served a similar function (Bozzola in Brescia prints Palestrina's first book of masses in 1581 as his first music book), though even as late as 1640, Vincenzo Bianchi in Rome printed an edition of Arcadelt as one of his first half-dozen volumes.

44. The following instances are cited in Fulin, "Documenti", at Nos.59, 62, 64, 71, 73, 74, 90, 100, 108, 127, 129, 130, and 185. Three are discussed in Agee, *Privilege*, pp. 40–43; Bridges, *Publishing*; and (more significantly) in Duggan, *Italian*.

45. ASV, Collegio, Notatorio, Registro XIV (1489–1499), f.149(153)v.

46. ASV, Collegio, Notatorio, Registro XIV, ff.149(153)v.

47. Agee, *Privilege*, pp. 41–42. These volumes are interesting from both a bibliographical and a textual viewpoint: there are many signs of the great care that had been taken with the textual and musical content, including the use of a prototypical form of white-out to make corrections.

48. Fulin, "Documenti", p. 56. This privilege is discussed in Horatio Brown, *Venetian*, p. 41.

49. ASV, Collegio, Notatorio, Registro XIV (1489–1499), ff.164(168)v.

50. ASV, Collegio, Notatorio, Registro XV (1499–1507), ff.17(19)r.

51. ASV, Collegio, Notatorio, Registro XVII (1512–1514/15), ff.11(13)v.

52. Grendler, *Roman*, pp. 170–71.

53. ASV, Collegio, Notatorio, Registro XIII (1499–1509), f.141r. The privilege is transcribed below; it is also printed in Schmid, *Petrucci*, pp. 12–13; Brown, *Instrumental*, pp. 11–12;

Castellani, *Stampa*, pp. 79–80; Fulin, "Documenti", No.147; Ness, *Herwarth*, pp. 350–51 (with an English translation on pp. 351–52); and Vernarecci, *Petrucci*, pp. 103–104 (incomplete).

54. Again, it is not clear whether this means 10 ducats for each copy or for each title.

55. Chapman, *Antico*, pp. 21–22.

56. Agee, *Privilege*, p. 37.

57. Ness, *Herwarth*, in chapters 6 and 7, presents the only coherent discussion of Marco's style and its sources.

58. In *Herwarth*, specifically on p. 327, although this is merely a statement of a much longer argument.

59. ASV, Collegio, Notatorio, Registro XVII, f.78(80)r. The document is transcribed in chapter 20. Earlier transcriptions are in Fulin, "Documenti", no.189 (incomplete); Castellani, *Stampa*, pp. 81–82; Duggan, *Italian*, pp. 487–88. English translations can be found in Chapman, *Antico*, p. 23; Gehrenbeck, *Corona*, p. 51.

60. This possible interpretation would suggest that he became Petrucci's outlet for printed music in the Veneto. Unfortunately, no evidence that Ungaro became a *libraio* seems to survive, nor can any be found in the extant copies of Petrucci's editions; in addition, it seems unlikely that a Scotto would cede this commercial responsibility to someone else.

61. See Sorbelli, "Mago", p. 119. Duggan, *Italian* builds an important case on Ungaro's presence in Aldus's shop.

62. The testament is dated 27 March 1506: "Lasso che siano distribuiti docento cinquanta ducati in deci donzelle da maritare, a vinticinque ducati per una: le quali siano, quatro figliole de mio compatre, magistro Jacomo todesco, gettator de lettere" (from Castellani, *Stampa*, p. 93). The will is transcribed in a number of places, including Fulin, "Documenti", No.155.

63. Duggan, *Italian*, p. 243.

64. Ibid., pp. 132–35.

65. See, especially, Lowry, *World*, pp. 86–91.

66. Ibid., p. 91.

67. ASV, Collegio, Notatorio, Registro XVII (1512–1514/15), ff.92(94)r. This is printed in Schmid, *Petrucci*, pp. 19–20; Castellani, *Stampa*, pp. 82–83; Vernarecci, *Petrucci*, pp. 146–49; Sartori, pp. 19–20; and translated into English in Gehrenbeck, *Corona*, pp. 53–54.

68. The first position is taken in Chapman, *Antico*, p. 23. Both possibilities are suggested in Agee, *Privilege*, p. 38.

69. See chapter 1 for a mention of these petitions, and (in fn.114 below) citation of the sources.

70. Although the original privilege does refer specifically to printing and gains a ban on printing or publishing books in the specified languages, when it turns to banning the import of books into the republic, there is no specific reference to printing.

71. We do not know when Niccolò di Raphael died. In chapter 1, I have mentioned the later will of a Maria Antivari, widow of Niccolò di Raphael, presumably this man, though it gives no further clue. It is found in ASV, Notarile Testamento, 63 (atti Bartoli), No.87.

72. Horatio Brown, *Venetian*, p. 56, mentions another similar case. He cites the supplication of Filippo Pincio made on grounds of the "miserabil caso che brusò la casa cum libri et ogni sua facultade".

73. This document is printed in Fulin, "Nuovi", pp. 92–93.

74. In 1518 Antico's Book 2 of frottole was signed "per Iacomo Mazochio Ad insta[n]tia di Iacomo Gionta", and his Book 3 "per Iacobum Mazochium ad Impensis Iacobi de Gionta". This Mazzochi was a well-known printer in Rome and should be distinguished from the Giovanni Mazzocchi described as Scotto's agent in the 1516 contract between Scotto and Antico. The latter was perhaps the small-time printer discussed in Norton, *Italian*, 100. For the contract, see Chapman, *Antico*, pp. 448–49, with a following translation. A major study of the various copies of Antico's second book, which clarifies their dating, is Luisi, *Secondo*.

75. This suggestion has already been made in Miller, "Antico". I can see no other logical explanation of the pattern of the dates on Antico's editions. It also makes more sense of the references to his sacred books, now only known through Colón's citations. For this, see my review of Picker, *Motet*, p. 288.

76. Fulin, "Documenti", No.228. This is discussed in Agee, *Privilege*, pp. 44–45.

77. This is *RISM* [ca.1520][7] which unfortunately lacks the last folios, and thus the colophon. Both Colón and Gesner refer to a volume that is assumed to be this one. Gesner's title (Bernstein, "Bibliography", No.249) corresponds exactly to that of the extant book in I-Fc and adds that the book was printed in Venice. Colón also cites a book, which is probably that referred to by Gesner, and states that it was printed in Venice in 1520 (Chapman, "Printed", No.55).

78. Current thinking on the question of early authorial privileges, and of authors' relations with printers, is most developed in the study of French fifteenth- and sixteenth-century literature. There it is argued that authors saw the printer as to some extent replacing the patron who had previously promoted the production of a manuscript. The parallels drawn in this mode of thought are distinct from those in which the printer is directly related to the scribe of the manuscript. In this context, the possibilities of printing and publishing are seen as allowing the author to retain some of the rights over a text that had previously been ceded to the patron— and to negotiate with the printer accordingly. These rights are presumed to lead to the lawsuits between author and printer that occurred in Paris soon after the turn of the century. For a detailed and wide-ranging discussion of this issue, see Cynthia Brown, *Poets*.

79. Fulin, "Documenti", No.232: also transcribed in Sartori, *Petrucci*, p. 4, and cited in Agee, *Privilege*, p. 177. An interesting sidelight on the situation in 1523 is that Cavazzoni gained privileges from both Venice and the papal court. The Venetian privilege was to run for ten years, whereas the Roman was effective only for six. Equally significant is that the published book, although printed in Venice, carried the text of the Roman privilege, above the colophon. (The book, *RISM* C1574, has been published in facsimile, as Cavazzoni, *Recerchari*.) This seems to argue either (and implausibly) that the Venetian privilege was less effective, or (and more probably) that the book was expected to sell well within the area of the Papal States.

80. See Agee, *Privilege*, especially pp. 176–90.

81. ASV, Senato, Terra, Registro XXXII (1542–1543), f.68(90)*r–v*. The whole grant is transcribed in Agee, Privilege, p. 211.

82. I do not think that it refers to the special formes that Lewis proposed for musical editions—for placing the staves. Rather I believe that Petrucci (and probably many of his predecessors printing liturgical music) had already had some device for ensuring correct register between staves and notes.

83. ASV, Senato, Terra, Filza 2 (1545), and Registro XXXIV (1545–1546), f.87(119)*v*. Both documents are transcribed in Agee, *Privilege*, pp. 217–19, from which my quotations are taken.

84. For a discussion of the unsigned editions, and a presentation of the evidence tying them to Scotto's press, see Bernstein, "Burning". Bonicello's petition is discussed in Bernstein, *Printing*.

85. ASV, Senato, Terra, Registro XXIX (1536–1537), f.33(54)*v*. Transcribed in Schmid, *Petrucci*, pp. 121–22; Castellani, *Stampa*, pp. 83–84; and Agee, *Privilege*, p. 207. Translated into English in Chapman, *Antico*, and Agee, *Privilege*, pp. 69–70. Interestingly enough, Marcolini petitioned for a privilege for a spiritual manual later in the same year.

86. See my discussion of this letter in chapter 1.

87. ASV, Senato, Terra, Registro XXX (1538–1539), f.9(30)*r–v*. Transcribed in Agee, *Privilege*, pp. 208–209, and discussed there on pp. 76–78.

88. The contract between Carpentras and de Channey, and the subsequent negotiations, which took the greater part of 1531, are transcribed in Pansier, *Histoire*, iii, Nos.108–109; a detailed summary of the process is in Heartz, *Attaingnant*, pp. 110–17. Again, the discussions in Brown, *Poets*, add much to our understanding of Carpentras's position and reinforce the fact that his actions in France precede similar ones in Italy.

89. ASV, Senato, Terra, Registro XXIX (1536–1537), ff.53*r–v* (new 74*r–v*): transcribed in Agee, "Privilege", pp. 207–208: discussed in Thibault, "Notes", pp. 61–65; and Agee, "Privilege", pp. 73–75.

90. In addition to the privileges awarded to Tromboncino and Cavazzoni, another was given to Aaron for a book of music theory, in 1522/23.

91. Norton, *Italian*, pp. xxviii–xxix. Norton points out that some papal privileges ap-

plied in Florentine territory. D'Accone, *Civic*, p. 605, gives a later Sienese privilege, dated 1545.

92. These books are recorded in *RISM* as W1103 (1536), R3047 (1542) and 1543[3].

93. See Norton, *Italian*, p. 100. This man is referred to above in connection with Antico's contract with Scotto.

94. Agee, *Privilege*, p. 169.

95. Fumagalli, *Lexicon*, p. 143; Chapman, *Antico*, pp. 46–48; Picker, "Florentine". These earlier studies seem to have been unknown to Carter, who mentions the privilege in his otherwise excellent study, *Printing*, at p. 39. He, like the others, assumes that nothing was printed under the privilege.

96. None is given, for example, in D'Accone, *Civic*. See also Norton, *Italian*, p. 115, citing Riemann, "Notenschrift", and Vogel.

97. Jeppesen, *La Frottola*, i, pp. 61 and 159, draws attention to plausible biographical ascriptions for certain composers, including Nicolo Piccolomini and Nicolo Pifaro, both of whom were employed in Siena at the time. More details are given in Fusi, *Frottole*; and D'Accone, *Civic*, p. 699.

98. Norton, *Italian*, pp. 109–115, describes the printers active in Siena between 1500 and 1520; he makes the repeated point that they concentrated on local material, translations of early authors by Sienese scholars, or local vernacular verse and plays. In many ways, the Sambonettus volume should be seen as within the latter category.

99. The evidence of commercial motivation, and of a profitable outcome, in the production of the *Libro Primo de la Salamandra* (1526) is most instructive here. For details, see Blackburn, "Printing".

100. With the establishing of a permanent Holy Office—the Sacra Congregatio Romanae et Universalis Inquisitionis—in 1542, documents concerning papal privileges and licenses to print were kept there, with those concerning the Index of Prohibited Books, in the Archivio Segreto Vaticano. See Boyle, *Survey*, pp. 85–86. The archives of the Holy Office have only recently been opened to the public. It is presumed that some documents from earlier years are also preserved there—although it is possible that the *Breves* of privilege are all the documents that survive, with the addition of the one petition from Petrucci. Cusick, *Dorico*, p. 144, fn.1, notes that she was told that there are no such documents in the Archivio Segreto.

101. The best survey to date of this information for the first decades of the century is to be found in Norton, *Italian*, pp. xxvii–xxviii, from which what follows has been drawn. Agee, *Privilege*, p. 172, fn.303, lists several later privileges mentioned in Vogel, *Bibliothek*, while Cusick, *Dorico*, p. 95, notes that Morales was required to gain a privilege for publishing his volume of masses in 1544. Sadly, the otherwise excellent study of Roman printers in the second half of the sixteenth century, Masetti-Zannini's *Stampatori*, while mentioning some contracts for musical volumes (see p. 195), does not cover privileges.

102. The full text is transcribed in chapter 20, as is Bembo's letter to Paulus, confirming the grant of the privilege, and dated 1 May 1513.

103. According to Boyle, *Survey*, p. 52, this formulation makes the document strictly a *Breve*. Boyle further points out, p. 150, that the original letter of supplication was often preserved, in the *Registra Supplicationum*, while the *Breve* giving the concessions would be preserved in the register of *Breves*, the *Brevia Lateranensia*. Richard Sherr has discovered the formal copy of the original petition for Petrucci's privilege of 1513 in the former archives; see below.

104. Documentation for this may be found, not only in Norton, *Italian*, but also in Leicht, "Editore". See also the references to privileges accorded to Aldus in Venice, given in Renouard, *Annales*, p. 505–508. Similarly, Morales's privilege for his 1544 book of masses, mentioned in fn.101 above, was to include the "Kingdom of Naples and the Republic of Venice as well as the Papal States" (Cusick, *Dorico*, p. 95).

105. Norton, *Italian*, p. xxvii; Grendler, *Roman*, pp. 170–81 and elsewhere.

106. The formal document is preserved in ASV, Provveditori di Comun, Busta 1, 444*v*.

107. The first book is *RISM* 1510, dated 9 October of that year. The first edition of the second book is lost, as is an edition of 1516 cited by Colón, and we only have an edition of 1518 (printed by Mazzocchi) and one that can be dated in 1520—for which, see Luisi, *Secondo*.

The third book, which carries this privilege on its last folios, is dated 15 October 1513, according to Colón. For the details, see Chapman, *Antico*, where they are presented synoptically on pp. 414–21.

108. Reproduced in Luisi, *Secondo*, p. 77. See Chapman, *Antico*, p. 40, and the translation, pp. 445–46. The text is given in full, with an English translation, in Gehrenbeck, *Motetti*, pp. 44–46.

109. Taken from the printed version of the privilege in Antico's third book of frottole, *RISM* 1513[1]. The phrase reads, in Chapman's translation: "[The above books] which you now have in hand and have edited and which hereafter will be printed by you in this way".

110. The privilege is transcribed in full in Vernarecci, *Petrucci*, pp. 140–46; Sartori, pp. 164–65; Gehrenbeck, *Motetti*, pp. 47–49; and in chapter 20. A translation is in Chapman, *Antico*, pp. 453–54.

111. I-Rvat, Archivio Secreto Vaticano, Registrum Supplicationum 1430, f.22r. As Sherr, "Relationship" points out, the usual signature by Bembo has been replaced by a reference to Leo X himself.

112. In the phrase adopted in Gehrenbeck, *Motetti*, p. 44.

113. Unlike the Venetian privileges, the Roman actually specifies that the penalty is for each book, rather than infraction.

114. This letter is printed in translation in Chapman, *Antico*, pp. 446–47.

115. It appears on folio DD6r, above the colophon. It is transcribed in Sartori, *Petrucci*, pp. 22–23, and translated in Chapman, *Antico*, pp. 447–48.

116. "Quocirca Venerabili fratri hyeronimo episcopo Asculano, et dilecto filio Amadeo electro Augustensi et pro tempore existentibus Camere apostolice Auditori et dicte Urbis Gubernatori ac eorum loca tentibus et eorum cuilibet committimus et mandamus quantus tibi in premissis efficacis defensionis presidio assistentibus faciant te concessione huiusmodi pacifice frui et gaudere, non permittente per dictum octavianum et quoscumque alios impressores et personas quacumque auctoritate fangentes in persona seu bonis desuper quomodolibet molestare inquietari vel perturbari".

117. The list of his publications in Miller, "Antico", p. 146, makes this evident for Antico's Roman years.

118. It is possible that Antico, acting in a similar manner, printed no books of motets while in Rome. The reference in Colón's catalogue to "Motetti libro primo. . . . Impressum rome per andream antiquum de mantua anno 1518 .15. maij" (Chapman, "Columbus", No.51) is problematic in its ascription of the book to Antico. Earlier Roman editions of the same year had used Antico's woodblocks, but had been printed by Mazzocchi: these include the second book of frottole (15 January), the third book (27 February), and probably the lost fifth book (25 January). These editions and dates suggest that Antico had moved to Venice by the beginning of 1518 and begun to prepare for the burst of editions that would be issued in October and November 1520. As a result, I believe that the motet book, while using Antico's woodblocks, was actually printed by someone else, probably Mazzocchi.

119. Transcribed in Sartori, *Petrucci*, pp. 23–24, and translated in Chapman, *Antico*, pp. 452–53.

Chapter Three

PETRUCCI'S MATERIALS

n order to start (and continue) printing music and other books, Petrucci needed to acquire a range of technical resources. These obviously included typographical material of various sorts, for music, text, and decoration: they also included both ink and paper, and physical apparatus, principally the press. Apart from the paper, and the ink impressed on it, none of these survives: the only direct evidence lies in the printed books themselves, although there is indirect evidence from other printers' work and from some peripheral sources. Discussions of the evidence for each of these elements of book production fill this chapter, while the next outlines the evidence for normal house procedures.[1]

We know relatively little about the materials and technology for printing in Italy during its first century, and almost all has been gathered from a study of the printed books themselves, from illustrations of presses and printing shops, or from descriptions or legal documents.[2] There are few illustrations of printing shops before 1600: one of the most useful is that engraved by Johannes Stradanus, in *Nova Reperta*. Although this book appeared in Amsterdam in 1600, Moran[3] has shown that many details of the engraving reflect a practice that was probably common in the first half of the sixteenth century. Also useful is the famous series of devices used on books printed in Paris by Badius Ascensius early in the century. These tend to concentrate on the press, but also show the typesetter, as does the first extant picture of a printing house, dated 1499.[4]

The earliest Italian descriptions of printing technique were written long after Petrucci had finished work.[5] Indeed, the "first comprehensive manual in any language"[6] is the printing section of the *Mechanick exercises* by Joseph Moxon, published in 1683:[7] there is no Italian manual of printing practice or techniques until well into the eighteenth century. Fortunately, there had been some simple discussions or illustrations prior to this. They were not aimed at instruction, how-ever, as much as illustration. Leonardo Fioravanti, in his *Dello specchio di scientia universal* of 1567,[8] discusses something of the technique of printing, and, in the same year, the only sixteenth-century discussion of printing procedures, *Le premier et la seconde partie des dialogues françois*, was published in the Netherlands by Plantin.[9]

Paper

Evidently, paper is one of the principal ingredients Petrucci used for printing his books. Paper for printed volumes has always been rather different in its attributes from that destined for manuscript use, and the paper used for early incunables was often of a thickness and opacity that suggests it was meant to bear comparison with parchment. Even while papers became thinner and more commercial in character, the opacity and whiteness of the surface were important elements of their quality, as were the exact degree of absorbency that suited printing ink best.[10] The quality of the paper and the manner in which it took ink play a major part in the elegant appearance of Petrucci's first volumes, and both, not surprisingly, seem to have become less important to him late in the 1510s.

Nonetheless, the cost of paper was a major part of the expenses incurred in producing any printed book. This cost in general declined during the late fifteenth and the whole of the sixteenth centuries, but its proportional cost, commencing at as much as 50 percent of the total cost of a book, remained high, having only declined to no less than one-third of that cost by the end of the sixteenth cen-tury.[11] Paper therefore was a major expense, and decisions about its quality for any given book may be seen as reflections of the status of the book and its purchasers. Stockpiling paper would have been a major investment: a large print-run coupled with slow sales would tie up a major part of most printers' capital.[12] Thus, the patterns of purchasing paper become significant for the historian trying to reconstruct the economic profile of a printing or publishing venture.

The standard size of a sheet of paper bought by Petrucci is now hard to judge. Almost all the extant copies have been trimmed for binding at one stage or another, as is evident from the state of the watermarks. Because the books are printed in landscape (oblong) quarto format, the marks straddle the top center of two folios and thus are susceptible to a loss of twice the amount trimmed by the binder.

One or two copies do survive untrimmed. Among them is that of Josquin's first book of masses (1516), now at the Sibley Music Library in Rochester; al-though the pages have been cut, they seem not to have been trimmed. Gathering A, in particular, seems to have survived with virtually nothing lost at any side. The two sheets have almost exactly the same size: 347 × 482 mm and 347 × 481 mm. The copy of *Frottole V* at the Bibliothèque Sainte Geneviève in Paris, which appears not to have lost anything at the common edges of folios, has evidently been cut on the other two sides; it now shows pages measuring 167 × 221 mm, providing minimal sizes for a full sheet of at least 334 × 442 mm.[13]

There is also the possibility of estimating the size of the sheet when marks are not strictly centered on the half-sheet, or when the sheet was laid off-center on the press. In such cases, two apparently identical versions of a mark may, between them, preserve enough of the different parts of the mark to indicate clearly its overall size. If one of the relevant pages also contains a deckle edge, an estimate of the true size of the untrimmed sheet can be gleaned. Among the cases in which this can be done with a reasonable degree of optimism is the Bologna copy of Josquin's second book of masses (the 1505 printing), where the height of the sheet was probably about 345 mm, and the surviving width is 476 mm (after some trimming).

The results of these analyses are surprisingly consistent. The average size of a sheet of paper as received by Petrucci from the stationer and presented to the press, seems to have been about 347 × 482 mm. This corresponds to the size most commonly called *Mezana*. Briquet cites this size as about 345 × 500 mm, Labarre gives ca.345 × 515 mm, and Needham calls it "Median", with a size of approximately 35 × 52 cm.[14]

Different conclusions may be drawn from the evidence of the last books of music printed by Petrucci. The volume of music by Pisano (1520) seems to have been printed on half-sheets of paper in octavo format, with horizontal chain-lines. It has trimmed pages, measuring 113 × 170 mm, which would produce a whole sheet of paper with a minimum size of 340 × 450 mm. Not surprisingly, the paper carries a watermark which is also found in earlier editions. The paper was probably of the same size as that used for the earlier editions. The different trimmed size as preserved, however, reflects more closely the size of Florentine partbooks, as will be shown later.

The final books, from the 1530s, have papers of a different size. The earlier, the "*Musica XII*", was also not cut at the common edges of the pages, when first discovered. The two folios have a combined height of 279 mm, and a maximum width of 405 mm; it appears, however, that they have been cut down and that both measurements should be larger than this. The other, the *Motetti del Fiore* of 1538, survives in two fragmentary exemplars: the sheet in the Archivio di Stato at Pesaro measures 334 × 443 mm and is apparently untrimmed. According to Gialdroni and Ziino,[15] the other sheet, in private possession, is the same size and has the same watermark.

Petrucci's earliest papers are of admirable quality. They were certainly bought in Venice, for the marks they contain conform to those most frequently found in Venetian documents[16] and are similar to those in Aldus's or other printers' work of the time. The patterns of paper use confirm, too, that Petrucci was following standard buying patterns. The paper that monopolizes his second title, the *Canti B* of early 1502, is also found in the first edition of *Odhecaton A*. The paper that begins to appear with the next book—*Motetti A*—is found in several of the following volumes. This paper has been subdivided in my analysis of watermarks into three different possible papers. They all contain the same basic mark in the countermark position, consisting of a capital letter A with a bar across the top. The modern observer cannot always be sure whether this bar is actually a thicker laid line, or really part of the mark, whether the bar extends on both sides or only one, or even, sometimes, whether there is a bar at all. Thus, I have divided the mark up into three different classes, according to how it looked at the time I studied the individual copy. Probably, all three are variants of one pair of marks and represent supplies purchased from the same *cartolaio*.[17] They seem to confirm a pattern whereby Petrucci bought large batches of paper, from a *cartolaio* rather than from the makers, with the intention of having on hand enough paper for at least one book. Indeed this group of papers lasts, with few exceptions, for seven editions, until *Motetti B* of mid-1503.

Thereafter, the patterns of paper use seem at times more complex. Fewer books are printed with only one paper. Several show patterns suggesting that Petrucci used more than one batch of paper, rather than stock bought specifically for the book. Most clear-cut in this respect is the pattern of paper use in the 1504 edition of *Canti C*. (See table 3-1).

The pattern of watermarks suggests that the book was printed in layers.[18] Two aspects of other evidence are important here. First, there seem to be layers of content that match some of the layers of paper: gathering A contains the table of contents and so was probably printed last. The second is drawn from other books; the preceding volume, of masses by La Rue, was printed with paper 6 and 8 in the Superius and Tenor, and paper 11 in the Altus and Bassus; the immediately succeeding volumes (the masses of Agricola and the last edition of *Odhecaton A*) are printed entirely on papers 11 and 12. I am inclined to believe that Petrucci's *cartolaio* was supplying him with batches of both papers 6 and 11 during 1503, and that he replaced paper 6 with paper 12 during 1504. This theory explains why the papers appear consistently through several gatherings and then are changed, while there is no evidence of changes in the house practice for the music printed on them.

At other times, Petrucci appears to have bought a stock with a specific book in mind. The batches of paper found in *Frottole III* (1505) or the frottola editions of 1506–07 are clear examples. More obviously, a special batch was purchased for the 1513 edition of Paulus's book, the *Paulina*. All these papers tend to be white and opaque, and to produce good impressions. The *Paulina*, at least, is probably an example of an apparently common phenomenon, whereby the author or commissioner of a volume was also responsible for supplying the paper. There is no evidence, however, that this happened for any of the books of music.

Before he left Venice Petrucci had taken to using paper of a less consistent quality: this may suggest no more than that he was buying from different stationers, or that his stationers were buying from different mills. But it also seems to

TABLE 3-1 Watermark distribution in the various copies of *Canti C*

Gatherings		A	B	C–E	F–H	J–P	Q	R	S–X
Copy:	A-Wn	12	6	11	6	9	13	6	11–12[a]
	F-Pc	11–12[b]	6	11	6–11[c]	9	13	6	11–12[d]
	I-TVcap	11–12[b]	6	11	11–6[e]	9	13	6	11–12[f]

A number of the sheets with mark 6 also have a countermark 11.

[a] S (both sheets) and T outer sheet on paper 11, the rest on paper 12.

[b] outer sheet on paper 11 and inner sheet on paper 12.

[c] G inner sheet, only, on paper 11.

[d] both sheets of S on paper 11, the rest on paper 12.

[e] F outer sheet, only, on paper 11.

[f] T inner sheet, only, on paper 12.

reflect a gradual decline in the high standards with which he had set out in 1501. Books printed toward the end of that first decade more often contain an amalgam of papers, and also more often contain paper of variable colour, thickness, and quality of finish. The variable finish ensures that the papers take ink with varying degrees of success, and that certain sheets or pages present images that are largely grey or even partially missing.

Once in Fossombrone and printing music regularly (in 1514), Petrucci seems for a while to have had difficulty in acquiring regular stocks of good paper. The quality of paper does not match that of either many Venetian editions or the non-musical books of 1513. There is a relatively large number of papers in the surviving musical volumes, and many of these seem to be job-lots, for they are used only slightly. These papers are often not of good quality: each is markedly less consistent in thickness, acid content, absorbency and quality of the vatman's work, varying not only from sheet to sheet, but also across the width of a single sheet. It seems unlikely that Petrucci did not have access to good paper; Fabriano, the most important center for high-quality Italian paper, was nearby, and also within the Papal States. I suspect that the music-publishing business was not as successful as Petrucci had hoped; he would have had to develop new outlets to sell the early musical volumes of 1514 and 1515, and to ship much of his stock to major but distant centers, including Venice. As a result, I believe that the paper patterns of these years suggest that he could not afford to lay in large stocks of high-quality paper, and was experimenting with a series of cheaper papers from other *cartolai* and mills (perhaps including the one he was later to buy in Fossombrone).

The exceptions are the books by Paulus de Middelburgh and Castiglione. The paper for the first, the *Paulina de recta paschae*, was almost certainly supplied specifically for this volume. The second book, Castiglione's Epistle to Henry VIII, seems to have used stock left over from the printing of the earlier, more ambitious volume. These two books account for the only appearances in Petrucci's editions of two (closely related) papers, each with a mark of a balance within a circle, and surmounted by a bird. A similar mark with a balance but without the bird had been used by Petrucci for some time during 1503–05, and this is also one of his better-quality papers. The third non-musical volume, again by Paulus, the *Parabola Christi* of 1516, also uses a paper not found elsewhere in Petrucci's output: in this case the mark is a gauntlet.

The last musical editions and re-editions of 1519–20 are printed on a paper that can vary from an opacity and density so great that chain lines are scarcely visible to other sheets so flimsy that they are nearly translucent. These papers are of variable consistency, can carry no mark at all or show marks in virtually the same condition, and can even appear side-by-side in a printed edition. Despite their differences, they apparently had come from the same supplier.

In the early sixteenth century, the leading center for papermaking was still Fabriano. Papermakers in the hinterland of the Veneto, however, had become prolific suppliers of paper for the city. It is not surprising that modern-day scholars have begun to be able to distinguish papers which circulated principally in the Veneto or in Venice from those that found their principal uses in the Marche or in Tuscany, and that appear to have originated more commonly in Fabriano. Yet it is clear that many makers in different centers used very similar marks, and this is partly a reflection of the function of marks. Whereas some marks (those with initials no doubt among them) were intended to indicate the maker of the paper, others seem to have been used more as an indication of the quality and size of the paper, or of the stationer or *libraio* who had ordered the batch.[19] In this situation it is no wonder that similar marks could appear all over Italy. The series of anchor marks studied by Mošin have diverse provenances, even when many details of the marks are similar.[20] Papers with anchor marks and circulating in the Veneto will have looked, to the stationer's eye, very similar to other papers circulating farther south. Petrucci's editions carry seven different marks showing anchors within circles, and these are found at quite different periods of his work. We can assume that some were purchased in Venice, and others after his return to Fossombrone, and indeed the provenances suggested by Briquet and other authorities support such a view.

Beside the anchor, Petrucci's papers carry other marks familiar to the modern scholar. The pair of crossed arrows on paper used in Petrucci's earliest volumes, the six-pointed star in a circle, the tower, the merman, and the half-moon—all these are classes of mark found in many Italian editions of the period and often cited in modern studies. Similarly common are some of the marks found in the lower corner of a sheet, at the position of the countermark: these include initials, or a pair of small flowers (one a fleur-de-lys). Such marks perhaps indicated papers of general utility, for they are found in manuscript as well as printed documents of the period.

Petrucci's practice seems to have consisted (with the exceptions mentioned above) of buying a bulk supply of paper at one time and using it up as he needed it, rather than buying just enough paper to print a single title. Thus, marks that seem to be the same tend to appear in two or more books in close succession, to be replaced by new marks in the final gatherings of the last of these books or in subsequent books. A good example lies in the use of the papers with a simple countermark (here called Nos.3, 4, and 5), which seem to have been the basis for many of Petrucci's editions of 1507–08. In other cases, a relatively small batch of paper will appear in one or two volumes and disappear; even the exceptional papers bought for the *Paulina* were also used for the subsequent book by Castiglione.[21]

While Petrucci's pressmen were working down the piles of paper from the stationer, they could well come to the end of one batch in the middle of a press-run and simply switch to a new paper. This might happen once or more often in a single title, depending on the state of the paper stock: perhaps there were relatively few reams left of several papers, all of which could be employed for one volume; alternatively, a new batch of paper might recently have arrived, and this would predominate in a single volume.

Occasionally, two or more papers will run in tandem through a sequence of books. There are two possible implications of this pattern. One is that the formes for two books were being prepared simultaneously, with different compositors working on each. (The book of La Rue's masses may be an example.) The other is that two presses, each with its own supply of paper, were being used to print these books, in which case the books could have been prepared either simultaneously or consecutively, again presumably by two compositors. In the majority of cases, it is not possible to tell which of these options was followed, although other ranges of evidence lead me to believe that two books were sometimes printed at the same time.[22]

Then there are volumes in which several papers appear to have been used in a haphazard manner. In these cases, it is not unusual to find different papers in different copies of the same sheet; all copies nonetheless show the same setting of type. Such cases argue for Petrucci having built up a collection of tail-ends of stocks of papers, all of which could be piled together and used at once. This probably explains the pattern of papers found in *Motetti B.*

The result of these patterns of paper distribution is as might be expected. It is quite typical to find more than one paper in any edition printed by Petrucci. The patterns of occurrence, however, are still worthy of analysis. Patterns of paper change in a single volume may well indicate the order of work, perhaps that the first gathering was printed later, especially if that first gathering contains an index to the volume. I have referred to this pattern in the edition of *Canti C* (1504), where both sheets of the first gathering are printed on one of the two papers also used for the last four gatherings of the book. One of these papers had been used in the last gatherings of the previous volumes, but the other is new with this title.

If the change of paper can be found in one gathering for some copies and in the next for others, this probably tells us something slightly more complex. In such cases, the presence of other changes between copies adds force to any argument that might be made: an instance involving Ghiselin's masses is discussed in the next chapter.

In other books, one batch of paper was being finished, and another started, and the two seem to have become mixed at the press. The 1503 edition of La Rue's masses (A–B^8; C^{10}; D–E^8; F^{8}G^6) shows the following pattern (see Table 3-2).[23]

This clearly indicates that there was not enough of a stock of paper 6 to finish the book; paper 11 was used for the last four gatherings, D–G. However, paper 6 did not even complete three gatherings, for some stock of paper 8 was added to it. It seems to me that stacks of papers 6 and 8 were picked up at random from the paper stock, resulting in an apparently haphazard appearance of one or the other in the surviving copies. Both papers had been used in the preceding

TABLE 3-2 Watermark distribution in the various copies of *Misse Petri de la Rue* (1503)

Gatherings	A–B	CI	CII	CIII	D–G
A-Wn	6	8	6	8	11
E-Bc					11
GB-CW					11
GB-Lbl	6	6	6	8	11
I-Ac	6	6	6	8	11
I-Bc	6	8	8	6	11
I-Mc		8	8	8	11
I-Rvat	6	6	8	6	11
PL-Kj	6	8	6	8	11
US-CA		6	6	6	
US-NH	6				

editions. The extreme example of this situation, when several batches of paper were being finished up, is less susceptible of this form of analysis, for we cannot tell that any one paper (as indicated by its watermarks) was present in only one consistent batch.

These extreme examples, however, should not blind us to the point that there are very few cases in which one paper appears in only one book, and that it must have been normal for Petrucci's men to change paper stock during a volume. One curious case is the appearance of a very large mark, a castle with banners flying, found only in three gatherings of the Munich copy of *Frottole VIII* (1507). Why this paper should have been used here, I cannot imagine. I suspect that Petrucci, whose shop was in the middle of a most prolific phase, found himself suddenly short of paper stock and borrowed a few reams from another printer.

One or two other apparent cases of very brief uses of paper may have a different explanation. With the evidence that there were so many "hidden" editions (evidence introduced step by step and discussed in detail in chapter 5), we have to recognise that many more editions may be lost, and that there are probably fewer pauses in Petrucci's output (at least in Venice) than we have previously thought. It is likely, therefore, that some slight appearances of individual marks are a reflection of their use to a much greater extent in a volume now lost. An example occurs in *Canti C* (1504), where gathering Q of every copy is printed on a paper not found elsewhere in Petrucci's output; there are gaps in Petrucci's production in the surrounding months, which (while I cannot suggest specific titles) may have been filled by some lost editions or partial printings. Another example may be the merman mark found in the Rochester copy of Josquin's third book of masses (dated 1514).

Finally, once these paper patterns and their significance are grasped, we can use anomalies in their appearances to look for cancels or sophisticated editions. This is a slightly more complex issue, for it is always possible that a few sheets of a stock of paper may have languished in the shop for months or even years, only to be used later. The issue is discussed in chapter 5, though I mention one clear-cut instance here. One copy (at Vienna) of the edition of Ghiselin's masses stands apart from the others, for it is printed on quite different papers. These papers are found only in later volumes, beginning in 1507, but most significantly used in early Fossombrone printings. It does not take a detailed comparison of the Viennese copy of Ghiselin with the other copies to confirm that it represents an entirely different setting of type, one that went through the press years later.

Typographical Material

This is the second principal component without which Petrucci could not have proceeded. Although his type was unusual in a few ways, not least in that it was designed for printing music, it seems to have conformed in most respects to normal practice for the period. Thus, I shall not dwell at length on the general principles governing each category of typographical material, discussing only those aspects that are of relevance to this study.

There are several early descriptions of how type was made. The first is apparently by Biringuccio in 1540.[24] The composition of type metal given by this author has been translated as 92.3 percent fine tin, 3.85 percent black lead, and 3.85 percent fused marcasite of antimony. Fioravanti, in his book of 1567 mentioned above, refers to a "mistura che ui entra stagno, piombo negro, antimonio, marcasita, rame, & ferro"—that is of tin, black lead, antimony and marcasite, copper and iron.[25]

The actual elements used in Petrucci's type and their proportions cannot be guessed at now. It seems that the introduction of antimony as an ingredient of type-metal was fairly new at the turn of the century, and it may be, as suggested in chapter 1, that this is the distinctive feature that allowed Petrucci to use such fine music sorts. A number of elements of his material were finely cast; flats and ledger lines, in particular, appear to be very thin.

In distinguishing the different ingredients of a printed page, it is important to remember that Petrucci used a multiple-impression process, in which the music and the staves on which it appeared were printed at different runs through the press. At times, the text was also printed at a different, third run. As a result, each of these layers had to be of different typographical material, for each would be set in its forme at a different time.

In fact, there are five different ranges of typographical material to be found in Petrucci's books. These correspond first to the different levels of content—staves, notes, and text—and second to the two different levels of decoration—initial letters and decorative blocks. In addition, there are ranges of material that produce white space on the page, the spacing sorts and the furniture.

This section discusses each of these ranges of type and blocks in turn, showing how they were organised to make the production of Petrucci's editions as simple as possible, how they changed over his productive years, and how they can be used for bibliographical analysis. But first it is necessary to make a few comments on the issue of measurements—or rather, on the two related issues of the level of accuracy of my given measurements and our knowledge of the amount of paper shrinkage. Since the paper was expected to be moist during printing, so that the ink would penetrate the fibers and become a permanent part of the paper,[26] there was always the certainty that it would shrink slightly as it dried out. I have seen different measurements given for paper shrinkage after printing, and it clearly varied.[27] McKerrow says that "it may be worth while to warn beginners in bibliography that they must be prepared for considerable variations, amounting to 4 or 5 percent linear measurement, in the size of prints from the same block".[28] It is evident, even from the measurements that follow, that such variations are possible, and indeed to be expected.

Throughout the following discussion of Petrucci's typographical material, as well as in many places in the bibliographical descriptions, I give measurements that are correct at least to the nearest millimeter, and sometimes to tenths of a millimeter, that is, to lower than 1 percent accuracy.[29] It might seem, given the previous comments on paper damping and shrinkage, that such precision is not valuable, indeed is perhaps harmful. I would agree that there is little point in making comments about many of the slight variations that occur, from copy to copy or edition to edition, in measurements of the same feature. A clear example lies in the series of measurements I give, in the bibliographical descriptions, of the vertical spread and distance apart of sets of staves. Here, slight differences have generally been ignored.

Yet there are two reasons why I do present measurements to a degree of accuracy finer than the 5 percent allowed for variation. One is that there are some patterns of change in measurements that can be shown to be statistically significant, even when they appear to lie within or about at the 5 percent limit; the most obvious of these is that of the lengths of sets of staves. The other is that *all* the paper in a book was subject to shrinkage, and thus the variation between features should be less than 5 percent. Indeed, the presentation of these more precise figures gives the reader a chance to determine the variation *between copies*, rather than that from a dry to a dampened sheet. This will, in turn, give us some idea of how much we should actually allow for the *variation* in paper shrinkage, a much more useful figure.

Music Staves

Staves would seem to be the most straightforward part of Petrucci's material, simple blocks constructed to fill the width of the text-block on each page. Each block was probably made of wood, with the stave-lines inserted in ready-made grooves in the block. The lines themselves would have been fairly thin and made of type-metal, and would necessarily have been rather fragile. Although they must have been prepared from rolled rather than cast metal, the manner in which they deform does not suggest the use of a hard alloy.

This pattern of having staves mounted in long blocks to cover the whole width of the page was not new. While many liturgical printers used short segments of staves, some did have sets of full-width staves. Much depended on the range of liturgical books being printed. With some books, the music was so frequently interrupted by rubrics, or in such short sections, that long stave-blocks would find little use. A prolific printer of liturgical books, like Hamman, possessed both.[30] For Petrucci, the consistency of the layout of his books made long blocks more convenient.

Since the staves and the music could never be set and printed at the same time (for they overlapped one another), the details of the size and placing of the staves were critical: they had to match exactly the details of the size and placing of the musical notation. If each stave was the same length, all would fit into the same text-block. Also, if each was the same height on the page, that is, the individual stave-lines were the same distance apart, they could be thought to be interchangeable. Further, if each stave was placed in the forme accurately, the musical notation would be aligned correctly. The same condition had to apply for the distance between staves, so that the pitches of one system could be aligned as accurately as those of the one above.

Indeed, at the simplest level of analysis, that of visual observation, these two conditions seem to be fulfilled almost all the time. The notation of pitches is rarely ambiguous. Although there are instances in which the notation extends beyond the length of the stave, these are clearly less critical for the user: as long as the only elements outside the stave are the clef at one end or the *custos* at the other, the musical notation remains entirely legible and usable.

Once detailed measurements are taken, however, it is apparent that the staves are not always the same. They vary in length from about 173 mm to about 180 mm. This variation is not haphazard, but rather seems to reflect a habit of keeping distinct and identifiable sets of staves in separate formes, ready for use. All the staves found on one page will measure between 178 and 181 mm in length; all those on another cover between 173 and 175 mm. Further, the staves of one page correspond in length to those of the other pages of the same forme, so that the whole of one side of a printed sheet will have staves of approximately the same length.[31]

Table 3-3 gives the measurements, in millimeters, for the lowest stave on all the pages in the Bassus partbook (signatures F and G) of Josquin's second book of masses (30 June 1505), as preserved at the Biblioteca Marucelliana in Florence.

This is perhaps more usefully arranged according to the formes in which the staves would be laid out for the press: the outer sheet (FI and GI) had two formes, for folios 1r, 2v, 7r, and 8v, and for 2r, 1v, 8r, and 7v. The inner sheet similarly had formes for folios 3–6 (the pattern is explained fully in chapter 4).

The pattern of two consistently used formes of staves is exceptionally clear, even allowing for what are presumably slight variations in paper shrinkage. These sets of staves must have corresponded with formes prepared for the music, so that the alignment of the two could be precisely controlled. Certainly the pattern is intended to be consistent. Long sets of staves were meant to be printed on the same pages as long formes for the music. The two were therefore presumably set up in formes that also matched. This simple decision would help to ensure the accurate alignment, or register, of the different impressions.

The correspondence, although certainly planned, was not always maintained. In several titles, long musical formes appear on pages that have short stave formes, resulting in a clef at one end, and a *custos* (occasionally even a note) at the other,

TABLE 3-3 Stave-lengths in the Bassus book of *Missarum Josquin Liber Secundus* (1505) (copy at I-Fm)

	1r	1v	2r	2v	3r	3v	4r	4v	5r	5v	6r	6v	7r	7v	8r	8v
F	—	175	175	180	180	175	175	180	180	175	175	181	179	175	174	189
G	178	175	175	179	179	175	175	180	180	174	175	181	179	175	174	—

TABLE 3-4 Rearranged by formes

Forme:	Outer	1r	2v	3r	4v	Inner	2r	1v	4r	3v
FI		—	180	179	180		175	175	174	175
FII		180	180	180	181		175	175	175	175
GI		178	179	179	—		175	175	174	175
GII		179	180	180	181		175	175	174	175

lying in the white space beyond the end of the stave. The vertical dimensions seem to have been the same for all formes, for the pitches are not in doubt in these cases.[32]

The measurements indicate that Petrucci always maintained, from 1503, at least two sets of such staves, and often more. It is also evident that they were normally kept in the forme. While not an integral part of the forme, for individual staves could be removed and replaced when they became damaged, the staves of one forme reappear in a consistent relationship to each other over long periods. Sequences of minor damage to individual staves can be followed from sheet to sheet of an individual printed book, and from one book to the next.

For example, the staves found on A3v of the Oxford copy of *Motetti IV* reappear on B3v and C3v, and also on A7v and B1v of the outer sheets of these gatherings. The staves on B1r and B2v of *Frottole XI* reappear on C3r and C4v, and on D1r and D2v. Indeed, some of the sets of staves used in this volume had also been used in the first edition of the first book of *Motetti de la Corona*, some months earlier. The interruptions in this kind of pattern are sometimes no more than a result of damage to or the deterioration of individual staves, but they are occasionally a product of a change in procedure or a sudden urgent need. The detailed analysis of these patterns will be found in chapter 4, with a discussion of some conclusions that can be drawn from them.

However, Petrucci had set out in 1501 with a more complex sequence of staves. Even a casual glance at the *Odhecaton A* of 1501 shows that some staves were considerably shorter. These were intended to occupy the first line of the upper voice of a composition, leaving a space at the left end of the line, into which the initial letter could be inserted. Petrucci needed only two of these staves, one for the top of each verso on a forme. In practice he seems to have had four (and possibly more), which allowed him to set up two formes of staves, or to employ capital letters that occupied the height of two staves at once.[33] These staves did not last long. By his second title, *Canti B* of February 1502, he had abandoned them and the practice that required them.[34]

This cannot be an indication of the durability of Petrucci's staves. I have not done a thorough study of their decay, or of their replacement with new sets, but the little evidence I have collected tends to suggest that they lasted for perhaps seven or eight editions. This evidence lies in the span of time during which specific patterns of staves may be traced through different editions, and in the replacement of individual staves. Such a short life span should not surprise us, for the staves were evidently relatively fragile. Although at times they do produce thick impressions on the printed page,[35] they must have comprised very thin pieces of typemetal, in long units, and therefore susceptible to bending and cracking. Indeed, there are relatively few pages in which no single stave-line shows a bend or corner at one end or the other—already an indication of the thinness and potential weakness of the lines.

Petrucci seems to have kept the same basic pattern from 1502 until 1520. All the staves are the same height, and they lie the same distances apart on the page. The introduction of the slightly longer set of staves (which I have mentioned above, and which were *ca.* 180 mm in length) occurred during 1503. These staves do not affect the procedure in any way; indeed, as I have remarked, they could be printed on the same pages as the narrower sets of music formes without any problems for printer or reader.

This slight difference apart, there was every reason for Petrucci to maintain the same detailed layout for the staves. He could then be sure that they would provide good register with the formes of music. In almost all of the double-impression volumes, the spacing between staves and lines of text is very consistent. The implication is that Petrucci's men had developed some method of ensuring this consistency, either through the use of designated pieces of furniture, or from some more subtle application of the technology.

Thus, it is surprising that the last three editions (the 1520 edition of music by Pisano, the volume I have called "*Musica XII*", and the 1538 *Motetti del Fiore*) use different sets of staves. These are shorter (only 122 mm long in the Pisano book, and 156–58 mm long in the other two) and slightly narrower (9.7 mm high). In this respect, as in the size of paper, these volumes are anomalous and will be discussed further in chapter 5.

There is one instance of Petrucci printing a stave without using one of these blocks. The short lowest stave on f.I3v of *Frottole XI* (1514) is evidently made up of five separate rules, of the sort Petrucci was using for leger lines. Each is about 112 mm long, but they are not equidistant from each other. None is straight, and the middle one is very curved. I assume that they were printed as an addition to the page, in a separate press-run after the normal two impressions. In this case, the impression of staves and text must have preceded the musical, for it was presumably only after the music had been printed that Petrucci discovered the need for a fifth stave.

Petrucci also developed a series of six-line "staves", for lute music. These seem to have been similar to the standard staves in their construction, and to have been used in the same manner.

Type

Some things are known about the general shape and character of early type fonts, drawing on a diverse range of evidence, the most obvious, being the surviving punches and matrices. In most cases, these give us no more than an idea of the dimensions of the face itself. We cannot tell whether these sorts were mounted on larger bodies, nor can we learn anything of the sizes of those bodies.

A second level of information comes from the many instances in which the edges of type sorts have taken ink and left impressions on the page. The implications of these data are twofold. They give us the actual face size of the sort— that is, how much space it occupied on the page. This can be valuable when there are problems of spacing (lack of alignment between music and text, for example), or when there is the possibility of printing "double-stops" at one impression. The data also show whether the sorts might be kerned—a feature of considerable value in multiple-impression printing, and discussed in detail below.

A third range of data comes from those occasional sorts that have "pulled" during printing—that is, sprung or been drawn from the forme—and lie on top of the rest of the type. They then take ink when subsequent copies are printed and leave a distinctive black shape on the page. A number of examples have been studied for the incunable period, and several collected and illustrated by Schol-derer,[36] among others. Some show a groove across one side of the body, a feature found in hand-press type to the present day and intended to ensure that no sorts are printed with the character upside down. In practice, when setting type, all the sorts in a line of text should show the groove, appearing along the line, as a guarantee that all have been placed in the forme with the letters in the same direction.

There is one such pulled sort visible in Petrucci's extant copies. In the Bod-leian copy of *Motetti libro quarto*, on f.A4v, a black impression appears to represent a broken piece of type, almost certainly from the text font. The area is about 3.0 × 12.3 mm, with a marked indentation on the upper surface, probably from such a groove. There is a crack, probably a break in the sort, and the impression shows only part of the whole type-sort. The majority of examples of pulled sorts have a long measurement of over 20 mm, representing the height-to-paper.[37] Schold-erer's plates, for example, include measurements of 22 and 27 mm, and those of the Type Face Society show measurements of 24 mm.[38] When Scholderer has a shorter measurement, he suggests, and the plate confirms, that the sort was broken when it was pulled. This is probably true also for the Petrucci example.

For Petrucci's music type, we unfortunately have no such evidence. Indeed, there is no reason to believe that his type was cast with a groove; grooves were not used by all typecasters this early[39] and would have had limited use for setting music, since each flagged sort (from *minima* down) had to be capable of being printed so that the impression had its tail up or down.

MUSIC TYPE

As far as I can tell, Petrucci used basically the same set of music type throughout almost all his active life. New versions of some notes, especially *minimas*, appear during his Fossombrone years, but these look to be no more than heavier versions of the earlier forms. It seems probable therefore that Petrucci kept the punches for the music sorts and had new matrices made and sorts cast as he needed them. Indeed, this makes sense of the situation in the 1520s and 1530s, when some of his type-sorts appear in Roman editions; although he retained the punches, the matrices could be sold or loaned.[40]

Petrucci used a full and normal range of sorts,[41] void notes with values from *maxima* to *semifusa*, colored notes for the *longa*, *brevis*, and *semibrevis*, rests for all values from the perfect *longa* to the *semifusa*, and a series of two-note ligatures. All the normal ancillary signs were available, some in more than one version: these included the three standard clefs and a gamma-ut clef; several mensuration signs, accidentals, leger lines, *custodes*, single bar-lines and bar-lines with repeat dots.

In addition, at some point in 1505 or 1506, Petrucci developed a complete series of signs for lute tabulature. This involved rhythm signs, numerals to indicate the pitches, and different bar lines to cover the larger staves. The pitch numerals included "x" for the 10th fret, and a similar "x" with one or two dots above it, for the next two frets. These tabulature sorts seem to have been similar to the music sorts in every respect and used in a similar manner.

It is not certain that all the signs were printed from orthodox typesorts, cast in metal from matrices. The mensuration sign for perfect tempus, perfect prolation—a circle with a dot in the center—may have been made from a woodblock, although several examples of it look suspiciously similar. Indeed, in a case of two examples on the same page, one looks to be an inverted image of the other, suggesting that both were cast from the same matrix.

The other symbols for musical notation were available as normal movable type. As such they were cast on standard bodies, although probably without the groove on one side. Not only are various note sorts (and *sb/m* rests) inverted whenever needed, even some *cum opposite proprietate* ligatures seem occasionally to have been inverted and used for the notation of an ascending ligature *cum proprietate et cum perfectione* (*b,l*).

Other elements might be thought to have been easily available from text fonts: the numerals for proportion signs, or those for frets in tabulature. The latter, however, certainly did not come from the punches and matrices that Petrucci used for his text font (for the sizes are quite different), and in any case many more sorts were cast for each numeral, in order to be able to set more than one forme of tabulature. The three numerals used for proportion signs, either singly or in combination, also do not appear in any of his text fonts, and seem to have been cast especially for the music font. The zero is small and not well formed, while the "3" and "2" are larger elegant figures.

The whole font is, as has often been remarked, peculiarly elegant, for it uses elongated diamond heads and long tails to the notes. The treatment of flags on fusas and smaller values is in accordance with the proportions of the basic design. Much of the character of this font is reminiscent of northeastern Italian scribal practice at the end of the previous century. Of course, it is not particularly like the hands displayed in the less formal work of the Milanese Gafori or (later) Bolognese Spataro manuscripts, where tails tend to be shorter, notes less precisely angled, and the whole vertical effect more compact.[42] Indeed, by 1500 this had become the character of many north Italian hands. Exceptions, which look much closer to the font designed for Petrucci, seem to be associated with the court of Ferrara: for example, the manuscripts I-MOe α.M.1.11–12, I-MOe α.M.1.13, and the musical fragments in I-MO as (the latter two, in particular) lie close in style to Petrucci's font.[43] These are formal hands, of course, and it is significant, though not surprising, that Petrucci should have chosen to imitate such a hand. Although they were also about twenty years old by the time Petrucci began to print,[44] similar hands continue to be found in northern Italy, for example in manuscripts from Verona. The hand in I-VEcap DCCLVII,[45] though again informal, has proportions much closer to those of Petrucci, even though, since the notes are more generously spaced across the page, the total effect is at first sight quite different. Once Petrucci had begun printing, similar hands were to be found in many centers in northern Italy. It seems likely that his typeface was modeled closely on, and then influenced, the style used in the area. Formal hands, such as that in I-Pc A17, and informal ones, as found in I-Vnm it.cl.IV.1795–1798, show the same long note-tails, larger bass clefs, and more vertical approach to the whole ductus.[46]

Given the range of symbols, and their diverse graphical content, few elements of Petrucci's font strike the reader as incongruous; this is true even when allowance is made for the changes in proportion that result from damage to the tails of notes, clefs, and *custodes*. These last, in particular, seem to suffer a great deal from damage, no doubt due to being kerned sorts.

This aspect of type, that it could be kerned, was increasingly commonplace from the late fifteenth century. I have mentioned, in chapter 1, the evidence for Aldus Manutius's use of kerned type, and the probability that Francesco Griffo had something to do with its development.[47] A kerned sort is one in which the symbol (to be printed) projects beyond the edge of the body of the type. One essential element of the beauty of a font is the manner in which different letters are different distances apart. The descender of a letter "y" can remove the body of the letter too far from the preceding letter; a sequence of letters "m" will look too close together if they are mounted on their bodies in the same manner as a sequence of letters "i"; finally, letters such as "f" or, particularly, capitals "Q", "T", or "R" (especially if they are cut with flair, approaching swash letters) will seem to be too far from the following letters. This problem of spacing can be partially overcome by mounting some letters off-center on their bodies, and by having ligatures—"ct", "fi", "ft", or "st" are common examples. The other solution is to kern some letters; then, the top of an "f" or the elegant tail of a capital "R" could project beyond the body of the sort and rest on the body of the next sort, or even on the leading or furniture. As a result, the effect of ligatures could be achieved without having to cast special sorts. At the same time, however, the kerned parts of these sorts were fragile and prone to damage during use or even when lying in the case.

The evidence suggests that most of Petrucci's shorter note values were mounted on small bodies, with the tails kerned. Three pieces of evidence point to this conclusion, one circumstantial and two more concrete. The most effective evidence lies in the patterns of damage that these sorts undergo. There are the normal traces of damage, of course, gashes across the tails of notes (now showing as white space), bruised corners of note heads, and splayed ends to the tails. In addition, there is a different and highly indicative form of damage. The further parts of a considerable number of the tails either are broken off or bent out of the straight line. Both these elements of change suggest that the tails were freestanding and not part of the body of the type, that is, that they were kerned. Even more significantly, in a great number of cases, this damage tends to occur at consistent distances from the body of the note: one particular distance, at about 3.7 mm from the top of the note head of *minimas*, *semiminimas*, and *fusas*, is so frequent, especially in the Fossombrone volumes, that it seems to indicate the point at which the notational tail left the body of the type-sort and became kerned. Clear examples can be seen in, for example, the third book of Josquin's masses of 1514 (see folio G3ν, stave 2, in the copy at B-Br), and his second book in the 1515 edition (in which there are several instances on ff.B1r and B2ν of the copy at GB-Lbl).

A second point concerns some evidence of the spacing sorts used for music. These sorts, which will be discussed in detail below, sometimes times give a vague indication of the dimensions of the musical sorts they are supporting. For example, there are occasional lines of ink traces, beyond the stave, in which each small patch of ink aligns itself with an individual note symbol or blank space on the stave. The evidence from these sorts can be used to determine the body size of sorts with notation on them, and also to distinguish the edge of the space allocated to music in the skeleton forme. Even more occasionally, the same pattern of marking can be seen within the stave, sometimes crossing the area that usually shows note tails. The presumption that follows is that the notes themselves are on small bodies and that the tails are kerned beyond these marks.

Finally, there is the evidence of the intrusion of the music on the space reserved for text. Although the music and the text were printed at different impressions, so that there is no intrinsic reason why they should not at times overlap,[48] there are reasons for suggesting that this overlap is an indication of the use of kerned sorts. The skeleton formes that ensured the correct alignment of music and staves will be discussed below. But one corollary of the multiple-impression process is that the music of each system would have been allocated a specific space, one corresponding exactly to that allocated to the staves in their skeleton forme. The boundary of this space is probably indicated by the lines of inking of spacing sorts, when they are outside the stave area. These lines are always at about the same distance below the text and are occasionally crossed by notes whose tails ascend or descend particularly far.

An immediate implication of the small body-size is that the music sorts had to be set in the forme in a manner diametrically opposed to that adopted for single-impression music. In the latter, all the sorts are the same height on the page, and all occupy the space of (and indeed carry) a five-line staff, plus however much space is allocated above and below the staff for tails. As a result, all the sorts can be entered in a straight line, occupying the same amount of vertical space in the forme (and hence on the page). A sort could indicate an erroneous pitch only if the wrong sort were inserted, or if the correct one were inserted upside down (producing a g' instead of a d" with a treble clef, for example). This is directly analogous to the manner in which text type was set and errors introduced.

With Petrucci's font, a completely different process was involved. For a music sort to be set in the forme at the right pitch, it had to be supported by spacing sorts above and below it; the number and size of these sorts would vary according to the musical pitch desired. The result would be a mosaic of sorts, spacers and symbols, in which each adjacent pitch would produce a different pattern of spacers.[49] This procedure must have been more laborious for the compositor; and errors by which a pitch was misplaced by a second or a third proportionally more likely to have occurred.

There is one element of the musical notation that seems always to have been printed with the text—the leger line. It would of course be impossible to print these lines at the same time as the music, for the only times they were needed were exactly those when the music would occupy the same space in the forme. Thus they had to be either inserted by hand or printed with the text. At first sight, they seem to have been done in manuscript. Many of the lines are far from straight, many seem to typify the sort of curve that hand-drawn "straight" lines often acquire, and many seem to be simply too distorted to have been the result of impressing a piece of type. However, there are two reasons for my conviction that they were printed: comparison of different copies often shows identical curvature of the same lines, even curvatures that seem implausible; and there are many cases in which the leger line is actually too far to the right or left to be superimposed on the relevant notes. This second phenomenon is most unlikely to have arisen from insertion of lines by manuscript, and is in any case also to be found in diverse copies of the same page. Both these patterns are typical of the details of printed material.

The leger lines must have been thinner than the stave lines, probably thin enough to be squeezed into the normal text forme without needing to adjust the leading of the text. In fact, I suspect that the leger lines were made of the same material as the leading. Such rules, still occasionally used, though more often as wafer-thin leading than to take ink, would necessarily be rather fragile and flexible. I believe they show distortion because they were made of type-metal, were exceedingly thin, and projected above the body of the surrounding furniture and sorts, and thus had to take the full burden of the weight of the press.

One other piece of evidence is pertinent here, for it suggests that, late in the 1510s, Petrucci began to experiment with music type mounted on full-length bodies. These sorts would have reached from below the stave to above it and thus obviated the need for spacing sorts above and below the notational symbol. Although this would seem to be an advantage, leading to faster setting, it also would have necessitated a much larger font, for each note value and other pitched symbol would have to have been stored in individual sorts for every possible pitch on the stave. The evidence that Petrucci may have turned to this style of type is slight, but suggestive. It involves a number of damaged sorts in some of his latest volumes. For example, a pair of damaged minim sorts recurs at the same pitches on every sheet of the bass partbook of the *Motetti de la Corona Libro primo* as preserved at D-LEu (which is from the last printing of this title). Similarly, an unusual semiminim, with a narrower flag can be seen both in the last reprints of *Corona* editions, and in the 1538 *Motetti del Fiore*. While this tells us something about the amount of type Petrucci had to hand, the significant feature is that each of these sorts appears only at the same place on the stave: one example of the minim, with a down tail, is to be found only in the top space of the stave, and the semiminim appears only on the second line, reading downward.[50] This seems too much of a coincidence, given the number of sorts in a case.

The most plausible conclusion is that each of these sorts *could* only be printed at a specific pitch, and therefore that each was on a full-sized body, not only not kerned, but occupying the whole height of the musical setting space. If the evidence is interpreted this way, and (it has to be stressed) there is not much evidence, then it represents a major change in Petrucci's techniques. It is, in specific ways, looking forward to the single-impression fonts of the future.

TEXT FONTS

The appearance of roman text fonts in the fifteenth century allowed printers to match a common pattern in contemporary manuscripts, whereby humanistic texts, classical and modern literature, were mostly presented in roman characters, while theological and liturgical, legal and scientific texts regularly appeared in the more traditional Gothic faces.[51] This pattern, which was maintained for much of the earlier sixteenth century, meant that all printers kept a range of fonts with both characteristics. If Petrucci seems to have had fewer fonts of each style than many of his contemporaries, that is merely a result of the limited range of subjects he was printing. His musical volumes required standard sizes of text fonts, to fit between the staves; the lateral spacing of these fonts was also conditioned to some extent by their need to relate to well-spaced music printed above them. Apart from the text underlaid to the music, he had relatively little need for text fonts. The dedicatory letters in *Odhecaton A* make up the largest block of prose before the instruction pages found in the lute volumes. After these latter pages, the only large-scale use of a text font in music books lies in the continuing reprinting of his Roman privilege, from 1514 to 1519 and later.

Petrucci did use other fonts in his music books. There are one or two uses of a pair of larger fonts, which I shall discuss below. But the principal reason for other fonts was in response to the commissions of Paulus de Middelburgh, in the second decade of the century. Even the roman fonts that had appeared in his frottola volumes were unsuitable for a serious scholarly text, or for the letter from Castiglione to Henry VIII of England. For these, Petrucci needed roman type of a larger size, in a style that would bear comparison with the distinguished fonts being used by his contemporaries elsewhere in the Marche, Soncino among them. This is the font that was probably designed and cut for Petrucci by Francesco Griffo, who was also surely responsible for the Greek font (though not for the Hebrew) necessary for a number of sections of Paulus's *Paulina*.

The descriptive details and measurements for each font will appear in chapter 15. Here I wish merely to indicate the general character of the fonts and the manner in which Petrucci used them.

Rotonda Fonts

In common with most Italian printers of the early sixteenth century, Petrucci had, as a central Gothic text font, one which would now be called rotonda or bastarda. This font is small, compared with many text fonts of the time, with an 'x' height of a mere 2.2 mm. However, it is elegant, typical of Venetian fonts of the end of the fifteenth century, with long ascenders and descenders. It is ideal for use below music, for it is a laterally compressed font, so that more characters could fit under each individual note symbol.

The font has the standard twenty-two–letter alphabet, with a number of letters represented by two forms. Among these, of course, are "r", "s", and "u"/ "v", but "a", "i", and "m" also appear in two designs, not apparently intended to be distinguished. A number of ligatures were cast for this font, although relatively few were called for in musical texts.

There is also a large number of contractions, although these rapidly diminish through use. It is possible that they were somewhat more fragile, although I tend to the view that the typesetters were merely keeping abreast of a pattern among scribes and other compositors, under which the great diversity of abbreviation signs was rapidly eroded. In any case, the majority of such contractions does tend to occur where they would most easily be interpreted—that is in settings of the Ordinary of the Mass and in prose sections—for example, the colophon.

In addition, there were two larger rotonda fonts, each with a special function. The smaller of the two was used rarely. It was probably acquired in or about 1514 (perhaps even at the same time as the fonts for the *Paulina*), for it appears for some rubrics in, for example, the edition of Mouton's masses, and for parts of the 1520 volumes. Otherwise, it seems not to have been used at all.

The larger, although it was not used to underlay music, was used more regularly. It is the font that carries the titles for a number of volumes, from the first *Odhecaton A* into the later second decade. At the same time, it was used regularly to indicate the part-names when books are in choirbook layout. As such, it clearly was a font and not a series of blocks or specific characters. Although the greatest need was for the symbols that made the words *Altus*, *Bassus*, *Tenor*, and sometimes *Contra*, the rest of the alphabet was also available. The font also apparently included some ligatures and abbreviations. In particular, the double "s" of the word *Bassus* was regularly printed with a ligature. This font has very similar characteristics to those of the smallest rotonda font; it has the same approach to balance and to verticals, modified (of course) by the greater size and blackness of the type. It may well have been cut by the same man.

Roman Fonts

Petrucci also had roman fonts throughout his career. The first appears in the prose at the front of *Odhecaton A*. This stylish font is typical of its period. It is fairly dense and is set with small spaces between words. It contains the regular alphabet, with the normal variant forms, and has a number of ligatures and contractions. This font seems only to be used on these pages, in all the extant editions.

One of the same pages has a few Greek words, in each edition. In the first edition, the type for these was almost certainly borrowed from Aldus Manutius and represents part of his third Greek font. Apart from the known fact that Aldus was very protective of his type and its style, Petrucci would not have had type cast for so little material, for he would have had no further use for it. In addition, the third edition uses a different Greek face, from Aldus's fourth font. Petrucci's typesetter allocated space for it when setting up the roman face, but the new Greek face was more compact, and white space is left after both the insertions.[52] On the other hand, it seems unlikely that the roman font was borrowed, even though it disappears from Petrucci's output. It is the same in all editions—and Petrucci may well have anticipated further uses for it.

A more important roman font appears in the books of frottole. This is much more compact than the first, but is stylish, with attractive small serifs. It is laterally dense, with little white space between letters; several letters have kerned ascenders, and there is a small number of ligatures. The ampersand is surprisingly spacious in its design.

A third appears for the first time in any quantity in the instruction pages to the lute volumes. It is more compact and is not particularly attractive. In common with a number of small roman fonts of the time, it does not have distinctive forms or any great contrast in blackness. This makes large blocks of text difficult to read. For underlaying to music, however, it would seem to be ideal. The font remains in use throughout the rest of Petrucci's career, with many replacement sorts as needed. This font also has numerous abbreviations, which, again, appear more frequently in well-known texts or lengthy non-musical prose sections within music books.

A final and much more important roman font was used for the books by Paulus and Castiglione and is mentioned below.

Uses of Roman and Rotonda

The pattern of using roman and rotonda fonts for different purposes, found in most Italian printing of the period, is reflected in Petrucci's books. In his first, the *Odhecaton A*, Petrucci used rotonda sorts for the tavola, for the colophon, and for the text incipits to all musical pieces. On the other hand, a roman font was used for the two initial letters of dedication and praise, as befits their humanist pretensions.

This pattern is retained throughout the early volumes. Since there were no further uses for dedicatory epistles for some years, the roman font languished for a while. Both the three chanson volumes and those of religious or liturgical music were printed with a rotonda font for the underlay. This casts an interesting light on the Italian view of the status of chanson texts, especially since Petrucci immediately adopted the roman font for the first volume of frottole. French texts cannot have been thought to have the humanistic value accorded even to recent frottola texts.

Once Petrucci began to use the roman font for underlay, his frottola and lute volumes were regularly printed with that face. The sacred books retained the use of the (Gothic) rotonda face until the last few editions. At that point, in 1519, it seems probable that Petrucci had decided not to replace a tired and worn rotonda font, which was no longer worth using (and, indeed, had been showing increasing signs of wear), and abandoned it altogether. From then on, all books were printed with the roman font, regardless of content. The editions of the three *Motetti de la Corona* volumes that first appeared in that year, are all set in roman. Further, late editions of earlier Fossombrone titles (masses by Josquin, Févin and Mouton, or the first book of *Motetti de la Corona*) should be dated after the last rotonda edition preceding 1519 (the first book of Josquin's masses, of May 1516), simply on the basis of the use of this roman font. Other information helps to place them more closely; in particular, one paper that was evidently only in use for a short time, contains some sheets printed with the rotonda font and others printed with the roman. None of the editions concerned are true first editions, and all have to be dated in late 1516 at the earliest.

The Fonts for Paulus, Etc.

In chapter 1, I have shown that Francesco Griffo, in Fossombrone during parts of 1511 and 1512, was probably responsible for the design of these fonts, the most important of which was one in a roman face, used for the bulk of the text. This font, which has been described in the standard literature,[53] is almost consciously elegant. The letters have fine serifs, are elegantly shaded, and have effective risers and descenders. I suspect that the sorts are mounted on bodies of a good size, rather than leaded in the forme. The result is a well-spaced page, not too black, and highly legible.

In addition, Petrucci had a small font of Greek characters made for this book. The font includes most necessary characters, although he probably had few sorts of each, for Greek text is used sparingly in the book, and usually in small sections. Finally, there was a little Hebrew in the book. There is no evidence that this was set from type. Indeed, the look of the characters suggests strongly that they were cut in small woodblocks, for insertion into the type forme where needed. This made sense, for there is not enough Hebrew text to warrant a font, or even to justify approaching a printer such as Soncino for the loan of the necessary sorts.

Spacing Sorts for Text and for Music

When he discussed the making of type, Fioravanti said that the typefounders

> fanno le lettere dell'alfabeto, & oltra le lettere fanno certi pezzeti grandi: che li chiamano quadrati, per empire doue non uanno lettere: & ne fanno d'una altra sorte che non hano lettera, e questi si chiamano spatij, che si mettono fra una parolla e l'altra, per accomodar le righe.[54]

It is obvious that spaces between words need to be filled when setting type, for, if they are not, the typeset words will be free to move around in the forme under the pressure of the press. These spaces are supplemented by other longer spacing sorts, which Fioravanti called "quadrati". They are still called "quads" by modern printers, and are used to fill in larger spaces. They will be used for the inset of a new paragraph, for example, or for the end of the last line of a paragraph, if that is short. They are also clearly invaluable for the setting of poetry. For Petrucci, too, these sorts were of especial value, for, as we should expect, his underlay was frequently not continuous. He thus must have had a large assortment of quads of various sizes, to cover the various lengths of space left between words or at the ends of short lines of text.

Ideally, there should be no evidence on the printed page of the use of such sorts. They are not supposed to be high enough in the bed of the press either to take ink or to make an impression on the page. However, a few of these spacing sorts have left ink on the page. Both quads and the shorter spacing sorts that broke up words were occasionally driven up in the forme, rising to a level nearer that of the text face; on such occasions they could take ink, and leave an impression on the printed page. Even more frequently, quads used to fill up an incomplete last line of a page would leave a blind or partially inked image if the sheet of paper were allowed to sag at all during impression. Thus, in a number of cases, we can see the use of spacing sorts; as a result, we can tell their size, and therefore the size of the bodies of the text sorts, which must correspond to that of the spacing sorts.

Even more important for the precision of the finished product were the spacing sorts for music. I have mentioned these above, when drawing together the evidence for the body size of music sorts, and the extent to which they were kerned. A result of the small body size is that a wide range and a large stock of these spacing sorts would have been required. Every note put in the forme had necessarily to be accompanied by at least one such sort (above or below) and many (especially *semibreves*, rests, and accidentals) would have had more than one. In addition many stretches of music as set in the edition have spaces inserted between the notes, allowing them to be spread more spaciously across the page and to align more closely to the text in such settings as frottole. The measurements of these sorts had to correspond to those of the music sorts, for they had to coexist.

CAPITAL LETTERS

Petrucci had many individual letters, separately designed and cut, and intended to be used primarily as initials on title pages or at the heads of individual compositions or mass sections. In this, he was like all other sixteenth-century printers. The earlier and widespread practice of printing guide letters, allowing a scribe or artist to enter manuscript initials, had become rare by the end of the fifteenth century and seems not to have occurred to Petrucci. He therefore, in common with other printers, must have commissioned a series of initial letters before he set up shop.

The first sets of initials purchased by Petrucci included the most famous and beautiful of them all—those used for the title pages of *Odhecaton A* and the other early volumes. They comprised only three letters, "A", "B", and "C", probably ordered at the same time. The styles are very similar—and the use of the letter "A" on the first title page displays Petrucci's intention of publishing more volumes of the same character, using the other letters. On the other hand, the fourth volume of motets was called *Motetti libro quarto* and not *Motetti D*; presumably, Petrucci had not commissioned letters in this series beyond "C".

The design of these letters is quite remarkable, in the level of ornamentation displayed, and in the treatment of the verticals. The "A" is the most interesting, with its fluid motion toward the right, engendered by the downward extension of the left vertical. While the roots of both this letter and the "B" seem to lie in a northern, specifically French, tradition of initials, the "C" has a balance of clean and decorated sides that points away from the late Gothic profusion of ornament.

Each of these letters was unique, a single copy designed for a specific purpose, and each took up so much space that it could not have been intended to appear anywhere other than on a title page. Both the "A" and "B" were in fact later used within lute volumes, where they had a similar special function. There was no need to have more than one copy of each, for no letter would have been used more than once in a volume.

But these three initials, while the largest, are also rather special cases, for Petrucci had to have many smaller, decorative letters, to introduce each piece. Each of these smaller letters was also unique, cut to an individual design and mounted on its block. The evidence of the damage that these letters sustain argues for their being cut in wood, not metal. In either case, however, multiple copies could not be made from a matrix, for each was an individual process.

Often a printer could survive with a single alphabet of ornate woodblock letters available at any one time, for they were used to introduce new chapters and were rarely to be found in close juxtaposition to each other.[55] Petrucci's letters, however, were called on much more frequently than those of other printers. He could often be sure that one large and decorative initial would appear on almost every opening of a volume. In the case of frottole books, there were sometimes two to an opening—with a different piece on each page. Some mass volumes had them even more frequently, especially if the Tenor book involved *cantus firmus* settings.

One result is evident. Petrucci would sometimes have to use the same initial in two formes of the same gathering, or even the two formes of the same sheet. This appears to imply that Petrucci developed a pattern in which the initials could be inserted into the forme at a fairly late stage,[56] for he did not, for the first volumes at least, own more than one version of most letters, one letter "E", one "F", and so on.

When Petrucci bought his first three large initials, therefore, he also acquired an alphabet for the initial letters of all the compositions in these volumes. The letters that appear at the heads of pieces in *Odhecaton A* probably stand for a series of twenty initials, not all of which were required in that volume. Of the twenty-three letters in the Renaissance Italian alphabet, there is no evidence that Petrucci ever commissioned initial letters for "X", "Y", or "Z".[57] Four other letters were not required in this first edition, but were presumably ordered at the same time and soon appear: these are "E" and "O" (both found in Petrucci's second edition, the first of *Canti B*), and "K" and "Q", which appear in *Motetti B* and *Misse Josquin*. However, three letters, "C", "L", and "S", seem to have been cut in two versions at once.

These letters, about 26–27 mm high, show a basic consistency of design, overlaid by much freedom in varying the structural form, with several combinations of details of ornamentation.[58] Fundamental to the designs is a treatment in which verticals are usually curved, normally backward, coupled with strapwork or garlands on their left, to provide visual support. All lines are reinforced by lighter parallels, which add weight while creating a flow around the basic structure. The most common ornaments of line consist of teeth designs and small balls on a continuous hairline. Both of these are smaller versions of decoration already seen on the first three, larger initials. Indeed, the structures of this whole alphabet depend directly from those letters. The two sets were probably designed by the same man, for each shows a flair in variety, a boldness of execution, and a subtle balance between form and choice of ornamentation that is of the highest standard. There is nothing mechanical about the sequence.

Particularly elegant are the initials "F", "G", "S", and "V"; the least successful are probably the "K", "M", and "R" (the last of which feels a little constricted). The early volumes of mass settings placed considerable demands on some of this initial series of letters, especially in Tenor partbooks. For one thing, there would normally be five uses of the letters "K", "E", "P", "S", and "A" in any one partbook (although there were exceptions—the use of an "F" for a Gloria part starting later, or an "L" in the Credo). Since a pattern quickly developed whereby partbooks in mass volumes comprised two gatherings of eight folios, that is four sheets of paper, there was the certainty that at least one sheet would use the same letter twice; these two appearances might or might not be in the two formes of the sheet. In Tenor books, often much shorter, it was much more likely that the same initial would appear more than once in the same forme. For example, the Tenor book of the third volume of Josquin's mass settings required twenty-one initial letters (including the "T" of the title) on merely fifteen pages, that is, four formes.

Therefore, to start each of the five movements of a cycle with a large initial, Petrucci would have to order more copies of the five relevant letters. Neither the *Misse Josquin* of 1502 nor the *Misse Obreht* of 1503 shows such a range of new letters (although a new letter "A" does appear in the second edition of the *Odhecaton A*, the book before the Obrecht masses). In the Josquin volume, there are few places where Petrucci was unable to insert a large initial from his existing stock—largely because of the spacious layout adopted for this edition. However, in the Obrecht book there is no large initial for one or more voices at the starts of many movements—over twenty, in fact. Petrucci must have realised that he would not be able to continue publishing music for the mass, and preserve his standard of using decorative initials, with the stock that he then possessed.

A third set of letters was therefore commissioned, comprising only further copies of the five essential letters for these mass volumes; it is easily distinguished by its size. It is the first of several sets of smaller letters, each involving the inset of only one stave. The initials of the new series are about 18 mm high and appear first in the volume of Brumel's masses of 17 June 1503. This book, with its immediate successor of Ghiselin's masses (published on 15 July 1503), occupies an unusual position in Petrucci's output, involving the change from triple- to double-impression, as will become apparent in the next chapter. It is possible that the circumstances surrounding the production of these books also stimulated the preparation of the new set of letters. However, the stimulus is more likely to have been the evident shortage of initials felt during the printing of *Misse Obreht*. The new letters do not appear in the intervening volume, the *Motetti de passione . . . B* (10 May 1503), and were perhaps not ready then: an "A" could have been employed, for example, on f.H4*v*, which lacks a large initial. However, they were ready by the beginning of presswork for the Brumel volume and are retained in use even into the Fossombrone years.

Petrucci acquired several sets of letters during his career. Although many of those used in Venice are of a consistent size, about 26–27 mm high, the letters bought in Fossombrone were all smaller. The first set, bought for the *Paulina,* is completely different in style from anything Petrucci had used before. Instead of the open-work letters with flourishes and decorative supporting lines, these letters are simpler, roman in form with some strapwork, on black grounds within frames.[59] These designs were prepared in three different sizes, were probably cut by Griffo, and perhaps reflect the more classical taste of Paulus de Middelburgh.[60]

The other three alphabets of initials bought in Fossombrone show a linear deterioration in quality of design and execution. It is reasonable to assume that the last two, at least, were commissioned from local craftsmen.[61] A final set of letters appears in the fragmentary remains of Petrucci's 1538 edition of the *Motetti del Fiore.* This series is quite different in style and reflects a different background.

These new sets of letters, from Venice and Fossombrone, have been identified (in chapter 15) in part by the dates on which they first appear, and primarily by the details of design—not only size, but also the role of ornament and the balance between form and decoration. Implicit in this identification has been the assumption that each letter is unique, that in no case did two examples of exactly the same design exist side by side. There are three strands of evidence confirming the validity of this assumption. One is that the details of size and style can be imitated in subsequent sets, but they are never the same; indeed, to have tried to make them identical would have seemed an alien concept to a letter-cutter.[62]

Second is the pattern of damage. Many of these letters show different levels of damage. The most general, and most to be expected, is the presence of hairline cracks, particularly across the finer lines of a letter. These cracks, beginning as fine white gaps in a line, often gradually expand, until they may be as much as one millimeter wide. Some are simple cracks, caused no doubt by the repeated pressure of the press on the wood of the letter; others seem the result of something sharp falling on the block, for the white line traverses several black lines of the printed initial. Some letters show more serious damage. Among them is a letter "C", which loses a major part of its lower portion and is withdrawn soon after. Other letters show more gradual and progressive damage, often to swirls and figures-of-eight on their outer edges.[63] These signs of damage have to be distinguished from traces of poor inking, a badly cut frisket, or the effect of the block lying lower in the press than surrounding type.[64] Once that is done, the patterns of damage are always in one direction, from the better condition to the worse: if there had been two copies of any letter, that would not happen.

Third, as a point of confirmation of the uniqueness of these initials, is the evidence that a single letter is never repeated within a forme and indeed rarely in adjacent formes. If an initial had appeared twice in the same forme, it would necessarily imply the presence of two such letters—for the whole forme was set up and printed at the same time. Indeed, as noted above, there are cases when Petrucci was unable to use an initial at all, for he did not have a second copy of the requisite letter.[65]

When a new alphabet arrived and was adopted by Petrucci's compositors, the other, older sets were downgraded. None seems ever to have been abandoned entirely, although a number of letters cease to appear after a certain point.[66] In practice, however, old alphabets were retained, the best becoming now the second best, the second demoted to third, and so on. The result is that the adoption of a new alphabet, while providing a *terminus post quem* for the use of the new, does not provide a corresponding *terminus ante quem* for use of the older sets. Instead they became available for those occasions when Petrucci needed more examples of the same letter at the same time. This meant not only that Petrucci could more easily handle those instances of two examples of "A" or "E" in the same forme; it also meant that he could set initials of the same letter in concurrent though different formes, the inner and outer of the same sheet, for example, thus avoiding delays in production.

Analyses of the use of the different sets of letters in different titles show clearly that letters from "semi-retired" alphabets were called on primarily when the corresponding letters of the newest sets were already in place on another page or forme. In later years, however, Petrucci's new alphabets seem to have pleased him less. For many volumes produced at Fossombrone, it is evident that the most recent alphabet, far from being the first choice, is actually reserved as a last choice. The new set of letters—series 8—first appearing in 1514, demonstrates this rather well. It seems to have been ordered when Petrucci decided to continue music publishing and began to be used in the first edition of the third book of Josquin's masses. In this book, an initial letter A appears twenty-two times in the four partbooks, but the latest block, from the new alphabet, is used only five times. The new letter "E" is used only twice, each time as a matter of real necessity. One initial, on f.D7r, is omitted from Table 3.5 for it is on a folio printed later as a cancel leaf, in all surviving copies.[67]

The only two cases where the letter "E" is needed twice on the same forme are in gathering C. In both cases, the new letter is used. In other cases, however, it is carefully avoided, even though one of the other two blocks would have to be lifted from one forme and placed in the other, presumably already set; see, as an example, folios A1v and A7r.

The appearance of an unexpected initial can be a critical factor in dating a number of impressions and cancels and is perhaps more useful than the patterns of paper distribution. We cannot say that an anomalous paper *must* be later, even if all other appearances of that paper are later, for it may have been part of a lost batch, or a single sheet that was mixed into a batch of some other paper. However, an appearance of an anomalous initial is different: it is not possible that this initial could have been used before it was made. We can therefore sometimes use the appearance of an initial letter in the dating of a sheet that does not actually belong with the rest of an edition.

I have already mentioned the case of the inner sheet of gathering F in the Bologna copy of Josquin's first book of masses (1502 edition), for it is printed on a paper not otherwise found in that edition. In addition, this single sheet employs two initial letters that do not belong to the rest of the edition. The "P" on folio F3r and the "S" on F4r are "alien", for they do not appear anywhere else before the series emerging in the Brumel and Ghiselin volumes of 1503. I believe that this sheet was probably printed at the end of the year, after the volume of La Rue's masses.

Similarly important are the two series of small letters that appear in 1519 and 1520. These letters are also found, in many cases already damaged, in copies of

TABLE 3-5 Initial letters used in *Missarum Josquin Liber Tertius* (1514, first edition)

Gathering	A			B			C					
folio	1v	4v	7r	1v	4r	7r	1v	3r	4v	6v	8v	11r
forme	Ii	IIo	Io	Ii	IIi	IIo	Ii	IIo	IIo	IIIo	IIIo	Io
style	E4	E3	E4	E4	E4	E3	E3	E10	E4	E10	E4	E4

Gathering	D		E			F			G		
folio	1v	4r	1v	4v	8r	2r	4v	7r	1v	4v	7v
forme	Ii	IIi	Ii	IIo	IIi	Ii	IIo	Io	Ii	IIo	IIi
style	E4	E4	E3	E4	E3	E3	E4	E4	E4	E3	E4

titles first printed in 1514—in *Motetti de la Corona Libro primo*, for example. Taken with the pattern of paper use, some of these are clearly later impressions, printed either late in 1519 or in 1520.

These patterns of the adoption of new sets of letters, as much as the evidence of growing damage to individual blocks, can be used for studying the chronology of "hidden" editions and of cancel leaves. In much the same argument that has been advanced for the appearance of initials before their time, evidence of a damaged state preceding a cleaner state can be used for attempting to discover and arrange in order these problem sheets.

Blocks

In addition to the initial letters, Petrucci used a number of other blocks at various times. By far the most important of these was the device printed at the end of his books, which served as an identifying mark.[68] This block, which measures 91 × 53 mm, is typical of printers' devices of the period, in both its simplicity and its form. While the Manutius family used the famous anchor device of the Aldine Press and the Giuntas the fleur-de-lys to represent their Florentine origins, the stylised circle or heart with a surmounted cross is found as the mark of many Italian printers, from the earliest. The Scotto device was at various times a circle with a double-barred cross, with the initials OSM (for Octavianus Scotus de Modoetia) within the three sections of the cross.

Music printers such as Scotto and Gardano changed the block showing their device regularly, presumably replacing a worn one with a newly designed and cut version. Petrucci kept the same block in use for twenty years. Even in its first extant appearance, in his second title, it shows the damage to the lower left corner that, appearing in every subsequent use, confirms that the same block was retained. This damage is but one more reason why the disappearance of the last folios in the unique copy of Petrucci's first book is a sad loss.

A second version of his device was prepared for the 1538 edition. Given the importance of a printer's device, we can assume that Petrucci had abandoned the first version. The new was modeled on the old, though not as elegantly cut, and now in black on a white ground. Like the first, it has damage in its first (and in this case only) appearance.[69]

If the device was the most important of Petrucci's blocks, the most elegant were those prepared for the *Paulina de recta Paschae* of 1513. Reference to the decorative elements in this book has already been made in the biographical chapter, in connection with the life of Francesco Griffo da Bologna. The presence in the book of Francesco's work (if it is indeed his) argues for the prestige with which both author and printer wished to invest it, and it should be no surprise that the volume also carries excellent decorative blocks.

The borders for the four major decorated pages, as well as a block below the privilege, are of a similar style: representative for their period, the side panels are typical vertical "garden" designs, with putti and fountain-like pieces balanced one above the other, surrounded by foliage. The lower borders bear heraldic devices— of Paulus, (the author),[70] Pope Leo X, and the Emperor Maximilian; all are done in white on black criblé grounds and within borders.

The remaining page, an engraving of the author's vision of Good Friday, is in a completely different style. In a tripartite form, with the crucified Christ dominating the lower two panels, and Mary in heaven central to the larger top section, the page has something of the form of an altarpiece.[71] I have suggested earlier that this block was probably designed and cut by a local craftsman, perhaps the one employed to cut the other blocks to designs supplied by Griffo.

Petrucci occasionally used other small blocks for decoration. There is, for example, a block that apparently shows crossed swords, used to mark the presence of the *Missa l'homme arme super voces musicales* in editions of Josquin first book of masses. Also, on folios C6*v*–C7*v* of the third book of Josquin's masses (all editions, all dated 1514), Petrucci inserts rather crudely cut blocks of the faces of two dice; these signal proportional ratios to be adopted in performing the Tenors of Josquin's *Missa Di dadi.*

These blocks imply some sort of recognition of the two works. Both masses are by Josquin, but other works of his that would seem to offer similar opportunities for decoration are not awarded their own blocks. The *Missa la sol fa re mi* (in book 1), *Missa Hercules dux ferrarie*, or *Missa una musque de buschaya* (both in book 2), or even the *Missa de beata Virgine* (of book 3) would all seem to be amenable to similar simple ornamental designs—and they at least are among Josquin's better works. It is not sufficient to argue that Petrucci was merely reflecting a design found in his source. Although that may be true, and indeed be the sole reason for the presence of the two designs, Petrucci would still have had to commission the two blocks, have more than one copy made, and then have adjusted the forme to leave room for them.

A third similar block, though with a different function, is that of the crown that graces the title-pages of Superius parts for the four books of *Motetti de la Corona*. This block seems to represent a conscious decision on the part of Petrucci to indicate the importance of the crown in the title. This was the first time Petrucci had chosen to use such a title, decorative or symbolic in its function, rather than the merely descriptive phrases that had characterised even the longer titles of earlier volumes. The presence of the block seems to stress the reference to the crown and raise it to a level at which it was related to the planning of the volume. This is discussed later, in chapter 9. Here it is enough to remark that the crown is well cut, unlike the blocks in the Josquin volumes. While it is possible that it is the work of Francesco, I believe that a different hand was at work here.

Furniture and the Structure of the Forme

A necessary part of any printer's stock was what is now called "furniture". Holme, in his list of "Several other things belonging to the Art of Printing", speaks of "Furniture, by which is meant all the Wood work used in the Chase, to keep the Form of Letter fast Wedged therein, as Head Sticks, Foot Sticks, Side Sticks, Gutter Sticks, Riglets, Quoins and Scabbords".[72] Since more than one page is printed at a time, there is need for some material to fit between the pages in the forme, but lying low enough not to take ink, even if the frisket were absent. This furniture was usually made of wood, placed around the pages on all sides, and then forced into a rigid framework with the use of wedges.

There is some evidence of this furniture in a number of copies of Petrucci's books, largely because of the special nature of his material and of the way it was laid out. In many cases, the content, either the music alone, or also the staves, did not go to the foot of the page, and only four or five staves were present or filled with music. In such cases, the staves could be left in the forme and printed or masked. For the music forme, however, there was little point in using normal spacing sorts to fill several lines of the page: although type, or bearers, could be used, it was obviously easier to use furniture to block off the rest of the page. Occasionally, the paper has sagged a little in the press, and the furniture has left an impression on the page. This shows that these blocks of wood had a cross-hatched pattern on their face.

A related issue concerns the actual shape of the forme. As I have remarked, Petrucci was able to ensure that the forme of music and the forme of staves were aligned so precisely that their contents would correspond exactly when printed. The vertical register, or alignment of the two or three impressions is very rarely out enough to cause doubt over the pitches printed, even though there was more latitude in the horizontal. There are two elements to achieving this level of precision. One requires that the alignments within the formes of staves and of music are the same, and the other that they are printed at the same place on the page. The former produces the same relative positions for the same pitch on different systems of the page, and the latter ensures that all the lines are not displaced by the same interval. The second requirement is more easily met: when the paper is placed on the tympan ready for printing, it is impaled on a pair of points, metal spikes, which (with the frisket) keep it in place as the tympan is folded over onto the type. All that is required is that the paper is carefully placed for the second impression so that the points occupy the same holes, automatically aligning the paper in exactly the same position in the press. At the same time, the locked-up formes of type are similarly aligned.

More difficult is to understand how the staves and notes were set in exactly the same positions within the two formes. Mary Lewis has proposed a possible solution—that the formes had some sort of a sawtooth design along the sides, so that a line of staves and the corresponding line of notes would be required to fit into a preset indentation.[73] For Petrucci, these formes (if they existed) could be made in pairs, one for the staves and one for the notation.

Indeed, the evidence presented earlier in this chapter, showing two series of staves, of slightly different lengths, seems to indicate that the staves were kept in the forme permanently. That they were not integral parts of the formes is clear from the manner in which individual staves could disappear and be replaced, but I can see no reason why they should not have been kept in the forme. Support for this contention comes once two impressions, rather than three, had become the normal method of work. As will appear, the text was then set with the staves in the same forme. However, identical stave patterns continue to appear in consecutive gatherings, and even in consecutive books. This argues strongly that the staves were kept in the forme, in a continuing and constant internal arrangement, for long periods of time.[74]

There is also the evidence showing that there were two different lengths for the music formes, matching those of the staves. These formes for the music were not actually kept together with the stave formes, for on occasion the longer music forme appears with the shorter stave forme (so that the music extends beyond the stave), or vice versa. All four formes (or more when more were used) apparently had precisely the same vertical distribution—height of individual staves and distance between them—for they were interchangeable in this respect. A standardised skeleton forme was essential, but so would be standardised furniture.

Ink

Recipes for printing inks are much rarer than those for inks for manuscript work. Fioravanti, the writer whose work on printing has been mentioned, did produce a recipe for printer's ink, though it was not printed until 1581.[75]

Despite Petrucci's claims in his petition to be admitted to the Guild of Cestieri, his ink does not seem to be exceptional. The requirements—that ink should have a good intense blackness, that it should be consistent and transfer easily to the paper, and that it should not smear or offset onto neighbouring sheets when drying on the page—seem to have been fulfilled for most editions of the fifteenth century, as they evidently were for Petrucci.[76] In addition, his craftsmen seem to have been experienced in distributing the ink evenly over the forme, with ink balls, at least while he was working in Venice, for it is normally consistent from page to page of an edition, and it is still very black and glossy in most cases.

The few pages on which the impression has gone grey are usually the result not of the ink itself fading, but rather of a faulty impression in the first place. This is particularly evident when both impressions have taken poorly, suggesting that the paper was perhaps not well sized. I believe that this may explain most of the poor impressions in the last year or two of Petrucci's work, when the paper was definitely of a poorer quality. Those pages that are thicker or marginally better often also have blacker and more continuous impressions from the type. Alternatively, the paper may not have been adequately damped. Little could be done about that once the sheet had been printed—and, in any case, it is probable that the difference in dampness between adjacent sheets was not easily detectable during presswork.

In other cases, one impression has taken less well than the other. When this occurs in later Fossombrone editions, it seems as though the pressman wielding the ink balls was not very careful about covering the whole of the forme. In other instances, the ink itself may not have been of quite the right composition. The blackening elements in a supply of ink would tend to settle with time, which may help to explain those good but grey impressions in a number of editions. This should have been spotted by the pressman, of course; indeed, it may have been, for we do not have enough copies of any afflicted page to see if other copies were better printed.

As it should, the ink spreads slightly beyond the actual symbol to be impressed. This spreading is seldom very much but it is enough for the edge of the sorts to be seen in the paper. If viewed through a magnifier, the edges of the type-metal can be seen as lighter lines near the edge of the inking of a symbol, showing where they had bitten into the paper under the pressure of the press, while the ink spread slightly beyond, to give a richer impression.[77]

In the same way, the first impression of the two sometimes impresses the paper so much that the second does not take as well. For example, some stave-lines seem to have very short white spaces immediately on either side of the notes that cross them. This is almost certainly a result of a note having been printed first, having indented the paper heavily, and therefore having prevented that short segment of stave from impressing so clearly.

The Printing Press

Nothing is known about Petrucci's press, and very little can be deduced from the evidence of the surviving printed books, although that yields no indication of unconventional features. Our knowledge of early presses in general is heavily dependent on reproductions, for the descriptions that survive from this period are seldom clear enough for one to be able to reconstruct a press without these illustrations. Moran has attempted to trace the early history of the printing press, largely from forty or so illustrations from before 1600.[78]

Perhaps the only matters that need to be discussed here are those which have left traces on the extant copies. These traces can be divided into three phenomena, each of which reflects in some way on the press and presswork, and sometimes also on the work of the compositor:

1. edges of friskets and the apparent loss of material;
2. inked furniture;
3. blind impressions of bearer sorts.

The key to much of the quality of a printed impression resided in the hands of the pressman and his assistant. The forme had to be inked evenly and consistently, which also meant that it needed to be wiped well between pulls; once it was mounted in the bed of the press, those parts that were not to be printed needed to be masked, using a frisket.

This frisket was a piece of card or leather, cut to leave open the material to be printed once it was laid over the forme. It rested against the paper, not the forme, and was lowered to the press with each sheet of paper to be printed.[79] In special cases, specially shaped friskets were cut; this was essential, for instance, when printing liturgical books in two colours from one setting of type. The text rubrics, to be printed in red, and the actual spoken texts, printed in black, were set up and run under the press together. Thus, two friskets were needed, one to mask the text to be printed in red while a black impression was being made, and the other to mask the black in a similar manner.

The normal frisket merely provided a frame around each page of the forme, leaving holes the size of the content of each page. This seems to have been the practice followed by Petrucci. There was no need to mask parts of any of the pages, for everything in each forme was to be printed. However, the hole in the forme had to be large enough to ensure that everything to be printed was exposed to the paper.

In practice, there are occasional instances where the hole was not quite large enough; these show up on copies when some content of the page appears to have been cut across, and only a part is present. The immediate reaction of the modern reader is that some type was damaged and failed to print properly. However, the straightness of the line, coupled with the reappearance of the same sorts or blocks elsewhere in an undamaged state, confirms that the apparent loss is only the result of careless cutting of a frisket.

I have found no instances where the music itself was obscured by a frisket cut too small, but other matter, nearer the edge of the page, does show the phenomenon. This includes left edges of initial letters, ascriptions when entered in the left margin, a headline or the lowest line of text, and occasionally even signatures.

In practice, Petrucci seems to have used a consistent size of frisket. This is suggested by the number of pages where empty blank staves also show the shadowy impression of the furniture covering that space in the musical forme. This furniture should not normally have had any ink on it and should have been wiped each time the forme was cleaned. But this wiping process probably moved a little ink from the rest of the forme (the parts that *were* to be printed) onto the furniture in places. In addition, the paper ideally should not have sagged in the press enough to come into contact with the furniture, which after all, lay at a lower height than the type to be printed. However, dampened paper did regularly distort a little during the impression, so that there are a great many such traces of the furniture.

When, however, a major part of a forme, perhaps a whole page, was to be left blank, furniture was not sufficient. The paper would certainly sag and pull the rest of the sheet out of alignment—a particular problem when multiple impressions had to be precisely correlated. Typesetters therefore resorted to putting some typographical material, bearer sorts, in the otherwise blank areas. The material necessarily had to be either something that would not be needed or a symbol of which there were many unused sorts. Thus, we find the initial letters that had graced *Odhecaton A* and *Canti B*, and also sets of ligatures, used for this purpose. The result is a blind impression, an indentation in the paper showing exactly the shape of the sort or block in the press. In one or two cases, this impression shows that the typesetter used a line of musical type, taken from some other page that had already been printed.[80] Even after nearly 500 years, these blind impressions show frequently in the surviving copies, especially in those that have been little used.

In other words, the press seems to have functioned like any other press of the period, and the craftsmen were more than competent. Even the falling off in visual quality in the last few years hardly affects the overall quality more than occasionally.

I suggest therefore that the materials used by Petrucci were rarely unusual. The only remarkable feature lay in the music font itself, which imposed the need for multiple impressions. Petrucci's books were also printed in a manner that closely approximated the normal procedures, as far as we can now tell. Here again, the biggest deviations from standard practice were a direct result of the nature of the musical font and its relationship to the staves on which the characters had to sit. This, with a description of the normal procedures, and the normal appearances of a volume printed by Petrucci, will occupy the next chapter.

Notes

1. Rather than giving a survey of our present state of knowledge of early typefounding or of the structure of the printing press as found in Italy at the end of the fifteenth century, this chapter focuses on the elements that relate to Petrucci's output. Reference is made to more detailed studies or to the primary literature where it is relevant.

2. Much the same point is made in Allen, "Contemporary", although it makes no reference to the value of legal documents. That study also refers to the descriptions of printing offered by Fioravanti (1567), Le Roy (1579), and François (1622).

3. Moran, *Printing*, pp. 26–28.

4. This comes from an edition of the Dance of Death (Huss: Lyons, 18 Feb. 1499). The best reproduction of this particular woodcut known to me can be found in Berry and Poole, *Annals*, at p. 72, where the assertion is made that this is the earliest such picture.

5. There is a growing bibliography on early printers' manuals, among which perhaps the most useful is Gaskell, Barber, and Warrilow, "Annotated". See also Allen, "Contemporary"; Fahy, "Descrizioni"; Gaskell, *New Introduction*; Romani, "Lessico".

6. Gaskell, Barber, and Warrilow, "Annotated", p. 13.

7. This section has been reprinted in an excellent modern edition, the work of Herbert Davis and Harry Carter. See Moxon, *Mechanick*.

8. This work was published in Venice by Valgrisi and reprinted at least twice in the same city, by Ravenoldo in 1567 and by the heirs of Sessa in 1572. Fioravanti was primarily a writer of several books on medical matters; in his other more general volume, *Del compendio de i secreti rationali* (first printed by Valgrisi in 1564, and frequently reprinted), he includes a method for making printer's ink (on folio Y8 of the 1581 Sessa edition). For a biography of Fioravanti and a discussion of his writings, see Furfaro, *Vita*.

9. See Clair, *Plantin*; Vogt, *Golden*. An English translation of the relevant section of Plantin's *Dialogues français pour les jeunes enfans* of 1567 has been translated by Roy Nash, as *An Account*.

10. Detailed discussions of a number of these issues can be found in Labarre, *Dictionary*, under several relevant entries. For a discussion of how far one could go in the technical description of paper when preparing a bibliographical study of a printed book, see Tanselle, "Bibliographical".

11. This assertion is based on the discussion in Hirsch, *Printing*, pp. 38–40. Voet, *Golden*, ii, pp. 379–85, shows that for Plantin, the cost of the paper was even higher, as much as 65 percent of the total.

12. This factor must be taken into account when assessing edition size, the number of copies printed. Unless a printer could be sure that a large and lavish book would sell well and fast, he would know that it could bankrupt him in short order. Hence the desire for contracts in which the author or a promoter paid a large part of the cost of, or actually supplied, the paper. Hence also the emerging pattern of frequent reprinting of titles. On other hand, every printer seems to have accepted the probability of slow sales for a number of titles. (This must have been true for Petrucci and can also be confirmed from the contents of the Gardano catalogue discussed in Agee, *Gardano*.) As a result, the selection of titles had to be carefully balanced with the size of the print-run. It is not enough to assert that a number of contracts specify certain edition sizes, and that therefore these were standard sizes of print-run. Instead, we should be thinking of the probable size of the potential market, the size of the book itself (the number of sheets used for each copy), the presence (and date) of later editions, and the character of other books printed at about the same time by the same printer—as well as by others. Certainly, the presence of dedications is another factor, as are the name and function of

the dedicatee, but the relationship between dedicatee and edition size—the issue of a "vanity edition"—is by no means as simple as it has been made to appear. This matter will need some discussion later, in chapter 5, where I will take issue with current statements about edition size.

13. A copy of the first gathering of Petrucci's third edition of Févin masses has survived at Northwestern University Library (Evanston, Illinois) with top edges uncut, so that A1 and A2 are joined, as are A3 and A4, etc. These sheets were used as binding strips and therefore have been trimmed on the other sides.

14. See Briquet, Nos.364 and 783, and the commentary to No.6289. Labarre, *Dictionary*, pp. 246–72, uses the term *Meçane*. Needham's statement, in the course of a discussion about cataloguing incunables, appears in his "ISTC", p. 41.

15. Gialdroni and Ziino, "New Light", p. 501.

16. The standard sources for watermarks from this area continue to be the classic ones: Briquet, *Filigranes*; Mošin, *Anchor*; Zonghi and Zonghi, *Watermarks*. The splendid new volume by Woodward, *Catalogue*, includes a few marks similar to those used by Petrucci, but covers a later repertoire. A useful "Checklist of books and articles containing reproductions of watermarks", which includes a number of musical studies, has been prepared by Pulsiano.

17. This point is made most clearly in Naiditch, *Catalogue*, i, p. xxiii.

18. Paper 13 is the most unusual element here, for it is found nowhere else in Petrucci's output. Since gathering Q has other anomalies, this instance will have to be discussed elsewhere. The papers are defined by their watermarks, which are described in chapter 15.

19. The same point is made about Italian eighteenth-century papers in Selfridge-Field, *Vivaldi*, p. 794. The appearance of different forms of the letter "A" as a countermark in many of Petrucci's Venetian editions is probably a similar indication of paper that he had bought from the same wholesaler of paper, but that the wholesaler had ordered from different paper mills.

20. Mošin, *Anchor*.

21. It is important to recognise that the value of watermark study in printed books is rather different from the benefits to be gained when studying manuscripts. There are several reasons for this. Perhaps the most important lies in the bulk use of paper implicit in the printing process, coupled with the manner in which adjacent sheets of a single copy are related. It is evident that an edition of 100 copies will use one hundred times as much paper as will a manuscript copy with the same number of folios. That implies a different purchasing pattern, different patterns of storage in the shop and of removing paper from the store; it also implies that any two adjacent sheets in such a printed edition will be printed on sheets of paper that were originally on average 100 sheets apart as they came from the paper mill or stationer. (I say "on average" for there is no guarantee that the copies of consecutive printed sheets will be stored in the same order of printing, or sold in the same order. Nor is there any guarantee that the whole pile of sheets printed on one side will be returned to the press in order when the time comes to perfect them.)

As the press-man came to the end of a pile of paper at the press, drawn from the stock in the storehouse, he would need to collect another similar pile of paper from store. This new pile might, in an orderly shop with only one press-man, continue exactly from the pile used previously, but that is by no means certain. It is not even certain that it would be from the same batch of paper. That might be exhausted, so that a new batch had to be adopted; the original might have been used at another press; the pressman might have been using up the tail ends of several batches; and so on.

As a result, the analysis of paper use in a printed book is different from that which has recently been shown to be so valuable in the study of manuscripts. There is usually little point, for example, in trying to follow the deterioration (or change) of a single mark through a single copy of a printed book, for the reasons I have just advanced. There *is* value, however, in attempting to confirm that the various bifolia in quarto or octavo are truly cut from the same original sheet. That remains one of the most useful manners of detecting cancels or other replacement sheets. Coupled with study of type and other features of the printed page, it will often indicate whether the replacement of a bifolium took place at the printer's shop, or later (e.g., at the bindery).

Even more valuable is the study of watermark patterns across a book; changes in watermark, the intrusion of an "alien" mark in an otherwise straightforward context, or patterns of two or more marks in one book, are all indicative of some event in the production of the book. In this respect, the work of Allan Stevenson is most instructive, and his conclusions often brilliant. Certain speculative approaches to the evidence, which he has advanced in various articles, will be discussed later.

I wish to stress the conclusion that the bibliographer's use of paper and watermark evidence is intrinsically different from that of the paleographer, primarily as a result of the voracious demands for paper made by the press. Thus, while statements made in the preceding paragraphs will sound familiar to the student of manuscripts, the actual conclusions that can be drawn from the evidence will be quite different.

22. For the special case of the editions of Brumel and Ghiselin masses, which were certainly produced simultaneously, see the next chapter.

23. This table uses the shorthand for naming sheets and formes in a gathering outlined in the preface: roman numerals joined to a signature letter indicate the different sheets within a gathering; "I" represents the outer sheet (ff.1, 2, 7, and 8 in a normal gathering); and, when a gathering contained more than eight folios, "III" indicates the innermost.

24. Biringuccio, *De la pirotechnia*.

25. Fioravanti, *Del compendio*, f.62*v*, as quoted in Allen, "Contemporary", p. 167. Allen also quotes, on p. 169, Ashley's 1594 translation of Le Roy's description of typecasting, in his *De la vicissitude ou varieté des choses en l'univers* (of 1579), which calls for "lead, tinglasse, antimony, and other mixed maters to the end to harden them and that they may endure longer".

26. Holme, *Academy* (dated 1688), pp. 113–27, when describing the equipment and the art of printing, defines the term "Wetting of Paper" as "to Wet it Quire by Quire in fair Water, to prepare it for the Press, laying it all on a Heap on the Paper Board". (This section of Holme's book has been reprinted: see Nuttall and Perkin, "Reprint".) Statements of this type, apparently derived from Moxon's similar instructions, are very general. Even earlier, Fioravanti, *Del compendio*, f.63*v*, states that, in order to print, "hanno carta inhumidita con acqua, & cosi sotto quel torcolo la stampano".

It is generally stated that dampened paper needs less ink to make a fine impression—see, for example, Rummonds, *Printing*, p. 247. With sized papers, this dampening ensured that the paper would be more responsive to the pressure of the press. The later slight shrinkage of paper, and therefore of the printed impression, gave to the image greater sharpness and blackness.

27. Labarre, *Dictionary*, under the entry "Expansion", pp. 92–93, points out that paper expands and shrinks as the humidity of the surrounding air varies. His figures, which are for modern machine-made papers, suggest that the expansion would always be considerably less than 1 percent in each direction. For hand-made papers, this figure is probably likely to be somewhat low, as the following reference suggests. However, since the paper was in any case dampened when being prepared for the press, it seems reasonable to suppose that any figure for expansion and shrinkage was fairly consistent across a batch of papers printed at the same time— and was also perhaps more consistent across all the production of a given press, following the same pattern of dampening for all its output.

28. McKerrow, *Introduction*, p. 151, fn. which also points out that the amount of expansion and shrinkage will tend to be different for measurements made along and across the chain lines.

29. The great majority of these measurements have been taken using only two specific implements: a small jeweller's loupe with a field of view of twenty millimeters graduated in tenths of a millimeter, and also having screens for measuring the thickness of lines and the sizes of angles; and one specific plastic ruler, graduated in millimeters. It is possible that neither implement is entirely accurate. The readings given here, however, are at least consistent, with the result that the reader can be sure that variations in the readings from one copy to another are indicative of real variations between the copies, rather than of variations between different implements.

30. A detailed study of this aspect of liturgical printing, among others, can be found in Duggan, *Italian*, pp. 163–219.

31. There is one problem with measuring the lengths of staves, one that apparently could throw my conclusions into doubt. It is evident that less care was taken with the actual printing

of the staves, particularly in lifting the printed sheets from the bed of the press. In a large number of cases there is a "drag" of the stave lines beyond their limits at one end, producing a distinct tailing off effect, often veering up or down. This can make it appear that the printed staves were longer than the type must have been, although accurate measurements can usually be taken. For a particularly good example of this "drag" effect, see F2v.vi of the Barcelona copy of the Altus book of the first edition of Mouton's masses (1515).

32. An example can be seen in the Vivarelli and Gulla facsimile of the copy at I-Ac, Petrucci, *Missarum*, on the inner sheet (folios 3–6) of gathering H of Agricola's masses.

33. These staves and a problem in placing them in the forme are discussed in Boorman, "First".

34. These short staves are also missing on the latest pages of the unique copy of the *Odhecaton A* preserved at Bologna. However, as I have shown, these folios are later than *Canti B*. I believe that the last cancel folios for the first edition were printed at around the time of *Motetti A*, whereas the other folios are of sheets printed as part of the second edition, from January 1503. There are inset staves for initials in the 1520 book devoted to Pisano's music. These, however, are not distinctive staves, but merely the standard ones that have been partially masked with a special frisket.

35. This is, of course, a product of the ink's character and density.

36. Scholderer, "Shape".

37. This term defines the height of the type when it is standing in the press. There are two sets of measurement needed to describe pieces of type. One set involves the measurement of the face of the type, that is its height and width on the page. The other involves the vertical measurements of the type as a physical object and includes its height-to-paper.

38. Scholderer, "Shape", pls.1 and 2; Type Face Society, pl.1909c.

39. Scholderer's plate No.1, from Venice in 1490, shows a sort without such a groove, but with a chamfer at the foot, which, the author suggests, might have served the same function. Sorts in the new music font found in Petrucci's last editions could not be inverted, and these sorts may well have had a groove or chamfer.

40. It also makes sense of the document from the end of his life, in which he sought to regain a set of matrices that had been hired by another printer. See Gialdroni and Ziino, forthcoming.

41. Formal descriptions of all the fonts can be found in chapter 15.

42. I recognise that the more informal nature of these hands had a direct effect on the shaping of the note-heads; however, the proportions of note to tail, and of clefs and rests to the stave as a whole are quite different. See Brown, *Milan*, for a facsimile of the former, and Tirro, *Spataro*, pp. 808–14 for illustrations of the latter.

43. Single reproductions of pages from all three can be found in Lockwood, *Ferrara*, plates 8–10.

44. Ibid., p. 216.

45. This hand has been dated about 1500 by Kanazawa. For a facsimile, see Brown, *Verona*.

46. The first of these was written for Padua Cathedral in 1522 by the new *maestro da cappella*, Passetto. The second is probably not a Venetian manuscript, but from farther south, probably in the Marche. See, for the Padua manuscript, Constant, *Padua*; RISM, BIV/5, pp. 310–17; and Blackburn, "Petrucci"; for the second, Luisi, *Apografo*; Fenlon and Haar, *Madrigal*; and Boorman, "Bibliography", pp. 245–46.

47. The relationship between Aldus Manutius, Francesco Griffo, and Jacomo Ungaro may be relevant here. Since Ungaro presumably cast the type that Francesco had designed, he would be very familiar with kerned sorts. This might help to support the supposition that he had something to do with Petrucci's font, discussed in Duggan, *Italian*, and here in chapter 2.

48. Indeed, this overlap is one of the most obvious demonstrations that Petrucci did use a multiple-impression process.

49. Much the same processes were adopted for some fonts in the later eighteenth century, though here the small sorts would contain fragments of stave lines, at times only one, sometimes two or more. Examples can be seen in the work of Breitkopf and Härtel, and in type specimens of the nineteenth century (Poole and Krummel, "Printing", p. 246). A simpler version, in which

most sorts had two or three lines on them, has been called nested type (Krummel, *English*, p. 50) and can be seen in the work of Petreius, of Le Roy and Ballard (Barksdale, *Printed*, p. 76), and of Day (Krummel, *English*, p. 48) among others. It can also be seen in many editions of lute tabulature produced in England around 1600. (Among convenient facsimiles is Dowland, *Varietie*.)

The particular character of Petrucci's type means that the standard typecases for music, depicted in some early treatises, would not be suitable, for they were designed for single-impression type and supplied a number of compartments for each note-value. Two such cases from 1733, one for the then old-fashioned font for church music, and one for a newer style of notation, are illustrated in Ernesti, *Wol-eingerichtete*, pp. 54–55.

50. This sort can be seen in the reproduction of pages from this source, in Gialdroni and Ziino, "New Light", pp. 522–23. It is notable that the sort is apparently not invertible, to be printed on the fourth line down.

51. Analysis for the fifteenth-century appears in Bühler, "Roman": further details, with a warning about making too glib a generalization, can be found in Hirsch, *Printing*, pp. 114–17. Writing over 100 years ago, Horatio Brown (in *Venetian*, p. 19) already noted that Jensen "reserves his Roman type chiefly for the classics, . . . the Gothic for sacred and Canon Law". The use of the word "Gothic" for this and similar types raises some questions. Since Petrucci's font is certainly not a true Gothic, I have followed a more current approach, reflecting early sources in calling it a "rotonda" face.

52. This is evident in the facsimile of the Treviso copy of this third edition, Petrucci, *Odhecaton*. The two sets of Aldine Greek type are well illustrated in Barker, *Aldus*, plates 24 and 26: their measurements are discussed in the same volume, in chapter 6.

53. See, for example, Isaac, *Index*; and Mardersteig, "Aldo". In this article, Mardersteig proposes that Petrucci used in his *Odhecaton A* one of the fonts that Griffo had prepared for Aldus.

54. See fn.8 above.

55. In fact, there were situations where many initials appeared frequently, often several to a page; these include the text of the litany in liturgical books, question-and-answer formats in theological and other treatises, or treatises such as those of Bonaventura da Brescia or the series of *Compendia musices*. In these cases, most paragraphs were begun with a large two-line type initial, cast in multiple copies just like the ordinary characters. Such initials were usually fairly simple, characteristically Lombard in style, or with some simple swirl to the letter. A few letters of this sort do appear in the work of Petrucci: the font used for part names in choirbook format apparently had enough letters that he could occasionally use them as initials for major sections of compositions; see, for example, the first book of Lamentations.

56. It is implausible to assume that Petrucci's compositors would have chosen to delay setting a whole page until the initial was ready. Instead, even if the same letter (e.g., a "K" in a mass volume) were needed in both formes of a sheet, the one forme would normally have been started before the other went to press. As I shall show below, there is little evidence that the text for such volumes was carefully cast off in advance of typesetting. It would, as a result, be difficult for the compositor to delay work on one whole forme until the other had been printed. Therefore, it seems more logical to suggest that the initial letters might have been inserted into a partly set forme at a later stage. Examples of this practice appear below. Fortunately, Petrucci soon realised that there was a simpler solution to this problem—one that incidentally helped other things—and had a second set of some of the most commonly needed letters prepared. Even so, there were occasions when he did not have sufficient letters: Dalza's fourth book of lute intabulations (1508) requires sequences of letters "P" (for Pavana) and "C" (for Calata). For each of these sequences, he used only two letters and evidently had to lift them from one forme for placing in the next.

57. Indeed, on the one occasion when Petrucci could have used an initial letter "Z", on folio A6v of *Frottole libro ottavo*, he had to use a type initial.

58. This alphabet is reproduced, evidently from approximate tracings, in Castellani, *Arte*, ii, p. 96; on the same page is a tracing of the "A" in the series of three title-page initials.

59. They are illustrated in, among other places, Brown, *Venetian*; and Castellani, *Arte*, ii, p. 71.

60. Castellani, *Arte*, shows many sets of initials of similar design and cut in Venice during the preceding decades. This would, of course, support an attribution to Francesco Griffo, who had worked there for several years, with Aldus. Since Griffo also worked for Soncino, it is interesting to compare these initials—and also the borders in the *Paulina*—with those in Soncino's editions printed in the Marche, which, although not the same, have similar aesthetic premises.

61. Examples of these are illustrated and discussed in Boorman, "Cancels".

62. This point can be reinforced by examining the initials used in Roman editions of the 1520s. Many initials in these editions imitate Petrucci's letters closely, but careful examination reveals that they are invariably copies, indeed sometimes made from defective originals. This probably reflects a deliberate attempt at reflecting the character of the original and would be an indication of the prestige in which his editions were held.

63. Patterns of deterioration are illustrated in Boorman, "Cancels".

64. Apparently, some letters were cut on blocks that were not exactly the same height-to-page as was the font of type. The appearance of poor inking of the edges of initials leads to a supposition that the letters lay rather low in the press; similarly, poor inking of material immediately to the right of an initial suggests that the letter stood too high.

65. Detailed analyses demonstrating this point, and including charts for a number of editions, can be found in Boorman, *Petrucci*, pp. 383–93, and Boorman, "Cancels". The numbers assigned there to the different initials do not correspond with those in the present study.

66. In certain cases, such as the letter "L" that had appeared in 1501, it is clear that the damage had reached a point when Petrucci wished to retire the letter. In this case, the damage was so bad that the letter could easily have been read as an "I". In others, when the letter was still clearly recognizable, I assume that further damage had occurred after the last extant use of the letter; in yet others, Petrucci seems merely to have preferred the new letter.

67. The numbers assigned to initials correspond to those of the various sets described in chapter 15 and illustrated on plates 2–3. Attempts at using such tables to reveal the order of work quickly run into problems, not so much of producing possible conclusions, but rather of arriving at real solutions. As Peter Davison stressed in "Printers", our intellectual constructs built on such evidence always ignore the probability of disturbance and disorder within the printing house, as well as the certainty of a disjunction between the mind-set of the early shopmaster and that of the present-day scholar. For this reason, I have tended not to pursue some apparently fruitful lines of analysis, knowing that they can never be demonstrated to accord with Petrucci's methods of work.

68. Reproduced here as a frontispiece. It is also reproduced in many other places, including Castellani, *Arte*, ii, p. 97; Kristeller, *Italienischen*, as No.259; and Zappella, *Marche*, fig.427. Some reproductions are taken from copies of Paulus's book of 1513, the *Paulina*: among these are Davies, *Devices*, No.180, on p. 545; and Vaccaro, *Marche*, as figure 83 (and see p. 105).

69. This is reproduced in Gialdroni and Ziino, "New Light", p. 508. An extended discussion of early printers' devices in Italy is in Zappella, *Libro*, pp. 559–622. Stevens and Gehl, in "Eye", point out that a device was more than an identifier, but also stood as a guarantee of quality.

70. One of the two pages bearing this block is reproduced in Castellani, *Arte*, ii, p. 71; and Mortimer, *Italian*, ii, p. 529.

71. This page is reproduced in Mortimer, *Italian*, ii, p. 530.

72. Holme, *Academy*, p. 117. Each of the first four terms reflects a place in the forme, which may be filled by identical pieces of furniture, although head- and foot-sticks will often be of different lengths from those at the side or in the gutter. Riglets are defined as furniture of specific sizes, corresponding to the different sizes of fonts in use, and must therefore have had specific functions within the page or sheet. Quoins are wedge-shaped pieces of furniture, with the particularly important function of firmly locking the rest of the furniture in place.

73. Lewis, *Gardano*, i, pp. 66–67. I have problems with the likelihood of this solution for Gardano, and I am also doubtful that it is actually supported by the evidence. I suspect that the

inking that Lewis detects and believes indicates the edge of these special formes is actually from individual spacing sorts. First, I would expect the forme to lie farther away from the content of the page than she suggests, allowing space for initials and, at the other end of the line, *custodes*. Second, for the forme to ink the page, either the page would have had to sag onto the forme, or the forme itself would have risen in the press. The latter is manifestly unlikely, for the forme was the rigid framework that kept the rest in place and would normally lie lower in the press even than the furniture. But the paper is also unlikely to sag onto the forme at that point, for it is about to disappear behind the frisket. It seems much more likely that the inking comes from individual spacing sorts, which could certainly rise up during a press-run.

Then, too, I can see no need for such a forme. Both music and text were set in straight lines, exactly as the text would be for standard, nonmusical volumes. The only difference lay in the need for furniture between each line; if the printer wanted a consistent height-on-the-page for each stave of music (itself by no means necessary for single-impression printing), he merely needed to preserve standardised pieces of furniture. The placing of headlines and of text lines relative to the music argues that this method represents a more probable solution.

However, a printer using double-impression methods, whether for music or not, always needed some means of ensuring that the two formes could be easily set and still produce consistent impressions. While this presupposes a consistent pattern of spacing sorts and of alignment, it need not have presumed some special skeleton forme. Printers of liturgical books had been solving the problem for a number of years before Gardano (or even Petrucci) began work.

74. We cannot hypothesise that staves and music were set into the same formes, one after the other. Apart from the practical inconvenience to the typesetter (and the inevitable delays involved while type was distributed), there would be no reason for him to return the staves to the forme in the same sequence each time: yet that is what we see.

75. Fioravanti, *Del compendio*, on f.Y8. A detailed discussion of printing ink, with early recipes for its manufacture, is in Bloy, *History*.

76. There are a few cases where Petrucci's ink has smeared across a page, which seem usually to be a result of dragging the sheet of paper slightly as it is placed with other printed sheets to dry. They do not resemble the sorts of slurred impression that result from a careless use of the tympan and frisket, nor do they appear to be the result of later moisture attacking the completed book.

77. This impression is always the best evidence for detecting the actual shape of individual pieces of type. I have used it, in Boorman, "Salzburg", to identify the earliest single-impression music type. Don Krummel has used similar evidence to determine when music sorts were made from twice-struck matrices. See Krummel, "Early German".

78. Moran, *Printing*, p. 25. The first chapter of this invaluable book covers the earliest period and includes a number of useful reproductions. Most surviving handpresses come from a period when the main body of the press was made of iron; for these, the best discussion is that in Rummonds, *Printing*, where the point is generally made that the manner of working the press was not significantly different from that employed on a wooden press, dating from before the late eighteenth century. An important discussion of a wooden hand-press, albeit much later than Petrucci's, can be found in Harris, *Common*.

79. There are several good illustrations of the way in which tympan and frisket were attached to the press; see, for example, Moran, *Printing*, p. 35, or (in a modern diagram), Rummonds, *Printing*, p. 22. The earliest illustrations of the press show a frisket, and Moran, *Printing*, p. 23, argues that one was already in use by 1487. Given the pattern of single settings of type for liturgical books, its adoption must have been inevitable.

80. A recent interesting paper, demonstrating the same practice on the part of Aldus Manutius's typesetters, was read by Neil Harris at the 2000 SHARP Conference in Mainz.

Chapter Four

NORMAL PRINTING-HOUSE PROCEDURES

his chapter is concerned almost exclusively with the music books printed by Petrucci. The three other books that have survived with his name attached (and that, I argue, represent the whole of his non-musical output) are in their own way more typical of the period in which they were printed and are discussed in chapter 7.

I. The Appearance of the Book

The great majority of the musical books present to the reader a largely consistent outward appearance.[1] They are oblong, in landscape format, normally about 165 × 236 mm in size,[2] with six staves to a full page (although frequently fewer are present), printed with an elegant musical typeface, and with ornate initial letters for almost every composition or mass movement. Each has a title page that conforms to the new practice, prevalent since late in the previous century, of giving in simple form the contents of the book, and sometimes the name of its author. Almost every book that is an anthology contains a tavola or index, usually on the *verso* of the title page, and almost all end with a colophon, a register of gatherings, and Petrucci's device. From time to time and from book to book there is variation in details of these aspects—for example, whether or not part-names are indicated on the title-pages, or Petrucci's device is included—but the basic plan is straightforward. Few books have dedications, and each that does is thereby made more significant. The books with lute tabulature, either solo or as accompaniment to the voice, open with a series of instructions for reading the notation.

If, as Hirsch stated, "the physical appearance of the early printed book followed the manuscript tradition",[3] we should ask how far this was also true for

Petrucci's musical books. In some respects, his patterns were more typical of printed books of the period. The form of the title-page, the presence and location of an index, the form of colophon, all are typical of early printed sources. In addition, the pattern of including a register of gatherings had become a typical Italian feature. In one respect, however, Petrucci's books were unusual. His layout, the shape and proportion of the page, was unknown in earlier printed material, but that is hardly relevant: no previous printer had attempted to address such a repertoire. However, it was also rather rare, perhaps novel, in manuscript sources.[4]

Before 1520, all Petrucci's secular music—French and Italian—was printed in choirbook layout, following the prevailing Italian custom in which the Tenor was entered below the Superius.[5] The pattern was established from the beginning, with the first edition of the *Odhecaton A*. In a number of ways, that book followed a long manuscript tradition (with the principal exception of adopting the new landscape format): chansons were spaced as lavishly as in any of the late-fifteenth-century chansonniers. Blank staves abound (as also in the following two volumes of the series), and no attempt was made to fill the lower parts of scarcely used pages. Only twice, on M2*v*–3*r* and M6*v*–7*r*, did Petrucci even put two compositions on an opening; yet these compositions are scarcely shorter than others in the volume. In several places only six of the possible twelve staves are employed,[6] and it is a rare opening that has no blank staves or spaces left where staves were not inked at all. Many of the elegantly designed initials that open pieces take up parts of two staves in height. This approach to space, lavish and opulent in itself, would have appealed to potential purchasers familiar with the manuscript tradition. Not surprisingly, it is followed in *Canti B*. Even in *Canti C*, where the pages tend to be fuller, reflecting the different musical styles represented, the pattern holds true, with the exception of a small section that may represent a problem in the printer's shop.[7] Almost without exception,[8] these three volumes give no more than the incipit of the text. The Superius will rarely have the whole of a poetic line, and the lower voices often have even less. In this, Petrucci or his supplier was merely following a pattern that had become common in Italian sources of secular music in the French styles. Many manuscripts, by this date, have no more than an incipit for almost all their pieces. The significance of this lack of text in these sources has been discussed with increasing frequency in recent years, and I shall return to it in chapter 8, in a discussion of the relationship between the appearance and organisation of Petrucci's volumes and his intended market.

Some aspects of this presentation remain constant in later volumes and for different repertoires: in particular, most of the technical features change only occasionally. There is always (until 1520) space for a maximum of six staves; blank staves (or white space in their place) continue to be found—truly crowded openings are rare, and therefore bibliographically significant; pieces are introduced with elegant capitals; title pages are usually similarly laconic; text setting (though varying from one repertoire to another) tends to be informal and often not complete.

Although the frottola volumes also maintain a choirbook layout, the appearance on the page tends to be rather different. There are more openings with one piece on each page, and many others tend to look fuller. But the critical difference in the appearance of the page is a response to the relative treatment of the poetry. Not only is the text regularly fully underlaid to the Superius part, there are often additional strophes supplied at the foot of the page. The difference is extreme: a number of frottole have as many as three columns of text set out at the foot of a page of music, and the text sometimes overflows from the verso to the succeeding recto.[9] This is also in keeping with the manuscript tradition: there are few frottola manuscripts with music that do not include underlaid text, reflecting the different perception of the two repertoires, "French" and "Italian".

The change in 1520 to partbook arrangement for the two surviving secular volumes is only one of a series of anomalous features of these books, which will have to be addressed in some detail later. This particular feature would have had something to do with the manner in which secular music in Italy had evolved in the nearly twenty years since the French chanson volumes,[10] with changes in its performance style and milieu, and probably also with the impact of the closely Florentine source of the new repertoire.[11]

Almost all the sacred music—masses and motets, so-called—was printed in separate partbooks, while maintaining the oblong landscape format. The first two books, *Motetti A* and *Motetti B*, had been printed in the more conservative choir-book layout, although this was then abandoned. Already, before *Motetti B* was printed, two volumes of mass settings by Josquin and Obrecht had been printed in separate partbooks. Thereafter this layout became the normal practice. The different arrangement might have been adopted because Petrucci did not like putting long movements into choirbook arrangements, when they would take many openings; significantly, there is only one piece or *pars* in either *Motetti A* or *Motetti B* that takes more than two openings—Pesenti's *Tulerunt Dominum meum* on folios D6v–E1r of *Motetti B*. This could explain, if not the retention of choir-book layout for *Motetti B*, certainly the adoption of partbooks for the Josquin volume. A more probable explanation, however, can be sought (and surely found) in the intended market for the volumes: the secular volumes—and the first two books of motets—were not intended for the choirs that presumably would be the only regular purchasers of settings of the Ordinary of the Mass.[12] This issue, too, will be explored further in chapter 8.

Interestingly, the books of laude and Lamentations are printed in choirbook layout. For the laude this seems almost obvious: their intended market was clearly not the professional choirs that would buy liturgical settings, but rather confraternities, private individuals, and groups, and perhaps some professionals who were regularly employed by the fraternities. Indeed, the market would often represent a technical ability not very different from that for the frottola volumes. For the Lamentations, I believe there is a different reason, to which I shall return.[13]

The identification of each book for the bookseller and purchaser is, as we would expect, to be found on the title page. In the case of the anthologies, this definition of the contents is usually very brief: *Canti C*, *Frottole libro primo*, *Motetti a cinque libro primo*, or *Laude Libro secondo*.[14] The exceptions to this pattern are always of interest. A title such as *Motetti De passione De cruce De sacramento De beata virgine et huiusmodi. B* sets out to describe the contents in a specific manner. The same can be said for the title to the fourth book of frottole—*Strambotti, Ode, Frottole, Sonetti. Et modo de cantar versi latini e capituli. Libro quarto.*—and Dalza's fourth book of intabulations—*Intabulatura de Lauto Libro Quarto. Padoane diuerse. Calate a la spagnola. Calate a la taliana. Tastar de corde con li soi recercar drietro. Frottole. Joanambrosio.* In each of these three cases, we may speculate that the editor or publisher was concerned that the market for the contents was not well defined and needed the encouragement of a more detailed title. In the case of *Motetti B*, for example, the details almost suggest that the book was aimed at potential buyers of Laude, which also emphasise the Cross, the Sacrament, and the Virgin Mary. The fourth book of frottole represents the first of a group of three books intended to be organised in a new manner. In the case of the lute book, it is reasonable to presume that Dalza also wanted to emphasise the presence of material that could not be found in the preceding volumes of the series.

The intabulations of Bossinensis also give more detail on the style of the contents: *Tenori e contrabassi intabulati col sopran in canto figurato per cantare e sonar col lauto Libro Primo. Francisci Bossinensis Opus.* In this case, there is every reason to give such detail, merely to alert the customer to the genre and performance medium. This voice-and-lute form of presentation of frottole, however common it was in performance, was apparently very rare in the sources; it had not been printed and seems to exist in very few manuscripts of the period, the principal of which is probably from the Veneto.[15]

All the volumes devoted to the music of a single composer have more detailed title pages. These are volumes of masses with merely five or six compositions in them.[16] Therefore they list the works on the title-pages and dispense with a tavola. This principle is also extended to the *Missarum diversorum auctorum Liber primus*. It is reasonable here to argue that the probably different market for these volumes affected the make-up of the title-page. If indeed professionals or their institutions were the likely purchasers, then the details of the specific pieces included would help to ensure both a wider circulation and a lower chance of institutions duplicating their manuscript holdings.

In the early years of partbook editions, the lower books were not given a formal title at all; it seems to have been enough to indicate the name of the part with a single initial letter—"T", "A", or "B". This must have led to confusion in the warehouse, where there would have been as many as nine sets of partbooks by the middle of 1505, all with each lower voice indicated solely by the relevant letter. Nonetheless, Petrucci did not at that stage turn to a pattern of printing titles on all the lower voices as well as on the Cantus book. Two volumes of 1505, the second book of Josquin's masses and the *Fragmenta Missarum*, survive with some copies having fuller titles, stamped onto the title pages after presswork. The only Venetian edition that shows these additions as part of the original typesetting is the *Missarum diversorum auctorum* of 1508. Other books retain the practice of single letters, indicating the part, until 1515 with the Fossombrone edition of Josquin's second book of masses; thereafter, all new volumes have complete titles on all parts, and even the third edition of the first book of *Motetti de la Corona* has full titles.

The colophon and its accompaniments also supplied essential information, although this was not aimed at the potential purchaser. Appearing at the end of all Petrucci's books, the colophon gave the name of the printer, the city in which he was working, and a date—which we assume was the date on which production was finished and the book became available, that is, was "published". Sometimes, the colophon also included a statement of privilege or of protection by the local authority. During the Fossombrone years, the whole privilege was usually printed.

The dates included in the colophon are apparently always expressed in terms of the local calendar. In Venice, most public documents intended for internal consumption followed the *more veneto*, a style in which the new calendar year began two months later than in modern usage, on the first day of March.[17] Thus, the first edition of *Canti B* is dated, in the colophon, "die 5 Februarij Salutis anno 1501". This practice provoked some speculation among earlier scholars, as I have said, as to whether this edition preceded the extant first edition of the *Odhecaton A*, with its dedication dated in May of 1501. As bibliographical analysis confirms, however, the date of *Canti B* is written in *more veneto* and should be read as referring to 1502, according to our modern understanding of dates. The same is true for the second edition of *Odhecaton A*, to be dated in January of 1503 (n.s.), the only edition of *Canti C*, of February 1504 (n.s.), the first of *Frottole libro secondo*, January 1505 (n.s.), and so on. All these dates have been recognised by modern scholars for the best part of one hundred years. One of Petrucci's Venetian volumes, however, has recently been mis-assigned: the *Missarum diversorum auctorum Liber primus* carries the date "1508. Die. 15 Martij". If Petrucci were using *more veneto* at the time, as I believe and as the typographical evidence confirms, this book should be assigned to 1508 and not 1509.[18] It is possible that the confusion arose from the presence in a number of Venetian documents of the phrase "anno incarnationis", which would normally imply that the New Year was to start on the Feast of the Annunciation, 25 March. According to Cappelli, however, Venetian notaries used this formula even while beginning their new year on 1 March.[19]

In Fossombrone, Petrucci, as a resident of the Papal States, would have been under the aegis of the Roman court. There is no evidence to suggest that Urbino followed any practice other than the Roman. Unfortunately, Roman practice seems to be less than clear. Apparently the prevailing custom was to use a calendar beginning with the Nativity of Christ, so that the new year began on 25 December. However, so-called Florentine style, which used the Incarnation (25 March) as the new year, was also prevalent at times and used for a number of papal documents. As it happens, two events in Petrucci's work fall within that part of the year. Josquin's third book of masses was printed on 1 March 1514, and appears to fit there rather than in 1515, on the basis of the state of the material. The colophon to Calvo's manuscript translation of Hippocrates states that it was printed by Petrucci on 1 January 1519. Since Petrucci was in Rome in August 1518 to protest the delays in receiving copy, 1519 seems a more likely modern date than 1520. We can therefore probably assume that dates for Petrucci's Fossombrone years follow modern usage.

In many volumes, the page with the colophon also included an impression of the printer's device. This design, unique to each printer, was traditionally employed as an indicator of his identity. For some printers, such as Antonio Barré or Antonio Gardano, the device could appear on the title-page. In the case of many non-musical printers, it might appear on both title and final pages and act as an identification of the printer, while the actual name was reserved for the colophon. In other volumes, two devices appear, one for the printer, usually associated with the colophon, and the other for the publisher. This situation prevails in several of Antico's volumes, which have his device, as well as that of Mazzocchi or Giunta, for example.

The colophon was almost always accompanied by a register. This element was essential to almost all the book's handlers, for it gave details of its make-up. The register took the form of a statement of the signing pattern of the gatherings, and the number of bifolia involved in each. It did not say, and did not need to say, whether the volume was in one unit or was a set of partbooks.[20] For book-sellers and binders, this register statement was the only available evidence as to whether the set of printed sheets before them was complete or lacking a gathering or two.[21] Coupled with the signatures, it also ensured that the gatherings were arranged in order, and that gatherings containing more than one folded sheet of paper were arranged correctly. The absence of a register is one more anomalous feature of Petrucci's last book, the *Motetti del Fiore* of 1538.

The format described by the registers was standard throughout Petrucci's musical output. All gatherings were set in landscape format, in quarto, and the normal full gathering contained two sheets of paper, one folded inside the other to make eight folios.[22] For that reason, such a gathering could be described in the *Registrum* as a quaternion—four bifolia. Many gatherings would use a half-sheet at their center, either in addition to the inner sheet, or as a substitute for it. The former was a quintern, yielding five bifolia, and the latter a ternion, with three bifolia, six folios.[23]

Once he had settled into a standardised practice, after the first volumes of chansons and Josquin's masses, Petrucci tended to favour books made of seven or eight gatherings. In frottola volumes, for example, this would yield fifty-six or sixty-four folios. In partbooks, each voice part could occupy two gatherings, which would be of sixteen folios unless extra or fewer were needed for a specific part. It seems that most partbook after 1502 were planned with the Superius in mind, and that the Superius was expected to fill sixteen folios; the deviations from this pattern tend to fall in the lower voices.[24] Some variation in the length of Superius books for mass volumes is to be expected, since Petrucci was planning to include five masses in each, and the length of these works could vary greatly. Thus the Superius of Ghiselin's masses is printed on eighteen folios, and that of the Agricola edition on twenty, but even here, 1505 sees an approach toward consistency.

Petrucci indicated the order of sheets and folios with two normal practices, in common with almost all printers of the period. The more important comprised the pattern of signatures, always found at the right foot of the *recto*. These are completely orthodox throughout Petrucci's output, although he did develop two minor modifications, both followed by many subsequent music printers. One was to employ different patterns of signing for different titles. This was almost neces-sary when so many volumes contained similar, and similar-looking, output, and no more than the part-initial on the first recto of lower voice parts. Petrucci, as well as his booksellers and their binders, had to be able to distinguish gathering B of de Orto's masses from that of Brumel.[25] If one fell on the floor of the stockroom, it needed to be immediately identifiable. Petrucci therefore began to adopt dif-ferent signature patterns with his edition of *Motetti B*, which, instead of using a simple capital letter as signature, used doubled letters; thereafter, almost all volumes had distinctive patterns: *Motetti B*: "AA"; Brumel's masses: "Aa"; La Rue's masses: "Aaa"; *Canti C*: "Aa"; Agricola's masses: "AAA"; *Motetti C*: "+A", etc.

Later printers followed suit in one of two ways. One was exactly like Petrucci's and can be found in the work of Tylman Susato among many others. The other was to present a shortened version of the book's title next to the signature, on what is called the Direction Line (and by many musical bibliographers, the Signature Line). This practice, found already in books printed by Antico, became the more normal Italian solution and would be followed consistently by both Gardano and Scotto.

Petrucci's other modification to standard signature practice was to sign the different partbooks of a single title sequentially. This was clearly convenient if the signature style also differed from title to title. Gatherings of the Tenor book could be signed with the letters "C" and "D" (if the Superius had used only "A" and "B") in the same style as the letters of the Superius and therefore clearly belong to the same title. Only once did Petrucci not follow this practice. In *Motetti C*, he had decided to precede each signature letter with a small cross, thus distinguishing this volume from others. But each partbook was signed with the same letters, from "A" to "D"; the problems that this could raise must have become clear, for Petrucci had to indicate in the *Registrum* that the different partbooks could be distinguished by looking for the part name, printed at the head of each page. For most of his career, he did not fall into this trap again. Indeed, why it should have happened here is a mystery: Petrucci had already published six volumes of mass settings, all signed sequentially through the various partbooks. Yet Petrucci apparently did exactly the same again in his last books: in the two fragmentary titles from the 1530s, the extant lower partbooks are signed from the letter A. Again, the part name appears on each page, acting as a secondary aid to the binder.

The standard second manner of indicating the order of folios, that of numbering them in sequence, was used less often by Petrucci. Many partbook sets have no foliation at all, particularly if they contain masses; indeed the only mass books with pagination are those with works by Obrecht, Brumel, and Ghiselin (the first edition only), and the *Fragmenta Missarum* (although the book of La Rue's masses starts out with a paginated first gathering). Other sets of parts are numbered consecutively through the parts, again with the exception of *Motetti C*, which has four partbooks each foliated from the number 1. Choirbooks and lute volumes are almost always foliated, and usually in the top outer corner of the *recto*. (This is because each of these books also has a tavola, carrying folio numbers.) Petrucci rarely used roman numerals, and in each case the pattern is a little unusual: for the two books of Bossinensis intabulations, he used roman foliation for the texted pieces, and arabic for the final group of ricercars. Roman numerals also appear in the first four books of frottole—though not in the second editions—and in the third edition (only) of the first book of *Motetti de la Corona*. I can see no obvious reason for any of these decisions.

Foliation was primarily of value to the reader. Numbers gave him a point of reference, and they allowed him to consult an index of the contents of anthology volumes. By contrast, the signatures were almost exclusively of value to professionals in the book trade. The bookseller and binder used them, as I have said, to ensure that all the sheets of a book were present and in the correct order. For the binder, the *Registrum* also indicated which signature letters corresponded to half-sheets. For the printer, the signatures had the same significance, but they were also an integral part of the process of placing the music in the correct layout in the forme, and thence on the bed of the press.

Petrucci's landscape format, oblong in orientation, and in quarto, with two sheets to a gathering, involved four formes, one for each side of each sheet, for each impression.[26] This imposed a certain layout of the pages in the forme, which, in a normal gathering of eight folios on two sheets of paper, was as shown below.[27]

Much bibliographical analysis depends on a perception of which elements were (or were not) part of the same forme at any given time, and of the order in which the different formes were prepared. Particularly in the case of Petrucci, using more than one sheet to a gathering, the possible relationships between different pages of a gathering could be quite diverse. The implications of these relationships depend on the order in which Petrucci's compositors set up the type and the consequent order in which the formes were sent to the press. Therefore, I propose to use a standard formulation throughout the rest of this study, to indicate the various formes in a gathering. The sequence of sheets will be indicated by capital Roman numerals, starting with the outermost sheet: the two formes of any sheet will be indicated with an "o" and an "i", for outer and inner formes. These symbols correspond to the various pages of the gathering (see Table 4-1).

When the inner folios of such a gathering only need half a sheet, that is, when a gathering occupies only six folios, the pattern is as shown in Table 4-2.

Io

7ī	2v̄
8v	1r

Ii

2ī	7v̄
1v	8r

IIo

5ī	4v̄
6v	3r

IIi

4ī	5v̄
3v	6r

DIAGRAM 4-1 The arrangement of pages by formes in a normal quarto-in-eights two-sheet gathering

TABLE 4-1 Relationship of formes and folios in a
normal quarto-in-eights two-sheet gathering

Forme	Pages			
Io	1r	2v	7r	8v
Ii	1v	2r	7v	8r
IIo	3r	4v	5r	6v
IIi	3v	4r	5v	6r

(It will sometimes be necessary to indicate the order of pages of the inner
forme in the same order as those of the outer, for example as 2r-1v-8r-
7v. Such a pattern will always be indicated clearly.)

TABLE 4-2 Relationship of formes and folios in a six-
folio gathering

Forme	Pages			
Io	1r	2v	5r	6v
Ii	1v	2r	5v	6r
IIo	3r	4v		
IIi	3v	4r		

Sometimes, as will be shown, the two half-formes of the inner sheet could
be printed on the same side of a sheet, in a process called "work and turn". When
that happens the inner sheet comprised only one forme, laid out (and referred to
here) as: II 3r, 4v, 4r, 3v.

In a similar manner, the formes of a twelve- or ten-folio gathering can be
shown clearly, with the addition of entries using the roman numeral "III" for the
central sheet.

These patterns make clear a feature that is essential for understanding how a
compositor worked with the material before him. In any gathering, the forme
containing the first recto also contained the last verso. The larger the gathering,
the further apart these would be; further, if the type were set sequentially from
the beginning of the gathering to the end, the first forme to be commenced, that
with the first recto, would also be the last to be finished and ready for the press.
Indeed, in a normal eight-folio gathering, no forme was ready for the press until
the compositor had set up and placed in the relevant forme the material for the
recto of folio 6 (the eleventh page of the gathering), completing the forme IIi of
my tabulation. The compositor therefore needed to have available to him at least
enough of every sort of type to set up eleven pages. In practice, he needed rather
more, for he would begin work on the first page of a new gathering while some
type was still at the printing press, printing the last formes of the previous gathering. Many compositors would need enough type to set at least fifteen pages (if
only one forme from the previous gathering was still set-up) and probably nineteen pages.

For most printers, this was not likely to be a problem, at least for the more
common type sorts. However, if several pages used less common sorts (in verbal
terms, if there were an excess of the letter "q", for example), the compositor
might well run out. This seems to have happened occasionally with Petrucci. I

shall cite below a case in which his font apparently did not contain enough different sorts of the ligature *cum opposite proprietate* descending a single pitch.

The easiest way to avoid the problem, however, was to cast off the text in advance, so that a compositor could then set, not sequentially, but by formes. Some printers' manuscripts of the period do show evidence of casting off, alongside other editorial decisions.[28] There is no good evidence that Petrucci cast off before setting commenced, especially for volumes of mass or lute music, where the content was continuous for several pages. Whether he did or not, his men must have experienced some of the benefits of casting off in advance, if only because he employed a multiple-impression process. Even if the compositor set up the first impression sequentially, the second impression was in effect cast off for him, for he had to follow the spacing and layout of the first.

These, then, are the structural features of the normal Petrucci volume. The elegance of the earliest editions, in which he not only employed the best of material in pristine condition, but also was willing to undertake labour-intensive processes, gradually gives way to a more mundane product, wherein even the replacements for the earlier materials are less stylish and the presswork almost descends to the sloppy.

The last three extant editions show a different face to the reader. They are one of Pisano's music (1520), one that I call "*Musica XII*", and the 1538 *Motetti del Fiore*. All three are smaller, in both page size and printed area. Pisano's book has only four staves to the page and uses a different text font. It was certainly published by Petrucci; it uses his music font and a number of his initials; and it has a colophon which gives his name, though in an unusual manner.[29] It is closer in size and style to contemporaneous Florentine manuscripts, though this is not sufficient to explain the unusual form of the colophon. Given the evidence that Petrucci was actually turning away from printing and moving to Sora, it seems plausible to argue that responsibility for the book should be assigned to an assistant or apprentice in the shop. In that case, this person may have provided the contacts with Rome, perhaps fostered in the aftermath of the Calvo debacle, and he would himself have moved to Rome or supplied Pasoti with some of Petrucci's typographical material.[30]

The last two volumes, of the 1530s, are different again. They have in common the staves, the text font, and Petrucci's music font. Both also have signatures for the lower voices (all that survive) beginning with "A", a practice otherwise found in Petrucci only with the *Motetti C* of 1504. They almost certainly represent a different set of craftsmen, perhaps with little input from Petrucci himself, then in his seventies. They do not present an identical picture, for certain details differ, most notably with a completely new set of initials for the *Motetti del Fiore*.

The appearance of Petrucci's volumes and the technical consistency, these three titles apart, are the product of procedures followed with continuing skill by his craftsmen. They had standardised practices, which can be largely deduced from details in the extant volumes. These practices provide an explanation for many of the visual features, musical as well as bibliographical, which distinguish Petrucci's editions, and open the door to an understanding of the possible stimuli for the many anomalies found there. The rest of this chapter is therefore devoted to a description of some aspects of Petrucci's normal practices. Chapter 5 draws on these patterns to explain a number of the anomalies, while chapter 8 uses the same material (as well as that from chapters 5 and 6) to draw a picture of what Petrucci may have seen as his role as a printer of music.

II. Preparing the Book: The Bibliographical Evidence

It is not my intention to present a detailed description of the normal manner in which a book was prepared for the press in early-sixteenth-century Italy. Many of the procedures are not very different from those of the preceding, much more heavily studied half-century, the period of incunable printing. Apparently, the processes of actually printing the text on the paper, and the presses with which these processes were implemented, remained constant into the seventeenth century. The details given by Bodoni's craftsman probably correspond to detailed aspects of Petrucci's work. In the same way, the practices of typesetting, the skills of the compositor, were much the same throughout the handpress period. The available literature on these is enormous, and there is nothing new to be added to them from the evidence in Petrucci's books.[31]

There *are* ways in which Petrucci's processes were less usual—among them the consistent use of multiple impressions. In addition, there are several features of Petrucci's editions that throw new or additional light on specific details of printing technique during the period—the use of type sorts to act as uninked "bearers" is an example. Finally, there is a number of features of technique that need to be understood before the rest of this study will make sense. I have in mind here the manner in which type was not left standing, or the pattern of deterioration of sorts and blocks.

The remainder of this chapter therefore does not present a primer for music printing by multiple impressions, or a description of how the musical and verbal text, delivered to Petrucci in manuscript, arrived in its present printed state. Instead, I propose to discuss a number of issues of varying importance, each of which has some bearing either on the history of printing or on musical or bibliographical issues to be discussed later.

Format

The standard layout of the average Petrucci book has been described above. The presence of two sheets per gathering, one folded inside the other, while making the book easier to bind, did have an effect on the typesetter's work, while providing additional evidence for the bibliographer.

I have remarked that Petrucci seems normally to have aimed to have books with whole sheets—that is with multiples of four folios. In fact, all the books set in choirbook format, and all the lute books do use complete sheets; there is even some evidence, to be mentioned below, of the addition of pieces to round out a gathering.

This consistency was not always possible when the music was set in partbooks; in the mass volumes, in particular, Petrucci was circumscribed by the lengths of the works he was publishing. Sometimes, the music would fit conveniently into a whole number of sheets, sometimes it needed an extra two folios, or half-sheet. This was quite acceptable: the half-sheet, once folded, could be bound into a gathering, and there were ways of ensuring that the other half-sheet was not wasted. Sometimes, of course, the music required only one or three extra folios. Since an odd folio could not be bound, Petrucci then had to waste another folio, the one that would normally be conjugate, which survives as a blank. Both these features are apparent even in the first volume printed in separate parts, Josquin's [first] book of masses (1502): the Superius is printed on twenty-four folios, three complete gatherings or six sheets. But each of the other parts has a different structure. The Altus needed only nineteen folios, so is printed on twenty, using five sheets, with the last folio completely blank. The Tenor needed even fewer, a mere thirteen folios. It is laid out accordingly, but the single extra folio had to be conjugate with something, and so the book takes fourteen folios— three and one-half sheets, and the one-half sheet is bound inside the last full gathering. A similar problem is resolved in a like manner in the Bassus.[32]

In other books, Petrucci tried to standardise the format. This becomes evident in 1508 with the two anthology volumes *Missarum diversorum auctorum* and *Motetti a cinque libro primo*, and it is clearly policy for partbooks thereafter. He seems to have begun with the Superius, for in every case this contains exactly two eight-folio gatherings. In only one case,[33] however, do all the other parts also have this standard collation. In all others at least one of the books is longer or shorter.

Number of Impressions

Perhaps the feature of Petrucci's technique most commonly addressed in present-day writings is the multiple-impression process. More than any other aspect, writers have concerned themselves with whether he printed with three or two impressions, and have asserted one or the other. I know of no contemporary report suggesting either, and the only support for such assertions lies entirely within the surviving editions, principally to be detected by one of only a few simple methods. The same evidence regularly indicates which elements on the printed page were (or, more clearly, were not) printed together.

On the most obvious level, symbols that overlap on the page cannot have been printed at the same time; this includes not only notes and staves, but also initial letters and staves, and (surprisingly often) notes and words. Secondly, when two copies of the same book can be placed side by side, it is evident that there are slight variations between them in the exact relationship of a syllable to a note, or of a stave line to the initial letter that opens a composition. Thirdly, when one element of a page has taken ink less well, either over the whole page or, more usefully, in a smaller area, then it is possible to see which parts of the content were printed at the same impression. Finally, there are occasional aspects of house practice that suggest (and rarely more) some detail of the pattern of impressions.

These ranges of evidence show that, for the earliest editions, Petrucci was using three impressions, with the staves printed separately. Indeed, he seems to have begun with only one set of staves, for the same forme of staves can be traced on both the inner and outer formes of every sheet, in volumes printed up to early 1503.[34]

The basic elements of the three impressions evidently were the music; the staves; and the text. I have already pointed out that the pattern of lengths of the staves, as well as the damage to be seen on them, shows that they were kept in the forme. It might seem possible, therefore, to print many pages of staves in advance, ready for use in any book whatsoever. This is certainly possible in the triple impression phase of Petrucci's work, although only under certain conditions, which are not normally fulfilled. Three such conditions stem from the need for the book to have the same patterns of staves on every page: that nothing else (signatures, foliation, etc.) should be on the formes; that any pattern of the need for short staves should be the same for every sheet, for every opening; and that no staves could be left uninked, in blind.

The first condition is obvious: it is the principal reason why staves could not have been printed in advance once double-impression printing was adopted. The second is equally clear: indeed, it might seem to be the reason why the inset staves were abandoned so early, after only one edition. I doubt, however, that the staves even for this edition, the first of the *Odhecaton A*, were printed in advance. In three instances, the inset staves are wrongly placed in the forme, and do not appear at the start of the verso of a folio but elsewhere. This seems unlikely to occur if the staves alone had been printed in bulk. The third condition assumes that the printer could not project in advance how many folios would need six staves, and how many would need only five, or four. It also fails to allow for pages that were to contain the title page and tavola, or the colophon, as well as any extra blank pages at the end of a book.

For these practical reasons, therefore, I believe that the staves were printed "on demand", as it were, as one more impression at the time of printing the book. Fortunately, the evidence does confirm that they were still printed separately until the middle of 1503. In *Motetti B* (the last book printed entirely from three impressions, in May 1503), the distance of staves from text in different copies is very variable. A comparison of almost any pages in the copies at London and Paris will show this quite clearly. Similar evidence can be found in any early title for which more than one copy survives. Therefore the staves were still being printed at a different time—that is, we are still seeing a triple-impression process.

Yet with the first edition after *Motetti B*, a different situation prevails. This, the volume of Brumel's masses, is a special case in several ways, and has to be discussed in connection with its own successor, containing Ghiselin's masses.[35] The two are dated 17 June and 15 July 1503, respectively. The sum of evidence in these books, involving watermarks, and stave patterns and deterioration, argues that the two were printed concurrently, at least in part.

The Brumel was started with three impressions, for it begins with a single forme of staves, the one that had been used in *Motetti B* and before. The staves are used for the Superius and Tenor, and then abandoned. Thereafter, two sets of staves are used. One of these is made up with part of the old set (it retains three of the four pages of staves in one forme, replacing the other), while the second is made of four completely new pages of staves. These two new sets of staves are used consistently through the rest of this book and for all the Ghiselin edition.

At the same time, the pattern of paper-use argues that the first three sheets of the Ghiselin book were printed before the lower voices of the Brumel volume; they are printed on a paper also found in the upper voices of the Brumel, with the addition of a few extra sheets from elsewhere. The paper that is used for the lower voices of the Brumel is then found in the rest of the Ghiselin edition.

Taken together, these two pieces of evidence suggest that the idea of a change from one set of staves to the new second and third sets was developed while the first two partbooks of the Brumel were being printed; the paper used to start the Brumel was soon exhausted, and a new paper was introduced. The new formes of staves could not have been used while these Brumel gatherings were at press, for they contain some of the same staves. They were prepared after these gatherings were printed and tried out on the first sheets of the Ghiselin edition, using the ends of the first batch of paper. They proved satisfactory; the technique of two impressions that they permitted also seems to have been satisfactory; and so the rest of both titles was printed. Probably the Brumel edition was finished first. The dates in the colophons suggest it; the slight changes in state for some initials support the idea; and the last sheets of Ghiselin's Altus and the whole of the Bassus show the beginnings of damage to both new sets of staves.

The sequence of printing, as demonstrated by this evidence, is shown in Table 4-3.

This argument implies that the introduction of two sets of staves was concurrent with the introduction of the quicker process, using only two impressions. Whatever the changes that occurred here, there is no doubt that the Ghiselin book was undertaken in something of a rush. It seems unlikely that a new technique would have been advanced here, during the printing of another book, unless there were a reason outside the mere exploration of the technique. I have suggested elsewhere that the reason for the hurry was that Ghiselin, who had been reappointed by Ferrara, was about to arrive there from the north. The court probably commissioned the volume, and Petrucci was required to produce it in time for Ghiselin's arrival, entailing a delay in finishing the edition of Brumel.[36]

However that may be, the evidence also argues that the introduction of two formes of staves was cause or product of the introduction of a process using only two impressions. For as long as the staves were to be printed separately, there was no need for two sets, or to alternate them. But once staves and text were to be printed from the same forme, more than one forme of staves became essential;

TABLE 4-3 The order of printing the editions of Brumel's and Ghiselin's masses (1503)

1.	Stave pattern	Paper	Gatherings
2.	1st forme:	paper "1"	Brumel: A-C, DI, DII
3.	1st forme:	paper "2"	Brumel: DIII
4.	2nd & 3rd formes:	paper "1"	Ghiselin: A, BI[a]
5.	2nd & 3rd formes:	paper "2"	Brumel: E-J
6.			Ghiselin: BII, BIII, C-D, EI
7.	2nd & 3rd, damaged:	paper "2"	Ghiselin: EII, F-H

[a] In several copies, odd sheets of paper from other batches appear in these three sheets. They do not make a consistent pattern, and they suggest that paper "1" was nearly exhausted. This, too, argues that these sheets were printed as experiments, after paper "2" had already been adopted, to finish the books.

one would be available for the addition of text, while the other stave-and-text forme was at the press.

The evidence again consists of all the ranges listed at the start of this section. Among many examples are the following early instances:

> text and staves are aligned identically in both the London copies of the Superius of *Motetti C* (15 September 1504), while their alignment with the music varies slightly;
>
> both text and staves are poorly inked in many places, while the music is clear: early examples include the Paris copy of *Canti C* (10 February 1504), K4*v* and K5*r*; the Budapest copy of the second edition of *Motetti A* (10 February 1505) in several places; the Oxford copy of *Motetti libro quarto* (4 June 1505) in gatherings A, C, and D;
>
> both text and staves are smudged in some places: see, for example, *Motetti libro quarto*, the copy at Wolfenbüttel, on folio N3*r*.

Further, there is the evidence that one forme of staves, consistently used for an inner forme through most of a title, can suddenly appear as an outer forme. If this happened in only one copy, there would be no doubt that the staves were printed separately; the anomaly would have been the result of handling the stock of papers with pre-printed staves. When it happens, as it does, in every copy, the pattern is a result of typesetting and not of press-work.[37]

With only two formes to set for each page of content, the typesetter could decide how to distribute all the various elements of a page. Some were almost predetermined: the large initial letters could not be printed with the staves, for they occupied the same space, once the shorter staves had been abandoned during 1502. Text and music could not be printed together, for the ascenders of many letters intruded on the space reserved for the tails of notes. Other elements could be printed in either forme: these include the headline, containing the voice part-name when in part-books, the composer's name, any title or rubric, and a folio number; part-names in the margins of books in choirbook format; and the signatures at the foot of pages. Certain decisions were more logical than others: initial capitals would be set with the music; folio numbers would be printed with the headline. This usually implied that signatures would be printed with the text. With signatures and foliation set up in different formes, compositor and press-man had an indicator of layout and sequence of folios in each forme.

This procedure produces a fairly logical pattern, which indeed emerges using the sorts of evidence that have been advanced above—places where two elements overlap, the alignment of details in different copies, and the quality of inking: one impression contained the music, initial capital letters, the signatures, and part-names found in the left margin; the other contained the staves, text, and the headline, including foliation.

There are one or two slight and necessary exceptions. In a number of cases, text appears in the space allotted to the stave lines—when, for example, it comprised a rubric within a mass setting, or a tacet instruction in a set of Lamentations—and it must have been set in the musical forme. The same holds for the extra verses of text for frottole, which lie in space normally occupied by staves;

although the staves are not printed, the blind impression of their presence in the forme is often very clear.

As we might expect, Petrucci's compositors normally set up the music first. The logical reason is that it is frequently much more dense on the page than is the text. As did scribes, Petrucci's compositors could easily have changed their patterns. They did, after all, follow the patterns of placing text phrases that were current in manuscripts: individual phrases were often set as in normal prose, fol-lowed by white space until the next phrase was due.[38] Particularly in the volumes of sacred music, there are many lines where the text is rather sparsely spread. Without following a copy of the music as printed, it would have been impossible to place the text accurately. This argues strongly that the text could not have been placed even as accurately as it was unless the music had already been set and run off, with a copy in front of the typesetter.[39]

Although there is no reason to believe that this sequence was followed reli-giously, especially in second or later editions, I have not found any convincing evidence that the text was set before the music—except for one or two cases where the musical impression seems to have drawn ink from the text, as if printed over it. There is also the case, on one folio (D1v) of the Lisbon copy of Josquin's first book of masses (1502), where the indentation of the three impressions suggests that in fact the music was last. Both cases are susceptible of alternative interpre-tations, however.

The stronger evidence lies on the other side: there are cases where the text is cramped, where excessive numbers of abbreviations are suddenly used, or where several phrases of text have to be run together—each indicating that the music had taken less space than was needed for the text. In late editions, the staves are often not inked much beyond the end of the music—suggesting again that the typesetter and pressman already knew exactly how much of the stave would be needed, and a suitable frisket was then cut.[40]

There is another form of multiple impression in Petrucci's work, one which is much more typical of printing of the period. In the *Paulina*, there are many pages with tables where some figures are in red and others in black. These different elements were set together in the same forme, just as text and rubrics would be in chant books of the period. The forme was then run through the press twice: once for the text printed in red, with a frisket cut to mask the material intended to be in black. A different frisket (the reverse of the first) was then placed over the type, and the black text could be printed. The evidence for this is different and consists of shadows of one colour on the edges of letters that were printed in the other, the result of a frisket being slightly misaligned.

Casting off

An important question about preparing the (musical and verbal) text for printing concerns the order in which the contents of a volume were set up in type. Did the compositor work right through one part at a time, or did he set pieces, working with all the voice parts, one after the other? Did he work straight through a part or a piece, or did he set the material forme by forme?[41] These questions involve consideration of the process of casting off, by which a typesetter or his foreman planned the layout page by page (and line by line) and marked up the manuscript copy to indicate his decisions. This is a pre-requisite for setting by formes, unless each composition fits onto a single page or an opening, and any space at the foot of a page is left blank.

I know of no theoretical evidence for casting off in sixteenth-century Italian music printing, and we are therefore reduced to such internal evidence as we may be able to glean from the extant printed sources.[42] For example, Mary Lewis has shown that, given the right circumstances, Gardano's compositors practiced what she has called "vertical setting", setting the first forme in each partbook, before proceeding to the second forme in any of them.[43] This involves making some decisions (in advance) about the music that will lie on each page of each partbook, but it seems to have been used almost exclusively in volumes where each composition took the same amount of space in each partbook, particularly when that space could be deemed to be one page (or rarely two) for each. The decisions were therefore more akin to arranging the pieces in order, rather than actually casting off the text.

There is very little internal evidence in Petrucci's books to suggest that he cast off copy before setting it in type. Indeed, it seems rather unlikely for almost all his books. However, even without a formal casting off, some of the music to be printed would have been susceptible of being set by formes. In the volumes of frottole, as well as the early three of chansons and the two volumes of laude, the majority of pieces take one opening, while the exceptions (shorter, to fit on one page; or longer, for two openings) were obvious from the start. Thus, it would be quite possible to decide exactly which pieces would lie on which openings (in the manner adopted by Gardano), without formally casting off text. Notably, however, these are all books that were set in choirbook layout. Since, for these, the music at the top of the second page of an opening, the recto, was not a continuation of that on the preceding verso, but began with the first notes of a different voice-part, almost all pages could be set without reference to the preceding page. Such books could, therefore, easily have been set by formes.[44]

But, as a result, there is almost no indication of whether this in fact happened. There is one strong evidence that might possibly indicate that the books were set straight through. It is a coincidence that the majority of paper changes in these books occur at the beginning of a gathering, with the outer sheet, while the inner uses paper found in earlier gatherings. The value of this evidence is weakest when only one copy survives, as in the first book of all, but it can be found in books with more than one copy, such as *Canti C* and *Frottole IX*. This evidence suggests that the books were set straight through, so that the first forme in any gathering to go to the press was one from the inner sheet, which exhausted the stock of the older paper. The outer sheet (with its two formes) would be ready later and therefore be printed with the newer paper. Without further evidence of a different character, however, this should be seen as mere speculation.

The other repertoires presented different problems for any foreman wishing to cast off copy. In the case of the motet volumes (whether set in choirbook or in parts), all the mass volumes, and the lute books, it would have been very difficult to set by formes unless the music were most carefully cast off in advance. Since these pieces regularly take more than one page, and since new numbers often start in the middle of a page, no composer could have guessed at the first notes of a new forme. Fortunately, there are some strands of evidence suggesting that the music was not cast off in advance. First is the frequent recurrence of blank pages at the ends of volumes. In some cases, if the content had been cast off in advance, earlier pages could have been more generously spaced, using up these spare pages. In others, it is apparent that a volume could have been printed on one less half-sheet, if the calculations had been made in advance. I give one example of each. The Superius book of *I Motetti de la Corona* starts out with a compact setting. The composer seems to have realised, however, that he could not quite fit the part onto three and one-half sheets. He therefore developed a more spacious arrangement for the last part of the volume and used the whole of the final sheet. In the Bassus of Pisano's *Musica*, the reverse seems to have happened, as the typesetter realised that he would be able to save a half-sheet.

In addition, there is the curious collation of the book of Isaac's masses, to be mentioned shortly. Equally interesting is the case of the edition of La Rue's masses, printed in 1503 (AB⁸;C¹⁰;DE⁸;F⁸G⁶). Every mass in every partbook starts at the head of a page, except for two occurrences in the Bassus book, both in the first gathering, F. This suggests that Petrucci gained from the experience of setting the upper voices and calculated that the Bassus could be set on fourteen folios. This not merely saved half a sheet of paper for each copy printed, but it also allowed him to print the middle bifolio of gathering G with that of C, by work and turn. But it does imply that the decision was not reached before typesetting began.

All these instances suggest that the material of the first impression was not cast off in advance. Almost certainly, then, the music in these books was normally set consecutively through a part, beginning with the title page and continuing piece by piece and page by page.

The text-and-stave formes need not have been set in the same manner as the music, however.[45] Once the music had been printed, whether sequentially or not, all the other material could be prepared by formes, working from the layout on the printed music pages. This is why I stated earlier that Petrucci received some of the benefits of casting off, even though he did not practice it for the music. Indeed, there is some evidence from the patterns of staves to suggest that Petrucci's composer did indeed set the text-and-stave layer by formes, to be discussed later in this chapter.

For the music, however, we can assume that the compositor set sequentially through the book. Therefore, no formes of any gathering could go to the press until the compositor had set folio 6r, completing the inner forme of the inner sheet of a normal gathering. One more page, 6v, would complete another forme, the outer of the same sheet, while the last two formes would not be ready until the last folio of the gathering. Therefore, the order in which the music formes of an ordinary gathering went to press was normally IIi–IIo–Ii–Io. This will reveal something about the typographical material that Petrucci owned, about compositors' work habits, and, surprisingly, about some anomalous readings. I shall therefore return to the issue on occasion below, for example, when discussing the use of decorative initial letters, or the presence of two compositors.

The preceding paragraphs have tacitly assumed that only one compositor worked through a volume. Clearly, if two were involved, the pattern should be more complex. But, without a preliminary casting-off of copy, there were few places where work could be accurately divided between two men. In the case of books of frottole and laude, the division could be effected at the end of a gathering, provided that there were two single-page pieces on that opening—or, at least, the different voice parts of a single-opening composition. With partbooks, the situation is obviously simpler, for the two craftsmen could be assigned different voice-parts.

Indeed, everything that has been said here must be taken to relate to one partbook at a time; there is no evident implication that books were set in the standard order of S-T-A-B. A few strands of evidence suggest otherwise: the Barcelona copy of the third book of Josquin's masses (1514) shows a single wrong signature, where D1 is signed F3: this suggests that the Altus was printed before the Tenor and a signature was simply not changed. Secondly, there is the curious collation of the book of Isaac masses: A^8B^{10}; C^6D^4; EF^8; G^8H^6. In every other case (some twenty-six times in sets of partbooks), ten folios were printed as a single gathering. If, in this case, the Tenor book were set after the Altus (and perhaps also after the Bassus), then signatures for it would already have been assigned, and the ten folios divided between two gatherings.[46]

Type-setting

Even when more than one compositor was involved on a title, the procedures adopted by both were very similar. The differences were slight, whether they concerned either the actual content of the book, or reflected discretionary decisions about how to handle some element of the supporting peripheral text or of the layout.[47]

The principal functions of the compositor were, of course, the same as those with other books and presses; this is inevitable, given the nature of type, and the craft or guild character of the process. Setting the text lines would have been standard, no different from the work of any other printer. Setting the music would have been somewhat different, though I believe that a number of fonts for chant raised the same issues.

Central is the fact that, for most of Petrucci's career, the bodies of individual sorts for the notes, rests, and other musical characters were not the same size as a full five lines of stave. They were always shorter, indeed, were small enough that the note tails of *minimas* and smaller values were kerned. This meant that the notes could not be set in a composing stick in a single straight line, as could the text. Almost all notational symbols needed spacing sorts of the same width above and below them,[48] serving to place the symbol at the correct pitch on the stave.

Once the line had been set, it would have to be placed in the forme, one line at a time for either music or text. For the music, this would almost have been essential, for there were so many small spacing sorts; however, in both cases, each line of type was separated from the next by the space needed for the other element—the text area when setting music and vice versa. Once each line of music had been inserted in the forme, furniture would have been placed below it, as far as the space allotted for the next line of music; this would not only ensure that each was placed correctly, it would also help prevent the spacing sorts from moving around. Finally, when all lines were in place, the signatures could be added at the foot of the relevant folios, and the whole forme filled with bearers and locked up ready for printing.

The act of setting the text pages was essentially the same, although here the process was easier, since the text could lie in a straight line. The only novel requirement was that the words or phrases should be so spaced that they would lie underneath the correct notes when printed.

There was one other slight complication: several pages in any edition had no music on them. If the page was to be blank, the staves could be printed, or could be left in the forme and not inked, printed in blind. Yet a number of these pages did have text on them; these normally included the title, the tavola (if present), and the page bearing colophon, register, and device. In some cases, there were more pages—the instruction pages in lute volumes for instance. In these cases the normal division of work between the two impressions was disrupted. Rather than removing the staves from the text forme, the compositor set up the text in the music forme. This meant that the staves could remain, as they normally did, in place and would print in blind. Evidence for this practice shows in a number of places, especially when the staves have left traces across Petrucci's device.

Blind Impressions

The normal procedure of protecting white space was to use furniture to cover blank areas in the forme. As I observed in chapter 3, the sizes of these blocks and the designs on their surfaces can often be seen from traces of ink on the printed page. These impressions result from the manner in which the paper tended to sag within the frisket, whenever there was no type to keep it in place, so that even furniture, lying lower in the forme, could make an impression on the page.

These traces of ink demonstrate the advantage of leaving staves standing in the forme even when they were not to be inked. Since staves stood higher in the press, at the level of the rest of the type, they would both keep the paper level (preventing sagging and hence distorted alignments) and keep it white. At the same time, the staves exerted the same amount of pressure on the page, and they therefore left a visible indentation—a blind impression. Clear examples can be found in many editions, from *Canti B* (1502), folio G8r, to *Motetti de la Corona III* (1519), on B2r and B8v.[49]

This procedure was not possible in the impression of music, where there were no staves already in the forme. Instead, pieces of type or blocks could be inserted in the areas where no content was to be printed, and then left uninked. The effect would be the same, though the process was more laborious: instead of merely inserting furniture or one large bearer to cover the area of a single stave (or leaving the stave in place), the compositor had to insert a series of notes. Since these sorts occupied a much larger and more easily defined area, perhaps a whole page in the forme, the inker could easily keep completely away from them, and they would not receive even the traces of ink showing on the furniture. However, they do still impress the paper and leave indentations. Since these often show clearly on all copies, they must have been part of the press-work and not some other process, such as weighting down a pile of copies in a storeroom. The frequency with which such sorts can be seen (from the first editions to the latest), not only when whole pages (quarter-sheets) were blank but also for single staves, shows another aspect of the concern Petrucci felt for maintaining high standards.

In many cases, these lines of characters involve only one or two note values, set many times over: for example, the first edition of *Odhecaton A* shows a vertical line of *fusas* on folio A1r and K6r; the first edition of *Canti B* shows lines of *fusas* on D4r, and of *minimas* on both A1r and F7r; the first edition of the first book of Josquin's masses (1502) shows ligatures on H4r.[50] Sets of ligatures were particularly valuable for this purpose, for they had larger surfaces, which could be in contact with more of the paper, and they were less likely to be needed in a hurry. Any composer, looking ahead, could see whether he was likely to need a great number of *c.o.p.* ligatures while a given forme was being set up and printed.

There are two variations on this process. One involves using a block of type from elsewhere in the same or another book, as it was set up, but locked into the new forme and meant to be left blank. This has been recorded in some other volumes,[51] but I have found it only rarely in Petrucci's output. In *Misse Obreht* (1503), some of the music of folio E5r was used as bearer type on the next recto; and in Pisano's *Musica* (1520), the music from H3r was used to support the paper on H10v.

More interestingly, the large initial letters, *A*, *B*, and *C*, prepared for Petrucci's first editions, served a similar, and less laborious, function. Each letter could be placed to occupy a large part of the center of a page and obviate the need for other bearers. In several cases the blind impression can be seen quite clearly. The large letter "B", in particular, seems to have been cut with a number of sharp fine lines, which have left obvious ruts in the surface of pages and can even affect inking on the other side of the leaf.

Compositors

Much of the appearance of a Petrucci edition depends on the quality of the materials used—the elegance of the note shapes and initial letters, for instance—or on the basic design of a page. But much also depends on the skill and behaviour of the typesetter. He was responsible for the detailed balance of black and white on a page, for the amount of unused space—white space or blank staves, for the clarity of the musical and verbal text, and for many details of the transmission. These details are significant enough that, if more than one compositor were involved in preparing the same book, the two would tend to produce slightly different results—on both the aesthetic and the textual level.

It is therefore important, from both a bibliographical and a musical point of view, to try and discover whether more than one compositor was involved in a volume. The evidence for this aspect of production hinges on the presumption that typesetters behaved like scribes when transmitting a text. However much they were concerned with being accurate, they also made a number of changes—sometimes deliberate, sometimes accidental, representing either error or unconscious transformation. The musical scribe was particularly prone to making such changes, for his text represented to him not something sacrosanct, but rather the stimulus for a performance—which he was probably hearing in his head as he copied. This could lead to error, to omissions and mistranscriptions; it could just as easily lead to transformations of readings, either in the process of making them more like what the scribe would himself sing, or as a result of the creative urge that was an essential component of the make-up of all Renaissance musicians.

Evidence suggests that a typesetter would behave in a similar manner.[52] We do not know that any of Petrucci's craftsmen were active, much less professional, musicians. But it is evident that all were fluent in notation, and that they (or a house editor) seem to have had a grasp of performance style. This is manifested both by the notational and musical variants that recur throughout the twenty years of editions and by the manner in which the limitations of the printed medium were overcome.[53]

The actual evidence is, like much else in this chapter, somewhat vague and dangerous to interpret. It might seem that any of the following, if they show two different patterns in different parts of a book, would indicate the presence of two craftsmen setting type: changes in layout; different type fonts; different habits of spelling either the text or the music;[54] different approaches to spacing the text; different forms of signatures, running heads, or other peripheral matter;[55] or specific alternations of two papers. In practice, however, any one of these, or even several together, could indicate a number of other possibilities, ranging from the presence of two different editions in a sophisticated copy to the presence of two presses working for one typesetter, to the influences of one or more exemplars on the typesetter. For these reasons, I have been reluctant to assign two craftsmen to most of Petrucci's editions. The evidence is simply too slight; there is often not enough to make a convincing case: however, one relatively clear case for two craftsmen can be made.

Throughout the period from the first edition of *Motetti de la Corona I* (1514) until sometime in 1519, Petrucci seems to have had two compositors available.[56] Suggestive evidence lies in habits of (musical and textual) spelling rather than in patterns of layout and organisation. For example, two different typesetters seem to have spelled a number of words differently: for one, certain words were spelled as "polens" and "vale", as "michi" and "franchorum", as "alleluya" and "martyrio", and as "iherusalem"; the other man saw them as "pollens" and "valle", as "mihi" and "francorum", as "alleluia" and "martirio", and as "hierusalem". These patterns seem consistent enough that we may assert that one typesetter set certain sheets, while the second worked on the others. Once those work assignments are made, it becomes apparent that the two craftsmen also had different musical preferences: when both had to use the proportion sign "3", the first would tend to add a small circle (for perfect tempus) above the numeral. The same man was more prone to retain (or add) ligatures to his notation, while the second tended to employ *minor color* when possible. The first seems to have been not only more fluent in ligature usage, but also more expert in the handling of the notational implications of triple mensurations or proportions. The second man, apparently "younger" in his understanding of the rules and their application, could create infractions of the standard rules.

Order of Setting through a Book: The Evidence
of the Initials and Staves

One aspect of the order of setting Petrucci's books has already been discussed—the possibility that the copy text was cast off in advance. This is very unlikely for the majority of Petrucci's editions, even in those books where some equivalent practice would have been possible.[57]

Thus, in my view, the musical formes, which were usually the first to be printed, were intended to be set up sequentially through all Petrucci's first editions. This means that we will rarely find any convincing evidence of deviations from this pattern, since the pattern leaves no defining evidence. I have found damaged sorts and traced some of them through several appearances in a book, but they usually seem to indicate the expected procession of formes.[58] The type for the text formes need not have been set sequentially, as I have asserted, but rather by formes.

The few exceptions that I have found have already been cited for one reason or another: the possibility that the first gathering was printed last, in *Canti C*, to accommodate the tavola; the hiatus in printing Brumel's masses, as a response to the commission for Ghiselin's volume; and the interval in the middle of the edition of Bossinensis's second book, the first published after his removal from Venice to Fossombrone. Many of the other apparent anomalies in individual copies, which might bear on the order of printing—for example, the presence of two different text typefaces in copies of Josquin's first book of masses, or curious patterns of watermarks in a number of books—turn out rather to be indicators of sophisticated copies, or the traces of two editions or of cancel leaves.

The best evidence for sequences of printing will lie in one of only two places. One involves the patterns of recurrence of initial letters in a series of music formes; the other concerns staves, in the other series of formes: these are the two sets of material for which Petrucci did not keep a large number of copies. While he normally worked with at least two sets of staves, for the two sides of a sheet, he did not attempt to hold large numbers of initial letters. Therefore, any pattern of increasing damage, for staves or initials, can be used to demonstrate the sequence of work. With the initials, there is an additional aspect: since each was unique, any one that had been inserted in a forme could not be used elsewhere until that forme was printed and the type redistributed in the case. Therefore the pattern of their use should help to confirm sequential setting for the music formes.

A first example comes from the use of the letter "S" at a stage when Petrucci had only one example of this letter, in the Superius of the first edition of Obrecht's masses (using the copy at Munich).

TABLE 4-4 The presence of the initial letter S in the Superius of
Misse Obreht (1502)

Gathering:	A			B		C
forme	Io	IIi	Ii	IIo	IIi	Io
folio	1r	4r	7v	3r	5v	1r
letter present?	y	n	n	y	n	y

The letter "S" was inserted on A1r, for the title. Since this was on forme Io, sequential setting would render it unavailable for all other formes in gathering A—for Io would be the last to the press. Indeed, no initial is printed on A4r or A7v, and this initial next appears on B3r, in forme BIIo. This prevents its appearance on B5v (forme BIIi), which would be printed sooner, though set later. However, forme BIIo would be distributed while BIi and BIo were going through the press. The initials would then be available for the first page of gathering C. (Both of these assumptions allow two formes to have been in use at a time, one being set or distributed while the other was at the press.) If the text had been set by formes, it would be reasonable to expect that the letter could have appeared twice in gathering A, whatever the order of setting: the three places where "S" was needed lie on different formes (Io, Ii, and IIi), and one would probably have been distributed before at least one of the others was set. Similarly, if we assume that setting by forme proceeded in order (Io–Ii–IIo–IIi), as would be probable, it is unlikely that the initial in gathering B (on forme IIo or IIi) would have been available for C1r.[59]

Petrucci had similar problems during the printing of the first edition of the first book of *Motetti de la Corona* (1514). At this stage, he had only one initial "B"; it necessarily appears on the title page of the Bassus partbook, folio G1r. As a result it was not available elsewhere in the same forme, though needed twice on G8v; Petrucci's typesetter inserted two versions of the letter "G" instead.

While printing his edition of Bossinensis's second book (1511), Petrucci had the same difficulty. In some cases, this required the use of type initials, of which he apparently had a good supply. The sequence of *Recercare* titles at the end of the volume, from G7v, provides a good example. Nine initial letters "R" were needed on just fifteen pages. He used R3 once, and R6 twice, once in each gathering. The other instances were set with type letters. In one or two other cases in the same book, his typesetter apparently lifted an initial from one forme as the type was being distributed and inserted it straight into another: this applies to the letter "O" on G6v (forme GIIo) and G7r (forme GIo); to "Q" on F1r (FIo) and F3v (FIIi); and to "V" on C2v (CIo) and C3v (CIIi). None of these provide evidence for the order of work, for none involve adjacent formes, in setting either sequentially or by formes, although one instance (the first) is only two formes apart. However, appearances of two letters "A" suggest sequential setting: A4 is found on F7v (Ii) and then on G3r (IIo), while A6 is used on G1r (Io). If F had been set by formes, A4 should have been available again by the first folio of gathering G.

More significant is the pattern of initials for letter "S" in this same book (see Table 4-5).

The pattern here is more complex. Gatherings A and B raise no problems, nor does gathering F, even though the letter "S" was used twice in each of two

TABLE 4-5 The presence of the initial letter "S" in Bossinensis' second book (1511)

Folio	A5v	A6v	B2r	D2v	D5r	D7v	E3r	F4r	F6r	F7r	F8v	G6r
Forme	AIIi	AIIo	BIi	DIo	DIIo	DIi	EIIo	FIIi	FIIi	FIo	FIo	GIIo
Initial	S4	S3	S4	S4	S3	S3	S4	S4	S3	S4	S3	S3

formes. Whether the text was set sequentially or by formes, the first forme would have been distributed before the second was set, and both letters were probably ready for use in gathering G. But the pattern in D is more interesting: if the text were set sequentially, forme DIIo would have been returned to the press in time for S3 to be used again on D7v: S4 would still be set up and ready for printing, on D2v. With setting by formes, however, I would have expected D5r to have character S4, distributed from the first forme to be set. This again suggests sequential setting.

If the music gathering were set sequentially, the stave-and-text formes could still set by formes, supposing them to have been set after the music (as would surely be probable for many books). But there are also occasions when it appears that the music, with the initials, may also have been set by formes. In chapter 3, I showed that the new set of initials cut in 1514 (series 8) was not Petrucci's first choice when printing the third book of Josquin's masses (1514). Nonetheless, as that discussion showed, they had become necessary if he were to continue printing, and especially for volumes of mass music. By this stage, however, Petrucci's craftsmen appear to be setting the music gathering by formes; whether this means that the musical text was cast off, or that it was set second (after the verbal formes), cannot always be determined. The Tenor partbook is set in one gathering of twelve folios—three sheets, six formes. The principal initials appear as shown in Table 4-6.[60]

Any hypothesis of consecutive setting raises problems in understanding the typesetter's decisions. The letter "A" could have been set that way, for the inner formes would have been distributed before A4 and A6 were needed at the end of the gathering. For each of the other letters, we cannot explain the appearance of initials in formes IIIo and IIIi.

A pattern of setting by formes, however, makes a good deal of sense; there is only one case where the same version of a letter appears in consecutive formes. In every other case, the letter would have been part of a distributed forme before it appeared again. This evidence occasionally also shows which letters were pre-

TABLE 4-6 The patterns of initial use in *Missarum Josquin Liber Tertius* (1514, first edition), Tenor book

Forme	Io	Io	Ii	IIo	IIi	IIIi	IIIi	
Folio	2v	11r	12r			6r	8r.	
Initial A	10	6	4	—	—	4	6	
Forme	Io	Ii	IIo	IIo	IIi	IIIo	IIIo	IIIi
Folio	11r	1v	3r	4v		6v	8v	
Initial E	4	3	10	4	—	10	4	—
Forme	Io	Io	Ii	IIo	IIi	IIIo	IIIo	IIIi
Folio	2v	11r	1v	4v		6v	8v	
Initial K	6	4	2	6	—	4	2	—
Forme	Io	Ii	IIo	IIi	IIIo	IIIo	IIIi	
Folio	11r	1v	3r		5r	7r	9v	
Initial P	4	6	4	—	2	4	2	
Forme	Io	Ii	Ii	IIo	IIi	IIIo	IIIi	IIIi
Folio		2r	12r	10v	3v		5v	7v
Initial S	—	4	10	3	4	—	4	10

ferred by Petrucci and his typesetters; here, for example, E4 and S4 seem more popular than other versions of the letters. By the time of the second printing, however, E10 had become preferable to E4.

Finally, these patterns of the use of initials can help detect cancel leaves. As I remarked in chapter 3, the adoption of a new set of initials acts as a *terminus post quem* for its appearance. This means that variant sheets can sometimes be arranged in order, with the later using initials not yet purchased at the time of the earlier. The third book of the *Motetti de la Corona* was first printed before the acquisition of the new and smaller sets of initials used in Petrucci's last active years, and the inner sheet of gathering A exists in two versions, with initials as shown in Table 4-7.[61]

The use of letters in series 11 and 12 is confirmation that the cancel leaves in this copy are later than the rest of the volume; they have to be dated after the first appearance of these letters in other books, for they already show signs of damage.

My second range of evidence for the sequence of printing concerns the staves, material that was retained in the forme from gathering to gathering. This set of material is among the most valuable for bibliographical analysis; any change in the pattern indicates clearly that something unusual had happened.

The evidence that Petrucci had two sets of staves, from the middle of 1503, has been cited several times and has been drawn on for a number of different conclusions.[62] In chapter 3, I showed that these were consistent sets of staves, which can be distinguished by both their different lengths and the detailed damage and bending apparent at the ends of individual stave lines.

Even though the staves were probably printed at the second impression, and therefore need not have been sent to press in the same order as the music formes, the pattern by which they recur can indicate the order in which parts of a book were prepared, or the presence of a hiatus in the work; it can signal a major change in Petrucci's printing technique (as it did with the change from three to two impressions); and it can be one more piece of evidence for the date of undated volumes or parts of volumes.

I shall start, however, with a straightforward example: the sequence of sets of staves in the *Misse henrici Izac* (20 October 1506), copy at I-Bc. (The numbers assigned to each set are arbitrary.)[63]

This pattern shows, as we would expect, that the two formes of staves then in use (and adopted during the printing of Brumel's and Ghiselin's masses in 1503) were alternated, one on each side of every sheet of paper. Apparently, the compositor did not have the four formes of staves that would allow him to set a whole gathering at once, consecutively. It suggests that he was compelled to set the staves and text (at least) by formes, so that he could use a set of staves as soon

TABLE 4-7 The pattern of initials in gathering A of *Motetti de la Corona III* (1519, first edition and cancel)

Folio	1r	1v	2r	2v	3r	3v	4r	4v	5r	5v	6r	6v	7r	7v	8r	8v
edition	—	—	H10	P3	A10	—	—	A6	A[b]	R3	—	S10	S[b]	—	—	M3
cancel					A4	—	—	A11	A12	R11	S11[a]					

[a]: this letter is inverted

[b]: these are letters cast as type, and not part of the decorative series

TABLE 4-8 The pattern of staves in *Misse henrizi Izac* (1506)

Forme	Gathering							
	A	B	C	D	E	F	G	H
Io	1	1	2	1	1	1	1	1
Ii	2	2	1	2	2	2	2	2
IIo	1	1			1	1	1	
IIi	2	2			2	2	2	
II/III		1	2					1

as it came back from the press. (As a corollary, these formes were surely set second, after the music.) Equally convincing is the evidence that he proceeded from Superius to Tenor to Altus to Bassus, and from the outermost forme of each gathering to the central one. Any other sequence would have produced different solutions as soon as the half-sheet formes at the centers of gatherings B and C had been set.

An additional implication seems to be that the whole series of text formes was not begun until the bulk of the music had been printed, so that the typesetter could work through the formes in sequence. If text formes had been set as music formes came back from the press (and pages were available to guide the typesetter in aligning the text), each gathering would have proceeded from the innermost forme to the outermost, resulting in several short disruptions in the pattern. The other solution is more likely.

A very similar situation prevails in the *Misse Gaspar* (7 February 1507) (see Table 4-9).

The first gathering seems distinctive, but once the typesetter began on gathering B, he progressed through the book forme by forme, without any deviation. Even when there is a half-sheet at the middle of a gathering, the next book begins with the other set of staves.

This simple pattern is by no means consistently followed, as the following example demonstrates: the use of staves in the copy of La Rue's masses (31 October 1503) at PL-Kj (see Table 4-10).

Here, again, staves are used systematically by formes, although evidently from the centers of gatherings out, which must mean that the text was set sequentially as the music formes returned from the press. For each gathering, the music formes would have come back in an order represented by reading up each column. The text formes were apparently set using each music forme as a guide once it returned from the press. This is the best explanation for the pattern of moving from gath-

TABLE 4-9 The pattern of staves in *Missae Gaspar* (1507)

Forme	Gathering						
	A	B	C	D	E	F	G
Io	2	1	2	1	1	2	2
Ii	1	2	1	2	2	1	1
IIo	1	1	2	1	1	2	2
IIi	2	2	1	2	2	1	1
III		1	2		1		

TABLE 4-10 The pattern of staves in *Misse Petri de la Rue* (1503)

Forme	Gathering						
	A	B	C	D	E	F	G
Io	1	1	2	2	2	2	2
Ii	2	2	1	1	1	1	1
IIo	1	1	2	2	2	2	
IIi	2	2	1	1	1	1	
II/III			2				2

ering B to C, and from C to D. The half-sheet at the center of gathering G does not disrupt the pattern, for it would have been set in the same forme as the half from gathering C, using work and turn.[64]

Other examples could be taken from the *Missarum diversorum auctorum* or the *Fragmenta Missarum*, both of which show almost consistent patterns, with one or at most two changes in the order of formes. Apparently more complex is the sequence found in the Krakow copy of Ghiselin's masses (see Table 4-11).[65]

This edition has been discussed several times already, for it shared with the volume of Brumel's masses in the emergence of double-impression printing. In my earlier analysis, I suggested that both sheets of A and the first of B were printed earlier than the rest, as an experiment; that the main run of printing began with sheet II of B; and that there was a change in the state of the staves between the two sheets of E. It is not surprising, therefore, that the two longer, "non-experimental" groups are internally consistent.[66]

A different form of evidence can be used to the same end in the 1504 edition of Agricola's masses. Occasionally, the pressure at the press was enough to make a deep impression on the page, producing a significant raised area on the verso. On one page (J2*v*), these raised areas have taken ink from the furniture in the forme. This must indicate that one impression on this page, part of the outer forme, was printed after the music on the other side of the leaf, the inner forme. I assume that this impression (on J2*v*) was that of staves and text.

Each of these cases has also suggested that partbooks were normally set up in sequence, as well, following the order Superius—Tenor—Altus—Bassus. There is one apparent exception to this, in the book that also has an unusual signature pattern, *Motetti C*, printed in 1504. The significant feature here is that the same change of paper occurs in all partbooks at approximately the same place. It appears that the four books were prepared a gathering at a time—all the gatherings B before C, and those before D—and that the new paper had to be introduced

TABLE 4-11 The pattern of staves in *Joannes Ghiselin*: Misse (1503)

Formes	Gathering							
	A	B	C	D	E	F	G	H
Io	1	1	2	2	2	1	1	1
Ii	2	2	1	1	1	2	2	2
IIo	2	1	2	2	1		1	1
IIi	1	2	1	1	2		2	2
III		1	1					1

TABLE 4-12 *Pattern of paper distribution by watermark in* Motetti C (1504)

Sheet:		AI	AII	BI	BII	CI	CII	DI	DII
Papers:	Superius	14	11	11	11	11	11	−/3/11	−/3/11
	Tenor	14	11	11	11	11	11	−/11	−/3
	Altus	14	11	11	11	11	11	−/3	−/3
	Bassus	14	14/11	11	11	3/11	11	−/3/14	−/3

toward the end of gathering C of the Bassus book. The move to this gathering does not occur in the same musical situation in the four partbooks, and so this cannot be a function of the content. For two partbooks, the same piece starts at the beginning of the gathering; for the other two, different pieces are involved. This offers a strong hint that two compositors were involved with preparing this book.

The details of the pattern of papers used in the last gathering of each book (presented in the bibliographical description) suggest that in this case the supply of one paper (numbered 11) was virtually exhausted, and a different stock was used to finish the work.[67]

Much of the evidence for casting off, then, lies in the area of the staves, which were more often than not part of the second impression, following the music. Given that the first was already printed, casting off would seem to have been a logical thing to do. But the evidence for casting off the music is, as I say, much more ambiguous, and such a conclusion seems implausible, except in one or two special cases, including reprintings of earlier editions.

Stocks of Type

Even though there were few sets of staves, and sometimes a scarcity of the necessary initials, stocks of the basic typographical material seem to have been ample for almost all situations. By counting numbers of sorts on whole formes, sheets or gatherings, one can demonstrate the possible minimal numbers of different sorts, though the exercise is exceedingly laborious, and almost always futile. It is only of value if it leads to the suggestion that a musical or textual reading had to be changed because of a temporary shortage.

In a very few cases we can detect this kind of shortage, where one sort, musical or textual, seems to be in specially urgent demand. For example, there may have been a shortage of the letter "s" when setting the tavola for the second edition of the *Odhecaton A*. The evidence consists of a changing pattern through the columns of a page, in which the long "ʃ" and the numeral 5 are increasingly used instead of the conventional form.[68]

A more interesting case involves a ligature. In the *Motetti de la Corona* version of Josquin's *Christum ducem,* the essentially triple-meter nature of much of the material in the Superius is reinforced by the use of *c.o.p.* ligatures. A great many of these represent a pattern of a falling second, and this evidently created a problem for the typesetter. After a certain point (on the fourth line of the page), the compositor was apparently running low on versions of the symbol, almost completely stopped using them, and restricted their use to the few occasions when underlay might have been ambiguous. The same ligature pattern could have been used on other pages of the forme, but none are present. The twelve appearances of this particular ligature with this interval probably represent nearly the total number available.[69]

This is a very unusual situation, occasioned by the particular nature of the composition being set. For most type symbols, the actual quantities can only be guessed at, and that not very successfully. Many symbols seem never to have been in short supply, and quick counts of some sorts show that there were many, even of the more obscure symbols. For example, there are fifty-two examples of a *pausa* on one sheet in *Motetti B*.

But it has to be stressed that these numbers are almost meaningless. They indicate an absolute minimum number of sorts, and presumably even the actual minimum must have been somewhat larger than the figures given here; otherwise, the typesetter might already have been looking for alternatives. For most notational situations that used less common characters (*minor color*, ligatures, *fusas*, and similar), the compositor would feel that it was within his competence to change the notation if it became necessary. We would not be able to detect whether the motive was musical, a general preference on the part of the compositor, or a shortage of special sorts.

Further, the evidence of stave patterns suggests that the compositors were used to working with only two formes for the text, and perhaps also for the music. This means that an adequate supply of the more common sorts would always be returning from the press. With one exception, no formes of type, once printed, were kept standing. Petrucci, in common with other printers of the period, did not have so much type that he could afford to lock up a portion in formes that might perhaps be needed for a later repeat impression. Thus, music and text were redistributed immediately after being used. The one exception is the page, found at the end of most editions printed in Fossombrone, giving a copy of Petrucci's papal privilege. Whereas the publication date and collation were redistributed each time, the privilege itself was kept standing, for it would be used regularly. It was not likely to put any particular burden on the text font; text was always relatively sparse in these editions.

Work and Turn

When a printer needed to include a half-sheet in a book, because the content did not fit into a round number of whole sheets, he had more than one way of printing it. All involve making the best possible use of the other half of the sheet of paper. One was to combine that half-sheet with another, taken perhaps from a different partbook. The content for one half-sheet could then be set at one end of two formes (inner and outer), and the other imposed at the other end. For Petrucci, this would have been possible in a number of titles, for there are several instances where two parts needed extra half-sheets. However, he seems to have done this rarely; I have suggested it for the edition of La Rue's masses.

A second alternative involved setting the half-forme at one end of a forme, and leaving the other end blank. Two copies could then be printed, by running the sheet under the press, and then turning it around to print the other end. The disadvantage with this procedure was that it involved double the number of impressions, or pulls at the press, for each forme.

The third alternative, and the one followed by Petrucci, involved no extra pulls. In this, the two half-formes, inner and outer,[70] were set together in a single forme, one at each end. One pull at the press, therefore, produced two imperfected half-sheets: if the paper were then turned around as it was turned over, a second pull would perfect both half-sheets at once. This process, called "work and turn", is the most efficient means of producing two complete half-sheets. The two need only two pulls.

Petrucci used work and turn consistently. It is thought to be a standard procedure for other printers, but its detection is particularly difficult. Only the presence of two impressions, with the manner in which one uses recurring formes of staves, allows the modern analyst to detect the process in Petrucci's work,[71] because the two half-formes utilise parts of the same set of staves, even though they appear back-to-back on the printed sheet.

Numbers of Workers

The normal printing shop employed workers at several levels of skill and salary. Lowest on the scale were the assistants at the press, men who operated the ink-balls and ensured that the type was evenly re-inked after each pull. They worked alongside the *torculatores*, or pressmen. These craftsmen were responsible for the press, for its condition and the quality of impression. They operated the press, sometimes alone, sometimes in pairs.[72] According to Hirsch, larger printing shops maintained a full-time employee whose sole function was to keep a steady supply of newly mixed ink.[73] Still higher paid were the *compositores*, or typesetters. While the *torculatores* had to be skilled at their craft, as well as physically fit, the *compositores* were also expected to be competent in the texts they worked with, at least to a level that would avoid too many errors in setting. Over these was a foreman, who was often also an *intagliatore* or typefounder. Larger shops could afford to keep a foreman active in making new types from the matrices, replacing damaged sorts as needed. Most printing shops would keep twice as many press-men as typesetters. In practice, this often meant three men for each press in the shop.

No data exist for the size of Petrucci's shop. There is a little evidence for the shops of some contemporaries, although it is rarely complete and always circumstantial. Census and tax records for Venice and Rome give the numbers of people in households. For printers, these would normally include all the employees, but they would also include the family members and household servants. From various pieces of evidence, Lowry reckons that Aldus Manutius employed about fifteen workmen for perhaps four presses,[74] which was a reasonable number for an active and flourishing shop. My analyses have found no trace of more than two teams (in fact, two typesetters) in Petrucci's work, and that not consistently throughout his career. Indeed, I think it highly unlikely that he could have justified running more presses. It seems probable, therefore, that his whole shop (even in its most flourishing phases) contained no more than perhaps seven employees: two compositors, two pressmen, two inkers, and perhaps one for making ink, acting as stockman for paper and printed copies, and other chores, including damping the paper. I assume that Petrucci was the "proof-reader" when Petrus Castellanus was not available, as well as being the business manager.

It may be, too, that Petrucci's work patterns were slightly different. This difference is not a result of the multiple impressions per se, but of the fact that the impression containing text and staves usually contains much less material, and therefore would normally be set up much more quickly than normal in the trade. Even the musical forme contained less matter than a full forme of prose, although the jigsaw-like fitting together of music symbols and spacing sorts probably made it slower to set. These two formes would have taken much less time to prepare than would two of a normal book.

Whether this circumstance implies that more compositors were needed to keep the press busy depends entirely on the size of the print-run. A smaller edition size would allow pressmen to keep pace with the faster-moving compositors. This is part of an equation relating also to the time allocated to each new edition. The critical factor for Petrucci and his colleagues must have been the size of the print-run, for this governed directly how many copies were available for sale, and therefore the return that could be expected. For us, however, the only useful bibliographical data lie in known rates of work at the press, and the actual chronology of Petrucci's editions. These are hardly satisfactory, but they will be considered, with some circumstantial evidence, toward the end of the next chapter.

Notes

1. Much of what follows is simple description of the appearance of Petrucci's volumes and of the manner in which that external character changes over the years. Each of the elements mentioned here is of importance both for an understanding of Petrucci's place in printing and musical history, and for a grasp of his own view of his role and the character of his customers. The data presented here will be combined with information from chapters 5 and 6 in the discussions that form the basis of chapter 8.

2. The value of these figures is obviously rather general. The original pages were larger, trimmed for binding, and the resulting sizes can vary considerably. For more on this, see the discussion on "Paper", in chapter 3.

3. Hirsch, *Printing*, p. 1.

4. This point is discussed in chapter 8, when considering Petrucci's decisions on how to make his books attractive to buyers.

5. I intend to use the term *Superius* for the top voice throughout this study. It was the term understood by Petrucci, for the title pages of a number of partbooks carry the letter "S". The term *Cantus*, adopted soon enough by other printers, seems not to have had the meaning of "the top voice" at this time.

6. See, for example, K4*v*–5*r* or K6*v*–7*r*.

7. This section involves the end of gathering Q and much of gathering R. It is discussed in the commentary to the description of this edition.

8. The exceptions are all special cases and will be discussed in chapter 8.

9. There is even the case, in the ninth book of frottole, where additional text is supplied at the end of the volume. The piece concerned, *A la fama si va*, appears on folio B1*v* of the book, but the text is on folio G8*r*, forty-seven openings later.

10. The distinction between the frottola and the madrigal, and the extent to which the latter cannot be seen as a development of the former, have been well revealed by James Haar. For the latest statement of this position, see Fenlon and Haar, *Italian*.

11. For a discussion of the early sources of the incipient madrigal and its parallel genres

(in such sources as *Libro primo de la Croce*), see Fenlon and Haar, *Italian*, which should be read in conjunction with Boorman, "Bibliography", and Slim, *Gift*.

12. This probability has already been discussed, in Brown, "Mirror".

13. See chapter 9.

14. This pattern conforms to the practice of providing a "label-title", which Margaret Smith describes as most prevalent during the later 1480s and the following decade. However, Petrucci's titles are more advanced, in that they use a larger font of type than that employed in the body of the book and have therefore already progressed beyond serving as a mere label. See Smith, *Title-page*.

15. This is the manuscript formerly in the possession of Geneviève Thibault, la comtesse de Chambure, and now F-Pn Rés.Vmd.27. Lesure, *Tablature* is a facsimile of the whole manuscript, which is discussed in Meyer, *Sources*, i, pp. 113–16, and Thibault, "Manuscrit". Another similar source is I-Fn B.R.62(b), discussed in Fabris, "Frottola" and Underwood, *Renaissance*, 206–209. See my comments in chapter 9.

16. In this context, it would be interesting to know what actually appeared on the title page of the lost edition of Martini's hymns: Colón called it "Hymni de tempore et de sanctis liber primus". See Chapman, "Printed", No.28.

17. Cappelli, *Cronologia*, p. 11, defines the "stile veneto" as "cominciante dal 1^0 marzo, posticipando sul moderno, al quale corrisponde dal 1° marzo al 31 dic[embre]".

18. It is dated 1509 new style in *RISM* and assigned the siglum 1509[1]. It is correctly placed in 1508 by Sartori. Attention should be drawn, however, to the work of George Fletcher, who has shown that, in one particular instance, the Venetian printer Aldus Manutius dated a book in February 1503, apparently using the Roman (and modern) convention. See Fletcher, *New*, p. 107.

19. Cappelli, *Cronologia*, p. 10.

20. The only exception to this in Petrucci's output is found in the *Motetti C* of 1504, discussed below.

21. By Scotto and Gardano, and most of their followers, the colophon was replaced by a simpler device: the addition of the word "Finis" to the signature on the first folio of the final gathering.

22. As so often, I have to except the volume of music by Pisano, printed in 1520.

23. It is interesting to note here that Petrucci was followed in format, the use of landscape quarto, by Antico and most printers of music during much of the sixteenth century. The exceptions are almost always for some practical reason connected with the repertoire and the potential purchaser rather than with the press. Yet, there is one unusual anomaly. Pasoti and Dorico normally printed in landscape octavo, but occasionally they inserted what appears to be an quarto sheet in the middle of a book. For example, the second book of Josquin's masses, in 1526, has some "sheets" of vertical chain lines in the middle of a book otherwise printed with horizontal lines. (See, for example, ff.H3-6, easily visible in the copy at E-Bc.) The reasonable presumption is that these two "sheets" were printed together and at a different time. There is a similar anomaly in the paper pattern of the same printers' edition of *Motetti de la Corona Libro Primo*.

There were more or less standard patterns for deriving the proportion of text size to page size, and of the various margins. The extent to which these proportions were fairly consistent for each format and size of book becomes clear in comparing a number of contemporaneous editions. More recent analyses of these measurements are presented in Rummonds, *Printing*, pp. 91–101. Here I have attempted no analysis of the ratios adopted by Petrucci.

24. All five sets of motets after the 1505 *Motetti IV* have Superius books of sixteen folios; so do some mass volumes, the 1505 and 1515 editions of Josquin's second book, the *Missarum diversorum auctorum* of 1508, and the books of Mouton and Févin from 1515. For nine of these ten books, one or more of the other voices uses more or fewer than the four sheets of the Superius book.

25. The change to the titles of lower voice books, mentioned above, was no guide to internal sheets of a partbook.

26. For the moment, I am writing as if the content were printed at one impression. Since

two or three impressions were required, the figures in the following paragraphs need to be increased in proportion. However, the analyses that depend on the details and patterns presented here always concern one level of content at a time—the text formes or the music formes, for example. Indeed, the evidence argues that Petrucci's compositors concentrated on one at a time. Thus, the patterns and the shorthand abbreviations I am proposing to use can be applied to explain Petrucci's processes without imposing an unacceptable over-simplification.

27. The diagram shows the arrangement of pages as they appear on the printed sheet of paper. The arrangements as found in the forme are necessarily mirror images of the ones presented here. The earliest Italian description known to me of this procedure, two sheets of paper for each gathering, can be found in Host von Romberch's *Congestorium*, first printed in Venice in 1520. The relevant phrase comes at the end of a discussion of which pages appear in which positions in octavo and sedecimo formats. It appears at the head of folio n6*v* in the 1533 edition (printed by Sessa, also in Venice) and refers to "complicationes . . . si folium in quattuor plicetur & in illius medio ponantur alius quaternus".

28. See, for example, Bertoli, "Segni"; Bond, "Printer's"; Hellinga, "Problems"; and Hellinga, "Dissemination". The last is interesting in that it concerns the use of printed exemplars and typesetters' habits, showing specifically how they may be reflected in the new edition. Scapecchi, "New Light", describes what is probably a fairly normal situation, in which the principal printer's annotations appear to be indications of page ends. Most important is Trovato, "Censimento", which discusses different types of evidence for printer's copy (and for proof correction), draws on a wide variety of sources, and includes a valuable bibliography.

29. This book was not the last printed before the end of that phase of his career. The presence of several of the same initials in undated re-editions of earlier titles, though in a worse condition, argues that Petrucci printed these editions after the Pisano, even though they use the traditional format, staves, text and music fonts, and initials. This is discussed in Boorman, "Some New".

30. The evidence for this is presented in chapter 11. For all intents and purposes, this book has to be regarded as the work of Petrucci, even as studio work is associated with the master in art-historical description, especially in the absence of any certain name within the "studio", the printing shop, to which they can be attributed (despite the issues raised in chapter 11).

31. Basic information on almost all these matters can be found in many of the books cited in this study: useful discussions or guides include Allen, "Contemporary"; Bartoli, "Segni"; Biringuccio, *Pirotechnia*; Blayney, *Texts*; Bond, "Printer's"; Brown, *Venetian*; Carter, *View*; Concetta et al., *Scrittura*; Crapulli, *Trasmissione*; Donati, "Fregi"; Enschedé, *Typefounders*; Fahy, "Correzioni"; Fletcher, *New*; Hellinga, "Notes"; Hellinga, "Problems"; Hellinga, *Copy*; Hinman, *Printing*; Janssen, "Notes"; Rummonds, *Printing*; Scholderer, "Red"; Scholderer, "Further"; and Veyrin-Forrer, "Fabriquer".

32. In fact, the Superius needed only twenty-three folios, but this necessarily entailed using twenty-four.

33. The *Motetti de la Corona Libro primo* of 1514.

34. If the text had been printed with only one forme of staves, it would have been impossible to set one forme until the other had been printed and returned from the press. This is clearly not an economical use of time. It would be easier to have two formes of staves, so that the second could be used for setting up the second forme of text while the first was being printed.

35. The details of this analysis were first presented in Boorman, "Work and Turn".

36. Boorman, "Printed". This argument, and its implications for other volumes, will be developed in chapter 9.

37. Each of these ranges of evidence can be detected throughout the rest of Petrucci's output, and many instances are cited in the bibliographical descriptions.

38. This pattern is not consistent, of course, and the various manners of laying out the text will be considered in chapter 7. The present statement is sufficient to make the following point about work patterns.

39. On the majority of pages the alignment of text and music is surprisingly accurate. There are few where the text placing changes drastically across a page, vis-à-vis the music, so

that we might doubt whether it could have been followed in performance. Instead, there are several cases where all the text of a line is displaced, by the same small distance, to the right or left. If this problem were to exist for all the lines in a forme, and only in a single copy, then we could argue that the page had been misplaced on the press, that the register was slightly off. However, when only one or two lines are so displaced, and when they are found in all extant copies, it is clear that the cause lies in the typesetting. If, for example, the starts of all text phrases on a line are 2 mm to the left of the starts of all musical phrases, then the compositor must have been working from a printed copy of the music and have merely miscalculated the starting point when setting the text line. Examples of this problem can be found, in particular, in editions printed at Fossombrone.

40. Here, again, the books of frottole may provide an exception. The spacing of the music does vary from piece to piece, in a way that seems to correspond with the density of the text. On occasion, it looks as if the compositor merely spaced the music more widely, rather than worked to a preprepared text setting.

41. The traditional argument is that setting by formes allowed for a smaller case of type and maintained a smoother flow of formes from the compositor to the press. Technically, both of these are true. Setting by formes, in Petrucci's format, required a minimum of eight pages' of type material, while setting linearly through the text required at least twelve. In each case, the calculation is for the minimum needed to send the first two formes to the press, which, in consecutive setting would not occur until folio 6*v* had been set. Thereafter, with formes returning from the press, the stock of type sorts would be regularly replenished. In practice, however, more would be needed in each case, simply to allow for special demands on some sorts. Further, in Petrucci's pattern, the first two formes of a book included a title page and often a tavola thereby reducing the total number of music sorts needed. As a result, the difference between the two methods of setting is not very great.

The second point, that setting by formes allowed a smoother flow of formes to the press, is hardly relevant in Petrucci's case. With the need for formes for text and for music, and with one of those (the one with text) containing little material to be set, there would always be set-up formes available for printing. Indeed, the question seems rather to be whether there were two presses for each compositor, in order to keep him busy.

42. Bernstein, *Music*, p. 57, implies, without advancing any evidence, that music printers regularly cast off copy before setting. I believe that she is confusing true casting off with the ability to arrange single-page pieces such as madrigals (or two-page works such as motets) in order, and then to set by formes. A number of the entries in her bibliography strongly argue that there was no attempt at casting off copy for longer works, or in those cases where their length was variable.

43. Lewis, *Gardano*, pp. 68–75.

44. It is probable that the frequent appearance of single-page compositions at the gathering joins of frottola volumes is part of the same practice.

45. I am writing here as if the music was always set first, and that the text-and-stave formes followed. This is convenient, for the sake of the argument, and was probably normally true. Strictly, however, the reference here should be to the second setting, which does not have to be prepared in the same manner as the first.

46. This is surely also a demonstration that Petrucci had not tried to cast off the content of each partbook. He had merely assumed the size of the Tenor book.

47. I have discussed this issue—essentially one of trying to discover the practice of the individual compositors, rather than the more generally applicable house practice—in Boorman, "Type-setters".

48. The possible exceptions comprise clefs and bar-lines. These are the longest sorts, and I have not seen any evidence of spacing sorts above or below them. Further, following the evidence outlined in chapter 3, suggesting that the type was cast on long bodies in Petrucci's later editions, typesetting would be much simpler for those editions.

49. The procedure seems to become more general during the later years. Petrucci was perhaps less willing to leave blank inked staves in his books as they were published. Whereas many such staves appear in the early editions of chansons and mass settings, later books tend to

leave the space white—or at least white in intention. The slacker press-work often results in faint impressions of staves that were apparently meant to be printed in blind.

50. More examples are cited in the bibliographical descriptions. No doubt there are many more, but the light has to be at a suitable angle before they can be viewed in the modern library. See also plate 1.

51. See the example in *BMC*, vi, p. 805, where the text meant to be left in blind was accidentally inked. Other examples have been cited in Paisey, "Blind", and Harris, "Blind". More interesting for the musical bibliographer, there are examples in musical editions: in Pasoti and Dorico's 1526 edition of *Il Motetti de la Corona*, a blind impression of music, as well as staves, shows very clearly on F4r of all extant copies. The place of the last two staves is filled with the music from the same place on the previous *recto*, uninked, and impressing in blind. Even more important, in the same book, on I6r, all staves have notes, but not taken from a single page. While the first three staves have music from the previous *recto* and the last seems to have the music of the first stave of I3r, stave iv has the music of the last stave of I2r. This line of music is *not* aligned with any stave, and it confirms, if confirmation were needed, that Pasoti and Dorico were using a multiple-impression process.

52. See, for example, the evidence advanced in Kirsop, "Habitudes", and the excellent bibliography given there.

53. One aspect of this latter point, the way in which Petrucci dealt with ligatures, is discussed in Noblitt, "Textual", pp. 208–14.

54. A valuable study of the manner in which spelling may be analysed and reveal compositor's habits is Hill, "Spelling".

55. Gabler, "Cupid", presents an interesting example, in which two compositors reveal the manner in which they collaborated in setting up the text through their different patterns of spelling and different running headlines.

56. The comments in the following section are abbreviated from analyses in Boorman, *Petrucci*, pp. 108–19, and Boorman, "Type-setters", pp. 249–54.

57. The presence of two typesetters in many volumes does not affect this issue, for the individual partbooks could still be set linearly. Yet there remains the question of whether two such typesetters were working on their partbooks at the same time.

58. The classic study of damaged sorts as indicators of printing-house practice remains Hinman, *Printing*.

59. It is interesting that Petrucci did not require his typesetters to lift the letter and insert it into each new forme. He had done this in earlier volumes, not least in the first edition of *Odhecaton A*. The letter "P" was required there, on both C1v and C2v, an "A" was needed on D1v and D4v, and also on E1v and F3v, as was a "J" on F2v and F4v. In each of these cases, the same initial was used and must have been lifted from one forme as soon as it left the press, ready for use in the next.

60. In addition, a letter "T" appears on the title page for the part, and a "Q" on C4r.

61. A first presentation of some of the following material was made in Boorman, "Cancels".

62. The evidence of working habits at other shops suggests that more sets of staves and other recurring material were needed than would deal with only one gathering. There is also the evidence of skeleton formes employed by non-musical printers; see Boorman, "Use". However, so many formes of staves may not have been necessary in Petrucci's shop, with its double- or triple-impression process. His men would already be effectively in the position of having four (or six) formes to work with at any one time.

63. The indicator II/III refers to the half-sheet at the center of a gathering: in C and H it comprises folios 3 and 4 of a six-folio gathering; in gathering B, folios 5–6 of 10.

64. Any other interpretation requires an interruption in the work. If we consider that the staves were set by formes, then the interruption would fall after the Superius was set, and perhaps similarly after the Tenor (unless the half-sheet CIII was set up and retained, waiting for the half-sheet from gathering G). If the book was set in order, but the Tenor was prepared before the Superius, there is again a break after the latter book. However, there is no sign in any other

evidence (e.g., the watermarks) of a break in the work after the Superius, or after the Tenor, was set.

65. This is an instance where the two sets of staves show relatively consistent measurements, despite the variable paper shrinkage. The actual measurements are given in the bibliographical description. They show two clear sets, one with staves approximating 174–175–175–175 mm, and the other 179–180–179–180, or 178–178–179–180 mm.

I do think that the two longer sets of stave measurements could represent different sets of staves. But it is not possible, merely by measuring, to decide whether the example in HIII (measuring 179–180–179–179) is the first version, or a form of the second imposed upside down (in which the first and second pairs of measurements would simply change places).

66. Again, the two half-sheets in the first long sequence of printing, at BIII and CIII, were each printed by work and turn.

67. The mark 3 is a countermark and is often heavily cropped; in a number of cases where no mark is visible, the paper appears to be that of mark 3 (following the chain lines), with the mark completely trimmed away. This supposition would reinforce the general argument.

68. Details are presented in the bibliographical description.

69. See Boorman, *Petrucci*, p. 96. I note the basic structure of the musical notation and its implications for underlay in Boorman, "Notational", p. 70.

70. If the half-sheet involves folios 3 and 4 of a six-folio gathering, the outer half-forme contains 3r and 4v, and the inner 3v and 4r.

71. For a discussion of this process and the manner in which Petrucci used it, as well as its application to the issue of the number of impressions in his printing, see Boorman, "Case".

72. Apparently, in many shops the two men at the press were equal in status. The pressman and the inker would then change places at regular intervals.

73. Hirsch, *Printing*, p. 36. This function seems unlikely for Petrucci's shop, even at its busiest.

74. Lowry, *World*, p. 95. Lowry cites the authorities on which he bases his analysis.

Chapter Five

PROBLEMS OF CHRONOLOGY

Editions and Impressions, Cancels and Sophisticated Copies

f Petrucci and his craftsmen had followed the patterns outlined in the previous chapter whenever they set about making a book; if they had been able to control exactly the number of copies of each sheet printed perfectly, as well as the storage and distribution of each; if, finally, Petrucci had invariably dated each new edition with its true date: if all these conditions had held true, then the received bibliography of his work would be more complex than it has so far been seen to be. On the other hand, it would still be much less complex than this study proposes as the true picture of Petrucci's output.

There are several reasons for this statement. Until some thirty years ago, the bibliography of Petrucci set out to provide individual entries for each dated edition. Scholars assumed that Petrucci dated each new edition of a title: for example, there were three recognised editions of *Odhecaton A*, each of which carried a separate date, but only one of the *Motetti de la Corona I*, for all the dated copies carry the same date. The growth in the perceived bibliography before the late 1970s was therefore largely a result of the discovery or rediscovery of copies demonstrably worthy of addition, by virtue either of being new titles or of carrying new dates for known titles.

With several studies from the 1970s and early 1980s,[1] the presence of a number of "hidden" editions was revealed. These editions, carrying the date of an earlier edition and masquerading as part of that edition, were only discovered and distinguished as a result of the diligent comparison of individual copies and their watermarks. Thus, if Petrucci had given these editions their actual date of publication, every report of his output would have included them from the beginning,[2] and his reported bibliography would have been larger (and also more interesting, if only from the point of view of an analysis of the popularity of individual volumes or of the printer's lack of experience or foresight).

This would have been the situation, therefore, if all three conditions proposed at the head of this chapter had held true. Even then, however, few printers arranged for the separate storage of a series of editions of the same title in their shop, or sold them scrupulously in sequence. This should not surprise us, for in practice, all the editions were thought of as the same book: the text was intended to be the same, the layout was often the same, the ends of gatherings came at the same places, and the typefaces were normally the same. As a result, there was little need to take care that each complete copy sold was made up only of sheets printed at the same time. Indeed, most printers do not seem to have considered that possibility, and with good reason (for it made their life easier, without discommoding the purchaser). The result is that many surviving copies of popular sixteenth-century books are "sophisticated", made up of sheets drawn variously from one or another of the extant and available editions. Almost forty years ago, H. K. Andrews pointed this out for the editions of Byrd's *Psalmes, Sonets and Songs*,[3] and it seems to have been normal practice in music, as elsewhere. As she remarked, the practice did not mean merely that each complete partbook could belong bibliographically to a different edition; sections of a partbook could also come from different editions. Indeed, the only limitation is that a whole sheet would normally be of one edition; the adjacent sheet could be from any of the others still available to the printer.

In the case of Petrucci, this practice resulted in the deeper concealment of individual "hidden" editions. Not only did some editions lie behind false dates, but sheets taken from them could also hide behind first sheets of a known edition. Indeed, what seems to modern scholars to be a complete edition may not survive with any title-pages at all, but exist solely in sheets and gatherings behind title-pages of other dates. Here, already, the bibliography of Petrucci takes on new dimensions, incorporating a description of sophisticated copies from the standpoint of the different editions of which each copy contains representatives.

However, my third condition was not the only one to be unfulfilled. It is evident, from a cursory study of almost any copy of almost any edition, that the craftsmen in the shop did not always follow their practice faithfully. There were slips, errors in preparing the printed text, errors in laying out the pages in the forme, and errors in presswork. In addition, there is no reason to believe that exactly the same numbers of every sheet in a book were printed; nor should we forget to allow for accidents in the shop, for damp (especially in Venice), or for any of the other hazards that were as prevalent then as now for any commercial enterprise. The two results of these actual and potential problems are that some sheets of a printing would be exhausted before others (necessitating new printings), and that some sheets would be found defective in some way (and therefore need replacing), while others were both satisfactory and sufficient.

This situation creates yet another level of complexity for Petrucci's bibliography. Not only do we see that Petrucci printed a number of editions, and that each copy could be made up of sheets from any possible permutation of those editions. We also have to face the probability that not all new printings were strictly complete editions. If the shop ran out of sheets of one or two gatherings, it might be sufficient to reprint only those, and relying on the remaining stock of the rest of the book for the time being; if the whole stock of only one sheet were lost through rain or fire, then only that one sheet need be reprinted; if a gross error were discovered in one sheet, then again only that one sheet would be replaced. It is possible, therefore, that a copy might be made up not merely of parts of whole printings (that is, editions) of the book, but might also contain copies of a special printing of one sheet.

In this case, the new sheet is here regarded as a *cancel*. Some cancels may have been intended as deliberate replacements of faulty sheets, and be cancels in the strict sense of the term: other similar sheets may not have been replacements of copies with defective text. They may just as easily have been intended to replace lost or damaged copies of such sheets, or prepared because the supply was exhausted. We often cannot tell, particularly with the low rate of survival for many of Petrucci's books. However, whatever the motive may have been, I propose to call all such sheets cancels in the present study.[4]

At a further level, when working in quarto, it was not always necessary to print the whole sheet: a single bifolium—half a sheet—could always be printed as a cancel, a quicker and cheaper process. While it required setting type for half a sheet and cutting the original sheets (as well as the newly printed replacements) in half, this would have been less laborious than setting up the whole sheet in type, especially where double-impression printing was involved.[5]

When a whole sheet is involved, one cannot tell whether the replacement was intended to cover gross error or for some other reason: but I believe that all replacements of half-sheets were true cancels. It must be improbable that only one end of a pile of sheets was damaged or despoiled in some way, while the stock of no half-sheet could have been exhausted before that of the other half. Therefore, the most plausible reason for printing a half-sheet seems to be to correct an error in the text of the originally printed sheet. The number of such cancels in Petrucci's output is quite large: I have already discovered nearly three dozen, involving either a whole or a half-sheet, and I am sure that there are more, often not detectable with present techniques.

We arrive finally at the level of analysis required for a detailed description of the printing history and chronology of Petrucci's output.[6] In it, there are two sets of information to lay before the reader. One comprises the printer's work as it survives: editions, printings of the whole of a book, whether dated overtly by the printer or analytically by the bibliographer; and impressions of parts of a book, single sheets and bifolia, never dated by the printer (for they are clearly intended as replacements), sometimes datable by the bibliographer, and here always called cancels. The second set of information comprises the extant copies, each with its own particular amalgam of parts of editions and cancel sheets. These clearly supply the data for the first set of information, but they remain distinct. They interlock with the first in the manner of a crossword, providing the horizontal words, while the first set contains the vertical solutions.

The two sets of data should be seen as distinct for a further reason: Petrucci, in common with all printers and publishers, would have had a view of the character of each book, as displayed in its form and contents. The book's appearance would have included the size and format, the character of the content and the version to be presented, how the content was to appear on the page, the points at which accuracy was or was not essential, the level of decoration and the impact of the ornate initial letters, and so on.[7] Some of these matters involved artistic judgment, and others were the responsibility of the craftsman. But the combination of the two produce what is now called the "ideal copy". This, a bibliographical fiction, is a copy as the printer wished it to appear. (As such, it does not have to be an accurate, or even complete, copy; it is merely a reflection of the point at which he regarded the work of preparation to be satisfactorily completed.) If all the extant copies of a title are sophisticated, no single copy can stand as an ideal copy; indeed, an ideal copy may well not exist. But the bibliographer wishes to describe it, for he then does more than merely list the printer's failings and frustrations; he also tries to describe the printer's hopes and aspirations for his edition, and thereby reach closer to the printer's view of his public and its taste and needs.[8]

For all these reasons, some the product of advances in the application of bibliographical techniques to music printing, some the need to distinguish the artifact from the art it is trying to represent, the present study offers a bibliographical history of Petrucci's work that is much more complex than that found in any previous exploration.

This chapter seeks to bring a semblance of order to the chaos threatened by the preceding pages. It presents the evidence for detecting "hidden" editions, impressions of parts of a book, and cancel leaves and sheets; and it demonstrates the possibilities that exist for arranging these (often newly reported) printings in chronological order.

The simplest means of detecting new editions or impressions is to compare each page of every copy of a title with the same page of every other copy. As I have discussed in the preceding chapter, Petrucci was unable to keep type standing after he had seen a forme through the press. The type was needed for the pages that were to be set up next. Therefore, each new printing must have been started from scratch, and every detail of the text would have been set up again.

In a number of cases, this is immediately evident. For example, during Petrucci's time at Fossombrone, he abandoned his rotonda text font; books of sacred music that had been set with that font were then reset with a roman face. The difference is obvious. In other instances, change can be just as evident, for the decorative initial letters change from one setting of type to another.

Often, the new typesetter would slightly modify the layout on a page. First editions tend to be less well spaced than later ones: although the craftsman might have been experienced at judging the music's requirements, there would have been cases in a first edition where a line or page was slightly cramped, while an adjoining one had space to spare, or where the alignment between text and music was poor. A typesetter preparing a second edition from the first could then adjust the layout to produce a more pleasing result. Even page-turns could occur in different places in the musical text, particularly if a typesetter were working in partbooks. The clearest example of this is the way in which the 1516 edition of Josquin's first book of masses changes the layout of the 1502 edition.

In a majority of cases, however, there is no such obvious change. Most typesetters, working from an earlier edition that seems attractively laid out, would tend to follow it closely, copying line ends, spacing and (sometimes) details of notation or spelling. Fortunately for the modern student, however, even when a typesetter copies a previous edition most carefully, there are always minor changes on a page, whether or not the content or layout is complex. Lines have to be justified by inserting small spacing sorts, and it is very unlikely that two typesetters would reach exactly the same sequence of decisions about these sorts for every line of a page. For music and its textual underlay (especially in a multiple-impression process), the possibilities are more varied, and the chance of slight changes of alignment correspondingly greater. Note tails might go in the opposite direction, rests sit on a different line of the stave, syllables sit just to the right or left of the notes involved, and so on.

Finally, given the nature of music copying in the Renaissance, and the manner in which compositors behaved like scribes, it is not surprising that many pages of a later printing show minor changes in the notation, or in the spelling of the text. These range from changes in ligatures and patterns of coloration to changes in the use of proportion signs; text spellings show different dialect traditions, or levels of awareness of the humanistic attempts at adopting classical spellings of Latin. The impact of these changes on our understanding of changes in notation, performance practice, the intended use of the source, and even the background of individual typesetters is a subject for chapter 8.[9] Here, I need merely note that such changes almost invariably signal a separate printing of the folios on which they appear. When more than one copy of any sheet survives, therefore, it is possible to detect different printings by the simple process of comparison. This does not necessarily give an accurate view of their relative chronology, but it will certainly show their presence.

Unfortunately, a number of titles or partbooks exist in single copies. In these cases, comparison is clearly impossible. Others seem to have the same pattern of setting throughout all the extant copies: here comparison has not yielded any useful evidence. In such cases, we cannot tell, without other evidence, whether we have copies of only a first or a later printing. There then remain three other methods that can be used to detect cancel sheets or later editions: one involves watermarks; a second searches for evidence of changes in house practice; and a third requires study of the condition of the type and blocks.

Watermarks were discussed in detail in chapter 3, for they are the prime evidence for any patterns of paper use. Our main concerns then were to show the manner in which Petrucci acquired and used paper, to indicate those occasions when it seemed that he laid in a special stock of paper for a specific edition and those others when editions were printed from whatever paper lay to hand, and to suggest that paper patterns can confirm that apparent gaps in production were probably filled with editions that are now lost. At that point, mention was made of the possibility of using the same evidence to reveal (or at least to suggest) the presence of cancels and later "hidden" printings of earlier editions. It is time now to take up that issue.

As was remarked in chapter 3, a few sheets of paper might lie around in the shop for a while, after the rest of the batch had been used for printing, and then be incorporated into a mixed batch of papers, used for a later volume. For that

reason, it is difficult to be sure that the *later* appearance of a watermark is necessarily evidence of a sophisticated copy—of the presence of sheets from an otherwise unknown earlier printing—without other supporting evidence. An example from the New York copy of *Odhecaton A* is discussed below, and there are
other instances where the evidence does point in the same direction.

However, the reverse situation is much more valuable. It is intrinsically unlikely that a few sheets of paper would appear significantly *before* the rest of the
batch was employed. If there were reason to believe that Petrucci was concerned
about the varieties of paper that he used, we might suspect that such an occurrence
represented a test of new paper. The general evidence of paper use suggests,
however, that he acquired papers as they were available and apparently trusted
his *cartolaio*. The unexpectedly early appearance of a few sheets must therefore be
significant—and the most simple solution is (and always appears to be) that they
are not earlier, but represent a later printing of those sheets, one which can be
shown to be contemporaneous with other uses of the same paper.

A simple example can be seen in the first edition of the *Misse Josquin* (Book
I), published in 1502. Almost all copies are printed on the same pair of papers
(paper Nos.3 and 4), using forms of the letter "A" in the countermark position.
However, a single sheet in each of the copies at Berlin and Bologna, the inner
of gathering F, is printed on one of the papers with an anchor mark (No.6), a
paper that does not surface anywhere else for nine months. It is first found elsewhere in the edition of Brumel's masses and is then used consistently, though not
exclusively, for another eight editions. The presumption has to be that the single
sheet in the Bologna copy of Josquin's masses is a later "cancel" sheet, printed
during the period of normal use of the paper in 1503, an assumption that can be
confirmed from other evidence.

Another straightforward example is the appearance of a couple of unexpected
papers in copies of *Motetti B*, dated 10 May 1503. The bulk of every copy is
printed on papers (probably) drawn from a single batch, with one version of the
letter "A" in the countermark position (Nos.3 and 4), which had been in use for
the immediately previous editions. However, there are anomalous papers on several formes (see Table 5-1).

This appears to be the only occurrence of paper 14 for sixteen months, and
of paper 15 for thirty months. Paper 8, however, does appear elsewhere: it is used
in the next book, of music by Brumel, and in some subsequent volumes. The
evidence seems to suggest that the gatherings of *Motetti B* that are printed on
these papers are parts of later reprintings of the original material, some fairly soon,
perhaps at the end of the year, and others during 1505. Conveniently, there are

TABLE 5-1 Pattern of watermarks in three gatherings of *Motetti B*
(1503)

Library	AI	AII	HI	HII	JII
F-Pc	15			14	15
GB-Lbl		8	14	14	8
H-Bn			14		
I-Bc				8	

gaps in Petrucci's output at those times, and study of the type and initial letters suggests that these pages do indeed belong there.

The pattern of watermarks appearing in the Fossombrone musical editions is equally informative. The small number of five marks can be found in many copies (and follow the pattern of paper use seen in Petrucci's Venetian period); and there is the surprisingly large number of eleven others that appear to have very limited use. This extravagant display of various papers was noted in chapter 3, and the suggestion was made there that it represents a casting around on Petrucci's part for a good supply of paper, which has some bearing on the present issue. It is obviously difficult to assign dates to papers used only once for two or three sheets in a single title—sometimes, even, in a single copy.

Among the five papers that are used more freely, the most important are one with a half-moon mark (No.35), and one without any mark. These characteristically appear together in the editions of 1519, and no other papers appear to be used in that year. However, both papers can also be found in copies or parts of copies of all the titles dated during the years 1514–16, alongside other papers. Several copies seem to contain these and other less common papers in random orders, and different copies of the same title have the half-moon mark, for example, on different sheets.[10]

The sheets with these two marks have to be assigned to a later date (ca. 1519), partly on the strength of the presence and pattern of appearance of these papers, and also for other reasons addressed below. The pattern of use of many other papers is not as clear-cut as these examples would suggest, however. A cursory glance at the inventory of watermarks presented in chapter 15 shows that several generic marks were used over a considerable period of time. It might be possible to show exactly the evolution of these marks, and to place their occurrences more closely; the present state of watermark research is not conducive to this kind of investigation, however. Few libraries can provide accurate life-size watermark reproductions—for example with beta-radiographs—and few of the reference volumes provide necessary measurements of marks or chain- and laid-lines. Something of the magnitude of the problem for a long-lived sequence of the "same" watermarks can be seen from the series of measurements I have given for marks 3 and 4 in chapter 15. These marks are closely related; indeed, it is not always possible to tell them apart, for some examples of what may be mark 3 look like mark 4 with a heavy laid-line at the crucial point. For that reason, I tend to think that we are here dealing with a number of discrete batches of paper, all with the same watermark design, but with marks actually resulting from different molds with different versions of the design, and different thicknesses of the crucial laidline. These batches would have been bought by Petrucci at different times and as separate consignments, even if from the same paper mill or *cartolaio*.[11] This hypothesis seems to be confirmed by the patterns of occurrence of mark 3. There are runs of volumes where it appears: from *Misse Josquin* of 27 September 1502 to *Motetti B* of 10 May 1503; from the first book of Spinacino's intabulations (February 1507) to *Frottole libro septimo* of 6 June 1507; and again from the reprint of *Frottole libro secondo* (29 January 1507/8) to *Frottole libro nono* of 22 January 1508/9. The paper does appear elsewhere (and one such occurrence will be discussed immediately below), but these runs of editions suggest distinct bulk purchases in each case. The marks on the different runs of paper cannot be easily distinguished one from another, however, without many beta-radiographs from many libraries, nor can they (at present) be distinguished from or associated with those found on other batches used outside these sequences of editions.

Similar, though probably simpler, is the group of editions on paper showing a countermark of a calvary, a small hill with a cross (No.20). This mark first appears in late 1505 and is used freely throughout much of the following two years. Again, the mark seems to be very variable, and measurements, while indicating the presence of twins in some volumes, also produce contradictory results elsewhere, presumably again indicating the presence of a single *cartolaio* buying from different mills.

This pattern of paper use works against the scholar in two ways: one of these marks, found in a book made up largely of a completely different paper, cannot be as easily dated as less common marks; at the same time, different versions of the "same" mark might produce evidence of further cancel sheets, similar to the evidence described above, but only if the marks on all pages were to be photographed and measured.[12]

A difficult example involves a particular group of papers with a version of mark 3, those that appear in books published in 1504—the third edition of *Odhecaton A* (RISM 1504²), *Motetti C* (RISM 1504¹), and *Frottole libro primo* (RISM 1504⁴). In each case, the appearance of this paper is restricted to only a few sheets (see Table 5-2). (The example of *Motetti C* was mentioned in chapter 3, although merely to indicate that the late change of paper suggested that the four partbooks were set up simultaneously.)

The presence of this paper in so small a group of editions, dated closely together, argues for the relevant sheets having been printed at about the same time, around the date of the latest edition of which they now appear to form part. If that were so, all would have been printed during 1504, probably between the second and the third of these editions. However, other evidence shows that

TABLE 5-2 The presence of watermark 3 in three editions of 1504

Book	Copy	Sheets Involved	
Odhecaton A: 25 May 1504	US-NYp	FI	
	other copies		Not present
Motetti C: 15 September 1504	D-Mbs		Not present
	D-Mu	Bassus: CI	
	D-W	Cantus: DII	
		Tenor: DII	
		Altus: DI; DII	
		Bassus: CI; DI; DII	
	GB-Lbl (Hirsch)	Cantus:	Not present
	GB-Lbl(K.1.d.4)	Cantus: DII	
	I-Bc	Cantus:	Not present
	I-Vnm	Cantus: DII	
		Altus: DI; DII	
		Bassus:	Not present
	US-Tm	Cantus: DI; DII.	
Frottole I: 28 November 1504	A-Wn	AII; BI; EI	
	D-Mbs		Not present

all were not printed at the same time. To begin with, and fortunately, the patterns of typesetting confirm that these sheets are anomalous in two of the titles. The whole of the outer sheet of F in the New York copy of *Odhecaton A* shows a different setting of type from that found in the other extant copies. In fact, it turns out to be part of the same edition as that represented at Seville and therefore printed earlier than any of the others, in early 1503.[13]

In the same manner, the three sheets showing mark 3 in the Vienna copy of *Frottole I* present different details, when compared with the sheets in the Munich copy. Although these were printed after the Munich sheets, that is, in 1505 at the earliest, yet, because of the distribution of this paper through other editions between 1502 and 1509, there is no easy way to tell from the watermarks alone when the sheets might have been printed. We have to turn to other evidence for that. However, it is clear that the watermarks in both these volumes act as signals that the relevant sheets were printed at a different time. It so happens that one instance represents an earlier printing, while the other (acting like a cancel) indicates a later one.

In the case of *Motetti C*, the evidence of all the papers, taken together, suggests what is confirmed by the state of the type and blocks: that the change of paper was a result of necessity and not an indication of a separate impression; the sheets on paper 3 were part of the same process represented by those on other papers.

The fact remains that, once again, the presence of an apparently anomalous paper within a volume has to be treated cautiously; it may well mean that we can assert the presence of cancel leaves, as in the earlier examples. But it may equally indicate something quite different; either the exhaustion of the primary paper stock for a volume, or the presence of sheets from an *earlier* printing. In these, as in a few other, less common situations, a study of the pattern of using the papers will help—as in the example of *Motetti C* here, or in that of the Brumel and Ghiselin mass volumes discussed in chapters 3 and 4. Finally, an anomalous paper will rarely provide concrete dates for the relevant layers of a copy, even though it will often suggest a range of months or years.

Of the other two forms of evidence that can be used for detecting and placing reprintings, sophisticated copies, and cancels, the second—variations in house practice—presents many of the same problems of interpretation encountered in studying the distribution of papers. We can rarely be sure that detectable changes represent conscious decisions or changes in house policy, on the part of Petrucci or his typesetters, rather than merely indicating temporary change or simple error. We cannot be sure how many of the patterns represent responses to different repertoires or diverse technical and musical problems, rather than mere procedural changes. Nor can we always be certain that the evidence signals more than the presence of two or more compositors in the printing shop, each with his own tendencies and practice.

That is not to say that house practice cannot be useful as an indicator of a chronological hiatus, or of the presence of a cancel. Much of my argument about the layers of Petrucci's first book, the Bologna copy of the *Odhecaton A*, hinged on details of house practice.[14] The details do not need to be repeated here, but they involve simple aspects of layout, the habits for indicating signatures or captions, and similar "peripheral" matters.

The third element most easily used for the detection of cancels or sophisticated copies, and thus for the existence of "hidden" editions, is the actual typographical material itself. This is useful on two levels, and both directly assist in any attempt at dating the cancel. First is the adoption of new material; anything showing that material must of necessity postdate its purchase. The second involves the continual use of individual sorts and blocks; after a while each is liable to become damaged. The deterioration of any element, its damage or simple erosion after many passes through the press, is irreversible, and the presence of such damage or erosion again acts as a *terminus post quem* for subsequent, equally damaged appearances.

There seem to have been few changes in the typefaces, for either music or text. Although new sorts were apparently cast, as older ones became worn and damaged, few clear patterns can be detected, which suggests that, for the music font at least, Petrucci kept his own matrices or punches. This practice would have allowed him to replace damaged or tired sorts with new ones made from the same patterns.

The most obvious change comes when the rotonda text typeface is abandoned, between the first Fossombrone edition of Josquin's masses, Book 1 (29 May 1516) and that of *Motetti de la Corona II* (17 June 1519). Jeremy Noble[15] has already shown that a number of the Fossombrone titles survive in different, "hidden" editions printed before and after the change, that is, editions printed in rotonda and others in roman. The two sets of copies of Fossombrone editions of Josquin's masses held at A-Wn show this clearly. One set (S.A.77.C.20) preserves copies printed before this transition, with the text in rotonda; the other (S.A.77.C.19) comprises later copies, with the roman text font. This distinction, easily visible to the naked eye, caused *RISM* to record one set erroneously, as coming from the earlier Venetian editions. Similarly, the two different editions of the first volume of *Motetti de la Corona* preserved at Bologna show the same transition, for the later one (Q 74) is printed in roman type, and the first (Q 70) is in rotonda. The third edition, surviving elsewhere, is also in roman. In fact, all the volumes of sacred music printed before 1519 began life with a rotonda text font, but those with later, "hidden" editions were transferred to the roman font.

These different printings and their respective text fonts are represented in the extant copies of Fossombrone titles in as confused a manner as possible. As a result, at even a casual glance, a number of copies can be seen to be sophisticated. Each of the British Library copies of the Fossombrone editions of Books 1 and 2 of Josquin's masses has a single sheet set with the rotonda text type, while the rest of each book is set in Roman.

Here is another feature allowing the various printings to be separated chronologically, for all those with roman text fonts lie later than do those with rotonda text. (The change itself is, of course, no proof of chronological order; other evidence supports this conclusion.) Yet this feature provides no date for the editions. It acts as no more than a segregator for the appearance of roman editions, and on this evidence alone, there is no reason to argue either for or against any of the later editions, in roman type, being dated before the edition of *Motetti de la Corona II.* All that can be said is that they date from after May 1516. On the basis of other evidence, much more can be said: certain titles show more than one edition in roman type. If the evidence of watermarks is taken into account, and with the further evidence of the initial letters, to be addressed below, the probable order of all the printings can be determined. This order is given in chapter 13, and the justification for the relative dating of individual editions, in the bibliographical descriptions.

There is no such clear change in the use of the music font. The lack of any clear patterns is probably partly a result of the kerned nature of the sorts, especially *minimas*, *semiminimas*, and *fusas*, which resulted in damage tending to happen at the same places on the sorts. Some sorts do show idiosyncratic damage; among them would be certain mensuration signs, F clefs, and *custodes*. I have made attempts at following some of these sorts through individual titles, and on to subsequent books. The method and what may be learned from it have been presented with a spectacular blend of industry and flair in studies by Hinman and Blayney[16]. To my chagrin, I have had little of the success with this particular technique that has attended these scholars. My work on stave patterns is analogous in methodology, but the study of individual sorts has not yielded convincing conclusions about either the order of work within volumes or the chronology of series of copies and volumes.

The study of the decorative initial letters that grace Petrucci's volumes has been more fruitful. As I have shown in chapters 3 and 4, each of these was unique, each was acquired as part of a specific purchase of letters (which can be approximately dated), each was used as a principal letter for a while and then relegated to a secondary position, and each shows continuing damage to its design—sometimes delicate, at times almost gross enough to conceal the identity of the letter represented.

The adoption of each set of letters provides a *terminus post quem* for their use (even if it does not provide any control for the dates of abandoning other letters)—much in the manner that the adoption of roman type for sacred volumes does. This has valuable implications in a number of cases. The manner in which this form of evidence confirms the presence of a cancel bifolio in the first edition of Josquin's first book of masses (Bologna copy) has already been discussed in chapter 3.

In the same manner, a number of the copies of *Motetti de la Corona I* have to be placed considerably later than 1514, for they employ initial letters that are otherwise not found until after October 1519. In practice, the argument is a little more complex than this: with the sole exception of *Frottole libro XI*, all the Fossombrone titles dated in 1514, 1515, and 1516 exist in more than one edition. The point has already been made that a later edition for each survives with the Roman text font. None of the rotonda-text editions show initials out of keeping with a simple chronological pattern. But a number of the roman text editions contain new, small, and ugly initials: these do not appear in the first printings of the 1519 continuation of the *Motetti de la Corona* series. The presumption must be that these initials were first used after that series was finished, that is, after October 1519. Fortunately, this conclusion is supported by the evidence of the papers.[17]

Of the other examples of sheets with unexpected watermarks discussed above, one or two confirm immediately that they represent different settings of the content, by presenting different sets of initial letters. This is true, for example, of the single sheet in the New York copy of *Odhecaton A*, and of the odd sheets in *Frottole I*. In the former case, the initials suggest what the watermarks had only made possible, but a detailed study confirms that this sheet is taken from the *earlier* second edition, otherwise principally found in Seville; in the latter, they do no more than signal a complete resetting.

These initials were prone to damage, for they were woodblocks. Such damage, once it happens, cannot be undone, and becomes a permanent feature of the letter. Any use of the letter showing damage must always postdate uses without it. Unfortunately, things are not quite as simple as that, especially in the last few editions. Letters made of wood and with delicate carving take ink with varying degrees of success, depending on the cleanliness of the block, the state of the weather, and the quality of the ink; they also give different impressions depending upon the moisture content of the paper. These impressions can be faint enough to present blank sections of the letter, simulating wear and damage, or heavy enough to obscure the cracks that are most valuable for dating; the blocks can also appear to have lost major sections at the left or along the top if the frisket was poorly cut or the tympan carelessly aligned. Even the right side can give a poor impression when it is placed in the forme too close to the clef that follows it. Further, the letters are prone to gather dust or pieces of the ink balls in small corners, producing blurred and thickened impressions.

However, with caution, the pattern of increasing damage can be read. As the damage progresses, we can write a history of the letter, and thus a chronology of the sheets on which it appears. This chronology then reveals sheets that do not belong with their neighbours, but that are part of an earlier or a later printing.[18]

Throughout the preceding description of the evidence for "hidden" printings, I have been referring to individual folios, bifolios, and sheets. This has been necessary, for the evidence surfaces at specific places, rather than generally. There are, indeed, cases where the evidence suggests that only one bifolium or one sheet was involved in a specific printing. In such a case, we have to assume that this represented a cancel for the original bifolio or sheet, rather than part of a larger printing, now otherwise lost.

However, many of the instances discussed here and in the bibliographical descriptions are parts of larger processes. Once comparisons are made with other copies, we can decide whether an individual copy is made up of portions of two editions. This is why the headline to this chapter includes a reference to the modern condition—the sophisticated copy—alongside references to the original activity of the printer—editions, impressions, and cancels.

The distinction is an obvious one, yet it is fundamental. If only a single copy of a title survives, it may be very difficult for the modern scholar to determine which he has in front of him—for there is no immediate analytical difference between a cancel leaf and a leaf taken over from another edition. Either will be evident only from the bibliographical evidence, but that evidence is of the same nature for both.

One can speculate and perhaps reach a correct informed judgment. But the presence of even one other copy of the "same" edition would make the whole process much more precise:

The outer sheet of gathering E of *Frottole libro VII* (1507) is alone in having a different watermark. There is no obvious difference in house practice or use of initials, and the unusual paper is also found in other books of the period. Nonetheless, I suspect that this is a true cancel leaf: almost all the frottola volumes are very consistent in both their appearance and their materials. Without another copy, I cannot be sure;

In the second of Bossinensis's books of intabulations (1511), the one copy previously known (in Milan) shows an anomalous paper for the final sheet, the outer of gathering H. Prior to the recent discovery of a second copy, it seemed likely that this sheet (with watermark 2) was printed some time after the rest of the book. The second copy, printed on consistent papers, confirms that the anomalous sheet in the Milan copy is indeed a later cancel;

The example of one bifolium in Josquin's first book of masses (1502), which I have discussed before, is a case in which both paper and initials argue convincingly that the anomalous page must have been printed later. It is probably a cancel, rather than part of a whole edition;

The copy of Févin's mass volume (1515) surviving in Vienna is a case of a single copy certainly reflecting two editions. The Bassus partbook, which carries the correct date, is printed on paper that seems to belong to 1515. The rest of the set is on very different paper, which corresponds with the paper in other surviving bassus books, and which Petrucci did not use until much later;

The unique copy of Dammonis's book of laude (dated in 1508) is also sophisticated; two sheets are printed on a different paper, whose stock had been exhausted sometime before. They confirm the existence of an earlier edition, one which pre-dated the book called *Laude libro secondo*;

The instance of the first edition of the *Odhecaton A* is well known and much cited. There are four stages present in the one copy, of which the first is of the true first edition. The second and third are, I believe, separate short printings, effectively cancels. The fourth layer turns out to be part of the true second edition. But this is evident only because other copies of that edition have survived;

The last of the four books of *Motetti de la corona* (1519) is printed on a paper that shows no watermark, and it has a consistent set of initials, and consistent house practice. One sheet, the same one, in two of the surviving copies has a watermark. This is not a cancel, for a comparison of this sheet with that in other copies shows the contents to be the same. However, another bifolio, surviving in only one copy and printed on the main paper, turns out to be a cancel sheet, after the same comparison. This could not have been detected without the existence of the other copies.

There is a remarkable number of cancels, reprintings, and complete new editions, as will be apparent. Some of these are significantly later than the original edition. In that case, we cannot know, without studying all the musical readings, whether the previous state was being rejected, or whether the stock had been exhausted. This applies as easily to single sheets as it does to whole editions. There is reason to assume that the same number of copies of each sheet hardly ever survived the whole process from printing to final sale; it may be that printers rarely printed the same number of copies of each sheet;[19] it is very likely that the various other processes, from drying newly printed sheets to transporting copies to the bookshop, would have been subject to accidents and miscalculations. Therefore, the need to print a few sheets to make up stock could easily befall any printer—and this no doubt has something to do with the complex bibliographical history of the first book of Josquin's masses.

Other reprintings seem to have taken place very soon after the original edition, and they always involve only a few sheets or one gathering. Although accidents could befall the whole stock of a single sheet, most of these printings must have been true cancels. Unfortunately, the closer in time they lay to the original printing, the less chance do we have of finding a copy of the unaltered sheet.

In addition, we cannot be sure that they represent correction. In the case of *Odhecaton A*, I think it likely; the book was the first of Petrucci's output, he was taking great pains with it, and he needed to satisfy both his partners and his editor, Castellanus—who was surely concerned about the quality of the musical readings. I also suspect that Petrucci's stock was as little liable to have been damaged then as at any time in his career. In the case of the cancel sheet to *Motetti de la Corona III*, at the other end of his career, we again cannot be sure. The significant changes to the content are slight and could have as easily been done by pen.

Thus, the cancel is of less value for our understanding of Petrucci's processes, judgments, and musical standards than is the new complete edition. This latter shows how Petrucci felt about the popularity of his music and publication, and its contents tell us a great deal about the care and attention to detail of his typesetters, while allowing us insight into their ranges of freedom to change. In-house manuscript corrections (for which see the following chapter) specifically indicate that one reading was to be rejected, and that it was regarded in a serious enough light that Petrucci was willing to expend the labour. Cancels could have functioned as either of these did, but we usually have no way to tell which.

The detailed chronology of all these different cancels, reprints of sheets and more, and hidden editions is given in chapter 13, in the second, analytical part of this study. However, despite all the available information, there are two reasons why some dates can be no more than conjectural. The first concerns the editions and partial editions that were printed following the edition of Pisano's *Musica*, of 1520. In theory, each of these could have been printed at any time before Petrucci's edition of the *Motteti dal Fiore* of 1538. In practice, of course, that is implausible, for the repertoire would have ceased to have been of sufficient interest. In any case, Pasoti and Dorico reprinted a number of these titles in 1526, so we may assume that the final Petruccian reprintings were earlier than that. In practice, it seems to me that they must antedate the Giunta edition of the *Missarum Decem*, dated in May 1522, in part because I believe (and argue in chapter 14) that Giunta's book probably represents material that had been submitted to Petrucci and not printed by him. Whether or not that is true, it is equally significant that so much of Petrucci's typographical material surfaces in Rome at this time. Therefore, I believe that the seven printings listed in chapter 13 immediately following the edition of Pisano have to be dated within a period of less than two years after that edition appeared; but it is impossible to be more precise.

The second reason applies particularly to cancels. A single bifolio or sheet will often not carry enough bibliographical data to distinguish it from its neighbours in a chronological list. These reservations are indicated in the bibliographical descriptions of each title concerned. However, it should be evident from the number of such printings that Petrucci cared about the quality of his readings, and that he managed to run a thriving business.

There are two further issues, related to the presence of so many new editions, impressions and cancels, both of which are addressed in later chapters. One concerns the question of how far patterns of paper use, themselves also the result of the analyses discussed here, can illumine the question of the sizes of Petrucci's editions. This is a particularly thorny problem, and I will discuss it in chapter 10, in connection with the evidence for their distribution.[20] The second issue is that of Petrucci's standards, both in absolute terms, and as a picture of those areas where he and his craftsmen felt some freedom to change without compromising those standards. This is an issue for chapter 8.[21] However, the patterns of in-house correction provide essential support for any conclusions and form the topic of the next chapter.

Notes

1. Boorman, "Motetti"; Boorman, "New"; Boorman, *Petrucci*; Noble, "Petrucci". Sparks, *Bauldeweyn*, pp. 18–22, was one of the first studies to take note of the different readings surviving in different copies of a single Petrucci "edition".

2. This would only be true, of course, insofar as extant copies included the last folios of the book, that is, included the colophon with its date. The extent to which this is so can be seen from the misdating of one of the sets of Josquin's mass volumes held at Vienna, mentioned below. This resulted from three factors: the evident differences when it was compared with the other copies; the lack of the Bassus book, and therefore of a date; and the state of knowledge at the time, assuming that there were only two editions. As a result, copies in this set had to be assigned to the editions of 1502 and 1505, although (on subsequent examination) they clearly do not belong there.

3. Andrews, "Printed", especially pp. 5–6. A much more detailed study of these and related volumes has since appeared, as Smith, "Hidden".

4. As I return to cancels later in the present chapter, I will consider particular cases where textual problems may be discerned, as well as others that may well be sheets printed for another reason.

5. Preparing a half-sheet cancel would be evidently less labour-intensive if copies were printed using the "work-and-turn" process. See the preceding chapter, and also Boorman, "Case".

6. At this stage, I am taking no account of corrections made to the copies during or after presswork; these clearly do not affect the chronology of printing. Their place in a bibliographical description is also subsidiary (even while their role is paramount in assessing the printer's measure of accuracy and taste), for they lie below the level of "Edition", "Issue", and "Impression", and at the level of "State".

7. No doubt a number of these details were marked (or hinted at) on the printer's copy, so that the compositor would know at once what he was expected to do. As pointed out in the previous chapter, however, no such exemplars survive for Petrucci's titles.

8. The bibliographical meanings of the various terms used here are discussed in chapter 16, especially as they refer to music printed from movable type and in partbooks. The impli-

cations of the concept of ideal copy for our view of Petrucci and his market are explored in chapter 8. Here, I need only mention that, for the purposes of this volume, the description of an ideal copy includes those manuscript changes that were made in the printing shop. Even though they were not printed, they represent a part of the book as Petrucci wanted it to appear, and as he tried to ensure it would appear.

9. The discussion of similar evidence in chapter 4 had a significant difference. There the point was to examine these types of change as they appeared in different partbooks; in chapter 8, the concern is the evidence of change in different copies of the same books.

10. The books concerned are *Motetti de la Corona I*, and mass volumes by Févin, Mouton, and Josquin (Books I and II). The details of all these patterns are given in the bibliographical descriptions.

11. These small countermarks appear to refer to the *cartolaio* who placed an order for paper at the mill, more often than they refer to the mill itself. (For the most succinct statement of that position, see Nicholas Barker, in Naiditch, *Catalogue*, i, p.xxiii.) This would imply that Petrucci had a fairly stable relationship with his *cartolaio* for several years.

12. This is one point at which the different patterns of paper use in printed and manuscript sources need to be borne in mind. Slight changes in a mark, when found in a manuscript, can be used to reveal something of the source's copying history—which is normally not true for printed sources, where each sheet in the book represents many sheets at the paper mill, according to the size of the printrun.

13. Note that this is well within one of the batches of editions using paper 4 outlined above. This case happens to be an instance of an anomalous sheet that does come from an earlier printing. In this situation, as in all such, the sheet cannot be a cancel, and its chronological position can only be deduced from other evidence, from other copies with identical typesetting, or from the state of the type and blocks.

14. See the discussion in Boorman, "First".

15. See Noble, "Petrucci", which groups some copies on the strength of their use or abandonment of the rotonda face, there called "black-letter", as well as on the basis of divergent watermark patterns.

16. See Hinman, *Printing*, especially chapter 3.A; and Blayney, *Texts*, chapter 4.

17. A detailed discussion of this evidence can be found in Boorman, "New".

18. Ibid., pp. 136–42.

19. Rummonds, *Printing*, gives figures for wastage at the modern handpress, and they are probably comparable to those from earlier periods.

20. Aspects of the discussion in chapter 9, concerning the repertoire and its probable provenances and markets, will also bear on this issue.

21. It will become evident that the issues discussed in chapter 6 are at least as relevant, and the evidence presented there as useful, as are those discussed in this chapter.

Chapter Six

OTHER PATTERNS OF

IN-HOUSE CORRECTION

n chapter 4, when outlining what seem to have been Petrucci's normal procedures, I omitted any discussion of proofreading or other in-house manners of correcting the printed text. In chapter 5, I discussed one such method, the use of a newly printed cancel bifolium or sheet. In practice, it is not usually possible to tell whether a cancel represents the correction of error in the earlier version, the *cancelland*, or a replacement copy for stock that had in some manner been lost or damaged, or, even, no more than the result of a shortfall in the number of copies of that sheet.

However, there are other cases in which we can be absolutely sure that the change indicates a concern for improving the readings. These are the cases where both the original and the corrected versions survive, and where the change consists solely in altering a single specific reading. In common with many other printers of the period, Petrucci was apparently quite willing to undergo labour-intensive procedures to correct errors of faulty text or clefs, erroneous pitches or rhythmic values, or wrong folio numbers or signatures.

Apart from the use of cancel leaves, seven ways of correcting the text seem to have been practiced during the sixteenth century, and all but the first four are laborious in the extreme:[1]

1. true proof-pulls, with the type then corrected in the forme;
2. stop-press correction;
3. an errata list, printed at the end of the book;
4. a second run through the press, to add omitted details;
5. manuscript correction, erasing all or part of the printed reading when necessary, and adding the corrected version in ink (the use of something

akin to white-out to cover the offending notes is also occasionally observed);[2]

6. correction involving type, manually stamped onto the page at the correct place, after presswork;

7. a printed slip, containing the corrected reading, pasted over the erroneous one.

Of these, Petrucci seems not to have used the first or the last.[3] The last was widespread by the end of the sixteenth century (and found frequently in the work of music printers)[4] and was certainly in use by Petrucci's time. For example, the *Missale Pataviense*, printed in Vienna by Winterburg in 1513, has two pasteovers (neither of which is musical: one corrects a folio number),[5] and both Ferrari in Milan (1509) and Guillery in Rome (1515) are known to have used this method of correction.[6]

One or more of the other practices, however, can be found in almost all copies of Petrucci's books.[7] Errata lists and complete second impressions on already printed pages are rare, for reasons that will become obvious. But the other practices—stop-press correction, manuscript correction, and stamped-in corrections—are found freely in most of the musical volumes. Many of these changes, not merely the manuscript ones, but also those involving stamped-in type and even a second impression, could be made at any time before the last copies were sold and be effected on all the copies remaining in the shop.

Such changes rarely survive in all extant copies of a title. For one thing, once a copy had been sold and left Petrucci's shop, he was clearly unable to make any further changes to it. Secondly, while some changes, especially purely manuscript alterations, could be made to all the copies then in the printer's shop, stop-press corrections could no longer be made once the press-run for that forme was complete. It is thus evident that a stop-press correction would survive only on that percentage of the copies still to be printed when the correction was made. Indeed, we find examples where different copies of a single sheet have different patterns of stop-press correction for the outer and inner forme.[8]

Occasionally, all or almost all copies of a title show all the extant corrections, however they were made. In Agricola's mass volume, it is tempting to see a pattern by which the book was checked for errors more carefully than usual, and all that were caught were immediately corrected. As a corollary, the presumption that an early impression of every sheet of the edition was read with this intense care is equally tempting.

In most cases, however, we cannot use the number of copies with and without corrections to give any guide as to how early in the process copy was read; the rate of survival for all these editions is so low that even the existence of a stop-press correction in all or all but one of the extant copies is of no statistical significance.[9]

Proofreading and stop-press correction both involved a single process (changing the type in the forme), which thereafter produced a stream of corrected copies: by contrast, the last three types of changes in the list given above (manuscript and stamped-in corrections, and paste-overs) involved operations that had to be conducted on individual sheets, one at a time. These changes could not be mechanised in any way (through the use of the press, for instance) and thus were clearly labour intensive. All such changes required that each sheet be taken, the point of change located, and either an erasure or a new entry or both made, or the paste-over attached. Most also involved allowing the copy to dry again before it could be stacked. For these reasons, such changes must be seen to carry great significance for Petrucci, as presumed to add to the value of his products in the eyes of potential purchasers.

In the case of small errors (removing an extraneous rest), or necessary changes discovered only after the presswork was completed (correcting a single misplaced note), these processes, involving manuscript or stamped-in type corrections, were the most practicable ones available to Petrucci. They could only be made on copies as yet unsold; it may be that some were made almost immediately after presswork, for they survive on all extant copies. I repeat that the number of surviving copies is never enough to justify making this assertion with any confidence, but it is bolstered by those cases where both stop-press changes and in-house manuscript changes occur for the same variant, although in different copies. This fairly common pattern demonstrates that the error involved was found during presswork, and that it was major enough (musically or in some other way) for all copies (including those already printed) to need changing, without being large enough (physically) to support the preparation of a cancel leaf.

Since the different methods have different implications for procedure during printing, since they involve different practices within the printing shop, and since it is not always easy to determine the criteria by which Petrucci chose one over the other, I propose to discuss them separately and then briefly illustrate some examples that involve a combination of two elements.

There is one important distinction to be made at the outset, a distinction between the methods of correcting type in the forme (the first two on the list above) and those others that involved making corrections on the printed copies.

Stop-press Correction

There is considerable evidence that contemporary printers employed "correctors", often full time. Contracts regularly included a specific requirement on the accuracy of the text, or on the need to employ a reader, and many printers record the presence of correctors, although by no means all were employees of the shop.[10] Petro Loslein is described as a corrector in colophons of books printed in partnership with Ratdolt and Pictor in Venice, in 1476–78, and he may have been a regular employee. On the other hand, Chalcondylas and his partners budgeted for a proof-reader for Greek texts in 1499.[11] Still in the fifteenth century, Soncino employed one Gabriele Strasburgo, a rabbi, as corrector for Hebrew texts,[12] while he cites Guido de Sancto Leone and Francesco Armillino as correctors of his 1516 edition of Vigerius's *Decachordum christianum*.[13] The author Lodovico Dolce was employed as a house corrector by Giolito in the 1550s, and not only for his own editions of the great poets (Ariosto, Boccacio, Dante, and Ovid, among others). Dolce clearly read copy as it came off the press, for corrections were made during presswork. These include not only normal stop-press corrections of individual errors, but even resettings of complete pages or formes. These are not cancel leaves for the versos of both the original and the reset pages have the same setting of type.[14]

Dolce also wrote an attack on other printers and proof-readers in a letter to the reader printed in Giolito's 1552 quarto edition of Boccaccio's *Il Decamerone*. In this, he is typical of other authors, Brant, Erasmus, Filelfo, Melanchthon, or Reuchlin among them. In many cases, the word "corrector" seems to have covered the duties we would now assign to an editor, especially when the new edition claimed scholarly standards in presenting a humanist or classical text; the term did sometimes also include the duties of a proof-reader.[15] The practice of employing such a corrector, on one basis or another, seems to have been fairly widespread during the first half of the century,[16] and I have already mentioned the name of Posthumus in connection with Petrucci's edition of *Paulus de recta Paschae*.

It is often not clear just when the corrector read the printed copy. There is a distinction to be made between the act of pulling true proof-sheets, which were then read for errors *before* the rest of the sheets were printed, and the (apparently much more common) act of merely reading an early copy from the press-run.

True proof-reading did take place. Proof-sheets themselves have survived—providing the only possible physical evidence, for all the other copies should have been corrected.[17] In many cases, the sheets can be detected because they contain marks of correction—and these were followed in type in the other copies. The marks are not likely to be similar to the manuscript corrections of readings that can be found in many copies of all books; these latter often try to be inconspicuous, involving careful erasure, imitation of the style of the printed material, and careful placing to aid reading. Corrector's marks, on the other hand, need to be obvious and seen at a glance: they are in the margin, and there usually cannot be any erasures at the point of error. In addition, it is often assumed that true proof copies were printed only on one side of the page.[18] Even when this condition is not met, there are other signs that a sheet bound into a modern copy was printed at a preliminary pull: in some cases, the pen corrections appear in only one forme of the sheet.[19] There is almost no evidence of this sort in any surviving edition from Petrucci.[20]

The second procedure is easier to detect: if two groups of copies, when compared, show almost entirely the same setting of type, but include some slightly different readings, we must assume that the press was stopped during the run, that an early pull was read, and that corrections were made as a result. Such changes can be found in virtually every edition of an early book that is studied in enough detail, and discussions of examples abound in the bibliographical journals.[21]

Similar traces are being found just as generally in music books.[22] The best documentary reference from sixteenth-century Italy is probably that in the contract between Girolamo Scotto and Don Benedetto of the monastery San Giorgio Maggiore in Venice, signed in 1565. In it, Scotto agreed to supply 500 copies of Paolo Ferrarese's music printed in a large font on "commune" paper and corrected according to the supplied copy—"stampati in stampa grosseta, et corretti in carta commune, secondo gli Esemplari".[23] The contract goes on to say that, if by chance there should be folios with errors—"se per caso venissero li fogli scorretti", Scotto would be required to have them reprinted at his own cost: "obligato à farli ris-tampare à spese sue". This implies that cancel leaves might be necessary, but the contract says nothing about the manner or time of correcting the original printing.

But the evidence for stop-press correction is strong, not only for later music printers, but also for Petrucci. First is the reference made on the last pages of the *Paulina*. Although the corrector does not say that the press was stopped and corrections made, for he is too busy excusing himself for other errors, a number of these changes were indeed made in some copies.

There are also some rare cases in which we can see stages of the correction in progress. The earliest is that of the foliation of D1r and D7r in the third (1504) edition of *Odhecaton A*. These two folios, which form part of the same (outer) forme of the outer sheet of the gathering, would be correctly numbered 25 and 31. The numbers were originally interchanged, so that D1r was apparently first numbered 31, and D7r numbered 25. This inaccurate numbering survives in the copies at Paris and Washington. The corrected version is in the New York copy. However, the copy at Treviso apparently was pulled during the process of reading and correcting this sheet. D1r is still erroneously numbered 31, but the incorrect number 25 has been pulled from the forme for D7r. That folio now carries no number. For D7r, therefore, we can say that the process of correction began before the Treviso sheet was pulled and was completed later,[24] but before the sheet now in New York was pulled. The correction of D1r appears to have taken place a little later. (See Table 6-1 below.)

This sort of pattern argues strongly for press changes being effected during the press-run rather than before it (as would occur if a true proofsheet had been pulled).[25] It is evident that different corrections occur at different points during the press-run. There were similar problems and similar stages of correction in the outer sheet of gathering D of the edition of Obrecht's masses.

The strongest evidence for regular reading of copy lies in the number of stop-press corrections that have surfaced during study of the editions. All those so far discovered are given in the bibliographical descriptions of the various volumes. While many of these have been spotted only because they correspond to manuscript corrections in other copies, their existence is a sure indication that some reading was undertaken in the printing shop. It is also evidence that this kind of reading was not allowed, of itself, to stop the press-run: the only reason for that would be the discovery of some gross error needing immediate correction.[26]

The presence of these stop-press corrections, with their implications for a costly delay in the printing process, suggests that the errors thus corrected were seen to be crucial to the use of the book and its contents. This is something that I suspect cannot be said about corrections merely deferred until the next edition.

TABLE 6-1 Patterns of correcting foliation in the third edition of *Odhecaton A* (1504)

Copy:	F-Pc	US-Wc	I-TVcap	US-NYp
D1r	31	31	31	25
D7r	25	25	[nil]	31

It elevates *these* changes to the level of significance also held by the true cancel sheet, with the added advantage (when dealing with stop-press corrections) that we can be sure about which reading Petrucci wanted to see changed.[27]

Thus, a study of the elements of the book that were changed in stop-press corrections, and of the types of readings that were altered, provides the first group of evidence we have seen so far that clearly illustrates Petrucci's priorities. The extent to which the changed material is purely musical or textual, and the extent to which it includes peripheral elements, such as folio numbers, is of considerable importance.

We are accustomed to thinking that every printer and publisher put the quality of the text above everything else—even when we feel that they have not succeeded. Our presumption is that page numbers, foliation or signatures, the index, and other preliminary or marginal material were less important. Yet, this hierarchy is a product of our own view of the relationship between printed text (music and words) and performance. In a musical culture such as ours, where the first presumption is that a good performance must follow the text implicitly, the integrity of the text is paramount. But, in one such as we recognise the Renaissance musician to have inhabited, the text was less sacrosanct, both in performance and (as a result) in written or printed transmission. I do not mean to suggest that Petrucci could be willingly and grossly inaccurate, or that he did not want to present a careful text. Indeed, much of the evidence suggests that he sought to be very accurate, and I shall discuss that evidence in chapter 8, which is primarily concerned with questions of the quality and consistency of the book and its readings as printed. Yet, I believe it is valid to argue that Petrucci's priorities were notably different from ours.

Faulty (bibliographical) signatures are elements that seem to have been regularly corrected, and by stopping the press if the error were spotted in time:

> the signature to folio H2 of the third edition of the *Odhecaton A* (1504) is lacking in some copies, but present in a stop-press addition in those at New York and Washington;
> the erroneous signature on folio e2 of *Paulus de recta paschae* (1513) is corrected in at least eleven of the extant copies;
> there are similar corrections in Ghiselin's masses (1503) and in *Motetti de la Corona III* (1519).

When the error was not spotted in time, it was later corrected in manuscript, as in all surviving copies of *Canti C* (1504).[28] Even when there was a stop-press correction, other copies were often corrected in some other way, as will appear below. Other apparently marginal elements could also be changed; I have already mentioned folio numbers. Initial letters, ascriptions, and titles were occasionally incorrect or omitted, and these were among the elements changed by stop-press work:

> the letter "K" had to be added to folio C7r of the edition of La Rue's masses and survives in several copies;
> the headline of G8r of Agricola's masses originally read "Secnndi toni" (pre-

sumably as the result of an "n" finding its way into the "u" slot in the
case) and was corrected before the copies at Bologna and Krakow were
printed;

an ascription to "Compnre" on B1r of the *Fragmenta Missarum* (1505) is
corrected in copies at Bologna and Venice.

However important it was to have the indications of format and foliation correct,
or to present composers' names correctly, the majority of stop-press corrections
still concerned musical details.

By 1503 at the latest, these changes, which Petrucci must have considered
important improvements, became a normal part of his procedure. The standard
changes regularly involved the simplest possible alterations: only one or two notes,
from a *semiminima* to a *minima* on folio L1v of Obrecht's masses (1503); or from
two *minimas* to two *semibreves* on D2v of *Canti C* (1504); or pitches c and d
corrected to B and c in the second edition of *Motetti de la Corona I* (f.H5v), dated
1514. By the same criteria, ligatures could be changed just as easily, for example,
from a ligature *sine proprietate et cum perfectione* to one *cum proprietate et cum perfectione*
in the edition devoted to De Orto's masses (1505).

Relatively few such changes were made to the verbal text. While there is
often less text in any given volume, Petrucci seems to have cared less about the
spelling, the placing and spacing of syllables, or detailed accuracy.[29] Of the few
stop-press changes to text that I have noticed, some do affect the spelling or
accuracy, while others correct simple typographical problems:

in the third edition of *Odhecaton A* (1504), a real error in the index of the
Paris copy (folio A1v, line 9: "temis") is corrected in all the other copies
(to "meas");

on folio E6r of the volume of La Rue's masses (1503), some text that is
inverted in all other copies is correctly printed in the Bologna copy.

Normally, there seems to have been one limitation on the use of stop-press
corrections: that the new reading should take no more space than the old.[30] With
changes that took more or (even) less space, the whole line would have to be
reset: although this was of course possible, and other printers included such
changes, Petrucci seems normally to have adopted one of the available forms of
manuscript correction in those cases where setting the whole line would otherwise
have been necessary. The result is that even small changes such as the insertion
of a point of addition are not usually introduced at the stage of a stop-press
alteration, but are reserved for manuscript change. The only exceptions are a few
changes that occur at the right end of a line, when clearly the problem does not
arise. A probable example is in the first book of *Lamentations* (1506): on folio D7r,
the end of the fourth stave shows a lengthy alteration; while the original is not
legible in the London copy (for it is covered with a partly stamped in and partly
manuscript correction), it does seem to be shorter than the stop-press change
found in other copies.[31]

More stop-press changes will certainly emerge with closer study of all the
copies of individual titles. It is clear that this was one of the most common

methods of making corrections for all printers of the period, second only to the use of errata lists. For Petrucci, too, I have consistently found additional stop-press corrections whenever I have done a detailed comparison of every symbol in different copies of the same title. There is every reason to expect that more will surface. The majority of those discussed here have been discovered by comparing points at which some copies include manuscript or stamped-in corrections. These, after all, often correspond to stop-press corrections in other copies, being entered in sheets that had been run through the press before the error was noticed. Without comparing every note of every copy of every edition, one will certainly miss a number of other similar corrections, if they happen not to correspond to some more obvious feature in other copies. As a result, the listings of stop-press corrections in the following bibliography represent a minimum number, which are perhaps not even representative, in that they often concentrate on those important enough to warrant manuscript changes in other copies.[32]

Errata Lists

The errata list, as far as the printer is concerned, is clearly the simplest method of indicating errors and their corrections. Once the errors have been discovered, by reading an early copy of each sheet, they need only be listed and eventually set in type. The procedure is found quite often in both fifteenth- and sixteenth-century books: the famous Aldine edition of Bembo's *Gli Asolani* (1505), for example, has a list of *Errore fatti nel stampare* on folios n1r–v.

Petrucci only used errata lists twice, the first being in Bossinensis's first book of intabulations. This list gives only four errors, each in the verbal phrase setting the first pitch for the voice. For example, one of the entries reads: "Io non compro piu speranza uuol esser scripto cosi La uoce del sopran il canto uodo"—for the piece "Io non compro . . ." the rubric should read "the soprano's first pitch is given by the open top string".

The other appearance of an errata list is at the end of *Paulus de recta Paschae* (1513). I have suggested that this list was a special case, in that the book was the *magnum opus* of Paulus de Middelburgh and was to be his *entrée* to the Lateran Council and papal favour. If Paulus took particular interest in the book, he would have wanted to ensure that the text was as accurate as possible. The corrector, Hieronymus Posthumus, provides a long list of corrections to the text, especially corrections to the tables that provide the core of the argument. He also lays the blame at the door of the chalcographer.

Not surprisingly, there are no errata lists for musical errors. The difficulties involved in indicating musical readings are obvious enough; especially for Petrucci's multiple-impression technique, they introduced two problems, one for the reader, and the other for the printer. The first lies in the difficulty of indicating the point at which the error lies. The manner of signaling this which is adopted in the following bibliographical descriptions is convenient for the bibliographer, or for the musical scholar studying the readings. It is exceedingly tedious, as any similar algebraic formulation would be, for the performer.

The obvious alternative procedure is that of indicating the error with musical notation, printing both the erroneous and the corrected readings. This procedure is useful for the performer, always provided that the erroneous reading does not occur twice in the same line of music (one of them perhaps correctly entered), and the notation can be interpreted without ambiguity. The latter becomes a problem when the total duration of the notes in the two versions is not the same, if, for example, the only change is the insertion of a point of addition, or the change of a rest from a *semibrevis* to a *minima*. In such cases, the example has to be extended to include enough notation on either side of the corrected reading to make clear its incorporation into the rest of the musical text.

Two examples of this use of musical notation are known to me: the earlier, and relevant, example is found in the third volume of Isaac's *Choralis Constantinus* (1555), where the last *recto* of the Tenor book carries two corrections for the second volume. The first is relatively simple, referring to a faulty intonation in the Discantus part of a specified mass, and therefore giving merely the correct version. The second is more complex. It reads: "In Missa 22. de Sancto Martino in Alto, in fine vltimi versus prosæ erratum sic corrige, pro [music example] Cane [second example]". Both versions contain a note before and one after the change; indeed, since the two versions are of different lengths, this is the only possible way of demonstrating how the new version should be inserted. These two changes take up two complete staves of a five-stave page.[33]

But for Petrucci the real difficulty of this apparently elegant solution would have lain in preparing it for print. It would require several short segments of stave to show "before" and "after", presenting both versions on an additional page. Apart from the simple point that there is not always an extra blank page or folio at the end of a volume, this method consumes vast amounts of space. If the examples were to be clear, it is unlikely that Petrucci could have fitted more than six corrigenda to a single six-stave page. If he had the space and the special staves,[34] it is questionable whether he would have thought the effort worthwhile, and dubious that his readers would have found it much easier to use. Petrucci never tried to indicate musical errors in lists of errata and indeed never used errata lists in any musical volume other than the first by Bossinensis. Even in that volume, notational corrections were made while the press-run was stopped, or by hand.

Re-impression of Printed Sheets

The most unusual of these methods of correction was that of running sheets through the press again, and its adoption can be detected in only one or two special cases. It was useless for making corrections to material already printed, for example, and could only be of value for an addition of some significance or size.

There is a simple reason why any extra impression is hard to detect. An additional impression had to be aligned as precisely as the previous ones, and in precisely the same place. In this, Petrucci seems to have been consistently successful, especially in the vertical dimension. The result is that there may be a number of places where omissions were restored to the page as a result of an additional impression, but would be difficult to detect without precise measurement.

There are many places where a few letters seem to have slipped from the line of type and have printed a little higher or lower on the page. We normally assume that these, with their surrounding furniture, moved slightly under the pressure of repeated pulls at the press. In some cases, though, the internal alignment of the individual notes or letters seems to remain consistent, even while the whole group moves relative to the rest of the printed text. In these cases, the misaligned symbols might equally be the result of a later insertion by means of additional impression.

One case seems fairly clear-cut. The compositor of the *Missarum diversorum auctorum liber primus* (1508) apparently omitted the composer's name for the last mass when setting up the title-page. As a result, the phrase "Piero de la rue" was added later. The internal arrangement of the letters in this addition is absolutely consistent, indicating that they cannot have been stamped in separately. At the same time, the alignment of the phrase differs slightly from copy to copy and is never exactly in accord with the rest of the title. Yet it is never so different that the results suggest a handheld block of type. It appears that the whole phrase was set up and printed as one unit, presumably at a second, special run through the press.

A second group of changes, which are almost certainly the result of a later impression, comprises additions to previously printed title pages for the lower voices of a number of books. Petrucci seems to have originally planned not to present any title on the front pages of the Tenor, Altus, and Bassus books of mass and motet volumes. Thus the lower voices of the first volumes to appear in separate parts bear only the initial letter "T", "A", or "B" on these pages. The first set of partbooks to have a descriptive title for the lower voices is for the second book of masses by Josquin (1505). The next title printed, the *Fragmenta Missarum*, also contains descriptive titles for the lower voices: in this case, however, their alignment is not consistent from copy to copy, although the internal arrangement of the letters is precisely maintained. My belief is that the whole line of text was mounted in a new forme and printed on the title pages at a second run. That would have been quicker than trying to stamp a set of seventeen letters and one space on each copy.

This addition makes excellent sense, and I am surprised that Petrucci did not use it more often. He already had in his storeroom several sets of partbooks where the lower voices had no title to indicate what they contained. Although he surely filed each title separately, and tried to ensure that there was no confusion, yet this simple addition would have helped not only himself but also his purchasers. Indeed, a few early owners did add a composer's name to the title pages of these lower voices: for an example, see the copies, now in Krakow, of the masses of Agricola and Ghiselin, coupled with the Berlin copies of Josquin (1502) and La Rue. It seems clear that, once the idea had occurred to Petrucci (or rather, once it has occurred to the modern bibliographer), other examples might be discovered, if a detailed enough series of measurements were taken.

Manuscript Correction

It is manifestly dangerous to argue that manuscript alterations found on surviving copies of Petrucci's books were added by someone in the printer's shop. Yet there are many instances where this assertion can be made with absolute confidence, and many others where it remains more than a probability. Each of these fulfills two requirements: (1) that the correction is found in more than one copy, is made in each with the same ink and a similar pen, in a closely similar writing and correcting style, and (as a result) plausibly by the same hand; (2) that the copies have demonstrably different provenances, in particular, early ownership patterns. This second condition eliminates the possibility that some early owner or user corrected more than one copy—a greater possibility, as well as of more significance, for music than for many other printed texts. These two conditions are met often enough when studying copies of Petrucci's editions that it seems reasonable to argue that the printer regularly used manuscript correction as an alternative to stop-press or other manners of improving the printed text.

These changes are of the greatest value for the student of early texts. They must represent readings that were important either to the author or to the printer. They are readings that needed to be corrected before the book was issued—or at least before the remaining stock was sold;—and the printer was prepared to devote much time and energy to correcting them. As such they form an integral part of the text as the printer wished to see it issued, of an "ideal copy". Further, unlike some stop-press changes, in these instances the direction of change is immediately evident.

In holding to this position and presenting the arguments that follow I am reflecting an emerging view among students of Renaissance printing.[35] Scholars of particularly important texts have compared multiple copies of the most significant editions, among them the *editio princeps*. Bibliographers, seeking to understand the transmission of a text and its place in the techniques of printing, have also come across many situations that can only be explained in this manner. We continue to find patterns of manuscript corrections appearing in multiple copies of the same edition, and to argue that these were made by the same hand.

Thus, Aldus Manutius's first edition of Caesar's *Commentarium de bello gallico* (1513) has manuscript corrections to the captions of two plates, in the same hand.[36] Mazzocchi's 1521 Roman edition of *Epigrammata antiquae* has the same corrections in several copies.[37] A similar pattern appears in Aldus's edition of Benedetti's *Diario de bello carolino*.[38] The tradition continues throughout the century: an edition of 1557 from the press of Paolo Manuzio shows twelve manuscript corrections, all of which are incorporated in the later edition of the same year.[39] Clearly, there is a tradition of having some sorts of corrections made by hand.[40] On occasion, the corrections were even made by the author himself. Juan de Ortega's *Suma de arithmetica* was printed by Guillery in Rome in 1516; the errata page includes a list of the corrections made by the author in copies of the edition.[41]

The easiest way of demonstrating that certain changes were made by one of Petrucci's employees is to present examples of the same relatively complex change, made in the same manner, by the same hand, in copies with completely different provenances. Among the clearest examples are those involving whole words:

the addition of "pier zu*n* quarti toni" in four copies of the Superius of the second edition of Févin's masses (1515) seems to have been made by the same hand in each case. These four copies (comprising all the extant Superius books) are now in Bergamo, London, Paris, and Vienna, and there is no reason to argue that they were ever the property of the same owner; the manuscript phrase "Bñdictus | tacet", found in five copies of the Bassus of Agricola's mass edition (1504), is similarly consistent. These occurrences are probably in the same hand that entered "Bñdict₉ | tacet" in two other copies. Between them, these seven copies account for all the surviving Bassus books.

In both cases, the presence of such a specific and unnecessary textual addition in several copies seems enough to imply in-house correction.

We should also believe in one scribe altering all the copies when the addition or change comprises musical notation. The assumption is that an identical musical change, if it involves more than one or two notes, could not easily have occurred to a number of different musicians. Significantly, in a number of Petrucci's editions, we can find different copies with identical musical changes involving several notes. These changes also often appear to be in the same hand:

in the Bassus of the edition of *Missarum diversorum auctorum* of 1508, there is a major change—four notes and a rest changed to a *punctus additionis*, six notes and a rest—in four copies. This change could not have been made with type, for the new material would then take up more space than the original;

the 1507 edition of Gaspar's masses has an elegant solution to a problem in the Altus. On folio E10*r*, the typesetter apparently ignored a new clef, presumably present in the exemplar. As a result, a new clef and a (cautionary) custos were entered in manuscript and can be found in all the extant copies.

Many such changes are listed in the following bibliographical descriptions. They are sufficient for us to assert that, in Petrucci's mind, this was a perfectly normal procedure. The decisive features, in each case, are the uniformity in style and pen position, often coupled with ink apparently of an identical hue.

This consistency of correction can sometimes also be found in copies belonging to completely different editions. When the correction is large and distinctive enough, and when the copies have not traveled together (i.e., do not have the same pattern of provenance), there is little room for doubt that the changes were made in-house: the word "Resolutio" is added to the left margin of folio C3*r* of the unique copy of the second edition of Ghiselin's masses, and in two copies of *Motetti de la Corona III*. These changes are convincingly the result of work in Petrucci's shop. There is no other possible explanation for the uniformity of the new readings, or of the presentation of these readings, when coupled with the dissemination of the copies.

Following from this argument, I believe we have to add a considerable number of other—though less identifiable—changes, each also made in the same style in various copies: they include changes to mensuration signs, custodes and clefs, added accidentals, deletions of passages of dittography, a number of "double-stops", the bibliographical (rather than musical) signatures,[42] and changes in double bars:

> in *Canti C* (1504), the bibliographical signatures on folios Q3 and Q4 were erroneously printed on Q5 and Q6. This is a simple problem of layout in the forme, but was one of the elements critical to the binder, and therefore one that Petrucci would want to correct. The three extant copies all have the same style of entry on Q3 and Q4 and of striking through on Q5 and Q6;
>
> in the fourth book of *Motetti de la Corona* (1519), the Bass clef is entered at the wrong pitch on folio G8*v*. The manner of correcting this in three copies seems to be identical;
>
> a *signum congruentiae* is entered in several editions in a manner consistent throughout, and in the characteristic ink of many of Petrucci's changes: there is an example in *Frottole I* (1504), on folio B2*r*.

Many of these are relatively small changes, and it might seem that they cannot provide enough evidence to confirm that the changes were made by the same hand. However, as before, a comparison of similar changes in different copies and, even more important, in copies from different editions yields an exceptionally consistent pattern. The manner of deleting dittographies is a good example. This regularly involves drawing a bar line on either side of the repeated section, and writing below it the word "vacat":

> in *Frottole III* (1505), on G7*v* in the unique copy;
>
> in *Frottole V* (1505), on folio C3*v* in both the extant copies;
>
> in *Missarum diversorum auctorum* (1509), on all six extant copies of folio C7*v*.

Similarly, the manner of adding the numeral "3" to proportion signs in several places even in one copy seems consistent enough to argue for it having been done in-house. A clear example lies in the various treatments of this change in the unique copy of the first edition of *Motetti de la Corona I* (1514) at Bologna (Q70).

In these, as in other cases, the pattern of changes, the number of them, the extent to which they seem to be identical in different places, taken together suggest strongly that we are dealing with the practice of making changes in manuscript in the printing house.

Perhaps less clear-cut are one or two changes where the hand and ink *seem* to be the same, even when there is not really enough material to be sure:

> the addition of the mensuration sign ø in the Bassus in three Italian copies of *Misse Ghiselin* (1503);
>
> many of the changes found in all three copies of Dalza's fourth book of tabulature (1508), even though they seldom comprise more than the change of a numeral or a rhythm sign;
>
> the addition of a single bar-line on folio G8*v* of the second 1514 edition of

the Josquin's masses book 3, surviving in exactly the same manner in four different copies.

To push this line of argument to its furthest possible point, there are cases where the same erasure can be found in several copies of a title. Clearly, without some form of detailed chemical analysis, we could not argue that the same razor was used. If there is any support for saying that these might have been executed in-house, it can only lie in similar patterns of erasure when accompanied by a clear manuscript or stamped-in addition. For example, some instances show a partial erasure of an item, such as a note head, and the incorporation of the remainder into a new symbol:

> on the third stave of folio J8*v* of the first edition of Josquin's Masses, Book I (1502), the nineteenth note was printed as an *f*: in two copies (at Bologna and Milano) the top was erased and a new base was added, to make the pitch *e*;
> in both copies of *Frottole libro quinto* (1505), an erasure of a symbol on folio B3*r* is accompanied by a careful touching up of the damaged stave lines.

Each of these cases may have been done in-house, both because of the similarities of style and because, as I suggest, of the colour of the ink.

In other cases, I have chosen to be more circumspect in suggesting that the changes may have been made in-house: these would include many erasures when there is no new insertion. A considerable number of these seem to be done in a similar manner to each other, and also to reflect the manner adopted in cases where an addition also appears. However, the nature of Petrucci's notation and the often close spacing of musical elements make further speculation risky. It seems impossible to say who effected the erasure of a *longa* tail to produce a *brevis* in three copies of Isaac's masses (folio E6*v*) or half of a *longa* rest in four copies of Gaspar's masses (folio A8*r*), or carefully changed a *semiminima* to a *minima* by erasing the center on folio F6*v* of La Rue's masses. It is risky to assert that these were done by Petrucci's men. But there are so few corrections made away from the printing shop[43] that it is tempting to speculate about even these.

In practice, I do believe that we can sometimes go as far as this and argue that some minor changes were made in-house, even though they could never be shown to be identical in style. The corrections which I have so far proposed for Petrucci's workmen are (almost without exception) written in an ink that has faded, consistently, to an attractive gingery-brown colour. This raises the possibility that other corrections, also apparently in the same, now ginger-coloured, ink, may have been effected in-house. I have therefore tentatively included some of these among the in-house changes, even when they appear in only one source, or when there is not enough evidence to identify a correcting style.

This is, I recognize, a very dubious practice: many black inks of the period may have faded to a very similar shade, and I have not regularly been able to put many copies side by side. However, over the years, I have come to recognize one particular shade of ginger that appears consistently in copies of many titles.

This shade is regularly found in corrections that I am confident in ascribing to Petrucci's house—those which are idiosyncratic and in several sources, or where enough is present to help identify a hand or style—and it is regularly used for other similar patterns of change. In most cases, those corrections that I believe were not the work of Petrucci's men tend to have been done in inks that are now either still black, occasionally a pale grey, or a rich and dark brown. If this distinction dare be made, there are several changes that might justifiably be included among those made by Petrucci's men:

on folio D8*v* of *Canti B* (1503), surviving in one copy, a *minima* is erased, and two notes and a rest are inserted, in the same ink that touches up the staves;

the unique copy of the second edition of Ghiselin's masses (1514) contains a correction on folio C6*r*. This involves an erasure and drawing a double bar line with repeat dots on both sides. The same style of notating a repetition can be found in other editions;

all the surviving copies of the Bassus of Book Two of Josquin's masses (1505) have the same correction on folio F2*v*. A *minima* is erased on the fourth system, and the stave lines are touched-up in brown ink. This deletion is necessary, though not obvious when reading the single part;

in the first book of *Lamentations* (1506), a *minima* on C7*v* (first stave) has a *punctum additionis* added in brown ink.

The support for these examples becomes more and more dubious as one moves from the drawing of rests and note heads to even slighter changes, such as the insertion of dots of addition.

However, there are the four changes made in the half-sheet of "*Musica XII*" now preserved at Fossombrone. One is stamped in and is mentioned below. But three are manuscript changes. One, the erasure of a single *longa* rest, could not otherwise have been attributed to Petrucci's shop with any semblance of responsibility; another, the provision of a large initial letter, is not found elsewhere in Petrucci's work. Since this sheet was apparently never issued, but kept with the printer's stock, and passed directly from there to a binder, it would seem that all these corrections must have been made in-house.

Not all in-house changes were made in the same ink. In some cases, two correctors were involved in applying the manuscript changes: this is indicated by the manner in which some corrections were effected in the same manner in one colour of ink and also survive in a second. In the volume of Agricola's masses (1504), some are most frequently in ink that is still black (with some copies altered in brown), while others are usually in a now-brown ink (with other copies changed in black). Since most copies of this volume show the majority of the corrections, in one colour or the other, in manuscript or by some other method, it seems that, for once, Petrucci was under some pressure, to ensure either that as many corrections as possible were entered, or that the books were completed as soon as possible. Two of his men were committed to the task.[44]

In the twenty years of his active career, Petrucci must have employed more than one corrector, and probably there were other cases where two worked side by side on a single book. Thus, the corrections for the volume of De Orto's masses (1505) show two different inks and styles: a number are done in brown ink, while some others are written in black and appear to be intended to imitate the printed note exactly. Each change is consistently written in the same ink and the same manner in all the copies in which it is found.

In at least one case (the description of changes to the unique copy of the first edition of *Motetti de la Corona I*), I have attempted to list all the changes that might possibly be assigned to in-house manuscript correction. This gives some idea of the possibilities for other titles. It also puts purely manuscript corrections on the same level as those using stamped-in characters. The latter often survive in only one copy, as many manuscript corrections must do.

There is one other special case of manuscript corrections that should be discussed here, that of the large number of detailed tabulature changes, all made in the same ink, in the two volumes of music intabulated by Spinacino. All (except for one on A4r of Book I) seem to be done in the same hand, in the same ink, and in the same manner, and they show a concern for correcting all the erroneous readings, to a level not normally found in Petrucci's other books. In those other books, it is clear that Petrucci cared about making corrections, but that he made them only as they were discovered and managed to miss quite a few (which presumably were never revealed to him by the "proof-reader" or by his circle of acquaintance). Here, however, a large number of corrections were made at one time. In addition, these are of a particularly detailed nature and required an especially careful hand to execute them so well.

All these corrections seem to have been made early in the sixteenth century and must have been the work of either a member of Petrucci's shop or an early user of the book. Given the pristine condition of the volume as well as the appearance that all the changes were made at the same time (to judge from the consistency of ink and manner), it seems more likely that the changes were made in Petrucci's house. It is also significant that the same hand changes one signature in the second volume. This change (from "F3" to "fF3") does not affect the binder's view of the sequence of binding and would normally not have been made by either an owner or Petrucci.[45] Coupled with the other changes, it argues for someone in Petrucci's circle who was familiar with the music, who was expected to "proof"-read the whole book, but who was not particularly familiar with Petrucci's house practice. The most likely candidate for this, given that Petrucci was, for the first time, dealing with printed tabulature, is Spinacino himself.

It should be evident that manuscript corrections made in-house must carry the same weight as corrections made with type (stamped-in, or as cancels). Both represent the printer's attempts at presenting the best possible readings. We must therefore be cautious about attributing to Petrucci the acceptance of any error, when there is a probability that a specific difficult reading may have been changed in some other copy. We must be equally cautious in ascribing, on the basis of manuscript changes, musical ability or experience to the purchasers of annotated copies.

Stamped-in Correction

The idea of stamping material into each printed copy, by hand, seems to have been known during the fifteenth century. Donati has shown that it was used for the decorative borders of a number of Italian incunables.[46] In these instances, the division between printed and stamped-in was planned by the printer. But the process was equally available for inserting omissions in the text, if they were not too large. Any single piece, a woodblock or a single typesort, could easily be stamped-in, in one or many copies, and even small groups of type sorts—single words, for example—could be tied up and stamped together.

One example can be seen in the *Paulina de recta paschae*, printed in 1513. Part of a word has been inserted at the foot of folio A8*v*, as if a catchword, because it was omitted from the opening of B1*r*. The entry, "anti-", is usually assumed to have been stamped in.[47] The alignment of the four letters, with each other and with the text above, is not entirely consistent, though it looks as though they were tied and stamped together.

Petrucci not only used this technique for inserting omissions, but was also able to make corrections to the text, with erasures and stamped-in symbols. As I have said, the first three titles of Petrucci's output show no trace of in-house corrections. However, with the printing of the first book of Josquin's masses in 1502, manuscript changes appear, as do examples of stamped-in corrections. After presswork, someone decided to move the first note of the fourth stave of D8*r* to the end of the previous stave. This is apparently a classic example of the sort of change made by a performer, for its only value can be to assist in fluency of reading, by completing the *tactus* at the end of a stave. But the correction must have been made in-house, for it involved erasing part of the custos, stamping in a new note with type, and adjusting the end of the custos by hand. This change survives in only one copy.

Unlike those made in manuscript, these corrections were necessarily made in-house. The type sorts used, either text or musical symbols, always correspond to those belonging to Petrucci's fonts, and the inks seem to be printing inks. In that respect, the interpretation of these corrections is easy: they cannot belong to later changes. For volumes that survive in single copies, especially some of the frottola collections, these provide the best evidence we have. Interpretation is also easier, as it is for manuscript correction (but in contrast to the situation with stop-press changes), in that these changes can have happened in only one direction: the "error" or the omission can easily be determined.

It is interesting to note how many of these changes, as also the manuscript changes, do not concern the content of the book, but instead clarify its structure and layout. Among these are additions of folio numbers in, for example, *Motetti B* (1503), the third edition of *Odhecaton A* (1504), *Lamentationes I* (1506), and *Frottole libro settimo* (1507), and of signatures in *Motetti de la Corona IV* (1519). Some of these indicate a surprising problem found elsewhere with stamped-in symbols, that they can be upside down: the folio number 3 in the book of La Rue's masses is inverted (when present), and numerals are inverted on folio 41 in some copies of the second book of *Lamentations*.

In *Misse Ghiselin* (1503), the signature for A2 was incorrectly printed with the letter "B". In the copies at Bologna and Krakow, this is corrected with a stamped-in signature, alongside the original printed one: a stop-press correction appears in the copy at Assisi. This is again confirmation that some errors, even though corrected in stop-press changes, were considered so important that they had to be corrected by hand in all the copies printed before the correction had been effected.

As with manuscript changes, there are fewer changes to the verbal text than there are to the musical, though some are present. A whole word is stamped into the newly discovered copy of the 1503 edition of *Motetti B*, but there are very few other such changes. Petrucci is careful, however, to correct inappropriate initial letters. It may seem surprising that such a bold feature of the printed page could be the subject of typesetter's errors, and yet every printer seems to have experienced them, sometimes even on the title page. Petrucci had to correct initials or enter missing ones several times, in *Fragmenta Missarum* and *Frottole libro quinto* (both of 1505), *Misse Gaspar* (1507), and the first edition of *Motetti de la Corona II* (1519).

By contrast, there are a great many stamped-in corrections to the musical text. These include a number of omitted mensuration signs in the third edition of *Odhecaton A*, and, at the other end of Petrucci's career, in the second edition of Mouton's masses and the third 1516 edition of Josquin's first book (both actually printed after the 1519 edition of *Motetti de la Corona IV*). The majority of the other errors corrected in this manner are simple ones of one or two pitches, erased and then correctly stamped in, or occasionally of a wrong note value, frequently a *semibrevis* replaced by a *brevis*. Similar corrections are made to the rhythm signs and pitch numerals in the tabulature volumes.

Some of these changes are extremely small and often hard to detect. While there are examples as slight as the addition of a single *punctus additionis* in the 1503 edition of *Canti B*, the scholar can be sure that he has not seen everything, and that more such changes will surface as Petrucci's volumes continue to be studied.

Other changes show Petrucci and his craftsmen as thoughtful about the easiest and tidiest ways to make them. The correction of *minimas* and *semiminimas* at the wrong pitch often involved an erasure merely of the note head; a new note head was stamped in (using a *semibrevis*) and associated with the original tail. Sometimes, a manuscript line is drawn from the note head to the old tail, for the alignment of stamped-in notes was necessarily a little less precise than that of the originally printed items. In *Misse Obreht* (1503), the pitches of two *semiminimas* are changed by using colored *semibreves*. In *Canti C* the tail of an erased flat sign is used with a stamped-in *semibrevis* to create a new *minima*.

When discussing stop-press corrections, I suggested that Petrucci tended to restrict that resource to changing readings where both versions were of the same length; clearly, the length is an even more rigorous restriction for stamped-in alterations. It is true that many lines of music use small spacing sorts between most notes, and that therefore it should have been possible to insert three notes, for example, in the space of two original ones. However, Petrucci seems to have done this only rarely, perhaps because it was harder to place the impression from a handheld piece of type as precisely as could be achieved with a manuscript entry. One of the rare examples occurs on F1r of *Frottole libro nono* (1509), where two *minimas* were replaced by a *semibrevis*, a *minima*, and a *semibrevis*. Others occur at the end of a stave, when there is clearly more flexibility, as in the first (1502) publication of Josquin's masses. An interesting example is on folio G6r of *Frottole libro tertio* (1505), where one note and a final double bar are converted to two notes and a single bar line: the new final *longa* is created with a *brevis* stamped to touch the first bar line.

This is typical of the ways in which Petrucci's men made clever use of the existing printed material. One already mentioned is the manner in which the tail of a *minima* could be retained while the new note-head alone was stamped in. The *semibrevis* was easier to align exactly than was the *minima*, for it was mounted on a smaller body.

Mixes of Manuscript and Stamped-in

A variety of corrections involving stamped-in changes also required the addition of elements by hand. At first sight, this might seem surprising. After all, Petrucci had all the sorts he might need and could presumably arrange to use one sort with or instead of another. However, several types of correction involve both manuscript and type. Perhaps the most common are those in which the stamped-in note had to be preceded by an erasure of something else. Quite frequently in such cases, the stamped elements would necessarily be accompanied by a manuscript touching-up of the stave lines, always in the common ginger-brown ink.

There are other similar cases, patterns of the combination of manuscript and stamped-in elements. Among these is a group that confirms a preference (mentioned in the preceding paragraph) for using *semibreves* rather than *minimas*, for correction whenever possible. In several cases, a note with a tail (a *minima* or a *semiminima*) was completely erased so that a *semibrevis* could be stamped in, and a manuscript tail added to convert it to the shorter note-value. Examples can be found in the editions of Agricola's masses (1504) in the copies at Bologna and Vienna, or De Orto's masses (1505), or the first book of *Lamentations* (1506)—except for the London copy. Similar preferences for smaller type-sorts when making corrections appear in the Venice copy of *Motetti IV* (1505). A *custos* on folio D2v was erased so that a *minima* could be stamped in before it. The re-entered *custos* was entered in manuscript.

By far the most obvious situation that encouraged this double process is the presence of chords—"double-stops". Here, quite frequently, one of the lines of music was not printed but entered in manuscript. While the small bodies of sorts for notes did allow for two to be printed on the same stave, it seems at times to have been easier to insert one set after presswork. There are two examples in *Canti C* (both on folio R8r) that show a combination of printed, stamped-in, and manuscript notes. Interestingly, in both examples, the pattern of added material—which notes are stamped and which entered in manuscript—is different in the different copies. It appears that this was a complex (and therefore slow) enough series of changes to require more than one member of the shop for its timely execution. *Canti C* is therefore another in the small number of books (including that of Agricola's masses, already discussed) that provide evidence for two men occasionally having to undertake correction of a pile of copies, those where different copies carry the same change, sometimes stamped in, and sometimes in manuscript. Another case involves the first issue of the third volume of Josquin's masses (1514).

More examples will probably surface with further study, but even these few, coupled with the evidence of the imaginative combinations of stamped sorts and manuscript additions, confirm that Petrucci used all the resources at hand to make as correct an edition as possible, and to get it out to market as soon as possible. The balance between those two needs is part of the self-image of the printer, to be discussed in chapter 8. The following section merely reinforces what should already be apparent—that the quality of the printed text (both verbal and musical) was of considerable importance.

Stop-press Changes Reflected by Manuscript or Stamped-in Changes in Other Copies

By the nature of the process of stop-press correction, as I have outlined it above, a number of copies of a forme would have been printed before the error was even spotted by the reader, much less corrected. For some printers, these were just as viable as the amended copies, for they appear in present-day collections alongside other copies bearing the stop-press alterations. This does not often seem to have been true for Petrucci. There were certainly some changes that he seemed content to ignore in the finished copies, and several have already been mentioned. But the majority of those I have discovered were also corrected by hand in copies that had been already printed.[48]

I have so far discovered about thirty examples of stop-press changes corrected by other means in other copies, and all but a few concern musical readings. Two of the others, in the *Misse Ghiselin* and in *Motetti de la Corona III*, involve erroneous signatures, and a third is the name of the composer Compère, in the *Fragmenta Missarum*. (All these examples have already been mentioned.) But the majority concern musical changes. Many of these were important:

> in the first book of *Lamentations* (1506), a change on folio D7r concerns five symbols, two of them ligatures, and is entered as a stop-press correction in all but one copy. In the London copy, there is a complicated blend of erasures, stamped-in type symbols, and manuscript adjustments;
> the first 1516 edition of Josquin's first book of masses has a similar (though shorter) correction on folio G2r. In the copy at I-Rvat, the new reading is stamped-in, although it appears as a stop-press correction in that at I-Bc;
> two chords are changed in the first book of Bossinensis's intabulations (1509).

Others were apparently no less worthy of attention, although they might concern a smaller change, of one rhythm or one pitch—from a *minima* to a *semibrevis* (as in the third 1516 edition of Josquin's first masses); or from a *minima* rest to a *semibrevis* rest (as in the 1506 edition of Isaac's masses). Such changes were relatively simple and could as easily have been made by pen in all copies; some, indeed, would only have required a single pen stroke:

> on folio M2v of *Canti C* (1504), a *brevis* was changed to a *longa*, by a stop-press correction in the Treviso copy. The change was made in manuscript in that at F-Pn;
> on folio C2r of the edition of De Orto's masses (1505), a ligature change has already been mentioned. Although this required a single pen down-tail, as in the copy at Bologna, it was changed with a stop-press correction (found in the copy at Güssing);
> in the first book of Bossinensis's intabulations (1509), a slur is moved one measure on folio C2r. A stop-press change in the Vienna copy is mirrored by a manuscript change in the copy at Chicago.

Other changes—for example, moving a flat key signature from the pitch c to the correct pitch B in the *Missarum diversorum auctorum* of 1508—could have been left to the intelligence of the users. Yet each is made by a stop-press correction in at least one of the extant copies. This raises surprising points about Petrucci's criteria for accuracy and about the speed with which copy was read. If the press could be stopped in time to make changes that would have required a single line in ink, and if it was still advantageous to Petrucci to correct in this manner, we should assume that the stopage was early in the print-run. While a majority of the run still had to be impressed, it would no doubt have seemed more economical to stop the press; if, on the other hand, a small percentage of the sheets were still unimpressed, Petrucci would no doubt have settled for manuscript changes (since he would, in any case, have to use manuscript to correct those copies that *had* been printed). Indeed, I assume that some of the changes that survive only in manuscript or stamped-in versions were actually discovered while the press was still running, but too late to justify stopping the run.

However, the great majority of those editions that survive in more than one copy do show evidence of stop-press corrections on one or more of their sheets. This suggests that the normal pattern was to read copy at once, from one of the first copies off the press, and to have errors noted in time to stop the press and make type corrections. Clearly, this has bearing on the size of the print-run, although (equally clearly) there is a circular argument here. The slower the presses ran, and the larger the print-run, the slower or later could copy be read before Petrucci would decide to correct all copies in manuscript. The sooner copy was read, the smaller a print-run may have been. This point is taken up elsewhere, in the discussion of the size of editions.

Related to this issue is the question of Petrucci's regard for accuracy, and, indeed, what that term may have meant to him. The series of observations that have formed the core of this chapter, and especially those on stop-press and manuscript versions of the same correction, are obviously central to any examination of this question: as such, they are considered in chapter 8. Here it is enough to point out that Petrucci apparently did care a great deal about the musical readings he was transmitting. I have already argued for accuracy as a concern in the transmission of certain levels of the content—for example, pitches and rhythms, if not notation; and content of the text, if not spelling. The evidence advanced here is drawn so widely from his output that it also bears out my argument that precision in the music's detailed content was a major concern for Petrucci, apart from any interest expressed by the suppliers of his music.

Notes

1. Rummonds, *Printing*, p. 85, quotes John Smith, writing *The Printer's Grammar* (1755): "Correcting is the most disagreeable work that belongs to Compositors". He is here referring to the more routine methods of correcting, the first two in my list. It should be added that the printer using woodblocks faced different problems and had different solutions. Any corrections made after press-work could be handled in the same way, but for Antico with woodblock music, stop-press corrections to the notation were virtually impossible. There are occasional signs of changes to the blocks, and even of small sections being replaced, but these can hardly have been effected during the press-run.

I am here tacitly making the assumption that the "corrector" or proof-reader compared his "proof" with the printer's copy: this is an unsafe assumption, for we have no examples of printer's copy for Petrucci's editions. In his edition of Shakespeare's *Much Ado about Nothing*, Charlton Hinman says (pp. viii–ix) "that none of the changes made in any of the formes now known to be press-variant implies reference to the copy by the proofreader, and that a good many of these changes are at best mere sophistications". Many of the corrections and changes made on Petrucci's editions have the same limitation: corrections of spellings of the mass text, of clefs and "key signatures", or of the incidentals on the page (the "meta-text") did not require reading the exemplar. However, given the nature of a musical text, and the use of choirbook or partbook layouts, it is evident that Petrucci's in-house reader did sometimes check the printed version against a manuscript exemplar. For this reason, we do not need to look to the "corrector" to explain changes in readings, but have to assume that such changes represent a return to readings dating from an earlier stage, and found in the exemplar. This has some bearing on the editorial processes adopted in Petrucci's shop, an issue to be raised in a later chapter.

2. There are several uses of a white paste to cover errors, over which a correct reading could be stamped in, or entered in manuscript. The earliest examples of this, definitely from the printing shop, that I have seen are in the famous *Graduale Romanum* edited by Francesco de Brugis, printed by Emerich for Giunta in 1499 and 1500 (Bohatta, No.704; Hain-Copinger, No.7844; Meyer-Baer, *Liturgical*, 20; Duggan, *Italian*, No.17). Massera, *Mano*, is a modern edition of Francesco's preface to this edition.

3. My assumption that Petrucci did not pull a formal proof copy, and then correct the type before printing the full run, is based on the pattern of surviving corrections. These corrections are so extensive and often so obvious to a superficial eye, that it is difficult to argue that proof was read (in particular, read against copy) and corrections made before the print-run proper was commenced. The correction of folio numbers and signatures tends to suggest that they were also not checked before press-work.

4. Forney, *Susato*, p. 160, says that Susato actually preferred this method of correction. For an example in the work of Gardano, an edition of Verdelot, see Lewis, *Gardano*, pp. 299–300. Examples are also mentioned in Bernstein, *Scotto*. For examples in the work of Barré, see Buja, *Barré*.

5. The copy of this book, which I have consulted, is at GB-Cu, SSS.1.1, and the two pasteovers are on folios N4r and N5v. For further discussion of this edition and its musical contents, see Boorman, "Salzburg".

6. Both of these are cited in Mortimer, *Italian*. The first is No.514 in her catalogue (vol.ii, pp. 711–12) and concerns a cancel initial letter pasted over the incorrect letter; the second is No.331 (ii, pp. 483–84) and involves a folio number. This volume, Ortega's *Suma de arithmetica*, will be mentioned again below.

7. It is perhaps not surprising that the first titles printed by Petrucci are among the

few that show no sign of in-house corrections. For one thing, the single extant copy of the first edition of *Odhecaton A* includes several sheets printed later (which may or may not be cancels to correct major errors). For a second, we may be sure that Petrucci set out to preserve the highest possible standards, and these would certainly have included standards of typesetting.

8. These differences should not be surprising, for it is very unlikely that the sheets would be run through the press in the same order (or even an exactly reversed order) for both formes. However, if a stop-press correction in some copies is matched by a manuscript correction in others, Petrucci probably planned to make that particular change in all copies. This issue has been discussed recently, in Milsom, "Tallis".

9. For this reason, I am reluctant to follow the arguments proposed by Allan Stevenson, in "New", p. 154.

10. Lenhart, "Pre-Reformation", includes a discussion of over 700 correctors named during the fifteenth century; he stresses how many of them were not professionals—full-time employees in a printer's shop—but other learned men, presumably with a specific interest in the text being read.

11. Brown, *Venetian*, pp. 30–31; Lowry, *World*, p. 99.

12. See Manzoni, *Annali*, part 1, pp. 15, 35, and 79.

13. "Sacrae Theologiae magistris Guido de Sancto Leone et Francisco Armillino de Serra comitum eiusdem ordinis Correctoribus" (GB-Lbl, 3833.d.12, f.F10*v*). The reference to "the same order" is to the Franciscans, to which author of the book belonged. There are many copies of this splendid book, printed in Fano, which has more than once been compared with Petrucci's *Paulina* as among the most splendid productions of the area and time. Indeed, Manzoni, *Annali*, part 2, vol.i, p. 118, regards this book as the stimulus for Petrucci's and other elegant volumes, in the richness and quality of the decorative borders. See also Johnson and Scholderer, *Short-Title Catalogue*, p. 725; Mortimer, *Italian*, ii, No.537, pp. 743–44; Servolini, "Edizioni", pp. 112–15.

14. For a discussion of this in the 1553 Giolito edition of Ovid's *Le trasformationi*, see Bongi, *Annali*, i, pp. 395–401, and for an example preserved at Harvard, see Mortimer, *Italian*, ii, No.342, pp. 494–96.

15. This is discussed in Richardson, "Print", particularly pp. 10–11, 24, and 26.

16. See, for example, references such as that in the Venice, de Sabbio, 1533 edition of Amadis de Gaule, where Francisco Delicado is named as corrector.

17. The important early study, Simpson, *Proof-reading*, needs to be updated in the light of recent work. Hellinga, *Copy*, gives a number of examples of proof-sheets, some of which also show the corrector's annotations; the evidence presented in Bühler, "Pen", has close parallels with Petrucci's books; Hellinga, "Proof-reading", shows how proof sheets appear in bound-up copies; and Plantin's instructions to his proof-readers are discussed in Vervliet, "Instruction", and Boghardt, "Instruktionen". There is also at least one Italian reference to copy being read before printing. In Corio's *Patria historia*, printed by Minuziano in Milan in 1503, the list of errata ends with a statement informing the reader that many had been corrected before the forme was sent to the press—"Avisandoti che molte ne sono state corecti prima che la forma fosse comita de imprimere". See Mortimer, *Italian*, No.137, i, p. 195. This may be an unusual practice: Rogers, "Glimpse", records a fifteenth-century German document indicating that the pages were put into formes and complete sheets were printed before a proof copy was read; this seems to be the practice for Petrucci's printers also. For another early reference, implying reading against the exemplar, and even a further reading of the corrected sheets, see Gerritsen, "Printing".

18. Needham, "Cambridge", discusses some sheets, used in a full copy, which have corrections already printed on the recto but in manuscript on the verso.

19. For an example, see Mortimer, *Italian*, No.457, p. 634.

20. I exclude the surviving fragments of "*Musica XII*", which I shall discuss below. It is possible to see this as a sheet containing notations for the errors found at the stage of reading copy; unfortunately, however, there simply is not enough conclusive evidence.

21. See, for example, Bühler, "Stop-press"; Fahy, "Ariosto"; and several references in Mortimer, *Italian*. The extensive studies of Shakespeare and of the presses that worked on editions

of his plays have produced much detailed evidence of the practice of proofreading in England, ca. 1600. See, for example, Craven, "Proof-reading"; and Hinman, *Printing*.

22. See, for example, Forney, *Susato*, p. 161. Many bibliographies of music do not go into sufficient detail on individual copies to be able to assert that we are dealing with stop-press copies rather than a cancel leaf, or even a stamped-in correction. Sometimes the presence of stop-press corrections, however, can be deduced from lists of variant readings: see examples in Lewis, *Gardano*; and Vanhulst, *Catalogue*.

23. This quotation is taken from Agee, "Contract", p. 1. See also Agee, *Privilege*, p. 335.

24. This is theoretically possible, if the pull was of a half-sheet at a time, as was normal. Then, one correction could be made, while copies would be pulled of the other half-sheet only. There is no record of this procedure (rather than that of pulling the two half-sheets consecutively for each exemplar), and it seems easier to suggest that the two errors were not noticed at the same time.

25. Interesting figures demonstrating just this, that the corrections were made during the press-run, are provided in Bühler, "Stop-press", p. 140.

26. Since the press-run continued until the error was found, any given correction would appear on only some copies; the later the page was read, or the error spotted, the more "incorrect" copies would have been printed. Since the timing varied from sheet to sheet, we can never say that we have a copy bearing corrections to *all* the errors found in an edition. Indeed, if all copies *do* have identical readings for a single sheet, we still cannot know whether some stop-press corrections were made or whether all the extant copies were printed before or after these corrections were effected at the press.

27. We do know that a reading was to be changed at a given place on the page, but we cannot always be sure that we know the direction of change. In this respect, again, stop-press correction is unlike other forms of in-house change: when both versions exist, they seem to have equal validity. On many occasions, the solution is clear: a faulty page number or signature is immediately evident; a faulty clef or key signature is spotted as an error after scoring a few measures of the piece; the same is true for some erroneous pitches or rhythms. But in others, as in many instances of change between editions, we cannot strictly be sure of the superiority of one reading over the other.

28. It is reasonable that this last error might not be seen at once, for it (in which the folio numbers are also wrong) involves an imposition error, which would not be detected until the sheet were folded. The other mistakes mentioned here, the absence of a signature or an erroneous entry, would be evident at once, whether the sheet were open or folded.

29. Volumes of mass settings often present remarkable errors in the text; presumably the printer recognized that the correct text would be well known to virtually all users of such books.

30. This is a less stringent restraint for verbal errors. For one thing, the text was often less closely packed in a line, and therefore the only extra change would be to the spacing sorts adjacent to the changed word. This also meant that there was available space, into which a longer correction could intrude.

31. However, there are other similar situations in which Petrucci relies exclusively on manuscript changes. One has been mentioned above, and a few others will appear in the commentary to various editions.

32. Even without this caveat, I regard stop-press corrections as a significant part of the preparation of almost any early-sixteenth-century book. They seem to represent a significant effort on the printer's part to reach nearer to an ideal copy, insofar as his understanding of that ideal included the text printed. For that reason, I have chosen to include these corrections under the descriptions of the ideal copy (rather than the individual copies) in my bibliographical material. They may not be present in every copy (which is no reason to abandon them), or even in every copy sold, but they do stand as part of the printer's response to preparing the edition.

33. These books have been reproduced in facsimile, in Isaac, *Choralis*. The two sites to be corrected are in the Discantus on m2*v*, and in the Altus on pp3*r*. The other example comes from much later in the century: an errata page is found at the end of the Tenor book of Demantius, *Trias precum vespertinarum à4–6* (Nürnberg: Konrad Agricola [Katharina Dietrich],

1602), *RISM* D1533. Here again, Dietrich prints a correction using a line of music, preceded by the rubric "l. pag.1. fac.2. lin.2. post 16. Notam sequentes sic corrig": [i.e., f.l1*v*, line 2, after the sixteenth note, substitute the following]. It is notable that the correction does not say when the singer should return to the original version. Other corrections on this page are presented without notation and follow a pattern very similar to the one adopted in my bibliographical entries for showing changes in copies. For example: "ff. pag.4. fac.1. lin.6. Note 8. in | G. seminimima pro minima", which can be interpreted as meaning that ff4r [in the Altus], line 6, note 8, which is a G, should be sung as a *semimimina* rather than a *minima*, or, in the formulae adopted here, "ff4r.vi.8: *sm* → *m*". The presence of these two examples argues that others probably also exist, but have not been noted, either by me or in the literature.

34. In practice, Petrucci would not have needed special staves. He could have used an ordinary forme, with a specially prepared frisket to mask unwanted parts of the staves. In that way, two staves, one above the other, could be arranged to show the pairs of readings. However, I am doubtful that Petrucci could easily have fitted more than two variants on each system, given that the erroneous readings would have to be long enough to be immediately unambiguous. It seems to me that the novelty of this method, coupled with its extravagance in execution, militates against Petrucci having even considered it as a mode of correction.

35. See, for example, the statements made in Bühler, "Stop-press": "Since the corrections are always identical in form, written in at the same time and with the same ink, and many are certainly supplied by just one hand, it is certain that these alterations are not the diligent corrections of individual scholars but 'wholesale' emendations made at the printing house" (p. 139); and "it is my contention that such manuscript alterations *made by the printer or in his shop in several copies* form an integral part of the book. Since it is clear that such corrections were considered by Aldus as essential in the presentation of the text as he wished it to appear" (p. 139, emphasis in the original). Since I discussed this issue in my dissertation (1976), it has been increasingly noted by other describers of musical books, among them Agee, Bernstein, Gustavson, and Lewis.

36. Mortimer, *Italian*, No.96, i, p. 134.

37. Ibid., No.297, i, p. 436.

38. Bühler, "Stop-press". Bühler made something of a specialty of examining copies for changes made in-house, and discussions of instances can be found in a number of his articles, reprinted in Bühler, *Early*.

39. See Bühler, "Pen", for the details.

40. Once again, study of the comments about individual copies in Lewis, *Gardano*, reveals that his house also resorted to this practice on occasion: see, for example, the comments to her No.47, *RISM* 1543[18].

41. Mortimer, *Italian*, No.331, ii, p. 483. According to Mortimer, the copies at Harvard and at the British Library have the same manuscript corrections.

42. Interestingly, signatures were also added in manuscript in the 1532 editions of Calvo's *Simulachrum*, a book mentioned in chapter 1 as providing part of a long-distance link between Petrucci and Dorico.

43. I except here those copies that are heavily corrected, ones that belonged to Glareanus among them. These are obviously exceptional and do not negate the striking lack of later correction in many other copies.

44. The black ink used in this volume is dense and seems very like the ink used for the printed material. If, indeed, it should prove to be printer's ink, this would confirm that those corrections were made in-house. The same ink does surface in other titles, for example, in the second book of *Lamentations* (1506).

45. Petrucci's changes in signatures are significant and appear whenever a misleading signature was printed. However, this particular instance would not mislead anyone.

46. Donati, "Fregi". In this case, it seems likely that the borders were stamped-in by hand because they were made on woodblocks. These blocks could withstand less pressure in the press than the metal type and so might have been more prone to damage if printed with the text.

47. See, for example, in Mortimer, *Italian*, ii, No.363, p. 529.

48. That Petrucci was not alone in this is demonstrated in Bühler, "Stop-press".

Chapter Seven

THE NON–MUSICAL BOOKS

hile Petrucci's musical output lies at the center of the present study, and was indeed the initial stimulus, the three extant non-musical volumes (with one other that was probably not published) are also of considerable importance. Indeed, there have been many bibliographers over the last two centuries who have written as if unaware of any of the musical publications. For every writer who discussed the role of Petrucci in the dissemination of music, there were several others who knew of his production of the *Paulina*, his (indirect) contacts with the Lateran Council, or his place in the publishing history of Castiglione's work; even more knew Paulus through his incunable publications.[1]

What Petrucci himself thought of these three volumes we can no longer tell; nor can we deduce much from the actual quality or presence of the books. There is perhaps a strand of evidence in the proposal to publish Calvo's translation of Hippocrates suggesting that his contemporaries thought highly of the craftsman-ship in his edition of the *Paulina*. But this is no more than a straw in the wind, a suggestion that he had reached a certain standard, one which was probably not possible for contemporary Roman printers.[2] On the other hand, it is probable that he saw these books merely as commercially convenient; two were commis-sions from a powerful local patron.

What is certainly evident, however, is that each played a significant role in the shaping of Petrucci's career at Fossombrone. It is not too much to say that his musical output in the city might have been significantly smaller in scope, and have taken a different direction but for the intervention of each of these editions (including the planned Hippocrates). Each, therefore, deserves consideration for its place in Petrucci's professional biography.

Paulus de Middelburgh: *Paulina de recta*
Paschae, 8 July 1513

When Petrucci returned to his hometown from Venice, there was presumably
little incentive for him to continue any long-term plan for music publishing. He
did apparently bring all his typographical material with him, and probably also
the press (although that was not an expensive item to replace). But the general
situation would hardly have encouraged him to launch into new volumes. He
had lost contact with his immediate suppliers of music as well as his outlets. His
two partners in Venice show no signs of commercial contacts in the Marche,[3] and
indeed relations between Venice and Rome were not such as to encourage to a
Venetian printer or bookseller in exploration of the Papal States.[4]

It might be thought that Petrucci, for whom the market was so specialised,
would have had direct contacts with many of his purchasers. The cathedrals and
chapels of the Veneto and surrounding states, as well as the court circles that
welcomed the frottola editions, could have bought directly from Petrucci in Venice. I suspect, however, that Niccolò and Scotto were more likely agents for
selling and distributing Petrucci's books. Further, it is significant how many of
the surviving collections of his books consist wholly or largely of editions published in one or the other city. Once Petrucci had returned to Fossombrone, the
local courts and courtiers may perhaps have bought one hundred copies of a
frottola volume—but there were not that many choral institutions within the area.
Thus, however well Petrucci knew his local contacts from his Venetian days, they
would hardly have promised a commercially viable print-run of liturgical polyphony. Further, the actual record of Petrucci's editions at this stage argues that he
was aware of the problem.

In fact, the commission to print Paulus de Middelburgh's volume, intended
to sway the sitting Lateran Council, could not have come at a more convenient
time. In May 1511, Petrucci had finished the second book of Bossinensis's intabulations—a book that, I suggest, he had decided to print before he left Venice.
The only other music book to appear from his press during the next three years
(in fact, thirty-four months), was the tenth book of frottole, which, following the
citation of Colón, was printed sometime in 1512, and which, I believe, was also
probably the result of planning during the Venetian years. These two books were
not enough to provide an adequate income, to build up commercial contacts
from his new base, or indeed to allow him to keep a competent staff on hand.
Paulus de Middelburgh's decision to publish his *Paulina* with Petrucci was most
opportune.

Paulus was born in 1446 in Middelburg on Walcheren, in the south of the
present-day Netherlands, and studied philosophy, theology, and medicine at the
University in Louvain.[5] After a spell in Middelburg, where he held a canonry, he
taught in Padua during 1477 and 1478 and was called to the chair of mathematics
there in 1479. He visited Urbino and other local towns in 1479 and was established at the Urbino court by 1481, as doctor and later also as astrologer.[6] His
Prognosticon of 1481 calls him "illustrissimi principis Federico, ducis Urbini . . .
physicorum ninimis", and he dedicated a book to the duke in 1486. He also had
the support of the Emperor Maximilian, to whom he dedicated his *Prenostica ad*

vigenti annos of 1484.[7] He returned to Louvain briefly in 1484, but was back in Italy before the end of the following year. He was Abbot of Castel Durante (present-day Urbania) before being translated to the see of Fossombrone, apparently on the recommendation of Maximilian. Appointed to the new see on 30 July 1494 (following the death of Hieronymus de Santuciis of Pavia five days earlier), he remained there until he resigned on 16 December 1524.[8] He died in Rome in 1534. Vernarecci suggests, somewhat implausibly, that he may have procured northerners' music for Petrucci.

Paulus was keenly interested in astrology and published a number of books entitled *Prognosticon*, intended for different years. The book for 1482 was published in 1481 by Ratdolt in Rome, and by Vydenast in Perugia; that for 1523, published by Ruff in Augsburg, also saw an Italian edition, which has been attributed erroneously to Petrucci.[9] Paulus was also an important writer on questions of astronomy and the calendar. He sided with Copernicus in the dispute over the solar system and is mentioned by the scientist in his treatise, *De revolutionibus*, printed in 1543. Among Paulus's studies is a pseudo-scientific exploration, *De numero atomorum totius universi*, published in 1518 by Silber in Rome.[10]

More important are his studies of the calendar, and of its reform, two of which were published by Petrucci. Earlier, in 1511, Paulus had published a tract on the reform of the calendar: his *Parabola Christi de correctione Kalendarii* appeared anonymously but probably from the press of Silber in Rome. This apparently drew the author to the attention of Pope Julius II, although he was already well known as a leading writer on astrological questions. Nearly fifteen years earlier, in his *Responsiones in disputationes Johannes Pici* (Florence, 1498), Lucia Bellanti had referred to the "excellentissimus ille vir Paulus, forosemproniensis episcopus" (f.109r), and his book as the "prognosticum singularis viri Pauli theutonici" (f.94v). Even earlier, Luca Pacioli had referred to Paulus in his *Summa de Aritmetica* (Venice 1494), and other contemporary commentators mentioned his skill as mathematician and astrologer.

Pope Julius II had summoned a council, which sat at San Giovanni in Laterano, as a political maneuver to counteract the Council of Pisa, called by the King of France to put pressure on the pope. The Lateran Council opened on 10 May 1511 and had presented the pope with a strong diplomatic victory before his death. The new pope, Leo X, not particularly interested in the political issues that had originally stimulated the summoning of the council, nonetheless allowed it to continue in session until early in 1517, with its first session under him, the sixth overall, meeting on 27 April 1513. Among the topics to which it now devoted its attention, and which interested Leo X more, was reform of the liturgical calendar, which would eventually lead to the secular calendrical changes associated with the name of Gregory XIII. Paulus must have ensured that the pope knew of his work in this field and perhaps had already sent him a copy of the 1511 *Parabola Christi*. Apparently, he also sent to Leo X parts (perhaps even sheets from the forthcoming edition) of his major work, the *Paulina de recta Paschae*, before it was published by Petrucci, for the volume, dated 8 July 1513, carries the text of a papal breve of 29 April of the same year.[11] Paulus was summoned to Rome, by a breve of 16 February 1514,[12] to advise the Lateran Council on calendar reform, and he attended the ninth session, on 5 May 1514 (continuing to attend until the close of the council in 1517).[13] The pope then established a commission on the subject, with Cardinal Vigerio as its chairman (and Paulus as *de facto* secretary), and wrote to various universities for technical advice. Paulus published two reports during the council's sessions, a *Compendium correctionis Calendarii* (in 1514) and a *Secundum Compendium* (in 1516), both of which have been attributed to the press of Silber in Rome. He also published a second *Parabola Christi* in 1516, by the hand of Petrucci. Paulus is generally held to have been the one scholar most responsible for setting in motion the reforms that followed.[14]

The book for which Paulus is now best known is also his largest work, the *Paulina de recta Paschae*, printed by Petrucci. Technically, the content is complex, for it involves sections in Greek and Hebrew, a number of tables, and additional tabular sections to be printed in two colours. Since both the alphabets and a number of other features (including the folio format) were new to Petrucci, he would have needed to prepare his shop and expand his resources before commencing work. The resulting book is a most elegant volume, often cited as among the most stylish of early-sixteenth-century Italy. It uses a new text font and new decorative elements. It is significant, therefore, that one of the best-known typecutters in Italy, Francesco Griffo, resided in Fossombrone during late 1511 and much of 1512.

Griffo is an important figure in the history of the printed book, albeit one whose life and even identity are still obscure. Indeed, in assigning the name Griffo to the typecutter under discussion, I am perhaps going further than some scholars would wish. Lowry rightly points out that the evidence that Griffo was the surname of Francesco da Bologna, the man under discussion, is only circumstantial.[15] Francesco had worked for Aldus Manutius at the turn of the century, and Aldus himself praised his work in the edition of Virgil published in 1501, which introduced the first italic font.[16] Soncino reported in 1503 that he had hired Francesco from Aldus, and also praised his types. The reference appears in the dedication of his famous edition of Petrarch (published in Fano), addressed to Cesare Borgia, and is worth quoting here for the light it throws on Francesco:

> Per el che essendo stato da sua .R.S. benignamente exaudito; ho voluto observare quanto da me era stato promesso. E per mia exhortatione non solo sonno venuti quivi li compositori tanto notabili, et sufficienti, quanto sia possibile adire; ma anchora un nobilissimo sculptore de littere latine, graece, et hebraice, chiamato .M. Francesco. da Bologna. l'ingeno del quale certamente credo che in tale exercitio non troue unaltro equale. Perche non solo le usitate stampe perfectamente sa fare: ma etiam ha excogitato una nova forma de littera dicta cursiva, o vero cancellaresca, de la quale non Aldo Romano, ne altri che astutamente hanno tentato de le altrui penne adornarse. Ma esso .M. Francesco è stato primo inventore et designatore. el quale e tucte le forme de littere che mai habbia stampato dicto Aldo ha intagliato, e la praesente forma. con tanta gratia e venustate, quanta facilmente in essa se comprende.[17]

The evidence here that Soncino brought in his compositors from outside Fano is not surprising, given the known mobility of printers and printing establishments during the period. Nor is it surprising that a type designer and type-founder would have to follow an itinerant career, for even Venice would be unlikely to keep him fully employed. But Francesco is given an outstanding en-comium. (The implication of dishonesty on Aldus's part is touched on below.) Despite this, he largely disappears from our view for several years hereafter. By 1516 he was printing for himself in Bologna, but he produced few titles[18] and was dead by 1519, probably executed as a result of murdering his son-in-law.

In 1512 Griffo is thought to have been working for Soncino again, but had recently worked for the Venetian printer Bernardo Stagnino and was resident at that time in Fossombrone.[19] He seems to have been in Fossombrone by the first of October 1511 and to have been there still in August of the following year. Stagnino sent payment to him via a bookseller and a printer in Perugia, and Francesco was required to attest through a notary that he had received it.

There can be little doubt that Francesco, who evidently had acquired con-siderable fame within the profession (at least), would spend much of a year in a small city in the Marche only if there were some professional contact or advantage. It is not surprising, therefore, that Petrucci's major work for Paulus de Middel-burgh, appearing only months after the last reference to Francesco's residence in Fossombrone, should show new typefaces of great elegance. The *Paulina* also uses new initial letters of a decorative floral style, and new woodblock borders that recall closely the style found in Venetian editions of the time. If these were also the work of Francesco, as is quite feasible, then he ceases to be merely a type-designer and punch-cutter. The initials (which may in any case have lain within the normal province of a type-designer) are well-balanced letters with floral spray-work within frames. In the same way, the work on the decorative borders is of a very high order, using elegantly balanced criblé grounds. The only slightly weaker element is the full-page block of Paulus's vision of the crucifixion. This image, which betrays an old-fashioned approach to construction and some crude-ness of drawing, is in a completely different style and is surely the work of a different craftsman.

Since all these elements were new to Petrucci and since Soncino had also produced a number of books with exceptionally beautiful borders and well-balanced typography, it is reasonable to see the hand of Francesco in the other new elements of this book.[20] Indeed, this seems the only valid reason, apart from a possible close friendship, for Francesco to have spent at least ten months in Fossombrone.[21]

Apparently, Petrucci had enough influence to attract Francesco to Fossom-brone. True, the designer may have been willing enough to take any work, and Paulus may have been willing to act as a particularly generous patron. There is, however, another possibility. Francesco had been in Venice and working as a type-designer and -cutter during the very years when Petrucci was preparing to set up shop, between the grant of his privilege in 1498 and the appearance of his first edition in 1501. Petrucci's first sets of initials are again elegantly designed, with pleasing asymmetries and exceptional control of density: a number of them, in particular, one form of "S", also show considerable flair in their conception. It is tempting to speculate that Francesco had worked for Petrucci in those first years, while preparing his initial letters and perhaps also his musical type.

If this seems merely fanciful, there is one piece of possibly relevant evidence. As discussed in chapter 3, Petrucci's music types rely heavily on kerned sorts, and on the careful nesting together of several different sorts—in his case, usually of notes whose tails could overlay the small spacing sorts used to give them the correct pitch on the stave. Significantly, although kerned fonts can be shown to have existed before 1500, Francesco seems to have resolved the problems of printing Greek for Aldus Manutius by just the same process, placing the accents and breathings on kerned sorts, so that they could hang over the top of the sorts holding the actual letters, bringing the two closer together and making the font much more legible. Aldus, in a privilege supplication of 14 October 1502, specifically mentions kerned sorts.[22]

That application must have been made shortly after Griffo left Aldus and Venice to work for Soncino. It has been suggested that Aldus tried, in his supplication and elsewhere, to take the credit for a method of creating a usable Greek font that was actually the invention of Griffo.[23] If so, it seems at least possible that Francesco Griffo also had something to do with the creation of Petrucci's music font, and perhaps also his set of initials. In his petition, Petrucci claimed that the invention was his; perhaps Francesco who realised its execution and then turned the idea to use in a Greek font. It certainly explains why Francesco should have been willing to spend so long in Fossombrone, working for a former colleague, producing material for a printer who must have seemed, if not dormant, at least no longer very active.

If Francisco Griffo did indeed design the ornamental blocks for Paulus's book, that should not surprise us. The bishop would have wanted this volume to be as attractive as possible, to impress the pope and Council with its appearance as much as its content. He must have begun work on it immediately after publishing his first *Parabola Christi* in 1511, intending it to be a more comprehensive statement.[24] Although Paulus could not have foreseen that, only two years later, a new pope, Leo X, would launch an active consideration of calendar reform and the dating of Easter, he found himself ideally positioned to take advantage of that interest. As a provincial bishop now in his mid-sixties, Paulus must have felt that this was perhaps his last chance for promotion to a more lucrative and significant see, perhaps even to the cardinalate.

Little over a month after Leo's election, therefore, Paulus wrote to him, apparently sending copies of parts of his new book and seeking a privilege for its publication. The book must have been already at press by the time Paulus received the papal breve and privilege (dated 29 April 1513), for it appeared on 8 July. The result was the call to Paulus to attend the Lateran Council.

Paulus must have planned from the beginning (in 1511) how to make the *Paulina* an elegant, well-produced volume. As was customary, he would have supplied the paper and probably met other costs.[25] Without such support, a book of this type would have been a very large venture for a small printer in a small city. Someone would have paid Francesco, as well as the type-founder, not only for the Roman font, but also for a small range of Hebrew (cut in woodblocks), and a font of Greek, with a number of special characters. Petrucci had to have the blocks cut, and to lay in the large stock of good quality paper. Further, the complexity of some parts of the book meant that typesetting was far from straightforward. Finally, Petrucci was evidently expected to give the book a careful proof-reading, and to correct it thoroughly.[26]

This operation was on a much larger scale than that involved in Petrucci's normal musical volumes. In addition to the complexity and detail of the text, the book's size required a much greater commitment: it took 396 folios, using twelve times as much paper for each copy as did the average sixty-four quarto leaves of a music book. It is reasonable to assume that Petrucci hired additional men to prepare the book, even though it may have been several months at press. Finally, the proofreading was indeed thorough: a number of corrections were made, or listed in the errata leaf at the end of the volume; part of a word, omitted at the end of A8*v*, was stamped in each copy; and a cancel leaf survives in a number of copies. The complaint that the reader, Hieronimus Posthumus, had printed at the end of the volume is well known. It accuses an "ethiop" chalcographer of being responsible for a great number of typographical errors in the text.[27]

Once printing began, however, Petrucci would have faced few new problems. Books in folio, with the large font used here, were among the most common ranges of work faced by his contemporaries, and the craftsmen he hired should have been experienced in the format. The two-colour printing would also not have caused any difficulty, although the procedure was different from that used in the double-impression music books. Here, there are no overlaps of content, and the type for both impressions was imposed in the same forme, printed with the aid of special friskets. The only tedious part probably lay in the many pages containing lengthy tables—and indeed the poor vertical alignment of columns is one of the very few weak aspects of the volume.

Paulus must have been satisfied, for he returned to Petrucci in 1516 for another book; some members of the Lateran Council were also satisfied, perhaps even impressed, for they did add Paulus to their number and brought him closer to the center of church influence; they seem to have preferred his arguments to those of his rival Petrus de Rivo (whom he attacked in his treatise). Finally, Petrucci was probably satisfied, with both the impressive result and the evident fact that he could not have been left out of pocket.

Baldassare Castiglione: *Ad Henricum* . . .
Epistola, 29 July 1513

As he reached the last stages in the production of the *Paulina*, Petrucci must have had to look around for new work. He could have laid off his craftsmen, but he would then have had no return on his other investments, in type fonts, for example; in addition, these men were clearly well qualified, and, although there was always a large itinerant population of printers in Italy, additional work would be to Petrucci's benefit. Further, he evidently had some paper left over. Thus, it was fortunate that Castiglione's text was available to be printed. It would make a short pamphlet, easy to sell and probably profitable.

Castiglione was of course an important member of the Urbino court circle; during the years 1513–15, he was ambassador to the court at Rome for Duke Francesco Maria I della Rovere, who had ascended to the duchy in 1508. In earlier years he had been confidante and ambassador for the previous duke, Gui-dobaldo Montefeltro. Indeed, Castiglione had been chosen by Guidobaldo to go to England in 1506, to receive from Henry VIII the insignia of the Order of the Garter, as proxy for the duke. Castiglione claimed to have begun writing *Il Cortegiano* (which he set at the same court of Urbino) in 1508, following the death of his patron, and to have worked on it for ten years, although it would not be published until another ten years had passed.[28]

It seems probable that the *Epistola* published by Petrucci was a preliminary work,[29] not so much a sketch for *Il Cortegiano*, as a self-sufficient panegyric that inspired the greater work. Its text seems to have been written soon after the death of the duke in 1508, and the extant dedication copy was written and decorated by the Urbino scribe Federico Veterani.[30] There is some evidence to suggest that Castiglione intended the work for Henry VIII from the beginning, and the il-lumination of the dedication page in the autograph supports this.

How the text came into Petrucci's hands is not clear. I think it is improbable that Castiglione himself promoted the edition. Apart from the probability that he was already working on the larger volume, he would surely have gone to a printer in a more significant center, in all likelihood Venice, and would not have allowed the printer to include a preface such as that contributed by Petrucci. It is possible that Paulus was the conduit: he was newly in Rome, where Castiglione was already based, and they would have known each other from earlier days at the Urbino court. However, there is no reference to Paulus anywhere in the printed edition, and Petrucci's letter to the reader would have been an ideal place to acknowledge his patron's assistance. Perhaps, equally implausibly, Bembo sug-gested the project; Castiglione was apparently close enough to Bembo to show him drafts of *Il Cortegiano*, and the latter was one of those who urged its publi-cation. It is more probable that a member of the Urbino or Fossombrone aris-tocracy promoted the edition; if so, the most likely names are those of Biagio Benverardo of Urbino or Cristoforo Piero Gigas of Fossombrone. The former wrote a valedictory epistle at the end of the *Paulina*, but is not otherwise known; the latter appears in both the *Paulina* and Castiglione's *Epistola*, and also in Spi-nacino's first book of 1507. In 1514 he was recorded in the acts of Fossombrone as "magister ludi litterarij",[31] and was probably familiar with both Castiglione's and Petrucci's circles; it is possible that he would have suggested this work to Petrucci and then written the laudatory epistle. The book may even have been timed to coincide with Castiglione's departure from Urbino in 1513 as the ducal ambassador to Rome.[32]

Indeed, the timing of this edition was of the greatest value to Petrucci. It provided some immediate employment for his men, following the publication of Paulus's book, and it also must have given him additional direct return for the investment in type fonts and materials. Even more conveniently, he was evidently able to use some of the paper stock that had been bought for the larger volume. The shortness of Castiglione's text, the great savings resulting from using paper already in hand (and probably paid for by Paulus), and from continuing work directly after the *Paulina*, coupled with a probable guaranteed sale within the Duchy of Urbino (and perhaps also in Rome), all must have made the *Epistola* a well-nigh irresistible project. It resulted in a small quarto volume of only sixteen folios, presenting a consistent face to the reader, with a regular number of lines to the page, good typesetting, and a good balance between text and white space. Petrucci need not have regarded it as anything special (indeed, the lack of decoration suggests that he did not), but it is an exemplary model of the better work turned out by many of the best printers of the time, in a number of different centers.

It seems that Petrucci's occupation with non-musical printing for so many months was enough by itself to induce him to return to music printing. Apparently, as the Castiglione edition left the press, Petrucci still had no musical volumes planned; there is a gap of seven months before the first such—the third book of Josquin's masses, published in 1514. However, he still had all his material, and a group of trained craftsmen, and his new privilege from Leo X is dated two months after the *Epistola* had appeared. As I suggested earlier, this new privilege of 1513 seems to have caused Antico some concern (given the wording of the latter's 1516 privilege). The grants from the pope distinguish the two printers, name both, and refer to specific repertoires. But, equally certainly, Petrucci's privilege seeks to draw lines between his activity and that of Antico, as if to allow both to continue working. It is hard to see Petrucci's privilege, or his return to music printing, as a response to the possibility of Antico monopolizing the market. To the extent that this may be true, therefore, we can see the combination of a large and lavish commission—from Paulus—and a subsequent small and more profitable volume— by Castiglione—as encouraging Petrucci to use the materials at hand and to turn again to publishing music.

Paulus de Middelburgh: *Parabola Christi*, 20 November 1516

The burst of editions that followed the resumption of musical work with Josquin's third book in 1514 lasted for no more than two years. From May 1516, for three years, Petrucci dated no new musical editions. In fact, as the bibliographical analyses make clear, he did continue to print music, but concealed each new edition under an earlier date. I have already argued (in chapter 1) that this habit was a reflection of a sense of political insecurity that Petrucci probably shared with many within the Duchy of Urbino. It is significant, therefore that the one book correctly dated within these three years is not musical in content and does not carry the name of the city Fossombrone in its colophon.

Paulus was doing well. He was apparently secretary to the papal Commission on reforming the church calendar, he was in the process of publishing his second report of the commission's deliberations, and he could see a successful future for his proposals. The two official reports from the commission were both printed in Rome, probably from the press of Silber, as would be expected. Significantly, however, Paulus returned to Petrucci for the edition of his own text, which suggests that Paulus had been well pleased with the edition of his *Paulina*; it is just as likely that the commission's reports were paid for out of the council's funds, while Paulus would have had to find his own money for his own book. In addition, Petrucci's labor costs would surely have been lower.

While the bishop was secure in the favour of the present Pope, and therefore perhaps not in any danger, this could hardly be said of Petrucci. Personally, his position appeared secure: less than three months earlier (on 7 September 1516), while serving as Anziano, he had been chosen by the Fossombrone city council as one of three citizens bringing congratulations to Lorenzo de' Medici as he assumed the Duchy of Urbino. Vernarecci records that Petrucci was cited as "già commendato dal Pontefice Leone X".[33] The vote to send a delegation was however a close one, and Fossombrone itself seems to have been regarded as antipathetic to the new duke. Indeed, most cities in the duchy were,[34] but Fossombrone was also the site of a crucial bridge crossing the Metauro. The chance to print a book relevant to the deliberations of the Lateran Council was therefore opportune.

For Petrucci, it was also convenient. He could keep his press active and ensure a financial return in an overt manner. However, given the state of the Duchy, it is perhaps not surprising that Petrucci's colophon should read: "Impressum per Octavianum petrutium habita licentia a deputatis iuxta decretum lateranensis concilii".

The book itself is very similar to Castiglione's *Epistola*, though even shorter and simpler. It uses the same font (prepared for the *Paulina*) on its twelve folios, and also one of the initials cut for that volume. It has no laudatory epistle, but a simple dedication from Paulus to the pope. Like the earlier book, it is neatly executed and stylish within the limited conventions of its genre.

Hippocrates: *Opera*, 1 January 1519

More significant is a project, mentioned earlier, that does not seem to have come to fruition. Among the rich treasures of Renaissance scholarship in the Vatican libraries there is a translation of the works of Hippocrates, made by a significant member of the Roman intellectual élite, Marco Fabio Calvo, and written in his hand.[35] This manuscript, Vat.lat.4416, was apparently given to the Vatican library by its author and scribe in 1526.[36] It carries the following inscription, also in Calvo's hand, on folio 2r, beneath a pasteover:

> Hoc in operis fine imprimatur
> Fabius Calvus civis ravennis Qui hoc hippocratis opus latinitate donavit ac Manens leontinus physicus civis fluentinus, qui sua pecunia ut per octavium petrucium forosemproniensis ex solertissimis impressoribus non postremum imprimendum curavit. Ex urbium principe Roma legendum omnibus latinum Hippocratem emiserunt Mox et graecum Daturi Deo optimo maximo Favente Die vero Ianuarij primo Millesimo quingentesimo ac insuper Decimo Nono.

The evidence of this document is that there was a plan to print the translation, and that Calvo expected the plan to be fulfilled; the wording also suggests that the text was ready to print before the inscription was entered. In the manuscript, Calvo dates various parts of the translation between 1510 and 1515, although the document itself is probably later. He also in effect says that a printer's copy was ready, when reporting that Manente Leontini had paid Petrucci to print it. In fact, however, the book seems not to have been printed.

There had been a contract, involving at least Petrucci and Leontini. On 19 August of the previous year, Petrucci had attended Lorenzo de' Medici's palace in Rome to lodge a complaint against Leontini. Petrucci brought with him two "character witnesses", Barnabo Pontio and Francesco "de Bono Laicis" in the diocese of Piacenza, and swore his complaint before a notary, Bartolomeo Benivolo, himself a citizen of Fossombrone.[37] Petrucci's complaint, that he had sought Leontini at his normal residence in Lorenzo's palace, and that he had not found him, continues with the lament that he therefore could not move to print the edition, with a resulting great inconvenience and loss of money. (This point is probably entirely valid; the sack of Fossombrone would almost certainly have involved the destruction of Petrucci's shop, and the prospect of a large and well-financed volume—one on the level of Paulus's *Paulina*—would have encouraged Petrucci to make the considerable investment of setting up again.[38]) Finally, Petrucci demanded the penalties laid out in the original contract, which are not here specified.

Leontini was a member of Lorenzo's household, and probably his personal physician. He may be the Manente di Ugolino di Manente who matriculated in medicine in 1507 and is certainly the man cited in a number of letters from or about Lorenzo, not only as his physician but also as familiar with his political designs.[39] The doctor was called from Rome to Florence in late 1518 when Lorenzo caught his final illness, which explains his absence when Petrucci sought him out.

Leontini himself was interested in the text of Hippocrates. In 1517 he had borrowed a Greek text from the Vatican library and (probably during the next two years) made a Latin translation of the *Epidemie*.[40] Apparently, this translation was itself highly regarded, for a copy was made, illuminated by Boccardi, and presented to Leo X.[41]

Just what the relationship with Calvo's work was has not been determined. Calvo claims priority of translation, by dating sections of his work in the early years of the decade. He went on to make a translation of Galen's commentary on the *Epidemie*, which he dated between 1516 and 1518.[42] Leontini's translation of the *Epidemie* was presumably not finished, at least, until some time after he borrowed the Vatican's Greek manuscript. In his dedication copy, he asserts that it is his first work of the sort, adding that he intends to continue and translate Galen's commentary.

It seems to me likely that Calvo's work was indeed finished before 1518, that the original contract was probably signed at least a year before Petrucci's complaint, that is, in the first half of 1517. That contract may have been for the complete translation of Hippocrates, and not merely for the *Epidemie*. Leontini perhaps borrowed the Vatican manuscript to check on Calvo's work, or even to edit it for publication. If it were not for the existence of Leontini's own manuscript, we could believe that the problem merely lay in a slow rate of progress on Leontini's part, perhaps exacerbated by Lorenzo de' Medici's illnesses. However, the presence of a dedicatory manuscript of Leontini's translation, coupled with his promise to translate the commentary of Galen, tends to suggest a more sinister motive for the problem: it looks as though Leontini had decided that he could do scholarly work as well as Calvo could, and so delayed the publication. There is additional support for this view: on 15 April 1519, the Venetian Senate considered an unusual request. The Apostolic Legate in Venice, acting on letters received from Lorenzo de' Medici, requested the Senate to issue a privilege to Manente, that no one else in Venice could print the translation of Hippocrates made by Fabio Calvo. The senate co-operated, adding the rider that Manente should himself print the book, in Venice.[43]

Perhaps it is no coincidence that Calvo's edition did not see print at all until 1525, when it appeared as *Hippocratis coi Medicorum omnium*.[44] This text, which was printed by Francesco Minizio Calvo,[45] was not the only publication with which Calvo had problems. Nor was it his only contact with Fossombronese craftsmen. In 1527 he published his *Antiquae urbis Romae cum regionibus simulacrum*, a series of plans of Rome in the time of Pliny, indicating its classical layout and the sites of the major monuments. This volume, whose publishing history was complicated in part by the Sack of Rome, was apparently produced as part of Raphael's plan to restore the glories of ancient Rome. The artist had persuaded Calvo to undertake a translation of Vitruvius into Italian, and to work with Fulvio on the topography of the classical city. Calvo's eventual contribution was this volume, comprising a series of large woodblocks, with brief supporting text. Each block was cut by Ptolomeo Egnatio, a chancery scribe in the papal curia, another citizen of Fossombrone and associate of Petrucci. The edition was printed by Ludovico Arrighi Vicentino, himself a chancery scribe, and best known as the writer and publisher of the writing book, *La Operina*, which appeared in 1522, and *Il modo de temperare le penne* of the following year.[46] He probably also designed the lettering and layout of the *Simulacrum* of Calvo.

This latter volume also has another point of interest for music historians. The first printing was presumably largely lost in the Sack of 1527. When the book was reprinted, in 1532, it was printed by Blado and published by Valerio Dorico.[47] Thus, coincidentally, Calvo provides a link between Petrucci and Dorico, a link which can probably be paralleled, as I argue in a later chapter, by those of the printers and their craftsmen.

The Hippocrates text would, like Paulus's *Paulina*, have resulted in a large and expensive book. Petrucci apparently still had the necessary typefaces (and probably a series of borders) surviving from the earlier edition, and he no doubt also had the men standing by. The book would therefore have served a similar function to that of the *Paulina*, in furthering Petrucci's career. It did provide him with an incentive to use both materials and men, and apparently encouraged him to return to the repertoire that he had made his specialty. The date of the first musical edition, June 1519, suggests that Petrucci waited a little longer than necessary before abandoning the translation project. With a press set up and music type that evidently survived the Sack of Fossombrone, it would not have taken him six months to prepare a musical volume. Productivity at Fossombrone was slower than it had been in Venice, but he had produced a volume in about three months more than once and was about to print the fourth volume of *Motetti de la Corona* considerably faster. Thus it seems likely that he did not move on the first musical book of 1519 until after the New Year.

It may be more significant that he waited until after the death of Lorenzo de'Medici, in 1519. Although Petrucci had represented Fossombrone in Rome and had acquired a professional reputation among the circle of the Urbinese usurper, he seems (like his city) to have remained loyal to the rightful duke. This statement does not conflict with the evidence (discussed in chapter 9) that much of the repertoire for these last volumes came from Rome (or Florence). Given the location of Fossombrone, and the decline of music in Ferrara, that would almost be inevitable, whatever the printer's political affiliations.

It is apparent that all four planned non-musical books served important functions in Petrucci's career. Each evidently helped to keep his craftsmen employed, and both the first and the last seem to have acted as direct stimuli, encouraging Petrucci to return to music printing. The two smaller volumes filled important economic niches at crucial times. The books also serve important functions in our view of Petrucci's career, his repertorial contacts, and his outlets. They direct our eyes away from Venice and northern Italy, toward Rome and its contacts with Florence. It is now time, having examined the nature of Petrucci's books (musical and non-musical), to turn to their contacts and presentation, to explore Petrucci's view of his market, and its interests and taste—in both music and the style of books.

Notes

1. Given the extent of interest in incunabula, and the descriptions, catalogues, and library inventories that have appeared, this is inevitable.

2. Roman printers did not, it seems, match the quality of work regularly achieved by the best Venetian presses. Barberi, in his study of the major Roman printer, Stephan Guillery, working during the same period as Petrucci, remarked that standards improved in the third decade of the century, with the work of Giacomo Mazzocchi. (See his "Stefano Guillery", pp. 18–20 of the reprint.) Several commentators make the point that Roman production was much more limited in scope, with an emphasis on official documents and works of interest to the Curia, expanding into anti-Lutheran tracts. In addition to Barberi's work, see Ascarelli, *Annali*; Blasio, "Privilegi"; Norton, *Italian*; Rhodes, "Further notes"; and (for an up-to-date view of the types of books published in Rome) *Le Cinquecentine Romane*. An invaluable collection of material relating to later in the century can be found in Masetti-Zannini, *Stampatori*. The literature on early music printers and publishers in Rome is cited elsewhere in this volume. Among the extensive literature on fifteenth-century Roman printing, reference should be made to Concetta et al., *Scrittura*.

3. The Scotto family did, of course, have contacts with other parts of Italy, in particular with Florence, but there is no sign of any significant interest in the eastern coast of Italy.

4. The political details that lead easily to such an observation when discussing Petrucci's reasons for returning to Fossombrone are outlined in chapter 1.

5. For details of Paulus's life, see Baldi, *Vita*; Gams, *Series*, p. 698; *Hierarchia*, ii, p. 172 and iii, p. 214; Marzi, *Questione*, pp. 39–52; and Struik, "Paulus". An autograph copy of Baldi's collection of lives of mathematicians that contains this *Vita*, and that served as the basis for Marzi's edition, was at one time in the collection of Baldassare Boncompagni. See Narducci, *Catalogo*, Nos.63 and 65. The latter is apparently a copy, while a third copy, entered at No.66 in that catalogue, seems not to have Paulus's biography included.

6. His name appears in the late copy of a list of Federigo's court "family", now in GB-Lbl Add.Ms.22027, 131r–36r. Vespasiano di Bisticci stated, in his *Vita di uomine illustri*, that Paulus taught mathematics to the duke.

The most complete list of Paulus's publications known to me is in Vernarecci, *Petrucci*, pp. 121–24. There has been some disagreement about a number of his publications over the years; one, which has been wrongly attributed to Petrucci's press, is discussed later in this book. Others are discussed elsewhere, for example, in Moranti and Moranti, "Arte", pp. 1–5.

7. Charles Parron, the Italian astrologer to Henry VII, "criticized a fellow-astrologer, Paul of Middelburg, for making the pope and emperor, who were Paul's patrons, superior to the influence of the stars" (Armstrong, "Astrology", p. 450).

8. The date is taken from Gams, *Series*, p. 698. Paulus's own successor was Joannes Guidiccioni, elevated on 18 December 1524. However, Marzi, *Questione*, p. 48, fn.3, questions the succession, stating that Paulus continued to receive concessions calling him bishop, until November of 1534.

9. The evidence for this assertion is advanced in the chapter on "Ghosts".

10. Manuscript copies of Paulus's writings, sent to Popes Innocent VIII and Leo X, survive in the Vatican libraries, as Vat.Lat.3684, Vat.Lat.7046, and Ottob.Lat.370. A treatise by him on algebra is extant in I-Ma Q.72.sup.s.XVI. He also owned a collection of medical recipes, which is now GB-Lbl Sloane Ms.981.

11. See the bibliography of this volume, below, for the text, and chapter 20 for the letter accompanying the breve, signed by Bembo. Note that there are manuscripts copies of parts of this book, now in the Vatican library and cited in Kristeller, *Iter*.

12. Cited in Hergenroether, *Leonis*, No.6851, and found in I-Rvat Vat.ms.3364, f.142v. Reprinted in Bembo, *Opere*, vii, p. 56, No.18.

13. The details of Paulus's attendance at the council can be found in Labbei and Cossarti, *Concilia*, passim.

14. For details of the council, see Hefele, *Conciles*, vii, pp. 445–51, and Kaltenbrunner, *Vorgeschichte*, passim. Further details appear in Creighton, *Papacy*, v, pp. 170–270. Paulus's role in the council is described in Baldi, *Vita*, while the history of the debate on reforming the calendar is outlined in Marzi, *Questione*. Significantly, the discussions on the calendar do not appear in the acts of the council, published as *Sanctum Lateranense Concilium novissimum* (Rome: Mazzocchi, 1521). Marzi suggests (*Questione*, p. 72) that, since the acts are in any case incomplete, there may have been strong disagreement over the proposals for reform, and that all the discussions may have taken place outside the principal sessions, in the committee headed by Cardinal Vigerio. The second reason seems more likely.

Paulus's first *Compendium* includes, at the end, a *Primo Sommario*, which he had earlier prepared for submission to the council. It contains fourteen different heads on the correction of the calendar. It was criticised in Antonio Dolciati's *De Kalendario correctione* (I-Fl, Med.Laur.II, pl.XXIX), which was submitted to Leo X on 13 December 1514 and is discussed in Marzi, *Questione*, pp. 112–23. Marzi also lists other criticisms of Paulus's draft proposals. After the tenth session of the council (which met in May of 1515), Paulus prepared a *Secondo Sommario*, which is similarly printed in his *Secundum Compendium* of 1516. These probably acted as official documents, perhaps paid for from Vatican funds, which would explain why they were printed in Rome.

15. Lowry, *World*, pp. 87–88. Lowry presents the basic evidence for the various identifications, and for Francesco's life, although he appears to be unaware of the typecutter's sojourn in Fossombrone. His study is particularly valuable in stressing the importance of Francesco's work for Aldus Manutius, in suggesting that Francesco was probably more than just a commissioned freelance craftsman where Aldus was concerned, and in drawing the lines of Francesco's contribution to both the success of Aldus's editions and the development of typefaces at the end of the fifteenth century. There is a large literature on the actual name and biography of Francesco, much of it from the last century. It is outlined in Manzoni, "Francesco"; Rossi, "Ultima"; Sorbelli, "Mago"; Sorbelli, *Storia*, pp. 91–94; Norton, *Italian*, pp. 8–10; Mardersteig, "Aldo"; Scholderer, *Greek*, pp. 6–7. A very synoptic view of Francesco's activities as type designer can be found in Funke, *Buchkunde*, pp. 41 and 46.

There is an additional detail that may have bearing on Francesco's life and name. Among the records of the Venetian *zecca* (or mint) are several references to two men called Griffo or Grypho. One, Sylvester, apparently became a master punch-maker or "stampatore" active by 1490 and called "ex principali*um* ma*gister*is stampar*um*" in July 1499 (ASV, Capo dei Consiglio de' Dieci, Notatorio, Reg.1 and 2, passim). There are other references to members of a Griffo family in the same archive, which includes *ex gratia* payments to state employees (among them one Hieronymo Griffo) and the grant of a pension in 1498 to the daughter of a Francesco Griffo, whom it is tempting to associate with the Franciscus de Bononia commissioned in 1475 to copy two fonts of Jensen. The same file, in its references to the *zecca*, seems to document connections between Venetian printers and the craft skills required in the mint, but does not indicate why either Francesco of Bologna should be associated with the name Griffo.

16. In grammatoglypta laudem.

> Qui Graiis dedit Aldus, en Latinis
> dat nunc grammata sculpta Daedaleis
> Francisci manibus Bononiensis.

The text is quoted in Renouard, *Annales*, p. 380; also in Orlandi, *Aldo*, i, p. 49, with a reproduction as plate 5, opposite p. xxxii. Griffo referred to cutting type for Aldus in the preface to his own edition of Petrarch's *Canzoniere et triomphi*, published in Bologna in 1516. A discussion of the Aldine italic font and its sources can be found in Barker, *Aldus*, pp. 109–16.

17. Taken from Manzoni, *Annali*, pt.2, i, pp. 27–28. "And with my encouragement there came here [to Fano] not only the most notable and competent typesetters that it was possible to attract; but also a very great type designer for latin, greek and hebrew, called M. Francesco da Bologna, of whose skill in this craft I truly believe one could not find an equal. Because not only does he know how to make the more usual sorts perfectly, but also has devised a new style of letter, called cursive or cancellaresca, which neither Aldus nor any other who tried to create with their own pens [= skill]. But this M. Francesco is the first creator and designer of it, and has cut the shapes of all its letters (never yet printed by the same Aldus), with such grace and beauty".

18. Among the books are one or two famous titles: in addition to the edition of Petrarch cited in fn.16, he printed Bembo's *Gli Asolani* and Sannazaro's *Archadia*, also in 1516. Each of these seems to be in small octavo format.

19. Vernarecci, *Petrucci*, p. 128, fn., gives the relevant extracts.

20. I do not wish to imply that Francesco cut the woodblocks himself. Indeed, that would seem to be very unlikely. I suppose him to have acted strictly as designer and as punch-cutter, but that the act of design included constructing the initials and the borders, which were later cut from his designs by someone else, for whom we can supply no name, but for whom we would have to look among the woodblock cutters of the Marche. Further, it seems likely that this cutter was also the artist of the Crucifixion scene.

21. In fact, Griffo cannot have cut all the blocks at that time. One block displays the device of Pope Leo X and must therefore postdate Leo's election in 1513. It is possible that this was a later addition. The block appears by itself, on folio a1*v*, below the privilege, and then again on a2*r*, as the lowest of four units. The other three units, however, are repeated elsewhere in conjunction with the arms of Paulus himself and of Maximilian. Thus we could plausibly argue that the Leonine arms were only cut after Leo ascended the papal throne, and as a replacement for another block, perhaps the arms of Leo's predecessor, Julius II.

That being so, it is tempting to push the speculation further. One line of thought argues that a craftsman who could also act as artist must surely have illustrated other books before he prepared the blocks for Petrucci's editions. I know of no such books, nor have I come across references to a signature or set of initials that might refer to Francesco. However, this is an avenue that lies outside the scope of the present study.

22. See Fulin, "Documenti", item 127.

23. Barker, *Aldus*, is a detailed discussion of the manuscript roots of Aldus's various Greek types and argues that Griffo did cut each font. Although it has also been assumed that Griffo was responsible for the italic type that more than any other typeface is now associated with Aldus, some scholars believe that other influences were at work here. Wardrop, *Script*, argues

that the scribe San Vito was possibly the inspiration (and even the designer) of this first italic font, while Barker, *Aldus*, leans toward Aldus himself.

24. The book was at least as old-fashioned in its methods as were the prognosticons: its manner was fast becoming obsolete in its dependence on medieval authority, and it displays an obsessive attention to detail, for example, in the manner in which it presents charts of the dates for Easter for centuries to come.

25. Jane Bernstein has discussed the extent to which musical books were subsidised in a similar manner: see Bernstein, "Financial", and Bernstein, *Venetian*.

26. It is unfortunate that no contracts exist for this volume. Even after the bishop had paid for a large part of the outlay, Petrucci would have had to meet salaries and other costs, from whatever payments the bishop made to him. In return, Paulus would have received at least the major proportion of the printed copies, and Petrucci might have been faced with small return after the bishop's payments.

27. It is possible, given the high level of other aspects of the book, that there was a rush at the end of production, in order to have it ready before the bishop could lose his chance of influencing the council.

28. Castiglione's manuscript survives in I-Fl, and the earliest edition appeared from Aldus's press in 1528. There is a point in the fourth book of *Il Cortegiano* where the author makes Ottavio Fregoso remark that Castiglione writes from England in praise of Henry VIII and promises to tell more on his return, thereby setting the scene in 1506.

29. See Michelini Tocci, "Manoscritto", p. 274, quoting Cian as calling the *Epistola* "quasi il necessario preludio". A further discussion of the evolution of the later book is Ghinassi, "Fasi".

30. See Michelini Tocci, "Manoscritto", p. 274, for a discussion of the origins of this text and a description of the manuscript. In his first paragraph, the author refers to Giovanni Mardersteig, who "studiava con amorosa acutezza le particolarità dei caratteri tipografici usati da Ottaviano Petrucci". Mardersteig's study, unfortunately, does not seem to have been published.

31. ANF, Atti de' Consigli Municipali, 1513–20, 16r, dated 26 February 1514. Gigas's own letters and songs are collected in I-PApal Pal.555, ff.415–505, with another in I-VEcap CCLVII, 270r–v, dedicated to Domitius Calderinus (Kristeller, *Iter*, ii, pp. 36 and 296). One Girolamo Giganti was apparently also from Fossombrone and served as a criminalist and consulting lawyer to the Council of Ten in Venice during the 1520s. He may also have been the man who wrote *Tractatus de residentia episcoporum* (Venice: Bascarini, 1548). See Vernarecci, *Petrucci*, p. 218.

32. However, Castiglione was apparently back in Urbino in late September, for Cardinal Bibbiena wrote to him there. See Bibbiena, *Epistolario*, ii, pp. 7–8.

33. Vernarecci, *Petrucci*, p. 160. Papal awareness of Petrucci may not have been so much from his printing of the *Paulina*, but more from his diplomatic visits to Rome.

34. Gubbio may have been an exception. See the details given in Mazzatinti, "Gubbio", pp. 89–95.

35. The manuscript was discussed, and much of the following evidence first presented, in Campana, "Manente". Many more details are available in Mercati, "Notizie".

36. So says a dedicatory letter in the manuscript. Other manuscripts of Hippocrates owned by Calvo came to the Vatican after his death, as gifts of his nephew, Timotheo Calvo. These include Vat.gr.278, the autograph for Calvo's translation, also in his hand, and dated 24 July 1512, which is discussed in Mercati, "Notizie", pp. 68 and 70.

37. The document was published in Vernarecci, *Petrucci*, p. 192, fn., and in Campana, "Leontini", pp. 514–15. The location given there, the Roman Archivio Urbano, lib.inst.xxxviii, folio 72v, has no modern equivalent. I am grateful to Francesco Izzo for attempting to discover a modern interpretation of the siglum. For this study, I have relied on the published transcriptions.

38. Much of the typographical material used in the 1519 editions is the same as that used before the sack of the city; coupled with the plans to print Calvo's translation, this argues that Petrucci was able to salvage a fair proportion of his material from destruction.

39. Many of these letters appear in Corsini, *Malattia* (which also cites the matriculation record, on p. 128), and in Giorgetti, "Lorenzo".

40. Both these details are taken from Campana, "Manente", pp. 499–502.

41. The presentation manuscript is now in the Biblioteca Laurenziana in Florence, at Plut.LXXIII, 12. The dedication to Leo, which is not dated, has been published, in Campana, "Manente", pp. 513–14. For the attribution of the illuminations to Giovanni Bocardi, see D'Ancona, *Miniatura*, No.1621. This attribution, of course, brings forward another name of interest to musicologists, for Boccardi was also the illuminator of the Newberry partbooks and the Cortona-Paris partbooks. An outline of Boccardi's career and a partial list of his work is published in Slim, *Gift*, i, pp. 27–40. To the datable manuscripts listed there can be added a Psalter for Lorenzo de' Medici and Madeleine de la Tour d'Auvergne, necessarily written at about the same time as the Hippocrates translation, during 1518 or perhaps 1519 (D'Ancona, No.1629: see Perkins, "Review", p. 265, fn.8). Campana's dating for Leontini's manuscript is tighter than that offered by D'Ancona and is based on the evidence of the borrowing register for the Vatican library. Leontini seems to have kept on loan the library's Greek Hippocrates for over two and one-half years from December 1517.

42. His autograph manuscript of this translation is also in the Vatican library, as Vat.lat.2396. A copy of his translation of Galen's *De rebus bini malive succus libellus* is manuscript CCXXXVI in I-VEcap, dedicated to Bernardo Dovizi, that is, Bibbiena.

43. The privilege, which I have not seen, is reported in Fulin, "Documenti", as No.220 on p. 193.

44. The book also carries references, though not on the title page, implying that Calvo had finished translating by 1515; the following details are taken from the copy at I-Vnm 79.D.49. In full, the title reads:

> [A frame of four blocks, making a triumphal arch above a frieze: above, the Medici stemma: the whole 289 × 191 mm Within:] HIPPOCRATIS | COI MEDICORVM OMNIVM | longe Principis, octoginta Volumina, quibus | maxima ex parte, annorum circiter duo mil | lia Latina caruit lingua, Græci uero, Arabes, | & Priſci noſtri Medici, plurimis tamen utilibus | prætermiſſi, ſcripta ſua illuſtrarunt, nunc | tandem per .M. Fabium Caluum Rhauenna | tem uirum undecunq*ue* doctiſſ imum latinita- | te donato, CLEMENTI .VII. Pont. Max. | dicata, ac nunc primum in lucem ædita, quo | nihil humano generi ſalubrius fieri potuit.
>
> The colophon, PPP7*v*, reads:] ROMAE EX AEDIBVS | FRANCISCI MINITII | CALVI NOVOCOMENSIS | ANNO A PARTV | VIRGINIS | MDXXV. [There are statements of a ten years' privilege from Clement VII, on the verso of the title page and the recto preceding the colophon.
>
> The second preliminary gathering opens with an index, in which Calvo refers to 1515:] ELENCHUS | Octoginta librorum | Hippocratis Coi: | Quos M. Fabius Caluus | ciuis Rhauennas. Milleſi= | mi Quingenteſimi: quintiq*ue* | decimi: Men ſis Julij die | octauo Romae conuertit: | Milleſimi Quingenteſimi | decimique inſuper: menſis | Aprilis die tertio auſpica= | tus quorum ordo ſequitur.
>
> Similarly, the first of the final three pages contains the following:] M. FABIVS CALVVS RHAVENNAS | CVM CAETERIS HIPPOCRATIS | OCTAGINTA VOLVMINIBVS | ROMAE VERTEBAT XIX CALEN. | SEPTEMB. MILLESIMO | QVINGENTESIMO AC INSVPER | QVINTO ET DECIMO.

Both of these citations suggest that Calvo's translation was indeed completed by 1515; as with the manuscript, however, they were prepared long after and may well reflect his need to justify himself. The reference to an edition of 1520, made in passing in Jammes, "Chefd'oeuvre", p. 308, seems to be in error.

45. A brief outline of this printer's career, with a list of his publications, is in Barberi, "Edizioni".

46. A survey of Vicentino's life, with a translation of the *Operina*, appears in Osley, *Scribes*, pp. 70–80. The original treatise has been reprinted in facsimile in Ogg, *Three Classics*, pp. 3–62, and its publishing history is discussed in Hofer, "Variant".

47. The different issues and editions of this book imply a complicated history of relationships between the responsible parties. For a discussion of the evidence, see Jammes, "Chefd'oeuvre", and Ruysschaert, "Différents".

In the copy at I-Vnm, Misc.1592.22, the colophon reads:] ANno a Partu Virginis. MDXXXII. Menſe Aprili | Valerius Dorichus Brixienſis Romæ impreſſit. Quod opus | Ptolomæo Egnatio Foroſempronienſi antea Fabius Cal|uus Rhauenn. coelandum dederat. || CAVTVM EST SVB GRAVISSIMIS POENIS | EDICTO CLEMENTIS .VII. PONT. MAX. | Ne quis hoc Opus intra proximum Decennium Imprimat. | aut Impreſſum vendat.

Other copies are at GB-Lbl 139.h.2; I-Bu AVM.IV.7; and I-Pu 67.b.12, according to the *Index Aureliensis*, No.130.306.

Chapter Eight

IDEAL COPY

Petrucci's View of the Book, Its Character,

Function, and Destination

his chapter, with the next two, attempts to address one of the more thorny questions in the history of music printing, namely, who was expected to buy the printed books. I have tried to divide the issue into three sections, each of which, I believe, needs separate consideration. In this chapter, I want to examine what Petrucci and his employees did with the content of a book to make it useful and appealing. Thus, I shall examine the in-house decisions concerning matters such as format and layout, levels of responsibility about readings and accuracy, and some special features (for example, incomplete mass texts) found in the books. These should help us to detect Petrucci's view of the users of his book. This is logically the first of the three chapters, for it ties in most closely with the bibliographical part that precedes it.

In the next chapter, I shall look at the actual repertoire: what was selected, and how it helps us define Petrucci's understanding of the market for printed music. I also shall try to determine the possible and probable sources for much of the repertoire. Finally in chapter 10, I shall turn to who seems actually to have bought the books, and how Petrucci might have arranged for the books to be available to them.

Simply put, chapter 8 is about bibliographical and textual matters, reflecting Petrucci's attempts to make people like his books after they bought them; chapter 9 is about repertorial matters, revealing Petrucci's attempts to supply content that would also appeal; chapter 10 is about commercial matters, Petrucci's attempts to make a living from his books.

While this may seem to view the issues in reverse order, I believe that the specialist printer of the Renaissance had to think in these ways: his methods of presenting texts were the elements that made his versions of those texts acceptable

247

to the public and kept him in business. Only after that had been achieved could he hope to continue to explore new texts within the same field. Only after he had acquired a name for these texts, did the issue of disseminating his copies become a problem, as he began to reach outside his own (or his patron's) local circles.

We can learn no more than a limited amount about Petrucci's view of his books, and almost all of that is necessarily derived from a study of the details of presentation. Layout on the page, treatment of page-turns, levels of indexing, even the phrasing of title-pages reveal a great deal.[1] But we can often learn more from levels of editing, types of correction, the use of cancels, or the concern for accuracy in later printings. Some of these issues belong in earlier chapters; some will appear in chapter 9, for the titles of the books and the extent to which composers' names are stressed are both features of Petrucci's salesmanship. Other features belong here.

The most useful place to start is with an analysis of what Petrucci would have seen as an Ideal Copy. This bibliographical concept has become central to most analyses of printed sources, whether bibliographical or textual. The concept exists to distinguish the individual copies, as they survive—with missing pages, incomplete sets of in-house corrections, and all the accretions deriving from later owners—from the form of a copy as it was intended to be issued by the printer or publisher. This latter is the ideal copy, a copy that may well not exist in practice.[2] If, for example, Petrucci were to make ten in-house corrections in different copies of a title, and no one copy contained all ten corrections, then there would be no copy that completely fulfilled his intentions in that respect. A description of an ideal copy, however, would take account of all ten. Evidently, such a copy represents more closely the "intentions" of the printer.

The word "intention" is, of course, a dangerous one. I am not claiming to describe an aesthetic position that Petrucci may have held, whereby landscape format was more pleasing than portrait, or the initials of the early title pages more attractive than other possible styles. Nor dare I make many suggestions about his musical judgments or expectations. All one can say is that certain elements of the finished book commanded more attention than others, and that some decisions, usually the purely practical ones, seem to have had a commercial implication. We surely are right in assuming that any aspect of the book of particular concern to Petrucci was also, in his estimation, important to the purchasers or their agents, including not only the musicians but also binders, librarians, and scribes. These aspects of the book are therefore important for us in analyzing Petrucci's work.

An ideal copy contains elements that seem to lie on both sides of a crucial divide, that between details that the printer and publisher required to be present and in a certain form, and others where flexibility and variation were tolerated, perhaps even encouraged.[3] For the modern reader, not least a reader of music, the actual content of the book should belong among the most rigidly controlled features, where editor, typesetter (or engraver), and proof-reader should exercise the most scrupulous attention, the first to provide accurate copy, the second to follow it precisely, and the third to ensure success in the endeavour. I have already clearly stated that this was not the practice in the sixteenth century, and have discussed some of the implications elsewhere.[4] At the same time, the limits of the compositors' freedom were carefully circumscribed, as is revealed both by the types of changes permitted in a second edition and by the ranges of corrections made in-house.

Other features in the book concern the modern reader less (and, indeed, are no longer of value to binder or bookseller): Petrucci and his fellow publishers seem to have regarded these features as demanding the highest level of accuracy.

Of course, both ranges of material were treated differently by different printers and authors or editors. But certain decisions about what was essential, and therefore represented in an ideal copy, must have been obvious. The title-page had to announce the contents of a volume, and the contents had to conform to the resulting expectation: those contents (whatever their level of accuracy) had to be legible, visually pleasing, and presented in the most convenient manner for use; where possible, authority for the contents should be assigned, for example, with a composer's name (representing part of the process of making the contents attractive); and evidence of the bibliographical structure and completeness of the book had to be presented clearly. Each of these ranges of decisions would influence the commercial success of the volume to be printed, and even decisions that were apparently simple, and that Petrucci followed throughout his career, need to be examined for what they reveal about Petrucci's priorities.

All Petrucci's music was produced in landscape format. This should not surprise us, for, near the end of the fifteenth century, north Italian sources for domestic use were turning toward this shape. Among them were I-Bc Q17, I-Fn Magl.XIX.178, and (especially significantly) I-MOe α.F.9,9. Each of these manuscripts was probably prepared before 1500, the first two in Florence, and the last perhaps in Padua.[5] They were followed by several similar manuscripts prepared in the early years of the next century, including I-Bc Q18 (from Bologna), I-Fn Panc.27 (from Mantua), I-VEcap DCCLVII from Verona, and I-Fc Basevi 2439 which, though written in Flanders, was intended for a Florentine recipient.[6]

Given the probability, to be discussed in detail in chapter 9, that the *Odhecaton* and its series of "Canti" volumes were aimed at a domestic rather than an institutional market, it is significant that several of these manuscripts contain a similarly varied repertoire. Alongside a basically secular repertoire, they include works, not merely in Latin, but even composed with liturgical functions in mind. Further, all were arranged in a choirbook layout, with all voices on an opening, despite their relatively diminutive size. It is notable that one of the earliest, I-MOe α.F.9,9, is also one of the smallest, and that its size corresponds very closely with that of the two books now in Milan, I-Ma Trotti 519 (112 × 160 mm) and I-Mt 55 (112 × 165 mm). It is significant that Bologna Q18 is double the size (at 168 × 240 mm). Given that the Modena manuscript was copied in Padua, this northern group suggests a fairly standard size for the sheet of paper.[7] Perhaps not surprisingly, the size of the unique copy of the first edition of *Odhecaton A* is closely similar, at 164 × 237 mm.[8]

As I say, the early landscape-format books were choirbooks in layout. By contrast, the earliest manuscript partbooks were, when not related to the rotulus, almost always in portrait format,[9] for that provided more lines to the page, with fewer notes to the line. Among the earliest sets of landscape partbooks seem to be the set now divided between Cortona and Paris (from the second decade), I-Ma Trotti 519 (also after 1500), and of course Petrucci's later books.

Therefore, it probably seemed logical to Petrucci that he should launch his two series of Canti and Motetti in small landscape-format choirbooks. He must have had contact, presumably through Castellanus, with an up-to-date circle of musicians, who would have advised him that this was the newly fashionable way to present music for domestic and amateur use.

Interestingly, this arrangement, especially in the smaller sizes, made it relatively harder for four musicians to use the book for performance at the same time. Nonetheless, it apparently does reflect a move toward portability—the book being usable in the hand—a pattern that I suggest is related to the decline in rehearsal that I have posited from analysis of other ranges of evidence.[10] This move is shown in other books, by other and more distinguished printers: Aldus, in his 1501 edition of Juvenal, describes his new octavo-format books as planned to be comfortable to hold in the hand—"ut commodius teneri manibus",[11] and in his second advertisement list (of 1503), he calls them "libri portatiles".[12] Martin Lowry has pointed out[13] that these books were not therefore any cheaper nor designed for a mass-market; they were simply more compact and "portable" and therefore more convenient versions of the still common folio editions, often without the commentary and apparatus.

That Petrucci seems to have felt the same may be deduced from the manner in which he maintained the format throughout his career, and from the evidence of the prices of his books (discussed in chapter 10). Petrucci maintained this format even when he started using partbooks in 1502, with the first book of Josquin's masses. Gallico has assumed that the transition in layout represents a transition in intended market: "sono passati dal solo intento di trasmettere i testi, a quello di fornire anche i materiali per l'esecuzione corale".[14] This is almost certainly partly true. I agree, and develop the point in chapter 9 that Petrucci was selling volumes of mass settings to institutions that intended choral performance. This seems self-evident. Although mass movements can be found in some of the contemporary (largely secular) landscape-format choirbooks, such as I-Bc Q18, Petrucci's mass volumes present complete cycles. This must have intended a different function—a liturgical, or at least an institutional setting.

One of the two areas where I disagree slightly with Gallico[15] is in the simple act of using landscape format for the partbooks, and keeping them the same size as the earlier volumes. I have mentioned the absence of landscape-format partbooks for liturgical music dating from before Petrucci.[16] Petrucci must have had to face a decision about format and size, as soon as he decided to print Josquin's masses, in 1502. If he had wanted to mirror the fashionable sources for mass settings, as he had done for the secular repertoire, he would have had to produce choirbooks of a much larger size, essentially in folio, as Antico would soon do in his *Liber Quindecim Missarum* (1516). Petrucci, however, decided otherwise, and this decision to produce music for choirs and for liturgical use in small landscape partbooks may therefore be one real innovation in Petrucci's output. However, it was probably financially motivated, rather than a thought-out aesthetic decision.

Scotto, with his expertise as a publisher, may well have played a crucial part in this decision, which saved Petrucci the expense of acquiring materials for choir-books. This expense would have been considerable, entailing new sets of fonts for the music and text, and initials, and rearranging the press to print in folio rather than in quarto. At the same time, setting type in choirbook layout would also introduce new complexities: whereas Petrucci's earlier repertoires had tended to sit comfortably on few pages, and (for most pieces) the various voice parts had contained related numbers of notes, rests, and so on, neither was true for Josquin's masses. Petrucci himself must have welcomed the decision.

Once this decision was made, Petrucci kept the format and basic layout for the rest of his career, with the minor changes necessary for frottole and lute music. Within that pattern, partbooks could be used for masses, and (in less than two years) for the more serious anthologies of motets that corresponded to the masses in effective destination. Choirbook format was retained for the frottola books, as we might expect. The only significant exceptions come in the last books, Pisano's *Musica* and two from the 1530s, where Petrucci adopted partbooks for a secular repertoire. Here Gallico[17] is right in seeing a reflection of the different status accorded to madrigalian music, when compared with the frottola. The change is also a reflection of the different source (and perhaps destination) for the music in these two volumes.

The second feature most likely to be noticed by a prospective purchaser was the title-page. On a purely verbal level, the contents of these pages are typical of the late fifteenth century: brief and to the point, they define the contents, set the information in a stylish rotonda typeface, and are placed above center on an otherwise empty page. The absence of any ostentatious display of ornament, and even of the name of printer or publisher, is standard. The pattern was also followed in Petrucci's non-musical books, even the otherwise elegantly decorated edition of Paulus's *Paulina*. The ornamental borders and blocks, which we associate with the glories of Venetian sixteenth-century printing, seem at this time to have been largely reserved for books in folio.[18]

Also typical is the inclusion of the composer's or author's name in the phrase that made up the title. Petrucci gives the name in all volumes dedicated to a single composer; he even anticipates patterns from later in the century, by putting Févin's name on what is in fact an anthology. The presence of the names of several composers on the title page of the *Missarum diversorum auctorum* (1509) is, to my eye, a reflection of the special status of books of masses—destined for performing institutions that would already have collections of such music that they might not want to duplicate. This title-page is paralleled by those of other mass volumes, detailing the full contents of the book.

In all respects, then, the style of title presentation was standard, that is, until the *Motetti de la Corona*. Why Petrucci should have put a block of a crown on the title-page of these volumes is not yet clear. The reason must relate directly to the actual title of the book, and thence to some aspect of its promotion, and will therefore be addressed in chapter 9; but the idea of adding an illustration of a crown is quite possibly also a reaction to some of Antico's title-pages.

Related to the presence of attributions on title-pages is the pattern of attributions at the heads of pieces, or in the various *tavole*. In his letter to the reader in Spinacino's first book of intabulations, Petrucci claimed that ascribing pieces correctly was important to him, and that he was offended by assertions otherwise. The evidence suggests that it did indeed matter: all masses and a great majority of the motets have ascriptions.[19] But when we turn to the volumes of "Canti", of frottole, and of laude, the situation is very different. A large number of the frottole are anonymous, even though many others do have attributions to minor, even insignificant figures. Names are attached to all works in Book I (even in the last, miscellaneous, gathering), and to almost all of Books VII and XI. At the other extreme is Book VI (which is anomalous in other ways), where less than one piece in three is attributed. More typical is the pattern best demonstrated by Books III and IV; there, sequences of assigned pieces are interrupted by sequences of anonyma.

As did the masses and motets, frottole apparently tended to travel with a name attached. In Book I, Petrucci went further, and headed a number of the pieces with the rubric *Michaelis* [Pesenti] *Cantus et Verba*.[20] A similar phrase attaches to one more work by Pesenti in Book VIII, to one by Cara in Book V (*M.C.C.V.*), and to five in Book V by Paulo Scotto (*Pauli Scoti Cantus & verba*). Petrucci seemed to regard this as important, more so than signaling texts written by Serafino or Bembo or Petrarch. It is part of what we see as the nature of frottole, that they were above all performance art, and the composer's name was attached to the performance—hence to the edition. It is probable, too, that the names of the poets of many verses were well known in some circles, perhaps the very circles that Petrucci expected to buy the books. The presence of so many anonyma must tell us something about Petrucci's sources.

Attributions in the *tavole* at the fronts of various books must have been as effective a purchasing lure as the title page itself and probably gave Petrucci as much concern. While, for Book V (in particular) of the frottole, Petrucci did add to the index some attributions not found in the body of the book, the pattern of composers' names in the tables of the three "Canti" volumes is much more interesting. The list of contents for the first of these, the *Odhecaton A*, is revealing of Petrucci's assessment of his purchasers' musical knowledge. Almost all the works with composers' names are cases where more than one piece in the book had the same textual incipit. This, of course, allowed the reader to select which one to perform. But there are two additional cases: the setting of *Se congie pris* ascribed to *Japare* [*sic*], and Isaac's very widely known *Benedictus*. It is apparent that the other pieces, those without composer's names, did not raise problems of authorship in the minds of the editor or typesetter—or (as they assumed) in the minds of the purchasers. However, the presence of two settings with the same incipit, or of only one setting in cases where other settings of the same text were likely to be well known to purchasers (that is *Se congie pris* or the *Benedictus*), was enough to make the editor wish to have a composer's name inserted. It seems probable, therefore, that these works, at least, were known by both the textual incipit and the composer's name.

Other works in this anthology were associated sufficiently with the incipit and did not need a composer's name in the tavola. Petrucci, or his supplier, knew the name, for it is often found at the head of the music, later in the volume. But he apparently also knew that purchasers and performers associated this setting, and only this one, with the given incipit. The presence of Japart's name for *Se congie pris* in the tavola is indicative of this understanding; a composer's name was associated strongly enough with a setting even when there were other, equally well-known settings.

This I believe, is quite distinct from the manner in which motets and masses traveled. The concordance patterns for late-fifteenth-century chansons[21] show a concentration on individual pieces—this popular work by so-and-so, that marvelous piece by someone else, this beautiful work by a relative nonentity. By contrast, the pattern for masses shows a concentration on composers—the works of Josquin or La Rue. Lesser composers circulate less widely, even with their best works. I recognise that this is in part a reflection of the nature of many manuscripts of mass settings, compiled as they were for local use or as a gift, and therefore containing works of local composers. But I believe it is also a function of the kinds of performance for each of these repertoires ca.1500. Chansons were increasingly being sung by amateurs, who "knew what they liked—and liked what they knew". Masses remained the province of professionals who knew who the best composers were, or at least who the favourites of their patrons were.

Petrucci certainly worked toward this end, by making sure that composers' names were prominently displayed on the mass volumes (even the *Missarum diversorum auctorum*) and entered as fully as possible in collections of motets and the *Fragmenta Missarum*. Indices to the chanson volumes, on the other hand, give a composer's name only when it would help the reader to distinguish one popular setting of a text from others, whether in the same book or not.

The tavola is interesting in another way. Typically, and especially in the frottola volumes, it was arranged in the standard Renaissance pattern: works were grouped according to their initial letters, but within these groups in the order in which they appear in the book. There are few exceptions, mostly with other repertoires. Thus, *Laude II* lists the works in the order in which they appear in the edition. Even more significantly, some books show adaptations of the pattern. The volume of Dammonis's laude seems to have an index arranged in true modern order, at least as far as folio 54 of the contents. Thereafter, the pieces are added at the end of each letter: they apparently represent a series of later additions.

All these elements—format, title statement, index, and attributions—are essential features of Petrucci's view of an ideal copy; so are others that do not affect content, even at the level of the "paratext". These involve principally the character of the decorative initials and of the notational symbols.

The initials—especially those particularly grand examples of the early title-pages—immediately announced that the books would be of good quality and expensive. These initials were a luxury (and not very common) addition to their title-pages. They represent a considerable expense in preparation; the work of a master designer, as well as a skilled craftsman,[22] they are paralleled by similar, smaller initials throughout the volume. These internal initials exceed in frequency and therefore often in actual number the initials that contemporary printers were regularly placing at the beginnings of chapters, in place of the small rubricators' guides of earlier books.[23]

In the early volumes, this recurrent use of elegant initials would immediately announce to the browser a level of workmanship that could be expected throughout the book. As I have shown earlier, the standard of the initials themselves, as well as the care with which they were impressed, begins to decline even before Petrucci left Venice, and both suffered a marked decline during his last years. This decline is reflected, as will become evident, in other changes in his view of an acceptable ideal copy. But in the early volumes in particular, those in which Petrucci was laying down the standards his customers could expect, the initials were an announcement that these books would not be cheap, and were a way of casting light on the level to be expected in other, less obvious, features.

The same is true for the notation. Petrucci retained the diamond-headed note shapes of the previous century, as still did a majority of other sources. But for many secular sources, the precision of the angles in a note head was less and less well maintained. Increasingly, the right side of a note head began to resemble a curved continuation of the downstroke of the tail, while the left side became a more emphasised arc.[24] While diamond-shaped heads were still used by some scribes in secular anthologies—for example, in I-MOe α.F.9,9—they were still (and were to remain for many decades) the norm for large choirbooks and formal collections of sacred music. Petrucci, therefore, was following the more formal end of notational design at the time. In one respect, perhaps, he was a little behind the times: the design shows a tighter angle at the apex of a note head and a slightly longer tail. Both these features are more reminiscent of the 1470s or 1480s, and perhaps also of French rather than Italian copying. They are also features we admire as giving an additional level of elegance to the appearance of the music on the page. Indeed, everything discussed so far in this chapter has reflected Petrucci's view of the taste and knowledge of the purchaser, as musician and book-buyer.

A number of other details central to the production of an ideal copy have been discussed in chapter 4. The features that would have been of first importance for the bookseller and the binder include title-page details, and similar indicators for the lower partbooks;[25] sets of signatures, distinguishing not only the different sheets and parts but also different titles; a register at the end of the book (alongside the colophon) to confirm that all the gatherings were to hand; and foliation.[26] Although these were not all of interest to most users of the book, they were essential for ensuring that every user had a complete copy. In earlier chapters, I have shown that Petrucci was very concerned with these features, requiring that all should be correct.

At a slightly lower level of significance is the presence, in editions published in separate voice parts, of the part name in the running head. The names were of no value to the binder, except in a case such as *Motetti C*, where Petrucci used the same signing pattern in each book; and they were hardly necessary for the user (who knew already which book he was holding). But Petrucci continued to print them throughout his career; perhaps in his mind (if not that of the user), they served the function of running heads giving chapter numbers.

These elements were apparently central to Petrucci's view of an ideal copy; not only their presence but also their accuracy and consistency were important. Other features were less important, or perhaps less amenable to detection and correction. At the top of any list of this material lies the music itself. In chapter 6, I have discussed the various methods of correcting the music, giving examples of each adopted by Petrucci. Needless to say, the presence of in-house manuscript corrections in each of several copies, apparently the most tedious of all the options open to Petrucci, implies a real concern on his part (or that of his editor or patron) that the correction be made available to as many purchasers as possible.

It is notable that the most important corrections, judging from the care with which they are executed, seem to be those that affect the duration of a phrase of music. The removal of a redundant extra note or a section of dittography is often effected in a number of copies—one wants to say "as many as possible". Erroneous clefs or rests are similarly corrected very generally. These would also have affected the ability of an ensemble to stay together during performance.

Single erroneous pitches are corrected, though less often than one might expect. Different versions of the music itself are virtually never changed—unless another error is also apparent in the sheet. In making this last assertion, I wish to imply that these different versions do not all reflect Petrucci's exemplar. I am apparently claiming to be able to recognise when Petrucci's compositors deviated from the readings in their exemplars, even though these exemplars no longer exist.[27] If I am right in this claim, then we can discover much about how Petrucci viewed the musical readings he presented. This needs further discussion.

In practice, I believe that there are two occasions when we can say something about how Petrucci's versions do differ from those he was given—apart from the obvious errors corrected in-house. One involves those cases where second and third editions and printings survive. In the case of later editions, it can be shown that they were prepared from copies of earlier ones. This is to be expected, of course, for the original exemplars would often have been returned to their previous owners.[28] Further, the earlier edition would provide solutions to questions of layout, spacing, page turns, and so on. As a result, any changes between the editions become indicators of actions taken (consciously or not) by the compositor, exactly in the way that manuscripts show evidence of scribal initiative—and they provide criteria for other possible changes.

The second occasion of "scribal" activity on the part of compositors consists of patterns of difference between readings in different partbooks of the same edition. There are occasions when two parts show distinct patterns, setting them off from the other two. I have used this evidence in the past, to argue for the presence of two compositors, working alongside each other on different books.[29] There are several ranges of evidence pointing in this direction. One involves features of the "para-text"—patterns of presenting foliation and captions. More important are patterns of text spelling, especially in a period when spelling was not completely standardised. In Italy, the impact of Tuscan theories of etymology and spelling were slowly spreading, and we can see, in the work of many scribes, patterns that are not purely local or regional preferences, but that also point to levels of humanist awareness.[30] Local spellings that include the Venetian uses ("z" for "g", etc.) are well known, and other examples of different practices are discussed above, in chapter 4. These evidently reflect the tastes of different compositors working on different parts, or different issues, of the same title.[31]

As with literary texts, the scholar will find that the same variants are not invariably selected by the same craftsman. The compositor's preference is just that—a preference—and no more. If his copy-text offers the alternative spelling, he will occasionally follow that exemplar. But as can be shown more easily for anthology manuscripts,[32] when preferences reach across layers that represent different exemplars they provide convincing evidence of the copyist's or typesetter's preferences.

This is where printed partbooks are particularly valuable, when not prepared according to Mary Lewis's "vertical-setting" procedure.[33] The natural division of work between two typesetters working simultaneously—especially if dealing with pieces of variable lengths (that is, motets and masses)—is to assign them different partbooks. Any differences in practice between partbooks suggests the different thinking of two compositors.

Textual alternatives such as those given in earlier chapters can be used, often alongside choices among alternatives in the "para-text", to suggest when more than one typesetter was employed, and for which partbooks and gatherings. More significant is the extent to which similar analyses can be made of the musical notation and its readings. The only edition in which I have pursued this analysis extensively is the first of *Motetti de la Corona Libro Primo* (I-Bc Q74); I have discussed the manner in which triple mensurations are handled differently in the partbooks and drawn attention (in chapter 6) to the extent to which some manuscript changes were made in-house.[34]

To a limited extent, this argument can be supported by other notational features. In the same edition, one typesetter used ligatures more freely than did the other, clarifying underlay and making strategic distinctions in accentuation;[35] the same man seems to have a clearer knowledge of detailed rules for the treatment of perfections in triple mensurations.[36] Not surprisingly, perhaps, this typesetter, with his more conservative grasp of notation (using $\frac{\text{O}}{3}$ and with a thorough ability to use coloration "correctly" in triple mensurations), also has a more flexible awareness of its possibilities (more extensive ligature usage to indicate underlay). It seems likely that he was an older man, or at least trained in a more conservative school of musical notation.

Similar ranges of conclusions can be reached for both the principal Fossombronese editions of Josquin's second book of masses. The evidence suggests that one of the two typesetters of the second edition, working from a copy of the first, had a clear idea of the value of *minor color* for the performer—as indicator of underlay, complex accentuations across the tactus, or rhythmic complications with other voices. He added indicative examples to his notation, while removing others for which I (and perhaps he) could see no value. The other compositor apparently liked the appearance of coloration on the page and tended to add it, even when it seems to have no significative value.

All these changes concern the notation or text-music relationships. Although they may affect the performance, they do not change the actual notes. Indeed, the pitches seem almost to have been sacrosanct. In moving from one edition to the next, the compositor tried to follow all the pitches exactly, even though he was free to change how they were notated. Between the first two editions of *Motetti de la Corona I*, for example, there are only nineteen musical differences. All but three of the new readings in the second edition correspond to brown-ink in-house manuscript changes made in the unique copy of the first edition. This confirms that Petrucci's compositors for the second edition worked with a copy of the first and argues that they used a "file-copy", which had been kept up-to-date with corrections.

Indeed, this practice of using a first edition for the second implies that we do have exemplars for many later printings of Petrucci's titles. Here the evidence for what Petrucci valued is much less subject to interpretation. When he changed an attribution for a composition (as he did in the editions of *Odhecaton A* and some frottola volumes), we can assume that this was important to him; when his compositors made noticeable improvements in the layout of the page, we are justified in assuming that the visual appearance continued to be a significant issue; and when they copied pitches as exactly as possible from edition to edition, we know that Petrucci required of his men a high level of accuracy.

This evidence of practices in second and third editions can then be extended back to first editions. Even though, in these cases, we have no exemplar, there is no reason to believe that either Petrucci or his craftsmen employed a double standard.

These arguments allow us to gain a rough picture of how Petrucci wanted his ideal copy to look, and the levels of presentation and accuracy of content that concerned him. His decisions must have reflected his knowledge of how the books would have been used by musicians. Indeed, he would have had to have been woefully ignorant of performance practice not to know that every performer would to some extent adapt what he read. We must next turn from what constrained his decisions to where his freedom to change can be found, and ask a different series of questions. Did Petrucci specify that Castellanus and his other suppliers give him an edited musical text? Did he himself have opinions about the extent, the detailed placing, even the spelling of the verbal texts? Can we separate his opinions and wishes from those of the supplier of the music?

This last question must of course come first, and the obvious answer is that we can barely separate Petrucci from his supplier. When there is a first or an only edition, we can never know who made which decisions. I have argued that, for the first edition of *Odhecaton A*, there is some evidence of editorial decisions, and that they seem to be fairly consistent; Willem Elders has also drawn attention to a number of changes that he believes were made for this edition.[37] Given the avowed role of Castellanus, it seems reasonable to suppose that he undertook some editorial work. How far we can extrapolate from that to other editions, I am not sure. It depends in part on how far we think Castellanus remained involved in Petrucci's output (a question which I shall address in chapter 9). It also depends on there being enough anomalies in Petrucci's versions, and sufficient sources with which to compare them. Some books do appear to be better edited than others, and much of the evidence concerns detail, or matters of presentation. But some of this evidence might derive from the activities of different typesetters.

The only sure evidence for separating any editorial intervention on Petrucci's part, rather than that of Castellanus and other suppliers, again lies in the treatment of second and third editions. It seems unlikely that these suppliers would take an active role in later editions, beyond correcting any serious blunders that had not already been changed. From what I have stated above, these editions closely follow the earlier, with the mere corrections of "error" (and, of course, the occasional creation of new "error"). Other levels of change mainly fall within the responsibility of the compositor, rather than an editor. I believe, therefore, that Petrucci took little active part in editorial decisions about the music, at least for later editions. This view should, again, be extended to first editions, rather than suggesting that he had different approaches in different contexts.

This argues for what in any case seems most probable: that Petrucci's view of an ideal copy of the musical contents represents a desire to reproduce the content of the exemplar handed to him.[38] The only freedoms were those that a normal scribe would have been expected to take. (The implication, incidentally, is that Petrucci's compositors were competent musicians, apparently experienced in singing the relatively complex polyphony of the masses and motets, where they would have found the greatest opportunity for this sort of freedom.)

If this assertion is true, then any editorial influence was exerted almost exclusively by the supplier of the music. Castellanus, at least, had sufficient experience and expertise, and parts of my argument in chapter 9 will hinge on his successors having similar abilities. We can deduce a little about the activities of the music's suppliers and putative editors.

Outside music, there is a fair range of evidence, principally in the form of printer's copy (*Druckvorlage*) or of manuscripts evidently used for preparing that copy. When compared with the surviving editions, these manuscripts indicate a wide range of concerns and care. Many manuscripts, when being prepared for the printer, show little more than mere scribal alterations, editing involving misspellings, improvements of layout, or the introduction of headings. Sometimes, such simple editing can involve author's manuscripts; Pontanus, when presenting his *De Prudentia* to the press of Mayr in Naples in 1508, seems to have done no more than correct scribal mistakes.[39] At the same time, the house editor, Summonte, added many instructions to the printer—details of layout, the wording of the running title, instructions to insert large capital initial letters, and similar details. (Apart from the few changes to the text made by Summonte, this is the sort of work I would expect to assign to Petrucci.) Finally, the printer, or more probably the shop foreman, made a series of other markings. His most important markings involve casting off the text. He seems to have calculated how many lines of the manuscript would equal a page of printed text and then marked off the beginning of each page. He also indicated the number of the page in each gathering, allowing the typesetter to set by formes, rather than sequentially through the text.

These last markings are the surest indicator of a *Druckvorlage*. Lotte Hellinga reports that the surviving fifteenth-century examples indicate that casting-off was common, and that setting by formes was perhaps the norm.[40] Carter likewise discusses later evidence and draws a similar conclusion.[41]

But in the present context, the most interesting manuscript exemplars are ones in which the editor or publisher claims to have edited the text, and among these, the sources for editions by Petrucci's contemporary Aldus Manutius are pre-eminent. He claimed for himself the role of a "scholar-editor", and his claims have generally been respected—until recently. Martin Lowry[42] has taken a number of his manuscript sources, compared them with contemporary and earlier respected sources for the texts, and with Aldus's own editions. His conclusions are significant, for they highlight the extent to which "the easy attitudes of the manuscript-age died a hard death, and . . . authors not only condoned, but expected, a large amount of intervention from their publishers". Lowry necessarily draws on the work of other scholars and argues that Aldus's editing decisions were rarely made with any clear understanding of textual principles, or with a consistent view of where the author's authority lay. He concludes that Aldus's co-editors were often haphazard in their behaviour, showing an uneven approach to emending an annotating the text, and apparently only slowly learning how to communicate with their "press-operators".

What is most important about Lowry's analyses and conclusions is that we cannot use the term "editor" in any modern sense, and that the word's current meanings are hopelessly anachronistic. The late-fifteenth-century editor's role was to provide an acceptable text for the printing operation, one which an author would not feel the need to reject, which the compositor could himself adapt (within defined parameters) according to his own taste, and which a reader would accept as responsible.

This situation did not last long. We can reasonably speak of the later "death of a manuscript-age", largely achieved through the devastating power of a printed edition that imposed implicit consistency and apparent authority, ensured that readers and performers (and scholars) would come to think that they had the same version, and gradually even cut back on the range of manuscript glosses found in printed books.[43] At the same time, authors—and, it can be admitted, printers' editors—began to insist on a specific version of the text to be circulated. The famous musical example of Carpentras at Avignon (and his similar behaviour at Rome)[44] only slightly precedes the evidence of the relationships between readings presented by Moderne and Petrucci, or by Moderne and Gardano.[45] In music, these instances seem to grow in importance once we reach the 1530s, and to come first from France or from musicians who had worked there. Outside music, the pattern also appears in Paris, where authors began to assert their authority over the printer, even before 1500.[46]

My belief is that Castellanus and Petrucci's other suppliers conformed to the earlier model. This does not mean that Castellanus did nothing; the editors of this phase were often quite active, although their actions may often seem to us limited or unsatisfactory. However active Castellanus may have wanted to be, and however inconsistent his efforts were, the nature of polyphonic music provided some restraint. I have already mentioned Elders's (and my) belief that editorial changes were made to the musical text of the *Odhecaton A*, and it is surely true that Dammonis would have edited part of his book of laude, that Dalza and Spinacino would have provided edited versions of their own lute music, and that Bossinensis edited, while creating, his lute and voice versions of frottole. But all these were probably rather haphazard operations, not aimed at any standard of editorial consistency, of style and presentation, and not guided by any great knowledge of printing-house problems.

Nowhere is this more apparent than with the verbal texts. A general principle seems to have been applied: that each musical genre had its own standard of textual treatment. The works in the "Canti" volumes generally had only an incipit, while frottole were supplied with a full underlay and additional strophes alongside or below the music; masses were usually given abbreviated texts, while motets normally could not be treated in the same way.

These broad criteria were evidently part of Petrucci's view of an ideal copy, although it is hardly possible to discern the sources for the criteria or their results. If Castellanus controlled the texting in the exemplars of the early editions, then he, as a practicing musician, was probably the source for Petrucci's opinions. In later books, the supplier probably took the same role, for it seems unlikely that Petrucci would have asked for extra text in, for example, the frottola volumes. In any case, most of these broad criteria reflect what was being offered in contemporary manuscripts.

David Fallows has traced the manner in which French texts are presented in Italian fifteenth-century manuscripts.[47] He argues that a radical change took place around the mid-century, after which scribes often "show ignorance of the most rudimentary features of the [French] language". He suggests that French texts were unusable, being replaced by Latin or Italian, or largely omitted. In this, Petrucci and Castellanus follow the pattern of the manuscripts. Castellanus had probably acquired the works in this condition.

Significantly, in all three volumes of the "Canti" series, the only text supplied (after a brief incipit) is to pieces with Latin words. In the *Odhecaton*, they are added to the first piece, de Orto's *Ave Maria*, and to single voice-parts of two motet-chansons by Compère: the Contra to *Le Corps* reads *Corpusque meum licet*; and that to *Male bouche* is *Circumdederunt me*. Three other pieces with only a Latin text lack added text, as do two more song-motets: they are *Benedictus* (Isaac); *L'heure/Circumdederunt* (Agricola); *Mater patris* (Brumel); *Royne de ciel/Regina celi* (Compère); and *Si dedero* (Agricola). In *Canti B*, of four Latin-texted works, only the opening piece, Compère's *Virgo celesti*, has a complete text, and that in two voice parts. Apparently, Petrucci's view of the place of text is clearly not simply controlled by the language used; some compositions with Latin incipits—Agricola's *Si dedero* and Brumel's *Mater patris*—were perhaps stylistically so close to French pieces that they also did not need texts. But we can certainly say that, while his purchasers might have been able to perform a Latin text (or even one in French), the text itself was evidently not essential to the success of the book.

Texting patterns for the books containing other repertoires are more straightforward. To be acceptable, frottole apparently needed the full text. Petrucci even included additional verses on a different blank page, when necessary. The underlaid text tends to be presented in a traditional manner, as a string of words to be sung to the notes; this is not surprising, given the largely syllabic text setting.

Motets similarly needed to be texted. These texts were essential to the success of the volumes, at least from *Motetti C* onward. Although some texts were standardised and well known, by no means all were. Further, the style of text setting was more flexible than in frottole; it required that Petrucci attempt to show roughly where syllables lay—or at least where there were correspondences between new phrases of text and new phrases of music.

For both these repertoires, we can say that Petrucci's view of an ideal copy required that the text be present, and that it could be sung from the copy. In keeping with contemporary manuscript practice, this did not require that every syllable be placed under the note to which it belonged, but merely that enough guidance was given for the singer to apply his experience and produce a musical result.[48] Additional support for this claim lies in the various in-house corrections made to the text, which rarely concern alignment.

The treatment of text in the volumes of mass settings is more interesting. Here the patterns are often inconsistent, involving wide variation in the amount of text and the care taken in its placing. In this case, Petrucci's practice is somewhat removed from that of many manuscripts. For most masses printed by him, the Gloria and Credo are presented with more or less complete texts. But there are exceptions, and sometimes we can see inconsistencies in the pattern across a single volume. In the book of Agricola's masses (1504) four are well texted, but for the Gloria and Credo of the third mass, *Malheur me bat*, the Superius has only the following: "ET in terra pax . . . Qui tollis . . . suscipe" and "PAtrem omnipotentem . . . Crucifixus . . . [Et resurrexit Tacet] . . . Et ascendit in celum".

Even more extreme is the case of the book *Missarum Diversorum auctorum* of 1509. The details of the extent of texting for each mass are presented in the bibliographical description. But the radical differences between masses, and between partbooks for some masses, point strongly to a series of separate sources for the music, sources representing different scribal traditions. This evidence (with many similar though lesser occurrences) is so clear that one cannot presume the presence of an overriding editorial position. It strongly suggests that any editing undertaken on the mass volumes did not involve the text. To Petrucci and his editors, the mass settings were primarily musical, and the texts were presented as they reached the editor.

Petrucci's view of the importance of texting for an ideal copy therefore varied, as of course we would expect, from genre to genre. The inconsistency in the mass volumes adds another layer to our interpretation: there were points where a consistent pattern was sought and these include texting in the frottola repertoire, as well as the general lack of text in the "Canti" series; there were others where it did not matter, and Petrucci apparently took whatever was given to him.

It is now time to turn, therefore, to what may be deduced about what *was* given to him, where it came from, and why he, his editor, and his patrons decided to publish it.

Notes

1. Many of these features have become part of what is now called the "Paratext", following on from Genette, *Seuils*; and Brown, *Poets*. In that argument, these features are as important for the history of books and of "The Book" as are the texts themselves and the care taken over them. I shall attempt to use aspects of these arguments here, for I believe that all printers or publishers must have taken them into account in trying to be successful. In Petrucci's case, I like to think that the issues were particularly important, not merely because he was launching an essentially new repertoire-in-print, but also because he seems to have started out with high artistic standards. Therefore, the manner of impagination and other related details would surely have concerned him. Hence the need for the present chapter.

Although there has been considerable recent discussion of the issue of paratext in the context of literature, and principally French literature, it seems not to have been discussed for music. Yet the patterns of presentation of printed music in the various "nations" of the sixteenth century are significant. Some of the differences are obvious and have been remarked; many are directly related to the place of each "nation" in the history of music printing. The presentation of the book and of its contents can then be seen as a reflection of the extent to which a market for printed music, for particular repertoires, or for specific composers had already developed and affected the expectations of the purchasers. This is perhaps obvious in many cases: the head start for music printing in Venice, the Papal States, and Catholic Germany; the importance of music printing in Protestant German lands, related of course to the functions of music in reformed society; the parallel bursts of activity in the Low Countries, including printers in Catholic areas feeding Protestant purchasers; the remarkably late start for music printing in England. Each of these is well known, and simple answers, ranging from religious to economic reasons, have been advanced. Equally important is the manner in which the music is presented. I have recently remarked on the different treatment of music printing in Venice and Antwerp, and how it reflected the available market, in Boorman, "Music Publisher's View". In the present chapter, other issues, format and layout, style and "finish", will be considered.

2. See Bowers, *Principles*, p. 113; Tanselle, "Ideal"; Fahy, "Concetto". See especially the definition by Bowers, and the manner in which Tanselle tries to adapt it (on p. 46).

3. It will not be surprising that I refer only to "printer and publisher", leaving aside the composer. With the possible exception of Spinacino, the composer's views seem to have been irrelevant during these decades. I have also chosen to omit the "editor", for, in most cases, we can have little idea of what effect he may have had on the book. In the present context, his input can hardly be distinguished from that of Petrucci, despite my suggestions elsewhere about purely musical matters.

4. Boorman, "Type-setters", and "Musical Text".

5. My comments here are derived from the *Census-Catalogue*, as are the following measurements: I-Bc Q17: 115 × 190 mm; I-Fn Magl.XIX.178: 114 × 165; I-MOe à.F.9,9: 112 × 166. See also the study of the Modena manuscript, La Face Bianconi, *Strambotti*, and the facsimile, d'Accone, *Modena*.

6. The measurements of these manuscripts are, according to the *Census-Catalogue*, as follows: I-Bc Q18: 168 × 240 mm; I-Fn Panc.27: 153 × 214; I-VEcap DCCLVII: 217 × 325; I-Fc, Basevi 2439: 168 × 240. See also Weiss, *Manuscript* for Q18; and Meconi, *Basevi* and Brown, *Verona*, for facsimiles of the last two sources.

7. This size seems slightly smaller than that used in Florence. A measurement of about 120 × 170–90 for the folio is found in I-Bc Q17, I-Fn Magl.XIX.178, and the Cortona-Paris partbooks; double-sized folios, ca.170 × 240, are used for I-Fn Magl.XIX.107bis and Magl.XIX.117. This is also, incidentally, the size of Basevi 2439, suggesting that the Flemish scribes were well informed as to current Florentine taste, not merely in music, but also in presentation.

8. Equally unsurprising is the size of the folio in Petrucci's edition of Pisano's *Musica* (of 1520), which corresponds to the Florentine size: the unique copy has a page size of 113 × 170 mm.

9. See Owens, "Stimmbuch".

10. See Boorman, "Two Aspects".

11. Renouard, *Annales*, p. 29.

12. Davies, *Aldus*, p. 46.

13. Lowry, *World*, pp. 142–47.

14. The partbooks "had passed from the simple intention of providing the [musical and verbal] texts, to that of also providing the material for a choral performance". Gallico, "Laboratorio", p. 196.

15. The other, to which I shall return at other points in this discussion, is the implication that the earlier "secular" choirbooks were solely concerned with "transmitting the texts of works", without concern for performance.

16. See the list of early sources in Owens, "Stimmbuch".

17. See fn.14.

18. The only recent study of the early development of the title-page since 1929 is Smith, *Title-Page*. Earlier writings include Pollard, "Last". Many scholars have, reasonably, been interested in the emergence and exploitation of decorative titles, with borders or illustrations. By far the most important of these studies, for Venetian printing is Essling, *Livres*. A brief commentary with additional material appears in Barberi, "Frontespizi"; and an introduction to the subject,

with some comments on the earliest period, is in Johnson, "Title Pages". Coupled with these is the use of historiated initials in printed books, which became common in musical volumes by the middle of the century. See Isaac, *Ornamentation*, in which Rawles, "Description", is a sad demonstration of method; see also Petrucci Nardelli, "Lettera".

19. It is not relevant that we believe some of these ascriptions to be wrong. Petrucci could only have been acting on what he and his suppliers knew, and the "erroneous" ascriptions can be used to tell us a great deal about those suppliers and their ranges of knowledge.

20. This, or an abbreviated version, is attached to seven of Pesenti's twenty-three compositions in this volume alone.

21. See Fallows, *Catalogue*, which demonstrates clearly how important core repertoires were, and how many other pieces fell outside these selections.

22. While welcoming Mary Kay Duggan's arguments, discussed in chapter 2, that Ungaro was involved in making Petrucci's music type, I feel it is probably stretching the evidence to assert that he therefore was also involved with the initials. The two skills and the materials were somewhat different.

23. Each of Petrucci's small non-musical pamphlets of the second decade uses only one initial. Even the edition of the *Paulina* often has no initial on any sequence of openings. This fact and its implications for Petrucci, as well as for the bibliographer, have been discussed earlier.

24. This change does not seem to be restricted solely to informal manuscripts, or to sources copied in haste, for it can be found in "elegant" sources as well. It is evidently an aesthetic change, even while also a direct result (as well as a cause) of a change in the number of pen-strokes used to make notes with tails. A good series of examples of this change during the previous decades is presented in the plates in Brown, *Florentine*. More examples, with a contrasting series showing the more geometric notational style employed in large-format choirbooks, are found in Besseler and Gülke, *Schriftbild*.

25. This is paralleled by the later addition of La Rue's name to the title page of the *Missarum diversorum auctorum liber primus* of 1508—although in that case, the motivation was clearly different: it was designed to appeal to the purchaser.

26. In common with many of his contemporaries, Petrucci did not at first see the need for all these elements. But as time went on, he saw the advantages of using different signature patterns for different titles, as Attaingnant did, from the beginning. The direction line was adopted rather later.

27. Without a proven exemplar, it is not usually possible to assert that a specific instance represents a deviation, but we can develop criteria for *types* of deviation, for probable changes, and thereby identify readings that are more likely to represent the activities of the typesetter.

28. I am sceptical that special printer's copies were made for many of Petrucci's editions, in the way that they were occasionally made for other repertoires. From an extensive literature, see especially Hellinga, "Three Notes"; HellingaW, *Copy*; Trovato, "Censimento".

29. See Boorman, *Petrucci*; Boorman, "Type-setters"; and Boorman, "Notational".

30. The classic statement about the early stages of this development is Ullman, *Origin*. It has been supplemented by a number of studies, especially by Albinia de la Mare. See also Wardrop, *Script* and, for musical sources, Frankel, *Phonology*, chapters 6 and 7.

31. The full discussion of these cases appears in Boorman, *Petrucci*. Much detailed work on typesetters' spelling habits has been conducted by scholars of the early editions of Shakespeare.

32. See Boorman, "Limitations".

33. For the most detailed explanation of this procedure, see Lewis, *Gardano*, i, pp. 68–75.

34. The patterns of manuscript changes might make an argument for two typesetters as proof-readers of their own work. I think it is more likely that the typesetter was responsible, not for reading the "proof"-pull, but for making the necessary manuscript corrections, and that the craftsman who had set the Superius and Tenor was also responsible for ensuring that the "o" was added.

35. The case of Josquin's *Christum ducem* has been discussed in an earlier chapter. It shows one danger, both for the compositor's ability to make changes in notation, and for the modern scholar's ability to produce an accurate analysis.

36. For examples of these, see Boorman, *Petrucci*, pp. 114–17.

37. See Boorman, "First", last few pages; Elders, "Frage". Of course, when Elders argues for the changes to have been made by Petrucci, we should probably substitute Castellanus, or even the copyist of his exemplar.

38. I have extended this argument to suggest that Petrucci rarely, if ever, made decisions in response to issues of performance practice. See Boorman, "Did Petrucci".

39. This example, including the details that follow, is discussed in Bond, "Printer's". Further information on the history of the edition can be found in Lowry, *World*, pp. 221–22 and 248.

40. Hellinga, "Notes". On the same issue, Haebler, in *Handbuch*, p. 77, points out that the varying numbers of lines per page and variations in the width of the text block may both be explained by casting-off text and setting by formes; both are the result of a need to squeeze extra text into a given forme. This evidence has been used by a number of other scholars examining different repertoires, and I have occasion to refer to it in my discussion of Paulus de Middelburgh's *Paulina*.

41. Harry Carter, in his foreword to Simpson, *Proof-reading*.

42. Lowry, *World*, pp. 217–56. The following quotation comes from p. 227, and the end of this paragraph reflects Lowry's thinking, especially on pp. 237–38.

43. An important discussion of the effect of this on readers' responses to printed material is found in Johns, *Nature*, pp. 28–33.

44. See Sherr, "Notes".

45. See Pogue, "Editor".

46. See Brown, "Confrontation"; and Brown, *Poets*.

47. Fallows, "French", cf. pp. 437–38 for the following.

48. It is tempting to see this practice as further evidence that motet volumes from *Motetti C* onward were primarily aimed at professional singers.

Chapter Nine

PETRUCCI'S REPERTOIRE AND ITS SOURCES

onsidering the impact Petrucci's publications have had, not only on the history of musicological scholarship or on the history of music printing and publishing, but also on the dissemination of music during the mid-Renaissance,[1] it is surprising how little we know of the sources on which he was able to draw for his repertoire.

In a recent article, Bonnie Blackburn drew attention to the musical contacts of Petrus Castellanus, the supplier of music for Petrucci's *Odhecaton A*.[2] Her argument that Petrus continued to supply Petrucci with music for many of his subsequent editions would provide a very attractive solution to the problem of Petrucci's sources, even though it would then raise the logical next question: what were Castellanus's own sources? This will need consideration in the present chapter.

Equally appealing would be a presumption that, after the first few publications had been successful, Petrucci found himself at the center of a group of patrons and musicians, willing to offer him material to be published, or wanting to disseminate the repertoire they already owned. There are some signs that might be taken to point in this direction: the sudden expansion into frottole in late 1504; the phase, during the years 1506–08, which saw two volumes each of Lamentations and laude, and also a series of intabulations; or the publication of volumes entitled *Liber primus* or *Libro primo,* but for which no second book seems to exist.[3] Each of these strands of evidence suggests that there were specific and different plans about the repertoire to be published, at different stages of Petrucci's career. This might indicate merely an acute business sense on the publisher's part, or that of Petrus Castellanus. But, as I shall suggest, certain signs instead point to a varied group of suppliers of music.

Yet, it will appear that the evidence for probable, or even presumptive, sources for much of the music is very slim. Too much of it relies on possible connections in musical readings, or on coincidences in the careers of composers or performers.[4] In the past, I have made a case for the production of Petrucci's edition of Ghiselin's masses being directly related to the composer's relations with the Ferrarese court chapel;[5] my evidence was largely bibliographical and as such entirely circumstantial. Even earlier, I suggested that the first volume of the *Motetti de la Corona* (1514) was intended as a gift on the betrothal of Giuliano de'Medici to Filiberta of Savoy:[6] this is exactly the sort of case that it is dangerous to construct. Even more marginally, Lewis Lockwood has suggested that the inclusion of the second mass, the *Missa Hercules Dux Ferrariae*, in the second book devoted to Josquin (published on 30 June 1505) was perceived (and perhaps intended) as a tribute to the recently deceased duke.[7]

Unlike later printers, Petrucci was reticent about the genesis of his volumes; there are few dedications or letters to users, virtually no uses of allusive woodblocks or other illustrative material, and few volumes in which the repertoire has highly specific extramusical origins—*Staatsmotetten* or wedding music, for example. Even those cases for which we think we can assign a work to a specific occasion, including some works published by Petrucci, there is no reason to believe that his editions (or, normally, their exemplars) had any specific connection to that occasion.[8] In this respect, Petrucci is still part of the fifteenth century, reflecting those early stages when printing did not actively shout its origins or patrons. Antico, however, already belongs to the next age of music printing and publishing. If Petrucci had produced a few title-pages similar to Antico's for the *Liber Quindecim Missarum* or his fourth book of frottole,[9] we would probably know much more about his repertoire's origins.

The non-musical volumes have the clearest provenances,[10] for the evidence is inscribed in the books themselves, or lies in the proximity of author and printer. There are few musical volumes, however, for which we can confidently accept the available internal evidence as indicating probable sources. Among these few is the first edition of all. Budrio's letter in the *Odhecaton A* says that the music contained in that book came from the collections of Petrus Castellanus.

Three other people who almost certainly supplied music to Petrucci are Francesco Bossinensis, Innocentio Dammonis, and Francesco Spinacino; reasons for this assertion are advanced below. In each case, however, we can reasonably assume that a collusion between printer and composer/arranger resulted in the edition; that is, that the likely motives that stimulated the published works of these three men were rather different from those that may have occasioned other volumes.

In chapter 8, I was concerned with how Petrucci might have thought about both content and presentation. The concept of ideal copy proved to be useful there, for it helped to determine when the printer considered the book ready for sale. At that point, he must have believed that he had done as much as possible, not only to make the text satisfactory, but also to make it as attractive as possible.

Of course, I recognise immediately that the task of impressing the reader or potential purchaser should have become easier as time progressed. If a purchaser had been happy with the content of several of Petrucci's editions, he was more likely to look with enthusiasm on the latest new title. The existence of a series of eleven frottola volumes argues that the first few satisfied buyers. Not only did those early books contain music that was needed or approved; not only must they have been a financial success for the printer; they would also have provided excellent guidelines for the content of any future volumes in the series. The problems Petrucci faced were lessened in some respects (those of format and editing style, for example) and increased in others (those of balance between the proven repertoire and the need for new works and composers).

This impact of what we might call the track record may have spilled over into different repertoires. It is possible that the perceived excellence of the chanson volumes, suggested by the number of reprintings, encouraged the preparation of the first book of frottole; that the success of two books of Lamentations reassured Petrucci when considering two of laude; or that the apparent success of four books of lute intabulations made him willing to try out two of intabulations for lute and voice from the hand of Bossinensis. In each of these cases, however, it is equally plausible that the success of the first group stimulated the interest and generated the plans of someone other than Petrucci—that Bossinensis came to Petrucci with his two volumes of intabulations, or that Dammonis (and others) thought the lauda would sell well. In the last accounting, of course, decisions were financial, and there is virtually no evidence as to whether Petrucci could act as a vanity press, requiring a Dammonis or a Bossinensis to pay for the whole cost of production.[11] On the other hand, there is the suggestion that Petrucci found these books successful, in the extent to which he undertook further, similar volumes.

We do, therefore, have some evidence for how Petrucci and his backers may have thought about his market, and what its musical requirements or interests may have been. This evidence will need to be evaluated. The comments in chapter 8, after all, were written from the perspective of making the books attractive and easy to use, that is, Petrucci's view of the market *after* it had bought his books. His view (more probably, the view held by his backers) of the character of that market clearly influenced decisions about future repertoire.[12]

The bulk of the present chapter is concerned with the immediate stimuli for Petrucci's books—patronage, outside events, or individual promotion, while a final brief section looks at the contents of the books as epitomes of public taste. The chapter attempts to draw Petrucci's picture of his musical market, as he made his business decisions. This will lead, in the next chapter, to a discussion of the known purchasers of Petrucci's books and the spread and influence of the books and their contents. These issues of choice and market are important, for they were the factors which decided Petrucci (with Castellanus and his other suppliers or patrons) to publish music at all, and to select specific repertoires.

There are several clear divisions in Petrucci's output; some of which have been visible since the earliest accountings, while others are more subtle. The obvious ones assume distinctions between sacred and secular, masses and motets, or vocal and instrumental. They extend further: to separate Fossombronese volumes from those printed at Venice, and partbooks from choirbooks. But, in practice, these divisions are somewhat misleading. They need to be modified, within and across repertoires, to take account of differences in style and in choice of composers, as well as the sequence of publication dates, and apparent gaps in what looks to have been a series of titles.

Much of the rest of this chapter attempts to view Petrucci's output as a series of decisions, about repertoire and about market. I believe that each of the following groups represents an initial decision to publish one or more volumes of a given type, or a continuation of a plan, reflecting the success of the first volume(s). In some cases, I have also tried to hypothesise a potential reason for turning away from the series of books.

> Group 1: The chanson volumes:
>   *Harmonice Musices Odhecaton A*: [1501]; 14 Jan. 1503; 25 May 1504
>   *Canti B*: 5 Feb. 1502; 4 Aug. 1503
>   *Canti C*: 10 Feb. 1504
> The early motet volumes:
>   *Motetti A*: 9 May 1502; 13 Feb. 1505
>   *Motetti de passione de cruce . . . B*: 10 May 1503

The motives that led Castellanus to seek publication of his "100" untexted pieces, mostly chansons, cannot now be reconstructed. However, they probably should not be separated from Petrucci's motives in seeking a privilege for music printing in 1498. Although it is possible that Petrucci was merely protecting an intellectual discovery (and once again the fact that he did not call himself a "stampator"—printer—is significant), it seems more likely that he was already looking toward at least one specific publication, and probably a small series.[13]

Castellanus himself had probably made the decision to have parts of his own collection published. We no longer know the extent of the whole collection, although the evidence laid out by Blackburn about Castellanus's life and contacts supports an idea that the collection was sizeable.[14] It seems to me unlikely that a member of the Ferrarese (or any other) court approached Castellanus, with the desire of having the music published, and asked him to draw on the materials he already had collected. I have two, admittedly not very strong, reasons for this. One is that Petrucci needed the financial backing of Amadeo Scotto and Niccolò di Raphael. This implies that neither he nor Castellanus had some other patron willing to sponsor the volume. The second reason is that we can plausibly argue that not all the music collected and then printed by Petrucci came from a single source. It is fairly clear that someone (surely Castellanus) went through the *Odhecaton* material and edited it for publication.[15] Indeed, Budrius says as much when he states that Castellanus had "cuius opera et diligentia centena haec carmina expurgata".[16] This implies that Castellanus had collected the material from various sources, in various conditions and with various musical characteristics, and that he felt the need to "correct" it, to edit it for the press.

It is also doubtful that a Ferrarese courtier would have chosen the repertoire that appeared in *Odhecaton A*. There are, unfortunately, no sources of secular music for the Ferrarese court between I-Rc 2856[17] and *Canti B*. But the pattern of concordances between the earlier manuscript, *Odhecaton A*, and the north Italian

sources from the turn of the century suggests that the Ferrarese part of the repertoire preserved by Petrucci was not of particular interest to other collectors by
1501.[18] Of the eighteen works found in both the Casanatense manuscript and
Petrucci's first book, relatively few were popular in other contemporary sources.
The concordance tables at the end of this volume show this clearly: while Agricola's *Si dedero*, Caron's *Helas que poura devenir*, Hayne's *Alles regrets* and *De tous bien
plaine*, and Congiet's *Je cuide se ce temps* are found in a number of these sources,
they are exactly the pieces we would expect to find, internationally popular and
still remembered into the sixteenth century. Even these, however, are not all
transmitted in a manner that argues for a Ferrarese connection, via Petrucci's
edition. Petrucci presents a four-voiced version of *De tous bien plaine*, which is
not preserved in any other north Italian source, even I-Rc 2856; his four-voiced
version of Caron's *Helas*, which is present also in three of the north Italian sources,
has a different text incipit in the Ferrarese manuscript; and his source for *Je cuide*
knew no composer, whereas Ferrara knew it as by Japart (who had worked there
until at least 1481). This last situation also prevails for Ockeghem's *Malheur me
bat*, which I-Rc 2856 attributes to Malcort. In the same vein, if Ferrara had been
Castellanus's source, it would be surprising if he could not have named the composer of either Busnois's *Accordes moy* or Hayne's *Mon souvenir*.

Even more significant is the choice of De Orto's *Ave Maria* as the work that
opens the volume. If the volume had presented a collection of Ferrarese pieces,
then surely Castellanus or his patron would have opened it with a work from a
composer honored at court.[19] In other words, some parts at least of his repertoire
probably did not come from Ferrara. But others may well have done so, for they
are found in I-Rc 2856 and then seem to have disappeared from view (apart from
Castellanus's collection); there are no other sources as late as this for Agricola's *Le
heure est venue*, Busnois's *Accordes moy* or *Je ne demande*, Colinet's *Cela sans plus*
(printed in *Canti B*), Hayne's *Amours amours*, or (outside northern Europe) Ockeghem's *Ma bouche rit*. Japart's *Amour fait mult* appears with all three texts only in
the earlier I-Fr 2794 (probably French) and the same Ferrarese source.

Although this last range of works draws some of Castellanus's material closer
to Ferrarese circles, it highlights what is apparent from a reading of the contents
of *Odhecaton A*: that some parts of the collection are notably old-fashioned. All
six works of Busnois, the two by Ockeghem, several by Hayne and Japart, and
Urrede's *Nunque fue pena maior* (copied into I-VEcap DCCLVII from Petrucci)
had effectively disappeared by the time Petrucci printed them. Alongside these
are more up-to-date layers, groups of pieces for which Petrucci's edition is among
the earliest sources: works by composers who were still active, including Agricola
and Compère, but also a few pieces by representatives of the next generations,
Mouton, Bruhier, or Ghiselin.

These features are enough to suggest that the choices for *Odhecaton A* were
made by someone with a large collection of music, which had been acquired
over a period of time. This person seems to have been little concerned to reflect
only the latest trends and most famous composers of the moment, preferring
(apparently) to choose a group of favorite pieces, regardless of date, origin, or
contemporary prestige. The only candidate for this role is, of course, Petrus Cas

tellanus, and the further implication is that he drew on the results of at least two decades of collecting music.

The collection was successful, however, from the bibliographical evidence for reprintings. Assuming that Castellanus was to some extent reflecting his own taste, I believe that he was also a mirror of the taste of a significant part of the musical public. This public must be seen as one that is not largely represented by the surviving manuscript sources, even those that are more informal in character. It is hard to believe that the level of performer or patron who could afford a manuscript chansonnier, of the quality of most surviving today, would also need to buy a published edition, for he presumably already had his own personal collection. It is equally difficult to assume that professional performers did not have access to similar collections, either their own or those of their patrons. While some professionals would have wanted to buy Petrucci's edition, they were not likely to have been numerous enough to justify the costs of production. Castellanus (and Petrucci) must have had reason to argue that others, principally amateurs, would be willing to buy the book for the sake of the music, and that there were enough of these to make an edition viable. Scotto and Niccolò, professionals in the printing and publishing field, were apparently convinced.

A feature of the collection that has attracted some attention, and that must have been discussed by the collaborators, is the general lack of text. The presence of incipits, without further text, is not unusual at this time: a number of the north Italian manuscripts, including I-Rc 2856, have no more than an incipit; I-VEcap DCCLVII goes even further, often presenting pieces without any indication. Rather than suggesting that this always meant instrumental performance—as was true for the Ferrarese manuscript[20]—or the rather implausible implication (for this repertoire and market) of memorised texts,[21] I prefer to suggest that the absence of full (or even partial) texts in a *printed* edition (where a much wider dissemination is implicit) argues for a large market that was unable to cope with French texts. This seems reasonable. While courtiers, and no doubt virtually all musicians, would have been capable of pronouncing French (if not translating it),[22] these people are surely among those who would already have had access to manuscript sources of the music. Once again, any estimate of the smallest practical print-run has to assume that Petrucci was selling (in large part) outside these circles, to businessmen, amateurs, and so on, people who need not necessarily have known any French. In other words, Petrucci's edition may have resulted in instrumental performance, but that was effect rather than cause.

This market was new—not in the sense that it had not bought (non-musical) books before, or that it had only recently learned to read music. But it had not made a practice of buying manuscripts of music. I do not want to assert that such people did not have access to copies of chansons; they must have been able to see or hear the music, and probably perform it, for that would be a principal precondition for buying Petrucci's editions. But I presume that they were not in a position to contact the composers or their patrons, and therefore could not acquire a large collection. They must instead have relied on an informal network of contacts, among whom people such as Castellanus would have played an important role. Presumably, evidence of the viability of printed music, gathered in this way by Castellanus and Petrucci, also allowed them to pursue the sale of copies.

Given what we know of how slowly many books moved, as well as the novelty and specialised character of the music, this is the only way we can explain why Petrucci, Scotto, and Niccolò were willing to undertake a second title so soon. It is true that the use of the letter "A" on the title page of the *Odhecaton* implies that Petrucci, at least, was planning a series; nonetheless, these men would not have invested in a second volume until they were sure that the first had sold well enough to suggest that there was a market for the next.

It is no surprise, therefore, that *Canti B* would have basically the same range of contents as the *Odhecaton*. Perhaps Petrucci went back to Castellanus and asked for "more of the same". In practice, the evidence confirms that the first book contained a range of Castellanus's "favorites", for the second (while presenting a smaller percentage of music by some of the same composers) expands the range of styles and adds more recent music. Busnois, de Orto, and Hayne do have one composition each, but they are easily outstripped by the generation of Compère. The stylistic variety is significant; Lowinsky has drawn attention to the "wide gulf between the performer-oriented art of De Orto's canonic tour de force and the audience-oriented art of the Ninot, Compère, Lourdault generation".[23] But the first things that a prospective purchaser saw on opening the volume would have served to reassure him; Petrucci placed at the head a piece by Josquin (albeit a canon), followed by music of Compère and Obrecht.

The smaller size of *Canti B* may indicate that Castellanus already had fewer pieces of the requisite type; certainly, many of these pieces seem to have been less well known, if the pattern of extant concordances is any guide. There is also some tentative evidence, mentioned in the bibliographical description of this volume, that Castellanus may have drawn on relatively fewer sources. More probably, the size of the book means no more than that Petrucci was willing to print only a smaller volume. *Odhecaton A* was, after all, a large investment—one of the longest books he put out—and a second volume, whatever the evidence of sales seemed to suggest, must have represented something of a risk.

Whichever factor influenced the practical decisions, it had clearly been resolved by the time of *Canti C*. The real difference in repertoire between this and the earlier volumes has been noted often enough. But, from the point of view of Petrucci and his potential purchasers, it can easily be overstated. Petrucci apparently expected to reach the same market, for, in using the title *Canti C*, he stressed the continuity of the series; and the average purchaser would have seen a similar type of content on many pages when making his decision to buy. Indeed, it was a shrewd decision to place Obrecht and Agricola first in the volume, with an *Ave regina* and two settings of *Fors seulement*.

The size of *Canti C* is impressive. With 139 chansons, requiring 42 sheets of paper for the 168 folios, it is the largest music book Petrucci published[24] and is on the scale of many text volumes from contemporary Venetian presses. This represents a very large investment, for, given the low cost of labor, the relationship of total production costs (and therefore investment) to the cost of paper is not far short of linear—even for a multiple-impression volume. Petrucci must therefore have expected to reach a fair percentage of the purchasers of the earlier editions of *Odhecaton A* and *Canti B*, and even of the third edition of *Odhecaton A*, which was to appear less than fourteen weeks after *Canti C*.

This pattern of multiple editions also suggests that Petrucci was beginning to measure the size of his audience for this repertoire with some accuracy. *Odhecaton A* went to three editions, and *Canti B* to two, while only one is known of *Canti C*. The implication is that the first printing of *Odhecaton A* was relatively fairly small (as we might expect) and probably on about the same scale as the first of *Canti B*. Both lasted for about eighteen months before a new edition was needed. Since the second of *Canti B* followed the second of *Odhecaton A* by over half a year, and could be planned with the additional sales information, it probably had a longer print-run, with *Canti C* an even larger one.

However, by the time of *Canti C*, even by the second editions of the first two volumes in the series, Petrucci had already launched out in two new directions, one significantly different, the other only apparently so. In choosing to make *Motetti A* his third title, Petrucci was not really branching out very far. Some years ago, Howard Mayer Brown made the point that almost all the contents of this volume were intended for private devotional performance, or for domestic ensembles, rather than for chapels and liturgical occasions.[25] (The analogy with Books of Hours, when compared with missals, antiphonals, and similar books is clear.) This is true for a large proportion of the volume, for the compositional styles, the texts, and in particular the choices of composers draw this book closer to the contents and users of the chanson volumes. Indeed, a number of pieces of this type had already appeared in Petrucci's first two volumes, and not only as obligatory opening works.[26]

Alongside these works in *Motetti A* are other, larger-scale, liturgical works, and even an occasional piece: Compère's *O genitrix gloriosa* and perhaps his *Ave Maria*, Josquin's *Ave Maria* and *Virgo prudentissima* were also copied into liturgical manuscripts. Compère's *Quis numerare queat* is thought to have been composed for the Peace of Bagnolo.[27] But these few pieces cannot have deterred the purchasers, for a second edition was needed.

We can safely assume that Castellanus was involved with this edition. But we do have to ask whether Petrucci and Castellanus were right in trying to associate this volume with the chanson series. While Brown certainly was correct in drawing the parallels, the patterns of concordances for pieces in *Motetti A* tell a slightly different story. Few of the works surface in manuscript anthologies of French-texted music, and those mainly copied elsewhere, alongside a few in I-VEcap DCCLVII or the Grey manuscript now in Cape Town:[28] by far the largest group is to be found in I-Fn Panc.27. This north-Italian manuscript followed Petrucci's editions by a few years, and many of the numbers in it seem to have been copied from his versions; thirteen of the pieces in *Motetti A* are copied into this manuscript, arguing that the scribe felt they belonged alongside the chansons. But he must have been exceptional; the only other sources that show any numbers of concordances with *Motetti A* and would support such a view of the collection come from north of the Alps: CH-SGs 643, D-Mu Mus.8°.322–325, and Egenolff's *RISM* [1535][14].

Nonetheless, Castellanus and Petrucci seem to have felt that there was some continuity. Castellanus had, as we know, a collection of liturgical settings and could include a large number in the material with which he appears to have supplied Passetto in Padua. The decision to avoid such pieces must have been almost entirely deliberate. We can see that he tried to select works that tended to emphasise the continuity with the first two volumes of the *Canti* series, or (at least) that probably appealed to the same purchasers.

Motetti A, like *Canti B*, went to a second edition, though not nearly as soon. Indeed, I believe that the motivation for the second edition lay not in the success of the book with purchasers of the *Canti* series, but with the recent production of *Motetti C*, to which I shall turn later. The sales of the book, however, were sufficient to encourage Petrucci to prepare a second book, *Motetti B*.

Like the *Odhecaton*, *Motetti B* opens with a composition suggesting a Roman connection: *Non lotis manibus* is a work by Crispin van Stappen, who had by then been in the papal chapel for a number of years. Nine of the next ten compositions seem to support this connection: they are by Josquin, van Weerbeke, De Orto, and Vacqueras.[29] Much of the rest of the volume confirms the pattern, with more works by van Weerbeke, Josquin, and van Stappen, as well as by the older Regis. However, not everything can have come from the Vatican: pieces by Pesenti and (probably) Martini would more surely have been collected in northern Italy; and I am about to stress the Ferrarese interest in Brumel and Agricola. Nonetheless, this volume (unlike its predecessors) does provide solid confirmation of Blackburn's argument that Castellanus had acquired music from Rome.[30]

Castellanus's selections for this volume seem to move further away from the chanson repertoire, in style, and particularly in the range of liturgical functions that they fulfill. But the long cycles of movements—Josquin's *O Domine Jesu Christe* and *Qui velatus*, or Compère's *In nomine Jesu*—remain simple in construction and easily accessible to amateurs and devotional groups. This is even more true of pieces such as Vacqueras's setting of *Domine non secundum peccata nostra*.

Even more significant are the ties between this volume and the second book of laude (1508). Individual laude in that volume are made up of extracts from Weerbeke's *Panis angelicum* and *Verbum caro*, as well as the anonymous *Sancta Maria quesumus*, all with new texts. The whole of the anonymous *Gaude virgo mater Christi* is treated in the same manner.[31] Weerbeke's *Anima Christi* (in *Motetti B*) is a setting of a popular lauda text. Indeed, while the range of compositional style is sometimes rather different from that of works in *Motetti A*, the level of skill required for performance is much the same.

Despite the progression of style seen in both sets, this group of five titles represents one ongoing set of commercial decisions. Petrucci and his backers decided that there was a viable market; they had their judgment amply confirmed, and they produced the five titles in just two years. The books contained a total of 286 works in the chanson series, and 69, some of considerable size, in the two books of "motetti". In total, the books carried a significant proportion of the whole active repertoire, outside liturgical settings and frottole, and compared well with the largest Italian manuscripts of similar repertories. It is true that I-Fn B.R.229 contains 268 compositions, and later sources from across the Alps grew even larger. More typically, though, the north Italian sources are definitely smaller: I-Bc Q18 contains ninety-two works, I-VEcap DCCLVII has sixty-four, and F-Pn Rès.Vm⁷.676 rather more than one hundred. These figures tend to be typical; they suggest that Petrucci and Castellanus had effectively exhausted the needs of the market. Few collectors or performers would have wanted as many pieces as the 350 that made up this repertoire, and it is notable that the last editions of *Odhecaton A* and *Motetti A* were to bracket two new endeavors—*Motetti C* and the first three books of frottole.

But both these new repertoires had already been preceded by a radical new venture, the second of the two new directions already mentioned, and one which reinforces the extent to which the first two motet volumes stand alongside the three of chansons.

> Group 2: The first series of mass volumes:
>   *Misse Josquin*: 27 Sept. 1502; [1506] (also Fossombrone)
>   *Misse Obreht*: 24 March 1503
>   [*Misse*] *Brumel*: 17 June 1503
>   [*Misse*] *Joannes Ghiselin*: 15 July 1503 (also Fossombrone)
>   *Misse Petri de la Rue*: 31 Oct. 1503
>   *Misse Alexandri agricole*: 23 March 1504

The decision to print a volume of masses—liturgical music based on highly formal stylistic and constructional principles—and furthermore to print it in part-books, represented as serious a challenge as had the original decision to launch the press. The decision to choose Josquin as the composer to be presented would have followed the initial decision and presumably was an easier one to make.

There must have been a fairly strong impetus to produce this volume, and the first person to persuade must have been Castellanus.[32] His musical knowledge was certainly greater than that of anyone else involved in the business, and he probably already had copies of all the masses to be included. He would have known that Josquin was highly regarded by the musically literate of all northern Italy, and that, if anyone's masses would sell, Josquin's would.

But Castellanus would also have known (as would Amadeo Scotto) that such music was aimed at a very different audience from the purchasers of the earlier series. Although there is ample evidence that liturgical music and motets were performed outside their normal occasions, at dinner and for entertainment, texted or not,[33] it is difficult to imagine these books or their contents being used by the amateurs who had purchased Petrucci's earlier volumes. The new titles are pre-sented differently (in partbooks), and the musical styles are very different: each movement is longer, the structure of the music is consistently more complex (with fewer clear-cut cadences, very variable phrase lengths, and fewer traces of a stan-dardised chordal movement), and there are many more performance problems. Succinctly, the music was composed for professionals, and perhaps also accessible (at this time) only to the most skilled and most adventurous amateurs.

As a "music-lover", Castellanus may have been enthusiastic, but Amadeo Scotto was probably sceptical. Whatever contacts Petrucci and his partners had used to distribute his first editions to their intended purchasers, this volume and its successors would require a different approach. Scotto was a member of a pub-lishing house with a history of producing liturgical books with music,[34] mostly missals described as "Romanum" and therefore sold by commercial exercise, rather than specially commissioned and distributed by a bishop or abbot. As a result, Scotto would have known the numbers and locations of professional choral and liturgical institutions, and probably also exactly which of them would have been capable of performing and purchasing polyphonic masses; this in addition to the crucial part he may have made in the decision to issue the volume in separate partbooks, using the same format as the earlier books. As I have suggested in chapter 8, this decision was surely influenced by financial factors.

So, without outside support, the practical and commercial decisions would not have been easy. In particular, the market must have *looked* smaller. The evidence we have for laymen—the purchasers of the earlier *Canti* and *Motetti* volumes—performing sections of masses seems to concern only trios and duos, sections that were often not merely simpler in texture, but also harmonically or imitatively clear-cut, and usually relatively short.[35] Isaac's "Benedictus" is a good example. Now Petrucci was about to produce a volume of complete masses. All this argues that there was some external encouragement, that a patron proposed or requested the volume and perhaps provided financial support. I believe it also argues for a patron other than Castellanus.[36]

In my earlier discussions of paper use, I drew attention to the manner in which work on the volume of Brumel's masses—the third in this series—was suspended so that a volume of works by Ghiselin could be produced. This interruption was apparently the incentive to bring on line a more speedy process—using two impressions rather than three. Evidently, Petrucci was under pressure to produce the Ghiselin edition, apparently at short notice, and to have it available as soon as possible. Someone, outside the partnership, had made a decision that he needed this book at once, and that person had the influence, political or financial, to make it happen.

As I have said, the most plausible reason for this decision lies in the plan to hire Ghiselin for the Ferrarese court chapel. He had been in Ferrara for a short period over ten years earlier and had maintained his contacts, sending Ercole d'Este music from Paris in 1501.[37] He apparently traveled with Josquin, on the latter's journey from France to take up his position in Ferrara in 1503, but, as Lockwood points out,[38] Ghiselin did not actually reach Ferrara with Josquin. In April, however, both men had traveled as far as Lyons, and Petrucci had begun work on his volume of Brumel. The only likely incentive for him to stop work on this volume and suddenly start on music by Ghiselin must have been the impending visit of the composer to Italy. The book was begun while Ghiselin was en route, was produced rapidly, and was finished in time for any welcome that might have been planned for the composer.

In this scenario, it does not matter whether or not Ghiselin actually took up a post in Ferrara. The implication of the bibliographical evidence is that someone (presumably at Ferrara) wanted to flatter him, to encourage him to think he would be highly esteemed in Italy. It seems probable, therefore, that a member of the Ferrarese court turned to Petrucci and asked him to produce the edition; as a result, Ghiselin's music would circulate widely—much more than could be achieved with manuscript production—and glory would be reflected back on the court. At least, that would have been the plan. This seems a reasonable hypothesis, partly because a similar tactic is the simplest explanation for the decision to produce the first in Petrucci's series of mass volumes, that by Josquin. Here, again, the timing of the volume is significant.

Lockwood has published a series of letters about the possibility of hiring Josquin for Ferrara, one of which includes the famous comparison between Josquin and Isaac.[39] The first letter of relevance here was sent to Ercole on 14 August 1502, favouring Josquin, with a strongly opposing view presented in a second letter of 2 September. Among the points that Lockwood makes, two are significant in the present context: one, that the first letter claims that Alfonso d'Este, as well as the singers, was in favor of Josquin's appointment; and second, that the two views represent something of a personal rivalry between the writers. (Much later in the same discussion, he points out that Josquin's stay at Ferrara fell between the dates of Petrucci's first two books of his masses.)

It seems to me probable that the production of the first book was a carefully aimed salvo in the dispute in the court over whether to hire Josquin or Isaac. Someone in the Ferrarese court—specifically, in Alfonso's circle—pushed Castellanus and Petrucci to prepare the book of masses as a weapon in the dispute. Supporting this argument is the nature of the works chosen for this book. The masses are without exception among the more virtuosic in their technical achievement and represent a cross-section of the skills in common use: the solmisation ostinato of *Missa La sol fa re mi* (less virtuosic than in the Hercules mass, which, if already composed, perhaps could not have been included in an edition intended to support rather than announce a partisan position);[40] the use of an entire plainsong in the *Missa Gaudeamus*; the contrasting treatments in the two *L'homme armé* masses; and the presence of a popular art song as a *cantus firmus*, in the *Fortuna Desperata* mass. This range of works was unlikely to appeal to the average purchaser of the *Canti* series: the pleasures of the two repertoires lie in very different directions. Indeed, Petrucci and his business partners, sceptical as they must have been, may well have driven a hard bargain with their unknown patron.

Most of the problems we face in trying to understand the decision to branch out in this way—new repertoire, new format, new marketing strategies—disappear if one assumes the influence of a Ferrarese courtier. This person, probably associated with Alfonso rather than the duke himself, may not have subsidised the whole edition, though he may have paid for the small block of crossed swords that decorates the first mass. He would also certainly have undertaken to pick up a number of copies; distributing them would be part of the strategy. The chapel choir, allegedly already in favour of Josquin's appointment, could be persuaded to sing the music. Other copies could be given to members of other courts—Mantua is an obvious possibility—whence people might write to Ferrara and praise the music.

Such a direct Ferrarese stimulus is supported by the choices for the other volumes included in Petrucci's first mass series. Second, after the Josquin volume, came a book of masses by Obrecht. This should not surprise us; he was another favourite with the court. Lockwood refers to him as "Obrecht, whose music [the duke] had been collecting since the early 1480s".[41] Further, when Josquin left in 1504, Obrecht was to be the choice for the next head of the chapel. Yet there is no reason to believe that this volume was planned at the same time as that for Josquin. It did not appear until six months later; more crucially, although the Josquin edition had shown a need for additional decorative initials (to start each movement of the mass), they were apparently not ordered before the Obrecht book was planned. At that point, evidently, Petrucci recognised that he might continue to face the special pattern of initials in mass books, in at least one more book.

The third volume of masses, which contains music by Brumel, continues the Ferrarese connection and strengthens the possibility that Alfonso's circle at court was responsible for the whole series. On his ascension to the dukedom in 1505, Alfonso released Obrecht and appointed Brumel in his place. At the same time, the choice of Brumel may reflect the esteem that he was held in by the supplier of the music. His Latin-texted works had been well represented in earlier volumes: *Mater patris* in *Odhecaton A*; *Ave ancilla trinitas* and *Noe noe* (as well as two French-texted pieces) in *Canti B*. He was the only composer to have more than one Latin-texted work in these two volumes.[42] In addition he was represented by *Ave stella matutina* and *Regina coeli letare* in *Motetti A*, and, finally, the large-scale *Lauda syon salvatorem* in *Motetti B*. The inclusion of Brumel among the composers represented in this first series of mass volumes seems to be merely an extension of that pattern.

The fourth book is of music by Ghiselin, produced while the composer was on his way to Ferrara. But for the last two volumes, the picture is not as clear: La Rue (represented by the fifth book) had no known contacts with Ferrara, or indeed with any center in Italy.[43] It is possible that the impetus for a mass series had slowed, or that Ferrara had no plans for more volumes. A second edition of *Canti B* preceded the book of La Rue's masses, and the massive edition of *Canti C* came between it and the book devoted to Agricola. It may be that La Rue was of interest to Castellanus rather than promoted in Ferrara.

Agricola was certainly known in Ferrara, for he had visited the city almost thirty years earlier, and his music continued to be well known there and was included in earlier Petrucci editions. The mass for which fragments survive at the Modena Archivio di Stato[44] is included in Petrucci's volume twenty years later.

The Agricola book was the last in a series of six, each devoted to a single composer, published in a period of just eighteen months, and it appeared a mere six weeks after the last in the series of chanson and motet volumes. That series of five titles had taken nearly three years to appear, even though they had been popular: there were new editions, and the music was soon known in Germany as well as in Italy. The mass books, on the other hand, were not reprinted (at least not for some years, and some not at all). We have to assume that they moved more slowly. Even with a smaller print-run (which was likely for at least the later volumes in the series of six), the immediate demand was apparently fully satisfied by the available number of copies. Further, Petrucci apparently had copies available for sale long after they were printed; a sheet from the edition of La Rue's masses (1503) was still in his shop when he retired in 1520.[45] And yet Petrucci printed six such volumes in short order.

Given the dates of publication, Petrucci can hardly have waited to see how the first mass volume sold, but, from the second on, he pressed ahead with the series. The whole series must have been, to a greater extent than we can guess, promoted and distributed by means of patronage and gift. The Ferrarese patron whom I propose, having scored a minor coup with his edition of Josquin (and won the debate over whom to hire as *maestro*), had gained enough prestige to decide to continue the series of mass volumes, probably selecting the names of the composers to be included.

The music itself also presumably came from Ferrara.[46] While the proposed courtier patron may merely have suggested (or requested) that Castellanus find masses by particular composers to give to Petrucci, there is no reason to believe that the patron did not also arrange for Castellanus to have specific compositions for inclusion. I have already pointed out how the selection of Josquin's works emphasises his contrapuntal and organisational skills, even at the expense of his more lyrical gifts. The other volumes similarly show a range of styles that seem to represent each composer well.

A second series of masses, which begins a year later, suggests a different range of composers and interests. It opens with De Orto, representing a style and generation (as well as musical centers) notably lacking in the first series; it also includes Isaac, not appointed to Ferrara when Josquin's supporters, and his music, won the day. It would seem that, with the first six volumes, my proposed Ferrarese patron had exhausted the range of composers that would serve him well in the competition for prestige at court. With one exception, the few remaining significantly popular composers, among them Japart, were not notable for their sacred music; the exception is Martini, whose masses were already well represented in Ferrarese sources. Thus, it is reasonable to look elsewhere for the stimulus for the second cycle.

In the meantime, Petrucci turned back to volumes entitled "Motet", although with a rather different look to them, and he also started on frottole. The pressure, apparently stemming from Ferrara, for mass settings had evaporated.

> Group 3: The new motet books:
>   *Motetti C*: 15 Sept. 1504
>   *Motetti Libro Quarto*: 4 June 1505

The most visible difference between the first two motet books and this pair is that the new volumes are printed in part-books. This is symptomatic of a larger change. In chapter 8, I pointed out that the landscape-format small choirbook was unsuitable for ensemble performance from the book, and I cited Gallico as arguing that one reason for the change to part-books was the perceived need of larger choral ensembles.[47] This (with its attached implication of professional trained singers) was a reasonable assumption when printing complete mass settings, and it is valid for the present context also and helps to distinguish the two new motet books from the earlier ones.

There are superficial resemblances between the two pairs of books. Both of the present volumes also have high concentrations of works in honour of the Virgin Mary—more than half of *Motetti IV*; indeed, each opens with a series of Marian compositions. These are joined by a number of works honoring popular saints, Anne, Catherine, and Sebastian, as well as Christ and the Trinity. Both, again, have works that were commonly attributed to Brumel, Josquin, or Weerbeke, with single works by Agricola; alongside them are pieces from the composers that have made up the bulk of Petrucci's earlier books—Compère, Ghiselin, Isaac, and others.

The differences are perhaps more significant. These two new books have a higher preponderance of works that seem to be designed for professional performance, either because of their liturgical function (as in psalm settings or a work for the dedication of a church), or perhaps from the structure and style of the work (as in the *Liber generationis* attributed to Josquin, or Obrecht's *O beate Basili*). This would go hand-in-hand with the decision to print the volumes as part-books. Nonetheless, there is no evidence of any plan behind the choice of works, such as an attempt at providing a range of works to meet liturgical needs; despite the presence of a few such compositions, the general picture is of pieces that happened to please the collector, or at least were available.

There is also a slight difference between the two books, a difference that does not give any guidance about the sources for the music. It is notable that the great majority of the works in *Motetti C* is anonymous; in fact, the only attributions appear in the first gathering, where every piece is accorded a composer. This is surely a phenomenon of the printing process, rather than of the copy supplied. As the paper patterns confirm, the first gathering was certainly printed last, for it contains an index to the volume.

Little more needs to be said about these two volumes; the ranges of composers and works suggest a silhouette for the selector of the works similar to that for the first books: an interest in a wide range of composers and styles, including some that might now seem to have been out of date.[48] At the same time, the expansion, both in styles and (more particularly) in length and complexity found in some compositions, argues that this pair of volumes was prepared more as a response to the success of the first series of mass volumes; in publishing these two motet books in parts, Petrucci (presumably with Castellanus) was directing them at the purchasers of those books.

There may have been some hesitation after *Motetti C* while waiting to see how well it sold; almost nine months elapsed before *Motetti IV* appeared. Perhaps, too, the absence of a large-scale letter "D" almost encouraged Petrucci to think in terms of sets of three. Certainly, between these two volumes, Petrucci launched into two new endeavours. The first, the early books of frottole, seems again to have been planned as a set of three volumes, whereas the second, new mass volumes, was more probably an extension of the old series and developed into a series as time passed.

> Group 4: The first frottole books:
> *Frottole Libro primo*: 28 Nov. 1504
> *Frottole Libro secondo*: 8 Jan. 1505; 29 Jan. 1508
> *Frottole Libro tertio*: 6 Feb. 1505; 26 Nov. 1507

As with the mass group, this series introduces a significantly different repertoire and also a clearly different mode of presentation.

It is true that Petrucci was again printing a secular repertoire in choirbook layout, but he faced new issues. On one hand, layout was simplified: most frottole took a single page or a single opening, more consistently even than did the contents of the *Canti* volumes. Petrucci could plan ahead; he and his suppliers could set out to fill a specified number of gatherings in an orderly manner—as is shown in a number of ways, some of which are relevant here. Among others is the opportunity (usually taken) to follow a single-page composition by another, or by one taking three pages, thus filling complete openings.

A more important new feature concerns the treatment of the texts. Whatever we may say about the performance of the texts in the *Canti* series, these frottole were regularly sung with the words. This is to be expected: the essence of the frottola genres lay in the texts, and only rarely did the music seek to compete— even in those many cases where the music shows considerable artistry.

First, the Cantus part, almost without exception, has at least one complete strophe and refrain of text underlaid. In some cases, including a few where Michele Pesenti is assigned both words and music, the lower voices are also given a full text. These texts were normally set by the composer much more syllabically than were those of the motets and masses found in Petrucci's recent volumes. This means that the printer, faced with more than partial text or textual cues, had to govern his musical space more carefully, and in accordance with the spacing of the text; text spacing dominated that of the music, for the whole of each book. While this probably affected the sequence of operations in the printing shop, it presented no real problems for the compositor.[49]

The decision to present all the text, that is, including additional strophes, for many pieces, is more interesting. This produces a real technical change, requiring that the additional verses be printed in space normally occupied by staves. Since the staves remained in the skeleton formes,[50] the additional verses of text had to be set in the same forme as the musical notation.

This change in procedure merely stresses just how important the full text was for the purchasers of the books—or at least for the editor's view of the potential purchasers. In this, Petrucci was following the view of the scribes of earlier manuscripts. In chanson sources, the presentation of Italian texts had tended to follow the patterns of presentation for chansons. Sometimes this meant that the words were loosely laid under the top voice, with additional text set into a separate space on the page; sometimes, as with I-Bc Q18, it meant very little text at all. The early sources devoted to frottole are much more consistent: I-MOe α.F.9,9, a Paduan source probably written before Petrucci began work, and perhaps the earliest of the central sources for the repertoire, gives the complete text, underlaid to the top voice, with additional strophes copied between the parts. The other three voices have only textual incipits, often extending to the length of a full line of verse. This manuscript is also in the landscape format adopted by Petrucci.

Of the early-sixteenth-century sources with significant numbers of frottole, the great majority follow this pattern: they include I-Fc Basevi 2441, I-Fn B.R.230, I-Mt 55, GB-Lbl Egerton 3051, and F-Pn Rès.Vm⁷.676. These sources come from various centers in Italy, and all were probably copied by 1513; some may even predate Petrucci's first book of frottole. But what they certainly do indicate is that this pattern of texting was a norm, virtually obligatory, for frottole. Petrucci must have felt required to follow the pattern, reflecting what his supplier and purchasers would have expected.

It is significant, therefore, that both Petrucci's editions and these manuscripts present frottole as if composed for (three or) four separate lines, hardly independent, but laid out as if to be performed by separate people. This confirms, if confirmation were needed, that the great court presenters of frottole, lutenist-singers, were indeed improvisers, and that this side of their skill did not translate easily to other performers. Those others needed clear-cut parts that would allow them to re-create the chordal progressions used by the improvisers, without having to acquire the skills, of either creation or lute- or viola-playing. Given the general absence of text for the lower voices, in both manuscripts and printed editions, it is plausible to suggest that individual lines could easily be taken on lutes or violas, with amateurs playing single parts, rather than the whole harmonic web.

Some years ago, Claudio Gallico remarked that, in effect, Petrucci's editions present the first affirmation of the significance of an Italian genre.[51] It is true that the frottola was the first genre, alongside the lauda, both to use the Italian language and to be accessible to more than merely court circles—the latter point distinguishes it from the trecento repertoire. Given the total number of copies of all Petrucci's frottola volumes that were printed and sold (whatever that number may have been), it is evident that they reached more widely than could all the extant manuscripts; with the total number of frottole actually included in those volumes, they also presented a much larger repertoire. The first three alone, apparently produced as a set, included 177 compositions. By contrast, while there are 187 works in I-Fn Panc.27 (though less than half have Italian texts), and 156 in I-Fn B.R.230, there are only 64 in I-Mt 55 and 65 in I-VEcap DCCLVII.

It is also true that few of these manuscripts appeared before Petrucci's books.[52] Nonetheless, Petrucci must have been responding to a previous affirmation of the frottola's significance. It may be that he and his partners were influenced by the relatively recent appearance from Venetian publishers of editions of texts by Boiardo, Cornazano, Serafino Aquilano, and Tebaldeo, among others.[53] But, whatever the stimulus, Petrucci's first three books were published within ten weeks, immediately after *Motetti C*. In committing themselves at once to the set of three books, Petrucci and his partners must not have doubted that there was a ready market for printed sources of frottole; nor could the promoter of the series.

There is no clear evidence of whom that promoter might have been. We have few enough sources from the crucial years leading up to Petrucci's editions, and those sources show little relationship to his repertoire, in either the range of composers favoured, or the actual pieces chosen. If the opening piece in a volume is presumed to be significant,[54] it is notable that Petrucci's first book begins with a single work by Giovanni Brocco; the other work by him in this book calls him "Ioannes Brocchus Vero". The most important composers (Cara, Tromboncino, and Pesenti, in this order) are also given a Veronese appendage to their names, at their first appearance (except in the case of Michele Pesenti, for which see below), even though they were no longer resident in the city.

I have previously drawn attention to the arrangement of compositions in this book[55] and argued that it implies a change of plan, involving added compositions, after the first four gatherings were completed. These four are almost evenly divided between Cara and Tromboncino, with two works by Brocco, and two by Pesenti, named simply "Michael.". There is then a sudden shift to two gatherings devoted solely to works by Pesenti, who is then presented (with the first piece of these gatherings) as "Michael Pesentus Vero.". After this series, which extends into the seventh gathering (on G1*r*), a mixed bag of composers is used to round out the last gathering. These include another Veronese, "Georgius de la Porta Vero"., as well as Josquin, and composers announced as from Brescia and Venice. This last group of seven compositions, after the previous six gatherings, is apparently a make-weight, included to round out the collection to the size that was viable for Petrucci. (There was probably no other composer from Verona who could supply a gathering of six to seven compositions.)

I suspect that the same holds true for the collection of Pesenti's works. Even by the end of the fourth gathering there is some evidence of the breakdown of an organised structure. While the first two gatherings are well ordered, so that they begin and end with Brocco (two single-page pieces, on A2*r* and B8*r*), the second pair do not work as well. Tromboncino's works begin on B8*v*, and the group does end on D8*r*, but the two "Michael." pieces are inserted on D3*v* and D8*v*, apparently to help complete a gathering. Only after that is the long sequence of Pesenti pieces introduced, as if the decision to include a series of his works was made later in the planning stage. In practice, it does not matter whether the music for three gatherings (E–G), or only for the last, was the afterthought; the pattern clearly indicates some sort of later addition on the part of the supplier of the music.

These features do not mean that Pesenti or Brocco supplied the music for the volume. But they do imply that the supplier was interested in providing a group of "Veronese" compositions (perhaps to offset the Ferrarese emphasis of earlier volumes), and that he did not know how much music would fill seven gatherings. Petrucci's editions may follow the layout of contemporary frottola manuscripts, but they regularly use more staves to the page, and the added text takes up less space.[56] Both of these factors (the apparent organization by composer, and the implication of inexperience in the spacing of printed books) argue against Castellanus being the supplier of the music, for Book I at least. Indeed, all the evidence, while not pointing at anyone in particular, is indicative of a different pattern of collecting and presentation (see Table 9-1).

Books II and III followed closely on Book I. It is reasonable to assume that they are related; indeed, Book II starts out in a similar vein. After a first composition attributed to "R.M"., it announces two groups of works, the first filling two gatherings with works by "Franciscus Venetus Orga".—Francesco d'Ana, the organist at San Marco, who had died in 1498.[57] This is followed by two gatherings of largely anonymous works, with a few attributions to two more "Veronese"

TABLE 9-1 Distribution of composers by gathering in the first two books of frottole (1504 and 1505)

Bk I:	A–B:	Cara (bracketed by Brocco)
	C–D:	Tromboncino (with some Pesenti)
	E–F:	Pesenti
	G:	miscellany
Bk II:	A–B:	d'Ana
	C:	anonyma
	D:	Veronese composers
	E:	anonyma
	F:	Honophrius Antenoreus
	G:	Nicolo Patavino

composers, Peregrinus Cesena and Antonius Rossetus, to B. T[romboncino], and finally (on D7ν–8r) to Rossinus Mantuanus. This Rossinus is probably the "R.M". who opened the book, suggesting a pattern similar to that of the first book—in this case, four gatherings of music, framed by a single composer. The rest of the book is anonymous, at least in the first edition. The second edition shows that it contained a series of pieces by Honophrius Antenoreus, occupying the sixth gathering, and by Nicolo Patavino, which fill the seventh and last. Since Honophrius is probably the same man as the Honophrius Patavinus of later Petrucci volumes, this book effectively ends with two gatherings of music by Paduan composers. Once again, the emphasis is on music by composers from the Veneto, by and large advertised as such at the heads of their compositions. This follows the pattern of the first volume, in gathering together small collections of works by a single composer, and then presenting them in sequence, each with an acknowledgment of his city of origin. Equally important is the extent to which each collection approximately fills a gathering. While some start or end on the first or last complete opening of a gathering, others bridge the joins; but all seem to be designed to meet the practical needs of a book printed in eights. Because of this connection between content and bibliographical structure, Petrucci could easily have assigned different material to different typesetters, which is probably how he managed to produce all three books so quickly.

Book III does not work in this manner. There are few runs of a single composer's works (unless one includes "Anonymous", with the sequence that is contained largely in gathering F), and those that do exist do not correspond to the gathering structure. The group of works by Tromboncino forms a significant part of gathering C, and that by Cara crosses from D to E. The other composers are mainly the same as in the first two books, although no stress is laid on their origins, and their music is not grouped into sets. In other words, this volume much more closely resembles a miscellany of pieces collected from various sources. Whereas the first book had six (or perhaps four) consistent gatherings, with the seventh filled out with a mixture of pieces; and the second was planned for seven gatherings (assuming that the two groups of anonyma are homogeneous in some manner); this third book is made up of eight gatherings, not one of which could be seen as an organised unit. It rather looks as though the three books represent the larger part of a single private collection, with Book 3 collecting the remnants, after two organised collections.

To summarise: the books' promoter came to Petrucci with over 150 pieces, many of them arranged in a manner that reflects the patterns of collecting Italian music by composer, known since the fourteenth century. These were organised into two books, with an emphasis on Veronese origin for the composers in the first, and a strong collection of Venetian and Paduan composers in the second. At this point, the music filled an odd number of gatherings (thirteen), and the last (G) of the first book was made up with pieces from the remaining miscellaneous collection. This left enough pieces to fill a slightly larger third book, as it turned out. In fact, there is the same number of pieces, sixty-four, as the first book, but those for the third include fewer that could be fitted onto a single page, and a few, including a group of works by Cara, that required two openings.

This provides a second significant reason why these books should be associated, and also why they should be separated from the next. They were not only produced in short order, but also show a progressive decline in the level of organization, until the end constitutes a collection of whatever the promoter wanted to include. It is not surprising, therefore, that there is a gap before the fourth book appears. That will also be significant for the different manner in which it advertises itself.

> Group 5: the next series of mass volumes:
> *Misse de Orto*: 22 March 1505
> *Missarum Josquin Liber secundus*: 30 June 1505 (also Fossombrone)
> *Fragmenta Missarum*: 31 Oct. 1505
> *I Missarum Josquin*: second edition [Aug. 1506]
> *Misse Henrici Jzac*: 20 Oct. 1506
> *Misse Gaspar*: 7 Jan. 1507

These volumes evidently took time to reach the press, for they cover a span of nearly two years. It is probable that each represents a distinct decision, given this length of time, and especially the gap of almost a year between the *Fragmenta Missarum* and the new edition of Josquin's first book. It is true that a fair amount of the time was spent in continuing other established series, or reprinting earlier books. Apparently unless one of these new mass volumes had been urgently demanded by a patron willing to support its production, it would always take second place to a book with a guaranteed sale, such as a new edition of a successful title. More urgent, and therefore more likely to delay the production of a new title, would be a commissioned volume, or any cancel leaves needed for books currently in stock.

Immediately after the production of De Orto's collection, cancel leaves were prepared for the extant editions of *Motetti B* and *Motetti C* (originally from May 1503 and September 1504). With the directly preceding second edition of *Motetti A*, there was evidently a market for these books. The cancels were followed by *Motetti IV*, which also would be likely to sell, if it could be related to the preceding motet volumes. Between the second book of Josquin's masses and the *Fragmenta Missarum* came the first of the next series of frottole volumes, Book IV. Books I–III must have been selling well, for we know that two of them were to be reprinted; Book IV also reached a second edition, in just about two years. In addition, Petrucci seems not to have worked continuously during this period. This may be related to Castellanus's absence from Venice during the summer of 1505,[58] though there is no corresponding gap in Petrucci's output.

It is reasonable, therefore, to assume that the mass series had become, not a set of books like the first three frottola volumes (or even the first set of mass books), but an ongoing series, to which new volumes could be added if the market seemed ready and when the music was available.

The most likely source for the music in the first of these books, that of de Orto's masses, would seem to have been Rome, though probably at more than one remove, and yet few of these works have any Italian concordances. Only one of the five (his *Missa L'homme arme*) is also represented in any Sistine manuscript (in Cap.Sist.64, probably copied after the composer's service in the papal chapel).[59]

One other, the *Missa Dominicalis*, survives in I-VEcap DCCLXI, which carries a repertoire standing at the early end of Petrucci's output—Binchois, Busnois, Faugues—alongside Brumel, Josquin, Martini, and van Weerbeke. Christopher Reynolds has argued for a close connection between this manuscript and Vatican sources.[60]

Discussing de Orto's life and output, Martin Picker has drawn attention to the way that sources for his music divide into an Italian group (with Sistine manuscripts pre-eminent), and a northern group, largely with different works.[61] Picker points out that Petrucci's editions seem to bridge the gap in sources and suggests "that the printer made a special effort to obtain representative works of De Orto, including some written after the composer left Italy". Apart from the point, which I have stressed several times, that Petrucci himself seems to have done little to collect music for his editions, I am sceptical that any collector of music for Petrucci would have sought music from north of the Alps. The concordance pattern also suggests that few other Italians were really interested in collecting de Orto's music; there are few concordances for any of his works. Castellanus, however, seems to have had an interest in the composer: he put de Orto first in the *Odhecaton A*, thirteen of the composer's twenty-eight extant works are included in Petrucci's books before the end of 1506; and these include the first work in the future *Fragmenta Missarum*. Further, if Martin Picker is right in believing that the five masses printed by Petrucci cover a span of over twenty years before 1500, the relative conservatism of some aspects of the works may have made them more attractive to Castellanus. Indeed, I believe that this interest on Castellanus's part, rather than the activities of any patron, led to the publication of the present book.

I am not convinced, however, that Castellanus was the initiator of the second book of Josquin's masses. Josquin had left Ferrara more than a year before it was published, and at first sight it may be seen merely as a response to the good sale of the first Josquin book. However, Duke Ercole had died in January of 1505, and Lewis Lockwood argues that "there is no doubt" that the inclusion of Josquin's *Hercules dux Ferrariae* mass "was seen publicly as a tribute by a great composer to a famous patron".[62] It is probably safer to argue that the whole edition was a tribute to the late duke. The selection of works is quite different from that of the first volume. The mass *Ave maris stella* can be seen as reflecting a particular Marian interest on the part of the duke; his *Corona Beatae Mariae Virginis*, a sequence of prayers, begins with this text.[63] No doubt the mass opens Petrucci's volume as a prayer on the duke's behalf. It is followed by the mass on his name. The remaining four masses are based on French tunes; two of these chansons (Ockeghem's *Malheur me bat* and Josquin's own *Une musque de buscaya*) had already appeared in Petrucci's chanson series, and both are also present in the Ferrarese I-Rc 2856. It is likely that the set of four reflect ducal, or at least Ferrarese, taste in some way.

This one volume, therefore, must be associated with members of the Ferrarese court circle. While it may be that Castellanus wanted to make his own tribute to the duke, that must be unlikely, partly because the book appeared soon after he had left for Recanati, and partly because I would have expected him to arrange for Petrucci to print it earlier in the year. Instead, the music probably came directly from Ferrara. If my view of the genesis of Petrucci's first book of Josquin masses is correct, it would seem very likely that the same patron would have commissioned this new book. The patron may well have been in Alfonso's circle, as I propose above, for Alfonso himself ascended to the duchy on Ercole's death.

After this book, Petrucci began the second series of frottola volumes. That sequence, again of three books, was interrupted once Castellanus returned from Recanati, and work was begun on the *Fragmenta Missarum*. The repertoire of this book presents some interesting features, not least the strong series of works by Josquin, which may reflect a response on Castellanus's part to the stimuli for the preceding second book of masses. The book opens, somewhat unusually for any Italian source of music for the mass, with two settings each of three different liturgical texts. For the first two, *Asperges me* and *Vidi aquam*, settings by well-known composers (Compère and Brumel) are preceded by works by Fortuila. Whoever he was,[64] he must somehow be associated with the sources for the music, but these works seem to be unique to this edition. Both texts, with the third, *Salve sancta parens*, could be used for festal masses, matched by the final work in the edition, a *Haec dies*, intended for the Easter liturgy.

In between are two layers; first are settings of the Ordinary, although the organization of the collection is far from straightforward. After a single Kyrie—by de Orto—and a Gloria by Stockem,[65] there is a group of seven Credos, by seven different composers. At this point, there is an evident change of plan: nine consecutive pieces—a Gloria, five Credos, one *Missa Ferialis*, and two Sanctus settings—are attributed to Josquin. It appears that the supplier of the music (and I believe it was still Castellanus) had planned two groups of music, first, an anthology comprising a group of Propers and a group of Credo settings, to be followed by the selection of works by Josquin. This would have completed the book, perhaps with the addition of the single *Haec Dies* and would have filled two normal gatherings in both the Superius and Bassus books (allowing room for the device and colophon in the latter). The Tenor book, however, would not have filled a second gathering, while the Altus would have run into a third gathering. At this point, two more settings of the Credo were added, by Agricola and van Weerbeke, both already represented in the earlier layers of the edition.

A second feature of the anthology is the number of these works that do not appear to survive in any other extant source; this includes the first thirteen works—almost all the first layer, as I have proposed it. Only the last two of that layer, by Nicasius de Clibano and Compère, are also found in Vatican manuscripts (and the former also in I-VEcap DCCLXI). Josquin's movements, which seem to have had a very limited circulation, especially before Petrucci's edition, are also extant elsewhere principally in Vatican manuscripts.

It would seem logical to assert that the collection came to Castellanus directly from Roman sources. Among the contents, however, are two sets of conflicting attributions. Josquin's Patrem on *La belle se siet* is attributed to Robert de Févin in I-Rvat Cap.Sist.41: this is surely a preferable attribution, if only because of the Sistine choir's awareness both of other works by the lesser Févin and of the production of Josquin. Josquin's *Missa Ferialis* is anonymous in I-Rvat Cap.Sist.35, an earlier source that should have reflected any attribution to Josquin more accurately. (Again, it is also in I-VEcap DCCLXI.) Both of these instances suggest that Castellanus did not receive this music directly from Rome, or at least not from authoritative sources. The second work is, perhaps reliably, ascribed to Martini in I-MOe α.M.1.13.

If the Josquin anthology may have had Roman antecedents (however distant), it is harder to assert this for the first collection of Credos. With so many unica, the presence of the last two works is hardly sufficient evidence; it does not have to be, for the picture of the volume as a whole implies that it is a composite of more than one collection, and therefore probably of more than one source.

However, the best name to suggest for Petrucci's supplier remains that of Petrus Castellanus. He had been back from Recanati long enough to supply the music for this edition, and he probably had the standing to persuade Petrucci to put the current series of frottola volumes on one side, to print this volume. After it, however, Petrucci did return to the frottole, printing Books V and VI of the series; he also printed two books of Lamentations, and the first of laude, before returning to masses. It is possible that the *Fragmenta Missarum* was intended to close the series of mass volumes, presenting isolated movements, especially Credos, and summing up Josquin's work in the genre. The gap following the *Fragmenta Missarum*, a period of several months before the next mass book, certainly confirms that the books of Isaac's and van Weerbeke's masses represent independent publishing decisions. Indeed, they may well represent a surge of interest in purchasing settings of the mass.

The reprint of the first book of Josquin's masses must be placed somewhere in the summer of 1506. The combination of papers,[66] as much as the timing of the dated editions, argue that late July or August was the most likely time. Unusually, sheets from this reprint could not be sold with sheets from the first edition. Petrucci changed the layout of each voice part to a more economical one that corresponded closely to that of other mass books of the period. This implies that the first edition had been completely distributed by the middle of the year; while it is tempting to think that much (perhaps all) of the first printing was taken by the patron I have proposed, nonetheless the intervening mass volumes must have sparked an interest in purchasing printed editions of mass settings. This edition would then have led to an assumption that Isaac's and van Weerbeke's were viable.

It is plausible that the music for both these last two volumes also came from Castellanus. In many ways, both were almost inevitable choices for a continuation of the series. Isaac's position as a (unwitting) rival of Josquin for the position in Ferrara had probably excluded him from inclusion in the first series of books. His absence there is another factor in my belief that Alfonso d'Este's circle had much to do with the early mass volumes. But Isaac's international fame, stature in Florence, and prestige in Ferrara would all have required that he now be included. His book seems to have sold well; as Staehelin remarked years ago, the book was reprinted.

Equally inevitable was the choice of van Weerbeke. This was the last mass volume to be devoted to a single composer before 1514 and the completely different situation in Fossombrone. Castellanus had already shown his interest in the composer, including a number of his pieces in earlier volumes; he would have been reflecting the composer's standing in both Rome and Milan.

Attempts at deciding the provenance of the music for these two volumes run into the same problems faced when considering the immediately previous ones. There are too few concordant sources: every significant variant in readings suggests only that the two principal sources do not have a close connection, without clearly pointing elsewhere; every significant agreement may be meaningless when there are no other sources to act as controls. There is no reason to believe that the music for both volumes did not come from Rome, at least indirectly; nor is there enough reason to be obliged to accept a Roman provenance.

These five new volumes of masses, coupled with the first series of six, give a revealing picture of what the partnership thought would sell. To a certain extent, the choice of composers reflects those who appeared most frequently in the early volumes of *Canti* and motets. This is particularly evident in the first series. Agricola and Josquin were the best represented in the secular volumes, alongside Compère, and followed by Busnois and Japart. Presumably, there was no prospect of a set of masses from any of these last three, although a Credo by Busnois is notable as probably the earliest work in the *Fragmenta Missarum*, and another work is by Compère. Equally popular with Castellanus were Brumel, Ghiselin, and Obrecht, well represented in the motet volumes. This list almost completes the names chosen for the first series of mass volumes. It also comprises most of the leading composers who were employed in Italy during the years around 1500, and who had a wide dissemination of their music. The one exception, as I have said, is Pierre de la Rue.

The second series of mass volumes follows a similar pattern: three of the four single-composer volumes—by Josquin, Isaac, and van Weerbeke—extend interests already evident in earlier editions. The one exception is the book devoted to de Orto, and this probably reflects the conservative side of Castellanus's tastes.

> Group 6: The second group of frottola books:
> *Strambotti, Ode, frottole . . . Libro quarto*: [Aug. 1505]; 31 July 1507
> *Frottole Libro quinto*: 23 Dec. 1505
> *Frottole Libro sexto*: 5 Feb. 1506

This series of frottola volumes looks quite unlike the first: there is no sign of the clear organization that marked the first two books of the earlier series. The present set was started in a gap in the sequence of mass volumes and was itself suspended while the book of *Fragmenta Missarum* was published. This tends to suggest that Castellanus had nothing to do with these frottola volumes, and that, as a senior member of the production team, he could interpose the liturgical book, once he had returned from Recanati.

The first of these new books, volume IV, distinguishes itself from the earlier volumes by its title. Instead of merely announcing a book of frottole, it is called *Strambotti, Ode, Frottole, sonette, Et modo di cantar versi latini e capituli*, adding the *Libro quarto* at the end to indicate that it is part of the larger series.[67] The tavola for this edition is also unusual, listing the contents according to the principal categories given in the title: the "Sonetti" list, containing a small group of pieces, also includes "Aer de Capituli", alongside an "Aer de cantar versi latini" and a "Modo de cantar sonetti".

This arrangement by content, suggested by the tavola, is the principal level at which one can see any semblance of organization in the volume. The bulk of gathering F is dedicated to odes, and most of G contains frottole by Lurano. But some examples of these two forms are placed according to different criteria: a group of frottole by "Ant Cap[reolus]" at the center of the first gathering has an ode attached to it; the same composer has another group of frottole and a single strambotto as the second half of gathering E. A small group of frottole by "N.P.". (Nicolo Patavino) and another by "F.V." (d'Ana) occupy gathering C. The rest of the volume does not present any clear structure. In particular, the so-called Sonetti and Capituli are placed apparently at random through the volume.

This suggests that the anthology was put together by someone other than the collector of the material for Books I–III, and that it was put together from a series of small collections. The supplier of the music selected pieces while working through each of these smaller collections and did no further arranging or sorting.

Much the same has probably to be said for Book V. There is no overall organizational principle; composers are often only mentioned in the tavola—and, in two cases, the name found there disagrees with that entered on the musical page. Four of the six gathering joins (A–B, B–C, D–E and F–G) have single-page pieces on both the verso and the recto. They are joined by a fifth (E–F), where a three-page composition ends the first gathering, and a single-page work opens the second. This suggests that the supplier of the music provided small batches, probably representing his own exemplars, and that Petrucci himself then played a small role in arranging the printed order of the pieces in order to divide the work between two compositors.[68]

Somebody certainly rearranged the opening gathering of Book VI. The analysis in my bibliographical description[69] shows how the index for the book was compiled in two stages. The first contains all the works from the beginning of gathering B; those in gathering A were added later. At the same time, the paper evidence argues that the outer sheet of gathering A (the one that contains the tavola) was printed late in the process. Finally, this first gathering has works by composers who otherwise only appear in the last gathering, alongside (more particularly) the small group of four three-voiced settings that are unique in Petrucci's repertoire for the melismatic character of the upper voice. The decision to redo the gathering was probably not made in order to insert the one or two pieces that were left over from the last gathering—works by Lurano and Honophrius [Antenoreous] Patavinus. The motive for the change was surely a wish to add these unusual three-voiced justiniane.

James Haar has convincingly shown that there are ways in which these three-voiced pieces lie outside the patterns of fifteenth-century justiniane settings.[70] His argument that they do not represent written-out improvisations, but rather lie in a peculiarly Venetian memory of the genre, associated with the memory of Giustiniani himself, fits well with the presentation of these pieces at the front of the book. He suggests that the three-voiced version was prepared for Petrucci, working from an earlier two-voiced version (and that this would correspond to the practice of adding an Altus part to otherwise three-voiced up-to-date frottole).

One is tempted to see here the same didactic mentality that controlled the indications of genre in Book IV, and an interest in "helping the amateur" by giving examples of this style. Such a view would be reinforced by the unusual heading given to the tavola of this volume: "Frottole Sonetti Stramboti Ode. Iustiniane numero sesante sie [*sic*]", corresponding to the organised tavola of Book IV. Apart from these features, the book is bibliographically straightforward. Every gathering begins and ends with a piece occupying only a single page, taking the arrangement of Book V even further, and suggesting that the whole content of the book could have been supplied to Petrucci in stages.

All three books impress by the manner in which any principle of organisation can have worked only on the smallest scale, at the level of perhaps five to six works. For all, it seems as if the compiler drew from collections at hand, selecting them in the order in which he came across them. This, coupled with the evidence of gathering-ends, suggests that the compiler may not have supplied all of any complete book at one time, rather providing a gathering or two of material as Petrucci needed it. This does not correspond at all with the way that the first three books were arranged. Although the last of those books was not so clearly structured, the set as a whole does show that there was an initial plan. This does not seem to be true for Books IV–VI. The two series of three frottola volumes must have had different suppliers, people with different interests and priorities. The approach to the first volumes, implying an interest in having a corpus arranged by composer and his origins, has perhaps given way here to an interest in genres and performing approaches to the various poetic forms.

These two sets also contain different repertoires. The extensive series of short settings of strambotti, the sonnet and ode settings, and particularly the two reciting tones, for sonnets and for "versi latini", mark off the first of the new series and indeed distinguish it from all the other frottola books to come. In this sense, the additional details on the title-page are essential. They would have told the purchaser that he was getting, not merely a continuation of the repertoire in the first books, but rather a manual of suitable melodic material, and a guide to performing additional texts. If nothing else, Book IV confirms that the supplier saw himself as supplying amateur musicians, those who knew of the repertoires being printed and wanted to expand their own expertise alongside their musical repertoire. This approach is matched by the presentation of the tavola in Book VI and argues that these two books at least came from the same supplier. There is even a little similar evidence in Book V, where the first pieces in both gatherings A and B are given formal designations: the heading on B1*r* reads "Per sonetti", suggesting that the music on that page is a model for use in other situations. Given the brief gaps between the three volumes (and the long gap before Book VII), one is justified in calling them a set, intended to complement the first set of three books, and make the whole repertoire more accessible to musicians wishing to learn basic performing skills—reciting poetry musically, embellishing vocal parts, and recalling a specifically Venetian tradition.[71]

This organizational (perhaps didactic) approach again does not suggest the mentality that had been guiding Castellanus. He had shown no desire to arrange works in any obvious sequence; Latin and Italian pieces are mixed in with the French in the *Canti* volumes, and there is no sense of organization by genre. (The only possible exception to this generalization lies in the volume of *Fragmenta Missarum*, and yet that volume lies closer to the other mass books, in both intention and organization.) For these reasons, it is difficult to argue that he might have been responsible for either set of three frottola volumes—the first because of the clear organization of the contents, the second because of the approach to the market. In addition, the second set opened with a book that was probably prepared while Castellanus was away from Venice, in Recanati.

Nonetheless, the most likely source for the music in Books IV–VI is Venetian, even apart from the specifically Venetian connotations for the justiniane, noted by Haar. D'Ana, well represented (particularly in Book IV), was, of course, in Venice; and Andrea d'Antiquis is called Venetian by Petrucci. Both Philippo de Lurano and Nicolo Patavino would be in Rome during the next decade, but both had close contacts with Cividale and received benefices there.[72] Further, the general shortage throughout these three books of pieces by Cara[73] should be coupled with the presentation of "model" settings to argue that the collector and supplier of the music was probably not related to any courtly or aristocratic milieu.

The books were, as I say, printed quickly. Even with the interjection of the *Fragmenta Missarum*, they appeared in under six months. No more frottola volumes were to be published for well over a year; either the supplier of the music had largely exhausted his stock (which seems possible, given the high proportion of anonyma in Book VI), or Petrucci had made the decision to produce three volumes as a group, to match the first three. Whatever the reason (and there are, of course, other possibilities), the speed with which these three books were produced argues strongly that the first set of three had sold well, and to a market that was looking for yet more. After Book VI, however, Petrucci immediately turned to other repertoires: two books of Lamentations appeared in the next four months, and the last two of the second series of mass books (discussed above), with the first of laude at the end of the year.

> Group 7: The two books of Lamentations:
> *Lamentationum prophete Jeremie Liber primus*: 8 April 1506
> *Lamentationum Liber secundus*: 29 May 1506

Once again, we see Petrucci starting a new repertoire with the expectation that it will include more than one book. Once again, given the short period elapsing between these two, he cannot have waited to see how the first volume sold before starting to print the second: the two were planned as a pair from the start. Indeed, he must have had much of the music for both volumes in hand before he started work on the first.

There is every reason to believe that the music in these books came from Castellanus. The content shows more than one style and compositional approach and is organised for the demands of the text and its liturgical occasion. All the settings, for two, three, or four voices, are straightforward, responsive to the formal structure of the text and often to the chant used for the Hebrew letters and for the verses proper.[74] Pieces tend to be grouped together, apparently largely to group similar composers, and these groupings also reveal basic stylistic divisions. Indeed, these two books together show a wider range of stylistic possibilities than any other book in Petrucci's output: from the melodic fifteenth-century writing of Ycart to the complex polyphony of Erasmus, and from the two-part decoration of a traditional solo version to Tromboncino's often treble-dominated frottolesque works, a suitable composition could have been found for ensembles of any size and ability.

This was surely a deliberate policy on the part of Petrucci and Castellanus. They could hope to sell a book of settings of Lamentation texts to many institutions that might not buy large-scale polyphonic masses or motets. The solemnity of Holy Week liturgies would encourage the use of simple polyphony in many institutions where it was not customary, if they could find singers to hire. The nature of Tenebrae, usually sung in the dark, required that the singers should be able to learn their music, and as a result that some of the settings should be easy to remember.

This must be why Petrucci and his colleagues were happy to publish the books in choirbook format—the first with Latin texts laid out thus since *Motetti B*. The music would not and could not be performed from the book during the liturgy. In practice, too, Book I worked much better in choirbook layout. With its mix of works for two, three, and four voices, any part-book arrangement would have been decidedly complicated; the Tenor book would have presented no problems, but the other parts, Altus and Bassus (and even the Superius in some of the three-voiced works), would have required a solution of the sort eventually adopted for the *Motetti à cinque*.

This is primarily true for the first book, which opens with an eye-catching piece, a single-page setting of the lauda text *Adoramus te Christe*, almost entirely homophonic and syllabic, with an harmonic bass moving as for a frottola. The rest of the book contains two quite different repertoires. The first half has six settings, whose composers can be related to the music of the *Canti* and earlier motet volumes. In addition to the Neapolitan repertoire of Tinctoris (from whom one chanson had already been published) and Ycart, there are works by Agricola and de Orto, both of whom had received mass volumes from Petrucci's hand. Each of their works is a relatively short setting of a group of verses, presumably to be associated with a single celebration. Although their style is more complex than that of the first two motet books, it should, with its frequent cadences and repetitions of sections for the Hebrew letters, have been within the reach of singers of the same ability. This repertoire probably came from the same source as those motets, the courts and choirs that had supplied Castellanus from the beginning.

The second half seems quite different. It comprises an extended series of two-voice settings, probably by de Quadris, and perhaps composed in the 1460s.[75] The whole series in this two-voiced section fills a clear liturgical need: in addition to the Lamentation setting itself, there are three texts needed for the Good Friday vigil, also composed by de Quadris. Although the musical basis of this series of movements was monophonic, and evidently widely disseminated, his setting is certainly from the Veneto. The last piece in the volume is also Venetian, a laudalike setting for four parts of *Passio sacra*, composed by Francesco d'Ana, late of San Marco. It is quite reasonable to suggest that this half of the volume represents a traditional Venetian repertoire, for it is known that the de Quadris setting was sung at San Marco through much of the sixteenth century.

Although a number of the movements appear to be anonymous, most can be related stylistically to the schools followed by the named composers in each part of the book; indeed, Elmer Thomas has ascribed a number of the anonyma in the second part to De Quadris,[76] although it is at least as likely that they were composed by other musicians, working in Venetian institutions, but forgotten by 1506.

The second book also has few attributions. Significantly, three names are listed on the title page, and the book's organization suggests that they composed all the music in it. First is Tromboncino, followed by Gaspar van Weerbeke, and Erasmus.[77] While these names suggest a connection with the first part of Book 1, there is a significant difference. Here the two principal composers are represented by long sequences of movements, to be performed on more than one day. Indeed, the set from Tromboncino is probably liturgically complete. Although this set, like the other works in Book II, is not musically complex, it clearly requires a different ensemble, and different skills, from those of the set by de Quadris, in Book I.

It is notable, however, that both books present a seemingly incongruous juxtaposition of composers and styles: whereas the first book has works by Flemish composers followed by a much simpler Italian setting, the second reverses the order, both of composing background and of stylistic complexity. The first book appeared just four days before Easter, on the Wednesday that would have required some of the music it contains. With nine weeks since the previous publication, Petrucci should have been able to produce it sooner, and there may therefore have been some problem with the supply of music. This could be the best explanation for the unusual pairing of music in the two books. The music by de Quadris and d'Ana (in Book I) takes roughly the same space as that by van Weerbeke and Erasmus (in Book II). It is tempting to suggest that there was a delay in providing Petrucci with the music by van Weerbeke (who was soon to be accorded a volume in the mass series): this could have resulted in a change in the order of music in the two books, moving de Quadris's setting out of its intended place in the second half of Book II, into Book I. It would have made more sense to have planned the two books to be distinguished clearly by repertoire—one containing more complex music by northern composers, and the other with simple works by Tromboncino and de Quadris (with d'Ana). This would make each more consistent, not only by composer's origins but also stylistically, while providing a self-contained and comprehensive pair of volumes. These volumes were followed by the last two in the series of volumes of masses (discussed above), between which Petrucci was apparently commissioned to undertake a new venture.

Group 8: Dammonis: *Laude I*: [Summer 1506]

The sole surviving copy of this edition carries a date of 7 July 1508; it followed the second book of laude by almost six months. For all but two sheets, the bibliographical evidence supports the date. The state of the initials and the paper usage both confirm this, and the colophon has an identical setting of type to that found in the second book, with merely a change of date. It might seem that the signature pattern, using single letters "A" in the second book, and doubled letters "AA" in Dammonis's volume, implies that his edition was the later.

However, this was not unusual at this stage of Petrucci's career; during 1506, Petrucci had signed the two books of Lamentations according to the same pattern. He also used the "AA" sequence in other books during the same period, for example, in the Gaspar masses in early 1507.

Some years ago, Jonathan Glixon proposed that there should have been an earlier first edition, preceding the publication of the second book, in 1508.[78] Indeed, the bibliographical evidence confirms his suggestion, for the unique copy preserves two sheets that must have been printed earlier. They place the book certainly in 1506, and probably in the middle of the year, at about the same time as the second edition of Josquin's first book of masses.[79]

Glixon has investigated the contents of Dammonis's book in some detail.[80] The composer, whom Glixon identifies as a member of the Canons Regular of San Salvatore, opens his book with a dedication, to Seraphinus Venetus, prior of the church of San Salvatore in Venice, and a recent Prior General of the order.[81] Dedications are rare in Petrucci's output: apart from those in the *Odhecaton A*, there is only one other, in Spinacino's first volume. Like that, this dedication implies that the signer was a prime mover in having the book published. Dammonis would have seen that the earlier books of Lamentations (of the same year), containing settings that were technically very simple, could sell well: for the same reason, Petrucci would have been receptive to his proposal.

The collection probably represents a number of years' production. It opens with two relatively complex pieces, both canonic, no doubt intended to set a high musical tone. Glixon points out the wide range of musical styles, reflected in the various manners of underlaying texts. He also discusses the texts, and the extent to which they reveal Florentine, as well as Venetian and other, more neutral, contexts. His data show that the compositions reflecting these various backgrounds are not presented in groups, but freely intermingled across the volume. There is other evidence suggesting that Dammonis drew from different parts of his personal collection, without any particular concern for internal consistency. Adjacent pieces honouring the Virgin Mary may have different captions: *De beata virgine*, *Ad beatam virginem*, or *Gaudia beate virginis*.

This case is even stronger, for there is evidence, discussed in the bibliographical commentary, suggesting that the second edition was expanded at a late stage in its preparation. In brief, this lies in the ordering of the tavola and in the use of headlines describing the texts that were set. It appears that the book was originally planned (and the first edition presumably executed) to be seven gatherings long, but that a gathering was added to the end of the new edition late during its production. This would tend to confirm that Dammonis was directly involved with the production of the book, and that he retained this interest even with the second edition. This interest would explain the presence of the book in Petrucci's output; after it, he produced the last of the group of mass books, devoted to Weerbeke, before exploring ways to fulfill his right to print tabulature.

Group 9: The four lute books:
    Spinacino: *Intabulatura de Lauto Libro primo*: [27 Feb.] 1507
    Spinacino: *Intabulatura de Lauto Libro secondo*: 31 March 1507

Alemannus: *Intabulatura de Lauto Libro tertio*: 20 June 1508
Dalza: *Intabulatura de Lauto Libro quarto*: 31 Dec. 1508

This set clearly represents more than one publishing decision. The gap between the second and the third is long enough (and filled with enough other volumes) that we cannot assume that the last two were planned when the first two were printed. Further, despite the impact of Marco dall'Aquila's petition of 1505, Petrucci had not reacted at once, rushing into print with lute music. Part of the delay, of course, involved preparing the special type for lute tablature; another part probably resulted from seeking suitable music to print, and a lutenist competent to present it to the press and oversee any necessary corrections.

Perhaps it is not surprising that Petrucci finally turned to a compatriot. We cannot be sure that Spinacino was from Petrucci's home town, although the epigram in his praise (included in his first book) was written by Cristoforo Gigas, another citizen and office-holder of Fossombrone. Spinacino was clearly an expert lutenist; he would be praised by Philippo Oriola da Bassano, at the end of the next decade, as one among the most eminent of late-fifteenth-century lutenists, and, in the edition itself, Gigas compares Spinacino with Orpheus.[82]

There is some evidence that these books represented something special for Spinacino. The use of the *Odhecaton* title-page initials for the incipits of the first piece in each book seems to be an unusual statement, for nowhere else does Petrucci arrange pieces to make this possible. He had to make minor changes to the layout of the page in order to use the letters.[83] Further evidence of Spinacino's interest lies in the extreme care taken over correcting these volumes. As I say elsewhere, the style of correcting is the same throughout, and it looks to have been done at the time of printing.[84] These two features seem to argue that Spinacino had some contact with the preparation of the volumes. Perhaps he even paid for them in part; Petrucci did not wait to see whether lute music sold, but immediately printed both.

The contents also confirm at least a temporary connection between Spinacino and Petrucci. For the first book, Spinacino concentrated on intabulations of works already published by Petrucci (with the exception of a transcription of a different *Jay pris amours*, perhaps a piece already in his repertoire). The second book expands the range of compositions; over a third of the works intabulated there had not previously appeared in one of the *Canti* volumes produced by Petrucci. Each book concludes with a series of ricercars of Spinacino's own composition; in Book I, the first two of these are fantasias on chansons also published by Petrucci, but the remaining fifteen are intended to show the lutenist's musical abilities.

This first Spinacino volume has a curious letter from Petrucci to the reader. As I have suggested in chapter 1, this letter reads as distinctively defensive and intended as a response to suggestions that Petrucci had not been giving the correct composers' names for works he had printed. The most likely place for this to have happened lies in the recent series of frottola books, especially Book VI.

A year later, Petrucci decided to publish more books of lute music. The first two must have sold well enough, so that Petrucci could have seen their commercial viability before making this decision. The new books represent both new intabulators and new repertoire. Kent Underwood makes the point that "each of Petrucci's lutenists had a specialty: for Franciscus Bossinensis, it was the *frottola*; for Dalza, the popular dance; and for Spinacino, the Franco-Flemish *chanson*".[85] It is clear enough that it looks as if Petrucci planned the series from the beginning, stretching the plan as far as Bossinensis's volume, published two years after the first book by Spinacino. However, as I say, the dates of the books argue that Petrucci did not plan a series. Further, the first volume was not devoted to the genres that already had been most freely published by Petrucci—masses, motets, frottole—but to the chanson, which the publisher had abandoned some three years before. It seems reasonable to assert, therefore, that the Spinacino volumes reflect the sort of special situation that I propose here, and that the gap of fifteen months before the production of Book III represents a chance to evaluate the success of the two books before considering more material.

This third book, with music intabulated by "Alemannus", then, was not related to the first two. Nonetheless, Petrucci felt it worthwhile to link it to them, calling it *Libro tertio*, and probably arranging to begin it with the large "C" from *Canti C*, introducing *Comme femme*.[86] From the limited evidence provided by Colón, this book looks as though it would have continued the pattern of repertoire laid out in the two books by Spinacino, beginning with a chanson intabulation, and ending with at least one ricercar. This immediately weakens any argument that Petrucci was planning to survey the range of lute repertoire. I believe that Alemannus probably came to Petrucci, offering the volume, and Petrucci accepted it, as extending what was apparently already a successful venture.

The fourth volume, with music by Dalza, is completely different, for it contains no intabulations of vocal compositions. Instead, it has only instrumental works, including a series of dance suites. The movements of the suites are deliberately associated, by both Dalza and Petrucci: "Nota che tutte le pauane hanno el suo saltarello e piua".[87] In the same way, there is a group of *Tastar de corde*, each associated with a ricercar. The book ends with four pieces given titles, as if intabulations of texted pieces, but even these do not correspond to the selection favoured in the earlier books. Here, there are two frottole by Tromboncino, and two settings of anonymous laude.

For this volume, as for the others, it is tempting to see the lutenist as the instigator. If Petrucci wanted more lute music at all, he must have welcomed a change from the intabulations of chansons and short motets with ricercars, which dominated the first two volumes (and probably the third). Since the fourth book presented another facet of the lute repertoire, it would have appealed to the same purchasers, lutenists, probably amateur, wanting to have the sort of repertoire they could play at home or to friends—an almost guaranteed market, supposing the first two volumes to have sold well. The alternative is that all four books were promoted and partly financed by the lutenists themselves (or their anonymous patrons). My inclination is to believe that the truth comprises a mixture of the two, with the first pair representing Petrucci's need to show he could print tabulature, and the second pair offered to him by the lutenists themselves.

After the early months of 1507, we can see more clearly that Petrucci began to run several series of publications concurrently. This is particularly evident when we take into account those volumes (including the lost ones) that say "Libro Primo" on the title page, but which are not, as far as we know, followed by a second. Previously, most of the small series of titles he had published had only been interrupted by reprints of earlier titles, and the few exceptions can often be explained by some external pressure—such as I propose for the first book of Josquin's masses. That tends to argue that there was only one influence on repertoire, one provider of music, at any given time. The only significant exception had been in 1505, when the fourth, fifth, and sixth books of frottole interrupted the mass series, but I have argued above that the books of masses represented more of an ongoing possibility rather than a planned series. In any case, it is reasonable to assume a spell in 1505 when Castellanus, away from Venice in Recanati, was not supplying Petrucci with music.

Now, increasingly, sets begin to appear alongside each other. As a result, we must look further afield for the suppliers of Petrucci's music, as we see the publisher exploring new possibilities. I have already argued this for the pair of volumes supplied by Spinacino and suggested it earlier, with the books of frottole. But, now, this point of view becomes essential. Petrucci, becoming better known, with his elegant musical publications circulating in Venice and throughout northern Italy, was being offered and was undertaking diverse repertoires. The way in which these repertoires overlap, then, is evidence of the extent to which his reputation was drawing out proposals from other musicians.

That was also, of course, a financial necessity. With the end of the mass series and the inevitable decline in sales of the early chanson and motet books, Petrucci was increasingly dependent on expanding his markets. Two books of lute music would not have kept him in business, nor would two of Lamentations or three new ones of frottole. But by issuing books of different types intermingled with each other, he was increasing the chances of not making a disastrous loss on any one.

Therefore, the pattern is not surprising. Taking the date of February 1508 as a dividing line, one finds that most of the then current series include publications on both sides of the divide (even though it is likely that the frottole books do not really represent one series) (see Table 9-2):

Group 10: More frottole:
 Frottole libro octavo: 21 May 1507
 Frottole libro septimo: 6 June 1507

These two volumes might have been planned at the same time as Books IV–VI of the series, though I think that is unlikely. The intervening time was largely

TABLE 9-2 Patterns of publishing different genres on either side of February 1508

Before 1508	After 1507
Lute: Spinacino, two books (iii.1507)	Lute: Alemannus and Dalza (vi.1508; xii.1508)
Frottole VII and VIII (v–vi.1507)	Frottole IX (and perhaps X)(i.1509 and later)
Magnificats; Martini's Hymns (?; x.1507)	Missarum diversorum; Motetti á5 (iii.1508; xi.1508)
Dammonis' Laude I [1506]	Laude II (11.i.1508)

filled, as we have seen, with special productions—Lamentations and lute music, coupled with two more books of masses. The most curious feature in these books is the pair of dates. Book VII apparently appeared later than Book VIII.[88] In the year 1507, 6 June fell on a Sunday: Book VII is one of five books with Sunday publishing dates. Apparently, Petrucci printed the whole book in the two weeks following the completion of Book VIII, a supposition supported by the pattern of paper use at the time. The unique copy of Book VIII is largely made up of paper 23 (with five sheets of paper 31, from a later printing); that of Book VII is largely on paper 20, with one sheet on paper 23. Table 9-3 shows how these two books fit into the pattern of paper use during the surrounding months.

The two principal papers, 23 and 20, are similar in quality and distinguished only by the countermarks they carry. This suggests that Petrucci's *cartolaio* supplied him with batches that happened to come from different makers, perhaps himself changing from the maker of paper 20 to that of paper 23 during this period.

I find it unlikely that the surviving copy of Book VII is a second edition, and that the first is lost, as almost happened with Dammonis's book of laude. If so, the first would have been printed after 5 February 1506, the date of Book VI, and before February of 1507; after that, there is no convenient break in publication before the date of the surviving copy. It is true that there is room for an edition during the summer, alongside the first edition of Dammonis's laude, and the second of Josquin's first book. That would imply, however, that a second edition was needed within a year, and no frottola book was reprinted in under thirty months—with the sole exception of Book IV, itself exceptional in its character, which reappeared after two years. It seems to me more likely, therefore, that the first (and only) edition of Book VII did indeed appear after Book VIII.

Apart from this issue, there is little to distinguish either book; both open with a single work (by Zesso and Paulo Scotto), and both contain ranges of works by very minor composers. Perhaps Zesso had something to do with the collection of the music, for he both opens and closes Book VII, and also closes Book VIII.

TABLE 9-3 Patterns of watermarks in book published during 1507 and 1508

Date		Book	Paper
1506	20.x.	Isaac: *Misse*	17 and 22
1507	7.i.	Gaspar: *Misse*	20, with 17 and 22
	[Feb]	Spinacino: Book I	Mostly 23: three sheets of 20
	31.iii.	Spinacino: Book II	Only 23
	21.v.	*Frottole VIII*	Only 23
	6.vi.	*Frottole VII*	Only 20: one sheet of 23
	31.vii.	*Frottole IV*	Only 20
	[—]	Martini: *I Hymnorum*	not extant
	14.x.	*Magnificats I*	not extant
	26.xi.	*Frottole III*	Only 23
1508	11.i.	*Laude II*	Only 23
	29.i.	*Frottole II*	Only 23
	15.ii.	*Missarum diversorum auctorum I*	Only 23
	7.vii.	Dammonis: *Laude I*	Only 23 (for the second edition sheets)
	20.xi.	*I Motetti 3*	Only 23
	31.xii.	Dalza: *Intabulatura IV*	Only 23

In between, there are suggestive patterns, principally the importance of Tromboncino: each book has a short run of his works immediately following the first piece—twelve of the next fourteen in Book VII and a mere five pieces in Book VIII. For the compiler, he was certainly more popular than Cara with twenty (perhaps twenty-one) to ten (perhaps 11) in Book VII, and eleven to six (perhaps seven) in Book VIII. Tromboncino had also featured in the two collections of Lamentations, and it is possible to suggest that the same person supplied all four books. Certainly a Venetian provenance for the music in the frottola volumes seems the most likely, with works by Paulo Scotto and d'Ana, alongside other minor figures.[89] There are, additionally, a few interesting couplings of names: in Book VII the three works by "A. d'Antiquis" are grouped alongside works by Tromboncino; in Book VIII, Antenoreus is closely linked with Nicolo Pifaro (in a group of pieces beginning with f.C1*v*), and Stringarius with Lodovico Milanese. These combinations merely highlight the wide geographical spread of composers in the two volumes. The first (and last) composer, Zesso, was perhaps in Padua, where Peregrinus Cesena had been maestro; the Bolognese Demophon was in Ferrara with Cardinal Ippolito, Scotto in Venice, and Giacomo Fogliano in Modena. For Book VIII, there is a greater spread: while Veneto composers reappear (with Brocco and d'Ana), Pesenti was in Ferrara, Pifaro was probably the Sienese composer also found in Sambonettus's 1515 edition of *Canzone*, and Lodovico Milanese was soon to be (if not already) in Lucca.[90] It is as if Petrucci commissioned some unknown person to find additional pieces that would allow him to extend the frottola series.

Despite the apparent connections in repertoire with *Frottole IX*, I do not think that book was planned at the same time. It appeared over eighteen months later, and there were at least two gaps in Petrucci's production during 1508. Either of these would have been adequate for the production of a new book of frottole, if it had already been planned. Instead, Petrucci launched into a number of books of new liturgical repertoire, of laude and intabulations, with new editions of early frottole books. First among these was the second edition of *Frottole IV*, but that was followed by the first books in a new venture—hymns and Magnificats.

> Group 11: Expanded liturgical repertoire:
>   Martini: *Hymni de tempore . . . Liber primus*: 1507
>   *Magnificat Liber primus*: 14 Oct. 1507
>   *Missarum diversorum auctorum Liber primus* 15 March 1508
>   *Motetti a cinque libro primo*: [28 Nov. 1508]

These four books seem to belong together; they expand the previously printed repertoire in similar ways, and they were all called "Book 1", apparently seen as possibly opening the way for more similar volumes. However, I do not think they were part of an integral plan. It could be argued that Petrucci and his suppliers were trying to fill the repertoire bought by choral institutions. But rather than seeing the series as having been planned from the beginning, it is easier to see each book as part of a vague undefined agenda, in which music that filled a gap was supplied as it became available. The "Liber primus" designation is not of any great significance here. The only volumes that had been published without any indication of a possible following series had been those of mass settings, when dedicated to a single composer. Petrucci was, as stated in chapter 1, increasingly confident that he had a ready market for his productions, and that he could continue in business.

Unfortunately, the two most interesting titles, the first two, no longer survive. We know from Colón's catalogues that the "first book" of Magnificats appeared on 14 October 1507.[91] Both Colón and Bottrigari confirm that the book of hymns was also published in 1507.[92] The only reasonable gap in Petrucci's output during that year lies before the Magnificat volume, in the almost eleven weeks following the second edition of *Frottole IV*. Since, as one would expect, second editions seem normally to have taken less time than first,[93] it is possible that the book of hymns was even begun before the frottola reprint was finished.

Given this probability, we face two expansions of the liturgical repertoire, to be marketed at effectively the same time. They were probably conceived as a pair, each potentially beginning a new series. They are most interesting in the manner in which they explore important parts of the liturgical repertoire. Both Magnificats and hymns were central fifteenth-century polyphonic liturgical genres, with the mass,[94] and both were widely disseminated. They were to remain for a while longer significantly more important than psalm settings, and on a par with the Marian texts featured in Petrucci's earlier volumes.

It is doubly unfortunate, then, that both volumes have been lost. There would be no similar editions for just twenty-five years, until Carpentras put out his editions in Avignon in 1532.[95] It is notable that Carpentras's four volumes contain the same genres that Petrucci's advisors had concentrated on up to this time: masses, Magnificats, hymns, and lamentations.

In a manner similar to that employed by Carpentras, Petrucci and his supplier seem to have been planning to prepare volumes expanding the range of printed polyphony available to choral foundations. Only five months later, they published the book *Missarum diversorum auctorum*, and that summer a *Motetti à cinque*. These two may not actually extend the range of genres, but they do both signal important moves. The mass volume keeps largely to composers who had already appeared in the earlier series, allowing Petrucci to indicate that he had available more pieces from these men—whose books were presumably still selling, if slowly. At the same time, it introduces a new composer, Philippe Basiron. For this composer, whether Basiron or Philippon,[96] we do not have (and presumably Petrucci's supplier did not have) enough masses to complete a volume. But the present book could easily suggest to musicians that other composers' works would be accepted for publication, and that a potential series would have interesting contents. Not only Castellanus, but a number of other potential suppliers, could have offered masses, by Gaforius, Martini, and composers employed at other Italian centers.

The *Motetti à cinque* are notable in a different way. In many respects the contents are very old-fashioned for the early sixteenth century. There are seven works with a clear-cut *cantus firmus* structure and at least two texts, to which the Obrecht *Factor orbis* should probably be added. Two of these (in addition to one work with only one text) are by Regis; he had been dead about twenty years and was probably known primarily in Italy through Dufay in Rome and Tinctoris in Naples. One of his pieces was certainly composed by 1477, for *Clangat plebs* is praised in the *Liber de arte contrapuncti* for its contrapuntal skill.[97] The others were probably composed no later than that. Rob Wegman suggests that Obrecht's *Laudemus nunc* may have been composed during the 1490s.[98] With *Factor orbis*, it was known in Rome, for both were copied into Cap.Sist.42, compiled around the same time as the Petrucci book. Strohm connects the same composer's *O preciosissime sanguis* with his stay in Bruges, which ended in 1491.[99]

As to the source of the music, the supplier for Petrucci, there are few straws. It is certainly significant that Weerbeke's *Dulcis amica dei* is dedicated to "Leonardo [Loredan] duce nostro", Venetian doge from 1501 to 1521. The concordant source, I-Rvat, Cap.Sist.15, copied earlier, carries a dedication to "N. papa". That manuscript also contains Josquin's *Illibata dei virgo*, and his *Homo quidam fecit* is in Cap.Sist.42, alongside the Obrecht works. Apart from these few concordances, there is little evidence of the presence of any works of *Motetti à 5* in Italy before the Petrucci edition. More critically, few of them can be related to specific events, despite their frequently old-fashioned style.

With fourteen *cantus firmus* pieces, from a total of eighteen, the book seems to be breaking new (or rather old) stylistic ground for Petrucci. There had been few parallel works in the earlier motet series: Compère's *Quis numerare queat* in *Motetti A*, and a few four-voiced *cantus firmus* pieces, including Obrecht's *Mille quingentis*[100] in *Motetti C*. Petrucci and his supplier were therefore, by and large, looking to a different motet tradition in the present volume, and they were illustrating this tradition with a number of older pieces alongside the more recent.

The source for all four volumes was probably the same. They act, with the books of Lamentations of 1506, as an apparently deliberate series of expansions of the available repertoire. But while the 1506 volumes were designed for a specific need, were able to fill almost all that need, and were apparently meant to have been published in time for Holy Week, these new volumes provided music for a wider array of liturgical occasions. Magnificats, more masses, and many of the motets could be sung on a number of occasions in any year. While we cannot know the textual contents of the volume of Martini's hymns, beyond Colón's reference to the first piece (*Conditor alme syderum*), we can safely assume that a book of thirty-seven hymns (*de tempore et de sanctis*) would cover a significant portion of the church calendar.

Given this relatively consistent approach, we probably have to look back once more to Castellanus. He would certainly have been able to supply Martini's hymns, from his long-standing connection with Ferrarese music. He would also have been able to produce works that seem to have been known best in Rome (among Italian centers), including the Regis compositions, while the selection of five-voiced motets suggests a collector interested in the technical as well as the musical or religious aspects of composition. Finally, the supplier almost certainly has to be in Venice, given the textual reference in Weerbeke's *Dulcis amica dei*. Unfortunately, this can only be guesswork at present. There is no other likely contributor on the horizon, unless an avid musician and collector is discovered in Venice itself, or copies of the missing books should surface.

In the interval between the two pairs of volumes, Petrucci reprinted two books of frottole and also printed the third in his series of lute music, by Alem-manus. This emphasises the manner in which he needed (and also met the needs of) a diverse group of purchasers. From the professional singers of Magnificats and masses (and their institutions) to the amateurs, merchants, middle-class musicians and courtiers purchasing frottole and lute music, he was building on small bases of support and a much larger group of more occasional purchasers.

The one new venture during this period produced the second book of laude, designed for those who had bought the first book. There were evidently enough of these professionals who sang for a confraternity or scuola, or the casual singers within the confraternity, who could follow a text and struggle with the music.

Group 12: The second book of laude:
    Laude Libro secondo: 11 Jan. 1508

The decision to publish this book may have belonged with those involved in the previous group of editions. In this instance, however, there is no expansion in repertoire or genres; instead, the book seems to have been designed to capitalise on the success of the first book, by Dammonis, which indeed would be reprinted later in the year.

Book II, however, almost certainly did not come directly from Dammonis, or from any single musician. One reason for this assertion lies in the existence of four pairs of settings, for each of which effectively the same music is used for two different texts. In one case (nos. 19 and 52), the composition is ascribed to different people. This pattern surely indicates that the contents were collected from several sources: we cannot even assume that the opening group of works was of any size, for the first repetition of music concerns numbers 4 and 13 in the book. However, it is likely that all the sources were Venetian, given the pattern of words with Venetian orthography (e.g., *zorno* for *giorno*, and *ziglio* for *giglio*).[101] The book therefore represents small collections of laude from several places in Venice, presumably different confraternities. As I suggest in the bibliographical commentary, a logical place to look for such a group of collections would be one of the friaries to which several scuole were attached, not least because compositions are ascribed to *Frater petrus* and *Frater Benedictus Bella Busca*.[102] This volume probably reflects more closely what was sung in Venetian confraternities than does the collection of his music put out by Dammonis: when it repeats a composition, and when it takes an extract of a simple motet by van Weerbeke and adapts it to a lauda text, the volume reveals that these works were popular enough in Venice that they could be found in more than one of the working anthologies, presumably sung in more than one scuola. This would not have mattered to Petrucci: indeed, it would have reinforced his evident belief that this repertoire would also sell, even as it confirms for us that he played at most an insignificant part in the detailed musical decisions involved.

Group 13: Two more books of frottole:
    Frottole Liber nono: 22 Jan. 1509
    Frottole Libro decimo: 1512

This pair of books, like the pair of Bossinensis's intabulations to be discussed next, was printed partly in Venice and partly in Fossombrone. The dates of the two frottole books, compared with those of the two prepared by Bossinensis, suggest that Petrucci's first plan in his home town was merely to finish work on Bossinensis's second book; the tenth book of frottole represents a later decision. On the other hand, he must have been able to sell not only the Bossinensis book but also copies of some Venetian titles; the Ghiselin mass volume and perhaps parts of *Frottole IX* were reprinted in Fossombrone sometime during 1514.[103]

Petrucci's activities before the edition of the *Paulina* in 1513 suggest, however, that he was about to give up producing music books. He purchased a new font of text type and made contact with Francesco Griffo: the commissioned non-musical book by Paulus, followed by one written by Castiglione, probably represents his new intentions. If this is true (and especially since there is no significant pattern of hidden editions and printings), then we should assume that the plan for *Frottole X* also came with Petrucci from Venice. Having printed the second book of Bossinensis's intabulations, and waiting for Paulus to supply the text for his *Paulina*, Petrucci was able to keep his craftsmen employed by printing *Frottole X*. The decision, in other words, was a practical one, rather than a desire to publish specific compositions.

The range of composers in Book IX is similar to that of the seventh and eighth Books in the series. While there are some new composers—Cariteo, Diomedes, and Timoteo—the main range of names follows the earlier pattern. The extant references to the lost Book X suggest a similar pattern of new and recurring composers: Bottrigari names Filippo Mantuano, Jo. Hesdin, Jo. Scrivano, Franciscus, G. B. de Ferro, Dionisius da Mantova, and Pietro da Lodi, few of whom appear elsewhere in Petrucci's frottola books. As I suggest in chapter 1, this pattern argues that the music for both books was collected and submitted to Petrucci, probably at the same time, while he was in Venice. After his move to Fossombrone, he must have wondered about the economics of distributing his books. Even if Scotto and Niccolò were still active as distributors and salesmen for him (as the 1514 petition for a renewal of his privilege argues), the cost of shipping books to them in Venice and then of onward distribution would have cut the profit margins for Petrucci himself and his partners. Apparently, the second book of Bossinensis's intabulations suggested that business was still viable, even in the Marche.[104]

Undoubtedly, Petrucci and his colleagues were aware of Antico's first book of frottole, published in 1510. That volume may have been produced when it was because Antico thought that Petrucci had finished publishing. Antico's second volume was also probably produced before Petrucci put out his tenth book.[105] It may be, therefore, that Petrucci was making a statement about his privilege and priority in the field, as well as stressing the availability of his editions. He was apparently successful in both endeavours: Antico decided to seek a papal privilege in 1513, and Petrucci needed to undertake several re-editions during the following years.

Group 14: Bossinensis's intabulations:
Tenori e contrabassi intabulati . . . Libro primo: 27 March 1509
Tenori e contrabassi intabulati . . . Libro secondo: 10 May 1511

Petrucci moved back to Fossombrone between these two books, one published in Venice and the other in his home town. As I have shown, however, the second book was probably at least partly planned before Petrucci left Venice.

The first book represented a new departure on Petrucci's part, in moving away from the choirbook layout of frottole and pre-supposing a market for a different performing convention. There are illustrations of, and literary references to the practice of performing frottole with one voice accompanied by lute or viola: it is, in any case, the logical manner of presenting the genre, given its performing roots in the previous century.

However, that manner of presenting a frottola in the sources was very unusual. Only two contemporary manuscripts of this type and with a similar provenance are known to me, alongside two later editions—the volumes of intabulations of frottole by Tromboncino and Cara, and of Willaert's intabulations of Verdelot madrigals.[106] One manuscript is similar in format and date, a single leaf, folio 35, in a *konvolut*, I-Fn B.R.62, containing one frottola, *Chi dal ciel non ha favore*, with the soprano notated on a staff and below it a reduced intabulation of the lower voices. As with the intabulations in Bossinensis's editions, the three vocal parts (as they survive in a Petrucci frottola edition) are mostly reduced to two, or (here) even one. As pointed out by Dinko Fabris,[107] however, the intabulation in this manuscript concentrates on the Altus and Bassus. Fabris also suggests that the spellings of the text in the manuscript suggest a different line of transmission, from Rome or southern Italy, and independent of that for the Petrucci edition of the same piece.

The second source is also important. A manuscript formerly in the collection of Geneviève Thibault, written in Italy, probably in the Veneto, in the very early sixteenth century,[108] contains both motets and frottole intabulated, alongside a number of instrumental dances and other pieces. The manuscript is relevant in the present context because a long series of intabulations of frottole does not include the top vocal part. In other words, they seem to be for the accompaniments of a singer. They are, however, different from the Bossinensis settings in more than one way. The notation is normally defective, lacking rhythm signs, and usually without bar lines, which has led Prizer[109] to regard the manuscript as an *aide-memoire*. This view is supported by Underwood, who also argues that it was not written by a professional, but rather by someone who had learned the music and was not highly competent in notation.[110] Finally, the form of the intabulation varies: some pieces are presented simply, without much ornamentation, in the manner of the Bossinensis transcriptions, whereas others use the lower parts of the "vocal original" as the stimulus for a flowing, melismatic version.

There are, then, two other sources, different in origin or form, that suggest the Bossinensis volumes may have been related to an active manuscript tradition. Neither can be tied to Petrucci's editions—or his sources—but taken together, they imply that there were already enough musicians to ensure the success of this kind of volume. Yet this edition's lengthy title suggests otherwise. I do not believe that all the specific details were given merely to distinguish this from the other frottola volumes. Rather, I suspect that Petrucci, his editor, or Bossinensis felt that the volume had to be advertised very clearly, with all the details. This implies that the market was (at best) undefined, and I believe that to be largely true. In earlier comments, I have assumed that this book was aimed at dilettante lutenists, able to entertain and to sing. The presumption is based on the technical level of the intabulations, as much as on the title-page. In that case, the potential purchaser probably did need to be wooed by the book title: he (or she) needed to know that it was not one more in the ongoing series of books arranged for four voices and instruments, largely useless to the single lutenist. It looks as if Petrucci did not know how many such potential purchasers there were.

It seems, therefore, that Petrucci had to be persuaded to publish at least the first volume. Given the apparent success of the frottola volumes, he may have received suggestions that books of music in this format would be valued, or he may have been encouraged by Bossinensis himself. The latter appears more likely, again given the details presented on the title page. Bossinensis was from Bosnia, but apparently resident in Venice, for he dedicates the first volume to Geronimo Barbarigo, the Apostolic Protonotary in Venice,[111] perhaps at Petrucci's suggestion.

I suspect that Bossinensis had an agreement for two books, in the manner that (I argue) had occurred more than once in Petrucci's career—most notably with Spinacino's two books of intabulations.[112] It is likely that work on the second book was begun in Venice, immediately after the end of Book I, and copy or even possibly some printed pages were taken to Fossombrone on Petrucci's removal to that city.[113] We do not therefore have to assume that the first sold well enough to stimulate demand for a second. The continuing lack of sources giving the music in this form suggests rather that the two books did not sell particularly quickly. The first book did, it is true, reach a second edition while Petrucci was in Fossombrone, which may reflect a steady, slow sale; it probably does not imply the loss of the remainder of the first edition during Petrucci's move, because other books from his Venetian period certainly were transported to Fossombrone.

In the year after the second book of Bossinensis's intabulations of frottole, Petrucci printed Book X of the vocal settings. During the next year, he produced both Paulus's *Paulina de recta Paschae* and Castiglione's epistle; given the chronology of Paulus's connections with the Lateran Council and the amount of work involved in producing his book, there is no reason to believe that Petrucci planned any more music at this stage. He seems rather to have been thinking about branching into general printing, starting with Castiglione's letter. I suspect, too, that he would have been the printer for some of the official documents that every court, bishopric, and city needed to circulate.

At the same time, though, he was continuing to sell from his stock of music books. This is the only possible conclusion to be drawn from the presence of later undated printings of Ghiselin's book of masses and both Bossinensis's books of intabulations.[114] These could easily have been fitted into any number of gaps in output between finishing work on Castiglione and the middle of 1516.

Group 15: Starting up again, in 1514:
  Missarum Josquin Liber Tertius: 1 March 1514
  Motetti de la Corona: 17 August 1514
  Frottole Liber undecimo: 24 Oct. 1514

It is likely that the resumption of music printing was a direct result of printing the two non-musical books of 1513. Undoubtedly, the *Paulina* would have brought Petrucci, as well as Paulus, recognition, and the subsequent pamphlet of Castiglione probably brought some financial return. In addition, Petrucci would have had a full crew of trained men, resident in Fossombrone; these men would, as was customary, have moved on unless they could be offered more work at once. It is possible that Petrucci was involved in printing official documents for the duchy, though none have survived. Yet, *librai* were apparently still asking for copies of his musical editions, for he would have to reprint some during the years 1514–16. This would have been a second incentive to look for new editions to print. The immediate question is whether Petrucci sought out the music for these three new editions, or whether someone brought the music to him, as a commission.

Each book of this group raises interesting questions. To start, the volumes were almost certainly not planned together as a group. Although they fall fairly close together, each has distinctive characteristics, in repertoire and presentation. It is easier to regard each of these musical books as the result of some strong external stimulus. Given the range of composers involved in the eleventh book of frottole, in particular, we have to suspect that the same stimulus may not have prompted all three. Further, I believe that each was initially seen as a single volume; even when (as in the cases of the Josquin masses and the frottole) they continued a series begun in Venice, they were not seen as leading to a further extension of the series.

Despite that, we have to presume that the three were somehow related, in sources for the music, and in the intent to reach purchasers from Petrucci's base in Fossombrone. Conventionally, it is assumed that the music for the second, at least, was collected in Rome, and that Petrucci's Roman contacts were enough to encourage him to start printing the repertoire. The difficulty with this lies not in the individual compositions chosen but in deciding the character of any person or persons in Rome who might want to see not merely an edition of the motets in *Motetti de la Corona,* but also a collection of frottole, and a motley group of masses by Josquin. The last, particularly, is significant, given the fact that Antico, in Rome, must already have been cutting blocks for his *Liber Quindecim Missarum*, which would contain three of the same masses.

The book of *Motetti de la Corona* is both the easiest and the hardest to understand. I have already pointed out one or two of its special features: it was originally not intended to be the first of a set, for the *Libro primo* designation was not present in the first printing; it was most unusual among Petrucci's musical editions, in having both an evocative (rather than a descriptive) title and a decorative block on the title page; and it contains a new set of composers and works, apparently representing a strong Roman influence on the selection of music. These three features must be considered together, of course, and I have previously advanced a possible explanation in the political situation in Urbino.[115] Publishers of later volumes with similar titles—*Motetti de la Croce, Motetti de la Salamandra, Motetti del Fiore*—appear to use them more as advertising slogans, and means of making distinctions between different books, or of suggesting that a series builds on a specific reputation. I doubt that these motives were true in the present case.

For one thing, this is the first such title in music publishing and should therefore have had some special stimulus; a second reason is that the choice of a crown suggests that it was specific political stimulus.

The crown would be described as "open", that is without arches, and carries eight fleurs-de-lys alternating with eight balls.[116] There seems no reason to doubt that this crown was meant to represent France. Richard Sherr has recorded that Louis XII used an open crown, although François I adopted the closed crown.[117] An illustration of the open form appears in a manuscript recording the English King Henry VI being crowned King of France in 1485,[118] while the closed form is illustrated in I-Rvat, Sist.63, 75r. Both carry the same basic design of the crown used by Petrucci. The implication is that the book is related to an event in France, one of importance to an Italian center, or to an Italian Mycaenas.

The only two possible events are the wedding of the French heir-apparent, François, to Claude, daughter of King Louis XII, on 28 May 1514, and the betrothal of Giuliano de'Medici to Filiberta of Savoy. The first of these seems to me unlikely: it took place during the period of mourning for the Queen, Anne of Brittany, who had died on 11 January; everyone wore black, and the bride apparently wept. If the book had been designed to commemorate this wedding, I would expect that it would contain, somewhere in the volume, the lament for Anne, Mouton's *Quis dabit oculis nostris*, itself based on the funeral oration. Further, the motet probably written for Claude, *O desolatorum consolator* by Divitis, although present, is buried in the middle of the book, and apparently did not have a special significance in its compilation.

On the other hand, this is the time when Leo X, Louis XII, and Charles of Savoy were settling Giuliano's marriage, and a volume of music reflecting French taste would be an admirable gift for a musical nobleman about to marry into the French royal family.[119] Already, in mid-1513, the pope had begun a plan to give Giuliano a state in northern Italy,[120] and on 13 August Lorenzo de'Medici took on all Giuliano's Florentine offices. By the end of the year, Leo X began to weaken in his enthusiasm for the attack on France represented by the Treaty of Mechelen,[121] probably in part because of Louis XII's renunciation of the Council of Pisa (which had been an overt political attack on the papacy).[122] Another factor may have been the influence of Giuliano de'Medici, whom the French regarded as their ally at the papal court.[123] The moves to marry Giuliano to Filiberta probably began late in 1513. On 23 January 1514, the new Florentine ambassador to France, Francesco Pandolfini, was given credentials for Savoy and a specific mission to the duke.[124] Giuseppe Fatini remarks that Leo X had already reached an agreement with Louis XII by February, and that he had the support of Luisa of Savoy.[125] The plan was hatched early in the year, for on 6 April Giuliano agreed to the marriage, according to a "procura" signed in Turin on his behalf.[126] That same day, Pietro Bembo wrote on behalf of the pope to Charles, Duke of Savoy, saying that he would be delighted if Filiberta should marry Giuliano, for it would make them relatives.[127] On 21 June Bembo (that is, the pope) wrote again to the duke, thanking him for his response, and the diplomatic details were apparently settled soon thereafter. This would allow just enough time for the music to be collected, and for Petrucci to print and have the book published in late August. It is true that the wedding itself did not take place until 25 January 1515.[128] But there seems to be no other event that affected the necessary centers (Rome, Florence, and Paris) and also involved a crown.

If this conclusion is reasonable, it is much harder to decide who might actually have commissioned the book from Petrucci. Among the possibilities are Leo X, his brother Giulio (now a Cardinal in Rome), perhaps Lorenzo de'Medici, or less obviously Francesco Maria of Urbino (still holding onto his position as a result of Giuliano's intercession).[129] But it is also difficult to see why any such person should think that a printed book of polyphony would be a worthy gift. For that reason, I tend to view the edition itself not as a gift, but as a by-product, a volume printed to commemorate the event, spreading abroad a repertoire that was copied into a now-lost manuscript.

The repertoire points directly at the French court. The book opens with Mouton's *Gaude Barbara beata*, followed by music of Josquin, Carpentras, de Silva, Therache, and Févin, and the connection is even clearer when the texts are examined. I have already mentioned the motet dedicated to St. Cloud and probably written for Claude. In addition, there are Févin's *Gaude francorum regia* and *Adiutorium nostrum*, referring to Louis XII and Anne of Brittany: the latter is a plea for an heir. Each of these would have been recent works when Petrucci printed the volume. Still relatively recent were the opening work, dedicated to the patron saint of gunners (and apparently a plea for protection in battle), Mouton's *Laudate Dominum in sanctis* (which Lowinsky has suggested was another plea for a male heir for Louis and Anne),[130] and Févin's *Benedictus Dominus Deus* (which appears to refer to Louis returning triumphant from war). Each work suggests a close contact with Parisian court musicians or patrons. The presence of a work for Claude argues that the contact was more than a casual single event, or even the exchange of music between performers, for her wedding had taken place less than three months before Petrucci's book appeared.[131]

Lockwood has drawn a picture of the extent of Italian court awareness of French music and musicians.[132] Although the focus of his work has been Ferrara, he clearly shows that this court was not alone in welcoming composers from the north, or in acquiring their compositions. Ferrara, however, seems an unlikely starting point for Petrucci's anthology; among the composers he included are de Silva, Therache, Divitis, and Hylaire (probably Turleron rather than Penet),[133] none of whom seem to have had contacts with Ferrara. Although this does not mean that their music was unknown there, it is significant that they were better known in Rome. Leo's interest in French music and musicians is well known, as is his recruitment of composers appearing in Petrucci's book (in particular, the recently promoted Carpentras), but it is difficult to argue that this collection came from music at the Vatican, for there are few concordances for specific pieces in any of the Vatican manuscripts. Further, the priority of Mouton in the book, rather than Carpentras, suggests that the supplier was not particularly close to the Sistine singer.

In addition, there is the curious feature of the spelling of Mouton's name. At some point in the transmission to Petrucci, it had been transformed into "Monton" and appears as such for all eight of his works. Although this was corrected in Petrucci's later editions (by which time Carpentras's name also underwent some transformations), it resurfaces in the Superius book of Pasoti and Dorico's 1526

edition, and also for the first time in their edition of the second book of the
Corona series. This feature supports a direct connection between their Roman
press and Petrucci. It is more significant, however, that the spelling (sometimes
with an abbreviation sign for the first "n") is found in few other sources. It appears
once, for example, in each of the later sources, I-Rvat Cap.Giul.XII,2, I-TVcap
8, and I-VEaf 218: once in D-Mbs Mus.76 and F-Pc Rès.F.41. None of these
need be related to Petrucci's exemplars. It is also found at the head of two works
in the Medici Codex, but more significantly, the name was consistently entered
as "Moton" in ascribing sixteen works in I-Bc Q19.[134] This is paralleled by the
spelling of "Molu", again without the letter "u". Lockwood's comments on this
manuscript[135] present it as a paradigm for the circulation of music in northern
Italy; while remarking that it was not copied in Ferrara (but "more than likely
in Bologna or another musical center of Emilia or Romagna"), he maintains that
its contents show a strong awareness of Ferrarese taste and repertoire. The list of
composers found in this manuscript is longer and more diverse than that of Petrucci's book (which is hardly surprising, for there are nearly four times as many
works), but it betrays the same pattern, with the importance of Mouton and the
inclusion of similar minor composers.

This tends to remove both Giulio and Lorenzo de'Medici from the list of
possible promoters of Petrucci's book, and rather to require a search in central
northern Italy. As a result, I believe that Petrucci was probably commissioned by
a member of the court of Urbino, perhaps by Francesco Maria himself. The two
most suitable reasons for this possibility are clear: one is that the duke felt himself
indebted to Giuliano for his own continued life and position, a situation that was
in danger of changing even during these months; and the other that the court
would have known about Petrucci's activities, probably from the *Paulina*, but also
probably from the presence of Castiglione in Urbino in late 1513, some months
after the publication of his *Epistola*.[136] A source at this court would well explain
the contents of the volume: works known in Rome, or by composers (such as
Carpentras) favored there, alongside works by composers known or favoured in
Ferrara.[137] Mouton's place at the head of the volume would fit either circle of
interest, while the presence of so many works celebrating or referring to events
in France would accord well with Giuliano's interests in the French court and his
forthcoming wedding to Filiberta. Finally, Giuliano had himself been an honoured
member of the Urbino court circle,[138] and this collection may well have been
designed to represent his own taste as much as that of Francesco Maria or his
wife, Eleonora Gonzaga.

While later Fossombrone titles show increasingly strong connections with
Rome, this book seems to have a different genesis. We then need to look at the
two other volumes produced in 1514—the third of Josquin's masses and the eleventh of frottole—to see whether they confirm such a hypothesis.

Of the six masses found in the third book of Josquin's settings, only three
are also in Sistine manuscripts, with another in Antico's *Liber quindecim missarum*
of 1516. Despite this, there is no strong reason why Petrucci's versions should
have come from the Vatican, and Sherr has pointed out that for the *Missa de Beata
Virgine* all except the Gloria must have originated elsewhere.[139] If one removes
the Vatican sources from consideration, this particular group of masses has sur-

prisingly few concordances with Italian provenances: Florence II.I.232 (a Medicean source); I-Rvat Pal.lat.1980–1981 (for Giulio de'Medici in Rome); I-MOd IV (for Modena Cathedral, and later); and I-MOe α.N.1.2-3 (Estense court, and perhaps earlier).[140] Perhaps not surprisingly, the little evidence that this offers points away from Roman liturgical centers, to Giuliano or Giulio de'Medici, or to northern Italy. There is a consistency in this picture with the one I have drawn for the first book in the Corona series, which is very attractive. On the other hand, there is an inconsistency in the style and nature of the contents, which suggests that the compiler (having taken account of Petrucci's previous two Josquin books) did not have a large selection to draw upon. Indeed, he included all but one of the remaining masses known in Italy at the time, the exception being the *Missa Pange Lingua*. That mass was certainly known in Medicean Rome, and survives in a number of manuscripts now in the Vatican library.[141] It seems reasonable to assume that Petrucci's supplier thought he was completing a monument to the work of Josquin, adding all the remaining masses known to be by the master, but perhaps did not know of the *Missa Pange Lingua*—and thus may not have had direct access to the Sistine sources.

The frottola book, the eleventh in the series, shows a series of groupings of pieces, similar in manner to those in earlier frottola books. The section devoted largely to the two Eustachio composers, Roman and French, is preceded by a single opening gathering, containing six works by Tromboncino, one by Cara, and one by Honophrius. After these, there are groups of works by Antonius Patavus and by Joannes Lulinus Venetus, and a final section mostly by Tromboncino and Alauro. Partly because of the range of composers, this book has fewer than usual concordances with contemporary sources. One composition by Lurano had appeared in Petrucci's *Frottole IV*, and therefore in other sources: four other works are in Antico's editions, and also elsewhere, and one was to be printed in Sambonettus's 1515 collection.[142] One of the Lulinus works appears in I-Vnm 1795-8, and in this is joined by seven of the Tromboncino works, two by Cara, and one by Piero da Lodi.[143] I suspect that this manuscript is not actually Venetian in origin, but comes from central Italy, perhaps from the Marche.[144] Given the presence of Roman pieces (by the Eustachios), it seems plausible that Petrucci was drawing on a central Italian repertoire.

As a conclusion, therefore, I believe that all three of these books represent a central Italian collection, not Venetian or Florentine, and probably not Bolognese.[145] Few of the other courts or cathedrals for which we have sources show any pattern of concordances with these three books, and I believe that we are reduced to looking to a new center for the stimulus.[146] Given the special nature of the title to the *Motetti de la Corona*, and the arguments I have made above, I believe that all three books must be related to Urbino. Each looks slightly different, though that is largely a result of the chosen repertoires, which, taken in toto, would give a cross-section of the genres favoured at the court.

> Group 16: Expansion of the mass series:
> *Missarum Joannis Mouton Liber primus*: 11 Aug. 1515
> *Misse Antonii de Févin*: 22 Nov. 1515

with new editions of masses:
    Ghiselin: [*Misse*]: [late 1514]
    Missarum Josquin Liber secundus: 11 April 1515
    Liber Primus Missarum Josquin: 29 May 1516

The presence of new editions of the first two books of Josquin's masses draws attention to issues of the size of the market and the level of Petrucci's commitment to publishing music. The easiest explanation, of course, is that the earlier, Venetian editions had only recently sold out—and that the appearance of Book 3 encouraged new buyers to look for these earlier books. This, together with the hidden new edition of Ghiselin's masses, also from Fossombrone, and evidence that Petrucci had unsold copies of La Rue's masses, suggests that Petrucci was selling (directly or indirectly through agents) to a new range of institutions and purchasers, a suggestion that is supported by evidence presented in chapter 10. In particular, an attractive hypothesis is that he was selling to a number of the clerics at the Lateran Council, alerted to his abilities by Paulus and his editions, and not yet able to buy Antico's forthcoming *Liber Quindecim Missarum*.

Nonetheless, these re-editions can be taken, with the two new titles, to indicate that Petrucci was finally beginning to launch into a fuller career of producing music. Certainly he had put out three musical editions within eight months in 1514, but they must be seen as having some special stimuli. Alongside them, the hidden second editions and added sheets represent commercial necessity. But now Petrucci began to produce more books, three titles and some reprints in seven months of 1515; for a while, these would have represented something close to full-time activity, though this did not continue. Further, he was active in city government during this period, visited Rome as a city delegate, and was in 1516 "già commendato dal Pontefice Leone X".[147]

This Roman recognition, perhaps partly because of his political activities, perhaps partly because of the elegance of his edition of the *Paulina*, surely had some bearing on the books he printed in 1515 and 1516. He felt more confident of his prospects; his edition of Mouton's masses was entitled *Libro primo*, and the same rubric was added to the *Motetti de la Corona* when he reprinted the book in 1516. Alongside these, he printed masses, new editions of three Venetian books, and a book avowedly devoted to music by Févin.[148]

It is tempting to see in this program of publishing not merely the group of new purchasers I have mentioned, but a specific market among the cardinals, bishops, and others attending the Lateran Council. Much of the music in the two new books seems to come from Rome: this is particularly clear for Févin's volume. Two of the masses, the *Missa Sancta Trinitas* (No.1) and Robert de Févin's *Missa Le vilain jaloys* (No.4), appear in only one other source with Sistine or Medici connections.[149] The other two attributed to Antoine de Févin, the masses *Ave Maria* and *Mente tota*, are also found in contemporary Sistine manuscripts, as well as in Antico's *Liber Quindecim Missarum* of 1516. Although the second of these is also in early sources from northern Europe, as is the final mass in the book, La Rue's *Missa Quarti toni* (or *Sub tuum presidium*), there is almost no evidence that any of these masses circulated widely elsewhere in Italy before Petrucci printed them. By far the most probable source for all of them should be sought in Rome, among the many musicians recently acquired by Leo X for his chapel, and those in the chapels of patrons in residence for the council.

The evidence for the five masses by Mouton, also printed in 1515, is similar. Three appeared in Roman manuscripts before, or at about the time that they were printed by Petrucci.[150] A significant feature, however, is the absence of the first two masses from Roman sources. Indeed, neither appears anywhere in Italy before Petrucci's editions, and when they do surface in manuscripts, the sources seem to have Ferrarese connections.[151] I am sceptical, however, that this indicates a potential source for these two works: the political situation in the Urbino duchy required a strong orientation toward Rome, to keep some support from the pope; the bishop of Fossombrone was looking to Rome and indeed was resident there during the council; and Petrucci would have been well aware that any future for himself and his commercial activities would lie within the papal sphere.

The most likely stimulus for all five books therefore is a Roman or conciliar one. Any patron, or supporter, in Rome would have been able to encourage Petrucci with the prospects there and would probably also have been able to obtain the new music. The stimulus is unlikely to be papal, or even from members of the curia or the Sistine Chapel. These would have known of Antico's impending mass volume, and probably of his intention to present it to the pope. A conciliar connection, however, would still allow for the gathering of all these works, indeed for collecting them from a number of different sources, chapels of cardinals, for instance, each representing a different background and stemmatic history.

At the same time, the pope (or his counselors) was probably aware of the possibility of Petrucci's editions. The various privileges gained by Antico and Petrucci were worded so that each was clearly perceived to be dancing around the other, neither offending nor conceding ground. Any Roman awareness of the publishing program of each, however, need not have involved awareness of the individual masses to be included. Thus Antico could plan to include works that he thought had not been printed, and Petrucci could be offered works that he thought (equally innocently) to promise a good sale in Rome.[152] This has bearing on the ghost allegedly published by Petrucci in 1515, and discussed below in chapter 14.

Unfortunately for Petrucci, however, his political world turned over just at this time. On 18 August 1516, Lorenzo de'Medici was formally installed as Duke of Urbino. The ongoing war in the duchy included a sack of Fossombrone, as well as divided loyalties on all sides. Petrucci stopped printing new books and putting new dates on later editions of earlier books. These later editions included the papal privilege and a colophon; significantly, the colophon included the name and titles of the rightful duke, alongside the original date of publication, when he was still in position. If this was a statement of where Petrucci's loyalties lay, it would be matched by the timing of his next musical publications.

Group 17: The final conventional volumes:
   Motetti de la Corona Libro secondo: 7 June 1519

Motetti de la Corona Libro tertio: 7 Nov. 1519
Motetti de la Corona Libro quarto: 31 Oct. 1519

These books appeared immediately after the death of the usurping Duke of Urbino, before Leo X had the opportunity even to decide on whom he would bestow the title. In fact, the pope would make Urbino a part of the papal territory, rather than return it to the Della Rovere. Petrucci might seem to have been fairly closely associated with the pope and Roman circles, more than with the evicted duke; he had been involved in the abortive project to print Calvo's translation of Hippocrates, which was connected with Manente Leontini, Lorenzo de'Medici's doctor. He also had been in Rome more than once during the intervening years. Yet, he had stopped printing new musical volumes as soon as Lorenzo became duke and before the war reached Fossombrone.[153]

It is generally assumed that Petrucci's repertoire in these three new volumes came from Rome, and therefore probably from one of its major institutions, or from a Medici contact. This indeed seems likely: he had already been printing music that had a Roman connection, if my analysis of the books of 1515 and 1516 holds true. He had no reason to expect to find music from the supplier of the 1514 volumes, whoever that was; in any case, the first book of *Corona* motets was originally intended as a single volume, not the first of a series. The supplier covered the repertoire that interested him, in that one volume.

It is not surprising, then, that the second book shows a different group of composers, though it seems to divide into two layers. Mouton is still there, with eleven compositions, but it is notable that he does not appear in the first layer, comprising eleven motets. That contains a different group of composers, among them Therache, Jacotin (3), Acaen (3), Richafort, Lupus, Mr. Jan, and (last) Eustachius de Monte Regali. But of the second layer, with fourteen compositions, eleven were written by Mouton. The concordance pattern also suggests that this book contains two separate collections of music. The first eleven works have fewer than a dozen Italian concordances: these include two in the Medici codex (with the same ascriptions) and two in I-Pc A17 (both anonymous there). The series of Mouton's works (of which two do not appear in other Italian sources of the period) were much more widely disseminated, with virtually three dozen concordances; even the works by other composers found in this second layer have concordances. Equally significantly, seven of the eight concordances in I-Pc A17 are again anonymous. This argues against any direct connection with Castellanus. While the readings in Petrucci's editions are often very close to those in the Paduan manuscript, it is difficult to explain why one source should have so many ascriptions and the other so few, if they are indeed connected.[154] Other sources in northern Italy also tend to lack ascriptions for these pieces.[155] Sources from Ferrara always have ascriptions that correspond to those in Petrucci, and so do some connected to Florence.[156]

These works, the second layer of the edition, seem more likely to have come from Roman or Florentine sources. With only a few concordances in any Vatican source, the contact was, once again, probably not with the Sistine choir or a Vatican dignitary. This is confirmed by the names of the three composers who appear alongside Mouton in this second layer—L'Héritier, La Fage, and Eustachius (again closing the section). The sequence of composers in the first layer seems to point in a different direction: Therache is first, it is true, but he is followed by a group of composers who refer, if anywhere, to northern Italy, with both Jacotin and Mr. Jan. The mix is also more unusual.

Given these two, quite diverse groups of works, a logical source for this selection of music would be someone with connections to both northern Italy and Florence or Rome. While Cardinal Ippolito I d'Este is an obvious choice, no Medici really seems to fit well. Another possibility, apparently remote at this point, is that the supplier was a member of the Strozzi family. I shall be drawing attention, when discussing Petrucci's next book, to their possible involvement with Petrucci's suppliers.

Whoever it was, it is difficult to see how the same person supplied music for all three books published in 1519. After Book II, there is a gap of almost three months before the next appeared, but that and the last were produced quite quickly and should be considered together, as products of the same plan. Apparently someone, Petrucci or a patron, saw that Book II was selling and decided to venture into new books.

Book III has a much more traditional look. It opens with Josquin—four of his large-scale works, with two more following a single composition by Lebrun. These works are all for five or six voices, while the remainder (including two more by Josquin) are for four. This inclusion of an ordered arrangement of pieces for different scorings, to become typical of many later editions, was a new feature for Petrucci. In laying these pieces out on the page, he faced an additional problem in that the Tenors for the first and third pieces are *cantus firmus* parts in long note values. He solved the problem in an elegant manner.

Again, however, it is possible to see the book as containing two different repertoires: it is not only the scoring, but the scale and complexity of the pieces that separate the first seven (or perhaps eight) from the rest. The first layer shows Josquin at his most formal and constructive, skillful in treating his pre-existing material. Works in the second layer employ more straightforward compositional styles. Nonetheless, the two repertoires probably come from the same source, certainly Roman.[157]

Not surprisingly, the fourth book also seems to contains more than one repertoire and taste; it almost certainly includes the end of the collection represented by Book III. The choices suggest that the collector was exhausting his stock of suitable music. There is little consistency in the repertoire or in the number of voices. Opening with a large-scale work by Festa, and following it with Willaert's *Verbum bonum*, again for six voices, Petrucci might have been thought to be presenting the latest repertoire favored by the Ferrarese, and indeed neither work survives in earlier Italian sources. This view is not supported by the seven following works, all of which have survived (if at all) in Florentine or Sistine sources of the surrounding years. As in Book III, these present a collection of music by Josquin; again his work is central to the choice of music. Yet the last six pieces have nothing in common with these. They are largely anonymous and survive elsewhere in Italy (if at all) in northern sources.[158]

The overall conclusion must be that these last two volumes represent the taste of a supplier, rather than a series of decisions about popularity and commercial viability. That supplier perhaps had some sort of contact with Ferrara and could collect the latest works from that court; at the same time, he seems to have had access to music performed in Rome and above all had an interest in Josquin's music. Perhaps this consistency should not be surprising. The two books were produced together, without waiting to see how Book III would sell, apparently trading on a success that must have attended Book II. Nonetheless, one can hardly argue that the supplier was able to choose freely from the repertoire at these major centers. Sherr has pointed out that the transmission is not clear, and he feels that the attributions "may not be entirely reliable".[159]

Perhaps a solution may be found in the re-use of the title "de la Corona", taken from the first book of 1514. Evidently, the second book, at least, was intended to show to the world a face similar to that of the first—and to imply a similar stimulus or repertoire. If the first reflected a Roman or a French repertoire, so then did the second; if the first was a picture of musical culture at Ferrara or Urbino, then the second extended that picture—so the argument must have been intended to run. I suggested above that the most likely patron or supplier for the first book was in Urbino, part of the court circle. If the timing of the second book of the series, immediately after Lorenzo's death, is significant, there is justification for a view of the adoption of the title as a conscious reflection of Urbino, released from Medici control and (hopefully, though not for some time) returned to Della Rovere control. Indeed, this use of the "Corona" title reinforces a notion that the first book did indeed derive from Urbino, in repertoire and in conception.

Group 18: New repertoire and format:
    Musica di meser Bernardo pisano: 23 May 1520

Everything about this volume points toward an origin for the music among Florentine circles resident in Rome, and a similar destination for the printed copies, and the same is true for the later "*Musica XII*". In this, they follow earlier volumes, but there is a difference in that the repertoire is more closely tied to Florentine composers and taste. Indeed, it is so securely Florentine that one might wonder whether the patronage of the Pisano volume was based in that city, rather than in Rome. There was no active printer in Florence (despite the 1515 petition discussed above), and Sambonettus would not have appealed to the Florentine "nobility" (for the visual appearance if nothing else). Petrucci, however, was on hand. Yet with the composer already in Rome,[160] a Roman origin is more likely. By 1520 Antico, living and working in Venice, was long gone from Rome.[161] Any patron wanting to see music printed would have turned first to Petrucci.

Although Pisano clearly owed much to the Medici family, both in gaining his position in Florence and in becoming a papal singer (in 1514) under Leo X, he also seems to have kept close contacts with the Strozzi, and to have moved in their literary circles.[162] Pisano's edition of Apuleius, published in 1522 and dedicated to Filippo Strozzi, is thought to have been based on real philological study of the extant sources, including one manuscript, I-Fl Med.68.2, which was in the Medici collections. This may have bearing on the manner in which Petrucci acquired the music for the volume, or the possible patron.

Maria Miggiani[163] discusses the texts in the edition, noting that fewer than half of them—only seven—have been shown surely to be by Petrarch. She adds that the Petrarch texts have readings that do not correspond with those in the most famous edition, Aldus's of *Le cose volgari* in 1501, or the Giunta edition of 1504.[164] Miggiani suggests[165] that the presence in first place of a poem by G. B. Strozzi—attributing *Fondo le mie speranze* to that young son of Lorenzo Strozzi—may have been intended as a compliment to his father, who was also Pisano's protector. She recognises, however, that this is one of the poems attributed to Petrarch at various times.[166] On the other hand, there are also four poems by Lorenzo himself—numbers 2, 3, 14, and 15. It is at least possible, therefore, that the first group of three poems was seen, by the patron of the edition, to refer specifically to Lorenzo Strozzi.[167] This then raises problems of how Petrucci acquired the music. He does not seem to have had any contacts with Florence, for, at this time, his principal activities outside Fossombrone seem to have involved Rome. Perhaps the easiest explanation of the stimulus for him to print the book lies in the presence of Filippo Strozzi in Rome.[168] There would be at least a graceful compliment implied in the order of pieces if Filippo himself arranged for the publication, including his brother's and nephew's works in strategic positions.[169]

This was the last of the main series of publications. Petrucci appears to have stopped producing new editions when he decided to go to Sora and establish a paper mill there, perhaps even with the intention of publishing books there.[170] The surviving evidence argues that Petrucci was not in Fossombrone when this book was planned, much less published, and explains the unusual wording of the colophon as well as the freedom to adopt a new format, one more in line with the size and shape of partbooks carrying the Florentine repertoire.

> Group 19: A third start:
> [*Musica XII*]: [ca.1533]
> *Motetti del Fiore*: (1538)

The surviving fragments of these last two volumes raise many questions, a number of which cannot be answered, given our present state of knowledge. Neither advertises the source of its music in any convincing manner; the motives for publishing either are obscure; even the date of the first is largely conjectural; and both show connections to Fossombrone in the manner in which the fragments have survived.

The first book has been known for some time, for the few leaves found in the Biblioteca Passionei of Fossombrone were mentioned by Vernarecci and have been the subject of several subsequent discussions.[171] For some time, I believed that they had been printed in or about 1520, since it was not known that Petrucci had ever returned to printing, while some of his typographical material had surfaced in Rome in the following year. More recent research and the fortunate discovery of fragments of a book dated in 1538 have rendered that hypothesis unnecessary. While Pasoti and Dorico certainly did have access to Petrucci's type, Petrucci may still have retained the punches. Indeed, only in the 1530s does he seek the return of matrices from another printer.[172]

This discovery allows us to move the date of the Fossombrone fragment to fall any time between 1521 and 1538. Gialdroni and Ziino have discussed the repertoire in detail and concluded that the book should be "dated rather late (1537–38?)".[173] They recognise that the presence of a villotta does tend to place the repertoire close to Roman editions of the 1520s, and I would add that the mixture of repertoire, styles, and composers reflects the commercial insecurity to which I allude in chapters 10 and 11. Perhaps more significant is the pitch of the Verdelot madrigal, *Non po far morte*. In Petrucci's edition, it lies a fourth lower than in all other editions, beginning with that by Antico and Scotto in Venice in 1534. Two manuscript sources use the pitch that survives in the other editions: one, I-Fc 2495, has been dated 1530 or soon after and associated with the Strozzi, as perhaps were the earliest editions in Venice; the other, I-Fn 122-25, was also copied in Florence, though probably somewhat later.[174] Petrucci's pitch is only found in one other source, the manuscript I-MOe, γ.L.11.8, which still contains some frottola repertoire and which, it has been argued, was copied in northern Italy ca.1530.[175] Thus, Petrucci's edition and the Modena manuscript stand apart from the main transmission of the work, both geographically and in pitch. At the same time, the very existence of the later book of *Motetti del Fiore* indicates that, by the second half of the decade, Petrucci (or a supplier of his music) was in touch with up-to-date taste and sources. It seems more likely therefore, that Petrucci published this version before Antico's editions began to circulate through Italy, drawing his copy from a source unconnected with the Florentine transmission reflected in Antico's reading. This places the Fossombrone fragment no earlier than 1533, the year in which Petrucci seems to have returned to the city. The book might have appeared in 1534 or early 1535, but probably no later.

The dating of the second book, the *Motetti del Fiore*, is also of interest. Like the Fossombrone fragment, it precedes a more successful edition, but not by much. The Italian interest in French secular music, traced by Lawrence Bernstein,[176] is evident throughout the 1530s. It is manifest not merely in the number of editions to which Bernstein can refer, or in the existence of reprintings of some titles, but also in Torresano's petition of 1536,[177] stating that he had been importing editions of chansons from Paris, apparently from Attaingnant's shop. All the Italian editions were printed in Venice, where Torresano was also based, and their wide circulation was therefore assured. But printers in the Papal States had already shown that they could sell music books from Rome and had maintained a consistent, if irregular, presence in the market. It seems likely that Petrucci and Egnatio were attempting to break into that market again, with a repertoire that they could see was gaining in popularity. In choosing motets, they were avoiding direct conflict with the Venetian editions, and perhaps even attempting to cater more closely to Roman needs. In copying music from Lyons, rather than from Paris, they were also avoiding duplication, while in fact directly anticipating a major source of Gardano's early editions.

It is perhaps significant that neither of these two late books seems to have been known to an early collector or bibliographer: neither is cited anywhere, and the survival of each seems to be the result of copies being used as waste paper. On the other hand, neither can be dismissed as merely a non-commercial exercise, as an exercise in training a new craftsman or a demonstration of local patronage; each uses new typographical material, and the appearance of a new version of Petrucci's device implies a more serious intent. Indeed, so does the timing of each book; if the one containing Verdelot can be placed before Antico's editions, it occupies a position very similar to that of Petrucci's *Motetti del Fiore*. Each would have appeared not long before an edition from Venice, put out by a more significant house; each would reflect an awareness on the part of Petrucci or Egnatio that the repertoire was becoming increasingly popular and that there was a niche in the musical market waiting to be filled. Given this situation, the absence of any subsequent volumes coming from Fossombrone, as much as the absence of early references to these books, does assume some significance: it suggests that these books may have had short print-runs, that they were to some extent "trial balloons" sent up to see whether Petrucci could return to center stage. Other books from the 1530s may yet surface, but on the present evidence of two books in a period of some years, each surviving only as waste paper and close to home, it appears that Petrucci's earlier trade outlets and contacts had moved on, and that his mantle had passed to a younger generation.

The preceding discussion is an attempt at showing whence Petrucci may have acquired the music he printed and also suggesting possible stimuli for individual volumes. These have ranged beyond the classic view of the place of patronage—as providing the contents of and paying for the printing of a whole book; as rewarding the composer or other promoter of a book; or as a commercial venture by a bookseller or other agency. Examples of each surely exist among Petrucci's work, and I have pointed to some possibilities above. But I hope to have made clear that several volumes must have been speculative ventures, on the part of Petrucci and his partners, a collector (such as Castellanus), or a composer (such as Spinacino).

Each such volume would only have been undertaken if Petrucci, with Niccolò and Scotto, felt that there would be an adequate return on their investment. I argue that on occasion (not only with Spinacino, but also for Josquin's first book and the book of Ghiselin masses, perhaps also for Dalza and Bossinensis) they would have been satisfied that the costs would be met by someone else. In others, I believe they followed the sorts of thought processes I have outlined.

It is now hard to determine how far they were successful. I shall argue in chapter 12 that there was no great expansion in the market for printed music during the first three decades of the century, and this might be seen as a measure of failure. However, Petrucci *was* the first to try to sell printed polyphony, and his continued career must equally be viewed as a measure of success.

For us, the only evidence for this success lies in the pattern of editions and re-editions. On that basis, we can assert that some parts of his output sold well, and others hardly at all. On the positive side, there may be the following four distinct repertoires that succeeded, or there may be only the first of the following:

1. Frottole. There can be no doubt that Petrucci's editions sold well. No
   publisher would go through eleven different volumes of any repertoire
   unless the first few had established a pattern of sale and profit. Notably,
   the early volumes went into second editions, while the later ones did not.
   This probably means no more than that Petrucci could gauge the probable
   sale more accurately as time went on and adjust the print-run accordingly.

2. Motets. From *Motetti C* until his return to Fossombrone, Petrucci seems
   to have been able to sell books of motets, though not particularly well.
   Apparently, he did not regard these as sure-fire sellers and probably only
   printed collections that were proposed to him, by Castellanus and others.
   On the other hand, he certainly was willing to publish such books, when
   they were proposed. The Fossombrone editions of *Motetti de la Corona*
   seem to present a different picture. We cannot know the size of the print-
   run, but the sequence of reprintings of these books within six years suggests, tentatively, that Petrucci was able to find an ongoing sale for them.

3. *Canti*, and the first two books of motets. It is difficult to say that these
   sold well. There were second editions (and even a third of the *Odhecaton
   A*), but these tell us nothing. Here I repeat the point that second editions
   merely indicate that the first was sold out and no more. Much is contingent on the print-run, the size of each edition. It must be assumed, as I
   say, that the first editions of these earliest books had small runs—and it
   is notable that *Canti C* did not go to a second edition. Equally significant
   is the fact that Petrucci dropped the repertoire after 1504: this may partly
   reflect a change in taste, despite the evidence advanced by Lawrence
   Bernstein, showing the importance of French-texted pieces in Italy during the following decades. It is questionable, therefore, whether this group
   of pieces was a success, or merely viable.

4. Masses. Before Petrucci's return to Fossombrone, only one of his mass
   editions went into a second edition. Editions remained on sale for at least
   ten years after they had been printed, and the fragments of the La Rue
   edition that survive in Fossombrone suggest that some never sold out.
   Once again, the Fossombrone sale pattern presents a different picture, one
   in which reprintings became necessary.

   On the other side of the coin, there are two repertoires that probably
   did not represent a success for Petrucci.

5. Miscellaneous Latin-texted works. There is virtually no evidence here.
   Two most important books, of hymns and Magnificats, have not survived
   at all, and others apparently did not require second printings. Further, the
   second book of Lamentations can arguably be shown to have been compiled with the first and thus not reflect any success that the first might
   have had.

6. Lute music. It must be remembered that these editions were almost certainly special cases, promoted by the lutenist himself, or the response to
   a political situation in the printing world—a rival privilege. Only one
   seems to have gone to a second printing, suggesting that Bossinensis's
   settings were more popular. These were, in any case, closer to the frottola
   repertoire than to solo lute writing.

7. Finally, there are the two, very different, editions of the 1530s. Whenever
   the first of these is dated, close to 1538 or not, we have no evidence to
   suggest that either was successful. They seem rather to represent oppor-

tunistic attempts at breaking into the market again, attempts that (as far as we know) were not followed by second editions.

The first four groups probably made a significant profit for Petrucci—either directly through sales, or because they were proposed and paid for by someone else.[178] Even so, once Petrucci had been able to gauge the size of the market for a first edition, few books regularly went to second editions. But it seems unlikely that the rest were profitable; although they may have broken even, they did not encourage him to produce many new editions: this is another strand of evidence arguing that few of these books were speculative ventures on Petrucci's past.

Again, it must be stressed that the situation at Fossombrone during the 1510s was slightly different, in that some types of books that had rarely been reprinted in Venice seem to have demanded second editions. Evidence presented in the next chapter will argue that this was a direct reflection of a change in the market— of a number of new purchasers.

But the general pattern is in keeping with a particular view of the character of the market for printed music: that there were, at least at first, barely enough professional institutions to support a publisher of polyphonic liturgical settings, while the amateur and perhaps the court secular musician tended to look to printed sources; further, that amateurs seem to have been willing to buy series of books of the same type of repertoire, effectively building up their collection exclusively in printed editions. On the other hand, the professional institution that wanted to buy printed books would either look to fill holes in its collection, or be one, perhaps a new foundation, without a large collection of manuscripts.

These generalisations have been based exclusively on the patterns of editions and re-editions, that is on the decisions the publisher made, based on his view of the market. The next chapter looks at the actual purchasers, and which ranges of books they bought.

Notes

1. See the next chapter for details of what we can tell about the diffusion of Petrucci's music. Whatever we think of the impact of Petrucci's editions on modern scholarship, they must represent something real from the sixteenth century, for they drew on the collections of a number of musicians and patrons whose musical interests would be less well documented without their survival.

2. Blackburn, "Petrucci".

3. For example, the first book of Magnificats and the first of Martini's hymns (both of 1507 and both now lost), the *Missarum diversorum auctorum Liber primus* and the *Motetti a cinque libro primo* (both of 1508), and the *Missarum Joannis Mouton Liber primus* (1515). Other titles with the relevant phrase and followed by later volumes include *Frottole libro primo* (1504), *Lamentationum Jeremie prophete Liber primus* (1506), *Intabolatura de Lauto Libro primo* (1507), *Laude libro primo* (1508) and Bossinensis's first book of 1509. One should also add here the first editions of *Harmonice Musices Odhecaton A* (1501) and *Motetti A* (1502), for the distinguishing letter surely implies a plan to initiate a series of publications. Two titles apparently were not expected to lead to the series of volumes that they in fact produced, for they did not have the qualifying clause added to the first issue: these were the *Misse Josquin* (1502) and the *Motetti de la Corona* of 1514. I shall present cogent reasons for both instances.

The presumed implication is that *Libro primo* books were expected to lead to subsequent volumes, forming a series. However, there may have been no such expectation on the part of the printer or publisher; the willingness may have lain solely with the composer or the supplier of the music. It certainly must be true that many such "first" volumes from the second half of the century were promoted by the composer, as "vanity" publications. The implication of a forthcoming series was merely an attempt at self-promotion. The lack of subsequent volumes might imply that the composer achieved his object with the first volume (gaining tenure, as it were), or perhaps that there were not enough works for a second book, or merely that the first made a loss and the composer could not afford a second. (Of course, there were series that were the work of a publisher—perhaps with encouragement or subsidy from an editor or patron; the various *Motetti del Fiore* volumes are an example.) This argument can be applied equally well to Petrucci, provided that Petrucci himself and his supplier are taken to stand for "the composer" in the preceding sentences.

4. For thoughtful comments on the extent to which we should trust the pattern of personal contacts as guiding the pattern of stylistic dissemination (or even the transmission of specific works from one center to another), see Wathey, "Peace". Assuredly, the situation was very different by the early sixteenth century, for many Italian individuals and institutions were lusting after polyphonic ensembles and fully fledged northern repertoires to perform. The results of that newly developing pursuit (for which "lust" is hardly too strong a term) were that whole repertoires could be transferred from one center to another, and a maestro at a center such as the cathedral of Bergamo, Casale Monferrato, or Padua, could be required to create a full year's polyphony as soon as possible. In such a situation, the new maestro must have drawn on as many sources as he could, pulled strings, and sought the repayment of past favours to acquire music wherever he could. Yet we should not always point to direct personal contact as the sole stimulus for the spread of specific pieces. The repertoire of the Sistine Chapel continuously makes that point. Fortunately for the study of Petrucci, there are few known contacts, for both himself and the musical circles of the Marche (once he had returned to Fossombrone), that we need to adopt other methods of determining the sources from which he worked.

5. Boorman, "Work and Turn". The bibliographical evidence is outlined in chapter 3, and in the bibliographical entry for the book. I return to this case below.

6. Boorman, *Petrucci*, pp. 173–78. More recently, Sherr, *Sixteenth-Century*, iv, pp. xiv–xv, draws attention to Carpentras's travels to Paris and back in 1513 and hypothesises a visit to Rome by Petrucci. During 1513, Petrucci had held two of the most important positions in Fossombrone: he was selected Anziano in 1513 and Revisor Viarum at the end of the year. However, as we have seen in chapter 1, this would not have precluded a journey to Rome.

7. Lockwood, *Ferrara*, p. 207. There is some reason to assert that the whole volume commemorated the duke, in which case the contents may more closely reflect the taste of the Ferrarese court, with a series of four masses based on French chansons.

8. I include in this such works as Josquin's *Missa Hercules Dux Ferrariae*, for, even if Petrucci acquired his works from Castellanus, or directly from Ferrara, there is no reason to believe that the edition commemorated the event for which the mass was composed. Indeed, Elders's recent argument (in "New Light") plausibly places the mass considerably earlier.

9. For comments on the evidence offered by the title pages of these two volumes, see Boorman, "Raphael".

10. These volumes were discussed in more detail in chapter 7. Given their local origin, we would be justified in considering Fossombrone, or (more plausibly) Urbino, as the center from which Petrucci drew music for his last volumes. Unfortunately, we know virtually nothing about music in Fossombrone at the time (see my comments in chapter 1) and not a great deal more about music at the court of Urbino. But, as I shall argue, Urbino itself seems a likely center as the source for some of the Fossombrone editions.

11. The presence of dedicatory epistles in the Spinacino and Bossinensis volumes may indicate that the books were in the nature of "vanity" publications.

12. For my views on this issue, see, in particular, Boorman, "Market"; Boorman, "Bibliography"; and Boorman, "Music Publisher's View". It should be evident from what follows, I do not entirely agree with the view of the character of a purchaser of music books as expressed in Lewis, *Gardano*, i, pp. 11–16.

13. It is worth mentioning again that many printers or publishers can now only be asso-

ciated with one surviving book, and that there is no reason to believe that any of the smaller printing establishments provided a complete income for their owners.

14. Blackburn, "Petrucci". This paper rightly draws attention to the implications of a large collection of music in the connection between Castellanus and Passetto, the scribe of Padua A17.

15. See Boorman, "First", specially the last few pages.

16. Blackburn, "Petrucci", p. 17 for the translation. See also her "Lorenzo".

17. For the dating of this manuscript, see the *Census-Catalogue*, and more particularly Lockwood, *Ferrara*, pp. 204–206. Lockwood discusses the evidence for lost Ferrarese manuscripts of secular music on pp. 218–19.

18. The manuscripts are F-Pn Rès.Vm⁷.676, I-Bc Q18, I-Fn Panc.27, and I-VEcap DCCLVII. All these later northern Italian secular manuscripts (to which E-Se s.s. could perhaps be added) tend to show a similar repertoire, with frequent concordances between them, and to relate to Petrucci's volume to a greater or lesser extent. Whether this relationship is directly to Petrucci's readings or to Castellanus's collection remains to be seen, though Blackburn has recently argued for a direct connection with Castellanus in the case of I-Pc A.17; and I see direct copying from Petrucci's edition in the manuscripts now in Paris and Verona.

19. De Orto seems to have had no connection with Ferrara, and his music there may not have been known at all well. Petrucci, however, published a volume of his masses, which I shall discuss below, and this argues for knowledge of his music on the part of Castellanus. Blackburn, "Petrucci", p . 29, posits a process by which Castellanus collected music from Rome (although here note Sherr, "Relationship"), which could certainly include works by de Orto, who had been there for some fifteen years before returning north. See Picker, "Career", for the latest survey of the composer's life.

20. See Lockwood, *Ferrara*, pp. 226 and 269–71, for support for this assertion and an analysis of its implications.

21. For this possibility with a different repertoire, see Kmetz, "Singing".

22. See Fallows, "French", for a discussion of the linguistic abilities of Italian courtiers.

23. Lowinsky, in the introduction to Helen Hewitt's edition of *Canti B*, p. xv.

24. The nearest contenders were soon to appear, *Motetti C*, with thirty-two and one-half sheets of paper, and *Motetti IV*, with thirty-two. Of course, Paulus de Middelburgh's *Paulina* is considerably larger.

25. Brown, "Mirror".

26. In *Odhecaton A*, which opens with De Orto's *Ave Maria*, there are also a *Mater patris* by Brumel and a *Si dedero* by Agricola. Isaac's *Benedictus* probably should not be included here, for it seems to have acquired a rather different status, more akin to the *In Nomine* in England. In *Canti B*, there are another five works: *Ave ancilla trinitas* and *Noe noe* by Brumel (the second perhaps also different in character), *Cela sans plus* "in missa" and *Si sumpsero* by Obrecht, and *Virgo celesti* by Compère.

27. See Dunning, *Staatsmotette*, pp. 9–14. However, Wegman, *Born*, p. 317, rightly draws attention to features one might expect in a text celebrating a peace treaty, but are lacking here. At the same time, in a footnote on p. 310, he suggests a similar occasion in 1492 as the possible cause of Obrecht's setting of the same text.

28. The details are in the concordance tables: Tinctoris's *Virgo Dei throno* is in I-Fn B.R.229, with Richafort's *O genitrix gloriosa* in I-Fr 2794; Ghiselin's *Anima mea* and *O florens rosa* are in the Flemish I-Fc Basevi 2439; and Agricola's *O quam glorifica* in the French source, F-Pn f.fr.1597. Of north Italian sources, Verona DCCLVII contains Tinctoris's work, and ZA-Csa Grey 3.b.12 has three works: Weerbeke's *Mater digna Dei* and *O pulcherrima mulierum*, and the anonymous *Da pacem Domine* (also found in F-Pn f.fr.1597).

29. The fourth piece, *Secundum multitudinem dolorum*, is anonymous and appears to survive only in Petrucci's edition. It, too, could well be Roman in origin.

30. Indeed, given the age of some of these pieces, it also argues for a direct connection, rather than one through intermediaries.

31. We have no way of knowing which came first, even in the case of the fragments taken from Weerbeke's pieces, for the style allows the shorter pieces to seem self-sufficient.

32. Even if the following argument is discounted, Castellanus would still have had to produce reasons that could persuade Petrucci and his partners.

33. See Cummings, "Toward".

34. Duggan, *Italian*, pp. 102–106, lists the volumes with music published by the Scotto family before 1501 and mentions that the house printer, Locatello, published a noted missal in 1501.

35. These movements were popular and became more so as the sixteenth century wore on, with the growth of amateur performers. A number of mass movements printed by Petrucci survive elsewhere with new contrafactum texts, stressing their independent existence. However, the popularity of these individual movements does not invalidate an assumption that their performers would not buy a book of masses.

36. It is for these, basically commercial, reasons that I doubt the importance of a Roman source for these works, hinted at in Blackburn, "Petrucci", pp. 29–30. I also see the Josquin book as having the same external stimuli as the rest of this group of titles.

37. Gottwald, *Ghiselin*, p. 14; Lockwood, *Ferrara*, p. 202.

38. Lockwood, "Josquin", p. 109, fn.19. Gottwald, in his article on Ghiselin in *The New Grove*, vii, pp. 340–41, assumes that Ghiselin did reach Ferrara and took up a position there. Lockwood's interpretation of the documents suggests that the "Messer Johane fiamengo" listed in Ferrarese records from 1503 to 1509 was a different singer. Whichever solution is correct, it seems that the Ferrarese were expecting Ghiselin to come to the city.

39. The letters are reproduced and discussed in Lockwood, "Josquin", and Lockwood, *Ferrara*, pp. 203–205. See also Lockwood, "Virtuoso".

40. See the statement of position and a new theory in Elders, "New Light".

41. Lockwood, *Ferrara*, p. 207.

42. The composers with one Latin-texted work were Agricola, De Orto, and Isaac in *Odhecaton A*, and Compère and Obrecht in *Canti B*.

43. For the latest discussion of this question, see Meconi, "Free".

44. *RISM*, BIV⁵, p. 256. Lockwood, *Ferrara*, pp. 222–24, advances reasons for suggesting that the manuscript from which these fragments come was copied ca.1481.

45. See the description of this fragment in the bibliographical entry for this edition.

46. Haar, in a recent study of Josquin's masses as they survive in Roman sources, points out that these are in "versions differing from Petrucci's sources" (Haar, "Josquin", p. 214). For example, discussing the *Missa La sol fa re mi*, he draws attention to variants that "set the Cappella Sistina redaction distinctly apart from Petrucci's version" (p. 219); even for those masses copied in Rome after Petrucci's edition, Haar believes that the printed edition was not a primary source, with the possible exception of the *Missa L'homme arme super voces musicales*. This leaves Ferrara as the most likely source for Petrucci's versions, with or without the intervention of Castellanus. Incidentally, both the *Missa L'homme arme super voces musicales* and the *Missa Fortuna desperata* can be found in I-MOe α.M.1.2, a Ferrarese manuscript.

47. Gallico, "Laboratorio".

48. The most obvious example is Ockeghem's *Ut heremita solus*, in *Motetti C*.

49. This does not mean, of course, that we see a close alignment between the music and text spacing; that would not happen for some decades. But it does mean that Petrucci had to approximate the spacing, allowing the text to be more or less continuous, and therefore spacing the music more generously. Extreme examples were to come in the volumes of Bossinensis, where the lute tablature complicated the situation even more.

50. There is considerable evidence for this practice. One clear-cut case is in the A-Wn copy of *Frottole I*: see the bibliographical entry.

51. This statement from Gallico, "Laboratorio", p. 200, has been discussed elsewhere in the present study. James Haar, in "Petrucci", p. 14, makes a similar statement, though about the repertoire (rather than the publications): "To an Italy long impressed by French musical culture and recently awed by French military strength, the *frottola* represented an indigenous music, an art song to be placed alongside the century-long dominant chanson".

52. Although we cannot date most of them precisely, several show traces of having taken individual pieces from Petrucci.

53. I have not made a systematic search for Venetian editions of these and similar poets, or of volumes of canzone or frottole, for the years 1495–1502. The rather fortuitously discovered evidence suggests that the market for printed editions of these works began to develop only in the years after 1498: Bonelli, de Pensis, and Rusconi issued editions during the following four years.

54. This position was probably not true in the traditional sense for any book published by Petrucci up to this time; there is no indication of dedicatory compositions or of works with topical allusions. First pieces, however, were certainly designed to attract potential purchasers, and scholars have been able to use them on occasion as a guide to probable sources for the repertoire.

55. Boorman, "Printed", pp. 2597–98.

56. A number of works that take only one page in Petrucci's editions require a full opening in the contemporary manuscripts I-Fc Basevi 2441 and F-Pn Rès.Vm⁷.676.

57. Quaranta, *Oltre*, p. 359.

58. The documentation for Castellanus's absence from Venice, on a visit to Recanati, is given in Blackburn, "Petrucci", p. 21, and shows that he was back in Venice by 1 August. Further details can be found in Quaranta, *Oltre*.

59. Brauner, *Parvus*, pp. 243–55.

60. Reynolds, "Origins".

61. Picker, "De Orto", p. 538, which includes the following quotation.

62. Lockwood, *Music*, p. 207. While I agree with the sentiment expressed here, I doubt that the publication of this one mass was associated specifically with any sentiment on Petrucci's (or Josquin's) part. The mass had been composed long before, although not yet widely disseminated, and its publication was probably seen more as a reflection of the late duke's interests, as, I propose, was also the first mass.

63. Lockwood, *Music*, p. 199. Lockwood draws attention to the edition of the *Corona Beatae Mariae Virginis*, written by the duke and printed for him.

64. He had already appeared once, in *Canti C*, unfortunately surrounded by anonymous compositions.

65. Picker, in "De Orto", links these two, suggesting that both were composed ca.1487.

66. This dating was first proposed in Noble, "Ottaviano". I am grateful to David Fallows for discussing this edition, and the first edition of Josquin's second book.

67. Perhaps the phrase "Libro quarto" was an editorial addition, reflecting an in-house decision to link this book with the earlier group of three.

68. Details of the patterns of attributions and other relevant evidence are in the bibliographical description for this volume.

69. The evidence was presented in outline in Boorman, "Printed", pp. 2588–90.

70. Haar, "Petrucci".

71. Further confirmation of this approach may perhaps be found in the presence of instructions in the lute volumes that began to appear in early 1507.

72. Nicolo was probably not the "Nicolo de Chimento pifaro", entered as a member of the Scuola Grande di Santa Maria della Misericordia at the Frari (alongside other, mostly windplaying, musicians) by 1505. See Quaranta, *Oltre*, p. 322.

73. The figures are instructive: in the three books, Cara is represented by five, four, and two works. While Tromboncino is a significant contributor (with eleven, twelve, and six works), it is equally notable that there are twenty-two works by Lurano, and fifteen by D'Ana.

74. Thomas, *Petrucci*, is a discussion and edition of the music in these books.

75. See the biographical details and conclusions reached in Bent, "Emiliani".

76. Thomas, *Petrucci*.

77. The oddity in this volume is the presence of Erasmus, presumably the Lapicida also found in *Motetti IV*. Given his appearance with a simple Italian-language piece in *Frottole IX*, we may have to assume that the gap in his biography before 1510 included a visit to northern Italy. Othmar Wessely, in *The New Grove*, x, p. 465, remarks that Lapicida's German pieces, with their "frottola-like" traits and flowing melodic lines, suggest that he had some contact with

Italian influences. This Lamentation setting, coupled with the frottola, suggests that the influence was received at first hand.

78. Glixon, "Polyphonic", pp. 34–38. His reasons are not really satisfactory; the extant copy of Dammonis's edition is more accurate than Book 2, not because it is a second edition, but because the composer probably had to act as reader of an early copy of the first as it came from the press. Petrucci's second editions tend to follow the first very closely: even so, the book does have in-house corrections.

79. The details are given in the bibliographical description of the volume.

80. Glixon "Polyphonic": for earlier studies, see the literature cited there.

81. Glixon, "Polyphonic", p. 22. I find this identification preferable to the suggestion in Luisi, *Laudario*, i, pp. 441–45. Reynolds, *Papal*, pp. 55–6, suggests that the Baldasar cited as a composer in *Laude II* may be a Seraphinus Baldesarius, himself perhaps the Serafinus paid in the Vatican during 1485–9. The retention of the dedication in the second edition is a practice followed by the various editions of Petrucci's *Odhecaton A*. The later practice of withdrawing a dedication for later editions, which reflects a view of those editions as purely commercial transactions, would emerge only once music publishing itself became a routine commercial business, in which privately promoted editions (with their accompanying dedications) represent one of a number of possible situations, alongside speculative ventures on the part of composer or publisher.

82. The Oriola poem is translated and discussed in Slim "Musicians"; Gigas's epigram is translated in Schmidt, *First*, ii, p. vi.

83. This may be another indication that Spinacino was from Fossombrone, or at least was a friend of Petrucci.

84. It is probably significant that, in the first volume, the corrections stop at about the point that the series of ricercars begins, though what the significance of that is cannot be determined. Since only one copy survives we cannot exclude any of the following: that the book was sold before all the corrections were entered; that the corrector became tired of correcting all the copies; that the recercars were part of Spinacino's standard repertoire and therefore more accurately copied, while the intabulations were specially prepared for this edition (not impossible given the preponderance of works already published by Petrucci in vocal form).

85. Underwood, *Renaissance*, p. 6.

86. This speculation derives from Colón's description of the volume, which includes the phrase "prima Cantilena .I. Come feme". I suspect that this was a transcription of one of the settings by Agricola, perhaps the one already transcribed by Spinacino.

87. "Note that all the pavanes have their own saltarellos and pivas". This point is made in Moe, *Dance Music*.

88. Einstein, in the revision of Vogel, *Bibliothek*, p. 611, assumes that 1507 is an error for 1508.

89. One piece of evidence might suggest otherwise: *Voi che passati*, No.21 in Book 7, is there assigned to "B.T." In Bossinensis's intabulation of 1509, it is assigned to "F.V.", that is, D'Ana. Given that Petrucci was working in Venice, the latter ascription would seem more plausible.

90. Giovanni del Lago mentions Zesso, his teacher, as being from Padua (see Blackburn et al., *Correspondence*, p. 819); both Demophon and Pesenti are in Cardinal Ippolito's accounts (see Lockwood, "Adrian", pp. 97–99 and 110–12); for the other composers, see the references in Jeppesen, *Frottola*, i, pp. 143–63.

91. Colón's entry in his catalogue includes the phrase "Impressum Venetijs per octauianum petrucium. anno. 1507. 14. octobris". See Chapman, "Columbus", No.29.

92. Unfortunately, neither gives more than the year "1507", and so perhaps the book did not either. See Chapman, "Columbus", No.28. There is not much reason to believe that the book of hymns contained only works by Martini. His few surviving hymns (at I-MOe) would not fill even a single volume, though we cannot know how many have been lost.

93. For example, the second edition of the *Odhecaton A* took only eighteen days including weekends, as did the second of *Frottole II*. The second of *Canti B* took twenty days. In these cases, it is reasonable to assign the whole period to the one volume.

94. Strohm, *Rise*, pp. 585–86, stresses this point.

95. Even after those volumes, such printed editions were still rare. (See the pattern of sources in Kirsch, *Quellen*; for hymns, there is no similar catalogue, though Ward, *Polyphonic*, indicates the extent of manuscript sources at the time of Petrucci's edition.) Attaingnant, who had published an anthology of keyboard intabulations of Magnificats in 1530, added two volumes to his motet series, in 1534 (*RISM* 1534[7] and 1534[8]). In Germany there were books of Magnificats by Dietrich in 1535 (published by Schöffer) and by Senfl in 1537 (from Formschneider's press), as well as several hymn settings for reformed congregations. But the next Italian editions of both genres appeared in 1542—Morales's of Magnificats, and Willaert's of hymns.

96. See Higgins, "Tracing".

97. See Tinctoris, *Opera Theoretica*, p. ii.

98. Wegman, *Born*, p. 317.

99. Strohm, *Music*, p. 145.

100. Wegman, *Born*, p. 23, dates this work to 1489.

101. For this reason, while Prizer's suggestion (in "Courtly", p. 27) that the collection may have been music from the Chapel of S. Maria dei Voti in Mantua is attractive, I doubt this was the source of the versions printed by Petrucci.

102. Bella Busca was apparently Benedetto Bellabusta, a friar at S. Elena in Venice. See Blackburn, *Correspondence*, p. 982.

103. My description of *Frottole IX* raises this possibility, though with some scepticism.

104. Petrucci's situation was of course different from that of Soncino and others in the Marche, who published books that would have been of interest to any humanist. All printers in the area probably earned some sort of living from official documents; some seemed to have made them a specialty. But music was always different: see Boorman, "Market".

105. This book of Antico is no longer extant, but it is probable that it had already appeared by then. Book 3 appeared in 1513. For Book 2, see Luisi, *Secondo*.

106. These are *RISM* [ca.1520][7] (the date of which is confirmed by Colón: see Chapman, "Columbus", No.55, p. 68) and V1224=W1104 (of 1536, with a reedition of 1540: *RISM* V1225=W1105).

107. Fabris, "Frottola", p. 5, fn.2. I am grateful to Dr. Fabris for sending me a copy of this article and for discussing the implications of the manuscript with me. See also Underwood, *Renaissance*, pp. 207–209, which provides a transcription.

108. The manuscript is now F-Pc, Rés.Vmd.27, and has been reproduced in facsimile, in Lesure, *Tablature*. It is discussed in Thibault, "Manuscrit". The spelling of the text incipits is clearly Venetian, but Mme. Thibault argues, convincingly, that the unknown copyist probably did not have access to sources closely related to those used by Bossinensis. See also Underwood, *Renaissance*, pp. 113–54.

109. Prizer, "Frottola", p. 28.

110. Underwood, *Renaissance*, pp. 118–20.

111. Barbarigo was the supporter of Petrucci's complaint about not being admitted to the Cestieri in 1504.

112. Other similar cases are the first three of frottole, and the two of Lamentations.

113. See the reasoning in chapter 1, especially the precise dating of political events. In addition, there is no reason to believe that Petrucci kept in touch with Bossinensis, or any other of the lutenist suppliers (except perhaps the Fossombronese Spinacino), once he had left Venice.

114. It is possible that the books bought by Colón in Rome in 1512 were supplied from Fossombrone rather than Venice.

115. Boorman, *Petrucci*, pp. 48–52 gives a synoptic history of the period, primarily as it concerns Urbino and its duke; see also Sherr, *Sixteenth-Century*, p. iv.

116. Gehrenbeck, *Corona*, p. 147.

117. Sherr, *Papal*, pp. 165–66.

118. GB-Lbl, Cot.Jul.IV.Art.vi, f.24r.

119. It would seem less appropriate for a gift to the French king, even as a part of the politics surrounding the betrothal; for that, one would expect a higher level of extravagance—parchment, illumination—as well as a much more specific opening composition. It is significant

that there would be another printed volume produced to commemorate a marital alliance; the *Libro primo de la Serena* does not include motets, but otherwise can be compared with the present book. See Campagnolo, "Libro".

120. For this point, see the letter of 26 July 1513, from the Archdeacon of Gabbioneta to Francesco Gonzaga, quoted in Luzio, "Isabella", pp. 121–22, according to which it was a Mantuan proposal.

121. This had been signed on 5 April 1513, and Emperor Maximilian, Henry VIII of England, and Ferdinand of Spain agreed to attack France from all sides. Leo was apparently a reluctant participant at first, but became an active member of the group on 25 May when he agreed to pay for Milanese mercenaries. In late June, he made his position publicly clear, also revealing himself opposed to Venice. Pastor, *History*, vii, p. 50; Giovio, *Historiarum*, xi, p. 161; Sanuto, *Diarii*, xvi, pp. 223, 225, 227, 270, 292, 295, and 305.

122. Pastor, *History*, vii, p. 67.

123. The Bishop of Marseilles had arrived in Rome on 24 July as the French ambassador, and "turned especially to Giuliano de'Medici, who was his King's friend". See Dufayard, *Seyssel*, p. 22; Pastor, *History*, vii, p. 66; and Sanuto, *Diarii*, xvi, p. 548.

124. Lupi, *Relazioni*, p. 302. At the same time, the pope was trying to discourage Louis from marrying Renée to the Archduke Ferdinand.

125. Fatini, *Giuliano*, preface, p. lxix.

126. The documents for the betrothal are in the Archivio di Stato di Torino, Sezione Corte, Matrimoni, Mazzo 18. This is first in the file and is followed by the contract of 10 May, mentioned below, and Giuliano's ratification of the contract, dated 12 October. I am grateful to Professor Giorgio Pestelli for drawing my attention to these documents.

127. Bembo, *Opere*, iv, p. 464, No.20. On the same day, the pope wrote via Bembo to Filiberta herself, telling her that he was sending a message to the duke. See the next entry in Bembo's *Opere*. The letter of 21 June, cited next, is No.24 on the same page.

128. This date is given in Roscoe, *Vita*, v, p. 80. But Ardinghelli, scribe for Cardinal Giulio de'Medici, and then in Rome, wrote to Giuliano on 1 February, in response to a letter from him dated 26 January, saying that he had not yet heard that the wedding took place. See Guasti, *I Mss Torrigiani*, pp. 227–28. Other dates proposed by modern scholars include 10 February (Fatini, *Giuliano*, p. lxxiiii), 15 February at Turin cathedral (Luzio, "Isabella", p. 161); and 25 February (Nitti, *Leone*; and Pastor, *History*). On the other hand, Francesco Vettori writes to Florence on 8 February discussing the journey "di Giuliano e la consorte" (I-Fa, VIII.Prat. Cart.Resp.xi, p. 445). In any case, the wedding would have been commemorated with formal parallel ceremonies in Florence and other centers on the route from Paris.

129. Guicciardini, *Historie*, p. 510 reports of Francisco Maria della Rovere that "*Iulian, . . . could not endure to see him deprived by them of the Duchie wherein he had been entertained and honored*". Castiglione also included Giuliano in the circle at court, suggesting in his *Il Cortegiano* that he was knowledgeable in music theory, and perhaps also capable as a musician. See Castiglione, *Book*, pp. 69 and 94.

130. Lowinsky, "Boleyn", pp. 177–80.

131. We can hardly assert that the piece was written for the wedding itself. The text begins "O desolatorum consolatio, captivorum liberator, resurrectio mortuorum, lumen cecorum, auditus surdorum, mutorum eloquium". With its continuing pleas to S. Cloud to intercede for those "in hac valle miserie", it seems rather to refer to that earlier period, especially during 1513, when Claude's marriage was opposed by Anne, who still hoped to prevent François ascending to the throne.

132. Lockwood, "Jean Mouton".

133. The last was a young singer, only recently sent from Paris to the pope.

134. For a facsimile of this manuscript, see Owens, *Bologna*. The total of sixteen instances includes two where the name was later changed to that of Moulu. It is curious that Cosimo Bartoli calls the composer "Giouanni Monton", on folio 36 of his *Ragionamenti accademici* of 1567. Bartoli, of course, was a Florentine and was involved in the printing of Vasari's famous *Vite de'più excellenti pittori* of 1550. See Bryce, *Bartoli*.

135. Lockwood, "Jean Mouton", pp. 234–41: the following quotation appears on p. 240.

136. Bibbiena, *Epistolario*, ii, pp. 7–8.

137. The number of concordances that the first book of the *Corona* has with I-Pc A17 (seven) might suggest that there was a common source for the music. That manuscript was the one compiled by Passetto, apparently from music supplied by Castellanus (see Blackburn, "Petrucci"), and so perhaps indirectly from Ferrarese contacts. This seems enough to suggest that the two may have had distant common origins, but not that there was any closer contact. See also fn.146 below.

138. See fn.129, above.

139. Sherr, "Relationship"; and I cite again Haar, "Josquin", with the evidence that Petrucci did not receive his copies of Josquin's masses from Rome. I find it unlikely that Petrucci would receive only one movement from Rome and incorporate it into a version of the whole mass from a different source. Further, I see little indication that he had an editorial eye, at any time in his career. Thus, although I find Sherr's suggestion that Petrucci was the first to combine the Gloria with other movements to make a complete mass to be very attractive, I doubt that Petrucci himself would have done so. Instead, I regard it as the action of the local patron who supplied the music. This does not negate the thrust of Sherr's argument.

140. I leave aside Antico's 1516 edition, for I presume that compiler to have drawn on Vatican sources.

141. These include two with attributions to Josquin—Cap.Sist.16 and Pal.lat.1982, as well as three slightly later that preserve the work anonymously: I-Rsm 26, C.G.XII,2, and Pal.lat.1980–1981. It is also possible that two later ascriptions to Josquin reflect a general opinion held during at least the 1510s. Both masses are in I-Ma Mus.E.46; they are an otherwise unknown *Missa Quem dicunt homines* (perhaps a later work) and La Rue's *Missa Cum iocunditate* (which was attributed correctly in the Vatican Cap.Sist.45).

142. One other, *Aqua non e'l humor*, is known elsewhere only in the Antico edition of intabulations of Tromboncino and Cara, *RISM* [1520]⁷.

143. Of these, the Lulinus work is also in the Roman *Fior de motetti e canzoni nove* of 1523 (*RISM* [1526]⁵); one by Tromboncino is also found in Florentine manuscripts with various attributions; and four by Tromboncino are intabulated in Antico's 1520 edition.

144. Boorman, "What Bibliography", p. 246.

145. It is possible that Francesco Griffo, moving to Bologna, and later to print on his own account, might have suggested the repertoire to Petrucci, or even acted as an intermediary for some Bolognese notable. Certainly, Bologna would be a feasible center from which to gather the majority of this repertoire. However, there are few concordances with Bolognese sources, which significantly weakens any such argument, given the extent of the San Petronio collection.

146. It has been suggested (Blackburn, "Petrucci") that Petrucci was still receiving music from Castellanus. Blackburn's argument is based on Castellanus's travels during this time, and on the closeness between some Petrucci readings and those found in I-Pc A17. The first factor is valid, but I believe the second is not. Castellanus did send music to Passetto at Padua; some of the readings are very close. But there is no reason to believe that Passetto copied only from Castellanus's manuscripts, nor is there any reason to believe that Castellanus was the only suitable person in his circle of acquaintance. In other words, it is possible that Petrucci's edition supplied some of the material in the later I-Pc, A17, and equally that he drew on the same sources that had supplied Castellanus himself. See also the discussion of Group 17, below.

147. Vernarecci, *Petrucci*, p. 160. See also Sherr, "Relationship".

148. In addition, he printed a pamphlet by Paulus de Middelburgh.

149. The first in I-Rvat, Pal.lat.1982 and the fourth in Cap.Sist.23, definitely written before Petrucci set out to print the work.

150. These are the masses *Alma redemptoris mater*, *Dictes moy*, and *Regina celorum*. Two of these are also in Antico's *RISM* 1516¹, alongside the two masses in Févin's book.

151. The first is in I-RE s.s., and the second in I-MOd IV.

152. An attractive scenario would involve Bishop Paulus recommending Petrucci to other members of the council, perhaps even acting as an intermediary, for when they wished to have

a largely Roman repertoire printed for their own ends. The absence of dedicatory letters, however, argues against this hypothesis.

153. Apart from the various hidden editions and additional sheets, Petrucci did print Paulus's short pamphlet, six months after the last avowed edition, in late 1516.

154. The closeness of the readings has been discussed in Boorman, *Petrucci*.

155. They include I-Bsp 38 (one work), I-CF LIX (one), I-CMac (various sources, with three concordances).

156. Ferrarese sources: I-Mod IX (three works), GB-Lbl Add.19583 (one), I-MOe α.N.1.2 (one), and also the later GB-Lcm 2037, with four concordances. Roman/Florentine sources: I-Fl, Acq. e doni.666 (five concordances), I-Fn II.i.232 (one). Other Roman sources do not have similar patterns of ascription: among those are the Vatican manuscripts Pal.lat.1980 (one work), Cap.Sist 26 (one), Cap.Sist.46 (one of the two concordant works), and the later C.G.XII,4 (one).

157. The first layer (with the exception of the one work by Lebrun) is widely distributed in Italian sources; the only early concordances are either Sistine or Medicean (I-Fn, II.I.232), with some concordances in Antico's 1520 editions. The second layer is not as well distributed, but again includes Medicean sources (Cortona-Paris). A few concordances with Ferrarese sources (I-MOe α.F.2.29 and GB-Lbl Add.19583) do not really change the pattern.

158. Only three works from this layer have attributions; two of those have Italian concordances: No.14, by Févin survives anonymously in I-Bc Q27, I-Bc R142, I-Pc A17, and I-VEcap DCCLX, none of which precedes the edition by Petrucci; No.15, Bauldeweyn's *Quam pulchra es*, has two, both anonymous and later: GB-Lbl Add.19583 and I-MOe α.F.2.29. This contrasts with the relatively large number of concordances for pieces 3–9 in the edition.

159. Sherr, "Notes", p. 68.

160. Pirrotta, "Florence from Barzelletta", pp. 17–18, makes the point that "much of the content of the 1520 [Pisano] print was composed in [Rome] under the auspices of his Medici protector, Leo X".

161. I have argued earlier that he went to Venice in 1518, rather than in 1520.

162. His biography has been most recently summarised in D'Accone's article in *The New Grove*.

163. Miggiani, "Petrucci", pp. 35–49.

164. A detailed study of other editions would seem to be in order, though Miggiani does remark that the textual readings of those also found in I-Fn, Magl.XIX.164–67 are identical in the two sources. Since these are, of course, the same settings, this observation does little more than associate the two sources in the transmission.

165. Miggiani, "Petrucci", pp. 66–67, fn.12. Pirrotta also wonders about how powerful the impact of the Strozzi family was on Pisano, and this could relate to my statements in "What Bibliography".

166. See also Petrarch, "Disperse", p. 285.

167. The musical interests of Lorenzo have been studied in D'Accone, "Transitional", and a few additional documents are cited in Agee, "Filippo", p. 227, fn.2.

168. See Bullard, "Filippo". The musical activities of Filippo have been discussed in a number of places; see Brown, "Chansons"; Brown, "Music"; and Agee, "Filippo", with the literature cited there.

169. This point raises a significant question about the Roman editions of the 1520s, and particularly about the emergence of the madrigal, in editions and manuscripts. Some editions seem to show Strozzi (rather than Medicean) influence; many argue for a distinctively Roman view of the repertoire. This repertoire would, of course, include much that was Florentine, even after Leo X's death, but it also included other styles and genres; in particular, it is reflected in the curious organization of the printed editions, containing several different repertoires (motets and madrigals, even a mass) in the same volume.

170. As Gialdroni and Ziino show, in "New Light", the documents discovered by Mariani reveal that the city was looking to hire Petrucci as much for his reputation as a printer as for the opportunity to build a paper mill.

171. Vernarecci, *Petrucci*, pp. 127–28. The fragments were first discussed in Ceccarelli and

Spaccazocchi, *Tre Carte*, and then reproduced in Coviello, *Tradizione*: I dated them in my "Petrucci . . . some new", p. 147, on the basis of other typographical evidence. More recent discussions, in Fenlon and Haar, *Italian*, pp. 201–202, and Gialdroni and Ziino, "New Light", have allowed us to propose a date for the editions more in keeping with the probable dates of the music.

172. For this and other documents concerning Petrucci's technical material, see Gialdroni and Ziino, "New Light", and also their forthcoming article.

173. Gialdroni and Ziino, "New Light", pp. 511–14.

174. Slim, *Gift*, discusses the possible connection of I-Fc 2495 with the Strozzi family, while Agee, "Filippo", and Agee, "Ruberto", relate the Strozzi interest in the madrigal. Haar, "Madrigals", discusses the dating of the second source.

175. See Fenlon and Haar, *Madrigal*.

176. Bernstein, "La Couronne".

177. This petition is discussed in chapter 2.

178. Here, of course, one must add the two editions of Paulus de Middelburgh's writings.

Chapter Ten

THE DISSEMINATION

OF PETRUCCI'S BOOKS

AND REPERTOIRE

Prices

It is generally accepted that Petrucci's music books were more expensive than those of his successors. Chapman took this position and based her opinion on the evidence of the catalogues compiled by Ferdinando Colón. In comparing the prices he paid for different editions of music, published by Petrucci, Antico, Sambonettus (1515), and de Frizis (1519), she concluded that "there was a dramatic difference".[1] In presenting the following table, I have expanded it to include a number of musical treatises and a few non-musical books when they provide additional data. The first column gives the catalogue entry number in Colón's *Registrum* B[2]; the last gives the value in terms of 100ths of the "ducado de oro", based on the values given by Colón himself. (In the following discussion, I have used the term "soldo" to represent 1% of the ducato: this is a practical convenience, for the relationship did vary.)[3] Petrucci's editions are entered in bold type.

There are several significant layers of evidence in this table. Foremost, of course, is the range of prices demanded for Petrucci's editions: the collection of books purchased in Rome in September 1512 seems to have prices related to the repertoire. The cost per folio was consistent for the three volumes of lute music, at rather less than half a soldo. (This translates to about one and three-quarters soldo for a complete sheet of paper.) Colón could buy the first edition of Bossinensis at a lower price (a third of a soldo), perhaps reflecting the smaller market for songs with lute, as opposed to lute solos. Four months later, in February 1513, he bought a copy of *Motetti C* at the higher rate, and he had to pay a similar price for the second book of laude, when he bought it in Perugia in 1530. This suggests that the retail price remained fairly constant throughout Petrucci's career, although the price he would have been able to charge booksellers and middlemen

Reg.B Title	(Publisher, date): format and length	Purchased	Price	% of a ducato d'oro	% per folio	% per sheet
2580	**Spinacino: *Intabulatura de Lauto I*** (Venice: Petrucci, 1507): 4⁰ 56 ff.	Rome, ix.1512	76 quatrines	24.8	0.443	1.77
2581	**Spinacino: *Intabolatura de Lauto II*** (Venice: Petrucci, 1507): 4⁰: 56 ff.	Rome, ix.1512	74 quatrines	24.1	0.430	1.72
2582	**Alemannus: *Intabolatura deI Lauto III*** (Venice: Petrucci, 1508): 4⁰:	Rome, ix.1512	110 quatrines	35.8		
2543	**Dalza: *Intabolatura de Lauto IV*** (Venice: Petrucci, 1508): 4⁰: 56 ff.	Rome, ix.1512	76 quatrines	24.8	0.443	1.77
3803	**Bossinensis: *Tenori . . . intabulati I*** (Venice: Petrucci, 1509): 4⁰: 64 ff.	Rome, ix.1512	70 quatrines	22.4	0.350	1.40
2563	Sadoleto: *De Bello suscipiendo* [?Rome: Mazzocchi, 1509]: 4⁰:	Rome, ix.1512	24 quatrines	7.8		
3803	**Bossinensis: *Tenori . . . intabulati II*** (Fossombrone: Petrucci, 1511): 4⁰: 64 ff.	Rome, ix.1512	96 quatrines	31.2	0.4875	1.95
3798	Urceo: *Orationes* (Bologna: Platonides, 1502): fol.: 168 ff.	Rome, ix.1512	125 quatrines	40.7	0.242	0.45
2772	*Canzoni nove* (Rome: Antico, 1510): 4⁰: 44 ff.	Rome, x.1512	75 quatrines	24.5	0.557	2.23
2828	Balbi: *Regule brevis musice* (s.l.: s.n., s.d.): 4⁰: 14 ff.	Rome, x.1512	2 quatrines	0.65	0.046	0.184
2777	Bonaventura da Brescia: *Regula musicae planae* (Pesaro: Capha, s.d.): 4⁰: ??16 ff.	Rome, x.1512	8 quatrins	2.61	0.163	0.65
2773	Pontanus: *De fortitudine* (Naples: Moravus, 1490): 4⁰: 100 ff.	Rome, x.1512	45 quatrines	14.67	0.147	0.588
2776	Russus: *Thesaurus musices* (Messina: de Brugis, 1500): 4⁰: 8 ff.	Rome, x.1512	3 quatrines	0.98	0.1225	0.49
3885	Sannazaro: *Arcadia* (Milan: Mantegatus, 17.ii.1509): 4⁰: 92 ff.	Rome, x.1512	30 quatrines	9.78	0.107	0.427
3886	Spataro: *Honesto defensio* (Bologna: de Benedictis, 1491): 4⁰: 50 ff.	Rome, x.1512	15 quatrines	4.89	0.098	0.39
3872	Colonna: *Hypnerothomachia Poliphili* (Venice: Aldus, xii.1500): fol.: 234 ff.	Rome, xii.1512	200 quatrines	48.5	0.207	0.415
2895	***Motetti C*** (Venice: Petrucci, 1504): 4⁰: 130 ff.	Rome, ii.1513	247 quatrines	60.9	0.468	1.87
2896	Collenuccio: *Plinia defensio* (Ferrara: Belfortis, [1493]): 4⁰: 52 ff.	Rome, vi.1513	3 quatrines	0.98	0.019	0.075
2897	Plutarch: *Proemium in musicam* (Brescia: Britannico, 1507): 4⁰: 30 ff.	Rome, vi.1513	8 quatrines	2.61	0.087	0.35
3737	Calpurnius, T, & Nemesian: *Bucolicum Musicae* (Bologna: Mazzocchi, 1504): fol.: 96 ff.	Rome, ix.1515	47 quatrines	15.9	0.166	0.322
	Giustiniani: *Laude* (Venice: de Cellere, 1483): 4⁰: 54 ff.	Rome, ix.1515	15 quatrines	5.07	0.094	0.376
3459	**Paulus: *Paulina de recta Paschae*** (Fossombrone: Petrucci, 1513): fol.: 396 ff.	Rome, xi.1515	315 quatrines	102.6	0.259	0.52
	Dominici: *Trattato della sanctissima charita* (Siena: di Nicolo & di Alexandro, 1513): 4⁰: 24 ff.	Rome, xi.1515	6 quatrines	1.84	0.077	0.307
	Castellanus: *Evangelij si cantano la quaresima* (Florence: for F. di Jacopo, 1514): 4⁰: 26 ff.	Rome, xii.1515	8 quatrines	2.456	0.094	0.388
	La passione de nostro Signore Jesu Christe (Pesaro: Soncino, 1513): 4⁰: 18 ff.	Rome, xii.1515	6 quatrines	1.84	0.102	0.408
6775	*Canzone . . . libro primo* (Rome: Antico, 1515): 8⁰: 52 ff.	Venice, vii.1521	10 soldi	7.45	0.143	1.14
5867	*Canzoni . . . libro tertio* (Rome: Antico, 1513): 4⁰: 56 ff.	Venice, vii.1521	10 soldi	7.45	0.136	1.08
	Chansons a troys (Venice: Antico [Giunta], 1520): 4⁰: 72 ff.	Venice, vii.1521	10 soldi	7.45	0.105	0.84

(continued)

Reg.B Title	(Publisher, date): format and length	Purchased	price	% of a ducato d'oro	% per folio	% per sheet
?5084	*I Frottole intabulate* (Rome: Antico, 1517): 8⁰: 40 ff.	Venice, vii.1521	10 soldi	7.45	0.186	1.48
5929	*Frottole libro quinto* (Rome: [Mazzocchi/Antico, 1518): 8⁰:	Venice, vii.1521	10 soldi	7.45		
4975	**Magnificat Liber Primus** (Venice: Petrucci, 1507): 4⁰:	Venice, vii.1521	26 soldi	19.4		
6222	*Motetti libro primo* (Naples: de Frizis, 1519): 8⁰:	Venice: x.1521	12 soldi	8.96		
348	Cochlaeus: *Tetrachordum musices* (Nürnberg: Peypus, 1520): 4⁰: 28 ff.	Nürnberg, xii.1521	3 craicer	3.5	0.14	0.56
1496	Glareanus: *Isagoge in musicen* (Basel: Froben, 1516): 4⁰: 20 ff.	Nürnberg, xii.1521	5 craicer	5.81	0.29	1.16
1439	Koswick: *Compendaria musice artis* (Leipzig: Stöcker, 1519): 4⁰: 16 ff.	Nürnberg, xii.1521	2 craicer	2.33	0.14	0.56
1471	Ornithoparchus: *Musice active micrologus* (Leipzig: Schuman, 1519): 4⁰: 54 ff.	Nürnberg, xii.1521	28 fenins	8.14	0.15	0.60
712	Paulus de Middelburgh: *Protonotariomastix* (Louvain: 1484): 4⁰: 24 ff.	Nürnberg, xii.1521	1 craicer	1.16	0.48	0.19
905	Quercu: *Opusculum musices* (Landshut: Weyssenburger, 1516 *or* 1518): 4⁰: 54 ff.	Nürnberg, xii.1521	3 craicer	3.5	0.15	0.60
946	Torrentinus: *Sequentie et Hymni* (Cologne: Quentell, 1509): 4⁰: 34 ff.	Nürnberg, xii.1521	11 fenins	3.2	0.095	0.38
922	Virdung: *Musica getuscht* (probably Augsburg: Öglin, 1511): 4⁰: 56 ff.	Nürnberg, xii.1521	6 craicer	7.96	0.142	0.58
90	Lefevre d'Etaples: *In hoc libro . . . Musica* (Paris: Estienne, 1514): fol.: 24 ff.	Nürnberg, xii.1521	15 craicer	17.44	0.409	0.82
2586	Odonis, G.: *Expositio cum questionibus* (Venice: Luere, 1500): fol.: 172 ff.	Nürnberg, xii.1521	42 craicer	48.8	0.284	0.568
1552	Conrad von Zabern: *Ars bene cantandi* (Mainz: Heuman, 1509): 8⁰: 28 ff.	Frankfurt, i.1522	4 fenins	1.39	0.050	0.40
	Burchard: *Hortulus Musice* (Magdeburg: Lotter, [1514]): 4⁰: 12 ff.	Frankfurt, i.1522	4 fenins	1.39	0.115	0.46
1474	Bogentanz: *Collectanea utriusque cantus* (Cologne: s.n., 1515): 4⁰: 26 ff.	Köuln, ii.1522	8 fenins	2.71	0.104	0.42
1305	Faber: *Musica rudimenta* (Augsburg: Miller, 1516): 4⁰: 18 ff.	Köuln, ii.1522	6 fenins	2.03	0.113	0.45
1359	Tzwyvel: *Introductorium musice practice* (Cologne: Quentell, 1513): 4⁰: 29 ff.	Köuln, ii.1522	4 fenins	1.35	0.465	1.87
137	Mauburne: *Rosetum exercitiorum spiritualium* (Paris: Petit & Scabeler, 1510): fol.: 344 ff.	Köuln, ii.1522	130 fenins	43.9	0.124	0.25
2495	Gidij, P.: *Threnodia . . . Maximilian cantis . . . Maximilian* (1519): 4⁰:	Louvain, iv.1522	4 negmits de mediado			
4701	**Laude II** (Venice: Petrucci, 1508): 4⁰: 56 ff.	Perugia, ix.1530	105 quatrines	25.0	0.446	1.78
4716	**Frottole Libro XI** (Fossombrone: Petrucci, 1514): 4⁰: 72 ff.	Perugia, ix.1530	100 quatrines	23.8	0.330	1.32
	Spataro: *Dilucide et probatissime* (Bologna: de Benedictis, 1521): 4⁰: 4 ff.	Bologna, ix.1530	2 quatrines	0.44	1.10	4.4
	Bonini: *Acutissime observationes* (Florenze: Zanetti, 1520): 4⁰: 18 ff.	Bologna, xi.1530	12 quatrines	2.44	1.36	5.46
	Hemicovius: *Musica choralis* (Cologne: Quentell, 1522): 4⁰: 24 ff.	Köuln, vii.1531	10 haler	1.63	0.68	2.72
11937	*Livre plaisant et tres utile* (Antwerp: Vorsterman, 1529): 4⁰: 38 ff.	Brussels, viii.1531	12 negmit	3.75	0.98	3.92
	Abbreviatio statutorum ([?Lyons: s.n.,] 1518): 4⁰: 20 ff.	Montpellier, vii.35	8 dineros	1.42	0.70	2.8

would of course have been lower.[4] Apart from the lower price for the first volume of Bossinensis's settings, there are two other exceptions, both easily explicable. The first concerns the purchase of Petrucci's eleventh book of frottole, also bought in Perugia in 1530, which was priced at a mere one-third of a soldo per folio. This price should hardly surprise us; by 1530 the frottola was well on the wane as a repertoire, especially in the Papal States,[5] where the early madrigal had largely replaced it as a viable repertoire. The demand for the volume must similarly have declined.[6]

The other exceptional volume is the one non-musical title from Petrucci's press purchased by Colón: the *Paulina* is priced substantially lower than the music books, at one-quarter of a soldo per folio. this price also should not surprise us, for two reasons: a book should become marginally cheaper per sheet as the book gets longer; more relevantly, a large part of this book could be printed at a single impression, not using any red-inked type. As a result, each sheet of the book should cost between a half and two-thirds of the cost of a sheet of a music volume, printed by double impression.[7] This supports the hypothesis that a figure of about 45% of a soldo per folio is representative of the price of Petrucci's music volumes.[8]

Comparisons between Petrucci's music books and others bought by Colón during the same period are revealing: Antico's *Canzoni nove* of 1510, bought in Rome soon after the first Petrucci purchases, cost about a quarter as much again, at 55% of a soldo per folio. But by the time Colón was again buying (and listing the prices of) Antico's editions, in Venice in July 1521, each folio cost about a third of the price of Petrucci's editions, and a quarter of that of Antico's first book.[9] These figures are not entirely parallel to those for Petrucci, since Antico's books were printed in octavo; the figures should be doubled to compare them with books printed in quarto. Although they cost more per sheet than did Petrucci's edition of the *Paulina*,[10] they still remain cheaper, even per sheet of purchased paper, than the musical editions of Petrucci. Perhaps they were bought directly from Antico in Venice.

When these prices are compared with other book prices of the same period, they serve to place both Petrucci's and Antico's editions in a hierarchy of expense—one that can be directly related to function and destination. For example, Glareanus's *Isagoge in Musicen*, printed by Froben in 1516, cost less than Bossinensis's first book (in 1521), while Tzwyvel's *Introductorium musicum* (from Quentell in 1513) was slightly more expensive in 1522 than the Spinacino edition. It is notable that both these were also in quarto. It seems that scholarly books were relatively expensive (a not-unknown phenomenon, even in the present day). The alternative assumption that German booksellers were charging more is offset by other data: Torrentinus's collection of *Sequentie et Hymni* (printed in 1509) cost less than a tenth of a soldo per folio, and Burchard's *Hortulus musice* not much more. These figures suggest (and the additional data for editions of Conrad von Zabern, Gaudensi, and Faber confirm) that the more practical a volume, the lower the price. The format seems to have little relationship to the price, although the cheapest of all these, Conrad's treatise, was printed in octavo.[11] These prices correlate directly with those being charged for Antico's books in Venice in the early 1520s, arguing that his repertoire—and its presentation—was seen as "literate culture", rather than "courtly" or "high culture".

These prices need to be compared with those from other presses of the time. The best evidence survives for editions from the Aldine press: in both 1498 and 1503 Aldus issued catalogues of some of his works: the first had printed prices, the second had them added in manuscript.[12] A few examples follow. (See Table 10-2.)

The last two of these were among the famous series of octavo editions, "Libelli portatiles" as Aldus called them, all of which were given the same price in the 1503 catalogue, regardless of the number of folios. Apart from this practice, Aldus's pricing more closely reflected the number of folios (the "thickness" of the book) than the number of sheets of paper required to print a copy. For non-musical books, this is reasonable. A book in quarto or octavo (or even more in 16°) involved more time in setting, using a smaller typeface, and extra labor in making up the forme. This is not a factor when comparing Antico with Petrucci, since Antico used woodblocks and Petrucci type.

More significantly, Petrucci's books are all cheaper than those put out by Aldus; even his edition of Paulus's treatise, at just over a ducat, was significantly cheaper than Aldus's Aristotle (although nearly twice as long). Similarly, his quarto books cost little more than a third of the cost of an Aldine quarto. In this respect, Aldine editions relate to Petrucci's musical volumes in much the same manner as do the more serious texts from German and other printers.

Table 10-1 reveals another factor—that there was a dramatic inflation in the cost of some books by the 1530s. Indeed, the figures suggest that, by 1530 and 1531, Colón was paying four times as much (in terms of his ducato d'oro) for his purchases. The figures are given above, but it is worth noting that a volume such as Spataro's *Dilucide* cost about four times as much as Glareanus's *Isagoge*, and that a pamphlet was similarly more expensive. This throws a different light on the prices paid for Petrucci's books in 1530. If we can assume that the inflation in Perugia was similarly fourfold, then the prices paid for a Petrucci edition are directly comparable with those that Colón had paid for his copies of Antico's editions. This makes a good deal of sense; it explains how Petrucci's could seem (to us) still to be expensive, while maintaining the relatively lower price of the book of (probably obsolescent) frottole.

This evidence is critical, for it is initial support for an argument that prices of polyphonic music did not fall drastically during the first three or four decades of the century. It is certainly true that they must have been cheaper by mid-

TABLE 10-2 Prices cited in Aldus' catalogues of 1498 and 1503, and relative costs

Title	Format	Size	Price	% of a ducat	
				per folio	per sheet
Aristotle: *Logica* (1495)	folio	234 ff.	1498: "aureo & semis" 1503: 1 ducat, 3 livre	0.641	1.28
Lascaris: *Erotemata* (ca.1495)	4⁰	166 ff.	1498: 4 Marcellis 1503: 3 Marcellis	1.20 0.90	4.82 3.61
Office of the *BVM* (1497)	16⁰	112 ff.	1497: 2 Marcellis	0.89	14.29
Catherine of Siena (1500)	folio	514 ff.	1503: 1 Ducat	0.195	0.391
Virgil (1501)	8⁰	228 ff.	1503: 3 Marcelli	0.658	5.26
Juvenal (1501)	8⁰	78 ff.	1503: 3 Marcelli	1.92	15.38

century and probably continued to stay cheap. Evidence for this can be found in archival data from the Accademia Filarmonica in Verona, and by extrapolating from the contract signed by Girolamo Scotto and a representative of the monastery of San Giorgio Maggiore.[13] Bernstein maintains that the Accademia paid about one lira and four soldi for a set of partbooks during the 1540s.[14] If we could assume that the ducat was worth about as many lire as it had been when Colón was buying, one arrives at a cost for a set of about 26 soldi. That is a dangerous assumption, but nonetheless the sets of parts seem to have cost more than the early Antico frottola books, although these were smaller exercises. It would also have been significantly less than Colón paid in 1530 for Petrucci's editions, again assuming that inflation had had no impact on the value of the lira vis-à-vis the ducat.

Conclusions about the relative prices of Petrucci's books are therefore rather more complex than has been thought. They were more expensive than most Antico editions (given the exception of his first book, and the probable exception of the volume of masses), but this differential did not last. Petrucci had the advantage of an effective commercial monopoly and was able to charge what he thought the market would bear, until at least sometime after 1512, when Antico perhaps was beginning to charge less. At the same time, a bookseller in Rome was charging these relatively high prices in 1521, perhaps because he thought the Roman market would bear what the Venetian apparently would not, or perhaps because he had bought his stock at the higher prices and needed to recoup his costs. However, Petrucci's books were not necessarily expensive when put alongside the work of other high-quality printers. The prices asked by Aldus, and the apparent relationship between press (and quality of work) and price are important here. Petrucci's books should be placed not alongside the editions of Antico and his successors but alongside the works of the scholarly presses of the 1490s and 1500s. By those standards, his books were not excessively priced.

This must weaken any argument derived from the alleged luxury status of the volumes. While they were at the more expensive end of the market, they were evidently within the reach of professional musicians or any institution that might have wished to acquire them. This brings us, inevitably, to a discussion of the purchasers of his books, how many there might have been, and how far they form a distinct group or series of groups.

Types of Purchasers

We know very little about specific purchasers of early books. Library lists, occasional booksellers' accounts, and letters requesting books sometimes give clues, but the best evidence remains that of the owners' inscriptions found in the books themselves. Reading these, and collecting the known information for the incunable period, Hirsch was able to suggest that "the earliest customers were mostly clergymen, teachers and students and an unidentified medley of townspeople".[15] This pattern probably continues to be relevant for the first third of the sixteenth century, with a few modifications. It is evident that courts and courtiers should be added to the list, especially in Italy, as well as doctors and lawyers, and that the burgeoning merchant classes also bought books.[16]

We can probably be confident that some circles, while buying the occasional book, would have had no intention of buying music. Many of the groups of people recently investigated, in particular, would seem neither to have been able to read music nor to have needed to replace their oral repertoire. Thus, while Natalie Zemon Davis can draw attention to peasant circles where many people could read and own one or two books, she recognizes that such groups would not even buy books apparently aimed at them, when the content would do no more than supersede their own oral tradition.[17] She adds that many who might own books, even among townsfolk, restricted their purchasers to very precise repertoires.[18]

These points should be taken over to the dissemination of printed music. While I do not wish even to hint that rural purchasers might have bought printed music, I do wish to draw the parallel; we should not assume that townsmen bought frottole or popular music, either, when they already had a strong oral tradition and a ready repertoire in their memory.[19]

For this reason, when considering the situation during the first two decades of the sixteenth century, I have tended to draw the circle of potential purchasers of printed music with a smaller radius than might seem possible.[20] I have necessarily limited it to those who could read music, those who employed others to read and perform it for them, or their agents. This includes, from the start, professional institutions and professional performers. Yet, even here, I have reservations. Many liturgical institutions did not practice this sort of polyphony; as Gallo says: "Up until the beginning of the 16th century sacred mensural polyphony is, in Italy, the preserve of a few culturally and economically privileged circles, rather than a general rule of liturgical practice".[21] No doubt the situation reflected in the collections of books at San Giacomo in Padua in 1559 was more typical: among forty-one titles there are solely "Un messale stampato in Milan nel 1480" and "Dui breviarii secundum Curiam et de la stampa del Jonta [= Giunta] del 1504".[22] We must not forget that the development of an interest in complex polyphony in many cathedrals of northern Italy—among them Bergamo, Casale Monferrato, Cividale del Friuli, and Padua—was a phenomenon of the decades after the end of Petrucci's principal activity.

The existence, even the probable prevalence, of *cantus planus binatim* is also relevant here.[23] Many institutions where this repertoire was performed would have had virtually no use for any of the music put out by Petrucci. (The only editions with music even approaching that style are the first of Lamentations and the two of laude.) Others probably practiced a form of arrangement and adaptation, as represented in the earlier I-Vnm cl.it.IX,145,[24] which would again preclude the use of printed sources. Indeed, the connections between music in that manuscript and some items in Dammonis's collection of laude highlight this very point.

I also doubt that all the institutions that practiced mensural polyphony, sacred or secular, saw the need for buying printed sources. The famous dictum concerning the Duke of Urbino[25] is not strictly relevant here, but other institutions, especially ecclesiastical ones, were probably content with their manuscript sources.

With the number of institutions restricted in this manner, it is equally important to recognize that many professional musicians would not have needed to buy any polyphony (much less printed anthologies) when the employing institution could be persuaded to meet their needs.[26]

However, as we discover more about musical taste and the general interest in music during the early sixteenth century, it becomes evident that a wider range of people than has previously been believed was actively interested in acquiring copies of music. I stress "acquiring copies", for we have to try to draw a fine distinction between the collectors of the music itself and the collectors of musical manuscripts or editions. I have already discussed the former group, those who could afford to retain performing groups at their command—because either they were courtly or religious patrons with the money for a permanent salaried cappella, or they could draw on friends and perhaps professional musicians to come and perform for them. These people acquired musical manuscripts and printed music, of course, but the owning and study of these sources was not the prime function of their acquisition. They bought music primarily so that it could be performed. Performance, indeed, was the central issue, and the acquisition of copies of music was merely a necessary adjunct.

We are beginning to realize, however, that there was a large number of purchasers for whom institutional performance was not necessarily the sole (or even the primary) reason for acquiring music.[27] When Glareanus bought copies of Petrucci's titles, there is no evidence that he expected them to be used regularly in performance; when the Strozzi or Isabella d'Este asked for and obtained copies of compositions, they were probably thinking of performance, but almost certainly the pleasure of the performance, rather than some formalized presentation of the work. And when Girolamo Donato (the dedicatee of the *Odhecaton A*) received a volume of music by Isaac, from Lorenzo de'Medici in 1491, it is unlikely that the prime reason was so that some permanent group could have access to it for a formal rehearsed performance. Girolamo's letter of thanks to Lorenzo[28] suggests no more than that he was an ardent listener to music—"whenever it is time for music (which is every day) . . .".

While "amateurs" and devotees of music and musical performance have always been recognized as an important part of the market for keyboard or lute music, and while they have been presumed to be purchasers of the *Tenorlied* in Germany or the lauda and the frottola in Italy, I think we have to recognize that a number of them were also interested in "real" polyphony, in the motets and masses of Isaac and other composers, in the chansons published by Petrucci and his successors, and very soon in the emerging madrigal. Without such a market, I fail to see how any of the surviving editions can have been commercially viable. Some of these purchasers would have been clerics, purchasing for their own pleasure rather than for the institution they served, but others were certainly laymen, nobles, merchants, and bankers, who enjoyed music for its own sake and could read it well enough to understand what was going on in a composition.[29]

I have written in earlier chapters as if we could restrict the potential market for any of Petrucci's editions to a single branch of the musical world. No doubt this was true to a certain extent, in that the majority of probable purchasers for any edition would tend to lie within a small range of people and institutions:

settings of the mass were bought primarily by cathedrals and court chapels; lute music by those who could both read and perform the notation; laude by confraternities and churches with an active processional life; and so on. Petrucci and his backers would have had to have a clear view of each such majority and have made their decisions as if it comprised the only significant group of purchasers for a book. This view would influence not only decisions about repertoire (addressed in chapter 9), but also a series of parallel decisions (discussed in chapter 8) about the appearance and presentation of the book. Indeed, the student of printers' and publishers' decisions has to focus on these majorities, almost to the exclusion of other, perhaps casual, buyers. Nonetheless, for all these repertoires, those (potential and actual) purchasers who fell outside this majority group could form a significant proportion of the total. Glareanus was an obvious example; equally significant is the purchase of frottole by the Fuggers in Augsburg, or the apparent purchase of a set of *Motetti de la Corona III* by the Accademia Filarmonica of Verona.

Until we have for Italy a reference volume emulating Ker's superb work on medieval libraries in England,[30] we will no doubt miss many references to small collections of books. This may be particularly true for music, since the institutional collection of this repertoire was rarely preserved or catalogued alongside the traditional library, and the private library hardly ever catalogued in sufficient detail, if at all. Indeed such catalogues as survive give us an unbalanced view of the purchasers of almost any practical (and widely disseminated) repertoire—books of Hours, elementary encyclopedias, or manuals of behavior, as much as music.[31] On the other hand, and perhaps as a balancing factor, the liturgical and musical repertoire of many institutions has been preserved more carefully than the general library.

Therefore, if we try to go beyond these institutions and their members as the basis for a market for printed music, we run into difficulties. Undoubtedly, a number of the lettered—Hirsch's "clergymen, teachers and students"—bought a little polyphony (as opposed to treatises on music), either for themselves or to enjoy with guests; equally certainly, there were circles in Italy corresponding to that of the Amerbachs in Basel, one or more members of which would have bought music. But the evidence is scanty; some ownership ascriptions survive, though we can rarely reconstruct a collection of music.[32]

Occasionally there is a more detailed description of an early library, or a major collection can be in part reconstructed, even though neither may contain music for practical purposes. The most famous collections in Italy are two which have been the subjects of detailed study—those of Cardinal Bessarion and San Marco in Florence, established by the Medici.[33] But attempts have been made at reconstructing other princely libraries of the time.[34]

Even more rarely, we find information with a closer bearing on the present subject, that of the dissemination of music, as opposed to texts about music. But most reports of libraries or of ownership date from later in the century and seem to refer to later editions and manuscripts.[35] Few make mention of musical books from the Petrucci generation. One is the inventory of books given by Luca Gaurico, the distinguished astrologer and former Bishop of Civitate (1545–50), to his presumed birthplace, Gauro, near Giffoni to the northeast of Salerno: the gift was made in 1557, the year before his death (though apparently the books had been acquired many years earlier), and required the town to make the collection available for free study. Dennis Rhodes, in his study of this inventory,[36] describes a surprisingly wide-ranging collection. Among the predictable items is a copy of Paulus de Middelburgh's *Paulina*, the only book evidently printed by Petrucci. In addition, there are several books of or about music:

> Among the "Libri magni"
>   Franchini musica theoricalis
>   Franchini musica praxis
>   Ludouici Foliani musica
>   Gulielmi de Podio musica.
>   Musica vulgaris noua
>
> Among the "Libri mediocres"
>   Musices libelli plurique
>   Beroaldi carmina

The last of these, the songs of Beroaldi, is almost certainly not a musical volume. Beroaldus, humanist and scholar at the beginning of the century, was only marginally a poet. His carmina, or poems, were published several times in the years around 1500, but always with his orations.

Gafori's two volumes are presumably the *Theorica musice* of 1492 (or perhaps the earlier *Theoricum opus musice*) and the *Practica musice* (probably in one of its later editions, called *Musice utriusque cantus practica*, appearing until 1512). De Podio's treatise was published in 1495, whereas the latest of these books, Fogliano's *Musica theorica*, appeared in 1529.

The remaining two entries are considerably more interesting. "Musices libelli" almost certainly refers to printed music, partly because of the format, corresponding to that of partbooks, rather than folio or pocket-sized volumes. We may regret that no further details were supplied in the inventory—, a regret that is compounded when we turn to the last of the "Libri magni". If this is indeed the famous *Musica nova* of Willaert, then we have one further suggestion of an early publication date.[37] The greatest weakness in reading this title as the Willaert item lies in the date of the other books in the catalogue. There is no musical volume less than twenty-five years old by the time the gift was made. Perhaps some of the lost "libelli" were also of more recent music. The value of this inventory for our purposes, apart from mentioning one more lost copy of Paulus's magnificent volume, lies in the indication of another member of a most significant group of collectors for the history of music, a scholarly book collector, resident in an obscure part of the world,[38] who also had books of notated music.

For Petrucci's music books, there is very little information of this sort.[39] Only one collection of a contemporary individual lists in its catalogues any of Petrucci's musical books—the library amassed by Ferdinando Colón.[40] His collection has already been used here for discussing the price of Petrucci's books; I shall return to it later in the chapter, for other reasons.

Apart from this well-known series of purchases, I know of only four other citations which might specify the purchase of Petrucci's editions during his life-time. One concerns the collection of books now at the Milan conservatory, which perhaps represent those purchased for the chapel of Cardinal Ippolito I d'Este, then resident in Ferrara. According to Lewis Lockwood,[41] the cardinal bought a book of motets and one of *Canti* in 1508; in 1517 he bought nine books of masses, which (as Lockwood remarks) were probably the nine books published by Petrucci and later in the collection of Santa Barbara, Mantua, from whence they passed to the Conservatorio in Milan. An alternative version relates these books to an attempt by an agent of the Gonzaga to buy music in Venice in 1511.[42] The circumstantial details added to Lockwood's comment tend to suggest that at least some of the extant books did originally come from Ferrara. The manner in which the books survive implies that they may actually be parts of two purchases, perhaps one for Mantua and the other for Ferrara.

A second instance is the probable purchase of a Petrucci edition for the Casa Santa in Loreto: a book of motets was bought at Recanati on 23 September 1515.[43] Although the Petrucci edition is not specified, it was probably the first of the *Motetti de la Corona* series.

The third is the ownership ascription in the Vendrogno copy of *Motetti C*. This copy was then in the possession of a priest in a small town of northern Italy. Whether he intended to use the book in performance cannot be determined, but it is significant that there are both a series of corrections and the later addition of a four-voiced *falso bordone* progression.

The last of these four instances is less plausible: on 4 August 1536, the effects of a priest, Tristan, of Mugla Regini in Friuli, were inventoried, following his death.[44] The inventory records a large library of books, listed in sections by sub-ject. A short section is headed "Item Libros Musice" and contains five items:

> Librum Aron de practica musice vulgarem ligatum cartono
> Item librum Franchini de musica cartono ligatum novum
> Item Tractatus tonorum musice non ligatum
> Item octo libellus musice Iosquini et aliorum
> Item madrigali verde lot

While the first three of these items clearly represent theoretical works, the first at least must be a manuscript, a translation into Italian of Aron's *Toscanello*. The last two refer to notated music; the last is an early reference to a volume of Verdelot's madrigals. The reference to small books of music by Josquin and others seems to point to two sets of four-voiced music in partbooks. If these books were printed, then it is likely that one was the third book in the series of *Motetti de la Corona*. But we can hardly select between the Petrucci editions of the 1510s and the Pasoti and Dorico reeditions of the 1520s; while the latter are closer in time to the date of the inventory, the former were printed in Venice, the plausible source of the Verdelot and Gafori editions, and of an edition employed for trans-lating Aron's work.

Apart from these instances, representing perhaps four or five purchases of books published by Petrucci, the only evidence consists of citations in early in-ventories, or copies with early annotations. In each case, these entries suggest that the books were in the relevant institution or nearby, in early years. As a result, they tell us something about the distribution of the books, rather than about the pattern of original purchasers. Table 10-3 lists all of these institutions.[45]

Certain entries in this table stand out for their importance in tracing both the distribution of Petrucci's editions and the use of the music they contained. In common with the earlier examples, all the Italian entries but one seem to imply that the music would be used. The books listed under S. Giovanni Laterano in Rome are only known to have been in the possession of Girolamo Chiti, maestro at the Lateran during the mid-eighteenth century. Chiti corresponded with Padre Martini, reported his ownership of these books in letters of 1746, and supplied Martini with some editions.[46] It is probable that these copies had been in the archive of the Lateran since the sixteenth century, although we cannot say that they were bought for performance there. The only other set with an early Roman provenance would have been the three books owned by S. Luigi dei Francese,[47] none of which seems to have survived.

The set cited here as from Split was another series of editions collected by Padre Martini. According to Anne Schnoebelen,[48] these books were acquired by Martini from a Venetian, Domenico Maria Cavallini, as a set and had originally come from an institution in Split. The whole set belonged together, even though Cavallini did not mention them all: they have uniform edge colors, and they are continuously numbered through the set of volumes.[49] Split may be regarded as having been securely in the Venetian orbit at the time, and the books were very probably bought in Venice.

To these should be added two names, which will appear in Table 10-4, of individual owners. The Bishop of Pienza, Francesco Maria Piccolomini, would not have owned four books of polyphonic masses for use in his own private chapel; they would more probably have come from an institution he served. The same is probably true for the set of books owned by Muti of Bergamo; this set comprises all five books of masses and the four of motets that Petrucci put out while in Fossombrone. Evidently, some institution, presumably also in Bergamo, decided to establish a polyphonic choir and bought a basic repertoire directly from one of Petrucci's outlets. It would be attractive to relate these books to the increasing importance of Gasparo de Albertis at S. Maria Maggiore in the city.

The sum of Italian evidence argues that Petrucci's mass books, in particular, were of interest to major performing institutions—though not, apparently, to all. The cathedral at Milan, San Petronio in Bologna, or the Sistine Chapel[50] evidently already had enough music in manuscript, for there is no sign that they bought any Petrucci edition. Other institutions, however, beginning to build up their polyphonic repertoire, bought settings of the mass in bulk. It is surprising that so few of these centers also bought books of motets. The Bergamo set is one exception; another is Loreto, and it is possible that the Santa Casa, as an important pilgrimage center, rarely sang a polyphonic mass, but relied instead on frequent spoken repetitions of the rite.

Outside Italy (and Dalmatia), there is considerably less evidence. The most important is that of the Heidelberg catalogue of the Neuburg (Pfalz) collection of Ottheinrich,[51] which lists not only Petrucci's editions, but also the manuscripts into which individual works were copied. Like the Bergamo set, this includes all

TABLE 10-3 Institutions owning copies of Petrucci's editions in the 16th century

ITALY

Assisi: Convento di S. Francesco: these are all now at I-Ac
Ghiselin: *Misse* (1503); La Rue: *Misse* (1503); Agricola: *Misse* (1504); Josquin: *III Missarum* (1514); Josquin: *II Missarum* (1515); Josquin: *I Missarum* (1516)

Ferrara: chapel of Cardinal Ippolito I d'Este: some of all of these copies may be the ones now at I-Mc, from the collection of Sta Barbara in Mantua. It is certainly significant that none of the books was printed after 1508

Loreto: Santa Casa
I Motetti de la Corona (1514) (not certain: now lost)

Mantua: Sta Barbara: these are all now at I-Mc
Josquin: *Misse* (1502); Brumel: *Misse* (1503); La Rue: *Misse* (1503); Obrecht: *Misse* (1503); *Motetti IV* (1505); De Orto: *Misse* (1505); Josquin: *II Missarum* (1505); Isaac: *Misse* (1506); Gaspar: *Misse* (1507); *Missarum diversorum auctorum* (1508)

Monte Cenis (Col du), Savoy or perhaps Grosskanizsa (now Nagykanizsa in Hungary): *house of Mauritani*
I Motetti à5 (1508) (now in PL-Kj)

Padua: Fratelli Reverendi di Zuane Padin
I Lamentationes (1506) (now in I-Pca)

Rome: S. Luigi dei francesi: all these are now lost
Ghiselin: *Misse* (1503); *I Motetti à5* (1508); *I Motetti de la Corona* (1514)

Rome: S. Maria de Scala Urbij
Paulus: *Paulina de recta Paschae* (1513) (now in I-Rn)

Rome: S. Giovanni Laterano: all these are now in I-Rvat
Ghiselin: *Misse* (1503); La Rue: *Misse* (1503); Agricola: *Misse* (1504); Josquin: *III Missarum* (1514); Josquin: *II Missarum* (1515); Josquin: *I Missarum* (1516)

Split: certainly later in Venice, and now in I-Bc
Josquin: *Misse* (1502); Brumel: *Misse* (1503); Obrecht: *Misse* (1503); Agricola: *Misse* (1504); De Orto: *Misse* (1504); Isaac: *Misse* (1506); Gaspar: *Misse* (1507); *I Missarum diversorum auctorum* (1508); *I Fragmenta missarum* (1509)

Venice: S. Pietro in Castello (Duomo)
Paulus de Middelburgo: *Paulina de recta Paschae* (1513) (now lost)

Venice: S. Salvatore
Paulus de Middelburgo: *Paulina de recta Paschae* (1513) (now in GB-Lbl)

Verona, Accademia filarmonica
III Motetti de la Corona (1519) (still in I-VEaf)

Italian, perhaps a monastic house
Bossinensis: *Intabulatura I* (1509) (now in US-Cn); Bossinensis: *Intabulatura II* (1511) (now in I-Mb)

NORTHERN EUROPE

Augsburg: S. Anna
For the inventory of this collection, see Schaal, "Inventar". The frottola volumes appear to have come from Herwart.
Fragmenta Missarum (1505); *Frottole VI* (1506); *Frottole VII* (1507); *Frottole VIII* (1507)

Munich: Bavaria Ducal Library
The two books of mass music have different provenances, from each other, and from the rest: all are now in D-Mbs
Frottole I (1504); *Frottole II* (1505); *Frottole III* (1505); Frottole IV (1505); *Frottole V* (1505); *Frottole VI* (1506); *Frottole VII* (1507); *Frottole VIII* (1507); *Missarum diversorum auctorum I* (1508) (*see* Moncill: Table 10-4); *Frottole IX* (1509); Josquin: *I Missarum* (1516)

Neuburg: Ottheinrich's Court Chapel: all now lost
Ghiselin: *Misse* (1503, presumably the reprint); Josquin: *II Missarum* (probably the 1515 edition); Josquin: *III Missarum* (1514); *I Motetti de la Corona* (1514); Févin: *Misse* (1515); Mouton: *I Missarum* (1515); Josquin: *I Missarum* (presumably 1516 edition); *II Motetti de la Corona* (1519); *III Motetti de la Corona* (1519); *IV Motetti de la Corona* (1519)

Szambothely: Seminary: still at H-SY
Paulus de Middelburgo: *Paulina de recta Paschae* (1513)

(continued)

TABLE 10-3 *(continued)*

perhaps from the Austro-Hungarian orbit: all now at A-GÜ
    Ghiselin: *Misse* (1503); Obrecht: *Misse* (1503); Agricola: *Misse* (1504); De Orto: *Misse* (1505);
    Fragmenta Missarum (1505); Isaac: *Misse* (1506); *I Missarum diversorum auctorum* (1508); Josquin:
    III Missarum (1514); Josquin: *II Missarum* (1515)
perhaps also Austro-Hungarian (see below, under Widman): all now at H-SY
    Josquin: *III Missarum* (1514); Josquin: *II Missarum* (1515); Mouton: *I Missarum* (1515); Josquin:
    I Missarum (1516)
perhaps a German institution: these are all related by the additional inscription on their title-pages.
    All are now in D-B.
    Josquin: *Misse* (1502); Ghiselin: *Misse* (1503); Obrecht: *Misse* (1503); Agricola: *Misse* (1504); De
    Orto: *Misse* (1505)
SPAIN and PORTUGAL
    Alcobaça: Cistercian monastery
    Josquin: *Misse* (1502) (now lost)
    Lisbon: Library of João IV
        See the facsimile and study in Sampaio Ribeiro, "Livraria". In the commentary to this edi-
    tion, Damiao Peres suggests (pp. 156–159) that the Josquin editions are probably all of the 1526
    editions from Pasoti and Dorico in Rome. I suspect that the same is true for the *Motetti de la
    Corona*, even though three other mass books must presumably come from Petrucci. The Obrecht
    volume is paired in the catalogue with that of Ghiselin's masses: this would seem to preclude it
    being a copy of the undated edition put out by Mewes in Basel.
        Professor Calvin Elliker reports (in a personal communication) that there is no evidence that
    any of the books purchased by the King from Queen Christina might have included the follow-
    ing titles:
    Obrecht: *Misse* (1503); Ghiselin: *Misse* (1503); De Orto: *Misse* (1505) Lost

Petrucci's Fossombrone editions of masses and motets, if we assume that the copy
of Ghiselin is of the second (hidden) edition, probably of 1513. Ottheinrich's
biography suggests that he would not have needed any chapel music before 1522,
when he returned from a pilgrimage to the Holy Land.[52] By 1528 he did employ
an organist, Michael Wünnckler, although no other editions seem to have been
acquired before the late 1530s.

   The other interesting set of books is the one currently in a Franciscan monastery at Güssing (Burgenland). Although the binding style appears to be Venetian,
the books were reportedly near the Austro-Hungarian border early in their life.[53]
The set opens with the second and third books of Josquin's masses, each in a
Fossombrone edition. The rest of the series of nine volumes date from 1508 or
earlier. Given the absence of Josquin's first book, and its imminent new edition
in 1516, it is tempting to speculate that the whole set was bought in 1515 or
early 1516, before that book had appeared—and also before stocks of the books
of Mouton and Févin had reached the bookseller. The only other mass editions
from Petrucci's house that were not part of this set are those devoted to Brumel,
Gaspar, and La Rue—none of which appear regularly alongside Fossombrone
editions: of those, only one, of La Rue, was certainly still available, for we know
that Petrucci still had at least one sheet, and that Assisi bought a copy, probably
during Petrucci's Fossombrone years.

   Federhofer, in his announcement of this set, attempted to draw connections
with the set of four mass books surviving nearby, in the bishop's seminary at
Szombathely.[54] These have several ownership marks, of which the earliest is for
a Paul Widman of Geras in Styria. Whatever the provenance of these two sets,

they argue for two more institutions in southern Austria that practiced polyphony at a high level early in the sixteenth century. The exclusive presence of many mass settings is reminiscent of the requirements in the endowment of the parish church at Hall (Tyrol), that a polyphonic mass be sung every Sunday and feast day.[55]

There is disappointingly little Iberian evidence. The major collection, that of the Portugese King João I in Lisbon, probably had very few Petrucci editions.[56] In the catalogue, which survives (while the books themselves were destroyed by fire), several entries could correspond to Petrucci's titles. Damiao Peres, however, has suggested[57] that the Josquin mass volumes were probably all of the 1526 editions from Pasoti and Dorico in Rome. I suspect that the same is true for the listed copies of the *Motetti de la Corona*, even though three other books of masses must presumably have come from Petrucci. The Obrecht volume is paired in the catalogue with that of Ghiselin's masses; this seems to preclude it being a copy of the undated edition put out by Mewes in Basel.

Given the survival of so many manuscripts of liturgical music from Spanish cathedrals and monasteries, it would seem unlikely that many of Petrucci's editions were purchased specifically for use in those institutions.

Compared with the barely two dozen institutions that certainly acquired Petrucci's books, Table 10-4 reveals a longer list of individual owners.[58] One or two of these men have been mentioned already, as perhaps reflecting institutional needs or purchases. For most of the rest, there is little to be said. Colón, of course, stands head and shoulders above the rest; it is unfortunate that so many of his copies have been lost.[59] Nearly as important as a collector was Ercole Bottrigari. According to Gaspari's transcription[60] of his notes, Bottrigari owned twenty-one different Petrucci editions, including copies of two books that have completely disappeared: the tenth book of frottole and Martini's collection of hymns. Apart from the frottola book, Bottrigari apparently owned no editions published in Fossombrone: for example, he had the first two books of Josquin's masses (in Venetian editions), but not the third. This must be significant, since he probably did not obtain all these copies from the same source.[61] On the other hand, he numbered the sequence of mass volumes, which suggests that he probably acquired at least those in a single binding.

Glareanus's copies are interesting for the range of annotations they include, which repay detailed study. But among the other northern names, that of the Fugger family stands out. If their library had survived intact, it would include the largest collection of Petrucci's editions—thirty-three in all, including the otherwise incomplete 1520 edition of Pisano's *Musica*. The apparent attempt at acquiring as much printed music as possible seems to have two omissions: there is no evidence of editions dated before the middle of 1503,[62] and there are no editions dating in the period between Bossinensis's first book of 1509 and Févin's mass volume of 1515.[63] In addition, Books II, III, and IV of frottole are represented by the later second editions. Despite these patterns, it seems likely that the Fugger used an agent in the Fondaco dei Tedeschi in Venice, as indeed we would expect.

The one piece of evidence for an awareness in England of Petrucci's editions comes from the library catalogue (dated 1609) of the collection of John, Lord Lumley.[64] Lumley's copy of the *Paulina* probably came to him from Thomas Cran-

TABLE 10-4 Individuals owning copies of Petrucci's editions in the 16th to 18th centuries

---

Alomanno, Pirro
> *II Motetti de la Corona* (1519) (now at PL-Kj)

Altovisi, Franciscus: all now at D-Mbs
> It is tempting to see in this name some connection with the Roman family of Altoviti. These were associated with the Accademia degli Amici, and with G.B. Strozzi. However, the possibility of a connection is a little far-fetched.
> > Obrecht: *Misse* (1503); *Motetti C* (1504); *I Missarum diversorum auctorum* (1508)

Arundel, Earl of: all now at GB-Lbl
> > Josquin: *I Missarum* (1516); *II Motetti de la Corona* (1519); *III Motetti de la Corona* (1519); *IV Motetti de la Corona* (1519)

Bataliensi de Musonis, Pietro Antonio, priest in Muggiasca
> > *Motetti C* (1504) (now at I-VENsl)

Battiferri, Antonio Vergili
> Battiferri was an archdeacon at the Cathedral of Urbino during the 16th century, and related to the poetess, Laura Battiferri, who was settled in Florence, and was highly regarded for both her poetry and her beauty. The archdeacon called himself "pronepote" to the writer Polydore Vergil.
> > Castiglione: *Epistola* (1513) (now at I-Rvat)

Bottrigari, Ercole
> These details come from Bottrigari's notes in his copy of Galilei, and transcribed by Gaspari. All these books seem to be lost.
> > Josquin: *Misse* (1502); *Odhecaton A* (second edition, 1503); Obrecht: *Misse* (1503); Josquin: *II Missarum* (1503); *Motetti de Passione . . . B* (1503); Brumel: *Misse* (1503); Ghiselin: *Misse* (1503); *Canti B* (1503); Agricola: *Misse* (1504); *Motetti A* (1504); *Frottole V* (1505); Isaac: *Misse* (1506); *Frottole VIII* (1507); *Frottole VII* (1507); *Frottole IV* (1507); Martini: *I Hymnorum* (1507); *Laude II* (1507 sic); *Missarum diversorum auctorum* (1508); Dammonis: *Laude I* (1508); *Frottole IX* (1508); *Frottole X* (1512)

Brebilla, Tiburtio, rector of S. Giorgio in Ravagnate
> > *Motetti C* (1504) (now at I-VENsl)

Bressa, Vincislao, of Treviso: both these are now at I-TVcap
> > *Canti C* (1504); *Odhecaton A* (1504);

Castiglione, Camillo
> Son of the author Baldassare Castiglione.
> > Castiglione: *Epistola* (1513) (now at US-CA)

Colón, Fernando
> The status of Colón as a source of information for early printed music is well known. Chapman ("Printed") has laid out most of the evidence for musical editions, and much supplementary information is available in studies by Anglés and Plamenac. (See Anglés, "Música", and Plamenac, "Excerpta".) Parenthetical numbers refer to the entries in Chapman's list: all are lost unless a location is given)
> > *Canti B* (1502) (at F-Pc); *Odhecaton A* (1503) (at E-S); Obrecht: *Misse* (1503); *Motetti de passione . . . B* (1503); Ghiselin: *Misse* (1503); *Canti B* (1503) (at F-Pc); La Rue: *Misse* (1503); *Canti C* (1504); Agricola: *Misse* (1504); *Odhecaton A* (1504) (at F-Pc); *Motetti C* (1504); *Frottole I* (1504); De Orto: *Misse* (1505); *Motetti IV* (1505); *Fragmenta Missarum* (1505); *Frottole V* (1505); *Frottole VI* (1506); *Lamentationes I* (1506); *Lamentationes II* (1506); Isaac: *Misse* (1506); Gaspar: *Misse* (1507); Spinacino: *Intabulatura I* (1507); Spinacino: *Intabulatura II* (1507); *Frottole VIII* (1507); *Frottole VII* (1507); *Frottole IV* (1507); Martini: *I Hymnorum* (1507); *I Magnificats* (1507); *Frottole III* (1507); *Laude II* (1508) (now at E-S); *Frottole II* (1508); *I Missarum diversorum auctorum* (1508); Alemannus: *Intabulatura III* (1508); Dammonis: *Laude I* (1508) (now at E-S); *I Motetti à5* (1508); Dalza: *Intabulatura IV* (1508); *Frottole IX* (1509); Bossinensis: *Intabulatura I* (1509) (now at E-S); Bossinensis *Intabulatura II* (1511); *Frottole X* (1512); Paulus: *Paulina de recta Paschae* (1513) (now at E-S); *Frottole XI* (1514) (now at E-S); Mouton: *I Missarum* (1515); Févin: *Missa* (1515); Pisano: *Musica* [c.1533] (now at E-S)

Cranmer, Thomas
> He was the probable owner of one book that passed to John, Lord Lumley.
> > Paulus de Middelburgo: *Paulina de recta Paschae* (1513) (now at GB-Lbl)

Doni, Antonfrancesco
> He may possible have owned *Lamentationes I* (1506). This is unlikely: see Haar, "Libraria", p. 117.

(continued)

Egenolph, Johannes
    He acquired these two titles from Glareanus: they are now at D-Mu
        Motetti C (1504); *I Missarum diversorum auctorum* (1508)
Fabri, Johannes, Bishop of Vienna
        Paulus de Middelburgo: *Paulina de recta Paschae* (1513) (now lost)
Fugger family
    For an early inventory of this music collection, see Schaal, "Musikbibliothek". All copies are lost
    unless otherwise indicated
        Odhecaton A (edition unknown); *Motetti A* (1502 or 1505); Ghiselin: *Misse* (1503); La Rue: *Misse*
        (1503); *Canti C* (1504) (now in A-Wn); Agricola: *Misse* (1504); *Motetti C* (1504); *Frottole I*
        (1504) (now in A-Wn); De Orto: *Misse* (505); *Motetti IV* (1505); *Fragmenta Missarum* (1505);
        Frottole V (1505) (now in A-Wn); *Frottole VI* (1506) (now in A-Wn); *Lamentationes I* (1506);
        Lamentationes II (1506); Gaspar: *Misse* (1507); *Frottole VIII* (1507); *Frottole IV* (1507) (perhaps
        the copy from Suenulus, now in A-Wn); Martini: *I Hymnarum* (1507); *Frottole III* (1507) (now
        in A-Wn); *Frottole VII* (1507) (now in A-Wn); *Laude II* (1508); *Frottole II* (1508) (now in A-
        Wn); *I Missarum diversorum auctorum* (1508); Dammonis: *Laude I* (1508); *Frottole IX* (1509) (now
        in A-Wn); *I Motetti de la Corona* (1514) (now in D-Mbs); Févin: *Misse* (1515); Josquin: *I Missa-
        rum* (1516) (now in A-Wn); *II Motetti de la Corona* (1519) (now in D-Mbs); *III Motetti de la
        Corona* (1519) (now in D-Mbs); *IV Motetti de la Corona* (1519) (now in D-Mbs); Pisano: *Musica*
        [c.1533]
Gagliardi, Giovanbatista
    Later possessor of the copies from Hieronymi Muti de pappazuris.
Gaurico, Luca, bishop of Civitate
        Paulus: *Paulina de recta Paschae* (1513) (now lost)
Glareanus, Heinrich
    His copies passed to Egenolph: they are now at D-Mu
        Motetti C (1504); *I Missarum diversorum auctorum* (1508)
Heintzen, Wolff, of Halle: these copies are now all at D-W
        Motetti C (1504); *Motetti IV* (1505); Josquin: *II Missarum* (1505); *Fragmenta Missarum* (1505)
Herwart family
    The frottola volumes appear to have been given to S. Anna, Augsburg, at the end of the century.
        Frottole VI (1506); *Frottole VIII* (1507); *Frottole VII* (1507); Spinacino: *Intabulatura I* (1507); Ale-
        mannus: *Intabulatura III* (1508)
Lehner, Petrus and *Jacob Lehner*
        These copies are now at H-SY. Their original owner was Paul Widman.
Lumley (and Arundel)
    Details of the library of John, Lord Lumley, according to the early seventeenth-century cata-
    logue, are given in Jayne & Johnson, *Lumley*, and Milson, "Nonsuch". These copies are now all
    at GB-Lbl
        Paulus: *Paulina de recta Paschae* (1513); Josquin: *I Missarum* (1516); *II Motetti de la Corona* (1519);
        III Motetti de la Corona (1519); *IV Motetti de la Corona* (1519)
Magagnico, Piero Antonio
        Paulus de Middelburgo: *Paulina de recta Paschae* (1513) (now at I-BGc)
Maren, Prospero, di San Leo
        Fevin: *Missarum* (1515) (now at I-BGc)
Martini, Giambattista, Padre.
    Not strictly an early owner, but on the same level as Agostino Chiti. All the copies presently at I-
    Bc were acquired by Martini at some time. His correspondence (for which see Martini, *Carteggi*;
    Rostirolla, "Corrispondenza"; Schnoebelen, *Padre*) gives many details about his acquisition of
    these and other books. These include the items listed under "Split" in Table 10-3. The following
    list is of those cited in Martini's letter of 22.vii.1746 (See Chapter Twenty)
        Canti B (1502); Brumel: *Misse* (1503); Obrecht: *Misse* (1503); Agricola: *Misse* (1504); de Orto:
        Misse (1505); Isaac: *Misse* (1506); Gaspar: *Misse* (1506); *I Missarum diversorum auctorum* (1508);
        Josquin: *III Missarum* (1514); Josquin: *II Missarum* (1515); Josquin: *I Missarum* (1516)
Medici family
        Fragmenta Missarum (1505) (now at E-Bbc); Josquin: *I Missarum* (1516) (now at E-Bbc); Josquin:
        I Missarum (1516) (now at US-R). Perhaps also the copy of De Orto: *Misse* (1505) bound with
        the other books at E-Bbc

(continued)

TABLE 10-4 *(continued)*

Moibam, Johannes of Passau
　　I Missarum diversorum auctorum (1508) (from Moncill: now at D-Mbs)
Moncill, Soranus: all now at D-Mbs
　　Obrecht: *Misse* (1503); *Motetti C* (1504); *I Missarum diversorum auctorum* (1508)
Muti de pappazuris, Hieronymi
　These books, which passed to Giovanbattista Gagliardi, are bound together, with a following
　manuscript appendix: they are in I-BGc
　　　Josquin: *III Missarum* (1514); *I Motetti de la Corona* (1514); Josquin: *II Missarum* (1515); Mouton:
　　　I Missarum (1515); Févin: *Misse* (1515); Josquin: *I Missarum* (1516); *II Motetti de la Corona*
　　　(1519); *III Motetti de la Corona* (1519); *IV Motetti de la Corona* (1519)
Petrucci, Ottaviano. These fragments, now in I-FBR, probably came from Petrucci's shop, either as
　parts of complete copies, or as damaged sheets
　　La Rue: *Misse* (1503); Josquin: *I Missarum* (1516); *IV Motetti de la Corona* (1519);
　　[*Musica XII*] [c.1533]
Piccolomini, Francisco Maria, Bishop of Pienza. These copies are now all at D-B
　　Josquin: *I Missarum* (1516: not the Altus); Josquin: *II Missarum* (1515); Mouton: *I Missarum*
　　(1515); Josquin: *III Missarum* (1514)
Qualile, Dominus
　These books, which were bound together, seem to have belonged at some time to a monastic
　house. See Sartori, "Little".
　　　Bossinensis: *I Intabulatura* (1509) (now at US-Cn); Bossinensis: *II Intabulatura* (1511) (now at I-
　　　Mb)
S, B. A.
　　I Motetti de la Corona (1514) (copy now at CH-Zz: this provenance may well relate to the
　　other books in the same binding)
Schuyt, Cornelis
　When he died, his books were auctioned in 1617, and included a "Missae Iosquin, quatuor voll."
　(See Rasch and Wind, "Music", p. 345, who suggest that the books came from "pre-
　Reformation Leiden ecclesiastical possession": I suspect they may well be one of the volumes
　printed by Petrucci, in an edition from his press or that of Pasoti and Dorico.)
Seiletio, Scipione
　　Paulus de Middelburgo: *Paulina de recta Paschae* (1513) (now at US-CA)
Shremi, Petri: a later owner of the copies, now at H-SY, originally owned by Paul Widman.
Suenulus, Andreas
　　Frottole IV (1507) (now at A-Wn)
Tamer (Tanner), Georg: a later owner of the copies, now at H-SY, originally owned by Paul Wid-
　man.
Ventura, Giovanni Battista
　　Motetti A (1502) (now at I-Bc)
Widman, Paulus, of Geras (Styria)
　These copies are now bound with a number of other later titles. They passed from Widman to
　Tanner, Schremi and Lehner, and are now at H-SY
　　　Josquin: *III Missarum* (1514); Josquin: *II Missarum* (1515); Mouton: *I Missarum* (1515); Josquin:
　　　I Missarum (1516)

mer, after his political fall.[65] The four books of music, however, were certainly among those which Lumley received from his father-in-law Henry Fitzalan, the Earl of Arundel, for they are signed with both names. Arundel seems to have collected a number of music books during the 1540s, including chansons published by Attaingnant in 1540 and Susato in 1543, motets from Scotto in 1541 and Susato in 1546, and madrigals from 1541. He probably acquired the Petrucci editions at about the same time. It is notable that the four are among the last titles printed by Petrucci before 1520, and that two (the first book of Josquin masses, and the second of the *Motetti de la Corona*) survive as examples of the later hidden editions. There was apparently no attempt at completing either set of books, with the other Josquin volumes, or the first of the motet series: this suggests that an earlier owner bought them in Italy, from whatever a *libraio* happened to have in stock at a given moment, rather than as part of a larger collection.

A few other references are similar to those for the Lisbon Royal Library, for they may be to Petrucci's editions or to the later printings by Dorico. Among these is the report of copies of Josquin's masses—"Missae Iosquin, quatuor voll".—owned by Cornelis Schuyt and auctioned off 1617.[66] A similar uncertainty also applies to some of my examples of copying from Petrucci's editions, and of their influence on later scribes and theorists.

Several sets of books show that they were originally bound together. I have already mentioned that the set of books that Martini acquired from Cavallini have uniformly painted edges and sequential foliation.[67] They are not alone in this, as Table 10-5 shows.

The Roman set is the one described by Chiti when writing to Martini. The most significant feature of this table is the sequence of numberings of the Viennese copies, to which two now in Venice should be appended. Unfortunately, the books are in modern bindings, so that there is no additional information about their provenance; however, since two are now in Venice, it is possible that all were originally in Italian collections and gathered up by Schmid when making his study of Petrucci during the nineteenth century. This is a remarkable series of books, for it contains a copy of one edition of every mass volume put out by Petrucci,[68] and it is notable just how many of the early collections had that orientation. At least as significant is the extent to which this collection (with a few others) is unusual in containing books from both the Venetian and Fossombronese periods of Petrucci's activity.

Early Knowledge of His Editions

A number of other collections concentrate on editions published before 1509, while Petrucci was in Venice, or else on those published later, once he had returned to Fossombrone. Clearly someone whose buying needs were fulfilled by 1511 would not own any editions printed in Fossombrone. Thus it may not mean anything that only Venetian editions are featured in the collection now held in Milan's Conservatorio, in the one formerly at Split (surely associated with Venetian suppliers), or in the collection listed by Bottrigari. However, a collection that only features Fossombrone editions presumably did not have access to editions printed in Venice, especially if that collection comprises more than just one or two titles; examples of this pattern include the series of nine volumes owned by Muti de Pappazuris, the six from S. Francesco in Assisi, the four mass editions owned by the Piccolomini Bishop of Pienza, the ten bought for Neuburg,[69] and the four owned by Widman in Styria. Given this pattern, some collections of Venetian editions may also be significant, especially the large group sold to Martini by Cavallini.

Even more remarkable is the pattern of knowledge of Petrucci's editions on the part of the German bibliographers. With one exception, and that problematic,

TABLE 10-5 Manuscript foliations and piece numberings

Foliations Library	Title (Date)	Edges	Superius	Tenor	Altus	Bassus
B-Br	Obrecht: *Misse* (1503)		53–72	37–50	[27]90–110	47–65
B-Bc	Brumel: *Misse* (1503)			51–53 …		
B-Br	Agricola: *Misse* (1504)		111–130		113–130	101–116
D-B	Isaac: *Misse* (1506)		1–18	1–10	1–16	1–14
GB-Lbl	Josquin: *I Missarum* (1516)				1–12	
H-SY	Josquin: *II Missarum* (1515)					1–16
I-Bc	*Odhecaton A* (1501) *Canti B* (1502)		1–63 …			
I-Bc	Agricola: *Misse* (1504)	gold	[0],1–19	[0],1–13	[0],1–17	[0],1–15
I-Bc	De Orto: *Misse* (1505)	gold	20–37	14–29	18–35	16–33
I-Bc	Gaspar: *Misse* (1507)	gold	38–55	30–39	36–53	34–49
I-Bc	Isaac: *Misse* (1506)	gold	56–73	40–49	54–69	50–63
I-Bc	Brumel: *Misse* (1503)	gold	74–93	50–[59]	70–89	64–79
I-Bc	Obrecht: *Misse* (1503)	gold	94–113	60–73		80–99
I-Bc	*I Missarum diversorum* (1508)	gold	114–129	74–83	112–127	100–113
I-Bc	*Fragmenta Missarum* (1505)	gold	130–147	84–98	128–147	114–131
I-Bc	La Rue: *Misse* (1503)	brown green	37–52	27–36	[40s–50s]	[30s–40s]
I-Bc	Obrecht: *Misse* (1503)	green			51–72	
I-Bc	Ghiselin: *Misse* (1503)	brown green	93–110		93–112	83–100
PL-Kj	Gaspar: *Misse* (1507)	red/br. green	131–148		131–148	117–132
I-Bc	Josquin: *Misse* (1502)	brown green	149–172		149–168	133–150
I-Bc	Josquin: *Missarum II* (1505)	brown green	173–188		169–180	151–166
I-Bc	Josquin: *I Missarum* (1516)					i,1–35
I-Rvat	Josquin: *I Missarum* (1516)		1–18	1–11	1–18	1–16
I-Bc	Josquin: *II Missarum* (1515)		19–34	12–21	19–36	17–32
I-Bc	Josquin: *III Missarum* (1514)		35–51	22–33	37–53	33–50
I-Bc	LaRue: *Misse* (1503)		52–67	34–43	54–69	51–64
I-Bc	Agricola: *Misse* (1504)		68–87	44–57	70–87	65–80
I-Bc	Ghiselin: *Misse* (1503)		88–105	58–67	88–106	81–97
P-Ln	Josquin: *Misse* (1502)		—	1–13 …		
D-LEu	*I Motetti de la Corona* (1514)					49–

(continued)

Library	Title (Date)	Superius	Tenor	Altus	Bassus
Pagination:					
I-Bc	Josquin: *I Missarum* (1516)			[0],1–35	
I-Bc	Josquin: *II Missarum* (1515)			36–71	
I-Bc	Josquin: *III Missarum* (1514)			72–100,1001,	
				[102–107]	
Piece Numberings					
Library	Title (Date)				
A-Wn,20	Josquin: *Misse* (1506)	1–25			
A-Wn,20	Josquin: *II Missarum* (1515)	30–59			
A-Wn,20	Josquin: *III Missarum* (1514)	60–89			
A-Wn	Mouton: *Misse* (1515)	90–114			
A-Wn	Fevin: *Misse* (1515)	115–139			
A-Wn	Ghiselin: *Misse* (1503)	140–164			
A-Wn	Agricola: *Misse* (1504)	165–188			
A-Wn	Brumel: *Misse* (1503)	190–214			
A-Wn	La Rue: *Misse* (1503)	215–238			
A-Wn	Obrecht: *Misse* (1503)	240–264			
A-Wn	Isaac: *Misse* (1506)	265–289			
[A-Wn	De Orto: *Misse* (1505)]				
A-Wn	Gaspar: *Misse* (1507)	315–339			
I-Vnm	*Missarum diversorum auctorum* (1508)	340–364			
I-Vnm	*Fragmenta Missarum* (1505)	365–393			
I-Vnm	*I Motetti de la Corona* (1514)	1–26			
I-Vnm	*II Motetti de la Corona* (1519)	27–51			
I-Vnm	*III Motetti de la Corona* (1519)	52–67			
I-Vnm	*IV Motetti de la Corona* (1519)	68–83			
D-Mbs	*I Motetti de la Corona* (1514)	150–175			
D-Mbs	*II Motetti de la Corona* (1519)	176–200			
D-Mbs	*III Motetti de la Corona* (1519)	201–216			
D-Mbs	*IV Motetti de la Corona* (1519)	217–232			

Gesner, Draudius, and Bolduanus seem to have known only Venetian editions. The best informed was also the earliest, Conrad Gesner.[70] Writing in 1548, he cited twenty editions as printed by Petrucci; the first is the questionable edition of *Missarum decem à clarissimis Musicis*, which Gesner states was printed in Fossombrone in 1515.[71] The next section, of "Libri de cantu figurato in Italia impressi", contains both the early chanson and motet books and a group of the first books of masses. The list comprises one edition of every title printed by Petrucci before the *Motetti C* of 1504, with the sole exception of the book of masses by Brumel.[72] This section is followed by an appendix of additional items, with a number of repetitions of earlier entries, and which in general follows the actual titles of books much more closely. It includes one book of laude and five of frottole, as well as the following: "Iosquini & aliorum diuersis locis et temporibus impressi Motettorum libri 4". I am sceptical that this might refer to the *Motetti de la Corona*.[73]

Much less well-informed were the two principal bibliographers of the early seventeenth century, Paul Bolduanus and Georg Draudius. The former, in his

Bibliotheca Philosophica (1616),[74] cites only four books printed by Petrucci, in two entries. Both entries present problems; the first, on p. 204, reads: "Concentus jucundiss. 8.6.5.4. vocum Harmonicæ Musices Odhecaton. Venet". This refers to two separate books, of which the second is the *Odhecaton*.[75] The second entry is as follows: "Mottetæ A. num.33. In. Cantus 50. Cantus B. 50. Cantus C. 150. Venetiis". This appears to me to refer to four separate books, of which the second may be a printer's error (a dittography) or a reference to a lost book, while the other three are certainly by Petrucci.[76]

Draudius evidently based his Petrucci entries on earlier scholarship. An entry in his *Bibliotheca Classica* of 1611, under the rubric "Librorum Musicorum", would be followed in Bolduanus's second entry. In the 1625 edition of his *Bibliotheca Classica*, under the same rubric, he copies Bolduanus's first entry precisely,[77] though later in the same book, he presents a new entry: "Cant. var. & modus cantandi versus Ln. & capitula. Liber II. 4, 5, 6. Venet. apud Octav. Petrucium". This is another problematic entry: Petrucci's *Frottole II* has no pieces for five or six voices; nor does it have a title in this form. His *Frottole IV* does have a similar title, though again no pieces for more than four voices. Nonetheless, Draudius evidently knew the title of Book IV, and this entry probably represents that book.

The sum of evidence argues that none of the German bibliographers had seen the books they described, nor did they know of any Fossombrone editions.[78]

There is, therefore, a case for arguing that Petrucci changed some of his outlets once he moved to Fossombrone. The local sales, including to Assisi, to Loreto, and perhaps to whoever bought the Lateran and Pienza copies, appear to be concentrated on the Fossombrone editions. This probably does not exclude sales to other centers, through his partners in Venice, who would have sent his books throughout the Italian and German book-buying world. But the patterns of acquisition and knowledge suggest that there were significant changes in the other agencies by which Petrucci's editions were distributed.

Distribution and Sale

We do not, and probably never will, know enough about how printers and publishers of music managed to bring their books to the attention of potential purchasers during the first two-thirds of the sixteenth century. Indeed, there is not really sufficient evidence for the printers and publishers of other repertoires, and such evidence as survives is sporadic and not necessarily representative.[79] The same can be said for the other side of the coin, how purchasers found out about new books.

It would be historically simplistic to discuss whether the extant evidence bearing on these questions represents a typical situation, or whether it has survived merely because it demonstrates the unusual occurrence, worthy of memorial. However, the potential significance of that evidence forms the present section of this chapter. The aim is to present the current state of knowledge, both for musical printing and publishing, and for the same functions in other repertoires, and to see how far it illumines the procedures that might have been available to Petrucci.[80]

The first and most obvious means by which either a printer or a publisher could dispose of books, supposing them not to have been printed under contract to a patron who was to take all the copies, was to run his own bookshop. Many Italian printers seem to have done this; the evidence of Nicolas Jenson's will, dated 1480, shows that he had such a shop, for he made a bequest to a bookseller in the company.[81] Torresano was also active as a bookseller, as well as printer and publisher, for many years, both before and after his alliance with Aldus.[82] This manner of operating was ideal for texts that would have a good sale within Venice, pamphlets, chapbooks, popular literature of all sorts (which was probably not seen as largely an export commodity), as well as scholarly texts intended for the university and the various schools flourishing within the city, and official documents.

Many texts, however, were not intended primarily for sale in Venice: liturgical books for other dioceses are an obvious example, though the sheer bulk of Venetian printing suggests that there were many others—and many more would have been intended from the start to have a larger sale than Venice could sustain. This last must have been true for humanistic, legal, and medical texts, and also for all the editions printed by Petrucci. It is remotely possible that there were enough purchasers in Venice to justify an edition of laude or even of frottole. I regard it as unlikely that there were enough to take most of an edition of lute music. But it must have been impossible that Petrucci could sell within Venice an edition of, for example, De Orto's masses, in enough numbers to justify printing it. I have already addressed, in the previous chapter, the extent to which Petrucci may have acquired the music for some editions (directly or indirectly) from patrons or institutions outside Venice, and even certain occasions when a court or religious institution may have sponsored an edition. But whatever the sources of the music, Petrucci and his partners would have to have been sure of an adequate return on their capital, in other words, of an adequate sale. Thus, they must have been looking to geographically dispersed markets.

Books had been widely circulated long before the end of the incunable period. The evidence of known owners indicates that Venetian books were soon available in Britain,[83] that those from the German presses were available in the east of the Empire, at Prague and Vienna, and also at cities in southeastern, northeastern, and northwestern Europe,[84] and that many Italian editions, from cities other than Venice, could be purchased north of the Alps.[85] The evidence of printed liturgical books provides direct support for the argument that this was the normal pattern. Books for the Use of Paris, Prague, or Salzburg could be printed in Venice, those for the Use of Sarum in Venice or Rouen or Paris, and those for Hungarian churches in several centers of Western Europe.[86] This surely implies that the bishops and archbishops who promoted, and often paid for, these editions were already familiar with books printed and published in Venice and the other centers, already regarded them as being of more than adequate quality and accuracy, and already had access to trade routes and perhaps even specialist book transporters and dealers. Therefore we can say with confidence that many books and their publishers were widely known throughout Europe, and that these publishers had the means of disseminating their books widely. These means must concern us for a while.

There seem to have been four means available to the Italian publisher of the first half of the century: mutual relationships with printers and publishers in other cities; relationships with booksellers acting as agents, and even with itinerant booksellers, the so-called *colporteurs* of later centuries; selling through the large fairs on the Italian peninsula (and elsewhere, leading to the great German book fairs); and advertising books by means of printed catalogues.

As to the first, we have little information for music printers and publishers, although information from other fields exists. There are several cases where we know that one publisher was selling, and even listing as for sale, the books of other publishers. The catalogue issued by Hamman by 1498 will be mentioned below. But, for example, the catalogue issued by Koberger of Nürnberg in 1480 includes books printed or supplied by Rusch of Strassburg.[87]

Perhaps the most interesting case in the present context is revealed through the petition made by Torresano to the Venetian Senate, in September 1536. Torresano's request for a privilege to print several titles is supported by his claim that he had been importing certain books and maps from Paris, but that they were lost in Turin.[88] The shipment comprised a number of bales of various books made in Paris, with some maps or designs of France place by place with the distances— "alcune balle di diuersi libri fatti in Paris con alcune carte ouer desegni di tutta la franza a loco *per* loco con le sue misure"; several of the titles were listed in the application for privilege, and these include a little music book of twenty-nine songs from Paris—"uno libreto di canto canzon 29 de paris". It seems clear that the Aldine house, of which Torresano was by then the proprietor, was importing books in bulk; if they had been imported in single copies, Torresano would scarcely have sought a privilege to print his own copies.[89] By the time of Torresano's petition, of course, the picture had changed from that of the 1500s and 1510s: the market was larger, if the pattern of music printing in the immediately following years is any guide. Indeed, within a few years it appears that shipping music from France (the press of Moderne) was probably much harder than printing it (by Gardane) in Italy.[90]

This Torresano petition is likely to be representative of the situation in which the remote publisher was acting as a dealer and bookseller, rather than as a mutual partner with a specific French publisher. For one thing, there is no evidence that Attaingnant ever published either maps of France or the classical texts for which Torresanus sought privilege; someone was therefore acting as an exporting bookseller, dealing with a number of publishers. This also appears to be the situation in the case of Hamman and Silber, in or before 1498. When Silber, in Rome, produced a catalogue of his recent titles, the Venetian house of Hamman printed the same list, apparently being willing to supply Silber's editions. Other printers did the same; Kunne of Memmingen, for instance, listed Venetian books in his catalogue.[91]

There is also evidence of publishers employing agents in distant cities. Fust and Schöffer already had an agency in Paris by 1470, and the Kobergers maintained an office in Lyons, which was responsible for Spain and northern Italy.[92] Even more interestingly for the present study, the Roman printer Francesco Minizio Calvo (whom we have already mentioned), in 1517 during his Milan years, wrote to Froben suggesting a mutual contract, offering books which he could supply at discount, and enclosing a list of those he sought, also at a discount, from Froben's house, to sell in Italy.[93]

This active use of distant booksellers or agents is perhaps the most obvious means of disseminating newly printed books. Aldus left books for sale on commission in Augsburg, Basel, Paris, and Vienna. The Kobergers apparently acted as booksellers for many other printers, stocking books from presses as far afield as Amsterdam, Gdansk, and Venice. At the same time, their accounts at the closing of the firm in 1509 show that they were owed money by booksellers in Paris, Lyons, Milan, Florence, Venice, Augsburg, Leipzig and Prague, among other cities.[94] When contracting with Antico for the *Liber Quindecim Missarum*, Scotto agreed to be responsible for sales "tam in urbe quam in illis mittendis extra eam etiam in Gallia et aliis partibus ultramontanis"—for Rome and outside the city, for France and elsewhere across the Alps.[95] Petrucci had a similar pattern, for he retained his contact with the Venetian Scotto and Niccolò after he returned to Fossombrone.

There is also evidence of books offered for sale to the general public at local fairs. The best early musical reference for this may be the purchase of music for the Casa Santa at Loreto during the annual fair of 1515 at Recanati.[96] In some cases, such books would have been carried to fairs by itinerant booksellers. These *colporteurs* almost certainly would have divided themselves into different groups: while some would have sold popular literature to all and sundry, others would have dealt with booksellers in the cities through which they passed and would have carried appropriate stock. But printers themselves also visited fairs and relied on the contacts made there. The big fairs at Recanati and Foligno seem to have been important, as part of a network of cities and business places along the eastern half of Italy,[97] where printers could sell books to both each other and the public, and also make arrangements with agents covering other parts of the peninsula. In his recent work on the book trade in Perugia, Jeremy Potter has shown how, for that city (no more easily accessible than Fossombrone), the fairs allowed printers outside the big commercial cities to disseminate their production.[98] Some incidental evidence for the success of this system may lie in the patterns of books purchased by Colón in different cities.

This evidence (even when combined with the other details offered here) is necessarily sparse, and not plausibly representative, but it precedes the well-known instances of the German book fairs, especially those at Frankfurt and Leipzig. The catalogues for these latter fairs, which did not begin until 1564,[99] were perhaps begun as no more than a recognition of the international nature of the book trade, and of the necessity of wide publicity for publishers. Even so, they publicized trade fairs, in which publishers looked at the work of their colleagues and competitors, and decided on the books they could well print and those they might just as satisfactorily buy from other publishers on commission. For this reason, publishers were willing to cooperate in the preparation of these catalogues. They would send lists of their books in advance, so that the catalogue would be available at the start of the fair.

This brings us to the existence of published catalogues of books, prepared by the publisher or, as in the Roman case above, by a bookselling agent. The best survey of catalogues prepared by music printers and publishers is that of Mischiati,[100] although the author can cite no examples as early as the time of Petrucci. However, occasional catalogues were already known, and Pollard and Ehrman have provided a survey of those extant from the years before 1800.[101] They remark that the Aldine catalogues were unusual in being made in booklet format.[102] Much more frequently, broadsheets were used; these contained not so much a catalogue of a publisher's output as a list of recent publications. As a broadsheet, such a page would be useful at fairs and for itinerant sellers, immediately notable by its size.

Few of these catalogues have survived, as is hardly surprising, for they would not have been thought worth keeping. However, many must have been prepared, for Gesner, in his *Bibliotheca universalis* (1548), could remark that many printers and booksellers prepared broadsides and lists of their books. He reports that he used catalogues to help him prepare his own bibliographies.[103] The up-to-dateness of many catalogues is in doubt, for there is some evidence[104] that they remained in use for up to twenty years, not being reprinted, but supplemented by manuscript additions. This is enough to suggest that, in many cases, the catalogue was not strictly a widely disseminated list of the latest works, but rather a true publicity device for the press and its general output.

We cannot tell how successful any of these methods truly was. Apparently, for example, Torresano was doing well with his practice of importing books from France, or he would not have bothered to seek a privilege that cited those he had lost. Presumably, too, advertising by catalogue was a satisfactory device, for the practice continued. On the other hand, the evidence that catalogues continued to be used for up to twenty years makes a different and equally relevant point: that books also remained in print for many years. This is only one strand of evidence here; the same point can be made after a study of the Colón catalogues.[105] Surviving stock lists also seem to show a slow movement of books.[106]

On the other side, we do occasionally know of the methods pursued by purchasers, scholars and others, to ensure that they were aware of new publications. Both Offenbacher and Lowry draw attention to the manner in which Pirckheimer of Nürnberg managed to keep in touch with the latest books.[107] He remarked "that there were always one or two of his Imhof relatives at the Fondaco dei Tedeschi who would be glad to act as agents".[108] He had a relative who was for some years a law student at Padua, and at one point he enquired specifically for editions of Greek texts printed in Milan.

Many other collectors and scholars used agents in Italy, and the tenants of the Fondaco dei Tedeschi in Venice were ideally placed for such activity. When the Elector Frederick the Wise decided to expand his own library to make it the nucleus of the Wittenberg University library, he turned to Georg Burkhard, who arranged for Frederick to receive Aldus's catalogues. When an agent bought the books, he provided an inventory of 153 titles: these were by no means all Aldine editions, but seem to have come from a great many Italian presses.[109]

We know much less about individual collectors of music. We have to assume that the Amerbachs, the Fuggers, Glareanus, or Ottheinrich's agent were active in discovering new titles. Later in the century, it is evident that Gardano was able to see what Moderne was publishing,[110] and the same must have been true for Petrucci or Egnatio. Susato, Phalèse, Morley, and others were alert to Italian editions and apparently saw them soon after they came off the press.[111] In Germany a wide range of collectors seems to have been willing to keep contacts with Italian dealers or with middlemen. Morell has shown that even in Gdansk a collector of music from the end of the century was able to keep abreast of the latest Italian music.[112] By then, of course, books had acquired the status of many other commodities, and (perhaps as a result of Reformation musical practices) polyphonic volumes seem to have been freely available in many centers, or through many contacts.

We cannot tell how many of the methods mentioned here were followed by Petrucci or his purchasers. I am sceptical that he ever printed a catalogue. His "list" was never very extensive, and its appeal must have been somewhat limited—however willing we are to assume that courtiers and humanists sought his frottole and motets. Nor do I believe that he would have worked out mutual contracts or agreements with printers in other cities. There *were* no other printers of polyphony with whom he could deal;[113] and printers of other repertoires would surely have looked first to similarly inclined or more active printers in Venice. Once Petrucci was in Fossombrone, buried in the Marche, the benefits of such an arrangement would have seemed even more dubious to any colleague in another center.

On the other hand, there is some evidence that he did distribute his books to *librai* and booksellers in other cities. I refer again to the purchase of books of polyphony at the Recanati book fair, to be used at the Santa Casa in Loreto. Despite the fame of this fair, I doubt that books of polyphony would be carried around by an itinerant bookseller. Such men would spend a considerable amount of their time on the road, passing through villages and small country towns before reaching the next major center. These places may have produced some literate purchasers, and the many monastic establishments that a *colporteur* would have used for hospitality would have yielded purchasers; yet I doubt that polyphony would have been worth carrying around. I assume that the Loreto purchase at Recanati was more in the nature of taking delivery of books previously ordered. Since, as Potter shows, printers and publishers did travel to the major fairs, Petrucci may have taken the books himself—or he may have used one of the other printers or booksellers from the Marche.[114]

This series of observations brings us hardly any closer to conclusions. I am forced to believe that Scotto was the principal outlet for Petrucci's books, and that he circulated information about them to specific purchasers and *librai*—the sacred repertoire to the institutions that bought chant, the rest to courts and to any who were also buying humanistic literature.

Availability and Reprints

So far in this chapter, I have been concerned with how Petrucci's books reached their intended purchasers: whether they were priced to sell, and how they might have been distributed. Now, I propose to turn to an equally critical question—, that of what may have actually happened: whether the books sold as he had hoped, and whether they had much of an impact.

A significant issue here hinges on the question of how long music and other books remained available. If Petrucci's books were on the market (perhaps only in a few bookshops) for twenty years or so, then clearly the implications for his business reputation are different.[115] Not only could we surmise less about how Petrucci himself distributed the books, but we could also be less sure of how early purchasers thought of them. By the 1530s, much of his music would have seemed out-of-date, or at least old-fashioned.[116]

I have discussed the patterns whereby books could travel great distances across Europe in the span of a year or two, and I have mentioned those few cases in which we can assume that the probable provenances of Petrucci's books include very early ownership. Unfortunately, most of those instances allow for a gap of even decades between the printing and the first surmised owners. This should not surprise us, for the presence in publishers' catalogues of old books, often twenty years old, has been remarked by musicologists, and is highlighted by some evidence in Mischiati's collection of transcriptions.[117] While all of this evidence comes from much later in the century, there is parallel evidence in the catalogues compiled by Colón.

Colón bought a few of Petrucci's volumes long after they were published: his copy of *Motetti C* (published in 1504) was acquired in Rome in 1513, and the now lost copy of the 1507 book of Magnificats, in Venice in 1521. The second book of laude, published in 1508, and the 1514 edition of the eleventh book of frottole, were both bought in Perugia in 1530. In addition, based on its location in Colón's catalogues, Chapman believed that his copy of the 1504 edition of the *Motetti A* was bought in Bologna in 1530, over twenty-five years after its publication; most of his other Petrucci editions were acquired during the same "voyage", from August 1529 to October 1531.[118]

This pattern was not restricted to polyphonic music, of course. Among the few titles of interest to musicologists so far cited in the new catalogue of Colón's books are the following, bought in Nürnberg in 1521: Tritonius's *Melopoiae* (Augsburg in 1507); Faber Stapulensis's *Epitome . . . Arithmeticos* (Paris: Estienne, 1510); Virdung's *Musica getuscht* (Basle: 1511); and Schlick's *Tabulaturen* (Mainz: Schöffer, 1512). More extreme is the case of a *Directorium Constantiense* (Basle: Wenssler, 1481), bought in Nürnberg in 1522.[119] This can be matched by other volumes: Spataro's *Honesto Difensio* of 1491 bought in Rome in 1512, or Gafori's *Practica musice* of 1496, also bought in Rome, in 1515.[120]

Even further afield, the evidence is more convincing: the famous 1483 edition of Giustiniani's lauda texts, bought in Rome in 1515;[121] a Venetian 1498 edition of Abiosius, a Brescia 1500 edition of sermons and a Brescia 1505 edition of B. Castileonus, all acquired in Trento in 1521; a Venice 1484 edition of Leto, and a Milan 1495 edition of Albert of Brudzewo, bought in Nürnberg in 1521. Interesting for our study is the purchase of a copy of Paulus de Middelburgh's 1484 *Protonotariomastix*, also in Nürnberg in 1521.[122] These examples could be extended almost endlessly. Although among the more extreme cases, they highlight the general point—that many books were relatively slow-moving commodities. Some must have sold fast, and no doubt printers and publishers wanted to move their stock, to recoup their investment. But books were held by *librai* and other dealers for a relatively long time.[123]

The interest for Colón of the musical books was presumably the same as that of any other of his purchases, not necessarily one of content at all. With careful study, we may be able extrapolate from his purchases to argue which repertoires sold fast or slowly. But at present we can only assert with confidence that none of Petrucci's books moved fast; once they had left his shop, or his partners' hands in Venice, delivered to a bookseller in some other city, they might have waited years for their first purchasers.

However, some of his books did remain of interest to purchasers in Italy for several years after he finished production. The evidence lies in the re-editions bought out by Pasoti and Dorico in 1526 and 1527.[124] The proposed direct link between Petrucci and Pasoti would have ensured that the latter had access to Petrucci's editions. Indeed, as I have suggested earlier, Petrucci probably waived his rights under his Roman privilege, which still had a few years to run. It is possible that he passed at least part of his stock to Pasoti, for sale from Rome, although Colón did not purchase any there. However, Pasoti and Dorico were apparently correct in seeing that there was still a need for editions of Josquin's masses, and of the *Motetti de la Corona*. Perhaps not surprisingly, the other Fossombrone editions, those of Mouton and Févin, were not reprinted, and neither were any of Petrucci's Venetian editions, by then already fifteen and more years old. In particular, there can hardly have been any serious interest in frottole by 1526, even in central Italy; the eleventh book was being sold at a discount when Colón bought a copy in Perugia in 1530.

The sequence of editions put out by Pasoti and Dorico also implies that Petrucci's books and their content had acquired enough of a reputation that they were still sought out. It is not evident that the other Roman books published in the 1520s had the same cachet, even though some would be reprinted after a number of years.

If books moved so slowly, then printers and publishers could face problems in recouping their investment. With paper making a larger proportion of the cost than labor, more capital was necessarily tied up in unsold copies. This explains in part the enthusiasm they had for partnerships in other cities. A publisher could unload a batch of copies on another distributor or a bookseller and be paid for them, whether or not they reach final purchasers. This necessarily affects our view of how many copies were actually purchased (especially in the years immediately following publication) for the need to reprint does not imply that all the extant copies had already been sold by librai; but it also has a critical bearing on a different decision:, that of the size of the print-run, that is, the number of copies that the publisher decided was financially viable.

Costs and Profit

Having decided to publish a specific edition, the publisher faced the difficult decision of the number of copies to be printed. Apart from the obvious question of the size of the market for the content, this decision also required an equation between the cost of labor (relatively fixed, regardless of the edition size) and of materials (in direct proportion to the number of copies), and the number of copies that could be immediately sold or otherwise unloaded (to agents, bookshops, and dealers).[125] I have discussed the first aspect elsewhere.[126] Here, my interest is in how large an edition had to be to make a profit, given the state of the market.

In the contract for his *Liber Quindecim Missarum* of 1516, Andrea Antico arranged for a mark-up of a third, the difference between the wholesale price (for his partners) and the retail price.[127] Unfortunately, we do not know what the book cost to produce, although at least one copy in the Marche sold for thirty-two carlini.[128] The internal price, however, would also surely have led to a small profit. In the case of the contract for the *Libro primo de musica de la Salamandra* (Rome, 1526),[129] the value on each copy set for the purposes of internal accounting was about 6 hundredths of a ducato d'oro, just about 10.1 percent above cost. As Bonnie Blackburn remarks in her analysis of this contract, the retail price would certainly have been much higher. If we assume a mark-up similar to that proposed by Antico, the retail price of the book would have been about 8 hundredths of a ducato d'oro. When Colón bought Antico's frottole volumes in Venice in 1521, he paid ten soldi for each one; this was then just below 7.5 hundredths of a ducat: at the same time, his copy of de Frizis first book of motets cost 9 hundredths.[130] If, therefore, we assume that 8 hundredths was a plausible price for the *Salamandra*, then costs would have been met after the sale of only 350 copies, of an edition of 500. Indeed, the cost of paper was so great a part of the whole, that they would have made a profit even if they had printed only 300 copies.

Two conclusions can be drawn: first, that the partners had made a decision about the number of copies booksellers would take—setting that figure at 500 copies, and thereby increasing their profit; second, that they could have allowed copies beyond the first 350 to sell more slowly. If Petrucci's prices were set at three times as much per folio as were Antico's, but his expenses were effectively only a little more than one and one-half times as much,[131] he should begin to make a profit after fewer copies, perhaps fewer than 200. This has direct bearing on the problem of the size of his print-run.

Print-run, or Edition Size

Essentially, when no archival evidence survives to reveal specifically how large an edition was planned, there are only fragmentary strands of other evidence. One involves the known rates of work in printing houses, the normal number of sheets printed in a day, and the normal number of pulls at the press in the same time; another involves the number of days that it took to complete a book; a third might involve the patterns of paper use, and the normal sizes of bales, reams, and quires. None of these is conclusive in any instance, and all can to some extent be fitted together to produce a series of possibilities. In Petrucci's case, we do have plausible data on the second—the length of time available for an edition. The following figures give the number of sheets per copy and the number of days involved, for some periods when his shop may have been working at full stretch; second and third editions, and also cancels, are marked with an asterisk.[132]

Not surprisingly, these figures do not give a constant ratio of numbers of

TABLE 10-6 Numbers of days per edition and rates of work: this assumes a six-day week, with an extra day off for Easter (indicated by [a]), for Ascension ([b]) and for All Saints ([c]). Second editions are marked with an ★.

Date of Edition:	Title	Number of Sheets	Number of Days Available	Rate of Work (Days per Sheet)
Friday, 24.iii.1503	Misse Obreht			
Wednesday, 10.v.1503	Motetti B	18	39[a]	2.17
Saturday, 17.vi.1503	Misse Brumel	16 + 1 half	32[c])	
Tuesday, 15.vii.1503	Misse Ghiselin	15 + 3 halves	24) 74	1.58
Friday, 4.viii.1503	★Canti B	14	17)	
Tuesday, 31.x.1503	Misse La Rue	13 + 2 halves	75	
Saturday, 10.ii.1504	Canti C			
Saturday 23.iii.1504	Missa Agricola	16 + 2 halves	36	2.12
Saturday, 25.v.1504	★Odhecaton A	26	53[a]	2.04
[no date: cancels for	★Misse Agricola	1 + one half	)	
Sunday, 15.ix.1504	Motetti C	32 + one half	) 96[b]	2.82
Thursday, 28.xi.1504	Frottole I	14	62[c]	4.43)
Wednesday, 8.i.1505	Frottole II	14	35)	)
Thursday, 6.ii.1505	Frottole III	16	25) 66	1.67) 2.21
Thursday, 13.ii.1505	★Motetti A	14	6)	)
Saturday, 22.iii.1505	Misse De Orto	16 + 3 halves	32	1.83
[no date: cancels for	★Motetti B	3	)	
[no date: cancels for	★Motetti C	8 + 1 half	) 63[ab]	1.45
Wednesday, 4.vi.1505	Motetti IV	32	)	
Monday, 30.vi.1505	Josquin II	14 + 2 halves	22	1.47
[no date]	Strambotti IV	14	)	
[no date: cancels for	★Motetti A	3	) 106	3.03
Friday, 31.x.1505	Fragmenta Miss.	17 + 2 halves	)	
[no date: cancel for	Fragmenta Miss.	1	) 45[c]	3.00
Tuesday, 23.xii.1505	Frottole V	14	)	
Thursday, 5.ii.1506	Frottole VI	14	44	3.14
Wednesday, 8.iv.1506	Lamentations I	12 + 1 half	64	5.12
Friday, 29.v.1506	Lamentations II	13	42[ab]	3.23
Thursday, 7.i.1507	Misse Gaspar			
[Saturday, 27.ii.1507]	Spinacino I	14	)	
Wednesday, 31.iii.1507	Spinacino II	14	) 71	2.54
Friday, 21.v.1507	Frottole VIII	14	42[ab])	
			) 56	2.00
Sunday, 6.vi.1507	Frottole VII	14	14)	

working days to sheets. Each series of editions seems to give a reasonably consistent rate, for a few months, perhaps suggesting changes in the craftsmen involved. But we can sometimes advance a reason for the bigger anomalies. I have already pointed out that the Brumel and Ghiselin editions of 1503 overlapped in their production, and that they indicate the point at which Petrucci introduced double-impression techniques.[133] The longer time taken over the first book of frottole may be because it involved real differences in layout on the page, and perhaps even new decisions about what went in each forme; in addition, the three books may have been partially prepared, or at least planned, at the same time. It is reasonable that the two books of settings by Spinacino were planned at the same time—there was not enough time to see if the first was selling well before work must have started on the second. These two books might easily have taken slightly longer than the earlier volumes, for lute tabulature was also new to the typesetters.

A slight problem with these figures lies in the possibility that work was occasionally rushed in order to complete some books by significant dates. It is probably not a coincidence that *Misse De Orto* is dated on the day before Easter 1505; *Fragmenta Missarum* on the day before All Saints', also in 1505; the two volumes of Lamentations just before Easter and Whit-Sunday respectively, in 1506. This pattern may affect the accuracy of the work-rates; so will the setting of cancels and later editions, all of which must necessarily have proceeded rather faster than a first edition. It is also reasonable to assume that cancels, at least, would be printed in smaller runs.

Nonetheless, it appears that, under pressure, Petrucci's shop could complete both impressions of a single sheet in two days. The Venetian copyright law of 3 January 1533/34 required a rate of work of one folio per day for work in progress.[134] In 1565 Scotto was expected to print at least a sheet per day: Don Benedetto of San Giorgio Maggiore stipulated "et non voglio, che se ne faccia meno d'un foglio al giorno".[135] All these refer to single-impression processes.

This would allow us to calculate possible numbers of copies for an edition, if we knew the average rates of work at the press, the number of copies of a sheet printed in a day. Unfortunately, there is little evidence on rates of work during the early sixteenth century, and less for music printing. Stevenson cites a document showing that "already in 1458–9 Gutenberg, Fust, and Mentelin were printing 300 sheets a day".[136] Later printers were faster than this: Le Roy, in his English account,[137] suggests that pressmen could pull 1,250–1,300 perfected sheets a day, which is consistent with figures from other sources of the time.[138] Since Petrucci was printing with two impressions, any figures would need to be halved; but the implication seems clear, that (unless he had more than one team of craftsmen, for which there is not enough evidence) he could not normally have printed editions of more than about 500 copies at any time. Among the tacit assumptions in this figure are that he employed a full team of men, for textsetting as for presswork, that they were not working on other books at the same time, and (which seems to me to be the most questionable) that the shop was committed to full-time printing. Given that Petrucci petitioned for admission to the guild of *cestieri*, we must assume that he, and perhaps some of his men, spent time in that craft as well as printing, and this would immediately lower the ceiling considerably. In addition, the differing figures in Table 10-6 may reflect in part different lengths of print-run for different titles. I conclude, therefore, that 500 copies was probably the largest print-run Petrucci could have achieved: as I now show, the likely figure was normally smaller.

This runs counter to the evidence from outside music; it is generally assumed that Venetian editions of the first half of the sixteenth century averaged about 1,000–1,500 copies, taking into account those contracts that have survived, as well as the economics of running a printing shop.[139] A number of scholars have argued that smaller runs were often expected; Scholderer assumes an average of about 250 during the fifteenth century,[140] though I do not see that this is much of a guide to the sale of music, even immediately after 1500.

It is clear that the surviving contracts are not a great deal of help.[141] So few exist for the whole of Italian sixteenth-century printing, and they cover such a wide range of situations and repertoires, that it is hard to argue that they are representative. For one thing, there must have been a great deal of variation in edition size, related to the type of book, and we cannot now tell the reasons. It is reasonable to assume that the edition size for commissioned books represented a compromise between the wishes of the promoter and the potential of the market. This situation may be represented by the so-called vanity publication, in which (typically) a composer sought to have a volume of his music published. He could then claim that he had achieved the status of being printed, and use this for some other purpose—for career advancement or financial return. Such editions can hardly have been economically viable for the composer, though the printer would have protected his own interests. There would have been similar volumes, though of different characters, for which the number of recipients precisely conditioned the size of the edition: even at the end of the nineteenth century, it was possible to commission an edition to be given away at a wedding, or a liturgical calendar for an obscure diocese.[142] No doubt most of these volumes had contracts, specifying the number of copies to be received by the composer or patron, and whether the printer and publisher might keep any for sale. Probably similar clauses were attached to a number of more standard books, new translations, scholarly and legal texts, and no doubt most liturgical books.[143] These are among the repertoires most often mentioned in privilege applications.

But many other editions would not have had any specific contract. Among them might have been those covered by a blanket arrangement between author and publisher, or (more frequently) between publisher and printer;[144] those where the publisher was house printer for a local government, and therefore obliged to follow orders;[145] those where the publisher, having fulfilled the requirements of a first edition, was able to print a second;[146] and, most importantly, all editions that the publisher or printer undertook as a speculative venture.[147] For these groups, unlikely to have had contracts, we have no evidence as to the potential size of the edition.[148]

The problem is even more acute for musical books during these first decades, and is currently insoluble. My present opinion is that, before the 1540s, most musical editions were small, usually no more than 300–500 copies, and that even this number was an increase over the figures for the first two decades of the century. There are several strands of evidence, none of any real substance, six of which follow.

Firstly, I believe the books had a clearly defined market. Here it is important to distinguish the various repertoires from each other. Books of masses and motets present the most easily measurable evidence, although even here we know too little. But given the current state of knowledge about polyphonic establishments, it is inconceivable that there were at this time as many as 1,008 institutions (enough to buy out Antico's 1516 edition) performing polyphony during the liturgy, even throughout Europe.[149] Further, the great number of such institutions would not continue to purchase books of masses, not needing further volumes, after acquiring perhaps two or three. But Petrucci printed many and frequently. In addition, if one is optimistic, perhaps one hundred or so might have been bought by lay organizations, by composers, foreigners, or other interested amateurs or theorists; and they may have been more willing to continue buying more editions of the same mass repertoire.

With frottole, there is less ground for any useful assertion, although I suspect that the books did not have as wide a sale for performance as we might wish. The claims, based on Castiglione's assertions—that every courtier was expected to be able to sing, that they could all sing in a three- or four-voiced setting, and read their parts from a small quarto-format book—seem to me poorly founded.[150] Even if these assertions do turn out to be sound, there is no reason to believe that such courtiers would all buy their own copies of music books, and there are too many manuscript books containing this repertoire to argue that everyone sang from printed editions once they became available. On the other hand, it is possible that some copies were sold, not so much for the music as for the verse, which was otherwise not easily available. The contacted number of 500, with fifty additional copies, for the *Libro primo de la Salamandra*, represents as large a figure as seems conceivable, especially if we assume that *librai* were able to sell all of them.

Even more difficult to assess are the lute books: those by Spinacino and Dalza contain music of much greater complexity than is found in the later Bossinensis arrangements of frottole, even though simpler than the music composed by, for example, Marco dall'Aquila. Although music by Marco was not printed by Petrucci (or apparently by Marco himself, despite his privilege: see chapter 2), the works Petrucci did print were presumably used by skilled players, rather than by the dilettantes suggested by Castiglione, and supplied with music by Bossinensis.

A second strand of argument stems from the evidence that no other Italian printer made a full-time career of music books before the last years of Petrucci's own career. This suggests that the market willing to buy on a regular basis was not very large. The few volumes published by Antico between 1510 and 1521, if anything, support this argument by the way in which they pick up on the repertoires explored by Petrucci at times when he might have been thought not to be publishing. Antico may not have been competing, so much as trying to find his own series of niches. In this connection, it is worth remembering that Petrucci himself was probably not really a full-time printer. Not only must he have been involved with the craft of the *cestieri*, he was also frequently in Fossombrone and acting as a town official.

Third, is the probability that a majority of the early editions were specially commissioned, which would immediately affect the size of a print run. For Petrucci, I have discussed this in chapter 9, arguing that some books present clear examples of patronage. In addition, it can be argued that the pattern of publishing pairs of books in close succession means that the second of each pair could not have been a reaction to the commercial success of the first. These arguments can also be advanced for some of Antico's volumes.[151] Such books must lie outside the patterns of commercial promotion. It may be that a patron commissioning a book would demand an excessive number of copies (or equally an uncommercially small number)—and the printer would certainly comply, for the patron would have met all the costs. The existence of these books, alongside others that were speculative undertakings, even by Petrucci or Antico,[152] must immediately affect decisions about print-run. The costs of those other books would have been properly calculated by printer and publisher, and we can be sure that the expected rate of sale (and therefore of return) was part of that calculation. Given this variety of circumstance, the surviving contracts cannot be seen as providing norms for the size of the print-run for many editions.[153]

Fourth, there is the evidence of the number of in-house corrections, particularly the possibility, which I advanced earlier, that Spinacino himself corrected the two lute books appearing under his name. It is not a strong argument, given the fact that many printers seem to have used manuscript correction, rather than (or later than) stopping the press during the print-run. The argument is weak, because similar corrections have been found in editions that presumably were large, surely of more than 500 copies. It is slightly strengthened in Petrucci's case, because there are no manuscript corrections in the one large-scale edition he put out, his *Paulina*. This book must have circulated to all the most significant players in the deliberations at the Lateran Council, and it apparently was widely bought by religious houses elsewhere, to judge by the number of surviving copies. It is notable that there are cancel and stop-press corrections, and even two that are stamped in by hand after the presswork, but there appear to be no corrections in manuscript that originate from the printing house. The easiest explanation would be that this volume had a much larger print-run than did the music books.

Fifth is the evidence of the use of Petrucci's editions by copyists working for Italian institutions. There is surprisingly little evidence of direct copying, given the number of manuscripts with similar repertoires or identical compositions that survive from the same years.[154] Indeed, many copies show clearly different lines of transmission. Any argument for a large-scale and wide distribution of Petrucci's editions seems weakened by this evidence.

Finally, there is the evidence of the number of subsequent editions, public and concealed, appearing in short order, sometimes within a couple of years. In these cases, which are evidently the majority of reprints, the first print-run cannot have been large, whatever the size of the second. This is a particularly intractable point, and one I have addressed elsewhere.[155] In essence, all one can assert is that the edition size was smaller than the market size. Given the length of time that some of Petrucci's editions were available and the pattern of frequent reprinting of others, it would seem that Petrucci did not yet have a detailed view of his market. For some books, he (perhaps deliberately) underestimated the demand; with others, he or his contacts still had stock many years later. It is possible, following this line of reasoning, that the edition size, the print-run, was fairly consistent for editions within each genre. There is partial support for this in the figures for rates of work, given above.

But despite this, the frequent reprintings mean that we have to take the size of the possible market as definitely larger than the print-run. It seems improbable that Petrucci could saturate the market for Josquin's masses in his first printing, and then need to reprint his book several times within fifteen years. I recognize that it is during these very decades that the expansion in the number of performing institutions began to appear; but that expansion was not yet anything like sufficient to justify several complete editions with large print-runs, for each one apparently failed to satisfy demand.

All in all, then, the evidence suggests—and no more—that edition sizes remained small. The print-run for the second volume in some series (such as *Canti B* or the second book of Josquin's masses) may have been rather larger, since Petrucci would have had some reassurance by the time he prepared it (although, again, there are later second editions). In other cases, however, it was probably smaller than the average. My suspicion is that an outside number was considerably smaller than the average for later books. I suspect that for Petrucci an initial print-run of any music book was never more than 300; in many cases, I submit, it was significantly smaller.

But even if we could know the actual edition size for any of these books, that would not provide us with an approximate figure for the size of the market. Publishers who sent books on consignment did not need to know whether they sold or not, for payment was still due from the receiving agent. As we know, many books did not sell for years, even decades, and print-runs seem to have been calculated with that in mind. This has to be the explanation for the additional printing cited in the contract for the *Libro Primo de la Salamandra*: all 500 printed copies that the contracting parties had not themselves sold had been sent on to agencies and *librai*; hence the need for another fifty copies. But we cannot assert that 550 people actually bought the book; and we certainly cannot say that they bought copies during the first few months or years.

The Impact of Petrucci's Editions

For the past 150 years, we have accorded Petrucci a central importance in the history of music. There is no need to repeat any of the information in the introduction to this study, for music historians have assumed that he must have been as influential for his particular field as we assume Gutenberg was in general. Each apparently liberated the circulation of material otherwise reserved for those able to purchase (often to commission) manuscripts. Even surveys of Renaissance music, aimed at a general reader, devote a section to the "importance of the invention". Similarly, we assume that Petrucci's editions must have brought a series of compositions to a much wider audience than before, drawing on the patterns of circulation of many works, for example, by Josquin, and the copying of Petrucci's versions, in both editions and manuscripts.

There is in fact little direct evidence of Petrucci's musical impact at the time.

This may not significantly weaken his significance in our eyes, for we are dependent on the survival of later sources carrying signs of his readings or selection of compositions. For at least the first two decades of the sixteenth century, however, this survival tended to follow patterns already established during the preceding century. These patterns militate against evidence of a rapid expansion in the market for printed music.

Institutional collections of manuscripts are the best represented, whether they come from an Italian or Spanish cathedral or the Imperial court circle. These collections often fail to show clear influence of Petrucci's editions. First, they necessarily reflect the local requirements, both in the selection of motets, and even, as in Milan, in the larger aspects of liturgical usage.[156] Second, many of the most popular works—by Josquin, of course, but also such pieces as Févin's *Sancta Trinitas*—survive so widely and often so consistently that a true stemmatic tree is difficult to construct. Indeed, the new compositional techniques developed under the influence of Josquin contrive to produce a style in which the surviving variants are often not at the level of significant readings.

Private manuscripts continue to survive, too, though rarely in the same important constellations of sources; as a result, it is often harder to place each one in the circle of its probable original owner. At the same time, the secular repertoires printed by Petrucci had a much shorter "shelf-life" than did the sacred. The works in the "Canti" books were fast becoming dated—this is even true of the newer repertoire in *Canti C*[157]—and the frottola repertoire was largely replaced within ten years of Petrucci's last edition, by settings of the Pisano type, and then immediately by the emerging madrigal.

There are, it is true, some groups of manuscripts that compare, in the way they interrelate, with the Italian sources of the late-fifteenth-century chanson.[158] But it so happens that most of these do not relate to Petrucci's editions. They either contain these new genres, or revolve around each other and a different series of exemplars, as do the German (and often Reformed) manuscripts transmitting motets from Josquin's and succeeding generations.

On the other hand, we should expect Petrucci's musical influence to be most evident where there was no pre-existing self-supporting tradition: among sources prepared by or for dilettantes and amateurs, new ecclesiastical institutions, or intabulators looking for new repertoire. But with a few exceptions,[159] these are not the sources that tend to survive in great numbers. As a result, valuable evidence is necessarily sporadic. The following examples, which could easily be multiplied, are representative of the probable situation, that Petrucci's influence was patchy, but in some places quite strong.

Occasionally, we can be sure that a Petrucci edition was used for surviving sources, without any intermediary. Among these is S-Uu Vok.mus.hdskr.76e, apparently copied in Frauenburg in Prussia during the second half of the sixteenth century: this contains complete copies of Petrucci's editions of masses by Isaac and Gaspar van Weerbeke.[160] Equally convincing, and more significant, is the entry on f.4r of CH-Bu F.VI.26d, which records the contents of Petrucci's 1503 editions of Obrecht and Brumel masses. If, as John Kmetz suggests,[161] the manuscript was written before 1520, then this is an early example of Petrucci's books being (not merely bought, but) consulted north of the Alps. Although the Obrecht titles are not listed in Petrucci's order, and there are some spelling variants, yet the scribe must have had a copy, or a list of contents before him. Significantly, a copy of Brumel's *L'homme arme* mass, apparently prepared from Petrucci's edition, survives in a related fragment in the same library, F.VI.26e.[162]

The first four masses in Petreius's *Liber Quindecim Missarum* (*RISM* 1539[1]) probably came from Petrucci's first book of Josquin's masses, for they are preserved in the same order; the two Mouton masses in D-Mbs Mus.Ms.66[163] are equally likely to have come from the 1515 edition; and there are other instances.[164] Initially, this northern market seems to have been more interested in secular music. Most significant is the re-publication of Petrucci's *Canti B* by Schöffer in 1513.[165] This reflects not merely knowledge of the Venetian edition, but also a belief in a market for the music, north of the Alps. The same should be said of the extent to which Öglin copied from Petrucci's editions for his books published around 1535.[166] These imply that the market continued to be substantial, well into the 1530s. Several northern manuscripts also show evidence of copying from Petrucci's editions: among them are D-Mbs Mus.1516,[167] probably copied after 1530; and D-Z LXXVIII,3, also copied after Petrucci had finished work.[168] A number of pieces in the Sicher Liederbuch appear to have come from the *Odhecaton*;[169] and Marx maintains that Sicher used Petrucci's editions, alongside others, as sources of the music that he intabulated, and that the exemplars may have come from Sicher's teacher, Buchner.[170] Further, a long sequence of works in Hans Newsidler's *Ander Theil*[171] was apparently prepared from Petrucci's editions, though not necessarily directly.

If this betrays an ongoing interest in Petrucci's music, and use of his editions, in northern Europe, there is less evidence for a similar interest in Italy, and what is there is more localized. A group of northern Italian sources from the years after 1500 shows clear influence of Petrucci's editions. The principal sources are of secular music, comprising F-Pn Rés.Vm⁷.676,[172] I-Bc Q18,[173] I-Fn Panc.27,[174] and ZA-Csa Grey 3.b.12.[175] Coupled with these, E-SE s.s.,[176] though probably written in Spain, seems to show an awareness of Petrucci's *Odhecaton*. As a whole, these sources work as a large-scale unit, transmitting music from one to another, collecting compositions from similar sources, and (with the exception of an interest in religious themes in the South African source) concentrating on a similar range of musical and textual genres.[177]

It is interesting to note Pirrotta's remarks about a Florentine awareness of the frottola in the years around 1500–10.[178] He argues that the occasional appearances of frottole in Florentine manuscripts of the period "may have resulted from the arrival in Florence of isolated copies of some of the Petrucci prints". But he also shows a pattern whereby the interest shown in Petrucci's first book (with some thirty pieces in Florentine sources) waned rather rapidly.[179] This reflects, more than anything, the directions in which Florentine taste had been going and would continue to move, but it also suggests that the first book was bought by at least one person in Florence, even while the repertoire was not appealing enough for the trade to continue.

Manuscripts of sacred music in Italy show even less evidence of Petrucci's influence. While the question whether I-Pc A17 was drawn from Petrucci or Castellanus, or from a third, intermediary copyist may have to remain open,[180]

Joshua Rifkin has shown that one of the Milan codices copied Petrucci's edition of Josquin's *Missa L'homme armé sexti toni*.[181] There are other similar individual instances; but combined with the short span of evident interest in Petrucci's secular repertoire, this highlights the extent to which his editions had only a short-term influence in Italy.

This discussion of practical sources presents a different picture from the one evident when we turn to theoretical sources. Here, undoubtedly Petrucci's editions were widely used: this should not be surprising, for they provided a ready source of new materials for any theorist. North of the Alps, the sequence of writers who relied on Petrucci for their material begins with Sebald Heyden, and his *De arte canendi* of 1537.[182] He was followed by Glareanus, in his *Dodecachordon* of 1547,[183] Zanger, with *Practicae musicae praecepta* (Leipzig: Hantzsch, 1554),[184] Finck, in his *Practica Musica* (Wittenberg: Rhau, 1556), and perhaps Wilphling-seder, in the *Erotemata musices practicae* (Nürnberg: Heussler, 1563). Italian writers similarly relied on Petrucci's editions; this would be almost inevitable, even for a theorist such as Gafori with a ready supply of music, for they would provide new compositions, as well as new versions (both textual and notational) of pieces they had seen elsewhere. Recent studies have shown that Aaron used Petrucci's music in 1525 and 1529,[185] and at the other end of the century Zacconi was still citing music from his edition of Obrecht masses.[186]

The extant evidence argues, therefore, that Petrucci's influence on musical dissemination and taste was diffuse and occasional. Some manuscripts show awareness of his readings; parts of some editions derive directly from his editions; and theorists drew on his editions as a large collection of examples to be used. In some places, primarily German-speaking, the influence was strong, but there was nothing like the widespread influence that has been tacitly assumed. On the other hand, his influence on the techniques of music printing, and indeed on music printing itself during the 1520s, is much greater than has been presumed: that is the subject of the next chapter.

Notes

1. Chapman, "Printed", pp. 51–52.

2. This catalogue is published in facsimile in Huntington, *Catalogue*. Much more information will become available through the continuing publication of Marin Martinez et al., *Catálogo*. The table expands considerably on that in Chapman, "Printed", and can add a value for the Perugia quatrine in terms of the ducat, among other data. On the other hand, a number of volumes owned by Colón are not listed, since I have no evidence of the price he paid for them.

3. In his entries, Colón ends many items with the comment "and the [local currency] is worth so many gold ducats". There were notionally 100 soldi to each ducat, although in 1500 the rate was about 103 soldi to the ducat. See Munro, "Coinages", pp. 674–5, and the bibliography cited there, as well as fn.12, below. The resulting figures do not take account of inflation during the period covered, although the relative inflation of other currencies vis-à-vis the ducat is necessarily present, given the nature of Colón's citations.

4. For music, the only contemporary evidence for wholesale pricing seems to be in the contract for Antico's 1516 mass volume, and in that recently discussed in Blackburn, "Printing".

5. It had never been very popular in Florence, of course, as has been argued in various places, including D'Accone, *Civic*: its decline in Rome is an incidental topic in Fenlon and Haar, *Madrigal*, and this is a factor in our assessment of Roman editions of the 1520s.

6. It is interesting to speculate whether this volume, bought in Perugia, had come from Petrucci's stock at Fossombrone, rather than via his partners in Venice. There is evidence, mentioned in previous chapters, that Petrucci had retained a stock of other (Venetian) titles during his years in Fossombrone.

7. While the labor would be doubled, in both typesetting and presswork, multiple impression printing would not cost twice as much as a single-impression volume, for it used the same sheet of paper, and paper was a major part of the cost.

8. This observation, as well as what follows, assumes that sets of partbooks were priced in parallel with single volumes in choirbook. I can see no reason why that should not be true, so long as the books were sold unbound.

9. Although it seems likely that Antico was able to reduce costs as he became more fluent and experienced in the trade, there is another possible solution, reflecting on the extent to which Venetian books were available in Rome and Roman books in Venice. While the first is certainly true and would allow Antico to price his 1510 volume accordingly, the second does not follow. The evidence of the table above shows that Colón's purchase of Roman volumes of music were made in Venice after Antico had arrived there. The books were plausibly brought from Rome by Antico himself. Similarly, as I shall argue below, Petrucci's editions purchased (by various institutions) after his return to the papal states reveal a very different distribution from those sold while he was in Venice.

10. It may be that the comparative price of Antico's and Petrucci's books could be used to show the proportion of the cost of a book represented by the paper, as opposed to labor. Gerritsen, "Printing", has collected some evidence showing that the retail price for a book tended to be about three to four times the cost of the paper.

11. This suggests setting the format, as well as pricing, by market, rather than merely by cost.

12. These catalogues are transcribed in Renouard, *Annales*, pp. 329–32: the first is reproduced in facsimile in Davies, *Aldus*, p. 21. Davies (pp. 115–6) works to a relationship of soldo and ducat which is rather different from that given in fn.3 above, suggesting that in 1503 one ducat was slightly larger (by four soldi) than six lire or two marcelli. The lira was worth twenty soldi. The ducat, as an internationally employed coin, had value from its gold content, and therefore moved against local currencies.

13. The Accademia account books are discussed, and a number presented, in Turrini, *Accademia*, passim. The Scotto contract is published in Agee, "Venetian", and discussed further in Bernstein, *Music*, pp. 116–17. At that point, Bernstein assumes a mark-up of 100 percent from wholesale to retail price, citing Grendler, *Roman*, p. 15, in support. In fact, neither statement offers any supporting evidence, and both must be seen as speculative. The evidence in the two contracts already mentioned points in a much more moderate direction.

14. See Bernstein, *Music*, p. 117.

15. Hirsch, *Printing*, p. 15.

16. The market for books of commercial arithmetic confirms this, in addition to the evident market for books of popular religion, given the many editions of the works of S. Catherine of Siena.

17. Davis, *Printing*, pp. 197–201. We probably have to make an exception to this argument, at least for the second half of the century, for the many Protestants in northern Europe who bought noted psalters and related books. The vast output of such editions, whatever the size of the individual print-runs, argues that many people bought them, even though they would not have bought any other music.

18. Ibid., pp. 210–11.

19. This argument has particular bearing on the sale of the books of laude, which must have been aimed as much at individuals wishing to sing the repertoire as at institutional purchasers. Both Jeppesen, *Mehrstimmige*, and Luisi, *Laudario*, provide evidence that reinforces this point, for example, in pointing out the interrelationship of texts and music in different compositions.

20. See Boorman, "Working".

21. Gallo, "Practice", p. 13.

22. Barzon, "Note".

23. Gallo, "Practice", pp. 18–22, lists a number of fifteenth- and early-sixteenth-century Italian manuscript sources. Cattin adds a number of sources, in particular printed editions, in various articles, among them "Canti"; *Processionale*; and "Sconosciuto".

24. For this manuscript, see Cattin, *Manoscritto*.

25. The relevance of this story to the career of Petrucci has been discussed in chapter 1; there I suggested that the duke was probably less opposed to printing and printed editions than many have supposed.

26. It is fair to say that the situation in Italy seems to have changed radically during the 1530s. The advent of *Accademie*, the emergence of the madrigal with its approachable style, the dissemination of the ideas of Castiglione, and (either as stimulus or response to these other changes) the development of single-impression printing, all made the growth of a middle-class market for polyphony inevitable.

27. I am leaving out of issue those who received musical manuscripts as gifts. The gift of an Alamire manuscript to the Elector of Saxony is not really relevant to the present issue, even though it has considerable bearing on the role of music at the Saxon court, and on the prestige that a fine music manuscript carried with it.

28. Quoted in Blackburn, "Petrucci".

29. We do not have to presume that they could read a score, or hear the whole of a composition in their heads. These are modern concepts, not valid in years when the score (insofar as it existed at all) was apparently a tool for composition or analysis. (For further information on early scores, see Owens, *Composers*, and the bibliography cited there.) But I do not think it far-fetched to believe that a musical layman of the first years of the Italian sixteenth century could distinguish different styles from a perusal of one voice-part. Indeed, one voice-part was all the casual reader had available to him. In the bookstore, preparing for a performance in the choir loft, or when singing with friends, each musician was restricted to one part at a time. The importance of this point, its impact on the design of books, on changes in taste, and on questions of the longevity of certain styles, has barely begun to be discussed. See Boorman "16th-Century".

30. Ker, *Medieval*.

31. Among the many references to music books in private collections, one is not widely known: the inventory of Lucantonio delli Alessandri of Urbino, dated 1625, examined in Moranti and Moranti, *Librarie*, pp. 340–42, listed the following:

No.247. "Item un libretto di Canto, dove vi è scritto in quattro carte alcuni Madrigale, scritto a mano con le coperte à cartone".

No.266. "Fior Angelico di Musica del patre Fra Angelo da Picitono".

No.277. "Libri sei de Musica et diversi altri libretti che contengano Indulgentie, Horationi, Meditationi, la Pratica di dire l'Officio divino et altre opere sante".

No.282. "Un quinterno grosso di varii et diversi libri di musica tanto stampati quanto scritti a mano".

It is tempting to see in the first item, so far into the history of madrigals, a late copy of Arcadelt's music, paralleling the seventeenth-century editions. More certainly, the six books of the third item contained sacred music. Sadly, of course, such entries rarely give enough information, and, indeed, the wording of the last item merely emphasizes the problem.

32. Here, of course, the collection of Colón is not relevant, and many other early collections are basically too late for the present context. The private collections of Amerbach, Fugger, and Herwart, for example, already represent the next generation: where they contain earlier books, those from the start of the century, the relationship of these books to the rest of the collection is not always clear.

33. For San Marco in Florence, see Ullman and Stadter, *Public*. A list of other private libraries, for which published catalogues appeared during the sixteenth century, is in Serrai, *Storia*, ii, pp. 76–106. On p. 141, Serrai asserts that the first published catalogue of an institutional library is that of Leiden University in 1595.

34. The attempt most relevant to the present study is Clough, "Library", discussing the collections of the Dukes of Urbino.

35. This late dating is true, for example, of the series of Veneto libraries discussed in Ongaro, "Library", and of the references in Bernstein, "Buyers", and Lewis, "Printed".

36. Rhodes, "Unknown".

37. For the latest study of this famous volume, see Owens and Agee, "Stampa". The present citation does not, it is true, indicate anything specific about when the book might have been published; however, this would be the most recent book in the list, whatever its date, and an earlier date seems more likely. An alternative interpretation of the citation, Antico's *Canzoni nove*, would yield a publication date more in accord with the other books in the list.

38. Civitate is now a tiny city on the Adriatic flank of Italy, north of Foggia.

39. All the details that support the following are presented in the descriptions of the individual copies, in the bibliographical catalogue.

40. The short list of Petrucci's books owned by Ercole Bottrigari is different; it is merely an outline list, and it dates from much later in the century.

41. Lockwood, "Adrian", p. 99.

42. Prizer, "Cappella", and the entry in Chambers and Martineau, *Splendours*, p. 158.

43. See Grimaldi, *Cappella*, p. 91.

44. Rozzo, "Biblioteche", p. 13.

45. The evidence for each of these statements is provided in the full descriptions of the books and their editions.

46. Rostirolla, "Corrispondenza", pp. 261–65.

47. For these, see Perkins, "Notes".

48. Schnoebelen, *Padre*, items numbered 1110, 1245, and 1250.

49. This range of evidence for relating sets of books now bound separately is touched on below.

50. The copies presently in the Sistine collection at I-Rvat are those formerly owned by Chiti. For Chiti's donation, see the description of the 1516 edition of Josquin's second book of masses.

51. The catalogue is transcribed and analysed in Lambrecht, *Heidelberger*. The earlier study by Hermelink, "Musikalienverzeichnis", appears in a volume of essays devoted to Ottheinrich. These books were probably bought after the end of Petrucci's career. The only other editions listed as dating from before the late 1530s are Antico's 1516 *Liber quindecim Missarum* and the 1522 (or perhaps earlier) *Liber decem Missarum*. It is likely that the copy of Josquin's first book of masses comes from the later edition (despite Lambrecht's tacit assumption that all printed books were represented by their first editions), for the volume number is mentioned in the Heidelberg inventory. With the evidence that Ghiselin's mass book was reprinted at Fossombrone, it becomes probable that the copy of Josquin's second book also comes from the Fossombrone edition, and that all the books were acquired at about the same time, ca.1522. (The presence of the Ghiselin edition makes it unlikely that the other titles were of Pasoti and Dorico's editions.)

52. Lambrecht, *Heidelberger*, i, pp. 25–32, outlines Ottheinrich's life.

53. Federhofer, "Petrucci".

54. Werner, "Szombathely"; Werner, "Rarità".

55. Strohm, *Rise*, p. 523, citing a study by Walter Senn.

56. See the facsimile and study in Sampaio Ribeiro, *Livraria*, and Vasconcelles, *Primeira*. Although a large part of the King's library was purchased from Queen Christina of Sweden, Professor Calvin Elliker has reported (in a personal communication) that the evidence suggests that music volumes were not among those books.

57. In the preface to Sampaio Ribeiro, *Livraria*, pp. 156–59.

58. This table lists only names that survive, on the copies or elsewhere. A number of other copies do show evidence of the geographical area of early ownership: for example, the Paris copy of the second book of Lamentations (1506) has manuscript annotations in Italian; and the London copy of La Rue's masses (1503) was probably bound in Cologne, ca.1538. Other sets, including those at Chatsworth, at the Marucelliana in Florence, and at Zurich, have probably been together since the sixteenth century. For more on this point, see below, with Table 10-5.

59. David Fallows has confirmed (in a private communication) that the three *Canti* books

now in Paris were originally part of Colón's collection. It is also possible that the copies of the first three frottola volumes now in private possession in Madrid come from the same source. I have not been able to see these books, but they are apparently bound with a manuscript collection of Spanish music, in a manner typical of the Colombina.

60. The text is transcribed in the chapter of documents. This series of bifolia, all written by Gaspari, were originally bound in the library's copy of Schmid, *Petrucci*, at I-Bc, P. 59. The fifth bifolium contains various notes on Petrucci editions as well as the transcription of comments by Bottrigari included here. Other bifolia also contain notes on printed music: the second concerns Scotto and later music; the third includes a transcription of the title page of Schmid, *Petrucci*, and references to the *Gazzetta Musicale di Milano*, viii (nos.40 and 43) (1850), where "il Sigr. Malfatti diede copiose notizie di Ottaviano Petrucci"; the fourth contains references to Petrucci in Zacconi's, *Prattica*, i, ch.79, p. 84, and to Draudius, *Bibliotheca classica*; while the sixth lists Petrucci's editions held in I-Bc at the time.

61. This seems likely given the spotty representation, for example, of frottole volumes.

62. The earliest necessary date is 31 October 1503, for La Rue's mass collection. All the earlier titles are either missing (Josquin's first book, *Canti B*, masses by Obrecht and Brumel, *Motetti B*) or could be represented by later editions (*Odhecaton A, Motetti A*, masses by Ghiselin).

63. There is a copy of the first book of *Motetti de la Corona*, with the date of 1514, but it is also identified as a *Libro Primo*, which means that it comes from one of the later re-editions.

64. This catalogue was studied in detail in Jayne and Johnson, *Lumley*. A more recent examination of the musical entries, and of Lumley's collection, is Milsom, "Nonsuch".

65. Selwyn, *Library*, traces the history and dispersal of Cranmer's library. On p. 9 he remarks that Cranmer "had an unusually comprehensive collection of almanacs and treatises on the sphere".

66. See Rasch and Wind, "Music", p. 345. The authors speculate that these books may have come from "pre-Reformation Leiden ecclesiastical possession" (p. 339).

67. Apparently Cavallini omitted to mention the second book of Josquin's masses. It is evident, from the different colors of the page-edges, that the Josquin volumes were at one time separate from the rest of the set. When they were combined, there was probably a divider-folio between the last of the original series, the *Fragmenta Missarum*, and the first of the Josquin.

68. More than any other evidence (e.g., the lack of citations in early sources, or the contents of Colón's collection), this suggests that there are no new books of mass settings yet to be discovered.

69. This number is true if, as seems probable, the Ghiselin and Josquin copies come from Fossombrone printings.

70. The list of musical works in Gesner's *Pandectae* has been transcribed and studied by Lawrence Bernstein, in "Bibliography".

71. I have grave problems with this entry, and with the implication that it represents a specific publication by Petrucci. For a detailed discussion, see chapter 14.

72. The details are given with the other documents, transcribed in chapter 20. All the titles in this section suggest that Gesner had not seen any of the books; his informant was aware of the books and also of their contents, but was not concerned to represent the titles accurately.

73. This reference was suggested by Lawrence Bernstein in his study; to me, the implication is of a reference to four editions published in different places, and at different times. In addition, this title does not correspond to any published by Petrucci.

74. Krummel, *Bibliotheca* presents a facsimile and commentary on the musical sections of this bibliography.

75. Despite the layout of the entry, I assume that it contains two items. The first, *RISM* 1545², is a close fit for the *Concentus octo, sex, quinque & quatuor vocum, omnium iucundissimi* (Augsburg: Ulhard, 1545).

76. Krummel, *Bibliotheca*, p. 93, identifies this entry as having only three components. However, following Bolduanus's normal practice, the phrase "In. Cantus 50". should refer to a separate item. It is tempting to suggest that it referred to the edition of Martini's hymns, but Bolduanus never uses the abbreviation "In" to refer to hymns.

Further, Krummel sees the first item as referring to the *Odhecaton*, thereby relating it to the last two in the entry. However, the wording, as well as the mention of thirty-three items, clearly implies that the writer was referring to *Motetti A*: the connection of "Motettæ" and "Cantus" in this entry may relate to a German use of the two terms.

77. The entries from Draudius have been taken from Heussner and Schultz, *Collectio*, p. 18.

78. One Italian bibliographer may have referred to editions by Petrucci: James Haar, in "Libraria", p. 115, notes a reference in Doni's *Prima Libraria* (Venice: Giolito, 1550) to "Messe Di Iosquino cinque libri". Haar remarks that this might refer to editions from Petrucci's press or from Pasoti and Dorico (in 1526). Given Haar's point that Doni seems to have been aware of Gesner's bibliography, I think it more likely that Doni took this reference from the earlier writer. Gesner's reference to "Misse quinque" could then be taken by Doni to refer to five books, rather than five masses.

On p. 117 of the same article, Haar rightly doubts that Doni's reference to "di diversi a 4 et a cinque parecchi libri Magnificat & lamentationi" might relate to Petrucci's editions.

79. The surviving evidence for Aldus Manutius's contacts with his market, for example, is hardly likely to have been typical of the patterns adopted by other printers. This is certainly known to be true for the manner in which Aldus prepared his catalogues of books.

80. There is little point in discussing here the many editions of local ordinances, city statutes, or practices for religious orders that were printed by an establishment based in the city or commissioned by a leader within the order. In these cases, the dissemination of the edition rested more with the patron—the city or order—than it did with the printer. The patron would, after all, have commissioned the edition and probably have paid for it *en bloc*, taking all the copies for direct sale or distribution. This situation is also exemplified not much later by much of the output of Blado or others appointed as Printer to the Vatican or Printer in another city.

81. For the life of Jenson, see Lowry, *Nicholas*.

82. Perhaps not so different was the manner in which Madonna Paola, who had taken as her second husband the printer Rinaldus of Nijmegen, then married off her daughter to an important bookseller, Gaspar of Dinslaken. These parties lived and worked in Venice at the time.

83. See, for example, the evidence of the early inventory of Corpus Christi College, Cambridge, given in Fletcher and McConica, "Inventory". The list includes books printed not only in Venice, but also in Paris, Lyons, and Basel, which the authors believe were acquired by the library soon after publication, as well as other books from Nürnberg, Strasburg, Cologne, Freiburg, and Milan. There is much similar evidence elsewhere: a copy of the Venetian 1499–1500 edition of Saxoferrato was owned by the Abbot of Cambuskenneth, residing in Edinburgh, before 1517 (Donaldson, "Cambuskenneth", p. 4); the British Library's copy of a Cicero *Epistolae*, printed by Spira in 1471 was in Britain by the end of the century (*BMC*, v, p. 158); Cicero's *Epistolae ad familiares*, the work of the 1480 Martial printer, was in Leyston near Aldeburgh early in its life (*BMC*, v, 296); and an undated Isocrates was bound with a 1503 edition of Juvenal by Spierinck in Cambridge (*BMC*, v, 475). Then, too, many of the books in the Lumley collection seem to have reached Britain fairly early: see Jayne and Johnson, *Lumley*. Here, as in the other footnotes to the present paragraph, my examples are no more than samples, taken from one or two secondary sources to illustrate a pattern that has been demonstrated much more thoroughly in many studies within the bibliographical literature. Finally, there is the evidence advanced in Needham, "Continental", with the advantage of being both dated and specific.

84. Many examples of early ownership of this kind can be found in early library catalogues and even more clearly in surviving copies. The few dated examples are particularly interesting: some can be found in volume 2 of the *BMC*, and in the manuscript annotations to it that appear in the undated lithographic reprint, published in the 1960s. See, as an example, the copy of the *Buch der Weisheit der alten Weisen*, printed in Ulm by Dinckmut in 1485, owned by "Closter Vieborg" in Jutland, Denmark (p. 534). Archbishop William Scheves of St. Andrews in Scotland bought a copy of the 1485 Basel edition of S. John Cassian in Louvain in 1491 (Cherry, "Library", p. 63). The British Library copy of Balbi's *Catholicon*, printed in Nürnberg in 1483, was apparently in England soon after (see *BMC*, ii, p. 424). Less convincing are the many citations of ownership dating from some time after the book was printed. A typical example is the copy

of Koberger's Nürnberg (1486) edition of Pius II's *Epistolae familiares* in the British Library, which has seventeenth-century annotations from Bratislava (*BMC*, ii, p. 430).

85. The same catalogue of the incunables in the British Library includes examples of this. Here I list a few only where there are dates of both printing and possession (giving the two dates, and the page number in *BMC*): Milan editions: in Baden (1475, 1481: ii, p. 730); and in Buxheim (1479, s.d.: ii, p. 740). Bolognese editions: in Flügelsberg (1494, 1496: ii, p. 827); and in Ulm (1489, 1503: ii, p. 824). Three Treviso editions, printed in 1476 (ii, p. 887), 1478 (ii, p. 893), and 1482 (ii, p. 898), are found in Ingolstadt by 1516. William of Occam's *Sumulae physicorum* (Bologna, Hector, 1494) was bound for the monastery of Tergensee, with books from Lyons and Memmingen, printed the same year (ii, p. 606).

Many Venetian editions reached northern Europe and had been bought within a few years (and are listed in volume 5)—at Augsburg (1491, 1493: p. 326), Bruges (1475, 1479: p. 193), Erfurt (1470, 1472: p. 154), the Buxheim Charterhouse (p. 155), Fürstenfeld (1484, 1491: p. 288), Lilienfeld (1479, 1483: p. 272), Munich (1498, 1502: 387), Prüfening (near Regensburg: 1500, 1502: p. 331), Regensburg (1484, 1486: 398), and Tegernsee (1493, 1496 and 1496/97, 1497, among others: pp. 392 and 531). The evidence of bindings, of institutional ownership marks from later but implying an ongoing possession of the book, or of undated entries would increase the amount of detail in this picture considerably.

86. Fifteenth-century examples with music are provided in Meyer-Baer, *Liturgical* (or, for Italian printers, in Duggan, *Italian*), and the next century is being covered by David Crawford's database, RELICS. From the years in which Petrucci was preparing to print, as well as those of his early activity, the following provide a representative sample:

> 1498 Agenda for Passau (Venice: Hamman); Breviary for Cologne (Venice: Hamman)
>
> 1499 Missals for Esztergom (Venice: Emerich) and for Pècs (Venice: Emerich)
>
> 1500 Missals for Salisbury (Paris: Higman and Hopyl) and for Segovia (Venice: Emerich)
>
> 1501 Manual for Salisbury (Rouen: Olivier and de Lorraine)
>
> 1502 Breviary for Salzburg (Venice: Liechtenstein); Missal for Hereford (Rouen: Olivier and Mauditier)
>
> 1503 Missal for Prague (Nürnberg: Stuchs)
>
> 1504 Missal for Augsburg (Venice: Emerich for Giunta)
>
> 1505 Missal for Bratislava (Augsburg: Lotter)

In fact, there are many other editions of the Sarum Missal, printed in Paris and Rouen during this period. In addition, other, non-musical, parts of the liturgy were also often printed on the Continent for British dioceses: for example, at least four Breviaries for Salisbury and one for York were printed in Venice before 1500.

87. See the description of this catalogue in *BMC*, ii, pp. 417–18.

88. ASV, Senato, Terra, Reg.XXIX. f.53r–v (new 474r–v). The document has been recorded before and is discussed in Agee, *Privilege*, pp. 73–75 (with a transcription on pp. 207–208). See also Thibault, "Notes", pp. 61–65; Heartz, *Attaingnant*, pp. 124–25; Bernstein, "Couronne" (1973), p. 58; Glixon, *Music*, i, p. 228.

89. I go rather further than Agee, *Privilege*, pp. 74–75, in believing that the musical reference is to *RISM* 1536[4]. There is no reason to doubt that Torresano or anyone else could have received books from Paris within a few months of their first appearance in that city. I find the application strange in a number of ways. First, Torresano does not appear to have printed any of the texts for which he sought a privilege; there is no evidence that he ever printed maps or music; the demand for maps of France ("desegni di tutta la franza") cannot have been any greater than that for chansons; some of the non-musical texts had been printed by Aldus, and presumably the remaining stock had passed to Torresano; finally, two volumes of *Canzone francese* had recently appeared in Venice, from the hand of Antico and the press of Scotto. I am tempted to believe that Torresano had no intention of actually printing any of the volumes listed in his application, but was merely trying to ensure that no one else would print or import them before he could receive replacement copies from Paris. It is notable, in this context, that the restriction and punishment are repeated in the approval that follows the petition as copied in the manuscript,

whereas normally the rubrics merely affirm the terms of the petition. Perhaps a member of the Senate or a scribe to that body was in close contact with Torresano.

90. The instances of Gardano printing the French repertoire might suggest that few copies were being shipped from one end of the line to the other, thereby making the new editions viable. I believe that they argue, instead, that a number of copies of the earlier French editions, and of related volumes, had appeared in Italy, and that they had stimulated an active interest in the repertoire concerned and therefore encouraged the Venetian printers in their belief that their editions would be commercially viable.

91. Pollard and Ehrman, *Distribution*, p. 25.

92. Ibid., pp. 7–8. The latter instance is probably one of mutual interaction between the Koberger's and their agency.

93. Barberi, "Calvo"; Hirsch, *Printing*, pp. 75–77. The section of Calvo's letter containing his list of requests is reproduced in Hirsch, *Printing*, opposite p. 112.

94. Pollard and Ehrman, *Distribution*, p. 25. Raven, "Selling", p. 5 points out that most local shops selling books were not specialist book-shops, but general stores. He uses this point to emphasise the importance of traveling salesmen.

95. See Chapman, *Antico*, pp. 451–52.

96. See Grimaldi, *Capella*, p. 90.

97. In 1676 Codogno provided a list of the most important fairs in Italy and elsewhere, specifically as a service to merchants and others who were reading his book. Among the fifty-three that he cited for Italy, Recanati stands out for its long duration. Many fairs, even in major centers, lasted between three and eight days, and others for up to fifteen days. The fair at Recanati, however, ran for two full months, from 15 September "fino alli 15. di Novembre", and was matched only by that at Osimo (southwest of Ancona), which ran from "1 d'Apr. e dura tutto Magg[io]". The nearest in length were those at Pesaro, from 15 November (immediately after Recanati) "e dura fino à Nat[ale]", Foligno, from 25 April "e dura per tutto Maggio", Rimini, from 20 June "fino a S. Giacomo" (presumably James the Greater, in late July), and Cesena and Faenza (both lasting for the whole of a month, August and September respectively). (See Codogno, *Nuovo Itinerario*, pp. 441–48.) It is notable that these particularly lengthy fairs lie in an arc in the eastern half of Italy, and had been within the Papal States. Although Codogno was describing the situation nearly two hundred years later than Petrucci's time, by then these fairs had long histories, and the Recanati fair, in particular, was known throughout the central peninsula. The best study of Italian fairs remains Zdekauer, *Fiera*.

98. Potter, "Zoppino", pp. 139–42. Elsewhere in this article, Potter also demonstrates the Venetian use of the group of cities down the Adriatic coast, and a series of potential connections between Venetian printers and Perugian printers, craftsmen, and authors. Fogelmark, *Flemish*, p. 74, makes the unsubstantiated remark that "we know that at the book fairs in Frankfurt and Lyon, not only publishers, printers, and stationer/bookbinders were present, but also representatives of other trades connected with book production, such as typefounders and suppliers of bookbinding equipment". I am sure that this was also true for the Marche in the sixteenth century, a period when many jobbing printers were trying to earn a living in one or another of the nearby cities.

99. Göhler, *Verzeichnis*. See also the important comments in Raven, "Selling", on the significance of the earlier fairs.

100. Mischiati, *Indici*.

101. Pollard and Ehrman, *Distribution*. See especially the tables on pp. 32–39 and the details on pp. 282–88. Additional information for the earlier years appears in Hirsch, *Printing*, pp. 63–65, while a recent survey of sale catalogues of "Tipografici, Editoriali, di Librai, Bibliotecari" is given in Serrai, *Storia*, iv, 5–75.

102. Two of Aldus's catalogues are reproduced in facsimile in Orlandi, *Aldo*, as plate 9 (opposite p. 22), and plates 10–13 (between pp. 78 and 79). The second of these is particularly interesting for it carries Aldus's own annotations of prices.

103. Gesner, *Bibliotheca universalis, Pandectarum libri XXI* (Zurich, 1548), f.21r. It seems to me that the sporadic representation of music in Gesner's books suggests that he had not had

good access to catalogues listing musical editions. For a discussion and presentation of the musical entries in his bibliographies, see Bernstein, "Gesner".

104. Presented in Pollard and Ehrman, *Distribution*, p. 281.

105. Comments about the durability of music editions are made below. Here it is sufficient to point out that the same pattern seems to hold for other titles as well. The rapid turnover of editions that we assume from the competitive applications for privileges entered in the Venetian archives is probably not a true reflection of the state of affairs. At this point, it becomes necessary to reconsider the profitability of the book trade as a whole. Clearly, stock *did* move slowly, and its retention in the publishing house or the *libraio's* store apparently did not represent an intolerable burden on the accounts.

106. See, for example, the stocklist printed in Brown, *Venetian*.

107. Offenbacher, "Bibliothèque"; Lowry, *World*, pp. 274–76.

108. Using the translation in Lowry, *World*, p. 274.

109. Buchwald, "Archivalische", pp. 7–10.

110. Pogue, "Editor" is a discussion of the relationship between editions from these two houses.

111. The evidence for this lies most clearly in the dates of publication of Venetian editions and of their northern counterparts.

112. Morell, "Knoff". Incidentally, there is no reason to believe that this was in any way exceptional. Some measure of the existence of a similar market in England is provided by the study of an Oxford bookseller, Robert Martin, in Krummel, "Venetian".

113. I except Antico, whose relations with Petrucci can hardly have allowed for this sort of cooperation. It is possible that Caneto or de Frizis in Naples was an agent or contact for Petrucci, which might explain the attempt each made to print on his own account. It might also relate to the evidence that Petrucci lent some typographical material to a Neapolitan: see Gialdroni and Ziino, "New Light".

114. Potter, "Zoppino" suggests, on p. 140, that Perugian printers went to Recanati on occasion.

115. There are also implications for the financial side of his business, for the number of copies that would turn a profit, and for the number that might actually be printed.

116. Here, as often, an exception has to be made for German-speaking lands. There the well-documented interest in music of Josquin's generation would have made Petrucci's books still of interest to musicians: among interested musicians was Glareanus, who prepared some of the examples in his *Dodecachordon* (1547) from Petrucci's editions.

117. Mischiati, *Indici*. See also the evidence offered in Agee, *Gardano*, pp. 361–405, transcribing Angelo Gardano's 1591 catalogue, and the patterns indicated in Vanhulst, "Balthasar"; and Vanhulst, "Plantin". The first item in Krummel's analysis of the Martin catalogues (Krummel, "Venetian") is a treatise that was seventy years old when advertised: this alongside another that had been out for nearly fifty, and music that had been published for sixteen, nineteen, twenty, or forty-four years—and much more that was hot off the press.

118. Chapman, "Printed", pp. 44 and 48.

119. Marín Martinez et al., *Catálogo*, nos.79, 96, 922, 426, and 160.

120. See Plamenac, "Excerpta", pp. 681–82 and 684–85.

121. This book survives in the Colombina, as 6-3-26 (13), one of a collection of thirty-five books of Italian verse, all bought in late 1515, and mostly in Rome. The entry from Colón's *Registrum B* is transcribed in Plamenac, "Excerpta", p. 675.

122. Marín Martinez et al., *Catálogo*, nos.362, 362, 523, 546, 444, and 712.

123. To my knowledge, no one has discussed the possibility that a number of the books bought by Colón were really second-hand, bought from earlier owners or from dealers who themselves had bought from owners. The first volume listed in the *Registrum B* (reproduced in Huntington, *Catalogue*) is Albertus of Padua's *Expositio evangelorum*, printed in Venice in 1476 and bought by Colón in London in 1522. During the same month, he bought a 1481 edition from Louvain of William of Occam's *Epitoma*. (This is no.6 in the same catalogue.) The general evidence of the slow movement of printed books, including musical volumes, does not invalidate this possibility: it means that it is in general unlikely, while remaining possible in individual

cases. But many of the manuscripts he bought must surely have been "secondhand"; in such cases, as in any concerning printed books, the prices may well have been set on a different scale.

124. These books have been discussed in Cusick, *Dorico*. This interest in "old" music continues throughout the century. There is clear-cut evidence in Angelo Gardano's catalogue (see fn. 117, above) not only that old editions remained available but, in several cases, that old music was still being actively reprinted. I have discussed this interest in Boorman, "Bibliographical".

125. The word "immediately" is dangerous here, of course. A successful publisher could take a longer view than could many smaller printers and arrange for one important but slower-moving volume, to be balanced by a more popular book, a local decree, or a commissioned work.

126. Boorman, "Bibliographical".

127. Chapman, *Andrea*, pp. 451–52. The price was twenty giulii, or fifteen for wholesale purchases.

128. A Magister Simon bought "un libro di 15 messe in canto figurato" at the fiera di Recanati on 3 October 1516 (Grimaldi, *Cappella*, p. 90).

129. The details are presented in Blackburn, "Printing".

130. There are not enough data for us to know why there was a difference: whether because the book came from Naples, or because it contained "motets". Size was not the most significant factor; the books by Antico were priced identically, even though they ranged from forty to seventy-two folios.

131. Of course, this is an exercise in fanciful accounting. We have no way of knowing how Petrucci, or Antico or anyone else, estimated the costs of equipment, of setting up and maintaining the shop, of depreciation, or of any of the many items that affected pricing. Here, I am tacitly assuming that each printer and each publisher worked to a similar set of criteria, and that, therefore, the figures quoted by Blackburn can be used as a yardstick for other editions.

132. This table assumes a six-day working week, and the exclusion of a few particular feasts, Christmas Day, Good Friday, All Saints' Day. Some writers assume as many as fifty worker's holidays each year in sixteenth-century Venice. One or two of Petrucci's editions are actually dated on Sundays, and this may imply a full seven-day week. See, for this table, *Canti C* and *Motetti C* in 1504, and *Frottole VII* in 1507.

133. Earlier editions moved more slowly, simply because they involved a third impression. But the editions of 1502 and early 1503 show a marked increase in speed:

Date of Edition:	Title	Number of Sheets	Number of Days Available (Days per Sheet)	Rate of Work
Saturday, 5.ii.1502	*Canti B*			
Monday, 9.v.1502	*Motetti A*	14	78	5.6
[no date: cancel leaves for	*Odhecaton A*	2	)	
			)121	5.4
Tuesday, 27.ix.1502	*Misse Josquin*	24 2/2	)	
Saturday, 14.i.1503	*Odhecaton A★*	26	92	3.5
Friday, 24.iii.1503	*Misse Obrecht*	18 1/2	59	3.2

Although it is dangerous to interpret these figures, they do suggest a group of craftsmen slowly learning the business of printing music. The end result is not far from the standard rate of one sheet per day, given the need for three impressions at this time.

134. Brown, *Venetian*, p. 76. This rate seems to have been an industry norm for most books. Stevenson, *Problem*, p. 316, fn.IX.14, states that it was normal after the 1470s. Gerritsen, "Printing", p. 154, gives some data about the number of typesorts that might be set in a day.

135. "And I do not wish that he should print less than one folio per day". Agee, "Contract", pp. 59–61. The word "foglio" here means a complete sheet and presumably refers to both formes. Scotto apparently took fourteen weeks over the book, if he received his final

payment a mere two days after completing the book, for that was made ninety-nine days after the due date for beginning work. At a six-day week, that implies eighty-four sheets for all of the parts. At twenty-one sheets per partbook, this would imply a massive volume. However, it is unlikely that Scotto worked at this, or any other book, full time, but rather divided his men between several books.

There were of course many exceptions to this pattern. Callierges printed his 1500 edition of Galen between 7 September and 5 October: this results in 117 folios in (presumably) twenty-four working days, or five folios per day (Brown, *Venetian*, p. 44, fn.6). Other exceptions no doubt involve the division of work between two or more teams of craftsmen.

136. Stevenson, *Problem*, p. 316, fn.IX.14.

137. See Povey, "Variant".

138. See the citations in Gaskell, *New*, pp. 139–41.

139. Gaskell, *New*, presents interesting figures to illustrate the relative costs of labor and materials, and the risks of tying up too much capital in a stock of printed copies. He also draws attention to the point that the print-run for specially commissioned editions could always be much smaller. For the middle of the century, Grendler, *Critics*, pp. 179–80, has some figures and suggests that "one can infer that the works of Landi, Franco, and Doni published by large, active printers such as Giolito and Marcolini possibly ran to about 2,000 copies while editions by small Venetian and non-Venetian printers were probably smaller, running from a few hundred to a little over a thousand". His figures include 1,800 for Dolce's translation of Ovid's *Metamorphoses* (Giolito, 1553), and a mere 300 for Lando's *Forcianae Quaestiones*, printed in Naples in 1536. See also McKenzie, "Printers".

140. Scholderer, "Printers and Readers", p. 205, where he adds that this "is possibly an understatement". Bühler, in *University*, p. 18. notes an edition of 500 copies for Johannes de Imola's *Repetitiones super capitulo*, printed by Malpigi at Bologna in 1476, and that 184 copies were still unsold in 1484. He adds that the copy in US-NYpm was bought in 1502.

Stevenson has developed an elegant method of attempting to determine the possible range of edition sizes, based on the distribution of different papers in two volumes. While he reaches no conclusions, his argument does provide a series of possibilities, which can be weighed with other evidence. See Stevenson, *Problem*, pp. 86–91. Given the number of cancels and supplementary printings already apparent, the method seems inconclusive for Petrucci's output.

141. Agee, "Venetian Music", with the addition of Blackburn, "Printing".

142. An example of the first can be seen in the bibliography to the present work, in Gentile, *Nozze*. I am sure that it was no less true for the editions of music for the wedding celebrations of 1539 or 1589. As an instance of the second, the Bishop of Fossombrone commissioned a calendar of Saints' days for the diocese, as late as 1952.

143. This must have been particularly true of those many liturgical books commissioned of Venetian or other printers by bishops and cardinals from dioceses far away.

144. These arrangements seem to have been particularly characteristic of the pattern of publishing psalters and lay tune-books in the Low Countries. I am sure that there was a verbal agreement to make the next edition one of so many copies, but I doubt that it needed a full-blown contract.

145. Among those publishers there were some who also prepared musical editions, including Blado in Rome, and Baldini in Ferrara.

146. This must surely apply to those Venetian editions put out by Petrucci, when he decided to reprint them in Fossombrone.

147. No printer would have sought a contract if he were about to produce a speculative edition of Arcadelt's madrigals or the Gero duos. Indeed, printers seem to have seen those books as sure moneymakers, and a good way to start up a business in music.

148. The last two of these are instances in which calculations of the minimum number of copies that would yield a profit would be most valuable. The printer or publisher had no outside commitment, and (especially if he were experienced in the field) his calculation of the edition size should be more directly related to the size of the potential market. I have drawn attention to the role of editions of Arcadelt's madrigals as speculative ventures and have dis-

cussed the implications of many editions for estimates of edition size, in "Bibliographical evidence", a forthcoming conference paper.

149. Antico printed 1,008 copies of his *Liber Quindecim Missarum* in 1516. He, like Petrucci, would have benefited from the presence of many senior churchmen and some of their establishments, at the Lateran Council, and we know that he reached similar buyers. The Fugger owned a copy and so did the Casa Santa at Loreto. (See Schaal, "Musikbibliothek", 1/18, and Grimaldi, *Cappella*, p. 90.) Churches including S. Giovanni Laterano (the copy now in I-Rvat) and S. Luigi dei Francesi in Rome had copies and so did Guatemala Cathedral. (See Perkins, "Notes", p. 60, and Stevenson, *Renaissance*, p. 50.)

150. These claims appear in various places. I am more of the opinion that every courtier was expected to be able to perform verse in a musical manner, and perhaps provide a very simple accompaniment. There is little here to affirm that each one could also read notation, or hold a part in a contrapuntal setting.

151. I am thinking here not of the *Liber Quindecim Missarum*, but of some of his frottola volumes, and especially that of keyboard arrangements.

152. On the other hand, I suspect that all the musical volumes published in Rome between 1519 and 1527 by anyone other than Pasoti and Dorico were probably commissioned books. This is the only sensible explanation for the pattern of isolated books (which would still hold even if twice as many were to be discovered).

153. We need to remember that, compared with a composer, an editor or a patron, the printer or publisher was in a strong position in almost all situations: he could require delivery of paper before being willing to print; having printed the copies, he could demand payment before releasing them; and failing payment, he could himself dispose of the copies. The commissioner of a volume, however, could not force the printer to print before payment.

154. Bonnie Blackburn's recent work on Castellanus, in her "Petrucci", strengthens this point. When writing my dissertation, I was still able to argue that Padua A17 was probably copied from Petrucci's editions. Given Castellanus's biography, it is much more likely, as she argues, that Petrucci's music came from the same sources as did Padua, with Castellanus as the intermediary in each case. This reduces significantly the number of manuscripts that can be shown to have been copied from Petrucci's books of liturgical music.

155. See my review of Weaver, *Waelrant*, in the *Journal of the Royal Musical Association* 122 (1997), pp. 119–27.

156. There are cases where a motet can be adapted, so that the name of a local saint chosen by the composer is replaced by a different one, chosen by the scribe to reflect the new needs of the new institution. There are even cases where this happens with motets published by Petrucci. But these are in the minority—both because the majority of Latin texts are for the universally commemorated occasions, and because singers could evidently change the name of a saint during rehearsal and performance.

157. Bernstein, "Couronne" is valuable here.

158. This is the group of manuscripts with which Atlas developed musical applications of stemmatic theory: see Atlas, *Cappella*.

159. The most obvious group of exceptions concerns the new polyphonic foundations in cathedrals such as Bergamo, Casale Monferrato, or Padua; these institutions, while looking for new repertoire, also preserved their sources in the manner of older foundations. They can be paralleled by a few private collections, most notably that collected by the Amerbach family.

160. See Stevenson, "Toledo".

161. Kmetz, *Handschriften*, pp. 54–57.

162. Ibid., p. 58. According to Kmetz, both sources come from the same area within reach of Basel and should be dated between 1503 and 1520.

163. Bente, *Neue*, pp. 147–48, makes it clear that these two masses were part of an independent fascicle, probably copied ca.1515, and later bound into this manuscript.

164. Thomas Noblitt, in "Textual", proposed a number of stemmata with northern manuscripts directly descending from Petrucci's editions. He suggests that Josquin's *Missa Fortuna Desperata* was copied from the first book of his masses (1502) into *RISM* 1538[1] and indirectly into *RISM* 1539[1], that his "little" *Ave Maria* was transmitted from *Motetti A* to CH-SGs

463, D-Mbs Mus.Ms.322–325 (and thence to the *Dodecachordon*) and D-Usch 237[a-d], as well as I-Fn II.I.232; and that Petrucci's version of Obrecht's *Missa Je ne demande* was the basis for the citations in Heyden, Faber (1553), and Wilphlinseder's *Erotemata* of 1563.

165. See Senn, "Sammelwerk"; Staehelin, "Petrucci".

166. These three books are *RISM* (ca.1535)[14]. A sequence of seventeen works in the first book comes from Petrucci's *Canti B*; and much of the third is based on that edition and the *Odhecaton*. Something of the impact of Öglin's editions can be seen in the extent to which they were used in the preparation of D-HB X.2, a manuscript appendix to *RISM* 1541[2], probably copied ca.1550 in Frankfurt. See Siegele, *Musiksammlung*, pp. 42–48.

167. Pieces 1–12 and 122–27 are apparently copied directly from Petrucci's *Canti C*. On this manuscript, see Bente, Göllner, and Wackernagel, *Chorbücher*, 92–101; Whisler, *Munich*.

168. Fallows, *Catalogue*, p. 52, asserts that this scribe copied specific works from Petrucci, and others can be added to his list. For the manuscript, which was owned by Stephen Roth, ca.1533–45, see Brown, "Zwickau"; and Vollhardt, *Bibliographie*.

169. For this manuscript, CH-SGs 461, see Geering, *Vokalmusik*, and Fallows, *Songbook*.

170. Marx, "Neues". The manuscript is CH-SGs, 530, now edited as Marx and Warburton, *St. Galler*. See also Nef, *St. Galler*.

171. *RISM* 1536[13]=N522; Brown, *Instrumental*, 1536₇. The sequence of pieces from no.2 to no.31 is based on Petrucci's editions, with the single exception of no.10, which is an organ piece. It may be that Petrucci was the immediate source for Newsidler, and that his published anthology merely reflects the ordering of pieces in his manuscript collection of intabulations.

172. Bridgman, "Manuscrit".

173. *RISM* BIV[5], pp. 45–50; Atlas, *Giulia*; Torchi, *Monumenti*; Weiss, "Bologna"; Weiss, *Manuscript*.

174. *RISM* BIV[5], pp. 141–50; Becherini, *Catalogo*, pp. 118–22; Jeppesen, *Frottola*, ii, pp. 37–42.

175. Cattin, *Italian*; Cattin, "Nuova fonte"; Cattin, "Tradizione".

176. Anglès, "Manuscrit"; Baker, *Segovia*; Perales de la Cal, *Cancionero*.

177. Incidentally, there is reason to believe that Antico took a number of the compositions in his first book, the *Canzoni Nove* of 1510, from earlier editions by Petrucci, especially Books 4 and 7. In particular, this is likely for many of the pieces numbered 20–33 in Antico's edition, given the pattern of abbreviations in attributions.

178. Pirrotta, "Florence", pp. 7–8. The quotation in the next sentence comes from p. 8.

179. This waning interest can be confirmed from the tables of contents and concordances laid out in Jeppesen *Frottola*, volume 2.

180. There remains the issue of the curious pattern of attributions in this manuscript and Petrucci's sources, suggesting the presence of an intermediary.

181. See Fallows, "Josquin", p. 75, fn. acknowledging Rifkin's work.

182. Heyden, *De arte* (both the edition and the facsimile); Teramoto and Brinzing, *Katalog*, no.3.

183. Glareanus, *Dodecachordon*.

184. H. Finck, *Practica musica*.

185. Judd, "Reading"; Bent, "Accidentals".

186. Zacconi, *Prattica*, f.84*v*.

Chapter Eleven

PETRUCCI'S TECHNICAL LEGACY

he patterns of dissemination of Petrucci's editions and the manner in which later printers and scribes repeated and changed his repertorial decisions are important aspects of his legacy. Equally important, however, is the manner in which his technical innovations and procedures spread, in Italy and other parts of Europe. These issues are, of course, related to the larger question of printing music at all, and that topic is discussed a little in the next chapter. Here, the concern is solely with technical issues.

It is significant, if not surprising, that Antico printed exclusively from woodblocks. He called himself *miniator*,[1] presumably a decorator (perhaps even an illuminator) of manuscript and printed pages. Although his hand has not been identified in any manuscripts (and there is no evidence to allow us to identify it), he probably had copied manuscripts for some time before his first publication in 1510. This would explain the competence in both notation and presentation found in his first volume, and account for the fluency of the borders and designs of his *Liber Quindecim Missarum* (1516), as well as the elegant impagination.

I doubt that we can say that Antico avoided using type in response to the power of Petrucci's privileges. He need not have worried much about the effect of any Venetian privilege, especially once he gained his own from the papal authorities. Indeed, the history of the two men's privileges argues that Antico carefully built his own base of protection during his time in Rome. Further, his choice of repertoire, at least in the first books, shows a conscious imitation of the most popular side of Petrucci's output—frottole.[2] We must therefore assume that Antico chose to ignore Petrucci's technical advances, preferring to follow his own strength and stay with single-impression woodblocks. In this, he would be followed by Sambonettus, in a single volume printed in Siena.

A number of the next books, however, do not follow Antico's practice. This is particularly true of some of the books produced in Rome after Antico's departure. Table 11-1 covers these, with other music books; in order to highlight the interrelationships, the entries are arranged not chronologically but according to the technique used and the characteristics of the staves.[3]

It is immediately obvious that group II, of five books, follows Antico in a number of respects. Indeed the first of these, printed by Mazzocchi in 1518 and published by Giunta, used Antico's own blocks. This book is distinguished from three of the next four by the repertoire; they try to be inclusive, with both motets and secular works. The last was, according to Colón, printed in Venice[4] and can be discounted for the moment. The other three are distinctive however: not only do they have a mixed repertoire, printed from woodblocks, they also use four

TABLE 11-1 Bibliographical details for some early editions

Date	RISM	Short Title	Printer	Texts[a]	Technique	Format	Staves[b]		
I									
1517	1517²	*Canzoni IV*	Antico/Giudici	I	Blocks[d]	4⁰, 8⁰	4	117	8-26-62
1520	1521¹	*I Missarum*	Antico	L	Blocks	4⁰, 4s	5	126	8-25-77
1521	1521³	*I Motetti*	Antico	L	Blocks	4⁰, 16s	5	117	8-26-81
II									
1518	1518	*III Canzoni*	Mazzocchi (Giunta)	I	Blocks[d]	8⁰, 4s	5	117	8-26-81
1520	[1521]⁶	*I Motetti e Canzone*	?	L/I	Blocks[e]	4⁰, 16s	4		10-32-72[c]
1521	1521⁴	*II Motetti*	?	L	Blocks[e]	8⁰, 4s	4	123	10-30-74
1523	[1526]⁵	*Fior de Motetti . . .*	?	L/I	Blocks[e]	4⁰, 4s	4	132	10-31-73
1524	[1521]⁷	*Motetti novi/canz.*	(Venice)	L/F	Blocks[e]	4⁰, 4s	5	122	8-26-75
III									
to 1519			Petrucci		Multiple[e]	4⁰, 8s	6	173-7	10-28-113
1520	P2451	*Pisano: Musica*	Petrucci	I	Multiple[e]	8⁰, 8s	4	131	10-31-73
?1533	—	*[Musica XII]*	Petrucci	I	Multiple[e]	4⁰, ?8s	5	157	10-30-97
1538	—	*[Motetti del Fiore]*	Petrucci	L	Multiple[e]	4⁰, 8s	5	157-8	10-32-96
IV									
?1526	[1530]¹	*I de la Fortuna*	[Giudici]	L/I/F	Multiple[e]	4⁰, 4s	4	115	12-33-75
1526	—	*Messe Motetti*	Giudici	L/I	Multiple[e]	4⁰	4	115	12-33-75[f]
1526	—	*Bosco: la Salamandra*	Giudici	?L		?8⁰			
V									
1521	E889	*Eustachio: Musica*	Pasoti	Inst.	Multiple[d]	4⁰, 4s	5	174	10-31-92
1522	1522	*Missarum Decem*	Pasoti (Giunta)	L	Multiple[e]	4⁰, 4s	5	173-4	10-31-92
1526	J669	*Josquin: I Missarum*	Pasoti & Dorico (Giunta)	L	Multiple[e]	4⁰, 8s	5	174	10-30-90
1526	1526⁶	*I de la Croce*	Pasoti & Dorico (Giunta)	I	Multiple[d]	4⁰, 4s	5	174	10-30-90
1526	1526¹	*I de la Corona*	Pasoti & Dorico (Giunta)	L	Multiple[e]	4⁰, 8s	5	174	10-30-90
?1530	[1530]²	*I de la Serena*	[?Pasoti or Dorico]	I	Multiple[e]	8⁰, 4s	4	134	10-30-70
1531	1531⁴	*II de la Croce*	Dorico (Giunta)	I	Multiple[d]	4⁰, 4s	5	175	10-30-90

[a] The letters stand for the languages used: F = French; I = Italian; and L = Latin.
[b] The colums for staves give the following data: normal number per page; average overall length; heights, of one stave, of two (with the text space between them), of all on the page. A blank in one of these columns indicates that I do not have the measurements.
[c] The distances between staves, and even their heights, vary considerably across the book.
[d] Choirbook format.
[e] In part-books.
[f] Jeppesen, "Unknown" asserts that the dimensions are the same as for the previous book.

staves per page, and the staves are approximately the same size. The earliest, the *Motetti e canzone libro primo* (*RISM* [1521]⁶), was clearly not prepared by Antico,⁵ although it shows a close awareness of his work, in the decorative elements in particular. A number of the initials are very close copies of those found in his earlier frottola volumes, and the G clef is also a direct imitation. These copies are so precise that the blockcutter must have had a copy of an Antico edition in front of him while preparing the new letters and clef. We have to assume that he did not have the actual blocks: for one thing, if he had had access to them, the printer could have used them; for another, they were probably already in Venice with Antico.⁶

Two people in Rome had had experience in producing an earlier Antico edition and might also have been inclined to attempt to emulate it: they were Giacomo Mazzocchi and Giacomo Giunta. The first had printed and signed two new editions of Antico's titles, the second and third books of frottole, in 1519 and 1518, respectively; the second had subsidised the 1518 edition. Either man is likely to have had some copies of one of these editions in hand. In addition, either (or both) probably estimated that there was an ongoing market for printed music in Rome; they would have known that Antico was planning to publish in Venice, for he took the blocks for the second book of frottole for his own edition, which can be dated in 1520.⁷ Indeed, this action ensured that they could not compete directly with him. However, the need for these second editions of the frottola books would have made them think that the market was large enough to support their editions as well. At the same time, they must also have known that Petrucci was back in business for secular music as well as sacred. His edition of Pisano's *Musica* had appeared in May, he had recently finished three books of motets, and he was reprinting earlier titles.

I suspect, however, that Mazzocchi was not responsible for preparing the edition of *Motetti e canzone libro primo*, although Giunta may have been willing to underwrite the volume to some extent.⁸ The printer would have been inclined to follow Antico's design and practice, for this was his only experience with music, and he would have required both special materials and skilled craftsmen if he were to have adopted Petrucci's methods. The printer of this book, however, follows a different plan, different sizes of staves and of pages.⁹ Further, the repertoire betrays a significantly different mind at work: it contains works by the same Roman favourites that Petrucci had recently presented—Mouton, Brumel, Moulu, de Silva, and Costanzo Festa—alongside "Eustachi", Rufino da Padova, Michele Pesenti, and Tromboncino. With the exception of Rufino, these last four composers had been represented in editions of secular music by both Petrucci and Antico.¹⁰ But this new printer attempted to keep away from Antico's current interests in secular music (the Tromboncino work is an *Ave Maria*) and avoided duplicating any compositions appearing in Petrucci's motet volumes.

Musically the most interesting aspect of the volume is the combination of sacred and secular in one collection. This cannot be compared with Petrucci's occasional inclusion of Latin-texted works in secular volumes, for those works are always on the level of private devotion or lauda-like compositions. Here, though, the book begins with a canonic six-voiced setting by Mouton (on the text *Salva nos domine*) and continues with a wide range of styles. In this respect, the book is unlike anything published previously: it seems to be attempting to catch as wide a market as possible, and to be tailored to Roman interests.

Whoever the printer of this book was, I believe he was also responsible for the *Fior de motetti e Canzone novi* of three years later.[11] (Again the stave measurements given above vary, within about 2 percent from page to page.) This book has the same approach to repertoire, including both sacred and secular, and again publishes works by composers featured in the last Petrucci volumes.[12] Further, it uses the same techniques, both in presswork and in blockcutting. Yet, there are two small developments. One is a new range of initial letters, which incorporate imitations of Petrucci, rather than those of Antico: some are newly cut (and one, at least, is modeled on Antico),[13] whereas others had appeared (apparently from the same blocks) in the earlier *Altus liber secundus* (1521).[14] The imitations of Petrucci's initials are very close, carefully cut, and clearly intended to summon up a connection in the minds of potential purchasers. It is notable that the staves have a spacing and height that follows Petrucci's pattern, although they are not as long. This book has been tentatively assigned to Giunta,[15] although he was a publisher and not a printer.

These three books were apparently related, in the minds of the printer and publisher; they present a similar face to the purchaser, in terms of the size and proportions of the staves, and of the style of decoration. This face seems designed to reflect Petrucci's approach to the musical layout, while adding echoes of Antico's books, through imitation of his letters.

The presence, in the *Fior de motetti e Canzone novi*, of a dedication, from Francesco Seraphin to Pomperio Colonna, a Roman cardinal, gives all three books a specifically Roman colour. In this connection, it is important that only one book in this group (or indeed among those attributable to Giudici) had a tightly defined repertoire; the implication must be that the market which Petrucci had reached (and that was to be addressed by Pasoti and Dorico) was no longer very well defined in the first years of this third decade, and that there were not enough purchasers of any single repertoire, at least in the Papal States, to support more than an occasional volume.

Two more books that attempted to sell a mixed repertoire came from the press of Nicolo Giudici, and are listed as section V of Table 11-1. They are the *Libro Primo de la Fortuna* and the book of *Messa Motetti Canzonni*, both of 1526,[16] to which must now be added the lost book of Bosco's *Musica de la Salamandra*.[17] These books are notable in that each is called a *Libro primo*, each that survives has a macaronic repertoire, and each imitates Petrucci in the use of a double-impression technique and in the style of some initials. Although the two extant books do not use any of Petrucci's material, indeed have a different proportion to the page, they seem again to attempt to capitalise on his reputation. In common with the earlier books, these are all in partbook format, no doubt largely because of the presence of the Latin-texted pieces as the first works.[18]

It seems likely, on technical and visual grounds, that these books, both those printed between 1520 and 1524 and the three new titles of 1526, represent two series of publishing ventures, even though all have either a similar view of the size and interests of the Roman market[19] (when there was not an editor [Seraphino] or composer [Bosco] interested in putting out a specific repertoire). It is difficult to see a single person might have been behind the two ventures. Giunta was probably not the man, despite his importance as a bookseller and publisher in Rome. As publisher, whenever he paid the costs of some volumes, he made sure that they bore his name or mark.[20] In addition, already in 1522, he had turned to Pasoti to print for him, and he probably had something to do with the lost editions of *Canzone de la Croce*. Whoever the backers were, they were probably the ones who decided on the imitations of Antico and Petrucci, decided that the market was not large enough for complete books of motets or masses (or even secular pieces), and commissioned the individual volumes.

It is unlikely that Giudici was the promoter of all the books.[21] His books are important for the history of music printing, for they are printed with a double-impression process, as is evident even from the photographs reproduced by Jeppesen.[22] The pattern of running the stave lines through the initial letters is highly indicative. In addition, it is possible to see that music sorts are cast and consistent, unlike wood-cut symbols. The significant feature is that sorts are distinctive according to their height on the stave. Thus, the *custodes* are not all identical, but all in the top space correspond to each other, as do those on the middle line. Similarly, the C clefs vary according to the line on which they are placed. This development is a crucial step in the emergence of single-impression printing in Italy; it required a much larger font, but allowed for typesetting in a straight line, without all the small pieces of spacing and furniture required by Petrucci. I have suggested that Petrucci had begun to experiment with sorts that were specific for each height on the stave, in his latest edition. This simple development bridged one of the two gaps between Petrucci's normal process and true single-impression printing; it removed the problem of the mosaic-like setting of the notation, without resolving the issue of overlapping notes and staves.[23]

But this was not the first multiple-impression printing after Petrucci's career had ended. Pasoti had printed two books, in 1521 (Eustachio Romano's *Duos*) and 1522 (*Missarum decem*), both using the technique. He then stopped and may have produced nothing until his collaboration with Dorico in 1526. This hiatus appears to correspond with the production of other Roman editions, ones I have already discussed, almost as if Pasoti's backers had switched allegiance, to other printers and other techniques. We know, however, of a lost group of three books of *Canzone de la Croce*, with Book III appearing in 1524,[24] and it is likely that Pasoti was involved in these three books, possibly with Dorico. The pair did print the second edition of Book 1 in 1526, with Giunta as publisher. This tends to support a theory that Giunta's interest did not spill over to supporting the other, woodblock editions, and it is possible that the printer of those editions had moved to Venice (where he prepared the 1524 *Motetti nove e canzone*), leaving Pasoti in Rome.

Pasoti is important for Petrucci's legacy.[25] Not only did he use double-impression printing, he also used some of Petrucci's materials in both the Eustachio *Duos* and the *Missarum decem*.[26] He did not have access to the whole of Petrucci's font, though this need not surprise us. Pasoti apparently had to have a number of new rests cast, for they have square ends quite unlike those used by Petrucci; for the *Duos*, he also had to use some sorts that Petrucci had needed very rarely—the void *fusa* and *semifusa*; and he evidently made his own clefs.

(Interestingly, clefs came to be seen as something of a fingerprint of a printer's font, although there is no reason to believe that printers would think in that manner for some years.) Other sorts are clearly cast from the same matrices as were Petrucci's: these include *minimas* with both ascending and descending tails, and colored *fusas*, whose measurements are identical to the older man's sorts. Certain clefs, the *signum congruentia*, many *custodes*, and the "3" used to indicate triplets seem to correspond to Petrucci's sorts. The staves also appear to have been Petrucci's, some even showing the same signs of distortion.[27] Finally, the manner of making ligatures is the same. Most ligatures are of two notes butted together, as one might expect, but many others have lines joining the two notes in an ink necessarily used in-house, and similar to Petrucci's.

The text font does not seem to correspond. This is not surprising, for such fonts were easy to acquire, and the older man is known to have retained some materials. But for Pasoti to be able to use many of Petrucci's matrices for music sorts would have been a great saving in labour and time. This kind of font was not otherwise available, and he would have to have commissioned one from a skilled designer, a craftsman cutter, and a typefounder.

This opportunity for Pasoti to use at least some of Petrucci's materials was significant for the future of music printing in Rome. It is even more significant for the bridge it provides between Petrucci and Dorico. Antico was not long gone from Rome, and examples of his work had been produced there in 1518 and 1519. At the same time some other publishers produced at least one book a year in 1520, 1521, and 1523. To launch into music during the same years, Pasoti must have had some practical experience, as well as an idea of the size and interests of the market, and (most importantly) some contacts with possible patrons and distributors. Remembering that Petrucci had visited Rome often enough, and that his last editions were probably sponsored by Romans, the presence of his type in Pasoti's workshop suggests a closer connection between the two men. So perhaps does the *Missarum decem* of 1522 (for which see chapter 14).

We know nothing of Pasoti's biography before he appears in 1521 with the first of his two early editions, so that it is conceivable that he (or one of his workmen) was in Petrucci's employ in Fossombrone. While this seems far-fetched, it is notable that printing craftsmen were famously mobile during the sixteenth century, moving anywhere they might find work. Given the inferior craftsmanship of Petrucci's last editions, and the curious pattern of different sets of staves in 1520, it is probable that he had hired a new craftsman. This man does not have to have been Pasoti. As I noted in chapter 1, Gialdroni and Ziino propose that it may have been Bartolomeo Egnatio, the papal chancery scribe who would later collaborate with Petrucci in at least one volume, and also acted for Petrucci's widow.[28] There is here a small nexus of relationships drawing Petrucci and Dorico closer, via Pasoti and Egnatio. Egnatio may indeed have been the direct contact between Petrucci and the new Roman press, but I am inclined to think that Pasoti must also have had earlier contacts with Petrucci; without them, it is difficult to understand why Petrucci's type materials should have passed to him, rather than Egnatio.

The *Missarum decem* uses some new typographical material. Many of the in-itials are imitations of Petrucci's, though the initials for the title pages follow the style of Antico's letters. It would not be surprising if Petrucci did not let these major artistic products out of his shop. Suzanne Cusick has argued plausibly[29] that Giunta supplied the new music font, for his name is prominently featured on the Cantus title page, while Pasoti's is only found in the colophon. In that case, Giunta must have been planning to launch a new series of editions of music, competing with other printers and publishers in Rome. He was probably also responsible for publishing the lost three books of *Canzoni de la Croce*, especially if Pasoti was involved in their production.

But the most obvious connection between Giunta, Pasoti and Dorico, and the best known between those two and Petrucci, is the series of volumes that they put out in 1526 and 1527. This comprised new editions of all three books of Josquin's masses and of all four books of the *Motetti de la Corona*. Again, we are faced with questions about the size of an edition and of the market. Evidently, the stock of Petrucci's editions had sold, and presumably were also unavailable from his Venetian partners. I believe that here, also, Petrucci must have allowed some of his unsold stock to go to Pasoti, or to whoever went from Fossombrone to Rome. This would explain why the Roman printers knew to publish all seven books.[30] The selection also provides an early sign of the pre-eminence of Josquin and the decline in repute of his contemporaries.

Significantly, one work was added to the series of *Motetti de la Corona*. Franciscus Seraphin provided a five-voiced setting of the *Ave Maria*, appended to the end of the second book in the series. It was probably added because of the different layout of Pasoti and Dorico's editions. With their different format, each voice-part of the second book went part-way into a third gathering: the material from Petrucci's edition would have ended on the third recto of the Bassus, and on the third verso of the Tenor. Seraphin's composition takes only one page and uses paper that would otherwise have been left blank.

Seraphin had appeared earlier, as the provider of two compositions and a dedication in the *Fior de Motetti* (1523). He had apparently built a connection with Pasoti and Dorico during the intervening time, and he may well have encouraged them to reprint the series. These activities make clear that he was probably resident in Rome, where he both could influence the earlier edition with its dedication, and persuade the new printers to add a work of his to the later one. This confirms the point made by Blackburn,[31] arguing that he was probably not the Seraphin who wrote to Del Lago. He may still be the man who appears in I-PEc 431, or the one whose music also survives in I-VEcap DCCLX.[32] This is another name to add to the small nexus of musicians and printers active in Rome in the years before the Sack.

The other seven books put out by the partnership during 1526 and 1527 have the same contents as the first editions, as far as we can tell.[33] All books show Petrucci's influence, even though more of the typographical material is now new. All also show the same care over presentation that had marked Petrucci's work: there are in-house corrections involving erasure and stamped-in readings, corrections in brown ink and apparently done in-house, some probable cancel leaves, and care over the visual appearance of the page. There is also the evidence of at least one re-edition, of the third book of the Corona series, in the following year.[34]

Thus it appears that Petrucci's most direct legacy was through the printer Pasoti, his collaboration with Giunta, and the later partnership with Valerio Dorico. This looks forward to the 1530s and even further, for Dorico later took up single-impression printing and was still publishing after Gardano and Girolamo Scotto had begun their Venetian activities. But the first appearance of two simultaneous music-publishing ventures in the same city was not theirs; it had already occurred in Rome in 1526. For, alongside the three editions (that we know of) put out by Nicolo de Giudici in 1526, there are the eight extant from the press of Pasoti and Dorico (perhaps with another lost edition), all reprintings of earlier books.

Clearly, music printing seemed as if it ought to be flourishing, and Rome was in a fair way to overtake a Venice which was already in economic decline.[35] In April 1527, Pasoti and Dorico put out another book, and then disaster struck, in the form of the Sack of Rome by the Emperor Charles V, early in May. Many printers lost their equipment, many booksellers lost their stock, and Pasoti may have even lost his life, for he disappears at this stage.[36]

By 1531 at the latest, Dorico was back in business, for he produced a new edition of the second book of the "Croce" series. In 1532 he published two books, neither of them musical—one was the edition of Calvo discussed above.[37] Only one year later, however, Antico (in Venice) persuaded Scotto to support his edition of Verdelot's madrigals, printed by the de Sabbio brothers. This was the real beginning of the Scotto family's successful career in music printing,[38] though it is notable that Antico managed to prevail on them to concentrate on printing with woodblocks—his own production—even after single-impression music printing had been adopted by Gardano and printers in other centers.

The later years of the fourth decade show the beginnings of rivalry in music printing. Marcolini tried to establish a successful business in Venice in 1536 using the multiple-impression process, and Gardano was about to appear, in 1538. Outside Venice and Rome, music publishing began in Naples, Milan, and Ferrara. Clearly, at last, there seemed room for more than one music publisher to make a profit—and single-impression type must have played a part in the transition. Multiple-impression type continued to be used in Milan, by Castiglione and (even later in 1555) the two Moschenio brothers. These types produced elegant editions, finer than those of the leading firms of Gardano and Scotto: but for all that they could not compete with the much more efficient type and general methods being developed in Venice.

North of the Alps, Petrucci's clearest legacy lay in southern Germany. Both Öglin and Peter Schöffer (the Younger) used a double-impression process, directly related to that adopted by Petrucci in 1503. Öglin, working in Augsburg, would surely have seen copies of Petrucci's editions, probably from among those bought for the Fugger collection, for his division of work into impressions follows that of Petrucci, even though the layout on the page is different. The note shapes and some other type designs resemble those of Petrucci, though the custos, the corona, and the flat were newly designed. Öglin's first edition, that of Tritonius's settings of Horace's odes,[39] was apparently set with so many errors that a second had to be prepared almost immediately. The presswork, however, was of a high standard, for the results bear comparison with those of Petrucci. The edition largely used breves and semibreves to interpret the Horatian meters, but Öglin retained the types and expanded the range of note values when he printed at least two more books, in 1512 and 1513.[40]

Schöffer had certainly seen Petrucci's editions; his types are closer to those of the Italian, and even the *custodes* look very similar. More significantly, he published a new edition of Petrucci's *Canti B* in Mainz, also in 1513.[41] This copied the work closely, with few textual changes, and with similarly skillful craftsmanship; it is, however, significantly different and follows a stronger German tradition, in being in partbooks. Schöffer printed one other set of partbooks with these types in 1513,[42] a mere three weeks later, and retained them in his travels. In 1535 they were still in good condition and employed for his edition of Frosch's *Rerum musicarum opusculum*.

A completely different set of type was used by Grimm and Wyrsung in Augsburg, for their edition of the *Liber selectarum cantionum* (1520), edited by Ludwig Senfl. This large choirbook is superbly printed.[43]

Two impressions were used elsewhere. In London, the edition of *XX Songes* (1530), also in partbooks, used notes with elongated tails, though other features of the font are distinctive. Don Krummel has suggested that it may have been modeled after the font used by Schöffer.[44] Finally, the editions of music by Carpentras, prepared by Jean de Channey in Avignon in 1532, also used a double-impression font, although the design is very different.[45] It is famous as one of the first appearances of a rounded note-head: the tails of up-tailed notes descend with flair directly to the right of the note head, as if written in a single stroke of the pen. The *custos* is similar to that employed by Öglin, but the font was certainly cut in France, by Etienne Briard working at Bar-le-Duc.[46]

By then, of course, single-impression printing had been around for several years. The earliest examples known to me comprise a small number of notes in otherwise double-impression liturgical fonts. They can be found in editions of the missal for the archdiocese of Salzburg. In 1510 the Viennese printer Winterburg created a small range of true single-impression sorts for printing in red, improving on a 1507 innovation of Liechtenstein in Venice.[47] However, these sorts do not comprise a font, but are rather individual sorts to meet special needs. The first font capable of printing a full composition appeared ca.1525 in England, in editions of Rastell's work.[48] Whatever the sources of this font, there is no reason to think that Rastell ever saw anything from Petrucci; there are really no features in common, and he could more easily have seen the few books with short sections of music in woodblocks that were printed in Germany during the early decades of the century.

Within a few years, Attaingnant launched single-impression music printing in earnest, with a clear small font and a format which more closely reflected the style of Antico's early books than that of Petrucci.[49] This marks the effective end of Petrucci's technical influence, for not only the type but other aspects of his technique (including the need to maintain accurate register) were now redundant. In other ways, too, the age of Petrucci was past. Daniel Heartz has called Attaingnant "the first music publisher to achieve a true mass production",[50] and indeed he had launched an ambitious program of publishing while the Scottos were still tentatively responding to Antico's proposals.

Petrucci's influence on the technique of music printing lasted the best part of thirty years; in Germany, it lasted longer. But the new directions were those of Attaingnant in France, and of Gardano and Scotto in Italy. It is time to ask whether Petrucci was the influence that changed the direction of music dissemination, or whether he was the prophet who announced the changes effected by his successors.

Notes

1. In Antico's 1513 privilege for secular music, Pope Leo calls him "Dilecto filio Andreae Antiquo Miniatori de Montona", doubtless following Antico's own description of himself. In the contract for the *Liber Quindecim Missarum*, he was "Andreas Antiquus de Montona miniator et impressor in urbe". See Chapman, *Antico*, p. 451.

2. I have suggested in the previous chapter that he even took some of his music for this edition from Petrucci's earlier frottola books. If that is true, then he carefully buried these pieces in the middle of his own book.

3. Cusick, *Valerio*, pp. 36–37, offers a similar table, adding measurements for a number of musical sorts. Her conclusions correspond to those reached here.

4. Following Chapman, "Printed", no.74. Colón's catalogue reads: "Moteti e canzone franzose de Jusquin et altri. V. 1524. *6169*. 8 [and] Moteti novi e canzone franzose de Jusquin et altri. V. 1524. 8 *6169*. [and] Nesciens mater nesciens mater virgo viru*m* peperiti. *6169*". It is interesting to note the extent to which this book tried to emulate the look of Antico's works, although it clearly was not cut by him. However, the staves and their impagination reflect his layout, and the initials seem to imitate his. Chapman, *Antico*, pp. 106–109, says this is not Antico, but perhaps the cutter who did Caneto's 1519[4]. I agree that it cannot have been cut by Antico, but I would rather associate it with the earlier Roman editions.

5. Chapman, "Printed", no.67, quotes Colón's catalogues as follows: "Moteti et canzone li°. p°. Jo. mouto*n* et alioru*m* autoru*m* n°.21 7307. R. 1520. 8". It is a little troubling that Colón's other reference to same the catalogue number, 7307, cites a work "In omni tribulatione et angustia succurrat", as if that is the first in the book, following his normal custom; in fact, it is the third and begins (in the Superius part from which Colón took the book's title) low on f.2*v*. (This was also noted in Fenlon and Haar, *Italian*, p. 205, fn.7.) There is, however, no other candidate for this description. The book was assigned to Antico by the editors of *RISM*. Chapman, *Antico*, pp. 110–12, rightly says that it is not his work; Einstein, "Supplement", agrees and thinks it must have been published by Giunta or Scotto. (See also Einstein, "Dante".) Jeppesen, "Unknown", merely asserts that it was probably Roman from 1520. Fenlon and Haar, *Italian*, p. 205, follow Einstein.

6. Although we know that printers did lend decorative blocks to each other (for which, see Rhodes, "Alcuni"), the years 1520 and 1521 were busy ones for Antico, and I doubt that he would have sent the blocks to Rome for the relatively extended period that would be involved.

7. See Luisi, *Secondo*, for a detailed investigation of the various editions of this title. The common design elements confirm that Antico did not immediately take all his material to Venice, leaving both the blocks and initials for Mazzocchi's editions, before claiming them, in 1520. That may also have been the point at which he decided to sell some of his material.

8. We know that Giunta was interested in continuing to support music. He was responsible for the *Missarum decem . . . Liber Primus* (1522), printed by Pasoti, to whom I shall return. The initial letters defining the Altus and Bassus partbooks of that title are also close copies of Antico's letters.

9. It is notable that he emulates the spacing and size of staves manifested in Petrucci's edition of Pisano, which appeared in the same year.

10. The preponderance of composers found in Petrucci's later volumes is apparent: it confirms a Roman connection for those books and suggests that the printer of the present book perceived that they had sold well in Rome and nearby centers.

11. This title is discussed in Fenlon and Haar, *Italian*, pp. 207–209, with references to the earlier literature. We should associate with these works the book of *Moteti nove e canzone francese* (*RISM* 1521[7]), which Colón calls variously "Moteti e canzone franzose de Jusquin et altri. V. 1524" and "Moteti novi e canzone franzose de Jusquin et altri". Although he calls this a Venetian publication, it has parallels with these Roman books, in repertoire, and in some decorative and formal elements, including at least one initial that is very close to some found in *RISM* 1521[4]. Assuming Colón is correct in assigning it to a Venetian printer, one is tempted to look to a direct contact with the creator of the Roman editions, both for technical reasons and because it is another macaronic collection. This probably means that the Roman printer or publisher was now in Venice, rather than that he loaned material to a Venetian printer; just possibly, a Venetian publisher could have approached the Roman printer to work for him, since Antico had apparently decided to stop work.

12. The absence of attributions for the Italian pieces is not necessarily a reflection on their sources; the last of the Latin-texted works, *Lydia bella*, is also anonymous. There are only attributions for the first three gatherings of the Superius, and *Lydia bella* begins the last gathering. Having abandoned attributions, the typesetter included none in the lower voices.

13. See the letter "A" on f. J1r.

14. *RISM* 1521[4]. Chapman, "Printed", favours no.68: "Moteti li°. 2°. n°.16. diversor*um* autor*um*. p° Jo. mouton ulti[a] anton de viti. 6215. R. 1521. 8".

15. Lowinsky, *Medici*, iii, p. 122. I doubt this suggestion.

16. These two have been closely associated in Jeppesen, *Frottola*, i, pp. 70–75, and Jeppesen "Unknown".

17. See Blackburn, "Printing", for details of the contract to publish this book, and earlier literature. It is a measure of the close connections between the various Roman printers and publishers, as well as the extent to which music was an occasional activity for many of them, that the same Giudici had been involved in publishing Antico's fourth book of frottole, nine years earlier, in 1517.

18. Petrucci's practice of putting sacred music into partbooks and frottole into a choirbook format was followed by Antico during 1520 and 1521, by Pasoti and Dorico, and by all the books I have discussed so far. The change in Petrucci's book of 1520 is paralleled by a change in *Madrigali de la Serena*; the implications here are repertorial, lifting the "madrigal" above the canzoni and frottole, rather than bibliographical. The most recent discussion of this last book, attempting to make it into an occasional volume, is Campagnolo, "Libro".

19. The details of the contracts concerning the *Musica de la Salamandra* imply that 500 copies of the book were distributed in under eight months. As Blackburn ("Printing", p. 354) remarks, almost all the copies had probably been sold to booksellers, or to other distributors.

20. See for details of his career, Pettas, *Giunti*; Pettas, "International"; and Renouard, *Annales*.

21. Giudici had already worked with woodblocks for Antico, as printer of *Canzoni . . . IV* (*RISM* 1517[2]). However, I suspect two different promoters, for the two sets of editions (of 1520–23 and of 1526) use different proportions for the notation.

22. See his *Frottola*, i, pls.XXIII and XXIV.

23. These books precede Attaingnant's work in France, though probably not Rastell's in England (for which, see King, "Significance"). Both of these printers, of course, achieved true single-impression printing, but it is very unlikely that anyone in Italy knew of Rastell's few efforts, or even of any experiments being conducted in France.

24. This book is cited in Colón's catalogue as: "Canzoni stramboti ode frotole soneti et modo de cantar versi latini. li°. 3°. de la croce. *4970*. R. 1524 4b n°.22. [and] Canzoni stramboti ode frotole soneti et modo de cantar versi latini libro 3°. de la croce *4970*. Ro. 1524 4ab n°.22". (See Chapman, "Printed", no.73.) It implies, of course, two earlier volumes, presumably in 1522–24; these would serve to highlight the contrast discussed here.

25. The best treatment of Pasoti's place in printing history is in Chapman, *Andrea*, pp. 114–

20, followed by Cusick, *Valerio*, pp. 16–18. He is briefly mentioned in Barberi, "Dorico", and omitted from Krummel and Sadie, *Printing*. He apparently came from Monticello, near Reggio Emilia in the diocese of Parma, according to his colophon in Eustachio's *Musica Duorum* (see p. 6 of the modern edition).

26. This suggestion was first made in Chapman, *Andrea*, pp. 115–16, and rejected in Cusick, *Valerio*, p. 16.

27. Cusick, *Valerio*, p. 34, states that the stave length is less important, since pieces of staff "were deliberately designed to be broken off wherever necessary to fit the horizontal dimensions of the page". However, this does not apply to all staves in a book, but only to certain exceptional situations. Further, no printer could afford to destroy his long staves gradually in this way. Finally, the normal length of a stave in a book is directly related to the area within the forme to be filled by each page. Thus the length of staves is a significant feature, as much as are the patterns of distance between pairs of staves.

28. See Vernarecci, *Petrucci*.

29. See Cusick, *Valerio*, p. 17.

30. We cannot tell whether they actually had copies of many of Petrucci's editions. Petrucci did keep at least a few sheets of some titles, for they survive in fragmentary state in the Fossombrone Biblioteca Passionei. But, quite plausibly, he had appointed someone in Rome, the nearest big city of easy access, to act as his agent and bookseller. That person was most likely to be the same individual who would use his typographical materials and reprint his editions.

31. Blackburn, *Correspondence*, p. 1014.

32. Jeppesen, *Italia*, i, p. xiv, and pp. 87–89. Reynolds, *Papal*, pp. 55–56, draws attention to a "Serafinus" who was in papal service during 1485–89. He suggests that this may be the Seraphinus of the Perugia manuscript.

33. No first edition survives for the first of the "Croce" series, but this was one of the firm's own first editions, so that a change seems unlikely.

34. There is also evidence in the 1526 editions of the other books in the series, suggesting that there was more reprinting than would represent merely a cancel.

35. Music publishing in Venice had virtually ceased once Antico stopped cutting blocks in 1521. Cavazzoni published his edition of keyboard music in 1523, and one book (listed in Table 11-1) appeared in 1524. In addition, in 1523 there was at least one edition of the *Regula musicae planae* attributed to Bonaventura da Brescia (put out by Tacuino) and one of the *Cantus monastici formula* (published by L. A. Giunta). The Rusconi brothers published another edition of the pseudo-Bonaventura text the next year. Apart from treatises and books of chant, nothing musical appears from any Venetian press thereafter until 1530, with a Giunta edition of the *Cantorinus*. Venetian presses had effectively abandoned polyphony completely, until the first edition in Antico's renewed burst of activity (Verdelot's first book) appeared in 1533.

In Rome, by contrast, there had been music published in each year from 1520 to 1524, supplemented by new ventures of 1526. Despite the number of editions, however, the pattern suggests more ambition than success. Pasoti and Dorico's volumes reflect a continuing interest in some of the music produced by Petrucci and presumably also the status of the editions. The other books are significant in the extent to which their planners tried to capture as many parts of the market as possible with each edition.

36. Cusick, *Dorico*, p. 49, proposes that Pasoti may have survived the sack of Rome and have been involved in preparing the second edition of the *Libro Primo de la Serena* in 1530. This is not impossible, for Dorico does not resurface until the following year. But it is noteworthy (as Cusick records on p. 37) that the impagination of this edition lies much closer to that of the earlier woodblock editions, even though it seems to use the same font of music type as the earlier editions. It is easier to assume that Pasoti had died, and that Dorico hired another craftsman, one whose experience in music stemmed from those earlier editions.

37. Details are given in Barberi, "Dorico", p. 132. The list of editions beginning on this page shows how music printing became much less important for Dorico.

38. The edition is *RISM* 1533^2=V1218, and it was followed by a number of other editions cut by Antico. For the career of Girolamo Scotto, see Bernstein, *Music*.

39. This is *RISM* T1250, followed by T1249.

40. They are *RISM* 1512[1] and [ca.1513][3]. Details of Öglin's career can be found in Benzing, *Buchdrucker*, and the sole study of his later books is Eitner, "Liederbuch".

41. This book is not listed in *RISM*. A single Tenor partbook survives at A-Iu and is described in Senn, "Sammelwerk".

42. This is *RISM* 1513[2]=*B.VIII* 1513[02]. In the previous year, Schöffer had printed Schlick's *Tabulaturen etlicher Lobgesang*.

43. *RISM* 1520[4]. A reproduction of part of a single page can be seen in Barksdale, "Printed", p. 70. At various times, it has been asserted that this was printed from woodblocks (as, e.g., in the entry on Grimm and Wyrsung in Krummel and Sadie, *Music*, p. 270), but details of technique as much as the repetition of certain sorts argue that it was printed from type.

44. The book is *RISM* 1530[6], and Brown, *Instrumental,* 1530[6]. The comment on the typeface can be found in Krummel, *English*, p. 81, and is certainly reasonable. There is considerable evidence that typefonts traveled up and down the Rhine and across the English Channel, sometimes with printers, sometimes as a commercial undertaking.

45. These four books are *RISM* G1571-1574. The first book appeared in 1532; the others have been assigned various dates between 1532 and 1536.

46. Carter and Vervliet, *Civilité*, p. 22, fn. regard the types as related to the Civilité fonts cut for Granjon during the 1550s. Despite evident similarities in basic design, it seems to me unlikely that Granjon's font was based on de Channey's.

47. See Boorman, "Salzburg".

48. See King "Significance", and the illustration in King, *Four hundred*, pl.XI.

49. The standard work on Attaingnant remains Heartz, *Pierre*. Significant bibliographical aspects of his books are discussed in Heartz, "Typography".

50. In Krummel and Sadie, *Music*, p. 155.

Chapter Twelve

CODA: EARLY MUSIC PRINTING

AS AN AGENT OF CHANGE

n a recent study of Russian printing during the eighteenth century, Gary Marker argued that the traditional view of printing as
an "instrument of progress" is insufficient, and that he needed to
discuss a more basic series of questions: "Was printing simply an
object of larger developments [by which he means responding to
patterns and changes in society] or did the process and structure of printing come
to influence important features of Russian society?"[1] Of course, Russian society
during and after the reign of Peter the Great was very different from that of Italy
during the sixteenth century, even given the desire for censorship and control
that existed in most Italian states. There are ways, however, in which publishing
in the first half of the sixteenth century does seem to show parallels. Among these
are the apparent power of the church and local rulers to control not only what
was printed, but also how the content was presented;[2] the gradual shift in control
over the material printed, from the printer or publisher to the author, including
the emergence of something akin to copyright;[3] and the expansion in both numbers of books and types of repertoire contained in them.[4] For music, the closeness
of the parallels (especially for the second and third points) is enhanced by the
presence of a specialised market, involving both particular reading (and performing) skills and (often) particular classes of purchasers. Taken together, these various
elements make more relevant the question of whether music printing "merely"
responded to developments in musical society, or whether (and how) it seriously
influenced those developments.[5] Perhaps we may have to decide whether the
innovation of printed polyphony had much impact at all, at least for some decades.

In this context, the questions posed by Marker need to be addressed at three
different points. First is the issue of how far Petrucci himself was reacting to a
perceived demand, or how much he created a future demand and defined its

character; second is the problem of how extensive was the role of music printers of the first two-thirds of the century in the growth of a music-buying public in Italy, whose beginnings can be securely traced to the 1530s; and third is the matter of how far music printing affected the music itself, its composition and performance. Traditionally (as I was able to show by quotation in the introduction to the present volume), Petrucci has been seen as a major agent of change, largely responsible for the actions that led to the expansion of musical literacy during the sixteenth century. Such a historically significant position is often accorded any pioneer, for scholars love to find the first occurrence of anything, and then push back the causes and origins of large humanistic developments to as early a date as possible.

In practice I think that this position needs serious questioning. It has long seemed to me much more likely that Petrucci was not the creator of a large new market for printed music, and also that he did not set up the pattern that led to the later, definite expansion. The evidence of hidden and public later editions from his press (and even of the editions put out by Dorico and Pasoti in the 1520s) does show that there was a measurable public, and that this public was larger and more diverse than it had been under a purely manuscript culture. But it does not follow that it was intrinsically large, that it covered any representative cross-section of society, or that it was expanding significantly after the two decades of Petrucci's work.

I have several reasons for holding this view: first, throughout his career, Petrucci seems to have had little idea of how well his books would sell; second, many of his first editions were the direct response to some sort of external stimulus, and not the product of commercial speculation; a third is that his books were rather expensive, and not comparable even with treatises or popular editions of "good literature"; and a fourth has to be that so few other printers attempted to compete with him. My first three points have been addressed above, and there is little need to say more on them here. I merely wish to stress that the evidence of the repertoires that he printed, and of their probable provenances, suggests that he was not reacting to popular demand, but simply to specific opportunities as they arose. This is most certainly true for the few non-musical works that he published (or nearly published), and I have suggested that it was equally true for many of the musical volumes. Also, the apparent pricing of these books, though well within the reach of scholars and book collectors—and of course of financially responsible institutions—would not have encouraged exploratory purchases.

The market for notated music in 1501 was a fragmented one: there were patrons and institutions looking for liturgical and para-liturgical settings, for devotional music of various sorts, for secular music—both in the chanson tradition and as settings of the courtly or the popular frottola—and for instrumental settings. In addition, there was a range of *dilettanti*—music lovers, merchants, and courtiers, and some from other levels of society[6] (particularly north of the Alps)—who bought music for their own private domestic or social consumption. While, certainly, some purchasers would have bought manuscripts representing more than one kind of music, most would have concentrated on one or two facets of the total repertoire. Thus, there are few concordances for *Motetti A* or its successor among manuscripts compiled for liturgical institutions; similarly, few of the concordant sources for frottole contain more than the most famous works found in the *Odhecaton* series. This is not surprising, for each patron would, under a manuscript culture, also keep to particular collecting (and performing) interests.[7]

Petrucci necessarily had to look beyond those patrons of manuscript culture if he was to have any financial success. This is, of course, why he (and his various editors and encouragers) gradually worked through almost all of the available repertoires. But there is little evidence that he was able to persuade his purchasers to expand their own tastes (indeed, why should they have done so?), or that he expanded to any great extent the general pool of purchasers.[8]

The principal reason why I doubt that he achieved either of these (no doubt historically imposed) aims is that there was so little competition from other printers. Regardless of the actual print-run for Petrucci's editions, if he had been expanding the market and increasing the interest in notated music (printed or manuscript), there would have been other printers seeking to enter the field and compete for his profits. This is certainly true for a city like Venice, where the number of specialised printers was so great, and the lines of commercial dissemination already so well established. It is significant that all the other early attempts began outside Venice, all were distinctive in one way or another, and all (with two significant exceptions) seem not to have been successful.[9]

One of the exceptions concerns a sequence of Roman editions, from 1521 to the early 1530s.[10] This includes, on one hand, the new editions of Petrucci's books (put out by Pasoti and Dorico), which argue for the reputation he and his editions had acquired: on the other, there is the series of odd volumes, put out by various printers, none apparently promising a lucrative future to printer or publisher. To judge from the record of surviving editions, even Giunta was not consistently successful, despite his economic strength.

The principal exception was Andrea Antico. After his first three books of frottole, which appeared between 1510 and 1513, he had done well enough to be able to continue printing in Rome. True, his *magnum opus* was a specifically Roman volume, aimed at the papal curia and (probably) the Lateran Council, but the five books of frottole and one of intabulations and at least one book of motets[11] speak to a reliable market, whatever its size.

Both the number and range of Antico's editions (in Venice as well as in Rome) and the sequence of editions of Petrucci's music prepared by Pasoti and Dorico in Rome argue that Petrucci did not saturate the market. There were still purchasers wanting polyphony; indeed, by 1526, there were enough potential purchasers to stimulate new editions. It is notable, however, that Antico turned to sacred music for his new Venetian editions and that the majority of Giunta's promotions from the 1520s were of liturgical music. Antico put out motets and masses; Giunta's editions were of Josquin's masses and the *Motetti de la Corona*.[12] These editions reflect the growth in choral institutions in cathedrals and chapels throughout Italy, and these institutions were probably the principal purchasers of printed editions.

But we cannot say that the emergence of the new institutions, or their demands for complex polyphony, were the result of Petrucci's activities, or of music printing in general. They were more a result of the increasing wealth of Italy in general, the despondency resulting from war and plagues, and a desire to compete with their most famous rivals—in other words, from a view that polyphony was a desirable accompaniment to a lavish and well-endowed church life. Nor can we say that there was a rapidly increasing demand for secular music. The surviving editions from the 1520s do not seem to have inspired any publisher with the confidence that this would be a thriving market.

I believe, therefore, that we have to assert that music printing did little to expand the market for musical sources during the first twenty-five or thirty years of the century. We cannot speak of real competition or success when printers or publishers were often content (or compelled) to restrict themselves to one or two volumes.[13] In this respect the work of Pasoti and Dorico is also indicative, for the larger part of their early production consisted of new editions of books originally published by Petrucci.

In previous publications, I have argued that the beginnings of the expansion in the Italian market for printed music fell in the years immediately before Gardano started work.[14] The evidence for this statement is fairly clear. The willingness of the Scottos to launch into music, early in the fourth decade of the century (albeit first using materials prepared by Antico), was soon followed by the first signs of real competition in northern Italy—Marcolini in Venice, and then Buglhat and company in Ferrara.[15] This competition, especially in the case of Marcolini, must imply that the actual market was already thought to be larger, regardless of the size of the print-runs for these editions, for otherwise no printer would have wanted to consider risking his capital with a series of titles.

And yet there must still be doubts about how far this expansion continued through the following decades. Even once Scotto and Gardano were both working at full speed and turning out the majority of Italian editions of music in the 1540s, the number of rivals (and even more significantly the number of editions from their presses) remains depressingly low. The competitors before the 1550s must have been seen as insignificant: Casteleone and Flamengho in Milan; Marcolini, and Ganassi publishing his own works, in Venice; Caneto (and de Frizis) in Naples; the Ferrarese group. Each was a limited venture, related to a particular composer, a specific genre of music, or a local patronal stimulus.

Only after mid-century did any printers begin to look as though they might emerge as rivals to the two Venetian houses. The first three worked in Rome, exploring the particular benefits of working in a city that was again becoming rich in patronage, for the Sack of Rome was twenty-five and more years past. These were Barré (1555–64), and Dorico (1555–66) each with over a dozen editions, and the Blados (1551–77) with at least eight.[16] At the same time, Moschenio, working in Milan (1554–66), produced about a dozen editions; and the beginnings of a Venetian attempt at supporting a third music publisher can be seen in the production of Pietrasanta in 1557, leading to Rampazetto, Merulo, Angelieri, Bariletto, and Guglielmi.[17] With the exceptions of Rampazetto and Merulo, none of these produced enough music to earn a living, and none seem to have stayed with music for long. Indeed, the first successful rivals to Scotto and Gardano did not appear until Gerolamo Scotto had been dead for ten years. Vincenti and Amadino burst into activity in 1583 and changed our picture of the market for music radically, but their emergence and the flurry of new editions they produced must raise speculation about the size of the market in the previous sixty years.[18]

Perhaps, then, with the absence of other printers making a profit from music, we should doubt whether the great number of editions pouring from the houses of Scotto and Gardano did signal a large and continually expanding market for the music. Even if the privilege system had prevented others from printing titles that were already successful (and the evidence of editions of Arcadelt, Gero, and Lassus, among others argues against such a premise), there were enough composers, both new and famous, for any printer to establish his own repertoire. Indeed, that is exactly what Vincenti and Amadino were to do in the 1580s. It is certainly what Barré and Moschenis tried to do in their own cities—although they seem to have found the local market not big enough to support an expansive musical operation.

There seem to me to be two possible explanations for the pattern of printers and production. One is that Scotto and Gardano managed to effect a virtual monopoly, presumably through economic pressures. In this model, they would be able to hold down costs (by using poorer paper, for example, and streamlining production methods), and also develop close and binding contacts with *librai* and representatives at the many fairs. I find this explanation difficult to believe; there is no support for it, for smaller printers printed similar titles and presumably must have circulated them to similar buyers, through similar agencies. Further, any such hypothesis would require that the two Venetians tried to control major markets such as Rome and Milan, as well as the more local Ferrara and Verona. Yet, it is in these cities that the few, relatively feeble, rivals do appear. Finally, no evidence for similar behaviour has surfaced in other fields of printed matter.

The alternative explanation is that the market was rather smaller than we would like, and that it was fairly stable in size, at least from late in the 1530s until well into the 1550s.[19] This was not true for markets north of the Alps, which were constructed in quite different ways, and required increasing numbers of musical books—including those from the south, as the taste for things Italian increased.[20] But, in Italy, there need not have been a vastly increased market for printed music. This explains simply and plausibly why there was no room for a third competitor turning out enough musical volumes to maintain a complete printing shop; : at the same time, it raises interesting questions about the numbers of different titles that were printed, and the sizes of the print-runs.[21]

It appears that some purchasers were rapacious in their collecting; the Accademia Filarmonica acquired more music than could possibly have been performed, and the Fuggers in Augsburg (like the later Knoff in Gdansk) seems to have bought anything they could lay hands on.[22] This was surely true for other collectors, but they must have remained in a minority. Most purchasers continued to buy a relatively small selection of books, suitable for their own needs and abilities. In this respect, they followed the buying patterns of many religious institutions, for whom manuscripts remained important. Other books, especially those devoted to a minor local composer, probably never reached further than a small locality, perhaps with a smattering of copies sent by the publisher or an alert dealer to the few omnivorous collectors.

If some such scenario is possible, then the history of printed music in sixteenth-century Italy looks different. It fits more comfortably into what we know of the sizes and tastes of courts, the numbers of church institutions, and the practice of private music. In this view, music printing ceases to be, to use Eisenstein's phrase, the "agent of change",[23] a grand force that revolutionised musical practice. Certainly, it did change a few things: it allowed some individuals to amass large collections of polyphony; gradually it permitted institutions to buy more music than they needed, with the option to select from anthologies those few pieces that more closely fitted their needs; it allowed the commemorative volume of madrigals to be seen and admired by more people; and it no doubt encouraged composers to seek publication as a means to "career advancement", and patrons to support them without involving any long-term commitment. But none of these points represents a radical change in the market for music, in its size or its behaviour. That change was about to happen of its own accord, and for quite different reasons.

I repeat that there was certainly growth in the size of the market early in the second quarter of the century. Antico saw it, and persuaded Scotto to publish; Gardano saw it and set up shop in Venice. But that growth seems to a large extent to have slowed again, so that few other attempts to make profits from music publishing seem to have succeeded.[24] At the same time, the market was being defined—sacred institutions knew what they wanted, secular institutions had their own tastes in secular music, and amateurs similarly favoured specific genres and styles. For Petrucci's generation, this had probably not been true, at least as far as buying printed music was concerned. But by the 1540s, buyers were beginning to know what to look for, and to understand what the different printed title-pages represented in the way of texts and styles. Gardano and Scotto were astute enough and capable enough to provide the guidance for this new market, at the same time as they fulfilled almost all its needs.

That they could take advantage of the opportunity the market offered was in large part due to the invention of single-impression type. At the same time, the streamlining of production processes finally made small print-runs significantly cheaper than manuscripts, and the new patterns of patronage allowed printers to publish other titles, ones they could not otherwise have afforded.

But there was one significant manner in which the act of printing music changed the musical world, and it involved the reader's view of the music and its perfor-mance. The classic argument runs something like this: a printed edition was dis-tributed to a great many readers; the act of printing imposed some sort of uni-formity on the content; there was an increasing uniformity in the way many readers reacted to this content; commentaries on printed texts tended to respond to the same details in the content; as a result, readers began to assume that the content carried authority, at one level or another; at the next stage, authors were increasingly concerned that the details of content should reflect their own wishes; by a circular process, the printed editions did indeed have increased authority and credibility.[25] The assumptions behind this series of arguments are particularly dan-gerous for music, where the whole issue of the authority of a printed or written text was always more complex.

On one hand, we can discern how far printed editions were used (and not merely bought) only in those instances where we have evidence, of their use—corrections and annotations—or of copying from them. But in studying both these forms of evidence, and particularly the second, we assume that the preserved readings already carried extreme authority. This is the assumption that justifies examining later annotations, and the one on which the whole study of textual transmission is based. Without it, we cannot tell whether the "accurate" copies were the only ones actually to use the same exemplar.

On the other hand, we assume that performances did not follow the written transmission—that variation, embellishment and ornamentation were the norms, and that these quasi-improvisational skills were held in high esteem by all professional performers. As modern historians, therefore, we face an implicit contradiction: did the transmitted text have authority, or was it merely the most convenient way of stimulating a performance of the transmitted work?[26]

We need to put alongside these issues another central factor: the apparent interest among amateurs and less qualified musicians in owning and using copies. Some evidence for this expansion in the types of consumers can be found in the earliest music printing:

    editions of laude and similarly simple polyphony, and particularly the reprinting of Dammonis's book: later evidence includes the emergence of books of *napoletane* and similar repertoires;

    simplified performing editions of some repertoires: in Petrucci's output, this includes Bossinensis's arrangements of frottole;

    different levels of care about performance details when printing different repertoires. For Petrucci, this care is reflected in the different treatments of texts for masses and for frottole: not primarily in the patterns of texting, but rather in patterns of inconsistency;

    and decisions about printing in partbooks rather than choirbook layout. I suspect that frottole were printed in choirbooks because the musicians were expected to learn their music, rather than gather round a single copy. (Alternatively, they may have been expected to copy their own parts, but this would not affect our argument.)

It will be apparent that the less competent readers of music books would have benefited from some of these details. Yet by the same token, these are the very readers who would have taken the printed text as authoritative and tended to sing and play exactly what was written. They did not kill off the practice of ornamentation, but many of them would have found it beyond their abilities. It is not surprising that ornamentation became a feature of German treatises on music during the first half of the century.

Nor is it surprising that composers began to take an active interest in music publishing. I have mentioned earlier the interest of French poets in controlling what was printed,[27] and musicians were not far behind. Whether Tromboncino (in 1521) and Festa (in 1538) were merely trying to control the circulation of their music, or were particularly concerned with the versions being circulated, we cannot be sure.[28] But it is significant that Tromboncino's repertoire, like that protected by Cavazzoni in 1523, was one more easily available to amateurs.

By the 1520s, therefore, some professional musicians and publishers were aware of a market among purchasers who did not possess the highest technical performing skills. It is unlikely that these new purchasers were a large part of the market; the mixed contents of books published in Rome during the 1520s argue against that. But they were becoming a significant proportion and were no doubt establishing a pattern of performance conduct in which the printed (or written) note was followed ever more closely.

We cannot tell whether these patterns preceded changes in musical style, or went hand-in-hand with those changes. Indeed, it is hardly a useful question, largely because the printed repertoire of the 1530s (in particular) concentrates on so few genres. But it is notable how the early madrigal (and also numbers of liturgical works) developed clear periods, predictable harmonic movements, and simpler text-setting. It is more significant that composers of longer settings (and not only for professional institutions) were able to vary to a greater extent their style within individual compositions. Florid or contrapuntal sections could be controlled, inserted when needed, and placed alongside more syllabic sections. This practice speaks to a decline in the freedom to embellish—or at least to an increase in controlling when and how much, through manipulation of the individual voice parts. This must be seen as part of an increase in the authority of the notated text. Even the most skilled singers were expected to be able to see, in the details of musical style, how far they could stray from the text at any given moment. In the same way, text placing was clarified: phrases and words were broken up into syllables, which were more carefully aligned with the notation, and repetitions of text phrases clearly indicated. Again, the printed version asserted its own greater authority, while assisting the inexperienced to achieve acceptable results, and the professional to perform with less and less rehearsal.

I suspect that some of these changes stem directly from the emergence of printed music. Once publishers decided that money could be made from polyphony, they would, of course, seek out the largest market. This might be, in 1500, among the professional institutions, or (more probably, as I argue) with trained courtiers and secular musicians. But we can also see the emergence of a measurable group of willing singers and players who had not previously bought music on any regular basis. The steps I have described, designed to make musical books easier to use and the content simpler to comprehend, would have tapped into this market. In the 1520s, Roman publishers were still uncertain how large it was, and so they produced the types of anthologies I have described. But in the 1530s, with the emergence of the Scotto as a powerful music-publishing force, repertoires are clearly separated: the first books are almost entirely of madrigals and *canzone francese*.[29] It is true that, in their early years (from 1538), Antonio Gardano and Girolamo Scotto published a number of books of liturgical settings—almost certainly mostly commissioned or supported; but they soon seem to have realised where the bigger profits might lie, and (as the work of Lewis and Bernstein has shown) the majority of their editions lay in secular music.[30] These editions can be further broken down into genres and stylistic categories that reveal a series of smaller markets.

The existence of these books and the authority apparently invested in their contents by many readers provide prime evidence for the changing character of the market. The changes would eventually have happened without printed music, simply because of the relative affluence of the merchant classes and their desire to "ape their betters". But the extent to which different parts of the musical world could develop different tastes (and performing patterns) was fostered by the easy accessibility of a variety of printed editions.

Petrucci could not have taken part in that transition; nor was he an active player in the expansion of the market. He was, for much of his career, too concerned with quality—of readings, of presentation, and of repertoire. He was also working at a time when the market had none of its later size or definition. Finally, his relationship with potential patrons still stood closer to that of the professional scribe, responding to individual interests and requests. What he did achieve was more subtle, and perhaps more powerful. He proved that there was a market for music aimed at the highest professional levels. At the same time, he revealed a demand for volumes intended for the other end of the spectrum, for amateurs, whether noble or not, who could at least cope with musical notation and create musical effects in ensemble. Finally, he demonstrated the viability of specialised volumes, books with a limited and specific function, such as collections of laude, Magnificats, or Lamentations. This last group was the most adventurous, the realm where Petrucci's successors were the slowest to follow him. They could print volumes of motets and even masses; they could sell hundreds of editions of madrigals, villanellas, and canzonettas; but they rarely ventured into books with more specific social or liturgical function. Here, more than in the other repertoires, Petrucci was ahead of the times; in these areas, he would not be followed for some decades, whereas his other editions continued to stimulate successors, even through the relatively barren 1520s, and eventually into the prolific 1540s and beyond.

   Modern scholars have increasingly shown an interest in the transition from manuscript culture to print culture. They have begun to point out that there was a long period of overlap—although it is not generally recognised that the musical overlap was of longer duration than for almost any other repertoire. Changes in patterns of patronage, of technique, of the "paratext" and the appearance of the book, and (of course) of repertoire, all gradually turned the late medieval book into something produced in the manner of a modern volume. Even if Petrucci was not the "first printer of music", or the establisher of a "new pattern of music dissemination", he was someone more significant: an entrepreneur taking risks with a new repertoire, gifted with a fine eye for artistic effect and an evident concern for quality, and working at exactly the right time to produce a large body of splendid and splendidly presented music. These are the reasons for the respect he has continued to receive, and they make him a rare and remarkable figure in the history of music and of printing.

Notes

1. Marker, *Publishing*, pp. 5–6. Marker's study takes both sides of this question seriously, examining as closely the impact of society on the details of printing and book trades as it does the effect of printed material on Russian society. The phrase "agent of change" in the heading to the present chapter comes from the title of the influential work, Eisenstein, *Printing*.

2. See Blasio, "Privilegi"; Bosisio, *Stampa*; Grendler, *Roman*.

3. For music, see Agee, *Privilege*; Bernstein, "Financial". In general, see Armstrong, *Before Copyright*; Blasio, "Privilegi"; Bosisio, *Stampa*; Brown, "Confrontation"; Brown, *Poets*; Castelain, "Histoire"; Schottenlohr, "Druckprivilegien".

4. Davis, "Printing"; Fenlon, *Music*; Gallico, "Laboratorio"; Noakes, "Development"; Richardson, *Print*.

5. Boorman, "Working".

6. For reflections of this point, see, for example, Leech-Wilkinson, "Libro", or Feldman, *City*.

7. Of course, this point does not apply to the courts (or similar institutions) with professional musicians attached, for they would need repertoires of music for different social situations—masses and motets as well as secular music. Nor in practice does it cover certain religious institutions, such as the Duomo in Verona, whose members (as we know) also collected secular music. But even here, within each large class of music, one might expect different tastes to predominate, for example, chansons or incipient madrigals as opposed to frottole.

8. This is an important point: to some extent we need to distinguish cultures that were exploratory in their musical tastes from those that remained circumscribed in one way or another. This cultural difference would be reflected in the music produced by local publishers, or displayed by local booksellers. Even more significant (and more clearly reflected in the printers' output) is the extent to which amateurs or the less skilled wished to explore new repertoires, and to build up their technical abilities. These two factors are represented in a number of ways—in the presence of didactic instruction in vocal books, the simplification of notations, the mixing of repertoires in anthologies, the marketing of different styles (either by introducing them in anthologies or by advertising them on title pages), and the deliberate addition of more complex styles to a booklist. I have used these types of evidence to argue that amateurs in the Low Countries were more adventurous than were those of Italy, at least during the second half of the sixteenth century. See my "Music Publisher".

9. The most distinctive example is the edition of frottole from Siena in 1515 (*RISM* 1515₂), for it bears little relation to the mainstream repertoire and was evidently prepared to honour local musicians. No other music seems to have come from this press. In Florence, the situation is even more extreme, for the single privilege for music appears not to have resulted in any editions.

Similarly, music printers and publishers in Naples apparently did not take an optimistic view of the prospect of profits, at the same time that they focused on a largely local repertoire. The repertoire of *RISM* 1519⁴ contains many local works, alongside nine (ascribed to Tromboncino and Cara) previously published by Antico. The printer of this book tried a second (*RISM* [ca.1516]²) the next year. The now-lost book of motets put out by de Frizis may have had a more mainstream repertoire: the four textual incipits given by Colón (for which see Chapman, "Printed", No.66) were each set by more than one composer, and two, *Beata dei genitrix* and *Sancti dei omnes*, had settings printed by Petrucci. In her dissertation, Chapman suggests, on p. 84, that Caneto was probably the publisher for this volume as well as for the frottola books: this makes excellent sense, and argues that there was, as in the other centers, only one music publishing activity at a time during the 1510s. For further work on the Neapolitan situation, see Pompilio, "Editorià": for the next burst of music printing, see Cardamone, *Canzone*; Cardamone, "Debut"; and Cardamone, "*Madrigale*".

10. A number of these are discussed in Fenlon and Haar, *Italian*; see also Blackburn, "Printing".

11. On Antico's motet volumes, see Picker, *Motet*; and Picker, "Motet". I believe that the repertoire for at least the second book was collected while Antico was in Rome. (See my review of Picker, *Motet*, in *Music & Letters* 70 [1989], pp. 285–88.) That he believed it would sell well when printed in Venice probably indicates two things: that he felt the repertoire was not exclusively Roman, and that he knew the Venetian *librai* and trade routes were much more effective than those in Rome.

12. For Antico, the most recent list is in Miller, "Antico": for the Giunta volumes, see Cusick, *Valerio*, chapter 2. While Antico reprinted a number of his Roman frottola editions in Venice in 1520 and even added a volume of intabulations (which is undated), he then produced

four volumes of motets and two of masses. For Giunta, whose books were produced by Pasoti (at first alone, and later with Dorico), one large sacred volume in 1522 balanced a smaller secular one in 1521, and the total of eight books (known to us) published in 1526–27 included only one with secular contents.

13. Again, Antico seems to be the one exception; however, we have to ask why Antico should have been so keen to move to Venice (for which I think we have simple answers), and why he should suddenly have stopped producing in 1521, when the Florentine Giunta was beginning to try out the Roman market (and here I can suggest no reliable answers). But both facts tend to argue against any general expansion of the market for printed music.

14. See, for example, my "Working".

15. It is true that both Marcolini (with a limited number of editions, and a claimed concentration on the music of Willaert) and the Ferrarese (with their interest in the local repertoire) might seem to belong with the earlier printers whom I have dismissed as not really competing with the major names: however, both enterprises would have needed to base their success on sales in Venice and the Veneto and would have been using the same trade routes exploited by Scotto. This cannot be said of the earlier Neapolitans and Romans.

16. For Barré, see Buja, *Antonio*; for Blado, see Bridges, "Antonio", and Cusick, *Valerio*, chapter 2; for Dorico, see Cusick, *Valerio*. None of these men was dependent on music printing for a livelihood. Barré was a professional musician, while for Blado or Dorico music represented an insignificant part of his duties as publisher.

17. On Rampazetto, see Nielsen, *Francesco*. Edwards, *Merulo*, pp. 199–205, points out that part of Merulo's typographical material passed to Angelieri, and that there was almost certainly a business agreement between the two. As she suggests, the music type did go even further and reappears in the work of both Bariletto and Guglielmi.

18. I am indebted to Beth Miller for observations on the manner in which they sought to enter the market, by exploring contacts and repertoire in under-represented parts of Italy.

19. I am not denying an expansion during the 1530s; I merely argue that it did not generate continuous growth, but established a new plateau in the size of the market.

20. Indeed, the steady (and faster) growth in the market for musical editions throughout Germany and the Empire (excluding Spain) helped the commercial success of both Gardano and Scotto. They may not have sent many separate copies of individual books to the fair (see Bernstein, *Venetian*, pp. 127–29), but their publications were avidly bought by individuals and institutions; and it is not until late in the century that printers north of the Alps began as a matter of course to print complete editions of Italian composers' work.

The other paramount feature in northern Europe was, of course, the Reformation. While manuscript studies have stressed the importance of Latin schools and reformed churches in the propagation and performance of art music, it must be stressed that the expectation that congregations would take part in the liturgy was equally important. This involved singing from the book, and encouraged a growth of amateur ensemble singing—as the wealth of editions aimed at a lower level of achievement affirms. In this respect, music printing and publishing in the Low Countries and in Germany present a very different picture (after about 1530) than in France or Spain or Austria, or (of course) Italy. See my "Music Publisher", and, in particular, Höweler and Matter, *Fontes*: this catalogue covers much more ground than does the equivalent volume for German editions in the *RISM* series, Ameln et al., *Deutsche*.

21. These questions directly concern the stimuli for books of music. Without getting embroiled in the question of patronage, I have to argue that we cannot know, merely from the presence of dedications, how many books were subsidised by a patron, and how many were paid for by a composer, relative, or colleague eager for the publicity. It seems evident that many books were put out as speculative ventures, and this presumably includes virtually all those in which the printer or publisher signed a dedicatory letter. Once again, the great many Arcadelt editions are prime evidence here and once again they raise the question of the size of print-runs, a still-unresolved issue that bears centrally on much of what appears here. At the same time, detailed study of local repertoires (Bologna, Ferrara, Mantua, Rome, or Venice), as well as of the stylistic and technical interests of composers and patrons, increasingly shows that many books reflect a special taste and local interest: a number of these were probably commissioned.

22. For the Accademia, see Turrini, *Accademia*, and Turrini, "Patrimonio"; an inventory of the Fugger collection is described in Schaal, "Musikbibliothek"; and a valuable study of Knoff's collection is Morell, "Georg".

23. This is part of the title for the influential study, Eisenstein, *Printing*.

24. One should probably except the Mezzogiorno. Music printing *did* expand in centers south of Rome during the second half of the century, and Vincenti and Amadino exploited southern composers when they set up shop, as a means of establishing a corner for themselves.

25. This line of argument lies behind many of the issues discussed in Eisenstein, *Printing*. It has been subjected to thoughtful criticism in Johns, *Nature*: see especially pp. 28–40.

26. Of course, the truth lies somewhere in between. Authority had to be accorded some aspects of a text, or else any ensemble work became unperformable; other aspects provided merely the support for a creative performance. I am concerned here with the changing balance between these two extremes.

27. See Brown, *Poets*.

28. For the Tromboncino and Festa applications, see above in chapter 2, with the literature cited there. But it seems likely that Carpentras was as much interested in readings as he was in publication itself, given his actions when he arrived at the Sistine Chapel: see Sherr, "Notes".

29. It is tempting to suggest that Marcolini's attempt at publishing Willaerts's sacred works came a few years too soon, and that he might have been more successful five or six years later.

30. For the most convenient depiction of this pattern, see the figure on p. 156 of Bernstein, *Music*.

BIBLIOGRAPHY

Chapter Thirteen

CHECKLIST OF PETRUCCI'S PUBLICATIONS,

IN CHRONOLOGICAL ORDER

his list includes all titles published by Petrucci, including cancels and hidden editions. In addition, it includes, in sequence, books which I have relegated to chapter 14 on "Ghosts". The numbers in the last column refer to the entry numbers in the following bibliographical descriptions.

All dates in parentheses are speculative; many are contingent on analyses of paper and typographical material. Several of these dates could therefore be moved by some months in either direction. Further, when several occur in succession, as in 1514–15 or 1519–20, it is possible that the order of individual items could be changed slightly, as a result of further research.

Date	Title	Edition	RISM	Number
VENICE				
[v.1501]	*Odhecaton A*	first edition	1501	1
[late 1501]	*Odhecaton A*	cancel leaves		1a
5.ii.1501/2	*Canti B*	first edition	1502²	2
19.v.1502	*Motetti A*	first edition	1502¹	3
[mid 1502]	*Odhecaton A*	cancel leaves		1b
27.ix.1502	Josquin: *Misse*	first edition	J666	4
27.xii.1502	Josquin: *I Missarum*	ghost		see Ch.14
14.i.1502/3	*Odhecaton A*	second edition	1503²	5
24.iii.1503	Obrecht: *Misse*	edition	O7	6
[iii–iv.1503]	Obrecht: *Misse*	cancel		6a
[iv.1503]	Josquin: *II Missarum*	ghost		see Ch.14
10.v.1503	*Motetti . . . B*	edition	1503¹	7
17.vi.1503	Brumel: *[Misse]*	edition	B4643	8
15.vii.1503	Ghiselin: *[Misse]*	first edition	G1780	9

(continued)

411

Date	Title	Edition	RISM	Number
4.viii.1503	*Canti B*	second edition	1503³	10
31.x.1503	La Rue: *Misse*	edition	L718	11
[xi.1503]	La Rue: *Misse*	cancel leaves		11a
[xi–xii.1503]	Josquin: *Misse*	cancel leaves		4a
[xii.1503]	Josquin: *III Missarum*	ghost		see Ch.14
[late 1503]	*Motetti . . . B*	cancel leaves		7a
10.ii.1503/4	*Canti C*	edition	1504³	12
23.iii.1504	Agricola: *Misse*	edition	A431	13
25.v.1504	*Odhecaton A*	third edition	1504²	14
[summer 1504]	Agricola: *Misse*	cancel leaves		13a
[?viii.1504]	*Motetti . . . B*	ghost		see Ch.14
15.ix.1504	*Motetti C*	edition	1504¹	14
28.xi.1504	*Frottole I*	edition	1504⁴	16
18.i.1504/5	*Frottole II*	first edition	1505³	17
6.ii.1504/5	*Frottole III*	first edition	1505⁴	18
13.ii.1504/5	*Motetti A*	second edition	—	19
22.iii.1505	De Orto: *Misse*	edition	O137	20
[i–iv.1505]	*Motetti . . . B*	cancel leaves		7b
[iv.1505]	*Motetti C*	cancel leaves		15a
4.vi.1505	*Motetti IV*	edition	1505²	21
30.vi.1505	Josquin: *II Missarum*	edition	J670	22
[viii.1505]	*Strambotti . . . frottole IV*	first edition	1505⁵	23
[ix.1505]	*Motetti A*	cancel leaves		19a
31.x.1505	*Fragmenta Missarum*	edition	1505¹	24 and 24a
[xi.1505]	*Fragmenta Missarum*	cancel leaf		24b
[28.xi.1505]	*I Motetti à 5*	ghost		see Ch.14
23.xii.1505	*Frottole V*	edition	1505⁶	25
5.ii.1505/6	*Frottole VI*	edition	1506³	26
[iii.1506]	*Fragmenta Missarum*	second printing	—	24c
8.iv.1506	*Lamentationum I*	edition	1506¹	27
29.v.1506	*Lamentationum II*	edition	1506²	28
[vii.1506]	Dammonis: *I Laude*	first edition	—	29
[viii.1506]	Josquin: *I Missarum*	second edition	—	30
20.x.1506	Isaac: *Misse*	edition and new settings	I88	31 and 31a
[xi.1506]	Isaac: *Misse*	cancel folios		31b and 31c
7.i.1506/7	Weerbeke: *Misse Gaspar*	edition	G450	32
[27.ii.]1507	Spinacino: *Intabulatura I*	edition	1507⁵	33
31.iii.1507	Spinacino: *Intabulatura II*	edition	1507⁶	34
21.v.1507	*Frottole VIII*	edition	1507⁴	35
6.vi.1507	*Frottole VII*	edition	1507³	36
31.vii.1507	*Strambotto . . . frottole IV*	second edition	1507²	37
[1507]	Martini: *Hymni de tempo I*	edition	—	38
14.x.1507	*Magnificat I*	edition	—	39
26.xi.1507	*Frottole III*	second edition	1507¹	40
[1507]	*Frottole VI*	ghost		see Ch.14
[1507]	*Odhecaton A*	ghost		see Ch.14
11.i.1507/8	*Laude II*	edition	1508³	41
29.i.1507/8	*Frottole II*	second edition	1508²	42
15.iii.1508	*Missarum diversorum I*	edition	1509¹	43
[v.1508]	*Frottole VII*	cancel		36a
20.vi.1508	Alemannus: *Intabulatura III*	edition	—	44
7.vii.1508	Dammonis: *I Laude*	second edition	DD833 I,1	45
[1508]	*Frottole I*	cancel leaves		16a
[28.xi.1508]	*I Motetti à5*	edition	1508¹	46
31.xii.1508	Dalza: *Intabulatura IV*	edition	D828	47
[1508]	Mouton: *Missarum*	ghost		see Ch.14
22.i.1508/9	*Frottole IX*	edition	1509²	48
[ii.1509]	*I Motetti à5*	cancel		46a

(continued)

Date	Title	Edition	RISM	Number
27.iii.1509	Bossinensis: *Intabulatura I*	first edition	1509³	49
[1509]	*Fragmenta Missarum*	ghost		see Ch.14
FOSSOMBRONE				
10.v.1511	Bossinensis: *Intabulatura II*	edition	1511	50
[1511]	Bossinensis: *Intabulatura II*	cancel		50a
[1512]	*Frottole X*	edition	—	51
8.vii.1513	Paulus: *Paulina*	edition	—	52 and 52a
29.vii.1513	Castiglione: *Epistola*	edition	—	53
[viii.1513]	Paulus: *Paulina*	cancel leaves		52b and 52c
[1513]	*Messa Corale*	ghost		see Ch.14
1.iii.1514	Josquin: *III Missarum*	first edition	J673–4	54
[v.1514]	Josquin: *III Missarum*	cancel leaves		54a
17.viii.1514	*I Motetti de la Corona*	first edition	1514¹	55
24.x.1514	*Frottole XI*	first edition	1514²	56
[xii.1514]	Ghiselin [*Misse*]	second edition	—	57
[1514]	Josquin: *I Missarum*	ghost		see Ch.14
[ii.1515]	Bossinensis: *I Intabulatura*	second edition	—	58
11.iv.1515	Josquin: *II Missarum*	first Fossombrone edition	J671	59
11.viii.1515	Mouton: *I Missarum*	first edition	M4015	60
[viii.1515]	Mouton: *I Missarum*	cancel		60a
22.xi.1515	Févin: *Misse*	first edition	1515¹=F689	61
[xii.1515]	*I Motetti de la Corona*	cancel leaves		57a
[1515]	Bossinensis: *Intabulatura II*	cancel leaves		50b
[1515]	*Missarum decem . . . Libri duo*	ghost		see Ch.14
29.v.1516	Josquin: *I Missarum*	first Fossombrone edition	J667–8	62
[vii.1516]	Févin: *Misse*	second edition	—	61a
[vii.1516]	*I Motetti de la Corona*	second edition	—	57b
[ix.1516]	Josquin: *III Missarum*	second Fossombrone edition	—	54b
20.xi.1516	Paulus: *Parabola Christi*	edition	—	63
[1516]	Josquin: *III Missarum*	ghost		see Ch.14
[i.1517]	Josquin: *I Missarum*	second Fossombrone edition	—	62a
[1517]	Josquin: *II Missarum*	second Fossombrone edition	—	59a
[1517]	Josquin: *II Missarum*	cancel	—	59b
[1517]	Josquin: *I Missarum*	third Fossombrone edition	—	62b
[1.i.1519]	Calvo: *Hippocrates*	[edition]	—	see Ch.7
17.vi.1519	*II Motetti de la Corona*	first edition	1519¹	64
7.ix.1519	*II Motetti de la Corona*	edition	1519²	65
31.x.1519	*IV Motetti de la Corona*	edition	1519³	66
[1520]	*I Motetti de la Corona*	third edition	—	57c
[1520]	Josquin: *I Missarum*	fourth edition	—	62c
23.v.1520	Pisano: *Musica*	edition	P2451	67
[1520]	*IV Motetti de la Corona*	cancel leaves		66a
[1520–1]	Févin: *Misse*	third edition	—	61b
[1520–1]	Févin: *Misse*	cancel		61c
[1520–1]	Mouton: *I Missarum*	second edition	—	60b
[1520–1]	Mouton: *I Missarum*	cancel		60c
[1520–1]	*II Motetti de la Corona*	second edition	—	64a
[1520–1]	*III Motetti de la Corona*	cancel sheet		65a
[1523]	*Tre Messe Corali*	ghost		see Ch.14
[1523]	Paulus: *Prognosticon*	ghost		see Ch.14
[c.1533]	[*Musica XII*]	edition	—	68
15.x.1538	*Motetti del Fiore*	edition	—	69

Chapter Fourteen

GHOSTS: BOOKS AND EDITIONS FALSELY

ATTRIBUTED TO PETRUCCI

iven the status of Petrucci in the history of music printing, and
the long sequence of eighteenth- and nineteenth-century bibliographical and musicological studies that include his books, it is
hardly surprising that he should have been assigned his fair number
of ghostly issues and titles. The following discussion tries to elim-
inate as many of these as possible from the future literature.

I have included lost editions among the entries in my bibliography when
they were cited by reliable writers such as Colón. There are, however, other
proposed editions for which I can find little or no justification, and they have
been relegated to the present chapter. Apart from the special case of Paulus de
Middelburgh's last title of 1523, the more obvious cases tend to fall into three
different categories:

1. announced editions that are merely the result of a misunderstanding of
   the Venetian calendar. Since these are always represented by copies that
   actually belong in a different year, they can all be safely rejected;
2. editions for which the only evidence is a citation in one or other of the
   secondary sources that have not earned respect for their accuracy. Among
   these are entries that appeared first in Fétis, *Biographie*, or Schmid, *Petrucci*,
   without any other evidence to confirm their existence. Although these
   editions are commonly cited in later literature, by Vernarecci, in particular, those references can normally be traced back to the citation of Fétis
   or Schmid;
3. editions that have been postulated in order to make Petrucci's output look
   more tidy. This is the case with the Viennese copies of the Fossombrone
   editions of Josquin's masses, where the restorers seem to have decided
   that the 1514 and 1516 dates must have belonged to Books I and III, in

that order. The same stimulus caused an allusion to a 1504 edition of *Motetti B*.

After these ghostly shadows of books have been removed, there remains a small, though much more troubling, group of references. None of these can be disposed of so simply: all might conceivably represent an edition which is now lost. If it should seem surprising that an edition cited only in the last 200 years might still disappear, the reader is encouraged to refer to the entries for "Lost Copies" in the following bibliography. A disappointing number of these copies have disappeared since the time of Fétis, having originally been cited in dealers' catalogues or in references by competent scholars who nonetheless omitted to mention where they had seen the book.

5 February 1501: *Canti B*

This was the date assigned to the first edition copy at Bologna, before scholars realised that the Venetian year did not begin until 1 March.[1]

27 December 1502: Josquin: *Misse* [Book 1]

Vernarecci[2] referred to two editions of Josquin's first book of masses, both from 1502. The first, *Misse Josquin* is my No.4. Vernarecci dated the second on 27 December 1502, and no copies of such an edition seem to exist. Sartori[3] argued that this is a ghost, and based his argument on the citations by Winterfeld, Schmid, and Fétis.[4] His case is strong, for there is no reason to believe that Winterfeld, who first cited this edition,[5] copied his colophon correctly; nor does he state that the title page defines the book as a *Liber primus*. Schmid's case must be weakened by the fact that the Vienna library still believes (as does *RISM*) that the second copy at Vienna is also of a 1502 edition, whereas it has to fit bibliographically with the newly described 1506 edition.

There are even other arguments on Sartori's side:

1. 27 December is an unusual date for a book. Petrucci has the habit of finishing, or at least dating, his books just *before* a holiday. In addition, it is at least a coincidence that each of the two editions, the known and the doubtful, should be dated on the 27th of its month;
2. if the date were correct, Petrucci would have had to work very fast to produce the next volume, the second edition of *Odhecaton A*, only two and a half weeks later. This production time was not impossible, for both books would be second editions, but it was certainly unusual;
3. there is no evidence of a copy of this date, even though Josquin's mass volumes have survived better than most other of Petrucci's titles.

Coincidentally, there was an early reprinting of at least one sheet of the extant edition. The inner sheet of gathering F survives in two copies in a later printing, datable to late 1503. I believe that this was a true cancel, rather than part of a new edition.

April 1503: *Missarum Iosquin Liber secundus*

At one point, Vernarecci refers to "Nuove produzioni di musica, sacra e profanna, si hanno dal Petrucci nel 1503: *Missarum Iosquin Liber secundus* e *Liber tertius*; *Canti C. N°. cento Cinquanta*", without giving any authority for his citation,[6] though Gaspari's transcription of Bottrigari's notes also suggests an edition of 1503.[7] Sartori, tracing the list of earlier authors who cite the book, believes the first to be a ghost.[8] I agree for a number of reasons. An analysis of the rate of work suggests that Petrucci probably could not, so early in his career, have produced two new books (this one and *Motetti B*) in forty-seven days, especially since the period included Easter.[9] Further, the edition of 1505 shows none of the expected signs of being copied from an earlier edition. Finally, the hypothesis, like that of a second edition of the first book in 1502, hinges critically on the mis-identification of the second copy at A-Wn.

The third book in Vernarecci's reference, *Canti C*, does exist, with a date of 10 February 1503 o.s., that is, in 1504.

1503: *Missarum Iosquin Liber tertius*

This title was cited by Vernarecci alongside the previous book, and Sartori treated it similarly.[10] As with the case for a second 1502 edition of the first book of Josquin's masses, much depends on the erroneous identification of the second copy at Vienna.

Sartori makes the point that the appearance of the third book in 1514 seems to have been a direct stimulus for the reprintings of the first two books. While this does not prove the absence of an earlier edition of Book III, it certainly helps.

8 January 1504: *Frottole Libro secondo*

Schmid[11] assigned the surviving edition to this year, on the strength of its Old Style date.

Before September 1504: *Motetti A*

Schmid[12] suggests this edition, probably because he did not know of the earlier editions of *Motetti A* or *Motetti B*. Presumably, he therefore believed both were printed in 1504, before the first edition of *Motetti C* in September. Schmid's reasoning is specious and is discounted by Sartori.[13] The copy of *Motetti A* now at H-Bn, and dated early in 1505 (n.s.), represents the edition cited by Colón. This edition further militates against another appearing only six or so months before.

Before September 1504: *Motetti B*

This edition was also proposed by Schmid,[14] who relied on the undated reference in Gesner. Ambros, when he saw the Bologna copy of the 1502 edition in 1866, inscribed it with a note stating that Fétis did not know of it.

1504: *Frottole IV*

Brunet[15] enters the undated edition of 1505 under this year.

1505: *Motetti a cinque Libro primo*

Fétis asserted that there was a volume with this title dated in 1505, and Schmid went even further, dating it 28 November 1505.[16] Sartori, in discussing the extant volume,[17] says that it should be assigned to 1508, in accordance with the citation in Colón's catalogues. The bibliographical analysis confirms that 1508 is the date of extant copies.

Vernarecci[18] reported that Bologna had a different edition of this book, unknown to Schmid, and "condotta in carattere tondo, mentre l'altra è in semigotico. Novera pagine 65: manca dell'*Alto* e del *Basso*; e, perchè imperfetta, non porge facile congettura dell'anno in cui uscisse alla luce". No trace of this copy could be found at I-Bc: it is probable that Vernarecci attempted to make a distinction between Schmid's use of "semigotico" and his own of "tondo", and therefore assumed that the two text fonts were different.

1505: *Harmonice Musices Odhecaton A*

Rosaria Boccadifuoco[19] regards the Treviso copy of the 1504 edition (No.14 here) as a separate edition, published in 1505. The copy conforms to others of 1504.

1507: *Harmonice Musices Odhecaton A*

Cerone, in *El Melopeo y Maestro*, cites an edition of this year. This is surely erroneous, as Sartori implies,[20] for there is no evidence that interest in Petrucci's chanson volumes lasted that long. It is true that other volumes from this year have been lost, but they would fill up the only significant gaps in production during the year.

1507: *Frottole Libro sexto*

A volume with this title at S. Anna, Augsburg, a gift of the Herwart, was catalogued in 1620.[21] It was then bound with Books VII and VIII, both published in 1507. The most likely explanation is that this was actually a copy of the 1506 edition. It seems unlikely that the cataloguer would have looked within the binding for the colophons of each book: if he had, he would have cited 1505 (o.s.) for Book VI, rather than merely looking at the end of the bound set, where the date of 1507 (for Book VIII) provided all that he needed.

1507: *Missarum diversorum auctorum Liber primus*

Abbiati[22] suggested an edition of this year, with a second edition in 1508. Sartori discounted the suggestion, surely correctly.

22 January 1508: *Frottole Libro nono*

Cited by a number of authorities, this title is certainly the edition of 1509, entered under its Old Style date.

1508: *Missarum Ioannis mouton Liber primus*

Vernarecci[23] states that a Tenor book of this edition exists at F-Pn, in this following Fétis. As Sartori points out, if only a Tenor part were available to Fétis, he should not have been able to suggest any date for the edition. No Tenor book of Mouton's masses is extant in Paris.

1509: *Fragmenta Missarum*

Vernarecci[24] cites Schmid as recording an edition of this year. Schmid presumably saw the copy that is now back in Venice. Although that copy does have a replacement sheet, in the Superius, it has the same date in the colophon as other extant copies. In any case, the new sheet was prepared immediately following the printing of the original.

1509: *Missarum diversorum auctorum liber primus*

RISM assigns the 1508 edition to this year. The date of issue is, however, 15 March, after the Venetian New Year, so that the volume should properly be entered in 1508.

1513: *Messa Corale*

This title was first recorded by Gianandrea[25] in 1881, and in the next year Vernarecci[26] followed his reference, describing the book as a "volume di 123 fogli,
di cui è noto serbarsi un esemplare nell'archivio della Cappella Pontificia in
Roma". As Sartori points out,[27] no such book is now extant in the Biblioteca
Vaticana. He continues that he can do no more than remark that many sources
have been lost.

I find the book to be very improbable. Petrucci owned no type for extended
passages of chant notation, nor does he seem to have planned this type of book
at any time. (As I have stated earlier, the simple reference to chant in Petrucci's
first application for a privilege seems to have had other motives.) If indeed he
had ever planned to print chant, then Venice, with its history of publishing noted
missals and similar volumes for many dioceses, would have been a more logical
place to start such an undertaking. The only plausible reason for Petrucci to
consider a book of chant in 1513 would have been the patronage of the local
bishop. However, Paulus was much more interested in his own speculative writings, and in any case, the diocese was firmly entrenched within the use of Rome.

1514: Josquin: *Missarum I*

This date, cited by Schmid,[28] resulted from confusion over the dates of the Fossombrone editions of Josquin's masses. Schmid, with others, seems to have assumed that the three books would have been issued in order, with the first book
in 1514. The confusion was compounded by the existence of two clearly distinct
copies at A-Wn. As a result, the copies there (and at US-R) of Josquin's first and
third books have had their colophon pages exchanged during an early restoration.
The error is repeated in *RISM*, where each title is given two reference numbers,
one for each date; the second date (and number) for this first book is even repeated
in Rosaria Boccadifuoco, *Bibliografia* (see Nos.1194 and 1997). In fact, although
both books went through several printings (as the bibliographical descriptions
show), each had only one date assigned to it during the Fossombrone years.
Haberl had already pointed out the error and was followed by Vernarecci.[29]

1515: *Missarum decem libri 2*

These books were cited by Gesner, in his *Pandectae* of 1548, as: "Miſſarum decem
à clariſſimis Muſicis | compoſitarum, necdum antea (exce-|ceptis tribus) ædi-
tarum, libri 2. im-|preſſi Foroſempronij 1515".[30] The citation has engendered
some discussion, usually starting from the assumption that it refers to one publishing endeavour.[31]

I have to say, at the outset, that I find the books to be implausible as cited,
and certainly as one single volume. It was unknown for Petrucci to include ten
masses in a volume: indeed to print ten polyphonic masses together would require
twice as many gatherings as normal, taking the signatures at least to the letter P.

Petrucci did, of course, print volumes with as many sheets of paper, but only in his early years (for example, with *Canti C*), and not in partbooks.

On the other hand, the reference is to "libri 2". This seems to stand for two volumes, not just for one, fitting more closely Petrucci's normal practice at this time. If we look for possible books by Petrucci, there are few candidates printed in 1515. One is the second volume of Josquin's masses: a dealer might have received copies of Books 1 and 2 bound together, and a bibliographer then dated them both by the colophon of the second. But since these books involve one composer, they would not merit the description "à clarissimis Musicis compositarum". More likely, perhaps, are the two other volumes of masses, one by Mouton and the other by Févin (including Robert Févin and Pierson). However, these two fail to meet Gesner's other criterion, that three of the masses should have appeared before.

The problem is made more complex by the survival of a single copy of an edition published by Giunta in 1522.[32] This book has a similar title, carrying the same phrase about reprinting three works:

MISSARVM DECEM A CLARISSIMIS MVSICIS COMPO|SITARVM. NEC DVM ANTEA. EXCEPTIS | TRIBVS. AEDITARVM. | LIBER PRIMVS [...] ROMAE IN AEDIB. IACOBI IVNCTAE. MENSE MAIO .M.D.XXII.

Evidently, either Gesner was copying this edition accurately (but conflating it with the Petrucci editions), or else the edition (and Gesner) repeats the title page of an edition of 1515. The contents of the 1522 book are:

1.	[Missa] de beata Virgine	Brumel
2.	[Missa] Ave Maria	Pierre de la Rue
3.	[Missa] Alma redemptoris	Jo. Mouton
4.	[Missa] Quem dicunt homines	Antonius Diuitis
5.	[Missa] de beata virgine	Joſquin
6.	[Missa] Faisant regretz	Joſquin
7.	[Missa] L'home arme	Pipelare
8.	[Missa] Pro defunctis	Brumel
9.	[Missa] Chantes sans pauses en sospir	Moulu
10.	[Missa] Baysez moy	Petrus Rosselli

Of these, Petrucci had already published No.3 in 1515, and Nos.5 and 6 in 1514. On the other hand, during 1516, Antico published his *Liber quindecim Missarum*, which contained all except Nos.4 and 9. As a result, the phrase implying that three were reprinted would seem to be appropriate only for an edition of late 1515 or early 1516, rather than for one of 1522.

This evidence has been discussed by Lockwood,[33] and his argument presumes that Giunta's edition of 1522 is a re-edition of a book that had appeared before Antico's of May 1516, thus following Gesner's dating. In following this interpretation, Lockwood draws attention to the number of Giunta-sponsored books that are re-editions of titles first printed by Petrucci; he also correctly asserts that

Giunta must have been aware of Antico's edition when he commissioned his own, for both were printed in Rome. As a result, Lockwood assumes that Giunta merely copied the wording, as well as the content of an earlier edition, therefore one published by Petrucci.

Of course, it is possible that Petrucci did indeed publish *two*, now lost, volumes of masses during 1515. They would contain the repertoire given above, divided equally between the two, thus conforming to his normal practice of five masses per volume.[34] Gesner perhaps saw a reference to both volumes. (As I argue in chapter 10, it is not likely that he actually saw any of the books he cited.)

A first objection to this hypothesis lies in the nature of the title, as quoted. It is unlike anything else that Petrucci printed, in both the detail given and the style of the language used. More significantly, there is the thorny question of why Petrucci should have reprinted three masses so quickly after their first editions. He very rarely reprinted any individual compositions; the few existing cases seem all to have been slips—several laude in 1508,[3] five frottole (two with contrafacta texts, and two with different textual incipits), and one motet in *Motetti de la Corona*. In no case does he seem to have intended to republish anything. However, this title states quite boldly that *all but three* were newly published, allowing the purchaser to deduce that those three were reprinted. This statement is unlike Petrucci's practices in every regard; it may reflect a response to the limitation in Petrucci's 1514 privilege, that he could not print material previously printed.

In fact, given the dates of Petrucci's editions in 1515, it would have been difficult for him to print this book at the end of the year, after the book of Mouton's masses (from which No.3 would have been reprinted), which appeared in August. That book was followed in November by an edition devoted to Févin, and then by a cancel sheet for *Motetti de la Corona I*. The ten weeks between the editions of Mouton and Févin would entail a rate of working (assuming that the two lost books were each of the normal length) that Petrucci could never achieve in Fossombrone, and that he maintained in Venice only for short periods of time. The sum of these arguments makes it very unlikely that Petrucci printed this title during 1515.

There remain a few other possibilities. One is that Gesner conflated two entries,[35] one of which referred to the surviving edition from Giunta (or to an earlier edition that it copied), while the other mentioned two editions, probably of Mouton and Févin, printed by Petrucci during 1515. At first sight, such a conflation seems quite plausible and it does address some of the problems. Indeed, as far as Petrucci is concerned, it resolves all the necessary issues.

But it does not explain the wording of Giunta's title. Apart from the references to earlier editions, which effectively seem to require a date of 1515, there is another curious phrase in Giunta's title: the reference to "Liber Primus". If we assume that Gesner's two volumes were divided equally (with five masses in each), the three masses that appeared earlier include ones that would appear in the different volumes: this weakens the precision of the title as printed, for the first book would only have two "re-printed" masses.

The printed title, therefore, contains several elements that work against each other, in either 1515 or 1522. Format and reprinting argue against 1515, while the title itself argues against 1522, as does the implicit reference to the possibility of a second book.

I believe therefore that in 1522 Giunta was working from a manuscript of a book (or a pair of books) that was *intended* to have been published in 1515. This manuscript, I propose, was offered to Petrucci, probably with some abbreviated version of the extant title.[36] As with the Calvo manuscript, the necessary details, including a colophon, were already entered. The manuscript was not printed, perhaps because Petrucci noted that he had already printed three of the masses. He may even have entered that himself on the submitted title-page, alongside a note that the manuscript would take two printed books, not one.[37]

The manuscript may then have stayed in the shop. As I have argued in chapter 11, Pasoti (the eventual printer of Giunta's edition) must have had connections with Petrucci's shop, perhaps even bringing typographical material with him to Rome: if he also brought a manuscript such as I propose, it would be an admirable subject for a book in 1522, following the edition of Eustachio Romano's Duos of the preceding year. It would have provided both printer and publisher with an entrée into the market explored and then abandoned by Antico. At the same time, both would have been happy to let the book look as if it were a second edition (retaining a title appropriate to 1515), thereby establishing a pattern that they would follow later in the decade, with reprints of Petrucci's books of motets and of masses by Josquin.[38]

29 March 1516: Josquin: *Missarum I*

Brunet[39] suggests an edition with this date, probably as a result of a simple misreading of the date on the colophon of the surviving edition.

9 May 1516: *Liber Quindecim Missarum*

Lichtenthal[40] refers to this Antico edition as if printed by Petrucci.

1516: Josquin: *Missarum III*

For this erroneous date, see the discussion (above) of references to a 1514 edition of Josquin's first book.

1 January 1519: Hippocrates: *Opera*

For the details of this planned edition, see chapter 7.

1523: *Tre Messe Corali*

Schmid and Vernarecci[41] record a copy in the Cappella Sistina. Vernarecci reports
Fétis as saying a copy was bought in Rome in 1829, that it was a very large folio
choirbook, and very fine. As Sartori says,[42] "poichè troppo spesso il Fétis è incorso
in errori, la sua affermazione troppo poco documentata non ci basta a credere alla
reale esistenza di questa [edizione]".

I suspect that this entry should be related to the suppositious *Messa Corale* of
1513, also allegedly surviving in Rome. One entry probably represents a misreading of the date in the other.

1523: Paulus de Middelburgh: *Prognosticon*

This book is unusually troublesome. It has been assigned to Petrucci at least since
the time of Vernarecci,[43] though none of the five editions known to me can be
ascribed to Petrucci's press. The most likely reason for the error lies in the conclusion of the text, which ends with a farewell from Paulus to Clement VII:
"Valeat Sanctitas tua, quam deus ad vota conservet. Ex Forosempronii calendis
Decembris MDXXIII". These words have been presumed to indicate that the
book was also printed in Fossombrone, though the second edition below confirms
that it was not. Vernarecci's description of the book that he assumed was published
by Petrucci corresponds to the first cited here. Brunet also believed that edition
to be by Petrucci, and he was followed by Sander, whereas Sartori relied on
Vernarecci for his attribution.[44]

1. This edition was certainly printed in Italy and perhaps in Rome.

A1*r*] Progno∫ticum R. p. d. Pauli de Mid|delburgo Epi∫copi
Foro∫empronien*sis*. | o∫tendens Anno. M. D xxiiii. | nullum neq*ue* vniuer∫ale
neq*ue* | prouinciale diluuium futu|rum. S. d*omi*no no∫tro Cle|menti Pape.
vii. | dicatum. | [block]

A1*v*] AD SANCTISSIMVM DOMINVM | no∫trum Clementem ∫ep-
timum Pauli de Middelburgo | dei & apo∫tolicœ ∫edis gratia Ep*iscop*i
Foro∫empronien∫is | Progno∫ticum q*uod* per coniunctiones o*mn*ium
Plane=|tas, nullum ∫ignificatur Diluuium | neq*uae* uniuer∫ale neq*uae* |
prouinciale.

A4*v*] Ex Forosempronii cale*n*dis Dece*m*bris MDXXIII.

Collation: Quarto: A⁴

Signature: only on] A ii

Font: Roman, thirty-six lines per page. Title in a rotonda gothic, similar
to Petrucci's, though clearly distinct.

Copy: private possession, Jaap van Benthem.[45]

Watermark: a gauntlet with a flower above.

Binding: probably eighteenth-century pressed paper, with a mottled paper spine.

Comments: this copy was apparently folded into four, sometime before
its binding.

Vernarecci described the block on the title page in a footnote: "Sotto il titolo pose il Petrucci un'incisione, che rappresenta un astrologo che dà lezione a tre scolari; innanzi ha un tavolo, su cui posa una sfera armillare: la camera, in fondo nero, è trapunta di stelle". The block is rather crudely cut and badly set on the page. The initial on A1*v* is a letter "I", intertwined with branches and leaves.

2. Published Rimini: Soncino, 1523. This edition was probably the first, for after Petrucci's apparent retirement, Soncino would be the only local printer who could continue the standards he had set in the *Paulina* (and which would be acceptable to Paulus). I have not seen this book, which Manzoni states was in his own possession. The following relies on his description,[46] which seems to imply that the text that had acted as a title in the first of these editions was not present.

a1*r*] Ad Sanctissimum Dominum nostrum Pon-|tificem maximum Clementem septimum Pau-|li de middelburgo dei et apostolice sedis gra|tia Episcopi Forosemproniensis prognosticum | quod per coniunctiones omnium planetarum in | signo piscium sequenti anno futuras nullum signifi|catur diluuium neque universale neque provinciale.

a4*r*] Text ends:] Ex forosempronii calendis Decembris M. D. XXiii. Arimini apud ieronimum soncinum.

 Collation: Quarto: a⁴
 Signed:] a [and] aii
 Font: rotonda, thirty-seven lines per page.

Assuming Manzoni to have transcribed the details correctly, this cannot correspond to either of the other Italian editions. In addition, Manzoni does not mention a block on the title page, either that of Vernarecci or that of the following source.

3. Published presumably in 1523 and assigned by the British Library to an unnamed Venetian press.[47]

A1*r*] Ad Sanctiſſimum Dominum noſtrum Pontificem maxi|mum Clementem ſeptimum Pauli de Middelbur-|go dei ˀ apoſtolicæ ſedis gratis. Epiſcopi Foro|ſempronienſis prognoſticum *quod* per *coniunctio*-|nes *omnium* planetarum in ſigno piſcium ſe|que*nti* anno futuras nulllum ſigni|ficatur diluuium neque vniuer-|ſale neq*ue* prouinciale. | [block of a bishop seated on a throne, holding his mitre, in an architectural setting] | [Text starts]: IAm multis annis . . . [etc.]

A4*r*] Text ends:] Valeat ſanctitas tua Quam Deus aduota con=|ſeruet Ex foroſempronii Calendis Decembris .M.D.xxiii.

 Collation: Quarto: A⁴
 Signed:] A [and] Aii
 Font: Roman, "20" = 80.2 mm, "x" = 2.0 mm: forty lines per page
■ The title is in rotonda, "x" = 2.9 mm ■ Lombard initials
 Text-block: 162 × 105 mm
 Technical comments: There is one ornate initial, an "I", with white strap-work on a black ground ■ The block on the title-page, of a bishop holding out a book, is in poor condition: it also appears on an edition of

Voragine's *Legendario de Sancti,* printed in Venice by Tacuino and dated 30 December 1504.[48]

Copy: GB-Lbl, 8610.c.35: No apparent watermark

4. This edition, published in Augsburg by Ruff in 1523, was probably based on the first one above.

A1*r*] PROGNOSTICVM R.P.D. PAV|li de Middelburgo Episcopi Foro-sempro|niensis, ostendens Anno. M.D.XX. | IIII. nullu*m,* neq*ue* universale neq*ue* | provinciale, diluuiu*m* fu-|turum S. domino | nostro Clemen|ti Pape. vij. dicatum.

A1*v*] [Dedication from Othmar Luscinius to R. Fugger, dated Augsburg, Ides of January 1524

B2*r*] Text ends:] Ex Forosempronij Kalendis De|cembris Anno M.D.XXIII.

Collation: Quarto: A⁴B²

Font: Roman, "20" = 108 mm, "x" = 2.3 mm: the dedication is in italic, with "10" = 42 mm

Text block: 157 × 97 mm: twenty-nine lines per page
Copies: A-Wn, 11.J.69; D-Mu, 4°.Astr.P.90 h/7; GB-Lbl, 8610.bb.35

5. Published Augsburg: Ruff, 1524.
Translated into German by Luscinius (= Nachtigall).
Copy: GB-Lbl, C.71.k.14 (2)

1526: *Motetti de la Corona IV*

Reese[49] states that a copy of this title was printed in Rome in 1526, and that this evidence that Petrucci continued printing that late. In fact, the edition was printed by Pasoti and Dorico.

No date, but after 1520: Virgil: *[Opera?]*

According to Vernarecci,[50] a Monsignor Castracane reported that he had "veduto in Olandia un Virgilio impresso superbamente in Fossombrone". This relates to Schmid's assertion that Petrucci worked on various Latin classics in the last years, after 1520: the question of Petrucci's activity in those years is discussed in chapter 1.

Notes

1. Catelani, "Due stampe"; Haberl, "Drucke". See also Fétis, *Biographie,* vii, p. 13.
2. Vernarecci, *Petrucci,* p. 82.
3. Sartori, *Petrucci,* pp. 48–50.
4. Fétis, *Biographie,* vii, p. 14.
5. Winterfeld, *Gabrieli,* ii, p. 200.
6. Vernarecci, *Petrucci,* p. 85. As a result, on p. 105, he calls the 1505 edition a "ristampa".
7. See the reference in chapter 10.

8. Sartori, *Petrucci*, pp. 51–52. He cites the following earlier secondary sources: Brunet, *Manuel*, ii, p. 649; Fétis, *Biographie*, vii, p. 14; Schmid, *Petrucci*, p. 28.

9. It is true that, in the same year and immediately after the volume of Brumel masses of 17 June, Petrucci seems to have printed two books (Ghiselin's masses on 15 July, and the new edition of *Canti B* on 4 August) in forty-eight days. As I have shown above, however, the volume of Ghiselin was in fact in preparation during the production of the Brumel book: while relieving the apparent pressure on the months of June and July, this actually increases *pressure* on April and May.

10. See fns. 7 and 8 above.

11. Schmid, *Petrucci*, p. 57.

12. Ibid., p. 28.

13. Sartori, *Petrucci*, pp. 81–82.

14. Schmid, *Petrucci*, pp. 28 and 36.

15. Brunet, *Manuel*, ii, col.1413.

16. Fétis, *Biographie*, viii, p. 15; Schmid, *Petrucci*, p. 28.

17. Sartori, *Petrucci*, p. 130.

18. Vernarecci, *Petrucci*, p. 105. Further on this matter, see Jeppesen, "Neuentdeckter", p. 74, and Jeppesen, *Italienische*, p. 57.

19. Rosaria Boccadifuoco, *Bibliografia*, No.1731.

20. Sartori, *Petrucci*, p. 144.

21. Schaal, *Inventar*, p. 30, cites the 1620 catalog.

22. Abbiati, *Storia*, i, p. 33: the discussion by Sartori appears in *Petrucci*, pp. 136–37.

23. Vernarecci, *Petrucci*, p. 166, and Sartori, *Petrucci*, p. 178.

24. Vernarecci, *Petrucci*, p. 105.

25. Gianandrea, "Ottaviano", p. 182.

26. Vernarecci, *Petrucci*, p. 140. The book is also mentioned by other writers, although there is no sign that any of them had actually seen a copy. See, for example, Schmid, *Petrucci*, p. 28, and Fétis, *Biographie*, p. 14.

27. Sartori, *Petrucci*, p. 161.

28. Schmid, *Petrucci*, p. 28.

29. Haberl, "Drucke", pp. 97–98; Vernarecci, *Petrucci*, p. 149, fn.2. See also Noble, "Petrucci", and Boorman, "New".

30. Gesner, *Pandectae* (1548), VII, folio 82v, under the rubric "TITVLVS IIII. DE CAN-|tionibus ecclesiaticis". See Bernstein, "Gesner", No.130. Other potential references by Gesner to Petrucci's editions are cited in chapter 10.

31. See Sartori, *Petrucci*, No.54; Schmid, *Petrucci*, p. 28.

32. *RISM* 1522. The unique copy survives at I-Nn, SQ XXVII L 40–43, though another copy was purchased by Colón, whose catalogue entry agrees with the date and place of publication of the surviving copy. (See Chapman, "Printed", No.70, p. 71.) Given the extent to which Colón covered music printing during the second and third decade of the century, this merely makes the problem of the 1515 citation all the more acute.

33. Lockwood, "A View", pp. 65–77. Lockwood is primarily concerned at this point in his study with the dating of Divitis's *Missa Quem dicunt homines*. In assigning the Giunta to a reprint of a lost Petrucci edition of 1515, he can assert not only that all the contents must predate that year, but also that they represent a close contact with the French court.

34. The relative lengths of the masses as printed might seem to confirm this: the first five masses of the 1522 edition take a whole number (five) of gatherings in the Superius partbook.

35. This is not at all impossible. Indeed, in chapter 10, I show that both Draudius and Bolduanus did exactly that while referring to Petrucci's *Odhecaton A*.

36. It is notable that the extant Bassus of the 1522 edition has a completely different title, one that reads like a Roman adaptation (with the phrase "In alma urbe nuper impressa*rum* & correcta*rum*") of an earlier title. It is also more in keeping with Petrucci's style, especially once one removes the flowery phrases that came to characterise Roman music printing of the 1520s.

37. The different Bassus title-page has no mention of the three masses: in addition, it refers to "Liber decem missarum", and does not include the "Liber Primus" of the other parts.

38. When Pasoti and Dorico began their series of reprints of Petrucci's books in 1526, Petrucci's Roman privilege was still in effect. He must at that point have waived his rights and allowed the younger men to publish. (This is not surprising, for he was already active in Sora.) However, the printing of the present book four years earlier, in 1522, suggests that it did not fall under the earlier privilege.

39. Brunet, *Manuel*, ii, col.649.

40. Lichtenhthal, *Dizionario*, p. 359.

41. Schmid, *Petrucci*, p. 28; Vernarecci, *Petrucci*, p. 213.

42. Sartori, *Petrucci*, p. 192.

43. Vernarecci, *Petrucci*, pp. 215–16.

44. Brunet, *Manuel*, iv, col.453; Sander, *Livre*, No.5473, apparently described the same block seen by Vernarecci; Sartori, *Petrucci*, p. 193. The book is illustrated in Sander, Plate no.742.

45. I am very grateful to Professor van Benthem for allowing me access to his copy of this edition.

46. Manzoni, *Soncino*, vol.4 (= part 2, vol.2), pp. 56–59, no.119.

47. Johnson and Scholderer, *Short-Title*, p. 495.

48. I am grateful to Dennis Rhodes for pointing out this edition to me.

49. Reese, "First", p. 39.

50. Vernarecci, *Petrucci*, p. 217.

Chapter Fifteen

PETRUCCI'S TYPE, INITIAL LETTERS,

AND WATERMARKS

n these inventories, I do not set out to give all the information necessary to conduct research into Petrucci's printing. They are intended merely to meet two needs: to supply the data that will allow readers to use the bibliography and the prose chapters, in other words, to illustrate the arguments made there; and to supply sufficient data for researchers in libraries to be able to identify the material before them.

Because these needs have been seen as paramount, as they should be for all bibliographical writing, many details are omitted here. There is no analysis, for example, of exactly which letters in the fonts of text type exist in ligatures; nor are measurements given for the chain-lines of the papers, or indeed for all the marks themselves.

Type fonts

The fonts of music and text type are discussed in chapter 3. Here I give only basic descriptions for each.

Music type

Petrucci used one font of music type throughout his career. He apparently kept the matrices, and perhaps also the punches, for a number of sorts do show slight changes at different stages. For example, the tails of minims vary in thickness, presumably reflecting a new series of castings. The basic note, however, remains the same, and these changes rarely do more than affect some notes at any time.

A number of the sorts could be inverted. In theory, they all could, but there would never be a reason to invert a clef or a custos, a flat or a proportion numeral. The mensuration sign "C" could be inverted, when it would be reversed, and some *c.o.p.* ligatures were used in the inverted form, at the end of a composition. But the most commonly inverted sorts were the minima and fusa. Since neither had a piece of stave line on them, they could be used at any pitch, with the tail up or down. In the early volumes, the notes were used so that tails mostly ascend, and it was only gradually that Petrucci's typesetters increased the number of down-tails.

There are some sorts in the font that seem not to conform to the general style: for example, in the proportion signs, the "o" is a small and ugly symbol, most evident when used alongside the "2" and "3".

Given these exceptions, the character of the font is distinctive, especially when compared with those of his successors. I have discussed earlier the relationship of the font to contemporary manuscript sources. Its distinctive visual appearance lies in a heavy contrast between thick and thin strokes, and in the elongation of many of the sorts, in both note-heads and tails: internal angles of the shorter note-values balance their elongated tails, as does the shaping of flats and custodes. Since these tails are always kerned, they are frequently damaged, and the most obvious effect lies in the shortened custodes. Nonetheless, there is no sign, before the last books, that any sorts were cast with a shorter tail.

The last volumes do seem to show a technical change. If the slight evidence can be read correctly, the change involved casting the notes on bodies of a full height—that is, occupying at least the height of the five-line stave. Since the new sorts apparently used the same punches and matrices as the earlier, the only evidence for this new approach to musical printing lies in sorts with tails and flags, the minima and shorter values, and (furthermore) only in the presence of distinctive sorts, especially if slightly deformed or damaged: as a result any conclusions can only be tentative. These sorts, however, seem to appear first in 1519 and support the suggestion that a younger craftsman was taking over some of the duties. They would have significantly changed the work of the typesetter and considerably assisted in ensuring the stability of the composed type in the forme. This evidence does not change the basic elements of the font, which are as follows:

Notes: maxima (*max*): 5.5 mm wide; another form, with dog-teeth on the horizontal edges ■ longa (*l*): 2.5 × 2.5: both up and down tails, of variable lengths ■ brevis (*b*): 2.5 × 2.0; outside height with the serifs, 4.3 ■ semibrevis (*sb*): diagonals 2.0 × 2.3, 3.8 high ■ minima (*m*): diagonals 2.0 × 2.3, 11.2 high ■ semiminima (*sm*): the same measurements, though the inner angles seem to be slightly more open, at 45° and 135° ■ fusa (*f*) ■ semifusa (*sf*): found very rarely, for example, on F2r of the edition of Agricola's masses.

Colored notes: with the same measurements as the void: longa ■ brevis ■ semibrevis.

Rests: perfect longa: 9.2 mm high ■ imperfect longa 5.9 high ■ brevis: 3.4 high ■ semibrevis: 2.2 high ■ minima: 2.2 high ■ semiminima: 2.2 high ■ fusa ■ semifusa.

Ligatures: Cum opposite proprietate (*c.o.p.,* 2 *sb*): in a quadrate form, for ascending intervals from a second to the octave (excepting the seventh), and descending for the second to the fifth, with the octave; in the oblique form, for a descending second ■ *Cum proprietate et sine perfectione* (2 *b*): for ascending intervals of the second to the fifth, and the octave; for the descending second ■ *Cum proprietate et cum perfectione* (*b*, *l*): for the ascending second and fourth, and the descending second ■ *Sine proprietate et cum perfectione* (*l*, *l*): only used freely at cadences, it was prepared for descending second and fourth.

Other symbols: clefs: G clef; C clef (2.4 mm wide: variable height, presumably because of damage to the kerned sections); F clef; gamma-ut clef ■ mensuration signs (*m.s.*): C; ₵; ℭ; ○; ⏀; ☉ ■ proportion numerals: 2, 3, o ■ sharp; flat ■ *punctum;* custos (in two forms); bar line; double line; double line with repeat dots; short triple line with repeat dots; *pausa; signum congruentiae;* leger lines; staves.

Spacing sorts: these were essential to provide for the varying distances between notes. They existed in various widths, but all were 19.5 mm high, reaching about 5 mm above the stave, and about 4 mm below.

Lute notation

This font was obviously designed to display a similar style to that of the music font. The rhythm signs are again elongated, though they seem not to be kerned. This is reasonable, for they do not normally have to fit around sorts for a verbal text, though they must have been mounted close to the lower edge of the bodies, so that they could be aligned with the symbols for pitch. This alignment also explains why the rhythm signs move up and down "on the stave", following the highest notated pitch symbols. The latter are necessarily on the smallest possible bodies; whenever notating a chord, their bodies could be no larger than the distance between two "stave" lines.

Rhythm signs: longa; brevis; semibrevis; minima; semiminima; fusa ■ *Pitch numerals:* numerals 1–9, x, ẋ, ẍ ■ *Other signs:* six-line staves; ties for lute tablature; bar line.

Text fonts

Petrucci used both rotonda and roman fonts for much of his career following traditional manners of distinguishing when to use each.[1]

ROTONDA:

1. The largest of the rotonda fonts, this had originally a very specific group of purposes; it was to be used for title-pages, and for part-names in choir-book format. Apart from that, it occasionally appears in the word "tavola"; it also supplies the sorts for initials of individual works, when one of the large initial blocks was not available. Finally, it was also used in Petrucci's edition of the *Parabola Christi* (1516). The font has an 'x'-height of 4.8 mm and corresponds to one mentioned in Isaac, *Italy*, as having a twenty-line measurement of 160 mm.

   This is an elegant font, very black, and with strong contrasts. It has no serifs and virtually no other decoration. Some of the capitals are stylish, with doubled verticals and occasional decoration based on the serif. There are few ligatures: the most prominent is the doubled long s, ∬, used in the word *Bassus*.

Similar fonts were owned by many printers in the late fifteenth century and after 1500 and were used for title-pages. Many are illustrated in various places: for a particularly close example, see Joh. Ferrarienses, *Liber de coelesti vita* (Venice: Matteo di Codeca Capcasa, 1494).[2]

2. Found in all sacred music books (before the latest editions), and in the chanson volumes, for text underlay, this font is also sometimes used for the tavola. It is a simple font, without decoration, and laterally compact; sorts have relatively tall bodies, with long ascenders and descenders. While the font is typical of Venetian fonts of the late fifteenth century, its proportions make it particularly useful for underlay in musical editions, while remaining clear and easy to read.

The font has an 'x'-height of 2.2 mm (twenty lines measure 77 mm) and is a complete series, including two forms of a number of letters, *a*, *d*, *i*, *m*, *r*, and *s*, and both forms of *u* and *v*. These are typical of contemporary rotonda fonts, including *d* with both straight and curved ascenders, and also the long *s*. However, the two forms of *a*, *i*, and *m* may not have been cut at the beginning, for they were not apparently designed to be distinctive. Indeed, they cannot always be easily distinguished before the editions printed in Fossombrone.

There is a large number of ligatures in the font, including *ff*, *ij*, *ʃi*, *ʃʃ*, *ʃt*, and *tr*. In addition, many of the standard contraction signs seem to have been cast on the same body as the letter: this means that the font was considerably larger than a modern one—also a typical feature for the time. Among the contractions are the following: a*n*, e*n*, o*m*, u*n*, u*s*; co*n*, ne, pa*tre*, pe*r*, p*ro*, prop*ter*, q*uae*, q*ua*, q*uem*, q*ui*, q*uoniam*, se*r*, and vi*r*. Finally the font has a few other signs, including æ, Æ, the ligature œ, the Tironian signs for final "m" and for "et" (resembling full-sized subscript numerals 3 and 7) and a small numeral 5 used as a final *s*.

3. This font was not much used and was apparently not owned by Petrucci until some years after he arrived in Fossombrone. It appears for some rubrics in volumes of masses, and in the late book of Pisano's settings. It is larger than the regular font, having an 'x'-height of 2.8 mm. A complete font, however, cannot be reconstructed, for it has a relatively limited use. Indeed, it may never have been complete, for Petrucci could well have bought it to eke out the regular font as he neared the end of his career.

ROMAN:

1. Found only in the introductory texts to *Odhecaton A*, this is an attractive font, suitable for humanistic texts, though by no means as elegant as many of its contemporaries. It has a large number of contractions, ligatures, and diphthongs. The measurements are: '20' = 83 mm, 'x' = 2.8 mm.

2. Found in all the Venetian frottola volumes, where a roman font was required, this font had first appeared in the lists of contents of the chanson volumes. This is a compressed font, suitable for underlay. The serifs are small, ascenders and descenders are not significant, and there is little difference in the weight of different parts of a letter. There is a full range of capitals, and a number of ligatures and contractions. It has an 'x'-height

of 1.7 to 1.8 mm, and a twenty-line height of 57 mm. In this respect, although it seems to have a slightly larger face than the next font, it is mounted on smaller bodies, as befits a typeface apparently designed from the start to be used for underlay.

3. This font first appears in the instruction pages attached to the front of Bossinensis's first book of intabulations (1509). It is another small font, constricted vertically, though mounted on taller bodies. Thus there is actually more space between lines. It has short serifs and not a great deal of contrast. There is a small range of abbreviations, basically only the most commonly found. It has the following measurements: 'x'-height, 1.6 mm; twenty-line measure, 66 mm.

The font may have been intended to serve primarily for any use of Roman other than underlay. Yet by the end of the second decade, it is an all-purpose roman font, used for both privileges and underlay. During these years, a number of letters appear to develop two forms, although these are almost certainly merely because Petrucci had new sorts cast. He would have owned the punches and matrices, for new sorts only differ in details of the thickness of line or aspect of the serif. The new and the old appear side-by-side in later Fossombrone editions.

4. Found only in the non-musical books, by Paulus and by Castiglione, this is the font which was probably designed and cut by Francesco Griffo da Bologna.

This is a very full font, with more contractions and ligatures than are to be found in the fonts designed for music books. For example, the subject matter required the presence of diphthongs æ and œ, not found in the other Roman fonts; it also demanded a fuller range of punctuation, including parentheses, the hyphen and both colon and semicolon. There are rather slight serifs, tapered, and heavily sloped at the tops of letters.

The font has an 'x'-height of 2.1 mm, and a twenty-line height of 108–110 mm, which argues for either a large type body or consistent leading. Isaac[3] finds a closely similar font in Petrucci's edition of the *Parabola Christi* (1516), to which he gives a twenty-line height of 109 mm, as compared with his '110 mm' for the present font. I believe that the two are identical.

Greek fonts

Different Greek fonts appear in each edition of the *Odhecaton A*. Since they were used very little, and Petrucci could not have expected to have regular use for them, he certainly would have borrowed them from other printers. The font used in the first edition appears to correspond with Aldus's fourth Greek font,[4] which Petrucci may have been able to borrow through his connection with either Ungaro or Griffo. Those for the other two editions are different: that in the third is significantly more compressed laterally, leaving white space after it in the line. This confirms that the font was not in Petrucci's house, but collected and inserted after the rest of the page have been set.

A fourth Greek font appears freely in the *Paulina*. This fits exactly with the basic roman font of the book and was probably prepared at the same time and by the same person.

Hebrew font

There is also some use of a Hebrew font in the *Paulina,* on a mere eighteen pages. Petrucci certainly did not own this font. It must have been loaned to him, most probably from Soncino, working nearby at the time. This font, like the Greek in the same book, measures 110 mm for twenty lines.

Confirmation that the font had been borrowed can be found in the existence, on Z1*r* (and repeated on Z4*r*), of a single woodblock carrying a few Hebrew characters. This block implies that the font was no longer in Petrucci's house.

Initial letters

These have been discussed in chapter 3, where the salient points about their adoption, decay, and replacement have already been made, as well as the essential fact that all are unique, apparently all cut from woodblocks.

Here, they are numbered according to the chronology of the adoption of a new set, although few of the numbers actually refer to alphabets that can be termed complete, even by Renaissance standards. For example, there was never more than one letter Q in Petrucci's house.

Even so, some of the allocations of letters to series are necessarily conjectural. It has seemed probable that Petrucci would order at the same time a series of all the letters he felt he needed, rather than ordering them individually. This belief is bolstered by the evidence of those occasions on which there is a significant change in the size or the design of letters. Nonetheless, there are several occasions where one or two letters appear for the first time in a book with no other new letters. In such cases, it is usually possible to associate these letters with others that had been introduced in the previous few books—and I have therefore assumed (with one exception) that they were ordered at the same time and accorded them the same number in the following tables.[5] Representative illustrations of these initials appear on plates 2–3.

1. The set of three initials, *A*, *B*, and *C*, cut for the title pages of the chanson volumes. They appear on the early motet books and at the front of the two volumes by Spinacino, and are also used as uninked furniture on otherwise blank pages. The letter *A* is 92 mm high, and the other two are in proportion.

   These initials were surely ordered at the same time, even though they are not entirely consistent in design. I believe that, even when Petrucci was planning his first book, he already hoped to be able to continue with a series, and that this is why he ordered three initials. If the venture had not been successful, he certainly would have been able to sell these letters to another Venetian printer.

2. The first series of initials commissioned for heading compositions, surely ordered at the same time as the large initials, and from the same artist, for some imitate details of the first three. They stand about 26–27 mm high on the page. Almost all (*A*, *B*, *C*, *D*, *F*, *G*, *H*, *J*, *L*, *M*, *N*, *P*, *R*,

S, T, and *V*) are to be found in the first edition of the *Odhecaton A.* A few others, first appearing in the next book, seem to conform stylistically and have therefore been incorporated here. They are *E, O,* and *Q.* This provides almost a complete standard alphabet (only lacking *K, X, Y,* and *Z,* with the normal exclusions, *I* and *U*—represented by *J* and *V,* and of course *W*). Indeed, despite all the new blocks cut later, only one letter of the alphabet was added, and that was the *K* that would become essential for mass volumes.

In addition, three letters, *C, L,* and *S,* seem to have been cut twice. Both forms of *L* and *S* appear in the earliest sheets of *Odhecaton A,* and so must have been cut at the very beginning. While one *C* is clearly modeled on that in series 1, the other is very close in design to the *E* and *G* of the present series. It is possible that some of these letters were damaged very early on. The form of *C* closest to the *E* and *G,* and one of the two forms of *L* do not seem to survive in perfect condition: the *L,* in particular, becomes ambiguous in meaning, for it soon loses almost all of its horizontal foot. There is no such obvious explanation for the two forms of *S:* one, while very elegant is, in effect, a capital long *S,* and this may well have been abandoned by Petrucci. It appears only once in each of two titles, the *Odhecaton A* and Josquin's first book of masses, of the following year.

This set was probably not the work of a single man, but rather of a studio: there are slight differences in style, among them varying treatments of the slender supporting verticals; the extent of dog-tooth decoration along principal verticals; the occasional addition of decoration that threatens to distract from the basic shape; and even some slightly eccentric designs. Similar letters can be found in a number of other humanistic editions of the time. See the elegant large examples in Livy, *Decades* (Venice: Vercellense for Giunta, 11 Feb. 1493).[6]

It seems probable that this alphabet was constructed with the precise contents of the *Odhecaton A* in mind. That would explain the duplication of a few letters; it would also make some business sense. If the music-publishing venture did not succeed, there were still copies of all the letters normally needed by a printer, with a minimum number of duplications. On the other hand, if the venture were to continue, it would be easy to commission more letters, as indeed happens.

3. A few new initials first appear during 1502, in or immediately after the Josquin edition. These are again 26–27 mm high, though they are less consistent in design, and some are distinctly less attractive, being unbalanced. Others, among them an *S,* are lavish in design, with many ornamental lines; the *K,* which now becomes essential for the mass books, is much simpler and makes a bold statement on the page, perhaps as befitting the start of a new mass. The initials were probably the work of a single man, though not executed at the same time, but rather as Petrucci began to see the need for them.

4. Another set of supplementary letters was surely commissioned as a result of Petrucci's experience with the early mass volumes of Josquin and Obrecht. These continue to be about 26 mm high and may have been ordered soon after the book of Obrecht. They comprise just those that would be needed, the *A, E,* and *S* that typically open movements of a

setting of the Ordinary, and begin to appear with the book of Brumel's masses in mid-1503.[7]

5. At about the same time, Petrucci had commissioned a set of five smaller initials, each about 20 mm high. These were apparently intended to serve for mass movements that began further down the page. As such, they avoided the imbalance in weight on the page that resulted from a large and heavy initial appearing opposite the fourth or fifth stave and removed the need to inset the music on at least two staves. They first appear in the 1503 edition of Brumel's masses and are used thereafter, not only in mass books, but also in *Motetti C* and *Motetti IV*. An attractive example of the pattern of use can be found in the two printings of the *Fragmenta Missarum*. At the tops of pages, the larger initials *P* are often not the same in both editions, since more than one was available: but the smaller letter was consistently used in both, whenever an initial *P* was needed further down the page. Although they do not supplant the larger initials in general, they remain in use throughout Petrucci's career, the *P*, in particular, still being in reasonable condition almost twenty years later. They imply strongly that Petrucci knew by then that he would be publishing more books of mass music.

6. When Petrucci began to publish the series of lute intabulations in 1508, he seems to have commissioned a single letter *R*. At about the same time, a few additional letters begin to appear in his books. They may have been commissioned with the *R*, or separately within a short period. They include letters *A*, *B*, *K*, *R*, and *S*. None of these letters are nearly as attractive as the early series. Both the *A* and *R*, for example, are heavy and rather unbalanced, while the *K* makes an aggressive statement that tends to dominate the page.

7. A new series of initials was cut for Paulus's *magnum opus* of 1513. These are significantly different from those of the music volumes; this is to be expected, for they had a different function—introducing chapters and major sections of the book, rather than announcing new musical works. As a result, they had to be less assertive, and their density more in keeping with that of the type font. They come in perhaps four sizes, all were intended to be square, and most are framed by rules. Decoration is restrained, often consisting of floral devices supporting a basically simple roman letter.

   These letters were not much used outside the *Paulina*. Both the non-musical pamphlets (by Castiglione in 1513 and by Paulus in 1516) open with an initial from this series, as would be appropriate, for they also use the same text font as the *Paulina*. But the initials are not really suitable for use in the musical volumes, although both the *D* and the *I* make an appearance in the late editions.

8. A new series of letters was commissioned sometime during 1514, specifically for the musical volumes. Much of this series is less elegant than before: the letters have ornamental elements that were meant to copy earlier letters, but the proportions are rarely satisfactory. In particular, a letter *R* seems to be leaning far forward and off-balance. A common ornamental feature consists of a small cross-figure, like the design for a sharp, with points in the open corners. This feature, with a heavy figure-of-eight figure, tends to unbalance the designs. The set comprised at

least ten letters, with two examples of *C*. (Both the earlier large forms of *C* had deteriorated: one was not used after 1508, and the other apparently suffered serious damage during the move to Fossombrone.)

9. An important set of initials first appears in 1519 with the series of *Motetti de la Corona*, and can then be used to date a number of the later reprints. The need for this series must have been apparent to Petrucci, who had printed nothing but settings of the mass since 1514, and would have needed to replace some of the letters that had decayed but not been needed during those years. Letters *C* and *J* appear in the second book of the series, and the *J* in particular was (apparently) most urgently needed. Other letters followed and come to predominate in the last of the reprinted editions, alongside those of series 10.

    The letters are 19–20 mm high, and most are modeled on earlier designs, though never very closely. They are relatively crude in execution, with haphazard decoration of the basic design, and they often take ink rather poorly. They must have been the work of a local craftsman.

10. A further, still smaller, series of basically unattractive initials appears in the sequence of reprints that Petrucci produced around the time of the Pisano edition of 1520. They are about 16 mm high and are again mostly modeled on earlier designs. Decoration has been reduced to a series of occasional swirls, and there is little contrast of blackness in the various lines. These initials are still available to Petrucci in the 1530s, for they are used in [*Musica XII*].

11. A different group of initials appears in the *Motetti del Fiore* (1538). These are unlike any others from his press; key to the design is a very heavy basic letter, clearly articulated, and usually outlined with a parallel framing of significant parts of the letter's shape. Additional ornamentation is simple. The letters are about 18 mm high and are reproduced in Gialdroni and Ziino, "New Light".

Watermarks

This section provides an inventory of all the watermarks found in Petrucci's output. The numbers that appear to the left of each item are those used throughout the descriptive bibliographies. The parenthetical citations of reference sources are no more than guides to similar marks, allowing a design to be identified, without asserting that Petrucci's paper is "the same" as the one cited.[8]

The word "countermark" here signifies a mark in the second half of a sheet of paper, always to be found (unless otherwise specified) in the lower outer corner. Such a mark is often the only mark on the sheet. I have used the term merely as a shorthand to indicate its location.

In a number of my descriptions of copies, the indications of papers are followed by a letter "a" or "b". These are used whenever the twin versions of a mark are particularly clear, as an indication to any reader who may be interested in observing that distinction.

1. Long bow and arrow in a circle (similar to Zonghi 522–23, dated 1504). Used in Petrucci's first two books.

2. Crossed arrows (cf. Briquet 6281, dated Florence, 1515–16; Zonghi 1212–13). Petrucci bought a paper with this mark several times during his career. It appears in his first two books and again from late 1514 until mid-1516, during which time it may have been his only paper. The mark also appears during 1509, alongside some other papers. Given the difficult situation facing Venice at the time, it is possible that Petrucci was having to use whatever papers he could find.

3. This may be indistinguishable from the next two marks: all three are countermarks and comprise versions of a capital letter "A". This one has a horizontal cross-bar on both sides of the upper point (cf. Briquet 499, found in Verona and dated 1519, and Briquet 7919). It is sometimes difficult to tell, however, whether the cross-bar was actually a part of the mark, or merely a marginally thicker part of a laid-line. In addition, all three tend to appear in the same or adjacent volumes, suggesting that they were at least part of the same purchases from a *cartolaio*, whether or not they came from the same paper mill. They have a similar range of sizes, from about 21–22 × 19–20 mm, to about 23–24 × 21–22. The two sizes are evidently twins, as can be seen most clearly in copies of the 1502 edition of Josquin's masses. All three marks appear in *Motetti A* of 1502 and are freely used until the *Motetti B* of 1503. Apparently a small second batch was bought in 1504, for it can be seen in *Motetti C* and the first book of frottole, both of that year.

4. This is closely similar to the previous mark, though it appears to have only half of the upper cross-bar, to the right of the apex of the letter "A" and was used at the same time.

5. This is the third of a set of marks, in this case without any solid trace of a cross-bar at the apex of the letter "A", but used alongside Nos. 3 and 4.

6. An anchor in a circle, surmounted by a star, one of a group of anchor marks used by Petrucci and usually found with a countermark, No. 7. The anchor does not touch the top of the circle, and there is no small circle below the star (perhaps close to Briquet 478—Bergamo, 1502— or 493—Udine, from 1524). It can measure 49 or 52 mm at its widest point. This mark first appears in 1503 in the books of Brumel and Ghiselin and was available into the next year. A second batch of this paper was bought in 1509 and was used for Petrucci's last two books in Venice. Finally, Petrucci bought a third batch sometime in 1515 and 1516, for it was used in the second edition of Bossinensis's first book and the first printing of the Fossombrone edition of Josquin's first book. This evidence helps with the dating of several cancels.

7. This is a countermark, normally found with papers 6 and 8. It comprises two elements, the outer of which is another capital letter "A", apparently with no upper cross-bar. Inside that is a capital letter "B" (cf. Briquet 502–03).

8. An anchor in a circle, without a star above, centered on a chain line, usually accompanied by mark 7 as a countermark (cf. Briquet 475). The anchor's barbs appear to be only on the inner side of each arm, and the mark is 45 mm at the widest point. This paper was bought sometime in mid-1503 and first appears in some sheets of Brumel, but it lasted only a few months and does not seem to predominate in any edition.

9. This paper has a small countermark, with two flowers on stalks: the outer has five petals, and the inner is a fleur-de-lys. The two stalks lie on chain lines. The height of both is 22 mm: they are 7 and 9 mm high respectively, and 35 or 39 mm apart. Petrucci bought this paper in mid-1503; it appears freely in the two books printed together, Brumel's and Ghiselin's masses, as well as in the 1503 edition of *Canti B,* and in *Canti C* of 1504, probably as remnants of paper.

10. An anchor, not enclosed by a circle, and 36 mm wide and more than 33 mm high (cf. Briquet, No.437). This paper appears only on four sheets in Petrucci's output, two at the end of a single copy of Brumel's masses (1503), one in the 1503 edition of Ghiselin's masses, and the other in a later printing of the Fossombrone edition of Josquin's second book (dated 1515).

11. First bought in 1503, this has a mark of a pair of scales within a circle. The top of the holder projects beyond the top of the circle and ends in two small oval loops. The mark, which is about 35 mm wide, is similar to Briquet 2538. It appears in a number of editions from *Canti B* (1503) to *Frottole I* (1504), with some relics used in *Frottole II* and *Motetti A* (both of 1505). The principal uses represent more than one purchase, as is evident from the pattern of its use in *Motetti C:* the mark on the Koper copy of this edition, f.A4, is a mere 31 mm wide. Another small batch appears in the *Fragmenta Missarum* (1505).

12. This paper was evidently in use for a very short time, and Petrucci may not have had free access to it. The mark is a six-pointed star in a circle, looking like a sand-dollar, and about 29 mm wide (cf. Briquet 6085). It is found in three books of 1504—*Canti C*, Agricola's masses, and the third edition of *Odhecaton A*. In each it appears only in the same specific places, in every copy; it may therefore have been supplementary stock, even borrowed from another printer.

13. This paper appears only once in Petrucci's output, for both sheets of gathering Q in *Canti C* (1504). It is possible therefore that these sheets were printed separately, after the rest of the book, though there is no clear bibliographical evidence to support such a hypothesis. The mark is a countermark, of a flower with a capital letter A; in this it seems to resemble other similar marks and indeed may come from the same mill. But here the A is inside the flower and is in an ornamental style, rather than the more normal roman character.

14. This mark is a flower on a stalk, which curls round to form an inverted P, measuring about 36×14 mm. It was probably only in use for a short time, in late 1504 or early 1505. This raises doubts about the brief appearance of the paper in *Motetti B* of May 1503 (see the comments to that edition).

15. This is similar to mark 6, with a star above the anchor and circle, although here the anchor does touch the top of the circle (cf. Briquet 481 and 484). It is normally about 51 mm wide, and in the 1505 edition of Josquin's second book it has a total height on 71 mm. It was bought in that year, more than once, appearing early in the year in the *Misse De Orto* and also in three other books. It was used for the 1505 cancel leaves for *Motetti B.* Evidently another stock was bought in Fossombrone and used in the new edition of Bossinensis's first book.

16. Another paper with a mark of an anchor in the circle, again just touching the top of the circle. Above the circle is another, much smaller circle, itself surmounted by a six-pointed star. The mark varies in size, apparently indicating different purchases: different versions are 61 mm or 52 mm wide in *Motetti IV*, and 44.5 mm wide in the Bossinensis first book. The mark is similar to Briquet No.497 (Vicenza, 1505; Treviso, 1514–19). Petrucci apparently bought three separate batches of this paper: one appears in two books of 1505, a second is found in some sheets of Bossinensis's first book as well as in one cancel bifolium to the *Motetti a cinque* (both of 1509), and the third appears in two of the later Josquin editions.

17. A countermark, evidently related to 18, 21, and 22. This has an initial capital A with no cross-bar, but a horizontal at the top, and to its right a two-petaled flower on a stalk, resembling a letter B on its side. It appears in 1505, remains in use into 1507, and represents more than one purchase.

18. This is related to 17, though the sequence of the two designs is reversed, with the flower nearer the edge of the sheet. It compares with Briquet 481 or 484 (found in Treviso, ca.1510). It appears in 1505, starting as did 17 in *Motetti IV*, and continuing into the next year.

19. This mark is very similar to mark 6, though it seems not to be the same paper. This version is only used in two books in 1505.

20. A countermark of a small hill, a calvary, surmounted by a cross, and with a longer line at its base. One of the twins measures 38 × (5)12(17) in 1505, and 39 × (5)16(17) in 1506; the other measures 38 × (5)21(11) in 1506. It was apparently bought in several batches, for it was used in 1505–06 and again in 1507. This is critical for the dating of one copy of Josquin's first book, and the two remaining sheets of the first edition of Dammonis's *Laude*.

21. This is probably another version of 17, for it is identical except that there is no line at the apex of the letter A. As with the group of papers numbered 3–5, this line may have been a dense chain line, though the marks are distinguished here. This version appears in two books of 1506, *Lamentations II* and the second edition of Josquin's first book. Mošin says that this is a Venetian mark.

22. This is related to mark 18, in exactly the manner that 21 is related to 17. It appears only in 1506 and 1507.

23. This mark and the next three have essentially the same designs as Nos.3–5 and present the same problems of differentiation. They probably came from the same mill as the others, although they carry marks from new molds: the new marks are generally larger, measuring 25–27 × 24 and 27–28 × 27 mm. This particular form, with a cross-bar on both sides of the apex of the "A", seems to have been bought early in 1507 and was used for a number of volumes early in that year. It, with its companions, was evidently bought again at the end of the year, for it reappears in January 1508 and is used until the first book of 1509.

24. This is closely similar to the previous mark: it again has a cross-bar only on the right of the apex of the "A". It appears in the same books as the previous mark, and the two papers, with the next, were presumably parts of the same batch.

25. This is the third of three closely related marks, a capital "A", but without a cross-bar at the apex. It is found alongside the previous two marks.

26. A pair of crossed arrows with a line from the crossing up to a six-pointed star. Similar marks can be found in Briquet 6289 (Pistoia, 1511) and the following designs. In Petrucci's work, this mark appears only in the second book of Bossinensis's intabulations, dated 1511.

27. A single large capital letter "P", similar to marks in Briquet and Zonghi (cf. Zonghi, 1666, found in 1501). It is only found in copies printed in Fossombrone, beginning with the later layers of Bossinensis II, dated 1511; it also appears in cancels that must be dated in late 1514 or early 1515.

28. This and the next evidently are two sets of marks from the same *cartolaio*, probably even from the same mill. This paper has a mark of a balance within a double circle: the upper extension of the balance beyond the circle is capped by a small bird (Zonghi 1162, dated 1515: cf. Briquet 2480 or 2517). The basic size is 55–56 × 41 mm. Chain lines are 34 mm apart. The two papers were bought for Paulus's *De recta Paschae* (1513) and appear indiscriminately throughout the book. More of the paper survives in the next edition, of Castiglione's *Epistola*.

29. This mark is very similar; the extension of the balance is longer and capped by a small figure-of-eight perch for the bird (Briquet 2478; Zonghi 1155–1156). The mark is therefore larger, sometimes 88 × 44 mm. This appears in both books, alongside No.28.

30. A mark of a merman, close to Zonghi 1065 (dated Fabriano 1513). This is only found in a few sheets of the first edition of Josquin's third book of masses (1514).

31. This has a large design of a castle, or a fortified tower or gatehouse with banners at the top corners, measuring a number of different sizes (cf. Briquet 15891). In *Frottole VIII* (1507), the marks measure 54 × 36 mm or 42 × 37 mm: in Fossombrone editions, it is larger, measuring 59 × 32 mm. It appears that a small batch was bought in late 1507, and a different batch sometime after mid-1514.

32. A gloved hand, with the fingers together, and two double bands across the palm, similar to Briquet 11148. This was bought for the 1516 edition of Paulus and not used elsewhere.

33. An anchor touching the top of an enclosing circle, itself surmounted by a bird on a simple perch. It is reasonable to assume that this and the next paper came from the same mill that made the paper for Petrucci's editions of Paulus and Castiglione. It appears in later editions of books published in 1515 and 1516, and since it carries settings that use both rotonda and roman typefaces for underlay, it precedes the editions of 1519.

34. This is another anchor in a circle, surmounted by a line with two small oval loops. Like the previous paper, it appears in later editions of books from 1515 and 1516.

35. A mark of a crescent moon (Briquet 5213 or 5209). More than one paper carries this mark, with more than one size: in 1519, some marks are 23 × 12 mm, while Pisano's book of 1520 has a mark of 26 × 22 mm. Compare Briquet 5211—Venice in the 1520s, though there with a countermark. Petrucci first bought these papers during 1519, for one

appears in the first edition of his *Motetti de la Corona II*. The mark continues to appear in later editions of other (earlier) Fossombrone titles, apparently returning after a period of using a paper without a mark.

36. A crown surmounted by a deformed cross, or perhaps a low fleur-de-lys, measuring 31 × 65 mm is found in the 1538 edition. Gialdroni and Ziino, "New Light", fn.3, associate this mark with Briquet No.4839.

—. Paper without a mark becomes a fundamental resource in the latest editions of titles from the 1510s. It is found in 1519 alongside No.35 and was used exclusively for a while in these later editions.

Evidently, some of these dates for purchases of paper must be speculative. Complete editions have been lost, distorting the evidence. At the same time, incomplete editions and printings often carry no date, and their dating is dependent on the state of the typographical material, but at least as much on the presumed sequence of paper use. It is notable, however, that Petrucci rarely stayed with one paper for long enough to establish a consistent pattern over many volumes. This suggests that his press was not seen as consistently full time, and therefore to be regularly supplied from the same mill, even if it did receive papers from the same *cartolaio*.

A second interesting feature concerns the patterns of paper in the years 1515 and later, that is, while Petrucci had ownership of the land and paper mill at Aqua Santa. The papers in use in 1514 and 1515 are ones that he had used previously, sometimes in Venice or Fossombrone, rather than new paper that could plausibly be associated with the mill. It may be that the mill made papers that were not of the quality and character required for printing. In 1516, however, there is a significant change: papers 33, 34, and (in particular) 35 appear for the first time, alongside the paper without a mark. I suspect that the last two of these could indeed come from the Fossombrone paper mill. Since they first appear at the moment when Petrucci was planning to move to Sora, to erect a mill there, he may have decided to simplify one aspect of the production process at Fossombrone, by arranging for a continuous local supply of paper—from the mill he owned. Equally plausibly, the manager who took over the day-to-day responsibility of the printing shop may have decided to use the local paper: these papers are consistently of a poorer quality than those that had been used in earlier editions. In either case, it is plausible to argue that the half-moon mark, as well as the unmarked paper, represents the product of the mill at Aqua Santa.

Notes

1. See the discussion of this in chapter 3.
2. This book is illustrated in Bertieri, *Editori*, pl.XXVIII.
3. See the entry for Petrucci in Isaac, *Index*.
4. See Barker, *Aldus*, and Proctor, *Printing*.
5. It should be noted that these numbers do not always correspond to those in Boorman, "New", and Boorman, *Petrucci*.
6. This famous book is illustrated in Bertieri, *Editori*, pl.XCVIII, and Essling, *Livres*, i, p. 47.
7. I regard this belated appearance of some initials as a crucial reason for arguing that the

Josquin book was originally not seen as the first of a series of mass volumes, and that it was not until the Obrecht book was decided on that the new initials were ordered. Taken with the appearance of series 5, the K and P of series 2 and 3 were sufficient for most situations.

8. These sources are cited in the bibliography: see Briquet, *Filigranes*; Mošin, *Anchor*, Zonghi, *Zonghi*.

Chapter Sixteen

BIBLIOGRAPHICAL CONCEPTS

AND TERMINOLOGY

he remainder of the present volume gives the (primarily biblio-graphical) data that support the conclusions drawn in the first part. Bibliography is necessarily a historical study: the data it accumu-lates are solely of value insofar as they are put at the service of the history of the book trades, of the contents of the books, or of the dissemination of those contents. In that sense, what follows, although it comprises a major part of the book, and although it will probably be referred to more often by many users, is ancillary to what has gone before.

Nonetheless, the craft of bibliography has a long and distinguished history in its own right, and its practitioners have spent countless hours and many bottles of ink on developing methods for making the results of their work as clear as possible. The methodological studies of McKerrow, Bowers, Tanselle, and Krum-mel, among others[1] have developed a corpus of procedures, both for analysing the printed book and for laying out the results of that analysis. This corpus is generally accepted among bibliographical scholars, and one departs from it at one's peril, not merely because it *is* generally accepted, but also because it is the result of long and careful thought and testing.

However, music printing and publishing is in some ways a special case; music printing of the Italian sixteenth century raises even more particular issues; and the output of Petrucci produces further problems, whichever detailed variation of the general approach one adopts. The function of the present chapter is to discuss some of these problems, as they affect my current practice of bibliographical description.[2]

As the first part of this volume has made clear, Petrucci expended consid-erable effort on preparing accurate copies—accurate within his own terms. The sequence of patterns of correction, outlined in chapters 5 and 6, led to different sets of readings (deriving directly from the printing house) in virtually every extant copy. One can rarely be sure of the point at which Petrucci felt he had finished tinkering with the text-as-printed, that is, the point at which we can believe that we have a true "ideal copy" in our hands, or in our bibliographical sights.

Petrucci also appears to have been content to employ short print-runs, with the concomitant necessity of frequently re-setting type, for whole volumes or individual series of sheets. As a result, few extant copies of any of his titles can truly be described as bibliographically straightforward, as not sophisticated in one way or another. This complexity further affects our view of the "ideal copy", but it also makes much more complex our use of the standard terms by which copies are normally situated within the publishing history of a title. It is difficult to locate a copy within an edition when we cannot really be sure at what point Petrucci placed it. The terms *issue* and *state* also acquire additional resonances, in which almost every copy belongs to its own state, and many copies seem to involve a distinct "version" as put on the market.

The present chapter contains more than a mere introduction to the bibliographical descriptions and their presentation: it discusses some concepts as they can be applied to early music printing, and to Petrucci's output in particular; and it seeks to justify the consciously hybrid manner in which certain categories of data have been arranged in the following bibliography. Chapter 13 lists all the surviving editions and impressions, of books and parts of books, in chronological order, and thereby acts as a chronological index to the bibliography and a guide to the history of Petrucci's output, designed for the bibliographer.

Edition and Issue

The function of the terms *edition* and *issue*, coupled with that of two others—*impression* and *state*—is to place every extant copy of a book within a simple hierarchy. This strategy takes cognisance of the distinction between the book's printing history and its publishing history. The term *issue* relates directly, almost solely, to the pattern of publishing of a book: the term *edition*, for a bibliographer, refers primarily to the printing history, but is usually related in some way to the pattern of publication.

A single issue comprises all the copies of a book that were put on sale under the same arrangements. A change in any of these circumstances—price (if on the copy), printer's or publisher's address, or date—is enough to indicate that copies are from a new issue. Clearly, we cannot always assert that all the copies of one issue were actually put on sale at the same time: the printer or publisher may have held a part of the stock in the warehouse for a while, waiting to measure the fortunes of the title. These copies are, of course, part of the same issue. In the same manner, we cannot assume that all the copies were printed in one process: if additional copies of a book were printed to supplement an issue that had sold especially well, those books could belong to the same issue, merely enlarging it. Even so, such additional copies might need to be described as a different edition, if they were printed from newly set-up type.

This requirement might arise because of the definition of an edition, which is seen as made up of all the copies prepared from one setting of type.[3] For almost all typeset material, and certainly for Petrucci's editions, this meant that every copy of each sheet had to be run off at the same time, before the type was distributed again. The type for each of the various levels of printing was set up in one series of processes: the presswork proceeded as the type was ready, and all the copies of each sheet of that edition were the result of one set of operations. The few cases where I can argue that there was a hiatus in the printing process do not affect this point: all the copies of each sheet were still run off together.

It would be possible to prepare an edition intended to contain two or more issues. Indeed such editions exist: there are examples of copies from the same printing, but with different publisher's names on the title page; of editions containing some copies with a dedication, and others without, apparently intended for different distribution; and of other editions containing copies printed on vellum, apparently again not for ordinary sale, but for donation to patrons and dedicatees. In each of these cases, a single edition comprises more than one issue.

None of these instances has arisen in the study of Petrucci's volumes. Indeed, the opposite is not only present but common—in which a single issue incorporates more than one edition. I have already remarked, and the bibliographical descriptions will make it clear, that almost all the books printed in Fossombrone after 1513 survive in more than one edition—but that the different editions of a single title always carry the same publication data. In this instance, the later editions were intended to be sold under the same arrangements as the earlier. They were, therefore, part of the same issue.[4]

The editions can be distinguished because they are not produced from the same setting of type. Each involved a repetition of the whole process of printing the book, from editing the text (as I believe) through typesetting to presswork. As a result, each is easily distinguished from the next, for the appearance on the page is always, at least slightly, different.

In practice, the situation is a little more complex than that. A printer might need to reprint one sheet of a book, while the rest of the volume continued to be made up of sheets from the original printing. In this case, the change is (relatively) so slight that it would be ludicrous to consider the ensuing copies part of a new edition. The printer might then need to reprint a different sheet, and then another, and a fourth, and so on, each done at a different time. The point will come at which all the sheets are new, and by this time, we are, of course, already dealing with a second edition. Alternatively, a copy of the new edition might contain one sheet from the earlier, in order to use up surplus stock: another copy might have two sheets, another three, and so on. At some point along the line, the scholar needs to be able to assert that a transition from the first to the second has been achieved.

Scholars have taken different positions on marking the critical point. Some suggest a specific percentage of the whole, after which a new edition is deemed to be in place.[5] The most useful position for the case of Petrucci is that taken by Bowers: that the bibliographer, wishing to place a given composite copy, should try to divine the printer's intention. Does it look as though the new sheets in the copy represent an attempt at supplementing the earlier edition? Or is it more likely that they represent a new edition, using up some sheets from the earlier?

This might seem a dangerous process: we have no way of determining with certainty what the printer or publisher was thinking. In the case of Petrucci, however, it is usually not difficult. There are many cases in which single sheets, pairs, or small groups of sheets were printed and added to the earlier edition. In the following bibliography I have always related these additions to that earlier edition. There are also cases in which a major part of a separate typesetting exists: these must represent more than merely filling in cracks in the earlier edition. They are, to my eye, representative of building a new one.

For this reason, I have chosen to take a fairly generous line in deciding when a printing represents a complete edition. For example, whenever two complete partbooks from a set of four exist in a specific printing, even though they comprise only half of the entire volume, they almost certainly do represent a new edition. Even when rather less than half of the set of partbooks survives, we can sometimes be confident in assigning this to a new edition. Sections of all partbooks, or a small component of an edition earlier than any other extant, have been understood to indicate the intention of making, not supplementing, an edition,—as in the case of the surviving copies of Févin's masses.

Impression and State

An impression is normally regarded as a separate printing from a given setting of type. If the type is kept set up, it becomes possible to make a new impression at any time after the original. This is obviously normal for all forms of plates, for the plates themselves can be kept, sometimes for centuries. In these instances, a single edition may comprise a large number of impressions, and these may also have different conditions of sale, thus representing different issues.

For Petrucci, only one example exists of more than one impression from the same typesetting of type.[6] As we might expect, elsewhere Petrucci's craftsmen broke down the forme and redistributed the type immediately after the press-run. As a result, every new impression required setting up the type again, whether for a single sheet or for a whole edition.

In Petrucci's output, the term *state* also has limited usefulness, in its traditional context. As a term, it always refers specifically to the content, and is the only one of these terms to do so. Any copies of a book with identical readings of the text (and peripheral matter) are said to be of the same state. As soon as any change is made—a stop-press correction, a cancel sheet, even an in-house manuscript change—subsequent copies belong to a new state.

Therefore, virtually every copy of every musical title printed by Petrucci seems to belong to a different state of that book. Even though we can determine the direction of a number of in-house changes and note what seems to have been Petrucci's preferred version, we have to acknowledge all the surviving states.

However, there is one, rather different, use for these terms: to apply them to the individual page, half-sheet, or sheet. Every book is an amalgam of these smaller units, each of which also survives in different impressions and states. Part of the reason for the bibliographic complexity of Petrucci's editions lies here. There is no evidence that Petrucci intended to preserve a strictly consistent edition, once the first printing had been finished. Rather, he made changes as they became necessary or desirable.[7]

Therefore, the individual sheet might be transformed, printed from a new setting: in that case, it is probably reasonable to refer to the new sheet as a second impression of that part of the book. Of course, this stretches the customary meaning of the word "impression": and yet, we cannot assign the copy to a second edition if the change concerns only one sheet; it is, even more certainly, not part of a new issue. Nor do I want to assign that sheet to a new state when the whole sheet has been reset. Indeed, *impression* seems to be the best term: the sheet has been printed from a new setting of type.[8]

New states of sheets also exist and are easier to discuss. They contain different textual content, perhaps stop-press changes or some of the various in-house modes of correction. To change a single reading in a whole book is to introduce a new state of the whole: to describe all such changes as new states is self-defeating. By being used for virtually every copy, the term becomes meaningless. Indeed, it becomes misleading. In every copy of a sixteenth-century book, there are sheets that show the latest possible state of corrections, and other (often adjacent) sheets that remain in their original state. Indeed, the two faces of a single sheet can lie at different points along the continuum of new states. As a result, the concept of a single "state" for a whole book is meaningless chronologically—for the copy will comprise both early states for some sheets, and later for others.

If, on the other hand, we use the term *state* for each separate sheet (or even forme), as it is changed, we regain some value for the practice. Then we can see the number of times that a sheet was changed, arrange them in order, and become aware of the relative strength of, for example, the pattern of stop-press changes as opposed to manuscript changes.

However, I have avoided the terms *impression* and *state* in these sorts of context.[9] For one thing, it is often impossible to arrange states in order: even when this can be done (because a particular sort of change can have occurred only in one direction), laying out the variants in this manner adds an additional and unnecessary layer to what is already a complex arrangement. Instead, by listing all the in-house corrections in one place, under the initial description of each book, I show where all these changes lie, and which copies present them.

Cancels

Although I have tended to use the word *cancel* for almost all new impressions of one or two sheets, I recognise that this is almost certainly not correct. A cancel was, after all, a page or sheet deliberately intended to *replace* another. This carries the implication that the *cancelland* bore some defect that caused it to be rejected. A cancel does not merely supplement the stock of the original, but replaces it entirely.

In a number of cases there are enough differences in readings for us to believe that the new sheet was truly a cancel; in as many others, there seem to be few differences between the two versions—differences that are not troublesome to the user. The replacement sheet in some copies of Paulus's *Paulina,* although it does have differences in readings, contains nothing that affects the content. In other cases, a sheet that was evidently prepared later than the rest of the book survives in every extant copy: in those cases, the new sheet may well be a true cancel, for Petrucci *may* have chosen to discard all copies of the original. But, here again, I am using the term *cancel* without a strict justification.

It might have been preferable to use the word *impression* for all of these new sheets—were it not for the potential confusion caused thereby. Self-evidently, the word *cancel* does imply a specific replacement for the named sheets. The reader merely needs to be aware that the additional implications of the term are not necessarily present in any given case.

Ideal Copy

The manner in which bibliographers understand the concept of the *ideal copy* has undergone considerable rethinking in recent years.[10] Nonetheless, the central point remains that an ideal copy represents a book as issued by the printer and publisher, once they were satisfied that the details of appearance and content were as they wished to see them. This does not necessarily mean that the book was perfect, either as regards the content or as regards the bibliographical structure. It only implies that they intended to issue the book in the form described here as an ideal copy. This also means that an ideal copy may not exist: for example, in the case of sets of partbooks, there may be no extant copy with all parts. However, the ideal copy has to be described, for that is how the printer intended the book to be bought.

In some cases, we have to go further: not only is there no complete copy of Petrucci's *Motetti a cinque Libro primo* (1508), there is none at all of the second Contratenor part. Here, of course, one cannot reconstruct the whole of a lost partbook, but its presence in an ideal copy must be noted, and, where possible, its structure or constituents projected.

For the present study, the term *ideal copy* has been interpreted in a slightly idiosyncratic manner. As is evident in the first part of the book, I have made a case for a large number of extant corrections (including those made in manuscript) having been effected in the printing shop. For that reason, I have felt that these corrections represent part of the version of the book-and-text as Petrucci wished it to be published.[11] Therefore, I have included such corrections in the description of the ideal copy whenever I have felt confident that they were made in the printer's shop—even when they may not survive in every extant copy. In this way, I have tried to represent a copy that I believe Petrucci regarded as the best he could present at the time the copies left the shop—effectively at the time the latest and most extensively corrected copies were sent to agents or purchasers.

On the other hand, later correction sheets, cancels, and others do not belong with the ideal copy. The book was published without them, so that we must assume that Petrucci thought he was producing something approaching an ideal copy. These sheets are rather an indication of a later decision by Petrucci that he had failed in some manner.[12]

As a result, each of the following bibliographical entries begins with a description of what I believe was, in Petrucci's eyes, an ideal copy, including any in-house corrections that survive. That is followed by a description of the individual copies, with notes of the ways in which each copy diverges from the ideal, as well as other features specific to the copy, including binding, ownership marks, and musical variants introduced by later users. In addition, each entry notes which in-house variants are present: after which it should theoretically be possible to note the order in which the surviving formes went through the press, and the order in which individual sheets left the printing shop. This work is of significance only when many copies survive, and has little value, given the pattern of survival of Petrucci's editions.

Notes

1. Bowers, *Principles*; Krummel, "Citing"; Krummel, "Functions"; McKerrow, *Introduction*, Tanselle, "Bibliographical"—among others of his writings cited here. I would also list here Blayney, *Texts*; Hinman, *Printing*; and the works of Bühler, Fahy, Hellinga, Rhodes, and Stevenson cited in the bibliography.

2. I have discussed some of these issues, or at least laid out my conclusions, in various entries in Boorman, "Glossary".

3. It goes without saying that the word *type* in this instance always includes engraved plates, off-set plates, or the materials for any other process. There are many places in the history of music printing where the terminology used in the study of type-set music cannot be translated directly to music printed by other processes. Since all of Petrucci's work is the result of a letter-press process, these issues do not arise.

4. This point is different from the position prevailing in the later editions of the earliest Venetian titles. Here, Petrucci placed a new date on the new printing, making of it not only a new edition, but also a new issue.

5. Among these are Krummel, *Guide*.

6. This single exception to the general rule concerns the page carrying the papal privilege, which appears in a number of volumes printed at Fossombrone. The evidence suggesting that this was kept in standing type for some periods has been mentioned in chapter 8.

7. I assume that many new impressions—settings and printings—of formes for sheets or half-sheets were seen as necessary, but we cannot distinguish between the two most probable reasons—a shortfall of stock, and a drastic error in content. Yet, I assume that many in-house corrections—stop-press, stamped in, or manuscript—were also considered desirable. The distinction might seem arbitrary, but I doubt that the labour of setting up a forme would be undertaken if there were many usable copies, on many sheets of valuable paper.

8. It is even possible to have a new impression of only one side of a sheet of paper, if the press had to be stopped during the run of the second forme, so that a new forme could be prepared. I know of no example of this in Petrucci's output.

9. The word *impression* has, of course, been used in a general sense throughout this study. While writing about a multiple-impression process, it has been easiest to refer to the distinct layers (stave and text as opposed to music) as impressions, indicating not only different formes, but the whole sequence of one series of formes used in a book, as opposed to the other.

10. For recent discussions of the issue, see Fahy, "Concetto", and Tanselle, "Ideal".

11. The same position is taken in Bühler, "Stop-press", p. 139; the author says that "it is clear that such corrections were considered by Aldus as essential in the presentation of the text as he wished it to appear".

12. We also have to look at these sheets in the same terms manner looking for an ideal copy of each.

Chapter Seventeen

BIBLIOGRAPHICAL DESCRIPTIONS

 ithin a given entry, the details for the earliest extant edition (with all its copies) are presented first, followed by discussion of cancel leaves for that edition. Any subsequent edition, or any partial reprinting, which Petrucci regarded as part of this issue — and which, as a result, musicologists have traditionally associated with it — is then presented under the same overall entry.

This method produces some inconsistencies. The various editions (of frottole and chanson volumes, in particular) that carry different dates are entered at different places in this catalogue. In addition, some "new" editions that have survived without colophon (and therefore date) are entered at their presumed date: this applies, for example, to the second editions of Josquin's *I Missarum*, Ghiselin's *Misse*, and the first book by Bossinensis. It also means the insertion of a first edition of Dammonis's *Laude* during 1506. The justification for this decision lies in Petrucci's evident practice of re-dating editions that he produced in Venice, as well as first Fossombrone editions of Venetian titles. (There seems to be one exception to this rule, in the Fossombrone edition of Bossinensis's first book.)

In Fossombrone, however, he abandoned this practice during 1514. Therefore, different editions (mostly of sacred music) were produced with the same date. These editions, and almost all "cancels", are entered with the first printing, under the same number, which should not produce much inconvenience, for I have made as many cross-references as I can to explain the relationships of different entries.

For each edition or cancel, an entry proceeds from the description of an ideal copy to the description of the individual extant copies. Entries in the bibliography are arranged in the following manner:

REFERENCE DATA

1. Running number. This sequence includes all titles and editions definitely or plausibly printed and published by Petrucci.

2. The running number is followed by a short title and composer's name. Both are conventional in form, merely acting as identifiers of the book discussed.

3. The following line includes the official date of the edition to be described, followed by a *RISM* number. This number is entered solely for identification purposes: since more than one issue and edition can be found under the same *RISM* number, or two numbers can represent a single title, the number can be no more than a locator for the average user, and an easy means of association between these entries and discussions elsewhere in the literature.

4. When more than one printing is included in an entry, an overview of editions or cancels is supplied: on occasion, this may include notes on the distribution of copies between editions.

5. If there is more than one printing, a line follows indicating the edition being described first.

IDEAL COPY

6. A transcription of the principal title-page, with all others insofar as they are different, with an indication of the folios from which they have been transcribed. Abbreviated letters in the source are indicated here by italics: omitted letters are placed within parentheses.

7. This is always followed by a transcription of the colophon and register, with an indication of the folio on which they appear.

8. A transcription of any other introductory matter — dedication, instructions for the lute, etc. A transcription of the Tavola, if it is of significance, or the details are markedly different from those given on the pages and recorded here under the Contents.

9. An indication of the format, the number of folios and the collation of an ideal copy.

10. Indication of the style and pattern of signatures, with a listing of all variants and omissions. After a pattern example of the signatures, an opening bracket leads to a description of its use: thus "[$4 • − A1 • + B5" indicates that all gatherings are signed on folios 1-4, with the exception of A1, and with the addition of B5.

11. The original foliation, with all anomalies: "t.r.r." indicates "top right recto" as the place of the numbering.

12. When there is a running head line, this is indicated next. For some books, details of nonrecurrent headings are also given.

13. Part names. When these are not part of the running head line, but appear within the page (as they normally do in the choirbook format favoured by Petrucci for secular music), the next entry gives an analysis of the pattern of spelling and placing of these names, as an aid to the analysis of patterns of content and typesetting.

14. Fonts. This is a fairly mechanical entry for most volumes. It records whether Petrucci's normal music font is used; it records the number of staves per page with their basic dimensions; and it lists the text fonts used in each volume.

The details of stave measurements are as follows: the lengths are extremes, unless there is some significant pattern to be described. The height is recorded as three numerals, e.g., 10-91-110: the height of the lowest stave on a page (from bottom to top, usually at the righthand end) — the height from the bottom to the top of the second stave — the height of a complete set of staves. (This allows for a measurement of the height of the single stave, as well as of the spacing between staves.) When there are recurring patterns of stave arrangement throughout a volume, that is reserved for discussion under "Technical comments," either at the level of the ideal copy, at the level of the individual copy, or in the final commentary.

The text identifications refer to the basic descriptions of the text fonts given in chapter 15.

15. Textual comments: these usually consist of unusual spelling errors, or similar textual oddities.

16. Technical comments: these include any comments on special sorts, or on matters of technical procedure that can be seen in copies of this title.

17. In-house corrections. This lists all the corrections I believe to have been made in the printing shop and to be the result of Petrucci's desire to improve his editions. The format followed is as follows:

folio number.stave number (lower case roman numerals).note number (arabic numerals): notation before the change and notation after (using italics for the rhythmic value and Helmholtz's signs for the pitch): copies concerned.

Notes are counted continuously along a line, with each note in a ligature being counted: rests and other signs are not counted.

l = longa; b = breve; sb = semibreve; m = minim; sm = semiminim; f = fusa; sf = semifusa; r = rest; d = dotted; $c.o.p.$ = ligature cum opposite proprietate.

Thus:] A5v.iv.14: $ma^1 \rightarrow sbc^2$, erased and entered in brown ink: D-Mbs, GB-Lbl [indicates that the fourteenth note on the fourth stave of A5v was printed as a *minima* at a^1: this was corrected as described, to a semibreve at c^2, and the correction survives in the copies in Munich and London.

The format for tabulatures is slightly different:

folio number (arabic numerals).stave number (roman).bar number (arabic).vertical event [= chord] (arabic number): notation before change and notation after. The notation is indicated by showing the whole event from the bottom of the stave upward: thus, 24//2/ indicates that a figure 2 is on the bottom line, a 4 on the next line, and a 2 on the fifth, with no indication on the others, producing (with a G tuning) a chord of d, f#', a'. The signs for 10, 11, and 12 (using an "x" with the necessary number of points above it) are here presented as arabic numerals. The sign • is used to indicate the point that appears below a chord in many tabulatures. Rhythm signs are given before the chord and follow our normal understanding of their values, using | for a sb.

The phrase "stamped in" means that I believe Petrucci used a type sort, inked, to stamp in the symbol named.

18. Contents. This accounts for all pages of each volume and part, including blanks. Wherever possible, the details of text incipits are taken from the cantus

part, and follow the orthography in the same manner as the transcription of title pages. Minor variations between parts are not listed, although all differences of attribution or significant spelling are included for books printed in separate parts: in choirbook format, these differences have not seemed to be so important.

The designated folio is followed by an indication of stave if the item does not start at the head of the page. An asterisk at this point indicates that the item begins somewhere other than at the beginning of the stave.

All compositions are assumed to be for four voices, unless otherwise indicated.

Concordant sources are not listed here: the intent of this list is to indicate what may be found in the source, and how it is spelled there. For concordances, the reader is directed to Part III, where all citations, including those to Petrucci's editions, are found in one place.

INDIVIDUAL COPIES. FOR EACH COPY, DATA FOR ITEMS 19 TO 27 MAY BE GIVEN:

19.   Library; call number; state of completeness.

20.   Size of the page of a copy.

21.   The distribution of watermarks in the copy. The marks are referred to by the numbers explained in chapter 15. Since each mark spans the top edge of two folios, originally adjacent on the sheet, each cited occurrence of a mark normally involves two folio numbers, separated by a dash, thus A6-3. These are always given with the top of the mark indicated first. Where only part of the mark appears, on one page, there will be no number on the other side of the dash: thus A-3 indicates that the top of the mark is not present on folio 6, either because the mark was trimmed off in binding, or because folio 6 is a cancel folio. All marks in the lower outer corner, which I have indiscriminately called "countermarks", appear on only one folio.

22.   Textual comments. Any necessary remarks about individual readings in the copy, whether of text or of music.

23.   Technical comments. These will include any evidence of technical details only to be seen (or only noticed by the writer) in the copy under description.

24.   Corrections and changes. These are divided into ones plausibly made in the printing shop, and ones clearly made after the copy left the shop.

The discovery of these variants is an on-going process: my examination of each new copy of any of these titles has always yielded new minor changes, so far undetected in previous copies. On returning to earlier copies, however, once alerted and looking for them I have often found the same changes. This listing must therefore be regarded as only an indication of what I have seen to date and not an exclusive checklist. It is probable that an examination of any one copy with the list of variants in *all* copies at hand would yield more changes than listed here.

25.   Binding: this does not aim to be a technical description of the binding, much less an attempt at placing it. It gives general comments and associates the binding with others where that can be easily done. It will also indicate a) other volumes bound with this one, and b) the presence of fly-leaves or paste-downs.

26.   Provenance. For a study of printed music, this is exceedingly important. Unfortunately, the evidence for most of these volumes is sketchy, and there are many leads which I have chosen not to follow up, rather than take another lifetime on the present study.

27.   The description of each copy ends with any bibliographical citations of that copy. Library catalogues are usually not listed, but assumed: exhibition catalogues or an article on the discovery of a book will be found here.

At this point the process will resume for the next surviving copy, repeating items 19 to 27.

After all copies of this edition or impression have been discussed, the next edition, impression, or series of cancels is introduced; the process then returns to step 6, above, though some of the categories may not be relevant. This is again followed by a discussion or listing of each copy.

28.   After the description of each edition, cancel, and copy comes a listing of other, now lost, copies whose ownership was once known.

29.   Other early references are listed next, among them citations in, for example, Gesner or Zacconi, with modern bibliographical references.

30.   Other editions of the book are listed, with catalogue entry numbers when printed by Petrucci; otherwise *RISM* numbers are given.

31.   The analytical part of each entry ends with a bibliography. This does not pretend to cover all the references to the music contained in a book, or indeed all those to the book itself. For many of Petrucci's volumes, such a listing would be very long. Instead, it is divided into five sections:

    (a) standard musical reference works: Sartori, *Petrucci*; Brown, *Instrumental*; Jeppesen, *La Frottola*; Vogel, *Bibliografia*;

    (b) standard (nonmusical) bibliographical references: Isaac, *Index*; Sander, *Livre*; *Index Aureliensis*; Essling, *Livre*; etc.;

    (c) facsimiles of the whole volume. Here may also be included some reproductions of individual pages, if they are easily accessible or valuable;

    (d) editions of the volume as a whole, normally excluding editions of parts of the book;

    (e) literature specifically on the book as a whole. Literature on specific copies tends to be cited at the end of the description of the copy, rather than here.

32.   *Commentary*. This addresses any issues of significance, either bibliographical, historical, or repertorial, which arise from the evidence presented. For example, here is laid out the evidence suggesting that the music printed in the second book of *Laude* came from Venetian confraternities; a discussion of the paper and bibliographical evidence suggesting that Ghiselin's book of masses was printed as a special commission; the analysis of implications of traits indicating the transition from triple to double impression; or the evidence for dating an undated printing, edition, or cancel.

    Among the comments at the end of each entry I include some samples of detailed data, measurements of stave lines, and the like, which would take up too much space in the standard description or in one of the earlier chapters.

★   ★   ★

A few general conventions need to be noted:

1. I have followed the then-conventional order of partbooks, always placing the Tenor second in descriptions, followed by Altus and Bassus.

2. A colon followed by a closing bracket, thus, :] is used to indicate that what precedes is comment, and what follows is a quotation from the specified document or source. If further comment is needed after the quotation, the bracket is reopened. For example:

    Signatures:] A II [$4

    or On the first fly-leaf:] Lumley [written in dark brown ink

    This formulation also allows me to indicate when there is punctuation at the end of the quoted material.

3. I have invariably used signatures to locate every item: many books do not have foliation or pagination, and those that do often present errors. In each case, I use a "correct" signing, so that errors on Petrucci's page (though listed) are not used for description.

4. Certain lengthy texts appearing in more than one book are not repeated each time: this applies to the dedicatory letters in the *Odhecaton A*, to the instructions pages in the lute volumes, and to the privilege printed in many of the Fossombrone titles. Each appears only the first time, while variants (including changes in line ends) are listed subsequently.

5. In the same manner, I have not usually given a detailed list of contents for cancels and later impressions, unless the manner of arranging or presenting the contents is visually distinct.

6. As I have explained, it is impossible to make a clear distinction between in-house manuscript corrections and changes made by later owners or users. I have tended to be conservative here, normally including in a list of changes only those that appear in more than one copy, and in a very similar manner. It is likely, therefore, that some of the changes found under individual copies would have been made by one of Petrucci's men: the reverse is also probably true.

7. It should be noted that, in a number of instances, full stops have not taken ink in individual copies. For some reason, this is particularly pronounced in head lines. Nonetheless, the description of these entries uses the full stop: exceptions, where the stop is in blind, are usually noted under the individual copies.

8. Conventional signs adopted here:

    | a line end in transcribed material;

    •   used to separate items in a sequence, for example of manuscript corrections or bibliographical citations.

No. 1. *Odhecaton A*

[1501]   *RISM* 1501

There are three individually dated editions of this book. The unique copy of this first edition survives incomplete and includes two later impressions of sections, as well as parts from the second edition.

This bibliography separates the other editions, entering them under the appropriate dates (as Nos.5 and 14), since they are given distinct dates. The various layers of the first edition are treated here: those parts of the unique copy at Bologna which are of the second edition are discussed there.

First edition

A1r]   Harmonice Muſices | Odhecaton | A

N8r]   [this folio, which certainly carried the colophon, does not survive]

A1v]   Octauianus Petrutius foroſempronienſis Hieronymo Donato patricio | Veneto Felicitatem.   1

NOVERAM iam pridem te ſummum uirum Hieronyme: ſummum patronum. Extant enim ingenii | tui monumenta egregia: quibus tuarum uirtutum quaſi effigiem dum intuemur ſic animis noſtris | imprimeris et inheres: ut cum de diſciplinis: et bonis artibus ſermo incidit: uel cogitatio ſubit: | ſtatim occurras. Sed et Bartholomæus Budrius utraque lingua clarus: & tui ſtudioſiſſimus   5 me | aſſidua predicatione tuarum laudum: quamque caſte ſanctiora illa totius philoſophiæ ſtudia muſice | temperes: in admiratione tui ita confirmauit: ut mihi non eſſet diu deliberandum: cui potiſſimum | meas delicias: meos amores committerem: cui perpetuo dedicarem. Non pridem uir clariſſime | animaduerteram rei impreſſoriæ artifices certatim ex omnibus diſciplinis noui aliquid quottidie | proferre: muſicam uero illam numeroſam ſiue diſcantum malis ſine qua non deum   10 optimum | maximum propiciamus: non nuptiarum ſolennia celebramus: non conuiuia: non quicquid in uita iucum|dum tranſmittimus: ab hiſdem opificibus neglectam iacere. Mox edoctus ingenioſiſſimos ui-|ros difficultate uictos ſepius ab inceptis deſtitiſſe hoc ego erectus ſi me quoque poſſem tollere | humo: latinum uero nomen et Venetum imprimis: ubi hæc parta & perfecta forent: hac quoque | noſtri inuenti gloriola uirum uolitare per ora: conſilio uſus ipſius Bartholomei   15 uiri optimi | rem ſum: puto feliciter agreſſus: tam arduam: quam iucundam: quam publice profuturam mortalibus. Si | quidem diuinus ille plato: eas demum beatiſſimas fore ciuitates iudicauerit in quibus ado-|leſcentes ſolida hac: qualemque ipse ſecutus cæteris uideris preſcripſiſſe: muſica delectati: ſordi-|dis illis uoluptatibus renunciauerint. Quod breui futurum nobis maxime ſperandum. Commoda | enim carminum huiuſmodi occaſione ingenui adoleſcentes   20 inuitati: et dicatura ipsa in admira-|tionem tui erecti: ad imitationem quoque non degeneri emulatione excitabuntur. Paululum mo|do ſentiant tibi induſtriam noſtram non improbari. Vale ac nos noſtraque quo potes patrocino libens | tutare. Venetiis decimo octavo cal. iunias. Salutis anno. MDI.   23

A2r]   Bartholomúus Bndrius Iuſtinopolita. Hieronymo donato patricio Veneto. S.   1

SOLEO Hieronyme clariſſime ac omnium bonarum artium cumulo eminentiſſime: tacita ad-|miratione: qua hominum ingenia proſequor iucundiſſime affici: huiuſque declarandæ quamuis | occaſionem auidiſſime arripere. ita enim ſentio & conſcientiæ: & profeſſionis teſtimonio (quod | poſſum) ingrati animi ac malignitatis crimen effugere. Quod tum cæteris: tum uero tibi impri-|mis   5 maxime probatum uelim. quem ita admiramur: ita ſuſpicimus: ut contemplatione tui receptiſ||ſimum illud quaſi oraculum. αλλ᾽ οὔ πωδαμα πάντα Θεοὶ δόιαν ανθςωποιοι. ſapientiſſimi uatis animum | deluſiſſe uideatur: illud uero haud quaquam pulcherrime. n. in te. ιοφό τι χρημ᾽ ὠνθρωποι omnia. n. tibi | pariter cum ſapientia. quæ ne ſingula proſequitur. & tui pudoris: & meæ imbecillitatis ratio facit: cum | & alioqui ſuſcepti negotii ampliſſimum mihi fructum propoſuerim: ſi nouus hic tuæ   10 urbis fœ|tus: communem patriam tecum nobilitaturus: me quoque deprecatore in chorum tuarum muſarum re|cipiatur. quem fœcunda parens ingeniorum natura iam diu parturiens. poſt aliquot abortus tan|dem Octauiani petrutii ſolertiſſimi uiri ope ſubnixa: omnibus numeris abſolutiſſimum edidit | dignus profecto & hic uir: quem omnes admirentur: uel ob hoc: qui rem pulcherrimam ſepe a sum|mis ingeniis infeliciter tentatam ſolus perfecerit: dignus: quem tu ita   15 ſuſcipias. ut & cæteri in-|telligant: eidem non plus ingenii in nouo inuento perficiendo: quae iudicii in patrocinio deligen|do ſuperfuiſſe. En igitur tibi primitiæ camenarum prouentus: ex uberrimo: ac numeroſiſſimo | ſeminario Petri Caſtellani e predicatorum familia: religione: & musicæ diſciplina memoratiſſi|mi. cuius opera: & diligentia centena hæc carmina repurgata: & profeſſione ſummorum aucto|rum: & imprimis que tibi dicata inuidia maiora: tuis auſpiciis publicum captura dimittimus. — 20

A2v   Tavola, in four columns

A quatro.		A.tre.			
		Jay pris amours. Ja-			
		part — 24.			
Aue maria. Folio — 4.	James iames. — 39.	Ales regres: Agricola — 54.	Me doibt. — 51.
Amours amours. — 12.	Je nay dueul. — 43.	Ales regres: hayne. — 63.	Male bouche. — 52.
Adieu mes amours. — 17.	Jay pris amours. Buſno	Ales mon cor. — 71.	Ma bouche rit. — 54.
Amours amours amo-	is — 45.	Benedictus Yzac. — 83.	Mes penſees. — 65.
urs. — 26.	Je ne demande. — 48.	Cela ſans plus: Josquin. — 67.	Mater patris. — 68.
Alons ferons la barbe. — 20.	Lenzotta mia. — 10.	Crions noel. — 82.	Malor me bat. — 69.
Amor fait molt. — 34.	Lo ſeraie dire. — 32.	De tous biens: bourdon. — 80.	Madame helas. — 72.
A cordes moy. — 36.	Le ſeruiteur. — 38.	Diſant adiu madame. — 93.	Mon ſouuenir. — 91.
Alaudienche. — 99.	La turatu — 101	Eſt il poſſible. — 79.	Margaritte. — 92.
Brunetta. — 8.	Mon mignault. — 20.	Fortuna per ta cruelte. — 66.	Mais que ſe fuſt. — 93.
Bergerette ſauoyene. — 13.	Meſkin es hu. — 103.	Fortuna dun gran tempo. — 81.	O uenus bant. — 85.
Ceſt mal charche. — 15.	Nunqua fue pena maior. — 7.	Gariſſes moy. — 64.	Penſif mari. — 49.
Cela ſans plus. — 27.	Noſtre cambriere. — 35.	Gentil prince. — 93.	Pius que de uous. — 0.
Dit le bourguignon. — 21.	Nous ſomes delorde. — 41.	Helas: Yzac — 56.	Royne de fleurs. — 61.
De tous biens. — 23.	Pour que non. — 18.	Helas: Tinctoris. — 58.	Roy de ciel. — 91.
De tous biens. Joſquin. — 103.	Pour quoy ie ne puis di-	Ha traitre anours. — 93.	Se mieulx. — 57.
E qui la dira. — 14.	re. — .19.	Jay bien a huer. — 96.	Si dedero. — 62.
Gratieuſe. — 20.	Rompeltier. — 28.	La morra. — 50.	Siator on mablamee. — 77.
Hor oires. — 6.	Se congie pris. Japare. — 25.	L homme banni. — 53.	Tant ha bon oeul. — 74.
Helas. Caron. — 16	Tmeſkin uas iunch. — 30.	La ſtangetta. — 55.	Tandernaken. — 75.
Helas ce neſt pas. — 22.	Tan bien mi ſon penſa. — 37.	La plus de plus. — 70.	Uenus regres. — 59.
Helas qui il eſt amon gre — 33.	Tſat een meſkin. — 97.	Le corps. — 73.	Uenus tu ma pris. — 94.
Ho logeron nous. — 46.	Uray dieu damours. — .19.	Le grans regres. — 79.	
Je cuide. — 5.	Ung franc archier. — 31.	Le renuoy. — 84.	
Jai pris amours. — 9.	Uoſtre bargeronette. — 47	Lalfonſina. — 88.	
Je ne fay plus. — 11.		Le eure e uenue. — 89.	

Format and collation: Choirbook: landscape quarto-in-eights. 104 folios: A–N⁸, on the evidence of later editions

Signatures: Aiii [$4 • -A1, A2

Foliation: top centre recto:] [1–3], 4–8, [9–16, a later impression], 17–25, [26, lost], 27–30, [31–32, lost, 33–40, a later impression], 41–48, [49–50, lost], 51–54, [55–57, lost], 58–63, [64, missing], 65–74, [75–78, a later impression], 79–80, [81–95, later impression, 96–104, lost]

No running heads • The composers' names are found in the head-line

Part-names:

recto:]	Contra Baſſus	[A4-8, C1-D1, D3-6, F1-8
	Contra	[G3-6, H2-7, J1-K2, K7-8
	[Nil:	A1-3

verso:]	Tenor	[A3-4,6,8, C1-D1, D3-6, F1-8, G3-6, H2-7, J1-K2, K7-8
	Tenor Tenor	[A5,7
	[Nil:	A1-2

When the data from the cancels and second edition sheets are added to this, they produce a remarkably clear group of captions, with no errors or strange uses of letters. The layout is simple and is retained consistently throughout

Fonts: Music: Petrucci's normal music type

Staves: six per page: 10-91-110 high, 175 mm long: short staves normally appear at the top of each verso

Text: Rotonda, used for all incipits, etc • Roman, used on A1v-2r only • Greek, on A2r, only: Aldus Manutius's fourth Greek font

Textual comments: A2r. The name Budrius reads] Bndrius • In the Tavola the numerals for the folios are all (except for three, to Nos.16, 101, and 47) in arabic, with following points. As with the part-names in the book, there is no use of a "5" for a final "s"

Technical comments: Type, probably a row of fusas, was used as bearer sorts on A1r and K6r • The sixth stave was sometimes completely uninked, or only partially inked • The initial capital "D" is omitted on C6v • No inset was left in the stave for the initial letter on F1v or F3v • The signature on K1r is above v, though music goes onto vi

There appear to be no in-house corrections

Contents: presented for the whole volume, on the basis of the surviving Tavola and the evidence of the later editions: the third column gives the page number to be found on the recto of the relevant opening:

	A1r		[Title]		
	A1v		[Dedication]		
	A2r		[Letter from Budrius]		
	A2v		[Tavola]		
	A3r		[blank staves]		
1	A3v	4	AUe maria gratia plena		De orto
2	A4v	5	JE cuide [e ce tamps me dure		[Congiet/Japart]
3	A5v	6	HOr oires une chanzon	à5	[Anon.]
4	A6v	7	NUnqua fue pena maior		[Urrede]
5	A7v	8	BRunette	à5	Jo.Sthokem
			[Tav:] Brunetta		
6	A8v	9	JAy pris amours		[Anon.]
7	B1v		[Tav:] Lenzotta mia		[Japart]
8	B2v		[Tav:] Je ne fay plus		[Busnois]
9	B3v		[Tav:] Amours amours		[Hayne]
10	B4v		[Tav:] Bergerette savoyene		[Josquin]
11	B5v		[Tav:] E qui le dira		[Isaac]
12	B6v		[Tav:] Cest mal charche		[Agricola]
13	B7v		[Tav:] Helas [que pourra devenir]		[Tav:] Caron.
14	B8v	17	[A:] Adieu mes amours		[Josquin]
15	C1v	18	POr quoy non		Pe.de la rue.
			[Tav:] Pour que non		
16	C2v	19	POr quoy ie ne puis dire		Jo.Sthokem
			[T:] Uray diu damours		
			[Tav:] Pour . . . [and] Uray dieu damours		

17	C3v	20	MOn mignault [T, A, Tav:] Gratieuſe		[Busnois]
18	C4v	21	DIt le bourguygnon		[Anon.]
19	C5v	22	HElas ce neſt pas ſans rayſon		Sthokhem
20	C6v	23	De tous biens playne [A headed:] Si placet		[Hayne]
21	C7v	24	JAy pris amours		Japart
22	C8v	25	SE congie pris		Japart [Tav:] Japare.
23	D1v		AMours amours		Japart
24	D2v	27	[A:] Cela ſans plus		[Japart]
25	D3v	28	ROmpeltier		Ja.Obreht
26	D4v	29	ALons ferons la barbe		Compere
27	D5v	30	TMeiſkin [Tav:] Tmeiſkin uas iunch		Jſac
28	D6v		VNng franc archier		Compere
29	D7v		[Tav:] Loſeraie dire		[Anon.]
30	D8v		[Tav:] Helas que il eſt a mon gre		[Japart]
31	E1v		[Tav:] Amor fait mult [/ Il est de bonne heure / Tant que vostre argent]		[Japart]
32	E2v		[Tav:] Nostre cambriere		[Ninot]
33	E3v		[Tav:] Acordes moy		[Busnois]
34	E4v		[Tav:] Tan bien mi ſon pensa		[Japart]
35	E5v		[Tav:] Le ſeruiteur		[Buſnoys]
36	E6v		[Tav:] James james		[Mouton]
37	E8v	41	[A:] Nous sommes [de lordre]		[Compere]
38	F2v	43	JE nay dueil		Agricola
39	F4v	45	JAy prius amours tout au rebours [Tav:] Jay pris amours		Buſnoys [Tav:] Buſno|is.
40	F5v	46	HE logeron nous [Tav:] Ho . . .		[Isaac]
41	F6v	47	VOſtre bargerenette		Compere
42	F7v	48	JE ne demande aultre de gre		Buſnoys
43	F8v		PEnſif mari	à3	Ja.Tadinghen
44	G1v		[Tav:] La morra	à3	[Isaac]
45	G2v	51	[CT:] Me doibt	à3	[Compſre]
46	G3v	52	MAle bouche	à3	Compere
47	G4v	53	LHome banni	à3	Agricola
48	G5v	54	ALes regrets	à3	Agricola
49	G6v	[55]	LA ſtangetta	à3	Uuerbech
50	G7v		[Tav:] Helas	à3	[Tav:] Yzac
51	G8v		[Tav:] Se mieulx	à3	[Compſre]
52	H1v	58	[CT:] Helas	à3	[Tav:] Tinctoris.
53	H2v	59	VEnis regrets	à3	Compere
54	H3v	60	MA bouche rit	à3	Okenghem
55	H4v	61	ROyne de fleurs	à3	Alexander

N8*r*   [probably Colophon; Register; device]
N8*v*   [probably blank]

Extant copy:

I-Bc, Q51. The incomplete remains of this copy are bibliographically sophisticated. The following table gives the extant leaves and their place in the history of this title:

Folios:	A1-8	B1-8	C1-8	D1,3-6	D2,7-8	E1-8	F1-8	G1-2,7-8	G3-6	H1,8
Edition, etc.:	1	2	1	1	Lost	1a	1	Lost	1	Lost

	H2-7	J1-8	K1-2,7-8	K3-6	L1-2,7-8	L3-6	M1-7	M8	N1-8
	1	1	1	1b	1b	2	2	Lost	Lost

Impressions 1a and 1b are seen here as part of the first edition and are described below, as Cancels 1 and 2. Edition 2 is described in full later, at 14.i.1503 (No.5).

Size of page: 164 × 237 mm.

Watermarks:

Folios:	A2-1	A5-6	C2-1	C4-3	D6-5	F1-2	F3-4	G4-3	H2-	H3-4	J6-5	J8-7	K7-8
Mark:	1	1	2	2	2	1	1	1	2	2	2	2	1

Later changes: 16th-century ms foliation:] 1–14, [15–30 = D6], [31–38 = E8], 39–63[= J7]. This implies that folio D2 was then present, but that D7-8, G1-2, G7-8, H1 and H8 were already missing • J6*r*.i.43–44: ligature, B,a → A,a, erasure and manuscript

Binding: 19th-century marbled boards • One fly-leaf and one paste-down at each end

Bibliography: Boorman, "First" • Fava, *Primo*, pp. 36–37 (exhibition catalogue, Bologna, 1929) • Fenlon and Dalla Vecchia, *Venezia*, pp. 71–72 (exhibition catalogue, Venice, 2001) • Gaspari, *Catalogo*, iii, p. 200 • Haberl, "Drucke", pp. 50–55

No. 1a. *Cancel sheets 1.*

There exists only gathering E printed at this stage

Signatures:] EII [$4 • E4 signed] E IIIi
Foliation: 23 [*recte* 33], 34–40
Part-names: in the left margin, to be read vertically from the top:

  recto:] Altus Ba∫∫us [E1-8
  verso:] Tenor   [E1-8

Textual comments: The wrong initial [D] is printed on E8*v*

Technical comments: The problems with the imposition of the outer sheet, revealed by the choice of stave at the start of E7*v*, are discussed in Boorman, "First"

For other details see the description of the first edition, above

Contents:

30	E1*r*	23 [= 33]	[A:] Helas que il e∫t a mon gre	[Compère]
31	E1*v*	34	AMor fait mult tant que argen dure	[Japart]
			[T:] Il e∫t de bonne heure ne	
			[B:] Tant q*ue* uo∫tre argent dura	
32	E2*v*	35	NO∫tre cambriere ∫i mala	[Ninot]
33	E3*v*	36	ACordes moy ce*que* yepen∫∫e	[Busnois]
34	E4*v*	37	TAn bien mi∫on pen∫a	Japart
35	E5*v*	38	LE ∫eruiteur	Bu∫noys

36	E6ν	39	JAmes iames iames		[Mouton]
37	E8ν	41	DOus ſommes de lordre de ſaynt babuyn		Compere
			[recte Nous . . .]		

Extant copy:

I-Bc, Q51. These sheets are bound up as part of the copy described above
    Watermarks: No.2 on ff.E2-1 E4-3
    Later changes: Manuscript foliation, following on from that in the first edition folios:] 31–38
    Bibliography: Boorman, "First"

No. 1b. *Cancel sheets 2.*

Two sheets, K inner and L outer, are extant from this stage. They make up K3-6 and L1,2,7,8

Signatures:] K III [$4
Foliation: 75–78; 81–82, 87–88
Part-names: in the left margin, to be read vertically from the top:
    recto:]   Contra   [K3-6, L1-2, L7-8
    verso:]   Tenor   [K3-6, L1-2, L7-8
Technical comments: These cancel pages have abandoned the use of inset staves to leave space for
    an initial letter
For other details, see the description of the first edition, above

Contents:

69	K3r	75	[CT:] Tander naken	à3	[Obrecht]
70	K4ν	77	SI a tort on ma blamee	à3	[Anon.]
71	K5ν	78	LEs grans regres	à3	[Hayne]
72	K6ν	79	ESt poſſible quelhome peult	à3	[Anon.]
. . .					
74	L1r	81	[CT:] Fortuna	à3	[Joſquin]
75	L1ν	82	CRions nouel	à3	Agricola
76	L2ν	[83]	BEnedictus	à3	Jſac
. . .					
79	L7r	87	[Ma seule dame — ending	à3	[Anon.]
80	L7ν	88	LA alfonſina	à3	Jo.ghiſelin
81	L8ν	[89]	LEeure e venue	à3	Agricola

Extant copy:

I-Bc, Q.51. These sheets are bound up with the rest of the Bologna copy, described above
    No watermarks are visible
    Later changes: L1r: Three-voiced setting, apparently of a frottola, added in manuscript
    Bibliography: Boorman, "First"

Lost copies: The copy in the Fugger collection may have been of this edition (Schaal, "Musikbibliothek", I/70)

Early references: Reference to one of the editions, not necessarily this one, was made by Bolduanus, Draudius, and Gesner. Their texts are transcribed in chapter 20

Other editions: The second edition is of 14.i.1503 (No.5), and includes some sheets from the Bologna copy described above: B1-8, L3-6 and M1-7 • The third is of 25.v.1504 (No.14)

Bibliography:

    (a) Sartori, *Petrucci*, No.1 • Brown, *Instrumental*, 1501₁ • Jeppesen, *Frottola*, Pe.A • Vogel, *Bibliografia*, 1501₁

    (c) Note that the published facsimiles are not of this copy

    (d) Hewitt, *Odhecaton*

    (e) Becherini, "Alcuni" • Blackburn, "Petrucci" • Boorman, "First" • Castellani, "Petrucci" • Catelani, "Bibliografia" • Cauchie, "A propos" • Cauchie, "Odhecaton" • Disertori, "Margine" • Fétis, "Note" • Haberl, "Drucke" • Marix, "Odhecaton" • Reese, "First" • Vogel, "Erste"

Commentary:

1. Many of the bibliographical complexities of this volume have been sorted out in recent years: see Boorman, "First", and Boorman, *Petrucci* (1976), pp. 144–49. There seems to be no good reason to believe that the first extant printing was not Petrucci's first effort. The problems he encountered with layout and arrangement of the contents, as well as the pristine state of the blocks and typographical material, suggest that he was new to printing polyphony. Despite this, the artistic level and the details of presentation show a very high level of both design and presswork. Petrucci's craftsmen cannot themselves have been new to printing, but merely to the present repertoire. Further, the dedication to Donato offers not only the present volume, but also all future books from the press. This, while explaining the absence of dedications in other musical volumes, also tends to argue that this was indeed the first title printed by Petrucci.

2. It is reasonable to assume that the book was published soon after the date of the dedicatory letter — early summer of 1501. Certainly, the first edition appeared before the first of the *Canti B*, in February 1502: indeed, it must have appeared some time before, for the first set of cancel leaves also predates that second title. But we cannot assume, as do many writers, that it appeared on the date of the dedication. (See, for example, Geldner, *Inkunabelkunde*, p. 128.) It is true that the *Tavola* appears on the outer sheet of gathering A, and that this sheet, including the dedication, was therefore almost certainly printed last. However, given that this book is the first from Petrucci's shop, it seems to me more likely that the dedication was written before any press-work began: the book would therefore probably have appeared at sometime early in the summer of 1501.

3. Bonnie Blackburn (in "Lorenzo") has pointed out that the form of the date in the dedication is not correct, that "18 Kalends June" did not exist in a Roman calendar. However, it is relatively easy to find other similar errors in printed books of the period, and there is no proposed alternative reading of the printed date which would allow for a simple error on the part of the typesetter.

4. The fact that this volume is labelled with the letter A, even in the earliest edition, is suggestive. It may be that Petrucci was doing no more than signal that this was indeed the first *ever* volume of printed polyphony. However, it seems more likely that he and his backers were already thinking in terms of subsequent volumes in the series, those now labelled *Canti B* and *Canti C*, for instance. This argument is reinforced by the probability that the three large initials, *A*, *B*, and *C*, were designed and cut at the same time. The issue is discussed further in chapter 1.

5. Other transcriptions of the dedication and letter by Budrius can be found in Catelani, "Bibliografia", pp. 9–15 (with Italian translation); Haberl, "Drucke", pp. 50–52; Sartori, *Petrucci*, pp. 34–35; Vernarecci, *Petrucci*, 48–55 (with Italian translation).

6. There is some evidence, in the layout, the spacing of incipits and of the introductory text, and in the arrangement of rests and other notational features, to suggest that the compositor was working from copies that were sometimes in a different layout. This also resulted in occasional overcrowding and other infelicities of spacing. These are all corrected or improved in the later editions.

7. Mardersteig, "Aldo" states that Petrucci used a fount cut by Francesco Griffo for the Roman type used in the dedications. Since the Greek fount is one from Aldus' press, also cut by Griffo, this argues that Petrucci had the support of the more famous publisher, as well as of Scotto.

8. This book uses a series of short staves to provide an inset for the initial letters. These staves, which would normally occur as the first on a verso, in fact do not always appear in the correct place. This supports an argument that the staves were printed separately, thus implying a triple-impression process. For an analysis of the anomalies, see Boorman, "First".

9. The six gatherings of four-voiced pieces are followed by six of three-voiced, and a final single gathering of four-voiced works. It appears that Petrucci and Castellanus planned the volume as a series of discrete fascicles, each made up of complete gatherings. Indeed, the first two layers end on a final recto, which could have allowed for a colophon and device on the last verso of the gathering. However, the generous spacing for many pieces argues that Petrucci was not actually sure how much music could fill an opening: he could even have saved an opening on occasion.

10. It is possible that the last gathering represents a later addition to the planned volume. It contains a small group of four-voiced pieces, destroying the clear earlier structure of four-voiced works followed by three-voiced. Marginal support for this might be seen in the inclusion of one piece by Bruhier — otherwise only represented in Petrucci's work by a single piece early in *Canti B*. More significant is the point that *Canti B* also moves from a layer of four-voiced works to one of pieces for three. Therefore, when printing the *Odhecaton A*, Petrucci may have asked for one more gathering of music, and Castellanus then produced four-voiced pieces.

   Despite the loss of gathering N from the first edition, there is no reason to believe that these pieces were only added to the second edition. With the possible exception of Dammonis' volume of laude, there is no place in Petrucci's re-editions where he changed the musical contents of the first edition.

11. The pattern of ascriptions in the index is of some interest for the view that Petrucci's editor (and by extension purchasers of the volume) apparently had of the importance of authorship, as compared with the need to identify pieces sufficiently clearly. The works with composer's names in the Tavola are those where more than one piece has the same textual incipit, with two exceptions: *Se congie pris* of Japare (*sic*) and the Benedictus by Isaac. The implications of this pattern for the manner in which chansons were transmitted are discussed in Chapter Eight.

12. The assumption has been, until recently, that the compositions were all vocal, with the corollary that the performers would have known the texts well enough. Sartori, *Bibliografia*, p. 38 suggests that the extensive ranges of some parts implies a use *per cantare e suonare*. More generally, the pattern of texting found here is by no means uncommon, and has led to a discussion about the probability of instrumental performance, or of *contrafacta*. For discussion of this issue, see Chapter Nine.

13. The history of awareness of this edition is interesting. Catelani, seems to have been the first to mention it, and his references were taken over in Fétis, "Note" and Gianandrea, "Ottaviano",

and published with acknowledgement in Haberl, "Drucke". A detailed listing of various opinions about the surviving copies and their dates is given in Sartori, *Petrucci*, pp. 39–41.

14. The first cancel must be dated before the appearance of Petrucci's second book, the *Canti B* of February 1502, for it still uses the shorter staves which would allow for initial letters. The staves were abandoned after this cancel, perhaps because Petrucci's craftsmen still had problems with ensuring that the impressions with content (music or text) were imposed to correspond with the placing of the shorter staves in their forme.

15. The second series of cancels follows this rejection of the shorter staves. Unfortunately, no watermark is visible in the unique copy of these sheets. They can therefore only be dated on the strength of the condition of the type and blocks of initials. On this basis, it appears that the cancel sheets were printed after *Motetti A*, but before the *Misse Josquin*, that is, during the summer of 1502.

No. 2. *Canti B*

5.ii.1501/2   *RISM* 1502²

First edition

A1r]   Canti .B. numero | Cinquanta | B

G8r]   Impreſſum Uenetijs per Octauianum Petrutium Foroſempronien|ſem die 5 Februarij Salutis   1
anno 1501 Cuʒ priuilegio inuictiſſi|mi Dominii Uenetiarum quae nullus poſſit cantum Figuratum Im|primere ſub pena in ipſo priuilegio contenta. | Regiſtrum ABCDEFG. Omnes quaterni. | [Petrucci's device]

A1v   Tavola: in two columns]

A quatro		Mon pare ma mariee.		.21
A qui direlle ſa penſee	19	Min morghen.		.22
Amor me troten ſur la pance	.37	Mon pare ma done marj.		.45
Auant auant.	.41	Noe noe. .29		
Bon temps	18.	Orſus bouier.		.40
Baſies moy. Joquin.	.38	Pour quoy fu fait.		.37
Baſies moy. .A ſej.	.41	Reuellies vous.		.13
Ceneſt pas.	.11	Se ſuis trop ionnette		.10
Cela ſans plus .Obreht.	.71•	Tous les re gres		.26
Cela ſans plus. Lannoy.	.20	Uirgo celeſti		.3
Coment peult hauer yoye	.23	Uray dieu qui me confortera		8
Coment peult.	.24	Ue ci la danſe		.27
Dung aultre amer .Orto.	.28	Una moza		.30
En chambre polie.	.14	Ua vil ment		.39
E la la la.	.31	A tre		
E dunt reuenis vous.	.33	Aue ancilla		.42
Fors ſeulement.	.32	Adieu fillette		.49
Fortuna dun tran tempo. Deuigna	36	Aqui dirage		52
Helas helas. Ninot.	.25	Chanter ne puis		50.
Jay pris amours .Obreht.	.4	De tous biens. Ghiſelin		46

Format and collation: Choirbook: landscape quarto-in-eights. 56 folios: A-G⁸

Signatures:] A II [$4 • -A1

Foliation: t.r.r.:] [1], 2–31, 32 [with inverted "2"], 33–40, 35 [*recte* 41], 42–46, 37 [*recte* 47], 48–55, [56]

No running heads. Composers' names and rubrics for canons in the head-line

Part-names:

recto:]
Tenor Altus Baſſus	[A2
Altus Baſſus	[A3-C3, C5-D3, D5-E1, E3,5,7, F5
Contra Contra	[C4
Contra Baſſus	[D4, E4
Altus Contra	[E2
Tenor Altus Baſſus	[E6
Tenor Baſſus	[E8-F1
Contra	[F2-4, F6-G7
[Nil:	A1, F8

verso:]
Tenor | Secundus [and] Tenor | Primus	[A2
Tenor	[A3-E2, E4,6, F1-G6
Tenor Contra	[E3, G7
Tenor Altus Baſſus	[E5,7
Tenor Baſſus	[E8
[Nil:	A1, G8

Founts: Music: Petrucci's normal music type

Staves: six per page, 178 mm long: 10-91-111 mm high

Text: Rotonda throughout • Roman numerals used in the colophon

Textual comments: No capital letters on A2r [intentionally] or F1r [A]

Technical comments: Uninked minims used as bearer sorts on A1r and F7r: either minims or semiminims on D4r • Uninked staves have left a blind impression on G8r • For comments on the arrangement of the voice-parts, see below

No apparent in-house changes

Contents:

	A1r	[Title]		
	A1v	[Tavola]		
1	A2r	Lomme arme		.Joſquin.
		[Headed:] Canon. Ed ſic deſingulis		
2	A2v	VIrgo celeſti	à5	Compere
3	A3v	JAy pris amours		.Obreht.
	A5v	2/ Jay pris amours		
4	A7v	VRay dieu qui me confortera		[Bruhier]
5	A8v	LOurdault lourdault		Compere

6	B1*v*	SE ſuis trop ionnette		[Raulin]
7	B2*v*	CE neſt pas		Pe.de.la rue.
8	B3*v*	LAutrier q*ui* paſſa		.Buſnoys.
9	B4*v*	Reuelies vous		[Anon.]
10	B5*v*	EN chambre polie		[Anon.]
11	B6*v*	JE ſuis amie du forier		[Compère]
12	B7*v*	MOn mari ma deffamee		.De.Orto.
13	B8*v*	CEla ſans plus	à4 ex 2	.Obreht In miſſa.
14	C1*v*	BOn temps		[Anon.]
15	C2*v*	A Qui direlle ſa penſe [A:] ... penſee		[Anon.]
16	C3*v*	CEla ſans plus		[Colinet] [Tavola:] La*n*noy.
17	C4*v*	MOn pere ma mariee		[Anon.]
18	C5*v*	MYn morghen ghaf		[Anon.]
19	C6*v*	COoment peult hauer ioye [A:] Coment ...	à4 ex 3	.Joſquin.
20	C7*v*	COomment peult [A:] Comment peult		[Anon.]
21	C8*v*	HElas helas helas		.Ninot.
22	D1*v*	TOus les regres		Pe.de.la rue
23	D2*v*	VEci la danſe barbarj		Uaqueras.
24	D3*v*	DUng aultre amer [T:] Quartus confortatiuus [CT, B:] Obelus quinis ſedibus ip*s*e volat		De orto.
25	D4*v*	NOe noe noe		.Brumel.
26	D5*v*	VNa moza falleyo		[Anon.]
27	D6*v*	E La la la [T, B:] Fates lui bona chiera		[Ninot]
28	D7*v*	FOrs ſeulement		Pe.de.la rue
29	D8*v*	ET do*n*t reuenes vous [A:] Et dunt ...		Compere
30	E1*v*	JAy pris amours {Headed:] Fit aries piſcis in licanoſypathon:	à4 ex 3	.Japart.
31	E2*v*	JE cuide [T, B:] De tous biens		.Japart.
32	E3*v*	FRanch cor quaſtu [A:] Fortuna [Tavola:] Fortuna du*n* gra*n* te*m*po. Deuigna		.De.Uigne.
33	E4*v*	AMours me trote*n*t ſur la pance		.Lourdoys.
34	E6*r*	BAſies moy	à4 ex 2	.Joſquin
35	E6*v*	VAuilment [A:] Vanilment		.Obreht.
36	E8*r*	OR ſus orſus bouier [Headed:] In ſubdiateſſaron	à4 ex 3	.Bulkyn.
37	E8*v*	BAſies moy [Headed:] Fuga In diateſſaron	à6 ex 3	[Josquin]

38	F1*r*	[A]Uant auant	à4 ex 3	[Anon.]
		[Headed:] In ſubdiateſſaron		
39	F1*v*	AUe ancilla trinitatis	à3	.Brumel.
40	F2*v*	SI ſumpſero	à3	Obreht.
41	F4*v*	MOn pere ma dona mari		[Anon.]
42	F5*v*	DE tous biens	à3	Ghiſelin.
43	F6*v*	POur quoy fu fiat ceſte empriſe	à3	[Anon.]
	F7*v*	2/ Pour quoy fu fiat ceſte empriſe		
		[Omitted from the Tavola]		
44	F8*v*	ADieu fillette de regnon	à3	[Isaac]
45	G1*v*	CHanter ne puis	à3	.Compere.
46	G2*v*	JE vous impire	à3	.Agricola.
		[CT:] Je vous empire		
47	G3*v*	AQui dirage mes penſees	à3	[Compère]
48	G4*v*	LA regretee	à3	.Hayne.
49	G5*v*	EN amours que cognoiſt:	à3	.Brumel.
50	G6*v*	JE deſpite tous	à3	.Brumel.
51	G7*v*	LE grant deſir	à3	.Compere.
	G8*r*	[Colophon; Privilege; Device]		
	G8*v*	[blank]		

Extant copy

I-Bc, Q.52. Complete

> **Page size:** 165 × 237 mm.
>
> **Watermarks:** Mark 1 on folios A5-6, A7-8, B2-1, B4-3, C6-5, C8-7, D6-5, D8-7, E6-5, E8-7, F5-6, F8-7, G4-3 and G8-7
>
> **Technical comments:** A spacing sort for text appears on F5*r* • The stave patterns show a progression through the book • In a number of cases, the last stave of a page is not inked: this becomes more frequent, including almost whenever possible, towards the end of the book, and implies that the staves were printed after the music formes
>
> **Later changes:** Folio numbers have been corrected on F1*r* and F7*r*, in the hand employed for foliation in the Bologna copy of *Odhecaton A* (No.1)
>
> **Binding:** 19-century marbled boards (with the same paper as that found in the copy of *Odhecaton A*) • One paste-down and one flyleaf, both modern, at the front: one modern paste-down and one 18th-century flyleaf at the back
>
> **Provenance:** This copy is cited in Martini's letters to Chiti of 2.iv.1746, 7.v.1746, and 22.vii.1746 (See Martini, *Carteggio*, pp. 177, 190 and 204; and Schnoebelen, *Padre*, Nos.1245 and 1250, pp. 144–145) • The evidence of manuscript foliation suggests that this was originally owned and bound with the Bologna copy of *Odhecaton A*
>
> **Bibliography:** Fava, *Primo*, p. 37 (exhibition catalogue, Bologna, 1929) • Fenlon and Dalla Vecchia, *Venezia*, p. 72 (exhibition catalogue, Venice, 2001) • Gaspari, *Catalogo*, iii, p. 200 • Haberl, "Drucke", pp. 55–57

Lost copies: A copy was owned by Colón (Chapman, "Printed", No.5)

Early references: The citations by Bolduanus, Draudius, and Gesner are quoted in chapter 20. It is interesting that Draudius gives a date for his edition, whereas the others do not specify either edition

Other editions: A second edition was published in 1503 (No.10, below) • A third came from the press of Schöffer in Mainz, dated 7.ii.1513

Bibliography:

(a) Rosaria Boccadifuoco, *Bibliografia*, No.544 • Sartori, *Petrucci*, No.2 • Vogel, *Bibliografia*, 1502₁

(c) Petrucci, *Canti B*

(d) Hewitt, *Canti B*

(e) Boorman, *Petrucci* (1976), p. 149 • Catelani, "Di due" • Hewitt, "Chansons"

Commentary:

1. The pattern of distribution of parts on the page confirms the trend, already evident in the first book (although it is less clear here) towards settling the four-part layout as S and T on the verso, with A and B on the recto: the only exceptions are on C3v-4r and E3v-4r (with two Contras), and D3v-D4r (with Contra and Bassus). In a similar manner, the majority of the three-voiced pieces retain the Contra and Tenor designations.

2. The variations in scoring and in naming the parts seem to suggest that much of the music was collected (by Castellanus) from a relatively small number of sources. (The following deliberately excludes the names of composers, so that the pattern of distribution can be clearly seen.)

Four-voiced works	taking a whole opening:	taking one page:
Tenor, Altus, Bassus:	A3v-C3r	A2r
Tenor, Contra, Contra:	C3v-4r	
Tenor, Altus, Bassus:	C4v-D3r	
Tenor, Contra, Bassus:	D3v-4r	
Tenor, Altus, Bassus:	D4v-E1r	
Tenor, Altus, Contra:	E1v-2r	
Tenor, Altus, Bassus:	E2v-E3r, E4v-E5r, E6v-E7r	E5v-6r, E7v
Tenor, Altus, Bassus:	F4v-F5r	
Three-voiced works		
Tenor, Contra:	F1v-F4r, F5v-G7r	G7v
Tenor, Bassus		E8r, E8v, F1r
Other pieces:		
Tenor, Tenor, Altus, Bassus:	A2v-3r	
Tenor, Contra, Contra, Bassus:	E3v-4r	

This should imply that, however many sources were used for the layers leading to E3r (and I believe that there was more than one), the rest of the edition was collected from a number of sources, each adding only one or two pieces.

3. The scoring also presents a pattern similar to that of the *Odhecaton A*, in which four-voiced pieces precede those for three. In this instance, there are considerably more works for four, already initiating a change which will be much more pronounced in *Canti C*, with its more modern repertoire. It is interesting that there is a small batch of canonic pieces in close proximity. They may well have come from the same prior source.

4. Apparently, Petrucci ran off enough staves at one time to cover several sheets. The first set of staves was enough for five sheets, as far as the outer of gathering C: the second also appears on five sheets, from inner C to inner E, while the third was used for the last four sheets, gatherings

F and G. Since the lowest stave is occasionally not inked, it is likely that he ran the staves last, after the music (and probably the text) for each set of gatherings was prepared and printed.

5. The pattern of adding points to page numbers on the Tavola is very erratic, suggesting that a number of aspects of house practice were not yet settled. In the next book, *Motetti A*, practice is much more consistent.

6. The pattern of attributions in the Tavola corresponds to that found in *Odhecaton A*, and again reflects the presence of popular settings, or of cases where known settings existed from the hand of more than one composer.

7. This book was originally assigned to 1501, for example in Gianandrea, "Ottaviano", pp. 125–126, raising problems with the dating of the known copies of the *Odhecaton A*.

No. 3. *Motetti A*

9.v.1502   *RISM* 1502^1

First Edition

A1*r*]   Motetti. A. numero. | .trentatre. | A

G8*r*]   Impreſſum Uenetijs per Octauianuʒ Petrutiu*m* Foroſempronie*n*|ſem die 9 Madij Salutis anno 1502 Cuʒ priuilegio inuictiſſi|mi Dominij Uenetiaru*m* q*uae* nnllus [*sic*] poſſit cantum Figuratuʒ Im|primere ſub pena in ipſo priuilegio contenta. | Regiſtrum ABCDEFG. Omnes quaterni. | [Petrucci's device]

A1*v*   Tavola: in one column]

Aue maria. Joſquin.	3.
Adonay	16.
Aue maria. Compere.	28.
Aue maria	35.
Aue ſtella matutina. Brumel	36.
Aue do*m*ina ſa*n*cta maria. Gaſpar	39.
Aue vera caro xpi	44.
Aue ſtella matutina. Gaſpar.	52.
Anima mea. Ghiſelin	53.
Benedicta ſit creatrix	19.
Crux triumphans	9.
Chriſti mater aue	51.
Deſcendi in ortum meum	14.
Du*n*g aulter amer: Uictime	17.
Da pacem	46.
De tous biens. Joſquin	56.
Ecce video.	25.
Ibo mihi. Gaſpar.	38.
La ſpagna. Ghiſelin.	32.
Mater digna dei. Gaſpar	55.
O genitrix glorioſa	5.

O qua3 glorifica. Agricola	15.
O florens rofa.	34.
O pulcherrima. Gafpar.	41.
Propter grauamen.	11.
Quis numerare queat: Da pacem	47.
Regina celi	20.
Surge propera. Pinarol.	7.
Scile fragor.	27.
Stella celi.	42.
Uirgo maria	22.
Uidi fpeciofa.	43.
Uirgo dej trono.	50.
Uirgo prudentiffima Jofquin	8.

Format and Collation: Choirbook: landscape quarto-in-eights. 56 folios: A-G⁸

Signatures:] .AII. [$4 •-AI • The second point is raised (perhaps an inverted sort) on C1-2, D2-3, E1-4 and F1-4

Foliation: t.r.r.:] [1], 2–55, [56]

No running head-line

Part-names: entered in left margin, reading vertically from top to bottom:

recto:]	Altus [and] Baffus	[A3-B6, B8-C6, D3-G1, G3-G7
	Baffus	[B7
	Contra	[C7-D2, G2
	[Nil:	A1-2, G8
verso:]	Tenor	[A2-G6
	Tenor et Contra	[G7
	[Nil:	A1, G8

Fonts: Music: Petrucci's music type

Staves: six per page: ca.165 mm long, 10-92-112.5 mm high

Text: Rotonda throughout

Technical comments: This book already abandons the shorter staves, which Petrucci had used in the *Odhecaton A* to leave space for initials • The stave patterns indicate that there were only two formes of staves available during the printing of this volume. All of gatherings A, B, and G are printed with one set (on both sides of the sheet) and C-F with the other set • Uninked *fusas* were used as bearer sorts on folio D1r • Part of the unused sixth stave has taken ink on folios D1r and G2r, suggesting an inaccurately cut frisket • The evidence of the use of quadrate descending *c.o.p.* ligatures of two pitches a tone apart suggests that there were no more than 40 such sorts in the case: 39 are used in gathering C, while there are places on folio C4r where more could have been used, especially in the Bassus. The same analysis may be valid for ascending one-step *c.o.p.* ligatures: 48 are used in gathering C, although many had been used in B also

No evident in-house corrections

Contents:

	A1r	[Title]	
	A1v	[Tavola]	
1	A2r	[untexted canon: the rubrics read] Canon:	[Anon.]
		mifericordia ꝯ veritas obuiauerunt fibi:	
		[and] Canon. iufticia ꝯ pax obfculate funt:	

2	A2v	AVe maria gratia plena		Jo∫quin.
3	A4v	O Genitrix glorio∫a mater		[Comp∫re]
	A5v	2/ Ave virgo glorio∫a		
4	A6v	SUrge propera amica mea		.Jo.de pinarol.
5	A7v	VIrgo prudenti∬ima		Jo∫quin.
6	A8v	CRux triumphans decus potentiam		Compere.
	B1v	2/ Je∫us nomen dignuʒ		
7	B2v	PRopter grauamen ꝫ tormentuʒ		Compere.
	B3v	2/ Memento nostri		
8	B5v	DE∫cendi in ortum meuʒ		[Anon.]
9	B6v	O Quam glorifica	à3	Agricola
10	B7v	ADonay ∫ancti∬ime domine deus		Ga∫par
11	B8v	DUng aultre amer		.Jo∫quin
		[T:] Victime pa∫cali		
	C1v	2/ De tous biens / Dic nobis		
12	C2v	BEnedicta ∫it creatrix		[Josquin]
13	C3v	REgina celi letare		.Brumel.
	C4v	2/ Re∫urrexit ∫icut dixit		
14	C5v	VIrgo maria non est tibi simili5		.Ga∫par.
15	C6v	O Florens ro∫a [untexted]	à3	.Jo.ghi∫elin.
16	C8v	ECce video celos apertos: [untexted]	à3	.Craen.
17	D2v	SCile fragor		.Compere.
	D3v	2/ Su ∫cipe dei mater		
18	D4v	AVe maria gratia plena . . . benedicta tu		.Compere.
	D5v	2/ Sancta michael ora pro nobis		
19	D7v	LA ∫pagna [untexted]		Jo ghi∫elin:
20	E2v	AVe maria gratia plena . . . benedicta tu		[Craen]
21	E3v	AVe ∫tella matutina		Brumel
	E4v	2/ Tu es area compluta		
22	E5v	IBo mihi ad montem		Ga∫par
23	E6v	AVe domina sancta maria		Ga∫par.
	E7v	2/ Tu peperi∫ti creatorem		
24	E8v	[A:] O pulcherima mulierum		.Ga∫par.
25	F1v	STella celi extirpauit		[Anon.]
26	F2v	VIdi ∫pecio∫am		Ga∫par
27	F3v	AVe vera caro christi		[anon.]
	F4v	2/ Salve sancta caro dei		
28	F5v	DA pacem domine		[Anon.]
29	F6v	QVis numerare queat	à5 ex 4	Compere
		[T:] Da pacem		
	F7v	2/ AUdivit / [S:] Da pacem		
	F8v	3/ FUndat prece5 / [T:] Da pacem		
30	G1v	VIrgo dei troni digna [untexted]	à3	Tinctoris
31	G2v	Chri∫ti mater aue		Ga∫par
32	G3v	AVe ∫tella matutina		Ga∫par
33	G4v	ANima mea liquefacta est		Ghi∫elin
	G5v	2/ Tulerunt palium meum		

34	G6ν	MAter digna dei	[Weerbeke]
		[Tav:] Ga[par	
35	G7ν	De tous biens [untexted]	Jo[quin [lower voices only]
	G8r	[Colophon: Register: Device]	
	G8ν	[blank]	

Extant Copy:

I-Bc, Q53. Complete

> **Page size:** 165 × 235 mm.
>
> **Watermarks:** Twin marks in the lower outer corner:
>
> A2   A6   B3   B7   C4   E3   G7   (no other marks visible)
>
> 4   4   4   4   3   3   3
>
> **Later changes:** A number of 19th-century annotations on the index — mostly of composers' names
>
> **Binding:** Bound with eleven folios of 19th-century printed manuscript paper, containing scores of Josquin's *Ave Maria* "a car= 3", Tinctoris' *Virgo dei trono*, Pinarol's *Surge propera*, and Gaspar's *Adonay sanctissime*. The last is signed:] Fortunato Santini li 12 Febraio 1850 • Bound in 19th-century marbled boards • One fly-leaf and one paste-down at each end, on wove paper. The back flyleaf has a watermark of] P L MMA[paper edge
>
> **Provenance:** Presumably owned by Santini, but in Bologna by 1866, when Ambros saw it • G8ν, inverted:] que[to libro e de giovan bati[ta ventura
>
> **Bibliography:** Fava, *Primo*, p. 37 (exhibition catalogue, Bologna, 1929) • Haberl, "Drucke", pp. 92–94

Lost copies: A copy was in the Fugger collection (Schaal, "Musikbibliothek", I/74)

Early references: It is not clear which is the edition of this title referred to in German citations, by Bolduanus, Draudius, and Gesner, all quoted in chapter 20. The assumption by Krummel, *Bolduanus*, No.618, that the author was referring to *Odhecaton A* seems unlikely: I take it to be a reference to the present volume, especially in the light of the point, well made in Sartori, *Petrucci*, p. 46, that this was long thought to be the earliest Petrucci edition

Other editions: Printed by Petrucci, 13.ii.1505 (No.19, below)

Bibliography:

> (a) Rosaria Boccadifuoco, *Bibliografia*, No.2337 • Sartori, *Petrucci*, No.3 • Brown, *Instrumental*, 1502₁
>
> (b) Brunet, *Manuel*, iii, 1924
>
> (c) Petrucci, *Motetti A*
>
> (d) Drake, *First* • Sherr, *16-Century*, i
>
> (e) Brown, "Mirror" • Brunet, *Manuel*, iii, p. 2 • Catelani, "Di due" • Schmid, *Petrucci*, pp. 28–33

Commentary:

1. This edition was long thought to be the first production of Petrucci. Caffi (*Storia*, ii, p. 205) said as much in 1755, and the same line was therefore taken by several subsequent scholars, including Schmid among music historians, and Brunet among bibliographers.

2. The pattern of ascriptions in the Tavola follows that of the *Odhecaton A*, in that many pieces apparently did not need an attribution. It may be that this is another piece of evidence in favour of Howard Brown's argument (Brown, "Mirror") that the volume was intended for private devotion. Further on this, see chapter 9.

3. The evidence of the division of staves by gatherings might argue for a division between two typesetters. In practice, though, with the staves being printed separately, this has no bearing on whether two men were involved in setting the content. It may imply that Petrucci had access to two presses and was able to print the two sets of staves simultaneously.

4. *Virgo prudentissima*, the last piece in the Tavola, appears to have been added after other works beginning with the letter "V". More probably, the Tavola was made up last (as usual), and from the other sheets already printed. The addition of this last piece would then result from it also being on the outer sheet of gathering A.

5. With the abandoning of the shorter staves for the heads of pieces, Petrucci produced a result in which the decorative initials were overlaid by stave lines. This represents his first artistic compromise, and apparently the only one for a number of years.

No. 4. Josquin: *Misse*

27.ix.1502   *RISM* J666

There is a cancel for the inner sheet of F, and later Venetian and Fossombronese editions (Nos.30 and 62)

First Edition

A1r]   Miſſe Joſquin | Lomme arme. Super voces muſicales | La.ſol.fa.re.mi. | Gaudeamus. | Fortuna deſperata. | Lomme arme. Sexti toni. | S

D1r]   T

F1r]   A

J1r]   B

K9r]   Impreſſum Uenetijs per Octauianum Petrutium Foroſemproni | enſem die 27. ſetembris anno 1502 Cu3 priuilegio inuictiſſimi Do | minij Uenetiarum quae nullus poſſit cantum Figuratum Impri- | mere ſub pena in ipſo priuilegio contenta. | Regiſtrum ABCDEFGHJK Omnes. quaterni. praeter E que est | ternus H duernus K quinternus | [Petrucci's device]

Format and collation: Partbooks: landscape quarto-in-eights. [S] 24 folios: A-C⁸; [T] 14 folios: D⁸E⁶; [A] 20 folios: F-G⁸H⁴; [B] 18 folios: J⁸K¹⁰

Signatures:] AIIII [$4 • − A1 • + K5 signed] K 5 • K3 signed] k iii • K4 signed] K iiii

No foliation or pagination: no running heads

Fonts: Music: Petrucci's normal music type

Staves: Six per page: 174–176 mm long, 10-92.5-111.5 or 10-91.5-112 high.

Text: Rotonda throughout

Textual comments: D6r.iii.text:] Qui tullis [D-B, P-Ln and US-CA • K5r.iii.text:] Pleni [nut [for sunt: D-B • K7v.iv.text:] Santtus [D-B

Technical comments: Capital letters missing on D1v [K], D2v [P], D4r [K and E], D4v [P], D5r

[S], D5*v* [A], D8*r* [E], E2*r* [A], F8*r* [A], F8*v* [E], J2*v* [P], J7*v* [A], J8*r* [K and E], K2*v* [A], K5*v* [A] K6*r* [K], and K8*r* [A]. There are none missing in the Superius part • Only five staves are inked on A6*r*, C4*v*, E5*r* and E6*r* • The manner in which the *m.s.* for perfect tempus and major prolation shows the dot in two positions argues that the sort was on a small body, which could be inverted • Final points do not always take ink • The additional text on C4*v* is printed over the second stave • Similarly, text is printed over K5*v*.vi • The tail directions are sometimes strange: see B2*v* and B5*v*

This edition has clear evidence of blind impressions from type, used as bearer sorts. A row of *c.o.p.* ligatures was used on H4*r*, and lies at right angles to the staves. The sequence is clearest on the copies at D-B and I-Bc, and seems to be as follows: 2 oblique ligatures descending a 2nd; 5 quadrate, descending a 3rd; 3 ascending a 4th; 5 ascending a 5th; 2 quadrate descending a 6th; 1 oblique, descending a 2nd; 2 quadrate descending a 3rd; two more descending a 4th; a final ligature perhaps a ternaria; one minim with a down tail • A similar long row of notes printed in blind on H3*v* can be clearly seen in the copy at D-B: this begins with 34 *m*, followed by one *c.o.p.* ligature ascending a 3rd, one *sb*, one custos, and one *c.o.p.* ligature ascending a 5th. A row of notes was used for the same purpose on C4*v*: reading from the right, they begin *m,m,b,m,m,b,sb,m,m*, [etc.]. A clear example is in the copy at P-Ln. There is a similar row on E5*r*, visible in the copies at I-Mc and US-CA • Two rows of notes printed in blind on J1*r*, both about 66 mm long, one perhaps with twenty-six notes in it, are clearly visible in the copy at I-Fm

In-house corrections:

> **Stop-press corrections:** A5*v*.iii.start: two rests from imperfect *l* to perfect *l*, by a stop-press correction in D-B, in manuscript in P-Ln, and uncorrected in I-Bc

> **After press-work:** A5*v*.iii.start: mensuration sign from ¢ to cut circle 2: P-Ln • B3*r*.iii.46: *sb*a' → *dsb*a': the note erased, except for the right corner, converted to a dot, and stave lines touched up in brown ink, and a new *sb* stamped in: D-B, I-Bc and P-Ln • D8*r*.iii.end: custos e' → *sb*d' and changed end of custos; erasure and new note stamped in: D-B, I-Mc, P-Ln, and US-CA • D8*r*.iv.start: *sb*d' erased: D-B, I-Mc, P-Ln, and US-CA • G5*v*.v.25: *sb*, g → f, erased and stamped in: D-B and I-Bc • G5*v*.v.37: colored *sb*, e' → f': erased and stamped in: D-B and I-Bc • J8*v*.iii.19: f → e, top erased and new base: D-B, I-Bc, and I-Mc • K3*v*.iv.after 15: erasure perhaps of a *mg*: D-B, I-Bc, and I-Fm

> > The following may also have been an in-house correction: K7*r*.iv.after rests after bar line: erased high b flat: D-B, I-Bc, and I-Mc

Rubrics: A5*v*:] Clama ne ceſſes • B7*v*:] Creſcat In duplum • B7*v*.iii, reading down:] Reſolutio • B8*r*.iii-iv, reading up:] Reſolutio • B8*v*.iii, reading down:] Reſolutio • C6*v*:] Fuga ad minimam: • D1*v*.iii-iv, reading down:] Reſolutio. • D2*r*.iv, reading down:] Reſolutio. • D2*v*.iii, reading down:] Reſolutio. • D3*v*.ii, reading down:] Reſolutio. • D6*r*:] Undecies canito pauſas | linque*n*do priores

Contents: The contents for the inner sheet of F are taken from the cancel leaves:

	A1*r*	D1*r*	F1*r*	J1*r*	[Title]
1	A1*v*	D1*v*	F1*v*	J1*v*	Joſquin ſup*er* voces muſichales
	A2*r*	D2*r*	F2*r*	J2*r*	[Gloria]
	A3*r*	D2*v*	F3*r*	J2*v*.v	[Credo]
	A4*r*	D3*r*	F4*r*	J3*v*.iv	[Sanctus]
	A5*r*	D3*v*	F4*v*.iv	J4*v*	[Agnus]
2	A6*r*	D4*r*.iii	F5*v*	J5*v*	Joſquin. La.ſol.fa.re.mi.
	A6*v*	D4*r*.v	F5*v*.iv	J5*v*.iii	[Gloria]

	A7v	D4v.iii	F6v	J6r.iii	[Credo]
	A8v	D5r.iii	F7v	J7r	[Sanctus]
	B1v	D5v.iii	F8r.iii	J7v.v	[Agnus]
3	B2r	D6r	F8v	J8r	Jo[quin [uper gaudeamus
	B2v	D6r.iii	F8v.v	J8r.iv	[Gloria]
	B3v	D6v	G1v	J8v.v	[Credo]
	B5r	D6v.v	G3r	K2r	[Sanctus]
	B5v	D7r.iv	G3v	K2v.iii	[Agnus]
4	B6r	D8r	G4r	K3r.iii	Jo[quin fortuna de [perata
	B6v	D8r.iii	G4v	K3v	[Gloria]
	B7v	D8v	G5r.iii	K4r.iii	[Credo]
	C1r	E1v	G6r.iii	K5r	[Sanctus]
	C2r	E2r.iv	G6v	K5v.v	[Agnus]
5	C2v	E3r	G7r	K6r.iv	Jo[quin. [L'homme arme sexti toni]
	C3r	E3r.iv	G7v	K6v	[Gloria]
	C4r	E3v.v	G8v	K7r	[Credo]
	C5v	E4v.iv	H1v.iv	K7v.v	[Sanctus]
	C6r	E5r	H2r.ii	K8r.v	[Agnus]
6	C7r	E5v	H3r	K8v	Jo[quin.de.pre[. [A:] Ecce tu pulchra es
				K9r	[Colophon; Register; Device]
	C7v–8v	E6v	H4r–v	K9v–10v	[blank]

Extant copies:

The copy listed in *RISM* as at US-R is in fact of the 1516 edition (No.62).

D-B, Mus.ant.pract.D224. Four parts, complete. The inner sheet of F is a cancel, for which see below.

Size of page: 241 × 171 mm.

Watermarks: No.3 on A5, A8, B6, B7, C1, C4, D2, E6, F7, G1, G6, H1, J1, J5, K1, and K3 • No.5 on D4

Technical comments: F8v.iii: a text spacing sort, before the word *Kyrie*, measuring 3.8 × 0.3 mm • G2r.iii: the words] Verte folio [printed in the stave area, clearly show from their inking that they were printed with the music • G5v.v.rest after 9: perhaps meant to be a *sb*, is actually an inverted *sm* • The use of music sorts as bearers, revealing blind impressions, is clear on folios C4v, H3v, H4r, and J1r. The details are given above • K9r, the uninked staves used as furniture went through the press before the colophon, and were retained for K10r, as was the colophon, both uninked

Corrections and changes:

In-house: A5v, B3r, D8r, D8r, G5v, J8v, and K3v: see above

Later: Inscriptions on title pages of lower voices:] Mi[[e Jo[quin • For the Sanctus of the first mass, in each voice part, there are small brown strokes to indicate each complete perfect *sb*: folios A4v, D3r, F4v and J4r • A7v.i.m.s.: line drawn through the circle, in brown ink • D8v.vi.after 45: rests *sb,m* → *b,sb,m*, in ink • F1v.v.40: *m* d → e, with brown "ears" to the note-head • G5v.v.4: *dm*d': the dot erased • K7r.iv.after rests after bar line: erased high b flat

Binding: 19th-century white leather, with a gold serpentine rule • One paste-down and one fly-leaf at each end of each part

Provenance: With the library's copies of *Misse Obreht* (1503, No.6), *Misse Ghiselin* (1503, No.9), *Misse La Rue* (1503, No.11), and *Misse Agricola* (1504, No.13): all have similar annotations on the title-pages of the lower voices, in the same hand

I-Bc, Q.54. Superius, Altus, and Bassus, complete. F3-6 is a cancel sheet, for which see below.

Size of pages: 170 × 237: Bassus 162 × 237 mm.

Watermarks: The twin marks are particularly clear in this copy:

A5	A7	B2	B6	C1	C6	F2	G5	G8	H1	J1	J4	K4	K5	K10
3a	3a	3a	3a	3b	3b	3b	3a	3a	3b	3a	3a	3b	3b	3a

Technical comments: The text spacing sort on J8v.vi corresponds to that in the copy at I-Fm

Corrections and changes:

    In-house: J8v and K3v: see above

    Later: 16th-century manuscript pagination: [S] 149–172; [A] 149–163; [B] 133–150 • C3r.i.47–54: 16th-century inking, with ginger ink, of poorly impressed note-heads • K7r.iv.after rests after bar-line: erased high b flat

Binding: Modern slip-case • Fore-edges are coloured: Superius and Bassus are brown; Altus is green

Provenance: Martini • On the evidence of the manuscript pagination, this was originally to be found with the Bologna copy of La Rue's masses

Bibliography: Fenlon and Dalla Vecchia, *Venezia*, pp. 73–74 • Haberl, "Drucke", p. 94

I-Fm, R.u.115³. Bassus, complete

Size of page: 164 × 232 mm.

Watermarks: No.3 on J6, K3 and K6 • No.5 on J8 and K1

Technical comments: The order of printing certain pairs of formes can be detected from the inking on some folios: J2v before J2r; J7r before J7v; J8v before J8r; perhaps K1v before K1r; probably K6v before K6r • K9r, the uninked staves used as furniture went through the press before the colophon, and were retained for K10r, as was the colophon, both uninked • The use of music sorts as bearers, revealed by blind impressions, is clear on folio J1r • Text spacing sorts: J8v.vi: 0.6 × 1.2 mm; K2v.ii: 0.6 × 4.1 mm: both seem to suggest that the edges of the sorts were higher, from the clearer inking • There is clear evidence of the text moving within the forme, probably during press-work, at the end of J8r.v

Corrections and changes:

    In house: K3v: see above

    Later: modern stamped foliation, b.r.r.:] 32–49

Binding: with the Petrucci edition of Agricola's masses (No.13)

Provenance: From the Landau-Finaly collection

Bibliography: Damerini, *Esposizione*, pp. 25–26 (exhibition at Florence, 1949); Fanelli, *Musica*

I-Mc, S.B.178/9a. Tenor and Bassus, complete

Page size: 169 × 134 and 169 × 135 mm.

Watermarks: No.3 on D7 and K8 • No.5 on D6, E2, J5, J7 and K9

Technical comments: Many of the technical details, such as of blind impressions, are as in the copy at I-Fm

Corrections and changes:

    In-house: D8r and J8v: see above

    Later: Modern pencil foliation: 35–48 and 51–68 • D1v.iii.28: *col.l* scratched void • D2v.v.2: *mb* → c', by a large circle in brown ink • D3v.v.before 34: a flat or signum • E3r.ii.5 back: *sbc'* colored in brown ink • E3r.iii.3: *sba* c' • K7r.iv.after rests after bar line: erased high b flat

Binding: with Josquin, *II Missarum* (No.22)

Provenance: Mantua, Sta Barbara • perhaps Ferrara, the chapel of Cardinal Ippolito d'Este

Bibliography: Damerini, *Esposizione*, pp. 25–26 (exhibition at Florence, 1949) • Lockwood, "Adrian", p. 99 • Prizer, "Cappella"

P-Ln, Res.377. Superius and Tenor, lacking C8. Many pages have small patches on them, occasionally obliterating some material

Page Size: 164 × 235 mm.

Watermarks: No.3 on A6, A8, C5, C7, D1 and E5 • No.5 on B1, B5, C5 and D4

Technical Comments: C4*v*: row of notes used as bearers: reading from the right they begin *m,m,b,m,m,b,sb,m,m,* etc. The same pattern may appear on A6*r*.vi • In many places, large pieces of furniture, marked with an X, have taken ink and impressed. See, for examples, A2*r*.v-vi; A3*r*.vi; A4*r*.v-vi, etc. • D6*r*.top margin: two furniture sorts, one certainly, and the other probably, 8.5 mm wide; both at least 2.5 mm high • Evidence of three impressions: D1*v*: the music indents more than the text, and text more than the staves: the music was last • Stave lengths are given in the commentary

Corrections and changes:

> **In-house:** A5*v*, B3*r* and D8*r*: see above

> **Later:** Early 16th-century foliation in the Tenor, t.r.r.:] [1], 2–7, [7a], 8–12, [13, torn corner to the folio] • The masses are numbered in the inner margin of each part-book, in a 19th-century pencil • A2*r*.iii.above 24: brown ink custos, f' • A3*r*.iv.right end: patch where something has been removed, possibly in an attempt to change *fb,fa* • A4*r*.ii.41: g', *m → sb*: tail partly erased • A5*v*.iii.start: part of clef and first rests erased and redrawn in brown ink: the clef not changed, the two rests from imperfect *l* to perfect *l* • A7*v*.i.m.s.: line through the circle, in brown ink • D1*v*.iii.28: *col.l* scratched void • D1*v*.iii.m.s.: line through the circle, in brown ink • D2*r*.i.40: signum, in brown ink • D2*r*.iv.40 [= resolutio]: signum, in brown ink • D3*v*.v.above 35: a signum, in grey-brown ink • D8*v*.vi.after 45: rests *sb,m → b,sb,m*

Binding: Of the 19th or early 20th century • One paste-down with a conjugate, of patterned paper, at each end. At the front there is also a leaf (probably of the 18th century), with watermark]$^A_C{}^G$

Provenance: On A1*r* and D1*r*] de Alcobaça Gerez • D1*r*: the stamp of] LIVRARIA DE AL-CABACA • Front flyleaf has a 19th-century note, signed] J de R • These books belonged to the Cistercian abbey of Alcobaça until the suppression of the monasteries in 1834

Bibliography: Stevenson, "Josquin", p. 225

US-CA, Mus.786.2.501(2). Tenor, lacking E6

Page Size: 162 × 223 mm.

Watermarks: No.3 on E1 • No.5 on D5 and D7

Technical comments: D6*r*, in top margin: two furniture sorts, one certainly, and the other probably, 8.5 mm wide: both at least 2.5 mm high • E5*r*: a line of minims used as bearers, at two pitches a fifth apart • There is clear evidence that this book was printed from three impressions: D1*v*: the music indents more than the text, and text more than the staves • D5*v* and D7*r*: text printed over the staves • Stave lengths are given in the commentary

Corrections and changes:

> **In-house** D8*r*: see above

> **Later:** D1*v*.iii.28: *col.l* scratched void • D2*r*,lower outer corner: 3 *m* in manuscript • D8*v*.vi.after 45: rests *sb,m → b, sb,m*, in ink

Binding and Provenance: With Josquin, *III Missarum* (1514, No.54)

No. 4a. *Cancel.*

A single sheet, for F3-6

Signatures:] FIII [$4
Other bibliographical details as above

———

Extant copies:

D-B, Mus.ant.pract D224. For the rest of this copy, see above
>   **Watermark:** No.6 on F4-3

I-Bc, Q54. For the rest of this copy, see above
>   **Watermark**: No.6 on F6-5
>   **Textual comments:** F4*v*.iii.end: text:] vt [u[pra
>   **Technical comments:** Stave lengths here confirm a pattern of two sets of staves:

3*r*	4*v*	5*r*	6*v*		4*r*	3*v*	6*r*	5*v*
177	176	178	177		180	181	181	182

———

Lost copies: A copy was apparently once owned by Bottrigari, for Gaspari's transcription of his notes mentions the year. See chapter 20 • The copy cited in the catalogue of João IV may be of a Venetian edition, or possibly from Petrucci's Fossombrone edition, but is more likely to have been printed by Pasoti and Dorico in Rome.

Early references: This is unlikely to be the edition referred to Gesner. Bernstein, "Gesner", No.137, argues that the reference could be to the third book, and I suspect it to refer to the 1526 edition • Doni probably followed Gesner: see chapter 10.

Other editions: This title was reprinted more than once by Petrucci, beginning in 1506: see Nos.30 and 62, below • It was further reprinted, from copies of one of the 1516 editions, by Pasoti and Dorico in 1526, *RISM* J669

Bibliography:

(a) Rosaria Boccadifuoco, *Biblbiografia*, No.1192 • Sartori, *Petrucci*, No.4

(d) This edition was used by Smijers for his collected Josquin edition • See also the New Josquin Edition

(e) Elders, "Problème" • Haas, "Josquin" • Noble, "Petrucci" • Sartori, "Nuove", p. 177 • Winterfeld, *Gabrieli*, i, p. 200 • See also the citations in chapter 14, for a ghost edition in the same year

Commentary:

1. The decision to launch into a volume of masses must have been a serious one for Petrucci. All three earlier volumes had been aimed at a similar market, but this represented a significant change. The implications are either that Petrucci or his partners believed that they could reach enough new purchasers, or that the book was promoted by an outsider. My reasons for believing the second to be the case are discussed in chapter 9.

2. The long gap between the previous book and this one was only partially filled by the cancel sheets for the *Odhecaton A*. No doubt, some of the delay was occasioned by the transition to partbooks, with the different approach to layout implied by the much longer individual movements.

3. Three impressions were certainly used for the first edition, and the staves were printed separately. In addition, the text printed over the staves on C4v and K5v was evidently not set in the same forme as the music.

4. Apparently Petrucci introduced a second set of staves during this edition. Although individual staves can be traced through the book (for example, the damaged stave-end on H3v.vi can be seen on other sheets), yet the pattern of stave lengths on J1–8 shows that different sets were in use:

	1r	2v	7r	8v		2r	1v	8r	7v		3r	4v	5r	6v		4r	3v	6r	5v
D-B	—	177	178	176		177	177	178	176		177	178	178	177		178	177	178	177
I-Bc	—	176	174	176		175	176	175	176		174	177	174	176		173	176	174	175
I-Fm	—	175	174	173		174	175	175	173		173	175	173	173		173	174	175	173

Allowing for paper shrinkage, this shows different patterns in the different copies:

D-B	α	α	α	β
I-Bc	β	β	β	β
I-Fm	α	α	β	α

This evidence not only demonstrates that there was more than one set of staves: it also confirms that the staves cannot have been printed with either the text or the music. They were run off at a separate run, probably employing two presses at the same time.

There is similar evidence in the P-Ln copy of the higher part-books, showing for example, the presence of one set in which one of the inner staves "2v" or "3r" was slightly longer:

	1r	2v	7r	8v		2r	1v	8r	7v		3r	4v	5r	6v		4r	3v	6r	5v
A	—	178	177	177		177	177	178	176		178	178	177	176		178	178	177	177
B	177	177	178	177		177	176	178	177		177	177	178	176		177	178	178	177
C	176	178	178	—		177	177	—	—		176	177	177	177		177	177	178	176
D	—	177	178	176		176	177	178	176		176	178	177	177		177	177	178	176
E	176	177	177	—		176	177	176	177		176	177	178	177					

These figures can be compared with those for the Tenor gathering D at US-CA, which also shows the same pattern, despite the slight changes in paper shrinkage:

	1r	2v	7r	8v		2r	1v	8r	7v		3r	4v	5r	6v		4r	3v	6r	5v
D	—	177	177	176		177	177	178	177		176	177	177	176		176	177	177	176

5. The order of impressions can sometimes be detected: the evidence of D1v, in the copies at P-Ln and US-CA, argues that the music was printed first.

6. The changes made in-house to folio D8r suggest a concern, found elsewhere in Petrucci's early editions, for completing a *tactus* on one line, rather than breaking it up over two lines.

7. The large number of missing initial letters was a direct result of the fact that Petrucci had had only one copy cut for most of the alphabet. If this book were a special commission, as I propose, the lack may not have concerned the patron or recipients, for it would find analogies in both manuscript and printed books of the time. It is significant for my view that this book was commissioned that Petrucci did not order new initials in time for the volume of Obrecht's masses, six months later.

8. The cancel leaves are very crowded in places: it seems likely that something was omitted in the first printing, for which no copy of these pages survives.

9. The dating of the cancel sheet is briefly addressed in chapter 5. There it is pointed out that paper 6 was not used before the middle of 1503, with the edition of Brumel. The stave measurements show that two sets were used, and this confirms that the sheet was printed after the editions of Brumel and Ghiselin in 1503. Finally, the initial letters on this sheet first appear in the edition of Brumel: their condition implies that the sheet was printed even later, probably during November or December of 1503.

10. The stave lengths for this cancel, given above, show that Petrucci had not yet adopted the "work and turn" process that was soon to become normal in his house. Again, if the book were a special commission, there would have been no reason to adopt any labour-saving device in its preparation.

11. The relatively spacious layout adopted for this edition continues the pattern of the first editions of secular music. However, this was abandoned in the later editions of this title, as it was soon to be for other mass books.

No. 5. *Odhecaton A*

14.i.1502/3   *RISM* 1503[2]

Second Edition

A1r]   Harmonice Mu∫ices | Odhecaton | A

N8r]   Impre∫∫um Uenetiis per Octauianum Petrutium Foro∫empronien|∫em 1502 die 14 Januari. Cu3 priuilegio inuicti∫∫imi Dominij | Uenetiarum q*uae* nullus po∫∫it cantum Figuratum imprimere | ∫ub pena in ip∫o priuilegio contenta. | Regi∫trum ABCDEFGHJKLMN. Omnes quaterni. | [Petrucci's device]

A1v]   Octauianus Petrutius foro ∫empronien∫is Hieronymo Donato patricio | Veneto Felicitatem. [etc. For variants with the first edition, see below, under "Textual Comments"

A2r]   Bartholomæus Budrius Iu∫tinopolita. Hieronymo donato patricio Veneto. S. [etc. For variants with the first edition, see below, under "Textual Comments"

A2v   The Tavola is again arranged in four columns. There are few textual changes, most changes being to the presentation. Thus, "Tintori5" and "Royne de fleur5" are spelled with the final "5" which Petrucci begins to employ more often, and other words (among them "regre∫") end with the long "s" which was normally reserved for use within words. Both suggest that the fount had lost a number of sorts of the short "s". More obviously, the Tavola largely uses roman numerals to identify folios (— with the exception of those in the last column, which are primarily in arabic form). There does not seem to be a consistent pattern to the decision whether or not to use roman numerals: most numbers above 70 are in arabic, as are most of those in the 40s, but there are exceptions. Both pieces of evidence, however, suggest that the Tavola was set up in columns, rather than in lines.

Format and collation: Choirbook: landscape quarto-in-eights. 104 folios: A–N⁸

Signatures: A IIII [$4 •-A1, A2

Foliation: top centre recto:] [1–3], 4–24, [25, stamped in later in the corner], 26–30, [31, also later], 32–103, [104]. The two later numbers are in the same forme

No running heads • Composers' names and *si placet* instructions appear in the head line

Part–names:

recto:]	Altus Ba∫∫us	[A4-B3, B5-F8, N1-N2, N5-6
	Ba∫∫us Altus	[B4
	Contra	[G1-M2, M4,6,8, N7
	Tenor Contra	[M3,5,7
	Contra Ba∫∫us	[N3-4
	[Nil:	A1-3, N8

verso:]	Tenor	[A3-4,6, A8-M1, M3,5, M7-N6
	Tenor Tenor	[A5,7
	Tenor Contra	[M2,4,6
	Tenor Altus Baſſus	[N7
	[Nil:	A1-2, N8

Note that the group of changes in gathering M follows the pattern of formes: single page pieces, with the extra lay-out problems, are on M2ν-3r, M4ν-5r, and M6ν-7r — the outer formes for each sheet.

Fonts: Music: Petrucci's normal music type

Staves: six per page. See the Commentary to this edition

Text: Rotonda, "20" = 78 mm, "x" = 2.0.mm, on A2ν • Roman, for A1ν-2r only • Greek, on A2r: a different fount from those found in the first and third editions

Textual comments: A1ν: the following textual changes are made from the first edition: line 6: ſanctiora → ſantiora • 10: numeroſam → numeroſa: • 10: malis → malis. • 11: celebramus: → celebramus. → 13: ui- | ros: → ui | ros • 13: deſtitiſſe → deſtitiſſe: • 14: imprimis: → imprimis: • 21: inuitati: → inuitari:

A2r: the following textual changes are made from the first edition: 1: Bndrius → Budrius • 12: iam diu → iamdiu • 18: religione: → religione: • 21: dimittimus. → dimitimus.

A5r.ii.start: a different reading in this edition • B8r/C1r: in this edition, the end of the page comes at a different place in the music • G5ν.text: the first "e" in "regrets" is inverted • H5r.text: the Contratenor incipit reads] Royne de flenrs [sic] • Opening initials are lacking on C6ν [D, where a small initial is present, as part of the text incipit] and E8ν [N]

Technical comments: When parts continue from verso to recto, the indication is sometimes omitted: a cross on each page appears on L1ν-2r and L7ν-8r. There is no sign on G1ν-2r, G7ν-8r, H4ν-5r, H8ν-J1r, J8ν-K1r, or L8ν-M1r • B4r.i.35–36: this ligature looks rather as if it was poorly cast from two single sorts • The short staves that allowed space for the opening initials are not used in this edition

In-house corrections: D1r: folio number 25 stamped in later • D7r: folio number 31 stamped in later

Rubrics: N7r.below CT:] Canon Petrus ꝛ Joannes currit Jn puncto

Contents: The last column gives the folio numbers to be found in the Tavola:

	A1r	[Title]			
	A1ν	[Dedication]			
	A2r	[Letter from Budrius]			
	A2ν	[Tavola]			
	A3r	[blank staves]			
1	A3ν	AUe maria gratia plena		De orto	iiii
2	A4ν	JE cuide ſece tamps me dure		[Anon.]	v.
3	A5ν	HOr oires vne chanzon	à5	[Anon.]	vi.
4	A6ν	NUnqua fue pena maior		[Anon.]	vii
5	A7ν	BRunette	à5 ex 4	Jo.Sthokem	viii
		[Tav:] Brunetta			
6	A8ν	JAy pris amours		[Anon.]	viiii
		[A,B:] De tous biens			
7	B1ν	NEnciozza mia		Japart	x
		[Tav:] Lenzotta mia			
8	B2ν	JE ne fay plus		[Anon.]	xi

9	B3ν	AMours amours	Hayne	xii
10	B4ν	BErgerette ſauoyene	Joſquin	xiii
11	B5ν	E Qui le dira	[Anon.]	xiiii
12	B6ν	CEſt mal charche	Agricola	xv
13	B7ν	HElas que poura deuenir	Caron.	xvi
			[Tav:] Caron.	
14	B8ν	ADiu mes amours	Joſquin	xvii
		[A,B,Tav:] Adieu . . .		
15	C1ν	POr quoy non	Pe.de la rue.	xviii
		[Tav:] Pour quoy non		
16	C2ν	POr quoy iene puis dire	Jo.Sthokem.	19
		[T:] Uray diu damours		xviiii.
		[Tav:] Pour . . .		
17	C3ν	MOn mignault	[Anon.]	xx
		[T, A:] Gratieuſe		xx.
	C4ν	DIt le bourguygnon	[Anon.]	xxi
19	C5ν	HElas ce neſt pas ſans rayſon	.Sthokem	22.
20	C6ν	De tous biens playne	[Anon.]	xxiii
21	C7ν	JAy pris amours	Japart.	24
			[Tav:] Japart	
22	C8ν	SE congie pris	Japart.	xxv.
			[Tav:] Japart	
23	D1ν	AMours amours	Japart	xxvi
24	D2ν	CEla ſans plus	[Anon.]	xxvii.
25	D3ν	ROmpeltier	[Anon.]	xxviii
		[Tav:] Ronpeltier		
26	D4ν	ALons ferons barbe	Compere	xxviiii
27	D5ν	TMeiſkin	[Anon.]	30.
		[Tav:] Tmeſkin uas iunch		
28	D6ν	VNg franc archier	Comper [sic]	xxxi
29	D7ν	LO ſeray dire	[Anon.]	xxxii
		[Tav:] Lo ſeraie dire		
30	D8ν	HElas que il eſt amongre	Japart	xxxiii
31	E1ν	AMor fait mult tant que argen dure	[Anon.]	xxxiiii
		[T:] Il eſt de bonne heure ne		
		[B:] Tant que noſtre argent dure		
32	E2ν	NOstre cambriere ſi malade eſtoit	[Anon.]	xxxv
33	E3ν	ACordes moy ceque yepenſſe	[Anon.]	xxxvi
34	E4ν	TAn bien miſon penſa	Japart	xxxvii
		[Tav:] . . . mi ſun		
35	E5ν	LE ſeruiteur	[Anon.]	xxxviii
36	E6ν	JAmes iames iames	[Anon.]	xxxviiii
37	E8ν	[N]Ous ſommes de lordre de ſaynt babuyn	Compere	41
38	F2ν	JE nay dueul	Agricola	xxxxiii
39	F4ν	JAy prius amours tout au rebours	Buſnoys:	45.
		[Tav:] Jay pris amours	[Tav:] Buſnois	
40	F5ν	HElogeron nous	[Anon.]	46.

41	F6*v*	VO∫tre bargerenette		Compere.	47
		[Tav:] Vo∫tre bargeronette			
42	F7*v*	JE ne demande aultre de gre		Bu∫noys.	48.
43	F8*v*	PEn∫if mari	à3	Ja. Tadinghen	49.
44	G1*v*	LA morra	à3	Yzac	50
45	G2*v*	ME doibt	à3	Compere.	51.
46	G3*v*	MAle bouche	à3	Compere	lii
		[T:] Circundederunt me			
47	G4*v*	LHome banni	à3	Agricola	liii
48	G5*v*	ALes regrets	à3	Agricola	liiii
		[Tav] Ales regres			
49	G6*v*	LA ∫tangetta	à3	[Anon.]	lv.
50	G7*v*	HElas	à3	Yzac	lvi
51	G8*v*	SE mieulx	à3	Compere	57.
52	H1*v*	HElas	à3	Tintoris.	lviii
53	H2*v*	VEnis regrets	à3	Compere	lviiii
54	H3*v*	MA bouche rit	à3	Okenghem	60.
55	H4*v*	ROyne de fleurs	à3	Alexander	lxi
56	H5*v*	SI dedero	à3	Alexander	62.
57	H6*v*	ALes regres	à3	Hayne	lxiii
58	H7*v*	GAri∫∫es moy	à3	Compere.	lxiiii
59	H8*v*	MEs pen∫ees	à3	Compere.	lxv
60	J1*v*	FOrtuna per ta crudelte	à3	Uincinet	lxvi
61	J2*v*	CEla ∫ans plus	à3	Jo∫quin	lxvii
62	J3*v*	MAter patris	à3	Brunel	68.
63	J4*v*	MAlor me bat	à3	Okenghen:	69.
64	J5*v*	LA plus des plus	à3	Jo∫quin	70.
65	J6*v*	ALes mon cor	à3	Alexander	71.
66	J7*v*	MAdame helas	à3	[Anon.]	72.
67	J8*v*	LE corps	à3	Compere	73.
		[CT:] Corpus*que* meu*m* lic*et*			
68	K1*v*	TAnt ha bo[n] oeul	à3	Compere	74.
69	K2*v*	TAnder naken	à3	Obreht	75.
70	K4*v*	SI a tort on ma blamee	à3	[Anon.]	77.
71	K5*v*	LEs grans regres	à3	[Anon.]	78.
		[Tav:] Le grans regres			
72	K6*v*	ESt po∫∫ible que lhome peult	à3	[Anon.]	lxxviiii
		[Tav:] E∫t il po∫∫ible			
73	K7*v*	DE tous biens	à3	Pe.bourdon	lxxx.
				[Tav:] bourdo*n*	
74	K8*v*	FOrtuna dum gran tempo	à3	[Anon.]	81.
		[Tav:] Fortuoa du*n* . . . [*sic*]			
75	L1*v*	CRions nouel	à3	Agricola	82.
76	L2*v*	BEnedictus	à3	Jzac	83.
				[Tav:] Yzac	
77	L3*v*	LE renuoy	à3	Compere.	84.
78	L4*v*	O Uenus bant	à3	Jo∫quin	85.

79	L5v	MA ſeule dame	à3	[anon.]	86.
80	L7v	LA alfonſina	à3	Jo.ghiselin:	88
81	L8v	LE eure e venue	à3	Agricola	89
		[CT:] Circundederunt			
82	M1v	PUis que de vous	à3	[Anon.]	90.
83	M2v	MOn ſouenir	à3	[Anon.]	91.
		[Tav:] Mon ſouunir [sic]			
84	M3r	ROyne du ciel	à3	Comper e	91.
		[CT:] Regina celi			
85	M3v	MArguerite	à3	[Anon.]	92.
		[Tav:] Margaritte			
86	M4v	HAtraytre amours	à3	Jo.ſtoken	93
		[S:] Harraytre amours			
87	M5r	MAis que ce fuſt	à3	Compere	93.
88	M5v	VEnus tu ma pris	à3	De Orto	94.
89	M6v	DIſant adiu madame	à3	[Anon.]	94.
					[recte 95]
90	M7r	GEntil prince	à3	[Anon.]	95.
91	M7v	JAy bien ahuer	à3	Agricola	lxxxxvi
		[CT:] Jay bien ahner [sic]			
92	M8v	TSat een meſkin		Obreht.	97.
93	N2v	ALa audienche		Hayne	99.
94	N4v	LAtura tu.		[Anon.]	101.
95	N6v	DE tous biens playne	à4 ex 3	[Anon.]	103
				[Tav:] Joſquin	
96	N7v	MEſkin es hu		[Anon.]	103.
	N8r	[Colophon; Register; Device]			
	N8v	[blank]			

Extant copies:

The copy listed in Vogel, *Bibliografia*, at I-TVcap as being of this edition is in fact of the third (No.14)

E-Sc, 12-1-29. Complete

Size of page: 234 × 165 mm.

Watermarks: No.3 on B1, B6, C1, C3, D4, E3, E7, F5, G7, H2, J8, L6 and M1 • No.5 on A2, A6, D8, F1, G5, H3, J5, K1, K3, L8, M3 and N2 • In one or two cases (D8 and M1, in particular), it is difficult to determine which of the two marks is represented

Technical comments: Text spacing sorts appear on A1v.i.near end, measuring 3.2 × 0.5 mm; and on A2r, at the end of the page, measuring 4.0 × 0.6 mm • It is evident that Petrucci was still using three impressions: see, for example, the various inkings on B2v, F2v or F7v • There are many traces of the large pieces of furniture with an x-shaped design on the face: see, for example, D3v, E4r, E4v, E7v, E8r, F3v, G3r, G4r, L1r or M2r. The frequency of this suggests either an over-zealous inking, or poor cleaning of the forme between impressions. Given other evidence, I lean toward the latter • L5r.iii: the stave is present in blind for its whole length. It has taken hardly any ink

Corrections and Changes:

In-house: see above

Later: B6r.i.45: *sm* → *colsb*, by erasing the tail • C6v.ii.*custos*: a → b, by erasing the head, and redrawing it, using a black ink

Binding: "encuadernación de la época en madera recubierta de piel negra repujada" (Anglés "Colombina", p. 26, No.82). Leather-covered double-thickness boards, each with two panels within a floral border. Fittings for four clasps on each board. Re-backed • One paste-down and two fly-leaves, of wove paper, at each end. Also at each end a fly-leaf of earlier paper, with a watermark of a gauntlet with a letter A in the palm and a flower above

Provenance: Has various call numbers associated with the Colombina collections: on A1r. 3049 [struck through and replaced by] 3051 [. Also] 6856 [and] 104 [and] C . . . GG . . . Tab. 175 . . . No . . . 12 [with the last numeral struck through and replaced by 30 • On the old fly-leaf: the call number 12 . . . 1 . . . 29 [and] Harmonice Musices Hyeronymi Donati. [with the name struck through, and replaced by] Petri Castellani • From the collection of Colón. Chapman believes that Colón bought this copy in Venice, in 1530

Bibliography: Anglés, "Colombina", No.82 • Arboli y Farando, *Biblioteca*, ii, pp. 51–52 • Chapman, "Printed", No.1

I-Bc, Q51. Five sheets only: B1-8, L3-6, and M1-8, lacking M8. These sheets form part of the copy of the first edition at I-Bc: for other details, see that copy (No.1), issued in 1501, above
Size of page: 164 × 237 mm.
Watermarks: No.3 on B2, B3 and M3: No.5 on L4

US-NYp, Mus.Res.*MN/P497. Only one sheet, F1-2,7-8. This forms part of a complete copy, described here under edition three (No.14), below
Page size: 162 × 221 mm.
Watermark: No.3 on F2

Lost copies: A copy was apparently once owned by Bottrigari. See chapter 20.
Early references: Zacconi, *Prattica di Musica*, f.84r • In addition, a number of the references cited under the first edition (No.1, above) might well be to this edition
Other editions: First edition: 1501 (No.1) • third edition: 1504 (No.14)
Bibliography:
In addition to the citations under entry No.1, see the following:
(a) Rosaria Boccadifuoco, *Bibliografia*, No.1729 (dated 1502) • Sartori, *Petrucci* No.5 • Brown, *Instrumental*, 1503₁ • Vogel, *Bibliografia*, 1503ᵃ
(e) Hewitt, *Odhecaton*, pp. 6–8 • Jeppesen, "Neuentdeckten" • Marix, "Odhecaton" • Reese, "First" • Trend, "Musikschätze", p. 503

Commentary:

1. The stave lengths and the reappearance of specific individual staves, taken together, imply that staves were kept in the forme from one sheet to the next, but that Petrucci only ran off enough paper for a few gatherings at a time. After each session, he seems to have dismantled the forme, since new patterns seem to emerge every few sheets. Thus the staves on the versos of A5-8 and B5 seem to be identical, as do those on the rectos of F1-4 and G1-2. In these cases, it seems that only one forme of staves was in use: the same may be true for the versos of J5-8, K5-8 and L6-8, or the rectos of J5-8, or of L3-4, M1 and M3-4. The figures that follow (from the copy at E-Sc), therefore, provide as much information on paper shrinkage as they do on the retention of

staves from forme to forme. (The two columns of single numbers indicate the papers for each sheet.)

		1r	2v	7r	8v	2r	1v	8r	7v		3r	4v	5r	6v	4r	3v	6r	5v
A	5	—	—	177	175	—	—	177	176	5	176	177	178	177	177	177	177	176
B	3	177	178	178	177	176	178	178	178	3	176	176	177	176	175	177	177	176
C	3	176	177	177	176	176	177	177	176	3	177	177	177	177	176	177	177	177
D	5	176	177	177	176	176	176	178	176	3	176	177	177	176	177	177	177	176
E	3	176	177	178	176	176	177	178	176	3	176	178	177	177	177	177	177	177
F	5	177	177	178	176	176	177	178	177	3	176	177	177	176	176	177	178	176
G	3	176	177	177	176	176	177	178	177	5	177	176	178	176	176	177	178	177
H	3	176	177	177	176	176	177	177	176	5	176	177	176	176	176	176	177	176
J	3	176	177	177	176	177	176	177	176	5	176	177	177	176	176	177	177	176
K	5	177	177	[—]	176	177	177	176	[—]	5	176	177	177	175	176	176	176	176
L	5	177	177	178	175	176	177	177	175	3	176	177	177	176	176	177	177	176
M	3	177	178	178	177	177	177	178	177	5	176	176	175	176	176	177	177	176
N	5	176	177	177	—	176	177	—	176	5	176	177	177	176	176	177	177	176

Taken with the watermark evidence, this pattern might seem to suggest that there were two stages of printing the book, one exclusively on paper with watermark 3, and one with a mix of staves and watermark 5. However, there is no other evidence arguing against a single printing of all the surviving sheets. Secondly, the few sheets that survive in more than one copy do not always have the same mark. (Since these two marks are hardly to be distinguished, and may well have travelled together, this is not surprising.) Further, Petrucci already seems to have had more than one set of staves when printing the previous edition, the first of Josquin's masses. It is more likely therefore that this evidence represents only different stages of printing the staves, associated with the printing of the other material.

2. The same evidence does confirm that Petrucci was still using three impressions.

3. The Greek font used in this volume, on A2r, is different from that in the other two editions. It appears, as one would expect, that Petrucci borrowed the font from another printer. The typesetter apparently set up the Latin text of the rest of the page, leaving a space into which the Greek was to be fitted. The space is the same length in all three editions.

4. Some pieces of evidence suggest that more than one typesetter worked on this book. There is the pattern of layout of parts in gathering M; the two omitted folio numbers in gathering D; and the omission of signs for parts continuing from verso to recto. None of this is enough to prove the case, either way, though it is suggestive.

5. The two missing initials are both the result of necessity: in each case (C6v and E8v), the same initial had been required earlier in the same forme. Petrucci still had not made plans to order any further initials.

6. There are several changes of authorship between this and the first edition, which have been noted elsewhere (Hewitt, *Odhecaton*, p. 8; Sartori, *Petrucci*, p. 53):

			FIRST EDITION	SECOND EDITION
25	D3v	ROmpeltier	Ja.Obreht	[Anon.]
27	D5v	TMeiſkin	Jſac	[Anon.]
35	E5v	LE ſeruiteur	Buſnoys	[Anon.]
49	G6v	LA ſtangetta	Uuerbech	[Anon.]
66	J7v	MAdame helas	Joſquin	[Anon.]
74	K8v	FOrtuna dum gran tempo	Joſquin	[Anon.]

All these changes suggest what Petrucci (or Castellanus) wanted his readers to believe: that he was taking care to assign correct and full authorship details wherever possible. This relates to the Letter that he would add in the first books of transcriptions by Spinacino (see chapter 8 above).

The list given by Sartori is longer than necessary, for it includes works which were on the lost folios of the Bologna copy: for all these, the index happens not to give an author. They are the following:

			First edition: Tavola	Second edition
30	D8*v*	HElas que il e∫t amongre	[Anon.]	Japart
44	G1*v*	LA morra	[Anon.]	Yzac
45	G2*v*	ME doibt	[Anon.]	Compere.
59	H8*v*	MEs pen∫ees	[Anon.]	Compere.
92	M8*v*	TSat een me∫kin	[Anon.]	Obreht
93	N2*v*	ALa audienche	[Anon.]	Hayne.

Given the points that I have made above (in the discussion of the first edition) about the patterns of ascribing pieces to composers in the index to this volume, there is no reason to believe that these would have been treated differently in the different editions.

No. 6. Obrecht: *Misse*

24.iii.1503   *RISM* O7

There is a cancel for the outer sheet of gathering A

Edition

A1*r*]   Mi∫∫e obreht. | Je ne demande. | Grecorum. | Fortuna de ∫perata. | Malheur me bat. | Salue diua parens. | S

D1*r*]   T

F1*r*]   A

J1*r*]   B

L3*r*]   Impre∫∫um Uenetijs per Octauianum Petrutium Foro∫empronien | ∫em 1503 die 24 Martii. Cu3 priuilegio inuicti∫∫imi Dominij | Uenetiarum q*uae* nullus po∫∫it cantum Figuratum imprimere | ∫ub pena in ip∫o priuilegio contenta. | Regi∫trum ABDFGJK Quaterni EH Terni CL Duerni | [Petrucci's device]

Format and collation: Part-books: landscape quarto-in-eights. [S] 20 folios: A-B⁸C⁴; [T] 14 folios: D⁸E⁶; [A] 22 folios: F-G⁸H⁶; [B] 20 folios: JK⁸L⁴

Signatures:] A 2 [$4 • − A1, C3, C4, D1, D4, H4, L1, L2 • + F1 and J1

Foliation: t.r.r:] [S] [1], 2–4, 6 [*recte* 5], 6–18, [19–20]; [T] 21–26, 28–29 [*recte* 27–28], 29–33, [34]; [A] 35, [36], 37–56; [B] 57–74, [75–76] • This includes a correction from 25 to 21, 31 to 29 [*recte* 28], and 36 to 35: the patterns are given below • In addition, some folio numbers were probably usually present, but very poorly inked, perhaps because they sat very low in the forme. The numbers 19 and 20 are present in the copy at B-Br: the number 34 is barely visible in the same copy, and is present in that at D-B

No running heads or part-names

Fonts: Music: Petrucci's normal music type

Staves: Six per page, 176 mm long, 10-92-112 mm high

Text: Rotonda • Roman for dates in the colophon

Textual comments: A8*r*.ii.text:] Plni • G1*r*.i.text: Agnns dei

Technical comments: The book uses only one block for each initial, with the exception of an occasional type-letter. This results in many blank spaces where initials should have been used to open movements • E6*r*: the music of E5*r* was used as furniture for this page, and has shown in blind on the copies at D-B, D-Mbs, and I-Bc

In-house corrections: B4*r*.signature: stamped in later: all copies • B8*r*.iv.41–42: *smb'*,*sma'* → *sma'*,*smb'*: the note-heads erased and two colored *sb* stamped in D-Mbs and I-Bc; as a stop-press correction in D-B • D1*r*.folio number: 25 → 21: the original number is in the copy at I-Mc: the change is in manuscript in the copies at D-B and I-Bc, and by stop-press correction in the copies at A-GÜ, A-Wn and B-Br • D4*r*.iii.16: *sbe'* → *mc'*: a stop-press correction: D-B; partly erased and stamped-in: A-Wn; unchanged: D-Mbs • D8*r*.folio number: 31 → 29 by stop-press correction: the original number: I-Mc, and also D-Mbs, with the correct number 28 stamped over it; stop-press correction: A-GÜ, A-Wn, B-Br, D-B, and I-Bc • F1*r*.folio number: 36 in B-Br, D-Mbs, and I-Bc: corrected by a stop-press change to 35 in the copies at A-Wn, D-B • J1*v*.iv.last *m*: d → e, note head erased and a new *sb* stamped in: D-B, D-Mbs, I-Bc, and I-Mc • J4*r*.vi.last *l*: A → c, erased and stamped in: B-Br, D-B, D-Mbs, I-Bc, and I-Mc • L1*v*.ii.29: *sm* → *m*, by erasure of the tail in the copy at D-Mbs; by a stop-press change in the copies at D-B and I-Bc

Contents:

	A1*r*	D1*r*	F1*r*	J1*r*	[Title]
1	A1*v*	D1*v*	F1*v*	J1*v*	Obreh.t [up*er* Jene demande.
	A1*v*.iv	D1*v*.iv	F1*v*.v	J1*v*.vi	[Gloria]
	A3*r*	D2*r*	F2*v*.iii	J2*v*.iii	[Credo]
	A4*r*.v	D2*v*	F4*r*	J3*v*.v	[Sanctus]
	A5*r*.iv	D2*v*.i	F5*r*	J4*v*	[Agnus]
2	A6*r*.ii	D3*r*.v	F6*r*	J5*r*	Jaco: Obreht [T:] Grecorum
	A6*r*.v	D3*v*.iii	F6*v*	J5*r*.v	[Gloria]
	A7*r*.ii	D4*r*.ii	F7*r*.ii	J6*v*	[Credo]
	A7*v*.vi	D4*v*.ii	F8*r*	J6*v*.vi	[Sanctus]
	A8*v*.iv	D4*v*.iv	G1*r*	J7*v*.ii	[Agnus]
3	B1*r*.iii	D5*r*.iii	G1*v*	J8*r*.ii	Jacobus | obreht [T:] fortuna de[perata]
	B1*v*.iii	D5*r*.vi	G2*r*.ii	J8*v*.ii	[Gloria]
	B2*v*	D5*v*.iv	G2*v*.v	K1*v*.ii	[Credo]
	B3*r*.iv	D6*r*	G3*v*.iii	K2*r*.iii	[Sanctus]
	B4*r*	D6*v*	G4*v*.iii	K3*r*	[Agnus]
4	B4*v*.iii	D7*r*	G5*v*.iv	K4*r*	Ja.obreht [up*er* Malheur me bat:
	B4*v*.vi	D7*v*	G6*r*.iii	K4*r*.v	[Gloria]
	B5*r*.v	D8*v*	G7*r*	K5*r*.ii	[Credo]
	B5*v*.iii	E1*v*	G8*r*	K6*r*	[Sanctus]
	B5*v*.vi	E2*r*.iii	G8*v*.iii	K6*v*.iii	[Agnus]
5	B6*v*	E3*r*	H1*v*	K7*r*.iv	Ja.obreht. [up*er* [alue diua parens
	B6*v*.vi	E3*r*.v	H2*r*	K7*v*.ii	[Gloria]
	B8*r*.i	E4*r*	H3*r*	K8*r*.v	[Credo]
	C1*r*.i	E4*v*.iv	H4*r*	L1*r*.v	[Sanctus]

C2r.iii	E5v	H5r.iii	L2r.iii	[Agnus]
			L3r	[Colophon; Register; Device]
C3r				[blank]
C3v–4r	E6r	H6r	L3v–4r	[blank staves]
C4v	E6v	H6v	L4v	[blank]

Existing copies:

A-GÜ, s.s. Tenor, lacking folios D4, D5 and E6. The top outer corner of E5 has been cut away, to remove the initial letter on the verso.

> **Size of page:** 165 × 235 mm.
>
> **Watermarks:** No.5 on D3, D7 and E3
>
> **Corrections and changes:**
>> **In-house:** D1r and D8r: see above
>>
>> **Later:** D1r: signature in manuscript
>
> **Binding and Provenance:** With Josquin, *II Missarum* (1515, No.59)
>
> **Bibliography:** Federhofer, "Petrucci"

A-Wn, SA.77.C.13. Three complete parts, lacking the Bassus

> **Size of page:** 162 × 229 mm.
>
> **Watermarks:** No.3 on A6, C3, F2, F4, G6, and H2 • No.5 on A8, B5, B8, D5, D8, E5, G8, and H3
>
> **Corrections and changes:**
>> **In-house:** B4r, D1r, D4r, D8r and F1r: see above
>>
>> **Later:** manuscript numbering of movements:] 240–264 [in brown ink • Binder's marks on A1r
>>
>> • D1r: manuscript signature added
>
> **Binding:** Of the Austrian National Library
>
> **Provenance:** From the later numbering, originally bound with Josquin, *Misse* (1506, No.30)

B-Br, Fétis 1639 A. Complete, except for folio H6, blank. For the cancel sheet, the outer of gathering A, see below • This copy seems to have been cleaned, and in-house corrections largely removed.

> **Size of page:** 158 × 228 mm.
>
> **Watermarks:** No.3 on A6, B1, B3, C2 and D6 • No.5 on D2, E6, F2, F4, G1, G3, H4, J3, J7, K2, K4, and L4 • These are not very clear, and it is possible that some could be changed from 3 to 5 or vice-versa
>
> **Textual comments:** L1r: signature lacking
>
> **Corrections and changes:**
>> **In-house:** B4r, D1r, D8r and J4r: see above
>>
>> **Later:** Manuscript foliation: [S:] 53–72 [including the cancel]; [T:] 37–40; [A:] 90–100, 111, 102–110, [111]; [B:] 47–65. Coupled with this, the printed numbers have been struck through in all but the Altus book, in a light brown ink • D2r: some touching-up of the notation in brown
>
> **Binding:** Now in four mid-19th-century bindings of leather over boards. Each book has a red marker ribbon. The four books slip into a spine sleeve, with a label, which seems to be of an earlier date in the 19th century. The whole is now kept in a green slip-case • Marbled paste-downs conjugate with single fly-leaves at each end. The fly-leaf is glued to the outer of two paper flyleaves: the inner paper fly-leaf at the front of the Cantus book has a mark reading] L & C 1857

Provenance: Probably the Gaspari copy, probably bought by Fétis in Paris. • A recent owner has been a very heavy smoker • The set probably belonged with the copy of Brumel's masses, now in B-Bc, given the early foliation

Bibliography: Fétis, *Biographie*, vii, p. 14 • Potier, "Gaspari", p. 24

D-B, Mus.ant.pract.O40. Complete

Size of page: 173 × 242 mm.

Watermarks: No.5 on A2, A5, B5, B8, C2, D1, D4, E2, F2, F6, G2, G5, H1, H4, J4, J8, K5, K8 and L1

Textual comments: Apparent corrections on folios D3*v* and D7*r* appear to be stains or defects in the paper.

Technical comments: D2*r*.ii.text: a spacing sort, measuring 4.8 × 0.6 mm • E6*r*.iii: music from E5*r*.iii was used as bearer sorts, and has printed in blind

Corrections and changes:

In-house: B4*r*, B8*r*, D1*r*, D4*r*, D8*r*, F1*r*, J1*v*, J4*r*, and L1*v*: see above

Later: A6*r*.above ii:] Jaco: Obreht [in manuscript • D1*r*.] Miſſe hobrecht [in manuscript • D1*r*. signature added in manuscript • F1*r*.] Miſſe hobrecht [in manuscript • G7*v*.iii.38: now *gb*: it may have had a short tail erased • J1*r*.] Miſſe hobrecht [in manuscript • L1*v*.ii.33: *m → sm*, in brown ink

Binding: 19th-century white leather with a gold serpentine rule as a border • One paste-down and one fly-leaf at each end of each book

Provenance: The additions on the title page seem to be in the same style as those in the Berlin copy of Josquin's first book

D-Mbs, 4°.Mus.pr.160/1. Complete

Size of page: 165 × 235–237 mm.

Watermarks:

A3	A8	B1	B4	C3	D2	D5	E3	E6	F4	F8	G4	G8	H5	J4	J8	K6	K8	L1
5	3	3	4	5	5	5	5	5	5	5	5	5	5	5	5	5	5	4

Technical comments: The music of some pages can be shown to have been printed before that of their versos: F8*v* before F8*r*; G8*r* before G8*v*; H1*r* before H1*v*

Corrections and changes:

In-house: B4*r*, B8*r*, D1*r*, D8*r*, F1*r*, J1*v*, J4*r*, and L1*v*: see above

Later: D1*v*: manuscript signature • D2*v*.vi.after 43: erased p.d. • H6*r*: later manuscript music, probably 16th-century, headed] Fuga • L1*v*.ii.33: *m → sm*, in brown ink • L3*r*.text: the word] pronie*n* is expanded, above the abbreviation

Binding and Provenance: With *I Missarum diversorum auctorum* (1508, No.43)

I-Bc, Q.55. Complete • The Altus comes from a different set than the other books

Page size: Altus: 167 × 240 mm.; the other books: 162 × 240 mm.

Watermarks:

A5	A8	B6	B8	C3	D1	D5	E1	F1	F4	G2	G5	H4	H6	J3	J8	K6	K7	L4
3	4	3	3	5	3	5	5	5	4	3	5	5	5	5	5	5	5	4

Technical comments: E6*r*: the music of E5*r* is used as bearer sorts for this folio

Corrections and changes:

In-house: B4*r*, B8*r*, D1*r*, D8*r*, F1*r*, J1*v*, J4*r*, and L1*v*: see above

Later: A2*r*-B1*r*: the folio numbers are erased. Manuscript foliation: [S] 94–113, [T] 60–73, [A] 51–72, [B] 80–99 • D1*r*. signature added in manuscript

Binding: Modern slip-case and folder • Fore-edges painted in gold (S, T, B) or green, perhaps originally gilded (A)

Provenance: Martini • On the evidence of the manuscript pagination, this was originally to be found with the Bologna copy of Agricola's masses

Bibliography: This copy is cited in Martini's letters to Chiti of 7.v.1746 and 22.vii.1746. See Schnoebelen, *Padre*, Nos.1245 and 1250, pp. 144–145

I-Mc, S.B.178/6. Tenor and Bassus, complete

Page size: 169 × 234; 169 × 235 mm.

Watermarks:

D1	D6	E4	E5	J5	J7	K4	K8	L1
5	3	5	5	5	5	5	5	5

Textual comments:

Technical comments: D2*v*: the text on the staves was printed with the music • D5*r*.vi.end: partially inked] Verte foliu*m* [apparently retained in the forme from D6*r*

Corrections and changes:

In-house: J1*v* and J4*r*: see above

Later: modern pencil foliation: 1–14, and 1–20 • D1*r*: manuscript signature • L1*v*.ii.33: *m* → *sm*, filled in, in brown ink

Binding: with Josquin, *II Missarum* (No.22)

Provenance: Mantua, Sta Barbara • perhaps Ferrara, the chapel of Cardinal Ippolito d'Este

Bibliography: Exhibited in Florence in 1949. Damerini, "Esposizione", p. 25

No. 6a. *Cancel sheet.*

One copy exists of a cancel for A1,2,7,8

A1*r*]   Mi∬e obreht. | Je ne demande. | Grecorum. | Fortune de∫perata. | Mal heur me bact. | Salue diua parens. | S

This sheet has been reset throughout: other details correspond to those of the edition, described above

———

Existing copy:

B-Br, Fétis 1639 A. For the rest of this copy, see above

Watermark: No.3 on A2

Textual comment: The head-line for A1*v* reads] .Obreht [up*er* Jenedemande.

———

Lost copies: A copy was apparently once owned by Bottrigari. Gaspari, in transcribing Bottrigari's notes on his copies of Petrucci's editions, cites this edition • Colón owned a copy, bought in Milan in 1531 (Chapman, "Printed", No.2) • A volume of Masses labelled "De Obrehet.", and No.247, is cited in the library of João IV (Sampaio Ribeiro, *Livraria*, p. 50). It is more likely that this is of the Petrucci edition than that it is of the undated edition published by Mewes in Basel (for which, see Lodes, "Anderen")

Early references: Gesner, as cited in chapter 20

Bibliography:

(a) Sartori, *Petrucci*, No.6

(c) Obrecht, *Misse*

(d) Obrecht, *Werken*, i; Obrecht, *Opera Omnia*, i, fasc.1–5

(e) Noblitt, "Problems" • Sartori, "Nuove", p. 177

Commentary:

1. The gathering structure for the Superius is a little strange. Given that the last two folios, C3-4, are completely blank, it would have been possible to print the book as two gatherings, A⁸B¹⁰. This would be the normal practice elsewhere in Petrucci's output. The evidence is that Petrucci was not yet casting off his material. Thus he did not know, as late as starting B5r, just how much space the rest of the music would take. This is supported by the frequency with which new masses (and not merely new movements) begin part way down a page.

2. The unwanted inking of the phrase] Verte folium [on D5r also argues that the music, at least, was set sequentially in the Tenor book.

3. The absence of so many initials follows the pattern of the first edition of Josquin's masses, of six months earlier: in that description, I suggest that the Obrecht book had not yet been planned, supporting the argument of chapter 9. However, this edition seems to have persuaded Petrucci that he had to own more than one copy of many letters, particularly if he were to continue publishing books of mass settings. Certainly, he had enough by the time of the *Misse Brumel*, dated only three months later.

4. It is not clear that the cancel is to be found in the Brussels copy, rather than in all the others. The Brussels title page has a unique spelling of the fourth mass, while the other copies have an anomalous head-line on A1v. However, since the typographical material seems to be in the same state for both copies, the cancel will have been printed immediately after the edition, at the very end of March or the beginning of April.

No. 7. *Motetti B*

10.v.1503   *RISM* 1503¹

There appears to be only one printing of this edition: however, see the remarks about gathering H, in the comments, below.

A1r]   Motetti De paſſione De cruce De ſacramento | De beata virgine et huiuſmodi. | B

J8r]   Impreſſum Venetijs per Octauianum Petrutiuȝ Foroſempronien|ſem 1503 die 10 Maij. Cum priuilegio inuictiſſimi Dominij | Uenetiarum q*uae* nullus poſſit cantum Figuratum imprimere | ſub pena in ipſo priuilegio contenta. | Regiſtrum ABCDEFGHJ Omnes quaterni | [Petrucci's device]

A1v]

Aue ver*um* Joſquin.	18
Aue domina.	36
Aue ver*um* corpus Gaſpar.	43
Aſpice domine	45
Anima xpi.	46
Aue ver*um* Gregoire.	56
Adoro te.	57
Aue maria Regis	60
Aue pulcherrima	61
Aue decus.	63
Aue maria Criſpini	65

Domine non ſecunduȝ Deorto	22
Domine non ſecunduȝ Uaqueras	25
Domine non ſecunduȝ Josquin	28
Gaude virgo.	66
Hec eſt illa.	64
Lauda ſyon.	38
Officiuȝ de paſſione Joſquin.	3
Officiuȝ de cruce Compere	47
Parce domine Obreht	34
Pange lingua.	35
Parce domine Franci.	37
Panis angelicus	42
Quis dabit.	70
Secunduȝ multitudinem	15
Sancta maria	62
Salue regina.	68
Tenebre.	17
Tulerunt dominum meuȝ	31
Tu ſolus Joſquin.	58

Format and collation: Choirbook: landscape quarto-in-eights. 72 folios: A-J⁸

Signatures:] AA II [$4 •— A1

Foliation: top right recto:] [1–2], 3–27, 28 (as stamped-in addition), 29–71, [72]
No running head-lines

Part-names: in left margins reading vertically from top to bottom:

recto:]	Tenor Altus Baſſus	[A2
	Altus Baſſus	[A3-C1, C4-D1, D3-F3, F5-H2, H6-J2, J4, J6-7
	Tenor	[C2-3, H5
	Baſſus	[D2 (Altus omitted)
	[Nil:	F4, H3-4, J3, J5
verso:]	Tenor	[A2-B8, C3-F2, F4-H1, H5-J1, J3, J5-6
	Contra	[C1-2, H4
	Tenor Baſſus	[D1
	Baſſus	[H3
	[Nil:	F3, H2, J2, J4, J7

It is probable that some of these represent errors in inking or typesetting, rather than deliberate changes of pattern • J2v-3r and J4v-5r both have small type initials, acting like guide letters for illuminators

Fonts: Music: Petrucci's music type

Staves: Six per page: 173–175 mm long, 10-91-111.5 high

Text: Rotonda, used throughout: "20" = 77 mm • Roman, used for numerals in the colophon
   The rotonda text fount includes the symbols for the abbreviated forms of tur (G2v, G3r, J6r), l with a line through it (H4r), and v with the line (virgo, H4v) • Brief counts of the appearance of some ligatures in the first gatherings reveals minimum numbers for different sorts of c.o.p. ligature: ascending 2nd: 34; ascending 3rd: 8; ascending 4th: 9; descending 2nd: 17; descending 3rd: 9

Textual comments: F1v.caption] Terminuȝ [has the first "m" inverted: GB-Lbl, H-Bn • F3v-F4r:

the part names are lacking: F-Pn, GB-Lbl • H2*v*-H3*r*: the part names are lacking: F-Pn, GB-Lbl • No capital initial on H4*r* [A] • J2*v*-J3*r*: the part names are lacking: F-Pn, GB-Lbl • J4*v*-J5*r*: the part names are lacking: GB-Lbl

Technical comments: A3*r*.iv.10: the chord of a *colb* and a void *b* is printed from one impression: see the alignment of the individual components • G2*v*.i.text: after the word] tertiar*um* [there is an extraneous letter R on its side, apparently used as spacing, visible in the copies at GB-Lbl and H-Bn • H4*r*.i and H4*v*.i: space left for a large initial letter. The occurrence on H4*r* is rather problematic, for the Altus is not usually given a large capital. This opening contains music à3, and perhaps the typesetter decided that a large initial was therefore needed for the Tenor voice • There seem to have been only one forme of staves throughout: the evidence is most clear in the copy at GB-Lbl • Petrucci is still printing with three impressions: the distance of staves from text is very variable, when the same page in the copies at F-Pc and GB-Lbl is compared

In-house corrections:

    Stop-press: A2*r*.folio number: added to I-Bc • D8*r*.folio number: 31 (GB-Lbl) → 32 (other copies)

    After press-work: D4*r*.folio number: 28 stamped in: all extant copies • E7*v*.vi.text: stamping-in of the word] ta*n*tu3 [: H-Bn • F5*v*.iv.14: *sb*, a → b, erased and stamped in: GB-Lbl • F5*v*.vi.14: *sb*, D → E, erased and stamped in: GB-Lbl • H1*r*.iv-vi.clef: F$_4$ → F$_3$, black ink: all extant copies

Contents:

	A1*r*	[Title]		
	A1*v*	[Tavola]		
1	A2*r*	Non lotis manibus		Cri∫pi*n*.
		[Not in the Tavola.]		
2	A2*v*	O D*o*m*i*ne Jesu xpe . . . pe*n*dente3		Jo∫quin
		[Tavola:] Officium de pa∫∫ione		
	A3*v*	2/ O domine . . . in cruce		
	A4*v*	3/ O domine . . . in ∫epulcro		
	A5*v*	4/ O domine . . . pa∫tor bone		
	A6*v*	5/ O d*o*m*i*ne . . . pro*p*ter illam		
3	A7*v*	QUi velat*us* fui∫ti		Jo∫quin
		[Not in the Tavola]		
	A8*v*	2/ Hora q*ue* duct*us*		
	B1*v*	3/ In flageli5 potu*m* felli5		
	B1*v*.ii	4/ Honor ꝯ ben*e*dictis		
	B2*v*	5/ In amara crucis		
	B3*v*	6/ Qui iacui∫ti mortuus		
	B4*v*	7/ Christu*m* duce3 redemit nos		
4	B6*v*	SEcundu3 multidune*m* dolor*um* meorum		[Anon.]
5	B8*v*	TEnebre facte ∫unt		Ga∫par
6	C1*v*	AVe veru3 corpus natum	à3	Jo∫quin
	C1*v*.ii	2/ Vere pa∫∫u3 immolatum		
	C1*v*.iii	3/ Cuius latus p*er*foratu3		
	C2*v*	4/ E∫to nobis pregu∫tatum		
7	C3*v*	VErbu3 caro factu*m* e*st*		Ga∫par
		[Not in Tavola]		
	C4*v*	2/ [T:] Cuius lat*us* p*er*foratu3		

8	C5v	DOmine [T:] Non ſecundu3 peccata nostra		De:Orto
	C6v	2/ [A:] Domine [S:] Ne memineris		
	C7v	3/ Adiuua nos deus ſalutaris		
9	C8v	[T:] Domine non ſecundu3 peccata nostra	à2	Vaqueras
	D1v	2/ Domine ne memineris	à2	
	D2v	3/ Adiuua nos deus ſalutaris	à4	
10	D3v	DOmine Non ſecundu3 peccata noſtra		Joſquin
	D3v.ii	2/ Domine ne memineris		
	D4v	3/ Adiuua nos deus ſalutaris		
11	D6v	TUlerunt dominum meum		[Pesenti]
	D7v	2/ Scio enim quae redemptor		
12	E1v	PArce domine parce populo tuo		Obreht
13	E2v	PAnge lingua glorioſi		[Anon.]
14	E3v	AVe domina sancta maria		[Anon.]
15	E4v	PArce domine parce populo tuo		[Anon.]
				[Tavola:] Franci.
16	E5v	LAuda ſyon ſaluatorem		Brumel
	E6v	2/ [A:] In hac menſa noui regis		
	E7v	3/ Sub diuerſis ſpeciebus	à2	
	E7v.i	4/ A ſumente non conciſſus	à2	
	E7v.ii	5/ Sumunt boni ſumunt mali		
	E7v.ii	6/ Fracto demum ſacrum		
	E8v	7/ Ecce panis angelorum		
	E8v.ii	8/ Bone paſtor panis vere		
17	F1v	PAnis angelicus		Gaſpar
18	F2v	AUe verum corpus natu3		Gaſpar
19	F4v	ASpice domine quia facta eſt		.Pe.biaumont.
20	F5v	ANima xpi ſanctifica me		Gaſpar
21	F6v	IN nomine Jesu omne genuflectatur		Compere
		[Tavola:] Officium de cruce		
	F7v	2/ Adoramus te christe		
	F8v	3/ Patris ſapientia		
	G1v	4/ Hora prima ductus eſt		
	G2v	5/ Crucifige crucifige		
	G3v	6/ Hora ſexta Jeſus eſt in cruce		
	G4v	7/ Hora nona dominu5 Jeſus		
	G5v	8/ De cruce deponitur		
	G6v	9/ Hora completorij datur		
22	G7v	AUe verum corpus natum		Gregoire
23	G8v	ADoro te deuote latens		[Anon.]
24	H1v	TU ſolus que faciſ mirabilis		Joſquin
	H2v	2/ Nobis eſſet falatia		
		[S & B:] Dung aultre amer		
25	H3v	AUe maria . . . benedicta tu	à3	Regis
26	H4v	[A]Ue pulcherrima regina	à3	Agricola
27	H5v	SSancta maria quesumus		[Anon.]
		[other voices:] Sancta		

28	H6*v*	AUe decu5 virginale		Jo.marti.
29	H7*v*	HEc *est* illa dulcis ro[a		[Anon.]
30	H8*v*	AVe maria gratia plena . . . benedicta tu		Cri[pinns [*sic*]
31	J1*v*	GAude *virg*o mater xpi		[Anon.]
32	J3*v*	[T:] SAlue regina mat*er* mi[ericordie		[Anon.]
	J4*v*	2/ Et ie[u3 benedictum		
33	J5*v*	QUis dabit capiti meo aquam		[Isaac]
34	J7*v*	SIc vnda impellitur vnda	à5 ex 1	[?Moulu]
		[Not in Tavola]		
	J8*r*	[Colophon; Register; Device]		
	J8*v*	[blank]		

Extant copies:

F-Pc, Rés.861. Lacks folios D1 and D8, and the lower outside corner of G1

> **Size of page:** 164 × 231 mm.
>
> **Watermarks:**
>
> | A1-2 | B1 | B4 | F1 | F6 | H3 | H8 | J1 | J4-3 |
> |---|---|---|---|---|---|---|---|---|
> | 6 | 4 | 4 | 3 | 3 | 14 | 3 | 4 | 6 |
>
> **Technical comments:** J8*v* shows the impress of uninked staves kept in the forme • Spacing sorts for text: E7*v*.below v: 3.85 × 0.4 mm; and for music: G2*v*.iii.right end: 18.8 × 0.9 mm
>
> **Corrections and changes:**
>
> > **In-house:** D4*r* and H1*r*: see above
> >
> > **Later:** An index of the contents of the manuscript appendix has been added to A1*v* • Various marks on C2*r*, C3*v*, C6*r* in black ink • J8*r*. Folio number 72 in manuscript
>
> **Binding:** with Ms. appendix, Rés.862 • In brown calf, rebacked (probably during the 19th century), with 4 medallions of a bust, facing left, surrounded by a laurel wreath, on each board (No medallion this small is recorded in Hobson, *Humanists*, though it is evidently in an Italian style, and probably from the 1510s or 1520s) • One paste-down and a modern flyleaf at the front followed by an early fly-leaf with an Italian watermark of the 16th century: at the end, three fly-leaves plus paste-down, all modern.
>
> **Provenance:** A2*r* has the number 155 plus a poorly copied inscription in Greek • Conservatory accession number 32712
>
> **Bibliography:** Bridgman, "Clandestins"

GB-Lbl, K.1.d.2. Complete

> **Page size:** 169 × 233 mm.
>
> **Watermarks:**
>
> | A6 | A7-8 | B6 | B7 | C3 | C7 | D2 | D4 | E6 | E7 | F1 | F5 | G2 | G3 | H3 | H8 | J1 | J5-6 |
> |---|---|---|---|---|---|---|---|---|---|---|---|---|---|---|---|---|---|
> | 3 | 6 | 3 | 5 | 5 | 3 | 3 | 3 | 3 | 5 | 5 | 5 | 3 | 3 | 14 | 14 | 3 | 6 |
>
> **Technical comments:** G2*v*.i.text: see above • The pattern of only one set of staves, retained in the forme, is very clear in this copy. There is a general trend of deterioration, but this is not consistent, as should be expected from the use of one forme on both sides of the sheet • Spacing sorts for music: G2*v*.iii.right end: 18.8 × 0.9 mm.
>
> **Textual comments:** D8*r*: foliated 31
>
> **Corrections and changes:**
>
> > **In-house:** D4*r*, F5*v*, H1*r*: see above
> >
> > **Later:** C4*v*.i.29: *sb*, colored and scratched void, possibly not an error, but an unclean sort •

F1r.iv.17: leger line in brown ink • F1r.v.23: leger line in brown ink • H3v.vi.14: *sb*, c' → d', erased and drawn in black ink

Binding: Oak boards with a wide ½-leather spine, decorated with stamps and rolls in blind. Four damaged metal clasps • One early paste-down, pasted to the outer of a later bifolium, front and back

Provenance: J1v: British Museum stamp, dated] 19 JY [18]94 • A1r:] della Chiesa di … [with, written over the last word:] Doria

Bibliography: Johnson & Scholderer, *Short-Title*, p. 454 • Barclay Squire, "Petrucci"

H–Bn, ZR 523 (2). Lacking folios J1 and J8

Size of page: 169 × 240 mm.

Watermarks:

A4	A7	B1	B3	C6	C8	D1	D5	E8	F1	F6	G1	G3	H4	J3	J7
3	3	3	3	3	3	3	[?]3	3	3	3	3	3	6	7	3

Textual comments: F1v. caption: the first "m" is inverted in] terminu3

Technical comments: In two places, what appears to be an erasure is actually the result of a small piece of extraneous material having been present during inking: D8v.v.8 and F4v.v.9 • G2v: see above • for stave lengths, see below

Corrections and changes:

In-house: D4r, E7v, H1r: see above

Later: A6r.v.custos: d → e, very careful erasure and dark brown ink: it is possible that the original was printed at F, and a double layer of correction is present • F1r.iv.17: leger line in manuscript • F1v.v.23: leger line in manuscript • J2v.i.after 15: added *sb* rest, in light brown ink

Binding: With the library's copy of *Motetti A* of 1505 (No.19)

Provenance: On the title page is a seal stamp, now illegible, of a coat of arms, within a wreath • According to Professor Murányi, this came to the library from a priest at Pécs, in 1960

Bibliography: Murányi, "Unbekannte", p. 292

I–Bc, Q56. Lacks folios A1 and A8

Page size: 165 × 234 mm.

Watermarks:

A5	B4	B8	C2	C4	D1	F6	F8	G6	G8	H5-6	H8	J4
5	3	5	3	3	3	3	3	3	5	8	3	3

Technical comments: G2v.iii.right end: a spacing sort for music, 18.8 × 0.9 mm

Corrections and changes:

In-house: A2r, D4r and H1r: see above

Later: Ambros made an annotation on this copy when visiting Bologna in 1866

Binding: Contemporary black leather, with floral stamps: the central rosette wreath has been removed, and an eagle with wings outstretched has been drawn on the board in red • Three flyleaves and one paste-down, probably of the 18th-century, at the front

Bibliography: Fava, *Primo*, p. 37 (exhibition catalogue, Bologna, 1929) • Haberl, "Drucke", pp. 95–96

Lost copies: A copy was apparently once owned by Bottrigari. Gaspari, in transcribing Bottrigari's notes on his copies of Petrucci's editions, gives] Mott. de Passione. 1503. [I-Bc, (I). P. 59, bifolio [1] • A copy is recorded in Colón's catalogue, as purchased in 1530, perhaps in Venice: see Chapman, "Printed", No.3, p. 59 • A copy is recorded in Liepmannsohn's sale catalogue

No.162 of 1907: this is not the copy now in London, as had been suggested in Sartori, *Petrucci*, p. 58

Early references: Cited by Gesner: see chapter 20

Bibliography:

(a) Rosaria Boccadifuoco, *Bibliografia*, No.2345 • Sartori, *Petrucci*, No.7

(e) Drake, *First* • Sartori, "Nuove", p. 177 • Schmid, *Petrucci*, 28 • Vernarecci, *Petrucci*, p. 86

Commentary:

1. The following notes on stave lengths and formes come from the copy at H-Bn

	1r	2v	3r	4v		2r	1v	4r	3v		paper
Ao	—	176	175	175	β/X	177	—	175	175	β	4
Ai	178	177	174	175	X	175	178	175	175	α	4
Bo	175	175	175	176	τ	178	175	175	175	β	4
Bi	175	174	175	174	τ	174	176	175	175	τ	4
Co	175	178	175	176	α	175	177	175	175	α	4
Ci	174	177	175	176	α	174	177	176	176	α	4
Do	175	178	175	175	α	174	177	175	175	α	4
Di	174	176	176	176	τ	174	176	175	175	α	4
Eo	174	177	175	175	α	174	177	175	175	α	4
Ei	174	177	175	176	α	174	177	176	176	α	?
Fo	174	177	175	176	α	174	177	175	175	α	4
Fi	174	177	175	176	α	174	177	175	176	α	4
Go	174	177	175	176	α	174	178	175	176	α	4
Gi	175	177	176	176	α	174	177	176	176	α	4
Ho	175	177	176	177	X	174	177	177	177	α	?
Hi	175	177	176	176	α	174	177	175	176	α	7
Jo	[-]	176	175	[-]	X	178	[-]	[-]	175	β	4
Ji	174	177	175	175	α	174	177	175	176	α	7

2. Despite the patterns of papers, there appears to be only one extant printing for any sheet of this title. The anomalous appearance of paper 14 in gathering H, accompanied by papers 7 and 8 in other copies, raises the probability that these sheets were printed later. However, the outer sheet of H in the London copy seems to be of the same setting of type as that presented in the Bologna and Paris copies. It seems to me probable that these are later printings, true cancels, which happen to survive in every copy. However, I have found no concrete evidence for arguing that all three were printed later. These folios therefore remain part of the original printing, until further evidence surfaces.

3. There is interesting evidence in support of this position, as well as on the order of work, in the state of the initial letters: the letter A on C1v is in a better condition that in F2v, which corresponds to that on H3v and with subsequent uses. The T on B8v is in a better condition than that on D6v, itself better than that on H1v: however, the S on H5v appears to be in the same state as found elsewhere in the book. Similarly, the stave patterns do not suggest that these two gatherings H and J), or even the sheets using exceptional papers, are later than the rest of the book.

4. Large numbers of a *pausa* are used on certain pages: there are 39 on B1v and B2r with another on B7v; 30 on B8v with four more on B2v; and 52 on E3v-4r.

5. There are similarly large numbers of *c.o.p.* ligatures with intervals of a second on the inner sheet of B:

	outer forme	inner forme
ascending quadrate	15	16
descending quadrate	17	21
descending oblique	2	7

6. The literature on this edition has tended to suggest that there were two sets of variant sheets. Barclay Squire, "Petrucci", suggested that the Bologna and London copies are different: I have been unable to find such differences, admittedly without checking every single note. Similarly, Bridgman, "Clandestins" points out that the London and Paris title-pages are different: the only difference seems to lie in the addition, in the Paris copy, of an index to the manuscript appendix to this volume. Finally, Sartori, in his description of this book, suffered from a printing anomaly, in which several lines of his transcription of the London Tavola were displaced to the head of the list.

No. 8. Brumel: *Misse*

17.vi.1503   *RISM* B4643

A1*r*]   Brumel | Je nay dueul | Berzerette ſauoyene. | Ut re mi fa ſol la | Lomme arme. | Victime paſchali | S

D1*r*]   T

E1*r*]   A

H1*r*]   B

J8*r*]   Impreſ ſum Uenetijs per Octauianum Petrutiuჳ Foroſempronien|ſem 1505 die 17 Junij. Cum priuilegio inuictiſſimi Dominij | Uenetiarum q*uae* nullus poſſit cantum Figuratum imprimere | ſub pena in ipſo priuilegio contenta. | Regiſtrum ABEFHJ q*u*aterni D q*u*intern*us* CG duerni. | [Petrucci's device]

Format and collation: Part-books: landscape quarto-in-eights. [S] 20 folios: AB⁸C⁴; [T] 10 folios: D¹⁰; [A] 20 folios: EF⁸G⁴; [B] 16 folios: HI⁸

Signatures: Aa II [$4 • + D1, E1, H1, D5 (in form Dd IIIII) • − A1, C3, C4, G3, G4 • J1 printed] Ji [at I-Bc

Foliation: [C] [1], 2–20; [T] 21–30; [A] 31–45, 36 [*recte* 46], 45–48 [*recte* 47–50]; [B] 49–63, [64] No running heads or part-names

Fonts: Music: Petrucci's normal music type
Staves: Five line: ca.177 mm long, 10-92-112 mm high
Text: Rotonda throughout

Textual comments: The initial letter *P* is missing from folio A3*r* • F5*v*.v.text:] Et iucarnatus

Technical comments: For the history of the printing of this book, and the change in technique during its production, see chapter 4

In-house corrections, after press-work: E4*v*.i.28: f → g, in brown ink: A-Wn and B-Bc • H8*v*.vi.43; a badly-impressed note head is touched up in brown ink: A-Wn and I-Mc

Contents:

A1*r*	D1*r*	E1*r*	H1*r*	[Title]
1 A1*v*	D1*v*	E1*v*	H1*v*	[T:] [Missa] Je nay dueul
A2*r*	D1*v*.v	E2*r*	H1*v*.vi	[Gloria]
A3*r*	D2*r*.v	E2*v*.iii	H2*v*	[Credo]

A4r.ii	D2v.v	E3v	H3r.iv	[Sanctus]
A5r	D3r.iii	E4r.iii	H3v.iii	[Agnus]
2 A5v	D3v.ii	E4v.iii	H4r.iii	[T:] [Missa] Berzerette Sauoyene
A5v.iii	D4r	E5r.ii	H4v	[Gloria]
A6v.ii	D4r.iii	E6r	H5r.iv	[Credo]
A7v.ii	D4v.iii	E7r.ii	H6r.ii	[Sanctus]
A8v.iii	D4v.v	E8r	H7r.ii	[Agnus]
3 B1v	D5r.ii	E8v.iii	H7v.iv	[T:] [Missa] Ut re mi fa ſol la
B1v.vi	D5r.iii	F1r	H8r.ii	[Gloria]
B2v.iv	D5r.v	F1v.v	H8v.v	[Credo]
B3v.v	D5v.ii	F2v.v	I1v.iv	[Sanctus]
B4v.iii	D5v.iv	F3v.iii	I2r.v	[Agnus]
4 B4v.v	D6v	F4r.v	I2v.iii	[T:] [Missa] Lomme arme
B5r.iv	D6v.iii	F4v.iv	I3r	[Gloria]
B6r	D7r	F5v	I3v.ii	[Credo]
B7r.ii	D7v	F6v	I4v	[Sanctus]
B7v.iv	D7v.iii	F7r.iv	I5r.ii	[Agnus]
5 B8r.iv	D7v.v	F7v.iv	I5r.v	[T:] [Missa] Uictime paſcali
B8v.iii	D8r	F8r.iii	I5v.iii	[Gloria]
C1v	D8r.iv	G1r	I6r.v	[Credo]
C2v	D8v.ii	G2r.ii	I7r.ii	[Sanctus]
C3v	D9r	G3r	I7v.ii	[Agnus]
			I8r	[Colophon: Register: Device]
C4r	D9v-10v	G3v-4r		[blank staves]
C4v		G4v	I8v	[blank page]

Extant copies:

As Sartori, *Petrucci*, p.63, points out, the reference by Fétis to a copy at I-Vnm is probably an error

A-Wn, S.A.78.C.10. Four part-books, complete

Size of Page: 163 × 223 mm.

Watermarks:

A2-1	A3-4	B2-1	B3-4	C1-2	D1-2	D4-3	D5	D7	D10	E3	E8
6	6	6	6	6	6	6	7	7	7	9	9

F5	F8	G3	H6	H8	I1	I5
9	9	9	9	9	9	9

Technical comments: The state of the printer's device on I8r is very close to that in the copy of *Canti C* at A-Wn

Corrections and changes:

In-house: H8v: see above

Later: The pieces are numbered, in MS, in all books: 190–214 • In the Bassus, all the printed folio numbers have been struck through • Binding instructions can be seen on the inner margin of some folios, in brown ink, suggesting that at one time the first gathering of the Cantus book was the eighth in a series of books: c.f. A1r, B1r and C1r • A3r: a word seems to have been erased before the first word of text

Binding: Of the Austrian National Library

Provenance: Given the piece numbering, the book was certainly at one time bound as part of a set opening with one of the library's copies of the first book of Josquin's masses (No.4)

Bibliography: This is probably the copy cited by both Eitner, *Quellenlexikon*, ii, p. 211, and Fétis, *Biographie*, as being at I-Vnm.

B-Bc, Litt.A, no.27.635. Superius and Altus complete: Tenor has only ff.D1-3 with the rest of the gathering supplied in manuscript: the Bassus, missing, is also present in a scrupulous manuscript facsimile • I am grateful to Prof. Anne Gross for examining this copy

Size: 153 × 228 mm.

Watermarks:

A2-1	A3-4	B2-1	B3-4	B6	C3-4	D2	E3	E7	F5	F8	G3
6	6	6	6	9	6	9	9	9	9	9	9

Textual comments: F5v: see above • The Bassus facsimile has the reading on J2r also found in I-Bc

Corrections and changes:

In-house: E4v: see above

Later: D1-3.folio numbers: 21–23 struck through and 51–53 entered in brown ink, prior to the binding

Binding: Recent dark leather, with decoration: stamped on the front board with] Brumel • Messes [and the part-name • End-papers watermarked with a capital initial D

Provenance: Prof. Wagener, and thence to Prof. H. Strahl, of Giessen • Given the manuscript foliation, probably originally bound with the copy of Obrecht's masses (1503, No.6) now in the Bibliothèque royale in Brussels

Bibliography: Eitner, *Quellenlexikon*, ii, p. 211

I-Bc, Q57. Four part-books, lacking only D10.

Size: 162 × 240 mm.

Watermarks:

A1-2	A8	A4-3	A5	B1-2	B8	B6-5	B3	C4-3	C1	D-9	D1
8	7	8	7	8	7	8	7	8	7	8	7

D4-3	D7	D5-6	E1	E5	F4	F7	G3	H5	H8	I2	I6
8	7	[7]	9	9	9	9	9	9	9	10	10

Textual comments: J2r.end of page: for *Verte*] veert

Later changes: All parts have manuscript foliation: [S] 74–93; [T] 50–58; [A] 70–89; [B] 64–79 • Folio numbers are erased throughout the Superius, and to No.38 in the Altus

Binding: Modern wrappers of marbled paper • All fore-edges are painted gold

Provenance: Given the manuscript foliation, this was originally bound with the library's copy of Agricola masses (No.13) • Perhaps from Split

Bibliography: Martini's letters to Chiti of 7.v.1746 and 22.vii.1746 (see Schnoebelen, *Padre*, Nos.1245 and 1250, pp. 144–145)

I-Mc, S.B.178/8. Tenor and Bassus, both complete

Size of Page: 169 × 234 mm.

Watermarks:

D1-2	D3	D6	D8-7	H3	H7	I4	I7
8	7	9	8	9	9	9	9

Corrections and changes:

In-house: H8v: see above

Later: Modern pencil foliation: 25–34; 35–50, [51] • H7v.v.45: f → g, the base of the note erased and a new top drawn in brown ink • J3*v*.i.penultimate: struck through in modern pencil

Binding: with Josquin, *II Missarum* (No.22)

Provenance: Mantua, Sta Barbara • perhaps Ferrara, the chapel of Cardinal Ippolito d'Este

Bibliography: This copy was exhibited in Bologna in 1949 (see Damerini, *Esposizione*, 25)

Lost copies: A copy was apparently once owned by Bottrigari (see chapter 10) • A different copy was owned by Gaspari (Potier, *Gaspari*), and lacked part of the Tenor: this is not the copy now at I-Bc • A copy was owned by Fétis: see his *Biographie*, vii, 14 • The copy listed as at D-B by Sartori does not seem to be either at D-B, or at PL-Kj

There are no other editions of this book

Bibliography:

   (a) Rosaria Boccadifuoco, *Bibliografia*, No.515 • Sartori, *Petrucci*, No.8

   (d) Brumel, *Opera Omnia*

   (e) Boorman, "Work and turn" • EitnerQ, ii, 211 • Sartori, "Nuove", p. 177 • Winterfeld, *Gabrieli*

Commentary:

1.   Despite the patterns of watermarks in Cantus and Tenor, in which the copies at A-Wn and B-Bc appear to use different papers from those found at I-Bc and I Mc, this is apparently composed of only one printing. Part of the reason for the paper distribution is certainly that Petrucci was changing technique during this period, and that this book was interrupted to start the book of Ghiselin's masses. Further, paper 8 was only in use for a short time, and may have been bought with paper 6: both sometimes show the same countermark in the outer corner.

2.   As a result, the pattern of paper use may suggest that Petrucci already had two presses available to him, and that each worked to its own stock of paper.

3.   The significance of the change to paper 9, and of changes in stave patterns, during the production of this book, is discussed earlier in this book (see chapter 5), and in Boorman, "Work and Turn". The stave patterns for the two books are as follows, where each numeral represents a particular page of staves:

Forme		Io	Ii	IIo	IIi	III
Brumel	A	-234	1234	1234	1234	
	B	1234	1234	1234	1234	
	C	123-	1234			
	D	12--	1234	1234	1234	1234
	E	-534	6789	1534	6789	
	F	1534	6789	1534	6789	
	G	15--	67--			
	H	-534	6789	1534	6789	
	I	153-	67-9	1534	6789	
Ghiselin	A	-789	1534	1634	6789	
	B	678-	1534	6789	1534	6789
	C	-53-	6789	1534	6789	6789
	D	-534	6789	1534	6789	

E	1534	6789	1534	6789
F	67--	15-4		
G	-789	1534	6789	1534
H	678-	15--	6789	1534	6789

4. This book is able to take advantage of the new set of initials prepared specifically for mass books. These initials, not available for the Obrecht edition (dated nearly three months earlier), must have been ordered after that book, when it became apparent that there would be more books of mass music.

5. Copies of this book were to be found in some early collections (that from S. Barbara, Mantua, or the Bologna copy, perhaps from Split). Nonetheless, it is notable that no early bibliography cites the book, and that Colón does not seem to have acquired it. Maybe it did not sell well: certainly there is no trace of a later printing.

No. 9. Ghiselin: *Misse*

15.vii.1503   *RISM* G1780

There are two editions of this title extant: for the second, no Bassus (and therefore no colophon or date) survives. For the actual date of the later edition, see below, at No.57.

First Edition

A1r]   Joannes ghiſelin. | La bellaſeſiet | De les armes. | Gratieuſa. | Narayge. | Jenay dueul. |
　　S

C1r]   T
D1r]   A
G1r]   B

H9v]   Impreſ ſum Uenetijs per Octauianum Petrutiuȝ Foroſempronien|ſem 1503 die 15 Julij. Cum priuilegio inuictiſ ſimi Dominij | Uenetiarum q*uae* nullus poſ ſit cantum Figuratum imprimere | ſub pena in ipſo priuilegio contenta. | Regiſtrum ADEG q*ua*terni BCH q*ui*nterni F duern*us* | [Petrucci's device]

Format and collation: Part-books: landscape quarto-in-eights. [S] 18 folios: A⁸B¹⁰; [T] 10 folios: C¹⁰; [A] 20 folios: DE⁸F⁴; [B] 18 folios: G⁸H¹⁰

Signatures: Aa 3 [$4 • − A1, but + other titles • − F3, F4 • + B5, C5, H5 • A2 signed] Bb

Foliation: [S] [1–2], 3–18; [T] 19–28; [A] 26 [*recte* 29], 30–48; [B] 49–65, [66]. Note the corrections in various copies, listed below

No running heads

Fonts: Music: Petrucci's normal music type
　　Staves: six per page. For details, see the discussion under the previous entry (No.8), for Brumel's Masses
　　Text: Rotonda • Roman used for dates in the colophon

Textual comments: Capital letter omitted on C7v [P]

Technical comments: The stave patterns are clear and provide the data listed under Brumel: they have been taken from the copy at I-Ac • There is a peculiar reappearance of the practice of occasionally using a two-stave capital letter, with two inset music lines, a practice Petrucci had effectively abandoned since the earliest volumes

In-house corrections: A2r.signature: corrected signature, stamped in alongside the incorrect (I-Bc and PL-Kj), or as a stop-press correction (I-Ac and I-Bc) • B2r.signature: stamped in later: PL-Kj • D1r. stop-press correction to the folio number: PL-Kj • G6r.iv.after 11: the mensuration sign ¢ is entered in brown ink: I-Ac, I-Bc, I-Fm, and I-Rvat

Contents:

	Aa1r	Cc1r	Dd1r	Gg1r	[Title]
1	Aa1v	Cc1v.i	Dd1v	Gg1v	[Missa La bella se siet]
	Aa2r.ii	Cc1v.vi	Dd2r	Gg2r	[Gloria]
	Aa2v.iii	Cc2v	Dd2v.iv	Gg2v.iii	[Credo]
	Aa3r.vi	Cc3r.ii	Dd3r.vi	Gg3r.v	[Sanctus]
	Aa4r.iv	Cc3v.ii	Dd4r.vi	Gg4r.iii	[Agnus]
2	Aa5r.ii	Cc4r.iii	Dd5r.v	Gg4v.vi	[Missa de les armes]
	Aa5v	Cc4r.iv	Dd5v.v	Gg5r.v	[Gloria]
	Aa6r.vi	Cc4r.vi	Dd6v.iv	Gg6r.ii	[Credo]
	Aa7v	Cc4v.iii	Dd7v.vi	Gg7r	[Sanctus]
	Aa8r.v	Cc4v.iv	Dd8v.v	Gg8r	[Agnus]
3	Bb1r	Cc5r.v	Ee1v.v	Gg8v.iv	[Missa Gratieusa]
	Bb1v	Cc5v	Ee2r.v	Hh1r.iii	[Gloria]
	Bb2r.v	Cc6r	Ee3r.iv	Hh2r	[Credo]
	Bb3r.vi	Cc6v.ii	Ee4v	Hh3r	[Sanctus]
	Bb4r.vi	Cc6v.v	Ee5v	Hh3v.v	[Agnus]
4	Bb4v.v	Cc7r	Ee6r	Hh4r.v	[Missa Narayge]
	Bb5r.iii	Cc7r.iv	Ee6r.v	Hh4v	[Gloria]
	Bb5v.iii	Cc7v.iii	Ee6v.iv	Hh5r	[Credo]
	Bb6v.ii	Cc8r.iii	Ee7v.iv	Hh5v.iv	[Sanctus]
	Bb7r.iii	Cc8v	Ee8r.v	Hh6r.iv	[Agnus]
5	Bb7v	Cc8v.iii	Ee8v.iii	Hh6v	[Missa Je nay dueul]
	Bb7v.v	Cc9r	Ff1r	Hh7r	[Gloria]
	Bb8v	Cc9v	Ff1v.v	Hh7v.ii	[Credo]
	Bb9r.iv	Cc9v.vi	Ff2v.v	Hh8r.v	[Sanctus]
	Bb10r	Cc10riii	Ff3r.iii	Hh9r	[Agnus]
				Hh9v	[Colophon; Register; Device]
			Ff4r		[blank staves]
	Bb10v	Cc10v	Ff4v	Hh10r-v	[blank]

Extant copies:

A-GÜ, s.s. Tenor book, lacking folio C2

  Size of page: 165 × 235 mm.

  Watermarks: No.9 on C6, C7 and C10

  Technical comments: C7v.i: a number of the colored notes appear to show void centres, as if poorly-inked void notes • The same is true on C9v.v

  Later changes: C10r.i.m.s.: C over 3; the 3 erased

  Binding and Provenance: With *II Missarum Josquin* (1515, No.59)

  Bibliography: Federhofer, "Petrucci"

I-Ac, Stamp.N.189 (2). Complete

> **Page Size:** 168 × 232 mm.
>
> **Watermarks:** The twin versions of mark 9 can be clearly distinguished: one, for example, is on D2, the other on D4

A1-2	A5-6	B5	B7	B9-10	C1	C8	D2	D4	E4	E8	F1	G3	G8	H3	H10
10	6	9	9	6	9	9	9	9	9	9	9	9	9	9	9

> **Corrections and changes:**
>
>> **In-house:** A2r and G6r: see above
>>
>> **Later:** A modern pencil foliation, bottom centre recto, continues from the volume of Agricola
>
> **Binding:** With the library's copy of Agricola's masses (1504, No.13)
>
> **Provenance:** San Francesco at Assisi
>
> **Bibliography:** Petrucci, *Missarum*

I-Bc, Q58. Three part-books, lacking the Tenor

> **Page size:** 169 × 239 mm.
>
> **Watermarks:**

A2-1	A7	A6-5	A3	B10-9	B1	B6	B7	D3	D8	E3	E7	F4	G5	G8	H6	H7	H10
6	7	6	7	6	7	9	9	9	9	9	9	9	9	9	9	9	9

> **Technical comments:** H5r: the signature line was printed with the text
>
> **Corrections and changes:**
>
>> **In-house:** A2r and G6r: see above
>>
>> **Later:** Manuscript foliation: [S] 93–110; [A] 93–112; [B] 83–100 • The printed foliation is lightly struck through in the Bassus, and perhaps also the Altus • E1v.vi.mensuration sign after 30: the upper numeral is touched up, in brown ink
>
> **Binding:** Slip case and folder, of marbled boards • All edges are coloured: [S and B] brown; [A] green
>
> **Provenance:** Possibly originally bound with the library's copy of La Rue's masses (see Table 10-5)

I-Fm, R.u.115⁴. Bassus book, lacking folios H9 and H10

> **Page size:** 164 × 232 mm.
>
> **Watermarks:** No.9 on G5, G7, H1, H4 and H5: those on G5 and H5 represent one "twin", with the other on the remaining sheets
>
> **Technical comments:** G1r: there seems to be no evidence of notes being used for furniture • G1v and G2r show smudges from the house, though in different directions • The order of work for staves and text shows in some places, as a result of deep impressions on one side of the leaf affecting the impression on the other: G7r before G7v; H4r before H4v and H6r before H6v; H7r before H7v • The stave pattern is very clear here: for details, see below
>
> **Corrections and changes:**
>
>> **In-house:** G6r: see above
>>
>> **Later:** Modern stamped foliation, b.r.r.:] 50–65
>
> **Binding:** With Agricola's masses (1504, No.13)
>
> **Provenance:** From the Landau-Finaly collection
>
> **Bibliography:** Fanelli, *Musica*

I-Rvat, Sist.235–238. Complete. The end of the Altus is badly damaged, with only fragments of the last folio

> **Size of page:** 233–235 × 169 mm.

Watermarks:

A3	A7-8	B1-2	B5	B4	C3	C5	C10	D4	D8	E3	E8	F3	G1	G3	H4	H10
9	10	6	9	9	9	9	9	9	9	9	9	9	9	9	9	9

Corrections and changes:

> **In-house:** G2r: see above

> **Later:** Has manuscript foliation: S: 88–105; T: 58–67; A: 88–106B: 81–97

Binding and Provenance: with Josquin, *I Missarum* (1516, No.62)

Bibliography: Baini, *Palestrina*, i, p. 244, n.234

Pl-Kj, Mus.ant.pract.G.535. Complete

Size of page: 171 × 238 mm.

Watermarks:

A2	A5	A7-8	B2	B7	B9-10	C2	C4	C6	D2	D5	E2	E3	F4	G5	G8	H1	H4
7	9	6	7	6	6	9	9	9	9	9	9	9	9	9	9	9	9

B5-6 and H5-6, without marks, seem to be on paper 10.

Textual comments: A8r.v:] Agnns dei • The rubric] vt ſuſpra [*sic*, is found on C3v.ii; D4r.v; D8v.iv; E5r.vi; E8r.iv; F3r.ii; G4r.ii; H5r.iii • H3r.i.last two are both *m*: the tails are present, though in blind

Technical comments: For the pattern of stave lengths, see the first part of this study, under chapter 3, and also the details entered in the preceding description, of the *Misse Brumel*

Corrections and changes:

> **In-house:** A2r, B2r, D1r: see above

> **Later:** C1r: in MS. in the hand of the Agricola additions:] Miſ ſe Joannes ghiſelin • C1v.ii.15–16: probably *m,m* → *sm,sm*, colored by hand • C5r.i.rubric: the "du" of "dupluȝ" is struck through and "tri" added above, probably in the hand found on C1r • C9v.vi.after 38: inserted *b* r, dark brown ink • C9v.vi.after 39: erased *b* rest • D1r: as on C1r • G1r: as on C1r • G6r.iv.after 11: m.s. added of cut C, dark brown ink • G6v.ii.31: *m*, f → g, note head erased and a new one drawn, dark brown ink

Binding: the binding and the end-papers are as the Krakow copy of Agricola's masses (1504, No.13)

Provenance: Ex Berlin

Lost copies: Copies of this edition were owned by Colón (Chapman, "Printed", No.14) and Bottrigari. Other copies, owned by the Fuggers (Schaal, "Musikbibliothek", No.I/49), by the chapel of Ottheinrich at Pfalz-Neuburg (Lambrecht, *Heidelberger*, i, p. 110), and by King John IV of Portugal (Sampaio Ribeiro, *Livraria*, p. 50) could have been of either edition • There was perhaps also a copy at Rome, S. Luigi dei Francesi. The inventory records a volume of] Messe sligate di Jo. Ghiselin [and later a] Misse Jois Ghiselin [See Perkins, "Notes", 64

Early References: Cited by Gesner: see chapter 10

Other editions: A second edition, printed by Petrucci at Fossombrone, is listed here as No.57

Bibliography:

> (a) Rosaria Boccadifuoco, *Biblbiografia*, No.1610 • Sartori, *Petrucci*, No.9

> (c) Petrucci, *Missarum*

> (d) Ghiselin, *Opera Omnia*

> (e) Boorman, "Work and Turn" • Noble, "Petrucci", the first to notice the presence of two editions, and to suggest an approximate date for the second • Sartori, "Nuove", pp. 177–78

Commentary:

1. There are enough blank staves in the Bassus to suggest that Petrucci might have been able to fit the contents of that part onto two normal 8-folio gatherings. The blanks are G6r.vi; G7v.vi; H2v.vi; H4v.vi; H6v.v-vi; H7v.vi; H8v.v-vi. This may be evidence against casting-off text during the initial planning of the part-book

2. The change in the technical processes during the printing of this book has been discussed at length earlier in this volume (see chapter 4). Evidence from several copies of both this book and that by Brumel was laid out there. In addition, the detailed distribution of stave sets is shown at the end of the previous entry (No.8). Here, I give the measurements for the staves in the Krakow copy:

Forme Sheet	Outer 1r	2v	3r	4v		Inner 2r	1v	4r	3v	
AI	—	180	179	180	α	174	176	175	175	β
AII	174	176	176	175	β	180	180	179	180	α
BI	179	180	179	—	α	174	175	175	175	β
BII	179	180	179	180	α	173	175	175	175	β
BIII	178	179	178	178	α					
CI	—	175	175	—	β	178	178	179	180	α
CII	174	176	174	174	β	179	180	179	180	α
CIII	179	179	178	179	α					
DI	—	175	174	174	β	179	179	179	179	α
DII	174	175	175	175	β	179	179	179	180	α
EI	174	176	175	175	β	179	180	179	180	α
EII	179	179	179	180	α	174	176	175	175	β
FI	179	180	179	—	α	175	176	175	175	β
GI	—	179	180	180	α	175	176	176	175	β
GII	180	179	179	180	α	174	176	175	175	β
HI	179	179	179	—	α	176	175	—	—	β
HII	179	179	180	180	α	174	176	175	175	β
HIII	179	180	179	179	α					

The Greek letters α and β distinguish the two obviously different patterns of stave lengths, one lying between 178 and 180 mm in length and the other between 174 and 176. The slight differences fall within the limits of variation in paper shrinkage: and the measurements for the Bassus copy at I-Fm conveniently demonstrate what those limits might be:

Forme Sheet	Outer 1r	2v	3r	4v		Inner 1v	2r	3v	4r
GI:	—	178	178	179		176	174	174	175
GII:	178	179	178	179		175	173	175	175
HI:	178	179	—	—		176	174	—	—
HII:	178	178	178	179		175	173	174	175
HIII:	178	179	178	179					

3. The Assisi copy shows evidence in a number of places that the staves of the inner forme were printed before those of the outer.

4. The anomalous use of paper 10 for two copies of the first sheet of paper (A outer) is matched by its appearance for single copies of two sheets in the Brumel edition: all seem to carry the settings of type found in other copies of those sheets.

5. The second edition lacks a Bassus part, and so carries no date. The evidence of the watermarks puts it clearly into Petrucci's Fossombrone production, probably at the end of 1514: in accordance

with Petrucci's normal practice, it probably carried a new date. It is therefore discussed in a separate entry, No.57.

No. 10. *Canti B*

4.viii.1503   *RISM* 1503³

Second Edition

A1r]   Canti. B. numero | Cinquanta. | B

G8r]   Impreſſum Uenetijs per Octauianum Petrutiȝ Foroſempronien|ſem 1503 die 4 Auguſti. Cum priuilegio inuictiſſimi Dominij | Uenetiarum q*uae* nullus poſſit cantum Figuratum imprimere | ſub pena in ipſo priuilegio contenta. | Regiſtrum ABCDEFG Omnes q*u*aterni. | [Petrucci's device]

A1v   Tavola: in two columns]

A quatro		Mon pare ma mariee	xxi
A qui direlle ſa penſee	19	Min morghen	22
Amourȝ me troct ſur la pance	37	Mon pere ma done mari	xxxxv
Auant auant.	41	Noe noe	29
Bon temps	xviii	Or ſus bouier.	xxxx
Baſies moy. Joſquin.	38	Pour quoy fu fait.	xxxvii
Baſies moy .Aſei.	41	Reuellies vous	13
Ceneſt pas.	xi	Se ſuis trop ionnette.	x
Celaſans plus. Obreht	xvii	Tous les regreȝ	26
Cela ſans plus. La*n*noy	20	Uirgo celeſti	3
Come*n*t peult hauer yoye	23	Uray dieu qui me *con*fortera	8
Come*n*t peult.	24	Ueci la dan ſe.	27
Dung aultre amer.Orto	28	Una moza	30
En chambre polie	xiiii	Uavilment	39
Ela la la.	xxxi	Atre	
E dunt reuenis vous	xxxiii	Aue ancilla	xxxxii
Fors ſeule ment.	32	Adieu fillette	xxxxviiii
Fortuna du*n* gra*n* te*m*po. Deuigna	36	Aqui dirage	2
Helas helas. Ninot	25	Chanter ne puis	50
Jay pris amours.Obreht	iiii	De tous biens. Ghiſelin	xxxxvi
Je ſuis amie	xv	En amourȝ	liiii
Jay pris amours .Japart	xxxiiii	Je vous emprie	51
Je cuide: de tous biens	35	Je deſpite tous	lv
Lomme arme	2	La regretee	liii
Lourdault.	9	Le grant deſir	lvi
Lautrier q*ui* paſſa	xii	Si ſumpſero	xxxxiii
Mon mari ma deffamee	xvi		

Format and collation: Choirbook: landscape quarto-in-eights. 56 folios: A-G⁸

Signatures:] A II [$4 • — A1

Foliation: t.r.r.:] [1], 2–8, 6 [*recte* 9], 10–46, 48 [*recte* 47], 48–55, [56]

No running heads. Composers' names in the head line.

Part-names:

recto:]	Tenor Altus Ba∬us		[A2
	Altus Ba∬us		[A3-C3, C5-D3, D5-E1, E3,5,7, F5
	Contra Contra		[C4
	Contra Ba∬us		[D4, E4
	Altus Contra		[E2
	Tenor Altus Ba∬us		[E6
	Tenor Ba∬us		[E8-F1
	Contra		[F2-4, F6-G7
	[Nil:		A1, F8
verso:]	Tenor	Secu *n*dus [and] Tenor	Primus	[A2
	Tenor		[A3-D2, D4-E4,6, F1-G6
	Tenor Contra		[E3, G7
	Tenor Altus Ba∬us		[E5,7
	Tenor Ba∬us		[E8
	[Nil:		A1, D3, G8

Not surprisingly this follows the pattern of the first edition, with the omission of a "Tenor" on D3*v*

Fonts: Music: Petrucci's normal music type

Staves: 6 per page: 180 mm long, 10-92-110 high

Text: Rotonda

Textual comments: For No.24, the following rubrics: T:] Quartus con∫ortatiuus [and A and B:] Obelus quinis ∫edibus ip*se* volat

Technical comments: The pattern of arabic or roman numerals in the index is not strictly random: almost all entries between B2 and C2, all from F2 to F8, and G5-8 are in roman, but so are one or two others • Capital letter omitted on C5*v* [M]

In-house corrections, after press-work: These are all in the unique copy: C6*v*.iv.19: point is later addition, in type • D8*v*.v.46: *m*c' erased → *m*c',*m*c',*r*m in ginger ink • D8*v*.v.50: *m*d' erased: stave touched up in ginger ink

Contents: The last column gives the folio numbers as they appear in the Tavola:

	A1*r*	[Title]			
	A1*v*	[Tavola]			
1	A2*r*	Lo*m*me arme		Jo∫quin	.2
		[Headed:] Canon. Et ∫ic de ∫ingulis			
2	A2*v*	VIrgo cele∫ti	à5	Compere.	.3
3	A3*v*	JAy pris amours		Obreht.	iiii
	A5*v*	2/ Jay pris amours			
4	A7*v*	VRay dieu qui me *con*fortera		[Anon.]	8
5	A8*v*	LOurdault lourdault		Compere.	.9
6	B1*v*	SE ∫ui5 trop ionnette		[Anon.]	x
7	B2*v*	CE ne∫t pa5		Pe.de.la rue.	xi
8	B3*v*	LAutrier q*ui* pa∬a		Bu∫noys.	xii
9	B4*v*	REuellies vous		[Anon.]	.13
10	B5*v*	EN chambre polie		[Anon.]	xiiii
11	B6*v*	JE ∫uis amie du forier		[Anon.]	xv

12	B7*v*	MOn mari ma deffamee		.De. Orto.	xvi
13	B8*v*	CEla ſans plus	à4 ex 2	.Obreht In miſſa.	xvii
14	C1*v*	BOn temp5		[Anon.]	xviii
15	C2*v*	A Qui direlle ſa penſe		[Anon.]	19
		[A:] . . . penſee			
16	C3*v*	CEla ſans plus		[Anon.]	.20
				[Tavola:] Laɴnoy.	
17	C4*v*	MOn pere ma mariee		[Anon.]	.21
18	C5*v*	[M]Yn morghen ghaf		[Anon.]	.22
		[Tavola:] Min morghen			
19	C6*v*	COment peult hauer ioye	à4 ex 3	.Joſquin.	.23
20	C7*v*	COmment peult		[Anon.]	.24
21	C8*v*	HElas helas helas		.Ninot.	.25
22	D1*v*	TOus les regres		Pe.de la rue	.26
23	D2*v*	VEci la danſe barbarj		Uaqueras.	.27
24	D3*v*	DUng aultre amer		De Orto	.28
				[Tavola:] .Orto.	
25	D4*v*	NOe noe noe		.Brumel.	.29
26	D5*v*	VNa moza falle yo		[Anon.]	.30
27	D6*v*	E La la la		[Anon.]	xxxi
		[T, B:] Fates lui bona chiera			
28	D7*v*	FOrs ſeulement		Pe.de.la rue	.32
29	D8*v*	ET dont reuenis vous		Compere	xxxiii
		[Tavola:] E dunt reuenis vous.			
		[A:] Et dunt . . .			
30	E1*v*	JAy pris amours	à4 ex 3	.Japart	xxxiiii
		[Headed:] Fit aries piſcis in licanoſypathon:			
31	E2*v*	JE cuide		apart. .35	
		[T, B:] De tous biens			
32	E3*v*	FRanch cor qua ſtu		.De.Uigne.	36
		[T:] Fortuna dun gran tempo			
				[Tavola:] Deuigna	
33	E4*v*	AMours me trotent ſur la pance		Lourdoys.	.37
34	E6*r*	BAſies moy	à4 ex 2	Joſquin	.38
35	E6*v*	VAuilment		Obreht.	.39
36	E8*r*	ORſus orſus bouier	à4 ex 3	.Bulkyn.	xxxx
		[Headed:] In ſubdiateſſaron			
37	E8*v*	BAſies moy	à6 ex 3	[Anon.]	.4i
		[Headed:] Fuga in diateſſaron			
		[Tav:] A ſei			
38	F1*r*	AUant auant	à4 ex 3	[Anon.]	.4i
		[Headed:] In ſubdiateſſaron			
39	F1*v*	AUe ancilla trinitatis	à3	Brumel.	xxxxii
40	F2*v*	SI ſumpſero	à3	Obreht.	xxxxiii
41	F4*v*	MOn pere ma dona mari	à3	[Anon.]	xxxxv
42	F5*v*	DE tous biens	à3	Ghiſelin.	xxxxvi

43	F6*v*	POur quoy fu fiat ce[te empri[e	à3	[Anon.]	xxxxvii
	F7*v*	2/ Pour quoy fu fiat ce[te empri[e			
		[Omitted from the Tavola]			
44	F8*v*	ADieu fillette de regnon	à3	[Anon.]	xxxxviiii
45	G1*v*	CHauter ne puis	à3	Compere.	50.
46	G2*v*	JE vous emprie	à3	Agricola.	5i
47	G3*v*	AQui dirage mes pen[ees	à3	[Anon.]	52
48	G4*v*	LA regretee	à3	.Hayne.	liii
49	G5*v*	EN amours que cognoi[t:	à3	Brumel	liiii
50	G6*v*	JE de[pite tous	à3	.Brumel.	lv
51	G7*v*	LE grant de[ir	à3	Compere.	lvi
	G8*r*	[Colophon; Privilege; Device]			
	G8*v*	[blank]			

———

Extant copy:

F-Pc, Rés.539. Complete

> **Page size:** 160 × 221 mm.

> **Watermarks:**

> | A4-3 | A8-7 | B5-6 | B7-8 | C3 | C7 | D5-6 | D8-7 | E2-1 | E3-4 | F1-2 | F3-4 | G1-2 | G3-4 |
> |---|---|---|---|---|---|---|---|---|---|---|---|---|---|
> | 8 | 6 | 8 | 8 | 9 | 9 | 11 | 11 | 8 | 11 | 8 | 11 | 8 | 8 |

Technical comments: E5*v*.above iv and below v: spacing sorts • F4*r*. the folio number was printed with the text, not the music • G3*r* and K1*r*. text and staves printed together

Corrections and changes:

> **In-house:** see above

> **Later:** C3*v*: headed] de Lannoy [in blue pencil • F1*v*.iv.2nd rest after 6: *sb m*, erasure and brown ink • F2*v*: manuscript direction hand — the same style as that in the Paris copy of *Odhecaton A* • F5*v*.last note: f → g with partial erasure and the same ink as that found on F1*v* • H3*v*.iv.rest, was across the line: partial erasure and now *sb*

Binding: With the library's copy of *Odhecaton A* (1504, No.14)

Provenance: On A1*r*, Conservatoire stamp and accession number:] 21775 • From Seville and Colón: see *Odhecaton A* (No.14), and Chapman, "Printed", (No.5)

Bibliography: Vernarecci, *Petrucci*, p. 86

———

Lost copies: A copy was originally owned by Bottrigari: see chapter 20

Early references: There is no reason to believe that some of the early references (cited in the description of the first edition) may not apply to this volume, especially since the first edition was not generally known before the 19th century

Other editions: The first edition of this title appeared in 1502 (No.2)

Bibliography: In addition to the entries supplied for the first edition (No.2), see

> (a) Rosaria Boccadifuoco, *Bibliografia*, No.545 • Sartori, No.10 • Nuovo Vogel 15031

> (d) Hewitt, *Canti B* is of the first edition

> (e) Cauchie, "Odhecaton" • Sartori, "Nuove", p. 178

Commentary:

1. It is tempting to suggest that the use of paper 11 for only four sheets in the middle of the volume represents a later impression of those sheets. This paper first appears elsewhere in the next book printed for Petrucci, the *Misse La Rue*, dated almost three months later. In that volume it is used consistently for the Altus and Bassus books, and not at all in the Cantus and Tenor. After that, it reappears during 1504 and 1505, as one of a number of papers which Petrucci was apparently buying at the time.

    If the four sheets in this book, Do, Di, Ei, and Fi, are indeed later, they presently show no evidence of it. This means that they can hardly be later than the end of 1503. The gap between the volume of La Rue masses and the appearance of *Canti C* is only a little over three months (including Christmas): the latter volume was very large, and would have taken much time; and I already believe that cancel sheets prepared for the *Misse La Rue* and the first book of Josquin's masses were printed during that time. It seems unlikely therefore that these sheets are later than the rest of the run of *Canti B*.

    Instead, it is better to argue that two presses (with two compositors) were working for Petrucci during the second half of 1503. They would have divided the work on *Misse La Rue* by partbooks. Given the nature of the repertoire in *Canti B*, it would have been possible to divide work up here by sheets.

2. If indeed two teams worked on this edition, it seems that each compositor set a line for the Tavola as he completed each piece. This is the most logical explanation of the pattern of numbers there. It would imply that most of the roman numerals were the work of one man, and the arabic produced by the other. However, this seems to be one of the situations envisioned in McKenzie, "Printers", in which there is no simple logical explanation: such a division of work does not correspond with any other evidence, and (in particular) works against the pattern of paper use.

    At the moment, all that can be said is that there does not seem to have been a consistent pattern of house-practice at any level of detail.

No. 11. La Rue: *Misse*

31.x.1503   *RISM* L718

There is a cancel for D3,6, discussed below. In addition, there are slight traces of another later printing, in the survival of a few fragments

Edition

A1r]   Miſſe Petri de la Rue. | Beate virginis | Puer natus | Sexti. Ut fa | Lomme arme | Nunque fue pena maior | S

C1r]   T

D1r]   A

F1r]   B

G6r]   Impreſ ſum Uenetijs per Octauianum PetrutiƷ Foroſempronien|ſem 1503 die 31 Octobris. Cum priuilegio inuictiſ ſimi Dominij | Uenetiarum quae nullus poſ ſit cantum Figuratum imprimere

| [ub pena in ip [o priuilegio contenta. | Regi[trum ABDEF quaterni C quinternus G ternus. |
[Petrucci's device]

Format and collation: Part-books: landscape quarto-in-eights. [S] 16 folios: A-B⁸; [T] 10 folios:
C¹⁰; [A] 16 folios: D-E⁸; [B] 14 folios: F⁸G⁶

Signatures:] Aaa IIII [$4 • − A1, G4 • + C1, D1, F1 and C5 • C5 in the form] Ccc IIII

Foliation: t.r.r. only [S]: [1], 2, [3], 4–6 [and none thereafter. See below for f.3

There are no running heads: Petrucci had not yet adopted the pattern of including the part-name at
the head of each page. The actual head lines are listed in the commentary, at the end of this
entry

Fonts: Music: Petrucci's normal music type

Staves: Six per page: 175–80 mm long, 10–91.5–112 mm high.

Text: Rotonda throughout • Roman used for dates in the colophon

Textual comments: E6r.vi.text:] ⁊ homo [is all inverted in most copies (see below) • G3r.right
margin, reading downwards:] Re [olotio

Technical comments: A small capital letter is used on D4v [P] • Bassus gathering F is the only place
not to start a new mass at the top of a page, regardless of spacing. This suggests that Petrucci
was gaining experience in calculating the length of musical text, and had realised that the book
could be made to fit into 14 folios • The staves were certainly retained in the forme, from sheet
to sheet: A3-4 matches A7-8, B3-4, B7-8, etc.

In-house corrections:

Stop-press corrections: C5v.ii.text: "tu sobus" corrected to "tu solus": GB-Lbl • C7r.i: the
initial letter "K" stamped in later: GB-Lbl, PL-Kj and US-CA • E6r.vi.text:] the inverted
text is corrected: E-Bc and I-Bc

Corrections after press-work: A3r. folio number 3 stamped in, inverted: GB-Lbl, I-Bc, PL-
Kj, and US-NH • F6v.iii.6 back: sm → m, by erasure: this correction appears in many copies:
it may therefore have been undertaken in-house, although there is no way to demonstrate
that

Contents:

	A1r	C1r	D1r	F1r	[Title]
1	A1v	C1v	D1v	F1v	[Missa] De beata virgine
	A1v.v	C1v.iii	D1v.v	F1v.iv	[Gloria]
	A2v	C2r.ii	D2r.iv	F2r.iii	[Credo]
	A3r.iv	C2v.iii	D2v.v	F2v.iv	[Sanctus]
	A4r	C3r	D3v	F3r.v	[Agnus]
2	A4v	C3v	D4r	F3v.iii	[Missa] puer natus.
	A4v.v	C3v.iii	D4r.v	F4r	[Gloria]
	A5v	C4r	D4v.v	F4v	[Credo]
	A6v	C4v	D5v	F5r.iii	[Sanctus]
	A7r.iii	C4v.iii	D6r.ii	F5v.v	[Agnus]
3	A7v	C5r	D6v	F6r.iii	[Missa] Sexti. ut fa.
	A7v.iv	C5r.iv	D6v.v	F6v	[Gloria]
	A8v	C5v.iv	D7v	F7r	[Credo]
	B1r.iv	C6r.ii	D8r.iv	F7v.iv	[Sanctus]
	B1v.v	C6v	E1r	F8v	[Agnus]
4	B2v	C7r	E2r	G1r	[Missa] Lomme arme
	B2v.vi	C7r.iii	E2r.iv	G1v	[Gloria]

B3v	C7v	E3r	G2r	[Credo]
B4r.vi	C8r.iii	E4r	G2v.iv	[Sanctus]
B5r.ii	C8v	E4v.iii	G3r.iii	[Agnus]
B6v	C9r	E5r	G3v	[Missa] Nu*n*qua[m] fue pena maior
B7r	C9r.iv	E5v	G4r	[Gloria]
B7v.iii	C9v.ii	E6r.ii	G4v	[Credo]
B8r.iii	C10r̃ii	E7r	G5v	[Sanctus]
			G6r	[Colophon; Register; Device]
		E8r		[blank staves]
B8v	C10v	E8v	G6v	[blank]

(row marked "5" in left margin at B6v)

Rubrics: C7r.headline:] Re ſolutio ex baſſo • C7r, above ii:] Reſolutio ex baſſo • C8v, above iii:] Reſ olutio • G3r.right margin, reading downwards:] Reſolotio

---

Extant copies:

A-Wn, S.A.77.C.11. Superius, Tenor, and Altus, complete, with a 19th-century manuscript copy of the Bassus • This copy contains the cancel bifolium at D3,6, for which see below.

Page size: 163 × 227 mm.

Watermarks:

A2-1	A3-4	A6	A7	B1-2	B3-4	B6	B8	C3	C5	C7-8	C10-9	D-4	D7-8	E5-6	E8-7
6	6	7	7	6	6	7	7	7	8	6	8	11	11	11	11

Textual comments:

Technical comments: The cancel is demonstrated by the distribution of the watermarks on D3 and D4, as well as the pattern of stave lengths:

folios	1/3r	2/4v	7/5r	8/6v		1/3v	2/4r	7/5v	8/6r
D outer	—	180	179	180		176	175	175	175
D inner	180	179	178	181		181	174	175	180
E inner	179	180	179	—		176	175	175	176
E inner	179	179	179	180		175	175	176	176

Later changes: Movements numbered in later brown ink:] 215–238 • No apparent changes to the content • E1r. a binding initial, perhaps "F", at the top of the page

Binding: Of the Austrian National Library

Provenance: This must have been bound with the library's copy of the first book of Josquin's masses (1502, No.4)

E-Bbc, M.115 (6). Altus • This copy contains the cancel bifolium for D3,6, see below

Page size: 174 × 230 mm.

Watermarks: No.11 on D5-, D7-8, E4-3, and E7-8

Corrections and changes:

In-house: E6r. see above

Later: E4r.iv.51: *sb*, f → e, erasure and black ink • E5r.i.1: perhaps was originally colored and has been scratched void

Binding: Bound with the library's copy of Josquin's first book (1516) (No.62, below)

Provenance: E8v.top left:] 56 [and below:] Aulimi quel | torato Auch

Bibliography: Pedrell, *Catálech*, No.427

GB-CW, s.s. Altus part-book, complete. It has the cancel bifolio, D3,6, discussed below

Watermarks: No.11 on D1-2, D5-, E1-2 and E6-5

Technical comments: This copy is very close in its condition to that at I-Ac

Later correction: F6v.iii.6 back: *sm* → *m*, by erasure

Binding and Provenance: With the first book of Josquin's masses (1516, No.62)

GB-Lbl, K.1.d.1. Complete. This copy has the cancel bifolium D3,6, discussed below

Page size: 159 × 216 mm.

Watermarks:

A1–2	A3–2	A6	A8	B1	B4–3	B5	B8–7	C2–1	C4–3	C5–	D2–1	D4–
6	6	7a	7b	7a	6	7a	6	8	8	8	11a	11a

E1–2	E3–4	F2–1	F5–6	G1–2	G3–
11a	11b	11a	11b	11a	11b

The two letters for marks 7 and 11 indicate the presence of the twin marks

Textual comments: A2r. folio number 2 was probably present but barely inked • B2v.vi.text:] homib*us*

Technical comments: Spacing sort on the head-line of A7v, and of F8v • The poor impression of both text and staves on some folios confirms that these elements were printed at the same impression: cf. B3v or C7v

Corrections and changes:

    In-house: A3r and C5v: see above

    Later: Pencil foliation in the Tenor:] 25–34 • E4r.iv.51: *sb*, f → e, erasure and black ink, carefully drawn • F6v.iii.6 back: *sm* → *m*, by erasure

Binding: Original boards with, on each board, two blind-stamped blocks, apparently placed separately within rolled borders, rebacked in 1928. Both blocks have a monogram, of a cross on a hill, with the initials I P. On the front board, the left block shows a statue of] LVCRESIA [between two columns and below a grape arbour. At the top is inscribed in roman:] IN-GENIVM VOLENS NIHIL NON [and at the foot, in italic:] Claruit aît ine[sia a*n*nis 528 [The right column has the date 1534 and the left a monogram. The right block shows a man looking up at a cross, with the words] Spes [at the top right,] Chari | tas [at the left foot, and] Fides [at the center foot. In addition, the left side reads, in italic:] In te do*m*ine [pe | raui no*n* con | fundar in | eternum, | in iu [titia | tua libera | me & eri | pe me. P [al: | 70 [Around the border, in roman: QVONIAM IN | ME SPERAVIT LIBERABO | EVM PROTEG | AM EVM QVO Ec. PSA: 90 [These texts both follow the Septuagint.] On the back board, the sequence of the two blocks is reversed. [The block has been identified as the work of Jacob Pandelaert, of Louvain, working in the mid-16th-century. See Goldschmidt, *Gothic*, No.179 • One bifolium of marbled card at each end, with the outer sheet pasted down on the board, and the inner sheet pasted to the outer of a bifolium of laid paper fly-leaves

Provenance: See the notes on the binding

Bibliography: Johnson and Scholderer, *Short-Title*, p. 369

I-Ac, Stampati.No.189(3). Complete. This copy has the cancel bifolium at D3,6, for which see below

Page size: 168 × 232 mm.

Watermarks:

A2	A5–6	A7–8	B2–1	B3–4	B6	B7	C1–2	C3	C5–	C8–7	D5–	D8–7
7	6	6	6	6	7	7	6	7	8	6	11	11

E2–1	E4–3	F4–3	F8–7	G–3	G5–6
11	11	11	11	11	11

Later changes: Modern manuscript foliation, continuing from the Agricola edition •

Binding: With Agricola's masses (No.13)

Provenance: S. Francesco, Assisi

Bibliography: Petrucci, *Liber* (facsimile)

I-Bc, Q.59. Complete • This copy has the cancel leaf at D3,6, for which see below

   Page size: 169 × 236 mm.

   Watermarks:

A2	A4-3	A5	A7-8	B2-1	B4	B5-6	B7	C2-1	C4-3	C5-	C6-	D5-	D8-7
7	6	7	6	6	7	6	7	8	8	7	6	11	11

E6-5	E8-7	F4-3	F7-8	G-3	G6-5
11	11	11	11	11	11

   Technical comments: Spacing sort on the head-line of A7*v* • G1*r*.iv-v: furniture visible

   Corrections and changes:

      In-house: A3*r*, E6*r*: see above

      Later: Manuscript pagination, [C] 37–52; [T] 2[7]-36, with a number of the second digits trimmed off; [A] in the 40s and 50s, almost all gone; [B] in the 30s and 40s • F6*v*.iii.6 back: *sm → m*, by erasure

   Binding: Modern card wrappers, with paper flyleaves. All within a folder of marbled card. Painted edges: S and B, brown; T and A, green

   Provenance: Given the pagination, and edges, this was originally bound behind some now lost volumes, and before the library's copy of Obrecht's masses (No.6)

I-Mc, S.B.178/7. Tenor and Bassus, complete

   Size of page: 169 × 234 and 169 × 235 mm.

   Watermarks:

C6	C8-7	C9-10	F5-6	F8-7	G1-2	G-4
8	8	8	11	11	11	11

   Technical comments: C7*r*.i: lacks the large initial K • F8*v*.head-line: text spacing sort is visible, 3.4 mm high • G1*r*.iv-v: furniture has taken light impressions

   Later corrections and changes: Modern pencil foliation:] 15–24; 21–34 • C7*v*.iv.rests before 3 back: *sb → 2sb*, in light brown ink • F6*v*.iii.6 from end: *sm → m*, by erasure

   Binding: with Josquin, *II Missarum* (No.22)

   Provenance: Mantua, Sta Barbara • perhaps Ferrara, the chapel of Cardinal Ippolito d'Este

   Bibliography: This copy was exhibited in Florence in 1949 (see Damerini, "Esposizione", p. 25) and in London in 1981–82 (see Chambers and Martineau, *Splendours*) • Prizer, "Capella"

I-Rvat, Sist.235–238. Complete. This copy has the cancel leaf at D3,D6, for which see below

   Watermarks:

A2	A4	A5-6	A7-8	B2	B4-3	B5	B7-8	C2-1	C3	C-5	C8-7	C9
7	7	6	6	7	6	7	6	6	7	6	8	7

D5-	D7-8	E4-3	E8-7	F2-1	F4-3	G-3	G5-6
11	11	11	11	11	11	11	11

   Later corrections and changes: Foliated [S] 52–67; [T] 34–43; [A] 54–69; [B] 51–64 • F6*v*.iii.6 from end: *sm → m*, by erasure

   Binding and Provenance: with Josquin, *I Missarum* (1516, No.62)

PL-Kj, Mus.ant.pract.L115. Complete. This copy has the cancel leaf at D3,6, for which see below

   Size of page: 171 × 238 mm.

   Watermarks:

A1-2	A4-3	A5	A8	B1-2	B3-4	B6	B8	C3-4	C5-	C8	C10-9	D1-2	D-4
6	6	7	7	6	8	7	7	6	8	7	8	11	11

E3-4	E8-7	F6-5	F8-7	G3-	G6-5
11	11	11	11	11	11

Technical comments: A7r.i.rest after 34: not erased, merely poorly inked • The pattern of staves is significant, not only showing a pattern of "work-and-turn" production, but also certain other details: for the measurements, see the Commentary, below

Corrections and changes:

    In-house: A3r. see above

    Later: B2v.iii.above rest after 22: a small cross in brown ink. Similar crosses can be found on B2v-4r, C8r-9r, and E2r-3v. They are apparently rehearsal cues • C1r. in a 16th-century manuscript hand, also found on *Misse Ghiselin*:] Mi[[e petri de la rue • C4r.iv.9: touched up in dark brown, as a result of a poor impression • D1r. as on C1r • E4r.iv.51: *sb*, f → e, almost all erased, and new note drawn • F1r. as on C1r • F6v.iii.6 back: *sm* → *m*, by erasure

Binding: Berlin bindings, within a 19th-century slip-case. All part-books bound in early 19th-century parchment with gold rolled border • One fly-leaf and one paste-down at each end of each part-book

Provenance: From Berlin. The stamp, in red] Ex | Biblioth. Regia | Berolinen[i. [appears on A1v and C1v

US-CA, Mus.786.2.501 (3). Tenor, complete. This copy looks to have been washed at some time. See, for example, C5riii.19–22, which have a number of brown spots around them, hinting at early manuscript changes. As printed, they read *lg,la,*ligature *ba+bb*

Size of page: 162 × 223 mm.

Watermarks:

C1-2	C3	C-5	C6	C7-8	C10
6	7	6	7	8	7

Technical comments: For the stave lengths, see the end of this description.

In-house correction: C7r. see above

Binding and Provenance: With Josquin *Missarum III* (1514, No.54)

US-NH, Music Deposit No.52. Superius, complete

Size of page: 151 × 221 mm.

Watermarks:

A2	A4-3	A5	A7-8	B2-1	B4-3	B5	B7
7	6	7	6	6	6	7	7

Textual comments: A2r. folio number 2 was probably present, but there is merely a smudge, apparently from the lower edge of the sort • B2v.vi.text:] homib*us*

Technical comments: A7v. headline: the same spacing sort seen in the copy at I-Bc • B6r.i.text: large spacing sort, ca.2.8 × 3.5 mm.

Corrections and changes:

    In-house: A3r. see above

    Later: A modern foliation has been started on the first two folios • B6v.vi.text: there may be an erasure at the abbreviation for *con* in the word] con[b[tantiale*m* [*sic*]

Binding: Modern red leather, with gold rolls on the inside edges, and blind rules on the borders. • One modern paste-down and conjugate flyleaf at each end, the flyleaf pasted to the outer of two conjugate 18th-century flyleaves

Provenance: From the collection of Commer, *via* W. H. Cummings, *via* A. Rosenthal • A1r. the book-plate of F. Commer, with a manuscript comment on Petrucci • Bought by the John Herrick Jackson Fund in 1963

Bibliography: Barclay Squire, "Petrucci"

No. 11A. Cancel bifolium for folios D3 and D6

Most details correspond to those of the edition, as described above

Running heads:

.De beata virgine.	[D3r,3v
.Puer natus.	[D6r
.Pe de la rne. Sexti vt fa.	[D6v

Technical comments: The pattern of points in the head-lines is different on these pages

Contents: As for the main edition, above

———

Extant copies:

For further details on all these copies, see above

A-Wn, S.A.77.C.11

    Watermark: Mark 11 on D3-

    Technical comments: Stave lengths are given below

E-Bc, M.115 (6)

    Watermark: Mark 11 on D6-

GB-CW, s.s.

    Watermark: Mark 11 on D6-

GB-Lbl, K.1.d.1

    Watermarks Mark 11 on D3-

    Technical comments: Stave lengths are given below

I-Ac, Stamp.No.189 (3)

    Watermark: Mark 11 on D6-

    Technical comments: Stave lengths are given below

I-Bc, Q 59

    Watermark: Mark 11 on D6-

    Technical comments: Stave lengths are given below • The pattern of running heads is different on this sheet

I-Rvat, Sist.235–238

    Watermark: Mark 11 on D6-

PL-Kj, Mus.ant.pract.L115

    Watermark: Mark 11 on D3-

    Technical comments: Stave lengths are given below

No. 11B. Fragmentary additional printing

Three fragments from a different printing survive in Fossombrone. They can be distinguished from the principal edition, as described below

———

Extant material:

I-FBR, s.s. Three fragments removed from bindings: parts of the lowest two systems of B3

    Sizes: 32.5 × 67 mm; 27 × 23 mm; 30 × 30 mm.

    No watermarks are visible

    Textual comments: Several of the tails appear to go in the other direction to those of the main edition: the alignment of text and music is also different

Provenance: These have probably been in Fossombrone since the beginning, and were remains of material disposed of after Petrucci finished his active career

Bibliography: Coviello, *Tradizione*

———

Lost copies: A copy existed in the Colón collection (see Chapman, "Printed", No.6, p. 59) • A copy was in the Fugger collection (see Schaal, "Musibibliothek", No.I/61)

Early references: Gesner: see chapter 10

Bibliography:

(a) Rosaria Boccadifuoco, *Bibliografia*, No.1827 • Sartori, *Petrucci*, No.11

(c) Coviello, *Tradizione* • Petrucci, *Missarum*

(d) La Rue, *Opera Omnia*

(e) Auda, "Transcription"

Commentary:

1. The pattern of paper use suggests that the book was divided between two sets of craftsmen, one of whom was responsible for the first two parts (Superius and Tenor), and the other for the Altus and Bassus. I have found no other bibliographical reason to assert this. It is notable however that paper 11 (used for Altus and Bassus) had already come into use during the printing of the previous book, *Canti B*, while the supply of the papers used for the Superius and Tenor seems to be exhausted with this title.

2. The pattern of staves in the formes of the copy at PL-Kj are indicative. The following measurements are of the length of the lowest stave on each page:

Forme	outer				inner			
A I	—	176	175	175	180	180	180	180
II	174	176	175	175	180	179	180	179
B I	175	176	174	—	180	179	180	179
II	174	176	174	175	180	179	180	178
C I	—	180	179	—	176	174	175	175
II	179	179	178	179	176	174	175	174
III	179	180	179	180				
D I	—	179	178	180	176	174	174	174
II	179	179	179	180	179	174	174	178
E I	178	179	178	—	174	174	174	173
II	179	179	178	180	175	174	175	174
F I	—	179	178	180	176	174	175	174
II	178	180	178	180	176	175	175	174
G I	179	180	178	—	176	176	176	—
II	179	180	178	179				

There are three points to make:

(a) this clearly shows the retention of staves in the skeleton forme, in sets which can be used without movement;

(b) The pattern reverses at the beginning of gathering C. The patterns of watermarks in the various copies indicate that this does not represent a hiatus in production: it must therefore be a reflection of the pattern of setting. I suspect that the inner formes of text usually went to the press first, following the normal pattern of sequential setting. Then the staves for the inner forme of BII would be ready before those of the outer: these staves would then be ready for the innermost forme of gathering C, that on CIII. Since this was only a half sheet, printed by work and turn, the pattern would necessarily shift.

(c) The anomalous forme DII is not strictly so, but the result of the cancel.

3.   The single gathering C at US-CA shows the same pattern, but, in its larger measurements, also indicates the extent to which paper shrinkage can affect the readings.

C I	—	181	180	—	177	176	176	177
II	180	181	180	182	178	176	177	177
III	182	181	181	183				

4.   The head-lines, only comprising the name of the mass concerned, show every sign of being reset on each page. The following is taken from the copy at I-Ac (easily available in facsimile, as part of Petrucci, *Liber.*) The variety of added full stops is notable, although a pattern can be discerned, of adding a stop between "Pe" and "de la rue". Other points are more haphazard, although a comparison of copies shows that many were present but did not print. Any two copies will present a seeming variety of added and removed points, although they in fact contain the same setting of type.

recto:] De beata virgine. [A2, F2,3 • .De. beata.virgine. [A3 • De beata virgine [A4, C2 • De.beatvirgine [C2 • De.beata virgine [D2 • .De beata virgine. [D3

.Puer.natus. [A5 • Puer natus [A6,7, C4, F5 • .Pe.de la rue.Puer natus [D4 • Puer natus. [D5, F4,6 • .Puer natus. [D6

Sexti vt fa [A8, B2, C5,6 • Sexti.vt fa [B1 • Sexti vt fa. [D7-E1, F7,8

Lomme arme. [B3-5, E3,4 • Lomme arme [C7,8 • .Lomme arme. [G2,3 • Pe. de la rue. Lomme arme. [E2, G1

Nun qua.fue [B6 • Nunqua fue [B7, C10 • Nunqua fue. [B8, E6,7, G5 • Nunqua fue pene maior [C9 • .Nunqua fue. [G4 • Pe. de la.rue. Nunqua fue. [E5

[Nil A1, C1, D1, E8, F1, G6

verso:] Pe.de.la.rue.De.beata.virgine. [A1 • De beata virgine [A2,3, C2, D2 • De Beata virgine [C1 • Pe.de la rue De beata virgine [D1, F1 • .De beata virgine. [D3 • De beata virgine. [F2,3

.Pe.de la rue. .puer natus. [A4 • Puer natus. [A5, D5, F4,5 • Puer natus: [A6 • Puer natus [C3,4 • .Puer.natus [D4

.Pe de la rue. Sexti.vt fa. [A7 • Sexti vt fa [A8, C5,6 • Sexti.vt fa. [B1, F8 • Sexti vt fa. [D7-E1, F6,7 • .Pe.de la rue. Sextivt fa. [D6

Pe.de.la rue.Lomme arme [B2 • Lomme arme [B3, C7,8, E3 • Lomme arme. [B4, E2,4, G2 • .Lomme ar me. [G1

Pe.de la rue. Nunqua fue pena maior: [B5 • Nunqua fue. [B6, E5,7, G4 • Nun qua.fue [B7 • Nunqua fue [C9 • .Nunqua fue. [E6 • Pe. de la rue. Nunqa fue. [G3 • Nunqua fue. [G5

[Nil B8, C10, E8, G6

Despite the variety of solutions to be found here, it is clear that these head-lines could not have been kept in the forme as a normal practice. On the other hand, there were evidently occasions when the compositor left the heading in place: some cases of consecutive uses of the same style that appear above can also be shown to comprise exactly the same setting. Among these are, on rectos: B3 and 5, E6 and 7, and F4 and 6; and on versos: D2 and 3, E6 and 7, and F6 and 7. This shows that the compositors were aware of the possibility.

5.   There are only two places in the volume where Petrucci does not begin a new mass on a new page: both fall in the Bassus, and allow that book to be printed on six folios, instead of seven

(requiring eight). This suggests that Petrucci's foreman might have begun to acquire the skill needed to cast off polyphonic music, and to calculate the required number of pages.

6.   There are typographical reasons for asserting that the half-sheet D3,6 was the cancel, rather than D4,5:

(i) folios 4 and 5 would not need the small initial P on 4*v*, since the large initial (on D3,6) would not be in use;

(ii) the A on 3*v* has some damage at the top of the letter, on both sides, when compared with elsewhere in the volume, suggesting that this page was printed later;

(iii) while the stave lengths on D4,5 follow the normal pattern, those on D3,6 show a pattern of printing by work-and-turn. All extant copies have the same group of staves:

A-Wn	180	181	180	181
GB-Lbl	179	180	178	180
I-Ac	179	181	179	181
I-Bc	180	180	180	181
PL-Kj	179	179	178	180

7.   The cancel bifolio must have been printed very soon after the edition. It survives in all copies, and the typographical material seems to be in much the same state as in the edition.

8.   The fragmentary remains of another printing cannot be dated: coming as they do from the foot of a page, they do not contain watermarks or large initials. It is tempting to suggest that they were printed in Fossombrone (where they survive), rather than in Venice. However, that would presume a new edition: while there is the example of the new edition of Ghiselin, printed around New Year 1515, it is significant that no copy of such a La Rue edition survives, while the first edition was widely preserved.

No. 12. *Canti C*

10.ii.1503/4 *RISM* 1504[3]

A1*r*]   Canti. C. N° cento | Cinquanta. | C

X8*r*]   Impreſ ſum Uenetijs per Octauianum Petrutiʒ Foroſempronien|ſem 1503 die 10 Februarij. Cum priuilegio inuictiſ ſimi Dominij | Uenetiarum q*uae* nullus poſ ſit cantum Figuratum imprimere | ſub pena in ipſo priuilegio contenta. | Regiſtruʒ ABCDEFGHJKLMNOPQRSTUX Omnes quaterni. | [Petrucci's device]

A2*r*]   [**Tavola**: in four columns, set in roman, with roman numerals, all with final points

Format and collation: Choirbook: landscape quarto-in-eights. 168 folios: A-X[8]

Signatures:] Aa II [$4 •-A1, Q3, Q4 • C2-C4, D2 signed with arabic numerals • Q5 and 6 signed] Qq III [and] Qq IIII • all J and U signed with the letters] Ji [and] Uv

Foliation: t.r.r.:] [1-2], 3–102, 101–102 [*recte* 103–104], 105–109, 1010–1022, 1025–1026 [*recte* 123–124], 1023–1024 [*recte* 125–126], 1027–1046, 147–150, 1051–1052, 153–167, [168] • For in-house corrections, see below

No running heads • Composers' names and references to second *partes* appear in the head-line

Part names: in the left margin, to be read vertically from the top:

recto:]   Contra Baſ ſus   [A3-6, A8-G1, G3,4, G6-J8, K3-L3, L5-M7, N1-Q7, R4

	Contra	[G2,5, L4, R8, S8, T3, T7-V4, V6-V8, X3,5
	Contra Contra	[K1,2
	Contra Contra Baſ ſus	[M8
	[All three, some in the stave:	Q8, R2,3
	Tenor Contra Baſ ſus	[R1,5, T4,5
	Tenor Contra	[R6,7, S1-7, X1,2
	Tenor	[T1,2, T6, V5, X4
	[Nil:	A1,2,7, R5, X6-8
verso:]	Tenor	[A2-7, B1-F8, G2,3, G5-L2, L4-O1, O3-Q6, R7, S7,8, T2, T6-V3, V5-7, X2, X4-6
	Tenor Baſ ſus	[G1,4, L3, R1
	Tenor Tenor	[O2
	[all three, some in the stave:	Q7,8, R2
	Tenor Contra Baſ ſus	[R4
	Contra	[T1,5, V4, X3
	[Nil:	A8, R3,5,6, R8-S6, T3,4, V8-X1, X7,8

The part-names seem to be erroneous on some of S8-T2

Fonts: Music: Petrucci's normal music type

Staves: six per page, 178 mm long, 10-92-112 high

Text: Other texts in Rotonda • Tavola in Roman

Textual comments: F8v and M7v: the text is spaced out as if the exemplar were texted • J1v: ascription is to:] Josqnin • K7v: Tenor text incipit is a line too high

Technical comments: Small capital letters used on A5v [F] • No capital letter on J7v [J], V6v [V, guide letter present] • This is one of the volumes where extra notation and a second custos are entered after the final custos of a page • The music for O8r was printed before O8v, from evidence in the copies at F-Pc and I-TVcap • The inner sheet of gathering Q was apparently imposed with the two formes reversed, as indicated by both signatures and page numbers: see the Commentary below

In-house corrections:

Stop-press corrections: B4r.folio number: 21 (F-Pc, I-TVcap) → 12 (A-Wn) • D2v.iv.21 and 37: both originally m and changed to sb: the change by stop-press correction in I-TVcap, and in manuscript in F-Pc • D5r.folio number: 26 (I-TVcap) → 29 (A-Wn) • D7r.folio number: 32 (I-TVcap) → 31 (A-Wn) • M2v.i.23: b → l: by stop-press in I-TVcap; by manuscript in F-Pc • T2r.folio number: 1056 (I-TVcap) → 1046 (A-Wn, F-Pc) • T3r.folio number: 1047 (F-Pc) → 147 (others) • T5r.folio number: 1049 (F-Pc) → 149 (others)

Corrections after press-work: C4r.iv.after 16: flat and mf → mf,mg, using original tails, and 2 sb stamped in over erased heads: F-Pc and I-TVcap • D3v.i.1: me' → mf', note head erased and new one stamped in with type: A-Wn and I-TVcap • F1r.iv-v.clefs: from F4, to F3, partly by erasure and partly with a sb stamped in: F-Pc; the new head is in manuscript: A-Wn and I-TVcap • G4v.iv.21-22: sb,sb stamped in over b,b: I-TVcap • L1v.iv.9-10: sbf,mf → sbf,mrest,mf,sbf, with a stamped in note-head, and ginger ink: A-Wn • L7r.v.10: b → l, by addition of tail in brown ink: A-Wn and I-TVcap • O4r.iv.19-22: bg,sbc,bg → sbg,sbd,sbg,sbf, by erasure of the bg and sbc, and new note-heads stamped in with type: A-Wn and I-TVcap • O4v.iv.20-22: dsbG, bc, bB → erased dot, and sb stamped in over each b, then touched up with brown ink: A-Wn • Q3r,4r: signatures added, in brown ink: A-Wn, F-Pc, and I-TVcap • Q4r.iv.20-22: originally dsbG, bc, bB; the dot erased and two sb stamped over the second and third notes, at the same pitches: I-TVcap • Q5r,6r: signatures struck through, in brown ink: A-Wn, F-Pc and I-TVcap • R3r.v.36–39: *smb,mc',smd',me'*: now all black notes, *sbb,mc',sbd',me'*, by erased tails, and black ink; stave-lines redrawn in ginger: I-TVcap • R8r.v.final three chords: upper notes all printed normally; first two lower notes stamped in, and then colored with brown ink; last lower note drawn in brown ink: A-Wn and I-TVcap: F-Pc, four chords were created, as follows: the original notes were all void — *bA,sbA,bG,lc*: the others — *bc,sbE,bB,bA* (sharing the *l* tail) — are all stamped in: all currently black notes were filled in with ink • R8r.vi.final three chords: lower three notes all printed, then colored with brown ink; first two upper notes stamped in, and final notes drawn in brown ink: A-Wn and I-TVcap. At F-Pn: from *sbA,bB,bB*. First two removed, and replaced by stamped in colored *sbA,bB*, with, above them stamped in *4sb* a,g,g,f. Then, in ginger ink, the following changes: low Aflat is filled in, upper notes have the rhythms changed to *dsb,m,m,m* and a final *lA* added, using part of the double-bar as a tail • T6v.ii.22–23: *dme*," *smd*" → *md*",*smc*", erased note-heads and dot; new note-heads stamped in, with ginger ink dot and touched-up stave lines • V5r.i.33–34: struck through, in brown ink: A-Wn and I-TVcap

Contents

20	D8*v*	QUi ueult ioner de la queue	[Anon.]
		[other vv:] iouer	
21	E2*v*	CHeſcun me crie	[Anon.]
22	E4*v*	MOn enfant	[Anon.]
23	E5*v*	FOrſeulement	Ghiſelin
24	E7*v*	SE congie pris	[Anon.]
25	E8*v*	JAy pris amours	[Anon.]
26	F1*v*	VNg franc archier	[Anon.]
27	F2*v*	HElas helas fault il	[Anon.]
28	F3*v*	GEntils galaus ananturiers	[Anon.]
		[other vv:] galans avanturiers	
29	F4*v*	MOn mari ma defamee	[Anon.]
30	F5*v*	LOſeraige dire ſe Jame per amoure	[Anon.]
31	F7*v*	POur quoy tant	[Anon.]
32	F8*v*	ALba celumba	Infantis
		[other vv:] columba	
33	G1*v*	ELogeron nous	[Anon.]
34	G2*v*	A Uous ie vieng	[Anon.]
35	G3*v*	FOrſeulement	[Anon.]
36	G4*v*	FOrtuna dun gran tempo	Japart
37	G5*v*	LOier mi fault vag carpentier	Japart
38	G6*v*	JAy pris amours	[Anon.]
39	G7*v*	LE ſecond Jour dauril	[Anon.]
40	G8*v*	LAutrier ie men aloye iouer	[Anon.]
41	H1*v*	ICh byn zo elende	[Anon.]
42	H2*v*	BErzeretta ſauoyena	[Anon.]
43	H3*v*	ALeure que ie vous pri.x.	Joſquin.
		[Headed:] Canon: Ad nonam canitur baſſus hic tempore lapso:	
		[B:]Reſolutio ex ſupremo.	
44	H4*v*	LE bon temps que ianoy	[Anon.]
45	H5*v*	SUr le pont dauignon	[Anon.]
		[Capital U inverted]	
46	H6*v*	DAmer ie me veul intremetre	.Jo.Fortuila.
47	H8*v*	LAutre iour men cheuauchoye	[Anon.]
48	J1*v*	JEſey bien dire	Joſqnin [*sic*]
49	J2*v*	MOn pere ma done mari	Compere
50	J4*v*	FOrtuna deſperata	.Jo.pinarol
51	J5*v*	LA fleur de biaulte	Jo.martini
52	J6*v*	ET marion la brune	[Anon.]
53	J7*v*	[J]E ne me peus tenir damer	[Anon.]
54	J8*v*	FAult il que beur ſoy	.Jo.martini
55	K2*v*	GEntil galans de gerra	Criſpin.de ſtappen
56	K3*v*	HElas le poure iohan	[Anon.]
		[CT,B:] . . . ioan	
57	K4*v*	PAr vng iour de matinee	Yzac.
58	K5*v*	EN lombre dung buſſinet	[Anon.]
		[Tav:] Eulombre . . . buſſiuet	

59	K6*v*	IL e∫t de bone heure ne		Jo.Japart
		[B:] Lo*m*me arme		
60	K7*v*	DE tous biens		Jo.Japart
		[above K8*r*:] Canon. Hic dantur antipodes.		
61	K8*v*	POur pa∫ ∫er temps		Jo.Japart
		[T:] Plu5 ne cha∫ccray ∫ans ga*n*s		
62	L1*v*	ELeue vous		[Anon.]
63	L3*v*	DE tous biens		Agricola
64	L4*v*	MOn ami mauoyt promis		[Anon.]
65	L6*v*	QUant vo∫tre ymage		[Anon.]
66	L7*v*	VIrtutu3 explu∫us terris		Cri∫pinus de ∫tappen
67	L8*v*	DE tous biens planye [*sic*]		[Anon.]
68	M1*v*	JAy pris amours		[Anon.]
69	M2*v*	LA tourturella Jaco.Obreht		
70	M3*v*	UNe fillere∫∫e		[Anon.]
		[T:] Uo∫tre amour		
		[CT:] Sil ya compagnon en la *com*pagnie		
71	M4*v*	AMours ne ∫t pas		[Anon.]
72	M5*v*	JE nay deul		Okenghem
73	M6*v*	JE ne ∫uis mort ne nief		[Anon.]
74	M7*v*	VRay dieu damours	à5	Jo.Japart
		[CT1:] *Sa*nate iouanes bapti∫ta		
		[CT2:] Ora *pro* nob*is*		
75	M8*v*	QUis det vt veniat		Agricola
76	N1*v*	PRe∫tes le moy		Jo. Japart
77	N3*v*	ROyne de ciel		Compere
	N4*v*	2/ [no incipit]		
78	N5*v*	NEnccioza		Jo.martini
79	N6*v*	DE v*os*t*re* deul		[Anon.]
	N7*v*	2/		[no incipit]
80	N8*v*	QUe vous madame		Agricola
		[B:] Je [*sic*] pace In idip∫um		
81	O1*v*	COrps digne		Bu∫noys
		[T, CT, B:] Dieu quel mariage		
82	O2*v*	JE ∫uy dalemaygne	à5	[Anon.]
		[T1:] Jolietteme*n*t me*n* vay		
83	O3*v*	COmme feme de∫confortee		[Anon.]
84	O5*v*	VIlana che ∫a tu far		[Anon.]
85	O6*v*	DE tous biens		[Anon.]
86	O7*v*	JAy pris mo*n* bourdon		Sthokem
87	O8*v*	ENtre vous galans		[Anon.]
		[CT:] Je mi leuay hier au matin		
88	P1*v*	EN de∫pit de la be∫ogna		[Anon.]
		[T:] Aduegna q*ue* aduenir poudra		
89	P2*v*	TRes doulx regart		[Anon.]
90	P3*v*	QUe∫ta ∫e chiama		Jo.Japart
91	P4*v*	SEruiteur ∫oye		Jo.Sthokem

92	P5ᵥ	MAyntes femmes	à4 ex 3	Buſnoys
		[S:] Canon: Odam ſi protham teneas in remiſ ſo diapaſon		
		cum paribus ter augeas		
93	P6ᵥ	SIl vous playſiſt		Jo.Regis
94	P7ᵥ	JE ſui dalemagne		Jo.Sthokem
95	P8ᵥ	LE deſproueu infortune		[Anon.]
96	Q1ᵥ	ROſa playſant		Philipon.
97	Q2ᵥ	CEnt mille eſcuts		[Caron]
98	Q3ᵥ	TArt ara mon cor		Molinet
99	Q4ᵥ	PEtite camuſete		Okenghem
100	Q5ᵥ	AYmy aymy		[Anon.]
101	Q6ᵥ	FOrtuna deſperata		[Anon.]
102	Q7ᵥ	JAy bien nouri		[Anon.]
103	Q8r	VIure ou mourir		[Anon.]
104	Q8ᵥ	CElux qui font la gorre		[Anon.]
		[T:] Il ſon byen pelles		
105	R1r	JE ne ſuis pas a ma playſache		[Anon.]
106	R1ᵥ	VNa muſque de buſcgaya	à4 ex 3	Joſquin
		[Headed:] Quieſcit qui ſupreme volat | Uenit poſt mequi in puncto clamat		
107	R2r	E Uray dieu que payne		Compere
108	R2ᵥ	EN vroelic		[Anon.]
109	R3r	LInken van beueren		[Anon.]
110	R3ᵥ	VIue le roy		Joſquin
111	R4ᵥ	EN lombre dung biſ ſonet	à4 ex 2	Joſquin
112	R5r	AUant a moy	à4 ex 2	[Anon.]
		[Headed:] Fuga in diateſ ſeron ſuperius		
113	R5ᵥ	ALma redemptoris mater	à3	[Anon.]
	R6ᵥ	2/ Uirgo prius		
		[B:] Aue regina celorum		
114	R7ᵥ	LE ſeruiteur	à3	[Anon.]
115	R8ᵥ	TArtara	à3	Yzac.
116	S2ᵥ	JOli amonrs [sic]	à3	Jo.Ghiſelin
117	S4ᵥ	JOli amours	à3	:Cor:De:Uuilde:
118	S6ᵥ	DE tous biens playne	à3	[Anon.]
119	S7ᵥ	DE tous biens	à3	[Anon.]
120	S8ᵥ	TAndet naken	à3	Agricola
		[T:] Tander naken		
121	T2ᵥ	COomme feme	à3	Agricola
		[T,CT:] Comme feme		
122	T3ᵥ	LA ſpagna	à3	[Anon.]
123	T5ᵥ	SI aſcendero in celum	à3	Nico.Craen
124	T6ᵥ	FAuus diſtilans	à3	Jo.Ghiſelin
125	T7ᵥ	LA hault dalemaigne	à3	Mathurin
126	T8ᵥ	TAnder naken	à3	Licide
127	V3ᵥ	VUeit ghy	à3	[Anon.]
128	V4ᵥ	SE mieulx ne vient damours	à3	Agricola

129	V5v	LA bernardina	à3	Jo∫quin.
130	V6v	[U]Na mai∫tre∫∫e	à3	Brumel
131	V7v	VO∫tre a iamays	à3	Ghi∫elin
		[CT:] Je nay dueul		
132	V8v	SE iay requis	à3	Ghi∫elin.
133	X1v	BElle ∫ur toute5	à3	Agricola
		[CT:] Tota pulcra es		
134	X2v	HElas hic moet my liden	à3	Ghi∫elin.
135	X3v	VOus dont fourtune	à3	[Anon.]
136	X4v	TOus les regrets	à3	[Anon.]
137	X5v	LE ∫eruiteur	à2	
		[T:] Le ∫eruiteur		Ja.Tadinghen
138	X6v	LE ∫eruiteur	à2	
		[T:] Le ∫eruiteur		.Hanart
139	X7v	PRennes ∫ur moy	à3 ex 1	Okenghem
	X8r	[Colophon; Register; Device]		
	X8v	[blank]		

Extant copies:

A-Wn, 47.355. Complete

> **Size of page:** 159 × 230 mm.
> **Watermarks:**

A1-2	A3-4	B1	B3	B6-5	B8-7	C1-2	C4-3	D1-2	D5-6	E5-6	E7-8
12	12	7	7	6	6	11	11	11	11	11	11

F1-2	F6-5	G2-1	G4-3	H5-6	H8-7	J2	J4	K2	K5	L6	L8
6	6	6	6	6	6	9	9	9	9	9	9

M6	M7	N1	N4	O2	O4	P2	P5	Q2	Q4	R2-1	R3-4
9	9	9	9	9	9	9	9	13	13	6	6

R6	R7	S4-3	S7-8	T8-7	T3-4	V3-4	V7-8	X5-6	X7-8
7	7	11	11	11	12	12	12	12	12

> **Technical comments:** E2v.i: text spacing sort • K6v.vi.start: a music spacing sort, measuring
> 6.0 x 8.7 mm
> **Corrections and changes:**
>> **In-house:** B4r, D3v, D7r, F1r, L1v, O4v, Q3r,4r, Q5r,6r, R8v.v, R8r, V5r: see above
>> **Later:** G4v.iii.last: $m \rightarrow sb$, by erasure of the tail • H4r.iv.clef: descenders poorly impressed
>> and redrawn in ink • H8r.v.last note: lower part of note and stave line failed to take
>> ink, and were touched up with brown ink • R3r.iv.47: sb, b → a, in black ink, perhaps
>> stamped • R8r.iv.custos: changed in brown ink
> **Binding:** Late 17th-century, with the Imperial arms on the spine • At present there is a bifolium
> of grey paper at each end, one leaf used as a paste-down, and a white paper folio between
> it and the book
> **Provenance:** From the Fugger collection. A piece of leather from an earlier binding, with the
> Fugger crest, is mounted inside the front board
> **Bibliography:** Ambros, *Geschichte*, p. 196

F-Pc, Rés.540. Complete

> **Page size:** 160 × 221 mm.

Watermarks:

A1-2	A5-6	B3	B6-5	B8-7	C1-2	C3-4	D2-1	D3-4	E6-5	E7-8
11	12	7	6	6	11	11	11	11	11	11

F3-4	F7-8	G6-5	G7-8	H2-1	H4-3	J6	J7	K6	K8	L2	L5
6	6	11	6	6	6	9	9	9	9	9	9

M1	M5	N6	N8	O3	O8	P1	P6	Q2	Q4	R1-2	R6-5
9	9	9	9	9	9	9	9	13	13	6	6

S1-2	S5-6	T3-4	T7-8	V5-6	V7-8	X1-2	X3-4
11	11	12	12	12	12	12	12

Textual comments: A8r: folio number is lacking

Technical comments: Evidence of the order of impressions: E6v music before E6r; K4v text, stave and composer name in one impression; part name, capital and music in the other; O8r music before O8v • The initial letter "T" on Q3v shows damage on later pages (R8v, S8v, T8v, X4v). It is worst on A6v — no doubt set last to include the Tavola • E2v.i.incipit: a text spacing sort, 3.9 × 0.5 mm; sorts of the same size are to be seen on J2r.iv, L8r.iv, M7r.i, and N6v.iv • Q8r.v.5 and rest: apparently printed well, but covered with a piece of rag paper, perhaps while drying

Corrections and changes:

> **In-house:** C4r, D2v.iv.21 and 37, F1r, L1v, Q3r,4r, Q5r,6r, R8r.v, R8r.vi, T6v, V5r: see above

> **Later:** D2v.iv.before 18: added *m* rest, ginger ink • D2v.iv.24: *sb* → *m*, ginger ink tail • D2v.iv.before 34: added *m* rest, ginger ink • D2v.iv.40: *sb* → *m*, ginger ink tail • D3r.i.rests after 11: were *sb,b,b,sb*: second *b* erased • D3r.iv.rests after 1: were *l,l,l,l*: last *l* changed to a *b* by erasure • G4v.iii.last: *m* → *sb*, by erased tail • H1v.v.penultimate: was black, centre erased • M2v.i.23: ?*b* → *l*, with black ink • S8r.iii.after 42: rests were *sb,m*: *l* added, in ginger ink

Binding: With the library's copies of the third edition of *Odhecaton A* (No.14, *q.v.*) and the second edition of *Canti B* (No.10)

Provenance: Has the Conservatoire stamp, acquisition number of 21775, on A1r and X8v • Seville and Colón: see *Odhecaton A* (third edition, No.14) • Cited in Colón's catalogues (see Chapman, "Printed", No.7)

I-TVcap, Stampa Mus.n.6. Complete

Size of page: 169 × 235 mm.

Watermarks:

A-2	A-6	B2	B3	B6-5	B7-8	C1-2	C3-4	D3-4	D8-7	E1-2	E3-4	F1-2	F4
11	12	7	7	6	6	11	11	11	11	11	11	6	7

F5-6	F8	G2	G3	G6-5	G7-8	H1	H4	H5-6	H8-7	J4	J7	K2	K6
6	7	7	7	6	6	7	7	6	6	9	9	9	9

L2	L5	M2	M5	N7	O5	O8	P3	P8	Q4	Q7	R2-1	R4-3	R5
9	9	9	9	9	9	9	9	9	13	13	6	6	7

R7	S6-5	S7-8	T5-6	T7-8	V2-1	V6-5	X6-5	X7-8
7	11	11	12	11	11	11	11	11

Technical comments: The same evidence of order of impressions found on O8v in the copy at F-Pc • E2v.i: a text spacing sort • K2r: a text spacing sort at the level of the direction line

Corrections and changes:

> **In-house:** C4r, D3v, G4v, L7r, O4v, Q3r,4r,5r,6r, V5r: see above

> **Later:** F1r.iv and v. clef: C₄ → C₃, in black ink • G4v.iii.last note: *m* → *sb*, by erasure •

H8r.v: part of the last note and the stave line touched up in brown ink • J8r.vi.clef and signature: C_4 and flat at c → F_4 and flat at B, in brown ink • R3r.v.34: erased *ma* • R3r.v.35–38: *sm,m,sm,m,* → *sb,m,sb,m,* all colored, by erasure • S8r.iii.after 42: rests were *sb, m: l* drawn in ginger ink

Binding: 16th-century, corresponding to that of the library's copy of *Odhecaton A* (No.14, *q.v.*) • One paste-down at each end of the book

Provenance: Given to the Biblioteca Capitolare in 1700 by Canon Agapito Burchelliati (Sartori, *Petrucci*, p. 69)

Bibliography: d'Alessi, "Cappella", p. 187 • Cosenza, *Biographical*, p. 482 still repeats the report of Fumagalli, *Lexicon*, that this copy is of an otherwise lost 1500 edition

---

Lost copies: Sartori, *Petrucci*, p. 69, states that a copy of Vogel, *Bibliothek* with author's annotations reported a copy of this edition in a library at Bordeaux. This was quite plausibly the copy now in F-Pc: the Paris copy of the 1504 edition of *Odhecaton A* (originally owned by Colón) was reportedly bought from a dealer in Bordeaux. No other corrresponding copy has surfaced

Early references: Bolduanus, Draudius and Gesner: see chapter 20

Bibliography:

(a) Rosaria Boccadifuoco, *Bibliografia*, No.546 • Sartori, *Petrucci*, No.12; BrownI 1504_1; Jeppesen; Nuovo Vogel 1503^2

(b) Brunet, *Manuel*, i, col.1550

(c) Petrucci, *Canti C* • The colophon is reproduced in Castellani, "Arte", ii, p. 97

(e) Cauchie, "Odhecaton" • Dalmazzo, *Libro*, p. 185 • Fétis, "Specimen", p. 3 • Sartori, "Nuove", p. 178

Commentary:

1. Fétis, "Specimen", p. 3, asserts that this was the first book printed by Petrucci. He was followed in this by Dalmazzo, *Libro*, p. 185

2. This may be another case of a book created in layers: the watermark patterns tend to coincide with layers of content. See, for example, the change at the end of H, and perhaps one around gathering C. This may reflect the use of two teams of craftsmen in Petrucci's shop, since it would be relatively easy to divide up a repertoire of this sort.

3. The crowding in gathering R, so that some pieces need the music of lower voices to start in the middle of a line, is not characteristic of the Odhecaton series, which have tended to be generous of space. This again suggests that some of the work had been divided up in advance, and gathering S had been assigned to a different compositor, working simultaneously.

4. For gathering Q, it appears that both the signatures and the foliation were "wrong", although only the signatures were corrected. Both formes seem to have been rotated when being setup, i.e., the pages were inserted in the wrong sequence: instead of

5r	4v
6v	3r

and

4r	5v
3v	6r

they were set as

3r	6v
4v	5r

and

6r	3v
5v	4r

This is a simple enough error: but it seems to imply that the page numbers and signatures were left in the forme, and updated at the end of the process. If they had been set as part of the text page, then they would have corresponded to the correct texts, and it would have been hard to get the result that survives.

5.   Once again the pieces scored for three voices are collected separately, clearly reflecting a view of the distinction to be made betwee three- and four-voiced compositions. The same does not appear to hold true for those à5, although there are generally too few to be sure.

6.   It is tempting to assert that Petrucci employed new and relatively inexperienced typesetters, beginning with this volume. Coupled with other features remarked here, there is a large number of in-house corrections, spread fairly evenly across the volume.

7.   In fact, the list of in-house changes made after press work, given above, has been made comprehensive rather than restrictive. However, all these changes were almost certainly made in-house: it is also probable that many similar changes in other editions, which I have listed as "Later", were also made before the copies left the house.

8.   The practice of entering additional notation and a second custos, at the page turn, is common in this book. They can be found on A7*v*-8*r*, B1*v*-2*r*, B4*v*-5*r*, C7*v*-8*r*, D1*v*-2*r*, D8*v*-E1*r*, E2*v*-3*r*, E5*v*-6*r*, F5*v*-6*r*, J2*v*-3*r*, L1*v*-2*r*, O3*v*-4*r*, R8*v*-S1*r*, S2*v*-3*r*, S4*v*-5*r*, S8*v*-T1*r*, T3*v*-4*r*, T8*v*-V1*r*, and V1*v*-V2*r*. This represents all the occasions where (a) the music continues onto the next opening, and (b) there is no bar-line, *corona*, or *signum congruentiae*. The additional notation and custos are lacking on some openings that do have one of these features: C2*v*-3*r* (with a *corona*), D4*v*-5*r* (with a *signum*), L4*v*-5*r* (with a *signum*), and N1*v*-2*r* (with a *signum*).

No. 13. Agricola: *Misse*

23.iii.1504   *RISM* A431

There is a cancel for a half-sheet in gathering H

Edition

A1*r*]   Mi∫ ∫e Alexandri agricole | Le ∫eruiteur | Je ne demande | Mal heur me bat | Primi toni | Secundi toni | S

D1*r*]   T

F1*r*]   A

H1*r*]   B

J8*r*]   Impre∫ ∫um Uenetij5 per Octauianu3 Petrutiu3 Foro∫empronien | ∫em 1504 die 23 Martij. Cu3 priuilegio inuicti∫ ∫imi Dominij | Uenetiarum q*uae* nullus po∫ ∫it cantum Figuratum imprimere | ∫ub pena in ip ∫o priuilegio contenta. | Regi∫tru3 ABDFHJ q*ua*terni C duern*us* E tern*us* G quintern*us* | [Petrucci's device]

Format and collation: Partbooks: landscape quarto-in-eights. [C] 20 folios: AB⁸C⁴; [T] 14 folios: D⁸E⁶; [A] 18 folios F⁸G¹⁰; [B] 16 folios: HJ⁸

Signatures:] AAA II [$4 • − A1, C3, C4, E3 • + G5 • G5 signed] GGG IIII

No printed foliation or pagination

Headlines are not retained in the forme

Fonts: Music: Petrucci's normal music type

Staves: Five line: 175 or 180 mm long: 10-91.5-112 mm high

Text: Rotonda throughout

Textual comments: E2r.head-line:] Prmi toni [in the copies at A-GÜ, I-Ac, I-Bc and PL-Kj •
H7r.headline: the letter e in "ne" is inverted

Technical comments: This edition uses demi-semi fusas, on F2r

In-house corrections:

Stop-press correction: G8r.headline: Secundi (I-Ac) → Secundi: I-Bc, I-Rsc and PL-Kj •
H4r.i.text:] Beuedictus (GB-Lbl, I-Bc and PL-Kj) → Benedictus (B-Br)

Corrections made after press work: A3v.i.40–41: c.o.p. ligature, b,c' → b,d', in brown ink:
A-Wn, B-Br, I-Ac, I-Bc and I-Rvat; in black ink: I-Rsc and PL-Kj • A4r.ii.34–35: originally
probably a sbb, now sba, dsbb, in ginger ink: B-Br, I-Ac, I-Bc, I-Rvat and PL-Kj: at I-Rsc,
the two notes are in black ink, and the dot in brown • A5v.iv.6; bc' → bd', stamped-in: A-
Wn, I-Ac, I-Bc, I-Rsc, I-Rvat and PL-Kj: in brown ink at B-Br • A6r.ii.38–39; mb
erased → sbc',ma stamped in, with a m tail added to the c' in brown ink: A-Wn, I-Bc I-Rsc
and I-Rvat: at I-Ac, B-Br and PL-Kj, the changes are made in manuscript • E3r.v.after 20:
sbrest erased: A-GÜ, A-Wn, I-Ac, I-Bc, I-Rvat and PL-Kj: also at I-Rsc, where a brown
ink sb b has been entered • E3v.ii.23: sbg partly erased, sbf stamped in:all copies • F3r.v.26–
27: from ?sbg, sbf → sba, sbf, in brown ink: I-Bc; the original notes struck through in brown
ink: A-Wn, I-Ac and PL-Kj; the original notes erased: B-Br and I-Rvat; at I-Rsc, sbg,sbf
are printed, and rung round and struck through in brown ink • F3r.vi.18: sb → m, brown
ink tail: B-Br, I-Ac, I-Bc, I-Rsc, I-Rvat and PL-Kj • F3r.vi.25: sb → b, stamped-in change:
B-Br and I-Rsc • F4v.v.30: colored dm → sb, by erasure: at A-Wn, B-Br, I-Ac, I-Bc, I-Rsc,
I-Rvat and PL-Kj • F4v.v.33: f → sm by erasure: A-Wn, B-Br, I-Ac, I-Bc, I-Rsc, I-Rvat
and PL-Kj • F5v.v.30–31, c.o.p. ligature: from f,b to f,d by erasure and black ink: I-Ac, I-
Bc and PL-Kj; similarly in B-Br, I-Rsc and I-Rvat, though the ink is brown • F6r.vi.m.s:
brown ink "2" added: B-Br, I-Ac, I-Bc, I-Rsc, I-Rvat and PL-Kj • G4r.iii.after38: rest m
to sm with brown ink: I-Bc and I-Rvat; unchanged at B-Br • G5v.vi.14–15: originally one
note, sbc: now two notes, a stamped-in sbd with a black-ink m tail, and a stamped-in sbB:
B-Br, I-Ac, I-Bc, I-Rsc, I-Rvat and PL-Kj • G8r.iv.10: sb → m, with a black ink tail in the
copy at I-Rvat, and as a stop-press change in the copy at I-Bc • J2r.vi.right end:] Bñdict₉ |
tacet [: I-Bc and I-Fm;] Bñdictus | tacet [: B-Br, GB-Lbl, I-Ac, I-Rvat and PL-Kj;] Bñdictu[
tacet [: I-Rsc

Contents:

	B5*r*	D8*v*	G4*r*.iii	J2*v*	[Agnus]
4	B5*v*.v	E1*r*	G5*r*	J3*r*.ii	[Missa] Primi toni
	B6*r*	E1*r*.iii	G5*r*.iv	J3*r*.iv	[Gloria]
	B6*v*	E1*v*.iv	G5*v*.iv	J3*v*.ii	[Credo]
	B7*v*	E2*v*.iii	G6*v*.v	J4*v*	[Sanctus]
	B7*v*.vi	E2*v*.vi	G7*r*.vi	J4*v*.vi	[Agnus]
5	B8*r*	E3*r*	G7*v*	J5*r*	[Missa] Secundi toni
	B8*v*.iii	E3*v*	G8*r*.ii	J5*v*.i	[Gloria]
	C2*r*	E4*v*	G9*r*	J6*v*	[Credo]
	C3*r*	E5*r*.iii	G10*r*	J7*r*.iii	[Sanctus]
	C3*v*.iv	E5*v*.iv	G10*v*.v	J7*v*.v	[Agnus]
				J8*r*	[Colophon: Register: Device]
	C4*r*	E6*r*			[blank staves]
	C4*v*	E6*v*		J8*v*	[blank]

Extant copies: The copy cited by Sartori as at D-B is now at PL-Kj

A-GÜ, s.s. Tenor, lacking E6

> **Size of page:** 165 × 235 mm.
>
> **Watermarks:** No.11 on D2-, D5-6, E-4 and E-5
>
> **Textual comments:** E2*r*, the headline reads] Prmi toni
>
> **Technical comments:** D3*r*: the signature is almost entirely uninked
>
> **Corrections and changes:**
>> **In-house:** E3*r*, E3*v*: see above
>>
>> **Later:** D6*r*.v.7: brown *sm* tail added to the pitch d
>
> **Binding and Provenance:** With Josquin's *Missarum II* (1515, No.59)
>
> **Bibliography:** Federhofer, "Petrucci"

A-Wn, S.A.77.C.16. Lacks the Bassus, present in a 19th-century copy

> **Size of page:** 163 × 229 mm.
>
> **Watermarks** No.11 on A3-4, A7-8, B2-1, B5-6, C3-4, D2-1, D3-4, E1-2, E3-, F2-1, F4-3, G2-1, G4-3, and G-6
>
> **Technical comments:** Size of staves: 175–180 mm long: 10-92-113 mm high
>
> **Corrections and changes:**
>> **In-house:** A3*v*, A5*v*, A6*r*, E3*r*, E3*v*, F3*r*, F4*v* and F4*v*: see above
>>
>> **Later:** All movements numbered in manuscript, in brown ink: 165–188
>
> **Binding:** of the Austrian National Library
>
> **Provenance:** Given the manuscript numbering, presumably originally with Josquin: *Misse* (1502, No.4)

B-Br, Fétis 1640 A. Three part-books, lacking the Tenor. H2 and H7 are a cancel, for which see below

> **Size of page:** 160 × 237 mm.
>
> **Watermarks:** No.11 on A2-1, A6-5, B2-1, B-4, C3-4, F5-6, F8-7, G3-4, G6- and G9-10 • No.12 on H1-, H3-4, J1-2 and J3-4
>
> **Textual comments:** F2*v*.i.text: mu*n*di has an inverted letter "m" • F4*v*.i.text: Benadictus
>
> **Corrections and changes:**
>> **In-house:** A3*v*, A4*r*, A5*v*, A6*r*, F3*r*, F4*v*, F5*v*, F6*r*, G4*r*, G5*v*, H4*r*, H8*r*, and J2*r*: see above
>>
>> **Later:** Manuscript foliation, t.r.r., in pale brown: 111-130; 113-130; 101-116 • A2*r*.i–ii: much touching up of poor impressions • B1*v*.ii: several poorly impressed colored notes

have been filled in, with black ink • F4*r*.iii.48: *sb*, f → a, erased and entered in grey ink • F5*v*.ii.5–6: *sb,sb* → *m,m*, with brown ink tails • H8*v*.iii.last note: A, *b* → *l*, with a tail in brown ink

Binding: Modern half-leather over boards • One paste-down and two fly-leaves at each end

Provenance: Perhaps the copy from Gaspari's collection (Potier, "Gaspari") • Later owned by Fétis • Possibly connected with the library's copy of Obrecht's masses (1503, No.6), on the basis of manuscript foliation

Bibliography: Fétis, *Biographie*, vii, p. 14 • Potier, "Gaspari", p. 24

GB-CW. Altus, complete

Watermarks No.11 on F3-4, F8-7, G3-4, G-6 and G10-9

Technical comments: This copy appears to be in the identical state to that of the copy at I-Ac, using the same leger-line patterns and even the same strengths of ink • G2*r* and G4*r* at the foot have used leading within the area of the last stave line, for the impression of the music

Binding and Provenance: With Josquin, *I Missarum* masses (1516, No.62)

GB-Lbl, K.1.d.3. Bassus, complete. For the cancel, H2,7, see below

Size of page: 156 × 217 mm.

Watermarks: No.12 on H1-, H3-4, J5-6 and J7-8 • Both examples of the *a* mould of paper 12 have filled in rays, presumably from felt or something in the mould. This can also be seen in other uses of this paper

Corrections:

In-house: J2*r*. see above

Later: H8*v*.iii.last 2, joined together by a line to make a ligature, in pencil or charcoal • J1*r*.v.7: *sb* ra *m*, with a brown ink-tail

Binding: Modern British Museum binding of white parchment, with gold rolls and stamps, dated 1897 • There are marbled end-papers at each end, pasted to flyleaves

Provenance: Acquired by the British Museum, and dated 17 No [18]96, on J8*v*

Bibliography: Johnson and Scholderer, *Short-Title*, p. 10

I-Ac (sf). Stampati N. 189 (1). Complete set of four part-books. For H2 and H7, see the description of the cancel, below

Size of page: 232 × 168 mm.

Watermarks: No.11 on A-43, A7-8, B1-2, C3-4, D6-5, D7-8, E1-2, E-4, F6-5, F7-8, G2-1, G3-4 and G-5 • No.12 on H1-, H5-6, J1-2 and J3-4

Textual comments: G8*r*, the headline reads] Secnndi toni

Technical comments: The evidence of leading found on ff.G2*r* and G4*r* of the copy at GB-CW is also clearly visible here

In-house Corrections: A3*v*, A4*r*, A5*v*, A6*r*, E3*r*, E3*v*, F3*r*, F4*v*, F4*v*.v.33, F5*v*, J2*r*. see above

Technical comment: Stave lengths, 175 or 180 mm. • Both staves and text have impressed poorly on parts of D5*r*, E1*v* and G7*r*

Binding: This is the first of six books bound together, all editions printed by Petrucci: (1) This book; (2) Ghiselin: *Misse* (1503, No.9); (3) La Rue: *Misse* (1503, No.11); (4) Josquin: *I Missarum* (1516, No.62); (5) Josquin: *II Missarum* (1515, No.59); (6) Josquin: *III Missarum* (1514, No.54) • Original leather boards, with a small repeating floral design, incorporating the part letter, all stamped, and with a special stamp in the centre of each board • Four holes for tie-strings on each board. The front board of the Cantus part is now detached • A paste-down at each end of each book

Provenance: The book belongs to the Convento of San Francesco, Assisi, and is in the care of the Biblioteca Comunale. There is now the stamp of the Biblioteca Comunale on all first rectos

Bibliography: Petrucci, *Missarum* (facsimile)

I-Bc, Q60. Complete set of four part-books. The cancel bifolium H2,7 is discussed below

Size of page 162 × 238 mm.

Watermarks: No.11 on A3-4, A7-8, B1-2, B4-3, C1-2, D3-4, D7-8, E1-2, E-3, F2-1, F4-3, G2-1, G3-4 and G-5 • No.12 on H3-4, H8-, J3-4, and J7-8

Technical comments: The evidence of minimas used as furniture can be seen on D1r • G2r and G4r, show leading within the area of the last stave-line, for the impression of the music

Corrections:

> **In-house:** A3v, A4r, A5v, A6r, E3r, E3v, F3r, F3r, F4v, F4v, F5v, F6r, G4r, G5v, J2r. see above

> **Later:** Manuscript foliation in all part books, beginning on the second recto: [C] 1–19; [T] 1–13; [A] 1–17; [B] 1–15 • D6r.v.7: pale brown *sm* tail added to the pitch d

Binding: Now in modern card covers in a card folder • All the books have gold fore-edges • This book was apparently the first in a long series, all now at I-Bc, which were originally bound together. This is indicated by the sequences of manuscript folio numbers, as well as the painted edges of the pages:

	S	T	A	B	
Agricola: *Misse*	[0] 1–19	[0] 1–13	[0] 1–17	[0] 1–15	gold
de Orto: *Misse* (1505, No.20)	20–37	14–29	18–35	16–33	gold
Gaspar: *Misse* (1507, No.32)	38–55	30–39	36–53	34–49	gold
Isaac: *Misse* (1506, No.31)	56–73	40–49	54–69	50–63	gold
Brumel: *Misse* (1503, No.8)	74–93	50–58	70–89	64–79	gold
Obrecht: *Misse* (1503, No.6)	94–113	60–73		80–99	gold
I Missarum diversorum (1508, No.43)	114–129	74–83	112–127	100–113	gold
Fragmenta missarum (1505, No.24)	130–147	84–98	128–147	114–131	gold

The Tenor series is lacking the last folio of the volume of Brumel: the Altus part for the Obrecht book does exist at I-Bc, but has a different series of manuscript numbers, and different coloured edges.

Of other copies at Bologna, the Superius, Altus, and Bassus of the first two books of Josquin's masses look, in their numbering, to belong to the same series, assuming that a single sheet divider was inserted before them: however, they have different coloured edges, brown for the Superius and Bassus, and green for the Altus:

Josquin: *Misse* (1502, No.4)	149–172	149–168	133–150	
Josquin: *Missarum II* (1505, No.22)	173–188	169–180	151–166	

It is more likely that these two books belonged with others, also painted in brown (Superius and Bassus) and green (Tenor and Altus), and even possibly with the copy of Gaspar's masses now at PL-Kj (red on Superius and Bassus, green on Altus):

La Rue: *Misse* (1503, No.11)	37–52	27–36	[40s–50s]	[30s–40s]
Obrecht: *Misse* (1503, No.6)			51–72	
Ghiselin: *Misse* (1503, No.9)	93–110	93–112		83–100
Gaspar: *Misse* (1507, No.32)	131–148		131–148	117–132

Provenance: This copy is cited in Martini's letters to Chiti of 7.v.1746 and 22.vii.1746 (See Schnoebelen, *Padre*, Nos.1245 and 1250, pp. 144–45) • Old call numbers appear as follows: 34: in Tenor, Altus, and Bassus. This number was certainly originally 1034, for there are traces of old guard strips next to the surviving number; 767: in all books; 1034: in the

Superius • This is almost certainly the set of volumes bound together, described in a letter sent to Martini by Domenico Maria Cavallini, and dated from Venice on 8.iii.1738. Schnoebelen, *Padre*, No.1110, p. 125, quotes the relevant section: " . . . quattro Libri di Messe di Autori francesi stampati del 400 li Autori sono Alessandro Agricola, de Orto, Enrico Izac, Brumel, Obret, etc. Sono di une bellissima stampa, e molto ben conservati." Schnoebelen's abstract of the letter suggests that these volumes came from Split, now in Croatia

I-Fm, R.U.1151 (*olim* 4.A.VI.118[1]). Bassus, lacking folios J1 and 8. H2,7 is a cancel, for which see below

Size of pages: 164 × 232mm. • If watermark 12 was circular, then just over 10 mm were trimmed from the join between H3 and H4, and rather less from that between J3 and J4. That gives a minimum height to the sheet of *ca.*339 mm.

Watermarks: No.11 on J7- • No.12 on H3-4, H8-, and J3-4

Technical comments: The width of some type sorts is indicated by the width of the inking on the lower edge of some occurrences: for example:- *sb*, H4*v*.iii: 2.4 mm; *sb* rest, H4*v*.iii: 1.4 mm • The height of the stave block may be 12 mm, from the ink left by it on H3*v*.vi • Blank staves appear on H3*v*.vi; H4*v*.iv–vi; H5*r*.v–vi; H6*v*.vi; J6*r*.vi; J7*v*.vi • Two rows of notes (perhaps *sm* sorts) used as furniture on either side of the initial letter have left an impression on H1*r*. The right colums seems to have 22 sorts, and the left is of about the same length • There may be some evidence as to which forme was printed first: e.g., furniture has printed ink on some folios only at the point of the impress of material from the other side of the folio. Thus J2*r* was printed before J2*v*

Corrections:

> **In-house:** J2*r*. see above

> **Later:** J6*r*.i.40: flat sign above *dsb*b • 19th-century title of] Canto figurato da Messa • Modern foliation continues through the whole volume: for Agricola it comprises 1–14, with 15 on the following fly-leaf

Binding: Bound as the first of four books: (1.) This book; (2.) Josquin: *II Missarum* (1505, No.22); (3.) Josquin: *Misse* (1502, No.4); (4.) Ghiselin: *Misse* (1503, No.9)

> Early leather panels, front and back, now mounted on modern boards: decorated with a simple daisy-pattern stamp and rolled rules, all in blind • Paste-downs are from a printed book, probably an incunable, using a roman type measuring "x" = 2.7 and "20" = 125. The back paste-down includes a chapter heading:] Cap.si. In quos praecipe sit humanitas | exercenda. & in quibus liberalitatibus ima|ginariis pereant opera & quae impensa praestantis • There is one fly-leaf between this and the contents • Three holes for a stab-binding are evident in gathering H and much of J

Provenance: On H2*v*, the stamp of] DSA • On H1*r* the old call number of] C[3].I.114 [with the date] 11.6.[19]13 [probably that of acquisition by the Marucelliana, whose stamp is on the same page

Bibliography: Damerini, "Esposizione", 26 (exhibition at Florence in 1949); Fanelli, *Musica*

I-Rsc, G.CS.3.B.30. Complete, except for last folio of Bassus

Size of page: 169 × 234 mm.

Watermarks: Mark 11 except in gatherings H and J, which have mark 12.

In-house Corrections: A3*v*, A4*r*, A5*v*, A6*r*, E3*r*, E3*v*, F3*r*, F3*r*, F3*r*, F4*v*, F4*v*, F5*v*, F6*r*, G4*r*, G5*v*, G8*r*, J2*r*. see above

Binding: Dark leather, with decorative rolls, as a border and making a diamond shape within each. Also stamps of a vase in each corner • One paste-down and one flyleaf at each end.

I-Rvat, Sist.235–238. Complete. Folios H2 and H7 are cancel leaves

Watermarks: No.11 on A2-1, A5-6, B1-2, B5-6, C2-1, D6-5, D7-8, E4-, E6-5, F4-3, F8-7, G1-2, G-43 and G-1 • No.12 on H1-, H3-4, J3-4, and J7-8

Textual comments: F4*v*.i. the text includes:] Benadictus

Corrections and changes:

> **In-house:** A3*v*, A4*r*, A5*v*, A6*r*, E3*r*, E3*v*, F3*r*, F3*r*, F4*v*, F4*v*, F5*v*, F6*r*, G4*r*, G5*v*, G8*r*, J2*r*. see above
>
> **Later:** D2*v*: stave lines touched up in ginger ink • D6*r*.v.7: pale brown *sm* tail added to the pitch d • F3*r*.vi.25: *b* to *sb* with black ink, and no erasure • G8*r*.iv.10: from *sba* to *m* with a black ink tail • Manuscript foliation [S] 68–87; [T] 44–57; [A] 70–87, [B] 65–80

Binding and Provenance: with Josquin, *I Missarum* (1516, No.62)

PL-Kj, Mus.ant.pract.A 100. Complete. Folios H2 and H7 are cancel leaves: see below

Size of page: 171 × 239 mm.

Watermarks: No.11 on A2-1, A4-3, B1-2, B3-4, C2-1, D2-1, D3-4, E-2, E4-, F2-1, F6-5, G2-1, G4-3 and G6- • No.12 on H1-, H3-4, J1-2 and J4-3

Textual comments: D2*r*.i.text:] Laudaus te • E2*r*, the headline reads] Prmi toni • F2*v*.i.text:] mu*n*di [, with an inverted "m" • F4*v*.i. the text includes:] Benadictus • H2*r*.iii.text:] pecacta •

Technical comments: G4*r*. leading within the area of the last stave line, for the impression of the music • The evidence of minims used as bearers can be seen on D1*r* • Only five staves are inked on E6*r* • Two rows of notes (perhaps *semiminime*) used as bearers on either side of the initial letter have left an impression on H1*r*

Corrections and changes:

> **In-house:** A3*v*, A4*r*, A5*v*, A6*r*, E3*r*, E3*v*, F3*r*, F3*r*, F4*v*, F4*v*, F5*v*, F6*r*, G5*v*, G8*r*, J2*r*. see above
>
> **Later:** C2*v*.ii.above 40: modern pencil cross • D1*r*, above title letter:] Mi[[e Allexandri agricola [in 16th-century brown ink, in the hand found in *Misse Josquin* (1502) • E2*v*.i.1: *sb* → *m*, with a brown ink tail • F1*r*. as D1*r*, except] allexandri • F4*r*.iii.48: *sb*, g → f, erasure and brown ink • F5*v*.ii.5–6: *sb,sb* → *m,m*, with brown ink tails • G8*r*.iv.10: from *sba* to *m* with a black ink tail • H1*v*: as D1*r*

Binding: Berlin bindings, within a 19th-century slip-case. All part-books bound in early 19th-century parchment with gold rolled border • One fly-leaf and one pastedown at each end of each part-book

Provenance: From Berlin. The stamp, in red] Ex | Biblioth. Regia | Berolinen[i. [appears on each title page • Probably originally with the D-B copy of Josquin, *Misse* (1502, No.4)

No.13A. *Cancel Bifolio.*

A half-sheet of the second paper appears in several copies, to replace the second bifolium of gathering H. The need for the cancel seems to have been seen very early on, for the new paper is consistent with that used for the last sheets of the book

Running heads:

Le [eruiteur	[H2*r*-H2*v*
.Je ne demande.	[H7*r*
Je ne demande	[H7*v*

Stop-press corrections: H2*r*.iii.text: pecacta (PL-Kj) peccata (GB-Lbl)

For other details, see the description of the edition, above

Extant copies: for each of the following copies, see above for details of the rest of the book

NO. 13. AGRICOLA: MISSE 541

B-Br, Fétis 1640 A
  Watermark: No.11 on H-2
GB-Lbl, K.1.d.3.
  Watermark: No.11 on H-2
  In-house correction: H2r: see above
I-Ac (sf). Stampati N. 189 (1).
  Watermark: No.11 on H7-
I-Bc, Q60.
  Watermark: No.11 on H7-
I-Fm, R.u.115[1].
  Watermark: No.11 on H7-
I-Rvat, Sist.235–238.
  Watermark: No.11 on H-7
Pl-Kj, Mus.ant.pract.A 100
  Watermark: No.11 on H2-

Lost copies: Copies were owned by Colón (see Chapman, "Printed" No.8), Fugger (Schaal, "Musikbibliothek", I/47) and Bottrigari • A copy was owned by Fétis: see his *Biographie*, vii, 14
Early references: Gesner: see chapter 20
Bibliography:
  (a) Rosaria Boccadifuoco, *Bibliografia*, No.25 • Sartori, *Petrucci*, No.13
  (c) Petrucci, *Missarum*
  (d) Agricola, *Opera Omnia*
  (e) Sartori, "Nuove", p. 178

Commentary:

1. There seems to have been a real effort to correct as many copies as possible of this title. Most of the extant in-house corrections survive in most of the copies, and some show the pattterns of different types of correction which we have seen elsewhere, though less frequently. Note also the use of black ink for some of the corrections: this is unusual, and suggests that two people were involved in making some of the corrections. This may be an indication of a need for speed.

2. The lengths of staves show clearly the pattern of formes in use, as the following samples (from the copy at I-Bc) indicate:

	Io				Ii				IIo				IIi			
	1r	2v	7r	8v	2r	1v	8r	7v	3r	4v	5r	6v	4r	3v	6r	5v
F	—	175	175	175	180	180	180	180	175	175	175	175	178	180	178	180
H	—	175	175	180	175	175	175	175	175	175	175	175	180	180	178	180
J	175	175	175	—	180	180	—	180	175	175	175	175	180	180	178	180

  This indicates that there were certainly three, and probably four, sets of staves: one, probably a pair of formes, had staves that were all 175 mm long; forme three had staves measuring 180 mm; and a final forme had staves of 178 and 180 mm (as used on 3v,4r,5v,6r).

3. The central half-sheet in gathering G (ff. 5–6) has staves 175 mm in length on all pages, confirming that it was printed with work and turn: this may be the first occurrence of the technique in Petrucci's output.

4. The stave-lengths for the bifolio H2,7 confirm that it was a cancel, also printed by work and turn:

	2r	7v	7r	2v		1r	8v	8r	1v
I-Bc	175	175	175	175		—	180	175	175
I-Fm	175	175	175	175		—	180	175	175
PL-Kj	176	175	174	175		—	180	175	176

The related figures for the outer bifolio confirm that all three copies were printed with the two formes of staves that should be expected. It is only the inner that is anomalous.

5. There is some typographical evidence that supports this conclusion: the initial "A" appearing on H7v is not found elsewhere in the book; the treatment of note-tails is unusual on both H2 and H7, in that virtually all are up-tails, regardless of where the note lies on the stave.

6. Head-lines were certainly not kept in the forme, as the following tabulation confirms:

Alexander: Le ſeruiteur [F1v • Alexander .Leſeruiteur. [H1v • .Le ſeruiteur. [A1v-2r, A3v-4r, H3r-H4v • Le ſeruiteur [A2v-3r, A4v-5r; D1v-D3r; F2r-F5r; H2r-H2v

.Alexander. .Jene.demande. [A5v • Alexander: Je ne demande. [F5v • .Alexander Je ne de-mande. [H5r • .Jene.demande. [A6r • .Je ne.demande. [A6v-7r, A8r-A8v • .Je ne demande. [D3v-4r, D5v-6r; H5v-H7r • .Je nedemande [F6v • Je ne.demande. [A7v, B1r • Je ne demande. [F7v-Fr • Je ne demande [D4v-5r; F6r, F7r, H7v

Alexander Mal heur me bat [B1v; H8r • Alexander: Mal heur me bat [F8v • Mal heur me bat [B2r-B5v; D6v-8v; G1r-G2v, G3v-G4r • .Mal heur me bat. [G3r, G4v; J1r-J2v • .Mal heur me bat [H8v

Alexander: Primi toni [E1r; G5r • .Alexander Primi toni [J3r • .Primi toni. [E1v • .Prmi toni. [E2r • Primi toni [B6r, B7r, E2v; G5v-G6v; J3v-J4v • Primi tonj [B6v, B7v • Primi ton [G7r

.Alexander. Secundi toni. [E3r • Alexander Secondi toni [B8r, G7v • .Secundi.toni. [E5v • .Secundi toni. [G9v-G10r, J5r-J6r, J6r-J7v • Secondi toni [B8v • Secandi toni [C1r • Secundi toni [B8v, C1v-C3v; E4v-5r; G8r, G9r • Secnndi toni [J6v • Secundi toni. [E3v; G10v • Secundi toni [E4r; G8v

Nil: A1r, C4r-C4v; D1r, E6r-E6v; F1r, H1r, J8r-J8v

7. The cancel must have been printed very soon after the completion of the book. The paper is not used much, appearing occasionally in the editions that bracket this edition, *Canti C* and *Odhecaton A*. I suspect that the cancel was printed after the *Odhecaton*, given the use of the different initial "A".

No. 14. *Odhecaton A*

25.5.1504   *RISM* 1504²

Third Edition

A1r]   Harmonice Muſices | Odhecaton | A

N8r]   Impreſ ſum Venetijɜ per Octauianuɜ Petrutiuɜ Foroſempronien | ſem 1504 die 25 Maij. Cuɜ priuilegio inuictiſ ſimi Dominij | Venetiarum *quae* nullus poſ ſit cantum Figuratum imprimere | ſub pena in ipſo priuilegio contenta. | Regiſtruɜ ABCDEFGHJKLMN Omnes quaterni. | [Petrucci's device]

A1ν]   Octauianus Petrutius foro[empronien[is Hieronymo Donato patricio | Veneto Felicitatem. [etc.
         For variants with the first edition, see below, under "Textual Comments"

A2r]   Bartholomæus Budrius Iu[tinopolita. Hieronymo donato patricio Veneto. S. [etc. For variants
         with the first edition, see below, under "Textual Comments"

A2r   The Tavola is again in four columns: almost all the numerals are now in arabic characters

Format and collation: Choirbook: landscape quarto-in-eights. 104 folios: A-N⁸

Signatures:] A IIII [$4 • — A1, A2 • There is apparently a capital "N" to the left of the signature
    on C1r

Foliation: top centre recto:] [1–2], 3–20, 21 [both elements inverted], 22, 23 [the "2" inverted], 24–
    61, 62 [the "2" inverted], 63–83, 48 [*recte* 84], 85 [86], 87–103, [104] • For details of variations
    in this pattern, see below, "In-house corrections"

No running heads: composers' names appear in the head-line

Part-names:

recto:]	Altus Ba[[us	[A4-F8, N1-2,5-6
	Contra	[G1-M2, M4,6,8, N7
	Tenor Contra	[M3,5,7
	Contra Ba[[us	[N3-4
	[Nil:	A1-3, N8
verso:]	Tenor	[A3-4,6, A8-G8, H2-M1,3,5, M7-N6
	Tenor Tenor	[A5,7
	Teno	[H1
	Tenor Contra	[M2,4,6
	Tenor Altus Ba[[us	[N7
	[Nil:	A1-2, N8

Fonts: Music: Petrucci's normal music type

    Staves: six per page: 176 mm long, 10-92-113 long

    Text: Rotonda; Roman for A1ν-2r; Greek, only on A1ν, using a new font

Textual comments: A1ν: the following textual changes are made from the first edition: line 1:
    Petrutius → petrutius • 9: animaduerteram → animaduerteram • 10: qua non → qua non • 13:
    de[titi[[e → de[titi[[e: • 15: quoque → quoque • 16: publice → publice. • 18: ado-|le[centes →
    ado = |le[centes • 18: qualemque ipse → qualemque ip[e • 19: delectati: [ordi-|dis → delectati
    [ordi|dis • 23: patrocino → patrocinio

    A2r: the following textual changes are made from the first edition: 1: Bndrius → Budrius •
    4: con[cientiæ: → con[cientiæ: • 4: profe[[ionis → profe[[ionis • 8: in te. → inte. • 9: cum | → cum
    | • 11: in chorum → in. chorum • 12: re|cipiatur. quem → re[|cipiatur. quem • 12: partu-
    riens. → parturiens: • 12: aliquot → aliquod • 13: tan|dem → tan-|dem • 14: ab[oluti[[imum →
    ab[oluti[[imum • 14: admirentur: → admirentur. • 16: [u[cipias. → [u[cipias: • 16: in-|telligant: →
    in = |telligant: • 17: deligen|do → deligen|do • 18: Ca[tellani → Ca[tellani • 18: musicæ → mu[
    icæ • 19: diligentia → diligentia •:

    Composer ascriptions do not consistently have final points: they are found on the versos of
    B1,7, C1,2,5,7,8, F6,7, G4, and H1. The ascription on L7ν has a final colon

    C4ν-5r.text incipits to No.18: [S,T:] Dit le burguygnon [A:] Dit le bourgyugnon [B:] Dir
    le bourguygnon [where the "b" and second "u" are inverted • D4r. Incipits:] Rompletier [spelled
    (A):] Rompletir [and (B):] Rompltir

Technical comments: A1ν.line 1: spacing sort at right end • C4ν.below v: a series of tops of sort-bodies, probably spacing sorts corresponding to the notation above, have taken ink. They give measurements for the widths of some sorts and spacers. They are visible in all copies except I-TVcap • C6*v*.initial: lacking; supplied to the text • The sixth stave is increasingly seldom inked as the book progresses: this occurs on the following rectos: G4, H1,2,4,7, J2-8, K3,5–8, L1,3–7, M2,4,6 • The stave pattern is far from clear: it appears that staves were not kept consistently in the forme. However, the fifth stave on many rectos seems to be the same block

In-house corrections:

> **Stop-press changes:** A1*v*.9.first word: from] temis [(F-Pc) to] meas [other copies • A4*r*.page number (missing in I-TVcap): added in F-Pc, US-NYp, US-Wc • A7*v*.v.14: *sbc'* → *sbe'*, using black ink: F-Pc and I-TVcap • C5*r*.folio number: usually inverted but the second numeral has been corrected: I-TVcap • D1*r*.page number:] 31 [F-Pc, I-TVcap, US-Wc] → 25 [US-NYp • D7*r*.page number:] 25 [F-Pc, US-Wc → nil, I-TVcap] → 31 [US-NYp] • H2*r*.signature: [nil →] H [US-NYp, US-Wc] • H5*v*.head-line:] Alexander [the second "e" is inverted only in I-TVcap and US-NYp, and corrected in US-Wc • N8*r*.colophon: reads] Fero[emp*ro* niensem [with the first "e" inverted: F-Pc; corrected by a stop-press change: other copies
>
> **Other corrections:** B3*r*.i.mensuration sign: omitted and stamped in later: F-Pc, I-TVcap, US-NYp, US-Wc • C1*r*,uv,text;] Adien mes . . . [with an apparent attempt at correcting the first word: F-Pc and I-TVcap • D2*v*.iv.14: e → f, in manuscript: I-TVcap, US-NYp and US-Wc; with a stamped-in note-head: F-Pc • D5*r*.iv.45: e → d, in manuscript: I-TVcap and US-NYp • F5*v*.v.last: f → g, in manuscript: I-TVcap, US-NYp and US-Wc • L6*r*.folio number: 86 stamped in: F-Pc, US-NYp and US-Wc • N4*r*.iv.33: *sbf, mc* → *mc*, *sbf*, by erasure and stamped-in *sb*: US-NYp

Contents: The last column gives the folio numbers as found in the Tavola:

	A1*r*	[Title]			
	A1*v*	[Dedication]			
	A2*r*	[Letter from Budrius]			
	A2*v*	[Tavola]			
	A3*r*	[blank staves]			
1	A3*v*	AUe maria gratia plena		De orto	iiii
2	A4*v*	JE cuide [ece tamps me dure		[Anon.]	5
3	A5*v*	HOr oires vne chanzon	à5	[Anon.]	6
4	A6*v*	NUnqua fue pena maior		[Anon.]	7
5	A7*v*	BRunette	à5	Jo.[tokem	8
		[Tav:] Brunetta			
6	A8*v*	JAy pris amours		[Anon.]	9
7	B1*v*	NEnciozza mia		Japart.	x
		[Tav:] Lenzotta mia			
8	B2*v*	JE ne fay plus		[Anon.]	xi
9	B3*v*	AMours amours		Hayne	xii
10	B4*v*	BErgerette savoyene		Jo[quin	xiii
11	B5*v*	E Qui le dira		[Anon.]	xiiii
12	B6*v*	CE[t mal charche		Agricola	xv
13	B7*v*	HElas que poura deuenir		Caron.	xvi
				[Tav:] Caron.	
14	B8*v*	ADiu mes amours		Jo[quin	xvii

15	C1v	POr quoy non		Pe.de larue.	xviii
		[Tav:] Pour quoy non			
16	C2v	POr quoy iene puis dire		.Jo Sthokem.	19
		[T:] Uray diu damours xviiii			
		[Tav:] Pour . . . [and] Veray . . .			
17	C3v	MOn mignault		[Anon.]	20
		[T, A:] Gratieuſe			20
18	C4v	DIt le burguygnon		[Anon.]	xxi
19	C5v	HElas ce neſt pas ſans rayſon		.Sthokem.	22
20	C6v	De tous biens playne		[Anon.]	23
21	C7v	JAy pris amours		Japart.	24
				[Tav:] Japart	
22	C8v	SE congie pris		.Japart.	25
				[Tav:] Japart	
23	D1v	AMours amours		Japart	xxvi
24	D2v	CEla ſans plus		[Anon.]	27
25	D3v	ROmpeltier		[Anon.]	28
26	D4v	ALons ferons barbe		Compere	29
27	D5v	TMeiſkin			xxx
		[Tav:] Tmeſkin uas iunch			
28	D6v	VNg franc archier		Compere	xxxi
29	D7v	LO ſeray dire		[Anon.]	xxxii
30	D8v	HElas que il eſt amongre		Japart	xxxiii
31	E1v	AMor fait mult		[Anon.]	34
		[T:] Il eſt de bonne heure ne			
		[B:] Tant que nostre argent dure			
32	E2v	NOstre cambriere ſi malade eſtoit		[Anon.]	xxxv
33	E3v	ACordes moy ceque ye penſſe		[Anon.]	36
34	E4v	TTan bien miſon penſa		Japart	xxxvii
35	E5v	LE ſeruiteur		[Anon.]	xxxviii
36	E6v	JAmes iames iames		[Anon.]	39
37	E8v	[N]Ous ſommes de lordre dsaynt babuyn		Compere	41
38	F2v	JE nay dueul		.Agricola.	43
39	F4v	JAy pris amours tout au rebours		Buſnoys	45
				[Tav:] Buſnois	
40	F5v	HE logeron nous		[Anon.]	46
41	F6v	VOſtre bargeronette		.Compere.	47
42	F7v	JE ne demande aultre degre		Buſnoys.	48
43	F8v	PEnſif mari	à3	Ja.Tadinghen	49
44	G1v	LA morra	à3	Yzac	50
45	G2v	ME doibt	à3	Compere	51
46	G3v	MAle bouche	à3	Compere	lii
47	G4v	LHome banni	à3	.Agricola.	53
48	G5v	ALes regrets	à3	Agricola	54
49	G6v	LA ſtangetta	à3	[Anon.]	55
50	G7v	HElas	à3	Yzac	56

51	G8*v*	SE mieulx	à3	Compere	57
52	H1*v*	HElas	à3	Tintoris.	58
53	H2*v*	VEnis regrets	à3	Compere	59
54	H3*v*	MA bouche rit	à3	Okenhe	60
55	H4*v*	ROyne de fleurs	à3	Alexander	lxi
56	H5*v*	SI dedero	à3	Alexander	62
57	H6*v*	ALes regres	à3	Hayne	63
58	H7*v*	GAri∫∫es moy	à3	Compere	64
59	H8*v*	MEs pen∫ees	à3	Compere	65
60	J1*v*	FOrtuna per ta crudelte	à3	Uincinet	66
61	J2*v*	CEla ∫ans plus	à3	Jo∫quin	67
62	J3*v*	MAter patris	à3	Brumel	68
63	J4*v*	MAlor me bat	à3	Okenghen.	69
64	J5*v*	LA plus des puls	à3	Jo∫quin	70
65	J6*v*	ALes mon cor	à3	Alexnder	71
66	J7*v*	MAdame helas	à3	[Anon.]	72
67	J8*v*	LE crops [T:] Le corps [CT:] Corpusq*ue* meu*m* licet	à3	Compere	73
68	K1*v*	TAnt habo[n] oeul	à3	Compere	74
69	K2*v*	TAnder naken	à3	Obreht	75
70	K4*v*	SI a tort on ma blamee	à3	[Anon.]	77
71	K5*v*	LEs grans regres	à3	[Anon.]	78
72	K6*v*	E∫t po∫∫ible que lhome peult [Tav:] E∫t il po∫∫ible	à3	[Anon.]	79
73	K7*v*	DE tous biens [Tav:] Bourdo*n*	à3	[Anon.]	80
74	K8*v*	FOrtuna dum gran tempo	à3	[Anon.]	81
75	L1*v*	CRions nouel	à3	Agricola	82
76	L2*v*	BEnedictus [Tav:] Yzac	à3	Jzac	83
77	L3*v*	LE renuoy	à3	Compere	84
78	L4*v*	O Uenus bant	à3	Jo∫quin	85
79	L5*v*	MA ∫eule dame	à3	[anon.]	86
80	L7*v*	LA alfon∫ina	à3	.Jo.ghiselin:	88
81	L8*v*	LE eure e venue [CT:] Circundederu*n*t	à3	Agricola	89
82	M1*v*	JAy bien ahuer	à3	Agricola	90
83	M2*v*	MOn ∫ouenir	à3	[Anon.]	91
84	M3*r*	ROyne du ciel [CT:] Regina celi	à3	Compere	91
85	M3*v*	MArguerite	à3	[Anon.]	92
86	M4*v*	HAtraytre amours	à3	.Jo.∫token	93
87	M5*r*	MAis que ce fu∫t	à3	Compere	93
88	M5*v*	VEnus tu ma pris	à3	De Orto	94
89	M6*v*	DI∫ant adiu madame	à3	[Anon.]	94 [recte 95]
90	M7*r*	GEntil prince	à3	[Anon.]	95

91	M7v	PUis que de vous	à3	[Anon.]	90
					[recte 96]
92	M8v	TSat een me[kin		Obreht	97
93	N2v	ALaudienche		Hayne	99
94	N4v	LAtura tu		[Anon.]	101
95	N6v	DE tous biens playne	à4 ex 3	[Anon.]	103
				[Tav:] Jo[quin	
96	N7v	ME[kin es hu		[Anon.]	103
					[recte 104]
	N8r	[Colophon; Register; Device]			
	N8v	[blank]			

Extant copies:

E-Bprivate. I have not been able to trace this copy, which was formerly in the Medinaceli collection, in Madrid

F-Pc, Rés.538. Complete

> **Page size:** 160 × 221 mm.
>
> **Watermarks:**
>
> A3-4 A7-8 B1-2 B3-4 C3-4 C7-8 D3-4 D8-7 E3-4 E7-8 F5-6 F7-8 G2-1 G5-6
> 11   11   11   11   12   12   11   11   11   11   12   11   11   11
>
> H4-3 H8-7 J2-1 J5-6 K1-2 K5-6 L2-1 L5-6 M1-2 M4-3 N1-2 N3-4
> 11   11   11   11   11   11   11   11   11   11   11   11
>
> **Textual comments:** A1v.first word: meas] temis
>
> **Technical comments:** D7v.iv.2: A piece of furniture, implying three impressions
>
> **Changes and corrections:**
>
> > **In-house:** A4r, A7v, B3r, C1r, D2v, L6r and N8r. see above
> >
> > **Later:** A8r.ii.7: bc' → sba" by erasure • A series of manuscript additions on the versos of B7, B8, C6, G1, G6, G7, H3, H5, J1, J3, L2, and L3
>
> **Binding:** Modern red leather, with gold-stamped flower heads and petals, and gold rolls. The same binding contains *Canti B* (1503) and *Canti C* (1504) • Three end-papers of marbled paper at each end, the outer one used as a paste-down
>
> **Provenance:** Bought from the bookseller Léfébure of Bordeaux in 1879. Léfébure claimed to have acquired it from a Spaniard named Miro • On the other hand, Gianandrea, "Ottaviano", p. 124 asserts that Weckerlin bought the copy in Spain • This is the former Colón copy (see Chapman, "Printed", No.9), reaching Paris with copies of *Canti B* and *Canti C*, as suggested by Sartori (*Petrucci*, pp. 77 and 80) and Fallows
>
> **Bibliography:** Weckerlin, "Bibliothèque", pp. 372–400 (listing the three books of the series as if one) • Bridgman "Clandestins"

I-TVcap. lacks folio N8

> **Size of page:** 169 × 235 mm.
>
> **Watermarks:**
>
> A5-6 A8-7 B2-1 B3-4 C2-1 C6-5 D3-4 D7-8 E1-2 E6-5 F3-4 F7-8 G3-4 G7-8
> 11   11   11   11   12   12   11   11   11   11   12   12   11   11
>
> H2-1 H6-5 J4-3 J7-8 K4-3 K8-7 L4-3 L7-8 M5-6 M7-8 N4-3 N7-
> 11   11   11   11   11   11   11   11   11   11   11   11

Technical comments: Several pieces of spacing sorts can be seen on A1*v*: they confirm that the text type was not leaded

In-house corrections and changes: A1*v*, A7*v*, B3*r*, C1*r*, D1*r*, D2*v*, D5*r* and F5*v*: see above

Binding: as the Treviso copy of *Canti C*

Provenance: Inside the front board:] Vincislao Bressa Tv°

Bibliography: Catelani, "Bibliografia" • Castellani, *Arte*, pp. 96–97 (facsimiles of A1*r* and A3*v*), and p. 65, fn • Rosaria Boccadifuoco, *Bibliografia*, No.1731 dates this copy 1505

US-NYp, Mus.Res.*MN/P497. Complete • The outer sheet of gathering F is from the second edition, and is described there (No.5, above)

Page size: 162 × 221 mm.

Watermarks:

A1-2	A5-6	B3-4	B7-8	C5-6	C7-8	D4-3	D8-7	E2-1	E4-3	F5-6	G2-1	G5-6
11	11	11	11	12	12	11	11	11	11	12	11	11

H1-2	H3-4	J2-1	J5-6	K1-2	K5-6	L1-2	L3-4	M4-3	M7-8	N1-2	N4-3
11	11	11	11	11	11	11	11	11	11	11	11

Technical comments: A3*r*: clear blind impression of musical sorts, as in the copy at US-Wc • The music for A8*v* was printed before the line of furniture on A8*r*, itself probably printed with the music of that page • E1*v* was later through the press than for the copy now at I-TVcap

Changes and corrections:

In-house: A1*v*, A4*r*, B3*r*, D1*r*, D2*v*, D5*r*, D7*r*, F5*v*, H2*r* and N4*r*: see above

Later: A8*r*.i.custos: a → b, in manuscript • L8*r*.iv.6: *colsb* scratched void

Binding: Early parchment, originally painted white, with two leather tie strings. On the spine:] Musica de adgecaton • One end paper at each end, with a stub of the conjugate inside the adjacent gathering. The final end paper has a watermark of a gauntlet with a star above

Bibliography: Reese, "First"

US-Wc, M1490.P4 Case. Complete

Watermarks:

A5-6	A8-7	B5-6	B8-7	C1-2	C3-4	D5-6	D7-8	E1-2	E6-5	F1-2	F3-4	G5-6	G7-8
11	11	11	11	12	12	11	11	11	11	12	12	11	11

H1-2	H6-5	J3-4	J7-8	K6-5	K8-7	L5-6	L8-7	M1-2	M3-4	N3-4	N8-7
11	11	11	11	11	11	11	11	11	11	11	11

Technical comments: The width of some sorts can be seen: on D4*r*.iv: *sb*, 2.5 mm; *b*, 3.25 mm; *sbr*, 0.1 mm. • A3*r*: clear blind impression of musical sorts, as in the copy at US-NYp • H5*r*.iv.after flat: vertical space, 18.85 mm high gives the total space between staves, and indicates the amount of kerning • L4*r*.vi: rows of *sm* used as bearer sorts in the area of the stave: 20 at one pitch, and 25 one pitch higher • L6*r*: as L4*r*

Corrections and changes:

In-house: A1*v*, A4*r*, A7*v*, B3*r*, D2*v*, F5*v*, H2*r*, H5*v* and L6*r*: see above

Later: A1*v*: manuscript parentheses around two entries • K2*v*: note values written above the music, in manuscript • L2*v*.i.iv: addition of *2b* rest before other rests, in both voices • L3*r*.i: *2b* rest added, in manuscript • L3*r*: addition of a fourth voice, with a manuscript extra stave

Binding: Early brown calf, with four holes for tie-strings on each board • One early flyleaf and one later at the front. None at the back

Provenance: From the Gottschalk collection • Inside front cover:] Pgongs/~ [(presumably a dealer's price code), followed by the Library of Congress accession number and the date 20 Jy [19]43 • On A1r is an inscription in Greek

Bibliography: Barksdale, *Printed*, No.69 (Toledo exhibition, 1957)

———

Lost copies: Reese, "First", p. 47, reports another copy, at J. C. Adler of Berlin, and thence to Munich

Early references: It is possible that some of the references cited under the first edition refer in fact to this edition

Other editions: 1501 (No.1) • 14.i.1503 (No.5)

Bibliography:

In addition to the citations under entry No.1, see the following:

    (a) Rosaria Boccadifuoco, *Bibliografia*, Nos.1730–1731 • Sartori, *Petrucci*, No.14 • Brown, *Instrumental*, 1504₂ • Vogel, *Bibliografia*, 1504^1

    (c) Boorman, *Harmonice* • Petrucci, *Harmonice* (of the copy at I-TVcap) • Petrucci, *Odhecaton* (of the copy at US-Wc)

    (e) Hewitt, *Odhecaton*, pp. 6–8 • Marix, "Odhecaton" • Reese, "First"

Commentary:

1.   The Greek text on A2r is again set in a different fount. As before, the typesetter, when he set up the page, left a space for its insertion: in this instance however, the fount has a significantly narrower body-width, and white space is left at the end of the phrase.

2.   Apparently, the introductory texts were set from a copy of the first edition, rather than from the second. There is some evidence that the music was also copied from the first edition. This implies that Petrucci kept a "house-copy", into which corrections and errors could be noted, for any future edition. The same conclusion can be reached about the editions of *I Motetti de la Corona*.

3.   Despite the pattern of watermarks in gatherings C and F, those sheets seem to have been set in type at the same time as the rest of the book. In each case, there are initials which can be seen to have deteriorated by the time they are used in later gatherings.

No. 15. *Motetti C*

15.ix.1504   *RISM* 1504^1

There is a cancel bifolium for Cantus ff.C1 and C8, discussed below
The copy in HR-Ssf (Bassus book) has not been consulted

Edition

S: A1r]   Motetti. C. | C

T: A1r]   T

A: A1r]   A

B: A1r]   B

B: D8r]   Impre∬um Uenetijs per Octauianum Petrutiȝ Forosempronien∫em 1505 die 15 | Setembris.
Cum priuilegio inucti∬imi [*sic*] Dominij Uenetiarum q*uae* nullus po∬it ca*n*tuȝ | Figuratum
imprimere ∫ub pena in ip∫o priulegio [*sic*] contenta. | Regi∫trum.
.+A.+B.+C.+D.+A.+B.+C.+D.+A.+B.+C.+D. | +A.+B.+C.+D. Om*n*es qu*a*terni
prae*ter* .+D. alti q*ui* e∫t q*ui*ntern*us*. Nota q*uae* q*ue*libet | pa*rs* di∫tinguit ab alia p*er* rubrices: quia pars:
tenoris: habet: tenor: pars alti habet | altus 7 ∫ic de ∫ingulis | [Petrucci's device]

1*v* of each part-book: Tavola: reset for each book. The following is taken from the Bassus:

Aue maria de Jo∫quin.	2.	Mi∬us e∫t de Jo∫quin	7.
Aue celo*rum* do*m*ina.	2.	Mi∬us e∫t.	14.
Alma rede*m*ptoris.	15.	Miles mire p*ro*bitatiȝ	15.
Aue regina celo*rum*: O dec*us*	16.	Mi∫erere mei	22.
Aue maria: O bone ꝫ dulcis.	14	Magnus es tu do*m*ine	3.
		Mittit ad vi*rg*ineȝ	30.
Beata dei genitrix.	7.		
		O bon*e* ꝫ d*u*lcis: Pat*er* n*oste*r: Aue ma*ri*a	14.
Concede	8.	O dec*us* in noce*n*tie: Aue regina	16.
Ciuitateȝ	12.	O ∫acruȝ co*n*uiuiuȝ	17.
Confitemini.	19.	O admirabile	18.
		O dulci∬ime	20.
Dauitica.	6		
		P∫alite noe	10.
Ergo ∫ancti martires.	8.	Pat*er* n*oste*r: Aue ma*ri*a: O bon*e* ꝫ d*u*lcis	14.
		Profitentes	21.
Factuȝ e∫t aut*em*.	4.	Planxit aut*em*	23.
Filie reguȝ in honore.	21.		
		Requieȝ	9.
Gloria laus.	26.	Re∫pice me in feliceȝ	20.
Gaudeammus.	27.	Rogam*us* te	25.
Gaude vi*rg*o mater xpi	27.		
Gaude quia magi dona.	27.	Si oblit*us*	11.
Gaude quia tui nati.	28.	Sancti deɪ om*n*es	18.
Gaude que po∫t ip∫*um*.	28.	Sibona ∫u∫cepim*us*	22.
		Saluatoris mater pia	30.
Huc om*n*es pariter.	29.		
		Tota pulcra es	5.
In violata.	25.	Trinitaȝ deitas	20.
Inlectulo.	31.		
		Virgo precellenȝ	17.
Liber generationis.	3.	Ut hemerita	12.

Format and collation: Landscape format: quarto-in-eights. [S:] 32 folios: A-D⁸; [T:] 32 folios: A-
D⁸; [A:] 34 folios: A-C⁸D¹⁰; [B:] 32 folios: A-D⁸ • For the Altus foliation, see below

Signatures:] + A IIII [$4 • + DIIIII • − *S:*A 1 • *A:* C4 signed B IIII (and corrected); D4 signed D
III

Foliation: top centre recto:] [S] [1], 2–32; [T] [1], 2–25, 25 [*recte* 26] 27–32; [A] [1], 2–30, 29–32
[*recte* 31–34]; [B] [1], 2–31, [32]

Running heads:

recto:	S:]	Sup*ranus*	[A2–B8, C3,5,7, C8–D8
		Snp*ranus*	[C1
		ſup*ranus*	[C2,4,6
		[Nil:	A1
	T:]	Tenor	[A2–D8
		[Nil:	A1
	A:]	Altus	[A2, A4–C3,5, C7–D10
		Alt*us*	[C4,6
		[Nil:	A1,3
	B:]	Baſſus	[A2–D4, D6,7
		[Nil:	A1, D5,8
verso:	S:]	Sup*ranus*	[A2–B8, C1,2,4,6, C8–D7
		ſup*ranus*	[C3,5,7
		[Nil:	A1, D8
	T:]	Tenor:	[A2–D7
		[Nil:	A1, D8
	A:]	Altus	[A2–C2, C4, C6–D9
		Alt*us*	[C3,5
		[Nil:	A1, D10
	B:]	Baſſus	[A2–C1, C3–D4, D6,7
		Beſſus	[C2
		Baſſuſ	[D5
		[Nil:	A1, D8

Fonts: Music: Petrucci's normal music type

Staves: Six per page: 175–179 mm long, 10–91.5–112 long

Text: Rotonda, "x" = 2.0 mm, "20" = 76 mm • Title font: "x" = 12.3 mm.

Textual comments: This volume shows the habit of adding extra notes after the first *custos* on many rectos: it follows a complex pattern of: *custos*, *Verte*, notation, *custos*: S: A6, B1, B6, C2, C5; T: A6, B1, B4, D4; A: A6, A7, B7, C1, C2, C4; B: A5, B4, B7, C3; • Initial letters are omitted on Superius C8v [M] and Bassus A7r [B] • S:A8v.text] Co*n*nede [*sic*] • A number of movements are very sparsely texted, often with no more than an incipit

Technical comments: The Tavola appears to have been reset for each part-book • The evidence of the watermarks in each book suggests simultaneous work on all books by different men. For a detailed discussion, see below • The pattern of starting a number of pieces or *partes* on new pages results in a large number of blank last staves on preceding pages: 24 such pages can be found in the Superius book, for example. In contrast to the practice in other, later titles, however, these blank staves are here inked and impressed • The pattern of use of capital letters here confirms their uniqueness: thus the letter M on (Superius) C1v cannot reappear on C7v (the other forme for that sheet); nor the O of (Superius) C3v on C4r; the capital letter B on (Bassus) A1r cannot appear on A7r, where in fact the initial is omitted entirely • The evidence of stave lengths (given below for the copy at I-Vnm) shows that the half-sheet at the centre of gathering D (Altus) was printed by work-and-turn

In-house corrections: S: B1v.vi.53: *sba'* erased: D-Mbs, D-W, GB-Lbl (both: very carefully done in K.1.d.4), I-Bc, I-Vnm, US-Tm • B3v.iii.13: g', *sb* → *m*, with erased tail, and addition of *m* rest in brown ink: D-Mbs, D-W, GB-Lbl (both), I-Bc, I-Vnm, US-Tm • B4r.vi.50–52: originally *lg*', double bar: now reads *bg*' with an erased tail, *bf*', *lg*', double bar: in the copy at D-W, the second note is in manuscript and the third and bar-lines are stamped in; in both copies at GB-Lbl, and at I-Bc and I-Vnm, all is in manuscript. In other copies the *bf*' has a *corona*: at D-Mbs and US-Tm, all is stamped in, with type • B8v.iii.22: *sb* → *m*, with tail added in the same brown ink: D-Mbs, GB-Lbl (both), I-Bc, US-Tm • C4r.iii.2: *b* → *l*, with a brown ink up-tail: D-Mbs, GB-Lbl (both), I-Bc, I-Vnm

T: B3v.vi,last 3: probably originally *lg,ld*: now *bg* with erased tail,*ba* and *corona* stamped in,*bg* stamped in with a *l* tail in brown ink, and double bar; line and staves touched up in brown ink: D-Mbs, D-Mu, D-W, I-VENsl • B6v.iv.34: *sb* → *m*, with a tail in brown ink: D-Mbs and D-Mu • B6v.iv.41: *m* → *dsb*, by erasure and a dot in brown ink: D-Mbs and D-Mu • B6v.iv.51: *m* g → f, erased note-head, stamped in new *sb*, and a brown ink link to the original tail: D-Mbs, D-Mu • B6v.v.9: d' → c', erased and stamped in: D-Mbs, D-Mu • B7v.i.k.s: a flat to b flat, erasure and brown ink: D-Mbs, D-W

A: Foliation:] 1–28, 29, 30, 29–32: I-FPfanan, I-VENsl and SI-Ka: corrected in the other copies • B7r.vi.end: *sbf*', *bg*' and the word *Verte* were removed in a stop-press correction: they were present (now erased) in the copies at D-W and I-FPfanan, SI-Ka, while that at I-Vnm was printed after a partial correction (with the word *Verte* again erased) • C1r.iv.42–43: *dm,sm* → *sb,colsb,colm*, by erasure and stamped in notes: D-Mbs, D-W, I-FPfanan, I-Vnm, I-VENsl • C1r.iv.46–47: *dm,* → *sm sb,colsb,colm*, by erasure and stamped in notes: D-Mbs, D-W, I-FPfanan, I-Vnm, I-VENsl • C1v.i.33–37: a rule on either side: in brown ink in I-Vnm: in addition, a repeat sign above, printed in the copy at D-Mbs, and in manuscript in that at D-W: in the copies at I-FPfanan, I-VENsl and SI-Ka, both the rule and the repeat sign are printed • C4r.signature: B IIII → C IIII, by stop-press correction: D-W and I-FPfanan • C4v.v.53–56: a brown ink rule on either side: stamped in double bar and repeat dots, below the stave, in the copies at D-Mbs, I-FPfanan, I-Vnm, I-VENsl and SI-Ka; above the stave in that at D-W • D3r.i: the *m.s.* was stamped in later: I-VENsl • D8v.i: between 5 and 6 from the end: *sm*, d', stamped in: I-VENsl

*B:*A4r.iv.6: *b*, G → A, as a stop-press correction. The original form exists in copies at D-Mbs and I-VENsl, with an in-house stamped-in correction: the revised version is in the copy at D-Mu • B5r.ii.11: *m*, d → e, erased and a new note-head stamped in: D-Mbs, D-Mu, I-Vnm, I-VENsl • B7r.i.48: *m*,a → *dm*,b: erasure, new note-head stamped in, and the dot added in brown ink: D-Mbs, D-Mu, D-W, I-Vnm, I-VENsl: in the copy at D-W, the erasure has left a hole in the page, resulting in a replacement of a *mA* on the other side of the sheet • B7v.i.13: G → F, erasure and stamped in: D-Mbs, D-Mu, I-Vnm • B7v.iii.1–2: *dm,sm* → *dsb,m*, by erasures and a new stamped-in second note: D-Mu, D-Mbs, D-W, HR-Ssfa, I-Vnm, I-VENsl • C1v.iii.25: *b*,d, stamped in, though there is no evidence of an erasure: I-VENsl • C4r.iii.2: *b* → *l*, with a brown ink up-tail: D-Mbs, I-Vnm • C4v.iv.1 *?b?A* → *sbG*, erasure and new note stamped in: D-Mu, D-Mbs, I-Vnm • C7v.i-v.signatures: c → B, partial erasure and new brown ink heads: D-Mbs, D-Mu, D-W, I-Vnm • C7v.i.3: *b*, b → a, erased and new note stamped in: D-Mbs, D-Mu, D-W, I-Vnm, I-VENsl • C8r.i.signature: c → B, partial erasure and new brown ink top: D-Mbs, D-Mu, D-W I-Vnm, and I-VENsl • D3v.v.last *l*: E → *bG* and a *l* tail, brown ink: D-Mbs, D-Mu and I-VENsl • D6r.i.6–7: *signum* above 7 struck through, and entered above 6 in brownish-grey ink: D-Mbs, D-Mu and I-VENsl

Rubrics: The rubrics for the Tenor part of *Ut heremita solus* read as follows:
Entered in the stave of each part, between the notes:]
Ue [...] bes [...] es [...] te [...] es go [...] per͡o que
[Below the *prima pars* is entered, laid out in this manner:]
Canon | |

per vtraq3 | Quamlib3 in∫picias notulam qua claue locetur |

parte | Tunc deniq*ue* ∫ocios in eadem concine tentos |

              Pro qual3 littera duo tu tempora pau∫a

Canon   Sed vere pr*o*lationes no*n* petu*n*t pau∫ationes

                Sed ∫unt ∫igna generis:

[Below the *secunda pars*, in two long lines:]

Canon | Littera5 caute notabis pr*o* qual3 tu pau∫abi5 vni*us* pau∫a3 tempori5

            | Sed vere pr*o*lationes no*n* petu*n*t pau∫ationes ∫ed ∫u*nt* ∫igna generis

Contents: Ascriptions appear only in the first gathering of the Cantus

	S	T	A	B		
	A1*r*	A1*r*	A1*r*	A1*r*	[Title]	
	A1*v*	A1*v*	A1*v*	A1*v*	[Tavola]	
1	A2*r*	A2*r*	A2*r*	A2*r*	AVe Maria	.Josquin.
2	A2*v*	A2*v*	A2*v*	A2*v*	AVe celorum domina	.Brumel.
3	A3*r*	A3*r*	A3*r*	A3*r*	LIber generationis	.Josquin.
	—	A3*v*	A3*v*	A3*v*	2/ Salomon autem à3	
	A3*v*	A4*r*	A4*r*	A4*r*	3/ Et po∫t tran∫migrationem	
4	A4*r*	A4*v*	A4*v*	A4*v*	FActum e∫t autem	.Josquin.
	A4*v*	A4*v*.iv	A4*v*.v	A4*v*.iv★	2/ Qui fuit heli	
	A5*r*	A5*v*	A5*v*	A5*r*.iii★	3/ Qui fuit obeth	
5	A5*v*	A6*r*	A6*r*	A5*v*.iii	TOta pulchra es	.Nico.
						Craen
	A5*v*.iv	A6*r*.iv	A6*r*.iv★	A5*v*.vi★	2/ Flores aparuerunt	
6	A6*r*.iii	A6*v*.iii	A6*v*.iv	A6*r*.iv	DAvidica ∫tirpe maria	[Anon.]
	A6*v*.i	A7*r*	A7*r*.iii	A6*v*.i	2/ Ergo omnium mulierum	
7	A7*r*	A7*v*	A7*v*.iii	A7*r*	BEata dei genitrix	[Anon.]
	A7*r*.iv	A7*v*.iii	A8*r*.i	A7*r*.iii	2/ Ora pro populo	
8	A7*v*	A8*r*	A8*v*	A7*v*	MI∫∫us e∫t angelus gabriel	.Josquin.
					[A.B:] . . . gabriel angelus	
					[Tav:] Mi∫∫us e∫t de Josquin	
9	A8*r*	A8*v*	B1*r*	A8*r*	ERgo ∫ancti martires	[Agricola]
10	A8*v*	B1*r*	B1*v*	A8*v*	COncede nobis domine	[Anon.]
	B1*r*	B1*r*.iii	B2*r*	A8*v*.iii	2/ Electi dei pontifices	
11	B1*r*.v	B1*v*.ii	B2*v*	B1*r*.ii	REquiem eternam	[Obrecht]
	B1*v*.ii	B1*v*.iii	B2*v*.v	B1*v*	2/ [no text]	
12	B2*v*	B2*r*	B3*v*	B2*r*	PSalite noe iudei credite	[Ninot]
	B3*r*	B2*v*	B4*r*	B2*v*	2/ Puer nobis na ∫citur	
13	B3*v*	B3*r*	B4*v*	B3*r*	SI oblitus fuero	[Ninot]
	B4*r*	B3*v*	B5*r*	B3*v*	2/ Decantabant populus	
14	B4*v*	B4*r*	B5*v*	B4*r*	CIuitatem i∫tam	[Anon.]
	B5*r*	B4*r*.v	B6*r*	B4*r*.v	2/ Tua e∫t potentia	
15	B5*v*	B4*v*.iv	B6*v*	B4*v*.iv	UT heremita ∫olus	[Ockeghem]
					[Text incipit only]	
					[T:] Expecto donec veniat	
	B6*r*.iii	B5*r*	B7*r*.iii	B5*v*	2/ [no text]	
					[T:] Expecto donec veniat	
16	B7*r*	B5*v*	B7*v*.iv	B6*r*.iii	O Bone et dulcis domine	[Josquin]

					[T:] Pater noſter		
					[B:] Ave Maria gratia plena		
17	B7v	B5v.iv	B8r.iv	B6r.iii	MIſſus eſt angelus		[Josquin]
	B7v.v	B6r.i	B8v.ii	B6v	2/ Splendor inextinguibilis		
18	B8v	B6v	C1r.iv	B7r	ALma redemptoris mater	à3	[Isaac]
	C1r	B6v.iii	C1v.iii	B7r.v	2/ Tu que genuisti		
19	C1v	B7r	C2r.iii	B7v.iv	MIles mire probitatis		[Anon.]
	C1v.iv	B7v	C2v.ii	B8r.i	2/ In nocte scis		
20	C2r.iii	B8r	C3r	B8v	O Decus innocentie		[Anon.]
					[T, B:] Ave regina celorum		
	C2r.v	B8r.ii	C3r.iii	B8v.ii	2/ O mater egregie		
21	C2v.iii	B8r.iv	C3v	C1r	VIrgo precellens		[Anon.]
	C2v.iv	B8r.v	C3v.ii	C1r.ii	2/ Anna te mundo genuit		
	C3r	B8v	C3v.iv	C1r.iii	3/ Pacis in terris		
	C3r.iii	B8v.ii	C3v.v	C1r.iv	4/ Ergo te noſtre		
	C3r.v	B8v.iv	C4r	C1r.vi	5/ Jam mine fere fileant		
22	C3v	C1r	C4r.iii	C1v.ii	O Sacrum conuiuium		[Anon.]
					[T:] QUi pacem ponit		
23	C4r	C1v	C4v.ii	C2r	O Admirabile commercium		[Anon.]
24	C4r.v	C2r	C5r	C2r.v	SAncti dei omnes		[Mouton]
	C4v.iv	C2v	C5v	C2v.iii	2/ Chriſte audi nos		
25	C5r.iv	C3r	C6r	C3r.iii	COnfitemini domino		[Anon.]
	C5v.ii	C3v	C6r.v	C3v.i	2/ Qui diuiſit mare rubrum		
26	C6r.ii	C4r	C6v.iv	C4r	REſpice me in felicem		[Anon.]
27	C6v	C4v	C7r.iii	C4v	TRinitas deitas		[Anon.]
	C6v.iv	C4v.iii	C7v	C4v.iii	2/ Tu uertux ⁊ apex		
					[T, A, B: no text]		
28	C7r	C5r	C7v.iv	C5r	PRofitentes unitatem		[Compère]
	C7r.iv	C5r.v	C8r	C5r.iv	2/ Digne loque de perſonis		
29	C7v	C5v ii	C8r.iv	C5v	FIlie regum in honore tuo		[Anon.]
	C7v.iii	C5v.iii	C8v	C5v.iii	2/ In ueſtitu de aurato		
30	C7v.vi	C6r	C8v.iv	C6r	MIſerere mei		[Anon.]
31	C8r.iii	C6v	D1r	C6v	SI bona ſuſcepimus		[Anon.]
	C8r.vi	C6v.iv	D1r.iv	C6v.iii	2/ [T:] Adeſto domine		
32	C8v.iii	C7r	D1v.ii	C7r	MAgnus es tu domine		[Josquin]
	D1r	C7r.iii	D1v.iv	C7r.iv	2/ Tu pauperum refugium		
33	D1r.iv	C7v	D2r.ii	C7v	PLanxit autem Dauid		[Josquin]
	D1v.ii	C8r	D2v	C7v.vi	2/ Montes gelboe		
	D1v.v	C8r.iii	D2v.iii	C8r.iii	3/ Sagitta ionathe		
	D2r.ii	C8v.ii	D3r.ii	C8v.ii	4/ Doleo ſuper te		
34	D2v	D1r	D3v	D1r	ROgamus te pijſſima		[Isaac]
					[T:] O Maria O regina		
	D2v.iii	D1r.i	D3v.iv	D1r.iv	2/ O Maria O regina		
35	D3r	D1r.iv	D4r	D1v	INuiolata integra		[Anon.]
	D3r.i	D1r.vi	D4r.ii	D1v.ii	2/ Que es effecta		
	D3r.ii	D1v	D4r.iii	D1v.iii	3/ O mater alma chriſti		

	—	—	D4r.iv	D1v.v	4/ Suſcipe pia laudem	à2
	D3r.iii	D1v.i	D4r.v	D1v.vi	5/ Noſtra ut pura pectora	
	D3r.iv	D1v.ii	D4v	D2r.i	6/ Te nunc flagitant	
	D3r.v	D1v.i	—	—	7/ Tua per precata	à2
	D3r.vi	D1v.iii	D4v.ii	D2r.ii	8/ Nobis concedas	
	D3v	D1v.iv	D4v.iv	D2r.iii	9/ O benigna	
	D3v.ii	D1v.v	D4v.v	D2r.iii	10/ O regina	
	D3v.ii	D2r	D4v.vi	D2r.v	11/ O Maria	
	D3v.ii	D2r.i	D5r	D2r.v	12/ Que ſola inuiolata	
36	D3v.iv	D2r.iii	D5r.ii	D2v	GLoria laus et honor	[Anon.]
	D4r	D2r.iv	D5r.iii	D2v.ii	2/ Iſrael es tu	
	D4r.ii	D2v	—	D2v.ii	3/ Cetus in excelſis	à3
	D4r.iv	D2v.iii	D5r.v	D2v.iv	4/ Plebs hebrea	
37	D4v	D3r	D5v.ii	D3r	GAudeamus omnes	[Anon.]
	D4v.v	D3r.v	D6r	D3v	2/ Gaude uirgo mater	
	D5r	D3v	D6r.iii	D3v.iii	3/ Gaude quia magni dona	
	D5r.iii	D3v.iv	D6r.v	D4r	4/ Gaude quia tui nati	
	D5v	D4r	D6v.iii	D4v	5/ Gaude que poſt ipſum	
38	D6r	D4r.v	D7r	D5r	HUc omnes pariter	[Anon.]
	D6r.ii	D4v.ii	D7r.iv	D5r.iv	2/ Splendor quo regitur	
39	D6r.iv	D5r	D7v.ii	D5v	O Dulciſſiuma pulcra	[Anon.]
					[S:] . . . plucra	
	D6v	D5r.iii	D7v.iv	D5v.iii	2/ O mea ſponſa de libano	
40	D6v.iv	D5v	D8r	D6r	MIttit ad uirginem	[Josquin]
	D7r.iii	D6r	D8v	D6r.iv	2/ Accede nuntia	
					[T:] Accide	
41	D7v	D6v	D9r	D6v	SAluatoris mater pia	[Anon.]
	D8r	D7r	D9v	D7r	2/ O maria ſtella matris	
	D8r.iii	D7r.iii	D9v.iii	D7r.iii	3/ Aue uirgo meo	
42		D7v	D10r	D7v	IN lectulo meo	à3 [Anon.]
			D8r		[Colophon; Register; Device]	
		D8r			[blank staves]	
	D8v	D8v	D10v	D8v	[blank]	

Extant copies:

D-Mbs, 4°.mus.pr.160/2. Complete. This copy has the cancel at Superius C1,8, discussed below
  Size of page: 165 or 167 × 235 mm.
  Watermarks:

S:	A3-4	A7	B3-4	B7-8	C-2	C4-3	T:	A5-6	A7-	B3-4	B8-7	C2-1	C6-5
	11	14	11	11	11	11		11	14	11	11	11	11

A:	A5-6	A1	B2-1	B6-5	C2-1	C5-6	B:	A6-5	A7	B3-4	B8-7	C5-6	D1
	11	14	11	11	11	11		14	14	11	11	11	14

Textual comments: *A:* B5r.ii: the word] cantorib*us* [did include the "a": it has printed, but
  only in blind • *B:* A5v: the erased version may suggest that the typesetter did not understand
  the notational practice of the proportion 03 in the exemplar

Technical comments: *S:* A1*r* shows the impress of uninked staves used as furniture • B2*r.* only five staves were inked • D7*r.* the text was printed before the text of D7*v* • *T:* A2*v*, the music was printed before the staves

Corrections and changes:

In-house: *S:* C4*r*, B1*v*, B3*v*, B4*r*, B8*v*; *T:* B3*v*, B6*v* (4 changes), B7*v*; *A:* foliation, C1*r* (2 changes), C1*v*, C4*v*; *B:* A4*v*, B5*r*, B7*r*, B7*v* (2 changes), C4*r*, C4*v*, C7*v* (2 changes), C8*r*, D3*v*, D6*r.* see above

Later: *T:* B1*v*.ii.10: brown ink *sb* over printed *b*, both colored • B6*v*.iv.50: *m* → *sb*, by erasure • C2*v*.iv.4: *sb* → *m*, with added tail • C8*r*.vi. near end: a modern pencil mark through a point • C8*v*.iv.6: *f* → *sm*, by erasure

> *A:* A3*v*.i.17: a black ink line through the tail to strike it out: the line and the rest of the tail later erased • B4*r*.ii.22: dot erased from *sb* • B4*v*.i.23: *?m* → *sm*, in very pale brown ink • B7*r*.vi.*r* end: *Verte* erased • D4*r*.iv.36: *b* written above the *sb*, in 16th-century brown ink • D4*r*.iv.39: *sb* written above the *b*, in the same ink • D5*r*.v.after bar-lines:] cet*us* tac*et* [in brown ink • D6*v*.v.first rests: *sb*, *l*, *l*, *l* → *sb*, *l*, *l*, *b*, by erasure • D8*v*.i.before 5 from end: *smd'*, in brown ink and untidy

> *B:* A5*v*.i.first rests: *l* to *b*, *sb*, *sb*, by erasure and additions in brown ink • A5*v*.i.v: *db*: the dot erased • A6*r*.iii. right end:] de Vorda [in 16th-century dark ink • C1*r*.ii.10: *?sm m* • C4*v*.iii.*custos*: A → G, in brown ink • D1*v*.v.16–18: *sb*, *b* + *b* in ligature: below first a *b*, below the last a *sb*, both in ginger ink • D2*r*.iii.4: *l* → *b*, by erasing the tail

Binding: With *Missarum diversorum I* (1509, No.43)

Provenance: With *Missarum diversorum I* (1509) • An inscription on Cantus A1*r* perhaps reads] Soranus moncill

D-Mu, Cim.44ᵐ (2). Tenor and Bassus, complete

Size of page: 171 × 229 and 168 × 233 mm.

Watermarks:

T:	A3-4	A2	B6-5	B7-8	C1-2	C5-6		*B:*	A2	A4-3	B4-3	B8-7	C1-	C6-5	D8
	11	14	11	11	11	11			14	11	11	11	3	11	14

Technical comments: *B:* C4*r*.ii: text spacing sort, 3.9 × 2.7 mm • The part-names seem to have been printed with the staves: c.f. *B:* D4*r*

Corrections and changes:

In-house: *T:* B3*v*, B6*v* (4 changes); *B:* A4*r*, B5*r*, B7*r*, B7*v* (2 changes), C4*v*, C7*v* (2 changes) and C8*r.* see above

Later: *T:* Three ascriptions against the Tavola • Modal indications are entered against the pieces • A3*r*.iii.15 from the end: added *signum*, black ink • A3*v*.iii.34: added *signum*, black ink • A3*v*/4*r*.top, and A4*v*/5*v*.top:] Secu*n*da | Pars [and] Tertia pars [in an early hand, but not that of the modal indications • A8*v*.i.7–8: ligature: b,a → g,f, probably in the hand of the modal indication on the same page • B6*v*.headline:] Henricus Isaac [perhaps in Glarean's hand • C8*v*.iv.6: *f* → *sm*, by erasure • D5*v*.head:] Petrus de Therache [perhaps in Glarean's hand

> *B:* A3*r*.iii: *signum* below stave in black ink • A3*v*.iii: *signum* below stave in black ink • A4*r*.iii: another *signum*, entered below 13, erased and re-entered below 18 • A7*r*.ii.6 back: has a black ink "V" before it • B7*r*.heading:] Isaac [as in the Tenor • B7*v*.iv.right:] No 77 [in brown ink • C7*v*.iii.8 from end: *signum* in black ink • D2*r*.iii.4: *l* → *b*, by erasure of tail • D3*v*.v.last *l*: ?F or ?A → *bG* and a *l* tail, brown ink • D6*r*.i.6–7: *signum* above 7 struck through, and entered above 6, in brownish-grey ink

Binding: With *Missarum diversorum I* (1509, No.43)

Provenance: Glareanus • Egenolph

D-W, 2.8.Musica-2.8.3.Musica (3). Complete. This copy includes the cancel bifolium at C1,8, for which see below

Size of page: 173 × 244 mm.

Watermarks:

S:	A6-5	A7	B2-1	B4-3	C4-3	C-7	D5	D8-7	T:	A5-6	A7	B4-3
	11	14	11	11	11	11	3	11		11	14	11

B8-7	C5-6	C7-8	D3	D8-7	A:	A2	A4-3	B5-6	B7-8	C4-3	C8-7	D2	D8
11	11	11	3	11		14	11	11	11	11	11	3	11

B:	A6-5	A7	B2-1	B4-3	C6-5	C7	D3	D7-8
	11	14	11	11	11	3	3	14

Textual comments: *B:* D4*v.*first word:] Gande

Technical comments: The recurring use of staves remaining in the forme is evident in this copy: f.6*v* of all gatherings shows the same pattern, identical with that of 8*v* for all gatherings except *B:*C and D, where it is to be found on f.7*v* • *C:* A1*r* uses staves as uninked furniture • *T:* C3*v.*iv: spacing sort for the music

Corrections and changes:

In-house: *S:* B1*v*, B3*v*, B4*r*; *T:* B3*v*, B7*v*; *A:* foliation, B7*r*, C1*r* (2 changes), C1*v*, C4*v*; *B:* B7*r*, B7*v*, C7*v* (2 changes) and C8*r.* see above

Later: *S:* A1*v.*Tavola: added ascription] ij∫aac [not in the hand of the ownership ascription. The same hand enters the composer's name on the Tavola and relevant folio of each part-book, as listed below • B8*v.*head-line:] ijsaac [in brown ink

T: A1*v.*Tavola: added ascription] ij∫aac [in brown ink • B3*r.*ii.32: *sb*, probably merely over-inked, scratched void • B6*v.*head-line:] ijsaac [in brown ink • C7*v.*head-line:] 2.Reg*ni* j. [brown ink

A: A1*v.*Tavola: added ascription] ij∫aac [in brown ink • A3*v.*i.17: line through tail • B4*r.*ii.22: f', *dsb* → *sb*, by erasure • C1*r.*head-line:] ijsaac [in brown ink • C4*r.*signature: corrected • D5*r.*v.right margin: written] Ce*tus* tacet [in ink

B: A1*v.*Tavola: added ascription] ij∫aac [in brown ink • B7*r.*head-line:] ijsaac [in brown ink

Binding and Provenance: With *Fragmenta Missarum* (1505, No.24)

GB-Lbl, Hirsch.III.984. Cantus, complete. For the cancel leaves C1 and C8, see below

Size of page: 158 × 227 mm.

Watermarks: No.11 on A3-4, B1-2, B6-5, C-2 and C5-6 • No.14 on A7

Textual comments: A8*v*:] Co*n*nede [*sic*]

Technical comments: A1*r* and A1*v* both show the impress of uninked staves • B2*r.* spacing sorts, about the size of ems, have impressed in the space of the bottom stave

Corrections and changes:

In-house: B1*v*, B3*v*, B4*r*, B8*v*, C4*r.* see above

Later: C1*v.*ii.after 26: *sb* rest, in brown ink • C8*r.*iii.22: g' → a', by erasure and black ink

Binding: 16th-century Italian calf over boards. Stamped with seven copies of a maze design, in a cruciform pattern, within a border made of a repeated stamp, all in blind • Two conjugate end-papers at each end, with a watermark of a wheel (width 5.4 mm) on the first of each pair

Provenance: From the Hirsch collection • Inside the front board:] E.S.126[a]

Bibliography: Johnson and Scholderer, *Short-Title*, p. 454; Meyer and Hirsch, *Katalog*, iii. 984

GB-Lbl, K.1.d.4. Cantus, complete. For the cancel leaves C1 and C8, see below

    Size of page: 167 × 232 mm.

    Watermarks: No.11 on A3-4, B1-2, B3-4, C3-4 and C-7 • No.14 on A7-8 • No.3 on D3

    Textual comments: A8*v*:] Co*n*nede [*sic*].

    Technical comments: This copy is very close in condition to the other part-book at GB-Lbl
      • A1*r* and A1*v* both show the impress of uninked staves

    Corrections and changes:

      In-house: B1*v*, B3*v*, B4*r*, B8*v*, C4*r*: see above

      Later: There are several MS headings to pages, all in the same hand: A3*v*:] tertia pars [A4*r*:]
        Luca .3. prima pars [A4*v*:] Secu*n*da pars [A5*r*:] Tertia pars [and B8*v*:] ISAAC • C8*r*.iii.22:
        g' → a', by erasure and black ink

    Binding: Contemporary parchment over boards: three tie strings • One flyleaf, conjugate with
      a paste-down, at each end

    Provenance: British Museum stamp on D8*v*:] 19 JY [19]62 [• Earlier call numbers: inside front
      board:] 4'78 [and on f.[i]v:] A.633

    Bibliography: Johnson and Scholderer, *Short-Title*, p. 454

HR-Ssf. This copy has not been seen

    Technical comments: C2*r* lacks the opening initial • pieces of text furniture appear on A4*v*,
      B2*r*, B7*v* (headline) and C4*r* • Inking is inconsistent in several places

    Corrections and Changes:

      In-house: B7*v*: see above

      Later: Modern foliation, 33–64

    Binding: Bound with *Motetti IV* (No. 21)

I-Bc, Q.61. Cantus, complete. For the cancel C1,8, see below

    Size of page: 170 × 236 mm.

    Watermarks: No.11 on A4-3, B1-2, B6-5, C-2, C6-5 and D3-4 • No.14 on A8

    Technical comments: The impress of uninked staves on A1*r* and A1*v*

    In-house corrections and changes: B1*v*, B3*v*, B4*r*, B8*v* and C4*r*: see above

    Binding: Same modern wrapper and folders as found in the Bologna copy of Agricola's masses

    Provenance: Old call no. 1005

    Bibliography: Fava, "Primo", p. 38 (exhibition in Bologna in 1929) • Vernarecci, *Petrucci* p. 103

I-FPfanan. Altus, complete.

    Size of page: 158 × 228 mm.

    Watermarks: No.11 on B1-2, B5-6, C5-6 and C8-7 • No.14 on A8 • No marks in gathering
      D

    Corrections and changes:

      In-house: B7*r*, both on C1*r*, C1*v*, C4*r* and C4*v*: see above

      Later: Modern foliation, including the first flyleaf • A2*v*.iv.20: the stave-line is touched up,
        and the *sb* may have been changed, perhaps from e' to the present d' • D5*r*.v.over the
        clef:] cot⁹ tacet [in pale brown ink, but not in Petrucci's style • D6*v*.v.rests after 9: the
        last rest, *l* → *b*

    Binding: Bound with the Contratenor Primus of the *Motetti a cinque* (No.46) • Italian binding,
      perhaps Venetian, first half of the 16th-century, with a new spine • one paste-down and one
      flyleaf at each end, both modern

    Provenance: bought from a Parisian dealer in the 1960s • Front flyleaf verso has a call-mark of]
      F-I-3

I-Vnm, Mus.200–202. Cantus, Altus and Bassus, complete. Cantus C1,8 is a cancel: see below • It is possible that there is also a cancel at Bassus ff.D1,8. The only evidence for this is the pattern of stave-lengths, and perhaps the pattern of chain-lines in the paper. Since this evidence is not conclusive, these two folios are described here

Size of page: 170 × 236 mm.

Watermarks:

C:	A4-3	A7-8	B1-2	B4-3	C-2	C5-6	D3	A:	A3-4	A7	B5-6	B8-7	C1-2
	11	14	11	11	11	11	3		11	14	11	11	11

	C5-6	D2	D7	B:	A2	A6-5	B1-2	B6-5	C4-3	C1
	11	3	3		14	11	11	11	11	14

Technical comments: For the stave measurements in this copy, see below

Corrections and changes:

In-house: S: B1v, B3v, B4r, C4r; A: foliation, B7r, C1r (2 changes), C1v, C4r; B: B5r, B7r, B7v (2 changes), C4r, C4v, C7v (2 changes) and C8r: see above

Later: S: C8r.iii.22: b, g' → a', erased and black ink • A: A3v.i.17; line through tail • C4r.signature corrected

Binding: From the Austrian National Library • One paste-down and one flyleaf at each end

Provenance: The A-Wn call number] SA.77.C.24 [inside the front board is partly concealed by the new I-Vnm call number: an A-Wn library stamp appears in the books (cf. Coggiola, "Ricupero") • There are also the numbers A.N.47.D.24, with the number 47 changed to 24, and the whole struck through and replaced by 35.E.121

Bibliography: Fenlon and Dalla Vecchia, *Venezia*, p. 76 (exhibition catalogue, Venice, 2001)

I-VENsl, s.s. Tenor, Altus, and Bassus books, complete, though defective. Skillfully restored by the Abbazia di Viboldone. I am grateful to Massimo Gentili Tedeschi for arranging my access to this copy

Size of page: 167 × 237 mm.

Watermarks: A number of folios, including much of the Altus, are damaged in the area of the watermark, resulting in gaps in the following table:

T:	A5-6	A7	B6-5	B7-8	C2-1	C4-3	D4	A:	A3-4	B1-2	B3-4	C1-2	C5-6
	11	14	11	11	11	11	11		11	11	11	11	11

	D6-	B:	A2-1	A4-3	B2-1	B4-3	C5-6	D1-
	11		14	14	11	11	11	14

Textual comments: T: C6r. foliation reads] 2 • B: a damaged *m* tail, with a pronounced curve to the left, can be seen in several places, including B4v and C6v

Technical comments: B: C4r.ii: a text spacing sort, measuring c.4 × 2 mm.

Corrections and changes:

In-house: T: B3v; A:: C1r, C1v, C4v and D3r; B: A4v, B5r, B7r, B7v, C1v, C4v, C7v, C8r, D3v, and D6r: see above

Later: T: B4v.iv.34: *sb* → *m*, with up-tail in ginger ink • B4v.iv.41: e', *m* → *dsb*, with an erased tail, and a ginger ink point • B4v.iv.50–51: originally *2m*, g,f: the first has the tail erased, and the second the note-head erased, implying *sbg* • D8 is largely missing: the recto shows clefs on staves iii–v, and the start of a word below stave iv: all in ginger ink

A: C3v.ii.35: erased *sb*, f' • D5r.v: added word in brown ink] Cotᵃtnor • D6v.v.rests after 9: *sb,l,l,l*: last *l* → *b*, by erasure • D9v.ii.9: the ink line through the note was an accident: see the blot in the next system • D10v: at the top of the page is a single stave with a four-voiced cadential figure: it presents three chords in black notation, on c, f and d. This appears to be in a later 16th-century hand

B: A3*v*.iii.after 16: an added *m*,g, in a different brown ink from that used elsewhere • D2*r*.iii.4: *l* → *b*. by erasure

Binding: Original leather covers to boards are glued to a modern binding. Each carries the part-initial in gold on the front and back, inside plain panels, probably stamped • Originally three tie-strings for each board, leaving merely holes in the boards • The boards themselves are detached and loose, apparently made of about 12 layers of paper • An original fly-leaf bifolio for the Tenor is also detached: one for the Bassus is bound in

Provenance: *A:* flyleaf:] Antonius nomine | Petrus Hunc po[sidet | Librum | de Musonis [and] Hunc po[sidet libru*m* Antonius no*m*ine | petrus de Musonis • D10*v*:] Hic liber intere[t mea[?] p*re*bite*r*i petri Ant*onio* bataliensis de Musonis | de Mugia[cha

B: flyleaf:] 1523 Ildi 9. a nov 22 de Julio novite D. pre Thiburtío Brébilla rector de S^to | Georgio in rauagnate. • *B:* D4*r*, foot:] Hic liber po[sidetur a p*re*sbite*r*o petro Ant*onio* bataliensi de Musonis | de Mugiascha

Muggiasca is the present name of the area around the town of Vendrogno, taking its name from a nearby Mount Múggio, and lying east of the Lecco branch of Lake Como. Rovagnate is a small town between Lecco and Milan

SI-Ka, s.s. Altus, complete.

Size of page: 169 × 239 mm.

Watermarks: No.11 on A4-3, B2-1, B3-4, C2-1 and C6-5 • No.14 on A7-8 • No.3 on D1

Technical comments: A2*v*: the music was printed before the text • A number of text spacing sorts are visible, e.g. on A4*v*.v and C5*v* • B1*r*: the head-line was printed with the text and staves

Corrections and changes:

In-house: B7*r*, C1*v* and C4*v*: see above

Later: B4*r*.ii.22: *dsb*,f: the dot erased • B5*v*.iii.53: after the note, a dividing rule, in pale brown ink • D4*v*.vi.4: the original note, ?*m*,g': now filled in and a small black *sb*,f' added after, all in black ink • D5*r*.v, above bar-lines and m.s.:] Cont*ra*tenor [in brown ink

Binding and Provenance: Bound behind an Altus of *Motetti Libro quarto* (1505, No.21)

US-Tm, Acc.55.30. Cantus, complete. For the cancel leaves, see below

Size of page: 169 × 238 mm.

Watermarks: No.11 on A-43, B1-2, B5-6, C-2, and C3-4 • No.14 on A7-8 • No.3 on D2 and D3

Corrections and changes:

In-house: B1*v*, B3*v*, B4*r*, and B8*v*: see above

Binding: 19th-century red half-leather over marbled paper boards. The spine stamped in gold with a fleur-de-lys and] MOTET | TI | SEC. | XVI • At each end a marbled paper pastedown and conjugate fly-leaf. At the front, a further fly-leaf, perhaps 18th-century, with a mark of a double turreted tower and the letters] M S

Provenance: Inside the front board, the bookplate of Landau-Finaly, and the number 6419 • A price in Lire appears on D8*r* • Bought by Toledo from the auction XXV (26.v.1955) of L'Art Ancien S.A. of Zurich, Lot no.582

Bibliography: Exhibited at Toledo, OH, in 1957. See Barksdale, *Printed*, No.70, with one page illustrated

No. 15a. *Cancel*

A bifolium printed as a cancel for Cantus folios C1 and C8

Technical comments: The stave lines show a consistent layout, indicating that the half-sheet was printed by work and turn

In-house corrections: C1*v*.ii.after 26: a second *sb* rest was added in a stop-press correction: the uncorrected version is at GB-Lbl (both copies), I-Bc and US-Tm (all with a manuscript correction, probably made in house), and the corrected is in the copy at D-Mbs • C8*r*.iii.22: *sb* → *b*, a manuscript change in the copies at D-W, I-Bc and I-Vnm, but stamped-in in the copies at D-Mbs, GB-Lbl (both copies), and US-Tm

———

Extant copies: For the rest of each copy, see the descriptions above

D-Mbs, 4°.Mus.pr.160/2

No watermark visible.

In-house changes: C1*v* and C8*r*: see above

D-W, 2.8.Musica (3)

Watermark: No.14 on C8.

In-house changes: C8*r*: see above

GB-Lbl, Hirsch.III.984

No watermark visible.

In-house changes: C1*v* and C8*r*: see above

GB-Lbl, K.1.d.4

No watermark visible.

Technical comments: C8*v* lacks its initial capital letter [M].

In-house changes: C1*v* and C8*r*: see above

I-Bc, Q.61

Watermark: No.14 on C8

In-house changes: C1*v* and C8*r*: see above

I-Vnm, Mus.200

Watermark: No.14 on C8

In-house changes: C8*r*: see above

US-Tm, Acc.55.30

No watermark visible

In-house changes: C1*v* and C8*r*: see above

———

Lost copies: A copy was bought by Colón in Rome, ii.1513 (Chapman, "Printed", No.10) • There was a copy in the Fugger collection (Schaal, "Musikbibliothek", No.I/51)

Early references: Aaron cites this book specifically, in Chapter 6 of his *Trattato* (1525) (see Judd, "Reading")

Bibliography:

(a) Rosaria Boccadifuoco, *Bibliografia*, No.2354 • Sartori, *Petrucci*, No.15

(b) Brunet, *Manuel*, iii, cols.1924–1925

(c) Petrucci, *Motetti C*

(d) Sherr, *16th-Century*, ii

(e) Adamson, *Petrucci* • Jeppesen, "Neuentdeckte", p. 76 • Sartori, "Nuove", pp. 178–81

Commentary:

1. The evidence of the distribution of papers argues that the four part-books were set simultaneously.

Sheet	Copy	AI	AII	BI	BII	CI	CII	DI	DII	DIII
Superius:	D-Mbs	14	11	11	11	11	11	—	—	
	D-W	14	11	11	11	11	11	11	3	
	GB-Lbl (1)	11	14	11	11	11	11	—	—	
	GB-Lbl (2)	11	14	11	11	11	11	—	3	
	I-Bc	14	11	11	11	11	11	—	11	
	I-Vnm	14	11	11	11	11	11	—	3	
	US-Tm	14	11	11	11	11	11	3	3	
Tenor:	D-Mbs	14	11	11	11	11	11	—	—	
	D-Mu	14	11	11	11	11	11	—	—	
	D-W	14	11	11	11	11	11	11	3	
Altus:	D-Mbs	14	11	11	11	11	11	—	—	—
	D-W	14	11	11	11	11	11	3	3	—
	I-Vnm	14	11	11	11	11	11	3	3	—
Bassus:	D-Mbs	14	14	11	11	11	11	14	—	
	D-Mu	14	11	11	11	3	11	14	—	
	D-W	14	11	11	11	3	11	3	3	
	I-Vnm	14	11	11	11	14	11	—	—	

    I suspect that two typesetters were involved, one having responsibility for the first two parts, and the other dealing with Altus and Bassus. In both cases, the outer sheet of gathering A will have been sent to the press last (whenever the bulk of it was set in type), for it contains the Tavola with folio numbers. This helps to explain the presence of paper 14 here and in the cancel, as well as at the end of the Bassus. This paper was, in any case, new to Petrucci.

2. The appearance of paper 3 and an apparently unmarked paper, late in the book, represents no more than a shift in paper stock as paper 11 ran low. The change in papers occurs at different places, with the Altus and Bassus running out of paper 11 first. This also suggests two presses, probably working one for each typesetter. After the stock of paper 11 was exhausted, the presses apparently used up various other stocks, for different copies have different papers for the same sheets, in the same settings.

    Further, it is not possible to argue that either paper represents a later series of cancels. They both appear on the outer sheet of the Bassus gathering D, which includes the colophon carrying this date.

3. The pattern of setting in this manner explains the foliation mistake in the Altus: the numbers were retained from one part to the next, and no allowance was made for the extra half-sheet needed in that part-book.

4. The pattern of staves in the Venice copy shows that there were probably only two formes in use for this title:

    α) 179 180 179 181:   *S:* AIo; AIIo; BIo; BIIo; CIo; CIIo; DIo; DIIo
                            A: AIo; AIIo; BIo; BIIo; CIo; CIIo; DIo; DIIo; DIII
                            B: AIo; AIIo; BIo; BIIo; CIi; CIIo; DIi; DIIo

    β) 176 176 176 175   *S:* AIi; AIIi; BIi; BIIi; CIi; CIIi; DIi; DIIi
                            A: AIi; AIIi; BIi; BIIi; CIi; CIIi; DIi; DIIi
                            B: AIi; AIIi; BIi; BIIi; CIo; CIIi; DIo; DIIi

The detailed measurements are as follows:

	1r	2v	7r	8v	2r	1v	8r	7v	3r	4v	5r	6v	4r	3v	6r	5v
S: A	—	180	179	181	177	—	176	176	179	181	179	180	176	176	175	176
B	179	180	179	181	176	176	175	176	179	181	179	181	175	176	175	176
C	179	180	179	181	176	181	179	176	179	181	179	181	176	176	175	177
D	179	180	179	—	176	176	176	177	179	180	179	180	176	176	176	176
A: A	—	179	179	18	177	—	176	177	179	180	179	181	176	176	175	176
B	179	181	180	179	176	176	176	177	179	181	179	181	176	177	176	177
C	[—]	180	180	[—]	176	[—]	[—]	176	180	180	179	181	175	176	175	176
D		(9r	10v)			(10v	9r)			(7r	8v)			(8r	7v)	
	179	180	179	—	176	176	176	176	179	180	179	181	176	176	175	176
	(5r	5v	6r	6v)												
	179	180	179	181												
B: A	—	180	179	181	176	—	176	176	179	181	179	181	176	176	175	176
B	180	181	179	181	176	176	176	176	179	181	179	181	176	176	175	176
C	176	176	176	176	179	181	179	181	180	180	179	180	175	176	175	176
D	176	176	176	—	179	176	—	181	179	180	179	180	176	176	176	177

The pattern suggests a very simple and straightforward sequence of work throughout the book, consisting of the alternation of two formes, with a minor change at the end of the Bassus. That this change is not very significant can be inferred from the point already made, that the first sheet of gatherings A of all books were printed last, coupled with the fact that the normal sequence returns for these sheets.

It is rather surprising that only two formes of stave should be used throughout a volume. However, there is relatively little text set for this repertoire (and, indeed, some pages have no more than a verbal incipit), so that the setting of a page with staves already in the forme and few words of text would take very little time, especially when put beside the time required for setting the music. It is therefore plausible that each forme of text could have been set and run off during the setting of the same forme of music.

5.   One significant implication of the use of only two formes of staves is that it seems to require some measure of casting-off. In fact, there is some other evidence to support this idea. The late setting of the outer sheet of each gathering A is supported by the distribution of the music on those pages. Each part-book begins every part of the motets on a fresh page as far as folio A4v, despite the waste in unused staves (five each in Superius and Bassus): the same pattern prevails for folios A7-8. However, the middle of the gathering shows a very different pattern. In each voice, parts begin in the middle of lines and pieces in the middle of pages. The evidence suggests that an attempt at casting off was made, leaving folios A1,2,7,8 unset. The material for the middle four folios (the inner sheet) was set, loosely at first, but increasingly tightly towards the end. (Neither the Altus or the Bassus has any blank staves on these folios.) There is similar, though much weaker, evidence from the later gatherings. It is possible, too, that the pattern of the adoption of paper 3 implies cast-off text and setting by formes in gatherings D of each part-book.

6.   The same pattern of staves indicates that the half-sheet at the centre of Altus gathering D was printed by work and turn, using the forme with long staves.

7.   The one anomaly in the chart of stave lengths lies in the Cantus outer sheet of gathering C, where there was evidently a cancel. The following lists two additional copies for that bifolio:

	C1r	C8v	C1v	C8r	C2r	C7v	C2v	C7r
GB-Lbl	177	178	177	178	174	173	178	177
I-Bc	178	178	178	179	175	175	180	178
I-Vnm	179	181	179	181	176	176	179	179

This is a classic example of the effect of producing a work-and-turn cancel bifolium. The stave-lengths on C2,7 show the patterns of a set of long staves backed by a set of shorter ones, that characterise Petrucci's work at this stage. The patterns for C1,8 imply the same set of staves on both sides.

8.   There seems to be a surprising number of penitential and "release-from-trouble" motets. Among them, in particular, is the anonymous No.14, whose text refers to a city in trouble. *Civitatem istam tu circunda domine et angeli tui custodiant muros eius. Exaudi domine populum tuum cum misericordia avertatur furor tuus domine a populo tuo et a civitate sancta tua.* An obvious candidate for such an anonymous work would be Venice itself, still reeling from the effects of the naval battle of Zonchio, and facing increasing hostility from the great powers.

9.   A number of works or *partes* are very poorly texted. There is no text beyond an incipit, for example, for the Bassus of No.11, or the second pars of No.10.

10.   The presence of a four-part figure, looking like a *falsobordone* sequence, on the last folio of the Altus of the books at I-VENsl, suggests that these books were used in a performing institution. Since the books were in small hill-towns east of Lake Como, certainly by 1523, and have been there ever since, it seems that polyphony may have been practised in these towns: with the music notated at the back of a book of complex settings, we can not restrict that polyphony to simple *cantus planus binatim* and *falso bordone*. The notation is certainly from later in the 16th-century, and is possibly in the same ink as the addition to the Bassus G3*v*, and the blot on the Altus D9*v*.

No. 16. *Frottole I*

28.xi.1504   *RISM* 1504[4]

There are cancel sheets for A inner, B outer and E outer, described below

Edition

A1*r*]   Frottole libro | primo.

G8*r*]   Impreſſum Venetiis per Octauianum Pe-|trutium Foroſempronienſem. Die. xxviii. No- | uembris Salutis anno M.ccccciiii. Cu*m* pri-|uilegio inuictiſſimi Dominii Venetiar*um* q*uae* nul | lus poſſit cantum Figuratum imprimere ſub | pena in ip ſo priuilegio contenta. | Regiſtrum. | ABCDEFG Omnes quaterni. | [Petrucci's device]

A1*v*]   [Tavola:] Numero ſeſantadoi

Format and collation: Choirbook: landscape quarto-in-eights. 56 folios: A-G[8]

Signatures:] Aii [$4 • -A1

Foliation:] [I], II-LV, [LVI]

Composers' names appear in the head-line

Part-names: in the left margin, to be read downwards from the top of the page:

recto:]	Tenor Altus Baſſus	[A2, B5-6, B8, F4-7
	Altus Baſſus	[A3-B4, B7, C1-F3, F8-G7
	[Nil:	A1, G8
verso:]	Tenor	[A2-B3, B6, B8-F2, F7-G6

Tenor Altus Ba∫∫us   [B4-5, B7, F3-6, G7

[Nil: A1, G8

Fonts: Music: Petrucci's normal music type

Staves: In theory, six per page, 178–180 mm long, 10-92.5-113 high: in practice almost always only five staves are printed

Text: Roman, for all except title: "x" = 1.7.mm, "20" = 57 mm.

Textual comments: A8r. the text reads] ue*n*duto [and] ∫pera*n*za • B8r.text: que ∫ta

Technical comments: The appearance of a small type initial for the start of a composition on F4r is the result of having only one "I" in the case, which had been used on F3v • The staves are consistently used in two formes throughout the volume: there is some evidence that gathering A was printed last, at least for the impression of staves and text • The composer's names are at a consistent height above the staves, and may have been part of that forme, with texts

In-house corrections: B2r.iv.33: added in ink: both copies • B2r.v.5 and 9: touched up in brown ink: both copies • B2r.v.18: *signum* in brown ink: both copies

Contents: The final column shows the folio number as entered in the Tavola:

	A1r	[Title]		
	A1v	[Tavola]		
1	A2r	ALma ∫uegliate hormai	IO.BROC.	ii
2	A2v	OIme el cor oime la te∫ta	MARCVS CARA VERO.	iii
3	A3v	NOn e tempo da∫pectare	M.C.	iiii
4	A4v	DEfecerunt donna hormai	M.C.	v
5	A5v	O Mia cieca e dura ∫orte	M.C.	vi
6	A6v	HOr uenduto ho la ∫peranza	M.C.	vii
7	A7v	SE no*n* hai per∫erueranza	M.C.	viii
8	A8v	SE de fede hor uengo a meno	M.C.	ix
9	B1v	IO no*n* co*m*pro piu ∫peranza	M.C.	x
10	B2v	IN eterno io uoglio amarte	M.C.	xi
11	B3v	GLie pur gionto el giorno aime	M.C.	xii
		[A:] Non ual aqua al mio gran foco		
12	B4v	VDite uoi fine∫tre	M.C.	xiii
13	B5r	Si come chel bia*n*cho cigno	M.C.	xiii
		[S:] COme chel bia*n*cho . . .		
14	B5v	CHi me dara piu pace	M.C.	xiiii
15	B6r	PIeta cara ∫ignora	M.C.	xiiii
16	B6v	DEh ∫i deh no deh ∫i	M.C.	xv
17	B7v	LA fortuna uoi co∫∫i	M.C.	xvi
18	B8r	AYme che doglia e que∫ta	IOANNES BROCCHVS VERO.	xvi
19	B8v	SCopri li*n*gua el cieco ardore	BARTHOLOMEVS TRVMBONCINVS VERO.	xvii
		[T,A,B:] Scopri o lingua		
20	C1v	NOn ual aqua al mio gra*n* foco	B.T.	xviii
21	C2v	SE ben hor no*n* ∫copro	B.T.	xix
22	C3v	SE mi e graue el tuo pa*r*tire	B.T.	xx
		[Tav:] Se mi e grato . . .		
23	C4v	VAle diua mia ua in pace	B.T.	xxi
24	C5v	POi chel ciel co*n*trario	B.T.	xxii
25	C6v	CRudel come mai pote∫ti	B.T.	xxiii

26	C7*v*	DEh perdio non me far torto	B.T.	xxiiii
27	C8*v*	POi che lalma per fe molta	B.T.	xxv
28	D1*v*	EL conuera chio mora	B.T.	xxvi
29	D2*v*	BEn che amor mi faccia torto	B.T.	xxvii
30	D3*v*	[T:] DAl lecto me leuaua	MICHAEL.	xxviii
		[S: line 2] ALhor quando		
31	D4*v*	AH partiale e cruda morte	B.T.	xxix
32	D5*v*	LAqua uale al mio gran foco	MICHAEL.	xxx
33	D6*v*	PIu che mai o fofpir fieri	B.T.	xxxi
34	D7*v*	A La guerra	B.T.	xxxii
35	D8*v*	ARdo e brufcio e tu noi fenti	MICHAEL PESENTVS VERO.	xxxiii
36	E1*v*	DIme un pocho che uol dire	MICHAEL.	xxxiiii
37	E2*v*	SEmpre le come effer fole	MICHAELIS Cantus & u	xxxv
38	E3*v*	POi chel ciel e la fortuna	MICHA. C. & V.	xxxvi
39	E4*v*	SIo fon ftato a ritornare	MICHA. C. & V.	xxxvii
40	E5*v*	O Dio che la brunetta mia	MICHA. C. & V.	xxxviii
41	E6*v*	FVggir uoglio el tuo bel uolto	MICHA. C. & V.	xxxix
42	E7*v*	SI me piace el dolce foco	MICHA. C. & V.	xl
		[Headed:] A uoce mutate		
43	E8*v*	QVefta e mia lho fatta mi	MICHAELIS C. & V.	xli
44	F1*v*	AIhme chio moro	MICHA.	xlii
45	F2*v*	NOn mi doglio gia damore	MICHA.	xliii
46	F3*v*	IN hofpitas per alpes	MICHA.	xliiii
47	F4*r*	INteger uitae fcelerifque	MICHA.	xliiii
48	F4*v*	PAffando per una rezolla	MICHA.	xlv
49	F5*r*	TRifta e noiofa forte	MICHA.	xlv
50	F5*v*	SE in tutto hai deftinato	MICHA.	xlvi
51	F6*r*	BEn mille uolte al di	MICHA.	xlvi
		[Headed:] MODVS DICENDI CAPITVLA.		
52	F6*v*	VNa legiadra donna	MICHA.	xlvii
53	F7*r*	TV te lamenti a torto	MICHA.	xlvii
54	F7*v*	VIeni hormai non piu tardar	MICHA.	xlviii
55	F8*v*	ADio fignora adio	MICHA.	xlix
56	G1*v*	IN te domine fperaui	IOSQVIN DASCANIO	l
57	G2*v*	DOnna afcolta el tuo amatore	D. ANTONIO RIGVM.	li
58	G3*v*	SE me amafti quanto io te amo	GEORGIVS DE LA PORTA VERO.	lii
59	G4*v*	NAqui al mondo per ftentare	FRANCISCVS ANNA VENETVS.	liii
60	G5*v*	SE me e grato el tuo tornare	PHILIPPVS DE LVRANO	liiii
61	G6*v*	VOglio gir chiamando morte	GEORGIVS LVPPATVS	lv
62	G7*v*	POi che per fede mancha	ANTONIVS CAPREOLVS BRIXIENSIS	lv
	G8*r*	[Privilege; Colophon; Device]		
	G8*v*	[blank]		

Extant copies:

A-Wn, S.A.77.C.2 (1). Complete. Three sheets, A inner, B outer, and E outer, are cancels, and are described below

    Size of page: 166 × 237 mm.

Watermarks: No.11 on A2-1, B3-4, C1-2, C4-3, D6-5, D7-8, E6-5, F4-3, F8-7, G3-4 and G7-8

Textual comments: B8r.text: que[ta

Technical comments: Six staves only printed on D3v-4r, G5r and G6v-7r, four staves on F3v-7r and G1r

In-house Corrections: B2r. see above

Binding: Fugger binding. On front board:] FROTT: L: PR • One fly-leaf and conjugate paste-down at each end, bearing a watermark also found in the Fugger copies of Josquin's masses

Provenance: From the Fugger collection

Bibliography: Fenlon and Dalla Vecchia, *Venezia*, pp. 74–75 (exhibition catalogue, Venice, 2001)

D-Mbs, Rar.878/1. Complete

Size of page: 159 × 228 mm.

Watermarks: No.11 A6-5, B2-1, B6-5, C4-3, C7-8, D2-1, D4-3, E2-1, E6-5, F2-1, F5-6, G4-3 and G8-7

Technical comments: B8r. the part name Ba[[us has not taken ink properly • D2r.i.text: spacing sort, measuring 2.7 × 1.3 mm • F2r.signature line: spacing sort, measuring 2.8 × 0.8 mm • G2v: extra text printed with the music, on the evidence of the quality of impression

Corrections and changes:

In-house: B2r. see above

Later: Modern pencil foliation:] 1–56 • B2r.v.21: apparently *m* tail erased and redrawn, brown ink • B2r.v.26: *l*, B → d, erasure and brown ink • B4v.iii.13: *sm* → *m*, by erasure • B6v.v.before 13 from end: bar-line in grey-brown ink • C4r.i.before 8 from end: bar-line in grey-brown ink • F4r.i.after 6 from end: rule in grey ink • F4r.ii.5 from end: *m*, tail struck through, and rule on either side of notes 4 and 5, grey ink • F4r.iii.4 and 5 from end: 2*m* tails struck through, grey ink • F4r.iv.after last note: *sb*g and initials • G5r.iv. after 4 from end and before rule: *sb*A, in grey-brown ink

Binding: Books 1–9 of frottole are bound together in two volumes (1–5 and 6–9) in original dark calf Bavarian bindings, with rolls and flowers in the corner • One modern paste-down and conjugate fly-leaf, plus one early fly-leaf at front

Provenance: Bookplate of the Elector of Bavaria's library inside front board • Bookplate of the Duke of Bavaria, dated 1618, inside back board • Earlier call nos: Mus.Inc.4; 4°.Mus.pr.120; Mus.N.74

E-Mprivate. I have not been able to consult this copy, which is apparently bound with copies of the second and third books of frottole, and a manuscript of Spanish secular music

No. 16A. *Cancel.*

Sheets for A inner, B outer and E outer: contents and layout as above

Technical comments: Only four staves are inked on B7v • Minims used as bearer sorts for the musical forme at the level of the sixth stave on B7r, and perhaps also on other rectos • The differences between the original version of these pages and the cancel are mainly technical: the most obvious are the redistribution of the material on B7v so that there is no blank stave between the Tenor and the Altus, and the changed initials on B8r, B8v and E7v

Textual comments: A5r.iv: the addition of the word "Defecerunt" • For textual changes from the first issue of these sheets, see Schwartz, *Ottaviano*

For other details, see above

Extant copy:

A-Wn, S.A.77.C.2 (1). Three sheets, A inner, B outer and E outer. For the rest of the volume, see above

> **Watermarks:** Paper 23 on A5, B2 and E8
>
> **In-house Corrections:** B2r.iv.33: added, in ink • B2r.v.5 and 9: touched up in brown ink • B2r.v.18: *signum* in brown ink
>
> For other details, see above

Lost copies: Colón had a copy:] Frotole li°. p°. n°. 62. V. 1504. 4a [Chapman, "Printed", No.11 • According to Fétis, a copy was owned by a Herr Butsch, bookseller of Augsburg, and another was in Landsberg

Bibliography:

(a) Rosaria Boccadifuoco, *Bibliografia*, No.1451 • Sartori, *Petrucci*, No.16; Jeppesen, *La Frottola*, Pe I; Vogel, *Bibliografia*, 1504[1]

(b) Brunet, *Manuel*, ii, col.1412

(d) Cesari, *Frottole* (1954); Schwartz, *Ottaviano*

(e) Jeppesen, *La Frottola*, i, 15–19 and 78–81 • Vogel, *Bibliothek*, p. 604, lists minor variants in the copy at A-Wn, which "prove it a later publication". The same information is in Schwartz, *Ottaviano*, p. v and Jeppesen, *La Frottola*, i,16

Commentary:

1. This publication launches a new aspect of Petrucci's output, that of the series of frottole volumes which occupied him intensively at times, and were to become a significant part of his normal activities. This first volume should therefore give us some idea of the stimuli to the series, and perhaps also of the outside sources for his music. This issue is discussed in detail in chapter 9, where I suggest a new supplier, rather than Castellanus, and one particularly interested in music of Veronese composers, with the addition of others working in the Veneto. (Apart from d'Ana, Lupato may also be Venetian, for a Pietro Lupato was later employed at San Marco, according to Luisi, *Laudario*, i, p. 456.) Equally important is the pattern of arrangement of the music itself, which suggests that the last gathering represents an addition to the original plan (for which see also Boorman, "Printed", pp. 2597–2598). Even the first layers, devoted to a single composer, were probably drawn from more than one earlier source, for there is no sign of an internal arrangement.

2. The pattern of providing ascriptions wherever possible is significant. I have already remarked, in commenting on the *Odhecaton A* of 1501, that Petrucci (or his editor) was following a pattern in which most pieces were associated primarily with their textual incipits, and not automatically with their composers. This does not seem to be true for the frottole, at least as far as Petrucci's house was concerned. It must be unlikely that all these texts had been set so often that each setting needed to be associated with its composer. Nor can we argue, as might have been possible not many years earlier, that the compositions were largely the work of the poets of the texts. We therefore have here one more sign of the manner in which the frottola held a position very different, in the minds of musicians and audience, from that of the chanson — and also, incidentally, from that of the early madrigal.

3. The pattern of using notes as bearer sorts on rectos does not carry over to the versos, because

added text was printed there. Apparently the additional verses were not printed in the same forme as the underlaid text (where they would clash with uninked staves retained in the forme), but with the musical impression: cf. the inking on A2v, A3v, B7v, etc. See also E3v, where the added text under stave v could not have been printed with the stave: the text font has a body height of *ca*.2.95 mm, but the three words *Per un cor* are only 2.5 mm above the stave-line below.

4. The in-house changes on the first sheet of gathering B survive in both copies, even though that sheet in the Vienna copy is of a later impression. All the common changes appear on one page, B2r, so that it might appear that only the outer forme of that sheet had been reset. However, a cursory glance confirms that, as the paper evidence suggests, the whole sheet was set and printed later. This is further evidence that Petrucci's men used sheets from earlier editions as copy for later ones.

5. The cancel leaves were printed sometime during 1507 or 1508. There is not really enough evidence to locate them more closely, but 1507 was a busy year in Petrucci's output. In assigning these leaves to the late summer of 1508, I am guided principally by the pattern of paper use during that year: it seems to me most likely that these sheets would have been used for cancels at a time when they were in plentiful supply in the shop. In effect, this means in the early months of 1508 or during the summer of the same year. At the beginning of the year, Petrucci's shop was busy with new editions, whereas there is a significant gap after the production of the second edition of Dammonis's *Laude*, and before the first book of five-voiced motets. This paper was in use for both those editions, as well as for books on either side of them. In the absence of stronger evidence (for example, from the state of the initials), I have placed these leaves in that empty period.

6. As a result, we should ask whether these sheets are the sole remains of a complete second edition. Books II, III and IV had all received second editions within the previous twelve months or so, and it is evident, from the presence of Book IX early in 1509, that the genre was continuing to sell. On the other hand, while Colón bought copies of the second editions of the other three books, he had the 1504 edition of Book I. This tends to argue that Petrucci and his suppliers were still selling that edition, in other words that a second had not yet become necessary.

No. 17. *Frottole II*

8.i.1504/5 *RISM* 1505[3]

First Edition

A1r] Frottole libro | secondo

G8r] Impre[[um Venetiis per Octauianum Pe-|trutium Foro [empronien [em. Die .viii. Ianua-|rii Salutis anno M.ccccciiii. Cum priui-|legio inuicti[[imi Dominii Venetiarum quae nul-|lus po[[it cantum Figuratum imprimere [ub | pena in ip[o priuilegio contenta. | Regi[trum. A B C D E F G Omnes quaterni. | [Petrucci's Device]

A1v] [Tavola:] Numero cinquantatre

Format and collation: Choirbook: landscape quarto-in-eights. 56 folios: A-G[8]
Signatures:] aA IIII [$4 • -A1
Foliation: top right recto:] [I], II-LV, [LVI]
Part-names:

    recto:]   Tenor Altus Ba[[us   [A2, D3,4, F8-G1, G3

	Altus Baſſus	[A3-D2, D5-F7, G2,4-7
	[Nil:	A1, G8
verso:]	Tenor	[A2-D1, D4-F6, G1,3-6
	Tenor Altus Baſſus	[D2,3, F7,8, G2,7
	[Nil:	A1, G8

In a number of cases, smaller initial letters are used for the part-names. For example, a small capital B for the word Bassus appears on ff.2r and 4r of all gatherings

Fonts: Music: Petrucci's music type

Staves: Six per page, though often fewer

Text: Roman

Technical comments: D2v: the text incipits and staves were not set with the added text

In-house corrections, after press work: All these are extant in the unique copy: B6r.i.11: f' → f, by erasure and stamping in • B6r.ii.3: f' → f, by erasure and stamping in • B6r.ii.17: m, e → d, erasure and stamping in • B6r.v.24: b, c → B, erasure and stamping in

Contents: The last column gives the folio number entered in the Tavola:

	A1r	[Title]		
	A1v	[Tavola]		
1	A2r	DA poi chel tuo bel uiso	R.M.	II.
2	A2v	LA mia uita liberale	FRAN.VENE.ORGA.	iii.
	A3v	2/ A tuo modo affligi e stratia		
3	A4v	QVeſte quel locho amore	FRANCISCVS VENE ORGA.	v.
4	A5v	SOn quel troncho ſenza foglia	[Anon.]	vi.
5	A6v	SPero hauer felicita	[Anon.]	vii.
6	A7v	NOn ſo perche non mora	P.C.V.	viii.
7	A8v	COn la rete cogli el uento	FRAN.VENE.ORGA.	ix.
8	B1v	NAſce laſpro mio tormento	FRAN.VENE.ORGA.	x.
9	B2v	VEdo ben chio perdo el tempo	[Anon.]	xi.
10	B3v	OCchi mei troppo guardaſti	[F]RANCISCVS VENE. ORGA.	xii.
	B4v	2/ Ligiermente o cor credeſti		
11	B5v	OCchi dolci oue prendeſti	FRANCISCVS VENETVS ORGA.	xiiii.
	B6v	2/ Sel mio ben da uoi deriua		
12	B7v	FAmme pur quel che ti pare	[Anon.]	xvi.
13	B8v	GLiochi toi macceſel core	FRAN.VEN.ORGA.	xvii.
14	C1v	SErra dura mia partita	[Anon.]	xviii.
	C2v	2/ Sel partir me ferra forte		
15	C3v	Occhi mei al pianger nati	[Anon.]	xx.
16	C4v	SE lamor in te e pocho	[Anon.]	xxi.
17	C5v	ITe caldi ſuſpiri mei	[Anon.]	xxii.
18	C6v	DIo ſa quanto me doglio	[Anon.]	xxiii.
19	C7v	VIuo lieto nel tormento	[Anon.]	xxiiii.
20	C8v	SI non poſſo il cor placarte	[Anon.]	xxv
		[Tavola:] Sio . . .		
21	D1v	OChii mei frenati el pianto	PEREGRINVS CESENA VERONENSIS	xxvi.
22	D2v	HAi laſſa me meſchina	P.C.V.	xxvii.
23	D3r	OYme che ho per ſo il core	P.C.V.	xxvii.
24	D3v	O Dolce diua mia	P.C.V.	xxviii.
25	D4r	CHe piu felice ſorte	ANTONIVS ROSSETVS VERONENSIS.	xxviii.

26	D4v	LA pieta chiuſo ha le porte	B.T.	xxix.
	D5v	2/ Certo naſcer non douea		
27	D6v	TV me uoi crudel laſſare	[Anon.]	xxxi.
28	D7v	LIrum bililirum	ROSSINVS MANTVANVS	xxxii.
		[Headed:] Vn ſonar de piua in fachineſco		
29	D8v	GLiochi toi mhan poſto	B.T.	xxxiii.
	E1v	2/ Gliocchi toi		
30	E2v	MOrir uoglio in la mia fede	[Anon.]	xxxv.
31	E3v	POi che a tal condutto mhai	[Anon.]	xxxvI.
32	E4v	PAce hormai ſu	[Anon.]	xxxvii.
33	E5v	PIu uvolte fra me ſteſſo	[Anon.]	xxxviii.
34	E6v	REſta in pace diua mia	[Anon.]	xxxix.
35	E7v	GVarda donna el mio tormento	[Anon.]	xl.
36	E8v	HAime che non e un giocho	[Anon.]	xli.
37	F1v	VIua e morta uoglio amarte	[Anon.]	xlii.
38	F2v	EL te par che man chi in fede	[Anon.]	xliii.
39	F3v	REſta in pace o diua mia	[Anon.]	xliiii.
40	F4v	HAi promeſ ſe dolce e amare	[Anon.]	xlv.
41	F5v	SEgua pur ſeguir chi uole	[Anon.]	xlvi.
	F6v	2/ Vidi gia ne la ſua corte		
42	F7v	MI parto a dio	[Anon.]	xlviii.
43	F8r	E Queſta quella fede	[Anon.]	xlviii.
44	F8v	PIangeti mecho amanti	[Anon.]	xlix.
45	G1r	MAl fai ſignora mia	[Anon.]	xlix.
46	G1v	AMor ſempre me dimoſtra	[Anon.]	l.
47	G2v	LAmentomi damore	[Anon.]	li.
48	G3r	NOn e tempo de tenere	[Anon.]	li.
49	G3v	SEl te piacque un tempo farmi	[Anon.]	lii.
50	G4v	SE da poi la tua partita	[Anon.]	liii.
51	G5v	SE non uoi penſar in tutto	[Anon.]	liiii.
52	G6v	TE lamenti & io mi doglio	[Anon.]	lv.
53	G7v	SE non poi hor riſtorarmi	[Anon.]	lv.
	G8r	[Colophon; Register; Device]		
	G8v	[blank]		

Extant copies:
D-Mbs, Rar.878/2. Complete
   Size of page: 159 × 228 mm.
   Watermarks: Only one is visible: No.11 on G6-5
   Textual comments: B3v: the capital letter "F" has not taken ink
   Technical comments: The capital letter "O" is lacking on B5v • There are normally only five
      staves inked on many pages. Six staves are inked on C6v, D5v, D6v, D7v and E4v; four
      staves on C7v, D2v-3r and D8v
   Corrections and changes:
      In-house: See above
      Later: Modern pencil foliation, t.r.r.:] 57–112 • B6r.ii.1: sb → m, with an ink tail • B6r.ii.11:
         sb → m, with an ink tail • B6v.iv.after 30: rest struck through, initialled R.J. • B7r.i.22:

sb → *m*, tail in brown ink • B7r.i.29: *sb* → *m*, tail in brown ink • b7r.i.30: *m* → *sb*, with erased tail • B8r.iv.after 9: bar-line in brown ink • B8r.iv.after 17: originally two symbols: now *b*A plus repeat bar-lines • C6v.iv.5: *sb* → *m*, tail in dark brown ink, initialled R.J. • D1r.i.after 10: added *sbe*', in dark brown, initialled R.J. • D6r.i.before 8 notes from end: rest *m* → *sm*, in black, initialled g.c. • E2v.ii.before 12 notes from end: inserted repeat bar-lines, in black, initalled g.c. • E5r.ii.after last note: added *p.d.*, initialled R.J. • E5v.v.before 12 notes back: *m* rest struck through, *sb* rest added, in black, initalled g.c. • E7v.ii.after 17: *mc'*,*mc'* → *sbc'* only, by erasure • G6v.ii.before 11 notes back: *m* rest struck through, *sb* rest added, in black, initalled g.c.

Binding and Provenance: with *Frottole I* (1504, No.16)

E-Mprivate. I have not been able to consult this copy

––––––––

Early references: Gesner cites this edition, and Draudius has a reference which may be to one or other edition of this book. See chapter 20

Other editions: Another edition was published in 1508 (No.42, below)

Bibliography:

(a) Rosaria Boccadifuoco, *Bibliografia*, No.1454 • Sartori, *Petrucci*, No.17 • Jeppesen, *La Frottola*, Pe II • Vogel, *Bibliografia*, 1504[3]

(b) Brunet, *Manuel*, ii, col.1412

(d) Cesari, *Frottole* (1954)

(e) Ambros, *Geschichte*, iii, p. 200 • Jeppesen, *La Frottola*, i, 19–21 • Sartori, "Nuove", pp. 181–83

Commentary:

1. This book seems to be directly related to the first of frottole, as argued in chapter 9.

2. The pattern of ascriptions varies by gathering, and by sheets. For example, the name of Franciscus is given in full on inner sheets and abbreviated on the outer. This pattern seems to suggest that the work was divided between different typesetters. In particular, it is notable that there are no ascriptions at all in gatherings C, E, F, or G.

3. The initials added to various corrections and changes in the unique copy at D-Mbs can also be found in other frottole books in that collection. Both sets of initials are clearly later, plausibly 19th-century, and both presume a close performing (or editing) reading of the corrected works.

No. 18. *Frottole III*

6.ii.1504/5   *RISM* 1505[4]

First Edition

A1r]   Frottole Libro | tertio.

H8r]   Impreſſum Venetiis per Octauianum Pe-|trutium Foroſempronienſem. Die. vi. Februarii | Salutis anno M.ccccciiii. Cum priuilegio in-|uictiſſimi Dominii Venetiarum *quae* nullus poſ-|ſit

cantum Figuratum imprimere [ub pena | in ip[o priuilegio contenta. | Regi[trum. | A B C D E F G
H Omnes quaterni. | [Petrucci's device]

Format and collation: Choirbook: landscape quarto-in-eghts. 64 folios: A-H⁸

Signatures:] AA II [$4 • — A1 • Signature on F2 possibly stamped in later

Foliation: top right recto:] [I], II-LXIII, [LXIIII] • All the letters are small capitals, except for the *L*,
   which is in lower case

No running heads: composers' names appear in the head-line

Part-names:

verso:]	Tenor	[A2-4, A6, B1-D2, D4-F3, F5-7, G1-7, H1-6
	Tenor [within the stave:	A5
	Tenor Altus Ba[[us	[A7-8, D3, F4, F8, G8, H7
recto:]	Altus Ba[[us	[A3, A5, A7, B3, B5-D1, D3, D5-F4, F6-8, G2-8, H2-7
	Altus Ba[[us	[B2, B4, D2
	Altus [with Ba[[us within the stave: A4, A6	
	Tenor Altus Ba[[us	[A2, A8-B1, D4, F5, G1, H1

Small capital letters are used in a number of cases:

verso:]	Tenor	A2,4, B2,4,5,7, C2,4,5,7, D2,4,5,7, E2,4,5,7, F2,4,5,7,
		G2,4,5,7, H2,6,7
recto:]	Bassus	A2,4,6,8, B2,4, C2,4, D2,4, E2,4, F2,4, G2,4, H2,3

Fonts: Music: Petrucci's normal music type

   Staves: six per page, though usually fewer

   Text: Roman throughout.

Textual comments: A8r. an erroneous capital letter [A for P]

In-house corrections: All these are present in the Munich copy: A7r.i.after 9: bar-line in brown
   ink • E3r.i.7: *sba*' erased and *b* stamped in over the space • E3r.v.9: colored, in brown ink •
   E5r.i.penultimate: *sbf*' erased, and *sbe*' stamped in: stave lines touched up in brown ink • G6r.ii.last
   two notes: were one note, *lb*: that erased and two stamped in, *sbd'*,*bb*, with the breve using part
   of the double bar-line to act as a longa: stave-lines touched up in ink • G7v.iii. from the rest
   after 5 to 13: struck through, with the word] vacat [in brown ink, in Petrucci's house hand

Contents: The last column gives the folio number as entered in the Tavola:

	A1r	[Title]		
	A1v	[Tavola] Numero [e[anta una.		
1	A2r	POi che [on [i [fortunato	A.DE ANTIQVIS	ii.
2	A2v	POi che amor con dritta fe	[Anon.]	iii.
3	A3v	VOl[i oime mirar troppo alto	B.T.	iiii.
4	A4v	SOn fortuna omnipotente	F.D.L.	v.
5	A5v	NAque al mondo per amare	B.T.	vI.
6	A6v	TAnto po quel fare trato	FRAN. ORGA.	vii.
7	A7v	POi che ho prouato ognarte	[Anon.]	vIIi.
8	A8r	PIangeti occhi mie la[[i	[Anon.]	viii.
		The Cantus begins] AIngeti		
9	A8v	VIuero patiente forte	PHI.DE LV.	ix.
10	B1r	SIa felice la tua uita	MICHA.	ix.
11	B1v	Per che fai donna el gaton	ROSSI. MAN:	x.
	B2v	2/ Gnao gnao gnao vo cridando		
12	B3v	NOn bi[ogna che contra[ta	P.C.	xII.

13	B4v	LA ſperanza col timore	B.T.	xIII.
14	B5v	OYme che io ſento al core	IO.BRO.	xIIII.
15	B6v	LA mia fe non uene ameno	IO.BRO.	xv.
16	B7v	LIeta e lalma poi che ſciolta	IO. BRO.	xvI.
17	B8v	SE a un tuo ſguardo ſon areſo	B.T.	xvii.
18	C1v	MHa pur gionto el troppo amarte	B.T.	xvIII.
19	C2v	POi che uolſe la mia ſtella	B.T.	xIx.
20	C3v	TRoppo e amara e gran faticha	B.T.	xxviii. [recte xx]
21	C4v	DEbbio chieder guerra o pace	B.T.	xxI.
22	C5v	SE mi duol eſſ er gabato	B.T.	xxii.
23	C6v	SE alcun ſpera nel ſuo amore	[Anon.]	xxiii.
24	C7v	SE ogni donna fuſſe il credo	R.M.	xxiiii.
25	C8v	NOn poſſ o abandonarte	P.C.	xxv.
26	D1v	SE per mio fidel ſeruire	N.P.	xxvi.
27	D2v	CHi dal ciel non ha fauore	N.P.	xxvII.
28	D3v	SE non ſon degno donna	IO.BRO.	xxviii.
29	D4r	IO mi uoglio lamentare	IO.BRO.	xxvIII.
30	D4v	ITe caldi ſuſpiri	IO.BRO.	xxIx.
		[Headed:] El modo de dir ſonetti		
31	D5v	OGni ben fa la fortuna	M.C.	xxx.
	D6v	2/ Pone un baſſo e laltro in cielo		
32	D7v	PErſo ho in tutto hormai la uita	M.C.	xxxii.
	D8v	2/ Mia crudele e iniqua ſorte		
33	E1v	FOrſi che ſi forſi che no	M.C.	xxxIIII.
	E2v	2/ Forſi chi ode non intende		
34	E3v	QVei che ſempre han da penare	M.C.	xxxvi.
	E4v	2/ Lor fur quelli che mirando		
35	E5v	FVgitiua mia ſperanza	M.C.	xxxvIII.
	E6v	2/ Io ſo ben che al tuo diſpecto		
36	E7v	LIber fui un tempo in foco	M.C.	xl.
	E8v	2/ Credo ben pero che me ama		
37	F1v	PIango el mio fidel ſeruire	[Anon.]	xlii.
38	F2v	BEn chio ſerua a cor ingrato	[Anon.]	xlIII.
39	F3v	TV me ſtrugi e dai tormento	[Anon.]	xliiii.
40	F4v	NOn poi per che non uoi	[Anon.]	xlv.
41	F5r	HAime che graue doglia	[Anon.]	xlv.
42	F5v	SI morſi donna el tuo labro ſuaue	[Anon.]	xlvi.
		[Headed:] Per ſonetti		
43	F6v	ARda el ciel el mondo tutto	[Anon.]	xlvII.
44	F7v	LA ſperanza me tien uiuo	[Anon.]	xlvIII.
45	F8v	IO mi moro e chi potria	[Anon.]	xlIx.
46	G1r	PRendi larme ingrato amore	[Anon.]	xlix.
47	G1v	QVel chio poſſo io tho donato	[Anon.]	l.
48	G2v	ALa fe ſi ala fe bona	[Anon.]	li.
49	G3v	SOn tornato e dio el ſa	PHILIPPVS DE LVRANO.	lII.
50	G4v	ALdi donna non dormire	F.D.L.	lIII.

51	G5v	SE non dormi donna a[colta	[Anon.]	lIIII.
52	G6v	CHi [e fida de fortuna	B.T.	lv.
53	G7v	DE dolce diua mia	[Anon.]	lvI.
54	G8v	LA tromba [ona	[Anon.]	lvII.
55	H1r	NVnqua fu pena magiore	B.T.	lvII.
56	H1v	CHi [e pa[ce de [peranza	B.T.	lvIII.
57	H2v	FA chio [o hor [u fa pre[to	[Anon.]	
		[Omitted from the Tavola]		
58	H3v	VOx clamantis in de[erto	B.T.	lx.
59	H4v	PAce e gloria al gentil lauro	[Anon.]	lxi.
60	H5v	EL grillo e bon cantore	IOSQVIN DASCANIO.	lxii.
61	H6v	SE conuiene a un cor uillano	ENEAS	lxiii.
62	H7v	Signora anzi mia dea	B.T.	lxiii.
	H8r	[Colophon: Register: Device]		
	H8v	[blank]		

Surviving copies:

D-Mbs, Rar. 878/3. Complete

> **Size of pages:** 195 × 228 mm.
>
> **Watermarks:** No.14 on A1, A5-6, B3, D6, D8, E3, E7-8, F6-5, F7, G2, G5-6, H1-2, and H5
>
> **Technical comments:** On D6v, the leger-line was evidently printed with the staves • E3r.i: a spacing sort for music, 2.8 mm wide, has taken ink above the stave
>
> **Corrections and changes:**
>
> > **In-house:** See above
> >
> > **Later:** Foliated in modern pencil, 113–176 • A5r.i.51: md' tail struck through, initialled] R J • D4v.ii.after 10: bar-line in modern pencil • E3r.i.35: sbg has added tail, initialled] g.c. • E7v.ii.penultimate: mg' tail struck through, initialled] R J • F6r.ii.10: whited-out tail to m • G4v.iv.after 41: added sbg, initialled] R J • G8r.iv.33: bg struck through, ba written, initialled] g.c. • H1v.iii.14: mf' struck through, initialled] g.c. • H6r.ii.after 14: added sbd', initialled] g.c. • H7r.iv.16: bA struck through, sbA written and then struck through, and a dotted line stet indication under the breve, initialled] R J
>
> **Binding and Provenance:** With Frottole I (1504, No.16)

E-Mprivate. I have not been able to consult this copy

Other editions A later edition in 1507 (No.40)

Bibliography:

> (a) Rosaria Boccadifuoco, *Bibliografia*, No.1459 • Sartori, *Petrucci*, No.18; Jeppesen, *Frottola*, Pe III; Vogel, *Bibliografia*, 1504[4]
>
> (d) Cesari, *La Frottola*, ii (1954)
>
> (e) Jeppesen, *Frottola*, i, 21–24 and 84–87 • Sartori, "Nuove", pp. 183–86

Commentary:

1. This book is one gathering longer than the are the first two of frottole. The three were certainly prepared as a set, for they appeared within twelve weeks, a period that included Christmas and

the New Year. As I argue in chapter 9, the arrangement of composers in the first two books, coupled with the disorganised appearance of this one, suggests that the supplier of the music had presented Petrucci with a complete collection — in which the contents of this book were the remnants and miscellaneous "other pieces".

2. The evidence of small initial letters for the part-names seems to confirm very clearly that these names were kept in the skeleton forme, throughout much of the work, even when other part-names (Altus on *rectos,* for example) were changed.

3. The pairs of initials attached to a number of the changes seem to be 19th-century: see the comments to *RISM* 1505³ (No.17)

No. 19. *Motetti A*

13.ii.1504/5   Not in *RISM*

Second Edition

Three sheets of this edition are tentatively assigned to a later impression, here called a cancel impression (following my convention in this volume). They are the outer sheets of C, D, and E: see below

A1r]   [Lacking:] Motetti A Numero trentatre [following Colón]

G8r   ]Impreſſum Uenetijs per Octauianum | Petrutium Foroſempronienſem. Die 13 | Februarij Salutis anno 1504. Cum pri | uilegio inuictiſſimi Dominij Uenetiarum: | q*uae* nullus poſſit cantum Figuratum impri | mere ſub pena in ipſo priuilegio contenta. | Regiſtrum. | A B C D E F G Omnes quaterni. | [Petrucci's device]

Format and collation: Choirbook: landscape quarto-in-eights. 56 folios, A-G8. The unique copy lacks gathering A, and three sheets are listed below, as cancels

Signatures:] .B II. [$4

Foliation: including the cancels: t.r.r.] [1–8, lost], 9–55, [56]

Part-names: including the cancels:

recto:]	Altus Baſſus	[B1, B3-6, C1-6, D3-F1, F3-7, G1, G3-7
	Altus Baſſus	[with a small B: B2, B8, F2, F8
	Baſſus	[B7
	Contra	[C7-D2, G2
	[Nil:	G8
verso:]	Tenor	[B1-7, C1-G6
	Tenor	[with a small T: B8
	Tenor et Contra	[G7
	[Nil:	G8

Fonts: Music: Petrucci's normal music type

Staves: 176–181 mm long. 10-92-112 high

Text: Rotonda

Textual comments: B8*v*.i.after 42: the flat printed below the stave is in front of a *b* an octave higher, for which it is redundant, but seven notes before one at the lower pitch, for which it is necessary.

Technical comments: Only five staves are inked on B7r and G2r • F5v: a piece of furniture appears in place of the ascription • The folio numbers were printed with the staves: cf. the inking on C3r and E3r

No apparent in-house changes

Contents: including the cancel leaves:

6	B1r	[end of Crux triumphans		Compere]
	B1v	2/ Jeſus nomen dignum		
7	B2v	PRopter grauamen ꝛ tormentum		Compere.
	B3v.ii	2/ Memento nostri		
8	B5v	DEſcendi in ortum meu3		[Anon.]
9	B6v	O Quam glorifica	à3	Agricola.
10	B7v	ADonay ſanctiſſime		Gaſpar
11	B8v	DUng aultre amer		Joſquin
		[T:] Victime paſcali		
	C1v	2/ De tous biens / Dic nobis		
12	C2v	BEnedicta ſit creatrix		[Anon.]
13	C3v	REgina celi letare		.Brumel.
	C4v	2/ Reſurrexit ſicut dixit		
14	C5v	VIrgo maria non est tibi simili5		.Gaſpar
		[other vv.] Virgo ...		
15	C6v	O Florens roſa [untexted]	à3	.Jo.ghiſelin.
16	C8v	ECce video celos apertos: [untexted]	à3	.Craen.
17	D2v	SCile fragor ac verborum		.Compere.
	D3v	2/ Suſcipe dei mater		
18	D4v	AUe maria gratia plena ... benedicta tu		Compere.
	D5v	2/ Sancta michael ora pro nobis		
19	D7v	LA ſpagna [untexted]		.Jo.ghiſelin:
20	E2v	AVe maria gratia plena ... benedicta tu		[Craen]
21	E3v	AVe ſtella matutina		.Brumel.
	E4v	2/ Tu es area compluta		
22	E5v	IBo mihi ad montem mirrhe		.Gaſpar.
23	E6v	AVe domina sancta maria		.Gaſpar.
	E7v	2/ Tu peperiſti creatore3		
24	E8v	[T:] O pulcherima mulierum		.Gaſpar.
25	F1v	STella celi extirpauit		[Anon.]
26	F2v	VIdi ſpecioſa3		.Gaſpar
27	F3v	AVe vera caro christi		[Anon.]
	F4v	2/ Salve sancta caro dei		
28	F5v	DA pace3 domine		[Anon.]
29	F6v	QVis numerare queat	à5 ex 4	.Compere.
		[T:] Da pacem		
	F7v	2/ Audiuit / [S:] Da pacem		
	F8v	3/ FUndant preces / [T:] Da pacem		
30	G1v	VIrgo dei troni digna [untexted]	à3	Tinctoris
31	G2v	Chriſti mater aue		Gaſpar
32	G3v	AVe ſtella matutina		.Gaſpar.

33   G4*v*   ANima mea liq*ue*facta *est*   .Ghi∫elin.
     G5*v*   2/ Tuleru*nt* plaiu3 meum [*sic*]
34   G6*v*   MAter digna d*e*i   [anon.]
35   G7*v*   DE tous biens   Jo∫quin [lower voices only]
     G8*r*   [Colophon: Register: Device]
     G8*v*   [blank]

————

Extant copy:

H-Bn, ZR 523. Lacks gathering A. For three sheets, see the discussion of a probable cancel, below

Size of page: 169 × 240 mm.

Watermarks: No.14 on B6, B8-7, C6-5, D6, E5-6, F2-1, F3-4, G4-3 and G8

Technical comments: The folio numbers on E3 and E4 [35 and 36] are present, though not inked • B5*v*.iv.text: a text spacing sort has taken ink, about 3.8 mm high; a similar sort can be seen on G3*r*.ii • F7*v*.i.right end: inked edge of furniture

Corrections and changes:

   Later: B4*r*.v.rests after 9: *sb,m* → *sb*, by erasure • G2*r*.below v:] Anna a suos p*a*rens [in brown ink • G6*v*.iii.above 16: an erased blot or symbol, perhaps a note • G7*r*.v.28: leger line in brown ink

   Binding: Dark brown leather, lifted and mounted on new boards. Stamps and rolls in blind, looking like north Italian workmanship • One paste-down and one flyleaf at each end. All have vertical chainlines and the back flyleaf has a watermark] REGEST • According to Murányi, "Unbekannte", p. 292, this was originally bound with the library's copy of *Motetti B* of 1503

   Provenance: Pasted to the inner front flyleaf is a slip of paper with] V34/1682/1970 [and] B1850/1960 [According to Robert Murányi, the former is the acquisition number of the library. The library acquired the book from a priest in Pécs. It cannot always have been there, for the city was razed by the Turks in 1526.]

   Bibliography: Murányi, "Unbekannte", pp. 292–93

No. 19A. *Cancel Sheets.*

Three sheets (C, D, and E outer) are provisionally entered as a later printing
For most details, including the contents, see àbove

Technical comments: Only five staves are inked on C8*r*, D1*r* and D2*r* • See below for evidence suggesting that these sheets are later than the rest of the volume

————

Extant copy:

H-Bn, ZR 523. For the rest of this copy, see above

Watermarks: No.11 on C7-8, D1-2 and E8-7

Technical comments: Large furniture pieces have taken ink, showing an X design, on C8*r*, D1*r*, D2*r* and E1*v* • C2*v*.v: a text spacing sort has taken ink

Later corrections and changes: C1*r*.ii.4: *ba* → *smb,ba*, by erasure and then all being entered in manuscript, in dark ink

————

Lost copies: Copies were owned by Colón (Chapman, "Printed", No.12) and Bottrigari: see chapter 20.

Other editions: The first edition appeared in 1502 (No.3)

Bibliography:

(e) in addition to literature cited under the first edition, see Murányi, "Unbekannte"

Commentary:

1. The existence of this edition, only recently discovered and announced by Robert Murányi, throws an interesting light on the popularity of Petrucci's earliest volumes. It falls nearly a year after the last edition of any of Petrucci's chanson volumes — the third of the *Odhecaton A* — and is probably the only second edition of any of the early motet books. The need for this re-edition suggests that the chanson volumes, as well as *Motetti B*, were still finding new purchasers.

2. The marking on the right end of F7v lies 5.5 mm above the top of the stave, at about the level of the foot of a text line. For this reason, it cannot be the edge of the text sorts, or even furniture designed to align the text: it is also unlikely to be the edge of a marker for the staves in the forme. It seems, therefore, to be evidence of some furniture used for setting the music.

3. Analysis of the patterns of watermarks and stave-groupings suggests that the two papers represent different stages of work:

Sheet	Mark	1r	2v	3r	4v		2r	1v	4r	3v	
B.I	14	181	181	181	181	α	179	177	176	176	β
B.II	14	180	181	180	181	β	178	176	176	177	α
C.II	14	180	181	180	181	α	178	176	176	176	β
D.II	14	180	181	180	180	α	178	176	175	176	β
E.II	14	180	181	181	182	τ	181	181	181	181	α
F.I	14	180	181	181	182	τ	178	176	176	176	β
F.II	14	181	181	180	181	α	181	182	180	181	τ
G.I	14	181	181	181	—	α	178	176	177	—	?β
G.II	14	179	180	180	181	τ	180	181	180	181	α
C.I	11	180	182	180	180	?α	180	181	180	180	α
D.I	11	180	181	180	181	α	180	182	180	181	α
E.I	11	180	180	180	181	α	180	181	180	181	α

The evidence argues that the main printing of the book involved three formes of staves: while work started with only two, the last stages show a pattern of three formes being rotated. The three sheets on the different paper show a different pattern, in which only one forme of staves was employed. This evidence is supported by the presence, noted above, of inked blocks of furniture on four of these formes. This evidence is not entirely convincing, since there is no other sign, for example in the typographical material, that these three sheets are notably later.

4. For the dating of the cancel, it is significant that the volume of *Fragmenta Missarum* (No.24, dated 31. X .1505) seems to use the same blocks of staves as in this edition: it also uses paper with watermark 11 as one of its principal papers, apparently exhausting the stock before the end of the book. I have therefore tentatively dated the cancel leaves in the months before that edition, probably in September of 1505.

No. 20. de Orto: *Misse*

22.iii.1505   *RISM* O137

A1r]   Misse De Orto. | Dominicalis. | Jay pri∫amours | cu*m* duobus patre*m*. | Lo*m*me arme. | La
          bella ∫e ∫ied. | Petita camuseta. | S

C1r]   T

E1r]   A

G1r]   B

H9v]   Impre∫∫um Uenetijs per Octauianum | Petrutium Foro∫empronien∫em. Die 22 | Martij
          Salutis anno 1505. Cum pri-|uilegio inuicti∫∫imi Dominij Venetiarum: | *quae* nullus po∫∫it cantum
          Figuratum impri-|mere ∫ub pena in ip∫o priuilegio contenta. | Regi∫trum ABCDEGFH O*mne*s |
          quaterni pr*ae*ter BFH q*ui*nterni. | [Petrucci's device]

Format and collation: Partbooks: landscape quarto-in-eights. [S] 18 folios: A⁸B¹⁰; [T] 16 folios: C–
D⁸; [A] 18 folios: E⁸F¹⁰; [B] 18 folios: G⁸H¹⁰

Signatures:] .A iiij. [$4 • + B5, F5 • − A1, G1 • A2 signed] .A II. [• B5 and F5 signed with an
arabic numeral 5

No foliation

Heads: Two components: a part-name, apparently retained in the forme; and a title, reset on each
page. For details of the latter, see below

recto:]	Sup*erius*.	[A2-B10
	Tenor.	[C2-D8
	Altus	[E2-4, F1-5
	Altus.	[E5-8, F6-10
	Bassus.	[G2, G4-H9
	Bassus•	[G3
	[Nil:	A1, C1, E1, G1
verso:]	Sup*erius*.	[A1-B9
	Tenor.	[C1-D7
	Altus.	[E2-3,5-8, F2,4,6–9
	Altus•	[E4, F1,3,5
	Bassus.	[G1-8, H1-5,7
	Bassus	[H6,8
	[Nil:	B10, D8, E1, F10, H9,10

Fonts: Music: Petrucci's normal music type

Staves: six per page: 175–180 mm long, 10-92-112.5 mm long

Text: Rotonda

Technical comments: Only five staves are inked on A4v, D2r, D7v and G7v • B3v.iv: the mensuration sign is apparently a wood-block, 6.5 × 5.5 mm. • E7v and F6v: the head-line is very low,
barely above the stave • The colophon seems to be taken from an earlier edition, using standing
type, with the date changed

Rubrics: F2r.left margin:] Re∫iduu*m* pr*i* mi | *con*tra tenoris

F2v.v:] Canon | [block of 4 swords] | Primu*s* *con*tra te*n*oriza*n*s

In-house corrections: A7r.ii.28–30: leger line in manuscript: A-Wn, D-Mbs, F-Pn, I-Bc and I-Mc
• C2r.ii.32–33: ligature, *l*+*l* → *b*+*l*, with added down tail: in brown ink in the copy at I-Bc; a
stop-press correction in that at A-GÜ • C5r.vi.rests after 1: the second *sb* rest erased and re-

entered one stave line lower: A-GÜ, in dark brown ink, and D-Mbs, in black ink • C6*v*.iv.24: *dsbs* → *dm*, tail added in printer's ink: D-Mbs • G3*v*.v.51: *smd* erased and *sbd*,*sbc*, stamped in with *m* tails added in ginger ink: D-Mbs, F-Pn, GB-Lbl, and I-Bc • H6r.iv.3: *sb*, e → f, erased and manuscript, imitating print: D-Mbs, F-Pn, GB-Lbl, and I-Bc • H7r.iii.30: *m*, B → A, erasure and manuscript in black ink, retaining the old tail, and imitating print: D-Mbs, F-Pn, GB-Lbl, and I-Bc

Contents:

	A1r	C1r	E1r	G1r	[Title]
1	A1*v*	C1*v*	E1*v*	G1*v*	De orto [Missa] dominicalis
	A2r	C1*v*.iv	E1*v*.vi	G1*v*.v	[Gloria]
	A2*v*.iii	C2r.iv	E2*v*.ii	G2*v*.i	[Credo]
	A3*v*	C3r	E3*v*.ii	G3r.vi	[Sanctus]
	A4r.iv	C3r.iv	E4r.vi	G4r.i	[Agnus]
2	A5r	C3*v*.iv	E5r	G4*v*	[Missa] Jay pri[amours
	A5r.iv	C3*v*.vi	E5r.iv	G4*v*.iv	[Gloria]
	A5*v*.v	C4r.iv	E5*v*.iv	G5r.iv	[Credo]
	A6*v*.v	C5r.iv	E6*v*.iv	G6r.iii	[Second Credo]
	A7*v*	C6r	E7*v*.ii	G6*v*.v	[Sanctus]
	A8r	C6*v*	E8r.ii	G7r.iv	[Agnus]
3	A8*v*	C7r	E8*v*	G8r	De Orto [Missa] Lomme arme
	B1r	C7*v*	F1r	G8r.vi	[Gloria]
	B1*v*.iii	C8r	F1*v*.iv	H1r	[Credo]
	B2*v*	D1r	F2*v*.iii	H1*v*.v	[Sanctus]
	B3r.v	D1*v*	F3*v*	H2*v*.ii	[Agnus]
4	B4r	D2*v*	F4r.v	H3r	De orto: [Missa] La bella [e [ied
	B4*v*	D2*v*.iv	F4*v*.iv	H3*v*	[Gloria]
	B5r	D3r.iii	F5r.iii	H4r	[Credo]
	B5*v*.iv	D4r	F5*v*.vi	H4*v*.iii	[Sanctus]
	B6*v*	D4*v*.iii	F6*v*.ii	H5r.v	[Agnus]
5	B7r	D5*v*	F7r.iv	H6r	De Orto: [Missa] Petita Camu[eta
	B7r.v	D5*v*.iv	F7*v*.ii	H6r.iv	[Gloria]
	B8r	D6r.iii	F8r.iii	H7r	[Credo]
	B9r.ii	D7r.iii	F9r.iii	H8r.iv	[Sanctus]
	B9*v*.vi	D7*v*	F9*v*.vi	H9r	[Agnus]
				H9*v*	[Colophon; Register; Device]
		D8r			[blank staves]
	B10*v*	D8*v*	F10*v*	H10r-*v*	[blank]

Extant copies:

A-GÜ. Tenor, lacking last folio

    Size of page: 165 × 235 mm.

    Watermarks: No 14 on C2-1, C5 and D4

    Corrections and changes:

        In-house: C2r and C5r. see above

        Later: • C8*v*.foot: in pale brown] [olon*us* [?]

    Binding and Provenance: With Josquin, *Missarum II* (1515, No.59)

    Bibliography: Federhofer, "Petrucci"

A-Wn, S.A.77.C.7. Superius, Tenor, and Altus, complete

Size of page: 162 × 227 mm.

Watermarks:

A6-5	A7-8	B8-7	B9-10	C5-6	C7	D1-2	D4-3	E2-1	E3-4	F2-1	F3-4	F-6
14	14	14	14	14	14	14	14	14	14	15	15	15

Corrections and changes:

In-house: A7r: see above

Provenance: It is probable that this book completed the set at A-Wn (and I-Vnm), all originally bound together behind a copy of Josquin: *Misse* (1506: No.30)

D-Mbs, 4°.mus.pr.57. Four part-books, lacking only H10 (blank)

Watermarks: In the following list a number of marks are indicated solely with an "x". In these instances, it is not possible to tell, because of the loss of part of the mark through trimming, whether the mark was originally of type 15 or type 16:

A6	A7	B2	B3	B5	C5	C8	D2	D4-3	E1-2	E5-6
14	14	14	14	14	14	14	14	14	16	14

F1-2	F3-4	F5-	G6-5	G8-7	H5-	H3-4
x	x	16	15	x	16	x

Technical comments: A2v.i.text: spacing sorts have taken ink

Corrections and changes:

In-house: A7r, C5r, C6v, G3v, H6r, and H7r: see above

Later: B3r.iii.leger line: in manuscript • B3v.iv.m.s.: in manuscript • C1r. head-line:] Misse de orto [in a German 16th-century hand; then, in a different hand:] Vol quarta [the numeral struck through and, above it, probably in a 19th-century hand:] tertia • C2r.i.right end: rests perhaps have an added *b* rest, very light brown • E1r. head-line:] Misse de orto [German 16th-century hand: then, in a different hand] Vol tertia [the numeral struck through and, in a third hand] secunda • G1r. head-line: as E1r

Binding: Modern leather binding

E-Bbc, M.115 (7). Altus, complete

Size of page: 174 × 230 mm.

Watermarks:

E6	E8	F2	F-5	F8-7	F10-9
14	14	14	15	15	15

No corrections or changes visible

Binding and Provenance: Bound with Josquin *I Missarum* (1516, No.62)

Bibliography: Pedrell, *Catálech*, No.427

F-Pn, Rés.Vm¹.229. Complete

Watermarks:

A3-4	A7-8	B7-8	B9	C4-	C8-7	D4-3	D7-8	E1	E3	F3-4	F5-
14	14	14	14	14	14	14	14	14	14	15	15

F10-9	G2-1	G6-5	H5-	H7-8	H9-10
15	15	15	15	15	15

Technical comments: The impress of uninked staves on D7v.vi and H10r • The impress of an uninked large capital B (as used for the title page of *Motetti B*) on D8r

In-house corrections and changes: A7r, G3v, H6r, and H7r: see above

Provenance: Perhaps the copy from the Gaspari collection

Bibliography: Potier, "Gaspari" • Sartori, *Petrucci*, p. 97

GB-Lbl, K.1.d.5. Superius, complete, and Bassus, lacking last folio

Size of page: 157 × 220 mm (Superius) and 157 × 215 mm (Bassus)

Watermarks:

A6-5	A7-8	B2	B-5	B7	G1-2	G4-3	H3-4	H-5	H-9
14	14	14	14	14	15	15	15	15	15

Corrections and changes:

> **In-house:** A7r, G3v, H6r and H7r: see above
>
> **Later:** B3r.iii: manuscript leger line

Binding: Different bindings: for the Superius, see "Provenance" • The Bassus has a British Museum binding, with the Museum stamp, dated 17 NO [18]96 [on H9v • One flyleaf conjugate with one pastedown at each end

Provenance: The two books have different provenances. The Superius has a binding with the inscription] H VIII [on the spine, indicating that it came from the old Royal Library. On B10v it has the old British Museum stamps, and on A1r, the call] No 1281

Bibliography: Johnson and Scholderer, *Short-Title*, p. 478

I-Bc, Q.62. Complete

Size of page: 160 × 240 mm.

Watermarks:

A2-1	A3-4	B5-	B8	B10	C3-4	C8-7	D2-1	D5-	E3-4	E8-7
14	14	14	14	14	14	14	14	14	14	14

F1-2	F4-3	F-6	G2-1	G4-3	H-6	H7-8	H10-9
15	15	15	15	15	15	15	15

Technical comments: A5r: clear evidence that text and staves were inked together • B3v.iv: the mensuration sign is clearly a woodblock

Corrections and changes:

> **In-house:** A7r, C2r, G3v, H6r and H7r: see above
>
> **Later:** Manuscript foliation: [S] 20-37; [T] 14-29; [A] 18-35; [B] 16-33

Provenance: This copy is cited in Martini's letters to Chiti of 7.v.1746 and 22.vii.1746 • Old call number 1006 in the Superius • Apparently originally bound behind the book of Agricola's masses (No.13)

Bibliography: Schnoebelen, *Padre*, Nos.1245 and 1250, pp. 144–45

I-Mc, S.B.178/4. Superius, complete

Size of page: 164 × 223 mm.

Watermarks: No.14 on A6-5, A7-8, B-6, B8-7 and B10-9

Technical comments: B7r.ii.text: spacing sorts, measuring 2.4 × 0.8, and 2.4 × 1.7 mm.

In-house Change: A7r: see above

Binding: With Josquin *II Missarum*, q.v.

Provenance: Sta. Barbara, Mantua • Perhaps the Chapel of Cardinal Ippolito d'Este

Bibliography: This copy was exhibited at Florence in 1949. Damerini, "Esposizione", p. 25 • Prizer "Cappella" • Lockwood, "Adrian"

───────

Lost copies: Copies were owned by Colón (Chapman, "Printed", No.13), by the Fuggers (perhaps that now at A-Wn, Schaal, "Musikbibliothek" I/52), and by King João IV of Portugal (Sampaio Ribeiro, "Livraria", p. 5)

Bibliography:

a) Rosaria Boccadifuoco, *Bibliografia*, Nos.2249 and 2430 • Sartori, *Petrucci*, No.20

Commentary:

1. The manner in which mass titles and part-names are presented in the head-lines argues convincingly that the part-names had become part of a skeleton forme: see in particular the Altus book. On the other hand, the mass titles were not, as we would expect, for they changed too frequently:

     recto:] Dominicalis. [A2-4, C2 • Dominicalis. [C3, E4, G2-3 • .Dominicalis. [E2,3 • Jay pris amours. [A5-8, E5-8, G5,7 • Jay prif amonrs. [C5 • Jay pris amours· [G6 • Jay prif amours. [C4,6 • De orto Lomme arme [C7, G8 • Lomme arme. [B1-3, C8, F2 • Lomme arme. [D1,2, F1,3,4, H1,2 • De orto: La bella fe fied. [B4 • De orto La bella fe fied. [H3 • La bella fe fied. [B5,6, D3-5, F5-7, H4,5 • De Orto: Petita Camuseta. [B7 • De orto Petita Camusetta [H6 • Petita. [B8-10, D6,7, F8-10, H7-9 • Nil: A1, C1, E1, G1

     verso:] De orto dominicalis. [A1 • De orto Dominicalis. [C1 • De orto Dominicalis. [E1, G1 • Dominicalis. [A2,4 • Dominicalis [A3, G4 • Dominicalis. [C2,3, E2-4, G2,3 • De orto Jay pris amours. [G6 • Jay pris amours. [A6,7, E6,7, G5,7 • Jay prif amours. [A5, C4,6 • Jay prif amours. [C5 • De orto Lomme arme [E8 • De Orto Lomme arme [A8 • Lomme arme. [B1,2, C7 • .Lomme arme. [B3 • Lomme arme. [C8-D1, F1-3, G8-H2 • De orto La bella fe fied. [D2 • La bella fe fied. [B4-6, D3-4, F4-6, H3-5 • De orto Petita Camusetta. [D5 • Petita. [B7-9, D6-7, F7-9, H6-8 • Nil: B10, D8, E5, F10, G7, H9,10

2. The pattern of in-house corrections is a little unusual in two respects: one is the presence of changes apparently meant to imitate printed notation, alongside occasional use of what appears to be printer's ink for other changes; the second is the appearance of some changes in different colours. While the latter would suggest a need for haste in correcting (at least) some of the copies, the former implies that more time was available. Since the imitative corrections all lie in the Bassus book, it may mean no more than the presence of a different corrector, who indulged in imitating the printed forms.

No. 21. *Motetti IV*

4.vi.1505   *RISM* 1505[2]

A1r]   Motetti libro | quarto.
E1r]   T
J1r]   A
N1r]   B
Q8r]   Impreffum Uenetijs per Octauianum | Petrutium Forofempronienfem. Die 4. | Junij Salutis anno 1505. Cum pri-|uilegio inuictiffimi Dominij Uenetiarum: | *quae* nullus poffit cantum Figuratum impri-|mere fub pena in ipfo priuilegio contenta. | Regiftrum. | A B C D E F G H J K L M N | O P Q Omnes quaterni. | [Petrucci's device]

Tavola: A2*v*, reset for each book, always in two columns. Taken from the Superius:

	Numero cinquantacinque.	
Jofquin.	O maria virgo Jo.moton	4.
Ave regina: Alma redemptori5 2.	O quam fulges Jo.motom.	7.
Ave virginum gemma Bulkin. 7.	O gloriosa domina Jo.ghifelin	10.

Alma redemptoris	16.	O bone iesu o *dulcis* Ninot	13.
Aue Je[u *christe verbum patris*	25.	O beate [eba[tia*ne* Jo.martini	16.
Aue m*ater* o*mn*ium Ga[par	29.	O beate [eba[tiane Ga[par.	20.
		O potens magni	21.
Beata es maria Brumel.	9.	O clauiger regni celoru*m*	22.
Beata es maria Ja.obreth	23.	O [tclliferi *conditor* orbi5	24.
Beata gens cuius e[t	29.	Ob[ecro te *virgo* dulci[[ima	24.
		O beate ba[ili Jaco. obreth	26.
Co*n*cept*us* hodiern*us* Brumel	25.	O maria nullam ta*m* grave3	28.
Christe fili dei mundi	28.	Ora pro nobis [ine termi*no*	28.
Confirma: Hoc deus	30.	Brumel.	
Decantemus in hac die	11.	Panagiricu*m*: Aue *virgo* glorio[a	2.
		P*ater* me*us* agri. A tre Alex.	18.
Fe[tivitate*m* Jero. *de* clibano	19.		
Factus e[t repente de celo	30.	Quis nu*m*erare Ja oberti	5.
Gaude *virgo* Josqu*in* de pre5	12.	Regina celi Jo.ghi[elin	18.
Gloria laus 7 ho. Brumel.	17.	Regina celi letare	30.
Joannes ghi[elin.			
		Salue regi*na* Petr*us* *de* la rue	4.
In patie*n*tia: Mi[er*er*e A tre	8.	Stabat mater: Turplin	15.
Inuiolata Jo.ghi[elin	14.	Salue *virgo* virginum Jo. aule*n*.	22.
Inviolata Philip.ba[yro*n*	20.	Ga[par i*n* honore*m* *sancti* sp*iritu*s.	
Intemerata virgo	27.	Spiritus d*omi*ni repleuit orbe*m*	29.
		Si bibero crathere pleno	32.
Laudes chr*isto* J a.obreth.	11.		
Leuate capita Jo.martini	15.	Ut plebi radij5 Jo[qu*in*.	6.
Loquebant*ur* varijs linguis	30.		
		Virgo [alutiferi	14.
Maria *virgo* *semper* Jo. ghi[elin	3.	Vultum tuum Josqu*in* de pre5	27.
Me*n*te tota tibi [upplicam*us*	28.	Veni [ancte [piritus	29.
		Era[mus lapicide.	
Natiuita5 vnde Brumel	17.	Virgo prudenti[[ima	31.
Era[mus lapicide.			
Natiuitas tua dei genitrix	31.		

Format and collation: Partbooks: landscape quarto-in-eights. [C] 32 folios: A-D⁸; [T] 32 folios: E-H⁸; [A] 32 folios: J-M⁸; [B] 32 folios: N-Q⁸

Signatures:] A ij [$4 • − A1 • + E1, J1, N1 • B4 is set very high, above the last line of text, and far to the right • L1 also has, on the direction line:] Uerte

Foliation: t.r.r. [C] [1], 2–11, 12 [with 2 inverted], 13–32; [T] [33], 34–57, 68 [*recte* 58, f.H2r], 59–63, [64]; [A] [65], 66–96; [B] [97], 98–127, [128]

Running heads: In addition to the running head-line of the part-name, the same line carries composer's names, and titles when necessary: see below

recto:] Supe*rius*. [A2-D8

Tenor. [E2

Altus. [J2, J4-M8

	Altus	[J3
	Baſſus.	[N2-4,6,8, O2,4-8, P2, P4-Q4, G6,7
	Baſſus	[N5
	Baſſuſ.	[N7, O1,3, P1,3, Q5
	[Nil:	A1, E1, H8, J1, N1, Q8
verso:]	Superius.	[A2-D7
	Tenor.	[E2
	Altus.	[J2-M7
	Baſſuſ.	[N2,4, P1,3, Q2,4
	Baſſus.	[N3, N5-O8, P2, P4-Q1, Q3,5-7
	[Nil:	A1, D8, E1, H8, J1, M8, N1, Q8

Fonts: Music: Petrucci's normal music type

Staves: six per page: 175-180 mm long, 10-91-112 mm high.

Text: Rotonda

Technical comments: Initial "O" omitted on K7*v*, and N6*v* • Small capital letters are used on A8*v* [M], B2*r* [O], C4*r* [O], G5*r* [O], G6*v* [O], L3*r* [O], O1*v* [O], P4*r* [O], P8*r* [O] and Q7*v* [V] • Five staves only are inked on E2*r*, G8*r*, H1*v*,3*v*,4*r*,6*v*,7*r*, M6*v*, N5*r* and Q7*v* • Fusas seem to have been used for furniture in the last stave of H1*v*, H3*v*, H4*r* and H7*r*: they are particularly clear in the copy at D-W

In-house corrections: D2*v*.last: *custosc'* → *mc"* (stamped in) and *custosc"* (brown ink manuscript): I-Vnm • G5*v*.v.2-3: *sbe,sbf* → *sbf,sbe*, notes erased and stamped in: I-Mc • P2*v*.v.3: *b* stamped in over *sb*: I-Mc

Contents: Note that all attributions appear only in the Superius book:

	A1*r*	E1*r*	J1*r*	N1*r*	[Title]	
	A1*v*	E1*v*	J1*v*	N1*v*	[Tavola] Numero cinquantacinque.	
1	A2*r*	E2*r*	J2*r*	N2*r*	ALma redemptoris	Joſquin.
					[T,A] AUe regina celorum	
2	A2*v*	E2*v*	J2*v*.ii	N2*v*	AVe virgo glorioſa	Brumel.
					[Headed:] Panagiricum.	
	A3*r*	E3*r*	J3*r*.ii	N3*r*	2/ O regina pietatis	
3	A3*v*	E3*v*	J3*v*.iv	N3*v*	MAria virgo semper letare	Jo.ghiſelin.
4	A4*r*	E3*v*.iv	J4*r*.iii	N4*r*	SAlue regina miſericordia	Petrus de la rue.
	A4*r*.iv	E4*r*	—	N4*r*.iii	2/ [T] Eya ergo	
	A4*v*.ii	E4*r*.iii	J4*v*	N4*v*	3/ Et Jeſum benedictum	
5	A4*v*.vi	E4*v*	J4*v*.iv	N4*v*.iv	O Maria virgo pia	Jo.moton.
	A5*r*.ii	E4*v*.iii	J5*r*	N5*r*	2/ O maria templum dei	
6	A5*v*	E5*r*	J5*r*.v	N5*v*	QUis numerare queat	Jacobus oberti.
	A5*v*.iv	E5*r*.iii	J5*v*.ii	N5*v*.iv	2/ [A] Audiuit ipse tamen	
	A6*r*.i	E5*v*	J6*r*	N6*r*	3/ [A] Fundant preces	
7	A6*r*.vi	E5*v*.iv	J6*r*.iv	N6*r*.v	UT phebi radijs	Joſquin.
	A6*v*.iii	E5*v*.iv	J6*v*.ii	N6*r*.vi	2/ Latius in numerum	
8	A7*r*	E6*r*	J7*r*	N6*v*	O quam fulges in etheris	Joannes moton.
9	A7*v*.ii	E6*v*.iii	J7*v*.iii	N7*r*.ii	AVe virginum gemma catherina	Bulkyn.
	A8*r*	E6*v*.v	J8*r*	N7*v*	2/ [A] Aue virgo ſpecioſa	
10	A8*v*	E7*r*	—	N8*r*	MIſerere domine [á3]	Joannes ghiſelin.
					[T,B] IN patiencia veſtra	
	B1*r*	E7*v*	—	N8*v*	2/ Tu domine	

11	B1v	E8r	J8v	O1r	BEata es maria virgo dulcis	Brumel.
12	B2r	E8v	K1r	O1v	O Gloriosa domina	Joannes ghiselin.
	B2r.v	E8v.v	K1r.v	O1v.v	2/ O domina sanctissima	
13	B3r	F1v	K2r	O2v	LAudes christo redemptori	Ja.obreht.
	B3v	F2r	K2r.v	O2v.v	2/ Hec est dies	
14	B3v.vi	F2v	K2v.v	O3r.v	DEcantemus in hac die	[Anon.]
	B4r.iii	F2v.iv	K3r.ii	O3v.ii	2/ Salue virgo labe carens	
15	B4v	F3r.ii	K3v	O4r	GAude virgo mater christi	Josquin: de pres.
16	B5r	F3v	K3v.v	O4r.v	O Bone Jesu O dulcis Jesu	Ninot.
	B5v.i	F4r.i	K4r.v	O4v.v	2/ O bone Jesu si merui	
17	B6r.v	F4v.iv	K5r	O5v.iii	VIrgo salutiferi	[Anon.]
	B6v	F4v.v	K5r.ii	O5v.v	2/ Adsis o nostri custos	
18	B6v.iii	F5r	K5r.iv	O6r	INviolata integra ꝫ casta	Jo.ghiselin.
19	B7r	F5r.iii	K5v.iv	O6v	STabat mater	Turplin.
	B7r.i	F5v.i	K6r.ii	O6v.iv	2/ Eya mater	
20	B7r.iv	F6r	K6v.iii	O7r.iii	LEuate capita vestra	[Anon.]
	B7v.i	F6v	K7r	O7v	2/ Dum ortus fuerit	
21	B8r	F6v.v	K7r.v	O8r	O Beate Sebastiane	Jo.martini.
	B8r.iii	F7r	K7v.i	O8r.iv	2/ Libera nos	
22	B8v	F7r.iii	K7v.v	O8v	ALma redemptoris mater	[Anon.]
23	C1r	F7v	K8r.iv	P1r	NAtiuitas vnde gaudia	Brumel.
	C1r.i	F7v.iv	K8v.ii	P1r.iv	2/ Cernere diuinum	
24	C1r.iii	F8r.ii	L1r	P1v.iii	GLoria laus ꝫ honor	Brumel.
	C1r.v	F8r.iii	L1r.iii	P1v.iv	2/ Hij tibi passuro	
	C1v	F8r.v	L1r.v	P1v.v	3/ Plebs ebrea	
	—	F8v	L1v	P2r	4/ Dauidis	
	C1v.i	F8v.ii	L1v.iii	P2r.iii	5/ Hij placere	
	C1v.ii	F8v.iii	L1v.v	P2v.iv	6/ Israel es tu	
	C1v.iv	F8v.vi	L2r	P2v.v	7/ O dauitica plebs	
25	C2r	G1r	L2r.iii	P3r	REgina celi Letare	Jo.ghiselin.
26	C2r.v	G1r.iii	—	P3r.iv	PAter meus agricola est	Alexan.Agricola
	C2v.iii	G1v.i	—	P3v.i	2/ [untexted]	
27	C3r.v	G2r.v	L2r.vi	P3v.ii	FEstiuitatem dedicationis	Jero. de Clibano.
	C3v.ii	G2v.ii	L2v.iv	P3v.v	2/ Sit igitur ad ipsum	
28	C4r	G3r	L3r.iii	P4r.iv	O Beate Sebastiane	Gaspar.
	C4r.iv	G3r.iii	L3v	P4v.i	2/ Libera nos	
29	C4v	G3v	L3v.iv	P4v.iv	INuiolata integra ꝫ casta	Philippus Basyron.
30	C5r	G4r	L4r.ii	P5r.ii	O Potens magni	[Anon.]
	C5v	G4v	L4v	P5v	2/ Cui de nomen fuit	
31	C6r	G5r	L5r	P5v.vi	O Clauiger regni celorum	[Anon.]
	C6r.iv	G5v	L5r.v	P6r.iii	2/ Qui regni claves	
32	C6v.iii	G6r	L5v.iii	P6v	SAlue virgo virginum	Joannes:Aulen
	C7r.i	G6r.iv	L6r.i	P6v.iv	2/ Salue lux fidelium	
33	C7v	G6v	L6v	P7r.iii	BEata es maria virgo	Jacobus obreth.
	C7v.iv	[repeat]	L6v.iii	P7r.v	2/ Aue maria virgo clemens	
34	C8r	G6v.iv	L7r	P7v	O Stelliferi conditor orbis	[Anon.]
	C8r.v	G7r	L7r.v	P7v.vi	2/ O iam miseras	

35	C8v	G7r.iii	L7v	P8r.iii	OB[ecro te virgo dulci[[ima	[Anon.]
	C8v.iv	G7r.vi	L7v.iv	P8r.vi	2/ Gaudeat plebs	
36	D1r	G7v.iii	L8r.ii	P8v.iii	COnceptus hodiernus marie	Brumel.
	D1r.v	G8r	L8v	Q1r.i	2/ Maria plena gratia	
37	D1v.iii	G8v	L8v.v	Q1r.v	AUe Jesu christe verbum patris	[Anon.]
	D2r	G8v.ii	M1r.iii	Q1v.ii	2/ Aue Jesu christe splendor	
38	D2v	H1r	M1v.ii	Q2r	O Beate ba[ili confe[[or	Jaco.Obreth.
	D2v.iv	—	M1v.iii	Q2r.iv	2/ O beata pater ba[ili	
	D2v.v	H1r.ii	M2r	Q2v	3/ O virum digne	
39	D3r	H1v	M2v	Q2v.iv	VUltum tuum deprecabuntur	Jo[quin de pres
	D3v	H1v.ii	M2v.iii	Q3r	2/ Sancta dei genitrix	
	D3v.iii	H2r	M3r	Q3r.iii	3/ INtemerata virgo	
	D4r	H2v	M3r.v	Q3v	4/ O Maria nullam	
	D4r.iv	H2v.iv	M3v.iii	Q3v.iv	5/ MEnte tota tibi	
	D4v.ii	H3r	M4r	Q4r.ii	6/ ORa pro nobis	
	D4v.v	H3r.iv	M4r.iv	Q4r.v	7/ CHri[te dei mundi	
40	D5r	H3v	M4r.vi	Q4v	AUe mater omnium	Ga[par.
41	D5r.iv	H4r	M4v.iii	Q4v.iv	SPiritus domini repleuit	Ga[par
					[Headed:] in honorem sancti spiritus.	
	D5v	H4v	M5r	Q5r.ii	2/ VEni sancte spiritus	
	D5v.iv	H4v.ii	M5r.ii	Q5r.v	3/ BEata gens cuius e[t	
	D6r	H5r	M5v	Q5v	4/ Confirma	
	D6r.iv	H5v.iv	M5v.iv	Q5v.iv	5/ Loquebatur	
	D6v	H6r.ii	M6r.ii	Q6r	6/ FActus est repente	
42	D6v.iv	H6v	M6v	Q6r.iv	REgina celi letare	[Anon.]
43	D7r.iii	H6v	M7r	Q6v.ii	NAtiuitas tua dei genitrix	Era[mus lapicide.
44	D7v	H7r	M7v	Q7r	VIrgo prudenti[[ima	Era[mus lapicide.
45	D8r	H7v	M8r	Q7v	SI bibero crathere pleno	[Ninot]
				Q8r	[Colophon; Register; Device]	
		H8r			[blank staves]	
	D8v	H8v	M8v	Q8v	[blank]	

Extant copies:

D-W, 2.8-2.8.3.Musica (4). Complete

    Size of page: 173 × 244 mm.

    Watermarks:

A1-2	A3-4	A7	B1-2	B4-3	B6	B7	C2	C3-4	C5	C8-7	D2-1	D4-3	E1	E4-3	E6
16	16	17	16	16	18	18	17	16	18	16	16	18	16	17

E7-8	F2-1	F4-3	F8	G1-2	G4	G6-5	G7	H2-1	H3-4	H5	H8	J2-1	J4	J6-5	J8
16	16	16	17	16	17	16	17	16	16	17	17	16	17	16	17

K2-1	K4	K6-5	K8	L2-1	L4	L6-5	L8	M2-1	M4	M6-5	M8	N1-2	N3-4	N5	N7
16	17	16	17	16	18	16	17	16	18	16	17	16	16	18	18

O1-2	O3	O5-6	O7	P2-1	P4-3	P5	P8	Q1	Q4	Q6-5	Q7-8
16	17	16	17	16	16	18	17	17	18	16	16

    Some of the Nos. 16 are probably No.6

Technical comments: N3*v*: staves and text are both smudged • Q2*r*: signature and music both smudged

Corrections and changes:

  In-house: D2*v*: see above

  Later: Q6*r*.i.clef: F$_4$ → F$_3$, in manuscript

Binding and Provenance: with *Fragmenta Missarum* (1505, No.24)

GB-Ob, Don.d.12. Superius, lacking ff.B4-5

  Watermarks:

A2-1	A4	A6-5	B1-2	B-6	B7	C1-2	C4-3	C6	C7	D2-1	D4	D6-5	D8
16	18	16	16	16	18	16	16	18	18	16	18	16	18

  Technical comments: There are some patterns of stave repetitions: for example, A3*v* → B3*v* → C3*v* and B7*v* → C7*v*

  Later changes: A7*v*.ii.signature: upper flat is touched up in brown ink • D2*v*.vi: custos erased

HR-Ssf. Altus and Bassus. This copy has not been seen

  Technical comments: N3*r*.v: text spacing sort • O7*v*.v and P1*v*.iii: music spacing sorts

  Later Changes: Modern pencil foliation: [1], 2–32

  Binding: contemporary with rolls and a diamond-shaped stamp • Bound with *Motetti C* (No.15)

I-Mc, S.B.178/10. Tenor and Bassus. Lacking folio H8, blank

  Size of page: 169 × 235 and 169 × 235 mm.

  Watermarks:

E1	E3-4	E5	E7-8	F1	F4	F6-5	F7-8	G1-2	G3	G5-6	G7	H2-1	H6-5
17	16	17	16	18	18	16	16	16	18	16	18	16	16

N6-5	N7-8	O2	O4	O6-5	O8-7	P1-2	P4-3	P7	Q3-4	Q5	Q7-8
16	16	17	17	16	16	16	16	17	16	18	16

  Corrections and changes:

  In-house: G5*v* and P2*v*: see above

  Later: G2*r*.iv.12: *corona* in brown ink • O3*r*.ii: stave line added in brown ink • O5*r*.iv.after 5: an erasure, possibly of a flat • P3*v*.i.penultimate note has a *corona* below it, in grey ink

  Binding: With Josquin, *II Missarum*

  Provenance: Mantua, Sta. Barbara • perhaps the Chapel of Cardinal Ippolito d'Este

  Bibliography: Exhibited at Florence in 1949: Damerini, "Esposizione", 25 • Prizer, "Cappella" • Lockwood, "Adrian"

I-Vnm, Mus.197–199. Superius, Altus, and Bassus, complete. In 1990, the Superius could not be found

  Size of page: 169 × 234 mm.

  Watermarks:

A2-1	A3-4	A6	B3-4	B5	B8-7	C1	C4-3	C6	C7-8	D2	D3-4	D5	D8-7
16	16	17	16	17	16	18	16	17	16	18	16	18	16

J2-1	J4-3	J6	J8	K2-1	K4	K6-5	K8	L2-1	L4-3	L6	L8	M1	M3	M5-6	M7-8
16	16	17	17	16	17	16	17	16	16	17	17	18	18	16	16

N2	N4	N6-5	N8-7	O2	O3-4	O5	O8-7	P1-2	P3	P5-6	P7	Q4-3	Q6	Q7-8
18	18	16	16	17	16	17	16	16	18	16	17	16	17	16

Technical comments: N3*r*.v: a text spacing sort, 1.6 mm wide • N5*r*.i.after 21: a music spacing sort, 0.8 mm wide, extends 5.3 mm above the top of the stave • N5*v*.vi: a text spacing sort, 0.8 mm wide, is 3 mm high • N6*r*.v: a line of tops of the spacing sorts shows above the stave, at a height of about 5 mm: no tops show for the music sorts • Q8*r* shows the blind impress of staves

Corrections and changes:

In-house: D2*v*: see above

Later: A7*v*.ii.signature: upper flat is touched up in brown ink • O3*v*.v.1–3: now three *colb*: not well printed and filled in, in ink • O5*v*.v.last 2: *bg*, *sbg*, now colored, perhaps in black ink

Binding: From the Vienna Nationalbibliothek • Both books have 19th-century and modern flyleaves

Provenance: The A-Wn call number] SA.77.C.23 [is pasted inside the front board of each book: A separate label reads] AN 47.D.23 [with the last three elements struck through and, written below:] 35.E.123 • On the first 19th-century flyleaf is written] Inv.N°.20584 • This is one of the copies taken from Venice to Vienna so that Schmid could study them: it was returned in 1919 (see Coggiola, "Recupero")

Bibliography: Fenlon and Dalla Vecchia, *Venezia*, pp. 77–78 (exhibition catalogue, Venice, 2001)

SI-Ka, s.s. Altus, complete. I am grateful to Dr. Metoda Kokole for arranging for me to consult this copy

Size of page: 169 × 239 mm.

Watermarks:

J2-1	J4-3	J6	J8	K2-1	K4-3	K6	K8	L1-2	L4	L6-5	L7	M2-1	M3	M6-5	M8
16	16	18	18	16	16	18	17	16	18	16	18	16	17	16	17

Technical comments: J1*r*: the blind impress of three lines of notes, probably all *sm*, on either side of the initial • J1*v*: the blind impress of staves iii-vi • J8*v*: the staves were apparently printed before the notation • M6*v*.vi: the impress of notes in the area of the uninked stave No apparent corrections or changes

Binding: the first of four books: (1) This book; (2) *Motetti C* (1504, No.15); (3) *I Motteti del Fiore á4* (Moderne, *RISM* 1532[10]); (4) *II Motteti del Fiore à5* (Moderne, *RISM* 1532[9]) • Dark leather, now very worn, with a blind-stamped and rolled design, probably Italian. Original three tie-strings on each face, none now extant

Bibliography: Radole, *Capodistria*, p. 19 • Radole, *Istria*, p. 147 • In a letter of 8.i.1980 kept with this copy, Professor Lilian Pruett relates it to the copy now held in Split

---

Lost copies: Copies were owned by Colón (Chapman, "Printed", No.14) amd the Fuggers (Schaal, "Musikbibliothek" I/64)

Bibliography:

(a) Rosaria Boccadifuoco, *Bibliografia*, No.2347 • Sartori, *Petrucci*, No.21

(b) Brunet, *Manuel*, iii, col.1925

(d) Sherr, *16th-Century*, iii

(e) Lockwood, *Music*, pp. 314–15

Commentary:

1.   The Tavola claims that there are fifty-five pieces, implying that those *partes* of *Vultum tuum* and *Spiritus Domini* listed in the index are counted as pieces. This tends to confirm the pattern of

dissemination of these movements, whereby different *partes* do surface as independent compositions.

2.   There is no obvious reason why only five staves are inked on certain folios: in many other places, both the fifth and sixth staves are inked but not used for notation.

3.   The pattern of added information in the head-line is clear: for most works, an attribution is supplied, but only in the Superius book. There are few comments in the lower parts: for the two compositions with two texts, a cue is given in the lower voices; for the first, the presence of a second *pars* is noted; and for the second work, an added caption is provided:

recto:] Aue regina. Jo∫quin. [A2 • Secunda pars [A3 • Petrus de la rue. [A4 • Joannes moton. [A7 • Joannes ghi∫elin. [B2 • Ja.obreth. [B3 • Ninot. [B5 • Turplin. [B7 • Jo.martini. [B8 • Brumel. [C1, D1 • Jo.ghi∫elin. [C2 • Ga∫par. [C4, D5

verso:] Panagiricum. Brumel. [A2 • Jo.ghi∫elin. [A3 • Jacobus oberti. [A5 • In patientia Joannes ghi∫elin. [A8 • Brumel. [B1 • Jo∫quin:de pre5. [B4 • Philippus Ba∫yron. [C4 • Jacobus obreth. [C7 • Jaco. Obreth. [D2 • Era∫mus lapicide. [D7

Lower voices: recto:] Alma redemptoris [E2, J2 • Comme femme [G1 • Aue regina [N2 • Secunda pars. [N3

verso:] Panagiricum: [E2 • Panegiricum [J2 • Ave virginum gemma [J5, above iii • Panagiricum. [N2

4.   These copies show relatively little correction, and appear to have been sent out largely as printed. The few corrections that I have listed as possibly in-house may well have been made by early owners, for they survive in only one copy each.

No. 22. Josquin: *Missarum II*

30.vi.1505   *RISM* J 670

A1*r*]   Mi∫∫arum Jo∫quin | Liber ∫ecundus. | Aue maris ∫tella. | Hercules dux ferrarie. | Malheur me bat. | Lami baudichon. | Una mu∫que de bu∫caya. | Dung aultre amer.

C1*r*]   Libri ∫ecundi Mi∫∫arum Jo∫quin. | T

D1*r*]   Libri ∫ecundi Mi∫∫arum Jo∫quin. | A

F1*r*]   Libri ∫ecundi Mi∫∫arum Jo∫quin. | B

[For the Bassus at I-Bc, see below, "In-house changes"]

G8*r*]   Impre∫∫um Uenetijs per Octauianum | Petrutium Forо∫empronien∫em. Die vlti-|mo Junij Salutis anno 1505. Cum pri-|uilegio inuicti∫∫imi Dominij Uenetiarum: | quae nullus po∫∫it cantum Figuratum impri-|mere ∫ub pena in ip∫o priuilegio contenta. | Regi∫trum. | ABCDEFG Omnes quaterni | preter CE quinterni. | [Petrucci's device]

Format and collation: Partbooks: landscape quarto-in-eights. [S] 16 folios: A-B⁸; [T] 10 folios: C¹⁰; [A] 18 folios: D⁸E¹⁰; [B] 16 folios: F-G⁸

Signatures:] aAa ij [$4 • − A1 • + C5 and E5, both signed with an arabic numeral

No foliation or pagination

Running heads: The head-line has two components: part-names were apparently kept in the forme, and are listed here. The names of the masses were reset each time, and are listed in the Commentary, below

recto:]   Superius.   [A2-B8

	Tenor.	[C2–C10
	Altus.	[D2–E10
	Baſſus.	[F2–G7
	[Nil:	A1, C1, D1, F1
verso:]	Superius.	[A1–B7
	Tenor.	[C1–C9
	Altus.	[D1–E9
	Baſſus.	[F1–G7
	[Nil:	[B8, C10, E10, G8

Fonts: Music: Petrucci's normal music type. Includes a *maxima* without the dog-tooth pattern: cf. C9*v*.v.last note

Staves: six per page: 175–180 mm long, 10-92-112 mm high

Text: Rotonda

Technical comments: B7*v*.last chord: the edge of the note must go right to the edge of the sort: this is evident in the copies at D-W and I-Bc

In-house changes: A5*v*.iv.22: *sb*, a' → g', erasure and perhaps stamped in: I-Bc, I-Mc and US-R • C1*r*. the phrase:] Libri ſecundi Miſſarum Joſquin. [has been added later, at a further run through the press: D-W and I-Mc • D1*r*. as C1*r*: D-W and I-Bc • F1*r*. as C1*r*: D-W, I-Fm and I-Mc • F2*v*.iv.after 22: *m*d erased: stave lines touched up in brown: I-Bc, I-Fm and I-Mc

Contents:

	A*r*	C1*r*	D1*r*	F1*r*	[Title]
1	A1*v*	C1*v*	D1*v*	F1*v*	Joſquin. Ave maris ſtella.
	A1*v*.iv	C1*v*.iii	D1*v*.iv	F1*v*.iv	[Gloria]
	A2*r*.iv	C2*r*	D2*r*.iv	F2*r*.iv	[Credo]
	A3*r*	C2*v*.ii	D3*r*	F3*r*	[Sanctus]
	A3*v*.ii	C2*v*.iv	D3*v*.iv	F3*v*.iii	[Agnus]
2	A4*r*	C3*r*	D4*r*.v	F4*r*	Joſquin. Hercules Dux ferrarie.
	A4*r*.v	C3*r*.ii	D4*v*.v	F4*r*.iv	[Gloria]
	A4*v*.v	C3*r*.iv	D5*r*.iii	F4*v*.iv	[Credo]
	A5*r*.ii	C3*v*	D6*r*.ii	F5*v*	[Sanctus]
	A6*r*	C3*v*.iii	D6*v*.iii	F6*r*	[Agnus]
3	A7*r*	C4*r*	D7*v*	F7*r*	Joſquin. Mal heur me bat.
	A7*v*	C4*r*.iv	D7*v*.vi	F7*r*.iv	[Gloria]
	A8*r*	C4*v*.ii	D8*r*.vi	F7*v*.iv	[Credo]
	A8*v*	C5*r*.vi	E1*r*.iv	F8*v*	[Sanctus]
	B1*r*.vi	C6*r*.ii	E2*r*	G1*r*	[Agnus]
4	B2*r*	C6*v*.v	E3*r*	G1*v*.ii	Joſquin. Lami baudichon.
	B2*r*.iv	C7*r*	E3*r*.iv	G1*v*.iii	[Gloria]
	B2*v*.iv	C7*r*.iii	E3*v*.v	G2*r*.iv	[Credo]
	B3*v*.iii	C7*r*.vi	E4*v*.iv	G3*r*	[Sanctus]
	B4*r*.iv	C7*v*	E5*r*.iv	G3*r*.iv	[Agnus]
5	B4*v*	C7*v*.iii	E5*v*	G3*v*	Joſquin. Una muſque de buſchaia.
	B4*v*.iv	C8*r*	E5*v*.v	G3*v*.v	[Gloria]
	B5*v*	C8*r*.v	E6*v*	G4*v*	[Credo]
	B6*r*.v	C8*v*.v	E7*v*	G5*v*	[Sanctus]
6	B7*r*	C9*r*.v	E8*v*	G6*v*	Joſquin. Dung aulter amer.
	B7*r*.iii	C9*v*	E8*v*.iv	G6*v*.iii	[Gloria]

B7*v*	C9*v*.iii	E9*r*	G7*r*	[Credo]
B8*r*	C10*r*	E9*v*	G7*v*	[Sanctus]
B8*r*.v	C10*r*.v	E9*v*.iv	G7*v*.v	[Agnus]
			G8*r*	[Colophon; Register; Device]
		E10*r*		[blank staves]
B8*v*	C10*v*	E10*v*	G8*v*	[blank]

Extant copies: The copy cited by both Sartori (*Petrucci*, p.103) and *RISM* as being at Vienna is of an edition dated 1515, and is described with No.59

D-W, 2.8–2.8.1.Musica (2). Complete

    Size of page: 173 × 244 mm.

    Watermarks:

A1-2	A4	A6-5	A7	B1	B3	B5-6	B7-8	C2	C3-4	C6-	C7
15	17	15	18	18	18	15	15	17	15	15	17

C10-9	D1-2	D3	D5-6	D7	E2	E4	E-5	E8-7	E10-9	F1-2	F3-4
15	15	18	15	18	18	18	15	15	15	15	15

F5	F7	G2-1	G4	G6-5	G8
18	18	15	17	15	17

    Textual comments: This has the addition to the title-pages of the lower voices

    Corrections and changes:

        In-house: C1*r*, D1*r* and F1*r*: see above

        Later: D5*r*.outer margin: erasure, probably of inked impressions from furniture • E9*r*.vi.22–23: first struck through in brown ink: then the ink between the notes erased, so that the 4 *m* become 4 *f* • F4*v*.iv.17: *sb*, apparently has a tail scratched in drypoint • F8*v*.i.mensuration sign, C: has a brown ink tail

        Binding and Provenance: With *Fragmenta Missarum* (1505, No.24)

I-Bc, Q.63. Three complete part-books, lacking the Tenor

    Size of page: 169 × 236 mm.

    Watermarks: No.15 on A2-1, A5-6, B2-1, B6-5, D4-3, D7-8, E1-2, E4-3, E5-, F1-2, F3-4, G1-2 and G4-3

    Textual comments: This shows the addition to the Altus title-page, while the Bassus has the original form

    Corrections and changes:

        In-house: A5*v*, D1*r* and F2*v*: see above

        Later: Manuscript pagination: [S] 173–188; [A] 169–180; [B] 151–166

    Binding: Same wrappers as used for Agricola's masses (No.13) • Edges painted brown (S and B) or green (A)

    Provenance: Old call number 1007 on A1*r* • With the Agricola volume

    Bibliography: See No.13

I-Fm, R.u.115². Bassus, complete

    Size of page: 164 × 232 mm.

    Watermarks: No.15 on F1-2, F5-6, G2-1 and G3-4 • No.17 on F7 and G8

    Textual comments: Has the addition to the title-page

    Technical comments: G8*r*: the letter B from title-pages used as a bearer, leaving a blind impression • For the stave patterns, see below • There is strong evidence for two impressions on F1*r*. The head-line, initial letter, staves and text from F1*v* have made the same deep

impression into the folio. Only the music give a different effect • The evidence of F2*v*
suggests that the signature on F2*r* was printed at the same impression as the music • Blank
staves: F1*v*.vi; F6*r*.vi; F6*v*.iii & vi; G6*r*.v-vi; G6*v*.vi; G7*r*.vi

Corrections and changes:

In-house: F1*r* and F2*r*: see above

Later: Modern stamped foliation:] 16–31

Binding and Provenance: With the book of Agricola masses (No.13)

Bibliography: Fanelli, *Musica*

I-Mc, S.B.178/1 aba. Superius, Tenor, and Bassus, all complete

Size of page: 164 × 223; 169 × 234; 169 × 235 mm.

Watermarks:

A3-4	A7-8	B5-6	B8-7	C2-	C3-	C5-	C7-8	C10-9	F6-5	F8-7	G2-1	G5-6
15	15	15	15	17	17	15	15	15	15	15	15	15

Textual comments: Has the addition to the Tenor and Bassus title-pages

Technical comments: F3*v*.vi: furniture in the stave area has taken ink

Corrections and changes:

In-house: A5*v*, C1*r*, F1*r* and F2*v*: see above

Later: Modern foliation: [S] 1–16; [T] 49–58; [B] 69–84 • A3*v*.above i]: sanctus bami [in-
verted, in brown ink • A3*v*.i.12: *l* → *b*, by erasure • F4*v*.iv.17: *sb* → *m*, with added tail
in brown ink

Binding: These are bound in three different books, one with different contents from the other
two, and all with distinct tools and rolls for ornamentation.

Superius: 164 × 223 • Four modern tie strings • One original paste-down and one
modern fly-leaf at each end, the latter with a stub one gathering into the book:

Contents:	foliation
1. Josquin: *II Missarum*	1–16
2. Gaspar: *Misse* (1507, No.32)	17–34
3. Isaac: *Misse* (1506, No.31)	35–37, [37a], 38–51
4. De Orto: *Misse* (1505, No.20)	52–58, [58a], 59–68
5. *I Missarum diversorum* (1508, No.43)	69–84

Tenor: 169 × 234 • One paste-down and one fly-leaf at each end. The front paste-
down has a watermark of an anchor in a circle with a star above, similar to those found
in the printed pages of other Petrucci titles • Rhythmic notation on the *recto* of the first
flyleaf, and staved notation on the recto of the back paste-down.

1. Obrecht: *Misse* (1503, No.6)	1–14
2. La Rue: *Misse* (1503, No.11)	15–24
3. Brumel: *Misse* (1503, No.8)	25–34
4. Josquin: *Misse* [I] (1502, No.4)	35–48
5. Josquin: *II Missarum*	49–58
6. *Motetti IV* (1505, No.21)	59–89

Bassus: 169 × 235 • One paste-down and one fly-leaf at each end, all original. Back
fly-leaf has the watermark found in the Tenor book • Inside front board, a chart of
mensuation values

Contents:	foliation
1. Obrecht: *Misse* (1503, No.6)	1–20
2. La Rue: *Misse* (1503, No.11)	21–34

3. Brumel: *Misse* (1503, No.8)		35–50
4. Josquin: *Misse* [I] (1502, No.4)		51–68
5. Josquin: *II Missarum*		69–84
6. *Motetti IV* (1505, No.21)		85–106

Provenance: Mantua, Sta. Barbara. The name of] S. Barbara. [is entered on the title pages of the two Obrecht parts • Possibly Cardinal Ippolito d'Este

Bibliography: Damerini, "Esposizione", p.25 (exhibition at Florence, 1949) • Lockwood, "Adrian", p. 99 • Prizer, "Cappella"

US-R, ★★MI490.D424.MI.c.2. Superius, lacking A1,2,6,7,8

Watermarks: No.15 on A3-4, B1-2 and B6-5

Technical comments: A4r: the outer upper corner has taken ink very poorly, but all text seems to be present

In-house correction: A5v: see above

Binding and Provenance: With fragments of Josquin, *I Missarum* (1516, No.62)

Lost copies: This may be the edition owned by Bottrigari, although Gaspari gives a date of 1503 in his transcribed notes • It is unlikely to be the edition owned by João IV of Portugal

Other editions: Petrucci published a later series of editions dated 1515 (No.59) • An edition was put out by Pasoti and Dorico in 1526

Bibliography:

   (a) Rosaria Boccadifuoco, *Bibliografia*, No.1193 • Sartori, *Petrucci*, No.22

   (c) Josquin, *Missarum*

   (d) Josquin Werke

   (e) Noble, "Josquin" • Sartori, "Nuove", p. 186

Commentary:

1. The stave pattterns are particularly clear in the copy at I-Fm: the measurements show the presence of different formes of staves on *recto* and *verso* of each sheet, and this is confirmed by the state of individual stave lines:

	1r	2v	7r	8v		2r	1v	8r	7v		3r	4v	5r	6v		4r	3v	6r	5v
F	—	180	179	180		175	175	174	175		180	180	180	181		175	175	175	175
G	178	179	179	—		175	175	—	174		179	180	180	181		175	175	175	174

This pattern is so consistent that it seems that Petrucci intended, for many volumes, to have sets of staves that approximately corresponded to lengths of 175–176 mm or 180–181 mm. (Paper shrinkage yields the figures here.) In many books, it is apparent that there was more than one set of staves with one or other of these general measurements. However, there must have been some practical reason, within the structure of the skeleton forme, for Petrucci to adhere to these general measurements.

2. The names of the masses were entered in the head-lines as follows:

   recto:] Ave [A3 • Ave. [C2, D2-3, F2-3 • Jo[quin. Hercules Dux ferrarie. [A4 • Hercules Dux ferrarie. [C3, D4 (stave iv) • Hercules dux Ferrarie. [F4, D4 • Hercules. [A5-6, D5-7, F5-6 • Jo[quin. Malheur me bat. [A7 • Malheur me bat. [C4, F7 • Malheur. [A8-B1, C5-6, D8-E2,

F8-G1 • Jo[quin. Lami baudichon. [B2 • Lami baudichon. [B3-4, C7, E3-5, G2-3 • Una musq*ue*. [B5-6, C8-9, E6-8, G4-6 • Du*n*g aulter amer. [B7-8, C9 (stave iv) C10, E9, G7 • Nil: A1,2, C1, D1, E10, F1, G8

verso:] Jo[quin. Ave maris stella. [A1 • Ave maris stella. [C1, D1, F1 • Ave [A2-3 • Ave. [C2, D2-3, F2-3 • Hercules. [A4-5, C3, D4-6, F4-6 • Hercules. cum sex vocibus. [A6 • Malheur me bat [D7 • Malheur. [A7-B1, C4-6, D8-E2, F7-G1 • Lami baudichon. [B2-3, C6 (stave iv), C7, E3-4, G1 (stave i), G2 • Jo[quin. Una musq*ue* de buschaia [B4 • Una musq*ue* de buschaia [C7 (stave iii), E5, G3 • Una musq*ue*. [B5-6, C8, E6-7, G4-5 • Jo[quin. Du*n*g aulter amer [B7 • Du*n*g aulter amer [C9, E8-9, G6-7 • Nil: B8, C10, E10, G8

There is in general a higher level of consistency of presentation than in earlier volumes. This is clearest in the practice of entering relatively full names on the first appearance of a mass, and then shortening them for the following pages.

3. Josquin is the only composer for whom Petrucci ventured a second (and even a third) volume of masses. (The title-page for the Mouton edition of 1515 does imply that a second book might be published: but this seems merely to be in line with Petrucci's practice of the time.) This might be seen as a reflection of Josquin's stature at the time, and a result of the sales of the first book. However, I believe that both the Josquin books were probably reflections of particular situations in Ferrara, and have argued for this in chapter 9. In this connection, it is notable that the first book went into a new edition in the following year, as if the special circumstances surrounding its first edition had precluded large general sales, which only began to follow the publication of the second book.

No. 23. *Frottole IV*

[viii.1505]   *RISM* [1505][5]

First Edition

A1*r*]   Strambotti, Ode, Frot= | tole, Sonetti. Et mo | do de cantar *u*er= | [i latini e ca= | pituli. | Libro quarto.

[G8: Lacking in the unique copy]

A1*v*]   [Tavola] Numero nonanta una [arranged in three columns, in roman with roman page numerals: the works are grouped in typical alphabetical order of first letter, under captions. Under] STRAMBOTTI. [are Nos.1, 9, 11–18, 20, 22, 24–27, 29–50, 52–58, 67 and 78; under] ODE. [are Nos.6, 8, 68–77, 79 and 82; under] FROTTOLE. [Nos.2–5, 59–61, 63–66, 80, 81 and 83–90; under] SONETTI. [are Nos.7, 10, 19, 21, 23, 28, 51, 62 and 91

Format and collation: Choirbook: landscape quarto-in-eights. 56 folios: A–G[8].

Signatures:] .AA ij. [$4 • – A1

Foliation: t.r.r.] [I], II–III, iiii, V–XI, xii, XIII, XiIII, XV–XVII, XViii, XIX–XX, XXi, XXii, XXIII, XXiIII, XXV, XXVi–XXXii, XXXIII–Xl, Xli, Xlii, XlIII–XlV, XlVi, XlVii, XlVIIi, [49 missing], l–lv, [56 missing]

No running heads: composers' names in the head line

Part-names:

verso]   Tenor   [A2-5, B2-3, E2, E4-7, F7, G2-6

	Tenor Altus Baſſus	[A6-7, B1, B5-8, C3, C5-8, D3, D5-6, D8-E1, E3, E8, F3, F5-6, F8, G7
	Tenor [in stave] Altus Baſſus	[A8
	Tenor Altu5 Baſſus	[B4, C1, C4 D2, D4, F1-2, F4
	[all three, in stave as needed:	C2, D1, D7
recto]	Tenor Altus Baſſus in stave:	[A2, E1
	Altu5 Baſſus	[A3, A6, E3, E8, F8, G4
	Altus Baſſus	[A4-5, B3-4, E5-7, G3, G5-7
	Tenor Altus Baſſus	[A7-B2, B6-8, C2, C4, C6, D2, D4, D6, D8, F2-3, F5-7
	Tenor Altus Baſſu	[C8
	Tenor Altu5 Baſſus	[D1, D3, E4, F1, F4
	[all three, in staves as needed:	B5, C1, C3, C5, C7, D7, E2, G2
	Altus Tenor Baſſus	[D5

Small incipit letters are used in several part-names:

verso: Tenor: A2,4,5,6,7; B1,2,3,5,7; D6,7,8; E2,3,5,6,7; F1,5,6,8; G2,4,5,6,7
          Altus: A6,8; B1,6; C2,3,5,8; D1,3,7; E8; F1,3
          Bassus: A7; B4,5,7,8; C1,4,6,7; D2,3,4,5,6,7,8; E3; F1,2,4,5,6,8; G7
recto: Tenor: A2,7; B5,6,8; C2,3,4,5,6,7,8; D1,3,4,5,7,8; E1,4; F1,3,4,5,7
          Altus: A3,5,6,7; B5,6,7,8; C1,3,8; D1,3,5,6,7; E1,3; F1,3,4,5,7,8; G3,4
          Bassus: A3,4,6,8; B1,2,3,4,5; C1,2,3,4,7; D1,2,3,7; E3,5,6,7; F1,2,4,6; G2,4,5,6,7

Fonts: Music: Petrucci's normal music type

Staves: Six per page were intended, though not often printed

Text: Roman throughout

Technical comments: Small capital letters used on C4r [M], D8r [D], E3v [T], F5v [O], G2v [D] • No capital letter on E4r

In-house corrections: All to be found in the unique copy: A6v.iv.22: erased note, perhaps a b, and stamped-in *sbf*, with touched-up stave lines • A6v.iv.35: erased note, perhaps a b, and stamped-in *sbf*, with touched-up stave lines • D2v.iv.34: *b*, G erased and A stamped in • D8r.iii.9: *colsb*, d' erased and c' stamped in • F6r.iii.3: *sba*' erased and *sbb*' stamped in

Contents: The last column gives the folio number as entered in the Tavola:

	A1r	[Title]		
	A1v	[Tavola] Numero nonanta una		
1	A2r	IO ſon locel che ſopra i rami doro	MARCVS CHARA. VERO	ii.
2	A2v	OGni amor uol eſſer uero	ANT.CAP.	iii.
3	A3v	QVeſto oime pur mi tormenta	ANT.CAP.	iiii.
4	A4v	POi che mia ſincera fede	ANT.CAP.	v.
5	A5v	RItornata e la ſperanza	ANT.CAP.	vi.
6	A6v	VAga zioioſa e biancha	ANT.CAP.	vii.
		[T,A,B:] zioioſa e bella		
7	A7r	VA poſa larcho e la pharetra amore	[Anon.]	vii.
8	A7v	SE la gran fiamma ardente	[Anon.]	viii.
9	A8r	MOrte te prego che de tanti affanni	B.T.	viii.
10	A8v	LI angelici ſembianti e la beltade	[Anon.]	ix.
11	B1r	VAna ſperanza mia che mai non uiene	PHILIPPVS.L.	ix.
		[Tavola:] . . . ueue		
12	B1v	DEus in adiutorium meum intende	B.T.	x.

13	B2r	NOn fu ſi crudo el dipartir de Enea	[Anon.]	x.
14	B2v	A Che affligi el tuo ſeruo	B.T.	xi.
15	B3v	OChi mei laſſi poi che perſo	M.C.	xii.
16	B4v	SI ſuaue mi par el mio dolore	[Anon.]	xiii.
17	B5r	DEl tuo bel uolto amor	B.T.	xiii.
18	B5v	VEdo ſdegnato amor crudel e fiero	F.V.	xiiii.
19	B6r	[Heading:] Modo de cantar ſonetti	[Anon.]	xiiii.
20	B6v	O Caldi mei ſuſpiri	M.C.	xv.
21	B7r	BEnche inimica e tedioſa ſei	[Anon.]	xv.
		[Headed:] Sonetto.		
22	B7v	LAſſa el cieco dolor che ti tranſporta	[Anon.]	xvi.
23	B8r	MEntre che a tua belta	M.C.	xvi.
		[Headed:] Sonetto.		
24	B8v	TV mhai priuato de ripoſo e pace	[Anon.]	xvii.
25	C1r	LA fiamma che me abruſcia	N.P.	xvii.
26	C1v	TI par gran maraueglia	N.P.	xviii.
27	C2r	MI fa ſol o mia dea	N.P.	xviii.
28	C2v	PEnſa donna chel tempo fuge	N.P.	xix.
		[Headed:] Sonetto		
29	C3r	SContento me ne reſto	[Anon.]	xix.
30	C3v	ME ſteſſo incolpo e me ſteſſo	[Anon.]	xx.
31	C4r	MErce ha per mi ſpento ognun ſuo lume	[Anon.]	xx.
32	C4v	NOn bianco marmo non candida pietra	F.V.	xxi.
33	C5r	Se per humidita daque ſacoglie	F.V.	xxi.
34	C5v	AMor a chi non ual forza	F.V.	xxii.
35	C6r	AMor con le tue faze e larcho	F.V.	xxii.
36	C6v	SE laffanato core in focho iace	F.V.	xxiii.
37	C7r	PAſſo paſſo pian pian apocho	F.V.	xxiii.
38	C7v	EL cor un altra uolta me fugito	F.V.	xxiiii.
39	C8r	QVeſto sol giorno	B.T.	xxiiii.
40	C8v	RInforzi ognhor piu mia dura ſorte	M.	xxv.
41	D1r	LA nocte aquieta ogni animale	[Anon.]	xxv.
42	D1v	LInfermo alhor piu ſe conſuma	[Anon.]	xxvi.
43	D2r	RIſeno i monti el mar moſtro bonaza	[Anon.]	xxvi.
		[T:] Montes exultauerunt		
44	D2v	SVrge cor laſſo hormai dal ſonno	B.T.	xxvii.
45	D3r	COme potu temer che mai te laſſi	[Anon.]	xxvii.
46	D3v	SIlentium lingua mia ti prego	B.T.	xxviii.
47	D4r	NOn te ſmarir cor mio ua paſſo	[Anon.]	xxviii.
48	D4v	NOn temo de bruſciar	B.T.	xxix.
49	D5r	DIlecto albergo e tu beato nido	M.C.	xxix.
50	D5v	SE hogi e un di chogni defunto iace	B.T.	xxx.
51	D6r	CHi uede gir la mia dea	[Anon.]	xxx.
52	D6v	SVſpir ſuaui o mio dolce tormento	[Anon.]	xxxi.
53	D7r	DA poi che non ſi po piu ritrouare	[Anon.]	xxxi.
54	D7v	DAl ciel deſceſe amor	F.V.	xxxii.

55	D8r	DI focho ardente adeſſo	B.T.	xxxii.
56	D8v	HAi pretioſa fe ſi laccerata	[Anon.]	xxxiii.
57	E1r	LA nocte quando ognun ripoſa [Tav:] Le notte . . .	[Anon.]	xxxiii.
58	E1v	SE ne gli affanni non creſceſſe [Tav:] Se nelli	[Anon.]	xxxiiii.
59	E2r	QVanto piu donna te dico	PHI.DE LV.	xxxiiii.
60	E2v	ROmpe amor queſta cathena	PHI.DE LV.	xxxv.
61	E3v	TVtto el mondo chiama e crida	PHI.DE LV.	xxxvi.
62	E4r	[Headed:] Aer de uerſi latini [Tav:] Aer de cantar uerſi latini	ANTONIVS CAPREOLUS BRIXIEN.	xxxvi.
63	E4v	OGnun fuga fuga amore	ANT.CAP.	xxxvii.
64	E5v	TAnto mi e il partir moleſto	ANT.CAP:	xxxviii.
65	E6v	FVggi pur da me ſe ſai	ANT.CAP.	xxxix.
66	E7v	DIo lo ſa quanto me ſtrano	ANT.CAP.	xl.
67	E8v	SE ho ſdegnato la tua mente altera	ANT.CAPREO.	xli.
68	F1r	SColtatime madonna	[Anon.]	xli.
69	F1v	EL laccio che la mane	[Anon.]	xlii.
70	F2r	COn pianto e con dolore	[Anon.]	xlii.
71	F2v	LAchrime e uoi ſuſpiri	[Anon.]	xliii.
72	F3r	O Mia ſpietata ſorte	[Anon.]	xliii.
73	F3v	ECcome qui hormai Fa di me	[Anon.]	xliiii.
74	F4r	O Tanti mei ſuſpiri	[Anon.]	xliiii.
75	F4v	EL cor che ben diſpoſto	[Anon.]	xlv.
76	F5r	COme po far el cielo	[Anon.]	xlv.
77	F5v	O Dolce e lieto albergo	[Anon.]	xlvi.
78	F6r	QVando per darme nel languir	[Anon.]	xlvi.
79	F6v	LA dolce diua mia	[Anon.]	xlvii.
80	F7r	CHe fa la ramacina	COMPERE	xlvii.
81	F7v	SCaramella fa la galla	[C]OMPERE	xlviii.
82	F8v	O Mia infelice ſorte	[Anon.]	xlix.
83	G1r	[Donna contra la mia voglia]	[PHI.DE LV.]	xlix.
84	G1v	[Donna questa e la mia voglia]	[PHI.DE LV.]	l.
85	G2r	FAmmi almen una bona cera	PHI.DE LV.	l.
86	G2v	DAmmi almen lultimo uale	PHI.DE LV.	li.
87	G3v	NOn mi dar piu longhe hormai	PHI.DE LV.	lii.
88	G4v	VIen da poi la nocte luce	PHI.DELV.	liii.
89	G5v	VAle hormai con tua durezza	PHI.DE LV.	liiii.
90	G6v	FAmmi quanto mal te piace	PHI.DE LV.	lv.
91	G7v	VN ſolicito amor una gran fede [Headed:]	PHI.DE LV. Aer de Capituli.	lv.
	G8r	[Privilege: Colophon: Device]		
	G8v	[blank]		

Extant copy:

D-Mbs, Rar.878/4. Lacks G1 and G8

Size of page: 159 × 228 mm.

Watermarks: No.15 on A1-2, A3-4, B1-2, B6-5, C1-2, C5-6, D1-2, D4-3, E4-3, E7-8, F5-6, F7-8, G5-6 and G7-

Technical comments: A2*v*.i: text spacing sort, suggesting that the top of the type came to the very edge of the body

Corrections and changes:

    In-house: A6*v*, D2*v*, D8*r* and F6*r*: see above • The following may also have been executed in-house: B3*v*.vi.after 10: 3 *m* erased: now *mc'*,clef C$_4$,flat,*md'*,*mb*, all in light brown ink • B5*r*.i.last note: *b* → *l*, with an ink tail • B5*r*.vi.9 from end: *m* pitch from d to c, in light brown ink • C3*r*.iv.before 10 from the end: *sb*, erased c' and replaced d', light brown ink • C3*r*.iv.7-8 from end: *m*, *m*, changed to *sm*, *sm*, in light brown ink • C3*r*.iv.5-6 from end: *mb* erased and *md'*, *mb* entered in light brown ink

    Later: Foliated in modern pencil: 177–230 • A8*r*.ii.before 11 back: *sb* rest added, initialled RJ • B5*r*.i.*l*: tail added in ink, initialled RJ • B7*r*.i.1: manuscript tail added, initialled RJ • B7*r*.i.6: erased tail • B8*r*.iii: *m* rest added after bar-line, initialled RJ • C3*v*.iii.after 21: first *r* struck through, and the deletion itself struck through, initialled RJ • E4*r*.iv.last 2, from a, a to g, g, in manuscript initialled c.g. • E8*v*.iii.5 from end: from *sb* to *b*, in ink, initialled g.c. • F7*r*.v.rests before 13: from *b*, *m* to *b*, *sb*, in manuscript, initialled g.c.

Binding and Provenance: with *Frottole I* (1504, No.16)

———

Lost copies: A copy existed in the Fugger collection, perhaps the copy of the second edition, now at A-Wn (see Schaal, "Musikbibliothek", I/71)

Early references: The book is cited by Gesner (Bernstein, "Gesner", No.245) • This is perhaps the book cited by Draudius in his *Bibliotheca classica* (1625).] Cant. var. & modus cantandi versus Ln. & capitula. | Liber II. 4, 5, 6 | Venet. apud Octav. Petruvium [Heussner and Schultz, from whom I take this reference, believe that it refers to one of the editions of *II Frottole*: I think it is more likely that the numeral is in error, and that this is a reference to one of the editions of the present volume

Other editions: A second edition appeared in 1507 (*RISM* 1507², No.37)

Bibliography:

    (a)   Sartori, *Petrucci*, No.19 • Jeppesen, *Frottola*, Pe.IV • Vogel, *Bibliografia*, 1505¹

    (b)   Brunet, *Manuel*, ii, col.1413 (dated 1504)

    (d)   Schwartz, *Ottaviano*

Commentary:

1.   The date of this volume is conjectural, for the colophon is missing in the uniquely surviving copy. A first edition of Book IV must have appeared between February and December of 1505, when the third and fifth books appeared, respectively. During the intervening months, Petrucci published *Motetti A* (13 February), *Misse de Orto* (22 March: 70 folios), *Motetti libro quarto* (4 June: 128 folios), *Missarum Josquin II* (30 June: 60 folios) and *Fragmenta Missarum* (31 October: 72 folios). The papers for these books suggest that the present volume was published after the stock of paper 11 was finished (for it had been used intensively for a few books) — that is, after the *Misse de Orto*. Table 10-6 (above), while intended to provide information regarding rates of work, does also suggest a place for the present volume: it is hard to see a specific place in the first half of

the year into which to insert the 56 folios of *Frottole IV*. After the summer, however, there is more space: the most likely solution would be sometime in August. Paper 15 reappeared in the preceding volume, the second of Josquin's masses, and was exhausted in the succeeding one, the *Fragmenta Missarum*.

2. Petrucci's use of small initials for part-names in this edition tells us much less about printing-house practice than it did in *Frottole III*. That is because the distribution of parts on the opening is itself so inconsistent. It is, as a result, unlikely that the typesetter was ever able to retain part names in the forme, even though there are occasional repetitions of distinctive sorts in consecutive gatherings.

3. Both the title and the Tavola indicate that genre was an important aspect of this volume: as I argue in chapter 9, this draws it away from the first three books and toward Book VI, in particular. The strong presence of Strambotti (just over half the total) reflects the general popularity of that form. But it is notable that, after a single-page strambotto, the book immediately presents a group of frottole, as well as representatives of the other forms. After that strambotti take over, especially once we reach the end of gathering B. From here, for two complete gatherings, the sequence is almost uninterrupted. The less popular forms, frottola and oda, also have short sequences of pieces, in gatherings E and F respectively. Only the sonetto settings are spaced at random through the book. But there are very few of these: in the Tavola they are augmented by the insertion of the three overtly didactic pieces.

    The intention seems to be that the purchaser should have a guide to performing the various forms, and also groups of examples on which to practice.

4. However, the detailed arrangement of pieces shows a balance between this criterion of form and grouping by composer. (A preliminary approach to this issue is in Boorman, "Printed", pp. 2598–99.) For example, there is an ode in the group of works by Capreolus in gathering A; similarly a strambotto is included in the same composer's frottole in gathering E. The ordering in the Tavola is therefore not the primary means of arranging the pieces in the book. Instead, it can be argued that the music was collected in a series of small batches, some of which concentrated on individual forms, and others on specific composers. Thus, after a single piece by a flag-ship name, Cara, there is a small group of works by Capreolus. The great bulk of gathering F is comprised of anonymous works in similar styles; the whole of gathering G is devoted to works by Lurano. Then the music in gathering C is almost entirely by Nicolo Patavino or Francisco d'Ana; and gathering B is similarly committed to music by Cara and Tromboncino. Significantly, the changes between these groups of works coincide precisely with gathering joins, regardless of the number of single-page pieces involved. This is not strictly true for the grouping by form: apparently the small collections from which this book was drawn were ordered primarily by composer.

5. The book has a surprisingly large number of works occupying just one page. In particular, there is a long run of 44 such pieces from B4*v* to E2*r* (largely coinciding with the group of strambotti): and, in total, only 17 works are of the normal length of frottole in other volumes. This is a direct reflection of style, and of the level of repetition in the musical settings: perhaps it also reflects another aspect of the intent of the unusual title.

6. It is notable that this was the first of the frottola books to be reprinted, about two years later. It was to be followed three months later by Book III, and then Book II, and possibly even Book I, as I suggest above (see No.16). But the greater popularity of Book IV is attested both by this priority, and by the fact that the other books had to wait nearly three years for their second editions. No doubt, the didactic intent of the present book (perhaps supported by the presence of so many shorter and simpler pieces) helped it sell among new purchasers, and also drew their attention to the earlier books.

No. 24. *Fragmenta Missarum*

31.X.1505   RISM 1505[1]

There were apparently two printings of this book, although neither survives complete. The second was printed not long after the first, though not necessarily all at the same time. It is entered here, because all copies use the same final sheet, and therefore have the same date of publication • There is a cancel for the first printing.

Edition.

One sheet (H1,2,7,8) and the half-sheet J5-6 do not survive from this printing

For the title-pages of the lower voices, see "Technical Comments", and "In-house Corrections"

A1r]   Fragmenta Miſſarum. | S

C1r]   Fragmenta Miſſarum | T

E1r]   Fragmenta Miſſarum | A

H1r]   Fragmenta Miſſarum | B

J10r]   Impreſſum Uenetijs per Octauianum | Petrutium Foroſempronienſem. Die vlti- | mo Octobris Salutis anno 1505. Cum pri- | uilegio inuictiſſimi Dominij Uenetiarum: | quae nullus poſſit cantum Figuratum impri- | mere ſub pena in ipſo priuilegio contenta. | Regiſtru3. ABCDEFGHJ Omnes | quaterni praeter B J qui sunt quinterni 7 G duernus. | [Petrucci's device]

Tavola: This is a synoptic presentation, giving the text and page numbers of the Superius: the page numbers for the other voices are given at the right end of each line: the rest of the setting was changed for each partbook

		S	T	A	B
A1v]	Aſperges:De Fortuilla	2	19	36	56
	Aſperges:Compere	2	19	36	56
	Et in terra:De beata virgine Stokem	4	22	38	58
	Et in terra:De beata virgine Joſquin	9	27	45	64
	Hec dies.	18	34	53	71
	Kyrie de beata virgine:De orto	3	21	38	58
	Miſſa ferialis.Joſquin	14	31	49	68
	Patrem:De buſnoys.Uilayge	4	22	39	58
	Patrem de:Regis.Uilayge	5	23	40	59
	Patrem:Cardinale.Gaſpar	6	23	40	60
	Patrem:Agricola:Uilayge	7	24	41	61
	Patrem:De brumel.Uilayge	7	25	42	61
	Patrem:De clibano.Uilayge	8	26	43	62
	Patrem:Compere:Mon pere	9	27	44	63
	Patrem La bella ſa ſied Joſquin	9	28	45	64
	Patrem:De tous biens.Joſquin	10	28	46	65
	Patrem:Uilayge. Joſquin	12	29	47	66
	Patrem:Uilayge Euſde3	13	30	48	67
	Patre3: Ciaſchun me crie.Joſquin	13	30	49	67

Patrem:Agricola.Jene vis	16	33	52	70
Patrem: Ga[par.	17	33	53	71
Salue [ancta parens:	3	21	37	69
Salue [ancta parens a Fuga	3	21	38	69
Sanctus:De pa[[ione.Jo[quin	15	32	51	57
Sanctus:Dunc aultre amer Jo[quin	16	32	51	57
Uidi aquam:De fortuilla	2	20	36	56
Uidi aquam:De brumel	3	21	37	57

Format and collation: Partbooks: landscape quarto-in-eights. [S] 18 folios: A^{8}B^{10}; [T] 16 folios: C–D^8; [A] 20 folios: E–F^{8}G^4; [B] 18 folios: H^{8}J^{10}

Signatures:] aAa iij [$4 • − A1, G3 and G4 • + B5 and J5 • B5 signed:] bBb 5 • A2, D2 and H2 all signed with] ii • C2 signed:] cCc tj • J5 signed:] iJi iiiij

Foliation: [S] [1], 2–18; [T] 19–26, 29 [*recte* 27], 28–32, 31 [*recte* 33], 34; [A] 35–54; [B] 55–60, [61–62, not extant], 63–71, [72]

Running heads: top left corner (and including the folios only found in the second printing):

Sup*erius*   [A2r-3r, A4r-B7v, B8v-10r (outer corner on A3r,5r)

Tenor   [C2r-4r, C5r-D5v, D6v-8r

Altus   [E2r-G1r, G2r-4r

Ba[[us   [H2r-J5r, J6r-9v

[Nil: A1r,1v, B8r,10v, C1r,1v,4v, D6r,8v, E1r,1v, G1v,4v, H1r,1v, J5v,10r,10v

Fonts: Music: Petrucci's normal music type

Staves: Six per page: 175 or 180 mm long: 10-92-112 mm high.

Text: Rotonda

Textual comments: B1r.above iii:] Compnre • E2r.iv: the initial letter "D" is missing: E-Bbc

Technical comments: The assertion that the phrase "Fragmenta Mi[[ar*um*" was stamped in later on the title pages of the three lower voices stems from evidence of differing alignment in different copies of the same part-book • A7v and B9r, the marginal caption reads upwards • Only five staves inked on D8r • The blank staves on G3v lie in the middle of a composition

In-house corrections: C1r, E1r and H1r: the phrase] Fragmenta Missarum [was stamped in later: present in all extant copies • A5v.ii.35: *f* → *sm*, changed by an erasure, in D-W and I-Bc • C5r.ii.40: *l* → *b*, by a manuscript correction in the copy at I-Vnm, and after a stop-press change in those at D-W and I-Bc • F1v.i.29: *m* → *sb*, by stop-press correction: the corrected version in I-Vnm: the uncorrected, changed by an erasure, in D-W, E-Bbc and I-Bc • F3r.ii.end: a major change: now *mf'*,*me'* (with MS. tail),*sbg*,*mf* (with MS. tail),*sbe'*,*sbd*,*sbg*,custos a: all note-heads seem to be in type: stave lines and custos are in brown ink: present in the copies at D-W, E-Bbc, I-Bc, and I-Vnm • F5r.iv.27: ?*smc"* erased and *smb'* stamped in over leger line: brown ink tail later erased and custos g' added: present in the copies at D-W, E-Bbc, I-Bc, and I-Vnm • G1r.i.6-7: *sbd*,*mc* → *md* and space: tail added in brown ink and second note erased: present in the copies at D-W, E-Bbc (using black ink) and I-Vnm • It is quite probable that the alteration made on C4r was also executed in-house, although there is not really enough evidence to confirm this

Contents (including the folios of the second printing): Attributions are from the Superius:

A1r	C1r	E1r	H1r	[Title]
A1v	C1v	E1v	H1v	[Tavola]

1	A2r	C2r	E2r	H2r	ASperges me	Jo Fortuila
2	A2r.iv	C2r.iv	E2r.iv	H2r.iv	ASperges me	Compere
3	A2v.ii	C2v.ii	E2v.ii	H2v.ii	Vidi aquam [S:] EGredientes	Fortuila
4	A3r	C3r	E3r.iv	H3r.iii	Vidi aquam [S:] Egredientes	.A.Brumel
5	A3v	C3r.vi	E3v.v	H3v.iii	SAlve [ancte parens	Gap[ar [sic] [Tav: anon.]
6	A3v.iii	C3v.ii	E4r	H3v.v	SAlve [ancte parens	[Anon.]
7	A3v.v	C3v.iv	E4r.iii	H4r	KYrie In honorem beati[[ime virginis	De orto
8	A4r.ii	C4r	E4v	H4r.iv	ET in terra	Jo.Stokem
9	A4v.iv	C4v	E5r.v	H4v.v	PAtrem [Vilayge]	[margin:] A Bu[nois
10	A5v.v	C5v	E6r.iv	H5v.iii	PAtrem [Vilayge]	Jo.regis.
11	A6r.iv	C5v.v	E6v.iii	H6r.ii	PAtrem [Cardinale]	[margin:] Gaspar cardinale.
12	A7r.ii	C6v.iv	E7v.v	H7r	PAtrem [Vilayge]	.Agricola.
13	A7v.v	C7v.iii	E8v.iv	H7v.v	PAtrem [Vilayge]	[margin:] A.Brumel
14	A8v	C8r.iv	F1v.ii	H8v.ii	PAtrem [Vilayge]	Nica[ius de Clibano
15	B1r.iii	D1r	F2r.iv	J1r.iv	PAtrem	Compnre Mon pere.
16	B1v.v	D1v.ii	F3r	J2r	ET in terra	[Anon.] De Beata Uirgine [Tav:] Josquin
17	B2v.ii	D2r.iii	F3v.v	J2v.iii	PAtrem [La bella se sied]	Jo[quin La bella [e [ed
18	B3v.ii	D2v.iii	F4v.iv	J3v	PAtrem	super De tous biens [Tav:] Josquin
19	B4r.iii	D3r.iv	F5r.v	J4r.iii	Patrem [vilayge]	Jo[quin
20	B5r	D4r.v	F6r.iii	J5r	Patrem [vilayge]	[Tav:] Eusde3
21	B5v.iii	D4v.v	F7r	J5v	Patrem [ciaschun me crie]	[Tav:] Jo[quin
22	B6v B6v.iv B7r.iii	D5v	F7v.v	J6r.iii	MIssa Ferialis Sanctus Agnus	[Tav:] Jo[quin
23	B7v.iii	D6r.v	G1r.iii	J7r.v	SAnctus	Depa[[ione [Tav:] Josquin
24	B8r	D6v.ii	G1v	J7v.ii	SAnctus	Dung aultre amer [Tav:] Josquin
25	B8r.v	D7r	G2r	J8r	PAtrem [Je ne vie]	Agricola
26	B9r.iv	D7r.iv	G3r G3v	J9r	PAtrem [blank staves]	[margin:] Gaspar
27	B10r	D8r	G4r.iii	J9v.iii J10r	Hec dies [Colophon; Register; Device]	[Anon.]
	B10v	D8v	G4v	J10v	[blank]	

Extant copies:

A-GÜ, s.s. Tenor, lacking D8 • D1,2,7 is a cancel: see below • D4v: the initial letter is cut away, resulting in some loss of text on both sides of the folio

   Size of page: 165 × 235 mm.

   Watermarks: No.11 on C1-2, C6-5, D6-5

Technical comments: C8*v*.i.after 36: a music spacing sort, projecting ca.6 mm above the stave, is 1.2 mm wide

Corrections and changes:

In-house: C1*r*: see above

Later: C4*r*.i.m.s.: something erased, probably a circle-slash, and a circle entered, in black ink

Binding and Provenance: With Josquin *II Missarum* (1515, No.59)

Bibliography: Federhofer, "Petrucci"

D-W, 2.8-2.8.3 Musica (1). Complete: for D1,2,7,8, H1,2,7,8 and J3-8, see below

Size of page: 173 × 244 mm.

Watermarks:

A1-2	A4-3	B4-3	B-6	10-9	C2-1	C5-6	D6-5	E1	E5-6	E7-8	F4	F6-5
11	11	11	11	11	11	11	11	17	11	15	18	15

F7-8	G2	G4-3	H5-6	J2	J10-9
11	17	15	15	17	15

Textual comments: B1*r*.above iii:[Compnre mo*n* pere [*sic*]

Corrections and changes:

In-house: A5*v*, C1*r*, C5*r*, E1*r*, F1*v*, F3*r*, F5*r* and G1*r*: see above

Later: A2*v*.last note: *l*, partially erased • A5*v*.ii.35: *f* → *sm*, by erasure • C4*r*.i.after bar line: mensuration sign has had a tail removed • F1*v*.i.29: *m* → *sb*, by erasure • Inside each front board: a 16th-century index of all four books in this binding

Binding: Original calf over wooden boards, with paper borders. Blind border rolls and diagonal cross: the tenor has an additional border roll of flowers: five bosses on each board, and two clasps from back to front. S, A, and T recently rebacked • The part-names have been entered in black ink on each front cover • One paste-down with conjugate stub at front and back of all books, with the watermark of a bull's-head tau with snake on the cross (cf. Tromanin, 334, 680, 682 and 900) on at least one folio in each book • Red stained edges to the folios • The set comprises: (1) This book; (2) Josquin: *II Missarum* (1505, No.22); (3) *Motetti C* (1504, No.15); (4) *Motetti IV* (1505, No.21)

Provenance: Tenor, inside back board:] Dise vier | partes [ind Wolff Heintzens zu Halle [and] 1542 | u | bringen [: inside back board of Bassus:] Dis 4 bücher sindt | Wolff Heintzen zü Hall [and] 1542

E-Bbc, M.115 (8). Tenor, lacking G4

Size of page: 162 × 226 mm.

Watermarks: No.11 on E5-6, E8-7, F2-1, F6-5

In-house Corrections and changes: F1*v*, F3*r*, F5*r*, and G1*r*: see above

Binding and Provenance: Bound with Josquin, *I Missarum* (1516, No.62)

I-Bc, Q.64. Complete. For B1-8 and H1,2,7,8, see below

Size of page: 162 × 238 mm.

Watermarks:

A5-6	A7-8	C5-6	C8-7	D6-5	D8-7	E1-2	E4-3	F3-4	F7-8	G1-2
15	11	11	11	11	11	15	11	15	11	15

H4-3	J3-4	J10-9
15	15	15

Corrections and changes:

   In-house: F1v, F3r, F5r and J5r: see above

   Later: Manuscript foliation: [S] 130–147; [T] 84–98; [A] 128–147; [B] 114–131 • A5v.ii.35: $f \rightarrow sm$, by erasure • C4r.i.after bar-line: mensuration sign has had a tail removed

Binding: 19th-century folder with marbled paper cover • All four sets of edges are coloured gold

Provenance: Liceo stamp on A1r

Bibliography: Exhibited at Bologna in 1929. Fava, "Primo", p. 36

I-Vnm, Mus.206–208. Superius, Tenor, and Altus, complete. For folios A3–6 and B3–8, see below

   Size of page: 161 × 223 mm.

   Watermarks:

A2-1	B10	C3-4	C7-8	D2-1	D5-6	E1-2	E6-5	F6-5	F7-8	G1-2
11	15	11	11	11	11	?15	11	15	11	15

   Technical comments: B4r.vi: text spacing sort, approx 3.0 × 1.8 mm

   Corrections and changes:

      In-house: B1v, C5r, F1v, F3r, F5r, and G1r: see above

      Later: Pieces numbered in manuscript, all books:] 365–393 • A1r.signature: erased • C4r.i.after bar-line: mensuration sign has had a tail removed • C5r.ii.40: ?l with short tail: the tail erased • G1r.i.6-7: sbd,$mc \rightarrow m$d and space: tail added in brown ink and second note erased

   Binding: From Austrian National Library • One fly-leaf and one paste-down at each end of each part

   Provenance: One of the copies sent to Vienna for Schmid to study, and returned to Venice in 1919

   Bibliography: Coggiola, "Recupero" • Fenlon and Dalla Vecchia, *Venezia*, p. 77 (exhibition catalogue, Venice, 2001)

No. 24A. *Reprinting in gathering A.*

The inner forme of the inner sheet (3v,4r,5v,6r) exists in two different settings of type. This is not a cancel, for the outer forme contains the original setting

Extant copy:

I-Vnm, Mus.206–208. Folios A3–6: for the rest of the book see elsewhere in this description

   No watermark is visible

   Textual comments: For the variants between this and the earlier printing, see below

   Technical comments: A5v.i.9 from end: music spacing sort, 0.9 mm wide, projects 3.5 mm below the stave • A6v.iv-v: music spacing sorts have taken ink

   For other details, see above

No. 24B. *Cancel*

The outer sheet of gathering D in the copy at A-GÜ is in a different setting. It is a very close copy of the original setting, differing in the use of two different initials and a series of different forms of standard abbreviations. The layout is very close to the original

Extant copy:

A-GÜ, s.s. Tenor book lacking D8

   Watermark: No.11 on D-7

No. 24C. *Second Printings.*

I am reluctant to call these a full edition, even though a large percentage of the book is included. In various copies, they comprise the following sheets, Ai, Bo, B2, Bi, Do, Ho, and J2, that is, 26 folios of a total of 72.

Foliation: As for the first printing, except that H7,8 are erroneously numbered 57 and 58, instead of 61 and 62

Textual comments: B1r.above iii:] the reading of] Compnre [is corrected in this printing

In-house corrections: H1r. the phrase] Fragmenta Missarum [was stamped in later: present in both copies • J5r. the initial P was originally omitted, as in the copy at D-W, and later stamped in, in the copy at I-Bc

———

Extant copies: For the rest of these copies, see above

D-W, 2.8-2.8.1 Musica (1). Folios D1,2,7,8, H1,2,7,8 and J3-8 are of this printing
    Watermarks: Mark 20 on D2, H1 and J7
    In-house corrections: H1r. see above

I-Bc, Q.64. Folios B1-10, H1,2,7,8 and J5-6 are of this printing
    Watermarks: No.20 on B2, B8 and H1
    In-house corrections: H1r and J5r. see above

I-Vnm, Mus.206–208. Folios B3-8 are of this printing
    Watermarks: No.20 on B4 and B6

———

Lost copies: Copies were owned by Colón (Chapman, "Printed", No.15) and by the Fuggers (Schaal, "Musikbibliothek", I/48) • The copy at S. Anna, Augsburg was given by Herwart in 1596, and catalogued in 1620 (Schaal, *Inventar*, p. 45)

I know of no other early references to this book

Bibliography:
    (a) Rosaria Boccadifuoco, *Bibliografia*, No.1415 • Sartori, *Petrucci*, No.23
    (c) Petrucci, *Fragmenta*
    (e) Vernarecci, *Petrucci*, p. 105

Commentary:

1. It was usual for Petrucci's edition not to give a title on the title-page of lower voices, reserving it for the Superius book. This edition marks a point of change in his output, in that he added the title to the lower voices after press work. However, he did not do it immediately, since the addition survives in copies of both printings, in the Tenor and Altus for the first, and in the Bassus for the second.

2. The stave-lengths of the Venice copy confirm that (with the exception of the inner sheet of gathering A), the book was printed using two formes of staves, one on each side of a sheet:

	1r	2v	3r	4v		1v	2r	3v	4r
A outer	—	177	177	177		—	180	182	181
A inner	180	181	180	182		181	180	182	180
B outer	177	177	176	—		181	180	182	180
B second	177	177	177	178		181	180	182	181

B inner	178	178	177	178 (printed by work-and-turn)				
C outer	—	177	178	177	—	180	182	180
C inner	177	177	178	177	181	180	182	181
D outer	177	177	177	—	180	180	181	180
D inner	177	177	177	177	181	180	182	180
E outer	—	177	177	177	—	180	181	180
E inner	177	177	177	177	181	180	181	180
F outer	177	177	177	177	181	180	181	180
F inner	178	178	177	177	181	180	181	180
G	177	178	177	—	180	180	182	181

There is no reason to hypothesise the existence of more than two skeleton formes of staves, although it is unlikely that there were only two for the music.

3. The presence of a page of blank staves in the middle of the penultimate composition, G3v of the Altus book, suggests a mistake in imposing the formes for that sheet.

4. Given the clear evidence of the second printing using paper 20, it might seem that paper 15 also represented a different printing. However, I am unable to find any reason to argue for that, and am reduced to supposing that the two papers were blended in the shop.

5. For the Venice copy, the inner sheet of gathering A was, following the evidence of the staves (above), printed by work and turn. However, the readings of the outer forme of that sheet correspond to those of other copies, while the inner forme was completely reset. A sample of the variants follows:

	D-W	I-Vnm
A3v.title	Gaſpar	Gaſpar
A3v.v.text	Chrıste	Chrrste
A3v.v.14–15	*dm,sm*	*colsb,colm*
A4r	Jo.Stokem:	Jo Stokem.
A5v	Jo.regis.	Jo.Regis
A5v.i.43–44	ligature	two separate notes
A5v.ii.35	*f*, erased tail	*sm*
A6r.margin	reads downwards	reads upwards

This must reflect a problem with the type of the inner forme, and presumably one larger than merely suggested by these variants. The problem will have emerged while the sheet was being perfected, and therefore while the type was at the press: whatever it was, the press had to be stopped and the forme reset, so that the rest of the sheets could be perfected.

6. The cancel was almost certainly printed at once, following the edition.

7. The second large-scale printing may have comprised a full edition, for it contains over a third of the book, made up of sheets in different copies. However, it cannot have been prepared in response to a large sale of the first printing: too many sheets of the first survive, including among them the outer sheet of J with the colophon and date.

8. The new printings may not have taken place all at the same time, but represent small groups of replacement pages. Nonetheless, they were probably prepared soon after the first edition, and I have (somewhat arbitrarily) assigned them the first vacant space in the following year. They certainly should fall before the newly described first edition of Dammonis's laude and the second edition of Josquin's first book, both of which precede the mass volumes of the end of the year.

No. 25. *Frottole V*

23.xii.1505   *RISM* 15056[6]

A1r]   Frottole Libro | quinto.

G8r]   Impre∬um Venetiis per Octauianum Pe-|trutium Foro∫empronien∫em. Die. XXIII Decembris | Salutis anno M.ccccc v. Cum priuilegio | inuicti∬imi Dominii Venetiarum q*uae* nullus | po∬it cantum Figuratu*m* imprimere ∫ub pena | in ip∫o priuilegio contenta. | Regi∫trum. | ABCDEFG Omnes quaterni. | [Petrucci's device]

A1v   [Tavola:] Frottole numere Se∫anta.

Format and collation: Choirbook: landscape quarto-in-eights. 56 folios: A-G[8]

Signatures: aaa II [$4 • − A1

Foliation:] [1], 2–55, [56]

Part-names:

recto:]	Tenor Altus Ba∬us	[A2, B1, C1, D2, E1
	Altus Ba∬us	[A3,5,8, B5,7, C3-5,7, D1,4–5,8, E2-7, F2,4–8, G2-4,6–7
	Altu5 Ba∬us	[A4,6, B2,4,6,8, C2,6
	Altu5 Ba∬u5	[A7, D6, E8, F3
	Tenor Alt Ba∬usus	[B3
	Altu5 [with inverted *A*] Ba∬us	[C8 [See below: In-house corrections]
	tenor [in stave] Altus Ba∬us	[D3
	Tenor [in stave] Altus Ba∬us	[D7
	Tenor Altu5 Ba∬u5 Ba∬us	[F1
	Tenor Altu5 Ba∬u5	[G1,5
verso:]	Tenor	[A2-7, B1,3–7, C1,3–8, D3-5,7, E1-7, F1-7, G1-2,5–7
	Tenor Altus Ba∬us	[A8, B2,8, D2, G4
	tenor [in stave:	C2, G3
	Tenor Altu5 Ba∬u5	[D1
	Tenor Altu5 Ba∬us	[D6
	tenor [in stave] Altu5 Ba∬us	[D8, E8
	tenor [in stave] Altus Ba∬us	[F8

Small initial letters are used in a number of cases:

recto:]	Altus	[A5,6,8, B5-8, C4,7,8, D1,6, E6,8, F6,8, G6
	Altus Bassus	[A2,4,7, B2,4, C2,3,5,6, D1,3,4,8, E2,3,4, F2,3,4, G2,4
	Bassus	[A3, B1,3, C1, G3
	Tenor Altus	[D2
	Tenor Altus Bassus	[E1, F1, G1,5
verso:]	Tenor	[A2,4,6, B1,3,4,6, C1,4,5 [in D-Mbs],6,8, D3,4,7, E1,3,4,6, F1,3,4,6, G1,2,6
	Tenor Altus	[A8, G4
	Tenor Altus Bassus	[B2,8, D2,6
	Altus Bassus	[D8, E8, F8

Fonts: Music: Petrucci's normal music type

Staves: six per page, 178 mm long, 10-92-113 mm long

Text: Roman

Textual comments: Gatherings seem to have been seen as discrete units. In five out of six cases, the piece on the last verso of the gathering does not extend onto the next gathering

Technical comments: The sixth stave is only occasionally inked • B2*v*: the sixth stave is displaced to the left, and was probably a later addition • Capital letter missing on D8*v* [D] • Small capital used on G5*v* [I] and G7*v* [H]

In-house corrections: B3*r*.iii.8 from end: *m* → *sb*, by erasure: stave lines touched up in brown: all copies • C3*r*.i.from after 8, rest to after 12: 2 brown bar-lines and the word *vacat*: A-Wn and D-Mbs • C8*r*. the initial letter of the part-name Altus is inverted in the copies at D-Mbs and F-Psg, but has been corrected in stop-press in that at A-Wn • D1*v*.vi.30: *b c' d'*, part erasure, and part in brown ink: A-Wn and D-Mbs • D7*r*.initial: letter *D*, lacking in the copy at A-Wn, is stamped in: D-Mbs

Contents: The last column gives the folio number as cited in the Tavola

	A1*r*	[Title]		
	A1*v*	[Tavola]		
1	A2*r*	SI come fede ſe de pinge biancha [Headed:] Stramotto.	[Anon.]	ii
2	A2*v*	AHime laſſo ahime dolente	.MI.C.	iii
3	A3*v*	IL iocondo e lieto aſpecto	[Anon.]	iiii
4	A4*v*	O Bon eglie bon	.M.C. [Tav:] DM	v
5	A5*v*	ALa fe per la mia fe	[Anon.] [Tav:] P.C.	vi
6	A6*v*	HHor passata e lasperanza	[Anon.] [Tav:] B.T.	viiii [*recte* vii]
7	A8*v*	NOn de tardar chi uol a piacer [Headed:] Stramoto	[Anon.]	viiii
8	B1*r*	PIu uolte me ſon meſſo [Headed:] Per ſonetti.	[Anon.]	viiii
9	B1*v*	OGni uermo al ſuo ueneno	[Anon.] [Tav:] N.P.	x
10	B2*v*	MA de cancher le pur uero	[Anon.] [Tav:] F.V.	xi
11	B3*r*	IL ciel natura e amor	[Anon.]	xi
12	B3*v*	NOn pigliar tanto ardimento	.B.T.	XII
13	B5*v*	ITe in pace o ſuſpir fieri	.B.T.	xIIIi
14	B7*v*	PAce hor mai che adiſcoprire	[Anon.]	xvI
15	B8*v*	AMor Poi che non poi	.MICAEL.	xvII
16	C1*r*	BEn che ſoletto uado	[Anon.]	xvI
17	C1*v*	OGni impreſa fia felice	[Anon.]	xviii
18	C2*v*	SE mai fo tuo	[Anon.]	xviiii
19	C3*v*	SE me dol el mio partire [A,B:] Se me duol . . .	[Anon.]	xxi [*recte* xx]
20	C4*v*	PVr al fin conuien ſcoprire	[Anon.]	xxi
21	C5*v*	DIcha ognun chi mal dir uole	[Anon.]	xxII

22	C6*v*	NOn ſe muta el mio uolere	[Anon.]	xxiii
		[Tav:] Noɴ ſi . . .	[Tav:] T.	
23	C7*v*	SEl mio cor piu chaltra aſſai	[Anon.]	xxIIii
24	C8*v*	EL focho e rinouato	[Anon.]	xxv
			[Tav:] B.T.	
25	D1*v*	SEl partir mincrebe e dolſe	[Anon.]	xxv
26	D2*r*	DAl ciel crudo imperio e peruerſo	[Anon.]	xxvi
			[Tav:] F.V.	
27	D2*v*	PO piu un ſdegno aſſai	[Anon.]	xxvii
		[Tav:] Po piu un sguardo aſai		
28	D3*r*	DEl partir e gionto lhora	[Anon.]	xxvii
29	D3*v*	VEro amore uol ferma fede	[Anon.]	xxviii
30	D4*v*	SE noɴ mami a che ſtentarmi	[Anon.]	xxvIIIi
			[Tav:] F.V	
31	D5*v*	IO ti laſſo doɴna hormai	[Anon.]	xxx
		[Tav:] Io te laſo . . .	[Tav:] F.D.L.	
32	D6*v*	COme ti ſofre il core	[Anon.]	xxxI
		[Tav:] Come te ſofri		
33	D7*r*	DE no de ſi de no	[Anon.]	xxxi
34	D7*v*	POcha pace e molta guerra	[Anon.]	xxIi
			[Tav: .T.]	[*recte* xxxii]
35	D8*v*	[D]Olce amoroſo focho	[Anon.]	xxxIIi
			[Tav:] F.L	
36	E1*r*	IO ſon quel doloroſo e triſto	A.DE ANTIQVIS.	xxxiii
		[Tav:] . . . quello . . .		
37	E1*v*	PRendi larme o fiero amore	.A.DE.A.V:	xxxIIIi
38	E2*v*	A Ti ſola ho dato el core	A. DEANTIQVIS VENETVS.	xxxv
39	E3*v*	REſta horſu madoɴna in pace	.A.DE.A.V:	xxvi
40	E4*v*	QVeſta amara aſpra partita	A.DE.A.V	xxxvii
41	E5*v*	VAle iniqua uale hormai	A.DE.A.V.	xxxvilI
42	E6*v*	SE gran feſta me moſtraſti	[Anon.]	xxxviiii
			[Tav:] T.	
43	E7*v*	PEr pietade ho dite hormai	[Anon.]	xxxx
			[Tav:] T.	
44	F1*r*	BEnedetto chi te adora [à5]	[Anon.]	
		[omitted from Tavola]		
45	F1*v*	AMa pur donna ſpietata	[Anon.]	xxxxii
			[Tav:] F.A.V.	
46	F2*v*	A La abſentia che me acora	M.C.C.V.	xxxxiii
47	F3*v*	DIſperato fin amorte	[Anon.]	xxxxIIIi
48	F4*v*	ROcta e laſpra mia cathena	M.C.	xxxxv
		[Tav:] Rotta . . .	[Tav:] M.	
49	F5*v*	FErmo ho in cor ſempre dmaarte	[Anon.]	xxxxvI
		[other vv.] . . . damarte		
50	F6*v*	SE damarti non ſon degno	[Anon.]	xxxxxvIi
51	F7*v*	SI egua pur chi uol amore	A.DE A.	xlvIIi
		[Tav:] Segua pur chi . . .	[Tav:] T.	

52	F8*v*	DE ſerviti al tuo diſpecto	PHI.DE L.	xxxxvIIII
		[Tav:] De ſervirte al tuo ...	[Tav:] F.D L	
53	G1*r*	O Selue ſparſe egregie	[Anon.]	xxxxvIIIi
54	G1*v*	HOr iuo ſcoprir el focho	B.T.	l
55	G2*v*	EL colpo che mede tuo ſguardo	[Anon.]	lI
			[Tav:] B.T.	
56	G3*v*	IO ſon quello che fu mai	B.T.	lii
57	G4*v*	SOn pur congionto a tanto	[Anon.]	lii
		[Tav:] Son pur gionto ...		
58	G5*r*	SIo ſedo alombra amor	MARCHETO	lIIi
		[Headed:] Sonetto	[Tav:] B.T.	
59	G5*v*	IO non poſſo piu durare	Aron	liIIi
60	G6*v*	SVſpir io themo	B.T.	lv
61	G7*v*	HOr chio ſon de preſon fora	B.T.	lvI
			[Tav:] T.	
	G8*r*	[Colophon; Register; Device]		
	G8*v*	[blank]		

Extant copies:

A–Wn, S.A.77.C.2 (5). Complete

> **Size of page:** 162 × 234 mm.
>
> **Watermarks:** No.20 on A3, A8, B5, B7, C2, C4, D1, D4, E4, E7, F3, F7, G4, and G7
>
> **Textual comments:** The capital letter on D7*r* [D] is lacking
>
> **Technical comments:** *Sm* used for furniture on D6*r*, E7*r*, E8*r*, F6*r*, F8*r*, and G6*r*, all on stave vi
>
> **Corrections and changes:**
>> **In-house:** B3*r*, C3*r*, C8*r* and D1*v*: see above
>>
>> **Later:** A3*r*.ii. 5 and 6 from end: struck through • E5*r*.i.after 14: *m* rest erased
>
> **Binding:** A Fugger binding, labelled on the spine:] FROT. L QVIN.
>
> **Provenance:** Fugger

D–Mbs, Rar.878/5. Complete

> **Size of page:** 159 × 228 mm.
>
> **Watermarks:** No.20 on A5, A7, B2, B3, C2, C4, D3, D8, E4, E8, F4, F8, G6, and G7
>
> **Textual comments:** C8*r*: the initial letter of the part-name Altus is inverted
>
> **Technical comments:** Notes, perhaps minims, used as bearer sorts on A1*r* (two vertical rows), and E6*r* and F7*r* (horizontal rows)
>
> **Corrections and changes:**
>> **In-house:** B3*r*, C3*r*, D1*v*, and D7*r*: see above
>>
>> **Later:** A3*r*.ii. 5 and 6 from end: struck through and initialled RJ • A3*r*.iii.9–10: struck through, initialled g.c. • A5*v*.iv.custos: g or a → b, in brown ink • C8*r*.ii.5: struck through, initialled g.c. • D5*r*.ii.after 30: inserted *sb* c, initialled g.c. • E5*r*.i.after 14: *m* rest erased • F1*r*.vi.clef: f₄ → F₃, initialled g.c. • F1*v*.v.10 from end: *m* tail struck through, initialled RJ • F4*v*.v.30: *b, p.d.* added, initialled RJ • G2*r*.v.16: tail added, initialled RJ • G5*r*.i.before 10 from the end: added *mg'*, initialled RJ •
>
> **Binding and Provenance:** With *Frottole I* (1504, No.16)

F–Psg, Vm.49. Only three sheets, folios B1 to C2, C7, and C8

> **Size of page:** 167 × 221 mm.

Watermarks: No.20 on B1, B6 and C1

Textual comments: C8r: the initial letter of the part-name Altus is inverted

Technical comments: The stave lengths seem to confirm the continued use of only two formes of staves:

		1r	2v	3r	4v	2r	1v	4r	3v
B	outer	175	176	176	176	179	181	179	181
	inner	176	176	174	176	181	180	181	180
C	outer	176	175	175	176	181	179	181	180

Corrections and changes:

>   **In-house:** B3r: see above

>   **Later:** C8r.iv.12: perhaps a dot was erased here

Binding: Bound as the last in five books, the others all quintus parts:

>   1. Lassus: *I modulorum quinis vocibus*. 1571. (*RISM* L845)
>   2. Lassus: *II modulorum quinis vocibus*. 1571. (*RISM* L847)
>   3. Lassus: *Moduli quinis vocibus*. 1571. (*RISM* L843)
>   4. Lassus: *Livre de chansons nouvelles*. 1571. (*RISM* L848)
>   5. *Frottole V* (Petrucci)

>   Presumably the frottola volume was merely bound in because it was otherwise unbound
>   • Dark brown leather over card boards. A gold rolled border, and a gold medallion on both boards, with the inscription] QVINTA PARS. [on the front board. The boards measure 174 × 226 mm. • Five sewing bands on the spine, with a floral medallion in each panel • Three end-papers and one paste-down at each end, forming a single sheet of paper. Each has parts of a watermark of an unidentifiable flower

Provenance: The Lassus books at least, and probably the Petrucci (to judge from the evidence of water stains and binding) were in the library before 1753

Bibliography: Garros, "Exemplaire" • Garros and Wallon, *Catalogue*, No.478

Lost copies: Copies were owned by Colón (Chapman, "Printed", No.16), and Bottrigari: see chapter 20

Early references: Gesner (See Bernstein, "Gesner", No.246)

Bibliography:

>   (a) Rosaria Boccadifuoco, *Bibliografia*, No.1453 • Sartori, *Petrucci*, No.24
>   (b) Brunet, *Manuel*, ii, col.1413
>   (e) Sartori, "Nuove", pp. 186–89

Commentary:

1. As with earlier frottole volumes, the content is here arranged in a manner which suggests some patterns of the earlier manuscript sources. The most obvious features are two:

>   (i) the manner in which every gathering join but one (C to D) presents single-page pieces on both pages of the opening;

>   (ii) the sudden effloresence of compositions by Antiquis in gathering E.

In addition,

>   (iii) the double gathering C to D is notable for containing a miscellaneous collection of essentially anonymous works;

(iv) both gatherings A and B begin with works indicating their form;

(v) there are relatively few concordances to any pieces in this book (only 17 out of 61 pieces, if we exclude Bossinensis's volumes), and these tend to be grouped together: there are none for works in gathering A, and only one (in a later copy) for any in gathering G; there is one for gathering E (and that for one of the last two pieces added after the Antiquis collection); the only concordances in gathering F (to Nos.45, 50 and 52) are found in the Florentine manuscript B.R.337; the only works with any sign of popularity — Nos.16, 31, 34, and 35 — are found in the group in gatherings C and D: the last three are the only ones with more than two concordances, but even these are largely north Italian — GB-Lbl Eg.3051; F-Pn Rés.Vm⁷.676; I-Bc Q18; and I-Fn Panc.27.

The conclusion has to be that the majority of these works were fairly little known — perhaps that Petrucci's editor was beginning to run low on material (for which point see my comments on the sixth book of frottole, and chapter 9).

More significantly, the editor had small groups of material which he had organised in his own collections, and which were transferred to Petrucci as material for separate gatherings. This explains my first two points above. Gathering F and the first six works of gathering E represent two such groups. In the case of gathering F, we cannot tell whether the editor had more similar works or not: in the case of gathering E, we can probably tell, for he finished the gathering with more compositions similar to those that had filled gatherings C and D, which must be considered a unit, despite the concordance pattern.

2. The evidence of "fascicle exemplars" is to some extent confirmed by the pattern of part-names in various parts of the book. But the pattern of use of small initial letters for these part-names is indicative of how these names were kept in skeleton formes: it is obvious, from the pattern of the word Tenor alone, that the names were kept in place whenever possible. This is an advance in technique.

3. This book appeared in short order with Books IV and VI, and about a year after the first three. However, there is a significant gap before the next two Books (VII and VIII) are published, in mid-1507. If, as I suggest, material was running low, it may be significant of the popularity of these pieces that this is one of the few frottole books that shows no sign of having been reprinted.

4. The copy now in Paris may well have been in France during the 16th century, to judge from the books with which it shares a binding. If so, it represents perhaps the only evidence of Petrucci's books having circulated in France at the time.

No. 26. *Frottole VI*

5.ii.1505/1506   *RISM* 1506³

A1r]   Frottole libro | Sexto

G8r]   Impreſſum Venetiis per Octauianum Pe-|trutium Foroſemproniensem. Die. v Februarii | Salutis anno M. cccccv. Cum priuilegio | inuictiſſimi Dominii Venetiarum quae nullus | poſſit cantum Figuratum imprimere ſub pena | in ipſo priuilegio contenta. | Regiſtrum. | A B C D E F G Omnes quaterni.

A1v   [Tavola:] Frottole Sonetti Stramboti Ode. Iuſtiniane numero ſeſanta ſie.

Format and collation: Choirbook: landscape quarto-in-eights. 56 folios: A-G⁸

Signatures: Aa iiii [$4 •-A1

Foliation:] [1], 2–26, 29 [*recte* 26], 27–55 [56]

Part-names:

recto:]	Tenor Altu5 Ba∫∫u5	[A2, B5
	Tenor Ba∫∫us	[A3-4,6
	Tenor Ba∫∫u5	[A5
	Altus Ba∫∫us	[A7-8, B2,6,8, C2-4,6,8, D2,4,6,8, E2-4,6,8,
		F2,4,6,8, G2,4,6
	Tenor Altus Ba∫∫us	[B1,4, C1, D3, E1,5, F3, G1
	tenor [in stave] Altus Ba∫∫us [in stave:	B3
	Altus Ba∫∫u5	[B7, D5, E7, F5,7, G5
	Altu5 Ba∫∫u5	[C5,7, D7
	Tenor Altus Ba∫∫us [in stave:	D1
	tenor [in stave[Altus Ba∫∫us	[F1, G3
	Ba∫∫u5	[G7
verso:]	Tenor	[A6-7, B1, 5–7, C1-6, D1,3-7, E1-3,5–7,
		F1,3–7, G1,3–6
	Tenor Altu5 [both in stave] Ba∫∫us	[A8
	Tenor Altu5 Ba∫∫us	[B2-3,8, E4, F2
	Tenor Altus Ba∫∫us	[B4, G2
	tenor [inset in the stave:	C7
	tenor Altu5 Ba∫∫us [all in stave:	C8
	tenor [in stave] Altu5 Ba∫∫us	[D2, E8, F8
	tenor [in stave] Altus Ba∫∫us [instave:	D8
	Tenor Ba∫∫us	[G7

These patterns are informative as to the retention of part-names in the forme. Small initials used for part-names:

recto:]	Tenor	A7
	Altus	A7,8; B3,8; C3,6,8; D6,8; E5,6,8; F6,8; G1,3,6
	Altus Bassus	B2,6; C2,4,5,7; D2,4,7; E2-4; F2,4; G2,4;
	Bassus	A4; B7; D5; E7; F5,7; G5,7
	Tenor Altus	B1,4; C1; D1,3; E1; F3
	Tenor Bassus	A5,6; G2
	Tenor Altus Bassus	A2r; B5
verso:]	Tenor	A6,7; B1; C1-4,6; D1,3,4; E1-3; F1,3,4; G1,3,4
	Altus	C8
	Altus Bassus	B8; D2; E8; F8
	Bassus	G7
	Tenor Bassus	B4
	Tenor Altus Bassus	A8; B2,3; E4; F2

Fonts: Music: Petrucci's normal music type

Staves: six per page, 178 mm long, 10-91-112 mm high.

Text: Roman

Textual comments: The part name of Tenor on G1r has the letter *r* inverted in the copy at A-Wn
• Note the large number of in-house corrections, many in both copies

Technical comments: Although six staves are clearly the normal pattern, the last stave is actually inked fairly rarely in this edition. (It appears only on A2v-3v,4v-6v,7v,8v, B1r,2v-3r,4v, C4v,6v-8r, D6v, E3r, and G1v,3r,7v.) However, the pattern of normalcy is evident from the number of cases where the music forme has uninked notes as bearer sorts in the space of the lowest stave

In-house corrections: B5r.iii.21: d → e, and dot of the *corona* redrawn, brown ink: both copies • C2v.i.33: b' → c'', stamped in: both copies • D3r.i.11 from end: d' → e', erasure and stamped in: both copies • D3r.iii. last seven notes: *sba,sba,bb,rm,mb,me',be'la*, all erased → *sbf,sbf,bg,rm,mb, sbe,be',lc'* all stamped in: D-Mbs • D5r.i.before bar-line: *bc'* → d', stamped in: both copies • D6v.ii.20: rest erased and *ld'* and redrawn rest inserted: both copies • E7r.i.18: *sb* → *b*, stamped in: both copies • G5r.ii.39: *sb* → *b*, stamped in: both copies • G7v.v.5 rests after 38: the second rest, *m*, added by stop-press correction: A-Wn (note the ms. change in the copy at D-Mbs)

There are several alterations, made in manuscript or merely as erasures, which appear in both copies, but which can not be securely assigned to work done in the printing shop. They are listed under the individual copies

Contents:

	A1r	[Title]		
	A1v	[Tavola]		
1	A2r	NOn ſom quel che ſolea	PHI.D.L.	ii.
		Tavola: Non ſon quello che ſolea		
2	A2v	CHui diceſe	à3	[Anon.]	iii.
3	A3v	MOro de doglia	à3	[Anon.]	iiii.
4	A4v	AIme cha torto	à3	[Anon.]	iii. [recte v]
5	A5v	AIme ſoſpiri	à3	[Anon.]	vi.
6	A6v	SEruo haime ſenza mercede	HONOPHRIVS PATAVINVS	vii.
7	A7v	MAledecto ſia la fede	[Anon.]	viii.
8	A8v	QVesto uiuer a ſperanza	HONOPHRIVS PATAVINVS	ix.
9	B1r	TV dormi io ueglio	[Anon.]	ix.
10	B1v	BEn che la facia al quanto lieta	[Anon.]	x.
		[Headed:] per ſonetti		
11	B2v	STauaſi in porto la mia nauicella	[Anon.]	xi.
12	B3r	VIſto ho piu uolte	[Anon.]	xi.
13	B3v	O Suaue e dolce dea	[Anon.]	xii.
14	B4r	AIme chio ſon ſcaciato	[Anon.]	xii.
15	B4v	REſuegliate ſu ſu	[Anon.]	xiii.
16	B5r	COme el piombin quel ſimplice	[Anon.]	xiii.
17	B5v	SEl te chara la mia uita	NICOLO PIFAR.	xiiii.
18	B6v	FOra ſon dogni ſperanza	NICOLO.PIFAR.	xv.
19	B7v	AQua aqua al focho al focho	NICOLO PIFAR.	xvi.
20	B8v	POi che gionto el tempo el loco	P.D.LV.	xvii.
21	C1r	VAna ſperanza incerta la mia uita	B.T.	xvii.
22	C1v	DOnna hormai fammi contento	[Anon.]	xviii.
23	C2v	SOn infermo recaduto	N.P.	xix.
24	C3v	CHi non ſa chi non intende	B.T.	xx.
25	C5v	SE ben fugo el tuo bel uolto	B.T.	xxii.
26	C6v	LAſſa donna i dolci ſguardi	[Anon.]	xxiii.
27	C7v	SV ſu ſu ſu mia ſpeme	M.C.	xxiiii.
28	C8v	NOn ſon ciecho che non ueda	[Anon.]	xxv.
29	D1r	VAle iniqua e deſliale	[Anon.]	xxv.

30	D1*v*	PAga el datio do*n*na chai	[Anon.]	xxvi.
		[other vv:] . . . dacio . . .		
31	D2*v*	PAn de miglio caldo	[Anon.]	xxvii.
32	D3*r*	INgrata do*n*na a la mia pura fede	[Anon.]	xxvii.
		[Headed:] Per [onetti.		
33	D3*v*	SE le carti me [on contra	F.V.	xxviii.
34	D4*v*	DVn partir na[co*n* doi parte	PHI.D.L.	xxix.
35	D5*v*	DOnna daltri piu che mia	[Anon.]	xxx.
36	D6*v*	SE col [guardo me dai mo*r*te	B.T.	xxxi.
37	D7*v*	SIo [on da te lontano	[Anon.]	xxxii.
		[Tavola:] Se son . . .		
38	D8*v*	O Che dio no*n* maiute mai	[Anon.]	xxxiii.
		[Tavola:] . . . me aiute . . .		
39	E1*r*	BEn cogno[co el tuo cor finto	F.V.	xxxiii.
40	E1*v*	DOnna hormai no*n* piu dolore	[Anon.]	xxxiiii.
41	E2*v*	Con[umatu*m* e[t hormai	B.T.	xxxv.
		[T:] Comn[uatum [*sic*] . . .		
42	E3*v*	SIo di[m]o[tro al uiso el focho	[Anon.]	xxxvi.
43	E4*v*	SE hora el tempo nol co*n*cede	[Anon.]	xxxvii.
44	E5*r*	PIu non uoglio contra[tare	[Anon.]	xxxvii.
45	E5*v*	HOr[u correr uoglio a morte	[Anon.]	xxxviii.
46	E6*v*	O Mi[chini o[iagurati	[Anon.]	xxxviii.
		[T:] . . . o[ciagurati		
		[Tav, A, B:] . . . e[iagurati		
47	E7*v*	PA[[ero la uita mia	[Anon.]	xl.
48	E8*v*	ADio [iati chiome ne uo	[Anon.]	xli.
49	F1*r*	SE [ei dami lontano	[Anon.]	xli.
50	F1*v*	QVa*n*to ardor [ta chiu[o	[Anon.]	xlii.
51	F2*v*	SE ben el fin de la mia uita	M.CARA	xliii.
52	F3*r*	CHe te gioua [eruir cor mio	[Anon]	xliiii.
		[Tavola:] [ervir co*n* fe		
53	F3*v*	FOre[tieri ala uentura	[Anon.]	xliiii.
54	F4*v*	ADognhor cre[ce la doglia	[Anon.]	xlv.
55	F5*v*	VEnimus en romeria	[Anon.]	xlvi.
56	F6*v*	NOn po[[o hauer pacientia	[Anon.]	xlvii.
57	F7*v*	NOn [i po quel che [i uole	PHI.D.L.	xlviii.
58	F8*v*	DE fo[[e la qui mecho	[Anon.]	xlix.
59	G1*r*	O Cara libertade	[Anon.]	xlviiii.
60	G1*v*	SEd libera nos a malo	HONOPHRIVS PATAVINVS.	l.
61	G3*r*	NEl mouer de quei dolci	[Anon.]	li.
62	G3*v*	GIa fui lieto hor gio*n*cto el me[e	[Anon.]	lii.
63	G4*v*	POi cho per[o i giouen anni	[Anon.]	liii.
		Tavola:] . . . i gioueni enni		
64	G5*v*	TAci lingua el non el tempo	[Anon.]	liiii.
65	G6*v*	OGni co[a ha el [uo locho	à3	[Anon.]	lv.
66	G7*v*	DVm bel matin che	à3	[Anon.]	lvi.

G8*r*   [Colophon; Register; Device]

G8*v*   [blank]

Extant copies:

A-Wn, S.A.77.C.2.(6). Complete.

>   **Size of page:** 166 × 235 mm.
>
>   **Watermarks:**
>
> | A6 | A7 | B4 | B8 | C2 | C6 | D1 | D6 | E3 | E8 | F4 | F8 | G2 | G6 |
> |----|----|----|----|----|----|----|----|----|----|----|----|----|----|
> | 20 | 17 | 20 | 20 | 20 | 20 | 20 | 20 | 17 | 20 | 20 | 20 | 20 | 20 |
>
>   **Technical comments:** Rows of notes are used for bearer sorts in the space of stave vi on B2*r*,6*r*,7*r*,8*r*, C4*r*,6*r*, D2*r*,6*r*, E2*r*,4*r*,7*v*,8*r*, F2*r*,4*r*,6*r*,8*r*, and G6*r*
>
>   **Corrections and changes:**
>
>   >   **In-house:** B5*r*, C2*v*, D3*r*.i.11, D5*r*, D6*v*, E7*r*, G5*r* and G7*v*: see above
>   >
>   >   **Later:** All these are also in the copy at D-Mbs, and may have been done in-house: C6*r*.i.23: *bb,sbc'* → *bb* • C6*r*.ii.before last note: *ba* erased • F6*v*.v.last: *l* → *b*, by erasure of tail • G5*r*.ii.43: *m* → *sb*, by erasure
>
>   **Binding:** From the Fugger collection. Spine labelled:] FROT: L: SEX: • One paste-down and one fly-leaf at each end
>
>   **Provenance:** From the Fugger collection

D-Mbs, Rar.878/6. Complete.

>   **Size of page:** 164 × 228 mm.
>
>   **Watermarks:**
>
> | A5 | A7 | B1 | B4 | C3 | C8 | D6 | D8 | E4 | E6 | F2 | F3 | G6 | G7 |
> |----|----|----|----|----|----|----|----|----|----|----|----|----|----|
> | 20 | 17 | 20 | 20 | 20 | 20 | 20 | 20 | 20 | 17 | 20 | 20 | 20 | 20 |
>
>   **Technical comments:** A6*r* and B8*r*, the edges of sorts for the part-names confirm that these were not blocks • The staves on D8*r* reappear on E8*r* • F8*v*, music offset from elsewhere
>
>   **Corrections and changes:**
>
>   >   **In-house:** B5*r*, C2*v*, D3*r* (twice), D5*r*, D6*v*, E7*r* and G5*r*: see above
>   >
>   >   **Later:** A5*v*.iii.13: a question mark above the reading, initialled g.c. • B3*v*.head of page: perhaps an attribution to] C.d. • B3*v*.iii.4: *m* → *sb*, tail struck through, initialled A.E • B3*v*.iii.13: *mg'* struck through and then reinstated, initialled g.c. • C6*r*.i.23: *bb,sbc'* → *bb* • C6*r*.ii.before last note: *ba* erased • C6*v*.v.11 before bar line: struck through from here to the bar-line, initialled g.c. • D2*r*.iv.after 35: rest *l* → *b*, by erasure • D7*r*.ii.19: *l* → *b*, by erasure: stave line touched up in brown • E4*v*.iv.11,14, 24 and 27: four notes *sm* → *m*, initialled g.c. • E7*r*.ii.6 from end: ?, initialled g.c. • E8*r*.ii.8: ? initialled g.c. • F6*v*.v.last: *l* → *b*, by erasure of tail • G3*r*.i.rest after 14: struck through, initialled RJ • G3*r*.iii.rest after 17: struck through, initialled RJ • G4*r*.ii. 5 from end: tail added, initialled RJ: the addition struck through, initialled g.c • G5*r*.ii.43: *m* → *sb*, by erasure of tail • G7*v*.v.5 rest after 38: *b* struck through, *rm* added, initialled g.c. (note that the copy at A-Wn has both rests printed) • G7*v*.vi.20: *sb* → *b*, initialled RJ: later struck through
>
>   **Binding and Provenance:** The first item in a second volume of frottole: see *Frottole I* (1504, No.16)

Lost copies: Copies were owned by Colón (Chapman: "Printed", No.17), and by Herwart (which he gave to S. Anna, Augsburg) (Schaal, *Inventar*, p. 30)

Early references: Gesner (See Bernstein, "Gesner", No.246)
Bibliography:

(a) Rosaria Boccadifuoco, *Bibliografia*, No.1458 • Sartori, *Petrucci*, No.25

(b) Brunet, *Manuel*, ii, col.1413

(d) Marcon, *Libro*

(e) Haar, "Petrucci" • Sartori, "Nuove", pp. 189–92

Commentary:

1. Books 4–6 appeared within a very short period, and clearly represent a continuous printing project: this is evident from the pattern of repertoire as much as from the dates. See the discussion in chapter 9.

2. Once again there are single-page pieces at the joins of gatherings.

3. The order of entries in the Tavola is of interest: it shows that all the entries for gathering A were entered after everything else. It looks as though the contents of gathering A were radically changed: it now contains the unusual works à3 and most of the compositions by Honophrius. In addition two pieces are entered out of order in letter "V": perhaps the works on B3r and C1r were moved from gathering A when the change was made. (For details, see Boorman, "Printed".)

4. The appearance of paper 17 on two gatherings in both copies does not seem to represent a different printing. The paper was in use in previous books, although not in the most recent, and was to reappear two books later. If it represents a later printing, that must have been within a few months, since there is no other evidence to support such a conclusion.

5. The initials "R.J." and "g.c." had appeared in the Munich copies of earlier frottola volumes: the initials "A.E" are new, though probably also of the 19th-century.

6. James Haar's discussion of the Justiniane settings (see Haar, "Petrucci") highlights the special character of this book. In ways that are discussed above, in chapter 9, it can be seen to correspond with *Frottole IV*, not only in the presence of these potentially didactic creations, but also in the organisation of the Tavola — again stressing the genre of various pieces. This is confirmation that the two books, with the intervening fifth volume, comprise a set showing a consistent mentality on the part of the collector (and provider) of the music.

No. 27. *Lamentationes I*

8.iv.1506   *RISM* 1506[1]

A1r]   Lamentationum Jeremie | prophete Liber primus.

F10r]   Impreſſum Venetijs per Octauianum | Petrutium Foro ſempronienſeʒ: Die Octaua | Aprilis Salutis anno 1506. Cum priuile|gio inuictiſſimi Dominij Venetiarum | quae nullus poſſit cantum Figuratum impri-|mere ſub pena in ipſo priuilegio contenta. [To right of last three lines:] Regi ſtruʒ. ABCDEF Omnes | quaterni praeter F qui eſt quinternus

Tavola: A1v]

Adoramus te christe	1
Lamê: Tinctoris	2
Lamê. Ber: ycart	8
Lamê. cum tribus vocibus	13

Lamê. Alexandri cu*m* trib*us* vocib*us*	16
Lamê: Alexa*n*dri cu*m* q*u*atuor vocib*us*	22
Lamê. de. orto.	28
Lamê. Jo. de quadris. duo.	30
Popule meus eiusdem. duo.	45
Cu*m* aut*em* veni[[ent. eiu [deʒ. duo.	47
Sepulto. do*m*ino. eiu [deʒ. duo.	47
Pa[[io [acra .Fran. veneti	48

Format and collation: Choirbook: landscape quarto-in-eights. 50 folios: A-E⁸F¹⁰

Signatures:] AA II [$4 • − A1 • + FF 5, signed with an arabic numeral

Foliation: t.r.r. [1], 2–40, [41], 42–50. For folio 41, see below

No running heads

Part-names:

verso:]	Tenor	[A2-7, B1-7, C6-D5, F8-9
	Tenor Altu5 Ba[[u5	[A8
	Contra	[B8-C5
	[Nil:	A1, D6-F7, F10
recto:]	Tenor Altus Ba[[us	[A2
	Altus Ba[[us	[A3-B5, C7-D6, F9-10
	Contra	[B6-8
	Tenor	[C1-2, C4-6, D7-F8
	Teonr [*sic*]	[C3
	[Nil:	A1

Fonts: Music: Petrucci's normal music type

Staves: Six per page, 175–180 mm long, 10-92-112.5 high

Text: Rotonda throughout, "5" = 16.7 mm, "x" = 2.1 mm.

Textual comments: The layout of the opening at A8*v*-B1*r* is remarkable. All four voices of the setting of the letter Aleph are presented on A8*v*, while the four voices of the continuation and the letter Beth are laid out normally in choirbook format — for the Superius and Tenor following the setting of the letter, and for the Altus and Bassus on the facing page. There is no evident reason for this, although the fact that it occurs at a gathering join is significant • B5*v* part-name:] Teonr • C3*r*.part-name:] Teonr • E6*v*-7*r*: the Superius incipit reads] Fecit do*m*in*u*s [while that of the Tenor reads] Fecit deus • F1*v*-2*r*: although a rubric reads "ut supra", the first few notes of the music are given

Technical comments: Erroneous duplication of the capital letter on A6*v* and D6*v*: in each case, both letters were set with the text • Only five staves were inked on several rectos: B5-8; C1-6; D1-4; E1-3; and F1,3,6-8,10 • In a number of these cases, a row of notes, fusas or minims, has taken ink or left a slight impression: see the comments below

In-house corrections: B2*r*.iv.56: *b*, G → A, erased carefully and stamped in: GB-Lbl • C3*r*.signature: the letters CC are stamped in (I-Pca) or printed as a stop-press correction (GB-Lbl) • C7*v*.i.22: *mb*' has an added point in brown ink: GB-Lbl • D7*r*.iv.45 to end of line: a stop-press correction, reading *lg* with up-tail, *c.o.p.* ligature d' + f' (formed of a *b,b,* ligature with a ms. tail), *sbe*', *c.o.p.* ligature d' → a, *sb*d': all in type except for the up-tails to the *l* and following ligature, in brown ink: the uncorrected original (perhaps of a *c.o.p.* ligature g' + f', under the first of these ligatures) exists in GB-Lbl, with a stamped-in change to the correct reading, while the corrected form survives in the other copies • D8*r*.v.after 1: *sb* rest and dot struck through, in brown ink: GB-Lbl • E4*r*.signature: the second E is inverted in the copy at F-Pc, and corrected in that at GB-Lbl • F1*r*.

the folio number 41 appears to have been stamped in, in all surviving copies of that folio. In the copies at GB-Lbl and I-Pca the first numeral is inverted, while both are in the copy at I-Bc

Contents: There are potential problems in deciding where a new work begins. Thomas, *Petrucci*, chooses to regard a new composition as beginning after any singing of "Jerusalem, convertere". However, some of these settings should be grouped into larger sets, and not merely because they would be sung liturgically on the same occasion, or because they are by the same composer and appear to travel together (when there are any concordances at all). Petrucci's index clearly indicates what he felt to be separate units, and by implication, how he expected his readers to use the book. That pattern has been followed here:

	A1r	[Title]		
	A1v	[Tavola]		
1	A2r	ADoramus te	à4	[Anon.]
2	2v	[Lamentations]	à4	Tinctoris.
		ALeph. Quomodo ſedet		
	A3v	Beth Plorans plorauit		
	A4v	Gimel Migrauit iudas		
	A5v	Jeruſalem *con*uertere		
3	A6v	IIncipit lame*n*tatio Jheremie	à4	B. ycart.
		[In the index, this is cited as on the next folio]		
		[B:] Aleph. Quomodo ſedet		
		[A:] Beth. Plora*n*s plorauit		
	A7v	Gimel Migrauit iudas		
		[T:] Jeruſalem conuertere		
3(a)	A8v	ALeph. Quomodo obtexit	à4	B. ycart.
		Beth.		
	B1v	[A:] Precipitauit nec pepercit		
		Theth		
	B2v	Defixe ſunt in terra3		
		[T:] Jeruſalem conuertere		
3(b)	B3v	REcordare do*m*ine	à4	
4	B5v	[Lamentations]	à3	[Anon.]
		ALeph Quomodo ſedet		
		Beth ſicut | Aleph [no music]		
	B6v	Plorans plorauit		
		Gimel ſicut | Aleph [no music]		
	B7v	Migrauit iudas		
		Jeruſale3 ieruſalem *con*uertere		
5	B8v	[Lamentations]	à3	Alexander Agricola
		[Aleph] QUomodo ſedet ſola		
		Beth Plorans plorauit		
	C1v	Gimel Migrauit iudas		
	C2v	Deleth Uie ſion lugent		
		1[T:] Om*n*es porte eius		
	C3v	He Facti ſunt hoſtes		
	C4v	Vau. Et egreſſus eſt		
	C5v	Zay Recordata eſt		
6	C6v	[Lamentations]	à4	Agricola

		AAleph	Quomodo obtexit		
	C7ν	[A:] Beth	Precitipauit dominus		
		Jeruſalem ierusale3 conuertere			
	C8ν	Gimel	Confregit in furore		
	D1ν	Deleth ſuper | Beth [no music]			
			Tetendit arcu3		
		Hee:			
	D2ν		Factus eſt dominus		
		Jeruſalem | vt ſupra [no music]			
	D3ν	Vau	Et diſipauit		
		Jeruſalem [no music]			
7	D4ν	INcipit lamentatio ieremie		à4	De orto.
		Aleph	Quomodo ſedet ſola		
		Beth | vt ſupra [no music]			
			Plorans plorauit		
	D5ν	Gimel | vt ſupra [no music]			
			Migrauit iudas		
		Jeruſalem ieru ſalem conuertere			
8	D6ν	IIncipit lamentacio ieremie		à2	Jo.De quadris.
		Aleph	Quomodo ſedet ſola		
		Beth | vt ſupra [no music]			
			Plorans plorauit		
		Gimel | vt ſupra [no music]			
			Migrauit iudas		
		Deleth | vt ſupra [no music]			
	D7ν		Uie ſion lugent		
		Jeruſale3 ieruſalem conuertere			
		Teth. [sic]	Facti ſunt hoſtes		
		Vau. | vt ſupra [no music]			
			Egreſſus est		
		Zay vt | ſupra [no music]			
	D8ν		Recordata eſt		
		Eth. | vt ſupra [no music]			
			Peccatu3 peccauit		
		Jeruſalem ieru ſale3 conuertere			
	E1ν	TEth.	Sordes eius		
		Joth vt | ſupra [no music]			
			Manu3 ſua3 miſit		
		Caph. vt | ſupra [no music]			
			Omnis populus eius		
		Lamech. | vt ſupra [no music]			
	E2ν		O uos omnes qui tranſitis		
		Jeruſalem ieruſalem conuertere			
8(a)		BEth. [sic] Cogitauit dominus			
		Teth | vt ſupra [no music]			
	E3ν		Defixe ſunt in terra		
		Joth | vt ſupra [no music]			

		Sederun*t* in terra		
		Caph. | vt ſup*ra* [no music]		
		Defecerunt		
		Jeruſale3 ieruſale3 conuertere		
	E4*v*	LAmech Matrib*us* ſuis dixerunt		
		Mem | vt ſup*ra* [no music]		
		Cui comp*er*abo te		
		Num | vt ſup*ra* [no music]		
		Prophete tui		
		Samech. | vt ſup*ra* [no music]		
	E5*v*	Plauſeru*nt* ſuper te		
		Jeruſale3 ieruſale3 conuertere		
		PHe. Aperuerunt ſup*er* te		
		Ain. vt | ſupra [no music]		
	E6*v*	Fecit d*omin*us		
		[T:] Fecit deus		
		Sade. vt | ſupra [no music]		
		Clamauit cor eor*um*		
		Reſe vt | ſupra [no music]		
		Uide d*om*ine		
		Jeruſale3 ieruſale3 conuertere		
8(b)	E7*v*	Caph. No*n* e*ni*3 humiliauit		
		Men | vt ſupra [no music]		
		Quis eſt iſte		
		Num | vt ſupra		
		Scrutemur vias		
		Samech. | vt ſupra [no music]		
	E8*v*	Operuiſti in furore		
		Ayn. Cu3 aduc ſubſiſtenerem*us*		
		[T:] . . . adhuc ſubſtinerem*us*		
		Jeruſale*m* ieruſale3 conuertere		
	F1*v*	SAde vt *supra* [giving the musical incipit]		
		Lubricauerunt		
		Caph. vt | ſupra [no music]		
		Uelociores fuerunt		
		Res vt | ſupra [no music]		
		Sp*iritu*s oris		
	F2*v*	Sen. Gaude 7 letare		
		Tau. | vt ſup*ra* [no music]		
		Completa *est*		
		Jeruſalem ieruſalem conuertere		
8(c)	F3*v*	REcordare d*om*ine	à2	
8(d)	F5*v*	Venite et ploremus	à2	
9	F5*v*	POpule meus	à2	[Anon.]
				[Tav:] eiusdem [= de Quadris]
10	F7*v*	CUm aut*em* veniſſem	à2	[Anon.]
				[Tav:] eiusdem [= de Quadris]

11		SEpulto do*mi*no		à2	[Anon.]
					[Tav:] eiusdem [= de Quadris]
12	F8*v*	PA∬io ∫acra		à4	Fran. Vene.
	F10*r*	[Colophon; Register]			

Extant copies

F-Pn, Rés.Vm^c.17. Lacks C7, F1 and F9-10

> **Size of page:** 169 × 236 mm.
>
> **Watermarks:** No.20 on A4, A8, B4, B7, C1, C3, D3, D5, E5, E7, and probably F7
>
> **Textual comments:** E4*r*, signature: the second "E" is inverted
>
> **Technical comments:** A row of *m* sorts used as bearers in the space of stave vi on B6*r*,7*r*,8*r*, C2*r*,4*r*,5*r* and F6*r* • E2*v*.vi.text:] Teth [apparently masked by wool from the ink-ball during impression
>
> **Corrections and changes:**
>
>> **In house:** F1*r*: see above
>>
>> **Later:** C4*r*.iv-v: additional text in manuscript • C6*r*.iv: a few manuscript notes, perhaps in the hand found on C4*r* • F6*v*-7*r*: manuscript music, perhaps late 16th- or early 17th-century
>
> **Binding:** 16th-century binding, with the second book • Calf with rolls of acanthus leaf for border and an internal design of rolls and stamps, in blind • One paste-down and one fly-leaf at each end: the stub of each flyleaf is inside the nearest gathering. Watermark of letters:] C Z | G
>
> **Provenance:** From Rosenthal, catalogue 22, p. 4

GB-Lbl, K.1.d.6★ (1). Lacks A1

> **Size of page:** 172 × 239 mm.
>
> **Watermarks:** No.20 on A6, A7, B5, B7, C1, C4, D2, D3, E6, E8, F3, F6, and F10 • The twin marks show clearly here: one is on A6, B7, D3, E6, E8, F3, and F6: the other examples are of its twin
>
> **Technical comments:** Furniture sorts, with a cross pattern on their face, have taken light ink on B6*r*,8*r*, C2*r*,3*r*,5*r*
>
> **Corrections and changes:**
>
>> **In-house:** C7*v*, D7*r*, D8*r* and F1*r*: see above
>>
>> **Later:** D6*v*.i.27: brown ink numeral 2 above the note • D6*r*-E1*r*, and other places (including E5*r*, E82 and F12) all have added numerals indicating the durations of notes and ligatures: these begin with De Quadris's setting • D7*r*.ii.after 40: *sb* rest added, in brown ink • E1*r*.iv.40: f', *sb* → *b*, in brown ink, with numeral "2" • E7*r*.i.second word:] deus [changed with brown ink to] do*mi*nus • E7*v*.ii.text: after] homi*nu*3 [added in the same brown ink] ut converteret • E8*r*.iii.after 8: added *sb* rest, in same brown ink • F4*v*.iii and F5*r*.ii: extra rules below the stave, to mark a section end • F5*v*.i.17–18: *dmc*",*sbc*",*sba*': crude erasure of dot and second note, so that music on the recto appears, as a *ma*' • F6*r*.i.17: dot erased
>
> **Binding:** Bound with *II Lamentationes* (No.28) • Original parchment, the lower part of a bifolium from a fifteenth-century Italian liturgical manuscript • Modern end-papers, one paste-down and two flyleaves at each end
>
> **Provenance:** British Museum stamp of] 16 JUL [19]26
>
> **Bibliography:** Johnson and Scholderer, *Short-Title*, p. 101

I-Bc, Q.66. Complete

Watermarks: No.20 on A1, A3, B5, B7, C3, C7, D2, D4, E3, E7, F3, and F9

Textual comments: F8*v*: the part-name *Tenor* lacks the last letter

Technical comments: A row of *m* used as furniture for the 6th stave on F6*v* and F7*r*

In-house changes: D8*r* and F1*r*: see above

Provenance: This copy is cited in Martini's letters to Chiti of 7.v.1746 and 22.vii.1746 (see Schnoebelen, *Padre*, Nos.1245 and 1250, pp. 144–145)

Bibliography: Fava, "Primo", p. 38 (exhibition at Bologna, 1929) • Fenlon and Dalla Vecchia, *Venezia*, pp. 78–79 (exhibition catalogue, Venice, 2001) • Gaspari, *Catalogo*, iii, p. 170

I-Pca, III.C.1185. Lacking E3*r*, roughly torn out, leaving a stub

Size of page: 173 × 238 mm.

Watermarks: No.20 on A1, A6, B4, B8, C2, C4, D5, D8, E8, F2, F6, and F7 • The twin marks are again very clear: one mark is on A1, B8, C2, D5, D8, E8, and F6

Technical comments: Lines of fusas were used as bearers on B6*r*.vi, B7*r*.vi, B8*r*.vi, and F7*r*.vi

Corrections and changes:

   In-house: C3*r* and F1*r*: see above

   Later: A8*v*.iv.before 10: perhaps the traces of a natural sign, in brown ink • D7*r*.iv,text: addition of] Hae [(in margin) and] He [below stave, correcting the original] Teth

Binding: Original black leather over wood, rolled and stamped in blind. Three metal clasps, all lost on the front board, all present on the back • No end papers: there are two stubs of 16th-century paper after A8, which were probably conjugate with the front end-papers

Provenance: A1*v*:] adi 8 FebO 1624 comprati dali *Frateli Reverendo* di Juane padin [in brown ink

———

Lost copies: Copies were owned by Colón (Chapman, "Printed", No.18) and by the Fuggers (Schaal, "Musikbibliothek", I/57): see chapter 20.

Early references: There is the remote possibility that this volume was cited by Doni, in his *Prima Libraria* (see Haar, "Libraria", p. 117, where it is argued that this is rather unlikely)

Bibliography:

   (a) Rosaria Boccadifuoco, *Bibliografia*, No.1824 • Sartori No.26

   (c) Petrucci, *Lamentationum Jeremie*

   (d) Cattin, *Quadris* • Herman, *Two Volumes* • Thomas, *Petrucci*

   (e) Bent, "Pietro" • Cattin, "Sconosciuto" • Sartori, "Nuove," p. 192 • Thomas, *Petrucci*

Commentary:

1. I accept the view adopted in Thomas, *Petrucci*, by which de Quadris was the composer of the long cycle of settings, mostly not attributed, which form the core of the second half of this volume. This is perhaps supported by the use of the word "eiusdem" for the following texts. In addition, these works, whether overtly by him or not, are given many more ornate initial letters (opening internal sections) than is the rest of the book.

2. The importance of de Quadris in the transmission of early settings of Lamentations texts is underscored here. His settings are by far the earliest music in any of Petrucci's volumes (being perhaps 50 years old at the time): with the additional initials, it is evident that they held a central place in the repertoire collected for this volume.

      In chapter 9, I propose an arrangement of this and the second volume which reflects a change of plan. In that, de Quadris's settings may originally have been intended for Book 2, so that each of the two books would have had works of a more consistent style. Nonetheless, the two books were evidently planned together, and de Quadris's works would have held a significant place in either book.

3. A number of the settings (Tinctoris, Anonymous, and De Orto) involve the first readings for the first Nocturn on Thursday of Holy Week, sometimes with the same reading for Friday (Ycart and Agricola). The setting by de Quadris probably represents a complete cycle, especially when accompanied by the final texts. Notably, this contrast follows both the stylistic differences and the status of the composers, and the positions they held.

4. As a note on the size of the musical font, there are 71 *coronas* on the forme A1*v*,2*r*,7*v*,8*r*.

No. 28. *Lamentations II*

29.v.1506   *RISM* 1506²

A1*r*]   Lamentationum liber | Secundus. Auctores | Tronboncinus | Ga ſ par. | Era ſmus.

G3*v*]   Impreſſum Uenetiis per Octauianum Pe-|trutium Foro ſempronien ſem. Die. XXIX Madii | Salutis anno M.ccccc vi. Cum priuilegio | inuictiſſimi Dominii Uenetiarum q*uae* nullus | po ſſit cantum Figuratu*m* imprimere ſub pena | in ip ſo priuilegio contenta. | Regi ſtrum. | A B C D E F G Omnes quaterni. Preter G. | qui eſt duernus. | [Petrucci's device]

Format and collation: Choirbook: landscape quarto-in-eights • 52 folios: A-F⁸G⁴

Signatures:] A 2 [$4 • − A1, G3, G4 • B2 signed B II • E2 has an inverted "2" • F2 and F3 both signed F 3

No foliation, or running heads

Part-names: in the left margin, reading vertically from the top:

    verso:]   Tenor   [A1-G2
    recto:]   Altus Baſſus   [A2-G3

Fonts: Music: Petrucci's normal music fount

    Staves: six per page, 178–180 mm long and 10-93-113 mm high

    Text: rotonda throughout, "x" = 2.1 • colophon in roman: "x" = 1.5 = 1.6, "5" = 14.3 mm.

Technical comments: The part-names seem to have been part of the skeleton forme: one setting of the word *Tenor* can be traced through the volume, reappearing on 1*v* and 3*v* of gatherings B-E. In the same way, the setting on B4*v* can be seen on each 2*v* and 4*v* to the end of the volume. • Even clearer evidence can be seen in the patterns of setting the part-names *Altus* and *Bassus*: for example, the same initial *B* is used on the rectos of A2, A4, A6 and A8, B3, and B5, and thereafter on rectos 1, 3, 5, and 7, of each gathering, until G1. • Similar evidence can be seen in the retention of staves in the forme: the second and third staves on A1*v* reappear on A3*v* and B4*v*, and thereafter on 2*v* and 4*v* of each gathering to the end of the book. The staves are in their best state in gathering B, and gradually deteriorate through the rest of the book, with A presenting the worst state. • The reappearance of the same damaged sort more than once in the same gathering is unusual: the damaged bar-line on B1*r*.i is also on B4*r*.iii: another bar-line on B4*v*.iv appears on B6*r*.i, and perhaps also on C4*r*.vi • The chords on E5*v*.vi and E6*r*.iii are printed at one impression

In-house corrections: B7*r*.v.22: *l* c' → d', part erasure and manuscript addition, with new point for corona, done in printing ink, in all extant copies • F2r.ii.42: second note of ligature, d' → e', part erasure and printing ink, in all extant copies

Contents:

	A1r	[Title]	
1	A1v	INcipit lamentatio	Bartho. T.
		Aleph. Quomodo ſedet	
	A1v.iii	Beth. Plorans ploravit	
	A2v.ii	Gimel. Migrauit iudas	
	A3v	Deleth. Uie syon lugent	
		Jeruſale3 conuertere	
	A4v	HEe. Facti ſunt hoſtes	
	A5v	Vau. Et egreſſus eſt	
	A5v.ii	Zai. Recordata eſt	
	A6v	Hieruſale3 conuertere	
	A7v	HEth. Peccatum peccauit	
	A7v.ii	Teth. Soroles eius	
	A8v.ii	Joth. Manum ſuam miſit	
	B1v	Caph. Omnis populus eius	
	B2v	Lamech. Quos omnes	
		Jerusalem conuertere	
	B3v	SEquitur de lamentatione Jeremie	[Anon.]
	B3v.i	Mem. De excelſo niſit	
	B4v	Nun. Uigilauit inqu3	
	B5v	Samech. Abſtulit omnes	
	B6v	Ain. Id circo ego	
		Jeruſale3 conuertere	
	B7v	SAde. Juſtus eſt dominus	
	B8v	Caph. Uocaui amicos meos	
	C1v	Res. Uide domine	
	C1v.ii	Sin. Audierunt quia	
	C3v	ALeph. Quomodo obtexit	
	C3v.iii	Beth. Precipitauit dominus	
	C4v.ii	Gymel. Confregit	
	C5v	Deleth. Tetendit arcum ſuum	
		Jeruſale3 conuertere	
	C6v	HEe. Factus eſt domimus	
	C6v.iii	Vau. Et diſſipauit	
	C7v.ii	Zay. Repulit dominus	
	C8v	Heth. Cogitauit dominus	
		Jeruſale3 conuertere	
	D1v	TEth. Defixe ſunt	
	D2v	Joth. Sederunt in terra	
	D3v	Caph. Deffecerunt pre lacrimis	
	D4v	Lamech. Matribus ſuis	
		Jeruſalem conuertere	
2	D5v	INcipit oratio Jeremie prophete.	[Anon.]
		Recordare	

3	E1*v*	BEnedictus dominus deus i∫rael	[Anon.]
	E2*v*	2/ Ut ∫ine timore de manu	
4	E3*v*	INncipit lamentatio ieremie	
		Aleph. Quomodo ∫edet Ga∫par.	
	E3*v*.ii	Beth. Plora*ns* plorauit	
	E5*v*	Deleth. Uie ∫yon luge*nt*	
	E5*v*.ii	He. Paruuli eius	
		Jeru∫ale3 co*n*uertere	
	E6*v*	VVau. Et egre∫∫us e∫t	
	E6*v*.ii	Zay. Recordata e*st*	
		Jer*usalem* co*n*uertere	
	E7*v*	BEth. Mi∫erficordie d*om*ini	
	E7*v*.ii	Heth. Noui diluculo	
	E7*v*.ii	Teth. Bonus e∫t d*omin*us	
		Jeru∫alem conuertere	
	E8*v*	ALeph. Quomodo ob∫curatu*m* e∫t	
	E8*v*.ii	Gimel. Sed ꝩ lamie	
		Jeru∫alem conuertere	
	F1*v*	INcipit oratio Jeremie . . . Recordare	
5	F3*v*	INcipit lamentatio ieremie	Era∫mus.
		Aleph. Quomodo ∫edet	
	F4*v*	Beth. Plora*ns* plorauit	
	F5*v*	Gimel. Mig*r*auit iudas	
	F6*v*	Deleth. Uie ∫yon luge*nt*	
	F7*v*	He. Facti ∫u*nt* ho∫tes	
	F8*v*	Vau. Et egre∫∫*us est*	
	F8*v*.ii	Zay. Recor*d*ata e*st*	
6	G2*v*	BEnedictus dominus deus i∫rael	[Anon.]
	G3*v*	[Colophon; Register; Device]	
	G4*r–v*	[blank]	

Extant copies

F-Pn, Rés.Vm^c.18. Lacking gathering A

> **Size of page:** 169 × 236 mm.

> **Watermarks:**

B1	B5	C3	C7	D4	D7	E1	E5	F5	F7	G2
20	21	21	20	17	20	20	17	20	20	20

> **Corrections and changes:**

>> **In-house:** B7*r* and F2*r*: see above

>> **Later:** All these changes seem to be in the same brown ink: Manuscript pagination from B2*r*.] 18–24, [i–ii, B5*v*–6*r*], 25–26, 28, 28–32, 33 (with 41 above), 34–42, [iii–iv, C7*v*–8*r*], 43–48, [v–vi, D3*v*–4*r*], 50–95, [96]. This pagination was apparently entered before the loss of gathering A, and excluded one page (probably the title) from that gathering • Manuscript music additions, B1*v*.iii and vi; B8*v*.iii; C1*r*.iii; D1*v*.vi; and D2*r*.vi • B1*r*.vi.10: *b*, *c'* → *d'*, erasure and brown ink • B3*v*.caption:] Secondo giorno P*r*ima Lame*n*t*atio* • B7*v*.caption:] Secondo giorno seconda Lame*n*t*atio* • C1*v*.caption:] Terzo

giorno Prima Lamen*ta*tio • C6*v*.caption, probably reads] Terzo di • D1*v*.caption:] Terzo di • G4*v*.caption:] Lamentacio libri secundus

Binding and Provenance: With *Lamentations I* (No.27)

GB-Lbl, K.1.d.6* (2). Lacking ff. G3-4

Size of page: 172 × 239 mm.

Watermarks:

A6	A7	B3	B7	C2	C5	D5	D8	E2	E3	F1	F5	G2
20	22	20	21	21	20	20	17	21	20	17	22	20

Corrections and changes:

> **In-house:** B7*r* and F2*r*. see above
>
> **Later:** B1*r*.vi.10: *b*,c' → d', erasure and black ink • B8*r*.iv.last note: *lc*' → *b*d', erasure and black ink • D1*v-2r*. wine stains!

Binding and Provenance: With *Lamentations I* (No.27)

Bibliography: Johnson and Scholderer, *Short-Title*, p. 101

I-Bc, Q.67. Lacking folio G4

Size of page: 168 × 237 mm.

Watermarks:

A4	A8	B2	C6	C8	D1	D4	E1	E3	F6	F7	G2
20	21	21	20	17	17	20	21	20	21	21	17

Corrections and changes:

> **In-house:** B7*r* and F2*r*. see above
>
> **Later:** B8*r*.iv.last note: *lc*' *b*d', erasure and brown ink

Binding: 19th-century marbled paper over boards, as for *Lamentations I* at I-Bc • One paste-down and one flyleaf at each end

Provenance: Old call number] 267 [at top left of A1*r* and at the top right in a different hand and ink] A2

Bibliography: Fava, "Primo" p. 38 (exhibition at Bologna, 1929)

Lost copies: Copies were owned by Colón (See Chapman, "Printed", No.19) and the Fuggers (Schaal, "Musikbibliothek", I/58): see chapter 20

Bibliography:

> (a) Rosaria Boccadifuoco, *Bibliografia*, No.1824 • Sartori, *Petrucci*, No.27
>
> (c) Petrucci, *Lamentationum liber secundus*
>
> (d) Herman, *Two Volumes* • Thomas, *Petrucci*
>
> (e) Sartori, "Nuove," p. 192 • Thomas, *Petrucci*

Commentary:

1. Thomas, *Petrucci*, suggests that the anonymous works (No.2, 3, and 6) were composed by the writers of the preceding cycles — Tromboncino and Erasmus. This seems quite plausible.

2. As with the first book, this can be divided into two repertorial sections: the first represented by Tromboncino, and the second by Weerbeke and Erasmus. The possibility that the content of both books was rearranged is discussed in chapter 9. The music in this second book was apparently

less well known, however. The only concordance is that in I-Fn Panc.27, a north Italian source in part copied from Petrucci's editions.

2.   There are some unusual bibliographical features of the book: the retention of the part-names as part of a skeleton forme had not been Petrucci's recent custom. On the other hand, he had published few books in which the layout had been as consistent as here, with its simple and regular choir-book format for four voices. Petrucci had sometimes retained a part-name as a running head-line: but that was easier to do than the present practice, where the retained elements are in the left margin of the page. Coupled with the evidence (much less remarkable) of the retention of staves in the forme, this argues that Petrucci used only two skeleton formes for most of the book, at least from the inner sheet of gathering B, and probably for A also.

3.   The evidence of increasing distortion in stave-lines, progressing from gathering B to the end, with gathering A representing the worst state, argues that Petrucci set up the first gathering last. This common practice would not have been necessary, for there is no table of contents: it suggests that the first gathering had to be reprinted at the end of the process.

4.   It is also surprising to find the same musical sorts in both formes of a single sheet. This may signify that the book was set up in formes (rather than straight through), which would certainly be possible, given the repertoire and planned lay out. I do not think that the evidence implies that the type setter was short of bar-lines.

5.   This is another book which apparently did not see any reprinting at all: although the paper patterns seem confused (see below), they in fact suggest no more than the blending of two stocks. One is represented by paper 20: the other comprises all the remaining marks, which are all of the same type. Both are found in other books printed at this stage of Petrucci's career.

Forme:	Ao	Ai	Bo	Bi	Co	Ci	Do	Di	Eo	Ei	Fo	Fi	G
F-Pn			20	21	20	21	20	17	20	17	20	20	20
GB-Lbl	22	20	21	20	21	20	17	20	21	20	17	22	20
I-Bc	21	20	21	—	17	20	17	20	21	20	21	21	17

6.   The pattern of in-house corrections also suggests that there was no new edition. All the copies have the same corrections. In addition, of the two substantive corrections that I have called "later", one is present in all three copies, and the other in two of them. Both of these may well be in-house corrections, although (since they were effected in different inks) I am unable to assert that with any confidence. Nonetheless, this pattern does argue (at least) that all the extant copies represent a single setting of type.

No. 29. Dammonis: *Laude I*

[1506]   Not in *RISM*

This is the incomplete first editon of Dammonis's book. Only two sheets survive, D outer and F inner. There is no date, for the only extant colophon is attached to the rest of the unique copy, for which see No.45, below.

    The first edition probably had the same title and dedication as does the second: in keeping with Petrucci's Venetian custom, the colophon would have had a different date.

The title-page, A1r, probably read:

    Laude Libro Primo. | Jn. dammonis. | Curarum dulce lenimen.

Format and collation: Choirbook: landscape quarto-in-eights. Probably 64 folios: A-H⁸

Signatures:] DD 2 [$4

Foliation: t.r.r.] 25, 26, 31, 32, 43–46

Fonts: Music: Petrucci's normal music font

    Staves: six per page (although six are inked on few pages)

    Text: Roman throughout, "20" = 57 mm, on B2r

Technical comments: A small initials was used on D1r [O]

There are no apparent in-house corrections

Contents:

26	D1r	O Maria diuina [tella
		[Headed:] De beata virgine
27	D1v	O Madre [ancta o luce
28	D2v	O Madre del [ignore
		[Headed:] Te matrem
		. . .
32	D7r	MAria madre de dio
		[Headed:] Ad beatam virginem
	D7v	[verse:] Vergine [acre e figlia del tuo figlio
33	D8v	SAlue regina di mi[ericordia [upper voices only]
		[Head-line cropped: [Ad beatam] virginem
		. . .
42	F3r	DAmmi il tuo amore [lower voices only]
43	F3v	PEccatori perche [eti tanto crudi
		[Headed:] De pa[[ione
44	F4r	HVmilmente tenuocho Ie[u
45	F4v	PIanzeti chri[tiani Il dolor de maria
		[Headed:] De pa[[ione [Tavola: Piangeti . . .
46	F5v	DE piangeti amaramente
		[Headed:] De pa[[ione eiu[dem verba
47	F6v	POpul mio popul ingrato [upper voices only]
		[Headed:] De pa[[ione

Extant copy:

E-S, 12-1-4. These two sheets are bound up with the complementary sheets of the second edition: a description of the copy is given there

    Watermarks: No.20 on D7 and F3

    Provenance: From Colón, with the sheets of the second edition (Chapman, "Printed", No.35)

Lost copies: Copies of the second edition were owned by the Fuggers (Schaal, "Musikbibliothek", I/73) and by Bottrigari

Other editions: The second edition was published in 1508 (No.45)

Bibliography:

    (a) Sartori, *Petrucci*, No.42 describes the unique copy as one edition

    (c) Luisi: *Dammonis*

(d) Jeppesen: *Mehrstimmiger*, referring to the second edition

(e) Glixon, "Polyphonic"

Commentary:

1. This first edition of this volume has to be presumed, from the presence of two sheets definitely earlier than the rest of the unique copy. Those two sheets are on a paper (No.20) that was in use twice during the critical period, the first during the first half of 1506. This included editions of the fifth and sixth books of frottole (December 1505 and February 1506) and of both books of Lamentations (April and May). By the time of the last of these, the stock was running down, and Petrucci was using new papers. These new papers, alongside some remnants of paper 20, can be found in the masses of Isaac, in October. Between May and October, there are no known and dated editions, though I have placed the second edition of Josquin's first book there. Paper 20 does reappear briefly in the first two editions of 1507, and also in two books of frottole in the middle of that year: but I do not believe that there is sufficient room for a complete edition of a new book at either stage. Unfortunately, there is not enough bibliographical evidence to make a final decision, but the most likely answer seems to me to be that this book was printed during the summer of 1506, perhaps before the Josquin edition.

2. The first serious suggestion that an earlier edition might survive appeared in Glixon, "Polyphonic".

3. The fact that no early owner mentions a copy of this edition suggests that it may have had a particularly small print-run: the alternative, equally viable, is that Dammonis took the greater part of the edition himself, for distribution to friends, colleagues, and other local institutions.

No. 30. Josquin: *I Missarum*

[1506]   Not in *RISM*

Second Edition

A1r]   Liber primus Miſſarum Joſquin | Lomme arme. Super voces muſicales | La. ſol. fa. re. mi. | Gaudeamus | Fortuna deſperata | Lomme arme.Sexti toni. | S

C1r]   Liber primus Miſſarum Joſquin. | T

E1r]   Liber primus Miſſarum Joſquin. | A

The Bassus is not extant

Format and collation: Partbooks: landscape quarto-in-eights. [S:] 18 folios: A⁸B¹⁰; [T:] 12 folios: C⁸D⁴; [A:] 18 folios: E⁸F¹⁰; [B: presumably 16 folios: G-H⁸]

Signatures:] aaA II [$4 • − A1 • + B5, with an arabic numeral

No foliation or running heads

Fonts: Music: Petrucci's normal music type

Staves: six per page: 177 mm long, 10-92-113 mm high

Text: Rotonda throughout, "x" = 2.2.mm • Rotonda for Superius title, "x" = 3.6 mm.

No evidence of in-house corrections

Technical comments: Only five staves are inked on A4*v*,5*r*, B9*r*, C1*v*, F9*v*, 10*r*, and B8*v* (stave three for added text)

Rubrics: B4ν:] Cre∫cat In duplum • B4ν.iii, reading down:] Re∫olutio • B5r.iii, reading down:] Re∫ olutio • B5ν.iii, reading down:] Re∫olutio • C6ν:] Fuga ad minimam: • C1ν.iii-iv, reading down:] Re∫olutio. • C2r.iv, reading down:] Re ∫olutio. • C2ν.iii, reading down:] Re∫olutio. • C3ν.ii, reading down:] Re∫olutio. • F3r.iii, reading down:] Super fortuna de∫perata

Contents:

	A1r	C1r	E1r	[Title]
1	A1ν	C1ν	E1ν	Lomme arme ∫uper voces mu∫icales
	A2r	C2r	E2r	[Gloria]
	A2ν.iv	C2ν	E2ν.v	[Credo]
	A3ν.iv	C3r	E3ν.iv	[Sanctus]
	A4ν	C3ν	E4ν	[Agnus]
2	A5ν	C4r.iii	E5r.iv	Jo∫quin. La.∫ol.fa.re.mi.
	A5ν.iv	C4r.v	E5ν	[Gloria]
	A6r.v	C4ν.iii	E6r	[Credo]
	A7r.iv	C5r.iii	E7r	[Sanctus]
	A8r	C5ν.ii	E7ν.iii	[Agnus]
3	A8r.v	C5ν.iv	E8r	Jo∫quin ∫uper gaudeamus
	A8ν.iii	C5ν.vi	E8r.v	[Gloria]
	B1r.v	C6r.iii	F1r	[Credo]
	B2ν.ii	C6ν	F2r.iv	[Sanctus]
	B3r	C6ν.vi	F2ν.iv	[Agnus]
4	B3ν	C7r.iv	F3r.iii	Jo∫quin fortuna de∫perata
	Bν.v	C7r.vi	F3ν	[Gloria]
	B4ν	C7ν.ii	F4r.iii	[Credo]
	B6r	C8ν	F5r.iii	[Sanctus]
	B6ν.iv	D1r.iv	F5ν	[Agnus]
5	B7r.ii	D1ν.iv	F6r	[Reading down:] Jo∫quin
				T:] Lomme arme.
	B7ν	D2r	F6ν	[Gloria]
	B8r.iii	D2ν	F7ν	[Credo]
	B9r	D3r.iv	F8ν.iv	[Sanctus]
	B9ν	D3ν	F9r.ii	[Agnus]
6	B10r.iii	D3ν.iii	F10r	Jo∫quin de pre∫.
				A:] Ecce tu pulchra es
		D4r		[blank staves]
	B10ν	D4ν	F10ν	[blank]

Extant copy:

A-Wn, S.A.77.C.20. Superius, Tenor, and Altus, complete

   Size of page: 164 × 233 mm.

   Watermarks:

A3	B10	C5	D3	E3	F3	F5
21	20	21	20	21	22	21

   Technical comments: The sixth stave is not inked on folios A4ν,5r, B9r, C1ν, F9ν,10r; and the third is uninked on B8ν

   Later changes: Movements numbered in manuscript throughout all three volumes of Josquin:] 1–89 • D1ν: appended to] Lomme arme [in manuscript:] sexti toni

Binding: Modern, followed by Josquin's *II Missarum* (1515, No.54) and *III Missarum* (1514, No.59)

Provenance: With the other books in this binding

Bibliography: Noble, "Petrucci"

Lost copies: See the notes under the first editon (No.4)

Other editions: The first edition appeared in 1502 (No.4 above): the book was reprinted more than once in Fossombrone (No.62) • It was further reprinted, from copies of one of the 1516 editions, by Pasoti and Dorico in 1526, *RISM* J669

Bibliography: Apart from the entries under the first edition (No.4), see also Noble, "Petrucci". This edition was not known to Sartori

Commentary:

1. The dating of this second edition has already been discussed by Jeremy Noble (in "Petrucci"). He points out that the papers place the edition in 1506, and indeed all three are only available together during that year. While paper 20 had been in used since late in 1505, it disappeared from Petrucci's editions with the second book of Lamentations (29.v.1506), and was running low even then, for additional papers were needed, and new papers are in use until early in 1507. There was still some stock of paper 20, for it appears on the fragments of Dammonis's first edition, as well as here. But the other papers in this book are only found as additional stock in the book of Lamentations (paper 21), or in the next two volumes, of Isaac and Gaspar (paper 22). The implication is that the present edition fits into the five-month gap between the second book of Lamentations, and the book of Isaac's masses (20. x .1506).

2. It is significant that this second edition follows a more compact layout than that adopted for the first. The first edition was unnecessarily extravagant of space, probably because it had been sponsored by an outside patron: even this one leaves a number of blank stave-lines at various places. But by now Petrucci had prepared almost thirty editions, including nine of masses and movements, and his men will have been much more experienced at gauging the space required for a movement.

3. This is another edition that was not known to any early owner or bibliographer. It is difficult to argue, as one could for the edition of Dammonis's Lamentation settings, that the edition was probably closely controlled by the composer. Instead, one must suggest that the first edition, as a sponsored book, was at least in part reserved by the patron: the remaining stock, put on the market, apparently did not exhaust the needs of the market.

No. 31. Isaac: *Misse*

20. × .1506   *RISM* I 88

Some pages and formes were reset during the printing of the edition: they are discussed under No.31a. In addition, there are two cancels, on B4-5 and F1,8, entered as Nos.31b and 31c.

Edition

A1*r*]   Mi∫∫e henrici Jzac | Charge de deul | Mi ∫ericordias domini | Quant yay au cor | La ∫pagna
| Comme feme

C1*r*]   T

E1*r*]   A

G1*r*]   B

H6*r*]   Impre∫∫um Uenetijs per Octauianum Pe | trutiuȝ Foro∫empronien∫em. 1506. Die .xx. |
Octobris. Cum priuilegio inuicti∫∫imi Domi | nij Uenetiarum quae nullus po∫∫it cantum Figura | tum
imprimere ∫ub pena in ip∫o priuilegio | contenta. | | Regi∫trum. | | AaA BbB CcC DdD EeE FfF |
GgG HhH Omnes quaterni. Preter | BbB quinternus CcC HhH terni DdD | duernus.

Format and collation: Partbooks: landscape quarto-in-eights. [S] 18 folios: A⁸B¹⁰; [T] 10 folios:
C⁶D⁴; [A] 16 folios: E-F⁸; [B] 14 folios: G⁸H⁶

Signatures:] AaA 2 [$4 • − A1, C4, D3, D4 and H4 • + B5

No Foliation

Head-lines comprise only the name of the mass, without part-names. See below

Fonts: Music: Petrucci's normal music font

Staves: Six per page, 175–180 mm long, 10-92-112.5 mm high

Text: Rotonda

Textual comments: C3*r*.i] Krie [D-B; GB-Lbl • C8*r*.iii] Agnns [D-B; not GB-Lbl • The wrong
initial appears on F3*v*: K for P. [D-B, GB-Lbl

Technical comments: Only five staves are inked on B9*v* (A-Wn, D-B) and D3*v* (all copies): only
four are inked on H6*r* • There seem to be at least ten *longas* in the font: there are seven (of which
one has the dog-tooth sides) on D2*v*, with 2 on D1*r* and one on D3*r* • The mensuration sign
"cut C dot" is apparently a block: the same sign appears on A7*v*, C5*r*, E7*v*, G6*v* • The evidence
of the stave lengths, GB-Lbl copy, show that the half-sheet in B and the half-sheet in C were
both printed by work-and-turn, rather than being set up together: that in B has all long staves,
while that in C is printed with the shorter ones • B1o*r*: the large initial letter *B*, used for the
title-page of *Canti B*, is here used as furniture and printed in blind. It is visible in the copies at
A-Wn, D-B, and I-Mc, and lightly visible on B1o*v* in the copy at GB-Lbl • F1*r* and *v* are both
very crowded, and give a suggested type-width of 2.6-2.7 mm.

In-house corrections: A1*v*.i.after 35: p.d., *m* rest → *sb* rest, p.d.: unchanged in the copies at D-B
and GB-Lbl: the change is in manuscript in that at I-Mc, and the result of a stop-press correction
in that at I-Bc • E6*v*.v.32–33: *sbe'*,*sbd'* → *sbf'*,*sbe'*, erased and stamped in: D-B, GB-Lbl and I-Bc
• E6*v*.vi.15: *l* → *b*, by erasure of tail: A-Wn, D-B, GB-Lbl, and I-Bc • F3*v*.iii.54: *mf* note head
erased, and *sbg* stamped in to make a *mg*: D-B, GB-Lbl, and I-Bc

Rubrics: D3*v*.top right:] Tenor ∫ecundus. • G2*v*.v-vi.margin, reading upwards:] De∫cendit in
dyate∫∫aron • G4*r*.iv-v.margin, reading downwards:] De∫cendit in vndecimam

Contents:

	A1*r*	C1*r*	E1*r*	G1*r*	[Title]
1	A1*v*	C1*v*	E1*v*	G1*v*	[Missa] Charge de deul
	A1*v*.vi	C1*v*.iii	E1*v*.v	G1*v*.v	[Gloria]
	A2*v*.iii	C2*r*	E2*v*.iii	G2*v*.ii	[Credo]
	A3*v*.iii	C2*v*	E3*v*.iii	G3*r*.vi	[Sanctus]
	A4*v*	C2*v*.iii	E4*r*.v		[Agnus]
2	A4*v*.v	C2*v*.v	E4*v*.iv		[Missa] Mi∫ericordias domini

	A5r.iii	C3r.iii	E5r.ii	G4v.iv	[Gloria]
	A5v.iv	C3v.iii	E5v.iii	G5r.iv	[Credo]
	A6v	C4r.v	E6v	G5v.v	[Sanctus]
	A6v.vi	C4v.iii	E7r	G6r.iv	[Agnus]
3	A7r.v	C5r	E7v	G6v.iii	[Missa] Quant jay
	A7v.iii	C5r.iv	E7v.v	G6v.vi	[Gloria]
	A8r.iv	C5v.iii	E8r.vi	G7r.vi	[Credo]
	B1r.iv	C6r	F1r.v	G8r.iv	[Sanctus]
	B2r	C6r.iii	F2r	G8v.v★	[Agnus]
4	B2v.iii	C6r.vi	F2v	H1r.ii	[Missa] La [pagna
	B3r.iii	C6v.i★	F2v.vi	H1v.i	[Gloria]
	B3v.iv	C6v.v	F3v.ii	H2r	[Credo]
	B4v	D1r.iv	F4r.iii	H2v	[Sanctus]
	B5r.v	D1v	F4v.vi	H2v.vi	[Agnus]
5	B6r.ii	D1v.iv	F5v.iii	H3r.v	[Missa] Comme femme
	B6v	D2r.ii	F6r	H3v.ii	[Gloria]
	B7r.iv	D2r.vi	F6v.iii	H4r.iii	[Credo]
	B8r.iii	D2v.iv	F7v.ii	H4v.v	[Sanctus]
	B9r	D3r.ii	F8r.iv	H5r.vi	[Agnus]
				H6r.[vi]	[Colophon; Register]
	B10r	D4r			[blank staves]
	B10v	D4v		H6v	[blank]

Extant copies:

A-GÜ. Tenor, lacking C1, D1, D3 and D4

    Size of page: 165 × 235 mm.

    Watermarks: No.17 on f.C3

    No corrections or changes visible

    Binding and Provenance: With Josquin Masses II (1515)

    Bibliography: Federhofer "Petrucci"

A-Wn, S.A.77.C.14. Superius, Tenor, and Altus, complete. For the cancel bifolio at F1,F8, see below

    Size of page: 162 × 229 mm.

    Watermarks:

A1	A4	B2	B7	C2	D1	E3	E8	F6
22	17	22	22	22	22	17	17	17

    Corrections and changes:

      In-house: E6v: see above

      Later: Movements numbered in MS, brown ink:] 265–289 • F6r.iv.text: manuscript addition, brown ink:] Qui tollis

    Binding: Austrian National Library binding

    Provenance: With the library's copy of Josquin's masses, given the numbering of movements

D-B, N.Mus.ant.pract.11. Complete. For the reset pages E2v,7r, and the cancel bifolium F1,8, see below

    Size of page: 169 × 233 mm.

    Watermarks:

A1	A3	B1	B3	C5	D1	E1	E4	F2	F5	G1	G6	H1	H3
17	22	22	17	17	22	17	22	22	17	17	17	17	17

Technical comments: G8*v*.v.after 2nd bar-line:] a music spacing-sort, 16.2 × 0.6 mm: this projects above the stave 2.3 mm, and 3.3 mm below

Corrections and changes:

In-house: E6*v*, E6*v* and F3*v*: see above

Later: Manuscript foliation:] 1–18; 1–10; 1–16; 1–14 • F3*r*.ii.5: d', dotted *b*: the point erased • F3*r*.iv.mensuration sign: from cut circle to cut C, erasure • H2*r*.ii.40: *bc*: point added, in brown ink

Binding: Newly rebound in red linen, with red leather spines, in a slip-case • Grey paper paste-downs and end-papers • The second gathering of the Tenor is misbound, in the order ff.2, 1, 4, 3

Provenance: There are presently no ownership marks, though a library stamp has been cleaned from all the title-pages. This is presumably the copy stolen from the East Berlin library, and later (in 1962) offered for sale by Witten

GB-Lbl, K.1.d.7. Complete. For the cancel bifolium F1,8, see below

Size of page: 155 × 224 mm.

Watermarks: Some of those noted here as No.22 might plausibly No.18: this does not affect the chronology of those pages.

A5	A7	B1	B3	C4	C6	D2	E3	E8	F3	F7	G3	G8	H2
22	22	17	17	22	17	17	22	17	17	17	22	17	17

Technical comments: A6*v*.iii.above 25: a spacing sort for music, 1.8 mm wide. The note below is a *sb*, 1.6 mm wide: perhaps the sort shows the size of the body • Stave lengths are given below in the commentary • Uninked staves appear on both B10*r* and D4*r*

Corrections and changes:

In-house: E6*v*.v.32–33: *sb*e', *sb*d' → *sb*f', *sb*e', erased and stamped in • E6*v*.vi.15: *l* → *b*, erased tail • F3*v*.iii.54: *mf* note head erased, and *sb*g stamped in to make a *mg*

Later: F3*r*.ii.5: d', dotted *b*: the point erased • F3*r*.iv.mensuration sign: from cut circle to cut C, erasure • H2*r*.ii.40: *bc*: point added, in dark brown ink

Binding: British Library binding • Marbled paste-down and conjugate fly-leaf, at each end: two additional fly-leaves at the front, and one at the back • The edges are painted gold

Provenance: Old call number on A1*r*.] 7AAc

Bibliography: BM STC Italian, p. 341

I-Bc, Q.68. Complete. For the reset page A5*r*, see below

Size of page: 165 × 242 mm.

Watermarks:

A1	A3	B7	B10	C5	D4	E2	E5	F1	F6	G3	G7	H3	H5
17	22	22	22	17	17	17	22	22	22	17	17	22	22

Textual comments: Wrong capital letter on F3*v* [K for P]

Technical comments: There are at least seven longas in the fount, of which six have dog-teeth: cf. D2*v*, with 3 more on D1*r* and D3*r*

Corrections and changes:

In-house: E6*v*.v.32–33: *sb*e', *sb*d' → *sb*f', *sb*e', erased and stamped in • E6*v*.vi.15: *l* → *b*, erased tail • F3*v*.iii.54: *mf* note head erased, and *sb*g stamped in to make a *mg*

Later: Manuscript foliation:] [S] 56–73; [T] 40–49; [A] 54–69; [B] 50–63 • E6*v*.vi.15: *l* → *b*, erased tail • F3*r*.iv.mensuration sign: from cut circle to cut C, erasure

Binding: Bound in a folder, with the same marbled paper used in the folder of Agricola's masses. Each part in a buff card folder • All edges are painted gold

Provenance: This copy is cited in Martini's letters to Chiti of 7.v.1746 and 22.vii.1746.

See Schnoebelen, *Padre*, Nos.1245 and 1250, pp. 144–145 • Old call number on A1r.]
1011
Bibliography: Fenlon and Dalla Vecchia, *Venezia*, p. 79 (exhibition catalogue, Venice, 2001)
I-Mc, S.B.178/3. Superius book, complete. For the reset page A5r and the cancel bifolio B4,5, see below
    Size of page: 164 × 223 mm.
    Watermarks:

        A2   A3   B3   B10
        22   17   18   22

    Later corrections and changes: Modern pencil foliation, f.r.r:]: 35–37, [37*bis*], 38–51 •
    A1*v*.i.after 35: *sb* rest and p.d. → p.d. and *m* rest, changed in manuscript
    Binding: With Josquin Masses II, *q.v.*
    Provenance: Mantua, Sta Barbara
    Bibliography: Exhibited at Florence in 1949. Damerini, "Esposizione", p. 25 • Prizer

————

No. 31A. *Reset pages.*

Formes for page A5r, and for pages E2*v* and 7r, seem to have been reset during the printing process. The rest of the forme in each case seems to be of the same setting of type in all copies.

The differences on A5r are insignificant, and involve only the music forme. It appears that the second stave, in particular, suffered some slight damage during press-work, and had to be reconstructed in the forme.

The change in gathering E is more immediately evident. The large initial on E2*v* is different in the two settings: but in fact both music and text formes were completely reset. The differences are much less obvious on E7r, though detailed examination shows that the music forme was again reset.

Given the slight extent of these changes, it is reasonable to assume that the new settings were the result of technical problems, rather than of problems in the readings.

Extant copies: The rest of each copy is described above, including watermarks for these pages
D-B, N.Mus.ant.pract.11. Pages E2*v* and E7r
I-Bc, Q.68. Page A5r
I-Mc, S.B.178/3. Page A5r

No. 31B. *Cancel bifolium for B4 and B5*

Extant copy:
I-Mc, S.B.178/3. For the rest of this copy, see above
    Watermark: No.18 on B5

No. 31C. *Cancel bifolium for F1 and F8*

Extant copies:
A-Wn, S.A.77.C.14. For the rest of this copy, see above
    Watermark: The top of what is probably No.15 on F1
D-B, N.Mus.ant.pract.11. For the rest of this copy, see above
    No watermark visible.

Technical comments: The stave lengths demonstrate that this half-sheet was printed by the work-and-turn method:

F1*r*	F1*v*	F8*r*	F8*v*
178	178	178	178 mm.

GB-Lbl, K.1.d.7. For the rest of this copy, see above.

Watermark: The top of what is probably No.16 on f.F1

Technical comments: The stave lengths, although different from those in the copy in D-B (probably merely as the result of paper shrinkage), carry the same message:

F1*r*	F1*v*	F8*r*	F8*v*
176	175	174	175 mm.

———

Lost copies: Copies were owned by Colón (Chapman, "Printed", No.20) and Bottrigari. See chapter 20 • A copy was owned by Gaspari (Potier, "Gaspari")

Bibliography:

(a) Rosaria, Boccadifuoco, *Bibliografia*, No.1769 • Sartori, *Petrucci*, No.28

(d) Isaac, *Messe* • Isaac, *Opera Omnia*

(e) Blackburn, "Lorenzo" • Feldmann, "Divergierende" • Sartori, "Nuove", p. 192 • Staehelin, *Messen*

Commentary:

1. Note that Petrucci's device is not printed in this book, although there is room for it on the blank H6*v*.

2. The head-lines giving names of works are as follows:

    recto:] Charge [A2-4, C2, E2-4, G2-4 • Miſericordias [A5-7, C3-4, E5-7, G5-6 • Quant jay [E8-F2 • Quant Jay [A8-B2, C5, G7-8 • Quant Jay [C6 • La ſpagna [B3-5, D1, F3-5, H1-3 • Comme feme [B6-9, D2-3, F6-8, H4-6 • Comme femme [B7-9, D2-3, F6-8, H4-6 • [Nil: A1, B10, C1, D4, E1, G1

    verso:] Charge de deul [A1, C1, E1, G1 • Charge [A2-4, C2, E2-4, G2-3 • Miſericordias [A5-6, C3-4, E5-6, G4-6 • Quant Jay [A7-B1, C5, E7, F1, G7-8 • Quant jay [B2, E8 • La ſpagna [B3-5, C6-D1, F2-4, H1-2 • Comme femme [B6-9, D2-3, F5-8, H3-5 • [Nil: B10, D4, H6

3. The collation of the Tenor book is unusual: in most cases, a book of ten folios would have been printed as a quintern, rather than as two gatherings. It seems that the decision resulted in some problems. The Gloria of the Mass *La Spagna* on C6*v* is very crowded: the two Tenors of the second Agnus of the Mass *Comme femme* are on D3*r* and D3*v*, and therefore cannot be sung together. There is no evidence of setting by formes, either in these places or elsewhere in the title: it may therefore be that the reasons for the crowding and the unusual format lie in a division of work by present gatherings.

4. Further evidence of dividing the typesetting between two craftsmen may be found elsewhere. The pattern of overcrowding of the Gloria on C6*v* also survives in places in gathering F. F1*r* and F1*v* are both very crowded. There are stretches of notes on F1*r*, staves 2 and 3, which seem to have been set with no spacing sorts at all. One stretch on F1*r*.iii, in particular, contains 16 notes, all of which seem to have a body-width of 2.6 mm.

    Another strand in the same pattern is the manner in which masses do not start at the beginning of pages, and some movements even start in the middle of lines: in parallel with the other evidence, this argues that earlier attempts at casting-off were abandoned, perhaps because Petrucci was dividing the work of each part-book between two men, each assigned a different and complete gathering.

5. It is notable that the two Tenor parts for Agnus II of *M. Comme femme* cannot be sung together. This is very unusual for Petrucci, who is careful about maintaining standard layout patterns.

6. The patterns of stave repetitions, as seen in the copy at GB-Lbl, argue that Petrucci was using four sets of staves. These comprise two that measure about 180 mm and two that measure about 175 mm. Consistently, the printers retained the formes of longer staves for the outer forme of a sheet, with two exceptions: one is in the already anomalous gathering C; the other is the result of printing all half-sheets by work and turn.

   As examples, the staves of A2*v* can be seen to return on A4*v*, B2*v*, C1*v*,3*v*, D2*v*, E2*v*,4*v*, F2*v*,4*v*, G2*v*,4*v*, and H2*v*,3*v*. Similarly, the staves on A3*v* re-appear on B1*v*,3*v*, C2*v*, D1*v*, E1*v*,3*v*, F1*v*,3*v*, G1*v*,3*v*, and probably H1*v*.

7. The patterns of repeating staves suggest that the books were printed in the order Tenor, Bassus, Altus, and Superius.

8. The two cancels must have been printed immediately after the edition. The same pattern of staves is present: for example, the staves of A2*v* can also be found on B4*v* and 5*v*.

No. 32. Gaspar van Weerbeke: *Misse*

7.i.1506/7   *RISM* G 450

A1*r*]   Miſſe Gaſpar | Aue regina celor*um* | O venus banth | E trop penſer | Octaui toni | Se
           mieulx ne vient
C1*r*]   T
D1*r*]   A
F1*r*]   B
G8*r*]   Impreſſum Uenetijs per Octauianum Þe | trutiu3 Foroſempronienſeiii .1506. Die .vij. |
           Januarij. Cum priuilegio iñuictiſſimi Domi | nij Uenetiar*um* q*uae* nullus poſſit cantum Figura | tum
           imprimere ſub pena in ipſo priuilegio | contenta. || Regiſtrum. || AA BB CC DD EE FF GG |
           Omnes quaterni preter B C E q*ui*nterni.

Format and collation: Part-books: landscape quarto-in-eights. [S] 18 folios: A⁸B¹⁰; [T] 10 folios:
   C¹⁰; [A] 18 folios: D⁸E¹⁰; [B] 16 folios: F-G⁸
Signatures:] AA 2 [$4 • − A1 • + B5, C5 and E5
No Foliation.
Running heads: The headline has two components: the part-name, which was probably kept in the
   forme, and the piece title, which was not • For the latter, see the end of this entry. The part-
   name is at the top outer corner of each page:

Super*ius*	[A1*v*-B9*v*: set to the left margin on A8*r*
Tenor	[C1*v*-C9*v*
Altus	[D1*v*-E10*r*
Baſſus	[F1*v*-G8*r*
[Nil:	A1*r*, B10*r*-*v*, C1*r*, C10*r*-*v*, D1*r*, E10*v*, F1*r*, G8*v*

Fonts: Music: Petrucci's normal music type

Staves: Six per page: 175–178 mm long, 10-91.5-112 mm high

Text: Rotonda. The signatures use a Roman fount

Textual comments: F4r: the head-line] Ba∫∫us [lacks the final "s" in some copies: for example, it is present in that at GB-Lbl, but missing in the copy at I-Bc: it probably was present, but in blind

Technical comments: Only four staves are inked on G8r • The text-and-stave formes, which must have followed the music formes, were probably set by formes: see the Commentary, below • The colophon apparently uses the setting of type found in Isaac's *Misse*

In-house corrections: A8r.i.after 10: rests: *sb, l,* → *sb, b,* by erasure: all extant copies • B2r.signature: the first letter B stamped in later: I-Bc and PL-Kj • E10r.vi.42–44: after 42, clef C$_1$; after 43, a *custos* a third above the following pitch, to activate the new clef: both are entered in pale brown ink, in all extant copies • It is possible that the changes at E2v.vi.after 16 were also made in-house

Contents:

	A1r	C1r	D1r	F1r	[Title]
1	A1v	C1v	D1v	F1v	[Missa] Ave regina celor*um*
	A2r	C1v.iv	D2r	F1v.vi	[Gloria]
	A2v.iii	C2r.ii	D2v.iv	F2v.ii	[Credo]
	A3v.iii	C2v	D3v.iv	F3v	[Sanctus]
	A4r.vi	C2v.v	D4v	F4r.iv	[Agnus]
2	A5r.ii	C3r.iii	D5r.iv	F4v.vi	[Missa] O venus banth
	A5v.ii	C3r.v	D5v.iv	F5r.v	[Gloria]
	A6r.v	C3v.iii	D6v	F5v.vi	[Credo]
	A7r.iii	C4r	D7r.v	F6v.iii	[Sanctus]
	A7v.vi	C4r.iv	D8r.iii	F7r.v	[Agnus]
3	A8v	C4v	D8v.v	F7v.vi	[Missa] E trop pen∫er
	B1r	C4v.iii	E1r.v	F8r.vi	[Gloria]
	B1v.v	C4v.vi	E2r.iii	G1r.ii	[Credo]
	B2v.v	C5r.iv	E3r.iii	G1v.vi	[Sanctus]
	B3v	C5r.vi	E3v.vi	G2r.vi	[Agnus]
4	B3v.vi	C5v.ii	E4r.vi	G2v.v	[Missa] Octavi [toni]
	B4r.iv	C5v.vi	E4v.iv	G3r.iii	[Gloria]
	B4v.v	C6v	E5r.v	G3v.iv	[Credo]
	B5v.ii	C7r.iv	E6r	G4r.vi	[Sanctus]
	B6r.ii	C7v.iv	E6v	G4v.v	[Agnus]
5	B6v	C8r.iv	E6v.v	G5r.iii	[Missa] Se mieulx ne vient
	B6v.vi	C8r.vi	E7r.iv	G5v	[Gloria]
	B7v.iv	C8v.iv	E8r.ii	G6r.iii	[Credo]
	B8v.iii	C9r.iii	E9r.ii	G7r	[Sanctus]
	B9r.v	C9v	E9v.v	G7v.iii	[Agnus]
		C9v.v		G8r.iv	[blank staves]
				G8r.v	[Colophon; Register]
	B10r	C10r			[blank staves]
	B10v	C10v	E10v	G8v	[blank]

Extant copies:

Sartori, *Petrucci*, p. 118, remarks that Fétis knew of a copy at I-Vnm, which no longer existed. Fétis was probably confusing this with the Viennese copy, given the pattern of moving Italian copies for the benefit of Schmid's research

A-Wn, S.A.77.C.9. Superius, Tenor, and Altus, complete

> **Size of page:** 162 × 224 mm.
>
> **Watermarks:**
>
> | A3 | A8 | B2 | B5 | B7 | C2 | C4 | C6 | D1 | D3 | E4 | E10 |
> |----|----|----|----|----|----|----|----|----|----|----|-----|
> | 17 | 20 | 22 | 17 | 22 | 20 | 20 | 20 | 20 | 20 | 27 | 27 |
>
> **Corrections and changes:**
>
> > **In-house:** A8r, E10r: see above
> >
> > **Later:** Movements numbered in manuscript in each book:] 315–339 • A symbol is visible at the top of D1r and E1r, presumably a binder's mark: that at the top of E1r could be a "B"
>
> **Binding:** Modern binding of the Austrian National Library
>
> **Provenance:** From the manuscript pagination, this was originally bound with the library's copy of Josquin: *Misse* (1506: No30)

D-B, N.Mus.ant.pract.50. Altus complete

> **Size of page:** 159 × 223 mm.
>
> **Watermarks:** No.20 on D1; No.27 as a countermark on E7
>
> **Technical comments:** The signature on D3 was printed with the music • Many of the initial capitals have left very poor impressions
>
> **Corrections and changes:**
>
> > **In-house:** E10r: see above
> >
> > **Later:** E2v.vi.after 16: originally perhaps a *c.o.p.* ligature, b+d', and a rest *sb*; now a *sb* rest, and touched up stave lines, in brown • On the final flyleaf, verso, a series of note shapes, in order, from *maxima* to *minima*
>
> **Binding and Provenance:** Bound with *Missarum diversorum I* (No.43) • Early 16th-century parchment, with a new spine. Remains of four tie-strings of leather • One paste-down and two flyleaves at each end, all original. On the second final fly-leaf is a watermark of a radiant sun with a face, similar to Briquet 13963 (Parma 1543) or Heawood 3889

GB-Lbl, K.1.d.6. Bassus, complete

> **Size of page:** 156 × 218 mm.
>
> **Watermarks:** No.20 on F5, G6 and G7 • No.27 on F1
>
> **Textual comments:** F1v.caption:] Aue regiua [sic]
>
> No corrections or changes visible
>
> **Binding:** British Museum white parchment binding, 1897 • Gold fore-edges
>
> **Provenance:** British Museum stamp on G8v:] 17 NO [18]96
>
> **Bibliography:** Johnson and Scholderer, *Short-Title*, p. 318

I-Bc, Q.65. Complete.

> **Size of page:** 161 × 240 mm.
>
> **Watermarks:**
>
> | A3 | A8 | B2 | B4 | C2 | C3 | D1 | D6 | E2 | E7 | F5 | F7 | G4 | G8 |
> |----|----|----|----|----|----|----|----|----|----|----|----|----|----|
> | 22 | 20 | 22 | 17 | 22 | 22 | 22 | 27 | 27 | 27 | 22 | 27 | 22 | 22 |
>
> **Technical comments:** The signatures were not printed with the text: cf. B1r, where the two overlap • The Superius of Missa *O venus banth* has an exceptional number of up-tails

Corrections and changes:

    In-house: A8*r*, B2*r*, E10*r*: see above

    Later: Manuscript foliation: [S] 38–55; [T] 30–39; [A] 36–53; [B] 34–49 • E2*v*.vi.after 16: some sort of an erasure, perhaps of two notes, and an inserted *sb*, in brown ink

Binding: Each part in a buff paper wrapper, and all in a board folder, covered as in the copy of Agricola's masses. Edges painted gold, all parts

Provenance: This copy is cited in Martini's letters to Chiti of 7.v.1746 and 22.vii.1746 • A1*r*: old catalogue number:] 1008 • According to the manuscript pagination, the copy was originally bound with Agricola: *Misse* (1504, No.13)

Bibliography: (See Schnoebelen, *Padre*, Nos.1245 and 1250, pp. 144–45)

I-Mc, S.B.178/2. Superius, complete.

    Size of page: 164 × 233 mm.

    Watermarks: No.17 on A5 and A8 • No.22 on B3 and B10

    Technical comments: Stave lengths indicate work-and-turn for B5-6: see the comments, below

    Corrections and changes:

        In-house: A8*r*: see above

        Later: Modern manuscript foliation:] 17–34

    Binding: With Josquin, *II Missarum* (1505, No.22)

    Provenance: Mantua, Sta. Barbara • Perhaps the Chapel of Cardinal Ippolito d'Este

    Bibliography: Damerini, "Esposizione", p. 25 (exhibition at Florence in 1949) • Lockwood, "Adrian", p. 99 • Prizer, "Cappella"

PL-Kj, Mus.ant.pract.G 290. Three parts, complete: lacking the Tenor

    Size of page: 167 × 238 mm.

    Watermarks:

A6	A7	B7	B10	D3	D7	E2	E3	F1	F6	G5	G7
17	20	17	22	27	20	27	27	27	20	20	20

    Technical comments: The patterns of repeating staves are particularly clear in this copy: they confirm that a complete set was kept in the forme: A1*v* = A4*v*, B5*v*, D2*v*,4*v*, E2*v*,5*v*, F3*v*, G3*v*: similarly, A5*v* = D5*v*; E7*v* and E9*v* = F6*v*, and F8*v* = G6*v*

    Corrections and changes:

        In-house: A8*r*, B2*r*, E10*r*: see above

        Later: Manuscript foliation: [S] 131–148; [A] 131–148; [B] 117–132 • A2*v*.v.37–38: *sb*c', *m*d': both colored and scratched void • E2*v*.vi.after 16: erasure of a ligature or two notes: *sb* rest inserted and stave lines touched up, in brown ink [16 = *bb*, "17–19" = *sb*f', *m*f', *m*d'] • E9*v*.v.after 51: ?*m* rest erased → *sb* rest entered in light brown

    Binding: Modern white parchment covers for each part-book, kept in a 20th-century box • One paste-down and one end-paper at each end of each part • Edges painted red (S and B) or green (A)

    Provenance: From Berlin. Stamp of the Berlin library on A1*r* and D1*r* • Probably to be associated with copies now in I-Bc: see Table 10–5

Lost copies: Copies were owned by Colón (Chapman, "Printed", No.21) and the Fuggers (Schaal, "Musikbibliothek", I/46) • Another copy was in the Gaspari collection (See Fétis, "Biographie" and Potier, "Gaspari")

Bibliography:

(a) Rosaria Boccadifuoco, *Bibliografia*, No.3360 • Sartori, *Petrucci*, No.29;

(e) Sartori, "Nuove", p. 193

Commentary:

1. The sequence of using sets of staves argues that the impressions with staves and texts were set forme by forme, rather than sequentially. This issue is discussed in chapter 4.

Forme	Outer	1r	2v	3r	4v	Inner	2r	1v	4r	3v
I-Mc:										
A.I	α	—	180	177	179	β	174	174	173	174
A.II	β	176	175	174	174	α	179	180	179	180
B.I	β	174	174	174	—	α	178	177	177	179
B.II	β	177	176	175	175	α	179	180	178	180
B.III	β	176	173	174	175					
PL-Kj:										
A.I	α	—	180	179	180	β	176	175	175	174
A.II	β	176	176	175	175	α	180	180	179	180
B.I	β	176	175	175	—	α	179	178	180	179
B.II	β	176	176	174	175	α	179	180	179	180
B.III	β	177	176	176	176					
D.I	β	—	175	175	174	α	180	180	180	181
D.II	β	176	175	175	176	α	180	180	180	181
E.I	β	177	176	175	—	α	181	181	180	181
E.II	β	177	175	174	175	α	179	180	179	181
E.III	β	176	174	175	174					
F.I	α	—	181	179	180	β	176	175	174	175
F.II	α	178	179	178	171	β	176	174	174	174
G.I	α	180	180	179	—	β	176	176	175	175
G.II	α	178	180	178	180	β	176	176	174	174
GB-Lbl:										
F.I	α	—	182	180	181	β	178	178	177	178
F.II	α	180	182	182	182	β	178	177	177	178
G.I	α	181	187	181	—	β	177	178	176	178
G.II	α	180	182	182	182	β	177	178	177	178

    It is notable that the pattern of using set β for the outer formes changes with the innermost sheet of E. This sheet was apparently printed by work and turn.

2. The pattern of staves confirms a visual examination, indicating that the book went through only one setting. This setting used an unusually large and complex range of papers: papers 17 and 22 had been in use for a while, and this was the last book in which they would appear. Petrucci had also been purchasing stocks of paper 20 since 1505, and would continue to use it for some more months. The assumption is that this book used whatever papers were to hand, rather than a batch specially purchased with it in mind.

3. As might be expected, the mass titles could not be retained in the forme, even from one part-book to another. The evidence argues that they were freshly set for each page:

    recto:] Ave [A2-4, C2-3, D2-5, F2-4 • O venus banth. [A5 • O venus banth [A6-8, C4, D6-8, F5-7 • E trop penſer [B1-3, E1, E3, F8-G2 • Etrop penſer [C5, E2, E4 • Octaui [B4-6,

C6-8, E5-6, G3-5 • Se mieulx ne vient [B7-9, C9, E7-10, G6-8 • Nil: A1, B10, C1, C10, D1, F1

verso:] Ave regina celor*um* [A1, C1 • Ave regina [D1, F1 • Ave [A2-4, C2, D2-4, D5 (in error), F2-4 • O venu5 banth. [A5 • O venus banth. [A6 • O venus banth [A7, C3, D6-8, F5-7 • E trop pen[er [A8-B3, C4, E1-2, F8-G2 • Etrop pen[er [E3 • Octaui [B4-5, C6-7, E4-6, G3-4 • Octaui toni [C5 • Se mieulx vient [B6 • Se mieulx ne vient [B7-9, C8-9, E7-9, G5-7 • Nil: B10, C10, E10, G8

4.   This is one of few mass volumes which saw no additional printings: there seem to have been no cancels or replacement sheets, much less a second edition.

No. 33. SPINACINO: *Intabolatura I*

after 27.ii.1507   *RISM* 1507⁵

A1r]   Intabulatura de Lauto | Libro primo.

G8r, at foot of page]   [Two lines at left:] Impre[[u3 Uenetijs: Per Octauianu3 Petrutiu*m* Foro[empronien[e3: 1507. Cu*m* priuilegio inuicti[[imi | Dominij Venetiar*um*: q*uae* nullus po[[it imprimere intabulaturam lauti. vt in [uo priuilegio contine*tur*. [Two lines at right:] A B C D E F G | Omnes qua terni.

A2r]   Regula pro illis qui canere ne[ciunt.   1

Intelligendu3 est primo q*uae* in pre[enti intabulatura [unt [ex ordines cordar*um* prout in lauto. Suprema linea [tat pro contra|ba[[o 1 sic per ordine*m*. Que debent tangi in [uis ta[tis secundum numer*um* in ip[is [ignatu*m*. Q*ua*ndo inuenis .o. tangitur corda illa vacua | 1 q*ua*ndo inuenis .1. tangitur in primo tastu. 1 [ic de [ingulis. Aduerte q*uae* i[ti numeri [unt [ignat per vnam littera3   5 roma*ni*. [cilicet. 10 11 12 [ic | X Ẋ Ẍ. Et quia quia cantileni vt habeant earum perfectionem voces non debent e[[e equales: ideo inuenta [unt infra-|[cripta [igna que [unt loco notar*um* **Γ Γ₣₣** quor*um* primu3 valet pro [emibreui: [ecu*n*dum pro minima: 1 [ic de [ingulis. Et | [ic [ecu*n*du3 valet pro medietate primi: tertiu*m* pro medietate [ecu*n*di: et [ic per ordine*m*. Sunt 1 queda*m* [ignis que dicu*ntur* | [igna proportionu*m*: 1 [u*nt* i[ta. **Ρ ꞵ** tria ex primo ponu*n*tur pro i[to **|** 7   10 secu*n*dum pro medietate primi. Su*nt* 1 alia huiu[-|modi **ꟼꟼ** quor*um* [ecu*n*dum valet pro medietate primi: 1 quinq*ue* ex [ecundo pro tali **|** Item [ciendu*m* q*uae* quando inuenis pu*n*ctum | [ub littera illa corda debet moueri [ur[um omnes alie deor[um. Soli Deo Laus honor 1 gloria.

Regole per quelli che non [anno cantare.

Prima deue intendere che in la pre[ente i*n*tabulatura [onno [ei ordine de corde co*m*mo in lo   15 lauto. La linea de [opra e per | el co*n*traba[[o: e co[i va [eguitando per ordine. Le qual [e ha*n*no a tochare in li lor ta[ti [eco*n*do [onno in e[[i [ignati li numeri | Quando [era [ignato .o. [ignifica che [e tocha quella corda doue e tal [igno voda. Et qua*n*do e [ignato .1. [e mette el deto in | lo primo ta[to: E co[i del re[to de li numeri. Et per che a X [egnar .10.11.12. per e[[er doi letere po[[ea fare confu[ione e [ta | me[[o per .10. X. per .11. Ẋ. per .12. Ẍ. E anchora da   20 [apere che le co[e che [e [onano per hauer la [ua perfectio*n*e le botte no*n* [e | da*n*no equali per tanto [onno [ta fatti [opra li ditti numeri li infra[cripti [ignali quali [onno [egni de notte redutte *in* tal for|ma: accio che etiam quelli che non ſanno cantar poſſino anchora loro participar de tal uirtu: li quali ſi ſe acco|modaranno a tegnir tal meſura ſonaranno tutte le coſe intabulate perfectiſſimamente: Queſti ſonno li ſegni **❘ ⌐ ⸠ ⸡** | El primo ſignifica la meſura che deue   **25** tegnir: a qual biſogna pigliarla ſi larga che in quel tempo tu poſſi dare le botte del | numero diminuto: perche lo ſecondo ſegno vale per la mita del primo. El terzo per la mita del ſecondo. El quarto per la | mita del terzo. El quinto per la mita del quarto. Et quando tu trouerai vno ponto apreſſo al primo ouer al ſecondo ſegno | quel tal ponto vale per la mita de quel ſegno apreſſo al qual e meſſo. Sonno anchora certi ſegni de meſura che | ſe dimandano ſegni de proportione che   **30** ſonno queſti **Ρ Β** Tre del primo vale tanto quanto queſto **❘** El ſecondo per | la mita del *primo* el terzo *per* la mita del ſeco*n*do. So*n*no etia*m* de altra ſorte **⌐ ⌐** de li quali el ſecondo vale per la mita del *pri*|mo E cinque del ſecondo vale *per* vno tal ſegno **❘** Item nota che tutte le botte ſonno ſenza ponto de ſotto ſe danno | in giu: e quelle dal ponto ſe danno in ſu: excepto quando ſonno piu de vna che ſe pizzichano non eſſendo de ſotto el ponto | che biſogna darle tutte in ſu   **35**

A2*v*]   OCtauianus Petrutius Foroſempronienſis Lectori Sal*ute*. Cum mihi a natura inſitum eſſe   **1** ſemper nouerim: & preſentibus: & | posteris vel prodeſſe velle: vel placere quam*uis* ingenio ſim debilis: omni ſtudio enixus ſum obſeruare. ne in aliquo refragari | nature muneri dici queam. Quapropter quicquid ingenii in me fuit hactenus impendi & non inuitus tot uoluminibus | in arte Muſices a me impreſſis: qua*n*tum aute*m* in his profecerim alioru*m* relinquitur iudicio. & ſano: **5** quibus huiuſmodi ars maxime | eſt cordi: & q*uando* cantui ſonus eſt amicus: & adeo illi co*n*nexus videtur: vt diſſolutione*m* nequaqua*m* patiatur: aggreſſus ſum opus & ſa-|ne difficile: quem vero auctorem in hoc libro ſim ſecutus eius nomen cantiones in fro*n*te gerunt. Et ne aliqui ſorte ſint qui vana | ſuſpitione ducantur: me falſum nomen in caput cuiuſlibet poni iuſſiſſe: illis ſancte: ſi opus eſt: recipio omnia proprii auctoris ma-|nu notata me habuiſſe: & ad unguem conſtare. Nolim   **10** preterea que*m* piam incredulum latere: q*uae* quicquid in futurum emiſſurus | ſum veri auctoris nomine id numqua*m* fraudare velle meam eſſe ſententiam: & quem omnium excellentiſſimum fama canat nec | ſumptu: pareens *[sic]* inueniam. nam fallere iniqui eſt hominus & obeſſe volentis. Ego autem pro virili parte omnibus prodeſſe vel | ſaltem placere ſtudeo. Tu igitur Lector rerum nouarum auidiſſime postquam vetiora veris que dixi eſſe no*n* ignorabis. ſi ſtatim mihi | gratias non egeris.   **15** Spero noſtrorum librorum paulatim non parcus laudator euades Vale. Venetiis. III. Calendas Martias. Anno | Salutis. M.D.VII. |

[3 columns: the right two are taken by the] Tabula. [The left one reads:]

    Chriſtophorus Pierius Gigas Foroſempro-|nienſis in Laude*m* Franciſci Spinacini.

      Eſt natura quidem Spinis non omnibus vna

      Tacta roſas que fert pungere na*m*q*ue* ſolet   **20**

      Non hec ſpina manu*m* ledit: ſed concitat aures

      Mellifluo cantu: Threiciaq*uae* Lyra.

      Orpheus hac quo*n*dam mouit cu*m* co*n*iuge ditem.

      Inimites parcas ſpina mouere potest

[Column 2:]

Aue Maria Franceſco Spin.	.iii.
Adiu meſamours Fra*n*. Sp.	XXXIII.
Benedictus Fra*n* Spi.	IIII.
Baſſadanza	XXIX

Come feme Fra*n*. Sp.	VI.
De tous biens Fra*n*.	XVI.
Fortuna p*er*te crudele	XXXVI.
Fortuna du*n* gran tempo F.S.	Vii.
Iuli amours Fra*n*. Spi.	Xi
Iene fay Fra*n*. Spi.	XXi.

[Colu*m*n 3]

Iay pris amours Fra*n*. Spi.	XXIiIi
Le Deproueu fortune Fra*n*. Spi.	V.
La bernardina de Io[qu*in* F.S.	XIX.
La mora Fra*n*. Spi.	XXVI
La bernardi*n*a de Io[qu*in* F.S.	XXVIII.
Mabucherit	XXXi.
Nu*n*quam fuit pena mairo	XXXiii.
Non [ouenir	XXXV.
O uenus banth Fra*n*, Spi.	XXVII.
Vna mai[tres Fra*n*. Sp.	iX.
Recercare Numero diece[ette	

Format and collation: Tabulature: landscape quarto-in-eights. 56 folios: A-G⁸

Signatures:] A 3 [$4 • − A1

Foliation: t.r.r.] [1–2], 3–17, [18], 19–23, [24], 25–41, 43 [*recte* 42], 43–56

No running heads • Composer's name in head-line

Fonts: Music: Petrucci's tablature font

    Staves: Six-line: four per page, 175–177 mm long. 17-79-110 mm high

    Text: All in Rotonda. The initial A on A3*r* is 93 × 73 mm.

Technical comments: Uses the A of the title page of *Odhecaton A* for the first piece • Small capital on F4*r*

In-house corrections: It seems probable that many of the corrections made to the musical text are in the hand of Spinacino: see the notes in the description of the unique copy at PL-Kj, and the assessment in the Commentary to this entry

Contents:

	A1*r*	[Title]			
	A1*v*	[blank]			
	A2*r*	Regula . . .			
	A2*v*	[Letter to the reader; Encomiastic poem;]		Tabula	
1	A3*r*	AVe Maria de Jo[quin		France[co Spinacino	[Josquin]
2	A4*r*.iii	BEnedictus de I[ach		France[co Spinacino	[Isaac]
3	A5*r*.ii	LE de[proueu infortune		Francesco Spinacino	[Caron]
4	A6*v*	COme feme		France[co Spinacino	[Agricola]
5	A8*r*.ii	FOrtuna du*n* gra*n* tempo		France[co Spinacino	[Josquin]
6	B1*r*	VNa mai[tres		France[co Spinacino	[Brumel]
7	B2*r*.ii	VO[tre a Jamays		France[co Spinacino	[Ghiselin]
8	B3*r*	JUli amours	[Duet]	France[co Spinacino	[Ghiselin]
	B5*r*.iii	Secunda pars			
9	B8*r*.iii	DE tous biens	[Duet]	France[co Spinacino	[Hayne]
10	C3*r*	LA Bernardina de Jo[quin	[Duet]	France[co Spinacino	[Josquin]

11	C5r.iii	JE ne fay	[Duet]	Franceſco Spinacino	[Busnois]
	C6v	Secunda pars			
12	C7v	JAy pris amours	[Duet]	Franceſco Spinacino	[Anon.]
	C8v.iii	Secunda pars			
13	D2r	LA Mora		Franceſco Spinacino	[Isaac]
14	D3r.ii	O Uenus banth		Franceſco Spinacino	[Weerbeke]
15	D3v.iii	LA Bernardina de Joſquin		Franceſco Spinacino	[Josquin]
16	D4v	Baſſadans		[Anon.]	
17	D7r.ii	MAbucherit		[Anon.]	[Ockeghem]
18	D8v	ADiu meſamours		[Anon.]	[Josquin]
19	E1v.iii	NUnquam fuit pena maior		[Anon.]	[Urrede]
20	E3v	NOn ſouenir		[Anon.]	[Hayne]
21	E4v	FOrtuna per te | crudele		[Anon.]	[Vincenet]
22	E5v	REcercare de tous biens		Franceſco Spinacino	
23	E6r.iii	REcercare a Juli amours		Franceſco Spinacino	
24	E7r	REcercare [3]		Franceſco Spinacino	
25	E7v	REcercare [4]		[Anon.]	
26	E8v.iii	REcercare de tutti li Toni		[Anon.]	
27	F2v	REcercare [6]		[Anon.]	
28	F3r.iii	REcercare [7]		[Anon.]	
29	F4r	REcercare [8]		[Anon.]	
30	F4v.ii	REcercare [9]		[Anon.]	
31	F6v	REcercare [10]		[Anon.]	
32	F7r	REcercare [11]		[Anon.]	
33	F7v.ii	REcercare [12]		[Anon.]	
34	G1r.ii	REcercare [13]		[Anon.]	
35	G2r	REcercare [14]		[Anon.]	
36	G3r	REcercare [15]		[Anon.]	
37	G4r.ii	REcercare [16]		[Anon.]	
38	G5v	REcercare [17]		[Anon.]	
	G8r foot	[Colophon: Register]			
	G8v	[blank]			

Extant copy: Sartori, "Nuove", p. 193 corrects his assertion, in *Petrucci*, p. 119, that there was a copy at A-Wn

PL-Kj, Mus.ant.pract.P 680. Complete (*RISM* records the photographic copy held at F-Pn)

Size of page: 168 × 232 mm.

Watermarks:

A4	A7	B2	C4	C7	D3	D8	E4	E7	F3	F7	G4	G8
20	23	20	23	20	23	23	23	23	23	23	23	23

Technical comments: D1r suggests that the notation was printed before the staves • The notation of F5r and F8v was printed before the staves of F5v and F8v • E5v.iv.8,4 is hardly inked: it appears to read //2///

Corrections and changes:

In-house: E3v.iv.2,3.rhythm sign: *m* → *sm*, erasure and stamped in

Perhaps by Spinacino: All the following are in brown ink, with erasures where needed: for my reasons for attributing these to Spinacino, see below • A3v.ii.2,1: //6/// → //

67// • A4*v*.i.2,1: /3/20/ → /2/20/ • A5*r*.i.6,1: 03//2/ → /35/2/ • A6*r*.iii.4,5: ///01/ → ////0/ • B1*r*.iv.7,5: 75/X// → 75//7/ • B1*v*.iii.3,1: 85///7 → 85/7// • B2*v*.iv.5,5: 85/5// 85/7// • B4*v*.iii.3,1: ///3// → ///2// • C5*v*.ii.1,4: //1/// → /1//// • D2*r*.i.1,2: 2///// → 6///// • D2*r*.i.4,1: 51/4// → 52/4// • D2*v*.iii.5,1: /?//2/ → ////2/ • D8*v*.i.4,2: /?//// → /1//// • D8*v*.i.6,5: ////2/ → ////3/ • E1*r*.iii.3,2: /6//// → //// 3/ • E3*v*.iv.2,5: /35/// → /35/2/ • E7*r*.iv.7,5: /1?/0/ → /11/0/ • E8*r*.iii.3,5: /1//// → /2//// • There seem to be no corrections after E8*r*, that is, for most of the ricercars • There are fingerprints on E2*r*, apparently in the same ink as used for these corrections. It is tempting to suggest that they may have been made by Spinacino!

Later: A4*r*.i.4,1–2: both 01/21/ → 0//21/0, by poor erasures

Binding: Leather, probably of the 19th century, bound with Spinacino's second book. Gold rules and inscription] EX COLLECTIONE | G. POELCHAU • Black panel on the spine with title • Marbled paste-downs at each end, the conjugate is pasted to the outer of two fly-leaves at each end. The inner flyleaves are watermarked, that at the front reading] EPER-STEIN | G | GERMAR • With Book 2 by Spinacino (No.34)

Provenance: From Berlin. The Berlin library stamp is on A1*r* • From the Poelchau collection • The verso of the first front flyleaf has an inscription:] Aus Florenz 1822

———

Lost copies: A copy was bought by Colón in Rome, ix.1512 (see Anglés, "Colombina", pp. 27–28; Chapman, "Printed", No.22; Plamenac, "Excerpta", p. 679) • There was a copy in the Herwart collection (Martinez-Göllner, "Herwart", p. 47)

Bibliography:

(a) Sartori, *Petrucci*, No.30 • Brown, *Instrumental*, 1507₁

(b) Brunet, *Manuel*, iii, col.446

(c) Spinacino, *Intabulatura* • Apel, *Notation*, 63 (of page 39)

(d) Buetens, *Lute*

(e) Nordstrom, "Ornamentation" • Sartori, "Nuove", p. 193 • Schmidt, *First* • Underwood, *Renaissance*, 6–87 • Wolf, *Handbuch*, ii, 66

Commentary

1. The date of this volume is not entirely clear. The letter to the reader is dated III Kalends March 1507, i.e., 27 February. Since the Venetian New Year fell on 1 March, this could be interpreted either as the more habitual interpretation, third day of the kalends of March 1507, or as the third day of the kalends, but falling in 1507 (i.e., 1508 n.s.). It seems to me that the formulation, unusual in Petrucci's work, is a reference to March of 1507, rather than March of 1508. This may also help to explain why the date in the colophon, most unusually, gives neither day nor month.

2. This is the first source to mention the important, and presumably new, playing technique of alternating the thumb and index finger in rapid passages. The practice would be a natural response to the development of finger technique, without a plectrum. The alternation is indicated by the presence or absence of a point beneath the tablature symbols, as is made clear in the prefatory *Regula*. This technique is discussed in a number of places. Among them, and one of the first to draw attention to Petrucci's rules and their relationship to later similar rules, is Heartz, "Premières", p. 83. Binkley, "Luth", p. 27, calls it the most important new technique of the time.

3. Despite the evidence of the papers in the unique copy, there is no reason to believe that any parts of this book were printed at a different time. For one thing, the stave patterns are consistent within the limits discussed in chapter 3 above, as is evident from the following table of top staves for each page. Further, the pattern of corrections is consistent throughout the early gatherings.

Sheet	Forme									
	Outer	1r	2v	3r	4v	Inner	2r	1v	4r	3v
A.I		—	—	175	176		—	—	175	175
A.II		177	176	175	177		176	175	176	176
B.I		176	176	176	175		176	176	175	176
B.II		176	176	176	176		177	176	176	176
C.I		176	176	175	176		176	176	175	176
C.II		176	176	175	176		176	175	175	175
D.I		176	176	175	176		176	176	175	176
D.II		176	175	175	175		176	175	175	176
E.I		176	175	175	175		175	176	175	176
E.II		176	175	175	176		176	175	175	176
F.I		176	175	175	176		175	176	175	176
F.II		176	176	175	175		176	175	175	176
G.I		176	177	176	—		176	176	175	176
G.II		176	175	175	176		176	175	175	176

4. The pattern of manuscript corrections in this volume, as well as in Spinacino's second book, is highly significant. All (except for one on A4r) seem to be done in the same hand, in the same ink, and in the same manner, and all show a careful concern for correcting all erroneous readngs, a concern not normally found in Petrucci's other books. In these others, it is clear that Petrucci cared about making corrections, but that he made them only as they were discovered, and managed to miss quite a few (which presumably were never revealed to him by the in-house reader or by his circle of acquaintance). Here, however, a large number of corrections were made at one time. In addition these are of a particularly detailed nature, and require a peculiarly careful hand to execute them as unobtrusively as here.

All these corrections seem certainly to be made early in the 16th-century, and must have been the work of either a member of Petrucci's shop or an early user of the book. Given the probability that all were made at the same time (to judge from the consistency of ink and manner), as well as the pristine condition of the volume, it seems more likely that the changes were made in Petrucci's house. It is also significant that the same hand changes one signature in the second volume. This change (from F3 to fF3) does not affect the binder's view of the sequence of binding, and would normally not have been made either by an owner or by Petrucci. Coupled with the other changes, it argues for someone in Petrucci's circle who was familiar with the music, who was expected to proofread the whole book, but who was not particularly familiar with Petrucci's house-practice. The most likely candidate for this, given that Petrucci was dealing with printed tabulature for the first time, is Spinacino himself.

No. 34. Spinacino: *Intabolatura II*

31.iii.1507   *RISM* 1507[6]

A1r]   Intabulatura de Lauto | Libro ſecondo.

G8r]   Impreſſum Venetijs: Per Octauianu3 | Petrutium Foro ſempronienſem: Cum pri|uilegio inuictiſſimi dominij Uenetiarum: | q*uae* nullus po ſſit intabulatura3 Lauti impri|mere: ſub penis in ipſo priuilegio contenti5. | Die vltimo Martij 1507. Regi ſtrum. | AA BB CC DD EE FF GG | Omnes quaterni. [To right: Petrucci's device]

A1v]   Regole per quelli che non ſanno cantare. [etc. as in the first book, No.33]

[Below the instructions, in three columns (all numerals except l are in small capitals):]

Tabula.

Agnus de vt re mi fa sol la	v.
Aleregretz	xxi.
Amours amours	xxii.
Bergerette ſauoyene	ii.
Baſſadanza	xxxi.
Chri ſte de ſi dedero	iiii.
Cent mil eſcus	xvii.
Coment peult auoye ioye	xix.
Dung autramer	xx.
Fortuna deſperata	xxxviii.

[column 2:]

Harai tre amours	xv.
Helogeron nous	xxiiii.
Iene cuide	iii.
Iene demande	ix.
Iay pris amours	xiii.
Iene fay cont damer	xlii.
In pace	xlv.
Kyrie delez armes	xxv.
Leure et venue	x.
Le ſouenir	xiiii.
Lom e bani	xxxv.
La ſtanghetta	xxxvii.

[column 3:]

La mignonne	xliii.
Malor me bat	xviii.
Mo mari ma defame	xxiii.
Marguerit	xxvi.
Motetto o dulcis Ieſu	xxvii.
Mater patris & filia	xxxiii.
Palle de Iſach	xvi.
Penſif meri	xxxvi.
Si dedero	xxix.
Si fays viey	xli.

Tandernaken   vii.
Recercare Numero diece

Format and collation: Tabulature: landscape quarto-in-eights. 56 folios: A–G⁸

Signatures:] AA 2 [$4 • − A1

Foliation: t.r.r.]   [1], 2–56

No running heads: composers' names usually in the head-line

Fonts: Music: Petrucci's tablature font

Staves: six-line, 175–177 mm long. 17-79-110 mm high

Text: Rotonda throughout • The initial B on A2*r* is 77 × 54 mm, and is the initial found on the
title pages of *Canti B* and *Motetti B*

In-house corrections: See the notes below in the description of the copy at PL-Kj

Contents:

	A1*r*	[Title]		
	A1*v*	Regola . . . Tabula.		
1	A2*r*	Bergirette sauoyene	France[co Spinacino	
2	A3*r*.iii	JE ne cuide	France[co Spinacino	[?Congiet]
3	A4*v*	CHri[te de[idedero	France[co Spinacino	[Obrecht]
4	A5*v*	AGnus de vt re mi fa [ol la	France[co Spinacino	[Brumel]
5	A7*r*	TAndernaken	France[co Spinacino	[Agricola]
6	B1*r*	JE ne demande	France[co Spinacino	[Busnois]
7	B2*v*	LEure et venue	France[co Spinacino	[Agricola]
8	B5*r*.iii	JAy pris amours	France[co Spinacino	
9	B6*v*	LE [ouenir	France[co Spinacino	[Morton]
10	B7*v*.ii	HAray tre amours	France[co Spinacino	[Stockem]
11	B8*r*.ii	PAlle de y[ach	France[co Spiancino	[Isaac]
				[Tav:] Isach
12	C1*v*	CEnt mil e[cus	France[co Spinacino	[Caron]
13	C2*v*	MAlor mebat	France[co Spinacino	[Ockeghem]
14	C3*v*	COment peult auoir Joye	France[co Spinacino	[Josquin]
15	C4*v*	DUng autramer	France[co Spinacino	[Ockeghem]
16	C5*v*	ALeregretz	France[co Spinacino	[Agricola]
17	C6*v*.ii	AMours amours	France[co Spinacino	[Hayne]
18	C7*v*.iv	MO mari ma defame	France[co Spinacino	
19	C8*v*	HElogeron nous	France[co Spinacino	[Isaac]
20	D1*r*.iii	KYrie delez armes	France[co Spinacino	[Ghiselin]
21	D2*r*	MArguerit	France[co Spinacino	
22	D3*v*	MOtetto o dulcis Je[u de [opra el pater no [tro	France[co Spinacino	
23	D5*v*	SI dedero	France[co Spinacino	[Agricola]
24	D7*r*	BA[[adanza	France[co Spinacino	
25	E1*v*	MAter patris ꓱ filia	France[co Spinacino	[Brumel]
26	E3*r*	LOm e bani Bordon de[cordato	Fran.Spi.	[Agricola]
27	E4*v*.ii	PEn[i che mai	France[co Spinacino	[Tadinghem]
28	E5*v*.iii	LA [tanghetta	France[co Spinacino	[Weerbeke]
29	E6*v*.iii	FOrtuna de[perata [Duet]	France[co Spinacino	[Busnois]
30	F1*v*	SI fays viey	France[co Spinacino	[Agricola]
31	F2*v*	JEne fay cont damer	France[co Spinacino	

32	F3*v*.ii	LA Mignonne con lo bordon de[cordato	France[co Spinacino	[Agricola]
33	F5*v*.iii	IN pace in idip[um	France[co Spinacino	[Josquin]
34	F7*r*	REcercare [1]	France[co Spinacino	
35	F8*r*	REcercare [2]	France[co Spinacino	
36	F8*r*.iv	REcercare [3]	France[co Spinacino	
37	G1*v*	REcercare [4]	France[co Spinacino	
38	G2*v*	REcercare [5]	France[co Spinacino	
39	G3*v*.iii	REcercare [6]	France[co Spinacino	
40	G4*v*	REcercare [7]	France[co Spinacino	
41	G5*v*.ii	REcercare [8]	France[co Spinacino	
42	G6*v*	REcercare [9]	France[co Spinacino	
43	G7*v*	REcercare [10]	France[co Spinacino	
	G8*r*.[ii]	[Colophon; Register; Device]		
	G8*v*	[blank]		

Extant copies: Sartori, "Nuove", p. 193 corrects his assertion, in *Petrucci*, p. 119, that there was a copy at A-Wn

PL-Kj, Mus.ant.pract.P 680 (2). Complete

    Size of page: 168 × 232 mm.

    Watermarks: Mark 23 on A3, A7, B3, B8, C4, C7, D2, D4, E4, E7, F5, F7, G3, and G7

    Technical comments: G8*v*: a very clear row of *minima* used as bearers. There are 31 notes, though set at varying heights • E4*r*.iv: Spacing sort above the bar-line, 6.5 × 2.0 mm, and extending 8 mm above the stave. This probably delineates the edge of the forme for music and rhythm signs • The stave on G8*r* is a later addition: it presumably reflects a miscalculation of the length of the piece, which overflows from G7*v*

    Corrections and changes:

        Possibly by Spinacino: For notes on this possibility, see the commentary to Spinacino's first book • A6*r*.iv.3,5: /?/?// → //45// • A6*v*.iii.3,8: ////2/ → ///2// • B2*r*.iii.5,5: 85/ //3 → 85//3/ • B3*r*.iii.2,6: //2/// → ///2// • B7*r*.iii.5,3: 7/5/// → 7//5// • B8*v*.iii.7,5: ///1// → //1/// • B8*v*.iv.2,2: ?//0// → 5//0// • B8*v*.iv.5,5.rhythm sign: *sf* → *f* • C1*r*.i.7,1-3: each /132/1 → /133/1 • C1*r*.ii.2,4: /122// → /1/2// • C2*r*.ii.3,1: 3/123 → 3/1/3/1 • C2*r*.ii.6,4: /?/02/ → ///02/ • C7*v*.iii.1,1: /3?[perhaps3]5// → /3/ 5// • C8*v*.ii.7,3: 5/?4// → 5-34// • C8*v*.iv.4,4: 7/3/// → 73//// • C8*v*.iv.6,4: 857/// → 85/7// • D4*v*.i.8,3: ///1// → //1/// • D7*v*.iv.1,7: ////0/ → /1//0/ • E1*v*.iv.5,3: // 3/// → ///3// • F3*r*.i.2,2: /0//0/ → 0///0/ • F3*r*.signature: F3 → fF3 • F8*r*.ii.7,6: 2/// // → 0///// • G5*r*.iv.2,2: //2/// → //3/// • G7*v*.iv.5: /3////: the numeral poorly inked and touched up

    Binding and Provenance: With Spinacino's first book (No.33)

Lost copies: A copy was bought by Colón in Rome in ix.1512 (Anglés, "Colombina", p. 28; Chapman, "Printed", No.23; Plamenac, "Excerpta", p. 679)

Bibliography:

    (a) Sartori, *Petrucci*, No.31 • Brown, *Instrumental*, 1507₂

    (b) Brunet, *Manuel*, iii, col.446

    (c) Spinacino, *Intabulatura*

(d) Buetens, *Lute*

(e) *Renaissance*, Sartori, "Little-known" • Sartori, "Nuove," p. 193 • Schmidt, *First* • Underwood, 6–87

Commentary:

1. The choice of *Bergerette savoyenne* as the first piece is deliberate. It allows Petrucci to use the capital letter B which had graced the opening of *Canti B*, thus following the pattern of using the A of *Odhecaton A* for the first piece of Spinacino's first volume.

2. The pattern of corrections suggests, as it did for Spinacino's first book, that the lutenist himself was responsible for reading and correcting the musical text.

3. In contrast with the practice in the first book, all the recercars have attributions to Spinacino himself. This seems more likely to reflect the presence of Spinacino in the shop than it does the possibility of a different lutenist composing works in Book 1.

No. 35. *Frottole VIII*

21.v.1507   *RISM* 1507[4]

A1r]   Frottole Libro octauo.

G8r]   Impreſſum Venetiis per Octauianum Pe-|trutium Foroſempronienſem. M.D.vii. Die xxi. | Madii Cum priuilegio inuictiſſimi Dominii | Venetiarum quae nullus poſſit cantum Figuratum | imprimere ſub pena in ipso priuilegio contenta. | Regiſtrum. | A B C D E F G Omnes quaterni. | [Petrucci's device]

A1v   [Tavola] Frottole numero cinquanta ſei

Format and Collation: Choirbook: landscape quarto-in-eights. 56 folios: A–G⁸

Signatures:] X A 2 [$4 •– A1

Foliation: top right recto: [1], 2–55, [56]

No running heads. Composers' names in the head-line

Part-names:

recto:]	Altus Baſſus	[A3-6, A8, B2, B4, B8, E2, E6, E8, F3-4, F6, F8-G3
	Altus Baſſus	[B3, B5, B7, C1-D1, D4-E1, E3, E5, E7, F7, G5, G7
	Altus	[with Bass⁹ in stave line: B6
	Tenor Altus Baſſus	[B1, D2, F5
	[all three, in stave lines as needed: A7, D3	
	Tenor Altus Baſſus	[A2, E4, G4, G6
	Concordans Baſſus	[F1-2
verso:]	Tenor	[A2-5, A7, B1-C8, D3-E2, E4-E7, F2-3, F5-G1, G4, G6
	Tenor Altus Baſſus	[A6, A8
	Tenor Altus Baſſus	[D1-2, E3
	Tenor Altus	[E8-F1
	Tenor Altus	[with Bass⁹ in the stave: F4
	Tenor Quintus	[G2
	all three, in the stave as needed: G3, G5, G7	

small initials are used as follows

recto:]	altus	A6,8
	bassus	A3,7, B5-8, C5-8, D1,2,5-8, E5,7, F1,2,4,5,7, G2,5,7
	altus bassus	A2,4, B3, C1-4, D1,3,4, E1-4, F3r, G1,3
	tenor bassus	G4
	tenor altus bassus	B1, D2
verso:]	altus	G3,5
	tenor	B2,4, E1,3, F1,3, G1
	altus bassus	6v,8v, F4v

the letter *u* is inverted in some instances:

| | altus | A8v,B2r,4r,6r,8r, D1v, E3v,8r,8v, F1v,4r |
| | bassus | B5r |

Fonts: Music: Petrucci's normal music type

Staves: Six per page were in the forme throughout

Text: Roman throughout

Technical comments: No capital initial on A6v [Z] • Small guide letter capital used on D2v [D] • The sixth stave was rarely inked: it appears only on A4r,6v-7r, B3v,5v,6r, C2r,6v-7v, D4v,6v, E2r,4r,5r-7r,8r-8v, F5v,7v-8v, G2v,6v: part of the stave is inked on C4r • Only four staves are inked on D2r and D3r

There are no evident in-house corrections

Contents:

The last column gives the folio numbers entered in the Tavola:

22	C4v	ALa bruma al giatio al vento	NI.PI.	xxi
		[Tav:] Ala bruma al ghiaccio e al vento		
23	C5v	PEr amor fata ſolinga	NICOLO PIFARO	xxii
	C6v	2/ Son diſpoſto anchio cantare		
24	C7v	SE io ti dico el mio gran danno	HONO.ANTE.	xxiv
25	C8v	PEr memoria di quel giorno	NI.PI.	xxv
26	D1v	LA colpa non e mia	NICOLO PIFARO	xxvi
27	D2r	O Sola mia ſalute	NICOLO PIFARO	xxvi
28	D2v	DApoi che cuſi pate	NICOLO PIFARO	xxvii
29	D3r	SE mai nei mei pochanni	B.T.	xxvii
30	D3v	PIu ſperanza non apreggio	ANTONIVS STRINGARIVS PATAVINVS	xxviii
31	D4v	POi chio ſon in libertate	ANTONIVS PATA.	xxix
32	D5v	AMeni colli	LVDOVICO MILANESE	xxx
33	D6v	CHi non ſa chel cor	ANTONIVS PATA.	xxxi
	D7v	2/ Chi non ſa che io ardo in foco		
	D8v	3/ Chi non ſa chel cor gli ho dato		
34	E1v	SVm piu tua che non ſum mia	M.C.	xxxiiii
		[Tav:] Son piu tua che non son mia		
35	E2v	NOn pigliar madona aſdegno	FRAN.ORGA.VENETVS	xxxv
36	E3v	VSciro di tanti affanni	FRAN.ORGA.VENETVS	xxxvi
37	E4r	APe de la montagna	ROSIN MANTOVANO	xxxvi
38	E4v	SCopri lingua el mio martire	[Anon.]	xxxvii
39	E5v	DOnne habiati voi pietate	M.C.	xxxviii
40	E6v	AI maroni ai bei maroni	B.T.	xxxix
41	E7v	FAte ben gente corteſe	B.T.	xxxx
42	E8v	FVgga pur chi vol amore	M.C.	xli
	F1v	2/ Mai non perſi la ſperanza		
43	F2v	PEr ſeruite perdo i paſſi	N.BROCVS	xliii
44	F3v	POi che in te donna ſperaui	N.B.	xliiii
		[Headed:] RESPOSTA		
45	F4v	O tiente alora	N.B.	xlv
46	F5r	IO ſon locello	B.T.	
		[Omitted from the Tavola]		
47	F5v	DEh chi me fa dir nouella	MI.C.&.V.	xlvi
	F6v	2/ Poi che far del monaſtiero		
48	F7v	SE non fuſſela ſperanza	M.C.	xlviii
	F8v	2/ Queſta ſpeme e vna bona herba		
49	G1v	IO ſon locel	D.MI.	l
50	G2v	NVi ſiamo ſegatori	Antonius ſtringarius patauinus	li
51	G3v	ALme celeſte che ripoſo date	LVDOVICO MILANESE	lii
52	G4r	QVando mimoſtra amor	LVDOVICO MILANESE	lii
53	G4v	SEra chi per pieta	LVDOVICO MILANESE	liii
54	G5v	VEdo ogni ſelua riueſtir	M.C.	liv
55	G6r	CHi vi dara piu luce occhi	B.T.	liv
56	G6v	NOn e penſier chel mio ſecreto	D.MI.	lv

57 G7*v*   DEh no*n* piu no no*n* piu [pietata   IOANNES B. GESSO   lvi
           [Headed:] AERE DA CAPITOLI
     G8*r*   [Colophon; Register; Device]
     G8*v*   [blank]

_____

Surviving copy:

D-Mbs, Rar.878/8. Complete

  Size of page: 164 x 228 mm.

  Watermarks: No.23 on A4, A7, B4, B7, C1, C3, D3, D7, and G5 • No.31 on E3-4, E7-8, F3-4, F7-8, and G2-1

  Technical comments: Furniture has taken ink on G1*v*

  Later corrections and changes: A3*v*.ii,clef: C₁ → C₂, in pencil • C6*v*.ii.15 from end: *colsb* → *colm*, initialled c.g. • D2*r*.iii.16: *colsb* struck through, void *sb* entered, in brown ink • D4*v*.vi.after 31: point struck through, initialled RJ • E7*r*.i.15 from end: *colsb* struck through, void *sb* entered, in brown ink • F1*v*.v.25: brackets added around *sb*d, initialled R.J. • G1*v*.iv.after 3rd *l* rest: added *b* rest, initialled R.J. • G7*r*.ii: bar-line → clef C₃, initialled R.J.

  Binding and Provenance: With *Frottole VI* (1506, No.26)

_____

Lost copies: Copies were owned by Colón (Chapman, "Printed", No.24), by the Fuggers (Schaal, "Musikbibliothek", I/72), by Herwart (later given to S. Anna, Augsburg, with Books VI and VII: see Schaal, *Inventar*, p. 30), and by Bottrigari

Bibliography:

  (a) Rosaria Boccadifuoco, *Bibliografia*, No.1450 • Sartori, *Petrucci*, No.32 • Jeppesen, *La Frottola*, Pe.VIII • Vogel, *Bibliografia*, 1507².

  (b) Brunet, *Manuel*, ii, col.1413

  (d) Boscolo, *Frottole* • A manuscript copy survives at A-Wn, alongside the printed copies of other frottola volumes

  (e) Jeppesen, *La Frottola*, i, 107–108 • Sartori, "Nuove", pp. 193–96 • Vogel, *Bibliothek*, p. 611, assumes that 1507 is an error for 1508

Commentary:

1. It is not possible to study patterns of paper use during 1507: all the extant copies remain in single copies, and (more importantly) two editions from the middle of the year have not survived at all. At present, it looks as though Petrucci went through a number of batches of paper during the year: thus, despite the fact that paper 31 does not reappear until the first edition of Bossinensis's intabulations, almost two years later, it seems that the sheets here do belong to 1507. There is no good reason to argue that the present, unique, copy contains material from some years later than the recorded date.

2. It seems likely that the formes containing the head-lines were not set in order: these formes normally contained the staves and text. There is little evidence, but the order in which composers' names are set in full or abbreviated, in gatherings C and D, is a little strange: so is the use of lower-case letters for names on B8*v* and G2*v*.

No. 36. *Frottole VII*

6.vi.1506/7   *RISM* 1507³

There is a single cancel sheet, E outer, in the unique copy

Edition

A1r]   Frottole Libro | Septimo.

G8r]   Impreſſum Venetiis per Octauianum Pe-|trutium Foroſempronienſem. M. D. vii. Die. vi. | Iunii. Cum priuilegio inuictiſſimi Dominii | Venetiar*um* q*uae* nullus poſſit cantum Figuratum | imprimere ſub pena in ip*s*o priuilegio co*n*tenta. | | Regiſtrum. | | A B C D E F G Omnes quaterni. | | [Petrucci's device]

Format and collation: Choirbook: landscape quarto-in-eights. 56 folios: A-G⁸

Signatures:] A 2 [, with all letters inverted • $4 • − A1

Foliation: t.r.r.] [1], 2–9, 10 [inverted], 11–47, 40 [*recte* 48], 49–55, [56]

Part-names:

recto:]	Tenor Altus Baſſus	[A2,6, B8, C3,6, D2,4,7, E4,6, F4,7, G1
	Altus Baſſus	[A3,5,7, B1-2,4–7, C1-2,4–5,7–8, D1,3,5–6,8, E3,5, F1-3,5–6, G2-7
	tenor Altu5 [both in stave] Baſſus	[A4
	Tenor Altus Baſſus [in stave	A8
	tenor [in stave] Altus Baſſus	[B3, F8
	[Nil:	A1, G8
verso:]	Tenor	[A2,4,6, B1,3–6,8, C1,3–4,6–8, D2,4–5,7, E4, F1-2,4–5, G1-6
	Tenor Altus Baſſus	[A3,5, B2,7, C2,5, D1, E3,5, F3,6,8, G7
	Tenor [in stave] Altus Baſſus	[A7
	tenor [in stave]	[A8
	tenor Altu5 [in stave] Baſſus	[D6
	tenor [in stave] Altus Baſſus	[D8, F7
	tenor Altu5 Baſſus [all in stave	E6
	Tenor [in stave] Altus Baſſus [in stave]	D3
	[Nil:	A1, G8

Small initial letters are used for part names as follows:

recto:]	Baſſus:	A3,5,7,8 B1,4,6,7, C1,4,6,7, D2,3,5,8, E3,5, F1,3,5,7, G3,5,7
	Altus	A4, B2,3, F4, G2,4
	Altus Bassus	D37, E7,8
	Tenor Bassus	G1
verso:]	Baſſus:	A3,5,7, E5, F7
	Tenor:	A2,4,6, B3,5,8, C3, D4, E4, F2,4, G2,4,6
	Altus Bassus	C5, D3,6, E3,6
	Tenor Bassus	A7, B2
	Tenor Altus	F8
	Tenor Altus Bassus	C2, D1, F6

Fonts: Music: Petrucci's normal music type

   Staves: six per page, though normally only five are inked

   Text: Roman throughout

Textual comments: It is noticeable that this volume has a larger than usual number of three-page pieces • The placing of M.C. pieces in D is interesting: on D2*v*–3*r* and 6*v*–7*r*, that is across the joins of the two sheets • The letter *u* is inverted in the part-name Bassus on G3*r*, although correct in the Altus

In-house corrections: All the following are in the unique copy: A4*r*.ii.18: d' → c', erasure and stamped-in note • F8*r*.folio number: 8 stamped over the erroneous 0 • F8*r*.iii.26: *sb*, c' → b, erasure and stamped in • F8*r*.v.21 from end: *sb*, c → e, erasure and stamped in

Contents: The final columns gives folio numbers from the Tavola • The contents of the cancel folios have been included here

	A1*r*	[Title]		
	A1*v*	TABVLA. Numero ſeſantaſette.		
1	A2*r*	IO tho donato il core	IOANNES BAPTISTA ZESSSO.	ii.
2	A2*v*	AFflicti ſpirti miei	B.T.	iii.
3	A3*v*	SE il morir mai de gloria	B.T.	iiii.
4	A4*r*	ACcio che il *tempo* e i cieli	B.T.	iiii.
5	A4*v*	SI e debile il filo	B.T.	v.
6	A6*r*	A Prender la mia donna	B.T.	vi.
7	A6*v*	POi che vſcitomi e di	[Anon.]	vii.
8	A7*v*	SE io te adima*n*do	B.T.	viii.
9	A8*r*	CReſce la pena mia	B.T.	viiii.
10	A8*v*	NOn ſi uedra gia mai	A.C.	ix.
11	B1*v*	POi chio vado in altra parte	B.T.	x.
12	B3*r*	PRegoui fro*n*de fiori acque	B.T.	xi.
13	B3*v*	COme va il mondo	B.T.	xii.
14	B4*v*	POi chel ciel e mia ve*n*tura	B.T.	xiii.
15	B5*v*	CHe debbio far	B.T.	xiiii.
16	B6*v*	CRedul cor per che credeſti	M.C.	xv.
17	B8*r*	NOn temer chio ti laſſi	PAVLI SCOTI Cantus & verba	xvi.
18	B8*v*	A Che ſon hormai conducto	ALEXANDRO DEMOPHON	xvii.
19	C1*v*	PEr che mhai abandonato	[Anon.]	xviii.
20	C2*v*	LAmor do*n*na chio te porto	[Anon.]	xix.
21	C3*r*	VOi che paſſati	B.T.	xix.
22	C3*v*	OChi mei mai non reſtati	A.DE ANTIQVIS.	xx.
23	C4*v*	SPenta mai del pecto amore	DOM MICHIEL.	xxi.
24	C6*r*	DOnna mia qua*n*to diſpecto	[Anon.]	xxii.
25	C6*v*	DAltro hormai voglio hauer cura	NICOLO PIFARO.	xxiii.
26	C7*v*	COnſumato ha amor el dardo	[Anon.]	xxiiii
27	C8*v*	POi chel ciel e la fortuna	[Anon.]	xxv.
28	D1*v*	SI ſi ſi taruo taruo	[Anon.]	xxvi.
29	D2*r*	TVr lu ru la capra e moza	PAVLI SCOTI Cantus & verba	xxvi.
30	D2*v*	NOn pecca*n*do altro ch*e*l core	M.C.	xxvii
31	D3*v*	DAmor che me leuaua	IOANNES.B.ZESSO	xxviii.
		[Tav., T,A,B:] Dun bel matin damor		
32	D4*r*	ECco che per amarte	B.T.	xxviii.

33	D4v	REgi & guidi ogni human ſtato	[Anon.]	xxix.
34	D5v	QVeſta longa mia ſperanza	[Anon.]	xxx.
35	D6v	LArdor mio graue e aſſimilante	M.C.	xxxi.
36	D7r	DEh dolce mia ſignora	M.C.	xxxi.
37	D7v	SIl diſſi mai chi venga	B.T.	xxxii.
38	D8v	MAl vn mute pereffecto	M.C.	xxxiii.
39	E1r	CHi lo ſa e chi nol ſa	E.DVPRE	xxxiii.
40	E1v	CHia martello dio glil toglia	E.DVPRE	xxxiiii.
41	E2v	QVel chel ciel ne da per ſorte	A.DE ANTIQVIS	xxxv.
42	E3v	O Suſpir ſuaui	B.T.	xxxvi.
43	E4r	QVel foco che mi poſe	B.T.	xxxvi.
44	E4v	QVaſi ſempre auanti	[Anon.]	xxxvii.
45	E6r	DOgni altra haria penſato	M.C.	xxxviii.
46	E6v	EL penſier andra col core	[Anon.]	xxxix.
47	E7r	LA virtu mi fa guerra	E.DVPRE	xxxix.
48	E7v	BEn ben ben tu mahi laſa	PEREGRINVS CESENA	xl.
49	E8v	IO non lho perche non lho	M.C.	xli.
50	F1v	BOna dies bona ſera	M.C.	xlii.
51	F2v	IO ſon lieto nel aſpecto	[Anon.]	xliii.
		2/ Io ſon lieto nel aſpecto		
52	F4r	HA bella e freſca etade	PHILIPPVS DE LVRANO	xliiii.
53	F4v	Deh non piu deh non piu mo	M.C.	xlv.
54	F5v	SEgue cuor e non reſtare	IACOBVS FOGLIANVS	xlvi.
55	F6v	CAde ogni mio penſier	B.T.	xlvii.
56	F7r	HAime perche mhai priuo	[Anon.]	xlvii.
57	F7v	EL baſiliſcho ha lochio	PIETRO DA LODE	xlviii.
58	F8r	ROtto ho al fin el duro nodo	PAVLI.S.Cantus & verba.	xlviii.
59	F8v	AIutami chio moro	M.C.	xlix.
60	G1r	DEh prendi homai conforto	PAVLI.S.Cantus & verba	xlix.
61	G1v	VIdi hor cogliendo roſe	ALEXANDRO DEMOPHON.	l.
62	G2v	O Deſpietato tempo	P.ZANIN BISAN.	li.
63	G3v	HAria voluto alhor	PIETRO DA LODI	lii.
64	G4v	IO cercho pur la inſupportabil doglia	B.T.	liii.
65	G5v	PIu nonſon pregion damore	B.T.	liiii.
66	G6v	QVeſto tuo lento tornare	A.DE ANTIQVIS	lv.
		[Headed:] Reſpoſta de Sio ſon ſtato aritornare		
67	G7v	E Quando andaretu al monte	IO.BA.ZESSO.	lv.
	G8r	[Colophon; Register; Device]		
	G8v	[blank]		

Extant copy:

D–Mbs, Rar.878/7. Complete: for the outer sheet of E, see the cancel, below
    Size of page: 164 × 228 mm.
    Watermarks: Paper 20 on A3, A8, B1, B6, C2, C6, D3, D8, E5, F3, F8, G4, and G7
    Corrections and changes:
        In-house: see above
        Later: A6r.v.bar-line after 10: struck through and moved to after 12, initialled RJ • A7r.v.6:

sm → *m*, by erasure, initialled g.c. • E4r.v.after 20: *b*G and *b*A, struck through, initialled g.c. • F5r.ii.after 9: *sb*a added, initialled g.c. • F5r.ii.23: an illegible change, initialled c.g.

Binding and Provenance: With *Frottole VI* (1506, No.26)

No. 34A. *Cancel.*

A single sheet, for E1,2,7,8

Part-names:

verso:]	Tenor	[E1-2,7–8
recto:]	tenor [in stave] Altus Ba∫∫u5	[E1
	Altus Ba∫∫u5	[E2
	Tenor Altus Ba∫∫us	[E7
	Altus Ba∫∫us	[E8

Technical comments: It is notable that there is almost no use of the small initials for part-names

Extant copy:

D-Mbs, Rar.878/(7). For other details, see above

    Watermark: No.23 on E8

    Later correction: E1*v*.ii.18: struck through, in brown, and initialled RJ, and also c.g.

Lost copies: Copies were owned by Colón (Chapman, "Printed", No.25), by Herwart (given to S. Anna, Augsburg: see Schaal, *Inventar*, p. 30), and by Bottrigari: see chapter 20

Bibliography:

  (a) Rosaria Boccadifuoco, *Bibliografia*, No.1457 • Sartori, *Petrucci*, No.33 • Jeppesen, *La Frottola*, Pe.VII • Vogel, *Bibliografia*, 1507[1]

  (b) Brunet, *Manuel*, ii, col.1413

  (d) A manuscript copy exists at A-Wn, alongside printed copies of other frottola books

  (e) Jeppesen, *La Frottola*, i, 30–31, 102–105 • Sartori, "Nuove", pp. 196–198

Commentary:

1. It is not clear why this should have been dated 16 days after Book VIII. Bibliographically, this copy does seem to belong here, where it is dated. Further, there is no reason to believe that this might be a second edition. Any first edition would presumably have appeared after February of 1506, the month of Book VI. There are really only two possible places for such an edition, if my speculative dating of other books (the first edition of Dammonis's *Laude* and the second of Josquin's first book of masses) is accepted: they are immediately after Book VI, in March 1506, or in April 1507. The earlier date seems unlikely, for that would presume that this book should be associated with Book VI, in repertoire and planning. As I have shown in chapter 9, that is very implausible. However, a planned date in April 1507 seems much more likely: first, it would put Book VII immediately before Book VIII, where it seems to belong; second, if the book were planned for April, this would explain how it could be prepared in such a short period. I believe, given the patterns of paper use (also discussed in chapter 9), that this is the true first edition, but that much of the planning had been completed before Book VIII was printed.

It is possible, given the motley array of composers in the last pair of gatherings, that there was a problem with the supply of music for this edition. However, given the pattern of composers represented in Book VIII, that can be no more than speculation.

2. The cancel must have been printed soon after the main edition. The paper on which it appears was not used for the next edition (*Strambotti . . . IV* of the following month), and first appears in *Frottole III*, nearly six months later. However, two editions from the intervening months have been lost, so that it is not clear when Petrucci bought the next batch of this paper. Since the evidence of the type and initials is inconclusive, I have placed the cancel, somewhat arbitrarily, early in 1508, after the *Missarum diversorum auctorum I*.

3. One advantage of placing the cancel here lies in one pattern of house-practice. Many of Petrucci's frottola books show patterns of using small capital initials for the part-names, and the full edition of this book is no exception. However, the cancel leaves seem not to do this to the same extent. Since, as I propose, they were printed at a time when Petrucci was publishing no new frottola editions, and indeed had just published a collection of masses, it is possible that the typesetters were not in the habit of using the smaller letters.

Of course, an alternative explanation could be that, since only a single sheet was involved in this cancel, there was no shortage of the standard initial capital letters.

No. 37. *Frottole IV*

31.vii.1507 *RISM* 1507²

Second Edition

A1*r*]   Strambotti Ode Frot|tole Sonetti. Et mo|do de cantar uer|[i latini e ca|pituli. | Libro quarto.

G8*r*]   Impre[[um Venetiis per Octauianum Pe|trutium Foro[empronien[em .M.D.vii. Die vlti-|mo Iulii. Cu*m* priuilegio inuicti[[imi Dominii | Venetiaru*m* q*uae* nullus po[[it cantum Figuratum | imprimere [ub pena in ip*s*o priuilegio co*n*tenta. | | Regi[trum. | | ABCDEFG Omnes quaterni.

Format and collation: Choirbook: landscape quarto-in-eights. 56 folios: A-G⁸

Signatures:] .AA 3. [$4 • − A1 • A2 signed without points

Foliation: t.r.r.] [1], 2–55, [56]

No running heads • Composers' names in the head-line

Part-names:

verso:]	Tenor	[A2-5, B2-3, E2, E4-7, F7, G2-6
	Tenor Altus Ba[[us	[A6-7, B1, B4-C1, C3-8, D2, D4-6, D8, E8, F2, F4-6, F8-G1
	Tenor Altu5 Ba[[us	[D3, E1, E3, F1, F3, G7
	Tenor Altu5 [in stave] Ba[[us	[C2, D1
	[all three, in stave as needed:	A8, D7
recto:]	Tenor Altus [Bassus in stave:	A2
	Altu5 Ba[[us	[A6, G4
	Altu5 Ba[[us	[A3-5, B3-4, E3, E5-8, F8, G3, G5-7
	Tenor Altus Ba[[us	[A7, B1-2, B6-8, C2, C4, C6, C8-D6, D8, E4, F1-7, G1

Tenor Altu5 Ba∬us   [A8

[all three, in staves as needed: B5, C1, C3, C5, C7, D7, E1-2, G2

Small initials are found in part-names as follows:

verso: Tenor   [A2-4,6; B2-4; C1-4; D2-4; E1-5,7; F1-5,7; G1-4

        Altus   [A8; B6,8; C1-3,8; D1,3,5,7; E1,3; F1,3,5; G7

        Bassus   [A6,7; B1,4,5,7; C1,3–5,7; D1-5,7; E1,3; F1,3,5,6,8; G1

recto: Tenor   [A7, C2,4, D2,4, G1

        Altus   [A3,6,8; B1,3,5; C1,3; D1,3,7; E1,3,6,8; F1,3,8; G1,3,4

        Bassus   [A4-8; B5-8; C6-8; D5-8; E5-8; F5-8; G2,4–7

Fonts: Music: Petrucci's normal music type

    Staves: Five-line, ca 180 mm long, 10-92-112 high

    Text: Roman throughout. Rotonda for title page has an "x" of 4.8.mm.

Technical comments: Small capital letters used on C4r [M], D8r [D], E3v [T], F5v [O], G2v [D] • No capital letter on E4r. That this is the same pattern as that found in the first edition is a convincing argument for this copy having been prepared from that edition

In-house correction: A5r.iii.19: *md'* → *mc'*, erasure and stamped in, in the only surviving copy

Contents: The last column gives the folio number entered in the Tavola:

	A1r	[Title]		
	A1v	[Tavola] Numero nonantuna.		
1	A2r	IO ∫on locel che ∫opra i rami doro	MARCVS CHARA VERO.	ii.
2	A2v	OGni amor uol e∬er uero	ANT.CAP.	iii.
3	A3v	QVe∫to oime pur me torme*n*ta	ANT.CAP:	iiii.
4	A4v	POi che mia ∫incera fede	ANT.CAP.	v.
5	A5v	RItornata e la ∫peranza	ANT.CAP.	vi.
6	A6v	VAga gioio∫a e bia*n*cha	ANT.CAP.	vii.
		[Tav:] . . . zoio∫a		
7	A7r	VA po∫a larcho e la pharetra amore	[Anon.]	vii.
8	A7v	SE la gra*n* fia*m*ma ardente	[Anon.]	viii.
9	A8r	MOrte te prego che de ta*n*ti affanni	B.T.	viii.
10	A8v	LI angelici ∫embianti e la beltade	[Anon.]	ix.
11	B1r	VAna ∫peranza mia che mai non viene	PHILIPPVS.L	ix.
12	B1v	DEus in adiutoriu*m* meu*m* inte*n*de	B.T.	x.
13	B2r	NOn fu ∫i crudo el dipartir de Enea	[Anon.]	x.
14	B2v	A Che affliggi el tuo ∫eruo	B.T.	xi.
15	B3v	OChi mei la∬i poi ch*e* p*er* ∫o	M.C.	xii.
16	B4v	SI ∫uaue mi par el mio dolore	[Anon.]	xiii.
17	B5r	DEl tuo bel volto amor	B.T.	xiii.
18	B5v	VEdo ∫degnato amor crudel e fiero	F.V.	xiiii.
19	B6r	[Heading:] Modo de cantar ∫onetti.	[Anon.]	xiiii.
20	B6v	O Caldi mei ∫u∫piri	M.C.	xv.
21	B7r	BEnche inimica e tedio∫a ∫ei	[Anon.]	xv.
22	B7v	LA∬a el cieco dolor che ti tran∫porta	[Anon.]	xvi.
23	B8r	MEntre ch*e* a tua belta	M.C.	xvi.
24	B8v	TV mhai priuato de ripo∫o e pace	[Anon.]	xvii.
25	C1r	LA fia*m*ma che me abru∫cia	N.P.	xvii.
26	C1v	TI par gra*n* maraueglia	N.P.	xviii.
27	C2r	MI fa ∫ol o mia dea	N.P.	xviii.

28	C2v	PEnſa donna chel tempo fuge	N.P.	xix.
29	C3r	SContento me ne reſto	[Anon.]	xix.
30	C3v	ME ſteſſo incolpo e me ſteſſo condanno	[Anon.]	xx.
31	C4r	MErce ha per mi ſpento ogni ſuo lume	[Anon.]	xx.
32	C4v	NOn biancho marmo non candida pietra	F.V.	xxi.
33	C5r	Se per humidita dacque ſacoglie	F.V.	xxi.
34	C5v	AMor a chi non val forza	F.V.	xxii.
35	C6r	AMor con le tue faze e larcho e larme	F.V.	xxii.
36	C6v	SE laffanato core in focho iace	F.V.	xxiii.
37	C7r	PAſſo paſſo pian pian apocho	F.V.	xxiii.
38	C7v	EL cor vn altra volta me fugito	F.V.	xxiiii.
39	C8r	QVeſto ſol giorno	B.T.	xxiiii.
40	C8v	RInforzi ogni hor piu mia dura ſorte	M.	xxv.
41	D1r	LA nocte aquieta ogni animale	[Anon.]	xxv.
42	D1v	LInfermo alhor piu ſe conſuma	[Anon.]	xxvi.
43	D2r	RIſeno i monti el mar moſtro bonaza	[Anon.]	xxvi.
44	D2v	SVrge cor laſſo hormai dal ſonno	B.T.	xxvii.
45	D3r	COme potu temer che mai te laſſi	[Anon.]	xxvii.
46	D3v	SIlentium lingua mia ti prego hormai	B.T.	xxviii.
47	D4r	NOn te ſmarir cor mio va paſſo	[Anon.]	xxviii.
48	D4v	NOn temo de bruſciar per alcun focho	B.T.	xxix.
49	D5r	DIlecto albergo e tu beato nido	M.C.	xxix.
50	D5v	SE hoggi e vn di chogni defuncto iace	B.T.	xxx.
51	D6r	CHi vede gir la mia dea	[Anon.]	xxx.
52	D6v	SVſpir ſuaui o mio dolce tormento	[Anon.]	xxxi.
53	D7r	DA poi che non ſi po piu ritrouare	[Anon.]	xxxi.
54	D7v	DAl ciel deſceſe amor per darme pace	F.V.	xxxii.
55	D8r	DI focho ardente adeſſo	B.T.	xxxii.
56	D8v	HAi pretioſa fe ſi lacerata	[Anon.]	xxxiii.
57	E1r	LA nocte quando ognun ripoſa e tace	[Anon.]	xxxiii.
58	E1v	SE ne gli affanni non creſceſſe amore	[Anon.]	xxxiiii.
59	E2r	QVanto piu donna te dico	PHI.DE LV.	xxxiiii.
60	E2v	ROmpe amor queſta cathena	PHI.DE LV.	xxxv.
61	E3v	TVtto el mondo chiama e crida	PHI.DE LV.	xxxvi.
62	E4r	[Heading:] Aer de verſi latini.	ANT. CAPREO. BRIXIEN.	xxxvi.
63	E4v	OGnun fuga fuga amore	ANT.CAP.	xxxvii.
64	E5v	TAnto mi e il partir moleſto	ANT.CAP.	xxxviii.
65	E6v	FVggi pur da me ſi ſai	ANT.CAP.	xxxix.
66	E7v	DIo lo ſa quanto me ſtrano	ANT.CAP.	xl.
67	E8v	SE ho ſdegnato la tua mente altera	ANT.CAPREO.	xli.
68	F1r	SColtatime madonna	[Anon.]	xli.
69	F1v	EL laccio che la mane	[Anon.]	xlii.
70	F2r	COn pianto e con dolore	[Anon.]	xlii.
71	F2v	LAchrime e voi ſuſpiri	[Anon.]	xliii.
72	F3r	O Mia ſpietata ſorte	[Anon.]	xliii.
73	F3v	E Come qui hormai Fa di me	[Anon.]	xliiii.
74	F4r	O Tanti mei ſuſpiri	[Anon.]	xliiii.

75	F4v	EL cor che ben di∫po∫to	[Anon.]	xlv.
76	F5r	COme po far el cielo	[Anon.]	xlv.
77	F5v	O Dolce e lieto albergo	[Anon.]	xlvi.
78	F6r	QVando per darme nel languir	[Anon.]	xlvi.
79	F6v	LA dolce diua mia	[Anon.]	xlvii.
80	F7r	CHe fa la ramacina	COMPERE	xlvii.
81	F7v	SCaramella fa la galla	COMPERE	xlviii.
82	F8v	O Mia infelice ∫orte	[Anon.]	xlix.
83	G1r	DOnna contra la mia voglia	PHI.DE LV.	xlix.
84	G1v	DOnna que∫ta e la mia voglia	PHI.DE LVRA.	l.
		[Headed: Ri∫po∫ta]		
85	G2r	FAmmi almen vna bona cera	PHI.DE LV.	l.
86	G2v	DAmmi almen lultimo vale	PHI.DE LV.	li.
87	G3v	NOn mi dar piu longhe hormai	PHI.DE LV.	lii.
88	G4v	VIen da poi la nocte luce	PHI.DE LV.	liii.
89	G5v	VAle hormai con tua durezza	PHI.DE LV.	liiii.
90	G6v	FAmmi quanto mal te piace	PHI.DE LV.	lv.
91	G7v	VN ∫ollicito amor vna gran fede	PHI.DE LV.	lv.
		[Headed:] Aer de Capitoli.		
	G8r	[Privilege: Colophon: Device]		
	G8v	[blank]		

Extant copy:

A-Wn, S.A.77.C.2 (4). Complete

> **Size of page:** 166 × 229 mm.
>
> **Watermarks:** No.20 on A5, A8, B6, B8, C5, C8, D3, D7, E1, E5, F1, F3, G3, and G7
>
> **Technical comments:** The signatures were not printed with the staves, but with the music: cf. C2r • A row of *sm* used as bearers for the area of the sixth stave have left blind impressions on E5r and E7r
>
> **Corrections and changes:**
>
> > **In-house:** A5r: see above
> >
> > **Later:** C2r.iii.40: *m*g' note-head erased and f' drawn in, with tail touched up • G8v: manuscript music for O *liebe böchin* . . . , à3, dated 1545
>
> **Binding:** Austrian National Library
>
> **Provenance:** G8r:] Andreas suenulus | hunc italice mû∫ices | comparauit librum | non nûmo at per = | mûtatione cuiusdam | imaginis virginis | Marie quam pretij | loro venditori contribuit. [and at right:] 1522

Lost copies: Copies were owned by Colón (Chapman, "Printed", No.26), by the Fuggers (Schaal, "Musikbibliothek", I/71), and by Bottrigari: see chapter 20

Early references: There are citations to one or other edition of this title in Gesner and, perhaps, Draudius

Other editions: The first edition appeared in 1505 (No.23)

Bibliography:

(a) Sartori, *Petrucci*, No.34 • Jeppesen, *La Frottola*, Pe.IV • Vogel, *Bibliografia*, 1507[3a]

(d) Schwartz, *Ottaviano*

(e) Ferand, "Neuer" • Ferand, "Two Unknown" • Sartori, "Nuove", pp. 198–199

Commentary:

1. There are many differences between this edition and the first, 1505⁵, at Munich, though few are significant. The style in the following partial list is the one used for "In-house corrections", in which the entry before an arrow represents the first edition, and one after indicates the present one. (References to "stanza 2", etc. are to the specified stanza counting solely the added text.)

   A1r. reset • A1v: re-set • A2r.i.text: lamento → lame*n*to • A2r.iii.44–45: a,b c.o.p.ligature *sb*, • 2 × *sb* • A2v.i.text: Ben chei tuo cangi → Be*n* chi tuo ca*n*gi • A3r.part-name: Altu5 → Altus • A3v.i.text: gran → gra*n* • A3v.ii.text: tien → tie*n* • A3v.iv.text:tormenta → tormenta • A4r.i & iv.text: torme*n*ta → tormenta • A4v.iii.text: twice ama*n*do → amando • A4v.v.31: d': *sm* → *m* [in error] • A5r.iii.19: *m*c' → *m*d' [changed in-house] • A5v.i.text: spera*n*za . . . anchor → speranza . . . anchor • A5v.i.text: pe*r*severanza → perseueranza • A5v.ii.text: agiunge → agiu*n*ge • A5v.ii.text: qu*e*lla . . . co*n*forto → quella . . . conforto • A6r.stanza 3.vi: sta*n*za → stanza • A6r.stanza 4.iii: spera*n*do → sperando • A6v.i.text: zoiosa e biancha → gioiosa e bia*n*cha • A6v.i.text: colu*m*bella → columbella • A6v.ii.text: diua [omitted in 2| • A6v.iii–v.text: zoiosa → gioiosa • A6v.stanza 2.iv: Et → E • A6v.stanza 3.iv: i*n*felice → infelice • A6v.stanza 4.i: felice → infelice • A6v.stanza 4.iii: felici → felice • A6v.stanza 7.ii: amando → ama*n*do • A6v.stanza 9.i: qua*n*do → quando • A6v.stanza 10.111: premio → premio • A7r.stanza 3.iii: pe*r* → per • A7r.stanza 4.i: facto → fatto • A7v.i.text: arde*n*te → ardente • A7v.iii.15: c', *m* → *sm* [in error] • A7v.stanza 2.i: che → chel • A7v: last stave uninked in 2| • A8r.part-name: Altus → Altu5 • A8r.ii.after 33: rest omitted: added in ms. → rest present • A8v.i.text: p*r*eda → preda • A8v.stanza 2.i: fove*n*te → fovente • A8v.stanza 2.ii: pare*n*do → parendo • A8v.stanza 3.ii: pecto → petto • A8v.stanza 4.ii: p*r*esume → presume • A8v.stanza 5.i: qua*n*to → quanto • A8v.stanza 5.ii: co*n*funde e ta*n*to me*n* → confunde e tanto men • A8v.stanza 5.iii: Quanto . . . ragi → Quanto . . . raggi • A8v.stanza 6.i: ta*n*to → tanto • A8v.stanza 7.iii: Sobito → subito • B1r.i.text: spera*n*za . . . no*n* → speranza non

   B1r.stanza 2.i: el bene → il bene • B1r.stanza 3.i: tene → tiene • B1v.i.text: i*n*tende → intende • B1v.iii.text: adiutoriu*m* → adiutorium • B1v.text incipits: u*n*der staves iv and v, in error: under v–vi • B1v.added text: El regno → El legno [in error] • B2r.i.text: cossi → cosi • B2r.ii–iii.text, twice: No*n* → Non • B2v.i.text: affligi . . . ap*r*e∬o → affliggi . . . apre∬o • B2v.ii.text: non . . . sequitar → no*n* . . . sequitar • B2v.iii.text: arge*n*to . . . ha*n*no → argento . . . hanno • B2v.iv.text: affligi → affliggi • B3r.i.text: affligi → affliggi • B3r.iv.text: affligi → affliggi • B3v.i.text: mantiene → ma*n*tiene • B3v.ii.text: be*n* → ben • B3v.iii.text: afflitto → afflicto • B3v.vi.music: the clef-change entered in manuscript in 1| is followed in 2|, though in a different manner • B4v.v.part-name: Altu5 → Altus • B5r.i–ii: different line-ends • B5r.part-name: Al-tus → Atu5 • B5r.vi.9 back: *m*d [changed in ms] → *m*c, correctly • B5v.i.29: c": *l* with a *pausa* → *b* with a *pausa* • B5v.iv.42–43: *sb,sb* → *b* [the other voices have 2 × *sb*] • B5v.stanza 2.i: ligi-ero → legiero • B5v: last stave uninked in 2| • B6v.i.text: co*m*pagni → compagni • B6v.stanza 4.i: setrei → serrai • B7r. the .heading] Sonetto. [is lacking in 2| • B7r.i.6: *m* [changed in MS] → *sb* [correctly] • B7r.i.text: qualch . . . no*n* → qualche . . . non • B7r.iv.text: Be*n*che → Benche • B7r.stanza 2.i: tocha → toccha • B7v.i.text: tra*n*sporta Che → transporta Che • B7v.ii.text, twice: ciecho → ciecco • B7v: last stave uninked in 2| • B8r. the heading] Sonetto [is lacking in 2| • B8r.i.text: che → ch*e* • B8r.text.col 3.iii: dentro el focho . . . sempr*e* → de*n*tro el fuoco . . . sempre • B8v.iv.text: priuato [added in 2| • B8v.stanza 2.ii: be*n* → ben

C1r.part-name: Altus → Altu5 • C1r.stanza 2.i: toi → tuoi • C1r.stanza 2.ii: de altrui con → daltrui con • C1v.i.text: laqui → laq*ui* • C2r.i.text: ste*n*to → stento • C2r.iii.40: m f' → g' [see above • C2r.stanza 4.ii: ado*n*que → adonque • C2v: the heading] Sonetto [is lacking in 2| • C2v.i.text, twice: u*n* → un • C2v.iii.text: do*n*na chel te*m*po → donna chel tempo • C2v.iv.text: te*m*po → tempo • C2v.stanza 1.i: co*n* → con • C3r.iii.45–6: g,a, *colsb,colm* → *dotted sb,m* • C3r.iv.5– 6: *m*b [changed in ms → *m*d',*m*b • C3r.v.text: sconte*n*to → contento • C3v.i.text: con- dino → condino • C4r.i–v.text, three times: p*er* → per • C4v.i.text: no*n* ca*n*dida → non candida • C4v.ii,iv.text: no*n* bia*n*cho → non biancho • C4v.stanza 4.i: sepulcro → sepulchro • C4v.stanza 4.ii: fia*m*ma → fiamma • C5r.i.text: daque → dacque • C5r.v: the text, far to the left in 1|, has been correctly aligned in 2| • C5r.stanza 3.ii: iocho → giocho • C5v.i.text: ingegno → i*n*gegno • C5v.iii.text: non → no*n* • C6r.iii,v text, twice: co*n* → con • C6r.stanza 2.ii: co*n* → con • C6r.stanza 3.i: cognoscho → cognosco • *etc.*

Few of these changes are of much significance, even those involving errors in one or the other edition. The much larger number of abbreviations in the text of the earlier edition are indication of the wider bodies of Petrucci's earlier text fonts. The changes cannot be taken to imply editorial intervention in the preparation of the second edition: instead, they are to be seen as a measure of the license accorded the typesetter. For that reason, the changes in spellings that could be interpreted as dialect variants are of some interest as possibly telling us something about the men involved. The change from *zoiosa* to *gioiosa* is perhaps the most obvious: however, that from *Et* to *E* and from *pecto* to *petto*, or those from *ragi* to *raggi* and from *affligi* to *affliggi*, or *cognoscho* to *cognosco*, *tocha* to *toccha*, *ciecho* to *ciecco*, and *daque* to *dacque*, among others, are significant. The implication has to be that a different typesetter was involved with much of the second edition. However, the pattern is not consistent: *sepulcro* is changed to *sepulchro*, and *afflitto* to *afflicto*. These patterns, as much as the evidence of spellings which were not changed from edition to edition, suggest that, as usual, Petrucci was using two typesetters, and dividing the work up between them.

No. 38. Martini: *Hymns*
1507

Not extant, but the title probably read:]
Hymni de tempore et de sanctis liber primus

Format: Landscape quarto, probably in eights
Contents: According to Colón, there was some kind of prefatory material, followed by a setting of
Conditor alme syderum

———

Lost copies: A copy was owned by Colón, and listed in his Abcedarium B:] hymni de tempore et de sanctis liber primus de canto. n°. 37. 4974. V. 1507. 4b
A copy is listed in the inventory of the Fugger collection:] Hymnor. Lib. 1°. [which was bound with the first book of Magnificats and the two of Lamentations:] In Blaw Leder bund. Sein mit einem Spago alle 4 zusamen bunden.

A copy is listed in Gaspari's transcription of Bottrigari's notes on his own collection:] 21 Hymnorum Lib p^{us}. 1507. Jo. Martini

Bibliography:

(a) Sartori, *Petrucci*, No.36

(e) Chapman, "Printed", No.28 • Schaal, "Musikbibliothek", I/56 • Vernarecci, *Petrucci*, p. 112

Commentary:

1. The book was certainly printed in choirbook format, rather than in part-books: the books of Lamentations (Nos.27 and 28) with which it was bound for the Fuggers were printed in choir-book. The hymns were probably laid out on the page like frottole or the laude (of which the first edition of Book 1, by Dammonis) had already appeared.

2. The formula devised by Colón for his entries ends with "4b" which states that the book was in quarto and contained prefatory material: this last was most probably a dedicatory letter of some sort. I have suggested, in chapter 9, that this book preceded the other lost volume from the same year, that of Magnificats, and that both represent something of a deliberate plan to expand the liturgical repertoires covered in Petrucci's editions. While Petrucci might have signed a dedication (as he did for the first book of Spinacino's intabulations), it is more likely that it would have been written by the supplier of the music.

3. It must be unlikely that these works correspond to any of those in the pair of Ferrarese manu-scripts, I-MOe α.M.1,11–12: those were all written for double choir. Nor need we believe that all Petrucci's works were composed by Martini. Neither Colón's catalogue nor Fugger's inventory mentions a composer, implying that no name appeared on the title-page. Presumably the first composition, the *Conditor alme siderum* cited by Colón, was composed by Martini, for Bottrigari will have drawn the composer's name from somewhere.

No.39. *Magnificat I*

14.x.1507

Not extant. The title probably read as follows:
Magnificat liber primus de quolibet tono duo diversorum auctorum

Format: Landscape quarto, probably in eights.
Contents: Apparently the first work was a Magnificat à4 by Agricola

_____

Lost copies:

Colón bought a copy in Venice in 1521, and apparently had another copy at one time: there are two sets of entries in his catalogues:] Octavij petrucii magnificat liber primus. *1985* [and, in Registrum A, No.1985:] Magnificat liber primus de quolibet tono duo diversorum auctorum et In toto opere nil aliud continetur nisi magnificat variorum auctorum cum .4. vocibus et prima est agricole est Impressum Venetijs per octauianum petrucium. anno .1507. 14. octobris est In quarto Costo en Venetia .26. sueldos a cinco de Julio 1521 y el ducado val .134. sueldos

The second series includes, in the Abecedarium B:] Magnificat liber primus de quolibet tono duo 4975. V. 1507. 4 [and] Et exultavit sp*iritus* meus in deo salutare. 4975. [Chapman, "Printed", No.29. Huntington, *Catalogue* does not show this book at number 1985, but reads] Libri diṇirandi facti di paladinij Iṇtitulato Veṇdetta de falconeto . . . [printed in Venice in 1513.

A copy was at one time owned by the Fugger family and is listed in the inventory:] Magnificat Lib. 1° [which was bound with Martini's hymns, and the two books of Lamentations:] In Blaw Leder bund. Sein mit einem Spago alle 4 zusamen bunden.

Bibliography:

(a) Sartori, "Nuove", p. 202, No.36 bis

(e) Chapman, "Printed" • Jeppesen, "Neuentdeckter", p. 81 • Schaal, "Musikbibliothek", I/55

Commentary:

1. The book was certainly printed in choirbook format, rather than in part-books: the books of Lamentations (Nos.27 and 28) with which it was bound for the Fuggers were printed in choir-book.

2. It is reasonable to assume that this book had a layout similar to that for the four-voiced movements in the books of Lamentations. By now, Petrucci was controlling the lengths of his books more closely, and most that were published in this format comprised seven gatherings. Certainly the price paid for the book by Colón suggests that it was at least five gatherings long.

3. The title as given by Colón states that there were two Magnificats for each mode, composed by different composers. This implies ten or twelve Magnificats (for mode seven was relatively rarely set, and even mode five was less common than the others). Given the probable size of the book, it means that the musical style will have been at the simpler end of the spectrum (for otherwise part-books would have been more practical). The works were probably arranged in modal order, for the practice seems to be becoming established at this time: I–Rvat S.P. B.80 has a modally ordered sequence, interrupted only by one piece in second mode (by Dunstable); the sequences of 14 settings in I–Rvat C.S.15 and of 11 in I–Rvat C.S.44 are in strict order. The first two of these manuscripts were copied before Petrucci's edition, while the last is roughly contemporary. (For details, see Sherr, *Papal*, and the literature cited in chapter 19 here. Note also that the 18 Magnificats in the roughly contemporary D–Ju 20, copied in the Netherlands, are also in sequence.) On the other hand, none of the collections of Magnificats in I–Mfd 2269 or I–VEcap (in manuscripts DCCLVIII and DCCLIX) are arranged in order, although these sources are more informally arranged in general. But the contents of Petrucci's edition would (like those of any printed book) be ordered from the beginning, and therefore be more likely to be arranged in a manner similar to that of the more formal Sistine manuscripts.

4. Given the probability that the works were in order, and the statement by Colón that the first Magnificat was by Agricola, that work was likely to have been in the first mode. Only three Magnificats can be securely attributed to the composer (with details in Kirsch, *Quellen*, pp. 275–76), alongside two with stronger attributions elsewhere: one of these is in mode 1, found in I–Rvat C.S.44, where it is also first in order.

5. If that work was indeed the one printed by Petrucci, the other Magnificats in the Sistine manuscript becoming potential contents for Petrucci's volume: they include all three Agricola works, two by Brumel and Prioris, and single settings by Compère, Escribano, and Josquin, with one

anonymous setting in mode 4. The earlier C.S.15 contains an earlier repertoire, with a setting by Dufay and three by Martini, but it also has works by Brumel, Compère, and Weerbeke. Taken together, these manuscripts probably give a good picture of the composers from whose works Petrucci's anthology was drawn: Agricola, Brumel, and Josquin, perhaps with Compère or Weebeke, were already known to sell well, and any group of them should have provided a marketable selection.

I stress that this is all speculation, bolstered solely by an understanding of Petrucci's house-style and marketing practices, with the presumption that this book, in presenting a new repertoire, did not move far from what had already been shown to be successful.

No. 40. *Frottole III*

26.xi.1507   *RISM* 1507[1]

Second Edition

A1r]   Frottole Libro | tertio.

H8r]   Impreſſum Venetiis per Octauianum Pe-|trutium Foroſempronienſem .M.D.vii. Die xxvi | Nouembris Cum priuilegio inuictiſſimi Domini | Venetiarum quae nullus poſſit cantum Figuratum | imprimere ſub pena in ipso priuilegio contenta. | Regiſtrum. | A B C D E F G H Omnes quaterni. | [Petrucci's device]

A1v   [Tavola:] Numero ſeſantuna.

Format and collation: Choirbook: landscape quarto-in-eights. 64 folios: A-H[8]

Signatures:] AA iiii [$4 • − A1 • On B2, the numerals have only printed in blind, appearing as] BB

Foliation: [1], 2–62, 36 [*recte* 63], [64].

Part-names:

verso:]	Tenor	[A2-4, A6, B1-D2, D4-F3, F5-G7, H1-H6
	Tenor [in stave]	[A5
	Tenor Altus Baſſus	[A7-8, D3
	Tenor Altus Baſſus	[F4
	Tenor Altu5 Baſſu5	[G8
	Tenor Altu5 Baſſus	[H7
recto:]	Tenor Altus Baſſus	[A2, B1, D4, F5, G1, H1
	Altus Baſſus	[A3, A5, A7, B2-5, B7, C1-5, C7, D1-D3, D5, D7, E1-E5, E7, F1-F4, F7, G2-G5, G7, H2-H5, H7
	Altus Baſſus [in stave]	[A4,6
	Tenor Altu5 Baſſus	[A8
	Altus Baſſu5	[B6, B8, C6, C8, D6, D8, E6, E8, F8
	Altu5 Baſſus	[F6, G6, G8, H6

Fonts: Music: Petrucci's normal music type

Staves: Six per page, 175–76 or 178 mm long, 10-92-113 mm high

Text: Roman

Textual comments: The captions are in capitals in A,B,D,G, and H, are with initials in C and E, and are lacking in F

In-house corrections: G6r.v.37: f → g, erased note-head and a *sb* stamped in: both copies

Contents: The last column gives the folio numbers cited in the Tavola

	E6*v*	2/ Io ſo ben che al tuo diſpecto		
36	E7*v*	LIber fui un tempo in foco	M.C.	xl.
	E8*v*	2/ Credo ben pero che me ama		
37	F1*v*	PIango el mio fidel ſeruire	[Anon.]	xlii.
38	F2*v*	BEn chio ſerva a cor ingrato	[Anon.]	xlIII.
39	F3*v*	TV me ſtrugi e dai tormento	[Anon.]	xliiii.
40	F4*v*	NOn poi per che non voi	[Anon.]	xlv.
41	F5*r*	HAime che graue doglia	[Anon.]	xlv.
42	F5*v*	SI morſi donna el tuo labro ſuaue	[Anon.]	xlvi.
		[Headed:] Per ſonetti		
43	F6*v*	ARda el ciel el mondo tutto	[Anon.]	xlvII.
44	F7*v*	LA ſperanza me tien uiuo	[Anon.]	xlvIII.
45	F8*v*	IO mi moro e chi potria	[Anon.]	xlIx.
46	G1*r*	PRendi larme ingrato amore	[Anon.]	xlix.
47	G1*v*	QVel chio poſſo io tho donato	[Anon.]	l.
48	G2*v*	ALa fe ſi ala fe bona	[Anon.]	li.
49	G3*v*	SOn tornato e dio el ſa	PHILIPPVS DE LVRANO.	lII.
50	G4*v*	ALdi donna non dormire	F.D.L.	lIII.
51	G5*v*	SE non dormi donna aſcolta	[Anon.]	lIIII.
52	G6*v*	CHi ſe fide de fortuna	B.T.	lv.
53	G7*v*	DE dolce diua mia	[Anon.]	lvI.
54	G8*v*	LA tromba ſona	[Anon.]	lvII.
55	H1*r*	NVnqua fu pena magiore	B.T.	lvII.
56	H1*v*	CHi ſe paſce de ſperanza	B.T.	lvIII.
57	H2*v*	FA chio fo hor ſu fa preſto	[Anon.]	
		[Omitted from Tavola]		
58	H3*v*	VOx clamantis in deſerto	B.T.	lx.
59	H4*v*	PAce e gloria al gentil lauro	[Anon.]	lxi.
60	H5*v*	EL grillo e bon cantore	IOSQVIN DASCANIO	lxii.
61	H6*v*	SE conuiene a vn cor uillano	ENEAS.	lxiii.
		S:] Se conuine a vna . . .		
62	H7*v*	SIgnore anzi mia dea	B.T.	lxiii.
	H8*r*	[Colophon: Register: Device]		
	H8*v*	[blank]		

_____

Extant copies:

A-Wn, S.A.77.C.2 (3). Complete

> **Size of page:** 165 × 234 mm.
>
> **Watermarks:** No.23 on A4, A7, B3, B8, C6, C8, D3, D7, E5, E8, F2, F6, G1, G6, H4, and H8
>
> **Textual comments:** B2*r*. see above
>
> **Technical comments:** Notes, perhaps *sm*, used as bearer sorts in place of the sixth stave on A7*r*, B6*r*, B7*r*, and C8*r*
>
> **In house correction:** G6*r*.v.37: see above
>
> **Binding:** Fugger binding. On front board:] FROT: L: TERCIO
>
> **Provenance:** Fugger collection

D-Rp, B.33–35. Complete
> **Size of page:** 168 × 232 mm.
> **Watermarks:** No.23 on A1, A3, B1, B3, C2, C4, D2, D3, E6, E8, F6, F8, G3, G8, H1 and H4
>> • The twins can be seen quite clearly
> **Textual comments:** B2r: see above
> **Technical comments:** Strong impressions of different sequences of groups of notes used as bearer sorts, on most rectos. See below • Spacing sorts for music have left clear traces on B4v.vi, B5r.i, D1r.iv, and E3r.ii. The edges of the sorts lie 5 mm above the stave or 4 mm below it • The title-page shows particularly clear impressions of bearer sorts: these include sequences of notes, but also letters from the font Petrucci used for title-pages
> **Corrections and changes:**
>> **In-house:** G6r.v.37: see above
>> **Later:** A4r.ii.32–40: annotation in 19th-century pencil, suggesting a deletion • A4v.top: the contemporary annotation] nota placet. [in the hand found in *Frottole II*
> **Binding and Provenance:** With *Frottole II* (1508, No.42)

Lost copies: Colón owned a copy (Chapman, "Printed", No.27)
Other editions: The first edition was in 1505, No.18, above
Bibliography:
> (a) Rosaria Boccadifuoco, *Bibliografia*, No.1460 • Sartori, *Petrucci*, No.35; *Nuovo Vogel*, 1507[4]
> (b) Brunet, *Manuel*, ii, col.1413
> (e) Sartori, "Nuove", pp. 199–202

Commentary:

1. The pattern of part-names shows that they were retained in the forme for as long as possible. This is most evident from the recurring placement of the numeral "5" as a final "s": from the beginning of gathering B the two inner formes both show the same sequence, on *6r* and *8r*.

2. The same pattern, at the point where it changes, in gathering F, seems to imply that the outer sheet was printed before the inner. Since this is a second edition, it would in fact be easier to set type by formes, and hence by sheets.

3. The pattern of using sequences of notes as bearer sorts in place of the sixth stave implies that they were left in the forme from sheet to sheet. A particularly clear sequence can be seen in the Regensburg copy, where the notes on A7r can also be seen on B5r, B7r, D5r, D7r, E7r and (probably) F7r: similar sequences appear on other pages of the formes.

4. Unusually, in this edition, the letter "y" looks as though it was added to the text font after the rest had been cast, for it is cut according to a different weight.

5. Confirmation that the added verses of text were printed with the music can be seen on A2r, especially in the Regensburg copy. Here, the first line of the second strophe overlaps with the text underlaid to stave five.

No. 41. *Laude II*

11.i.1507/8   *RISM* 1508³

A1r]   Laude Libro ſecondo

G8r]   Impreſſum Venetiis per Octauianum Pe-|trutium Foroſempronienſem. M.D.vii. Die xi | Ianuarii Cum priuilegio inuictiſſimi Dominii | Venetiarum quae nullus poſſit cantum Figuratum | imprimere ſub pena in ipso priuilegio contenta. | Regiſtrum. | A B C D E F G Omnes quaterni. | [Petrucci's device]

A1v]   Laude numero ſeſanta [Tavola, arranged in two columns in the order of pieces in the book. At the end, the word:] Finis

Format and collation: Choirbook: landscape quarto-in-eights. 56 folios: A-G⁸

Signatures:] A 2 [$4 • − A1

Foliation: t.r.r.] [1], 2–34, [35 probably present, but cropped in the only surviving copy], 36–55, [56] No running heads. Composers' names entered in the head-line

Part-names: in the left margin, set vertically, reading from the top:

verso:]	Tenor	[A2-5,7, B1-4, B6-C2, C4-7, D1-5, D7-E4, E6-G1, G3-7
	tenor [within the stave:	B5
	Tenor Altus	[E5
	Tenor Altuſ Baſſuſ	[C3, D6
	Tenor Altuſ Baſſuſ	[C8
	Tenor Altuſ Baſſus	[G2
	[All three, set within staves as needed:	A6,8, G7
recto:]	Tenor Altus Baſſus	[A2, B1, C4, D7
	Tenor Altuſ Baſſus	[A7
	Tenor Altus Baſſuſ	[E6
	Altuſ Baſſus	[A3-5, B5,7, C6,8, D5,8, E5,8, F5,7, G5,7
	Altus Baſſus	[A4,6,8, B2-4, B8-C3, C5,7, D2-4,6, E1-4, F1,3–4,6, G1-2,4
	Altus Baſſus	[F8, G6
	Altus [and Baſſus within the stave:	B6
	[all three set within staves as needed:	D1, E7, G3
	Baſſus Primus Baſſus Sˢ	[E6
	Altus Contra Primus Contra Sˢ	[F2

Fonts: Music: Petrucci's normal music type

Staves: Six in the forme, though not often printed

Text: Roman throughout

Textual comments: A5v.v.30–32: double use of the sign "3", as proportion sign, and as indicator of triplets, for the same three notes • F5v: this piece once had an ascription, for there are the traces of type: the most likely solution seems to be Tromboncino, although Petrucci uses the initials B.T. on adjacent folios

Technical comments: Small capital letter used as initial on C5v [D] • No initial capitals at all on E7r [O], G5v [O] • The last stave is only partly inked on G1v • The added verses of text are printed with the staves, not with the music • The colophon looks to have been the same setting as that for Dammonis' book, with white space in places, such as after the word "Ianuarii"

In-house corrections: Both in the unique copy: F4*v*.end of stave v:] pro alijs verbis require in fine librj • F8*v*.v.40: *b*, a → g, erased and stamped in

Contents:

40	E4ν	LEgno ſancto e glorioſo		Piero da lodi
41	E5ν	STella celi extirpauit	à5	Piero da lodi
42	E6ν	ANima mia diletta		I.B.Z.
		[Headed:] Oda		
43	E7r	OOgnun driza al ciel el viſo		[Anon.]
		[Other vv:] Ognun . . .		
44	E7ν	AVe maria gratia plena		B.T.
45	E8ν	AVe maria Regina in cielo		B.T.
46	F1ν	AVe maria gratia plena	à5	Marchetto
47	F2ν	ANima chriſti ſanctifica me		[Anon.]
48	F3ν	AVe maria gratia plena		Frater petrus
49	F4ν	TV ſei quella aduocata		B.T.
50	F5ν	AVe maria Gratia plena		[Anon.]
51	F6ν	AVe maria Gratia plena		B.T.
52	F7ν	AVe maria gratia plena		B.T.
53	F8ν	A Te drizo ogni mio paſſo		Ludouico milaneſe
54	G1ν	VErgine inmaculata alma regina		Marchetto
55	G2ν	CHriſtus factus eſt pro nobis		[Anon.]
56	G3r	O Inextimabilis dilectio caritatis		[Anon.]
57	G3ν	NE le tue braze o vergene maria		F.D.L.
58	G4ν	ANima chriſti ſanctifica me		Antonet
59	G6ν	AVe noſtra ſalus ieſu chriſte		[Anon.]
	G6ν.ii	2| Salue ſalus mundi		
60	G7ν	AVe verum corpus christi		Fr Benedictus Bella Busca
	G8r	[Colophon: Register: Device]		
		[second column, additional text for *Tu ſei quella aduocata de peccanti*]		
	G8ν	[blank]		

Extant copy:

E-S, 12-1-3. Complete

> **Size of page:** 161 × 230 mm.
>
> **Watermarks:** No.23 on A5, A7, B1, B4, C2, C6, D3, D8, E5, E7, F1, F4, G6 and G8 • The two twin marks are clearly visible in this copy: one appears on A5, A7, B1, C2, C6, D3, D8, E5, and G8
>
> **In-house changes:** See above
>
> **Binding:** Parchment wrapper, with three sewing bands: two ties on either side, one of those on the back cover now lost • Traces of an old label on the spine • Front cover now detached • One paste-down and flyleaf at each end, of the same Spanish paper found in Dammonis' binding
>
> **Provenance:** This copy was purchased by Colón in Perugia in 1530 • G8ν:] Eſte libro coſto en peruſo .105. qua-|trines a .2. de Setienbre de 1530. | y el ducado de oro vale | 420 quatrines [It is also cited in Colón's catalogues (Chapman, "Columbus", No.32) • Front flyleaf verso:] Cantionela [and] R 9700 • A1r: old call numbers of] L .KK Tab 175 Nº 16 [and] E . . . GG | Tab . . . 175 | N . . . 33 [and] 3096 [and] 4701
>
> **Bibliography:** Arboli y Farando, *Biblioteca*, iv, pp. 220–21 • Jeppesen, *Mehrstimmiger* • Jeppesen, "Neuentdeckter" • Trend, "Musikschätze", p. 499

Lost copies: A copy was once owned by Bottrigari, and another was in the Fugger collection (Schaal, "Musikbibliothek", I/73)

Early references: Gesner, *Pandectae* (1548) (Bernstein, "Gesner", No.244)

Bibliography:

(a) Sartori, *Petrucci*, No.39 • Vogel, *Bibliografia*, 1507[1a]

(d) Jeppesen, *Mehrstimmiger*

(e) Jeppesen, "Neuentdeckten", p. 73 • Luisi, *Laudario* • Sartori, "Nuove", pp. 202–3 • Trend, "Musikschätze", p. 499

Commentary:

1. Some of the compositions (Nos. 4 and 13, 14 and 40, 19 and 52, and 20 and 51) have identical or closely related music. In those cases where there are minor changes, it is not always possible to determine which versions might have been the earlier.

    Nos. 14 and 40 are essentially the same composition, in text and music. Most of the changes are very minor: major changes involve the last few bars, and the order of additional verses. However, the lesser changes all seem to suggest that No.14 is the earlier version, and that No.40 represents a smoothed-out series of readings: they involve, for example, the substitution of pitches by rests (to avoid a dissonance between Altus and Tenor), or breaking up one note into two different pitches (giving a clearer harmonic structure). Two words are changed in the text of the first verse, apparently reflecting use of the *lauda* for meditation on the Procession to Calvary rather than the Crucifixion itself:

    No.14: Legno *sancto* e glorioso Che tenesti el dolce figlio De maria quel suave ziglio Suo dilecto e humel speso . . .

    No.40: Legno sancto e glorioso Che portasti el dolce figlio De maria quel fresco ziglio Suo diletto e humil speso . . .

    The case of Nos.19 and 52 is more interesting, in that the two versions of the same piece are attributed to different composers. Unfortunately, there is not enough evidence to decide, either between Cara (No.19) and Tromboncino (No.52), or between the two versions. At one point only, No.52 has a minor variant which makes the text much harder to underlay.

2. However, the presence of these repeats argues strongly that the collection was not reproduced from a single manuscript source, or, indeed, probably from one institution. There is considerable evidence from the spellings that the texts were taken from Venetian sources: No.2 uses both *zorno* (for giorno) and *hozi* (for oggi); both No.14 and 40 use *ziglio* (as shown above); and the list could be extended. In looking for a possible source among the *scuole* in Venice, the texts give a few not very precise clues: there is a strong preponderance of texts centered on the Cross (and the Crucifixion) or on the Virgin Mary. Not surprisingly, these do not seem to break into discrete groups, for most *scuole* would have had an interest in the BVM, and most would have used the Cross as an emblem during their processions. Indeed, No.2 opens with a comment on those who do not follow the cross in procession.

    It is tempting to look at those *scuole* asociated with one of the friars' churches in Venice, and not only because it was a Friar who had first edited music for Petrucci. While most of the compositions are assigned to known composers from elsewhere, and presumably represent *contrafacta* of secular songs, two or three have more significant attributions. Apart from the attribution to *D. Philippo* for the first piece in the book, there are two compositions apparently assigned to friars: No.48 is attributed to *Frater petrus* and the last to *Fr. Benedictus Bella Busca* (whom Blackburn, in *Correspondence*, p. 982, identifies as a friar at Santa Elena). These associations are appropriate, for friars certainly promoted lay religious culture, and their houses played host to, and guided, the religious activities of various *scuola*. Several *scuole* were in fact attached to such churches as the Frari and SS. Giovanni e Paolo (a Dominican house).

But I doubt that Castellanus collected and provided the music, even though he was at SS. Giovanni e Paolo. The duplications (with the conflicting attribution) argue against such a hypothesis, as does the character of the music, and even the range of composers represented. Instead, it seems more likely that Petrucci (no doubt responding to assertions from Dammonis) decided that a second anthology would sell. He did not rely on Dammonis, but went to Venetian musicians, who could provide repertoire from a number of *scuole* or church collections.

3. Prizer, "Courtly", p. 27, notes that some of the compositions in this collection seem to be associated with Mantua. In addition to drawing attention to the works by Tromboncino and Cara, he suggests that "Don Philippo" may be Filippo Lappacino, "attached to Francesco's *cappella*". He suggests that these works were sung in the Chapel of S. Maria dei Voti. This is certainly reasonable, though I doubt that Petrucci acquired the music directly from Mantua.

4. Glixon ("Polyphonic", pp. 34–38) sees this second book as having been prepared in haste, both because of the errors that it carries, and because of the repetition of pieces. Certainly, there are errors, although a number of the variants cited by Jeppesen, *Mehrstimmige*, lvx–lxx (and mentioned by Glixon) are rather on the order of "revisions", "performing variants", or "re-compositions". It may be that the works were collected together rather rapidly, but the press-work seems to be of as good a quality as in other editions of the period.

No. 42. *Frottole II*

29.i.1507/8   *RISM* 1508²

Second edition

A1r]   Frottole Libro ſecondo

G8r]   Impreſſum Venetiis per Octauianum Pe-|trucium Foroſempronienſem. M.D vii. Die xxix | Ianuarii Cum priuilegio inuictiſſimi Dominii | Venetiarum quae nullus poſſit cantum Figuratum | imprimere ſub pena in ipſo priuilegio contenta. | Regiſtrum. | A B C D E F G Omnes quaterni. | [Petrucci's device]

A1v]   [Tavola:] Numero cinquantatre. [in two columns: all numerals in lower case roman]

Format and collation: Choirbook: landscape quarto-in-eights. 56 folios: A–G⁸
Signatures:] aA iiii [$4 • − A1
Foliation: t.r.r.] [1], 2–55, [56]
No running heads
Part-names:

recto:]	Altus Baſſus	[A4,6,8, B1-4, C1-4, D1,2, E1-4, F1-4, G2,4,6
	Altu5 Baſſus	[A3,5,7, B5-8, C5-8, D5-8, E5-8, F5-7, G5,7
	Tenor Altus Baſſus	[A2, D3-4, G1
	Tenor Altu5 Baſſus	[F8, G3
	[Nil:	A1, G8

verso:]	Tenor	[A2–D1, D4–F6, G1,3-6
	Tenor Altus Baſſus	[D2, F7, G2
	Tenor Altu5 Baſſus	[G7
	Tenor Altus Baſſus	[D3, F8
	[Nil:	A1, G8

Small initials are used in some part names:

recto:]	Bassus	A3,5-8; B1,3,5,7; C1,3,5,7; D1,3,5,7; E1,3,5,7; F1,3,5,7,8; G1,3,5,6,7
	Altus	A3; B6,8; C6,8; D3,6,8; E1,3,6,8; F1,3,6,8; G1,3,
verso:]	Tenor	A2,3,4; B1,3; C1,3; D1,3,4; E1-4; F1-4; G1-4
	Bassus	D2,3; G2
	Altus	F7; G7

The letter "u" is inverted in some part-names:

| | Bassus | 2r and 4r of all gatherings |
| | Altus | A6r,8r, D2v |

Fonts: Music: Petrucci's normal music type

Staves: Six per page, though usually fewer are inked • 10-92.5-113, and 175–76 or 178 mm long

Text: Roman

Textual comments: B2v.ii.text:] ſerute [in both copies • B4v, D5v and E1v: the annotation for the Seconda pars has an inverted first "S" • D1v-2r: the opening notation, showing rests and bar-lines, seems to be aimed specifically at performers

Technical comments: Signatures are at the same height throughout, and were therefore not necessarily set with the text • The style of ascriptions seems to vary according to formes. See the details at the end of this entry • Small capital on B5v [O] • The capital letter O on D1r, D3 etc. is in a better condition than the same letter in *Frottole IX*, A-Wn and better than *I Motetti à5*, f.A6r • Six staves are rarely inked in this volume

In-house corrections: A4v.v.after 16: bar line, brown ink, to correspond with the other voices: both copies • D2v.v.26: *b*, *c* → *d*, the note erased, and a new one stamped in, with the staves touched up in brown ink: D-Rp

Contents:

The folio numbers as given in the Tavola do not have final points

	A1r	[Title]		
	A1v	[Tavola:] Numero cinquantatre.		
1	A2r	DA poi chel tuo bel viſo	R.M.	ii
2	A2v	LA mia vita liberale	FRAN.VENE.ORGA.	iii
	A3v	2/ A tuo modo		
3	A4v	QVeſte quel locho amore	FRANCISCVS VENE.ORGA.	v
4	A5v	SOn quel troncho ſenza foglia	[Anon.]	vi
5	A6v	SPero hauer felicita	[Anon.]	vii
6	A7v	NOn ſo perche non mora	P.C.V.	viii
7	A8v	COn la rete cogli el vento	FRAN.VENE.ORGA.	ix
8	B1v	NAſce laſpro mio tormento	FRAN.VENE.ORGA.	x
9	B2v	VEdo ben chio perdo el tempo	[Anon.]	xi
10	B3v	OChi mei troppo guardaſti	FRANCISCVS VENETVS ORGA.	xii
	B4v	2/ Ligiermente o cor credeſti		
11	B5v	OCchi dolci oue prendeſti	FRANCISCVS VENETVS ORGA.	xiiii
	B6v	2/Sel mio ben da voi deriua		

12	B7v	FAmme pur quel che ti pare	[Anon.]	xvi
13	B8v	GLiochi toi macceſel core	FRAN.VEN.ORGA.	xvii
14	C1v	SErra dura mia partita	[Anon.]	xviii
	C2v	2/ Sel partir me ſerra forte		
15	C3v	OChi mei al pianger nati	[Anon.]	xx
16	C4v	SE lamor in te e pocho	[Anon.]	xxi
17	C5v	ITe caldi ſuſpiri mei	[Anon.]	xxii
18	C6v	DIo ſa quanto me doglio	[Anon.]	xxiii
19	C7v	VIuo lieto nel tormento	[Anon.]	xxiiii
20	C8v	SI non poſſo il cor placarte	[Anon.]	xxv
		[A,B,Tav:] Sio . . .		
21	D1v	OChii mei frenati el pianto	PEREGRINVS CESENA VERONENSIS	xxvi
22	D2v	HAi laſſa me meſchina	P.C.V:	xxvii
23	D3r	OYme che ho perſo il core	P.C.V.	xxvii
24	D3v	O Dolce diua mia	P.C.V:	xxviii
25	D4r	CHe piu felice ſorte	ANTONIVS ROSSETVS VERONENSIS	xxviii
26	D4v	LA pieta chiuſo ha le porte	B.T.	xxix
	D5v	2/ Certo naſcer non douea		
27	D6v	TV me voi crudel laſſare	[Anon.]	xxxi
28	D7v	LIrum bililirum	ROSSINVS MANTVANVS	xxxii
		[Headed:] Vn ſonar de piua in fachineſco		
29	D8v	GLiochi toi mhan poſto	B.T.	xxxiii
	E1v	2/ Gliochi toi		
30	E2v	MOrir voglio in la mia fede	[Anon.]	xxxv
31	E3v	POi che a tal condutto mhai	[Anon.]	xxxvI
32	E4v	PAce hormai ſu non piu guerra	[Anon.]	xxxvii
33	E5v	PIu volte fra me ſteſſo	[Anon.]	xxxviii
34	E6v	REſta in pace diua mia	[Anon.]	xxxix
35	E7v	GVarda donna el mio tormento	[Anon.]	xl
36	F8v	HAime che non e vn giocho	[Anon.]	xli
37	F1v	VIua e morta voglio amarte	Honophrius Antenoreus	xlii
38	F2v	AL te par che manchi in fede	Honophrius Antenoreus	xliii
39	F3v	REſta in pace ingrata hormai	Honophrius Antenoreus	xliiii
40	F4v	HAi promeſſe dolce e amare	[Anon.]	xlv
41	F5v	SEgua pur seguir chi vole	Honophrius Antenoreus	xlvi
	F6v	2/ Vidi gia ne la ſua corte		
42	F7v	MI parto a dio	Honophrius Antenoreus	
43	F8r	E Queſta quella fede	Honophrius Antenoreus	xlviii
44	F8v	PIangeti mecho amanti	Nicolo Patauino	xlix
45	G1r	MAl fai ſignora mia	Nico.Pa.	xlix
46	G1v	AMor ſempre me dimoſtra	Nico.Pa.	l
47	G2v	LAmentomi damore	Nico.Pa:	li
48	G3r	NOn e tempo de tenere	NI.PA:	li
49	G3v	SEl te piacque vn tempo farmi	NI.PA.	lii
50	G4v	SE da poi la tua partita	NI.PA.	liii
51	G5v	SE non voi penſar in tutto	NI.PA	liiii

52	G6*v*	TE lamenti & io mi doglio	[Anon.]	lv
53	G7*v*	SE non poi hor ri[torarmi	Ni.Pa.	lv
	G8*r*	[Colophon; Register; Device]		
	G8*v*	[blank]		

Extant copies:

A-Wn, S.A.77.C.2 (2). Complete
  Size of page: 166 × 235 mm.
  Watermarks: No.23 on A6, A8, B1, B5, C4, C7, D3, D7, E3, E8, F1, F6, G5, and G7
  Corrections and changes:
    In-house: A4*v*: see above
    Later: C7r.v.16: struck through, pale brown ink
  Binding: Fugger binding:] FROTTO: L: SE • One paste-down and one fly-leaf at each end
  Provenance: From the Fugger collection • A2r. stamp:] BIBLIOTHECA PALAT. | VINDO-
    BONENSIS

D-Rp, B.33–35. Complete
  Size of page: 168 × 232 mm.
  Watermarks: No.23 on A6, A8, B2, B4, C2, C4, D4, D8, E6, E7, F2, F3, G2 and G5
  Technical comments: C1*v* and C2r. many traces of the furniture, from a poorly cleaned forme
    • C4r.ii: a text spacing sort, measuring about 3 × 2 mm. • C8*v*: the initial has a curious black
    patch over it, almost certainly a piece of felt from the ink-ball
  Corrections and changes:
    In-house: A4*v*, D2*v*: see above
    Later: There is a series of annotations from an early owner, at the heads of versos, and
      expressing approval of specific works: for example, A5*v* reads] placet [and E4*v* reads]
      bonu*m* [: similar annotations appear on A6*v*, A8*v*, E3*v*, F1*v*, F2*v*: further comments
      have been erased on A4*v*, F3r • A very faded inscription, probably in the same hand,
      appears on A1r, beginning with the word] Mu[ica •
  Binding: Contemporary full calf binding, with stamped repetitions of a simple cross-over design,
    and rolled borders, all in blind • Each board originally had four green tie-strings, though all
    that remains is a trace inside the board • The binding is completely detached and the spine
    is badly damaged and mostly lost • One paste-down inside each board, but the fly-leaf is
    not extant
  Provenance: Bought by Proske from the antiquarian Butsch
  Bibliography: Vogel, *Bibliothek*, ii, p. 370

Lost copies: Colón owned a copy (Chapman, "Printed", No.33)
Other editions: The first edition appeared in 1505 (No.17)
Bibliography:
  (a) Rosaria Boccadifuoco, *Bibliografia*, No.1455 (dated 1507) • Sartori, *Petrucci*, No.40 • Jeppesen,
    La Frottola, Pe II • Vogel, *Bibliografia*, 1507[3]
  (d) Cesari, *Frottole* (1954)
  (e) Ambros, *Geschichte*, p. 196 • Sartori, "Nuove", pp. 203–5

Commentary:

1. The style of ascriptions seems to vary according to formes:

Gathering	1r,2v,7r,8v	1v,2r,7v,8r	3r,4v,5r,6v	3v,4r,5v,6r
A	capitals	initials	capitals	initials
B	capitals	capitals	none needed	capitals
C	none given	none given	none given	none given
D	initials	capitals	initials	capitals
E	none given	none given	none given	none given
F	lower case	lower case	none given	lower case
G	lower case	lower case	capitals	capitals

Since this is a second edition, it would be reasonable for the book to have been set by formes, and even divided betweeen two craftsmen. This evidence might argue for more than two men, each having a distinctive manner of indicating the composer: however, the information is derived from the earlier edition, and there is no other convincing evidence for the number of typesetters involved.

2. It is clear, on D2*v* and D3*r*, in particular, that added verses of text were set with the music: this shows both in the quality of the impression, and when comparing alignments in the two extant copies.

No. 43. *Missarum Diversorum auctorum I*

15.iii.1508   *RISM* 1509¹

A1r]   Miſſarum diverſor*um* | auctoru3 Liber | primus. | Si dedero Obreth. | De fra*n*za Philippus baſiron. | Dringhs Brumel. | Naſtu pas Gaſpar. | De ſancto Antonio Piero de | la rue.

C1r]   Libri primi miſſarum Diuerſoru3 autor*um* | T

D1r]   Libri primi miſſar*um* Diuerſoru3 autor*um* | A

F1r]   Libri primi miſſar*um* Diuerſoru3 autor*um* | B

G6r]   Impreſſum Uenetijs per Octauianum Pe|trutiu3 Foroſempronienſem. 1508. Die. 15 | Martij. C*um* priuilegio i*n*uictiſſimi Dominij | Uenetiarum q*ua*e nullus poſſit cantu*m* Figura-|tum imprimere ſub pena in ipſo priuilegio | contenta. Regiſtru*m*. AA BB CC DD | EE FF GG O*mn*es quaterni pr*ae*ter BB CC | q*ui* su*nt* quinterni ꝫ GG qui eſt ternus. | [Petrucci's device]

Format and collation: Part-books: landscape quarto-in-eights. [C] 16 folios: A⁸B⁸; [T] 10 folios: C¹⁰; [A] 16 folios: D⁸E⁸; [B] 14 folios: F⁸G⁶ • Note that the Register, as printed by Petrucci, wrongly states that gathering B has ten folios

Signatures:] X AA 2 [$4 • − A1 and G4 • + C5

No foliation or pagination

Headlines: These were evidently not kept in the forme, but reset for each page

verso:] Jacobu5 obreth Si dedero [C1 • Obreth Si dedero. [D1 • Jacob*us* obreth Si dedero [F1 • Si dedero. [A2-5, D2-5 (the point does not always show) • Si dedero [C3, F2-5 • Philippus Baſiron. Meſſa de franza. [A6 • Philipus baſiron [C3 • Meſſa de franza. [A7-8, D7 • La meſſa de franza [C4 • Meſſe de franza. [D6-7 • Meſſa de franza [F6-7 • De dringhs. [B1-2 • Brumel De dringhis [D8 • De dringhis [E2, F8 • De dringhi5 [E1 • Gaſpar. Naſtu pas. [B3 • Gaſpar naſtu pas

[G1 • Naſtu pas. [B4 • Naſtu pas [C7-8, E3-4, G2 • Piero de la rue. De ſancto Antonio. [B5 • Piero de la rue De ſancto anthonio [G3 • Piero de la rue. De ſancto anthonio [E5 • De ſancto antonio. [B6 • De ſancto antonio. [B7 • De ſancto Anthonio [C9 • De ſancto anthonio [E6-7, G4,5 • Nil: A1, B8, C5,6,10, E8, G6

recto:] Jacobus obreth. Si dedero. [A2 • Si dedero. [A3-6, D2-5 (the point does not always show) • Si dedero [C2-3, F2-5 • Meſſa de franza. [A7-8 • La meſſa de franſia [C4 • Meſſe de franza. [D6 • Meſſa de franza [D7, F6-7 • Meſſe franza. [D8 • Antonius Brumel. De dringhs. [B1 • De dringhs. [B2-3 • Dringhs [C7 • De dringhis [E1,3, F8, G1 • De dringhi5 [E2 • Naſtu pas. [B4-5 • Naſtu pas [C8, E4-5, G2-3 • Piero de la rue De ſancto anthonio [C9 • De ſancto antonio. [B6 • De ſancto antonio. [B7-8 • De ſancto Anthonio [C10, G5 • De ſancto anthonio [E6-8, G4 • Nil: A1, C1,5,6, D1, F1, G6

One caption is in the left margin, to read vertically from the top:] Gaſpar Naſtu pas [C7r

Others are tucked in at the head of a piece:] Gaſpar Naſtu pas [E3r • Philipus baſiron Meſſa de franza [F5v • A. Brumel De dringhis [F7v

Fonts: Music: Petrucci's normal music type

Staves: Six per page, 175–180 mm long, 10-92-112 mm high

Text: Rotonda

Textual comments: The Altus is very short of text throughout: though see the Commentary below
• B4v.i: the music is very widely spaced out

Technical comments: The practice of not inking the last, unused stave of a page, common in other titles, is not followed here: thus there are blank sixth staves on nine pages • A small capital is used on G5r [S] • The different customs of using points in the headlines tend to point to the presence of two typesetters • D4r: the rubric of] Verte [appears on the direction line, rather than with the last stave

In-house corrections: A1r: the phrase] Piero de | la rue. [is a later addition, apparently printed at a second run through the press: in all copies • C1r, D1r and Fr: the phrase] Libri primi miſſar*um* Diuerſoru3 autor*um* [is a later stamped-in addition in all copies except that at D-Mu • C4v.i.24: b, d in the copy at I-Vnm (changed to f in manuscript): stop-press correction to f in those at A-GÜ, GB-Lbl and I-Bc • C7v.v.33–43: a line at each side, and the word] vacat [below: A-GÜ, D-Mbs, D-Mu, GB-Lbl, I-Bc and I-Vnm • D4v.iii.11–18: an added leger line, after a stop-press correction in the copy at D-B, and as later manuscript additions in those at GB-Lbl and I-Bc • E4v.vi.after 50: an added *m* rest in faint brown ink: D-B, D-Mbs, GB-Lbl and I-Bc • F2v.iv.after 29: four tailed notes, f,g,a,f, with *m* rest → dot,*smd,me,dmf,smg,ma,mf,m*rest, all in brown ink: D-Mbs, D-Mu, GB-Lbl and I-Bc • F3r.v.55: *sb*, f → g, erased and stamped in: GB-Lbl • F3r.v.53–56: ligature *bg+ba,sbf,bf* → ligature *dbg+ba* (dot in brown ink),*sbf,sb*rest in brown ink,*bf*: D-Mbs • F3r.v.53–57: ligature *bg+ba,sbf,bf,b*rest,*sbg*: all but the first two erased → ligature *dbg+ba* (dot in brown ink),*sbg,bf,b*rest (all three stamped in),*sb*rest (by erasure),*sbg* (untouched): D-Mu (with a further change by Glareanus) • F3v.v.3: g, *sb* → *m*: as a stop-press correction in the copies at GB-Lbl and I-Bc, as a stamped-in correction in that at D-Mbs, and as a later manuscript correction in that at D-Mu • F4r.iii.k.s.: c → B: as a stop-press correction in the copy at I-Bc, and corrected later by hand in that at GB-Lbl • G3r.ii.24: *sb*, d → c, erased and stamped in, in the copies at D-Mbs, D-Mu, and I-Bc: erased and manuscript addition in that at GB-Lbl

Contents:

	A1r	C1r	D1r	F1r	[Title]	
	A1v				[blank]	
I	A2r	C1v	D1v	F1v	[Missa] Si dedero	Jacobus obreth.
	A2v.iii	C1v.ii	D2r.iii	F2r	[Gloria]	

	A3v	C1v.iii	D3r	F2v.vi	[Credo]	
	A4v	C1v.iv	D4r.ii	F3v.iv	[Sanctus]	
	A5v.iii	C1v.vi	D5r.iii	F4v.v	[Agnus]	
		C2r.iv			[The same Tenor:] Ad longum	
		C2r.vi			[Gloria]	
		C2v.iii			[Credo]	
		C3r			[Sanctus]	
		C3r.iv			[Agnus]	
2	A6v	C3v	D6r	F5v.iii	Messa de franza	Philippus Basiron
	A6v.v	C3v.iv	D6r.v	F5v.vi	[Gloria]	
	A7r.vi	C4r.iv	D7r	F6r.v	[Credo]	
	A8r.i	C4v.v	D7v.iii	F6v.v	[Sanctus]	
	A8v.iv	C5r.v	D8r.iv	F7r.v	[Agnus]	
3	B1r.iii	C5v.ii	D8v.ii	F7v.iv	[Missa] De dringhs	Antonius Brumel
	B1r.v	C5v.v	D8v.v	F8r	[Gloria]	
	B1v.iv	C6r.iii	E1r.v	F8r.v	[Credo]	
	B2v	C6v.v	E2r.iii	G1r	[Sanctus]	
	B3r.iv	C7r.ii	E3r	G1r.iv	[Agnus]	
4	B3v	C7r.iv	E3r.v	G1v	[Missa] Nastu pas	Gaspar
	B3v.iv	C7v	E3v.ii	G1v.iv	[Gloria]	
	B4r.iii	C7v.v	E4r	G2r.ii	[Credo]	
	B4v.iv	C8r.vi	E4v.ii	G2v.iii	[Sanctus]	
	B5r.iii	C8v.iv	E5r.ii	G3r.iii	[Agnus]	
5	B5v	C9r.ii	E5v	G3v	[Missa] de sancto Antonio	Piero de la rue
	B5v.vi	C9r.iv	E5v.v	G3v.v	[Gloria]	
	B6v	C9v.iii	E6v	G4v	[Credo]	
	B7r.v	C10r	E7r.iv	G5r.iii	[Sanctus]	
	B8r	C10r.iv	E8r	G5v.iii	[Agnus]	
				G6r	[Colophon; Register; Device]	
	B8v	C10v	E8v	G6v	[blank]	

Extant copies:

A-GÜ, s.s. Tenor part, complete

   Size of page: 165 × 235 mm

   Watermarks: No.23 on C2, C4 and C5

   In-house changes: C7v: see above

   Binding and Provenance: With Josquin, *II Missarum* (1515, No.59)

   Bibliography: Federhofer, "Petrucci"

D-B, N.Mus.ant.pract.51. Altus complete

   Size of page: 159 × 223 mm.

   Watermarks: No.23 on D2, D5, E3 and E8. It measures 28 × 28 mm on D2

   Technical comments: D1v.left margin: a large piece of furniture, 18.8 × 2.2 mm and with a grid pattern on the surface, has taken ink • E3r.vi.10: the leger line was printed before the note, making a deep impression and preventing the centre of the note from impressing the paper

   Corrections and changes:

      In-house: E4v: see above

Later: D2r.ii.rest after 3: *b → m*, with a crude erasure • D4v.i.4 from end: *m → sb*, erased tail: stave-lines touched up in brown • D5v.iii.6: a, *dsb → sb*, by erasure of the point • E3r.iii.51: c', *sm → m*, scratched void • E3v.ii-E4r.vi: added text to the Gloria and Credo of the *Missa Nastu pas*, in brown ink. The German hand uses a great many abbreviations: after the printed words] ꝛ re[urrexit [the manuscript reads] 3ᵃ die 2ᵐ [etc • E5v.iv.4: b, *sm → m*, scratched void

Binding and Provenance: With *Misse Gaspar* (1507, No.32)

D-Mbs, 4°.mus.pr.160. Complete

Size of page: 165 × 235/237 mm.

Watermarks: No.23 on A2, A3, B4, B8, C7, C10, D2, D3, E6, E7, F5, F8, G1, and G3

Technical comments: C1r. a vertical line of uninked notes, perhaps *semiminims*, has left a blind impression on each side of the page • D1v.left margin: the large piece of furniture seen on the Berlin copy has also taken ink here

Corrections and changes:

> **In-house:** C7v, E4v, F2v, F3r, F3v and G3r. see above
>
> **Later:** Roman pencil numeration at the start of each mass • A2r.i.after 36: rest, *b → sb*, by erasure • B3v-4r. modern rhythm signs, in pencil • D2r.ii-iii: apparently pen doodles • D3v.ii.5 from end: *b*, apparently an erased p.d. • D4v.i.4 from end: *m → sb*, erased tail • D6v.v.10: *l*, ?e → f, erasure and brown ink • E1v.ii.below bar-line:] duo [in brown ink, and smudged onto E2r • E3v.v.16: *sb*, apparently colored by hand • F4r.vi.end: *me*, *mf*, *sbg*, *sbd*, *lG → mf* erased, *mg* with a brown tail • F5v.iii.1-2: p.d.erased after 1 and added after 2, brown ink

Binding: With *Misse Obreht* and *Motetti C* • Original pale vellum, with two sewing bands per book. On each top board, the relevant part-name is entered • Each book except the Superius has two fly-leaves at the front, and each has two at the back. In addition, one leaf is bound in after the *Misse Obreht*

Provenance: From the Electoral library. Previously in the possession of Johannes Moibam of Passau (or possibly Padua), 1551, and perhaps of Franciscus Altovisi, potentially a member of the Florentine family of Altoviti (c.f. inscriptions on the Bassus book).

> Superius: Inside front board: part of the bookplate:] EX ELECTORALI BIBLIO-|THECA SERENISS. VTRIVSQ*VE* | BAVARIAE DVCVM • On A1r:] Di[s z. zü[smen 30. | Sum [. . .] | Patavij 1551 • verso of back fly-leaf:] Soranus [twice] • [Inside back board:] Amor actio ac la[[o ormai son [ta rietro | Amor mio te ho vi[to tanto da lontano • [on A1r of *Motetti C*:] Soranus monsill[?]
>
> Tenor: Inside front board: full electoral book-plate • On A1r:] Sum [. . .] | Patavij 1551 • On back board: a list of the contents of Petrucci's *Misse Josquin*, in a different order, and an Italian poem
>
> Altus: inside front board: the bookplate has been removed • On A1r:] Sum [. . .] | Patavij 1551 • On back board:] lauro
>
> Bassus: front board outside has some illegible Italian text • Inside front board: book-plate has been removed • first fly-leaf, recto:] domine deu[no[tra [icut abra*ham* a[. . .] ego | in sechulo [and musical doodles • A1r:] Sum Johannis Moibam, | Patavij 1551 • back fly-leaf, verso, written several times, inverted:] [orgorra *per* Dio al mis*ser* Corry • Back board, inverted:] Fran^cus Altovi[i [and] Muovodoni[?]

D-Mu, Cim.44ᵐ (1). Tenor and Bassus, complete

Size of page: 171 × 229 and 168 × 233 mm.

Watermarks: No.23 on C1, C4, F3, F8, G1, and G4

Corrections and changes:

> **In-house:** C7*v*, F2*v*, F3*r*, F3*v* and G3*r*: see above
>
> **Later:** C1*r*.after T:] ENOR • C1*v*.margin:] Hypiastius • C3*r*.i.15: *signum*, in ink •
> C3*v*.margin:] Hypodorius • C3*v*.vi.after 13: bar-line, in dark brown ink • C5*v*.margin:]
> Hypodorij • C7*r*.margin:] Hypoionia | & Tm • C9*r*.margin:] Aeolius uno super|ne
> definiens tono quem in[true|muerit • F1*r*.after the letter B:] ARYTONANS • F1*v*.foot,
> probably a binding instruction:] .N. • F2*r*.ii.1: *signum*, in ink • F2*v*.vi − F5*v*.ii: flat sig-
> nature struck through on all systems, with two lines in brown ink • F3*r*.v.9 from end
> to the end (see Petrucci's change above): dots above all notes, and (in Glareanus's hand)
> a different version in the margin: *lg*, ligature *bg+ba,lf,brest,sbg,dsbg,smf,sme,custos* •
> F4*r*.vi.4 from end: tail erased and later redrawn • F5*v*.iii.1−2: p.d. erased after 1 and
> redrawn after 2, in grey ink • G2*r*.i.under first rests: dots beneath, and, in a faint brown
> ink and in Glareanus's hand, in the margin: rests, probably *b,sb,sb,m,m* • G2*v*.i.before 6
> from end: first rest, *b* → *sb*, by erasure • G6*r*. The note that B is a quintern has been
> struck through

Binding: Bound with *Motetti C* • Leather binding, typical of Glareanus's bindings (according to
librarians at D-Mu) • One paste-down and three fly-leaves at each end of each book • Tenor,
on the front paste-down: the Sanctus of the *Missa Si dedero*, notated by Glareanus *ad longum*
• Bassus, on the front paste-down: the Sanctus of the *Missa Si dedero*, notated by Glareanus
ad longum, inscribed] In Mis[a Si dedero ad longam [and] Sanctus

Provenance: Glareanus • Bookplate of Joannes Egenolphus

GB-Lbl, K.1.d.8. Complete

Size of page: 159 × 219 mm.

Watermarks: No.23 on A1, A3, B5, B8, C5, C8, C9, D4, D8, E5, E7, F5, F7 and G6

Technical comments: The added section on A1*r* lies 0.3 mm too low • A3*r*.iv: spacing sort in
the left margin, 2.5 × 3.5 mm • D1*v*.left margin: furniture, 18.8 × 2.2 mm, as in the Berlin
copy • F1*r*: the initial B has a manuscript addition at the foot to replace damage to the letter

Corrections and changes:

> **In-house:** A1*r*, C4*v*, C7*v*, E4*v*, F2*v*, F3*r*, F3*v*, F4*r* and G3*r*: see above
>
> **Later:** A few of these correspond to in-house changes in other copies, but do not seem to
> have been done by Petrucci's shop: B6*v*.ii.2: *sm*, b' → c'', with a touched-up leger line,
> in dark brown ink • Tenor has pencil pagination:] 63–72 • D4*v*.iii.11–18: ink leger line
> • E3*r*.iii.51: c' *sm* → *m*, scratched void • E3*r*.iii.58: end of leger line erased, and a new
> one drawn, to change the pitch from e to d: the letter "C" added in dark ink, later •
> F2*v*.iv.after 29: a significant erasure has been replaced by d*sm,em,fdm,gsm,asb,fm,m* rest,
> to be followed by the original d*m,em,fm* • F3*v*.ii.27: *sb*, colored and centre erased •
> F3*v*.ii.31: ?*sm* → *m*, scratched void • F3*v*.v.after the rest after 56: added *sb* rest •
> F4*r*.iii.signature: flat, c → B, erasure and black ink • G3*r*.ii.24: *sb*, ?d → c, in black
> ink

Binding: British Museum binding, dated 1905 • Three British Museum flyleaves and one earlier
at the front, two at the back

Bibliography: Johnson and Scholderer, *Short-Title*, p. 425

I-Bc, Q.69. Complete

Size of page: 164 × 237 mm.

Watermarks: No.23 on A3, A8, B4, B8, C1, C4, D1, D3, E1, E3, F6, F7, and G1 • The twin
marks are very clear in this copy, one being on A8, B4, B8, D3, and F6, and the other on
all other folios

Corrections and changes:

> **In-house:** C7*v*, E4*v*, F2*v* and G3*r.* see above

> **Later:** Manuscript pagination: [S] 114–129; [T] 74–83; [A] 112–127; [B] 100–113 • A1*r.* a repeated ascription to] de La Rue [using a rebus, entered twice • A2*r.*i.after 36: rest*b* → *sb*, by erasure • D4*v*.iii.11–18: ink leger line • F3*v*.ii.27: *sb*, colored and centre erased • F3*v*.ii.33: *b*, colored in manuscript • G6*r.* The note that B is a quintern has been struck through

Binding: Each part in a buff card wrapper, all held in a folder like that used for Agricola's masses • All edges painted gold

Provenance: This copy is cited in Martini's letters to Chiti of 7.v.1746 and 22.vii.1746 • Old catalogue number 1012 • From the pagination, originally bound with Agricola's *Misse* (1504, No.13)

Bibliography: Schnoebelen, *Padre*, Nos.1245 and 1250, pp. 144–45

I-Mc, S.B.178/5. Superius, complete

Size of page: 164 × 233 mm.

Watermarks: No.23 on A4, A7 and B5

Later corrections and changes: Modern pencil foliation:] 69–84 • B6*v*.ii.6 from end: c', *m* → *sb*, by erasure • B6*v*.ii.4 from end: *m*, either f' or e', erased

Binding: With Josquin, *II Missarum* (1515, No.59)

Provenance: Sta Barbara, Mantua • perhaps the Chapel of Cardinal Ippolito d'Este

Bibliography: Damerini, "Esposizione", p. 25 (exhibition at Florence, in 1949) • Lockwood, "Adrian", p. 99 • Prizer, "Cappella", p. 275

I-Vnm, Mus.209–211. Superius, Tenor and Altus, complete

Size of page: 161 × 230 mm.

Watermarks: No.23 on A6, A8, B4, B8, C4, C9, D5, D7, E1, and E5

Technical comments: B1*r.* the signature was apparently printed with the music forme • E3*r*.vi.10: see the comments under the copy at D-B • Stave-lines are described below

Corrections and changes:

> **In-house:** C4*v* and C7*v*: see above

> **Later:** Manuscript piece numbers in each book:] 340–364 • 19th-century thick pencil annotations on A4*r*.v; A5*v*.vi; A6*r*.v.34; C2*r*.ii.28; C7*v*.v-vi.43–45; C10*r*.i.1–2; D3*v*.end; D5*r*.i; and E2*v*.v • A4*v*.iv.28–29: c.o.p. ligature, g'-g: the linking line between the notes appears to have been drawn by hand • C3*r*.above iv: in brown ink:] B*enedictu*s tacet

Binding: Austrian National Library binding. One paste-down and one fly-leaf at each end of each book • The Tenor also has two folios from earlier bindings: the first has horizontal chainlines and no mark, and is probably 18th-century; the second is perhaps 16th-century, has vertical chainlines and shows the lower half of a mark of an anchor in a circle. Both these have worm holes corresponding to those in the book

Provenance: One of the volumes taken to A-Wn: the Austrian call-mark label shows inside the front board:] S.A.77.C.10 • Acquisition number on the front board:] 20585 • From the pagination, originally bound with Josquin: *Misse* (1502, No.4)

Bibliography: Fenlon and Dalla Vecchia, *Venezia*, pp. 81–82 (exhibition catalogue, Venice, 2001)

Other copies: A copy of the Discantus was offered by the Antiquariat Hans Schneider, in Catalogue 330, as No.19

Lost copies: Copies were owned by Colón (Chapman, "Printed", No.34) and Bottrigari • It is probable that there was a copy in the Fugger library (Schaal, "Musikbibliothek", I/60)

Bibliography:

(a) Rosaria Boccadifuoco, *Bibliografia*, No.2246 • Sartori, *Petrucci*, No.41

(c) Apel, *Notation*, 183 (folio C1v only) and 185, other voices of the Sanctus of No.1 • Petrucci, *Missarum diversos*

(e) Sartori, "Nuove", p. 205

Commentary:

1. This title should be entered under 1508, following Sartori. The Venetian New Year began on 1 March.

2. The printed texting in this volume is very old-fashioned. It often gives no more than the incipits of phrases, and shows much less concern for accuracy than in previous volumes. That this reflects the exemplar rather than the craftsman is suggested by the changes in pattern. The figures for additional phrases of text that follow are necessarily to some extent arbitrary: it is difficult in some cases to decide whether the presence of words represents one phrase or two, and the use of, for example, *Pleni* rather than *Pleni sunt*, has not been distinguished if the two words are set close together. For the Agnus, therefore, the presence of either "Agnus" or "Agnus Dei" (when without an extended space between the words) has been regarded as one occurrence. The columns are numbered in sequence: 1 = Kyrie; 2 = Et in terra; 3 = Qui tollis; 4 = Patrem; 5 = Crucifixus; 6 = Sanctus; 7 = Pleni; 8 = Osanna; 9 = Benedictus; 10 Agnus:

	1	2	3	4	5	6	7	8	9	10
Missa Si dedero										
Cantus	0	0	0	0	0	1	0	0	0	2
Tenor	0	0	0	0	0	1	0	0	0	1
Altus	0	0	0	0	0	0	-	0	-	1
Bassus	3	0	0	0	0	0	0	0	0	2
Missa De Franza										
Cantus	0	7	9	6	8	4	1	1	2	3 + 4
Tenor	0	7	11	0	1	0	0	0	0	0
Altus	0	4	1	2	3	0	0	1	0	0
Bassus	0	4	1	2	3	1	0	1	0	0
Missa De dringhs										
Cantus	0	9	8	10	14	7	4	1	4	5
Tenor	0	8	12	0	1	0	0	0	0	0
Altus	0	2	1	2	10	3	2	0	0	0
Bassus	0	1	3	3	4	0	-	0	-	0
Missa Nastu pas										
Cantus	0	6	7	8	11	4	2	1	3	7
Tenor	0	8	12	0	1	0	0	0	0	0
Altus	0	0	0	7	6	1	1	0	1	3
Bassus	0	3	4	6	6	3	1	-	0	0
Missa S. Antonio										
Cantus	0	11	13	10	17	1	2	0	4	0
Tenor	1	3	4	6	9	0	-	0	2	0

Altus	o	9	3	8	11	o	2	o	4	o
Bassus	o	11	6	8	9	o	1	o	o	o

Thus, in most sections of the *Missa Si dedero*, only the first word is given. In the other masses, phrases of text are regularly inserted within sections. For the last mass, there are nearly as many inserted phrases in the lower voices as in the Cantus, and the *Missa de Dringhs* has much additional texting for the Gloria or Credo in Tenor and Altus. The other masses show similarly distinct patterns of texting. These results can not be correlated with the patterns of treating running head-lines, discussed below, which seem to suggest the presence of two craftsmen. Therefore, it seems much more likely that the pattern presented here points to each mass being drawn from a different exemplar, each representing a different scribal practice.

3. Note that the titles are set as are those of *Fragmenta Missarum*. That is, that the part-initial seems integral to the printing, but, in the lower voices, the title of the book is a later addition, in a small fount which is used in later books to indicate the title. The evidence of this later impression is particularly clear in the copy of the Altus at D-B: while the "A" has impressed quite lightly, the rest of the page (including the signature) has left a much heavier impression on the verso.

    The change is not found on every copy of the present title, although it does survive on every extant copy of the *Fragmenta Missarum*, printed some three years earlier. However, the few intervening titles published in part-books (masses of Isaac and Gaspar — late 1506 and early 1507 respectively) do not have the full titles on the lower parts. Nor does the 1508 edition of motets for five voices. It is very tempting therefore to suggest that the change in title-page practice took place during 1508, and was largely a response to the need to distinguish the two anthology books of mass music.

4. Stave lines (measured from the bottom line of each page in the copy at Venice) indicate that by this time Petrucci had four skeleton formes, two pairs of similar lengths:

	1r	2v	3r	4v	1v	2r	3v	4r
A outer	—	179	179	179	—	176	176	176
A inner	179	179	180	180	176	176	176	176
B outer	180	180	180	—	177	176	176	176
B inner	179	179	180	179	176	177	175	176
C outer	—	177	176	—	179	179	180	179
C second	177	176	176	176	179	179	179	180
C inner	179	179			180	179		
D outer	—	180	180	179	176	177	176	176
D inner	179	180	180	181	176	176	176	176
E outer	180	180	180	—	176	176	177	177
E inner	179	179	180	181	176	176	177	177

For the longer pair of staves, there is one for which both the later pages are marginally longer than the earlier, and another in which the last is shorter than the third; for the shorter pair, the evidence is inconclusive. Once again, the presence of a half-sheet in a gathering affects the sequence by which they are used.

5. Points at the ends of running head-lines are found in all entries in the Superius, and most of gathering D of the Altus; there are no points in the Tenor or Bassus or gathering E of the Altus. In addition, there are no head-lines at all in the inner half-sheet of gathering C. Although there is so far no other evidence to support this, it does suggest that two typesetters were involved.

No. 44. Giovanni Maria Alemannus: *Intabulatura III*

20.vi.1508

Not extant.

The title probably read as follows (adapting Colón's entry to conform with the other lute volumes):]

    Intabulatura di Lauto, Libro Tertio Joannis marie alemanij

An alternative title would follow the form of the citation for Herwart's copy:

    Di Joanmaria intabulatura de lauto libro terzo

Format: Landscape format: probably quarto in eights

Contents:

	[The same introduction found in Spinacino, in Italian]	
	[The same, in Latin]	
1	Comme femme	
25	Recercar	Giouan maria

———

Lost copies: Copies were owned by Colón (Anglés, "Colombina", p. 28; Chapman, "Printed", No.30; Huntington, *Catalogue*; Jeppesen, "Neuentdeckten", p. 81; Plamenac, "Excerpta", p. 679) and Herwart (Martinez-Göllner, "Herwart", p. 47)

Bibliography:

    (a) Sartori, *Petrucci*, No.37; Brown, *Instrumental*, [1508]₁.

    (e) Sartori, "Nuove", p. 202 • Vernarecci, *Petrucci*, p. 112

Commentary:

1.   It is tempting to think that the first piece was introduced with the same large initial that had been found on the title-pages of *Canti C* and *Motetti C*. The opening compositions of the first and second books of this series (the work of Francesco Spinacino) had been chosen so that they might use the initials *A* and *B*, respectively

No. 45. Dammonis: *Laude I*

7.vii.1508   *RISM* D 833 I,1

There were two editions of this book: for the first, see No.29, above

Second Edition

A1r]   Laude Libro Primo. | Jn. dammonis. | Curarum dulce lenimen.

H8r]   Impreſſum Venetiis per Octauianum Pe-|trutium Foroſempronienſem. M.D.viii. Die vii |

Iulii Cum priuilegio inuictiſſimi Dominii | Venetiarum quae nullus poſſit cantum Figuratum | imprimere [ub pena in ipso priuilegio contenta. | Regiſtrum. | AA BB CC DD EE FF GG HH Omnes quaterni. | [Petrucci's device]

A1v]   F. Innocentius Dammonis reuerendo in Chriſto patri Seraphino Veneto eiuſdem | regularium Canonicorum Congregationis Diui Saluatoris Viſitatori digniſſi- | mo patri plurimum obſeruando. S.P.D.

Et religionis noſtræ uinculo quod apud me maximi [emper momenti fuit: & tua in | me animi inductione [ingulari pater optime omnia mea tibi debeo: & quamuis | tibi alii quoque omnes conſecranei mei debeant: quicquid poſt uotum nuncupa- | tum habere uideantur: ego tamen neſcio quo pacto & ea tibi debeo quæ cæteri | & aliquid etiam amplius: quo fit ut cum laudes quaſdam [ubitario quodam ca- | lore a me æditas: diuerſis quoque numinibus nuncupatas muſica ratione comtexi[- | ſem: dicandas tibi illas præcipuo quodam ardore duxerim. Cui enim dicari meli | us poterant quam parenti meo? quam uitæ inſtitutori? quam omnis [anctitatis | & pietatis exemplari mirifico. Canes igitur tu interdum iſtæc dum aliquod defa | tigati animi oblectamentum queres: non [olum quod muſica ars optimum quem- | que [emper decuit: [i modo [ancta [i uirilis [i casta illa fuerit: [ed quod deo: quod | eius genitrici: quod aliis numinibus iſtæ concinuntur: qui & uerborum uim & | cum uerbis modulatam quandam cantilenam exigunt adeo ut religionis no- | [træ columina tum ueteris tum noui inſtrumenti magnum [ibi hinc & pietatis | in deum & in homines religionis argumentum [perarint. Vale.

A2r]   Tavola: In three columns in roman type. Arranged in approximately modern alphabetical order. The sequence strives for true alphabetical ordering (with some anomalies) until the entry for folio 54 (G6r). Thereafter, titles are appended to the relevant letter

Format and collation: Choirbook: landscape quarto-in-eights. 64 folios: A-H⁸

Signatures:] AA 2 [$4 • − A1

Foliation: t.r.r.] [1], 2-9, [10], 11–21, [22, probably present, but page cropped], 23–37, [38, ?present], 39–63, [64]: this includes folios 25, 26, 31, 32 and 43–46, which are sheets of the first edition, but preserved in the unique copy

Part-names: in the left margin

Fonts: Music: Petrucci's normal music type

Staves: six per page (although six actually appear on only about 15 pages)

Text: Roman throughout, "20" = 57 mm, on B2r. A Rotonda font is used for the title-page. A large Roman font is used for the Dedication: "10" = 54 mm and "x" = about 2.2 mm.

A hand is used to indicate the placement of the continuation of a part, on A5v and A6r

Textual comments: A significant number of gathering joins (— A-B, B-C, C-D, G-H —) have single-page pieces on each face of the opening

Technical comments: The feature of starting a three-page piece on a recto, found on C1r, D5r, D7r and G7r, is a little unusual. The implication is strong that the house editor or the typesetter was aware of the refrain-and-verse structure of the texts • The initial capital letter is missing on D4v [M]: a small initial was used on D6v [M] • The absence of the folio number on B2r is almost certainly because there was also no music on the page. Thus the part of the music forme containing this page was not inked at all.

In-house corrections: All these are in the unique copy: A2v: the phrase] Canonis dy[tichon [has been stamped in later • A6r.iii.42–44: 3 × xsb, e',e',e' → d',d',d': erased and stamped in • A8v: the Bassus texted seems to have been inserted later • B3r.i.12: sb, originally void, filled in with printer's ink • B3r.i.14: sm → m, by scratching clear the center of the note-head

Contents: including the contents of the leaves from the first edition:

	A1r	[Title]	
	A1v	[Dedication]	
	A2r	[Tavola:] Laude numero lxvii [*recte* 66]	
1	A2v	TE invocamus te adoramus	à6 ex 4
		[Headed: A. 6. F. Innocentii Dammonis ceter*eque* ſequentes	
		[T,A,S2:] Trinitas deitas epualis [*sic*] vnitas	
		[Canon:] Canonis dyſticon. Tres ſunt perſonæ ac vna	
		eſt ſubſtantia ſimplex | Prima per octauam (duplex fuga) & altera	
		quartæ	
2	A3v	ADoramus te Christe	à6 ex 5
		[Canon:] Secundi cantus canon tenor loquitur | Quem mecum	
		reſonare iuuat duo tempora pauſet | Octaua ſuperans me &	
		ſuperans erit.	
3	A4v	SPirito ſancto amore	
4	A5v	VBi caritas & amor	à3
5	A6v	DA che tu mhai idio il cor ferito	
6	A7v	DA che tu mhai ieſu moſtra la via	
7	A8v	POi che da me partiſti	
		[Headed:] Eiuſdem verba]	
8	B1r	AIme dolce mio dio	
9	B1v	IEſu dulcis memoria	
10	B2v	SAlue mundi ſalutare	
		[Headed:] Ad crucifixum	
11	B3v	VErbu*m* caro factum eſt	
	B4v	2/ Sine viri copula	
	B5v	3/ Ab angelis pſallitur	
12	B6v	VErbum caro factum eſt	
13	B7v	LAudiam lamor diuino	
		[Headed:] De natiuitate	
14	B8r	TVtti debiam cantare	
		[Headed:] De natiuitate	
15	B8v	AMor ieſu diuino	à5
16	C1r	CVm iubili damore	
		[Headed:] De natiuitate	
	C1v	2 | Andiam tutti cantando	
17	C2v	AVe maria gratia plena	
		[Headed:] Ad beatam virginem	
		2| S*an*cta maria mater dei	
18	C3v	O Glorioſa vergine maria	
		[Headed:] Ad beatam virginem	
19	C4r	STabat mater doloroſa	
		[Headed:] Ad beatam virgine*m*	
20	C4v	VErgine benedecta Del ciel imperatrice	
		[Headed:] Ad beatam virginem	
21	C5v	AVe virgo glorioſa par[a]diſi rubens roſa	
		[Headed:] Ad beatam virginem	

22	C6r	GAude virgo mater chriſti	à3
		[Headed:] Gaudia virginis	
23	C6v	GAude virgo mater chriſti	
		[Head-line cropped, probably ends:] virginis	
24	C7v	GAude flore virginali	
		[Headed:] Gaudia beate virginis	
25	C8v	AL bel fonte ſacro e degno	
		[B:] Al del fonte	
26	D1r	O Maria diuina ſtella	
		[Headed:] De beata virgine	
27	D1v	O Madre ſancta o luce	
28	D2v	O Madre del ſignore	
		[Headed:] Te matrem	
	D3v	2| Spoſa del padre eterno noi ſapemo	
29	D4v	[M]Adre che feſti collui	
		[Headed:] Ad beatam virginem	
	D5v	2| Porzi ſoccorſo o verzene gentile	
30	D5r	MAria del ciel regina	
		[Headed:] De beata virgine	
31	D6v	MAria miſericordia	
		[Headed:] Ad beatam virginem	
32	D7r	MAria madre de dio	
		[Headed:] Ad beatam virginem	
	D7v	[verse:] Vergine ſacre e figlia del tuo figlio	
33	D8v	SAlue regina di miſericordia	
		[Head-line cropped: [Ad beatam] virginem	
34	E1v	SAlve regina o germinante ramo	
		[Headed:] Laus beate virginis	
35	E2v	MAria drentalla tua corte	
		[Headed:] Ad beatam virginem	
36	E3v	VIrtu che fai in queſto miſer mondo	
		[Head-line completely cropped]	
	E4v	2| Superbia & auaritia	
37	E5v	COmo dinanzi a chriſto fuzirai	
		[Tavola:] Come denanzi xpo fu zera:	
38	E6v	SEmpre te ſia in diletto	
39	E7v	FVzite chriſtiani	
		[Headed:] De contemptu mundi	
		[Tavola:] Fugiti . . .	
40	E8v	O Vero amor celeſte	
		[Headed:] De inferuorato chriſti amore	
41	F1v	SOl mi ſol diſſe holoferno	
		[Headed:] De ſuperbia luciferi a uoce mudade eiuſdem verba	
42	F2v	DAmmi il tuo amore	
		[Headed:] De chriſti amore	
43	F3v	PEccatori perche ſeti tanto crudi	
		[Headed:] De paſſione	

44	F4*r*	HVmilmente tenuocho Ieſu
45	F4*v*	PIanzeti chriſtiani Il dolor de maria
		[Headed:] De paſſione [Tavola: Piangeti . . .
46	F5*v*	DE piangeti amaramente
		[Headed:] De paſſione eiuſdem verba
47	F6*v*	POpul mio popul ingrato
		[Headed:] De paſſione
48	F7*v*	O Peccatore ti mouerai tu mai
		[Headed:] De paſſione
49	F8*v*	O Croce alma mirabile
		[Headed:] De cruce
50	G1*v*	NOſtra interna & vera pace
		[Headed:] De pace Eiuſdem verba
51	G2*v*	CHi uol pace nel ſuo core
		[Headed:] De pace
52	G3*v*	DA poi che te laſciai
		[Tavola:] . . . lassai
53	G4*v*	SAlue regina glorie Maria ſtella maris
		[Headed:] Ad beatam virginem
54	G5*r*	O Stella matutina
		[Headed:] Ad beatam Virgine*m*
55	G5*v*	ADoramus te o ieſu chriſte
56	G6*v*	ANima beneditta
		[Tavola:] benedetta
57	G7*r*	ANima che del mondo uo fugire
	G7*v*	2| Guarda ſe le cagion
58	G8*v*	SE voi guſtar lamore
59	H1*r*	LAmor a me venendo
60	H1*v*	NEl to furore
		[Tavola:] Nel tuo . . .
61	H2*v*	IO ſon q*ue*l miſero ingrato
62	H3*v*	O Ieſu dolce o infinito amore
		[Omitted from the Tavola]
63	H4*v*	PEccatori ad vna voce
64	H5*v*	QVeſta e q*ue*lla croce grande
65	H6*v*	IEſu fami morire
66	H7*v*	LAſſo io moro
	H8*r*	[Colophon; Register; Device]
	H8*v*	[blank]

———

Extant copy:

E-Sc, 12-1-4. Complete. D outer and F inner are from the first edition.

> **Size of page:** 166 × 226 mm, but not cut square
>
> **Watermarks:** No.23 on A6, A7, B2, B5, C5, C8, D3, E4, E7, F8, G2, G3, H5, and H7
>
> **Technical comments:** A1*r*. a line of notes is used on either side of the title, to act as bearer
>> sorts, impressing in blind • A4*r*.vi and H7*r*.vi: a line of notes, perhaps *m*, is used as bearers
>
> **In-house corrections and changes:** see above

Binding: Parchment wrapper, with three sewing bands: two ties on either side, one of those on the back cover now lost. Traces of an old label on the spine. Front cover now detached • One paste-down at the front: at the back a paste-down and flyleaf, of Spanish paper

Provenance: Bought by Colón (Chapman, "Printed", No.35) • Front paste-down has the call number] R 9701 • On A1*r* are the call marks:] E KK | Tab 175.N°.45 [and] E . . . GG | Tab . . . 175 | n° . . . . 34 [and] 3045

Bibliography: Arboli y Farando, *Biblioteca*, ii, pp. 239–40 • Chapman, "Printed" • Fenlon and Dalla Vecchia, *Venezia*, pp. 80–81 (exhibition catalogue, Venice, 2001) • Jeppesen, "Neuentdeckten" • Trend, "Musikschätze"

———

Lost copies: Copies were owned by the Fuggers (Schaal, "Musikbibliothek", I/73) and by Bottrigari

Bibliography:

(a) Sartori, *Petrucci*, No.42

(c) Luisi, *Innocentius*

(d) Jeppesen, *Mehrstimmiger* • Luisi, *Laudario*

(e) Glixon, "Far una bella" • Glixon, "Polyphonic" • Luisi, *Laudario*

Commentary:

1. The first edition of this volume has to be assumed, from the presence of two sheets definitely earlier than the rest of the unique copy. The evidence is addressed in describing the remnants of that edition (No.29, above). The hints in the second edition of late changes and of the composer's continuing influence are unusual, but the evidence for the earlier edition is conclusive.

2. There is no problem with the date of the second edition: for example, Petrucci's mark (on H8*r*) is certainly in a worse state than as found in *Laude II*.

3. There are interesting signs that the second edition was expanded at a late stage in its preparation. In the Tavola, the last works, from G5*v*, seem to have been added later. Significantly, none of these works was given a heading, as had been common for almost all the preceding compositions. (Some of the earlier pieces probably had headlines, which were lost in the severe cropping of the book for binding: however, there is ample room for such a heading on the last folios of gathering G.) One of these last works is not even listed in the Tavola.

    It is unlikely that these features would be carried over to a second edition from the first: this is surely particularly true of the arrangement of the Tavola.

    In addition, this book, rather unusually, has eight gatherings. Of the nine frottola books published in Venice, only one (Book III of 1505 with eight) did not have seven gatherings: all three extant books of tabulature, the first of Bossinensis's settings, and one of Lamentations also had seven. (The first book of Lamentations only had six gatherings, although I have suggested that there was some anomaly in preparing this book.) Given that this volume has the other signs of a change in gathering G, it appears that this edition was expanded from the first.

4. This adds another issue: it argues that Dammonis was still able to influence Petrucci's decisions. Perhaps the book had been particularly successful, perhaps Dammonis (or even Petrucci) had been asked to include specific additional works, or perhaps Petrucci was merely short of competent readers to check the printed text, and Dammonis did the work. Certainly, Dammonis has to be seen as still associated with Petrucci himself. This is particularly interesting given the view

expressed by both Jeppesen (*Mehrstimmige*, lxx–lxx) and Glixon ("Polyphonic", pp. 34–38), that Book II (published only six months before this second edition of Book I) is unusually inaccurate.

No. 46. *I Motetti à5*

[28.xi.1508]   *RISM* 1508[1]

A1r]	Motetti a cinque Libro │ primo.
C1r]	T B
F1r]	Contratenor primus
H1r]	Contratenor secundus: not extant
perhaps J6r]	Colophon, register, mark: not extant
A1v	[Tavola:]

Motetti acinque numero xviii

Aue maria Pipelare.	xii
Aue maria. Regis.	xvi
Aue ſctiſſima. Diniſet	xvii
Clangat. Regis.	I
Dulcis amica dei. Gaſpar	iii
Exaudi nos filia. Criſpin	xv
Factor orbis. Obreth	II
Homo quidam. Ioſquin	v
Hodie ſcietis. Iſac	xviii
Illibata. Ioſquin	iiii
Inuiolata. Iſac	vii
Laudemus nunc dominuȝ. Obreth	Ix
Lux ſolempnis. Regis	xi
Mater patris. Obreth	xiiii
O precioſiſſime Obreth	xiii
O decus eccleſie. Iſac	vi
Requiem. Ioſquin	viii
Salue ſponſa. Regis	x

Format and collation: Partbooks: landscape quarto-in-eights. [S] 16 folios: A-B[8]; [T and B] 20 folios: C-D[8]E[4]; [CT I] 14 folios: F[8]G[6]; [CT II probably H[8]J[6]]

Signatures:] AAA 2 [$4 • − A1, E3, E4 • + C1

Foliation: t.r.r.] [S] [1], 2–16; [T B] [17], 18–36; [CT I] [41], 42–53, 53 *[recte* 54]; [CT II, presumably numbered [55], 56–69, [70]]

Piece numbering:] I-XIII, IXV [*recte* XIV], XV-XVIII

Part-names: In the Superius and Contratenor I parts, these are in the head-line:

S:]	Sup*erius*	[A2*r*–B8*r*, at the outer corner except on A2*r*
	Nil:	A1*r*, A1*v*, B8*v*
CT I:]	Contra tenor primus	[F1*v*, G1*v*, at the top left
	Contra tenor p₂imus	[F2*r*–G1*r*, G2*r*-6*r*, at the top left
	Nil:	F1*r*, G6*v*

In the Tenor-Bassus book, they are entered in the left margin, reading downwards:

Tenor	[C1*v*,6*v*,8*v*, E2*v*
Ba∫∫us Secundus	[C2*r*
Ba∫∫*us*	[C3*r*
Ba∫∫u5	[C7*r*,8*r*
Ba∫∫us	[D1*r*, E2*r*,3*r*
Tenor Ba∫∫us	[C4*v*-6*r*,7*v*, D1*v*,2*v*-3*v*,4*v*,5*r*,7*r*-8*r*, E1*r*,3*v*
Tenor [in head] Ba∫∫us	[D2*r*
Tenor Ba∫∫u5	[D4*r*, E4*r*
Tenor Ba∫∫us Tenor Ba∫∫*us*	[D5*v*
Tenor Ba∫∫*us*	[D6*v*,8*v*
Tenor Ba∫∫us Tenor	[E1*v*
Secu*n*da pars	[C3*v*, C4*r*
Nil:	C1*r*, D6*r*, E4*v*

Fonts: Music: Petrucci's normal music type

    Staves: Six per page

    Text: Rotonda

Textual comments: Roman numerals for each piece, for the first time in his career • No.14 is numbered IXV in all parts

Technical comments: Small capital letters on F5*v* [I] and G4*v* [E] • The rubrics in the margin read vertically:

    from top:]   A2*r*,3*r*,5*r*,6*v*,8*v*, B4*v*; C1*v*-D5*v*, D6*v*-E4*r*; F1*v*,5*r*,7*r*,7*v*,8*v*, G1*v*,2*v*-5*v*

    from bottom:]   A4*r*, B2*r*,4*r*,5*r*,5*v*,6*r*,6*v*,7*v*; F2*r*, G6*r*

    [Nil: D6*r*, E4*v*.

    The layout is very simply conceived, even though there appear to be a large number of different solutions.

In-house corrections: G4*r*.i.11: ?e′ → d′, erased and stamped in: A-Wn, D-Mbs and I-FPfanan

Contents: all ascriptions are from the Tavola:

	A1*r*	C1*r*	F1*r*	[Title]		
	A1*v*			[Tavola]		
I	A2*r*	C1*v*	F1*v*	CLangat plebs	à5	Regis
				[T:] SIcut lilium		
		C2*r*		[B:] CUm cantu claro		
	A2*r*.vi	C1*v*.ii	F1*v*.iv	2/ Carmina cude*n*te3 tibi		
				[T:] Sic anima mea		
				[CT1, B:] Carmina tibi florida		
II	A2*v*.vi	C2*v*	F2*r*.i	FActor orbis	à5	Obreth
				[T:] CAnite tuba		
				[CT1:] VEni do*m*ine ꝫ noli tardare		
		C3*r*		[B:] NOe . . . ecce		
	A3*r*.vi	C3*v*	F2*r*.vi	2/ Spiritus do*m*ini ∫uper me		

				[T:] Erunt praua indirecta		
				[CT1:] Hodie [cietis quia veniet		
		C4r		[B:] Bethleem e[t ciuitas		
III	A3v.v	C4v.iv	F2v.v	DUlcis amica dei	à5	Ga[par
		C4v		[T:] DA pacem domine		
	A4r.iii	C5r.iii	F3r.iii★	2/ Rogamus te pii[[ima uirgo		
		C5r		[T:] Da pacem domine		
IIII	A4v.iii	C5v	F3v.i	ILlibata dei virgo	à5	Jo[quin
	A5r.ii	C6r	F3v.vi	2/ Ave virginu3 decus		
V	A5v	C6v	F4r.iv	HOmo quidam [S untexted]	à5	Jo[quin
	A5v.v	C6v.iii	F4r.vi	2/ Venite comedite [S untexted]		
VI	A6r	C7v	F4v	O Decus eccle[ie [untexted]	à5	Jsac
	A6v.ii	C7v.ii	F5r	2/ [untexted]		
VII	A7r.v	C8v	F5v.iiv	INviolata integra 1 ca[ta	à5	Isac
VIII	A7v.iv	D1v	F6r	REquiem	à5	Jo[quin
IX	A8r	D2r.ii	F6r.v	LAudemus nunc dominum	à5	Obreth
		D2r		[T:] NOn est hic aliud		
	A8v.ii	D2v.iii	F7r	2/ Cantemus nunc domino		
		D2v		[T:] Uidit iacob [calu3		
				[CT1:] Cantemus domino canticum nouu3		
X	B1r.ii	D3r	F7v	SAlue [pon[a tui genitrix	à5	Regis
	B1r.vi	D3v	F7v.iv	2/ Nil eua officiet		
XI	B1v.iii	D4r.iii	F8r	LUx [olempnis	à5	Regis
		D4r		[T:] REdempti [unt		
	B2r.iii	D4v.iv	F8v.ii	2/ Nec miru3 [i tanta		
		D4v		[T:] Pro vt [piritus sanctus		
XII	B2v.iii	D5r	G1r.iv	AUe maria	à5	Pipelare
	B2v.vi	D5r̃★	G1v	2/ Et benedictus fructus		
	B3r.iii	Tacet	G1v.iii	2/ Tu parui	à3	
	Tacet	Tacet	G1v.iv★	3/ Tu floris 1 roris	à2	
	B3r.v	D5v	G1v.v★	4/ Tu ciuitas		
	B3v	D5v.ii	G2r	5/ Ergo maris [tella		
XIII	B3v.iii	D5v.v	G2r.iii	O Precio[i[[ime [anguis	à5	Obreth
	B4r.iv	D6v	G2v.iv	2/ Guberna tuos [untexted]		
	B4v.i	D7r	G3r	3/ Te ergo que[umus [untexted]		
XIV	B4v.iii	D7v.iii	G3r.vi	MAter patris nati nata	à5	Obreth
		D7v		[T:] SAncta dei genitrix		
	B5r.iii	D8r.iii	G3v.iv	2/ Ab eterno genitura		
		D8r		[T:] Sancta dei genitrix		
	B5v	D8v	G4r.ii	3/ Virgo mater dei		
XV	B6r	E1r.iii	G4v	EXaudi nos filia	à5	Cri[pin
		E1r.ii		[T:] UIrgo maria		
	B6r.iv	E1v.ii	G4v.iv	2/ Ora pro populo tuo		
		E1v		[T:] Uirgo maria		
XVI	B6v	E1v.iv	G5r	AUe maria	à5	Regis
		E2v	G5r.v	2/ Tu floris et roris		
XVII	B7r.iii	E3v	G5v.iii	AUe [ancti[[ima maria	à5	Dini[et

XVIII	B7v.iii	E4r	G6r.ii	HOdie [cietis quia veniet	à 5	Isac
		B8r.iii		[blank staves]		
				[Colophon, Register		
	B8v	E4v	G6v	[blank]		

Extant copies:

A-Wn, S.A.77.C.22. Superius, T-B, and Contratenor I, complete

> **Watermarks:** No.23 on A2, A3, B1, B3, C6, C7, D5, D8, E1, F6, F7, G2, and G4

> **Technical comments:** Five staves only were printed on B8r, C1v,2v,3v,6v,7v, D3v

> **In-house correction:** G4r: see above

> **Binding:** Of the Austrian National Library

D-Mbs, 4°.mus.pr.168. Superius and Contratenor I, complete

> **Size of page:** 163 × 241 and 165 × 239 mm. The same sizes as other books at D-Mbs

> **Watermarks:** No.23 on A5, A7, B1, B4, F3, F8, and G2

> **Corrections and changes:**

>> **In-house:** G4r: see above

>> **Later:** A number of attributions have been added to the starts of works in the CT I book • A4r.i.after 5: *sbb* erased • A4r.ii.28: f, *sm* → *m*, by erasure • F6r.ii.48: f, *b* → *l*, addition of tail in brown ink • G3v.v.leger line: looks to have been drawn in ink

> **Binding:** Now in marbled boards, with half cloth • These books were originally bound with other books, for they have tabs near the foot of first pages: these are aligned as if to follow the four books of *Motetti de la Corona*, which would themselves have been preceded by something else

GB-Lbl, K.1.d.5*. Superius, complete

> **Size of page:** 157 × 225 mm.

> **Watermarks:** No.23 on A4, A7, B5 and B8

> **Technical comments:** Only five staves are inked on B8r

> Apparently no corrections or changes

> **Binding:** Modern parchment binding • A 19th-century fly-leaf and conjugate paste-down at each end

> **Provenance:** British Museum stamp on B8v, dated] 20 JU 1918 • Pencil call number, inside front cover:] ES 226[b] • The same call number on B8v, in pencil, with the annotation:] LIB XIX 330592

> **Bibliography:** Johnson and Scholderer, *Short-Title*, p. 454

I-FPfanan. Contratenor primus, complete. There is a cancel in gathering G, see below. I am grateful to Dottore Fanan for bringing his copy to my attention and allowing me to study it in detail

> **Size of page:** 158 × 228 mm.

> **Watermarks:** No.23 on F5, F8 and G3

> **Corrections and changes:**

>> **In-house:** G4r: see above

>> **Later:** F6r.ii.48: f, *b* → *l*, addition of tail in brown ink

> **Binding and Provenance:** with *Motetti C* (No.15)

PL-Kj, Mus.ant.pract.P 670. Tenor/Bassus book, complete

> **Size of page:** 153 × 229 mm.

> **Watermarks:** No.23 on C1, C4, D2, D4 and E3

> **Technical comments:** Only five staves are inked on 1v,2v,3v,6v,7r, and D3v

> **Binding:** 19th-century cloth over boards • One paste-down and one fly-leaf at each end

Provenance: From Berlin • Inside front board:] 14,009 • On C1r.] Vun.67. [and] Ex. Lib. Cani[. Ord. Maurit. [the second entry in a 16th-century German hand: also part of a red wax seal, bearing the words] JESUS | MARIA

No. 46a. *Cancel.*
A bifolium for folios G1 and G6: there seems to be no change in the readings
    Signature: GGG 1

Extant copy:
I-FPfanan
    Watermark: the lower part of No.16 on G1

———

Lost copies: Colón owned a copy (Chapman, "Printed", No.31) • There was probably a copy at S. Luigi dei Francesi in Rome, in 1583 (Perkins, "Notes", 64) • Vernarecci, *Petrucci*, p. 105, reported that there was a copy in Bologna, which he (probably wrongly) regarded as distinct from the copy reported by Schmid. No trace of that copy can be found
Bibliography:
    (a) Rosaria Boccadifuoco, *Bibliografia*, No.2353 • Sartori, *Petrucci*, No.38
    (e) Schmid, *Petrucci*, p. 81

Commentary:

1. This is a very old-fashioned anthology, containing works dating back perhaps fifty years, and others (alongside those) composed with techniques and in styles which were fast becoming obsolete (or reserved for special events). There are eight (perhaps nine, with composition No.2 by Obrecht) using multiple texts and a rigid *cantus firmus*: Nos.1 (Regis), 3 (Weerbeke), 9 (Obrecht), 11 (Regis), 12 (Pipelare), 13 and 14 (Obrecht), and 15 (Crispin). Six works have a similarly rigid *cantus firmus*, though with only one text: they are Nos.4 and 5 (Josquin), 6 (Isaac), 8 (Josquin), 10 (Regis: and note the Bassus line in the first *pars*), and 17 (Diniset), Nos.16 and 18 both show an old-fashioned feature in their use of an opening duo. Emphasising this conservative approach to repertoire is the strong presence of Regis.
2. Perhaps this pattern helped Petrucci to decide not to print another five-voiced anthology. There are very few à5 pieces in his later books: the few in the last *Motetti de la Corona* books are already much more advanced in style.
3. The selection surely argues for a different taste from that represented in the earlier motet and mass volumes. If we are to assume that Castellanus had anything to do with the volume, then he must have deliberately put it out as a monument to past glories. It might be seen as a reflection of his Roman residence. But I am much happier in asserting some other contact — someone for whom this repertoire represented a high point of style, and one which he felt (perhaps sadly) was not reflected in more recent work.
4. For the first time, Petrucci used roman numerals to number compositions in a book. This is probably a reflection of his view of the repertoire.
5. The Tenor part, by itself, would have taken only 14 pages (including the title-page) and could have been printed in one 8-folio gathering. The Bassus would then have involved one 12-folio volume. Thus the two separately would have used the same amount of paper as together. There

is no good reason for them to be together, unless Petrucci was expecting the Tenor to be almost all *cantus firmi* pieces-i.e., had not necessarily received everything when he started.

6. The fact that Tenor and Bassus *are* printed together says something about the expected use of this book. The two obvious alternatives are (i) that the music would be sung one to a part — although even then the Tenor and Bassus book is fairly small; or (ii) that the music would be used in institutions that would copy it into manuscript books. The latter seems to me to be the more likely solution. Brown's remarks (in Brown, "Mirror") about the private and devotional nature of the early motet volumes makes the distinctive character of this book all the more obvious.

7. As a result, it is not surprising to find no manuscript changes in the book carrying the Tenor and Bassus parts, for corrections would have been made when these parts were copied onto separate sheets, or into separate part-books.

8. For the Tenor-Bassus book, at least, only one forme of staves seems to have been used almost consistently: this is unusual at this late date, but is probably a product of the special nature of the book–involving two voice-parts, one of which was very compressed for much of the time. This certainly did cause some problems with layout, and so probably led to the book being set up outside the normal patterns of work. The following data come from the copy at Krakow:

Forme: Outer	1r	2v	3r	4v	Inner	2r	1v	4r	3v
C.I	—	175	174	176		175	175	173	174
C.II	175	175	174	176		176	175	175	176
D.I	174	174	174	175		175	174	173	175
D.II	175	175	174	176		175	175	174	175
E.I	175	175	174	—		175	175	174	176

9. There is no date anywhere on the surviving copies. It has usually been assumed that the reference in Colón's catalogue to an edition of 1508 covers the surviving copies. The literature which has in the past assigned them to 1505 is discussed in the chapter on Ghosts.

In fact, the bibliographical evidence does support a date of late 1508. Many of the initial letters in the Vienna copy can be compared directly with the library's copy of Petrucci's next book, Dalza's book of tabulature. The initials are in very similar states, and (in one or two cases) marginally better in condition, in this book. The paper on which the present book was printed is of a common type, found often throughout Petrucci's work, in one of its forms (numbered 3–5 or 23–25). However, there seems to have been a change in the dimensions of the watermark during 1508: a larger mark appears in the first edition from Spinacino (1507) and in the *Missarum diversorum auctorum I* of March 1508.

10. The cancel bifolium seems to have been printed during 1509, and represents one of Petrucci's last activities in Venice: he bought this paper, No.16, more than once during his career — in 1505, in 1509 and in Fossombrone. Its appearance in the first book of Bossinensis's arrangements seems to represent the end of a batch of paper, for it (with No.2) is replaced by another paper for the later gatherings. Since this cancel does not seem to fit among the Fossombrone editions, and the type and initials seem to fit in 1509, I assume that it was printed not long before the Bossinensis edition.

No. 47. Dalza: *Intabulatura IV*

31.xii.1508   *RISM* D 828

A1r]   Intabulatura de Lauto | Libro Quarto. | Padoane diuerſe. | Calate a la spagnola. | Calate a la taliana. | Taſtar de corde con li | ſoi recercar drietro. | Frottole. | Joanambroſio.

G8r:]   Impreſſum Venetijs: per Octauianuƺ | Petrutium Foroſempronienſem: Cum pri | uilegio inuictiſſimi dominij Venetiarum: | *quae* nullus poſſit intabulaturaƺ Lauti impri | mere: ſub pena in ipſo priuilegio contentiſ. | Die vltimo Decembris .1508. | Registrum. AA BB CC DD EE FF GG

A1v]   Regole per quelli che non ſanno cantare. [etc., as for the first book of Spinacino's Intabulations, No.33: Followed by four columns:]

[Column one:]

   Tauola ce la preſente opera compoſta | per lo excelente muſico e ſonator de | lauto. Ioanambroſio dalza milaneſe | Acomplacentia de quelli deſiderano | dare principio atal virtu. Pero ha | dato principio a coſe facile e da mol | te deſiderate. Per lo aduenir dara coſe piu maiſtreuele e difficile per | ſatiſfare etiam aquelli ſonno exercitati | in tal ſcientia.

[Column two:]

Galdibi caſtigliano	ii
Calata a doi lauti	xli
Calata dito zigonze	xliii
Calata de ſtrambotti	xlv
Calata	xlv
Calata	xlvi
Calata	xlvii
Calata	xlvii
Calata ala ſpagnola	xlviii
Calata ala ſpagnola	xlix
Calata ala ſpagnola	xlix
Calata ala ſpagnola	l
Calata ala ſpagnola	l
Calata ala ſpagnola	li

[Column three:]

Laudate dio	lvi
Calata ala ſpagnola	ix
Pauana ala venetiana	ix
Pauana ala venetiana	xii
Pauana ala venetiana	xiiii
Pauana ala venetiana	xvii
Pauana ala venetiana	xviii
Pauana ala ferrareſe	xxi
Pauana ala ferrareſe	xxv
Pauana ala ferrareſe	xxviii
Pauana ala ferrareſe	xxxiii
Poi chel ciel contrario aduerſo	lii
Poi che volſe la mia ſtella	liiii

[Column 4:]

Recercar	iii
Recarcer	vii
Recercar	viii
Recercar	viii
Saltarello e piua con doi lauti	xxxvii
Ta[tar de corde	iii
Ta[tar de corde col [uo recer car	iii
Ta[tar de corce col [uo recer car	iiii
Ta[tar de corde col [uo recercar	v
Ta[tar de corde col [uo recer car	vi

Format and collation: Tabulature: landscape quarto-in-eights. 56 folios: A-G⁸

Signatures:] X AA 2 [$4 •-A1

Foliation:] [1], 3 [*recte* 2], 3–54, 5, 56

Fonts: Music: Petrucci's tablature font. Uses *sf*, and signs for 11 and 12 which appear to have the points mounted on the same sort as the x

Staves: six-line, four per page: 176–177 mm long, 17.5 mm high

Text: Rotonda • Tavola in Roman • Title uses Rotonda, " X " = 7.8 and " X " = 4.2 mm.

Technical comments: Evidence suggesting that text and stave lines were not printed together appears on D3*v*.ii and G8*r*.iv

In-house corrections: A3*r*.ii.9,4: 1 → 2 in brown ink: all copies • A5*r*.iv.11,1: /3/3/1 → /3/3/0, erasure and brown ink: A-Wn and B-Br • B2*r*.i.7,1: 2002// → 2003//, in brown ink: all copies • B3*v*.iv.10: //2104 → //2103, erasure and stamped in symbol: present in A-Wn and US-Cn, in brown ink in B-Br • B4*r*.i.10.3–6: rhythm signs all from triplet *f* to triplet *sm*, by erasure: all copies • B4*v*.iii.1,1–4: rhythm signs all from triplet *f* to triplet *sm*, by erasure: all copies • B4*v*.iii.7,3–6: rhythm signs all from triplet *f* to triplet *sm*, by erasure: all copies • B5*r*.ii.4,3–6: rhythm signs all from triplet *f* to triplet *sm*, by erasure: all copies • B7*v*.ii.12,3: now 2//42/, the 4 stamped in over an erased symbol, perhaps a 3: all copies • C1*v*.iii.7,1: rhythm sign, triplet *sm* → *m*, by erasure, apparently by a different, less careful hand: all copies • E5*v*.iii.5,3: //3/// → //2///, in brown ink: all copies • F8*r*.iii.7,3: rhythm sign, *f* → *sm*, by erasure: all copies

Contents: There are no attributions in the body of the book

	A1*r*	[Title]
	A1*v*	Regula per quelli che non [anno cantare. [followed by a Tavola]
1	A2*r*	CAldibi ca[tiglione
2	A3*r*.ii	REcercar
3	A3*v*	TAstar de corde
4	A3*v*.ii	TAstar de corde
5	A3*v*.iv	REcercar dietro
6	A4*r*.iii	TAstar de corde
7	A4*v*	REcercar dietro
8	A5*r*.ii	TAstar de corde
9	A5*v*	REcercar dietro
10	A6*r*.iii	TAstar de corde
11	A6*v*.ii	Finis seguite il recercar
12	A7*r*.ii	REcercar

13	A8*r*	REcercar
14	A8*r*.iii	REcercar
15	B1*r*	PAuana alla venetiana
	B1*v*.iii	Saltarello
	B2*v*.iii	Piua
16	B3*v*.iii	PAuana alla venetiana
	B4*v*.ii	Saltarello
	B5*v*.i	Piua
17	B6*r*.iii	PAuana alla venetiana
	B6*v*.iv	Saltarello
	B7*v*.i	Piua
18	B8*v*	PAuana alla venetiana
	C1*r*	Saltarello
	C1*r*.iv	Piua
19	C2*r*	PAuana alla venetiana
	C3*r*.ii	Saltarello
	C4*r*.iii	Piua
20	C5*r*	PAuana alla ferrareſe
	C6*r*.iii★	Saltarello
	C7*v*.ii★	Piua
21	C8*v*	PAuana alla ferrareſe
	D1*v*.iii	Saltarello
	D2*v*.iii★	Piua
22	D3*v*.ii	PAuana alla ferrareſe | Accordasi il contra basso octa [etc]
	D5*v*.ii★	Saltarello
	D7*v*.ii★	Spingardo
	D8*v*.iv	[blank stave]
23	E1*r*	PAuana alla ferrareſe col contra baſſo acordato ottava col tenor
	E2*v*.i★	Saltarello
	E4*r*.i★	Spingardo
24	E5*r*.ii	SAltarello [for two lutes. [Headed:] Tenor e contra; ſaltarello con due liuti
		Suprano del ſaltarello
	E7*r*.i★	piua [for two lutes]
25	F1*r*	CAlata [for two lutes]
26	F3*r*	CAlata dito zigonze
27	F4*v*	CAlata de ſtrambotti
	F4*v*.iii	Secunda pars
28	F5*r*	CAlata
29	F6*r*	CAlata
30	F6*v*	CAlata
31	F7*r*	CAlata
32	F7*v*	CAlata ala ſpagnola.
33	F8*v*	CAlata ſpagnola.
34	G1*r*	CAlata ala ſpagnola
35	G1*v*	CAlata ala ſpagnola
36	G2*r*	CAlata ſpagnola

37	G2*v*	CAlata ala ſpagnola ditto terzetti di znan [*sic*] ambroſo dalza
38	G4*r*.iii	POi che ciel co*n*trario aduerſo
39	G5*v*.ii	POi che volſe la mia ſtella
40	G6*r*.iv	PAtientia ognun medice
		[Not in the Tavola]
41	G7*v*.iv	LAudato dio.
	G8*r*.[iv]	Colophon; Register
	G8*v*	[blank]

Extant copies: The copy listed in *RISM* as being at GB-HAdolmetsch is in fact a series of photo-graphs of the copy now at A-Wn

A-Wn, S.A.77.C.26. Complete

Size of page: 160 × 228 mm.

Watermarks: No.23 on A1, A5, B3, B8, C6, C8, D5, D7, E5, E7, F6, F7, G4, and G7

Technical comments: Evidence suggesting that text and stave lines were not printed together appears on D3*v*.ii and G8*r*.iv

Corrections and changes:

> **In-house:** A3*r*, A5*r*, B2*r*, B3*v*, B4*v*, B5*r*, B7*v*, C1*v*, E5*v* and F8*r*: see above

> **Later:** A6*v*.ii.5,2: erased *sb* sign and o on top string • A6*v*.iv.1,1: 2/23// → 2/////, by erasure • B7*r*.iii.right end: pencil mark • C1*v*.iii.7,1: *f* → *sm*, by erasure • C8*v*.initial: 20th-century pencil number • E5*v*.iii.5,3: mensuration sign, 3 → 2, erasure and brown ink • G4*r*.iii.1,1–2: ///587, ///587 → //5/87, //5/87, by erasure and brown ink addition • G4*r*.iii.6,2: ////10: perhaps a rhythm sign erased after this chord

Binding: Early calf simple binding, identical to that of Bossinensis's first book, at A-Wn. Edges of pages gauffered and painted gold • One fly-leaf and one paste-down at each end

B-Br, Fétis 2893 A L.P. Complete

Size of page: 171 × 238 mm.

Watermarks: No.23 on A2, A4, B1, B5, C1, C3, D2, D5, E1, E4, F6, F7, G3, and G7

Technical comments: The initial letter C shows similar damage on F5*r*, F6*r*, G2*v*, etc. • G1*r*.i.10,1: Music spacing sort, measuring 3.0 × 3.5 mm, just large enough for one stave line in height

Corrections and changes:

> **In-house:** A3*r*, A5*r*, B2*r*, B3*v*, B4*v* (three times), B5*r*, B7*v*, C1*v*, E5*v* and F8*r*: see above

> **Later:** A6*r*.i.3,3: a point erased below the symbol 3 • A6*r*.ii.5,2: erased *sb* sign and o on top string • A6*v*.iv.1,1: 2/13// → 21/3//, by erasure and grey ink • B8*v*.ii.7: rhythm sign, *sm* → *m*, by erasure • D8*v*.iii–iv.after the music: inserted unrhythmicised tablature, visible in the Minkoff facsimile • G1*v*.ii.,2: /////1/ → ////2/, in ginger ink • G4*r*.iii.1,1–2: both ///587 → //5/87, erasure and ginger ink

Binding: Early 19th-century parchment over boards • One paste-down and two fly-leaves at each end

Provenance: From the Fétis collection • Has a lavish coat of arms on A1*r*, though it is now illegible

Bibliography: Huys, *Grégoire*, No.41 (exhibition at Brussels, 1966) • Fétis, *Catalogue*, No.2893 • Dalza, *Intabulatura* is a facsimile of this copy

US-Cn, Case-Vm.140.D.15i. Lacks gathering G

Watermarks:

A1	A5	B1	B3	C3	C7	D5	D7	E1	E3	F1	F3
24	23	24	23	23	23	24	23	24	23	23	23

Corrections and changes:

    In-house: A3*r*, B2*r*, B3*v*, B4*v* (three times), B5*r*, B7*v*, C1*v*, E5*v*, and F8*r*: see above

    Later: A6*r*.i.3,3: perhaps a point erased below the note • A6*r*.ii.after 17: *sm* 3/////: the signs erased • A6*v*.iv.1,1: 2/23// → 2/////, by erasure • A8*r*, inner margin: a hand, in brown ink • B8*v*.ii.7: rhythm sign, *sm* → *m*, by erasure

Binding: Modern

Provenance: ex A. Rosenthal: according to a label:] Purchased from the Jane Oakley Fund

Bibliography: Krummel, *Newberry*, 382 • Exhibited at Toledo, OH, in 1957. See Barksdale, *Printed*, No.71, with one page illustrated

———

Lost copies: Colón owned a copy, bought in Rome in 1512 (Chapman, "Printed", No.36; Huntington, *Catalogue*; Plamenac, "Excerpta", 679): see chapter 20

Bibliography:

    (a) Rosaria Boccadifuoco, *Bibliografia*, No.1048 • Sartori, *Petrucci*, No.43 • Jeppesen, *La Frottola*, PeK • Brown, *Instrumental*, 1508₂

    (b) Brunet, *Manuel*, iii, col.446 • *Index Aureliensis*, No.149.354

    (c) Dalza, *Intabulatura* • one page in Huys, *Gregoire*, No.41, and another in Barksdale, *Printed*, No.71

    (d) Buetens, *Lute* • Dalza, *Intavolatura* • Snow, *Petrucci*

    (e) Chiesa, "Storia" • O'Dette, "Quelques" • Underwood, *Renaissance*, pp. 88–106

Commentary:

1. This is the first source clearly to associate the various movements of the sets of dances: *Nota che tutte le pauane hanno el suo saltarello e piua*. These "suites", and the relationships between the movements, are discussed in detail in Moe, *Dance*.

2. It is also the first to indicate the association of a ricercar with a preceding freer movement. The phrase on the title-page reads *Ta[tar de corde con li | [oi recercar drietro*. Schrade has shown that the *Tastar de corde* is in effect an early manifestation of the toccata. See Schrade, "Beitrag", p. 610. These pieces are discussed further in Murphy, "Fantaisie".

3. The presence of the *Laudate Dio* in I-MOe α.F.9.9 is perhaps significant. It suggests another connection with the Ferrara circle.

4. Moe, *Dance*, p. 20 points out that there are two examples of scordatura in this volume. Nos. 22 and 23 imply it from their titles. The first of these, according to Moe, involves a retuning of both the *Bordon* and the *contrabasso*.

5. For a discussion of the term *Calata*, and of its use by Dalza, see Moe, *Dance*, pp. 56–59: this is followed by a discussion of the Piva, pp. 59–61, and of the Spingardo, p. 61. There is also a discussion of the musical forms associated with Dalza's terms, in his chapter 3.

6. There is a preponderance of in-house corrections, in particular from the first three gatherings, which survive in all three copies. I am also inclined to add to the list a number of corrections which I have listed above, for caution's sake, as being later changes: these would include those on A6*r*.ii, A6*v*.iv, E5*v*.iii, and G4*r*.iii.

It is tempting to see here the situation which I propose for the editions of Spinacino, in which the lutenist himself was the corrector. That argument would make equal sense here, where many of the changes are relatively slight and might not be easily evident to a non-lutenist, even while many appear in all copies.

7.   Apparently Petrucci was willing to allow his typesetters to lift initial letters from one forme for immediate insertion into another. This was perhaps partly necessary because of the number of repeated initials: but it suggests that Dalza (or someone else) was concerned that the book should present an attractive face to the reader: the letter "R" on A3r reappears on A7r and A8r, the "P" on B1r is found on B3v, C5r, C8v, D3v, and E1r, while a different "P" is on B6r, B8v, and C2r; the "C" on F1r is also, on F5r and F6r, while another is on F4v, F7v, and F8v.

No. 48. *Frottole IX*

22.i.1508/9   *RISM* 1509²

A1r]   Frottole Libro | Nono.
G8r]   Impre[[um Venetiis per Octauianum Pe- | trutium Foro[empronien[em. M.D.viii. Die xxii | Ianuarii Cum priuilegio inuicti[[imi Dominii | Venetiarum quae nullus po[[it cantum Figuratum | imprimere [ub pena in ip[o priuilegio contenta. | Regi[trum. | AA BB CC DD EE FF GG Omnes quaterni | [Petrucci's device]

Format and collation: Choirbook: landscape quarto-in-eights. 56 folios: A-G⁸
Signatures:] X AA II [$4 • − A1 • On D1, the "D" is inverted
Foliation: t.r.r.:] [1], 2–29, 32 [*recte* 30], 31–55, [56]
Running heads:
Part-names:

recto:]	Altus Ba[[us	[A4, B2,4–8, C2,5,7, D2,4–5,8, E2-4,6–8, F2-3,5–6,8r, G2,4,6–7
	Altus Ba[[u5	[A5-6, B3, C3, D6, E1,5, F4,7, G1,3,5
	Aluts Ba[[us	[A8
	Tenor Altus Ba[[us	[C4, D1,3
	Tenor Altus Ba[[u5	[B1, C1, D7
	Tenor Altu5 Ba[[us	[C6
	Tenor Altu5 [both in stave] Ba[[u5	[A7
	Tenor [in stave] Altus Ba[[us	[A2
	Tenor [in stave] Altus Ba[[u5	[F1
	Tenor Altu5 [both in stave] Ba[[us	[A3
	Tenor Altus Ba[[us [all in stave]	[C8
verso:]	Tenor	[A3-5,7, B1,3-7, C1-2,4,6, D1,3-5, D7-E7, F1-G6
	Teonr	[B2
	Tenor Altus Ba[[us	[A2,8, B8, C3,5,8, E8
	Tenor Altu5 Ba[[us	[C7, D2
	Tenor Altus [both in stave] Ba[[us	[A6
	Tenor [in stave] Altus Ba[[us	[G7
	Tenor [in stave] Altu5 Ba[[us	[D6

The letter "u" is inverted surprisingly frequently in this volume • Small initials are often used in part-names:

recto:] Tenor   [B1, C4, D3
          Altus   [A3,7, B2,4, C2,4, D3,5,8, E2
          Bassus [A2-7, B2-8, C1-5,7, D1,4-8, E1-3,5-8, F1,4-8, G1,3,5-7
verso:] Tenor   [B1,3, C1,3, D5,7,8, E2,3, F2,3, G2,4
          Altus   [C5,8, D2
          Bassus [A2,6,8, B8, D2, G7

Fonts: Music: Petrucci's normal music type

Staves: six per page: 176–77 or 180 mm long, 10-92-112 mm high.

Text: Roman

Technical comments: All gathering joins except D-E contain single-page pieces • No capital initial on D2*v* [N] • Small capital letters used on B3*v* [I], C4*v* [J], E4*v* [F] and F8*v* [I]: a type sort for the initial on C4*r* [V]. • The signatures have two sizes of the symbol X, the smaller on A2-4, E1-4, and F3,4

In-house corrections: A5r.iv.2: c' → d', erased and stamped in: both copies • A6*v*.i.last 2: g, f → f, e, erased and stamped in note-heads, with a manuscript line through the tails: both copies • C1r.iv.penultimate note: a → g, erased and stamped in, with an ink connection to the original tail: both copies • C6*v*.ii.before 4 from end: *sbc*" added in a stop-press correction, in the copy at A-Wn • D5r.ii.17–18: note-heads struck through, in brown ink, in both copies • D6r.i.9: *m*, d' erased → c' stamped in, with an ink connection to the original tail: copy at D-Mbs; changed in black ink, possibly printer's ink, in the copy at A-Wn • F1r.iv.33–35: was *mf*, *mg*: now *sbf*, *mg*, *sb*a, all stamped in: both copies

Contents: the last column gives the folio numbers as they appear in the Tavola:]

	A1r	[Title]		
	A2r	[Tavola:] Frottole numero sessantaquatro		
1	A2r	QVercus iuncta columna est	Luranus numeros faciebat carmina faustos.	ii
2	A2v	NAsce la speme mia [Headed:] Aer de capitoli	M.C.	iii
3	A3r	DOlermi sempre voglio	B.T.	iii
4	A3v	SOn disposto de seguire	[Anon.]	iiii
5	A4v	PIeta cara signora [T,A,B:] La pieta ha chiuso	Rasmo	v
6	A5v	LA mia vaga tortorella	HE.dupre	vi
7	A6v	QVesto mondo e mal partito	B.T	vii
8	A7r	SE lontan partir mi fa	[Anon.]	vii
9	A7v	BEn chel ciel me thabbi tolto	B.T	viii
10	A8v	O Tempo o ciel volubil	[Anon.]	ix
11	B1r	A La fama se ua	B.T.	ix
12	B1v	CHi la castra la porcella	M.C.	x
13	B2v	DE la impresa mia amorosa	M.C.	xi
14	B3v	ITe caldi o mei suspiri	B.T	xii
15	B4v	OStinato vo seguire	B.T.	xiii
16	B5v	VNa legiadra nimpha	A.C.	xiiii
17	B6v	POrta ognun al nascimento	[Anon.]	xv
18	B7v	OChi dolci o che almen scorto	M.C.	xvi

59	G2*v*	LA in[uportabil pena	A.D.A.	li
60	G3*v*	SE con vo[tra alma belleza	[Anon.]	lii
61	G4*v*	LA mi la [o la [o la mi Gia	[Anon.]	liii
62	G5*v*	SEmpre haro quel dolce focho	Diomedes	liiii
63	G6*v*	CHie pregion del ciecho amore	[Anon.]	lv
64	G7*v*	AMando e de[iando	CARITEO	lv
	G8*r*	[left: Colophon; Register; Device]		
		[right:] Que[te [onno el re[to de le parole de la frottola |		
		A la fama [i ua per uarie schale		
	G8*v*	[blank]		

Extant copies:

A-Wn, S.A.77.C.2 (9). Complete

    Size of page: 167 × 237 mm.

    Watermarks:

A5-6	A8-7	B5	B8	C1	C6	D6	D7	E1	E6-5	F1-2	F5-6	G1-2	G4-3
2	2	24	24	23	23	24	24	23	2	2	2	2	2

    Technical comments: A row of notes, probably *sm*, used as bearer sorts on the 6th stave of A6*r*, E1*r*, E3*r*, E4*r*, F4*r*, F6*r*, and F8*r* • There appear to be slightly different groups of capital letters on the pages printed on paper 2, as opposed to other pages

    Corrections and changes:

        In-house: A5*r*, A6*v*, C1*r*, C6*v*, D5*r*, D6*r*, and F1*r*: see above

        Later: B5*r*.v.30: *l* → *b*, erased tail • D3*r*.v.after 6: *sba* added, *ma* → *sba* by erasure, *sbg* → *mg* with added tail • D5*r*.ii.28: *m* → *sb*, by erased tail • F1*r*.i.after 35: rest *l* → *b*, by erasure. Note that some of these appear in both extant copies

    Binding: Fugger binding, with remains of tie-strings. Inscribed:] FROT: L: IX:

    Provenance: From the Fugger collection

D-Mbs, Rar.878/9. Complete

    Size of page: 164 × 228 mm

    Watermarks:

A1-2	A3-4	B6	B8	C6	C7	D6	D7	E4-3	E8-7	F3-4	F8-7	G5-6	G7
6	6	23	23	23	23	23	23	6	6	6	6	6	23

    Corrections and changes:

        In-house: A5*r*, A6*v*, C1*r*, D5*r*, D6*r* and F1*r*: see above

        Later: A7*v*.iv.21: dot added, initialled RJ • B5*r*.v.30: *l* → *b*, by erasure • B6*r*.ii.30 *corona* erased and moved one to the right: *sba* added, initialled RJ • C6*v*.ii.before 4 from end: *sbc"* added, initialled RJ • D3*r*.v.after 6: added *sba*, *sb* a → *ma*, *sba* → *ma*, *sbg* → *mg*, with added tails, initialled RJ • D5*r*.ii.28: e, *m* → *sb*, erasure of tail • E2*v*.i.14: *dsm* → *dm*, by erasure, initialled g.c. • E4*r*.ii.14: *sb* → *m*, with added down-tail, initialled RJ • F1*r*.i.after 35: rest, *l* → *b*, by erasure, leaving a hole in the page • F8*r*.ii.after 9 before double bar: *sba* added, initialled RJ • G4*v*.iv.end: added *sba* over the *custos*, *sba*, initialled g.c. • G5*r*.ii.27: *sb* → *m*, with downtail, initialled g.c. • G7*r*.ii.penultimate note: struck through, initialled RJ: then the initials struck through in pencil

    Binding and Provenance: With *Frottole VI* (1506, No.26)

Lost copies: A copy was owned by Colón (Chapman, "Printed", p. 64), and another by Bottrigari.

Early references: Gesner, *Pandectae* (1548), VII, under the heading De cantionibus Italicis, vel in Italia impressis praesertim Venetiis:] Liber nonus ibidem. [= Petrucci. See Bernstein, "Gesner", No.248

Bibliography:

    (a) Rosaria Boccadifuoco, *Bibliografia*, No.1449 • Sartori, *Petrucci*, No.44 • Jeppesen, *La Frottola*, Pe IX • *Nuovo Vogel*, 1508[1]

    (b) Brunet, *Manuel*, ii, col.1413

    (d) Facchin, *Frottole*

    (e) Jeppesen, *La Frottola*, i,32 and 108–9 • Sartori, "Nuove", pp. 206–9

Commentary:

1. The evidence of the pattern of part-names suggests that names were kept in the forme, but fairly freely adjusted. That would be necessary, given the number of compositions occupying a single folio.

2. The presence of two forms of the letter "X" for the signature is interesting: it does not appear to indicate separate printings, for the pattern is the same in both copies, and does not correlate with that of the papers.

3. The pattern of papers ought to suggest that more than one printing is represented in the two copies. However, they appear to carry identical printings of every folio. It must be, therefore, that Petrucci was unwilling to order a complete batch of paper for this edition, preferring to use stocks already in-house, or smaller stocks that he could easily find at a *cartolaio*. The same situation seems to prevail for the cancel leaf to the *Motetti à cinque*, and the following book, his last in Venice.

No. 49. Bossinensis: *Tenori e contrabassi intabulati, I*

17.iii.1509   *RISM* 1509[3]

There are two editions of this title, each carrying the same date. For the second, see No.58, below.

First Edition

A1r]   Tenori e contrabaſſi intabu|lati col ſopran in canto fi|gurato per cantare e ſo|nar col lauto Li|bro Primo. | Franciſci Boſſinenſis | Opus.

G8r]   Impreſſum Venetijs: Per Octauianuʒ | Petrutium Foroſempronienſem: Cum pri|uilegio inuictiſſimi dominij Venetiarum: | q*uae* nullus poſſit intabulaturaʒ Lauti impri|mere: ſub penis in ipſo priuilegio contentiſ. | Die 27. Martij. 1509. | Regiſtrum. ABCDEFG O*mne*s quaterni | [Printer's device] [in a second column alongside the device:] Errori fatti ſtampando | [see below]

A1v]   Tavola ſlaid out in two columns. Each item is preceded by a letter, which does not indicate the mode or pitch centre, but relates to the table in the third column. This table is introduced as follows:] Recercar li quali ſerueno ale frottole ſecondo | lordine de le littere ſottoſcripte.

      A   1. 5. 8. 10. 12. 13. 19.

      B   2. 4. 9. 14. 15. 24.

C   3. 17. 22.

D   6. 7. 11. 16. 21. 25.

E   18. 20.

F   23.

G   26.

A2r]   Regula per quelli che non sanno cantore. [etc., giving the Italian version found in Spinacino's first book, No.33, above]

A2v]   Reuerendo in Chriſto Patri Domino. D. Hieronymo Barbadico Prothonotario apoſtolico ac   1
primicerio .S. Marci Venetiarum di-|gniſſimo patrono ſingulari Franciſcus boſſinenſis. S. P. D.

Grande & incredibile laude ſoleno li mortali a quelli attribuire li quali ogni loro ſtudio &
induſtria in commune hanno conferito | concioſia che non ſolum ad ſe medeſimi ma ancora ad
altri ſe hanno ſforciato giouare coſa in vero laudabile ſecondo la ſententia | di Platone qual dice: 5
niuno ad ſi ſolo douer eſſer nato: il che conſiderando molte volte ho in la mente diſcorſo la
infinita copia de ſcri-|ptori li quali in diuerſi modi de ſcriuer di ſe memoria hanno laſciato: niento
dimeno mai compoſitione ho viſto. Qual nuoua dire ſe po-|teſſe: per il che deſideroſo ancora io
laſſare ali poſteri parte de le fatiche mie: exiſtimando eſſe future vtile ſi per la nouita ſua ſi
etiam dio | per eſſer di ſorte che molti ſopiti ingegni per eſſe ſi accenderanno. Deliberai in   10
quanto potea la debilita del ingegno mio cum ogni cura | & ſollicitudine a mi poſſibile ritrouar in
muſica alcuno modo di compoſitione: qual nuouo & vtile iudicar ſi haueſſe. Et cuſi tal mio |
inuento ho publicato. Al qual ſi cum diligentia ciaſcaduno di muſica amatore dara opera: ſon certo
in breue vltra la incomparabile vti-|lita di eſſo reportera incredibile ſara la iocundita del animo e la
volupta de li ſenſi. Per la qual coſa hauendo con perfetto examino pen|ſato: a cui tal mie vigilie in   15
principio driccia ſſi niuno altro con piu ragione mi e occorſo di tua ſignoria. Qual cognoſco in ogni
liberal | arte delectarſi: & maxime in muſica quanto la dignitade tua rechiede. Donde prego non ſi
ſdegni tua Signoria con aliegro animo le | fatiche dil ſeruitore ſuo acceptare. Perche ſotto vmbra &
protectione ſua voglio ſtiano: cognoſcendo per la grandezza dil ingegno suo | niuna compoſitione
eſſerli occulta o inexperta. Interponendo adunque alcuna quiete ale vrgenti facende tue non gli   20
diſpiaccia di | queſta mia opera prender delectatione. Per che piacendo a ti ſignor preclaro: potra
etiam ali altri ſatiſfare: non reſguardando ali nomi | varii de li compoſitori: perche ſi come in li
altri libri impreſſi ho trouato coſi in queſto mio gli ho poſti. Si cognoſcero adotica queſte |
fatiche mie eſſerti grate: Sappia ad maiora ſempre ſara acceſo da tua Signoria qual deſidero felice
in queſto ſeculo & beata in laltro | vedere. Vale Decus Venetiarum.   25

Per moſtrar opra inuſitata & noua

De miei dolci anni con gran ſtenti lhore

Trappaſſate ho: non per diſio de honore

Che dentro del mio cor punto non coua

Ma per che il ben operar continuo gioua   30

E per che in uer ognun e debitore

A diſpenſar la uirtu con amore

A ciaſcum che qui giu viuo ſi troua

A cordatho col canto il ſuon ſoaue

Con ogni ingegno mio miſura & arte   35

Non piu ſcritto atal modo anoſtri tempi

Si che ſignor mio car non ve ſia graue

Veder questopra che ho pinti in ſue carte

De mie fatiche auoi tre primi exempi

B. M. F.   40

In this edition, the sonnet is set in two columns

Format and Collation: Score: landscape quarto-in-eights. 56 folios. A-G^8

Signatures:] A 2 [$4 • − A1

Foliation: t.r.r.:] [I-II], III-XXIX, [XXX], XXXI-XLIX, 50–55, [56] (including IIII, IX and XL) •
As with Book 2, the change from roman to arabic numerals occurs at the end of the texted pieces
No running head-line

Fonts: Music: Petrucci's music type; also a series of rhythm signs. Numerals used for tablature come
from a text font
Staves: Five-line for vocal part: 178 mm long, 10 mm high • Six-line for tablature: 178 mm long,
17 mm high • Two pairs of staves per page, total height, 93.5 mm
Text: Rotonda, " x " = 7.4 mm, for title page • Rotonda, " x " = 2.1 mm, for A2r, G8r, signatures and for some material on A1ν • Roman, " x " = 1.7 mm, "20" = 57 mm, for texts
and Tavola

Textual comments: There is a redundant ascription to] D. M. [at the head of F3ν, which is retained
in the second edition

Technical comments: The slurs are very rare and rather formless: but they appear to be in printer's
ink, and may be similar to the leger lines, in being very thin rules • A3ν.iii-iv and C8r.iii-iv:
short staves, 125 mm long, so as to accommodate added text • Certain ascriptions are entered in
the smaller rotonda, which is larger than the normal roman face: they are on B6ν, C4r, C4ν,
C7ν, D7r, E1r, E2ν, E4r, E5r, E7ν, and F5ν • Additional text was inserted in the music forme,
rather than in the one containing text and staves. It over-runs the staves in places, e.g., on B2ν

In-house correction: A list of errors appears on G8r.]
Errori fatti ſtampando
Tu dormi io ueglio ala tempeſta e uento vuol | eſſer ſcritto La voce del ſopran al terzo taſto |
de la ſottana
Chi vi dara piu luce occhi miei laſſi de franceſco | varoter fanno diſmenticato ſcriuer la voce del
| del [sic] ſopran qual ſcriuereti coſi La voce del ſopran | il canto vodo
Sio gel dico che dira vuol eſſer ſcritto coſi | La voce del ſopran al terzo taſto del canto
Io non compro piu speranza vuol eſſer ſcripto | coſi La voce del ſopran il canto vodo.

Contents:

	A1r	[Title]	
	A1ν	[Tavola]	
	A2r	Regula per quelli che non ſanno cantare.	
	A2ν	[Dedication]	
1	A3r	AFflitti ſpirti miei ſiati contenti	B.T.
2	A3ν	SEl morir mai de gloria	B.T.
3	A4r	ACcio chel tempo e i cieli empi & aduerſi	B.T.
4	A4ν.iii	O Dolce e lieto albergo	[Anon.]
5	A5r	SI e debile il filo a cui fattene	B.T.
6	A6r.iii	COn pianto e con dolore	[Anon.]
7	A6ν	SIl diſſi mai chio venga in odio	B.T.
8	A7ν	CHe debo far che me conſegli amore	B.T.
9	A8ν.iii	HAime per che mhai priuo	[Anon.]
		[Tav:] Haime per che mai priuo	
10	B1r	VOi che paſſate qui firmate il paſſo	F.V.
11	B1ν	NOn peccando altri chel core	B.T.
12	B2ν	CAde ogni mio penſier cade ogni ſpeme	B.T.

13	B3r	A La fama ſi ua per varie ſcale	B.T.
14	B3v	CHi in pregion crede tornarmi	B.T.
15	B4v	SPargean per laria le anno date chiome	B.T.
16	B5r.iii	ZEphyro ſpira e il bel tempo rimena	B.T.
17	B6r	HO ſcoperto il tanto aperto	B.T.
18	B6v.iii	DEh non piu deh non piu mo	M.C.
19	B7v.iii	O Deſpietato tempo	P. Zanin Biſan.
20	B8v	IO cerco pur la inſuportabil doglia	B.T.
21	C1r.iii	CHi lharebbe mai creduto	[Anon.]
22	C1v	ARma del mio valor	M.C.
23	C2r.iii	LAgrime e voi ſoſpiri	[Anon.]
24	C2v	NAſce laſpro mio tormento	F.V.
25	C3r.iii	O Mia cieca e dura ſorte	[Anon.]
26	C4r.iii	SE per chieder merce gratia ſimpetra	M.C.
27	C4v.iii	OStinato vo ſeguire	B.T.
28	C6r	TV dormi io veglio a la tempeſta e vento	B.T.
29	C6v	DEus in adiutorium meum intende	B.T.
		[This is a macaronic text]	
30	C7r	MIa benigna fortuna el uiuer lieto	[Anon.]
31	C7v.iii	Come chel bianco cigno per natura al coſtume	M.C.
32	C8r	AQua aqua aiutal foco al foco i ardi	B.T.
33	C8v	SEra forſi ripreſo il penſier mio	B.T.
34	D1r	CHi vi dara piu luce ochi miei laſſi	F.V.
35	D1v	SOm pi[u] tua che non ſon mia	M.C.
		[Tav:] Son piu . . .	
36	D2v	CHi vi dara piu luce ochi miei laſſi	B.T.
37	D3r	POi che volſe la mia ſtella	B.T.
38	D4r	Deh ſi deh no deh ſi	B.T.
39	D4v	SIo gel dico che dira	B.T.
40	D5v.iii	CRudel come mai poteſti	[Anon.]
41	D6v	SCopri lingua el cieco ardore	B.T.
42	D7r.iii	SE de fede vengo a meno	M.C.
43	D8r	OIme il cor oime la teſta	M.C.
44	D8v	NOn e tempo daſpetare	M.C.
45	E1r.iii	HOr vendu[to] ho la ſperanza	M.C.
46	E2r	IO non compro piu ſperanza	M.C.
47	E2v.iii	LA fortuna vol coſi	M.C.
48	E3r	INhoſpitas per alpes	D.M.
49	E3v	SE me grato il tuo tornare	PHI.DE LV.
50	E4r.iii	INteger vite ſceleriſque purus	D.M.
51	E4v	BEn chamor me faci torto	B.T.
52	E5r.iii	OGnun fugga fugga amore	Ant. Cap.
53	E6r	POi chel ciel contrario aduerſo	B.T.
54	E6v.iii	In te domine ſperavi	Joſquin Daſcanio
55	E7v	A La guerra a la guerra Chamor non uol	B.T.
56	E8r	EL conuera chio mora	B.T.
57	E8v.i★	ODite voi fineſtre	M.C.

58	F1r	POi che per fede manca	Ant. Cap. BRIXIENSIS
59	F1v	AIme chio moro	D.M.C.
60	F2v	BEn chel ciel me thabbi tolto	B.T.
61	F4r.iii	O Cara libertade	[Anon.]
62	F4v	PIu non tamo aibo aibo	M.C.
63	F5v.iii	SE laffannato cor in foco giace	F.V.
64	F6r	TI par gran maraueglia	N.P.
65	F6v	CHi me dara piu pace	M.C.
66	F7r	PIeta cara signora	M.C.
67	F7v	NOn ſon quel chio ſolea	PHI.D.L.
68	F8r	SE ben il fin de la mia vita	M.C.
69	F8v	Non ſi po quel chi ſi vole	PHI.D.L.
70	G1r	DE che parlera piu la lingua mia	M.C.
71	G1v	REcercar primo	[Anon.]
72	G1v.iii★	[Recercar] 2	[Anon.]
73	G2r	[Recercar] 3	[Anon.]
74	G2r.ii	[Recercar] 4	[Anon.]
75	G2r.iii★	[Recercar] 5	[Anon.]
76	G2v.iii	[Recercar] 6	[Anon.]
77	G3r	[Recercar] 7	[Anon.]
78	G3r.ii★	[Recercar] 8	[Anon.]
79	G3r.iii★	[Recercar] 9	[Anon.]
80	G3r.iv★	[Recercar] 10	[Anon.]
81	G3v.ii★	[Recercar] 11	[Anon.]
82	G4r	[Recercar] 12	[Anon.]
83	G4r.ii★	[Recercar] 13	[Anon.]
84	G4r.iii★	[Recercar] 14	[Anon.]
85	G4r.iv★	[Recercar] 15	[Anon.]
86	G4v.ii	[Recercar] 16	[Anon.]
87	G4v.iii★	[Recercar] 17	[Anon.]
88	G5r.i★	[Recercar] 18	[Anon.]
89	G5r.ii★	[Recercar] 19	[Anon.]
90	G5v	[Recercar] 20	[Anon.]
91	G5v.iii	[Recercar] 21	[Anon.]
92	G6r.iii★	[Recercar] 22	[Anon.]
93	G6r.iv★	[Recercar] 23	[Anon.]
94	G6v.iii★	[Recercar] 24	[Anon.]
95	G7r	[Recercar] 25	[Anon.]
96	G7r.iii	[Recercar] 26	[Anon.]
	G7r	El reſto de le parole Ala fama ſe va per | varie ſcale	
		El reſto de le parole Afflitti ſpirti mei ſiati	
		El reſto de le parole de Zephiro ſpiara [= spira]	
	G8r	[Colophon: Register: Device: List of errors]	
	G8v	[blank]	

Extant copies:

A-Wn, S.A.77.C.25. Complete

 Size of page: 160 × 228 mm.

 Watermarks:

A2-1	A4-3	B1-2	B6-5	C4-3	C7-8	D2-1	D6-5	E2-1	E4-3	F1-2	F5-6	G5-6	G8-7
31	31	2	2	2	2	2	2	31	31	31	31	31	31

 Corrections and changes:

  In-house: C8*v*: see above

  Later: C6*r*: 20-century annotations

 Binding: Same as the library's copy of Dalza (No.47) • All edges gauffered and gilded • One fly-leaf and one paste-down at each end

E-S, 12-1-5. Complete

 Size of page: 178 × 236 mm.

 Watermarks:

A2-1	A3-4	B2-1	B3-4	G6-5	C8-7	D6-5	D7-8	E2-1	E3-4	F2-1	F5-6	G4-3	G8-7
31	31	16	16	16	16	16	16	31	31	31	31	31	31

 Technical comments: D7*v*.iv.4.8: A spacing sort for the tablature: 0.8 × 3.3 mm. The proportions are necessarily very different from that for the music

 Later changes: B1*v*.iv.1.3: rhythm sign, from three flags to two, by erasure

 Binding: As with other copies in this collection, a parchment wrapper, with two tie-strings (the lower now lost) on each face. Remains of a label on the spine • One paste-down and one fly-leaf at each end, with a Spanish watermark

 Provenance: Bought by Colón in Rome in 1512, with the second book (Anglés, "Colombina", 24; Chapman, "Printed", Nos.38–39; Huntington, *Catalogue*; Plamenac, "Excerpta", 683–84) • G8*v*:] Esto libro costo en Roma .70. quatrines. Anno. 1512 por set*iembr*ᵉ uale un ducado de oro .307. quatrines. Esta Registrado 3803.

 Bibliography: Arboli y Farando, *Biblioteca*, i, pp. 279–80

F-Pc, Rés.432. The inner sheet of gathering D: for the rest of the copy, see the second edition, here dated to 1515 (No.58)

 Watermark: No.16 on D5-6

Private possession. Complete

 Size of page: 163 × 228 mm.

 Watermarks:

A5-6	A7-8	B3-4	B8-7	C1-2	C3-4	D3-4	D7-8	E1-2	E5-6	F6-5	F7-8	G6-5	G7-8
31	31	16	16	16	16	16	16	31	31	31	31	31	31

 Technical comments: D7*v*.iv.4.8: The spacing sort for the tablature found in the Seville copy is also apparent here

 Later changes: B1*v*.iv.1.3: rhythm sign, from three flags to two, by erasure

 Binding: ¼ leather over lightly marbled boards, certainly of the 18th century. The spine has one word entered in gold:] ARIE Both boards detached. One paste-down and two fly-leaves at the front, one and one at the back, all of an 18th-century paper. Bound with Bossinensis' Book 2 (No.50)

 Provenance: Sold by Sotheby's in their London rooms on 5 December 2003, as Lot 145. The book contains manuscript ownership notes for Robert Bolling of Virginia on A1*r* and G8*v* (which records the death of his wife in child-birth in 1748). Inside the front board is the inscription:] Questo libro appartiene | ad Signor | Roberto Bolling | di | Buckingham. | 1764. [Additional annotations in the same hand on A2v, B4r and G1r. Further details can be found in the Sotheby catalogue, which illustrates one annotation on the first folio of Bossinensis' second book

Bibliography: Sotheby's catalogue for the London sale of 5 December 2003, Lot 145

Bibliography:

(a) Rosaria Boccadifuoco, *Bibliografia*, No.494 • Sartori, *Petrucci*, No.45 • Brown, *Instrumental*, 1509$_1$ • Jeppesen, *Frottola*, Pe.E • Vogel, *Bibliografia*, 1509^1

(b) Brunet, *Manuel*, iii, cols.446–47 • *Index Aureliensis*, 122.660

(c) Bossinensis, *Tenori* only of the sheet found in Paris: the rest of the facsimile is of the second edition

(d) Disertori, *Frottole*

(e) Disertori, "Contradiction" • Sartori, "Little-known" • Underwood, *Renaissance*, 155–205.

Commentary:

1. The presentation of frottole in this format, new to Petrucci, presupposed a market for solo settings: this is discussed in chapter 9. But the manner of presentation also required new solutions on Petrucci's part — combining lute tabulature with staff notation on the same page. The technical problems were slight, but they did involve abandoning a structure within the forme that must have become almost mechanical for his craftsmen.

2. The patterns of papers in the two copies confirms that Petrucci had two presses in action at this time.

3. The manner of transcribing the original models for voice and lute is very mechanical. The Tenor and Bassus are taken into the lute part, usually with little change, while the Altus is abandoned. However, as Disertori has pointed out (Disertori, "Contradiction"), there is one exception. In *Amando e Desiando*, Bossinensis shows a greater awareness of the sonorous limitations of the lute, and of its potential for rhythmic activity by means of displacing notes to create a more active texture. In addition, this work shows a certain amount of melismatic writing.

4. The manner of relating the ricercars to the frottole, using letters with no modal implications, is interesting. From the layout of the Tavola, it is clear that the letters were assigned from the ricercars, and not from the frottole. Presumably, each ricercar was composed to be attached to a specific frottola, and then its application merely extended to others.

5. The presence of a later edition implies that the market was larger than Petrucci had expected.

No. 50. Bossinensis: *Tenori e contrabassi II*

10.v.1511   *RISM* 1511

There are cancel leaves in the copy at I-Mb, at F1,8 and H1,2,7,8

Edition

A1r]   Tenori e contraba ſſi intabu|lati col ſopran in canto fi|gurato per cantar e ſo|nar col lauto Li|bro Secundo. | Franciſci Boſſinenſis | Opus.

H8r]   Impreſſum in Foroſempronii per Octauia-|num petrutium Foroſempronienſem Anno domini | M D XI Die io Madii | Regiſtrum | AA BB CC DD EE FF GG HH Omnes quaterni | [Petrucci's device]

A1v]   [Tavola, set in three columns:]

B	Aime laſſo aime dolente	li
A	Ameni colli aprici monticelli	xlix
B	Ala fe per la mia fe	xlviii
D	Amando e deſiando	xii
C	Ai ceco et crudo amore	xxxiii
B	Coſi confuſo e il ſtato ondio ſon drento	xl
A	Chi non fa chi non intende	xxxiii
B	Chi promette e debitore	xxxvi
B	Come ua il mondo fior tu che beato	xxiii
A	Con pianto e con dolore	xx
B	Dolce amoroſo foco	xli
B	Deh chi mi fa dir nouella	xiiii
B	Seh per dio non mi far torto	liii
A	Dopoi lunghe fatiche e lunghi affanni	xi
B	Dolermi ſempre uoglio	xliii
B	Ele nata Aime colei	xv
B	Fuggitiua mia ſperanza	xxxix
B	Felice fu quel di felice il punto	iii
D	Fate ben gente corte ſe	xxvii
B	Ite caldi o miei ſoſpiri	xlv
B	Ite impace o ſoſpir fieri	xxv
F	I non manchai di fede et ſo imbando	xxi
B	Il buon nochier ſempre parla de uenti	v
B	I tho donnato il core	v
A	Liber fui un tempo in foco	xxxi
A	Non e penſer chel mio ſecreto intenda	l
A	Non ua laqua al mio gran foco	xxiiii
B	Non ſi uedra gia mai ſtanca ne ſatia	xxviii

[column two:]

B	O bon eglie bon o bon	xxiii
B	Occhi mei laſſi mentre chio ui giro	viii
A	O ſelue o ſparſe gregge	lv
A	O tempo o ciel uolubil che fuggendo	lv
D	Poi chel ciel ela fortuna	xvi
B	Poi che mia ſincera fede	xxii
B	Pregoui frondi fior frutti aque et herbe	xvii
A	Per fugir damor le punte	ix
A	Per dolor mi bagno il uiſo	iiii
B	Paſſato e il tempo	xviii
F	Quei che ſempre han da penare	xxvii
B	Quella bella e bianca mano	xliiii
F	Quando andaratu al monte bel pegotaro	xlii
F	Sio sedo alombra amor mi porge il ſtrale	xlix

A	Si oportuerit me teco mori non te negabo	ix
A	Se mai per maraueglia alzando il uiſo	vi
A	Se per colpa dil uoſtro fero ſdegno	x
B	Spinta mhai dil petto amore	xxix
F	Soſpiri i temo ma piu teme il core	xlvi
F	Se mai ne miei pochi Anni	xlvii
E	Sel partir mincrebbe e dolſe	xxvii
B	Sotto un uerde Alto cupreſſo	xxxv
A	Sio ſon ſtato aritornare	xxxii
B	Son pur gionto a tanto	liiii
B	Staralla ben coſi	xliiii
B	Vale diua uale impace	liii
B	Vidi hor cogliendo roſe hor gigli	xix
B	Venimus eromerira	xx

[column three:]

Recercar li quali ſerueno ale frottole ſecondo
    lordine de le littere ſottoſcripte.

A	.5.6.8.13.
B	1.9.12.14.15.16.18.20.
C	5.6.7.8.11
D	2.10.18.19.
E	3.4.6.8.9.11.17.
F	2.13.15.

A2r]   Regula per quelli che non ſanno cantare. [etc., giving the Italian version found in Spinacino's first book, No.33, above]

A2v]   Dedication to G. Barbadico, Apostolic Protonotary, as in No.49, with the following variants: 4: conferito → conferito • 5: ſententia → ſententia • 7: copia de → copia di • 8: compoſitione → compoſitione • 11: ſollicitudine a mi → ſolicitudine a me • 15: vigilie → voglie • 18: aliegro → alegro • 19: cognoſcendo → cognoſcendo • 21: prender delectatione → prender delectatione • 25: vedere. → vedere: • 25: Venetiarum → Venetiarum • 34: soave → suaue

Format and collation: Score: landscape quarto-in-eights. 64 folios: A-H⁸

Signatures:] AA 2 [\$4 • − A1

Foliation: top right recto] [1–2], III–X, XIII [*recte* XI], XII, XI [*recte* XIII], XIV–XVI, XXIII [*recte* XVII], XVIII–XXII, XVII [*recte* XXIII], XXIIII–XXXIII, XXIXV [*sic*], XXXV–XL, [XLI, not extant], XLII–XLVII, [XLVIII, not extant], XLIX–LV, 56–63, [64] • The two folios reported as not extant survive only in a later cancel sheet (see below)

No running heads. Composers' names are in the area of the head-line

Fonts: Music: Music type for texted vocal parts. Tabulature type for accompanying parts and for recercars

    Staves: Five-line for vocal parts: six-line for lute parts. Four per page, two pairs for the vocal items

    Text: Rotonda: for Regula, f.A2r • Roman, for texts and all else

Technical comments: Initial letter omitted on B4v [D], D1r [I] • Small guide letters are used on D3r [F], G1v [N], G5r [D] • The initial "R" on H1v.iv and on H2r.ii is a letter "B" with the lower horizontal masked: this is corrected in the cancel • The right end of last staves is not fully inked on several folios

No evident in-house corrections

Contents: This follows the voice part throughout, except when a letter or syllable is repeated in the
source for clearer underlay

	A1r	[Title]	
	A1v	[Tavola]	
	A2r	Regula per quelli che non ſanno cantare.	
	A2v	[Dedication; Sonnet]	
1	A3r	FElice fu quel di felice il ponto	[Anon.]
2	A3v	PEr dolor me bagno il uiſo	B.T.
3	A4v.iii	IL bon nochier ſempre parla de venti	[Anon.]
4	A5r	IO tho donato il core	IO.BA.ZE.
5	A5v	Se mai per maraueglia alzan dol uiſo	[Anon.]
6	A6v	SI oportuerit me teco mori	M.C.
7	A7v	O Chi mei laſſi mentre chio vi giro	B.T.
8	B1r	PEr fuggir damor le punte	M.C.
9	B2r	SE per colpa dil uostro fero	[Anon.]
10	B3v	AMando e deſiando	CARITEO
11	B4v	[D]o poi longe fatiche & longi affanni	[Anon.]
12	B5v	DEh chi me sa dir nouella	D.MI.C.& V.
13	B7r	HEle nata aime colei	PIE.DA LODI
14	B8r	POi chel ciel e la fortuna	MICHEL.V.
15	C1r	PRegoui frondi fiori aque & herbe	B.T.
16	C1v	COme ual mondo fior tu che beato	T.B.
17	C2r.iii	PAſſato el tempo tempo io condo	[Anon.]
18	C2v	VI di hor cogliendo roſe	ALEXAN. DEMOPHON
19	C3v	VEnimus e romeria	[Anon.]
20	C4r.iii	COn pianto e con dolore	[Anon.]
21	C4v	IO non manchi di ſede e ſono in bando	IO.BA.ZE.
22	C5v	POiche mia ſincera fede	ANT.CAP.
23	C7r	O Bon eglie bon	M.C.
24	C8r	NOn ual aqua al mio gran foco	B.T.
25	D1r	[I]Te in pace ſuſpir fieri	B.T.
26	D2v	SEl partir mincrebe e dolſe	[Anon.]
27	D3r.iii	FAte ben gente corteſe	[Anon.]
28	D4r	NOn ſi vedra mai ſtanca	A.C.
29	D5r	SPenta mhai del petto amore	D.M.
30	D6v	LIber fai un tempo in foco	M.C.
31	D7v.iii	SIo ſon ſtato a ritornare	D.MI.
32	D8v	AI cieco & crudo amore	HELIAS DVPRE
33	E1r	CHi non fa chi non intende	b.t.
34	E3r	SOto vn verde e alto cupreſſo	ANTO.CAPRI.
35	E4r.iii	CHi promete e debitore	[Anon.]
36	E5r	QUei che ſempre han da penate	M.C.
37	E6v	FVggiti ua mia ſperanza	M.C.
38	E7v.iii	COſi con fuſo e il ſtato	B.T.
39	E8v	DOlce amoroſo foco	[Anon.]
40	F1r	QVando andaratu al monte	IO.PIE.MAN.

41	F2*v*	DOlermi ſempre voglio	B.T.
42	F3*v*	QVella bella e biancha mano	A.C.
43	F4r.iii	STarala ben cuſſi	IO.BA.ZE.
44	F4*v*	ITe caldi o mei ſuſpiri	B.T.
45	F6r	SVſpir io themo me piu theme il core	B.T.
46	F7r.iii	SE mai nei mei pochi anni	[Anon.]
47	F7*v*.iii	A La fe per la mia fe	PELE.CESENA
48	F8*v*	SIo sedo a lombra amor	M.C.
49	G1r	AMeni colli aprici monticelli	LVDO.MILA.
50	G1*v*.iii	NOn e penſer chel mio ſecreto intenda	[Anon.]
51	G3r	AHime laſſo ahime dolente	MI.C.
52	G4*v*	VAle diua uale im pace	B.T.
53	G5r.iii	DEh per dio non mi far torto	[Anon.]
54	G6r	SOn pur con gio[n]to a tanto	[Anon.]
55	G6*v*	O Selue o ſparſe gregge herbete	AN.PATTAVINVS
56	G7r	O Tempo o ciel volubil che fugendo	PAVLI SCOTTI
57	G7*v*	REcercar primo	[Anon.]
58	G7*v*.iii	[Recercar] 2	[Anon.]
59	G8r.iii	[Recercar] 3	[Anon.]
60	H1r.ii	[Recercar] 4	[Anon.]
61	H1*v*.iv	[Recercar] 5	[Anon.]
62	H2r.ii	[Recercar] 6	[Anon.]
63	H2r.iv	[Recercar] 7	[Anon.]
64	H2*v*.ii	R[ecercar] 8	[Anon.]
65	H2*v*.iv	[Recercar] 9	[Anon.]
66	H3*v*.iii	[Recercar] 10	[Anon.]
67	H4r.iv	R[ecercar] 11	[Anon.]
68	H4*v*	[Recercar] 12	[Anon.]
69	H4*v*.ii	[Recercar] 13	[Anon.]
70	H4*v*.iii	[Recercar] 14	[Anon.]
71	H5r.i	[Recercar] 15	[Anon.]
72	H5*v*.ii	[Recercar] 16	[Anon.]
73	H6r.iii	[Recercar] 17	[Anon.]
74	H6*v*.ii	[Ricercar] 18	[Anon.]
75	H7r.iii	R[icercar] 19	[Anon.]
76	H7*v*.ii	R[icercar] 20	[Anon.]
	H8r	[Colophon; Register; Device]	
	H8*v*	[blank]	

Extant copy:

I-Mb, A.P.XVI.40. Complete. Folios F1 and F8 and the sheet H1,2,7,8 are cancels: see below

Watermarks:

A2–1	A5–6	B6–5	B8–7	C3–4	C7–8	D6–5	D7–8	E6–5	E7–8
26	26	26	26	26	26	26	26	26	26

F–2	F6–5	G5–6	G7–8	H3–4
27	27	27	27	27

Later corrections and changes: C1r and C2v: badly smudged imitations of the capital initials • C8v.iv.after music: *dmb,smg,mb,mb*, in ink • F1r.margin:] [?]Dominus Qualile [in ink • F8v: start of an imitation of the capital initial • H7v.foot: numeral:] 373555

Binding: Originally bound with the copy of Bossinensis's first book now at US-Cn • Modern parchment • Three fly-leaves at each end

Provenance: From the de Marinis collection (see Plamenac, "Toma Cecchini") • According to Sartori, *Petrucci*, pp. 158–59, a Professor Vatielli of Bologna saw this book in 1935, and reported that it came from a monastic house, and that it was then for sale from a book-dealer. In 1938, continues Sartori, it was on sale from De Marinis and Breslauer, and was bought by the Brera in 1943

Bibliography: Bonamo Schellembri, "Due recente" • Doná; "Musica", No.17 (exhibition at Milan in 1963) • Doná, "Musiche" • Fenlon and Dalla Vecchia, *Venezia*, pp. 82–83 (exhibition catalogue, Venice, 2001) • Vatielli, "Mostra" (exhibition at Bologna in 1935)

Private possession. Complete.

Size of page: 163 × 228 mm.

Watermarks:

A2-1	A6-5	B2-1	B6-5	C1-2	C5-6	D6-5	D7-8	E1-2	E6-5
26	26	26	26	26	26	26	26	26	26

F3-4	F7-8	G1-2	G4-3	H3-4	H8-7
27	27	27	27	27	27

Textual comments: A1r. the final point on the title has not taken any ink in this copy

Technical comments: D2r.iv: a clear set of spacing sorts beneath tablature notation, each about 0.5 mm wide.

Later changes: A4v.ii.4.5: ////1/ → ///1//, by erasure and with brown ink: this is similar to in-house corrections elsewhere

Binding: bound with Bossinensis' first book (No. 49)

Provenance: with Bossinensis' first book (No. 49) • A1r has the inscription:] Maria Bolling! | Ah fui di tanto | Tesoro Poſseſsor! | RB [namely Robert Bolling]

Bibliography: Sotheby's catalogue for the London sale of 5 December 2003, Lot 145

No. 50A. *Cancel.*

A bifolium for folios F1 and F8

Technical comments: the staves on F8 show a different inking pattern from that of the original edition Other details as above

———

Extant copy:

I-Mb, A.P.XVI.40. For the rest of this copy, see above

No watermark, or traces of change

No. 50B. *Cancel.*

The outer sheet of gathering H.

H8r]   Impreſſum in Foro ſ empronii per Octauia-|num petrutiu*m* foro ſ empronien ſ em Anno do*m*ini | M D XI Die io Madii | Regiſtrum | AA BB CC DD EE FF GG HH O*mn*es quaterni | [Petrucci's device]

Textual comments: the initial letter R for the fourth Ricercar, H1r.ii. is present.

Technical comments: the initial on H1ν.iv and H2ν.ii is correctly an "R"• H7ν: stave iv is not inked

Extant copy:
I-Mb, A,P.XVI.40. For the rest of this copy, see above
    Watermark: No 2 on H7-8

Lost copies: A copy was owned by Colón (Anglés, "Colombina", 24; Chapman, "Printed", Nos.38–39; Huntington; Plamenac, "Excerpta", 683–84)

Bibliography:
    (a) Rosaria Boccadifuoco, *Bibliografia*, No.495 • Sartori, *Petrucci*, No.46 • Jeppesen, *La Frottola*, Pe.F • Brown, *Instruemtal*, 1511₁ • Vogel, *Bibliografia*, 1511[1]
    (b) Brunet, *Manuel*, iii, cols.446–47 • *Index Aureliensis*, 122.661
    (c) Bossinensis, *Tenori*
    (d) Disertori, *Frottole*
    (e) Plamenac, "Toma Cecchini" • Sartori, "Little-known" • Sartori, "Bossinensis"

Commentary:

1. The connection between frottola and ricercar is presented in the same manner as in volume 1.

2. It is notable that the change in foliation from roman to arabic numerals occurs with the change from texted frottole to recercars, that is, in the middle of a gathering. Since this is also the point at which five-line staves stop, it may be that the change is a result of spacing in the forme, although it is possible that a different craftsman was involved.

3. Given the layout of the music, this book must have been set more or less linearly, without any attempt at setting by formes. That is the probable explanation for the use of small type letters as initials for the start of many compositions.

4. I have argued, in chapter 1, that this book was at least planned before Petrucci left Venice. The biographical evidence is presented there. Despite the change in papers at the beginning of gathering F, there is slight reason to believe that the book was printed in two layers. The pattern of staves seems to be consistent through the book, and the only change in type consists of an insignificant shift in the choice of initials "A" with the new paper. It is more probable that Petrucci had access to a relatively limited selection of paper, and that the "hiatus" at the beginning of gathering F represents a relatively small break in the work.

    The alternative solution requires that a second edition was printed in the first half of 1515. While this would make convenient good sense of the use of paper 27, there is not really strong enough evidence for such an assertion.

5. The cancel in gathering F seems to have been printed rather soon after the adjoining folios, i.e., at Fossombrone, and probably during the summer of 1511. The basic character of work is the same, and the absence of a watermark is probably coincidental, given that only half a sheet was used.

6. The second cancel is certainly significantly later, for Petrucci would only use this paper for a period of less than two years, during 1514–1516. With the limited evidence available, I have merely placed it at some point during 1515.

No. 51. *Frottole X*

1512

Not extant.

A1r]   [According to Colón, this may have read] Frottole Libro Decimo numero settanta cinque

Format: Landscape quarto, presumably in eights
Contents: The book opens with an "Exaudi preces meas", according to Colón: following Bottrigari, it also contained works by Filippo Mantuano, Jo. Hesdin, Jo. Scrivano, Franciscus, G.B.de Ferro, Dionisius da Mantova and Pietro da Lodi

———

Lost copies: Copies were owned by Colón (Chapman, "Printed" No.40) and Bottrigari: see the texts in chapter 20
Bibliography:
    (a) Sartori, *Petrucci*, No.47: Jeppesen, *La Frottola*, i
    (e) Jeppesen, "Review" • Jeppesen, "Neuentdeckten" • Vogel, *Bibliothek*, 616

Commentary:

1.   I have suggested, in chapter 9, that this book was probably originally thought of as a pair with *Frottole IX*; that Petrucci left Venice before printing it; and that it was eventually only published because the second book of Bossinensis settings showed that music could be sold from Fossombrone, and because Petrucci was stating his position in the face of Antico's emergence in Rome. In addition, I suspect that Petrucci had to keep his men busy while waiting for Paulus's *magnum opus*, or they would have moved on to other work elsewhere.

2.   The list of composers cited in Bottrigari helps to characterise this title as lying apart from the early frottola books, and closer to the last Venetian volumes in the series. However, I find Colón's statement, that the first work in this book was texted "Exaudi preces meas o mater gloriosa del tuo", to be very curious. This text looks much more like that of a lauda, and Petrucci had not previously opened a frottole volume with such a text.

3.   There are two folios at I-FBR, which have regularly been ascribed to this volume: see Vernarecci, *Petrucci*, p. 271; Jeppesen, "Review", p. 84; Sartori, "Nuove", p. 209. For the true place of those folios in Petrucci's output, see below at No. 68.

No. 52. Paulus de Middelburgh: *Paulina de recta Paschae*

8.vii.   1513

There are two cancels in this volume, one at the bifolium b1 and b6, and the other a single folio, A7. In addition, A1v was reset during printing. For all these, see below.

a1r]   PAVLINA | DE RECTA PASCHAE | CELEBRATIONE: | ET DE DIE PASSIONIS | DOMINI NOSTRI | IESV | CHRISTI:-

a1*v*] ¶Priuilegium conce∫∫um autori operis a ∫ancti∫∫imo domino | no∫tro Leone decimo q*uae* 1
nullus po∫∫it imprimere, neq*ue* imprimi | facere, neq*ue* uendere hoc opus de recta pa∫chæ
celebratione, & de | die pa∫∫ionis domini no∫tri Ie∫u Chri∫ti intitulatum, ∫ine licen-|tia autoris
ip∫ius libri Pauli de Middelburgo Epi∫copi foro∫em|pronien∫is, quoad uixerit, ∫ub pœna
excommunicationis latæ ∫en|tentiæ & ami∫∫ionis librorum ut patet in breui apo∫tolico ∫u-|per hoc 5
confecto, cuius exemplar hoc e∫t. | [block, 62 × 102 mm, of two angels supporting the arms of
Leo X]

¶LEO PAPA DECIMVS.

¶Venerabili fratri Epi∫copo Foro∫empronien∫i.

¶Venerabilis frater ∫alute*m* & apo∫tolica*m* benedictione*m*: Egregiam i*n* | omni prope 10
di∫ciplina doctrina*m* tuam plurimarum*que* optimarum artiu*m* | præ∫tante*m* ∫cientiam maximi ∫emper
fecimus facturiq*ue* i*n* dies magis ac | magis ∫umus: Quamobre*m* excelle*n*s tuu*m* ingeniu*m* pro∫equi
fauore cu|pie*n*tes libros de pa∫chæ obseruatione, pa∫∫ioni∫q*ue*, domi*n*icæ die quos | noui∫∫ime
co*n*feci∫ti, esq*ue* (ut i*n*telleximus) editurus, uolum*us* & ∫ub | excommunicationis latæ sententiæ
libroru*m*q*ue* amitte*n*dorum pœ-|na mandamus, ne quis imprimere po∫∫it, imprimiue facere, aut | 15
impre∫∫os uendere quoad uixeris præter te, ut utilitatem aliqua*m* | ex tuis laboribus hac etiam ex
parte percipias, & ip∫iq*ue* tui libri di|ligentius impre∫∫i in lucem prodeant: Datum Romæ apud San-
| ctum Petru*m* ∫ub Anulo Pi∫catoris. Die .xxix. Aprilis .M.D.xiii. | Pontificatus No∫tri Anno Primo.

¶Petrus Bembus. 19

a2*r*] [Within a frame of four blocks:] ¶Ad ∫ummu*m* chri∫tianæ ari∫tocratiæ principe*m*,
maxi|mu*m*q*ue* ∫acroru*m* anti∫titem, Leonem decimu*m*: Pauli ger|mani de Middelburgo dei &
apo∫tolicæ ∫edis gratia | epi∫copi foro∫empronien∫is i*n* libros ∫uos de recta pa∫|chæ
ob∫eruatione, & de die pa∫∫ionis Chri∫ti præfatio | in qua exponit cau∫am, quæ eu*m* ad
∫cribendu*m* impulit. | [text starts] | [the lower block is of two angels with Leo's arms, as found
on a1*v*]

GG4*v*] ¶Hieronymus Po∫thumus Foro∫empronien∫is lectori .*Salute*.

¶Si qua lector candidi∫∫ime i*n* hoc opere errata offendes, ea correctori | no*n* ad∫cribas uelim,
∫ed chalcographis: qui cu*m* docti no*n* ∫int, ∫æpe nume|ro literas i*n*uertant, dictiones pro dictionibus,
& ∫ub∫ulta*n*tes ∫yllabas | reponant nece∫∫e e∫t. In∫uper ne ne∫cius omniu*m* exi∫tas, ∫cire debes
Ioa*n* | ne*m* Bapti∫tam æthiopem adule∫ce*n*tulum imberbem excu∫oriæ artis tyrocinium | in hoc opere
exercui∫∫e. quicquid igitur male & perpera*m* impre∫∫um in|ueneris calami cu∫pide tran∫fodies, ac
iugulabis. Et ∫i error aliquis | in tabulis & numeris earu*m* commi∫∫us fuerit, habes canone*m* per
que*m* ta|bulas corrigere, & nouas tabulas co*m*ponere poteris.

¶Annotabimus tamen errores aliquos in tran∫cur∫u inuentos, | in quibus impre∫∫ores
hallucinati sunt. [There follow 27 lines with 52 corrections.]

GG5*r*] ¶Chri∫tophorus Pierius Gigas Canonicus | Foro∫empronien∫is.

¶AD LECTORES.

Quod clari ingenio na∫cantur ubiq*ue* per orbem
  Auctores: nulli e∫t (credite) res dubia.

Hic e∫t e multis ∫olus qui uicerit omnes
  Paulus, cui ∫tudium ∫cire futura dedit.

Quid Phœbus Phœbeq*ue* ualent: quid ∫idera cœli
  Omnia ab ingenio peruia facta ∫uo.

Erratum nullus Chri∫ti qui dogmata ∫eruat
  Nouerat: id clare te docet i∫tud opus.

Numine proq*ue* coli ut po∫∫et res defuit una
  Sum natus latio dicere nanq*ue* nequit.

¶Hieronymus Poſthumus Foroſempronienſis.

Perfectum quis carpet opus? ceſſabit acerbus
    Liuor, nam Pauli ſum liber altiloqui.
Ingenium natura dedit cui noſcere curſus
Aſtrorum, & magno ſcribere digna deo.
Me toto inſpecto dices pro Iuppiter, unus
    Omnia ſcire poteſt? liuide triſtis abi.

¶Blaſius Benuerardus Vrbinas.

Non hic inuidiæ rabies, neque dura laboret
    Cenſura, eſt omni parte opus eximium.
Mome procul fuge & ad latebras, & ad horrida teſqua,
    Iſta tua non eſt indiga falce ſeges.
Tu lolium legere, & lappas, tribuloſque ſuetus,
    Hiſce nouis abſunt quæ mala gramina agris.
Ergo late, aut ſi non potes hoc, confuſus honora,
    Poſtquam omni exiuit parte opus egregium.

GG5ν]   ¶ Regiſtrum libri:
        a b c d e f g h i k l m n o p q r ſt | A B C D E F G H I K L M N O W P Q R S | T V X Y Z
    AA BB CC DD EE FF GG
        ¶ Omnes ſunt quaterni præter .b. .W. & .GG. qui ſunt terni. & | t. eſt quinternus.
        ¶ Impreſſum Foro ſempronii per spectabilem uirum Octauianum petru|tium ciuem
    Foroſempronienſem impreſſoriæ artis peritiſſimum Anno | Domini.M.D.XIII. die octaua Iulii.
    cum priuilegio a | summo pontifice Leone decimo autori operis conceſ-|ſo, que nullus poſſit
    imprimere neque imprimi facere | neque uendere dictos libros ſine licentia au|toris ſub
    excommunicationis latæ | ſententiæ librorumque amittendorum | pœna: quemadmodum patet in |
    breui apostolico ſuper | hoc confecto, cuius | exemplar in prin-|cipio operis | poſitum | eſt. | + |
    [Petrucci's device]

Format and collation: Portrait folio. 396 folios, a⁸b⁶c-r⁸ſt¹⁰A-O⁸; Œ⁶P-Z,AA-FF⁸GG⁶
Signatures:] a ii [$4 • − a1, b4, W4, GG4 • + t5 • For e2 and e3, see below
No foliation
Text-block: 39 lines: 213 (223) × 125 mm.
Fonts: Roman text, "x" = 2.1 mm; "20" = 108mm. • Greek text: on c6r-7ν, f3r-5ν, f8ν-g3r, g8r-ν, i5r, k6ν, k8r, l2r, n3r, ſ8r, A5r, B3ν, B6r-B7r, C3ν-C4ν, D4r-ν, D5ν-D6r, E1ν, E2ν-E3r, E4ν-E5r, E6r, H6r, M2ν, P1ν, Z1r, Z2r, Z8r, AA4ν, BB5ν, CC7r, DD6r-DD7r, GG4r. • Hebrew text on B7r-ν, C4r, D2r, D7r, D8r, M1r, M2ν, M4ν, N2r-N5ν, GG4r. also, with much larger characters, cut on a single block, on Z1r and Z4r, using the same block • The volume also has new sets of initials • Isaac, *Index*, No.14040, calls the three fonts, Roman, Greek, and Hebrew, all 110 mm
Blocks: a block of the arms of Pope Leo X, with angel supporters, 62 × 102 mm: on a1ν.foot and a2r.foot • a head-piece with two dolphins, 33.5 × 101.5 mm: on a2r, b5ν, A1r and A2r • a column with a fountain and two individuals, 269 × 26 mm: on a2r, b5ν, A1r and A2r, on the left, except for b5ν, where it is on the right • a column with a fountain and several individuals, 269 × 43 mm: on a2r, b5ν, A1r and A2r, on the right, except for b5ν, where it is on the left • a block, 62 × 102 mm, with the arms of the author, with a miter for his rank as Bishop of Fossombrone, a stemma designed to show his interest in astronomy: at the foot of b5ν and A2r • a block with

the arms of the Emperor Maximilian (illustrated in Castellani, *Arte*, ii, p. 181), 61 × 102 mm: at the foot of A1 • P5r: a whole-page block of the author's vision of the Crucifixion

Running heads: Although these appear on many pages, they do not seem to have been retained in the forme. The following folios have no running head: a1r-b6v, t10v, A1r, A2r, P5r, GG3v-Gg6v. Of these, headlines should appear on b6r, b6v, and t10v

     verso:] Liber [c1-GG2, except as follows • Liber. [e6,7, E3,6, F3,6, G2,4,5, H2,4,5,8, I2,5,7, K1,3-6,8, P8, Q1-Q4,7,8, R1-R3,5,8, S1,4,7, T2-T4,6,8, X1,2,4-6,8, Y1-Y3,5,8, Z2-Z5,7, AA1,2,4-6,8, BB2,3,5,7,8, CC4-CC6 • Procemium. [X3

     recto:[Primus. [c1-d1, A3-B4 • Secundus. [d2-e6, B5-D3, D5,6 • Secunduss [D4 • Tertius. [e7-f6, f8-g3, D7-E6 • Tertius [f7 • Quartus. [g4-h3, E7-F7 • Quintus. [h4-i4, G1-G7 • Sextus. [i5-k2, F8, G8-H2, H4,5,8, I2,4,7, K1,3-6,8 • Sextus [H3,6,7, I1,3,5,6,8, K2,7 • Septimus. [k3-k8, L1-L8 • Octauus. [l1-l5, M1-N8 • Nonus. [l6-n2, O1-W6 • Decimus. [n3-o1, P1-P4, P6-Q4 • Vndecimus. [o2-r1, Q5, Q7-R1, R3-R6 • Vndecimns. [Q6r • Vndecimus [R2 • Duodecimus. [r2-s5, R7-S5, S7-T1 • Duodecimus [S6 • Tertiu[decimus. [s6-t2, T2-V2 • Quartu[decimus. [t3-t5, t9, t10, V3-X3 • Quartu[decimus [t6-t8 • Procemium [X4 • Quintu[decimus. [X5-Y5 • Sextu[decimus. [Y6-AA6 • Decimu[[eptimus. [AA7-CC3 • Decimu[octauus. [CC4-EE4 • Decimu[nonus [EE5-GG3

     Errors occur on t2r, t3r, B5r, F8r, and EE4r

Catchwords: On the verso of the fourth or last sheet of many gatherings: a4, c4,8, d4, g8, i4, l8, t5, A4, B4, C4,8, E4, F4,8, G4, H4,8, I4,8, K4,8, M4, O4, P8, Q4,8, R4,8, S4,8, T4,8, X4,8, Y4,8, Z4, AA4,8, BB4,8, CC4,8, DD4v • For A8v, see under "In-house corrections"

Textual comments: o7r.21: the year should be 1502. This correction is listed in the Corrigenda on GG4v. It still reads 1504 in many copies, including the copies at A-Wn and E-Sc, and all three at GB-Lbl

Technical comments: This uses red and black printing on many folios: d6v-e1r, e3v-e6r, f3r-f5v, f8v-g3r, g5r-g7v, h2v, and F1r • Similar material (perhaps intended to be in red) is printed in black on e8v-f2v, h2r, i7r, l3r-6r, m2r-4v, m6r, m7r-n1v, n7r-8r, o7r-r1v, etc. • A sign like a crescendo sign on e8v-f2v, o7r-r1v, V6v-8v • f6r: an initial S is damaged in some copies

In-house corrections: a3r.22: religioe → religione (A-Wn, all three copies at GB-Cu, GB-Lbl 472.e.8 and GB-Lbl 696.l.15, I-Ra, I-Rvat Ferraioli and I-Rvat Liturgia) • b3v.37–38: aggre[[am aggre[[i (GB-Cu, F★.8.27 and I-Rvat Liturgia) • e2r.signature: cii (A-Wn, all copies at GB-Cu, GB-Lbl 216.d.15, GB-Lbl 472.e.8, I-Ra, I-Rn 69.1.d.1, P-Ln, I-Rvat Ferraioli and US-CA Typ.525.13.675F) → eii, by stop press change (both at B-Br, D-B, E-Mmarch, E-Sc, GB-Lbl 696.l.15, GB-Ob – all three copies, I-Rvat Liturgia, and US-CA ★fNC.P2863.513p) • e3r.signature: stamped in: A-Wn, GB-Cu F★.8.27, GB-Cu G.2.16, GB-Lbl 216.d.15, GB-Lbl 696.l.15, I-Ra, I-Rvat Liturgia • o7r.21:] 1504 → 1502 (GB-Cu F★.8.27 and GB-Cu G.2.16) • p2r.signature: may have been added as a stop-press correction, although it seems to appear in almost all copies: it is in manuscript on the copy at D-B, although this is more likely to be the result of a poor impression • t2r.head-line: Quartu[decimus (for example, A-Wn, two copies at GB-Cu and two at GB-Lbl) → Tertiu[decimus, by a stop-press change (including GB-Cu Norton.a.23 and GB-Lbl 696.l.15) • A8v.signature line: stamped-in catchword "anti-" (actually an insertion, for this part of the word "anticipatam" is missing on B1r): B-Br (two copies), D-B, E-Mmarch, E-Sc, GB-Cu (three copies), GB-Lbl (three copies), H-SY, I-Ra, I-Rn (three copies), I-Rvat Ferraioli, I-Rvat Liturgia, P-Ln, US-CA (two copies). It is particularly easy to see this in those libraries containing more than one copy, for the alignment is often different: see the two copies in Brussels or the three at GB-Lbl for particularly clear examples • F1r.18.last column:] d [stamped in (A-Wn, E-Sc, I-Ra, I-Rn 69.1.d.1 and US-CA ★fNC.P2863.513p) or in manuscript (in the other two I-

Rn copies, I-Rvat Ferraioli and US-CA Typ.525.13.675F). In all three copies at GB-Cu, all three
at GB-Lbl and I-Rvat Liturgia, it is printed normally probably as the result of a stop-press correction
• Q6*v*.30: perii → *imperii* (all copies at GB-Lbl, I-Ra, I-Rvat Ferraioli and I-Rvat Liturgia) • R3*r*.1:
] indicarem → iudicarem (A-Wn and I-Rvat Liturgia) • R6*r*.1:] bandm → bandum (A-Wn and I-
Rvat Liturgia) • R7*v*.21: iibro → libro (all the copies at GB-Cu, all three at GB-Lbl, I-Ra and I-
Rvat Ferraioli) • V5*r*.3: neneris → ueneris (GB-Cu Norton.a.23, GB-Lbl, 696.l.15, I-Ra and I-
Rvat Ferraioli) • X7*v*.4: deutronomii → deuteronomii (all three copies at GB-Cu, all three at GB-
Lbl, I-Ra, I-Rvat Ferraioli and I-Rvat Liturgia) • Z7*v*.12: con[entaneam → con[entaneum (A-Wn,
all three copies at GB-Cu, I-Rvat Ferraioli and I-Rvat Liturgia) EE4*r*.head-line: Decimu[nonus → Decimu[
octaus, [*sic*: in GB-Cu Norton a.23 • GG4*v*.4–5:] sæpen ume | ro → sæpe nume | ro [by stop-press
correction in the copies at B-Br III.47,758.C and E-Sc. The original is in A-Wn, GB-Cu, G.2.16,
all three copies at GB-Lbl, and US-CA Typ.525.13.675f • GG4*v*.8:] Tra[fodies → tran[fodies [in
many copies. The original can be found in all three copies at I-Rn and in US-CA Typ.525.13.675F.
The correction is in, for example, A-Wn, B-Br III.47, E-Sc, all three copies at GB-Cu, all three
at GB-Lbl, I-Rvat Ferraioli, and I-Rvat Liturgia

   It is probable that many of the corrigenda listed on GG4*v* were subject to stop-press correction: a few examples are noted above

Contents:

a1*r*   [Title]

a1*v*   [Privilege]

a2*r*   [Letter to Leo X]

a3*r*.18   ¶Ad eundem [ummum pontificem Leonem decimum: Pauli de mid | delburgo epi[copi
             foro[empronien[is exhortatio, ut legitimam | pa[chæ celebrationem, defectu calendarii
             abolitam, in u[um reuo- | cet: & in pri[tinum [tatum reducat.

a7*v*   [Letter to Maximilian:]
             ¶Ad [acrati[[imam cæ[aream maie[tatem epi[tola exhortato- | ria pro recta pa[chæ
             celebratione & calendarii correctione.
             ¶Paulus germanus de middelburgo, dei & apo[tolicæ [edis gra | tia epi[copus
             foro[empronien[is, [erenii[imo romanorum regi | Maximiliano imperatori electo
             [emper augu[to fœlicitatem optat.

b1*r*.19   [Letter to the College of Cardinals:]
             ¶Ad apo[tolicum cœtum et chri[tianæ religionis reipublicæ [ena- | tum pro calendarii
             emendatione exhortatio, ut legitima pa[chae ce | lebratio errore calendarii abolita in u[um
             reuocetur.

b2*v*.23   [Letter to the Council:]
             ¶Ad [acro[anctum lateranen[e concilium pro calendarii emenda | tione exhortatio, ut
             legitima pa[chæ ob[eruatio errore calendarii | abolita in u[um reuocetur:

b4*r*   Ad illu[tri[[imum principem Franci[cummariam urbini ducem | almæ urbis
             præfectum, [anctæque romanæ eccle[iæ uexilliferum epi[tola.

b4*v*   ¶Ad eundem Leonem decimum pontificem maximum, operis de recta pa[| chæ
             celebratione & calendarii emendatione dedicatio.

b5*v*   [Within a frame of four blocks] ¶ Libri de paschae celebratione exordium eiu[que
             diui | [io in partes quatuordecim: diuinique numinis inuocatio. [Text starts]

c1*r*   [Book I:] ¶ Liber primus Chri[ti [aluatoris ad discipulorum eius pa[cha | lem
             ob[eruationem continet: pri[corumque doctorum de pa[chæ | celebratione opiniones
             [uccincte & breuiter narrat; & ob[erua- | tiones antiquas u[que ad celebrati[[imam
             illam nicœnam [ynodum | exponit: inqua confutata, & extirpata opinione

quartadecimano | rum (qui una cum iudæis paſcha faciebant) canon orthodoxorum | confirmatus fuit.

A1r   [Part II.]

[Within a frame of four blocks] ¶ Ad ſacratiſſimam cæſaream maieſtatem, libri de | die paſſionis domini noſtri Ieſu Chriſti dedicatio.

¶Paulus de Middelburgo, dei & apoſtolicæ ſedis | gratia epiſcopus foroſempronienſis, ſereniſſimo roma | norum regi Maximiliano imperatori electo ſemper | auguſto fœlicitatem optat.

A2r   [Within a frame of four blocks] ¶ Secunda pars operis dominicæ paſſionis & reſurrectio- | nis diem indagat, & iudæorum ſuper hoc argumenta confutat.

G8v.25   [first letter from Petrus de Rivo:]

¶Paulus de middelburgo zelandiæ doctiſſimo viro ſacræ theologiæ | profeſſori eximio, magiſtro Petro de riuo: ſalutem dicit.

I5r.18   ¶ Sequitur alia epiſtola eidem magiſtro Petro de riuo tranſmiſ | ſa in qua ſcripta eius de cyclo lunari, ad decemnouenali confutantur.

I5v   ¶ Paulus de Middelburgo Zelandiæ doctiſſimo uiro magiſtro Pe | tro de riuo ſacræ theologiæ profeſſori eximio ſalutem dicit.

GG3r.33   FINIS. | LAUS. DEO. AETERNO.

GG3v   Totius operis peroratio.

GG4r.20   ¶ Finis & deo gloria. | ¶ Τελος χαῖ θεῶ δο ξα.. | ¶ הם דכשלמ תללו'ה. | ¶ Tam ueniſlam haleluia. [sic]

GG4v   Hieronymus Poſthumus Forosemproniensis lectori .S. [and errata: see above]

GG5r   [Verses to the reader, transcribed above]

GG5v   [Register; Colophon; Device]

GG6r-v   [blank]

Extant copies: This is by far the most commonly found of all Petrucci's titles: there are, for example, almost 20 copies in the US (as recorded in the NUC) alone, more than survive in the whole world for any other of his books. Therefore, I am sure that this is not a complete list of all extant copies, and the *Index Aureliensis* is some time from reaching this author. Nor have I attempted to see many copies, concentrating on those which happen to be available in libraries or cities which I have visited for other reasons

A-Wn, 74.N.10. Complete

    Size: 319 × 208 mm.

    This copy is very tightly bound and watermarks are difficult to see. The evident ones are Nos.28 and 29

    Corrections and changes:

       In-house: a3r, e3r, F1r, R3r, R6r, and GG4v: see above

       Later: a3r.18] potificem → pontificem [in brown ink

    Binding: ¼-leather over wooden-boards. The leather panel has blind rolls front and back. There are incisions for two metal clasps • Guard strips inside the boards come from a fifteenth-century liturgical manuscript, with texts for Holy Week • In addition there are two fly-leaves, front and back

B-Br, III.47,758.C. Lacks the last blank folio

    Size: 308 × 200 mm.

    Watermark: Nos.28 and 29 throughout

    Corrections and changes:

In-house: e2*r*, A8*v*, GG4*v*.4–5, and GG4*v*.9: see above

Later: Red ink markings against some lines of text

Binding: Original brown leather over wood, with five sewing bands. Blind rolls to delineate compartments on the spine. Rebacked • All fore-edges painted red. The numeral 60 on the front edge • A later, probably 20th-century, panel on the spine, of green leather, inscribed:] PAVLINAE | DE RECTA PASCHÆ | CELEBRATIONE • One later fly-leaf and paste-down at each end: both flyleaves have the watermark] Baujoz & Cie

Provenance: A French-language sale catalogue entry inside front board

B-Br, V.H. 15,154. C. L.P. Complete. For the cancel bifolium b1,6, see below

    Size: 310 × 211 mm.

    Watermark: Nos.28 and 29 throughout

    Corrections:

        In-house: e2*r* and A8*v*: see above

        Later: Some errata have been corrected, following the printed list, and additional emendations have been made, in brown ink

    Binding: Original brown-stained leather over boards, with six sewing-bands. Both boards and each spine panel outlined with three gold rules. The second panel reads] PAVLINA • All edges gilt and gauffered • One fly-leaf and one paste-down at each end. Each fly-leaf has the watermark of a bunch of grapes

    Provenance: a1*r*.] Bibliotheæ Colbertinæ • Inside the front board are the book-plates of] C. VAN HULTHEN [and of] BIBLIOTEHCÆ MEERMANNIANÆ [Inside the back board is a bookplate of an engraving of a female St. Jerome in her study, a quotation from Cicero, and signed] *B Dauiuier Brugensis del^r* 1806.

D-As, 2 Chron.13. Not seen

D-As, 2 Chron.13a. Not seen

D-B, 4°.Ds.6550. Lacks the last blank folio

    Size of page: 312 × 197 mm.

    Later changes: A number of manuscript annotations and side-lining, on, for example, a3*v*-a4*r*, d4*v*, and e7*r*

    Binding: Modern, dated 1988. One modern paste-down and one flyleaf at each end

D-Mbs, P.lat.1136. Not seen

    Binding: Bound with Scaliger, *Opus Movum* (Paris, 1583), according to Lorenz Welker

    Provenance: "sum ex bibliotheca Joh. Georgii à Werdenstein."

D-Mbs, P.lat.1136a. Not seen

    Provenance: from the library of the Premonstratensian Monastery in Steingarden

D-Mbs, Res.2°.Liturg.327. Not seen

    Provenance: St. Ulrich and Afra, Augsburg

E-Mmarch, 51/4/13. Complete

    Size of page: 318 × 203 mm.

    Watermarks: Nos. 28 and 29 throughout

    Corrections and changes:

        In-house: A8*v*: see above

        Later: Many later manuscript annotations

    Binding: Modern

E-Sc, 1–4–12. Lacks f.GG6. Has a cancel folio at A7

    Size: 328 × 210 mm.

    Watermarks: Nos.28 and 29 throughout

Binding: Limp parchment, with 4 tie-strings per cover. Three sewing bands • Red edges, and the word PAVLVM in black ink on all three • One paste-down and conjugate fly-leaf at each end. Watermarked with a bull on one half-sheet, with the word QVARTINO, and a mounted spearman on the other

Provenance: a1r.] old call number:] C . . . S . . . Tab . . . 106 . . . N° . . . 2 • Purchased, according to Colón's *Registrum*, in Rome in November 1515, for 315 quatrines:] Pauli de midelburgo paulina in .2. partes diuiſa prima | eſt de recta paſche celebratione [. . .] Imp. foroſempronij 8ª Julij .1513. coſto en Roma | 315 quatrines por Noujembre de 1515. es en folio

Bibliography: Moreno Maldonado, et al. *Biblioteca*, v, p. 103 • *Registrum*, No.3459 • Chapman, "Printed", No.40

F-Pn, F.B.8148. Not seen

F-Pn, Rés.G.147. Not seen

GB-Ctc. Incomplete, lacking c3-6 and GG6. Not seen

GB-Cu, F*.8.27

> **Size of page:** 320 × 206 mm.

> **Corrections and changes:**

>> **In-house:** b3v, e3r, o7r, A8v, R7v, X7v, Z7v, and GG4v: see above

>> **Later:** a3r.18] potificem → pontificem [in brown ink • b2v-b3r. the Lateran dedication is ruled round and underlined • This has several layers of later annotation: in brown ink on a3r-a6v; in a faded pink on a3r-c4v and EE5r-FF3r; in pencil on c6v-7r; and in a different brown ink on B4r and C2r-7v

> **Binding:** 16th-century dark leather with simple border rolls and five sering bands • a panel on the spine reads] PAVLINA | DE. PASCHE | CELEBRAT. • Two parchment guard strips • two flyleaves at each end, with a watermark of a bunch of grapes

> **Provenance:** a1r, the bookplate of] *Academiæ Cantabrigien[is | Liber*

GB-Cu, G.2.16. Complete

> **Size of page:** 293 × 211 mm.

> **Watermarks:** Nos.28 and 29 throughout

> **Corrections and changes:**

>> **In-house:** o7r, e3r, A8v, R7v, X7v, Z7v, GG4r and GG4v: see above

>> **Later:** a3r.18] potificem → pontificem [in brown ink • b2v-b3r. the Lateran dedication is ruled round and underlined • An Italian 16th-century hand has added many marginalia, also underlining words

> **Binding:** Parchment, probably of the 17th-century, with 5 sewing bands • Edges painted red • On the spine, probably written in the Lyons (or Leiden) Academy:] P DE MIDDELBUR. | *RECTA*| *PASCHÆ* | *Celebratione.* | MDXIII. • On the fore-edge:] pauline

> **Provenance:** On top and bottom edges, the stampe] ACAD | LVGD • Inside the front board, the book-plate of] GEORGIVS D.G. MAG. BR. FR. ET HIB. REX. F.D. [and] MVNIFICENTIA REGIA 1715. [with the engraver's signature of] I.P.Sc.

GB-Cu, Norton.a.23. Complete

> **Size of page:** 321 × 211 mm.

> **Watermarks:** Nos.28 and 29 throughout

> **Corrections and changes:**

>> **In-house:** t2r, A8v, R7v, V5r, X7v, Z7v, EE4r, and GG4v: see above

>> **Later:** An early Italian owner, writing in a gingery ink, set out to correct all the errate listed on GG4v, striking through on that page all those that he corrected: only a few

are listed here, alongside others. He also marked many places with side-lines in the margins, and added annotations on many pages from a4v, though there are fewer after 18r. He was probably the paginator, entering numerals 1–121 on a2r–h8r.

a3r.18] potificem → pontificem [in brown ink • a7r.27:] aggreſſam → aggreſus [in brown ink • b2v–b3r: the Lateran dedication is ruled round and underlined • b3v.37 8:] ag-|greſſam ag-|greſſi [in brown ink • d2v.22:] uni — |cuiſque → uniuſ-|cu^{9}ſque [in brown ink • 07r.21: the erroneous year 1504 has been corrected in manuscript, to 1502 • t3r.head-line: Quartuſdecimus → Tertiuſdecimus [by erasure of the first five letters and manuscript insertion • F8r.head-line: Sextus → Quintus [by erasure of the first four letters, and insertion • R3r.1:] indicarem → iudicarem [in brown ink • R6r.1:] bandm → bandum [in brown ink • Y2r.4:] loo → loco [in brown ink

A different writer marked paragraph signs, in an ink now faded to pink, from c4r • GG5v, Petrucci's mark is touched up, with the following beneath it:] jnt.20 jnt.3 1/2

Binding: old vellum, with four sewing bands, and the remains of two tie-strings on each board • Edges were green • On the front board:] Paulus de midelburg de paſsione celebratione | de die paſsionis chriſti [and, later:] Paulina de recta Pasche celebrat. et de die passion. D. N. Jesu xpi | Ar mar° p° abbat° 3 muro n° 40 [On the spine:] Paulina de recta Paſche celeb < . . . > | de Die Paſſion. D. N. Jesu < . . . > • One blue paste-down at each end stubbed through to inside the fly-leaves. Four fly-leaves at the front, with a watermark of an anchor in a circle with a star above, 69 × 47 mm, on i and iv. Eight fly-leaves at the back, with the same watermark on vi, viii, x, and xii

Provenance: From the collection of F.J. Norton • on front paste-down: the book-plate of] Stephen Gaselee • a1r:] Ex bibli^{ca} Altemps^{na} • GG5v:] Rome 9 Martij 1534 | Sibi et amicis eius | Petrus de Son[. . .]

GB-DR, Palace Green Library, Routh 17.B.13. Complete. Not seen

GB-Lbl, 216.d.15. Complete

Size of page: 304 × 203 mm.

Watermarks: Nos.28 and 29 throughout • No.28 on a2,5,6; b1,3,5; d1,4,6,7; e5,6,7,8; f1,2,6; g4,6,7,8; h2,4,6,8; i3,4,7,8; k7; l6; n7; p1,5; q1,2,3; r6; B2; D1,5; E4; H1,6,7; I5,6,7,8; K2,5,6,8; L5,6,7,8; W4,6; P2,3,5,8; Q1,2,3,4; R1,3,4,7; S1,3,4,7; T1; V2,4; Y1; BB2; CC3,5; EE2,6; FF2,4,6,8; GG3,5,6 • No.29 on a8; c2,3,4,8; f5; k3,4; l1,2,5; m1,2,3,4; n4,6,8; o1,3,4,7; p6,7; q5; r1,4,7; s1,3,4,7; t1,3,6,7,9; A1,3,4,7; B3,4,8; C1,2,3,5; D2,3; E1,2,3; F2,3,4,8; G3,4,7,8; H5; M2,3,5,8; N2,3,4,8; O1,4,6,7; W5; T4,6,7; V6,8; X2,3,4,8; Y3,4,7; Z1,2,3,5; AA1,3,4,7; BB1,4,6; CC2,8; DD1,2,5,6; EE1,5

Corrections and changes:

In-house: e2r, p2r, A8v, F1r, Q6v, R7v, X7v and GG4v: see above

Later: At least two levels of 16th-century manuscript annotation. The first can be seen on, for example, a8r, b2r, and cc6r. The second, apparently especially interested in numerology, appears on c2r–7r, c8v–d5r, e1v–2v, E6v–H1r, etc.

Binding: Leather, bearing the arms of George III • At each end, a marbled paste-down conjugate to a fly-leaf, the latter pasted to the outer of two paper fly-leaves

Provenance: h3r: manuscript at foot of the page:] Iste liber est monasterij s. saluatoris. que$m$ reliquit R$_{mus}$ D. D. | Ant. Cont. patriarcha venetiarum pro cuius anima orave tenemus

Bibliography: Johnson and Scholderer, *Short-Title*, p. 495

GB-Lbl, 472.e.8. Lacking folio a1

Size of Page: 311 × 203 mm.

Watermarks: Nos.28 and 29 throughout

Textual comments: folio e3 is not signed

Corrections:

  In-house: e2r, p2r, A8v, F1r, Q6v, R7v, X7v, and GG4v: see above

  Later: Has 16th-century manuscript annotations, on a8v, and then frequently from c4r •
    07r.21: the erroneous year 1504 has been corrected in manuscript, to 1502 • A7r.31: a
    comma has been added in manuscript, after the word] horis • F8r.headline: the erro-
    neous] Sextus [struck through in ink • R5v–R6r: approbandum → approbandam • Y2r.4:
    loo → loco

  Binding: Late black leather • Gilt edges • At each end, a marbled paste-down and conjugate,
    the latter pasted to the outer of two fly-leaves. An additional fly-leaf at the front • A crown
    stamped on each paste-down

  Bibliography: Johnson and Scholderer, *Short-Title*, p. 495

GB-Lbl, 696.l.15. Complete

  Watermarks: Nos.28 and 29 throughout

  Corrections and changes:

    In-house: e2r, t2r, A8v, F1r, Q6v, R7v, V5r, X7v, and GG4v: see above

  Binding: Royal binding with the heraldic device, rebacked in 1934 • Green edges • At each
    end, marbled paste-down and conjugate, the latter pasted to the outer of two fly-leaves

  Provenance: a1r.] Lumley

  Bibliography: Jayne and Johnson, *Lumley*, No.703 • Johnson and Scholderer, *Short-Title*, p. 495

GB-Lv, A.L.I,406–1890. Not seen

GB-Ob, Byw.G 5.15. Complete

  In-house correction: A8v: see above

GB-Ob, F.19.Th.Seld. Complete

  In-house correction: A8v: see above

GB-Ob, Rigaud.c.14. Complete

  Watermarks: No.28 on a2,3,5, b1,4,5, d4,6,7,8, etc.: No.29 on a1, c1,3,5, etc.

  In-house correction: A8v: see above

H-SY, Ös.XXVII.I.(3). Complete

  Size of page: 307 × 196 mm.

  Watermarks: No 28 or 29 present throughout: it is not always possible to tell which mark is
    present, for the mark lies beneath the text, and the paper is sometimes fairly heavy. But, for
    example, mark 28 appears on d7, p5, D5, D8, GG4 and GG5; mark 29 is on m2, m3, n5,
    p8, q5, B3, and GG6

  In-house correction: A8v: see above

  Binding: Early white leather, with gilt fore-edges • One paste-down and one flyleaf at the front;
    only the paste-down at the back. The flyleaf has a mark of three flowers within a circle,
    with another flower above

  Provenance: A1r.] Cat. Eccle. Sabarum | Anno 1791. [This suggests that the book was in the
    Seminary at Szambothely from quite an early date

I-Fm, I.BB.IV.5. Lost

I-FBR. Not seen

I-FBR. Not seen

I-Mcap. Complete. Not seen

  Size of Page: 305 × 200 mm.

  Bibliography: Valentini and Malusardi, *Incunaboli*, p. 188

I-Rc. Not seen

I-Rli. Not seen

I-Rn, 69.1.d.1. Lacks f.GG6

> **Size of page:** 332 × 197 mm.
>
> **Watermarks:** Marks 29 and 28 throughout. For example, mark 29 on a2,8, b1, c2,5,6,8, etc; mark 28 on a4,6, b3,5, d3,4,7,8, e1,4,6,7, etc.
>
> **Corrections and changes:**
>
> > **In-house:** A8*v*: see above
> >
> > **Later:** a3*r*.18] potificem → po*n*tificem [in brown ink • b2*v*-b3*r*. the Lateran dedication is ruled round and underlined •
>
> **Binding:** Modern parchment binding and flyleaves
>
> **Provenance:** a1*r*.] Sanct*æ* Mari*æ* de Scala Urbij [i.e., in Rome]

I-Rn, 69.1.d.2. Complete

> **Size of page:** 318 × 204 mm.
>
> **Watermarks:** Marks 28 and 29 throughout: 28 on a4,6,7; b4,5,6; d2,3,5,8; e1,2,3,4; f3,5,7,8; g1,2,4,6; h1,3,7; i3,5,7,8; k2,4,6; l6; n7; p1,4; q2,6,8; r6; B7; D1,4; F8; G7; H1,5,6; I2,3,5,8; K1,2,4,6; L1,4,7; W1,4,5; P3,4,7,8; Q1,4,6,7; R2,3,4,8; S4,6,7; T3,8; V3,5,7; X4; Y1; BB2,8; CC2,4; EE1,6,7; FF3,5,7,8; GG1,2,3 • 29 on a8; c3,4,7,8; h5; k8; l5,7,8; m2,4,6,8; n1,4,6; o4,6,7,8; p3,7; q4; r2,5,8; s3,5,7,8; t1,2,5,7,8; A2,4,6,8; B4,6,8; C2,5,6,8; D6,7; E2,3,5,8; F4,6,7; G3,4,8; H7; M1,2,5,6; N4,6,7,8; O1,4,6,7; S8; T2,5; V8; X1,6,7; Y3,4,7; Z1,2,3,5; AA2,5,6,8; BB4,6; CC1,3; DD3,4,7,8; EE5
>
> **Corrections and changes:**
>
> > **In-house:** e2*r*, A8*v* and F1*r*: see above
> >
> > **Later:** r4*r*.25:] 1563 11 aprilis 11 aprilis 0 → 1563 11 aprilis 8 aprilis 3 • r5*r*.18:] 1600 → 1700 [in the same hand as that of r4*r*
>
> **Binding:** Hand-painted "marbled" leather. On the spine, an 18th-century panel, with a gold title. Below it, in 16th-century script:] Pauli Germa[...] | De Middel[...] • Blue painted edges • Paste-down and two flyleaves at the front: paste-down and one flyleaf at the back. There is a watermark on i and ii, of a crown and star in a circle, with the letter M below, measuring 79 × 49 mm: this mark is not to be found in the standard works
>
> **Provenance:** Earlier signatures, on front paste-down:] F.II.12 [and] 4.5.F.10 • a1*r*. book-plate of] D. SISTO | ABATE BENIGNI [and the oval stamp bearing the initials EVB • GG5*v*] Di piero Antonio | Magagnico | In foss.[ne]

I-Rn, 69.1.d.3. Complete

> **Size of page:** 308 × 204 mm.
>
> **Watermarks:** Marks 28 and 29 throughout
>
> **Corrections and changes:**
>
> > **In-house:** e2*r*, A8*v* and F1*r*: see above
> >
> > **Later:** On some folios, there are occasional markings
>
> **Binding:** Modern parchment. • One paste-down and one flyleaf at each end • All edges lightly carved in horizontal bands • On the top edge:] PAULINA DE RECTA PAS. OBSER.
>
> **Provenance:** a1*r*.] Ex Legato Ill[mi] Couini.

I-Ru, A.d.56. Complete

> **Size of page:** 291 × 201 mm.
>
> **Watermarks:** Marks 29 and 28 throughout
>
> **Corrections:**
>
> > **In-house:** A8*v*, e2*r*, e3*r*, A8*v*, F1*r*, R7*v*, Q6*v*, V5*r*, and X7*v*: see above
> >
> > **Later:** a3*r*.18] potificem → po*n*tificem [in brown ink • a6*v*.last:] exhortati → exhortari [in

dark brown ink • r5r.18:] 1600 → 1700 • R3r.1:] indicarem → iudicarem [in brown ink • R6r.1:] bandm → bandum [in brown ink

Bibliography: this is the copy used to reproduce Petrucci's mark in Vaccaro, *Marche*, p. 105

I-Rvat, Barberini Q.V.21. Not seen, in deinfestation

I-Rvat, Ferraioli II.262

> **Size of page:** 301 × 205 mm.
>
> **Watermarks:** Marks 28 and 29 throughout
>
> **Corrections and changes:**
>> **In-house:** a3r, e3r, A8v, F1r, Q6v, R7v, V5r, X7v, Z7v, and GG4v.8: see above
>
> **Binding:** 19th-century half leather, in green over brown boards • a red label reads] PAVLINA | DE RECTA PASCHÆ | CELEBRATIONE || FOROSEMPRONII | 1513 • One paste-down and one flyleaf at each end
>
> **Provenance:** on 1r.] Fabius Santutius Vrbinas [and] Soci S^{ti} Bernardini Vrbini 1622 [and the stamps of] COM B S HERCULES SILUA [and the] BIBLIOTECA FERRAIOLI

I-Rvat, Racc.I.II.816. Not seen, in deinfestation

I-Rvat, Racc.gen.Liturgia II.125. Complete. This copy is heavily infested with active bookworms

> **Corrections and changes:**
>> **In-house:** a3r, b3v, e2r, e3r, A8v, F1r, Q6v, X7v, Z7v, and GG4v.8: see above
>>
>> **Later:** b3v.37–38: a long manuscript comment, later struck through • A7v-D3r. occasional underlining or comments, in a later 16th-century hand, also seen on G8r and rarely elsewhere • GG1r.margin:] Pilatus erat Gallus | ex lugdunensis • GG1v.margin:] Nota delinqua latina
>
> **Binding:** In two volumes, in an 18th-century parchment binding • Labels on the spines, reading] PAUL. DE | MIDDEL. | OP. PASQ. | TOM. I. [and] PAUL. DE | MIDDELB. | OP. PASCH. | TOM. II.
>
> **Provenance:** inside the front board of each volume, the bookplate] EX LIBRIS FRANC. XAV. DE ZELANDA ARCHIEP. PETRÆ.

I-Rvat, Rossiana 3125. Not seen, in deinfestation

I-Uu, B.I.79. Not seen

I-Uu, B.II.81. Not seen

I-Vnm, Rar.173. Not studied

> **Binding:** Probably late 17th-or early 18th-century, parchment over boards. The spine is labelled] PAVL. DE PASC. CEL. • There is one paste-down and one flyleaf at each end. The back flyleaf has a watermark of a hand with a flower
>
> **Provenance:** Inside the front board, a bookplate inscribed] LEGATO | Nobile | GIROLAMO CONTARINI | 1843 [. An old call-number is at the head of the spine of the binding:] A V/233
>
> **Bibliography:** Fenlon and Dalla Vecchia, *Venezia*, pp. 88–89 (exhibition catalogue, Venice, 2001)

I-Vnm, Rar.175. Not seen

N-Ou, Inst. of theoretical astrophysics. Not seen

P-Ln, Res.386.V. Lacks folio GG6

> **Size of page:** 291 × 192 mm.
>
> **Watermarks:** Numbers 28 and 29 throughout. It is not always easy to tell which is which: however the following is probably correct. No.28 on a2,3,4,8; b2,3,6; c3,8; d2,3,5,8; e2,3,5; f3,4,7,8; g2,3,4,8; h4,6,7,8; i2,5,6,8; k1,2,3,4; l3,5,7; n2,5; o1,4; p1,4; q6,7,8; r3; s3,5,7,8; A1,7; B7; D2,8; E4; F4,8; G1; H1,3,5,7; I2,5,8; K2,4,6,8; L1,2,4; M1; œ3,5,6; P2,5,8; Q1,4,6,7; R1,2,3,5; S5,6,7,8; T8; V5,6,7; BB4,7,8; CC2,3,5,8; DD5; EE4,6; FF5,6,7,8;

GG1,4,5 • No.29 on c4,7; l8; m2,4,6,7; n1,6; o2,3; p2,3; q5; r2,4,8; t2,5,7,8,10; A4,6; B1,5,6; C2,4,6,8; D3,5; E2,6,8; F3,7; G2,5,6; I3; L6; M2,3,5; N4,6,7,8; O1,2,5,6; P6; T3,5,7; V1; X1,2,5,6; Y5,6,7,8; Z1,3,5,7; AA2,3,5,8; BB3; DD3,7,8; EE1,7

In-house correction: A8*v*: see above

Binding: 19th-century green morocco, with gilt lettering on the spine • The edges are gilt over marbling • Marbled paste-down and conjugate fly-leaf at each end, the latter pasted to the outer of two 18th-century paper fly-leaves

PL-Kj, Theol.11725. Not seen

US-BLl. Not seen

US-Cn, Ayer.★107.58.P3.1513. Complete

Technical comments: Certain letters, notable the capital "L", show damaged sorts which recur through the volume: c.f. l4*v*, l5*v* and l6*v* or g6*r*, and g7*r*

Binding: Original tooled half-leather over wooden boards

Provenance: Bookplate of William Horatio Campbell • a1*r*.] Liber e*st* R*e*verendi patris et D. D. Johannes Fabri Episcopi Vienne*n*sis [. . .] p*r*e*dicato*rijs | Et non Episcopat*us* pecunijs empt*us* et *postquam* morte*m* insigni | Bibliotheca Collegij sui S. Nicolai ad usu*m* inhabitantiu*m* | studentu*m* et studiosoru*m* iuxta sua*m* ordinatione*m* collocant*us* | Arte*m* Viennae 10 Januarij anno a Christo nato 1540 | Ex singulari mandato et ex | ora insig*nato* R*e*verendi Epi*s*copi Io*hannes* pfarr Sci. • There is a similar annotation on GG6*r*

US-Cn, fZP.535.P.445. Lacks ff.GG6

This appears to lie very close in its state to that of the copies at US-CA.

US-CA, Typ.525.13.675F. lacks ff.GG6. Has a cancel folio at A7

Size of page: 319 × 214 mm.

Watermarks: Nos.28 or 29 on the appropriate folios in each gathering throughout

Corrections:

In-house: A8*v* and F1*r*: see above

Later: Manuscript annotations in gathering Q • r4*r*, right margin against line 5 contains corrections in manuscript

Binding: Original parchment over boards, rebacked • One paste-down and conjugate fly-leaf, of modern paper, at each end. The back fly-leaf has the watermark] GERMANIA

Provenance: Gift to US-CA by Philip Hofer. A plate inside the back board records the acquisition date as 3.i.1939. • Inside front board: stamp of Bundesdenkmalamt Wien, and the bookplate of Philip Hofer • Inside the front board is an inscription of the late 19th-century, in German • a1*r*.] Questo libro ha dato M. Scipione Seiletio alloco de Capuci de S*a*. Vittoria | di no*stro* si possa le nav*e* del dett° loco • a1*r*. stamp of] Loci Capuccinorum Sancta Victoria.

US-CA, ★fNC.P2863.513p. Complete. Has a cancel folio at A7

Size of page: 307 × 205 mm.

Watermarks: Nos.28 or 29 on the appropriate folios in each gathering throughout

In-house Corrections: e2*r*, A8*v* and F1*r*: see above

Binding: Modern • One modern green paste-down and conjugate fly-leaf, plus one modern off-white fly-leaf at each end

Provenance: From the bequest of John Harvey Trent of Lawrence, MA, according to a plate inside the front board • A plate inside the back board records an aquisition date of 27.xi.1911 • Inside the front board, there is a catalogue entry in English, for Lot 114, priced at L4/4/-

US-CIhc. Not seen

US-DMu. Not seen

US-Lu. Not seen. Lacks ff.GG6

US-MSu. Not seen

US-NYcu. Has the cancel leaf on A7.

US-NYp. Not seen

US-NYts. Not seen

US-PROu. Not seen

US-SLc. Not seen

US-SM. Not seen

US-Wc. Not seen

In addition, copies appear on dealers' lists and auction catalogues with relative frequency. In 2001, the
Librairie Henri Godts of Brussels offered a copy in their sale of 1 December.

No. 50A. *Resetting of one page.*

a1*v* was reset more than once during press work. While each setting shows minor variants, the rest
of the bifolium shows only one setting of type. It is not really possible to decide which of these
versions was indeed the first to be set, and which the last. I have merely assumed that the increasing
number of changes implies a sequence of events. However, the sequence could as easily be reversed

Textual comments:

The variants between the original and a second version are as follows: 11: ſcientia*m* →
ſcientiam • 17: percipias, & → percipias,

Extant copies: Other details of these copies, including watermarks, are given above

GB-Cu, F*.8.27

GB-Cu, G.2.16

GB-Cu, Norton.a.23

———

Textual comments:

The variants between the original setting and a third version are as follows: 11: ſcientia*m* →
ſcientiam • 17: percipias, & → percipias, • 18: Petru*m* → Petrum

Extant copies: Other details of these copies, including watermarks, are given above

E-Sc, 1-4-12.

GB-Lbl, 216.d.15.

H-SY, Ös.XXVII.I.(3).

US-CA, Typ.525.13.675F.

US-CA, *fNC.P2863.513p.

———

Textual comments:

A fourth version has the following variants: 11: ſcientia*m* → ſcie*n*tiam • 17: percipias,
& → percipias, • 18: Petru*m* → Petrum • 18: Piſcatoris. → Piſcatoris

Extant copies: Other details of these copies, including watermarks, are given above

A-Wn

GB-Lbl, 696.l.15

I-Rvat, Ferraioli II.262

I-Rvat, Racc.Gen.Liturg.II.125

I-Ru

No. 50B. *Cancel 1*

A bifolium was used as a cancel bifolio for b1 and b6. This was discovered by comparison of the two Brussels copies. The version in V.H. 15,154 C. L.P. is probably the cancel, for it uses fewer hyphens than the other edition, and than adjacent folios. In addition, this copy has a line length of 127 mm for this bifolium, compared with 125 mm for the adjacent ones. The other copy has 125 mm lines on all local folios.

readings	III. 47,758 C.	V.H. 15,154 C. L.P.
b1r.i	calendarium	calendarium
b1r.ii	celebrandum	celebrandum
b1r.iii	tuae	tuæ
b1r.iv	tum . . . accepi)	tum . . . accepi(
b1v.v	lucubratiuncula	lucubratiuncula
b1v.xi	Celebritatem	Celeritatem
b1v.xxxvi-xxxvii	mun|do	mun|do
b6r.xxxvi	controuerſias	controuerſias
b6r.xxxii	utrumque	utrumque
b6v.iii	calendarii	calendarii
b6v.xxxvii	obſeruan	obſeruan

This cancel has not been sought in all copies: column 1 is found in those at A-Wn; B-Br, III. 47,758 C; D-B; E-Mmarch; E-Sc, 1-4-12; GB-Cu, F*.8.27; GB-Cu, G.2.16; GB-Lbl (all three copies); GB-Ob (all three copies); H-SY; I-Ra; I-Rn (all three copies); I-Rvat, Ferraioli II.262; I-Rvat, Racc.Gen.Liturg.II.125; P-Ln; and US-CA, Typ.525.13.675F: column 2 represents the copies at B-Br, V.H.15,154 C. L.P.; GB-Cu, Norton.a.23; and at US-CA, *fNC.P2863.513p. Apart from the instance on b1v.xi, there seem to be no substantive variants on these two sets of pages, despite the extra line-length in the second copy

Extant copies: for details, see above
B-Br, V.H. 15154 C. L.P.
GB-Cu, Norton.a.23
   Manuscript corrections: b1v.xi: Celeritatem → Celebritatem
US-CA, *fNC.P.2863.513p

No. 50C. *Cancel 2*

A single folio, apparently a cancel folio, has been used at A7 in some copies examined, and is glued to A8. It is not present in the copies at D-B, E-Mmarch, H-SY, and P-Ln

Textual comments:

   Two different readings have been detected so far: • A7r.39: nanque → namque (in the copy at E-Sc) • A7v.39: conſumatum man up → conſummatum ? nam ut (in all three at GB-Cu and all three at GB-Lbl)

Extant copies: Other details of these copies, including watermarks, are given above
E-Sc, 1-4-12
I-Ru, A.d.56
US-CA, Typ.525.13.675F

US-CA, *fNC.P2863.513p
US-NYcu

———

Lost copies: There must have been many copies in important collections or owned by liturgical or theological institutions. One instance was drawn to my attention by Jonathan Glixon: the Cathedral of S. Pietro di Castello in Venice bought and bound a copy in 1514. See Venice, ASV, Mensa Patriarcale, Busta 58, VIII (Entrate e spese, 1511–1514) 66r, right column, and 67r, right column; also Busta 62, A. (Registro Cassa, 1511–1514), 133r, left column • Another copy was in the gift made by Luca Gaurico, formerly Bishop of Civitate, to Gauro, in 1557 (See Rhodes, "Unknown", p. 224, and chapter 10 here) • In addition, Sander (No.5470) mentions 10 copies sold between 1914 and 1937. No attempt has been made at tracing these copies, or that sold at the dispersal of the Broxbourne Library, 15.xi.1977, Lot 174 • A copy was sold in Maggs Brothers's catalogue of 1992, with a provenance from the Dyson Perrins collection

Other editions: Baldi, *Vita*, mentions an edition of the book published at Louvain, ca.1600: Marzi, *Questione*, p. 54, in reporting this suggestion, adds that he has found no trace of such an edition, and I have also been unsuccessful. Given the late date, I suspect that it did not exist

Bibliography:

(a) Sartori, *Petrucci*, p. 192

(b) Adams, No.504 • Ascarelli and Menato, *Tipografia*, p. 204 • Brunet, *Manuel*, iv, pp. 451–52 • Essling, *Livres*, iii, 1776 • Fumagalli, *Lexicon*, pp. 162–64 • Isaac, *Index*, No.14040 • Maittaire, *Annales*, p. 242 • Panzer, *Annales*, vii, 50–51 • Sander, *Livre*, No.5470

(c) There are many reproductions of the two ornamented pages, A2r and P5r: see, as examples, Castellani, *Arte*, plate 181 • Essling, *Livres* • Fumagalli, *Lexicon* • Mortimer, *Italian*, ii, 530–31 • Sander, *Livre*, pl.741

(d) Baldi, *Vita*, pp. 240–46 • Marzi, *Questione*, pp. 53–72 • Struik, "Paulus"

Commentary:

1. The background to the production of this book has been outlined in chapter 7 of the present volume. The book itself was carefully organised, showing in various ways Paulus's interest in mathematical and arithmetical features. The first Part concerns the correct celebration of Easter, and therefore the necessary reform of the Calendar: the second discusses the morning of Christ's Passion. In his letter to Leo X, on a2r, Paulus states that the volume is in 33 books, divided into fourteen in Part I and nineteen in Part II: the total reflects the years of Christ's life, and the division represents the years spent under Augustus and Tiberius, respectively.

    Among Paulus's arguments for reforming the dates for Easter is one that Jews had mocked Christians for getting the date wrong: Paulus apparently felt that this was a strong argument, for it is raised in his second letter to Leo X, on a3r, as well as in his letters to the College of Cardinals, on b1r, and to the Duke of Urbino, on b4r.

2. With the exception of the full-page depiction of the Crucifixion, all the blocks are of a similar style. They were quite possibly designed by Francesco Griffo, while he was in Fossombrone, and evidently designing the type-face for this book. The one design with the arms for Leo X must have been executed later, for Griffo apparently left Fossombrone during 1512, before the previous

Pope, Julius II, had died. However, it would have been a simple matter to take his design for Julius and insert the new shield in place of the old.

3. The one unusual design is that of the Crucifixion. It is tempting to assume it was cut by a local craftsman. It does not look to be on the level of the work of Timoteo Viti, who painted for Fossombrone.

4. The privilege for this book is dated 29.iv.1513, on folio a1*v*. This is confirmed by the statement in the documents transcribed by Hergenroether: item 2315, dated 30.iv.1513.] Paulo Middelburgensi episcopo Forosemproniensium concedit privilegium pro ejus libro de Paschae celebratione, ita ut nemo praeter ipsum possit eum imprimere vel imprimi facere vel venundere.

5. Considerable care was taken over the production of this volume. Even the number of cancels and stop-press changes that I have discovered on a cursory examination of several copies is enough to confirm this assertion. The provision of a better quality paper, the purchase of a fount, and of new and decorative initial letters, the preparation of rather splendid blocks to decorate the title and preliminary pages, all are indications that Paulus was prepared to spend extravagantly: he must have seen the book as opening up the possibility of a more glorious career than merely Bishop of a provincial Italian diocese.

    Petrucci was equally on his mettle. The typesetting is of a high standard, with the care taken in aligning tables and marginal annotations very apparent. Paulus may well have read the text of each sheet as it was printed, in addition to the reading given by Hieronymus Posthumus: one or other of these also required an additional set of corrigenda, which are printed at the end of the volume.

6. Similar lists of corrigenda are not unknown during this period. However, it is a little unusual for one person, Posthumus, to blame another in the manner done here.

7. Comparison of the two copies at B-Br or at US-CA shows that the red and black text was set up in the same forme, and printed from different pulls, each inked with one colour and masked with a special frisket. Good examples can be seen on d7*r*, d8*r* and g5*r*.

8. The absence of catchwords can sometimes be explained by the content of the pages concerned:
    a table on both pages: d8*v*, e4*v*,8*v*, f4*v*,8*v*,, l4*v*, m8*v*, o8*v*, 4*v* and 8*v* of p-s, and N4*v*;
    a table on the page itself: m4*v*, n4*v*, and V8*v*;
    a table on the following page: g4*v*, n8*v*, and E8*v*;
    the page is the end of a *pars*: t10*v* and P4*v*.
    There remains no obvious reason for the omissions on the following pages: h4*v*, h8*v*, i8*v*, k4*v*, k8*v*, o4*v*, s8*v*, B8*v*, D4*v*, D8*v*, G8*v*, L4*v*, L8*v*, M8*v*, N8*v*, O8*v*, W3*v*, W6*v*, V4*v*, Z8*v*, DD8*v*, 4*v*, and 8*v*, of EE-FF and GG3*v*.

9. It seems likely that a new typesetter began at P1*r*. Although there is no obvious division of the text there, the presence of a short gathering, coupled with some slight changes in habit, argue for this.

10. The cancel pages were probably printed very soon after the edition was completed. It is true that I have seen them in relatively few copies: however, apart from the obvious fact that this is not statistically significant, I have not gone back to copies seen earlier, to check for their presence. But I would have expected Paulus to require their preparation as soon as he felt they had become necessary.

No. 53. Castiglione: *Ad Henricum Angliae Regem Epistola*

29.vii.1513

a1*r*] BALTHASARIS CASTILIONII | AD HENRICVM ANGLIAE REGEM | EPISTOLA DEVITA ET GES|TIS GVIDVBALDI | VRBINI | DVCIS.

d3*v*] ¶ Impre∫∫um Foro∫empronii per Octauianum Pe-|trutium ciuem Foro∫empronien∫em. Anno | Domini .M.D.XIII. IIII. Calendas Au|gu∫ti. Dominante inclito ac excellen|ti∫∫imo Principe: Domino Franci∫[-|comaria Feltrio de Ruere: | Vrbini Soraeque Duce: Pi|∫auri &c. Domino, Almae | Vrbis Praefecto, ac ex|ercitus. Sancta Romane | Ecclesie Imperato|re ∫emper | inuicto.

[each *ae* represents an e with a sedilla]

a1*v*] ¶ Octauius Petrutius ad lectorem.

¶ Libellum hunc qui in manus meas forte incidit, | imprimendum curaui, tum, que eleganti ∫tilo mihi con-|∫criptus e∫∫e ui∫us e∫t, tum etiam que clari∫∫imi princi-|pis, & de me optime meriti uitam & ge∫ta continet. | Atque ego & pietate & uirtute me ∫ati∫facere arbitra-|tus ∫um, ∫i boni ducis egregias dotes, quas diutina | aegritudo, & aduer∫a fortuna adeo oppre∫∫erant, ut | paucis admodum cognitae e∫∫ent, opera & labore meo | notas facerem.

d3*v*, above the colophon] ¶ Chri∫tophorus Pierius Gigas Canonicus Foro-|∫empronien∫is autori operis ∫alutem.

More tuo ∫cribens, ∫equeris uir docte lacones,

Principis & tanti facta minora canis.

Autor (for∫an ais) quis ∫cribere po∫∫et abunde?

Guido modum meritis noluit e∫∫e ∫uis.

Vera refers, tantum genitori ce∫∫it in armis

Ille ∫uo, in reliquis uicta Minerua tacet.

Format and Collation: Portrait quarto. 16 folios: a-d^4

Signatures:] a ii [$2 • − a1

No foliation

Text-block: 143 × 101 mm. 26 lines per page

Font: Roman text, " x " = 2.1mm, "20" = 110 mm. Title set in the same font

Technical comments:

a1*r* shows two double rows of type sorts used as bearer type, one at the top and one at the foot of the page, each with 25 sorts in each row, in the copies at I-Rn and US-NYpm. All the sorts, except the last in the lower row of the lower pair, are ampersands: the exception is a lower case letter "v". Thus, 99 ampersands are used on this page. There are 12 more used in the text printed on the other pages of this forme (a2*v*, a3*r*, and a4*v*), and another 15 on the other forme of the same sheet. This means that there were at least 111 sorts of the ampersand character in the font, and probably 126. The presence of the final "v" may be taken to indicate that there were no more ampersands • a2*r* uses an initial *V* from the set made for the *Paulina*: cf. f.AA7*r* of that volume • d4*r* uses standing type as furniture, probably taken from folio d1*r*, visible in the copies at I-Rn and US-NYpm • It is probable that the font had no semi colons: see the changes in punctuation made at the stop-press stage

No running heads or catchwords

Corrections and changes: See the notes for the copy at GB-Lbl

Stop-press: a2*v*.16:] compleuerint → compleuerunt [in GB-Cu, I-Ra and US-NYpm • b3*r*.19:]

prepare → prepon [in GB-Cu, I-Ra and US-NYpm • d2r.8:] *a*eterni → *a*eternu*m* [in GB-Cu, I-Ra, and US-NYpm

In addition, the following places, listed in the copy at I-Rn as having manuscript changes to the punctuation, are printed with colons, in the copies at GB-Cu and US-NYpm, rather than the comma in I-Rn or the semicolon in the manuscript reading (those marked with an asterisk are also found in the copy at I-Ra): a2r.3★; a2*v*.4★; a2*v*.6★; a2*v*.8; a2*v*.9; a2*v*.10★; a2*v*.13; a2*v*.14★; a2*v*.18; a2*v*.20; a2*v*.23★; a2*v*.26★; etc.

Possibly stop-press: each of these, found in the copies at GB-Cu, GB-Lbl, I-Ra, and US-NYpm, reflects a change when compared with the copy at I-Rn • a3r.2: printed] uita*m*: • a4*v*.8: printed] Et • c4r.21: printed] Audiebantur • c4*v*.10: printed] Garterii

In-house: c1*v*.5:] quoqu*e* → quo*modocumque* [with brown ink, in GB-Cu, GB-Lbl, I-Ra and US-NYpm

Contents:

A1*r*	[Title]
A1*v*	Octauius Petrutius ad lectorem.
A2*r*	[Text: headed] ¶ Baltha∫ar Ca∫tilionus charus ad ∫acrati∫∫imu*m* Bri | ta*n*niæ rege*m* Henricu*m* de Guidubaldo Vrbini duce.
D3*v*	[Verses by Christophorus Gigas]
	[Colophon.]
D4*r-v*	[blank]

———

Extant copies: The copy cited in the *Index Aureliensis*, as being at D-B, call number Rr.9327, is no longer there. Although it can be found in the pre-war library catalogue, neither Berlin library (on the Potsdamerstrasse or on Unter den Linden) can find any trace of the book

GB-Cu, F.151.c.2.6. Complete.

Size of page: 206 × 143 mm.

Watermarks: No.28 on c1-4 and d4-1; No. 29 on a3-2 and b1-4

Technical comments: the bearer sorts visible on a1*r* in the copy at I-Rn are also evident here

Corrections and changes:

Stop-press: a2*v*.16; b3*r*.19; and d2*r*.8: see above • In addition, the following places, listed in the copy at I-Rn as having manuscript changes to the punctuation, are here printed with colons, rather than the comma in I-Rn or the semicolon in the manuscript reading: a2r.3; a2*v*.4; a2*v*.6; a2*v*.8; a2*v*9; a2*v*.10; a2*v*.13; a2*v*.14; a2*v*.18; a2*v*.20; a2*v*.23; a2*v*.26; etc.

Possibly stop-press: as with the copy at GB-Lbl, each of these reflects a change when compared with the copy at I-Rn • a3*r*.2: printed] uita*m* • a4*v*.8: printed] Et • c4r.21: printed] Audiebantur • c4*v*.10: printed] Garterii

In-house: c1*v*.5, see above

Binding: modern half leather over marbled boards • a panel on the spine reads] CASTI | EPISTO • one end paper at each end

Provenance: c3*r* and c4*r* each has the stamp of] BIBLIOTECA DEL DVCA DI GENOVA

Bibliography: Adams C.944

GB-Lbl, 1199.c.3. Complete. Missing since 14 March 1998

Size of page: 195 × 139 mm.

Watermarks: No.28 on d3-2; one "twin" of 29 on a2-3, and the other on b3-2 and c1-4

Corrections and changes:

Possibly stop-press: Each of these reflects a change when compared with the copy at I-Rn: the relative status of the two copies has not been investigated • a3*r*.2: printed] uita*m*

• a4*v*.8: printed] Et • b1*r*.15: printed] cu*m* enim • b1*v*.13: printed] Garterii • c4*r*.21: printed] Audiebantur • c4*v*.10: printed] Garterii • d2*r*.8: printed] *a*eternu*m*

Later: c1*v*.5, see above

Binding: Modern, quarter cloth over marbled boards • One modern fly-leaf at the front, and two at the back, of which the inner is early

Provenance: On a1*v*: the mark and date:] C.$^{45}{}_{1729}{}^{28}$

Bibliography: Johnson and Scholderer, *Short-Title*, p. 156

I-Fn, Mcxl.14.cust. This copy cannot now be found.

I-FBR. Gianandrea, "Ottaviano", p. 181, and Vernarecci, *Petrucci* refer to a copy in the Fossombrone library. According to Gianandrea, it was previously in the Frari at Fossombrone

I-Rn, 69.4.A.103. Complete

Size of page: 205 × 150 mm.

Watermarks: No.28 on b4-1; No.29 on a2-3, c1-4 and d4-1

Technical comments: a1*r* and d4*r*: see above

Corrections and changes: These may well be all in-house: they are all, unless otherwise indicated below, in the same hand and ink. The text changes, whether indicated by an erasure and over-writing, or by an annotation in the margin, are almost all following earlier pencil underlinings and corrections. Those that I have called hand 2 use a different ink throughout.

The most interesting of the following changes are found on b2*r*.22; b3*r*.19; b3*r*.20; c3*r*.19–20; d1*v*.6; d2*r*.8; d2*r*.17. Others concern the pattern of adding capital letters to almost all proper names:

a1*v*.6.left margin:] pietati, et vir = |tuti [correcting Petrucci's pietate & uirtute • a2*r*.2.right:] VII [and an insertion sign after] Henricu*m* • a2*v*.11: erased letter before] Nunqu*am* • a2*v*.19:] [ub[equta → [ub[equ^{u}ta • a3*r*.2:] uita. → uita*m* • a3*r*.5:] m*an*tuae [has first letter changed to a capital • a3*r*.12: underlining, perhaps in a different hand • a3*v*.11.left margin:] animo [for text] animi • a3*v*.12–13: underlining • a4*v*.3–4:] mher-|cle → mehercule [in the margin • a4*v*.8:] Et → et • a4*v*.10: first letters changed to capitals on this line • a4*v*.12–13:] A[[eren|tes → a[[eren|tes • a4*v*.19:] iocunditate → iucunditate [in left margin • b1*r*.15.right margin:] eum [to insert between the words] cu*m in* • b1*r*.21:] uultus → -ultus [in the right margin • b1*v*.5–7:] braced together in both margins, in hand 2 • b1*v*.13:] ri[[imo Gasterii ordine [is underlined, and] erius ordo [is entered in the left margin, with some earlier letters lost by trimming. Hand 2 • b1*v*.15:] ne → nee [in left margin • b2*r*.12:] conferrebat → conferebat [in right margin • b2*r*.22:] dubio → studio [in right margin • b2*v*.1:] Extremo → extremo [erasure and correction • b2*v*.12:] Atq*ue* → atque [erasure and correction • b2*v*.17:] qui*n*ti → Qui*n*ti [erasure and correction • b2*v*.18:] In → in [erasure and correction • b3*r*.19:] quod prepare græci uocant [is underlined and] ποεπον [is entered in the right margin • b3*r*.20:] tamen trauli[mum pa [is underlined and] decens [is entered in the right margin • b3*r*.25:] ac [is struck through • b3*v*.16:] germani*ae* [has the first letter changed to G • b3*v*.19:] di[erebat → disserebat [in left margin • b4*r*.10:] dirruta → diruta [in right margin • b4*r*.15:] turcharu*m* [has the first letter changed to a capital: at the same time, the right margin carries] Turcarum • b4*r*.18:] Maumethanorumq*ue* → Mohemetanorum* [in right margin • b4*r*.22:] per[arum arabumq*ue* [has the initials erased and changed to capitals • b4*r*.26:] Multo → multo [erasure and change • b4*v*.7:] Te[tor → te[tor [erasure and change • b4*v*.14:] Percutabatur → percontabatur [in left margin • c1*r*.1:] Prae[ertim → prae[ertim [erasure and change • c1*r*.2:] Eodem → eodem [erasure and change • c1*r*.4–7, 9–10, 17:] underlining • c1*r*.7:] Tandiuq*ue* → tandiuq*ue* [erasure and change • c1*r*.11:] gallorum → Gallorum [erasure and change • c1*r*.14:] Imperatore [has the last letter erased • c1*r*.22:] capitals for three names, all written over the original initials • c1r.23:] erased colon before] precutinos [and the first letter changed to a capital • c1v.3:] ur∫inorum → Vr∫inorum [written over • c1v.4:] peru → Peru [by erasure and over-writing • c1v.5:] quoque → quo*modocum*que [and, in left margin] cumque • c1v.8:] uenetorum → Venetorum [over-written • c1v.15–16:] im|pedi∫∫e → impendi∫∫e [in left margin • c2r.18:] præfectum [has a capital over the erased initial • C2r.20:] Nouerat → nouerat [erasure and change • c2v.2–5: underlined references to Fossombrone, with, in the left margin, the end of the word [rusem*pron*ij. [in Hand 2 • c2v.7:] Quod → quod [erasure and change • c2v.11:] Nos → nos [erasure and change • c2v.15:] langorem → languorem [in left margin • c2v.18:] Ea → ea [erasure and change • c2v.22:] Nos [underlined in pencil, and something, now lost, was written in the margin • c2v.26:] attolens → attollens [erasure and change • c3r.3:] Et → et [erasure and change • c3r.5:] dum → Dum [erasure and change • c3r.15:] Ea → ea [erasure and change • c3r.19–20:] tem-|ptabat → tentabat [in right margin • c3r.23:] . Ne → ; ne [erasure and change • c3r.24:] Apriles → Aprilis [erasure and change • c3r.26:]. Idque → :idque [erasure and change • c3v.7:] Admonuit → admonuit [erasure and change • c3v.19:]. Adeo → : adeo [erasure and change • c4r.6:] ∫imulaac → ∫imulac [pencil deletion • c4r.7:] quod → quid [erasure and change • c4r.8:] At → at [erasure and change • c4r.12:] Omnes → omnes [erasure and change • c4r.18:] Amari∫∫imam → amari∫∫imam [erasure and change • c4r.19:] Comitabamur → comitabamur [erasure and change • c4r.21:] Audiebantur → audienbantur [erasure and change • c4r.22:] Occurrebant → occurrebant [erasure and change • c4r.23:] Occurrebant → occurrebant [erasure and change • c4v.7:] Excitum → excitum [erasure and change • c4v.10:] Gasterii in∫ ignibus [underlined • c4v.13:] Fata → fata [erasure and change • c4v.15:] : tot → , tot [erasure and change: part of the first "t" erased in error and replaced • c4v.19:] At → at [erasure and change • d1r.1:] Raptus → raptus [erasure and change • d1r.15:] Berardini: → Bernardini, [in right margin • d1r.15:] quam ip∫e Dux extruxe [underlined • d1r.20:] impediti: → impediti [by erasure • d1r.21:]. Vul → :uul [erasure and change • d1v.4:] Affixa → affi∫∫a [erasure and change • d1v.5:] Intra → intra [erasure and change • d1v.6:] quem [struck through, and] cum [in right margin • d1v.13–14 and 19–20: underlining • d2r.3–5: underlining • d2r.3:] odaxius → Odaxius [erasure and change • d2r.8:] aeterni → in *a*eternum [in right margin • d2r.12:] Nec → nec [erasure and change • d2r.13:]. Sed → : ∫ed [erasure and change • d2r.17:] temptat → tentat [in right margin • d2r.25:] Nam → nam [erasure and change • d2v.9:] ∫ordi∫∫ imis → sordidissimis [in right margin • d2v.13:] Nullam → nullam [erasure and change • d2v.14:] Extremo → extremo [erasure and change • d3r.6:]. Sed → : ∫ed [erasure and change • d3r.11:] Nos → nos [erasure and change

    In addition to the preceding list, there is a large number of changes to the punctuation as printed, in particular using colons and semicolons, adding commas and so on. For example, the first two pages alone of the text contain the following changes: a2r.3: full stop to semicolon • a2r.7: full stop erased • a2r.9: comma added after] animus • a2r.17: the comma after] dubitem [changed to a semicolon • a2r.17: comma added after] tamen • a2r.22: the full stop after] con∫titui [changed to a semicolon • a2v.4: full stop to semicolon • a2v.5: comma added after] ris • a2v.5: comma added after] incumbens • a2v.6: full stop to a semicolon • a2v.8: full stop to a semicolon • a2v.9: full stop to a colon • a2v.10: full stop to a semicolon • a2v.13: comma added after] ∫unt • a2v.14: full stop to a semicolon • a2v.15: comma added after] magnitudine*m* • a2v.16: Colon added after] compleuerint • a2v.17: comma to a colon • a2v.18: colon to a semicolon • a2v.20: full stop to a semicolon • a2v.22: full stop to a semicolon • a2v.23: comma added after] i*n*genio • a2v.26: full stop to a semicolon • [etc.]

Binding: Parchment, from a fifteenth-century manuscript, in a humanist script • One paste-down and one flyleaf at each end

Provenance: The old call-number of 944948, on f.d3*v*

I-Ru, Misc.Ant.XV.f.15.10. Incomplete, lacks a1 and a4. Patched on d2*r* and d4*v*

Page size: 195 × 140 mm.

Watermarks: No.29 on b4-1, c2-3 and d4-1

Corrections and changes:

Stop-press: a2*v*.16; b3*r*.19; and d2*r*.8: see above. Also the list of changes to punctuation

Possibly stop-press: as with the copy at GB-Lbl, each of these reflects a change when compared with the copy at I-Rn • a3*r*.2: printed] uita*m* • a4*v*.8: printed] Et • c4*r*.21: printed] Audiebantur • c4*v*.10: printed] Garterii

In-house: c1*v*.5, see above

Later: all these are in the same brown ink: c1*r*.10:] paulopo[t → Paulipo[t [erasure and brown ink • d1*r*.24: above] [exto nonas maias] is added] .26. april: • a colon is struck through at the following places: c1*r*.11; c1*r*.13; c1*r*.14 • the colon is changed to a semicolon at c1*r*.12; c1*r*.14 and c1*r*.18

I-Rvat, Riserv.IV.47. (*olim* Stamp.Barb.Z.V.55) Complete

Provenance: M. Antonio Vergili Battiferri, archdeacon of Urbino and "pronepote" of Polydore Vergil • Barberini

I-Vc. Not seen

I-Vnm, Cicogna 816.3. Not seen

Bibliography: Fenlon and Dalla Vecchia, *Venezia*, pp. 89–90 (exhibition catalogue, Venice, 2001)

US-CA, IC5.c2782.514a. Complete

Watermarks: No.28 on b4-1; No.29 on a3-2, c2-3 and d1-4

Binding: 20th century quarter-leather, over marbled boards • Paste-down and 3 fly-leaves at front; paste-down and one at the end

Provenance: a1*r*] Munus Ill. Do*minu*3 Comitu*m* Balthassaris | et Christophori filioru*m* multu*m* Ill. S. | Comitis Camilli filij Authoris huius | opusculi • On frontpaste-down: bookplate] EX | LIBRIS | LUIGI | CORA • On back paste-down:] Bequest of Mary P.C.Nash [with the date 1946 on the fly-leaf

US-NYpm, E2 47 A (PML 42127). Complete

Page size: 198 × 132 mm.

Watermarks: No.28 on b3-2 and c1-4; No.29 on a1-4 and d3-2

Technical comments: a1*r* and d4*r*: see above • d3*r* shows the blind impression of standing type used as bearer sorts, probably taken from d2*r*

Corrections and changes:

Stop-press: a2*v*.16; b3*r*.19; and d2*r*.8: see above

Possibly stop-press: those cited in the copy at GB-Lbl, with the exception of that at b1*r*.15

In-house: c1*v*.5, see above

Later: a number of annotations on folios a1*r*-3*r*, all in a tiny hand and very faded brown ink: most involve repetitions of words or comments in the text. For example:

a2*r*.top] Ca[tilioneus scriberem vnde apud nos celebrat*ur* xpophorus ca[tilioneus sub|tililitatu*m* princeps magni viri in legij ingenij at*que* au[piciis

a2*r*.i-ii:] Britaniae rege*m* Henricu*m* [is struck through

a2*r*.ii.left margin:] Guidubaldus

a2*v*.11.left margin:] Precor ingeniu*m*

a2*v*.11:] peruenire → perueniret

a2*v*.11.right margin:] peruenir^et lege

a3r.v.left margin:] Elisabeth | Gonzaga

Binding: Simple modern vellum, with a script label on the spine:] Castilione | De Guido Uba | Urbini Duc | Lib Raris. • Marbled paste-down at each end • four fly-leaves at the front: i*v*-iii*v* contain a long annotation in Italian, including a note that the writer acquired the book in 1847: at the end a later addition, in a similar hand, makes reference to Vernarecci's study of Petrucci • four fly-leaves, all blank, at the back

Provenance: The Library records Dominico Passionei (1682–1761), Gaetano Volpi (1689–1761), Jacopo Morelli (1745–1819), Andrea Tessier (1819–1896), and Don Pietro Bettio as previous owners. The implication of Passionei's ownership puts the book at Fossombrone during the 18th century. • Pierpont Morgan's bookplate on the front paste-down

Bibliography:

(b) *Edizioni*, No.C2027 • *Index Aureliensis*, 133.560

(d) Castiglione, *Lettere*, i, pp. 162–98 and 944–58

(e) Clough, "Baldassare" • La Rocca, "Storia" • Tocci, "Manoscritto"

Commentary:

1. The significance of Petrucci's letter to the reader is discussed in chapter 7.

2. It is tempting to assume that the wealth of changes in the I-Rn copy represent a move towards a second edition of the book. Certainly only a few carry real corrections to the text: the majority represent aspects of presentation style, punctuation, and the like, which might be important to an author concerned with the quality of his writing, especially in a climate of humanistic interest in literary style. However, some were apparently changed in some copies, apparently representing decisions about which should be changed at the proof stage, rather than the possibility of a new printing.

4. Since the evidence for possible stop-press changes appears in only two gatherings of the GB-Cu copy, it is more likely that they were in fact effected in the printing shop.

3. A late, perhaps 18th-century, copy of the text, with Petrucci's letter, survives at GB-Lbl, Add.Ms.22027, 150r-162*v*. In the early pages, at least, it carries the text as printed in the copy at GB-Lbl, without the changes proposed in the Roman copy.

No. 54. Josquin: *Missarum III*

I.iii.1514   *RISM* J 673 and J 674

There were two editions of this title printed in Fossombrone. For the first edition there is a cancel for folios A3 and A6 and one for folios D2 and D7

(1) comprises the copies at A-GÜ; A-Wn (S.A.77.C.20); D-B; E-Bbc; E-SI; GB-Lbl; I-Bc; I-PEc; I-Rsc; US-CA; US-Eu; US-R

(2) is represented by copies at A-Wn (S.A.77.C.19); B-Br; CH-Zz; H-SY; I-Ac; I-BGc; I-Rvat. Sartori mentions a copy at D-Mbs, which I have not been able to find

First Edition

A1r]   Miſſaru3 Joſquin | Liber Tertius | Mater patris | Fayſans regres | Ad fugam | Didadi | De beata virgine | Miſſa ſine nomine

C1r]   T

D1r]   A

F1r]   B

G10r]   LEO. pp. X.

        ¶ Dilecte fili ſalutem & apoſtolicam bene. Cum tu ſicut nobis nuper exponi feciſti alius Venetiis com[e]morans tua induſtria, et ſolertia | primus inueniſſes modum imprimendi libros Cantus figurati Propterea dilecti filii dux et Conſiliarii Ciuitatis Venetiarum | tibi tanquam primo inuentori priuilegium nequis illos infra uiginti annos ſub certis penis in ſuis terris auderet imprimere   5 aut | alios quam tuos libros in dictis Terris uenales habere conceſſerunt: Nuper uero cum in tuam patriam Foriſſempronii ad | habitandum ueneris, et aliquid noui ſemper excogitando Tandem maximo labore diſpendio: et temporis curſu eſt primus | modum imprimendi organorum intabulaturas per multos ingenioſos uiros in Italia & extra ut dicitur tentatum, et tanquam | opus deſperatum derelictum, inueneris: quod non parum decoris Eccleſiaſtice religioni, et ſtudere   10 uolentium commoditati fo- | re dinoscitur: Nec non alios libros alterius facultatis alias nunquam impreſſos in tua patria predicta: ac aliis Terris Eccleſie romane | mediate uel immediate ſubiectis imprimere deſideres: Nos tuis ſupplicationibus inclinati uolentes te tanquam inuentorem | et primum impreſſorem dummodo libri iuſto percio uendantur apoſtolicis gratiis et fauoribus proſequi ac de remedio pro- | uidere opportuno, ne ceteri impreſſores qui non laborarunt ex diſpendio, & labore tuo   15 ditentur, ut que ad alia eſt maiora fa- | cienda. promptuis inuiteris tibi tanquam primo inuentori et impreſſori dictorum operum, ne ceteri impreſſores, et biblipole ali- | quas organorum intabulaturas infra quindecim annos, ac alios libros alterius facultatis per te impreſſos et imprimendos per ali- | os tamen antea non impreſſos infra alios quindecim annos a die impreſſionis tuú Immediate currentes in omnibus Terris | nobis, et Eccleſie Romane mediate, et Immediate ſubiectis imprimere, aut alios   20 quam tuos uenales habetur ſub excommunicationis | late ſententie, ipsorumque librorum, et intabulaturarum amiſioñ ac quatuor ducatorum pro quolibet libro et intabulatura pro una fi- | ſco noſtro pro alia accuſatori, et alia tertia partibus executori applicandorum poenis: audeant ſeu preſumant concedimus, etiam in | dulgemus: Mandantes propterea auditori Camere et Alme urbis noſtre Gubernatori: Senatori: Bariſello ac omnibus, et | ſingulis aliis Gubernato. potestatibus,   25 officialibus, et executoribus in dictis Terris noſtris ubique exiſtentibus presentibus et futuris: quos tu uel | procurator tuus duxeritis eligendos ſub excommunicationis poena ipſo facto per ipſos incurrenda Quatenus tibi in permiſſis- | ſicari contrafacientes. quoſcunque et rebelles per cenſuras Eccleſiaſticas et poenas predictas appellatione remota conpeſcendo. In | uocato eſt ad hoc ſi opus fuerit auxilio brachii ſecularis, et alia faciendo et exequendo in premiſſis, et circa ea neceſaria et | 30 oportuna: uolentes eſt has noſtras literas imprimimi, et earum impreſſioni plenam adhiberi fidem in Iudicio et extra Incontrarium facientibus non ob- | ſtant. quibuſcunque. Datum Rome apud Sanctum Petrum ſub Annullo Piſcatoris Die xxii Octobris M.D.xiii Pontificatus no- | ſtri Anno Primo

        [left:] Dilecto filio domino Octauiano de | petrutiis de foroſempronii

        [right:] Petrus Bembus   35

        [between the two:] ¶ Impreſſum Foroſempronii per Octauianum | Petrutium ciuem Foroſempronienſem. Anno | Domini .MDXIIII. Die primo martii. Domi- | nante inclito ac excelenti∫∫imo Principe Domino | Franci∫comaria Feltrio de Ruere: Vrbini Soræ | que Duce: Pi∫auri &c. Domino: Alme Vrbis Præfecto: | ac exercitus Sanctæ Romanæ Ecclesiæ. Imperatore ∫emper inuicto.   **40**

Format and collation: Partbooks: landscape quarto-in-eights. [S] 18 folios: A⁸B¹⁰; [T] 12 folios: C¹²; [A] 18 folios: D⁸E¹⁰; [B] 18 folios: F⁸G¹⁰

Signatures:] AaA 2 [$4 • − A1 • + B5, C5, C6, E5 and G5 • For D1, see below

No foliation

Running heads: Two levels of heads:

recto:]	Sup*erius*	[A2, A7-B9
	Sup*erius*.	[A3-6
	Tenor	[C2-12
	Altus	[D2-6, E1-9. On D3r, at the inner corner.
	Altus.	[D7-8
	Ba∫∫us	[F2, G1-9
	Ba∫∫us.	[F3-5, F7. On F4 and F5, at the inner corner.
	Ba∫∫u5.	[F6, F8. On F6 and F8, at the inner corner.
	[Nil:	A1, B10, C1, D1, E10, F1, G10
verso:]	Suprano	[A1
	Sup*erius*	[A2, A4, A7-B8
	Sup*erius*.	[A3, A5-6
	Tenor	[C1-11
	Altus	[D2-7, E1-9
	Altus.	[D1, D8
	Ba∫∫us.	[F 1–8
	Ba∫∫us	[G1-9. On G9, at the inner corner.
	[Nil:	B10, C12, E10, G10

The bassus is the clearest of the patterns of different treatment, although it does not imply that the part-name was retained in the forme.

Fonts: Music: Petrucci's normal music type, with some newly cast forms

Staves: six per page, 174–180 mm long, 10.3-92-112 long.

Text: Rotonda, "x" = 2.2 mm • Roman, used for privilege and colophon, "20" = 166 mm. • Large Rotonda used for title, "x" = 4.9 mm.

Blocks: Dice, used on C6v-7v, apparently printed with the initials: five different forms, with 1, 2, 3, 4, or 6 spots

Textual comments: The title page does not have the points found on copies of the second edition • B9r: the text seems not to have been printed with either the staves or the music

Technical comments: There is evidence of two typesetters in this volume, rather than of two layers of work. The capitals follow the same pattern in all copies, and appear to be in the same state in all layers of work, on all papers

In-house corrections: A1v.head-line: Suprano, with an inverted "u", corrected by a stop-press change: D-B, I-PEc and I-Rsc • A5v.v.14: e', *m* → *sb*, by erasure: A-Wn, I-PEc and US-R • A5v.vi.14: d' *m* → *sb*, by erasure: A-Wn, D-B, GB-Lbl, I-Bc, I-PEc, I-Rsc, and US-R • A8v.iv.5 after bar-lines: *sb*, g' → c", erased and stamped in: D-B, GB-Lbl, I-PEc, and US-R • A8v.iv.37: *sb*, g' → c", erased and stamped in: A-Wn, D-B, GB-Lbl, I-Bc, I-PEc, I-Rsc, and US-R • D1r.signature: printed FfF3: this struck through in brown ink, and the correct DdD stamped in with type: E-Bc • D3r.ii.28–30: *sbf'*,*me'*,*lf* → *mg'*,*sba'*,*lg'*: all erased and stamped in, in the copies at D-B, GB-Lbl, I-Bc, and I-Rsc; in manuscript at A-Wn; in the copy at E-Bc, the error has been erased, but not replaced • D3*v*.ii.12: *m*, a → g, note head erased, and a new one stamped in: E-Bc • D3*v*.vi.23: *m* → *sb*: erased tail in the copy at I-Bc; changed with a stop-press correction in those at D-B, E-Bc, GB-Lbl, and I-Rsc • F7r.i.43: *b*, c → d, erased and stamped in: E-SI, GB-Lbl, I-Bc, and I-Rsc • F7*v*.ii.48–50: *mg*,*me*,*mf* → *dsbg*: erased tail, notes struck through, and brown ink dot: D-B, E-SI, I-Bc, I-Rsc, and US-R

It seems unlikely that the change at A5*v*.vi.12 was made in-house, even though found in copies at GB-Lbl and I-Bc

Rubrics: B7r, margin:] Tenor in diateſſaro*n* ſequentib*us* ſignis • B8r, margin:] Altus in diateſaro*n* liqu*en*do primam pauſam • C10r, margin:] Le derain va derriere • C10*v*:] Tenor CANON Vous Ieuneres les Quatre temps. de batavi*r*giene [*sic*] • C11r.] CANON Jeuneres les Quatre temps De beata vi*r*gine Tenor • E9r.] Tenor in diapente ſequentibus ſignis

Contents:

	A1*r*	C1r	D1r	F1r	[Title]
1	A1*v*	C1*v*	D1*v*	F1*v*	[Missa] Mater patris
	A1*v*.v	C1*v*.iii	D1*v*.iii	F2r	[Gloria]
	A2r.iv	C1*v*.vi	D2r	F2*v*	[Credo]
	A2*v*.v	C2r.v	D2*v*.ii	F3r.v	[Sanctus]
	A3*v*	C2*v*	D3r.vi	F3*v*.v	[Agnus]
2	A4r.iv	C2*v*.v	D4r	F4r.iv	[Missa] Fayſans regres
	A4*v*	C3r	D4r.iv	F4*v*	[Gloria]
	A5r	C3r.iv	D4*v*.v	F5r	[Credo]
	A5*v*.v	C3*v*.v	D5*v*.iv	F5*v*.iv	[Sanctus]
	A6*v*	C4r.iii	D6*v*	F6r.iv	[Agnus]
3	A7r	C4*v*	D7r	F7r	[Missa] Ad fugam
	A7r.iv	C4*v*.iv	D7r.iv	F7r.iv	[Gloria]
	A7*v*.iv	C5r.iii	D7*v*.iv	F7*v*.iv	[Credo]
	A8r.v	C5*v*.iii	D8*v*	F8r.v	[Sanctus]
	B1r	C6r.iii	E1r	G1r.ii	[Agnus]
4	B1r.v	C6*v*	E1r.iv	G1*v*	[Missa] Didadi
	B1*v*.ii	C6*v*.v	E1*v*	G1*v*.iv	[Gloria]
	B2r.iv	C7r.iii	E2r.iii	G2*v*	[Credo]
	B3r	C7*v*	E3r	G3r	[Sanctus]
	B3r.vi	C8r	E3*v*	G3*v*.iv	[Agnus]
5	B4r	C8*v*	E4*v*	G4r	[Missa] De beata virgine
	B4r.v	C8*v*.v	E4*v*.v	G4*v*.ii	[Glora]
	B5r.ii	C9*v*.iii	E5*v*.iii	G5*v*	[Credo]
	B6r	C10*v*	E6*v*.ii	G6*v*	[Sanctus]
	B6*v*.iii	C11r	E7r.v	G7r	[Agnus]
6	B7r	C11r.iii	E8r	G7*v*	[Missa sine nomine]
	B7r.v	C11r.iv	E8r.v	G7*v*.iii	[Gloria]
	B8r	C11r.v	E9r	G8r.iii	[Credo]
	B8*v*.v	C12r.iii	E9r.ii	G9r	[Sanctus]
	B9*v*	C12r.v	E9*v*	G9*v*	[Agnus]
				G10r	[Privilege, Colophon]

B10r		E10r		[blank staves]
B10v	C12v	E10v	G10v	[blank]

Extant copies:

A-GÜ, s.s. Tenor, lacking C12

   Size of page: 165 × 235 mm.

   Watermarks: No.2 on C5-6 and C9-10

   Textual comments: Some running heads are different, as follows: C3v:] fay[ans regres • C4v:] fay[ans regres • C6v:] Di dadi Supra naragie • C8v:] De beata virgine

   Technical comments:

   No evident corrections or changes

   Binding and Provenance: With Josquin, *II Missarum* (1515, No.59)

   Bibliography: Federhofer, "Petrucci"

A-Wn, S.A.77.C.20. Superius, Tenor, and Altus, complete. A3,6, and D2,7 are cancels: see below

   Size of page: 164 × 233 mm.

   Watermarks:

A2-1	A-4	B-6	B7-8	B9-10	C4-3	C8-7	C11-12	D5-6	D8-	E6-	E8-7	E10-9
2	16	2	2	2	2	27	30	16	16	2	2	2

   Corrections and changes:

     In-house: A5v.v, A5v.vi and A8v: see above

     Later: Movements numbered in manuscript in all parts, 60–89 • A5v.v.after 10: erased rest, perhaps a *m* • D3r.ii.28–30: *sbe',mf',lf'* → *mg,sba,lg* • D3r.iii.11: *md'* erased

   Binding and Provenance: With Josquin's *I Missarum* (1516, No.62)

D-Bds, Mus.ant.pract.D.227. Complete

   Size of page: 231 × 165 mm: the altus measures 226 × 153 mm.

   Watermarks:

A2-1	A4-	B2-1	B4-3	B-6	C1-2	C3-4	C8-7	D-1	D6-5	E-6	E7-8	E9-10
2	16	2	2	2	27	2	2	16	16	2	27	27

F4-3	F7-8	G-5	G8-7	G9-10
16	16	2	2	2

   Technical comments: C12r.vi: stave only partly inked

   Corrections and changes:

     In-house: F7v: see above

     Later: There are light pencil bar-lines in the *Missa Didadi*, B1v-B2v, C6v-C8r, E1r-E2v, G3v-G4r • A5v.v.rest after 9: *sb* erased, and *m* added in black ink • D3r.iii.11: *md'* struck through

   Binding and Provenance: With Josquin, *I Missarum* (1516, No.62)

E-Bbc, M.115 (3). Altus, lacking f.E10. The bifolium D2/7 is a cancel: see below

   Size of page: 174 × 230 mm.

   Watermarks:

D5-6	D8-	E4-3	E-5	E-9
16	16	2	2	2

   Corrections and changes:

     In-house: D1r.signature, D3r.ii.28–30, D3r.ii.12, D3v.vi.23: see above

Later: D3r.iii.11: *m*d' struck through, in brown ink • D8v.margin: a scribble, apparently with the name Saboell

Binding: With Josquin, *I Missarum* (1516, No.62)

Bibliography: Pedrell, *Catálech*, No.427

E-SI, R.73252. Bassus part, complete • I am grateful to Padre Lorenzo Maté for supplying me with photos of this recently discovered copy

Size of page: 166 × 228 mm.

In-house changes: F7r and F7v: see above

Technical comments: F5v.above i: spacing sort between the notes, 2.7 × 0.7 mm.

Later changes: F7v.iii.after 3: rest, *b* → *sb*, by erasure

Binding: Modern

Bibliography: *Edades*, p. 152

GB-Lbl, K.1.d.9. Complete. Bifolios A3,6 and D2,7 are cancels: see below

Watermarks:

A2-1	A-5	B1-2	B4-3	B-6	C1-2	C3-4	C5-6	D-1	D4-3	E6-	E8-7	E9-10
2	16	2	2	27	30	27	30	16	16	2	2	2

F1-2	F4-3	G2-1	G-6	G7-8
16	16	2	2	2

Technical comments: F5v.above i: spacing sort between the notes, 2.7 × 0.7 mm.

Corrections and changes:

> **In-house:** A5v, A8v, D3r and F7r: see above • On D3r, the new *m* may have been stamped twice, the first time with insufficient ink

> **Later:** A5v.vi.12: was perhaps a *b*: now *dsb*, in black ink • G1v.iii.14–16: 3 *b*, G, F, G, all colored in

Bibliography: Johnson and Scholderer, *Short-Title*, p. 214

I-Bc, Q.73. Complete. Bifolios A3,6, and D2,D7 are cancels: see below.

Size of page: 169 × 234 mm

Watermarks:

A8-7	A-5	B1-2	B3-4	B5-	C4-3	C7-6	C11-12	D-1	D4-3	E1-2	E-5	E7-8
2	16	2	2	2	2	30	30	16	16	2	2	27

F5-6	F7-8	G1-2	G3-4	G-6
16	16	2	2	2

Corrections and changes:

> **In-house:** A5v.vi, A8v, D3r, D3v, F7r, and F7v: see above

> **Later:** Manuscript foliation in pencil: [S] 1–18; [T] 19–30; [A] 31–48; [B] 49–67 • Manuscript pagination in the Altus:] 72–100, 1001, [102–107] • A2v.v.15: flat added, brown ink • A5v.ii.after 27: m.s. 3 has an added circle above, brown ink • A5v.vi.12: was perhaps a *b*: now *dsb*, in black ink • A6r.vi.after 20: m.s. 3 has an added circle above, brown ink • A8r.v.9: flat erased • B6r.v.after bar-line: m.s.cut C, 0/3, has the 0 erased • C3v.ii.after bar-line: flat erased • C9r.iii.after bar-line: flat erased • D3r.iii.11: *m*d' erased • D5v.i.before 32: flat erased • E8v.iii.41: *dsb*, the dot erased • E9v.iv.13: flat added, in brown ink • F4r.ii.before 41: m.s. 3 0/3, in brown ink • F5r.iv.before 1: flat erased • F5v.i.18, 22 and 26: dots erased • F6r.iii.14: dot erased • G1v.iii.14–16: three colored *b*, G, F, G: brown up-tail for the first, and brown line connecting the first two, as if in a c.o.p. ligature • G6r.v.34: *b*, colored in brown ink • G7r.v.40: *l* → *b*, by erasure of the tail

Binding: The same as that for the library's copy of *Motetti de la Corona I*

Provenance: Old call number 1016 on A1r

I-PEc, I.M.1079. Superius, lacking ff.B1 and B10

    Size of page: 230 × 160 mm.

    Corrections and changes:

        In-house: A1v, A5v.v, A5v.vi, and A8v: see above

        Later: A1r.] Venetiis *per* Octauianu*s* Petrutium anno d*o*mini 1514 [in the hand of the first
            work of the manuscript appendix • A5v.v.after 10: erased rest, perhaps a *m*

    Binding: Contemporary parchment, with traces of green cloth strings • With *I Motetti de la
        Corona* (1514), and a manuscript appendix

    Provenance: first flyleaf:] Hieronymi Muti de pappazuris [and later] Giouanbatista gagliardi

    Bibliography: Fenlon and Haar, "Fonti", 226–30 • Fenlon and Haar, *Italian*, 186–87

I-Rsc, G.CS.3.B.30. Lacks f.G10 • Folio B10 is badly damaged

    Size of page: 169 × 234 mm.

    Watermarks:

A1-2	A-5	B-5	B7-8	B10-9	C8-7	C9-10	C12-11	D1-	D6-5	E1-2	E4-3	E-6
2	16	2	2	2	30	2	2	2	2	2	27	2

F5-6	F8-7	G2-1	G-5	G7-8
16	16	2	2	2

    Technical comments: Only five staves were inked on F6v

    Corrections and changes:

        In-house: A1v, A5v.vi, A8v, D3r, D3v, F7r and F7v: see above

        Later: Modern pencil foliation • C12r.iii.after text: clef C_3, *b*a', brown ink • C12r.vi.end of
            stave: brown decorative hatching • C12v:] Aantonia Mog [in much later hand • D1v.iv.
            first rests: *l, b, m* → *l, b, sb, m*, in brown ink

    Binding: Dark leather, with decorative rolls, as a border and making a diamond shape within
        each. Also stamps of a vase in each corner • One paste-down and one flyleaf at each end.
        The inner flyleaf has the edge of a watermark, reading]RA • The Superius has red-stained
        edges

US-CA, Mus.786.2.501. Tenor, lacking C3, C10, and C12

    Size of page: 162 × 223 mm.

    Watermarks: No.2 on C-9 • No.27 on C7-8 and C-11

    Later change: C8r.ii.text:] secu*n*du*m* → secu*n*du3 [manuscript

    Binding: Bound with parts of Josquin, *Misse* (1502, No.4) and La Rue, *Misse* (1503, No.11) •
        The binding is of dark brown leather with three sewing bands: it has been rebacked, with
        a portion of the old spine preserved. Each face has two panels with a shared frame, and is
        made up of a complex series of double snaking rolls and stamps. The sale catalogue entry
        calls the binding "Spanische Arbeit, ca 1510" • One paste-down at each end, attached with
        a parchment guard strip to the adjacent folio of the contents. The back paste-down shows
        some traces of a manuscript in rotonda

    Provenance: Bought by the Elkan Naumburg Fellowship Fund, with the acquisition date of
        2.viii.1920 stamped on C1r • Inside the front board, a German sale catalogue entry • Beneath
        the sale catalogue is a 16th-century inscription, now illegible but plausibly in Spanish

US-Eu. Fragments of f.E9

    Size of page: fragments totalling 206 mm wide, showing only five staves.

    No watermarks visible

Provenance: Bought from Baron, London. Apparently the five strips were used for binding strips

US-R, ★★M.1490.D424 M3. Superius and Bassus. This copy is erroneously dated 1516 in *RISM*.

Watermarks:

A5-	A8-7	B4-3	B-5	B10-9	F1-2	F4-3	G2-1	G-6	G8-7
16	2	2	2	2	16	16	30	2	2

Corrections and changes:

In-house: A5*v*.v, A5*v*.vi, and A8*v*: see above

Later: A5*v*.v.25: *mc* → *sb*, by erasure • A5*v*.vi.20: *sb* → *m*, by erasure • B9*v*.ii.12: *m*, e → a, brown ink • F7r.i.57: *b*, e → d, by erasure, and brown ink • F7*v*.ii.6 from end: *mg,me,mf* → *dsbg* only, by erasure and brown ink • F7*v*.iii.after 3: rest, *b* → *sb*, by erasure • G1*v*.iii.14–16: now *sbG,sbF,bG* • G3r.iii.after 14 from end: rests, *sb* → *sb,m*, brown ink • G3r.iii.9 from end: *sb* → *m*, with brown ink tail • G6*v*.iii.29–30: ligature, g, e → g, d, by erasure and brown ink

Binding: The worm-hole on F2-8, which expands towards the end, is not at all present in gathering G: it may be that the two gatherings were not always kept together

Provenance: Gift of Hiram Sibley, 1937

Cancels

A half-sheet for ff. A3 and A6, and another for D2 and D7. For the rest of each copy described, see above

Technical comments: There is some additional space at the end of D2*v*.vi, apparently the result of a closer spacing on the cancel • Evidence drawn from the stave measurements in the copy at I-Rsc (and given below) suggests that the two cancel leaves were not prepared at the same time

---

Extant copies:

A-Wn, S.A.77.C.20

Watermarks: No.31 on A3- and on D2-

D-B, Mus.ant.pract.D227 (3)

Watermarks: No.31 on A-3 and on D7-

E-Bbc, M.115 (3). D2/7 only

Watermarks: No.31 on D-2

GB-Lbl, K.1.d.9

Watermarks: No.31 on A3- and on D-7

I-Bc, Q.73

Watermarks: No.31 on D7-. None visible on A3 or A6

Later change: A6r.vi.after 20: m.s. 3 has an added circle above, brown ink

I-Rsc, G.CS.3.B.30

Watermarks: No.31 on A6- and on D-2

US-R, ★★M.1490.D424 M3

Watermarks: No.31 on f.A6-

Second Edition

A1r]   Mi ſſarum Jo ſquin. | Liber tertius. | Mater patris. | Fayſans regres. | Ad fugam. | Di dadi. | De beata virgine. | Missa sine nomine.

C1r]   T
D1r]   A
F1r]   B
G10r]   ¶ Impre ſſum Foro ſempronii per Octauianum | Petrutium ciuem Foro ſempronien ſem. Anno | Domini .MDXIIII. Die primo martii. Domi-|nante inclito ac excellenti ſſimo Principe Domino | Franciſcomaria Feltrio de Ruere: Vrbini Sorǣque | Duce: Piſauri &c. Domino: Alme Vrbis Prǣfecto: | ac exercitus Sanctǣ Romanǣ Ecclesiǣ Imperatore. semper inuicto. [The differences from the first edition copies lie in "excellentiſſimo", the abbreviation in "Franciscomaria" and the line-break in "Sorǣque"]

Format and collation: Partbooks: landscape quarto-in-eights. [S] 18 folios: A^{8}B^{10}; [T] 12 folios: C^{12}; [A] 18 folios: D^{8}E^{10}; [B] 18 folios: F^{8}G^{10}

Signatures:] AaA 2 [\$4 • − A1 • + B5, C5, C6, E5 and G5 • G2 signed G

No foliation

Running heads: in two levels, as in the first edition:

recto:]	Superius.	[A1, B10, C1, QD1, E10, F1, G10
	Superius	[A6
	Tenor	[C2, C5-6, C11-12
	Tenor.	[C3-4, C7-10
	Altus.	[D2-3, D5-E6
	Altus	[D4, E7-9
	Baſſus.	[F2-6, F8-G2, G9
	Baſſus	[F7, G3-8
	[Nil:	A1, B10, C1, D1, E10, F1, G10
verso:]	Superius	[A1, A4, A8
	Superius.	[A2-3, A5-7, B1-9
	Tenor	[C1-C4, C11
	Tenor.	[C5-10
	Altus.	[D1-6, E1, E5-6
	Altus	[D7-8, E9
	Altus:	[E2-4, E7-8
	Baſſus.	[F1-4, F8-G2, G9
	Baſſus	[F5-7, G3-5, G7-8
	Baſſus:	[G6
	[Nil:	B10, C12, E10, G10

Fonts: Music: Petrucci's normal music type

Staves: Six per page

Text: Roman throughout • Title text in Rotonda, "x" = 5.1.mm.

Technical comments: The staves on G2r-5r.iv show damage of a typical range • Only five staves are inked on D6r, F6v and G9v

In-house corrections: G8v.i.after 41: bar-line, in brown ink: A-Wn, B-Br, CH-Zz, H-SY, I-Ac and I-Rvat

Contents:

	A1r	C1r	D1r	F1r	[Title]
1	A1v	C1v	D1v	F1v	Ioſquin. [Missa] Mater patris.
	A1v.v	C1v.iii	D1v.iii	F2r	[Gloria]
	A2r.iv	C1v.vi	D2r	F2v	[Credo]

	A2v.v	C2r.v	D2v.ii	F3r.v	[Sanctus]
	A3v	C2v	D3r.vi	F3v.v	[Agnus]
2	A4r.iv	C2v.v	D4r	F4r.iv	[Missa] Fay[ans regres.
	A4v	C3r	D4r.iv	F4v	[Gloria]
	A5r	C3r.iv	D4v.v	F5r	[Credo]
	A5v.v	C3v.v	D5v.iv	F5v.iv	[Sanctus]
	A6v	C4r.iii	D6v	F6r.iv	[Agnus]
3	A7r	C4v	D7r	F7r	Io[quin De Pres. [Missa] Ad fugam.
	A7r.iv	C4v.iv	D7r.iv	F7r.iv	[Gloria]
	A7v.iv	C5r.iii	D7v.iv	F7v.iv	[Credo]
	A8r.v	C5v.iii	D8v	F8r.v	[Sanctus]
	B1r	C6r.iii	E1r	G1r.ii	[Agnus]
4	B1r.v	C6v	E1r.iv	G1v	[Missa] Di dadi
	B1v.ii	C6v.v	E1v	G1v.iv	[Gloria]
	B2r.iv	C7r.iii	E2r.iii	G2v	[Credo]
	B3r	C7v	E3r	G3r	[Sanctus]
	B3r.vi	C8r	E3v	G3v.iv	[Agnus]
5	B4r	C8v	E4v	G4r	[Missa] De beata uirgine.
	B4r.v	C8v.v	E4v.v	G4v.ii	[Glora]
	B5r.ii	C9v.iii	E5v.iii	G5v	[Credo]
	B6r	C10v	E6v.ii	G6v	[Sanctus]
	B6v.iii	C11r	E7r.v	G7r	[Agnus]
6	B7r	C11r.iii	E8r	G7v	Io[quin [Missa sine nomine]
	B7r.v	C11r.iv	E8r.v	G7v.iii	[Gloria]
	B8r	C11r.v	E9r	G8r.iii	[Credo]
	B8v.v	C12r.iii	E9r.ii	G9r	[Sanctus]
	B9v	C12r.v	E9v	G9v	[Agnus]
				G10r	[Privilege, Colophon, Device]
	B10r		E10r		[blank staves]
	B10v	C12v	E10v	G10v	[blank]

Extant copies:

A-Wn, S.A.77.C.19. Complete. This copy is erroneously dated 1516 in *RISM*

> **Size of page:** 164 × 233 mm.

> **Watermarks:** None visible, but the evidence of the chain-lines confirms that the parts were printed on one paper throughout

> **Textual comments:** E5v.ii.text:] Amen [set as] Ame [with a sideways letter m

> **Technical comments:** D3r.vi: part of both stave and notes missing, apparently because something was on the page when it went through the press

> **Corrections and changes:**

>> **In-house:** G8v: see above

> **Binding:** Of the Austrian National Library.

B-Br, III 99.239A L.P. Bassus, complete

> **Size of page:** 152 × 227 mm.

> **Watermarks:** None visible, but the part is printed on the same batch of paper throughout

> **Technical comments:** Five staves inked on F6v and G9v • F6r.v: Text spacing sort, 2.8 × 0.6 mm • G3v.ii.29: *m* tail clearly distorted, at 3.8 mm above the top of the note-head

Corrections and changes:

>   **In-house:** G8*v*: see above

>   **Later:** F2*v*.i.28: *sb* → *m*, by erasing the tail • G1*v*.iii.16–17: G,F, colored *b* to colored *l*, with ginger ink up-tails • G2*r*.signature: the numeral "2", which has failed to print, has been added in pencil

Binding: A modern library binding, made by Vander Heyden of Brussels • Modern paste-down and end paper at each end • In an earlier binding, probably with the other two Fossombrone editions of Josquin's masses, books 2 (1515, No.59) and 1 (1516, No.62), this book had red edges

Provenance: Probably with Josquin, *I Missarrum* (1516, No.62)

CH–Zz, Mus.Jac.G.67₄. Bassus, complete

>   **Size of page:** 165 × 232 mm.

>   No watermarks visible

>   **In-house, corrections:** G8*v*: see above

>   **Binding:** With the first volume of Motetti de la Corona, *q.v.* • The last folio of this book is used as a back paste-down

>   **Provenance:** From the collection of Erwin Jacobi

>   **Bibliography:** Puskás, *Musikbibliothek*, item 159

H–SY, xx.8.b (3). Bassus, complete

>   **Size of page:** 153 × 215 mm.

>   No watermarks visible

>   **Technical comments:** Only five staves inked on F6*v*

>   **Corrections and changes:**

>>   **In-house:** G8*v*: see above

>>   **Later:** F1*r*.] Liber terti*us* Jo[qu: Miss*arum* • F2*r*–G1o*r*, all rectos, some form of] lib*er* 3 [and manuscript foliation, 1–17 • F8*v*.iv.44: *b*, colored, scratched void

>   **Binding:** With Josquin *I Missarum* (1516, No.62)

>   **Provenance:** With Josquin *I Missarum* (1516) • F1*r*.] Simbolum Petri Shremj | spes mea | Christe [alus hominum jam non moriture redemptor | Christe Deus pura virgine natus homo, | Es mea [pes, mea [pes fueras, mea, Christe maneti | spes, lux, pax, requies, dux, via vita, salus

I–Ac, St.n.189 (6). Complete. This copy is misbound, with the inner sheet of the Tenor preceding the other two sheets, producing the sequence of folios 5–8, 1–4, 9–12

>   **Size of page:** 168 × 232 mm.

>   **Watermarks:** None visible, but the part is printed on the same batch of paper throughout

>   **Corrections and changes:**

>>   **In-house:** G8*v*: see above

>>   **Later:** G1*v*.iii.16–18: now 3 col. *sb*, G, F, G

>   **Binding:** With Agricola, *Misse* (1504, No.13)

>   **Provenance:** From S. Francesco, Assisi

>   **Bibliography:** Petrucci, *Liber* (facsimile)

I–BGc, Cinq.4.984 (3). Superius, complete

>   **Size of page:** 169 × 235

>   No watermarks visible

>   **Technical comments:** A3*r*.vi: furniture has taken ink • B1o*r*: the blind impression of staves

>   **Binding:** With Josquin, *I Missarum* (1516, No.62)

>   **Provenance:** Cortesi • Mayr • Presumably with Josquin's *I Missarum* (1516)

I–Rvat, Sist.235–238. Complete

Size of page:

No watermarks visible

Textual comments: E5*v*.ii.text:] Ame*n* [set as] Ame [with a sideways letter m

Technical comments: There is a heavy impress of staves on A1*r*, apparently from before the title was printed. This implies that the title was in the music forme

Corrections and changes:

  In-house: G8*v*: see above

  Later: D3*r*.iii.11: struck through, dark brown ink • G1*v*.iii.16–18: now 3 col.*sb*, G,F,G

Provenance: formerly owned by Chiti. See Rostirolla, "Corrispondenza"

Bibliography: Rostirolla, "Corrispondenza", 261 and 265. On pp. 261–62, Rostirolla transcribes Leo X's privilege to Petrucci

---

Lost copies: A copy of one of the editions was in the library of King João IV. It seems more likely that this was of the edition of 1526. (See Sampaio Ribero, item 85) • A copy, probably of one of these editions, was in the collection of Ottheinrich' chapel at Pfalz-Neuburg, and is listed in the inventory of 1554, on folio 35*v*. (See Lambrecht, *Heidelberger*, i, p. 106)

Early references: Gesner's reference, in *Pandectae* (1548), VII, under Libri de cantu figurato in Italia impressi, to:] Missae quinque de Iosquin. [could perhaps refer to this volume, although it is more likely to mean Book I. It is unlikely that Gesner had actually seen a copy. See Bernstein, "Gesner", No.137 • It is tempting to think that Doni knew of the three volumes of Josquin's masses put out by Petrucci. He refers to] Messe | Di Iosquini cinque libri [and, as Haar, "Libraria", p. 115 remarks, a possible reading of this could be to Petrucci's work. Some support for this may be gleaned from Haar's comment (p. 101, fn.3) which suggests that Doni may have known of Gesner's work. Doni's citation could then be a modification of Gesner's (given above), and, from its form, could suggest that Doni had not actually seen the books

Other editions: Another edition was printed by Pasoti and Dorico in 1526 (*RISM* J675)

Bibliography:

  (a) Rosaria Boccadifuoco, *Bibliografia*, No.1195 • Sartori, *Petrucci*, No.48

  (c) Petrucci, *Liber*

  (d) editions; Josquin, *Werke*, Missen III

  (e) Noble, "Petrucci" • Boorman, "Cancels"

Commentary:

1. This volume represents a new venture on Petrucci's part. The only music printed since his arrival in Fossombrone had been the rest of Bossinensis's second book and the lost *Frottole X*. Both of these probably represent the end of the Venetian stage, in repertoire and in printing history. (I discount the reported volume of the *Messa Corale*, discussed elsewhere.) In 1513, Petrucci had published the two non-musical books catalogued before this volume. The decision to re-embark on music printing will have involved a search for a new supplier of music, and also (probably) a delay while the music type was refurbished.

2. The repertoire here is distinct from that found in the earlier volumes of Josquin's masses in one respect, in that it is much less integrated in style or chronology. Petrucci seems to have gathered together whatever was available.

   As Noble has said (Noble, "Josquin", 723), Petrucci's first volume is "the most homogeneous in style; the five works in it could all have been composed within the preceding 15 years". The second book has two groups of material, as I have suggested. This volume, however, is less clearly representative of any one person's taste. Both the canonic masses are here, as also are two based on early chansons, by Frye and Morton. Coupled with these are a middle-period setting based on a Brumel motet, and the much more recent *Missa de beata Virgine*. The impression given is that Petrucci gathered whatever was left and available to him: indeed, some of these works were not widely disseminated or well-known—they are found in very few sources, and do not provide material for later treatises and collections of duos and trios.

3. The evidence for two editions is clearly seen in three features:
    (a) the change from rotonda to roman type;
    (b) the patterns of watermarks (see below); and
    (c) the sequences of capital initials. Details of these can be found in Boorman, *Petrucci*, 387–90.

4. The ranges of paper used for the first edition seem to present a complex problem of analysis: the watermarks are as follows:

	Ao	Ai	Bo	B2	Bi	Co	C2	Ci	Do	Di	Eo	E2	Ei	Fo	Fi	Go	G2	Gi
A-GÜ					—	2	2											
A-Wn,20	2	16	2	2	2	30	27	2	16	16	2	2	2					
D-B	2	16	2	2	2	27	2	2	16	16	27	27	2	16	16	2	2	2
GB-Lbl	2	16	2	23	2	30	2	30	16	16	2	2	2	16	16	2	2	2
I-Bc	2	16	2	2	2	30	30	2	16	16	2	27	2	16	16	2	2	2
I-Rsc	2	16	2	2	2	2	2	30	2	2	2	27	2	16	16	2	2	2
US-CA					27	2	27											
US-Eu ?																		
US-R	2	16	2	2	2									16	16	30	2	2

The most likely solution is that both Altus and Bassus were begun at one press, using the paper 16. The Superius and Tenor were probably begun at a second press, using paper 2 at first. The shifts in pattern from one paper to another probably represent no more than changes in paper stock as it was drawn from store. There is certainly no other evidence either for interruptions in press work or for complex patterns of different typesetters.

5. There is a little evidence, in the state of initials and staves, to argue that the text forme (at least) was first set for the Tenor book. The two sheets, C1,2,11,12 and C5,6,7,8, use different papers, and also seems to have a pattern of initials that places them earlier. For example, the initial "S" is as found on C3*v* and C5*v*: that is better than on A2*v* (*cf.* the lower left of the letter), A5*v*, D2*v*, D5*v*, F3*r*, F5*v*, and F8*r*. This is particularly evident in the London copy.

6. Neither the titles of the masses nor the voice-names were kept in the forme. For the former, the evidence is presented here: for the latter, it was given above.

    recto:] Mater patris [A2, C2 • Mater patris. [A3-4, D2-3, F3-4 • .Mater patris. [F2 • Fayſans regres. [A4 (above iv), A5-6, D5, F4 (above iv), F5-6 • Fayſans regres [C3 • fayſans regres [C4 • Fayſant regres. [D4, D6 • Ad fugaʒ [A7-B1, G1 • Ad fugam. [D8, F7-8 • Ad fugam [C5-6, D7, E1 • Di dadi [B2, C7-8, E1 (above iv), E3-4, G2 • Di dedi [G4 • Didadi [B3, E2, G3 • De beata virgine [B4-5 • De beata virgine [B6, E5, E7, G5 • Debeata virgine [C9, G6-7 • De beata virgine [C10-11, E6, G4 (above v) • Joſquin [B7-9, C11 (above iii), C12, E9, G9 • Juſquin [E8 • Joſpuin [G8

    verso:] Mater patris [A1-3, C1-2 • Mater patris. [D1-3, F1-3 • Fayſans regres. [A5-6, F4-6 • .Fayſans regres. [A4 • Fayſan regres [C2 (above v) • fayſans regres [C3 • Fayſans regres [D4, D6 • Fayſant regres. [D5 • Ad fugaʒ [A7, C4, D8 • Ad fugam [A8, C5 • .Ad fugaʒ [D7 • Ad fugam. [F7 • Ad fugaʒ. [F8 • Didadi [B1-3 • Didadi Supra naragie [C6 • Di dadi [C7, E1-3, G1-3 • De

Beata virgine [B4 • De beata virgine [B5-6, E6-7 • De beata virgine [C8 • De beata virgine [C9, E4-5, G4, G6 • De betam virgine [G5 • Joſquin [B7v-9v, C11, E8-9, G7-9

This pattern, with its complexities, is sufficient to demonstrate that the head-lines were not normally retained within the forme. Even the part-names change too frequently and randomly. In fact, there are additional details which are not presented here, but which confirm this conclusion. Wojciech Typrowicz has taken this study somewhat further, and examined the various forms of the letters "d" and "r", which are not indicated separately above, as well as the occasions on which the part-name is nearer to or further from the spine than is the title of the mass. These additional details confirm that the forme did not contain this headline as a separate unit, without providing any clear evidence of the number of typesetters involved.

7. The paper used for the cancel bifolia in the first edition is unusual in Petrucci's output. It is otherwise only to be found in *Frottole Libro VIII* of 1507. There is no evidence that the use of this paper in that book represents a later impression: thus its appearance here is no help in dating the cancel bifolia. Without good grounds for saying so, I suspect that they were printed soon after the rest of the edition.

8. The evidence of the stave patterns on the cancels in gatherings A and D shows that both were printed by work-and-turn:

	1r	2v	7r	8v		2r	1v	8r	7v		3r	4v	5r	6v		4r	3v	6r	5v
A	—	176	176	178		180	180	180	181		176	178	176	178		181	178	178	182
D	—	178	177	182		177	178	177	177		179	178	178	177		181	182	181	183

There were evidently two sets of formes: one measuring consistently between 176 and 179 mm long, and the other measuring between 180 and 183 mm. The first was used for the original settings of the outer formes of AI, AII, and DII, and the inner of DI: the other for the other formes. However, the shorter forme was used consistently for both sides of both cancel sheets.

	3r	6v	6r	3v
A	176	178	178	178

	2r	7v	7r	2v
D	177	177	177	178

This argues strongly that they were not prepared at the same time. If they had been, they could have been printed simultaneously, with both formes used, one for each side of the sheet.

9. The second edition must lie after the change from rotonda to roman type, and therefore after the second Fossombrone edition of the first book of Josquin's masses. This puts it within the group of editions which appeared after the new edition of Josquin's first book, beginning late in 1516. None of these have correct dates attached to them, though this seems to be one of the first.

10. The pattern of captions is slightly different from that for the first edition:
recto:] Mater patris. [A2-4, C2, D2, F2-4 • Mater patris [D3 • Fayſans regres. [A5-6, C3-4, D4-6, F5-6 • Ioſquin De Pres. Ad fugam. [A7 • Ad fugam. [A8-B1, C5-6, D7-E1, F7-G1 • Di dadi. [B2-3, C7-8, E2-4, G2-4 • De beata uirgine. [B4-6, C9-11, E5, G5-7 • De beata uirgine: [E6 • De beata uirgine [E7 • Ioſquin. [B7-9, C12, G8-9 • Ioſquin: [E8-9
verso:] Ioſquin. Mater patris. [A1 • Mater patris. [A2-3, C1-2, D1-3, F1-3 • Fayſans regres. [A4-6, C3, D4-6, F4-6 • Ad fugam. [A7-8, D7-8, F7-8 • Ad fugam [inverted] [C4 • Ad fugam [C5 • Di dadi [B1-3, C6, G2-3 (the copy at I-Ac shows final points on B2-3) • Di dadi. [C7, E1, G1 • Di dadi: [E2-3 • De beata uirgine. [B4, C8-10, E4-5, G4-6 • De beta uirgine [B5 • De beata uirgine [B6, E5-7 • Ioſquin. [B7-9, C11, E8, G7-9 • Ioſquin: [E9

These patterns are over-simplified in the same manner as those for the first edition. In addition, there is a difficulty over the probable use of a colon instead of a point at the end of a number of captions. This colon does not seem to take ink at all well. While it is possible that some copies were printed with a colon and others with a point, yet the patterns of the two on different copies are not consistent from folio to folio of the same sheet

No. 55. *Motetti de la Corona I*

17.viii.1514   *RISM* 1514[1]

This title was published in more than one edition, of the same date.
   Edition 1: I-Bc, Q70
   Cancel for folios E2 and E7: I-Bc, Q70
   Edition 2: D-Mbs; I-Bc, Q74; I-Fn; I-Vlevi; PL-Kj
   Edition 3: CH-Zz; D-LEm; I-BGc; I-PEc; I-Vnm
   The copy listed in *RISM* as at A-Wn is in fact of RISM 1526[1]. The copy of 1526[1] which *RISM* records at I-Bc, is actually the copy with the siglum Q.74, listed here.

First Edition

A1r]   Motetti de la corona. | [crown]
C1r]   T
E1r]   A
G1r]   B
H8r]   LEO. p*a*pa. X. [etc. as in Josquin, *III Missarum*, No.54): followed by:]
         [left:] Dilecto filio do*mi*no Octauiano de | petrutiis de foro∫empronii
         [right:] Petrus Bembus
         [between the two:] ¶ Impre∫∫um Foro∫empronii per Octauianum | Petrutium ciuem Foro∫empronien∫em. Anno | Domini. MDXIIII. Die xvii. Augu∫ti. Domi-|nante inclito ad excellenti∫∫imo Principe Domino | Franci∫comaria Feltrio de Ruere: Vrbini Soræque | Duce: Pi∫auri &c. Domino: Alme Vrbis Præfecto: | ac exercitus. S*an*cte. R*om*ane. E*u*le∫i*u*e. Imperatore semp*er* inuicto.
A1v]   Tabula

	Supremus	Tenor	Altus	Ba∫∫us
A∫cendens *christu*s in altum	11	28	44	59
Bonitatem feci∫ti cum	4	19	35	51
Benedictus do*minu*s deus	8	25	41	56
Beata dei genitrix maria	8	25	41	57
Benedicat nos imperialis	9	26	42	57
Benedicta es celor*um* regina	12	28	44	59
Chri∫tum regem regum	10	27	43	58
Contremuerunt o*m*nia me*m*bra	11	28	44	59
Cele∫te beneficium	13	30	46	61
Chri∫tum ducem redemit	15	31	48	63
Dilectus deo₇ ho*mi*nibus	14	31	47	62
Ecce maria genuit nobis	8	24	40	56
Egregie chri∫ti confe∫∫or	14	30	47	62

Gaude Barbara beata	2	18	34	50
Gaude francorum regia	10	27	43	58
Letatus ſum in his que	5	21	37	52
Laudate deum in ſanctis	7	23	39	55
Laudate dominum de celis	15	32	48	63
Memor eſto verbi tui	3	18	34	50
Nos qui viuimus In enim	5	21	37	53
Nobilis progenie nobilior	7	24	40	55
O deſolatorum conſolator	10	26	42	58
Senatus apoſtolorum	6	23	39	54
Sancta trinitas vnus deus	9	26	42	57
Tempus meum eſt	12	29	45	60
Uulneraſti cor meum	13	29	46	61

Format and Collation: Part-books: landscape quarto-in-eights, each book of 16 folios. [S] A-B⁸; [T] C-D⁸; [A] E-F⁸; [B] G-H⁸

Signatures:] ⋆ A 2 [$4, − A1. On A3, the letter is inverted

Foliation: t.r.r., consecutively through all four books:] [S] [1], 2–16; [T] [17], 18–22, 15 [*recte* 23], 24–32; [A] 33–48; [B] 49–63, [64]

Running heads: including those of the cancel: top left unless otherwise indicated:

verso:	Sup*erius*		[A2-B5, B7
	Sup*erius*	Diſcantus	[B6: top left, and centre
	Tenor		[C1-D7
	Altus		[E1-F7
	Baſſus		[G1-H6
	[Nil:		A1, B8, D8, F8, H8
recto:	Sup*erius*		[A2,7,8, B1,2,7,8
			[A3,4,5,6, B3,4,5,: top right
	Tenor		[C2-D2, D7,8: top right
			[D3-6
	Altus		[E2-F8
	Baſſus		[G2-H7
	[Nil:		A1, B6, C1, E1, G1, H8

Fonts: Music: Petrucci's normal music type

Staves: six per page: 175–180 mm long, 10-91.5-112 mm high

Text: Rotonda: Roman used for the privilege and colophon

In-house corrections: These are all present in the unique copy: the mensuration sign o over 3 uses a manuscript o over a type 3 on A5*v*.iii; A7*v*.iii; B1*r*.ii; B2*r*.iii; C5*r*.vi; C6*r*.ii; C6*r*.v; D3*r*.i • B1*r*.v.12: *mg* → *ma*, erasing the note head and stamping in an *sb*, using the original tail • F1*v*.i.37: stamped in later • For further possible in-house corrections, see the list under the description of the unique copy

Textual comments: The Tavola is set in a single column, with four columns of arabic numerals as folio numbers for the various parts • The second *pars* of No.12 has the incipit] Regat me potentia . . .

Contents: including the contents of the cancel:

A1*r*	C1*r*	E1*r*	G1*r*	[Title]
A1*v*				Tabula

1	A2r	C1v	E1v	G1v	GAude barbara beata	Jo.Mouton
	A2r.iv★	C1v.v	E1v.iv★	G1v.iv★	2/ Gaude quia meruisti	
2	A2v.ii	C2r.iv	E2r.iii	G2r.ii	MEmor esto verbi tui	Josquin
	A3r	C2v.ii★	E2v.iv	G2v.ii	2/ Portio mea domine	
3	A3v	C3r.iv	E3r.v	G3r	[T:] BOnitatem fecisti	Carpantras
	A4r.i★	C3v.v	E3v.v★	G3v	2/ Manus tue domine	
4	A4v.ii	C4v	E4v	G4r	LEtatus sum in hiis que	Andreas de silua
	A4v.v★	C4v.v	E4v.iv★	G4r.iv★	2/ Fiat pax in virtute	
5	A5r	C5r	E5r	G4v	NOs qui uiuimus	Jo.Monton
	Tacet	C5v.ii★	E5v.ii	G5r	2/ [B:] Deus autem	
	A5v.i★	C6r.iii★	E6r.ii	G5v	3/ Dom[in]us memor fuit	
6	A6r.ii	C6v.v	E6v.iv	G6r.ii	[T:] CLare sanctorum	P.de therache
7	A6v.iii	C7r.v	E7r.iv	G6v.iii	LAudate deum in sanctis	Jo.Monton
	A6v.vi	C7v.ii	E7v.i★	G6v.vi	2/ Or cum clamarem	
8	A7r.iv	C8r	E7v.v	G7r.iv	NObilis progenie	Antonius de feuin
9	A7v	C8r.v	E8r.iii	G7v.ii	ECce maria genuit nobis	Jo.Monton
10	A7v.v	C8v.ii	E8v	G7v.vi	BEnedictus dominus deus	Ant.feuin
	A8r.ii★	C8v.v★	E8v.iv	G8r.iii★	2/ Omnes gentes plaudite	
11	A8r.v	D1r.iii	F1r	G8v	BEata dei genitrix maria	Jo.Monton
12	A8v.iv	D1v.ii	F1v	G8v.v	BEnedicat nos imperialis	Longheual
	B1r	D1v.iv★	F1v.v	H1r.ii	2/ Regat nos potentia	
13	B1r.iii	D2r	F2r	H1r.iv	SAncta trinitas vnus deus	feuin
14	B1v	D2r.v	F2r.v	H1v	O Desolatorum consolator	Diuitis
	B1v.iv	D2v.i★	F2v.ii	H1v.iii★	2/ [T:] Beate claudi	
15	B2r	D2v.v	F3r	H2r	GAude francorum regia	Antonius feuin
16	B2r.v	D3r.iii	F3r.v	H2r.iv	CHristum regem regum	Monton
17	B2v.iii	D3v	F3v.iv	H2v.ii	Contremuerunt omnia	[Anon.]
18	B3r	D3v.iv	F4r	H2v.v	Ascendens christus in altum	Hylaire
19	B3v	D4r.iii	F4r.v	H3r.iv	Benedictus es celorum regina	Jo. Monton
	B3v.iv★	D4r.vi	F4v.iii	H3v	2/ Per illud aue	
20	B4r	D4v.iii	F5r	H3v.v	Tempus meum est	Feuin
	B4r.iii★	D4v.v★	F5r.iii★	H4r.ii	2/ Viri galilei	
21	B4v	D5r.iii	F5v	H4v	Vulnerasti cor meum	[Anon.]
	B4v.iii	D5r.v	F5v.iii★	H4v.iii★	2/ Veni in ortum meum	
22	B5r	D5v	F6r	H5r	Celeste beneficium	Jo.Monton
	B5r.v	D5v.iv★	F6r.v	H5r.iv★	2/ Adiutorium nostrum	[Févin]
23	B5v.ii	D6r.ii	F6v.ii	H5v.ii	Egregie christi confessor	feuin
	B5v.iv★	D6r.v	F6v.v	H5v.iv★	2/ Ecce enim festus est	
24	B6r.iii	D6v.iii	F7r.iii	H6r.ii	Dilectus deo ꝫ hominibus	[Anon.]
25	B6v	D7r.ii	F7v	H6v	Christum ducem redemit nos	Josquin
26	B7r	D7v	F7v.v	H6v.v	Laudate dominum de celis	Brumel
	B7v.iii	D8r.ii	F8r.vi	H7r.v	2/ Laudate dominum in sanctis eius	
				H8r	[Privilege; Colophon]	
	B8v	D8v		H8v	[blank]	

Extant copy:

I-Bc, Q.70. Complete. The bifolio E2,7 is a cancel, for which see below

> **Size of page:** 163 × 227 and 169 × 234 mm.
>
> **Watermarks:** No.2 on A2-1, A6-5, B2-1, B3-4, C1-2, C5-6, D2-1, D4-3, E1-, E6-5, F6-5, and F8-7
>
> **Technical comments:** A1*r* and B8*v* both show the blind impress of uninked staves • B8*r* shows the impress of uninked musical notation
>
> **Corrections and changes:**
>
> > **In-house:** See above: in addition, the ink used for the mensuration signs appears to be used in the following changes, which may therefore also be in-house: C7*v*.v.30: f → g • D4*r*.i.50: f → g • E4*r*.vi.46: *l*, b → e' • E5*r*.i.after bar-line after 6: added rest • F2*v*.iv.24–25: *sb* → *m* • G2*v*.i.18: d → e • G2*v*.i.31–32: *sb,m* → *colb,sb* • G5*v*.iii.34–35: *sb*B,*sb*G → *colb*B,*sb*A • H2*v*.iv.13: *b* → *l*, with added tail • H5*v*.vi.after 39: rests, *b,sb* → *b,m* • H7*v*.iii.11: added point • H7*v*.iii.24: *b* rest → point • This ink appears also to be used to align text and notes on C5*v*.ii–iii; E5*v*-6*r*; and G5*r*
> >
> > **Later:** A1*v*: ascriptions added in ink • E3*r*.vi.after 21: erased g', probably *m* • E4*r*.vi.44–45: c.o.p. ligature, a, d' → original a and *sb*f' in black ink • E5*v*.ii: two added words at the start of the line • E5*v*.iii: added] ij • E5*v*.iv–E6*r*.i: lines linking words and pitches • F6*r*.ii.43: f → g, in grey ink • F8*v*.iii.20: *b* → *sb*, in grey ink • G4*r*.v.9: c → A • G5*r*.i-vi: added text and linking lines, as on E5*v* • G5*v*.i.after 27: *sbc*' erased • G7*r*.i.26: *ma* → *dmg*, in ink • H2*r*.iv.20–21: *b*A, *b*d with added dot for the A
>
> **Binding:** Modern, marbled boards, matching those for the volumes of Josquin's masses in I-Bc
>
> **Provenance:** This is perhaps the copy given to Martini by Chiti early in 1746 (See Martini, *Epistolario*, I/11/7–18, and Schnoebelein, *Padre*) • Early call-marks include, on title pages:] H863 [and on A1*r*.] 1013
>
> **Bibliography:** Fava, *Primo*, p. 39 (exhibition at Bologna in 1929)

No.59A. *Cancel.*

A half-sheet for folios E2 and E7 was printed soon after the first edition. For the rest of this edition, see above

Foliation:] 32 [and] 37

Extant copy:

I-Bc, Q.70.

> **Watermark:** No.2 on E7-

No.59B. *Second Edition*

A1*r*]   Motetti de la corona | [crown]

C1*r*]   T

E1*r*]   A

G1*r*]   B

H8*r*]   LEO. p*apa*. X. [etc. as for the first edition]

A1*v*]   [Tavola:]

	Supremus.	Tenor.	Altus.	Ba[[us.
A[cendens *christu*s in altum	xi	xxviii	xliiii	lix
Bonitate*m* feci[ti cum	iiii	xix	xxxv	li

Benedictus dominus deus	viii	xxv	xli	lvi
Beata dei genitrix maria	viii	xxv	xli	lvii
Benedicat nos imperialis	ix	xxvi	xlii	lvii
Benedicta es celorum regina	xii	xxviii	xliiii	lix
Chriſtum regem regum	x	xxvii	xliii	lviii
Contremuerunt omnia membra	xi	xxviii	xliiii	lix
Celeſte beneficium	xiii	xxx	xlvi	lxi
Chriſtum ducem redemit	xv	xxxi	xlviii	lxiii
Dilectus deo & hominibus	xiiii	xxxi	xlvii	lxii
Ecce maria genuit nobis	viii	xxiiii	xl	lvi
Egregie christi confeſſor	xiiii	xxx	xlvii	lxii
Gaude Barbara beata	ii	xviii	xxxiiii	l
Gaude francorum regis	x	xxvii	xliii	lviii
Letatus ſum in his que	v	xxi	xxxvii	lii
Laudate deum in ſanctis	vii	xxiii	xxxix	lv
Laudate dominum de celis	xv	xxxii	xlviii	lxiii
Memor eſto uerbi tui	iii	xviii	xxxiiii	l
Nos qui uiuimus in exitu	v	xxi	xxxvii	liii
Nobilis progenie nobilior	vii	xxiiii	xl	lv
O deſolatorum conſolator	x	xxvi	xlii	lviii
Senatus appoſtolorum	vi	xxiii	xxxix	liiii
Sancta trinitas unus deus	ix	xxvi	xlii	lvii
Tempus meum eſt	xii	xxix	xlv	lx
Vulneraſti cor meum	xiii	xxix	xlvi	lxi

Format and collation: Part-books: landscape quarto-in-eights, each book of 16 folios: [S] A-B⁸; [T] C-D⁸; [A] E-F⁸; [B] G-H⁸

Signatures:] ★ A 2 [$4 • In two sizes: larger on A2, B1-4, C1-2, G1-4, H1-4; the smaller on A3-4, C3-4, D1-4, E1-4, F1-4

Foliation: t.r.r.:] [S] [1], 2-16; [T] 17-32; [A] 33-48; [B] 49-63, [64]

Running heads: at the outer margin, though inside the numerals:

verso:]	Superius.	[A2-8, B1-7: at the inner margin on A3
	Tenor.	[C1-D7
	Altus.	[E1-F8
	Baſſus.	[G1,2,7,8, H1-7: centered on H4
	Baſſus	[G3,5,6
	Bſſus.	[G4
	[Nil:	A1, B8, D8, H8
recto:]	Superius.	[A2-8, B3-8: the "S" is inverted on A7 • centered on B6
	Superius	[B1,2
	Tenor.	[C2-D8
	Altus.	[E2,3, E5-F7
	Altus:	[E4
	Altus	[F8
	Baſſus.	[G2-7, H3-6: centered on H6
	Baſſus	[G8, H1,2,7
	[Nil:	A1, C1, E1, G1, H8

Fonts: Music: Petrucci's normal music type

Staves: six per page

Text: Roman, used throughout, "x" = 1.7 mm, "20" = 57 mm • Rotonda, for the word] Verte [on a few pages

Textual comments: A list of all variants (both textual and merely formal) between this and the first edition is given in Boorman, *Petrucci*, pp. 307–13. The most significant feature is the extent to which brown-ink alterations in the first edition are followed in print in the present one • It is notable that the numerals in the Tabula are not entirely consistent: most seem to be lower case letters — this applies to all the letter "l", "v" and "x", and some of the uses of "i". But many of the numerals 1 are printed with a capital "I". In both the copies at I-Vlevi and PL-Kj, the following use l.c. letters "i":

Ascendens   [T] xxviiI   [B] lix

Beata dei genitrix   [S] vIiI

Dilectus deo   [T] xxxi

O desolatorum   [A] xlii

Senatus apostolorum   [S] vi

Technical comments: The word "Verte" is set in two styles: rotonda on A4r,5r,6r, C3r,5r,6r, D2r,4r,6r, E2r,3r,5r,6r,7r, F6r; roman on A2r,3r, B2r,5r,7r, C1r,7r,8r, D1r, F2r,3r,4r,8r, G2r,3r,5r,6r,7r, H2r,3r,5r,7r • Small capital initial letters are use in a number of cases, in all but one because the previous piece did not allow for extra space at the beginning of the last line.

In-house corrections: B1v.vi.3–9: now reads printed sba',sbf',sbg', all these merely touched up: followed by sba',sb rest,sb rest,colsbe',colsbf',colbg',colba' → ba',sbb',ba',sbrest,sbg',a', all in brown ink. The first notes after the correction are sbd',dsba',mg',bg',sbf',mensuration sign: I-Vlevi • H5v.ii.5-4 from the end: 2m: printed as c, d in the copy at I-Fn, and corrected in manuscript: reading B, c after a stop-press correction in the copy at PL-Kj • H5v.iii.19: corrected in manuscript in the copy at I-Fn, and by stop-press in that at PL-Kj

Contents:

9	A7v	C8r.v	E8r.iii	G7v.ii	ECce maria genuit nobis	IO.MOVTON.
10	A7v.v	C8v.ii	E8v	G7v.vi	BEnedictus dominus deus meus	ANT.DE FEVIN.
	A8r.ii	C8v.v★	E8v.iv	G8r.iii★	2/ Omnes gentes plaudite	
11	A8r.v	D1r.iii	F1r	G8v	BEata dei genitrix maria	IO.MOVTON.
12	A8v.iv	D1v.i	F1v	G8v.v	BEnedicat nos imperialis	LONGHEVAL.
	B1r	D1v.iv	F1v.v	H1r.ii	2/ Regat nos potentia	
13	B1r.iii	D2r	F2r	H1r.iv	SAncta trinitas unus deus	ANT.DE FEVIN.
14	B1v	D2r.v	F2r.v	H1v	O Defolatrum confolator	DIVITIS.
	B1v.iv	D2v.i★	F2v.ii	H1v.iii★	2/ Ora pro nobis	
15	B2r	D2v.v	F3r	H2r	GAude francorum regia	ANT.DE FEVIN.
16	B2r.v	D3r.iii	F3r.v	H2r.iv	CHriftum regem regum	IO.MOVTON.
17	B2v.iii	D3v	F3v.iv	H2v.ii	COntremuerunt omnia membra mea	[Anon.] [A:] MOVTON.
18	B3r	D3v.iv	F4r	H2v.v	AScendens xps in altum	HYLAIRE.
19	B3v	D4r.iii	F4r.v	H3r.iv	BEnedictus es celorum regina [other vv:] BEnedicta . . .	IO.MOVTON.
	B3v.iv	D4r.vi	F4v.iii	H3v	2/ Per illud aue	
20	B4r	D4v.iii	F5r	H3v.v	TEmpus meum eft ut reuertar	ANT.DE FEVIN
	B4r.iii	D4v.v★	F5r.iii★	H4r.ii	2/ Viri galilei	
21	B4v	D5r.iii	F5v	H4v	VVlnerafti cor meum	[Anon.]
	B4v.iii	D5r.v	F5v.iii★	H4v.iii★	2/ Veni in ortum meum	
22	B5r	D5v	F6r	H5r	CElefte beneficium	IO.MOVTON.
	B5r.v	D5v.iv★	F6r.v	H5r.iv★	2/ Adiutorium nostrum	
23	B5v.ii	D6r.ii	F6v	H5v.ii	EGregie xpi confeffor	ANT.DE FEVIN.
	B5v.iv	D6r.v	F6v.v	H5v.iv★	2/ Ecce enim feftus eft nobis	
24	B6r.iii	D6v.iii	F7r.iii	H6r.ii	DIlectus deo & hominibus	[Anon.]
25	B6v	D7r.ii	F7v	H6v	CHriftum ducem redemit	IOSQVIN.
26	B7r	D7v	F7v.v	H6v.v	LAudate dominum de celis	BRVMEL.
	B7v.iii	D8r.ii	F8r.vi	H7r.v	2/ Laudate dominum in fanctis	
				H8r	[Privilege; Colophon]	
	B8v	D8v		H8v	[Blank]	

Extant copies:

D-Mbs, 4°.mus.pr.247. Superius and Altus, complete

    Size of page: 163 × 241 and 165 × 239 mm.

    Watermarks:

A-2	A4-3	B5-6	B7-8	E-4	E7-8	F4-3	F7-8
35	6	35	6	6	6	6	6

Textual comments: A8r: the initial is present, merely poorly inked • B4v, F2r, and F8r lack the folio numbers, again probably from poor inking

Technical comments: A5v.iii.8 from end: music spacing sort, 16.5 × 0.7 mm.

Later corrections and changes: A1v: manuscript ascriptions in pencil are supplied for many pieces • Pieces are numbered sequentially in manuscript, in the margin, from 150 to 175 • B5r.vi.33: c', sm → m, by erasure

Binding: 19th-century marbled boards in half-cloth. Leather tabs, mostly lost • Dark red stained edges, with a black pattern • One paste-down and one fly-leaf at each end

Provenance: This, with the rest of the set, is presumed to be a Fugger copy

I-Bc, Q.74. Superius and Tenor, complete

Size of page: 164 × 233 mm.

Watermarks:

A5-6	A7	B4-3	B8-7	C2	C6-5	D2-1	D4-3
35	6	35	35	6	35	35	35

Technical comments: A1r: ligatures have been used as furniture

Later corrections and changes: B1v.vi.9–10: touched up in ink • B5r.vi.33: c', sm → m, by erasure • B8r.iii.1: sbd" erased • D2v.left margin:] Ant de feuin [in a 16th-century hand

Provenance: Sent to Martini by Girolamo Chiti in 1745 or early 1746. See the letters from Chiti dated 3.xii.1745 (offering the books, although they lack the Bassus and Contratenor), from Martini dated 15.xii.1745, from Chiti dated 29.xii.1745 (sending the music), from Chiti on 13.i.1746 (repeating that he is sending the music), from Martini on 19.i.1746 (acknowledging its receipt) and from Martini on 26.ii.1746 (with further thanks). • Old call numbers 974 and 870 on A1r, and 1017 on C1r

Bibliography: Schnoebelen, *Padre*, Nos.1218–1221, 1223–1224 and 1230, pp. 138–41

I-Fn, Landau-Finaly 8. Bassus, lacking f.G3

Watermarks: No.35 on G1, G5-4, H2-1, and H4-3

Corrections and changes:

In-house: H5v: see above

Later: H7v.ii.7: f, b → sb • H7v.iv.10: g, sb → b

Binding: Contemporary Italian binding, rebacked • Bound with the other three volumes of the series of *Motetti de la Corona*

I-Vlevi, Ris.A.85. Superius only

Size of page: 165 × 235 mm.

Watermarks:

A1-2	A6-5	B2-1	B4-3
35	6	6	6

Textual comments: B5r.iv.text: Annanos, with the last letter very poorly inked

Technical comments: This copy shows many blind impressions: A1r, right side: a set of ligatures, apparently c.o.p., descending a sixth, in blind; B8r.vi: very clear blind impressions of music • B7v and B8r: the last stave is not inked

Corrections and changes:

In-house: B1v: see above

Later: A2r.ii.rest after 40: b → m, by erasure • A2r.iii.text: after] ui[itauit [is added] xps vita • A5v.i.31: B c' → d', erasure and a new brown ink note-head • B5v.ii.13: m f' → e', erasure and grey ink • B5r.vi.33: c', sm → m, by erasure • B7v.iv.after 121: rests b,b → b,m, by erasure • B8r.iii.1: before the preceding present dsbd" a sbd" was erased

Binding: 16th-century Italian brown leather over pasteboard, with rolls and stamps, including a *yhs* in the centre of both boards. Three holes on each for tie-strings • One pastedown and flyleaf at the front, one pastedown at the back. These are all early papers, but show no marks.

Provenance: B8*v*:] Die 15 Marcij. 1520

Bibliography: Fenlon and Dalla Vecchia, *Venezia*, pp. 83–84 (exhibition catalogue, Venice, 2001)

Pl-Kj, Mus.ant.pract.P 675. Three part-books complete, lacking the Tenor

Size of page: 150 × 224 mm.

Watermarks:

A2	A3–4	B1–2	B5–6	E2–1	E3–4	F–1	F6	G6–5	G–8	H–4	H8–7
6	35	6	6	6	6	35	35	35	35	35	6

Textual comments: E1*r*: the folio number 33 has not printed • F2*r* and F8*r* lack the folio numbers

Technical comments: Only five staves are inked on B7*v* and B8*r*

Corrections and changes:

> **In-house:** H5*v*: see above
>
> **Later:** A5*v*.i.31: *l*, *c'* → d' in ginger ink • B5*r*.vi.33: *c'*, *sm* → *m*, by erasure • B8*r*.iii.1: *sbd''*, struck through in pencil • E8*r*.i.rests after 37: *b*, *?sb* → *b*, *m*, by erasure and brown ink • G4*r*.ii rest after 38: *b* → *m*, by erasure • G4*r*.v.9: *m*, *?c* → A, erasure and brown ink • G4*v*.ii.last note: *sb*A → *m*A, *m*A, with brown ink • H7*v*.ii.7: f, *b* → *sb* • H7v.iv.10: g, *sb* → *b*

Binding: Three card covers, probably of the 19th-century • One paste-down and one flyleaf at each end of each part

Provenance: From Berlin: Berlin library stamp on A1*r* • Accession no. 17,945 on the verso of the fly-leaf of each part-book

No.59C. *Third Edition*

A1*r*]   Motetti de la corona | Libro primo | [crown]

    The Tenor is not extant

E1*r*]   Motetti de la corona | Libro primo | A

G1*r*]   Motetti de la corona | Libro primo | B

H8*r*]   LEO. p*apa*. X. [etc. as for the first edition]

Format and collation: Partbooks: landscape quarto-in-eights. [S] 16 folios: A-B⁸; [T not extant, presumably 16 folios: C-D⁸]; [A] 16 folios: E-F⁸; [B] 16 folios: G-H⁸

Signatures:] ★ A 2 [$4 • − A1

Foliation: t.r.r.:] [S] [I], II–XVI; [T not extant]; [A] XXXIII–XLVIII; [B] XLIX–LXIII, [64]. Dots are added after certain numbers: 49, 53, 55, 57, 58, 61

Running heads: The head-line comprises the composer's name, centered, the folio number at the outer corner of rectos, and a part-name, placed half-way to the outer corner:

verso:	Sup*erius*.	[A1-B5, B7
	Sup*erius*	Di[cantus. [B6
	Altus	[E1-F8
	Ba[[us	[G1-H7
	[Nil:	B8, H8
recto:	Sup*erius*.	[A2-B
	Altus	[E2-F8

Baſſus   [G2-H7

[Nil: A1, E1, G1, H8

Fonts: Music: Petrucci's normal music type

Staves: Six per page. 175 mm long, 10-92-112.5 mm high.

Text: Roman throughout

Technical comments: A complete list of variants with both the previous editions may be found in Boorman, *Petrucci*, pp. 315–20 • It is notable that *Nos qui vivimus*, on ff.G4v-5v, is very crowded, while *Clare sanctorum*, on G6r-v, is spaciously laid out

In-house correction: B4r.iv.20: *dm*, ?d' → c', erased and stamped in: I-BGc and I-Vnm

Tavola: As for the second edition

Contents:

				[Title]	
	A1r	E1r	G1r	[Title]	
	A1v			Tabula	
1	A2r	E1v	G1v	GAude barbara beata	Io. Mouton.
	A2r.iv★	E1v.iv★	G1v.iv★	2/ Gaude quia meruiſti	
2	A2v.ii	E2r.iii	G2r.ii	MEmor eſto verbi tui	Ioſquin
	A3r	E2v.iv	G2v.ii	2/Portio mea domine	
3	A3v	E3r.v	G3r	[B:] BOnitatem feciſti	Carpentras
	A4r.i★	E3v.v★	G3v	2/Manus tue domine	
4	A4v.ii	E4v	G4r	LEtatus ſum in hiis que	Andreas de ſilua
	A4v.v★	E4v.iv★	G4r.iv★	2/ Fiat pax in virtute	
5	A5r	E5r	G4v	NOs qui uiuimus	Io. Mouton
	Tacet	E5v.ii	G5r	2/ [B:] Deus autem	
	A5v.i★	E6r.ii	G5v	3/ Dom[in]us memor fuit	
6	A6r.ii	E6v.iv	G6r.ii	[B:] CLare ſanctorum	P. De therache:
7	A6v.iii	E7r.iv	G6v.iii	LAudate deum in ſanctis	Io. Mouton:
	A6v.vi	E7v.i★	G6v.vi	2/ Quia cum clamarem	
8	A7r.iv	E7v.v	G7r.iv	NObilis progenie	Ant. de feuin.
9	A7v	E8r.iii	G7v.ii	ECce maria genuit nobis	Io. Mouton.
10	A7v.v	E8v	G7v.vi	BEnedictus dominus deus	Ant. de feuin.
	A8r.ii★	E8v.iv	G8r.iii★	2/ Omnes gentes plaudite	
11	A8r.v	F1r	G8v	BEata dei genitrix maria	Io. Mouton.
12	A8v.iv	F1v	G8v.v	BEnedicat nos imperialis	Longheual.
	B1r	F1v.v	H1r.ii	2/ Regat nos potentia	
13	B1r.iii	F2r	H1r.iv	SAncta trinitas vnus deus	Ant. de feuin:
14	B1v	F2r.v	H1v	O Deſolatorum conſolator	Diuitis
	B1v.iv	F2v.ii	H1v.iii★	2/ [B:] Beate claudi	
15	B2r	F3r	H2r	GAude francorum regia	Ant. de feuin:
16	B2r.v	F3r.v	H2r.iv	CHristum regem regum	Io. Mouton.
17	B2v.iii	F3v.iv	H2v.ii	Contremuerunt omnia	[Anon.]
18	B3r	F4r	H2v.v	Ascendens christus in altum	Hylaire
19	B3v	F4r.v	H3r.iv	Benedictus es celorum regina	Io. Mouton.
	B3v.iv★	F4v.iii	H3v	2/ Per illud aue	
20	B4r	F5r	H3v.v	Tempus meum eſt	An. de feuin.
	B4r.iii★	F5r.iii★	H4r.ii	2/ Viri galilei	
21	B4v	F5v	H4v	Vulneraſti cor meum	[Anon.]
	B4v.iii	F5v.iii★	H4v.iii★	2/ Veni in ortum meum	

22	B5r	F6r	H5r	Cele[te beneficium	Io. Mouton.
	B5r.v	F6r.v	H5r.iv★	2/ Adiutorium no[trum	[Févin]
23	B5v.ii	F6v.ii	H5v.ii	Egregie christi confe[[or	Ant. de feuin.
	B5v.iv★	F6v.v	H5v.iv★	2/ Ecce enim fe[tus e[t	
24	B6r.iii	F7r.iii	H6r.ii	Dilectus deo & hominibus	[Anon.]
25	B6v	F7v	H6v	Christum ducem redemit nos	Jo[quin.
26	B7r	F7v.v	H6v.v	Laudate dominum de celis	Brumel.
	B7v.iii	F8r.vi	H7r.v	2/ Laudate dominum in [anctis eius	
			H8r	[Privilege; Colophon]	
	B8v		H8v	[blank]	

Extant copies:

CH-Zz, Mus.Jac.G.67/₁. Bassus, complete

> **Size of page:** 165 × 232 mm.
>
> **Watermarks:** The only visible marks are of type 35 on G-6 and H-8
>
> **Technical comments:** G2r.iv.text: spacing sort, 0.8 mm wide • H3v.caption: partly masked by a badly-cut frisket • H5r.ii.text: spacing sort 1.3 mm wide
>
> **Later corrections and changes:** G5r.v.3-9: manuscript leger lines • H4r.left margin: doodles in brown ink • H4r.ii.5: leger line in brown ink • H6r.iv-vi.signature: flat erased • H6v.iii. second rest after mensuration sign: *l* → *b*, by erasure
>
> **Binding:** With *Motetti de la Corona II-IV*, the masses of Mouton and Févin, and the third volume of Josquin's masses. Original dark calf, with four ties, now gone. A central design of three stamped mazes, within rolls of triple rules and of acanthus leaves, all in blind • One paste-down at the front, from a fifteenth-century printed volume, in large folio, with 2 columns of text, mentioning Justinian and manumission • the last folio of Josquin's third volume is pasted-down to the back board
>
> **Provenance:** From the collection of Erwin Jacobi • On the fore-edge are the initials] B A S
>
> **Bibliography:** Puskás, "Jacobi", 36

D-LEm, PM.1303. Bassus, lackng the last folio, with the colophon

> **Size of page:** 225 × 152 mm.
>
> **Watermarks:** Mark 35 on folios G5-6 and H-7. The paper is consistent throughout
>
> **Textual comments:** G4r. the head-line reads] Andreas de [ilue • G7v.vi. two text words] bellum bellun [with the"m" in the first word inverted • G7v.vi.right end: there is a curious sort, unlike any other in Petrucci's fount, and looking like a reversed numeral "2"
>
> **Technical comments:** G2r.iv.text: the spacing sort also found in the copy at CH-Zz • G2v.i, above notes 5–6, a music spacing sort, 1.2 mm wide, and with a minimum height of 3.5 mm • G6r.ii, above notes 34–35, a similar sort, 1.0 mm. wide • H1v.i, text spacing sort, 1.2 mm wide • H3v.caption: the same masking effect found in CH-Zz • H5r.iii.text: the spacing sort also found in the copy at CH-Zz • Two damaged sorts show a curious pattern of recurrence: a damaged *m* can be seen at G2v.v.31; G6r.iii.5; H2r.ii.1; H3r.vi.30: a different *m* at G6r.i.3; G7r.i.41; H6r.iv.13; H7r.vi.7: each always appears at the same height on the stave, in the top and second spaces respectively
>
> **Later corrections and changes:** Foliation, t.r.r.] 49- • G1v.ii.rest after 21: *sb* → *b*, in brown ink. The original rest was probably actually a *b*, merely printed too high • G1v.iv.1: *mf*, poorly printed, drawn in brown ink • G1v.v.rests after 15: *sb, l, l, sb* → *l, l, l, sb*, in brown ink • G2r.iv.13: *smb*, poorly printed, filled in with brown ink • G3v.iii.1: *sbA*, poorly printed, touched up in brown ink • G4r.ii.50: *mb*, poorly printed, touched up in brown ink • G4r.iv

and vi: stave lines poorly printed, touched up in brown ink • G5r.v.3 and 9: short leger lines in a ginger-brown ink • G7r.vi.12: A, *sb m*, using the ink found on G5r • H3v.v.after 2: erasure, perhaps of *sbc* • H4r.ii.5: leger line, brown ink • H5v.vi.after the *l* rest after 39: an erasure, perhaps of *sb*A, then a *m* rest, then the rest struck through lightly, all in the same ink • H6r.iv–vi.signature: a flat erased • H6v.iii.second rest after mensuration sign: *l* → *b*, by erasure

Binding: A modern binding, of pale brown leather, with titles in gold • One paste-down and one conjugate flyleaf at each end • The binding contains copies of the Bassus part for all four books of *Motetti de la Corona*

I-BGc, Cinq.4.987 (1). Superius
    Size of page: 169 × 235 mm.
    Watermarks: No.35 on ff. A8-7, B-1 and B4-3
    Technical comments: A3v.iii.before 19: music spacing sort, 18.5 × 1.3 mm, projecting 4.6 mm above and 3.8 mm below the stave
    In-house correction: B4r: see above
    Binding and Provenance: With Josquin *I Missarum* (1516, No.62)

I-PEc, I.M.1079 (2). Superius, lacking folio A1
    Size of page: 230 × 160 mm.
    Binding and Provenance: with Josquin *I Missarum* of 1516 (No.62)

I-Vnm, Musica 203–205. Superius, Altus, and Bassus, complete
    Watermarks: The only ones visible are of No.35 on A1-2, B2-1, B5-, E5-, E8-7, F1-2, F3-4, G-4 and H-2
    Corrections and changes:
        In-house: B4r: see above
        Later: Manuscript numbering of pieces in all parts:] 1–26 [continued in the other volumes of the set • E3v.vi.15: *b*, perhaps originally g, now c' • F7r.i.rests after 5: *sb,b* → *sb,b,m*, in ink
    Binding: Austrian National Library binding • With the other volumes of the *Motetti de la Corona*

Lost copies: It is not clear which edition is represented by any of the following entries: The Fugger owned a copy (Schaal "Musikbibliothek", No.I/50) • A copy was in the collection of Otthein-rich's chapel at Pfalz-Neuburg, and is listed in the inventory of 1554, on folios 38r-38v (Lam-brecht, *Heidelberger*, i, pp. 111–12) • A possible copy is listed in the Strozzi family inventory of 1573:] Un libro di mottetti in istampa della corona pecora bianco (d'Accone, "Transitional", p. 35, n.26). It is quite possible, given our knowledge of Strozzi interests, that this was the *Couronne et fleur des chansons* of 1536 • A copy was in the collection of João with copies of the other volumes of the series:] *Motteti de la corona.* | 107. Io. Mouton, & outros, a 4. lib.I. (Sampaio Ribeiro, *Livraria*, p. 148) • A copy was owned by S. Luigi dei Francesi:] Motetti della corona (Perkins, "Notes", p. 64). Since other entries in the 1682 inventory list the number of the volume, e.g.:] Philippo de Monte il 5° libro [this book may be of the first edition above) • A copy, entitled "Motetti de la Corona Musick itall", was sold in London in 4.xii.1682 (Coral, "Music", p. 277) • The copy owned by Siena Cathedral may more probably have been of the Pasoti and Dorico edition of 1526 (D'Accone, *Civic*, p. 298) • It is possible that this was the book of motets bought by Loreto on 23.ix.1515, along with a book of motets. • In addition, Colón owned a copy, but of the edition of 1526 (See Chapman, "Printed", Nos.77–80).

Early references: Gesner (*Pandectae*, VII, section headed "De cantionibus ecclesiasticis") cites the following books:] Iosquin & aliorum diversis locis et temporibus impressi Motettorum libri 4. [Bernstein, "Gesner", No.225, suggests that this reference might include the volumes of *Motetti de la Corona*

Other editions: Another edition was printed by Pasoti and Dorico in 1526 (*RISM* 1526¹)

Bibliography:

(a) Rosaria Boccadifuoco, *Bibliografia*, No.2338 • Sartori, *Petrucci*, No.49

(b) Brunet, *Manuel*, iii, cols.1925–1926

(d) Gehrenbeck, *Last* • partial edition in Sherr, *16th-Century*, iv

(e) Boorman, "Motetti" • Boorman, "Editions" • Boorman, *Petrucci* • Gehrenbeck, *Last* • Haberl, "Drucke" • Noble, "Petrucci"

Commentary:

1. The title of this edition is significant. Apart from the letter series of early titles (and presumably the last book, the *Motetti del Fiore*), this is the only case when Petrucci uses anything other than a strict description of the contents. I believe that the stimulus has to have come from outside his immediate circle, especially given the political situation at the time: I discuss this in chapter 9, and suggest a possible explanation.

2. This is one case where Sartori recognised the presence of different editions of the same title, with the same date. He states (*Petrucci*, p. 165): "Con questo volume ci troviamo di fronte a un caso per ora assolutamente unico nella produzione petrucciana. Di questo primo volume di *Motetti de la corona* troviamo infatti per lo meno due esemplari differenti, come si vedo anche dal frontespizio . . .". (In fact, he had already noted two versions of *Frottole libro primo*, which had been cited in previous literature: he seems not to regard them as truly different editions.) As will be seen from the descriptions of the various editions, above, Sartori is correct when he assumes that the copy which does not say *Libro Primo* is indeed from the first edition. He uses the Venetian copy as his paradigm for the other edition: he also notes that the second Bologna copy belongs to neither of these editions.

3. The number of potentially in-house corrections for the first edition should not be surprising. Unless Petrucci printed a number of unknown works (perhaps official documents), it must be likely that the craftsmen who had worked for Petrucci in 1511 and 1512 had left for employment elsewhere. If so, this would be only the second music book printed by a group of craftsmen who had presumably set the books by Paulus and Castiglione. The very different nature of the music type (not to mention the notation itself) would plausibly lead to a number of errors, as it had with the previous edition, of the third book of Josquin's masses.

4. There is some evidence in the first edition for the presence of two craftsmen setting type: most clearly this lies in the manner of paginating title-pages.

5. The cancel must have been set before the adoption of Roman type for all editions, which occurred sometime after May 1516. In fact, it seems to have been prepared after the 1515 edition of Févin's masses, perhaps at the end of the year, perhaps before the May 1516 edition of Josquin's first book.

6. The second edition retains the privilege and colophon of the first, apparently in the same typesetting. It seems that Petrucci kept the bulk of that page set up, ready for each edition from Fossombrone, only needing to change the date at the foot of the page.

   In the second edition, there is some evidence that Petrucci did not cast off type very precisely. The pattern of starting pieces on a new page is not consistent. Thus, for the Cantus, there is a change of pattern at B2*v*. Before that 6 pieces start a new page, 11 do not. Thereafter 7 start pages and 2 do not. However, of those seven, four could have started on the previous page, if following earlier practice. There seem also to be fewer symbols per line on these later pages. This suggests that the more concise setting of the earlier pages would not have led to the saving of a half-sheet of paper, and so was abandoned before the inner sheet of gathering B.

7. The second edition also shows stronger evidence for two typesetters. As the following table makes clear, there are distinct patterns of two signature styles and two fonts for setting the word *Verte*. The way in which these two patterns coincide implies two levels of work, divided between two men, working either consecutively or at the same time. Tending towards the latter interpretation is the presence of two anomalies — that of the two treatments of signature on the inner sheet of D and that of the *Verte* fount for the inner sheet of F. Both these are in the second gathering for a part-book, implying that the work was divided between two men, and that the man working with smaller signatures was slower: the other man would then have helped out on certain pages. The pattern of watermarks does not coincide with the typographical evidence, and this argues that the two settings were simultaneous. Two batches of paper were available, perhaps originally divided between two presses, and later distributed according to the pressmen's need. (Signature styles are "l" for large, and "s" for small: the word "Verte" is in either a roman or a rotonda face.)

sheet	AI	AII	BI	BII	CI	CII	DI	DII	EI	EII	FI	FII	GI	GII	HI	HII
signature	l	s	l	l	l	s	s	s	s	s	s	s/l	l	l	l	l
"Verte"	rom	rot	rom	rom	rom	rot	rot	rot rom	rot	rot	rot	rot	rom	rom	rom	rom
Watermarks:																
D-Mbs	35	6	6	35					6	6	6	6				
I-Bc,74	6	35	35	35	6	35	35	35								
I-Fn													35	35	35	35
I-Vlevi	35	6	6	6												
PL-Kj	6	35	35	35					6	6	35	35	35	35	6	35

8. The second edition probably has to be dated during the summer of 1516. In common with a number of other "hidden" editions, it lies after the first Fossombrone edition of Josquin's first book (29.v.1516), and before the books published in 1519. I incline to place these editions earlier rather than later, for two weak reasons: firstly that Fossombrone was sacked during May of 1517, and secondly that I expect that Petrucci would have produced shorter print-runs during 1515 and 1516, given the general insecurity of the times. This would lead to more frequent new editions. This second edition seems to be the first of the new books, given the state of the type and initials, as well as the use of a remaining stock of paper 6.

9. The third edition raises the possibility that Petrucci had been experimenting with a different style of music sorts. Each of the damaged sorts noted above in the description of the Leipzig copy appears each time at the same place on the stave, the first in the top space and the second in the second space. Unless a remarkable pattern of coincidence were at work, this would suggest that Petrucci had begun to mount his notes on bodies that were the full height of the stave. This would mean that he would have had notes for each value and each pitch, thus considerably enlarging the size of the fount: there seems to be no other simple explanation of the phenomenon.

10. These sorts are important for dating the third edition: they do not appear in the Leipzig copy of the second book of *Motetti de la Corona*, and only the second sort can be found in the third of the series. This provides some further evidence for the dating of this edition of the present book. In addition, the new late initials are now in use, and this puts the third edition no earlier than the last book of the *Motetti de la Corona*. I think, in fact, that this is the first of a small series of

late reprinted editions that followed the avowed edition of Pisano, in 1520, and before the appearance of some of Petrucci's type in Rome in September 1521. It probably appeared during July 1520.

No. 56. *Frottole XI*

24.x.1514   *RISM* 1514²

A1*r*]   Frottole Libro | undecimo
I8*r*]   LEO. p*a*pa. X. [etc., as in No.54: followed by:]
          [Left:] Registrum. ABCDEFGHI | omnes quaterni.
          [Centre:] Impre[[um Foro[empronii per Octauianum | Petrutium ciuem Foro[empronien[em. Anno | Domini .MDXIIII. Die xx. Octobris. Domi- | nante inclito ac excellenti[[imo Principe D*o*mino | Franci[comaria Feltrio de Ruere: Urbini Soræq*u*e Duce: Pi[auri &. D*o*mino: Alme Urbis Præfecto: ac exercitus. Sa. Ro. E. Imperatore [emper i*n*uicto
A1*v*]   Tabula [in two columns. Within each alphabetical letter, in order of appearance, with lower-case Roman numerals]

Format and collation: Choirbook: landscape quarto-in-eights. 72 folios: A-I⁸

Signatures:] XI A ii [$4 • − A1 • E1 signed D iii (and later corrected) • The signature exists in two forms, with and without a point after the roman XI: without on sheets Ao, Bo,i, Co,i, Do, and Eo; with on sheets Ai, Di, Ei, and F-I

Foliation: t.r.r.] [1], 2–17, 81 [*recte* 18, both sorts inverted], 19–23, 23 [*recte* 24], 52 [*recte* 25], 26–31, 23 [*recte* 32], 33, 34–71, [72]

No running heads

Part-names:

verso:]	Tenor	[A3, A5-6, A8-B4, B6-7, C1-D2, D4-E1, E3-F2, F4, F6-G1, G3, G5-H6, H8, J1, J3-6
	Tenor Altus Ba[us	[A7, B5, B8, D3, F3, F5, G2
	[in stave:] Tenor	[A4, G4, H7, J2
	Ba[[us [in staves:] Tenor Altus	[A3
	Altus Ba[[us [in stave:] Tenor	[E2
	Altus [in staves:] Tenor Ba[[us	[J7
	[Nil:	J8
recto:]	Altus Ba[[us	[A4-7, B1-5, B7-8, C2-D3, D5-E2, E4-F3, F5, F7-G2, G4-J7
	Tenor Altus Ba[[us	[A2, E3, F4, F6
	Altus Ba[[us [in stave:] Tenor	[A3, A8, C1
	Tenor Ba[us [in stave:] Altus	[B6
	[all in stave:] Tenor Altus Ba[[us	[D4, G3
	[Nil:	A1, J8

Fonts: Music: Petrucci's normal music type

Staves: six per page, 175 mm long, 10.2-92-110 mm high.

Text: Roman • Rotonda for] Verte: [and a smaller one for titles and part-names

Technical comments: I3*v*.v.stave: this short stave is not one of Petrucci's staves at all: it comprises five separate rules, of the sort used for leger lines. They are not evenly spaced, and the middle one is very warped

In-house corrections: All these in the unique copy • A5*v*.v.18: *m* → *sb*, by erasing the tail • B6*v*.v.37: flat added, in brown ink • B7*v*.ii.*custos*: c' d', partly erased and redrawn in black ink • B8*r*.iv.*custos*: f → g', partly erased, and corrected in printer's ink • C5*r*.i.54: *sm* → *m*, by erasing the center of the note-head • D2*v*.iv.after 35: rest, *sb* → *m*, by an erasure and a new rest drawn in brown ink • D4*v*.ii.before 9: m.s. ¢ stamped in after presswork • E1*r*: the signature corrected, by erasing the minims and stamping in an E • G2*r*.v.clef: C3 F4: the two lowest horizontals were erased, and two new ones added above in brown ink: the left component of the new clef was made by stamping in a *l* • H3*r*.iv.22: *sb*, c → d, with an erasure and a stamped in note • H7*v*.vi.58: *sb*, e → f, by erasure and stamping in • J6*v*.iv.l: *b*, f → g, by erasing the lower horizontal and adding a new upper one, in brown ink

Contents:

32	E1v	LA belta chogi e diuina	Pietro da lod.[*sic*]
33	E2v	DHe credete do*n*na a me	P.L.
34	E3r	FVi felice un te*m*po hayme	P.L.
35	E3v	E Dun bel matin damore	Ant. C.
36	E4v	DI[colorato hai morte el piu bel uolto	Antonius patauus
37	E5v	DAtemi pace o duri mei pen[ieri	A.P.
38	E6v	VAlle che de lame*n*ti mei [ei piena	A.P.
39	E7v	SOn piu matti i*n* que[to mo*n*do	.AP.
40	E8v	[B:] Don do*n* [S:] AL foco al foco [S Headed:] Don Don	A.P.
41	F1v	NOn al [uo ama*n*te piu diana piacque	A.P.
42	F2v	AMor qua*n*do fioriua	Ioannes Lulinus Venetus
43	F4r	NOn piu [aette amor no*n* piu hormai	A.P.
44	F4v	CHiare fre[che e dolce acq*ue*	Io. Lu. V.
45	F6r	POi che [on di [peranza al tutto priuo [Headed:] Aer da capitoli	Io. lu. V.
46	F6v	DI tempo in tempo mi [i fa me*n* dura	Io. lu. V
47	F8v	MEntre che gliocchi giro	Io. lu. Ve.
48	G1v	NEl te*m*po che riue[te il verde manto	Io. Lu. V.
49	G3r	NOn mi pe*n*to e[[er ligato	Io. Lu. V.
50	G3v	Hay bella liberta come tu mhai	Io. Lu. V.
51	G4v	OCchi piangeti a co*m*pagnate il core	Io. Lu. V
52	G5v	REndete amante le [agite amore	Io. Lu. V
53	G6v	Cchi [*sic*] non [a che [ial dolore	Io. Lu. V
54	G7v	SEl non fu[[e la [peranza	Io. Lu. V.
55	G8v	SVrge dalorizonte il biondo appolo	Io. Lu. V.
56	H1v	VAle iniqua hor uale uale	Io. Lu. V
57	H2v	Fvga ognu*n* amor proteruo	Io. Lu. V.
58	H3v	Non potra mai dir amore	Io. Lu. V
59	H4v	OCchi mei la[[i acompagnate il core	Io. Lu. V.
60	H5v	SEnto li [pirti mei che per la dogha	Du*n* Thimoteo.
61	H6v	DOnna no*n* mi tenete pregion	B.T.
62	H7v	QVe[ta lacri*m*e mie que[ti [u[piri	B.T.
63	H8v	LAura romanis decorata po*m*pis	Hie. A lauro.
64	J1v	Ca[o crudel ch*e* ogni mortal [tupi[[e [Superius:] EA[o . . .	Hie. Alauro
65	J2v	COme hauro du*n*q*ue* il frutto del [par[e [eme	Hie. a lauro
66	J3v	GIogia mea bo*n*da al cor ta*n*ta e [i pura [Tavola:] gioglia mabonda . . .	B.T.
67	J4v	DAme alme*n* lultimo uale	B.T.
68	J5v	AQue [tilante e riue [Tav:] Acque . . .	Hie. Alauro
69	J6v	CHe fai alma ch*e* fai	[Anon.]
70	J7v	AQua no*n* e lhumor che ver[an gliochi	B.T.
	J8r	[Privilege; Register; Colophon]	
	J8v	[blank]	

Extant copy:

E-Sc, 12-1-28. Complete

    Size of page: 227 × 165 mm.

    Watermarks: No.2 on A5-6, A8-7, B6-5, B8-7, C6-5, C8-7, D6-5, D7-8, E4-3, E7-8, F2-1, F5-6, G1-2, G4-3, H6-5, H7-8, J1-2, and J3-4

    Technical comments: D5r.i: a badly damaged stave at the right end: a type sort apparently was pulled and rested on it during presswork • F1r.i.after 12: a music spacing sort, reaching 5.0 mm above the stave • G3r.i.after the bar-line following 39: a music spacing sort, reaching 5.8 mm above the stave and 3.3 mm below

    Corrections and changes:

        In-house: See above

        Later: A1v: four modern crosses against pieces listed in the Tabula

    Binding: Parchment wrapper, with fragments of two tie-strings per face • One fly-leaf and one paste-down at each end, with a watermark of a mounted stallion: stubs for each pair inside the nearest gathering

    Provenance: Owned by Colón (Chapman, "Printed", No.41) • A1r. call numbers:] 3074 [and] 4716 [and] C KK Tab 175 No. 43 [and] E . . . GG | Tab . . . 175 | N . . . 32 • Inside front cover, the call mark:] R.9696 • J8v:] Este libro co[to en peru[o .100. quatrines a .3. de setienbre de .1530. y el ducado de oro | vale .420. quatrines

    Bibliography: Arboli y Farando, "Biblioteca", iii, 136–137 • Chapman, "Printed" • Trend, "Musikschätze"

Bibliography:

    (a) Rosaria Boccadifuoco, *Bibliografia*, No.1462 • Sartori, *Petrucci*, No.50 • Jeppesen, *La Frottola*, Pe.XI • Vogel, *Bibliografia*, 1514[1]

    (d) Bettanin, *Libro* • Luisi & Zanovello, *Frottole* • Maccarone, *Libro*

    (e) Einstein, "Elfte"

Commentary:

1.   Like a number of frottola volumes, this one shows something of the grouping of pieces in Petrucci's exemplars. Thus the collection of pieces largely by Tromboncino occupies only the first gathering (A2r-8r). It is followed by just two gatherings of music mostly by the two composers called Eustachius — de Monte Regali Gallus aand de M. Romanus (folios A8v-C8r). There is a small mixed section thereafter, apparently collecting together a remnant of pieces from the same collections as the previous pieces. Starting on E4v, there is a group of pieces by Antonius Patavus, followed by a long section of those by Joannes Lulinus. The link between these two sections is not as complex as it looks, for the last work by Antonius takes only a single page (a *recto*): it therefore has to be preceded by another taking either one or three pages. Since such a work from Antonius does not seem to have been available, one by Lulinus is inserted there. The last layer is again a mixed bag of works, and the return to Tromboncino at the end probably signals no more than the preference of the compiler.

2.   Petrucci apparently had some problems with fitting pieces onto single pages. This is evident from the number of times when one or more of the part-names has to be entered in the stave, rather than in the left margin, which would require the part to start on a new stave. Further, on several

occasions, the entries within the stave employ the small text rotonda font, thus saving yet more space. This confirms an argument about the music being supplied in batches.

3.   Colón's copy of this book may well have come from Petrucci, rather than from his partners in Venice. More interesting is the fact that it was much cheaper than the other Petrucci editions he bought. By 1530, it was probably enough out of date that it was being remaindered, if not actually a second-hand copy.

No. 57. Ghiselin: *Misse*

[late 1514]   see *RISM* G1780

This is a second edition, printed in Fossombrone: the first was dated 15.vii.1503, and is described here as No.9.

Second Edition

A1r]   Joannes ghiſelin. | La bella ſe ſiet | De les armes. | Gratieuſa. | Narayge. | Je nay dueul. | S
C1r]   T
D1r]   A
[The Bassus book is not extant, and no colophon survives]

Format and collation: Landscape format: quarto-in-eights. [S] 18 folios: A⁸B¹⁰; [T] 10 folios: C¹⁰; [A] 20 folios: D-E⁸F⁴. [B not extant]

Signatures:] Aa2 [$4. • − A1. A2 signed correctly

No foliation or running heads

Founts: Music: Petrucci's normal music type

    Staves: Six per page, 178 mm long; 10-92-113 mm high

    Text: Rotonda throughout

In-house corrections: See below

Technical comments: The absence of both foliation and head-lines argues that this edition was prepared, if not in a hurry, certainly without the normal attention to detail. It was clearly made from a copy of the first edition, as the pattern of punctuation on A1r demonstrates: but corners were apparently cut here and there. The large number of errors on specific pages also argues for a less committed concentration on the part of typesetter and/or reader. This would tend to fit into the historical pattern of the production of this book, outlined below • Only five staves are inked on C8r and E8v

In-house corrections: All these are to be found in the unique copy: A7v.v.1: e" → d", stamped in • C3r.iii.left margin:] Resolutio [in brown ink • C6r.i.after 11: from a 4-space line, a bar line, a *br* and a double bar, to a double 4-space line with repeat dots on either side and a double bar, done by erasure and with brown ink • D2v.vi.after 6: rest *m sb*, by erasure and brown ink • E3v.vi.last note: a → g, in brown ink • E7r.iii.41: g → a, in brown ink

Contents:

	Aa1r	Cc1r	Dd1r	[Title]
1	Aa1v	Cc1v.i	Dd1v	[Missa La bella se siet]
	Aa2r.ii	Cc1v.vi	Dd2r	[Gloria]

	Aa2v.iii	Cc2v	Dd2v.iv	[Credo]
	Aa3r.vi	Cc3r.ii	Dd3r.vi	[Sanctus]
	Aa4r.iv	Cc3v.ii	Dd4r.vi	[Agnus]
2	Aa5r.ii	Cc4r.iii	Dd5r.v	[Missa de les armes]
	Aa5v	Cc4r.iv	Dd5v.v	[Gloria]
	Aa6r.vi	Cc4r.vi	Dd6v.iv	[Credo]
	Aa7v	Cc4v.iii	Dd7v.vi	[Sanctus]
	Aa8r.v	Cc4v.iv	Dd8v.v	[Agnus]
3	Bb1r	Cc5r.v	Ee1v.v	[Missa Gratieusa]
	Bb1v	Cc5v	Ee2r.v	[Gloria]
	Bb2r.v	Cc6r	Ee3r.iv	[Credo]
	Bb3r.vi	Cc6v.ii	Ee4v	[Sanctus]
	Bb4r.vi	Cc6v.v	Ee5v	[Agnus]
4	Bb4v.v	Cc7r	Ee6r	[Missa Narayge]
	Bb5r.iii	Cc7r.iv	Ee6r.v	[Gloria]
	Bb5v.iii	Cc7v.iii	Ee6v.iv	[Credo]
	Bb6v.ii	Cc8r.iii	Ee7v.iv	[Sanctus]
	Bb7r.iii	Cc8v	Ee8r.v	[Agnus]
5	Bb7v	Cc8v.iii	Ee8v.iii	[Missa Je nay dueul]
	Bb7v.v	Cc9r	Ff1r	[Gloria]
	Bb8v	Cc9v	Ff1v.v	[Credo]
	Bb9r.iv	Cc9v.vi	Ff2v.v	[Sanctus]
	Bb10r	Cc10riii	Ff3r.iii	[Agnus]
			Ff4r	[blank staves]
	Bb10v	Cc10v	Ff4v	[blank]

Extant copy:

A-Wn, S.A.77.C.15. Three part-books • The Bassus is present in a 19th-century copy of the first edition

Page size: 163 × 225 mm.

Watermarks:

A4-3	A7-8	B1-2	B7-8	C5-	C7-8	C9-10	D1-2	D4-3	E6-5	E8-7	F2-1
31	27	27	31	27	27	27	31	31	27	27	27

Textual comments: The assumption that corrections listed above in brown ink were made in the shop is based on a comparison of colours, and on the manner of writing the word "Resolutio"

Corrections and changes:

> **In-house:** see above

> **Later:** Each of the following changes follows readings present as printed in the first edition: B9r.iv.54: e' → d', in black ink • B9r.v.9–10: c'', b' → a',g', in ink • C7r.ii.before 47: erased ligature c',?a • C7r.iii.14–15 ligature: tail erased • C7r.v.5–6: b,f → f,b, in black ink • C7r.vi.2–3: f,a → b, d', in black ink • D2v.vi.22: me → sbf, by erasure and black ink • D2v.vi.25–26: m,m, → sb,sb, with erasures • D2v.vi. 43: d → e, in black ink • D2v.vi.after 44: rest m → sb, in black ink • F1r.ii.11: d' → c', in pencil • The movements are numbered in manuscript in all three books:] 140–164 (see chapter 10)

Binding: Of the Austrian National Library

Provenance: With the library's copy of the first book of Josquin's masses (1502, No.4)

———

Lost copies: It is not clear which edition was represented by copies in the possession of the Fuggers (Schaal, "Musikbibliothek", No.I/49), the chapel of Ottheinrich at Pfalz-Neuburg (Lambrecht, *Heidelberger*, i, p. 110), and of King João IV of Portugal (Sampaio Ribeiro, *Livraria*, p. 50) • A copy of one edition may have been at Rome, S. Luigi dei Francesi. The inventory records a volume of] Messe sligate di Jo. Ghiselin [and later a] Misse Jois Ghiselin [See Perkins, "Notes", 64

Other editions: The first edition appeared in 1503: see No.9, above

Bibliography:

(a) Rosaria Boccadifuoco, *Bibliografia*, No.1610 • Sartori, *Petrucci*, No.9

(d) Ghiselin, *Opera Omnia*

(e) Noble, "Petrucci," the first place to notice the presence of two editions, and to suggest an approximate date for the second • Sartori, "Nuove", pp. 177–78

Commentary:

1. This second edition lacks a Bassus part, but it was certainly printed in Fossombrone: the two papers are only found in isolated spots within Venetian editions, and not more frequently in those from the later city. All the "Venetian" occurrences can be shown to be on later editions or cancel sheets, printed in Fossombrone. The appearances of paper 27 on eight sheets of Bossinensis's second book (dated 1511) all relate to a later printing: the paper is also found in cancel sheets to the third book of Josquin's masses, printed in 1514. While it is possible that the paper had been used in the lost tenth book of frottole (of 1512), I can see no reason why it would not then appear in the main printing of Josquin's third book, or of the first of the *Motetti de la Corona*. I prefer to see all the uses as belonging together, in the months on either side of New Year 1515.

No. 58. Bossinensis: *Tenori e contrabassi intabulati, I*

[perhaps ii.1515]   Not in *RISM*

Second Edition.

For the first, see No.49

A1r]   Tenori e contraba∫∫i intabu | lati col ∫opran in canto fi | gurato per cantare e ∫o | nar col lauto Li | bro Primo. | Franci∫ci Bo∫∫inen∫is | Opus.

G8r]   Impre∫∫um Venetijs: Per Octauianuʒ | Petrutium Foro∫empronien∫em: Cum pri | uilegio inuicti∫∫imi dominij Venetiarum: | q*uae* nullus po∫∫it intabulaturam Lauti impri | mere: ∫ub penis in ip∫o priuilegio conte*n*ti5. | Die 27. Martij. 1509. | Regi∫trum. ABCDEFG O*mn*es quaterni | [Printer's device] [in a second column alongside the device:] Errori fatti ∫tampando | [see below]

A1v]   Tavola [laid out in two columns. Each item is preceded by a letter, which does not indicate the mode or pitch centre, but relates to the table in the third column. This table is introduced as follows:] Recercar li quali ∫erueno ale frottole ∫econdo | lordine de le littere ∫otto∫cripte.

A   1. 5. 8. 10. 12. 13. 19.

B   2. 4. 9. 14. 15. 24.

C   3. 17. 22.

D   6. 7. 11. 16. 21. 25.

E   18. 20.

F   23.

G   26.

A2r]   Regula per quelli che non sanno cantore. [etc., giving the Italian version found in Spinacino's first book, No.33, above]

A2v]   Dedication to G. Barbadico, Apostolic Protonotary, as in No.49, with the following variants: 3: attribuire → atribuire • 4: induſtria → in duſtria • 5: in vero → in uero • 5: ſententia → ſententia • 6: nato: il che → nato il che • 6: conſiderando → conſiderando • 6: la mente . . . la nfinita → la mente . . . la infinita • 7: laſciato: → laſciato. • 8: ho viſto → ho uiſto • 9: vtile → utile • 10: accenderanno. → accenderanno. • 11: quanto potea → quanto potea • 11: del ingegno → de lo ingegno • 12: compoſitione: → compoſitione: • 12: vtile → utile • 12: Et cuſi → Et coſſi • 13: inuento → in uento • 13: diligentia → diligentia • 14: vti-|lita → uti-|lita • 14: iocundita → iocundita • 14–5: la volupta → la uolupta • 15: pen||ſato: → pen-|ſato: • 15: vigilie in → uigilie in • 16: con piu → con piu • 16: mi e occorſo → mie occorſo • 17: non ſi → non ſi • 18: aliegro → alegro • 18: fatiche dil → fatiche del • 18: vmbra & protectione ſua voglio → umbra & protectione ſua uoglio • 19: cognoſcendo → cognoſcendo • 19: niuna → aniuna • 20: occulta → oculta • 20: Interponendo → Interponendo • 20: vrgenti facende → urgenti faccende • 21: prender → prender • 22: riſguardando → reſguardando • 22: varii de li compoſitori: → uarii de li compoſitori: • 23: gli ho → glio • 23: adotica → adanca

Format and Collation: Landscape quarto-in-eights. 56 folios. A–G[8]

Signatures:] A 2 [$4 • A1 unsigned

Foliation: t.r.r.:] [1–9], [X], XI–XVIII, XXI [recte XIX], XX, XIX [recte XXI], XXII–XXXII, [XXXIII in ms], XXXIIII–XXXVIII, [XXXIX], XL–XLIX, 50–54, [55–56]

No running head-line

Fonts: Music: Petrucci's music font; also a series of rhythm signs. Numerals used for tablature come from a text font

Staves: Five-line for vocal part: 178 mm long, 10 mm high • Six-line for tablature: 178 mm long, 17 mm high • Two pairs of staves per page, total height, 93.5 mm.

Text: Rotonda, 'x' = 7.4 mm, for title page • Rotonda, 'x' = 2.1 mm, for A2r, G8r, signatures and for some material on A1v • Roman, 'x' = 1.7 mm, '20' = 57 mm, for texts and Tavola.

Textual comments: The redundant ascription to] D. M. [at the head of F3v is retained from the first edition • Different readings: E6v.iii.8.1: d" in this edition: in the first, c" tied to the previous note • E7r.i.1–2: these notes were tied in the first edition

Technical comments: This edition provides an excellent demonstration that the curved slurs and ties are printed and not drawn freehand: both the surviving copies show identical slurs, even with the most eccentric shapes, and they are quite distinct from those of the first edition • B3v.below iii: a text spacing sort

In-house corrections: C2v.iv.9.5–6: //2///, //2///: both numerals partly erased, but not replaced, in both copies • C7r.i.2.3–5: slur erased, in both copies • C8v.i.4.1: the added sharp was probably stamped in after presswork • F3v.iv.2.2: 0//1//: the "0" deleted, in both copies • F6r.ii.4.1: 0///2/ → /0//2/, in manuscript, but printer's ink: present in both copies • F7r.iv.6,4: 3///1/ → /3//1/, in manuscript, but printer's ink: present in both copies

A list of errors appears on G8r.]

Errori fatti stampando

Tu dormi io ueglio ala tempesta e uento uol esser scripto
    La uoce del sopran al terzo tasto de la sottana
Chi ui dara piu luce occhi miei lassi de francesco
    varoter sanno desmenticato scriuer la uoce del sopran
    qual scriuereti cosi La uoce del sopran il canto uodo
Sio gel dico che dira uuol esser scripto cosi La voce del
    sopran al terzo tasto dil canto
Io non compro piu speranza uuol esser scripto cosi La
    uoce del sopran il canto uodo

Contents:

	A1r	[Title]	
	A1v	[Tavola]	
	A2r	Regula per quelli che non ſanno cantare.	
	A2v	[Dedication]	
1	A3r	AFflitti ſpirti miei ſiati contenti	B.T.
2	A3v	SEl morir mai de gloria	B.T.
3	A4r	ACcio chel tempo e i cieli empi	B.T.
4	A4v.iii	O Dolce e lieto albergo	[Anon.]
5	A5r	SI e debile il filo	B T.
6	A6r.iii	COn pianto e con dolore	[Anon.]
7	A6v	SIl diſi mai	B.T.
8	A7v	CHe debo far che me conſigli	B.T.
9	A8v.iii	HAime per che mhai priuo	[Anon.]
10	B1r	VOi Voi che paſſate qui	F.V.
11	B1v	NOn peccando altri chel core	B.T.
12	B2v	CAde ogni mio penſier	B T
13	B3r	A La fama ſi ua	[Anon.]
14	B3v	CHi in pregion crede tornarmi	B.T.
15	B4v	SPargean per laria	.B.T
16	B5r.iii	ZEphyro ſpira e il bel tempo	B.T.
17	B6r	HO ſcoperto il tanto aperto	B.T.
18	B6v.iii	DEh non piu deh non piu mo	M.C.
19	B7v.iii	O Deſpietato tempo	P. Zanin
20	B8v	IO cerco pur la inſupportabil doglia	B.T.
21	C1r.iii	CHi lharebbe mai creduto	[Anon.]
22	C1v	ARma del mio ualor	M.C.
23	C2r.iii	LAcrime e uoi ſoſpir	[Anon.]
24	C2v	NAſce laſpro mio tormento	F.V.
25	C3r.iii	O Mia cieca e dura ſorte	[Anon.]
26	C4r.iii	SE per chieder merce	M.C.
27	C4v.iii	OStinato uo ſeguire	[Anon.]
28	C6r	TV dormi io veglio a la tempeſta	B T.
29	C6v	DEus in adiutorium meum	B.T.
		[This is a macaronic text]	
30	C7r	MIa benigna fortuna	[Anon.]
31	C7v.iii	Come chel bianco cigno	M.C.
32	C8r	AQua aqua aiutal foco	B.T.

33	C8v	Sera forſi ripreſo il penſier mio	B.T.
34	D1r	CHi vi dara piu luce	F.V.
35	D1v	SOm pi[u] tua che non ſon mia	M.C.
36	D2v	CHi ui dara piu luce	B.T.
37	D3r	POi che volſe la mia ſtella	B.T.
38	D4r	Deh ſi deh no deh ſi	B.T.
39	D4v	SIo gel dico che dira	B.T.
40	D5v.iii	CRudel come mai poteſti	[Anon.]
41	D6v	SCopri lingua el cieco ardore	B.T.
42	D7r.iii	[S]E de fede vengo a meno	M.C.
43	D8r	OIme il cor oime la teſta	M.C
44	D8v	NOn e tempo daſpetare	M.C.
45	E1r.iii	HOr uendu[to] ho la ſperanza	[Anon.]
46	E2r	IO non compro piu ſperanza	M.C
47	E2v.iii	LA fortuna uo o ol coſi	[Anon.]
48	E3r	INhoſpitas per alpes	D.M.
49	E3v	SE me grato il tuo tornare	PHI.DE LV.
50	E4r.iii	INteger uite ſceleriſque purus	D.M
51	E4v	BEn chamor me facci torto orto	B.T.
52	E5r.iii	OGnun fugga fugga amore	Ant. Cap
53	E6r	POi chel ciel contrario aduerſo	B.T.
54	E6v.iii	In te domine ſperaui	Joſquin Daſcanio.
55	E7v	A La guerra a la guerra Chamor non vol	B.T.
56	E8r	EL conuera chio mora	B.T.
57	E8v.iii	VDite uoi fineſtre	M.C.
58	F1r	POi che per fede manca	Ant. Cap. BRIXIENSIS.
59	F1v	AIme chio moro	D.M.C.
60	F2v	BEn chel ciel me thabbi tolto	B.T.
61	F4r.iii	O Cara libertade	[Anon.]
62	F4v	PIu non tamo aibo aibo	M.C.
63	F5v.iii	SE laffannato cor in foco giace	F.V.
64	F6r	TI par gran maraueglia	N.P.
65	F6v	CHi me dara piu pace	M.C.
66	F7r	PIeta cara ſignora	M.C.
67	F7v	NOn ſom quel chio ſolea	PHI.D.L
68	F8r	SE ben il fin de la mia uita	M.C
69	F8v	Non ſi po quel chi ſi uole	PHI.D.L.
70	G1r	DE che parlera piu la lingua mia	M.C.
71	G1v	REcercar primo	[Anon.]
72	G1v.iii	[Recercar] 2	[Anon.]
73	G2r	[Recercar] 3	[Anon.]
74	G2r.ii	[Recercar] 4	[Anon.]
75	G2r.iii	[Recercar] 5	[Anon.]
76	G2v.iii	[Recercar] 6	[Anon.]
77	G3r	[Recercar] 7	[Anon.]
78	G3r.ii	[Recercar] 8	[Anon.]
79	G3r.iii	[Recercar] 9	[Anon.]

80	G3r.iv	[Recercar] 10	[Anon.]
81	G3v.ii	[Recercar] 11	[Anon.]
82	G4r	[Recercar] 12	[Anon.]
83	G4r.ii	[Recercar] 13	[Anon.]
84	G4r.iii	[Recercar] 14	[Anon.]
85	G4r.iv	[Recercar] 15	[Anon.]
86	G4v.ii	[Recercar] 16	[Anon.]
87	G4v.iii	[Recercar] 17	[Anon.]
88	G5r.i	[Recercar] 18	[Anon.]
89	G5r.ii	[Recercar] 19	[Anon.]
90	G5v	[Recercar] 20	[Anon.]
91	G5v.iii	[Recercar] 21	[Anon.]
92	G6r.iii	[Recercar] 22	[Anon.]
93	G6r.iv	[Recercar] 23	[Anon.]
94	G6v.iii	[Recercar] 24	[Anon.]
95	G7r	[Recercar] 25	[Anon.]
96	G7r.iii	[Recercar] 26	[Anon.]
	G7r	El reſto de le parole Ala fama ſe ua per varie ſcale	
		El reſto de le parole Afflitti ſpirti mei	
		El reſto de le parole de Zephiro ſpira	
	G8r	[Colophon: Register: Device: List of errors]	
	G8v	[blank]	

Extant Copies:

F-Pc, Rés.432. Complete. For the sheet D3-6, see the first edition, of 1509 (No.49)

> **Watermarks:**

A3-4	A7-8	B6-5	B8-7	C2-1	C6-5	D7-8	E2-1	E4-3	F6-5	F7-8	G3-4	G8-7
6	6	2	6	6	2	2	2	6	6	6	6	2

> **Technical comments:** The blind impression of staves on G8r corresponds exactly with the staves printed on G2r • The staves on both the papers found in gathering G correspond with those found in earlier gatherings, on the same papers. Each set of stave formes is found on only one paper. The staves, however, were not in a special forme. They show different alignments on corresponding pages in different gatherings

> **Corrections and changes:**

>> **In-house:** C2v, C7r, C8v, F3v, F6r, and F7r: see above

>> **Later:** On the last verso there is a series of annotations on] *Mutationes* [probably in a 16th-century hand

> **Provenance:** On A1r.] Dal Card^e Pietro Mauandon f. all Ingrid[. . .] | 1746

> **Bibliography:** Facsimile: Bossinensis, *Tenori*

US-Cn, Case-VM.1490.B.74. Lacks A1-8 and B1

> **Watermarks:**

B2	B3-4	C2-1	C3-4	D1-2	D4-3	E6-5	E7-8	F1-2	F4-3	G2-1	G3-4
2	15	2	15	15	2	15	2	15	2	15	2

> **Technical comments:** G8r: the heavy blind impress of four uninked lute staves

> **Corrections and changes:**

>> **In-house:** C2v, C7r, F3v, F6r, and F7r: see above

>> **Later:** C2r.i.3-4: slur is erased and moved to bb.4-5 • D1r.left margin:] al canto | voto [in

brown ink • D4*v*.top right:] al quinto [struck through • D4*v*.margin:] al 3 [in a different ink • E1*r*.foliation:] XXXIII [in brown ink • E6*v*-7*r*. text deletions, in brown ink • E8*r*.foot:] mastro givan angelo a u [in ink

Provenance: Apparently originally bound with the copy of Bossinensis's second book, now at I-Mb (Plamenac, "Toma Cecchini", 101) • From A. Rosenthal • According to Sartori, *Petrucci*, pp. 158–159, the second book came from a monastic house

Bibliography: Plamenac, "Toma Cecchini"; Krummel, *Newberry*; Catálogo, i, 279–.

———

Bibliography: See the items entered under the first edition (No.49)

(c) Bossinensis, *Tenori*. This facsimile is of the Paris copy, and so contains one sheet (D3-6) of the first edition

Commentary:

1. This second edition is surprising, and implies that the market for this form of presenting frottole was larger than Petrucci and Bossinensis had expected. This edition of the first book also presumes that Petrucci still maintained good contact with the distributors from his Venetian years (presumably the partners mentioned in his privilege), and that they knew there was a market for more copies.

2. It is remarkable that this edition contains the sequence of errors and corrections also found in the first edition. It appears that the typesetters followed an uncorrected version of the first very closely, and then had to set the same errata.

3. This edition must lie in 1515, or perhaps very early in 1516: a number of the initials used here are new, not found before 1514. Specifically, the new letter "B" appears once in *Frottole XI*, of 24 October 1514: the letters "C", "H", and "O" used in this book are also new in the frottola volume. (It is true that all four also appear in copies of *I Motetti de la Corona*: however, they are not found in copies of the first edition, only appearing in the second, which is significantly later.) At the same time, some other type material, found here, seems to be in a worse condition than in the second (new) editions of Ghiselin's masses, and Bossinensis's second book. Both of these must also fall after the frottola volume, and there was not enough time to print all three books in 1514.

    The paper patterns suggest that the edition may have been printed early in 1516. The state of type and initials, however, argues that it was printed rather earlier, and the start of 1515 seems the most likely place.

    There is one other possibility, which is that the two copies represent parts of an ongoing process of printing replacement folios for an edition (the first) which was rapidly being exhausted. This would help to explain the different patterns of paper in the two copies. However, there is no other evidence of Petrucci having done this (with the possible exception of the Fossombrone editions of Josquin's first book, still to come), and there are other cases with similar patterns of paper use. For the moment, this should be considered a single edition, printed in 1515.

4. As such, it presents the only extant example of a Fossombrone edition carrying the date of its Venetian predecessor. It may be that the Fossombrone printing of layers of the book of Gaspar's masses would also have carried the old date: sadly, a colophon does not survive. But new editions in Fossombrone carry the date of the first Fossombrone edition, or, as in the case of the new editions of Josquin's first and second book (first printed in Venice) a new date.

No. 59. Josquin: *Missarum II*

11.iv.1515   *RISM* J 671

Two editions of this title were printed in Fossombrone, with a cancel bifolio to the second

First Fossombrone Edition

A1*r*]   Miſſarum Joſquin. | Liber ſecundus. | Aue maris ſtella. | Hercules dux ferrarie. | Malheur
me bat. | Lami baudichon. | Une muſque de buſcaya. | Du*n*g aulter amer.

C1*r*]   Libri ſecundi Miſſar*um* Joſquin. | T

D1*r*]   Libri ſecundi Miſſar*um* Joſquin. | A

F1*r*]   Libri ſecundi Miſſar*um* Joſquin. | B

G8*r*]   LEO. pp. X. [etc: as in Josquin, *III Missarum* (1514, No.54), followed by:]
¶Impreſſum Foroſempronii per Octauianum | Petrutium ciuem Foroſempronienſem. Anno
| Domini .MDXV. Die XI. Aprilis. Domi-|nante inclito ac excellentiſſimo Principe D*om*ino |
Franci*s*comaria Feltrio de Ruere: Vrbini Soræ*que* | Duce: Piſauri &c. Domino: Alme Vrbis
Præfecto: | [Left:] REGISTRVM. | ABCDEFG | Omnes quaterni preter CE | *qui* ſunt quinterni

Format and collation: Partbook: landscape quarto-in-eights. [S] 16 folios: A-B⁸; [T] 10 folios: C¹⁰;
[A] 18 folios: D⁸E¹⁰; [B] 16 folios: F-G⁸

Signatures:] aAa ij [$4 • − A1 • + C5 and E5, signed with an arabic numeral • gGg3 prints as gGg ii
No foliation

Running heads: In two sections, as in other editions of the period. There seems to be no underlying
pattern suggesting that the head-lines were retained in the forme. For the details, see the commentary at the end of this description

Fonts: Music: Petrucci's normal music type
Staves: Six per page: 175–180 mm long, 10.2-92-113 mm high
Text: Rotonda, used for underlay, "x" = 2.3 mm • Roman, used for Privilege and Colophon,
and for Benedictus on f.E5*r* • Rotonda, used for A4*r*, "x" = 4.8 mm.

Textual comments: A1*r*: the "u" in "Aue" is inverted • A3*v*.caption:] AAgn*u*

Technical comments: E1*r*: the initial letter "S" is inverted: A-Wn and D-B

In-house corrections: A3*v*.vi.penultimate: *sm* e' → f', the note-head erased and stamped in: D-B,
I-Ac • A6*r*.iii.49: *m*, c" → d", the note head erased and a *sb* stamped in: D-B, I-Ac • B8*r*.ii.5:
*sb*c" → *dsb*b': most of the note erased, and some retained to become a *p.a.*: the new note stamped
in: A-Wn, D-B, I-Ac, I-Bc • D5*r*.iii.46: d → f, old note-head erased, and a new one stamped
in: the stave touched up with the same brown ink: A-Wn, D-B, E-Bbc, I-Ac, I-Bc • D5*v*.i.29:
m, a → g, note-head and part of tail erased, new note-head stamped in: E-Bbc, I-Ac • E2*r*.iii.29:
d' → c', with a new note-head stamped in: D-B, I-Ac, I-Bc • E5*r*: the addition in a Roman
fount of the phrase] Benedictus | qui venit in nomine domini [: all copies

Contents:

	A1*r*	C1*r*	D1*r*	F1*r*	[Title]
1	A1*v*	C1*v*	D1*v*	F1*v*	Joſquin [Missa] Aue maris ſtella.
	A1*v*.iv	C1*v*.iii	D1*v*.iv	F1*v*.iv	[Gloria]
	A2*r*.iv	C2*r*	D2*r*.iv	F2*r*.iv	[Credo]
	A3*r*	C2*v*.ii	D3*r*	F3*r*	[Sanctus]
	A3*v*.ii	C2*v*.iv	D3*v*.iv	F3*v*.iii	[Agnus]

2	A4r	C3r	D4r.v	F4r	Joſquin [Missa] Hercules Dux Ferrarie.
	A4r.v	C3r.ii	D4v.iii	F4r.iv	[Gloria]
	A4v.iv	C3r.iv	D5r.iii	F4v.iv	[Credo]
	A5v.ii	C3v	D6r.ii	F5v	[Sanctus]
	A6r	C3v.iii	D6v.iii	F6r	[Agnus]
3	A7r	C4r	D7v	F7r	Joſquin. [Missa] Mal heur me bat.
	A7v	C4r.iv	D7v.vi	F7r.iv	[Gloria]
	A8r	C4v.ii	D8r.vi	F7v.iv	[Credo]
	A8v	C5r.vi	E1r.iv	F8v	[Sanctus]
	B1v.vi	C6r.ii	E2r	G1r	[Agnus]
4	B2r	C6v.v	E3r	G1v.ii	[Missa] Lami baudichon.
	B2r.iv	C7r	E3r.iv	G1v.iv	[Gloria]
	B2v.iv	C7r.iii	E3v.v	G2r.iv	[Credo]
	B3v.iii	C7r.vi	E4v.iv	G3r	[Sanctus]
	B4r.iv	C7v	E5r.iv	G3r.iv	[Agnus]
5	B4v	C7v.iii	E5v	G3v	Joſquin. [Missa] Una muſque de buschaia.
	B4v.v	C8r	E5v.v	G3v.v	[Gloria]
	B5v	C8r.v	E6v	G4v	[Credo]
	B6r.v	C8v.v	E7v	G5v	[Sanctus]
6	B7r	C9r.v	E8v	G6v	Joſquin. [Missa] Dung aultre amer.
	B7r.iii	C9v	E8v.iv	G6v.iii	[Gloria]
	B7v	C9v.iii	E9r	G7r	[Credo]
	B8r	C10r	E9v	G7v	[Sanctus]
	B8r.v	C10v.v	E9v.iv	G7v.v	[Agnus]
				G8r	[Dedication; Colophon]
			E10r		[Blank staves]
	B8v	C10v	E10v	G8v	[Blank]

Extant copies:

A-GÜ, s.s. Tenor part book only, complete

> **Size of page:** 165 × 235 mm.
>
> **Watermarks:** Mark 2 on folios C3-4 and C-6
>
> **Later correction:** C4r.v.47 (penultimate note): md' erased
>
> **Binding:** Bound as first in a set of nine books: (1) This book; (2) Josquin: *III Missarum* (1514, No.54); (3) Agricola: *Misse* (1504, No.13); (4) Ghiselin: *Misse* (1503, No.9); (5) Isaac: *Misse* (1506, No.31); (6) *I Missarum diversorum auctorum* (1508, No.43); (7) Obrecht: *Misse* (1503, No.6); (8) De Orto: *Misse* (1505, No.20); (9) *Fragmenta Missarum* (1505, No.24) Dark brown leather, 170 × 240 mm, with stamps and rolls suggesting a Venetian provenance • Three sewing bands, head and tail bands: the reinforcing strips at the spine are from an early religious text • One paste-down at each end: no flyleaves extant • Edges originally painted red • It is notable that the first book of Josquin masses is not (and probably never was) present, and that seven of the titles were at least seven years old when the first book in the set (the present title) was printed.
>
> **Provenance:** From a religious institution. A probably 17th-century hand entered a call number on the lost front flyleaf: the print-off on the adjacent page seems to read] H [. . .] 611 • Federhofer, "Petrucci" draws attention to the Szombathely copies to reinforce the possibility that this set of parts came from the same area. It is notable that both the Szom-

bathely and Budapest sets do seem to have provenances from the southern Austro-Hungarian Empire

Bibliography: Federhofer, "Petrucci"

A-Wn, S.A.77.C.20. Superius, Tenor, and Altus, complete

    Size of page: 164 × 233 mm.

    Watermarks: Mark 2 on A1-2, A4-3, B5-6, B7-8, C4-3, C6-, C9-10, D2-1, D5-6, E3-4, E6- and E9-10

    Technical comments: E1r: the initial letter "S" is inverted

    Corrections and changes:

        In-house: B8r, D5r: see above

        Later: The movements are numbered sequentially through all three part-books, 30–59 (ending at 57 in the Altus) • D2v.v.24: *m* tail partly erased • D5r.vi.clef: cleaned up • E2r.iii.29: d' → c'

    Binding and Provenance: With Josquin, *Misse* (1506, No.30) • Since the first book in this bound set is numbered 1–25, it would appear that a single manuscript mass was at one time bound between the two books

D-Bds, Mus.ant.pract.D.227. Complete

    Size of page: 231 × 165 mm: the altus measures 226 × 153 mm.

    Watermarks: No.2 on A1-2, A5-6, B6-5, B8-7, C1-2, C-5, C7-8, D1-2, D4-3, E1-2, E3-4, E-6, F1-2, F6-5, G4-3 and G8-7

    Textual comments: D3v.iv.12–13: not erasures, but poor impressions

    Technical comments: A7r: only five staves inked • C3r.ii: near the end a music spacing sort, ending at 5.3 mm above the stave

    Corrections and changes:

        In-house: A3v, A6r, D5r, 2r: see above

        Later: A4r.vi.37: *b, b'* → *g'*, the top of the note head erased, and a dark brown new base • D2v.v.24: *m* → *sb*, by erasing the tail • D2v.v.36: f, *sb* → *m*, with a brown ink tail • D4r.vi.18–19: an attempt at writing in over a poor impression has resulted in a hole • D5v.iv.35–37: *3m*, c',c',b → *sm*, in the same brown ink as on D2v • E8v.vi.last: the upper pitch e' → c', with an erased top, and a new base in the same brown ink • F7r.vi.*custos*: d → e, in brown ink

    Binding and Provenance: with Josquin, *I Missarum* (1516, No.62)

E-Bbc, 115 (2). Altus

    Size of page: 174 × 230 mm.

    Watermarks: No.2 on ff.D6-5, D8-7, E6-, E8-7 and E10-9

    Textual comments: E7r.v.6-7 from end: very messy but probably just ink-ball fluff

    Technical comments: D4r.ii.after 29: the proportion sign 3/2 has an inverted 2 • D5r.i.after 12: the sign 3/2 seems to have a 2 that was stamped in later • E4r.iii.12: *m*g', the note is strangely distorted

    Corrections and changes:

        In-house: D5r, E2r: see above

        Later: D2v.v.24: *m* → *sb*, erased tail • D2v.v.before 31: ?added *mf'* in brown ink • D2v.v.36: *sb* → *m*, with a tail in ginger ink • D5r.iii.47: *sb* f', with an added p.a. in brown ink • D6r.iii.35: something small was erased, probably a *punctum* • D7r.iii.39: added *signum congruentiae*, in brown ink • D8r.i.*custos*: b → d', the head erased, and redrawn in brown ink • E8v.vi.last 2 notes: f',d → d,d by erasing part of the first note, and adding a lower horizontal, in dark brown ink

Binding and Provenance: with Josquin, *I Missarum* (1516, No.62)

Bibliography: Pedrell, *Catàlech*, No.427

GB-Lbl, K.1.d.10. The outer sheet of D • For the rest of this copy, see below

Watermark: No.2 on D8-7

Later corrections: D2*v*.v.24: *m* → *sb*, by erasing the tail • D2*v*.v.rest after 30: *b* → *m*, by erasure

I-Ac, Stampati N.189 (5). Complete

Size of page: 168 × 232 mm.

Watermarks: No.2 on A5, A7-8, B2-1, B6-5, C1-2, C6-, C8-7, D4-3, D7-8, E1-2, E-5, F5-6, F7-8, G2-1 and G5-6 • Mark 10 on E8-7

Corrections and changes:

> **In-house:** A3*v*, A6*r*, B8*r*, D5*r*, D5*v* and E2*r*: see above

> **Later:** D2*v*.v.24: *m* → *sb*, erased tail • F6*v*.i.26–27: c.o.p. ligature → ligature *bl*, by erasing the tail • F7*r*.vi.*custos*: d → e

Binding: With Agricola, *Misse* (No.13)

Provenance: S. Francesco, Assisi

Bibliography: Petrucci, *Liber* (fascimile)

I-Bc, Q.72. Complete

Size of page: 169 × 236 mm.

Watermarks: Mark 2 on A5-6, A8-7, B2-1, B4-3, C1-2, C3-4, C-5, D1-2, D4-3, E2-1, E-5, F2-1, F3-4, G3-4 and G7-8 • Mark 27 on E4-3

Corrections and changes:

> **In-house:** B8*r*, D5*r* and E2*r*: see above

> **Later:** A8*v*.iii.16–17: erased, probably *mc*, *ma* • C4*r*.v.47: *md'* erased • D2*v*.v.24: *m* tail partly erased • D5*r*.vi.clef: cleaned up • F4*v*.iv.29: b, *sb* → *m*, with added brown ink tail • F6*v*.i.26–27: c.o.p. ligature → ligature *bl*, by erasing the tail • F7*r*.vi.*custos*: d → e

Binding: Card covers, as for Josquin, *III Missarum* (No.54)

Provenance: Mentioned in a letter from Martini, dated 22.vii.1746. Epistolario martiniano, I.11.35 • Old call number 1015 on A1*r*

US-R, *M1490.D424.M2. Superius and Bassus, complete

Watermarks: No.2 used consistently

Technical comments: Signature G3 was printed as gGg ii and has the final minim added in ink • F2*v*: staves were printed before the clefs

Later corrections and changes: A2*v*.vi: illegible • A6*r*.iii.before 1: an additional *l* rest, in ink • A6*r*.v.last 7 notes: *mc*,*sbe*,*md*,*mb*,*md*,*mc*,*ma*,*le* crossed through: the previous note *m* → *l*, with added bar-line • A6*r*.left margin:] Canit*ur* in sub dyapazo*n* [in 16th-century hand, plausibly German • A8*v*.iii.16–17: erased, probably *mc*, *ma* • B8*r*.ii.5: c" → b' • F4*v*.iv.29: b, *sb* → *m*, with added brown ink tail • F6*r*.ii.after 40 clef: C₄ → F₄, by adding the second component in manuscript • F6*r*.iii-v: same clef change: on stave vi, the original clef is completely erased • F6*r*.v.end: last five notes, *mc*,*me*,*md*,*mg*,*lf*, erased and replaced by *mc*,*me*,*md*,*mg*,*mf*,*sba*,*mg*,*me*,*mg*,*mf*,*md*,*la*,double bar-line, in brown ink • F6*v*.i.26–27: c.o.p. ligature → ligature *bl*, by erasing the tail • F7*r*.vi.*custos*: d → e

Binding: Early • A note on the binding of the Bassus, in a 19th-century German hand records that the two gatherings were then bound in reverse order

Provenance: From Hiram W. Sibley • Sibley's purchase is recorded on f.A2*r* in pencil:] 8 | 2 | 29 Liepmanssohn. M2250

No.59A. *Second Fossombrone Edition*

A1*r*] Mi∫∫arum Jo∫quin | Liber ∫ecundus. || Ave maris ∫tella. | Hercules dux ferrarie. | Malheur me bat. | La mi baudichon. | Una mu∫*que* de bu∫caya. | Du*n*g aultre amer

C1*r*] LIBRI SECVNDI MISSARVM IOSQVIN. | T

D1*r*] LIBRI SECVNDI MISSARVM IOSQVIN. | A

F1*r*] [L]IBRI SECVNDI MISSARVM IOSQVIN. | B

G8*r*] ¶ Impre∫∫um Foro∫empronii per Octauianum | Petrutium ciuem Foro∫empronien∫em. Anno | Domini .MDXV. Die xi. Aprilis. Domi-|nante inclito ac excellenti∫∫imo Principe D*o*mino | Franci∫comaria Feltrio de Ruere: Vrbini Sorúq*ue* | Duce: Pi∫auri &c. D*o*mino: Alme Vrbis Prúfecto: || REGISTRVM. | ABCDEFG. | Omnes uaterni preter CE | q*ui* ∫unt quinterni.

Format and collation: Partbooks: landscape quarto-in-eights. [S] 16 folios: A-B^8; [T] 10 folios: C^{10}; [A] 18 folios: D^{8}E^{10}; [B] 16 folios: F-G^8

Signatures:] aAa ij [$4 • − A1 • + C5 and E5 • B3 reads] bBb ij

No foliation

Running heads: In two sections, of part-name, in the outer corner, and title, in capitals and centered. The part-name was probably consistent: the following comes from the copy at GB-Lbl, but some final stops appear on different pages in other copies, as if they did not always take ink.

recto:]	Sup*erius*.	[A2-B8
	Tenor	[C2,4,6–8,10
	Tenor.	[C3,5,9
	Altus.	[D2-8, E1,3,4,6–9
	Altus	[E2,5
	Ba∫∫us.	[F2-G7
	[Nil:	A1, C1, D1, E10, F1, G8
verso:]	Sup*erius*.	[A1-B7
	Tenor.	[C1-6,8,9
	Tenor	[C7
	Altus	[D1,7, E4,9
	Altus.	[D2-6, D8-E3, E5-8
	Ba∫∫us.	[F1-G7
	[Nil:	B8, C10, E10, G8

Part-names:

Fonts: Music: Petrucci's normal music type

Staves: six per page, 175–178 mm long, 10-92-110 mm high

Text: Roman throughout, "x" = 1.6 mm, "20" = 66 mm

Textual comments: A list of variants between this and the first edition can be found in Boorman, *Petrucci*, pp. 328–32

Technical comments: A7*r*, B5*r*, C3*v*, stave vi not inked: A-Wn, GB-Lbl • E2*v*, stave vi not inked: GB-Lbl • E4*v*, E6*r*, stave vi partly inked: GB-Lbl • G5*r*, stave vi only partly inked: B-Br, GB-Lbl • G6*r*, stave vi not inked: B-Br, GB-Lbl • It may be only a coincidence that the signature on two copies of B3*r* shows the same defect

In-house corrections: A2*v*.ii.after pausa: bar-line in brown ink (— this was printed in the first edition): in all surviving superius parts except that at I-Rvat • A6*r*.iv.31: originally e" (I-Ac), and corrected by stop-press change (I-Rvat)

Contents: As the first edition

Extant copies:

A-Wn, S.A.77.C.19. Superius, Tenor, and Bassus, complete

> **Size of page:** 164 × 233 mm.
>
> **Watermarks:** No.35 on A6, A8, B2-1, B-3, F-6, F-7 and G4-3 • No.33 on C4-3 and C10-9
>
> **Textual comments:** The signature to B3r reads] bBb ij [probably as a result of poor inking at the press
>
> **Technical comments:** All the text seems to represent a late run through the press
>
> **In-house correction:** A2v.ii.after pausa: bar-line in brown ink
>
> **Binding:** Uniform with the binding of Josquin, *I Missarum* (1516, No.62) • 2 end-papers at each end of each part-book

B-Br, III.99.238 A L.P. Bassus, complete

> **Size of page:** 152 × 227 mm.
>
> **Watermarks:** No.35 on ff.F-1, F5-6 and G3-4
>
> **Textual comments:** F2r.signature: lacks the numeral (added in pencil)
>
> **Later corrections and changes:** F3r.iii.18: *mb* erased • F4r.v.45: c, *sm* → *m*, by erasing the center • F4v.iv.opening rests: now 3*l*, 2*sb*: second *l* in ginger ink • F4v.iv.17: B, *sb* → *m*, with a ginger tail • F5r.ii.after 18 [*md*]: erased dot • F6r.i.first rests: *l*, *l*, *b* → *l*, *l*, *m*, by erasure • F8v.vi.after 2: m.s.m C3 → ø, by erasure and a ginger stroke
>
> **Binding:** A modern library binding, made by Vander Heyden of Brussels • Modern paste-down and end paper at each end • In an earlier binding, probably with the library's copies of Josquin, *III Missarum* (1514) and Josquin *I Missarum* (1516), this book had red edges.
>
> **Provenance:** Probably the same at that of the library's copy of Josquin, *I Missarum* (1516, No.62)
>
> **Bibliography:** Huys, *Catalogue*, p. 133 (including reproduction of G8v)

GB-Lbl, K.1.d.10. Four parts, lacking the blank folio E10. For the outer sheet of D, taken from the first edition printing, see above

> **Watermarks:** No.35 on A1-2, A-4, B1-2, B-5, D-4, E4-, F3, F8, and G5-6 • No.6 on C4-3, C9-10, E5-, and E-9
>
> **Technical comments:** A2r. text spacing sort, 2.8 mm high • A3v.i: the mensuration sign is a damaged sort • E9r. capitals, running title and music all printed together, for all are blurred from the page being too damp • Several notes show damage to the tail, primarily revealed as a bent piece of metal, at about 3.5 mm above the body of the note. See, B1v.i.7; B1v.iv.36; B1v.vi.12; B1v.vi.25; B2r.iii.30; or B2r.iii.4 from the end. This pattern seems to indicate the extent to which the note-sorts were kerned
>
> **Corrections and changes:**
>
> > **In-house:** A2v.ii.bar-line: added in brown ink • A4v.iii.3: *dm* erased: *sm*a stamped in
> >
> > **Later:** C2v.iv.43: g → f
>
> **Binding:** Modern
>
> **Provenance** Earl of Arundel • Lord Lumley
>
> **Bibliography:** Johnson and Scholderer, *Short-Title*, p. 214; Jayne and Johnson, *Lumley*, No.2581

H-SY, XX.8.b (2). Bassus, complete

> **Size of page:** 153 × 215 mm.
>
> **Watermarks:** No.35 on F2-1, F4-3, and G-4
>
> **Later corrections and changes:** F1r.] Liber secundus Mi[sarum [in a 16th-century German hand • F1r. addition of the letter "L" to "IBRI" • Manuscript foliation in two layers: the earliest read] Lib.j. [and then numbering 1–16: a later hand, that of the inscription on F1r has changed the number "j" to "2" • F4v.iv.opening rests: now *l*, *l*, *l*, *sb*, *sb*. the second *l* is

in brown ink, perhaps merely touched up • F8*v*.vi.1: *sb*A erased. It is possible that the following *sb*G is stamped in

Binding and Provenance: with Josquin, *I Missarum* (1516, No.62)

I-BGc, Cinq.4.984 (2). Superius, complete. A3,6 is a cancel, for which see below

    Size of page: 169 × 235 mm.

    Watermarks: No.33 on A-4; No.35 on A7-8, B1 and B3-4

    Textual comments: The signature to B3 reads] bBb ij [probably as a result of poor inking at the press

    Technical comments: B2*v*.vi.9–10: actually 2 *sm*, very poorly inked • B7*r*.vi: inked furniture

    In-house changes: A2*v*.ii.after *pausa*: bar-line, in brown ink • A6*r*.iv..31: e" → d", stamped in

    Binding: with Josquin, *I Missarum* (1516, No.62)

    Provenance: Cortesi • Mayr

I-Rvat, Sist.235–238. Complete

    Size of page: 233–235 × 169 mm.

    Watermarks: No.35 on A2-1, B5, B8-7, C9, D2-1, D4, E8-7, F6 and G3 • No.33 on A5-6, C3-4, C5-, E5-, E9-10 and F7-8

    Technical comments: A7*r* and C3*v* have only five staves inked

    Corrections and changes:

        In-house: A2*v*.ii.after pausa: bar-line in brown ink • A6*r*.iv.31: e' → d", stamped in

        Later: The parts foliated [S] 19–34, [T] 12–21, [A] 19–36; [B] 17–32 • A1*r*. folio numbers written against the contents list • A4*v*.iii.12: *sb* → *m*, added tail in ink • A8*v*.iii.14–15: erased • D2*r*.ii.40: erased leger line • D2*v*.v.24: *m* → *sb*, with erased tail • D8*r*.iv.first rest after 29: *b* → *sb*, by erasure • E1*r*.ii.49–50: b, c' → c' d'

    Binding and Provenance: With Josquin, *I Missarum* (1516, No.62)

No.59B. *Cancel to the second edition.*

A single copy exists of a cancel bifolium, replacing A3,6.

Extant copy:

I-BGc, Cinq.4.984 (2). For the rest of this copy, see above

    Watermarks: No.33 on A-3

    Textual comment: A6*r*.iv.31: the e" of the first edition was corrected in this cancel

———

Lost copies: Copies of one or another edition were in the collections of João IV of Portugal (Sampaio Ribeiro, p. 19) and Ottheinrich (Lambrecht, *Heidelberger*, i, p. 106)

Early references: For the possible references to this volume, made by Doni and Gesner, see the citations in No.54

Other editions: Petrucci's first edition was in 1505 (No.22) • A later edition was published by Pasoti and Dorico in 1526 (*RISM* J672)

Bibliography:

    (a) Rosaria Boccadifuoco, *Bibliografia*, No.1196 • Sartori, *Petrucci*, No.51

    (c) Petrucci, *Missarum*

    (d) Josquin, *Werke*, Misse, Deel II.

Commentary:

1. The first of these Fossombrone editions is entirely consistent through all the extant copies, despite the occasional appearances of different papers in the Assisi and Bologna copies. Both papers 6 and 10 are rare in books at this time: nonetheless, they carry the same settings as sheets on paper 2.

2. The pattern of head-lines in these editions has been dismissed above as being suggestive that running heads were not retained in the forme. For the first edition, this is clear from the following:

    Jofquin Aue maris ſtella. [A1*v* • Aue maris ſtella [C1*v* • .Aue maris ſtella. [D1*v* • Aue maris ſtella [F1*v* • Aue [A3*r*,3*v*, D2*r*,4*r* • .Aue. [D2*v*,3*r* • Aue. [A2*v*, C2*r*,2*v*, D3*v*, F2*r*-3*v*

    Jofquin Hercules Dux Ferrarie. [A4*r* • Hercules dux Ferrarie [C3*r* • Hercules dux ferrarie. [F4*r* • Hercules. [A4*v*,5*r*,6*r*,6*v*, C3*v*, D4*v*,6*r*,7*r*, F5*r*-6*v* • Hercules [A5*v*, D5*r*-*v*, F4*v* • Hercules: [D6*v*

    Jofquin. Mal heur me bat. [A7*r* • Mal heur. [A7*v*-8*v*, B2*v* (in error), C4*v*-5*v*, F7*v*, G1*r* • Malheur me bat [C4*r*, D7*v* • Malheur [B1*v*, C6*r*, D8*r*-E2*v*, F8*r*,8*v* • .Malheur. [C6*v*, G1*v* • Mal heur me bat [F7*r*

    Jofquin. Lami baudichon. [B2*r* • Lami baudichon. [B1*r* (in error), B3*r*,4*r*, C7*r*,7*v*, E3*r*-5*r*, G2*r*,2*v* • Lami baudichon [B3*v*, G3*r*

    Jofquin. Una mufque de bufchaia. [B4*v* • Una mufque de bufchaia. [E5*v* • Una mufque de buſ chaia [G3*v* • Una muque [B5*r*, C8*r*-9*r*, E6*r*, G5*v*,6*r* • .Una mufque [E6*v* • Una mufque. [B5*v*-6*v*, E7*r*-8*r*, G4*r*-5*r*

    Jofquin. Dung aultre amer. [B7*r* • Dung aultre amer. [B7*v*, E8*v*-9*v*, G7*r* • Dung aultre amer [B8*r*, C9*r*, G6*v* • Dung aultre amer. [C10*r* • .Dung aultre amer. [G7*v*

    Nil: A1*r*,2*r*, B8*v*, C1*r*, F1*r*, G8*r*,8*v*

3. The faulty headlines on B1*r* and B2*v* suggest that there were still occasional problems in laying formes out correctly. They certainly imply that the head-lines were inserted independently of the content on those pages.

4. The attributions to Josquin only appear in the Superius book. This is not very unusual for Petrucci.

5. Perhaps unusually, the part-names were evidently not kept in the forme either: the following appear at the outer corner, unless otherwise noted:

recto:]	Superius.	[A2,7-B7
	Superius.	[inner corner: A3,4, B8
	Superius	[inner corner: A6
	Tenor.	[C2,4,5,9,10
	Tenor	[inner corner: C6-8
	.Tenor.	[C3
	Altus	[D8, E5,6,8
	Altus.	[D2-7, E1-4,7,9
	Baffus.	[F2-5,8, G1,2,7
	Baffus	[F6,7, G3
	Baffus	[inner corner: G4-6
	[Nil:	A1,5, C1, D1, E10, F1, G8
verso:]	Superius.	[A1-3,7-B5
	Superius	[A4,5, B7

Tenor.	[C1,3,4, C7-9
Tenor	[C2,5,6
Cum ſex vocibus. Sup*erius*	[A6
Altus	[D1,2
Altus.	[D4-E5, E7-9
Altu5	[E6
Baſſus.	[F1,2,7
Baſſus:	[F3
.Baſſus.	[F4
Baſſus	[F5,8, G1-7
Baſſus. Cum ſex vocibus	[F6
[Nil:	B6,8, C10, E10, G8

6.   Second edition headlines are more consistent than those of the first edition:

IOSQVIN. AVE MARIS STELLA. [A1*v* • AVE. [A2*r*,2*v*,3*v*, C2*v*, D2*r*-4*r*, F2*r*-3*v* • AVE
[A3*r*, C2*r* • AVE MARIS STELLA. [C1*v*, D1*v*, F1*v*

IOSQVIN. HERCVLES DVX FERRARIE. [A4*r* • HERCVLES DVX FERRARIE. [C3*r*,
F4*r* • HERCVLES. [A4*v*-6*v*, C3*v*, D4*v*-7*r*, F4*v*-6*v* • HERCVLES [D7*r*

IOSQVIN. MAL HEVR ME BAT. [A7*r* • MAL HEVR ME BAT. [C4*r*, D7*v*, F7*r* • MAL
HEVR. [A7*v*,8*r*, B1*r*, C5*r*-6*v*, D8*r*-2*v*, F7*v*-G1*v* • MAL HEVR [B1*v* • MAL. HEVR. [C4*v*

IOSQVIN. LA MI BAVDICHON. [B2*r* • LA MI BAVDICHON. [B2*v*4*r*, E3*r*-4*r*,5*r*, G2*r*-
3*r* • LAMI BAVDICHON. [C7*r* • LAMI BAVDICHON [C7*v*, E4*v*

IOSQVIN. VNA MVSQVE DE BVSCAIA. [B4 • VNA MVSQVE. [B5*r*-6*v*, C8*r*-9*r*, E7*r*-
8*r*, G4*r*-6*r* • VNA MVSQVE DE BVSCHAIA. [E5*v*-6*v*, G3*v*

IOSQVIN. DVNG AVLTRE AMER. [B7*r* • DVNG AVLTRE AMER. [B8*r*, C10*r*, E9*r*,
G6*v*-7*v* • DVNG AVLTRE AMER [B7, C9, E8 • DVNG AVLTRE AMER [E9

Nil: A1*r*, B8*v*, C1*r*, C10*v*, D1*r*, E10*v*, F1*r*, G8*r*,8*v*

7.   The privilege appears to be the same setting of type as that used in J III (GB-Lbl) and Mouton:
apparently kept standing.

8.   This second edition is clearly differentiated from the first: apart from the head-lines in capitals,
the text is now set in roman. This second change first appears after the second Fossombrone
edition of Josquin's first book (dated May 1516), and is used thereafter That book also uses paper
6, in much the same manner as here, to round out the stock of other paper. These two books
must therefore lie close together, and before any other Petrucci editions. For that reason, I have
dated both in 1517.

9.   The cancel was probably printed immediately after the edition. It comprises a single bifolio,
printed in the same manner and with the same materials, as the principal edition.

No. 60. Mouton: *Missarum I*

11.viii.1515   *RISM* M 4015

Two editions survive of this title: there is a cancel bifolium for each

First Edition.

Folio F1 is not extant

A1*r*]   Mi∫∫ar*um* Joannis Mouton. | Liber primus. | Missa ∫ine nomine. | Alleluya. | Alma redemptoris. | Ite3 alia ∫ine nomine. | Regina mear*um*.

C1*r*]   Mi∫∫ar*um* Jo. monton. Liber primus. | A

E1*r*]   Mi∫∫ar*um* Jo. monton. Liber primus. | A

G1*r*]   Mi∫∫ar*um* Jo. monton. Liber primus. | A

H8*r*]   LEO. p*a*p*a*. X. [etc. as in Josquin, *III Missarum*, No.54): followed by:]
¶ Impre∫∫um Foro∫empronii per Octauianum | Petrutium ciuem Foro∫empronien∫em. Anno | Domini. MDXV. Die xi. Augu∫ti. Domi-|nante inclito ad excellenti∫∫imo Principe D*o*mino | Franci∫comaria Feltrio de Ruere: Vrbini Soræ*que* | Duce: Pi∫auri &c. D*o*mino: Alme Vrbis Præfecto: | REGISTRVM. | ABCDEFGH | Omnes quaterni preter F | q*ui* e∫t quinternus

Format and collation: Partbooks: landscape quarto-in-eights. [S] 16 folios: A-B⁸; [T] 16 folios: C-D⁸]; [A] 18 folios: E⁸F¹⁰; [B] 16 folios: G-H⁸

Signatures:] A ij [$4 • – A1 • + C1, E1 and F5 (signed F iiiij)

No foliation

Head-lines: Two components: one at the corner of the page, giving the part-name: the other (for which see below) identifying the work
recto:] Sup*erius* [A3 • Superius. [A4-6, B1-7 • Tenor. [C2-8, D1,3–8 • Tenor [D2 • Altus. [E2,3,5,7, F3,4,6–10 • Alus. [E4 • Altus [E6,8, F5 • .Altus. [F2 • Ba∫∫us [G2,4,5 • Ba∫∫us. [A2,7,8, G3,6–8, H1-7 • [Nil: A1, B8, C1, E1, G1, H8
verso:] Sup*erius* [A4, B6 • Superius. [A3,5–6, B1-5,7 • Tenor [C1-5 • Tenor. [C2-8, D1-7 • Altus. [E1,2,4–6, F2-7,9,10 • Altus [E3,7,8, F8 • Ba∫∫us. [A1,2,7,8, G1-4,7,8, H1-4,7 • Ba∫∫us [G5,6 H5,6 • [Nil: B8, D8, H8

Fonts: Music: Petrucci's normal music type
Staves: Six per page, 176–178 mm. long
Text: Rotonda • Roman for the privilege

Textual comments: D4*r*.iii.text: at the right end the text is in two lines:] ∫edet ad | desteram p*a*tris • F9*r*.iii.end: the rests have an unusual layout, *b,sb,m,m*, given the mensuration sign

Technical comments: Blank staves on D2*r*.vi, D8*r*.vi, E1*v*.vi, E5*r*.vi, F2*v*.vi, F4*r*.v, H7*r* and H7*v* • The last stave on F4*r* was not printed

In-house corrections: D4*v*.ii.21: *sb*, f → a, erased and stamped in: D-B

Rubrics: E7*v*.left margin:] O∫anna ∫upra ∫uperiore*m*

Contents:

	A1*r*	C1*r*	E1*r*	G1*r*	[Title]
1	A1*v*	C1*v*	E1*v*	G1*v*	[Missa sine nomine] Io.mouton
	A2*r*	C1*v*.v	E2*r*.i	G1*v*.v	[Gloria]
	A2*r*.iv	C2*v*.ii	E2*v*.iv	G2*v*	[Credo]
	A3*v*.v	C3*v*.iii	E3*v*.v	G3*v*.ii	[Sanctus]
	A4*v*.ii	C4*r*.iv	E4*v*.iii	G4*r*.v	[Agnus]
2	A5*r*.iii	C4*v*.iii	E5*v*	G4*v*.iv	[Missa] Alleluya
	A5*v*	C4*v*.v	E5*v*.v	G5*r*	[Gloria]
	A6*r*	C5*v*	E6*r*.vi	G5*v*	[Credo]
	A6*v*.vi	C6*v*	E7*v*	G6*v*	[Sanctus]
	A7*v*.ii	C7*r*.iii	E8*r*	G7*r*	[Agnus]
3	A7*v*.v	C7*v*	E8*v*	G7*v*	[Missa] Alma redemptoris
	A8*r*.iv	C8*r*	F1*r*	G8*r*	[Gloria]
	A8*v*.v	C8*v*.ii	F1*v*.ii	G8*v*	[Credo]

	B1r.v	D1v	F3v	H1r.v	[Sanctus]
	B1v.iv	D2r	F4r	H1v.iv	[Agnus]
4	B2r.ii	D2v	F5r	H2r.iv	[Missa sine nomine II]
	B2v	D3r	F5v	H2v.iii	[Gloria]
	B3r.iii	D3v.iii	F6r.iv	H3r.iv	[Credo]
	B4r.ii	D4v.iii	F7r.iii	H4r	[Sanctus]
	B4v.iii	D5r.iv	F7v.iv	H4v	[Agnus]
5	B5r	D5v.iii	F8v	H5r	[Missa] Regina mearum
	B5v.v	D6r	F8v.iv	H5r.iii	[Gloria]
	B6r	D6v.iii	F9r.vi	H6r	[Credo]
	B7r	D7v	F10r.iv	H7r	[Sanctus]
	B7v	D8r	F10v.ii	H7v	[Agnus]
				H8r	[Privilege; Colophon]
	B8r–v	D8v		H8v	[blank]

Extant copies:

D-B, Mus.ant.pract.D.227. Three part-books, lacking the Altus • There is a cancel in gathering B

> **Size of page:** 165 × 231 mm.

> **Watermarks:** No.2 on A2-1, A3-4, B2-1, B-3, B-5, C1-2, C5-6, D2-1, D5-6, G1-2, G6-5, H5-6, H8-7

> **Technical comments:** B8v and C1r: staves stamped in blind • H8r has the lightly inked traces of the Odhecaton initial "A" over the privilege

> **Corrections and changes:**

> > **In-house:** D4v: see above

> > **Later:** A4r.iii.clef: C₁ → C₂, by erasure and in black ink • A5r.v.rests after 25: *l,b* → *l,m*, by erasure • A6r.v.last note: c″, *b* and *m* rest → *db*, in ink • B7r.i.m.s.: cut C → C, by erasure; C4v.iii.rest after 20: *sb*, shortened by erasing the base • C8r.i.rest after 7: *m*, which crossed the line, and the lower part erased • D5v.vi.k.s.: printed inverted: the head erased and a new one entered, in dark brown ink • G6v.iv.right end: now rests, *l,m*, in dark brown ink: previously perhaps a *sbg* •G6v.v. right end: originally *lg* and a double bar: now a ligature g,d, in brown ink, using the first line of the double bar

> **Binding and Provenance:** Fourth in a set of parts, bound with Josquin, *I Missarum* (1516, No.62)

E-Bbc, M.115 (5). Altus, lacking F1

> **Size of page:** 174 × 230 mm.

> **Watermark:** No.2 throughout

> **Technical comments:** E4r.v.9: actually a *dm*, though there seems to have been something else in the forme as well • F6v.i.after 7: part of a music spacing sort, ca 0.8 mm wide: the top is 4.0 mm above the stave

> **Later corrections and changes:** F4v.ii.after 9: rests, *l,sb* → *b,sb*, by erasure • F4v.v.*custos*: f′ → d′, by erasing the head, and using brown ink • F7r.ii.after 14: rest, *b* erased, and *sb* inserted in brown ink • F10r.iv.above stave:] Pleni Tacet [in brown ink, but not looking like Petrucci's house style

> **Binding and Provenance:** with Josquin, *I Missarum* (1516, No.62)

> **Bibliography:** Pedrell, *Catàlech*, No.427

No.60A. *Cancel for Edition 1*

There is apparently a cancel in gathering B of the unique copy of the Superius: the presence of two lower halves of the same watermark, on B3 and B5, argues that the two bifolia, B3,6 and B4-5, are not conjunct, drawn from the same sheet. It is not possible to tell which bifolio is the original and which is a replacement. For this reason, both are included in the preceding description of the first edition.

———

Extant copy
D-B, Mus.ant.pract.D.227.

> There is no evident anomaly on either bifolio

No.60B. *Second Edition*

A1r] Miſſarum Joannis mouton. | Liber primus. | Missa ſine nomine. | Alleluya. | Alma redemptoris. | Ite3 alia ſine nomine. | Regina mearum.

C1r] Miſſarum Jo. mouton. Liber primus. | T

E1r] Miſſarum Jo. mouton. Liber primus. | A

G1r] Miſſarum Jo. mouton. Liber primus. | B

H8r] [Privilege from Pope Leo X, followed by]

> ¶ Impreſſum Foroſempronii per Octauianum | Petrutium ciuem Foroſempronienſem. Anno | Domini. MDXV. Die xi. Auguſti. Domi-|nante inclito ad excellentiſſimo Principe Domino | Franciſcomaria Feltrio de Ruere: Vrbini Soræque | Duce: Piſauri &c. Domino: Alme Vrbis Præfecto: | REGISTRVM. | ABCDEFGH | Omnes quaterni preter F | qui eſt quinternus

Format and collation: Partbooks: landscape quarto-in-eights. [S:] 16 folios: A-B⁸; [T:] 16 folios: C-D⁸; [A:] 18 folios: E⁸F¹⁰; [B:] 16 folios: G-H⁸

Signatures:] A ii [$4 • − A1 • + F5 (in the form F iiiii)

No foliation

Head-lines: Two parts to the title:

recto:]	Superius.	[A2-B6
	Tenor	[C2-5, D2,4,6,8
	Tenor.	[C6-D1, D3,5,7
	Altus	[E2-F10
	Baſſus	[G2-H7
	[Nil:	A1, B7,8, C1, D8, E1, G1, H8
verso:]	Superius.	[A1-2, A4-B2, B4-7
	Superius:	[A3
	Superius	[B3
	Tenor	[C1v-3v, D1,6,7
	Tenor.	[C4-8, D2-5
	Altus	[E1-6, F8-9
	Altus.	[E7, F10
	Baſſus	[G1-H7
	[Nil	B8, D8, H8

> The most interesting pattern is that of gathering D of the Tenor

Fonts: Music: Petrucci's normal music type

    Staves: six per page: 175–180 mm long:

    Text: Roman, used for all text, "x" = 1.6 mm, "20" = 66 mm • Rotonda, used for title page of S, "x" = 4.9 mm • Rotonda, used for other titles, "x" = 2.8 mm.

In-house corrections: A3*v*.iii.7: now *mf* stamped in: US-Wc • A8*v*.v.mensuration sign: stamped in afterwards: I-BGc •B3r.ii.9–11 after the *m.s.*: stop-press change to 2 *colsb*, b,g, and *ba*: the original (not legible) in GB-Lbl (and corrected in pen), the corrected version in US-Wc • B3r.iii.11 from end: similar pattern of stop-press change to *smg'*: GB-Lbl • B3r.v.6 from end: similar pattern of stop-press change, to *md'*: GB-Lbl • B5*v*.v.penultimate note: *be'* → *sbf'*, erased and stamped in: I-BGc: US-Wc • H5r.iii.last note: *b*, f → g, erased base of note and new note stamped in: CH-Zz

Contents:

	A1r	C1r	E1r	G1r	[Title]
1	A1*v*	C1*v*	E1*v*	G1*v*	[Missa sine nomine] Io.mouton
	A2r	C1*v*.v	E2r.i	G1*v*.v	[Gloria]
	A2*v*.iv	C2*v*.ii	E2*v*.iv	G2*v*	[Credo]
	A3*v*.v	C3*v*.iii	E3*v*.v	G3*v*.ii	[Sanctus]
	A4*v*.ii	C4r.iv	E4*v*.iii	G4r.v	[Agnus]
2	A5r.iii	C4*v*.iii	E5*v*	G4*v*.iv	[Missa] Alleluya
	A5*v*	C4*v*.v	E5*v*.v	G5r	[Gloria]
	A6r	C5*v*	E6r.vi	G5*v*	[Credo]
	A6*v*.vi	C6*v*	E7*v*	G6*v*	[Sanctus]
	A7r.ii	C7r.iii	E8r	G7r	[Agnus]
3	A7*v*.v	C7*v*	E8*v*	G7*v*	[Missa] Alma redemptoris
	A8r.iv	C8r	F1r	G8r	[Gloria]
	A8*v*.v	C8*v*.ii	F1*v*.ii	G8*v*	[Credo]
	B1r.v	D1*v*	F3*v*	H1r.v	[Sanctus]
	B1*v*.iv	D2r	F4r	H1*v*.iv	[Agnus]
4	B2r.ii	D2*v*	F5r	H2r.iv	[Missa sine nomine II]
	B2*v*	D3r	F5*v*	H2*v*.iii	[Gloria]
	B3r.iii	D3*v*.iii	F6r.iv	H3r.iv	[Credo]
	B4r.ii	D4*v*.iii	F7r.iii	H4r	[Sanctus]
	B4*v*.iii	D5r.iv	F7*v*.v	H4r	[Agnus]
5	B5r	D5*v*.iii	F8*v*	H5r	[Missa] Regina mearum
	B5*v*.v	D6r	F8*v*.iv	H5r.iii	[Gloria]
	B6r	D6*v*.iii	F9r.vi	H6r	[Credo]
	B7r	D7*v*	F10r.iv	H7r	[Sanctus]
	B7*v*	D8r	F10*v*.ii	H7*v*	[Agnus]
				H8r	[Privilege; Colophon]
	B8r-*v*	D8*v*		H8*v*	[blank]

Extant copies:

A-Wn, S.A.77.C.18. Superius, Tenor, and Altus, lacking the blank B8. The bifolio B4-5 is a cancel (see below)

    Watermarks: No.35 on A3-4, A-7, B1, B3, C3-4, C8, D5-6, D8-7, E-1, E3-4, F1, F3, and F5

    Technical comments: Staves are not always inked to the far end

    Later changes: Manuscript numeration of movements in all parts, 90–114

CH-Zz, Mus.Jac.G.67$_5$. Bassus, complete

    Size of page: 165 × 232

    Watermarks: No.35 on folios G5-6 and H5

    Technical comments: Five staves inked on G7*v*; four on H7*r* and H7*v*. The blind impress of the last two is evident on H7*r*

    In-house correction: H5*r*: see above

    Binding: Bound with *I Motetti de la Corona* (1514, No.55)

    Provenance: From the collection of Erwin Jacobi

    Bibliography: Puskás, *Musikbibliothek*

GB-CW. Altus, complete

    Watermarks: No 35 on E2-1, E6-5, F2-1, F4-3 and F5-

    Binding: With the other Altus parts at Chatsworth

GB-Lbl, K.1.d.11. All four parts, lacking the blank G8

    Watermarks: No.35 on A-6, A8, B1-2, B4-3, C3-4, C-7, D-6, D8-7, E-2, E6-5, F-3, F-5, F9-, G3-4, G-7, H3 and H8-7

    Technical comments: Five staves inked on B7*r*, C5*r*, D2*r*,8*r*, E1*v*,5*r*, F4*r*, G7*v*; four only on H7*r* and H7*v* • A number of last staves are not inked to the right end: A1*v*, B6*r*, C6*r*, E3*v*,5*r*,8*r*, G5*r* and H5*r*

    Corrections and changes:

        In-house: B3*r*.ii, B3*r*.iii, B3*r*.v: see above

        Later: There is a certain amount of touching-up in this copy • B5*v*.vi.penultimate note: now *sb* d' • F7*r*.vi.margin:] Verte

    Bibliography: Johnson and Scholderer, *Short-Title*, p. 454

H-SY, XX.8.b (4). Bassus, complete

    Size of page: 153 × 215 mm.

    Watermarks: No 35 on G-1, G-6, H-2 and H-4

    Technical comments: Only five staves are inked on G7*v*, and only four on H7*r* and H7*v* • The last stave is not inked to the right end on G5*r* and H5*r* • The last two lines of the colophon appear to have shifted in the bed of the press, or perhaps to have been printed at a different time

    Later changes: G1*r*.] Comparavj ET IOSQVINi, ET MOVTONIS o*mniu*m atatum praestantiss. MUSICOR*UM* Cant[io]nes, quod celebrarimorum artificam iudicijs quib*us* cum Romæ cum pontificijs muſ[icis] | Peſaurj cum Dom*e*nico Phinotto, et [struck through] Ferrariæ cum Cypriano Rore et Venetijs cu[m] | Hadriano Willart amantes contulimus habitæ sint Excellentiss[im]ᵃ • Below it, perhaps in the same hand, though later:] Georgij Tamerj • Foliated, from 2*r*, in the hand of Tamer:] lib.4. folio 1.[-15.] • H4*v*.ii.18: *l* tail may have been added in manuscript

    Binding and Provenance: With Josquin, *I Missarum* (1516, No.62) • The name Georg Tamer appears on G1*r*

I-BGc, Cinq.4.985. Superius, complete

    Size of page: 169 × 235 mm.

    Watermarks: No.35 on folios A-5, A-5, B2-1 and B4-3

    Technical comments: Five staves inked on A1*v* and B7*r*. The lowest stave not inked to the end on A1*v* and B6*r* • B4*v*.v.end: music spacing sort, 5.5 × 1.2 mm.

    Corrections and changes:

        In-house: A8*v*, B5*v*: see above

        Later: B2*v*.i.5 from end: *m*, partly filled in, in ink

Binding and Provenance: With the library's copy of Josquin, *I Missarum* (1516, No.62)

US-Wc, M1490.M915. Complete

 Watermarks: No.35 on A-1, A-3, B-4, B-8, C-2, C-4, D-4, D-8, E2-1, E4-3, F2-1, F-6, F-7, G-2, G-3, H-2 and H-4

 Technical comments: Five staves inked on A1*v*, B7*r*, C5*r*, D2*r*,8*r*, E1*v*,5*r*, F4*r*, and G7*v*. Four inked on H7*r* and H7*v*. The last not inked to the end on B6*r* and E5*r* (the fifth)

 Corrections and changes:

  In-house: A3*v*, B5*v*: see above

  Later: A2*r*.vi.20: *b*, *l* with *pausa*, in ginger ink • A2*v*.i.*custos*: a' → g' • A2*v*.ii.*custos*: perhaps c" → b' • A2*v*.ii.end: added *m* rest • A3*r*.vi.rests after 36: *sb,m,l* → *sb,l,l*, in ginger ink • B2*v*.i.5 from end: *m*, filled in • B3*r*.i.rest after 20: *b* → *sb*, in brown ink • B6*v*.i.21: *m* → *sb*, with erased tail • D2*r*.iii.before 31: a note erased, ?was *md* • F7*r*.vi.margin:] Verte

 Provenance: From the Wolffheim collection

 Bibliography: Wolffheim, *Musikbibliothek*, ii, 400

No.60C. *Cancel for Edition 2.*

A cancel bifolio for B4-5 can be found in one copy

There are no significant differences in this cancel

———

Extant copy:

A-Wn, S.A.77.C.18. For the rest of this copy, see above

 Watermark: paper 35 on B4

———

Lost copies: Copies were owned by Colón (Chapman, "Printed", No.42) and by Ottheinrich's chapel at Pfalz-Neuburg (listed in the inventory of 1554, on folio 38r. See Lambrecht, *Heidelberger*, i, p. 111)

Bibliography:

 (a) Rosaria Boccadifuoco, *Bibliografia*, No.2357 • Sartori, *Petrucci*, No.52

 (d) Mouton, *Opera Omnia*, i.

 (e) Noble, "Petrucci" • Boorman, "Editions" • Boorman, *Petrucci* • Sartori, "Nuove," p. 209

Commentary:

1. The first edition probably involved a short print-run, no doubt reflecting the difficult political situation in the Marche at the time. It would have made sense for Petrucci not to tie up too much capital in sheets of printed paper, and indeed Fossombrone was to be sacked only two years later.

2. The surprising appearance of the wrong part-name (Ba[[us.) in both formes of the Superius gathering A probably reflects a pattern in which the Bassus was set immediately before the Superius. It is unlikely that Petrucci's men would have kept a forme standing, with the part-name in it, for the several months that had elapsed since the previous edition, of Josquin's second book.

3. In this first edition, it is not possible to tell which bifolio of gathering B is the cancel. Indeed, if it were not for the pattern of watermarks, the cancel would be invisible. The two bifolia are

on the same paper, and show typographical material in the same condition. Until a second copy of the Superius book surfaces, one can do no more than note that a cancel is present. This further implies that the cancel must have been printed immediately after the edition itself.

4.   The second component of the headlines was, as usual, entered for each page separately, centered on the page:

recto:] Jo. mouton. [A2, B4, E4,5, F8 • Jo. monton. [A3,4,6, B2,3, C2-4, D3-5, E2 • Jo. monton. Alleluya. [A5 • Alleluya. [A7, C5-7, E7 • Alma redemptoris. [A8, B1, C8, D1,2, F4 • Regina mear*um*. [B5-7, D6-8, F9,10 • Jo mouton. [E3, F6,7 • Alleluya [E6,8 • Alma redemptoris [F2,3 • Jo mouton [F5 • [Nil: A1, B8, C1, E1

verso:] Jo. mouton [A1 • Jo. mouton. [A2, B4, E3, F6,7 • Jo. monton. [A3-5, B2,3, C1,3,4, D2-4, E1 • Alleluya. [A6,7, C5,6, E7 • Alma redemptoris [A8, C8, F4 • Alma redemptoris. [B1, C7, D1, F2,3 • Regina mear*um*. [B5-7, D6,7, F8 • Jo. monton [C2, E2 • Jo. monton. Regina mear*um*. [D5 • Jo. monton. Alma redemptoris. [E8 • Jo mouton. [F5 • Jo. muoton. [E4 • Jo. mouton. .Alleluya. [E5 • Alleluya [E6,7 • Regina mear*um* [F9 • .Regina mear*um*. [F10 • [Nil: B8, D8

5.   The second edition has a number of differences:

recto:] Io.mouton. [A2,4–5, B2,4, C2-4, D3-5, E3-4,8, F5-7, H2 (above iv), H3 • Io.mouton [A3, E2,5 G2 • Io mouton. [B3 • Io:mouton. [F8, G3-4, H1 (in error) • Io:mouton [H4 • Alleluya. [A5 (margin), A6-7, C5-7, E6-8, G5-7 • Alma redemptoris [A8-B1, D2, F2,4 • Alma redemptoris. [C8-D1, F1,3, G8, H2 • Regina mar*um* [B5 • Regina mear*um* [B6, D8, H6 • Regina mear*um*. [B7, D6-7, F9-10, H5,6,7

verso:] Io.mouton. [A1,3,4, B2-3, C2-4, D2-5, E1-3,5, F5-7, G1,3,4,7, H2-4 • Io.mouton [A2, B4, C1, E4 • Io:mouton. [G2 • Io.mouton. Alleluya. [E5 • Alleluya. [A5-7, C4 (above iii), C5-6, E5-7, G4 (above iv), G5 • Alleluya [G6 • Io.mouton. Alma redemptoris [G7 • Alma redemptoris [A7 (above v), A8, C7, D1, E8, G8 • Alma redemptoris. [B1, C8, F1-4, H1 • Reginamear*um* [B5 • Regina mear*um* [B7, D5 (margin), D7 • Regina mear*um*. [B6, D6, F8-10, H5-7

6.   The second edition was apparently printed some time in 1520: it is on paper 35, and shows the free use of the earlier of the last two series of initials. The final, smallest series was apparently coming into use while it was printed, for the E and P of that series are used here, while the K is not.

7.   It is notable that the head-lines in the second edition are much more consistent than those of the first. In neither case were they retained in the forme, despite occasional strands of evidence suggesting otherwise. But apparently the typesetter of the second edition had a more consistent view of how to present the details. The evidence suggests that he was prone to add final points.

8.   The cancel to this second edition must have been printed soon after the edition itself. There is little difference between the two copies, and it is possible that we have instead a sophisticated copy made up with two half-sheets of the same printing.

No. 61. Févin: *Misse*

22.xi.1515   *RISM* 1515[1] = F689

This title was published in three editions, of the same date. The first two survive in fragmentary state. There is a possible cancel to the third edition, discussed below. Also see Addenda, p.1173

During their researches in the Archivio di Stato at Pesaro, Professors Teresa Maria Gialdroni and Agostino Ziino have recently discovered a fragment of the third edition of Févin's masses, comprising folios E5–6. They have kindly supplied me with photographs, from which the fragment appears identical to the same folios in the Paris copy: they reported that it has the same watermark. Their study of this fragment will appear as "Un altro frammento petrucciano della messa 'Mente Tota' de Févin", in *Fonti Musicali Italiane* 10 (2005).

> *Edition 1*: E-Bc (part)
> *Edition 2*: A-Wn (part); E-Bc (part)
> *Edition 3*: A-Wn (part); CH-Zz; F-Pn; GB-CW; GB-Lbl; I-BGc; US-Eu

Edition 1.
Only two sheets survive, comprising the first gathering of the Altus part

E1r]   Feuin. | A

Format and collation: Partbooks: landscape quarto-in-eights. [probably AB⁸; C⁸D⁴; E–F⁸; G⁸H⁶]
Signatures: EE ij [$4 • + E1
No foliation
Running heads: In two components: part-names at the outer margin:

　　　Altus.   [E1v,2v,3r,4r–5v,6v,7v–8v
　　　Altus   [E2r,3v,6r,7r

Piece titles, centered: Ant.feuin Sancta trinitas. [E1v • Sancta trinitas. [E2r–3r,4r • Sancta trinitas [E3v • Ant. feuin Mente tota. [E4v • Mente tota. [E5r,6r–7r • Mente tota [E5v • Aue maria. [E7v,8v • Ant. feuin Aue maria. [E8r

Fonts: Music: Petrucci's normal music type
　　　Staves: six per page: ca.177 mm long, 10–92–112.3 mm high
　　　Text: Rotonda
Technical comments: The stave lengths for the formes show the retention of two sets of staves: one appears on EIo and EIIi, and the other on the remaining two formes.

Forme	Outer				Inner			
Page	1/3r	2/4v	7/5r	8/6v	2/4r	1/3v	8/6r	7/5v
Outer sheet	—	183	183	184	179	179	178	179
Inner sheet	179	179	179	178	182	182	184	183

Contents: (as recorded in the unique Altus book)

	E1r	[Title]
1	E1v	[Missa] Sancta trinitas.
	E1v.v	[Gloria]
	E2v	[Credo]
	E3v	[Sanctus]
	E4r.iii	[Agnus]
2	E4v	Ant. feuin [Missa] Mente tota.
	E5r	[Goria]
	E5v	[Credo]
	E6v	[Sanctus]
	E7r	[Agnus]
3	E7v	[Missa] Aue maria.

E7*v*.v   [Gloria]
E8*v*   [Credo]

Extant copy:

E-Bbc, M.115 (4). Altus. Only Gathering E belongs to this edition: for gathering F, see edition 2

    Page size: 174 × 230 mm.

    Watermarks: No.2 on E1-2 and E4-3

    Technical comments: One or two notes which appear to be erased are merely covered with dirty white woolen stuff, presumably from the ink-ball: see, for example, E6r.iv.30 (*sbb'*), and E7*v*.v.1 (*dsbg*)

    Later change: E8*v*.vi.50: g, *m* → *dsb*, tail erased, and a brown ink punctus

    Binding and Provenance: with the rest of this copy, with Josquin, *I Missarum* (1516, No.62)

    Bibliography: Pedrell, *Catàlech*, No.427

No.61A. *Second Edition*

Only a complete Bassus and an incomplete second gathering of the Altus survive

G1*r*]   Feuin | B

H6*r*. below the music:]   Impreſſum Foroſempronij per Octauianuȝ Petrutiu*m* ciue*m* foroſempronien*ſem*. Anno | D*o*mini .MDXV. Die xxii Nouembris.Dominante Inclito ad excellentiſſimo Pri*n*cipe D*o*mino | Franciſcomaria Feltrio *de* Ruere: Urbini Duce: Pisauri ꝛc D*o*mino Alme Urbis p*re*fecto. | Impreſſum cu*m* priuilegio Leonis .X. Pont. Max. ne qua i*n*fra .XV. annos p*re*sens op*us* Im-| primere audeat i*n* terris ecclesias*ti*ci i*m*mediate v*e*l mediate ſubiectis ſub pe*n*a excomunicatio*n*is | ꝛ alijs penis tam imprime*n*tibus *quam* ve*n*dentibus impoſitis prout im priuilegio latius | continetur.

      [to right:] Regiſtrum. | A B C D E F G H. Om*n*es | quaterni p*re*ter D q*ui* eſt duer|nus ꝛ H ternus.

Format and collation: Partbooks: landscape quarto-in-eights. [probably AB⁸ and C⁸D⁴]; [A] 16 folios: E-F⁸; [B] 14 folios: G⁸H⁶

Signatures:] FF ii [$4 • − H4

No foliation

Running heads: In two components: part-names at the outer margin:

      Altus.   [F3*r*,3*v*,4*v*-8*r*

      Altus   [F4*r*

      Baſſus.   [G1*v*-8*r*, H1*r*,1*v*,2*v*,4*r*-6*r*. H4*r* is at the inner end

      Baſſus   [G8*v*, H3*v*

      .Baſſus.   [H2*r*,3*r*,4*r*. H3*r* is at the inner end

      [Nil: F8*v*, G1*r*, H6*v*

    Piece titles, centered: Sancta trinitas. [G1*v*-2*v*,3*v* • Mente tota. [G3*r* [in error], G4*v*-6*v* • Antonius feuin. Mente tota. [G4*r* • Aue maria. [G7*r*-H1*r* • Le vilayn ialoyos [F3*r* • Le vilayn ialoys. [F3*v*-4*v*, H1*v*, H2*v* • Lelayn ialoys. [F5*r* • Le vilayn ialoys [F5*v*, H2*r*,3*r* • Le vilayn ialoys. [H3*v* • Piero zon quarti. [F6*r*,6*v*,7*v*, H4*r*-5*r*,6*r* • Piero zon quarti [F7*r*,8*r*, H5*v* • [Nil: F8*v*, G1*r*, H6*v*

Fonts: Music: Petrucci's normal music type

    Staves: six per page: ca.177 mm long, 10-92-112.3 mm high

    Text: Rotonda

In-house correction: F3*r*.v.19–20: *mb*,*mc*' → *dmc*'pr,*smb*: the note-heads were erased and new ones stamped in: the dot is in brown ink

Contents: (the titles are taken from the Altus book, where it exists: otherwise from the Bassus)

		G1r	[Title]
1		G1v	[Missa] Sancta trinitas.
		G1v.v	[Gloria]
		G2r.v	[Credo]
		G3r.iv	[Sanctus]
		G3v.iv	[Agnus]
2		G4r	Ant. feuin [Missa] Mente tota.
		G4r.v	[Goria]
		G4v.v	[Credo]
		G5v.v	[Sanctus]
		G6r.iv	[Agnus]
3		G6v.iii	[Missa] Aue maria.
		G7r	[Gloria]
		G7v.ii	[Credo]
		G8v	[Sanctus]
		G8v	[Sanctus]
		H1r	[Agnus]
4		H1r.iii	[B: L. margin:] Robertus de feuin. | Le vilayn ialoys:
		H1v	[Gloria]
	F3r		[ending of the Gloria]
	F3v	H2r	[Credo]
	F4v	H2v.v	[Sanctus]
	F5r.v	H3v.ii	[Agnus]
5	F5v.iii	H3v.iv	Pier zon [Missa] Quarti [toni]
	F6r.ii	H4r.ii	[Gloria]
	F6v.iii	H4v.ii	[Credo]
	F7r.iv	H5r.iii	[Sanctus]
	F8r.iii	H6r	[Agnus]
		H6r.[vi]	[Colophon; Privilege]
	F8v	H6v	[blank]

Extant copies:

A-Wn, S.A.77.C.17. Bassus part only. The other parts are from the third edition, described below

    Size of page: 162 × 228 mm.

    Watermarks: Mark 33 on G-1, G-4, H3- and H-6

    Later changes: Movements numbered in manuscript, 115–139 • There is a bad smudge at H5v.i, as if an owner had intended to change the *m.s.*

    Provenance: Presumably originally bound as part of the set opening with Josquin, *I Missarum* (1506, No.30)

E-Bbc, 115 (4). Altus, gathering F, lacking F1-2. F7 has been bound as second folio of Josquin *II Missarum* (1515, No.59). For further details, see the notes on the first edition, above

    Page size: 174 × 230 mm.

    Watermarks: Mark 33 on F5-6

    Technical comments: F6r.vi.1: printed very low and looks like a b, but should probably be a c'

    Corrections and changes:

In-house: F3*r*.v.19–20: see above

Later: F4*v*.iii.*custos*: f → g, by erasing the head

Binding and Provenance: Bound with Josquin, *I Missarum* (1516, No.62)

Bibliography: Pedrell, *Catàlech*, No.427

No. 61B. *Third Edition*

A1*r*]   Mi∫∫e Antonii de Feuin. | Sancta trinitas. | Mente tota. | Aue maria. | Le vilayn ialoys. Roberti de feuin. | Quarti toni. Pier zon.

C1*r*]   FEVIN. | T

E1*r*]   FEVIN. | A

G1*r*]   FEVIN | B

H6*r*: below the music:]   Impre∫∫um Foro∫empronii per Octauianum Petrutium ciuem foro∫empronien∫em Anno | Domini .MDXV. Die xxii Nouembris. Dominante Inclito ad excellenti∫∫imo Principe Domino | Franci∫comaria Feltrio de Ruere: Vrbini Duce: Pisauri & c. Domino Alme Vrbis prefecto. | Impre∫∫um cum priuilegio Leonis .X. Pont. Max. ne quis infra .XV. annos presens opus Im- |primere audeat in terris ecclesiastice immediate vel mediate ∫ubiectis ∫ub pena excomunicationis. | & alijs penis tam imprimentibus quam vendentibus impo∫itis prout impriuilegio latius | continetur.

[to right:] Regi∫trum. | A B C D E F G H. Omnes | quaterni preter D qui e∫t duer- | nus & H ternus.

Format and collation: Partbooks: landscape quarto-in-eights. [S] 16 folios: A-B⁸, [T] 12 folios: C⁸D⁴; [A] 16 folios: E-F⁸; [B] 14 folios: G⁸H⁶

Signatures:] AA ij [$4 • − D3, D4 and H4

No foliation

Running heads: Two components: part-name, at the outer corner, and title, centered. For the title, see below, in "Comments"

Superius.	[A1*v*-B7*v*
Tenor	[C1*v*-D4*v*
Altus	[E1*r*-F8*r*
Ba∫∫us	[G1*v*-H6*r*
[Nil:	A1*r*, B8*r-v*, C1*r*, E1*r*, F8*v*, G1*r*, H6*v*

Fonts: Music: Petrucci's normal music type

Staves: six per page: 177 mm long: 10-93-114 mm high

Text: Roman • A Rotonda font is used for the title

Textual comments: A complete list of variants with the surviving Bassus of the second edition can be found in Boorman, *Petrucci*, p. 337

In-house corrections: B4*v*.margin:] pier zun quarti toni [added, in brown ink: A-Wn, F-Pn, GB-Lbl, I-BGc • H1*v*.v.rest after 23: *sb*, probably stamped in: CH-Zz

Contents:

	A1*r*	C1*r*	E1*r*	G1*r*	[Title]
1	A1*v*	C1*v*	E1*v*	G1*v*	Antonius de feuin. [Missa] Sancta trinitas.
	A2*r*	C1*v*.v	E1*v*.iv	G1*v*.v	[Gloria]
	A2*v*	C2*v*	E2*v*	G2*r*.v	[Credo]
	A3*v*	C3*v*	E3*v*	G3*r*.iv	[Sanctus]
	A4*r*	C4*r*	E4*r*.iii	G3*v*.iv	[Agnus]

2	A4*v*	C4*r*.iii	E4*v*	G4*r*	Ant. feuin. [Missa] Mente tota.
	A5*r*	C4*v*	E5*r*	G4*r*.v	[Gloria]
	A5*v*	C5*r*	E5*v*	G4*v*.v	[Credo]
	A6*r*.v	C5*v*.v	E6*v*	G5*v*.v	[Sanctus]
	A6*v*.iv	C6*r*.iv	E7*r*	G6*r*.v	[Agnus]
3	A7*r*.iii	C6*v*.iii	E7*v*	G6*v*.iii	[L. margin:] Ant. de feuin. [Missa] Aue maria.
	A7*v*	C7*r*	E7*v*.v	G7*r*	[Gloria]
	A8*r*	C7*v*	E8*v*	G7*v*.ii	[Credo]
	A8*v*.v	C8*v*	F1*v*	G8*v*	[Sanctus]
	B1*r*.v	C8*v*.v	F2*r*	H1*r*	[Agnus]
4	B1*v*.iii	D1*r*	F2*v*	H1*r*.iii	[margin:] Robertus de feuin. | [Missa] Le uilayn ialoys.
	B2*r*	D1*r*.iv	F2*v*.vi	H1*v*	[Gloria]
	B2*v*.ii	D1*v*	F3*v*	H2*r*	[Credo]
	B3*v*	D2*r*.ii	F4*v*	H2*v*.v	[Sanctus]
	B4*r*.iv	D2*r*.v	F5*r*.v	H3*v*.ii	[Agnus]
5	B4*v*.ii	D2*v*	F5*v*.iii	H3*v*.iv	Pierzon [Missa] Quarti. [toni]
	B5*r*	D2*v*.v	F6*r*.ii	H4*r*.ii	[Gloria]
	B5*v*.ii	D3*r*.v	F6*v*.iii	H4*v*.ii	[Credo]
	B6*v*	D4*r*.ii	F7*r*.v	H5*r*.iii	[Sanctus]
	B7*v*	D4*v*.iii	F8*r*.iii	H6*r*	[Agnus]
				H6*r*.[vi]	[Colophon; Privilege; Register]
	B8*r*–*v*		F8*v*	H6*v*	[blank]

———

Extant copies:

A-Wn, S.A.77.C.17. Superius, Tenor, and Altus, complete. The Bassus is of the second edition, for which see above

  Watermarks: No.35 on A2-1, A-6, B6-5, C5-6, C8, D2-1, E2-1, E6-5, F3-4, and F8

  Textual comments: A3*r*.caption:] ancta

  Corrections and changes:

   In-house: B4*v*: see above

   Later: Manuscript movement numbers, 115–139 • C3*v*.iii.beneath bar-lines:] Pleni | tacet [in manuscript

  Binding and Provenance: Bound with Josquin, *I Missarum* (1516, No.62)

CH-Zz, Mus.Jac.G.67₂. Bassus, complete

  Size of page: 165 × 232 mm.

  Watermarks: No.35 on folios G-1, G-5, and H-2

  Textual comments: G2*r*.caption:] Sacta trinitas

  Technical comments: G3*v*-4*r*: the inking confirms that stave and text were printed together

  Corrections and changes:

   In-house: H1*v*: see above

   Later: G2*r*.vi.10 from end: stave line drawn in brown ink • G3*r*.vi: stave line drawn in brown ink • G5*r*.i.rests after 2: a first rest of a *l* added in brown ink • H1*v*.v.after 22: erased note D, probably a *sb*

  Binding: With *I Motetti de la Corona* (1514, No.55)

  Provenance: From the collection of Erwin Jacobi

  Bibliography: Puskás, *Musikbibliothek*

F-Pn, Rés.416. Four parts, lacking the blank folio B8

> **Watermarks:** No.35 on A3, A8, B4, C1, C3, D3, E3, E8, F4-3, F8, G1-2, G3, H4, and H5 • The twins are again very clear: one appears on A8, C1, E3, G1-2, and H5

> **Technical comments:** A comparison of several pages of this copy with the corresponding pages in the copy at I-BGc reveals that they present very similar conditions for all details. There are some slight differences, of course: the inner forme of the outer sheet of A is more heavily inked in this copy, at least for the impression carrying text and staves: the same sheet shows evidence, in smudges to the music setting, that it was pulled across the bed of the press after printing. For the outer forme of the inner sheet of A, it appears that the text was printed later than that of the Bergamo copy. There is slightly more damage to several sorts. The alignment of music and text is not always exactly identical in these two copies, as one might expect. The shift seems always to be in the horizontal plane, so that actual pitches are never affected.

> **Corrections and changes:**
> > **In-house:** B4*v*: see above
> > **Later:** manuscript foliation, from 1 in each book

GB-CW. Altus, complete.

> **Watermarks:** No.35 on folios E5-6, E8-7 F-1 and F-5
> **Binding:** with the other Altus parts at Chatsworth

GB-Lbl, K.1.d.12. Four parts, lacking the blank folio B8

> **Watermarks:** No.35 on A5-6, A8, B-5, C-6, C8-7, D-3, E5-6, E-8, F-2, F-5, G5, G-8, H-4 and H6-5

> **Technical comments:** Several places have uninked sections of staves

> **Corrections and changes:**
> > **In-house:** B4*v*: see above
> > **Later:** Leger lines added, in brown ink, on G2r.vi and G3r.vi • G2*v*.ii.3: *sm* → *m*, by erasure • G4*v*.v.2: point added, in brown ink

> **Binding:** Modern
> **Bibliography:** Johnson and Scholderer, *Short-Title*, p. 249.

I-BGc, Cinq.4.986. Superius, complete

> **Size of page:** 169 × 235 mm.
> **Watermarks:** No.35 on folios A-3, A8-7, and B-3
> **Technical comments:** B8*r-v*: the impress of uninked staves can be seen on both folios

> **Corrections and changes:**
> > **In-house:** B4*v*: see above
> > **Later:** Manuscript leger lines, in brown ink, in B1*v*.iii,iv and vi; B2r.i,iii-vi; B2*v*.ii,v,vi; B7r.iii and B7*v*.i and v • A8*v*.foot: pen tries

> **Binding:** With Josquin, *I Missarum* (1516, No.62)
> **Provenance:** B1r.] Prospero Maren di | San Leono [in addition to the comments elsewhere on this set
> **Bibliography:** Fenlon and Dalla Vecchia, *Venezia*, pp. 84–85 (exhibition catalogue, Venice, 2001)

US-Eu. Folios A1-8 only, surviving as pairs of folios joined at the top — A1 to A2, A3 to A4, etc.

> **Size of bifolia:** A1-2: 311 × 212 mm; A3-4: 312 × 214 mm; A5-6: 313 × 214 mm; A7-8: 312 × 213 mm. There is extra material at the foot of f.A6, producing a total width of 233 mm, and implying that this particular folio was not conjugate with the copy of f.A3 in the same collection

Watermarks: No.35 is found on folios A3–4 and A8

Technical comments: The state of damaged sorts corresponds with that found in the copy at GB-Lbl

Later change: A7v: inverted annotations:] Bonaventura Caffarelli [and] Dom*inus* Caffi [and] Pauli [the last struck through

Provenance: Bought from Baron, London • Apparently used as binding strips for a printed book, since there is offset, which appears to come from a printed source, on A5r and A6v. On the other hand, offset definitely from a manuscript written in Latin (and perhaps used as more binding guards for the printed book), can be seen on A1r–2v

No.57C. *Cancel.*

Perhaps the outer sheet of gathering B.

It is difficult to argue for a cancel to this third edition. But it must be more than a coincidence that the only sheets without the half-moon mark comprise all the surviving copies of the same sheet. In addition, B7r has a unique form of the head-line.

If these pages, B1,2,7,8, do represent a cancel, it may even have been printed before the rest of the edition, for the initials in the copy at GB-Lbl seem to better in a better condition than those on surrounding pages. For example the "A" on B1r, is generally better than on C6r, D2r, E5r, and F8r, all of which have additional damage on the left lower half: and the "E" on B2r is definitely better than on A7v and G7r, both of which have real damage to the right raised foot, and to the lower left • In addition, two letters on this sheet do not appear elsewhere in the edition: they are the "P" on B2v and an "A" on B7v. Support for this possibility lies in the pattern by which Petrucci seems to have moved from paper without a watermark towards one, No.35, with a half-moon mark. This single sheet may therefore be another example (cf. Josquin's first book, 1516, No.62) where Petrucci built up the stock of one or more sheets, in anticipation of a complete new edition.

———

Lost copies: Copies were owned by Colón (Chapman, "Printed", No.43), by the Fugger family (Schaal, "Musikbibliothek", No.I/62) and by Ottheinrich (Lambrecht, *Heidelberger*, i, p. 110) • Lippmansohn had a complete copy in 1897 (Sartori, *Petrucci*, p. 178)

Bibliography:

(a) Rosaria Boccadifuoco, *Bibliografia*, No.1384 • Sartori, *Petrucci*, No.53

(d) Fevin, *Oeuvres* • R. Févin, *Collected*

(e) Noble, "Petrucci" • Boorman, "Editions" • Boorman, *Petrucci*

Commentary:

1. Very little survives of the first two editions. The single gathering of the Barcelona copy must be from the first edition. The paper on which it was printed ceased to be used during 1516, the little that was left being used alongside other papers in the first Fossombrone printing of Josquin's first book. This edition will correspond to the date in all the colophons.

2. The sequence of staves in the first two editions suggests that the text-stave pages were being set by sheets: the inner forme of the first sheet, coming back from the press first, would be available for the outer forme of the inner sheet.

3. The second edition was printed on a paper, 33, that was only used in three editions — all later

printings of books originally printed in 1515 and 1516. Even more significantly, it straddles the time when Petrucci moved from a rotonda to a roman font for underlay in his mass books. It therefore lies after the first edition of Josquin's first book, but before the spate of printings that use the half-moon watermark, No.35. I assume, therefore, that this edition was printed later in 1516.

4. The principal headlines in the third edition, giving the titles of the works, are given here: final points appear erratically, not always taking ink: they have been ignored here:

    Recto:] Sancta trinitas [A2-4, C2-4, E2-4, G2-3 • Mente tota [A5-7, C5,6, E5-7, G5-6 • Ant. de feuin. Mente tota [G4 • Aue maria [A8-B1, C7-8, E8, F1-2, G7-H1 • Le uilayn ialoys [B2-4, D2, F3-5, H2-3 • Robertus de feuin. Le uilayn ialoys [D1 • Pier zon quarti [B5-6, D3-4, F6-8, H4-6 • Quarti toni. Pier zon [B7 • [Nil: A1, B8, C1, E1, G1

    Verso:] Antonius de feuin. Sancta trinitas. [A1, C1, E1 • Sancta trinitas [A2-3, C2-3, G1-3 • Ant. feuin. Mente tota [A4, C6, E4 • Mente tota [A5,6, C4-6, 5-6, G4-6 • Aue maria [A7-B1, C7-8, E8, F1, G7-8 • Ant. de feuin. Aue maria [E7 • Le uilayn ialoys [B2-3, D1, F3-5, H1-3 • Robertus de feuin. Le uilayn ialoys [F2 • Pier zon quarti [B4-6, D2-4, F6-7, H4-5 • Quarti toni. Pier zon [B7 • [Nil: B8, F8, H6

5. This third edition is printed on the half-moon paper, which was in use through the hiatus in Petrucci's output that accompanied the Sack of Fossombrone, and the turbulent political situation, and picked up again later, after a spell of using unmarked paper. In fact, this edition looks to be one of those that followed the Pisano edition of 1520, even later than other editions of the time. Given the number of these editions, it may have appeared at the beginning of 1521.

6. The potential cancel sheet can hardly be dated: if it predates the edition, as I suggest, it must lie with the few editions on unmarked paper, including the fourth in the *Corona* series. This would put it securely in late 1519 or early 1520.

No. 62. Josquin: *I Missarum*

29.v.1516   *RISM* J 667 and J 668

This book must have remained popular, for there are four printings during Petrucci's years in Fossombrone, in addition to the two Venetian editions (Nos.4 and 30). The two copies cited by RISM at J667 should belong here. See the note under Josquin, *III Missarum* (1514, No.54), above.

The first two editions use a rotonda text font, while the last two use roman. Since many of the copies are sophisticated, often showing rotonda and roman typefaces on adjacent pages, an outline of their distribution across the printings is given here:

part:	Superius					Tenor			Altus					Bassus			
sheet:	A1	A2	B1	B2	B3	C1	C2	D1	E1	E2	F1	F2	F3	G1	G2	H1	H2
A-Wn, 19	4	4	4	4	4	4	4	4	4	4	4	4	4	4	4	4	4
B-Br														4	4	4	4
D-B	3	3	3	3	2	3	3	2	1	1	3	3	2	2	2	2	3
D-Mbs	3	3	1	1	2	4	4	4	4	4	4	4	4	2	3	2	1
E-Bbc									4	4	4	4	4				
GB-CW									4	4	4	4	4				
GB-Lbl	4	4	4	4	4	4	4	4	4	4	4	4	4	4	4	2	4
H-SY														4	4	4	4

I-Ac	4	4	4	4	4	4	4	4	4	4	4	4	4	4	4	4 4
I-Bc	1	1	1	1	1	1	1	1	1	1	1	1	1	1	1	1 1
I-BGc	4	4	4	4	4											
I-FBR							4									
I-Rvat	1	1	1	1	1	1	1	2	2	1	1	1	2	2	1	2 1
US-R, c.1	3	3	3	3	2									2	3	2 3
US-R, c.2	1	1	1	1	1											
US-Wc	4	4	4	4	4	4	4	4	4	4	4	4	4	4	4	4 4

First Fossombrone Edition.

This survives complete

A1r] Liber primus Miſſarum Joſquin. | Lomme arme. Super voces muſicales | La.ſol.fa.re.mi. | Gaudeamus. | Fortuna deſperata. Lomme arme. Seſti toni. | S

C12] Liber primus Miſſarum Joſquin. | T

E1r] Liber primus Miſſarum Joſquin. | A

G1r] Liber primus Miſſarum Joſquin. | B

H8r] Impreſſum Foroſempronij per Octauianuꝫ | Petrutium ciuem forosempronienſem. Anno | Domini .1516. Die 29. Mai Dominante inclito | ac excellentiſſimo Principe Domino Franciſco | maria feltrio de Ruere: Urbini Duces Piſauri: 7c. Domino Alme Urbis prefecto. | Regiſtrum. ABCDEFGH. Omnes quater|ni praeter BF qui ſunt quinterni 7 D duernus. | [Petrucci's device]

Format and collation: Partbooks: landscape quarto-in-eights. [S] 18 folios: A⁸B¹⁰; [T] 12 folios: C⁸D⁴; [A] 18 folios: E⁸F¹⁰; [B] 16 folios: G-H⁸

Signatures:] aaA II [$4 • + B5, with an arabic numeral • − A1 • B4 signed] bbB III

No foliation: no running heads or part-names. Titles in the head-line, as listed below

Fonts: Music: Petrucci's normal music type

Staves: six per page: 175–180 mm long, 10-92-112 mm high.

Text: Rotonda

Textual comments: Head lines:

Lomme arme ſuper voces muſicales. [A1v • Lomme arme ſuper voces muſicales [C1v, E1v, G1v

Joſquin. La.ſol.fa re.mi. [A5v • La.ſol.fa re.mi. [C4r.above iii • La.ſol.fa.re mi. [E5r • La. ſol.fa.re.mi. [G4r.above v

Joſquin ſuper gaudeamus. [A8r.above v • Super gaudeamus [C5v.above iv • Super gaudeamus. [E8r • Gaudeamus. [G7r.above iii

Joſquin fortuna deſperata. [B3v • Fortuna [C7r.above iv • Super fortuna deſperata [F3r, margin, reading down • Fortuna. [H2r.above iii

Joſquin [B7r, margin, reading down • Lomme arme. [D1v.above iv, H5r.above iv

Joſquin de pres. [B10r.above iii

Technical comments: Only five staves were inked on A4v,5r, C1v, F6r,9r,9v,10r, H4v, and B8v (where the space of the third stave was used for text): in the copy at I-Rvat, the sixth stave is also uninked on B5r

In-house corrections: G2r.i.22-24: a stop-press correction now reading *sm*d, p.d., *sb*e, *b*d, is present in the copy at I-Bc. In I-Rvat, it is present as a stamped-in correction over an erasure • G5r.v.23: ?*m*b → *sb*a, erasure and new note stamped in

Contents:

	A1r	C1r	E1r	G1r	[Title]
1	A1v	C1v	E1v	G1v	Lomme arme ſuper voces muſicales
	A2r	C2r	E2r	G2r	[Gloria]
	A2v.iv	C2v	E2v.v	G2v.v	[Credo]
	A3v.iv	C3r	E3v.iv	G3v	[Sanctus]
	A4v	C3v	E4v	G4r.ii	[Agnus]
2	A5v	C4r.iii	E5r.iv	G4v.v	Joſquin. La.ſol.fa.re.mi.
	A5v.iv	C4r.v	E5v	G5r	[Gloria]
	A6r.v	C4v.iii	E6r	G5v	[Credo]
	A7r.iv	C5r.iii	E7r	G6r.v	[Sanctus]
	A8r	C5v.ii	E7v.iii	G7r	[Agnus]
3	A8r.v	C5v.iv	E8r	G7r.iii	Joſquin ſuper gaudeamus
	A8v.iii	C5v.vi	E8r.v	G7v	[Gloria]
	B1r.v	C6r.iii	F1r	G8r.ii	[Credo]
	B2v.ii	C6v	F2r.iv	H1r.iii	[Sanctus]
	B3r	C6v.vi	F2v.iv	H1v.iv	[Agnus]
4	B3v	C7r.iv	F3r.iii	H2r.iii	Joſquin fortuna deſperata
	B3v.v	C7r.vi	F3v	H2v	[Gloria]
	B4v	C7v.iii	F4r.iii	H3r.iii	[Credo]
	B6r	C8v	F5r.iii	H4r	[Sanctus]
	B6v.iv	D1r.iv	F5v	H4v.v	[Agnus]
5	B7r.iii	D1v.iv	F6r	H5r.iv	Joſquin
					[T:] Lomme arme
	B7v	D2r	F6v	H5v	[Gloria]
	B8r.iii	D2v	F7v	H6r	[Credo]
	B9r	D3r.iv	F8v.iv	H6v.v	[Sanctus]
	B9v	D3v	F9r.ii	H7r.iii	[Agnus]
6	B10r.iii	D3v.iii	F10r	H7v	Joſquin de pres. AMica mea oculi
				H8r	[Colophon; Register; Device]

Extant copies:

D-B, Mus.ant.pract.D 227. Only gathering E at this stage. The rest of the copy is described with the second and third editions, below

> **Page size:** Altus: 226 × 153 mm. • Other parts, 231 × 165 mm.
>
> **Watermarks:** No.2 on E4-3 • No.6 on E7-8
>
> **Later changes:** E1v.v.40: d → e, note-head erased, and a new one in brown ink • E4v.v.21-22: a stmped-in *sb* g, later erased leaving a hole, followed by *m* → *sm* in ink
>
> **Binding:** The Altus has a modern binding • The other books have a (probably) Italian binding, with three blind rolled frames, and gold florets in the corners. Within the frames is a gold-stamped panel of floral design, and individual stamped letters within a cartouche, of the part name on the front board, and on the back] MI IOSQVIN • One paste-down at front and back
>
> **Provenance:** A1r] Francisci Marie Picolominej Episcopi Pientinj, et Ilcinensis. [also found on C1r and G1r • The Altus has no such ownership mark. It also has a different D-B mark

D-Mbs, 4°.Mus.Pr.194/9. Only the sheets comprising ff.B1-4,7-10 and H3-6. The rest of the copy is described in various editions, below.

Watermarks: No.34 on B3-4, B10-9 • No.35 on H5-6

Textual comments: Signatures: B2 reads bbB; B4 reads bbB III

Later change: H3*r*.iii.10: *b* printed void but not cleanly: scratched clear

Binding: Bound with nine other volumes, in original vellum, in four of a set of five part-books • The part-name is on the front of each book • The Altus and Tenor parts are bound into the opposite part-books. The set comprises: (1) Servin: *Psalmi Davidis* (Lyons: Pesnot, 1579); (2) Contini: *I Motetti à6* (Venice: Scotto, 1560); (3) Phinot: *I Motetti à5* (Beringen, 1547); (4) Phinot: *II Motetti à6-8* (Lyons: Beringen, 1548); (5) von Bruck: *Cantiones sacrae* (Antwerp: Plantin, 1579); (6) Rore: *Mottetti à4* (Venice: Scotto, 1563); (7) Carulli: *Mottetti à5* (Venice: Scotto, 1562); (8) *I Motetti del Frutto à4* (Venice: Scotto, 1562); (9) *Motetti de la Simia* (Ferrara: Buglhat . . . , 1539); (10) This book

I-Bc, Q.71. Complete

Size of page: 169 × 234 mm.

Watermarks:

A3-4	A7-8	B2-1	B4-3	B5-	C4-3	C8-7	E1-2	E5-6	F5-
2	16	16	16	16	2	6	6	2	2

F8-7	F10-9	H8-7	G6-5	G8-7	H8-7
16	6	2	2	6	6

Corrections and changes:

In-house: G2*r*, G5*r*: see above

Later: Text has been added in brown ink, on B2*r*.ii-iii, F1*r*.vi, F1*v*.i-iii, F2*r*.vi, F2*v*.i, G3*v*.iii-iv, G8*v*.i-iii, and H1*r*.v-vi • MS pagination of Altus, top outer corner:] [i], 1–2 [then at top centre] 3–35 • C2*r*.iv.after 3: p.d.erased • C2*r*.iv.after 41: p.d.erased • C2*r*.iv.after 49: p.d.erased • C2*r*.v.after 4, 10, 21, 28, 34, and 41: p.d.erased • C6*r*.iv-vi: some notes touched up in brown ink • E1*v*.v.40: d → e, note head erased, and drawn in brown ink • E2*r*.iv.after 32: p.d., in brown ink • F1*r*.v.5-6: *sm, sm → f, f*, with brown ink flags • F2*r*.iii.2-9: a brown ink bar-line on either side • G1*v*.iv.before 35: flat sign, brown ink • H6*v*.ii.before 35: E flat, in brown ink

Binding: As for Josquin, *II Missarum* (1515), with blue marbled boards • One modern pastedown and one modern fly leaf at each end of each book • Folios C6 and C7 have been reversed in this binding

Provenance: Martini letter I.II.35, of 22.vii.1746 • Old call number 1014 on A1*r*

I-Rvat, Cap.Sist.235-238. Complete. The following folios belong to the second edition, described below: D1-4, E1,2,7,8, F5,6, G1,2,7,8 and H1,2,7,8

Size of page: 233–235 × 169 mm.

Watermarks:

A6-5	A8-7	B2-1	B4-3	B5	C1-2	C5-6	E3-4	F7-8	F9-10	G4-3	H4-3
2	16	6	16	6	16	2	2	6	6	2	6

Corrections and changes:

In-house: G2*r*: see above

Later: Foliation in a 16th-century hand • The flyleaves of the Tenor, Altus, and Bassus books have a 16th-century index of all the volumes bound together • The Tenor book initially labeled the volume of LaRue masses as] Quarti libri [(i.e., of Josquin), which was corrected, probably immediately, to] Petri de la Rue [: the Bassus book has the forename] Giovanni [added to Ghiselin's name, probably in a later 16th-century hand] •

C4r.v.after 2; dot erased • C4r.v.after 35: dot erased • C4v.ii.after 4: *bg*, in brown ink • C6r. ii-iii, touched up poor impressions, in brown ink • C6r.iv.last ligature: numerals 2 and 4 above, in the same brown ink • C7r.v.last ligature: b, a → g, f, with new stave line, in ink

Binding: Bound with several other volumes,in original 16th-century leather over paper boards, decorated with rolls and stamps in blind • The paper board at the back of the Altus has been badly damaged, with the last page of the volume of Ghiselin masses. As a result, the text on one of the internal sheets can be read: it is printed, in two columns, apparently about 77.5 mm wide, with a rotonda font of "x" = 1.9 mm and "10" = 49 mm. The text reads, in part:] sine lice*n*tia iui pe*r*lati [. . .] | [. . .] [ed [i de facto te[tificat*ur* [ine lice*n*tia videtur | [. . .] • One paste-down at the front of the S, T, and A. The Altus has a watermark of a six-pointed star on a stem • The binding contains the following, with manuscript pagination:

	C	T	A	B
This book	118	111	118	116
		[+ 11a]		
Josquin *II Missarum* (1515)	19–34	12–21	19–36	17–32
Josquin, *III Missarum* (1514)	35–51	22–33	37–53	33–50
	[+ 51a]		[+ 53a]	
LaRue, *Misse* (1503)	52–67	34–43	54–69	51–64
Agricola, *Misse* (1504)	68–87	44–57	70–87	65–80
Ghiselin, *Misse* (1503)	88–105	58–67	88–106	81–97
			[+ 106a]	[+ 98a]

Provenance: A1*r*.] Hieronijmij Chiti in Lateranen*si* Ba[ilica Magister Capelle | Per Ill*ustrissi*^{mi} Dom*i*no Dominico Ricci Dono Dedit anno 1744. | Dominico inqual Ricci Magistro Cappellæ Pontificiæ etc | Libri quatuor Particulares in auctorib*us* vetu[tis, et Impre[sione Primaua • G1*r*.] I.M.I. | Per Ill*ustri*^ssi^{mo} Dom*i*^{no} Dominico Ricci Cantori ac Magistro Cappelle Pontificiæ | Libros istos Missar*um* Quatuor Vocibus: vetu[tate auctorum, et Impressionis Singulares | Donavit an .1744. Hieronijmij Chiti In Sacrosanc^{ta} Ba[ilica Laterana Capelle Magister

Bibliography: This set of books is described by Chiti in a letter to Martini, dated 28.iv.1746. See Schnoebelen, *Padre*, No.1243, p. 144

US-R, **M1490.D424.M1.c.2. Superius, lacking folios B1, B2, and B10

Size of page: 174 × 241 mm • Folios A3-6 appear not to have been trimmed at all: the resulting size of the sheet would be 482 × 348 mm.

Watermarks: No.2 on A6-5 • No.6 on A7-8 • No.16 on B3-4 and B6-

Technical comments: A5*v* and A6*v* show inking at right

Later correction: B3*v*.vi.*custos*: moved

Binding: Re-bound, wih a copy of Josquin Masses II (1505), No.22 • A single parchment sheet has been folded into oblong quarto and wrapped around the book inside the binding, as padding. It seems to have been part of a (possibly Venetian) scribe's notebook from the later fifteenth century: for example there are accounts on 2*r*, making reference to] Stefanij barberij [and to] Sancte Marci

Provenance: Bought of Liepmanssohn, apparently in 1930 • Acquisition number 150820

No.62A. *Second Fossombrone Edition.*

Just over a third of the 64 folios survive in this printing, B5-6, D1-4, E1,2,7,8, F5-6, G1-8, and H1,2,7,8. It probably did not represent a full edition, but rather a series of printings of individual sheets as needed.

E1*r*]   Liber primus Miſſarum Joſquin. | A
G1*r*]   Liber primus Miſſarum Joſquin. | B
H8*r*]   Impreſſum Foroſempronij per Octauianu3 | Petrutium ciuem forosempronienſem. Anno |
Domini .1516. Die 29. Mai Dominante inclito | ac excellentiſſimo Principe Domino Franciſco |
maria feltrio de Ruere: Urbini Duces Piſauri: 7c. Domino Alme Urbis prefecto. | Regiſtrum.
ABCDEFGH. Omnes quater|ni praeter BF quiſunt quinterni 7 D duernus. | [Petrucci's device]

Format and collation: Partbooks: landscape quarto-in-eights. [According to the colophon: S: 18 folios: A^{8}B^{10}; and T: 12 folios: C^{8}D^4]; [A] 18 folios: E^{8}F^{10}; [B] 16 folios: G-H^8

Signatures:] aaA II [$4 • + B5, with an arabic numeral • + A1 • B4 signed] bbB III

No foliation: no running heads or part-names. Titles in the head-line, as listed below

Fonts: Music: Petrucci's normal music type
Staves: six per page: 175–180 mm long, 10-92-112 mm high
Text: Rotonda

Headings: copied from the first edition

In-house corrections: G2r.i.22-24: a stop-press correction now reading *sm*d, p.d., *sb*e, *b*d, is present in the copies at D-B and I-Bc. In I-Rvat, it is present as a stamped-in correction over an erasure • G3r.i.g: *sb*, G → A, erased and stamped in: D-B

Contents: as for the first Fossombrone edition

———

Extant copies:

D-B, Mus.ant.pract.D 227. Folios B5,6, D1-4, F5-6, G1-8, and H1,2,7,8 belong to this printing
    Watermarks: No.2 on G3-4 • No.6 on B6-, D3-4, G8-7, and H7-8
    Corrections and changes:
        In-house: G3r. see above
        Later: D2*v*.vi.2: *mb* erased, and *ma* entered in pale brown • G3*v*.v.11, *m*, f → e, erased note-head and a new one in black ink • G4*v*.vi.rest after 22: *b* → *sb*, by erasure: this may have been originally a *sb* rest, lying low on the stave: G4*v*.vi.rest after 40: similar
    For other details, see the first and third Fossombrone editions

D-Mbs, 4°.Mus.Pr.194/9. Only the folios B5-6, G1,2,7,8 and H1,2,7,8 • The rest of this complete set is described under the relevant editions
    Watermark: No.34 of G8-7 • No.35 on H7-8
    Technical comments: The impress of uninked staves is visible on H8*v*
    For other details, see the first and third Fossombrone editions

GB-Lbl, K.1.d.13. Only sheet H1,2,7,8 belongs to this printing
    Watermarks: No.34 on H7-8
    For the rest of this copy, see the fourth edition, below

I-Rvat, Cap.Sist.235-238. Only the folios D1-4, E1,2,7,8, F5,6, G1,2,7,8 and H1,2,7,8 belong to this printing
    Size of page: 233–235 × 169 mm.
    Watermarks: No.6 on D4-3, E1-2, G7-8 and H8-7 • No.16 on F-6
    Corrections and changes:

In-house: G2r: see above

Later: G2r.i.after 2: *b* rest erased • G2r.i.after 4: *b* rest erased • G2v: touching-up in brown
ink

For other details, see the first Fossombrone edition, above

US-R, **M1490.D424.M1. Only three sheets from the two part-books, Superius and Bassus. They
comprise B5-6, G1,2,7,8 and H1,2,7,8.

Watermarks: No.33 on ff.B6-, G1-2 and H7-8

Later corrections and changes:

G1v.i.before 53: added flat, in brown ink • G7r.iv.59: ? → *db*d, brown ink

Binding: Original Medici binding: with oval Medici crest and the inscription:]
MED.PALAT.BIBL.CAES.

Provenance: A2r, in pencil:] 7/26/29 Gottschalk $1150 4v. [and, in a later hand] (lb.primus, 1-2
| lib tertius 1-2) • Acquisition number 154575–154576

For other details, see the third Fossombrone edition

No.62B. *Third Fossombrone Edition.*

Forty folios survive from this printing: A1-8, B1-4,7-10, C1-8, F1-10, G4-5 (presumably with G3
and G6) and H3-6. It is plausible to assume that they were intended to complement the second
printing, even though the inner sheet of G is found in both.

A1r]   Liber primus Miſſarum Joſquin. | Lomme arme. Super voces muſicales. | La. ſol. fa. re.
mi. | Gaudeamus. | Fortuna deſperata. | Lomme arme. Sexti toni.

C1r]   Liber primus Miſſarum Ioſquin. | T

Format and collation: presumably as other editions

Signatures:] aaA II [$4

No foliation or running heads. Some composer and work titles appear in the head-line, see below

Fonts: Music: Petrucci's normal music type

Staves: six per page

Text: Roman

No evident in-house changes

Textual comments: Head-lines:

Lomme arme Super uoces muſicales.	[A1v, C1v
Ioſquin. La. ſol. fa. mi re.	[A5v
La. ſol. fa. e. mi.	[C4r.above iii
Ioſquin. Super gaudeamus.	[A8r.above iv
Super gaudeamus.	[C5v.above iv
Ioſquin. Fortuna deſperata.	[B3v
Fortuna.	[C7r.above iv
Super fortuna deſperata.	[F3r, margin, reading down
Ioſquin.	[B7r, margin, reading down
Ioſquin de pres.	[B10r.above iii

Contents: As for the first edition

———

Extant copies:

D-B, Mus.ant.pract.D 227. Folios A1-8, B1-4,7-10, C1-8, F1-4,7-10 and H3-6 are of this edition.
No watermarks visible

Later correction: F8*v*.vi.51: d', *m* → *sb*, by erasure

For other details, see the first and second Fossombrone editions

D-Mbs, 4°.Mus.Pr.194/9. Only gathering A and ff.G3-6 belong with this edition

Size of page:

Watermark: No.34 on G5-6

Technical comments: A6*r*.i.before 1: music spacing sort, 18.2 × 0.6 mm

For other details, see the first and second Fossombrone editions

For other details, see above

US-R, ★★M1490.D424.M1. Of the Superius and Bassus books (lacking G3 and G6), folios A1-8, B1-4,7-10, G4-5, and H3-6 are part of this edition

No watermarks visible

Later corrections and changes: A3*v*.v.after 50: *sb* rest, in brown ink • B2*r*.ii.24: ? → *sba*, in brown ink • B2*v*.ii.68-69: *m*, *m* → *dm*, *sm* • B3*r*.ii.after Agnus Dei:] duo [in brown ink • G1*v*.i.before 53: added flat, in brown ink • G5*r*.ii.64: *smf* erased

For other details, see the second Fossombrone edition

No.62C. *Fourth Fossombrone Edition.*

This survives complete, and more widely than any of the others

A1*r*]   Liber primus Mi∫∫ar*um* Jo∫quin. | Lo*mme* arme. Super voces mu∫icales. | La. ∫ol. fa. re. mi. | Gaudeamus. | Fortuna de∫perata. | Lo*mme* arme. Sexti toni.

C1*r*]   Liber primus Mi∫∫arum Io∫quin. | T

E1*r*]   Liber primus Mi∫∫arum Io∫quin. | A

G1*r*]   Liber primus Mi∫∫arum Io∫quin. | B

H8*r*]   Impre∫∫um Foro∫empr*onii* per Octauianu3 | Petrutiu*m* ciue*m* Foro∫emproni*en∫em*. Anno | Do*mini* .1516. Die 29. Mai Dominante *inclito* | ac excelle*nti*∫∫imo Pri*n*cipe D*omino* Franci∫co | maria feltrio de Ruere: Urbini Duce: | Pi∫auri: 7c. D*omino* Alme Urbis pr*efecto*. | Regi∫tru*m*. ABCDEFGH. O*mn*es *quater*|ni pr*ae*ter BF qui∫unt *quin*terni 7 D duernus. | [Petrucci's device]

Format and collation: Partbooks. Landscape quarto-in-eights. [S:] 18 folios: A⁸B¹⁰; [T:] 12 folios: C⁸D⁴; [A:] 18 folios: E⁸F¹⁰; [B:] 16 folios. G-H⁸

Signatures:] aaA II [$4 • + bbB5, with an arabic numeral • − A • E3 reads] E III

No foliation or running heads. Some composer and work titles appear in the head-line, see below

Fonts: Music: Petrucci's normal music type

Staves: six per page: 10-92-113 mm.

Text: Roman, "x" = 1.6 mm • large Rotonda font, "x" = 2.7 mm, on H4*v* • Superius title: Rotonda, "x" = 4.9 mm.

Textual comments: Headlines:

Lo*mme* arme Super uoces mu∫icales. [A1*v* • Lo*mme* arme ∫uper uoces mu∫icale. [C1*v*, E1*v*, G1*v*

Io∫quin. La. ∫ol. fa. re. mi. [A5*v* • La. ∫ol. fa. re. mi. [C4*r*.above iii, E5*r*.above iv, G4*v*.above v

Io∫quin ∫uper gaudeamus. [A8*r*.above v • Super gaudeamus. [E8*r* • Super gaudeamus [C5*v*.above iv • Gaudeamus. [G7*r*.above iii

Io∫quin fortuna de∫perata. [B3*v* • per fortuna de∫perata. [F3*r*, margin, reading down • Fortuna. [C7*r*.above iv • Fortuna [H2*r*.above iii

Io[quin. [B7r, margin, reading down • Lomme arme. [D1v.above iv • Lomme arme: H5r.above iv • Io[quin de pres. [B10r.above iii

A number of signatures seem to have been very poorly inked: see, for example, B4 in the copies at D-Mbs and I-Bc, or G4 at H-SY • C2v.third phrase of text:] cancrizer • Rubric at the foot of H4v, in the stave area:]

Ingradus unde nos de[cendant multiplicantes

Con[imiliquae modo cre[cant antipodes uno

Technical comments: Only five staves are inked on the following pages: A5r,7v, B5r,9r, C3r, E1v,5r,5v,6v,7r,9r,9v, G2r, H4r,4v,5v,7v • Only four staves are inked on A4v, C1v, E6r and E10r • On other pages the lowest stave is only partially inked: the fifth on D2r and G1v; the sixth on B6v, C2r and H2r • In other cases there are blank staves: F8r.vi; F9v.v • H4v.v: this stave appears to have been printed at a different time, for it is not aligned with the others. This is particularly evident in the copies at B-Br, GB-Lbl, and US-Wc. This perhaps relates to the unusual typeface on this page

In-house corrections: A5r.iii.mensuration sign: originally reversed cut C: cut C stamped in, in the copies at I-Ac, I-BGc, and US-Wc, though in slightly different positions: in that at A-Wn, it was stamped in twice, the first time with insufficient ink • B3v.vi.33: $m \rightarrow sb$, by stop-press correction: the uncorrected version is in GB-Lbl (corrected by erasure), and the corrected in I-Ac, I-BGc, and US-Wc • C7v.v.last ligature: g,e g,f, by a stop-press correction, found in A-Wn, D-Mbs and US-Wc: other copies have the original reading, corrected in manuscript • F2v.vi.custos: c' → a, erased and stamped in, copies at D-Mbs and I-Ac

Contents: As for the first Fossombrone edition

Extant copies:

A-Wn, S.A.77.C.19. Complete

  Size of page: 164 × 233 mm.

  Watermarks: No.35 on A4, A8-7, B2-1, B5, B-7, C2-1, C4-3, D1-2, E6-, E8-7, F1-2, F5-, F-7, G-1, G3-4, H2-1, and H4-3

  Corrections and changes:

   In-house: A5r, C7v: see above

   Later: E5r.iii.start: ink smudges • G4r.i.18-21: manuscript stave-line

  Binding: Fugger binding: on Superius:] MISSE IOSQVIN | [double-headed eagle: shield, showing, left fleur-de-lys azure on or; right eagle or on azure, with above it] RF | LIB I [On back, the same shield. The other parts have the same shield, with the part-name added • One paste-down and two end-papers at each end

  Provenance: From Fugger

B-Br, III.99,237 A L.P. Bassus, complete

  Size of page: 152 × 227 mm.

  Watermarks: No.35 on ff.G6-5, G8-7, H5-6, and H-7

  Later changes: G4r.i.20: leger line in light brown ink • G4r.ii.last two notes: leger line in light brown ink • H4v.i.20: struck through in light brown ink • H6v.iii.after 17: m.s. of reversed C, in ginger ink

  Binding: A modern binding, made by Vander Heyden of Brussels for the library • Modern paste-down and end paper at each end • In an earlier binding, probably with the library's copies of Josquin II (1515) and Josquin I (1516), this book had red edges

  Provenance: On G1r, the letters] G.A.L. [surround the initial B

D-Mbs, 4°.Mus.Pr.194/9. Tenor and Altus, C-F, complete • For the other parts, see above

  Size of page:

  Watermarks: No.34 on C5 • No.35 on E-6, E8-7, F1-2, F4-3, and F5-

  Technical comments: A6r.i.before 1: music spacing sort, 18.2 × 0.6 mm • The impress of
    uninked staves is visible on H8v

  Corrections and changes:

    In-house: C7v, F2v: see above

    Later: C4r.v.after 2: d, struck through in pencil • F3r.v: leger line, in brown ink

  For other details, see above

E-Bbc, M.115 (1). Altus, lacking folios E1, E8, and F5-6

  Size of page: 174 × 230 mm.

  Watermarks: No.35 on E6, E8, F1, and F7-8

  Later corrections and changes: E4r: the leger line on i is printed: that on ii is in manuscript
    • F2v.vi.16 and 19: probably ink splats: the appearance is as if 16, *m* c', has been struck
    through, and 19, *sb* b, has been raised to c' • F3r.v: MS. leger line, in brown ink • F4r: the
    leger line on iv is printed: that on vi is in MS • F8v.vi.48-53: MS. leger line

  Binding: Bound in a set of Petrucci part-books: (1) This book; (2) Josquin: *Masses II* (1515,
    No.59); (3) Josquin: *Masses III* (1514, No.54); (4) Févin: *Masses* (1515, No.61); (5) Mouton:
    Masses (1515, No.60); (6) La Rue: *Masses* (1503, No.11); (7)/De Orto: *Masses* (1505, No.20);
    (8) *Fragmenta Missarum* (1505, No.24) • Contemporary brown leather boards, blind stamped
    with plain and floral rolls making a border, and a six-pointed star: within the star, the front
    board has a shield with 6 Medici balls, and the word ALTVS. The two boards have been
    mounted on a modern binding • The spine has been rebacked, and now reads] LIBRI
    MISSARVM • Three modern fly-leaves and a modern end-paper, at each end

  Provenance: Presumably Medici

  Bibliography: Pedrell, *Catàlech*, No.427

GB-CW. Altus, complete.

  Watermarks: No.35 on E-6, E8-, F1-2, F4-, and F-5 • The evidence of flaws in the paper
    indicates that these sheets were made at the same time as those in the GB-Lbl copy with
    the same mark, and confirms that they were part of the same impression

  Technical comments: All typography seems identical with that of the copy at I-Ac

  Binding: A modern binding has retained the original parchment covers: the top cover is in-
    scribed:] Missae Josquin quattuor vocibus | A • The single volume contains five titles, all
    by Petrucci: (1) This book; (2) Mouton: *I Missarum* (1515, No.60); (3) La Rue: *Misse* (1503,
    No.11); (4) Agricola: *Misse* (1504, No.13); (5) Févin: *Misse* (1515, No.61)

  Provenance: On front flyleaf: in an 18th-century hand:] Luigi [and] Purchased by S. Arthur
    Strong || All catalogued || 10/xii/24 [and the bookplate of Spencer Compton, 8th Duke
    of Devonshire

GB-Lbl, K.1.d.13. Four parts, lacking folio D4. For H1,2,7,8, see above

  Watermarks: No.35 on A-6, A7-8, B3-4, B6-, B-10, C-6, C-8, D-1, E6-5, E-8, F2, F5-, F-8,
    G3-4, G8-7, and H4-3

  Textual comments: The use of minor color is very pronounced on A2r

  Technical comments: B3v.vi.above notes: music spacing sort

  Later corrections and changes:

    Later: The Tenor book has pencil foliation:] [1], 2-11, [12] • B2r.v.12: f' → e' • B3v.vi.rest
      after 32: *l* → *b*, by erasure • B3v.vi.33: *m* → *sb*, by erasure • C7r.v.25-26: ligature:
      g,e → g,f, in manuscript • E4r.i-ii: manuscript leger lines • F2v.vi.custos: c' → a.

Binding: All parts have]Arundel XN6 [and] Lumley [and] 7.A Ac [on title-pages
Provenance: From the Lumley collection. Jayne & Johnson, *Lumley*, No.2581:] Missae Iosquin
   Fore Sempronii 1515. 4 volum.
Bibliography:
Jayne and Johnson, *Lumley* • Milson, "Nonsuch"
H-SY, XX.8.b. (1). Bassus, complete
   Size of page: 153 × 215 mm.
   Watermarks: No.35 on G3-4, G8-7, H2-1, and H6-5
   Textual comments: G4r.signature: reads ggG II, but the other letters may be present in blind
   Technical comments:
   Later changes: G3v.i.14-16: stave line in brown ink • G4r.i.19–21: stave line in brown ink •
      G4r.ii.last two notes: stave line in brown ink
   Binding: Renaissance white leather, blind stamped, restored in 1988. The surface is in a poor
      condition, though it appears that some of the stamps were pictures of saints. Four tie strings
      on each board, all new • At the front, one paste-down, glued to a modern one: at the back
      a torn 16th-century flyleaf and a paste-down • This binding antedates the inscription by
      Petre Shremi on G1r (for which see below), for it has offset on the paste-down • Bound
      with the following titles: (1) This book; (2) Josquin: *II Missarum* (1515, No.59); (3) Josquin:
      III Missarum (1514, No.54); (4) Mouton: *I Missarum* (1515, No.60); (5) Jhan: *Motetti* (Scotto,
      1543: *RISM* G269); (6) *I delle Muse à4* (Barré, 1555: *RISM* 1555²⁷); (7) Berchem: *I Motetti
      à4* (Scotto, 1555: *RISM* B1978); (8) Perego: *Motetti à4* (Scotto, 1555: *RISM* P1320); (9)
      Volpe: *I Motetti à4* (Scotto, 1555: *RISM* V2558); (10) Padovano: *I Recercare à4* (Gardano,
      1556: *RISM* A1250); (11) *II delle Muse à3* (Barré, 1557: *RISM* 1557²⁰); (12) *IV Armonia
      Celeste* (Gardano, 1556: *RISM* R3081); (13) *I delle Muse à5* (Gardano, 1555: *RISM* 1555²⁵).
      These seem to represent at least two separate purchases and collections. It is unlikely that
      the Josquin and Mouton were bought by the purchasers of the later volumes
   Provenance: Violet book stamp of] BIBLIOTHECA | CARD. HERZAN [a 19th-century
      prelate who is thought to have bought this book in Graz] • The names Georg Tanner or
      Tamer, Petre Shremi and Petre Lehner (probably in that order) appear in various places in
      the set. In this title: G1r: various scribbles, including:] Sum Georgij Tameri [and] Sum ex
      libris Petrj Shremj [and] Shremi [and] Der Gest von diese [inne | der er[te libris Petru
      Shremi | 56 40 Xx | [. . .] 30 [all in different hands. The name Tameri is struck through
      • On front paste-down:] Ex Libris est petre Lehner | Et parens est Jacobus Lehner • On
      back flyleaf in a different but German hand:] Ganzon di Archadelt • On back paste-down,
      a stave of music and the text] Paulus uidman conuentdiner zu Geras und Burger [thought
      by Werner to have been the first owner. Geras was a Premonstratensian house in Styria]
   Bibliography: Werner, "Szombathely"; Werner, "Rarità"
I-Ac, Stampati.N.189 (4). Complete
   Size of page: 168 × 232 mm.
   Watermarks: No.35 on A1, A5-6, B-1, B3, B4-, B-6, C4-3, C-7, D3-4, E2, E6-5, F2-1, F4-
      3, F5-, G5-6, G8-7, H4-3, and H8-7
   Corrections and changes:
      In-house: A5r, F2v: see above
      Later: B2r.v.12: f' → e' • B3v.vi.rest after 32: *l* → *b* by erasure • C7r.v.25-26: ligature: g,
         ?e → g, f • E4r.i-ii: manuscript leger lines • G4r.i: leger line, in brown ink
   Binding and Provenance: with Agricola, *Misse* (1504, No.13)
I-BGc, Cinq.4.984 (1). Superius, complete

Size of page: 169 × 235 mm.

Watermarks: No.35 on ff. A-4, A7-8, B2-1, B4-3, and B-6. The mark on B4-3 appears to be complete and measures 23 × 12 mm

Textual comments: A2r.ii.text:] noluntatis

Technical comments: Music spacing sort above B2r.vi: 2.2 mm high

Corrections and changes:

>   **In-house:** A5r, B3v: see above

>   **Later:** A2v.ii.3rd rest after 11: *b* → *m*, careful erasure • A5r.iv-v: manuscript music, a setting of *L'homme arme* as a *cantus firmus* • B3v.vi.rest after 32: *l* → *b*, by erasure.

Binding: Original calf, with a series of stamps and line rolls, originally with four tie-strings front and back. The front board is more heavily ornamented and carries the letter] S [for the part-name • One fly-leaf and one paste-down at the front, both stubbed through after f.A8: one paste-down at the back. On the front fly-leaf, in addition to the donation inscription, are two doodled alphabets • All edges painted yellow: tabs in top edge for each volume in the set • This book is bound with the Superius part of other Petrucci editions: (1) This book; (2) Josquin: *II Missarum* (1515, No.59); (3) Josquin: *III Missarum* (1514, No.54); (4) Mouton: *I Missarum* (1515, No.60); (5) Févin: *Misse* (1515, No.61); (6) *I Motetti de la Corona* (1514, No.55); (7) *II Motetti de la Corona* (1519, No.64); (8) *III Motetti de la Corona* (1519, No.65); (9) *IV Motetti de la Corona* (1519, No.66)

Provenance: On first fly-leaf, recto, is recorded the gift of the book from Simone Mayr to Fernando Cortesi in 1822 • On a separate leaf between books 2 and 3 of the *Motetti de la Corona*:] Colei per cui mi ace[si un di cantando | e che donato . . . el core | in vita in morte son el suo comando | Julio Xkshkokb laqual e | Tutto sono bene [where the name "Xkshkokb" is probably to be read as "Virginia"]

Bibliography:

I-FBR, s.s. The folio B6 with a part of B3, in one sheet

>   **Size of page:** The whole sheet measures 305 × 149 mm: folio B6r measures 225 × 149 mm. B6 is heavily trimmed at the top and lacks the outer corners; of B3 we have only ca.50mm of staves

No watermarks visible.

>   **Provenance:** From an unspecified binding in I-FBR: from the shape of the fragment, it was certainly used as a binding of a notarial document • This fragment was used in the same binding as the fragment of Petrucci's edition of La Rue's masses, and fragments from an early parchment manuscript. Both have offset on the Josquin fragment

>   **Bibliography** Facsimile in Coviello, *Tradizione*, pls. XVII and XVIII

US-Wc, M1490.D63M3.1516.Case. Four part-books, lacking folio D4

Watermarks: No.35 on A1-2, A6-5, B-4, B-6, B10-9, C2-1, C-6, D3-, E3-4, E8-7, F1-, F-7, G1-2, G-3, H4-3, and H8-7

Textual comments: Signatures: D2 signed ddDI; G4 is correct

Technical comments: The same leading to be found in the copy at GB-Lbl can be seen here on B3v and C7v • On B5r, the inking of the staves suggests that the music forme was the first through the press • This copy also suggests that the last stave on H4v was a later addition

Corrections and changes:

>   **In-house:** A5r: see above

>   **Later:** B1r.vi.rests after 49: *sb, sb* → *sb, b*, with addition in brown ink • B2r.vi.3rd rest after 39: *signum congruentiae* in ginger ink • B3v.vi.after 32: c" erased and rest from *l* to *b* • C1v.iv.added text:] Santa Fortuna [in ginger ink • C4r.v.2: point erased • C4r.v.after 4:

added *sb*a, in ginger ink • E3*v*.i: miscellaneous touchings-up, in ginger ink • E4*r*.ii.leger line: probably in manuscript, black ink • F2*r*.ii.35: above the point:] + [in ginger ink • F2*v*.vi.*custos*: c' → a, in manuscript • F4*r*.v-vi: leger lines in manuscript • F8*v*.vi.48–53: leger line, in ginger ink • G3*v*.i.14–18: leger line, in ginger ink • G4*r*.ii.end: leger line, in ginger ink • G6*r*.iii.6–8: notes touched up in brown • H4*v*.i.20: *m*d erased • H7*v*.v.end: added *l*G, in manuscript

Binding: 19th-century half-leather • Marbled paste-down and end-paper at each end: the flyleaf is pasted to the ouer folio of a 19th-century bifolium

Provenance: Landau-Finaly collection, sold at Sotheby in 1949 • Rosenthal, and thence to US-Wc

---

Early references: It is not clear whether the references cited in the first edition may refer to that, or this, or even the later Pasoti and Dorico editions

Other editions: Two Venetian editions were produced by Petrucci, in 1502 (No.4) and 1506 (No.30). A later edition was produced by Pasoti and Dorico in 1526.

Bibliography:
In addition to the bibliography cited in the first Venetian edition:
(a) Rosaria Boccadifuoco, *Bibliografia*, No.1193 • Sartori, *Petrucci*, No.54
(e) Noble, "Petrucci" • Boorman, "Editions" • Boorman, *Petrucci*

Commentary:

1. This title seems to have remained popular throughout Petrucci's last years, and into the Roman period of his successor. The first three printings were evidently not distinguished in the shop, but stored together, so that sophisticated copies seem to have been the norm. Only one copy of the first edition, now at I-Bc, survives intact. One other, that represented now only by the second Superius part at US-R, might originally have been made from one printing. But the other representatives were apparently sold alongside sheets from later printings.

2. It is doubtful that the second "edition" described above was truly a full edition. Only 24 folios (of a total of 64) survive from this printing, and they can be tentatively dated to sometime in 1517. They can probably be seen as printings of individual sheets replacing depleted stock. However, since copies of these sheets can still be found alongside sheets from the fourth printing, Petrucci must have printed large numbers for at least some of them. Fossombrone was sacked by Lorenzo's forces during May 1517, and it is possible that some of these sheets replaced material destroyed during the Sack.

3. The third printing survives in almost ⅔ of the total book, and can be accounted a true edition. It is notable that these sheets complement those that were printed earlier, perhaps in 1517. This reinforces the idea that the second "edition" had a larger print-run, so that sheets were available for use when a third edition had to be printed. That edition then went through a print-run that balanced the remaining sheets of the second.

4. The book continued to sell, perhaps better than anything else Petrucci printed. At the end of his career, it was completely reprinted for a sixth edition, the fourth at Fossombrone. Four copies of that edition survive virtually intact, with only two anomalous sheets in total. The other copies, all now lacking more than one part-book, might also have been consistent.

5. This fourth edition is late: the pattern of initials includes a preponderance of the new smallest

size letters, as well as a number of the intermediate size that had come into use gradually during 1519. This edition therefore belongs with the series of books printed in late 1520 or 1521. Its placing in that series is a result of study of the deterioration of type-sorts, and more particularly of the older initials.

No. 63. Paulus de Middelburgo: *Parabola christi*

20.xi.1516

A1*r*]   Parabola Chri∫ti | de correctione | calendarii.

C3*r*,foot] ¶ Impre∫∫um per Octauianum petru-|tiu*m* habita lice*n*tia a deputatis iuxta | decretum lateranen∫is conci-| lii. Die uige∫ima No-| uembris. | M. D. XVI.

A2*r*]   ¶ Ad ∫anctiſſimum .D.N. Leonem decimu*m* | Pauli de middelburgo dei & apo∫tolic*ae* ∫edis | gratia epi∫copi foro∫empronie*n*∫is ∫uper correc | tione calendarii parabola.

Format and collation: Portrait quarto. 12 folios: A–C⁴

Signatures:] A ii [$4 • − A1

No foliation

Text block: 28 lines per page

Font: Roman, "x" = 2.15 mm, "20" = 110mm • Title in the Rotonda used for the title of *Motetti de la Corona I*

Technical comments: The only ornamental capital initial is an "I", of a pattern which was used in Paulus's *de recta Paschae*, and which also appears in *Motetti de la Corona I*, third edition • The signature on C2*r* uses a cut-down letter G for the initial • The text font has a new form of long "s"

Contents:

A1*r*	[Title]
A1*v*	[blank]
A2*r*	[Dedication to Pope Leo X: text starts]
C3*r*, foot	[Colophon]
C3*v*–4*v*	[blank]

Extant copies:

No further copies of this title have been seen: it is probable that others exist

GB-Lbl, 3855.a.71. Complete

Size of page: 198 × 139 mm.

Watermarks: No.32 on A2-3, B1-4 and C1-4

No evidence corrections or changes

Binding: Modern • Five fly-leaves at the front and seven at the back. The last of those at the front is of an earlier paper, probably of the 19th-century.

Bibliography: Johnson and Scholderer, *Short-Title*, p. 495

I-PEc, Sc.15 Pl.3°.114. Not seen

This copy is cited in Vernarecci, *Fossombrone*, p. 198, fn

I-Rn, 69.4.D.14. Complete

Size of page: 201 × 132 mm.

Watermarks: No.32 on A2-3, B4-1, and C1-4. That on B4-1 is the twin of the others

Technical comments: A1r: set of initials from the series of rotonda capitals, used as bearers •
B1v.28: text spacing sort, measuring 5.5 × 0.7 mm

Later change: A4v.6:] haurixi [has the "x" struck through, and an "r" written above, in brown
ink

Provenance: A2r: an ownership stamp, including the letters EVB

I-Vnm, Rari 531.9. Lacks last, blank folio

Size of page: 215 × 145 mm.

Bibliography: Fenlon and Dalla Vecchia, *Venezia*, pp. 90–91 (exhibition catalogue, Venice, 2001)

Other editions: Vernarecci, *Petrucci*, p. 191 says that there is a 1523 Silber edition in the Biblioteca Alessandrina of Rome • Also according to Vernarecci, a Signor Narducci had a copy,
of which 8 folios corresponded to Petrucci's edition, and the last four were different

Bibliography:

(e) Marzi, *Questione* • Vernarecci, *Petrucci*

Commentary:

1. This volume presents no place of printing in the colophon. However, it is signed by Petrucci
    and should be assigned to him, on the basis of the type and initial used. Petrucci was in Fossom-
    brone throughout the year, and I can see no reason for believing that he would have been
    anywhere else when printing a work by the city's bishop, despite the frequent mobility of presses
    in Italy at this period.

2. The book presents no unusual features: it is a typical example of a well-printed pamphlet of the
    early 16th-century.

3. The circumstances of this printing are discussed in chapter 9. This book must have been another
    personal statement on the part of Paulus, for the documents of the Council's deliberations on the
    calendar, which he edited and signed, were published by Silber in Rome.

No. 64. *Motetti de la Corona II*

17.vi.1519   *RISM* 1519[1]

There are two editions of this title, both with the same date. The Tenor part-book cited by Sartori
and in *RISM* as being at A-Wn is actually from the edition of 1526, printed by Pasoti and Dorico

First Edition

A1r]   Motetti de la corona | Libro ſecondo. | [crown]

[C1r presumably reads as for the second edition]

E1r]   Motetti de la corona Libro ſecondo | A

G1r]   Motetti de la corona Libro ſecondo | B

H9r]   LEO. pp. X. [etc: as in Josquin, *III Missarum* (1514, No.54), followed by:]

[left:] Dilecto filio domino Octauiano de | petrutiis de forofempronii
[right:] Petrus Bembus
[centre:] [Impreſſum Foroſempronii per Octauianum | Petrutium ciuem
Foroſempronienſem. Anno | Domini .MDXIX. Die xvii Iunii. | | REGISTRVM. | A B C D E F G
H. Omnes quaterni preter | F H qui ſunt quinterni.

A1v]   Tabula.

Io.mouton	Amicus dei nicolaus	XV
Euſtachius de m.regali	Benedic anima mea domino	XI
Io.mouton	Corde & animo xpo	XIIII
Io.mouton	Congregate ſunt gentes	XVI
Lherithier	Dum complerentur	XXI
La faghe	Elizabeth zacharie	XXIIII
Io.mouton	Factum eſt ſilentium	XVIII
Io.mouton	Homo quidam fecit	XVIIII
Iacotin	Interueniat pro rege	II
Acaen	Iuduca me deus	VIII
Io.mouton	Illuminare illuminare	XII
Richafort	Miſeremini mei	IIII
Iacotin	Michael archangele	VI
Io.mouton	Maria uirgo ſemper letare	XX
Acaen	Nomine qui domini	III
Io.mouton	Non nobis domine non nobis	XXII
Io.mouton	Noe noe noe pſallite	XXIII
Maiſtre Ian	O benigniſſime domine Ieſu	X
Io.mouton	O chriſte redemptor	XIII
Euſtachius de m.regali	Omnes gentes plaudite	XXV
Lupus	Poſt quam conſumati ſunt	V
Io.mouton	Peccata mea domine	XVII
Iacotin	Rogamus te uirgo maria	VII
Acaen	Sanctificauit dominus	VIIII
Therache	Verbum bonum & ſuaue	I

Format and collation: Partbooks: landscape quarto-in-eights. [S] 16 folios: A-B⁸; [T not extant, presumably 16 folios: C-D⁸]; [A] 18 folios: E⁸F¹⁰; [B] 18 folios: G⁸H¹⁰

Signatures:] + A II [$4 • − A1

No foliation

Numbering of pieces: in Roman capitals:] I-XXV

Running heads: Include two components: one, centered, comprises the composer's name (as cited below) and piece number, in roman numerals; the other gives the part-name, at the outer corner:

Superius.	[A2r-B8r : on the inner corner on A4v, B6v
Altus.	[E1v,3r,4v,5r,6v,7r-8v
Altus	[E2r,2v,3v,4r,5v,6r, F1v-10r
Baſſus	[G1v-H6r, H7r-v,8v
Baſſus.	[H6v, H8r
[Nil:	A1r-v, B8v, E1r, F10v, G1r, H8v

Fonts: Music: Petrucci's normal music type.

Staves: six per page, 175–180 mm long, 10–92.112.5 mm high

Text: roman: rotonda, used for titles

Textual comments:

Technical comments: Five staves are inked whenever possible: see, in D-LEm, G3*v*, G5*r*, H1*v*, H6*r*, and H6*v*, with only four inked on H8*v* • The right end of the stave is not always fully inked, when the notation does not require it: see A7*r*.v; B1*r*.vi; B8*r*.*v*; F1or.iii

In-house corrections: A6*r*.i.19: *sb* → *b*, by erasure and stamping in, in the copy at I-Vnm: in that at D-Mbs, the change is entered in manuscript, probably later • B1*r*.iv.21: *b* → *l*, in brown ink: D-Mbs, I-Bc • B1*v*.v.43–49: originally *mc"*,*mb'*,*sba'*,*ma'mg'*,*sbe'*,*sbd'*: now *smc"*,*smb'*,*sba'*,*smg'*,*smf'*, *mg'*,*mf'*,*sbe'*,*sbd'*, all in brown ink: D-Mbs, I-Bc • B3*v*.iv.25–26: f",f" → g",g", erased and stamped in: D-Mbs, I-Bc • E5*v*.vi.37: e' → f', erased and stamped in: I-Vnm • G2*v*.v.21: G → A, erasure and manuscript: D-LEm, I-Fn, I-Vnm • G2*v*.vi.rest after 12: *b* (perhaps merely a poorly placed *m*) → *m*, by erasure: D-LEm, I-Fn, I-Vnm • G2*v*.vi.33: c → d: manuscript change in I-Fn, and a stop-press change in D-LEm • G3*r*.ii.23: G → A: manuscript change in I-Fn, and a stop-press change in D-LEm: in the latter there also seems to be a feint stamped-in *le* • • H7*v*: the wrong initial [S] was used: an "M" was later stamped in by hand: D-LEm

Contents:

	A	E	G	[Title]	
	A1*r*	E1*r*	G1*r*	[Title]	
	A1*v*			Tabula.	
1	A2*r*	E1*v*	G1*v*	VErbum bonum & ſuaue	Therache.
2	A2*r*.v	E2*r*	G1*v*.v	INterueniat pro rege nostro	Iacotin.
3	A2*v*.v	E2*v*.ii	G2*v*	NOmine qui domini	Acaen.
4	A3*r*.iii	E3*r*	G2*v*.v	MIſeremini mei	Richafort.
	A3*v*	E3*r*.iv	G3*r*.i★	2/ Cutis mea aruit	
5	A3*v*.iv	E3*v*	G3*r*.iv	POſtquam conſumati ſunt	Lupus.
6	A4*r*.ii	E3*v*.v	G3*v*	MIchael archangele	Iacotin.
	A4*v*	E4*r*.iii	G4*r*	2/ [A] In conſpectu angelorum	
7	A4*v*.iii	E4*v*	G4*r*.v	ROgamus te uirgo maria	Iacotin.
	A4*v*.v	E4*v*.iv	G4*v*.i★	2/ Vt proprium pro nobis	
8	A5*r*	E5*r*	G4*v*.iv	IVdica me deus	Acaen.
	A5*r*.iv★	E5*r*.iv	G5*r*.iii	2/ Ad deum qui letificat	
9	A5*v*	E5*v*.ii	G5*v*	SAnctificauit dominus	Acaen.
	A5*v*.v	E5*v*.vi	G5*v*.iv★	2/ O quam metuendus	
10	A6*r*.iv	E6*r*.v	G6*r*.ii	O Benigniſſime domine	Maiſtre Ian.
11	A6*v*.iii	E6*v*.v	G6*v*.iii	BEnedic anima mea domino	Euſtachius de monte regali.
	A7*r*.iii★	E7*v*	G7*r*.iv	2/ Non ſecundum peccata noſtra	
	A7*v*.ii	E7*v*.v★	G7*v*.ii	3/ Quoniam spiritus pertranſibit	
12	A8*r*.ii	E8*v*	G8*r*.iv	ILluminare illuminare hieruſalem	Io. mouton.
	A8*v*	E8*v*.iv	G8*v*	2/ Interrogabat magos herodes	
13	A8*v*.v	F1*r*.iii	G8*v*.v	O Chriſte redemptor	Io. mouton.
	B1*r*.iv	F1*v*.ii★	H1*r*.iv	2/ O excelſa trinitas	
14	B1*v*	F1*v*.vi	H1*v*	COrde & animo christo [xpo]	Io. mouton.
15	B1*v*.v	F2*r*.v	H2*r*	AMicus dei nicolaus	Io. mouton.
	B2*r*.iii	F2*v*.iii	H2*r*.v	2/ Ad ſacrum eius tumulum	
16	B2*v*	F3*r*	H2*v*.ii	COngregate ſunt gentes	Io. mouton.
	B2*v*.v	F3*r*.v	H2*v*.v	2/ Tu ſcis domine	
17	B3*r*.ii	F3*v*.ii	H3*r*.ii	PEccata mea domine	Io. mouton.

18	B3r.vi	F4r	H3v	FActum e[t [ilentium	Io. mouton.
	B3v.iii	F4r.iv★	H3v.iv	2/ Dum [acrum mi[terium	
19	B4r	F4v.iv	H4r.iii	HOmo quidam fecit	Io. mouton.
20	B4r.v	F5r.iii	H4v	MAria uirgo [emper letare	Io. mouton.
	B4v.iii	F5v	H4v.v	2/ Te laudant angeli	
21	B5r	F6r	H5r.iii	DVm complerentur	Lherithier.
	B5v	F6v	H5v	2/ Spiritus domini	
22	B6r	F7r	H6r	NOn nobis domine	Io. Mouton.
	B6r.v	F7v	H6v	2/ Lauda deum o renata	
23	B6v.iv	F8r	H7r	NOe noe p[allite	Io. mouton.
24	B7r.iii	F8v	H7v	ELizabeth zacharie magnum uirum	La faghe.
	B7r.vi	F8v.v	H7v.iv	2/ Inter natos mulierum	
25	B7v.iv	F9r.iv	H8r.ii	OMnes gentes plaudite manibus	Eustachius de monte regali.
	B8r.ii★	F9v.iv	H8v	2/ P[allite deo no[tro	
			H9r	[Privilege; Colophon]	
	B8v	F10v	H9v-10v	[blank]	

Extant copies:

D-LEm, PM.1303. Bassus, complete

Size of page: 229 × 156 mm.

Watermarks: No.35 on G-5, G-8, H2, and H4-3

Textual comments: G5r.above iii:] Secunpa Pars [i.e., with an inverted "d" • H1r.iv.text:] inmensa • H4r.v: the last note is not colored, but covered with something, probably from the ink-ball

Technical comments: G6r: the text forme was printed after that for G6v • G7r.vi.between 30 and 31: a music spacing sort, 0.8 mm wide • H7v: the initial on this page indicates that it went through the press before other copies of this edition

Corrections and changes:

In-house: G2v, G3r and H7v: see above

Later: G3r.i.40: a, sb → m, with a light ginger ink tail • G3r.i.42: f, sb → m, with a light ginger ink tail: it may have had an earlier printed tail, which was erased • G3r.v.last rests: l, l, b, m: the m struck through, and then re-entered, one space lower, in brown ink • H2r.v.custos: f → g, erasure and in manuscript • H6r.iii.rest after 3: b (i.e. a misplaced m) → m, by erasure • H6r.iii.rest after 22: b (i.e., a misplaced m) → m, by erasure • H7v.i-ii: signatures erased • H7v.i.23: m → sb, by erasure

Binding: A modern binding, of pale brown leather, with titles in gold • One paste-down and one conjugate flyleaf at each end

D-Mbs, 4°.Mus.pr.247/1. Superius and Altus, complete

Size of page: 163 × 241, and 165 × 239 mm.

No watermarks visible

Technical comments: B5v: only five staves are inked • A7v.vi: the left end of the stave is present only in blind • B2r.signature line: spacing sort, 2.4 mm high • E4r.iii.after 1: music spacing sort, 18.2 mm high

Corrections and changes:

In-house: B1r, B1v and B3v: see above

Later: The pieces are numbered in red ink:] 176–200 • A5v.iii.6 from end: sb → m, in brown ink • A6r.i.6: a', sb → b, in black ink • A6r.i..19: g', sb → b, in black ink • B1v.v 3,4,6 and 7 from end: all sm → m, by erasure of flag • B3r.v.clef: from? → C₃, in brown ink

• B3*v*.i.23: *m*, ?a' → c", in ink • B4*v*.ii.10–11: always were *m*, *m*, but over-inked and scratched void • E3*r*.iii.last note: a → c', erasure and brown ink

Binding and Provenance: With *i Motetti de la Corona* (1514, No.57)

I-Bc, Q.75. Superius, lacking folios A2–3. The Bassus is of the second edition, for which see below

Size of page 158 × 230 mm.

No watermarks visible

Corrections and changes:

  In-house: B1*r*, B1*v* and B3*v*: see above

  Later: A6*r*.i.19: *sb* → *b*, in black ink • B1*r*.ii.46: d" → e", in brown ink • B1*v*.vi.16–17: *m*, *m* → *sm*, *sm*, in brown ink • B2*r*.i.21: f' → g', in brown ink

Binding: Slip-case, etc., as for *I Motetti de la Corona* (1514, No.57), the copy I-Bc, Q70

Provenance: Old call number on A1*r*:] 1018

I-Fn, Landau-Finaly Mus 8 (2). Bassus, complete

Watermarks: No.35 on ff.G5-6, G7-8, H2, H7-8, and H5

Technical comments: The register of one impression was a little faulty for the outer forme of the outer sheet of gathering G, resulting in poor alignment of staves and notes: a few minor manuscript changes to G2*v* follow from this

Corrections and changes:

  In-house: G2*v* and G3*r*: see above

  Later: G4*v*.i.14: ?*me* erased • G6*v*.vi.33: erased • G7*r*.iii.rest after 12: *m* erased • All the following are in brown ink, apparently in the same hand as those entered in the copy at I-Bc: • G2*v*.vi.rest after 16: *b* → *sb* • G3*r*.iii.14–18: a bar-line on each side: the word] bis [below • G7*r*.iii.13: *m* → *sb*

Binding and Provenance: With *I Motetti de la Corona* (1514, No.57)

I-Vnm, Musica 203–205. Superius, Altus, and Bassus, complete

Watermarks: No.35 on G2, G3-4 H2, and H4

Corrections and changes:

  In-house: A6*r*, E5*v*, and G2*v*: see above

  Later: The pieces are numbered in manuscript in all part-books:] 27–51 • G7*r*.vi.rest after 12: erased • G7*v*.iii.13: *m* → *sb*, in manuscript

Binding and Provenance: With *I Motetti de la Corona* (1514, No.57)

Bibliography: Fenlon and Dalla Vecchia, *Venezia*, p. 85 (exhibition catalogue, Venice, 2001)

No.64A. *Second Edition*

A1*r*] Motetti de la corona | Libro ſecondo. | [crown]

C1*r*] Motetti de la corona Libro ſecondo. | T

E1*r*] Motetti de la corona Libro ſecondo. | A

G1*r*] Motetti de la corona Libro ſecondo. | B

H9*r*] LEO. pp. X. [etc: as in Josquin, *III Missarum* (1514, No.54), followed by:]

[left:] Dilecto filio domino Octauiano de | petrutiis de foroſempronii

[right:] Petrus Bembus

[centre: starting one line higher:] ſ Impreſſum Foroſempronii per Octauianum | Petrutium ciuem Foroſempronienſem. Anno | Domini .MDXIX. Die xvii Iunii. | REGISTRVM. | ABCDEFGH. Omnes quaterni preter | F H qui ſunt quinterni.

A1*v*] Tabula.

Io. mouton	Amicus dei nicolaus	XV
Euſtachius de m. regali	Benedic anima mea domiıno	XI
Io. mouton	Corde et animo *christo*	XIIII

Io. mouton	Congregate sunt gentes	XVI
Lherithier	Dum complerentur	XIX
La faghe	Elizabeth zacharie	XXIIII
Io. mouton	Factum eſt ſilentium	XVIII
Io. mouton	Homo quidam fecit	XVIIII
Iacotin	Interueniat pro rege	II
Acaen	Iudica me deus	VIII
Io. mouton	Illuminare illuminare	XII
Richafort	Miſeremini mei	IIII
Iacotin	Michael archangele	VI
Io. mouton	Maria uirgo semper letare	XX
Acaen	Nomine qui domini	III
Io. mouton	Non nobis domine non nobis	XXIX
Io. mouton	Noe noe noe pſalite	XXIII
Maiſtre Ian	O benigniſſime domine Ieſu	X
Io. mouton	O chriſte redemptor	XIII
Euſtachius de m. regali	Omnes gentes plaudite	XXV
Lupus	Poſt quam conſumati ſunt	V
Io. mouton	Peccata mea domine	XVII +
Iacotin	Rogamus te uirgo maria	VII
Acaen	Sanctificauit dominus	VIIII
Therache	Verbum bonum & ſuaue	I

Format and collation: Partbooks: landscape quarto-in-eights. [S] 16 folios: A–B⁸; [T] 16 folios: C–D⁸; A] 18 folios: E⁸F¹⁰; [B] 18 folios: G⁸H¹⁰.

Signatures:] + A II [$4. − A1. + F5 and H5, signed] + F IIIII, + H IIIII
No foliation

Numbering of pieces: in Roman capitals:] I–XXV

Running heads: Include two components: one, centered, comprises the composer's name (as cited below) and piece number, in roman numerals; the other gives the part-name, at the outer corner:]

Superius.	[A2r-B10r
Tenor	[C1v,2v-5v,6v-8v, D1r-8v
Tenor.	[C2r,6r
Altus	[E1v-F10r
Baſſus	[G1v-H8v
[Nil:	A1r,1v, B10v, C1r, E1r, F10v, G1r, H9r-10v

Founts: Music: Petrucci's normal music type

Staves: six per page, 173–5 mm long, 10-92-112 mm high.

Text: Roman, "x" = 2.6 mm, "20" = 55 mm. for the Tabula • Roman, "x" = 1.6 mm, "20" = 63 mm, for the Privilege • The two also seem to be used on the same pages • Rotonda, used for Superius title

Textual comments: Details of all variants between this and the first edition can be found in Boorman, *Petrucci*, pp. 349–350.

Technical comments: Five staves are inked when possible, leaving the sixth blind: A8r, B5r, E2v,4v; F5v,7r,7v, G3v, H6r,8v • The right end of the stave is not always inked if the music does not require it: cf. CH-Zz: G3v.v,8r.vi • GB-Lbl: A8r.v, B5r.v,8r.vi, E1r.iv,2v.v,4v.v, F5v.v,

7r.vi,7v.v,10r.iii, G3v.v,8r.vi • Note the use of a major prolation mensuration sign as clef on H3r

In-house corrections: B3v.iv.24–25: *dsb,m*, both f" → g", erased and stamped in, using the original tail: PL-Kj • B5r.v.end:] verte [added in manuscript: GB-Lbl, I-BGc • B8r.i.16: d → e, erased and stamped in: I-BGc • E3r.iii.last: *l*, a → c', note head erased and stamped in: PL-Kj • E4v.ii.24: *sb*, c' → a, erased and stamped in: PL-Kj • G4v.iv.33–34: d,e → e,f: stamped in for the copy at GB-Lbl, and printed after a stop-press correction in those at I-Bc and PL-Kj • G4v.vi.31: a → g: stamped in for the copy at GB-Lbl, and printed after a stop-press correction in those at I-Bc and PL-Kj

Contents:

	A1r	C1r	E1r	G1r	[Title]	
	A1v				Tabula.	
1	A2r	C1v	E1v	G1v	VErbum bonum & ſuaue	Therache
2	A2r.v	C1v.v	E2r	G1v.v	INterueniat pro rege noſtro	Iacotin.
3	A2v.v	C2r.vi	E2v.ii	G2v	NOmine qui domini	Acaen.
4	A3r.3	C2v.iv	E3r	G2v.v	MIſeremini mei	Richafort.
	A3v	C3r	E3r.iv	G3r.i★	2/ Cutis mea aruit	
5	A3v.iv	C3r.iv	E3v	G3r.iv	POſt quam conſumati ſunt	Lupus.
6	A4r.ii	C3v	E3v.v	G3v	MIchael archangele	Iacotin.
	A4v	C3v.v	E4r.iii	G4r	2/ In conſpectu angelorum	
7	A4v.iii	C4r.iii	E4v	G4r.v	ROgamus te uirgo maria	Iacotin.
	A4v.v	C4v	E4v.iv	G4v.i★	2/ [T] Vt proprium pro nobis	
8	A5r	C4v.iii	E5r	G4v.iv	IVdica me deus	Acaen.
	A5r.iv★	C5r	E5r.v	G5r.iii	2/ [T] Et introibo ad altare	
9	A5v	C5r.v	E5v.ii	G5v	SAnctificauit dominus	Acaen.
	A5v.v	C5v.iv	E5v.vi	G5v.iv★	2/ O quam metuendus	
10	A6r.iv	C6r.ii	E6r.v	G6r.iii	O Benigniſſime domine	Maiſtre Ian.
11	A6v.iii	C6v.iii	E6v.v	G6v.iii	BEnedic anima mea	Euſtachius de
	A7r★	C7r.iv	E7v	G7r.iv	2/ Non ſecundum peccata noſtra	monte regali.
	A7v.ii	C7v.iii	E7v.v	G7v.ii	3/ Quoniam spiritus pertranſibit	
12	A8r.ii	C8r.iv	E8v	G8r.iv	JLluminare illuminare	Io. mouton
	A8v	C8v.ii	E8v.iv	G8v	2/ Interrogabat magos herodes	
13	A8v.v	C8v.vi	F1r.iii	G8v.v	O Chriſte redemptor	Io. mouton
	B1r.iv	D1r.v	F1v.ii★	H1r.iv	2/ O excelſa trinitas	
14	B1v	D1v.ii	F1v.vi	H1v	COrde & animo christo	Io. mouton.
15	B1v.v	D2r	F2r.v	H2r	AMicus dei nicolaus	Io. mouton
	B2r.iii	D2r.v★	F2v.iii	H2r.v	2/ [T] Ad ſacrum eius tumulum	
16	B2v	D2v.iii	F3r	H2v.ii	COngregate ſunt	Io. mouton.
	B2v.v	D3r	F3r.v	H2v.v	2/ Tu ſcis domine	
17	B3r.ii	D3r.v	F3v.ii	H3r.ii	PEccata mea domine	Io. mouton.
18	B3r.vi	D3v.ii	F4r	H3v	FActum eſt ſilentium	Io. mouton.
	B3v.iii	D3v.v	F4r.iv★	H3v.iv	2/ Dum ſacrum miſterium	
19	B4r	D4r.iv	F4v.iv	H4r.iii	HOmo quidam fecit	Io. mouton.
20	B4r.v	D4v.ii	F5r.iii	H4v	MAria uirgo ſemper letare	Io. mouton.
	B4v.iii	D5r	F5v	H4v.v	2/ Te laudant angeli	
21	B5r	D5r.v	F6r	H5r.iii	DVm complerentur	Lerithier.
	B5v	D5v.iii	F6v	H5v	2/ Spiritus domini	

22	B6r	D6r.ii	F7v	H6r	NOn nobis domine	Io. mouton
	B6r.v	D6v	F7r	H6v	2/ Lauda deum o renata	
23	B6v.iv	D7r	F8r	H7r	NOe noe noe pſallite	Io. mouton.
24	B7r.iii	D7v	F8v	H7v	Elizabeth zacharie	La faghe.
	B7r.vi	D7v.v	F8v.v	H7v.iv	2/ Inter natos mulierum	
25	B7v.iv	D8r.iii	F9r.iv	H8r.ii	OMnes gentes plaudite manibus	Euſtachius de
	B8r.ii★	D8v.ii	F9v.iv	H8v	2/ Pſalite deo noſtro	monte regali.
				H9r	[Privilege; Colophon]	
	B8v		F10v	H9v-10v	[blank]	

———

Extant copies:

CH-Zz, Mus.Jac.G.67₂. Bassus, complete

> **Size of page:** 169 × 235 mm.
>
> **Watermarks:** No.35 on ff. G-1, G-5, H-5, H-7, and H-10
>
> **Textual comments:** H1r.iv.text:] inmensa
>
> **Technical comments:** H3r.below iii: inked edge of the music forme, lying 3.3 mm below the stave • H3v.iv.before 11: music spacing sorts, 1.1 mm wide.
>
> **Later changes:** Manuscript leger lines, all in brown ink, have been added to G3r.i, iv and vi; G3v.ii and iv; G4v.i; G6v.v; G7r.v-vi; G7v.i, iii and v; G8r.i; and H5v.ii
>
> **Binding:** With *Motetti de la Corona I* (1514, No.57)
>
> **Provenance:** From the collection of Erwin Jacobi
>
> **Bibliography:** Puskás, "Jacobi", p. 36

GB-Lbl, K.1.d.14. Four part-books, lacking the blank folio H10

> **Watermarks:** 35 on A6-5, A7-8, B-6, B-8, C-1, C3-4, D1-2, D-5, E6-5, E-7, F3-4, F-5, F9-10, G4-3, G7-8, H2, H6, and H8-7
>
> **Textual comments:** B5r.iv.26: col *sb*
>
> **Technical comments:** The outer forme of the outer sheet of A was apparently drawn across the bed of the press after printing, and shows smudging of initials and music on A2v, A7r, and A8v. The head-line is not smudged • A text space has taken ink on A2r.iii in the text space
>
> **Corrections and changes:**
>> **In-house:** B5r and G4v: see above
>>
>> **Later:** C7v.iv.21: added leger-line • H2v.i.24: *b* → *sb*, in manuscript • H7v.i-ii: signature erased • H7v.vi.29: leger line added
>
> **Binding:** Modern
>
> **Provenance:** From the Arundel and Lumley collections.
>
> **Bibliography:** BM STC Italian, p. 454 • Burney, *History*, ii, 447–448

I-Bc, Q.75. Bassus, complete. The Superius belongs to the first edition

> **Size of page:** 236 × 168 mm.
>
> **Watermarks:** No.35 on ff.G6-5, G8-7, H1, and H4-3
>
> **Technical comments:** All six staves are inked on f.G3v
>
> **Corrections and changes:**
>> **In-house:** G4v: see above
>>
>> **Later:** Brown ink leger lines have been added on the following pages, probably in the same hand noted elsewhere: G3r.iii and v; G3v.ii and iv; G4v.i; G6v.v; G7r.v and vi; G7v.i, iii and v; and G8r.i • H4v.v.32: a → g, in manuscript • H7v.i-ii: signature erased • H7v.vi.29: leger line added
>
> For other details, see the first edition, above

I-BGc, Cinq.4.987 (2). Superius, complete

    Size of page: 169 × 235 mm.

    Watermarks: No.35 on ff. A-2, A3-4, B6-5, and B7

    Textual comments: A2v: caption present

    Corrections and changes:

        In-house: B5r and B8r: see above

        Later: B4r.iii.35-36 and rest: now *me'*, *bf'*, *brest* • B7v.i.rest after 27: added *l*, in brown ink
            • B7v.iii.1-2: now *sbc"*, *sbb'*

    Binding and Provenance: With Josquin, *I Missarum* (1516, No.62)

Pl-Kj, Mus.ant.pract.P 676. Three complete parts, lacking the Tenor

    Size of page: 150 × 224 mm.

    Watermarks: No.35 on G1, G6, H-4, H-6, H10-9

    Technical comments: The privilege seems to be in the same setting of type found in the PL-Kj
        copy of Corona I • Inpress of uninked staves on A1v • A8r and G8r use the initial I found
        in the nonmusical books • B7v.vi.text: spacing sort about 3 mm high • F3v.v.13: a chord of
        two *sm*, f and d: the two were printed at the same impression.

    Corrections and changes:

        In-house: B3v, E3r, E4v and G4v: see above

        Later: A3v.vi.clef: C_1 in light brown ink, probably over a blind impression • A8v.ii.rest after
            27: $b \rightarrow sb$, by erasure • B1r.ii.46: *m*, d" $\rightarrow$ e", in brown, no erasure • B1r.vi.end: some
            decoration, in light brown • B1v.v.43-44 and 46-47: all $sm \rightarrow m$, by erasure • B2r.i.21:
            m, f' $\rightarrow$ g', in brown ink • B3v.ii.penultimate note: $sb \rightarrow m$, with a brown ink tail •
            B4v.vi.7: col$sb \rightarrow sb$, by erasure • B5v.iv.rests after 7: sb, b, $l \rightarrow b$, l, by erasure •
            B6r.vi.rests after last note: l, b, $?b \rightarrow l,b$, by erasure • E4r.v.clef: $C_2 \rightarrow C_3$, erasure and
            brown ink • F7v.iv.last: brown ink line through the tail of *lc'* • G2v.v.21: b, G $\rightarrow$ A,
            partial erasure and black ink • G2v.vi.33: sb, d $\rightarrow$ B, erasure and brown ink • G3$r$ii.14-
            18: struck through, a brown line before 14, and a double bar line with repeat signs after
            18, in brown ink • G7r.ii.after 12: *m* rest, *ma* $\rightarrow$ *sba*, erasure • H1r.ii.24-25: *dmc*,
            smd $\rightarrow$ *mc*, *md*: brown ink draws an extra large *m* head for the second note, so as to
            incorporate the dot • H2v.i.24: $bd \rightarrow sbd$, in brown ink • H4v.iii.rest after 34: $b \rightarrow sb$,
            by erasure • H6v.ii.final rests: l, $b \rightarrow l$, sb, *m*, erasure and brown ink: part of the *custos*
            is also erased, and a stave-line is touched up • H7v.i-iii.k.s.: flat erased • H7v.i.23:
            $m \rightarrow sb$, erasure

    Binding: Similar to that for Corona I at Pl-Kj, *q.v.*

    Provenance: From Berlin. Probably originally with Corona I, for this has the next acquisition
        number, 17,946 • F10v] Que[to libro e di pirro d'alamanno saluta3 ad amicor*um*

Lost copies: Copies were owned by Fugger (Schall, "Musikbibliothek", I.54) and the chapel of
    Ottheinrich at Pfalz-Neuburg (Lambrecht *Heidelberger*, i, pp. 113-114) • A copy of this or of
    the 1526 or 1527 edition was owned by King Joâo IV. The entry follows one for the first book:
    ] *de la corona*. De Terache, & outros, a 4. lib.1 [Sampaio Ribeiro, *Livraria*, p. 148 • According to
    Sartori, *Petrucci* p. 184, Gaspari reported that Conte Giacomo Manzoni of Bologna sold a Altus
    part-book to the Imperial Library in Vienna. That book does not seem to be there.

Other editions: A new edition was printed by Pasoti and Dorico in Rome in 1526 (*RISM* 1526²)

Bibliography:

- (a) Rosaria Boccadifuoco, *Bibliografia*, No.2341 • Sartori, *Petrucci*, No.56
- (b) Brunet, *Manuel*, iii, cols.25–1926
- (d) Gehrenbeck, *Motetti* • Sherr, *16th-Century*, v (partial edition)
- (e) Boorman, *Petrucci*

Commentary:

1. This is the first avowed edition after the death of Lorenzo de'Medici, usurper of the Urbino dukedom. The political situation, as much as the repertoire, has led me to argue that the immediate source for the music was not Roman, but further north. See chapter 9.

2. The first edition shows a pattern of paper use: watermark 35 can be seen in all three Bassus books, while the Superius and Altus books show no marks at all. This suggests that the work was divided between two presses. It also reinforces an argument that Petrucci was beginning to use paper 35 consistently.

3. The second edition shows a consistent use of Paper 35 throughout: at the same time, it employs both the sets of initials that appear after the beginning of 1519. The first set of these letters begins to be used during the three books of the *Corona* series: but the smallest initials, those that were designed at the end of Petrucci's career, do not appear in Book III or IV, in the earliest printings. They are also not found in Pisano's *Musica*. This puts the second edition into the last series of printings, put out late in 1520 or early in 1521, and, as I suggest, printed as a supply for Petrucci's successor. The detailed placing of this edition, among the others printed at about the same time, is contingent upon analysis of the state of the letters.

No. 65. *Motetti de la corona III*

7.ix.1519   *RISM* 1519²

There is a cancel for the inner sheet of gathering A. For details see below

Edition

Copy used for these data: I-VEaf

A1r]   Motetti de la corona | Libro tertio. | [crown]
C1r]   Motetti de la corona Libro tertio. | T
E1r]   Motetti de la corona Libro tertio. | A
G1r]   Motetti de la corona Libro tertio. | B
H9r]   LEO. pp. X. [etc: as in Josquin, *III Missarum* (1514, No.54), followed by:]
        [left:] Dilecto filio domino Octauiano de | petrutiis de foroſempronii
        [right:] Petrus Bembus
        [centre, one line higher:] ſ Impreſſum Foroſempronii per Octauianum | Petrutium ciuem
Foroſempronienſem. Anno | Domini .MDXIX. Die vii Septembris. || REGISTRVM. || A B C D
E F G H. Omnes quaterni preter | D qui eſt ternus & H quinternus.

A1*v*]   Tabula.

Io[quin	Aue nobili[[ima creatura	iii	a [ei
Io[quin	Aue maria gra*tia* plena	iiii	a cinque
Io[quin	Alma redemptoris	x	a quatro
Carpentras	Cantate do*mi*no canticum	xvi	a quatro
Io[quin	Domine ne infurore	xi	a quatro
	Ecce nunc benedicite	xiii	a quatro
	Felix namq*ue* es [acra	xv	a quatro
Io[quin	Huc me [ydereo	i	a [ei
Io[quin	Mi[erere mei deus	vii	a cinque
Loy[et	O bone iu[u illumina	xiiii	a quatro
Io[quin	Preter rerum [eriem	ii	a [ei
Io. mouton	Quis dabit oculis no*st*ris	viii	a quatro
Io. mouton	Quam pulchra es	xii	a quatro
Io. lebrung	Recu*m*bentibus undecim	v	a cinque
Io[quin	Stabat mater doloro[a	vi	a cinque
Pre michael de uer.	Tulerunt do*minu*m meum	viiii	a quatro

Format and collation: Part-books: landscape quarto-in-eights. [C] 16 folios: A-B⁸; [T] 14 folios: C⁸D⁶; [A] 16 folios: E-F⁸; [B]: 18 folios: G⁸H¹⁰

Signatures:] . + A II. [$4 • + H5 (as H IIIII) • − A1, D4

No foliation or pagination • Pieces numbered in Roman capitals

Running heads: Three components, the part-name, composer's name, and piece number. The first normally appears in the outer corner of the page

recto:]	Sup*erius*.	[A2-7, A8-B7
	Tenor.	[C2, C4-5, C8-D1, D4-D5
	Tenor	[D2-3
	Tenor [ecundus	[centered: C3, C6
	Tenor [ecundus.	[centered: C7
	Altus:	[E2-3, E6-8
	Altus	[F1, F3-8
	Altus.	[F2
	Secundus altus.	[centered on E4-5
	Ba[[us	[G2, G7, H2-8
	Secundus ba[[us	[centered on G3-6, G8-H1
	[Nil:	A1, B8, C1, D6, E1, G1, H9-10
verso:]	Sup*erius*.	[A2-B7: at the inner corner on A7
	Tenor.	[C1-4, C7-D4: at inner corner on C1, and centered on C2
	Tenor	[D5
	Tenor primus.	[centered on C5-6
	Altus:	[E1-2, E5, E7-8
	Altus	[E6, F2-7
	Altus.	[F1
	Primus altus.	[inner corner on E3-4

Ba∫∫us	[G1, G4, G6-7, H1-8: at the inner corner on H3
Prima uox	[nearer centre on G2
Primus ba∫∫us	[centered on G3, G5, G8
[Nil:	A1, B8, D6, F8, H9-10

Fonts: Music: Petrucci's normal music type

Staves: Six per page. 175 mm long, 10-90-112.5 mm high.

Text: Roman throughout

Technical comments: Only five staves are inked when possible, leaving the sixth blind: A4r-5r,6v-7v, B2r,3v,5r,6v,7v, C1v,4v-5r,7r,8r, D5v, E7r, F2r, G3v-G5r, and H1v,2v • In addition, the copies at GB-Lbl, I-BGc, and I-Vnm have only five staves inked on A2r • There are two sizes of symbols used to indicate when a part crosses a page-join:

the hand:	large: C1v	small: C2r
the cross:	large: C2v, E1v	small: C3r, E2r

In-house corrections: B5r.iv.36: b → c', erased and stamped in: I-Bc, I-BGc, I-Vnm, and I-VEaf • C3r.above v:] Resolutio [in brown ink: GB-Lbl and I-VEaf • H4v.vi.21: manuscript leger line: D-LEm, GB-Lbl, I-Fn, and I-Vnm

Contents:

	A1r	C1r	E1r	G1r	[Title]		
	A1v				Tabula.		
1	A2r	C1v	E1v	G1v	HVc me ∫ydereo	à6	Io∫quin
					[T:] Plangent eum		
	A2v	C2r	E2v	G2v	2/ Felle ∫itim magni		
					[T:] pla*n*gent eum		
2	A2v.v	C1v.iii	E3r	G2v.iv	PReter rerum ∫eriem	à6	Io∫quin
	A3r	C2v	E3r.iv★	G3v	2/ Virtus ∫ancti spiritus		
3	A3r.v	C2v.v	E3v	G4v	AVe nobili∫∫ima creatura	à6	Io∫quin
					[T:] Benedicta tu in mulieribus		
	A3v.v	C3r.v	E4v	G5v	2/ Tibi domina glorio∫a		
					[T:] Benedicta tu in mulieribus		
4	A4v	C3v	E5v	G6v	[T] VIrgo ∫alutiferi	à5	Io∫quin
					[S:] AVe maria		
	A4v.iii	C4r	E6r	G7r	2/ [T:] Tu potis es prime		
					[S:] Aue maria		
	A5r.iii	C4r.iv	E6r.v	G7r.iv	3/ Nunc celi regina		
					[S:] Aue maria		
5	A5v	C4v	E6v.ii	G7v	REcumbentibus undecim	à5	Iohannes
					[T:] Illi autem profecti		lebrung
	A6r	C4v.iii	E7r.iii	G8v	2/ [B] In nomine meo		
					[T:] Illi autem profecti		
	A6r.iv	C4v.iv★	E7v	G8v.iv	3/ Illi aute*m* profecti		
					[T:] Illi autem profecti		
6	A6v	C5r	E7v.iv	H1v	STabat mater	à5	Io∫quin
	A7v	C5r.iii	E8r.iii	H2r	2/ Eya mater fons amoris		
7	A8v	C5v	E8v.ii	H2v	MI∫erere mei deus	à5	Io∫quin
					[T2:] Mi∫erere mei deus		
	B1r.ii	C6v	F1r.iv	H3r	2/ [T:] Audi tui meo dabis		
					[T2:] Mi∫erere mei deus		

	B1ν	C7ν	F1ν.iv	H3ν	3/ Domine labia mea
					[T2:] Miſerere mei deus
8	B2r	C8ν	F2ν	H4r	QVis dabit oculis noſtris	Io. mouton.
	B2r.iv	C8ν.iv	F2ν.iv	H4r.iii	2/ Heu nobis domine
	B2ν	D1r	F3r	H4r.iv★	3/ Ergo eiulate
9	B2ν.iv	D1r.iv	F3r.iv	H4ν	TVlerunt dominum	Pre Michael de
	B3r.iii	D1ν.iii	F3ν.iv★	H4ν.v★	2/ Repoſita eſt	uerona.
10	B3r.v	D1ν.iv	F4r	H5r	ALma redemptoris mater	Ioſquin.
	B3ν.ii	D2r	F4r.iv	H5r.iv	2/ Tu que genuiſti
11	B4r	D2r.iv	F4ν	H5ν	DOmine ne in furore tuo	Ioſquin
	B4ν	D2ν.iii	F5r	H6r	2/ Cor meum conturbatum eſt
12	B4ν.v	D3r	F5r.v	H6r.v	QVam pulcra es	Io. mouton.
	B5r.iii	D3r.iv	F5ν.iii	H6ν.i★	2/ [T:] Labia tua
13	B5ν	D3ν	F6r	H6ν.v	Ecce nunc benedicite	[Anon.]
14	B6r	D4r	F6ν	H7r.v	O Bone Ieſu	Loyſet.
15	B6r.iv	D4r.iv	F6ν.iv	H7ν.ii	FElix namque es	[Mouton]
	B6ν.ii	D4ν.i★	F7r.ii★	H7ν.v★	2/ O maria mater dei
16	B7r	D4ν.v	F7ν	H8r.iii	CAntate domino canticum	Carpentras.
	B7ν	D5ν	F8r.ii★	H8ν.iii★	2/ Flumina plauden manu
				H9r	[Privilege; Colophon; Register]
	B8r-ν	D6r-ν	F8ν	H9ν-10r	[blank]

Extant copies:

The copy at A-Wn cited in *RISM* and Sartori, *Petrucci*, p. 186, is in fact of the 1526 edition

CH-Zz, Mus.Jac.G.67₃. Bassus, complete

Size of page: 165 × 232 mm.

No watermarks visible

Technical comments: The damaged sort at G6r.iii.23 and also at H2r.i.12 can also be seen in this library's copies of *Motetti de la Corona IV*, G6ν.ii.23 and of Févin's *Misse*, H4r • H6ν.i: a text spacing sort, 3.8 × 2.8 mm. • Staves are only inked to the end of the notation on G4r.v, G6r.vi, G7r.vi, G8r.vi, and G8ν.vi

Corrections and changes:

Later: G2ν.i.28: lightly struck through, pale brown ink • H4ν.vi.leger line, in manuscript, brown ink • H2r.iv.4 from end: an erasure, perhaps of an inverted "3" • H9r.privilege, below the word:] foroſempronij [is written] (Fossombrone) [in a 19th-century hand

Binding: With *Motetti de la Corona I* (1514, No.57)

Provenance: From the collection of Erwin Jacobi

Bibliography: Puskás, "Jacobi", p. 36

D-LEm, P.M.1303. Bassus complete

Size of page: 151 × 229 mm.

Watermark: No.35 on G-5

Technical comments: Text spacing sorts are visible on G3r.vi (3.1 × 5.0 mm) and G6ν.i (2.8 × 2.8 mm) • H6ν.i: a text spacing sort, 3.8 × 2.8 mm.

Corrections and changes:

In-house: H4ν: see above

Later: H9r: below the word] foroſempronij [a 19th-century hand has entered] Fossombrone

Binding: With *Motetti de la Corona I* (1514, No.57)

D–Mbs, 4°.Mus.pr.247/2. Superius and Altus, complete • For ff.A3–6, see the cancel sheet, below

   Size of page: 163 × 241 and 165 × 239 mm.

   Watermarks: No.35 on E6, E8-7, F1-2, and F-6

   Textual comments: The fact that the missing material on B6v was not added by hand may suggest that the other corrections were added in-house, and that this anomaly was not noticed

   Technical comments: B5r: apparently the frisket was designed to cover the area between the piece number and the part name, and here was cut too generously, so that it also covered part of the stave • Staves are only inked to the end of the notation on A8r.vi, F4v.vi, and F8r.vi

   Later corrections and changes: The pieces are numbered in red ink:] 201–216 • E7r.iii.32: f, $sb \rightarrow b$, new sides to the note, in grey-brown ink

   Binding and Provenance: With *Motetti de la Corona I* (1514, No.57) • Fugger

   Bibliography: Schaal, "Musikbibliothek", No.I/59

GB–Lbl, K.1.d.15. Four parts, lacking the blank folios B8, D6 and H10 • For the cancel sheet A3–6, see below

   Watermarks: No.35 on ff. C5-6, E6-5, E7-8, F-6, F8-7, G6-5, G-7 and H-6

   Technical comments: The following staves are only inked to the end of the notation: C1v.ii, F4v.vi, F8r.vi, G4r.v, G6r.vi, G7r.vi, G8r.vi, G8v, vi, and H1v.v • B5r.i: as in the copy at D–Mbs • C6r.vi: the stave is only inked to the end of the notation, but some ink has remained on the rest of the stave from an earlier impression • E7r.vi: the whole stave is only very lightly inked

   Corrections and changes:

      In-house: C3r and H4v: see above

      Later: B3v.v.13: *sm m*, possibly merely a case of over-inking, scratched void • E1v.v: manuscript stave-lines • F3r.vi.52–55: *sb*e, *sm*d, *sm*c, *sb*d → *m*a, *b*b, by erasure and in brown ink

   Binding: Modern, from the British Library

   Provenance: From the Arundel and Lumley collections

   Bibliography: Burney, *History*, ii, 447–448 • Jayne and Johnson, *Lumley* • Johnson and Scholderer, *Short-Title*, p. 454 • Milsom, "Nonsuch"

I–Bc, Q.76. Superius, complete

   Size of page: 156 × 230 mm.

   Watermarks: None visible

   Technical comments: Staves are only inked to the end of the notation on A7r.v and A8r.vi • The blind impress of stave lines is visible on B2r.vi and B8v

   Corrections and changes:

      In-house: A3r and B5r: see above

      Later: A6r.i.rests after 19: third *l* rest erased

   Binding: Modern, as for *Motetti de la Corona II* (1519, No.64)

   Provenance: With *Motetti de la Corona II* (1519)

   Bibliography: Fava, "Primo", p. 39 (exhibition in Bologna in 1929) • Damerini, *Esposizione*, p. 25 (exhibition in Florence in 1949)

I–BGc, Cinq.4.987 (3). Superius, complete • For the cancel sheet A3–6, see below

   Size of page: 169 × 235 mm.

   No watermarks visible

Technical comments: Staves are only inked to the end of the notation on A7r.v and A8r.vi •
The blind impress of staves is visible on B8r and B8v

In-house change: B5r: see above

Binding and Provenance: With Josquin *I Missarum* of 1516 (No.62)

I-Fn, Landau-Finaly, Mus.8³. Bassus, complete

Watermarks: No.35 on f.H6

Technical comments: A2r: only five staves are inked • Staves are only inked to the end of the
notation on G4r.v, G6r.vi, G7r.vi, G8r.vi and G8v.vi

In-house change: H4v.vi: see above

Binding and Provenance: With *I Motetti de la Corona* (1514, No.57)

I-Vnm, Musica 203–205. Superius, Altus, and Bassus, complete • For the cancel sheeet A3-6, see
below

Watermarks: No.35 on E1-2, E4-3, F-2, F-5, G3 and G5

Technical comments: Staves are only inked to the end of the notation on A7r.v, A8r.vi, F4v.vi,
F8r.vi, G4r.v, G6r.vi, G7r.vi, G8r.vi, G8v.vi and H1v.vi

Corrections and changes:

   In-house: B5r and H4v: see above

   Later: Pieces are numbered sequentially in all parts:] 52–67 • B3v.v.13: *sm* partly scratched
   void • E1v.v: added leger lines

Binding and Provenance: With *Motetti de la Corona I* (1514, No.57)

Bibliography: Fenlon and Dalla Vecchia, *Venezia*, pp. 85–86 (exhibition catalogue, Venice, 2001)

I-VEaf, Busta 205. Complete

Technical comments: Staves are only inked to the end of the notation on A8r.vi, C6r.vii,
F4v.vi, F8r.vi, G4r.v, G6r.vi, G7r.vi, G8r.vi, G8v.vi, and H1v.vi

Corrections and changes:

   In-house: B5r and C3r: see above

   Later: A6r.i.rests after 19: fourth *l* rest erased

Provenance: This copy is probably that cited in the inventory of 1543, as] Libri 4 de motteti
de iosquin

Bibliography: Turrini, *Accademia*, p. 27

No. 65A *Cancel sheet*,

prepared for the inner sheet of gathering A, folios A3-6

Signatures:] + A III [and] + A IIII

Running heads:

   verso:] Sup*erius*. [A3-6

   recto:] Sup*erius*. [A3-6

In-house corrections: A3r.signature: AII → AIII: stamped-in correction in the copy at D-Mbs

Textual comments: The following changes are made from readings in the first edition: A3r.caption:
Sup → Snp [both with abbreviation sig ns over the "p" • A3v.vi.text: hominibus → omnibus •
A4v.iv.text: milieribus → mulieribus • A6r.i.rests after 19: *l,l,l,l,m* → *l,l,l,m* • A6r.iii.text: sedet
dextera*m* dedal → sedet ad dexteram dei → A6r.v.text: sequentibus [with inverted first "e"] signis
saquentibus → seque*n*tibus signis seque*n*tibus • A6v.v.after the notation: the addition of] Verte

Technical comments: Six staves are inked on A4v and A6v • a different set of initials is used on this
cancel

Contents: As in the main edition

———

Extant copies: For the rest of each of these copies, see above

D-Mbs, 4°.Mus.pr.247/2
> **Watermark:** No.35 on A4-3
> **Technical comments:** A3*v*.ii: Two text spacing sorts, 3.0 × 2.7 and 3.0 × 1.1 mm
> **Corrections:**
> > **In-house:** A3*r*: see above
> > **Later:** A3*r*.headline: III → II, in pencil • A3*v*.v.12 from end: *dsb*, g' → a'

GB-Lbl, K.1.d.15
> **Watermark:** No.35 on f.A-6

I-BGc, Cinq.4.987 (3)
> **Watermark:** No.35 on f.A6

I-Vnm, Musica 203–205
> **Watermark:** No.35 on ff.A3-4
> **Later change:** A3*r*.iv.after bar-line: addition of d'*sm*, f'*sm*

———

Lost copies: Copies were in the collections of Ottheinrich's chapel at Pfalz-Neuburg (listed in the inventory of 1554: Lambrecht, *Heidelberger*, i, pp. 107–109), and of João IV (listed in the catalogue after books 1 and 2:] De la corona. Io[quim, & outros. a 4.5,& 6. lib.I.[*sic*] Sampaio Ribeiro, *Livraria*, p. 148

Other editions: Printed by Pasoti and Dorico in 1526 (*RISM* 1526³) and 1527 (*RISM* 1527)

Bibliography:
> (a) Rosaria Boccadifuoco, *Bibliografia*, No.2343 • Sartori, *Petrucci*, No.57
> (b) Brunet, *Manuel*, iii, cols.1925–1926
> (d) Gehrenbeck, *Motetti* • partial edition in Sherr, *16th-Century*, v
> (e) Boorman, *Petrucci*, pp. 274–85 and 352–57 • Kock, *Petrucci*

Commentary:

1. Staves are only inked as far to the right as necessary in many instances, although this does not seem to have been done with a frisket. Instead, given the weak impressions of stave-ends that appear in many places, and the inconsistency of the pattern, it seems to have been done with the ink-balls.

2. Note the layout of music in the Tenor part-book, for the six-voiced pieces. Since both Nos.1 and 3 are *cantus firmus* pieces, while all three present two voice parts in this book, Petrucci is able to use an unusual layout, without which the two voice parts of No.2 would not be so easily laid out. The two *partes* of No.1 are placed at the heads of ff.C1*v* and C2*r*, respectively, and those of No.3 at the foots of ff.C2*v* and C3*r*. Thus the two voices of No.2 can appear on facing pages, the first *pars* on the opening C1*v* and C2*r*, and the second on the next opening. This shows musical sensitivity on the part of house-editor or compositor.

3. The cancel sheet is decidedly later than the edition. It looks to be the last printing at Fossombrone, given the condition of the initial letters and staves, and the quality of presswork. Since some of Petrucci's material was in Rome by mid-summer, so that the book of music by Eustachio Romano could appear in September of 1521, this sheet could not have been printed much later

than early spring 1521. I suspect that it should be dated much closer to the turn of the year, given the need to establish a new press in Rome.

No. 66. *Motetti de la corona IV*

31. X .1519   *RISM* 1519[3]

There is a single surviving example of a cancel bifolium, for B3,6: see below

Edition

A1*r*]   Motetti de la corona | Libro quarto. | [crown]
C1*r*]   Motetti de la corona Libro quarto. | T
E1*r*]   Motetti de la corona Libro quarto. | A
G1*r*]   Motetti de la corona Libro quarto. | B
H7*v*]   [Privilege from Pope Leo X, followed by:]
       [Impreſſum Foroſempronii per Octauianum | Petrutium ciuem Foroſempronienſem. Anno | Domini.MDXIX. Die ultimo Octobris. | REGISTRVM. | A B C D E F G H. Omnes quaterni preter | D F qui ſunt terni.
A1*v*]   Tabula

	Deus in nomine tuo	viiii	a cinque
Io. lebrung	Deſcendi in ortum meum	x	a quatro
	Dulciſſima uirgo maria	xii	a quatro
Noel baultuin	Exaltabo te deus meus rex	xvi	a quatro
	Glorioſus dei apostolus Barth.	xi	a quatro
Ioſquin	Inuiolata integra & caſta es	vi	a cinque
Ioſquin	Lectio actuum appoſtolorum	v	a cinque
Ioſquin	Miſſus eſt angelus gabriel	iii	a cinque
Carpentras	Miſerere mei deus	vii	a quatro
Ioſquin	Miſericordias domini	viii	a quatro
	O crux aue ſpes unica	xiii	a quatro
	O pulcherrima mulierum	xiiii	a quatro
Noel baulduin	Quam pulchra es	xv	a quatro
Conſtantius feſta	Tribus miraculis	i	a ſei
Adrianus	Verbum bonum & ſuaue	ii	a ſei
	Verbum bonum & ſuaue	iiii	a cinque

Format and collation: Part-books: landscape quarto-in-eights. [S] 16 folios: A-B⁸; [T] 14 folios: C⁸D⁶; [A] 14 folios: E⁸F⁶; [B] 16 folios: G-H⁸

Signatures:] [A II [$4 • − A1, D4 and F4

No foliation

Running heads: top outer corner, except as noted

recto:]	Superius	[A2-B8
	Tenor	[C2-D6
	Altus	[E2-5, E7-F5

	Ba∬us	[G6-H3, H5-7
	Ba∬ns	[H4
	Secundus ba∬us	[G2-5
	[Nil:	A1, C1, E1, E6, F6, G1, H8
verso:]	Superius	[A2-4,6, A8-B4, B6-7
	Superius [inner corner]	[A5, B5
	Prima vox [centered]	[A7
	Tenor	[C2-D5
	Altus	[E1-F5
	Primus ba∬us	[G1,2,4
	Ba∬us	[G3, G5-H6
	[Nil:	A1, B8, D6, F6, H7-8

Fonts: Music: Petrucci's normal music type

Staves: six per page, 175 mm long, 10-30-112.5 mm high

Text: Roman • rotonda used for Superius title

Blocks: Crown: A1r • Hand: A2v, A3r, C3v, C4r

Technical comments: Staves are sometimes only inked to the end of the notation: see B2v, B5r, F2v, G8r, and H3r • The inner forme of DI (D1v,2r,5v,6r) shows smudging of music, capitals, and signatures: GB-Lbl

Textual comments: G2v.caption:] Ptimus ba∬us

In-house corrections: B1r: the signature is lacking: stamped in after press-work in the copy at I-Bc, and entered in manuscript in those at D-Mbs and GB-Lbl • C2v.ii.13: $b \rightarrow sb$, by erasure and stamped-in note: GB-Lbl • G2r.iv.31: $b \rightarrow sb$, by erasure and stamped-in note: GB-Lbl • G8v.ii.before 18: flat inserted, in brown ink: CH-Zz, D-LEm, GB-Lbl, I-Fn, and I Vnm

Contents:

	A1r	C1r	E1r	G1r	[Title]		
	A1v				Tabula		
1	A2r	C1v	E1v	G1v	TRibus miraculis	à6	Con∫tantius fe∫ta
	A2v	C2v	E2r	G2v	2/ Ab oriente venerunt magi		
2	A2v.v	C3v	E2v	G3v	VErbum bonum & ∫uaue	à6	Adrianus
	A3v.iii★	C3v.iv★	E2v.iv	G4v	2/Aue ∫olem genui∫ti		
3	A4v.ii	C4r	E3r	G5v	MI∬us e∫t angelus gabriel	à5	Io∫quin
					[A] Mi∬us e∫t gabriel angelus		
	A5v	C4r.iii★	E3v	G6r	2/ Hic erit magnus		
4	A6v	C4v	E4r	G6v	VErbum bonum & ∫uaue	à5	[Anon.]
	A6v.iv★	C5r			2/ Aue ∫olem genui∫ti	à2	
	A7v	C5r.iii	E4r.iv★	G6v.iv★	3/ Aue mater uerbi summi		
5	A8r	C5v	E4v	G7r	LEctio actuum appo∫tolorum	à5	Io∫quin
					[T2] DVm complerentur		
	A8v	C6v	E5r.i★	G7v	2/Facta autem hac uoce		
					[T2] Dum complerentur		
6	B1r	C7v	E5v.iii	G8r	Inuiolata integra & ca∫ta	à5	Io∫quin
	B1r.iv	C7v.iii	E6r	G8r.iv	2/ Que nunc flagitant		
	B1v	C7v.v	E6r.iii★	G8v	3/ O benigna o regina		
7	B1v.iv	C8r	E6v	G8v.iv	MI∫erere mei deus		Carpentras
	B2r.iv★	C8v	E7r.iii	H1r.iv★	2/ Cor mundum crea in me deus		
8	B3r	D1r.iii	E7v.v	H1v.v	MI∫ericordias domini		Io∫quin

	B3r.iv★	D1v	E8r.iii	H2r.ii	2/ Quoniam est dominus	
	B3v.i★	D1v.iv	E8v	H2r.iv★	3/ Miſerere noſtri domine	
9	B3v.iv	D2r	E8v.iv	H2v	DEus in nomine tuo	[Anon.]
	B4r.iii	D2v	F1r.iii	H3r	2/ Voluntarie sacrificabo tibi	
10	B4v.iii	D3r	F1v.iii	H3v	DEſcendi in ortum meum	Iohannes lebrung
11	B5r.ii	D3r.iv	F2r.iii	H3v.v	GLorioſus dei appoſtolus	[Anon.]
	B5v	D3v.iii	F2v.i★	H4r.iii★	2/Poſtquam licaoniam	
12	B6r	D4r.ii	F3r	H4v.ii	DVlciſſima uirgo maria	[Anon.]
13	B6r.iv	D4r.v	F3r.iv	H4v.v	O Crux aue ſpes unica	[Anon.]
14	B6v	D4v.ii	F3v.ii	H5r.iii	PVlcherrima mulierum	[Anon.]
					[T,A,B] O Pulcherrima mulierum	
15	B6v.v	D5r	F4r	H5v	QVam pulchra es	Noel baulduin
	B7r.i★	D5r.iii★	F4r.iv	H5v.iv	2/ Veni dilecte mi	
16	B7r.iv	D5r.v	F4v	H6r	EXaltabo te deus meus rex	Noel baulduin.
		D5v.iv★	F5r.i★	H6v	2/ [T:] Confiteantur tibi à3	
	B7v.v	D6r.iii★	F5v	H7r	3/ Aperis tu manum tuam	
				H7v	[Privilege; Colophon; Register]	
	B8v	D6v	F6r-v	H8r-v	[blank]	

Extant copies:

The copy cited in *RISM* and Sartori, *Petrucci*, p. 188, as being at A-Wn is in fact of the edition of 1526.

CH-Zz, Mus.Jac.G.67[4]. Bassus

Size of page: 165 × 232 mm.

No watermarks visible

Technical comments: The evidence of the change on G8v confirms that bass clefs consisted of two distinct sorts • G7r and H7r: the blind impression of stave vi • H8v: blind impression of all staves

Corrections and changes:

In-house: G8v: see above

Later: G3r.i.fifth rest: probably in ink • G8v.v.clef: first part erased and new one entered • There is possibly an erasure at H3r.i.after 11, where there is a separate down-tail

Binding: With *I Motetti de la Corona* (1514, No.57)

Provenance: From the collection of Erwin Jacobi

Bibliography: Puskás, "Jacobi", p. 36

D-LEm, PM.1303. Bassus, complete

Size of page: 151 × 229 mm.

No watermarks visible

Technical comments: G6r.v: the blind or lightly inked impressions of a row of *m*, at least 29 in number, and all at the same height • G7r and H7r: as in the copy at CH-Zz • H1v.vi.30–34: the lower edges of music spacing sorts have taken ink: they suggest a body width of 2.7 mm.

Corrections and changes:

In-house: G8v: see above

Later: G2v.iii.24–26: colored notes touched up, in ginger ink • H8r.right margin: doodles of note shapes, in brown and black inks

Binding: With *Motetti de la Corona I* (1514, No.57)

D–Mbs, 4°.Mus.pr.247/3. Superius and Altus, complete

    Size of page: 163 × 241 and 165 × 239 mm.

    No watermarks visible

    Technical comments: A5*v*.vi: blind impression of a stave • F2*r*.vi: two spacing sorts, 2.9 × 5.3 and 2.9 × 2.8 mm.

    Corrections and changes:

        In–house: B1*r*: see above

        Later: The pieces are numbered in red ink:] 217–232 • A4*r*.vi: leger line, brown ink • B4*r*.iv.15–16: *m,m* → *sb,sb*, by erasure • E4*v*.ii: leger lines, in brown ink • E5*r*.ii: leger line, in brown ink • E7*v*.vi.ligature: half-colored, in dark brown ink

    Binding and Provenance: Bound with *I Motetti de la Corona* (1514, No.57) • Fugger

GB–Lbl, K.1.d.16. Complete

    No watermarks visible

Technical comments: D1*v*,2*r*,5*v*,6*r* (i.e., a complete inner forme): smudged music, initials, and signatures

    Corrections and changes:

        In–house: B1*r*, C2*v*, G2*r* and G8*v*: see above

        Later: B4*r*.iv.15–16: *m,m* → *sb,sb*, by erasing the tails • C2*v*.ii.after 22: an erasure • E2*r*.iv: signature added, brown ink • G8*v*.v.clef: erased and inserted one pitch higher, brown ink

    Binding: Modern, from the British Museum

    Provenance: From the Arundel and Lumley collections

    Bibliography: Burney, "History", ii, 447–448 • Jayne and Johnson, *Lumley* • Johnson and Scholderer, *Short-Title*, p. 454 • Milsom, "Nonsuch"

I–Bc, Q.77. Superius and Tenor

    Size of page: 165 × 236 mm.

    Watermarks: No.35 on A6-5

    Corrections and changes:

        In–house: B1*r* and C2*v*: see above

        Later: A4*r*.vi: leger line in ink • B4*r*.iv.15–16: *m,m* → *sb,sb*, by erasing the tails • C2*v*.ii.after 21: *sbf* → *sb*rest • C3*r*.iv.1–2: colored in ink • D1*r*.v.21: probably c → d

    Binding: Modern, as for the I-Bc copies of Josquin's masses

    Bibliography: Fava, "Primo", p. 39 (exhibition at Bologna in 1929)

I–BGc, Cinq.4.987 (4). Superius, lacking folios B1, B7, and B8

    Size of page: 169 × 235 mm.

    Watermarks: No.35 on A2

    Corrections and changes:

        In–house: B6*v*: it is possible that the numeral] XV [was stamped in later

        Later: A2*r*.headline:] Con[tantius fe[ta [erased and] Adrianus [entered in brown ink • A4*r*.v: leger line, in brown ink • B4*r*.iv.15–16: *m,m* → *sb,sb*, by erasure of tails • B4*r*.iv.after 17: *sb*b' added, perhaps over an erasure

    Binding and Provenance: with Josquin, *I Missarum* (1516, No.62)

I–Fn, Landau-Finaly Mus.8⁴. Bassus

    No watermarks visible

    Corrections and changes:

        In–house: G8*v*: see above

     Later: G8*v*.v.clef: erased and redrawn, in brown ink
  Binding and Provenance: with *I Motetti de la Corona* (1514, No.57)
I-FBR, s.s. A fragmentary folio H5, only
  Maximum size of page: 147 × 195 mm.
  No watermark
  Provenance: With the fragments of [*Musica XII*] (No.68)
  Bibliography: Ceccarelli and Spaccazocchi, *Carte* • Jeppesen, "Frottola", i, 32 • Vernarecci,
     "Fossombrone", ii, p. 209 • Facsimile in Ceccarelli and Spaccazocchi, *Carte*, plates [1] and
     [2]
I-Vnm, Musica 203–205. Superius, Altus, and Bassus • For the cancel bifolium, see below
  Corrections and changes:
     In-house: G8*v*: see above
     Later: G8*v*.v.clef: erased and redrawn, in brown ink
  Binding and Provenance: with *I Motetti de la Corona* (1514, No.57)
  Bibliography: Fenlon and Dalla Vecchia, *Venezia*, p. 86 (exhibition catalogue, Venice, 2001)

Cancel

A single copy exists of a cancel bifolium for B3 and B6

The basic contents and presentation of this sheet correspond to the description above
Extant copy
I-Vnm, Musica 203–205.
  No watermark visible

————

Lost copies: Copies of this edition or the one put out by Pasoti and Dorico in 1526 were in the
    collections of the Fugger (Schaal, "Musikbibliothek," I/64), of John IV of Portugal (Sampaio
    Ribeiro, *Livraria*, pp. 148–49), and of Ottheinrich (Lambrecht, *Heidelberger*, i, p. 109)
Other editions: Reprinted by Pasoti and Dorico in 1526 (*RISM* 1526⁴)
Bibliography:
  (a) Rosaria Boccadifuoco, *Bibliografia*, No.2340 • Sartori, *Petrucci*, No.58
  (b) Brunet, *Manuel*, iii, cols.1925–1926
  (d) Gehrenbeck, *Motetti* • partial edition in Sherr, *16th-Century*, v
  (e) Boorman, *Petrucci*, pp. 135–40, 274–85 and 357–59 • Boorman, "New" • Sartori, *Petrucci*,
     pp. 188–89 • Sparks, *Music*

Commentary:

1. Like the previous book, this title did not achieve a second edition: but while it was reprinted,
    with all three other Corona volumes, by Pasoti and Dorico, the third also received a second
    edition from their press, so that the present book was the least reprinted of all the series. This is
    no doubt a reflection of the inconsistent nature of the repertoire. The first six of the seventeen
    works take over half the book: they are large-scale pieces for more than four voices, the first
    two (by Festa and Willaert) looking to present the latest style, and the rest (largely attributed to
    Josquin) providing the classic range of five-voiced grand works. This range of styles bears no

relation at all to that of the last six works. It is difficult to see why any institution interested in the first works would want the last ones: while those who could manage only to perform the simpler pieces would be dissuaded by the complexities and scoring of the first ones in the book. As I argue in chapter 9, the selection must represent the remnants of a collection of music that had also supplied the third Corona volume.

2. The clearest evidence that initials and signatures were printed with the musical impression is found in the London copy of this edition, with the smudging of the one forme of gathering D.

3. The staves are not consistently inked in the same manner from copy to copy. When the last stave on a page is not full of music, it may sometimes be inked only to the end of the text (set in the same forme). This is a product of inking, rather than of a specially cut frisket, since it varies from copy to copy.

4. This book marks the last traditional new edition in Petrucci's output. At the same time, by including a work of Willaert, it marks the key transition of the first twenty years of the century, from Josquin's generation (in Petrucci's first books) to his successors. While the content represents the end of the music supplied by one immediate source, the standard of printing also suggests that Petrucci's activity was winding down. After this, there is a series of small reprints, topping up the stock of a number of the earlier Fossombrone volumes — all of which may have suffered when the city was sacked in 1517. In addition, there is one new title, described in the next entry, distinguished from the earlier work by both repertoire and presentation — and, I believe, by the craftsmen involved. It is not particularly elegant, though better than the last reprints of earlier titles.

No. 67. Pisano: *Musica*

23.v.1520   *RISM* P2451

The Superius and Tenor parts are not extant: their title-pages probably followed the same form as those of the lower voices

Eɪr]   Musica de meſer Bernardo piſano | ſopra le Canzone del petrarcha. | A

Gɪr]   Musica de meſer Bernardo piſano | ſopra le Canzone del petrarcha. | B

H9r]   Impreſſum Foroſempronij per Octauianum | petrutium ciuem <F>oroſempronienſem: Anno | domini .152<o> Die 23. Mai. Regiſtrum. ABCDEFGH Omnes Quaterni | preter DFH qui ſunt quinterni.

Format and collation: Part-books: landscape octavo. [C] 16 folios: AB⁸; [T] 18 folios: C⁸D¹⁰; [A] 18 folios: E⁸F¹⁰; [B] 18 folios: G⁸H¹⁰. The paper has horizontal chain-lines • The proposed collation for the Cantus and Tenor is derived from the Register on H9r.

Signatures:] E II [$4 • + Eɪ, Gɪ • H5 signed] H IIIII

No foliation or pagination • The pieces are numbered

Running heads:

Altus	[Eɪv-F3v, F4v-F10r
Altu	[F4r
Baſſus	[Gɪv-H9r
[Nil:	Eɪr, F10v, Gɪr, H9v-10v

Fonts: Music: Petrucci's music type, possibly on full-length bodies

  Staves: four to a page, ca.131 mm long, and 10.3-52.3-73 high

  Text: Roman, "x" = 1.7 mm. The title-page is set in a Rotonda type, "x" = 3.0 mm.

Initials: This edition presents a haphazard mix of initials, including one floral letter "D", one large type-sort letter "P", and a group selected from among those that were new in 1519. The letter "D" is taken from the series designed for the *Paulina* (1513, No.52)

Technical comments: There is some inconsistency about whether unused or partially used staves are fully inked. Of unused fourth staves, all those in the Altus with, in the Bassus, G2r, G4rr, and G8r are inked, while G5r, G7r, and H8v are not. Similarly, staves that are largely unused are still inked, except for those on E4r, F9v (the second stave) and G6r: these contrast with a great majority that is uninked • On only one forme, the outer forme of the outer sheet of gathering E, the left end of a stave was not inked, but left blind, when an initial was to be inserted. This is clear on E8v, where the frisket actually leaves a little of the stave inked, and the initial was omitted in error • On H75 the caption lacks the last letter of "Bassus", apparently because something rested on the page during printing — a smoother patch still shows on the paper • The music was apparently printed before the staves: cf. E6v.i • Both title pages show the blind impression of rows of *sm* on either side of the title • There is the blind impression of music on H10v, possible taken from H3r

In-house changes: The following are all present in the unique copy: E2v.iii.after 7: rest, *?b → m*, erasure and stamping in • G3r.i.after 12: rest, *sb → m*, erased and stamped in • G5r.iii.12: this note stamped in, after presswork

Contents: Incipits taken from the Altus part-book:

	E1r	G1r	[Title]
I	E1v	G1v	FOndo le mie ſperanze in fragil uetro
II	E2v.ii	G2v	AMore quando ſperavo per fine
	E3r.ii	G2v.iv	2/ Tal chio pauento aſſai che la mia uita
III	E4r	G3v	PErche donna non uuol
	E4r.iv	G3v.iii	2/ In qualunche ama con perfecto amore
IIII	E5r.iii	G4v	DE perche in odio mhai ſi tamo piu di me
V	E6r.iii	G5v	AMore ſe vuol chi torni al giogo antico
VI	E7v	G6v	DOnna ben che di rado con riguardo
VII	E8v	G7v	SI e debile il filo a cui ſattiene
			[A: the initial S has not taken ink]
VIII	F1v	G8v	NElla ſtagion chel ciel rapido inclina
	F2v	H1r.iv	2/ Canzon ſe leſſer meco dal matin alla fera
VIIII	F3r.ii	H2r	SE mai prouaſti donna qual ſie amore
X	F4r	H2v.iii	LAſſo me chi non ſo in qual parte pieghi
XI	[?]	H3v	CHiare freſche e dolce acque
XII	[?]	H4r.iii	NOn la laſſar cor mio ſegui la ſorte
XIII	[?]	H5r.ii	TAnta pieta cor mio
XIIII	F7v.ii	H6r	COſil tuo ben fuſſi io
XV	F8r.iii	H6v.ii	SOn io donna qual moſtri ogni tuo bene
XVI	F9r	H7r.iii	CHe deggio fare che mi conſigli amore
			[B: caption:] Tenor loco Baſſu
	F9v.iii	H8r	2/ Fuggi fuggill ſereno el uerde
XVII	F10r.ii	H8v	SII diſſi mai chi uenga in odio a quella

H9*r*   [below one stave of music: Colophon; Register]

H9*v*-10*v* [blank]

Extant copy

E-S. 12-1-31 (1-2). Altus and Bassus only. Lacking folios F5-6

 Size of page: 113 × 170 mm.

 Watermarks: No.35 on E6-3 and H3. No others visible

 In-house corrections and changes: see above. There is no sign of later changes

 Binding: Bound in a series of books:

   (1) Pisano: *Musica* (Bassus)

   (2) Pisano: *Musica* (Altus)

   (3) *Motetti libro primo* (Rome: Antico, 1521: *RISM* 1521³) (Altus)

   (4) *Neuf basses danses* (Paris: Attaingnant, 1530) (Contratenor)

   (5) *Motetti novi libro tertio* (Rome: Antico, 1520: *RISM* 1520²) (Altus)

   (6) *Motetti novi libro secondo* (Rome: Antico, 1520: *RISM* 1520¹) (Altus)

   (7) *Madrigali . . . I de la Serena* ([?Rome: s.n.], 1530: *RISM* 1530²) (Altus)

Bound in a parchment cover, with 2 tie-strings on each face • One paste-down and one fly-leaf at each end • The two Pisano parts were not originally together, on the evidence of the worming

 Provenance: Owned by Colón (Chapman, "Printed", No.44) • Inside the front cover:] R.9702 • On the front fly-leaf: call numbers] 12-1-31 [and] 2885 [and] 6944 • Old call number:] GG Tab 175 NO 34

 Bibliography: Arboli y Farando, *Biblioteca*, v, p. 348 • Chapman, "Printed", No.44, p. 65 • Anglés, "Colombina", p. 25 • Jeppesen, "Neuentdeckten", 76 • Trend, "Musikschätze"

Lost copies: A copy was in the Fugger collection (Schaal, "Musikbibliothek", I/75)

Bibliography:

   (a) Sartori, *Petrucci*, No.59 • Jeppesen, *Frottola*, Pe.G • Vogel, *Bibliografia*, No.345 (dated 1620!)

   (d) Pisano, *Collected*

   (e) d'Accone, "Pisano" • Miggiani, "Petrarca" • Sartori, *Petrucci*, pp. 190–91

Commentary:

1. The relationship of Pisano to Florentine and Roman circles is outlined in chapter 9, where the relevant literature is cited. The pattern of texts by members of the Strozzi family make it plausible that the volume was collected by (or for) one of them, probably Lorenzo.

2. The appearance of this book — number and length of staves, typographical material, use of initial letters, and spacing of the material in the Bassus — all raise questions about the origin of the book. It does have a colophon attributing the work to Petrucci, although the form in which that is presented is also unusual. There is no reason to believe that the attribution to the publisher is false, and enough of his material is used that we should believe the book was indeed published by him. However, it is likely that the work was undertaken by a new craftsman, one not found (at least not in a position of authority) in earlier books. I suggest, in chapter 10, that this man may have been Pasoti, or else someone who may later have transferred from Fossombrone to work for Pasoti in Rome.

3.   The pattern of stave measurements seems to suggest that there was one set of staves, used through-out the book. Some examples are clear, even allowing for paper shrinkage: both formes of Eo, of Ei, of Fo, the outer forme of Fo and some in the other book seem to be the same throughout. Measurements given in brackets refer to those pages where the lowest stave is not inked:

		1r	2v	3r	4v	2r	1v	4r	3v
A:	Eo	—	131	132	131	131	131	132	131
	Ei	132	132	131	131	131	132	131	131
	Fo	131	131	132	131	131	132	131	131
	Fi	131	131	132	131	131	132	132	132
B:	Go	—	131	[130]	131	131	131	131	132
	Gi	131	132	[130]	131	131	132	131	131
	Ho	131	131	[131]	—	131	131	—	—
	H2	132	131	131	131	131	131	131	132
	H3	131	131	132	131				

4.   The Bassus has a second gathering of ten leaves, even though there is little enough music to allow for it to fit with comfort onto two normal gatherings of eight leaves. The 18 folios include three blank pages, H9v-10v, and the title page, G1r. The other 32 pages could contain 128 staves, but actually only have 119 staves with music. These would fit with comfort onto 30 pages. Such an arrangement would still allow for a title page and for the colophon to appear on the last verso. In practice, the additional blank space, sometimes with unused staves, sometimes blank, is spread through the volume, appearing at the foot of various pages, after the end of a piece.

    The evidence suggests several minor features of house practice:

    (i) there was a conscious move to avoid starting a new piece on the last stave of a page. This even applies to the last stave of a verso, *cf.* E3v, F3v, and F8v of the Altus;

    (ii) there was no attempt at casting off the musical text in advance to ensure that it would fill a convenient number of leaves. The need to have the blank stave at the foot of a page (rather than start a new piece) seems to have been more important than the need to save a half-sheet of paper;

    (iii) this last point may suggest that the volume was a special commission, in which the need to lay things out well was more important than the saving of paper supplied by someone else;

    (iv) it is apparent, even so, that the Bassus cannot have been the first volume set in type: the register on H9r states that the Cantus part book had two gatherings of eight leaves. It is probable that the Cantus was the first to be set, and acted as the control over how much music was contained in the volume.

No. 68. [*Musica XII*]

[ca.1533]   Not in *RISM*

No title extant

Collation and format: Partbooks: landscape quarto. Only one bifolio (half of the inner sheet of gathering A) is extant, joined at the head of each leaf, suggesting the normal Petrucci format.
Signature:] Aiiii
Foliation:] 3–4

No running heads or part-names

Fonts: Music: Petrucci. *minim* height = 3.5–11.0 mm

Staves: five per page: 156–157 mm long: 9.7–75.2–97 high. Not Petrucci's customary staves.

Text: Rotonda, "x" = ca.2.0 mm. This may be a different text font.

Technical comments: The size and use of the staves is very unusual for Petrucci

Contents:

A3*r*	. . . ro ſol lucenti rai ro ſe uermiglie	[Anon.]
A3*r*.iii	Se quanto in uoi ſe uede	[Anon.]
A3*v*.ii	La mi la so cantare	[Anon.]
A4*r*	Non po far morte el dolce riſo amaro	[?Verdelot]
A4*v*	Hai speranza . . . che premmetesti	[Anon.]

——

Extant copy:

I-FBR, s.s. Only folios A3-A4, damaged

Size of page: f.A3: 139 × 200 mm; f.A4: 140 × 205 mm

No watermarks visible

Technical comments: The capital on A4*v* was omitted, and added later in manuscript

Corrections and changes:

In house: A4*r*.iv.23: e' (erased) → c', stamped in

Later: A3*v*.i.14: b → g, in ink • A4*v*.i. Initial letter, suplied in brown ink, possibly in the printer's shop, since it is a copy of a Petrucci initial • A4*v*.iv.after 10: a perfect *l* rest erased • There are various doodles and arithmetical entries in later hands on both sides of the sheet.

Provenance: Taken from the binding of a volume belonging to Achille Ciurlo of Fossombrone in 1573. The manuscript passed to the Wool Merchants' Guild, and thence to the Biblioteca Passionei in 1882 • On the join of ff.3*v*-4*r*.] Il Latanzio amicho ca*rissi*mo salutem | co*n* inteso il tutto uoi mi dicieti | ch'io uj mandj quattro piantj | de tartofanj io li mandaró [taken from Ceccarelli and Spaccazocchi, "Carte", p. 5

Bibliography: Ceccarelli and Spaccazocchi, "Carte" • Fenlon and Dalla Vecchia, *Venezia*, p. 87 (exhibition catalogue, Venice, 2001)

——

No other copies or editions of this book are known

Bibliography:

(a) Sartori, *Petrucci*, No.47 • Jeppesen, *Frottola*, Fo.

(c) Ceccarelli e Spaccazocchi, *Carte* • Coviello, *Tradizione*, pls.V-VIII

(e) Boorman, "New" • Ceccarelli and Spaccazocchi, *Carte* • Fenlon and Haar, *Madrigal*, pp. 201–02 • Gialdroni and Ziino, "New Light" • Vernarecci, *Fossombrone*, ii, p. 209 • Vernarecci, *Petrucci*, p. 127

Commentary:

1. These folios have been known for a number of years. They were originally thought to have been part of the missing tenth book of Frottole, and are so assigned in a number of studies. They were then dated as following the end of the Fossombrone sequence of editions (that is, ca.1520), in Boorman, "New", followed with reservations in Fenlon and Haar, *Madrigal*, pp. 201–02. The

recent discovery of new fragments dated in 1538 has allowed the present fragments to be dated considerably later, more in line with the pattern of other sources for Verdelot's music.

2. The folios raise a number of bibliographical issues, even though the strong probability is that they were printed in Fossombrone, and with Petrucci's press:

(a) Some of the physical material is different. Like the book of Pisano's music and the later *Motetti del Fiore*, this uses new staves, not seen before in Petrucci's work. However, they are not the same as those used for the Pisano: nor are they merely cut-down versions of the earlier staves, for the stave-lines are somewhat closer together. Further, they appear to be in excellent condition, as if newly prepared for the purpose, while the earlier, longer staves continued to deteriorate in the final reprintings of the *Motetti de la Corona* volumes.

Secondly, the staves are spaced slightly differently on the page: this may not be serious, although it would involve extra, otherwise unnecessary, labour. The musical font, on the other hand, seems to be the one found in Petrucci's other books.

(b) There are significant changes in the house practice. The most immediately obvious is the size of the book, resulting in fewer staves on each page. But other features have changed:

the texts are set in a rotonda type-face. Petrucci had not used this for secular music since the early volumes of chansons, adopting the roman face for running text in all the frottola volumes (as in those of motets and masses);

text spacing also seems different, in this case more modern. Phrases are regularly broken up, with individual words set precisely under groups of notes. This is particularly evident in the last piece — *Hai speranza* — with its rather more melismatic style;

the custom had been to set each text with two initial capital letters, the first decorative and the second from the running font. In this case, the second letter of each text is set in lowercase;

the signature pattern is unusual: from the evidence of the one piece found elsewhere, *Non po far morte*, we assume that this is a Tenor book. Only once, in *Motetti C*, had Petrucci signed the Tenor with a letter A: but that was over twenty years earlier. Since then he had invariably followed the sequence Superius-Tenor-Altus-Bassus, though the *Motetti del Fiore* would also sign each part-book from A.

3. These features are all the probable results of two causes: the first is the length of time that had elapsed since Petrucci's Pisano book. The present volume relates to that one in its general size, again reflecting the new size of manuscripts of secular music: but Petrucci could no longer use some of the material that had been used in the Pisano and earlier books. This certainly applies to the staves: and a number of the notational symbols seem to be new, having been recast.

At the same time, it is evident that new craftsmen were involved. While the more up-to-date text placement might merely reflect changes in practice with the passage of time, other details of house-practice show different approaches to simple procedures. Implicit in this observation are the conclusions that a new house-editor was in place, making different decisions (the text font, for example), and also that the new typesetter had experience and his own standardised working patterns. Both are to be expected, for Petrucci was himself old, and in any case the craftsmen that he employed over ten years earlier will certainly have moved on to other printing shops.

4. There is no internal evidence for dating this book, beyond the requirement that it lie before the *Motetti del Fiore*, signed in 1538. The arguments of Gialdroni and Ziino are discussed above, in chapter 9, where I come to the conclusion that the edition should be dated sometime between 1533 and early 1535.

5. This sheet almost certainly reached the binder as waste paper from Petrucci's house. However,

it demonstrates the intention to sell the edition from which it comes, for it presents a revised state, including a stamped-in correction. The other corrections were presumably also made in-house, since the sheet did not leave Fossombrone, but they are not made in the customary bold manner of indicating proof changes: indeed, the drawn-in initial implies that the changes were made as if the sheet would be sold. However, the other doodles show that the sheet was not ever part of a completed copy, but remained loose until it was used as binding material: they are found on both sides of the sheet, and across the join of pages. The sheet probably represents part of Petrucci's unsold stock, which later became simple waste paper.

No. 69. [Motteti del Fiore]

15. × .1538   Not in *RISM*

No title extant

B:B6v]   Impreſſum In foroſempronio per Octauianum | Petrutium ₇ Bartholomeum Egnatium | Foroſempronienſes Die 15 Octobris | 1 5 3 8 | [second device]

Collation and format: Partbooks: landscape quarto. Only two sheets of paper survive: they imply a Tenor of A⁸B⁴ and a Bassus of A⁸B⁶

Signature:] B ii [$2, although probably signed to 4 and 3

Foliation:] t.r.r, in arabic numerals: Tenor:] 9-12; [Bassus:] 9-10, 13-14

Direction Line:] Mot dal Fio. [Tenor: B1
        Mot dal Fio [Tenor: B2; Bassus: B1, B2

Running heads: centered on every folio:]
    Tenor   [*T*: B1r-4v
    Baſſus   [*B*: B1r-2v,5r-6v

Fonts: Music: Petrucci. minim height = 3.5-11.0 mm
    Staves: five per page: 157-158 mm long: 9.7-73.6-95 or 96 high
    Text: Rotonda, "x" = ca.2.0 mm. This may be a new text font

Initials: These are completely new for Petrucci, more reminiscent of French styles: they measure ca.18 × 19 mm

Textual comments: The formulation for second *partes* is reversed here, reading] Pars | Secu*n*da • The underlay is more old-fashioned than that in the preceding Verdelot volume, following patterns of earlier Petrucci editions.
        Tenor: 9v.i.text:] iniquitatem [has the second "i" inverted • 10r.iv.17: a leger-line probably omitted • 10v.iv: note the spelling] hedificauerit

Technical comments: The headline was apparently printed with the staves and text • The music fount seems similar to that of the preceding volume, though the custos is the older, long form • Otherwise, the fount is the late one, with each note assignable to a specific pitch: cf. Tenor: 9r.ii.13; 9r.v.26; 10r.i.6; 11r.i.23 • Tenor: 11v.right end: a text spacing sort, apparently 3.3 mm high

In-house changes: 9v.i.text:] cu*m* opera [was stamped in later • 10v.v.37: *m* → *sb*, by erasure: the original may have been at pitch g', replaced by a stamped-in a'

Contents:

	Tenor	Bassus		
"1"		[ᵃ]	[Panis quem ego dabo]	[Lupus Hellinck]
		B1r.ii	2| Locutus eſt populus	
"2"	[ᵇ]	B1ν	Qui confidunt in domino	[L'Héritier]
	B1r.iv	B2r.iii	2| Bene fac domine	
"3"	B2r	B2ν.νᶜ	Dignare me laudare te	[Gombert]
	B2r.v		2| O regina poli	
"4"	B2ν.iv		Niſi dominus benedificauerit	[L'Héritier]
	B3ν	[ᵈ]	2| Cum dederit dilectis ſuis	
"5"	B4r.ii	B5r.iii	Aspice domine	[Gombert]
	B4ν.ii	B5ν.iv	2| Muro tuo inexpugniabili	
		B6r.v	[blank staves]	
		B6ν	[colophon and device]	

Extant copies:

I-PESas, Archivio Notarile di Fossombrone, Marcantonio Manasangui, volume for 1514-1563, ff.200 and 205. Only gathering B of the Tenor book, B1-4, unfoliated and wrapped around ff.201-204

Size: the sheet, apparently untrimmed, is 334 × 443 mm.

Watermark: No.36 on Tenor B2-1

Provenance: the uncut sheet surrounds a notarial agreement dated 1558, between Peranto Beccarini and Ser Francisco "Nuptium" [= Nuzzi], both of Fossombrone: the document does not refer to Petrucci or concern music. The sheet was apparently previously folded correctly, as if for binding

I-PESprivate. Only the outer sheet of gathering B of the Bassus book, B1-2,5-6. I have not seen this sheet: the following data are taken from Gialdroni and Ziino, "New Light"

Size: the sheet measures 334 × 443-444 mm.

Watermark: No.36

Later changes: there are many scribbled notes on both sides of the sheet, including at one point the date] 17 Iulij 1562

Provenance: The present owner is the Conte Carlo Stramigioli Ciacchi • The sheet had previously been used as a cover for a book or collection of documents

Professors Gialdroni and Ziino have also kindly notified me of their even more recent discovery of parts of two folios of Petrucci's *Motetti del Fiore,* now in the Archivio di Stato at Fano. These, folios A5–6 of the Tenor book, add further leaves and contents to the volume. Professor Ziino informs me that their contents are as follows:

---

a. The end of the Bassus of the prima pars is at the head of Bassus B1r
b. The end of the Tenor of the prima pars is at the head of Tenor B1r
c. Incomplete
d. The end of the Bassus of the secunda pars is at the head of Bassus B5r

A5r   *In convertendo* (Lupus)
A5v   *Qui seminant* (the second pars)
       Inviolata, integra et casta (Courtois): beginning
A6r   continuation
       O benigna (the second pars)
A6v   completion
       Pater noster (Willaert): opening.

Ziino assumes, surely correctly, that this first gathering concluded with the opening of L'Hériter's *Qui confidunt in Domino*, the rest of which is to be found on the Tenor fragment now in Pesaro.

————

No other copies of this edition are known, and no other edition from Petrucci's press. The edition
    is related to editions from the presses of Moderne and Gardano

Note: I am grateful to Professor Peretti for informing me of the Tenor fragment, and to Professors
    Gialdroni and Ziino for sending me many details of these folios before publication, and for
    facilitating my access to the Tenor sheet.

Bibliography:
    (e) Gialdroni and Ziino, "New Light"

Commentary:

1. The notarial file which now contains the Tenor fragment has documents from 1529 to 1576,
    despite the dates on the spine: it includes other documents for Fossombrone, including one for]
    Nicolaus Gigantes de Gigantibus de forosempronio [dated 1555.

2. The watermark does not seem to appear in the notarial file: a similar crown can be found (on
    folio 50 dated 1563), though surmounted with a star. Nor has the mark yet been found in other
    notarial files from Fossombrone.

3. The edition is remarkable in a number of ways: bibliographically, it follows the preceding Verdelot
    edition, retaining the staves and apparently the same notation: however, the custos is by no means
    the only new element. The initials are completely new, whereas the single one extant on the
    Fossombrone fragment is at least an imitation of the earlier ones, perhaps actually the same sort.

    The adoption of a direction line is also new: while this had become a normal practice in
    many editions of the time, Petrucci had never used one before.

    Similarly unusual is the absence of a Register, to accompany the colophon. This has been a
    normal feature of all Petrucci's books, while it was becoming increasingly rare elsewhere.

4. The pattern of signing more than one partbook from A is not unique here: it had happened in
    the preceding book, the Fossombrone fragment, and also in the much earlier *Motetti C*. It may
    be significant that the Scotto family also signed editions with every part starting from "A".

5. This book therefore stands as a link from the earlier work (including the Fossombrone fragment)
    to normal practices of the following decades. The manner by which that link was forged is
    addressed in chapter 10.

CONCORDANCE AND

DOCUMENTS

Chapter Eighteen

CONCORDANCE LISTS FOR ALL

PETRUCCI'S MUSICAL OUTPUT

his chapter contains concordance patterns for all works published by Petrucci, arranged in alphabetical sequence by language. Latin incipits are followed by Italian and French sequences, and then by the few titles in Dutch, German, and Spanish, and finally by a sequence of titles to instrumental or untexted pieces. Within the Latin series, complete masses are entered first, followed by mass ordinary movements and sections, and then an alphabetical series of other incipits.

At times the actual alphabetical sequence looks arbitrary. While titles show Petrucci's spelling, they are arranged in a sequence that corresponds to modern spellings.

With some 600 concordant sources, and more continuing to surface, it has proved impossible to check each source, and a number of the following entries are necessarily derived from the recent scholarly literature.

For each work, the entry comprises:

Headline, giving the title or incipit (usually in Petrucci's spelling), the composer's name (in standardised form) and the number of voices: when the spelling of the title varies from edition to edition, or issue to issue, the version of the first issue is given. Later versions are only given separate entries (as cross-references) if they are significantly different. The names of alternative composers (cited in concordant sources) are listed beneath Petrucci's (or the generally accepted) attribution, given on the headline.

This is followed, if necessary, by the titles or incipits of subsequent *partes*

1. a sequence listing Petrucci's sources, showing edition number (following the numbering in this bibliography); composition number in the edition, and folios

(except with part-books); in parentheses, attributions, and different text incipits, given in the spelling of the source;

Attributions, when in italics, are present in the source at the head of the piece (or in an index). Otherwise, they are taken from the title-page, thus drawing attention to the implicit (and dangerous) presumption that they apply to all pieces in the volume;

2. a similar sequence for other vocal or polyphonic printed sources. When these sources give a different text, this is indicated, and there is usually a cross-reference from that text to Petrucci's text. Attributions are treated as for Petrucci's editions;

3. a similar sequence for manuscripts concordances;

a list of reproductions or facsimiles, solely of Petrucci's editions;

Occasional remarks on the text, its authorship or sources, when particularly relevant to the work in question;

4. a list of editions of the piece. This does not aim to be complete, normally excluding ephemeral editions, and also editions of parts of works, particularly movements of masses;

Comments — these are restricted in scope, usually referring to questions of attribution or dissemination;

Literature — bibliographical citations to discussions of the work. This section cannot begin to be comprehensive, and only includes significant discussions which might impinge in some way on Petrucci's place in the dissemination of the piece;

These entries are followed by a similar sequence of categories for intabulations, which in many cases give important clues to the dissemination of Petrucci's editions. These are sorted according to the performing resources required. There has been no attempt to distinguish between different later intabulations for the same instrument, or to list editions for intabulations other than for those published by Petrucci.

Latin Texts

Missa Ad fugam   **Josquin**   4vv

1. **54**, No.3 (*Iosquin De Pres.*)

2. J675 (1526), No.3 (Josquin) • 1516¹, No.11, 129v-140r (*Josquin*)

3. D-Ju, 3, No.8, 105v-115r (*Josquin*. Headed *Missa diatessaron*) • D-Ju, 31, No.5, 67r-73r (Anon.) • I-Rvat, C.S.49, No.12, 129v-140r (Anon.)

4. Josquin, *Werken*, Missen, iii, 28

Intabulation: voice and vihuela

2. 1552³⁵ = P2448, No.60, 41r-45v (*Jusquin*. Pisador. Lacks Agnus II)

Cum sancto spiritu

Intabulation: vihuela

2. 1547²⁵ = V32, No.126, 84v (*Josquin*. Valderrábano)

Benedictus

2. Heyden 1537, p. 88 (Anon. Headed *Sequitur exemplum variarum Diminutionum*) • Heyden

1540, pp. 105–06 (Anon. Headed *Sequitur exemplum variarum Diminutionum*) • 1547[1], p. 219

Missa Agnosce o vicenti

see **Missa de Sancto Antonio**	**La Rue**	4vv

Missa Alleluya   Mouton   4vv

1. **60**, No.2 (Mouton)
3. D-Mbs, 65, No.1, 3*v*-30*r* (*Joannis Mouton*) • D-Mbs, 66, No.5, 97*v*-131*r* (Anon.) • I-MOd, IV, No.3, 4*r* and 8*r* (Anon. Only from the end of the Credo)
4. Mouton, *Missa* • Mouton, *Opera Omnia*, i, 1

Pleni

2. 1543[19], No.41, p. 26 (*Ian mouton*) • 1553[26], No.41, p. 26 (*Ian mouton*)

Osanna

Intabulation: vihuela

2. 1547[25] = V32, No.123, 83*v* (*Mouton*. Valderrábano)

Missa d'Allemaigne

see **Missa Regina mearum**	**Mouton**	4vv

Missa Alma redemptoris   Mouton   4vv

1. **60**, No.3 (Mouton)
2. 1516[1], No.3, 33*v*-46*r* (*Mouton*) • 1522, No.3 (*Joanes Mouton*)
3. F-CA, 4, No.7 • I-MOe, α.N.1.2–3, No.5, 74*v*-90*r* (*Jo. mouton*. Original number V) • I-Rvat, C.S.45, No.4, 48*v*-64*r* (*Jo. Mouton*) • NL-*SH*, 72c, 133*v*-153*r* (*Jo. Mouton*) • S-Uu, 76b, No.3, 25*v*-36*r* (Anon.)
4. Mouton, *Opera Omnia*, i, 37

Benedictus

2. 1543[19], No.37, p. 23 (*Ian mouton*) • 1553[26], No.37, p. 23 (*Ian Mouton*)
3. D-Mbs, 260, No.30, 21*v*-22*r* (Anon. Transposed a fourth lower)

Agnus II

2. 1543[19], No.63, p. 37 (*Ian mouton*) • 1553[26], p. 39 (*Ian Mouton*)

Missa Almana

see **Missa Regina mearum**	**Mouton**	4vv
see **Missa Sexti Ut fa**	**La Rue**	4vv

Missa Ave Maria   Févin   4vv

1. **61**, No.3. (Fevin)
2. 1516[1], No.8, 94*v*-104*r* (*Fevin*)
3. D-F, 2, 72*r*-83*v* (Anon. Incomplete) • D-Ju, 7, No.2, 17*r*-29*r* (*Josquin*) • D-Sl, 45, 23*v*-45*r* (Anon.) • I-Rsm, 26, No.9, 140*v*-154*r* (Anon.) • I-Rvat, C.G.XII.2, No.2, 32*v*-49*r* (*Ant. de Feuin*) • I-Rvat, C.S.45, No.3, 31*v*-47*r* (*Fevin*) • I-Tn, I.27, No.41, 69*v*-78*r* (Anon.) • S-Uu, 76c, 25*r*-33*v* (Anon.)
4. Clinkscale, *Févin*, ii, 1–71

Intabulation: lute

2. BB902 I,1 = 1546[22], No.1, 2*r*-16*v* (Antonio fevino. Barberiis)

Kyrie I

Intabulation: vihuela

2. M7725 (1546), No.41. ii, 18*r* (*Fevin*. Mudarra. Headed *Glosa sobre el primer Kyrie*)

Domine Deus

2. 1549[16], No.29 (Anon.)

Crucifixus

2. 1549[16], No.64 (Anon.)

Et resurrexit

2. 1549[16]. No.63 (Anon.)

Pleni

2. 1543[19], No.57, p. 34 (*Fevin*) • 1545[6], No.68 (*Antonius Fevinus*. Headed *Ne tardes converti ad Dominum*) • 1547[1], p. 355 (Headed *Hypoionici exemplum III Antonio Feum authore*)

Benedictus

Intabulation: keyboard

2. 1531[5], No.6, 97*v* (*Fevin*)

Agnus Dei II

2. 1545[6], No.61 (*Antonius Fevinus*. Headed *Quis est homo*) • 1549[16], No.52 (Anon.)

Missa Ave maris stella	Josquin	4vv

1. **22**, No.1 (*Josquin*) • **59**, No.1 (*Josquin*)

2. J672 (1526), No.1 (Josquin) • 1539[1], No.11 (*Josquin*)

3. A-Wn, 1783, No.11, 165*v*-175*r* (*Josquin*) • A-Wn, 4809, No.7, 123*v*-141*r* (*Josquin*) • B-Br, 9126, 1*v*-13*r* (Anon.) • CH-Bu, F.IX.25a-d, No.3 (*Josquin*) • D-F, 2, 18*r*-30*r* (Anon. Incomplete) • D-Ju, 3, No.3, 29*v*-43*r* (*Josquin des pres*) • D-Ngm, 83795 • D-Sl, 44, 29*v*-56*r* (Anon.) • E-Tc, 9, No.4, 35*v*-54*r* (*Jusquin*) • H-BA, 20 • H-BA, 24 • I-Bc, Q 25 • I-Bsp, A.XXXI, No.11, 127*v*-130*r* (Anon. Credo only) • I-Ma, 46, No.8, 72*v*-82*r* (*Jos*) • I-Mfd, 2267, No.13, 57*v*-66*r* (*Josquin:*) • I-Rsm, 26, No.3, 29*v*-42*r* (Anon.) • I-Rvat, C.S.41, No.6, 62*v*-72*r* (*Josquin* in the index) • I-Rvat, C.S.150 • S-Uu, 76c

4. Josquin, *Messe*, 1–34 • Josquin, *Werken*, Missen, ii, 15

Intabulations: vihuela

2. 1547[25] = V32, No.110, 75*v* (*Josquin*. Valderrábano. Headed *Fantasia acomposturada de cierta parte de la missa de Aue maris stella*) • 1552[35] = P2448, No.65, 63*v*-67*v* (*Jusquin*. Pisador. Lacking parts of Sanctus and Agnus Dei)

Benedictus

Intabulation: lute

2. 1552[29], No.80, p. 73 (Anon. Phalèse)

Intabulation: vihuela

2. 1547[25] = V32, No.132, 86*v* (Anon. Valderrábano)

Pleni

2. 1545[6], No.84 (*Josquin*. Headed *Nunquid oblivisci potest*)

Agnus

2. 1545[7], No.107 (*Ioskin*. Headed *Fuga in Epidiatessaron post tempus*. Texted *Diligam te Domine*)

3. E-Tc, 9.

Intabulation: keyboard

2. Baena 1540, No.10, 12*v* (Josquin) • Baena 1540, No.63, 61*r*-*v* (Josquin)

Qui Tollis

Intabulation: keyboard

2. Baena 1540, No.43, 44*r*-45*r* (Josquin)

Missa Ave regina celorum	Weerbeke	4vv

1. **32**, No.1 (Gaspar)

3. I-Mfd, 2268, No.33, 160*v*-175*r* (*Gaspar.*) • I-Rvat, C.S.14, No.5, 14*v*-27*r* (*Gaspar*)

4. Weerbecke, *Messe*, 95–147

Missa de Beata Virgine   **Josquin**   4–5vv
                                              (La Rue)

1. *54*, No.5 (Iosquin)

2. J675 (1526), No.5 (Josquin) • 1516¹, No.10, 114*v*-129*r* (*Iosquin*) • 1522, No.5 (*Josquin*) • 1539¹, No.5 (*Josquin*)

3. A-Wn, 4809, No.2, 23*v*-46*r* (*Josquin*. Titled *Missa de Domina*) • CH-Bu, F.VI.26h, No.1 (Anon. Incomplete) • D-Ju, 7, No.5, 61*v*-77*r* (*Josquin des Pres*) • D-Mbs, C, No.2, 41*v*-71*r* (*Josquin de P.*) • D-Mbs, 510, No.1, 1*v*-23*r* (Anon.) • D-Ngm, 83795, 67*r*-78*r* and 157*r*-166*r* (*Missa coronata Josquini*) • D-ROu, 49, Ser.2, No.6 (*Josquin*) • D-Sl, 44, No.3, 57*v*-84*r* (*Josquin*. Headed *M. Choral de Maria*) • D-W, A.Aug.2°, No.1, 1*v*-27*r* (*Josquin des Press*) • D-WRs, B, 76*v*-85*r* (*Petri de la Rue*: headed *Missa Coronata*) and 112*v*-118*r* (*Josquini*) • E-Tc, 16, 1*v*-20*r* (Anon.) • E-Tc, 23, No.4, 23*v*-45*r* (Anon: *Josquin* in index) • F-CA, 4, 232*v*-250*r* (Anon.) • F-CA, 18, No.15, 200*v*-218*r* (*Jossequin des Prez*) • H-BA, 20, No.58, 116*r*-119*r* and 91*v*-93*r* (*Officium Josquin*) • H-BA, Pr.6, Nos.16–19 (*Josquin*. Lacks the Credo) • I-Ma, 46, No.2, 11*v*-22*r* (*Josquin*. Headed *De nostra domina*) • I-Rvat, C.G.XII.2, No.5, 143*v*-159*r* (*Josquin*) • I-Rvat, C.S.45, No.1, 3*v*-17*r* (*Josquin des Prez*. Index: *Missa de domina nostra*) • I-Rvat, C.S.48, 143*v*-159*r* (*Josquin*) • I-Rvat, C.S.160, No.3, 33*v*-48*r* (*Iosquini Desprez*) • PL-Kj, 40013, 114*v*-131*r* (*Josquini*. Titled *Missa coronata*) • S-Uu, 76b, No.12, 97*v*-112*r* (Anon. Untexted) • S-Uu, 76c, 1*v*-10*r* (*Josquin des prez*)

4. Josquin, *Werken*, Misse, ii, 30

Intabulation: vihuela

2. 1552³⁵ = P2448, No.66, 68*r*-73*r* (*Jusquin*. Pisador. Lacking parts of Sanctus and Agnus Dei)

Kyrie and Gloria

3. D-Dl, Grimma 53, No.11 (*Josquin*) • D-EIa, Kantionale, 94*v*-100*r* (*Josquin de Pres*: the Kyrie headed *Kyrie coronatum*) • D-ROu, 40, No.3 (*Josquini*) • H-BA, 24, 41*r* (*Josquin*. Headed *In festa visitationis Mariae et Maria Magdalena*) • I-Bc, Q25, No.16 (Anon.)

Kyrie I

Intabulation: keyboard

2. V1108 (1557), No.100 (*Jusquin*. Venegas de Henestrosa. Headed *glosado*)

Intabulation: vihuela

2. M7725 (1546), No.25. Bk2, 4*r* (*Josquin*. Mudarra. Headed *glosado*)

Kyrie III

Intabulation: keyboard

2. V1108 (1557), No.101 (Anon. Venegas de Henestrosa)

Intabulation: vihuela

2. 1547²⁵ = V32, No.107, 73*v* (*Josquin*. Valderrábano. *Fantasia remedada al chirie postrero de la misa de Josquin, de beata virgine. Primero tono*)

Gloria

2. 1547¹, pp. 392–401 (Headed *Mixolydij Hypomixolydijq*(ue) *connexoru*(m) *exemplu*(m) *eiu*[*de*(m) *Iod.*)

3. D-Z, XIII,3, 6*r*-6*v* (Incomplete) • E-Bbc, 343, 59*v* (Anon. fragmentary) • I-Bsp, A.XXXVIII, No.23, 133*r*-135*r* (Anon. Incomplete) • I-Rvat, C.S.23, No.10, 134*v*-138*r* (*Josquini Desprez*)

2. Baena 1540, No. 42, 42*v*-43*v* (Josquin)

Intabulation: keyboard

Cum sancto spiritu

3. CH-Bu, F X 21, No.30, 33*v* (Anon.) • D-Dl, 1/E/24, No.41 (*Josquin*) • D-Dl, Grimma 52, No.53 (*Josquin*) • D-GRu, 640–641, No.1 (*Josquin*) • D-LEu, 49, No.102 (Anon.) • D-Mu, 718 • D-Usch, 237a-d, No.18, 34*r* (Anon.) • F-CA, 125–128, No.209, 141*r* (*Josquin de pres.*) • S-Uu, 89, 6*v* (Anon.)

Intabulations: keyboard

2. V1108 (1557), No.54, 33*r* (*Jusquin*. Venegas de Henestrosa. *Septimo tono sobre cum sancto Spiritu*) • 1578[24] = C1, No.71, 68*r* (*Jusquin*. Cabezón. *Tiento sobre Cum Sancto Spiritu*) • 1578[24] = C1, No.89, 103*r* (*Jusquin*. Cabezón) • 1583[22] = A939, No.70, 101*r* (Anon. Ammerbach)

Intabulations: lute

2. 1536[13] = N522, No.34, Z4*r*-Aa1*r* (*Joss Quin*. H. Newsidler) • 1552[29], No.69, p. 57 (Anon. Phalèse) • H4934 (1556), No.71 (*Josquin*. Heckel) • 1558[20] = O12, No.15, 31*v* (*Josquin de Pres*. Ochsenkuhn) • 1562[24] = H4935, No.71, p. 207 (*Josquin*. Heckel)

3. D-Mbs, 272, No.60, 73*v*-74*r* (Anon.)

Intabulations: vihuela

2. M7725 (1546), No.44. ii, 22*r* (*Josquin*. Mudarra. Headed *Glosa sobre el Cum Sancto Spiritu*) • 1547[25] = V32, No.127, 85*r* (*Josquin*. Valderrábano)

Credo

3. CH-Bu, F.VI.26h, 6a and 6b, No.1 (Anon.) • D-Ju, 36, No.5, 93*v*-98*r* (*Josquin des Pres*) • I-Bsp, A.XXXI, No.4, 15*v*-18*r* (Anon.) • I-MOd, IV, No.40, 92*v*-95*r* (*Jusquin des pres*) • I-MOe, α.N.1.2, No.13, 173*v*-178*r* (*Josquin*. Headed *Canon. Le premier va devant*) • I-Rvat, C.S.23, No.9, 129*v*-132*r* (*Josquin*. Headed *Credo de Village*) • I-TVd, 9, 106*v*-111*r* (Anon.)

Intabulation: voice and vihuela

2. 1554[32] = F2093, No.66, 73*v* (*Josquin*. Fuenllana)

Intabulation: two vihuelas

2. 1547[25] = V32, No.80, 51*v* (*Josquin*. Valderrábano. Headed *La primera parte del Credo*)

Benedictus

3. D-WRs, B, 115*v*-116*r* (*Josquin*)

Agnus Dei II

2. 1543[19], No. 61, p. 36 (*Iusquin*) • 1545[6], No.563 (*Iusquin*) • 1547[1], p. 305 • 1553[26], p. 33 (*Iusquin*)

3. D-WRs, B, 116*v*-118*r* (*Josquin*)

Missa de Beata Virgine	**La Rue**	4vv

1. **11**, No.1 (*Pe.de.la.rue.*)

3. A-Wn, 1783, 49*v*-60*r* (Anon: Discantus headed *Salve sancta parens*) • B-Amp, M 18.13, fragments 9–11 (Anon. Parts of the Credo) • D-Dl, Pirna IV, 96*v*-116*r* (*Petri de Larue. Missa super coronatum*) • D-Ju, 22, 18*v*-29*r* (Anon. *Petrus de la Rue: de beata Virgine* in the index) • I-Rvat, C.S.41, No.8, 73*v*-86*r* (*P. de la Rue*. In the index, *Perisson de la Rue*) • I-SUss, 248, No.2, 19*v*-37*r* (*Rue*)

4. La Rue, *Opera Omnia*, ii, 84–120 • La Rue, *Drei Missen*

Kyrie

3. D-EIa, Kantionale, 100*v*-102*r* (*Petrus de la Rue*. Headed *Kyrie coronatum*)

Credo

3. I-Bsp, A.XXXVIII, No.12, 23*v*-25*r* (Anon. *Patrem Cardinale*) • I-MOd, IV, No.13, 32*v*-34*r* (Anon.)

Pleni

    2. 1545[6], No.82 (Headed *In Hyperdiatessaron, post tempus*)

Missa Benedictus Dominus Deus   **Mouton**   4vv

    1. *60*, No.1 (Mouton)

    3. B-Br, IV.922, 42*v*-66*r* (*Johannes mouton.*) • D-Mbs, 510, No.7, 138*v*-159*r* (Anon. Imperfect) • E-Tc, 23, No.26, 239*v*-261*r* (*Johannes mouton*) • F-CA, 4, No.15, 197*v*-215*r* • I-RE, s.s., No.1, 2*r*-12*r* (Anon.)

    4. Mouton, *Opera Omnia* i, pp. 72–120

    Comments: Based on the motet by Févin, also published by Petrucci

Missa Berzerette savoyene   **Brumel**   4vv

    1. *8*, No.2 (Brumel)

    4. Brumel, *Opera Omnia*, i, 20–40 • Curtis, *Antoine*

    Comments: Based on the Superius of Josquin's chanson

Kyrie and Gloria

    3. D-Dl, 1/D/505, pp. 60–71 (Anon.)

Deus pater omnipotens

    2. Wilphingseder (1563), pp. 314–15 (Anon. Headed *Exempla de ternaria Notularum*)

Missa Cela sans plus   **Obrecht**   4vv

    3. PL-WRu, 428, 26*v*-41*r* (Anon.)

  see **Cela sans plus**   **Obrecht**   4 ex 2vv

Missa Charge de deul   **Isaac**   4vv

    1. *31*, No.1 (Isaac)

    3. CZ-HK, II.A.7, pp. 314–325 (Anon. Credo and Sanctus) • F-CA, 18, No.11, 137*v*-153*r* (Anon. Titled *Missa Sergies de doeul*) • I-La, 238, No.9, 35*v*-36*v* (Anon. Only fragments extant) • I-Mfd, 2268, No.32, 151*v*-159*v* (*Isac.* Lacking Kyrie and Agnus II) • PL-Wu, 58, 13*v*-16*r* and 17*v*-22*r* (Anon.) • S-Uu, 76e, No.1, 1*r*-11*v* (*Henrici Izac*)

    4. Isaac, *Messe*, 76 • Isaac, *Opera Omnia*, vi, 1–37

    Comments: This may have been the mass listed in the index of I-Bsp, A XXIX, as *Missa de Sarge de doglia*, for folios now missing • Based on an anonymous virelai

    Literature: Staehelin, *Isaac*, iii, 86–94

Kyrie

    3. ZA-Csa, Grey, No.83, 122*v*-123*r* (Anon. Texted *Homo cum in honore esset*)

Christe eleison

    3. E-SE, s.s., 179*r* (*Ysaac.* Incipit *Vostre amour*) • I-Fn, 178, No.48, 52*v*-53*r* (*Ysac.* Incipit *Amie des que*) • I-Fn, 229, No.16, 15*v*-16*r* (*Henricus Yzac.* Untexted) • ZA-Csa, Grey, No.63, 102*v* (Anon. Texted *Memento mei domine*)

    4. Brown, *Florentine*, music volume, 34–35 • Isaac, *Weltliche*, 63

Qui tollis

    3. DK-Kk, 1848, p. 447 (*Ysaac.* Texted *Or mauldist soyt*) • I-Fn, 178, No.65, 69*v*-70*r* (*Ycac.* Texted *O Fortune content*)

    4. Isaac, *Weltliche*, 64

Benedictus

    Intabulation: keyboard

    3. D-B, 40026, 49*v*-50*r* (Anon. Texted *La la he, In ut*)

Agnus Dei I

    3. I-Fn, Panc.27, No.81, 52*v*-53*r* (Anon. Incipit *Omnis laus in fine canitur*) • ZA-Csa, Grey, No.84, 123*v*-124*r* (*Jsaac.* Text *Omnis laus in fine canitur*)

Missa Comme femme   **Isaac**   4vv

    1. *31*, No.5 (Isaac)

    3. E-Boc, 5, No.3, 24*v*-33*r* (*Henericus Yzaac*) • I-Rvat, C.S.49, No.6, 69*v*-83*r* (Anon.) •
       S-Uu, 76e, No.5, 44*v*-55*r* (*Henrici Izac*)

    4. Isaac, *Opera Omnia*, vi, 38–77

    Comments: The cantus firmus is the Tenor of Binchois's rondeau

    Literature: Staehelin, *Isaac*, iii, 81–86

  Benedictus

    3. I-Rvat, C.G.XIII.27, 84*v*-85*r* (Anon. Texted *Gracias a vos donzella*) • US-Wc, Wolffheim,
       95*v*-96*r* (Anon. No text)

    4. Atlas, *Giulia*, ii, 51–52

Missa Coronata

  see **Missa de Beata Virgine**   **Josquin**   4–5vv

  see **Missa de Beata Virgine**   **La Rue**   4vv

Missa D'ung aultre amer   **Josquin**   4vv

    1. *22*, No.6 (*Josquin*) • *59*, No.6 (*Josquin*) • See also *Tu solus*

    2. J672 (1526), No.6 (Josquin)

    3. I-MOd, IV, No.7, 14*v*-19*r* and No.10, 25*v*-26*r* (Anon. The Sanctus is written first, with
       Tu solus qui facis mirabilia for the Benedictus. Then the Gloria and Credo. The Agnus is
       at No.10) • I-Rvat, C.S.41, No.13, 149*v*-155*r* (With a different Sanctus and *Tu solus qui
       facis mirabilia* for the Benedictus)

    4. Josquin, *Werken*, Missen, ii, 23 • *New Josquin Edition*, vii, 3

    Comments: Based on the chansons by Ockeghem, also published by Petrucci

  Sanctus

    1. *24*, No.24 (*Josquin* in index)

  see also **Tu solus qui facis mirabilia** (= Benedictus)

Missa Diatessaron

  see **Missa Ad fugam**   **Josquin**   4vv

Missa Dictes Moy   **Mouton**   4vv

    1. *60*, No.4 (Mouton)

    2. 1516[1], No.7, 80*v* 94*r* (*Jo Mouton*)

    3. D-Mbs, 510, No.5, 87*v*-113*r* (Anon.) • E-Tc, 16, 38*v*-62*r* (*Joannes Mouton*) • I-Rvat,
       1982, No.17, 151*v*-163*r* (*Jo Mouton*. Original number XVI) • I-Rvat, C.G.XII.2, No.3,
       87*v*-106*r* (*Jo Monton*) • I-Rvat, C.S.39, No.1, 1*v*-21*r* (Mouton) • I-RE, s.s., No.3, 13*v*-
       22*r* (Anon.) • NL-SH, 72C, 91*v*-112*r* (*Jo Mouton*)

    4. Mouton, *Opera Omnia*, ii, 1–50

    Comments: Based on Compère's chanson

Missa Didadi   **Josquin**   4vv

    1. *54*, No.4 (Iosquin)

    2. J675 (1526), No.4 (Josquin)

    4. Josquin, *Werken*, Missen, iii, 29 • *New Josquin Edition*, ix, 1

    Comments: Based on the Tenor of Morton's *N'aray je jamais*

    Literature: Brothers, "Vestiges", pp. 24–26 • Long, "Symbol"

  Agnus II

    3. D-Rp, B.220–222, 85*v*-86*v*/81*v*-82*r* (*Josquin*)

Missa Dominicalis de Orto 4vv
    1. **20**, No.1 (de Orto)
    3. I-VEcap, DCCLXI, No.7, 73*v*-89*r* (Anon.)

Missa De dringhs Brumel 4vv
    1. **43**, No.3 (*Antonius Brumel.*)
    3. I-Mfd, 2267, No.14, 66*v*-73*r* (*Brumel.* Gloria, Credo, and Sanctus only)
    4. Brumel, *Opera Omnia*, iv, 35–51
    Comments: Based on Brumel's chanson *Tous les regretz*
    Literature: Miller, "Musical"

  Pleni and Benedictus
    2. 1547¹, pp. 456–458 (Antonius Brumel)

  Agnus II
    2. 1547¹, pp. 458–459 (*Brumel*) • Wilphlingseder 1563, pp. 349–51 (*Anthonij Brumelij*)

Missa E trop penser Weerbeke 4vv
    1. **32**, No.3 (Gaspar)
    3. I-Rvat, C.S.41, No.14, 156*v*-174*r* (*Gaspar* in the index. Titled *Missa Trop penser* in the index)
    Comments: Based on the chanson by Bosfrin

Missa Elizabeth
  see **Missa Faysans regres** Josquin 4vv
Missa Faysans regres Josquin 4vv
    1. **54**, No.2 (Josquin)
    2. 1516¹, No.9, 104*v*-114*r* (*Iosquin*) • 1522, No.6 (*Josquin*) • J675 (1526), No.2 (Josquin)
    3. A-Wn, 4809, No.5, 90*v*-108*r* (Anon.) • A-Wn, 15495, No.3, 33*v*-47*r* (*Josquin des Pretz*) • D-HRD, 9821, No.8 (*Josquin*: Kyrie and Credo only) • D-Ju, 3, No.1, 1*v*-14*r* (*Josquin de Pres.* Headed *Missa Elizabeth*) • D-Mbs, 510, No.2, 24*v*-41*r* (Anon.) • E-Tc, 9, No.6, 83*v*-103*r* (*Jusquin*) • I-Rvat, 1980–1981, No.8, 48*r*-52*r* (Anon.) • I-Rvat, C.S.23, No.8, 118*v*-128*r* (*Josquin des Pres*)
    4. Josquin, *Werken*, Missen, iii, 27 • *New Josquin Edition*, viii, 1
    Comments: Based on the second *pars* of Frye's chanson, *Tout a par moy*
    Intabulation: voice and vihuela
    2. 1552³⁵ = P2448, No.59, 36*r*-40*v* (*Jusquin.* Pisador. Headed *Missa de Jusquin que va sobre fa re mi re.* Lacks Pleni, Osanna, and Agnus Dei)

  Kyrie I and III
    Intabulation: voice and vihuela
    2. 1554³² = F2093, No.75a and 75b, 91*v* (*Iosquin.* Fuenllana)

  Gloria
    Intabulation of part 1: voice and vihuela
    2. 1554³² = F2093, No.75, 91*v* (*Iosquin.* Fuenllana)
    Intabulation of part 2: vihuela
    2. M7725 (1546), No.10, 10*v*-12*r* (*Josquin.* Mudarra) • 1547²⁵ = V32, Nos.128–9, 85*v* (*Josquin.* Valderrábano)

  Sanctus and Osanna
    Intabulation: vihuela
    2. 1538²², No.16, 36*r*-38*r* (*josquin.* Narvaez)

Pleni

Intabulation: guitar

2. M7725 (1546), No.11, 12r–13r (*Iosquin*. Mudarra)

Missa ferialis   **Josquin.**   4vv
                                                     (Martini)

1. **24**, No.22 (*Josquin* in index)

3. I-MOe, α.M.1.13, No.13, 152v–159r (*Jo. Martini*) • I-Rvat, C.S.35, No.19, 170v–176r
   (Anon.) • I-VEcap, DCCLXI, No.17, 202v–208r (Anon. Without the Gloria and Credo)

Missa Fortuna desperata   **Josquin**   4vv

1. **4**, No.4 (Josquin) • **30**, No.4 (Josquin) • **62**, No.4 (*Josquin*)

2. J669 (1526), No.4 (Josquin) • 1539[1], No.4 (*Iosquin*) • 1539[2], No.2 (*Iosquin*)

3. A-Wn, 11778, No.4, 63v–83r (*Josquin*) • D-Mbs, Ms.3154, No.92, 172v–179r (*Josquin*) •
   E-Boc, 5, No.1, 1r–10r (Anon.) • I-MOe, α.M.1.2, No.7, 114v–127r (*Josquin*) • I-Rvat,
   C.S.41, No.5, 50v–61r (*Josquin des pres*) • S-Uu, 76b, No.11, 87v–96r (Anon. Mostly
   untexted)

4. Josquin, *Werken*, Missen, i, 13 • *New Josquin Edition*, viii, 2

Comments: Based on the Busnois chanson, also published by Petrucci

Literature: Antonowytsch, "Tendenzen"

Kyrie I

2. Glareanus 1557, H2v–H4r

3. D-Sl, HB.XVII.26, 69r (*Josquini*)

Christe

2. Zanger 1554, P3v–P4r

Credo

2. Heyden 1540, p. 124 (*Iosquin*. Ending only, with Superius and Tenor) • Finck 1556, Gg1v–
   Gg3v (Anon.) • Wilphlingseder 1561, D8v (*Iosquin*. Ending only, with Superius and Tenor)

Pleni

2. 1538[9], No.10, B3v (MS attribution in copy at D-Ju: *Joskin*)

Intabulation: vihuela

2. 1552[35] = P2448, No.67, 73v (*Jusquin*. Pisador)

Benedictus

Intabulation: voice and vihuela

2. 1552[35] = P2448, No.62, 52r–52v (*Jusquin*. Pisador)

Intabulation: keyboard

2. Baena 1540, No.23, 18v–19r (Josquin)

Agnus Dei I

2. 1547[1], pp. 388–91 (*Jodoco Prat.*) • Finck 1556, Hh3v–Hh4v (Anon.) • Wilphlingseder 1563,
   pp. 246–52 (*Jodoci Pratensi*)

Missa Fortuna desperata   **Obrecht**   4vv

1. **6**, No.3 (Obrecht)

2. O8 (s.d.), No.2 (Obrecht)

3. D-B, 40021, No.74, 150r–158r (Anon. Headed *O Fortuna*) • E-SE, s.s., No.6, 38v–45r.
   Jacobus Hobrecht. Lacks the Agnus) • I-MOe, α.M.1.2, No.6, 96v–114r (*Ja. Hobreth*)

4. Obrecht, *Collected Works*, iv, 49–91 • Obrecht, *Opera Omnia*, i/3, 113–69 • Obrecht,
   Werken, i, 85–135

Comments: Based on the Busnois chanson, also published by Petrucci

Literature: Antonowytsch, "Tendenzen" • Hudson, "Ferrarese"

Christe

    3. I-Fn, 107bis, No.33, 37*v*-38*r* (Anon.)

Kyrie II

    3. I-Fc, 2439, No.32, 33*v*-34*r* (*Jacobus Hobrecht*. Headed *Fortuna*)

Sanctus

    3. I-Fc, 2439, No.33, 34*v*-35*r* (*Hobrecht*. Headed *Fortuna*)

Pleni

    2. 1538^9, No.5, B1*v* (MS attribution in the copy at D-B: *Obrecht*. Untexted)

    3. I-Fn, 107bis, No.34, 38*v* (Anon.)

Osanna

    3. I-Fc, 2439, No.34, 35*v*-36*r* (*Ho*. Headed *Fortuna*)

    4. Newton, *Florence*, ii, 106–08.

Benedictus

    3. I-Fn, 107bis, No.35, 39*r* (Anon. Incomplete)

    Intabulation: keyboard

    3. CH-SGs, 530, 15*v*-16*r* (Anon. Incipit *Imprepel Frantaz*)

Agnus II

    3. I-Fn, 107bis, No.36, 39*v*-40*r* (Anon.)

Missa de Franza   **Basiron**   4vv

                                          (Philippon)

    1. *43*, No.2 (*Philippus Basiron.*)

    3. CZ-HK, II.A.7 (*Philippon*) • I-Rvat, C.S.35, No.15, 124*v*-135*r* (*.Phi.Basiron*)

Missa Fridericus dux Saxonie

  see **Missa Hercules dux Ferrariae**   **Josquin**   4vv

Missa Gaudeamus   **Josquin**

                                          (Ockeghem)

    1. *4*, No.3 (Iosquin) • *30*, No.3 (Josquin) • *62*, No.3 (*Josquin*. Titled *super Gaudeamus*)

    2. J669 (1526), No.3 (Josquin) • 1539^1, No.3 (*Iosquin*)

    3. A-Wn, 11778, No.3, 41*v*-62*r* (*Ockeghem*) • CH-Bu, F.IX.25a-d, No.2 (*Iosquin*) • D-Ju, 32, No.12 (Anon.) • D-Sl, 46, No.3, 103*v*-139*r* (*Iodocus de pratis*. Headed *Missa Josquini, musici excellentissimi, super Gaudeamus*) • E-Tc, 27, 85*v*-114*r* (Anon.) • F-CA, 18, No.7, 82*v*-97*r* (Anon.) • I-Rvat, C.S.23, No.3, 46*v*-60*r* (*Josquin des pres*)

    4. Josquin, *Werken*, Missen, i, 12

    Literature: Elders, "Gaudeamus"

    Intabulation: vihuela

    2. 1552^{35} = P2448, No.64, 57*v*-63*r* (*Jusquin*. Pisador. Lacks part of Sanctus and Agnus)

Benedictus

    2. Heyden 1537, p. 75 (Anon. Headed *Exemplum Proportionis Duplae.*) • Heyden 1540, pp. 88–89 (Anon. Headed *Exemplum Proportionis Duplae*) • 1547^1, p. 220 (Headed *in Missa Gaudeamus Tenor Benedictis eandem* [i.e., *Iodoci Pratensis*]) • A-Wn, 18832, No.8 (Anon.)

    Intabulation: keyboard

    2. Baena 1540, No.8, 11*v* (Josquin)

In nomine

    3. A-Wn, 18832, No.7 (Anon.)

    Intabulation: keyboard

    2. Baena 1540, No.7, 11*r*-*v* (Obrecht. Headed *Pleni Sunt celi:*)

Agnus Dei

Intabulation: vihuela

2. 1547²⁵ = V32, No.125, 84 (*Josquin.* Valderrábano)

Agnus Dei II

3. A-Wn, 18832, No.5 (*Josquin*) • D-Rp, B220-222, No.39, 71r-72r (*Josqn*)

Missa Gratieusa   **Ghiselin**   4vv

1. **9**, No.3 (Ghiselin); **57**, No.3 (Ghiselin)

3. A-Gla, 1 (Anon. Incomplete) • I-VEcap, DCCLVI, No.10, 122v-140r (Anon. Tenor is headed *Kyrie Gracieuse plaisant*)

4. Ghiselin, *Collected Works*, iii,

Comments: Based on Busnois's chanson *Mom mignault / Gratieuse*, also published by Petrucci

Gloria

2. Heyden 1537, p. 103 (Headed *Ghiselin. Canon Primo per ⅓. Secund per ½. Tertio ut iacet*) • Heyden 1540, p. 130

Qui tollis

2. Heyden 1537, p. 100 (Headed *Exemplum Ghiselini.* Tenor only) • Heyden 1540, p. 131 • Wilphlingseder 1563, p. 344

Patrem

2. Heyden 1537, p. 104 (Headed *Ghiselin. Patrem.* Tenor only) • Heyden 1540, p. 85 (Anon. Headed *Exemplum*)

Et iterum

2. Heyden 1537, p. 101 (Headed *Exemplum Sexti Canonis Et resurrexit. Ioannis Ghiselin.* Tenor only) • Heyden 1540, pp. 132–33 (Headed *Aliud exemplum Ghiselini*)

Sanctus

2. Heyden 1537, p. 105 (Headed *Sanctus Ghiselin.* Tenor only) • Heyden 1540, p. 84 (Headed *Exemplum Ghiselini.* Tenor only) • Wilphlingseder (1563), p. 150

Missa Grecorum   **Obrecht**   4vv

1. **6**, No.2 (Obrecht)

4. Obrecht, *Collected Works*, v, 1–33 • Obrecht, *Opera Omnia*, i/2, 69–111 • Obrecht, *Werken*, i, 49–84

Missa Hercules dux Ferrariae   **Josquin**   4vv

1. **22**, No.2 (*Josquin*) • **59**, No.2 (*Josquin*)

2. J672 (1526), No.2 (Josquin)

3. A-Wn, 4809, No.3, 47v-65r (Anon.) • B-Br, 9126, 72v-85r (Titled *Missa Philippus rex Castillie*) • CH-Bu, F.IX.25e-f, No.1 (*Josquin*) • D-F, 2 • D-Ju, 3, No.2, 15v-28r (*Josquin des Pres.* Headed *Missa Fridericus dux Saxonie*) • E-Tc, 27 • I-Bsp, A.XXXI, No.5, 18v-25r (Anon.) • I-Mfd, 2267, No.26, 141v-147r (.*Josquin.* Gloria, Credo, and Sanctus only) • I-Rvat, C.S.45, No.8, 116v-129r (*Josquin*)

4. Josquin, *Messe*, 65–85 • Josquin, *Werken*, Missen, ii, 17

Literature: Elders, "New Light"

Intabulation: voice and vihuela

2. 1552³⁵ = P2448, No.58, 31r-35v (*Jusquin.* Pisador. Lacks Pleni and Agnus Dei)

Et in spiritum

3. Faber 1550

Sanctus and Osanna

Intabulation: vihuela

2. 1538²², No.15, 38r (*josquin.* Narváez. Headed *Sanctus dela misa de faisan regres de josquin*)

Pleni

2. Heyden, 1537, p. 32 (*ex Hercule Iosquini*. Headed *Exemplum h durum partis infimae Systematis, sive Bassi. Fuga duorum in Epidiapente*) • Heyden, 1540, p. 38 (*Iosquini*. Headed *Fuga duorum, in Subdiatessaron*) • 1545[6], No.74 (*Ioskin*. Headed *In Hyperdiapente, post pausam semibrevem*. Texted *Numquid iustificari potest*) • 1547[1], p. 242 (Headed *Monados in Hypodorio prius exemplum ex Hercule Iodoci Pratensis*) • 1590[30] = P644, No.1, 3r (*D. Jodoci Pratensis vulgo Jusquin de pres*. Paix. Headed *Fuga in epidiapente*) • 1594[3] = P645, No.1, 3r (*D. Jodoci Pratensis vulgo Jusquin de pres*. Paix. Headed *Fuga in epidiapente*)

Intabulation: keyboard

2. Baena 1540, No.9, 11v-12r (Josquin)

Intabulation: vihuela

2. 1554[32] = F2093, No.1, 1r (*Josquin*. Fuenllana)

Agnus II

2. Heyden 1537, p. 110 (Headed *Exemplum Iosquini. Fuga trium, hic in Epidiapente ille in Subdiatessaron*) • 1540[7], No.103 • 1547[1], p. 221 (*ex Mi[[a Iodoci Praten[is*) • RISM 1558[10], No.1, f.1v (Transposed down a fifth. Headed *Trias in monade ad sex vocum deductionem Jodoci Pratansis: hic in epidiapente ille in subdiatessaron*) • Wilphlingsleder 1563 • 1590[30] = P644, No.34, 13v (*Jodoci Pratensis*. Paix, Headed *Fuga trium vocum, superius in epidiapente, Basis sub diatessaron incipit*) • 1594[3] = P645, No.32, 13v (*Jodoci Pratensis*. Paix. Headed *Fuga trium vocum, superius in epidiapente, Basis sub diatessaron incipit*)

Agnus Dei III   6vv

3. CH-SGs, 463, No.210, 74r and 135v-136r (*Josquin*. Headed *Dorius, idest primus*) • CH-SGs, 464, 7r (Anon.) • I-Bc, R142, No.48, 56v (*Josquin*) • I-MOd, IV, No.21, 47v-48r (Anon.)

Missa Jay pris amours   **de Orto**   4vv

1. **20**, No.2 (de Orto)

4. De Orto, *Works*, ii

Comments: Based on the anonymous rondeau, though not in the form published by Petrucci (see Fallows, *Catalogue*, 195–98)

Agnus Dei II

2. Heyden 1537, p. 32. *Ex Iay prys amours De Orto*. Headed *Exemplum bmolle partis infimae*) • Heyden 1540, p. 37 (*De Orto*. Headed *Fuga duorum in unisono*) • 1547[1], p. 320 (*Orto*. Headed *Monas in Hypoaeolio*)

Missa Je nay deul   **Brumel**   4vv

1. **8**, No.1 (Brumel)

2. 1539[1], No.6 (*Anthonii Brumel*. Headed *Festivale*)

4. Brumel, *Opera Omnia*, i, 119

Comment: Based on Agricola's chanson, also published by Petrucci

Crucifixus

2. 1538[9], No.73 (Anon. Untexted)

Pleni

2. 1549[16], No.4 (*ANTO. BRVMEL* Headed *Carmen in laudem musices*. Texted *Laeta graves abigit*)

3. A-Wn, 18832, No.88 (Anon. Untexted)

Benedictus

2. 1549[16], No.11 (*ANTO. BRVMEL* Texted *O ubi sancti rectores*)

3. A-Wn, 18832, No.52 (Anon. Untexted)

Qui venit

2. 1545[7] No.74 (Anon. Texted *Vac qui sapientis*) • 1547[1], p. 297 (*Antonij Brumel* Headed *Dyados in Dorio*) • Wilphlingseder 1563, pp. 44–45 (*Antonij Brumel.* Headed *Exemplum Mutationis [natural sign] durale*) • 1590[30] = P644, No.5, 4r (*Antonii Brumelii. Fuga in homophonia*)

3. A-Wn, 18832, No.87 (Anon.) • CH-SGs, 462, p. 140 (Anon. Headed *Duo*) • D-Mu, 322–325, No.11 (Anon. Untexted)

Missa Je nay dueul   **Ghiselin**   4vv

1. **9**, No.5 (Ghiselin); **57**, No.5 (Ghiselin)

3. A-Wn, 1783 • F-CA, 18, No.12, 153v–168r (Anon.)

4. Ghiselin, *Collected Works*, iii, 35–65.

Comments: Based on a chanson by Agricola or Ockeghem

Missa Je ne demande   **Agricola**   4vv

1. **13**, No.2 (*Alexander*)

3. D-LEu, 51, 38v–42r and 57v–62r (*Alexander Agricola*) • I-MOs, 221, No.3, pp. 3–6 (Anon. Original number XIIII. Parts of the Credo and Sanctus) • I-Rvat, C.S.23, No.2, 28v–45r (*Agricola*)

4. Agricola, *Opera Omnia*, i, 105

Comments: Based on Busnois's chanson, also published by Petrucci

Missa Je ne demande   **Obrecht**   4vv

1. **6**, No.1 (Obrecht)

Facsimile: Sadie, *New Grove*, iii, 480–81

3. A-Wn, 18742, No.6 • D-LEu, 51 (Lacks Agnus II and III) • D-Mbs, 3154, No.153, 370r–379v (Anon. Incomplete)

4. Obrecht, *Collected Works*, v, 35–84 • Obrecht, *Opera Omnia*, i, 1–64 • Obrecht, *Werken*, i, 1–48

Comments: Uses a *cantus firmus* derived from Busnois's chanson, also published by Petrucci

Literature: Blackburn, "Obrecht" • Burkholder, "Martini" • Noblitt, "Problems"

Kyrie I

2. Heyden 1537, p. 97 (Headed *Exemplum. Ie ne demande Oberti*)

Qui tollis

2. Heyden 1537, p. 83 (Headed *Exemplum in Ie ne demande Oberti*) • Heyden 1540, p. 101 (Headed *Exemplum in Ie ne demande Oberti. Qui tollis*) • Heyden 1540, p. 109 (Headed *Exemplum Oberti in Ie ne demande.* Superius and Tenor only) • Faber 1553 • Wilphlingseder 1563, pp. 243–245 (Tenor only) • Wilphlingseder 1563, p. 317 (Tenor and Bass for mm.111–25)

3. D-B, 1175, 38r (Anon. Tenor only)

Et in spiritum

2. Heyden 1537, p. 98 (Headed *Exemplum. Sanctus [sic] Ie ne demande Oberti*)

Missa La bella se siet   **Ghiselin**   4vv

1. **9**, No.1 (Ghiselin); **57**, No.1 (Ghiselin)

3. D-Dl, 1/D/506, 86v–93r (*Verbonnet*) • D-Ju, 32, 114v–133r (*Ghiselin*) • I-VEcap, DCCLVI, No.3, 33v–47r (Anon.)

4. Ghiselin, *Collected Works*, ii, 1

Comments: Based on the chanson by Dufay

Patrem

3. CZ-HK, II.A.7, No.22, d.12v–13r (*Verbonnet*)

Sanctus (incomplete)

    2. Heyden 1540, p. 129 (Headed *Exemplum ex Ghiselino*) • Wilphlingseder (1563), pp. 260–261 (*Ghiselin*)

Missa La bella se sied   **de Orto**   4vv

    1. *20*, No.4 (de Orto)

    Comments: Based on the chanson by Dufay

Agnus Dei III

    2. Heyden 1537, p. 104 (Headed *Alterum Exemplum. Agnus ultimum, ex La belle de Orto.* Superius only) • Heyden 1540, p. 134 (Headed *Agnus ultimum, ex La belle de Orto*)

Missa Lami baudichon   **Josquin**   4vv

    1. *22*, No.4 (*Josquin*) • *59*, No.4 (*Josquin*)

    2. J672 (1526), No.4 (Josquin)

    3. A-Wn, 11778, No.6, 108v-125r (Anon.) • D-Z, CXIX,1, No.14, 130v-133r (Anon. Kyrie, Gloria, and Credo, all incomplete) • I-Rvat, C.S.23, No.6, 96v-105v (*Josquin*) • I-VEcap, DCCLXI, No.6, 62v-73r (Anon.) • PL-Pu, 7022, II, No.1 (fragments)

    4. Josquin, *Werken*, Missen, ii, 20

    Literature: Brothers, "Vestiges," 26–29 • Fallows, *Catalogue*, 233–34

Gloria

    3. I-Sc, K.I.2, No.92, 212v-214r (Anon.)

Qui tollis

    3. D-Rp, B220-222, 75r (*Josquin*)

Credo

    3. CZ-HK, II.A.7, pp. 256–61 (Anon.)

Missa La Bassadanza

    see **Missa La Spagna**   **Isaac**   4vv

Missa La mi la sol   **Isaac**   4vv

    2. 1539[1], No.7 (*Henrici Isaac*)

    3. D-Rp, C.100, 118v-139r (*Isaac. Resoluta per Joannem Buechmayrum*: Titled *Missa O praeclara*)

    4. Isaac, *Messen*, 120

Patrem and **Et unam sanctam**

    1. *15*, No.34 (Anon. Texted *Rogamus te piisima virgo*. 2/ texted *O Maria, O regina*)

    3. CH-SGs, 461, 42–45 (*h.ysaac*. Untexted) • GB-Lbl, Add.31922, 7v-9r (Anon. Texted *La my*) • I-Bc, Q18, No.26, 26v-28r (Anon. Texted *La mi la sol*: part 1 only) • I-CF, LIX, No.21, 54v-56r (Anon. Texted *Rogamus te piisima virgo*) • I-Fc, 2439, No.37, 38v-40r (*yzaac*. Texted *La mi la sol*)

    4. Isaac, *Weltliche*, i, 87–89 • Newton, *Florence*, ii, 114–19 • Osthoff, *Theatergesang* • Sherr, *16th-century*, ii, 199–206 • Stevens, *Henry VIII*, 5–6

    Literature: Elders, "Frage"; Staehelin, *Isaac*

Missa La sol fa re mi   **Josquin**   4vv

    1. *4*, No.2 (*Iosquin*) • *30*, No.2 (Josquin) • *62*, No.2 (*Josquin*)

    2. J669 (1526), No.2 (Josquin) • 1539[1], No.2. (*Iosquin*)

    3. A-Wn, 11778, No.5 83v-107r (*Josquin*) • A-Wn, 11883, following No.17, 194v-195r (Kyrie and part of Gloria) • A-Wn, 15499, 244v-272r (Anon.) • D-B, 40091, No.8, 138v-157r (*Josquin des pres*) • D-Ju, 32, No.2, 21v-29r (Anon.) • D-Rp, C.100, No.7, 95v-118r (*Josquini*) • D-Sl, 44, No.5, 129v-157r (*Iosquin*) • E-Tc, 19, No.4, 71v-92r (*Josquin*) • F-Pn, 851, pp. 377–383 (*Josquin*) • I-Bsp, A.XXXI, No.2, 7v-14r (Anon.) • I-Ma, 46, No.9,

82*v*-88*r* (*Josquin*. Incomplete, lacking most of Sanctus and Agnus) • I-Rsm, 26, No.5, 62*v*-77*r* (Anon.) • I-Rvat, C.S.41, No.4, 38*v*-49*r* (*Josquin* in the index. Titled *Lesse faire a mi*)

4. Josquin, *Werken*, Missen, i, 11

Literature: Haar, "Some remarks"

Intabulation: vihuela

2. 1552³⁵ = P2448, No.63, 53*r*-57*r* (*Josquin*. Pisador. Lacks Pleni, Osanna, and Agnus Dei)

Kyrie

Intabulation: vihuela

2. 1554³² = F2093, No.76, 93*r* (*Josquin*. Fuenllana)

Qui tollis

Intabulation: voice and vihuela

2. 1554³² = F2093, No.73, 90*r* (*Josquin*. Fuenllana)

Agnus

Intabulation: keyboard

2. Baena 1540, No.61 59*v*-60*r* (Josquin)

Pleni

Intabulation: keyboard

2. Baena 1540, No.62, 60*r*-61*r* (Josquin)

Benedictus

Intabulation: vihuela

2. M7725 (1546), No.35. ii, 12*v*-13*v* (*Josquin*. Mudarra. Headed *Glosa sobre un Benedictus de una missa de Josquin que va sobre la sol fa re mi*)

Osanna II

2. Zanger 1554, K3*r*-K3*v* (*Josquini*)

Agnus Dei II

3. A-Wn, 18832, No.4, 10*r*-10*v* (Anon.) • D-Rp, B220-222, No.50, 30*v* (*Josquin*)

Missa La Spagna	Isaac	4vv

1. *31*, No.4 (Isaac)

3. E-Boc, 5, No.4, 33*v*-42*r* (*Henericus Yzac*. Headed *Missa sobre Castilla*) • I-Mfd, 2268, No.1, 0*v*-6*r* (*Enricus Isaac*. Titled *La Bassadanza*. Gloria, Credo and Sanctus only) • S-Uu, 76e, 33*r*-43*v* (*Henrici Izac*)

4. Isaac, *Messe*, 1–37 • Isaac, *Opera Omnia*, vii, 1–42

Literature: Staehelin, *Isaac*, iii, 37–40

Qui tollis

3. PL-Wu, 58, 22*r* (Anon. Texted as Agnus Dei. See Staehelin, "Isaac", i. 29)

Agnus II		3vv

3. D-LEu, 1494, 63*v* (Anon. Untexted) • I-VEcap, DCCLVII, No.5, 4*v*-5*r* (Anon. Untexted) • PL-Wu, 58, 38*r* (Anon. Untexted)

Missa super l'homme arme	Brumel	4vv

1. *8*, No.4 (Brumel)

3. CH-Bu, F.VI.26e, 1*r*-11*r* (*Brumel*) • D-Ju, 31, No.9, 109*r*-125*v* (Anon.) • I-Mfd, 2268, No.35, 191*v*-203*r* (*Antonius brumel*) • I-Rsm, 26, No.12, 183*v*-201*r* (Anon.) • I-Rvat, C.VIII.234, No.24, 199*v*-212*r* (*Brumel*) • I-Rvat, C.S.49, No.13, 144*v*-148*r* (Anon. Incomplete: parts of Kyrie and Credo) • I-VEcap, DCCLXI, No.14, 163*v*-179*r* (Anon.)

4. Brumel, *Opera Omnia*, i, 65–88

Missa L'homme arme sexti toni   **Josquin**   4vv

1. **4**, No.5 (*Iosquin*) • **30**, No.5 (Josquin) • **62**, No.5 (*Iosquin*)
2. J669 (1526), No.5 (Josquin) • J677 (1560), No.1 (Josquin)
3. A-Wn, 11778, No.2, 23v–41r (*Josquin*) • D-Ju, 31, No.14, 199v–211r (*Josquin des Prez*) • D-LEu, 51, 12v–16r (*Josquin*) • D-Sl, 47, 75v–90r (Anon., incomplete) • E-SE, s.s., No.2, 11v–18v (*Josquin Dupres*) • F-Pn, 851, p. 384 (*Josquin*) • I-CMac, M (D), No.15, 91v–100r (*Josquin de pres*) • I-Mfd, 2267, No.15, 135v–141r (*Josquin. Gloria, Credo and Sanctus only*) • I-Rvat, C.VIII.234, No.23, 191v–199r (*Josquyn. Incomplete, lacking Sanctus and Agnus*) • I-Rvat, C.S.41, No.3, 27v–37r (*Josquin*) • NL-L, 1443, No.28, 373r–384r (Anon.) • PL-Pu, 7022, III, No.3 (Anon. fragments)
4. Josquin, *Messe*, 35–64 • Josquin, *Werken*, Missen, i, 14

Kyrie III

2. Heyden 1537, p. 64 • Heyden 1540, p. 64 (Headed *Exemplum Iosquini ex Lhomme Arme sexti toni*). Tenor only • Wilphlingseder 1563, p. 234

Et resurrexit

Intabulation: lute

3. US-Cn, 107501, No.33, 53v–55v (Anon.)

Benedictus

2. Heyden 1537, p. 12 (Anon. Headed *Fuga in Subdiapente*) • Heyden 1540, p. 12 (Anon. Headed *Fuga in Subdiapente*) • 1547[1], p. 220 (*Iodoci Pratensis*) • Wilphlingseder 1561, B5r • Wilphlingseder 1563, p. 18 (*Josquini*)

Agnus Dei III

2. Heyden 1537, pp. 156–58 • Heyden 1540, pp. 156–58 (Headed *Exemplum Sexti Toni. Fuga ad minimam Iosquini in Lhomme arme Sexti Toni*) • Wilphlingseder 1563, pp. 156–58 (*Josquini*)

Missa L'homme arme super voces musicales   **Josquin**   4vv

1. **4**, No.1 (*Iosquin*) • **30**, No.1 (Josquin) • **62**, No.1 (Josquin)
2. J669 (1526), No.1 (Josquin) • 1539[1], No.1 (*Iosquin*) • 1539[2], No.5
3. A-Wn, 11778, No.1, 1v–22r (*Josquin des pres*) • CH-Bu, F.IX.25a–d, No.1. (*Josquin*) • D-F, 2, 1r–17r (Anon. Incomplete) • D-Ju, 32, No.1 (Anon.) • D-Rp, A.R.878–882, No.25, 59v–67v (Anon.) • D-Rp, C.100, No.10 • E-Boc, 5, No.6, 52v–55r (Anon. Incomplete, only Kyrie and Agnus III) • E-Tc, 9, No.3, 4v–35r (*Jusquin*) • F-Pc, 851, No.274 • I-Bsp, A.XXXI, No.13, 131v–138r and 148v–150r (Anon.) • I-MOe, α.M.1.2, No.8, 127v–142r (*Josquin*) • I-Rvat, C.G.XII.2, No.4, 125v–142r (*Jos*) • I-Rvat, C.S.154, No.1, 3v–29r (*Josquin des Prez: with a fifth voice for the third Agnus, attributed to Johannes Abbate*) • I-Rvat, C.S.197, No.1, 1v–12r (*Josquin*) • S-Uu, 76c, 10v–17r (*Josquin des Pres*)
4. Josquin, *Werken*, Misse, i, 10
Literature: Heikamp, "Struktur"
Intabulation: vihuela
2. 1552[35] = P2448, No.61, 46r–51v (*Jusquin. Pisador. Missa de super boze musicales. Lacks all from the Osanna*)

Kyrie I

2. Heyden 1537, pp. 125–126 (Two voices only) • Heyden 1540, p. 125 (Headed *Exemplum Primum Kyrie ex Lhomme arme Iosquini*: two voices only) • Zanger 1554, Q4r–Q4v • Finck 1556, H3v–H4r (Anon.) • Wilphlingseder 1563, pp. 336–37 (*Iosquini*)

Christe

2. Heyden 1540, p. 126 (Headed *Exemplum Christe eleyson ex Lhomme arme Iosquini*) • Faber 1550, Y1r-Y1v (*Josquini*) • Zanger 1554, Q4v-R1v • Dressler 1571, k2v-k4v (*Iosquini*)

Kyrie II

2. Finck 1556, H4v-I1r (Anon.)

Et in terra

2. Finck 1556, K2r-K4v (Anon.)

Patrem

Intabulation: keyboard

2. Baena 1540, No.64, 61v-63v (Josquin)

Sanctus

2. Zanger 1554, M1v-M3r • Finck 1556, N3r-N4v (Anon.) • Dressler 1571, I4r-I4v (*Josquin*. Tenor only)

Pleni

2. Zanger 1554, K4v-L1v

Intabulation: keyboard

2. Baena 1540, No.25, 20r-v (Josquin)

Osanna

2. Heyden 1537, pp. 160–61 • Heyden 1540, pp. 159–60 (Headed *Sequitur exemplum Septimi Toni Iosquini, ex Lhomme arme*) • Faber 1550, M1v-M2r (*Josquini*) • Zanger 1554, M4r-N1v • Finck 1556, Dd3v-Ee1r (Anon.) • Dressler 1571, H8r-I3r (Anon. Texted *Gaudet cum gaudentibus*)

Intabulation: keyboard

2. 1578[24] = C1, No.85, 96v-99r (*Jusquin*. Cabezón)

Benedictus

2. Heyden 1537, p. 86 (Headed *Exemplum Tertii Modi, per* [reversed C]. *Duo in unum Iosquini.*) • Heyden 1540, p. 103 (Headed *Exemplum Tertii Modi, per C cum* [reversed C]. *Duo in unum Iosquini*) • Finck 1556, O2r (Anon.)

Intabulation: keyboard

2. 1578[24] = C1, No.86, 98v-99r (*Jusquin*. Cabezón)

Qui venit

2. Heyden 1537, p. 85 (Headed *Exemplum Secundi Modi, per* [cut circle, cut c]. *Duo in unum Iosquini*) • Heyden 1540, p. 103 (Headed *Exemplum Secundi Modi, per* [cut circle] *cum* [cut c]. *Duo in unum Iosquini*) • 1547[1], p. 442 • Zanger 1554, L1v

In nomine

2. Heyden 1537, p. 85 (Headed *Exemplum primi Modi per C2. Duo in unum Iosquini*) • Heyden 1540, p. 103 (Headed *Exemplum primi Modi per C cum C2. Duo in unum Iosquini*) • 1547[1], pp. 442–43 (*De Iodoci pratensi*)

Qui tollis

2. Finck 1556, Ee1r-Ee3r (Anon.)

Agnus Dei II

2. Heyden 1537, p. 90 (*ex Lomme arme Iosquini.* Headed *Fuga trium vocum ex unica, quarum prima Proportionatum valorem: Altera Diminutum: tertia Integrum canit*) • Heyden 1540, p. 112 (Headed *Fuga trium. ex Lhomme arme Iosquini*) • 1547[1], pp. 442–43 (Headed *Ex una voce tres, ex eiusde*(m) *Iodoci Missa Lhome arme super voces musicales*) • Faber 1550, T1v (*Josquini*) • Zanger 1554, T1v-T2r • Finck 1556, Ff3v (Anon.) • 1590[30] = P644, No.13, 6r (*D. Jodoci*

Pratensis. Headed *Triados ex unica*) • 1594³ = P645, No.11, 6r (*D. Jodoci Pratensis*. Headed *Triados ex unica*)

   3. D-B, 1175, 86v-87r (*Josquin*) • GB-Lbl, Add.4911, 42v (*Josquini*) • I-MOd, IV, 49v-50r (Anon.)

   Intarsia: Piacenza, San Sisto

Agnus Dei III

   2. Finck 1556, Cc3v (Anon.)

   3. E-Tc, 21, No.16, 43v-47r (*Jusquin*. Headed *super vo*) • I-Rpol, a manuscript addition to *RISM* 1517³, third additional folio (Anon. Headed *Agnus voi clamo ne cesses*)

   Painting: Dosso Dossi, *Allegories of Music* (Florence, Museo Horne)

   Intabulation: keyboard

   2. 1578²⁴ = CI, No.84, 91v (*Jusquin*. Cabezón. Texted *Clama ne cesses*)

   Intabulation: vihuela

   2. 1547²⁵ = V32, No.7, 3v (*Josquin*. Valderrábano)

   Literature: Slim, "Dosso"; Stam, "Josquin"; van Benthem, "Musikintarsien"; van Benthem, "Kompositoriches"

Missa Lomme arme   La Rue   4vv

   1. *11*, No.4 (*Pe.de.la rue*)

   Facsimile: Apel, "Notation", 121 (the first Kyrie)

   3. A-Wn, 1783, 229v (*Rue*) • B-Br, 9126, 28v-43r (*Petrus de Rue*) • D-Ju, 22, 30v-42r (*Petrus de la Rue*) • D-LEu, 51

   4. La Rue, *L'homme arme*

Sanctus

   3. I-Rvat, 11953, No.24, 21v (Anon.)

Pleni

   2. 1545⁷, No.68 (Anon. Texted *Querite Dominum Deum*)

   3. D-Rp, B.220–222, 79v (Anon.)

Osanna

   3. I-Rvat, 11953, No.25, 22r (Anon.)

Agnus III

   2. Heyden 1537, p. 91 (*Petri de la Rue . . . ex Lomme arme*) • Heyden 1540. p. 112 (Headed *Tertium argumentum Petri de la Rue est*) • 1547¹, p. 445 (*Petri Platensis III vocum fuga ex unica ad Hypodorium.*) • 1590³⁰, No.18

   3. I-Rvat, 11953, No.23, 21r (Anon.)

Missa Lomme arme   de Orto   4vv

   1. *20*, No.3 (de Orto)

   3. I-Rvat, C.S.64, No.1, 3v-13r (*de Orto*)

   4. Feininger, *Monumenta*, I, i/7

Agnus Dei I

   2. Heyden 1537, p. 103 (Headed *Ex Lomme arme de Orto*)

Missa Le serviteur   Agricola   4vv

   1. *13*, No.1 (Agricola: *Alexander* in Altus and Bassus)

   3. A-Wn, 1783, No.8, 111v-126r (*Agricola* [with a rebus]) • D-Ju, 22, No.12, 128v-141r (*Alexander*) • I-Rvat, C.S.23, No.5, 76v-95r (*Agricola*)

   4. Agricola, *Opera Omnia*, i, 1–33

   Comments: Based on the chanson attributed to Dufay

Christe

    2. Heyden 1537, p. 113 (Headed *Exemplum. Fuga duorum Temporum ion Diatessaron Alexan. Agricolae*)

Missa Le vilayn ialoys   **R. de Févin**   4vv

    1. **61**, No.4 (*Robertus de feuin*)

    3. I-Rvat, C.S.23, No.7, 106r-117r (Anon.)

    4. Févin, *Collected Works*, pp. 75–110.

Missa de Les Armes   **Ghiselin**   4vv

    1. **9**, No.2 (Ghiselin); **57**, No.2 (Ghiselin)

    4. Ghiselin, *Collected Works*, ii,

Kyrie

Intabulation: lute

    1. **34**, No.20, 25r-25v (*Francesco Spinacino*)

    4. Schmidt, *Spinacino*, ii, 230–31

Christe

    3. I-Rc, 2856, 136v-137r (*Jo. Ghiselin.* Texted *Je lay empris*)

parts

    2. Wilphlingseder (1563), pp. 286 and 316.

Missa Malheur me bat   **Agricola**   4vv

    1. **13**, No.3 (*Alexander*)

    3. A-Wn, 1783, No.5, 65v-82r (*Allexander Agricola* [with a rebus]) • B-Br, 9126, 116v-134r (*Allexander*)

    4. Agricola, *Opera Omnia*, i, 66

Comments: Based on the chanson attributed to Ockeghem and others, also published by Petrucci

Kyrie I

    2. Heyden 1537, pp. 64–65 (*A Agricolae.* Headed *Exemplum*) • Heyden 1540, pp. 78–79 (*A. Agricola.* Headed *Exemplum. Kyrie ex Malheur me bat*) • Zanger 1554, N1v-3r

Crucifixus

    2. Heyden 1537, p. 109 (Headed *Exemplum Duo Alexand. Agric.*)

Et resurrexit

    3. A-Wn, 18832, No.9, 12r-12v (Anon.)

Benedictus

    3. A-Wn, 18832, No.1, 7v-8r (Anon.) • D-Mbs, 260, No.45, 29v-30r (Anon.)

Agnus I

    2. Heyden 1540, pp. 150–154 (*Alex. Agric.* Headed *Exemplum Quarti Toni*)

Missa Malheur me bat   **Josquin**   4vv

    1. **22**, No.3 (*Josquin*) • **59**, No.3 (*Josquin*)

    2. J 672 (1526), No.3. (Josquin)

    3. A-Wn, 4809, No.4, 66v-89r (*Josquin*) • A-Wn, 11883, No.1, 2v-11r (*Josquin des pres*) • B-Br, 9126, 82v-95r (*Josquin*) • CH-Bu, F.IX.25e-f, No.2 (*Josquin.* Titled *Malormebat*) • D-Ju, 3, No.5, 59v-73r (*Josquin des pres*) • D-LEu, 51, No.1 (*Josquin.* Lacks Agnus) • D-ROu, 40, No.5 (*Josquin.* Headed *Missa Quae est ista.* No Sanctus or Agnus Dei) • E-Tc, 9, No.5, 54v-83r (*Jusquin*) • I-Bsp, A.XXXI, No.15, 139v-148r (*Iosquin.* Incomplete) • I-Ma, 46, No.3, 22v-32r (*Josquin*) • I-Rvat, C.S.23, No.4, 61v-75r (*Josquin des pres*)

    4. Josquin, *Werken*, Missen, ii, 19 • *New Josquin Edition*, ix, 1

Comments: Based on the chanson attributed to Ockeghem and others, also published by
Petrucci

Kyrie and Gloria

3. I-MOd, IV, No.37, 88r–91v (Anon.)

Pleni

2. 1549[16], No.16 (*Josquin.* Texted *Quid tam solicitis*)

3. D-Rp, B.220–222, 73v–74r/68v–69v (*Josquin*) • GB-Lbl, Add.4911, 41v (*Josquini*)

Agnus II

2. Heyden 1537, p. 78 (Headed *Exemplum. Fuga duorum Iosquin*) • Heyden 1540, p. 92
(Headed *Exemplum. Fuga duorum. Iosquin*) • 1547[1], pp. 451–452 (Anon. Headed *Phrygij
phrasis ac systema superne semitonio inferne tono adiectis*) • 1590[30], No.31 (Anon.) • 1594[3],
No.31 (Anon.)

3. A-Wn, 18832, No.89 (Anon.) • D-Mbs, 260, No.56, 37v–38r (Anon.) • GB-Lbl,
Add.4911, 41v–42r (Anon. Texted *Per totium es elevatur tonus*) • I-MOd, IV, No.35, 74v–
75r (Anon.)

Missa Malheur me bat	**Obrecht**	4vv

1. *6*, No.4 (Obrecht)

3. D-B, 40021, No.97, 186r–192v (Anon. Headed *Officium mi .o. Mi fa mi ut re ut*) • D-LEu,
51, No.2 • PL-Kj, 40634, No.7

4. Obrecht, *Opera Omnia*, i/4, 173–225 • Obrecht, *Werken*, i, 141–88

Comments: Based on the chanson attributed to Ockeghem and others, also published by
Petrucci

Literature: Hudson, "Ferrarese"; Sparks, *Cantus Firmus*

Christe

2. 1538[9], No.85, L3r (Anon. Untexted)

4. Mönkemeyer, *Formschneyder*, ii, p. 123

Crucifixus

2. 1538[9], No.92, M2v (Anon. Untexted)

4. Mönkemeyer, *Formschneyder*, ii, pp. 133–34

Pleni

2. 1538[9], No.76, K3r (Anon. Untexted)

4. Mönkemeyer, *Formschneyder*, ii, pp. 111–12

Agnus II

2. 1538[9], No.93, M3r (Anon. Untexted)

4. Mönkemeyer, *Formschneyder*, ii, pp. 134–35

Missa Mater patris	**Josquin**	4vv

1. *54*, No.1 (*Iosquin*)

2. J675 (1526), No.1 (*Josquin.*)

3. I-MOd, IV, No.45, 107v–114r (Anon.)

4. Josquin, *Werken*, Missen, iii, 26

Comments: Based on Brumel's motet, also published by Petrucci • Adapted by Krzysztof
Borek, as No.7 in PL-Kk, I.1 (cf. Czepiel, *Music*, 85–89)

Literature: Antonowytsch, "Missa"

Benedictus

2. Heyden 1537, p. 28 *Iosquini.* Headed *Exemplum h durum acuti Systematis. Fuga*) • Heyden
1540, p. 30 (*Iosquin*) • 1547[1], p. 448 (*Iodocus.* Headed *Dorij Hypordorijque connexorum exemplum cum Semiditono superne*)

Pleni

 2. Heyden 1537, p. 26 (*Iosquin*. Headed *Exemplum bmolle acuti Systematis. Fuga*) • Heyden 1540, p. 28 (Headed *Fuga duarum vocum, quarum altera priorem post tempus sequitur, altior tono. Ios.*) • 1547[1], p. 446 (*ad Iodocum*. Headed *Ionici Hypoionicique connexorum exemplum finitum ut Phrygius*)

 3. GB-Lbl, Add.4911, 42*v* (*Josquin*)

Agnus Dei II

 2. Heyden 1537, p. 30 (*Iosquini*. Headed *Exemplum bmolle medii Systematis*) • 1547[1], p. 257 (Headed *Monados in Aeolio secundum exemplum Iodoci Pratensis*)

 3. D-Rp, B.220–222, 72*v*-73*r* (*Josquin*)

Missa Mente tota   **A. Févin**   4vv

 1. **61**, No.2 (*Ant. feuin*)

 2. 1516[1], No.4, 46*v*-57*r* (*Fevin*)

 3. A-Wn, 15495, No.2, 19*v*-33*r* (*Anthonius de fevin*) • D-Ju, 3, No.4, 43*v*-58*r* (*Anthonius de fevin*) • E-Bbc, 454, No.2, 4*v*-12*r* (*Anthonius Fevin*. Incomplete) • I-Rvat, C.G.XII.2, No.6, 175*v*-191*r* (*fevin*) • I-Rvat, C.S.16, No.4, 47*v*-60*r* (*Ant. de fevin*) • S-Uu, 76b, 50*v*-60*r* (Anon.) • S-Uu, 76c, 17*v*-25*r* (Anon.)

 4. Clinkscale, *Févin*, ii, 122–56 • Expert, *Maîtres*, ix, No.2

 Comments: Based on Josquin's motet

Benedictus

 2. 1545[6], No.40 (*Antonius Fevinus*. Headed *Ex Mente tota*)

 3. A-Wn, 18810, No.18 (Anon.) • D-Mbs, 260, No.57, 38*v*-39*r* (Anon.)

Pleni

 2. 1545[7], No.56 (Anon. Texted *Beatus homo*) • 1549[16], No.45

 3. A-Wn, 18832, No.20 (Anon. Untexted. Transposed a fourth lower) • D-Mbs, 260, No.58, 38*v*-39*r* (Anon. Transposed a fourth lower)

Agnus II

 2. 1545[6], No.41 (*Antonius Fevinus*. Headed *Ex Mente tota*)

 3. A-Wn, 18832, No.17

Missa Misericordias Domini   **Isaac**   4vv

 1. **31**, No.2 (Isaac)

 3. A-Wn, 11883, No.14, 145*v*-163*r* (*Henricus yzaac*) • S-Uu, 76e, 12*v*-21*r* (*Henrici Izac*)

 Comments: Parts of the opening of each movement, and of Agnus III are found as the secular work *In focho la mia vita* (See Staehelin, *Isaac*, iii, 104).

Missa Narayge   **Ghiselin**   4vv

 1. **9**, No.4 (Ghiselin); **57**, No.4 (Ghiselin)

 3. I-Bsp, A.XXIX, No.9, 64*v*-68*v* (Anon. Only as far as part of the Credo. In the index, *Missa de narai james*) • I-VEcap, DCCLVI, No.5, 64*v*-76*r* (Anon. Tenor is titled *Kyrie Narayme james mieulx*)

 4. Ghiselin, *Collected Works*, ii, 74–96

 Comments: Based on the rondeau by Morton

Kyrie I

 2. Heyden 1540, p. 122 (Headed *Exemplum ex Naraige Ghiselini*, and a second time Headed *Exemplo sint prioris exempli Diminutae voces, quibus si dimidum figurarum auferas, ita habebunt*) • Wilphlingseder 1561, D4*v* (Anon.)

Cum sancto

 2. Heyden 1537, p. 80 (Headed *Exemplum Ioannis Ghiselin*) • Heyden 1540, p. 94 (Anon.

Headed *Exemplum*) • 1547[1], p. 218 (Headed *Secundum exemplum* [of hemiola]. *Ioannes Ghi[elin author.*) • Finck 1556, X1v-2r (Anon.) • Wilphlingseder 1563, p. 288

Sanctus

2. Heyden 1540, p. 128 (Headed *Exemplum ex Naraige Iohannis Ghiselin*. Tenor and Bassus only) • Wilphlingseder 1563, pp. 200–01 and 235–37

Pleni

2. 1538[9], No.43 (MS attribution in the copy at D-Ju: *Joh. Ghyselin*) • 1542[8], No.36 (*Ghiselin*. Texted *Tota scriptura*)

3. D-LEu, 51, 83v-84r

Missa Nas tu pas	**Weerbeke**	4vv

1. *48*, No.4 (*Gaspar.*)

Credo

3. I-Rsm, 26, No.19. 253v-256r (Anon.)

Missa N'auray je jamais		
See **Missa Didadi**	**Josquin**	4vv
Missa Nunqua fue pena maior	**La Rue**	4vv

1. *11*, No.5 (*Pe.de la rue.*)

3. D-Ju, 22, No.5, 54v-67r (*Rue*) • D-Sl, 45, No.6, 95v-114r (*Petrus de la Rue*) • I-Rvat, C.S.45, No.9, 130v-145r (*Person de la rue*. Lacks the Agnus)

Comments: Based on the canción by Urrede (or Enrique), published by Petrucci in Spinacino's tabulature, and (in a different setting) in *Canti C*.

Missa O preclara		
see **Missa La mi la sol**	**Isaac**	4vv
Missa O sacer Anthoni		
see **Missa de sancto Antonio**	**La Rue**	4vv
Missa O Venus bant	**Weerbeke**	4vv

1. *32*, No.2 (Gaspar)

3. (all lacking some sections) CZ-HK, II.A.7, pp. 262–271 (Anon. Credo and Sanctus) • D-B, 40021, No.7, 23r-29r (Anon. Headed *Venuspandt*) • I-MOe, α.M.1.13, No.17, 207v-224r (*Guaspar Warbec*) • I-Rsm, No.7, 26, 98v-119r (Anon.) • I-Rvat, C.S.51, No.14, 132v-145r (*Gaspar*) • I-VEcap, DCCLVII, No.61, 63v-66r (Anon. Incomplete: only the Kyrie and part of the Gloria) • PL-Wu, 58, 120v-130r (Anon.) • S-Uu, 76e, No.2 (Gaspar)

Et incarnatus		3vv

3. D-LEu, 1494, 165v (*Vb*. Text *Respice virgo pura*) • I-Fn, 229, No.141, 145v-146r (Anon. Untexted)

4. Brown, *Florentine*, music volume, 141–142 • Gerber, *Mensuralkodex*, xxiii, 216

Pleni sunt caeli		3vv

3. I-Fn, 229, No.142, 146v-147r (Anon. Untexted)

4. Brown, *Florentine*, music volume, 296–97

Benedictus		3vv

3. I-Fn, 229, No.143, 147v-148r (Anon. Untexted)

4. Brown, *Florentine*, music volume, 298–99

Missa Octavi [toni]	**Weerbeke**	4vv

1. *32*, No.4 (Gaspar)

Agnus Dei III

2. Heyden 1537, p. 114 (Headed *Exemplum. Gaspar. Octaui.*) • Heyden 1540, p. 162 (*Gaspar*. Headed *Exemplum Octavi Toni*)

Missa Petita Camuseta	**de Orto**	4vv

 1. **20**, No.5 (de Orto)

 3. A-Wn, 1783, No.10 (*De Orto*. Titled *Officium My my*) • D-Ju, 32, No.3 (Anon.)

 4. Ambros, *Geschichte*, v, 198 (Agnus III only)

 Literature: Fitch, *Ockeghem*, 176–7

Missa Philippus rex Castillie

see **Missa Hercules dux Ferrariae**	**Josquin**	4vv
Missa Primi toni	**Agricola**	4vv

 1. **13**, No.4 (*Alexander agricola.*)

 4. Agricola, *Opera Omnia*, ii, 23–46

Missa Puer natus	**La Rue**	4vv

 1. **11**, No.2 (.*Pe.de la rue.*)

 3. A-Wn, 1783, No.18, 241r–261r (*Pierre de la rue*) • A-Wn, 16746, 3v (Anon.) • B-Amp, M 18.13, 15r–24v (Anon. Incomplete) • D-F, 2, 45r–58v (Anon.) • D-Ju, 22, No.4, 42v–54r (*Rue*) • D-Mu, 239, 1v–4r (*Petri Platensis*) • F-CA, 4, 124v–137r (Anon.) • I-Rvat, C.S.23, No.16, 208v–217r (*p. de la rue* in the index) • I-SUss, 248, No.3, 74v–109v (*La Rue*) • NL-L, 1443, No.29, 385v–389v (*De la rue*)

Missa Quant j'ay au cueur	**Isaac**	4vv

 1. **31**, No.3 (Isaac)

 3. A-Wn, 11883, No.5, 42v–51r (Anon. Lacking Agnus Dei) • D-B, 40021, No.56, 103r–112r (Anon.) • D-Ju, 31, No.3, 36r–50r (Anon.) • E-SE, s.s., No.7, 45v–54r (*Ysaac*) • I-Mfd, 2268, No.31, 144v–151r (*Ysac* in index. Gloria, Credo, and Sanctus only) • I-Rvat, C.S.35, No.6, 28v–37r (*ysaac*) • I-Sc, K.I.2, No.68, 137r–148r (Anon. Kyrie [incomplete], Gloria and Credo only) • PL-Wu, 58, 49r–57r (*ysaac*) • S-Uu, 76e, No.3, 22r–32r (*Henrici Izac*)

 4. Isaac, *Messe*, 38–73 • Isaac, *Opera Omnia*, vii, 43–83

 Comments: The *cantus firmus* is the tenor of Busnois's chanson

Kyrie II

 2. Heyden 1537, pp. 60–61 (Anon. Titled *Exemplum Prolationis maioris integrae, diminutae & proportionatae*) • Heyden 1537, pp. 68–69 (Anon. Titled *Aliud exemplum Temporis Perfecti, integri, diminuti & proportionati*) • Heyden 1540, pp. 68–69 (Anon. Titled *Exemplum Prolationis maioris integrae, diminutae & proportionatae*) • Heyden 1540, pp. 74–75 (Anon. Titled *Exemplum Temporis Perfecti, integri, diminuti & proportionati* • 1547[1], pp. 216–217 (Anon.) • Finck 1556, S2r–S2v (Anon.) • Wilphlingseder 1563, pp. 173–79 and 196–99 (Anon.)

 3. D-Bds, 1175, 6v–7r (Anon.) • GB-Lbl, Add.4911 (Anon.)

Et incarnatus

 3. PL-Wu, 58, 153r (Anon. Untexted)

Benedictus		3vv

 1. **1**, No.76 (*Izac: Yzac* in the index. Incomplete: f.83 in the unique surviving copy is of the second edition) • **5**, No.76 (*Izac*) • **14**, No.76 (*Izac*)

 2. [c.1535][14], iii, No.46 (Anon.) • 1538[9], No.30, E2r. (Anon: *H. Isac* in the D-Ju copy, in MS. Untexted)

 3. D-HB, X.2, No.9 (*Isaac*) • D-Rp, A.R.940–941, No.190 (Anon.) • D-Usch, 237a–d, 20r–22v (Anon.) • D-Z, LXXVIII,3, No.9 (*Isaac*. Untexted) • GB-Lbl, Add.31922, 3v–4r (Anon. Untexted) • I-Fn, 107bis, No.21, 20v (Anon.) • I-Fn, 229, No.10, 9v–10r (*Henricus Yzac*. Untexted) • I-Rvat, C.G.XIII.27, No.45, 50v–51r (57v–58r) (*Ysach*) • I-Tn, I.27, No.20, 35r (*Isach*) • US-Wc, Wolffheim, 88v–89r (Anon.)

The following sources are à4: CH-Bu, k.k.II.32, [43]*r* (Anon. Incomplete) • CH-SGs, 462, 7*v*-8*r* (*H.I.* Titled *Plytzgan*) • F-Pn, 676, 77*v*-78*r* (*Isach.* Texted *Absque verbis*) • GB-Lbl, Eg.3051, 88*v*-89*r* (Anon.) • I-Bc, Q18, No.62, 63*v*-64*r* (Anon. Texted *Absque verbis*) • I-Fn, Panc.27, No.21, 17*v*-18*r* (*Isachina Benedictus*) • I-VEcap, DCCLVII, No.30, 29*v*-30*r* (Anon. Untexted)

4. Brown, *Florentine*, music volume, 18–20 • Disertori, *Frottole*, 229–231 • Hewitt, *Odhecaton*, 379–380 • Isaac, *Messe*, 66 • Isaac, *Weltliche*, 42 • Mönkemeyer, *Formschneyder*, i, p. 51 • Plamenac, "Autour", 44–45 • Stevens, *Henry VIII*, 1 • Underwood, *Renaissance*, 148–53

Intabulations: keyboard

3. CH-Bu, F.IX.22, No.17, 30*v*-32*r* (*Isaac*) • CH-SGs, 530 • PL-Wn, 364 (destroyed), pp. 244–46 (Anon.)

Intabulations: lute

1. **33**, No.2 (*Benedictus de Jsach*)

2. 1536¹² = N521, No.49, p3*r*-4*v* (Anon. H. Newsidler) • H4934 (1556), No.19 (Anon. Heckel)

3. A-Wn, 18688, No.44, 31*v*-32*r* (Anon.) • D-B, 40632, No.14, 19*v*-20*r* (Anon.) • D-Mbs, 272, No.58, 71*v*-72*r* (Anon.) • D-Mu, 718, 136*v*-137*r*, 150*v* (Anon. Lower voices only) • F-Pn, 27, No.16, 21*r*-22*r* (Anon. The preceding *Recerchar* may be a prelude to this)

4. Disertori, *Frottole*, 229 • Schmidt, *Spinacino*, ii, 4–7.

Intabulation of lower voices: lute

3. F-Pn, 27, No.112, f.55*r*-55*v* (Anon.)

Intabulation: two lutes

2. 1562²⁴ = H4935, No.19, p. 46 (Anon. Heckel)

Missa Quarti toni	**La Rue**	4vv
(Missa Sub tuum presidium)	(Josquin)	

1. **61**, No.5 (*Pier zon*)

2. 1539² (*Josquin: Petrus de la Rue* in the contratenor)

3. A-Wn, 15496 (*Petrus de la rue*, with a rebus) • B-Br, 9126, (Titled *Missa sub tuum presidium*) • D-F, 2 (Anon.) • D-Ju, 12, No.3, 33*v*-50*r* (*Petrus de la Rue*) • D-PA, 9821 (Anon.) • I-Ma, 46, No.6, 50*v*-61*r* (*P. de la Rue*)

Comments: Attributed to La Rue in Kreider, "Works", pp. 110–12

Missa Regina mearum	**Mouton**	4vv
	(Josquin)	

1. **60**, No.5 (Mouton)

2. 1532³, No.2, 89*v*-102*r* (*Mouton*. Titled *Messe D'Allemaigne*) • 1546⁴, No.3 (*Io. Mouton.* Titled *Missa. Allemaigne*)

3. A-Wn, 4810. No.1, 1*v*-22*r* (*Josquin.* Titled *Missa de Venerabili sacramento*) • D-Mbs, 7, No.3, 31*v*-46*r* (*Joh. Mouton.* Titled *Missa de Almania*) • D-Mbs, 66, No.4, 67*v*-96*r* (Anon.) • D-Sl, 46, No.2, 39*v*-70*r* (*Joann Mutonis.* Titled *Regina Mearum*) • I-CF, LIII, No.10, 115*v*-128*r* (*Mouton.* Titled *Missa dallemaigne*) • I-Rvat, 1982. No.14, 122*v*-132*r* (*Mouton*) • I-Rvat, C.G.XII.2, No.10, 255*v*-270*r* (Anon.) • I-Rvat, C.S.26, No.6, 63*v*-76*r* (*Jo. Mouton*) • NL-SH, 72C, 154*v*-170*r* (*Jo. mouton.* Titled *Missa Dallemagne*) • P-Cu, 2, No.4, 50*v*-64*r* (The Kyrie is texted *Adieu solas, adieu joye*)

4. Mouton, *Opera Omnia*, iii, 65

Missa Salva nos	**Isaac**	4vv

2. 1539²

3. CH-Bu, F.IX.55, 9v-12r (*Isaac*) • I-VEcap, DCCLVI, No.9, 106v-121r (Anon.) • PL-Kj, 40634, 98v-105v (*Hennricus Isaac.* Lacking Agnus II and III)

For the sections of this mass that were used in Isaac's *Quis dabit capiti*, see under that title.

Kyrie

3. A-Wn, 15500, 331v-335r (Anon. Texted *Salva nos*) • D-Rtt, 76, 90v-92r (Anon. Only the Kyrie and part of the Agnus. See Staehelin, *Isaac*, i, 26)

Benedictus and **Osanna**

3. A-Wn, 15500, 335v-337v (Anon. Incomplete)

Agnus III

2. 1538[8], No.42 (*Petrus de la Rue.* Texted *Salva nos*)

3. D-Mu, 326–327, 19v (Anon. Incipit *Salva nos*) • D-Rtt, 76 (see above, under "Kyrie")

Missa Salve diva parens	**Obrecht**	4vv

1. **6**, No.5 (Obrecht)

3. A-Wn, 15495, 1v-18r (Anon.) • E-Boc, 5, No.2, 11v-24v (Anon.) • I-Rvat, C.S.51, No.24, 196v-215r (Anon.) • I-VEcap, DCCLXI, No.2, 7v-27r (Anon. Titled *Missa de Mimi alias Salve diva parens* in the index)

4. Obrecht, *Opera Omnia*, i/5, 229–84 • Obrecht, *Werken*, i, 193–244

Kyrie, Gloria, and **Credo**

3. D-LEu, 1494, 76v-83r (Anon.)

Qui cum patre

3. Heyden 1537, p. 33 (*Iac. Obrecht.* Headed *Exemplum tertium infimi Systematis, vulgatior Bassi formula. Fuga duorum in eadem clave*) • Heyden 1540, p. 36 (*Iacobi Obrecht.* Headed *Fuga duorum in unisono*) • 1545[6], No.106 • 1547[1], p. 257 (Headed *modandos in Aeolio primum exemplum Iacobi Hobrechthi*) • Faber 1553, p. 210 (*Jacob Obertus*) • 1590[30] = P644, No.6, 4v (*Jacobi Hobrecht.* Headed *Fuga in unisono*) • 1594[3] = P645, No.4, 4v (*Jacobi Hobrecht.* Headed *Fuga in unisono*)

3. A-Wn, 18832, No.13. (Anon.) • GB-LBl, Add.4911

Sanctus

3. A-LIs, 529 (Anon. Incomplete)

Pleni

2. 1538[9] (Anon. Untexted)

Missa Salve sancta parens

see **Missa de Beata Virgine**	**La Rue**	4vv
Missa Sancta Trinitas	**A. Févin**	4vv
	(Mouton)	

1. **61**, No.1 (Févin)

3. A-Wn, 15497, No.4, 27v-40r (Mouton) • I-Rvat, 1982, No.4, 28v-38r (*Jo. Mouton.* Original number III) • I-Rvat, C.S.160, 77v-89r (Anon.) • NL-SH, 72c, 47v-67r (*Jo. Mouton*) • P-Cu, 2, 87v-104r (Anon.)

4. Mouton, *Opera Omnia*, iv

Et resurrexit

3. D-Mbs, MS. 260, No.44, 28v-29r (Anon.)

Comments: Based on Févin's own motet, also published by Petrucci

Missa de sancto Antonio	**La Rue**	4vv

1. **48**, No.5 (*Piero de la rue.* Tenor headed *O sacer anthtni.*)

2. 1539[2], No.13 (*Petrus de la Rue*)

3. A-Wn, 1783. No.15 (*Rue.* Titled *O sacer Anthoni precibus pro nostra salute*) • B-Br, 9126,

44v–57r (*P de larue. Missa O sacer Anthoni*) • D-Ju, 22, No.1, 2v–18r (*Petrus de la Rue* with a rebus) • F-CA, 18, No.14, 183v–197r (Anon. Titled *Missa O sacer Anthoni*) • I-CF, LIX, No.1, 1v–9r (Anon.) • I-VEcap, DCCLVI, No.1, 1v–16r (Anon. The Tenor is labelled *Agnosce o Vincenti invictissime*)

    4. La Rue, *Opera Omnia*, iii, 58–96

Christe

    2. 1547[1], pp. 278–79 (*Petrus Platensis*)

    4. Glareanus, *Dodecachordon*, ii, 350–51.

Missa Se mieulx ne vient	**Weerbeke**	4vv

    1. *32*, No.5 (Gaspar)

    3. I-Rvat, C.S.35, No.16, 137v–148r (*Gaspar*)

    4. Gerber, *Mensuralkodex*, iii

Comments: Based on the rondeau by Convert, related to settings by Agricola and Compère, published by Petrucci

Missa Sarge de doglia

see **Missa Charge de deul**	**Isaac**	4vv
Missa Secundi Toni	**Agricola**	4vv

    1. *13*, No.5 (*Alexander*)

    4. Agricola, *Opera Omnia*, ii, 47–77

Missa Sergies de doeul

see **Missa Charge de deul**	**Isaac**	4vv
Missa Sexti. Ut fa.	**La Rue**	4vv

    1. *11*, No.3 (*.Pe de la rue.*)

    3. A-Wn, 1783, No.9, 126v–140r (*Rue*. Titled *Missa Almana*) • B-Br, 9126, 58v–72r (*P de la Rue* with a rebus) • B-TOs, Oud regime 183, 1r–1v (Anon. A fragment of the Gloria) • D-Ju, 22, No.14, 152v–163r • I-Rvat, C.VIII.234, No.21, 173v–186r (*P. de la rue*. Tenor is labelled *Missa almana*) • I-Rvat, C.S.45, No.6, 83v–97r (*Pe. de la rue* with a rebus. Titled *Missa Pourquoy non* in the index)

    4. La Rue, *Opera Omnia*, i

Missa Si dedero	**Obrecht**	4vv

    1. *43*, No.1 (*Jacobus Obreth*)

    3. D-LEu, 1494 • D-Mbs, 3154, No.186 275v–282r (*Ja. Obrecht*) • GB-Lbl, Add.11582 • S-Uu, 76e

Facsimile: Apel, *Notation*, 183 (the Tenor part) and 185 (the other voices for the Sanctus)

    4. Obrecht, *Werken*, iii, 1–54

Comments: Uses material from Agricola's motet, also published by Petrucci

Christe

    2. 1538[9], No.14, C1v (Anon. Textless)

    3. D-Mbs, 3154, 447v (*Ja. Obrecht*) • E-SE, s.s., No.104, 171r (*Jacobus Hobrecht*) • I-Fn, 107[bis], No.37, 52v–53r (Anon.)

Intabulations: lute

    1. *34*, No.3 (*Francesco Spinacino*)

    3. US-Cn, 107501, No.20, 35v–37r (Anon.)

    4. Disertori, *Frottole*, 238–242 • Schmidt, *Spinacino*, ii, 167–69

Sanctus

    3. D-Mu, manuscript copying of sections, in Glareanus's copy of the Petrucci edition

Pleni sunt coeli

   3. I-Fn, 107bis, No.38, 53*v*-54*r* (Anon.)

Benedictus

   3. I-Fn, 107bis, No.39, 54*v*-55*r* (Anon.)

Agnus II

   3. I-Fn, 107bis, No.40, 55*v*-56*r* (Anon.)

[Missa sine nomine]   **Josquin**   4vv

   1. *54*, No.6 (Josquin)

   2. 1516¹, No.11 (*Iusquin.* Titled *Ad fugam*) • J675 (1526), No.6 (Josquin)

   3. A-Wn, 4809, No.6, 109*v*-122*r* (*Josquin.* Headed *Missa in dyatessaron sequentibus signis*) • D-Ju, 3, No.8, 105*v*-115*r* (*Josquin.* Headed *Missa diatessaron*) • E-Tc, 9, No.7, 103*v*-127*r* (*Jusquin.* Titled *Ad fugam*) • I-CF, LIX, No.3, 15*v*-18*r* (*Josquin.* Titled *Ad fugam.* Incomplete, lacking end of Credo, Sanctus, and Agnus)

   4. Josquin, *Werken*, Missen, iii, 32

Credo

   3. I-MOe, α.N.1.2–3, No.XI, 166*v*-171*r*. (*Josquin.* Headed *Patrem de villaige.*)

Et incarnatus est

   3. US-NH, MS.710, 99*r* (*Jusquin*)

Cum sancto spiritu

   Intabulation: vihuela

   2. 1538²² = N66, No.17, 42*v*-44*r* (*iosquin.* Narváez. *Cum sancto spiritu de la missa de la fuga*)

Benedictus

   2. 1545⁶ (Texted *Nunquid oblivisci*)

Pleni

   2. Heyden 1537, p. 107 (Headed *Exemplum. Fuga duum Iosquini, in Subdiatessaron post duo tempora*) • 1545⁷, No.109 (Text incipit *Benedictus*) • 1547¹, p. 258 (Headed *Monados in Aeolio tertium exemplum ex eodem* [*i.e.*, Iodoci Praten[is].)

Agnus Dei

   Intabulation: keyboard

   2. Baena 1540 (Josquin. Assigned to the composer's *Missa Hercules Dux Ferrariae*)

Missa Sub tuum presidium

   see **Missa Quarti Toni**   **La Rue**   4vv

Missa Una Musque de Buscaya   **Josquin**   4vv

   1. *22*, No.5 (*Josquin.* Titled *Una musque de buschaia*) • *59*, No.5 (*Josquin.* Titled *Una musque de buscaye*)

   2. J672 (1526), No.5 (Josquin)

   3. A-Wn, 15495, No.7 (*Josquin des Prez*) • D-B, 40021, No.98, 193*v*-202*r* (*Iosquinus*)

   4. Josquin, *Werken*, Missen, ii, 22

   Comments: Based on the composer's chanson, also published by Petrucci

Missa Ut re mi fa sol la   **Brumel**   4vv

   1. *8*, No.3 (Brumel)

   3. D-Sl, 47, 114*r*-141*r* (Anon. Incomplete) • I-Rvat, C.S.45, No.10, 149*v*-68*r* (*A. Brumel*)

   4. Brumel, *Opera Omnia*, i, 41–64

Qui tollis

   3. I-Fn, 229, No.217, 234*v*-235*r* (Anon. Untexted)

   4. Brown, *Florentine*, music volume, 504–05

Credo

    3. I-PEc, 1013, No.2, 75*v* (Anon. Tenor only)

Benedictus   3vv

    3. I-Fn, 229, No.215, 232*v*-233*r* (Anon. Untexted)

    4. Brown, *Florentine*, music volume, 500–01

Intabulation: lute

    3. US-Cn, 107501, No.36, 60*r*-60*v* (Headed *Benedictus de bru.*)

Pleni sunt caeli   3vv

    3. I-Fn, 229, No.216, 233*v*-234*r* (Anon. Untexted)

    4. Brown, *Florentine*, music volume, 502–03

Agnus

    2. Heyden 1540, p. 82 (Anon. Headed *Exemplum pariter Prolationis, Temporis ac Modi Minoris*)

    3. I-Bc, Q18, No.84, 85*v*-86*r* (Anon.) • I-Sc, K.1.2, No.50, 103*v*-104*r* (Anon. Headed *Canon. Vado et venio sine pausis*) • I-VEcap, DCCLVII, No.22, 21*v*-22*r* (Anon.)

Intabulation: lute

    1. **34**, No.4, 5*v*-6*v* (*Francesco Spinacino*)

    3. US-Cn, 107501, No.22, 38*r*-41*r* (Anon. In the index as [Agnus] *Dei de brumel de la mesa de ut re mi fa sol la bel*^ma)

    4. Schmidt, *Spinacino*, ii, 170–74

Missa de Venerabile Sacramento	**Josquin**	
see **Missa Regina mearum**	**Mouton**	4vv
Missa Victime paschali	**Brumel**	4vv

    1. **8**, No.5 (Brumel)

    3. D-Ju, 31, No.11, 144*v*-163*r* (*Ant. Brumel*) • D-Sl, 44, No.1, 1*v*-29*r* (*Brumel*) • I-Rsm, 26, No.8, 119*v*-140*r* (Anon. Lacking the opening of the Kyrie) • I-Rvat, C.S.41, No.9, 87*v*-103*r* (*Brumel* in index) • I-VEcap, DCCLXI, No.15, 179*v*-193*r* (Anon.)

    4. Brumel, *Opera Omnia*, i, 89–113

Christe

    2. Heyden *Musica* (1540), p. 63 (*Brumel*. Gives the Tenor only) • Wilphlingseder 1563, pp. 231–33 (*Antonij Brumelij*)

Et iterum

    2. 1545^7, No.55 (*Anto Fevi.* Headed *In aeternum Domini*)

Et resurrexit

    2. 1545^7, No.59 (*Anto. Fevin.* Headed *Haec probantur coram*)

Et in spiritum sanctum

    2. Wilphlingseder 1563, pp. 159–161 (*Anthonij Brumelij*)

———

Kyrie in honorem beatissime Virginis	**de Orto**	4vv

    1. **24**, No.7 (*De orto*)

Et in terra De beata Virgine	**Josquin**	4vv

    1. **24**, No.16 (*Josquin* in the index of the I-Vnm copy)

    3. I-Fn, II.I.232, No.41, 124*v*-128*r* (*IOSQUIN*)

    4. Josquin, *Werken*, Missen, iv, 44 • *New Josquin Edition*, xiii, 7

Et in terra De beata Virgine	**Stokem**	4vv

    1. **24**, No.8 (*Jo Stokem*)

Patrem	Weerbeke	4vv

1. **24**, No.26 (*Gaspar*)

3. I-Rvat, C.S.51, No.20, 180*v*-183*r* (Anon.) • I-VEcap, DCCLXI, No.20, 217*v*-220*r*, Anon)

Patrem Cardinale	Weerbeke	4vv

1. **24**, No.11 *Gaspar*)

Patrem Cardinale

see **Missa de Beata Virgine**: Credo	La Rue	4vv
Patrem Ciaschun me crie	Josquin	4vv
	(Brumel)	

1. **24**, No.21 (*Josquin*)

3. A-Wn, 11778, No.8, 130*v*-135*r* (*Josquin des Pres*) • D-Mbs, 53, No.18, 205*v*-216*r* (*A.B.*) • F-CA, 18, No.19, 221*v*-224*r* (*Josquin*) • I-Rsm, 26, No.18, 250*v*-253*r* (Anon.) • I-Rvat, C.S.23, No.11, 140*v*-145*r* (*Josquin des pres*. Titled *des rouges nez* in the Index)

4. Brumel, *Opera Omnia*, iv, 99–105 • Josquin, *Werken*, Missen, iv, 50 • *New Josquin Edition*, xiii, 1

Literature: Hudson, "Josquin" • Sherr, "Josquin" • van Campen, "Conflicting"

Patrem De tous biens	Josquin	4vv

1. **24**, No.18 (*Josquin* in index)

3. I-Rvat, C.S.41, No.18, 185*v*-187*r* (*Josquin des pres*)

4. Josquin, *Werken*, Missen, iv, 44 • *New Josquin Edition*, xiii, 2

Comments: Based on the chanson by Hayne, also printed by Petrucci

Patrem Je ne vis	Agricola	4vv

1. **24**, No.25 (*Agricola*)

3. I-Rvat, C.S.41, No.16, 175*v*-180*r* (Agricola)

4. Agricola, *Opera Omnia*, ii, 94–102

Comments: Based on the chanson attributed to Dufay

Patrem La bella se sied	Josquin	4vv
	(R. Févin)	

1. **24**, No.17 (*Josquin*)

3. I-Rvat, C.S.41, No.17, 181*v*-184*r* (*Ro. de fevin* in the index)

4. Févin, *Collected Works*, pp. 123–136 • *New Josquin Edition*, xiii, 3

Comments: Based on the chanson by Dufay

Patrem Mon pere	Compère	4vv

1. **24**, No.15 (*Compere*)

4. Compère, *Opera Omnia*, i

Patrem de rouges nez

see **Patrem Ciaschun me crie**	Josquin	4vv
Patrem Vilayge	Agricola	4vv

1. **24**, No.12 (.*Agricola.*)

4. Agricola, *Opera Omnia*, ii, 114–24.

Comments: The Tenor is taken from Credo I

Patrem Vilayge	Brumel	4vv

1. **24**, No.13 (.*A. Brumel*; *De brumel* in the index)

4. Brumel, *Opera Omnia*, iv, 106–12

Patrem Vilayge	Busnois	4vv

1. **24**, No.9 (*A. Busnois*; *De busnoys* in index of the copy at I-Vnm)

Patrem Vilayge   **N. de Clibano**   4vv
   1. *24*, No.14 (*Nicasius de clibano*)
   3. D–Mbs, 3154, No.55, 78*v*–80*v* (Anon.) • I–Rvat, C.S.51, No.19, 178*v*–180*r* (Anon.)
     • I–VEcap, DCCLXI, No.21, 220*v*–222*r*, (Anon.)

Patrem Vilayge   **Josquin**   4vv
   1. *24*, No.19 (*Josquin*)
   4. Josquin, *Werken*, Fragmenta Missarum, p. 102 • *New Josquin Edition*, xiii, 5

Patrem Vilayge   **Josquin**   4vv
                                        (Brumel)
   1. *24*, No.20 (*Eiusdem* [= Josquin] in index)
   3. A–Wn, 11778, No.7, 125*v*–130*r* (*Josquin*) • D–Bga, 7, No.7, 21*v*–22*r* (Anon.) • D–Mbs,
     53, No.26, 182*v*–192*r* (*Antho: Brumel*) • I–CMac, L (B), No.7, 53*v*–55*r* (Anon.) • I–Rvat,
     C.S.23, No.12, 145*v*–150*r* (Anon. *Patrem de village* in the index)
   4. Brumel, *Opera Omnia*, iv, 87–91 • Josquin, *Werken*, Fragmenta Missarum, p. 118 • *New
     Josquin Edition*, xiii, 6
   Literature: Hudson, "Josquin"; Staehelin, "Einiger"; van Campen, "Conflicting"

Patrem Vilayge   **Regis**   4vv
   1. *24*, No.10 (*Jo.regis*; *de Regis* in the index of the copy at I–Vnm)
   4. Regis, *Opera Omnia*, i, 62

Patrem Vilayge
  see **Missa de Beata Virgine**: Credo   **Josquin**   4–5vv
   1. *24*, No.24 (*Josquin* in the index)
   Comments: Based on Ockeghem's chanson, published by Petrucci in Spinacino's intabulation

Sanctus D'ung aulter amer   **Josquin**   4vv
   1. *24*: No.24 (*Josquin* in index)
   4. Josquin, *Werken*, Missen, ii, p. 136 • *New Josquin Edition*, xiii, 10

Sanctus De passione   **Josquin**   4vv
   1. *24*, No.23 (*Josquin* in index) • [See also *Qui velatus facie fuisti*)
   4. Josquin, *Werken*, Missen, iv, 50 • *New Josquin Edition*, xiii, 11

Ab angelis psallitur
  3/ of **Verbum caro factum est**   **Dammonis**   4vv
Ab eterno genitura
  2/ of **Mater patris nati**   **Obrecht**   5vv
Ab oriente venerunt magi
  2/ of **Tribus miraculis**   **Festa**   6vv
Absque verbis   3vv
  see **Missa Quant j'ay au cueur**: Benedictus   **Isaac**   4vv
Accede nuntia
  2/ of **Mittit ad virginem**   **Josquin**   4vv
Ad sacrum eius tumulum
  2/ of **Amicus dei Nicolaus**   **Mouton**   4vv
Ad te solum confugimus
  2/ of **Tu solus qui facis mirabilia**   **Josquin**   4vv

Adesto dolori meo
2/ of **Si bona suscepimus**   [Anon.]   4vv
Adiutorium nostrum   **A. Févin**   4vv
                                      (Mouton)

1. **55**, No.22(a) (Anon in first issue: *IO. MOVTON* at head of second page in second issue)
2. 1526¹, No.22(a) (Anon: *Jo. Mouton* in Superius and Bassus)
3. GB-Cmc, 1760, No.14, 23*v*-25*r* (*A.de Fevin.*) • GB-Lbl, Roy.8.G.vii, No.3, 3*v*-5*r* (Anon.) • GB-Lcm, 1070, No.40, 128*v*-130*r* (Anon.) • GB-Ob, a.8 (Anon.) • I-Rvat, 1976–1979, No.34, 97*v*-99*r* (Anon.)
4. Braithwaite, *Introduction*, iii, 15–20 • Expert, Valois & Agnel, *Mouton*, 6–9 • Sherr, *16th-century*, iv, 118–23 • Shine, *Mouton*, 157–61

Comments: Petrucci published this work as the second part of Mouton's *Celeste beneficium*, *q.v.*, and was followed in this by the Giunta (Pasoti and Dorico) edition. The two are also linked in the London manuscript • This text is in honour of Louis XII and Anne of Brittany. The text is changed in each of the Burgundian manuscript sources, so that the names reflect the intended recipient of the manuscript: Henry VIII and Catharine of Aragon (GB-Lbl); Ferdinand and Anne of Bohemia (I-Rvat); perhaps Margaret of Austria herself, with a connection to Mechelen (GB-Ob)

Adiuva nos
3/ of **Domine non secundum peccata**   **Josquin**   4vv
3/ of **Domine non secundum peccata**   **de Orto**   4vv
3/ of **Domine non secundum peccata**   **Vacqueras**   4vv
Adonay sanctissime domine   **Weerbeke**   4vv

1. **3**, No.10 (*Gaspar*) • **19**, No.10 (*Gaspar*)
3. CH-SGs, 463, No.104, 35*v* and 95*v* (*Gaspar*. Headed *Hypodorius, idest secundus tonus*) • I-Fn, Panc.27, No.103, 70*v*-71*r* (*Gaspar*)
4. Drake, *First*, ii, 38–41 • Sherr, *Sixteenth-century*, i, 21–26
Intabulation: keyboard
3. CH-SGs, 530, No.101, 82*v*-84*r* (*Gaspar*)

Adoramus te Christe   [Anon.]   4vv
1. **41**, No.29 (Anon.)
4. Jeppesen, *Laude*, 42–43

Adoramus te Christe   **Dammonis**   6 ex 5vv
1. **45**, No.2 (Dammonis)
4. Luisi, *Laudario*, ii, 316–17

Adoramus te Christe   **Tromboncino**   4vv
1. **41**, No.33 (*B.T.*)
4. Jeppesen, *Laude*, 49

Adoramus te Christe
2/ of **In Nomine Jesu**   **Compère**   4vv
Adoramus te domine Jesu Christe   [Anon.]   4vv
1. **27**, No.1 (Anon.)
4. Thomas, *Petrucci*, 126–128

Adoramus te O Iesu Christe   **Dammonis**   4vv
1. **45**, No.55 (Dammonis)
4. Jeppesen, *Laude*, 148–50

Adoro te Devote [Anon.] 4vv
    1. *7*, No.23 (Anon.)
    4. Drake, *First*, ii, 259–61

Adsis o nostri custos
  2/ of **Virgo salutiferi** [Anon.] 4vv

Alba columba **Infantis** 4vv
    1. *12*, No.32 (*Infantis*. Superius incipit *Alba celumba*)

Aleph
  See **Lamentations**

Alleliua. Hodie
  see Italian texts: **Palle palle** **Isaac** 4vv

Alma redemptoris mater [Anon.] 3vv
  2/ *Virgo prius ac posterius* / *Ave regina celorum*
    1. *12*, No.113 (Anon.)
    3. D-LEu, 1494 • I-TRc, 91, No.163 [1319], 199*v*–200*r* (Anon.)
    4. Gerber, *Mensuralkodex*

Alma redemptoris mater **Isaac** 3vv
  2/ *Virgo prius ac posterius*
    1. *15*, No.18 (Anon: *Isaac* in the D-W copy, in MS)
    3. The following sources are à4, with a *seconda pars* which is texted *Tu que genuisti*: D-Dl, 1/D/505, pp. 466–469 (Anon.) • I-Fn, II.I.232, No.37, 113*v*–117*r* (*IZACH*) • I-Rvat, 1976–1979, No.32, 92*r*–96*r* (Anon.)
    4. Just, "Heinrich".

Alma redemptoris mater / Ave regina **Josquin** 4vv
  2/ *Tu que genuisti* / *Gaude virgo gloriosa*
    1. *21*, No.22 (Anon.)
    3. D-Usch, 237a–d, No.4, 6*r*–7*r* (Anon.) • F-Pn, 1817, No.31 (Anon.) • I-CT, 95/96, No.31, 27*v*–29*r* (Anon.) • I-Fn, II.I.232, No.39, 109*v*–111*r* (*Iosquin*) • I-Fn, 164–167, No.76 (Anon.) • I-Mfd, 2267, No.34, 178*v*–180*r* (*Jusquin despret*) • I-Rvat, C.S.15, No.53, 191*v*–198*r* (Anon.)
    4. Josquin, *Messe*, 86–94 • Josquin, *Werken*, Motetten, i, 7 • Sherr, *Sixteenth-century*, iii, 112–19

Alma Redemptoris mater **Josquin** 4vv
  2/ *Tu que genuisti*
    1. *65*, No.10 (*Josquin*)
    2. 1526³, No.10 (Josquin) • 1527, No.10 (Josquin)
    3. I-Bc, Q18, No.54, 55*v*–57*r* (Anon. Incomplete) • I-Fn, II.I.232, No.24, 77*v*–79*r* (*JOSQVIN*)
    4. Josquin, *Werken*, Motetten, ii, 21

Amicus dei Nicolaus **Mouton** 4vv
  2/ *Ad sacrum etius tumulum*
    1. *64*, No.15 (*Mouton*)
    2. 15262, No.15 (Mouton)
    3. A-Wn, 15941, No.15 (*Mouton* in the index) • I-Pc, A17, No.116, 168*v*–170*r* (Anon.) • S-Uu, 76b, No.17, 122*v*–124*r* (*Jo mouton*)
    4. Sherr, *Sixteenth-century*, v, 84–94 • Shine, *Mouton*, 16–25

Anima Christi sanctifica me   [Anon.]   4vv
    1. *41*, No.39 (Anon.)
    4. Jeppesen, *Laude*, 58–59

Anima Christi sanctifica me   [Anon.]   4vv
    1. *41*, No.47 (Anon.)
    4. Jeppesen, *Laude*, 71–72.

Anima Christi sanctifica me   **Antonet**   4vv
    1. *41*, No.58 (*Antonet*)
    4. Jeppesen, *Laude*, 93–95.

Anima Christi   **Weerbeke**   4vv
    1. *7*, No.20 (*Gaspar*)
    3. I-CF, LIX, No.17, 47*v*-48*r* (Anon.)
    4. Drake, *First*, ii, 235–238

Anima mea liquefacta   **Ghiselin**   4vv
  2/ *Tulerunt pallium*
    1. *3*, No.33 (*Ghiselin*) • *19*, No.33 (*.Ghiselin.*)
    3. D-Usch, 237a-d, No.3 (Anon.) • I-Fc, 2439, No.83, 92*v*-94*r* (*Ghiseling*)
    4. Drake, *First*, ii, 127–131 • Ghiselin, *Collected Works*, i, 24 • Josquin, *Messe*, 86–94

Anna nos cum filia
  2/ of **Celeste beneficium**   **Mouton**   4vv

Anna te mundo genuit
  2/ of **Virgo precellens**   [Anon.]   4vv

Aperis tu manum tuam
  3/ of **Exaltabo te Deus meus**   **Baulduin**   4vv

Ascendens Christus in altum   **Turleron**   4vv
    1. *55*, No.18 (*Hylaire*)
    2. 1526[1], No.18 (*Hylaire*.: anon. in Altus)
    3. I-Pc, A17, No.115, 167*v*-168*r* (Anon.)
    4. Févin, *Oeuvres*, iv, 36–42 • Gehrenbeck, *Corona*, 1452–1459 • Sherr, *Sixteenth-century*, iv,
      95–100
    Comments: The Hylaire is presumably not Penet

Asperges me Domine   **Compère**   4vv
    1. *24*, No.2 (*Compere*)
    4. Compère, *Opera Omnia*, iv,

Asperges me Domine   **Fortuilla**   4vv
    1. *24*, No.1 (*Jo Fortuilla*. The copy at I-Vnm has *De Fortuilla* in the index)

Aspice Domine   **Biaumont**   4vv
    1. *7*, No.19 (*Pe. beaumont*)
    3. CH-SGs, 463, No.134, 49*v* and 108*v* (*Petrus Biamont*. Headed *Hypoaeolius*)
    4. Drake, *First*, ii, 232–35

Aspice Domine quia facta est   **Gombert**   4vv
  2/ *Muro tuo unexpugniabili*
    1. *69*, No.5 (Anon)
    2. 1532[10], No.26 (*Nicolaus Gombert*) • 1534[4] • G2977 (1539), No.20 (*Gomberth*) • G2979
      (1541), No.14 (*Gomberth*) • 1551[2] = G2980, No.14 (*Gomberth*)
    3. D-Bga, 7, 91*v*-92*v* (*Con. Festa*) • D-Usch, 237a-d, 67*r*-68*v* (Anon) • E-Mmarch, R.6832,
      pp. 60–63 (*Nicolaus Gombert*)

4. Attaingnant, *Treize*, ii, 147 • Gombert, *Opera Omnia*, v, 86 • Morales, *Opera Omnia*, XX

Auditui meo dabis

    2/ of **Miserere mei Deus**   **Josquin**   5vv

Audivit

    2/ of **Quis numerare queat**   **Obrecht**   4vv

Audivit ipse tamen / Da pacem Domine

    2/ of **Quis numerare queat / Da pacem**   **Compère**   5 ex 4vv

Auxilium praesta

    See **Jay pris amours / De tous biens**   [Anon.]   4vv

Ave ancilla Trinitas   **Brumel**   3vv
                              (Mouton)

    1. **2**, No.39 (*Brumel*) • **10**, No.39 (*Brumel.*)
    2. *50 Carmina* (1513), No.39 (*Brumel*) • [c.1535][14], pt.iii, No.14 (Anon.) • 1541², No.46 (*Jo. Mouton.* Text *Ave Maria*)
    3. D-Mu, 322–325, No.17 (*Brumel* in altus) • E-SE, s.s., No.77, 156*v*-157*r* (*Anthonius brumel*)
    4. Brumel, *Opera Omnia*, v, 1–3 • Hewitt, *Canti B*, 201–4 • Hewitt, "An unknown", 77–80

Ave celorum domina   **Brumel**   4vv

    1. **15**, No.2 (*Brumel* in Superius)
    3. I-Rvat, C.S.42, No.4, 18*v*-21*r* (Anon. Texted *Ave cujus conceptio*. This appears as the last part of the original number III)
    4. Brumel, *Opera Omnia*, v, 3–6

Ave cujus conceptio   **Brumel**   4vv

    See **Ave celorum domina**   **Brumel**   4vv

Ave decus virginale   **Martini**   4vv

    1. **7**, No.28 (*Jo. marti.*)
    4. Drake, *First*, ii, 273–75

Ave Domina sancta Maria   [Anon.]   4vv

    1. **7**, No.14 (Anon.)
    4. Drake, *First*, ii, 213–15

Ave Domina sancta Maria   **Weerbeke**   4vv

    2/ *Tu peperisti creatorem*
        1. **3**, No.23 (*Gaspar*) • **19**, No.23 (*.Gaspar.*)
        4. Drake, *First*, ii, 91–94 • Sherr, *Sixteenth-century*, i, 51–59

Ave dulcis ave pia

    See **Popule meus quid feci tibi**   [Anon.]   4vv

Ave Jesu Christe splendor patris

    2/ of **Ave Jesu Christe verbum patris**   [Anon.]   4vv

Ave Jesu Christe verbum patris   [Anon.]   4vv

    2/ *Ave Jesu Christe splendor patris*
        1. **21**, No.37 (Anon.)
        3. D-B, 40021, No.67, 137*v*. (*H.F.*)
        4. Sherr, *Sixteenth-century*, iii, 213–26

Ave Maria   [Anon.]   4vv

    1. **41**, No.36 (Anon.)
    3. I-Fn, Panc.27, No.174, 146*v*-147*r* (Anon.)
    4. Jeppesen, *Laude*, 54–55

Ave Maria   [Anon.]   4vv

    1. *41*, No.49 (Anon.)

    4. Jeppesen, *Laude*, 78–79

Ave Maria   **Cara**   5vv
                               (Tromboncino)

    1. *41*, No.19 (*M.C.*) • *41*, No.51 (*B.T.*)

    3. I-Fn, Panc.27, No.4, 3*v*-4*r* (*Marcetus*)

    4. Jeppesen, *Laude*, 82–83

Ave Maria   **Cara**   5vv

    1. *41*, No.45 (*Marchetto*)

    4. Jeppesen, *Laude*, 68–70

Ave Maria   **Compère**   4vv

   2/ *Sancte Michael ora pro nobis*

    1. *3*, No.18 (.*Compere.*) • *7*, No.27 (Anon. Texted *Sancta Maria quesumus*) • *19*, No.18 (.*Compere.*)

    3. D-B, 40021, No.103, 206*v*-208*r* (Anon.) • E-Bbc, 454, No.57, 126*v*-128*r* (Anon.) • E-SE, s.s., No.38, 110*r* (Anon. Pars II, incomplete) • E-Tc, 21, 59*v*-61*r* (*Lysset*) • E-TZ, 2, 280*v*-282*r* (*LUISETH*) • I-Mfd, 2267, No.39, 187*v*-189*r* (*Loyset*) • I-Rvat, C.VIII.234, No.18, 140*v*-142*r* (*loyset com*pe, in index) • I-Rvat, C.S.15, No.51, 185*v*-187*r* (*Loyset Compere*) • I-Sc, K.I.2, No.57, 110*v*-112*r* (Anon. Incomplete) • I-VEcap, DCCLVIII, No.1, 2*v*-4*r* (Anon.) • PL-Wu, 58, 93*v*-95*r* (Anon.) • PL-WRu, 428, No.122, 206*v*-208*r* (Anon.)

    4. Compère, *Messe*, 157–164 • Compère, *Opera Omnia*, iv, 8–10 • Drake, *First*, ii, 68–73
    Intabulation: keyboard

    3. CH-SGs, 530, 69*v*-70*r* (Anon. Part 1 only)

    Intabulation: vihuela

    2. 1547²⁵ = V32, No.17, 10*v* (*Loyset*. Valderrábano)

Ave Maria   **Craen**   4vv

    1. *3*, No.20 (Anon.) • *19*, No.20 (Anon.)

    3. E-Boc, 5, No.7, 56*v*-57*r* (Anon.) • I-VEcap, DCCLVIII, No.50, 87*v*-88*r* (Anon.)

    4. Drake, *First*, ii, 80–82 • Sherr, *Sixteenth-century*, i, 37–43
    Intabulation: keyboard

    3. CH-SGs, 530, 88*v*-89*r* (*Nicholaus Craen*)

Ave Maria   **Dammonis**   4vv

   2/ *Sancta maria mater dei*

    1. *45*, No.17 (Dammonis. Headed *Ad beatam virginem*)

    4. Jeppesen, *Laude*, 114–16

Ave Maria   **Josquin**   4vv

    1. *3*, No.2 (*Josquin.*) • [Probably *19*, No.2: not extant]

    2. 1547¹, pp. 358–61 (Headed *Hypoionici quartum exemplum Idem Iodocus Pratensis author.*)

    3. CH-SGs, 463, No.148, 55*v* and 114*v* (*Josquinus Pratensis*) • CZ-HK, II.A.7, pp. 64–67 (Anon.) • D-B, 40021, No.18, 51*v*-52*r* (Anon. As *Verbum incarnatum*) • D-GOl, A.98, 100*v*-103*r* (Anon. As *Ave Maria . . . ne timeas* • D-LEu, 1494, 202*v* (Anon. Incomplete) • D-Mbs, 19, No.4, 38*v*-43*r* (*Josquin*) • D-Mbs, 41 No.17, 226*v*-238*r* (Anon. With two added voices) • D-Mbs, 3154, 147*v*-148*r* (*Josquin*) • D-Mu, 322–325, No.1 (*Jusquinus auctor*) • D-Mu, 326, 21*v*-22*r* (Anon.) • D-Ngm, 83795, 124*v* and 166*v* (Anon.) • D-Usch,

237a-d, No.2 (Anon. With four added voices) • E-Bbc, 454, No.56, 124*v*-126*r*. (*JVSQVIN* in the Index) • E-Boc, 5, 56*v*-57*r* (Anon.) • E-SE, s.s., No.17, 83*v*-85*r* (*Josquin dupres*) • GB-Lcm, 1070, No.10, 31*v*-33*r* (Anon.) • I-Fn, II.I.232, No.40, 111*v*-113*r* (*JOSQVIN*) • I-Fn, 164–167, No.77, 102*r*-103*v* (Anon.) • I-Mfd, 2266, No.11, 118*v*-120*r* (*Josquin*) • I-MOd, IX, No.11, 24*v*-26*r* (Anon. Damaged) • I-Rvat. C.S.42, No.5, 22*v*-24*r* (*Iosquini Desprez*. Original number IV) • PL-Kj, 40013, 170*v*-173*r* (Anon. As *Ave Maria . . . ne timeas*) • PL-Wu, 58, 7*v*-8*r* (Anon.).

4. Braithwaite, *Introduction*, iv, 106–13 • Glareanus, *Dodecachordon*, 436–42 • Josquin, *Werken, Motetten*, i, 2

Comments: Senfl's setting of *Ave Maria* is a parody of this work, as is an anonymous 8vv setting in I-VEaf, 218

Intabulation: keyboard

3. CH-SGs, 530, No.116, 92*v*-93*r* (Anon.)

Ave Maria	**Josquin**	4vv
	(Brumel)	

1. **15**, No.1 (*.Josquin.*)
3. I-Bc, R142, No.11, 12*r*-12*v* (*Brumel* in the index)
4. Josquin, *Werken, Motetten*, i, 2

Intabulation: lute

1. **33**, No.1 (*Josquin*)
4. Schmidt, *Spinacino*, ii, 1–4 • Disertori, *Frottole*, 243–47
Literature: Hudson, "Josquin" • Macey, "Josquin's Little"

Ave Maria	**Mouton**	3vv
See **Ave ancilla Trinitas**	**Brumel**	3vv
Ave Maria	**de Orto**	4vv

1. **1**, No.1 (*De orto*) • **5**, No.1 (*De orto*) • **14**, No.1 (*De orto*)
4. Ambros, *Geschichte*, v, 193 • Hewitt, *Odhecaton*, 219–21

Ave Maria	**Petrus**	4vv

1. **41**, No.47 (*Frater petrus*)
4. Jeppesen, *Laude*, 73–75
Comments: Blackburn suggests that Frater Petrus might be Petrus Castellanus

Ave Maria	**Pipelare**	5vv

2/ *Tu parvi et magni*
1. **46**, No.12 (*Pipelare*)
4. Pipelare, *Opera Omnia*

Ave Maria	**Regis**	5vv

2/ *Tu floris et rogis*
1. **46**, No.16 (*Regis*)
4. Regis, *Opera Omnia*, ii, 42–49

Ave Maria	**Regis**	3vv

1. **7**, No.25 (*Regis*)
3. CH-SGs, 463, No.16 (*Regis*. Headed *Dorius*) • D-Mu, 322–325, No.9 (*Regis*)
4. Drake, *First*, ii, 266–268 • Regis, *Opera Omnia*, ii, 60–62

Ave Maria	**Tromboncino**	4vv

1. **41**, No.20 (Anon.) • **41**, No.50 (*B.T.*)
3. I-Bc, Q18, No.19, 19*v*-20*r* (Anon.)

4. Jeppesen, *Laude*, 80–81

Comments: There are minor musical differences between Petrucci's two versions, suggesting different routes of transmission

Ave Maria   **Tromboncino**   4vv

    1. **41**, No.43 (*B. T.*)

    3. I-Fn, Panc.27, No.9, 7v–8r (*B. T.*) • ZA-Csa, Grey, No.58, 88v–89r (Anon.)

    4. Jeppesen, *Laude*, 64–65

Ave Maria   **Tromboncino**   4vv

    1. **41**, No.52 (*B. T.*)

    Intabulations: lower voices for lute

    3. F-Pn, 27, No.105, 52r (Anon.) • F-Pn, 27, No.113, 55r (Anon.)

Ave Maria   **van Stappen**   4vv

    1. **7**, No.30 (*Crispinus*)

    4. Drake, *First*, ii, 278–279 • Smijers, *Van Ockeghem*, No.60

Ave Maria

    See **Ave ancilla trinitas**   **Brumel**   3vv

    2/ of **Beata es Maria Virgo**   **Obrecht**   4vv

    2/ of **Gaude virgo mater Christi**   [Anon.]   4vv

    Bassus of **O bone et dulcissime Jesu**   [Anon.]   4vv

    Tenor of **Virgo salutiferi**   **Josquin**   5vv

Ave Maria virgo clemens

    2/ of **Beata es Maria virgo**   **Obrecht**   4vv

Ave mater omnium viri   **Weerbeke**   4vv

    1. **21**, No.40 (*Gaspar.*)

    2. Heyden 1540, p. 144 (*Gaspar.* Headed *Exemplum Secundi Toni*)

    4. Sherr, *Sixteenth-century*, iii, 227–31

Ave mater verbi summi

    3/ of **Verbum bonum et suave**   [Anon.]   5vv

Ave nobilissima creatura   **Josquin**   6vv

  2/ *Tibi Domina gloriosa*

    1. **65**, No.3 (*Josquin*)

    2. 1526³, No.3 (*Josquin*) • 1527, No.3 (*Josquin*)

    3. D-Mu, Art.410, Nos.18–19 (*Josquin*) • E-Tc, 13, 89v–102r (*Josquin*) • I-Bc, R142, No.46, 54v–55r (*Josquin*)

    4. Josquin, *Werken*, Motetten, ii, 18

    Literature: Elders, "Zusammenhänge"

Ave nostra salus   **Weerbeke**   4vv

    The last 14 mm. of **Verbum caro factum**   **Weerbeke**   4vv

    est (*q.v.*)

    1. **41**, No.58 (Anon.)

    4. Jeppesen, *Laude*, 96–98

Ave Panis angelorum   **Weerbeke**   4vv

    The first 21 mm. of **Panis angelicus** (*q.v.*)   **Weerbeke**   4vv

    1. **41**, No.9 (Anon.)

    4. Jeppesen, *Laude*, 15

Ave pulcherrima regina   **Agricola**   ?3vv

       1. *7*, No.26 (*Agricola*)

       4. Agricola, *Opera Omnia*, iv, 3–5 • Drake, *First*, ii, 268–71

Ave que sublimaris

     see French texts: **Comme femme**   **Agricola**   4vv

Ave regina celorum   **Obrecht**   4vv

     2/ *Funde preces ad filium*

          1. *12*, No.1 (.*Ja.Obreht.*)

          4. Ambros, "Geschichte", v, 20–28 • Obrecht, *Opera Omnia*, 2/ii, 75–81 • Obrecht, *Werken*, vi, 64–68

          Comments: Uses part of Frye's motet as a *cantus firmus*

Ave regina / O decus innocentie   [Anon.]   4vv

     2/ *O mater egregie*

          1. *15*, No.20 (Anon.)

          4. Sherr, *Sixteenth-century*, ii, 109–17

Ave regina

     Altus of **Alma redemptoris mater**   **Josquin**   4vv

     Bassus of 2/ of **Alma redemptoris mater**   [Anon.]   3vv

Ave rex regum ditissime

     See **Rosa playsant**   **Philippon**   4vv

Ave sanctissima maria   **Diniset**   4vv

          1. *46*, No.17 (*Diniset*)

Ave solem genuisti

     2/ of **Verbum bonum et suave**   [Anon.]   5vv

     2/ of **Verbum bonum et suave**   **Willaert**   6vv

Ave stella matutina   **Brumel**   4vv

     2/ *Tu es arca completa*

          1. *3*, No.21 (*Brumel*) • *19*, No.21 (.*Brumel.*)

          3. I-Pc, D27, No.35, 63*v*–65*r* (Anon.)

          4. Brumel, *Opera Omnia*, v, 8–11 • Drake, *First*, ii, 83–88

Ave stella matutina   **Weerbeke**   4vv

          1. *3*, No.32 (*Gaspar*) • *19*, No.32 (.*Gaspar.*)

          3. I-Fn, Panc.27, No.129, 99*v*–100*r* (*Gaspar*) • I-Mfd, 2269, No.80, 116*v*–117*r* (*Gaspar.*)

          4. Drake, *First*, ii, 123–26 • Weerbeke, *Messe*, 8–12

Ave sydus clarissimum

     See **Helas que poura devenir**   **Caron**   4vv

Ave vera caro Christi   [Anon.]   4vv

          1. *3*, No.27 (Anon.) • *19*, No.27 (Anon.)

          4. Sherr, *Sixteenth-century*, i, 83–89

Ave vera caro christi   [Anon.]   4vv

       1. *41*, No.35 (Anon.)

       4. Jeppesen, *Laude*, 52–53

Ave verum corpus christi   **Bellabusca**   4vv

       1. *41*, No.59 (*Fr. Bndictus Bella Busca*)

       4. Jeppesen, *Laude*, 99.

       Comments: Blackburn has discovered Bellabusca as a member of the Olivetan order, at Santa Elena in Venice

Ave verum corpus   **Josquin**   2–3vv

    2/ *Cujus latus*; 3/ *O dulcis, o pia*

        1. **7**, No.6 (*Josquin*)

        2. Heyden 1537, p. 77 (Anon. Headed *Quadrupla Proportio quam habet Notionem*. Part 2 only) • Heyden 1537, p. 114 (Headed *Exemplum. Iosquin. Duo*. Opening measures only) • Heyden 1540, p. 91 (Anon. No title) • 1547[1], pp. 288–89 (*Iodoci Pratensis*. Altus revised by Homer Herpol) • Wilphlingseder 1561, D2*v* (Anon. Texted *Miserere mei Deus*. With added parts) • Wilphlingseder 1563, pp. 188–90 (Josquin. As in the 1561 edition)

        3. CH-Bu, F.X.22–24, No.35 (*Josquin*) • CH-SGs, 463, No.27, 13*r* (*Josquinus Pratensis*. Headed *Ionicus*) • D-Mu, 322–325, No.10 (*Jusquin auctor*)

        4. Drake, *First*, ii, 171–73 • Glareanus, *Dodecachordon*, ii, 361 • Josquin, *Werken*, Motetten, i, 4

Ave verum corpus   **Weerbeke**   4vv

        1. **7**, No.18 (*Gaspar*)

        4. Drake, *First*, ii, 229–32

Ave verum corpus / Ecce panis angelorum /   **Gregoire**   4vv
Bone pastor / O salutaris hostia

        1. **7**, No.22 (*Gregoire*)

        4. Drake, *First*, ii, 258–59

Ave virginum decus hominum

    2/ of **Illibata Dei virgo nutrix**   **Josquin**   5vv

Ave virginum gemma catherina   **Bulkin**   4vv

    2/ *Ave virgo specie*

        1. **21**, No.9 (*Bulkyn.: Bulkin* in the index)

        3. I-Pc, A17, No.108, 162*v*-163*r* (Anon.)

        4. Sherr, *Sixteenth-century*, iii, 38–53

Ave virgo gloriosa   **Brumel**   4vv

    2/ *O regina pietatis*

        1. **21**, No.2 (*Brumel*. Headed *Panagiricum*)

        4. Brumel, *Opera Omnia*, v, 12–18

Ave virgo gloriosa   **Dammonis**   4vv

        1. **45**, No.21 (Dammonis. Headed *Ad beatam virginem*)

        4. Jeppesen, *Laude*, 120

Ave virgo gloriosa

    2/ of **O genitrix gloriosa**   **Compère**   4vv

Ave virgo gratiosa

    3/ of **Salvatoris mater pia**   [Anon.]   4vv

Ave virgo specie

    2/ of **Ave virginum gemma catherina**   **Bulkin**   4vv

Beata dei genitrix   [Anon.]   4vv

    2/ *Ora pro populo*

        1. **15**, No.7 (Anon.)

        4. Sherr, *16th-century*, ii, 31–40

Beata Dei genitrix   **Mouton**   4vv

        1. **55**, No.11 (*Jo. Monton: IO. MOVTON* in second and third issues)

        2. 1526[1], No.11 (*Jo. Mouton: Jo. Monton.* in the superius)

        4. Expert, *Mouton*, 33–37 • Sherr, *Sixteenth-century*, iv, 64–71 • Shine, *Mouton*, 106–11

Beata es Maria virgo   **Brumel**   4vv
    1. *21*, No.11 (*Brumel.*)
    3. F-Pn, 1597, 1*v-2r* (Anon.)
    4. Brumel, *Opera Omnia*, v, 18–21
    Literature: Bloxam, "Contenance"

Beata es Maria virgo   **Obrecht**   4vv
  2/ *Ave Maria virgo clemens*
    1. *21*, No.33 (*Iacobus obreth.*)
    4. Obrecht, *Werken*, vi, 69–74
    Literature: Bloxam, "Contenance"

Beata gens cuius est
  3/ of **Spiritus Domini replevit**   **Weerbeke**   4vv
Beate Claudi
  2/ of **O desolatorum consolator**   **Divitis**   4vv
Beati pacifici / De tous biens playne   **van Stappen**   4vv
    1. *12*, No.13 (*.C. de.stappen.*)
Beatus homo   **Fevin**   2vv
  See **Missa Mente tota**: Pleni   **Fevin**   4vv
Bene fac Domine
  2/ of **Qui confidunt in Domino**   **L'Héritier**   4vv
Benedic anima mea   **Eustache de Monte Regali** 4vv
                            (Isaac)
  2/ *Non secundum peccata nostra*; 3/ *Quem spiritus pertransibit*
    1. *64*, No.11 (*Eustache*)
    2. 1526², No.11 (*Eustache de monte regali*) • 1539⁹, No.7 (*H. Isaac*)
    3. NL-L, 1442, No.44, 118*v-126r* (Anon.)
    4. Gehrenbeck, *Corona*, 1460–1481 • Sherr, *Sixteenth-century*, v, 48–72

Benedicat nos imperialis   **Longueval**   4vv
  2/ *Regat nos potentiam*
    1. *55*, No.12 (*Longheval*: Tenor, *Longueval*, but *LONGHEVAL* in second issue, *Longheval* in the third)
    2. 1526¹, No.12 (*Longheval*)
    4. Gehrenbeck, *Corona*, 1482–1489 • Sherr, *Sixteenth-century*, iv, 72–81

Benedicta es celorum regina   **Mouton**   4vv
  2/ *Per illud ave*
    1. *55*, No.19 (*Jo. Monton. IO. MOVTON* in second and third issues)
    2. 1526¹, No.19 (*Jo. Monton.* and *Mouton.*) • M4017 (1555), No.4 (Mouton)
    3. E-Mmc, 607, No.10 (*Mouton*)
    4. Expert, *Mouton*, 38–44 • Morales, *Opera Omnia*, iii, 185–92 • Shine, *Mouton*, 118–23
    Intabulation: keyboard
    3. CH-SGs, 530

Benedicta sit creatrix   [Anon.]   4vv
                           (Josquin)
    1. *3*, No.12 (Anon.) • *19*, No.12 (Anon.)
    3. CH-SGs, 463, No.125, 46*v* and 105*v* (Anon. Headed *Hypomixolydius, idest octavus tonus*) • D-Mu, 322–325, No.4 (*Josquinus*)
    4. Drake, *First*, ii, 46–48 • Sherr, *Sixteenth-century*, i, 27–32

Intabulation: keyboard

    3. CH-SGs, 530, No.106, 86*v*-87*r* (Anon.)

Benedictus   3vv

    See **Missa Quant j'ay au cueur**: Benedictus   **Isaac**   4vv

Benedictus Dominus Deus   [Anon.]   4vv

                                                 (?Tromboncino)

    1. **28**, No.3 (Anon.)

    4. Thomas, *Petrucci*, 501–508

    Comments: Thomas, *Petrucci*, suggests that this is by Tromboncino

Benedictus Dominus Deus   [Anon.]   4vv

    1. **28**, No.6 (Anon.)

    4. Thomas, *Petrucci*, 577–79

    Comments: Attributed to Lapicida in *New Grove*, probably because it follows the *Lamentations*

Benedictus Dominus Deus   **A. Févin**   4vv

                                                 (Pope Leo X)

  2/ *Omnes gentes plaudite manibus*

    1. **55**, No.10 (*Ant. feuin*: *ANT.DE FEVIN* in the second issue)

    2. 1526¹, No.10 (*Ant de fevin.*)

    3. D-GRu, 640–641, No.22 (*Leo X*) • H-BA, 23, 10*v* (*Leo X*) • I-Bc, Q27, pt.ii, No.2. 8*r*-9*r* (Anon.) • I-Rvat, C.S.26, No.21, 152*v*-156*r* (*A de Fevin*) • NL-L, 1442, No.33, 74*v*-78*r* (Anon.) • S-Uu, 76c, 70*v* (Anon.)

    4. Clinkscale, *Févin*, ii, 320–326 • Févin, *Oeuvres*, iii, 62–69 • Mouton, *Opera Omnia*, i, 121–128 • Sermisy, *Opera Omnia*, v

    Comments: The basis of a mass by Mouton, also published by Petrucci

Bone pastor

    Tenor of **Ave verum corpus**   **Gregoire**   4vv

Bonitatem fecisti   **Carpentras**   4vv

                                               (Josquin)

  2/ *Manus tue Domine*

    1. **55**, No.3 (*Carpentras*: Cantus and Tenor *Carpantras*. In second issue, *CARPANTAS*, Cantus; *CARPENTRAS*, other voices: in third issue, *Carpantras*, Cantus: *Carpentras*, Tenor)

    2. 1526¹, No.3 (*Carpantras*:, Tenor, Altus, and Bassus: *Carpentras*.) • 1539⁹. No.XIX (*Carpentras*)

    3. CH-SGs, 463, No.89, 28*v*-29*r* and 88*v*-89*r* (*Josquin Pratensis*. Headed *Dorius*) • D-GRu, 640–641, No.4 (*Carpentras*) • D-Kl, 24, No.22 (*Josquin*) • D-LEu, 1494, No.181, 223*r*-223*v* (*Elzéar Genet*) • D-Rtt, 76 (*Josquin*) • I-Fn, II.I.232, No.61, 180*v*-185*r* (*Carpentras* in the index)

    4. Carpentras, *Opera Omnia*, v, 57–70 • Gehrenbeck, *Corona*, 1490–1509

    Comments: The concordance pattern fits the stylistic evidence of the ascription to Carpentras

    Intabulation: lute

    2. 1544²⁵ = N526, No.4, D2*v*-F3*r* (Anon. H. Newsidler)

Bonus et rectus Dominus

    See **Noe noe noe**   **Brumel**   4vv

Canite tuba

    See **Factor orbis**   **Obrecht**   5vv

Cantate Domine   **Carpentras**   4vv

  2/ *Flumina plaudent manu*

1. **65**, No.16 (*Carpentras*)

2. 1526³, No.16 (*Carpentras*) • 1527, No.16 (*Carpentras*) • 1537¹, No.43 (Anon.) • 1559², No.23 (Anon.)

3. I-Ma, 519, No.1, 1*r*-3*v* (Anon.) • I-Rvat, C.S.46, No.2, 7*v*-11*r* (*Carpentras*)

4. Carpentras, *Opera Omnia*, v. 1–11 • Gehrenbeck, *Corona*, 1510–1524

Cantemus nunc domine

2/ of **Laudemus nunc dominum**	**Obrecht**	5vv

Carmen in laudem

See **Missa Je nay deul**	**Brumel**	4vv

Carmina cadentem

2/ of **Clangat plebs / Sicut lilium**	**Regis**	5vv

Cecilie ad festum / Requiem aeternam

2/ of **Mille quingentis / Requiem**	**Obrecht**	4vv

Celeste beneficium

	Mouton	4vv

2/ *Anna nos cum filia*

1. **55**, No.22 (*Jo. Monton*: IO. MOVTON in the second and third issues)

2. 1526¹, No.23 (*Jo.Monton*.; *Jo, mouton*. in Altus)

3. A-Wn, 15941, No.7, f.32*r* (*Mouton* in the index. Incomplete) • GB-Lbl, Roy.8.G.vii, No.2, 2*v*-4*r* (Anon.) • I-Rvat, 1976–1979, No.6, 15*v*-16*r* (Anon.)

4. Braithwaite, *Introduction*, iii, 8–13 • Expert, *Mouton*, 6–9 • Sherr, *Sixteenth-century*, iv, 112–17 • Shine, *Mouton*, 152–56

Comments: Published by Petrucci and Giunta (Pasoti and Dorico) as if Févin's *Adiutorium nostrum* were a second part. The two are also found juxtaposed in GB-Lbl, Roy.8.G.vii; Shine, *Mouton*, i, 52–161 suggests that the two belong together. The attribution pattern, as well as the occurrence of Févin's motet as a separate unit, makes this unlikely, even though they were apparently both composed for Anne of Brittany and Louis XII

Cernere Divinum lumen / Hec resonet camenis aula

2/ of **Nativitas tua Dei genitrix**	**Brumel**	4vv

Cetus in excelsis

3/ of **Gloria laus et honor**	[Anon.]	4vv
2/ of **Gloria laus et honor**	**Brumel**	4vv

Christe audi nos

2/ of **Sancti Dei omnes**	**Mouton**	4vv

Christe redemptor

see **O Christe redemptor**	**Mouton**	4vv

Christe verbum fons amoris

alternative 2/ of **Stabat mater dolorosa**	**Josquin**	5vv

Christi fili Dei

7/ of **Vultum tuum deprecabuntur**	**Josquin**	4vv

Christi mater ave

	Weerbeke	4vv

1. **3**, No.31 (*Gaspar*) • **19**, No.31 (*Gaspar*)

3. I-Fn, Panc.27, No.99, 67*v*-68*r* (*Gaspar*) • I-Mfd, 2269, No.78, 114*v*-115*r* (*Gaspar.*)

4. Drake, *First*, ii, 121–22 • Weerbeke, *Messe*, 1–3

Christum ducem redemit

6/ of **Qui velatus facie fuisti**	**Josquin**	4vv

Christum regem regum

	Mouton	4vv

1. **55**, No.16 (*Monton*: lower voices, *Jo. Monton*: IO. MOVTON in second and third issues)

2. 1526¹, No.16 (*Jo. Mouton.*) • 1534⁶, No.13, 7*v* (Anon. Headed *De sancto andrea*)

3. I-Fn, II.I.232, No.54, 155*v*-157*r* (*Mouton* in the index) • I-Pc, A17, No.21, 35*v*-36*r* (Anon.)

4. Attaingnant, *Treize*, iv, 78–83 • Shine, *Mouton*, 176–81

Christus factus est pro nobis	[Anon.]	4vv

1. **41**, No.54, 50*v* (Anon.)

4. Jeppesen, *Laude*, 88–89.

Circumdederunt me

Tenor of **Lheure est venue**	**Agricola**	3vv
Tenor of **Male bouche**	**Compère**	3vv
Civitatem istam tu circunda	[Anon.]	4vv

2/ *Tua est potentia*

1. **15**, No.14 (Anon.)

4. Sherr, *Sixteenth-century*, ii, 62

Clama ne cesses

see **Missa L'homme arme super voces**	**Josquin**	4vv
musicales: Agnus Dei		
Clangat plebs / Sicut lilium	**Regis**	5vv

2/ *Carmina cadentem / Sic anima mea*; 3/ *Hac malaterge malis / Sicut lilium*

1. **46**, No.1 (*Regis*)

3. I-Rvat, C.VIII.234, No.38, 281*v*-284*r* (*Johannes Regis*. Parts 1 and 2 only) • I-Rvat, C.S.15, No.41, 163*v*-166*r* (Anon.) • I-Rvat, C.S.16, No.11, 150*v*-154*r* (*Regis*)

4. Regis, *Opera Omnia*, ii, 21–29

Literature: Brothers "Vestiges", 34–49 • Winkler, "Tenormotetten," 191–5

Clare sanctorum	**Therache**	4vv

1. **55**, No.6 (*P. de therache*)

2. 1526¹, No.6 (*P.de Therache*. Listed in the Cantus index as *Senatus apostolorum*)

4. Gehrenbeck, *Corona*, 1525–1533 • Sherr, *Sixteenth-century*, iv, 32–41

Concede nobis Domine	[Anon.]	4vv

2/ *Electi dei omnes*

1. **15**, No.10 (Anon.)

4. Sherr, *Sixteenth-century*, ii, 49–61

Conceptus hodiernus Marie	**Brumel**	4vv

2/ *Maria plena gratia stirpe*

1. **21**, No.36 (*Brumel.*)

4. Brumel, *Opera Omnia*, v, 21–27

Conditor alme syderum	**Martini**	

1. **38**, No.1 (Martini)

Comments: This comes from Colón's description of the volume.

Confirma hoc deus

4/ of **Spiritus Domini replevit**	**Weerbeke**	4vv

Confiteantur tibi

2/ of **Exaltabo te Deus meus**	**Baulduin**	4vv
Confitemini Domino	[Anon.]	4vv

2/ *Qui divisit mare rubrum*

1. **15**, No.25 (Anon.)

4. Sherr, *Sixteenth-century*, ii, 146–58

Congregati sunt   **Mouton**   4vv

   2/ *Tu scis Domine*

     1. **64**, No.16 (*Jo. Mouton*)

     2. 1520², No.9 (*Jo. mouton*) • 1526², No.16 (*Io. monton*)

     4. Picker, *Motet*, 277–285 • Shine, *Mouton*, 199–206

Contremuerunt omnia membra   [Anon.]   4vv

     1. **55**, No.17 (Anon.)

     2. 1526¹, No.17 (Anon.) • 1534⁶, No.14, 8r (Anon. Headed *De annunciatione .b. Marie*)

     3. I-Pc, A17, No.37, 58v-59r (Anon.)

     4. Attaingnant, *Treize*, iv, 84–88 • Expert, *Mouton*, 45–48 • Gehrenbeck, *Corona*, 1534–1538

Cor meum conturbatum est

   2/ of **Domine ne in furore tuo**   **Josquin**   4vv

Cor mundum crea in me

   2/ of **Miserere mei Deus**   **Carpentras**   4vv

Corde et animo Christi   **Mouton**   4vv

     1. **64**, No.14 (*Mouton*)

     2. 1520¹, No.13 (*J. mouton* in the Bassus Tavola) • 1526², No.14 (*Io. monton*)

     3. GB-Lcm, 2037, No.17, 26v (*Mouton*) • I-Bc, Q19, No.9, 6v-7r (*Jo. Moton*) • I-Fl, 666, No.19, 56v-58r (*Mouton*)

     4. Lowinsky, *Medici*, ii, 137–141 • Shine, *Mouton*, 207–12

Corpusque meum licet

   See French Texts: **Le corps**   **Compère**   3vv

Crucifige

   5/ of **In Nomine Jesu**   **Compère**   4vv

Crux triumphans   **Compère**   4vv

   2/ *Jesus nomen dignum*

     1. **3**, No.6 (*Compere*) • **19**, No.6 (Anon. Incomplete in the unique copy)

     2. 1538¹, No.5 (*Compere*. This is followed by *In nomine Jesu*, as if that were a third part of the same composition)

     3. CH-SGs, 463, No.94, 30v-31r and 90v-91r (*Compere*. Headed *Dorius, idest primus*) • F-Pn, 1597, 61v-63r (Anon.) • I-Fn, II.I.232, No.43, 118v-120r (*Loyset*) • I-Rvat, C.S.15, No.48, 179v-181r (Anon.) • I-VEcap, DCCLVIII, No.10, 20v-22r (Anon.) • PL-Wu, 58, 147v-148r (Anon.)

     4. Compère, *Opera Omnia*, iv, 11–13 • Drake, *First*, ii, 21–26 • Reich, *Selectae*, 101–07

Cui dei fuit usque

   2/ of **O potens magni**   [Anon.]   4vv

Cujus latus

   2/ of **Ave verum corpus**   **Josquin**   2-3vv

Cum autem venissem   **de Quadris**   2-4vv

     1. **27**, No.10 (*eiusdem*, i.e., de Quadris in the index. à2) • **41**, No.5 (Anon. à4)

     2. The following sources are à2: *Cantorino* (1523), 73v-76r (Anon.) • *Liber sacerdotalis* (1523), 267r-269r (Anon.) • *Cantorino* (1535), 58v-61r (Anon.) • 1563⁶, 115v-116r (Anon.)

     3. The following source is à1: I-Fd, 21, pp. 8, 10–11 and 12 (Anon. Set three times, to *Cum portaretur*, *Cum autem venissent* and *Cum vero venissent* [see Cattin, "Processionale", 80])

        The following sources are à2: I-Bc, Q13, No.1, 38v-44r (Anon.) • I-Bca, A.179, No.2, 183v-184r (Anon.) • I-PAVu, 361, No.8, 8v-9r (Anon.) • I-VEcap, DCXC, 53v-58r (Anon.) • US-Wc, ML.171.J.6, 122v-126r (Anon.)

The following sources are à3, though with different third voices: I-Fn, Panc.27, No.45, 28*v* (Anon.) • PL-Pr, 1361, No.5, 6*v*-7*r* (Anon.) • ZA-Csa, Grey, No.7, 19*v*-25*r* (Anon.)

The following source is à4: I-MC, 871, No.120, 138*v*-139*r* (pp. 408–09) (Anon.)

4. Cattin, "Canti polifonici", No.7 • Cattin, "Composizioni", 14 • Cattin, "Tradizione", 288–289 • Feicht, *Muzyka Staropolska*, 30 • Jeppesen, *Laude*, 8–9 • Johannis de Quadris, *Opera*, 71–72 • Morawski, *Sredniowiecze*, No.42 • Perz, *Sources*, 467–68 • Pope and Kanazawa, *Montecassino*, 479–82

Literature: Cattin, *de Quadris*, 35–43; Cattin, *Polifonia*, 96–102

Cum dederit dilectis suis

2/ of **Nisi dominus edificaverit**	**L'Héritier**		4vv

Cum defecerint ligna

See French Texts: **De tous biens playne**	**Hayne**		3vv

Cutis mea arvit

2/ of **Miseremini mei**	**Mouton**		4vv

Da pacem Domine

Tenor of **Quis numerare queat**	**Compère**		5 ex 4vv

Da pacem Domine   [Anon.]   4vv

1. *3*, No.28 (Anon.) • *19*, No.28 (Anon.)
3. I-Fn, Panc.27, No.51, 31*v*-32*r* (Anon) • I-Rvat, C.S.15, No.79. 266*v*-267*r* (Anon.)

   The following sources are à3: F-AM, 162, 2*r* (Anon.) • F-Pn, 1597, 2*v*-3*r* (Anon.) • I-Rvat, S.P. B.80, 18, 38*v* (Anon.) • ZA-Csa, Grey, No.69, 110*v*-111*r* (Anon.)
4. Cattin, *Italian* • Drake, *First*, ii, 106–108 • Sherr, *Sixteenth-century*, i, 91–95

Davidica stirpe maria   [Anon.]   4vv

2/ Ergo omnium mulierum

1. *15*, No.6 (Anon. Titled *Davitica* in the index)
4. Sherr, *Sixteenth-century*, ii, 14–30

Davidis

4/ of **Gloria laus et honor**	**Brumel**		4vv

De cruce deponitur

8/ of **In Nomine Jesu**	**Compère**		4vv

Decantabat populus

2/ of **Si oblitus fuero**	**Ninot**		4vv

Decantemus in hac die   [Anon.]   4vv

2/ Salve sancta christi parens

1. *21*, No.14 (Anon.)
4. Sherr, *Sixteenth-century*, iii, 54–66

Descendi in ortum meum   [Anon.]   4vv

1. *3*, No.8 (Anon.) • *19*, No.8 (Anon.)
3. CH-SGs, 463, No.118, 41*r* and 101*r* (Anon. Headed *Mixolydius, idest septimus tonus*)
4. Drake, *First*, ii, 33–36 • Sherr, *Sixteenth-century*, i, 13–19
Intabulation: keyboard
3. CH-SGs, 530, No.99, 81*v*-82*r* (Anon. Transposed down a fifth)

Descendi in ortum meum   **Lebrun**   4vv

1. *66*, No.10 (*Lebrung*)
2. 1526[4], No.10 (*Lebrun*)
4. Gehrenbeck, *Corona*, 1539–1544 • Sherr, *Sixteenth-century*, v, 174–80

Comments: Reese ("Renaissance" 278), among others, suggests that this is the second part of *O pulcherrima mulierum*, below. This is improbable, for that motet contains a different setting of these words.

Desolatorum consolator

  See **O desolatorum consolator**   **Divitis**   4vv

Deus autem noster

  2/ of **Nos qui viviums**   **Mouton**   4vv

Deus in adiutorium meum intende   **Tromboncino**   4vv

    1. **23**, No.12, 9v (B.T.) • **37**, No.12, 9v (B.T.)

    The text is macaronic

    4. Cesari, *Frottole*

    Intabulation: voice and lute

    1. **49**, No.29 (B.T.); **58**, No.29 (B.T.)

    4. Disertori, *Frottole*, 358–359

Deus in nomine tuo   **Carpentras**   4vv

                                        (Josquin)

  2/ *Voluntarie sacrificabo tibi*

    1. **66**, No.9 (Anon.)

    2. 1526⁴, No.9 (Anon.) • 1553⁵, No.2 (*Josquin*)

    3. I-Rvat, C.S.46, No.5, 19v-23r (*Carpentras*)

    4. Carpentras, *Opera Omnia*, v, 32–42 • Gehrenbeck, *Corona*, 1545–1559 • Josquin, *Werken. Motetten*, ii, 25

    Comments: The evident relevance of a Roman ascription to Carpentras, from the time of his residence in Rome, is supported by the stylistic evidence

Di gravi errori

  2/ of **Dolores mortis ne circundederunt**   **Diomedes**   4vv

Dignare me laudare te   **Gombert**   4vv

  2/ *O regina poli*

    1. **69**, No.3 (Anon.)

    2. 1532¹⁰, No.23 (*Nicolaus Gombert*) • G2977 (1539), No.21 (*Gomberth*) • G2979 (1541), No.18 (*Gomberth*) • 1551² = G2980 (*Gombert*), No.14 (*Gombert*)

    4. Gombert, *Opera Omnia*, v, 93

    Intabulation: lute

    2. 1546²³ = BB902 I,3, No.9 (Anon. Barberiis)

Digne loque de personis

  2/ of **Profitentes unitatem**   **Compère**   4vv

Dilectus Deo et hominibus   **A. Févin**   4vv

                                          (Josquin)

    1. **55**, No.24 (Anon.)

    2. 1526¹, No.24 (Anon. *Ant.de fevin.* in Altus) • 1538⁷, No.10 (*Josquin*) • 1538⁸, No.26 (*Anthonius Fevinus*)

    3. I-Pc, A17, No.117, 170v-171r (Anon.)

    4. Albrecht, *Symphoniae*, pp. 78–86 • Clinkscale, *Févin*, ii, 327–37 • Févin, *Oeuvres*, iii, 69–80

    Comments: The two German editions of 1538 both have an added *seconda pars*, texted *Christus purgavit*

Diligam te Domine		2vv
See **Missa Ave maris stella: Agnus**	**Josquin**	4vv
Dissimulare etiam sperasti	**Lurano**	4vv

      1. *35*, No.13 (*F.D.L.*)

      Text by Virgil, *Aeneid*, iv, 305–08

      4. Boscolo, *Frottole*, 137 • Disertori, *Frottole*, 164–66

Diva palestina		
See **Si ascendero**	**Craen**	3vv
Doleo super te		
4/ of **Planxit autem David**	**Josquin**	4vv
Dolores mortis ne circundederunt	**Diomedes**	4vv

    2/ *Di gravi errori*

      1. *41*, No.24 (*Diomedes*)

      4. Jeppesen, *Laude*, 34–36

Domine labia mea aperies		
3/ of **Miserere mei Deus**	**Josquin**	5vv
Domine ne in furore	**Josquin**	4vv

    2/ *Cor meum conturbatum est*

      1. *65*, No.11 (*Josquin*)

      2. 1526³, No.11 (*Iosquin*) • 1527, No.11 (*Iosquin*) • 1538⁶, No.19 (*Iosquin*) • 1553⁴, No.23 (*Josquin*)

      3. CZ-HK, II.A.21 • D-Dl, 1/D/6, No.11 (*Josquin*) • D-HB, XCIII–XCVI.3, No.19 (Anon.) • D-Rp, C.120, No.50, pp. 202–205 (Anon.) • D-Z, LXXXI,2, No.85 (Anon.) • F-Pn, 4599 • GB-Lbl, Add.19583, No.9, 20*v*-22*r* (*Josquin*) • I-Bc, Q20, No.45, 63*v*-65*r* (*Josquin*) • I-MOe, α.F.2.29, No.17, 12*r* and No.20, 13*v*-14*v* (*Josquin*. Incomplete) • NL-Uhecht, s.s.

      4. Josquin, *Werken*, Motetten, iii, 39

      Intabulation: lute

      2. 1544²⁵ = N526, No.5, F3*v*-H1*v* (Anon. H. Newsidler)

Domine ne memineris		
2/ of **Domine non secundum peccata**	**Josquin**	4vv
2/ of **Domine non secundum peccata**	**de Orto**	4vv
2/ of **Domine non secundum peccata**	**Vacqueras**	4vv
Domine non secundum peccata	**Josquin**	4vv

    2/ *Domine ne memineris*; 3/ *Adjuva nos*

      1. *7*, No.10 (*Josquin*)

      2. 1547¹, pp. 246–250 (*Hypodorij exemplum binarum uocum Iodoco Pratensi authore*, and for part 3, *Hypodorij IIII. uocum exemplum ex eodem Iusquino.*) • 1549¹⁶, No.80 (*Josquin*. Pts 1 and 2 only)

      3. CH-SGs, 463, No.97 (*Josquinus Pratensis*. Headed *Dorius, idest primus*) • CZ-HK, II.A.7 • D-Mu, 322–325, No.14 (*Jusquinus*) • D-Ngm, 83795 (Anon.) • E-Boc, 5, No.20, 67*v*-68*r* (Anon. Incomplete) • I-Rvat, C.S.35, No.2, 5*v*-7*r* (*Jodocus de pratis*) • I-Rvat, S.P. B.80, No.16, 32*v*-35*r* (*Jusquin*) • PL-Kj, 40013, 249*v*-252*r* (Anon.)

      4. Drake, *First*, ii, 194–201 • Glareanus, *Dodecachordon*, ii, 311 • Josquin, *Werken*, Motetten, i, 4

      Literature: Sherr, "Illibata"

Domine non secundum peccata   de Orto   4vv

2/ *Domine ne memineris*; 3/ *Adjuva nos*

    1. **7**, No.8 (*De: Orto*)

    2. The section beginning "Cito anticipent" appears in the following sources: Heyden 1537, p. 76 (Anon. Headed *Exemplum Proportionis Triplae.*) • Heyden 1540, 90 (Anon. Headed *Exemplum Proportionis Triplae*) • Wilphlingseder 1561, E1*v*-2*r* (Anon.)

    3. I-Rvat, C.S.35, No.22, 181*v*-184*r* (Anon.)

    4. Drake, *First*, ii, 179–88 • Obrecht, *Werken*, iv, 101

    Literature: Sherr, "Illibata"

Domine non secundum peccata   **Vacqueras**   4vv

2/ *Domine ne memineris*; 3/ *Adjuva nos*

    1. **7**, No.9 (*Vaqueras*)

    2. 1547[1], pp. 244–245 (*Hypodorij duarum uocum exemplum author Vaqueras*. Pts 1 and 2 only)

    3. CH-SGs, 463, No.98 (*Vaqueras*. Headed *Hypodorij duarum vocum exemplum*) • D-Mu, 322–325, No.10, 12*v*-13*r* (*Vaqueras*. Pts 1 and 2 only. Headed *Hypodorius* in the Tenor) • GB-Lbl, Add.12532, 35*r*-35*v* (*Vaqueras*) • I-Rvat, C.S.35, No.1, 2*v*-5*r* (*Vaqueras*)

    4. Drake, *First*, ii, 188–94 • Glareanus, *Dodecachordon*, ii, 308 • Vaqueras, *Opera Omnia*

    Literature: Sherr, "Illibata"

Dominus memor fuit

   3/ of **Nos qui vivimus**   **Mouton**   4vv

Dulcis amica Dei   [Anon.]   3-4vv

    1. **41**, No.2 (Anon.) à4.

    3. This work is not identical with, though it is closely related to, the setting by Prioris, found in many sources, including the following à3: 1538[8], No.3 (Anon. Texted *Qui credit in filium*) • 1540[2], No.2, 4*r* (Anon.) • 1546[1], No.2, 4*r* (Anon.) • DK-Kk, 1848. p. 413 (Anon.) • F-AM, 162, 117*v* (Anon.) • F-Pn, 2245, 31*v*-32*r* (Anon.) • GB-Cmc, 1760, No.4, 2*r* (*Prioris*. Transposed up a fourth) • GB-Lbl, 31922, 88*v*-89*r* (Anon.) • GB-Lbl, Add.35087, No.34, 61*v*-62*r* (Anon.) • S-Uu, 76a, No.56, 55*v*-56*r* (*prioris*) • US-Wc, La-borde, 139*v*-140*r* (Anon.)

        The following sources are à4, with different Altus parts: [c1521][7] (1524), No.19, 16*v* (Anon.) • CH-SGs, 462, 1*r*/5*r* (Anon. Texted *Dulcis Maria Dei*) • CH-SGs, 463, No.140, 52*r* and 111*r* (Anon. Headed *Ionicus, idest quintus*) • F-CA, 125–128, 133*v* (Anon.) • F-Pn, 1597, 4*v*-5*r* (Anon.) • I-Tn, I.27, No.21, 35*v* (Anon.)

    4. Jeppesen, *Laude*, 32 • There are many editions of the Prioris version, including Geering and Trümpy, *Liederbuch*, p. 3, and Prioris, *Opera Omnia*, iii, 45

    Extant intabulations are of the Prioris version:

    Intabulation: keyboard

    2. 1531[5], No.9, 106*v*-107*r* (Anon.)

    Intabulations: lute

    2. Brown 1529[3], No.6, 7*v*-8*r* (Anon.)

    3. US-Cn, 107501, No.8, 16*r*-17*r* (Anon. Titled *Sit nomen Domini benedictum nel tono del R[ecercar] 3° coe o dulcis amica mea.*)

Dulcis amica Dei   **Weerbeke**   5vv

2/ *Rogamus te piisima virgo*

    1. **46**, No.3 (*Gaspar*. Dedicated to "Leonardo [Loredan] duce nostro")

    3. I-Rvat, C.S.15, No.58, 204*r*-208*v* (*Gasparis*. Dedicated to "N. papa")

Dulcis conjugi bonum   **Agricola**   3vv

    See **Ales regres**   **Hayne**   3vv

Dulcissime virgo Maria   [Anon.]   4vv

    1. **66**, No.12 (Anon.)

    2. 1526⁴, No.12 (Anon.)

    3. GB-Lbl, Roy.8.G.vii, No.16, 25*v*–26*r* (Anon.)

    4. Braithwaite, *Introduction*, iii, 87–90 • Gehrenbeck, *Corona*, 1560–1563 • Sherr, *Sixteenth-century*, v, 194–97

Dum artis fuerit

    2/ of **Levate capita vestra**   **Martini**   4vv

Dum complerentur   **Lhéritier**   4vv

    2/ *Spiritus Domini replevit*

    1. **64**, No.21 (*Lheritier*)

    2. 1520¹, No.6 (*Jo. lheritier* in Bassus Tavola) • 1526², No.21 (*Lerithier*)

    3. E-Tc, 13, 43*v*–50*r*. *Lirithier*) • I-Bc, Q19, No.40, 57*v*–61*r* (*.Jo lheritier.*) • I-CMac, P (E), No.18, 119*v*–123*r* (Anon.) • I-Fd, 11, No.20, 89*v*–94*r* (Anon.) • I-Pc, A17, No.53, No.15, 78*v*–80*r* (Anon.) • I-Rvat, C.G.XII.4, No.17, 40*v*–44*r* (*Lheritier*)

    4. Gehrenbeck, *Corona*, 1564–1575 • Lhéritier, *Opera Omnia*, i, 52 • Picker, *Motet*, 135–49

Dum complerentur

    see **Lectio actuum**   **Viardot**   5vv

Dum ortus fuerit

    2/ of **Levate capita vestra**   **Martini**   4vv

Dum sacrum misterium

    2/ of **Factum est silentium**   **Mouton**   4vv

Dux Carlus

    See French texts: **Madame helas**   [Anon.]   3vv

Ecce enim factus est

    2/ of **Egregie Christe confessor**   **A. Févin**   4vv

Ecce Maria genuit nobis   **Mouton**   4vv

    1. **55**, No.9 (*Jo. Monton*: IO. MOVTON in second and third issues)

    2. 1526¹, No.9 (*Jo. Mouton.*: *Jo. Monton* in Superius)

    3. GB-Cmc, 1760, No.10, 16*v*–17*r* (*Io.Mouton.*) • GB-Lbl, Roy.8.G.vii, No.23, 40*v*–42*r* (Anon.) • I-Fn, II.I.232, No.53, 154*v*–155*r* (*JO. MOVTON*) • I-Pc, A17, No.97, 141*v*–142*r* (Anon.)

    4. Braithwaite, *Introduction*, iii, 137–41 • Expert, Valois & Agnel, *Mouton*, 49–51 • Sherr, *Sixteenth-century*, iv, 59–63 • Shine, *Mouton*, i, 245–49

Ecce nunc benedicite   [Anon.]   4vv

    1. **65**, No.13 (Anon.)

    2. 1526³, No.13 (Anon.) • 1527, No.13 (Anon) • 1539⁹, No.XXXV (Anon.)

    4. Gehrenbeck, *Corona*, 1576–1583 • Sherr, *Sixteenth-century*, v, 148–56

Ecce panis angelorum

    Altus of **Ave verum corpus**   **Gregoire**   4vv

Ecce tu pulchra es   **Josquin**   4vv

    1. **4**, No.6 (Josquin) • **30**, No.6 (Josquin) • **62**, No.6 (Josquin)

    2. J669 (1526), No.6 (Josquin)

    3. D-Usch, 237a-d, 12*v*–13*r* (Anon.) • E-Sc, 1, 84*v*–86*r* (*Josquin*) • F-Pn, 1817, No.48 (Anon.) • I-Bc, Q19, No.63, 100*v*–101*r* (*Josquim.*) • I-Bc, R142, No.18, 17*v*–18*r* (*Josquin*) • I-CT,

95–96, No.48, 58*v*-60*r* (Anon.) • I-Fn, II.I.232, No.68, 199*v*-299*r* (*IOSQVIN*) • I-VEcap, DCCLVIII, No.22, 40*v*-41*r* (Anon.) • I-VEcap, DCCLX, No.17, 18*v*-19*r* (*Jusquin de pres*)

4. Josquin, *Werken*, Motetten, ii, 16

Intabulation: voice and vihuela

2. 1552³⁵ = P2448, No.72, 78*r* (*Jusquin. Pisador.* Texted *Tota pulchra es*)

Literature: Cummings, *Florentine*, pp. 177–82

Ecce video celos apertos   **Craen**   3vv
                                                 (Josquin)

1. *3*, No.16 (.*Craen.*) • *19*, No.16 (.*Craen.*)

2. [c. 1535]¹⁴, iii, No.45 (Anon.) • 1538⁹, No.65, I1*v* (MS attribution in the copy at D-Ju: *Nicolaus Craen*) • 1547¹, pp. 326–27 (*Nicolaus Craen*)

3. CH-SGs, 463, No.20, 10*v* (*Craen.* Headed *Hypoaeolius*) • CZ-HK, II.A.20, pp. 97–98 (Anon.) • D-HB, X.2, 22*r* (*Craen*) • D-Kl, 53/2, No.32, 19*v*-20*r* (Anon.) • D-Mu, 322–325, No.5 (*Auctor Craen*) • D-Z, LXXVIII,3, No.4 (Anon.) • F-CA, 125–128, No.91, 85*v* (Anon. Texted *Osculetur me osculos*)

4. Drake, *First*, ii, 59–62 • Glareanus, *Dodecachordon*, ii, 404–06 • Mönkemeyer, *Formschneyder*, ii, 95–97

Intabulation: keyboard

3. CH-SGs, 530, 56*v*-57*r* (*Nicholaus Craen*) • PL-Wn, 364 (destroyed), pp. 336–40 (*Fuga Josquini*)

Intabulations: lute

2. 1536¹³ = N522, No.23, L4*v*-M3*v* (*N. Croen.* H. Newsidler)

3. A-Wn, 41950, No.12, 9*v*-10*r* (Anon.)

Egregie Christi confessor   **A. Févin**   4vv
                                                 (Mouton)

2/ *Ecce enim factus est*

1. *55*, No.23 (*Feuin: ant.evin* in altus: *ANT.DE FEVIN* in second and third issues)

2. 1526¹, No.23 (*Ant.de fevin.*)

3. A-Wn, 15941, No.24, 79*r* (*Mouton* in the index. Texted *Egregie Christi martyr*. Incomplete) • GB-Lbl, Roy.8.G.vii, No.25, 44*v*-48*r* (Anon. Texted *Egregie Christi martyr*) • I-Bsp, A.XXXVIII, No.6, 10*v*-12*r* (Anon.) • I-CMac, P (E), No.20, 128*v*-131*r* (Anon.)

Citation: Aaron, *Trattato* (1525)

4. Braithwaite, *Introduction*, iii, 149–57 • Clinkscale, *Févin*, 516–22 • Févin, *Oeuvres*, iv, 43–49 • Gehrenbeck, *Corona*, 1584–1592 • Sherr, *16th-century*, iv, 124–34 • Shine, *Mouton*, i, 250–58

Comments: The style seems more typical of the work of Févin • The copy in GB-Lbl is in honour of S. Christopher; that in I-Bsp, of "confessor petroni"; that in 1514¹, of S. Martin

Egregie Christi martyr

See **Egregie Christi confessor**   **A. Févin**   4vv

Electi Dei omnes

2/ of **Concede nobis Domine**   [Anon.]   4vv

Elizabeth Zacharie   **Lafage**   4vv
                                                 (Mouton)

2/ *Inter natos mulierum*

1. *64*, No.24 (*Lafage*)

2. 1520¹, No.4 (*De la fage* in the Bassus Tavola) • 1526², No.24 (*La faghe.*) • 1538⁸, No.28 (*Lafaghe*) • 1559², No.13 (*MOVTON.*)

3. D-Dl, 1/D/501, No.39 (Anon.) • D-LEu, 51, 77*v*-79*r* (Anon.) • D-Rp, A.R.861–862, No.13 (*Johannes Mouton*) • D-Rp, A.R.940–941, No.310a (*Johan. Mouton*) • D-Rp, C.120, No.17, p. 42 (Anon.) • I-Fl, 666, No.13, 41*v*-44*r* (*Lafage*) • I-MOd, IX, No.22, 41*v*-43*r* (*La fage*) • I-Pc, A17, No.66, No.63, 94*v*-96*r* (Anon.)

Sources of Part 2 only, both with a new *seconda pars* texted *Elisabeth impletum est*: I-Bc, Q20, No.6, 6*v*-8*r* (*Jo. Mouton*) • I-Rvat, C.S.46, No.33, 106*v*-108*r* (Anon.)

4. Albrecht, *Symphoniae*, pp. 93–98 • Gehrenbeck, *Corona*, 1593–1601 • Lowinsky, *Medici*, ii, 100–106 • Shine, *Mouton*, 259–66

Comments: The attributions to Mouton are, with the exception of that to Part 2 in I-Bc, Q20, all late and German. While the attribution of Part 1 to Lafage seems secure, it may be that the claims of Mouton to Part 2 depends on a confusion with his separate work with that incipit

Intabulations: lute

2. BB902,I,3 = 1546²³, No.10, 24*v*-27*r* (Anon. Barberiis)

3. D-Mbs, 266, No.148, 119*r* (copy of *RISM* BB902,I,3 = 1546²³)

Ergo eiulate pueri

3/ of **Quis dabit oculis nostris**	**Mouton**	4vv

Ergo omnium mulierum

2/ of **Davidica stirpe maria**	[Anon.]	4vv

Ergo sancti martires

	Agricola	4vv

1. *15*, No.9 (Anon.)

3. B-Br, 9126, 170*v*-172*r* (*Allexander*) • I-Fn, II.I.232, No.27, 84*v*-86*r* (*Agricola*)

4. Agricola, *Opera Omnia*, iv, 28–31 • Sherr, *Sixteenth-century*, ii, 41–48

Ergo te nostre

4/ of **Virgo precellens**	[Anon.]	4vv

Et benedictus fructus

see **Ave Maria**	**Pipelare**	5vv

Et introibo ad altare dei

2/ of **Judica me deus**	**Acaen**	4vv

Et Jesum benedictum

3/ of **Salve Regina**	[Anon.]	4vv
3/ of **Salve Regina**	**La Rue**	4vv

Et post transmigrationem

2/ of **Liber generationis Jesu Christe**	**Josquin**	4vv

Exaltabo te Deus meus

	Baulduin	4vv

2/ *Confiteantur tibi*; 3/ *Aperis tu manum tuam*

1. *66*, No.16 (*Baulduin*)

2. 1526⁴, No.16 (Baulduin) • 1553⁶, No.27 (*Noe Baulduin*)

3. D-Rp, B.220–222, 65–67 (*Noel Baulduinus*. Part 2 only)

4. Sherr, *Sixteenth-century*, v, 210–31

Exaudi nos filia

	van Stappen	5vv

2/ *Ora pro populo*

1. *46*, No.15 (*Crispin*)

Exaudi preces meas o mater gloriosa

	[Anon.]	

1. *51*, No.1 (Anon.)

Comments: According to Colón's catalogues, this seems to have been the first piece in Petrucci's lost *Frottole Libro Decimo*. The two references are cited in the bibliography, above: however, I am sceptical that this was indeed the first piece, and am more inclined to suspect another error in citing numbers on the part of Colón.

Exortum est in tenebris
    See **Fors seulement**   **Pipelare**   4vv

Eya ergo
    2/ of **Salve Regina**   [Anon.]   4vv
    2/ of **Salve Regina**   **La Rue**   4vv

Eya mater fons amoris
    2/ of **Stabat mater**   **Josquin**   5vv
    2/ of **Stabat mater**   **Turplyn**   4vv

Facta autem hic voce / Dum complerentur
    2/ of **Lectio actuum**   **Viardot**   4vv

Factor orbis / Canite tuba / Noe   **Obrecht**   5vv
    2/ *Spiritus domini / Erunt parva / Hodie*
        1. **46**, No.2 (*Obreth*)
        3. I-Fn, II.I.232, No.4, 17v-22r (*OBRET*) • I-Rvat, C.S.42, No.8, 36v-41r (*Obreck*. Original Number VI)
        4. Obrecht, *Opera Omnia*, II/ii, 41–57 • Obrecht, *Werken*, vi, 15–28
        Literature: Bloxam, "Obrecht"

Factum est autem   **Josquin**   4vv
    2/ *Qui fuit heli*; 3/ *Qui fuit obeth*
        1. **15**, No.4 (*.Josquin.*)
        3. GB-Lcm, 1070, p. 204 (Anon. Incomplete)
        4. Josquin, *Werken*, Motetten, i, 6 • *New Josquin Edition*, xix, 3

Factum est silentium   **Mouton**   4vv
    2/ *Dum sacrum misterium*
        1. **64**, No.18 (*Mouton*)
        2. 1521^5, No.5 (*Jo. Mouton*) • 1526^2, No.18 (*Io. monton*)
        3. A-Wn, 15941, No.14, 59v-61r (*Mouton* in the index) • F-Pn, 1817, No.52, 69r (Anon.) • I-CT, 95–96, No.52, 68r-70v (Anon.) • I-Fn, II.I.232, No.17, 48v-51r (*IO. MOVTON*) • I-MOd, IX, No.27, 50v-53r (*Jo Mouton*) • I-Pc, A17, No.89, 129v-131r (Anon.) • I-Rvat, C.S.46, No.31, 100v-103r (Anon.)
        4. Picker, *Motet*, 355–65 • Redmond, *Cortona*, 331–40 • Shine, *Mouton*, 296–302

Factus est repente
    6/ of **Spiritus Domini replevit**   **Weerbeke**   5vv

Favus distilans   **Ghiselin**   3vv
        1. **12**, No.124 (*Jo. Ghiselin*)
        4. Ghiselin, *Collected Works*, i, 1–2
        Intabulation: lute
        2. 1536^{13} = N522, No.17, G1r-2v (*Ghiselin*. H. Newsidler)

Felix namque es   **Mouton**   4vv
        1. **65**, No.15 (Anon.)
        2. 1521^3, No.10 (*Jo. mouton*) • 1526^3, No.15 (Anon.) • 1527, No.15 (Anon.)
        3. I-CMac, D (F), No.7, 19v-21r (Anon.) • I-Fn, II.I.232, No.10, 40v-43r (*Jo. Mouton*) • I-Fn, 164–167, No.80, 109r-111r (Anon.) • I-MOd, III, No.61, 154v-158r (*Jos mouton*) • I-Rvat, C.S.26, No.13, 132v-136r (*Mouton*)
        4. Picker, *Motet*, 76–87 • Shine, *Mouton*, 296–302

Felle sitim magni regis

    2/ of **Huc me sydereo**   **Josquin**   6vv

Festivitatem dedicationis   **J. de Clibano**   4vv

    2/ *Sit igitur ad ipsum templum*

        1. **21**, No.27 (*Jero.de Clibano*)

        4. Sherr, *Sixteenth-century*, iii, 120–32

Fiat pax in virtute tua

    2/ of **Letatus sum**   **de Silva**   4vv

Filie regum

    Tenor of **In honore tuo**   [Anon.]   4vv

Flores aparuerunt

    2/ of **Tota pulchra es**   **Craen**   4vv

Flumina plaudent manu

    2/ of **Cantate Domine**   **Carpentras**   4vv

Fundant preces

    3/ of **Quis numerare queat**   **Obrecht**   4vv

    3/ of **Quis numerare queat / Da pacem**   **Compère**   5 ex 4vv

Funde preces ad filium

    2/ of **Ave regina celorum**   **Obrecht**   4vv

Gaude Barbara beata   **Mouton**   4vv

        1. **55**, No.1 (*Jo. Mouton*: Altus and Bassus, *Jo. monton*: IO. MOVTON in all voices, second and third issues)

        2. 1526[1], No.1 (*Jo Monton.* and *Jo. Mouton.*)

        3. E-Mmarch, 6832, p. 6 (Anon.) • F-CA, 125–128, No.14, 1v-2r/2r-2v (Anon.) • F-Pn, 1817, No.53 (Anon.) • GB-Lcm, 1070, No.23, 72v-73r (Anon. Incomplete) • I-CF, LIX, No.25, 59v-61r (Anon.) • I-CT, 95–96, No.53, 70v-72r (Anon.) • I-Fn, II.I.232, No.56, 163v-166r (*Mouton* in the index. Transposed up a fifth) • I-Rvat, 1980–1981, No.11, 65v-66r (Anon.) • S-Uu, 76b, No.16, 120v-122r (Anon.)

        4. Gehrenbeck, *Corona*, 1622–1633 • Morales, *Opera Omnia*, vi • Shine, *Mouton*, i, 303–13

Gaude flore virginali   [Anon.]   4vv

        1. **41**, No.23 (Anon.)

        Text by Giustiniani

        4. Jeppesen, *Laude*, 33 • Luisi, *Laudario*, ii, 51–52

Gaude flore virginali   **Dammonis**   4vv

        1. **45**, No.24, 23v-24r (Dammonis. Headed *Gaudia beate virginis*)

        Text by Giustiniani

        4. Luisi, *Laudario*, ii, 49–50

Gaude Francorum regia   **A. Févin**   4vv

        1. **55**, No.15 (*Antonius feuin*: Tenor, *Anthonius de fevin*)

        2. 1526[2], No.15 (*Ant de feuin.*: *Mouton.* in Altus) • 1535[3], No.18, 12r (*Fevin*)

        4. Attaingnant, *Treize*, xi, No.18 • Clinkscale, *Févin*, 338–341 • Févin, *Oeuvres*, iii, 8–80

Gaude que post ipsum

    5/ of **Gaudeamus omnes**   [Anon.]   4vv

Gaude quia magi dona

    3/ of **Gaudeamus omnes**   [Anon.]   4vv

Gaude quia meruisti

    2/ of **Gaude Barbara beata**   **Mouton**   4vv

Gaude quia tui nati
  4/ of **Gaudeamus omnes**   [Anon.]   4vv
Gaude virgo mater Christi   [Anon.]   4vv
  2/ *Ave Maria . . . benedicta tu*
      1. *7*, No.31 (Anon.) • *41*, No.6 (Anon. Texted *Lauda Sion salvatorem*)
      4. Drake, *First*, ii, 279–82 • Jeppesen, *Laude*, 10–11
Gaude virgo mater christi   **Dammonis**   3vv
      1. *45*, No.22 (Dammonis. Headed *Gaudia virginis*)
      4. Luisi, *Laudario*, ii, 332
Gaude virgo mater christi   **Dammonis**   4vv
      1. *45*, No.23 (Dammonis. Probably headed *Gaudia virginis*, though largely cropped)
      4. Luisi, *Laudario*, ii, 333
      Compare: I-Bc, Q15, No.285, 280r (Anon. Texted *Gaude flore virginali*) • I-Bu, 2216, No.32,
          22r (Anon. Texted *Gaude flore virginali*) • I-Fn, Panc.27, No.48, 29v-30r (Anon.) • I-TRc,
          89, No.104 [618], 172v-173r (Anon.) • I-TRc, Feininger, No.2 (Anon.) • I-Vnm, IX,145,
          No.47, 127r-128r (Anon. à3)
      Literature: Feininger, "Neue"
Gaude virgo mater Christi   **Josquin**   4vv
      1. *21*, No.15 (*Josquin de pres.*)
      2. Faber 1553 (mm. 72–84 only)
      3. B-Br, 9126, 178v-180r (*Josquin*) • D-Usch 237a-d
      4. Josquin, *Werken*, Motetten, i, 7
Gaude virgo mater Christi
  2/ of **Gaudeamus omnes**   [Anon.]   4vv
Gaudeamus Omnes
                                                    [Anon.]   4vv
  2/ *Gaude virgo mater christi*; 3/ *Gaude quia magi dona*; 4/ *Gaude quia tui nati*; 5/ *Gaude que post
ipsum*
      1. *15*, No.37 (Anon.)
      4. Sherr, *Sixteenth-century*, ii, 242–65
Gaudeat plebs
  2/ of **Obsecro te virgo dulcissime**   [Anon.]   4vv
Gaudia beata virginis
  See **Gaude flore virginalis**   **Dammonis**   4vv
Gaudia virginis
  See **Gaude virgo mater christi**   **Dammonis**   3vv
Gloria laus et honor   [Anon.]   4vv
  2/ *Israel es tu rex David*; 3/ *Cetus in excelsis*; 4/ *Plebs hebrea*
      1. *15*, No.36 (Anon.)
      4. Sherr, *Sixteenth-century*, ii, 228–41
Gloria laus et honor   **Brumel**   4vv
                                          (Josquin)
  2/ *Hij tibi passuro*; 3/ *Plebs ebrea*; 4/ *Davidis*; 5/ *Hic placuere tibi*; 6/ *Israel es tu rex*; 7/ *O davidica plebs*
      1. *21*, No.24 (*Brumel.*)
      2. 1538³, No.43 (*Josquin* in index. With the following sections: 1/ *Israel es tu rex*; 2/ *Coetus
          in excelsis*; 3/ *Plebs hebraea tibi*; 4/ *Hi tibi passuro solvebat*; 5/ *Hi placuere tibi*; 6/ *Gloria*)

4. Brumel, *Opera Omnia*, v, 29–36

Literature: Hudson, "Josquin"

Gloriosus Dei apostolus Bartholomeus	[Anon.] (Baulduin)	4vv

2/ *Postquam licaoniam*

    1. **66**, No.11 (*Baulduin* in Altus only)

    2. 1526⁴, No.11 ⁇⁇

    4. Gehrenbeck, *Corona*, 1634–1644 • Sherr, *Sixteenth-century*, v, 181–93

Hac malaterge malis / Sicut lilium		
3/ of **Clangat plebs / Sicut lilium**	**Regis**	5vv
Hec dies quam fecit Dominus	[Anon.]	4vv

    1. **24**, No.27 (Anon.)

Hec est dies que illuxit		
2/ of **Laudes christo redemptori**	**Obrecht**	4vv
Hec est illa dulcis rosa	[Anon.]	4vv

    1. **7**, No.29 (Anon.)

    3. I-CMac, D (F), No.29, 54*v*-55*r* (Anon.)

    4. Drake, *First*, ii, 275–77

Haec probantur coram	**Févin**	2vv
See **Missa Victime paschali**: Et resurrexit	**Brumel**	4vv
Hec resonet camenis aula		
Tenor to 2/ of **Nativitas tua Dei genitrix**	**Brumel**	4vv
Heu nobis Domine		
2/ of **Quis dabit oculis nostris**	**Mouton**	4vv
Hi tibi passuro		
2/ of **Gloria laus et honor**	**Brumel**	4vv
Hic erit magnus et filius		
2/ of **Missus est angelus Gabriel**	**Mouton**	5vv
Hic placuere tibi		
5/ of **Gloria laus et honor**	**Brumel**	4vv
Hodie scietis quia veniet	**Isaac**	5vv

    1. **46**, No.18 (*Jsac*)

    3. I-MOd, IV, No.27, 60*v*-61*r* (Anon.)

    4. Crawford, *Modena*, 489–95

Homo cum in honore esset		
See **Missa Charge de deul**: Kyrie	**Isaac**	4vv
Homo quidam fecit	**Josquin**	5 ex 4vv

2/ *Venite comedite panem meum*

    1. **46**, No.5 (*Josquin*)

    3. D-Z, LXXIII,1 (Anon.) • E-Tc, 22 • GB-Lcm, 1070, No.39, 125*v*-128*r* (Anon.) • I-Rvat, C.S.42, No.34, 137*v*-139*r* (*Josquin des Pres*. Original number XXIII)

    4. Braithwaite, *Introduction*, iv, 372–83 • Josquin, *Werken*, Motetten, i, 9 • *New Josquin Edition*, xix, 4 • Lenaerts, *Kunst*, No.10

Homo quidam fecit	**Mouton**	4vv

    1. **64**, No.19 (*Mouton*)

    2. 1526², No.19 (*Jo. monton*) • 1534³, No.25, 16*v* (*Jo. Mouton*) • M4017 (1555), No.8 (Mouton)

3. E-V, 15, 17v-18r (Anon.) • GB-Lbl, Harl.5043, pp. 72–77 (*Mouton*) • GB-Lcm, 2037, No.16, 25v (*Mouton*) • I-CF, LIX, No.40, 80v-81r (Anon.) • I-Pc, A17, No.60, 87v-88r (Anon.)

4. Attaingnant, *Treize*, i, 196–201 • Shine, *Mouton*, 340–44

Hora completorii

| 9/ of **In Nomine Jesu** | **Compère** | 4vv |

Hora nona Dominus

| 8/ of **In Nomine Jesu** | **Compère** | 4vv |

Hora prima

| 4/ of **In Nomine Jesu** | **Compère** | 4vv |

Hora qui ductus tertia

| 2/ of **Qui velatus facie fuisti** | **Josquin** | 4vv |

Hora sexta Jesus

| 6/ of **In Nomine Jesu** | **Compère** | 4vv |

| **Huc me sydereo** | **Josquin** | 6vv |

2/ *Felle sitim magni regis*

1. **65**, No.1 (*Josquin*)

2. 1526³, No.1 (*Josquin*) • 1527, No.1 (*Josquin*) • 1538³, No.1 (*Josquin*) • J678 (1555), No.13 (Josquin) • 1558⁴, No.6 (*IOSQVIN.: Iosquin de Pres.* in the index)

3. B-Br, 9126, 172v-174r (*Josquin.* à5) • CH-SGs, 463, No.212, 74v and 137v-138r (*Josquin. Headed Aeolius, idest nonus tonus ex primo et quarto*) • CH-SGs, 464, No.2, 1v-2r (*Josquin*) • D-Rp, A.R.893, No.43 (*Josquin de Prees*) • DK-Kk, 1872, No.72, 71v (Anon.) • GB-Lcm, 1070, No.38, 121v-125r (*Josquin.* à5) • H-BA, Pr.6, No.13, 3v-4v (Anon.) • I-Bc, R142, No.45, 52v-54r (*Josquin*) • I-Fn, II.I.232, No.2, 8v-13r (*Josquin*) • I-Rvat, C.S.45, No.13, 183v-189r (*Josquin*) • NL-L, 1440, No.28, 246v-252r (*Josquin* in the index. à5)

Text by Vegius

4. Braithwaite, *Introduction*, iv, 354–70 • Josquin, *Werken*, Motetten, ii, 16

Comments: Originally written as a five-voiced work

Literature: Elders, "Zusammenhänge"

| **Huc omnes pariter** | [Anon.] | 4vv |

2/ *Splendor*

1. **15**, No.38 (Anon.)

4. Sherr, *Sixteenth-century*, ii. 266–75

Iam mine fere fileant

| 5/ of **Virgo precellens** | [Anon.] | 4vv |

| **Ibo mihi ad montem** | **Weerbeke** | 4vv |

1. **3**, No.22 (*Gaspar*) • **19**, No.22 (. *Gaspar.*)

3. I-Fn, Panc.27, No.130, 100v-101r (Anon.)

4. Drake, *First*, ii, 89–91 • Sherr, *Sixteenth-century*, i, 45–49

Id est trophis

| See **Cest mal charche** | **Agricola** | 4vv |

| **Illibata Dei virgo nutrix** | **Josquin** | 5vv |

2/ *Ave virginum decus hominum*

1. **46**, No.4 (*Josquin*)

3. I-Rvat, C.S.15, No.70, 246v-250r (Anon.)

4. Josquin, *Werken*, Motetten, i, 9

Literature: Antonowycz, "Illibata" • Brothers, "Vestiges", pp. 29–49 • Elders, "Josquin" • Macey, "Thoughts" • Sherr, "Illibata" • Titcomb, "Josquin"

Illuminare hierusalem **Mouton** 4vv

   2/ Interrogabat magos

     1. **64**, No.12 (*Mouton*)

     2. 1526², No.12 (*Io. monton*)

     3. A-Wn, 15941, No.27 (*Mouton* in index) • I-Bsp, A.XXXVIII, No.15, 29*v* (Anon. Transposed down a fourth. Incomplete) • I-CMac, D (F), No.37, 69*r*-70*r* (Anon. Incomplete) • I-CMac, L (B), No.10, 61*v*-63*r* (Anon.) • I-MOd, IX, No.8, 16*v*-18*r* (*Jo. Mouton*) • I-Pc, A17, No.3, 5*v*-7*r* (Anon.) • I-Rvat, 1976–1979, No.35, 99*v*-101*v* (Anon.) • I-Rvat, C.S.46, No.18, 55*v*-59*r* (Anon.)

        The following sources are á6: D-Mbs, 41, No.16, 212*v*-226*r* (Anon.) • S-Uu, 76c, 72*v*-73*r* (*Mouton*)

     4. Shine, *Mouton*, 343–53 • Sherr, *Sixteenth-century*, v, 73–83

In amara crucis ara

   4/ of **Qui velatus facie fuisti** **Josquin** 4vv

In conspectu angelorum

   2/ of **Michael archangeli** **Iacotin** 4vv

In eternum Domine **Fevin** 2vv

   See **Missa Victimae paschali**: Et iterum **Brumel** 4vv

In flagellis potum fellis

   3/ of **Qui velatus facie fuisti** **Josquin** 4vv

In honore tuo / Filie regum / Miserere [Anon.] 4vv

   2/ Miserere / In vestitu de aurato

     1. **15**, No.29 (Anon.)

     4. Sherr, *Sixteenth-century*, ii, 176–179

In lectulo meo per noctes [Anon.] 3vv

     1. **15**, No.42 (Anon.)

     4. Sherr, *Sixteenth-century*, ii, 298–302

In nocte scis

   2/ of **Miles mire probitatis** [Anon.] 4vv

In nomine Jesu **Compère** 4vv

Officium de Cruce

   2/ Adoramus te Christe; 3/ Patris sapientia; 4/ Hora prima ductus est Jesus; 5/ Crucifige; 6/ Hora sexta Jesus; 7/ Hora nona Dominus; 8/ De cruce deponitur; 9/ Hora completorii

     1. **7**, No.21 (*Compere*)

     2. 1538¹, No.5[b] (*Compere*. Printed as parts 3–9 of *Crux triumphans*)

     3. CH-SGs, 462, No.2, pp. 10–11 (Anon. Parts 1 and 2 only) • D-GRu, 640–641, 33*r*-36*v* and 35*v*-39*r* (Anon.) • D-Ngm, 83795, part 1, 140*v*-146*r* (Anon.) • D-Ngm, 83795, part 2, 97*v*-193*r* (Anon.) • D-Z, LXXIX-1, No.1 (Anon.) • I-Fn, II.I.232, No.48, 137*v*-146*r* (*LOYSE*) • PL-Kj, 40013, 277*v*-286*r* (Anon.) • PL-WRu, 428, No.124, 210*v*-219*r* (Anon.)

     4. Compère, *Opera Omnia*, iv, 14 • Drake, *First*, ii, 239–257 • Geering, *Heer*, No.2 (Parts 1 and 2) • Reese, *Renaissance*, 226 (Part 5) • Reich, *Selectae*, pp. 108–30

In pace

   Bassus of **Que vous madame** **Josquin** 4vv

In patientia vestra / Miserere domine   Ghiselin   3vv
    2/ *Tu Domine qui exterius*
       1. **21**, No.10 (*Ioannes ghiselin.*)
In summitate celorum
    See **O quam fulges**   Mouton   4vv
In te Domine speravi   Josquin   4vv
      1. **16**, No.56 (*Josquin Dascanio*)
    Facsimile: Cesari, *Frottole*, p. cxxii
      2. 1538[8], No.1 (*Joskin Dascanio*)
    Note that a number of the German sources abandon Josquin's macaronic barzelletta, and use
      Ps.30:1 for a text.
      3. CH-Bu, F.X.17–20, No.68 (Anon.) • CH-Bu, F.X.22–24, No.47 (Anon.) • CH-Sk, Tir
        84-7, 4*v* (Anon.) • CH-SGs, 463, No.25, 12*v* (*Josquinus Pratensis*. Headed *Ionicus*) • D-B,
        40196, No.1, 262*v*-263*r* (Anon.) • D-ERu, 473/4 • D-LEu, 51 • D-Mu, 326–327, 13*r*
        (Anon.) • D-PA, 9822/2–3, No.14 • D-Rp, A.R.940–941, No.42 (*Josquin Dascanio*) • E-
        Mp, 2-1-5, No.68, 56*r* (*Jusquin d'Ascanio*) • F-Pn, 676, 17*v*-18*r* (Anon.) • GB-Lbl,
        Eg.3051, No.45, 56*v*-57*r* (Anon.) • I-Bc, Q18, No.12, 12*v*-13*r* (Anon. Untexted) • I-Fc,
        2441, No.54, 56*v*-57*r* (Anon.) • I-Fn, 337, No.77, 72*v* (Anon.) • I-Fn, Panc.27, No.66,
        42*v*-43*r* (*Josquin D.*)
      4. Albrecht, *Symphoniae*, pp. 3–4 • Anglés, *Palacio*, ii, • Apel and Davison, *HAM*, 98 • Cesari,
        Frottole, 38–39 • Schwartz, *Frottole*, 37–38
    Intabulation: voice and lute
      1. **49**, No.54 (*Iosquin Dascanio*); **58**, No.54 (*Iosquin Dascanio*)
      4. Disertori, *Frottole*, 405–406
    Intabulations: lute
      2. 1544[24] = N524, No.34 (Anon. H. Newsidler) • 1547[26] = N527, No.31 (*Josquin des Prez*.
        H. Newsidler)
In vestitu de aurato
    3/ of **In honore tuo**   [Anon.]   4vv
Incipit lamentatio
    See **Lamentations**
Incipit orationem
    See **Lamentations**
Inhospitas per alpes   Michele [*?Pesenti*]   4vv
      1. **16**, No.46 (*MICHA.*)
    Facsimile: Cesari, *Frottole*, p. 44
      4. Cesari, *Frottole*, 34 • Schwartz, "Frottole", 33
    Intabulation: voice and lute
      1. **49**, No.48 (*D.M.*); **58**, No.48 (*D.M.*)
      4. Disertori, *Frottole*, 394–95
Integer vite scelerisque   Michele [*?Pesenti*]   4vv
      1. **16**, No.47 (*MICHA.*)
    Facsimile: Cesari, *Frottole*, p. 44
      3. I-Fn, Panc.27, No.61, 40*v* (Anon. Text *Io son de gabbia*. Tenor texted *Iste confessor Domini*)
      4. Cesari, *Frottole*, 35 • Schering, *Geschichte*, v, 72 • Schwartz, *Frottole*, 34
    Intabulation: voice and lute

1. *49*, No.50 (*D.M.*); *58*, No.50 (*D.M.*)

4. Disertori, *Frottole*, 393

Intemerata virgo

   3/ of **Vultum tuum deprecabuntur**   **Josquin**   4vv

Inter natos mulierum

   2/ of **Elizabeth Zacharie**   **Lafage**   4vv

Interrogabat magos

   2/ of **Illuminare hierusalem**   **Mouton**   4vv

Interveniat pro Gabriele

   see **Interveniat pro rege**   **Jacotin**   4vv

Interveniat pro rege nostro   **Jacotin**   4vv

   1. *64*, No.2 (*Jacotin*)

   2. 1520[1], No.14 (*Jacotin* on the Bassus Tavola. Texted *Interveniat pro Gabriele*) • 1526[2], No.2 (*Iacotin.*)

   4. Gehrenbeck, *Corona*, 1645–1652 • Picker, *Motet*, 188–97

   Comments: Cazaux, *Musique*, 361, associates this work with the death of Louis xii

Inviolata integra et casta   [Anon.]   4vv

2/ *Que es effecta*; 3/ *O mater alme christi*; 4/ *Suscipe pia laudum*; 5/ *Nostra ut pura pectore*; 6/ *Te nunc flagitant*; 7/ *Tua per precata*; 8/ *Nobis concede*; 9/ *O benigna*; 10/ *O regina*; 11/ *O Maria*; 12/ *Que sola inviolata*

   1. *15*, No.35 (Anon.)

   4. Sherr, *Sixteenth-century*, ii, 207–227

Inviolata integra et casta   **Basiron**   4vv

   1. *21*, No.29 (*Philippus Basyron.*)

   3. I-Rvat, C.S.15, No.71, 250*v*-252*r* (Anon.)

   4. Sherr, *Sixteenth-century*, iii, 143–49

Inviolata integra et casta   **Ghiselin**   4vv

   1. *21*, No.18 (*Jo. ghiselin* in the index)

   3. D-B, 40021, No.82, 169*v*-179*r* (Anon. Texted *Inviolata intemerataque virginitas*)

   4. Ghiselin, *Collected Works*, i, 31–36

   Comments: Uses the Tenor of Binchois's *Comme femme*

Inviolata integra et casta   **Isaac**   5vv

   1. *46*, No.7 (*Jsac*)

   3. D-Mbs, 3154, No.52, 74*v* (Anon. Incomplete)

   4. Noblitt, *Kodex*, 257–94

Inviolata integra et casta es   **Josquin**   5vv

2/ *Que nunc flagitant*; 3/ *O benigna o regina*

   1. *66*, No.6 (*Josquin*)

   2. 1520[4], 121*v*-128*r* (*Josquin de Press*) • 1521[3], No.15 (*Josquinus*) • [c.1521][7] (1524), No.2, 2*v*-3*r* (Anon.) • 1526[4], No.6 (*Josquin*) • 1538[3], No.11 (*Josquin*. Part 3 reads *O rex Christe, o redemptor*) • J678 (1555), No.9 (Josquin) • 1559[1], No.4 (*IOSQVIN. Josquin de Pres.* in the index. Part 3 reads *O rex Christe, o redemptor*)

   3. CH-SGs, 463, No.205, 71*r* and 131*v*-132*r* (*Josquin*. Headed *Hypoionicus, idest sextus*) • CZ-HK, II.A.26, p. 13 (Anon.) • CZ-HK, II.A.29, p. 484 (Anon.) • D-Mu, 326, 5*v* (Anon.) • D-Rp, A.R.891–892, No.33 (*Josquin de Prees*) • D-Rp, C.120, No.35, pp. 154–159 (*Josquin de Pres*) • D-ROu, 71/2, No.4 (Anon.) • DK-Kk, 1872 (*Josquin*) • E-Bbc, 681, No.12, 39*v*-40*r* (*Josquin*) • E-Sc, 1, 53*v*-62*r* (*Josquin*) • E-Tc, 10, 53*v*-60*r* • F-Pn,

4599 • GB-Lbl, Add.19583, 36v–37v (*Josquin*) • I-Fl, 666, No.35, 89v–92r (*Josquin*) • I-MOd, IX, No.9, 18v–21r (*Josquin*) • I-Rvat, C.S.24, No.5, 23v–27r (*Josquin*) • NL-L, 1442, No.34, 78v–81r (Anon.)

4. Josquin, *Werken*, Motetten, ii, 25 • Lowinsky, *Medici*, ii, 231–40

Comments: The basis of a mass by Daser, and an anonymous mass in E-Bbc, 1967

Intabulations: keyboard

2. 1578[24] = CI, No.91, 110v (*Jusquin*. Cabezón) • 1578[24] = CI, No.99, 134r (*Jusquin*. Cabezón)

Intabulations: lute

2. G1623 (1533), No.50, 90v–94r (Anon. Gerle) • 1558[20] = O12, No.5, 12v–14r (*Josquin de Pres*. Ochsenkuhn)

3. D-Mbs, 267, No.2, 2v–4r (*Josquin*)

Intabulation: vihuela

2. 1547[25] = V32, No.87, 60v– (*Josquin*. Valderrábano)

Inviolata intemerataque virginitas

    See **Inviolata integra et casta**   **Ghiselin**   4vv

Israel es tu rex David

    2/ of **Gloria laus et honor**   [Anon.]   4vv

    6/ of **Gloria laus et honor**   **Brumel**   4vv

Iste confessor Domini

    see **Integer vite scelerisque**   **Michele** [*?Pesenti*]   4vv

Jesu dulcis memoria   **Dammonis**   4vv

      1. **45**, No.9, 9v–10r (Dammonis)

      4. Jeppesen, *Laude*, 104

Jesu nomen dignum

    2/ of **Crux triumphans**   **Compère**   4vv

Judica me Deus   **Acaen**   4vv

                (Josquin)

    2/ *Et introibo ad altare dei*

      1. **64**, No.8 (*Acaen*)

      2. 1526[2], No.8 (*Acaen*) • 1538[6], No.XXI (*Josquin*) • 1553[4], No.27 (*Josquin*)

      3. A-Wn, 15500, 118v–123r (Anon.) • D-Dl, 1/D/6, No.14 (Anon.) • D-Kl, 24, No.36 (Anon.)

      4. Gehrenbeck, *Corona*, 1653–1660 • Kirsch, *da Silva*, 487–95 • Sherr, *Sixteenth-century*, v, 17–26

      Comments: Osthoff (*Josquin*, ii, 129) rejected this as a work by Josquin.

Labia distillantia

    2/ of **Quam pulchra es**   **Mouton**   4vv

Laeta graves abigit

    see **Missa Je nay deul**: Pleni   **Brumel**   4vv

Lamentations

Arranged in the order of settings opening with the *Incipit*, followed by those beginning with the *Aleph* verses, then settings of the *Recordare*. For many details, see Thomas, *Petrucci*; Cattin, *de Quadris*. Neither of Petrucci's sources is entirely clear as to how the texts are divided into *partes* according to musical or liturgical usage. It has seemed more useful here to indicate merely which verses are set to music, and note the presence of *Jerusalem convertere* or *Recordare* settings.

Incipit lamentatio ieremie   **Erasmus**   4vv
    1. **28**, No.5 (*Erasmus*)
    3. I-Fn, Panc.27, No.173, 144*v*-145*r* (Anon. With a 2/ *Aleph. Quomodo sedet*)
    4. Massenkeil, *Mehrstimmiger* • Thomas, *Petrucci*, 555–76

Incipit lamentatio ieremie prophete   **de Orto**   4vv
    2/ *Aleph. Quomodo sedet*; 3/ *Beth. Plorans ploravit*; 4/ *Ghimel. Migravit Judas*; 5/ *Jerusalem*
    1. **27**, No.7 (*de Orto*)
    3. ZA-Csa, Grey, No.60, 90*v*-95*r* (Anon.)
    4. Massenkeil, *Mehrstimmige*, 19–23 • Thomas, *Petrucci*, 245–58
    Comments: Cattin, "Nuova", p. 211, suggests that the two sources are independent.

Incipit lamentatio ieremie   **de Quadris**   2vv
    2/ *Aleph. Quomodo sedet*; 3/ *Beth. Plorans ploravit*; 4/ *Ghimel. Migravit Judas*; 5/ *Daleth. Viae Sion lugent*; 6/ *Jerusalem*; 7/ *He. Facti sunt hostes*; 8/ *Vau. Et egressus est*; 9/ *Zain, Recordata est*; 10/ *Heth. Peccatum peccavit*; 11/ *Jerusalem*; 12/ *Teth. Sordes ejus*; 13/ *Jod. Manum suam misit*; 14/ *Caph. Omnis populis ejus*; 15/ *Lamed. O vos omnes*; 16/ *Jerusalem*
    1. **27**, No.8 (*Io. De quadris*)
    3. I-Fd, 21, pp. 8–12 (Anon. à1. For details of the sections used, and the texts set to them, see Cattin, *Processionale*, 80)
        Sources also having the music for Friday (*Heth. Cogitavit*) and Saturday (*Caph. Non enim*), as one set (for details of the verses set, see Cattin, *de Quadris*, 32): I-Fn, II.I.350, Nos.35–43, 80*v*-90*r* (Anon.) • I-VIs, 11, 1*v*-10*r* (Anon.)
    4. Cattin, *Processional* • Cattin, *de Quadris* • Massenkeil, *Mehrstimmiger* • Thomas, *Petrucci*, 259–90
    Comments: This set travels with settings for Friday and Saturday, which are probably also by de Quadris. On the dating of the music, and of the Vicenza manuscript, see Bent, "Pietro".

Incipit lamentatio ieremie   **Tromboncino**   4vv
    This is apparently in 41 parts, and probably is liturgically complete
    1. **28**, No.1 (*Bartho. T.*; *Tromboncinus in the index*)
    4. Thomas, *Petrucci*, 386–509
    Literature: Croll, "Tromboncino"

Incipit lamentatio ieremie   **Weerbeke**   4vv
    In 18 sections, including the *Recordare*
    1. **28**, No.4 (*Gaspar.*)
    4. Schering, *Geschichte* • Thomas, *Petrucci*, 509–54

Incipit lamentatio   **Ycart**   4vv
    2/ *Aleph. Quomodo sedet*; 3/ *Beth. Plorans ploravit*; 4/ *Ghimel. Migravit Judas*; 5/ *Jerusalem*
    1. **27**, No.3 (*B.ycart.* Not listed in the index)
    4. Thomas, *Petrucci*, 145–57

Incipit oratio Jeremie prophete   [Anon.]   4vv
                            (?Tromboncino)
    1. **28**, No.2 (Anon.)
    4. Thomas, *Petrucci*, 485–500
    Comments: Thomas, *Petrucci*, suggests that this is by Tromboncino

Incipit oratio hieremie prophete
  See **Aleph. Quomodo sedet**   [Anon.]   3vv

Aleph. Quomodo obtexit   **Agricola**   4vv

2/ *Beth. Praecipitavit Dominus*; 3/ *Jerusalem*; 4/ *Ghimel. Confregit in ira*; 5/ *Daleth. Tetendi arcum suum*; 6/ *He. Factus est Dominus*; 7/ *Jerusalem*; 8/ *Vau. Et dissipavit*; 9/ *Jerusalem*

     1. **27**, No.6 (*Agricola*; *Alexandri* in the index)

     4. Agricola *Opera Omnia*, iii, 8–16 • Thomas, *Petrucci*, 219–44

Aleph. Quomodo obtexit   **Ycart**   4vv

2/ *Beth. Praecipitavit Dominus*; 3/ *Teth. Defixae sunt*; 4/ *Jerusalem*

     1. **27**, No.3(a) (*Ber: ycart* in the index)

     4. Thomas, *Petrucci*, 158–72

Aleph. Quomodo sedet   [Anon.]   3vv

                                            (?Ycart)

2/ *Beth. Plorans ploravit*; 3/ *Migravit Judas*; 4/ *Jerusalem convertere*

     1. **27**, No.4 (Anon.)

     3. ZA-Csa, Grey, No.61, 95*v*-101*r* (Anon. Text begins *Incipit oratio* . . .)

     4. Massenkeil, *Mehrstimmiger*, 14–18 • Thomas, *Petrucci*, 158–72

     Comments: Thomas, *Petrucci* suggests this is by Ycart • Cattin, "Nuova", p. 211, points out the differences between the two sources, suggesting that the manuscript represents a different embellishment of a model.

[Aleph] Quomodo sedet sola   **Agricola**   3vv

2/ *Beth. Plorans ploravit*; 3/ *Ghimel. Migravit Judas*; 4/ *Daleth. Viae Sion lugent*; 5/ *He. Facti sunt hostes*; 6/ *Vau. Et egressus est*; 7/ *Zain. Recordata est*

     1. **27**, No.5 (*Alexander Agricola*)

     3. I-Fr, 2794, No.66, 76*r*-78*r* (*Agricola*. Incomplete) • PL-Wu, 58, 132*v*-136*r* (Anon.)

     4. Agricola, *Opera Omnia*, iii, 1–7 • Jones, *First*, ii, 311–13 • Thomas, *Petrucci*, 197–218

Aleph. Quomodo sedet   **Tinctoris**   4vv

2/ *Beth. Plorans ploravit*; 3/ *Ghimel. Migravit Judas*; 4/ *Jerusalem convertere*

     1. **27**, No.2 (*Tinctoris*)

     4. Melin, *Tinctoris*, 463–478 • Thomas, *Petrucci*, 129–44

Caph. Non enim humilitavit   [Anon.]   2vv

                                         (?de Quadris)

2/ *Mem. Quis est iste*; 3/ *Nun. Scrutemur vias*; 4/ *Samech. Operuisti in furore*; 5/ *Ain. Cum adhuc*; 6/ *Jerusalem*; 7/ *Sade. Lubricaverunt*; 8/ *Caph. Velociores fuerunt*; 9/ *Res. Spiritus oris nostri*; 10/ *Thau. Completa est*; 11/ *Jerusalem*

     1. **27**, No.8(b) (Anon.)

     See *Incipit lamentatio ieremie: de Quadris*.

     4. Thomas, *Petrucci*, 323–47

     Comments: The pattern of layout in the edition suggests that this setting is by de Quadris

Heth. Cogitavit Dominus   [Anon.]   2vv

                                         (?de Quadris)

2/ *Teth. Defixae sunt in terrae*; 3/ *Jod. Sederunt in terra*; 4/ *Caph. Defecerunt prae*; 5/ *Jerusalem*; 6/ *Lamed. Matribus suis*; 7/ *Mem. Cui comparabo te*; 8/ *Nun. Prophetae tui*; 9/ *Samech. Plauserunt super*; 10/ *Jerusalem*; 11/ *Phe. Aperureunt super*; 12/ *Ain. Fecit Deus*; 13/ *Sade. Clamavit cor eorum*; 14/ *Res. Vide Domine*; 15/ *Jerusalem*

     1. **27**, No.8(a) (Anon.) • See *Incipit lamentatio ieremie: de Quadris*

     4. Thomas, *Petrucci*, 291–322

     Comments: The pattern of layout in the edition suggests that this setting is by de Quadris

Recordare Domine   [Anon.]   4vv
                                                        (?Ycart)

    1. **27**, No.3(b) (Anon.)

    4. Thomas, *Petrucci*, 173–81

    Comments: Thomas, *Petrucci* suggests that this setting is by Ycart

Recordare Domine   [Anon.]   2vv
                                                        (?Ycart)

    1. **27**, No.8(c) (Anon.)

    4. Thomas, *Petrucci*, 348–59

    Comments: Thomas, *Petrucci* suggests that this setting is by Ycart

Recordare Domine   **Weerbeke**

    See **Incipit lamentatio ieremie**   **Weerbeke**   4vv

Recordare Domine

    See **Incipit oratio Jeremie prophete**   [Anon.]   4vv

Latius in numerum

    2/ of **Ut phoebe radiis**   **Josquin**

Lauda Deum O renata

    2/ of **Non nobis, Domine**   **Mouton**

Lauda Syon salvatorem   **Brumel**   4vv

    Settings of odd-numbered verses, 1–23: v.1. *Lauda Sion salvatorem*; v.3. *Laudis thema specialis*; v.5. *Sit laus plena*; v.7. *In hac mensa*; v.9. *Quod in cena*; v.11. *Dogma datur*; v.13. *Sub diversis speciebus* (à2); v.15. *A sumente* (à2); v.17. *Sumunt boni*; v.19. *Fracto demum*; v.21. *Ecce panis angelorum*; v.23. *Bone pastor*

    1. **7**, No.16 (*Brumel*)

    3. CH-SGs, 463, No.122, 44*v*–45*r* and 103*v*–104*r* (*Antonius Brumel*. Headed *Mixolydii Hypomixolydiique, idest septimi et octavi toni connexio*)

    4. Brumel, *Opera Omnia*, v, 46–52 • Drake, *First*, ii, 218–27 • Smijers, *Van Ockeghem*, No.48

Lauda Sion salvatorem

    See **Gaude Virgo mater Christi**   [Anon.]   4vv

Laudate Deum in sanctis eius   **Mouton**   4vv

    2/ *Quia cum clamarem*

    1. **55**, No.7 (*Jo. Monton*: IO. MOVTON, in second and third issues)

    2. 1526[1], No.7 (*Jo. Monton* and *Jo. Mouton*.) • M4017 (1555), No.12 (Mouton)

    3. A-Wn, 15500, 279*v* (Anon.) • A-Wn, 15941, 68*v* (*Mouton*) • GB-Lbl, Harl.5043, pp. 108–11 (*Mouton*) • GB-Lcm, 1070, No.5, 15*v*–33*r* (Anon.) • I-Pc, A17, No.19, 32*v*–34*r* (Anon.)

    4. Braithwaite, *Introduction*, iv, 56–60 • Expert, Valois & Agnel, *Mouton*, 86–93 • Sherr, *Sixteenth-century*, iv, 42–52 • Shine, *Mouton*, i, 345–53

Laudate Dominum de celis   **Brumel**   4vv

    2/ *Laudate Dominum in sanctis eius*

    1. **55**, No.26 (*Brumel*)

    2. 1526[1], No.26 (*Brumel*.) • 1553[6], No.35 (*Brumel*)

    3. D-Sl, 34, 104*v*–130*r* (Anon.) • I-Fn, II.I.232, No.16, 62*v*–67*r* (*BRVMEL*) • I-Rvat, C.S.42, No.1, 3*v*–10*r* (*Brumel*)

4. Brumel, *Opera Omnia*, v, 53–62 • Forkel, *Geschichte*, i, 629 (part 1) • Gehrenbeck, *Corona*, 1669–1685 • Maldeghem, *Trésor*, religieuse, xi, 4 (part 1)

Intabulation: lute

2. 1536¹³ = N522, No.30, V1r–X3r (*Antonius Brumel*. H. Newsidler)

Laudate Dominum in sanctis eius

2/ of **Laudate Dominum de celis**   **Brumel**   4vv

Laudemus nunc dominum / Non est hic aliud   **Obrecht**   5vv

2/ *Cantemus nunc domine / Vidit Jacob*

    1. *46*, No.9 (*Obreth*)

    3. I-Rvat, C.S.42, No.44 162v–167r (*Obreck:*. Numbered XXX in the source)

    4. Obrecht, *Opera Omnia*, II/ii, 58–74 • Obrecht, *Werken*, vi, 49–63

Laudes christo redemptori   **Obrecht**   4vv

2/ *Hec est dies qui illuxit*

    1. *21*, No.13 (*Ia.obreht.*)

    4. Obrecht, *Werken*, vi, 75–84

Laura Romanis   **Alauro**   4vv

    1. *56*, No.63 (*Hie. Alauro*)

    4. Luisi & Zanovello, *Frottole*, 258

Laurus impetu fulminis

3/ of **Quis dabit capiti meo aquam**   **Isaac**   4vv

Lectio actuum / Dum complerentur   **Viardot**   5vv
                                              (Josquin)

2/ *Facta autem hic voce / Dum complerentur*

    1. *66*, No.5 (*Josquin*)

    2. 1520⁴, No.12, 143v–156r (Anon.) • 1526⁴, No.5 (Josquin)

    3. D-Mu, Art.401, Nos.42–43 (*Josquin*) • I-Rvat, C.S.42, No.31, 126v–130r (*Jo: Viardot:* as *Dum Complerentur* and without the first phrase. Numbered XXI in the source) • PL-Kj, 40272, 20r–22r/15r–15v (Anon.)

    4. Josquin, *Werken*, Motetten, No.41

    Literature: *New Josquin Edition*, xix, 12 • Sherr, "Notes", 235–36, suggesting that the work is by Viardot, with the first phrase added by Josquin.

Letatus sum   **de Silva**   4vv

2/ *Fiat pax in virtute tua*

    1. *55*, No.4 (*Andreas de silua*)

    Facsimile: de Silva, *Opera Omnia*, i, xix

    2. 1526¹, No.4 (*Andreas de Silva.*) • 1539⁹, No.XXIII (*A. de sylva: Andreas de Sylva.* in the Tavola)

    3. D-Dl, 1/D/6, No.19 (Anon.) • I-Ma, 519, No.2, 4r–5v (Anon.) • I-Rvat, C.S.46, No.22, 69v–72r (*A.de silva*)

    4. de Silva, *Opera Omnia*, i, 2–7 • Gehrenbeck, *Corona*, 1661–1668

    Intabulation: keyboard

    3. CH-SGs, 530, 133v–134r (*Andreanus Siluanus*)

    Intabulation: lute

    2. 1536¹³ = N522, No.28, R4r–S2v (*Andreas de Sylva.* H. Newsidler)

Levate capita vestra   **Martini**   4vv

2/ *Dum ortus fuerit*

    1. **21**, No.20 (*Io. Martini.*)

    4. Sherr, *Sixteenth-century*, iii, 89–102

Liber generationis Jesu Christe   **Josquin**   4vv

  2/ Salomon autem; *3/ Et post transmigrationem*

    1. **15**, No.3 (*.Josquin.*)

    Facsimile: Barksdale, *Printed*, 66

    2. 1538³, No.37 (Anon.) • 1547¹, pp. 376–87 (Headed *Phrygij Hypophrygijque connexorum eodem Iodoco*) • J678 (1555), No.1 (Josquin) • 1559², No.8 (*IOSQVIN DE PRES.: Iosquin de Prees.* in the Tavola)

    3. D-Dl, 1/D/505, pp. 416–421 (Anon.) • D-Mbs, 10, No.9, 127*v*-145*r* (*Josquin de press.*) • E-Tc, 23, No.1, iv*v*-7*r* (*Josquin despres*) • F-Pn, 1817, No.38 (Anon.) • GB-Lcm, 1070, No.31, 96*v*-102*r* (Anon.) • I-CT, 95–96, No.38, 39*r*-42*v* (Anon.) • I-Fn, II.I.232, No.18, 51*v*-57*r* (*IOSQVIN*) • I-Fn, 107ᵇⁱˢ, No.23, 24*v*-30*r* (Anon.) • I-Rvat, C.S.42, No.9, 41*v*-47*r* (Anon.) • S-Uu, 76c, 64*v*-67*r* (*Josquin des Pres*)

    4. Braithwaite, *Introduction*, iv, 284–307 • Glareanus, *Dodecachordon*, 454–469 • Josquin, *Werken*, Motetten, i, 6 • *New Josquin Edition*, xix, 13

Libera nos

  2/ of **O beate Sebastiane**   **Martini**   4vv

  2/ of **O beate Sebastiane**   **Weerbeke**   4vv

Locutus est populus

  2/ of **Panis quem ego dabo**   **Lupus Hellinck**   4vv

Loquebantur alleluya

  5/ of **Spiritus Domini replevit**   **Weerbeke**   4vv

Lux solemnis adest / Repleti sunt omnes   **Regis**   5vv

  2/ Nec mirum si tanta

    1. **46**, No.11 (*Regis*)

    3. I-Rvat, C.VIII.234, No.31, 257*v*-261*r* (Anon.)

    4. Regis, *Opera Omnia*, ii, 30–42 • Winkler, *Tenormotetten*

Magnificat   **Agricola**   4vv

    1. **39**, No.1 (Agricola)

    2. This piece was probably concordant with the following: B-Br, 9126, No.12, 144*v*-148*r* (*Allexander*) • D-Dl, 1/D/505, pp. 222–233 (Anon.) • I-Rvat, C.S.44, No.1, 2*v*-9*r* (*Agricola*)

    Comments: This attribution comes from Colón's description of the book. The work was probably in the first mode, and the only known first mode Magnificat by Agricola is found in these sources, and edited in Agricola, *Opera Omnia*

Magnus es tu Domine   **Josquin**   4vv

                                      (Finck)

  2/ Tu pauperum refugium

    1. **15**, No.32 (Anon.)

    2. 1538³, No.40 (*Hen. Finck*)

    3. A-Wn, 15500 • D-Rp, B.211–215 (*Josquin, aliis H.F.*)

    another version of part 1:

    2. 1547¹, pp. 272–75 (Headed *Hypophrygij Exemplum III. Jodocus a Prato author.*)

    3. CH-SGs, 463, No.112, 39*r* and 99*r* (*Josquinus Pratensis.* Headed *Mixolydii Hypomixolydiique, idest septimi et octavi toni connexio.*) • D-Mu, 322–325 (*Jusquinus*)

    4. Glareanus, *Dodecachordon*, 341–347 • Josquin, *Werken*, Motetten, i, 6

    Comments: Brown, "Hans Ott", p. 75, doubts the attribution to Josquin

Manus tue Domine

    2/ of **Bonitatem fecisti**   Carpentras   4vv

Maria plena gratia stirpe

    2/ of **Conceptus hodiernus Marie**   Brumel   4vv

Maria virgo semper letare   Ghiselin   4vv

        1. *21*, No.3 (*Jo. ghiselin.*)

        3. I-Mfd, 2267, No.33, 180*v*-181*r* (Anon.)

        4. Ghiselin, *Collected Works*, i, 20–23

Maria virgo semper letare   Mouton   4vv

                                      (Gascongne)

    2/ *Te laudant angeli*

        1. *64*, No.20 (*Mouton*)

        2. 1526², No.20 (*Io. monton*) • 1534³, No.10 (*Gascongne*)

        3. GB-Lcm, 1070, No.28, 87*v*-91*r* (Anon. Untexted)

        4. Attaingnant, *Treize*, i, 82 • Braithwaite, *Introduction*, iv, 262–73 • Sherr, *Sixteenth-century*,
            v, 95–107 • Shine, *Mouton*, 480–89

Mater digna Dei   Weerbeke   4vv

        1. *3*, No.34 (*Gaspar* in the index) • *19*, No.34 (Anon.)

        3. I-Fn, Panc.27, No.60, 39*v*-40*r* (Anon.) • I-Mfd, 2269, No.79, 115*v*-116*r* (*Gaspar*) • I-Pc,
            A17, No.107, 156*v*-157*r* (Anon.) • I-VEcap, DCCLVIII, No.9, 19*v*-20*r* (Anon.) • ZA-
            Csa, Grey, No.67, 107*v*-108*r* (Anon.)

        4. Drake, *First*, ii, 132–135 • Weerbeke, *Messe*, 4–7

Mater patris et filia   Brumel   3vv

        1. *1*, No.62 (*Brunel*) • *5*, No.62 (*Brunel*) • *14*, No.62 (*Brunel*)

        2. 1538⁹, No.55, H1*r* (Anon: *Ant. Brumel* in MS in the D-Ju copy, and *Henricus Brumel* in
            that at D-B)

        3. D-Mu, 322–325, No.18 (Anon.) • E-Sc, 5-5-20, No.11, 19*v*-20*r* (Anon.) • E-SE, s.s.,
            No.78, 157*v*-158*r* (*Anthonius brumel*) • I-Bc, Q18, No.74, 75*v*-76*r* (Anon.) • I-Fn, Panc.27,
            No.131, 101*v*-102*r* (*Brunel*)

        4. Brumel, *Opera Omnia*, v, 63–64 • Disertori, "Campane", 106–111 • Disertori, *Frottole*,
            232–237 • Hewitt, *Odhecaton*, 351–52 • Josquin, *Werken*, Motetten, iii, 29 • Mönkemeyer,
            Formschneyder, ii, pp. 81–82 • Smijers, *Van Ockeghem*, p. 138

    Comments: The basis for the mass by Josquin, also published by Petrucci

    Intabulations: keyboard

        2. Baena 1540, No. 32, 28*r*-29*v* (Compere)

    Intabulations: lute

        1. *34*, No.25 (*Francesco Spinacino*)

        2. 1536¹³ = N522, No.5, B4*v*-C1*r* (*Brumel*. H. Newsidler)

        4. Disertori, *Frottole*, 232–237 • Schmidt, *Spinacino*, ii, 254–58

Mater patris nati   Obrecht   5vv

    2/ *Ab eterno genitura*; 3/ *Virgo mater*

        1. *46*, No.14 (*Obreth*)

Memento mei domine

    See **Missa Charge de deul**: Christe   Isaac   4vv

Memento nostri piissima

    2/ of **Propter gravamen**   Compère   4vv

Memor esto verbi tui   Josquin   4vv

  2/ *Portio mea, Domine*

    1. **55**, No.2 (*Josquin*)

    2. 1526¹, No.2, (*Josquin.*) • 1539⁹, No.XVIII (*Iosquin*) • 1559², No.9 (*IOSQVIN. Iosquin de Prees.* in the index)

    3. CH-SGs, 463, No.88, 27*v*–29*r* and 87*v*–88*r* (*Josquinus Pratensis.* Headed *Dorius, idest primus tonus*) • D-Kl, 24, No.21 (*Josquin*) • D-Mbs, 19, No.3, 26*v*–37*r* (*Josquin*) • D-Mu, 322–325, No.7 (*Jusquinus*) • GB-Lcm, 1070, No.2, 5*v*–10*r* (Anon.) • I-Bc, R142, No.5, 4*v*–7*r* (*Josquin*) • I-Fn, II.I.232, No.60, 176*v*–180*r* (*IOSQVIN*) • I-MOd, IV, No.44, 98*v*–100*r* (Anon.) • I-Rvat, C.S.16, No.14, 165*v*–169*r* (*Josquin*) • NL-At, W.A. 208 F 7, No.2 (Anon.)

    4. Braithwaite, *Introduction*, iv, 18–36 • Gehrenbeck, *Corona*, 1688–1704 • Josquin, *Werken*, Motetten, ii, 16
    Literature: Macey, "Josquin"
    Intabulation: lute
    2. 1536¹³ = N522, No.29, S3*r*–T4*v* (*Josquin.* H. Newsidler)

Mente tota tibi supplicamus

  5/ of **Vultum tuum deprecabuntur**   Josquin   4vv

Michael Archangele paradisi   Jacotin   4vv

  2/ *In conspectu angelorum*

    1. **64**, No.6 (*Jacotin*)

    2. 1526², No.VI (*Iacotin*)

    4. Gehrenbeck, *Corona*, 1705–1713 • Sherr, *Sixteenth-century*, v, 6–16
    Intabulation: lute
    2. BB902,I,3 = 1546²³, No.7, 16*v* (*Jacotin.* Barberiis)

Miles mire probitatis   [Anon.]   4vv
                              (?Ockeghem)

  2/ *In nocte scis*

    1. **15**, No.19 (Anon.)

    4. Sherr, *Sixteenth-century*, ii, 93–108
    Comments: This work was attributed to Ockeghem by Ambros (*Geschichte*, iii, 179) and Pirro (*Histoire*, 114). Plamenac rejected the attribution (in his entry for Ockeghem in *MGG*)

Mille quingentis / Requiem aeternum   Obrecht   4vv

    1. **15**, No.11 (Anon. Text incipit: *Requiem aeternum*)

    3. E-SE., s.s., No.16, 81*v*–83*r* (*Jacobus Hobrecht*) • I-Fc, 2439, No.43, 47*v*–48*r* (*Obrecht.* Prima pars only. Titled [R]*equiem*)

    Text is a lament on the death of Obrecht's father in 1488

    4. Newton, *Florence*, ii, 142–47 • Obrecht, *Werken*, vi, 179–88
    Literature: Smijers, "Onbekende". For the latest assessment of the implications of the text for Obrecht's birthplace, see Wegman, "Music", pp. 199–201

Miseremini mei   Richafort   4vv
                              (Josquin, Mouton)

  2/ *Cutis mea arvit*

    1. **64**, No.4 (*Richafort*)

    2. 1520², No.2. (*Josquin*) • 1526², No.4 (*Richafort*) • 1534³, No.22, 15*r* (Anon.) • 1547¹, p. 322 (*Tertium Hypoæolij exemplum Author Joannes Mouton*)

3. A-Wn, 15941, 36v-37r (*Richafort* in the index) • CH-SGs, 463, No.136, 50v and 109v (*Joannes Mouton.* Headed *Hypoaeolius*) • CH-SGs, 464, 12r (Anon.) • D-Mbs, 16, No. 10, 61v-67r (*Mouton*) • I-Rvat, 1976–1979. No.20, 62v-64r (Anon.) • I-Rvat, 1980–1981, No.10, 64v-65r (Anon.) • NL-L, 1441, No.20, 66v-69r (Anon.)

4. Attaingnant, *Treize*, i, 176–182 • Glareanus, *Dodecachordon*, ii, 401–404 • Kabis, *Richafort*, ii, 257–261 • Picker, *Motet*, 217–224 • Shine, *Mouton*, 490–95

Comments: Picker, *Motet*, 39–40, gives a lucid description of the relevance of the various ascriptions. His preference for Richafort as the composer is supportable on stylistic grounds

Miserere Domine

cf. of **In patientia vestra**	Ghiselin	3vv

Miserere mei Deus . . . quoniam in te	[Anon.]	4vv

1. *15*, No.30 (Anon.)
3. I-CF, LIX, No.27, 64v-65r (Anon.)
4. Sherr, *Sixteenth-century*, ii, 184–88

Miserere mei Deus	Carpentras	4vv
	(Mouton)	

2/ *Cor mundum crea in me*; 3/ *Benigne fac domine*

1. *66*, No.7 (*Carpentras*: Part 3 is treated as a section of part 2)
2. 1526⁴, No.7 (Carpentras) • 1538⁶, No.XXIII (*Ioh. Mouton* in the index)
3. D-HB, XCIII-XCVI.3, No.11 (Anon.) • I-Fn, II.I.232, No.55, 157v-163r (*Carpentras* in the index) • I-Fn, 164–167, No.78, 103v-107v (Anon.)
4. Carpentras, *Opera Omnia*, v, 42–56 • Gehrenbeck, *Corona*, 1714–1733

Miserere mei Deus	Josquin	5vv

2/ *Auditui meo dabis*; 3/ *Domine labia mea aperies*

1. *65*, No.7 (*Josquin*)
2. 1520⁴, No.9, 103v-121r (*Josquin de Press*) • 1521³, No.2 (*Josquinus*) • 1526³, No.7 (*Josquin*) • 1527, No.7 (*Josquin*) • 1537¹, No.13 (*Josquin de Pres*) • 1553⁴, No.30 (*Josquin du Prees*) • 1559¹, No.3 (*IOSQVIN. Iosquin de Pres.* in the index)
3. CH-SGs, 463, No.213, 75v-76r and 138v-141r (*Josquin. à6*, with an added voice by Bidon. Headed *Hypoaeolius, idest decimus tonus seu secundus superior*) • D-Dl, 1/D/3, No.17 (*Josquin*) • D-Dl, Grimma 59a, No.13 (Anon.) • D-Kl, 24, No.15 (*Josquin*) • D-Mbs, 10, No.11, 158v-177r (*Josquin.*) • D-Mu, 326–327, 17v (Anon.) • GB-Lbl, Add.19583, No.17, 33v-36r (*Josquin.* Incomplete) • I-Fl, 666, No.41, 103v-112r (*Josquin*) • I-MOe, α.F.2.29, No.1, 1r-1v, and No.13, 8r (Anon. Incomplete) • I-Rvat, C.S.38, No.10, 41v-50r (*Josquin des pres*)
4. Braithwaite, *Introduction*, v, 51–55 • Josquin, Werken, Motetten, ii, 21 • Lowinsky, *Medici*, ii, 270–96

Comments: the basis of a mass by Parvus, and of motets texted *Peccantem me quotidie* by Berchem, Clemens, and Lassus • Other motets related to this setting are listed in Schlagel, *Josquin*, p. 251

Intabulation: organ

3. A-Kla, 4/3, 6v-11r

Intabulation: voice and vihuela

2. 1552³⁵ = P2448, No.76, 81r (*Jusquin.* Pisador)

Literature: Macey, "Inauthentic" • Macey, "Savonarola" • Novack, "Fusion"

Miserere mei Deus

    see **Ave verum corpus**   **Josquin**   2–3 vv

    see **In honore tuo / Filie regum**   [Anon.]   4vv

Miserere nostri Domine

    3/ of **Misericordias Domini**   **Josquin**   4vv

Misericordia et veritas

    See Untexted works

Misericordias Domini   **Josquin**   4vv

    2/ *Quoniam est Dominus*; 3/ *Miserere nostri Domine*

          1. **66**, No.8 (*Josquin*)

          2. 1526[4], No.8 (Josquin) • 1537[1], No.54 (*Josquin*) • 1559[2], No.6 (*IOSQVIN DE PRES.*)

          3. F-Pn, 1817, No.50, 64r (Anon.) • I-CT, 95–96, No.50, 63r-65v (Anon. In five *partes*) •
             I-Fn, II.I.232, No.57, 166v-170r (*Josquin* in the index. In five *partes*)

          4. Josquin, *Werken*, Motetten, ii, 25

          Literature: Macey, "Josquin's Misericordias"

Missus est angelus Gabriel   [Anon.]   4vv

    2/ *Splendor inextinguibilis*

          1. **15**, No.17 (Anon.)

          4. Sherr, *Sixteenth-century*, ii, 79–92

Missus est angelus Gabriel   **Josquin**   4vv

          1. **15**, No.8 (.*Josquin*. Altus and Bassus have the incipit *Missus est Gabriel angelus*)

          3. B-Br, 9126, 177v-178r (*Josquyn*) • D-As, 142a, No.41, 36v-38r (*Josquinus*. Texted *Missus est Gabriel*) • D-Usch, 237a-d, No.11, 12r-12v (Anon.) • E-Tc, 10, 31v-34r (*Jusquin*) • F-Pn, 1817, No.54 (Anon.) • GB-Lbl, Roy.8 G.VII, No.15, 23v-25r (Anon.) • I-Bc, R142, No.8, 9r-9v (*Josquin*) • I-CT, 95–96, No.54, 73r-73v (Anon.) • I-Fn, II.I.232, No.32, 94v-95r (*IOSQVIN*) • I-Fn, 164–167, No.79, 107v-108v (Anon.) • I-Rvat, C.S.63, No.7, 47v-48r (Anon. Texted *Missus est Gabriel*) • S-Uu, 76c, 67v-68r (*Josquin des Pres*)

          4. Josquin, *Werken*, Motetten, i, 6

Missus est Gabriel angelus   **Mouton**   5vv

                                 (Josquin)

    2/ *Hic erit magnus et filius*

          1. **66**, No.3 (*Josquin*)

          2. 1520[4], No.14, 165v-176r (*Mouton*) • 1526[4], No.3 (*Josquin*) • 1559[1], No.10 (numbered IX. *MOVTON. Ioannes Mouton* in the index)

          3. D-Mu, Art.401, Nos.40–41 (*Josquin. Muton* was entered in the Bassus, and then struck through. Text incipit reads *Missus est angelus Gabriel*) • I-Fl, 666, No.48, 132v-138r. (*Monton*. Text incipit reads *Missus est angelus Gabriel*. The tenor has the title *A une dame j'ay promis*) • I-Rvat, C.G.XII.4, No.45, 143v-147r (*Josquin*) • I-Rvat, C.S.19, No.15, 156v-162r (*Josquin despres*. The tenor reads *A une dame j'ay faict veu*)

          4. Josquin, *Werken*, Motetten, • Lowinsky, *Medici*, ii, 360–72 • Shine, *Mouton*, 495–511

          Comments: The Tenor uses Busnois's chanson tenor, *A une dame j'ay fait veu* • Perhaps composed in 1514 for the entry of Mary Tudor to Paris • Lowinsky (*Medici*, iii, 222–24) argues, on stylistic grounds, that the work is by Mouton. Braas, "Five-part" suggests it is by neither

Missus est Gabriel angelus

    See **Missus est angelus Gabriel**   **Josquin**   4vv

Mittit ad virginem   **Josquin**   4vv

    2/ *Accede nuntia*

       1. **15**, No.40 (Anon.)

       2. J678 (1555), No.6 (Josquin)

       3. GB-Lcm, 1070, No.9, 27*v*-31*r* (Anon.) • I-Rvat, C.S.46, No.35, 129*v*-133*r* (*Josquin.*)

       4. Braithwaite, *Introduction*, iv, 90–105 • Josquin, *Werken*, Motetten, i, 2

Montes exultaverunt

    See **Riseno i monti**   [Anon.]   4vv

Montes Gelboe

    2/ of **Planxit autem David**   **Josquin**   4vv

Muro tuo inexpugniabili

    2/ of **Aspice Domine**   **Gombert**   4vv

Nativitas tua Dei genitrix / Nativitas unde   **Brumel**   4vv
gaudia

    2/ *Cernere Divinum Lumen / Hec resonet camenis aula*

       1. **21**, No.23 (*Brumel.*)

       4. Brumel, *Opera Omnia*, v, 65–71

       Literature: Hudson, "Antoine"

Nativitas tua Dei genitrix   **Lapicida**   4vv

       1. **21**, No.43 (*Erasmus lapicide.*)

       4. Sherr, *Sixteenth-century*, iii, 268–73

Nativitas unde gaudia

    Tenor of **Nativitas tua Dei genitrix**   **Brumel**   4vv

    Tenor of **Stabat mater dolorosa**   **Turplin**   4vv

Ne tardes converti ad Dominum

    see **Missa Ave Maria**: Pleni   **Févin**   4vv

Nec mirum si tanta

    2/ of **Lux solemnis adest**   **Regis**   5vv

Nec resonat

    2/ of **Nativitas unde gaudia nobis**   **Brumel**   4vv

Nihil est opertum

    See **Fortuna par ta crudelte**   **Vincenet**   3vv

Nisi dominus edificaverit   **L'Héritier**   4vv

    2/ *Cum dederit dilectis suis*

       1. **69**, No.4 (Anon.)

       2. 1532[10], No.24 (*Lheritier*) • 1535[1], No.18 (*G. le heurteur*) • 1539[9], No.27 (*Lheriter*) • 1539[12], No.6 (*Leritier*) • 1545[4], No.6 (*Leritier*) • 1555[15] = L2316, No.7 (*G. Le Heurteur*) • 1564[6], No.6 (*Lerithier*)

       3. B-Br, Fétis 1782[A], No.7 (Anon) • D-Kl, 24, No.105 (Anon) • F-CA, 125–128, No.4 (*Claudin*) • NL-L, 1442, 31*v*-37*r* (Anon) • P-Cu, 48, 50*v*-52*v* (*Leritier*)

       4. L'Héritier, *Opera Omnia*, i, No.23

Nobilis progenie   **A. Févin**   4vv

       1. **55**, No.8 (*Antonius de feuin*)

       2. 1526[1], No.8 (*Ant.de fevin.*)

       3. GB-Cmc, 1760, No.13, 21*v*-23*r* (*Anth.de feuin.*) • I-Bsp, A.XXXVIII, No.5, 9*v*-10*r* (Anon.) • I-Pc, A17, No.95, 137*v*-138*r* (Anon.)

Text is a prayer to St. Francis of Assisi. The version in I-Bsp is dedicated to "pastor noster petronius": that in GB-Cmc to "pastor noster remigius"

    4. Braithwaite, *Introduction*, v, 129–33 • Clinkscale, *Févin*, ii, 373–376 • Févin, *Oeuvres*, iii, 105–109 • Gehrenbeck, *Corona*, 1734–1738 • Sherr, *Sixteenth-century*, iv, 53–57

Nobis concede

8/ of **Inviolata integra et casta**	[Anon.]	4vv

Noe

See **Factor orbis**	**Obrecht**	5vv

Noe noe noe

Brumel	4vv

    1. **2**, No.29 (*.Brumel.*) • **10**, No.29 (*.Brumel.*)

    2. *50 Carmina* (1513), No.29 (*Brumel*) • [c.1535][14], i, No.30 (Anon.)

    3. D-GRu, 640–641, No.5 (*Antonius Brummer.* Text *Bonus et rectus Dominus*) • I-Bc, Q18, No.22, 22*v*-23*r* (Anon.)

    4. Brumel, *Opera Omnia*, v, 84–85 • Hewitt, *Canti B*, 161–63

Noe noe psallite

Mouton	4vv

    1. **64**, No.23 (*Mouton*)

    2. 1526[2], No.23 (*Io monton*) • 1534[4], No.12, 8*v* (*Jo. Mouton*) • M4017 (1555), No.10 (Mouton)

    3. GB-Lbl, Harl.5043, pp. 85–91 (*Mouton*) • GB-Lcm, 2037, No.25, 39*v* (*Mouton*) • I-CMac, N (H), No.1, 2*v*-3*r* (Anon.) • I-MOe, α.N.1.2, No.23, 190*v*-192*r* (*Jo. mouton*) • I-Pc, A17, No.11, 19*v*-20*r* (Anon.) • I-Rvat, C.S.46, No.7, 28*v*-30*r* (*Jo.Mouton*)

    4. Attaingnant, *Treize*, ii, 86–92 • Shine, *Mouton*, 561–67

    Intabulations: lute

    2. B3772 (1548), No.23, f.11*v*-3*r* (*Jo. Moton.* Borrono) • Brown 1548[3], No.24 (*Jo Moton.* Borrono) • 1562[28] = A688, No.5, 13*v*-16*r* (Anon. de Rippe) • 1563[18], No.11 (Borrono)

Nomine qui Domini

Acaen	4vv

    1. **64**, No.3 (*Acaen*)

    2. 1526[2], No.3 (*Acaen*)

    4. Gehrenbeck, *Corona*, 1739–1743 • Sherr, *Sixteenth-century*, v, 1–5

Non diva parens

See **Adieu fillett**	**Isaac**	3vv

Non est hic aliud

C. f. to **Laudemus nunc Dominum**	**Obrecht**	5vv

Non lotis manibus

Crispin	4vv

    1. **7**, No.1 (*Crispi*)

    2. 1538[8], No.51 (*Crispinus*)

    3. D-Mu, 326, No.20 (Anon.)

    4. Albrecht, *Symphoniae*, 170–71 • Drake, *First*, ii, 138

Non nobis, Domine

Mouton	4vv
(Gascongne)	

  2/ *Lauda Deum o renata*

    1. **64**, No.22 (*Mouton*)

    2. 1526[2], No.22 (*Jo. monton*) • 1535[3], No.5 (*Gascongne.* The secunda pars is texted *Conserva regem Franciscum II*)

    3. GB-Lcm, 2037, No.19, 29*v* (*Mouton*) • I-Rvat, 1976–1979, No.24, 75*v*-78*r* (Anon.)

The text appears to honour Anne of Brittany. Cazaux, *Musique* 164, suggests that it was composed for the birth of Renée of France in 1510. The 1535 edition changes the text, perhaps to honour one of François's daughters.

    4. Attaingnant, *Treize*, ii, 38–47 • Kast, *Mouton*, 1–8 • Shine, *Mouton*, 583–92

Non secundum peccata nostra

2/ of **Benedic anima mea**	Eustache	4vv

Nos qui vivimus   Mouton   4vv

    2/ *Deus autem noster*; 3/ *Dominus memor fuit*

        1. **55**, No.5 (*Jo. Monton*: IO. MOVTON in second and third issues)

        2. 1526¹, No.5 (*Jo. Monton*.: *Mouton* in other voices) • 1539⁹, No.11 (*Ioh. Mouton*)

        4. Sherr, *Sixteenth-century*, iv, 1–31 • Shine, *Mouton*, 593–618

Nostra ut pura pectora

5/ of **Inviolata integra et casta**	[Anon.]	4vv

Nunc celi regina / Ave Maria

3/ of **Virgo salutiferi / Ave Maria**	Josquin	5vv

Numquam fuit pena

    see **Nunque fue pena maior** (Spanish texts)

Nunquid iustificari potest

see **Missa Hercules dux Ferrariae**: Pleni	Josquin	4vv

Nunquid oblivisci potest   Josquin   2vv

see **Missa Ave maris stella**: Agnus Dei	Josquin	4vv

O admirabile commercium. Creator   [Anon.]   4vv

        1. **15**, No.23 (Anon. Polyphony begins with the word *Creator*)

        4. Sherr, *Sixteenth-century*, ii, 139–45

O beate basili confessor domini   Obrecht   4vv

    2/ *O beate pater basili*; 3/ *O virum digne*

        1. **21**, No.38 (*Jaco: Obreth.*)

        3. I-Fn, II.1.232, No.49, 146*v*-150*r* (*OBRET*)

        4. Obrecht, *Werken*, vi, 85–94

        Comments: Uses the *cantus firmus* also found in Obrecht's *Missa de Sancto Donatiano*: for that reason, Strohm, *Music*, suggests that the work was written for Bruges

O beate pater basili

2/ of **O beate basili confessor**	Obrecht	4vv

O beate Sebastiane   Martini   4vv

    2/ *Libera nos*

        1. **21**, No.21 (*Io. martini.*)

        4. Sherr, *Sixteenth-century*, iii, 103–11

O beate Sebastiane   Weerbeke   4vv

    2/ *Libera nos*

        1. **21**, No.28 (*Gaspar.*)

        3. E-Bbc, 454, No.4, 16*v*-17*r* (*Gaspar*)

        4. Sherr, *Sixteenth-century*, iii, 133–42

O benigna O regina

9/ of **Inviolata integra et casta**	[Anon.]	4vv
2/ of **Inviolata integra et casta**	Josquin	5vv

O benignissime Domine   Mr. Jan   4vv

        1. **64**, No.10 (*Jan*)

2. 1526², No.10 (*Miastre Ian.*)

3. GB-Lbl, Add.19583, 30*v*-31*r* (*Maistre Jan*)

4. Gehrenbeck, *Corona*, 1744–1751 • Sherr, *Sixteenth-century*, v, 39–47

O bone et dulcis domine Jesu / Pater noster / Ave Maria   [Anon.]   4vv

(Josquin)

1. **15**, No.16 (Anon. Headed *Pater noster*)

2. [c.1521]⁷, No.3 (Anon.)

3. F-Pn, 1817, No.30 (Anon.) • I-CT, 95–96, No.30, 26*v*-27*r* (Anon.) • I-Fn, II.I.232, No.38, 117*v*-118*r* (*Josquin* in the index) • I-Fn, 164–167, No.81, 111*r*-112*v* (Anon.) • I-VEcap, DCCLVIII, No.26, 44*v*-46*r* (Anon.)

4. Josquin, *Werken*, Motetten, i, 6

Intabulation: lute

1. **34**, No.22 (*Francesco Spinacino*. Titled *Motetto o dulcis Jesu de sopra el pater nostro*)

4. Schmidt, *Spinacino*, ii, 236–41

Literature: Cummings, "Florentine", pp. 172–77

O bone Jesu   **Compère**   4vv

(Anchieta, Peñalosa, Ribera)

1. **65**, No.14 (*Loyset*)

2. 1526³, No.14 (*Loyset*) • 1527, No.14 (Loyset)

3. E-Bbc, 454, No.63, 135*v*-136*r* (*Penyalosa*) • E-Boc, 5, No.22, 69*r* (Anon.) • E-SE, s.s., No.33, 100*v*-101*r* (*Johannes Ancheta*) • E-TZ, 2, No.100, 273*v*-174*r* (*Antonio Ribera*) • Guatemala, Jacaltenango, Santa Eulalia, Archivo Musical, 7, pp. 66–68 (Anon.) • P-Cu, 12, No.57, 190*v*-191*r* (Anon.) • P-Cu, 32, No.18, 17*v*-18*r* (Anon.) • P-Cu, 48, No.21, 36*r*-36*v* (Anon.) • P-Cu, 53, No.94, 131*v*-132*r* (Anon.) • P-Ln, 60, No.8, 14*v*-16*r* (Anon.) • US-BLl, Guatemala, Music 8, 26*v*-27*r*, 58*v*-59*r* (Anon.)

4. Compère, *Opera Omnia*, iv, 27–28 • Gehrenbeck, *Corona*, 1782–1786 • Smijers, *Van Ockeghem*, iv, 116–18

Comments: The diverse endings of the Spanish versions of this piece tend to weaken the strength of any Spanish ascription

Intabulation: lute

2. 1536¹¹, No.35, 32*v*-33*r* (Anon. Francesco da Milano) • *II della Fortuna* (1536), No.25 (Francesco da Milano)

O bone Jesu o dulcis Jesu   **Ninot**   4vv

2/ *O bone Jesu si merui*

1. **21**, No.16 (*Ninot.*)

4. Ninot, *Collected Works*, 66–83

O bone Jesu si merui

2/ of **O bone Jesu O dulcis Jesu**   **Ninot**   4vv

O Christe redemptor   **Mouton**   4vv

(Maessens)

2/ *O excelsa trinitas*

1. **64**, No.13 (*Mouton*)

2. 1521⁵, No.7 (*Mouton*. Incipit *Christe redemptor*) • 1526², No.13 (*Io. monton*)

3. D-LEu, 49–50, No.47, 77*v*-78*r* (*Petrus Messens*) • D-Z, XXXIII,34, No.31 (Anon.)

4. Picker, *Motet*, 374–384 • Shine, *Mouton*, 170–75

O claviger regni   [Anon.]   4vv

2/ *Qui regni claves*

    1. *21*, No.31 (Anon.)

    3. I–Rvat, C.S.46, No.32, 103*v*–106*r* (Anon.)

    4. Sherr, *Sixteenth-century*, iii, 169–79

O crux ave spes unica   [Anon.]   4vv

    1. *66*, No.13 (Anon.)

    2. 1526[4], No.13 (Anon.)

    4. Gehrenbeck, *Corona*, 1757–1762 • Sherr, *Sixteenth-century*, v, 198–203

O Davidica plebs

   7/ of **Gloria laus et honor**   **Brumel**   4vv

O decus ecclesiae   **Isaac**   5vv

   2/ *Te laudant omnes*

      1. *46*, No.6 (*Isac*)

      3. D–B, 40021, No.92, 180*r*–182*r* (Anon. Untexted: *Vocum modulatio* in index) • D–LEu, 1494, No.96, 118*v*–121*r* (Anon. Untexted) • D–LEu, 1494, 177*v*–178*r* and 213*v*–214*r* and 257*v*–258*r* (Together, these make up a nearly complete reading. Anon)

      4. Gerber, *Mensuralkodex*, ii, pp. 155–62

O decus innocentie

   See **Ave regina / O decus innocentie**   [Anon.]   4vv

O desolatorum consolator   **Divitis**   4vv

   2/ *Beate Claudi*

      1. *55*, No.14 (*Diuitis*)

      2. 1526[1], No.14 (*Divitis*.: Altus is anonymous, though *fvin* is entered at the head of the page)

      3. I–Bc, Q27, pt.ii, No.9, 12*r*–12*v* (Anon. The incipit lacks the O)

      4. Divitis, *Collected Works*, pp. 221–30 • Gehrenbeck, *Corona*, 1673–1772 • Sherr, *Sixteenth-century*, iv, 82–92

      Comments: The Altus of 1526[1] shows a pattern of putting a new ascription at the head of a page, even when the piece begins on a lower stave. Despite this, the appearance of the name of Févin must be seen as a printing error • Composed in honour of Claude, wife of François I of France. Cazaux, *Musique*, 58–59, suggests that the work may have been written for their wedding in May 1514, although (as she adds) this may be too close to the date of Petrucci's edition

O Domina sanctissima

   2/ of **O Gloriosa Domina**   **Ghiselin**   4vv

O Domine

   See **Male bouche / Circumdederunt me**   **Compère**   3vv

O Domine Jesu Christe adoro te in cruce   **Josquin**   4vv
pendente

   Officium de passione

   2/ *O Domine Jesu Christe adoro te in cruce vulneratum*; 3/ *O Domine Jesu Christe adoro te in sepulchro*; 4/ *O Domine Jesu Christe pastor bone*; 5/ *O Domine Jesu Christe propter illam amaritudinem*

      1. *7*, No.2 (*Josquin*)

      4. Drake, *First*, ii, 139–48 • Josquin, *Werken*, Motetten, i, 4 • Schering, *Geschichte*, 58

O dominus libera animam meam

   See **Male bouche**   **Compère**   3vv

O dulcis Jesu

   See **O bone et dulcis domine Jesu**   [Anon.]   4vv

O dulcis, O pia

   3/ of **Ave verum corpus**   **Josquin**   2–3vv

O dulcissima pulcra   [Anon.]   4vv

     1. **15**, No.39 (Anon.)

     4. Sherr, *Sixteenth-century*, ii, 276–82

O excelsa trinitas

   2/ of **O Christe redemptor**   **Mouton**   4vv

O florens rosa   **Ghiselin**   3vv

     1. **3**, No.15 (.*Jo. ghiselin.*) • **19**, No.15 (.*Jo.ghiselin.*)

     3. CH-SGs, 463, No.18, 9*v*-10*r* (*Joannes Ghiselin.* Headed *Aeolii Hypoaeliique connexio*) • I-Fr, Basevi 2439, No.82, 90*v*-92*r* (Anon.)

     4. Drake, *First*, ii, 55–58 • Ghiselin, *Opera Omnia*, i, 3–5 • Gombosi, *Capirola*, No.34 • Newton, *Florence*, ii, 252–55

   Intabulation: lute

     3. US-Cn, 107501, No.34, f.55*v*-57*v* (Anon.)

O genitrix gloriosa   **Compère**   4vv
                                      (Richafort)

   2/ *Ave virgo gloriosa*

     1. **3**, No.3 (Anon.) • [Probably **19**, No.3: not extant]

     3. DK-Kk, 1848, pp. 286–87 (*Richafort*) • GB-Lcm, 1070, No.26, 83*v*-85*r* (Anon.) • I-Fr, 2794, No.8, 9*v*-11*r* (Anon.) • I-Mfd, 2267, No.9, 51*v*-52*r* (Anon. Part 1 only) • I-Mfd, 2268, No.10, 36*v*-37*r* (Anon. Part 2 only) • I-Mfd, 2269, No.89, 150*v*-151*r* (Anon. Part 2 only) • I-Rvat, C.S.46, No.26, 98*v*-100*r* (*L. Compere*) • I-Sc, K.I.2, No.72, 182*v*-184*r* (Anon.)

     4. Braithwaite, *Introduction*, iv, 244–52 • Compère, *Messe.* 148–149 • Compère, *Opera Omnia*, iv, 29–30 • Drake, *First*, ii, 10–14 • Jones, *First*, ii, 168–73 • Kabis, *Richafort*, ii, 208a–208e

O gloriosa Domina   **Ghiselin**   4vv

   2/ *O Domina sanctissima*; 3/ *O virgo virginum*

   Also texted as *O sacrum mysterium*; 2/ *Quam putas matris*; 3/ *Quam tristis et quam afflicta*

     1. **21**, No.12 (*Joannes ghiselin.* The third *pars* is here presented as part of the second)

     3. CZ-HK, Antiph. Franuse, 348*v*-349*r* (Anon.) • CZ-HK, II.A.7, pp. 286–91 (Anon.) • D-B, 40021, No.20, 53*v*-56*r* (Anon. Texted *O sacrum mysterium*) • PL-Wu, 58, 130*v*-131*r* (Anon. *O domina sanctissima* only) • PL-Wu, 58, 154*v*-155*r* (Anon. *O sacrum mysterium*: Part 1 only)

     4. Ghiselin, *Collected Works*, i, 39–48

O iam miseris respice

   2/ of **O stelliferi conditor orbis**   [Anon.]   4vv

O inestimabilis dilectio cavitatis

   mm. 1–26 of **Verbum caro factum est** (*q.v.*)   **Weerbeke**   4vv

     1. **41**, No.55 (Anon.)

     4. Jeppesen, *Laude*, 90–91

O intemerata Virgo

   See **Vultum tuum deprecabuntur**   **Josquin**   4vv

O Jesu fili David

   See French texts: **Coment peult**   **Josquin**   4 ex 3vv

O Maria

   11/ of **Inviolata integra et casta**   [Anon.]   4vv

O Maria nullam tuam
    4/ of **Vultum tuum deprecabuntur**   Josquin   4vv
O Maria, O regina
    2/ of **Rogamus te piisima virgo Maria**: see   Isaac   4vv
    Missa La mi la sol
O Maria stella maris
    2/ of **Salvatoris mater pia**   [Anon.]   4vv
O Maria templum dei
    2/ of **O Maria virgo pia**   Mouton   4vv
O Maria virgo pia   Mouton   4vv
    2/ *O Maria templum dei*
        1. *21*, No.5 (*Io.moton.*)
        4. Sherr, *Sixteenth-century*, iii, 17–27
O mater alma christi
    3/ of **Inviolata integra et casta**   [Anon.]   4vv
O mater Dei et hominis
    See **Tu solus qui facis mirabilia**   Josquin   4vv
O mater egregie
    2/ of **Ave regina / O decus innocentie**   [Anon.]   4vv
O mea sponsa de libano
    2/ of **O dulcissima pulcra**   [Anon.]   4vv
O potens magni   [Anon.]   4vv
    2/ *Cui dei fuit usque*
        1. *21*, No.30 (Anon.)
        4. Sherr, *Sixteenth-century*, iii, 150–68
O preciosissime sanguis   Obrecht   5vv
        1. *46*, No.13 (*Obreth*)
    Comments: Strohm, *Music*, p. 145, associates this work with Bruges
O pulcherrima mulierum   Bauldeweyn   4vv
        1. *66*, No.19. (*Noel baulduin*)
O pulcherrima mulierum   A. Févin   4vv
        (Festa, Mouton)
        1. *66*, No.14 (Anon.)
        2. 1526[4], No.14 (Anon.) • 1540[7], No.28 (*Antonius Fevin*. Part 2 only)
        3. A-Wn, 15941, No.31 (*A Fevin* in index) • E-Bbc, 454, No.20, 61*v*–64*r* (*Johannes Mouton*)
        • I-Bc, Q27, pt.ii, No.4, 9*v*–10*r* (Anon.) • I-Bc, R142, No.4, 3*v*–4*r* (*Con. Festa*) • I-Pc,
        A17, No.121, 176*v*–177*r* (Anon.) • I-VEcap, DCCLX, No.9, 9*v*–10*r* (Anon.)
        4. Clinkscale, *Févin*, 523–527 • Gehrenbeck, *Corona*, 1785–1790 • Sherr, *Sixteenth-century*, v,
        204–209 • Shine, *Mouton*, 644–46
    Intabulation: keyboard
        3. CH-SGs, 530, No. (*Mouton*)
O pulcherrima mulierum   Weerbeke   4vv
        1. *3*, No.24 (.*Gaspar.*) • *19*, No.24 (.*Gaspar.*)
        3. I-Fn, Panc.27, No.91, 59*v*–60*r* (*Gaspar*) • ZA-Csa, Grey, No.62, 102*r* (Anon. Incomplete)
        4. Drake, *First*, ii, 95–96 • Sherr, *Sixteenth-century*, i, 61–65
O quam fulges in etheris   Mouton   4vv
    2/ *Quis poterit eructare*; 3/ *In summitate celorum*

1. **21**, No.8 (*Joannes moton*. The *partes* are not indicated as separate)

3. I-Rvat, 1976–1979, No.11, 33*v*-36*r* (Anon.)

4. Sherr, *Sixteenth-century*, iii, 28–37

O quam glorifica luce   **Agricola**   3vv

  1. **3**, No.9 (*Agricola*) • **19**, No.9 (*Agricola*.)

  3. F-Pn, 1597, 6*v*-7*r* (Anon.) • I-Fn, Panc.27, No.95, 63*v*-64*r* (*Agricola*)

  4. Agricola, *Opera Omnia*, iv, 48–49 • Drake, *First*, ii, 36–38

  Comments: Based on the plainsong of the hymn

O quam in eternum

  2/ of **Sanctificavit Dominus**   **Acaen**   4vv

O regina

  See **La morra**   **Isaac**   3vv

O regina

  10/ of **Inviolata integra et casta**   [Anon.]   4vv

O regina pietatis

  2/ of **Ave virgo gloriosa**   **Brumel**   4vv

O regina poli

  2/ of **Dignare me laudare te**   **Gombert**   4vv

O rex Christe, o redemptor

  Alternative 3/ for **Inviolata integra et casta** **Josquin**   4vv

O sacrum convivium   [Anon.]   4vv

  1. **15**, No.22 (Anon.)

  4. Sherr, *Sixteenth-century*, ii, 132–38

O sacrum convivium   **Tromboncino**   4vv

  1. **41**, No.37 (*B. T.*)

  4. Jeppesen, *Laude*, 56–57

O sacrum mysterium

  See **O gloriosa Domina**   **Ghiselin**   4vv

O salutaris ostia   [Anon.]   4vv

  1. **41**, No.32 (Anon.)

  4. Jeppesen, *Laude*, 48

O salutaris hostia

  Bassus of **Ave verum corpus**   **Gregoire**   4vv

O stelliferi conditor orbis   [Anon.]   4vv

  2/ *O iam miseris*

  1. **21**, No.34 (Anon.)

  4. Sherr, *Sixteenth-century*, iii, 195–203

O ubi sancti rectores

  See **Missa Je nay dueul**: Benedictus **Brumel**   4vv

O virgo virginum

  3/ of **O Gloriosa Domina**   **Ghiselin**   4vv

Obsecro te virgo dulcissime   [Anon.]   4vv

  2/ *Gaudeat plebs*

  1. **21**, No.35 (Anon.)

  3. I-Rvat, C.S.46, No.29, 96*v*-98*r* (Anon.) • I-VEcap, DCCLVIII, No.3, 7*v*-9*r* (Anon.)

  4. Sherr, *Sixteenth-century*, iii, 204–12

Officium de Cruce

    See **In nomine Jesu**   **Compère**   4vv

Officium de passione

    see **O Domine Jesu Christe**   **Josquin**   4vv

Omnes gentes plaudite manibus   **Eustache de M.R.**   4vv

    2/ *Psallite Deo nostro*

        1. **64**, No.25 (*Eustache de Monte Regali*)

        2. 1526[2], No.25 (*Eustachius de monte regali*)

        3. I-Pc, A17, No.78, 113v-115r (Anon.)

        4. Gehrenbeck, *Corona*, 1773–1784 • Sherr, *Sixteenth-century*, v, 108–20

Omnes gentes

    2/ of **Benedictus Dominus Deus**   **A. Févin**   4vv

Omnis laus in fine canitur

    See **Missa Charge de deul**: Agnus I   **Isaac**   4vv

Ora pro nobis

    6/ of **Vultum tuum deprecabuntur**   **Josquin**   4vv

Ora pro nobis

    See **Vray dieu damours**   **Japart**   5vv

Ora pro populo

    2/ of **Beata dei genitrix**   [Anon.]   4vv

    2/ of **Exaudi nos filia**   **van Stappen**   5vv

Ortus de celo flos est

    See **La Stangetta**   **Weerbeke**   3vv

Osculetur me osculo oris sui

    See **Ecce video coelos apertos**   **Craen**   3vv

Pacis in terris

    3/ of **Virgo precellens**   [Anon.]   4vv

Pange lingua   [Anon.]   4vv

        1. **7**, No.13 (Anon.)

        4. Drake, *First*, ii, 211–12

Panis angelicus   **Gaspar**   4vv

        1. **7**, No.17 (*Gaspar*)

        4. Drake, *First*, ii, 228–29

    See also **Ave Panis angelorum**

Parce Domine   **Franci**[?*gena*]   4vv

        1. **7**, No.15 (Anon. *Franci* in the index)

        4. Drake, *First*, ii, 216–17.

Panis quem ego dabo   **Lupus Hellinck**   4vv

    2/ *Locutus est populus*

        1. **69**, No."1" (Anon.)

        2. 1532[10], No.18 (*Lupus*) • 1538[8], No.35 (*Lupus Hellink*) • 1539[12], No.4 (*Lupus*) • 1545[4], No.4 (*Lupus*) • 1555[11], No.29 (*Lupus*) • 1564[6], No.4 (*Lupus*)

        3. D-Kl, 43, No.28 (Anon.) • D-LEu 49/50, 287r-288r (Anon.) • D-Rp, A.R.844–848, No.V (*Lupus*) • D-Rp, A.R.863–870, No.5 (*Lupus*) • D-Rp, B.211–215, 19r-20v (Lupus) • F-CA, 125–128, No.70, 56v-57r (*Lupus noster hellinc*) • I-Bc, Q40, No.14, 59r-61v (Anon.) • I-Fd, 11, No.23, 102v-106r (Anon.) • I-MOe, γ.L.11.8, 68v-70r (Anon.) • I-

TVd, 7, 35*v*-37*r* (*Lupus*) • I-VEcap, DCCLX, 45*v*-47*r* (Anon.) • P-Cu, 48, 43*v*-44*r* (*Lupus*)

4. Clemens, *Opera Omnia*, vii, 123 • Lupus, *Opasa Omnia*

Comments: Used as the basis of masses by Clemens, Gheerkin, Marle, and Palestrina, as well as Lupus himself.

Parce Domine   **Obrecht**   4vv

    1. **7**, No.12 (*Obreht. à4*)

    2. [c.1521][7] (1524), No.20, 16*v* (Anon.)

    3. B-Br, IV.90, No.6, 8*v*-9*r* (Anon.) • B-Tv, 94, No.6, 9*r*-10*r* (Anon.) • CH-SGs, 463, No.128, 47*v* and 106*v* (*Jacobus Obrecht*. Headed *Aeolius tonus*) • D-Mu, 322–325, No.15 (*Hobrechtus auctor*) • I-Bc, Q18, No.83, 84*v*-85*r* (Anon.)

    The following sources are à3: *RISM* 1547[1], pp. 260–61 (*Triados in Aeolio exemplum Iacobi Hobrechthi*) • DK-Kk, 1848, 99*r* (Anon.) • F-AM, 162, 18*r* (Anon.) • GB-Cmc, 1760, No.26, 46*v*-47*r* (*Obrek* in the index) • GB-Lbl, Add.35087, No.4, 5*r* (Anon. Incomplete) • I-Bc, Q17, No.1, 2*r* (Anon. Incomplete) • I-Bc, R141, part 2, 16*v* (Anon.) • S-Uu, 76a, No.30, 26*v*-27*r* (Anon.)

    4. Besseler, *Cappella*, 9 • Braithwaite, *Introduction*, v, 195–97 • Drake, *First*, ii, 209–10 • Forkel, *Geschichte*, ii, 524 • Glareanus, *Dodecachordon*, ii, 327–328 • McMurtry, *Chansonnier*, 215–18 • Obrecht, *Werken*, vi, 95–96 • Vellenkoop, "Parce", 46–47

Intabulations: keyboard

    2. 1531[5], No.13, 117*r* (Anon.)

    3. CH-SGs, 530, No.15, 14*v* (Anon.) • CH-Zz, S.248/284a

Comments: Glareanus asserts that the Altus was a later addition, and probably not by Obrecht • The Bassus was used by Verdelot as the Quintus of his *Recordare Domine*

Literature: Buning-Jurgens, "More" • Vellenkoop, "Parce" • Vellenkoop, "Zusammenhänge"

Passio sacra nostri redemptoris   **Francesco** [?*d'Ana*]   4vv

    1. **27**, No.12 (*Fran Vene*; *Fran. veneti* in the index)

    4. Disertori, *Frottole*, 147–54, attributing the work to Francisc. de Dana Veneti dicti Varoter • Thomas, *Petrucci*, 378–85

Pater meus agricola est   **Agricola**   3vv

    1. **31**, No.26 (*Alexan. Agricola*)

    2. Heyden 1540, pp. 140–43 (*Alexander Agric*. Headed *Exemplum Primi Toni*)

    4. Agricola, *Opera Omnia*, v, 107–11

Pater noster

    Tenor of **O bone et dulcis domine Jesu**   [Anon.]   4vv

Patris sapientia

    3/ of **In Nomine Jesu**   **Compère**   4vv

Peccata mea Domine   **Mouton**   5 ex 4vv

    1. **64**, No.17 (*Mouton*)

    2. 1526[2], No.17 (*Io. monton*) • M4017 (1555), No.18 (Mouton)

    3. I-Bc, Q19, No.50, 78*v*-79*r* (*Jo. Moton*) • I-Bc, Q27, pt.i, No.47, 54*v*-55*r* (*Jo. mouton*. Transposed up a fifth) • I-Fl, 666, No.36, 92*v*-94*r* (*Mouton*) • I-Rvat, C.S.26, No.15, 138*v*-139*r* (*Mouton*. Rubric reads *Canon finis coronat*)

    4. Lowinsky, *Medici*, ii, 241–45 • Shine, *Mouton*, 667–72

Per illud ave

    2/ of **Benedicta es coelorum regina** **Mouton**   4vv

Planxit autem David   **Josquin**   4vv
                                                 (Ninot)

2/ *Montes Gelboe*; 3/ *Sagitta Jonathae*; 4/ *Doleo super te*

    1. **15**, No.33 (Anon.)

    2. 1547¹, pp. 418–429 (Headed *Ionici Hypoionicique connexorum Exemplum Iodoci Pratensis*) •
      J678 (1555), No.2 (Josquin)

    3. CH-SGs, 463, No.146, 53*v*–55*r* and 112*v*–114*r* (*Josquinus Pratensis*. Headed *Ionici Hypoion-
      icique, idest quinti et sexti connexio*) • D-Dl, 1/D/505, pp. 410–417 (*Josquin*) • I-Fn, II.I.232,
      No.19, 57*v*–62*r* (*Ninot* in the index) • I-Rvat, C.S.38, No.16, 63*v*–73*r* (*Josquin*)

    4. Glareanus, *Dodecachordon*, ii, 499–512 • Josquin, *Werken*, Motetten, i, 6

Plebs hebrea

    4/ of **Gloria laus et honor**   [Anon.]   4vv

    3/ of **Gloria laus et honor**   **Brumel**   4vv

Popule meus quid feci tibi   [Anon.]   4vv

    1. **41**, No.34 (Anon.)

    3. I-Fn, Panc.27, No.47, 29*v*–30*r* (Anon. Text incipit *Dolce regina*) • ZA-Csa, Grey, No.26,
      58*v*–60*r* (Anon. Text *Ave dulcis ave pia*)

    4. Cattin, *Canti polifonici*, No.26 • Jeppesen, *Laude*, 50–51

Popule meus   **de Quadris**   2vv

    1. **27**, No.9 (*eiusdem* [i.e., de Quadris] in the index only)

    3. I-Pc, C56, 62*v*–65*r* (Anon.)

    4. Thomas, *Petrucci*, 362–71

Portio mea, Domine

    2/ of **Memor esto**   **Josquin**   4vv

Postquam consumati sunt   **Lupus**   4vv

    1. **64**, No.5 (*Lupus*)

    2. 1526², No.5 (*Lupus*) • 1534³, No.23, 15*v* (*Lupus*) • 1545⁵, No. (*Johannes Lupi*) • 1555¹⁵,
      p. 30 (*Lupus*)

    3. I-BGc, 1209D, 51*v*–52*r* (Anon.) • I-Pc, A17, No.64, 92*v*–93*r* (Anon.)

    4. Attaingnant, *Treize*, i, 23 • Gehrenbeck, *Corona*, 1791–1795
    Intabulation: lute

    2. 1546²³ = BB902 I,3, No.4, 11*v* (*Lupus*. Borrono)

Postquam licaoniam

    2/ of **Gloriosus dei appostolus**   **Baulduin**   4vv

Precantibus

    see **Vavliment**   **Obrecht**   4vv

Preter rerum seriem   **Josquin**   6vv

2/ *Virtus sancti spiritus*

    1. **65**, No.2 (*Josquin*)

    2. 1520⁴, No.2, 13*v*–22*r* (*Josquin*) • 1526³, No.2 (*Josquin*) • 1527, No.2 (Josquin) • 1537¹,
      No.4 (*Josquin*) • J678 (1555), No.12 (Josquin) • 1558⁴, No.3 (*IOSQVIN.*)

    3. B-LVu, 163, 114*r*–115*v* (*Josquin*) • CH-SGs, 463, No.209, 73*r* and 135*v*–136*r* (*Josquin*.
      Headed *Dorius et Hypodorius, idest primus et secundus connexi*) • CH-SGs, 464, 1*r* (*Josquin*)
      • CZ-HK, II.A.29, p. 424 (Anon.) • CZ-RO, A.V.22a-b, 54*v* (*Josquin*)• D-B, Breslau 11,
      No.67 (Anon.) • D-B, Bohn 357 (i), No.19 *Iosquin de Pres*) • D-Dl, Glashütte 5, No.152
      (*Josquin*) • D-Dl, Grimma 57, No.18, 74*r* (*Josquin*) • D-Dl, Pirna IV, 10*v* (*Josquin*) • D-

GOl, A.98, 10v-15r (Anon.) • D-HO, 3713, F2r • D-Mu, Art.401, Nos.10–11 (*Josquin*) • D-Rp. A.R.775–777, No.56 (Anon.) • D-Rp, C.120, No.34, 148–153 (Anon.) • D-Z, XCIV,1, No.25 (Anon.) • DK-Kk, 1872, 87v (Anon.) • E-Sc, 1, 33v-42r (*Josquin*) • E-Tc, 23, No.8, 85v-89r. (Anon. *Josquin* in the index) • GB-Lcm, 1070, No.21, 63v-68r (Anon.) • H-BA, 2, 1r (*Josquin*) • I-Bc, R142, No.41, 45v-47r (*Josquin*) • I-Fd, 11, No.9, 39v-44r (Anon.) • I-Rpm, 23–24, No.44, 41v-42r (*Jusquin*) • I-Rsm, 26, 101v-106r • I-Rv, S¹ 35–40, No.50 (*Josquin*) • I-Rvat, 11953, No.29, 25v-26v (Anon.) • I-Rvat, C.G.XII.4, No.38, 109v-115r (*Josquin*) • I-Rvat, C.S.16, No.13, 160v-164r (*Josquin*. Original number III) • NL-L, 1440, 252v-268r (*Josquin* in the index) • NL-L, 1442, 142v-148r (*Josquin*) • PL-WRu, 39, 111v-112v (Anon.) • PL-WRu, 54, No.15 (*Josquin*) • S-Uu, 76b, No.15, 117v-120r (*Josquin*)

4. Braithwaite, *Introduction*, iv, 192–209 • Josquin, *Werken*, Motetten, iii, 18

Comments: Used as the basis of many masses, including works by Daser, Jistebnicky, La Hèle, Lassus, Le Maistre, and Rore: also for a Magnificat by Lassus and a motet by Calvisius

Intabulation: voice and vihuela

2. 1554³² = F2093, No.72, 88r (*Josquin*. Fuenllana)

Intabulations: lute

2. 1547²² = G2092, No.10, E2r-E4v (*Josquin* in the Tabula. Gintzler) • 1555³⁶, No.3, 8r-12v (*Josquin*. de Rippe) • 1558²⁰ = O12, No.2, 4v-6v (*Josquin de Pres*. Ochsenkuhn)

3. D-Mbs, 272, No.64, 80v-82r (Anon.) • Jelenia Gora, s.s., No.1 (Anon.)

Intabulations: keyboard

3. D-B, Bohn 6, No.27 • D-B, Bohn 357 (ii), No.2, 176v and 4r-5r (*Josquin de Prees*) • SK-Le, 13990a, 8v-10r (Anon.)

Primum querite regnum dei

see French texts: **Je cuide sece temps**   **Congiet**   4vv

Profitentes Unitatem   **Compère**   4vv

2/ *Digne loqui*

1. **15**, No.28 (Anon.)

3. GB-Lcm, 1070, No.25, 80v-83r (Anon.) • I-CF, LIX, No.29, f.67v-69r (Anon.) • I-Rvat, C.S.42, No.32, 130v-132r (*Louyset Compere*. Numbered XXII in the source)

4. Braithwaite, *Introduction*, iv, 232–42 • Compère, *Opera Omnia*, iv

Propter gravamen   **Compère**   4vv

2/ *Memento nostri piissima*

1. **3**, No.7 (*Compere*.) • **19**, No.7 (*Compere*.)

3. E-Bbc, 454, No.62, 133v-135r (Anon.) • F-CA, 125–128, No.81 (Anon. The second *pars* starts at *Et subveni*) • I-Fn, Panc.27, No.126, 95v-97r (*Compere*) • I-Rvat, C.S.15, No.54, 193v-196r (Anon.) • PL-WRu, 428, No.118, 196v-198r (Anon. The second *pars* starts at *Piissima mater misericordie*)

4. Compère, *Opera Omnia*, iv, 45–48 • Drake, *First*, ii, 26–32

Intabulation: keyboard

3. CH-SGs, 530, 78v-79r (*Compere*)

Psallite Deo nostro

2/ of **Omnes gentes**   **Eustache**   4vv

Psalite noe   **Ninot**   4vv

2/ *Puer nobis nascitur*

1. **15**, No.12 (Anon.)

3. I-Fn. II.I.232, No.23, 74*v*-77*r* (*Ninot* in the index) • I-Fn, 107bis, No.22, 21*v*-24*r* (Anon.)
• I-Rvat, C.S.42, No.10, 48*v*-52*r* (*Jo: le petit:*. Numbered VII in the source) • I-Sc, K.I.2,
No.79, 196*v*-197*r* (*Ninot le petit* in the index) • I-VEcap, DCCLVIII, 26*v*-30*r* (Anon.)

4. Ninot, *Collected Works*, 84–95

Puer nobis nascitur

2/ of **Psalite noe**	**Le Petit**	4vv

Quam pulchra es — **Baulduin** — 4vv

2/ *Veni dilecte mi*

1. **66**, No.15 (*Baulduin*)

2. 1526⁴, No.15 (*Baulduin*) • 1546⁸, No.11 (*Natalis Baudonin*)

3. A-Wn, 15941, 31–32 (*Noel*) • GB-Lbl, Add.19583, No.10, 22*v*-23*r* (Anon.) • I-MOe,
α.F.2.29, No.18, 12*v* (Anon. Incomplete) • I-Rvat, 1976–1979, No.30, 89*r*-90*r* (Anon.)

Painting: Caravaggio, *Rest on the flight into Egypt* (Collection Doria Pamphili, Rome), ca.1595

4. Braithwaite, *Introduction*, v, 35 • Gehrenbeck, *Corona*, 1796–1801

Comments: the basis of a mass by the same composer

Literature: Slim, "Caravaggio", pp. 244–46

Quam pulchra es — **Mouton** — 4vv
(Josquin, Moulu, Verdelot)

2/ *Labia destillantia*

1. **65**, No.12 (*Mouton*)

2. [ca.1521]⁷ (1524), No.4, 4*v*-5*r* (Anon.) • 1526³, No.12 (*Mouton*) • 1527, No.12 (*Mouton*)
• 1537¹, No.56 (*Josquin*, changed to *Petrus Mollu*) • 1559², No.4 (*IOSQVIN DE PRES.*)

3. CH-SGs, 463, No.119, 41*v* and 101*v* (*Petrus Moulu*. Headed *Mixolydius, idest septimus
tonus*) • CZ-HK, II.A.21 (Anon.) • D-LEu, 49, No.228 (Anon.) • D-Rp, B.220–222,
No.11 (*P. Moulu*) • D-Z, LXXXI,2, Series 2, No.4 (*P. Moulu*) • E-Tc, 10, 23*v*-28*r* (*Petrus
Molu* in the index. *Verdelot* at the head of the music) • F-CA, 125–128 (*Mouton*) • GB-
Lbl, Add.11582 • I-Bc, Q19, No.51, 79*v*-81*r* (*P.molu*: Owens, "Bologna", p. xi, points
out that this is entered over an erased *Jo. motu*) • I-Bc, R142, No.9, 10*v*-11*r* (*Jo. Mo.*) •
I-Ma, 519, No.11, 20*r*-21*r* (Anon.)

4. Shine, *Mouton*, 694–701

Comments: There is no reason to believe that this work is by Josquin. The ascriptions to
him are in late sources, and the style is that of Mouton (See Böker-Heil, "Josquin", p. 57)

Intabulations: lute

2. 1552²⁹, No.71, pp. 59–60 (Anon. Phalèse) • Brown 1563₁₂, No.102, 47*v*-48*r* (Mouton.
Phalèse)

Quam putas matris

Alternative 2/ of **O Gloriosa Domina**	**Ghiselin**	4vv

Quam tristis et quam afflicta

Alternative 3/ of **O Gloriosa Domina**	**Ghiselin**	4vv

Que es effecta

2/ of **Inviolata integra et casta**	[Anon.]	4vv

Que nunc flagitant

2/ of **Inviolata integra et casta**	**Josquin**	5vv

Que sola inviolata

12/ of **Inviolata integra et casta**	[Anon.]	4vv

Quem spiritus pertransibit

3/ of **Benedic anima mea**	**Eustache**	4vv

Quercus juncta columna est   **Luranus**   4vv

    1. **48**, No.1 (*Luranus*)

    Text is by Evangelista Capodiferro

    4. Facchin & Zanovello, *Frottole*, 109 • Luisi, *Cantar*, 398

Querite Dominum Deum   **La Rue**   2vv

    See **Missa L'homme arme: Pleni**   **La Rue**   4vv

Qui confidunt in domino   **L'Héritier**   4vv

    2/ *Bene fac domine*

      1. **69**, No."2" (Anon.)

      2. 1532[10], No.21 (*Lheritier* in the second issue) • 1535[1], No.16 (*L'heritier*) • 1539[9], No.25 (Anon.) • 1540[5] • 1555[15] = L2316, No.6 (*Lheritier*)

      3. I-Bc, Q20, No.34 (*Lheritier*) • I-CMac, N (H), 19*v* • I-VEcap, DCCLX, 62*v*-66*r* • US-Cn, VM1578, No.5 (*Lheritier*)

      4. Attaingnant, *Treize*, ix, 136 • Lhéritier, *Opera Omnia*, i, No.12

Qui divisit mare rubeum

    2/ of **Confitemini Domini**   [Anon.]   4vv

Qui fuit heli

    2/ of **Factum est autem**   **Josquin**   4vv

Qui fuit obeth

    3/ of **Factum est autem**   **Josquin**   4vv

Qui jacuisti mortuus

    5/ of **Qui velatus facie fuisti**   **Josquin**   4vv

Qui per viam pergitis

    See Italian texts: **Morte te prego**   **Tromboncino**   4vv

Qui regni claves

    2/ of **O claviger regni**   [Anon.]   4vv

Qui velatus facie fuisti   **Josquin**   4vv

    2/ *Hora qui ductus tertia*; 3/ *In flagellis potum fellis*; 4/ *In amara crucis ara*; 5/ *Qui jacuisti mortuus*; 6/ *Christum ducem redemit*

      1. **7**, No.3 (*Josquin*) • **55**, No.25 (*Josquin*. Part 6 only) • See also **24**, No.23: *Sanctus de passione* (extracted from part 3)

      2. 1526[2], No.25 (*Josquin*. Part 6 only)

      3. CZ-HK, II.A.7, pp. 296–299 (Anon. Part 6 only) • I-Pc, A17, No.22, 36*v*-37*r* (Anon. Part 6 only) • PL-WRu, 428, No.126, 224*v*-225*r* (Anon. Part 4 only)

      4. Drake, *First*, ii, 149–64 • Josquin, *Werken*, Motetten, i, 4

Quia cum clamarem

    2/ of **Laudate Deum in sanctis eius**   **Mouton**   4vv

Quis dabit capiti meo aquam   **Isaac**   4vv

    2/ *Sit turtur viduus solet*; 3/ *Laurus impetu fulminis*; 4/ *Sub cuius patula coma*

      1. **7**, No.33 (Anon.)

      3. F-Pn, 1817, No.42 (Anon.) • I-CT, 95–96, No.42, 48*v*-59*r* (Anon.) • I-Fn, II.I.232, No.25, 79*v*-81*r* (*YZACH*) • I-Rvat, C.G.XIII.27, No.60, 66*v*-68*r* (Anon.)

      Text: Poliziano's lament for the death of Lorenzo de'Medici in 1492

      4. Isaac, *Weltliche*, 45–48

      Literature: Atlas, *Giulia*, i, 155–60 • Atlas, "Note" • Sparrow, "Latin", 404–408 • Staehelin, *Isaac*, ii, 149

Comments: See Staehelin, *Isaac*, i, 26, for concordances between parts of this motet and parts of Isaac's Mass *Salva nos*

Quis dabit oculis nostris   Mouton   4vv

2/ *Heu nobis Domine*; 3/ *Ergo eiulate pueri*

  1. **65**, No.8 (*Mouton*)

  2. 1526³, No.8 (*Mouton*) • 1527, No.8 (*Mouton*) • M4017 (1555), No.2 (Mouton. Headed *Naenia in funere ANNAE BRITTANIAE Gallairum Reginae*) • 1559², No.12 (*IOANNES MOVTON.*)

  3. D-Rp, C.120, No.31, pp.126–131 (Anon.) • F-Pn, 1817, No.59, 67*v* (Anon.) • I-CT, 95–96, No.59, 66r-68r (Anon.) • I-Fn, II.I.232, No.62, 185*v*-187r (*Mouton* in the index) • I-Rvat, C.VIII.234, No.16, 136*v*-139r (Anon.)

  4. Festa, *Sacrae*, 113–119 • Expert, *Mouton*, 10–17 • Shine, *Mouton*, 712–22

The text is written in memory of Anne of Brittany, and makes reference to the funeral oration.

Quis det ut veniat   Agricola   4vv

  1. **12**, No.75 (*Agricola*)

  3. B-Br, 228, No.18, 19*v*-20r (Anon. Upper three voices have the text *Revenez tous regretz*) • B-Br, 11239, No.7, 11*v*-13r (*Alexand. Agricola*) • D-As, 142a, No.5, 50*v*-51r (Anon. Untexted) • I-Fc, 2439, No.4, 4*v*-5r (*Allexander*. the upper voice has the French text)

  4. Agricola, *Opera Omnia*, iv, 58–59 • Maldeghem, "Trésor", profane, XI (1875), 43–44 • Newton, *Florence*, ii, 12–14 • Picker, *Chanson*, 242–46

Quis est homo

  see **Missa Ave Maria**: Agnus Dei II   Févin   4vv

Quis numerare queat / Da pacem Domine   Compère   5 ex 4 vv

2/ *Audivit ipse tamen/Da pacem*; 3/ *Fundant preces / Da pacem*

  1. **3**, No.29 (*Compere*) • **19**, No.29 (.*Compere.*)

  3. CH-SGs, 463, No.192, 67r-67*v* and 123*v*-124r (*Compere*. Headed *Dorius, idest primus*) • CH-Sgs, 464, 4*v*-5r (*Compere*) • I-Rvat, C.S.15, No.58, 196*v*-199r (Anon.)

  4. Compère, *Opera Omnia*, iii, 9–14

Text perhaps for the Treaty of Bagnolo, in 1484

Literature: Dunning, *Staatsmotette* • Finscher, *Compère*, 121–124 • Wegman, *Born*

Quis numerare queat   Obrecht   4vv

2/ *Audivit ipse tamen*; 3/ *Fundant preces*

  1. **21**, No.6 (*Iacobus oberti.*)

  4. Obrecht, *Werken*, vi, 120–30

Text perhaps for the Treaty of Bagnolo, in 1484

Literature: Dunning, *Staatsmotette*, 9–14 • Wegman, *Born*

Quis poterit eructare

  2/ of **O quam fulges in etheris**   Mouton   4vv

Quomodo sedet sola   Agricola

  See **Lamentations**

Quoniam est Dominus

  2/of **Misericordias Domini**   Josquin   4vv

Quum autem venissem ad locum

  See **Cum autem venissem**   [Anon.]   2-4vv

Recordare domine

Last section of several settings of the Lamentations, *q.v.*

Recumbentibus undecim   **Lebrun**   5vv
   1. **65**, No.5 (*Lebrung*)
   2. 1526³, No.5 (*Lebrung*) • 1527, No.5 (*Lebrung*) • 1537¹, No.*xxx* (*J. Lebrun*)
   3. D-Mbs, 25, No.4, 49ᵃv-58r (Anon.) • D-Dl, 1/D/6, No.24 (*Joan. Lebrin*)
   4. Gehrenbeck, *Corona*, 1802–1824 • Sherr, *Sixteenth-century*, v, 121–47

Regat nos potentiam
  2/of **Benedicat nos imperialis**   **Longueval**   4vv

Regina celi letare   [Anon.]   4vv
   1. **21**, No.41 (Anon.)
   3. I-Rvat, C.S.42 (Anon. *Josquin* in the index)
  Literature: Noble, "Another"

Regina coeli letare   **Brumel**   4vv
  2/ *Resurrexit sicut dixit*
   1. **3**, No.13 (*.Brumel.*) • **19**, No.13 (*.Brumel.*)
   2. [1528]², No.6, 7v (Anon.)
   3. I-Fn, Panc.27, No.94, 61v-63r (*Brumel*) • I-Rvat, C.S.42, No.30, 123v-125r (*Brumel.* Numbered XX in the source) • I-VEcap, DCCLVIII, No.6, 13v-15r (Anon.)
   4. Ambros, *Geschichte*, v, 172 • Brumel, *Opera Omnia*, v, 95–99 • Drake, *First*, ii, 48–53
  Intabulation: keyboard
   3. CH-SGs, 530, 87v-88r (*Brumel*)

Regina celi letare   **Ghiselin**   4vv
   1. **21**, No.25 (*Io. ghiselin*)
   4. Ghiselin, *Opera Omnia*, i, 28–31

Regina celi letare
  See French texts: **Royne du ciel / Regina celi** **Compère**   4vv

Reple tuorum corda fidelium
  See Italian texts: **La morra**   **Isaac**   3vv

Repleti sunt omnes
  Tenor of **Lux solemnis adest**   **Regis**   5vv

Reposita est haec spes
  3/of **Tulerunt Dominum meum**   **Pesenti**   4vv

Requiem aeternam
  Tenor of **Mille quingentis**   **Obrecht**   4vv
  Tenor of **Nymphes des bois**   **Josquin**   5vv

Respice me infelicem   [Anon.]   4vv
   1. **15**, No.26 (Anon.)
   4. Sherr, *Sixteenth-century*, ii, 159–65

Respice virgo pura
  see **Missa O venus bant**: Et incarnatus   **Weerbeke**   4vv

Resurrexit sicut dixit
  2/of **Regina coeli letare**   **Brumel**   4vv

Rogamus te piisima virgo Maria
  See **Missa La mi la sol**: Credo   **Isaac**   4vv

Rogamus te piisima virgo
  2/of **Dulcis amica dei**   **Weerbeke**   4vv

Rogamus te, virgo Maria   **Jacotin**   4vv
  2/ *Ut proprium pro nobis*

1. **64**, No.7 (*Jacotin*)

2. 1526², No.7 (*Jacotin*)

3. I-Fl, 666, No.23, 66v–67r (*Jacotin*)

4. Gehrenbeck, *Corona*, 1825–1829 • Lowinsky, *Medici*, ii, 168–72

Sacris sollemnis

   6/of **Panis angelicus**   **Weerbeke**   4vv

Sagitta Jonathe

   3/of **Planxit autem David**   **Josquin**   4vv

Salomon autem

   3/of **Liber generationis Jesu Christe**   **Josquin**   4vv

Salva nos

   see **Missa Salva nos**: Kyrie and Agnus   **Isaac**   4vv

Salvatoris mater pia   [Anon.]   4vv

   2/ *O Maria stella maris*; 3/ *Ave virgo gratiosa*

      1. **15**, No.41 (Anon.)

      4. Sherr, *Sixteenth-century*, ii, 283–97

Salve lux fidelium

   2/of **Salve virgo virginum**   **Aulen**   4vv

Salve mundi salutare   **Dammonis**   4vv

      1. **45**, No.10 (Dammonis. Headed *Ad crucifixum*)

      4. Jeppesen, *Laude*, 105

Salve radix josophanie

   See **Le sovenir**   **Morton**   3vv

Salve Regina   [Anon.]   4vv

   2/ *Eya ergo*; 3/ *Et Jesum benedictum fructum*

      1. **7**, No.32 (Anon.)

      3. E-Bbc, 681, No.27, 80v–81r (Anon.)

      4. Drake, *First*, ii, 283–87

Salve regina   **La Rue**   4vv

   2/ *Eya ergo*; 3/ *Et Jesum benedictum*

      1. **21**, No.4 (*Petrus de la rue.*)

      3. B-Br, 9126, 136v–138r

      4. Sherr, *Sixteenth-century*, iii, 1–16

Salve regina di misericordia   **Dammonis**   4vv

      1. **45**, No.33 (Dammonis. Headed *Ad beatam virginem*)

      Text by Belcari

      4. Jeppesen, *Laude*, 136–37 • Luisi, *Laudario*, ii, 153–55

Salve regina glorie maria stella   **Dammonis**   4vv

      1. **45**, No.53 (Dammonis. Headed *Ad beatam virginem*)

      4. Luisi, *Laudario*, ii, 350

Salve regina o germinante ramo   **Dammonis**   4vv

      1. **45**, No.34 (Dammonis. Headed *Laus beate virginis*)

      Text by Giustiniani

      4. Jeppesen, *Laude*, 138–39 • Luisi, *Laudario*, ii, 121–23

Salve sancta Christi parens

   2/of **Decantemus in hac die**   [Anon.]   4vv

Salve sancta parens	[Anon.]	4vv

    1. *24*, No.6 (Anon.)

Salve sancta parens	**Weerbeke**	4vv

    1. *24*, No.5 (*Gaspar*)

Salve sponsa tui genitrix	**Regis**	5vv

    1. *46*, No.10 (*Regis*)

    4. Regis, *Opera Omnia*, ii, 1–4

Salve virgo virginum	**Aulen**	4vv

  2/ *Salve lux fide*

    1. *21*, No.32 (*Ioannes: Aulen*)

    4. Sherr, *Sixteenth-century*, iii, 180–94

Sancta Dei genitrix		

  2/ of **Vultum tuum deprecabuntur**   **Josquin**   4vv

Sancta Maria mater dei

  2/ of **Ave Maria gratia plena**   **Dammonis**   4vv

Sancta Maria ora pro nobis	[Anon.]	4vv

    1. *7*, No.27 (Anon.) (Texted *Sancta Maria quaesumus*) • *41*, No.8 (Anon. The first 37 mm. only)

    4. Drake, *First*, ii, 271–72 • Jeppesen, *Laude*, 13–14

Sancta Maria ora pro nobis

  See Italian texts: **Me stesso incolpo**   **Cara/Tromboncino**   4vv

Sancta Maria quaesumus

  See **Ave Maria**   **Compère**   4vv

  See **Sancta Maria ora pro nobis**   [Anon.]   4vv

Sancta Trinitas	**A. Févin**	4vv
	(Craen, Festa, Josquin, Morales, Mouton)	

    1. *55*, No.13 (*feuin*: Altus, *Antonius Fevin*)

    2. 1526¹, No.13 (*Ant de fevin.*)

    3. B-Tc, Missel de la Confrerie de la Transfiguration, 14*v* (Anon. Lost) • CH-SGs, 462, 110*v* (Anon.) • D-GM, 55, No.9 (*Fevin*) • D-Mbs, 1536, 315r-*v* (*Fevin*) • D-Sl, 25, 65*v*–72*r* (*Antoine de Fevin*) • E-Bbc, 454, No.90, 166*v*-167*r* (*Anthonius de fevin*) • E-SA, 34, 56*v*-57*r* (*Morales*) • E-Tc, 13, 25*v* (Anon.) • F-CA, 125–128, No.128, 118*r* (Anon.) • GB-Cmc, 1760, No.12, 19*v*-21*r* (*A.de fevin.*) • GB-Lbl, Roy.8.G.vii, No.7, 12*v*-14*r* (Anon.) • GB-Lcm, 1070, No.41, 125*v*-133*r* (Anon.) • I-Bc, Q27, pt.ii, No.8, 11*v*-12*r* (Anon.) • I-CF, LIX, No.42, 84*v*-85*r* (Anon.) • I-Fn, 117, No.52, 85*v*-87*r* (Anon.) • I-MOd, IX, No.20, 39*v*-40*r* (*A. fevin*) • I-Pc, A17, No.57, 83*v*-84*r* (Anon.) • I-Rvat, C.VIII.234, No.10, 87*v*-88*r* (*A de feuin*) • I-TVd, 5, 32*r* (*Constantus Festa*) • I-VEcap, DCCLX, No.41, 50*v*-51*r* (Anon.) • S-Uu, 76c, 71*v*-72*r* (*Fevin*)

    The following sources are à6: 1537¹, No.3 (Anon.) • 1555¹¹, No.7 (*Fevin*) • 1558⁴, No.10 (*FEVIN.*) • D-B, Bohn 5, No.155 • D-Dl, Glashütte 5, No.154 (*Fevin*) • D-Dl, Grimma 55, No.9 (Anon.) • D-EIa, Kantionale (*Josquin*) • D-ERu, 473/4, 33*v*-39*r* (Anon.) • D-Bga, 7, No.33 (*Craen*) • D-LÜh, 203, No.10 • D-Rp, A.R.70, No.7 (*Fevin*) • D-Rp, A.R.883–886, No.12 (*Antonius Fevin*) • D-Rp, A.R.940, No.234 (*Fevin*) • DK-Kk, 1872, 81*v* (Anon.) • DK-Kk, 1873, 100*r* (Anon.)

    4. Braithwaite, *Introduction*, iii, 39–44 • Clinkscale, *Févin*, ii, 382–86 • Févin, *Oeuvres*, iii,

114–119 • Févin, *Sancta Trinitas* • Geering & Trümpy, *Liederbuch*, 101–103 • Gehrenbeck, *Corona*, 1830–1835 • Gombosi, *Capirola*, p. 34

Comments: The basis for Févin's own mass, also published by Petrucci

Intabulation: keyboard

2. 1531[5], No.5, 92r (Anon.)

Intabulations: lute

2. 1536[13] = N522, No.32, Y2v–Z1v (*Jo. Muton.* H. Newsidler) • 1558[20] = O12, No.17, 33v (*Antoni Fevin.* Ochsenkuhn)

3. D-B, Bohn 3, No.41 • US-Cn, 107501, 22v–24r (Anon. Headed *Sancta trinitas basa el contrabaso in voce con el tenor quando voi sonate*)

Sancte iouanes baptista

  See **Vray dieu damours**   **Japart**   5vv

Sancte Michael ora pro nobis

  2/ of **Ave Maria**   **Compère**   4vv

Sancte speculum Trinitatis

  see French texts: **Fortune per ta cruelte**   **Vincenet**   3vv

Sancti Dei omnes   **Mouton**   4vv
                                (Josquin)

  2/ *Christe audi nos*

    1. **15**, No.24 (Anon.)

    2. M4017 (1555), No.7 (Mouton)

    3. E-Tc, 13, 1v–10r (*Josquin*) • GB-Lcm, 1070, No.17, 47v–51r (Anon.) • I-Bc, R142, No.17 (Anon.) • I-Bsp, XXXIX, 112v–115r (Anon.) • I-CF, LIX, No.28, 65v–67r (Anon.) • I-Mfd, 2267, No.33, 176v–178r (Anon.) • I-Rvat, C.S.42, No.2, 11v–15r (*Jo: Mouton* Numbered II in the source) • I-Rvat, C.S.76, 155v–161r (*Mouton*) • I-Sc, K.I.2, No.61, 116v–120r (Anon.) • I-VEcap, DCCLVIII, No.18, 32v–36r (Anon.) • I-VEcap, DCCLX, No.32, 35v–39r (Anon.)

    4. Braithwaite, *Introduction*, iv, 144–56 • Fano, *Motetti*, 102–13 • Josquin, *Werken*, Motetten, • Mouton, *Motetten*, 15–24 • Shine, *Mouton* 785–97

    Comments: the basis for an anonymous mass in D-Mbs, Mus. 66

Sanctificavit Dominus   **Acaen**   4vv

  2/ *O quam in eternum*

    1. **64**, No.9 (*Acaen*)

    2. 1526[2], No.9 (*Acaen*)

    3. I-Pc, A17, No.76, 110v–112r (Anon.)

    4. Gehrenbeck, *Corona*, 1836–1845 • Sherr, *Sixteenth-century*, v, 27–38

Scile fragor   **Compère**   4vv

  2/ *Suscipe dei mater*

    1. **3**, No.17 (.*Compere*.) • **19**, No.17 (.*Compere*.)

    3. CZ-HK, II.A.7, pp. 112–115 (Anon.) • E-Bbc, 454, No.61, 131v–133r (Anon.) • I-Rvat, C.VIII.234, No.37, 279v–281r (Anon.) • I-Rvat, C.S.15, No.53, 183v–185r (Anon.) • I-VEcap, DCCLVII, No.18, 17v–19r (Anon.)

    4. Compère, *Opera Omnia*, iv, 49 • Drake, *Petrucci*, ii, 62–67

Scio enim quod redemptor

  2/ of **Tulerunt Dominum meum**   **Pesenti**   4vv

Secundum multitudinem [Anon.] 4vv

    1. **7**, No.4 (Anon.)

    4. Drake, *First*, ii, 165–68

Sepulto domino **de Quadris** 2vv

    1. **27**, No.11 (*eiusdem* [i.e., de Quadris] in the index only)

    2. *Liber sacerdotalis* (1523), 268r–269r (Anon.)

    3. I-Pc, C56, 65v–67r (Anon.) • US-Wc, ML.171.J.6, 126v–128r • ZA-Csa, Grey, No.8, 25v–27r (Anon. à3)

    4. Cattin, *Canti polifonici*, No.8 • Thomas, *Petrucci*, 374–77

Si ascendero **Craen** 3vv

    1. **12**, No.123 (*Nico. Craen*)

    2. 1535[14], iii, No.37 (Texted *Diva palestina*)

    3. D-Mbs, 1516, No.127

    4. Smijers, *Van Ockeghem*, No.31

    Intabulation: lute

    2. 1536[13] = N522, No.2, B1r–2v (Anon. H. Newsidler. Titled *Trium Si ascendero*)

Si bibero crathere pleno **Ninot** 4vv

    1. **21**, No.45 (Anon.)

    3. I-Fc, 2439, No.87, 99v–101r (*Nino*)

    4. Ninot, *Opera Omnia* • Sherr, *Sixteenth-century*, iii, 281–86

Si bona suscepimus [Anon.] 4vv

  2/ *Adesto dolori meo*

    1. **15**, No.31 (Anon. Secunda pars untexted)

    3. I-Fn, II.I.232, No.36, 101v–103r (Anon.) • I-Rvat, C.S.42, No.45, 167v–169r (Anon.)

    4. Sherr, *Sixteenth-century*, iii, 189–98

Si dedero **Agricola** 3vv

    (Ghiselin, Obrecht)

    1. **1**, No.56 (*Alexander*) • **5**, No.56 (*Alexander*) • **14**, No.56 (*Alexander*)

    2. 1538[9], No.13. (Anon.: MS ascription to *Obrecht* in the copy at D-B: incipit *Si dedero* in the copy at D-Ju)

    3. B-Br, 11239, No.23, 32v–33r (Anon.) • CH-SGs, 462, 35v–36r (Anon.) • CH-SGs, 463, No.16, 8v (*Verbonet*. Headed *Hypomixolydius*) • D-GRu, 640–641, No.9 (Anon.) • D-Mbs, 3154, 454v (as part of the Obrecht mass based on this work) • DK-Kk, 1848, pp. 100–101 (Anon.) • E-SE, s.s., No.103, 170v (*Alexander Agricola*) • F-Pn, 1597, 7v–8r (Anon.) • I-Bc, Q16, No.117, 120v–121r (Anon.) • I-Bc, Q17, No.30, 34v–35r (*A Agricola* with a rebus) • I-Bc, Q18, No.69, 70v–71r (Anon: *Alexander* in a later hand) • I-Fn, 107[bis], 32r (Anon. This folio is lacking, but recorded in the index) • I-Fn, 178, No.27, 31v–32r (*Alexander*) • I-Fn, 229, No.68, 69v–70r (*Alexander Agricola*) • I-Fn, Panc.27, No.89, 57v–58r (*Alexi Agrice*) • I-Fr, 2356, No.61, 76v–77r (Anon.) • I-Fr, 2794, No.11, 14v–15r (Anon.) • I-Rc, 2856, No.78, 100v–102r (*Agricola*) • I-Rvat, C.G.XIII.27, No.17, 18v–19r (25v–26r) (*Agricola*) • I-VEcap, DCCLVII, No.25, 24v–25r (Anon. Untexted)

    The following sources are à4: E-Bbc, 454, No.43, 106v–107r (Anon.) • F-Pn, 676, 30v–31r (*Agricola*. The fourth voice is different from that in E-Bbc, 454)

    4. Agricola, *Opera Omnia*, iv, 50–51 • Brown, *Florentine*, music volume, 138–40 • Geering & Trümpy, No.39 • Gombosi, *Capirola*, p. 103 • Hewitt, *Odhecaton*, 339–40 • Isaac, *Weltliche*, 163 • Jones, *First*, ii, 183–86 • Maldeghem, *Trésor*, sacré, XIX (1883), No.6 • Mönkemeyer, *Formschneyder*, i, pp. 24–25 • Obrecht, *Werken*, iii, 55–57 • Picker, *Chanson*, 464–66

Comments: The basis for Obrecht's mass, also published by Petrucci

Intabulations: keyboard

2. Baena 1540, No.35, 31*v*-32*r* (obrecht)

3. CH-Bu, F.IX.22, No.9, 13*r*-15*v* (*Heinricus Isack*) • CH-SGs, 530, No.19, 17*v*-18*r* (*Alexander*)

Intabulations: lute

1. *34*, No.23 (*Francesco Spinacino*)

2. 1536[13] = N522, No.46, Ff2*v*-Ff4*v* (*Ja. Obrecht*. H. Newsidler)

3. US-Cn, 107501, No.35, 58*r*-59*v* (Anon.)

4. Schmidt, *Spinacino*, ii, 242–46

Si oblitus fuero tui Jherusalem   **Ninot**   4vv
                                      (Obrecht)

2/ *Decantabat populus*

1. *15*, No.13 (Anon.)

3. D-Dl, 1/D/505, pp. 460–463 (*Ja. Obrecht*) • D-Mbs, 3154, No. 131, 357*v*-358*r* (Anon. Part 1 only) • F-CA, 125–128, No.35, (Anon.) • F-Pn, 1817, No.35, 34*v* (Anon.) • I-CT, 95–96, No.35, 31*v*-34*v* (Anon.) • I-Fn, II.I.232, No.22, 70*v*-74*r* (*Ninot* in the index) • I-Fn, 107[bis] (Listed in the index) • I-Rvat, C.S.42, No.35, 139*v*-143*r* (*Jo. le Petit*. Numbered XXIV in the source) • I-Sc, K.I.2, No.80, 192*v*-196*r* (Anon.)

4. Shine, *Mouton*, ii, 798 • Ninot, *Collected Works*, 84–95 • Obrecht, *Werken*, vi, 97–107

Si oportuerit me teco mori   **Cara**   4vv

Intabulation: lute

1. *50*, No.6 (*M.C.*)

4. Disertori, *Frottole*, 466

Si sumpsero   **Obrecht**   3vv

1. *2*, No.40 (*Obreht.*) • *10*, No.40 (*Obreht*)

2. 50 *Carmina* (1513), No.40 (*Obreht*) • [ca.1535][14], iii, No.15 (Anon.) • 1538[9], No.12, B4*r* (MS attribution in the copy at D-Ju: *Jacobus Obrecht*. Transposed down a fourth)

3. B-Br, 11239, No.24, 33*v*-35*r* (Anon.) • CH-SGs, 463, No.24, 12*r* (Anon. Headed *Ionicus*) • D-As, 142a, No.35, 31*v*-32*r* and No.38, 34*v* (Anon. Incomplete) • D-GR, 640–641, No.11 (Anon.) • D-HB, X.2, No.8 (*Obrecht*) • F-Pn, 1597, 5*v*-6*r* (Anon.) • I-Fn, 107bis, f.33 (This folio is now lost, but recorded in the index)

4. Hewitt, *Canti B*, 204–208 • Maldeghem, *Trésor*, profane, XIX (1883), No.6 • Mönkemeyer, *Formschneyder*, i, 22–23 • Obrecht, *Werken*, vi, 175–78 • Picker, *Chanson*, 467–71 • Shipp, *Chansonnier*, 254–60

Intabulation: keyboard

2. Baena 1540, No.28, 22*v*-24*r* (Agricola)

3. CH-SGs, 530, No.21, 19*v*-20*r* (Transposed down a fourth) • D-B, 40026

Intabulation: lute

2. 1536[13] = N522, No.20, H4*r*-I2*r* (*Jacobus Obrecht*. H. Newsidler)

Sic anima mea

Tenor of 2/ of **Clangat plebs /Sicut lilium**   **Regis**   5vv

Sic unda impellitur unda   [Anon.]   3 ex IV
                               (Moulu)

1. *7*, No.35 (Anon. Untexted)

2. Heyden, 1537, p. 31 (Anon. Untexted. Headed *Exemplum hdurum medii Systematis. Fuga trium ex eodem*) • Heyden 1540, p. 35 (Anon. Untexted. Headed *Fuga trium in unisono*) •

1547[1], pp. 258–59 (*Monados in Aeolio quartum exemplum incerti authoris*. Untexted) • Zacconi 1592, i, 45r (*Pierre Moulu*. Headed *Trinitatis in unitate*)

   3. CH-SGs, 463, 4r (Anon. Untexted)

   4. Chapman, *Moulu*, ii, 313–16 • Drake, *First*, ii, 293–94 • Glareanus, *Dodecachordon*, ii, 325

Sicut lilium

| Tenor of **Clangat plebs** | **Regis** | 5vv |

Sine viri copula

| 2/ of **Verbum caro factum est** | **Dammonis** | 4vv |

Sit igitur ad ipsum templum

| 2/ of **Festivitatem dedicationis** | **J. de Clibano** | 4vv |

Sit turtur vi duus solet

| 2/ of **Quis dabit capiti meo aquam** | **Isaac** | 4vv |

Sol re ut re ut

| See **Adieu fillette** | **Isaac** | 3vv |

Spiritus Domini replevit   **Weerbeke**   4vv

2/ *Veni sancte spiritus*; 3/ *Beata gens cuius est*; 4/ *Confirma hoc deus*; 5/ *Loquebantur alleluya*; 6/ *Factus est repente*

    1. **21**, No.41 (*Gaspar*. Headed in *in honorem sancti spiritus*)

    3. I-Mfd, 2266, 120v–121r (Anon. Part 2 only) • I-Pc, A17, No.54, 80v–81r (Anon. Part 1 only) • I-Pc, A17, No.56, 82v–83r (Anon. Part 2 only)

Spiritus Domini replevit

| 2/ of **Dum complerentur** | **Lhéritier** | 4vv |
| 2/ of **Factor orbis / Canite tuba / Noe** | **Obrecht** | 5vv |

Splendor

| 2/ of **Huc omnes pariter** | [Anon.] | 4vv |

Splendor inextinguibilis

| 2/ of **Missus est angelus Gabriel** | [Anon.] | 4vv |

Stabat mater dolorosa   **Dammonis**   4vv

    1. **45**, No.19, 20r (Dammonis. Headed *Ad beatam virginem*)
    Text by Giustiniani

    4. Jeppesen, *Laude*, 118 • Luisi, *Laudario*, ii, 134–35

Stabat mater dolorosa   **Josquin**   5vv

2/ *Eya mater fons amoris*

    1. **65**, No.6 (*Josquin*)

    2. 1520[4], No.13, 156v–165r (*Josquin*) • 1526[3], No.6 (*Josquin*) • 1527, No.6 (*Josquin*) • 1538[3], No.10 (Part 2 texted *Christe verbum fons amoris*) • 1553[2]. f.4 (Josquin) • Faber 1553, pp. 116–39 (*Josquinus*) • J678 (1555), No.8 (Josquin) • 1559[1], No.1 (*IOSQVIN DE PRES*. Part 2 texted *Christe verbum fons amoris*)

    3. B-Br, 9126, 160v–164r (Josquin) • B-Br, 215.216, 39v–43r (Anon.) • B-LVu, 163, 4r (*Josquin*) • CZ-HK, II.A.26, p. 11 (Anon.) • CZ-HK, II.A.41, p. 4 (*Josquin*) • CZ-RO, A V 22a-b, 2r (Anon., with added sixth voice) • D-B, Breslau 11, No.138 (*josquin*) • D-Mbs, 12, No.8, 121v–132r (*Josquin*) • D-Mu, Art.401, Nos.44–45 (*Josquin*) • D-Mu, 327, 8v–9r (*Josquin*) • D-Rp, A.R.891–892, No.32 (*Josquin de Prees*) • D-Z, XXXIII, No.34, No.9 (Anon.) • DK-Kk, 1872, 4v (Anon.) • DK-Kk, 1873, No.37, 14v (Anon.) • E-Tc, 10, 11v–21r • E-V, 16, 8v–9v (Anon.) • E-V, 17, 116v–117r (*Josquin*) • GB-Lcm, 1070, No.8, 23v–27r (Anon.) • I-Fn, II.I.232, No.5, 22v–26r (*IOSQVIN*) • I-Rpm, 23–24,

No.45, 42*v*-43*r* (*Jusquin* • I-Rvat, 11953, No.41, 47*v*-51*r* (Anon.) • I-Rvat, C.G.XII.4, No.34, 94[ter]*v*-98*r* • I-Rvat, C.VIII.234, No.27, 241*v*-245*r* (*Josqyun* in the index) • NL-L, 1440, No.38, 258*v*-264*r* (*Josquin*) • NL-L, 1442, O*v*-4*r* (Anon.) • S-Uu, 76c, 60*v*-62*r* (*Josquin des Pres*)

    4. Braithwaite, *Introduction*, iv, 75–89 • Josquin, *Werken*, Motetten, ii, 21

Comments: The basis of a mass by Vinders

Intabulations: keyboard

    2. 1578[24] = C1, No.90, 105*r* (*Jusquin*. Cabezón) • 1578[24] = C1, No.98. 131*r* (*Jusquin*. Cabezón)

    3. A-Kla, 4/3, 11*v*-13*r*

Intabulations: lute

    2. 1536[11], No.33, 28*r*-29*v* (Anon. Francesco da Milano) • *II della Fortuna* (1536), 31*r*-32*v* (Anon. Francesco da Milano) • 1546[29], No.2, B1*v* (*Josquin*. Francesco da Milano. Headed *Stabat mater di Iusquin a 5*) • 1547[22] = G2092, No.13, G1*r*-G4*r* (*Josquin* in the index. Gintzler) • 1552[29], No.77, pp. 68–71 (*Josquin*. Phalèse) • 1558[20] = O12, No.4, 9*v*-11*v* (*Josquin de Pres*. Ochsenkuhn) • 1561[17], No.2 (*Jusqin*. Francesco da Milano) • 1563[20], No.2 (*Jusquin*. Francesco da Milano) • Brown 1563[12], No.105, 49*v*-51*r* (Anon. Phalèse) • 1568[23], No.119, 56*v* (*Josquin*. Phalèse. *Prima pars* only) • 1571[16], No.164, 94*v* (*Josquin*. Phalèse. *Prima pars* only)

    3. F-Pn, 429, No.12, 30*r*-38*v* (Anon. ?Neusidler) • F-VE, 698, No.96, 138*r*-140*r* (*Josquin de pres*)

Intabulation: voice and lute

    2. 1553[33], No.23, 14*r*-15*v* (Anon. Phalèse)

Stabat mater dolorosa / Nativitas unde gaudia   **Turplin**   4vv

    2/ *Eya mater fons amoris*

      1. **21**, No.19 (*Turplin*.)

      4. Sherr, *Sixteenth-century*, iii, 73–88

Stella coeli. Extirpavit   [Anon.]   4vv

      1. **3**, No.25 (Anon.) • **19**, No.25 (Anon.)

      3. I-Fn, Panc.27, No.102, 69*v*-70*r* (Anon.)

      4. Drake, *First*, ii, 97–99 • Sherr, *Sixteenth-century*, i, 67–73

Stella celi extirpavit   **P. da Lodi**   5vv

      1. **41**, No.40 (*Piero da Lodi*)

      4. Jeppesen, *Laude*, 60–61

Sub cuius patula coma

    4/ of **Quis dabit capiti meo aquam**   **Isaac**   4vv

Surge propera   **Pinarol**   4vv

      1. **3**, No.4 (.*Jo. de pinarol*.) • [Probably **19**, No.4: not extant]

      3. I-Fn, Panc.27, No.90, 58*v*-59*r* (*Jo. de Pinerol*)

      4. Drake, *First*, ii, 15–17 • Sherr, *Sixteenth-century*, i, 5–11

Suscipe pia laudum

    4/ of **Inviolata integra et casta**   [Anon.]   4vv

Tantum ergo sacramentum   [Anon.]   4vv

      1. **41**, No.31 (Anon.)

      4. Jeppesen, *Laude*, 46–47

Te invocamus Te adoramus / Trinitas deitas equalis unitas	**Dammonis**	6 ex 4vv

    1. **45**, No.1 (*F. Innocentii Dammonis cetereque sequentes*)

    4. Luisi, *Laudario*, ii, 354–56

Te laudant angeli		
2/ of **Maria virgo semper letare**	**Mouton**	4vv
Te laudant omnes		
2/ of **O decus ecclesiae**	**Isaac**	5vv
Te matrem		
See Italian texts: **O madre del signore**	**Dammonis**	4vv
Te nunc flagitant		
6/ of **Inviolata integra et casta**	[Anon.]	4vv
Tempus meum est	**A. Févin**	4vv

   2/ Viri Galilei aspicientis

    1. **55**, No.20 (*Feuin*: Altus and Bassus, *Ant. fevin*: *ANT.DE FEVIN* in the second issue)

    2. 1526¹, No.20 (*Ant. de fevin.*: anon. in Altus, with *Mouton.* at the head of the second page) • 1555¹⁰, No.10 (*Antonius Fevin*: Finot in the Tenor)

    3. A-Wn, 18825, No.9 23*v*–26*r* (*A. de fevin*) • CZ-HK, II.A.29 • D-Rp, A.R.69, No.10 • D-Rp, A.R.875–877, No.4 (*Antonius fevin*) • E-Tc, 23, No.19, 179*v*–183*r*. (Anon.: Fevin in the index) • GB-Lcm, 1070, No.16, 42*v*–46*r* (Anon.) • GB-Ob, a.8, 3*v* (*A. fevin*. Incomplete) • I-MOd, IX, No.18, 35*v*–37*r* (*A fevin*) • I-Rvat, 1976–1979, No.26, 80*v*–82*v* (Anon.) • I-Rvat, C.S.44, No.15, 87*v*–90*r* (Anon.)

    4. Braithwaite, *Introduction*, iv, 134–43 • Clinkscale, *Févin*, ii, 387–93 • Févin, *Oeuvres*, iii, 119–26 • Sherr, *Sixteenth-century*, iv, 101–11

    Comments: For the ascription to the Altus of 1526¹, see the note to *O desolatorum consolator*, above. This heading appears to be a similar error

Tenebre facte sunt	**Spataro**	4vv

    1. **41**, No.3, 3*v*–4*r* (*Io. Spatarius Bononiensis*)

    4. Jeppesen, *Laude*, p. 4–5

Tenebre factae sunt	**Weerbeke**	4vv

    1. **7**, No. 6 (*Gaspar*)

    3. ZA-Csa, Grey, No.57, 86*v*–87*r* (Anon.)

    4. Drake, *First*, ii, 168–70 • Smijers, *Van Ockeghem*, No. 51

Tibi Domina gloriosa		
2/ of **Ave nobilissima creatura**	**Josquin**	6vv
Tota pulchra es	**Craen**	4vv

   2/ Flores aparuerunt

    1. **15**, No.5 (*.Nico. Craen.*)

    4. Sherr, *Sixteenth-century*, ii, 1–13

    Intabulation: lute

    3. US-Cn, 107501, No.42, 72*v*–74*v* (Anon.)

Tota pulchra es		
Contra of **Belle sur toutes**	**Agricola**	3vv
Tota scriptura		
See **Missa Narayge: Pleni**	**Ghiselin**	
Tribus miraculis	**C. Festa**	6vv

   2/ Ab oriente venerunt magi

 1. **66**, No.1 (*Constantius Festa*)

 2. 1526⁴, No.1 (*Constantius Festa*)

 4. Festa, *Sacrae*, 59–77 • Gehrenbeck, *Corona*, 1846–1866

Trinitas deitas	[Anon.]	4vv

 2/ *Tu vertex et apex*

  1. **15**, No.27 (Anon.)

  3. I-CF, LIX, No. 26, 61*v*–63*r* (Anon.)

  4. Sherr, *Sixteenth-century*, ii, 166–75

Trinitas deitas equalis unitas

Three voices of **Te invocamus te adoramus**	**Dammonis**	6vv

Tu Domine qui exterius

2/ of **In patientia vestra / Miserere**	**Ghiselin**	4vv

Tu es arca completa

2/ of **Ave stella matutina**	**Brumel**	4vv

Tu floris et rogis

2/ of **Ave Maria gratia plena**	**Regis**	3vv

Tu parvi et magni

2/ of **Ave Maria gratia plena**	**Pipelare**	5vv

Tu pauperum refugium

2/ of **Magnus es tu Domine**	**Josquin**	4vv

Tu peperisti creatorem

2/ of **Ave Domina sancta Maria**	**Weerbeke**	4vv

Tu potis es prime / Ave Maria

2/ of **Virgo salutiferi / Ave Maria**	**Josquin**	5vv

Tu que genuisti

alternative 2/ of **Alma redemptoris mater**	**Isaac**	3vv
2/ of **Alma redemptoris mater**	**Josquin**	4vv

Tu scis Domine

2/ of **Congregati sunt**	**Mouton**	4vv
Tu solus qui facis mirabilia	**Josquin**	4vv

 2/ *Ad te solum confugimus*; 3/ *D'ung aultre amer nobis*

 From his *Missa D'ung aultre amer*

  1. **7**, No. 24 (*Josquin*) • **22**, No. 7 (Josquin) • **41**, No. 28 (Anon. Part 1 only: texted *O mater Dei et hominis*) • **59**, No.7 (*Josquin*)

  2. J672 (1526), No. 7 (*Josquin*)

  3. CH-SGs, 463, No.95, 31*v* and 91*v* and 91*v* (*Josquinus Pratensis*. Headed *Dorius, idest primus*) • I-Fn, Panc.27, No.115, 79*v*–80*r* (*Josquin*. Part 1 only) • I-MOd, IV, 15*v*–15*r* (*Josquin*. Part 1 only, within the mass) • I-Rvat, C.S.41, 155*v*–156*r* (Part 1 only, at the end of the mass) • I-RDMsm, s.s., 45*v*–46*r* (Anon.) • US-Wc, Wolffheim, 80*r*–81*r* (Anon. Part 1 only: texted *O mater Dei et hominis*)

  4. Drake, *First*, ii, 262–65 • Jeppesen, *Laude*, 40–41 • Josquin, *Werken*, Motetten, i, 4 • See also editions of the complete mass

  Comments: The manner in which this motet substitutes for the Benedictus apparently reflects a continuing tradition of using this text as part of the Sanctus (see Cummings, "Interpretation", p. 52)

Tu vertex et apex

2/ of **Trinitas deitas**	[Anon.]	4vv

Tua est potentia

2/ of **Civitatem istam tu circunda**   [Anon.]   4vv

Tua per precata

7/ of **Inviolata integra et casta**   [Anon.]   4vv

Tulerunt Dominum meum   **Pesenti**   4vv

(Isaac, Josquin)

2/ *Scio enim quod redemptor*, 3/ *Reposita est haec spes*

1. **7**, No. 11 (Anon.) • **65**, No.9 (*Pre. Michael de ver*)

2. 1526[3], No.9. (*Pre Michael de Verona*) • 1527, No.9 (*Pre Michael de Verona*) • 1547[1] pp. 314–19 (Headed *Phrygij Modi exemplum*. On p. 312, Glareanus writes *Authorem certumscire non potuimus*, while he says *quidam Isaac adscribunt* in the index)

3. CH-SGs, 463, No.111, 38r-38v and 98r-98v (*Josquinus Pratensis*. Headed *Phrygius, idest tertius tonus*) • D-Mu, 322–325, 9v-10v (*Jusquinnus*) • F-Pn, 1817, No.39, 43r (Anon.) • I-CT, 95–96, No.39, 42v-44r (Anon.)

4. Cesari, *Frottola*, xlvii–li • *Drake, First*, ii, 202–209 • Gehrenbeck, *Corona*, 1867–1879 • Glareanus, *Dodecachordon*, 391–98

Comments: The ascription to Michael (?Pesenti) seems to be the most reliable. The Florentine source, Cortona/Paris, significantly does not ascribe the piece to Isaac, and the conflict between Glareanus's edition and the related Munich manuscript is significant. Indeed (according to Miller, "Glareanus", 30), Glareanus changed the ascription to *Pre Michael de Verona* in a corrected copy sent to Johannes Aal

Tulerunt pallium

2/ of **Anima mea liquefacta est**   **Ghiselin**   4vv

Ubi caritas et amor   **Dammonis**   3vv

1. **45**, No. 4 (Dammonis)

4. Luisi, *Laudario*, ii, 357–60

Literature: Cattin, *Polifonia*, 88–89

Ut heremita solus   **Ockeghem**   4vv

2/ [Without text]

1. **15**, No.15 (Anon. Untexted)

Facsimile: *MGG*, ix, cols.1831–1834

2. Finck 1556, Kk1v-Ll1r (Anon. Prima pars only)

4. Lindmayr, "Rätseltenor" • Ockeghem, *Collected Works*, iii, 18–24 • Schering, *Geschichte*, 44–48

Comments: The attribution to Ockeghem derives from a reference in Crétin's *Déploration sur le trespas de feu Okergan*, where Hayne mentions "Ce motet, ut heremita solus"

Literature: Lindmayr, "Ockeghem" • Ockeghem, *Collected Works*, iii, xlvi–xlvii

Ut phoebe radiis   **Josquin**   4vv

2/ *Latius in numerum*

1. **21**, No.7 (*Josquin*.)

3. D-Usch, 237a-d (Untexted)

4. Josquin, *Werken*, Motetten, i, 7

Literature: ven Benthem, "A Waif"

Ut proprium pro nobis

2/ of **Rogamus te, Virgo Maria**   **Jacotin**   4vv

Vac qui sapientes

See **Missa Je nay dueul**: Qui venit   **Brumel**   4vv

Veni dilecte mi

   2/ of **Quam pulchra es**   **Baulduin**   4vv

Veni sancte spiritus

   2/ of **Spiritus Domini replevit**   **Weerbeke**   4vv

Venite amanti insieme   **Festa**   3vv

   see **Me doibt**   **Compère**   3vv

Venite comedite panem meum

   2/ of **Homo quidam fecit**   **Josquin**   4vv

Venite et ploremus   **[Anon.]**   2vv

     1. **27**, No.8(d) (Anon.)

     4. Thomas, *Petrucci*, 360–61

     Comments: Bibliographically, this appears in the edition to be the last section of a *Recordare* setting, but it comes after what should be the end — a *Jerusalem luge*. Thomas, *Petrucci* rightly regards it as a separate work. He suggests it might be by de Quadris.

Verbum bonum et suave   **[Anon.]**   5vv

                                      (Josquin)

  2/ *Ave solem genuisti*; 3/ *Ave mater verbi summi*

     1. **66**, No.4 (Anon.)

     2. 1526⁴, No.4 (Anon.)

     3. D-Mu, Art.401, Nos.46–48 (*Josquin* in the Tenor) • I-Fn, 125ᵇⁱˢ, No.18, 22*v*–23*v* (Anon.)

     4. Gehrenbeck, *Corona*, 1903–1919 • Sherr, *Sixteenth-century*, v, 157–74

Verbum bonum et suave   **Therache**   4vv

                           (Fèvin, La Fage)

     1. **64**, No.1 (*Therache*)

     2. 1521⁵, No.4 (*Therache: io de la fage* in the Tenor) • 1526², No.1 (*Therache.*)

     3. GB-Cmc, 1760, No. 6, 3*v*–5*r* (*P.de therache*: but *A de feuin* in the index) • GB-Lbl, Roy.8.G.vii, No.19, 30*v*–32*r* (Anon.) • GB-Lcm, 1070, No.14, 36*v*–38*r* (Anon.) • I-Fl, 666, No.12, 40*v*–41*r* (*Therache*)

     4. Braithwaite, *Introduction*, iii, 106–11 • Gehrenbeck, *Corona*, 1880–1885 • Lowinsky, *Medici*, iv, 95–99

Verbum bonum et suave   **Willaert**   6vv

  2/ *Ave solem genuisti*

     1. **66**, No.2 (*Willaert*)

     2. 1526⁴, No.2 (*Willaert*) • 1534¹⁰, No.8, 6*v* (*A. Wyllart*. Headed *De beata Maria*) • 1542¹⁰, No.4, p. 9 (*Adrian VV.*)

     4. Attaingnant, *Treize*, viii, 62–78 • Gehrenbeck, *Corona*, 1886–1902 • Willaert, *Opera Omnia*, iv, 16–24

Verbum caro factum est   **Dammonis**   4vv

  2/ *Sine viri copula*; 3/ *Ab angelis psallitur.*

     1. **45**, No.11 (Dammonis)

     4. Luisi, *Laudario*, ii, 212–20

Verbum caro factum est   **Dammonis**   4vv

     1. **45**, No.12 (Dammonis)

     4. Jeppesen, *Laude*, 106–107

     Compare: CZ-Pn, II.C7 • D-B, 190, No.5, 7*r* (Anon.) • GB-Ob, 213, 15*v*, 16*v*, (Anon.) • I-Bu, 2216, No.28, 19*r* (Anon. à3) • I-Fn, 112ᵇⁱˢ, No.35, 47*v* (*P.A. Janue*) • I-Fn, Panc.27, No.136, 104*v* (Anon.) • I-RAc, Libano, 194*r* • I-Tn, F.I.IV, 334*r* (Anon.) • I-TRc, 92,

No.10 [1374], 13r (Anon.) • Treviri, 724 • I-Vnm, IX, 145, No.1, 1r (Anon.) *and* No.65, 104r-104v (Anon.)

    4. van der Borren, *Polyphonia*, 49 • Jeppesen, *Laude*, No.20

Verbum caro factum est   **Weerbeke**   4vv

    1. **7**, No.7 (*Gaspar*) • **41**, No.56 (Anon. Only mm. 1–26, texted *O inestimabilis dilectio*) • **41**, No.59 (Anon. Only mm. 78–81, texted *Ave nostra salus*)

    4. Drake, *First*, ii, 174–78 • Jeppesen, *Laude*, Nos.52, 55 • Smijers, *Van Ockeghem*, No.50

Verbum incarnatum

  see **Ave Maria**   **Josquin**   4vv

Victimae paschali / D'Ung aultre amer   **Josquin**   4vv

    2/ Dic nobis Maria / De tous bien plaine

    1. **3**, No.11 (*Josquin*) • **19**, No.11 (*Josquin*)

    2. 1547¹, pp. 368–71 (Headed *Dorij Hypordorijque connexorum exemplum author Iodoci Pratensis*)

    3. CH-SGs, 463, No.100, 34v and 94v (*Josquinus Pratensis*. Headed *Dorii Hypodoriique, idest primi et secundi toni connexio*) • D-Mu, 322–325, No.3 (*Jusquinus auctor*) • E-Tc, 10

    4. Drake, *First*, ii, 41–45 • Glareanus, *Dodecachordon*, ii, 136 • Josquin, *Werken*, Motetten, i, 9

    Intabulation: keyboard

    3. CH-SGs, 530, No.104, 84v-85r (*Josquin*)

Vidi aquam egredientem   **Brumel**   4vv

    1. **24**, No.4 (*A. Brumel*)

    4. Brumel, *Opera Omnia*, iv, 80–83

Vidi aquam egredientem   **Fortuila**   4vv

    1. **24**, No.3 (*Fortuila: De fortuilla* in the index)

Vidi speciosam   **Weerbeke**   4vv

    1. **3**, No.26 (*Gaspar*) • **19**, No.26 (*Gaspar*)

    4. Drake, *First*, ii, 100–102 • Sherr, *Sixteenth-century*, i, 75–79

Vidit Jacob

  Tenor to 2/ of **Laudemus nunc dominum**   **Obrecht**   5vv

Virgine immaculata alma regina

  See **Vergine immaculata**   **Cara**   4vv

Virgo celesti   **Compère**   5vv

    1. **2**, No.2 (*Compere*) • **10**, No.2 (*Compere.*)

    2. *50 Carmina* (1513), No.2 (*Compere*)

    3. CH-SGs, 463, No.195, 68r and 125v-126r (*Compere*. Headed *Dorius, idest primus*) • CH-SGs, 464, 4v (*Compere*)

    4. Compère, *Opera Omnia*, iii, 20–21 • Hewitt, *Canti B*, 92–93 • Smijers, *Muziekgeschiedenis*, 114–15

Virgo Dei trono   **Tinctoris**   3vv

    1. **3**, No.30 (*Tinctoris*) • **19**, No.30 (*Tinctoris*)

    3. CH-SGs, 463, No.14, 7r (*Tinctoris*. Headed *Hypodorius*) • D-Mu, 322–325, No.6 (*Tinctoris*) • I-Bu, 2573, 1v-2r (*Joannes Tinctoris*) • I-Fn, 229, No.20, 19v-20r (*Jo. Tinctoris*) • I-VEcap, DCCLVII, No.7, 6v-7r (Anon. Untexted) • PL-Kj, 40098, No.258 (Anon.) • US-NH, 91, No.57, 80v-81r (*Jo. tinctoris*)

    4. Brown, *Florentine*, music volume, 42–43 • Drake, *First*, ii, 119–20 • Melin, *Tinctoris*, 481–82 • Perkins and Garey, *Mellon*, No.57 • Tinctoris, *Opera Omnia*, 126

Virgo Maria non est tibi similis   **Weerbeke**   4vv

    1. *3*, No.14 (*.Gaspar.*) • *19*, No.14 (*.Gaspar*)

    3. I-Fn, Panc.27, No.98, 66*v*-67*r* (*Gaspar*) • I-Sc, K.I.2, No.62, 120*v*-121*r* (Anon.)

    4. Ambros, *Geschichte*, v, 183 • Drake, *First*, ii, 54–55 • Lenaerts, *Kunst*, No.15 • Sherr, *Sixteenth-century*, i, 33–36

    Intablulation: keyboard

    3. CH-SGs, 530, 89*v* (*Gaspar*)

Virgo Mater

    2/ of **Mater patris nati**   **Obrecht**   5vv

Virgo precellens   [Anon.]   4vv

    2/ *Anna te mundo genuit*; 3/ *Pacis in terris*; 4/ *Ergo te nostre*; 5/ *Jam mine fere fileant*

    1. *15*, No.21 (Anon.)

    3. I-Mfd, 2267, No.43, 200*v*-203*r* (Anon.) • I-Rvat, C.S.15, No.66, 231*v*-235*r* (Anon.) • NL-SH, 73C, 39*v*-43*r* (Anon. Parts 1–3 only)

    4. Sherr, *Sixteenth-century*, ii, 118–31

Virgo prius ac posterius

    2/ of **Alma redemptoris mater**   **Isaac**   3vv

Virgo prius ac poste / Ave regina celorum

    2/ of **Alma redemptoris mater**   **Isaac**   3vv

Virgo prudentissima   **Josquin**   4vv
                                        (Isaac)

    1. *3*, No.5 (*Josquin*) • [Probably *19*, No.5: not extant]

    2. 1537[1], No.37 (*Isaac*) • 1559[2], No.24 (*ISAAC.: Henricus Isaac.* in the Tavola)

    3. CH-SGs, 463, No.99, 34*r* and 94*r* (*Josquinus Pratensis.* Headed *Dorii Hypodoriique, idest primi et secundi toni connexio*) • CZ-HK, II.A.7, pp. 342–43   (Anon.) • D-Di, 1/D/6 • D-Mu, 322–325, No.2 (*Jusquinus auctor*)

    4. Drake, *First*, ii, 18–20 • Josquin, *Werken*, Motetten, i, 9

    Intabulation: keyboard

    3. CH-SGs, 530, No.97, 84*v*-85*r* (*Josquin des Pres*)

Virgo prudentissima   **Lapicida**   4vv

    1. *21*, No.44 (*Erasmus lapicide.*)

    4. Sherr, *Sixteenth-century*, iii, 275–84

Virgo salutiferi   [Anon.]   4vv

    2/ *Adsis o nostri custos*

    1. *21*, No.17 (Anon.)

    4. Sherr, *Sixteenth-century*, iii, 67–72

Virgo salutiferi / Ave Maria   **Josquin**   5vv

    2/ *Tu potis es prime / Ave Maria*; 3/ *Nunc celi regina / Ave Maria*

    1. *65*, No.4 (*Josquin*)

    2. 1526[3], No.4 (*Josquin*) • 1527, No.4 (*Josquin*) • 1534[6], No.23 (*Josquin de pres.*: Headed *De beata Maria*) • 1559[1], No.7 (*IOSQVIN.*)

    3. D-Mu, Art.401, Nos.37–39 (*Josquin*) • GB-Lcm, 1070, No.22, 68*v*-72*r* (Anon. Incomplete) • I-Fl, 666, No.42, 112*v*-116*r* (*Josquin*) • I-Rvat, C.S.16, No.15, 172*v*-176*r* (*Josquin*) • I-Rvat, C.S.42, No.17, 99*v*-103*r* (*Josquin des pres.* Numbered XIII in the source)

    Text by Ercole Strozzi (See Lowinsky, *Medici*, iii, 199–200)

    4. Attaingnant, *Treize*, iv, 23 • Braithwaite, *Introduction*, iv, 211–25 • Josquin, *Werken*, Motetten, ii, 18 • Lowinsky, *Medici*, ii, 297–310

Intabulation of Part III: keyboard

2. 1578²⁴, No.96, 128ν (*Jusquin.* Cabezón)

Virgo sub etheris

    See French texts: **Comme femme**   **Agricola**   4vv

Viri Galilei aspicientes

    2/ of **Tempus meum est**   **Févin**   4vv

Virtus sancti spiritus

    2/ of **Preter rerum seriem**   **Josquin**   6vv

Virtutum explusus terris   **van Stappen**   4vv

    I. **12**, No.66, 87ν-88r (*Crispinus de stappen*)

Vox clamantis in deserto   **Tromboncino**   4vv

    I. **18**, No.58 (*B. T.*) • **40**, No.58 (*B. T.*)

    3. E-Mp, 2-1-5, 65r (Anon. à3)

Vulnerasti cor meum   [Anon.]   4vv

                                           (Rein)

    I. **55**, No.21 (Anon.)

    2. 1526², No.21.(Anon. *Ant. de fevin.* at the head of the Tenor page)

    3. D-Rp, A.R.940–941, No.30 (*Conradus Rein*) • E-Mmarch, R.6832, No.1 (Anon.) • I-Bc, Q19, No.57, 87ν-88r (Anon.) • I-CMac, L (B), No.9, 59ν-61r (Anon.).

    4. Gehrenbeck, *Corona*, 1920–1927 • Morales, *Opera Omnia* iii, 166–71

    Comments: I can see no justification for the assertion of Anglès (Morales, *Opera Omnia*, iii preliminary p. 41) that this work is by Mouton

Vultum tuum deprecabuntur   **Josquin**   4vv

2/ *Sancta Dei genitrix*; 3/ *Intemerata Virgo*; 4/ *O Maria nullam*; 5/ *Mente tota tibi supplicamus*; 6/ *Ora pro nobis*; 7/ *Christi fili Dei*

    I. **21**, No.38 (*Josquin de pres*)

    2. 1539². (Part 5) • 1559², No.11 (*IOSQVIN.* Part 5 only)

    3. CH-SGs, 463 (Anon. Part 5) • D-B, 40021, No.106, 217ν-218r (Anon. Part 5) • D-Mbs, 19, No.7, 58ν-63r (Anon. Part 5) • D-Rp, C.120, No.44, pp. 85–86. (Anon. Part 5, untexted) • D-Usch 237 a-d, 10r (Anon. Parts 2–6) • E-Bbc, 454, No.59, 128ν-130r (Anon. Parts 3–4) • E-SE, s.s., No.18, 85ν-87r (*Josquin Dupres.* Part 3) • F-CA, 125–128, No.93, 86ν-87r (Anon. Part 3, texted as *O intemerata* with a 2/ texted *O Maria nullam*) • I-Mfd, 2266, 104ν (Anon. Parts 3–6) • I-Pc, A17, No.122, 180ν-181r (Anon. Parts 1 and 2); No.2, 4ν-5r (Anon. Part 3); No.102, 154ν-155r (Anon. Part 5); No.120, 178ν-179r (Anon. Part 7) • I-Rvat, C.S.26, No.14, 136ν-138r (*Josquin.* Part 5) • Pl-Wu, 58, 92ν-93r (Anon. Part 5)

    4. Josquin, *Werken*, Motetten, i, 7

    Comments: Part 3 is the basis of masses by Forestier and Hellinck • Part 5 is the basis for Févin's mass, also published by Petrucci

    Literature: Macey, "Josquin's Little"

    Intabulations

    3. CH-SGs, 530 (Anon. Part 5 only) • D-B, 40026 (Part 5)

Italian Texts

A che affligi el tuo servo   Tromboncino   4vv
    1. *23*, No.14 (*B. T.*) • *37*, No.14 (*B. T.*)
    4. Schwartz, *Frottole*, 53

A che son hormai conducto   Demophon   4vv
    1. *36*, No.18 (*ALEXANDRO DEMOPHON*)
    4. Torchi, *L'Arte*, 5

A la absentia che me acora   Cara   4vv
    1. *25*, No.46 (*M.C.C.V.*)
    4. Prizer, *Courtly*, ii, 46–50

A la bruma al giatio al vento   Pifaro   4vv
    1. *35*, No.22 (*NI. PI.*)
    4. Boscolo, *Frottole*, 160 • Luisi, *Cantar*, 258–59

A la fama se va per varie schale   Tromboncino   4vv
    1. *48*, No.11 (*B. T.*: additional text on 55r)
    4. Facchin & Zanovello, *Frottole*, 131
    Intabulation: voice and lute
    1. *49*, No.13 (*B. T.*); *58*, No.13 (*B. T.*)
    4. Disertori, *Frottole*, 328–29

A la fe per la mia fe   Cesena   4vv
    1. *25*, No.5 (*P.C.* in index)
    Intabulation: voice and lute
    1. *50*, No.47, 47v-48r (*Pele. Cesena*)
    4. Disertori, *Frottole*, 566–67

A la fe si a la fe bona   [Anon.]   4vv
    1. *18*, No.48 (Anon.) • *40*, No.48 (Anon.)
    3. I-Bc, Q18, No.6, 6v-7r (Anon.)
    4. Cesari, *Frottole*, 131
    Intabulation: lute accompaniment to a Superius
    3. F-Pn, 27, No.77, 47r (Anon.)

A la guerra   Tromboncino   4vv
    1. *16*, No.34 (*B. T.*)
    3. I-Fc, 2441, No.21, 23v-24r (Anon.)
    4. Cesari, *Frottole*, 26 • Schwartz, *Frottole*, 24
    Intabulation: voice and lute
    1. *49*, No.55 (*B. T.*); *58*, No.55 (*B. T.*)
    4. Disertori, *Frottole*, 406–407

A ma donna spietata li rai novi
    see **Ama pur donna spietata**   d'Ana   4vv

A pe de la montagna   Rossino   4vv
    1. *35*, No.37 (*ROSIN MANTOVANO*)
    4. Boscolo, *Frottole*, 199 • Gallico, *Rimeria*, 167

A te drizo ogni mio passo   Ludovico   4vv
    1. *41*, No.52 (*Ludovico milanese*)
    4. Jeppesen, *Laude*, 84–85

A ti sola ho dato el core   **Antiquis**   4vv
    1. **25**, No.38 (*A. DE ANTIQVIS VENETVS*)
    4. Zupanovic, *Sedamnaest frottola*

A tuo modo affligi
  2/ of **La mia vita liberale**   **d'Ana**   4vv

Accio che il tempo   **Tromboncino**   4vv
    1. **36**, No.4 (*B. T.*)
  Intabulation: voice and lute
    1. **49**, No.3 (*B. T.*); **58**, No.3 (*B. T.*)
    4. Disertori, *Frottole*, 312–13

Ad ognhor cresce la doglia   [Anon.]   4vv
    1. **26**, No.54 (Anon.)
    3. I-Mt, 55, No.42, 42*v*-44*r* (Anon.)
    4. Jeppesen, *Frottola*, iii, 274–77

Adio siati chio me ne vo   [Anon.]   4vv
    1. **26**, No.48 (Anon.)
  Intabulation: lute accompaniment to a Superius
    3. F-Pn, 27, No.99, 50*v* (Anon.)

Adio signora adio   **Pesenti**   4vv
    1. **16**, No.55 (*MICHA.*)
    4. Cesari, *Frottole*, 38 • Schwartz, *Frottole*, 37

Adre che festi
  See **Nadre che festi**   **Dammonis**   4vv

Aer de capituli
  See **Li angelici sembianti**   [Anon.]   4vv
  See **Nesce la speme mia**   **Cara**   4vv
  See **Poi che son di speranza**   **Lulinus**   4vv
  See **Un sollicito amor una gran fede**   **Lurano**   4vv

Afflicti spirti miei   **Tromboncino**   4vv
    1. **36**, No.2 (*B. T.* Additional text on 55*r*)
  Intabulation: voice and lute
    1. **49**, No.1 (*B. T.*); **58**, No.1 (*B. T.*)
    4. Disertori, *Frottole*, 308–309

Ah partiale e cruda morte   **Tromboncino**   4vv
    1. **16**, No.31 (*B. T.*)
    4. Cesari, *Frottole*, 23 • Schwartz, *Frottole*, 22
  Intabulation: lute accompaniment to a superius
    3. F-Pn, 27, No.33, 38*r* (Anon. Incipit *Partiale e cruda morte*)

Ah vil cor piglia ardimento   [Anon.]   4vv
    1. **48**, No.36 (Anon.)
    4. Facchin & Zanovello, *Frottole*, 183

Ai cieco & crudo amore   **Dupre**   voice + lute
  Intabulation: voice and lute
    1. **50**, No.32 (*Helias Dupre*)
    4. Disertori, *Frottole*, 525

Ai maroni ai bel maroni   **Tromboncino**   4vv
    1. **35**, No.40 (*B. T.*)

4. Boscolo, *Frottole*, 208 • Gallucci, *Festival*, ii, 283–287

Comment: Prizer, "Facciamo", regards this as a carnival song from northern Italy

Aime ch'a torto   [Anon.]   3vv

  1. **26**, No.4 (Anon.)

  Text by Giustiniani: part 2 of *Io vedo ben ch'amore e traditore* (Cf. *Moro di doglia*)

  4. Disertori, *Frottole*, 255–59 • Haar, "Petrucci", 23–27 • Luisi, *Laudario*, ii, 230–33

Ahime ch'io moro   **Pesenti**   4vv

  1. **16**, No.44 (*MICHA.*)

  4. Cesari, *Frottole*, 33

  Intabulation: voice and lute

  1. **49**, No.59 (*D.M.C.*); **58**, No.59 (*D.M.C.*)

  4. Disertori, *Frottole*, 412–413

Aime ch'io son scaciato   [Anon.]   4vv

  1. **26**, No.14 (Anon.)

Aime dolce mio dio   **Dammonis**   4vv

  1. **29**, No.8 (Dammonis); **45**, No.8 (Dammonis)

  4. Jeppesen, *Laude*, 103

Aime el cor aime la testa

  See **Oime el cor oime la testa**   **Cara**   4vv

Ahime lasso ahime dolente   **Michele** [?Pesenti]   4vv

  1. **25**, No.2 (*.MI.C.*)

  Intabulation: voice and lute

  1. **50**, No.51 (*Mi. C.*)

  4. Disertori, *Frottole*, 572–74

Aime sospiri non trovo pace   [Anon.]   3vv

  1. **26**, No.5 (Anon.)

  3. cf. E-E, IV.a.24, 85*v*-86*r* (Anon.). The work is cited in I-Rvat, Ottob.251, 34*r*

  Text by Giustiniani, according to Luisi, although Pirrotta, "Ricercare", thinks not: Carboni and Ziino call it a "Canzonetta-Viniziana"

  4. Carboni and Ziino, "Composizioni", p. 456 • Disertori, *Frottole*, 260–63 • Haar, "Petrucci", 28–31 • Hanen, *Chansonnier*, 302–304 • Luisi, *Laudario*, ii, 268–69 • Rubsamen, *Justiniane*, 180–82

Aiutami chio moro   **Cara**   4vv

  1. **36**, No.59 (*M.C.*)

  4. Prizer, *Courtly*, ii, 63–64

Al bel fonte sacro e degno   **Dammonis**   4vv

  1. **29**, No.25 (Dammonis); **45**, No.25 (Dammonis)

  4. Jeppesen, *Laude*, 121

Al di donna non dormire   **Lurano**   4vv

  1. **18**, No.50 (*F.D.L.*) • **40**, No.50 (*F.D.L.*)

  3. GB-Lbl, Eg.3051, No.53, 60*v*-61*r* (Anon. Text *Odi donna el mie tormento*)

  4. Cesari, *Frottole*, 132

Al foco al foco

  See **Don don—al foco al foco**   **Stringari**   4vv

Al ombra dun bel velo   [Anon.]   4vv

  1. **56**, No.25 (Anon.)

  4. Luisi & Zanovello, *Frottole*, 158

Alhor quando arivava
   Line 2 of **Dal lecto me levava**   **Peseti**   4vv

Alma svegliate hormai   **G. Brocco**   4vv
     1. **16**, No.1 (*IO. BROC.*)
     3. I-Fn, Panc.27, No.17, 16*v*-17*r* (Anon.)
     4. Cesari, *Frottole*, 3 • Schwartz, *Frottole*, 1

Alme celeste che riposo   **Ludovico**   4vv
     1. **35**, No.51 (*LVDOVICO MILANESE*)
     4. Boscolo, *Frottole*, 237 • Disertori, *Frottole*, 145–46

Ama pur donna spietata   **d'Ana**   4vv
     1. **25**, No.45 (*F.A.V.* in the index)
     3. I-Fn, 337, No.18, 19*v* (Anon.)
     Intabulation: lute accompaniment to a Superius
     3. F-Pn, 27, No.60, 43*v* (Anon. Incipit reads *A ma donna spietata li rai novi*)

Amando e desiando io vivo   **Cariteo**   4vv
     1. **48**, No.64 (*CARITEO*)
     4. Facchin & Zanovello, *Frottole*, 254 • Luisi, *Cantar*, 113
     Intabulation: voice and lute
     1. **50**, No.10 (*Cariteo*)
     4. Disertori, *Frottole*, 478–79
     Literature: Disertori, "Contradiction"

Ameni colli   **Ludovico**   5vv
     1. **35**, No.32 (*LUDOVICO MILANESE*)
     4. Boscolo, *Frottole*, 183
     Intabulation: voice and lute
     1. **50**, No.49 (*Ludo. Mila.*)
     4. Disertori, *Frottole*, 570–71

Amero non amero   **Cara**   4vv
     1. **56**, No.21 (*M.C.*)
     4. Luisi & Zanovello, *Frottole*, 150 • Prizer, *Courtly*, ii, 130–32

Amor a chi non val   **d'Ana**   4vv
     1. **23**, No.34 (*F.V.*) • **37**, No.34 (*F.V.*)
     3. I-Mt, 55, No.14, 14*v*-15*r* (Anon.)
     4. Jeppesen, *Frottola*, iii, 207–208 • Schwartz, *Frottole*, 66

Amor con le tue faze   **d'Ana**   4vv
     1. **23**, No.35 (*F.V.*) • **37**, No.35 (*F.V.*)
     3. I-Mt, 55, No.13, 13*v*-14*r* (Anon. Text *Amor cum le faze*)
     4. Jeppesen, *Frottola*, iii, 205–206 • Schwartz, *Frottole*, 67

Amor Jesu divino   **Dammonis**   5vv
     1. **29**, No.15 (Dammonis); **45**, No.15 (Dammonis)
     4. Jeppesen, *Laude*, 110

Amor poi che non poi   **Michele** [?Pesenti]   4vv
     1. **25**, No.15 (*.MICAEL.*; *M.* in the index)
     2. 1510, No.18, 10*r* (*M.*)

Amor quando fioriva   **Lulinus**   4vv
     1. **56**, No.42 (*Ioannes Lulinus Venetus*)

Text by Petrarch, *Canzoniere*, CCCXXIV
    4. Luisi & Zanovello, *Frottole*, 199

Amore quando speravo   **Pisano**   4vv
  2/ *Tal chio pavento assai*
    1. **67**, No.2 (Pisano)
    3. I-Fc, 2440, No.39, 68*v*-71*r* (Anon.) • I-Fn, 164–167, No.8, 11*r*-12*r* (Anon.)
    Text by L. Strozzi
    4. Pisano, *Collected Works*

Amore se voi chi torni   **Pisano**   4vv
    1. **67**, No.5 (Pisano)
    3. I-Fn, 164–167, No.9 (Anon)
    Text by Petrarch, *Canzoniere*, CCLXX, 1–15
    4. Haar, *Chanson*, 219 • Pisano, *Collected Works*

Amor se voi chio torni   **Tromboncino**   4vv
    1. **56**, No.12 (*Bartholomeus Tromboncinus*)
    3. I-Vnm, IV.1795–1798, No.3 (Anon.)
    Text by Petrarch, *Canzoniere*, CCLXX, 1–15
    4. Luisi, *Apografo*, 7–8 • Luisi & Zanovello, *Frottole*, 127

Amor sempre me dimostra   **Nicolo**   4vv
    1. **17**, No.46 (Anon.) • **42**, No.46 (*Nico. Pa.*)
    4. Cesari, *Frottole*, 84

Andiam tutti cantando
  2/ of **Cum jubili damore**   **Dammonis**   4vv
Anima beneditta   **Dammonis**   4vv
    1. **29**, No.56 (*In. Dam.*); **45**, No.56 (*In. Dam.*)
    Text by Giustiniani
    4. Jeppesen, *Laude*, 151 • Luisi, *Laudario*, ii, 14

Anima che del mondo vo fugire   **Dammonis**   4vv
  2/ *Guarda se le cagion*
    1. **29**, No.57 (Dammonis); **45**, No.57 (Dammonis)
    Text by Belcari
    4. Luisi, *Laudario*, ii, 318–21

Anima mia diletta   **Zesso**   4vv
    1. **41**, No.41 (*I.B.Z..* Headed *Oda*)
    4. Jeppesen, *Laude*, 62

Aprender la mia donna   **Tromboncino**   4vv
    1. **36**, No.6 (*B.T.*)

Aqua aqua aiuto al foco   **Tromboncino**   4vv
    1. **48**, No.50 (*B.T.*)
    4. Facchin & Zanovello, *Frottole*, 216 • Gallico, "Dialogo", 210 • Luisi, *Del cantar*, 309
    Intabulation: voice and lute
    1. **49**, No.32 (*B.T.*); **58**, No.32 (*B.T.*)
    4. Disertori, *Frottole*, 364–65
    Literature: Gallico, "Dialogo"

Aqua aqua al focho   **Pifaro**   4vv
    1. **26**, No.19 (*NICOLO PIFAR.*)

Aqua aqua al foco   **Timoteo**   4vv
> 1. **48**, No.52 (*TIMOTEO*)
> 4. Facchin & Zanovello, *Frottole*, 220 • Luisi, *Cantar*, 309

Aqua non e lhumor   **Tromboncino**   4vv
> 1. **56**, No.70 (*B.T.*)
> 4. Boorman, *Frottole* • Einstein, *Elfte*, 620 • Einstein, *Madrigal*, iii, 318 • Luisi & Zanovello, *Frottole*, 278
> Intabulation: voice and lute
> 2. [c.1520][7], No.6, 9r-9v (*B.T.*)

Aque stilante   **Alauro**   4vv
> 1. **56**, No.68 (*Hie. Alauro*)
> 4. Luisi & Zanovello, *Frottole*, 272

Arbor victorioso arbor fecondo   **Tromboncino**   4vv
> 1. **41**, No.10 (*Tromboncino*)
> 4. Jeppesen, *Laude*, 16

Arda el ciel el mondo tutto   [Anon.]   4vv
> 1. **18**, No.43 (Anon.) • **40**, No.43 (Anon.)
> 3. F-Pn, 676, No.108, 119v-120r (Anon.) • I-Fc, 2441, No.8, 9v-10r (Anon.) • I-Fn, 337, No.22, 32v (Anon.) • I-Fn, Panc.27, No.43, 27v-28r (Anon.)
> 4. Cesari, *Frottole*, 27
> Intabulation: lute accompaniment to a Superius
> 3. F-Pn, 27, No.59, 43r (Anon. Titled *Grida el ciello*)

Ardo e bruscio e tu noi senti   **Pesenti**   4vv
> 1. **16**, No.35 (*MICHAEL PESENTUS VERO.*)
> 4. Cesari, *Frottole*, 27 • Schwartz, *Frottole*, 25

Arma del mio valor   **Cara**   4vv
> 1. **48**, No.19 (*M.C.*)
> 4. Facchin & Zanovello, *Frottole*, 153
> Intabulation: voice and lute
> 1. **49**, No.22 (*M.C.*); **58**, No.22 (*M.C.*)
> 4. Disertori, *Frottole*, 346–47

Ascoltame madona
> See **Scoltatime madonna**   [Anon.]   4vv

Audite vui fenestre
> See **Udite voi finestre**   **Cara**   4vv

Ave Maria. Regina in cielo   **Tromboncino**   4vv
> 1. **41**, No.44 (*B.T.* The index lists this as *Ave maria in cielo e in terra*)
> 4. Jeppesen, *Laude*, 66–67

Ave victorioso e sancto legno   **Cara**   4vv
> 1. **41**, No.18 (*MArcheto* [*sic*])
> 3. I-Fn, Panc.27, No.14, 14r (Anon.)
> 4. Jeppesen, *Laude*, 28–30.

Avendo in la mia mente   [Anon.]   4vv
> 1. **48**, No.40 (Anon.)
> 4. Facchin & Zanovello, *Frottole*, 192

Ay maroni ai bel maroni
> See **Ai maroni ai bei maroni**   **Tromboncino**   4vv

Ayme che doglia e questa   G. Brocco   4vv
    1. *16*, No.18 (*IOANNES BROCCHUS VERO.*)
    4. Cesari, *Frottole*, 14 • Schwartz, *Frottole*, 12

Ben ben ben tu mhai lassa   Peregrinus   4vv
    1. *36*, No.48 (*PEREGRINVS CESENA*)

Ben che ame si fiera e dura   Antenore   4vv
    1. *35*, No.20 (*HONO. ANTE.*)
    4. Boscolo, *Frottole*, 154

Ben che amor mi faccia torto   Tromboncino   4vv
    1. *16*, No.29 (*B.T.*)
    4. Cesari, *Frottole*, 22 • Schering, *Geschichte*, 68 • Schwartz, *Frottole*, 20
    Intabulation: voice and lute
    1. *49*, No.51 (*B.T.*); *58*, No.51 (*B.T.*)
    4. Disertori, *Frottole*, 398–399
    Intabulation: lute accompaniment to a Superius
    3. F-Pn, 27, No.34, 38r (Anon.)

Ben che inimica e tediosa sei   [Anon.]   4vv
    1. *23*, No.21 (Anon. Headed *Sonetto*) • *23*, No.51 (Anon. Text *Chi vede gir*) • *37*, No.21
       (Anon. Headed *Sonetto*) • *37*, No.51 (Anon. Text *Chi vede gir*)
    4. Schwartz, *Frottole*, 59

Ben che la facia al quanto   [Anon.]   4vv
    1. *26*, No.10 (Anon. Headed *Per sonetti*)

Ben che soletto vado   [Anon.]   4vv
    1. *25*, No.16 (Anon.)
    3. CH-Sgs, 463, No.169, 60r and 118r (Anon. Texted *Se ben soletto vado*. Headed *Hypoionicus,*
       idest sextus) • I-Fn, 121, 14v-15r (Anon. Texted *Se ben soletto vado*)

Ben chel ciel me thabbi tolto   Tromboncino   4vv
    1. *48*, No.9 (*B.T.*)
    4. Facchin & Zanovello, *Frottole*, 126
    Intabulation: voice and lute
    1. *49*, No.60 (*B.T.*); *58*, No.60 (*B.T.*)
    4. Disertori, *Frottole*, 414–16

Ben chio serva a cor ingrato   [Anon.]   4vv
    1. *18*, No.38 (Anon.) • *40*, No.38 (Anon.)
    3. F-Pn, 676, No.79, 88v-89r (Anon.) • I-Fn, 230, No.9, 10v-11r (Anon.)
    4. Cesari, *Frottole*, 124

Ben cognosco el tuo cor   d'Ana   4vv
    1. *26*, No.39 (*F.V.*)

Ben mi credea   Tromboncino   4vv
    1. *56*, No.7 (*B.T.*)
    3. I-Vnm, IV.1795–1798, No.4 (Anon.)
    Text by Petrarch, *Canzoniere*, CCVII, 1–13
    4. Luisi, *Apografo*, 9–11 • Luisi & Zanovello, *Frottole*, 114
    Intabulation: voice and lute
    2. [c.1520][7], No.33, 41r-43r (*F.T.*)

Ben mille volte al di **Pesenti** 4vv

    1. **16**, No.51 (*MICHA.* Headed *MODVS DICENDI CAPITULA.*)

    4. Cesari, *Frottole*, 36 • Haar, "Chanson", 211 • Schwartz, *Frottole*, 35

Ben sera crudel e ingrato **Nicolo** 4vv

    1. **41**, No.15 (*D. NICOLO*)

    4. Jeppesen, *Laude*, 22–23

Ben sera crudel e ingrato **Tromboncino** 4vv

    1. **41**, No.2 (*Tromboncino*)

    4. Jeppesen, *Laude*, 2–3

Benedetto chi te adora [Anon.] 5vv

    1. **25**, No.44 (Anon.)

Biageretta savoiana

  See **Bergerette savoyenne** **Josquin** 4vv

Bona dies bona sera **Cara** 4vv

    1. **36**, No.50 (*M.C.*)

    4. Prizer, *Courtly*, ii, 65–68

Cade egni mio pensier **Tromboncino** 4vv

    1. **36**, No.55 (*B.T.*)

  Intabulation: voice and lute

    1. **49**, No.12 (*B.T.*); **58**, No.12 (*B.T.*)

    4. Disertori, *Frottole*, 344

Candida rosa **Eustache Romano** 4vv

    1. **56**, No.14 (*Eustachius D. M. Romanus*)

  Text by Petrarch, *Sonnetti*, CCXLVI–CCXLVII

    4. Eustachio Romano, *Musica*, 145–48 • Luisi & Zanovello, *Frottole*, 132

Canzon se lesser meco

  2/ of **Nella stagion che ciel** **Pisano** 4vv

Caso crudel che ogni mortal **Alauro** 4vv

    1. **56**, No.64 (*Hie. Alauro*)

    4. Luisi & Zanovello, *Frottole*, 261

Cerchato ho sempre solitaria a vita **Eustache Romano** 4vv

    1. **56**, No.22 (*Eustachius D. M. R.*)

  Text by Petrarch, *Sonnetti*, CCLIX

    4. Eustachio Romano, *Musica*, 165–68 • Luisi & Zanovello, *Frottole*, 152

  Comment: Eustachio Romano, *Musica*, 18, attributes this work to him rather than to Eustachio de Monte Regali

Certo nascer non dovea

  2/ of **La Pieta chiuso ha le porte** **Tromboncino** 4vv

Che debbio far **Tromboncino** 4vv

    1. **36**, No.15 (*B.T.*)

    2. 1510, No.32, 31v-32r (*B.T.*)

    3. I-Fn, 164–167, No.36, 46v-47r (Anon. Text *Che deggio far*)

    4. Disertori, *Frottole*, 278–83 • Rubsamen, *Literary*, 57

  Intabulation: keyboard

    2. 1517³, No.7, 12v-13v (*B.T.*)

    4. Disertori, *Frottole*, 278–83

  Intabulation: lute

3. D-Mbs, 267, No.45, 50r (Anon.)

Intabulation: voice and lute

1. **49**, No.8 (*B. T.*); **58**, No.8 (*B. T.*)

4. Disertori, *Frottole*, 278–83 and 322–23.

Che debo far

    See **Che debbio far**   Tromboncino   4vv

Che deggio fare   Pisano   4vv

    2/ *Fuggi fugi*

1. **67**, No.16 (Pisano)

3. I-Fc, 2440, No.42, 74*v*-77*r* (Anon.) • I-Fn, XIX.164–167, No.12 (Anon.)

Text by Petrarch, *Canzoniere*, CCLXVIII

4. Jeppesen, *Neuentdeckten*, 86 • Pisano, *Collected Works*

Che deggio far

    See **Che debbio far**   Tromboncino   4vv

Che fa la ramacina   Compère   4vv

1. **23**, No.80 (*COMPERE*) • **37**, No.80 (*COMPERE*)

3. F-Pn, 1817, No.28 (Anon.) • I-Bc, Q17, No.57, 62*v*-63*r* (*Loyset Compere*) • I-CT, 95–96, No.28, 25*r* (Anon.) • I-Fn, 164–167, No.35, 46*r* (Anon.)

4. Compère, *Opera Omnia*, • Pannella, *Composizioni* • Schwartz, *Frottole*, 92 • Westphal, *Karnevalslieder*, 9

Che fa la ramacina

    Altus of **Fortuna dun gran tempo**   Fogliano   4vv

Che fai alma   [Anon.]   4vv

1. **56**, No.69 (Anon.)

4. Luisi & Zanovello, *Frottole*, 275

Che faralla che diralla   Michele Vicentino   4vv
                                                              (Tromboncino)

1. **56**, No.26 (*D.M.*)

2. 1513[1], No.27, 39*v*-40*r* • 1518, No.27, 39*v*-40*r*. (*D. Michael.V.*) • [c.1517][1] (1520), No.27, 39*v*-40*r* (*D. Michael Vicentino*) • 1563[6], 91*r* (For two voices: Anon.)

4. Einstein, *Canzoni*, 52–53 • Luisi, *Cantar*, 284–85 • Luisi & Zanovello, *Frottole*, 162

Intabulation: keyboard

2. 1517[3], No.21, 33*r*-33*v* (*B. T.*)

Intabulation: lute

3. US-Cn, 107501, No.5b, 10*r*-10*v* (Anon. Headed *Che farala per sua coda*, i.e., to *O mia cieca* by Cara)

Che piu felice sorte   Rosseto   4vv

1. **17**, No.25 (*ANTONIVS ROSSETVS VERONENSIS.*) • **42**, No.25 (*ANTONIVS ROS-SETVS VERONENSIS*)

4. Cesari, *Frottole*, 66

Che si fa cosi misto   Dupre   4vv

1. **48**, No.45 (*HE. Dupre*)

4. Facchin & Zanovello, *Frottole*, 201

Che te giova servir   [Anon.]   4vv

1. **26**, No.52 (Anon.)

Chi dal ciel non ha favore   Nicolo   4vv

1. **18**, No.27 (*N.P.*) • **40**, No.27 (*N.P.*)

4. Cesari, *Frottole*, 113 • Underwood, *Renaissance*, 207–209

Intabulations: voice and lute

3. I-Fn, 62(b), 1*r*. (Anon.)

4. Fabris, *Frottola*, 7 • Underwood, *Renaissance*, 207–209

Chi e pregion del ciecho amore   [Anon.]   4vv

  1. *48*, No.63 (Anon.)

  4. Facchin & Zanovello, *Frottole*, 252

Chi in pregion crede tornarmi   **Tromboncino**   4vv

  1. *35*, No.3 (*B.T.*)

  4. Boscolo, *Frottole*, 117

Intabulation: voice and lute

  1. *49*, No.14 (*B.T.*); *58*, No.14 (*B.T.*)

  4. Disertori, *Frottole*, 330–31

Chi la castra la procella   **Cara**   4vv

  1. *48*, No.12 (*M.C.*)

  4. Facchin & Zanovello, *Frottole*, 133 • Gallucci, *Festival*, ii, 293–96 • Gallucci, *Florentine* • Prizer, *Courtly*, 424

Comment: Prizer, "Facciamo", regards this as a carnival song from Mantua

Chi lharebbe mai creduto

  See **Chi lharia mai creduto**   **Cara**   4vv

Chi lharia mai creduto   **Cara**   4vv

  1. *48*, No.20 (*M.C.*)

  3. F-Pn, 676, 28*v*-29*r* (Anon.) • I-Fc, 2441, No.45, 47*v*-48*r* (Anon.)

  4. Facchin & Zanovello, *Frottole*, 155

Intabulation: voice and lute

  1. *49*, No.21 (Anon. Texted *Chi lharebbe mai creduto*); *58*, No.21 (Anon. Texted *Chi lharebbe mai creduto*)

  4. Disertori, *Frottole*, 345

Chi lo sa e chi nol sa   **Dupre**   4vv

  1. *36*, No.39 (*E. DVPRE*)

Chi me dara piu pace   **Cara**   4vv

  1. *16*, No.14 (*M.C.*)

  3. I-Fc, 2441, No.67, 69*v*-70*r* (Anon.)

  4. Cesari, *Frottole*, 11 • Schwartz, *Frottole*, 10

Intabulation: voice and lute

  1. *49*, No.65 (*M.C.*); *58*, No.65 (*M.C.*)

  4. Disertori, *Frottole*, 423

Chi non ha martel suo   [Anon.]   4vv

  1. *35*, No.11 (Anon.)

  4. Boscolo, *Frottole*, 124

Chi non sa che sial dolore   **Lulinus**   4vv

  1. *56*, No.53 (*Io. Lu. V.*)

  4. Luisi & Zanovello, *Frottole*, 231

Chi non sa chel cor gli ho dato   **Stringari**   4vv

  1. *35*, No.33 (*ANTONIVS PATA.*)

  4. Boscolo, *Frottole*, 186

Chi non sa chi non intende   **Tromboncino**   4vv
    1. *26*, No.24 (*B.T.*)
    Intabulation: voice and lute
    1. *50*, No.33 (*B.T.*)
    4. Disertori, *Frottole*, 528–31

Chi promette e debitore   [Anon.]   4vv
    1. *35*, No.14 (Anon.)
    4. Boscolo, *Frottole*, 140
    Intabulation: voice and lute
    1. *50*, No.35 (Anon.)
    4. Disertori, *Frottole*, 538–39

Chi propritio ha la so stella   **Capreolus**   4vv
    1. *48*, No.26 (*A.C.*)
    4. Facchin & Zanovello, *Frottole*, 168

Chi se fida de fortuna   **Tromboncino**   4vv
    1. *18*, No.52 (*B.T.*) • *40*, No.52 (*B.T.*)
    3. I-Fc, 2441, No.17, 19*v*-20*r* (Anon.)
    4. Cesari, *Frottole*, 134

Chi se pasce de speranza   **Tromboncino**   4vv
    1. *18*, No.56 (*B.T.*) • *40*, No.56 (*B.T.*)
    4. Cesari, *Frottole*, 136

Chi servir vol con speranza   [Anon.]   4vv
    1. *48*, No.55 (Anon.)
    4. Facchin & Zanovello, *Frottole*, 231

Chi vede gir la mie dea
    See **Ben che inimica e tediosa**   [Anon.]   4vv

Chi vi dara piu luce   **d'Ana**   voice + lute
    Intabulation: voice and lute
    1. *49*, No.34 (*F.V.*); *58*, No.34 (*F.V.*)
    4. Disertori, *Frottole*, 368–69

Chi vi dara piu luce   **Tromboncino**   4vv
    1. *35*, No.55 (*B.T.* Index and three lower voices read *Chi vi dira piu luce*)
    4. Boscolo, *Frottole*, 244
    Intabulation: voice and lute
    1. *49*, No.36 (*B.T.*); *58*, No.36 (*B.T.*)
    4. Disertori, *Frottole*, 372–73

Chi vol pace nel suo core   **Dammonis**   4vv
    1. *29*, No.51 (*In. Dam.* Headed *De pace*); *45*, No.51 (*In. Dam.*)
    4. Jeppesen, *Laude*, 145–46

Chia martello dio   **Dupre**   4vv
    1. *36*, No.40 (*E. DVPRE*)

Chiare fresche e dolce aque   **Eustache de Monte Regalo**   4vv
    1. *56*, No.15 (*Eustachius D. M. Regali Gallus*)
    Text by Petrarch, *Canzoniere*, CXXVI
    4. Luisi & Zanovello, *Frottole*, 135

Chiare fresche e dolce aque   **Lulinus**   4vv
    1. *56*, No.44 (*Io. lu. V.*)

Text by Petrarch, *Canzoniere*, CXXVI

    4. Luisi & Zanovello, *Frottole*, 203

Chiare fresche e dolce acque   **Pisano**   4vv

    1. **67**, No.11 (Pisano)

    3. I-Fn, 164–167, No.11, 15*v*–16*v* (Anon.)

    Text by Petrarch, *Canzoniere*, CXXVI

    4. Pisano, *Collected Works*

Chio lassi lalta impresa   [Anon.]   4vv

    1. **48**, No.51 (Anon.)

    4. Facchin & Zanovello, *Frottole*, 218

Cholei che amor cosi   **Cara**   4vv

    1. **48**, No.29 (*M.C.*)

    4. Facchin & Zanovello, *Frottole*, 173 • Prizer, *Courtly*, 427

Chui dicese e non lamare   [Anon.]   3vv

    1. **26**, No.2 (Anon.)

    Text possibly by Giustiniani (see Pirrotta, "Ricercare", 60)

    4. Disertori, *Frottole*, 248–51 • Haar, "Petrucci", 17–19 • Luisi, *Laudario*, ii, 271–73

Come havro dunque il frutto   **Alauro**   4vv

    1. **56**, No.65 (*Hie. Alauro*)

    Text by Pietro Barignano

    4. Luisi & Zanovello, *Frottole*, 263

Come chel bianco cigno   **Cara**   4vv

    1. **16**, No.13 (*M.C.*)

    3. I-Fc, 2441, No.15, 16*v*–17*r* (Anon. Text *Si como el bianco cigno*)

    4. Cesari, *Frottole*, XIII • Schwartz, *Frottole*, 10

    Intabulation: voice and lute:

    1. **49**, No.31 (*M.C.*); **58**, No.31 (*M.C.*)

    4. Disertori, *Frottole*, 362

Come denanzi christo

  See **Como dinanzi a christo fuzira**   **Dammonis**   4vv

Come el piombin   [Anon.]   4vv

    1. **26**, No.16 (Anon.)

    3. I-Bc, Q18, No.15, 15*v*–16*r* (Anon. Untexted) • I-Fn, 230, No.27, 26*v*–27*r* (Anon.)

    • I-Mt, 55, No.19, 19*v*–20*r* (Anon.)

    Text perhaps by Leonardo Corvino

    4. Jeppesen, *Frottola*, iii, No.19

Come po far el celo   [Anon.]   4vv

    1. **23**, No.76 (Anon.) • **37**, No.76 (Anon.)

    4. Schwartz, *Frottole*, 90

Come potu temer   [Anon.]   4vv

    1. **23**, No.45 (Anon.) • **37**, No.45 (Anon.)

    4. Schwartz, *Frottole*, 72

Come ti sofre il core   [Anon.]   4vv

    1. **25**, No.32, 30*v* (Anon.)

Come va il mondo   **Tromboncino**   4vv

    1. **36**, No.13 (*B.T.*)

    2. 1510, No.28, 27*v*–28*r* (*B.T.*)

Intabulation: voice and lute

1. **50**, No.16 (*T.B.*)

4. Disertori, *Frottole*, 490–91

Como dinanzi a christo fuzirai   **Dammonis**   4vv

1. **29**, No.37 (Dammonis); **45**, No.37 (Dammonis)

Text by Giustiniani

4. Luisi, *Laudario*, ii, 26–27

Con dolor vivo in piacere

See **Sel te chara**   **Pifaro**   4vv

Con iubili damore

See **Cum iubili damore**   **Dammonis**   4vv

Con la rete cogli el vento   **d'Ana**   4vv

1. **17**, No.7 (*FRAN. VENE. ORGA.*) • **42**, No.7 (*FRAN. VENE. ORGA.*)

4. Cesari, *Frottole*, 51

Con pianto e con dolore   [Anon.]   4vv

1. **23**, No.70 (Anon.) • **37**, No.70 (Anon.)

4. Schwartz, *Frottole*, 88

Intabulation: voice and lute

1. **49**, No.6 (Anon.); **58**, No.6 (Anon.)

4. Disertori, *Frottole*, 318

Intabulation: lute accompaniment to a Superius

3. F-Pn, 27, No.95, 50r (Anon. Incipit *Cum pianto e cum dolore*)

Con pianto e con dolore   [Anon.]   voice + lute

Intabulation: voice and lute

1. **50**, No.20 (Anon.)

4. Disertori, *Frottole*, 498

Comments: Despite Disertori, *Frottole*, 498, this setting of the same text is musically different
    from the preceding entry

Cono dinanzi a christo

See **Como dinanzi a christo**   **Dammonis**   4vv

Consumato ha amor el dardo   [Anon.]   4vv

1. **36**, No.26 (Anon.)

Consumatum est hormai   **Tromboncino**   4vv

1. **26**, No.41 (*B.T.*)

Cosi confuso e il stato   **Tromboncino**   voice + lute

Intabulation: voice and lute

1. **50**, No.38 (*B.T.*)

4. Disertori, *Frottole*, 544–45

Cosil tuo ben fussi

See **Son io donna qual mostri**   **Pisano**   4vv

Credo ben pero che me ama

2/ of **Liber fui un tempo in foco**   **Cara**   4vv

Credul cor per che credesti   **Cara**   4vv

1. **36**, No.16 (*M.C.*)

4. Ferand, *Improvisation*, 383 • Prizer, *Courtly*, ii, 69–73

Cresce la pena mia   **Tromboncino**   4vv

1. **36**, No.9 (*B.T.*)

Crescie e discrecie il mar   [Anon.]   5vv
    1. *35*, No.21 (Anon.)
    4. Boscolo, *Frottole*, 157

Crudel amore tu hai pur   **Antenore**   4vv
    1. *35*, No.19 (*HONO. ANTE.*)
    4. Boscolo, *Frottole*, 151

Crudel come mai potesti   **Tromboncino**   4vv
    1. *16*, No.25 (*B.T.*)
    4. Cesari, *Frottole*, 18 • Schwartz, *Frottole*, 17
    Intabulation: voice and lute
    1. *49*, No.40 (Anon.); *58*, No.40 (Anon.)
    4. Disertori, *Frottole*, 378–79

Cum iubili damore   **Dammonis**   4vv
  2/ *Andiam tutti cantando*
    1. *29*, No.16 (Dammonis. Headed *De nativitate*); *45*, No.16 (Dammonis)
    Text by Giustiniani
    4. Jeppesen, *Laude*, 111–13 • Luisi, *Laudario*, ii, 36–39

Da che tu mhai idio   **Dammonis**   4vv
    1. *29*, No.5 (Dammonis); *45*, No.5 (Dammonis)
    Text by Belcari
    4. Luisi, *Laudario*, ii, 180–81

Da che tu mhai iesu   **Dammonis**   4vv
    1. *29*, No.6 (Dammonis); *45*, No.6 (Dammonis)
    Text by Castellanus
    4. Jeppesen, *Laude*, 100–101 • Luisi, *Laudario*, ii, 322–24

Dapoi chai el mio core
  See **Tutto el mondo chiama**   **Lurano**   4vv

Dapoi che cusi pate   **Pifaro**   4vv
    1. *35*, No.28 (*NICOLO PIFARO*)
    4. Boscolo, *Frottole*, 175

Da poi che non si po   [Anon.]   4vv
    1. *23*, No.53 (Anon.) • *37*, No.53 (Anon.)
    4. Riemann, *Handbuch*, ii, 356 • Schwartz, *Frottole*, 76

Da poi chel tuo bel viso   **Rosso Mantovano**   4vv
    1. *17*, No.1 (*R.M.*) • *42*, No.1 (*R.M.*)
    Facsimile: Cesari, *Frottole*, p. 89
    4. Cesari, *Frottole*, 47

Da poi che te lasciai   **Dammonis**   4vv
    1. *29*, No.52 (Dammonis); *45*, No.52 (Dammonis)
    Text perhaps by Belcari or Terranuova
    4. Luisi, *Laudario*, ii, 328–29

Da poi lunghe fatiche
  See **Dopoi longhe fatiche**   [Anon.]   4vv

Dapoi nocte vien la luce   [Anon.]   4vv
    1. *35*, No.8 (Anon.)
    4. Boscolo, *Frottole*, 129

Dagdum dagdum vetusta
    Bassus of **Fortuna dun gran tempo**   **Fogliano**   4vv

Dal ciel crudo imperio e perverso   **d'Ana**   4vv
    1. **25**, No.26 (*F.V.* in index)
    4. Cesari, *Frottole*, p. II
    Comment: Cited in the catalogue for King João IV of Portugal in 1649

Dal ciel discese amor   **d'Ana**   4vv
    1. **23**, No.54 (*F.V.*) • **37**, No.54 (*F.V.*)
    3. I-Fn, 230, No.34, 33*v*-34*r* (Anon.)
    4. Schwartz, *Frottole*, 77

Dal lecto me levava   **Michael** [?Pesenti]   4vv
    1. **16**, No.30 (*MICHAEL*. The index gives the first words of the Cantus, *Alhor quando arivava*, the second line of text)
    Facsimile: Cesari, *Frottole*, p. LXVII
    4. Cesari, *Frottole*, 22 • Riemann, *Handbuch*, ii, 358 • Schwartz, *Frottole*, 20 • Torrefranca, *Segreto*, 434 • Westphal, *Karnevalslieder*, 7

Daltro hormai voglio haver cura   **Pifaro**   4vv
    1. **36**, No.25 (*NICOLO PIFARO*.)

Dame almen lultimo vale   **Tromboncino**   4vv
    See **Dammi almen lultimo vale**   **Lurano**   4vv

Dammi almen lultimo vale   **Lurano**   4vv
                                 (Tromboncino)
    1. **23**, No.86 (*PHI. DE. LV.*) • **37**, No.86 (*PHI. DE. LV.*) • **56**, No.67 (*B.T.*)
    3. GB-Lbl, Eg.3051, No.37, 42*v*-43*r* (Anon.) • I-Fn, 230, No.8, 8*v*-9*r* (Anon.) • I-Fn, 337, No.27, 37*v* (*P. d Lo.*)
    4. Luisi & Zanovello, *Frottole*, 270 • Schwartz, *Frottole*, 94
    Comments: Perhaps a response to *Fammi almen una bona cera*

Dammi il tuo amore   **Dammonis**   4vv
    1. **29**, No.42 (Dammonis. Headed *De christi amore*); **45**, No.42 (Dammonis)
    Text by Belcari
    Edition: Luisi, *Laudario*, ii, 325–27

Damor che me levava / Dun bel matin   **Zesso**   4vv
    1. **36**, No.31 (*IOANNES B. ZESSO*.)
    4. Disertori, *Frottole*, 162–63 • Rubsamen, "Frottole", 209–11

Dapoi . . .
    See **Da poi . . .**

Datemi pace o duri mei pensieri   **Stringari**   4vv
    1. **56**, No.37 (*A.P.*)
    Text by Petrarch, *Canzoniere*, CCLXXIV
    4. Brancacci, "Sonetto", 460 • Luisi & Zanovello, *Frottole*, 186

De che parlera piu la lingua   **Cara**   voice + lute
    Intabulation: voice and lute
    1. **49**, No.70 (*M.C.*: the first letter damaged); **58**, No.70 (*M.C.*)
    4. Disertori, *Frottole*, 429

Deh chi me sa dir novella   **Michele** [?Pesenti]   4vv
    1. **35**, No.47 (*MI. C. & V.*)
    4. Boscolo, *Frottole*, 225

Intabulation: voice and lute

    1. **50**, No.12 (*D. Mi. C. & V.*)

    4. Disertori, *Frottole*, 471–73

Dhe credete donna a me   **P. da Lodi**   4vv

    1. **56**, No.33 (*P. L.*)

    2. [c.1526]⁵ (1523), No.14 (Anon.)

    3. I-Vnm, IV.1795–1798, No.9, 10r (Anon.)

    4. Luisi, *Apografo*, 22 • Luisi & Zanovello, *Frottole*, 179

De dolce diva mia   [Anon.]   4vv

    1. **18**, No.53 (Anon.) • **40**, No.53 (Anon.)

Facsimile: Cesari, *Frottole*, p. CXXV

    3. I-Fc, 2441, No.28, 30v–31r (Anon.)

    4. Cesari, *Frottole*, 135

Deh dolce mia signora   **Cara**   4vv

    1. **36**, No.36 (*M.C.*)

    3. CH-SGs, 463–464, No.162, 58v and 116v (Anon. Headed *Hypoaeolius*)

    4. Prizer, *Courtly*, ii, 74–76

De fossela qui mecho   [Anon.]   4vv

    1. **26**, No.58 (Anon.)

    3. E-Mp, 2-I-5, 62r (Anon.) • F-Pn, 676, No.49, 57v–58r (Anon. Text *Dhe fusse pur qui meco*)

    4. Anglès, *Palacio*, No.98 • Barbieri, *Cancionero*, No.78

De fusse al men si nota   **Tromboncino**   4vv

    1. **56**, No.5 (*B.T.*)

    3. I-Vnm, IV.1795–1798, No.7 (Anon.)

    4. Luisi, *Apografo*, 18–19 • Luisi & Zanovello, *Frottole*, 108

Intabulations: voice and lute

    2. [c.1520]⁷, No.34, 43r-44v (*B.T.*)

Dhe fusse pur qui mecho

    See **De fossela qui meco**   [Anon.]   4vv

De non de si de no   [Anon.]   4vv

    1. **25**, No.33 (Anon.)

    4. Einstein, *Madrigal*, iii, 4

Deh non piu mo Non temer   **Cara**   4vv

    1. **36**, No.53 (*M.C.*)

Intabulation: voice and lute

    1. **49**, No.18 (*M.C.*); **58**, No.18 (*M.C.*)

    4. Disertori, *Frottole*, 338–339

Deh non piu no non piu spietate   **Zesso**   4vv

    1. **35**, No.57 (*IOANNES B. GESSO*. Headed *AERE DA CAPITOLI*)

    4. Boscolo, *Frottole*, 248 • Disertori, *Frottole*, 160–61

De paesi oltramontani   **Lurano**   4vv

    1. **48**, No.49 (*PHI D. L.*); **58**, No.49 (*PHI. D. L.*)

    4. Facchin & Zanovello, *Frottole*, 214 • Gallucci, *Festival*, ii, 303–304 • Luisi, *Musica*, 205–206

Comment: Prizer, "Facciamo", regards this as a carnival song from Rome

Deh per dio non mi far torto   **Tromboncino**   4vv

    1. **16**, No.26 (*B.T.*)

3. I-Bc, Q18, No.2, *2v-3r* (Anon.) • I-Fc, 2441, No.24, *26v-27r* (Anon.)

4. Cesari, *Frottole*, 19 • Schwartz, *Frottole*, 18 • Schwartz, "Nochmals", 5

Intabulation: voice and lute

1. **50**, No.53 (*B.T.*)

4. Disertori, *Frottole*, 578–79

De perche in odio mhai   Pisano   4vv

    1. **67**, No.4 (Pisano)

    3. I-Fn, 164–167, No.3 (Anon.)

    4. Pisano, *Collected Works*

De piangeti amaramente   Dammonis   4vv

    1. **29**, No.46 (Dammonis. Headed *De passione eiusdem verba*); **45**, No.46 (Dammonis)

    4. Luisi, *Laudario*, ii, 330–331

De porgi mano alla fanato ingegno   Eustachio Romano   4vv

    1. **56**, No.9 (*Eu. De. M. Romanus.*)

Text by Petrarch, *Sonnetti*, CCCLIV

    4. Eustachio Romano, *Musica*, 148–52 • Luisi & Zanovello, *Frottole*, 119

Deh prendi homai conforto   Scotto   4vv

    1. **36**, No.60 (*PAVLI. S. Cantus & verba*)

De scoprire el mio tormento

    See **Poi che gionto el tempo**   Lurano   4vv

De servirti al tuo dispecto   Lurano   4vv

    1. **25**, No.52 (*PHI. DE L.: F.D.L.* in the index)

    3. I-Fn, 337, No.10, *11v* (*P. d Lo.*)

Deh si deh no deh si   Cara   4vv
                                        (Tromboncino)

    1. **16**, No.16 (*M.C.*)

Facsimile: Cesari, *Frottole*, p. LXVI

    3. I-Bc, Q18, No.14, *14v-15r* (Anon.) • I-Fn, Panc.27, No.52, *32v* (Anon.)

    4. Cesari, *Frottole*, 12 • Einstein, *Unbekannte* • Schwartz, *Frottole*, 15

Intabulation: lute

    3. F-Pn, 27, No.22, *25v-26r* (Anon.)

Intabulation: voice and lute

    1. **49**, No.38 (*B.T.*); **58**, No.38 (*B.T.*)

    4. Disertori, *Frottole*, 363

De speranza hormai son fora   [Anon.]   4vv

    1. **48**, No.33 (Anon.)

    4. Facchin & Zanovello, *Frottole*, 179 • Luisi, *Del cantar*, 235

Debbio chieder guerra o pace   Tromboncino   4vv

    1. **18**, No.21 (*B.T.*) • **40**, No.21 (*B.T.*)

    4. Cesari, *Frottole*, 108

Defecerunt donna hormai   Cara   4vv

    1. **16**, No.4 (*M.C.*)

    3. I-Fc, 2441, No.20, *22v-23r* (Anon.) • I-Fn, Panc.27, No.37, *23v-24r* (Anon. Text *Defecerunt vedo hormai*)

    4. Cesari, *Frottole*, 4 • Schwartz, *Frottole*, 3

Intabulation: lute

    3. F-Pn, 27, No.63, *44r* (Anon.)

Del partir e gionto   [Anon.]   4vv
    1. **25**, No.28 (Anon.)
    Intabulation: lute accompaniment to a Superius
    3. F-Pn, 27, No.31, 37*v* (Anon.)

Del tuo bel volto   **Tromboncino**   4vv
    1. **23**, No.17 (*B. T.*) • **37**, No.17 (*B. T.*)
    4. Schwartz, *Frottole*, 57

Dela impresa mia amorosa   **Cara**   4vv
    1. **48**, No.13 (*M.C.*)
    4. Facchin & Zanovello, *Frottole*, 136 • Prizer, *Courtly*, 430

Di focho ardente   **Tromboncino**   4vv
    1. **23**, No.55 (*B. T.*) • **37**, No.55 (*B. T.*)
    4. Schwartz, *Frottole*, 78

Di servirti el mio tormento
    See **Donna hormai fammi contento**   [Anon.]   4vv

Di tempo in tempo mi si fa men dura   **Eustache de Monte Regali**   4vv
    1. **56**, No.20 (*Eu. D. M. Regali Gallus.*)
    Text by Petrarch, *Ballate*, CIL
    4. Luisi & Zanovello, *Frottole*, 146

Di tempo in tempo   **Lulinus**   4vv
    1. **56**, No.46 (*Io. lu. V.*)
    Text by Petrarch, *Ballate*, CXLIX
    4. Luisi & Zanovello, *Frottole*, 208

Dicha ognun chi mal dir vole   [Anon.]   4vv
    1. **25**, No.21 (Anon.)

Dilecto albergo e tu   **Cara**   4vv
    1. **23**, No.49 (*M.C.*) • **37**, No.49 (*M.C.*)
    3. F-Pn, 676, No.14, 21*v-22r* (Anon.)
    4. Schwartz, *Frottole*, 74

Dime un pocho che vol dire   **Michele** [?Pesenti]   4vv
    1. **16**, No 36 (*MICHAEL.*)
    3. I-Bc, Q18, No.11, 11*v-12r* (Anon.)
    4. Cesari, *Frottole*, 27 • Einstein, *Beispielsammlung* 3 • Schwartz, *Frottole*, 26 • Schwartz,
       "Nochmals", 6

Dio lo sa quanto
    See **Dio sa quanto me**   **Capreolus**   4vv

Dio sa quanto me   **Capreolus**   4vv
    1. **17**, No.18 (Anon.) • **23**, No.66 (*ANT. CAP.* Text *Dio lo sa quanto*) • **37**, No.6 (*ANT.*
       CAP. Text *Dio lo sa quanto*) • **42**, No.18 (Anon.)
    4. Cesari, *Frottole*, 62 • Schwartz, *Frottole*, 66

Discolorato hai morte el piu bel volto   **Stringari**   4vv
    1. **56**, No.36 (*Antonius Patavus*)
    Text by Petrarch, *Canzoniere*, CCLXXXIII
    4. Luisi & Zanovello, *Frottole*, 183

Disperato fin amorte   [Anon.]   4vv
    1. **25**, No.47 (Anon.)

Dogni altra haria pensato   Cara   4vv
> 1. *36*, No.45 (*M.C.*)
> 4. Prizer, *Courtly*, ii, 77–78

Dolce amoroso foco   Lurano   4vv
> 1. *25*, No.35 (*F.L.* in the index)
> 3. E-Mp, 2-I-5, 53r (Anon.) • GB-Lbl, Eg.3051, No.45, 52v–53r (Anon.)
> Intabulation: voice and lute
> 1. *50*, No.39 (Anon.)
> 4. Disertori, *Frottole*, 546–47
> Intabulation: lute accompaniment to a Superius
> 3. F-Pc, 27, No.65, 44v (Anon.)

Dolce regina
> See **Popule meus quid feci tibi**   [Anon.]   4vv

Dolermi sempre voglio   Tromboncino   4vv
> 1. *48*, No.3 (*B.T.*)
> 4. Facchin & Zanovello, *Frottole*, 112 • Prizer, *Courtly*, 560
> Intabulation: voice and lute
> 1. *50*, No.41 (*B.T.*)
> 4. Disertori, *Frottole*, 552–53

Don don—al foco al foco   Stringari   4vv
> 1. *56*, No.40 (*A. P.*)
> 4. Jeppesen, *Frottola*, ii, 304–306 • Luisi & Zanovello, *Frottole*, 194 • Osthoff, *Theatergesang*, ii, 172

Donna ascolta el tuo amatore   Antonio   4vv
> 1. *16*, No.57 (*D. ANTONIO RIGUM.*)
> 4. Cesari, *Frottole*, 39 • Schwartz, *Frottole*, 38

Donna bella el tempo pasa   [Anon.]   4vv
> 1. *48*, No.37 (Anon.)
> 4. Facchin & Zanovello, *Frottole*, 185

Donna ben che di rado   Pisano   4vv
> 1. *67*, No.6 (Pisano)
> 3. I-Bc, Q21, No.6 (Anon.) • I-Fn, 164–167, No.7 (Anon.)
> 4. Pisano, *Collected Works*

Donna contra la mia voglia   Lurano   4vv
> 1. *23*, No.83 (This folio is lacking in the unique copy) • *37*, No.83 (*PHI. DE LV.*)
> 3. GB-Lbl, Eg.3051, No.47, 54v–55r (Anon.) • I-Fn, 230, No.22, 21v–22r (*philipus de lurano*)
> 4. Ferand, *Improvisation*, 322
> Comments: Perhaps *Donna questa e la mia voglia* is a response to this setting

Donna daltri piu   [Anon.]   4vv
> 1. *26*, No.35 (Anon.)
> 3. I-Fc, 2441, No.31, 33v–34r (Anon.)
> Intabulation: lute accompaniment to a Superius
> 3. F-Pn, 27, No.96, 50r (Anon.)

Donna gentile
> See **La morra**   Isaac   3vv

Donna hormai fammi contento [Anon.] 4vv
  1. *26*, No.22 (Anon.)
  3. GB-Lbl, Eg.3051, No.29, 34*v*-35*r* (Anon. Text *Di servirti a tuo dispecto*)

Donna hormai non piu dolore [Anon.] 4vv
  1. *26*, No.40 (Anon.)

Donna mia quanto dispecto [Anon.] 4vv
  1. *36*, No.24 (Anon.)

Donna non mi tenete **Tromboncino** 4vv
  1. *56*, No.61 (*B.T.*)
  3. I-Vnm, IV.1795–1798, No.75, 58*v*-59*r* (Anon.)
  4. Luisi, *Apografo*, 159–60 • Luisi & Zanovello, *Frottole*, 251
  Intabulation: voice and lute
  2. [c.1520]⁷, No.25, f.30 (This folio is lacking in the unique copy.)

Donna questa e la mia voglia **Lurano** 4vv
  1. *23*, No.84 (This is folio lacking in the unique copy) • *37*, No.84 (*PHI. DE LVRA.* Headed
    Risposta)
  3. GB-Lbl, Eg.3051, No.48, 56*v*-57*r* (Anon.)
  4. Ferand, *Improvisation*, 324
  Comment: Perhaps a response to *Donna contra la mia voglia*

Donne habiati voi pietate **Cara** 4vv
  1. *35*, No.39 (*M.C.*)
  4. Boscolo, *Frottole*, 204 • Gallucci, *Festival*, ii, 305–310 • Prizer, *Courtly*, ii, 85–89
  Comment: Prizer, "Facciamo", regards this as a carnival song from Mantua

Donzella no men culpeys
  See French Texts: **Mais que ce fust** **Compère** 3vv

Dopoi longhe fatiche [Anon.] 4vv
  3. I-Vnm, IV.1795–1798, No.11, 11*v*-12*r* (Anon. Text starts *Dapoi*)
  Text by Galeotto del Carretto: *Canzona alla amante*
  4. Luisi, *Apografo*, 26–27
  Intabulation: voice and lute
  1. *50*, No.11 (Anon.)
  4. Disertori, *Frottole*, 480–82

Dum bel matin che fu sera de for [Anon.] 3vv
  1. *26*, No.66 (Anon.)
  3. I-Bc, Q18, No.66, 67*v*-68*r* (Anon. Text *Dun bel maitim*)
  4. Disertori, *Frottole*, 268–70

Dun bel matin
  Tenor to **Damor che me levava** **Zesso** 4vv
  See also **E dun bel matin damore** **Capreolus** 4vv

Dun partir nascon doi parte **Lurano** 4vv
  1. *26*, No.34 (*PHI. D. L.*)

E dun bel matin damore che mi levava **Capreolus** 4vv
  1. *56*, No.35 (*Ant. C.*)
  4. Boorman, *Frottole* • Jeppesen, *Frottola*, ii, 307–10 • Luisi & Zanovello, *Frottole*, 131

E quando andaretu al monte **Zesso** 4vv
  1. *36*, No.67 (*IO. BA. ZESSO*)
  4. Ambros, *Geschichte*, v, 534 • Disertori, *Frottole*, 159

E questa quella fede   **Antenore**   4vv

     1. *17*, No.43 (Anon.) • *42*, No.43 (*Honophrius Antenoreus*)

     4. Cesari, *Frottole*, 21

E qui le dira

     See French texts

E si son si son lassame

     Tenor of **Fortuna dun gran tempo**   **Fogliano**   4vv

Ecco che per amarte   **Tromboncino**   4vv

     1. *36*, No.32 (*B.T.*)

     Text by Serafino Aquilano

     4. Luisi, *Cantar*, 118

     Intabulation: voice and lute

     1. *49*, No.28 (*B.T.* Text *Tu dormi io veglio*); *58*, No.28 (*B.T.* Text *Tu dormi io veglio*)

     4. Disertori, *Frottole*, 357

     Compare with I-Vnm, IV.1795–1798, No.30 (Anon. Texted *Gli e pur*)

Eccome qui hormai   [Anon.]   4vv

     1. *23*, No.73 (Anon.) • *37*, No.73 (Anon.)

     4. Schwartz, *Frottole*, 89

El basilischo ha lochio   **P. da Lodi**   4vv

     1. *36*, No.57 (*PIETRO DA LODE*)

El colpo che mede tuo sguardo   **Tromboncino**   4vv

     1. *25*, No.55 (*B.T.* in the index)

El convera chio mora   **Tromboncino**   4vv

     1. *16*, No.28 (*B.T.*)

     3. F-Pn, 676, No.22, 29*v*-30*r* (Anon.) • I-Fc, 2441, No.27, 29*v*-30*r* (Anon.)

     4. Cesari, *Frottole*, 21 • Schwartz, *Frottole*, 19

     Intabulation: voice and lute

     1. *49*, No.56 (*B.T.*); *58*, No.56 (*B.T.*)

     4. Disertori, *Frottole*, 408–409

El cor che ben disposto   [Anon.]   4vv

     1. *23*, No.75 (Anon.) • *37*, No.75 (Anon.)

     2. 1510, No.20, 21*r* (Anon.)

     4. Schwartz, *Frottole*, 90

El cor un altra volta   **d'Ana**   4vv

     1. *23*, No.38 (*F.V.*) • *37*, No.38 (*F.V.*)

     4. Schwartz, *Frottole*, 69

El focho e rinovato   **Tromboncino**   4vv

     1. *25*, No.24 (*B.T.* in the index)

     2. 1510, No.9, 10*v*-11*r* (Anon.)

El foco non mi noce   [Anon.]   4vv

     1. *35*, No.9 (Anon.)

     4. Boscolo, *Frottole*, 132

El grillo e bon cantore   **Josquin**   4vv

     1. *18*, No.60 (*IOSQVIN DASCANIO*) • *40*, No.60 (*IOSQVIN DASCANIO*)

     Facsimile: Cesari, *Frottole*, p. 144

     4. Cesari, *Frottole*, 140 • Josquin, *Werken*, Wereldlijke, ii, 54 • Schering, *Geschichte*, 69

El laccio che la mane   [Anon.]   4vv
   1. *23*, No.69 (Anon.) • *37*, No.69 (Anon.)
   4. Schwartz, *Frottole*, 88

El mio amor e intiero amore   **Tromboncino**   4vv
   1. *48*, No.28 (*B. T.*)
   4. Facchin & Zanovello, *Frottole*, 171

El pensier andra   [Anon.]   4vv
   1. *36*, No.46 (Anon.)

El te par che man in fede   **Antenore**   4vv
   1. *17*, No.38 (Anon.) • *42*, No.38 (*Honophrius Antenoreus.* Incipit *El te par che manchi in fede*)
   4. Cesari, *Frottole*, 79

Es de tal metal mi gloria   **Eustache Eomano**   4vv
   1. *56*, No.16 (*Eustachius. M. Romanus.*)
   4. Eustachio Romano, *Musica*, 156–157 • Luisi & Zanovello, *Frottole*, 138

Eterno mio signor   **Tromboncino**   4vv
   1. *41*, No.17 (*TROMBONCINO*)
   2. 1510, No.24, 23v-24r (*B. T.* Texted *Quando fia mai quel di felice*)
   4. Jeppesen, *Laude*, 26–27

Fa chio so hor su   [Anon.]   4vv
   1. *18*, No.57 (Anon. Not cited in the index) • *40*, No.57 (Anon. Not cited in the index)
   4. Cesari, *Frottole*, 137

Fabbe e fasoi   [?]**Tromboncino**   4vv
   1. *56*, No.11 (*A. T.*)
   4. Luisi, *Cantar*, 297–98 • Luisi & Zanovello, *Frottole*, 125

Famene un pocho
   See **Questa se chiama**   **Japart**   4vv

Famme pur quel che ti pare   [Anon.]   4vv
   1. *17*, No.12 (Anon.) • *42*, No.12 (Anon.)
   4. Cesari, *Frottole*, 57

Fammi almen una bona cera   **Lurano**   4vv
   1. *23*, No.85 (*PHI. DE. LV.*) • *37*, No.85 (*PHI. DE. LV.*)
   3. GB-Lbl, Eg.3051, No.30, 35v-36r (Anon. Text *Fammi al manco buona cera*) • I-Fc, 2441,
      No.51, 53v-54r (Anon. Text *Fami pur una bona cera*)
   4. Schwartz, *Frottole*, 94
   Comments: Perhaps intended to be paired with *Dammi almen lultimo vale*

Fammi quanto mal   **Lurano**   4vv
   1. *23*, No.90 (*PHI. DE. LV.*) • *37*, No.90 (*PHI. DE. LV.*)
   4. Schwartz, *Frottole*, 98

Fate ben gente cortese   **Tromboncino**   4vv
   1. *35*, No.41 (*B. T.*)
   4. Boscolo, *Frottole*, 212 • Gallucci, *Festival*, ii, 311–13 • Osthoff, *Theatergesang*, ii, 157–58
   Intabulation: voice and lute
   1. *50*, No.27 (*B. T.*)
   4. Disertori, *Frottole*, 518–19
   Comments: Disertori calls this a *canto carnascialesco*, and Prizer, "Facciamo", suggests that it
      comes from northern Italy (Ferrara/Mantua)

Felice fu quel di   [Anon.]   voice + lute
    Intabulation: voice and lute
    1. *50*, No.1 (Anon.)
    4. Disertori, *Frottole*, 458

Fermo ho in cor sempre dmaarte [*sic*]   [Anon.]   4vv
    1. *25*, No.49 (Anon.)

Finira giamai mia sorte   Dupre   4vv
    1. *48*, No.46 (*HE. Dupre*)
    4. Facchin & Zanovello, *Frottole*, 204

Fondo le mie speranze   Pisano   ?4vv
    1. *67*, No.1 (Pisano. Incomplete)
    Poet: L. Strozzi

Fora son dogni speranza   Pifaro   4vv
    1. *26*, No.18 (*NICOLO PIFAR.*)

Forestieri ala ventura   [Anon.]   4vv
    1. *26*, No.53 (Anon.)
    4. Gallucci, *Festival*, ii, 314–18 • Haar, *Chanson*, 195–97 • Pirrotta, *Music*, 57–58
    Comment: Prize, "Facciamo", regards this as a carnival song, perhaps from Rome

Forsi che si forsi che no   Cara   4vv
  2/ *Forsi chi ode non intende*
    1. *18*, No.33 (*M.C.*) • *40*, No.33 (*M.C.*)
    Facsimile: Cesari, *Frottole*, p. CXXV
    4. Cesari, *Frottole*, 118

Forsi chi ode non intende
  2/ of **Forsi che si forsi che no**   Cara   4vv

Fortuna desperata   Busnois   4vv
    (Agricola, Felice)
    1. *12*, No.101 (Anon.)
    3. CH-Bu, F.X.10, No.17, 8r (Anon.) • CH-Sgs, 462, 6v-7r (Anon.) • CH-SGs, 463, No.144,
    53r and 112r (Anon. Headed *Ionicus, idest quintus*) • D-Z, LXXVIII,3, No.54, 39r (Anon.
    Untexted) • F-Pn, 676, 24v-25r (Anon.) • GB-Lbl, Add.31922, 4v-5r (Anon. Incipit *For-*
    tune esperee) • I-Bc, Q16, No.114, 132v-133r (Anon. With a different Altus) • I-Fn,
    Panc.27, No.36, 22v-23r (Anon. Texted *Poi che te hebi nel core*) • I-PEc, 431, No.17, No.59,
    84v-85r (Anon.) • ZA-Csa, Grey, No.50, 79v-80r (Anon. Texted *Poi che t hebi nel core*)
      The following source is à6: D-As, 142a, 46v-47r (*Allexannderr*)
      The following source is à5: I-Rvat, C.G.XIII.27, No.51, 63v-64r (*Felice*)
      The following sources are à3: E-SE, s.s., 174r (*Anthonius Busnoys*) • F-Pn, 4379,
    No.127, n11v-12r/40v-41r (Anon.) • GB-Lbl, Add.35087, No.9, 11v-12r (Anon.) • I-Fn,
    121, No.25, 25v-26r (Anon.) • I-PEc, 431, No.16, 83v-84r (Anon. Erased)
    4. Geering & Trümpy, *Heer*, 17–18 • Isaac, *Weltliche* • Josquin, *Werken*, Weltliche, ii, 53 •
    McMurtry, *Chansonnier*, 232–35 • Moerk, *Seville*, ii, 311–13 • Obrecht, *Opera Omnia* •
    Obrecht, *Werke*, i, 136–137 • Stevens, *Henry VIII*, 2 • Torrefranca, *Segreto*, 297–298
    There are many intabulations of this work
    Intabulation: two lutes
    1. *34*, No.29 (*Francesco Spinacino*)
    4. Schmidt, *Spinacino*, ii, 270–75

Comments: The basis for Obrecht's mass, also published by Petrucci

Literature: Atlas, *Giulia*, 134–36

Fortuna desperata   **Pinarol**   4vv

    1. *12*, No.50 (*.Jo.pinarol*)

Facsimile: Cesari, *Frottole*, p. VIII

    3. D-Mbs, 1516, No.4 (Anon.)

Fortuna dun gran tempo   **Japart**   4vv

    1. *12*, No.36 (*Japart*)

Fortuna dun gran tempo   **Josquin**   3vv

    1. *1*, No.74 (*Josquin*) • *5*, No.74 (Anon.) • *14*, No.74 (Anon.)

    2. [c.1535][14], iii, 10 (Anon.)

    3. I-Fn, Panc.27, No.139, 106v–107r (Anon.)

Facsimile: Besseler & Gülke, *Schriftbild*, 121

    4. Disertori, *Frottole*, 178–79 • Hewitt, *Odhecaton*, 366–67 • Josquin, *Werken*, Supplement •
    Torrefranca, *Segreto*, 458–60

Intabulations: keyboard

    3. CH-Bu, F.VI.26c, No.2, 7v–8v (Anon. Untexted) • CH-Bu, F.IX.22, 18r–19v (*Iosquin*) •
    D-B, 40026

Intabulation: lute

    1. *33*, No.5 (*Francesco Spinacino*)

    4. Disertori, *Frottole*, 176–79 • Schmidt, *Spinacino*, 17–19

Literature: Van Benthem, "Fortuna"

Fortuna dun gran tempo / E si son si son lassame / Che fa

la ramacina / Dagdum vetusta   **Fogliano**   4vv

    1. *48*, No.48 (*Ludovicus foglianus*)

Facsimile: Besseler & Gülke, *Schriftbilt*, 103

    4. Facchin & Zanovello, *Frottole*, 210 • Torrefranca, *Segreto*, 461

Fortuna dun gran tempo

    See French texts: **Franch cor quas tu**   **de Vigne**   4vv

Fuga ognun amor   **Lulinus**   4vv

    1. *56*, No.57 (*Io. Lu. V.*)

    4. Luisi & Zanovello, *Frottole*, 240

Fugga pur chi vol amore   **Cara**   5vv

    1. *35*, No.42 (*M.C.*)

    4. Boscolo, *Frottole*, 214 • Prizer, *Courtly*, ii, 90–98

Fuggi fuggil sereno

    2/ of **Che deggio far**   **Pisano**   4vv

Fuggi pur da me se sai   **Capreolus**   4vv

    1. *23*, No.65 (*ANT. CAP.*) • *37*, No.65 (*ANT. CAP.*)

    4. Schwartz, *Frottole*, 84

Fugi se sai fugir   **Cara**   4vv

    1. *48*, No.27 (*M.C.*)

    4. Facchin & Zanovello, *Frottole*, 170 • Osthoff, *Theatergesang*, ii, 161 • Prizer, *Courtly*, 433

Fuggir voglio el tuo bel volto   **Pesenti**   4vv

    1. *16*, No.41 (*MICHA. C. & V.*)

    4. Cesari, *Frottole*, 31 • Schwartz, *Frottole*, 30

Fugite christiani
  See **Fuzite christiani**   **Dammonis**   4vv
Fugitiva mia speranza   **Cara**   4vv
    2/ *Io so ben che al tuo dispecto*
       1. *18*, No.35 (*M.C.*) • *40*, No.35 (*M.C.*)
       4. Cesari, *Frottole*, 121
      Intabulation: voice and lute
       1. *50*, No.37 (*M.C.*)
       4. Disertori, *Frottole*, 540–43
Fui felice in un momento   **Capreolus**   4vv
       1. *35*, No.17 (*A.C.*)
       4. Boscolo, *Frottole*, 147
Fui felice un tempo   **P. da Lodi**   4vv
       1. *56*, No.34 (*P.L.*)
       4. Luisi & Zanovello, *Frottole*, 180
Fuzite christiani   **Dammonis**   4vv
       1. *29*, No.39 (Dammonis. Headed *De contemptu mundi*. Index reads *Fugite*);
        45, No.39 (Dammonis)
      Text by Giustiniani
       4. Luisi, *Laudario*, ii, 46–47
Gia fui lieto hor gioncto   [Anon.]   4vv
       1. *26*, No.62 (Anon.)
      Intabulation: lute
       3. F-Pn, 27, No.6, 14r (Anon.)
      Intabulation: lute accompaniment to a Superius
       3. F-Pn, 27, No.51, 41v (Anon.)
Gioia me abonda   **Tromboncino**   4vv
       1. *56*, No.66 (*B.T.*)
       3. I-Vnm, IV.1795–1798, No.44, 37v-38r (Anon. Titled *Giogia* in the index)
      Text by Bembo, *Rime*, LXXII
       4. Luisi, *Apografo*, 101–102 • Luisi & Zanovello, *Frottole*, 267
      Literature: Rubsamen, *Literary*, 29
Gionti siam ala vechieza   [Anon.]   4vv
       1. *48*, No.38 (Anon.)
       4. Facchin & Zanovello, *Frottole*, 187 • Gallucci, *Festival*, ii, 319–22
      Comment: Prize, "Facciamo", regards this as a carnival song from northern Italy
Glie pur gionto el giorno   **Cara**   4vv
       1. *16*, No.11 (*M.C.*. Altus texted *Non val aqua al mio gran foco*)
       4. Cesari, *Frottole*, 10 • Schwartz, *Frottole*, 8
Gliochi toi maccesel core   **d'Ana**   4vv
       1. *17*, No.13 (*FRAN. VENE. ORGA.*) • *42*, No.13 (*FRAN. VENE. ORGA.*)
       4. Cesari, *Frottole*, 57
Gliochi toi mhan posto   **Tromboncino**   4vv
       1. *17*, No.29 (*B.T.*) • *42*, No.29 (*B.T.*)
       4. Cesari, *Frottole*, 70
Gnao gnao gnao vo cridando
    2/ of **Perche fai donna el gaton**   **Rossino**   4vv

Gratia piu che virtu   [Anon.]   4vv

     1. *48*, No.35 (Anon.)

     Text has been ascribed to Serafino Aquilano

     4. Facchin & Zanovello, *Frottole*, 182

Guarda donna el mio tormento   [Anon.]   4vv

     1. *17*, No.35 (Anon.) • *42*, No.35 (Anon.)

     3. E-Mp, 2-I-5, 113r (Anon.) • GB-Lbl, Eg.3051, No.1, 2v-4r (Anon.) • I-Fc, 2441, No.35, 37v-38r (Anon.)

     4. Cesari, *Frottole*, 77

Guarda se le cagion

     2/ of **Anima che del mondo vo fugire**   **Dammonis**   4vv

Guardando alli ochi toi

     See **Se ben elfin de la mia vita**   **Cara**   4vv

Ha bella e fresca etade   **Lurano**   4vv

     1. *36*, No.52 (*PHILIPPVS DE LVRANO*)

Hai dispietato tempo

     See **O despietato tempo**   **Bisan**   4vv

Hai lassa me meschina   **Cesena**   4vv

     1. *17*, No.22 (*P.C.V.*) • *42*, No.22 (*P.C.V.*)

     4. Cesari, *Frottole*, 65

Hai pretiosa fe   [Anon.]   4vv

     1. *23*, No.56 (Anon.) • *37*, No.56 (Anon.)

     4. Schwartz, *Frottole*, 78

Hai promesse dolce e amare   [Anon.]   4vv

                                     (?Antenore)

     1. *17*, No.40 (Anon.) • *42*, No.40 (Anon.)

     4. Cesari, *Frottole*, 81

     Comments: This piece is perhaps by Antenore, from the layout of the surrounding pieces

Hai speranza che premetesti falace   [Anon.]   ?4vv

     1. *68*, 4v (Anon. Incomplete)

Haime che grave doglia   [Anon.]   4vv

     1. *18*, No.41 (Anon.) • *40*, No.41 (Anon.)

     4. Cesari, *Frottole*, 126

Haime che non e un giocho   [Anon.]   4vv

     1. *17*, No.36 (Anon.) • *42*, No.36 (Anon.)

     4. Cesari, *Frottole*, 78

Haime perche mhai privo   [Anon.]   4vv

     1. *36*, No.56 (Anon.)

     Intabulation: voice and lute

     1. *49*, No.9 (Anon.); *58*, No.9 (Anon.)

     4. Disertori, *Frottole*, 319

Haria voluto alhor   **P. da Lodi**   4vv

     1. *36*, No.63r (*PIETRO DA LODI*)

Hay bella liberta   **Lulinus**   4vv

     1. *56*, No.50 (*Io. Lu. V.*)

     Text by Petrarch, *Canzoniere*, XCVI

     4. Luisi & Zanovello, *Frottole*, 222

Hay lasso rimembrando il loco il giorno   [Anon.]   4vv
    1. *56*, No.28 (Anon.)
    4. Luisi & Zanovello, *Frottole*, 166

He le nata aime colei   **P. da Lodi**   voice + lute
    Intabulation: voice and lute
    1. *50*, No.13 (*Pie. Da. Lodi*)
    4. Disertori, *Frottole*, 486–87

Ho scoperto il tanto aperto   **Tromboncino**   4vv
    1. *35*, No.18 (*Tromboncino*)
    4. Boscolo, *Frottole*, 149
    Intabulation: voice and lute
    1. *49*, No.17 (*B.T.*); *58*, No.17 (*B.T.*)
    4. Disertori, *Frottole*, 336–37

Hogni Cosa val suo locho
    See **Ogni cosa ha el suo locho**   [Anon.]   3vv

Hor chio son de preson fora   **Tromboncino**   4vv
    1. *25*, No.61 (*B.T.*: *T.* in the index)
    3. F-Pn, 676, No.60, 69*v*–70*r* (Anon. Text *Or che son . . .*)
    4. Luisi, *Cantar*, 239

Hor ivo scoprir el focho   **Tromboncino**   4vv
    1. *25*, No.54 (*B.T.*)

Hor passata e la speranza   **Tromboncino**   4vv
    1. *25*, No.6 (*B.T.* in the index. Cantus incipit starts *Hhor*)

Hor sucorrer voglio amore   [Anon.]   4vv
    1. *26*, No.45 (Anon.)
    3. F-Pn, 676, No.43, 51*v*–52*r* (Anon. Text *Or su Corere voglio*) • I-Mt, 55, No.39, 39*v*–40*r*
    (Anon.)
    4. Jeppesen, *Frottola*, iii, 266–69

Hor venduto ho la speranza   **Cara**   4vv
    1. *16*, No.6 (*M.C.*)
    4. Cesari, *Frottole*, 6 • Schwartz, *Frottole*, 4
    Intabulation: voice and lute
    1. *49*, No.45 (*M.C.* Texted *Hor venduto la speranza*); *58*, No.45 (*M.C.* Texted *Hor venduto
    la speranza*)
    4. Disertori, *Frottole*, 388–89

Humilmente tenuocho Iesu   **Dammonis**   4vv
    1. *29*, No.44 (Dammonis. Headed *De passione*); *45*, No.44 (Dammonis)
    Text by Giustiniani
    4. Jeppesen, *Laude*, 142 • Luisi, *Laudario*, ii, 53

Il buon nochier sempre parla   [Anon.]   voice + lute
    Intabulation: voice and lute
    1. *50*, No.3 (Anon.)
    4. Disertori, *Frottole*, 462

Il ciel natura e amore   [Anon.]   4vv
    1. *25*, No.11 (Anon.)

Il iocondo e lieto   [Anon.]   4vv
    1. *25*, No.3 (Anon.)

In eterno io voglio amarte   **Cara**   4vv

    1. *16*, No.10 (*M.C.*)

    3. F-Pn, 676, No.62, 71*v*-72 (Anon. Text *La virtu si vole seguire*) • I-Fn, 230, No.4, 3*v*-4*r*
    (Anon. Text *In eterno voglio*) • I-Fn, 121, No.17, 17*v*-18*r* (Anon. Text *La virtu si vole
    seguire*) • I-Fn, Panc.27, No.148, 111*v*-112*r* (Anon. Text *La virtu si vole seguire*)

    4. Cesari, *Frottole*, 9 • Prizer, *Courtly*, ii, 227–30 • Schwartz, *Frottole*, 7

In eterno voglio amarti

    See **In eterno io voglio amarte**   **Cara**   4vv

    See **Ostinato vo seguire**   **Tromboncino**   4vv

In qualunque ama con perfecto amore

    2/ of **Perche donna non voi**   **Pisano**   4vv

In te Domine speravi   **Josquin**   4vv

    See Latin texts

Ingrata donna alamia   [Anon.]   4vv

    1. *26*, No.32 (Anon. Headed *Per Sonetti*)

Io cercho pur la insuportabil doglia   **Tromboncino**   4vv

    1. *36*, No.64 (*B.T.*)

    2. 1510, No.27, 26*v*-27*r* (*B.T.*)

    Intabulation: voice and lute

    1. *49*, No.20 (*B.T.*); *58*, No.20 (*B.T.*)

    4. Disertori, *Frottole*, 342–342

Io mi moro   [Anon.]   4vv

    1. *18*, No.45 (Anon.) • *40*, No.45 (Anon.)

    4. Cesari, *Frottole*, 129

Io mi parto el cor vi lasso   **d'Antiquis**   4vv

    1. *48*, No.57 (*A. D. A.*)

    4. Einstein, *Madrigal*, iii, 16 • Facchin & Zanovello, *Frottole*, 236 • Juverini et al, *Frottole*, 73
    • Zupanovic, *Sedamnaest frottola*

Io mi voglio lamentare   **G. Brocco**   4vv

    1. *18*, No.29 (*IO. BRO.*) • *40*, No.29 (*IO. BRO.*)

    3. E-Mp, 2-I-5, 284*v* (Anon. Text *Yo me vollo lamentare*) • F-Pn, 676, No.45, 53*v*-54*r* (Anon.)
    • I-Fn, Panc.27, No.65, 42*r* (*Bro*)

    4. Cesari, *Frottole*, 114

Io non compro piu speranza   **Cara**   4vv

    1. *16*, No.9 (*M.C.*)

    4. Cesari, *Frottole*, 8 • Schwartz, *Frottole*, 6

    Intabulation: voice and lute

    1. *49*, No.46 (*M.C.*); *58*, No.46 (*M.C.*)

    4. Disertori, *Frottole*, 390–91

Io non lho perche non lho   **Cara**   4vv

    1. *36*, No.49 (*M.C.*)

    2. 1510, No.29, 28*v*-29*r* (*M.C.*)

    Text by Poliziano

    4. Rubsamen, *Literary*, 39–41

Io non manchi di fede   **Zesso**   voice + lute

    Intabulation: voice and lute

1. **50**, No.21 (*IO. BA. ZE.*)

4. Disertori, *Frottole*, 502–503

Io non posso piu durare   **Aaron**   4vv

1. **25**, No.59 (*Aron*)

Io so ben che al tuo dispecto

2/ of **Fugitiva mia speranza**   **Cara**   4vv

Io son de gabbia

See **Integer vitae**   **Pesenti**   4vv

Io son lieto nel aspecto   [Anon.]   4vv

1. **36**, No.51 (Anon.)

Intabulation: lute accompaniment to a Superius

3. F-Pn, 27, No.52, 41*v* (Anon.)

Io son locel che con le debil ali   **Michele** [?Pesenti]   4vv

1. **35**, No.49 (*D. Mi.*)

4. Boscolo, *Frottole*, 241

Io son locello che non po   **Tromboncino**   4vv

1. **35**, No.46 (*B. T.*)

4. Boscolo, *Frottole*, 224 • Reese, "First", 162

Io son locel che sopra i rami   **Cara**   4vv

1. **23**, No.1 (*MARCVS CHARA. VERO.*) • **37**, No.1 (*MARCVS CHARA VERO.*)

3. F-Pn, 676, No.1, 9*r* (Anon.) • I-Fn, Panc.27, No.63, 41*r* (Anon.)

4. Schwartz, *Frottole*, 45

Io son quel doloroso   **Antiquis**   4vv

1. **25**, No.36 (*A. DE ANTIQVIS.*)

4. Zupanovic, *Sedamnaest frottola*

Io son quel misero ingrato   **Dammonis**   4vv

1. **29**, No.61 (Dammonis); **45**, No.61 (Dammonis)

Text by Lorenzo de'Medici

4. Luisi, *Laudario*, ii, 336–37

Io son quello che fu mai   **Tromboncino**   4vv

1. **25**, No.56 (*B. T.*)

3. GB-Lbl, Eg.3051, No.23, 26*v*-28*r* (Anon.)

Io sto male e vivo in stento

2/ of **Patientia ognum me dice**   [Anon.]   4vv

Io tho donato il core   **Zesso**   4vv

1. **36**, No.1 (*IOANNES BAPTISTA ZESSO.*)

4. Rubsamen, *Literary*, 47

Intabulation: voice and lute

1. **50**, No.4 (*Io. Ba. Ze.*)

4. Disertori, *Frottole*, 463

Io ti lasso donna hormai   **Lurano**   4vv

1. **25**, No.31 (*F.D.L.* in the index)

3. GB-Lbl, Eg.3051, No.51, 58*v*-59*r* (Anon.) • I-Bc, Q18, No.7, 7*v*-8*r* (Anon.) • I-Fn, 337, No.17, 27*v* (Anon.)

Io voria esser cholu   **Michele** [?Pesenti]   4vv

1. **48**, No.25 (*D.M.*)

4. Disertori, *Frottole*, 155 • Facchin & Zanovello, *Frottole*, 164

Ite caldi o mei suspiri   **Tromboncino**   4vv
    1. *48*, No.14 (*B.T.*)
    4. Facchin & Zanovello, *Frottole*, 139
    Intabulation: voice and lute
    1. *50*, No.44 (*B.T.*)
    4. Disertori, *Frottole*, 556–58 • Schwartz, "Nochmals", pp. 3–4

Ite caldi suspiri   [Anon.]   4vv
    1. *17*, No.17 (Anon.) • *42*, No.17 (Anon.)
    Text by Petrarch
    4. Cesari, *Frottole*, 61

Ite caldi suspiri   **G. Brocco**   4vv
    1. *18*, No.30 (*IO. BRO.* Headed *El modo de dir sonetti*) • *40*, No.30, (*IO.BRO.* Headed *El modo de dir sonetti*)
    Text by Petrarch
    4. Cesari, *Frottole*, 114 • Schering, *Geschichte*, 69

Ite in pace o suspir fieri   **Tromboncino**   4vv
    1. *25*, No.13 (*B.T.*)
    3. I-Fn, 230, No.5, 4v-6r (*Tromboncino*)
    Intabulation: voice and lute
    1. *50*, No.25 (*B.T.*)
    4. Disertori, *Frottole*, 512–15

Jesu benigno e pio   **Zesso**   4vv
    1. *41*, No.27 (*I.B.Z.*)
    4. Jeppesen, *Laude*, 39.

Jesu fami morire   **Dammonis**   4vv
    1. *29*, No.65 (Dammonis); *45*, No.65 (Dammonis)
    Text by Belcari
    4. Luisi, *Laudario*, ii, 334–35

Jesu summo conforto   **Scotto**   4vv
    1. *41*, No.25 (*Paulus scotus*)
    4. Jeppesen, *Laude*, 37

L amor a me venendo   **Dammonis**   4vv
    1. *29*, No.59 (Dammonis); *45*, No.29 (Dammonis)
    Text by Giustiniani
    4. Jeppesen, *Laude*, 152 • Luisi, *Laudario*, ii, 56

L amor donna chio te porto   **J.Fogliano**   4vv
    1. *36*, No.20 (Anon.)
    3. E-Mp, 2-I-5, 59r (Anon.) • F-Pn, 676, 110v-111r (*Ia.Fo.*) • I-Fc, 2441, No.36, 38v-39r (Anon.)
    4. Einstein, *Madrigal*, 5
    Intabulation: lute accompaniment to a Superius
    2. F-Pn, 27, No.94, 50r (Anon. Incipit *Lo amor donna*)

L aqua vale al mio gran foco   **Michael** [?Pesenti]   4vv
    1. *16*, No.32 (*MICHAEL*)
    4. Cesari, *Frottole*, 24 • Schwartz, *Frottole*, 23

L ardor mio grave Cara 4vv

    1. *36*, No.35 (*M.C.*)

    4. Prizer, *Courtly*, ii, 79–81

L infermo alhor piu se consuma [Anon.] 4vv

    1. *23*, No.42 (Anon.) • *37*, No.42 (Anon.)

    3. GB-Lbl, Eg.3051, No.10, 12*v*–13*r* (Anon.)

    4. Einstein, *Madrigal*, 6 • Schwartz, *Frottole*, 70

L oration e sempre bona

    See **Se ben hor non scopro el focho** Tromboncino 4vv

La alfonsina Ghiselin 3vv

    1. *1*, No.80 (*Io ghiselin.*) • *5*, No.80 (*Io.ghiselin:*) • *14*, No.80 (*.Io.ghiselin:*)

    2. [c.1535][14], iii, No.53 (Anon.) • 1538[9], No.49, G2*v* (MS attribution in the copy at D-Ju: *Joh. Ghiselin*)

    3. CH-SGs, 461, pp. 80–81 (*Jo. ghiselin*) • I-Fn, Panc.27, No.128, 98*v*–99*r* (*Io. ghiselin*)

    4. Ambros, *Geschichte*, v, 190 • Cesari, *Frottola*, xliv • Ghiselin, *Opera Omnia*, iv, 36–38 • Hewitt, *Odhecaton*, 387–88 • Mönkemeyer, *Formschneyder*, i, pp. 74–75

    Intabulation: lute

    2. 1536[13] = N522, No.15, F1*v*–2*v* (*Jo. Ghiselin. H. Newsidler*)

La belta chogi e divina P. da Lodi 4vv

    1. *56*, No.32 (*Pietro da lodi*)

    4. Jeppesen, *Frottola*, ii, 320–22 • Luisi & Zanovello, *Frottole*, 177

La bernardina Josquin 3vv

    1. *12*, No.129 (*.Josquin.*)

    2. 1538[9], No.16, C2*v* (MS attribution in the copy at D-Ju: *Joskin*)

    3. I-Bc, Q18, No.81, 82*v*–83*r* (Anon.)

    4. Josquin, *Collected Works*, xxvii, No.21 • Josquin, *Werken*, Wereldlijke, ii, 53 • Mönkemeyer, *Formschneyder*, i, p. 29 • Schering, *Geschichte*, 62 • Underwood, *Renaissance*, 25–29

    Intabulations: two lutes

    1. *33*, No.10 (*Josquin; Francesco Spinacino: Josquin* and *F.S.* in the index)

    4. Schmidt, *Spinacino*, ii, 45–49 • Underwood, *Renaissance*, 25–29

    Intabulations: lute

    1. *33*, No.15 (*Josquin; Francesco Spinacino: Josquin* and *F.S.* in the index)

    2. 1536[13] = N522, No.12, E2*r*–2*v* (*Jossquin. H. Newsidler*)

    4. Schmidt, *Spinacino*, ii, 66–68 • Schering, *Geschichte*, No.63a

La colpa non e mia Pifaro 4vv

    1. *35*, No.26 (*NICOLO PIFARO*)

    4. Boscolo, *Frottole*, 173

La dolce diva mia [Anon.] 4vv

    1. *23*, No.79 (Anon.) • *37*, No.79 (Anon.)

    4. Schwartz, *Frottole*, 91

    Intabulations: lute accompaniment to a Superius

    3. F-Pn, 27, No.80, 47*v* (Anon.) • F-Pn, 27, No.84, 48*v* (Anon.)

La fiamma che me abruscia Nicolo 4vv

    1. *23*, No.25 (*N.P.*) • *37*, No.25 (*N.P.*)

    4. Schwartz, *Frottole*, 61

La fortuna vol cossi Cara 4vv

    1. *16*, No.17 (*M.C.*)

4. Cesari, *Frottole*, 13

Intabulation: voice and lute

1. **49**, No.47 (*M.C.*); **58**, No.47 (*M.C.*)

4. Disertori, *Frottole*, 392

La insuportabil pena   d'Antiquis   4vv

1. **48**, No.59 (*A.D.A.*)

4. Facchin & Zanovello, *Frottole*, 241 • Luisi, *Cantar*, 131 • Juverini et al., *Frottole*, 77 • Zupanovic, *Sedamnaest frottola*

La mi la so cantare   [Anon.]   ?4vv

1. **68**, 3*v* (Anon. Incomplete)

La mi laso la sola mi Gia vol ici   [Anon.]   4vv

1. **48**, No.61 (Anon.)

4. Facchin & Zanovello, *Frottole*, 246

La mi la sol

See **Missa La mi la sol**   Isaac   4vv

La mia fe non vene   G. Brocco   4vv

1. **18**, No.15 (*IO. BRO.*) • **40**, No.15 (*IO. BRO.*)

4. Cesari, *Frottole*, 104

La mia impresa e vita biancha   [Anon.]   4vv

1. **48**, No.53 (Anon.)

4. Facchin & Zanovello, *Frottole*, 225

La mia vaga tortorella   Dupre   4vv

1. **48**, No.6 (*HE. dupre*)

4. Facchin & Zanovello, *Frottole*, 120

La mia vita liberale   d'Ana   4vv

2/ *A tuo modo affligi*

1. **17**, No.2 (*FRAN. VENE. ORGA.*) • **42**, No.2 (*FRAN. VENE. ORGA.*)

4. Cesari, *Frottole*, 47

La morra   Isaac   3vv

1. **1**, No.44 (These folios lacking) • **5**, No.44 (*Yzac*) • **14**, No.44 (*Yzac*)

2. [c.1535][14], iii, No.34 (Anon.) • 1538[9], No.29, E1*v* (MS attribution in the copy at D-Ju: H. Isac.)

3. CH-SGs, 462, pp. 136–137 (*Isaac*. Texted *O regina*, with the later addition of *La morra*. Different Altus) • CH-SGs, 463, No.176, 61*r* and 119*r* (*Henricus Isac*. Altus of CH-SGs, 462) • D-HB, X.2, No.14 (*Isaac*) • D-LEu, 1494, No.81, 85*v*-86*r* (*H. Y.*. Untexted) • D-LEu, 1494, 245*v* (Anon. Texted *Reple tuorum corda fidelium*) • D-Z, LXXVIII,3, No.25 (*Isaac*. Untexted) • DK-Kk, 1848, p.412 (Anon.) • E-SE, s.s., No.113, 175*v* (*Ysac*. Texted *Elaes*) • F-Pn, 676, 40*v*-41*r* (*Isach*. Title *La morra: Dona gentile*) • I-Bc, Q18, No.71, 72*v*-73*r* (Anon.) • I-Fn, 107bis, No.41, 56*v*-57*r* (*Izac*) • I-Fn, 178, No.25, 29*v*-30*r* (*Enrigus Yzac*) • I-Fn, 229, No.12, 11*v*-12*r* (*Henricus Yzac*. Untexted) • I-Fn, Panc.27, No.54, 33*v*-34*r* (Anon.) • I-Rvat, C.G.XIII.27, No.76, 90*v*-91*r* (*Ysach*. Text incipit *Dona gentil*) • I-VEcap, DCCLVII, No.39, 39*v*-40*r* (Anon. Untexted)

4. Brown, *Florentine*, music volume, 23–25 • Geering & Trümpy, *Liederbuch*, No.77 • Gerber, *Mensuralkodex*, 113 • Hewitt, *Odhecaton*, 315–16 • Isaac, *Weltliche*, 151–54 • Mönkemeyer, *Formschneyder*, i, p. 50 • Riemann, *Musikgeschichte*, 31

Intabulations: keyboard

3. CH-Bu, F.IX.22, No.18, 32*v*-34*r* (*Isacius author*) • CH-SGs, 530, No.117, 93*v*-94*r* (*Heinrich Isaac*)

Intabulations: lute

1. *33*, No.13 (*Francesco Spinacino*)

2. 1536¹² = N521, No.21, g3*r* (*Isaac. H. Newsidler*) • 1536¹² = N521, No.48, p1*v* (*Isaac. H. Newsidler*) • 1545²¹, No.8, 8*v* (*Isaac.* Titled *Benedictus*)

3. A-Wn, 41950, No.4, 6*r* (*Muteta Ysacc*) • D-Mbs, 272, No.59, 72*v*-73*r* (Anon. Headed *La Amora*) • F-Pn, 27, No.7, 14*v* (Anon.)

4. Schmidt, *Spinacino*, ii, 61–63 • Marx, *Tabulaturen*, 30

La nocte aquieta ogni animale [Anon.] 4vv

1. *23*, No.41 (Anon.) • *37*, No.41 (Anon.)

3. I-Fn, Panc.27, No.53, 33*r* (Anon.)

4. Schwartz, *Frottole*, 70

La nocte quando ognun riposa [Anon.] 4vv

1. *23*, No.57 (Anon.) • *37*, No.57 (Anon.)

4. Schwartz, *Frottole*, 79

La non vol esser piu mai Tromboncino 4vv
(Fogliano)

1. *56*, No.8 (*B.T.*)

2. 1515², No.16, 17*v*-18*r* (*Iac. Fo.*) • 1515², No.19, 20v-21r (Anon.: Incipit *Tua volsi esser*)

3. F-Pn, 676, 124*r* (Anon.: texted *Tua volsi esser*)

4. Luisi & Zanovello, *Frottole*, 117 • Prizer, *Courtly*, ii, 162–64

Intabulation: keyboard

2. 1517³, No.19, 31*r*-32*r* (*B.T.*)

La pieta chiuso ha le porte Tromboncino 4vv
2/ *Certo nascer non dovea*

1. *17*, No.26 (*B.T.*) • *42*, No.26 (*B.T.*)

Facsimile: Cesari, *Frottole*, p. 90

4. Cesari, *Frottole*, 67

La pieta ha chiuso le porte

See **Pieta cara signora** Erasmo 4vv

La speranza col timore Tromboncino 4vv

1. *18*, No.13 (*B.T.*) • *40*, No.13 (*B.T.*)

4. Cesari, *Frottole*, 102

La speranza me tien vivo [Anon.] 4vv

1. *18*, No.44 (Anon.) • *40*, No.44 (Anon.)

3. I-Fn, 337, No.21, 22*v* (Anon.) • I-Fn, Panc.27, No.34, 54*v*-55*r* (Anon.)

4. Cesari, *Frottole*, 128

La stangetta Weerbeke 3vv
(Isaac, Obrecht)

1. *1*, No.49 (*Uuerbech.* Incomplete) • *5*, No.49 (Anon.) • *14*, No.49 (Anon.)

2. [c.1535]¹⁴, iii, 54 (Anon.) • 1538⁹, No.44, F4*v* (Anon.)

3. D-HB, X.2, No.29 (Anon.) • D-Z, LXXVIII,3, No.18 (*Obrecht.* Untexted) • E-SE, s.s., No.106, 172*r* (*Ysacc.* Incipit *Ortus de celo flos est*) • I-Bc, Q16, 68*v*-69*r* (Anon. Texted *Ce nest pas*) • I-Fn, Panc.27, No.55, 34*v*-35*r* (Anon.)

4. Hewitt, *Odhecaton*, 325–26 • Mönkemeyer, *Formschneyder*, ii, pp. 68–69 • Obrecht, *Werken*, 45–47

Intabulations: lute
1. *34*, No.28 (*Francesco Spinacino*)
2. 1536[13] = N522, No.6, C1*v*-2*v* (Anon. H. Newsidler)
4. Schmidt, *Spinacino*, ii, 267–69
Comments: Kämper, "Stangetta" favours Weerbeke as the composer

La tourturella   **Obrecht**   4vv
1. *12*, No.69 (*Jaco. Obreht*)
3. I-Fn, 164–167, No.37, 47*v*-48*r* (Anon.) • I-Fn, 229, No.173, 182*v*-183*r* (*Jacobus Obrech*)
• I-Rvat, C.G.XIII.27, No.55, 67*v*-68*r* (*Jacobus Obrech*)
4. Ambros, *Geschichte*, v, 36–39 • Brown, *Florentine*, music volume, 173–75 • Obrecht, *Werken*, vii, 43–45

La tromba sona   [Anon.]   4vv
1. *18*, No.54, 56*v* (Anon.) • *40*, No.54, 56*v* (Anon.)
4. Cesari, *Frottole*, 135

La virtu mi fa guerra   **Dupre**   4vv
1. *36*, No.47, 39*r* (E. DVPRE)

La virtu si vole seguire
See **In eterno io voglio amarte**   **Cara**   4vv

Lachrime e voi suspiri   [Anon.]   4vv
1. *23*, No.71 (Anon.) • *37*, No.71 (Anon.)
4. Schwartz, *Frottole*, 71
Intabulation: voice and lute
1. *49*, No.23 (Anon. Text opens *Lagrime*); *58*, No.23 (Anon. Text opens *Lagrime*)
4. Disertori, *Frottole*, 348

Lamentomi damore   **Nicolo**   4vv
1. *17*, No.47 (Anon.) • *42*, No.47 (*Nico. Pa.*)
4. Cesari, *Frottole*, 85

Lassa donna i dolci sguardi   [Anon.]   4vv
                                            (Tromboncino)
1. *26*, No.26 (Anon.)
3. I-Fc, 2441, No.22, 24*v*-25*r* (Anon.)
Text by Galeotto del Carretto
Intabulation: lute accompaniment to a Superius
3. F-Pn, 27, No.55, 42*v* (Anon.)
Comments: This frottola is presumably the one cited in a letter of Cariteo (14.i.1497) to
   Isabella d'Este: *Lassa O Donna i dolci sguardi*
Literature: Einstein, *Madrigal*, i, 45–46

Lassa el cieco dolor   [Anon.]   4vv
1. *23*, No.22 (Anon.) • *37*, No.22 (Anon.)
4. Schwartz, *Frottole*, 59

Lasso io moro   **Dammonis**   4vv
1. *29*, No.66 (Dammonis); *45*, No.66 (Dammonis)
4. Jeppesen, *Laude*, 156

Lasso me chi non so   **Pisano**   ?4vv
1. *67*, No.10 (Pisano. Incomplete)
Text by Petrarch, *Canzoniere*, LXX

Laudate Dio   [Anon.]   4vv
     3. I-MOe, α.F.9.9, No.77, 75v-76r (Anon. Incipit *Laudate idio*)
     4. La Face Bianconi, *Strambotti*, pp. 363–65
     Intabulation: lute
     1. **47**, No.42 (Anon.)
     4. Disertori, *Frottole*, 228

Laudiam lamor divina   **Dammonis**   4vv
     1. **29**, No.13 (Dammonis. Headed *De nativitate*); **45**, No.13 (Dammonis)
     Text by Giustiniani
     4. Jeppesen, *Laude*, 108 • Luisi, *Laudario*, ii, 58

Legno sancto e glorioso   **P. da Lodi**   4vv
     1. **41**, No.14 (*PIERO DA LODI*) • **41**, No.39 (*Piero da lodi*)
     4. Jeppesen, *Laude*, 20–21
     Comments: The two settings are musically identical in the Superius, and have only very
         minor changes (including one error in the first setting) in the lower voices. The order
         of the additional four verses of text is different in the two versions.

Lenchioza mia
     See **Nenccioza**   **Martini**   4vv

Lenzotta mia
     See **Nenciozza mia**   **Japart**   4vv

Li angelici sembianti   [Anon.]   4vv
     1. **23**, No.10 (Anon. Labeled in the index, *Aer de capituli*) • **37**, No.10 (Anon.)
     4. Schwartz, *Frottole*, 51

Liber fui un tempo in foco   **Cara**   4vv
     2/ *Credo ben pero che me ama*
     1. **18**, No.36 (*M.C.*) • **40**, No.36 (*M.C.*)
     4. Cesari, *Frottole*, 122
     Intabulation: voice and lute
     1. **50**, No.30 *M.C.*)
     4. Disertori, *Frottole*, 522–24

Lieta e lalma   **G. Brocco**   4vv
     1. **18**, No.16 (*IO. BRO.*) • **40**, No.16 (*IO. BRO.*)
     4. Cesari, *Frottole*, 104

Ligiermente o cor credesti
     2/ of **Occhi mei troppo guardasti**   **d'Ana**   4vv

Lirum bililirum   **Rossino**   4vv
     1. **17**, No.28 (*ROSSINVS MANTVANVS*. Headed *Un sonar de piva in fachinesco*) • **42**, No.28
         (*ROSSINVS MANTVANVS*)
     Facsimile: Cesari, *Frottole*, p. CXXII
     4. Cesari, *Frottole*, 69

Lor fur quelli
     2/ of **Quei che sempre han da penare**   **Cara**   4vv

Ma de cancher   **d'Ana**   4vv
     1. **25**, No.10 (*F.V.* in the index)

Madre che festi collui   **Dammonis**   4vv
     1. **29**, No.29 (Dammonis. Headed *Ad beatam virginem*. The first letter of *Madre* is lacking);
       45, No.29 (Dammonis)

Text by Giustiniani

4. Jeppesen, *Laude*, 126–27 • Luisi, *Laudario*, ii, 61–62

Mal fai signora mia   **Nicolo**   4vv

   1. *17*, No.45 (Anon.) • *42*, No.45 (*Nico. Pa.*)

   4. Cesari, *Frottole*, 84

Mal un muta   **Cara**   4vv

   1. *36*, No.38 (*M.C.*)

   4. Prizer, *Courtly*, ii, 82–84

Maledecto sia la fede   [Anon.]   4vv

   1. *26*, No.7 (Anon.)

Maria del ciel regina   **Dammonis**   4vv

  2/ *Porzi soccorso o verzene gentile*

   1. *29*, No.30 (Dammonis. Headed *De beata virgine*); *45*, No.30 (Dammonis)

   Text by Giustiniani, with the incipit *Madre* . . .

   4. Jeppesen, *Laude*, 128–31 • Luisi, *Laudario*, ii, 63–66

Maria drentalla tua corta   **Dammonis**   4vv

   1. *29*, No.35 (Dammonis. Headed *Ad beatam virginem*); *45*, No.29 (Dammonis)

   4. Luisi, *Laudario*, ii, 338–40

Maria madre de Dio   **Dammonis**   4vv

  2/ *Vergine sacra e figlia del tuo figlio*

   1. *29*, No.32 (Dammonis. Headed *Ad beatam virginem*); *45*, No.32 (Dammonis)

   Text by Giustiniani

   4. Jeppesen, *Laude*, 133–35 • Luisi, *Laudario*, ii, 67–70

Maria misericordia   **Dammonis**   4vv

   1. *29*, No.31 (Dammonis. Headed *Ad beatam virginem*); *45*, No.31 (Dammonis)

   Text by Giustiniani

   4. Jeppesen, *Laude*, 132 • Luisi, *Laudario*, ii, 71–72

Me stesso incolpo   **Tromboncino/Cara**   4vv

   1. *23*, No.30 (Anon.) • *37*, No.30 (Anon.) • *41*, No.21 (*B.T. & M.C.* Text *Sancta Maria ora pro nobis*)

   Text by Serafino

   4. Jeppesen, *Laude*, 31 • Schwartz, *Frottole*, 64

   Comments: Given the sequence in which Paolo Scotto's works are ascribed to him *Cantus et verba*, it may be that Tromboncino wrote the music, and Cara the words for the lauda version.

Mentre che a tua belta   **Cara**   4vv

   1. *23*, No.23 (*M.C.* Headed *Sonetto*) • *37*, No.23 (*M.C.*)

   4. Schwartz, *Frottole*, 60

Mentre che gliocchi giro   **Lulinus**   4vv

   1. *56*, No.47 (*Io. lu. V.*)

   4. Luisi & Zanovello, *Frottole*, 213

Merce ha per mi spento   [Anon.]   4vv

   1. *23*, No.31(Anon.) • *37*, No.31 (Anon.)

   3. I-Mt, 55, No.9, 9v–10r (Anon. Text *Mercede ha* . . .)

   4. Jeppesen, *Frottola*, iii, 195–96 • Schwartz, *Frottole*, 65

Mha pur gionto   **Tromboncino**   4vv
    1. *18*, No.18 (*B. T.*) • *40*, No.18 (*B. T.*)
    4. Cesari, *Frottole*, 106

Mi fa sol o mia dea   **Nicolo**   4vv
    1. *23*, No.27 (*N.P.*) • *37*, No.27 (*N.P.*)
    4. Schwartz, *Frottole*, 62

Mi parto a dio   **Antenore**   4vv
    1. *17*, No.42 (Anon.) • *42*, No.42 (*Honophrius Antenoreus*)
    4. Cesari, *Frottole*, 83

Mia benigna fortuna   [Anon.]   4vv
    1. *48*, No.47 (Anon.)
    Text by Petrarch
    4. Facchin & Zanovello, *Frottole*, 208
    Intabulation: voice and lute
    1. *49*, No.30 (Anon.); *58*, No.30 (Anon.)
    4. Disertori, *Frottole*, 360–61

Mia crudele e iniqua sorte
    2/ of **Perso ho in tutto**   **Cara**   4vv

Morir voglio in la mia fede   [Anon.]   4vv
    1. *17*, No.30 (Anon.) • *42*, No.30 (Anon.)
    4. Cesari, *Frottole*, 72

Moro di doglia   [Anon.]   3vv
    1. *26*, No.3 (Anon.)
    Text by Giustiniani: 2/ of *Io vedo ben che'l buon servire* (Cf. *Aime ch'a torto*)
    4. Disertori, *Frottole*, 252–54 • Haar, "Petrucci", 20–22 • Luisi, *Laudario*, ii, 240–41.

Morte te prego che di tanti affanni   **Tromboncino**   4vv
    1. *23*, No.9 (*B. T.*) • *37*, No.9 (*B. T.*)
    3. ZA-Csa, Grey, No.45, 74*v*–75*r* (Anon.)
    4. Schwartz, *Frottole*, 50–51

Mostra lieto al tuo amatore   [Anon.]   4vv
    1. *56*, No.30 (Anon.)
    4. Luisi & Zanovello, *Frottole*, 169

Naque al mondo per amare   **Tromboncino**   4vv
    1. *18*, No.5 (*B. T.*) • *40*, No.5 (*B. T.*)
    Text by Calmeta
    4. Cesari, *Frottole*, 96 • Schwartz, *Frottole*, 40
    Intabulation: lute accompaniment to a Superius
    3. F-Pn, 27, No.58, 43*r* (Anon.)

Naqui al mondo per stentare   **d'Ana**   4vv
    1. *16*, No.59 (*FRANCISCUS ANNA VENETUS.*)
    4. Cesari, *Frottole*, 40

Nasce la speme mia   **Cara**   4vv
    1. *48*, No.2 (*M.C.*. Headed *Aer di capitoli*)
    4. Facchin & Zanovello, *Frottole*, 111 • Pirrotta, "Orfei", 95

Nasce laspro mio tormento   **d'Ana**   4vv
    1. *17*, No.8 (*FRAN. VENE. ORGA.*) • *42*, No.8 (*FRAN. VENE. ORGA.*)

3. GB-Lbl, Eg.3051, No.34, 39*v*–40*r* (Anon.) • I-Fn, 230, No.79, 77*v*–78*r* (Anon.) • I-Fn, 337, No.30, 40*v* (Anon.)

4. Ambros, *Geschichte*, V, 536 • Cesari, *Frottole*, 52

Intabulation: voice and lute

1. **49**, No.24 (*F.V.*); **58**, No.24 (*F.V.*)

4. Disertori, *Frottole*, 350–51

Intabulation: lute accompaniment to a Superius

3. F-Pn, 27, No.101, 51*r* (Anon.)

Ne le tue braze o vergene maria   **Lurano**   4vv

1. **41**, No.56 (*F.D.L.*)

Facsimile: Luisi, *Laudario*, pl.XIV

Text by Giustiniani

4. Jeppesen, *Laude*, 92 • Luisi, *Laudario*, ii, 79–80

Nel mover de quei dolci lumi   [Anon.]   4vv

1. **26**, No.61 (Anon.)

Nel tempo che riveste   **Lulinus**   4vv

1. **56**, No.48 (*Io. Lu. V.*)

3. I-Vnm, IV.1795–1798, No.10 (Anon.)

4. Luisi, *Apografo*, 23–25 • Luisi & Zanovello, *Frottole*, 216

Nel to furore   **Dammonis**   4vv

1. **29**, No.60 (Dammonis); **45**, No.60 (Dammonis)

4. Jeppesen, *Laude*, 153

Nella stagion chel ciel   **Pisano**   4vv

2/ *Canzon se lesser meco*

1. **67**, No.8 (Pisano)

3. I-Fn, 164–167, No.6, 7*v*–9*v* (Anon.)

Text by Petrarch, *Canzoniere*, L.

4. Pisano, *Collected Works*

Nenciozza mia   **Japart**   4vv

1. **1**, No.7 (*Japart.*) • **5**, No.7 (*Japart.*) • **14**, No.7 (*Japart.*) In all three editions, the incipit is given as *Lenzotta mia* in the index.

3. CH-SGs, 461, pp. 60–61 (*Japart.* Incipit *Ve mozza mia*) • I-Fn, 229, No.103, 105*v*–106*r* (*Jannes Japart*)

4. Brown, *Florentine*, music volume, 208–10 • Hewitt, *Odhecaton*, 233–34 • Schering, *Geschichte*, p. 66

Intabulation: keyboard

3. CH-SGs, 530, No.89 (Anon. Incipit *Lenziota mia*)

Nenccioza   **Martini**   4vv

1. **12**, No.78 (*Jo. martini*)

3. E-Sc, 5-I-43, No.158, q10*v*–r1*r*/130*v*–131*r* (Anon. Text incipit *Lenchioza mia*)

4. Martini, *Secular*, 55–57 • Moerk, *Seville*, ii, 390–92 • Strohm, *Rise*, 555–56

Noi lamazone siamo   **Lurano**   4vv

1. **48**, No.43 (*PHI. D. L.*)

4. Facchin & Zanovello, *Frottole*, 197 • Gallucci, *Festival*, ii, 337–40

Comment: Prize, "Facciamo", regards this as a carnival song from Rome

Noi . . .

See also **Nui** . . .

Non al suo amante   **Stringari**   4vv

    1. *56*, No.41 (*A. P.*)

    Text by Petrarch, *Canzoniere*, LII

    4. Luisi, *Cantar*, 455–56 • Luisi & Zanovello, *Frottole*, 196

Non biancho marmo   **d'Ana**   4vv

    1. *23*, No.32 (*F.V.*) • *37*, No.32 (*F.V.*)

    3. I-Mt, 55, No.10, 10*v*-11*r* (Anon.) • I-MOe, α.F.9.9, No.19, 21*v*-22*r* (Anon.)

    4. Jeppesen, *Frottola*, iii, 197–98 • La Face Bianconi, *Strambotti*, 243–45 • Schwartz, *Frottole*, 65

Non bisogna che contrasta   **Cesena**   4vv

    1. *18*, No.12 (*P.C.*) • *40*, No.12 (*P.C.*)

    4. Cesari, *Frottole*, 102

Non de tardar   [Anon.]   4vv

    1. *25*, No.7, 8*v* (Anon. Headed *Stramoto*)

Non e pensier chel mio secreto   **Michele** [?Pesenti]   4vv

    1. *35*, No.56 (*D. Mi.*)

    4. Boscolo, *Frottole*, 245

    Intabulation: voice and lute

    1. *50*, No.50 (*D. Mi.*)

    4. Disertori, *Frottole*, 559–61

Non e tempo daspectare   **Cara**   4vv

    1. *16*, No.3 (*M.C.*)

    3. I-Fc, 2441, No.18, 20*v*-21*r* (Anon. Transposed up a second)

    4. Cesari, *Frottole*, 3 • Schering, *Geschichte*, v, 70 • Schwartz, *Frottole*, 2

    Intabulation: voice and lute

    1. *49*, No.44 (*M.C.*); *58*, No.44 (*M.C.*)

    4. Disertori, *Frottole*, 386–87

Non e tempo de tenere   **Nicolo**   4vv

    1. *17*, No.48 (Anon.) • *42*, No.48 (*NI. PA.*)

    4. Cesari, *Frottole*, 86

Non fu si crudo el dipartir   [Anon.]   4vv

    1. *23*, No.13 (Anon.) • *37*, No.13 (Anon.)

    4. Schwartz, *Frottole*, 53

Non la lassar cor mio   **Pisano**   ?4vv

    1. *67*, No.12 (Pisano. Incomplete)

    4. Pisano

Non mi dar piu longhe   **Lurano**   4vv

    1. *23*, No.87 (*PHI. DE. LV.*) • *37*, No.87 (*PHI. DE. LV.*)

    4. Schwartz, *Frottole*, 95

Non mi doglio gia damore   **Michele** [?Pesenti]   4vv

    1. *16*, No.45 (*MICHA.*)

    4. Cesari, *Frottole*, 34 • Schwartz, *Frottole*, 33

Non mi pento esser ligato   **Lulinus**   4vv

    1. *56*, No.49 (*Io. Lu. V.*)

    4. Luisi & Zanovello, *Frottole*, 220

Non peccando altro chel core   **Cara**   4vv
                                                      (Tromboncino)

    1. *36*, No.30 (*M.C.*)

Intabulation: voice and lute

    1. *49*, No.11 (*B.T.*. Text reads . . . *altri* . . .); *58*, No.11 (*B.T.*)

    4. Disertori, *Frottole*, 326–27

Non pensar che mai te lassi   **Pelegrinus**   4vv

    1. *48*, No.42 (*D. PELEGRINVS*)

    3. I-Fn, 337, No.25, 35*v* (Anon.)

    4. Facchin & Zanovello, *Frottole*, 195

Intabulation: lute accompaniment to a Superius

    3. F-Pn, 27, No.35, 38*v* (Anon.)

Non pigliar madonna asegno   **d'Ana**   4vv

    1. *35*, No.35 (*FRAN. ORGA. VENETVS*)

    4. Boscolo, *Frottole*, 195

Non pigliar tanto ardimento   **Tromboncino**   4vv

    1. *25*, No.12 (*B.T.*)

    3. I-Fc, 2441, No.16, 17*v*-19*r* (Anon.)

Intabulation: lute

    3. F-Pn, 27, No.10, 17*r* (Anon.)

Intabulation: lute accompaniment to a Superius

    3. F-Pn, 27, No.44, 40*r* (Anon.)

Non piu saette amor non piu hormai   **Stringari**   4vv

    1. *56*, No.43 (*A. P.*)

Text by Antonio Tebaldeo

    4. Luisi, *Cantar*, 135 • Luisi & Zanovello, *Frottole*, 202

Non po far morte el dolce riso amaro   **Verdelot**   4vv

    1. *68*, 4*r* (Anon.)

    2. 1534[16], No.23 (*Verdelot*. Pitched a fourth higher) • 1536[7]˜1221, No.23 (Verdelot. Pitched a fourth higher) • 1537[10] = V1222, No.23 (Verdelot. Pitched a fourth higher) • 1540[20] = V1228, No.29 (*Verdelot*. Pitched a fourth higher) • 1541[18] = V1229, No.54, p. 49 (*Verdelot*) • 1544[18] = V1230, pp. 43–44 (*Verdelot*) • 1545[19] = V1231 • 1549[33] = V1232 • 1552[26] = V1233 • 1555[33] = V1234 • 1556[27] = V1235 • 1557[26] = V1236, pp. 43–44 (Verdelot) • 1565[20] = V1237 • 1566[22] = V1238

    3. I-Fc, 2495, No.26 (Anon. Pitched a fourth higher) • I-Fn, 122–125, No.12 (Anon. Pitched a fourth higher) • I-MOe, τ.L.11.8, No.25, 25*v*-26*r* (Anon.)

Text by Petrarch, *Sonnetti*

    4. Haar, "Early", 184–88 • Verdelot, *Madrigals*, xxix, 84–87

Comments: If in fact written by Verdelot, this is clearly his earliest printed madrigal, and affects our view of his activity as much as it does the provenance of the contents of Petrucci's edition.

Non po lolmo

  See **Se de fede hor vengo**   **Cara**   4vv

Non poi perche non voi   [Anon.]   4vv

    1. *18*, No.40 (Anon.) • *40*, No.40 (Anon.)

    4. Cesari, *Frottole*, 126

Non posso abandonarte   Cesena   4vv
> 1. *18*, No.25 (*P.C.*) • *40*, No.25 (*P.C.*)
> 4. Cesari, *Frottole*, 112 • Disertori, *Frottole*, 170–72

Non posso haver pacientia   [Anon.]   4vv
> 1. *26*, No.56 (Anon.)

Non posso liberar me   [Anon.]   4vv
> 1. *48*, No.34 (Anon.)
> 4. Facchin & Zanovello, *Frottole*, 181

Non potra mai dir amore   Lulinus   4vv
> 1. *56*, No.58 (*Io. Lu. V.*)
> Text by Poliziano
> 4. Luisi & Zanovello, *Frottole*, 243

Non se muta el mio volere   Tromboncino   4vv
> 1. *25*, No.22 (*T.* in the index)

Non si po quel che si vole   Lurano   4vv
> 1. *26*, No.57 (*PHI. D. L.*)
> Intabulation: voice and lute
> 1. *49*, No.69 (*PHI. D. L.*); *58*, No.69 (*PHI. D. L.*)
> 4. Disertori, *Frottole*, 430–31

Non si vedra gia mai stanca   Capreolus   4vv
> 1. *36*, No.10 (*A.C.*)
> Text by Bembo, from *Gli Asolani*
> Intabulation: voice and lute
> 1. *50*, No.28 (*A.C.*. Texted *Non si vedra mai stanca*)
> 4. Disertori, *Frottole*, 520–21 • Rubsamen, *Literary*, 63

Non si vedra mai stanca
>   See **Non si vedra gia mai stanca**   Capreolus   4vv

Non so perche non mora   Cesena   4vv
> 1. *17*, No.6 (*P.C.V.*) • *42*, No.6 (*P.C.V.*)
> 4. Cesari, *Frottole*, 51

Non son ciecho   [Anon.]   4vv
> 1. *26*, No.28 (Anon.)

Non son quel che solea   Lurano   4vv
> 1. *26*, No.1 (*PHI. D. L.*)
> Intabulation: voice and lute
> 1. *49*, No.67 (*PHI.D. L.*); *58*, No.67 (*PHI.D. L.*)
> 4. Disertori, *Frottole*, 426–27

Non tardar o diva mia   Antiquis   4vv
> 1. *48*, No.41 (*A. D. A.*)
> 3. I-Fn, 337, No.87, 94*v* (Anon. Untexted)
> 4. Facchin & Zanovello, *Frottole*, 193 • Juverini *et a*, *Frottole*, 71 • Zupanovic, *Sedamnaest frottola*

Non te smarir cor mio   [Anon.]   5 ex 4vv
> 1. *23*, No.47 (Anon. Tenor has the rubric *A fin et retro*) • *37*, No.47 (Anon. Tenor has the rubric *Ante et retro*)
> 3. GB-Lbl, Eg.3051, No.8, 10*v*–11*r* (Anon.)
> 4. Schwartz, *Frottole*, 73

Non temer chio ti lassi   **Scotto**   4vv

     I. *36*, No.17 (*PAVLI SCOTI CANTVS & VERBA*)

Non temer del vechio amore   **Tromboncino**   4vv

     I. *35*, No.4 (*B.T.*)

     4. Boscolo, *Frottole*, 120

Non temo de brusciar   **Tromboncino**   4vv

     I. *23*, No.48 (*B.T.*) • *37*, No.48 (*B.T.*)

     4. Schwartz, *Frottole*, 74

Non ti grava el mie partire

     See **Se me e grato el tuo tornare**   **Lurano**   4vv

Non val aqua al mio gran foco   **Tromboncino**   4vv

     I. *16*, No.20 (*B.T.*)

     Facsimile: Cesari, *Frottole*, p. LXVI

     3. GB-Lbl, Eg.3051, No.20, 22*v*-23*r* (Anon.) • I-Fc, 2441, No.7, 8*v*-9*r* (Anon.)

     4. Cesari, *Frottole*, 15 • Davidson and Apel, *HAM*, 97 • Schwartz, *Frottole*, 14

     Intabulation: voice and lute

     I. *50*, No.24 (*B.T.*)

     4. Disertori, *Frottole*, 510–11

     Intabulation: lute accompaniment to a Superius

     3. F-Pn, 27, No.72, 46*r* (Anon.)

Non val aqua al mio gran foco

     Altus of **Glie pur gionto el giorno**   **Cara**   4vv

Nostra interna & vera pace   **Dammonis**   4vv

     I. *29*, No.50 (Dammonis. Headed *De pace Eiusdem verba*); *45*, No.50 (Dammonis)

     4. Luisi, *Laudario*, ii, 341–43

Nui siam tutti amartelati   **Tromboncino**   4vv

     I. *48*, No.21 (*B.T.*)

     4. Facchin & Zanovello, *Frottole*, 156 • Gallucci, *Festival*, ii, 341–44 • Osthoff, *Theatergesang*, ii, 159–60

     Comment: Prize, "Facciamo", regards this as a carnival song from Ferrara or Mantua

Nui siamo segatori   **Stringari**   5vv

     I. *35*, No.50 (*Antonius stringarius patavus*)

     4. Boscolo, *Frottole*, 234 • Gallucci, *Festival*, ii, 345–48

     Comment: Prize, "Facciamo", regards this as a carnival song from northern Italy

Nunque fu pena magiore

     See Spanish texts

O bella man che me destrugi el core   **Eustache de Monte Regali**   4vv

     I. *56*, No.18 (*Eu. D. M. Regali Gallus.*)

     Text by Petrarch, *Sonnetti*, CIC

     4. Eustachio Romano, *Musica*, 168–70 • Luisi & Zanovello, *Frottole*, 141

O bon egli bon   **Cara**   4vv

                                               (Pesenti)

     I. *25*, No.4 (*D.M.* in the index)

     4. Haar, "Chanson", 254

     Intabulation: voice and lute

     I. *50*, No.23 (*M.C.*)

     4. Disertori, *Frottole*, 505–506

O caldi mei suspiri   Cara   4vv
     1. **23**, No.20 (*M.C.*) • **37**, No.20 (*M.C.*)
     4. Schwartz, *Frottole*, 58

O cara libertade   [Anon.]   4vv
     1. **26**, No.59 (Anon.)
     Intabulation: voice and lute
     1. **49**, No.61 (Anon.); **58**, No.61 (Anon.)
     4. Disertori, *Frottole*, 417

O celeste anime sancte   Cara   4vv
     1. **48**, No.31 (*M.C.*)
     4. Facchin & Zanovello, *Frottole*, 176 • Prizer, *Courtly*, 440

O che dio non maiute mai   [Anon.]   4vv
     1. **26**, No.38 (Anon.)

O croce alma mirabile   Dammonis   4vv
     1. **29**, No.49 (Dammonis. Headed *De cruce*); **45**, No.49 (Dammonis)
     Text by Giustiniani
     4. Luisi, *Laudario*, ii, 81–82

O despietato tempo   Bisan   4vv
     1. **36**, No.62 (*P. ZANIN BISAN.*)
     Intabulation: voice and lute
     1. **49**, No.19 (*P. Zanin Bisan.*); **58**, No.19 (*P. Zanin Bisan.*)
     4. Disertori, *Frottole*, 340–41
     Intabulation: lute accompaniment to a Superius
     3. F-Pn, 27, No.90, 49r (Anon. Incipit *Hai dispietato tempo*)

O Dio che la brunetta mia   Michele [?Pesenti]   4vv
                                                         (Festa)
     1. **16**, No.40 (*MICHA. C. & V.*)
     3. I-Fc, 2440, No.35, pp. 122–23 (Anon. Text *O me che la brunetta mia*) • I-Fn, 230, No.31, 30v–31r (*pre michele*) • I-Fn, 337, No.74, 82r (Anon. Text *Oime che la signore mia*) • I-Fn, 164–167, No.33, 44v–45r (Anon.)
     2. The following sources are à3: Festa 1543, No.21 (Festa) • 1547[15], No.21 (Festa)
     4. Cesari, *Frottole*, 31 • Schwartz, *Frottole*, 29

O dolce diva mia   Cesena   4vv
     1. **17**, No.24 (*P.C.V.*) • **42**, No.24 (*P.C.V.*)
     4. Cesari, *Frottole*, 66

O dolce e lieto albergo   [Anon.]   4vv
     1. **23**, No.77 (Anon.) • **37**, No.77 (Anon.)
     4. Schwartz, *Frottole*, 90
     Intabulation: voice and lute
     1. **49**, No.4 (Anon.); **58**, No.4 (Anon.)
     4. Disertori, *Frottole*, 314

O fallaca speranza   Scotto   4vv
     1. **35**, No.1 (*PAVLVS SCOTVS. C. & V.*)
     4. Ambros, *Geschichte*, V, 535 • Boscolo, *Frottole*, 113 • Westphal, *Karnevalslieder*, 10

O gloriosa colonna in cui sapoggia nostra speranza   Eustache de Monte Regali   4vv
     1. **56**, No.19 (*Eu. De. M. Regali gallus.*)

Text by Petrarch, *Canzoniere*, X

    4. Eustachio Romano, *Musica*, 168 • Luisi & Zanovello, *Frottole*, 143

O gloriosa vergine maria   **Dammonis**   4vv

    1. **29**, No.18 (Dammonis. Headed *Ad beatam virginem*); **45**, No.18 (Dammonis)

Text by Giustiniani

    4. Jeppesen, *Laude*, 117 • Luisi, *Laudario*, ii, 87

O iesu dolce o infinito amore   **Dammonis**   4vv

    1. **29**, No.62 (Dammonis. Not entered in the index); **45**, No.62 (Dammonis)

Facsimile: Luisi, *Laudario*, ii, pl.XIII

Text by Giustiniani

    4. Luisi, *Laudario*, ii, 91–92 • Wilson, *Music*, 277–78

O iesu dolce o signor benigno   **Baldasar**   4vv

    1. **41**, No.26 (*Baldasar*)

    4. Jeppesen, *Laude*, 38 • Ninot, *Collected Works*, 126

    Comment: Barton Hudson, *Grove 6*, xiii, 251, assigns this work to Ninot le Petit

O madre del signore   **Dammonis**   4vv

  2/ Sposa del padre eterno

    1. **29**, No.28 (Dammonis. Headed *Te matrem*. The index also lists the work under *Te matrem*;
        45, No.28 (Dammonis)

    4. Luisi, *Laudario*, ii, 344–46

O madre sancta o luce   **Dammonis**   4vv

    1. **29**, No.27 (Dammonis); **45**, No.27 (Dammonis)

    4. Jeppesen, *Laude*, 124–25

O Maria divina stella   **Dammonis**   4vv

    1. **29**, No.26 (Dammonis. Headed *De beata virgine*); **45**, No.26 (Dammonis)

    4. Jeppesen, *Laude*, 122–23

O me che la brunetta mia

  See **O Dio che la brunetta mia**   **Michele** [?Pesenti]   4vv

O mia cieca e dura sorte   **Cara**   4vv

    1. **16**, No.5 (*M.C.*)

    3. I-Fc, 2441, No.34, 36*v*–37*r* (Anon.) • I-Fn, 230, No.28, 27*v* 28*r* (Anon.)

    4. Cesari, *Frottole*, 5 • Schwartz, *Frottole*, 3

Intabulation: lute

    3. US-Cn, 107501, No.5, 9*r*–10*r* (Anon. Headed *O mia ciecha edura sorte seguita nel ton del
        secondo recerchar.* cf. also *Che faralla che diralla* by Cara)

Intabulation: voice and lute

    1. **49**, No.25 (Anon.); **58**, No.25 (Anon.)

    4. Disertori, *Frottole*, 352–53

O mia infelice sorte   [Anon.]   4vv

    1. **23**, No.82 (Anon.) • **37**, No.82 (Anon.)

    3. I-Fn, Panc.27, No.38, 23*v*–24*r* (Anon.)

    4. Schwartz, *Frottole*, 93

O mia spietata sorte   [Anon.]   4vv

    1. **23**, No.72 (Anon.) • **37**, No.72 (Anon.)

    2. 1510, No.22, 22*v* (Anon.)

    4. Schwartz, *Frottole*, 89

Intabulation: lute accompaniment to a Superius

    3. F-Pn, 27, No.93, 50r (Anon.)

O mischini osiagurati   [Anon.]   4vv

    1. **26**, No.46 (Anon.)

    4. Gallucci, *Festival*, ii, 349–53 • Luisi, *Cantar*, 216–17

    Comments: Prize, "Facciamo", regards this as a carnival song from northern Italy

O peccatore ti moverai tu mai   **Dammonis**   4vv

    1. **29**, No.48 (Dammonis. Headed *De passione*); **45**, No.48 (Dammonis)

    Text by Giustiniani

    4. Luisi, *Laudario*, ii, 96–98

O selve o sparse gregge

    See **O selve sparse egregie**   **Stringari**   4vv

O selve sparse egregie   **Stringari**   4vv

    1. **25**, No.53 (Anon.)

    Intabulation: voice and lute

    1. **50**, No.55 (*An. Pattavinus*)

    4. Disertori, *Frottole*, 580–81

O sola mia salute   **Pifaro**   4vv

    1. **35**, No.27 (*NICOLO PIFARO*)

    4. Boscolo, *Frottole*, 174

O stella matutina   **Dammonis**   4vv

    1. **29**, No.54 (Dammonis. Headed *Ad beatam Virginem*); **45**, No.54 (Dammonis)

    Text by Giustiniani

    4. Jeppesen, *Laude*, 147 • Luisi, *Laudario*, ii, 99–100

O suave e dolce Dea   [Anon.]   4vv

    1. **26**, No.13 (Anon.)

O suspir suave

    See **Suspir suave**   **Tromboncino**   4vv

O tanti mei suspiri   [Anon.]   4vv

    1. **23**, No.64 (Anon.) • **37**, No.64 (Anon.)

    4. Schwartz, *Frottole*, 89

O tempo o ciel volubil   **Scotto**   4vv

    1. **48**, No.10 (Anon.)

    4. Facchin & Zanovello, *Frottole*, 130

    Text by Petrarch

    Intabulation: voice and lute

    1. **50**, No.56 (*Pauli Scotti*)

    4. Disertori, *Frottole*, 582

O tiente a lora   **N. Brocco**   4vv

    1. **35**, No.45 (*N.B.*)

    4. Boscolo, *Frottole*, 223 • Torrefranca, *Segreto*, 515

    Literature: Luisi, "Il Tentalora"

O vero amor celesta   **Dammonis**   4vv

    1. **29**, No.40 (Dammonis. Headed *De infervorato christi amore*); **45**, No.40 (Dammonis)

    Text by Giustiniani

    4. Luisi, *Laudario*, ii, 101–104

Ochi dolce a che almen   **Cara**   4vv

    1. *48*, No.18 (*M.C.*)

    4. Facchin & Zanovello, *Frottole*, 150 • Prizer, *Courtly*, 435

Occhi dolci ove prendesti   **d'Ana**   4vv

  2/ Sel mio ben da voi deriva

    1. *17*, No.11 (*FRANCISCVS VENETVS ORGA.*) • *42*, No.11 (*FRANCISCVS VENETVS ORGA.*)

    3. GB-Lbl, Eg.3051, No.41, 46*v*-48*r* (Anon.)

    4. Cesari, *Frottole*, 55

    Intabulation: lute

    3. F-Pn, 27, No.20, 24*v* (Anon.)

    Intabulation: lute accompaniment to a Superius

    3. F-Pn, 27, No.81, 48*r* (Anon.)

Occhi mei al pianger nati   [Anon.]   4vv

    1. *17*, No.15 (Anon.) • *42*, No.15 (Anon.)

    4. Cesari, *Frottole*, 60

Ochii mei frenati el pianto   **Cesena**   4vv

    1. *17*, No.21 (*PEREGRINVS CESENA VERONENSIS.*) • *42*, No.21 (*PEREGRINVS CESENA VERONENSIS*)

    4. Cesari, *Frottole*, 64

Occhi mei lassi acompagnate   **Lulinus**   4vv

    1. *56*, No.59 (*Io. Lu. V.*)

    4. Luisi & Zanovello, *Frottole*, 246

Ochi miei lassi mentre   **Tromboncino**   4vv

    2. 1510, No.41, 41*v*-42*r* (*B.T.*)

    3. I-Vnm, IV.1795–1798, No.22, 20*v*-21*r* (Anon.)

    Text by Petrarch: *Canzoniere*, XIV

    4. Luisi, *Apografo*, 51–53

    Intabulation: keyboard

    2. 1517³, No.9, 16*v*-18*r* (*B.T.*)

    Intabulation: lute

    1. *50*, No.7 (*B.T.*)

    4. Disertori, *Frottole*, 284–89 and 468–470

Ochi mei lassi poi che perso haveti   **Cara**   4vv

    1. *23*, No.15 (*M.C.*) • *37*, No.15 (*M.C.*)

    4. Schwartz, *Frottole*, 55

Ochi mei mai non restati   **Antiquis**   4vv

    1. *36*, No.22 (*A. DE ANTIQVIS.*)

    4. Zupanovic, *Sedamnaest frottola*

Occhi mei troppo guardasti   **d'Ana**   4vv

  2/ Ligiermente o cor credesti

    1. *17*, No.10 ([F]*RANCISCUS VENETUS ORGA.*) • *42*, No.10 (*FRANCISCUS VENETUS ORGA.*)

    4. Cesari, *Frottole*, 54

Occhi piangeti   **Lulinus**   4vv

    1. *56*, No.51 (*Io. Lu. V.*)

Text by Petrarch, *Canzoniere*, LXXXIV
    4. Luisi & Zanovello, *Frottole*, 225

Odi donna el mio tormento
    See **Aldi donna non dormire**   **Lurano**   4vv

Odite voi finestre
    See **Udite voi finestre**   **Cara**   4vv

Ogni amor vol esser vero   **Capreolus**   4vv
    1. **23**, No.2 (*ANT. CAP.*) • **37**, No.2 (*ANT. CAP.*)
    4. Schwartz, *Frottole*, 45

Ogni ben fa la fortuna   **Cara**   4vv
    2/ *Pone un basso e lattro in cielo*
    1. **18**, No.31 (*M.C.*) • **40**, No.31 (*M.C.*)
    3. GB-Lbl, Eg.3051, No.22, 24v–26r (Anon.)
    4. Cesari, *Frottole*, 115

Ogni cosa ha el suo locho   [Anon.]   3vv
    1. **26**, No.65 (Anon.)
    3. I-Mt, 55, No.47, 49v–50r (Anon. Texted *Hogni Cosa val suo locho*)
    4. Disertori, *Frottole*, 264–67 • Giazotto, "Onde", 85–86 • Jeppesen, *Frottola*, iii, 288–90

Ogni impresa sia felice   [Anon.]   4vv
    1. **25**, No.17 (Anon.)

Ogni vermo al suo veneno   **Nicolo**   4vv
    1. **25**, No.9 (Anon: *N.P.* in the index)
    2. 1510, No.14, 15v–16r (Anon.)

Ogni volta crudel ch'io mi lamento   **Tromboncino**   4vv
    1. **56**, No.3 (*B.T.*)
    4. Luisi & Zanovello, *Frottole*, 103

Ognun driza al ciel el viso   [Anon.]   4vv
    1. **41**, No.42 (Anon.)
    4. Jeppesen, *Laude*, 63

Ognun fuga fuga amore   **Capreolus**   4vv
    1. **23**, No.63 (*ANT. CAP.*) • **37**, No.63 (*ANT. CAP.*)
    2. 1510, No.10, 11v–12r (*Ant. Cap.*)
    4. Riemann, *Handbuch*, 354 • Schwartz, *Frottole*, 83
    Intabulation: voice and lute
    1. **49**, No.52 (*Ant. Cap.*); **58**, No.52 (*Ant. Cap.*)
    4. Disertori, *Frottole*, 400–401

Oyme che ho perso il core   **Cesena**   4vv
    1. **17**, No.23 (*P.C.V.*) • **42**, No.23 (*P.C.V.*)
    4. Cesari, *Frottole*, 65

Oyme che io sento al core   **G. Brocco**   4vv
    1. **18**, No.14 (*IO. BRO.*) • **40**, No.14 (*IO. BRO.*)
    4. Cesari, *Frottole*, 103

Oime che la signore mia
    See **O dio che la brunetta mia**   **Pesenti**   4vv

Oime el cor oime la testa   **Cara**   4vv
    1. **16**, No.2 (*MARCUS CARA VERO.*)
    Facsimile: Besseler & Gülke, "Schriftbild", 129

3. F-Pn, 676, No.4, 11*v*-12*r* (*Marcheto*) • I-Fc, 2441, No.6, 7*v*-8*r* (Anon. à3) • I-Fn, Panc.27, No.3, 12*v*-13*r* (Anon.)

4. Cesari, *Frottole*, 3 • Schwartz, *Frottole*, 1 • Underwood, *Renaissance*, 234–35

Intabulation: voice and lute

1. **49**, No.43 (*M.C.* Text *Oime il cor*); **58**, No.43 (*M.C.* Text *Oime il cor*)

4. Disertori, *Frottole*, 384–85 • Reese, "First", 16

Intabulation: lute accompaniment to a Superius

3. F-Pn, 27, No.71, 46*r* (Anon. Incipit *Oime lo capo oime la testa*)

4. Underwood, *Renaissance*, 237

Oime il bel viso	**Eustachio Romano**	4vv

1. **56**, No.31 (*Eustachius. De M. Romanus.*)

Text by Petrarch, *Sonnetti*, CCLXVII

4. Eustachio Romano, *Musica*, 157–60 • Luisi & Zanovello, *Frottole*, 174

Oime lo capo oime la testa

See **Oime el core oime la testa**	**Cara**	4vv

Oime

See also **Aime, Ayme, Haime**

Or che son de preson

See **Hor chio son de preson**	**Tromboncino**	4vv

Or su corere voglio

See **Hor sucorrer voglio amore**	[Anon.]	4vv

Ostinato vo seguire	**Tromboncino**	4vv
	(Cara)	

1. **48**, No.15 (*B. T.*)

3. I-Fn, 337, No.12, 22*v* (*March*. Texted *In eterno io voglio amarte*)

4. Facchin & Zanovello, *Frottole*, 142

Intabulation: voice and lute

1. **49**, No.27 (*B. T.*); **58**, No.27 (*B. T.*)

4. Disertori, *Frottole*, 354–56

Pace e gloria al gentil Lauro	[Anon.]	4vv

1. **18**, No.59 (Anon.) • **40**, No.59 (Anon.)

3. GB-Lbl, Eg.3051, No.19, 21*v*-22*r* (Anon.)

4. Cesari, *Frottole*, 139 • Disertori, *Frottole*, 124–27

Pace hormai che adiscoprire	[Anon.]	4vv
	(Tromboncino)	

1. **25**, No.14 (Anon.)

Comments: This frottola is possibly the one cited in a letter of Cariteo (14.i.1497) to Isabella d'Este: *Pace hormai i miei sospiri*, attributed there to Tromboncino.

Literature: Einstein, *Madrigal*, 45–46

Pace hormai su non piu guerra	[Anon.]	4vv

1. **17**, No.32 (Anon.) • **42**, No.32 (Anon.)

4. Cesari, *Frottole*, 74

Pace non trovo	**Eustachio Romano**	4vv

1. **56**, No.10 (*Eustachius. De M. Romanus*)

Text by Petrarch, *Sonnetti*, CXXXIV

4. Eustachio Romano, *Musica*, 161–63 • Luisi & Zanovello, *Frottole*, 123

Pago el dacio donna   [Anon.]   4vv
    1. **26**, No.30 (Anon.)

Palle palle   Isaac   4vv
    3. CH-Bu, F.X.21, No.28, 32*v* (Anon. Headed *La bella*) • D-Ga, Königsberg 7 (Anon.
    Alleluia Hodie / Gloria tibi) • F-Pn, 1817, No.40 (Anon.) • I-CT, 95–96, No.37, 38*r*-39*r*
    (Anon.) • I-Fn, 107bis, No.27, 43*r* (Anon. Incomplete) • I-Fn, 117, No.51, 59*v*-61*r* (*Yzac*)
    • I-Rvat, C.G.XIII.27, No.1, 7*v*-9*r* (*H. Isach*) • US-Wc, Wolffheim, 82*v*-83*r* (Anon. Un-
    texted)
    4. Disertori, *Frottole*, 188–92 • Isaac, *Weltliche*, 98–99
    Intabulation: lute
      1. **34**, No.11 (*Palle de ysach*; and *Francesco Spinacino*)
      4. Disertori, *Frottole*, 188–92 • Isaac, *Weltliche*, 161–62 • Schmidt, *Spinacino*, ii, 203–206
    Literature: Atlas, *Giulia*, i, 49–55 • Atlas, "Palle"

Pan de miglio   [Anon.]   4vv
    1. **26**, No.31 (Anon.)
    4. Gallucci, *Festival*, ii, 354–56 • Luisi, *Cantar*, 211
    Comment: Prize, "Facciamo", regards this as a carnival song from northern Italy

Partiale e cruda morte
    See **Ah partiale e cruda morte**   Tromboncino   4vv

Passando per una rezolla   Michele [?Pesenti]   4vv
    1. **16**, No.48 (*MICHA.*)
    4. Cesari, *Frottole*, 35 • Schwartz, *Frottole*, 34

Passato el tempo iocondo   Tromboncino
    Intabulation: voice and lute
      1. **50**, No.17 (*B.T.*)
      4. Disertori, *Frottole*, 492

Passero la vita mia   [Anon.]   4vv
    1. **26**, No.47 (Anon.)
    Intabulation: lute accompaniment to a Superius
      3. F-Pn, 27, No.29, 37*r* (Anon.)

Passo passo pian   d'Ana   4vv
    1. **23**, No.37 (*F.V.*) • **37**, No.37 (*F.V.*)
    4. Schwartz, *Frottole*, 68

Patientia ognum me dice   [Anon.]   4vv
    2/ *Io sto male a vivo in stento*
      3. F-Pn, 676, 18*v*-19*r* (Anon.) • I-Fn, Panc.27, No.116, 80*v*-81*r* (Anon.) • ZA-Csa, Grey,
      No.51, 80*v*-82*r* (Anon.)
    Intabulations: lute
      1. **47**, No.41 (Dalza. Not listed in the index)
      3. F-Pn, 27, No.38, 39*r* (Anon.)

Peccatori ad una voce   Dammonis   4vv
    1. **29**, No.63 (Dammonis); **45**, No.63 (Dammonis)
    4. Jeppesen, *Laude*, 154–55

Peccatori perche seti tanto crudi   Dammonis   4vv
    1. **29**, No.43 (Dammonis. Headed *De passione*); **45**, No.43 (Dammonis)
    Text by Giustiniani
    4. Jeppesen, *Laude*, 140–41 • Luisi, *Laudario*, ii, 105–106

Pensa donna chel tempo   **Nicolo**   4vv
    1. **23**, No.28 (*N.P.*: Headed *Sonetto*) • **37**, No.28 (*N.P.* Headed *Sonetto*)
    4. Schwartz, *Frottole*, 62

Pensi che mai
  See **Pensif mari**   **Tadinghem**   3vv

Per amor fata solinga   **Pifaro**   4vv
    1. **35**, No.23 (*NICOLO PIFARO*)
    4. Boscolo, *Frottole*, 162

Per che mhai abandonato   [Anon.]   4vv
    1. **36**, No.19 (Anon.)

Per dolor mi bagno el viso   **Cara**   4vv
                                    (Tromboncino)
    1. **56**, No.23 (*M.C.*)
    2. Frottole II (1518), No.2, 4*v*-6*r* • [c.1516]² (1520), No.2, 4*v*-6*r* (*Marcheto carra*)
    4. Luisi, *Secondo*, ii, 7 • Luisi & Zanovello, *Frottole*, 154
    Intabulation: keyboard
    2. 1517³, No.16, 27*v*-28*r* (*M.C.*)
    Intabulation: voice and lute
    1. **50**, No.2 (*B.T.*)
    4. Disertori, *Frottole*, 459–61

Per fugir damor le ponte   **Cara**   4vv
    2. Frottole II (1518), No.4, 8*v*-10*r* (*M.C.*) • [c.1516]² (1520), No.4, 8*v*-10*r* (*Marcheto carra*)
    4. Luisi, *Secondo*
    Intabulation: voice and lute
    1. **50**, No.8 (*M.C.*)
    4. Disertori, *Frottole*, 474–75

Per memoria di quel giorno   **Pifaro**   4vv
    1. **35**, No.25 (*NI. PI.*)
    4. Boscolo, *Frottole*, 171 • Cesari, *Frottole*, xxxi • Disertori, *Frottole*, 173–75

Per pietade hodite hormai   **Tromboncino**   4vv
    1. **25**, No.43 (*T.* in the index)

Per quella croce ove spargesti el sangue   **Tromboncino**   4vv
    1. **41**, No.7 (*Tromboncino*)
    3. ZA-Csa, Grey, No.52, 82*v*-83*r* (Anon.)
    4. Jeppesen, *Laude*, 12

Per servite perdo i passi   **N. Brocco**   4vv
    1. **35**, No.43 (*N. BROCVS*)
    3. GB-Lbl, Eg.3051, 38*v*-39*r* (Anon.)
    4. Boscolo, *Frottole*, 219

Perche donna non voi   **Pisano**   4vv
  2/ In qualunque ama con perfecto amore
    1. **67**, No.3 (Pisano)
    3. I-Fc, 2440, No.38, 65*v*-68*r* (Anon.) • I-Fn, 164–167, No.10, 14*r*-15*r* (Anon.)
    Text by L. Strozzi
    4. Pisano, *Collected Works*

Perche fai donna el gaton   **Rossino**   4vv
  2/ Gnao gnao gnao vo cridando

1. *18*, No.11 (*ROSSI. MAN.:*) • *40*, No.11 (*ROSSI. MAN.*)

Facsimile: Cesari, *Frottole*, 143

4. Cesari, *Frottole*, 100

Perso ho in tutto hormai la vita   **Cara**   4vv

2/ *Mia crudele e iniqua sorte*

1. *18*, No.32 (*M.C.*) • *40*, No.32 (*M.C.*)

4. Cesari, *Frottole*, 116

Intabulations: lute accompaniment to a Superius

3. F-Pn, 27, No.87, 49r (Anon.) • F-Pn, 27, No.88, 49r (Anon. Headed *Idemque duj medesimi numeri*)

Piangeti christiani

See **Pianzeti christiani**   **Dammonis**   4vv

Piangeti mecho amante   **Nicolo**   4vv

1. *17*, No.44 (Anon.) • *42*, No.44 (*Nicolo Patavino*)

Text by Poliziano

4. Cesari, *Frottole*, 83

Piangeti occhi mie lassi   [Anon.]   4vv

1. *18*, No.8 (Anon. Cantus incipit starts *Aiangeti*) • *40*, No.8 (Anon.)

Text by Poliziano

4. Cesari, *Frottole*, 99

Piango el mio fidel servire   **Fogliano**   4vv

1. *18*, No.37 (Anon.) • *40*, No.37 (Anon.)

3. GB-Lbl, Eg.3051, No.42, 48v-50r (Anon.) • I-Fn, 230, No.2, 1v-2r (*Iacobus foglianus*)

4. Cesari, *Frottole*, 123

Pianzeti christiani il dolor de maria   **Dammonis**   4vv

1. *29*, No.45 (Dammonis. Headed *De passione*. The index reads *Piangeti christiani*); *45*, No.45 (Dammonis)

Text by Giustiniani

4. Jeppesen, *Laude*, 143–44 • Luisi, *Laudario*, ii, 109–10

Pieta cara signora   **Cara**   4vv

1. *16*, No.15 (*M.C.*)

3. I-Fc, 2441, No.29, 31v-32r (Anon.)

4. Cesari, *Frottole*, 12 • Schwartz, *Frottole*, 11

Intabulation: voice and lute

1. *49*, No.66 (*M.C.*) ; *58*, No.66 (*M.C.*)

4. Disertori, *Frottole*, 424–425

Intabulation: lute accompaniment to a Superius

3. F-Pn, 27, No.76, 47r (Anon.)

Pieta cara signore / La pieta ha chiuso le porte   **Erasmo**   4vv
(?Lapicida)

1. *48*, No.5 (*Rasmo*)

4. Facchin & Zanovello, *Frottole*, 117 • Luisi, *Cantar*, 264–265 • Prizer, *Courtly*, ii, 271–76

Piu che mai o sospir fieri   **Tromboncino**   4vv

1. *16*, No.33 (*B.T.*)

4. Cesari, *Frottole*, 25 • Schwartz, *Frottole*, 24

Piu non son pregion damore   **Tromboncino**   4vv

1. *36*, No.66 (*B.T.*)

Piu non tamo haybo   **Cara**   4vv
 1. *48*, No.22 (*M.C.*)
 4. Facchin & Zanovello, *Frottole*, 156
 Intabulation: voice and lute
 1. *49*, No.62 (*M.C.*); *58*, No.62 (*M.C.*)
 4. Disertori, *Frottole*, 418–20

Piu non voglio contrastare   [Anon.]   4vv
 1. *26*, No.44 (Anon.)

Piu speranza non apreggio   **Stringari**   4vv
 1. *35*, No.30 (*ANTONIVS STRINGARIVS PATAVINVS*)
 4. Boscolo, *Frottole*, 178

Piu volte fra me stesso   **Tromboncino**   4vv
 1. *17*, No.33 (Anon.) • *42*, No.33 (Anon.)
 Facsimile: Cesari, *Frottole*, p. CXXIII
 4. Cesari, *Frottole*, 75
 Intabulation: voice and lute
 2. [c.1520][7], No.8, 10*v*-11*v* (*B.T.*)

Piu volte me son messe   [Anon.]   4vv
 1. *25*, No.8 (Anon. Headed *Per sonetti*)

Po piu un sdegno assai   [Anon.]   4vv
 1. *25*, No.27 (Anon.)

Pocha pace e molta guerra   **Tromboncino**   4vv
 1. *25*, No.34 (*T.* in the index)
 3. F-Pn, 676, No.92, 102*v*-103*r* (*Trombetino*) • I-Fn, 337, No.14, 24*v* (Anon.) • I-Fn, Panc.27,
  No.150, 112*v*-113*r* (Anon.)
 Intabulation: lute accompaniment to a Superius
 1. F-Pn, 27, No.50, 41*v* (Anon.)

Poi che a tal condutto   [Anon.]   4vv
 1. *17*, No.31 (Anon.) • *42*, No.31 (Anon.)
 4. Cesari, *Frottole*, 73
 Intabulation: lute accompaniment to a Superius
 3. F-Pn, 27, No.68, 45*v* (Anon.)

Poi che amor con dritta   [Anon.]   4vv
 1. *18*, No.2 (Anon.) • *40*, No.2 (Anon.)
 Facsimile: Cesari, *Frottole*, p. CXXIV
 4. Cesari, *Frottole*, 93

Poiche da me partisti   **Dammonis**   4vv
 1. *29*, No.7 (Dammonis); *45*, No.7 (Dammonis)
 4. Jeppesen, *Laude*, 102

Poi che gionto el tempo   **Lurano**   4vv
 1. *26*, No.20*v* (*P.D.LV.*)
 3. I-Fc, 2441, No.58, 60*v*-61*r* (Anon. Text *De scoprire el mio tormento*) • I-Fn, 230, No.24,
  23*v*-24*r* (*philippus de lurano*. Text *De scoprire el mio tormento*) • I-Fn, 337, No.11, 21*v* (*P. de
  Lo*)
 4. Haar, "Petrucci", 34–35
 Intabulation: lute accompaniment to a Superius
 3. F-Pn, 27, No.70, 46*r* (Anon.)

Poi che ho provato [Anon.] 4vv
    1. *18*, No.7 (Anon.) • *40*, No.7 (Anon.)
    4. Cesari, *Frottole*, 99

Poi chel ciel contrario Tromboncino 4vv
    1. *16*, No.24 (*B. T.*)
    3. I–Bc, Q18, No.9, 9*v* (Anon.) • I–Fc, 2441, No.12, 13*v*–14*r* (Anon.)
    4. Cesari, *Frottole*, 18
    Intabulation: lute
    1. *47*, No.39 (Dalza)
    4. Disertori, *Frottole*, 225–27
    Intabulation: voice and lute
    1. *49*, No.53 (*B. T.*); *58*, No.53 (*B. T.*)
    4. Disertori, *Frottole*, 402–403
    Intabulation: lute accompaniment to a Superius
    3. F–Pn, 27, No.36, 38*v* (Anon.)

Poi chel ciel e la fortuna [Anon.] 4vv
    1. *36*, No.27 (Anon.)
    2. 1510, No.26, 25*v*–26*r* (Anon.)

Poi chel ciel e la fortuna Pesenti 4vv
    1. *16*, No.38 (*MICHA. C. & V.*)
    4. Cesari, *Frottole*, 29 • Schwartz, *Frottole*, 27
    Intabulation: voice and lute
    1. *50*, No.14 (*Michel. V.*)
    4. Disertori, *Frottole*, 483–85

Poi chel ciel e mia ventura Tromboncino 4vv
    1. *36*, No.14 (*B. T.*)
    4. Disertori, *Frottole*, 137–41

Poi che in te donna speravi N. Brocco 4vv
    1. *35*, No.44 (*N. B.*: headed *RESPOSTA*, *i.e.* to Josquin's *In te Domine speravi*)
    4. Boscolo, *Frottole*, 221

Poi chio son damor pregione [Anon.] 4vv
    1. *56*, No.29 (Anon.)
    4. Luisi & Zanovello, *Frottole*, 169

Poi chio son in libertate Stringari 4vv
    1. *35*, No.31 (*ANTONIVS PATA.*)
    4. Boscolo, *Frottole*, 180 • Luisi, *Cantar*, 233–34

Poi chio vado in altra parte Tromboncino 4vv
    1. *36*, No.11 (*B. T.*)

Poi che lalma per fe molta Tromboncino 4vv
    1. *16*, No.27 (*B. T.*)
    3. I–Bc, Q18, No.16, 16*v*–17*r* (Anon.) • I–Fc, 2441, No.19, 21*v*–22*r* (Anon.)
    4. Cesari, *Frottole*, 20

Poi che mia sincera fede Capreolus 4vv
    1. *23*, No.4 (*ANT. CAP.*) • *37*, No.4 (*ANT. CAP.*)
    4. Schwartz, *Frottole*, 47
    Intabulation: voice and lute

1. *50*, No.22 (*Ant. Cap.*)

4. Disertori, *Frottole*, 499–501

Poi che per fede mancha   **Capreolus**   4vv

1. *16*, No.62 (*ANTONIUS CAPREOLUS BRIXIENSIS.*)

4. Cesari, *Frottole*, 43 • Schwartz, *Frottole*, 43

Intabulation: voice and lute

1. *49*, No.58 (*Ant. Cap. BRIXIENSIS*); *58*, No.58 (*Ant. Cap. BRIXIENSIS*)

4. Disertori, *Frottole*, 411

Intabulation: lute accompaniment to a Superius

3. F-Pn, 27, No.102, 51*v* (Anon.)

Poi che perso i gioven anni   [Anon.]   4vv

1. *26*, No.63 (Anon.)

Poi che son di speranza   **Lulinus**   4vv

1. *56*, No.45 (*Io. lu. V.*: headed *Aer de capitoli*)

4. Einstein, *Madrigal*, 8 • Luisi & Zanovello, *Frottole*, 207

Poi che son si sfortunato   **Antiquis**   4vv

1. *18*, No.1 (*A. DE ANTIQVIS*) • *40*, No.1 (*A. DE ANTIQVIS*)

4. Cesari, *Frottole*, 93 • Zupanovic, *Sedamnaest frottola*

Poi che speranza e morta   **Lurano**   4vv

1. *48*, No.30 (*PH. D. L.*)

4. Disertori, *Frottole*, 167–69 • Facchin & Zanovello, *Frottole*, 174

Poi che tale e lamia sorte   [Anon.]   4vv

1. *35*, No.7 (Anon.)

4. Boscolo, *Frottole*, 127

Poi che te hebi

See **Fortuna desperata**   **Busnois**   4vv

Poi che uscito mi e di man   [Anon.]   4vv

1. *36*, No.7 (Anon.)

Poi che volse la mia stella   **Tromboncino**   4vv

1. *18*, No.19 (*B. T.*) • *40*, No.19 (*B. T.*)

4. Cesari, *Frottole*, 107 • Disertori, *Frottole*, 219–22

Intabulation: lute

1. *47*, No.39 (Dalza)

4. Disertori, *Frottole*, 223–24

Intabulation: voice and lute

1. *49*, No.37 (*B. T.*); *58*, No.37 (*B. T.*)

4. Disertori, *Frottole*, 219–22 and 374–75

Pone un basso e lattro in cielo

2/ of **Ogni ben fa la fortuna**   **Cara**   4vv

Popul mio popul ingrato   **Dammonis**   4vv

1. *29*, No.47 (Dammonis. Headed *De passione*); *45*, No.47 (Dammonis)

Text by Giustiniani

4. Luisi, *Laudario*, ii, 114–16

Porta ognun al nascimento   [Anon.]   4vv

1. *48*, No.17 (Anon.)

Text by Cammelli, *Filostrato e Panfila.*

4. Facchin & Zanovello, *Frottole*, 147 • Osthoff, *Theatergesang*, i, 131–43

Porzi soccorso o verzene gentile
    2/ of **Maria del ciel regina**   **Dammonis**   4vv

Pregovi fronde fiori acque   **Tromboncino**   4vv
    1. *36*, No.12 (*B.T.*)
    2. 1510, No.23, 23r (*B.T.*)
    4. Gallico, *Libro*, 137 • Rubsamen, *Literary*, 49
    Intabulation: voice and lute
    1. *50*, No.15 (*B.T.*)
    4. Disertori, *Frottole*, 488–89

Prendi larme ingrato amore   [Anon.]   4vv
    1. *18*, No.46 (Anon.) • *40*, No.46 (Anon.)
    4. Cesari, *Frottole*, 129

Prendi larme   **Antiquis**   4vv
    1. *25*, No.37 (*A. DE. A.V.*)
    4. Zupanovic, *Sedamnaest frottola*

Pur al fin convien   **Fogliano, J.**   4vv
    1. *25*, No.20 (Anon.)
    2. I-Fn, 230, No.3, 2v-3r (*Jacobus foglianus*)

Qual el cor non piangesse   [Anon.]   4vv
    1. *48*, No.56 (Anon.)
    3. I-Fc, 2441, No.1, 1v-3r (Anon.)
    4. Facchin & Zanovello, *Frottole*, 233

Quando quando andaratu al monte   **Joan Pietro**   voice + lute
    Intabulation: voice and lute
    1. *50*, No.40 (*Io. Pie. Man.*)
    4. Disertori, *Frottole*, 548–51

Quando andaretu al monte
    See **E quando andaretu al monte**   **Zesso**   4vv

Quando fia mai quel di felice
    See **Eterno mio signor po che per me**   **Tromboncino**   4vv

Quando lo pomo vien   **Tromboncino**   4vv
    (Cara, Pesenti)
    1. *56*, No.4 (*B.T.*)
    2. Frottole II (1518), No.6, 12v-13r (*M.C.*) • [c.1516]² (1520), No.6, 12v-13r (*Marcheto carra*)
    3. I-Fc, 2440, No.37, 64v-65r (*Pr. Michael*) • I-Fn, 230, No.66, 65r (Anon.) • I-Fn, 337, No.61, 69r (Anon.) • I-Fn, 164–167, No.32 (Anon.) • I-Vnm, IV.1795–1798, No.1, 3v (Anon.)
    4. Gandolfi, "Intorno", 537 • Luisi, *Apografo*, 3–4 • Luisi, *Secondo*, ii, 22–25 • Luisi & Zanovello, *Frottole*, 105 • Torrefranca, *Segreto*, 520–21

Quando mi mostra amor   **Ludovico**   4vv
    1. *35*, No.52 (*LVDOVICO MILANESE*)
    4. Boscolo, *Frottole*, 239

Quando per darme nel languir   [Anon.]   4vv
    1. *23*, No.78 (Anon.) • *37*, No.78 (Anon.)
    4. Schwartz, *Frottole*, 91

Quanto ardo sta chiuso   [Anon.]   4vv
    1. *26*, No.50 (Anon.)

Quanto la fiama
    See **Visto ho piu volte**   **Tromboncino**   4vv

Quanto piu donna   **Lurano**   4vv
    1. **23**, No.59 (*PHI. DE. LV.*) • **37**, No.59 (*PHI. DE. LV.*)
    4. Schwartz, *Frottole*, 80

Quasi sempre avanti   [Anon.]   4vv
    1. **36**, No.44 (Anon.)
    4. Disertori, *Frottole*, 128–32

Quei che sempre han da penare   **Cara**   4vv
    2/ *Lor fur quelli*
    1. **18**, No.34 (*M.C.*) • **40**, No.34 (*M.C.*)
    4. Cesari, *Frottole*, 120
    Intabulation: voice and lute
    1. **50**, No.36 (*M.C.*)
    4. Disertori, *Frottole*, 535–37

Quel chel ciel   **Antiquis**   4vv
    1. **36**, No.41 (*A. DE ANTIQVIS*)
    4. Zupanovic, *Sedamnaest frottola*

Quel chio posso io tho donato   [Anon.]   4vv
    1. **18**, No.47 (Anon.) • **40**, No.47 (Anon.)
    4. Cesari, *Frottole*, 130

Quel foco che mi pose   **Tromboncino**   4vv
    1. **36**, No.43 (*B.T.*)

Quella bella e biancha mano   **Capreolus**   4vv
    1. **35**, No.16 (*ANTO. CAPRIOLVS*)
    4. Boscolo, *Frottole*, 145
    Intabulation: voice and lute
    1. **50**, No.42 (*A.C.*)
    4. Disertori, *Frottole*, 554–55 • Schwartz, "Nochmals", 7

Questa amara aspra partita   **Antiquis**   4vv
    1. **25**, No.40 (*A. DE. A.V.*)
    4. Zupanovic, *Sedamnaest frottola*

Questa e mia lho fatta   **Michele** [?Pesenti]   4vv
    1. **16**, No.43 (*MICHAELIS C. & V.*)
    Facsimile: Cesari, *Frottole*, p. LXVII
    4. Cesari, *Frottole*, 33 • Schwartz, *Frottole*, 31

Questa e quella croce grande   **Dammonis**   4vv
    1. **29**, No.64 (Dammonis); **45**, No.64 (Dammonis)
    4. Luisi, *Laudario*, ii, 347–49

Questa longa mia speranza   [Anon.]   4vv
    1. **36**, No.34 (Anon.)

Questa se chiama   **Japart**   4vv
    1. **12**, No.90 (*Jo. Japart*)
    3. E-Sc, 5-I-43, No.156, 128v–129r/128v–129r (Anon. Text *Famene un pocho*)
    4. Moerk, "Seville", ii, 385–87

Queste lacrime mie   **Tromboncino**   4vv
    1. **56**, No.62 (*B.T.*)

3. I-Vnm, IV.1795–1798, No.39, 34*v*-35*r* (Anon.)

Text by Castiglione: *Tirsi*, "Canzone di Jola"

4. Luisi, *Apografo*, 90–91 • Luisi & Zanovello, *Frottole*, 254 • Osthoff, *Theatergesang*, ii, 60–63

Intabulation: voice and lute

2. [1520]⁷, No.27, 35*r* (Anon. Incomplete: The previous folios are lacking in the unique copy)

Queste quel loco　　　　　　　**d'Ana**　　　　4vv

   1. *17*, No.3 (*FRANCISCVS. VENE. ORGA.*) • *42*, No.3 (*FRANCISCVS VENE. ORGA.*)

Text by Niccolò da Correggio

4. Cesari, *Frottole*, 48 • Einstein, *Madrigal*, 9 • Rubsamen, *Literary*, 51

Comments: The first printed setting of a sonnet

Questo mondo e mal partito　　　**Tromboncino**　　　4vv

   1. *48*, No.7 (*B.T.*)

4. Facchin & Zanovello, *Frottole*, 122

Questo oime pur mi tormenta　　　**Capreolus**　　　4vv

   1. *23*, No.3 (*ANT. CAP.*) • *37*, No.3 (*ANT. CAP.:*)

   2. 1510, No.11, 12*v*-13*r* (*Ant. Cap.*)

4. Schwartz, *Frottole*, 46

Questo sol giorno　　　　　　**Tromboncino**　　　4vv

   1. *23*, No.39 (*B.T.*) • *37*, No.39 (*B.T.*)

   3. I-Fc, 2441, No.65, 67*v*-68*r* (Anon.)

4. Schwartz, *Frottole*, 69

Questo tuo lento tornare　　　**Antiquis**　　　4vv

   1. *36*, No.66 (*A. DE ANTIQVIS.* Headed *Resposta de Sio son stato aritornare*)

4. Zupanovic, *Sedamnaest frottola*

Questo viver asperanza　　　**Honophrius Antenore**　　　4vv

   1. *26*, No.8 (*HONOPHRIVS PATAVINVS*)

Regi & guidi ognun human stato　　　[Anon.]　　　4vv

   1. *36*, No.33 (Anon.)

Rendeti amanti　　　　　　**Lulinus**　　　4vv

   1. *56*, No.52 (*Io. Lu. V.*)

4. Luisi & Zanovello, *Frottole*, 228

Resta hor su madonna in pace　　　**Antiquis**　　　4vv

   1. *25*, No.39 (*A. DE. A.V.*)

4. Zupanovic, *Sedamnaest frottola*

Resta in pace diva mia　　　[Anon.]　　　4vv

   1. *17*, No.34 (Anon.) • *42*, No.34 (Anon.)

4. Cesari, *Frottole*, 76

Resta in pace ingrata hormai

  See **Resta in pace o diva mia**　　　**Antenore**　　　4vv

Resta in pace o diva mia　　　**Antenore**　　　4vv

   1. *17*, No.39 (Anon.) • *42*, No.39 (*Honophrius Antenoreus*. Incipit *Resta in pace ingrata hormai*)

4. Cesari, *Frottole*, 80

Resvegliate susu　　　　　[Anon.]　　　4vv

   1. *26*, No.15 (Anon.)

Rinforzi ognhor   **Cara**   4vv
    1. **23**, No.40 (*M.*) • **37**, No.40 (*M.C.*)
    4. Schwartz, *Frottole*, 69

Riseno i monti / Montes exultaverunt   [Anon.]   4vv
    1. **23**, No.43 (Anon. Listed in the index under *Montes exultaverunt*) • **37**, No.43 (Anon.)
    4. Einstein, *Madrigal*, 7 • Schwartz, *Frottole*, 43

Ritornata e la speranza   **Capreolus**   4vv
    1. **23**, No.5 (*ANT. CAP.*) • **37**, No.5 (*ANT. CAP.*)
    2. 1510, No.30, 29v-30r (*Ant. Cap.*)
    4. Schwartz, *Frottole*, 48

. . . ro sol lucenti rai   [Anon.]
    1. **68**, 3r (Any ascription is lacking. Incomplete)

Rocta e laspra mia cathena   **Cara**   4vv
    1. **25**, No.48 (*M.C.*; *M.* in the index)
    4. Prizer, *Courtly*, ii, 51–56

Rompe amor questa cathena   **Lurano**   4vv
    1. **23**, No.60 (*PHI. DE. LV.*) • **37**, No.60 (*PHI. DE. LV.*)
    2. 1510, No.21, 21v-22r (*Phi. De. Lu.*)
    4. Schwartz, *Frottole*, 81

Rotta e laspra mia cathena
    See **Rocta e laspra mia cathena**   **Cara**   4vv

Rotto ho al fin   **Scotto**   4vv
    1. **36**, No.58 (*PAVLI. S. Cantus & verba*)

Salve croce unica speme   **Nicolo**   4vv
    1. **41**, No.11 (*D. NICOLO*)
    4. Jeppesen, *Laude*, 17

Salve croce unica speme   **Tromboncino**   4vv
    1. **41**, No.12 (*Tromboncino*)
    4. Jeppesen, *Laude*, 18–19

Salve sacrata e gloriosa insegna   **Philippo** [?*Lapaccino*]   4vv
    1. **41**, No.1 (*D. philippo*)
    4. Jeppesen, *Laude*, 1
    Comments: Prizer, *Courtly*, p. 27, suggests Lapaccino, a member of Francesco Gonzaga's
      cappella, as the composer

Salve sacrata e gloriosa insegna
    Altus of **Salve victrice e gloriosa**   [Anon.]   4vv

Salve victrice e gloriosa insegna   [Anon.]   4vv
    1. **41**, No.16 (Anon. Altus incipit reads *Salve sacrata e gloriosa insegna*)
    4. Jeppesen, *Laude*, 24–25

Scaramella fa la galla   **Compère**   4vv
    1. **23**, No.81 (*OMPERE*) • **37**, No.81 (*COMPERE*)
    3. I-Fc, 2439, No.15, 16v-17r (*Compere*)
    4. Newton, *Florence*, ii, 44–45 • Riemann, *Handbuch*, 349 • Schwartz, *Frottole*, 92 • Torre-
      franca, *Segreto*, 522
    Intabulation: keyboard
    3. CH-Zz, 301, 59r

Scoltatime madonna   [Anon.]   4vv
    1. **23**, No.68 (Anon.) • **37**, No.68 (Anon.)
    4. Schwartz, *Frottole*, 87
    Intabulation: lute accompaniment to a Superius
    3. F-Pn, 27, No.86, 48*v* (Anon. Incipit *Ascoltame madona*)

Scontento me ne resto   [Anon.]   4vv
    1. **23**, No.29 (Anon.) • **37**, No.29 (Anon.)
    4. Schwartz, *Frottole*, 63

Scopri lingua el cieco ardore   **Tromboncino**   4vv
    1. **16**, No.19 (*BARTHOLOMEUS TRUMBONCINUS VERO*. All lower voices have the
       incipit *Scopri o lingua*)
    3. F-Pn, 676, No.101, 111*v*-112*r* (*Trombotino*)
    4. Cesari, *Frottole*, 14 • Schwartz, *Frottole*, 13
    Intabulation: voice and lute
    1. **49**, No.41 (*B.T.*); **58**, No.49 (*B.T.*)
    4. Disertori, *Frottole*, 380–81
    Intabulation: lute accompaniment to a Superius
    3. F-Pn, 27, No.25, 36*r* (Anon.)

Scopri lingua el mio martire   [Anon.]   4vv
    1. **35**, No.38 (Anon.)
    3. I-Fc, 2441, No.2, 3*v*-4*r* (Anon.)
    4. Boscolo, *Frottole*, 201

Se a un tuo sguardo son ateso   **Tromboncino**   4vv
    1. **18**, No.17 (*B.T.*) • **40**, No.17 (*B.T.*)
    4. Cesari, *Frottole*, 105

Se alcun spera nel suo amore   [Anon.]   4vv
    1. **18**, No.23 (Anon.) • **40**, No.23 (Anon.)
    4. Cesari, *Frottole*, 110

Se ben elfin de la mia vita   **Cara**   4vv
    1. **26**, No.51 (*M. CARA.*)
    3. GB-Lbl, Eg.3051, No.17, 19*v*-20*r* (Anon. Text *Guardando alli ochi toi*) • I-Fc, 2440, No.5,
       5*v*-6*r* (Anon.) • I-Fn, 230, No.1, 1*r* (Anon.)
    Intabulation: voice and lute
    1. **49**, No.68 (*M.C.* Text *Se ben il fin dela mia vita*); **58**, No.68 (*M.C.* Text *Se ben il fin dela
       mia vita*)
    4. Disertori, *Frottole*, 428

Se ben fugo   **Tromboncino**   4vv
    1. **26**, No.25 (*B.T.*)

Se ben hor non scopro el focho   **Tromboncino**   4vv
    1. **16**, No.21 (*B.T.*)
    3. D-B, 22048, 1*r* (Anon.) • GB-Lbl, Eg.3051, No.50, 57*v*-58*r* (Anon.) • I-Bc, Q18, No.3,
       3*v*-4*r* (Anon. Text *Se bene non schopro*) • I-Fn, 230, No.23, 22*v*-23*r* (*Tronboncino*) • I-Fn,
       Panc.27, No.93, 60*v*-61*r* (Anon.) • I-Mt, 55, No.32, 32*v*-33*r* (Anon.) • ZA-Csa, Grey,
       No.46, 75*v*-76*r* (Anon. Text *L oration e sempre bona*)
    4. Cesari, *Frottole*, 16 • Giazotto, *Musurgia*, 63–65 • Jeppesen, *Frottola*, iii, 249–50 • Schwartz,
       Frottole, 14–15 • Schwartz, "Nochmals", 8

Se ben il fin della mia vita

    See **Se ben elfin de la mia vita**   **Cara**   4vv

Se bene non scopro

    See **Se ben hor non scopro**   **Tromboncino**   4vv

Se ben soletto vado

    See **Ben che soletto vado**   [Anon.]   4vv

Se col sguardo   **Tromboncino**   4vv

    1. **26**, No.36 (*B.T.*)

Se con vostra alma belleza   [Anon.]   4vv

    1. **48**, No.60 (Anon.)

    4. Facchin & Zanovello, *Frottole*, 243

Se conviene a un cor villano   **Eneas**   4vv

    1. **18**, No.61 (*ENEAS*) • **40**, No.61 (*ENEAS*)

    3. I-Fn, Panc.27, No.85, 55*v*-56*r* (Anon.)

    4. Cesari, *Frottole*, 141

Se da poi la tua partita   **Nicolo**   4vv

    1. **17**, No.50 (Anon.) • **42**, No.50 (*NI. PA.*)

    4. Cesari, *Frottole*, 76

Se damarti non son degno   [Anon.]   4vv

    1. **25**, No.50 (Anon.)

    3. I-Fn, 337, No.19, 29*v* (Anon.)

Se de fede hor vengo   **Cara**   4vv

    1. **16**, No.8 (*M.C.*)

    3. I-Bc, Q18, No.10, 11*r*. (Incomplete, and lacking the ascription. Texted *Non po lolmo*, which is the third strophe of this text)

    4. Cesari, *Frottole*, 7 • Schwartz, *Frottole*, 6

    Intabulation: voice and lute

    1. **49**, No.42 (*M.C.* Texted *Se de fede vengo*); **58**, No.42 (*M.C.* Texted *Se de fede vengo*)

    4. **Disertori**, *Frottole*, 382–83

    Intabulation: lute accompaniment to a Superius

    3. Γ-Pn, 27, No.21, 36*r* (Anon.)

Se de fede vengo

    See **Se de fede hor vengo**   **Cara**   4vv

Se gran festa me mostrasti   **Tromboncino**   4vv

    1. **25**, No.42 (*T.* in the index)

    3. I-Fc, 2441, No.23, 25*v*-26*r* (Anon.) • I-Mt, 55, No.45, 46*v*-48*r* (Anon.)

    4. Jeppesen, *Frottola*, iii, 282–83

    Comments: This frottola is presumably the one cited in a letter of Cariteo (14.i.1497) to Isabella d'Este, as *Se gran festa mi mostrasti*, and attributed to Tromboncino.

    Literature: Einstein, *Madrigal*, 45–46

Se ho sdegnato   **Capreolus**   4vv

    1. **23**, No.67 (*ANT. CAPREO.*) • **37**, No.67 (*ANT. CAPREO.*)

    4. Schwartz, *Frottole*, 87

Se hogi e un di chogni defunto   **Tromboncino**   4vv

    1. **23**, No.50 (*B.T.*) • **37**, No.50 (*B.T.*)

    2. 1510, No.17, 18*v* (*B.T.*)

    3. I-Fc, 2441, No.64, 66*v*-67*r* (Anon.)

    4. Schwartz, *Frottole*, 75

Se hora el tempo   [Anon.]   4vv

    1. **26**, No.43 (Anon.)

Se il morir mai de gloria   **Tromboncino**   4vv

    1. **36**, No.3 (*B.T.*)

    Intabulation: voice and lute

    1. **49**, No.2 (*B.T.*); **58**, No.2 (*B.T.*)

    4. Disertori, *Frottole*, 310–11

Se in tutto hai destinato   **Pesenti**   4vv

    1. **16**, No.50 (*MICHA.*)

    4. Cesari, *Frottole*, 36 • Schwartz, *Frottole*, 35

Se io gliel dico che dira   **Tromboncino**   4vv

    1. **35**, No.2 (*B.T.*)

    3. I-Fn, 337, No.79, 86*v* (Anon.)

    4. Boscolo, *Frottole*, 114 • Prizer, *Courtly*, ii, 262–66

    Intabulation: voice and lute

    1. **49**, No.39 (*B.T.*); **58**, No.39 (*B.T.*)

    4. Disertori, *Frottole*, 376–77

Se io son la tua signora   [Anon.]   4vv

    1. **35**, No.10 (Anon.)

    4. Boscolo, *Frottole*, 133

Se io te adimando   **Tromboncino**   4vv

    1. **36**, No.8 (*B.T.*)

Se io ti dico el mio gran danno   **Antenore**   4vv

    1. **35**, No.24 (*HONO. ANTE.*)

    4. Boscolo, *Frottole*, 168

Se la gran fiamma   [Anon.]   4vv

    1. **23**, No.8 (Anon.) • **37**, No.8 (Anon.)

    4. Schwartz, *Frottole*, 50

Se laffanato core   **d'Ana**   4vv

    1. **23**, No.36 (*F.V.*) • **37**, No.36 (*F.V.*)

    4. Schwartz, *Frottole*, 68

    Intabulation: voice and lute

    1. **49**, No.63 (*F.V.*); **58**, No.63 (*F.V.*)

    4. Disertori, *Frottole*, 421

Se lamor in te e poche   [Anon.]   4vv

    1. **17**, No.16 (Anon.) • **42**, No.16 (Anon.)

    4. Schwartz, *Frottole*, 60

Se le carti me son contra   **d'Ana**   4vv

    1. **26**, No.33 (*F.V.*)

    4. Luisi, *Cantar*, 213–214

    Intabulation: lute accompaniment to a Superius

    3. F-Pn, 27, No.74, 46*v* (Anon.)

Se lontan partir mi fa   [Anon.]   4vv

    1. **48**, No.8 (Anon.)

    4. Facchin & Zanovello, *Frottole*, 124

Se mai fo tuo   [Anon.]   4vv
    1. *25*, No.18, 18*v*–19*r* (Anon.)

Se mai nei mei pochanni   **Tromboncino**   4vv
    1. *35*, No.29 (B.T.)
    4. Boscolo, *Frottole*, 176
    Intabulation: voice and lute
    1. *50*, No.46 (Anon.)
    4. Disertori, *Frottole*, 564–65

Se mai per maraveglia   [Anon.]   voice + lute
    Intabulation: voice and lute
    1. *50*, No.5 (Anon.)
    4. Disertori, *Frottole*, 464–65

Se mai provasti donna   **Pisano**   ?4vv
    1. *67*, No.9 (Pisano. Incomplete)
    4. Pisano, *Collected Works*

Se me amasti quanto in te amo   **La Porta**   4vv
    1. *16*, No.58 (GEORGIUS DE LA PORTA VERO.)
    4. Cesari, *Frottole*, 39 • Schwartz, *Frottole*, 39

Se me dol el mio partire   [Anon.]   4vv
    1. *25*, No.19 (Anon.)
    3. I-Fn, 230, No.15, 14*v*–15*r* (Anon. Text *Sel mi duole el . . .*)

Se mi duol esser gabato   **Tromboncino**   4vv
    1. *18*, No.22 (B.T.) • *40*, No.22 (B.T.)
    2. 1510, No.5, 6*v*–7*r* (B.T.)
    4. Cesari, *Frottole*, 109

Se me e grato el tuo tornare   **Lurano**   4vv
    1. *16*, No.60 (PHILIPPUS DE LURANO)
    3. I-Fn, 230, No.25, 24*v*–25*r* (philippus de lurano. Text *Non ti grava el mie partire*) • I-Fn, 337,
      No.16, 17*v* (P. d Lo.)
    4. Cesari, *Frottole*, 41 • Schwartz, *Frottole*, 40
    Intabulation: voice and lute
    1. *49*, No.49 (PHI.DE LV.); *58*, No.49 (PHI.DE LV.)
    4. Disertori, *Frottole*, 396–397
    Intabulation: lute accompaniment to a Superius
    3. F-Pn, 27, No.111, 54*v* (Anon. Text *Sel me grato*)

Se mi e grave el tuo partire   **Tromboncino**   4vv
                      (Lurano)
    1. *16*, No.22 (B.T.)
    3. F-Pn, 676, No.103, 114*v*–115*r* (Anon. Has a different Bassus) • I-Fn, 230, No.26, 25*v*–
      26*r* (philippus de lurano. Text *Se m'agrava*) • I-Fn, 337, No.15, 25*v* (B.T.)
    4. Cesari, *Frottole*, 16 • Schwartz, *Frottole*, 15
    Intabulation: lute accompaniment to a Superius
    3. F-Pn, 27, No.45, 40*r* (Anon.)

Se ne gli affanni   [Anon.]   4vv
    1. *23*, No.58 (Anon.) • *37*, No.58 (Anon.)
    4. Schwartz, *Frottole*, 80

Se no hai perseveranza Cara 4vv
 1. **16**, No.7 (*M.C.*)
 4. Cesari, *Frottole*, 7 • Schwartz, *Frottole*, 5

Se non dormi donna ascolta L.C. 4vv
 1. **18**, No.51 (Anon.) • **40**, No.51 (Anon.)
 3. F-Pn, 676, No.58, 67*v*-68*r* (*L.C.*) • GB-Lbl, Eg.3051, No.35, 40*v*-41*r* (Anon. Text *Se tu dormi*) • I-Fc, 2441, No.32, 34*v*-35*r* (Anon.) • I-Fn, Panc.27, No.145, 110*v*-111*r* (Anon.)
 4. Cesari, *Frottole*, 133

Se non fusse la speranza Cara 4vv
 1. **35**, No.48 (*M.C.*)
 4. Boscolo, *Frottole*, 228 • Prizer, *Courtly*, ii, 99–103

Se non mami a che stentarmi d'Ana 4vv
 1. **25**, No.30 (*F.V.* in the index)
 Intabulation: lute accompaniment to a Superius
 3. F-Pn, 27, No.61, 43*v* (Anon.)

Se non poi hor ristorarmi Nicolo 4vv
 1. **17**, No.53 (Anon.) • **42**, No.53 (*Ni. Pa.*)
 4. Cesari, *Frottole*, 88

Se non son sdegno donna G. Brocco 4vv
 1. **18**, No.28 (*IO. BRO.*) • **40**, No.28 (*IO. BRO.*)
 4. Cesari, *Frottole*, 114

Se non voi pensar in tutto Nicolo 4vv
 1. **17**, No.51 (Anon.) • **42**, No.51 (*NI. PA.*)
 4. Cesari, *Frottole*, 87

Se ogni donna fusse Rossino 4vv
 1. **18**, No.24 (*R.M.*) • **40**, No.24 (*R.M.*)
 4. Cesari, *Frottole*, 111

Se per chieder merce Cara 4vv
 1. **35**, No.12 (*M.C.*)
 4. Boscolo, *Frottole*, 136 • Prizer, *Courtly*, ii, 112
 Intabulation: voice and lute
 1. **49**, No.26 (*M.C.*); **58**, No.26 (*M.C.*)
 4. Disertori, *Frottole*, 349

Se per colpa del vostro altiero sdegno Tromboncino 4vv
 1. **56**, No.6 (*B.T.*)
 Text by Sannazaro
 4. Einstein, *Madrigal*, iii, 14–15 • Luisi & Zanovello, *Frottole*, 111

Se per colpa dil vostro fero sdegno [Anon.] voice + lute
 Intabulation: voice and lute
 1. **50**, No.9 (Anon.)
 Text by Sannazaro
 4. Disertori, *Frottole*, 476–77
 Comments: Disertori, *Frottole*, 476, assigns this to Tromboncino, perhaps in confusion with
  the previous item

Se per humidita daqua d'Ana 4vv
 1. **23**, No.33 (*F.V.*) • **37**, No.33 (*F.V.*)

3. GB-Lbl, Eg.3051, No.4, *6v-7r* (Anon.)

4. Lowinsky, *Medici*, iii, 210–11 • Schwartz, *Frottole*, 66

Se per mio fidel servire   **Nicolo**   4vv

   1. *18*, No.26 (*N.P.*) • *40*, No.26 (*N.P.*)

   4. Cesari, *Frottole*, 113

Se quanto in voi se vede   [Anon.]   ?4vv

   1. *68*, *3r* (Anon.)

   Text by Cassola

   Comments: Prizer, in "Cara", *New Grove*, assigns this work to Cara. He believes that it
     belongs with the Altus part of the anonymous work in *RISM* 1530[1], No.9

Se sei dami lontano   [Anon.]   4vv

   1. *26*, No.49 (Anon.)

Se son da te lontano

   See **Sio son da te lontano**   [Anon.]   4vv

Se tu dormi donna

   See **Se non dormi donna**   **L.C.**   4vv

Se un pone un fragil vetro   **Antenore**   4vv

   1. *56*, No.2 (*Honofrius Patavinus*)

   Text by Serafino Aquilano

   4. Luisi & Zanovello, *Frottole*, 101

Se voi gustar lamore   **Dammonis**   4vv

   1. *29*, No.58 (Dammonis); *45*, No.58 (Dammonis)

   Text by Francesco d'Albizo

   4. Luisi, *Laudario*, ii, 351

Sed libera non amalo   **Antenore**   4vv

   1. *26*, No.60 (*HONOPHRIVS PATAVINVS*)

   Comments: A macaronic text

Segua pur seguir chi vole   **Antenore**   4vv

   2/ *Vidi gia ne la sua corte*

   1. *17*, No.41 (Anon.) • *42*, No.41 (*Honophrius Antenoreus*)

   4. Cesari, *Frottole*, 81

Segue cuor e non restare   **J. Fogliano**   4vv

   1. *36*, No.54 (*IACOBVS FOGLIANVS*)

   2. 1510, No.16, *17v-18r* (*Iac. Foglianus*)

Sel mi duole el mio partire

   See **Se me dol el mio partire**   [Anon.]   4vv

Sel mio ben da voi deriva

   2/ of **Occhi dolci ove prendesti**   **d'Ana**   4vv

Sel mio cor Piu chaltra assai   [Anon.]   4vv

   1. *25*, No.23 (Anon.)

Sel morir mai de gloria

   See **Se il morir mai**   **Tromboncino**   4vv

Sel non fusse la speranza   **Lulinus**   4vv

   1. *56*, No.54 (*Io. Lu. V.*)

   4. Luisi & Zanovello, *Frottole*, 233

Sel partir me serra forte

   2/ of **Serra dura mia partita**   [Anon.]   4vv

Sel partir mincrebe e dolce   [Anon.]   4vv
    1. **25**, No.25 (Anon.)
    Intabulation: voice and lute
    1. **50**, No.26 (Anon.)
    4. Disertori, *Frottole*, 516–17

Sel pastor con affanno
    See **Stavasi in porta**   [Anon.]   4vv

Sel te chara la mia vita   **Pifaro**   4vv
    1. **26**, No.17 (*NICOLO PIFAR:*)
    2. 1515², No.13, 14*v*-15*r* (Anon. Text *Con dolor vivo in piacere*)

Sel te piacque   **Nicolo**   4vv
    1. **17**, No.49 (Anon.) • **42**, No.49 (*NI. PA.*)
    4. Cesari, *Frottole*, 86

Sempre haro quel dolce focho   **Diomedes**   4vv
    1. **48**, No.63 (*Diomedes*)
    3. I-Fc, 2441, No.46, 48*v*-49*r* (Anon.)
    4. Facchin & Zanovello, *Frottole*, 248

Sempre le come esser sole   **Pesenti**   4vv
    1. **16**, No.37 (*MICHAELIS Cantus & Verba.*)
    3. I-Fc, 2441, No.13, 14*v*-15*r* (Anon. Text *Sempre le qual esser*)
    4. Cesari, *Frottole*, 28

Sempre le qual esser sole
    See **Sempre le come esser sole**   **Pesenti**   4vv

Sempre te sia in diletto   **Dammonis**   4vv
    1. **29**, No.38 (Dammonis); **45**, No.38 (Dammonis)
    Text by Giustiniani
    4. Luisi, *Laudario*, ii, 125–27

Sento li spriti mei   **Timoteo**   4vv
    1. **56**, No.60 (*Dun Thimoteo*)
    4. Luisi & Zanovello, *Frottole*, 249
    Comments: A setting of the top voice is in I-PEc, 431, 120*v* (Anon.)

Senza te alta regina   **D. Nicolo**
    See **Vengo a te madre maria**   **J. Fogliano**   4vv

Senza te sacra regina   **Antiquis**   4vv
    1. **41**, No.31 (*Adam de antiquis. Venetus*)
    4. Jeppesen, *Laude*, 45

Sera chi per pieta   **Ludovico**   4vv
    1. **35**, No.53 (*LVDOVICO MILANESE*)
    4. Boscolo, *Frottole*, 240 • Disertori, *Frottole*, 142–44

Sera forsi ripreso   **Tromboncino**   4vv
    1. **48**, No.39 (*B.T.*)
    4. Facchin & Zanovello, *Frottole*, 190
    Intabulation: voice and lute
    1. **49**, No.33 (*B.T.*); **58**, No.33 (*B.T.*)
    4. Disertori, *Frottole*, 366–67

Serra dura mia partita   [Anon.]   4vv
    2/ *Sel partir me serra forte*

1. *17*, No.14 (Anon.) • *42*, No.14 (Anon.)

    4. Cesari, *Frottole*, 58

Servo haime senza mercede   **Antenore**   4vv

    1. *26*, No.6 (*HONOPHRIVS PATAVINVS*)

Si ben sto lontano   **Cara**   4vv

    1. *48*, No.44 (*M.C.*)

    4. Facchin & Zanovello, *Frottole*, 199 • Prizer, *Courtly*, 443

Si che la vo seguire   **Cara**   4vv

    1. *56*, No.1 (*M.C.*)

    3. I-Vnm, IV.1795–1798, No.36, 32r (Anon.)

    4. Luisi, *Apografo*, 84 • Luisi & Zanovello, *Frottole*, 99 • Prizer, *Courtly*, ii, 133–35

Si como el bianco cigno

   See **Come chel bianco cigno**   **Cara**   4vv

Si come fede   [Anon.]   4vv

    1. *25*, No.1 (Anon. Headed *Stramotto.*)

Si e debile il filo   **Pisano**   4vv

    1. *67*, No.7 (Pisano)

    3. I-Fn, 164–167, No.2, 2v-4r (Anon.) • I-Vc, B.32, No.29, 46r-47r (Anon.)

    Text by Petrarch, *Canzoniere*, XXXVII. This is the text recommended to Isabella d'Este by Nicolò di Correggio in 1504

    4. Pisano, *Collected Works*

Si e debile el filo   **Tromboncino**   4vv

    1. *36*, No.5 (*B.T.*)

    2. 1510, No.33, 32v-33v (*B.T.*)

    Text: See above

    4. Disertori, *Frottole*, 271–77 • Rubsamen, *Literary*, 53

    Intabulation: keyboard

    2. 1517³, No.8, 14r-15v (*B.T.*)

    Intabulation: voice and lute

    1. *49*, No.5 (*B.T.*); *58*, No.5 (*B.T.*)

    4. Disertori, *Frottole*, 271–77 and 315–17

Si egua pur chi vol amore   **Antiquis**   4vv
                                                       (Tromboncino)

    1. *25*, No.51 (*A. DE A.*; *T.* in the index)

    4. Zupanovic, "Sedamnaest frottola"

Si me piace el dolce foco   **Michele** [?Pesenti]   4vv

    1. *16*, No.42 (*MICHA. C. & V.*)

    4. Cesari, *Frottole*, 32 • Schwartz, *Frottole*, 30

Si morsi donna el tuo labro suave   [Anon.]   4vv

    1. *18*, No.42 (Anon. Headed *Per sonetti*) • *40*, No.42 (Anon. Headed *Per sonetti*)

    4. Cesari, *Frottole*, 127

Si non posso il cor placarte

   See **Sio non posso il cor placarte**   [Anon.]   4vv

Si oportuerit me teco mori   **Cara**   lute

    Intabulation

    1. *50*, No.6 (*M.C.*)

    4. Disertori, *Frottole*, 466–67

Si si si tarvo tarvo   [Anon.]   4vv
    1. *36*, No.28 (Anon.)

Si suave mi par el mio dolore   [Anon.]   4vv
    1. *23*, No.16 (Anon.) • *37*, No.16 (Anon.)
    4. Schwartz, *Frottole*, 46

Sia felice la tua vita   Michele [?Pesenti]   4vv
    1. *18*, No.10 (*MICHA.*) • *40*, No.10 (*MICHA.*)
    4. Cesari, *Frottole*, IX

Signora anzi mia dea   Tromboncino   4vv
    1. *18*, No.62 (*B.T.*) • *40*, No.62 (*B.T.*)
    Facsimile: Cesari, *Frottole*, p. 142
    3. I-Fn, Panc.27, No.147, 111*v*-112*r* (Anon.)
    4. Cesari, *Frottole*, 142 • Einstein, *Madrigal*, 7
    Comments: The anonymous setting of this text in I-Fn, Panc.27, No.149, 112*r* uses the
        Superius of the earlier setting in the same manuscript

Sil dissi mai chi venga   Pisano   ?4vv
    1. *67*, No.17 (Pisano)
    Text by Petrarch, *Canzoniere*, CCVI
    4. Pisano

Sil dissi mai chio venga   Tromboncino   4vv
    1. *36*, No.37 (*B.T.*)
    2. 1510, No.6, 7*v*-8*r* (*B.T.*)
    Text by Petrarch, *Canzoniere*, CCVI
    4. Einstein, *Madrigal*, 12 • Rubsamen, *Literary*, 60 • Underwood, *Renaissance*, 162–70
    Intabulations: voice and lute
    1. *49*, No.7 (*B.T.*); *58*, No.7 (*B.T.*)
    4. Disertori, *Frottole*, 320–21 • Underwood, *Renaissance*, 162–70

Silentium lingua mia   Tromboncino   4vv
    1. *23*, No.46 (*B.T.*) • *37*, No.46 (*B.T.*)
    3. GB-Lbl, Eg.3051, No.5, 7*v*-8*r* (Anon. Text *Silentio lingua mia*)
    Text by Serafino d'Aquila
    4. Schwartz, *Frottole*, 72

Sio dimostro al viso el focho   [Anon.]   4vv
    1. *26*, No.42 (Anon.)
    3. I-Fc, 2441, No.11, 12*v*-13*r* (Anon.)

Sio gel dico che dira
    See **Se io gliel dico che dira**   Tromboncino   4vv

Sio non posso il cor   [Anon.]   4vv
    1. *17*, No.20 (Anon.) • *42*, No.20 (Anon.)
    4. Cesari, *Frottole*, 64

Sio sedo al ombra amor   Cara   4vv
                             (Tromboncino)
    1. *25*, No.58 (*Marcheto: B.T.* in the index. Headed *Sonetto*)
    4. Einstein, *Madrigal*, i, 101
    Intabulation: voice and lute
    1. *50*, No.48 (*M.C.*)
    4. Disertori, *Frottole*, 568–69

Sio son da te lontano   [Anon.]   4vv
    1. **26**, No.37 (Anon.)

Sio son stato a ritornare   **Michele** [?Pesenti]   4vv
    1. **16**, No.39 (*MICHA. C. & V.*)
    4. Cesari, *Frottole*, 30 • Schwartz, *Frottole*, 28
    Intabulation: voice and lute
    1. **50**, No.31 (*D. Mi.*)
    4. Disertori, *Frottole*, 526–27
    Comments: According to 1507³, Antiquis's setting of *Questo tuo lento tornare* is a *risposta* to this work.

Sol mi sol disse holoferno   **Dammonis**   4vv
    1. **29**, No.41 (Dammonis. Headed *De superbia luciferi a voce mudade eiusdem verba*); **45**, No.41 (Dammonis)
    4. Luisi, *Laudario*, ii, 352–53

Som pi tua
    See **Sum piu tua**   **Cara**   4vv

Son disposto de seguire   [Anon.]   4vv
    1. **48**, No.4 (Anon.)
    4. Facchin & Zanovello, *Frottole*, 114

Son fortuna omipotente   **Lurano**   4vv
    1. **18**, No.4 (*F.D.L.*) • **40**, No.4 (*F.D.L.*)
    4. Cesari, *Frottole*, 95 • Gallucci, *Festival*, ii, 361–65 • Pirrotta, *Music*, 66–68 • Schwartz, "Nochmals", 1–2
    Comment: Prize, "Facciamo", regards this as a carnival song from Rome

Son infermo rechaduto   **Nicolo Pifaro**   4vv
    1. **26**, No.23 (*N.P.*)

Son io donna qual mostri   **Pisano**   4vv
    1. **67**, No.14 (Pisano)
    3. I-Fn, 164–67, No.4, 5*v*-6*r* (Anon.)
    Text by L. Strozzi
    4. Pisano, *Collected Works*

Son io donna qual mostri   **Pisano**   4vv
    1. **67**, No.15 (Pisano)
    3. I-Bc, Q21, No.3, 5*r*-5*v* (Anon.) • I-Fc, 2440, No.43, 77*v*-79*r* (Anon.) • I-Fn, 164–67, No.5, 6*v*-7*r* (Anon.)
    Text by L. Strozzi
    4. Pisano, *Collected Works*

Son piu matti in questo mondo   **Stringari**   4vv
    1. **56**, No.39 (*A.P.*)
    4. Luisi & Zanovello, *Frottole*, 192

Son piu tua
    See **Sum piu tua**   **Cara**   4vv

Son pur congionto a tanto   [Anon.]   4vv
    1. **25**, No.57 (Anon.)
    Intabulation: voice and lute
    1. **50**, No.54 (Anon.)
    4. Disertori, *Frottole*, 575

Son quel troncho senza foglia   [Anon.]   4vv

     1. *17*, No.4 (Anon.) • *42*, No.4 (Anon.)

     4. Cesari, *Frottole*, 49

     Comments: Einstein, *Madrigal*, i, 44, suggests that the text of this frottola was written by Isabella d'Este, following a letter written by Antonio Tebaldeo on 9.xii.1494

Son tornato e dio   **Lurano**   4vv

     1. *18*, No.49 (*PHILIPPVS DE LVRANO.*) • *40*, No.49 (*PHILIPPVS DE LVRANO.*)

     3. GB-Lbl, Eg.3051, No.36, 41*v*-42*r* (Anon. Text *Son tornato e lui*) • I-Fc, 2441, No.62, 64*v*-65*r* (Anon.) • I-Fn, 337, No.26, 36*v* (*P. d Lo.*)

     4. Cesari, *Frottole*, 131

Son tornato e lui

     See **Son tornato e dio**   **Lurano**   4vv

Sotto un verde e alto cupresso   **Capreolus**   4vv

     1. *35*, No.15 (*ANTONIVS CAPRIOLVS*)

     4. Boscolo, *Frottole*, 142 • Luisi, *Cantar*, 255–56

     Intabulation: voice and lute

     1. *50*, No.34, 35*r*-36*r* (*Anto. Capri.*)

     4. Disertori, *Frottole*, 532–34

Spargean per laria   **Tromboncino**   4vv

     1. *35*, No.5 (*B.T.*)

     4. Boscolo, *Frottole*, 123

     Intabulation: voice and lute

     1. *49*, No.15 (*B.T.*); *58*, No.15 (*B.T.*)

     4. Disertori, *Frottole*, 332–333

Spargo indarno el mio lamento   [Anon.]   4vv

     1. *48*, No.54 (Anon.)

     4. Facchin & Zanovello, *Frottole*, 228

Spenta mhai del pecto amore   **Michele** [?Pesenti]   4vv

     1. *36*, No.23 (*DOM MICHIEL.*)

     Intabulation: voice and lute

     1. *50*, No.29 (*D.M.*)

     4. Disertori, *Frottole*, 507–509

Spero haver felicita   [Anon.]   4vv

     1. *17*, No.5 (Anon.) • *42*, No.5 (Anon.)

     3. I-Fn, 337, No.23, 33*v* (Anon.)

     4. Cesari, *Frottole*, 50

Spirito sancto amore   **Dammonis**   4vv

     1. *29*, No.3 (Dammonis); *45*, No.3 (Dammonis)

     Text by Giustiniani

     4. Luisi, *Laudario*, ii, 128–30

Sposa del padre eterno

     2/ of **O madre del signore**   **Dammonis**   4vv

Starala ben cussi   **Zesso**   voice + lute

     Intabulation: voice and lute

     1. *50*, No.43 (*Io. Ba. Ze.*)

     4. Disertori, *Frottole*, 543

Stavasi amor   **Tromboncino**   4vv

    1. **56**, No.13 (*B.T.*)

    2. Frottole II (1518), No.8, 14*v*-15*r* • [c.1516]² (1520), No.8, 14*v*-15*r* (*Bartolomio tromboncino*)

    4. Luisi, *Secondo* • Luisi & Zanovello, *Frottole*, 130

    Intabulation: keyboard

    2. 1517³, No.12, 21*r*-21*v* (*B.T.*)

    Intabulation: lute

    3. US-Cn, 107501, No.10, 18*v* (Anon.)

Stavasi in porta la mia navicella   [Anon.]   4vv

    1. **26**, No.11 (Anon.)

    3. GB-Lbl, Eg.3051, No.12, 14*v*-15*r* (Anon. Text *Sel pastor con affanno*)

Su su su su mia speme   **Cara**   4vv

    1. **26**, No.27 (*M.C.*)

    4. Prizer, *Courtly*, ii, 57–62

Sum piu tua   **Cara**   4vv

    1. **35**, No.34 (*M.C.*)

    4. Boscolo, *Frottole*, 193 • Cesari, *Frottole*, xv

    Intabulation: voice and lute

    1. **49**, No.35 (*M.C.*); **58**, No.35 (*M.C.*)

    4. Disertori, *Frottole*, 370–371

Superbia et auaritia

    2/ of **Virtu che fai in questo miser mondo**   **Dammonis**   4vv

Surge cor lasso   **Tromboncino**   4vv

    1. **23**, No.44 (*B.T.*) • **37**, No.44 (*B.T.*)

    4. Schwartz, *Frottole*, 71

Surge dalorizonte   **Lulinus**   4vv

    1. **56**, No.55 (*Io. Lu. V.*)

    4. Luisi, *Cantar*, 278 • Luisi & Zanovello, *Frottole*, 235

Suspir io themo ma piu theme il core   **Tromboncino**   4vv

    1. **25**, No.60 (*B.T.*)

    4. Luisi, *Cantar*, 125–26

    Intabulation: voice and lute

    1. **50**, No.45 (*B.T.*)

    4. Disertori, *Frottole*, 562–63

Suspir suave o mio dolce tormento   **Tromboncino**   4vv

    1. **23**, No.52 (Anon.) • **37**, No.52 (Anon.) • **36**, No.42 (*B.T.* Text *O suspir suave*)

    4. Schwartz, *Frottole*, 76

Taci lingue e non el tempo   [Anon.]   4vv

    1. **26**, No.64 (Anon.)

Tal chio pavento assai

    2/ of **Amore quando speravo**   **Pisano**   4vv

Tanta pieta cor mio   **Pisano**   4vv

    1. **67**, No.13 (Pisano)

    3. I-Fn, 164–167, No.16, 22*v*-23*r* (Anon.)

    4. Pisano, *Collected Works*

Tante volte si si si   **Cara**   4vv

    1. **56**, No.24 (*M.C.*)

3. I-Vnm, IV.1795–1798, No.89, 70r (Anon.)

4. Luisi, *Apografo*, 193 • Luisi, *Cantar*, 293–94 • Luisi & Zanovello, *Frottole*, 157 • Prizer, *Courtly*, ii, 136–39

Tanto e lafano
  See French texts: **Le desporveu infortune**   Caron   4vv

Tanto mi e il partir   Capreolus   4vv
  1. **23**, No.64 (*ANT. CAP.*) • **37**, No.64 (*ANT. CAP.*)
  4. Schwartz, *Frottole*, 83

Tanto po quel faretrato   d'Ana   4vv
  1. **18**, No.6 (*FRAN. ORGA.*) • **40**, No.6 (*FRAN. ORGA.*)
  4. Cesari, *Frottole*, 98

Te lamenti & io mi doglio   [Anon.]   4vv
    ?Antenore
  1. **17**, No.52 (Anon.) • **42**, No.52 (Anon.)
  Facsimile: Cesari, *Frottole*, p. CXXIV
  4. Cesari, *Frottole*, 88
  Comments: From the layout of adjacent pieces, this can perhaps be attributed to Antenore

Ti par gran meraveglia   Pifaro   4vv
  1. **23**, No.26 (*N.P.*) • **37**, No.26 (*N.P.*)
  4. Schwartz, *Frottole*, 61
  Intabulation: voice and lute
  1. **49**, No.64 (*N.P.*); **58**, No.64 (*N.P.*)
  4. Disertori, *Frottole*, 422

Trista e noiosa sorte   Michele [?Pesenti]   4vv
  1. **16**, No.49 (*MICHA.*)
  4. Cesari, *Frottole*, 35 • Schwartz, *Frottole*, 35

Troppo e amara   Tromboncino   4vv
  1. **18**, No.20 (*B.T.*) • **40**, No.20 (*B.T.*)
  4. Cesari, *Frottole*, 108

Tu dormi io veglio   [Anon.]   4vv
  1. **26**, No.9 (Anon.)
  3. GB-Lbl, Eg.3051, No.7, 9v–10r (Anon.)

Tu dormi io veglio
  See **Ecco che per amarti**   Tromboncino   4vv

Tu me strugi e dai tormento   [Anon.]   4vv
  1. **18**, No.39 (Anon.) • **40**, No.39 (Anon.)
  4. Cesari, *Frottole*, 125

Tu me voi crudel lassare   [Anon.]   4vv
  1. **17**, No.27 (Anon.) • **42**, No.27 (Anon.)
  4. Cesari, *Frottole*, 68

Tu mhai privato de riposo e pace   [Anon.]   4vv
  1. **23**, No.24 (Anon.) • **37**, No.24 (Anon.)
  4. Schwartz, *Frottole*, 60

Tu mi tormenti a torto   [Anon.]   4vv
  1. **48**, No.32 (Anon.)
  4. Facchin & Zanovello, *Frottole*, 178

Tu sei quella advocata   **Tromboncino**   4vv
  1. *41*, No.48 (*B.T.*: Additional text on folio 56*r*)
  4. Jeppesen, *Laude*, 76–77

Tu te lamenti a torto   **Michele** [?Pesenti]   4vv
  1. *16*, No.53 (*MICHA.*)
  3. I-Fc, 2441, No.39, 41*v*–42*r* (Anon.)
  Text by Tebaldeo
  4. Cesari, *Frottole*, 37 • Schwartz, *Frottole*, 36
  Intabulation: lute accompaniment to a Superius
  3. F-Pn, 27, No.66, 452 (Anon.)

Turluru la capra e moza   **Scotto**   4vv
  1. *36*, No.29 (*PAVLI SCOTI Cantus & verba*)
  4. Luisi, *Cantar*, 241

Tutti debiam cantare   **Dammonis**   4vv
  1. *29*, No.14 (Dammonis); *45*, No.14 (Dammonis)
  4. Jeppesen, *Laude*, 109

Tutto el mondo chiama   **Lurano**   4vv
  1. *23*, No.61 (*PHI. DE. LV.*) • *37*, No.61 (*PHI. DE. LV.*)
  3. GB-Lbl, Eg.3051, No.28, 33*v*–34*r* (Anon. Text *Dapoi chai el mio core*)
  4. Schwartz, *Frottole*, 82

Udite voi finestre   **Cara**   4vv
  1. *16*, No.12 (*M.C.*)
  3. F-Pn, 676, No.46, 54*v*–55*r* (Anon. Text *Audite . . .*)
  4. Cesari, *Frottole*, 10 • Schwartz, *Frottole*, 9
  Intabulation: voice and lute
  1. *49*, No.57 (*M.C.* Texted *Odite . . .*); *58*, No.57 (*M.C.* Texted *Odite . . .*)
  4. Disertori, *Frottole*, 410

Un sollicito amor una gran fede   **Lurano**   4vv
  1. *23*, No.91 (*PHI. DE. LV.* Headed *Aer de Capituli*) • *37*, No.91, (*PHI. DE. LV.* Headed
     Aer de Capitoli)
  4. Schwartz, *Frottole*, 99

Una legiadra donna   **Michele** [?Pesenti]   4vv
  1. *16*, No.52 (*MICHA.*)
  4. Cesari, *Frottole*, 36 • Schwartz, *Frottole*, 36

Una legiadra nimpha   **Capreolus**   4vv
  1. *48*, No.16 (*A.C.*)
  4. Facchin & Zanovello, *Frottole*, 145

Uscirallo o resterallo   **Timotheo**   4vv
  1. *56*, No.27 (*D. Timotheo*)
  4. Luisi, *Cantar*, 287–88 • Luisi, "Commedia", 296 • Luisi & Zanovello, *Frottole*, 164

Usciro de tanti affanni   **d'Ana**   4vv
  1. *35*, No.36 (*FRAN. ORGA. VENETVS*)
  4. Boscolo, *Frottole*, 197 • Luisi, *Laudario*, ii, 188–89

Va posa larcho e la pharetra amore   [Anon.]   4vv
  1. *23*, No.7 (Anon.) • *37*, No.7 (Anon.)
  4. Schwartz, *Frottole*, 50

Va va iniqua
    See **Vale iniqua e desliale**   [Anon.]   4vv

Vaga zoiosa e biancha   **Capreolus**   4vv
    1. **23**, No.6 (*ANT. CAP.*) • **37**, No.6 (*ANT. CAP.* All voices read *Vaga gioiosa e bella*)
    4. Schwartz, *Frottole*, 49

Vale diva mia va in pace   **Tromboncino**   4vv
    1. **16**, No.23 (*B. T.*)
    4. Cesari, *Frottole*, 17 • Schwartz, *Frottole*, 16 • Underwood, *Renaissance*, 226–32
    Intabulation: voice and lute
    1. **50**, No.52 (*B. T.* Text reads *Vale diva vale in pace*)
    4. Disertori, *Frottole*, 576–77 • Underwood, *Renaissance*, 226–32
    Intabulations: lute accompaniment to a Superius
    3. F-Pn, 27, No.53, 42*r* (Anon.) • F-Pn, 27, No.69, 45*v* (Anon.)
    4. Underwood, *Renaissance*, 226–32

Vale diva vale im pace
    See **Vale diva mia va in pace**   **Tromboncino**   4vv

Vale hormai con tua durezza   **Lurano**   4vv
    1. **23**, No.89 (*PHI. DE. LV.*) • **37**, No.89 (*PHI. DE. LV.*)
    3. I-Fn, 337, No.28, 38*v* (*P. de Lo.*)
    4. Schwartz, *Frottole*, 97

Vale iniqua e desliale   [Anon.]   4vv
    1. **26**, No.29 (Anon.)
    3. I-Bc, Q18, No.8, 8*v*-9*r* (Anon. Text *Va va iniqua*)

Vale iniqua hor vale   **Lulinus**   4vv
    1. **56**, No.56 (*Io. Lu. V.*)
    4. Luisi & Zanovello, *Frottole*, 237

Vale iniqua vale hormai   **Antiquis**   4vv
    1. **25**, No.41 (*A. DE. A.V.*)
    4. Zupanovic, *Sedamnaest frottola*

Vale signora vale   **Lurano**   4vv
    1. **48**, No.24 (*PH. D. L.*)
    4. Facchin & Zanovello, *Frottole*, 163

Vale valde decora   **Lurano**   4vv
    1. **48**, No.23 (*PH. D. L.*)
    4. Facchin & Zanovello, *Frottole*, 162

Valle che de lamenti   **Stringari**   4vv
    1. **56**, No.38 (*A.P.*)
    Text by Petrarch, *Canzoniere*, CCCI
    4. Luisi & Zanovello, *Frottole*, 189

Vana speranza incerta   **Tromboncino**   4vv
    1. **26**, No.21 (*B. T.*)

Vana speranza mia che mai non   **Lurano**   4vv
    1. **23**, No.11 (*PHILIPPVS L.*) • **37**, No.11 (*PHILIPPVS L.*)
    4. Schwartz, *Frottole*, 52
    Intabulation: lute accompaniment to a Superius
    3. F-Pn, 27, No.79, 47*r* (Anon.)

Ve mozza mia
    See **Nenciozza mia**   **Japart**   4vv

Vedo ben chio perdo el tempo   [Anon.]   4vv
      1. *17*, No.9 (Anon.) • *42*, No.9 (Anon.)
      4. Cesari, *Frottole*, 53

Vedo negli ochi toi   [Anon.]   4vv
      1. *48*, No.58 (Anon.)
      4. Facchin & Zanovello, *Frottole*, 239

Vedo ogni selva   **Cara**   4vv
      1. *35*, No.54 (*M.C.*)
      4. Boscolo, *Frottole*, 242 • Prizer, *Courtly*, ii, 104–106

Vedo sdegnato amor   **d'Ana**   4vv
      1. *23*, No.18 (*F.V.*) • *37*, No.18 (*F.V.*)
      3. GB-Lbl, Eg.3051, No.2, 4v-5r (Anon. Text *Veggio sdegnato amore*) • I-Fn, 230, No.35,
          34v-35r (Anon.) • I-Mt, 55, No.2, 2r and 8v (Anon. Text *Vego sdegnato amor*)
      Text by F. Cintio Anconitani
      4. Jeppesen, *Frottola*, iii, 183–84 • Schwartz, *Frottole*, 57

Veggio sdegnato amore
    See **Vedo sdegnato amor**   **d'Ana**   4vv

Vengo a te madre maria   **J. Fogliano**   4vv
                                    (Nicolo)
      1. *41*, No.4 (*Iacobus Folianus Mutinensis*) • *41*, No.13 (*D. NICOLO*. Texted *Senza te alta
      regina*)
      4. Jeppesen, *Laude*, 6–7

Vergine benedecta Del ciel   **Dammonis**   4vv
      1. *29*, No.20 (Dammonis. Headed *Ad beatam virginem*); *45*, No.20 (Dammonis)
      4. Jeppesen, *Laude*, 119

Vergine immaculata alma regina   **Cara**   4vv
      1. *41*, No.53 (*Marchetto*. Altus and Bassus open with *Virgine*)
      4. Jeppesen, *Laude*, 86–87

Vergine sacra e figlia del tuo figlio
    2/ of **Maria madre de Dio**   **Dammonis**   4vv

Vero amore vol ferma   [Anon.]   4vv
      1. *25*, No.29 (Anon.)

Vidi gia ne la sua corte
    2/ of **Segua pur seguir chi vole** **Antenore**   4vv

Vidi hor cogliendo rose   **Demophon**   4vv
      1. *36*, No.61 (*ALEXANDRO DEMOPHON*.)
      Intabulation: voice and lute
      1. *50*, No.18 (*Alexan. Demophon*)
      4. Disertori, *Frottole*, 493–95

Vien da poi   **Lurano**   4vv
      1. *23*, No.88 (*PHI. DE. LV.*) • *37*, No.88 (*PHI. DE. LV.*)
      4. Schwartz, *Frottole*, 96

Vieni hormai non piu tardare   **Michele** [?Pesenti]   4vv
      1. *16*, No.54 (*MICHA.*)
      4. Cesari, *Frottole*, 37 • Schwartz, *Frottole*, 36

Vilana che sa tu far   [Anon.]   4vv
>   1. *12*, No.84 (Anon.)
>   3. E-Sc, 5-I-43, No.25, d10v–e1r/34v–35r (Anon.) • I-Fn, 229, No.180, 190v–191 (Anon. Untexted)
>   4. Brown, *Florentine*, music volume, 411–14 • Moerk, *Seville*, ii, 62–64

Virtu che fai in questo miser mondo   **Dammonis**   4vv
>   2/ *Superbia et auaritia*
>   1. *29*, No.36 (Dammonis. Heading completely cropped); *45*, No.26 (Dammonis)
>   4. Luisi, *Laudario*, ii, 361–65

Visto ho piu volte   [?*Tromboncino*]   4vv
>   1. *26*, No.12 (*T.B.*)
>   3. GB-Lbl, Eg.3051, No.11, 13v–14r (Anon. Text *Quanto la fiama*)

Viva e morta voglio amarte   **Antenore**   4vv
>   1. *17*, No.37 (Anon.) • *42*, No.37 (*Honophrius Antenoreus*)
>   3. I-Bc, Q18, No.18, 18v–19r (Anon. Untexted)
>   4. Cesari, *Frottole*, 78

Vivero paziente forte   **Lurano**   4vv
>   1. *18*, No.8 (*PHI. DE. LV.*) • *40*, No.8 (*PHI. DE. LV.*)
>   3. F-Pn, 676, No.97, 107v–108r (Anon.) • I-Fc, 2441, No.56, 58v–59r (Anon.)
>   4. Cesari, *Frottole*, 99
>   Intabulation: lute accompaniment to a Superius
>   3. F-Pn, 27, No.83, 48v (Anon.)

Vivo lieto nel tormento   [Anon.]   4vv
>   1. *17*, No.19 (Anon.) • *42*, No.19 (Anon.)
>   4. Cesari, *Frottole*, 63

Voglio gir chiamando   **Luppato**   4vv
>   1. *16*, No.61 (*GEORGIUS LUPPATUS*)
>   3. I-Mt, 55, No.58, 60v–61r (Anon. à3)
>   4. Cesari, *Frottole*, 42 • Jeppesen, *Frottola*, iii, 306–307 • Schwartz, *Frottole*, 41

Voi che passati   **Tromboncino**   4vv
                                        (d'Ana)
>   1. *36*, No.21 (*B.T.*)
>   3. GB-Lbl, Eg.3051, No.18, 20v–21r (Anon.)
>   Intabulation: lute
>   3. US-Cn, 107501, No.11, 19r (Anon. Headed *voi che pasati qui nel ton del r*[ecercar] *3°*)
>   Intabulation: voice and lute
>   1. *49*, No.10 (*F.V.*); *58*, No.10 (*F.V.*)
>   4. Disertori, *Frottole*, 324–325
>   Comments: Disertori, *Frottole*, ascribes this to Varoter [= d'Ana]

Voi mi ponesti in foco   **Eustache de Monte Regali**   4vv
>   1. *56*, No.17 (*Eu. De. M. Regali. Gallus.*)
>   Text by Bembo, *Gli Asolani*
>   4. Luisi & Zanovello, *Frottole*, 139

Volgi gli ochi o madre pia   **Antiquis**   4vv
>   1. *41*, No.30 (*A.DE.A.V.*)
>   4. Jeppesen, *Laude*, 44

Comments: Jeppesen ascribes this piece to Demophon, on the basis of a misreading of the ascription

Volsi oime mirar troppo alto   **Tromboncino**   4vv
    1. *18*, No.3 (*B.T.*) • *40*, No.3 (*B.T.*)
    4. Cesari, *Frottole*, 94

Zephyro spira e il bel tempo   **Tromboncino**   4vv
    1. *35*, No.6 (*B.T.*. Additional text on folio 55*v*)
    4. Boscolo, *Frottole*, 125
    Intabulation: voice and lute
    1. *49*, No.16 (*B.T.*); *58*, No.16 (*B.T.*)
    4. Disertori, *Frottole*, 334–35

French Texts

A la audienche   **Hayne**   4vv
    1. *1*, No.93 (Incipit *Alaudienche* in the index. These folios lacking in the unique surviving copy) • *5*, No.93 (*Hayne*) • *14*, No.93 (*Hayne*)
    3. I-Fn, 229, No.104, 106*v*-108*r* (Anon.)
    4. Brown, *Florentine*, music volume, 210–13 • Hayne, *Opera Omnia*, 1 • Hewitt, *Odhecaton*, 411–13 • Marix, *Musiciens*, No.66, p. 100
    Comments: The work is cited by Aaron, in his *Trattato* (1526) ch.6.

A la mignonne de fortune
    See **La mignonne**   **Agricola**   3vv
A le regretz
    See **Ales regrets**   **Agricola**   3vv
A leure que ie vous p.x.   **Josquin**   4vv
    1. *12*, No.43 (*Josquin.*)
    4. Josquin, *Werken*, Wereldlijke, ii, 53

Aqui dirage mes pensees   **Compère**   3vv
    1. *2*, No.47 (Anon.) • *10*, No.47 (Anon.)
    2. *50 Carmina* (1513), No.47 (Anon.) • [c.1535][14], iii, No.21 (Anon.)
    3. D-HB, X.2, No.24 (Anon.) • I-Bc, Q16, No.21, 15*v*-16*v* (Anon.) • I-Rc, 2856, No.80, 103*v*-105*r* (*Compere*) • S-Uu, 76a, No.67, 73*v*-74*r* (Anon.)
    4. Compère, *Opera Omnia*, v, • Hewitt, *Canti B*, 226–28 • Wolff, *Chansonnier*, ii, 276–79

Aqui direlle sa pense   [Anon.]   4vv
    1. *2*, No.15 (Anon.) • *10*, No.15 (Anon.)
    2. *50 Carmina* (1513), No.15 (Anon.) • [c.1535][14], i, No.24 (Anon.)
    3. D-Rp, C.120, No.9, pp. 22–23 (Anon.) • I-Bc, Q18, No.92, 93*v* (Anon. Incomplete)
    4. Hewitt, *Canti B*, 134–37
    Monophonic version: F-Pn, 12744, No.11, 9*r* (Anon.)

A une dame j'ay faict veu
    See Latin texts: **Missus est Gabriel angelus**   **Mouton**   4vv
A une dame j'ay promis
    See Latin texts: **Missus est Gabriel angelus**   **Mouton**   4vv

A vous je vieng [Anon.] 4vv
    1. *12*, No.34, 50*v*-51*r* (Anon.)

Acordes moy ce que ye pense **Busnois** 4vv
    1. *1*, No.33 (Anon.) • *5*, No.33 (Anon.) • *14*, No.33 (Anon.)
    3. F-Pn, 15123, 140*v*-142*r* (Anon. Texted *Accordes moy jay bien pense*) • I-Fn, 229, No.154, 160*v*-161*r* (Anon.) • I-Rc, 2856, No.115, 148*v*-149*r* (*Busnoys*)
    4. Boer, *Chansonvormen*, 54 • Brown, *Florentine*, music volume, 331-34 • Hewitt, *Odhecaton*, 290-91 • Wolff, *Chansonnier*, ii, 405-10

Accordes moy jay bien pense
    See **Acordes moy ce que je pense** **Busnois** 4vv

Adieu fillette **Isaac** 3vv
    (Agricola)
    1. *2*, No.44 (Anon.) • *10*, No.44 (Anon.)
    2. *50 Carmina* (1513), No.44 (Anon.) • [c.1535][14], iii, No.18 (Anon.) • 1538[9], No.33 (Anon. Untexted)
    3. D-B, 40021, No.10, 30*v* (Anon. Untexted, titled *Sol re ut re ut*) • D-Kl, 53/2 (Anon.) • D-Z, LXXVIII, 3, No.24 (*Isaac.* Untexted) • S-Uu, 76a, No.65, 67*v*-68*r* (*ysac.* Untexted)
    4. Hewitt, *Canti B*, 218-20 • Isaac, *Weltliche*, 120-21 • Mönkemeyer, *Formschneyder*, i, pp. 54-55
    Intabulation: keyboard
    3. CH-SGs, 530, 11*v*-12*r* (*Alexander Agricola.* Titled *Non diva parens*)
    Literature: Just, "Examinatio"

Adieu mes amours **Josquin** 4vv
    1. *1*, No.14 (*Josquin.* Incipit *Adiu mes amours*) • *5*, No.14 (*Josquin*) • *14*, No.14 (*Josquin*)
    2. [c.1535][14], i, No.4 (Anon.)
    3. CH-SGs, 462, 40*v*-41*r* (Anon.) • CH-SGs, 463, No.177, 61*v* and 119*v* (*Iosquinus Pratensis*) • D-Mbs, 1516, No.14, f.14*r* (*Iosquin.* Transposed down a fourth) • D-Rp, C.120, No.84, pp. 304-305 (*Iosquin*) • I-Bc, Q17, No.54, 59*v*-60*r* (*Iosquin*) • I-Bc, Q18, beneath No.33, 33*v* (Discantus only, erased) • I-Bc, Q18, No.77, 78*v*-79*r* (Anon.) • I-Fn, 107[bis], No.10, 9*v*-10*r* (*Iosquin.* Incipit *Adiu mens amors*) • I-Fn, 178, No.44, 48*v*-49*r* (*Josquin Depres.* Incipit *Adiu mens amors*) • I-Fn, 229, No.158, 164*v*-165*r* (*Josquin*) • I-Fr, 2794, No.56, 65*v*-66*r* (*Iosequin*) • I-Rc, 2856, No.118, 153*v*-155*r* (*Joskim*) • I-Rvat, C.G.XIII.27, No.6, 6*v*-7*r* (13*v*-14*r*) (*Iosquin*) • PL-Kj, Mus.Ms.40092, 13*r*-14*r* (Anon. às) • US-Wc, Wolffheim, 84*v*-86*r* [modern 5*v*-7*r*] (Anon. *Josquin des Pres* in a later hand)
    4. Ambros, *Geschichte*, v, 131 • Bernoulli, *Liederbüchern*, 63 • Brown, *Florentine*, music volume, 345-48 • Geering & Trümpy, *Liederbuch*, No.46 • Hewitt, *Odhecaton*, 249-251 • Isaac, *Weltliche*, 135 • Jones, *First*, ii, 290-292 • Josquin, *Werken*, Wereldlijke, iv, 1 • Lenaerts, *Kunst* • Lowinsky, *Josquin*, 665 • Obrecht, *Werken*, Messen, iv, 38-40 • Obrecht, *Collected*, i, p. xiii • Smijers, *Van Ockeghem*, 156 • Torrefranca, *Segreto*, 540-43 • Wolff, *Chansonnier*, ii, 423-28
    Monophonic version: F-Pn, 9346, No.83, 85v (Anon.)
    Intabulations: keyboard
    3. CH-Bu, F.IX.22, No.21, 40*v*-41*r* (*Isac*) • CH-SGs, 530, No.112, 90*v*-91*r* (*Josquin despres*) • D-B, 40026, 104*v*-105*r*.
    Intabulations: lute
    1. *33*, No.18 (Anon; *Fran. Spi.* in the index)
    2. G1623 (1533), No.31, 39*r*-40*r* (Anon. Gerle) • 1536[12] = N521, No.50, p4*v*-q1*v* (Anon.

H. Newsidler) • 1536¹³ = N522, No.37 (31), X3v-Y2r (*Joss Quin*. H. Newsidler) • 1556³², No.9, c3v-c4v (Anon. Drusina)

3. A-Wn, 41950, No.3, 5r-rv (*Ad.mes Morſs Yosquin*) • D-Mbs, 272, No.34, 52v-53r (Anon.)

4. Schmidt, *Spinacino*, ii, 81–84; Thibault, "Instrumental", 456–58

Comments: Used as the basis of a mass by Obrecht, and a *Salve Regina* by Divitis • Cited in the Neuburg catalogue as an intabulation

Adieu solas adieu joye

See Latin texts: **Missa Regina mearum**: Kyrie   **Mouton**   4vv

Ales mon cor   **Agricola**   3vv

1. **1**, No.65 (*Alexander*) • **5**, No.65 (*Alexander*) • **14**, No.65 (*Alexnder* [*sic*])

2. [c.1535]¹⁴, iii, No.11 (Anon.)

3. D-Z, LXXVIII,3, No.12 (*Agricola*. Untexted)

4. Agricola, *Opera Omnia*, v, 19–20 • Hewitt, *Odhecaton*, 357–58

Ales regrets   **Agricola**   3vv

1. **1**, No.48 (*Agricola*) • **5**, No.48 (*Agricola*) • **14**, No.48 (*Agricola*)

3. CH-SGs, 461, pp. 82–83 (*Agricola*) • I-Rvat, C.G.XIII.27, No.64, 71v-72r (78v-79r) (*Agricola*. Texted *No men canteys canteys ala prunera*)

4. Agricola, *Opera Omnia*, v, 20–21 • Hewitt, *Odhecaton*, 323–24

Intabulation: lute

1. **34**, No.16 (*Francesco Spinacino*. Incipit *A le regretz*)

4. Agricola, *Opera Omnia*, v, 20 • Schmidt, *Spinacino*, ii, 218–21

Comments: Uses the Tenor of Hayne's chanson, also published by Petrucci • The work is cited in Aaron's *Trattato* (1525), ch.6

Ales regres   **Hayne**   3vv

1. **1**, No.57 (*Hayne*) • **5**, No.57 (*Hayne*) • **14**, No.57 (*Hayne*)

2. [c.1535]¹⁴, iii, No.26 (Anon.) • 1538⁹, No.7, B2r (MS attribution in the copy at D-Ju: *Hayne*. Untexted)

3. B-Br, 11239, No.1, 2v-4r (Anon.) • B-Br, IV.90, No.1, 1v-2v (Anon. Incomplete) • B-Tv, 94, No.1, 1v-3r (Anon.) • D-LEu, 49/50, 211r-211v/210v-211r (*M. Agr.*. Texted *Dulcis conjugi bonum*, as the secunda pars of *Nuptiae factae sunt.* • D-Z, LXXVIII,3, No.11 (Anon. Untexted) • DK-Kk, 1848, No.243, p. 414 (Anon.) • E-SE, s.s., No.89, 163v (*Scoen Hayne*) • F-Pn, 1597, No.11, 11v-12r (Anon.) • F-Pn, 2245, No.16, 17v-18r (*Hayne*) • GB-Lbl, Roy.20.A.xvi, No.15, 20v-21r (Anon.) • GB-Lbl, Add.31922, No.3, 5v-6r (Anon.) • I-Bc, Q17, No.26, 30v-31r (*Hayne*) • I-Fn, 107ᵇⁱˢ, No.28, 43v-44r (Anon.) • I-Fn, 117, No.30, 38v-39r (Anon.) • I-Fn, 178, No.38, 42v-43r (*Hayne*) • I-Fn, 229, No.225, 242v-243r (Anon.) • I-Fn, Panc.27, No.127, 97v-98r (*Hayne*) • I-Fr, 2356, No.71, 91v-92r (Anon.) • I-Fr, 2794, No.50, 58v-59r (*Hayne*) • I-Rc, 2856, No.76, 95v-97v (*Haine*) • I-Rvat, C.G.XIII.27, No.19, 20v-21r (27v-28r) (*Hayne*) • I-Tn, I.27, No.8, 12v (Anon.) • I-VEcap, DCCLVII, No.29, 28v-29r (Anon. Untexted) • S-Uu, 76a, No.1, 1r (Anon. Lacking the Superius) • US-Wc, Laborde, No.101, 140v-142r (Anon.)

Text attributed to Jean II de Bourbon in F-Pn, 2245

4. Baker, *Segovia* • Becherini, "Alcuni", 344 • Brown, *Florentine*, music volume, 527–29 • Droz, Thibault, *Poètes*, p. 49 • Gombosi, *Capirola*, No.21 • Gombosi, *Obrecht*, No.3 • Hayne, *Opera Omnia*, 3 • Hewitt, *Odhecaton*, 341–42 • Jones, *First*, ii, 277–79 • Josquin, *Werken*, Missen, 83 • Litterick, *Manuscript*, 250–51 • Maldeghem, *Trésor*, profane, XIII (1877), No.13 • Mönkemeyer, *Formschneyder*, i, p. 16 • Picker, *Chanson*, 416–18 • Stevens, *Henry VIII*, 3 • Villanis, "Alcuni", supp., No.2 • Wolff, *Chansonnier*, ii, 262–64

Intabulations: lute

2. G1623 (1533), No.34, 43*v*-44*v* (Anon. Gerle)

3. D-B, 40026, No.15, 21*r*-22*v* (Anon.) • US-Cn, 107501, No.21, 37*v*-38*v* (Anon.)

Comments: The Tenor is used in Agricola's setting, among others. The basis for masses by
Compère, Prioris, Scompanius

Alons ferons la barbe   **Compère**   4vv

   1. **1**, No.26 (*Compere*) • **5**, No.26 (*Compere*) • **14**, No.26 (*Compere*)

   3. CH-SGs, 463, No.178, 61*v* and 119*v* (*Compere*. Text *Alons ferons barbe*) • DK-Kk, 1848,
No.3, p. 2 (Anon. Text *Alons faire nous barbes*) • F-Pn, 1817, No.11 (Anon. Text *Alons
fere no barbes*) • I-CT, 95–96, No.11, 10*r*-11*r* (Anon. Text *Alons fere no barbes*) • I-Fn, 107bis,
No.18, 17*v*-18*r* (Anon. Text *Alons fere une barbe*) • I-Fn, 164–67, No.65, 79*r*-79*v* (Anon.
Text *Alons feronus barbes*)

   4. Boer, *Chansonvormen*, No.12 • Compère, *Opera Omnia* • Hewitt, *Odhecaton*, 275–76

Amie des que

   See Latin texts: **Missa Charge de deul**: Christe **Isaac**   3vv

Amor fait mult / Il est de bonne heure /   **Japart**   4vv

   Tant que nostre   (Busnois / Pierson)

   1. **1**, No.31 (Anon.) • **5**, No.31 (Anon.) • **14**, No.31 (Anon.)

   3. B-Br, IV.90, No.14, 18*v*-19*v* (Anon. Incipit 1) • B-Br, IV.1274, No.2, 4*v*-5*v* (Anon.) • B-
Tv, 94, No.13, 18*v*-19*r* (Anon. Incipit 2) • CH-Bu, F.X.1–4, No.93, p. 111 (*Pirson*. Incipit
3) • D-Rp, C.120, p. 214 (Anon. Incipit 3) • I-Bc, Q17, No.58, 63*v*-64*r* (*A Busnois*.
Incipits 1 and 3) • I-Fn, 107bis, No.8, 7*v*-8*r* (Anon. Incipit 1) • I-Fn, 178, No.53, 57*v*-58*r*
(Anon. Incipit 1) • I-Fn, 229, No.157, 163*v*-164*r* (*Jannes Japart*. Incipits 1 and 3) • I-Fr,
2794, No.23, 26*v*-27*r* (Anon. All incipits) • I-Rc, 2856, No.121, 159*v*-160*r* (*Io. Iappart*.
All incipits) • I-Rvat, 11953, No.11, 9*r*-9*v* (Anon. Incipit 3) • I-Rvat, C.G.XIII.27, No.3,
10*v*-11*r* (Anon. Incipit 1)

   4. Becherini, "Alcuni", 340 • Brown, *Florentine*, music volume, 342–44 • Hewitt, *Odhecaton*,
286–287 • Jones, *First*, ii, 210–12 • Obrecht, *Werken*, vii, 99–100 • Torrefranca, *Segreto*,
544–46 • Wolff, *Chansonnier*, ii, 439–43

Amor me trotent sur la pance

   See **Amours me troct sur la pance**   **Braconnier**   4vv

Amours amours   **Japart**   4vv

                                                   (Busnois)

   1. **1**, No.23 (*Japart*. Incomplete) • **5**, No.23 (*Japart*) • **14**, No.23, (*Japart*)

   3. I-Bc, Q17, No.62, 67*v*-68*r* (*A. Busnois*) • I-Fn, 229, No.164, 172*v*-173*r* (Anon.)

   4. Brown, *Florentine*, music volume, 364–66 • Hewitt, *Odhecaton*, 271–72

Amours amours trop me fiers   **Hayne**   4vv

   1. **1**, No.9 (*Hayne*) • **5**, No.9 (*Hayne*) • **14**, No.9 (*Hayne*)

   3. The following sources are all à3: E-SE, s.s., No.129, 183*v* (*Scoen Heyne*) • F-Pn, 4379,
No.44, 10*v*-11*r*/17*v*-18*r* (Anon.) • F-Pn, 15123, 84*v*-85*r* (Anon.) • I-Bc, Q16, No.20, 27*v*-
28*r* (Anon.) • I-Fn, 229, No.264, 285*v*-286*r* (Anon.) • I-Fr, 2794, No.18, 21*v*-22*r* (Anon.)
• I-MC, 871, No.105, 152*v*-153*r* (pp. 382–383) (Anon.) • I-PEc, 431, No.60, 85*v*-86*r*
(Anon.) • I-Rc, 2856, No.43, 50*v*-51*r* (*Haine*) • I-Rvat, C.G.XIII.27, No.93, 107*v*-108*r*
(Anon.) • I-TRc, 89, 25*v*-26*r* [No.522] (*Heyne*) • PL-Kj, 40098, No.259 (Anon. Untexted)
• S-Uu, 76a, No.14, 11*v*-12*r* (Anon.) • US-Wc, Laborde, 93*v*-94*r* (Anon.)

   4. Brown, *Florentine*, music volume, 629–32 • Hayne, *Opera Omnia*, 5–6, 7 • Hewitt, *Odhecaton*, 237–39 • Jones, *First*, ii, 199–201 • Moerk, *Seville*, ii, 108–109 • Pope and Kanazawa,

Montecassino, 416–19 • Ringmann, *Glogauer*, 55 • *Trent*, vii, 257–58 • Underwood, *Renaissance*, 129–35 • Wolff, *Chansonnier*, ii, 147–49

Intabulation: lute

1. *34*, No.17 (*Francesco Spinacino*)

4. Schmidt, *Spinacino*, ii, 222–25 • Underwood, *Renaissance*, 129–35

Intabulation: lute accompaniment to a Superius

3. F-Pn, 27, No.108, 53*v*-54*r* (Anon. Headed *Tenor e ctra d'mors amors*)

Amours fait mult

See **Amor fait mult**   **Japart**   4vv

Amours me troct sur la pance   **Braconnier**   4vv

1. *2*, No.33 (.*Lourdoys*.) • *10*, No.33 (*Lourdoys*.)

2. *50 Carmina* (1513), No.33 (*Lourdoys*)

3. I-Fc, 2442, No.26, 42*v*-44*r* (*Lourdault*)

4. Hewitt, *Canti B*, 181–85

Amours nest pas   [Anon.]   4vv

1. *12*, No.71 (Anon.)

Au joly moys de may

See **Je ne fay plus**   **Busnois**   4vv

Avant a moy   [Anon.]   4 ex 2vv

1. *12*, No.112 (Anon. Rubric, above each voice: *Fuga in diatessaron superius*)

Avant avant   [Anon.]   4 ex 3vv

1. *2*, No.38 (Anon. Headed *In subdiatessaron*) • *10*, No.38 (Anon. Headed *In subdiatessaron*)

2. *50 Carmina* (1513), No.38 (Anon.)

4. Hewitt, *Canti B*, 199–200

Aymy aymy   [Anon.]   4vv

1. *12*, No.100, 125*v*-126*r* (Anon.)

Basies moy   **Josquin**   6 ex 3vv

1. *2*, No.37 (Anon. Headed *Fuga In diatessaron*) • *10*, No.37 (Anon. Headed *Fuga In diatessaron*)

2. *50 Carmina* (1513), No.21 (Anon.) • 1545[15], No.21, xiir (*Iosquin de Pres*) • J681 (1549), No.22, xiir (Iosquin des prez)

3. DK-Kk, 1848, p. 133 (*Josquin*)

4. Hewitt, *Canti B*, 195–98 • Josquin, *Werken*, Wereldlijke, i, 5

Basies moy   **Josquin**   4 ex 2vv

1. *2*, No.34 (.*Josquin*) • *10*, No.34 (*Josquin*)

2. *50 Carmina* (1513), No.34 (*Josquin*) • 1520[3], No.12, 17*v*-18*r* (Anon. *Beises moy* in the index) • [c.1535][14], i, No.33 (Anon.) • J681 (1550), No.22 (Josquin)

3. B-Br, IV.90, No.18, 23*v*-24*v* (Anon.) • B-Br, IV.1274, No.6, 10*r*-10*v* (Anon.) • B-Tv, 94, No.17, 22*v*-23*v* (Anon.) • F-Pn, 1817, No.2 (Anon.) • I-CT, 95–96, No.2, 2*r*-2*v* (Anon.)

4. Hewitt, *Canti B*, 186–187 • Josquin, *Werken*, Wereldlijke, i, 5

Monophonic version: F-Pn, 9346, No.102 (Anon.)

Belles sur toutes / Tota pulchra es   **Agricola**   3vv

1. *12*, No.133 (*Agricola*)

2. 1529[4], No.25 (Anon.) • 1538[9], No.84, L3*r* (MS attribution in the copy at D-Ju: *Agricola*. Only the French incipit)

3. CH-Sgs, 462, 37*r* (Anon.) • GB-Lbl, Add.31922, 99*v*-100*r* (Anon. à4) • I-Fc, 2439, No.58, 63*v*-64*r* (*Alexander Agricola*. Only the French text)

4. Agricola, *Opera Omnia*, iv, 52–53 • Geering and Trümpy, *Liederbuch*, 69–70 • Mönkemeyer, *Formschneyder*, ii, 122 • Newton, *Florence*, ii, 186–87 • Schering, *Geschichte*, 49 • Stevens, *Henry VIII*, 72–73

Intabulations: keyboard

3. CH-Bu, F.IX.22, No.25, 47v–48r (Anon.) • D-B, 40026

Berzeretta sauoyene [Anon.] 4vv

1. *12*, No.42 (Anon.)

4. Brown, *Theatrical*, 20–21

Bergerette savoyene Josquin 4vv

1. *1*, No.10 (*Josquin*) • *5*, No.10 (*Josquin*) • *14*, No.10 (*Josquin*)

3. CH-SGs, 463, 128v–129r (*Josquin dun pres.* Texted *Verginorette savosienne*) • E-SE, s.s., No.59, 128v–129r (*Josquin Dupres.* Texted *Verginorette sevosienne*) • I-Fn, 107bis, No.20, 19v–20r (*Iosquin.* Texted *Biageretta savoiana*)

4. Hewitt, *Odhecaton*, 240–41 • Brumel, *Opera Omnia*, v, 116–17 • Josquin, *Werken*, Wereld-lijke, ii, 53

Monophonic version: F-Pn, 12744, 9v (Anon.)

Comments: The basis for Brumel's mass, also printed by Petrucci

Bergirette Savoyene Spinacino lute

Intabulation: lute

1. *34*, No.1 (*Francesco Spinacino*)

4. Schmidt, *Spinacino*, ii, 160–63

Bon me larim bom bom

See **Corps digne / Dieu quel mariage** Busnois 4vv

Bon temps [Anon.] 4vv

1. *2*, No.14 (Anon.) • *10*, No.14 (Anon.)

2. *50 Carmina* (1513), No.14 (Anon.)

4. Hewitt, *Canti B*, 132–34 • Obrecht, *Werken*, iv, 126–27

Literature: Hewitt, "Chanson rustique"

Brunette Stockem 5vv

1. *1*, No.5 (*Jo. Sthokem*) • *5*, No.5 (*Jo. Sthokem*) • *14*, No.5 (*Jo. stokem*)

3. A-Wn, 18746, No.28 (Anon. Texted *Brunette mamiette*) • CH-SGs, 461, pp. 26–27 (*Io. Stockem*)

4. Hewitt, *Odhecaton*, 228–29 • Torrefranca, *Segreto*, 547–49

C'est mal charche Agricola 4vv

1. *1*, No.12 (*Agricola*) • *5*, No.12 (*Agricola*) • *14*, No.12 (*Agricola*)

3. DK-Kk, 1848, No.152, p. 225 (Anon.)

The following sources are à3: D-ISL, 124, No.43 (*Agricola.* Incomplete) • E-Sc, 5-I-43, No.152, q3v–4r/123v–124r (*Agricola*) • F-Pn, 1719, 29r–29v (Anon.) • GB-Lbl, Roy.20.A.xvi, No.6, 10v–11r (Anon.) • GB-Lbl, Add.35087, No.25, 37v–38r (*Agricola* [with a rebus]) • I-Fn, 178, No.16, 20v–21r (*Alexander.* Texted *Id est trophis*) • I-Fn, 229, No.64, 65v–66r (*Alexander Agricola*) • I-Rc, 2856, No.17, 19v–20r (*Agricola*) • I-VEcap, DCCLVII, No.27, 26v–27r (Anon. Untexted)

4. Agricola, *Opera Omnia*, v, 22–23 • Boer, *Chansonvormen*, No.6 • Brown, *Florentine*, music volume, 130–31 • Hewitt, *Odhecaton*, 244–45 • Litterick, *Manuscript*, 229–30 • Moerk, *Seville*, ii, 372–73 • McMurtry, *Chansonnier*, 280–83 • Wolff, *Chansonnier*, ii, 53–55

Comments: Cited in Aaron, *Toscanello* (edn. of 1529), apparently referring to the Odhecaton edition

Cest ung maves mal   [Anon.]   4vv
    1. *12*, No.16 (Anon.)
    4. Brown, *Theatrical*, 28–30

Cest vous
  See **Royne de fleurs**   **Agricola**   3vv

Ce nest pas jeu   **La Rue**   4vv
    1. *2*, No.7 (*Pe.de.la rue*) • *10*, No.7 (*Pe.de.la rue*.)
    2. *50 Carmina* (1513), No.7 (*Pe de la Rue*) • [c.1535]¹⁴, i, No.18 (Anon. Transposed down a fifth)
    3. B-Br, 228, No.4, 5v-6r (Anon.) • B-Br, 11239, No.16, 23v (*de la Rue*) • I-Rvat, 11953, No.13, 11v-12r (Anon.)
    4. Hewitt, *Canti B*, 114–16 • Maldeghem, *Trésor*, profane, XX (1884), 21–22 • Picker, *Chanson*, 188–91
  Intabulation: lute
    2. G1620 (1532), No.37, Q1v (Anon. Gerle. Titled *Cenespas*)

Ce nest pas
  See Italian works: **La Stangetta**   **Weerbeke**   3vv

Cela sans plus   **Colinet**   4vv
                    (Josquin)
                    Martini for Altus
    1. *2*, No.16 (Anon: *Lannoy* in the index) • *10*, No.16 (Anon: *Lanvoy* in the index)
    2. *50 Carmina* (1513), No.16 (*Lannoy*) • [c.1535]¹⁴, i, No.23 (Anon.)
    3. D-Rp, C.120, No.91, pp. 316–17 (Anon.) • I-Rc, 2856, No.117, 153v-154r (*Colinet de Lannoy*. The fourth voice, the same as that in 1502², is here attributed to *Jo. Martini*)
        The following sources are à3: E-Sc, 5-I-43, No.74, j4v-5r/54v-55r (Anon.) • I-Bc, Q16, No.42, 51v-52r (Anon.) • I-Bc, Q17, No.15, 19v-20r (*Colinet de Lannoy*) • I-Fn, 176, No.1, 0v-1r (Anon.) • I-Fn, 178, No.35, 39v-40r (*Iosquin*) • I-Fn, 229, No.98, 100v-101r (*Collinet de Lanoy*) • I-Rvat, C.G.XIII.27, No.72, 86v-87r (*Colinet*) • US-Wc, Wolffhiem, 91v-92r (Anon, ascription to *de Lannoy* in a later hand)
  Text cited by Molinet in *Le debat du viel gendarme*
    4. Brown, *Florentine*, music volume, 198–200 • Hewitt, *Canti B*, 137 39 • Martini, *Secular*, 5–7 • Moerk, *Seville*, ii, 179–80 • Obrecht, *Werken*, vii, 83–84 • Wolf, *Handbuch*, i, 395–97
  Intabulation: keyboard
    3. CH-SGs, 530, No.91, 65r (*Johannes Zela zens plus*)
  Literature: Warburton, "Sicher"
  Comments: The basis for Obrecht's mass, also printed by Petrucci, and for a mass by Martini. The tenor is also used in other settings

Cela sans plus   **Japart**   4vv
    1. *1*, No.24 (Anon. Incomplete) • *5*, No.24 (Anon.) • *14*, No.24, (Anon.)
    3. I-Fn, 229, No.108, 111v-112r (*Jannes Japart*)
    4. Brown, *Florentine*, music volume, 219–20 • Hewitt, *Odhecaton*, 272–73
  Intabulation: keyboard
    2. CH-SGs, 530, No.7 (Incipit *Zela sans plus non susipias*)

Cela sans plus   **Josquin**   3vv
    1. *1*, No.61 (*Josquin*) • *5*, No.61 (*Josquin*) • *14*, No.61 (*Josquin*)
    2. [c.1535]¹⁴, iii, No.8 (Anon.)

3. CH–SGs, 461, No.47, pp. 88–89 (*Josq-*) • D–Z, LXXVIII,3, No.13 (*Josquin*. Untexted) • I–VEcap, DCCLVII, No.47, 47*v*-48*r* (Anon. Untexted)

4. Boer, *Chansonvormen*, 82–83 • Hewitt, *Odhecaton*, 349–50 • Josquin, *Werken*, Wereldlijke, ii, 53

Comments: Cited in Aaron, *Trattato* (1525), ch.3 • See Fallows, *Catalogue*, p. 104, for suggested texts

Cela sans plus   **Obrecht**   4 ex 2vv

1. **2**, No.13 (.*Obreht In missa.*) • **10**, No.13 (.*Obreht In missa:*)
2. *50 Carmina* (1513), No.13 (*Obrecht*) • [c.1535][14], i, No.22 (Anon.)
3. PL–WRu, 428, 35*v*-36*r* (Anon. Texted as the Osanna of a mass on the chanson *Cela sans plus*, 26*v*-41*r*)
4. Hewitt, *Canti B*, 130–32 • Obrecht, *Werken*, vii, 12–13

Comments: The attributions in Petrucci are the only evidence for the authorship of the mass, preserved entire and anonymously in PL–WRu, 428

Literature: Staehelin, *Grüne*

Cent mille escus   **Caron**   4vv
                              (Busnois)

1. **12**, No.97 (Anon.)
3. D–W, 287, 63*v* (Anon.) • E–Sc, 5-I-43, No.55 (Anon.) • F–Dm, 517, No.127, 149*v*-150*r* (Anon.) • F–Pn, 15123, 10*v*-11*r* (*Busnoys*, trimmed) • F–Pn, 2973, No.22, 29*r*-30*r* (Anon.) • I–Bc, Q16, No.126, 146*v*-147*r* (Anon.) • I–Fn, 178, No.57, 61*v*-62*r* (Anon.) • I–Fn, 229, No.70, 71*v*-72*r* (*Busnoys*) • I–PEc, 431, No.27, 48*v*-49*r* (Anon.) • I–Rc, 2856, No.23, 26*v*-27*r* (*Caron*) • I–Rvat, C.G.XIII.27, No.31, 41*v*-42*r* (*Caron*) • I–VEcap, DCCLVII, No.59, 61*v*-62*r* (Anon. Untexted) • PL–Kj, 40098, No.272 (Anon. Untexted. Headed with the letter *P*)
4. Ambros, *Geschichte*, ii, 554 • Brooks, *Busnois*, ii, 297 • Brown, *Florentine*, music volume, 142–144 • Caron, *Oeuvres*, ii, 167 • Gutiérrez-Derhoff, *Wolfenbütteler*, 94 • Ringmann, *Glogauer*, iv, 67 • Thibault & Fallows, *Chansonnier*, 45 • Wolff, *Chansonnier*, ii, 76–79

Intabulation: lute
1. **34**, No.12 (*Francesco Spinacino*)
4. Schmidt, *Spinacino*, ii, 207–209

Ceulx que font la gorra
See **Il son bien pelles**   [Anon.]   4vv

Chanter ne puis   **Compère**   3vv

1. **2**, No.45 (.*Compere.*) • **10**, No.45 (*Compere*. The incipits of Superius and Contra, and the index entry all read *Chauter ne puis*)
2. *50 Carmina* (1513), No.45 (*Compere*) • [c.1535][14], iii, No.19 (Anon.)
3. D–HB, X.2, No.20 (*Compere*)
4. Compère, *Opera Omnia*, v, • Hewitt, *Canti B*, 221–22

Che letourmon gre
See **Helas que il est a mon gre**   **Japart**   4vv

Chescun me crie   [Anon.]   4vv

1. **12**, No.21 (Anon.)
3. F–Pn, 1817, 18*v*-19*r* (Anon.) • I–CT, 95–96, 15*r*-16*r* (Anon.)

Comme femme   [Anon.]

Intabulation: lute
1. **44**, No.1 (*Alemannus*)

Comments: This intabulation of an unspecified setting is cited from Colón's description of the book

Comme femme   **Agricola**   4vv

1. *12*, No.83 (Anon.)

3. D-B, 40021, No.64, 134*v*-135*r* (Anon. Texted *Ave que sublimaris*) • I-Fc, 2439, No.39, 42*v*-44*r* (*Allexander*)

4. Agricola, *Opera Omnia*, iv, 60-61 and v, 72-74 • Newton, *Florence*, ii, 127-31

Comme femme   **Agricola**   3vv

1. *12*, No.121 (*Agricola*)

2. 1538[9], No.26. (Anon. MS ascriptions to *Agricola* in the D-B and D-Ju copies. Untexted)

3. D-B, 40021, No.62, 131*v*-132*r* (Anon. Texted *Virgo sub etheris*) • F-Pn, 1597, No.27, 29*v*-30*r* (Anon.) • I-Fc, 2439, No.68, 74*v*-76*r* (*Alexander*) • I-Rc, 2856, No.98, 126*v*-128*r* (*Agricola*. Texted *Come fame*) • I-Rvat, C.G.XIII.27, No.95, 109*v*-111*r* (*Agricola*)

4. Agricola, *Opera Omnia*, iv, 62-63 and v, 75-76 • Ambros, *Geschichte*, v, 180-82 • Mönkemeyer, *Formschneyder*, i, pp. 41-42 • Newton, *Florence*, ii, 215-18 • Wolff, *Chansonnier*, ii, 341-45. • *EDM 77*

Text by Aeneis Silvius or Conrad Celtis (See Just, "Mensuralkodex", ii, 134)

Intabulation: lute

1. *33*, No.4 (*Francesco Spinacino*; *Fran.Spi.* in the index)

4. Schmidt, *Spinacino*, ii, 11-16

Comments: This, as the more popular setting, and in three voices, is possibly the chanson which was intabulated for the opening of Alemannus's third book of intabulations.

Comment peult   [Anon.]   4vv

1. *2*, No.20 (Anon.) • *10*, No.20 (Anon.)

2. *50 Carmina* (1513), No.20 (Anon.) • [ca.1535][14], i, No.28 (Anon.)

4. Hewitt, *Canti B*, 148-49

Coment peult haver ioye   **Josquin**   4 ex 3vv

1. *2*, No.19 (.*Josquin.*) • *10*, No.19 (.*Josquin.*)

2. *50 Carmina* (1513), No.19 (*Josquin*) • [ca.1535][14], i, No.27 (Anon.) • 1547[1], 356-57 (*Iodocus Pratensis*. Text *O Jesu fili David*)

3. I-Bc, Q17, No.53, 58*v*-59*r* (*Josquin*. Rubric: *Fuga duorum temporum per dyapason*) • I-Fn, 178, No.5, 7*v*-8*r* (*Josquin*. Text *O men pot auer yoye*) • I-Rvat, C.G.XIII.27, No.4, 11*v*-12*r* (*Josquin Despres*. Incipit *Ne come peult*)

4. Disertori, *Frottole*, 184-87 • Glareanus, *Dodecachordon*, ii, 434 • Hawkins, *History*, ii, 467-69 • Hewitt, *Canti B*, 145-47 • Josquin, *Werken*, Wereldlijke, ii, 54

Intabulation: lute

1. *34*, No.14 (*Francesco Spinacino*)

3. EIR-Dtc, D.3.30/I, No.152, pp. 168-9 (*per Francesca Spinakino*)

4. Disertori, *Frottole*, 184-87 • Schmidt, *Spinacino*, ii, 212-15

Corps digne / Dieu quel mariage   **Busnois**   4vv

1. *12*, No.81 (*Busnoys*)

3. D-B, 40021, No.24, 59*r* (*Busnois*. Untexted) • I-Fn, 229, No.182, 192*v*-193*r* (Anon. Incipit *Bon me larim bom bom*)

4. Brown, *Florentine*, music volume, 417-19 • Smijers, *Van Ockeghem*, i, 27

Crions nouel   **Agricola**   3vv

1. *1*, No.75 (*Agricola*) • *5*, No.75 (*Agricola*) • *14*, No.75 (*Agricola*)

4. Agricola, *Opera Omnia*, v, 54-55 • Hewitt, *Odhecaton*, 377-78

Damer ie me veul intremetre   **Fortuila**   4vv

    1. *12*, No.46 (*.Jo.Fortuila.*)

De la momera

    See **Petite camusete**   **Ockeghem**   4vv

De tous biens playne   [Anon.]   3vv

    (Hayne)

    1. *12*, No.118 (Anon.)

    2. 1538^9, No.60 (Anon: ascribed in the D-Ju copy to *Hayne*)

    3. I-Rvat, C.G.XIII.27, No.16, 24*v*-25*r* (Anon.)

    4. Gombosi, *Obrecht*, No.17 • Mönkemeyer, *Formschneyder*, ii, pp. 89–90

    Intabulations: keyboard

    2. D-B, 40026 (Anon. Headed *Carmen in fa*)

De tous biens   [Anon.]   3vv

    1. *12*, No.119 (Anon.)

    4. Gombosi, *Obrecht*, No.15

De tous biens playne   [Anon.]   4vv

    1. *12*, No.67 (Anon.)

De tous biens   [Anon.]   4vv

    1. *12*, No.85 (Anon.)

De tous biens playne   **Agricola**   4vv

    1. *12*, No.63 (*Agricola*)

    3. The following sources are á3: I-Rvat, C.G.XIII.27, No.63, 77*v*-78*r* (Anon.) • I-VEcap, DCCLVII, No.42, 42*v*-43*r* (Anon.)

    4. Agricola, *Opera Omnia*, v, 78–79 • Gombosi, *Obrecht*, No.18

    Comments: Uses the tenor of Hayne's chanson

De toulx bien   **Bourdon**   3vv

    (Agricola)

    1. *1*, No.73 (*Pe.bourdon*) • *5*, No.73 (Anon: *Bourdon* in the index) • *14*, No.73 (Anon: *Bourdon* in the index)

    3. E-SE, s.s., No.109, 173v (*Alexander Agricola*)

    4. Agricola, *Opera Omnia*, v, 123–124 • Gombosi, *Obrecht*, No.16 • Hewitt, *Odhecaton*, 373–74

    Comments: The *Cantus firmus* is taken from Hayne's chanson

De tous biens   **Ghiselin**   3vv

    1. *2*, No.42 (*Ghiselin*) • *10*, No.42 (*Ghiselin.*)

    2. *50 Carmina* (1513), No.42 (*Ghiselin*) • [ca.1535]^{14}, iii, No.16 (Anon.)

    3. D-Kl, 53/2, No.13 (Anon. Incomplete)

    4. Ghiselin, *Opera Omnia*, iv, 6–8 • Hewitt, *Canti B*, 212–14

    Intabulation: lute

    4. 1536^{13} = N522, No.9, D2*r*-D3*r* (*Ghiselin. H. Newsidler. Titled Tus Biens*)

De tous biens playne   **Hayne**   4vv

    1. *1*, No.20 (Anon.) • *5*, No.20 (Anon.) • *14*, No.20 (Anon.)

    3. I-Bc, Q18, No.47, 48*r* (Incomplete, with a different fourth voice)

        The following sources are à3: D-Usch, 237a-d, No.21, ff.17*r*, 15*r* 16*r* (Anon.) • D-W, 287, No.43, 52*v*-53*r* (Anon.) • DK-Kk, 291, No.5, 5*v*-6*r* (Anon.) • DK-Kk, 1848, p. 201, incomplete (Anon.) • E-Sc, 5-I-43, No.48, g3*r*/39*r*, incomplete (Anon.) • F-Dm, 517, No.10, 11*v*-12*r* (*Hayne*) • F-Pn, 15123, No.90, 105*v*-106*r* (Anon.) • F-Pn, 2973,

No.19, 25*v*-26*r* (Anon.) • F-Pn, 676, No.35, 42*v*-43*r* (Anon.) • GB-Lbl, Add.31922, No.36, 40*v*-41*r* (Anon.) • I-Bc, Q16, No.115, 133*v*-134*r* (Anon.) • I-Fn, 121, No.24, 24*v*-25*r* (Anon.) • I-Fn, 178, No.30, 34*v*-35*r* (*Hayne*) • I-Fn, Panc.27, No.40. 25*r* (Anon.) • I-Fr, 2356, No.22, 26*v*-27*r* (Anon.) • I-Fr, 2794, No.15, 18*v*-19*r* (Anon.) • I-MC, 871, No.85, 102*v* (p. 344) (Anon.) • I-PAVu, 362, No.18, 34bis*v*-35*r* (*Heyne*) • I-PEc, 431, No.48, 70*v*-71*r* (*Hayne*) • I-Rc, 2856, No.55, 66*v*-67*r* (*Haine*) • I-Rvat, C.G.XIII.27, No.52, 64*v*-65*r* (*Hayne*. Two different versions à3, using the same Superius) • S-Uu, 76a, No.18, 15*v*-16*r* (Anon.) • US-NH, 91, No.32, 42*v*-43*r* (*Heyne*) • US-Wc, Laborde, No.49, 62*v*-63*r* (Anon.) • ZA-Csa, Grey, No.54, 84*v*-85*r* (Anon. Texted *Cum defecerint ligna*)

Text cited by Molinet in several works.

4. Ambros, *Geschichte*, ii, 5 • Disertori, *Frottole*, 210–14 • Droz, Thibault, Rokseth, *Chansonniers*, No.11 • Gombosi, *Obrecht*, No.14 • Hayne, *Opera Omnia*, 14 • Hewitt, *Odhecaton*, 263–64 • Jeppesen, *Kopenhagener*, No.5 • Jones, *First*, ii, 194–96 • Moerk, *Seville*, ii, 117–18 • Perkins and Garey, *Mellon*, No.32 • Pope and Kanazawa, *Montecassino*, 320–23 • Smijers, *Van Ockeghem*, iv, 144–45 • Stevens, *Henry VIII*, 30 • Thibault and Fallows, *Chansonnier* • Underwood, *Renaissance*, 12–23 • Wolff, *Chansonnier*, ii, 186–88

Intabulation: lute

3. CH-Fcu, 527, 2*r*-2*v* (Anon.) • I-PESo, 1144, pp. 65–68 (Anon.) • US-Cn, 107501, No.13, 20*v*-22*r* (Anon. Headed *Detobiens plaene nel ton del p° Ric*[ercar])

Intabulation: two lutes

1. *33*, No.9 (*Francesco Spinacino*; *Fran* in the index) • See also *Recercare de tous biens*.

4. Disertori, *Frottole*, 210–14 • Schmidt, *Spinacino*, ii, 39–44 • Underwood, *Renaissance*, 12–23

Comments: It is perhaps significant of the fame of this version of the work, and of its role as a stimulus to others, that it is the only setting of this text not to have a composer's name attached to it in the index of 1501 • The work is cited in Aaron *Trattato* (1525), ch.4

De tous biens   **Japart**   4vv

1. *12*, No.60 (*Jo. Japart*)

3. E-SE, s.s., 173*v* (Anon.)

4. Gombosi, *Obrecht*, No.19

De tous biens playne   **Josquin**   4 ex 3vv

1. *1*, No.95 (*Josquin* in index. These folios are lacking in the unique copy) • *5*, No.95 (Anon: *Josquin* in the index) • *14*, No.95 (Anon: *Josquin* in the index)

2. 1547[1], pp. 452–53 (*Jodocus Pratensis*)

4. Glareanus, *Dodecachordon* • Hewitt, *Odhecaton*, 418–20 • Josquin, *Werken*, Wereldlijke, ii, 53

De tous biens   **Josquin**   3 ex 2vv

1. *3*, No.35 (*Josquin* is entered over the lower, canonic voice, with the rubric *Canon. Fuga per semibrevem in netesinemenon*. *Josquin* is also named in the index) • *19*, No.35 (*Josquin* as in the first edition)

4. Drake, *First*, ii, 135–36 • Osthoff, *Josquin*, ii, 395–96

De tous biens playne

See Latin texts: **Beati pacifici**	**van Stappen**	4vv
two voices of **Jay pris amours**	[Anon.]	4vv
Tenor of **Je cuide**	**Congiet/Japart**	4vv
See **Victime paschali**	**Josquin**	4vv

De votre deul   [Anon.]   4vv

    1. **12**, No.79 (Anon.)

    3. E-Sc, 5-I-43, No.78, j8v–9r/58v–59r (Anon.)

    4. Moerk, *Seville*, ii, 193–95 • Self, *Si placet*, No.8

Despitant fortune

    2/ of **Le eure est venue**   **Agricola**   3vv

Dieu damors

    See **Malor me bat**   **Ockeghem**   3vv

Dieu quel mariage

    lower voices of **Corps digne**   **Busnoys**   4vv

Disant adiu madame   **Compère**   3vv

    1. **1**, No.89 (Anon in the index. This folio in the unique surviving copy is of the second
edition) • **5**, No.89 (Anon.) • **14**, No.89 (Anon.)

    2. [c.1535]¹⁴, iii, No.57 (Anon.)

    3. F-Pn, 2245, No.7, 7v–8r (*Compere*)

    4. Compère, *Opera Omnia*, v, 18 • Hewitt, *Odhecaton*, 403

    Intabulation: lute

    2. 1536¹³ = N522, No.3, B3r (Anon. H. Newsidler)

    Comments: Cited by Aaron, *Trattato* (1525), ch.7 • Compare I-Fn, 229, No.115, 118v–119r
(*Compere*), texted *Ne vous hastem pas*. (See Brown, *Florentine*, the commentary to this
piece)

Dit le burguygnon   [Anon.]   4vv

    1. **1**, No.18 (Anon.) • **5**, No.18 (Anon.) • **14**, No.18 (Anon.)

    4. Hewitt, *Odhecaton*, 260

Du tout plongiet

    See **Fors seulement**   **Brumel**   4vv

Dung autramer   **Ockeghem**   3vv
                                        (Busnois)

    3. B-TOs, No.6, Cv (Anon. Incomplete) • D-F, VII 20 • D-W, 287, 33v–34r (Anon.) • DK-
Kk, 1848, No.88, p. 145 (Anon.) • DK-Kk, 291, No.28, 33v–34r/39v–40r (Anon.) • E-
Sc, 5-I-43, j1v–j2r/51v–52r (Anon.) • F-Dm, 517, No.35, 34v–40v/42v–43r (*Ockeghem*) •
F-Pn, 57, No.53, 66v–67r (*Okeghem*) • F-Pn, 2245, No.12, 13v–14r (*Okeghem*) • F-Pn,
15123, No.163, 189v–190r (*Busnoys*) • I-Bc, Q17, No.36, 40v–41r (*Jo. Ockeghem*) • I-Fn,
178, No.58, 62v–63r (Anon.) • I-Fr, 2356, No.58, 73v–74r (Anon.) • I-Fr, 2794, No.16,
19v–20r (*De okeghem*) • I-Rc, 2856, No.14, 16v–17r (*Jo okeghem*) • I-Rvat, C.G.XIII.27.
No.97, 112v–113r (Anon.) • US-Wc, Laborde, No.10, 18v–19r (Anon.)

    Text cited in Molinet's *Oroison a nostre dame* and *Colladaution a Madame Marguerite*

    4. Droz, Thibault, Rokseth, *Chansonniers*, No.36 • Guttiérez-Denhoff, *Wolfenbütteler*, 47 •
Jeppesen, *Kopenhagener*, No.28 • Josquin, *Werken*, Wereldlijke, xi, 140 • Smijers, *Van Ockeghem*, i, 3 • Taruskin, *D'ung*, 4–6

    Intabulation: lute

    1. **34**, No.15 (*Francesco Spinacino*)

    4. Schmidt, *Spinacino*, ii, 215–18

    Comments: For a series of citations and quotations, see Fallows, *Catalogue*, pp. 140–41 • Used
as the basis of Josquin's mass, also printed by Petrucci

Dung aultre amer   **de Orto**   4vv

    1. **2**, No.24 (*De orto.*) **10**, No.24 (*De orto*)

2. *50 Carmina* (1513), No.24 (*De Orto*)

4. Hewitt, *Canti B*, 159–161 • Taruskin, *D'ung*

Dung aultre amer

See Latin texts: **Tu solus qui facis mirabilia**   Josquin   4vv

See Latin texts: **Victimae paschali**   Josquin   4vv

E la la la Fates lui bona chiera   Ninot le Petit   4vv

1. *2*, No.27 (Anon.) • *10*, No.27 (Anon.)

2. *50 Carmina* (1513), No.27 (Anon.)

3. I-Fc, 2442, No.18, 25r-26r (*Ninot le petit*) • I-Fn, 164–67, No.53, 64r-65r (Anon.)

4. Hewitt, *Canti B*, 166–68 • Ninot, *Collected works*, 11–13

E leve vous   Ninot le petit   4vv

1. *12*, No.62 (Anon.)

3. F-Pn, 1817, No.8 (Anon.) • I-CT, 95–96, No.8, 7r-8r (Anon.) • I-Fc, 2442, No.10, 12r-13v (*Ninot le petit*)

4. Rubsamen, *Frottola*, 198–204 • Ninot, *Collected Works*

E qui le dira   Isaac   4vv

1. *1*, No.11 (Anon.) • *5*, No.11 (Anon.) • *14*, No.11 (Anon.)

3. B-Br, 11239, No.11, 17v-18r (*H. Ysac*) • CH-SGs, 461, No.38, pp. 70–71 (*H Isaacz*) • D-Rp, C.120, No.56, pp. 218–219 (*Isaac*) • I-Bc, Q18, No.85, 86v-87r (Anon.) • I-Fn, 107bis, No.7, 6v-7r (Anon.) • I-Rvat, 11953, No.6, 6r-6v (*Hen. Yzac*)

4. Hewitt, *Odhecaton*, 242–43 • Isaac, *Weltliche*, 12 • Picker, *Chanson*, 434–36 • Smijers, *Van Ockeghem*, 197–198

Monophonic version: F-Pn, 9346, 88v-89r

Intabulation: keyboard

3. CH-SGs, 530, No.111, 90r (*H. Isaac*)

Comments: For other settings of this melody and text, see Fallows, *Catalogue*, pp. 157–58

E vray dieu que payne   Compère   4vv

(Pipelare, Weerbeke)

1. *12*, No.107 (*Compere*)

3. F-Pn, 1817, No.34 (Anon.) • I-Bc, Q17, No.65, 71v-72r (Anon. Incipit *Vray dieu*) • I-CT, 95–96, No.34, 30v-31r (Anon. Incipit *Vray dieu*) • I-Fc, 2442, No.48, 85v-86r (*Gaspart*. Incipit *Vray dieu*) • I-Fn, 178, No.34, 38v-29r (Anon. Incipit *Vray diu*. à3) • I-Rvat, C.G.XIII.27, No.80, 87v-88r (94v-95r) (Anon. Texted *Quam diu che pena messe*)

4. Compère, *Opera Omnia*, v, 63–64 • Pipelare, *Opera Omnia*, i, 21

Intabulation: keyboard

3. CH-SGs, 530, No.74 (*Pipelare*. Incipit *Vray dieu*)

Elaes

See **Helas**

Elogeron nous

See **He logeron nous**   Isaac   4vv

En amours que cognoist   Brumel   3vv

1. *2*, No.49 (.*Brumel*.) • *10*, No.49 (*Brumel*)

2. [c.1535][14], iii, No.23 (Anon.)

3. D-HB, X.2, No.25 (*Brumel*)

4. Brumel, *Opera Omnia*, vi, 76–77 • Hewitt, *Canti B*, 232–34

En chambre polie   [Anon.]   4vv

1. *2*, No.10 (Anon.) • *10*, No.10 (Anon.)

2. *50 Carmina* (1513), No.10 (Anon.) • [c.1535][14], i, No.20 (Anon.)

4. Hewitt, *Canti B*, 123–25

En despit de la besogna   [Anon.]   4vv

  1. *12*, No.88 (Anon)

En lombre dung bussinet   [Anon.]   4vv

  1. *12*, No.58 (Anon.)

  3. Brown, *Theatrical*, No.26

En lombre dung bissonet   **Josquin**   4 ex 2vv
                                      (Ockeghem)

  1. *12*, No.III (*Josquin*)

  2. 1520³, No.13, 18v–19r (Anon.) • Attaignant No.3 [c.1528], pp. 33–42 (Anon.)

  3. D-HRD, 9820, No.3, 41r–43r (*Okenghem*) • D-Mbs, 1516, No.5 (Anon.) • F-Pn, 2245, No.24, 25v (*Josquin*) • I-Fr, 2442, No.3, 4r–4v (*Josquin des pres*) • I-Rc, 2856, No.101, 131r (*Boskun*. Incipit *A lumbre du bissonet*)

  4. Birmingham, *Chansonnier*, p. 130 • Brumel, *Opera Omnia*, iv, 127 • Josquin, *Werken*, Wereldlijke, ii, 54 • Wolff, *Chansonnier*, ii, 352–55

Entre vous galans / Je mi levay hier   [Anon.]   4vv

  1. *12*, No.87 (Anon.)

Est il possible que lhome peult   [Anon.]   3vv

  1. *1*, No.72 (Anon.) • *5*, No.72 (Anon. Incomplete) • *14*, No.72, (Anon.)

  4. Hewitt, *Odhecaton*, 372

Et dont revenis vous   **Compère**   4vv

  1. *2*, No.29 (*Compere*) • *10*, No.29 (*Compere*)

  2. *50 Carmina* (1513), No.29 (*Compere*)

  4. Compère, *Opera Omnia*, v, • Hewitt, *Canti B*, 171–73

Et leve vous

  See **E leve vous**   **Ninot le petit**   4vv

Et marion la brune   [Anon.]   4vv

  1. *12*, No.52 (Anon.)

  3. D-Mbs, 1516, No.9

  4. Whisler, *Munich*

Et raira plus la lune   **Gregoire**   4vv

  1. *12*, No.7 (*Gregoire*)

Faisans regres

  2/ of **Tout a par moy**   **Agricola**   4vv

Fates lui bona chiera

  Tenor and Bassus of **E la la la**   **le Petit**   4vv

Fault il que beur soy   **Martini**   4vv

  1. *12*, No.54 (*.Jo. martini*)

  4. Martini, *Secular*, 15–18

Forseulement   [Anon.]   4vv
                                      (Ghiselin; Josquin)

  1. *12*, No.35 (Anon.)

  3. CH-SGs, 461, pp. 6–7 (*Josquin Desprez*) • I-Fc, 2439, No.17, 18v–19r (*Ghisling*)

  4. Ghiselin, *Opera Omnia*, v, 11–13 • Gombosi, *Obrecht*, 18–20 • Newton, *Florence*, ii, 50–53 • Picker, *Fors*

Forseulement   **Brumel**   4vv
                                          (Agricola)

   1. *12*, No.3 (*Alexander*)

   3. B-Br, 228, No.17, 18*v*-19*r* (Anon. Texted *Du tout plongiet / Fors seulement*. Transposed a fifth lower) • CH-SGs, 461, pp. 16–17 (*Brumel*. Untexted. Transposed a fifth lower) • D-Mbs, 1516, No.2 (Anon.) • D-Rp, C120, No.92, pp. 324–25 (*An. Brumel*. Transposed a fifth lower) • I-Fc, 2439, No.19, 20*v*-21*r* (*Brumel*. Transposed a fifth lower)

   4. Agricola, *Opera Omnia*, v, 124–25 • Brumel, *Opera Omnia*, vi, 74–76 • Maldeghem, *Trésor, profane*, XXI (1885), No.13 • Newton, *Florence*, ii, 57–59 • Obrecht, *Werken*, vii, 85–87 • Picker, *Chanson*, 237–41 • Picker, *Fors* • Whisler, *Munich*

Forseulement   **Ghiselin**   4vv

   1. *12*, No.23 (*Ghiselin*)

   3. CH-SGs, 461, pp. 10–11 (*Verbonnet*) • D-Rp, C120, No.95, pp. 332–34 (*Verbonnet*) • I-Fc, 2439, No.16, 17*v*-18*r* (*Ghisling*) • I-Rvat, 11953, No.15, 13*v*-14*v* (Anon. Incipit *Fo soloment*)

   4. Gombosi, *Obrecht*, 16–18 • Newton, *Florence*, ii, 46–49 • Picker, *Fors*

Forseulement   **Obrecht**   4vv

   1. *12*, No.2 (*Ja. Obreht*)

   3. CH-SGs, 461, pp. 12–13 (*Obrecht*) • D-Rp, C120, No.91, pp. 320–333 (*Hobrecht*) • I-Fc, 2439, No.22, 23*v*-24*r* (*Hobrecht*)

   4. Ambros, *Geschichte*, v, 29–33 • Newton, *Florence*, ii, 67–70 • Obrecht, *Werken*, vii, 14–16 • Picker, *Fors*, 8–11

Comments: Cited in I-Rvat, Pal.Lat.1938, f.40

Fors seulement   **Pipelare**   4vv
                                          (La Rue)

   1. *2*, No.28 (*Pe.de la rue*) • *10*, No.28 (*Pe.de.la rue*)

   2. *50 Carmina* (1513), No.28 (*Pe de la rue*) • 1519[5], No.74 (Anon.) • [c.1535][14], i, No.31 (Anon.)

   3. B-Br, 228, No.16, 17*v*-18*r* (Anon.) • B-Br, IV.90. No.17, 22*v*-23*r* (Anon.) • B-Br, IV.1274, No.5, 9*r*-9*v* (Anon.) • B-Tv, 94, No.16, 22*r*-22*v* (Anon.) • CH-Bu, F.X.1–4, No.118 (*Mathias Pipilari*) • CH-SGs, 461, No.5 (*m. pipelare*) • D-Rp, C.120, No.96, pp. 336–337 (*Pipelare*) • E-Sc, 7.I.28, No.22, 92*r* (*Matheus Pipelare*. Texted *Exortum est in tenebris*) • F-Pn, 1597, 60*v*-61*r* (Anon.) • I-Bc, Q19, No.4, 1*v*-2*r* (*Piplare*) • I-Fn, 164–167, No.61, 75*r*-76*r* (Anon.)

   4. Bernoulli, *Liederbüchern*, 98–99 and 126–27 • Hewitt, *Canti B*, 168–71 • Maldeghem, *Trésor*, i (1865), 12 • Maldeghem, *Trésor*, xxi (1885), 25 • Obrecht, *Werken*, vii, 88–90 • Picker, *Chanson*, 233–36 • Picker, *Fors* • Pipelare, *Opera Omnia*, i, 11 • Seay, *Attaingnant*, 43 • Shipp, *Chansonnier*, 485

Intabulation: keyboard

   2. 1531[6], No.10, 18*v*-21*r* (Anon.)

Forseulement   **Reingot**   4vv

   1. *12*, No.15 (*G. Reingot,: rengot* in the index)

   3. Picker, *Fors*

Fortune per ta cruelte   **Vincenet**   3vv

   1. *1*, No.60 (*Vincinet*) • *5*, No.60 (*Vincinet*) • *14*, No.60 (*Vincinet*)

   3. D-As, 25, No.17, 10*v* (Anon. Incipit *Sancte speculum Trinitatis*) • E-Sc, 5-I-43, No.81, j11*v*-12*r*/61*v*-62*r* (Anon.) • F-Pn, 15123, No.143, 166*v*-167*r* (Anon.) • F-Pn, 2973, No.27,

34v-36r (Anon.) • I-Bc, Q16, No.113, 131v-132r (Anon. à4) • I-Bc, Q18, No.36, 37v-38r (Anon. à4, with a different Altus) • I-Fn, 229, No.51, 50v-51r (Anon.) • I-PEc, 431, No.67, 94v-95r (Anon. Headed *Fortuna vincinecta*) • I-Rvat, C.G.XIII.27, No.30, 40v-41r (*Vincinet*) • I-VEcap, DCCLVII, No.63, 66v-67r (Anon. Untexted) • PL-Kj, 40098, No.273 (Anon. Untexted, with an initial letter Q) • US-NH, 91, No.18, 23v-24r (*Vincenet*) • ZA-Csa, Grey, No.81, 121r (Anon. Text *Nihil est opertum*)

4. Brown, *Florentine*, music volume, 101–103 • Disertori, *Frottole*, 180–83 • Hewitt, *Odhecaton*, 347–48 • Moerk, *Seville*, ii, 198–99 • Perkins and Garey, *Mellon*, No.18 • Ringmann, *Glogauer*, No.275 • Thibault and Fallows, *Chansonnier* • Vincenet, *Collected works*, 167

Intabulations lute

1. *33*, No.21 (Anon.)

4. Disertori, *Frottole*, 180–83 • Schmidt, *Spinacino*, ii, 94–96

Intabulations: voice(?) and lute

3. I-Bu, 596, p. 2 (*Fortuna vincinecta*)

Comments: The *Fortuna vincineta* found in E-SE, s.s., 112r is not related to this piece

Fortune esperee

See **Fortuna Desperata**   **Busnois**   4vv

Franch cor quas tu / Fortune dun gran tempo   De vigne   4vv

1. *2*, No.32 (.*De. vigne*. Listed under *Fortuna dun gran tempo* in the index and ascribed to *De vigna*) • *10*, No.32 (.*De.Vigue.*: in the index as in first edition)

2. *50 Carmina* (1513), No.32 (*de vigne*)

4. Hewitt, *Canti B*, 179–81

Garisses moy   Compère   3vv

1. *1*, No.58 (*Compere*. Incomplete) • *5*, No.58 (*Compere.*) • *14*, No.58 (*Compere*)

2. 1538⁹, No.53, G4r (Anon. Untexted)

3. CH-SGs, 461, No.24, pp. 48–49 (*Compere*) • E-SE, s.s., No.144, 191v-192r (*Loyset Compere*) • I-Bc, Q18, No.89, 90v-91r (Anon.) • I-Tn, I.27, No.10, 13v-14r (Anon. Incipit *Guerrises moy du grant mal*)

4. Compère, *Opera Omnia*, v, 27 • Hewitt, *Odhecaton*, 343–44 • Mönkemeyer, *Formschneyder*, ii, p. 79

Gentil galans avanturiers   Ninot le Petit   4vv

1. *12*, No.28 (Anon.)

2. [c.1528]⁴, No.28 (Anon.)

3. I-Fc, 2442, No.12, 15r-16r

4. Ninot, *Opera Omnia*

Gentil galans de france

See **Gentil galant de gerra**   [Anon.]   4vv

Gentil galant de gerra   [Anon.]   4vv

1. *12*, No.9 (Anon.)

3. F-Pn, 1817, No.10 (Anon.) • I-CT, 95–96, No.10, 9r-9v (Anon. Incipit *Gentil galans de france*) • I-Fn, 164–167, No.63, 77r-78r (Anon. Incipit *Gentil galans de france*)

Gentil galans de gerra   van Stappen   4vv
                                                   (Prioris)

1. *12*, No.55 (*Crispin. de stappen*)

3. D-Rp, C120, pp. 318–319 (*Prioris*)

4. Prioris, *Opera Omnia*, iii, p. 121

Gentil prince   [Anon.]   3vv
    1. *1*, No.90 (Anon in the index. This folio in the unique copy is of the second edition) •
    5, No.90 (Anon.) • *14*, No.90 (Anon.)
    3. GB-Lbl, Add.31922, 49v-50r (*The Kynge H VIII.* à4)
    4. Hewitt, *Odhecaton*, 404 • Stevens, *Henry VIII*, 36
    Intabulation: lute
    3. US-Cn, 107501, No.31, 50v-51r (Anon.)

Gratieuse
    See **Mon mignault**   **Busnois**   4vv

Guerisses moy du grant mal
    See **Garisses moy**   **Compère**   3vv

Ha traitre amours   **Stockhem**   3vv
                                                     (Compère; Rubinet)
    1. *1*, No.86 (Anon in the index. This folio in the unique surviving copy is of the second
    edition) • *5*, No.86 (Anon.) • *14*, No.86 (Anon.)
    2. [c.1535][14], iii, No.31 (*Compere.* Untexted)
    3. I-Bc, Q17, No.38, 42v-43r (*Io. Stochem*) • I-Bc, Q18, No.79, 80v-81r (Anon. Texted
    Rubinet) • I-Fn, 121, No.8, 8v-9r (Anon. Incipit *A tratier amors*) • I-Fn, 178, No.29, 33v-34r
    (*Stochem*) • I-Fn, 229, No.23, 22v-23r (*Jannes Stochem*) • I-Rvat, C.G.XIII.27, No.36, 47v-
    48r (*Stochen*) • US-Wc, Wolffheim, 92v-93r (Anon. Untexted)
    4. Brown, *Florentine*, music volume, 48–49 • Hewitt, *Odhecaton*, 399 • Reese, *First*, 76
    Intabulations: lute
    1. *34*, No.10 (*Francesco Spinacino.* Incipit *Haray tre amours*)
    2. 1536[13] = N522, No.4, B3v-4r (Anon. H. Newsidler)
    4. Schmidt, *Spinacino*, ii, 201–202

Haray tre amours
    See **Ha traitre amours**   **Stockhem**   3vv

He Dieu qui me confortera
    See **Vray Dieu qui me confortera**   **Bruhier**   4vv

He logeron nous   [Anon.]   4vv
    1. *12*, No.33 (Anon.)

He logerons nous   **Isaac**   4vv
                                                     (Agricola)
    1. *1*, No.40 (Anon: *Isaac* added in a much later hand) • *5*, No.40, (Anon.) • *14*, No.40
    (Anon.)
    3. CH-SGs, 463, No.179, 62r and 120r (Anon.) • F-Pn, 1817, No.33 (Anon.) • I-Bc, Q17,
    No.44, 61v-62r (*Yzac*) • I-CT, 95–96, No.32, 29v-30r (Anon.) • I-Fn 107[bis], No.14, 13v-14r
    (Anon. Incipit *E loyere nos seans*) • I-Fn, 178, No.37, 41v-42r (*Yzac*) • I-Fn, 229, No.2,
    1v-2r (*Henricus Yzac.* Incipit *He logierons*) • I-Rvat, C.G.XIII.27, No.29, 39v-40r (*Ysach.*
    Incipit *Hellogaron cesalotesse*)
    4. Brown, *Florentine*, music volume, 3–4 • Hewitt, *Odhecaton*, 307–308 • Isaac, *Weltliche*, 76
    Intabulation: lute
    1. *34*, No.19 (*Francesco Spinacino*)
    4. Schmidt, *Spinacino*, ii, 228–29
    Intabulation: keyboard
    3. CH-Sgs, 530, No.119, 95r (*Alexander*)

| Helas ce nest pas sans rayson | Stockhem | 4vv |

1. *1*, No.19 (*Sthokhem*) • *5*, No.19 (.*Sthokem*) • *14*, No.19 (.*Sthokem.*)

3. CH-SGs, 461, p. 64 (*Stoken*) • I-Fn, Panc.27, No.97, 65*v*-66*r* (*Sthokhem*)

4. Hewitt, *Odhecaton*, 261–62 • Torrefranca, *Segreto*, 550–53

Helas dame		
See **Serviteur soye**	Stockhem	4vv
Helas helas fault il	[Anon.]	4vv

1. *12*, No.27 (Anon.)

| Helas helas helas | Ninot | 4vv |

1. *2*, No.21 (.*Ninot.*) • *10*, No.21 (.*Ninot.*)

2. *50 Carmina* (1513), No.21 (*Ninot*) • [c.1535][14], i, No.29 (Anon.)

3. D-Rp, C.120, No.10, pp. 24–25 (Anon.)

4. Hewitt, *Canti B*, 150–52 • Ninot, *Collected Works*, 23–25

Helas je suis mary		
See **Helas que devera mon cuer**	Isaac	3vv
Helas le bon temps	Tinctoris	3vv
	(Compère)	

1. *1*, No.52 (Anon: *Tinctoris* in the index. Incomplete) • *5*, No.52, (*Tintoris*.) • *14*, No.52 (*Tintoris*.)

3. D-Z, LXXVIII,3, No.21 (Anon. Untexted) • E-Sc, 5-I-43, No.54, g8*v*-9*r*/44*v*-45*r* (Anon.) • E-SE, s.s., No.130, 184*r* (*Loysette Compere*. Texted *Elaes Abraham*) • I-Fn, 229, No.198, 214*v*-215*r* (Anon.) • I-Fn, Panc.27, No.73, 47*v*-48*r* (*Tinctoris*) • PL-Kj, 40098, No.267 (Anon. Untexted. Headed with the letter *K*.)

4. Brown, *Florentine*, music volume, 460–62 • Gombosi, *Obrecht*, No.8 • Hewitt, *Odhecaton*, 331–32 • Melin, *Tinctoris*, 485–86 • Moerk, *Seville*, ii, 131–32 • Ringmann, *Glogauer*, iv, 63

| Helas le poure iohan | [Anon.] | 4vv |

1. *12*, No.56 (Anon.)

Helas mamour		
See **Helas que poura devenir**	Caron	4vv
Helas mon ceur		
See **Helas que poura devenir**	Caron	4vv
Helas que devera mon cuer	Isaac	3vv
	(Josquin)	

1. *1*, No.50 (*Helas: Yzac* in the index. These folios are lacking in the unique copy of this edition) • *5*, No.50 (*Yzac*) • *14*, No.50 (*Yzac*)

2. [c1535][14], iii, No.55 (Anon.) • 1538[9], No.3, A4*v* (Anon: MS attribution in the copy at D-Ju to *H.Isac*. Incipit *Helas je suis mary*)

3. CZ-HK, II.A.20, p. 101 (*H.I.* Untexted) • D-HB, X.2, No.31 (*Henri: Isaac*) • D-Z, LXXVIII,3, No.23 (*Isaac*. Untexted) • E-SE, s.s., No.116, 177*r* (*Ysaac*. Texted *Elaes*) • I-Bc, Q34, 6*v*-8*r* (*Josquini*) • I-Fn, 229, No.6, 5*v*-6*r* (*Henricus Yzac*) • I-Fn, Panc.27, No.167, 138*v*-139*r* (*Ysach*) • I-MOe, γ.L.11.8, No.69, 71*v*, incomplete (Anon.) • I-Rvat, C.G.XIII.27, No.69, 83*v*-84*r* (*Ysach*. Incipit *Hellas*) • I-VEcap, DCCLVII, No.21, 20*v*-21*r* (Anon. Untexted)

4. Brown, *Florentine*, music volume, 11–13 • Hewitt, *Odhecaton*, 327–28 • Isaac, *Weltliche*, 75 • Mönkemeyer, *Formschneyder*, ii, 12

Intabulation: keyboard

3. CH-SGs, 530, No.30 (*Heinrich Isaac*)

Comments: Based on Caron's *Helas que pourra*, also published by Petrucci

Helas que il est a mon gre   **Japart**   4vv

    1. *1*, No.30 (Anon. Incomplete) • *5*, No.31 (*Japart*) • *14*, No.31, (*Japart*)

    3. CH-SGs, 463, No.180, 62r and 120r (*Iapart*) • I-Fn, 107bis, No.12, 12r, incomplete (Anon. Untexted, listed in the index as *Elas que lata mon gre*) • I-Fn, 178, No.41, 45v-46r (Anon. Texted *Chel et a mon gre*) • I-Fn, 229, No.148, 152v-153r (Anon. Untexted) • I-Fn, Panc.27, No.96, 64v-65r (*Iapart*) • I-Rvat, C.G.XIII.27, No.42, 54v-55r (Anon.)

    Monophonic version: F-Pn, 12744, 3r (Anon.)

    4. Boer, *Chansonvormen*, No.8 • Brown, *Florentine*, music volume, 310–13 • Hewitt, *Odhecaton*, 284–85 • Torrefranca, *Segreto*, 554–57

Helas que poura devenir   **Caron**   4vv

    1. *1*, No.13 (*Caron.*) • *5*, No.13 (*Caron.*) • *14*, No.13 (*Caron.*)

    3. D-As, 25, No.7, 4r (Anon. Incipit *Dess mayen lust*) • F-Pn, 676, 12v (Anon.) • I-Bc, Q18, No.34, 35v-36r (Anon. Incipit *Helasso*) • I-Fn, Panc.27, No.56, 35v-36r (*Caron.* Incipit *Helas*)

        The following sources are à3: D-W, 287, 49v-50r (Anon.) • E-Sc, 5-I-43, No.49, g3v-4r/39v-40r (Anon.) • E-SE, s.s., No.43, 114v-115r (*Caron.* Headed *Elaes*) • F-Dm, 517, 78v-79r/81r-82r (*Caron*) • F-Pn, 15123, 33v-34r (Anon.) • I-Bc, Q16, No.110, 114v-114bisr (Anon.) • I-Fn, 229, No.206, 222v-223r (*Caron*) • I-PEc, 431, No.37, 59v-60r (Anon.) • I-Rc, 2856, No.38, 44v-45r (*Caron.* Incipit *Hellas mon ceur*) • I-Rvat, C.G.XIII.27, No.58, 71v-72r (*Caron*) • I-TRc, 89, No.255 [770], 416v-417r (Anon. Untexted) • I-VEcap, DCCLVII, No.20, 19v-20r (Anon. Untexted) • PL-Kj, 40098, No.8 (Anon. Title *Der Seyden schwantcz*, and texted *Ave sydus clarissimum*) • S-Uu, 76a, No.16, 13v-14r (Anon.) • SK-BRu, 33 • SK-BRu, 318-I • US-Wc, Laborde, 12v-13r (*Caron.* Texted *Helas mamour*)

    4. Brown, *Florentine*, music volume, 478–81 • Caron, *Oeuvres*, ii, 175 • Hewitt, *Odhecaton*, 246–48 • Lenaerts, *Kunst/Art* • Moerk, *Seville*, ii, 119–20 • Ringmann, *Glogauer*, 92 • Torrefranca, *Segreto*, 554 • *Trent*, vii, 248–49 • Wolff, *Chansonnier*, ii, 129–32

    Intabulation: Keyboard

    2. Baena 1540, No.34, 30r-31r (Caron)

Ho logeron nous

    See **He logeron nous**   **Isaac**   4vv

Hor oires une chanzon   **[Anon.]**   5vv

    1. *1*, No.3 (Anon.) • *5*, No.3 (Anon.) • *14*, No.3 (Anon.)

    3. CH-SGs, 461, pp. 28–29 (Anon.) • I-Fn, Panc.27, No.57, 36v-37r (Anon. Text incipit only) • I-VEcap, DCCLVII, No.46, 46v-47r (Anon. Untexted)

    4. Hewitt, *Odhecaton*, 224–25 • Torrefranca, *Segreto*, 558–60

Il est de bon heure / Lomme arme   **Japart**   4vv

    1. *12*, No.59 (*Jo. Japart*)

    4. Brown, *Theatrical*, 79–81

Il est de bon heure

    Tenor of **Amour fait mult tant**   **Japart**   4vv

Il son bien pelles / Celux qui font la gorre   **[Anon.]**   4vv

    1. *12*, No.104 (Anon. The Superius and Contra are given the incipits *Celux qui font la gorre* [*sic*], and the Tenor and Bassus read *Il son bien pelles*)

    3. DK-Kk, 1848, No.27, p. 44 (Anon.)

4. Brown, *Theatrical*, 89–92 • Christofferson, *French*, iii, 59

Monophonic version: F-Pn, 12744, 49r. (Anon.)

Comments: This is related to *Adieu mes amours* (cf. Hewitt, *Odhecaton*, p. 135)

James james james **Mouton** 4vv

    1. *1*, No.36 (Anon.) • *5*, No.36 (Anon.) • *14*, No.36 (Anon.)

    2. I-Fc, 2442, pp. 179–82 (*Mouton*. Text *Jamais Jacquez Bonhomme*)

    4. Hewitt, *Odhecaton*, 296–98

Jay bien huer **Agricola** 3vv

                        (Compère)

    1. *1*, No.91 (Anon in index. These folios either of the second edition or lacking) • *5*, No.91 (*Agricola*) • *14*, No.82 (*Agricola*)

    2. [c.1535][14], iii, 62 (Anon. Text incipit *Robert*)

    3. D-Z, LXXVIII,3, No.20 (*Agricola*. Untexted) • E-SE, s.s., No.126, 182r (*Loysette Compere*) • I-Bc, Q16, No.6, 13v–14r (Anon. Texted *Jay bien et honore*) • I-Fn, 178, No.15, 19v–20r (*Alexander*. Untexted) • I-Fn, 229, No.21, 20v–21r (Anon.) • I-Fr, 2794, No.35, 41v–42r (Anon.) • I-Tn, I.27, No.16, 19r (Anon.) • I-VEcap, DCCLVII, No.9, 8v–9r (*Agricola*. Texted *Jai biau haver amant*)

    4. Agricola, *Opera Omnia*, v, 28–29 • Brown, *Florentine*, music volume, 44–46 • Hewitt, *Odhecaton*, 392–93 • Jones, *First*, ii, 244–45

Intabulation: lute

    2. 1536[13] = N522, No.13, E3r-4r (*Alexander Agricola*. H. Newsidler. Titled *Jay vien ahur*)

Comments: The different location of this work in Petrucci's third edition is the result of a simple technical lapse, discussed elsewhere

Jay bien nouri [Anon.] 4vv

    1. *12*, No.102 (Anon.)

    3. D-Mbs, 1516, No.12

    4. Bernstein, "Notes", 306 • Whisler, "Munich"

Jay pris amours [Anon.] 4vv

    1. *12*, No.68 (Anon.)

    3. A-LIs, 529 • E-Sc, 5-I-43, No.135, 011v–12r/109v–110r (Anon.)

    4. Moerk, *Seville*, ii, 338–40 • Taruskin, *J'ay pris*

Jay pris amours [Anon.] 3vv

    3. F-Dm, 517, No.1, 7r (Anon. Incomplete) • I-TRc, 1947-4, No.5, 5v-6r (Anon. Untexted)

    4. Disertori, *Frottole*, 215–18 • Droz, Thibault, Rokseth, "Chansonniers", No.2 • Taruskin, *J'ay pris*

Intabulation: lute

    1. *34*, No.8 (*Francesco Spinacino*)

    4. Schmidt, *Spinacino*, ii, 194–97

Intabulation: two lutes

    1. *33*, No.12 (*Francesco Spinacino*)

    4. Disertori, *Frottole*, 215–18 • Schmidt, *Spinacino*, ii, 55–60

Comments: Disertori, *Frottole*, 278, suggests that the chanson is the work of Caron

Jay pris amours / De tous biens [Anon.] 4vv

    1. *1*, No.6 (Anon.) • *5*, No.6 (Anon.) • *14*, No.6 (Anon.)

    3. D-As, 25, No.11, 7v (Anon. Texted *Auxilium praesta nam*)

    4. Hewitt, *Odhecaton*, 230–32 • Taruskin, *J'ay pris*

Jay pris amours   **Busnois**   4vv
                                                  (Martini)

    1. *1*, No.39 (*Busnoys*) • *5*, No.39 (*Busnoys*) • *14*, No.39 (*Busnoys*)

    3. E-SE, s.s., No.39, 110*v*-111*v* (*Johannes Martini*)

    4. Martini, *Secular*, 38–40 • Hewitt, *Odhecaton*, 305–306 • Obrecht, *Werken*, vii, 96–98 •
    Taruskin, *J'ay pris*

Jay pris amours   **Ghiselin**   4vv

    1. *12*, No.38 (Anon.)

    4. Gombosi, *Obrecht*, No.23 • Taruskin, *J'ay pris*

Intabulations: lute

    2. 1536[13] = N522, No.14, E4*v* (*Jo. Ghiselin. H. Newsidler*)

Jay pris amours   **Isaac**   4vv

    1. *12*, No.25 (Anon: *Izac* in index)

    3. D-Rp, C.120, No.77, pp. 286–287 (Anon.) • I-Bc, Q18, No.58, 59*v*-60*r* (Anon.)

    4. Isaac, *Weltliche*, 77–78 • Taruskin, *J'ay pris*

Jay pris amours   **Japart**   4vv

    1. *1*, No.21 (*Japart*) • *5*, No.21 (*Japart.*) • *14*, No.21 (*Japart.*)

    4. Gombosi, *Obrecht*, No.24 • Hewitt, *Odhecaton*, 265–66 • Taruskin, *J'ay pris*

Jay pris amours   **Japart**   4 ex 3vv

    1. *2*, No.30 (*Japart. Rubric Fit aries piscis in licanosypathon*) • *10*, No.30 (.*Japart*)

    2. *50 Carmina* (1513), No.30 (*Japart*)

    3. I-Fn, 178, No.3, 4*v*-5*r* (*Japart. Superius* headed *Antiphrasis baritonat*; *Bassus* headed *Fit
    aries piscis in licanos ypathon*) • I-Fn, 229, No.52, 158*v*-159*r* (*Jannes Japart*. Rubrics *Anti-
    phrasis baritonat*; and *Canon. Ne sonitas amese Lycanosipaton summite*) • I-Rvat, C.G.XIII.27,
    No.54, 66*v*-67*r* (*Jo. Japart*. Rubric *Canon. Vade retro Sathanas*) • I-VEcap, DCCLVII,
    No.48, 48*v*-49*r* (Anon. Untexted)

    4. Brown, *Florentine*, music volume, 325–27 • Disertori, "Manoscritto", 15 • Hewitt, *Canti
    B*, 174–76 • Taruskin, *J'ay pris*

Jay pris amours   **Obrecht**   4vv

    1. *2*, No.3 (*Obreht*) • *10*, No.3 (*Obreht.*)

    2. *50 Carmina* (1513), No.3 (*Obreht*) • [ca.1535][14], i, Nos.17–20 (Anon.)

    4. Hewitt, *Canti B*, 94–105 • Obrecht, *Werken*, vii, 19–28 • Taruskin, *J'ay pris*

Jay prius amours tout au rebours

    See **Jay pris amours**   **Busnois**   4vv

Jay pris mon bourdon   **Stockhem**   4vv

    1. *12*, No.86 (*Sthokem*)

Je cuide sece tamps me dure   **Congiet**   4vv
                                                  (Japart)

    1. *1*, No.2 (Anon.) • *5*, No.2 (Anon.) • *14*, No.2 (Anon.)

    3. The following sources are à3: D-B, 40021, No.113, 226*v*-227*r* (Anon. Untexted) • F-Pn,
    676, No.41, 49*v*-50*r* (Anon.) • I-Bc, Q18, No.70, 71*v*-72*r* (Anon.) • I-Fn, 229, No.93,
    95*v*-96*r* (*P. Congiet*) • I-Rc, 2856, No.99, 128*v*-129*r* (*Io. Jappart*. Texted *Io quido*) • I-Rvat,
    C.G.XIII.27, No.49, 61*v*-62*r* (Anon.) • I-VEcap, DCCLVII, No.23, 22*v*-23*r* (Anon.
    Untexted) • ZA-Csa, Grey, No.53, 83*v*-84*r* (Anon. Text *Primum querite regnum dei*)

    4. Brown, *Florentine*, music volume, 187–89 • Hewitt, *Odhecaton*, 222–23 • Wolff, *Chanson-
    nier*, ii, 346–48

Intabulation: lute

1. **34**, No.2 (*Francesco Spinacino*. Incipit *Je ne cuide*)
4. Schmidt, *Spinacino*, ii, 164–66

Je cuide / De tous biens   **Japart**   4vv
  1. **2**, No.31 (*Japart*) • **10**, No.31 (*Japart*)
  2. *50 Carmina* (1513), No.31 (*Japart*) • [ca.1535]¹⁴, i, No.32 (Anon.)
  4. Hewitt, *Canti B*, 176–78

Je despite tous   **Brumel**   3vv
  1. **2**, No.50 (*.Brumel.*) • **10**, No.50 (*.Brumel.*)
  2. *50 Carmina* (1513), No.50 (*Brumel*) • [ca.1535]¹⁴, iii, No.24 (Anon.)
  3. D-HB, X.2, No.26 (Anon.)
  4. Brumel, *Opera Omnia*, vi, 83–84 • Hewitt, *Canti B*, 235–37

Je lay empris
  See Latin texts: **Missa de les armes**   **Ghiselin**   4vv

Je mi levay hier au matin
  Contra to **Entre vous galans**   [Anon.]   4vv

Je nay dueul   **Agricola**   4vv
  1. **1**, No.38 (*Agricola*) • **5**, No.38 (*Agricola*) • **14**, No.38 (*.Agricola.*)
  2. 1538⁹, No.73, K2r (Anon. Untexted)
  3. B-Br, 228, No.19, 20*v*-22*r* (Anon.) • D-Rp, C.120, No.86, pp. 308–11 (*Agricola*) • E-SE, s.s., No.42, 113*v*-114*r* (*Alexander Agricola*. Additional text in Contra 2, *Je ne demande*) • F-Pn, 1817, No.1 (Anon.) • GB-Lbl, Roy.20.A.xvi, No.19, 24*v*-26*r* (Anon.) • I-Bc, Q17, No.64, 69*v*-71*r* (*A. Agricola*) • I-CT, 95–96, No.1, 1*r*-2*r*. (Anon.) • I-Fn, 178, No.1, 0*v*-2*r* (*Alexander*) • I-Fn, 229, No.174, 183*v*-185*r* (*Alexander Agricola*) • I-Fr, 2794, No.25, No.25, 28*v*-30*r* (*Agricola*) • I-Rc, 2856, No.123, 162*v*-164*r* (*Agricola*) • I-Rvat, C.G.XIII.27, No.35, 45*v*-47*r* (*Agricola*. Incipit *Ge nay de duèl*) • I-VEcap, DCCLVII, No.35, 34*v*-36*r* (Anon. Incipit *Ja ne duil*)
  4. Agricola, *Opera Omnia*, v, 7–11 • Brown, *Florentine*, music volume, 392–96 • Brumel, *Opera Omnia*, i, 114–16 • Hewitt, *Odhecaton*, 302–304 • Jones, *First*, ii, 215–18 • Litterick, *Manuscript*, 261–65 • Maldeghem, *Trésor*, profane, XXI (1885), Nos.11 and 14 • Mönkemeyer, *Formschneyder*, ii, 107–108 • Picker, *Chanson*, 247–53 • Wolff, *Chansonnier*, ii, 451–59
  Comments: The basis for Brumel's mass, also printed by Petrucci
  Intabulation: keyboard
  2. CH-SGs, 530, No.95 (*Agricola*)

Je nay deul   **Ockeghem**   4vv
  1. **12**, No.72 (*Okenghem*)
  3. B-Br, 228, No.14, 15*v*-16*r* (Anon.) • B-Br, IV.90, No.20, 26*r*-27*r* (Anon.) • B-Br, IV.1274, No.8, 12*r*-13*r* (Anon.) • B-Tv, 94, No.19, 25*r*-26*r* (Anon) • GB-Lbl, Roy.20.A.xvi, No.18, 23*v*-24*r* (Anon.) • I-Bc, Q17, No.66, 72*v*-73*r* (Anon. With a different Altus) • I-Fc, 2439, No.29, 30*v*-31*r* (*Ockeghem*) • US-Wc, Laborde, 120*v*-121*r* (Anon.)
  4. Ambros, *Geschichte* v, 10–11 • Litterick, *Manuscript*, 258–60 • Litterick, "Revision", 43–48 • Maldeghem, *Trésor*, profane, XXI (1885), No.9 • Newton, *Florence*, ii, 90–92 • Ockeghem, *Collected*, iii, 67–69 • Picker, *Chanson*, 226–28
  Literature: Litterick, "Revision"

Je nay dueul
  Contra of **Vostre a iamays**   **Ghiselin**   3vv

Je ne cuide

    See **Je cuide**   **Congiet**   4vv

Je ne demande aultre de gre   **Busnois**   4vv

    1. *1*, No.42 (*Busnoys*) • *5*, No.42 (*Busnoys.*) • *14*, No.42 (*Busnoys.*)

    3. E-Sc, 5-I-43, No.133, 07*v*-9*r*/105*v*-107*r* (Anon.) • E-SE, s.s., No.41, 112*v*-113*r* (*Anthonius Busnoys*) • F-Pn, 15123, 153*v*-155*r* (*Busnoys*) • GB-Ctc, R.2.71, 1*r* (Anon. Incomplete) • I-Bc, Q18, No.38, 39*v*-40*r* (Anon.) • I-Fn, 229, No.147, 151*v*-152*r* (Anon.) • I-Rc, 2856, No.116, 151*v*-153*r* (*Busnoys*) • US-Wc, Laborde, 121*v* gives the text incipit, without music

    Citation: Tinctoris, *De arte contrapuncti*, ii, ch.33

    Text cited in Molinet's *Le debat du viel gendarme*

    4. Brown, *Florentine*, music volume, 306–309 • Hewitt, *Odhecaton*, 311–12 • Moerk, *Seville*, ii, 331–33 • Obrecht, *Opera Omnia*, i, 65 • Obrecht, *Werken*, i, Anhang, 1 • Wolff, *Chansonnier*, ii, 411–17

    Intabulation: lute

    1. *34*, No.6 (*Francesco Spinacino*)

    4. Schmidt, *Spinacino*, ii, 181–85

Je ne fay cont damer   [Anon.]   lute

    Intabulation

    1. *34*, No.31 (*Francesco Spinacino*)

    4. Schmidt, *Spinacino*, ii, 279–82

Je ne fay plus   **Busnois**   4vv
                                               (Compère; Mureau)

    1. *1*, No.8 (Anon.) • *14*, No.8 (Anon.)

    3. US-Wc, Wolffheim, 90*v*-91*r*. With fourth voice in a later hand, perhaps that of Weckerlin (see Brown, *Florentine*, text volume, 229)

        The following sources are à3: CH-SGs, 462, p. 85 (Anon.) • DK-Kk, 1848, p. 97 (Anon.) • E-Sc, 5-I-43, No.17, d1*v*-d2*r*/25*v*-26*r* (Anon.) • E-SE, s.s., No.125, 181*v* (*Loysette Compere*) • F-Pn, 2245, 23*v*-24*r* (*Mureau*) • F-Pn, 15123, 177*v*-178*r* (Anon.) • I-Bc, Q17, No.33, 37*v*-38*r* (*A. Busnois*) • I-Fn, 121, No.26, 26*v*-27*r* (Anon.) • I-Fn, 176, No.74, 73*v*-75*r* (*G. Mureau*) • I Fn, 178, No.36, 40*v*-41*r* (Anon.) • I-Fn, 229, No.55, 54*v*-55*r* (*Antonius Busnoys*) • I-Fr, 2356, No.2, 6*v*-7*r* (Anon. Incipit *Jenephai*) • I-Fr, 2794, No.43, 50*v*-51*r* (Anon.) • I-Rvat, C.G.XIII.27, No.12, 19*v*-20*r* (*Gil Mureau*) • I-Tn, I.27, No.27, 47*r* (Anon. Texted *Au joly moys de may*)

    4. Brown, *Florentine*, music volume, 109–10 • Geering & Trümpy, *Liederbuch*, No.44 • Hewitt, *Odhecaton*, 235–36 • Jones, *First*, ii, 262–63 • Moerk, *Seville*, ii, 42–43 • Underwood, *Renaissance*, 30–39

    Intabulation: keyboard

    3. D-B, 40026, 51*r* (Anon.)

    Intabulation: lute

    3. F-Pn, 27, No.9, 16*v* (Anon.)

    Intabulation: two lutes

    1. *33*, No.11 (*Francesco Spinacino*; *Fran.Spi.* in the index)

    4. Schmidt, *Spinacino*, ii, 50–54 • Underwood, *Renaissance*, 30–39

    Intabulation: lute accompaniment to a superius

    3. F-Pn, 27, No.109, 54*r* (Anon.)

    4. Thibault, "Manuscrit", p. 74 • Underwood, *Renaissance*, 137–41

Je ne me puis tenir damer   [Anon.]   4vv
                                                    (Josquin: Gombert)

   1. *12*, No.53 (Anon. Index reads *Je ne peus tenir*)
   2. J681 (1550), No.27 (Josquin)
   3. D-B, Breslau 12, No.6 (*Date siceram*) • D-Mbs, 1508 (*Date siceram*) • D-Mu, 326, No.6,
      8v (*Date siceram*) • D-Rp, A.R.1018, No.27 (Anon. *Date siceram*) • D-Rp, B211–215,
      No.30 (Anon. *Date siceram*) • H-BA, 23, No.140 (*Josquinus. Date siceram*)
   Intabulation: keyboard
   3. PL-Kp, 1716, 200v (*N.C.. Date siceram*)
   Intabulations: lute
   2. 1558²⁰ = O12, No.9, 19r (*Claudin. Ochsenkuhn. Date siceram*) • 1562²⁴ = H4935, No.68,
      p. 196 (Anon. Heckel. *Date siceram*)
   Intabulations: voice and vihuela
   2. M7725 (1546), No.50 (*Gombert. Mudarra.* Headed *Respice in me Deus*) • 1554³² = F2093,
      No.61, 65v (*Gombert. Fuenllana. Lauda syon*)

Je ne suis mort ne vief   [Anon.]   4vv
   1. *12*, No.73 (Anon.)

Je ne suis pas a ma playsach   [Anon.]   4vv
   1. *12*, No.105 (Anon.)

Je sey bien dire   **Josquin**   4vv
   1. *12*, No.48 (*Josquin*)
   4. Josquin, *Werken*, Wereldlijke, ii, 53

Je suis amie du forier   **Compère**   4vv
   1. *2*, No.11 (Anon.) • *10*, No.11 (Anon.)
   2. 50 *Carmina* (1513), No.11 (Anon.) • [ca.1535]¹⁴, i, No.21 (Anon.)
   3. F-Pn, 1817, No.9 (Anon.) • I-CT, 95–96, No.9, 8r–9r (Anon.) • I-Fn, 107ᵇⁱˢ, No.13, 12v–
      13r (Anon.) • I-Fn, 164–167, No.64, 78r–78v (Anon.) • I-Rvat, C.G.XIII.27, No.96, 111v–
      112r (*Compere*)
   4. Compère, *Opera Omnia*, v, 29 • Hewitt, *Canti B*, 125–28
   Intabulation: lute
   2. 1544²⁴, No.32, F2v (Anon. H. Newsidler)
   Comments: Brown, *Instrumental*, suggests comparison with 1562²⁴ = H4935 (Heckel),
      No.14, headed *Je suis ayme*

Je suy dalemaygne / Joliettement menvay   [Anon.]   5vv
   1. *12*, No.82 (Anon.)
   3. I-Fn, 229, No.162, 168v–170r (Anon. Incipit 1 only)
   4. Brown, *Florentine*, music volume, 357–60 • Brown, *Theatrical*, No.42

Je suy dalemagne   **Stockem**   4vv
   1. *12*, No.94 (*Jo. Sthokem*)
   3. I-Fn, 229, No.161, 167v–168r (Anon.)
   4. Brown, *Florentine*, music volume, 355–56 • Brown, *Theatrical.* No.41

Je suis trop jeunette
   See **Se suis trop ionnette**   **Raulin**   4vv

Je vous empire [= en prie]   **Agricola**   3vv
   1. *2*, No.46 (*.Agricola.* Superius incipit *Je vous impire*) • *10*, No.46 (*Agricola.*)
   2. 50 *Carmina* (1513), No.46 (*Agricola*) • [ca.1535]¹⁴, iii, No.20 (Anon.)
   3. F-Pn, 1597, 17v–19r. (Anon. Incipit *Se vous voulez*) • GB-Lbl, Roy.20.A.xvi, No.3, 5v–7r

(Anon. Incipit *Se vous voulez*) • I-Fn, 178, No.19, 23*v*-24*r* (*Alexander*. Incipit *Je vous vous eri*) • I-Fn, 229, No.255, 275*v*-277*r* (Anon.) • I-Fr, 2794, No.26, 30*v*-31*r* (*Agricola*. Incipit *Se vous voulez*)

4. Agricola, *Opera Omnia*, v, 17–18 • Hewitt, *Canti B*, 222–26 • Jones, *First*, ii, 219–21 • Litterick, *Manuscript*, 219–23 • Shipp, *Chansonnier*, 306–309

Joli amours   **Ghiselin**   3vv

    1. **12**, No.116 (*Jo. Ghiselin*)

4. Disertori, *Frottole*, 201–209 • Ghiselin, *Opera Omnia*, iv, 3–6

Intabulations: lute

    2. 1536[13] = N522, No.19, H1*v*-3*v* (*Ghiselin*. H. Newsidler. Incipit *Juli amors*)

Intabulation: two lutes:

    1. **33**, No.8 (*Francesco Spinacino*. Incipit *Juli amours*)

4. Disertori, *Frottole*, 201–209 • Schmidt, *Spinacino*, ii, 27–38

Joli amours   **Cor de Wilde**   3vv

    1. **12**, No.117 (*:Cor:De:Uuilde:*)

Joliettement menvay

    2 voices of **Je suy dalemaygne**   [Anon.]   5vv

Lamor de moy   [Anon.]   4vv

    1. **12**, No.5 (Anon.)

    3. CH-SGs, 462 • F-Pn, 1597, 71*v*-72*r* (Anon.) • I-CT, 95/96, No.24, 22*r*-22*v* (Anon.)

    4. Brown, *Theatrical*, 142–46 • Gerring and Trümpy

Lautre iour me chevanchoye   **Compère**   4vv

    1. **12**, No.47 (Anon.)

    3. F-Pn, 1817, No.27 (Anon.) • I-CT, 95–96, No.27, 24*r*-24*v* (Anon.) • I-Fc, 2442, No.33, 60*v*-61*v* (Anon.) • I-Fn, 164–67, No.62, 76*r*-77*r* (Anon.)

    4. Compère, *Opera Omnia*

Lautrier ie men aloye iouer   [Anon.]   4vv

    1. **12**, No.40 (Anon.)

Lautrier que passa   **Busnois**   4vv

    1. **2**, No.8 (*.Busnoys.*) • **10**, No.8 (*Busnoys.*)

    2. *50 Carmina* (1513), No.8 (*Busnoys*)

    4. Hewitt, *Canti B*, 117–20

Lheure est venue

    See **Le eure est venue** / [etc.]   **Agricola**   3vv

Lomme arme   **Josquin**   4vv

    1. **2**, No.1 (*.Josquin*. Caption: *Canon. Et sic de singulis*) • **10**, No.1 (*Josquin*. Caption *.Canon. Et sic de singulis*)

Facsimile: Hewitt, *Canti B*, 24 (of 1503[3])

    2. *50 Carmina* (1513), No.1 (*Josquin*)

    4. Disertori, "Mistificazione", 54 • Hewitt, *Canti B*, 91 • Josquin, *Werken*, Wereldlijke, ii, 53 • Maldeghem, *Trésor*, profane, XX (1884), No.8 • Smijers, *Van Ockeghem*, No.45

Lomme arme

    See **Il est de bon heure**   **Japart**   4vv

Lhome banni   **Agricola**   3vv

    1. **1**, No.47 (*Agricola*) • **5**, No.47 (*Agricola*) • **14**, No.47 (*.Agricola.*)

    3. CH-SGs, 461, pp. 84–85 (*Alexander*) • I-Bc, Q18, No.61, 62*v*-63*r* (Anon.)

4. Agricola, *Opera Omnia*, v, 89–90 • Bernoulli, *Liederbüchern*, App., No.18 • Hewitt, *Odhecaton*, 321–22

Intabulation: lute

1. *34*, No.26 (*Fran.Spi.* Titled *Lom e bani Bordon descordato*)

4. Schmidt, *Spinacino*, ii, 258–63

La fleur de biaulte   **Martini**   4vv

1. *12*, No.51 (*Jo. martini*)

4. Martini, *Secular*, 44–46

La hault dalemaygne   **Forestier**   3vv

1. *12*, No.125 (*Mathurin*)

La la he

See **Missa Charge de deul**: Benedictus   **Isaac**   4vv

La Mignonne   **Agricola**   3vv

3. D-B, 40021, No.3, 16*v* (Anon. Untexted. Headed *Trium*) • GB-Lbl, 20.A.XVI, No.2, 3*v*-5*r* (Anon. Incipit *A la mignonne de fortune*) • I-Fn, 229, No.127, 130*v*-132*r* (*Alexander Agricola*. Incipit *La mignone de fortune*) • I-Fr, 2794, No.62, 71*v*-72*r* (Anon. Incipit *La mignonne de fortune*) • I-Rvat, C.G.XIII.27, No.106, 121*v*-123*r* (Anon. Incipit *La mygnone de fortune*) • I-Tn, I.27, No.3, 8*v*-9*r* (Anon. Text incipit *A La mignonne*)

4. Agricola, *Opera Omnia*, v, 3–5 • Brown, *Florentine*, music volume, No.127

Intabulation: lute

1. *34*, No.32 (*Francesco Spinacino*. Headed *Con lo bordon descordato*)

4. Schmidt, *Spinacino*, ii, 283–88

La plus des plus   **Josquin**   3vv

1. *1*, No.64 (*Josquin*) • *5*, No.64 (*Josquin*) • *14*, No.64 (*Josquin*)

2. [c.1535][14], iii, No.12 (Anon.) • 1538[9], No.82, L2*r* (Anon.)

3. D-Z, LXXVIII,3, No.22 (*Josquin*. Untexted)

4. Hewitt, *Odhecaton*, 355–356 • Josquin, *Werken*, Wereldlijke, ii, 53 • Mönkemeyer, *Formschneyder*, ii, p. 120 • *New Josquin Edition*, xxvii, 22

Intabulation: lute

2. 1536[13] = N522, No.7, C3*r*-4*r* (*Jossquin*. H. Newsidler)

La regretee   **Hayne**   3vv

1. *2*, No.48 (*.Hayne.*) • *10*, No.48 (*.Hayne.*)

2. *50 Carmina* (1513), No.48 (*Hayne*) • [c.1535][14], iii, No.22 (Anon.)

3. F-Pn, 1597, 34*v*-35*r* (Anon.) • GB-Lbl, Roy.20.A.xvi, No.17, 22*v*-23*r* (*Heyne*) • S-Uu, 76a, No.20, 17*v*-18*r* (Anon. Incomplete)

4. Hewitt, *Canti B*, 229–32 • Litterick, *Manuscript*, 255–257 • Marix, *Musiciens*, 115–18 • Shipp, *Chansonnier*, 376–81

Las mi lares

See **Vous dont fortune**   **Ghiselin**   3vv

Latura tu   **Bruhier**   4vv
                                                 (?Bruguière)

1. *1*, No.94 (Anon in the index. These folios lacking in the unique extant copy) • *5*, No.94 (Anon.) • *14*, No.94 (Anon.)

3. I-Fc, 2442, pp. 37*v*-39*v* (*Bruhier*)

4. Boer, *Chansonvormen*, No.11 • Hewitt, *Odhecaton*, 414–17

Comments: The *New Grove* article on Bruhier suggests that some of his earlier pieces may be by Jean de la Bruguière.

Le bon temps que iavoy   [Anon.]   4vv
    1. *12*, No.44 (Anon.)

Le corps / Corpusque meum licet   **Compère**   3vv
    1. *1*, No.67 (Compere) • *5*, No.67 (*Compere*) • *14*, No.67 (*Compere*. Superius incipit *Le crops* [*sic*])
    4. Compère, *Opera Omnia* • Hewitt, *Odhecaton*, 361–63

Le desporveu infortune   **Caron**   4vv
    1. *12*, No.95 (Anon.)
    3. I-Bc, Q18, No.25, 25*v*-26*r* (Anon. Incipit *Tanto e lafano*. With a different contra)
        The following sources are à3: E-Sc, 5-I-43, No.72, j2*v*-3*r*/52*v*-53*r* (Anon.) • F-Pn, 15123, 139*v*-140*r* (Anon.) • I-Fn, 229, No.97, 99*v*-100*r* (*Caron*) • I-Rc, 2856, No.56, 67*v*-69*r* (*Caron*. Incipit *Tanto lafano*) • I-Rvat, C.G.XIII.27, No.28, 38*v*-39*r* (Anon. Incipit *Tante laffano*) • I-VEcap, DCCLVII, No.59, 62*v*-63*r* (Anon. Untexted) • PL-Kj, 40098, No.199 (Anon. Untexted. Headed *Undecimus*) • US-Wc, Laborde, 72*v*-73*r* (Anon.)
    4. Brown, *Florentine*, music volume, 196–98 • Caron, *Oeuvres*, ii, 179 • Moerk, *Seville*, ii, 175–76 • Ringmann, *Glogauer*, iv, 52 • Wolff, *Chansonnier*, ii, 189–91
    Intabulation: lute
    1. *33*, No.3 (*Francesco Spinacino*)
    4. Schmidt, *Spinacino*, ii, 7–11

Le grant desir   **Compère**   3vv
    1. *2*, No.51 (.*Compere*.) • *10*, No.51 (*Compere*.)
    2. *50 Carmina* (1513), No.51 (*Compere*) • [c.1535][14], iii, No.25 (Anon.)
    3. DK-Kk, 1848, p. 203 (Anon.)
    Monophonic version: F-Pn, 9346, No.25 (Anon.) • F-Pn, 12744, 93*v* (Anon.)
    4. Compère, *Opera Omnia* • Hewitt, *Canti B*, 237–38

Le eure est venue / Circumdederunt me   **Agricola**   3vv
  2/ Despitant fortune
    1. *1*, No.81 (*Agricola*. Incomplete) • *5*, No.81 (*Agricola*) • *14*, No.81 (*Agricola*)
    3. B-Br, 228, No.54, 62*v*-64*r* (Anon. Both texts) • F-Pn, 1597, 9*v*-10*r* (Anon. Both texts) • GB-Lbl, Roy.20.A.xvi, No.1, 1*v*-3*r*. (Anon. Text 1) • I-Bc, Q17, No.39, 43*v*-45*r* (*A Agricola*. Text 1) • I-Fn, 178, No.4, 5*v*-7*r* (*Alexander*. Texted *Lore venus*) • I-Fr, 2356, No.70, 89*v*-91*r* (Anon. Texted *Lore venus*) • I-Fr, 2794, No.28, 32*v*-33*r* (*Agricola*) • I-Rc, 2856, No.32, 37*v*-39*r* (*Agricola*) • I-Rvat, C.G.XIII.27, No.39, 50*v*-52*r* (Anon. Texted *Lore venus*)
    4. Agricola, *Opera Omnia*, iv, 54–57 • Boer, *Chansonvormen*, 79–81 • Hewitt, *Odhecaton*, 389–91 • Jones, *First*, ii, 224–28 • Litterick, *Manuscript*, 210–14 • Maldeghem, *Trésor*, profane, XXIII (1887), Nos.10–11 • Picker, *Chanson*, 399–403 • Shipp, *Chansonnier*, 277 • Wolff, *Chansonnier*, ii, 105–10
    Intabulation: lute
    1. *34*, No.7 (*Francesco Spinacino*)
    4. Schmidt, *Spinacino*, ii, 185–93

Le renvoy   **Compère**   3vv
    1. *1*, No.77 (Anon in the index. These folios in the unique surviving copy are of the second edition) • *5*, No.77 (*Compere*.) • *14*, No.77 (*Compere*)
    2. [c.1535][14], iii, No.9 (Anon.)
    3. D-Z, LXXVIII,3, No.15 (Anon. Untexted) • DK-Kk, 1848, No.46, p. 90 (Anon.) • I-Bc, Q17, No.23, 27*v*-28*r* (*Loyset Compere*) • I-Fn, 178, No.26, 30*v*-32*r* (Anon.) • I-Fn,

229, No.43, 42v-43r (Anon.) • I-Fr, 2794, No.46, 53v-54r (Anon.) • I-Rc, 2856, No.30, 34v-36r (*Compere*) • I-VEcap, DCCLVII, No.13, 12v-13r (Anon. Untexted)

4. Brown, *Florentine*, music volume, 85–87 • Compère, *Opera Omnia*, v, 33 • Christoffersen, *French*, iii, 87 • Hewitt, *Odhecaton*, 381–82 • Jones, *First*, ii, 268–69 • Wolff, *Chansonnier*, ii, 100–102

Comments. The Superius is used for the Agnus of Obrecht's *Missa Scoen lief*

Le second jour davril   Busnois   4vv

1. *12*, No.39 (Anon.)

3. I-Fc, 2439, No.28, 29v-30r (*Bunoys*. Texted *In myn zynn*)

Painting: Antoniszoon, Cornelis: *Banquet of Seventeen Members of the Civic Guard* (Amsterdam, Rijksmuseum), dated 1553. Fragments of the musical composition.

4. Lenaerts, *Nederlandse*, 24–26 • Newton, *Florence*, ii, 86–89 • Picker, "Newly discovered" • Taruskin, *In mynen zin*

Literature: Picker, "Newly discovered"

Le serviteur   [Anon.]   3vv

1. *12*, No.114 (Anon.)

3. D-As, 25, No.6 (Anon. Untexted) • E-Sc, 5-I-43, No.85, k3v-5r/65v-67r (Anon.)

4. Moerk, *Seville*, ii, 206–209

Le serviteur   Busnois   4vv

1. *1*, No.35 (*Busnoys*) • *5*, No.35 (Anon.) • *14*, No.35 (Anon.)

4. Hewitt, *Odhecaton*, 294–95

Le serviteur   Hanart   2vv

1. *12*, No.138 (*Hanart*, above Tenor)

3. I-Bc, Q16, 90, 98v-99r (Anon.)

Le serviteur   Tadinghem   2vv

1. *12*, No.137 (*Tadinghen*, above Tenor)

4. Schering, "Geschichte" • Underwood, *Renaissance*, 337–40

Le sovenir   Morton   3vv

3. D-W, 287, 47v-48r (Anon.) • DK-Kk, 291, No.20, 25r (Anon. Incomplete) • DK-Kk, 1848, p. 141 (Anon.) • F-Dm, 517, 87v-88r (Anon.) • F-Pn, 15123, No.18, 20v-21r (Anon.) • F-Pn, 2973, No.24, 30v-31r (Anon.) • I-Bc, Q16, No.118, 138v-139r (Anon.) • I-Fn, 176, No.36, 52v-53r (*Morton*) • I-Fr, 2356, No.36, 47v-48r (Anon.) • I-PEc, 431, No.55, 78v-79r (Anon. Later addition of a fourth voice) • S-Uu, 76a, No.23, 20v-21r (Anon.) • US-Wc, Laborde, No.43, 55v-56r (Anon.)

Text cited by Molinet in his *Le debat du viel gendarme*

4. Fallows, *Morton*, 2 • Jeppesen, *Kopenhagener*, No.20 • Morton, *Collected Works*, No.4 • Thibault and Fallows, *Chansonnier*

Intabulations: keyboard

3. D-Mbs, Cim.352b, No.250, 162r-162v (Anon. Titled *Salve radix josophanie*) • D-Mbs, Cim.352b, No.256, 165r-165v (Anon.)

Intabulation: lute

1. *34*, No.9 (*Francesco Spinacino*)

4. Schmidt, *Spinacino*, ii, 197–200

Le troys filles de paris   de Orto   4vv

1. *12*, No.11 (*De. orto.*)

3. I-Fc, 2442, No.30, 52v-56r (De orto)

3. Honegger & Dottin, "Chansons"

| Les grans regres | Hayne | 3vv |

(Agricola)

1. *1*, No.71 (Anon.) • *5*, No.71 (Anon.) • *14*, No.71 (Anon.)

3. B-Br, 11239, No.4, 7*v*-8*r* (*Agricola*) • B-Br, IV.90, No.2, 4*r* (Anon. Incomplete) • B-Tv, 94, No.2, 3*r*-4*r* (Anon.) • DK-Kk, 1848, No.49, p. 95 (Anon.) • F-Pn, 1597, 12*v*-13*r* (Anon.) • F-Pn, 2245, 19*v*-20*r* (*Hayne*) • I-Bc, Q17, No.32, 36*v*-37*r* (*Hayne*) • I-Fn, 107bis, No.29, 44*v*-45*r* (Anon.) • I-Fn, 117, No.32, 34*v*-35*r* (Anon.) • US-Wc, Laborde, 143*v*-145*r* (*Hayne*)

4. Agricola, *Opera Omnia*, v, 120–21 • Christoffersen, *French*, iii, 90–91 • Hayne, *Opera Omnia*, • Hewitt, *Odhecaton*, 370–71 • Maldeghem, *Trésor*, profane, XI (1875), No.16 • Marix, *Musiciens*, No.75 • Picker, *Chanson*, 422–24

| Lo seray dire | [Anon.] | 4vv |

1. *1*, No.29 (Anon in the index. These folios are lacking in the unique copy) • *5*, No.29 (Anon.) • *14*, No.29 (Anon.)

4. Hewitt, *Odhecaton*, 281–83

Monophonic version: F-Pn, 9346, No.17 (Anon. Texted *Ne loseray je dire*)

| Loier mi fault vag carpentier | Japart | 4vv |

1. *12*, No.37 (*Japart*)

| Loseraige dire se jame per amoure | [Anon.] | 4vv |

1. *12*, No.30 (Anon.)

| Lourdault lourdault | Compère | 4vv |

(Josquin; Ninot)

1. *2*, No.5 (*Compere*) • *10*, No.5 (*Compere*.)

2. *50 Carmina* (1513), No.5 (*Compere*)

3. CH-Bu, F.X.1–4, No.119 (*Josquin*) • D-Rp, C.120, No.68, pp. 260–61 (*Compere*) • F-Pn, 1597, 56*v*-57*r* (Anon.) • F-Pn, 1817, No.6 (Anon.) • I-Bc, Q17, No.55, 60*v*-61*r* (*Nino petit*) • I-CT, 95–96, No.6, 5*v*-6*r* (Anon.)

Monophonic version: F-Pn, 12744, No.71 (Anon.)

4. Ambros, *Geschichte*, v • Brown, *Theatrical*, 152–55 • Compère, *Opera Omnia*, v • Hewitt, *Canti B*, 108–109 • Jones, *First*, ii • Josquin, *Werken*, Wereldlijke, • Ninot, *Collected Works*, 127–29 • Obrecht, *Werken*, Missen • Shipp, *Chansonnier*, 466–70 • Smijers, *Van Ockeghem*, No.34 • Torrefranca, *Segreto* • Wolff, *Chansonnier*

Comments: Finscher, "Compère", *Grove 6*, iv, 598, regards this as only doubtfully by Compère

| Ma bouche rit | Ockeghem | 3vv |

1. *1*, No.54 (*Okenghem*. Listed as f.54 in the index) • *5*, No.54, (*Okenghem*) • *14*, No.54 (*Okenhem*)

2. 1538^9, No.86, L3*v* (Anon.)

3. D-Mbs, 810, 62*v*-64*r* (*Ockegheim*) • D-W, 287, 29*v*-31*r* (Anon.) • DK-Kk, 1848, 42*v*-44*r* (Anon. Prima pars only) • F-Dm, 517, 4*v*-6*r* (Anon.) • F-Pn, 57, 52*v*-54*r* (*Okeghem*) • F-Pn, 15123, 30*v*-32*r* (Anon.) • F-Pn, 4379, No.30, e5*v*-7*r*/4*v*-6*r* (Anon.) • F-Pn, 2973, 42*v*-44*r* (Anon.) • I-Fn, 176, No.24, 32*v*-34*r* (*Ochechem*) • I-Fr, 2356, No.23, 28*v*-29*r* (Anon.) • I-Rc, 2856, No.52, 61*v*-63*r* (*Okeghem*. Texted *Ma bouche frit*) • I-Rvat, C.G.XIII.27, No.62, 76*v*-77*r* (Anon.) • PL-Kj, 40098, No.265 (Anon. Untexted, with an initial letter *H*) • US-NH, 91, No.30, 38*v*-40*r* (*Okeghem*) • US-Wc, Laborde, 43*v*-34*r* (Anon.)

Text cited in Molinet's *Le debat du viel gendarme*, *Oroison a nostre dame*, and *Collaudation a Madame Marguerite*

4. Davison and Apel, *HAM*, i, 75 • Droz, Thibault, Rokseth, *Chansonniers*, 9–11 • Gombosi, *Obrecht*, No.5 • Hewitt, *Odhecaton*, 335–36 • Löpelmann, *Liederhandschrift*, No.142 • Martini, *Magnificat*, 29–31 • Mönkemeyer, *Formschneyder*, ii, pp. 124–25 • Moerk, *Seville*, ii, 75–77 • Ockeghem, *Collected*, iii, 73–74 • Perkins and Garey, *Mellon*, No.30 • Ringmann, *Glogauer*, 61 • Thibault and Fallows, *Chansonnier* • Wolff, *Chansonnier*, ii, 175–78

Intabulation: lute

1. *33*, No.17 (Anon. Incipit *Mabucherit*.)

4. Schmidt, *Spinacino*, ii, 77–80

Ma seule dame [Anon.] 3vv

1. *1*, No.79 (Anon. Incomplete: the other folios for this work in the unique surviving copy are of the second edition. The work is not entered in the index) • *5*, No.79 (Anon.) • *14*, No.79, (Anon.)

4. Boer, *Chansonvormen*, No.9 • Hewitt, *Odhecaton*, 385–86

Madame helas [Anon.] 3vv
(Josquin)

1. *1*, No.66 (*Josquin*) • *5*, No.66 (Anon.) • *14*, No.66 (Anon.)

3. CH-SGs, 463 (Listed in the index, but not entered) • D-Z, LXXVIII,3, No.17 (*Josquin*) • E-Sc, 5-I-43, No.153, q4*v*-5*r*/124*v*-125*r* (Anon. Untexted. à4) • I-Bc, Q16, No.125, 145*v*-146*r* (Anon. Titled *Dux Carlus*) • I-VEcap, DCCLVII, No.8, 7*v*-8*r* (Anon. Untexted)

4. Hewitt, *Odhecaton*, 359–60 • Moerk, *Seville*, ii, 374–77

Mayntes femmes Busnois 4 ex 3vv
2/ [No text incipit]

1. *12*, No.92 (*Busnoys*:. Rubrics: above piece: *Canon: Odam si protham teneas in remisso diapason cum paribus ter augeas*: and before the second *pars*: *Voces a mese non nullas usque licanosypatorecie singulas*)

3. E-Sc, 5-I-43, No.134, 09*v*-11*r*/107*v*-109*r* (Anon.)

4. Hewitt, "Bergerette" • Moerk, *Seville*, ii, 334–37

Mais que ce fust Compère 3vv
(Pietrequin)

1. *1*, No.87 (Anon in the index. This folio in the only extant copy is of the second edition) • *5*, No.87 (*Compere*.) • *14*, No.87, (*Compere*.)

3. DK-Kk, 1848, p. 130 (Anon.) • GB-Lbl, Add.35087, No.19, 29*v*-30*r* (Anon.) • I-Bc, Q17, No.14, 18*v*-19*r* (*Pierquin*) • I-Fn, 178, No.63, 67*v*-68*r* (*Pietraquin*. Incipit *Meschin che fuis secretament*) • I-Fn, 229, No.202, 218*v*-219*r* (Anon.) • I-Rc, 2856, No.110, 141*v*-142*r* (Anon. Untexted) • I-Rvat, C.G.XIII.27, No.41, 53*v*-54*r* (*Petrequin*. à4. Incipit *Donzella no men culpeys*) • US-Wc, Laborde, 114*v* (Anon. Incomplete)

4. Brown, *Florentine*, music volume, 469–70 • Compère, *Opera Omnia*, v, 67 • Hewitt, *Odhecaton*, 400 • McMurtry, *Chansonnier*, 265–67 • Wolff, *Chansonnier*, ii, 384–85

Literature: Atlas, *Giulia*, 113–120

Male bouche / Circumdederunt me Compère 3vv

1. *1*, No.46 (*Compere*) • *5*, No.46 (*Compere*) • *14*, No.46 (*Compere*)

2. 1542[8], No.41 (*Loyset Compere*. Texted *O Domine libera animam meam*)

3. CH-Bu, F.VI.26f, No.11, 8*r* (XVIIIr) (Anon.) • CH-SGs, 462, pp. 114–15 (Anon.)

4. Compère, *Opera Omnia*, v, 2 • Hewitt, *Odhecaton*, 319–20 • Noblitt, *Tricinia*, pp. 132–33

Malor me bat   **Ockeghem**   3vv
                                    (Malcort / Martini)

1. *1*, No.63 (*Okenghen*) • *5*, No.63 (*Okenghen:*) • *14*, No.63 (*Okenghen.*)
2. [c.1535]¹⁴, iii, No.58 (Anon.) • 1538⁹, No.91, M2*v* (Anon. Incipit *Malheur me bat*)
3. CH-SGs, 461, pp. 52–53 (*Ockeghem*) • I-Bc, Q16, No.14, 21*v*-22*r* (Anon. Texted *Dieu damors*) • I-Bc, Q18, No.72, 73*v*-74*r* (Anon.) • I-Fn, 229, No.11, 10*v*-11*r* (*Jannes Martini. Untexted*) • I-Rc, 2856, No.49, 57*v*-59*r* (*Malcort*) • I-Rvat, C.G.XIII.27, No.59, 72*v*-73*r* (*Io Martini*)
4. Anglès, *Carlos*, 52 • Brown, *Florentine*, music volume, 21–23 • Hewitt, *Odhecaton*, 353–54 • Josquin, *Werken*, Missen, viii, 66 • Martini, *Secular*, 53–55 • Mönkemeyer, *Formschneyder*, ii, pp. 132–33 • Obrecht, *Opera Omnia*, i, 226 • Obrecht, *Werken*, i, 189–90 • Ockeghem, *Complete Works* iii, • Wolff, *Chansonnier*, ii, 166–68

Intabulation: keyboard

2. V1108 (1557), No.43, f.26*r* (Anon. Venegas de Henestrosa. *Quarto tono sobre Malheur me bat*)

Intabulation: lute

1. *34*, No.13 (*Francesco Spinacino*)
4. Schmidt, *Spinacino*, ii, 210–12

Comments: Hudson, "Ferrarese" and Picker, *Ockeghem/Obrecht*, 37 attribute this work to Martini. Strohm, "Review", 553–54, makes a strong indirect case for attributing the song to Malcort. On Malcort, see Wegman, "Bergen", 240 and Haggh, *Brussels*, 627. • The basis for the masses by Agricola, Josquin, and Obrecht, also printed by Petrucci • Cited in Aaron, *Trattato della natura*

Literature: Atlas, *Giulia*, 149–53

Marguerite   [Anon.]   3vv
                                    (Josquin)

1. *1*, No.85 (Listed as *Margaritte* and anon in the index. These folios in the unique surviving copy are of the second edition) • *5*, No.85 (Anon.) • *14*, No.85 (Anon.)
3. I-Bc, Q34 10*v*-12*r* (*Josquini*)
4. Hewitt, *Odhecaton*, 397–98

Intabulation: lute

1. *34*, No.21 (*Francesco Spinacino*)
4. Schmidt, *Spinacino*, ii, 232–35

Me doibt   **Compère**   3vv
                                    (Festa)

1. *1*, No.45 (Anon. Incomplete) • *5*, No.45 (*Compere.*) • *14*, No.45, (*Compere*)
2. [c.1535]¹⁴, iii, No.52 (Anon.) • 1556²⁶ (*Festa. Incipit Venite amanti insieme*)
3. D-Z, LXXVIII,3, No.14 (Anon. Untexted) • F-Dm, 517, 186*v*-188*r* (*Loyset Compere*) • I-Bc, Q18, No.86, 87*v*-88*r* (Anon.) • I-Fn, Panc.27, No.59, 38*v*-39*r* (*Compere*)
4. Compère, *Opera Omnia*, v, 35 • Festa, *Opera Omnia* • Hewitt, *Odhecaton*, 317–18

Intabulation: lute

2. 1536¹³ = N522, No.8, C4*v*-D1*r* (*Compere.* H. Newsidler. Titled *Medobt*)

Mes pensees   **Compère**   3vv

1. *1*, No.59 (Anon. Incomplete) • *5*, No.59 (*Compere.*) • *14*, No.59 (*Compere*)
2. 1538⁹, No.18, C3*r*. (Anon. MS attribution in the copy at D-Ju: *L. Compere*)
3. D-Z, LXXVIII,3, No.19 (Anon. Untexted) • F-Pn, 1597, 8*v*-9*r* (Anon.) • F-Pn, 15123, 169*v*-170*r* (*Compere*) • GB-Lbl, Roy.20.A.xvi, No.27, 34*v*-35*r* (Anon.) • I-Bc, Q17,

No.12, 16*v*-17*r* (*Loyset Compere*) • I-Fn, 178, No.52, 56*v*-57*r* (*Loyset*) • I-Fn, 229, No.130, 134*v*-135*r* (*Loyset Compere*) • I-Fr, 2794, No.39, 46*v*-47*r* (Anon.) • I-MC, 871, No.115, 134*v*-135*r* (pp. 400–401) (*Loyset Compere*) • I-Rvat, C.G.XIII.27, No.87, 101*v*-102*r* (Anon.) • S-Uu, 76a, No.25, 22*v*-23*r* (Anon.) • US-Wc, Laborde, 106*v*-108*r* (Anon.)

    4. Boer, *Chansonvormen*, 60–62 • Brown, *Florentine*, music volume, 270–273 • Compère, *Opera Omnia*, v, 37 • Hewitt, *Odhecaton*, 345–46 • Jones, *First*, ii, 252–54 • Litterick, *Manuscript*, 283–86 • Mönkemeyer, *Formschneyder*, ii, pp. 31–32 • Pease, *Edition*, iii, 567–12 • Pope and Kanazawa, *Montecassino*, 459–65 • Shipp, *Chansonnier*, 271–76

    Intabulation: lute

    2. 1536[13] = N522, No.16, F3*r*-4*v* (*Compere*. H. Newsidler)

Mon amy mavoyt promis une belle chainture   **Ninot le Petit**   4vv

    1. *12*, No.64 (Anon.)

    2. [c.1535][14], i, No.15

    3. I-Fc, 2442, No.19

    4. Ninot, *Opera Omnia*

Mon enfant mon enfant   [Anon.]   4vv

    1. *12*, No.22 (Anon.)

Mon mari ma defamee   [Anon.]   4vv

    1. *12*, No.29 (Anon.)

Mo[n] mari ma defame   [Anon.]   3vv
                                        (Josquin)

    3. B-Br, IV.90, No.10, 13*v*-14*r* (Anon.) • B-Tv, 94, No.10, 15*r*-15*v* (Anon.) • GB-Lbl, Add.35087, No.13, 21*v*-22*r* (Anon.) • S-Uu, 76a, 24*v* (Anon. Incomplete)

    Monophonic version: F-Pn, 12744, 75*v*-76*r* (Anon.)

    4. McMurtry, *Chansonnier*, 249–53 • *New Josquin Edition*, xxvii, 27 • Schmidt, *Spinacino*, i, 26–29 • Van Benthem, "Josquin", 444–45

    Intabulation: lute

    1. *34*, No.18 (*Francesco Spinacino*)

    2. 1578[15], No.20, p. 16 (*Josquin*)

    4. Schmidt, *Spinacino*, ii, 226–27

Mon mari ma deffamee   **de Orto**   4vv

    1. *2*, No.12 (*.De.Orto.*) • *10*, No.12 (*.De.Orto.*)

    2. *50 Carmina* (1513), No.12 (*De Orto*)

    Monophonic version: F-Pn, 12744, 75*v* (Anon.)

    4. Hewitt, *Canti B*, 128–29

Mon mignault / Gratieuse   **Busnois**   4vv

    1. *1*, No.17 (Anon.) • *5*, No.17 (Anon.) • *14*, No.17 (Anon.)

    3. CH-SGs, 461, p. 65 (*Busnoys*. Incipits 1 and 2) • F-Dm, 517, 178*v*-179*r*/181*v*-182*r* (Anon. Texts 1 and 2) • I-Fn, 229, No.184, 194*v*-195*r* (*Antonius Busnois*. Untexted)

    4. Boer, *Chansonvormen*, No.3 • Brown, *Florentine*, music volume, 426–27 • Hewitt, *Odhecaton*, 258–259

    Comments: The basis of Ghiselin's mass, also printed by Petrucci

Mon pere ma dona mari   [Anon.]   4vv

    1. *2*, No.41 (Anon.) • *10*, No.41 (Anon.)

    2. *50 Carmina* (1513), No.41 (Anon.)

    4. Hewitt, *Canti B*, 208–11

Mon pere me done mari   **Compère**   4vv

    1. *12*, No.49 (*Compere*)

    3. E-SE, s.s., No.58, 127*v*-128*r* (*Loysette compere*) • I-Fc, 2442, No.34, 62*v*-63*r* (*L. Compere*)

    4. Compère, *Opera Omnia*, v, 38

Mon pere ma mariee   [Anon.]   4vv

    1. *2*, No.17 (Anon.) • *10*, No.17 (Anon.)

    2. *50 Carmina* (1513), No.17 (Anon.) • [c.1535]¹⁴, i, No.25 (Anon.)

    4. Hewitt, *Canti B*, 140-41

Mon sovenir   **Hayne**   3vv

    1. *1*, No.83. (Anon in the index. These folios in the unique surviving copy are of the second edition) • *5*, No.83 (Anon.) • *14*, No.83 (Anon.)

    3. DK-Kk, 1848, p. 122 (Anon.) and p. 364 (Anon.), *and* p. 450 (Anon.) • E-SE, s.s., No.90, 164*r* (*Scoen Heyne*) • F-Pn, 1597, 26*v*-27*r* (Anon.) • F-Pn, 2245, 1*v*-2*r* (*Hayne*) • GB-Lbl, Roy.20.A.xvi, No.21, 27*v*-28*r* (*Heyne.*) • GB-Lbl, Add.35087, No.18, 28*v*-29*r* (Anon.) • I-Bc, Q17, No.28, 32*v*-33*r* (*Hayne*) • I-Fn, 178, No.23, 27*v*-28*r* (*Ayne*) • I-Fr, 2356, No.4, 8*v*-9*r* (Anon.) • I-Fr, 2794, No.65, 75*v*, incomplete (*Heyne*) • I-Rc, 2856, No.96, 124*v*-125*r* (*Haine*) • I-Rvat, C.G.XIII.27, No.40, 52*v*-53*r* (Anon.) • S-Uu, 76a, No.28, 25*r* (Anon. Incomplete) • US-Wc, Laborde, 110*v*-111*r* (Anon.)

    4. Birmingham, *Chansonnier*, 76 • Gombosi, *Obrecht*, No.4 • Hayne, *Opera Omnia*, p. 34 • Hewitt, *Odhecaton*, 394 • Jones, *First*, ii, 310-11 • Litterick, *Manuscript*, 260-70 • Marix, *Musiciens*, No.76 • McMurtry, *Chansonnier*, 261-64 • Shipp, *Chansonnier*, 336 • Wolff, *Chansonnier*, ii, 335-37

    Intabulation: lute

    1. *33*, No.20 (Anon. Incipit *Non sovenir*)

    4. Schmidt, *Spinacino*, ii, 90-93

Nastu pas veu   [Anon.]   4vv

    1. *12*, No.17 (Anon.)

Ne come peult

    See **Coment peult**   **Josquin**   4 ex 3vv

Ne loseray je dire

    See **Loseraige dire**   [Anon.]   4vv

Nostra iamais

    See **Vostre a iamays**   **Ghiselin**   3vv

Nostre cambriere si malade estoit   **Ninot**   4vv

    1. *1*, No.32 (Anon.) • *5*, No.32 (Anon.) • *14*, No.32 (Anon.)

    3. I-Fc, 2442, No.16, 22*v*-23*v* (*Ninot le Petit. à3*) • I-164-167, No.50, 60*v*-61*v* (Anon. à4)

    4. Boer, *Chansonvormen*, No.10 • Ninot, *Collected Works*, 47-49 • Hewitt, *Odhecaton*, 288-89.

Nous sommes de lordre de saynt babuyn   **Compère**   4vv

    1. *1*, No.37 (*Compere. Cantus incipit Dous sommes*) • *5*, No.37 (*Compere. Cantus incipit ous sommes*) • *14*, No.37 (*Compere. Cantus incipit ous sommes*)

    4. Ambros, *Geschichte*, v, 186 • Compère, *Opera Omnia*, • Hewitt, *Odhecaton*, 299-301

Nymphes des bois / Requiem aeternam   **Josquin**   5vv

    1. *46*, No.8 (*Josquin. Only the Tenor texted*)

    2. 1545¹⁵, No.23, 13*r* (*Josquin de prez*)

    3. I-Fl, 666, No.46, 125*v*-127*r* (*Josquin*)

Text by Molinet: *Epitaphe de venerable Seigneur de bonne memoire, Obregam, tresorier de Tours.*
4. Josquin, *Werken*, Wereldlijke, i, 5 • Lowinsky, *Medici*, iv, 338–46

O Fortune content
　　See Latin texts: **Missa Charge de deul**: Qui tollis　　**Isaac**　　　　4vv

Or mauldict soyt
　　See Latin texts: **Missa Charge de deul**: Qui tollis　　**Isaac**　　　　4vv

Orsus orsus bovier　　　　　　　　　　**Bulkyn**　　　　4 ex 3vv
　　1. *2*, No.36 (.*Bulkyn.* Headed *In subdiatessaron*) • *10*, No.36 (.*Bulkyn.* Headed *In subdiatessaron*)
　　2. *50 Carmina* (1513), No.36 (*Bulkyn*)
　　4. Hewitt, *Canti B*, 193–94

Par ung iour de matinee　　　　　　　**Isaac**　　　　4vv
　　1. *12*, No.57 (*Yzac.*)
　　3. A-Wn, 18810, No.26 (*Henricus ijsaac*. Incipit *Hab mich lieb*) • D-Mbs, 1516 (Anon.) • D-Mu, 328–331, No.98, 111r (Anon. Texted *Hab mich lieb*)
　　4. Isaac, *Weltliche*, 101–02 • Whisler, *Munich*, 32–35

Pensif mari　　　　　　　　　　　　**Tadinghem**　　　3vv
　　　　　　　　　　　　　　　　　　　(Josquin)
　　1. *1*, No.43 (*Ja. Tadinghen*. Incomplete) • *5*, No.43 (*Ja. Tadinghen*) • *14*, No.43 (*Ja. Tadinghen*)
　　2. [c.1535]¹⁴, iii, No.7 (Anon.)
　　3. I-Bc, Q34, 5r-6v (*Josquini*)
　　4. Hewitt, *Odhecaton*, 313–14
　　Intabulation: lute
　　1. *34*, No.27 (*Francesco Spinacino*. Titled *Pensi che mai*. Index incipit *Pensif meri*)
　　4. Schmidt, *Spinacino*, ii, 262–66

Petite camusete　　　　　　　　　　**Ockeghem**　　　4vv
　　1. *12*, No.99 (*Okenghem*)
　　3. B-Br, 11239, No.13, 20v, incomplete (Anon.) • D-Mbs, 1516, No.11 (Anon.) • D-W, 287, 61v-62r (Anon. Texted *S'elle m'aymera / Petite Camusette*) • E-Sc, 7-I-28, 101v-102r (Anon. Texted *De la momera / Petit le camuset*) • F-Dm, 517, 161v-162r (Anon. Texted *S'elle m'amera / Petite Camusette*) • F-Pc, 57, 55v-56r (Anon. Texted *S'elle m'amera / Petite Camusete*) • I-Fc, 2439, No.30, 31v-32r (*Ockeghem*) • I-MC, 871, No.110, 160v (Anon.) • US-NH, 91, No.4, 4v-5r (*J okeghem*)
　　4. Gombosi, *Obrecht*, 256–58 • Haberkamp, *Vokalmusik*, No.87 • Newton, *Florence*, ii, 93–95 • Perkins and Garey, *Mellon*, No.4 • Picker, *Chanson*, 437–39 • Pope and Kanazawa, *Montecassino*, 438–41 • Querol Gavaldá, *Cancionero*, 90–91 • Whisler, "Munich" • Gutiérrez-Denhoff, *Wolfenbütteler* • Ockeghem, *Complete Works*, iii

Plus ne chasceray
　　Tenor of **Pour passer temps**　　　**Japart**　　　4vv
Pour passer temps / Plus ne chasceray　　**Japart**　　4vv
　　1. *12*, No.61 (*Jo. Japart*)

Pour quoy fu fait ceste comprise　　　[Anon.]　　　3vv
　　1. *2*, No.43 (Anon.) • *10*, No.43 (Anon. Incipit includes *fiat*)
　　2. *50 Carmina* (1513), No.43 (Anon.) • [c.1535]¹⁴, iii, No.17 (Anon.)
　　4. Hewitt, *Canti B*, 214–17

Por quoy je ne puis dire / Vray diu   **Stockem**   4vv

    1. *1*, No.16 (*Jo. Sthokem.*) • *5*, No.16 (*Jo. Sthokem.*) • *14*, No.16, (*.Jo Sthokem.*)

    4. Hewitt, *Odhecaton*, 255–57

Por quoy non   **La Rue**   4vv

    1. *1*, No.15 (*Pe. de la rue*) • *5*, No.15 (*Pe. de la rue*) • *14*, No.15 (*Pe. de la rue*)

    Facsimile: Barksdale, *Printed*, pp. 66–67 (from 1504²)

    3. B-Br, 228, No.10, 11*v*-12*r* (Anon.) • B-Br, 11239, No.12, 18*v-20r* (Anon.) • CH-Bu,
    F.X.1–4, No.110 (*Pirson*) • CH-SGs, 463 (Entered only in the index. *Petrus de La Rue*) •
    I-Bc, Q17, No.48, 53*v*-54*r* (*Pe de la Rue* [with a rebus]) • I-Fc, 2442, No.42, 75*v*-76*v* (*Pe
    de la Rue* [with a rebus]. á3) • I-Rvat, 11953, No.7, 7*r*-7*v* (*P. de la Rue*)

    4. Blume, *Josquin*, No.11 • Hewitt, *Odhecaton*, 252–54 • Maldeghem, *Trésor, profane*, XXI
    (1885), No.6 • Picker, *Chanson*, 211–14

    Intabulation: keyboard

    3. CH-SGs, 530, 75v-76r (Anon.)

Pour quoy tant   **La Rue**   4vv

    1. *12*, No.31 (Anon.)

    3. B-Br, 11239, No.14, 21*r* (Anon. Incomplete) • I-Fc, 2439, No.9, 10*v*-11*r* (*Rue: Perison* in
    index)

    4. Newton, *Florence*, ii, 28–30 • Picker, *Chanson*, 440–43

Prennez sur moy   **Ockeghem**   3 ex IV

    1. *12*, No.139 (*Okenghem*)

    2. Heyden 1537, p. 34 (*Okenghem. Headed Exemplum cantus ficti, sive bmollis iste fuerit, hduri.
    Fuga trium vocum, in Epidiatessaron, post perfectum tempus.*) • Heyden 1540, p. 39 (*Okeghem.
    Headed Fuga trium vocum in Epidiatessaron post perfectum tempus*) • 1547¹, p. 454 (*Okenheim.
    Headed Fuga trium vocum in epidiatessaron*) • Faber 1553, pp. 152–53 (*Okeghem. Headed
    Fuga trium partium*) • Wilphlingseder 1563, pp. 57–63 (*Okenheimius. Headed Fugra trium
    vocum in Epidiatessaron cum Resolutione*) • 1590³⁰, No.XV (*Okenhemius. Headed Fuga trium
    vocum in epidiatessaron*)

    3. DK-Kk, 291, 40*v* (Anon.) • F-Dm, 517, 1*r* (listed in the index but now missing)

    Intarsia: Mantua, Palazzo ducale, Studiolo d'Isabella d'Este (*Jo. Okenghem*)

    4. Ambros, *Geschichte*, 18 19 • Bockholdt, "Französische", 161–65 • Disertori, *Frottole*, 122–
    23 • Droz, Thibault, Rokseth, *Chansonniers*, 1–2 • Fallows, "Prenez" • Glareanus, *Dode-
    cachordon*, ii, 532–33 • Heyden, *De arte canendi*, 52 • Jeppesen, *Kopenhagener*, 62–63 •
    Levitan, "Ockeghem" • Ockeghem, *Complete Works*, iii, 80 • Reese, "Intarsie", 85–85 •
    Scherliess, *Musikalische Noten*, 79–81

       This work has often been transcribed as an example of musical ingenuity. A more
    complete list of editions since the later 18th-century can be found in Ockeghem, *Collected*,
    iii, lxxxvii-lxxxviii

    Literature: Dahlhaus, "Ockeghems" • Fallows, "Prenez" • Levitan, "Ockeghem" • Reese,
    "Intarsie" • Scherliess, *Musikalische Noten*

Prestes le moy   **Japart**   4vv

    1. *12*, No.76 (*Jo. Japart*)

Puisque de vous   [Anon.]   3vv

    1. *1*, No.82 (Anon in the index. These folios in the unique surviving copy are of the second
    edition • *5*, No.82 (Anon.) • *14*, No.91 (Anon.)

    4. Hewitt, *Odhecaton*, 405–406

Quant vostre ymage   [Anon.]   4vv
   1. *12*, No.65 (Anon.)

Que vous madame / In pace in idipsum   Josquin   4vv
                                          (Agricola)

   1. *12*, No.80 (*Agricola*)
   The following sources are à3:
   2. 1542[8], No.25 (*Alexander Agricola*. Text 2)
   3. B-Br, 11239, No.22, 31*v*-32*r* (Anon. Text 2) • CH-SGs, 463, No.31 (Anon. Text 2.
      Headed *Hypoionicus*) • E-SE, s.s., No.105, 171*v* (*Josquin des Pres*. Incipit 2) • F-Pn, 1597,
      45*v*-46*r* (Anon. Both texts) • GB-Lbl, Roy.20.A.xvi, No.24, 30*v*-31*r* (*Josquin*. Both texts)
      • I-Bc, Q17, No.31, 35*v*-36*r* (*Josquin*. Text 2) • I-Fn, 178, No.47, 51*v*-52*r* (*Josquin*. Text
      2) • I-Fn, 229, No.44, 43*v*-44*r* (*Josquin*. Text 2) • I-Rc, 2856, No.89, 114*v*-115*r* (*Joskin*.
      Text 2) • I-Rvat, C.G.XIII.27, No.11, 18*v*-19*r* (*Josquin*. Text 2) • PL-Wu, 58, 60*v* (Anon.)
      • US-Wc, Wolffheim, 89*v*-90*r* (Anon. Text 2)
   4. Agricola, *Opera Omnia*, v, 128–29 • Besseler, *Capella*, i, 22–23 • Brown, *Florentine*, music
      volume, 87–89 • Josquin, *Werken*, Wereldlijke, No.47 • Litterick, *Manuscript*, 275–77 •
      Maldeghem, *Trésor*, Religeuse, XIX, 6 • *New Josquin Edition*, xxvii, 33 • Noblitt, *Tricinia*,
      pp. 78–79 • Picker, *Chanson*, 461–63 • Shipp, *Chansonnier*, 420–23 • Wolff, *Chansonnier*,
      ii, 308–11
   Intabulation: keyboard
   2. Baena 1540, No.30, 25*r*-26*r* (Josquin)
   3. CH-Bu, F.IX.22, 2*r* (*Heinricue Yzaack*)
   Intabulation: lute
   1. *34*, No.33 (*Francesco Spinacino*. Titled *In pace*)
   4. Schmidt, *Spinacino*, ii, 289–92
   Comments: Lerner, in Agricola, *Opera Omnia*, v, p. xcvi, suggests that perhaps the fourth
      voice found in Petrucci's version was composed by Agricola

Qui veult iouer de la queue   [Anon.]   4vv
   1. *12*, No.20 (Anon.)
   3. I-Fc, 2442, No.39, 70*v*-72*v* (*Henricus Morinensis*)

Revelies vous   [Anon.]   4vv
   1. *2*, No.9 (Anon.) • *10*, No.9 (Anon.)
   2. *50 Carmina* (1513), No.9 (Anon.) • [1535][14], i, No.19 (Anon.)
   3. D-Rp, C.120, No.7, pp. 18–19 (Anon.)
   Monophonic version: F-Pn, 12744, No.138 (Anon.)
   4. Brown, *Theatrical*, 164–67 • Hewitt, *Canti B*, 120–23

Revenez tous regretz
   See Latin texts: **Quis det ut veniat**   Agricola   4vv
Robert
   See **Jay bien huer**   Agricola   3vv
Rosa playsant   Philippon   4vv
                                            (Caron / Dusart)
   1. *12*, No.96 (*Philipon.*)
   3. D-LEu, 1494, 169*v* (Anon. Text *Ave rex regum ditissime*) • F-Pn, 15123, 185*v* (Anon.) • I-
      Bc, Q16, No.112, 130*v*-131*r* (Anon.) • I-Fn, 229, No.219, 236*v*-237*r* (*Caron*. á3) • I-Rc,
      2856, No.74, 93*v*-95*r* (*Jo. Dusart*. á3)

4. Brown, *Florentine*, music volume, 508–10 • Caron, *Oeuvres*, ii, 192 • Gerber, *Mensural-kodex*, xxxiii, 223 • Smijers, *Van Ockeghem*, 62 • Wolff, *Chansonnier*, ii, 255–58

Royne de fleurs   **Agricola**   3vv

1. *1*, No.55 (*Alexander*) • *5*, No.55 (*Alexander*) • *14*, No.55 (*Alexander*)

3. F-Pn, 1597, 41*v*-42*r* (Anon.) • GB-Lbl, Roy.20.A.xvi, No.20, 26*v*-27*r* (Anon.) • I-Fn, 229, No.224, 241*v*-242*r* (Anon. Texted *Cest vous*)

Monophonic version: F-Pn, 9346, No.4 (Anon.)

4. Agricola, *Opera Omnia*, v, 11–13 • Brown, *Florentine*, music volume, 523–26 • Hewitt, *Odhecaton*, 337–38 • Litterick, *Manuscript*, 266–68

Royne du ciel   **Compère**   4vv

1. *12*, No.77 (*Compere*)

4. Compère, *Opera Omnia*, v

Royne du ciel / Regina celi   **Compère**   3vv

1. *1*, No.84 (Incipit *Roy de ciel*, anon. in the index. These folios in the unique surviving copy are of the second edition • *5*, No.84 (*Compere*) • *14*, No.84 (*Compere*)

3. I-Bc, Q17, No.6, 6*v*-7*r* (*Prioris*) • I-Fn, Panc.27, No.111, 77*r* (*Compere*. Texted *Regina celi*)

4. Compère, *Opera Omnia*, v • Hewitt, *Odhecaton*, 395–96

Rubinet

See **Ha traitre amours**   **Stockhem**   3vv

S'elle m'amera

See **Petite camusete**   **Ockeghem**   4vv

Se congie pris   **Agricola**   4vv

1. *12*, No.24 (Anon.)

3. CH-SGs, 461, pp. 62–63 (Anon. Untexted) • F-Pn, 1597, 30*v*-31*r* (Anon.) • I-Fc, 2439, No.69, 76*v*-78*r* (*Allexander*) • I-Tn, I.27, No.4, 9*v*-10*r* (Anon.)

Monophonic version: F-Pn, 12744, 35*v*-36*r* (Anon.)

4. Agricola, *Opera Omnia*, v, 1–3

Se congie pris   **Japart**   4vv

1. *1*, No.22 (*Japart*) • *5*, No.22 (*Japart.*) • *14*, No.22 (.*Japart.*)

Monophonic version: F-Pn, 12744, 30*v* (Anon.)

4. Boer, *Chansonvormen*, No.7 • Hewitt, *Odhecaton*, 267–69

Se jay requis   **Ghiselin**   3vv

1. *12*, No.132 (*Ghiselin.*)

2. 1538[9], No.64, 11*r* (MS attribution in the copy at D-Ju: *Jo. Ghiselin*. MS incipit in both copies: *Vostre a iamais*)

3. D-Mbs, 1516, No.126

4. Ghiselin, *Opera Omnia*, iv, 18–19 • Mönkemeyer, *Formschneyder*, ii, p. 94 • Whisler, "Munich"

Se je fay bien   **Agricola**   3vv

3. I-Fn, 178, No.55, 59*v*-60*r* (*Alexander*) • I-Fn, 229, No.81, 82*v*-83*r* (*Alexander Agricola*) • I-Fr, 2794, No.45, 52*v*-53*r* (Anon.) • I-Rvat, C.G.XIII.27, No.68, 82*v*-83*r* (*Agricola*)

4. Agricola, *Opera Omnia*, v, 35 • Brown, *Florentine*, music volume, No.81 • Jones, *First*, ii, 266–67

Intabulation: lute

1. *34*, No.30 (*Francesco Spinacino*. Incipit *Si fais viey*)

4. Schmidt, *Spinacino*, ii, 276–78

Se mieulx ne vient damours Agricola 3vv

    1. *12*, No.128 (*Agricola*)

    3. F-Pn, 1597, 31*v*-32*r* (Anon.) • GB-Ob, 831, 261*r* (Anon. Incomplete) • I-Fc, 2439, No.57, 62*v*-63*r* (*Allexander*)

    4. Agricola *Opera Omnia*, v, 32–34 • Newton, *Florence*, ii, 183–185

Se mieulx [ne vient damours] Compère 3vv

    1. *1*, No.51. (Anon in the index. These folios lacking in the unique copy) • *5*, No.51 (*Compere*) • *14*, No.51 (*Compere*)

    2. [c.1535][14], iii, 65 (Anon.)

    3. CH-SGs, 461, pp. 86–87 (*Compere*) • CH-SGs, 463 (Listed in the index: *Compere*)

    4. Compère, *Opera Omnia*, • Hewitt, *Odhecaton*, 329–30

Se suis trop ionnette Raulin 4vv

    1. *2*, No.6 (Anon.) • *10*, No.6 (Anon.)

    2. *50 Carmina* (1513), No.6 (Anon.)

    3. I-Fn, 176, No.73, 111*v*-113*r* (*Raulin*)

    4. Cauchie, "Odhecaton", 150–52 • Hewitt, *Canti B*, 111–13

    Monophonic version: F-Pn, 12744, 17*r* (Anon.)

Se vous voulez

    See **Je vous empire** Agricola 3vv

Serviteur soye Stockem 4vv

    1. *12*, No.91 (*Jo. Sthokem*)

    3. I-Fn, 229, No.153, 159*v*-160*r* (Text *Hellas dame*)

    4. Brown, *Florentine*, music volume, 328–30

Si a tort on ma blamee [Anon.] 3vv

    1. *1*, No.70 (Anon.) • *5*, No.70 (Anon.) • *14*, No.70 (Anon.)

    3. US-Wc, Laborde, 108*v*-109*r* (Anon.)

    4. Boer, *Chansonvormen*, No.4 • Hewitt, *Odhecaton*, 369

Si fais viey

    See **Se je fay bien** Agricola 3vv

Si je fet un cop apree

    See **Tan bien mi son pensa** Japart 4vv

Si je vo un chop apree

    See **Tan bien mi son pensa** Japart 4vv

Sil vous playsist Regis 4vv

    1. *12*, No.93 (*Jo. Regis*)

    3. F-Pn, 2973, 20v (Anon.) • I-Fn, 229, No.102, 104*v*-105*r* (*Joannes Regis. à3.* Text incipit *Si vous plait*)

    4. Brown, *Florentine*, music volume, 206–208 • Regis, *Opera Omnia*, ii, 62 • Thibault and Fallows, *Chansonnier*

Sil ya compagnon en la compagni

    Contra of **Une filleresse** Busnoys 4vv

Sur le pont davignon [Anon.] 4vv

    1. *12*, No.45 (Anon.)

    4. Christoffersen, *French*, i, 172–74

Tan bien mi son pensa Japart 4vv

    1. *1*, No.34 (*Japart*) • *5*, No.34 (*Japart*) • *14*, No.34 (*Japart*)

3. F-Pn, 1817, No.15, 16*v* (Anon. Texted *Si je fet un cop apree*) • I-Bc, Q17, No.71, 78*v*, incomplete (Anon.) • I-CT, 95–96, No.15, 13*v*-14*r* (Anon. Texted *Si je vo un chop apree*)

4. Hewitt, *Odhecaton*, 292–93

Tant ha bon oeul   **Compère**   3vv

1. *1*, No.68 (*Compere*) • *5*, No.68 (*Compere*) • *14*, No.68 (*Compere*)

3. I-VEcap, DCCLVII, No.14, 13*v*-14*r* (Anon. Textless)

4. Compère, *Opera Omnia*, v, • Hewitt, *Odhecaton*, 364–65

Tant que nostre argent durra   **Obrecht**   4vv

1. *12*, No.4 (*Ja. Obreht*)

3. D-Mbs, 1516, No.1 (Anon.) • I-Fc, 2442, No.54, 94*r*-95*r* (*Obrecth*)

4. Obrecht, *Werken*, vii, 36–38 • Whisler, *Munich*

Tant que nostre argent dure
Bassus of **Amour fait mult**   **Japart**   4vv

Tart ara   **Isaac**   3vv

1. *12*, No.115 (*Yzac.*)

4. Isaac, *Weltliche*, 107–108

Intabulations: lute

2. 1536¹³ = N522, No.18, G3*r*-H1*r* (*Henricus Isaac. H. Newsidler*)

3. A-Wn, 19286, 1*v*-3*r* (*Henricus Isaac*)

Tart ara   **Molinet**   4vv

1. *12*, No.98 (*Molinet*)

3. DK-Kk, 291, 8*v*-9*r* (Anon.) • F-Dm, 517, 82*v*-84*r* (Anon.) • F-Pc, 57, 78*v*-79*r* (Anon.) • US-Wc, Laborde, 138*v*-139*r* (Anon.)

The following sources are à3: F-Pn, 15123, 66*v*-67*r* (Anon.) • F-Pn, 4379, No.32, e8*v*-9*r*/7*v*-8*r* (Anon.) • I-Fn, 178, No.46, 50*v*-51*r* (Anon.) • I-Fr, 2356, No.60, 75*v*-76*r* (Anon.) • I-MC, 871, No.123, 141*v*-142*r* (Anon.) • I-Rc, 2856, No.81, 106*v*-107*r* (*Molinet*) • I-Rvat, C.G.XIII.27, No.79, 93*v*-94*r* (*Molinet*)

4. Droz, Thibault, "Poètes," 60 • Isaac, *Weltlicher*, • Jeppesen, *Kopenhagener*, 12–13 • Moerk, *Seville*, ii, 80–81 • Pope and Kanazawa, *Montecassino*, 489–93 • Wolff, *Chansonnier*, ii, 280–83

Tous les regrets   [Anon.]   3vv
                                              (?Ockeghem)

1. *12*, No.136 (Anon.)

4. Picker, "More", 97–101

Comments: Picker, "More", 86, suggests that this may be the work of Ockeghem

Tous les regres   **La Rue**   4vv
                                              (Josquin)

1. *2*, No.22 (*Pe.de.la rue*) • *10*, No.22 (*Pe. de larue*)

2. *50 Carmina* (1513), No.22 (*Pe de la rue*)

3. A-Wn, 18810, No.63 (*Petri.de.la.Rue*) • B-Br, 228, No.2, 3*v*-4*r* (Anon.) • B-Br, 11239, No.6, 9*v*-11*r* (*de la Rue*) • CH-Bu, F.X.1–4, No.109 (*Pirson alias Pe. de la Rue.*) • D-Rp, C.120, No.67, pp. 264–265 (*Josquin*) • I-Fc, 2442, No.43, 76*v*-77*r* (*P. de la Rue*) • I-Rvat, 11953, No.9, 8*v*-9*r* (*Rue*)

4. Hewitt, *Canti B*, 153–55 • Josquin, *Werken*, Wereldlijke, • Maldeghem, *Trésor*, profane, XX (1884), 16–17 • Picker, *Chanson*, 180–83

Intabulation: organ

3. D-B, 40026 (Anon.)

Comments: Kreider, "Works", attributed this to La Rue

Tout a par moy   **Agricola**   4vv

2/ *Faisans regres*

  1. **12**, No.12 (*Agricola*)

  3. D-As, 142a, No.54, 51*v*-53*r* (Anon.) • I-Fc, 2439, No.5, 5*v*-7*r* (*Allexander*)

  4. Agricola, *Opera Omnia*, v, 92–95 • Josquin, *Werken*, Missen • Smijers, *Van Ockeghem*

  Comments: Based on the tenor of Frye's chanson

Tres doulce fillete   [Anon.]   4vv

2/ *Tres doulce fillete*

  1. **12**, No.19 (Anon.)

  3. I-Fn, 164–67, No.55, 66*r*-67*r* (Anon.)

Tres doulx regart   [Anon.]   4vv

  1. **12**, No.89 (Anon.)

  3. I-Fn, 229, No.1, IIII*v*-1*r* (*Jannes Martini*. à3. Untexted)

  4. Brown, *Florentine*, music volume, 1–2 • Martini, *Secular*, 73–75

Une filleresse / Vostre amour / Sil ya compagnon   **Busnoys**   4vv

  1. **12**, No.70 (Anon.)

  3. I-Fn, 229, No.62, 63*v*-64*r* (*Busnoys*. First incipit only. Pitched a fifth higher)

  4. Brown, *Florentine*, music volume, 126–28

Una maistresse   **Brumel**   3vv

  1. **12**, No.130 (*Brumel*)

  3. D-Mbs, 1516, No.124 (Anon.)

  4. Brumel, *Opera Omnia* vi, 102–103 • Whisler, "Munich"

  Intabulation: lute

  1. **33**, No.6, 9*r*-10*r* (*Francesco Spinacino*)

  4. Schmidt, *Spinacino*, ii, 20–23

Una musque de buscgaya   **Josquin**   4 ex 3vv

  1. **12**, No.106 (*Josquin*. Rubric *Quiescit que super me volat Venit post me qui in puncto clamat*)

  3. E-Sc, 5-I-43, No.138, p3*v*-4*r*/113*v*-114*r* (Anon. Untexted) • F-Pn, 1817, No.33 (Anon. Incipit *Une*) • I-Bc, Q17, No.69, 75*v*-76*r* (*Josquin*) • I-Bc, Q18, No.73, 74*v*-75*r* (Anon.) • I-CT, 95–96, No.33, 30*r*-30*v* (Anon. Incipit *Une*) • I-Fn, 178, No.12, 16*v*-17*r* (*Josquin*. Rubric *Quiescit qui super me volat post venit que ante me factus est*) • I-Fn, 229, No.145, 149*v*-150*r* (*Josquin*. Rubric *Quiescit qui super me volat Post me venit qui in punctu clamat*) • I-Rc, 2856, No.67, 86*r* (*Josquin de pres*. Rubric *Quiescit qui super me volat venit post me qui in punctu clamat*) • I-Rvat, C.G.XIII.27, No.25, 34*v*-35*r* (*Josquin*. Rubric *Quiescit qui super me volat Qui in punctu clamat*)

  Monophonic version: F-Pn, 12744. 5*v* (Anon.)

  4. Brown, *Florentine*, music volume, 302–303 • Josquin, *Werken*, Missen x, 119 • Josquin, *Werken*, Wereldlijke, iv, 5 • Moerk, *Seville*, ii, 347–348 • Wolff, *Chansonnier*, ii, 231–34 •

  Comments: The basis for masses by Isaac and Josquin, the latter also printed by Petrucci

Une petite petite aquince   [Anon.]   4vv

  1. **12**, No.18 (Anon.)

Unne playsante fillete   **Compère**   4vv

  1. **12**, No.6 (*Compere*)

3. F-Pn, 1817, No.3 (Anon.) • I-CT, 95–96, No.3, 2*v*–3*v* (Anon.) • I-Fc, 2442, No.31, 56*v*–58*r* (*Loyset Compere*) • I-Fn, 164–167, No.69, 83*v*–84*v* (Anon.)

4. Compère, *Opera Omnia*,

Ung franc archier   [Anon.]   4vv

1. *12*, No.26 (Anon.)

4. Weckerlin, *Chanson*, 65–69

Ung franc archier   Compère   4vv

1. *1*, No.28 (*Compere*. The following folio is lacking in the unique surviving copy) • *5*, No.28 (*Comper*) • *14*, No.28 (*Compere*)

3. CH-Bu, F.X.5–9, No.7 (Anon. Text *Ong franck*) • I-Fn, 229, No.168, 176*v*–177*r* (Anon.)

4. Brown, *Florentine*, music volume, 373–76 • Compère, *Opera Omnia*, v, 57 • Hewitt, *Odhecaton*, 279–80

Intabulation: keyboard

1. CH-SGs, 530, No.78 (Anon. Incipit *Nunc franc*)

Veci la danse barbari   Vacqueras   4vv
(Compère)

1. *2*, No.23 (*Vaqueras.*) • *10*, No.23 (*Vaqueras.*)

2. *50 Carmina* (1513), No.23 (*Vaqueras*)

3. E-SE, s.s., No.56, 125*v*–126*r* (*Loysette Compere*) • I-Fn 107bis, No.15, 14*v*–15*r* (Anon. Headed *Vexilla danse barbare*)

4. Brown, *Theatrical*, 178–80 • Hewitt, *Canti B*, 156–58 • Vacqueras, *Opera Omnia*

Literature: Noblitt, "Problems"

Venis regrets   Compère   3vv

1. *1*, No.53 (*Compere*) • *5*, No.53 (*Compere*) • *14*, No.53 (*Compere*)

3. B-Br, 11239, No.2, 4*v*–6*r* (*Compere*) • B-Br, IV.90, 5*v*–7*r* (Anon.) • B-Tv, 94, 5*v*–7*r* (Anon.) • CH-SGs, 462, 39*v*–40*r* (Anon.) • D-Z, LXXVIII,3, No.16 (Anon. Untexted) • DK-Kk, 1848, pp. 124–25 (Anon.) • I-Bc, Q17, No.27, 31*v*–32*r*. (*Loyset Compere*) • I-Fn, 117, No.29, 31*v*–32*r* (Anon.)

4. Compère, *Opera Omnia*, • Geering and Trümpy, *Liederbuch* • Hewitt, *Odhecaton*, 333–34 • Maldeghem, *Trésor*, profane, XIII (1877), No.11 • Picker, *Chanson*, 419–421

Venus tu ma pris   de Orto   3vv

1. *1*, No.88 (Anon in the index. These folios in the only extant copy are of the second edition) • *5*, No.88 (*De Orto*) • *14*, No.88 (*De Orto*)

4. Hewitt, *Odhecaton*, 401–402

Verginorette savosienne

See **Bergerette savoyenne**   Josquin   4vv

Vive le roy   Josquin   4vv

1. *12*, No.110 (*Josquin*. Rubric for the tenor: *Vive le roy Fingito vocales modulis apteque subinde Vocibus his vulgi nascitur unde tenor Non vario pergit cur satiumque secundam Subushit ad primum per tetracorda modum*)

4. Josquin, *Werken*, Wereldlijke, ii, 53

Vivre ou mourir   [Anon.]   4vv

1. *12*, No.103 (Anon.)

3. D-Mbs, 1516

3. Whisler, "Munich"

Vostre a iamays / Je nay dueul   Ghiselin   3vv

1. *12*, No.131 (*Ghiselin*)

2. 1538⁹, No.62, H4*v* (Anon. Untexted)

3. CH-SGs, 463, No.51 (Anon. Texted *Nostre iamais*) • D-Mbs, 1516, No.125 (Anon.)

4. Ghiselin, *Opera Omnia*, iv, 16–18 • Mönkemeyer, *Formschneyder*, ii, p.92 • Whisler, "Munich"

Intabulations: lute

1. *33*, No.7 (*Francesco Spinacino*. In the index, this is titled *Vostre a maistres*)

2. 1536¹³ = N522, No.11, E1*r*-1*v* (*Ghiselin*. H. Newsidler)

4. Schmidt, *Spinacino*, ii, 23–26

Vostre a jamais		
See **Se jay requis**	**Ghiselin**	3vv
Vostre a maistres		
See **Vostre a iamays**	**Ghiselin**	3vv
Vostre amour		
See **Missa Charge de deul**: Christe	**Isaac**	3vv
Tenor of **Une filleresse**	[Anon.]	4vv
Vostre bargerenette	**Compère**	4vv

1. *1*, No.41 (*Compere*) • *5*, No.41 (*Compere.*) • *14*, No.41 (*.Compere.*)

3. F-Pn, 1817, No.7. (Anon.) • I-Bc, Q17, No.60, 65*v*-66*r* (*Loyset Compere*) • I-CT, 95–96, No.7, 6*r*-7*r* (Anon.) • I-Fn, 178, No.68, 73*v*-74*r* (*Loyset Comper*) • I-Rvat, C.G.XIII.27, No.37, 48*v*-49*r* (Anon.)

4. Compère, *Opera Omnia*, v, 61–62 • Hewitt, *Odhecaton*, 309–10

Vous dont fortune	**Ghiselin**	3vv

1. *12*, No.135 (Anon.)

3. I-Rc, 2856, No.105, 134*v*-136*r* (*Jo. Ghiselin*. Incipit *Las mi lares*)

4. Ghiselin, *Opera Omnia* • Wolff, *Chansonnier*, ii, 364–70

Vray dieu		
Tenor of **Por quoy je ne puis dire**	**Stockhem**	4vv
Vray Dieu damours / Sancte iouanes	**Japart**	5vv
baptista / Ora pro nobis		

1. *12*, No.74 (*Jo. Japart*)

4. Compère, *Opera Omnia*

Vray Dieu qui me confortera	**Bruhier**	4vv

1. *2*, No.4 (Anon.) • *10*, No.4 (Anon.)

2. *50 Carmina* (1513), No.4 (Anon.)

3. B-Br, 11239, No.10, 15*v*-17*r* (*A Bruhier*) • I-Rvat, 11953, No.12, 10*v*-11*v* (Anon.) • S-Uu, 76a, No.47, 46*v*-47*r* (Anon. Headed *He Dieu . . .*)

Monophonic version: F-Pn, 9346, No.57 (Anon.) • F-Pn, 12744, 83v (Anon.)

4. Hewitt, *Canti B*, 105–107 • Picker, *Chanson*, 430–33

Vray Dieu que pene		
See **E vray dieu que payne**	**Compère**	4vv

Dutch and German Texts

Andernaken
    See **Tandernaken**

De tusch in busch
    See **Tmeiskein was jongk**   **Obrecht**   4vv

Der seyden schwantz
    See **Helas que poura devenir**   **Caron**   4vv

Des mayen lust
    See **Helas que poura devenir**   **Caron**   4vv

En vroelic   [Anon.]   4vv
      1. *12*, No.108 (Anon.)
      3. D-Mbs, 1516
      4. Lenaerts, *Nederlandse*, p. (12) • Taruskin, *Een vrolic* • Whisler, "Munich"

Es sas ain Meitschi
    See **Tsat een meskin**   **Obrecht**   4vv

Hab mich lieb
    See **Par ung jour de matinee**   **Isaac**   4vv

Helas hic moet my liden   **Ghiselin**   3vv
      1. *12*, No.134 (*Ghiselin.*)
      3. D-Mbs, 1516, No.122 (Anon.)
      4. Ghiselin, *Collected Works*, iv, 27–28 • Lenaerts, *Nederlandse*, p. (20) • Whisler, "Munich"

Ich byn zo elend   [Anon.]   4vv
      1. *12*, No.41 (Anon.)
      4. Lenaerts, *Nederlandse*, p. (10).

In minen syn
    See **Le second jour davril**   **Busnois**   4vv

Linken van beueren   [Anon.]   4vv
      1. *12*, No.109 (Anon. Index reads *Lykken van beueren*)
      3. D-Mbs, 1516, No.7
      3. Lenaerts, *Nederlandse*, p. (13) • Whisler, "Munich"

Maule met
    see **Vavilment**   **Obrecht**   4vv

Meschin che fuis secretament
    See **Mais que ce fust**   **Compère**   3vv

Meskin es hu   **Obrecht**   4vv
      1. *1*, No.96 (Anon. in the index. This folio lacking in the unique surviving copy) • *5*, No.96 (Anon.) • *14*, No.96 (Anon.)
      3. CH-SGs, 463 (*Obrecht.* Listed in the index, but apparently not entered in the manuscript.) • E-SE, s.s., No.65, 134*v* (*Jacobus Hobrecht.* Additional incipit in the Tenor, *Wat heb dier mo te doene*) • I-Fn, 229, No.170, 179*v*–180*r* (*Jacobus Obrech.* Untexted) • I-Fn, 178, No.71, 76*v*–77*r* (*Jacobus Obret.* Texted *Adiu adiu*) • I-Fn, Panc.27, No.105, 72*v* (Anon. á3)
      4. Ambros, *Geschichte*, v, 34 • Brown, *Florentine*, music volume, 383–84 • Hewitt, *Odhecaton*, 421 • Obrecht, *Werken*, vii, 1–2
      Intabulation: keyboard
      3. CH-SGs, 530, No.103 (Anon.)

Myn hert heeft altyt **La Rue** 4vv
(Obrecht)

   1. *12*, No.10 (*De la rue.*)
   2. [c1535]¹⁴, ii, No.11 (Anon. Texted *Myn hert heft*) • 1538⁹, No.41 (Anon.)
   3. B-Br, 228, No.15, 16*v*-17*r* (Anon. Texted *Mijn hert altijt heeft*) • B-Br, IV.90, No.22, 29*r*-29*v*, incomplete (Anon. Texted *Myn hert heeft altyt*) • B-Br, IV.1274, No.11, 17*r*-18*r*, incomplete (Anon.) • B-Tv, 94, No.22, 29*v*-30*r* (Anon.) • CH-SGs, 463, No.73, 24*r* and 84*r* (*Jacobus Obrecht.* Texted *Min hertz tut.* Headed *Hypoaeolius, idest secundus superior seu decimus*) • D-Mbs, 1516, No.8 (Anon.) • D-Usch, 237a-d, (Anon. Transposed down a fifth) • F-CA, 125–28, No.52 (Anon. Texted *Mijn hert heeft*) • I-Fc, 2439, No.13, 14*v*-15*r* (*Rue.* Texted *Myn hetz altyt*) • I-Rvat, 11953, No.11, 10*r*-10*v* (Anon. Text incipit *Mein herz alzit.* Transposed down a fifth) • D-Bga, 7, D1*r* (Anon.)
   4. Maldeghem, *Tresor*, profane, XI (1875), No.14 • Maldeghem, *Tresor*, profane, XXI (1885), No.21 • Mönkemeyer, *Formschneyder*, i, 64–65 • Newton, *Florence*, ii, 39–41 • Obrecht, *Werken*, vii, 65–67 • Picker, *Chanson*, 229–32 • Smijers, *Van Ockeghem*
   Comments: The basis for a mass by Gascongne
   Literature: Schreurs, "Mijn hert"
   Intabulation: lute
   2. J687 (1523), No.32, h4*v* (*Obrecht.* Judenkünig) • 1536¹³ = N522, Ff1*r* (Anon. H. Newsidler)

Myn morghen ghaf [Anon.] 4vv
   1. *2*, No.18 (Anon.) • *10*, No.18 (Anon.)
   2. *50 Carmina* (1513), No.18 (Anon.) • [c.1535]¹⁴, i, No.28 (Anon.)
   3. I-Bc, Q18, No.87, 88*v*-89*r* (Anon.) • I-Rvat, 11953, No.19, 17*r*-17*v* (Anon. Untexted)
   4. Hewitt, *Canti B*, 143–145 • Lenaerts, *Nederlandse*, pp. (5)–(6)

O men potauer yoye
   See **Coment peult** **Josquin** 4 ex 3vv

O Venus bant [Anon.] 4vv
   1. *12*, No.8, 12*v*-14*r* (Anon.)
   4. Lenaerts, *Nederlandse*, p. (7) • Taruskin, *O Venus bant*

O Venus bant **Weerbeke** 3vv
(Josquin)

   1. *1*, No.78, 85 (Anon. in index. These folios in the unique surviving copy are of the second edition) • *5*, No.78 (*Josquin*) • *14*, No.78 (*Josquin*)
   3. CH-SGs, 463, No.48, 18*v* (*Iosquinus Pratensis.* Headed *Mixolydius, idest septimus*) • D-Mbs, 3154, 53*v* (Anon.) • E-Sc, 5-I-43, No.164, r5*v*-6*r*/135*v*-136*r* (*Gaspar*)
   4. Hewitt, *Odhecaton*, 383–84 • Moerk, *Seville*, ii, 404–405 • van Duyse, *Eenstemmig*, 165 • Taruskin, *O Venus*
   Intabulation: lute
   1. *33*, No.14 (*Francesco Spinacino*)
   4. Schmidt, *Spinacino*, ii, 64–65 • Taruskin, *O Venus*

Rompeltier **Obrecht** 4vv
   1. *1*, No.25 (*Ja.Obreht*) • *5*, No.25 (Anon.) • *14*, No.25 (Anon.)
   3. I-Fn, 121, No.3, 3*v*-4*r* (Anon.)
   4. Hewitt, *Odhecaton*, 274 • Obrecht, *Werken*, vii, 2–3
   Literature: Blackburn, "Carnival", 139–41

Tandernaken   **Agricola**   3vv

    1. *12*, No.120 (*Agricola*)

    2. 1538[9], No.99, N3r (*Alexander Agricola*. Incipit *To andernaken up dem Ryn*)

    3. E-SE, s.s., No.86, 161v–162r (*Alexander Agricola*. Texted *Tandernaken al up den Rijn*) Finck
       1556

    4. Agricola, *Opera Omnia*, v, 99–101 • Disertori, *Frottole*, 193–200 • Gombosi, *Obrecht*, No.25
       • Mönkemeyer, *Formschneyder*, ii, 144–45 • Taruskin, *T'Andernaken*

Intabulation: lute

    1. *34*, No.5 (*Francesco Spinacino*)

    2. 1536[13] = N522, No.26, O2v (*Alex.Agricola*. H. Newsidler. titled *Ander nacken up dem Rhin*)

    4. Disertori, *Frottole*, 193–200 • Schmidt, *Spinacino*, ii, 175–80

Tandernaken   **Lapicida**   3vv

    1. *12*, No.126 (*Lapicide*)

    4. Lenaerts, *Nederlandse*, p. (14) • Nowak & Koczirz, *Gesellschaftlied*, p. 52 • Taruskin,
       T'Andernaken

Intabulations: lute

    2. RISM 1536[12] = N521, No.24, h4v–i3r (Anon. H. Newsidler)

Tandernaken   **Obrecht**   3vv

    1. *1*, No.69 (*Obreht*) • *5*, No.69 (*Obreht*) • *14*, No.69 (*Obreht*)

    3. CH-SGs, 463, No.52, 19v (*Iacobus Obrecht*. Texted *Andernacken ligt ab dem Rhin*. Headed
       Aeolius, idest nonus, seu primus superior) • D-Z, LXXVIII,3, No.8 (Anon. Untexted)

    4. Hewitt, *Odhecaton*, 366–68 • Obrecht, *Werken*, vii, 3–7 • Taruskin, *T'andernaken*, 11–13 •
       van Duyse, "Oude", p. 1050

Intabulations: lute

    2. G1623 (1533), No.29, 33v–36v (Anon. Gerle. Titled *Der alt Tandernack*) • 1536[13] = N522,
       No.25, N3r–O1v (*Ja. Obrecht*. H. Newsidler. Titled *Ander nacken up dem Rhin*)

Comments: Bonda, "Tandernaken," 66, maintains that this was composed in the north.

Tmeiskin was jongk   **Isaac**   4vv
                              (Japart, Obrecht)

    1. *1*, No.27 (*Isac*) • *5*, No.27 (Anon.) • *14*, No.27 (Anon.)

    3. CH-Sgs, 463 (Entered in the index. Anon) • E-SE, s.s., No.36, 103r (*Jacobus Hobrecht*) •
       GB-Lbl, Add.35087, 52v–53r (Anon. à3) • I-Bc, Q17, No.63, 68v–69r (Anon. Texted *De
       tous in busc*) • I-Fn, 229, No.156, 162v–163r (Anon. Untexted) • I-Fn, 107bis, No.5, 4v–5r
       (Anon. Texted *De tusch in busch*) • I-Fn, 178, No.70, 75v–76r (*Iapart*. Texted *De tusche in
       busch*) • NL-L, 436, 58v, incomplete (Anon. Texted *Dat meyskin es jonck*)

    4. Brown, *Florentine*, music volume, 339–41 • Hewitt, *Odhecaton*, 277–78 • Isaac, *Opera
       Omnia*, vii, 138–39 • Isaac, *Weltliche*, 109 • Land, *Liedjes*, 11 • Lenaerts, *Nederlands*, 4–5

Intabulation: voice and lute

    2. 1512[2], No.23, p. 68 (*Isack*. Schlick. Titled *Metzkin*)

Comments: Picker, *Johannes*, 85, favours Obrecht as the composer

Tsat een meskin   **Obrecht**   4vv

    1. *1*, No.92 (Anon. in the index. These folios lacking in the only extant copy) • *5*, No.92
       (*Obreht.*) • *14*, No.92 (*Obreht*)

    3. CH-SGs, 461, pp. 90–93 (*Obrecht*) • CH-SGs, 463 (Only listed in the index, as *Obrecht*.
       Text incipit *Es sas ain Meitschi*) • E-SE, s.s., No.51, 121v–122r (*Jacobus Hobrecht*)

    4. Davison & Apel, *HAM*, i, 82–83 • Hewitt, *Odhecaton*, 407–10 • Obrecht, *Werken*, iv,
       7–11

Vavilment   **Obrecht**   4vv

   1. **2**, No.35 (*.Obreht.*) • **10**, No.35 (*Obreht.*)

   2. *50 Carmina* (1513), No.35 (*Obreht*)

   3. D-B, 40021, No.111, 225*v*-226*r* (Anon. Entered in the index as *Re mi fa sol mi*) • CZ-
HK, II.A.7, 340–341 (Anon. Incipit *Precantibus*) • CH-Bu, F.X.5–9, No.6 (Anon. Un-
texted) • E-SE, s.s., No.50, 120*v*-121*r* (*Jacobus Hobrecht*. Incipit *Wat willen wij*) • I-Rvat,
C.G.XIII.27, No.24, 32*v*-34*r* (*J. Obrech*. Incipit *Maule met*)

   Painting: Attributed to Cocke van Aelst, in I-Vc. Musical incipit *Wat willen*

   4. Hewitt, *Canti B*, 188–192 • Obrecht, *Werken*, vii, 38–42

   Literature: Slim, *Prodigal*

Wat heb dier mo te doene

   See **Meskin es hu**   **Obrecht**   4vv

Wat willen wij

   See **Vavilment**   **Obrecht**   4vv

Weit ghy   [Anon.]   3vv

   1. **12**, No.127 (Anon.)

   2. 1538⁹, No.59 (Anon.)

   4. Lenaerts, *Nederlandse*, p. (18) • Mönkemeyer, *Formschneyder*, ii, 87–88

Spanish Texts

Este conoscimiento

   2/ of **Nunque fue pena maior**   [Anon.]   4vv

Gracias a vos donzella

   See **Missa Comme femme**: Benedictus   **Isaac**   4vv

No men canteys ala prunera

   See **Ales regrets**   **Agricola**   3vv

Nunqua fue pena maior   [Anon.]   4vv

   2/ *Este conoscimiento*

   1. **12**, No.14 (Anon.)

Nunque fu pena magiore   **Tromboncino**   4vv
                                                        (Festa)

   1. **18**, No.55 (*B.T.*) • **38**, No.55 (*B.T.*)

   2. 1556²⁶ (Festa)

   3. I-Fc, 2441, No.25, 27*v*-28*r* (Anon.)

   4. Cesari, *Frottole*, 136 • • Festa, *Opera Omnia*, vii • Pisano, *Collected Works*

Nunqua fue pena maior   **Urrede**   4vv
                                                        (Enrique)

   1. **1**, No.4 (Anon.) • **5**, No.4 (Anon.) • **14**, No.4 (Anon.)

   3. CH-SGs, 463, No.161, 58*r* and 116*r* (Anon.) • GB-Ob, 831, 261*v*, incomplete (Anon.) •
I-Bc, Q16, No.116, 134*v*-135*r* (Anon.) • I-Bc, Q17, No.9, 11*r* (Anon. Lower voices only)
• I-Fn, 107bis, f.41 (This folio lacking: listed in index as *Nunquam fuit pena*) • I-VEcap,
DCCLVII, No.55, 57*v*-58*r* (Anon. Untexted)

     The following sources are à3: E-Mn, 2-1-5, No.1, 1*v*-2*r* (*Juan Urrede*) • E-Sc, 7-I-

28, No.9, 16v–17r (*Jo. Vrede*) • E-SE, s.s., No.167, 209r (Anon.) • F-Pn, 15123, 99v–100r (Anon.) • I-Bc, Q18, No.88, 89v–90r (Anon.) • I-Fn, 176, No.60, 91v–92r (Anon.) • I-Fn, 178, No.33, 37v–38r (Anon.) • I-Fr, 2356, No.20, 24v–25r (Anon.) • I-PEc, 431, No.54, 77v–78r (*Io. Vrede*) • I-Rvat, C.G.XIII.27, No.20, 28v–29r (*Enrique*)

Text by Don Garcia Alvarez de Toledo, 1st Duke of Alba

4. Anglès, *Palacio*, 1–2 • Barbieri, *Cancionero*, 239–40 • Gombosi, *Capirola*, 89–92 • Haberkamp, *Weltliche*, 135–36 • Hewitt, *Odhecaton*, 226–27 • Stevenson, *Columbus*, 228–29 • van der Straeten, *Musique*, 454

Intabulation: lute

1. *33*, No.19 (Anon.)

3. US-Cn, 107501, No.32, 51v–53r (Anon.)

4. Schmidt, *Spinacino*, ii, 85–90

Una moza falle yo	[Anon.]	4vv

1. *2*, No.26 (Anon.) • *10*, No.26 (Anon.)

2. *50 Carmina* (1513), No.26 (Anon.)

4. Hewitt, *Canti B*, 164–65

Venimus en romeria	[Anon.]	4vv

1. *26*, No.55 (Anon.)

Intabulation: voice and lute

1. *50*, No.19 (Anon.)

4. Disertori, *Frottole*, 496–97

Yo me vollo lamentare		
See Italian texts: **Io mi voglio lamentare**	**G. Brocco**	4vv

Instrumental and Untexted Works

Aere de Capituli		
See Italian texts: **Li angelici sembianti**	[Anon.]	4vv
See **Nasce la speme mia**	**Cara**	4vv
See **Poi che son di speranza**	**Lulinus**	4vv
See **Un solicito amor**	**Lurano**	4vv
Aer de versi latini	**Capreolus**	4vv

1. *23*, No.62 (*ANTONIVS CAPREOLVS BRIXIEN.*) • *37*, No.62 (*ANT. CAPREO. BRIXIEN.*)

4. Schwartz, *Frottole*, 82

Bassadans		
See **La Spagna**	[Spinacino]	lute
Calata	**Dalza**	2 lutes

Intabulation: two lutes

1. *47*, No.26 (Dalza)

4. Underwood, *Renaissance*, 97–101

Calata	**Dalza**	lute

Intabulation: lute

         1. **47**, No.29 (Dalza)

         4. Moe, *Dance*, 322

Calata	**Dalza**	lute

    Intabulation: lute

         1. **47**, No.30 (Dalza)

Calata	**Dalza**	lute

    Intabulation: lute

         1. **47**, No.31 (Dalza)

Calata	**Dalza**	lute

    Intabulation: lute

         1. **47**, No.32 (Dalza)

Calata ala spagnola	**Dalza**	lute

    Intabulations: lute

         1. **47**, No.33 (Dalza)

         2. J687 (1523), No.33 (Anon. Judenkünig)

Calata [ala] spagnola	**Dalza**	lute

    Intabulation: lute

         1. **47**, No.34 (Dalza)

Calata ala spagnola	**Dalza**	lute

    Intabulation: lute

         1. **47**, No.35 (Dalza)

Calata ala spagnola	**Dalza**	lute

    Intabulation: lute

         1. **47**, No.36 (Dalza)

Calata [ala] spagnola	**Dalza**	lute

    Intabulation: lute

         1. **47**, No.37 (Dalza)

Calata ala spagnola ditto terzetti di zuan ambroso dalza	**Dalza**	lute

    Intabulation: lute

         1. **47**, No.38 (Dalza)

Calata de strambotti	**Dalza**	lute

    Intabulation: lute

         1. **47**, No.28 (Dalza)

         4. Moe, *Dance*, 322–323

Calata dito zigonze	**Dalza**	lute

    Intabulation: lute

         1. **47**, No.27 (Dalza)

Caldibi castigliano	**Dalza**	lute

    Intabulation: lute

         1. **47**, No.1 (Dalza)

    Comments: Brown, *Instrumental*, p. 15, calls this a corruption of *Calvi vi valvi*.

La mi la sol

See **Missa La mi la sol**	**Isaac**	4vv
La Spagna	[Anon.]	3vv

         1. **12**, No.122 (Anon)

Intabulations: lute

    1. **33**, No.16 (Anon. Spinacino. Incipit *Bassadans*)

    3. A-Wn, 18688, No.1, 1v–5r (Anon.)

    4. Schmidt, *Spinacino*, ii, 68–76

La Spagna   **Ghiselin**   4vv

    1. **3**, No.19 (*.Jo ghiselin:*) • **19**, No.19 (*.Jo.ghiselin:*)

    2. Zanger (1554), E3v–E4v (*Io Gysselini*)

    3. I-Fn, Panc.27, 91v–94r (*Ghiselin*)

    4. Ghiselin, *Collected Works*, iv, 32–36

La Spagna   **Spinacino**   lute

Intabulation: lute

    1. **34**, No.24 (*Francesco Spinacino.* Headed *Bassadanza*)

    4. Schmidt, *Spinacino*, ii, 246–53

Comments: Based on the Tenor *Re di Spagna*

Misericordia et veritas obviaverunt sibi   [Anon.]   4vv

    1. **3**, No.1 (Anon.) • [Probably **19**, No.1: not extant]

    4. Drake, *Petrucci*, ii, 2–3 • Sherr, *Sixteenth-century*, i, 1–4

Comments: The title is a canon: the lower voices have the rubric *Canon: iusticia et pax obseulate sunt:* • This work is not listed in the Tavola

Modo de cantar sonetti   [Anon.]   4vv

    1. **23**, No.19 (Anon.) • **37**, No.19 (Anon.)

    4. Schwartz, *Frottole*, 58

Pavana alla ferrarese   **Dalza**   lute

   2/ *Saltarello* 3/ *Piva*

    Intabulation: lute

    1. **47**, No.20 (Dalza. This and the following three sets are linked together under the general title of *Pavan ala ferrarese*)

    4. Lowinsky, *Tonality*, 63

Pavana alla ferrarese   **Dalza**   lute

   2/ *Saltarello* 3/ *Piva*

    Intabulation: lute

    1. **47**, No.21 (Dalza)

Pavana alla ferrarese   **Dalza**   lute

   2/ *Saltarello* 3/ *Spingardo*

    Intabulation: lute

    1. **47**, No.22 (Dalza)

Pavana alla ferrarese   **Dalza**   lute

   2/ *Saltarello* 3/ *Spingardo*

    Intabulations: lute

    1. **47**, No.23 (Dalza. Headed *Pavana alla ferrarese col contra basso acordato ottava col tenor*)

    3. D-Mbs, 1511b, No.38, 13v–14v (Part 3 only) (Titled *Saltarello ala ferrarese col contra-Basso per ottava col Tenor*)

    4. Mönkemeyer, *Tabulatur*, viii, 22

Pavana alla venetiana   **Dalza**   lute

   2/ *Saltarello* 3/ *Piva*

    Intabulation: lute

1. **47**, No.15 (Dalza. This and the following four sets are linked together in the index as *Pavan ala venetiana*)

4. Moe, *Dance*, 319–22

Pavana alla venetiana   **Dalza**   lute

  2/ *Saltarello* 3/ *Piva*

    Intabulation: lute

      1. **47**, No.16 (Dalza)

Pavana alla venetiana   **Dalza**   lute

  2/ *Saltarello* 3/ *Piva*

    Intabulation: lute

      1. **47**, No.17 (Dalza)

    Facsimile: Barksdale, *Printed*, p. 67 (of the first page)

Pavana alla venetiana   **Dalza**   lute

  2/ *Saltarello* 3/ *Piva*

    Intabulation: lute

      1. **47**, No.18 (Dalza)

Pavana alla venetiana   **Dalza**   lute

  2/ *Saltarello* 3/ *Piva*

    Intabulations: lute

      1. **47**, No.19 (Dalza)

      2. J687 (1523), No.5, b3v-4v. (*Pavana alla venetiana*: Judenkunig)

Piva   **Dalza**   2 lutes

    Intabulation: two lutes

      1. **47**, No.25 (Dalza. In the index, this is linked with the preceding Saltarello, with which it belongs as a pair)

      4. Underwood, *Renaissance*, 91–93

Piva

  3/ of **Pavana** (several works)

Recercar   **Alemannus**

    Intabulation: lute

      1. **44**, No.25 (Alemannus)

    Comments: This citation comes from Colón's description of the book

Recercar primo   **Bossinensis**   lute

    Intabulation: lute

      1. **49**, No.71 (Bossinensis); **58**, No.71 (Bossinensis)

      4. Disertori, *Frottole*, 435

[Recercar] **2.**   **Bossinensis**   lute

    Intabulation: lute

      1. **49**, No.72 (Bossinensis); **58**, No.72 (Bossinensis)

      4. Disertori, *Frottole*, 436 and 447

[Recercar] **3.**   **Bossinensis**   lute

    Intabulation: lute

      1. **49**, No.73 (Bossinensis); **58**, No.73 (Bossinensis)

      4. Disertori, *Frottole*, 436 and 447

[Recercar] **4.**   **Bossinensis**   lute

    Intabulation: lute

    1. *49*, No.74 (Bossinensis); *58*, No.74 (Bossinensis)
    4. Disertori, *Frottole*, 436 and 448

[Recercar] **5.**   **Bossinensis**   lute
    Intabulation: lute
    1. *49*, No.75 (Bossinensis); *58*, No.75 (Bossinensis)
    4. Disertori, *Frottole*, 437 • Slim, *Keyboard*, ii, 605

[Recercar] **6.**   **Bossinensis**   lute
    Intabulation: lute
    1. *49*, No.76 (Bossinensis); *58*, No.76 (Bossinensis)
    4. Disertori, *Frottole*, 438 and 448

[Recercar] **7.**   **Bossinensis**   lute
    Intabulation: lute
    1. *49*, No.77 (Bossinensis); *58*, No.77 (Bossinensis)
    4. Disertori, *Frottole*, 438 and 449

[Recercar] **8.**   **Bossinensis**   lute
    Intabulation: lute
    1. *49*, No.78 (Bossinensis); *58*, No.78 (Bossinensis)
    4. Disertori, *Frottole*, 439

[Recercar] **9.**   **Bossinensis**   lute
    Intabulation: lute
    1. *49*, No.79 (Bossinensis); *58*, No.79 (Bossinensis)
    4. Disertori, *Frottole*, 439 and 449

[Recercar] **10.**   **Bossinensis**   lute
    Intabulation: lute
    1. *49*, No.80 (Bossinensis); *58*, No.80 (Bossinensis)
    4. Disertori, *Frottole*, 440

[Recercar] **11.**   **Bossinensis**   lute
    Intabulation: lute
    1. *49*, No.81 (Bossinensis); *58*, No.81 (Bossinensis)
    4. Disertori, *Frottole*, 440 and 450

[Recercar] **12.**   **Bossinensis**   lutc
    Intabulation: lute
    1. *49*, No.82 (Bossinensis); *58*, No.82 (Bossinensis)
    4. Disertori, *Frottole*, 440

[Recercar] **13.**   **Bossinensis**   lute
    Intabulation: lute
    1. *49*, No.83 (Bossinensis); *58*, No.83 (Bossinensis)
    4. Disertori, *Frottole*, 441

[Recercar] **14.**   **Bossinensis**   lute
    Intabulation: lute
    1. *49*, No.84 (Bossinensis); *58*, No.84 (Bossinensis)
    4. Disertori, *Frottole*, 441 and 450 • Ferand, *Improvisation*, 382

[Recercar] **15.**   **Bossinensis**   lute
    Intabulation: lute
    1. *49*, No.85 (Bossinensis); *58*, No.85 (Bossinensis)
    4. Disertori, *Frottole*, 441 and 451

[Recercar] **16.**   **Bossinensis**   lute
    Intabulation: lute
      1. **49**, No.86 (Bossinensis); **58**, No.86 (Bossinensis)
      4. Disertori, *Frottole*, 442 and 451 • Reese, *Renaissance*, 163

[Recercar] **17.**   **Bossinensis**   lute
    Intabulation: lute
      1. **49**, No.87 (Bossinensis); **58**, No.87 (Bossinensis)
      4. Disertori, *Frottole*, 442 and 452

[Recercar] **18.**   **Bossinensis**   lute
    Intabulation: lute
      1. **49**, No.88 (Bossinensis); **58**, No.88 (Bossinensis)
      4. Disertori, *Frottole*, 452

[Recercar] **19.**   **Bossinensis**   lute
    Intabulation: lute
      1. **49**, No.89 (Bossinensis); **58**, No.89 (Bossinensis)
      4. Disertori, *Frottole*, 443

[Recercar] **20.**   **Bossinensis**   lute
    Intabulation: lute
      1. **49**, No.90 (Bossinensis); **58**, No.90 (Bossinensis)
      4. Disertori, *Frottole*, 453

[Recercar] **21.**   **Bossinensis**   lute
    Intabulation: lute
      1. **49**, No.91 (Bossinensis); **58**, No.91 (Bossinensis)
      4. Disertori, *Frottole*, 443–44 and 453–54

[Recercar] **22.**   **Bossinensis**   lute
    Intabulation: lute
      1. **49**, No.92 (Bossinensis); **58**, No.92 (Bossinensis)
      4. Disertori, *Frottole*, 444 and 454

[Recercar] **23.**   **Bossinensis**   lute
    Intabulation: lute
      1. **49**, No.93 (Bossinensis); **58**, No.93 (Bossinensis)
      4. Disertori, *Frottole*, 445 and 455

[Recercar] **24.**   **Bossinensis**   lute
    Intabulation: lute
      1. **49**, No.94 (Bossinensis); **58**, No.94 (Bossinensis)
      4. Disertori, *Frottole*, 446 and 455 • Ferand, *Improvisation*, 382

[Recercar] **25.**   **Bossinensis**   lute
    Intabulation: lute
      1. **49**, No.95 (Bossinensis); **58**, No.95 (Bossinensis)
      4. Disertori, *Frottole*, 446 and 456

[Recercar] **26.**   **Bossinensis**   lute
    Intabulation: lute
      1. **49**, No.96 (Bossinensis); **58**, No.96 (Bossinensis)
      4. Disertori, *Frottole*, 456

Recercar primo   **Bossinensis**   lute
    Intabulation: lute

  1. **50**, No.57 (Bossinensis)
  4. Disertori, *Frottole*, 585 and 602

R[ecercar] **2**   **Bossinensis**   lute
 Intabulation: lute
  1. **50**, No.58 (Bossinensis)
  4. Disertori, *Frottole*, 585–86 and 602–603

[Recercar] **3**   **Bossinensis**   lute
 Intabulation: lute
  1. **50**, No.59 (Bossinensis)
  4. Disertori, *Frottole*, 587–88

R[ecercar] **4**   **Bossinensis**   lute
 Intabulation: lute
  1. **50**, No.60 (Bossinensis)
  4. Disertori, *Frottole*, 588–89

R[ecercar] **5**   **Bossinensis**   lute
 Intabulation: lute
  1. **50**, No.61 (Bossinensis)
  4. Disertori, *Frottole*, 590 and 604

[Recercar] **6**   **Bossinensis**   lute
 Intabulation: lute
  1. **50**, No.62 (Bossinensis)
  4. Disertori, *Frottole*, 590 and 605

[Recercar] **7**   **Bossinensis**   lute
 Intabulation: lute
  1. **50**, No.63 (Bossinensis)
  4. Disertori, *Frottole*, 605

R[ecercar] **8**   **Bossinensis**   lute
 Intabulation: lute
  1. **50**, No.64 (Bossinensis)
  4. Disertori, *Frottole*, 591 and 605–606

[Recercar] **9**   **Bossinensis**   lute
 Intabulation: lute
  1. **50**, No.65 (Bossinensis)
  4. Disertori, *Frottole*, 591–93 and 606–607

[Recercar] **10**   **Bossinensis**   lute
 Intabulation: lute
  1. **50**, No.66 (Bossinensis)
  4. Disertori, *Frottole*, 593–94 and 608

R[ecercar] **11**   **Bossinensis**   lute
 Intabulation: lute
  1. **50**, No.67 (Bossinensis)
  4. Disertori, *Frottole*, 609

R[ecercar] **12**   **Bossinensis**   lute
 Intabulation: lute
  1. **50**, No.68 (Bossinensis)
  4. Disertori, *Frottole*, 594 and 609

[Recercar] **13**   **Bossinensis**   lute
    Intabulation: lute
      1. *50*, No.69 (Bossinensis)
      4. Disertori, *Frottole*, 595 and 609

[Recercar] **14**   **Bossinensis**   lute
    Intabulation: lute
      1. *50*, No.70 (Bossinensis)
      4. Disertori, *Frottole*, 595 and 610

[Recercar] **15**   **Bossinensis**   lute
    Intabulation: lute
      1. *50*, No.71 (Bossinensis)
      4. Disertori, *Frottole*, 596–97 and 610–11

[Recercar] **16**   **Bossinensis**   lute
    Intabulation: lute
      1. *50*, No.72 (Bossinensis)
      4. Disertori, *Frottole*, 597–98 and 611–12

[Recercar] **17**   **Bossinensis**   lute
    Intabulation: lute
      1. *50*, No.73 (Bossinensis)
      4. Disertori, *Frottole*, 599

[Recercar] **18**   **Bossinensis**   lute
    Intabulation: lute
      1. *50*, No.74 (Bossinensis)
      4. Disertori, *Frottole*, 600 and 613

R[ecercar] **19**   **Bossinensis**   lute
    Intabulation: lute
      1. *50*, No.75 (Bossinensis)
      4. Disertori, *Frottole*, 601 and 614

R[ecercar] **20**   **Bossinensis**   lute
    Intabulation: lute
      1. *50*, No.76 (Bossinensis)
      4. Disertori, *Frottole*, 601 and 614 • Gallico, *Libro*, 137

Recercar   **Dalza**   lute
    Intabulation: lute
      1. *47*, No.2 (Dalza)

Recercar   **Dalza**   lute
    Intabulation: lute
      1. *47*, No.11 (Dalza. Listed in the Tavola with the preceding *Tastar de corde*)

Recercar   **Dalza**   lute
    Intabulation: lute
      1. *47*, No.12 (Dalza)
      4. Slim, *Keyboard*, ii, 603

Recercar   **Dalza**   lute
    Intabulation: lute
      1. *47*, No.13 (Dalza)

Recercar   **Dalza**   lute
    Intabulation: lute
    1. **47**, No.14 (Dalza)

Recercare [3]   **Spinacino**   lute
    Intabulation: lute
    1. **33**, No.24 (*Francesco Spinacino*)
    Facsimile: Apel, *Notation*, 63.
    4. Schering, *Geschichte*, No.63b • Schmidt, *Spinacino*, ii, 101–102

Recercare [4]   **Spinacino**   lute
    Intabulation: lute
    1. **33**, No.25 (Spinacino)
    4. Schmidt, *Spinacino*, ii, 103–106

Recercare [6]   **Spinacino**   lute
    Intabulation: lute
    1. **33**, No.27 (Spinacino)
    4. Körte, *Laute*, 129 • Schmidt, *Spinacino*, ii, 107–11

Recercare [7]   **Spinacino**   lute
    Intabulation: lute
    1. **33**, No.28 (Spinacino)
    4. Schmidt, *Spinacino*, ii, 114–15

Recercare [8]   **Spinacino**   lute
    Intabulation: lute
    1. **33**, No.29 (Spinacino)
    4. Schmidt, *Spinacino*, ii, 116–17

Recercare [9]   **Spinacino**   lute
    Intabulation: lute
    1. **33**, No.30 (Spinacino)
    4. Schmidt, *Spinacino*, ii, 118–23 • Slim, *Keyboard*, ii, 598

Recercare [10]   **Spinacino**   lute
    Intabulation: lute
    1. **33**, No.31 (Spinacino)
    Facsimile: Wolf, *Handbuch*, ii, 55
    4. Schmidt, *Spinacino*, ii, 124–25.

Recercare [11]   **Spinacino**   lute
    Intabulation: lute
    1. **33**, No.32 (Spinacino)
    4. Schmidt, *Spinacino*, ii, 126–27

Recercare [12]   **Spinacino**   lute
    Intabulation: lute
    1. **33**, No.33 (Spinacino)
    4. Schmidt, *Spinacino*, ii, 128–32

Recercare [13]   **Spinacino**   lute
    Intabulation: lute
    1. **33**, No.34 (Spinacino)
    4. Schmidt, *Spinacino*, ii, 132–34

Recercare [14]   **Spinacino**   lute
    Intabulation: lute

1. *33*, No.35 (Spinacino)

4. Schmidt, *Spinacino*, ii, 135–36

Recercare [15]   **Spinacino**   lute

Intabulation: lute

1. *33*, No.36 (Spinacino)

4. Schmidt, *Spinacino*, ii, 137–40

Recercare [16]   **Spinacino**   lute

Intabulation: lute

1. *33*, No.37 (Spinacino)

4. Schmidt, *Spinacino*, ii, 141–44

Recercare [17]   **Spinacino**   lute

Intabulation: lute

1. *33*, No.38 (Spinacino)

4. Schmidt, *Spinacino*, ii, 145–53

Recercare [1]   **Spinacino**   lute

Intabulation: lute

1. *34*, No.34 (*Francesco Spinacino*)

4. Schmidt, *Spinacino*, ii, 293–95

Recercare [2]   **Spinacino**   lute

Intabulation: lute

1. *34*, No.35 (*Francesco Spinacino*)

4. Schmidt, *Spinacino*, ii, 296–97

Recercare [3]   **Spinacino**   lute

Intabulation: lute

1. *34*, No.36 (*Francesco Spinacino*)

4. Schmidt, *Spinacino*, ii, 297–300

Recercare [4]   **Spinacino**   lute

Intabulation: lute

1. *34*, No.37 (*Francesco Spinacino*)

4. Schmidt, *Spinacino*, ii, 301–303

Recercare [5]   **Spinacino**   lute

Intabulation: lute

1. *34*, No.38 (*Francesco Spinacino*)

4. Schmidt, *Spinacino*, ii, 304–307

Recercare [6]   **Spinacino**   lute

Intabulation: lute

1. *34*, No.39 (*Francesco Spinacino*)

2. 1568[22], No.44, p. 87 (*Spinacino*. Becchi. Titled *Recercare accorda il lauto in altro modo*)

4. Schmidt, *Spinacino*, ii, 308–10

Recercare [7]   **Spinacino**   lute

Intabulation: lute

1. *34*, No.40 (*Francesco Spinacino*)

4. Schmidt, *Spinacino*, ii, 310–13

Recercare [8]   **Spinacino**   lute

Intabulation: lute

1. *34*, No.41 (*Francesco Spinacino*)

2. 1568²², No.42, p. 84

4. Schmidt, *Spinacino*, ii, 314–16.

Recercare [9]   **Spinacino**   lute

Intabulation: lute

1. *34*, No.42 (*Francesco Spinacino*)

2. 1568²², No.41, pp. 82–83 (*Spinacino*. Becchi)

4. Schmidt, *Spinacino*, ii, 317–19.

Recercare [10]   **Spinacino**   lute

Intabulation: lute

1. *34*, No.43 (*Francesco Spinacino*)

3. EIR-Dtc, D.3.30/I, No.92, pp. 102–3 (Anon.)

4. Gombosi, *Capirola*, p. xxxi • Schmidt, *Spinacino*, ii, 320–21

Recercare a Juli amours   **Spinacino**   lute

Intabulation: lute

1. *33*, No.23 (*Francesco Spinacino*)

4. Schmidt, *Spinacino*, ii, 99–100 • Slim, *Keyboard*, ii, 602

Recercare de tous biens   **Spinacino**   lute

Intabulation: lute

1. *33*, No.22 (*Francesco Spinacino*)

4. Schmidt, *Spinacino*, ii, 97–98 • Slim, *Keyboard*, ii, 601

Recercare de tutti li Toni   **Spinacino**   lute

Intabulation: lute

1. *33*, No.26 (Spinacino)

4. Körte, *Laute*, 129 • Schmidt, *Spinacino*, ii, 107–11

Recercar dietro   **Dalza**   lute

Intabulation: lute

1. *47*, No.5 (Dalza. Listed in the index with the preceding *Tastar de corde*)

Recercar dietro   **Dalza**   lute

Intabulation: lute

1. *47*, No.7 (Dalza. Listed in the index with the preceding *Tastar de corde*)

2. 1545⁷¹, No.11, f.10ν (Anon. Titled *Fantasia*)

4. Buetens, *Recercars*, p. 16

Recercar dietro   **Dalza**   lute

Intabulation: lute

1. *47*, No.9 (Dalza. Listed in the index with the preceding *Tastar de corde*)

Saltarello   **Dalza**   2 lutes

Intabulation: two lutes

1. *47*, No.24 (Dalza. In the index, listed with No.25, as *Saltarello e piua con doi lauti*)

Facsimile of the first opening: Huys, *Grégoire*, 63

Saltarello

See **Pavana**

Spingardo

See **Pavana**

Tastar de corde   **Dalza**   lute

Intabulation: lute

1. *47*, No.3 (Dalza)

4. Wolf, *Handbuch*, ii, 54

Tastar de corde   **Dalza**   lute

 Intabulation: lute

  1. **47**, No.4 (Dalza. In the index listed as *Tastar de corde col suo recercar*)

  4. Apel and Davison, *HAM*, No.99a

Tastar de corde   **Dalza**   lute

 Intabulation: lute

  1. **47**, No.6 (Dalza. In the index listed as *Tastar de corde col suo recercar*)

Tastar de corde   **Dalza**   lute

 Intabulation: lute

  1. **47**, No.8 (Dalza. In the index listed as *Tastar de corde col suo recercar*)

Tastar de corde   **Dalza**   lute

 Intabulation: lute

  1. **47**, No.10 (Dalza. In the index listed as *Tastar de corde col suo recercar*)

Chapter Nineteen

CONCORDANT SOURCES

his chapter lists the sources cited in the preceding chapter. The bibliographical citations given after sources are restricted to references to facsimiles, complete editions of the source, or studies giving complete inventories or important information on the provenance of the source. (No bibliographical citations are given here for editions printed by Petrucci, since they are listed *in extenso* in the descriptions, identified by the number at the end of each entry below.) The *Census-Catalogue* (*CC*) is a central bibliographical resource for the majority of the manuscripts mentioned below.

These citations are followed by reference to works in the source also found in Petrucci's edition: "**6**: 3" indicates that the third piece in edition No.6 of my catalogue is also found in this source, in one form or another. Further details can then be traced in chapter 18.

Printed Sources

RISM O8 (s.d.)	Obrecht: *Concentus harmonici quattuor missarum* ([Basel: Mewes], s.d.)
	Obrecht, *Opera Omnia: Editio altera*, i/3
	6: 3
1501	*Harmonice musices Odhecaton A* (Venice: Petrucci, [ded.15.v.1501]) (No.1)
1502¹	*Motetti A. numero trentatre* (Venice: Petrucci, 9.v.1502) (No.3)
1502²	*Canti B. numero cinquanta* (Venice: Petrucci, 5.ii.1501/2) (No.2)
J666 (1502)	Josquin: *Liber primus missarum* (Venice: Petrucci, 27.ix.1502) (No.4)
1503¹	*Motetti De passione . . . B* (Venice: Petrucci, 10.v.1503) (No.7)

1089

1503²	*Harmonice musices Odhecaton A* (Venice: Petrucci, 14.i.1502/3) (No.5)
1503³	*Canti B. numero cinquanta* (Venice: Petrucci, 4.viii.1503) (No.10)
B4643 (1503)	Brumel: *Misse* (Venice: Petrucci, 17.vi.1503) (No.8)
G1780 (1503)	Ghiselin: *Misse* (Venice: Petrucci, 15.vii.1503) (No.9)
L718 (1503)	La Rue: *Misse* (Venice: Petrucci, 1503) (No.11)
O7 (1503)	Obrecht: *Misse* (Venice: Petrucci, 24.iii.1503) (No.6)
1504¹	*Motetti C* (Venice: Petrucci, 15.ix.1504) (No.15)
1504²	*Harmonice musices Odhecaton A* (Venice: Petrucci, 25.v.1504) (No.14)
1504³	*Canti C. N° cento cinquanta* (Venice: Petrucci, 25.v.1503/4) (No.12)
1504⁴	*Frottole libro primo* (Venice: Petrucci, 28.xi.1504) (No.16)
A431 (1504)	Agricola: *Misse* (Venice: Petrucci, 23.iii.1504) (No.13)
1505¹	*Fragmenta missarum* (Venice: Petrucci, 31.x.1505) (No.24)
1505²	*Motetti libro quarto* (Venice: Petrucci, 4.vi.1505) (No.21)
1505³	*Frottole libro secondo* (Venice: Petrucci, 8.i.1504/1505) (No.17)
[1505]⁴	*Frottole libro tertio* (Venice: Petrucci, 6.ii.1504/5) (No.18)
Motetti A (1505)	*Motetti A* (Venice: Petrucci, 13.ii.1505) (No.19)
1505⁵	*Strambotti, ode . . . Libro quarto* (Venice: Petrucci, 1505) (No.23)
1505⁶	*Frottole libro quinto* (Venice: Petrucci, 23.xii.1505) (No.25)
J670 (1505)	Josquin: *Missarum liber secundus* (Venice: Petrucci, 30.vi.1505) (No.22)
O137 (1505)	de Orto: *Misse* (Venice: Petrucci, 22.iii.1505) (No.20)
Motetti A (1505)	*Motetti A* (Venice: Petrucci, 13.ii.1504/5) (No.19)
1506¹	*Lamentationum . . . Liber primus* (Venice: Petrucci, 8.iv.1506) (No.27)
1506²	*Lamentationum liber secundus* (Venice: Petrucci, 29.v.1506) (No.28)
1506³	*Frottole libro sexto* (Venice: Petrucci, 2.ii.1505/6) (No.26)
Dammonis (1506)	Dammonis: *Laude I* (Venice: Petrucci, [vii.1506]) (No.29)
I88 (1506)	Isaac: *Misse* (Venice: Petrucci, 20.x.1506) (No.31)
Josquin I (1506)	Josquin: *I Missarum* (Venice: Petrucci, [viii.1506]) (No.30)
Cantorino 1506	*Monastici cantus compendiolum* (Venice: Giunta, 1506)
	Cattin, "Canti polifonici"; Cattin, "Tradizione"
1507¹	*Frottole libro tertio* (Venice: Petrucci, 26.xi.1506) (No.40)
1507²	*Strambotti . . . Libro quarto* (Venice: Petrucci, 31.vii.1507) (No.37)
1507³	*Frottole libro septimo* (Venice: Petrucci, 6.vi.1507) (No.36)
1507⁴	*Frottole libro octavo* (Venice: Petrucci, 21.v.1507) (No.35)
Magnificats (1507)	*Magnificat I* (Venice: Petrucci, 14.x.1507) (No.39)
Martini (1507)	Martini: *Hymni de tempo I* (Venice: Petrucci, [1507]) (No.38)
1507⁵	Spinacino: *Intabolatura de lauto libro primo* (Venice: Petrucci, [27.ii].1507) (No.33)
	Lute tabulature
1507⁶	Spinacino: *Intabolatura de lauto Libro secondo* (Venice: Petrucci, 31.iii.1507) (No.34)
	Lute tabulature
G450 (1507)	Weerbeke: *Misse Gaspar* (Venice: Petrucci 7.i.1506/7) (No.32)
Magnificats (1507)	*Magnificat liber primus* (Venice: Petrucci, 14.x.1507)
Martini (1507)	Martini: *Hymni de tempore liber primus* (Venice: Petrucci, 1507)
1508¹	*Motetti a cinque libro primo* (Venice: Petrucci, 1508) (No.46)
1508²	*Frottole libro secondo* (Venice: Petrucci, 29.i.1507/8) (No.42)
1508³	*Laude libro secondo* (Venice: Petrucci, 11.i.1507/8) (No.41)

Alemannus (1508)	Alemannus: *Intabolatura de lauto . . . Libro terzo* (Venice: Petrucci, 20.vi.1508) (No.44) Lute tabulature
D828 (1508)	Dalza: *Intabolatura de Lauto. Libro Quarto* (Venice: Petrucci, 1508) (No.47) Lute tabulature
D833/2 (1508)	Dammonis: *Laude I* (Venice: Petrucci, 7.viii.1508) (No.45)
1509[1]	*Missarum diversorum auctorum liber primus* (Venice: Petrucci, 13.iii.1508/9) (No.43)
1509[2]	*Frottole libro nono* (Venice: Petrucci, 22.i.1508/9) (No.48)
1509[3]	Bossinensis: *Tenori e contrabassi Libro primo* (Venice: Petrucci, 27.iii.1509) (No.49) Voice with Lute tabulature
1510	*Canzoni nove* (Rome: Antico, 9.x.1510) Chapman, *Antico*, No.1 • Einstein, "Antico" • Jeppesen, *Frottola*, i *18/40*: 22 • *23/37*: 3, 5, 50, 60, 63, 72, 75 • *25*: 9, 15, 24 • *36*: 1, 12, 13, 15, 27, 37, 49, 54, 64 • *41*: 17 • *49/58*: 5, 7, 8, 20, 52 • *50*: 7, 15, 16
1511	Bossinensis: *Tenori . . . Libro secundo* (Fossombrone: Petrucci, 10.iii.1511) (No.50) Voice with Lute tabulature
Frottole X (1512)	*Frottole libro decimo* (Fossombrone: Petrucci, 1512) (No.51)
1512[2]	Schlick: *Tabulaturen* (Mainz: Schöffer, 1512) Keyboard tabulature • Brown, *Instrumental*, 1512[1] *1/5/14*: 27
1513[1]	*Canzoni sonetti . . . libro tertio* [Rome: Antico, 1513] Chapman, *Antico*, No.4 *56*: 26
50 Carmina (1513)	*Quinquagena carminum* (Mainz: Schöffer, 1513) Fallows, *Catalogue*, 9 • Senn, "Sammelwerk" *2/10*: all
—	Paulus: *Paulina* (Fossombrone: Petrucci, 8.vii.1513) (No.52)
—	Castiglione: *Epistola* (Fossombrone: Petrucci, 29.vii.1513) (No.53)
1514[1]	*Motetti de la Corona. Libro Primo* (Fossombrone: Petrucci, 17.viii.1514) (No.55)
1514[2]	*Frottole libro undecimo* (Fossombrone: Petrucci, 20.x.1514) (No.56)
J667 (1514)	This item is *recte* J668 (1516)
J673 (1514)	Josquin: *Missarum Liber tertius* (Fossombrone: Petrucci, 1.iii.1514) (No.54)
Ghiselin [1514]	Ghiselin: *Misse* ([Fossombrone: Petrucci, 1514]) (No.57)
Bossinensis [1515]	Bossinensis: *Tenori e contrabassi Libro primo* ([Venice: Fossombrone, 1515]) (No.58)
1515[1] = F689	Févin: *Misse* (Fossombrone: Petrucci, 22.xi.1515) (No.61)
1515[2]	*Canzoni sonetti . . . libro primo* (Siena: Sambonetti, 30.viii.1515) D'Accone, "Instrumental" • Fusi, *Frottole*; Jeppesen, *Frottola*, i *26*: 17 • *56*: 8
J671 (1515)	Josquin: *Missarum liber secundus* (Fossombrone: Petrucci, 11.iv.1515) (No.59)
M4015 (1515)	Mouton: *Misse* (Fossombrone: Petrucci, 11.viii.1515) (No.60)
1516[1]	*Liber quindecim missarum* (Rome: Antico, v.1516) Chapman, *Antico*, No.16 *54*: 2, 5, 6 • *60*: 3, 4 • *61*: 2, 3
[c.1516][2]	[*Frottole libro secondo* (Venice: Antico, 1520)]

	Chapman, *Antico*, No.30 • Luisi, *Secondo* • Jeppesen, *Frottola*, i
	50: 2, 8 • *56*: 4, 13, 23
J668 (1516)	Josquin: *Liber primus Missarum* (Fossombrone: Petrucci, 29.v.1516) (No.62)
J674 (1516)	This item is *recte* J673 (1514)
—	Paulus: *Parabola Christi* (Fossombrone: Petrucci, 20.xi.1516) (No.63)
[c.1517][1]	*Frottole libro tertio* ([Venice: Antico, 1520])
	Chapman, *Antico*, No.31 • Jeppesen, *Frottola*, i
	56: 26
1517[3]	*Frottole intabulate . . . I* (Rome: Antico, 13.i.1517)
	Keyboard score • Antico, *Frottolas* • Brown, *Instrumental* 1517[1] • Chapman, *Antico*, No.20; • Jeppesen, *Frottola*, i; Sartori, *Bibliografia*, pp. 1–2
	36/49/58: 5,15 • *50*: 2, 7 • *56*: 8, 13, 23, 26 • See also *4/30/62*: 1, found in the manuscript appendix to the copy at I-Rpol
1518	*Canzoni sonetti . . . libro tertio* (Rome: Mazzocchi [Antico], 1518)
	Chapman, *Antico*, No.23 • Einstein, *Canzoni*
	56: 26
Frottole II (1518)	*Frottole libro secondo* (Rome: Mazzocchi, 1518)
	Chapman, *Antico*, No.22 • Luisi, *Secondo*; • Jeppesen, *Frottola*, i
	50: 2, 8 • *56*: 4, 13, 23
1519[1]	*Motetti de la corona. Libro secondo* (Fossombrone: Petrucci, 17.vi.1519) (No.64)
1519[2]	*Motetti de la corona. Libro tertio* (Fossombrone: Petrucci, 7.ix.1519) (No.65)
1519[3]	*Motetti de la corona. Libro quarto* (Fossombrone: Petrucci, 31.x.1519) (No.66)
[1519][5]	*In diesem Buchlien findet man LXXV . . .* (Cologne: Arnt von Aich, [s.d.])
	Böker-Heil, Heckmann & Kindermann, *Tenorlied*, i, 17–23
	2/10: 28
1520[1]	*Motetti novi libro secondo* (Venice: Antico, 30.xi.1520)
	Chapman, *Antico*, No.37 • Picker, *Motet* (1987)
	64: 2, 14, 21, 24
1520[2]	*Motetti novi libro tertio* (Venice: Antico, 15.x.1520)
	Chapman, *Antico*, No.36 • Picker, *Motet* (1987)
	64: 4, 16
1520[3]	*Motetti novi e chanzoni franciose* (Venice: Antico, 15.x.1520)
	Chapman, *Antico*, No.35
	2/10: 34 • *12*: 111
1520[4]	*Liber selectarum cantionum* (Augsburg: Grimm & Wyrsung, 1520)
	Dunning, *Staatsmotette*, pp. 39–56 • Schlagel, *Josquin*, pp. 28–46
	65: 2, 6 • *66*: 3, 5, 6
[c.1520][7]	*Frottole . . . Tromboncino . . . Cara . . . tabulati* (Venice: Antico, [s.d.])
	Voice and lute tabulature • Brown, *Instrumental* 152?[1]; Chapman, *Antico*, No.33; Jeppesen, *Frottola*, i; Luisi, *Frottole*
	17/42: 33 • *56*: 5, 7, 61, 62, 70
P2451 (1520)	Pisano: *Musica* (Fossombrone: Petrucci, 23.v.1520) (No.67)
Frottole II 1520	See [1516][2]
Frottole III, 1520	See [c.1517][1]
1521[3]	*Motetti libro primo* (Venice: Antico, viii.1521)
	Chapman, *Antico*, No.38; Picker, *Motet* (1987)
	65: 6, 7, 15

1521[5]	*Motetti libro quarto* (Venice: Antico, viii.1521)
	Chapman, *Antico*, No.39; Picker, *Motet* (1987)
	64: 1, 13, 18
[c.1521][7]	[*Motetti e carmina gallica* (s.l.: s.n., 1524)]
	7: 12 • **15**: 16 • **41**: 22 • **65**: 12 • **66**: 6
1522	*Missarum decem a clarissimis musicis* (Rome: Pasoti [Giunta], v.1522)
	Lockwood, "A View"
	54: 2, 5 • **60**: 3
J687 (1523)	Judenkünig: *Ain schone kunstliche underweisung* (Vienna: Singreyner, 1523)
	Lute tabulature • Brown, *Instrumental* 1523₂
	12: 10 • **47**: 19, 33
Cantorino 1523	*Cantus monastici formula* (Venice: Giunta, 1523)
	Cattin, "Tradizione"
	27: 14 • **41**: 5
Liber sacerdotalis	*Liber sacerdotalis* (Venice: Sessa & de Ravanis, 1523)
	Cattaneo, "Rituale"
	27: 14, 15 • **41**: 5
Aaron 1525	Aaron: *Trattato della natura . . .* (Venice: Vitali, 1525)
	Judd, "Reading"
1526[1]	*Motetti de la Corona libro primo* (Rome: Pasoti & Dorico, xi.1526)
	Cusick, *Dorico*, No.8
	55: all
1526[2]	*Motetti de la Corona libro secondo* (Rome: Pasoti, viii.1526)
	Cusick, *Dorico*, No.6
	64: all
1526[3]	*Motetti de la Corona libro tertio* (Rome: Pasoti, iv.1526)
	Cusick, *Dorico*, No.2
	65: all
1526[4]	*Motetti de la Corona libro quarto* (Rome: Pasoti & Dorico, x.1526)
	Cusick, *Dorico*, No.7
	66: all
[1526][5]	*Fior de motetti e canzoni novi* ([s.l.: s.n., 1523])
	Fenlon & Haar, *Madrigal*, 207–209; Jeppesen, *Frottola*, i
	56: 33
J669 (1526)	Josquin: *Liber primus Missarum* (Rome: Pasoti and Dorico [Giunta], 1526)
	Cusick, *Dorico*, No.1
	4/30/62: all
J672 (1526)	Josquin: *Missarum liber secundus* (Rome: Pasoti and Dorico [Giunta], 1526)
	Cusick, *Dorico*, No.4
	22/59: all
J675 (1526)	Josquin: *Missarum liber tertius* (Rome: Pasoti and Dorico [Giunta], 1526)
	Cusick, *Dorico*, No.5
	54: all
1527	*Motetti de la Corona. Libro tertio* (Rome: Pasoti & Dorico, iv.1527)
	Cusick, *Dorico*, No.9
	65: all

[1528]²   *Motetz nouvellement composez* (Paris: Attaingnant [1529])
         Heartz, *Attaingnant*, No.11
           3/19: 13

[c.1528]⁴   *Trente chansons musicales à4* (Paris: Attaingnant [1528])
         Heartz, *Attaingnant*, No.8
           12: 28

Brown 1529₃   *Tres breve et familiere introduction* (Paris: Attaingnant, 6.x.1529)
         Lute, and voice and lute tabulature • Heartz, *Attaingnant*, No.13
           41: 22

1529⁴   *Quarante et deux chansons musicales a troys* (Paris: Attaingnant, 22.iv.1529)
         Heartz, *Attaingnant*, No.10
           12: 133

[c.1530]¹   *Libro primo de la fortuna* ([probably Rome, before 1526])
         Fenlon & Haar, *Italian*, pp. 218–20
           68: 3r

1531⁵   *Treze motetz musicaulx* (Paris: Attaingnant, iv.1531)
         Keyboard tabulature • Brown, *Instrumental* 1531₇; Heartz, *Attaingnant*,
         No.27; Rokseth, *Treize* (edition)
           7: 12 • **41**: 22 • **55**: 13 • **61**: 3

1531⁶   *Dixneuf chansons . . . tabulature des orgues* (Paris: Attaingnant, i.1530 [1531])
         Keyboard tabulature • Brown, *Instrumental* 1531₁; Heartz, *Attaingnant*, No.22
           2/10: 28

1532³   *Tertius liber tres missas continet* (Paris: Attaingnant, 1532)
         Heartz, *Attaingnant*, No.35
           60: 5

1532¹⁰   *Primus libre com quatuor vocibus. Motteti del Fiore* (Lyons: Moderne, 1532)
         Pogue, *Moderne*, Nos.4–5 (Note in particular the attribution pattern
           69: 1–5

G1620 (1532)   Gerle: *Musica Teusch* (Nürnberg: Formschneider, 1532)
         Lute tabulature • Brown, *Instrumental* 1532₂
           2/10: 7

G1623 (1533)   Gerle: *Tabulatur auff die Laudten* (Nürnberg: Formschneider, 1533)
         Lute tabulature • Brown, *Instrumental* 1533₁
           1/5/14: 14, 57, 69 • **33**: 18 • **66**: 6

[c.1533]   [*Musica XII* (Fossombrone: Petrucci, s.d.)] (No.68)

1534³   *Liber primus . . . motetos* (Paris: Attaingnant, iv.1534)
         Heartz, *Attaingnant*, No.46
           64: 4, 5, 19, 20

1534⁴   *Liber secundus . . . motetos* (Paris: Attaingnant, v.1534)
         Heartz, *Attaingnant*, No.47
           64: 23 • **69**: 5

1534⁶   *Liber quartus . . . modulos* (Paris: Attaingnant, vi.1534)
         Heartz, *Attaingnant*, No.50
           55: 16 • **64**: 16 • **65**: 4

1534¹⁰   *Liber octavus . . . motetos* (Paris: Attaingnant, xii.1534)
         Heartz, *Attaingnant*, No.57
           66: 2

1534[16] = V1220   Verdelot: *Secundo Libro de Madrigali* (Venice: O. Scotto, 1534)

Chapman, *Antico*, No.70

68: 4r

1535[1]   *Liber nonus . . . psalmos* (Paris: Attaingnant, i.1535)

Heartz, *Attaingnant*, No.60

69: 2, 4

1535[3]   *Liber undecimus . . . modulos* (Paris: Attaingnant, iii.1534/5)

Heartz, *Attaingnant*, No.63

55: 15; **64**: 22

[c.1535][14]   [Lieder (Frankfurt: Egenolff, s.d.)]

Berz, *Notendrucker*, No.6, p. 148; Böker-Heil, Heckmann & Kindermann, *Tenorlied*, i; Bridgman, "Egenolff"; Staehelin, "Egenolff"

1/5: 91 • **1/5/14**: 14, 20, 43, 44, 45, 49, 50, 51, 57, 62, 63, 64, 65, 74, 76, 77, 80, 86, 89 • **2/10**: 3, 7, 9, 10, 11, 13, 15, 16, 17, 18, 19, 20, 21, 28, 29, 31, 34, 39, 40, 42, 43, 44, 45, 46, 47, 48, 49, 50, 51 • **3**: 16 • **12**: 18, 64, 123 • **14**: 82 • **19**: 16 • **31**: 3 • **33**: 2, 5, 13, 18 • **34**: 10, 14, 27, 28

Cantorino 1535   *Cantus monastici formula* (Venice; Giunta, 1535)

Cattin, "Tradizione"

27: 15 • **41**: 5

1536[7] = V1221   Verdelot: *Secondo libro de madrigali* (Venice: Scotto, 1536)

Chapman, *Antico*, No.74

68: 4r

1536[11]   Francesco da Milano: *Intabolatura di liuto* (Venice: Marcolini, v.1536)

Lute tabulature • Brown, *Instrumental* 1536₃; Francesco da Milano, *Lute Music*

65: 6, 14

1536[12] = N521   H. Newsidler: *Ein newgeordnet künstlich Lautenbuch* (Nürnberg: Petreius, 1536)

Lute tabulature • Brown, *Instrumental* 1536₆; Teramoto & Brinzing, *Katalog*, No.1

1/5/14: 14, 44, 76; **12**: 126 • **31**: 3 • **33**: 2, 13, 18

1536[13] = N522   H. Newsidler: *Der ander Theil des Lautenbuchs* (Nürnberg: Petreius, 1536)

Lute tabulature • Brown, *Instrumental* 1536₇; Teramoto & Brinzing, *Katalog*, No.2

1/5: 91 • **1/5/14**: 14, 45, 49, 56, 59, 62, 64, 69, 80, 86, 89 • **2/10**: 40, 42 • **3/19**: 16 • **12**: 10, 38, 129, 115, 116, 120, 123, 124, 131 • **14**: 82 • **33**: 7, 8, 10, 15 • **34**: 5, 10, 25, 28 • **55**: 2, 4, 5, 13, 26

Il Fortuna (1536)   *Involatura de viola over lauto . . . Il Fortuna* ([Naples: Sulzbach], 1536)

Lute tabulature

65: 6, 14

1537[1]   *Novum et insigne opus musicum* (Nürnberg: Formschneider, 1537)

Gustavson, *Hans Ott*

3/19: 5 • **55**: 13 • **65**: 2, 5, 7, 12, 16 • **66**: 8

1537[10] = V1222   Verdelot: *Secondo libro de madrigali* (Venice: Scotto, 1537)

Chapman, *Antico*, No.81

68: 4r

Heyden 1537   Heyden: *Ars canendi* (Nürnberg: Petreius, 1537)

                    Heyden, *De arte*; Teramoto & Brinzing, *Katalog*, No.3

                          7: 35 • **12**: 139; cf.**4/30/62**: 1, 3, 5 • **6**: 1, 5 • **7**: 6, 8 • **9/57**: 3, 4 •

                          11: 4 • **13**: 1, 3 • **20**: 2, 3, 4 • **22/59**: 2, 3 • **31**: 3 • **32**: 4 • **54**: 1, 3, 6

1538[1]   *Selectae harmoniae* (Wittenberg: Rhau, 1538)

                    Reich, *Selectae* (edition)

                          3: 6 • **7**: 21 • **19**: 5

1538[3]   *Secundus tomus novi operis musici* (Nürnberg: Formschneider, x.1538)

                    Gustavson, *Hans Ott*

                          15: 3, 32 • **21**: 24 • **65**: 1, 6 • **66**: 6

1538[6]   *Tomus primus psalmorum* (Nürnberg: Petreius, ix.1538)

                    Teramoto & Brinzing, *Katalog*, No.4

                          64: 8 • **65**: 11 • **66**: 7

1538[7]   *Modulationes aliqout quatuor vocum selectissimae* (Nürnberg: Petreius, ix.1538)

                    Teramoto & Brinzing, *Katalog*, No.5

                          55: 24

1538[8]   *Symphoniae iucundae* (Wittenberg: Rhau, 1538)

                    Albrecht, *Symphoniae* (edition)

                        7: 1, 32 • **16**: 56 • **41**: 22 • **49/58**: 54; **55**: 24 • **64**: 24 • **69**: 1

1538[9]   *Trium vocum carmina* (Nürnberg: Formschneider, 1538)

                    Böker-Heil, *Tenorlied*; Brown, *Instrumental* 1538[2]; Mönkemeyer, *Form-schneyder* (edition)

                      1/5/14: 38, 44, 49, 50, 54, 56, 57, 58, 59, 62, 63, 64, 76, 80 • **2/10**: 40, 44 • **3/19**: 16 • **4/30/62**: 4 • **8**: 1 • **12**: 10, 118, 120, 121, 127, 129, 131, 132, 133; cf.**6**: 3, 4, 5 • **9/57**: 4 • **33**: 4, 7, 10, 15, 17 • **34**: 3, 5, 13, 25, 28 • **43**: 1

1538[22] = N66   Narvaez: *Los seys libros del Delphin* (Valladolid: Hernandez, 1538)

                    Vihuela tabulature • Brown, *Instrumental* 1538[1]

                      22/59: 2 • **54**: 2, 6

Motteti 1538   [*Motteti del Fiore*] (Fossombrone: Petrucci & Egnatio, 1538) (No.69)

1539[1]   *Liber quindecim missarum* (Nürnberg: Petreius, 1539)

                    Teramoto & Brinzing, *Katalog*, No.7

                      4/30/62: 1, 2, 3, 4 • **8**: 1 • **22/59**: 1 • **54**: 5

1539[2]   *Missae tredecim quatuor vocum* (Nürnberg: Graphaeus, 7.ii.1539)

                      4/30/62: 1, 4 • **7**: 33 • **48**: 5 • **61**: 5

1539[9]   *Tomus secundus psalmorum* (Nürnberg: Petreius, 1539)

                    Teramoto & Brinzing, *Katalog*, No.8

                      21: 38 • **55**: 2, 3, 4, 5 • **64**: 11 • **65**: 13 • **69**: 2, 4

1539[12]   *Primus Liber cum quatuor vocibus* . . . *Fior de Mottetti* (Venice: Gardano, xii.1539)

                    Lewis, *Gardano*, No.12

                      69: 1, 4

G2977 (1539)   Gombert: *Musica quatuor vocum* . . . *motecta liber primus* (Venice: Scotto, 1539)

                    Bernstein, *Music*, No.3

                      69: 3, 5

1540[2]   *Missarum musicalium* . . . *III* (Paris: Attaingnant & Jullet, 1540)

                    Heartz, *Attaingnant*, No.93

                      41: 22

1540⁷   *Selectissimae necnon familiarissimae cantiones* (Augsburg: Kriesstein, 1540)
    22/59: 2 • **66**: 14

1540²⁰ = V1228   Verdelot: *Tutti li madrigali* (Venice: Scotto, 1540)
    Bernstein, *Music*, No.14
    68: 4r

Baena 1540   Baena: *Arte novamente inventada pera aprender a tanger* (Lisbon: Galharde, 1540)
    Keyboard tabulature • Jas, "Ockeghem"; Knighton, "Newly"
    1/5/14: 13, 56, 62 • **2/10**: 40 • **4/30/62**: 1, 2, 3, 4 • **12**: 80 • **22/59**: 1, 2 • **54**: 5, 6

Heyden 1540   Heyden: *De arte canendi* (Nürnberg: Petreius, 1540)
    Teramoto & Brinzing, *Katalog*, No.13
    4/30/62: 1, 3, 4, 5 • **6**: 1, 5 • **7**: 6, 8, 35 • **8**: 3, 5 • **9/57**: 1, 3, 4 • **11**: 4 • **12**: 139 • **13**: 3 • **20**: 2, 4 • **21**: 26, 40 • **22/59**: 2, 3 • **31**: 3 • **32**: 4 • **54**: 1, 3

1541²   *Trium vocum cantiones* (Nürnberg: Petreius, 1541)
    Brown, *Trium* (facsimile); Teramoto & Brinzing, *Katalog*, No.15
    2/10: 39

1541¹⁸ = V1229   Verdelot: *Tutti li madrigali* (Venice: Gardano, 1541)
    Lewis, *Gardano*, No.27
    68: 4r

G2979 (1541)   Gombert: *Musica quatuor vocum* (Venice: Gardano, 1541)
    Lewis, *Gardano*, No.23
    69: 3, 5

1542⁸   *Tricinia* (Wittenberg: Rhau, 1542)
    Noblitt, *Tricinia* (edition); Teramoto, *Psalmmotettendrucke*
    1/5/14: 46 • **9/57**: 4 • **12**: 80 • **34**: 33

1542¹⁰ = W1112   Willaert: *Musicorum sex vocum* (Venice: Gardano, 1542)
    Lewis, *Gardano*, No.34
    66: 2

1543¹⁹   *Il primo libro a due voci* (Venice: Gardano, 1543)
    Lewis, *Gardano*, Nos.48 & 48a
    54: 5 • **60**: 2, 3 • **61**: 3

Festa (1543)   Festa: *Il Vero libro di madrigali a tre voci* (Venice: Gardano, 1543)
    Lewis, *Gardano*, No.41
    16: 40

1544¹⁸ = V1230   Verdelot: *A quatro voci* (Venice: Gardano, 1544)
    Lewis, *Gardano*, No.59
    68: 4r

1544²⁴ = N524   H. Newsidler: *Das erst Buch* (Nürnberg: Günther, 1544)
    Lute tabulature • Brown, *Instrumental* 1544₁
    2/10: 11 • **16**: 56 • **49/58**: 54

1544²⁵ = N526   H. Newsidler: *Das dritt Buch* (Nürnberg: Günther, 1544)
    Lute tabulature • Brown, *Instrumental* 1544₃
    55: 3 • **65**: 11

1545⁴   *Flos Florum Primus Liber cum quatuor vocibus* (Venice: Gardano, 1545)
    Lewis, *Gardano*, No.78
    69: 1, 4

1545[5]   *Officiorum .. de Nativitate . . . I* (Wittemberg: Rhau, 1545)
              64: 5

1545[6]   *Bicinia gallica, latina, germanica . . . I* (Wittemberg: Rhau, 1545)
              Bellingham, *Bicinia* (edition)
                     6: 5 • **11**: 1 • **22/59**: 1, 2 • **54**: 5, 6 • **56**, 5 • **61**: 2, 3

1545[7]   *Secundus tomus biciniorum* (Wittemberg: Rhau, 29.v.1545)
              Bellingham, *Bicinia* (edition)
                     8: 1, 5 • **11**: 4 • **22/59**: 1 • **54**: 6 • **61**: 2

1545[15] = J680   Josquin: *Le septiesme livre* (Antwerp: Susato, 1545)
              Meissner, *Susato*, ii, 39–43
                     2/10: 37 • **46**: 8

1545[19] = V1231 Verdelot: *Tutti li madrigali* (Venice: [O. Scotto], 1545)
              Bernstein, *Music*, No.54
                     68: 4r

1545[21]   *Des chansons reduictz en tabulature de lut I* (Louvain: Bathen & Velpen, 1545)
              Lute tabulature • Brown, *Instrumental* 1545₃; Vanhulst, *Catalogue*, No.1
                     1/5/14: 44: **33**: 13 • **47**: 7

1546[1]   *Missarum musicalium à4 liber primus* (Paris: Attaingnant, 1546)
              Heartz, *Attaingnant*, No.132
                     41: 22

1546[4]   *Liber tertius missarum quatuor vocum* (Antwerp: Susato, 1547)
              Meissner, *Susato*, ii, 54–55
                     60: 5

1546[8]   *Selectissimae symphoniae* (Nürnberg: Berg & Neuber, 1546)
                     66: 15

BB902 I,1 = 1546[22]   Barberiis: *Intabulatura de lautto IV* (Venice: [s.n.], 1546)
              Lute tabulature • Brown, *Instrumental* 1546₂
                     61: 3

BB902 I,3 = 1546[23]   Barberiis: *Intabulatura de lautto VI* (Venice: [s.n.], 1546)
              Lute tabulature • Brown, *Instrumental* 1546₄
                     64: 5, 6, 24 • **69**: 3

1546[29]   Francesco da Milano: *Intabolatura . . . Libro segundo* (Venice: Gardano, 1546)
              Lute tabulature • Brown, *Instrumental* 1546₇; Lewis, *Gardano*, No.85; Francesco da Milano, *Lute music*
                     65: 6

M7725 (1546) Mudarra: *Tres libros de música* (Seville: de Leon, 1546)
              Guitar and vihuela tabulatures • Brown, *Instrumental* 1546₁₄
                     4/30/62: 2 • **54**: 2, 5 • **61**: 3

1547[1]   Glareanus: *Dodecachordon* (Basle: Petri, ix.1547)
              Glareanus, *Dodecachordon*
                     1/5/14: 95 • **2/10**: 19 • **3/19**: 2, 11, 16 • **4/30/62**: 1, 3, 4, 5 • **6**: 5 •
                     7: 6, 9, 10, 11, 12, 35 • **8**: 1 • **9/57**: 4 • **11**: 4 • **12**: 139 • **15**: 3, 32, 33
                     • **20**: 2 • **22/59**: 2, 3 • **31**: 3; **34**: 14 • **43**: 3 • **48**: 5 • **54**: 1, 3, 5, 6 •
                     61: 3 • **64**: 4 • **65**: 9

1547[15]   Festa: *Il vero libro di madrigali a tre voci* (Venice: Scotto, 1547)
              Bernstein, *Music*, No.66
                     16: 40

1547²² = G2092   Gintzler: *Intabolatura de lauto . . . Libro primo* (Venice: Gardano, 1547)
    Lute tabulature • Brown, *Instrumental* 1547₃; Lewis, *Gardano*, No.108
       65: 2, 6

1547²⁵ = V32   Valderrábano: *Libro de música* (Valladolid: Fernandez de Cordova, 1547)
    Lute tabulature • Brown, *Instrumental* 1547₅
       3: 18 • **4/30/62**: 1, 3 • **7**: 27 • **19**: 18 • **22/59**: 1 • **54**: 2, 3, 5 • **60**: 2 •
       66: 6

1547²⁶ = N527   H. Newsidler: *Das erst Buch* (Nürnberg: Gutknecht, 1547)
    Lute tabulature • Brown, *Instrumental* 1547₄
       16: 56 • **49/58**: 54

B3772 (1548)   Borrono: *Intavolatura di lauto* (Venice: Scotto, 1548)
    Lute tabulature • Brown, *Instrumental* 1548₂; Bernstein, *Music*, No.68
       64: 23

Brown 1548₃   Francesco da Milano & Borrono: *Intavolatura di lauto* (Milan: Castelliono, 1548)
       64: 23

1549¹⁶   *Diphona amoena et florida* (Nürnberg: Berg & Neuber, 1549)
       7: 10 • **8**: 1 • **22/59**: 3 • **61**: 2, 3

1549³³ = V1232   Verdelot: *Tutti li madrigali* (Venice: Scotto, 1549)
    Bernstein, *Music*, No.85
       68: 4r

J681 (1549/1550)   Josquin: *Trente sixiesme livre . . . chansons* (Paris: Attaingnant, 1549)
    Heartz, *Attaingnant*, No.162
       2/10: 34, 37

Faber 1550   Faber: *Ad musicam practicam introductio* (Nürnberg: Berg & Neuber, 1550)
       4/30/62: 1 • **22/59**: 2

1551² = G2980   Gombert: *Motectorum.. Liber primus quatuor vocum* (Venice: Gardano, 1551)
    Lewis, *Gardano*, No.154
       69: 3, 5

1552²⁶ = V1233   Verdelot: *Tutti li madrigali* (Venice: Scotto, 1552)
    Bernstein, *Music*, No.115
       68: 4r

1552²⁹   *Hortus Musarum* (Louvain: Phalèse, 1552)
    Lute tabulature • Brown, *Instrumental* 1552₁₁; Vanhulst, *Catalogue*, No.13
       22/59: 1 • **54**: 5 • **65**: 6, 12

1552³⁵ = P2448   Pisador: *Libro de musica de vihuela* (Salamanca: Pisador, 1552)
    Vihuela tabulature • Brown, *Instrumental* 1552₇
       4/30/62: 1, 2, 3, 4, 6 • **22/59**: 1, 2 • **54**: 2, 3, 5 • **65**: 7

1553²   *Liber primus collectorum modulorum* (Paris: du Chemin & Goudimel, 1553)
    Lesure and Thibault, "Bibliographie . . . du Chemin"
       65: 6

1553⁴   *Psalmorum selectorum . . . Tomus primus* (Nürnberg: Berg & Neuber, 1553)
    Jackson, *Berg*
       65: 7, 11 • **66**: 8

1553⁵   *Tomus secundus Psalmorum selectorum* (Nürnberg: Berg & Neuber, 1553)
    Jackson, *Berg*
       66: 9

1553^6 *Tomus tertius Psalmorum selectorum* (Nürnberg: Berg & Neuber, 1553)
Jackson, *Berg*
55: 26 • **66**: 16

1553^{26} *I a due voci de diversi autori* (Venice: Gardano, 1553)
Lewis, *Gardano*, No.186
54: 5 • **60**: 2, 3

1553^{33} *Horti musarum secunda pars* (Louvain: Phalèse, 1553)
Lute tabulature • Brown, *Instrumental* 1553₁₀; Vanhulst, *Catalogue*, No.16
65: 6

Faber 1553   Faber: *Musices practicae Erotematum* (Basel: Petri, 1553)
6: 1, 5 • **12**: 139 • **21**: 15 • **65**: 6

1554^{32} = F2093   Fuenllana: *Libro de musica para vihuela* (Seville: Montesdoca, 1554)
Vihuela tabulature • Brown, *Instrumental* 1554₃
4/30/62: 2 • **22/59**: 2 • **54**: 5, 6 • **65**: 2

Zanger 1554   Zanger: *Practicae musicae praecepta* (Leipzig: Hantzsch, 1554)
3/19: 19 • **4/30/62**: 1, 2, 4 • **13**: 3

1555^{10} *Secundus tomus Evangeliorum* (Nürnberg: Berg & Neuber, 1555)
Jackson, *Berg*
55: 20

1555^{11} *Tertius tomus Evangeliorum* (Nürnberg: Berg & Neuber, 1555)
Jackson, *Berg*
55: 13; **69**: 1

1555^{15} = L2316   *Moteti de la Fama I à4* (Venice: Scotto, 1555)
Bernstein, *Music*, No.142
64: 5 • **69**: 2, 4

1555^{33} = V1234   Verdelot: *Tutti li madrigali* (Venice: Scotto, 1555)
Bernstein, *Music*, No.146
68: 4r

1555^{36} = A687   de Rippe: *Cinquiesme livre de tabulature de leut* (Paris: Fezandat, 1555)
Lute tabulature • Brown, *Instrumental* 1555₄
65: 2

J678 (1555)   Josquin: *Moduli à4–6, liber primus* (Paris: Le Roy & Ballard, 1555)
Lesure & Thibault, *Le Roy*, No.15*bis*
15: 3, 33–40 • **21**: 41 • **65**: 1, 2, 6 • **66**: 6

M4017 (1555)   Mouton: *Moduli . . . liber primus* (Paris: Le Roy & Ballard, 1555)
Lesure & Thibault, *Le Roy*, No.16*bis*
15: 24 • **55**: 7, 19 • **64**: 17, 19, 23 • **65**: 8

1556^{26} Festa: *I madrigali à3* (Venice: Gardano, 1556)
Lewis, *Gardano*, No.217
1/5/14: 45 • **18/40**: 55

1556^{27} = V1235   Verdelot: *Tutti li madrigali* (Venice: Gardano, 1556)
Lewis, *Gardano*, No.223
68: 4r

1556^{32} Drusina: *Tabulatura* (Frankfurt: Eichorn, 1556)
Lute tabulature • Brown, *Instrumental* 1556₂
1/5/14: 14

H4934 (1556) Heckel: *Lauten Buch* (Strasbourg: Wyss, 1556)
Lute tabulature • Brown, *Instrumental* 1556₅
1/5/14: 76 • *31*: 3 • *33*: 2 • *54*: 5

Finck 1556 Finck: *Practica musica* (Wittenberg: Rhau, 1556)
4/30/62: 1, 4 • *9/57*: 4 • *12*: 120 • *15*: 15 • *31*: 3;

Glareanus 1557 Glareanus: *Musicae Epitome* (Basel: Petri, 1557)
4/30/62: 4

1557²⁶ = V1236 Verdelot: *Tutti li madrigali* (Venice: Pietrasanta, 1557)
68: 4r

V1108 (1557) Venegas de Henestrosa: *Libro de cifra nueva* (Alcala: Brocar, 1557)
Keyboard tabulature • Brown, *Instrumental* 1557₂
1/5/14: 63 • *34*: 13 • *54*: 5

1558⁴ *Novum et insigne opus musicum* (Nürnberg: Berg & Neuber, 1558)
Brown, *Novum* (facsimile) • Jackson, *Berg*
55: 13 • *65*: 1, 2

1558¹⁰ *Premier livre des chansons a quatre parties* (Louvain: Phalèse, 1558)
Vanhulst, *Catalogue*, No.55
22/59: 2

1558²⁰ = O12 Ochsenkhun: *Tabulaturbuch auff die Lauten* (Heidelberg: Kohlen, 1558)
Lute tabulature • Brown, *Instrumental* 1558₅
54: 5 • *55*: 13 • *65*: 2, 6 • *66*: 6

1559¹ *Secunda pars magni operis musici* (Nürnberg: Berg & Neuber, 1559)
Brown, *Novum* (facsimile) • Jackson, *Berg*
65: 4, 6, 7 • *66*: 3, 6

1559² *Tertia pars magni operis musici* (Nürnberg: Berg & Neuber, 1559)
Brown, *Novum* (facsimile) • Jackson, *Berg*
3/19: 5 • *15*: 3 • *21*: 38 • *55*: 2 • *64*: 24 • *65*: 8, 12, 16

J677 [1560] Josquin: *Missa super Lhomme arme sexti toni* ([s.l.: s.n., s.d.])
4/30/62: 5

1561¹⁷ Francesco da Milano: *Intabolatura . . . Libro secondo* (Venice: Gardano, 1561)
Lute tabulature • Brown, *Instrumental* 1561₃
65: 6

Wilphlingseder 1561 Wilphlingseder: *Musica teutsch* (Nürnberg: Berg & Neuber, 1561)
Jackson, *Berg*
4/30/62: 4, 5 • *7*: 6, 8 • *9/57*: 4

1562²⁴ = H4935 Heckel: *Lautten Buch* (Strasbourg: Müller, 1562)
Lute tabulature • Brown, *Instrumental* 1562₃
1/5/14: 76 • *2/10*: 11 • *31*: 3 • *33*: 2 • *54*: 5

1562²⁸ = A688 de Rippe: *Cinquiesme . . . tabelature de luth* (Paris: Le Roy & Ballard, 1562)
Lute tabulature • Brown, *Instrumental* 1562₁₁; Lesure & Thibault, *Le Roy*
64: 23

Brown 1563₁₂ *Theatrum musicum* (Louvain: Phalèse, 1563)
Lute tabulature • Vanhulst, *Catalogue*, No.98
65: 6, 12

1563⁶ Razzi: *Laude spirituali* (Venice: Giunta, 1563)
27: 14 • *41*: 5 • *56*: 26

1563^{18} = B3773   Borrono: *La intabolatura de lauto* (Venice: Scotto, 1563)

           Lute tabulature • Brown, *Instrumental* 1563_3; Bernstein, *Music*, No.227

           64: 23

1563^{20} Francesco da Milano: *La intabolatura . . . secondo* (Venice: Scotto, 1563)

           Lute tabulature • Brown, *Instrumental* 1563_5; Bernstein, *Music*, No.245

           65: 6

Wilphlingseder 1563   Wilphlingseder: *Erotemata musices practicae* (Nürnberg: Heussler, 1563)

           4/30/62: 1, 4, 5 • **6**: 1 • **7**: 6 • **8**: 1, 2, 5 • **9/57**: 1, 2, 3, 4 • **12**: 139 •

           21: 24 • **22/59**: 2 • **31**: 3 • **43**: 3

1564^6 *I Motteti del Fiore* (Venice: Rampazetto, 1564)

           Nielsen, *Rampazetto*

           69: 1, 4

1565^{20} = V1237   Verdelot: *Tutti li madrigali* (Venice: Gardano, 1565)

           68: 4r

1566^{22} = V1238   Verdelot: *I madrigali del primo et secondo* (Venice: Merulo, 1566)

           68: 4r

1568^{22} = B1509   Becchi: *Libro primo d'intabulatura da leuto* (Venice: G. Scotto, 1568)

           Lute tabulature • Brown, *Instrumental* 1568_1; Bernstein, *Music*, No.300

           34: 39, 41, 42

1568^{23} *Luculentum theatrum musicum* (Louvain: Phalèse, 1568)

           Lute tabulature • Brown, *Instrumental* 1568_7; Vanhulst, *Catalogue*, No.123

           65: 6

Dressler 1571   Gallus Dressler: *Musicae practicae elementa* (Magdeburg: Kirchner, 1571)

           4/30/62: 1

1571^{16} *Theatrum musicum* (Louvain: Phalèse & Bellère, 1571)

           Lute tabulature • Brown, *Instrumental* 1571_6; Vanhulst, *Catalogue*, No.156

           65: 6

1578^{15} *II chansons á3* (Paris: Le Roy & Ballard, 1578)

           Lesure & Thibault, *Le Roy*, No.219

           34: 18

1578^{24} = C1   Cabezon: *Obras de musica* (Madrid: Sanchez, 1578)

           Keyboard tabulature • Brown, *Instrumental* 1578_3

           4/30/62: 1 • **54**: 5 • **65**: 4, 6 • **66**: 6

1583^{22} = A939   Ammerbach: *Orgel oder Instrument Tabulaturbuch* (Nürnberg: Gerlach, 1583)

           Keyboard tabulature • Brown, *Instrumental* 1583_2

           54: 5

1590^{30} = P644   Paix: *Selectae, artificiosae et elegantes fugae* (Lavingen: Reinmichel, 1590)

           Brown, *Instrumental* 1590_6

           4/30/62: 1 • **6**: 5 • **8**: 1 • **11**: 4 • **12**: 139 • **22/59**: 2, 3

Zacconi 1592   Zacconi: *Prattica di musica* (Venice: Polo, 1592)

           7: 35

1594^3 = P645   Paix: *Selectae, artificiosae et elegantes fugae* (Lavingen: Reinmichel, 1594)

           Brown, *Instrumental* 1594_{10}

           4/30/62: 1 • **6**: 5 • **22/59**: 2, 3

Manuscripts

A-Gla, 1	Graz, Steiermärkisches Landesarchiv, Musikalien Schuber 1
	ca.1500, perhaps in Styria • Federhofer, "Beiträge"; Staehelin, *Messen*, i
	9/57: 3
A-Kla, 4/3	Klagenfurt, Landesarchiv, GV 4/3
	Organ tabulature, c.1550
	65: 6, 7
A-LIs, 529	Linz, Bundesstaatliche Studienbibliothek, 529
	Austria, ca.1480–1490, perhaps from Sigismund's chapel at Innsbruck • Smith, "Inventory"; Strohm, "Native"
	6: 5 • **12**: 68
A-Wn, 1783	Vienna, Österreichische Nationalbibliothek, Cod.Vind.1783
	Netherlands court scribe, ca.1500–1506, for Manuel I and Marie of Portugal • Dixon, "Manuscript"; Kellman, *Treasury*, 140–141; Mantuani, *Tabulae* i, 289; van der Heide, "Symbolical"
	9/57: 5 • **11**: 1, 2, 3, 4 • **13**: 1, 3 • **20**: 4, 5 • **48**: 5
A-Wn, 4809	Vienna, Österreichische Nationalbibliothek, Cod.Vind.4809
	Netherlands court scribe, ca.1521–1525, for Raimund Fugger • Kellman, *Treasury*, 142–143
	22/59: 1, 2, 3 • **54**: 2, 5, 6
A-Wn, 4810	Vienna, Österreichische Nationalbibliothek, Cod.Vind.4810
	Netherlands court scribe, ca.1521–1525. Given to Raimund Fugger • Kellman, *Treasury*, 144–145
	60: 5
A-Wn, 11778	Vienna, Österreichische Nationalbibliothek, Cod.Vind.11778
	Netherlands court scribe, after ca.1520. Given to Raimund Fugger • Kellman, *Treasury*, 147–149
	4/30/62: 1, 2, 3, 4, 5 • **22/59**: 4 • **24**: 20, 21
A-Wn, 11883	Vienna, Österreichische Nationalbibliothek, Cod.Vind.11883
	Netherlands court scribe, early 16th century • Hudson, "Glimpse"; Kellman, "Josquin"; Kellman, *Treasury*, 150–151; Mantuani, *Tabulae*, vii, 72–73; Nowak, "Musikhandschriften"
	4/30/62: 2 • **22/59**: 3 • **31**: 2, 3 • **33**: 2
A-Wn, 15495	Vienna, Österreichische Nationalbibliothek, Supp.Mus.Hs.15495
	Netherlands court scribe, ca.1508–1511, for Maximilian I and Bianca Maria Sforza • Kellman, *Treasury*, 152–153
	6: 5 • **22/59**: 5 • **54**: 2 • **61**: 2
A-Wn, 15496	Vienna, Österreichische Nationalbibliothek, Mus.Hs.15496
	Netherlands court scribe, ca.1515–1516, for Charles of Austria • Kellman, *Treasury*, 15–155
	61: 5
A-Wn, 15497	Vienna, Österreichische Nationalbibliothek, Mus.Hs.15497
	Netherlands court scribe, ca.1515–1516, for Ulrich Pfintzing • Kellman, *Treasury*, 156–58
	61: 1

A-Wn, 15499   Vienna, Österreichische Nationalbibliothek, Mus.Hs.15499
       4/30/62: 2

A-Wn, 15500   Vienna, Österreichische Nationalbibliothek, Mus.Hs.15500
       German, dated 1544 • Kirsch, "Unbeachtetes"
       7: 33 • **15**: 32 • **55**: 7 • **64**: 8

A-Wn, 15941   Vienna, Österreichische Nationalbibliothek, Mus.Hs.15941
       Netherlands court scribe, ca.1521–1531, for the Fugger family • Kellman,
       "Josquin"; Kellman, *Treasury*, 159
       55: 7, 22, 23 • **64**: 4, 12, 15, 18 • **66**: 14, 15

A-Wn, 16746   Vienna, Österreichische Nationalbibliothek, Mus.Hs.16746
       11: 2

A-Wn, 18688   Vienna, Österreichische Nationalbibliothek, Mus.Hs.18688
       Lute tabulature by Craus, ca.1540: manuscript appendix to Judenkünig,
       1523 • Mantuani, *Tabulae*, x, 177–178; Meyer, *Sources*, iii, 125–127; *RISM*
       BVII, 352
       1/5/14: 76 • **31**: 3 • **12**: 122 • **33**: 2, 16

A-Wn, 18742   Vienna, Österreichische Nationalbibliothek, Mus.Hs.18742
       19th-century copy from Petrucci
       6: 1 • **48**: 5

A-Wn, 18743   Vienna, Österreichische Nationalbibliothek, Mus.Hs.18743
       19th-century copy from Petrucci
       15: 5

A-Wn, 18746   Vienna, Österreichische Nationalbibliothek, Mus.Hs.18746
       Signed Alamire, 1523. Given to Raimund Fugger • Kellman, *Treasury*, 160–
       62; van Benthem, "Einiger"
       1/5/14: 5

A-Wn, 18810   Vienna, Österreichische Nationalbibliothek, Mus.Hs.18810
       Munich Hofkapelle, ca.1524–1533, perhaps by Wagenrieder • Bente, *Neue*
       Wege, 264–70; Mantuani, *Tabulae*, x, 219–24; Robinson, "Vienna"; Schnei-
       der, *Collection* (facsimile)
       2/10: 22 • **12**: 57 • **61**: 2

A-Wn, 18825   Vienna, Österreichische Nationalbibliothek, Mus.Hs.18825
       Netherlands court scribe, before 1534. Given to Raimund Fugger • Kell-
       man, "Josquin"; Kellman, *Treasury*, 163
       55: 20

A-Wn, 18832   Vienna, Österreichische Nationalbibliothek, Mus.Hs.18832
       Netherlands court scribe, ca.1521–1525. Given to Raimund Fugger • Kell-
       man, *Treasury*, 164–65; Mantuani, *Tabulae*, x, 240–42
       4/30/62: 2, 3 • **6**: 5 • **8**: 1 • **13**: 3 • **22/59**: 3 • **61**: 2

A-Wn, 19286   Vienna, Österreichische Nationalbibliothek, Mus.19286
       Lute tabulature
       12: 115

A-Wn, 41950   Vienna, Österreichische Nationalbibliothek, Mus.41950 (*olim* D-WERl, 6)
       Lute tabulature, German notation: written by Adolf Blindhamer, ca.1525 •
       Kirnbauer, "A-Wn" (forthcoming); Meyer, *Sources*, ii, 301–302; Staehelin,
       "Egenolff"
       1/5/14: 44 • **3/19**: 16

B-Amp, M 18.13	Antwerp, Museum Plantijn-Moretus, M 18.13 (fragment 1) ca.1515 or later, Netherlands court scribe. Fragments used for binding • Kellman, *Treasury*, 166; van Benthem, "Alamire" **11**: 1, 2
B-Br, 228	Brussels, Bibliothèque royale Albert 1er, 228 1516–1523, Netherlands court scribe, for Margaret of Austria • *CC*, i, 91–92; Kellman, *Treasury*, 68–70; Picker, *Album* (facsimile); Picker, *Chanson* (1958); Picker, *Chanson* (1965) **1/5/14**: 15, 38, 81 • **2/10**: 7, 22, 28 • **12**: 3, 10, 72, 75 • **34**: 7
B-Br, 9126	Brussels, Bibliothèque royale Albert 1er, 9126 1505 and later: Netherlands court scribe, for Philippe the Fair and Juana of Spain • *CC*, i, 94; Kellman, *Treasury*, 72–73; van den Borren, "Inventaire", v, 70–71; van der Heide, "Symbolical" **11**: 3, 4 • **13**: 3 • **15**: 8, 9 • **21**: 4, 15 • **22/59**: 1, 2, 3 • **48**: 5 • **61**: 5 • **65**: 1, 6; *cf*. **39**: 1
B-Br, 11239	Brussels, Bibliothèque royale Albert 1er, 11239 ca.1500, probably Savoy • Picker, *Chanson* (1958); Picker, *Chanson* (1965); Picker, *Chansonnier* (facsimile); Picker, "New Look" **1/5/14**: 11, 15, 53, 56, 57, 71 • **2/10**: 4, 7, 22, 40 • **12**: 31, 75, 80, 99 • **34**: 23, 33
B-Br, 215.216	Brussels, Bibliothèque royale Albert 1er, 215.216 1503–1518: Netherlands court complex, for Charles de Clerc • *CC*, i, 91; Kellman, *Treasury*, 67; Robyns, "Musikhandschrift"; van den Borren, "Inventaire", v, 69–70 **65**: 6
B-Br, IV.90	Brussels, Bibliothèque royale Albert 1er, IV.90 Discantus book (companion to B-Br, IV.1274 and B-Tv, 94), copied in Bruges, 1511 • Huys, *Gregoire*, 34; Huys, "Recently"; Kessels, "Brussels" **1/5/14**: 31, 53, 57, 71 • **2/10**: 28, 34 • **7**: 12 • **12**: 10, 72 • **34**: 18
B-Br, IV.922	Brussels, Bibliothèque royale Albert 1er, IV.922 *Occo-Codex*, copied in the Alamire workshop, ca.1530, for Pompeius Occo • *CC*, iv, 297–98; Huys, "Unknown"; Huys, *Occo* (facsimile); Kellman, *Treasury*, 76–77 **60**: 1
B-Br, IV.1274	Brussels, Bibliothèque royale Albert 1er, IV.1274 Altus book (companion to B-Br, IV.90 and B-Tv, 94) • Huys, "Recently"; Kessels, "Brussels" **1/5/14**: 31 • **2/10**: 28, 34 • **12**: 10, 72
B-Br, Fétis 1782^A	Brussels, Bibliothèque royale Albert 1er, Fétis 1782^A A 1 L.P. (Suppl.MS.) ca. 1540 • Meyer, "Répertoire" **69**:4
B-LVu, 163	Louvain, Katholieke Universiteit van Leuven, Bibliotheek, 163 One partbook, dated 1546: destroyed in World War I **65**: 2, 6
B-Tc	Tournai, Chapitre de la Cathédrale, Archive, Missel de la Confrèrie de la Transfiguration

          Destroyed in World War II
             55: 13

B-Tv, 94   Tournai, Bibliothèque de la Ville, MS.94
          Companion to B-Br, IV.90 • Huys, *Gregoire*, 34; Huys, "Recently"; Kessels,
          "Brussels"; van den Borren, "Inventaires", 119–21
             1/5/14: 31, 53, 57, 71 • **2/10**: 28, 34 • **7**: 12 • **12**: 10, 72 • **34**: 18

B-TOs   Tongeren, Fonds Rijksarchirf Hasselt, St. Niklaas, *varia.*
          Tongeren, after 1470 • Fallows, "Tongeren"; Kellman, *Treasury*, 167;
          Schreurs, *Anthologie*; Schreurs, "Newly"
             11: 3 • **34**: 15

CH-Bu, F.VI.26c   Basel, Öffentliche Bibliothek der Universität, Musiksammlung, F.VI.26c
          Organ tabulature by Kotter, dated 1515 • *CC*, i, 26; Kmetz, *Basel*, 51–54
             1/5/14: 74 • **33**: 5

CH-Bu, F.VI.26d   Basel, Öffentliche Bibliothek der Universität, Musiksammlung, F.VI.26d
          Basel area, before 1520 • Kmetz, *Basel*, 54–57.
             6 and **8**: transcription of a list of the contents, from the title-pages

CH-Bu, F.VI.26e   Basel, Öffentliche Bibliothek der Universität, Musiksammlung, F.VI.26e
          Basel area, before 1520 • Kmetz, *Basel*, 57–59
             8: 4 [whole manuscript]

CH-Bu, F.VI.26f   Basel, Öffentliche Bibliothek der Universität, Musiksammlung, F.VI.26f
          Early 16th century • Kmetz, *Basel* 59–61
             1/5/14: 46

CH-Bu, F.VI.26h   Basel, Öffentliche Bibliothek der Universität, Musiksammlung, F.VI.26h
          Miscellaneous folios • Kmetz, *Basel*, 63–73
             54: 5

CH-Bu, F.IX.22   Basel, Öffentliche Bibliothek der Universität, Musiksammlung, F.IX.22
          Keyboard tabulature: Kotter and others in Basel and Freiburg in Breisgau,
          1513-ca.1535 • Kmetz, *Basel*, 75–84; Marx, *Tabulaturen*
             1/5/14: 14, 44, 56, 74, 76 • **12**: 80, 133 • **31**: 3 • **33**: 2, 5, 13, 18 • **34**:
          23, 28, 33

CH Bu, F.IX.25a-d   Basel, Öffentliche Bibliothek der Universität, Musiksammlung, F.IX.25a-d
          1500–1510, probably in Basel • Kmetz, *Basel*, 88–97
             4/30/62: 1, 3 • **22/59**: 1

CH-Bu, F.IX.25e-f   Basel, Öffentliche Bibliothek der Universität, Musiksammlung, F.IX.25e-f
          1500–1510, in the Basel area • Kmetz, *Basel*, 98–102
             22/59: 2, 3

CH-Bu, F IX 44   Basel, Öffentliche Bibliothek der Universität, Musiksammlung, F IX 44
          Organ tabulature: 1585–1589, Schleusingen, Saxony • Kmetz, *Basel*, 160–
          68
             65: 2

CH-Bu, F.IX.55   Basel, Öffentliche Bibliothek der Universität, Musiksammlung, F.IX.55
          Basel, ca.1500 • Kmetz, *Basel*, 176–80
             7: 33

CH-Bu, F.X.1-4   Basel, Öffentliche Bibliothek der Universität, Musiksammlung, F.X.1-4
          Basel, for Amerbach, dated 1522–1524 • *CC*, i, 29–30; Kmetz, *Basel*, 230–51
             1/5/14: 15, 31 • **2/10**: 5, 22, 28

CH-Bu, F.X.5-9   Basel, Öffentliche Bibliothek der Universität, Musiksammlung, F.X.5–9

Basel: in two layers, ca.1510 and dated 1535–1546 • *CC*, i, 30–31; Kmetz, *Basel*, 253–267

1/5/14: 28 • *2/10*: 35

CH-Bu, F.X.10   Basel, Öffentliche Bibliothek der Universität, Musiksammlung, F.X.10

Basel, owned by Ammerbach in 1510 • Kmetz, *Basel*, 268–71

12: 101 • *34*: 29

CH-Bu, F.X.17-20   Basel, Öffentliche Bibliothek der Universität, Musiksammlung, F.X.17–20

Perhaps Swiss, dated 1560 • Kmetz, *Basel*, 278–95

16: 56 • *49/58*: 54

CH-Bu, F.X.21   Basel, Öffentliche Bibliothek der Universität, Musiksammlung, F.X.21

Iselin Liederbuch, Basel, dated 1529–1575 • Kmetz, *Basel*, 296–310

34: 11 • *54*: 5

CH-Bu, F.X.22-24   Basel, Öffentliche Bibliothek der Universität, Musiksammlung, F.X.22–24

Amerbach Liederbuch, Basel, dated 1547–1551 • Kmetz, *Basel*, 311–17

7: 6 • *16*: 56 • *49/58*: 54

CH-Bu, k.k.II.32   Basel, Öffentliche Bibliothek der Universität, Musiksammlung, k.k.II.32

Supplement to *RISM* 1510. Basel, ca.1512 • Kmetz, *Basel*, 324–25

1/5/14: 7 • *31*: 3 • *33*: 2

CH-Fcu, 527   Fribourg, Bibliothèque cantonale et universitaire, Cap.Res.527

Italian lute tablature of one piece, perhaps ca.1470 • Meyer, *Sources*, i, 31

1/5/14: 20

CH-Sk, Tir.84-7   Sion, Archives du chapitre de la Cathédrale, Tir.84–7

Bassus part, perhaps from Breslau, after 1550 • Stenzl, "Musikheft"

16: 56 • *49/58*: 54

CH-SGs, 461   St. Gall, Stiftsbibliothek, 461

Fridolin Sichers Liederbuch: earlier than the date on the MS, 1545, but certainly after 1501, perhaps copied by Sicher • Fallows, *Songbook* (facsimile); Geering, *Vokalmusik*

1/5/14: 3, 5, 7, 11, 17, 19, 47, 48, 51, 58, 62, 63, 80, 92 • *2/10*: 28 • *12*: 2, 3, 23, 24, 35 • *15*: 34 • *34*: 13, 16, 26

CH-SGs, 462   St. Gall, Stiftsbibliothek, 462

Johannes Heers Liederbuch: written by Heer, of Glarus, ca.1510–1530 • Geering and Trümpy, *Liederbuch*

1/5/14: 8, 14, 44, 46, 53, 56, 76; *7*: 21 • *8*: 1 • *12*: 5, 101, 133 • *31*: 3 • *33*: 2, 11, 13, 18 • *34*: 23, 29 • *41*: 22 • *55*: 13

CH-SGs, 463   St. Gall, Stiftsbibliothek, 463

Aegidius Tschudis Liederbuch: compiled by Tschudi ca.1540 • Geering, *Vokalmusik*; Loach, *Tschudi*

1/5/14: 4, 10, 15, 26, 27, 31, 40, 44, 51, 56, 66, 69, 78, 92, 96 • *2/10*: 2, 40 • *3/19*: 2, 5, 6, 8, 10, 11, 12, 15, 16, 29, 30 • *7*: 6, 9, 10, 11, 12, 16, 19, 24, 25, 35 • *12*: 10, 80, 101, 131 • *15*: 32, 33 • *16*: 56 • *21*: 38 • *22/59*: 2, 7 • *25*: 16 • *33*: 7, 13, 14, 19 • *34*: 19, 23, 29, 33 • *36*: 36 • *41*: 22, 28 • *49/58*: 54 • *55*: 2, 3 • *64*: 4 • *65*: 1, 2, 7, 9, 12 • *66*: 6

CH-SGs, 464   St. Gall, Stiftsbibliothek, 464
                     Basel, from ca.1510 • Loach, *Tschudi*, 57–67
                     2/10: 2 • ***3/19***: 29 • ***22/59***: 2 • ***36***: 36 • ***64***: 4 • ***65***: 1, 2

CH-SGs, 530   St. Gall, Stiftsbibliothek, 530
                     Keyboard tabulature, copied by Sicher, ca.1512–1521 • Marx, "Neues";
                     Nef, *St Galler*; Warburton, "Fridolin"
                     1/5/14: 7, 11, 14, 15, 28, 33, 38, 40, 44, 50, 56, 76, 96 • ***2/10***: 16, 40 •
                     3/19: 2, 5, 7, 8, 10, 11, 12, 13, 14, 16, 18, 20 • ***6***: 3 • ***7***: 12, 27 • ***12***: 107
                     • ***21***: 38 • ***31***: 3 • ***33***: 2, 13, 18 • ***34***: 19, 23 • ***55***: 4 • ***55***: 19 • ***66***: 14

CH-Zz, S.248/284a   Zurich, Zentralbibliothek, S.248/284a
                     Keyboard tabulature, ca.1530: Supplement to Buchner's *Fundamentum*
                     7: 12

CH-Zz, 301   Zurich, Zentralbibliothek, Z.XI.301
                     Keyboard tabulature, by Hör, ca.1535
                     23: 81 • ***37***: 81

CZ-HK, Franuse   Hradec Králové, Státni vědecká knihovna, Antiphonale Jana Franuse
                     21: 12

CZ-HK, II.A.7   Hradec Králové, Státni vědecká knihovna, II.A.7
                     Specialnik. Bohemia, perhaps Prague, ca.1480–1540 • *CC*, iv, 405–406;
                     Černy, "Soupis", 40–41; Kozachek, *Repertory*
                     2/10: 35 • ***3/19***: 2, 5, 17 • ***7***: 3, 10 • ***9/57***: 1 • ***21***: 12 • ***22/59***: 4 • ***31***: 1
                     • ***32***: 2 • ***43***: 2 • ***55***: 25

CZ-HK, II.A.20   Hradec Králové, Státni vědecká knihovna, II.A.20
                     From a Confraternity at Hradec Králové, first half of the 16th century •
                     Černy, "Soupis", 52; Staehelin, "Obrechtiana"
                     1/5/14: 50 • ***3/19***: 16

CZ-HK, II.A.21   Hradec Králové, Státni vědecká knihovna, II.A.21
                     From a Confraternity at Hradec Králové, mid-16th-century • Černy,
                     "Soupis"
                     65: 11, 12

CZ-HK, II.A.26   Hradec Králové, Státni vědecká knihovna, II.A.26A
                     From a Confraternity at Hradec Králové, second half of the 16th century •
                     Černy, "Soupis"
                     65: 6 • ***66***: 6

CZ-HK, II.A.29   Hradec Králové, Státni vědecká, knihovna, II.A.29
                     From a Confraternity at Hradec Králové, dated 1556–1562
                     55: 13, 20 • ***65***: 2 • ***66***: 6

CZ-HK, II.A.41   Hradec Králové, Státni vědecká knihovna, II.A.41
                     From a Confraternity at Hradec Králové, second half of the 16th century •
                     Černy, "Soupis"
                     65: 6

CZ-Pn, II.C.7   Prague, Knihovna Národrího muzea, II.C.7
                     Canzoniere di Jistebnicz: 15th century • *Analecta Hymnodica*, i
                     29/45: 12

CZ-RO   Rokycany, Okresní muzeum, A.V.22a-b
                     From Rokycany, late 16th century or later
                     65: 2, 6

D-As, 25   Augsburg, Staats- und Stadtbibliothek, 4°.Cod.mus.25
                    ca.1500, probably Mindelheim, S. Germany • *CC*, i, pp. 14–15; Gottwald,
                    Augsburg, 220–22; Staehelin, "Augsburger"
                    1/5/14: 6, 13, 60 • *15*: 39 • *33*: 21

D-As, 142a   Augsburg, Staats- und Stadtbibliothek, 2°.Cod.142a
                    Augsburg, ca.1505–1514, once owned by Herwart • Bente, *Neue Wege*,
                    230–42; Böker-Heil, *Tenorlied*, 3–10; *CC*, i, pp. 12–13; Gottwald, *Augsburg*,
                    4–10; Jonas, *Augsburger*
                    2/10: 40 • *12*: 12, 75, 101 • *15*: 8 • *34*: 29

D-B, 190   Berlin, Staatsbibliothek zu Berlin Preussischer Kulturbesitz, Germ.oct.190
                    Probably from Utrecht, before 1500 • *RISM* BIV/3, 328–330; *CC*, i, 48–
                    49; Geering, *Organa*
                    29/45: 12

D-B, 1175   Berlin, Staatsbibliothek zu Berlin Preussischer Kulturbesitz, Mus.theor.1175
                    Treatise *De musica poetica*, by Heinrich Faber, ca.1550 • *CC*, iv, 251
                    4/30: 1 • *6*: 1 • *31*: 3 • *62*: 1 • *65*: 2

D-B, 22048   Berlin, Staatsbibliothek zu Berlin Preussischer Kulturbesitz, 22048
                    One folio, early 16th century, probably from Italy • *CC*, i, 50; Jeppesen,
                    Frottola, ii, p. 9
                    16: 21

D-B, 40021   Berlin, Staatsbibliothek zu Berlin Preussischer Kulturbesitz, Mus.40021
                    Compiled ca.1485–1500 in Torgau or Leipzig • *CC*, i, 51–52; Just, *Mensur-
                    alkodex*; Korth and Lambrecht, *Katalog*
                    1/5/14: 2 • *2/10*: 35, 44 • *3/19*: 2, 18 • *6*: 3, 4 • *7*: 27 • *12*: 81, 83, 121 •
                    21: 12, 18, 37, 38 • *22/59*: 5 • *31*: 3 • *32*: 2 • *33*: 2, 4 • *34*: 2, 32 • *46*: 6

D-B, 40026   Berlin, Staatsbibliothek zu Berlin Preussischer Kulturbesitz, Mus.40026
                    Keyboard tabulature by Kleber at Pforzheim, ca.1521–1524 • Kotterba, *Or-
                    geltabulatur*; Loewenfeld, "Kleber"
                    1/5/14: 8, 14, 74 • *2/10*: 22, 40 • *12*: 118, 133 • *21*: 38 • *31*: 1 • *33*: 5, 11, 18

D-B, 40091   Berlin, Staatsbibliothek zu Berlin Preussischer Kulturbesitz, Mus.40091
                    For S. Luigi dei Francesi, Rome, ca.1516 • *CC*, i, 53; Korth and Lam-
                    brecht, *Kataloge*; Staehelin, "Schicksal"
                    4/30: 2 • *62*: 2

D-B, 40098   see PL-Kj

D-B, 40196   Berlin, Staatsbibliothek zu Berlin Preussischer Kulturbesitz, Mus.40196
                    Roman, late 15th century: alternatively, after 1500, southern German or
                    Swiss • *CC*, iv, 269; Korth and Lambrecht, *Kataloge*
                    16: 56

D-B, 40632   Berlin, Staatsbibliothek zu Berlin Preussischer Kulturbesitz, Mus.40632
                    Lute tabulature, from Bavaria, ca.1570 • Boetticher, *Lauten*, 37–38
                    1/5/14: 76 • *31*: 3 • *33*: 2

D-B, Bohn 3   Berlin, Staatsbibliothek zu Berlin Preussischer Kulturbesitz, Bohn 3
                    Breslau. Keyboard tablature • Bohn, *Musikalische*
                    55: 13

D-B, Bohn 5   Berlin, Staatsbibliothek zu Berlin Preussischer Kulturbesitz, Bohn 5
                    Breslau, late 16th century • Bohn, *Musikalische*, 20
                    55: 13

D-B, Bohn 6   Berlin, Staatsbibliothek zu Berlin Preussischer Kulturbesitz, Bohn 6
                Keyboard tabulature, Wroclaw, dated 1567 • Bohn, *Musikalische*, 22–26
                    65: 2

D-B, Bohn 11   Berlin, Staatsbibliothek zu Berlin Preussischer Kulturbesitz, Breslau 11
                Breslau, in or before 1583 • Bohn, *Musikalische*
                    65: 2, 6

D-B, Bohn 12   Berlin, Staatsbibliothek zu Berlin Preussischer Kulturbesitz, Breslau 12
                    12: 53

D-B, Bohn 357 (i)   Berlin, Staatsbibliothek zu Berlin Preussischer Kulturbesitz, Bohn 357 (i)
                Charteris, *Newly*
                    65: 2

D-B, Bohn 357 (ii)   Berlin, Staatsbibliothek zu Berlin Preussischer Kulturbesitz, Bohn, 357 (ii)
                Charteris, *Newly*
                    65: 2

D-Bga, 7   Berlin, Geheimes Staatsarchiv, Pr. Kult, XX.HA StUB Königsberg Nr. 7 (*olim*
                Königsberg 1740) [another part may be in Vilnius]
                Copied 1537–1543, for the Königsberg court • *CC*, i, 250–251; Loge, *Messen*
                    12: 10 • **24**: 20 • **34**: 11 • **55**: 13 • **57**: 13 • **69**: 5

D-Dl, 1/D/3   Dresden, Sächsische Landesbibliothek, Musikabteilung, 1/D/3 (*olim* B.1270)
                ca.1550–1560, Wittenberg • Steude, *Dresden*, 20–24
                    65: 17

D-Dl, 1/D/6   Dresden, Sächsische Landesbibliothek, Musikabteilung, 1/D/6 (*olim* Oels 529)
                ca.1560–1580, in Silesia • Steude, *Dresden*, 24–28
                3/19: 5 • **55**: 4 • **64**: 8 • **65**: 5, 11

D-Dl, 1/D/501   Dresden, Sächsische Landesbibliothek, Musikabteilung, 1/D/501
                ca.1560, central Germany • Steude, *Dresden*, 33–35
                  64: 24

D-Dl, 1/D/505   Dresden, Sächsische Landesbibliothek, Musikabteilung, 1/D/505 (*olim* Anna-
                berg, 1248)
                St. Anna in Annaberg, or Wittenberg, ca.1530 • Noblitt, "Manuscript 505";
                Steude, *Dresden*, 221–33
                  8: 2 • **15**: 3, 13, 18, 33; *cf.* **39**: 1

D-Dl, 1/D/506   Dresden, Sächsische Landesbibliothek, Musikabteilung, 1/D/506 (*olim* Anna-
                 berg, 1126)
                St. Anna in Annaberg, or Wittenberg, ca.1530 • Noblitt, "Manuscript 506";
                Steude, *Dresden*, 233–41
                  9/57: 1

D-Dl, 1/E/24   Dresden, Sächsische Landesbibliothek, Musikabteilung, 1/E/24
                Dated 1571 • Steude, *Dresden*, 41–44
                  54: 5

D-Dl, Glashütte, V   Dresden, Sächsische Landesbibliothek, Musikabteilung, Glashütte, V
                1583–1600, in Saxony • *CC*, i, 177–178; Steude, *Dresden*, 53–61
                  55: 13, **65**: 2

D-Dl, Grimma 52   Dresden, Sächsische Landesbibliothek, Musikabteilung, Grimma 52
                Copied after 1565, probably near Leipzig • *CC*, i, 182–83; Steude, *Dresden*,
                88–89
                  54: 5

D-Dl, Grimma 53   Dresden, Sächsische Landesbibliothek, Musikabteilung, Grimma 53
ca.1560–75, Meissen, under Figulus • Steude, *Dresden*, 90–91
54: 5

D-Dl, Grimma 55   Dresden, Sächsische Landesbibliothek, Musikabteilung, Grimma 55
ca.1560–1580, Meissen • *CC*, i, 184–185; Steude, *Dresden*, 93–95
55: 13

D-Dl, Grimma 57   Dresden, Sächsische Landesbibliothek, Musikabteilung, Grimma 57
ca.1560–1580, in Meissen, with Figulus • *CC*, i, 186; Steude, *Dresden*, 101–102
65: 2

D-Dl, Grimma 59a   Dresden, Sächsische Landesbibliothek, Musikabteilung, Grimma 59a
Meissen, dated 1548–1550 • Steude, *Dresden*, 103–105
65: 7

D-Dl, Pirna IV   Dresden, Sächsische Landesbibliothek, Musikabteilung, Pirna IV
1554, for St. Marien, Pirna. ?Lost • *CC*, iv, 343–344; Hoffmann-Erbrecht,
"Chorbücher" • Steude, *Dresden*
11: 1 • **65**: 2

D-EIa   Eisenach, Stadtarchiv, Bibliothek, Kantionale
1540–1550, Eisenach • Schröder, "Eisenacher"
11: 1 • **54**: 5 • **55**: 13

D-ERu, 473/4   Erlangen, Universitätsbibliothek, 473/4
1540–1541, Heilsbronn, Cistercians • *CC*, iv, 364–365; Krautwurst, "Heils-bronner"
16: 56 • **49/58**: 54 • **55**: 13

D-F, 2   Frankfurt am Main, Stadt- und Universitätsbibliothek, Mus.fol.2
Copied in Flanders, ca.1520, • *CC*, i, 247; Hoffmann-Erbrecht, "Frank-furter"
4/30/62: 1 • **11**: 2 • **22/59**: 1, 2 • **61**: 3, 5

D-F, VII.20   Frankfurt am Main, Stadt- und Universitätsbibliothek, Fragm.lat.VII 20
Probably from the Dominican house, Frankfurt, ca.1500 • Fallows, *Catalogue*, p. 19
34: 15

D-GOl, A.98   Gotha, Forschungs- und Landesbibliothek, Chart.A.98
Dated 1545, for the Torgau court chapel, under the direction of Walter •
Blankenburg: "Verschlungenen"; Gerhardt, *Torgauer*
3/19: 2 • **65**: 2

D-GRu, 640–641   Greifswald, Universitätsbibliothek, BW.640–641 (*olim* lat.4°.67.Eb.133)
Manuscript appendix to *RISM* 1538[8], dated 1539–1588, perhaps copied
in Greifswald, by Joannes Soldeke • *CC*, iv, 395; Plamenac, "Libraries"
1/5/14: 56 • **2/10**: 29, 40 • **7**: 21 • **34**: 23 • **54**: 5 • **55**: 3, 10 • **65**: 2

D-HB, X.2   Heilbronn, Stadtbücherei, Musiksammlung, X.2
Manuscript appendix to *RISM* 1541[2]: in part a copy of the Bassus to *RISM*
[c.1535][14]. Probably ca.1550 in Frankfurt • Siegele, *Musiksammlung*, 42–48;
Staehelin, "Egenolff"
1/5/14: 44, 50, 76 • **2/10**: 40, 45, 47, 49, 50 • **3/19**: 16 • **31**: 3 • **33**: 2, 13

D-HB, XCIII–XCVI.3   Heilbronn, Stadtbücherei, Musiksammlung, XCIII–XCVI.3
                      After 1566, in Heilbronn • Siegele, *Musiksammlung*, 42–48; Staehelin,
                      "Egenolff"
                      65: 11 • **66**: 7

D-HEu, 318   Heidelberg, Universitätsbibliothek, cpg.318
                      Lambrecht, *Heidelberger*
                      4/30: 2 • **62**: 2

D-HO, 3713   Hof (Saale), Jean-Paul-Gymnasium, Paed.3713.Sbd
                      Treatise: manuscript part 2 of Faber's *Musica Practica*
                      65: 2

D-HRD, 9820   Arnsberg-Herdringen, Schlossbibliothek, 9820
                      olim Paderborn. Score: ca.1545–1550 • *CC*, iv, 402
                      12: 111 • **65**: 12 • **66**: 8

D-HRD, 9821   Arnsberg-Herdringen, Schlossbibliothek, 9821
                      olim Paderborn. Score: ca.1545–1550 • *CC*, iv, 402–403
                      56: 2 • **61**: 5

D-HRD, 9822/2–3   Arnsberg-Herdringen, Schlossbibliothek, 9822/2–3
                      olim Paderborn, mid-16th century • *CC*, iv, 404–405
                      16: 56 • **49/58**: 54

D-ISL, 124   Iserlohn, Evangelische Kirchengemiende, Varnhagen Bibliothek, IV 36 F 124
                      Binding fragments, dated 1544: perhaps Westphalia or Augsburg area • *CC*,
                      iv, 410–11
                      1/5/14: 12

D-Ju, 3   Jena, Thüringer Universitäts- und Landesbibliothek, Mus.3
                      1518–1520, Netherlands court scribe, for Frederick the Wise • Kellman,
                      Treasury, 86–89; Roediger, *Geistlichen*, 4–7
                      22/59: 1, 2, 3 • **54**: 2, 3, 6 • **61**: 2

D-Ju, 7   Jena, Thüringer Universitäts- und Landesbibliothek, Mus.7
                      ca.1513, Netherlands court scribe • Kellman, *Treasury*, 96; Roediger,
                      Geistlichen, 15–18
                      54: 5 • **61**: 3

D-Ju, 12   Jena, Thüringer Universitäts- und Landesbibliothek, Mus.12
                      ca.1520, Netherlands court scribe, for Frederick the Wise • Kellman, *Treasury*, 101; Roediger, *Geistlichen*, 24–28
                      61: 5

D-Ju, 22   Jena, Thüringer Universitäts- und Landesbibliothek, Mus.22
                      ca.1500–1505, Netherlands court scribe • *CC*, i, 294–295; Kellman,
                      Treasury, 106–109; Roediger, *Geistlichen*, 39–44; van der Heide, "Symbolical"
                      11: 12, 3, 4, 5 • **13**: 1 • **48**: 5

D-Ju, 31   Jena, Thüringer Universitäts- und Landesbibliothek, Mus.31
                      All Saints', Wittenberg, by 1520 • *CC*, i, 296; Roediger, *Geistlichen*, 73–79
                      4/30/62: 5 • **8**: 4, 5 • **31**: 3 • **33**: 2 • **54**: 3

D-Ju, 32   Jena, Thüringer Universitäts- und Landesbibliothek, Mus.32
                      All Saints', Wittenberg, ca.1500–1520 • Roediger, *Geistlichen*, 80–87
                      4/30/62: 1, 2, 3 • **9/57**: 1 • **20**: 5

D-Ju, 36   Jena, Thüringer Universitäts- und Landesbibliothek, Mus.36
        All Saints', Wittenberg, ca.1500–1520 • Roediger, *Geistlichen*, 175–79
         54: 5

D-Kl, 24   Kassel, Landesbibliothek und Murhardsche Bibliothek, 4°.Mus.24
        Kassel, dated 1534–1550 • Nagel, "Heugel", 102–105
         55: 2, 3 • **64**: 8 • **65**: 7 • **69**: 4

D-Kl, 43   Kassel, Landesbibliothek und Murhardsche Bibliothek, 4°.Mus.43
        Kassel, after 1550
         69: 1

D-Kl, 53/2   Kassel, Landesbibliothek und Murhardsche Bibliothek, 8°.Mus.53/2
        Copied by Heugel, upper Rhine. Dated 1534–1546.
         2/10: 42 • **3/19**: 32

D-LEu, 49/50   Leipzig, Universitätsbibliothek, Thomaskirche 49/50
        dated 1558, Thomaskirche • Orf, *Musikhandschriften*; Youens, *Music*
         1/5/14: 57 • **54**: 5 • **55**: 3 • **64**: 13 • **65**: 12 • **69**: 1

D-LEu, 51   Leipzig, Universitätsbibliothek, Thomaskirche 51
        Leipzig, ca.1550 • Noblitt, "Reconstruction"; Orf, *Musikhandschriften*
         4/30/62: 5 • **6**: 1, 4 • **9/57**: 4 • **11**: 4 • **13**: 2 • **16**: 56 • **22/59**: 3 • **49/58**: 54 • **64**: 24

D-LEu, 1494   Leipzig, Universitätsbibliothek, 1494
        Mensuralkodex des Magister Nicolaus Apel. Leipzig, before 1504 • Gerber, *Mensuralkodex*; Riemann, "Mensural"
         1/5/14: 44 • **3/19**: 2 • **6**: 5 • **12**: 96, 103 • **31**: 4 • **32**: 2 • **33**: 13 • **43**: 1 • **46**: 6 • **55**: 3

D-LÜh, 203   Lübeck, Bibliothek der Hansestadt, Mus.A.203
        Lübeck, after 1580
         55: 13

D-Mbs, C   Munich, Bayerische Staatsbibliothek, C
        Munich, ?by Wagenrieder, ca.1543 • Bente, *Neue Wege*, 198–206; Bente et al., *Chorbücher*, 58–59
         54: 5

D-Mbs, 7   Munich, Bayerische Staatsbibliothek, Mus.MS.7
        Bavarian court chapel. Alamire workshop, after 1511 • Bente, *Neue Wege*, 196–97 • Bente et al., *Chorbücher*, 66–67; Kellman, *Treasury*, 117
         60: 5

D-Mbs, 10   Munich, Bayerische Staatsbibliothek, Mus.MS.10
        Bavarian court chapel, ca.1520–1530 • Bente, *Neue Wege*, 66–68 • Bente et al., *Chorbücher*, 71–72 • Brown, *Munich* (facsimile)
         15: 3 • **65**: 7

D-Mbs, 12   Munich, Bayerische Staatsbibliothek, Mus.MS.12
        Bavarian court chapel, ca.1520–1530 • Bente, *Neue Wege*, 63–66 • Bente et al., *Chorbücher*, 74–75
         65: 6

D-Mbs, 16   Munich, Bayerische Staatsbibliothek, Mus.MS.16
        Bavarian court chapel, ca.1552–1556 • Bente, *Neue Wege*, 190–91 • Bente et al., *Chorbücher*, 83–85
         64: 4

D-Mbs, 19	Munich, Bayerische Staatsbibliothek, Mus.MS.19
	Bavarian court chapel, ca.1531, by Wagenrieder? • Bente, *Neue Wege*, 166–71 • Bente et al., *Chorbücher*, 87–91
	3/19: 2 • **21**: 38 • **55**: 2
D-Mbs, 25	Munich, Bayerische Staatsbibliothek, Mus.MS.25
	Bavarian court chapel, ca.1524 • Bente, *Neue Wege*, 161–64 • Bente et al., *Chorbücher*, 101–104
	65: 5
D-Mbs, 41	Munich, Bayerische Staatsbibliothek, Mus.MS.41
	Bavarian court chapel, after 1552 • Bente, *Neue Wege*, 191–93 • Bente *et al.*, *Chorbücher*, 160–62
	3/19: 2 • **64**: 12
D-Mbs, 53	Munich, Bayerische Staatsbibliothek, Mus.MS.53
	Bavarian court chapel. Italian origin, ca.1530 • Bente, *Neue Wege*, 62–63 • Bente et al., *Chorbücher*, 188–89
	24: 20, 21
D-Mbs, 65	Munich, Bayerische Staatsbibliothek, Mus.MS.65
	Bavarian court chapel, ca.1520 • Bente, *Neue Wege*, 160–61 • Bente et al., *Chorbücher*, 203–204
	60: 2
D-Mbs, 66	Munich, Bayerische Staatsbibliothek, Mus.MS.66
	Bavarian court chapel, ca.1515 • Bente, *Neue Wege*, 147–48 • Bente et al., *Chorbücher*, 204–205
	60: 2, 5
D-Mbs, 260	Munich, Bayerische Staatsbibliothek, Mus.MS.260
	Flemish, or German • Bellingham and Evans, *Bicinia* • Bente *et al.*, *Chorbücher*, 246–50
	13: 3 • **22/59**: 3 • **60**: 3 • **61**: 1, 2
D-Mbs, 266	Munich, Bayerische Staatsbibliothek, Mus.MS.266
	Lute tabulature, various sources, collected by Herwart • Göllner, *Bayerische*, 24–38 • Meyer, *Sources*, ii, 203–11; Ness, *Herwarth*; *RISM* BVII, p. 215.
	64: 24
D-Mbs, 267	Munich, Bayerische Staatsbibliothek, Mus.MS.267
	Lute tabulature, various sources, collected by Herwart • Göllner, *Bayerische*, 38–41 • Meyer, *Sources*, ii, 211–213; *RISM* BVII, p. 215
	36: 15 • **49/58**: 8 • **66**: 6
D-Mbs, 272	Munich, Bayerische Staatsbibliothek, Mus.MS.272
	Lute tabulature, German, perhaps Augsburg, after ca.1550 • Göllner, *Bayerische*, 45–49; Meyer, *Sources*, 217–219; *RISM* BVII, 217–18.
	1/5/14: 14, 44, 76 • **33**: 2, 13, 18 • **54**: 5 • **65**: 2
D-Mbs, 326	Munich, Bayerische Staatsbibliothek, Mus.MS.326
	7: 1, 33 • **16**: 56 • **49/58**: 54 • **66**: 6
D-Mbs, 352b	Munich, Bayerische Staatsbibliothek, Cim.352b (olim Mus.3725)
	Buxheim Orgelbuch: keyboard tabulature. Munich or Switzerland, ca.1460, with additions • Göllner, *Bayerische*, ii, 159–71; Wallner, *Buxheimer* (facsimile); Wallner, *Buxheim*
	34: 9

D-Mbs, 510   Munich, Bayerische Staatsbibliothek, Mus.MS.510
               For Cardinal M. Lang, before 1519 • Bente, *Neue Wege*, 206–207 • Bente
               et al., *Chorbücher*, 252–53
                   54: 2, 5 • *56*: 2 • *60*: 1, 4

D-Mbs, 810   Munich, Bayerische Staatsbibliothek, cgm 810 (formerly Mus.3232)
               Schedelsche Liederbuch: Nürnberg, ca.1456–1470, copied by Schedel • Bente
               et al., *Chorbücher*, 4–12 • Wackernagel, *Liederbuch* (facsimile)
                   1/5/14: 54

D-Mbs, 1511b   Munich, Bayerische Staatsbibliothek, Mus.MS.1511b
               Lute tabulature, Italian notation. ca.1550, perhaps Italian • Göllner, *Bayer-
               ische*, 79–84 • Meyer, *Sources*, ii, 221–23; Ness, *Herwart*
                   47: 23

D-Mbs, 1516   Munich, Bayerische Staatsbibliothek, Mus.MS.1516
               Probably after ca.1530, in Munich • Göllner, *Bayerische*, 92–101; Whisler,
               Munich
                   1/5/14: 14 • *12*: 3, 4, 10, 12, 50, 72, 99, 103, 108, 109, 111, 129, 130,
                   131, 132, 133, 134 • *33*: 6, 7, 10, 15, 18

D-Mbs, 1536   Munich, Bayerische Staatsbibliothek, Mus.MS.1536
               Bad Reichenhall, dated 1583 • Göllner, *Bayerische*, 101–21
                   55: 13

D-Mbs, 3154   Munich, Bayerische Staatsbibliothek. Mus.MS.3154
               Codex der Magister Nikolaus Leopold von Innsbruck. Late C15 to 1511 • Bente
               et al., *Chorbücher*, 299–311; Noblitt, "Chorbuch"; Noblitt, "Datierung"
                   1/5/14: 20, 56, 78 • *3/19*: 2 • *4/30/62*: 4 • *6*: 1 • *15*: 13 *24* :14 " *33*:
                   9, 44 • *34*: 3, 23 • *43*: 1 • *46*: 7

D-Mu, Art.401 Munich, Universitätsbibliothek, Art.401
               Appendix to Antico editions. Copied ca.1536–1545, perhaps in Augsburg
               • Gottwald, *München*, 102–11
                   65: 2, 3, 4, 6 • *66*: 3, 4, 5

D-Mu, 718   Munich, Universitätsbibliothek, Mus.4°.718
               Lute and viol tabulature, with a mathematical treatise, written by Jorg
               Wetzell of Ingolstadt, dated 1523–1524 • Gottwald, *München*, 55–62
                   1/5/14: 76 • *31*: 3 • *33*: 2 • *54*: 5

D-Mu, 239   Munich, Universitätsbibliothek, 2°.Art.239
                   11: 2

D-Mu, 322–325 Munich, Universitätsbibliothek, Mus.8°.322–325
               For Glarean, written by Besard, 1527 • Gottwald, *München*, 70–75
                   1/5/14: 62 • *2/10*: 39 • *3/19*: 2, 5, 11, 12, 16, 30 • *7*: 6, 9, 10, 11, 12,
                   25 • *8*: 1 • *15*: 32 • *34*: 25 • *55*: 2 • *65*: 9

D-Mu, 326–327 Munich, Universitätsbibliothek, Mus.8°.326–327
               Southern Germany, ca.1543 • Finscher, "Walter"; Gottwald, *München*, 75–
               79
                   3/19: 2 • *16*: 56; cf.*49/58*: 54 • *65*: 6, 7

D-Mu, 328–331 Munich, Universitätsbibliothek, Mus.8°.328–331 (= Cim.44c)
               Munich, copied by Wagenrieder, after 1523 • Bente, *Neue Wege*, 255–64;
               Gottwald, *München*, 83–97; Smithers, "Textual"
                   12: 57

D-Ngm, 83795   Nürnberg, Germanisches National-Museum, Bibliothek, 83795
    Torgau, ca.1539–1548, copied in part by Walter • Gerhardt, *Torgau*, 7–21
    3/19: 2 • *7*: 10, 21 • *22/59*: 1 • *54*: 5

D-Rp, A.R.69   Regensburg, Bischöfliche Zentralbibliothek, Proske-Musikbibliothek, A.R.69
    55: 20

D-Rp, A.R.70   Regensburg, Bischöfliche Zentralbibliothek, Proske-Musikbibliothek, A.R.70
    55: 13

D-Rp, A.R.775–777   Regensburg, Bischöfliche Zentralbibliothek, Proske-Musikbibliothek, A.R.775–777
    Regensburg, dated 1579
    65: 2

D-Rp, A.R.844–848   Regensburg, Bischöfliche Zentralbibliothek, Proske-Musikbibliothek, A.R.844–848
    Regensburg, dated 1573–1577
    69: 1

D-Rp, A.R.861–862   Regensburg, Bischöfliche Zentralbibliothek, Proske-Musikbibliothek, A.R.861–862
    Regensburg, dated 1577
    64: 24

D-Rp, A.R.863–870   Regensburg, Bischöfliche Zentralbibliothek, Proske-Musikbibliothek, A.R.863–870
    Regensburg, probably 1570s.
    69: 1

D-Rp, A.R.875–877   Regensburg, Bischöfliche Zentralbibliothek, Proske-Musikbibliothek, A.R.875–877
    Regensburg, dated 1568–1579
    55: 20

D-Rp, A.R.878–882   Regensburg, Bischöfliche Zentralbibliothek, Proske-Musikbibliothek, A.R.878–882
    Regensburg, dated 1569–1572
    4/30/62: 1

D-Rp, A.R.883–886   Regensburg, Bischöfliche Zentralbibliothek, Proske-Musikbibliothek, A.R.883–886
    Regensburg, dated 1573–1579
    55: 13

D-Rp, A.R.891–892   Regensburg, Bischöfliche Zentralbibliothek, Proske-Musikbibliothek, A.R.891–892
    65: 6 • *66*: 6

D-Rp, A.R.893   Regensburg, Bischöfliche Zentralbibliothek, Proske-Musikbibliothek, A.R.893
    65: 1

D-Rp, A.R.940–941   Regensburg, Bischöfliche Zentralbibliothek, Proske-Musikbibliothek, A.R.940–941
    Wittenberg, 1557–1559, by Wolfgang K•ffer • Brennecke, *Handschrift*
    1/5/14: 76 • *16*: 56 • *31*: 3 • *33*: 2 • *49/58*: 54 • *55*: 13, 21 • *64*: 24

D-Rp, B.211–215   Regensburg, Bischöfliche Zentralbibliothek, Proske-Musikbibliothek, B.211–215
    S. Germany or Austria, dated 1538–1543 • Mohr, *Handschrift*
    15: 32 • *69*: 1

D-Rp, B.220–222   Regensburg, Bischöfliche Zentralbibliothek, Proske-Musikbibliothek, B.220–222

Mid 16th century, perhaps from Salzburg • Mohr, *Handscrift*

4/30/62: 2, 3 • *11*: 4 • *22/59*: 3, 4 • *54*: 1 • *56*: 4 • *65*: 12 • *66*: 16

D-Rp. C.100   Regensburg, Bischöfliche Zentralbibliothek, Proske-Musikbibliothek, C.100 (*olim* A.R.773)

Regensburg, dated 1560

4/30/62: 1, 2 • *15*: 34

D-Rp, C.120   Regensburg, Bischöfliche Zentralbibliothek, Proske-Musikbibliothek, C.120

Pernner Kodex. S. Germany or Tyrol, early 1520s • Birkendorf, *Pernner*; Haberkamp & Scharnagl, *Bischöfliche*

1/5/14: 11, 14, 31, 38 • *2/10*: 5, 9, 15, 16, 21, 22, 28 • *12*: 2, 3, 23, 25, 55 • *21*: 38 • *33*: 18 • *64*: 24 • *65*: 2, 8, 11 • *66*: 6

D-Rtt, 76   Regensburg, Fürst Thurn und Taxis Hofbibliothek, 76

Saxony, ca.1530–1540 • Gottwald, "Neuentdeckte"

7: 33 • *55*: 3

D-ROu, 40   Rostock, Universitätsbibliothek, Mus.40

22/59: 3 • *54*: 5

D-ROu, 49   Rostock, Universitätsbibliothek, Mus.49

Hamburg, dated 1566, collected by Jacob Praetorius • Hoffmann, "Opus"

54: 5

D-ROu, 71/2   Rostock, Universitätsbibliothek, Mus.71/2

?Schwerin, after 1550

66: 6

D-Sl, 25   Stuttgart, Württembergische Landesbibliothek, Mus.fol.I.25

Stuttgart, ca.1540 • Gottwald, *Stuttgart*, 46–48

55: 13

D-Sl, 34   Stuttgart, Württembergische Landesbibliothek, Mus.fol.I.34

Stuttgart, ca.1540 • Gottwald, *Stuttgart*, 62–63

55: 26

D-Sl, 44   Stuttgart, Württembergische Landesbibliothek, Mus.fol.I.44

4/30/62: 2 • *8*: 5 • *54*: 5

D-Sl, 45   Stuttgart, Württembergische Landesbibliothek, Mus.fol.I.45

11: 5 • *61*: 3

D-Sl, 46   Stuttgart, Württembergische Landesbibliothek, Mus.fol.I.46

4/30/62: 3; *60*: 5

D-Sl, 47   Stuttgart, Württembergische Landesbibliothek, Mus.fol.I.47

Wittenberg, ca.1507. Gottwald, *Stuttgart*, 81–82

4/30/62: 5 • *8*: 3

D-Usch, 237a-d   Ulm, von Schermar'sche Familienstiftung, Bibliothek, 237a-d

German. Dated 1551, some earlier.

1/5/14: 20, 76 • *3/19*: 2, 33 • *4/30/62*: 6 • *12*: 10 • *15*: 8 • *21*: 7, 15, 22, 38 • *31*: 3 • *33*: 2, 9 • *54*: 5 • *69*: 5

D-W, A.Aug.2°   Wolfenbüttel, Herzog August Bibliothek, A.Aug.2°

Munich, for the court, dated 1519 and 1520

54: 5

D-W, 287   Wolfenbüttel, Herzog August Bibliothek, Guelf.287.extrav.
    France, 1460s • Gutiérez-Denhoff, *Wolfenbütteler*
    1/5/14: 13, 20, 54 • ***12***: 97, 99 • ***33***: 9, 17 • ***34***: 9, 12, 15

D-WERl, 6   Now at A-Wn, Mus.41950 (*q.v.*)

D-WRs, B   Weimar, Stadtbücherei, B
    Torgau, ca.1540–1544. Perhaps intended for Wittenberg • Gerhardt, *Torgauer*, 25–29
    54: 5

D-Z, XIII,3   Zwickau, Ratsschulbibliothek, XIII,3
    Perhaps Zwickau, after 1550
    54: 5

D-Z, XXXIII,34   Zwickau, Ratsschulbibliothek, XXXIII,34
    Zwickau, late 16th century
    64: 13 • ***65***: 6

D-Z, LXXIII,1   Zwickau, Ratsschulbibliothek, LXXIII,i
    Zwickau, late 16th century
    46: 5

D-Z, LXXVIII,3   Zwickau, Ratsschulbibliothek, LXXVIII,3
    Zwickau, owned by Stephen Roth, ca.1533–1545 • Brown, "Zwickau"; Vollhardt, "Bibliographie"
    1/5: 91 • ***1/5/14***: 44, 45, 49, 50, 52, 53, 57, 59, 62, 64, 65, 66, 69, 76, 77 • ***2/10***: 44 • ***3/19***: 16 • ***12***: 101 • ***14***: 82 • ***31***: 3 • ***33***: 2, 13 • ***34***: 28, 29 • ***46***: 5

D-Z, LXXIX,1   Zwickau, Ratsschulbibliothek, LXXIX,1
    Zwickau, before 1546
    7: 21

D-Z, LXXXI,2   Zwickau, Ratsschulbibliothek, LXXXI,2
    Wittenberg, before 1550 • Vollhardt, "Bibliographie", 33–38
    65: 11, 12

D-Z, XCIV,1   Zwickau, Ratsschulbibliothek, XCIV,1
    Dated 1590, perhaps in Zwickau • Vollhardt, "Bibliographie", 16
    65: 2

D-Z, CXIX,1   Zwickau, Ratsschulbibliothek, CXIX,1
    Zwickau, before 1546 • *RISM* BIV/3, 407–11
    22/59: 4

DK-Kk, 291   Copenhagen, Det kongelige Bibliotek, Thott.291.8°
    Copenhagen Chansonnier. France, ca.1470–1480 • *CC*, i, 162–63; Jeppesen, *Kopenhagener*; Thibault and Droz, *Chansonnier*
    1/5/14: 20 • ***12***: 98, 139 • ***33***: 9 • ***34***: 9, 15

DK-Kk, 1848   Copenhagen, Det kongelige Bibliotek, Ny.kgl.sam.1848.2°
    Lyons, 1520s • Christoffersen, *French*; Glahn, "Fransk"; Plamenac, "Postscript"; Stevenson, "Toledo"
    1/5/14: 8, 12, 20, 26, 37, 44, 53, 54, 56, 57, 71, 77, 83, 87 • ***2/10***: 37, 51 • ***3/19***: 3 • ***7***: 12 • ***12***: 104 • ***31***: 1 • ***33***: 9, 11, 13, 17, 20 • ***34***: 9, 15, 23 • ***41***: 22

DK-Kk, 1872   Copenhagen, Det kongelige Bibliotek, gly.kgl.sam.1872
    Dates of 1541–1543, for the Copenhagen court • *CC*, i, 164–165; van Crevel, *Coclico*, 324–40; Foss, "Stemmeböger"; Glahn, "Musik"
    55: 13 • ***65***: 1, 2, 6 • ***66***: 6

DK-Kk, 1873 | Copenhagen, Det kongelige Bibliotek, gly.kgl.sam.1873
1556 and after, for the Copenhagen court chapel • *CC*, i, 165–166; van Crevel, *Coclico*, 337–344
55: 13 • **65**: 6

E-Bbc, 454 | Barcelona, Biblioteca de Cataluña, 454
Has dates between 1525 and 1535 • *CC*, i, pp. 17–18; Anglès, *Música*, I, 112–115; Pedrell, *Catàlech*; Ros-Fàbregas, *Manuscript*
1/5/14: 56 • *3/19*: 2, 7, 17, 18 • *7*: 27 • *21*: 28, 38 • *34*: 23 • *54*: 5 • **55**: 13 • **61**: 2 • **65**: 14; **66**: 14

E-Bbc, 681 | Barcelona, Biblioteca de Cataluña, 681
Early 16th century, from Vich • *CC*, i, pp. 19–20; Anglès, *Música*, i
7: 33 • **66**: 6

E-Boc, 5 | Barcelona, Biblioteca Orfeó Català, 5
Late 15th century • *CC*, i, pp. 21–22; Anglès, *Música*, i, 115
3/19: 2, 20 • *4/30/62*: 1, 4 • **6**: 5 • **7**: 10 • *31*: 4, 5 • **65**: 14

E-E, IV.a.24 | El Escorial, Real Monasterio de San Lorenzo, IV.a.24
Milan or Naples, in 1460s • Hanen, *Chansonnier*; Kultzen, *Codex*; Pirrotta, "Alcuni"; Slavin, "Origins"; Southern, "El Escorial"
26: 5

E-Mp, 2-I-5 | Madrid, Palacio Real, Biblioteca y Archivo, 2-I-5
Cancionero de Palacio: Spanish, after 1500 • Anglés, *Music . . . Cancionero*; Ferrari-Barassi, "Alcune"
1/5/14: 4 • *16*: 56 • *17/42*: 35 • *18/40*: 29, 58**25**: 35 • **26**: 58 • *33*: 19 • *36*: 20 • *49/58*: 54 • *50*: 39

E-Mmarch, R.6832 | Madrid, private collection of March y Severa, R.6832 (*olim* E-Mmc, 607)
Spanish, late 16th century • Morales, *Opera Omnia*, xv, 57–59
55: 1, 19, 21 • **69**: 5

E-Sc, 1 | Seville, Biblioteca Capitular y Colombina, 1
Anglés, "Sevilla"
4/30/62: 6 • **65**: 2 • **66**: 6

E-Sc, 5-I-43 | Seville, Biblioteca Capitular y Colombina, 5-I-43
Belongs with F-Pn, nouv.acq.fr.4379. Neapolitan?, ca.1480. Owned by Colón • Boorman, "Limitations"; Moerk, *Seville*; Plamenac, "Facsimile"; Plamenac, "Reconstruction"
1/5/14: 8, 12, 13, 20, 42, 52, 60, 66, 78 • *2/10*: 16 • *12*: 68, 78, 79, 84, 90, 92, 95, 97, 106 • *33*: 3, 9, 11, 14, 21 • *34*: 6, 12, 15

E-Sc, 5-5-20 | Seville, Biblioteca Capitular y Colombina, 5-5-20
1/5/14: 62 • *34*: 25

E-Sc, 7-I-28 | Seville, Biblioteca Capitular y Colombina, 7-I-28
Cancionero musical de la Colombina: Spanish, perhaps in the 1490s • Haberkamp, *Weltliche*
1/5/14: 4 • *2/10*: 28 • *12*: 99 • *33*: 19

E-SA, 34 | Salamanca, Catedral, Archivo Musical, MS.34
55: 13

E-SE, s.s. | Segovia, Archivo Capitular de la Catedral, s.s.
Spanish, ca.1500, perhaps for Segovia • Anglès, "Manuscrit"; Baker, *Segovia*; Perales de la Cal, *Cancionero* (facsimile)

1/5: 91 • *1/5/14*: 4, 8, 9, 10, 12, 27, 38, 39, 42, 44, 49, 50, 52, 56, 57, 58, 60, 62, 73, 83, 92, 96 • *2/10*: 23, 35, 39 • *3/19*: 2, 18 • *4/30/62*: 5 • *6*: 3 • *7*: 27 • *12*: 49, 60, 80, 101, 120 • *14*: 82 • *15*: 11 • *21*: 38 • *31*: 1, 3 • *33*: 2, 11, 13, 19, 20, 21 • *34*: 3, 5, 6, 17, 23, 25, 28, 29, 33 • *43*: 1 • *54*: 6 • *65*: 14

E-Tc, 9   Toledo, Catedral, Archivo y Biblioteca Capítulares, 9
       Toledo, 1558
         4/30/62: 1 • *22/59*: 1, 3 • *54*: 2, 6

E-Tc, 10   Toledo, Catedral, Archivo y Biblioteca Capítulares, 10
       Toledo, ca.1544–1545
         3/19: 11 • *15*: 8 • *65*: 6, 12 • *66*: 6

E-Tc, 13   Toledo, Catedral, Archivo y Biblioteca Capítulares, 13
       Toledo, 1553–1554 • Lenaerts, "Manuscrit"; Stevenson, "Toledo"
         15: 24 • *55*: 13 • *64*: 21 • *65*: 3

E-Tc, 16   Toledo, Catedral, Archivo y Biblioteca Capítulares, 16
         54: 5 • *60*: 4

E-Tc, 19   Toledo, Catedral, Archivo y Biblioteca Capítulares, 19
         4/30/62: 2

E-Tc, 21   Toledo, Catedral, Archivo y Biblioteca Capítulares, 21
       Toledo, dated 1549
         3/19: 18 • *4/30/62*: 1 • *7*: 27

E-Tc, 22   Toledo, Catedral, Archivo y Biblioteca Capítulares, 22
         46: 5

E-Tc, 23   Toledo, Catedral, Archivo y Biblioteca Capítulares, 23
       Snow, "Toledo"
         15: 3 • *54*: 5 • *55*: 20 • *60*: 1 • *65*: 2

E-Tc, 27   Toledo, Catedral, Archivo y Biblioteca Capítulares, 27
       Toledo, dated 1550
         4/30/ 62: 3 • *22/59*: 2

E-TZ, 2   Tarazona, Catedral, Archivo Capitular, 2
       Sevillano, "Tarazona"
         3/19: 18 • *7*: 27 • *65*: 14

E-TZ, 8   Tarazona, Catedral, Archivo Capitular, 8
         65: 2

E-V, 5   Valladolid, Catedral, Archivo Musical, 5
       After 1550, Valladolid
         65: 12

E-V, 15   Valladolid, Catedral, Archivo Musical, 15
       After ca.1520, possibly Italian • Anglés, "Valladolid"
         64: 19

E-V, 16   Valladolid, Catedral, Archivo Musical, 16
       Mid-16th-century Spanish, perhaps Valladolid • Anglés, "Valladolid"
         65: 6

E-V, 17   Valladolid, Catedral, Archivo Musical, 17
       Late 16th century, perhaps Valladolid • Anglés, "Valladolid"
         65: 6

Eir-Dtc, D.3.30/I   Dublin, Trinity College, MS D.3.30/I
                      Lute tabulature. England, after 1600 • Ward, "Lute"
                           34: 14, 43

F-Am, 162   Amiens, Bibliothèque Municipale, 162
                      ca.1500, probably French • *RISM* BIV/3, 429–434; *CC*, i, p. 5; Hofmann-
                      Brandt, "Neue"
                           3/19: 28 • **41**: 22

F-CA, 4   Cambrai, Bibliothèque municipale, 4
                      ca.1526–30, from Cambrai • *CC*, i, 120–121
                           11: 2 • **54**: 5 • **60**: 1, 3

F-CA, 18   Cambrai, Bibliothèque municipale, 18 (20)
                      ca.1520, Cambrai cathedral • *CC*, i, 123; Cousssemaker, *Notice*; Josquin,
                      Werken, Missen, Deel iii, p. vi
                           4/30/62: 3 • **9/57**: 5 • **24**: 21 • **31**: 1 • **48**: 5 • **54**: 5

F-CA, 125–128   Cambrai, Bibliothèque municipale, 125–128
                      Dated 1542, perhaps Bruges • Bartha, "Bibliografisches"; Diehl, *Cambrai*
                           3/19: 7, 16 • **12**: 10 • **15**: 13 • **21**: 38 • **41**: 22 • **54**: 5 • **55**: 1, 13 • **69**:
                           1

F-Dm, 517   Dijon, Bibliothèque municipale, 517
                      France, the Loire valley, perhaps the Burgundian court, ca.1470–1475 • *CC*,
                      i, 168–169; Droz, Thibault & Rokseth, *Chansonniers*; Morelot, "Notice";
                      Picker, "Dijon"; Plamenac, *Dijon* (facsimile)
                           1/5/14: 13, 17, 20, 45, 54; **12**: 98, 99, 139 • **33**: 9, 12, 17 • **34**: 8, 9,
                           15

F-Pn, 27   Paris, Bibliothèque nationale, Département de la Musique, Rés. Vmd.27 (*olim*
                      Tl.1 in the possession of the Comtesse de Chambure)
                      Lute tabulature. Northern Italy, probably the Veneto, early C16 • Ivanoff,
                      Pesaro, 303–14; Lesure, *Tablature* (facsimile); Meyer, *Sources*, i, 113–16; Thi-
                      bault, "Manuscrit"; Underwood, *Renaissance*, 113–54
                           1/5/14: 8, 9, 44, 76 • **16**: 2, 4, 8, 15, 16, 19, 20, 22, 23, 24, 29, 31,
                           53, 60, 62, • **17/42**: 8, 11, 31 • **18/40**: 5, 8, 32, 43, 48 • **23/37**: 11,
                           68, 70, 72, 79 • **25**: 12, 28, 30, 34, 35, 45 • **26**: 20, 26, 33, 35, 47, 48,
                           62 • **31**: 3 • **33**: 2, 11, 13 • **34**: 17 • **36**: 20, 51, 62 • **41**: 52 • **47**: 39,
                           41 • **48**: 42 • **49/58**: 6, 24, 29, 38, 41, 42, 43, 49, 51, 53, 58, 66 • **50**:
                           24, 39, 52

F-Pn, 57   Paris, Bibliothèque nationale, Département de la Musique, Rés. Vmc.57
                      Chansonnier Nivelle de la Chaussée: France, ca.1460s–1470s • Higgins, *Chan-
                      sonnier* (facsimile)
                           1/5/14: 54 • **12**: 98, 99 • **33**: 17 • **34**: 15

F-Pn, 429   Paris, Bibliothèque nationale, Département de la Musique, Rés.429
                      Lute intabulation. Italian notation. ca.1560 • Meyer, *Sources*, i, 71–75; *RISM*
                      BVII, p. 269
                           65: 6

F-Pn, 676   Paris, Bibliothèque nationale, Département de la Musique, Rés.Vm[7].676
                      Northern Italy, probably Mantua, 1502 • Bridgman, "Manuscrit"
                           1/5/14: 2, 13, 20, 44, 56, 76 • **12**: 101 • **16**: 2, 10, 12, 19, 22, 28, 56

• **18/40**: 8, 29, 38, 43, 51 • **23/37**: 1, 49 • **25**: 34, 61 • **26**: 45, 58 • **33**: 2, 9, 13 • **34**: 2, 23, 29 • **36**: 20, 57 • **47**: 41 • **48**: 20 • **49/58**: 21, 41, 43, 54, 56

F-Pn, 851   Paris, Bibliothèque nationale, Département de la Musique, Rés.Vma.851

The Bourdeney manuscript: central Italy (?Parma), late 16th century • Bridgman & Lesure, "Anthologie"; Mischiati, "Bourdeney"

4/30/62: 1, 2, 5

F-Pn, 1597   Paris, Bibliothèque nationale, f.fr.1597

Lorraine, ca.1500–1508 • Bernstein, "Notes"; Couchman, "Lorraine"; Shipp, *Chansonnier*

1/5/14: 55, 56, 57, 59, 71, 81, 83 • **2/10**: 5, 28, 40, 46, 48 • **3/19**: 6, 9, 28 • **12**: 5, 24, 121, 128 • **21**: 11 • **33**: 4, 20 • **34**: 7, 23 • **41**: 22

F-Pn, 1817   Paris, Bibliothèque nationale, nouv.acq.fr.1817

Accompanies I-CT, 95–96 • *RISM* BIV/5, pp. 115–120; Atlas, *Giulia*; Cummings, "Giulio"; Gröber, *Liederbüchern*; Pannella, *Composizioni*; Renier, "Mazzetto"

1/5/14: 26, 34, 38, 40, 41 • **2/10**: 5, 11, 28, 34 • **4/30/62**: 6 • **7**: 11, 33 • **12**: 6, 9, 21, 47, 62, 106, 107 • **15**: 3, 8, 13, 16 • **21**: 22 • **23/37**: 80 • **34**: 11, 19, 22 • **55**: 1 • **64**: 18 • **65**: 8, 9 • **66**: 8

F-Pn, 2973   Paris, Bibliothèque nationale, Rothschild 2973

Chansonnier Cordiforme: Savoy or Geneva, 1470s • Kottick, *Music*; Thibault & Fallows, *Chansonnier*

1/5/14: 20, 54, 60; **12**: 93, 97 • **33**: 9, 17, 21 • **34**: 9, 12

F-Pn, 4379   Paris, Bibliothèque nationale, nouv.acq.fr.4379

The first part accompanies E-Sc, 5-I-43. Probably Neapolitan, ca.1480. Owned by Colón • Boorman, "Limitations"; Moerk, *Seville*; Plamenac, "Facsimile"; Plamenac, "Reconstruction"

1/5/14: 9, 54 • **12**: 98, 101 • **33**: 17 • **34**: 17, 29

F-Pn, 4599   Paris, Bibliothèque nationale, nouv.acq.fr.4599

Accompanies I-MOe, α.F.2.29, (*q.v.*)

65: 11 • **66**: 6

F-Pn, 9346   Paris, Bibliothèque nationale, f.fr.9346

Bayeux manuscript: France, ca.1500 • Gérold, *Bayeux*; Reese and Karp, "Monophony"; Rahn, *Melodic*

1/5/14: 14, 55, 71 • **2/10**: 4, 34, 51 • **33**: 18

F-Pn, 12744   Paris, Bibliothèque nationale, f.fr.12744

Monophonic songs. France, ca.1500 • Paris and Gevaert, *Chansons*; Rahn, *Melodic*

1/5/14: 10, 22, 31, 79 • **2/10**: 4, 5, 6, 9, 12, 51 • **12**: 24, 106 • **34**: 18

F-Pn, 15123   Paris, Bibliothèque nationale, f.fr.15123

Chansonnier Pixerécourt: Florence, before ca.1484 • Pease, *Edition*

1/5/14: 4, 8, 9, 13, 20, 33, 42, 54, 59, 60 • **12**: 95, 96, 97, 98 • **33**: 3, 9, 11, 17, 19, 21 • **34**: 6, 9, 12, 15, 17

F-VE, 698   Vesoul, Bibliothèque municipale, 698

Lute tabulature, Italian and French notations. German, ca.1598. Lost • Meyer, *Sources*, i, 162–70

65: 6

GB-Cmc, 1760   Cambridge, Magdalene College, Pepys 1760
　　　　　　　　ca.1510, France • Braithwaite, *Introduction*; Brown, *Cambridge* (facsimile);
　　　　　　　　Merritt, "Chanson"
　　　　　　　　　7: 11 • *12*: 10 • *41*: 22 • *55*: 8, 9, 13, 22a • *64*: 1

GB-Ctc, R.2.71   Cambridge, Trinity College, R.2.71
　　　　　　　　ca.1470–1480, French • *CC*, iv, 316–317; Fallows, "Johannes"
　　　　　　　　　1/5/14: 42 • *34*: 6

GB-Lbl, Eg.3051   London, British Library, Eg.3051
　　　　　　　　Belongs with US-Wc, 2.1.M 6 Case • Jeppesen, "Frottolenhandschriften";
　　　　　　　　Rifkin, "New"; Staehelin, "Florentiner"
　　　　　　　　　1/5/14: 76 • *16*: 20, 21, 56 • *17/42*: 8, 11, 35 • *18/40*: 31, 37, 49, 50,
　　　　　　　　　51, 59 • *23/37*: 18, 33, 42, 46, 47, 61, 83, 84, 85, 86 • *25*: 31, 35, 56
　　　　　　　　　• *26*: 9, 11, 12, 22, 51 • *31*: 3 • *33*: 2 • *35*: 43 • *36*: 21 • *49/58*: 10, 24,
　　　　　　　　　54, 68 • *50*: 24, 39 • *56*: 67

GB-Lbl, Harl.5043   London, British Library, Harleian MS. 5043
　　　　　　　　　55: 7 • *64*: 19, 23

GB-Lbl, Roy.8.G.vii   London, British Library, Roy.8.G.vii
　　　　　　　　Netherlands court, ca.1513–1525, eventually for Henry VIII and Catharine
　　　　　　　　of Aragon • Kellman, "Josquin"; Kellman, *London* (facsimile); Kellman,
　　　　　　　　Treasury, 110–111
　　　　　　　　　15: 8 • *55*: 9, 13, 22, 22a23 • *64*: 1 • *66*: 12

GB-Lbl, Roy.20.A.xvi   London, British Library, Roy.20.A.xvi
　　　　　　　　Paris, probably court, 1480s–1490s • Brown, *London* (facsimile); Litterick,
　　　　　　　　Manuscript; Urkevich, *Anne*
　　　　　　　　　1/5/14: 12, 38, 55, 57, 59, 81, 83 • *2/10*: 46, 48 • *12*: 72, 80 • *33*: 20
　　　　　　　　　• *34*: 7, 32, 33

GB-Lbl, Add.4911   London, British Library, Additional MS. 4911
　　　　　　　　Scottish Treatise, *The art of music*, dated 1558 • Maynard, "Heir"
　　　　　　　　　4/30/62: 1 • *6*: 5 • *22*: 3 • *31*: 3 • *56*: 1

GB-Lbl, Add.11582   London, British Library, Additional MS. 11582
　　　　　　　　Compiled by Burney
　　　　　　　　　43: 1 • *65*: 12

GB-Lbl, Add.12532   London, British Library, Additional MS. 12532
　　　　　　　　　7: 9

GB-Lbl, Add.19583   London, British Library, Additional MS. 19583
　　　　　　　　Probably Ferrara. Related to I-MOe, α.N.1.2, *q.v.* • Bernstein, "Cou-
　　　　　　　　ronne"
　　　　　　　　　64: 10 • *65*: 7, 11 • *66*: 6, 15

GB-Lbl, Add.31922   London, British Library, Additional MS. 31922
　　　　　　　　London, court, 1510s • Stevens, *Henry VIII* (edition)
　　　　　　　　　1/5/14: 20, 57, 76, 90 • *12*: 101, 133 • *15*: 34 • *31*: 3 • *33*: 2, 9 • *34*:
　　　　　　　　　29 • *41*: 22

GB-Lbl, Add.35087   London, British Library, Additional MS. 35087
　　　　　　　　Netherlands, ca.1505; scribal concordance with B-Tv, 94 • McMurtry, *Brit-
　　　　　　　　ish*; McMurtry, *Chansonnier* (facsimile)
　　　　　　　　　1/5/14: 12, 27, 83, 87 • *7*: 12 • *12*: 101 • *33*: 20 • *34*: 18, 29 • *41*:
　　　　　　　　　22

GB-Lcm, 1070   London, Royal College of Music, 1070
France, ca.1510–1515, with additions: perhaps for Marguerite d'Angoulême • Lowinsky, "Music Book"; Lowinsky, "1070"; Urkevich, *Anne*
3/19: 2, 3 • *15*: 3, 4, 24, 28, 40 • *46*: 5 • *55*: 1, 2, 7, 13, 20, 22a • *64*: 1, 20 • *65*: 1, 2, 4, 6

GB-Lcm, 2037   London, Royal College of Music, 2037
Lowinsky, *Medici*
64: 14, 19, 22, 23

GB-Ob, 213   GB-Ob, can.misc.213
North Italian, early 15th-century • Fallows, *Bodleian*
29/45: 12

GB-Ob, 831   Oxford, Bodleian Library, Ashmole 831
Burgundian court manuscript, early 16th century • Kellman, *Treasury*, 122
1/5/14: 4 • *12*: 128 • *33*: 19

GB-Ob, a.8   Oxford, Bodleian Library, Lat.lit.a.8
A fragment from a Burgundian court manuscript, probably after 1515 • Kellman, *London*, xii; Kellman, *Treasury*, 123
55: 20, 22a • *57*: 20

Guatemala   Jacaltenango, Santa Eulalia, Archivo Musical, 7
Has dates in the 17th and early 18th centuries • *CC*, i, 287
65: 14

H-BA, 2   Budapest, Országos Széchényi Könyvtár, Bártfá Mus.2
ca.1550, St. Aegidi, Bártfa • *CC*, i, 105–106
65: 2

H-BA, 20   Budapest, Országos Széchényi Könyvtár, Bártfá Mus.20
After 1570, St. Aegidi, Bártfa • *CC*, i, 110; Gombosi, "Musikalien"; Gombosi, "Quellen"
22/59: 1 • *54*: 5

H-BA, 23   Budapest, Országos Széchényi Könyvtár, Bártfá Mus.23
Dates in the 1540s, for St. Aegidi, Bártfa, possibly copied in Wittenberg • *CC*, i, 112; Albrecht, "Zwei"
55: 10

H-BA, 24   Budapest, Országos Széchényi Könyvtár, Bártfá Mus.24
Bártfa, after 1550 • *CC*, i, 113; Gombosi, "Musikalien"; Gombosi, "Quellen"
22/59: 1 • *54*: 5

H-BA, 26   Budapest, Országos Széchényi Könyvtár, Bártfá 26
Keyboard tabulature • Gombosi, "Musikalien"
65: 2

H-BA, Pr.6   Budapest, Országos Széchényi Könyvtár, Bártfá Mus.Pr.6
MS. additions to *RISM* L197 (1544): dated 1558, from Bártfa • Fox, *Liturgical*
54: 5 • *65*: 1

I-Bc, Q13   Bologna, Civico Museo Bibliografico Musicale G.B. Martini, Q13
Dated 1482, for S. Benedetto di Polirone, Mantua • *RISM* BIV/5, p. 15; Cattin, "Tradizione"; Cattin *Polifonia*, p. 96, asserting a Pomposa provenance
27: 14 • *41*: 5

I-Bc, Q15   Bologna, Civico Museo Bibliografico Musicale G.B. Martini, Q15
Copied ca.1410–1430, probably Vicenza • *RISM* BIV/5, pp. 16–33; Bent, "Pietro"
29/45: 23

I-Bc, Q16   Bologna, Civico Museo Bibliografico Musicale G.B. Martini, Q16
Dated 1487, later additions in 1490s. Probably Neapolitan • *RISM* BIV/5, pp. 33–40; *CC*, iv, 275–276; Fuller, "Additional"; Jeppesen, *Frottola*, ii, 10–16; Pease, "Report"; Pease, "Re-examination"
1/5: 91 • **1/5/14**: 4, 9, 13, 20, 49, 56, 60, 63, 66 • **2/10**: 16, 47 • **12**: 96, 97, 101, 138 • **14**: 82 • **33**: 9, 19, 21 • **34**: 9, 12, 13, 17, 23, 28, 29

I-Bc, Q17   Bologna, Civico Museo Bibliografico Musicale G.B. Martini, Q17
Before 1500, probably in Florence • *RISM* BIV/5, pp. 40–45; *CC*, i, 71–72; Smijers, "Muziekhandschriften"; Wexler, "Newly"
1/5/14: 4, 8, 14, 15, 23, 27, 31, 34, 38, 40, 41, 52, 56, 57, 59, 71, 77, 81, 83, 84, 86, 87 • **2/10**: 5, 16, 19 • **7**: 12 • **12**: 72, 80, 106, 107 • **23/37**: 80 • **33**: 11, 18, 19, 20 • **34**: 7, 10, 14, 15, 19, 23, 33

I-Bc, Q18   Bologna, Civico Museo Bibliografico Musicale G.B. Martini, Q18
ca.1502–1506, Bologna, partly in the hand of Spataro • *RISM* BIV/5, pp. 45–50; *CC*, iv, 276–277; Atlas, *Giulia*; Torchi, *Monumenti*; Weiss, "Bologna"; Weiss, *Manuscript*
1/5/14: 2, 4, 11, 13, 14, 42, 44, 45, 47, 56, 58, 60, 62, 63, 76, 86 • **2/10**: 15, 18, 29 • **7**: 12 • **8**: 3 • **12**: 25, 95, 106, 129 • **15**: 34 • **16**: 8, 16, 21, 24, 26, 27, 36, 56 • **17**: 37 • **18/40**: 48 • **25**: 31 • **26**: 16, 29, 66 • **31**: 3 • **33**: 2, 3, 10, 13, 15, 18, 19, 21 • **34**: 2, 6, 10, 13, 23, 25, 26 • **41**: 20, 50 • **42**: 37 • **47**: 39 • **49/58**: 38, 42, 53, 54 • **50**: 53 • **65**: 10

I-Bc, Q19   Bologna, Civico Museo Bibliografico Musicale G.B. Martini, Q19
ca.1518. Northern Italy, perhaps Bologna • *RISM* BIV/5, pp. 50–56; *CC*, i, 73–74; Lowinsky, *Medici*; Owens, *Bologna* (facsimile)
2/10: 28 • **4/30/62**: 6 • **24**: 27 • **55**: 21 • **64**: 14, 17, 21 • **65**: 12

I-Bc, Q20   Bologna, Civico Museo Bibliografico Musicale G.B. Martini, Q20
Probably soon after 1520, northern Italy • *RISM* BIV/5, pp. 56–60; *CC*, i, 74
64: 24 • **65**: 11 • **69**: 2

I-Bc, Q21   Bologna, Civico Museo Bibliografico Musicale G.B. Martini, Q21
ca.1525, Florence • *RISM* BIV/5, pp. 60–64; *CC*, i, 75; Gallico, *Canzoniere*; Jeppesen, *Frottola*
67: 6, 15

I-Bc, Q25   Bologna, Civico Museo Bibliografico Musicale G.B. Martini, Q25
ca.1540 (Pt.I) and ca.1520 (Pt.II) • *RISM* BIV/5, pp. 65–69; *CC*, i, 77; Lowinsky, *Medici*, pp. 114–115
22/59: 1 • **54**: 5

I-Bc, Q27   Bologna, Civico Museo Bibliografico Musicale G.B. Martini, Q27
Two manuscripts, the first ca.1530 and later, the second during the 1520s: both northern Italy, probably Bologna • *CC*, i, 78–79; Lowinsky, *Medici*, iii, 14–15
55: 13, 14, 18 • **64**: 17 • **66**: 14

I-Bc, Q34 Bologna, Civico Museo Bibliografico Musicale G.B. Martini, Q34
    Score. Copied by Mantuanus in Rome, dated 1613 • *CC*, iv, 281
      1/5/14: 43, 50, 85 • *34*: 21, 27

I-Bc, Q40 Bologna, Civico Museo Bibliografico Musicale G.B. Martini, Q40
      69: 1

I-Bc, R142 Bologna, Civico Museo Bibliografico Musicale G.B. Martini, R142
    ca.1525–30. north Italy • *RISM* BIV/5, pp. 72–76; Lowinsky, *Medici*, p. 177
      4/30/62: 6 • *15*: 1, 8, 24 • *22/59*: 2 • *33*: 1 • *55*: 2 • *65*: 2, 1, 3, 12 •
      66: 14

I-Bca, A.179 Bologna, Biblioteca comunale dell'Archiginnasio, A.179
    Northern Italy, later 15th century • *RISM* BIV/5, pp. 88–89; Gallo and
    Vecchi, *Antichi*
      27: 14 • *41*: 5

I-Bsp, A.XXIX Bologna, Archivio Musicale della Basilica di San Petronio, A.XXIX
    1512–1527, S. Petronio, Bologna • *RISM* BIV/5, pp. 76–77; Lowinsky,
    Medici, p. 115; Tirro, *Renaissance*; Tirro, *Spataro*
      cf.*31*: 1

I-Bsp, A.XXXI Bologna, Archivio Musicale della Basilica di San Petronio, A.XXXI
    1512–1527, S. Petronio, Bologna • *RISM* BIV/5, pp. 77–78; Tirro, *Renaissance*; Tirro, *Spataro*
      4/30/62: 1, 2 • *22/59*: 1, 2, 3 • *54*: 5

I-Bsp, A.XXXVIII Bologna, Archivio Musicale della Basilica di San Petronio, A.XXXVIII
    ca.1525–1527, S. Petronio, Bologna • *RISM* BIV/5, pp. 78–80; *CC*, iv, 286
      11: 1 • *54*: 5 • *55*: 8, 23 • *64*: 12

I-Bsp, A.XXXIX Bologna, Archivio Musicale della Basilica di San Petronio, A.XXXIX
    Dated 1552, for S. Petronio, Bologna • *CC*, iv, 286–87
      9/57: 4 • *15*: 24

I-Bu, 596 Bologna, Biblioteca Universitaria, 596.HH.2°
    Lute tabulature: late 15th century, perhaps Neapolitan. Binding fragments
    • Fallows, "Tablatures"; Slim, *Keyboard*, pp. 68–70
      1/5/14: 60 • *33*: 21

I-Bu, 2216 Bologna, Biblioteca Universitaria, 2216
    Before 1450, except for later additions, in the Veneto • *RISM* BIV/5,
    pp. 89–94; Besseler, "Manuscript"; Gallo, *Codice* (facsimile)
      29/45: 12, 23

I-Bu, 2573 Bologna, Biblioteca Universitaria, 2573
    Theoretical manuscript by Tinctoris • *RISM* BIV/5, pp. 94–96; *CC*, i, 89;
    Lowinsky, "Conflicting"; Tinctoris, *Opera Theoretica*
      3/19: 30

I-BGc, 1209D Bergamo, Biblioteca Civica Angelo Mai, 1209D
    Bergamo, ca.1545 • *CC*, iv, 249–250; Ravizza, "Gasparo"
      64: 5

I-CF, LIII Cividale del Friuli, Duomo, Archivio Capitolare, LIII
    Copied for the Cathedral, ca.1520–1530, or later • *RISM* BIV/5, pp. 112–
    113; *CC*, i, 153
      60: 5

I-CF, LIX   Cividale del Friuli, Duomo, Archivio Capitolare, LIX
Copied for the Cathedral, ca.1535–45 • *RISM* BIV/5, pp. 113–115; *CC*, i, 154

       15: 24, 27, 28, 30, 34 • **48**: 5 • **54**: 3, 6 • **55**: 1, 13 • **64**: 15, 19

I-CMac, D(F)   Casale Monferrato, Archivio Capitolare, Biblioteca, D(F)
ca.1521–1545, Casale Monferrato • *RISM* BIV/5, pp. 100–104; Crawford, *Casale*; Staehelin, "Wenig"

       7: 29 • **64**: 12 • **65**: 15

I-CMac, L(B)   Casale Monferrato, Archivio Capitolare, Biblioteca, L(B)
ca.1515–1525, Casale Monferrato • *RISM* BIV/5, pp. 97–98; Crawford, *Casale*

       24: 20 • **55**: 21 • **64**: 12

I-CMac, M(D)   Casale Monferrato, Archivio Capitolare, Biblioteca, M(D)
ca.1515, with later additions, Casale Monferrato • *RISM* BIV/5, pp. 96–97; Crawford, *Casale*

       4/30/62: 5 • **24**: 27

I-CMac, N(H)   Casale Monferrato, Archivio Capitolare, Biblioteca, N(H)
ca.1540, Casale Monferrato • *RISM* BIV/5, pp. 105–108; Crawford, *Casale*

       64: 23 • **69**: 2

I-CMac, P(E)   Casale Monferrato, Archivio Capitolare, Biblioteca, P(E)
ca.1521–1526, Casale Monferrato • *RISM* BIV/5, pp. 99–100; Crawford, *Casale*

       55: 23 • **64**: 21

I-CT, 95–96   Cortona, Biblioteca Comunale e dell'Accademia Etrusca, 95–96
Paired with F-Pn, n.a.fr.1817. Dateable ca.1514–1516, for Giuliano de'Medici, or later and for Giulio • *RISM* BIV/5, pp. 115–120; Atlas, *Giulia*; Cummings, "Giulio"; Gröber, "Liederbüchern"; Pannella, "Composizioni"; Renier, "Mazzetto"

       1/5/14: 26, 34, 38, 40, 41 • **2/10**: 11, 34 • **4/30/62**: 6 • **7**: 11, 33 • **12**: 5, 6, 9, 21, 47, 62, 106, 107 • **15**: 3, 8, 13, 16 • **21**: 22 • **23/37**: 80 • **34**: 11, 19, 22 • **55**: 1 • **64**: 18 • **65**: 8, 9 • **66**: 8

I-Fc, 2439   Florence, Conservatorio di Musica Luigi Cherubini, Biblioteca, Basevi 2439
Copied in the Netherlands, 1506–1514, perhaps by Bourgeois, for the Ciardi family of Siena • *RISM* BIV/5, pp. 120–125; Becherini, *Manoscritti*, 257–260; Kellman, "Josquin"; Kellman, *Treasury*, 78–79; Meconi, *Basevi* (facsimile); Newton, *Florence*; Staehelin, "Quellenkundliche"

       3/19: 15, 33 • **6**: 3 • **12**: 2, 3, 10, 12, 23, 31, 35, 39, 72, 75, 83, 99, 121, 128, 133 • **15**: 11, 34 • **21**: 45 • **23/37**: 81 • **33**: 4

I-Fc, 2440   Florence, Conservatorio di Musica Luigi Cherubini, Biblioteca, Basevi 2440
ca.1515–1520, Florence, probably associated with the Strozzi • *RISM* BIV/5, pp. 125–129; D'Accone, "Transitional"; Fenlon & Haar, *Madrigal*

       16: 40 • **26**: 51 • **49/58**: 68 • **56**: 4 • **67**: 2, 3, 15, 16

I-Fc, 2441   Florence, Conservatorio di Musica Luigi Cherubini, Biblioteca, Basevi 2441
Early 16th century, probably from Milan • *RISM* BIV/5, pp. 129–32; Becherini, *Manoscritti*, 264–266; Prizer, "Secular"; Rifkin, "Scribal", 306

       16: 2, 3, 4, 5, 13, 14, 15, 20, 24, 26, 27, 28, 34, 37, 53, 56 • **17/42**:

35 • *18/40*: 8, 43, 49, 51, 52, 53, 55 • *23/37*: 39, 50, 85 • *25*: 12, 42
• *26*: 20, 26, 35, 42 • *35*: 38 • *36*: 20 • *47*: 39 • *48*: 20, 56, 63 • *49/58*:
21, 25, 31, 43, 44, 53, 54, 56, 65, 66 • *50*: 24, 53

I-Fc, 2442   Florence, Conservatorio di Musica Luigi Cherubini, Biblioteca, Basevi 2442
Langres, and later in Florence for Filippo Strozzi: ca.1518–1527 • *RISM*
BIV/5, pp. 132–36; Becherini, *Manoscritti*, 266–268; Brown, "Chansons";
Brown, "Music"; Litterick, "Attribution"
1/5/14: 15, 32, 36, 94 • *2/10*: 22, 27, 33 • *12*: 4, 6, 10, 11, 20, 28, 47,
49, 62, 64, 107, 111

I-Fc, 2495   Florence, Conservatorio di Musica Luigi Cherubini, Biblioteca, Basevi 2495
ca.1530 or later, perhaps for the Strozzi, Florence • Becherini, *Manoscritti*,
268–70; Slim, *Gift*, 22–23
68: 4r

I-Fd, 11   Florence, Opera del Duomo, Biblioteca e Archivio, 11
Dated 1557 in Florence • *CC*, iv, 378; D'Accone, *Florence 11* (facsimile)
64: 21 • *65*: 2 • *69*: 1

I-Fd, 21   Florence, Opera del Duomo, Biblioteca e Archivio, Parte V, 21
Florence, begun in the 1480s, with additions of various dates • *RISM* BIV/
5, pp. 136–37; *CC*, iv, 380; Cattin, *Processionale*
27: 10, 14 • *41*: 5

I-Fl, 666   Florence, Biblioteca Medicea-Laurenziana, Acquisti e Doni 666
Dated 1518, and copied in Rome, probably for Lorenzo de'Medici • *RISM*
BIV/5, pp. 138–41; Lowinsky, *Medici*; Finscher, "Medici"; Rifkin,
"Scribal"
46: 8 • *64*: 1, 7, 14, 24 • *65*: 4, 7 • *66*: 3, 6

I-Fn, II.I.232   Florence, Biblioteca nazionale centrale, I-Fn, II.I.232
ca.1515, Florence • *RISM* BIV/5, pp. 203–208; Becherini, *Catalogo*, 21–23;
Cummings, *Florentine*; Kade, "Codex"
3/19: 2, 6 • *4/30/62*: 6 • *7*: 21, 33 • *15*: 3, 8, 9, 12, 13, 16, 18, 31, 33
• *21*: 22, 38 • *24*: 16 • *34*: 22 • *46*: 2 • *54*: 5 • *55*: 1, 2, 3, 9, 16, 26 •
64: 18 • *65*: 1, 6, 8, 10, 15 • *66*: 7, 8

I-Fn, II.I.350   Florence, Biblioteca nazionale centrale, II.I.350
Dated 1523, Florence, perhaps for the Cathedral • *RISM* BIV/5, pp. 213–
16; Becherini, *Catalogo*, 91–92; Cattin, *de Quadris*; d'Accone, "Pisano",
133
27: 10

I-Fn, 62(b)   Florence, Biblioteca nazionale centrale, B.R.62(b)
Voice and lute tablature, early 16th century • Fabris, "Frottola"; Underwood, *Renaissance*, 206–209
18/40: 27

I-Fn, 107bis   Florence, Biblioteca nazionale centrale, Magliabecchiana XIX.107bis
Florence, ca.1505–1513 • *RISM* BIV/5, pp. 151–54; Becherini, *Catalogo*,
42; Jeppesen, *Frottola*, ii, 58–59; Obrecht, *Collected*, iv, p. xxvi
1/5/14: 4, 10, 11, 14, 26, 27, 30, 31, 40, 44, 56, 57, 71, 76 • *2/10*:
11, 23, 40 • *6*: 3 • *15*: 3, 12, 13 • *31*: 3 • *33*: 2, 13, 18, 19 • *34*: 3, 11,
19, 23 • *43*: 1;

I-Fn, 112bis

Florence, Biblioteca nazionale centrale, Magliabecchiana XIX.112bis
Northern Italy, ca.1460, in part copied by Janue • *RISM* BIV/5, pp. 155–58; *CC*, i, 225; Becherini, *Catalogo*, 47–48; Besseler, "Studien", 238–39; Kanazawa, "Janue"
29/45: 12

I-Fn, 117

Florence, Biblioteca nazionale centrale, Magliabecchiana XIX.117
Florence, ca.1510–1518, perhaps begun in France • *RISM* BIV/5, pp. 159–61; Atlas, *Giulia*; Becherini, *Catalogo*, 51–52; Bernstein, "Florentine"; Rifkin, "Scribal", 109–10
1/5/14: 53, 57, 71 • *34*: 11 • *55*: 13

I-Fn, 121

Florence, Biblioteca nazionale centrale, Magliabecchiana XIX.121
Florence, early C16. Owned by Marietta Pugi • *RISM* BIV/5, pp. 162–64; Atlas, *Giulia*; Becherini, *Catalogo*, 52–54; Blackburn, "Carnival"; Ghisi, "Poesie"; Jeppesen, *Frottola*
1/5/14: 8, 20, 25, 86 • *12*: 101 • *16*: 10 • *25*: 16 • *33*: 9, 11 • *34*: 10, 29

I-Fn, 122–125

Florence, Biblioteca nazionale centrale, Magliabecchiana XIX.122–125
Florence, 1532–1537, apparently for a Medici • Haar, "Madrigals"
68: 4r

I-Fn, 125bis

Florence, Biblioteca nazionale centrale, Magliabecchiana XIX.125bis
Florence, ca.1530 • *RISM* BIV/5, pp. 164–166; Becherini, *Catalogo*, 55–56
66: 4

I-Fn, 164–167

Florence, Biblioteca nazionale centrale, Magliabecchiana XIX.164–167
Florence, ca.1520 or later • *RISM* BIV/5, pp. 166–71; Becherini, *Catalogo*, 67–71; Brown, *Florence* (facsimile); Pannella, "Composizioni"
1/5/14: 26, 32 • *2/10*: 11, 27, 28 • *3/19*: 2 • *12*: 6, 9, 19, 47, 69 • *15*: 8, 16 • *16*: 40 • *21*: 22 • *23/37*: 80 • *34*: 22 • *36*: 15 • *49/58*: 8 • *56*: 4 • *65*: 15 • *66*: 7 • *67*: 2, 3, 4, 5, 6, 7, 8, 11, 13, 14, 15, 16

I-Fn, 176

Florence, Biblioteca nazionale centrale, Magliabecchiana XIX.176
Florence, 1470s–1480s • *RISM* BIV/5, pp. 171–176; Becherini, *Catalogo*, 72–75; Rifkin, "Scribal"
1/5/14: 4, 8, 54 • *2/10*: 6, 16 • *33*: 11, 17, 19 • *34*: 9

I-Fn, 178

Florence, Biblioteca nazionale centrale, Magliabecchiana XIX.178
Florence, early 1490s • *RISM* BIV/5, pp. 176–181; Atlas, *Giulia*; Becherini, *Catalogo*, 75–77
1/5: 91 • *1/5/14*: 4, 8, 12, 14, 20, 27, 30, 31, 38, 40, 41, 44, 56, 57, 59, 77, 78, 81, 83, 86, 87, 96 • *2/10*: 16, 19, 30, 46 • *12*: 80, 97, 98, 106, 107 • *14*: 82 • *31*: 1 • *33*: 9, 11, 13, 14, 18, 19, 20 • *34*: 7, 10, 12, 14, 15, 19, 23, 30, 33

I-Fn, 229

Florence, Biblioteca nazionale centrale, B.R.229
ca.1492, Florence • *RISM* BIV/5, pp. 181–95; Becherini, *Catalogo*, 22; Bragard, "Manuscrit"; Brown, *Florentine*
1/5: 91 • *1/5/14*: 2, 7, 8, 9, 12, 13, 14, 17, 23, 24, 27, 28, 30, 31, 33, 38, 40, 42, 44, 50, 52, 55, 56, 57, 59, 60, 63, 76, 77, 86, 87, 89, 93, 96 • *2/10*: 16, 30, 46 • *3/19*: 30 • *8*: 3 • *12*: 69, 70, 80, 81, 82, 84, 89, 91, 93, 94, 95, 96, 97, 106 • *14*: 82 • *31*: 1, 3 • *32*: 2 • *33*: 2, 3, 11, 13, 18, 21 • *34*: 2, 6, 10, 12, 13, 17, 19, 23, 32, 33, 38

I-Fn, 230   Florence, Biblioteca nazionale centrale, B.R.230

ca.1510 or earlier, Florence • *RISM* BIV/5, pp. 195–203; *CC*, i, 221; d'Accone, *Florence 230* (facsimile); Ghisi, "Poesie"; Jeppesen, *Frottola*; Jeppesen, "Manuscript"

16: 5, 10, 21, 22, 40, 60 • **17/42**: 8; **18/40**: 37, 38 • **23/37**: 18, 54, 83, 86 • **25**: 13, 19, 20 • **26**: 16, 20, 51 • **49/58**: 24, 25, 49, 68 • **50**: 25 • **56**: 4, 67

I-Fn, 337   Florence, Biblioteca nazionale centrale, B.R.337

Florence, early 16th century • *RISM* BIV/5, pp. 208–213; Becherini, *Catalogo*, 109–11; Jeppesen, *Frottola*

16: 22, 40, 56, 60 • **17/42**: 5, 8 • **18/40**: 43, 44, 49 • **23/37**: 86, 89 • **25**: 31, 34, 45, 50, 52 • **26**: 20 • **35**: 2 • **48**: 15, 41, 42 • **49/58**: 24, 39, 49, 54 • **56**: 4, 67

I-Fn, Panc.27   Florence, Biblioteca nazionale centrale, Panc.27

Northern Italy, early 16th century • *RISM* BIV/5, pp. 141–50; Becherini, *Catalogo*, 118–22; Jeppesen, *Frottola*, ii, 37–42.

1/5/14: 3, 13, 19, 20, 31, 44, 45, 49, 50, 52, 56, 57, 62, 74, 76, 80, 84, 96 • **3/19**: 4, 7, 9, 10, 13, 14, 19, 22, 24, 25, 28, 31, 32, 34; **7**: 23 • **12**: 101 • **14**: 45 • **16**: 1, 2, 4, 10, 16, 21, 47, 56 • **18/40**: 29, 43, 44, 51, 61, 62 • **22/59**: 7 • **23/37**: 1, 41, 82 • **25**: 34 • **27**: 14 • **28**: 5 • **31**: 1, 3 • **33**: 2, 5, 9, 13 • **34**: 23, 25, 28, 29 • **41**: 5, 18, 19, 28, 34, 36, 43, 51 • **29/45**: 12, 23 • **47**: 41 • **49/58**: 38, 43, 50, 54

I-Fr, 2356   Florence, Biblioteca Riccardiana e Moreniana, 2356

Florence, 1480s with some later additions • *RISM* BIV/5, pp. 218–222; Atlas, *Giulia*; Jeppesen, *Frottola*; Plamenac, "Postscript"; Plamenac, "Second"; Rifkin, "Scribal"

1/5/14: 4, 8, 20, 54, 56, 57, 81, 83 • **12**: 98 • **33**: 9, 11, 17, 19, 20 • **34**: 7, 9, 15, 23

I-Fr, 2794   Florence, Biblioteca Riccardiana e Moreniana, 2794

France, 1480s–1490s, then to Florence • *RISM* BIV/5, pp. 222–27; Jones, *First*; Rifkin, "Pietrequin"; Rifkin, "Scribal", 318–20

1/5: 91 • **1/5/14**: 8, 9, 14, 20, 31, 38, 56, 57, 59, 77, 81, 83 • **2/10**: 46 • **3/19**: 3 • **14**: 82 • **27**: 7 • **33**: 9, 11, 18, 20 • **34**: 7, 15, 17, 23, 30, 32

I-Las, 238   Lucca, Biblioteca-Archivio Storico Comunale, 238

Bruges, ca.1470–1500 • *RISM* BIV/5, pp. 228–30; Strohm, *Bruges*; Strohm, "Chorbuch"

31: 1

I-Ma, 46   Milan, Biblioteca Ambrosiana, Mus.E.46

Italy, ca.1535–1540 • *RISM* BIV/5, pp. 233–234

4/30/62: 2 • **22/59**: 1, 3 • **54**: 5 • **61**: 5

I-Ma, 519   Milan, Biblioteca Ambrosiana, Trotti 519

ca.1520–1530, perhaps in Milan or Pavia • *RISM* BIV/5, pp. 235–36

55: 4 • **65**: 12, 16

I-Mfd, 2266   Milan, Archivio del Veneranda Fabrica del Duomo, 2266 (= Librone 4)

Milan, dated 1527 • Sartori, "Quarto"; Ciceri & Migliavacca, *Liber* (facsimile)

3/19: 2 • **21**: 38, 41

I-Mfd, 2267   Milan, Archivio del Veneranda Fabrica del Duomo, 2267 (= Librone 3)
                     Milan, ca.1500 • *RISM* BIV/5, pp. 248–251; Brown, *Milan* (facsimile); Jep-
                     pesen, "Gafurius"; Sartori, *Cappella*
                     3/19: 3, 14, 18 • *4/30/62*: *57*: 28 • *15*: 24 • *21*: 3, 22 • *22/59*: 1, 2 •
                     43: 3

I-Mfd, 2268   Milan, Archivio del Veneranda Fabrica del Duomo, 2268 (= Librone 2)
                     Milan, ca.1500 • *RISM* BIV/5, pp. 245–247; Brown, *Milan* (facsimile); Jep-
                     pesen, "Gafurius"; Sartori, *Cappella*
                     3/19: 3 • *8*: 4 • *31*: 1, 3, 4; *32*: 1 • *33*: 2

I-Mfd, 2269   Milan, Archivio del Veneranda Fabrica del Duomo, 2269 (= Librone 1)
                     Milan, ca.1490 • *RISM* BIV/5, pp. 237–45; Brown, *Milan* (facsimile); Jep-
                     pesen, "Gafurius"; Sartori, *Cappella*
                     3/19: 3, 31, 32, 34

I-Mt, 55   Milan, Biblioteca Trivulziana e Archivio Storico Civico, 55
                     RISM BIV/5, pp. 252–56; Jeppesen, *Frottola*, iii; Jeppesen, "Frottolenhand-
                     schriften"
                     16: 21, 61 • *23/37*: 18, 31, 32, 34, 35 • *25*: 42 • *26*: 16, 45, 54, 65

I-MC, 871   Montecassino, Monumento Nazionale di Montecassino, Biblioteca, 871
                     Neapolitan, ca.1480 • *RISM* BIV/5, pp. 301–308; Pope and Kanazawa,
                     Montecassino
                     1/5/14: 9, 20, 59 • *12*: 98, 99 • *27*: 14 • *33*: 9 • *34*: 17 • *41*: 5

I-MOas, 221   Modena, Archivio di Stato, 221
                     Ferrara, ca.1480 • *RISM* BIV/5, p. 256
                     13: 2

I-MOd, III   Modena, Biblioteca e Archivio Capitolare, III
                     Modena, for the Cathedral, ca.1520–1525 • *RISM* BIV/5, pp. 256–61;
                     Crawford, *Modena*; Roncaglia, *Cappella*, 21
                     65: 15

I-MOd, IV   Modena, Biblioteca e Archivio Capitolare, IV
                     Modena, for the Cathedral, ca.1520–1530 • *RISM* BIV/5, pp. 262–64;
                     Crawford, *Modena*; Rubsamen, "Research"
                     4/30/62: 1 • *7*: 23 • *11*: 1 • *22/59*: 2, 3, 6 • *24*: 24 • *41*: 28 • *46*: 18 •
                     54: 1, 5 • *55*: 2 • *60*: 2

I-MOd, IX   Modena, Biblioteca e Archivio Capitolare, IX
                     Modena, for the Cathedral, ca.1520–1530 • *RISM* BIV/5, pp. 264–68;
                     Crawford, *Modena*, 107; Rubsamen, "Research"
                     3/19: 2 • *55*: 13, 20 • *64*: 12, 18, 24 • *66*: 6

I-MOe, α.F.2.29   Modena, Biblioteca Estense, α.F.2.29
                     Ferrara. related to GB-Lbl, Add.19583 and F-Pn, f.fr.4599 • *RISM* BIV/5,
                     pp. 268–70; Bernstein, "Couronne" (1973); d'Accone, *Modena* (facsimile);
                     Lowinsky, *Medici*, 117–18
                     65: 7, 11 • *66*: 15

I-MOe, α.F.9.9.   Modena, Biblioteca Estense, α.F.9.9.
                     Padua, before 1500 • *RISM* BIV/5, pp. 270–275; D'Accone, *Modena* (fac-
                     simile); Jeppesen, *Frottola*; La Face Bianconi, *Strambotti*
                     23/37: 32 • *47*: 42

I-MOe, α.M.1.2   Modena, Biblioteca Estense, α.M.1.2 (olim lat.457.)
                   Ferrara, ca.1505 • *RISM* BIV/5, pp. 279–80; Lockwood, *Ferrara*
                   4/30/62: 1, 4 • *6*: 3

I-MOe, α.M.1.13   Modena, Biblioteca Estense, α.M.1.13 (olim lat.456.)
                   For Ferrara, ca.1480 • *RISM* BIV/5, pp. 288–89
                   24: 22 • *32*: 2

I-MOe, α.N.1.2   Modena, Biblioteca Estense, α.N.1.2
                   Probably Ferrara. Same scribe as in GB-Lbl, Add.19583 • *RISM* BIV/5,
                   pp. 290–91
                   54: 5, 6 • *60*: 3 • *64*: 23

I-MOe, τ.L.11.8   Modena, Biblioteca Estense, τ.L.11.8
                   Northern Italy, ca.1530 • *RISM* BIV/5, pp. 276–79; Fenlon & Haar, *Madrigal*
                   1/5/14: 50 • *68*: 4r • *69*: 1

I-Pc, A17   Padua, Duomo, Biblioteca Capitolare, A17
                   Copied by Passetto for the Cathedral, dated 1522 • *RISM* BIV/5, pp. 310–
                   17; Blackburn, "Petrucci"; Constant, *Padua*; Garbelotto, "Codice", liv,
                   297–98; Lovato, *Catalogo*, pp. 811–44
                   3/19: 34 • *7*: 3 • *21*: 9, 38, 41 • *55*: 7, 8, 9, 13, 16, 18, 24, 25 • *64*: 5,
                   9, 12, 15, 16, 18, 19, 21, 23, 24, 25 • *66*: 14

I-Pc, C56   Padua, Duomo, Biblioteca Capitolare, C56
                   Fifteenth-century processional for the Cathedral • *RISM* BIV/4, pp. 986–88
                   27: 17 • *41*: 34

I-Pc, D27   Padua, Duomo, Biblioteca Capitolare, D27
                   Copied by Passetto for the Cathedral, ca.1535 • *RISM* BIV/5, pp. 317–22;
                   Constant, *Padua*; Garbelotto, "Codice", liv, 298–299; Lovato, *Catalogo*,
                   pp. 844–67
                   3/19: 21

I-PAVu, 361   Pavia, Biblioteca Universitaria, Aldini 361
                   RISM BIV/5, pp. 324–325; Cattin, "Pavia"
                   27: 14 • *41*: 5

I-PAVu, 362   Pavia, Biblioteca Universitaria, Aldini 362
                   Savoy, ca.1470 or earlier • *RISM* BIV/5, pp. 326–28; d'Accone, *Pavia* (fac-
                   simile); Restori, "Codice"; Schavran, *Manuscript*
                   1/5/14: 20 • *33*: 9

I-PEc, 431   Perugia, Biblioteca Comunale Augusta, 431
                   Kingdom of Naples, perhaps Ortona, 1480s • *RISM* BIV/5, pp. 328–35;
                   Atlas, "Neapolitan"; Atlas, "Provenance"; Hernon, "Perugia"
                   1/5/14: 4, 9, 13, 29, 60 • *12*: 97, 101 • *33*: 9, 19, 21 • *34*: 9, 12, 17,
                   29 • *56*: 60

I-PEc, 1013   Perugia, Biblioteca Comunale Augusta, 1013
                   Venice, dated 1509, copied by Materanensis • *RISM* BIV/5, pp. 335–37;
                   Blackburn, "Lost"
                   8: 3

I-PESo, 1144   Pesaro, Biblioteca Comunale Oliveriana, 1144
                   Lute tabulature, Italian, ca.1500, with later additions • Ivanoff, *Pesaro*; Ivan-
                   off, *Zentrale*
                   1/5/14: 20

I-Rc, 2856   Rome, Biblioteca Casanatense, 2856
    Ferrara or Mantua, ca.1480 or ca.1490 • *RISM* BIV/5, pp. 337–45; Llorens, "Codice"; Lockwood, *Ferrara*; Wolff, *Chansonnier*
        1/5/14: 2, 9, 12, 13, 14, 20, 31, 33, 38, 41, 42, 54, 56, 57, 63, 77, 81, 83, 87 • ***2/10***: 16, 47 • ***9/57***: 2 • ***12***: 80, 95, 96, 97, 98, 105, 111, 121; ***33***: 3, 4, 9, 17, 18, 20 • ***34***: 2, 6, 7, 12, 13, 15, 17, 23, 33

I-Rpm, 23–24   Rome, private collection of Prince Massimo, VI.C.6.23–24
    Copied in Rome, between 1532 and 1534 • *RISM* BIV/5, pp. 345–48; Lippmann, "Musikhandschriften"
        65: 2, 6

I-Rsm, 26   Vatican City, Biblioteca Apostolica Vaticana, Santa Maria Maggiore, 26 (*olim* JJ.III.4)
    Roman, in two layers, ca.1520 and ca.1550 • *RISM* BIV/5, pp. 428–30; Hudson, "Neglected"
        4/30/62: 2 • ***8***: 4, 5 • ***22/59***: 1 • ***24***: 21 • ***32***: 2 • ***48***: 4 • ***61***: 3

I-Rv, S¹ 35–40   Rome, Biblioteca Vallicelliana, S¹ 35–40 (*olim* Vall.S.Borr.E.II.55–60)
    Florence, ca.1530 • *RISM* BIV/5, pp. 348–355; Lowinsky, "Newly-discovered"
        65: 2

I-Rvat, 1938   Vatican City, Biblioteca Apostolica Vaticana, Pal.lat.1938
    Inventory of Heidelberg sources, ca.1539
        12: 2

I-Rvat, 1976–1979   Vatican City, Biblioteca Apostolica Vaticana, Palatini latini 1976–1979
    Copied in the Netherlands court scriptorium, ca.1528–1534, for Anne of Hungary • *RISM* BIV/5, pp. 412–415; Kellman, "Josquin", 200–201; Kellman, *Treasury*, 130–32; Rubsamen, "Research", 44–46; Seeley, *Motets*
        15: 18 • ***21***: 8 • ***55***: 20, 22, 22a • ***64***: 4, 12, 22 • ***66***: 15

I-Rvat, 1980–1981   Vatican City, Biblioteca Apostolica Vaticana, Palatini latini 1980–1981
    Roman, for Giulio de'Medici, ca.1513–1523 • *RISM* BIV/5, pp. 415–17; Cummings, "Giulio"; Rubsamen, "Research", 46–48
        54: 2 • ***55***: 1 • ***64***: 4

I-Rvat, 1982   Vatican City, Biblioteca Apostolica Vaticana, Palatini latini 1982
    Roman, for Giulio de'Medici, ca.1513–1523 • *RISM* BIV/5, pp. 417–18; Rubsamen, "Research", 48–49
        60: 4, 5 • ***61***: 1

I-Rvat, 11953   Vatican City, Biblioteca Apostolica Vaticana, Vaticani latini 11953
    Several layers, from early 16th century, copied in Germany • *RISM* BIV/5, pp. 419–21; Casimiri, "Canzoni"; van den Borren, "Apropos"
        1/5/12: 11, 15, 31 • ***2/10***: 4, 7, 18, 22 • ***12***: 10, 23 • ***65***: 2, 6

I-Rvat, C.VIII.234   Vatican City, Biblioteca Apostolica Vaticana, Chigi C.VIII.234
    Flemish court scriptorium, ca.1498–1503, with later additions: originally for Philippe Bouton • *RISM* BIV/5, pp. 403–407; Kellman, "Origins"; Kellman, *Treasury*, 125–29; Kellman, *Vatican* (facsimile)
        3/19: 17, 18 • ***4/30/62***: 5 • ***7***: 27 • ***8***: 4 • ***11***: 3 • ***46***: 1, 11 • ***55***: 13 • ***65***: 6, 8

I-Rvat, C.G.XII.2   Vatican City, Biblioteca Apostolica Vaticana, Cappella Giulia, XII.2

Roman, for the Cappella Giulia, mostly ca.1520 • *RISM* BIV/5, pp. 430–
32; Llorens, *Giulia*; Rifkin, "Scribal", 307

        4/30/62: 1 • *54*: 5 • *60*: 4, 5 • *61*: 2, 3

I-Rvat, C.G.XII.4   Vatican City, Biblioteca Apostolica Vaticana, Cappella Giulia, XII.4

For the Cappella Giulia, copied by Parvus, with Ocho, in 1536 • *RISM*
BIV/5, pp. 436–39; Brauner, "Music"; Brauner, *Parvus*, 61–91; Llorens,
Giulia

        64: 21; No.34: *65*: 2, 6 • *66*: 3

I-Rvat, C.G.XIII.27   Vatican City, Biblioteca Apostolica Vaticana, Cappella Giulia, XIII.27

Florence, ca.1493 • *RISM* BIV/5, pp. 444–51; Atlas, *Giulia*; Llorens, *Giulia*,
43–48

        1/5/14: 2, 4, 8, 9, 13, 14, 20, 31, 38, 40, 41, 44, 48, 50, 54, 56, 57,
59, 60, 63, 76, 81, 83, 86, 87 • *2/10*: 11, 16, 19, 30, 35; *7*: 33 • *12*:
63, 69, 80, 95, 97, 98, 101, 106, 107, 118, 121 • *31*: 3, 5 • *33*: 2, 4, 9,
11, 13, 17, 18, 19, 20, 21 • *34*: 2, 7, 10, 11, 12, 13, 14, 15, 16, 17, 19,
23, 30, 32, 33, 39

I-Rvat, C.S.14   Vatican City, Biblioteca Apostolica Vaticana, Cappella Sistina, 14

Neapolitan, ca.1472–1481 • *RISM* BIV/5, pp. 357–58; Llorens, *Sistinae*;
Roth, *Studien*

        32: 1

I-Rvat, C.S.15   Vatican City, Biblioteca Apostolica Vaticana, Cappella Sistina, 15

Sistine Chapel, ca.1495–1501 • *RISM* BIV/5, pp. 358–63; Llorens, *Sistinae*;
Roth, *Studien*; Sherr, *Papal Chapel*

        3/19: 6, 7, 17, 18, 28, 29 • *7*: 27 • *15*: 21 • *21*: 22, 29 • *46*: 1, 3, 4

I-Rvat, C.S.16   Vatican City, Biblioteca Apostolica Vaticana, Cappella Sistina, 16

Sistine Chapel, ca.1515 • *RISM* BIV/5, pp. 363–65; Dean, *Scribes*; Llorens,
Sistinae; Rifkin, "Scribal," 308

        46: 1 • *55*: 2 • *61*: 2 • *65*: 2, 4

I-Rvat, C.S.19   Vatican City, Biblioteca Apostolica Vaticana, Cappella Sistina, 19

Sistine Chapel, ca.1535–1537 • *RISM* BIV/5, pp. 369–71; Brauner, *Parvus*;
Llorens, *Sistinae*

        66: 3

I-Rvat, C.S.23   Vatican City, Biblioteca Apostolica Vaticana, Cappella Sistina, 23

Sistine Chapel, ca.1497–1512 • *RISM* BIV/5, pp. 373–74; Dean, *Scribes*;
Llorens, *Sistinae*; Sherr, "Notes"; Sherr, *Papal*, pp. 132–44

        4/30/62: 3 • *11*: 2 • *13*: 1, 2 • *22/59*: 3, 4 • *24*: 20, 21 • *54*: 2, 5 • *61*:
4

I-Rvat, C.S.24   Vatican City, Biblioteca Apostolica Vaticana, Cappella Sistina, 24

Sistine Chapel, ca.1543–1550, copied by Parvus • *RISM* BIV/5, pp. 375–
77; Brauner, *Parvus*, 166–84; Llorens, *Sistinae*

        66: 6

I-Rvat, C.S.26   Vatican City, Biblioteca Apostolica Vaticana, Cappella Sistina, 26

Sistine Chapel, ca.1513–1521 • *RISM* BIV/5, pp. 377–78; Dean, *Scribes*;
Llorens, *Sistinae*, 54–56

        21: 38 • *55*: 18 • *60*: 5 • *64*: 17 • *65*: 15

I-Rvat, C.S.35   Vatican City, Biblioteca Apostolica Vaticana, Cappella Sistina, 35

Sistine Chapel, ca.1484–1503 • *RISM* BIV/5, pp. 379–81; Llorens, *Sistinae*, 69–72; Roth, "Datierung"; Sherr, *Papal Chapel*

7: 7, 8, 9, 10 • **24**: 22 • **31**: 3 • **32**: 5 • **33**: 2 • **43**: 2

I-Rvat, C.S.38   Vatican City, Biblioteca Apostolica Vaticana, Cappella Sistina, 38

Sistine Chapel, ca.1555–1563, copied by Parvus • Brauner, *Parvus*, 186–203; Llorens, *Sistinae*

15: 33 • **65**: 7

I-Rvat, C.S.39   Vatican City, Biblioteca Apostolica Vaticana, Cappella Sistina, 39

Sistine Chapel, ca.1560 • Brauner, *Parvus*, 186–203; Llorens, *Sistinae*

60: 4

I-Rvat, C.S.41   Vatican City, Biblioteca Apostolica Vaticana, Cappella Sistina, 41

Sistine Chapel, ca.1482–1512 • *RISM* BIV/5, pp. 383–84; Dean, *Scribes*; Llorens, *Sistinae*, 81–83; Sherr, *Papal*

4/30/62: 2, 4, 5 • **7**: 23 • **8**: 5 • **11**: 1 • **22/59**: 1, 6 • **24**: 17, 18, 25 • **32**: 3 • **41**: 28

I-Rvat, C.S.42   Vatican City, Biblioteca Apostolica Vaticana, Cappella Sistina, 42

Sistine Chapel, ca.1503–1512 • *RISM* BIV/5, pp. 384–388; Dean, *Scribes*; Llorens, *Sistinae*, 83–86; Sherr, "Notes"; Sherr, *Papal*

3/19: 2, 13 • **15**: 2, 3, 12, 13, 20, 24, 31 • **46**: 2, 5, 9 • **55**: 26 • **65**: 4 • **66**: 5

I-Rvat, C.S.44   Vatican City, Biblioteca Apostolica Vaticana, Cappella Sistina, 44

Sistine Chapel, ca.1503–1513 • *RISM* BIV/5, pp. 388–89; Llorens, *Sistinae*; Sherr, *Papal*

55: 20; *cf.* **39**: 1

I-Rvat, C.S.45   Vatican City, Biblioteca Apostolica Vaticana, Cappella Sistina, 45

Sistine Chapel, ca.1511–1514 • *RISM* BIV/5, pp. 389–91; Dean, *Scribes*; Llorens, *Sistinae*; Sherr, *Papal Chapel*

8: 3 • **11**: 3, 5 • **22/59**: 2 • **54**: 5 • **60**: 3 • **61**: 3 • **65**: 1

I-Rvat, C.S.46   Vatican City, Biblioteca Apostolica Vaticana, Cappella Sistina, 46

Sistine Chapel, ca.1507–1521 • *RISM* BIV/5, pp. 391–94; Dean, *Scribes*; Dean, *Vatican* (facsimile); Llorens, *Sistinae*, 94–98

3/19: 3 • **15**: 40 • **21**: 31, 35 • **55**: 4 • **64**: 12, 18, 23, 24 • **65**: 16 • **66**: 9

I-Rvat, C.S.48   Vatican City, Biblioteca Apostolica Vaticana, Cappella Sistina, 48

54: 5

I-Rvat, C.S.49   Vatican City, Biblioteca Apostolica Vaticana, Cappella Sistina, 49

Sistine Chapel, ca.1492–1504 • *RISM* BIV/5, pp. 394–95; Dean, *Scribes*; Llorens, *Sistinae*; Sherr, "Notes"; Sherr, *Papal*

8: 4 • **31**: 5 • **54**: 3

I-Rvat, C.S.51   Vatican City, Biblioteca Apostolica Vaticana, Cappella Sistina, 51

Naples, late 15th century, with later Roman layers • *RISM* BIV/5, pp. 396–97; Llorens, *Sistinae*, 103–105; Roth, "Datierung"; Roth, *Studien*

24: 14, 26 • **32**: 2

I-Rvat, C.S.63   Vatican City, Biblioteca Apostolica Vaticana, Cappella Sistina, 63

Copied ca.1480–1507 • *RISM* BIV/5, pp. 399–400; Dean, *Scribes*; Llorens, *Sistinae*; Sherr, *Papal*

15: 8

I-Rvat, C.S.64	Vatican City, Biblioteca Apostolica Vaticana, Cappella Sistina, 64
	Sistine Chapel, after ca.1538, with the de Orto mass from the late 15th
	century • Brauner, *Parvus*, 243–55; Llorens, *Sistinae*
	20: 3
I-Rvat, C.S.76	Vatican City, Biblioteca Apostolica Vaticana, Cappella Sistina, 76
	Sistine Chapel, after ca.1580
	15: 24
I-Rvat, C.S.150	Vatican City, Biblioteca Apostolica Vaticana, Cappella Sistina, 150
	22/59: 1
I-Rvat, C.S.154	Vatican City, Biblioteca Apostolica Vaticana, Cappella Sistina, 154
	Sistine Chapel, ca.1543–1560 (the Josquin mass, 1550–1555), copied by
	Parvus • Brauner, *Parvus*, 152–82; Llorens, *Sistinae*
	4/30/62: 1
I-Rvat, C.S.160	Vatican City, Biblioteca Apostolica Vaticana, Cappella Sistina, 160
	Netherlands court scribe, ca.1513–1520, for Pope Leo X • *RISM BIV/5*,
	pp. 400–401; Kellman, "Josquin", 212; Kellman, *Treasury*, 135–36; Llorens,
	Sistinae, 187–89
	54: 5
I-Rvat, C.S.197	Vatican City, Biblioteca Apostolica Vaticana, Cappella Sistina, 197
	Sistine Chapel, ca.1492–1495 • *RISM BIV/5*, p. 403; Llorens, *Sistinae*, 213;
	Sherr, *Papal*
	4/30/62: 1
I-Rvat, Ottob.251	Vatican City, Biblioteca Apostolica Vaticana, Ottoboni latini 251
	Fifteenth-century miscellany from northern Italy • Carboni and Ziino,
	"Composizioni"
	26: 5
I-Rvat, S.P. B.80	Vatican City, Biblioteca Apostolica Vaticana, San Pietro B.80
	Roman, for St. Peter's, ca.1474, with later additions • *RISM BIV/5*,
	pp. 421–28; Hamm, "Manuscript"; Reynolds, "Origins"; Reynolds, *Vatican*
	(facsimile)
	3/19: 28 • **7**: 10
I-RAc, Libano	Ravenna, Biblioteca Comunale Classense, MS. Monte Libano
	1412. perhaps for Ravenna
	29/45: 12
I-RDM, s.s.	Rocca di Mezzo, Chiesa Parrochiale di Santa Maria delle Neve, Museo, s.s.
	New Josquin Edition, commentary to vii, 3
	7: 24 • **22/59**: 7 • **41**: 28
I-RE, s.s.	Reggio Emilia, Biblioteca Capitolare, s.s.
	Ferrara, ca.1535
	60: 1, 4
I-Sc, K.I.2	Siena, Biblioteca Comunale degli'Intronati, K.I.2
	Siena Cathedral, ca.1500 • *RISM BIV/5*, pp. 452–57; d'Accone, "Late";
	d'Accone, *Siena* (facsimile); Ziino, "Appunti"
	3/19: 3, 14, 18 • **7**: 27 • **8**: 3 • **15**: 12, 13, 24 • **22/59**: 4 • **31**: 3 • **33**: 2
I-SUss, 248	Subiaco, Protocenobio di S. Scolastica, Biblioteca, 248

Copied in Alamire's workshop, ca.1521–1534 • *RISM* BIV/5, pp. 457–58; Kellman, "Josquin", 209; Kellman, *Treasury*, 124

11: 1, 2

I-Tn, F.I.IV Turin, Biblioteca Nazionale Universitaria, F.I.IV
Early C14 • *Analecta Hymnica*, xx

29/45: 12

I-Tn, I.27 Turin, Biblioteca Nazionale Universitaria, Ris.mus.I.27 (*olim* qm.III.59)
Probably Piedmont, ca.1500 • *RISM* BIV/5, pp. 458–61; d'Accone, *Turin* (facsimile); Villanis, "Alcuni"

1/5: 91 • **1/5/14**: 8, 57, 58, 76, 91 • **12**: 24 • **14**: 82 • **31**: 3 • **33**: 2, 11 • **34**: 32 • **41**: 22 • **61**: 3

I-TRc, 89 Trento, Castello del Buon Consiglio, Biblioteca, 89
Trent, copied by Wiser, ca.1460–1475 • *RISM* BIV/5, pp. 486–98

1/5/14: 13 • **29/45**: 23

I-TRc, 91 Trento, Castello del Buon Consiglio, Biblioteca, 91
Trent, probably mid-1470s • *RISM* BIV/5, pp. 514–22

12: 103

I-TRc, 92 Trento, Castello del Buon Consiglio, Biblioteca, 92
Two sections, the first probably ca.1435, the second copied by Lupi, ca.1443 with additions • *RISM* BIV/5, pp. 523–34

29/45: 12

I-TRc, 1947–4 Trento, Castello del Buon Consiglio, Biblioteca, 1947–4
Trent or Tyrol, ca.1500 • *RISM* BIV/5, pp. 548–49; Disertori, "Manoscritto"

33: 12 • **34**: 8

I-TRc, Feininger Trent, Biblioteca Musicale Laurence K.J. Feininger, s.s.
RISM BIV/5, pp. 547–48; Feininger, "Neue"

29/45: 23

Treviri, 724 Treviri, Biblioteca Comunale, 724
Dated 1482 • Geering, *Organa*

29/45: 12

I-TVd, 5 Treviso, Biblioteca Capitolare della Cattedrale, 5
Treviso, dated 1559–1572 • D'Alessi, *Cappella*; Ferrarese and Gallo, *Fondo*

55: 13

I-TVd, 7 Treviso, Biblioteca Capitolare della Cattedrale, 7
Treviso, dated 1558–1571 • D'Alessi, *Cappella*

69: 1

I-TVd, 9 Treviso, Biblioteca Capitolare della Cattedrale, 9
D'Alessi, *Cappella*; Ferrarese and Gallo, *Fondo*

54: 5

I-Vc, B.32 Venice, Conservatorio di Musica Benedetto Marcello, Torrefranca B.32
Tuscany, perhaps Pisa, ca.1525–1530 • Luisi, "Sconosciuta"; Fenlon & Haar, *Madrigal*

67: 7

I-Vnm, IX,145 Venice, Biblioteca Nazionale Marciana, cl.it.IX,145
Two sections, Venetian (perhaps Franciscan), first half of 15th century •

RISM BIV/5, pp. 550–54; Besseler, "Studien"; Cattin, *Laude*; Cattin, *Manoscritto*

29/45: 12;23

I-Vnm, IV,1795–1798   Venice, Biblioteca Nazionale Marciana, cl.it.IV,1795–1798 (now Mss.10653–10656)

The Marche or Veneto, ca.1520–1525 • *RISM* BIV/5, pp. 554–59; Jeppesen, "Frottolenhandschriften"; Luisi, *Apografo*

36: 32 • **49/58**: 28 • **50**: 11 • **56**: 1, 4, 5, 7, 12, 24, 33, 48, 61, 62, 66

I-VEcap, DCXC   Verona, Biblioteca Capitolare, DCXC

Northern Italy, ca.1500 • *RISM* B IV/4, pp. 1107–1110

27: 14 • **41**: 5

I-VEcap, DCCLVI   Verona, Biblioteca Capitolare, DCCLVI

From Alamire's workshop, ca.1508 • *RISM* BIV/5, pp. 561–62; Kellman, *Treasury*, 137–39; Preston, *Sacred*; Turrini, *Patrimonio*

7: 33 • **9/57**: 1, 3, 4 • **48**: 5

I-VEcap, DCCLVII   Verona, Biblioteca Capitolare, DCCLVII

Verona, ca.1490 or ca.1500 • *RISM* BIV/5, pp. 562–65, Brown, *Verona* (facsimile); Turrini, *Patrimonio*

1/5: 91 • **1/5/14**: 2, 3, 4, 12, 13, 38, 44, 50, 56, 57, 60, 62, 66, 68, 76, 77 • **2/10**: 30 • **3/19**: 17, 30 • **8**: 3 • **12**: 63, 95, 97 • **14**: 82 • **31**: 3, 4 • **32**: 2 • **33**: 2, 3, 13, 19, 21 • **34**: 2, 12, 23

I-VEcap, DCCLVIII   Verona, Biblioteca Capitolare, DCCLVIII

Verona, ca.1500 • *RISM* BIV/5, pp. 566–68; Kanazawa, "Vesper"; Preston, *Sacred*

3/19: 6, 13, 17, 18, 20, 34 • **4/30/62**: 6 • **7**: 27 • **15**: 12, 16, 24 • **19**: 18 • **21**: 35 • **34**: 22

I-VEcap, DCCLX   Verona, Biblioteca Capitolare, DCCLX

Verona perhaps ca.1530 • *RISM* BIV/5, pp. 573–76; Preston, *Sacred*; Turrini, *Patrimonio*, 5–15

4/30/62: 6 • **15**: 24 • **55**: 13 • **66**: 14 • **69**: 1, 2

I-VEcap, DCCLXI   Verona, Biblioteca Capitolare, DCCLXI

Verona, early 16th century • *RISM* BIV/5, pp. 576–78; Preston, *Sacred*; Turrini, *Patrimonio*

6: 5 • **8**: 4, 5 • **20**: 1 • **22/59**: 4 • **24**: 14, 22, 26

I-VIs, 11   Vicenza, Seminario Vescovile, Biblioteca, U.VIII.11

Vicenza, ca.1430–40 • Bent, "Pietro"; Bolcat & Zanotelli, *Fondo*, pp. 391–93; Cattin, "Sconosciuto"

27: 10

NL-At, 208 F 7   Amsterdam, Toonkunst-Bibliotheek, V.A. 208 F 7

Flemish, ca.1530–1550 • Jas, "Some"

55: 2

NL-L, 436   Leiden, Gemeentearchief, 436

1/5/14: 27

NL-L, 1440   Leiden, Gemeentearchief, 1440 (*olim* C)

65: 1, 2, 6

NL-L, 1441   Leiden, Gemeentearchief, 1441 (*olim* D)

	Brussels, dated 1565–1566 • Land, "Koorboeken"
	64: 4
NL-L, 1442	Leiden, Gemeentearchief, 1442 (*olim* E)
	Dated 1565–1566 • Land, "Koorboeken"
	55: 10 • **64**: 11 • **65**: 2, 6 • **66**: 6 • **69**: 4
NL-L, 1443	Leiden, Gemeentearchief, 1443
	4/30/62: 5 • **11**: 2
NL-SH, 72C	's Hertogenbosch, Archief van de Illustre Lieve Vrouwe Broedershap, 72C
	copied in the Alamire workshop for the Brotherhood, ca.1530 • *CC*, i, 269; Kellman, *Treasury*, 82–83; Smijers, "Meerstemmige", 17–18
	60: 3, 4, 5 • **61**: 1
NL-SH, 73	's Hertogenbosch, Archief van de Illustre Lieve Vrouwe Broedershap, 73C
	Copied at 's Hertogenbosch, 1544 • Maas, "Determinering"; Smijers, "Meerstemmige", 9–15
	15: 21
NL-Uhecht	Utrecht, private collection of Hecht, s.s.
	Perhaps Wittenberg, ca.1550 • Elders, "Handscrhiftlicher"
	65: 11
P-Cu, 2	Coimbra, Biblioteca Geral da Universidade, Mus.2
	After 1532, Coimbra • Rees, *Polyphony*, 133–47; Sampaio Ribero, "Manuscritos"
	60: 5 • **61**: 1
P-Cu, 12	Coimbra, Biblioteca Geral da Universidade, Mus.12
	Mid 16th century, Coimbra • Anglès, *Musica*; Rees, *Polyphony*, 185–94
	65: 14
P-Cu, 32	Coimbra, Biblioteca Geral da Universidade, Mus.32
	After 1539, Coimbra • Rees, *Polyphony*, 215–27
	65: 14
P-Cu, 48	Coimbra, Biblioteca Geral da Universidade, Mus.48
	Score. 1550s, Coimbra • Rees, *Polyphony*, 271–82
	65: 14 • **69**: 1, 4
P-Cu, 53	Coimbra, Biblioteca Geral da Universidade, Mus.53
	Late 16th century, Coimbra • Rees, *Polyphony*, 283–95
	65: 14
P-Ln, 60	Lisbon, Instituto da Biblioteca Nacional e do Livro, Colecèào Dr Ivo Cruz, MS.60
	Portugal, after 1521 • Rees, *Polyphony*, 431–36
	65: 14
Jelenia Gora	Jelenia Gora (Wroclaw), library of the Parish Church, s.s. (*olim*) Hirschberg 352
	Lute tabulature, from Silesia, dated 1537–1544 • *RISM* BVII, 370–71; Schneider, "Unbekannte"
	65: 2
Pl-Kj 40013	Kraków, Biblioteka Jagiellonska, 40013 (formerly Berlin)
	Torgau, ca.1540 • Gerhardt, *Torgauer*
	3: 2 • **7**: 10, 22 • **19**: 2 • **54**: 5
PL-Kj, 40092	Kraków, Biblioteka Jagiellonska, 40092 (formerly Berlin)

Discantus book, ca.1525

1: 14

PL-Kj, 40098   Kraków, Biblioteka Jagiellonska, 40098 (formerly Berlin)

Glogauer Liederbuch. From Glogau, ca.1480 • Owens, *Krakow* (facsimile); Ringmann, *Glogauer*; Ringmann and Klapper; Väterlein, *Glogauer* (edition)

1/*5*/*14*: 9, 13, 52, 54, 60 • *3*/*19*: 30 • *12*: 95, 97 • *33*: 3, 17, 21 • *34*: 12, 17

PL-Kj, 40272   Kraków, Biblioteka Jagiellonska, Mus.40272 (formerly Berlin)

German, dated 1563

66: 5

PL-Kj, 40598   Kraków, Biblioteka Jagiellonska, Mus.40598 (formerly Berlin)

Lute tabulature. German

65: 6

PL-Kj, 40634   Kraków, Biblioteka Jagiellonska, 40634 (formerly Berlin)

German, perhaps Stuttgart, before 1550

6: 4 • *7*: 33

PL-Kk, I.1   Kraków, Archiwum i Biblioteka Krakowskiej Kapituly Katedralnej, I.1

Written for the Cathedral at Kraków: 1550–1555 with later additions • Czepiel, *Music*, 76–100

54: 1

PL-Pr, 1361   Poznan, Mijska Biblioteka Publiczna im. Edwarda Raczynskeigo, 1361

15th century • Perz, "Handschrift"; Perz, *Sources* (facsimile and edition)

27: 14 • *41*: 5

PL-Pu, 7022   Poznan, Biblioteka Glówna Uniwersytetu im. A. Mickiewicza, 7022

From Lvov: late 15th century • Perz, "Lvov"

4/*30*/*62*: 5 • *22*/*59*: 4

PL-Wn, 364   Warsaw, Biblioteka Narodowa, Polinski 364

Keyboard tabulature, Krakow, dated 1548. Destroyed in World War II, formerly in S. Spiritus • Insko, "Krakowska" (edition); Jachimecki, "Polnische"; Jachimecki, "Tabulatura"

1/*5*/*14*: 76 • *3*/*19*: 16 • *31*: 3 • *33*: 2

PL-Wu, 58   Warsaw, Biblioteka Uniwersytecka, Rps.mus.58 (*olim* Breslau, 2016)

Silesia, ca.1500 • Feldmann, "Codex"; Feldmann, "Alte"

3/*19*: 2, 6, 18 • *7*: 27 • *12*: 80 • *21*: 12, 38 • *27*: 7 • *31*: 1, 3, 4 • *32*: 2 • *33*: 2 • *34*: 33

PL-WRu, 39   Wroclaw, Biblioteka Uniwersytecka, Brieg K.39

Brieg, late 16th century

65: 2

PL-WRu, 54   Wroclaw, Biblioteka Uniwersytecka, Brieg K.54

Brieg, dated 1578

65: 2

PL-WRu, 428   Wroclaw, Biblioteka Uniwersytecka, I.F.428

Grüne Codex: Frankfurt an der Oder, ca.1516 • Staehelin, *Grüne*

2/*10*: 13 • *3*/*19*: 7, 18 • *7*: 3, 21, 27

S-Uu, 76a   Uppsala, Universitetsbiblioteket, Vok.mus.hdskr.76a

France, perhaps Lyon, ca.1490–1510 • Brown, "New"; Brown, *Uppsala* (facsimile); Christoffersen, *French*, i, 325–34; Stevenson, "Toledo"

1/5/14: 9, 13, 20, 57, 59, 83 • *2/10*: 4, 44, 47, 48 • *7*: 12 • *33*: 9, 20 • *34*: 9, 17, 18 • *41*: 22

S-Uu, 76b   Uppsala, Universitetsbiblioteket, Vok.mus.hdskr.76b

French, early 16th century, with later lute music • MacCracken, *Manuscript*; MacCracken, *Uppsala* (facsimile)

4/30/62: 4 • *54*: 5 • *55*: 1 • *60*: 3 • *61*: 2 • *64*: 15 • *65*: 2

S-Uu, 76c   Uppsala, Universitetsbiblioteket, Vok.mus.hdskr.76c

Stevenson, "Toledo"

4/30/62: 1 • *15*: 3, 8 • *22/59*: 1 • *54*: 5 • *55*: 10, 13 • *61*: 2, 3 • *64*: 12 • *65*: 6

S-Uu, 76e   Uppsala, Universitetsbiblioteket, Vok.mus.hdskr.76e

Frauenburg, Prussia, C16 2/2: Copy of Petrucci editions of Isaac and Weerbeke masses • Stevenson, "Toledo"

31: all • *32*: all • *33*: 2

S-Uu, 89   Uppsala, Universitetsbiblioteket, Vok.mus.hdskr.89

54: 5

SK-BRu, 33   Bratislava, Univerzitná knižnica, Inc.33

Late 15th century, probably Košice. Now lost. Binding fragments • Brewer, "Historical"; *CC*, v, 292–93;

1/5/14: 13

SK-BRu, 318-I   Bratislava, Univerzitná knižnica, Inc.318-I

Late 15th century, probably Košice. Binding fragments • Brewer, "Historical"; *CC*, v, 293–94;

1/5/14: 13

SK-Le, 13990a   Levoča, Evanjelická a.v.cirkevná knižnica, Mus.13990a

Keyboard tabulature, begun 1603

65: 2

US-BLl, Guatemala 8   Bloomington, Indiana University, Lilly Library, Guatemala 8

From S.Juan Ixcoi, Guatemala, late 16th century • *CC*, i, 65

65: 14

US-Cn, VM1578   Chicago, Newberry Library, Case MS-VM1578.M91

Newberry Part-books • Slim, *Gift*

69: 2

US-Cn, 107501   Chicago, Newberry Library, 107501

Capirola lute book: Lute tabulature: ca.1517, in Venice • Cristoforetti, *Capirola* (facsimile); Gombosi, *Capirola* (edition)

1/5/14: 4, 20, 56, 57, 90 • *3/19*: 15 • *4/30/62*: 5 • *8*: 3 • *15*: 5 • *16*: 5 • *33*: 19 • *34*: 3, 4, 23 • *36*: 21 • *41*: 22 • *43*: 1 • *49/58*: 10, 25 • *55*: 13 • *56*: 13, 26

US-NH, 91   New Haven, Yale University Library, MS.91

Mellon Chansonnier: Naples, ca.1475 • Bukofzer, "Unknown"; Perkins and Garey, *Mellon* (edition)

1/5/14: 20, 54, 60 • *3/19*: 30 • *12*: 99 • *33*: 9, 17, 21

US-NH, 710   New Haven, Yale University Library, MS.710

Kyriale, from Spain, perhaps Burgos

54: 6

US-Wc, Laborde   Washington (D.C.), Library of Congress, Music Division, M.2.1.L 25 Case
Laborde Chansonnier. ca.1463–1471 with later additions • Bush, "Laborde";
Guttiérez-Denhoff, "Untersuchungen"
> ***1/5/14***: 9, 13, 20, 42, 54, 57, 59, 70, 71, 83, 87 • ***12***: 72, 95, 97, 98 •
> ***33***: 3, 9, 17, 20 • ***34***: 6, 9, 12, 15, 17 • ***41***: 22

US-Wc, Wolffheim   Washington (D.C.), Library of Congress, Music Division, M.2.1.M 6 Case
Wolffheim Chansonnier. belongs with GB-Lbl, Eg.3051 • Jeppesen, "Frot-
tolahandschriften"; Staehelin, "Florentiner"
> ***1/5/14***: 8, 14, 76, 86 • ***2/10***: 16 • ***7***: 24 • ***12***: 80 • ***22/59***: 7 • ***31***: 3, 5
> • ***33***: 2, 11, 18 • ***34***: 10, 11, 33 • ***41***: 28

US-Wc, 171.J.6   Washington (D.C.), Library of Congress, Music Division, ML.171.J.6
Benedictine, north Italy, ca.1465–1480 • *RISM* BIV/4, 1173; Cattin, *Polifonia*
> ***27***: 14, 15 • ***41***: 5

ZSA-Csa, Grey   ZA-Csa, Grey 3.b.12
Before 1506. northern Italy, Benedictine • Cattin, *Italian*; Cattin, "Nuova
fonte"; Cattin, "Tradizione"; Steyn, *Medieval*
> ***1/5/14***: 2, 20, 60 • ***3/19***: 24, 28, 34 • ***7***: 7 • ***12***: 101 • ***16***: 21 • ***23/37***:
> 9 • ***27***: 6, 9, 14, 15 • ***31***: 1 • ***33***: 9, 21 • ***34***: 2 • ***41***: 5, 7, 34, 43 • ***47***:
> 41

Chapter Twenty

DOCUMENTS

his chapter falls into three sections: first come documents relating to Petrucci's life and activity (Nos.1–25); a second section contains related documents — principally Venetian, details about citizenship, and other privileges (Nos.26–41); finally comes a small group of documents listing the contents of early collections, or specifically citing Petrucci's editions (Nos.42–54). This does not include ownership marks on extant copies, which can be traced through Tables 10-3 and 10-4.

The first section is not as complete as we would like. One principal reason is that, according to Don Ceccarelli, there are no longer any documents preserved in Fossombrone pertaining to dates before 1513. Some of the Notarial documents are now in the Archivio di Stato in Pesaro: other documents for the city from before 1513 were given to the Red Cross in 1952. Any references to such documents are taken from Vernarecci's work, unless otherwise stated.

Secondly, I have not included a number of the documents newly discovered by Gialdroni and Ziino, but not yet published. I am grateful to both scholars for allowing me to consult their work in progress, which has made my chapter 1 considerably more complete.

Finally, some important texts, such as Paulus's privilege, were printed in Petrucci's editions, and are therefore transcribed in the bibliographical descriptions: they are merely cited here.

Note that many of the documents in the ASV have new foliations, which are as visible as the old. In the following, the new are given in parentheses.

Checklist of documents:

BIOGRAPHICAL DOCUMENTS

1.   4.xi.1493: Petrucci sells property in Fossombrone.

2.   25.v.1498: Petrucci applies for a privilege.

3.   27.vi..1499: Petrucci appoints proxies for his Fossombrone affairs.

4.   19.iv.1501: record of Petrucci leasing his house in Fossombrone.

5.   15.iv.1504: Petrucci's appointment to the City Council of Fossombrone.

6.   18.x.1504: Petrucci petitions for admission to the guild of Cestieri.

7.   22.iii.1510: Petrucci's absence from his duties in Fossombrone.

8.   16.iv.1511: Petrucci leases a house in Fossombrone.

9.   22.i.1512: Francesco da Bologna is paid in Fossombrone.

10.   7.v.1512: Petrucci's salary as Captain of the Castles in Fossombrone.

11.   18.viii.1512: Francesco da Bologna, in Fossombrone, acknowledges receiving payment.

12.   1.iv.1513: Petrucci's salary as an Anziano in Fossombrone.

—.   29.iv.1513: Privilege for Paulus de Middelburgh (see Bibliography, No.52).

13.   1.v.1513: Bembo writes to Paulus de Middelburgh, confirming the grant of a privilege.

—.   22.x.1513: Petrucci's privilege from Leo X.

14.   1513–1514: Petrucci's activities as member of Fossombrone's ruling body.

15.   16.ii.1514: Leo X's letter requiring Paulus de M. to attend the Lateran Council.

16.   26.vi.1514: Petrucci's petition for a renewal of his Venetian privilege.

17.   1515–1516: Petrucci's activities as member of Fossombrone's ruling body.

18.   19.viii.1518: Petrucci's formal complaint against Leontini, presented at the house of Lorenzo de'Medici.

19.   1.i.1519: Calvo refers to Petrucci printing his translation of Hippocrates.

20.   17.i.1520: Petrucci is delegated to represent Fossombrone in negotiations with the Pope.

21.   1520: Petrucci leases a water-mill.

22.   17.x.1537: Petrucci nominates a procurator.

23.   12.i.1538. Petrucci seeks to recover type matrices that he had lent to others.

24.   1.xii.1538: The sale of the paper mill in Sora, Petrucci apparently being dead.

25.   3.i.1540: The sale of a paper mill from Petrucci's estate.

DOCUMENTS ON VENETIAN LAWS AND VARIOUS PRIVILEGES

26.   Venetian laws concerning the status of foreigners.

27.   Venetian laws concerning guild membership.

28.   30.vi.1496: Application by de Landriano for a Venetian privilege.

29.   5.iii.1497: Application by Stagnino for a Venetian privilege.

30.   15.vii.1498: Application by Terracina for a Venetian privilege.

31.   15.iii.1499: Moreto seeks a warning from the Venetian Council about breaking privileges.

32.   11.iii.1505: Petition of Marco dall'Aquila, for a privilege.

33.   31.v.1513: Petition for an extension of the Terracina privilege of 1498.

34.   26.ix.1513: Petition by Jacomo Ungaro.

35.   20.iv.1514: Petition of Juan de Brexa for a Venetian privilege.

36.   9.ii.1514/1515: Petition of Bernardo Benalius for a Venetian privilege, including "historie".

37.   27.i.1516. Antico's privilege from Leo X.
38.   1.vii.1536: Marcolini petitions for a Venetian privilege for music.
39.   11.ix.1536: Petition by Torresanus to be allowed to print books.
40.   14.x.1536: Marcolini petitions for a Venetian privilege for a religious book.
41.   v.1536: Marcolini refers to Petrucci's skill as a printer of lute music.

EARLY OWNERS OR CITATIONS OF PETRUCCI'S BOOKS

42.   Venice Cathedral
43.   Colón
—.   Heidelberg MS.
44.   Fugger family
45.   Herwart family
46.   Bottrigari
47.   John IV
48.   Martini
49.   Aaron
50.   Doni
51.   Gesner
52.   Draudius
53.   Bolduanus
54.   Zacconi

Biographical Documents

1.   4.xi.1493: Petrucci sells property in Fossombrone
     ASP, ANF, Notaio Ubaldo Azzi (No.228), Registro for 1486–1497, cc.146v-147r. Deed
     Numbered 203. Now probably lost: quoted from Vernarecci, *Fossombrone* pp. 197–98,
     and Gialdroni and Ziino, "Ancora".
     1493, Novembre 4
     In nomine Domini amen, Anno Domini MCCCCLXXXXIII, indictione XI tempore sanctissimi
     in Christo patris et domini domini Alexandri divina providentia Pape sexti, die vero quarta
     novembris. Actum Forossempronii [. . .] Sancti Maurentii iuxta suos notabiles fines, presentibus
     domino Christoforo de Bonifedis, domino Christoforo de Gigantibus, domino Berardino domini
     Petrini [one word in the margin:] exinactrese et domino Lucantonio magistri Christophori
     barbitonsor testibus &c Ibique cum fuerit et sit quod olim dominus Octavius Johannis Lodovici
     Baldi Petrucii olim vendiderit Francisco ser Rovelli de dicta civitate stipulanti pre se et vice et
     nomine Johannis eius fratris et nomine Elisabet eius matris et pro eorum heredibus medietatem
     pro indiviso cum ipso domino Octavio cuiusdam petie terre arative vineate et arborate site in
     curte Forissempronii in vocabulo Insule veteris iuxta viam a primo sive flumen Metauri mediante
     dicta via bona Iusti m*agistr*i a secundo bona Marrentii [. . .] a tertio et *IIII* bona ipsius domini
     Octavii [. . .] medietate alterius petie terre arative contigue predicte site in dicta curia et in
     vocabolo Plani Sancti Rinierii sive Sancti Antonii iuxta bon Iusti predicti, stratam publicam,
     bona ser Hieronimi ser Oddonis et dictam petiam terre ut supra venditam pro pretio quinqueginta
     duc*atorum* cum quod post dictam venditionem dictus Franciscus nominibus quibus supra
     promiserit dicto domino Octavio quandocumque voluerit sibi dictas res pro eodem pretio
     restituire [margin:] prout de dictis [. . .] patet publica venditionis manu mei notarii infrascripti

[text:] ea propter dictus dominus Octavius prima et ante omnia per se et eius heredes primo et ante omnia cassavit, irritavit et anullavit dictis Francisco et Johanni dictum contractum promissionis de rivendendo quod ex nunc habere voluit pro cassato, irritato et annullato postquam per se et eius heredes [margin:] ac vice et nomine domine Elisabet ei sororis pro qua deinceps promiserit alias promisit de suo tam de predicta quam etiam de presenti venditione [text:] iure emphiteotico episcopatus Forissempronii et cum licentia renovandi &c dedit et vendidit dictis Johanni ser Rovelli et domine Elisabet eius matri ibidem presentibus, stipulantibus et ementibus pro eis et eorum heredibus aliam medietatem dictarum petiarum terre quas habebat in comuni pro indiviso cum dictis Francisco et Johanni lateratarum et confinatarum ut supra ad habendum, tenendum &c et hoc pro pretio et nomine pretii ducatorum sexaginta monetis ad rationem XL bon. pro ducato, de quibus habuit et recepit illo tunc in contanti in quodam sacculo ducatos decem et octo vel videlicet octo ducatos auri et residuum in moneta argentea usque ad dictos decem et octo ducatos, residuum vero dicti pretii dictus venditor contentus et confessus fuit habuisse et recepisse &c Quas res &c promictens &c obligavit &c et maxime casu quo dicta eius soror se nollet ratificare tam presenti quam alteri ut supra facte venditionis obligavit bona hereditaria sibi pro parte tangentia que olim fuerunt Cechi Tamgnini, videlicet unum medietatem cuiusdam petie terre arative site quibuscumque situata &c renuntiavit &c rogavit quod me ad plenum cum pactis, utilibus ad sensum sapientis dictorum emptorum &c iuravit &c

2.   25.v.1498: Petrucci applies for a privilege

ASV, Collegio, Notatorio, Registro XIV (1489–1499), f.159/170r (new 174r)

Serenissimo principe, et Illustrissima Signoria siando fama celebratissima vostra serenitá cum sue concessio*n*, et privilegij | invitar, et excitar li inzegni ad excogitar ogni dì nove inventio*n*, qual habiano esser | acommodita, et ornamento publico da questa invitado Octavian de i petruci da foson-|bron habitator in questa inclyta Cita homo ingeniosissimo Cum molte sue spexe, et | vigilantissima cura ha trovado quello, che molti non solo in Italia, ma etiam dio de fuora | de Italia za longamente indarno hanno investigato che e stampar commodissamente | Canto figurado: Et per consequens molto piu facilmente Canto fermo: Cosa precipue à la | Religion Christiana de grande ornamento, et maxime necessaria: per tanto el soprascripto supplicante | recorri ali piede de vostra Illustrissima Signoria supplicando quella per solita sua clementia, et benignita | se degni concederli de gratia special chome á primo inventor che niuno altro nel dominio de | Vostra Signoria possi stampar Canto figurado, ne intabuladure dorgano et de liuto per anni vintj | ne anche possi portar, ne far portar ó vender dicte cosse in le terre et luogii de Excelsa Vostra | Signoria stampade fuora in qualunque altro luogo sotto pena de perder dicte opere stampade per altri, | over potade de fuora et de pagar ducati .X. per chadauna opera: la qual pena sia applicata per | la mita a lospedal de sancto Antonio, et laltra mita a la franchation del monte nuove, et questo di|manda de gratia singulare ^a^ Vostra Illustrissima Signoria a laqual sempre se ricommanda.

    .1498. Die XXV. Maij
Quod suprascripto supplicanti concedatur prout petit
    Consiliarij
    Ser Marinus leono
    Ser hieronimus vendramino
    Ser laurentius venerio
    Ser Dominicus bollanj.
l.margin:] Non data In tempore ૧.

3.   27.vii.1499: Petrucci appoints proxies for his Fossombrone affairs.

> *ASP, ANF, Notaio Ubaldo Azzi (No.228), ii (1487–1499), 402v-403r.* Deed numbered 228. Probably now lost: quoted from Vernarecci, *Fossombrone*, p. 198, and Gialdroni & Ziino, "Ancora"

In nomine Domini amen. Dictis millesimo indictione et tempore die vero XXVII iulii. Actum in civitate Forissempronii et in domo domini Christo*fori* de Gigantibus sita in quarterio Sancti Maurentii iuxta plateam bona I.D. Antonii de Monte Feretro et alia latera, presentibus Andrea Baldatii et Christoforo Bolsis testibus &c Ibique dominus Octavius quondam Johannis Lodovici Baldi Petrutii de dicta civitate omni meliori modo &c constituit, fecit et creavit supradictum dominum Christoforum et Bartolomeum Matei alias Bianchino ei*us* curatores, actores, factores &c ad omnia et ad omnes causas tam in agendo quam in deffendento et ad vendendum, tenendum et alienandum de eius bonis [ad eorum libitum] cum pote*re* etiam substituendi homines [. . .] et quod unus sive altero vel ambo insimul et in sollidum predicta facere possit et quia periculum . . . fuerit . . promictens &c obligans &c cum pleno mandato &c

Item contentus et confessus fuit penes se in depositum et nomine veri depositi habuisse et recepisse a dicto domino [. . .] presente et dictam confessionem acceptante et stipulanti per se et eius heredes ducatos octuaginta quinque ad rationem XL bon. pro ducato renuntians idem dominus Octavius exceptioni dicte quanti*tatis* non habite &c quo promisit tenere conservare &c omni eius pericolo &c et quos reddere et restituere ad omnem [. . .] petitionem& × obligavit &c renuntiavit &c iuravit &c rogans me ad plenum &c

4.   19.iv.1501: Petrucci leases out his house in Fossombrone

> [*Fossombrone, Archivio Comunale, Tecla V, Prot. VI, Rog. di Aldebrando di Francesco, f. 14*: from Vernarecci, *Petrucci*, p. 125, fn.]

Die 19 Aprilis 1501 actum Forosempronii in domo Domini Octaviani' Ludovici quam tenet ad pensionem Franciscus Iannetti de dicta civitate.

5.   15.iv.1504: Petrucci's appointment to the City Council of Fossombrone.

> [*Fossombrone, Archivio Comunale, Atti di città, 1504*: from Vernarecci, *Petrucci*]

Spectabiles dilecti nostri. Ve mandamo la lista del conseglio nuovo et li avemo aggionti quelli che mancavano per finire il numero de li trentasei. Le ben vero che in la lista non sono: sono trentacinque: perchè essendo del detto conseglio hieronimo de ser Oddo, lo avemo lassato sospeso infinchè sia resoluta la causa sua. Romae XV aprilis 1504. Guido Ubaldus Dux Vrbini.

> [In the list:] Dominus Octavius Petrutius.

6.   18.x.1504: Petrucci petitions for admission to the guild of Cestieri.

> *ASV, Collegio, Notatorio, Registro XV (1499–1507), 1322r*(new 134r). I am grateful to Giulio Ongaro for this reference.

Mccccciiij Die xviij octobris

Intellecta Supplicatione Fidelis n*os*tri octaviani Petrutij de fossimbruno petentis: Q*ui* cum | Ingenio, & Industria sua Invenerit quandam tinctura*m*: compositam ex mixtura qua*m* | ponit sup*ra* Cistellas finas: quas cum facere nesciat, et ob Id requisiverit, et quesierit Ingred*j* | scolam cistario*rum*, ut co*m*modius posset Intentione*m* suam mittere executionj, e gastaldio, & | Soc*ij* Id facere recusaverint p*re*textu certi Cap*itoli* contenti in eo*rum* matricula statuentis q*uod* nemo | possit eriger*e* appothecam nisi ab scolaribus scole no*n* fu*er*it p*ri*us aprobat*us* Quod [scriverit?] laborare misterium | ip*sum*[;] Dignemur sibi concedere: Q*uod* volente eo Ingredi scolam, & solvere factio*n*es ip*sorum* | p*ro*ut faciunt al*ij* magistri ip*s*e facere possit omne Id q*uod* facer*e* possunt Illi omnes, & quilibet existens | In dicta scola Cestariorum pro magistris non obstantj capitulo predicto, & visa responsione[?] virorum nobilium | Hieroni^imi barbarigo, & sociorum provisorum Comunis [Proveditori di Commune] Consulentium Id fierj posse, Infrascripti Domini Consiliarij, | Deliberaverunt, & Terminaverunt: Quod ipsi Petrutio fiat ut petivit, & sic Mandetur | ubi opus fuerit ut observerit.

Consiliarij

Ser andreas minoto

Ser Dominicus Benedicto

Ser Joannes Mocenigo

Ser andreas Venerio.

7.   22.iii.1510: Petrucci's absence from his duties in Fossombrone.

ANF, rogito di Giovan Paolo Mascioli, Teca V, Prot.XVII, p. 7: cited in Vernarecci, Petrucci, p. 125. The relevant section is also quoted in Gialdroni and Ziino, "Ancora", where the authors record that the document is not now to be found in the Archivio di Stato of Pesaro.

[22.iii.1510, records the actions of a substitute] in absentia tamen Domini Octavi Petrutii alterius correvisoris [. . .]

8.   16.iv.1511: Petrucci leases a house in Fossombrone.

ANF, atti di Cristoforo Cartari, Tec.II. Prot.XII, f.547 [now in Archivio di Stato, Pesaro]: cited by Vernarecci, Petrucci, p. 125, fn]

9.   22.i.1512: Francesco da Bologna is paid in Fossombrone.

ASP Rog. di Ercolano di Francesco, Prot. dal 1512 al 1515, f.13: from Vernarecci, Petrucci, 128, fn.

1512, 22.i.] Giuliano di Battista de'Pasquali da Bologna, stampatore in Perugia, riceve dal libraio Pietro di Michele Giannesi ducati venti d'ore per Bernardino Stagnino, con la promessa di pagarli a Fossombrone a Maestro Francesco da Bologna, e di ritirarne da lui formale quietanza da farsi in detta terra di Fossombrone per mano di notaio.

10.   7.v.1512: Petrucci's salary as Captain of the Castles in Fossombrone.

Fossombrone, Arch. Comunale, Libro di entrata e di uscita del Comune di Fossombrone dal 1504 al 1516, f.214: from Vernarecci, Petrucci, p. 153, fn.

Die VII maji 1512. A. M. Octavio petrutio capo de li castelli per li dicti sei mesi e per lui a [. . .] de pietro antonio ducati tre e bolognini trentotto per suo deputato salario de dicto capitaneato

11.   18.viii.1512: Francesco da Bologna, in Fossombrone, acknowledges receiving payment.

Ibid, f.74v: from Vernarecci, Petrucci, p. 128, fn

1512, 18.viii.] Lo stesso maestro Francesco, dimorante in Perugia, confessa d'aver ricevuto la detta somma nella terra di Fossombrone, in quo loco habitabat.

12.   1.iv.1513. Petrucci's salary as an Anziano in Fossombrone.

Fossombrone, Arch. Comunale, Libro di entrata e di uscita del Comune di Fossombrone dal 1504 al 1516, f.231: from Vernarecci, Petrucci, p. 153, fn.

Die 1° aprilis 1513. A M. Octavio petruzo dicati tre e bolognini trentotto per el suo anzianato de marzo e eprile.

—.   29.iv.1513. Privilege for Paulus de M.: see the transcription in the bibliographical descriptions, No.52, Paulus: *Paulina de recta Paschae* (Fossombrone: Petrucci, 8.vii.1513), a1*v*.

13.   1.v.1513. Bembo writes to Paulus de Middelburgh, confirming the grant of a privilege.
      Bembo epistolario: taken from Bembo, *Opere del Cardinale Pietro Bembo ora per la prima volta tutte in un corpo unite. Tomo quarto contenente i breve scritti a nome di Lione X* (Venice: Hertzhauser, 1729)

Paulo Germano Migdelburgensi Forosemproniensium Episcopo.

Egregiam in omni prope disciplina doctrinam tuam plurimarumque optimarum artium scientiam maximi semper feci. Quamobrem excellens tuum ingenium studio ac favore meo commendare aliqua nunc jam in re, atque prosequi cupiens libros de Pasche observatione ac mortis Dominicae die, quos novissime confecisti, volo, atque igni & aqua interdico, & mando, ne quis imprimere possit, imprimive facere, aut impressos venundare, quoad vixeris, praeter te: ut usum alique, ex tuis laboribus hac etiam ex parte percipias, ipsique tui libri diligentius impressi in lucem prodeant. Datis prid. Cal. Majas. M. D. XIII. Anno primo. Roma.

—.   22.x.1513. Petrucci's privilege from Leo X. See the transcription in the bibliographical descriptions, No.54, Josquin, *III Missarum* (Venice: Petrucci, 1.iii.1514)

14.   Documents from the Fossombrone Council during 1513 and 1514.

14a.   21.xii.1513. A list of the members of Fossombrone City Council.
      Fossombrone, Biblioteca Passionei, Atti de'Consigli Municipali, 1513–1520, f.5r-v (new 6r-v)

IN QVO quide*m* con∫ilio ferunt extractj infra∫criptj ad infra∫cripta | officia, vz. | [f.5*v*: list of the 4 Anziani, Notariles Custodie and ad Civila, and Apodimatores:]

Domin*us* Octauius petrutiu∫ &) Reui∫ore∫ viar*um*

Ser Jo. Ant*onius* bapti∫te   )

[etc.]

14b.   5.ii.1514. Petrucci and the Fossombrone City Council.
      Fossombrone, Biblioteca Passionei, Atti de'Consigli Municipali, 1513–1520, 6v (new 7v)

Convocato e cohaduriato con∫ilio generalij |

[The list includes two Antianj and 25 members of the Consilio of whom No.24 is]

Domin*us* Octauianu∫ petrutiu∫

[He is listed as present for meetings on 19 and 26 February, 2 and 19 April, 23 and 31 July, 8 and 15 August of the same year: on 18 June he was again elected a Revisor Viarum, and on 15 August Apodimatore: he was also present at meetings in 1515: 28.ii, 20.iii, 18.iv, 9.v, etc.]

14c.   26.ii.1514. Reference to Cristoforo Gigas in Fossombrone.
      Fossombrone, Biblioteca Passionei, Atti de'Consigli Municipali, 1513–1520, 16r (new 17r)

Secundo fuit propositu*m* qu*e* con*s*ultet*ur* quid age*n*dis sit super facto | do*m*inj Christofori gigantis magistri ludi litterarij qui dicit se infine | instantis men∫is [. . .]

14d.   18.vi.1514. Benedictus is to be paid to play the organ.
      Fossombrone, Biblioteca Passionei, Atti de'Consigli Municipali, 1513–1520 35v-36r (new 36*v*-37*r*)

[36*v*:] Ite*m* sup*er* supp*l*icatio[ne] do*m*ini Benedicti mu∫ici ꝫ haneva*n*tie potestis sibi amor' dei a commune | doctrinj aliquem mercede ad hoc ut possit commodius in hac civitate commemorare | ac etiam promidantis singulis festivis diebus pulsare organum in ecclesi͏ᵃ chatedalj huius civitatum pro ut [. . . : to be paid two florins per annum by the Commune]

15.   16.ii.1514. Leo X's letter requiring Paulus de M. to attend the Lateran Council.

I-Rvat, Vat.ms.3364, f.124v. From Bembo: Lettere . . . Leone X (Venice, 1552), p. 204.

Paulum Germanum Middelburgensem episc. Forosempronien. invitat, ut, quam primum fieri possit, se Romam conferat, cum ejus doctrina opus sit pro rebus Conc. Lateran., praesertim pro emendando Kalendario. "Quoniam et in temporum".

16.   26.vi.1514. Petrucci's petition for a renewal of his Venetian privilege.

ASV, Collegio, Notatorio, Registro XVII, (1512–1514/5), f.92r (New 94r).

Serenissi͏ᵐᵒ Principe & Illustrissi͏ᵐᵃ Signoria La sublimi͏ᵗᵃ vostra concesse á Octaviano di petruci da fossombron | presente supplican͏ᵗᵉ Como a primo Inventor de ſtampar librj de canto figurato per commodita. & orna- | mento de la religion Chriſtiana, et de tuti quellj ſono a tal scientia dediti: che altri che luj | non poteſſe stampar ditti librj de canto figurato, ne intabulature de lauto, & de organo, ne | anche poteſſe portar, ne far portar, o vendere de dicte ſorte de librj in le terre et luogi ſotto- | poſti a la Excellentissim͏ˢᵃ signoria vostra ſtampar da altri in qualunche loco ſotto pena, como in la gratia | a luj conceſſa si contiene. Et perche nel stampar de dicte opere era biſogno di gran capitale et non | ſi trouando Il ditto Octaviano il modo, ne commodita per eſſer pouer homo, tolſe per compagni Ser | Amadio Scoto mercadante de libri, & Ser Nicolo de Raphael, li qualj cum grandiſſima speſa, | summa diligentia, Induſtria, & vigilantia hano ſtampati molti volumj & diverſi de ditti librj, | ſperando conſeguirne qualche utile: ma per riſpetto de le guerre, et turbulentie ſono al pesennte, | non hano poſſuto dar expeditione a le ditte opere ſtampate, adeo che uengano ad hauer intrigato | el loro capitale cum grandiſſimo ſuo danno et iactura; et perche nel poco tempo che reſta de | ditta gratia, e Impoſſibile dare idonea expeditione a ditti librj, ma lj reſtariano a le spale | cum grandiſſimo detrimento de ditto octaviano, & compagni: et ſapendo loro che la sublimi͏ᵗᵃ vostra | non abandona quellj, che di continuo cercano excogitar noue inuention a ornamento de | queſta Inclyta Cita, come fidelissi͏ᵐⁱ ſubditi di vostra sublimi͏ᵗᵃ genibus flexis Ricorrano aj piedj | di quella, supplicando che di gratia special lj sia conceſſo, che a ditta gratia ſia prolungato Il | tempo per annj cinque, cum tuti li modi, & condition ne la ditta gratia dechiariti, azoche | poſſino, ſe non a tute al manco a bona parte de ditte opere Dar qualche bon fine per poter | fruire qualche beneficio de le ſue fatiche, et uigilie, eſſendo Ser Nicolo de Raphael di- | uentato mezo orbo, che non po piu exercitarſi ne le ſue ſolite mercantie, mediante le qual | ſubſtentaua la ſua fameglia; et azoche dittj supplicanti poſſino piu promptamente far | stampare molte altre opere noue de ditte faculta da loro racolte in diuersi loci cum grandis- | ſima ſpeſa, & fatica, et etiam excogitar altre noue inuention a ornamento & beneficio | de queſta inclyta Cita; Et queſto se rechiede de gratia spetial a Vostra Sublimi͏ᵗᵃ aj piedi | de la qual humiliter ſe ricommandano.

.1514. Die. xxvj Iunij.

Quod suprascriptis supplicantibus Concedatur prout petitur.

Consiliarij

Ser Petrus Capellus

Ser Hieroni͏ᵐᵘˢ Contarenus

Ser Donatus Marcellus

Ser Nicolau͏ˢ Bernardus.

17. Petrucci's activities in Fossombrone, during 1515–1516.

17a. 15.viii.1515. Petrucci elected first Anziano of Fossombrone.
  Fossombrone, Biblioteca Passionei, Atti de'Consigli Municipali, 1513–1520, 79v (new *80v*)
[the elected Anziani were:]
Dominus octauiu[petrutiu[| Ser Ga[par florimbenus | Ser Io: andrea[Ser Barthæ | Jo: bap*tis*ta magi[trij chri[tij

17b. 6.xi.1515. Payment to the Anziani of Fossombrone to go to Urbino.
  Fossombrone, Arch. Comunale, Libro di entrata e di uscita del Comune di Fossombrone dal 1504
  al 1516, ff.181–186
[1515, 6.xi. References to P as Anziano and his colleagues, f.181:] [to left:] M.Octavio | S. Gasparre | S. Giovanandrea | Giovanbaptista [a brace for all lines] [to right:] Antiani per tempo fiorini quattro e bolognini doi per una andata a Urbino de tre di per commissione del S. D. como lifo imposto pel commissario duchale.

17c. 17.ii.1516. Petrucci's appointment as Notary.
  Fossombrone, Biblioteca Passionei, Atti de'Consigli Municipali, 1513–1520, 94r (new *95r*)
[Petrucci in coucil, and elected:]
Not*arij* ad ciuilia per me*n*sib*us* Aperilis Maij et Junij

18. 19.viii.1518. Petrucci's formal complaint against Leontini, presented at the house of Lorenzo de'Medici.
  Rome, Archivio Urbano, LXVI,38, f.72v. Dated 19.viii.1518: from Vernarecci, *Petrucci*, 192,
  fn; Campana, "Manente", pp. 514–515
In nomine Domini amen. Anno ab eiusdem nativitate 1518, indictione sexta, tempore sanctissimi in Christo patris etc. domini Leonis divina providentia pape decimi, pontificatus sui anno quinto, die decimanona mensis augusti. In mei notarii etc. dominus Octavianus de Petrutiis de Foro Sempronio impressor librorum etc. requirens in edibus Ill*ustrissi*mi domini Laurentii ducis Medices Rome presentiam magistri Manentis florentini familiaris prefati Ill*ustrissi*mi domini ducis solitis habitationibus prefati domini Manentis, et non inveniens repertis ibidem barnaba pontio et francisco de bono laicis placentine diocesis qui asserebant se esse familiares dictarum edium protestatus fuit in presentia mei notarii et testium infrascriptorum ac dictorum familiarum contra dictum magistrum Manentem licet absentem vigore conventionis cuiusdam operis imprimende inite inter eos etc. de damnis expensis et interesse tam passis quam patiendis etc. et de pena contenta in instrumentis et conventionibus inter eos celebratis etc. offerens se omnia que promissa sunt per se servare etc. Rogans me notarium etc. Acta fuerunt hec Rome in edibus ill*ustrissi*mi domini ducis Laurentii Medices, sitisin regione Sancti Eustachii iuxta sua latera presentibus venerabilibus viris domino Petro Baldini canonico Forosemproniensi et fratre Guilelmo de Salvaterra ordinis Sancti Ieronimi Toletane diocesis testibus etc. Et ego Bartholomeus Benivolus notarius rogatus subscripsi etc.

19. 1.i.1519. Calvo refers to Petrucci printing his translation of Hippocrates.
  I-Rvat, Vat.lat.4416, 2 recto, beneath a paste-over
Hoc in operis Fine i*mprimatur*
Fabius Calvus *[two words inserted in the margin:] ciuis | raue*n*|nis Qui hoc hippocratis opus latinitate | donavit ac Manens leontinus physicus ciuis Flue*n*|tinus, qui sua pecunia ut per

octavi*um* petrucium | forosemproniensis ex solertissimi[∧ impr*essoribus* ∧ non postremu*m* | imprimendu*m* curauit. Ex urbiu*m* principe Roma | legendu*m* omnib*us* latinum Hippocratem emiseru*nt* | Mox et graecu*m* Daturi Deo optimo maximo | Favent*e* Die vero Ianuarij primo Millesi*mo* | quingentisi*mo* ac insuper Decimo Nono.

20.   17.i.1520. Petrucci is delegated to go to negotiate with the Pope.

   Fossombrone, Bibl. Passionei, Atti del Consiglio Municipale, 1520-, 4r.

Do*minum* octavium petrutiu*m* et) oratores ad po*n*tificum

xpofanu*s* canturin   ) sup*er* capse*it*

   [On 3.x.1520, this appointed was prolonged. see f.42v.:]

Conclu[u fuit q*ue* prologuntu*r* voto do*m*ini octavij et bapt*iste* sod|imeri oret*ur* Domi*n*u*m* The[aurariu*m* q*ue* faciat nobi[alignam | dilatione*m* in[olvendo tertiaria*m* [or territoria*m*] et [tatim ellectu*m* | orator ad tesaurariu*m* Domi*n*u*s* Bapt*iste* [tongus

21.   1520. Petrucci leases a water-mill.

   Fossombrone, Atti del Consiglio Municipale, 1520-. From Vernarecci, *Petrucci*, p. 215,
   fn. [According to Ceccarelli, this is probably from "gli antichi libri censarii" = catasto, of
   which there survives one in Pesaro]

Dominus Octavius Petrutius habet in curte Civitatis forisempronii et in vocabulo aque sancte iuxta bona Federici peruxini et heredes Ser Rovelli viam a capite et alia latera terrarum vineatarum tabulas sexaginta novem extensionis tor. decem sept . . . et terrarum scalabr. tabulas nonaginta extensionis torn . . . viginti etc.

22.   17.x.1537. Petrucci nominates a procurator.

   ASP, ANF, Notarile Fossombrone, Notario Girolamo Florinbeni (No.72), A (1518-1562), 243r,
   Deed numbered 210 in the left margin, with the word "extractu*m*".
   Also transcribed in Gialdroni & Ziino, "New Light", p. 527.

Die xvij oct*obris* 1537

Actum in ciuit*ate* foro[empronij in domo do*m*inj | hieronymi egnatij pr*esentibus* dicto domino hier|onymo et bart*olome*co alia[[euilla de bertgamo | te[t*ibus* &c Ibique[epctabil*is* uir do*minus* octaui|u[petrutius de d*i*cta ciuitate fori[empronii | om*n*i meliorj modo &c fecit suu*m* pro|curatore*m* &c leonardum thome de ricijs | de terra mondavij ducati urbinij ibide*m* pr*esentem* et acceptam &c cum pleno | [ptialj et gen*er*ali ma*n*dato &c roga*n* me | notaariu*m* &c

23.   12.i.1538. Petrucci seeks to recover type matrices that he had lent to others.

   ASP, ANF, Notario Girolamo Florinbeni (No.72), A (1518-1562), 248r-248v, Deed numbered
   214 in the left margin.
   Also transcribed in Gialdroni & Ziino, "New Light", pp. 527-528.

die 12 Januarij 1538

Actum in ciuit*ate* fori[empronij [ub porticu | domu[heredum [*er* berardinj gianectj de | d*i*cta ciuit*ate* ante apotectam aurelij | marioctij ius*ta* plateam magnam | et a;oa lat*era* pr*esentibus* benerabi*lis* uiris domino | petro antonio florimbeno et domino | hieroni*mo* egnatio cano*n*i*cis* dicte ciuit*ate* fori[empronii te[t*ibus* &c Ibiq*ue* per[onali*ter* con[t*itus* | dominus pctauius petruitius de d*i*cte | ciuit*ate* om*n*i meliorj modo &c | con[tituit [uu*m* procuratore*m* c | petrantonium alia*s* mazone de | d*i*cta ciuit*ate* ibidem pre[entem | et acceptente*m* &c ad exigendum | leuandumet recuperandum | [248v] qua[dam matrices lictera*rum* a quibuscumq*ue*| per[onis et hominib*us* cuiuscumq*ue* con|ditioni∫ et gradu∫ et maxime a | quodam d*o*m*i*no petro ambro∫ij | librarij comorantij in ciuitat*e* neapolj ∫eu in quocumq*ue* altro | loco &c et de ex actis et rece|ptis quietandum et ad ∫olue*n*|dum et ∫ati∫fatciendum et re|∫tituendum omnem qunatitat*em* | pecuniar*um* pro recuperandi∫ | et rihabendi∫ dictis matricib*us* | lictetar*um* et ad petendum et | re∫pendendu*m* et ∫ub∫tituendu*m* | unu*m* u*e*l plures procurat*ores* &c | promivt*ens* &c cum pleno et gener*a*ᵗⁱ | ma*n*dato &c rogans me &c

24.   1.xi..1538. The sale of the paper-mill in Sora, Petrucci apparently being dead.

    Taken from Gialdroni and Ziino, "Ancora", quoting Mariani, *Petrucci*, pp. 24–25.

    [. . .] libere vendidit dedit tradidit transtulit et assignavit Reverendo domino Mattheo de Cellis civi sorani [. . .] omnia et singula bona stabilia et mobilis sita in territorio civitatis Sore ubi dicitur Carnello, que fuerunt quondam magistri domini Octaviani de Petrutiis de Forosempronio civis sorani per ipsum quondam dominum Octavianum partim vendita ipsi domino Sebastiano [. . .] videlicet: Carteriam per ipsum quondam dominum Octavianum ibi constructam [. . .] quondam domino Octaviano primo patroni et fundatori [. . .] . [. . .] que fuerunt prefati quondam domini Octavian [. . .] . [. . .] partem respective tenebat et possidebat preftus quondam dominus Octavianus primus concessionarious et fundator ipsius carterie [. . .]

25.   3.i.1540. A paper-mill from Petrucci estate is sold.

    ASP, ANF, Notario Girolamo Florinbeni (No.72), A (1518–1562), 270r-271r, Deed numbered 232 in the left margin.

    Also transcribed in Gialdroni & Ziino, "New Light", p. 528.

    Die 3 Januarij 1540

    Actum In ciuitate Fori∫empronij in aula ∫iue | curte Ill*ustrissi*mj ducis vrbinj in introitu ∫olite | re∫identie Ill*ustrissi*me duce∫∫e, pr*esentibus*venerab*í*li viro | domino heiroymo egnatio canoni*co* ciuitat*is* | predicte et Bartholomeo eius fr*at*re carn*a*lj | te∫tib*us*, &c. Ibiqu*e* nobilis et circum∫pectus | vir d*o*min*u*s Seba∫tianus bonaiutus | al*i*as de li∫otta de vrbino p*er*sonali*ter* con∫ti|tutus no*n* ui no*n* dolo no*n* fraude neq*ue* ali|qua alia cau∫a circumunetus ∫e ∫ua | bona vera et ∫incera et libera uolu*n*tate | et eius liberalitate cum fuit et ∫it p*ro*ut | ip*s*a a∫∫eruit q*uod* ip*s*e d*o*min*u*s Seba∫tianus erat | verus creditor d*o*mini Octauianj petrutij de | dicta ciuitate foro∫empronij in ∫uma et | quantitat*e* octuaginta ∫cut*orum* airetor*um* | pro re∫iduo maioris sum*m*e de afflictu | [270*v*] naulo cottimo ∫iue pen∫io*n*e cuiusdam car|tarie ∫ite in curte de di∫trictu [blank space] qua cartaria | olim fuit vendita p*er* dictum d*o*minum octauum | *supra*dic*to* d*o*mino seba∫tiano et habita et retente | p*er* dic*tum* d*o*min*um* octauium a *supra*dic*to* | d*o*mino ∫eba|∫tiano ad cogttim*andum* et quia dic*tus*d*o*min*u*s | octauius et vita functus idcirco | *supra*dic*tus* d*o*min*u*s seba∫tianus ex eius ∫ponte|nea liberalitate ex nu*n*c prout ex | tunc et ex tunc p*ro*ut ex nu*n* dictum | ∫umma*m* et quantitatem octuaginta ∫cut*orum* | ∫imilium remi∫it et inreuicabiliter inter | viuos libera*m* donauit domi*n*e ypolite uxori | olim [*supra*dicti d*o*minj octauik ab∫enti et mihi | notario infra∫cripto ibidem pre∫enti | et ut publice p*er*∫one dictam donationem | et remi∫ionem acceptantij et ∫tipualn*ij* et recipien*ti* | pro vice et nomine dic*t*e domi*n*a ypolite | [271*r*] et om*n*ium alior*um* quor*um* intere∫t seu inter|e∫∫e peterit d*e* qua ∫um*m*a et quantitate | octuaginte ∫cut*orum* et om*n*ium et aliar*um* | rer*um* ex quacumq*ue* cau∫a interdic*tum* | sabatianu*m* [*sic*] et d*o*min*um* octauium dum | viueret negotiatam quietauit et | finem quietationem ut ∫upra*fecit | cum pac*t*is de ulterius no*n* pete*n*do | p*er* ∫e vel aliu*m* &c promic*t*d*n*s ᶜ obli|gans ᶜ renu*n*tians&c iurans &c | rogans me ad plenu*m* &c

Documents on Venetian laws, and various privileges

26.   Venetian laws concerning the status of foreigners.

26a.   The 1305 rules:

ASV. Cinque Savi alla Mercanzia, Busta 25 [= Capitolare 2], 1v.

[This is a 16th-century copy of earlier documents on the rights of citizens of Venice: in this case, of 4.ix.1304, 30 years' residence for foreigners to become citizens and 15 years' to trade]

MCCC V Die IIII Septembris.

IN Maiori Consilio.

Quod Omnes qui steterunt firmi habitatores Venetiarum à viginti = |quinque annis hactenus, et fecerunt, et facient factiones communis | Venetiarum debeant esse Veneti habitando Venetijs, vel in terris | subiectis Domino Venetiarum habendon in hoc illam meliorem pro = |visionem, quae haberi poteris scilicet quod tempore dictæ eorum habita = |tionis non defraudent, et si consilium, vel capitulare est contra, et cetera | et fuit captum per omnes sex Consiliarios, et trigintaduo de XLᵃ [i.e., the Council of 40].-

Item illi qui stetrunt, vel stabunt de castero Venetijs quindecim | annis, et fecissent, et facerent factionis communis, scilicet quod dictum est | superius, possint mercari Venetijs sicut alij, habitando Venetijs, vel in | terris subiectis dominio Venetiarum, habendo in hoc illam meliorem | prouisionem, quæ poterit haberi scilicet quod tempore eorum habitationis | non defraudent, et si consilium, vel capitulare est contra, sit revoca = | = tum quantum in hoc, et fuit captum per sex consiliarios et xxxiiij de XLᵃ.

26b.   Rules about foreigners.

ASV. Cinque Savi alla Mercanzia, Busta 25 [= Capitolare 2], 4r

[This is a 16th-century copy of earlier documents on the rights of citizens of Venice: in this case, of 23.iii.1382, referring to the 8-year provision for foreigners]

MCCCLXXXII. DIe XXIII. | Martij in Maiori Consilio.

Quia super omnia attendendum, et vigilandum est ad habitandum, et augendum terram nostram seguendo vestigia progenitorum nostrorum.-

Vadit pars quod sicut est ordo quod volentes fieri, vel esse cives Ve = | = netiarum de intus, debeant stare, et habitare Venetijs omni sua fami = | = lia per quindecim annos sustinendo onera, et factiones nostri communis, | Et volentes esse veneti, et cives de annis xxv. teneantur stare, et habitare in Venetijs cum sua familia per xxv. annos, et cetera sicut in illis ordinibus continetur. Item ordinetur in bona gratia que | omnes volentes esser cives de intus, teneantur stare, et habitare in | Venetijs cum uxore, vel sua familia per octo annos solum, sustinendo | onera, et factiones nostri communis reales, et personales, sicut alij | cives nostri. Ille vero, qui volent fieri, vel esse cives nostri de xxv. annis, teneantur stare, et habitare in Venetijs cum uxore | vel familia sua per xv. annos solum, sustinendo onera nostri communis, | et factiones reales, et personales, sicut alij cives nostri, quibus elapsis, | fiant eis privilegia sua secundum usum, Illi autem de conditionibus | prædictis, qui stetissent in Venetijs cum familijs suis per totum tempus | guerræ proximæ præteritæ, et fecissent, et sustinuissent onera, et | factiones nostri communis reales, et personales, sicut alij cives nostri, proban = | = do sic esse nostris provisionibus communis, si stetissent, et complevissent | tempus prædictum in Venetijs per modum superius annotatum, vel sta = | tim sicut complebunt ipsum tempus, expediantur pro civibus Vene = | = tiarum de Quindecim, vel Vigintiquinque annis, sicut erunt, et fiant eis privilegia secundum usum, et istud servetur, et intelligatur in illis; | qui Venetijs se præsentabunt, et facient se scripsi ad provisores communis | usque unum annum proximum et si Consilium et caetera.-

[This is followed by a series of rules allowing foreigners to sell *abroad* merchandise they make in Venice.]

26c.   Rules about foreigners.

ASV. Cinque Savi alla Mercanzia, Busta 25 [= Capitolare 2], 5r-5v.

[This is a 16th-century copy of earlier documents on the rights of citizens of Venice: in this case, of 5.vii.1407, referring to marrying a Venetian and thereby becoming a citizen.]

MCCCCVII. Die v. Iulij

In Maiori Consilio.

.   .   .

Quia una de rebus ad quas principaliter semper vigilarunt, et vigi = | = lare debent illi, qui rgunt, et dominantur civitates, fuit, et est ad | populandum, et implendum illas hominibus, quia dictæ civitates sunt | tantum divites, et potentes, quanto sunt populo copiose, quod si est | necessarium in aliqua civitate, est in nostra, quia est valde diminuta | populo propter mnortatlitates præteritas, et guerras, quæ multæ | fuerunt, et propterea bonum sit facere prouisionem superinde, ita | quod alie ingene habent causam, et materiam se reducendi ad habi = | [5v] = tandum civitatem nostram, quod multi libernter facient, si videbunt | posse gaudere beneficijs, quibus gaudent alijs cives nostri, et aggregari | in numero eorundem. Vacit pars quod ordinetur, et provideatur quod omnis illi forenses, | qui habitant, vel venient in coetero habitatum civitatem nostram Venetiarum, et acceperint in uxorem aliquam Venetam habitatricem | Venetiarum, ipso facto Venetijs cum sua familia habitando, sint | cives civitatis Venetiarum de intus tantum, et gaudeant omni pri = | = vilegio, et beneficio, quibus utuntur, et gaudent alij cives Venetiarum | de intus tantum cum omnibus cunditionibus aliorum civium Vene = | = tiarum de intus. quandiu Venetijs habitaverint, ut est dictum, et debeant presentare se nostris provisoribus communis, ut faciant | examinationem debitam, et postea accipiant sua privilegia, quæ | eis fiant per nostram cancellariam secundum usum.

Rules about foreigners.

26d.   *I-Vnm, Cl.It.VII,2451 (10130).*

[This is a further copy of documents from the Consilio Maggiore and the Consilio Rogatorum, regarding the rights of citiznes and foreigners in Venice. It includes the following items:

1r. 4.ix.1305. Consilio Maggiore. Citizenship for foreigners after 25 years. Transcribed above.

1v. 12.ix.1363. Consilio Rogatorum. That citizens could *navigare*, but foreigners could not, even after being made citizens.

2v. 15.iv.1374. Consilio Rogatorum. That certain *forestiere* could not trade through the *fondego dei tedeschi*, unless the rulers of the Fondego gave them a dispensation.

3v. 24.iii.1382/3. Consilio Maggiore. Transcribed above.

4r. 1.xii.1383. Consilium Rogatorum. Allows foreign artificers to sell goods relevant to their craft, if produced abroad. See below

4v. 16.vi.1385. Consilio Rogatorum. Amplifies the previous law, with the provision that the *Fontico Theutoni* can not be used.

5v: 5.vii.1407. Magiiore Consilio. A foreigner taking a Venetian wife is ipso facto a citizen. Transcribed above.

27.   Venetian law concerning membership in Guilds

   I-Vas, Provveditori di Comun, Busta 1, 86v and 236r.

   [Two laws enacting rules about guilds: the first allowed foreigners into guilds if they had a Venetian wife]

   M. ccclx Die septimo februarij in Conc° X^m [concilio de dieci]

   Che damo quanti tutti de l'arte di veluderi et samiterj i quali sono | nar∫udi de fore∫tieri in que∫ta cita et quelli ch*e per* habitation contegnuda | dalli ordenj nostrj dieno e∫∫er Tratadj p*er* cittadini dentro, et quelli, i quali | hano tolto mogier venetiana po∫∫ono e∫∫er Elleti, et e∫∫er gastaldj zu | deri *de* quelle arte, et participar dj honorj, beneficij grauezze, de quelle | scuole, et arte, et que∫to medesimo sia Intero, et os∫eruato p*er* tutti li | mestierj d*i* que∫ta n*ost*ra Citada, et se nelle sue mariegole alcuna consa | in contrario appares∫ee sia concelado, et scrito in le so marargole la p*rese*nte deliberation.

   [The second gave the rules of procedure for those who wished to enter a guild but were barred from entry. It is headed]

   Che quelli vorono Intrar nelli mestierj, et sarano repudiatj | p*er* quelli sono alle banch*i* d*e*lle schuole pos∫ino hauer | recorso alli prouediotrj de comun.

   M.D.XIX: Die XXIX Xmbris in Conso Xm: [text continues]

28.   30.vi.1496: Application by de Landriano for a Venetian privilege.

   ASV, Collegio, Notatorio, XIV (1489–1499), 144v (New 148v).

   [Landriano had only lived in Venice 5 years: perhaps not granted?]

   MccccLxxxxvj. Die Vltimi Junij

   Serenissi^mo Principe et Excel^a Signoria

   Humiliter Significa el Sp*ectabi*le Doctor di ragion Ciuile e canonica M*esser* Bernardin de | Landraino milanese come havendo lui dia per il tempo de'anni cinque passati in qu*e*sta | vostra inclita Cita de Venexia invigilato, et sostenuto gran fatiche in apostillare e far | additione a molte lecture Civile a Canonice, si per la publica utilitade come per | conseguirge qualche fruoto. Et far le altre opere a le lecture De Bartholo e dil speculo | come é notorio. Pare ad esso Supplic*ante* iusto, et honesto che del suo ben operar*um* lui hij riporti lo fruotto, et no*n* altri. Et per tanto priega la prelibata Sereni^ta et Sig*noria* v*ost*ra li vogli | conceder gra*n* special che niuno possi dicte opera stampare ne fare stampare cu*m* apostille | over additione del dicto M*esser* Bernardino fin ad anni .X. in questa Citade, ne inn loco | subdito al Dominio di v*ost*ra sig*noria*. Ne altrove stampate portare in dicti loghi a vender | sotto pena de duc*ati* .X. p*er* opera De ^la^qual la mita sia de lo accusator laltra mita | de lhospedal de la pieta. Et azio che v*ost*ra sig*noria* intendi che esso suppl*icato*r no*n* impetra tal | gratia azio che dicte opere se vendino piu care agli studenti come fano alcuni, Si offerisse | di no*n* la sorte vendere piu dil Solito, et fare ogni giorno Cosse utile di studenti in honor | di questa cita. et Exc*e∫*sa s*u*a alequal continue se ricomanda.

      Die ultimo Junij

      Q*uod* Dicto Supplicanti concedatur Sicut petit, et alijs q*uae* plurimis concessum fuit.

      Consil*io*

   S*er* Marinus De garzonib*us*

   S*er* Constant*ius* De priolis

   S*er* And*r*ea Dalege

Ser Ieronymus Bernardo.

[at right margin:] Non datum in temp[or]e

29.   5.iii.1497: Application by Stagnino for a Venetian privilege for chorales and liturgical books.

ASV, Collegio, Notatorio, XIV (1489–1499), 149v (new 153v).

MccccLxxxxvij Die Quinto Martij

Cum ad Communem Religiosorum utilitatem Thomasius venetibus sit Impressum Graduale, | Antiphonarium et psalmistum á choro, libros ad nome dicto é nomine impressos: ne ab | alijs hec eadem opera in futurum sorte imprimentibus, Cum [. . .] eis conficiendis. Ingentem sit | expensurus pecuniarum summam, tam insigni afficiatur factura. Domini Consiliarij | Infrascripsi nominaverunt Quod Hermini lixat tam venetis quam a localibus sub juristitionem Dominij Imprimere, vel imprimi facere dictos libros iusta decenium, vel alibi impressos | vendere, aut vendi facere sub pena omissionis librorum, et libri X. pro | quolibet volumine. Comnta presentem ordinem vendito vel reperto.

Consiliio

Ser Jacobus Leono

Ser Bartholomeus Minio

Ser Nicolaus Trivisano

Ser Benedictus de cà da pesaro

30.   15.vii.1498: Application by Terracina for a Venetian privilege for Arabic, etc.

ASV, Collegio, Notatorio, Reg.17, 49v (new 51v).

Serenissimo principj et exellentissimo Dominio Venetiarum humiliter supplica el fidel suo seruitor | & Citadin suo Venetian Democrito Terracina habitauer in uenetia. Cum sit | chel habia da far stampar alcune opere in lingua arabica, morescha, soriana, | Armenicha, Indiana et barbarescha cum grandissima et quasi Intollerabel | spexa et cum fadige et pericoli grandissimi et in utilita de la republica | christiana: et exaltation de la fede: et augmento de la scientia naturale et | ancor de la medicina per Conseruation de la salute de le anime et corpi de | molti et Infiniti fidel christiani che vsono le soprascripte lengue Considerata la | effrenata Cupidita de alcuni: et lo liuor: et inquieta de molti li quale non | resteriano uoler tuor el fructo de la Inzegno: et spexe: et fatiche del soprascripto | supplicante cum facti concorrentia de le soprascripte opere, poi che fusseno de si luntanj | paesi conducte in questa cita de venetia: pertanto supplica quella se degno | conciederli gratia che In termene de anni vintacinque proxime nisun ardisca stampar | o far stampar libri de qualunque sorte se siano in lettere de le lingue soprascripte ne que | in venetia ne in luochi subditi a la serenita vostra ne stampati in altri luogi | et terre: Ne in questa inclita Cita, ne nauigarli in vostri nauilij, ne di vostri | subditi portar: o vender, ne far vender in li soprascripti vostri luogi et terre | ne per el Colpho cum nauilij forestieri, soto pena ogni fiata de perder dicti | libri: et pagar ducati duxento doro: lamitta vadi al hospedal di sancto Antonio: | el Resto a I Auogadori de Comun: obligandosse lo soprascripto supplicante non stampar | mai libri: liquali tractino Cossa alcuna pertinente à la secta Maonettana | ne che siano in fauor de quella: ne contra la nostra sanctissima fede | ma tute in fauor: et augmento de la fede christiana.

Die XV. Iulij 1498

Quod dicto supplicati Concedatur quantum in supplicatione continetur.

Consilio

Ser francesco Marcello

Ser Marinus Leonus

Ser francesco valare[[o)Vice consil*ii*
Ser Vincentius Barbaro)
Ego Eneas Carpentus notarius Du. R^x autentia exemplarij.

31.   1499: Moreto seeks a warning from the Venetian Council about breaking privileges.

31a.   15.iii.1499: The original request
   ASV, Capi del Consiglio de'Dieci, Notatorio, Reg.2 (1491–1500), 155v (new 179v).
Per magnificos do*m*inos capita ex*c*ellentissi^{mi} consilij decem mandatur om*n*ibus et | singulis impressorib*u*s libror*um* et alijs ad quos spectat et spectare possit q*uo*d obser|verit et obseruare debeant antescriptam concessionem factam, | p*er* Ill*ustrussi*^{mu3} dominu$_3$ de impressione volumin*um* de scriptor*um* in supplicatione*m* | et no*n* andeant contrafacere sub pena specificata i*n* eadem suppli|catione, q*uo*ni*am* si ansi fuerint contrafacere irremisibili|ter punientur, et pena ab contrafactorib*u*s exigetur. Qu*oni*am intentio*n*is | et voluntatis eor*um* est, ut om*n*ia prefata concessio Ill*ustrissi*^{mi} dom*i*nij penitur obser|vetur sine aliquo impedimento et turbatio*n*e.
[l margin:] Sup*plicati*^{o} est in folio subscripto. ∧antonij moreto de brixia∧ p*er* dom*i*nos | consiliarios et postea seg*uu*ntur | in alio latere o*mn*iu*m* scriptu*m* mandatum.

31b.   3.iv.1499: the same request, with the printer's name inserted.
   ASV, Capi del Consiglio de'Dieci, Notatorio, Reg.2 (1491–1500), 157r (new 181r).
[Same document, completed with the printer's name, dated 3.iv.1499]
Per magnificos do*m*inos capita ex*c*ellentissi^{mi} consilij decem mandatur om*n*ibus | et singulis impressorib*u*s libror*um* et alijs ad quos spectat et spectare | possit, q*uo*d observerit et obseruare debeant concessionem, factam p*er* | Ill*ustrussi*^{mu3} dominu$_3$ de impressio*n*e [struck through:] libror*um* [clear:] volumin*um* de scriptor*um* in | supplicatione*m*, et no*n* andeant contrafacere sub pena specificata in eadem suppli|catio*n*e, q*uo*ni*am* siansi fuerint contrafacere, irremisi| biliter punie*n*tur, et pena a contrafactorib*u*s exigetur. Qu*oni*am intentio*n*is | et voluntatis eor*um* est ut o*mn*ia Prefata concessio Ill*ustrissi*^{mi} dom*i*nij penitur | observet*ur*, sine aliquo impedime*n*to et turbatio*n*e.
[l margin:] Sup*plicati*^{o} ∧antonij moreto de brixia∧ est i*n* folio | subscripto p*er* dom*i*nos consiliarios et | postea seg*uu*ntur in alio | latere o*mn*iu*m* scriptu*m* | mandatu*m*.

32.   11.iii.1505: petition of Marco dall'Aquila, for a privilege.
   ASV, Collegio, Notatorio, Registro XXIII (1499–1506), f.141v (new 143v).
Sere*n*issi^{mo} Principi: eiusq*ue* Sapientissimo Consilio:
Humilit*er* supplica el ser*ui*tor de la Subl*i*mi^{ta} V*o*stra Marco da laquila Cum sit che | cum gra*n*dissima sua fatica, et spesa no*n* mediocre se habii inzegnato à comune utilitate | de q*u*elli, che se delectaro*n*o sonar de Lauto nobilissimo Instrume*n*to p*er*tine*n*te a Varij Zentilho-|mini far stampar la tabullatura, et rasone de metter ogni Canto i*n* Lauto cu*m* summa | i*n*dustra, et arte: et cu*m* molte dispendio de tempo, et facultate sua: laq*u*el op*er*a no*n* maj | e sta stampata: Se degni la Ill*u*strissima Signor^a vostra concierder de sp*e*cial gra*t*ia al p*re*fato supplic*an*te | v*o*stro fidelissimo: che alcuno chi esser se vogli si i*n* q*u*esta Cita de Venetia, come i*n* tute | altre terre, et lochi nel Dominio de la Subl*i*mi^{ta} v*o*stra no*n* adisca, over prosuma far stampar | alcuna tabullatura de lauto de alcuna sorte, nec et*iam* se alcuno la stampasse extra dictionam Ill*ustrissi*^{mi} dom*i*nij V*o*strij, possi q*u*ella ve*n*der, over far vender i*n* q*u*esta Cita ne altrove nel p*re*dicto | Domi*n*io sotto pena, si aq*u*elli: che la stampasseno i*n* le terre de la Subl*i*mi^{ta} vostra, come aq*u*elli la co*n*ducessono à ve*n*der i*n* ipse terre de p*er*der Irremissibilit*er* le loro op*er*e et librj tabullatj, et

| *per* cadauno de q*u*elli stampatj, over ve*n*dutj pagar duc*ati* X. Il terzo delaq*u*el pena sia | del accusator, un terzo de q*u*el rector, over magistratto a chi sara facta la accusa | et lalt*r°* terzo de epso suppl*ican*^te acio el possi cu*m* tal grat*i*a de vo*s*tra Cel*situdi*^ne continuar a ve*n*der | le ditte op*er*e et librj tabullatj et ch*e* alcu*m* cum li togli la industria et utilita ch*e cum* tantj | sudorj, et vigilie el pr*e*fato fidel*issi*^mo suppl*ican*^te se ha acquistato: et q*ue*sta prohibitio*n*e se | i*n*tende valer p*er* an*n*i X come i*n* similibu*s* ad altr*i* esta co*n*cesso: Ai pied*i* delaq*u*al Sublim*i*^ta vo*s*tra | humilit*er* se ricom*m*anda.

Die ij Martij M D V.

Infra*s*crip*t*i Domi*n*j Consiliarij Intellecta sup*ra*scrip*t*a supplicatio*n*e terminaveru*n*t q*uo*d sup*ra*scrip*t*o | suppl*ican*ti fiat q*uo*d petit.

Consiliarij

S*er* franciscus barbadico

S*er* Nic*o*l*aus* Fosca*r*ino

S*er* Marcus de Molino

S*er* Andreas Grittj.

33.   31.v.1513: Petition for an extension of the Terracina privilege of 1498.

ASV, Collegio, Notatorio, Reg.17, 50r (new 52*r*).

Sere*nissi*^mo principi: et Ex*ellentissi*^moDoo*m*inio Venetiar*um*. humil*issi*me supplicano li fideli | sui seruitori et Citadini venetiani habita*n*ti in venetia leio: et paulo | Di Maximi. Cum sit che del 1498. adi xv. luio M*esser* Demochrito Terrazina, | cu[[i chiamado Barba de li decti suppl*ican*ti obtine[[e vna gratia de la Ill*ustrissi*^ma Signor*i*^a | Del Contrta[cripto Tenor. Et e[[endo occor[o chel dicto M*esser* Democrito per | volunta de la M*ae*s^ta Diuina sia defu*n*cto: et pa[[ado de que[ta pr*e*sente | vita sença dar' principio alcuno: ma solame*n*te habia facte de grande | et qua[i intollerabel spexe sença alcuna vtilita: et habia la[[ati li [opra[cripta | suppl*ican*ti videlicet lelio: et paulo di Maximi sui Neuodi fioli duno suo fratêllo: | I qualli humelme*n*te supplicano: et Dimandano che quella se degni confir-|-marli á loro decta gratia per an*n*i vinticinq*ue* proxi*me*: et che Ni[uno ardi[ca | stampar, ne far stampar dicti libri sotto le pene contra[cripte in om*n*ibu*s* et p*er* omnia.

Die vltimo Maij. 1513.

*Q*uod concedatur dictis supplicantib*us* quantum petet

Con[il*ii*.

S*er* Dominicus Benedicto

S*er* Petrus Marcello

S*er* Aloi[ius Sanuto

S*er* franc*escus* Bragadeno.

34.   26.ix.1513: Petition by Jacomo Ungaro.

ASV, Collegio, Notatorio, Registro XVII (1512–1514/5), 78r (new 80*r*).

Sere*nissi*^mo principi etc₇. per che suole la Ill*ustrissi*^mo Sig*n*oria remunerare q*u*elli ch*e* giouano. In | que[ta Inclita Cita cum qualche vtile et Ingenio[a Inventione: p*er*tanto have*n*do | el fidel*issi*^mo seruitor di q*u*ella Jacomo vngaro intagliatore de lettere et habita*n*te | za *quaran*^ta an*n*i in q*u*esta Ex*cellentissi*^mo Citade, trovato el modo de [tampare Canto figurato: et temendo da Altri. come accade. toglia el fructo de le sue fatiche. Supplica | a la Ex*cellentissi*^ma vo*s*tra de li piaqua Conciederli gratia che niuno altro po[[a stampar | o far stampare dicto Canto figurato in que[ta Citade, ne In lochi sotopo[ti | a q*u*ella per an*n*i xv. *p*roximi: ne alcune stampati portandi a vender in que[ta | Citade, o in lochi de q*u*ella. Soto pene de perder tuti li libri: et ducati Cento | per cadauna volta dal se Contrafaçia. De la qual pena sia la terſa parte | del hospitale de la pietate: laltra del Accusator: laltra del officio dove sia facta | la Conscientia. Et che sia licito al Accusator Andar a qualunche Officio | che li piaqua: de questa Inclita CIta et questo Dimando de gratia ala Illustrissima | Signoria vostra a laqual suppliciter semper se Racommanda.

       xxvj. Septembriſ 1513.

Quod fiat ut petitur cum hoc ne preiudicitur Concessionibus di que sorte facte | fuissens ante hac.

       Consiliarij

    Ser Zacharias Gabriel.

    Ser Petrus. Marcello.

    Ser Ludovicus grimani.

    Ser Andreas Dandulo viceconſilio

35.   20.iv.1514: Petition of Juan de Brexa for a Venetian privilege.

      ASV, Collegio, Notatorio, XVII (1512–1514/15), 87v-88r (new 89v-90r).

Serenissimo Principo

Humiliter et cum ogni debita reverentia supplicantia a la sublimita vostra el fidelissimo suo servitor | Zuan da Brexa depentor: cum sit che lui supplicante essendo studioso di la virtu habi | fatto uno desegno e quello fatto Intagliar in legno a sui nome nella qual | opera ha consumato molto tempo cum sua grande fatica et spesa per eſſere opera excellente | et tuto ha fatto volentiera per eſser desideroso de honor, et poi mediate le fatice | sue et industrie poter conseguir qualche utilita et emolumento de ditta sua opera la|qual è, la historia de Traiano Imperator: et havendo voluto lui supplicante far qual | che experien|tia de ditta sua opera, et veder come reusonia[??], ne'ha fatta stam-|par probare de quelle cum intention poi de farla stampar tuta, et perche in effecto | lo disegno et opera preditta è, bella e degna, e stat Immediatc folla da alcuni | altri, e hano commenzato voler quella stampar, laqual cosa seria contra | ogni debita de Justitia, et, a graue mio danno, che havendo lo stentato et fadigatome longo tempo in far ditta opera che altri devesse senza sua fa-|dica [. . . : seeks a privilege for 10 years, with a penalty set at 5 ducats: approved 20.iv.1514]

36.   9.ii.1514/1515: Petition of Bernardo Benalius for a Venetian privilege, including "historie".

      ASV, Collegio, Notatorio, XVII (1512–1514/15), 103r (new 105r).

A° Dmo xiiijmo. Die viiijmo Februarij

Serenissimo Princeps et Excelsa ac Illustrissima Signoria Reverentur ead Humilior supplicatur per el vostro fidelissimo | servitor: Bernardino Benalio stampador gia ongamente habitante in veniesia, exercitante larte | Impressoria: Cum sit chel ditto supplicante voglia stampare le opere del ſotino & li soi Conseglij | Cum molte additione che fin hora non sono piu stampate ne giu ne altrove, & le opere de tulio | cum li comenti, ★ etiam uno commento novo de baptista guirino elqual mai piu ci sa stampato. | Item el tiddo fa designare & intagiare molte Belle hijstorie denote çioe la submersione di pharaone | la hijstoria di susanna: la hijstoria del sacrifitio de abraham, et altre hystorie nove che non | sono mai piu stampate nel Dominio di Suo sublimita laqual opera & hijstorie ut supra esso | supplicante supplica che nisum altro che lui possi stampare, ne far intagliare per anni Diece proximi: | Et etiam se fosseno impresse fora del Dominio de lo Excellentissimo stato vostro sotto pene de Ducati | Dui per ogni opera óver hijstoria a chi conduca óver fara condur ó ver vendera & le volumi | ó ver hijstorie siano perſi contrafacendo ci la presenso gratia, ó Imparer ó presento: laqual pena vade | uno terço al Arsenal nostro, & un terço á lo accusador, laltro terzo ali vostri Signori De nocte. | Aliquali sia de la Commissione de exequire Contra o chi Contrafacasse ut supra, come in similibus | ei sta concesso per le signorie vostre á molti altri. Alla gratia de lequel reverentur & humilitatur Ricomandatum.

       Die viiijmo februarij 1514

Quod suprascripto supplicanti sint. Quod petit:

       Consiliarij.

   Ser Petrus leonio

   Ser Francescus Foscarino

   Ser Aloijsius Pisanus

   Ser Hieronijmus Pisaurens

37.   27.i.1516. Antico's privilege from Leo X.

       Liber quindecim missarum

      Leo Papa X:

      Dilecto Filio Andree Antiquo de Montona clerico Parnetinae dioceseos in Vrbe Commoranti.

DIlecte fili salutem et apostolicam benedictionem. Decorem domus dei, quam decet sanctitudo, et divini cultus augumentum intensis desideriis affectantes, Vptis illis gratu, prestamus assensum, per que christi fidelium devotio augeri, ac ecclesie et loca ecclesiastica ad laudem illius, qui in altis habitat divinis preconiis valeant iugiter resonare. Cum itaque, sicut fidedignorum relatione didicimus, tu in arte imprimendi libros Cantus figurati non parum expertus existas et artem seu liros huiusmodi in magno uolumine imprimendi inueneris, ac in alma Vrbe nostra similes libros in magnoi uolumine, pro quibus quingentorumducatorum auri de Camera nel circa exposuisti, et longe mairoes expensas te subire oportet, imprimi facere desidered, si tibi super hoc de aliquo oportuno remedio prouideatur, nos igitur te in huiusmodi laudabili proposito confouere, tibique super hoc oportune prouidere uolentes, tibi usque ad decennium quoscumque libros Cantus figurati in dicto magno uolumine ad regalibus Chartis in dicta Vrbe et extra eam et in quibuscumque aliis locis Romanae Ecclesiae mediate uel immediate subietcis, per te uel alium seu alios imprimendi et imprimi faciendi ac illos in Vrbe ad predictis et quibusuis aliis locis publice uendenti auctoritate apostoloica tenore presentium licentiam concedimus et facultatem: et nihilominus Vniuersis et singulis Archiepiscopis Episcopis Abbatibus et dilecto filio Octaviano de petrutiis de forosempronii et quibusuis aliis librorum impressoribus et personis tam ecclesiasticis quam secularibus etiam cuiuscumque dignitatis stats gradus ordinis et conditionis existentibus sub excomunicationis late sentenciae et ducentorum ducatorum similium Camere apostolice eoipso postquam presentibus contrauenerint absque alia declaratione applicandorum et librorum quos impresserint amissionis poenis, ne dicto durante decennio similes libros in dicto volumine regalis folii dumtaxat in Vrbe et locis praedictis absque tua expressa licentia imprimendi seuimprimi facere aut ad hoc auxilium consilium uel fauorem prestare quoquomodo presukmant districtius inhibemus. Quocirca Venerabili fratri hieronymo episcopo Asculano, et dilecto filio Amadeo electo Augustensi et pro tempore existentibus Camere apostolice Auditori et dicte Vrbis Gubernatori ac eorum cuilibet committimus et mandamus quantus tivi in premissis efficacis defensionis presidio assistentibus faciant te concessione huiusmodi pacifice frui et gaudere, non permittente per dictum octauianum et quoscumque alios impressores et personas quacumque auctoritate fungentes in persona seu bonis desuper quomodolibet molestari inquietari uel perturbari, Contradictores quoslibet et rebelles per censuras ecclesiasticas et alia opportuna iuris remedia, appellatione postposita, compescendo, ad cuiusmodi excommunicationis et alias penas totiens quotiens opus fuerit incurrisse declarando, inuvocato ad hoc si opus fuerit auxilio brachii secualris. Non obstantibus premissis ac constitutionibus et ordinationibus apostolicis etiam informa breuis per nos et sedem apostolicam etiam ad quorumuis aliorum impressorum et persomarum instantiam ac etiam motu proprio et iex certa scientia etiam concessis confirmatis et innouatis ac in posterum forsan concedendis et innovandis quibus omnibus, etiam si pro eorum sufficienti derogatione de illis eorumque totis tenoribus specialis specifica et expressa mentio habenda foret, eorum tenores presentibus pro expressis habentes, illis alias in suo robore permansuria, hac uice dumtaxa specialiter et expresse derogamus, Ceterisque contrariis quibuscumque. Per hoc autem quibusdam aliis in simili forma brevis litteris eidem octuiano, sub data videlicet. xxii. Octobris Pontificatus nostri Ano Primo, super impressione librorum nonullorum cantus figurati concessis, dummodo tecum super impressione librorum per te (ut prefertur) in dicto volumine folii reglais duntaxat imprimendorum dicto durante decennio non concurrat, nec tibi super hoc propterea aliquod preiudicium afferat, non intendimus in aliquo derogare. Volumus autem, quod postquam presentes littere per te impresse fuerint, illarum impressioni absque alia subscriptione aut decreti Iudicis appositione in indicio et extra illud plena et indubitata fides adhibeatur, prout adhiberetur eisdem presentibus originalibus litteris si forent exhibite vel ostense. Datum Florentie sub Anulo Piscatoris Die xxvii Ianuarii M.D.XVI. Pontificatus Nostri Anno Terio.

   Ja. Sadoletus.

38. 1.vii.1536: Marcolini petitions for a Venetian privilege for music.

   ASV, Senato, Terra, Registro XXIX (1536–1537/8), f.33v (new 54v).

Sere*nissi*mo Prin*cipe* et Ill*ustrissima* Signo*ria*

Sempre V*ostra* sub*liminita* é ſtata. et é larghiſsima donatrice delle gratie sue allj | fideliſsimi ſoi, che con sincerita q*u*elle dimandano, e par eſser circa | xxx. anni che fu uno Ottauiano da Foſsanbrono, che ſtampaua | musica nel modo, che se imprimono le *lettere*, et é circa xxv. anni | che tal opera non si fa, alla quale impresa si é meſso non pur la Italia | ma l'alemagna et la franza, é non l'hanno potuta retrouare. Io Fran*cisc*o | Marcolini ſuis ceratiſsimo Seruitor di quella eſsendomi affaticato molti | giorni, é non con poca ſpesa in ritrouar tal cosa, accio che io poſsá | godere il *bene*ficio d*e*l tempo, et denari ſpesi in tal faticha, richiedo di | ſpetial gratia, che per anni X. mi ſia conceſso che alcun'altro, che | Io fran*cisc*o servitor di q*u*ella, non poſsa ſtampar, ne far ſtampare muſica, et | intabolature con charatteri di ſtagno over di altra meſtura, ne in | alcun luogo ſtampado in tal modo si poſsa vendere, sj in queſta inclyta | Città, come D*omi*nio suo, ma sia in arbitrio di ogn'uno ſtampar in | legno, come alp*re*sente sj coſtuma, pur che non riſtampino le opre ſtampate | per me, ſotto pena alli contrafacenti di perder tutti li arctificij fatti p*er* | far tal opra, é tutti j libri se trouaſsero, li quali vengano in me | et pagar duc*ati* Doi p*er* volume, da eſser applicatio la mita alli hoſpital | di S*an*to Jouannipolo, et il reſto alli *officio* faciſse l'executione, Dando | podeſta et ampla liberta à cadauno officio sj di queſta Citta, come | D*omi*nio suo di far oſservar ditto priuilegio g*ra*tie et *cetera.*

   Die pri*mo* Julij

[l.margin:] Cons*ilio* om*nes* et | Cap*ite* de *quaran*ta.

[text:] Che p*er* auttorita di que[to Consi*li*o sia conceſso al ſopraſcri*tt*o supplica*nte* | quanto el domanda si come se contiene

In la suppl*icatio*n soprascritta.

   De parte   150

De Nò   7
Non significatio[?]   9

39.   11.ix.1536: Petition by Torresanus to be allowed to print books. Refers to the loss of books
       imported from Paris: 11.ix.1536.
              ASV, Senato, Terra, Reg.XXIX, f.53r-v (new 74r-v).
       Serenissi^mo Principe, et ex*cellentissi*^mi Signor^ie. Hauendo Io francesco d'Asola gia molti anni |
       con nostro padre fatto stampar infiniti libri in questa ex*cellentissi*^mo Città, et fatto | nouamente
       uenir alcune balle di diuersi libri fatti in Paris con alcune | carte ouer desegni di tutta la franza a
       loco per loco con le sue misure | et miglia particular, li quali desegni ſono ſta fatti per uno
       ex*cellentissi*^mo mathenatico | decto Orontio Delphinate, et per mia mala ſorte le balle
       capitorono in | Thurrino, doue imm*ediate* li quasconi intratti quelle sachizorno insieme con | li
       libri, Per la qual cosa eſsendomene domandate da infiniti nobeli di queſta | Città, ho deliberato
       de far di nouo stampar ditto desegno della franza | con aggiongerli molti et diuersi lochi lasciati,
       et max*ime*^e nella prouenza, | Item l'Antidotario grande di Nicolao Proclo tutto, et li Agrocoltori
       | greci, et Juba de Agricoltura greco mai piu ſtampati, Item molte | correttion[i], emendationi,
       et Tauole ſopra el libro de differentijs ſtirpium | ex Dioscoride, et commentaria Oribasij in
       Aphorismos Hippocratis, | et Tractatulus nouus Rhasis de curatione morborum particularium |
       [53/74*v*] et epitome Quintiliani authore iora, et uno libreto di canto canzon 29 | de paris,
       Pertanto, accio che altri noti habbino il frutto delle mie fatiche | suppl*ico* de gratia & sublimi^ta se
       degni concedermi gratia con il suo ex*cellentissi*^mo | Senato, che per anni XX dal di chel
       sopradetto desegno, et sopradetti | libri con le zonte et lochi che per me saranno ſta fatti
       stampar, niuno altr^o | che mi in questa città li possa stampar, ò ſtampati altroue possano |
       portarli nel Dominio de vostra subl*imita* sotto pena di perderli et duc*ato* uno per | cadauno
       desegno ouer libro, et duc*ati* tresento, da esser diuisi in tre | parte, una parte alla pietà, una
       parte all'accusator, et una parte | a quel magistrato fara l'executione, al qual sara fatta la
       conscientia, et alla gra*tia* et c*etera*.
              Die XI Septembr*is*.
       [l.margin:] Consil*io*
       Che al ditto suppl*icant*^e sia concesso, che per anni Diece alcuno altro | che lui non possa far
       stampar, ne stampate uender li desegni | et altre opere sporaſcript*e*, ne in questa Città, ne in
       alcuna delle | Terre et loci della Signoria Nostra sotto pena di perder li libri, et de pagar duc*ato*
       uno per libro, et de altri duc*ati* cento, la mita | delli qual sia del accusator, et l'altra mita del
       Arsenal, essendo | tenuto farle stampar con diligentia con diligentia in ottima carta, et ben
       correttij
              De parte   127
              De Non   6
              Non syni   5

40.   14.x.1536: Marcolini petitions for a Venetian privilege for a religious book.
              ASV, Senato, Terra, Reg.XXIX, 61v (new 82v).
       Serenissi^mo Principe, et excelso Concili^o uolendo lhumile seruidor di vostra sublimi^ta |
       Franceſco Marcolini al present*e* stampare una noua et molto util opera compoſto | dal
       Reveren^do padre frate hieronymo Malipiero de l'ordine de sancto francesc^o di | oſseruantia
       intitulata il petrarcha spirituale, et approbata come catholica, et | fidele dal Reverendissi^mo
       Monſignor Patriarca, si come appare nella licentia delli ex*cellentissi*^mi sign^or | Capi. fatta adi

21. di februario pro∫simamente pa∫sato, et douendo∫i far tale | impre∫sione in noua, et bella forma di letere nouamente fatte a que∫to | propo∫ito, et con noue figure rechiedendo co∫si la qualita dell'opera | et pero non con poca ma molta spe∫a; humilmente supp*lic*a il solito pri | uilegio, et gratia de u*o*stra sub*limi*ta uidelicet ch*e* per anni .x. niuno altr° | impre∫sore nel Dominio po∫sa stampare il prefato Petrarcha spiri | tuale, ne altroue stampato uender, eccetto e∫so supplicante de licen | tia del *presen*to auttore sotto pena di perder libri, et di pagare duc*ati* 25. | per ogni uolta ch*e*l fu∫se contrafatto da e∫ser di∫tribuiti per mitade à | lo accu∫ator, et all'hospital della pieta offerendo∫e et *cetera*.

[l. margin:] Con∫iliarij

Die xiiij. su*prascrip*ti

Che al so*prascrip*to supp*lican*te sia conce∫so quanto ch*e*l dima*n*da co*n* la condicion ch*e*l [. . .] uir^a la parte pre∫a in que∫ta conu°: /.

De parte———152———11———7.

41.   v.1536: Marcolini refers to Petrucci's skill as a printer of lute music.

RISM 1536[11]: *Intabolatura di liuto de diversi, con la bataglia, et altre cose bellissime, di M. Francesco da Milano* (Venice: Marcolini, v.1536). Unique copy at A-Wn, S.A.78.C.28. [References to Gianmaria Giudeo, il Te∫tagro∫∫a, and Taddeo Pi∫ano. . . .] Gentili∫∫imi Spiriti, benche tutti gli Stormenti di fiato, e di corde, per tener qualità de l'armonia che e∫ce da | le ∫phere mentre ∫i mouano i Cieli,[. . .] E perche l'unica vertù de i tre ∫opra detti innamora di ∫e ∫te∫∫a ogni bello intelletto de∫iderando∫i | d'imitargli, mancata la commodità, che ∫apea dargli il Fo∫∫ombrone, ne ∫apendo∫i trouar la uia u∫ata da lui, i nu | meri, e le note del ∫uono fino a qu con a∫∫ai tempo, e con molta ∫pe∫a ∫on ∫i intagliate in rame, et in legno. Ma | io, che ripo∫o quando mi afatico in ∫eruigio de i uertuo∫i hò mi∫o il piede for∫e piu oltre, che ne le ∫trade le quali | egli ∫i ∫ecrete fece, che non pensò fo∫∫er mai calpe∫te d'alcuno. [Marcolini declares his future plans.]

Early owners or citations of Petrucci's books

42.   Documents from the Cathedral of Venice. My thanks to Jonathan Glixon for drawing this to my attention.

42a.   24.vii.1514: the Cathedral buys a copy of the *Paulina*.

ASV, Mensa Patriarcale, Busta 58. VIII.Entrate e spese, 1511–1514, openings 66right and 67right.
[66] + Jesus maria M ccccc° xiiij adi 24 luio
[Item No.5 is headed] 31 [? the date]
P*er* conto de librij | [. . .] p*er* la paolina del vescove de fosimbro*n* de∫legate . . .[2 denarii]

[67] + Jesus marie a M ccccc° xiiij adi ii aogusto
[Item No.12] P*er* Conto de librj | & cop*er*tj p*er* un plauto p*er* frate anzolo, [. . .] p*er* ligadura de uno libro al ditto D 15 p*er* ligadura de ial° fabio et paulina del ep*iscop*o fosimbro*n* L4 D4 val.

42b.   8.xii.[1514]

ASV Mensa Patriarcale, Busta 62. A.Registro Cassa, 1511–1514, opening 133, verso
Conto de libri die dar[?] adi 8 dec*em*bro p*er* coperto p*r*imo libro | p*er* fra anzolo et p*er* le op*er*e del piego i*n* tutto

[4 lines]

adi 31 liuo per coperta perla paolina del episcopo di fosimbron allegata f 143 L − D 20

42c. Payments to] magistro bortholomio organista [for salary, on the same manuscripts, openings 9, 63, 106, 122, 148 and 152: the payments continue through the next MS: B.Registro Cassa, 1514–1517, on openings 20, 41, 62, 110 and 135.]

43. *Cristoforo Colón*: citations in his various catalogues, for editions by Petrucci. I have had access only to the facsimile of *Registrum B*. The other entries are taken from Chapman, "Printed": in that case, I have only taken her principal entry, in each case. (Numbers in parentheses are those of Chapman's entries.)

43a. Cristoforo Colón: *Abecedarium B*

col.66 Alexandri agricole misse quinque In cantu composite. I. le serviteur / Je ne demande malheur me bat primi toni. secundi toni. 5594. V. 1504. (No.8)

col.117 Antonij de fevin misse tres in cantu. 5960. Fo. 1515. 4c (No.43)

col.220 Bernardi pisani musica sopra le canzone del petrarcha 6944 in 4. partes. fo. 1520. 8a (No.44)

col.244 Canti. b. n°. 50. *4683*. V. 1503. 4a (No.5) [No.10]

col.244 Canti. c. numero 150. V. 1503. 4a 4653 (No.7)

col.606 Exaudi preces meas o mater gloriosa del tuo. 4967 (No.40)

col.647 Francisci bossinensis tenori et contrabassi liber primus et 2ᵃ. en toscano. 3803. 2287 (Nos.38,39)

col.676 Frotole li. 5°. n°. 6. *6547*. V. 1505. 4a [and] Si dome fede se dipinge biancha una candida. *6547*. (No.16)

col.676 Frotole li°. 6. n°. 6. *4690*. V. 1505. 4a (No.17)

col.691 Gasparis misse .5. scilicet ave regina celorum / o venus banth / e trop penser / octavi toni / se mieulx ne vient. 5598. V. 1506. 4 (No.21)

col.747 Harmonice musices odhecaton cantionum quod plurium in gallico. 6856. V. 1502. 4 (No.1)

col.747 [? . . .] et aloa n°.98. 5108. V. 1504. 4a (No.9)

col.781 hymni de tempore et de sanctis liber primus de canto. n°. 37. 4974. V. 1507. 4b (No.28)

col.893 Jo. ambrosii dalza intabulature de lauto libro quarto. 2543. 3054 (No.36)

col.936 Jo. guiselin misse quinque. V. 1503. 5090. 4 (No.4)

col.942 Jo. marie alemani intabulature de lauto libro tertio. 2582. 3053. 3203. 4a (No.30)

col.945 Jo. mouton missarum quinque in cantu liber primus. 5965. fo. 1515. 4 (No.42)

col.965 Isaac misse quinque. I. charge de deul / misericordias domini / quant Jai au coeur la spagna comme feme. 5599. V. 1506. 4 (No.20)

col.983 Liber primus n°.12. 4989. V. 1506. 4b (No.18)

col.983 Lamentationum liber secundus tromboncini gasparis et erasmi. 4980. V. 1506. 4 (No.19)

col.989 Laude libro p°. in. damonis curarum dulce lenimen. 6549. (No.35)

col.989 Laude libro 2°. n°.60. 4701. V. 1507. 4a (No.32)

col.1021 lomme arme cum aliis 49. in cantodorgano. *4683* (No.5)

col.1041 Magnificat liber primus de quolibet tono duo 4975. V. 1507. 4 (No.29)

"Misse in cantu" fragmenta n.27. 4695. V. 1505. 4 (No.15)

"Obreth" missa ie ne demande / grecorum / fortuna desperata / malheur me bat Salve diva parens in cantu. 9713. V. 1503. 4 (No.2)

—   Petri castellani harmonice musices odhecaton. 5108. V. 1504. 4a (No.9)

—   Petri de la Rue misse quinque in cantu composite. I. beate virginis / puer natus / Sexti ut fa / nunquam fue pena maior. 5593. V. 1503. (No.6)

—   Moteti. a. no°. 33. *8741.* V. 1504. 4 (No.12)

—   Misse de orto dominicalis jai prins amours lomme arme la bella se assied petita camuseta. *6545.* V. 1505. 4 (No.13)

43b.   Cristoforo Colón: *Registrum A*

1985   Magnificat liber primus de quolibet tono duo diversorum auctorum et In toto opere nil aliud continetur nisi magnificat variorum auctorum cum .4. vocibus et prima est agricole est Impressum Venetijs per octauianum petrucium. anno .1507. 14. octobris est iIn quarto Costo en Venetia .26. suelods a cinco de Julio de 1521 y e ducado val .134. sueldos. (No.29)

43c.   Cristoforo Colón: *Registrum B* (facsimile in Huntington, *Catalogue*)

2543   Intabulatura de lauto libro quarto Joannis ambrosij dalza .36. continens | cantiones quorum tabula e[t in principi° .Item e[t Regula pro ne[cientibus canere italice | .Item. prima deue. prima Cantilena .Item. galdibi ca[tigliano. ultimᵃ .Item. Laudate dio. Imp. | venetiis anno .1508. ultim° decembris e[t in 4°. ad longum. co[to enRoma .76. | quatrines por setienbre de .1512. (No.36)

2580   Intabulatura de lauto libro p° de *france[co Spinacino* in principi° e[t regulam | siue Canon ad docendum modum pul[andi ea que in libro [cripta [unt. | Latine et italice. liatine .Item. intelligendum e[t. italice .Item. Prima deue po|[ita et sequiturʳ epistola octauij petrutij .Item. Cum mihi. Item cri[tophori pierij | exha[ti con .Item. e[t natura. Item tabula cantilenarum totius operis prima .Item. aue | maria de Jo[quin. Ultimᵃ .Item. Recercare & tantum habentur principia Can-| tilenarum quw [unt .22. Imp. Venetiis anno .1507. e[t in 4°. ad longitudi | nem ligatus &in unaquaque pagina [unt .4°s ordines notularum | co[to en Roma .76. 1uatrines, por Setenbre. de .1512. (No.22)

2581   Intabulatura di Lauto libro [ecundo de *france[co Spinacino* continet | .34. Cantilenas [eu carmines principia quorum tabula e[t in principio prima .Item. berge|rette. ultimᵃ .Item. Recercare, In principi° e[t Regula pro illis qui Canere ne[ciunt | italice et latine. Italice .Item. prima deue. latine .Item. intelligendum e[t, | Imp. Uenetiis anno .1507. die Ultimᵃ martij est in .4°. ad longum | co[to enRoma .74. quatrines pro Setebre de .1512. (No.23)

2582   Intabulatura di Lauto, Libro Tertio, & opera que Continᵉᵗ sunt Joannis | marie alemanij cuius epistola .I. Come la mu[ica. cantilene [unt .25. | quorum tabulae[t in principio. Item Regula pro illis qui canere ne[ciunt Itali|-ce et Latine. Italice .Item. prima deue. Latine .Item. intelligendum e[t pri-| ma Cantilena .Item. come feme. Ultimᵃ .Item. Recercare giouan maria. Imp. | Venetijs Anno .1508. Junij .20. e[t in 4° ad longum. Co[to en Roma | .110. quatrines por Setenbrᶜ de .1512. (No.30)

2895 Libro de motetis de *Canto dorgano* y son .4. volumenes por*que* cada voz esta de
por soy en un libro. Imp. e*n* venecia por otavio petrucio anno .1504. septebris .15.
habet quelibet pa*rs* .49. Cantines seu motetos preter le typle q*uod* h*abet* solum .47.
q*uorum* tab*ula* alpha*betica* est in p*r*incipio. uniuscuiusq*ue* p*ar*tis dimidij folij .2. col.
La p*r*imera es ave maria Josquin y en las .3. p*ar*tes la postrimera es in lectulo meo
en el tiple la postrimera es dignitate singularis. costaro*n* las 4. p*ar*tes en Roma .247.
q*u*atrines anno .1513. por hebre*r*o. es en 4. ad longum. (No.10)

3459 Pauli de midelburgo paulina in .2. p*ar*tes diui*s*a p*r*ima | e*s*t de recta pa*s*che
celebratione et diuide*t* in .14. lib. | et lib. in enpr[?] ope*r*i. et Nume. p*r*imus lib. I*dest.*
No*n* veniet | Je*s*us *s*alue*r*e lege*m* .14. D. legitimum pa*s*cha Cu*s*todi*e*tur |
per*or*atio. *Id est.* habes lector et in hac p*er*seq*ue* Continentur cale*n* | daria & tabula
pro pa*s*chate inueniende. 2ª pars | e*s*t de die pa*ss*ionis *Christ*o e*s*t diui*s*a in
.29. lib. et lib. | in capo epitho. et *s*ermonis Author ep*istol*a .*Id est* Cogitati | mihi
p*r*imus lib .*Id est* et si multa *s*unt ragiome*n*to 19. et ult*erius* | D. nonfirmatum et
p*er*fectum e*s*t, in de*mo* libro e*s*t *Christi* | pa*ss*io depicta per*or*atio *Id est* habes
*s*ub Compe*n*dio in fine e*s*t | hieronj po*s*tumij ep*istol*a .*Id est* si qua Item*chri*[*s*tophori
gi | ij .*Id est* q*u*od Clari .*Item* aliud hieronymi po*s*thu | mj .*Id est* p*er*fectum e*s*t, Item aliud
bla*s*ij benuerardi .*Id est* | Non hic in p*r*im*is* totius ope*r*is
e*s*t Leonis .X. eplicit. *Item.* vene | rabilis f*r*ater Item alia autho. *Id est* Cum *s*acri.
Item alia conf[?] | .*Id est* *s*ola religione. Item alia *Id est* maximis e*ss*a. Item alia
.*Id est* | vera e*s*t. Item alia .*Id est* et similta. Item alia .*Id est* pudenda | nimis Itemalia .d
est proximi e*ss*e I. inuocatio .*Id est* cepit I. | *s*ub facere Imp. foro*s*empronij 8ᵘᵒ Julij
.1513. co*s*to e*n* Roma | 315 q*u*atrines por Nouimbᵉ de .1515. es in folio

3803 Tenori e Co*n*trabas*s*i intabulati col soprani in Canto figu- | rato p*er* ca*n*tar e sonar
col Lauto. e*s*t in toscan° cum suis | notulis diuiditu*r* in 2. lib. e*s*t author
fra*n*c*is*cus bo*ss*ine*n*s*s*is | in p*r*incipi° primj libri e*s*t tab*ula* alpha*betica* carminum.
I*tem.* regu*la*. In. | prima deue. Item autho*r*is ep*istol*a .*Item.* grande .*Item* Carmen.
I*tem.* per mo*s*trare | op*us* .*Item.* affliti spiriti mei. D. pre*s*e asdegno. Imp.
veneti*j*s | ano .1509. martij .27. in p*r*incipi° secu*n*di libri e*s*t tab*ula* car | minum
alpha*betica* .*Item.* regu*la* .*Item.* prima deue .*Item* autho*r*um ep*istol*a | .*Item.* grande
.*Item* Carmen .*Item.* per mo*s*trar. op*us* .*Item.* felice fu. D. anzi | bellarte. Imp. in
foro Sempronij. Anno .1511. maij .10. | e*s*t in q*u*arto° ad longum. El prim° co*s*to
.10. q*u*atrines el .2° .96. | en Roᵐᵃ por Seti*en*bre de .1512. (Nos.38,39)

43d.   Cristoforo Colón: *Supplementum*

Frotole li°. p°. n°.62. V. 1504. 4a (No.11)

Frotole li°. 2°. n°.53. 4720. V. 1507. 4 (No.33)

Frotole li°. 3°. 4365. V. 1507. 4a (No.27)

Frotole li. 5°. n°.6. 6547. V. 1505. 4a (No.16)

Frotole li°. 6.n°.66. 4690. V. 1505. 4a (No.17)

Frotole li°. 7°. 4366. V. 1507. 4a (No.25)

Frotole li°. 8°. n°.56. 5595. V. 1507. 4 (No.24)

Frotole li°. 9°. n°.64. V. 1508. 4a 4671 (No.37)

Frotole li°. 10. n°.75. 4967. fo. 1512. 4a (No.40)

Frotole li°. 11. n°.68. 4716. fo. 1512. 4 (No.41)

Intabulature de lauto li°. 4°. 36. cantionu*m* Jo. ambrosij [. . .] 2543. V. 1508. 4a (No.36)

Missarum diversorum n°.5. li.pª. 5596. V. 1508. 4 (No.34)

Misse de orto dominicalis jai prins amours lomme arme la bella se assied petita camuseta. 6545. V. 1505. 4 (No.13)

Moteti .a. n°. 33. 8741. V. 1504. 4 (No.12)

Moteti de passione de croce de sacrame2nto de b. virgine. n°.30. 5969. V. 1503. 4a (No.3)

Moteti in .4. partes n°.49 licet tipla licant solum 47. 2895. V. 1504. 4a (No.10)

Moteti lio. 40. no.55. 4645. V. 1505. 4a (No.14)

Moteti li°. p°. n°.18 a cinco. 6548. 4 (No.31)

Stramboti ode frotole soneti et modo de cantar versi latini ecapituli li°. 4°. 4675. V. 1507. 4a numero .91. (No.26)

— .   The inventory of the Chapel Library of Ottheinrich, at Neuburg (Pfalz), is now D-HEu, Cod.Pal.Germ.318. It has been studied by Lambrecht, *Heidelberger*, and references in chapter 10 are taken from her work.

44.   The Fugger family collection would have been one of the largest of Petrucci's editions, if it had survived intact. The inventory is edited in Schaal, "Musikbibliothek". Entries for Petrucci's editions appear in the first section, under the following heading:

Volgen truckhte Buecher auch mit 4 stimen

46.   Misse Gaspar. 4 Voc. In gelb Leder punden.

47.   Misse Alex. Agricole mit 4 Voc. In gelb Leder.

48.   Fragmenta missarum In gelb Leder.

49.   Misse Ghiselin In gelb Leder.

50.   Mutetti della Corona Lib 1° In Praun Led. punden.

51.   Mutetti C. In gelb Leder punden.

52.   Mutetti de Orto In gelb Leder punden.

53.   Misse Moutton Lib. 1.° In gelb Leder.

54.   Mutetti della Corona Lib. 2.° In Rot Praun Leder.

55.   Magnificat Lib. 1.°

[Nos.55–58 are bracketed together, with the annotation:] In Blaw Leder bund. Sein mit einem Spago alle 4 zusamen bunden.

56.   Hymnor. Lib. 1.°

57.   Lamentation. Lib. 1.°

58.   Lamentation. Lib. 2.°

59.   Mutetti della Corona Lib. iiii In Braun Rot Leder bund.

60.   Misse plures diuersi Author. Lib. 1.°

61.   Misse de la Rue.

62.   Misse Ant.° de Feuin.

63.   Mutetta 4 Voc. Isaac.

64.   Mutetta con 4 Lib. iiii.

[65.]

66.   Qunquaginta Carminum.

[67–69.]

70.   Harmonia musices Lib 1.° odhecaton

[Nos.70–74 are bracketed together, with the annotation:] sein zusamen bund mit Spago.

71.   Strambotti. ode. frottole. Sonettj. Lib. 4

72.   Frottole Lib. 8.

73.   Laude Lib. 1.° et 2.°

74.   Mutettj N° 33.

75.   Musica di Bernardo Pisano Sopra le Canzone del Petracha prue forme. In grien Leder bunden.

76.   Mutettj Lib. 2° De diuersi. In grien Leder.

45.   The Herwart family owned some books, which passed to S. Anna in Augsburg, and were there catalogued in 1620. Their books have been studied in Martinez-Göllner, "Augsburger," and Slim, "Music Library."

45a.   From Martinez-Göllner, "Herwart", p. 47
Di Joanmaria intabulatura de lauto libro terzo

45b.   From Schaal, *Inventar*, p. 30.
Gsanbuech in langquart in Pappen vndt braunen Leder vberzogen, gelb am schnit mit grienem bäntlein. Frottole libro sexto septimo et octavo Venetijs. 1507. 30 kr. (Entry in the S. Anna catalogue of 1620, with Books 7 and 8 of frottole: Schaal, *Inventar*, p. 30.)

46.   Bottrigari made notes on his own collection of early musical editions. These were transcribed by Gaspari, and an extract follows:

I-Bc, P59, [1]r

[1r] Le ſequenti parole di pugno del cav. Ercole Bottrigari ho | io letto in certe poſtille d'un opera del Galilei = (★) | Ho'io delle Canzoni o Barzellette in libri ſtampati | fin del 1480 in Venetia, = Forſe tali canzoni | erano ſtampate in tavole intagliate in legno. Il | medesimo Bottrigari poſsedeva parecchie opere muſicali d'antiche edizioni che trovanſi riferi = | te da lui ne'suoi mſs come qua ap | reſo:

1.   Libro di Canzᵉ Francᵉ 1502. De Orto, Jo. Stokem . . . Jo. Tadinghem . . .

2.   Laude lib. p° 1508.

3.   Laude lib. 2°. 1507.

4.   Mott. N°.33. 1504.

5.   Libro de Canti N°.50. 1503.

6.   Mott. de Passione. 1503.

7.   Libro 4°. Strambotti Frottole de Marc. Chara viso Ant. Capreolus, Philiippus di Lurano, Compere

[8–11: Frottole V, VII, VIII, IX]

12.   Lib. 10° 1512. Philippus Mantuanᵘˢ. Organ. Jo. Hesdi = | mitis, Jo. Scrivano, Franciſcuſ J. G.B.de Ferro | [1v:] Dionis dit Papin da Mantua, Pietro da Lodi.

[13–20: Miss.div.1, 1508; Miss 2. Obreth, 1503; Miss 3 Josquin II, 1503; Miss 4, Brumel, 1503; Miss 5, Ghiselin, 1503; Miss 6, Isaac, 1506; Miss.7 Agricola 1504; Miss 8, primus Josquin 1502]

21   Hymnorum Lib pᵘˢ. 1507. Jo. Martini

47.   The massive music library of King João IV of Portugal was given a printed catalogue in 1649.

Primeira Parte do Index da Livraria de Musica do Muyto alto, e poderoso Rey Don IOÃO IV. Nosso Senhor (1649) (from the facsimile and commentary (Sampaio Ribeiro, *Livraria*). The numbers are original.

85.   *Miſsarum* Iusquin. lib. primus. a 4. | Do mesmo. a 4. lib.2. | Do mesmo. a 4. lib.3.

.   .   .

[caption:]   *Miſsas.*

247.   De Obrehet. | Ioannis Ghiselin.

256.   De Orto, a 4.

.   .   .

         Motteti de la Corona.

607.   Io. Mouton, & outros, a 4. lib.I.

         De la corona. De Terache, & outros, a 4. lib.I.

         De la corona. Iosquin, & outros, a 4. 5, & 6. lib.I.

         De la corona. | Constantius Festa, & outros, a 4. 5. & | 6. lib.4.

48.   Giovanni Battista Martini made notes on his own collection, as well as writing about books to various other correspondents. For the latter, see Schnoebelen, *Padre.*

I-Bc, Epistolaria Martiniano, I.ii.35f.1r

Pongo qui la serie delle Opere più antiche che io mio trovo avere stampate da Ottavio Petrucio | Canti B. numᵒ 50 Mot a3.4. Voci di diuerſi Aut Venet. per Octav. Petrutius | 1501 in 8 biſl. | Brumel Miſse 4. Voc. Ven. per Octav. Petrutius 1503. in 8 biſl. | Obreht, Miſse 4. Voc. Ven. per Octav. Petrutius 1503. in 8 biſl. | Alex. Agricole Miſs. 4. Voc. Ven. per Octav. Petrutius 1504. in 8 biſl. | De Orto Miſse. 4. Voc. Ven. per Octav. Petrutius 1504. in 8 biſl. | Gaspar Miſse. 4. Voc. Ven. per Octav. Petrutius 1504. in 8 biſl. | Henr. Isac. Miſse 4. Voc. Ven. per Otcav. Petrutius. 1506. | Miſ. diverſ. Auct. lib.ib.1., li Auttori sono Obreht, Philippus Baſiron, Brumel, Faspar, Piero de la | Rue. Ven. per Octav. Petrutius 1508. in 8 biſl. | In fine le sopravenniete Opere qui è che il priuilegio della repubblica di Venet. e queſto | e disceſo, ma solamente Avennato. | Proſeguiſso Le Opere stanmpate dal Petrutio. | Lıbrı Miſs. Josquin 4 Voc. Forosemproniȷ per Octav. Petrutius ave Foroſempronienſe. | anno domini 1516. de 29. Maij. | [1v] Lib. 2. Miſs. Josquin 4. Voc. Impreſsum Foroſempronij per Octav. Petrutium. Anno Domino | MDXV. die XI. Aprilis. in queſt'Opera vi è disteſo il Priuilegio del Papa che incomincia. *Leo PP. X. dilecte fili Salute etpostolica*m *benedictione.* &c. *datum* | *Rome apud Saanctu*m *Petru*m *sub Annulo Piſcatoris. die XXII. Octobris M. D. XIII.* | *Pontificatus no*ſ*tri Anno Primo. Petru*ſ *Bembus.* | Miſse Josquin lib.3. . Voc. Impreſsum Foroſempronij per Octav. Petrutium. Anno Domino | MDXIIII. de primo Martij. vi è anche in queſt'Opera le soeſso Priuilegio | di Leone X. PP. come sopra. | Queſte sono le Opere oiù antiche, e prime stampate, che io mi trovo avere, ma di Andrea Antiquo [. . .] ne ho alcuna [. . .] Bologna li 22 Giugⁿᵒ 1746

49.   Aaron's reference to *Canti C.* (For more details, see Judd, "Reading".

Pietro Aaron: *Trattato della natura et cognitione di tutti gli tuoni* (Venice: Bernardo Vitali, 4.viii.1525) chapter 5, f.C1r

[in a discussion of third and fourth mode:] Per tanto si conclude che tal canti piu tosto saranno chiamati del quarto tuono per la discendente continuatione, come O maria rogamus te nel libro de motetti c et molti altri con questo modo facilmente potrai intendere

50. Antonfrancesco Doni: *Prima Libraria*

di diversi a 4 et a cinque parecchi libri Magnificat & lamentationi (see Haar, "Libraria", p. 117, where it is argued that this probably does not refer to Petrucci)

51. Gesner's list of Petrucci's editions.

Conrad Gesner: *Pandectae*, Book VII, under the heading] De cantionibus Italicis, vel in Italia impressis praesertim Venetiis [For details see, Bernstein, "Gesner": Bernstein's numbers are given here in parentheses

82*r*] "TITVLVS IIII. DE CAN- | tionibus ecclefiafticis"

Miffarum decem à clariffimis Muficis | compofitarum, necdum antea (exce- | ceptis tribus) æditarum, libri 2. im- | preffi Forofempronij 1515. (No.130)

Libri de cantu figurato in Italia im- | preffi.

Cantus centum fignati A. (No.131)

Cantus cinquaginta fignati B. (No.132)

Cantus centum quinquaginta figna- | ti C. (No.133)

83*r*] Motetti de piu forte fignati A. (No.134)

Motetti de paffione fignati B. (No.135)

Miffæ quinq*ue* de Obreth. (No.136)

Miffæ quinq*ue* de Iofquin. (No.137)

Miffæ quinq*ue* de Gifilim. (No.138)

Miffæ quinq*ue* Petri de la Rua. (No.139)

Miffæ quinq*ue* Alexandri. (No.140)

Below this section there is an appendix of additional items, which includes the following. With the exception of the first item, the titles given here are much closer to those of the extant books:

[Folio 84*r*.]

¶ Iofquini & alioru*m* diuerfis locis et tem | poribus impreffi Motettoru*m* libri 4. (No.225)

[Folio 84*v*:]

¶ De cantionibus italicis, uel in Italia imprefsis, | præfertim Venetijs.

Harmonicæ Mufices Odhecaton, im- | preffum Venetijs. (No.241)

Cantus B. numero quinquaginta, ibi- | dem. (No.242)

Cantus C. numero 150. Venetijs per O- | ctauianum Petrutium excufi. (No.243)

Laude liber fecundus, ibidem. (No.244)

Strambotti, ode Frottole, fonetti, & mo | dus cantandi uerfus Latinos, & capi | tula, liber 4. Venetijs apud Octauia- | num Petrucium. (No.245)

Frottole liber quintus, & liber fextus. (No.246)

Liber fecundus, apud eundem Petru- | cium. (No.247)

Liber nonus ibidem. (No.248)

[Folio 85*r*.]

Motetti A, numero 33. Latini, Venetijs | impreffi. (No.268)

52.   Draudius's lists of early editions (see chapter 10, above).

52a.   Georg Draudius: *Bibliotheca Classica* (Frankfurt: Kopf, 1611). (Facsimile by Ameln: see
       Heussner and Schultz, *Collectio*, whose numbers are cited here)
       No.1223   Cantus B. numero cinquanta 3–6 v. (No.97)
                  Motetti A. numero trentatre 3 & 4 v. (No.98)
                  Canti C. numero cento cinquanta 3–5 v. (No.99)

52b.   Georg Draudius, *Bibliotheca classica* (Frankfurt: Kopf, 1625) (with Heussner and
       Schultz's numbers)
       Concentus iucundiss. 8, 6, 5, 4 v. Harmonicae musices Odhecaton (No.96)
       Cant. var. & modus cantansi versus Ln. & capitula. | Liber II. 4, 5, 6 | Venet. apud Octav.
       Petrucium. (No.100)
                  Heussner and Schultz believe that this reference is to the second book of Frottole.
                  Despite the phrase "Liber II", I incline to think that it is more likely to be a reference
                  to Libro IV (My Nos.23 or 35), given the implication of "modus cantansi . . . ")

53.   Bolduanus's list of early editions.
                  Paulus Bolduanus: *Bibliotheca philosophica* (Jena: Weidner, 1616). Facsimile of the
                  music section in Krummel, *Bibliotheca*: both entries are discussed above, in Chapter Ten)
       p. 204   Concentus jucundiſs. 8.6.5.4. vocum Harmonicæ Muſi- | ces Odhecaton. Venet.
                 (No.454)
       p. 212   Mottetæ A. num. 33. In. Cantus 50. Cantus B. 50. Cantus | C.150. Venetiis.
                 (Nos.618–620)

54.   Lodovico Zacconi: *Prattica di Musica*, vol.1 (Venice: Polo, 1592), 84r, in a discussion of the
       use of the flat sign:
       Quello nel proua & manifesta, l'Odhecaton de Muſici stampato in Venetia l'anno 1503 |
       volume coſi chiamato che contiene aſſai beliſſime coſe de Muſici di quel tempo: [. . .]

BIBLIOGRAPHY

This listing includes all works cited anywhere in the preceding study: therefore it includes any that discuss Petrucci, or are fundamental to the study of music printing or the book trade during Petrucci's lifetime.

Aaron, Pietro. *Trattato della natura et cognitione di tutti gli tuoni* [facsimile]. Musica Revindicata. Utrecht: Joachimsthal, 1966.

Abbiati, Franco. *Storia della musica*. Milan: Garzanti, 1967–1968.

Acolea, Paola. "Il Libro VII di frottole edito da Ottaviano Petrucci (Venezia, 1507): trascrizione". Tesi di laurea, Università degli Studi di Padova, 1991.

Accoretti, G. "Ottaviano de'Petrucci da Fossombrone e la stampa musicale con caratteri mobili". *La Rassegna Marchigiana* 2 (1923–1924): 489–494.

Adami da Bolsena, Andrea. *Osservazione per ben regolare il coro dei Cantori della Cappella Pontificia*. Rome: A.Rossi, 1711; rpt. Lucca: Libreria Musicale Italiana, 1988.

Adamson, Amanda. "Petrucci's Motetti C: a critical edition and study of the anonymous motets". M.M. thesis, University of Auckland, 1991.

Adler, Guido, et al., eds. *Sechs Trienter Codices: Geistlicher und weltlicher Kompositionen des XV. Jahrhunderts*. Denkmäler der Tonkunst in Österreich, 7 (14–15), 11/1 (22), 19/1 (38), 27/1 (53), 31 (61). Vienna, 1900–1924; rpt Graz: Akademische Druck- und Verlagsanstalt, 1959.

Agee, Richard. "Filippo Strozzi and the early madrigal". *Journal of the American Musicological Society* 38 (1985): 227–237.

———. "The privilege and Venetian music printing in the sixteenth century". Ph.D. diss., Princeton University, 1982.

———. "A Venetian music printing contract and edition size of the sixteenth century". *Studi musicali* 15 (1986): 59–65.

———. "The Venetian privilege and music printing in the sixteenth century". *Early music history* 3 (1983): 1–42.

———. *The Gardano music printing firms, 1569–1611*. Eastman Studies in Music 11. Rochester, NY: University of Rochester Press, 1998.

Agricola, Alexander. *Opera Omnia*, ed. Edward R. Lerner. Corpus mensurabilis musicae 22. s.l.: American Institute of Musicology, 1961–1970.

Alamire, publisher. *Chansonnier of Marguerite of Austria* [facsimile]. Peer: Alamire, 1984.

Alberati, Anna. "La musica del XVI e XVII secolo nella Biblioteca Nazionale Marciana". *Miscellanea Marcian* 51 (1986): 179–221.

Alberti, Leandro. *Descrittione di tutta Italia*. Bologna: Giaccarelli, 1550. The edition consulted for this study was published in Venice, by Lodovico de Gli Avanzi, in 1561.

Albrecht, Hans. "Zwei Quellen zur deutschen Musikgeschichte der Reformationszeit". *Die Musikforschung* 1 (1948): 242–285.

Albrecht, Hans, ed. *Symphoniae jucundae atque adeo breves 4 vocum, ab optimis quibusque musicis compositae, 1538*. Georg Rhau: Musikdrucke aus den Jahren 1538 bis 1545 in prak- tischer Neuausgabe 3. Kassel: Bärenreiter, 1959.

Allaire, Gaston. "L'apport de la typographie et de la musique a la poésie française du début du seizième siècle". *Renaissance and Reformation* 7 (1978): 127–141.

Allen, Don. "Some contemporary accounts of renaissance printing methods". *The Library*, Ser.4, 17 (1937): 167–171.

Amati, Girolamo. *Bibliografia romana: notizie della vita e delle opere degli scrittori romani dal secolo XI fino ai nostri giorni*. Rome: Eredi Botta, 1880.

Ambros, August Wilhelm. *Geschichte der Musik*. 3rd ed. Leipzig: Leuckert, 1887–1911; rpt. Hildesheim: Olms, 1968.

Ameln, Konrad. "Ein Nürnberger Verlegerplakat aus dem 16. Jahrhundert". In *Musik und Verlag: Karl Vötterle zum 65. Geburtstag am 12. April, 1968*, ed. Richard Baum and Wolfgang Rehm: 136–142. Kassel: Bärenreiter, 1968.

Ameln, Konrad, Markus Jenny, and Walther Lipphardt. *Das Deutsche Kirchenlied*. Répertoire international des sources musicales, Ser B/VIII. Kassel: Bärenreiter, 1975–1980.

Amiani, Pietro Maria. *Memorie istoriche della città di Fano*. Fano: Leonardi, 1751.

Amram, David. *The Makers of Hebrew books in Italy*. London: Holland Press, 1963; rpt. 1988.

Andrews, Hilda K. "The printed part-books of Byrd's vocal music". *The Library*, Ser.5, 19 (1964): 1–10.

Anglés, Higinio. "El archivo musical de la Catedral de Valladolid". *Anuario musical* 3 (1948): 59–108.

———. "Un manuscrit inconnu avec polyphonie du XVe siècle conservé à la cathedrale de Ségovie (Espagne)". *Acta Musicologica* 8 (1936): 6–17.

———. "La música conservada en la Biblioteca Colombina y en la Catedral de Sevilla". *Anuario musical* 2 (1947): 3–39.

Anglés, Higinio, ed. *La música en la Corte de Carlos V*. Monumentos de la música Española 2. Barcelona: Consejo Superior de Investigaciones Cientificas, 1944.

———. *La música en la Corte de los Reyes Católicos: Polifonía religiosa, I*. Monumentos de la música Española 1. Madrid, 1941; 2nd ed., Barcelona: Consejo Superior de Investi- gaciones Científicas, Instituto Español de Musicología, 1960.

———. *La música en la Corte de los Reyes Católicos: Cancionero Musical de Palacio (Siglos XV– XVI)*. Monumentos de la música Española, 4. Barcelona: Consejo Superior de Inves- tigaciones Científicas, Instituto Español de Musicología, 1965.

Annibaldi, Claudio, ed. *La musica e il mondo: mecenatismo e committenza musicale in Italia tra Quattro e Settecento*. Bologna: Mulino, 1993.

Antico, Andrea. *Le frottole*, ed. Boris Jurevini et al. Bibliotheca istriana 13. Trieste: s.n., 1996.

———. *Frottole intabulate da sonare organi Libro Primo* [facsimile]. Bologna: Forni, 1972.

Antonowytsch, Miroslaw. "*Illibata Dei virgo*: a melodic self-portrait of Josquin des Prez". *Josquin des Prez: Proceedings of the international Josquin festival-conference*, ed. Edward E. Lowinsky with Bonnie J. Blackburn: 545–559. London: Oxford University Press, 1976.

———. "Die *Missa Mater patris* von Josquin des Prez". *Tijdschrift van der Vereniging voor Nederlandse Muziekgeschiedenis* 20 (1967): 206–225.

————. "Renaissance-Tendenzen in den Fortuna-desperata-Messen von Josquin und Obrecht". *Die Musikforschung* 9 (1956): 1–26.

Arboli y Farando, Servando *et al.* *Biblioteca Colombina, Catálogo de sus libros impresos.* 7 volumes: Seville: Raseo *and others*, 1888–1948.

Armstrong, C.A.J. "An Italian astrologer at the court of Henry VIII", *Italian Renaissance Studies*, ed. E.F. Jacob: 433–454. London: Faber and Faber, 1960.

Armstrong, Elizabeth. *Before Copyright: the French book-privilege system, 1498–1526.* Cambridge: Cambridge University Press, 1990.

Ascarelli, Ferdinando. *La tipografia cinquecentina italiana.* Florence: Sansoni, 1953.

Ascarelli, Fernanda. *Annali tipografici di Giacomo Mazzocchi.* Biblioteca di bibliografia italiana, 24. Florence: Sansoni, 1961.

————. *Le cinquecentine romane. Censimento delle edizioni romane del XVI secolo possedute dalle biblioteche di Roma.* Milan: Etimar, 1972.

Ascarelli, Fernanda, and Marco Menato. *La tipografia del '500 in Italia.* Biblioteca di bibliografia italiana, 116. Florence: Olschki, 1989.

Atlas, Allan. *The Cappella Giulia chansonnier (Rome, Biblioteca Apostolica Vaticana, C.G.XIII.27).* Musicological studies, 27. New York: Institute of Medieval Music, 1975.

————. "Conflicting attributions in Italian sources of the Franco-Netherlandish chanson, *c.*1465–*c.*1505: a progress report on a new hypothesis". In *Music in medieval and early modern Europe: patronage, sources and texts*, ed. Iain Fenlon: 249–293. Cambridge: Cambridge University Press, 1981.

————. "Heinrich Isaac's *Palle, palle*: a new interpretation". *Analecta musicologica* 14 (1974): 17–25.

————. *Music at the Aragonese court of Naples.* Cambridge: Cambridge University Press, 1985.

————. "A note on Isaac's *Quis dabit capiti meo aquam*". *Journal of the American Musicological Society* 27 (1974): 103–110. See also "Communications" from Martin Staehelin and Allan Atlas, in the same journal 28 (1975): 160 and 565–566.

————. "On the Neapolitan provenance of the manuscript Perugia, Biblioteca Comunale Augusta, 421 (G20)". *Musica Disciplina* 31 (1977): 45–105.

————. "La provenienza del manoscritto Berlin 78.C.28: Firenze o Napoli?". *Rivista italiana di musicologia* 13 (1978): 10–29.

Attaingnant, Pierre, publisher. *Treize livres de motets parus chez Pierre Attaingnant en 1534 et 1535*, ed. Albert Smijers and A. Tillman Merritt. Paris and Monaco: Editions de l'Oiseau-Lyre, 1934–1964.

Aubry, Pierre. *Les plus anciens monuments de la musique française.* Paris: Wetter, 1905.

————. "Les origines de la typographie musicale". *Le Bibliophile* 1 (1931): 142–148, 223–229; 2 (1932): 13–19.

Auda, Antoine. "La transcription en notation moderne du "Liber missarum" de Pierre de la Rue". *Scriptorium*, 1 (1946–1947): 119–128.

d'Auton, Jean. *Chroniques de Louis XII.* Publications de la Societé de l'Histoire de France, 245, 250, 264 and 273. Paris: Renouard, 1889–1895.

Baillie, Laureen, and Robert Balchin, eds. *The Catalogue of printed music in the British Library.* London: Saur, 1981–1987.

Bain, Susan. "Music printing in the Low Countries in the sixteenth century". Ph.D. diss., Cambridge University, 1974.

Baini, Giuseppe. *Memorie storico-critiche della vita e delle opere di Giovanni Pierluigi da Palestrina.* Rome, Società Tipografica, 1828; rpt. Hildesheim: Olms, 1966.

Baker, Norma Klein. "An Unnumbered manuscript of polyphony in the archives of the Cathedral of Segovia: its provenance and history". Ph.D. diss., University of Maryland, 1978.

Baldi, Bernardino. "Vita di Paolo di Middelburg". In Demetrio Marzi, *La Questione della riforma del calendario nel Quinto Concilio Lateranense (1512–1517)*, 27: 233–250. Pubblicazioni del R. Istituto di Studi superiori pratici e di perfezionamento in Firenze: Sezione di filosofia e filologia. Florence: Carnesechi & figli, 1896).

Barberi, Francesco. "I Dorico, tipografi a Roma nel cinquecento". *La Bibliofilia*, lxvii (1965): 221–261; rpt. in *Tipografi romani del Cinquecento: Guillery, Ginnasio Mediceo, Calvo, Dorico, Cartolari*. Biblioteconomia e bibliografia: Saggi e studi, 17: 99–146. Florence: Olschki, 1983.

———. "Le edizioni romane di Francesco Minizio Calvo (1523–1531)". In *Miscellanea di scritti di bibliografia ed erudizione in memoria di Luigi Ferrari*: 57–98. Florence: Olschki, 1952; rpt. in *Tipografi romani del Cinquecento: Guillery, Ginnasio Mediceo, Calvo, Dorico, Cartolari*. Biblioteconomia e bibliografia: Saggi e studi 17 (Florence: Olschki, 1983): 77–97.

———. "Frontespizi italiani incisi nel Quinquecento". *Studi di storia dell'arte, bibliologia ed erudizione in memoria di Luigi Ferrari*: 65–72. Florence: Olschki, 1960.

———. "Stefano Guillery e le sue edizioni romane (1506–1524). *Studi offerti a Roberto Ridolfi, direttore de "La Bibliofilia"*, ed. Berta Maracchi Biagiarelli and Dennis Rhodes: 95–145. Florence: Olschki, 1973; rpt. in *Tipografi romani del Cinquecento: Guillery, Ginnasio Mediceo, Calvo, Dorico, Cartolari*. Biblioteconomia e bibliografia: Saggi e studi, xvii (Florence: Olschki, 1983): 9–55.

Barbieri, Francisco Asienjo, ed. *Cancionero musical de los siglos XV y XVI*. Madrid: Los Huerfanas, 1890; rpt. Malaga: Departamento de Publicaciones del Centro Cultural de la "Generacion del 27", 1987.

Barblan, Guglielmo. "Aspetti e figure del cinquecento musicale veneziano". *La civiltà veneziana del Rinascimento (il Cinquecento)*. Storia della civiltà veneziana 4: 57–80. Florence: Sansoni, 1958; rpt. in the new edition 2: 247–257. Florence: Sansoni, 1979.

Barblan, Giuseppe. *Catalogo della Biblioteca del Conservatorio di Musica Giuseppe Verdi: Musiche della Cappella di S. Barbara in Mantova*. Florence: Olschki, 1972.

Barclay Squire, William. "Notes on early music printing". *Bibliographica* 8 (1897): 99–122.

———. "Petrucci's Motetti de Passione". *Monatshefte für Musikgeschichte* 27 (1895): 72–75.

Barker, Nicolas. *Aldus Manutius and the development of Greek script and type in the fifteenth century*. Sandy Hook: Chiswick Book Shop, 1985; 2nd ed., New York: Fordham University Press, 1992.

Barksdale, A. B., compiler. *The printed note: 500 years of music printing*. Toledo, OH: Toledo Museum of Art, 1957.

Bartha, Dénes von. "Bibliographisches Notizien zum Repertoire der Handschrift Cambrai 124". *Zeitschrift für Musikwissenschaft* 13 (1930–1931): 564–566.

Bartoli, Cosimo. *Ragionamenti accademici sopra alcuni luoghi difficili di Dante*. Venice: F. di Franceschi, 1567.

Bartoli, Gustavo. "I segni del compositore in alcune copi di tipografia di edizioni fiorentine del xvi secolo. Un pò di casistica". *La Bibliofilia* 91 (1989): 307–324.

Barzon, Antonio. "Note d'archivio: la libraria di un parroco di città, in Padova nell'anno 1559". In *Libri e stampatori a Padova: miscellanea di studi storici in onore di Mons. G. Bellini—tipografo editore libraio*, ed. Antonio Barzon: 325–334. Padua, Tipografia Antoniana, 1959.

Bautier-Regnier, Anne-Marie. "L'Édition musicale italienne et les musiciens d'outremonts au XVIe siècle (1501–1563)". In *Le Renaissance dans les provinces du Nord: Picardie, Artois, Flandres, Brabant, Hainaut*, ed. François Lesure: 27–49. Paris: Centre national de la recherche scientifique, 1956.

Becherini, Bianca. "Alcuni canti dell'‘Odhecaton’ e del codice fiorentino 2794". *Bulletin de l'Institut historique belge de Rome* 22 (1942–1943): 327–250.

———. *Catalogo dei manoscritti musicali della Biblioteca nazionale di Firenze*. Kassel: Bärenreiter, 1959.

———. "I manoscritti e le stampe rare della Biblioteca del Conservatorio "L. Cherubini" di Firenze: nuova catalogazione e reintegrazione". *La Bibliofilia* 46 (1964): 255–299.

Beck, Hans-Georg, Manoussos Manoussacas, and Agostino Pertusi, eds. *Venetia, centro di mediazione tra Oriente e Occidente (secoli XV–XVI): aspetti e problemi.* Civiltà veneziana, 32. Florence: Olschki, 1977.

Bellingham, Bruce, ed. *Bicinia gallica, latina, germanica Tomus I, II, 1545.* Georg Rhau: Musikdrucke aus den Jahren 1538 bis 1545 in praktischer Neuausgabe 6. Kassel: Bärenreiter, 1980.

Bellingham, Bruce and Edward Evans, eds. *Sixteenth-century Bicinia: a complete edition of Munich, Bayerische Staatsbibliothek, Mus. Ms. 260.* Recent researches in music of the Renaissance, 16–17. Madison, WI: A- R. Editions, 1974.

Beloch, Giulio. "La populazione di Venezia nei secoli XVI e XVII". *Nuovo Archivio Veneto,* n.s., 3 (1902): 1–49.

Bembo, Pietro. *Epistolarum Leonis X P.M. nomine scriptarum libri XVI.* Basel: Froben, 1547.

———. *Opere del Cardinal Pietro Bembo ora per la prima volta tutte in un corpo unite: IV. I breve scritti a nome di Leone X.* Venice: Hertzhauser, 1729.

Bent, Margaret. "Accidentals, counterpoint and notation in Aaron's *Aggiunta* to the *Toscanello in Musica.*" *The Journal of Musicology* 12 (1994): 306–344.

———. "Pietro Emiliani's Chaplain Bartolomeo Rossi da Carpi and the Lamentations of Johannes de Quadris in Vicenza". *Il Saggiatore Musicale* 2 (1995): 5–15.

———. "The Use of cut signatures in sacred music by Ockeghem and his contemporaries. In *Johannes Ockeghem: Actes du XIe Colloque international d'études humanistes,* ed. Philippe Vendrix: 641–680. Paris: Klincksieck, 1998.

Bente, Martin. *Neue Wege der Quellenkritik und die Biographie Ludwig Senfls.* Wiesbaden: Breitkopf und Härtel, 1968.

Bente, Martin, Marie Louise Göllner, H. Hell, and B. Wackernagel. *Chorbücher und Handschriften in chorbuchartiger Notierung.* Bayerische Staatsbibliothek: Katalog der Musikhandschriften 1. Munich: Henle, 1979.

Benzing, Josef. *Die Buchdrucker des 16. und 17. Jahrhunderts im deutschen Sprachgebiet.* Beiträge zum Buch- und Bibliothekswesen 12. Wiesbaden: Harrassowitz, 1963: second edition, 1982.

———. "Peter Schöffer der jüngere, Musikdrucker zu Mainz, Worms, Strassburg und Venedig (tätig 1512–1542)". *Jahrbuch für Liturgik und Hymnologie* 4 (1958–1959): 133–135.

Bernoni, Domenico. *Dei Torresani, Blado e Ragazzoni, celebri stampatori a Venezia e Roma nel XV e XVI secolo.* Milan: Hoepli, 1890; rpt. Farnborough: Gregg. 1968.

Bernoulli, Edouard. *Aus Liederbüchern der Humanistenzeit: eine Bibliographische und notentypographische Studie.* Leipzig: Breitkopf und Härtel, 1910.

Bernstein, Jane A. "The Burning Salamander: assigning a printer to some sixteenth-century music prints". *Notes,* 42 (1985–1986): 483–501.

———. "Buyers and Collectors of music publications: two sixteenth-century music libraries recovered". *Music in Renaissance cities and courts: Studies in honor of Lewis Lockwood,* ed. Anthony Cummings and Jessie Ann Owens: 21–33. Warren, MI: Harmonie Park, 1997.

———. "Financial arrangements and the role of printer and composer in sixteenth-century Italian music printing". *Acta musicologica,* 63 (1991): 39–56.

———. *Music printing in Renaissance Venice: the Scotto press (1539–1572).* New York: Oxford University Press, 1999.

———. "Printing and Patronage in sixteenth-century Italy". In *Actas del XV Congreso de la Sociedad Internacional de Musicología: "Culturas Musicales del Mediterraneo y sus Ramificaciones", Madrid, 3-10/IV/1992:* 2603–2613. Madrid: Sociedad Internacional de Musicología, 1993.

Bernstein, Lawrence. "The bibliography of music in Conrad Gesner's Pandectae (1548)". *Acta musicologica* 45 (1973): 119–163.

———. "*La Couronne et fleur des chansons a troys*: a mirror of the French chanson in Italy in the years between Ottaviano Petrucci and Antonio Gardano". *Journal of the American Musicological Society* 26 (1973): 1–68.

————. "A Florentine chansonnier of the early sixteenth century: Florence, Biblioteca Nazionale Centrale, MS Magliabechi 117". *Early Music History*, 6 (1986): 1–107.

————. "Notes on the origin of the Parisian chanson". *The Journal of Musicology* 1 (1982): 275–326.

Berry, W. Turner, and H. Edmund Poole. *Annals of printing: a chronological encyclopaedia from the earliest times to 1950*. London: Blandford, 1966.

Bertieri, Raffaello. Introduction to *Editori e Stampatori italiani del Quattrocento*. Milan: Hoepli, 1929.

Bertoli, Gustavo. "I segni del compositore in alcune copie di tipografia di edizioni fiorentine del XVI secolo. Un pò di casistica". *La Bibliofilìa* 19 (1989): 307–324.

Bertolotti, Antonino. *Musici alla Corte dei Gonzaga in Mantova dal secolo XV al XVIII: Notizie e documenti raccolti negli archivi mantovani*. Milan: Ricordi, 1890; rpt. Bologna: Forni, 1969.

Berz, Ernst-Ludwig. *Die Notendrucker und ihre Verleger in Frankfurt am Main von den Anfängen bis etwa 1630: eine bibliographische und drucktechnische Studie zur Musikpublication*. Catalogus Musicus, 5. Kassel: IAML and IMS, 1970.

Besseler, Heinrich. "The manuscript Bologna, Biblioteca Universitaria 2216". *Musica Disciplina* 6 (1952): 39–65.

————. "Studien zur Musik des Mittelalters: I. Neue Quellen des 14. und beginnenden 15. Jahrhunderts". *Archiv für Musikwissenschaft* 7 (1925): 167–252.

Besseler, Heinrich, ed. *Cappella: Meisterwerke mittelalterlicher Musik. I*. Kassel: Bärenreiter, 1950.

Besseler, Heinrich, and Peter Gülke. *Schriftbild der mehrstimmigen Musik*. Musikgeschichte in Bildern, Ser. 3: Musik des Mittelalters und der Renaissance, 5. Leipzig: VEB Deutscher Verlag für Musik, 1973.

Bettanin, Silvia. "Il Libro XI di Frottole edito da Ottaviano Petrucci (Venezia 1508): trascrizione et edizione critica". Tesi di Laurea, Università degli Studi di Padova, 1992.

Bibbiena, Bernardo Dovizi da. *Epistolario*, ed. G.L. Moncallero. Biblioteca dell'"Archivum Romanicum", Ser.1, 44. Florence: Olschki, 1955.

Binkley, Thomas. "Le luth et sa technique". In *Le luth et sa musique*, ed. Jean Jacquot. Colloques internationaux du Centre national de la recherche scientifique, 551: 24–36. Paris: Editions du Centre national de la recherche scientifique, 1976.

Biringuccio, Vanoccio. *De la pirotechnia. Libri X . . . quel che si appartiene a l'arte de la fusione ouer gitto de metalli . . .* , Venice: Roffinello for C. Navo e frateli, 1540. There were many later editions. Translated by Cyril Smith and Martha Gnudi. New York: The American Institute of Mining and Metallurgical Engineers, 1942. The section on typecasting appears in Book IX: Smith and Gnudi's translation of this part had been separately published by the Columbian Club of Connecticut in 1941.

Birkendorf, Rainer. *Der Codex Pernner: Quellenkundliche Studien zu einer Musikhandschrift des frühen 16. Jahrhunderts*. Augsburg: Wissner, 1994.

Birmingham, Hugh Myers. "A transcription into modern notation of a chansonnier (Fonds français 2245) of the Duke of Orleans, with commentary and concordance". M.M. diss., North Texas State University, 1955.

Blackburn, Bonnie J. "Two 'Carnival songs' unmasked: a commentary on MS Florence Magl.XIX,121". *Musica Disciplina* 35 (1981): 121–178.

————. "Johannes Lupi and Lupus Hellinck: a double portrait". *Musical Quarterly* 49 (1973): 547–583.

————. "Josquin's chansons: ignored and lost sources". *Journal of the American Musicological Society* 29 (1976): 30–76.

————. "A lost guide to Tinctoris's teaching recovered". *Early music history*, 1 (1981): 29–116.

————. "Lorenzo de'Medici, a lost Isaac manuscript, and the Venetian ambassador". In *Musica Franca: essays in honor of Frank A. D'Accone*, ed. Irene Alm, Alyson McLamore and Colleen Reardon: 19–44. Stuyvesant, NY: Pendragon, 1996; rpt. as ch.V in *Composition, Printing and Performance*. Aldershot: Ashgate, 2000.

————. "The Lupus problem". Ph.D.diss., University of Chicago, 1970.

————. *Music for Treviso Cathedral in the late sixteenth century: a reconstruction of the lost manuscripts 29 and 30.* Royal Musical Association monographs 3. London: Royal Musical Association, 1987.

————. "Obrecht's *Missa Je ne demande* and Busnoys's chanson: an essay in reconstructing lost canons". *Tijdschrift van de Koninklijke Vereniging voor Nederlandse Muziekgeschiedenis* 45 (1995): 18–32; rpt. as ch.IV in *Composition, Printing and Performance.* Aldershot: Ashgate, 2000.

————. "Petrucci's Venetian editor: Petrus Castellanus and his musical garden". *Musica Disciplina* 49 (1995): 15–45; rpt. as ch.VI in *Composition, Printing and Performance.* Aldershot: Ashgate, 2000.

————. "The Printing Contract for the *Libro primo de musica de la salamandra* (Rome, 1526)". *The Journal of Musicology* 12 (1994): 345–356.

————. "The sign of Petrucci's editor", paper read at the conference "Venezia 1501: Petrucci e la stampa musicale", Venice, 12 October 2001.

Blackburn, Bonnie J., Edward E. Lowinsky, and Clement A. Miller, eds. *A Correspondence of Renaissance musicians.* Oxford: Clarendon Press, 1991.

Blankenburg, Walter. "Die werschlungenen Schicksalswege des Codex Gothanus Chart. A.98: Ein kleines, absonderliches Kapital thüringischer Bibliotheksgeschichte". In *Quellenstudien zur Musik: Wolfgang Schmieder zum 70. Geburtstag,* ed. Kurt Dorfmüller and Georg von Dadelsen: 35–40. Frankfurt: Peters, 1972.

Blasio, Maria Grazia. "Privilegi e licenze di stampa a Roma fra Quattro e Cinquecento". *La Bibliofilia,* 90 (1988): 147–159.

Blayney, Peter. *The Texts of* King Lear *and their origins: I. Nicholas Okes and the First Quarto.* New Cambridge Shakespeare Studies and Supplementary Texts Series. Cambridge: Cambridge University Press, 1981.

Bloxam, M. Jennifer. " 'La contenance italienne': the motets on *Beata es Maria* by Compère, Obrecht and Brumel". *Early Music History* 11 (1992): 39–89.

————. "Obrecht as exegete: reading Factor orbis as a Christmas sermon". In *Hearing the Motet: essays on the motet of the Middle Ages and Renaissance,* ed. Dolores Pesce: 162–92. New York: Oxford University Press, 1997.

Bloy, Colin. *A History of printing ink, balls and rollers, 1440–1850.* London: Wynkyn de Worde Society, 1967.

Blume, Friedrich, ed. *Josquin Des Prés und andere Meister: Weltliche Lieder zu 3–5 Stimmen.* Das Chorwerk 3. Wolfenbüttel: Mäseler, 1930.

BMC. Catalogue of Books printed in the XVth century now in the British Museum. London: Trustees of the British Museum, 1908–1971.

Böker-Heil, Norbert. "Josquin und Verdelot: die Konfliktzuschreibungen". In *Proceedings of the International Josquin Symposium, Utrecht 1986,* ed. Willem Elders, with Frits de Haen: 55–58. Utrecht: Vereniging voor Nederlandse Muziekgeschiedenis, 1991.

Böker-Heil, Norbert, Harald Heckmann and Ilse Kindermann, eds. *Das Tenorlied: mehrstimmiger Lieder in deutschen Quellen 1450–1580.* Catalogus musicus 9. Kassel: Bärenreiter, 1979.

Boer, Coenraad L. W. *Chansonvormen op het einde van de XVde eeuw.* Amsterdam: A.J. Paris, 1938.

Boetticher, Wolfgang. *Handschriftlich überlieferte Lauten- und Gitarentabulaturen des 15. bis 18. Jahrhunderts.* Répertoire international des sources musicales, Ser.B, 7. Munich: Henle, 1978.

Boghardt, Martin. "Instruktionen für Korrekturen der Officina Plantiniana". In *Trasmissione dei testi a stampa nel periodo moderno: II. Il seminario internazionale, Roma-Viterbo, 27–29 giugno, 1985,* ed. Giovanni Crapulli: 1–16. Rome: Ateneo, 1987.

Bohatta, Hanns. *Liturgische Bibliographie des XV. Jahrhunderts mit Ausnahme der Missale und Livres d'Heures.* Vienna: Gilhofer and Ranschburg, 1911; rpt. Hildesheim: Olms, [1961].

Bohn, Emil. *Die musikalischen Handschriften des XVI. und XVII. Jahrhunderts in der Stadtbibliothek zu Breslau.* Breslau: Commissions-Verlag von Julius Hainauer, 1890.

Bolcato, Vittorio, and Alberto Zanotelli. *Il Fondo Musicale dell'Archivio Capitolare del Duomo di Vicenza.* Cataloghi di fondi musicali italiani 4. Turin: EDT, 1986.

Bolduanus, Paulus. *Bibliotheca philosophica, sive: Elenchus scriptorum philosophicorum.* Jena: Weidner, 1616.

Bonamo Schellembri, Maria. "Di due recenti acquisti della Biblioteca nazionale di Brera". In *Studi di bibliografia e di argomento romano in memoria di Luigi De Gregori*, ed. C. Arcamone: 46–56. Rome: Palombi, 1949.

Bond, W. H. "A printer's manuscript of 1508". *Studies in Bibliography* 8 (1956): 147–156.

Bonda, Jan Willem. "Tandernaken, between Bruges and Ferrara", In *From Ciconia to Sweelinck: donum natalicium Willem Elders*, ed. Albert Clement and Eric Jas. Chloe: Beihefte zum Daphnis, 21: 49–74. Amsterdam: Rodopi, 1994.

Bongi, S. *Annali di Gabriel Giolito de' Ferrari da Trino di Monferrato, stampatore in Venezia.* Rome: Vivarelli & Gulla, 1890–1897.

Bonime, Stephen. *Anne de Bretagne (1477–1514) and music: an archival study.* Ph.D. diss., Bryn Mawr College, 1975.

Boorman, Stanley. "Bibliographical evidence for the business end of music printing and publishing during the 16th century". Paper read at the New York Conference on Music and Business, 1999.

———. "A case of work and turn half-sheet imposition in the sixteenth century". *The Library*, Ser.6, 8 (1986): 301–321.

———. "Communication". *Notes*, 16 (1989–1990): 841–844

———. "Did Petrucci's concern for accuracy include any concern with performance issues?", *Basler Jahrbuch für historische Musikpraxis* 25 (2002): 23–37.

———. "Early music printing: an indirect contact with the Raphael circle". In *Renaissance studies in honor of Craig Hugh Smyth*, ed. Andrew Morrogh *et al*: 533–550. Florence: Barbèra, 1985.

———. "Early music printing: working for a specialized market". In *Print and culture in the Renaissance*, ed. Gerald Tyson and Sylvia Wagonheim: 222–245. Newark: University of Delaware Press, 1986.

———. "False relations and the cadence". In *Altro Polo: essays on Italian music in the Cinquecento*, ed. Richard Charteris: 221–264. Sydney: Frederick May Foundation for Italian Studies, University of Sydney, 1990.

———. "The 'first' edition of the *Odhecaton A*". *Journal of the American Musicological Society* 30 (1977): 183–207.

———. *Four frottole for voice and three instruments or four instruments.* North Harton: Alamire, 1972.

———. "Glossary". In *Music Printing and Publishing*, ed. D.W. Krummel and Stanley Sadie: 489–550. Grove Handbooks in Music. London: Macmillan, 1990.

———. "Limitations and extensions of filiation technique". In *Music in medieval and early modern Europe: patronage, sources and texts*, ed. Iain Fenlon: 319–346. Cambridge: Cambridge University Press, 1981.

———. "The music publisher's view of his public's abilities and taste: Venice and Antwerp". *Yearbook of the Alamire Foundation*, 2 (1995 [1998]): 405–429.

———. "Notational spelling and scribal habit". In *Datierung und Filiation von Musikhandschriften der Josquin-Zeit*, ed. Ludwig Finscher: 65–109. Wolfenbütteler Forschungen 26 = Quellenstudien zur Musik der Renaissance 2. Wiesbaden: Harrassowitz, 1983.

———. "Petrucci at Fossombrone: the Motetti de la Corona". In *Report of the eleventh congress [of the I.M.S.] Copenhagen 1972*: i, 295–301. Copenhagen: Hansen, 1974.

———. "Petrucci at Fossombrone: some new editions and cancels". In *Source materials and the interpretation of music: a memorial volume to Thurston Dart*, ed. Ian D. Bent: 129–153. London: Stainer & Bell, 1981.

———. "Petrucci in the light of recent research". Paper read at the conference "Venezia 1501: Petrucci e la stampa musicale", Venice, 13 October 2001.

————. "Petrucci at Fossombrone: a study of early music printing, with special reference to the 'Motetti de la Corona', 1514–1519". Ph.D. diss., London University, 1976.

————. "Petrucci's typesetters and the process of stemmatics". In *Formen und Probleme der Überlieferung mehrstimmiger Musik im Zeitalter Josquins Desprez*, ed. Ludwig Finscher: 245–280. Wolfenbütteler Forschungen 6 = Quellenstudien zur Musik der Renaissance 1 (Munich: Kraus International, 1981)

————. "Printed music books of the Italian renaissance from the point of view of manuscript study". In *Actas del XV Congreso de la Sociedad Internacional de Musicología: "Culturas Musicales del Mediterraneo y sus Ramificaciones", Madrid, 3–10/IV/1992*: 2587–2602. Madrid: Sociedad Internacional de Musicología, 1993.

————. Review of *The Motet books of Andrea Antico*, ed. Martin Picker. *Music and Letters* 70 (1989): 285–288.

————. "The Salzburg liturgy and single-impression music printing". In *Music in the German Renaissance: sources, styles, and contexts*, ed. John Kmetz: 235–253. Cambridge: Cambridge University Press, 1994.

————. "The 16th-century music publisher's impact on the history of music". Paper read at the conference "Legacies: 500 years of printed music", University of North Texas, 26 October 2001.

————. "Some non-conflicting attributions, and some newly-anonymous compositions, from the early sixteenth century". *Early Music History* 6 (1986): 109–157.

————. "Two aspects of performance practice in the Sistine Chapel of the early sixteenth century". In *Collectanea II: Studien zur Geschichte der päpstlichen Kapelle: Tagungsbericht Heidelberg 1989*, ed. Bernhard Janz: 575–609. Capellae Apostolicae Sixtinaeque Collectanea, Acta, Monumenta 4. Città del Vaticano: Biblioteca Apostolica Vaticana, 1994.

————. "Upon the use of running titles in the Aldus house of 1518". *The Library*, Ser.5, 27 (1972): 126–131.

————. "What bibliography can do: music printing and the early madrigal". *Music and Letters* 72 (1991): 236–258.

Boorman, Stanley, and Beth Miller. "La stampa musicale italiana tra Cinque e Seicento: lo stato delle ricerche". *Le Fonti musicali in Italia* 2 (1988): 35–51.

Borsa, Gedeon. *Clavis Typographorum Librariorumque Italiae 1465–1600*. Bibliotheca Bibliographica Aureliana 35. Baden-Baden: Koerner, 1980.

Boscolo, Lucia, ed. *Frottole Libro Octavo. Ottaviano Petrucci, Venezia 1507*. Octaviani Petrutii Forosemproniensis Froctolae 2. Venice; Comitato per la Pubblicazione di Fonti della Cultura Musicale Veneta, and Padua: CLEUP, 1999.

Bosisio, Achille. *La Stampa a Venezia dalle origini al secolo XVI. I privilegi, gli stampatori*. Trieste: LINT, 1973.

Bossinensis, Francesco. *Tenori e contrabassi intabulati col sopran in canto figurato per cantar e sonar col lauto: libro primo* [facsimile]. Geneva: Minkoff, 1978.

Bowers, Fredson. *Principles of bibliographical description*. Princeton: Princeton University Press, 1949; rpt. New York: Russell & Russell, 1962, and Winchester: St.Paul's Bibliographies, 1986.

Boyle, Leonard E. *A survey of the Vatican archives and of its medieval holdings*. Subsidia mediaevalia 1. Toronto: Pontifical Institute of Mediaeval Studies, 1972.

Braas, Ton. "The five-part motet *Missus est angelus Gabriel* and its conflicting attributions". In *Proceedings of the International Josquin Symposium, Utrecht 1986*, ed. Willem Elders, with Frits de Haen: 171–183. Utrecht: Vereniging voor Nederlandse Muziekgeschiedenis, 1991.

Bragard, Anne-Marie. "Un manuscrit florentin du quattrocento: le Magl.XIX,59 (B.R.229)". *Revue de musicologie* 53 (1966): 56–72.

Braithwaite, James. "The introduction of Franco-Netherlandish manuscripts to early Tudor England: the motet repertory". Ph.D. diss., Boston University, 1967.

Brambilla Ageno, Franca. *L'edizione critica dei testi volgari*. Medioevo e umanésimo 22. Padua: Antenore, 1975.

Branca, Vittore. "Ermolao Barbaro and late quattrocento Venetian humanism". In *Renaissance Venice*, ed. J.R. Hale: 218–243. London: Faber and Faber, 1973.

———. "L'Umanesimo veneziano alla fine del Quattrocento: Ermolao Barbaro e il suo circolo. In *Storia della cultura veneta* 3/1: 123–175. Vicenza: Branca, 1980.

Brancacci, Fiorella. "Il Sonetto nei libri di frottole di O. Petrucci (1504–1514). *Nuova rivista musicale italiana* 25 (1991): 176–215; 26 (1992): 441–468.

Braudel, Fernand. *Capitalism and material life, 1400–1800*, translated by Miriam Kochan. London: Weidenfeld and Nicolson, 1973.

Brauner, Mitchell P. "Music from the Cappella Sistina at the Cappella Giulia". *The Journal of Musicology* 3 (1984): 287–311.

———. "The Parvus manuscripts: a study of Vatican polyphony, ca.1535 to 1580". Ph.D. diss., Brandeis University, 1982.

———. "Traditions in the repertory of the Papal Choir in the fifteenth and sixteenth centuries". In *Papal music and musicians in late medieval and renaissance Rome*, ed. Richard Sherr: 168–178. Oxford: Oxford University Press, 1998.

Brecht, Martin. "Kaufpreis und Kaufdaten einiger Reformationschriften". *Gutenberg-Jahrbuch 1972*: 169–173.

Brennecke, Wilfried. *Die Handschrift A.R.940–941 der Proske-Bibliothek zu Regensburg: ein Beitrag zur Musikgeschichte in zweiten Drittel des 16. jahrhunderts*. Schriften des Landes-instituts für Musikforschung Kiel 1. Kassel: Bärenreiter, 1953.

Brewer, Charles. "The historical context of polyphony in medieval Hungary: an examination of four fragmentary sources". *Studia Musicologica* 32 (1990): 5–21.

Bridges, Thomas. "Blado, Antonio", In *Music Printing and Publishing*, ed. D.W. Krummel and Stanley Sadie: 176–177. Grove Handbooks in Music. London: Macmillan, 1990.

———. *The publishing of Arcadelt's first book of madrigals*. Ph.D. diss., Harvard University, 1982.

Bridgman, Nanie. "Christian Egelnoff, imprimeur de musique (A propos du recueil Rés. Vm⁷ 504 de la Bibl. nat. de Paris)". *Annales musicologiques* 3 (1955): 77–178.

———. "Un manuscrit italien du début du XVIᵉ siècle à la Bibliothèque Nationale (Dep. de la Musqiue, Rés. Vm⁷ 676)". *Annales Musicologiques*, 1 (1953): 177–267; 4 (1956): 259–260.

———. "Manuscrits clandestins: a propos du Ms. Rés. 862 de la Bibliothèque nationale de Paris, fonds du Conservatoire". *Revue de musicologie* 53 (1967): 21–27.

———. *Manuscrits de musique polyphonique: XVᵉ et XVIᵉ siècles*. Répertoire international des sources musicales, Ser.B/IV, 5. Munich: Henle, 1991.

———. "La typographie musicale italienne (1475–1630) dans les collections de la Bibliothèque nationale de Paris". *Fontes artis musicae* 13 (1966): 24–27.

Bridgman, Nanie, and François Lesure. "Une anthologie historique de la fin du XVIᵉ siècle: le manuscrit Bourdeney". In *Miscellánea en homenaje a Monseñor Higinio Anglés*: i, 161–172. Barcelona: Consejo Superior de Investigaciones Científicas, 1958–1961.

Briquet, Charles. *Les filigranes: dictionnaire historique des marques du papier dès leur apparition vers 1282 jusqu'en 1600*, ed. Allan Stevenson. Amsterdam: Paper Publications Society, 1968: the 1923 edition rpt. London: Martino, 1997.

Brothers, Thomas. "Vestiges of the isorhythmic tradition in mass and motet, ca.1450–1475". *Journal of the American Musicological Society* 44 (1991): 1–56.

Brown, Arthur. "The transmission of the text". In *Medieval and Renaissance Studies*, ed. John L. Lievsay: 3–28. Medieval and Renaissance Series, 2. Durham, N.C.: Duke University Press, 1968.

Brown, Cynthia J. "The confrontation between printer and author in early sixteenth-century France: another example of Michel le Noir's unethical printing practices". *Bibliothèque d'Humanisme et Renaissance* 53 (1991): 105–119.

———. "The interaction between author and printer: title pages and colophons of early French imprints". *Soundings: collections of the University Library* [of the University of California, Santa Barbara] 23 (1992): 33–53.

————. *Poets, patrons, and printers: crisis of authority in late medieval France*. Ithaca: Cornell University Press, 1995.

Brown, Horatio. *The Venetian printing press: an historical study based upon documents for the most part hitherto unpublished*. New York: Putnam, 1891.

Brown, Howard Mayer. "Chansons for the pleasure of a Florentine patrician: Florence, Biblioteca del Conservatorio di Musica, Ms. Basevi, 2442". In *Aspects of Medieval and Renaissance Music: A birthday offering to Gustave Reese*, ed. Jan LaRue *et al.*: 56–66. London: Oxford University Press, 1966.

————. "Hans Ott, Heinrich Finck and Stoltzer. Early sixteenth-century German motets in Formschneider's anthologies of 1537 and 1538". In *Von Isaac bis Bach: Studien zur älteren deutschen Musikgeschichte: Festschrift Martin Just zum 60. Geburtstag*, ed. Frank Heidlberger, Wolfgang Osthoff, and Reinhard Wiesend: 73–84. Kassel: Bärenreiter, 1991.

————. *Instrumental music printed before 1600: a bibliography*. Cambridge: Harvard University Press, 1965.

————. "The mirror of men's salvation: music in devotional life about 1500". *Renaissance Quarterly* 43 (1990): 744–773.

————. "The Music of the Strozzi chansonnier (Florence, Biblioteca del Conservatorio di Musica, Ms. Basevi 2442)". *Acta musicologica* 40 (1968): 115–129.

————. "Music for a town official in sixteenth-century Zwickau". *Musica antiqua, acta scientifica (Bydgoszcz)* 7: 479–491. Bydgoszcz: Filharmomica Pomorska im. Ignacego Paderewskiego, 1985.

————. "A 'New' chansonnier of the early sixteenth century in the University Library of Uppsala: a preliminary report". *Musica Disciplina* 37 (1983): 171–233.

————. *Theatrical chansons of the fifteenth and early sixteenth centuries*. Cambridge, MA: Harvard University Press, 1963.

Brown, Howard Mayer, ed. *A Florentine Chansonnier from the time of Lorenzo the Magnificent*. Monuments of Renaissance Music, vii (Chicago: University of Chicago Press, 1983)

Brown, Howard Mayer, intro. *Cambridge, Magdalene College, Pepys MS 1760*. Renaissance Music in Facsimile 2. New York: Garland, 1988.

————. *Florence, Biblioteca Nazionale Centrale, MSS Magl. XIX, 164–167*. Renaissance Music in Facsimile 5. New York: Garland, 1987.

————. *London, British Library, MS Royal 20 A.xvi*. Renaissance Music in Facsimile 10. New York: Garland, 1987.

————. *Milan, Archivio della Veneranda Fabbrica del Duomo, Sezione Musicale, Librone 1 (olim 2269)*. Renaissance music in facsimile 12/a. New York: Garland, 1987.

————. *Milan, Archivio della Veneranda Fabbrica del Duomo, Sezione Musicale, Librone 2 (olim 2268)*. Renaissance music in facsimile 12/b. New York: Garland, 1987.

————. *Milan, Archivio della Veneranda Fabbrica del Duomo, Sezione Musicale, Librone 3 (olim 2267)*. Renaissance music in facsimile 12/c. New York: Garland, 1987

————. *Munich, Bayerische Staatsbibliothek, Mus.Ms.10*. Renaissance Music in Facsimile 14. New York: Garland, 1986.

————. *Novum et insigne opus musicum, sex, quinque, et quatuor vocum, cuius in Germania hactenus nihil simile usquam est editum. Nunc quidem locupletatum plus centum non minus elegantibus carminibus, tum Josquini, tum aliorum clarissimorum symphonistarum tam veterum quam recentiorum, quorum quaedam antehac sunt edita, multa nunc primum in lucem exeunt. Nuremberg, Johann Berg and Ulrich Neuber, 1558–1559*. Renaissance Music in Facsimile 27–9. New York: Garland, 1986.

————. *Trium vocum cantiones centum, à praestantissimis diversarum nationum ac linguarum musicis compositae. Tomi primi. Nuremberg, Johannes Petreius, 1541*. Renaissance Music in Facsimile 26. New York: Garland, 1986.

————. *Uppsala, Universitetsbiblioteket, Vokalmusik i handskrift 76a*. Renaissance Music in Facsimile 19. New York: Garland, 1987.

————. *Verona, Biblioteca Capitolare, MS DCCLVII*. Renaissance Music in Facsimile 24. New York: Garland, 1987.

Brown, Patricia Fortini. *Venetian narrative painting in the age of Carpaccio*. New Haven: Yale University Press, 1988.

Brumel, Antoine. *Antonii Brumel: Opera Omnia*, ed. Barton Hudson. Corpus mensurabilis musicae 5. s.l.: American Institute of Musicology, 1969–1972.

Brunet, Jacques-Charles. *Manuel du libraire et de l'amateur de livres*. Paris: Didot freres, fils et cie, 1860–1865, with supplement, 1868–1880.

Bryce, J. *Cosimo Bartoli (1503–1572)*. Geneva: Droz, 1983.

Buchwald, G.. "Archivalische Mitteilungen über Bucherbezuge der Kurfurstlichen Bibliothek und Georg Spalatinus in Wittenberg". *Archiv für Geschichte des Deutschen Buchhandels* 18 (1896): 1–68.

Buetens, Stanley, ed. *Lute recercars by Dalza, Spinacino, Bossinensis, & Capirola*. Menlo Park: Instrumenta Antiqua, 1968.

Bühler, Curt. "Additional notes to Aldus Manutius and his first edition of the Greek Musaeus". In *Scritti sopra Aldo Manuzio*: 106–107. Florence: Olschki, 1955; rpt. in *Early books and manuscripts: forty years of research*: 167–169. New York: The Grolier Club and The Pierpont Morgan Library, 1973.

———. "The first edition of Valerius Maximus and a curious example of misprinting". *Gutenberg-Jahrbuch 1963*: 41–44.

———. "Manuscript corrections in the Aldine edition of Bembo's *De Aetna*". *Papers of the Bibliographical Society of America* 45 (1951): 136–142; rpt. in *Early books and manuscripts: forty years of research*: 170–175. New York: The Grolier Club and The Pierpont Morgan Library, 1973.

———. "Pen corrections in the first edition of Paolo Manuzio's 'Antiquitatem Romanorum liber de legibus' ". *Italia Medioevale e umanistica* 5 (1962): 165–170.

———. "Roman type and roman printing in the fifteenth century". In *Bibliotheca Docet: Festgabe für Carl Wehmer*: 101–110. Amsterdam: Erasmus, [1963]; rpt. in *Early books and manuscripts: forty years of research*: 284–298. New York: The Grolier Club and The Pierpont Morgan Library, 1973.

———. "Stop-press and manuscript corrections in the Aldine edition of Benedetti's *Diario de bello carolino*". *Papers of the Bibliographical Society of America* 43 (1949): 365–373; rpt. in *Early books and manuscripts: forty years of research*: 138–144. New York: The Grolier Club and The Pierpont Morgan Library, 1973.

Buja, Maureen. "Antonio Barré and music printing in mid-sixteenth century Rome". Ph.D. diss., University of North Carolina, 1996.

Bukofzer, Manfred. "An Unknown chansonnier of the 15th century". *Musical Quarterly* 28 (1942?): 14–49.

Bullard, Melissa M. *Filippo Strozzi and the Medici*. Cambridge: Cambridge University Press, 1980.

Buning-Jurgens, J.E. "More about Jacob Obrecht's *Parce Domine*". *Tijdschrift van de Vereniging voor Nederlandse Muziekgeschiedenis* 21 (1970): 167–169.

Burkholder, Peter. "Johannes Martini and the Imitation mass in the late fifteenth-century". *Journal of the American Musicological Society* 38 (1985): 470–523. See also "Communications" from Leeman Perkins and Peter Burkholder, in the same journal 40 (1987): 130–139.

Burney, Charles. *A General history of music, from the earliest ages to the present period*. London: for the author, 1776–1789. References are to the edition by F. Mercer, published New York: Harcourt, Brace, 1935.

Bush, Helen E. "The Laborde *chansonnier*". *Papers of the American Musicological Society, 1940* (1946): 56–79.

Caffi, Francesco. *Storia della musica sacra nella cappella ducale di San Marco in Venezia dal 1318 al 1799*. Venice: Antonelli, 1854–1855; rpt. Milan: Bollettino Bibliografico Musicale, 1931.

Call, Jerry M. "A chansonnier from Lyons: the manuscript Vienna, Österreichische

Nationalbibliothek Mus.Hs.18811". Ph.D. diss., University of Illinois at Urbana-Champaign, 1992.

Camerini, Paolo. *Annali dei Giunti*. Florence: Sansoni, 1962–1963.

Campagnolo, Stefano. "Il *Libro Primo de la Serena* e il madrigale a Roma". *Musica Disciplina* 50 (1996): 95–133.

Campana, Augusto. "Osservazioni sullo stampatore Nicolò Brentà da Varenna, con un nuovo documento riminese". In *Studi di bibliografia e di argomento romano in memoria di Luigi De Gregori*, ed. C. Arcamone: 57–64. Rome: Palombi, 1949.

———. "Manente Leontini fiorentino, medico e traduttore di medici greci". *La Rinascità* 4 (1941): 501–515.

Cappelli, Adriano. *Cronologia, cronografia e calendario perpetuo dal principio dell'era cristiana ai nostri giorni*. 3rd ed., Milan: Hoepli, 1969.

Caraci Vela, Maria, ed. *La Critica del testo musicale: metodi e problemi della filologia musicale*. Studi e testi musicale, n.s., 4. Lucca: Libreria Musicale Italiana, 1995.

Carboni, Fabio, and Agostino Ziino. "Un elenco di composizioni musicali della seconda metà del quattrocento". In *Musica Franca: Essays in honor of Frank A. D'Accone*, ed. Irene Alm, Alyson McLamore and Colleen Reardon: 425–487. Stuyvesant, NY: Pendragon, 1996.

Cardamone, Donna. *The canzone villanesca alla napolitana and related forms, 1535–1570*. Ann Arbor: UMI Research Press, 1981.

———. "The debut of the *Canzona villanella alla napolitana*". *Studi musicali* 4 (1975): 65–130.

———. "*Madrigale a tre et arie napoletane*: a typographical and repertorial study". *Journal of the American Musicological Society* 35 (1982): 436–481.

Cardamone, Donna G, and David L. Jackson. "Multiple formes and vertical setting in Susato's first edition of Lassus' 'Opus 1' ". *Notes* 46 (1989–1990): 7–24.

Caron, Philippe. *Oeuvres Complètes*, ed. James Thomson. Collected works 6. Brooklyn: Institute of Mediaeval music, 1976.

Carpentras (Genet, Elzear). *Elziarii Geneti (Carpentras) (c.1470–1548): Opera Omnia*, ed. Albert Seay. Corpus mensurabilis musicae 58. s.l.: American institute of musicology, 1972–1973.

Carter, Harry. *A view of early typography up to about 1600*. Oxford: Clarendon, 1969.

Carter, Harry, and Hendrik Vervliet. *Civilité types*. Monographs of the Oxford Bibliographical Society, n.s.,14 (1966).

Carter, Tim. "Music-printing in late sixteenth- and early seventeenth-century Florence: Giorgio Marescotti, Cristofano Marescotti and Zanobi Pignoni". *Early music history* 9 (1990): 27–73; rpt. as ch.XI in *Music, Patronage and Printing in late medieval Florence*. Aldershot: Ashgate, 2000.

———. "Music Publishing in Italy, c.1580–c.1625: some preliminary observations". *Royal Musical Association Research Chronicle* 20 (1986–1987): 19–37; rpt. as ch.X in *Music, Patronage and Printing in late medieval Florence*. Aldershot: Ashgate, 2000.

———. "Music-Selling in late sixteenth-century Florence: the bookshop of Piero di Giuliano Morosi". *Music and Letters* 70 (1989): 483–504; rpt. as ch.XII in *Music, Patronage and Printing in late medieval Florence*. Aldershot: Ashgate, 2000.

Carvell, Bruce Ray. "A practical guide to musica ficta: based on an analysis of sharps found in the music prints of Ottaviano Petrucci (1501–1519)". Ph.D. diss., Washington University, 1982.

Casali, S. *Gli annali della tipograficia veneziana di Francesco Marcolini da Forlí*. Forlí: Casali, 1861–1865; rpt. with an introduction by L. Servolini. Bologna: Gerace, 1953.

Casimiri, Raffaele. "Canzoni e Motetti dei sec. XV–XVI". *Note d'archivio* 14 (1937): 145–160.

Castelain, R. "Histoire de l'édition musicale: ou Du droit d'éditeur au droit d'auteur". *Bibliographie de la France 1957*, supplement to issues 4–7.

Castellani, Carlo. *L'Arte della stampa nel rinascimento Italiana: Venezia*. Venice: Ongania, 1894. Translated as *Early Venetian printing illustrated*. New York, 1895.

————. "Ottaviano dei Petrucci da Fossombrone e la stampa della musica in Venezia". In *La stampa in Venezia della sua origine alla morte di Aldo Manuzio seniore*: 61–68. Venice: Ongania 1889; rpt. Trieste: LINT, 1973.

————. *I privilegi di stampa e la proprietà letterarie in Venezia, dalla introduzione della stampa nella Città fin verso la fin del secolo XVIII.* 2nd ed., Venice: Visentini, 1889. Originally published in *Archivio Veneto* 18 (1888).

Castiglione, Baldassare. *The Book of the Courtier*, translated by George Bull. Harmondsworth: Penguin, 1967.

————. *Le Lettere*, ed. Guido La Rocca. Milan: Mondadori, 1978.

————. *Il libro del Cortegiano.* Venice: Aldus Manutius, 1528.

Catelani, Angelo. "Bibliografia di due stampe ignote di Ottaviano Petrucci da Fossombrone". *Gazzetta Musicale di Milano*, No.29404 (1856); rpt. in *Bollettino bibliografico musicale* for 1932.

Cattaneo, E. "Il Rituale romano di Alberto Castellani". In *Miscellanea liturgica in onore di S.E. il Card. G. Lercaro*: ii, 629–647. Città di Vaticano: Biblioteca Apostolica Vaticana, 1967.

Cattin, Giulio. "Canti polifonici del repertorio benedettino in uno sconosciuto 'Liber Quadragesimalis' e in altre fonti italiane dei secoli XV e XVI inc.". *Benedictina* 19 (1972): 445–537.

————. "Le composizioni musicali del Ms. Pavia Aldini 361". *L'ars nova italiana del trecento* 2: 1–21. Certaldo: Centro di Studi sull'Ars nova Italiana del Trecento, 1968.

————. "Contributi alla storia della lauda spirituale". Biblioteca di 'Quadrivium': serie musicologica 2. Bologna: Antiquae Musicae Italicae Studiosi, 1958. Also printed in *Quadrivium* 2 (1958): 45–75.

————. *Italian 'Laude' and latin 'unica' in MS Cape Town Grey 3.b.12.* Corpus mensurabilis musicae 76. s.l.: American Institute of Musicology, 1977.

————. *Johannes de Quadris, musico del sec.XV.* Biblioteca di "Quadrivium": seria musicologica 12. Bologna: Forni, 1971.

————. *Il manoscritto veneto Marciano Ital.IX.145.* Biblioteca di "Quadrivium": serie musicologica 3. Bologna: Antiquae Musicae Italicae Studiosi, 1962; rpt. from *Quadrivium* 4 (1960): 1–60.

————. "Nomi di rimatori per la polifonia profana italiana del secondo Quattrocento". *Rivista italiana di musicologia* 25 (1990): 209–311.

————. "Nuova fonte italiana della polifonia intorno al 1500 (Ms. Cape Town, Grey 3.b.12)". *Acta musicologica* 45 (1973): 165–221.

————. *Polifonia Quattrocentesca italiana del codice Washington, Library of Congress, ML 171 J 6.* Biblioteca di "Quadrivium": seria musicologica 11. Bologna: Forni, 1970.

————. *Un processionale fiorentino per la Settimana Santa: studio liturgico-musicale sul Ms.21 dell'Opera di S. Maria del Fiore.* Testi drammatici medioevali: A. Latini, 4. Bologna: Antiquae Musicae Italicae Studiosi, 1975.

————. "Uno sconosciuto codice quattrocentesco nell'Archivio capitolare di Vicenza e le lamentazioni di Johannes de Quadris". *L'Ars nova musicale italiana del trecento* 3: 281–304. Certaldo: Centro di Studi sull'Ars nova Italiana del Trecento, 1970.

————. "Tradizione e tendenze innovatrici nella normativa e nella pratica liturgico-musicale della congregazione di S. Giustina". *Benedictina* 17 (1970): 254–299.

Cattin, Giulio, ed. *Laudi Quattrocentesche nel Cod. Veneto. Marc.it.IX.145.* Biblioteca di "Quadrivium": seria paleografica, 10. Bologna: Antiquae Musicae Italicae Studiosi, 1958.

Cauchie, Maurice. "A propos des trois recueils instrumentaux de la série de l'Odhecaton". *Revue de musicologie* 9 (1928): 64–67.

————. "L'Odhecaton, recueil de musique instrumentale". *Revue de musicologie* 6 (1925): 148–156.

Cavallini, Ivano. "Irene da Spilimbergo: storia di una biblioteca di famiglia e la persistenza del repertorio frottolistico". Paper read at the conference "Venezia 1501: Petrucci e la stampa musicale", Venice, 12 October 2001.

Cavazzoni, Marc'Antonio. *Recerchari, Motetti, Canzoni Libro Primo. A Facsimile of the [Venice, 1523] Edition.* Monuments of Music and Music Literature in Facsimile, Ser.1, 12. New York: Broude, 1974.

Cazaux, Christelle. *La Musique à la cour de François 1er.* Mémoires et documents de l'École des Chartes 65. Paris: l'École des Chartes, 2002.

Ceccarelli, Giuseppe. *Notizie biografiche di Ottaviano De' Petrucci.* Fossombrone: Bartoloni & Aiudi, 1966.

Ceccarelli, Giuseppe, and Marco Spaccazochi. *Tre carte musicali a stampa inedite di Ottaviano Petrucci.* Fossombrone: s.n., 1976.

Cecchini, G. *Mostra dell'arte della stampa umbra.* Foligno: s.n., 1943.

Cellesi, Luigia. "Ricerche intorno ai compositori della 'Zibaldonaio musicale' Marucelliano". *Bollettino Senese di Storia Patria,* n.s., 2 (1931): 307–309.

Černy, Jaromir. "Soupis hudebnick rukopisů muzea v Hradci Králové". *Miscellanea Musicologica* 19 (1966): 9–240.

Cerretta, Florindo. "Luca Bonetti e l'arte della stampa a Siena nel Cinquecento". *La Bibliofilia* 71 (1969): 169–179.

Cesari, Gaetano and Raffaello Monterosso, eds. *Petrucci, Ottaviano dei: Le frottole nell'edizione principe. I.* Instituta e Monumenta 1. Cremona: Athenaeum Cremonense, 1954.

Ceulemans, Anne-Emmanuelle. "A Stylistic investigation of *Missa Une Mousse de Biscaye,* in the light of its attribution to Josquin Des Prez". *Tijdschrift van de Koninklijke Vereniging voor Nederlandse Muziekgeschiedenis* 48 (1998): 30–50.

Chaillon, Paule. "Le chansonnier de Françoise (MS. Harley 5242 Br. Mus.)". *Revue de musicologie* 35 (1953): 1–31.

Chambers, David, and Jane Martineau, eds. *Splendours of the Gonzaga* [Exhibition catalogue]. London: Victoria and Albert Museum, 1981.

Chapman, Catherine Weeks. "Andrea Antico". Ph.D. diss., Harvard University, 1964.

———. "Printed collections of polyphonic music owned by Ferdinand Columbus". *Journal of the American Musicological Society* 21 (1968): 34–84.

Chapman, James G. "The complete works of Pierre Moulu". Ph.D. diss., New York University, 1964.

Chartier, Roger. *The Cultural uses of Print in early modern France,* trans. L. Cochrane. Princeton: Princeton University Press, 1987.

Charteris, Richard. *Newly Discovered music manuscripts from the private collection of Emil Bohn.* Musicological Studies and Documents 43. Holzgerlingen: American Institute of Musicology and Hänssler, 1999.

Cherry, Alastair. "The Library of St. Mary's College, Blairs, Aberdeen". *The Bibliothek* 12 (1984): 61–69.

Chiarelli, Alessandra. *I codici di musica della Raccolta Estense: ricostruzione dall'inventario settecentesco.* Quaderni della Rivista italiana di musicologia 16. Florence: Olschki, 1987.

Chiesa, Ruggero. "Storia della letteratura del liuto e della chitarra—il cinquecento". *Il Fronimo,* i/4 (vii.1973): 20–25; i/5 (x.1973): 15–20; ii/1 (i.1974): 14–19.

Christoffersen, Peter Woetmann. *French music in the early sixteenth century: studies in the music collection of a copyist of Lyons, the manuscript Ny. kgl. Samling 1848 2° in the Royal Library, Copenhagen.* Copenhagen: Museum Tusculanum, 1994.

Chrysander, Friedrich. "A sketch of the history of music printing". *The Musical Times* 18 (1877): 265–268, 324–326, 375–378, 470–475 and 584–587.

Cian, Vittorio. "A proposito di un'Ambasceria di M. Pietro Bembo (Dicembre 1514): Contributo alla storia della politica di Leone X nei suoi rapporti con Venezia". *Archivio Veneto* 30 (1885): 355–407.

Ciliberti, Galliano. *Musica e società in Umbria ta medioevo e rinascimento.* Speculum Musicae 5. Turnhout: Brepols, 1998.

Cicero, Angelo, and Luciano Migliavacca, eds. *Liber Capelle Ecclesie Maioris: Quarto codice di Gaffurio* [facsimile]. Archivium Musices Metropolitanum Mediolanense 16. Milan: Veneranda Fabbrica del Duomo di Milano, [1968].

Cicogna, Emanuele. *Elenco di stampatori e librari tanto Veneti che forestieri e di quelli ad istanza dei quali si pubblicarono libri in Venezia dal 1469 al 1857.* Manuscript at I-Vc, 3044, with a copy (consulted for this study) at I-Vnm, It.Cl.VII.2040 (8481).

Cimarelli, Vincenzo Maria. *Istorie dello Stato d'Urbino.* Brescia: heredi de Bartholomeo Fontana, 1642; rpt. as *Historiae Urbium et Regionum Italiae Rariores* 56. Bologna: Forni, 1967.

Ciriacono, Salvatore. "Mass consumption goods and luxury goods: the de-industrialization of the Republic of Venice from the sixteenth to the eighteenth century". *The Rise and decline of urban industries in Italy and in the Low Countries (late middle ages-early modern times),* ed. Herman Van der Wee: 41–61. Studies in social and economic history 1. Leuven: Leuven University Press, 1988.

Clair, Colin. *Christopher Plantin.* London: Cassell, 1960.

Clinkscale, Edward. *The complete works of Antoine de Févin.* Ph.D. diss., New York University, 1965.

Clough, Cecil. "Baldassare Castiglione's 'Ad Henricum Angliae regem epistola de vita et gestis Guidubaldi Urbini ducis' ". *Studi Urbinati di storia, filosofia e letteratura* 47 (1973).

——. "Federigo da Montefeltro's patronage of the arts, 1460–1482". *Journal of the Warburg and Courtauld Institutes* 36 (1973): 129–144.

——. "The library of the Dukes of Urbino". *Librarium* 9 (1966): 101–108.

——. "Sources for the economic history of the duchy of Urbino, 1474–1508". *Manuscripta* 10 (1966): 3–27.

——. "Towards an economic history of the state of Urbino at the time of Federigo da Montefeltro and of his son, Guidobaldo". In *Studi in memoria di Federigo Melis,* iii: 469–504. Rome: Giannini, 1978.

Clulow, Peter. "Publication dates for Byrd's latin masses". *Music and Letters* 47 (1966): 1–9.

Codogno, Ottavio. *Nuovo Itinerario delle Poste per tutto il mondo.* Venice: Curti, 1676.

Coggiola, Giulio. "Il recupero da Vienna dei cimeli bibliografici italiani". *Emporium* 30 (1919): 198–217.

Cohen, Paul. "Die Nürnberger Musikdrucker im 16. Jahrhunderts". Diss., Friedrich-Alexander-Universität Erlangen, 1927.

Colón, Fernando. *Abedecarium B y Suplementum* [facsimile]. Madrid: MAPFRE América, 1992.

Compère, Loyset. *Messe, magnificat e mottetti,* ed. Dino Faggion. Archivium musices metropolitanum mediolanense 13. Milan: Veneranda Fabbrica del Duomo di Milano, 1968.

——. *Opera Omnia,* ed. Ludwig Finscher. Corpus mensurabilis musicae 15. s.l.: American Institute of Musicology, 1958–1972.

Compostella, Baldino. *I Petrucci di Vacone e di Siena: genealogica.* Bergamo, 1950.

Concetta, Bianca, Paola Farenga Caprioglio, Giuseppa Lombardi, Antonio G. Luciano and Massimo Miglio, eds. *Scrittura, biblioteche e stampa a Roma nel Quattrocento: aspetti e problemi. Atti del seminario 1–2 Giugno 1979.* Littera antiqua, ser.1, i–ii. Città di Vaticano: Scuola Vaticana di Paleografia, Diplomatica e Archivistica, 1980.

Constant, John G. "Renaissance manuscripts of polyphony at the Cathedral of Padua". Ph.D. diss., University of Michigan, 1975.

Copinger, W.A. *Supplement to Hain's Repertorium bibliographicum.* London: Sotheran, 1895, 1902.

Coppens, Christian. "A census of printers' and booksellers' catalogues up to 1600", *Papers of the Bibliographical Society of America* 89 (1995): 442–455.

Corsini, A.. *Malattia e morte di Lorenzo de'Medici duca d'Urbino.* Florence: Istituto micrografico italiano, 1913.

Cosenza, M. *Biographical dictionary of the Italian printers and foreign printers in Italy from the introduction of the art of printing in Italy to 1800.* Boston: Hall, 1968.

Couchman, Jonathan Paul. "The Lorraine Chansonnier". *Musica Disciplina* 34 (1980): 85–157.

Coussemaker, Charles. *Notice sur les collections musicales de la bibliothèque de Cambrai et des autres villes du département du Nord.* Paris: Techener, 1843; rpt. Hildesheim: Olms, 1970.

Coviello, Francesco. *Dalla tradizione manoscritta alll'invenzione dei caratteri mobili della musica: Ottaviano de' Petrucci, inediti della Biblioteca Passionei*. Fossombrone: Commune di Fossombrone, 1986.

Crapulli, Giovanni, ed. *Trasmissione dei testi a stampa nel periodo moderno: I seminario internazionale, Roma, 23–26 marzo, 1983*. Lessico intellettuale europeo 36. Rome: Ateneo, 1985.

Craven, Alan E. "Proof-reading in the shop of Valentine Simmes". *Papers of the Bibliographical Society of America* 68 (1974): 361–372.

Crawford, David. "A chant manual in sixteenth-century Italy". *Musica Disciplina* 36 (1982): 175–190.

———. *Sixteenth-century choirbooks in the Archivio Capitolare at Casale Monferrato*. Renaissance manuscript studies 2. s.l.: American Institute of Musicology, 1975.

———. "Vespers polyphony at Modena's cathedral in the first half of the sixteenth century". Ph.D. diss., University of Illinois, 1967.

Creighton, Mandell. *A History of the Papacy during the period of the Reformation*. London: Longman, Green & Co, 1882–1894.

Cristoforetti, Orlando, intro. *Compositione di Messer Vincenzo Capirola* [facsimile]. Archivum Musicum: Collana di testi rari 39. Florence: Studio per Edizioni Scelte, 1981.

Croll, Gerhard. "Zu Tromboncinos 'Lamentationes Jeremiae' ". *Collectanea historiae musicae* 2 (1957): 111–114.

Cummings, Anthony M. "A Florentine sacred repertory from the Medici restoration (Manuscript II.I.232 of the Biblioteca Nazionale Centrale, Firenze)". Ph.D. diss., Princeton University. 1980.

———. "A Florentine sacred repertory from the Medici restoration". *Acta Musicologica* 55 (1983): 267–332.

———. "Gian Maria Gudeo, Sonatore del Liuto, and the Medici." *Fontes Artis Musicae* 38 (1991): 312–318.

———. "Giulio de'Medici's music books". *Early Music History* 10 (1991): 65–122.

———. "Medici musical patronage in the early sixteenth century: new perspectives". *Studi musicali* 10 (1981): 197–216.

———. "Toward an interpretation of the sixteenth-century motet". *Journal of the American Musicological Society* 34 (1981): 43–59.

———. "The transmission of some Josquin motets". *Journal of the Royal Musical Association* 115 (1990): 1–32.

Curtis, Joseph. "Antoine Brumel's 'Missa Berzerette savoyenne': edition and commentary". DMA diss., Arizona State University, 2002.

Cusick, Suzanne. *Valerio Dorico: music printer in sixteenth-century Rome*. Ann Arbor: UMI Research Press, 1981.

Czepiel, Tomasz. *Music at the Royal court and chapel in Poland, c.1543–1600*. Outstanding dissertations in music from British universities. New York: Garland, 1966.

D'Accone, Frank. "Bernardo Pisano: an introduction to his life and works". *Musica Disciplina* 17 (1963): 115–135.

———. *The Civic Muse: Music and musicians in Siena during the Middle Ages and Renaissance*. Chicago: Chicago University Press, 1997.

———. "Instrumental resonances in a Sienese vocal print of 1515". In *Le Concert des voix et des instruments à la Renaissance: Actes du XXXIVe Colloque International d'Études Supérieures de la Renaissance, 1–11 juillet 1991*, ed. Jean-Michel Vaccaro: 333–359. Paris, 1995.

———. "A late 15th-century Sienese sacred repertory: MS K.I.2 of the Biblioteca Comunale, Siena". *Musica Disciplina* 37 (1983): 121–170.

———. "Transitional text forms and settings in an early 16th-century Florentine manuscript". *Words and Music: the scholar's view. A medley of problems and solutions compiled in honor of A. Tillman Merritt*, ed. Laurence Berman: 29–58. Cambridge, MA: Harvard University Press, 1972.

D'Accone, Frank, ed. *Music of the Florentine renaissance*. Corpus mensurabilis musicae 32. s.l..: American Institute of Musicology, 1966–1985.

D'Accone, Frank, intro. *Florence, Archivio Musicale dell'Opera di Santa Maria del Fiore, MS 11*. Renaissance Music in Facsimile 3. New York: Garland, 1987.

──────. *Florence, Biblioteca Nazionale Centrale MS Banco Rari 230*. Renaissance Music in Facsimile 4. New York: Garland, 1986.

──────. *Modena, Biblioteca Estense e Universitaria, MS alpha F.9.9*. Renaissance Music in Facsimile 13. New York: Garland, 1987.

──────. *Pavia, Biblioteca Universitaria, Aldini MS 362*. Renaissance Music in Facsimile 16. New York: Garland, 1986.

──────. *Siena, Biblioteca Comunale degli Intronati, MS K.I.2*. Renaissance Music in Facsimile 17. New York: Garland, 1986.

──────. *Turin, Biblioteca Nazionale Universitaria, MS Ris.mus.I.27 (olim qm III.59)*. Renaissance Music in Facsimile 18. New York: Garland, 1986.

D'Alessi, Giovanni. *La cappella musicale del Duomo di Treviso (1300–1633)*. Treviso: Ars et Religio, 1954.

──────. *Il tipografo fiammingo Gerardus de Lisa cantore e maestro di cappella nella Cattedrale di Treviso (1463–1496)*. Treviso: Vedelago, 1925.

D'Ancona, Paolo. *La miniatura fiorentina*. Florence: Olschki, 1914.

Dahlhaus, Carl. "Ockeghems 'Fuga trium vocum' ". *Die Musikforschung* 13 (1960): 307–310.

Dalmazzo, Gianolio. *Il libro e l'arte della stampa*. Turin: s.n., 1926.

Dalza, Joanambrosio. *Intabulatura de lauto* [facsimile]. Geneva: Minkoff, 1980.

──────. *Intavolatura de Lauto 1508*, ed. Helmut Mönkemeyer. Die Tabulatur 6 Hofheim am Taunus: Hofmeister, [c.1967].

Damerini, Adelmo, ed. *Esposizione nazionale dei Conservatori musicali e delle biblioteche: Palazzo Davanzati [Florence] 27 Ottobre 1949—8 Gennaio 1950*. Florence: Barbèra, 1950.

Dardo, Gianluigi. "Contributo alla storia del liuto in Italia: Johannes Maria Alemanus e Giovanni Maria da Crema". *Quaderni della Rassegna Musicale* 3 (1965): 143–157.

Daschner, Hubert. *Die gedruckten mehrstimmigen französischen Chansons von 1500–1600. Literarische Quellen und Bibliographie*. Diss., Universität Bonn, 1958.

Davidsson, Åke. *Bibliographie zur Geschichte des Musikdrucks*. Acta universitatis Upsaliensis: Studia musicologica Upsaliensia, nova Seria, 1. Uppsala: Almqvist & Wiksell, 1965.

Davies, Hugh William. *Devices of the early printers, 1457–1560: their history and development*. London: Grafton, 1935.

Davies, Martin. *Aldus Manutius: printer and publisher of Renaissance Venice*. London: British Library, 1995.

──────. "Two Book-lists of Sweynheym and Pannartz". In *Libri Tipografi Biblioteche: ricerche storiche dedicata a Luigi Balsamo*: 25–53. Biblioteca di bibliografia italiana 148. Florence: Olschki, 1997.

Davis, Natalie Zemon. "Printing and the people". *Society and culture in early modern France*. Stanford: Stanford University Press, 1975.

Davison, Archibald, and Willi Apel, eds. *Historical Anthology of Music*. Cambridge, MA: Harvard University Press, 1946–1950.

Davison, Peter. "Science, method and the textual critic". *Studies in Bibliography* 25 (1972): 1–28.

De Roover, Florence Edler. "New facts on the financing and marketing of early printed books". *Bulletin of the Business Historical Society* 28 (1953): 222–230.

Dean, Jeffrey. "The evolution of a canon at the Papal Chapel: the importance of old music in the fifteenth and sixteenth centuries". In *Papal music and musicians in late medieval and renaissance Rome*, ed. Richard Sherr: 138–166. Oxford: Clarendon, and Washington: Library of Congress, 1998.

──────. "The scribes of the Sistine Chapel, 1501–1527". Ph.D. diss., University of Chicago, 1984.

Dean, Jeffrey, intro. *Vatican City, Biblioteca Apostolica Vaticana, Cappella Sistina, MS 46*. Renaissance Music in Facsimile 21. New York: Garland, 1986.

Dennistoun, James. *Memoirs of the Dukes of Urbino, illustrating the arms, arts and literature of Italy, from 1440 to 1630*. London: Longman, Brown, Green and Longman, 1851.

Devonshire Jones, Rosemary. "Lorenzo de' Medici, Duca d'Urbino, 'Signore' of Florence?". In *Studies on Machiavelli*, ed. Myron P. Gilmore: 297–315. Biblioteca storica Sansoni, nuova serie, 50. Florence: Sansoni, 1972.

Diehl, George. "Ms. Cambrai 124 (125–128): a repertorial study". Ph.D. diss., University of Pennsylvania, 1974.

Disertori, Benvenuto. "Campane in un motetto del quattrocento". *Rivista musicale italiana* 44 (1940): 106–111

———. "Contradiction tonale dans la transcription d'un 'strambotto' célèbre ('Amando e Desiando' de Benedetto Cariteo, transcrit par Franciscus Bossinensis)". In *Le luth et sa musique*. ed. Jean Jacquot: 37–42. Colloques internationaux du Centre national de la recherche scientifique 511. Paris: Centre national de la recherche scientifique, 1976.

———. "La frottola nella storia della musica". *Petrucci, Ottaviano dei: Le frottole nell'edizione principe. I*, ed. Gaetano Cesari and Raffaello Monterosso: pp. VII–LXV. Instituta e Monumenta 1. Cremona: Athenaeum Cremonense, 1954.

———. "Il manoscritto 1947-4 di Trento e la canzone 'J'ay pris amours' ". *Rivista musicale italiana* 48 (1946): 1–29.

———. "In margine all'Odhecaton". *Rivista musicale italiana* 51 (1949): 29–42.

Disertori, Benvenuto, ed. *Le frottole per canto e liuto intabulate de Franciscus Bossinensis*. Istituzioni e Monumenti dell'Arte Musicale Italiana, n.s., 3. Milan: Ricordi, 1964.

Divitis, Antonius. *Collected works*, ed. B.A. Nugent. Recent Researches in the Music of the Renaissance 94. Madison: A-R Editions, 1993.

Dixon, Helen M. "The Manuscript Vienna, National Library, 1783". *Musica Disciplina* 23 (1969): 105–116

Donà, Mariangela. *La Musica nelle biblioteche milanesi: mostra di libri e documenti*. Milan: [Biblioteca nazionale Braidense], 1963.

———. "Musiche a stampa nella Biblioteca Braidense di Milano". *Fontes artis musicae* 7 (1960): 66–68.

———. *La stampa musicale a Milano fino all'anno 1700*. Biblioteca di bibliografia italiana 39. Florence: Olschki, 1961.

Donaldson, Robert. "The Cambuskenneth books; the Norris of Speke collection". *The Bibliothek* 15 (1988): 3–7.

Donati, Lamberto. "Discorso sulle stampe popolari italiane del xvi e xvii secolo". *Gutenberg-Jahrbuch 1965*: 233–241.

———. "Iniziali con le corona". *Gutenberg-Jahrbuch 1953*: 9–10.

———. "Le iniziali iconografiche del XVI secolo". In *Studi bibliografici: Atti del Convegno dedicato alla storia del libro italiano nel V centenario dell'introduzione dell'arte tipografica in Italia. Bolzano, 7–8 ottobre 1965*: 219–39. Florence: Olschki, 1967.

Doni, Antonfrancesco: *La Libraria*. Venice: Giolito, 1550.

Dowland, Robert. *Varietie of Lute-Lessons: a lithographic facsimile of the original edition of 1610*, ed. Edgar Hunt. London: Schott, 1958.

Drake, George Warren James. "The first printed books of motets, Petrucci's *Motetti A numero trentatre* (Venice, 1502) and *Motetti de Passione, de Cruce, de Sacramento, de Beata Virgine et huius modi* (Venice, 1503)". Ph.D. diss., Univeristy of Illinois, 1972.

Draudius, Georg. *Bibliotheca classica, Sive, Catalogus officinalis*. Frankfurt-am-Main: Hoffmann, 1611. The section "Librorum musicorum" is on pp. 1203–1236. In the edition of 1625 (Frankfurt-am-Main: Ostern), the music section is on pp. 1609–1654

Dreves, Guido, M. Blume and H.M. Bannister, eds. *Analecta hymnica medii aevi*. Leipzig, 1886–1922; rpt. New York: Johnson Reprint Corporation, 1961.

Droz, Eugénie, and Geneviève Thibault, eds. *Poètes et musiciens du XVe siècle*. Documents artistiques du XVe siècle 1. Paris: Jeanbin, 1924.

Droz, Eugénie, Geneviève Thibault and Yvonne Rokseth, eds. *Trois chansonniers français du XVe siècle*. Documents artistiques du XVe siècle 4. Paris: Droz, 1927.

Ducrot, Ariane. "Histoire de la Cappella Giulia depuis sa fondation par Jules II (1513) jusqu'a sa restauration par Gregoire XIII (1578)". *Mélanges d'Archéologie et d'Histoire* 75 (1963): 179–240 and 467–559.

Duggan, Mary Kay. *Italian music incunabula: printers and type*. Berkeley and Los Angeles: University of California Press. 1992.

———. "Italian music incunabula: printers and typefonts". Ph.D. diss., University of California at Berkeley, 1981.

———. "A system for describing fifteenth-century music type". *Gutenberg-Jahrbuch 1984*: 67–76

Dunning, Albert. *Die Staatsmotette, 1480–1555*. Utrecht: Oosthoek. 1970.

Las Edades del Hombre: La Musica en la Iglesia de Castilla y Leon. Leon: [s.n.], 1991.

Le edizioni italiane del XVI secolo: censimento nazionale. 2nd ed., Rome: Istituto centrale per il catalogo unico delle Biblioteche Italiane e per le Informazione bibliografiche, 1990–.

Edwards, Rebecca. "Claudio Merulo: servant of the state and musical entrepreneur in later sixteenth-century Venice". Ph.D. diss., Princeton University, 1990.

Einstein, Alfred. "Andrea Antico's *Canzoni Nove* of 1510". *The Musical Quarterly* 37 (1951): 330–339.

———. "Das elfte Buch des Frottole". *Zeitschrift für Musikwissenschaft* 10 (1927–1928): 613–624.

———. *The Italian Madrigal* (Princeton: Princeton University Press, 1949)

———. "Eine unbekannte Ausgabe eines Frottolen-Drucke". *Acta musicologica* 8 (1936): 154–155.

Einstein, Alfred, ed. *Beispielsammlung zu älteren Musikgeschichte*. Leipzig: Breitkopf und Härtel, 1917.

———. *Canzoni, sonetti, strambotti et frottole, libro tertio*. Smith College Music Archives 4. Northampton, MA: Smith College, 1941.

Eisenstein, Elizabeth. *The printing press as an agent of change*. Cambridge: Cambridge University Press, 1979.

Eitner, Robert. *Biographisch-bibliographisches Quellenlexikon des Musiker und Musikgelehrten des christlichen Zeitrechnung bis zur Mitte des 19. Jahrhunderts*. Leipzig: Breitkopf und Härtel, 1899–1904; rpt. New York: Musurgia, 1947 and Graz: Akademische Druck- und Verlagsanstalt, 1959.

———. "Ein Liederbuch von Oeglin". *Monatshefte für Musikgeschichte* 22 (1890): 214.

———. "Der Musiknotendruck und seine Entwicklung". *Facsimile: Zeitschrift für Bücherfreunde* 1 (1898): 630–636.

Elders, Willem. "Zur Frage der Vorlage von Isaacs Messe *La mi la so* oder *O praeclara*". In *Von Isaac bis Bach: Studien zur älteren deutschen Musikgeschichte: Festschrift Martin Just zum 60. Geburtstag*, ed. Frank Heidlberger, Wolfgang Osthoff and Reinhard Wiesend: 9–13. Kassel: Bärenreiter, 1991.

———. "Josquin des Prez en zijn motet *Illibata Dei virgo*". *Mens en melodie* 23 (1970): 141–144.

———. "Josquin's 'Gaudeamus' mass: a case of number symbolism in worship". *Studi musicali* 14 (1985): 221–234.

———. "New Light on the dating of Josquin's *Hercules* mass". *Tijdschrift van der Koninklijke Vereniging voor Nederlandse Muziekgeschiedenis* 48 (1998): 112–148.

———. "Le Problème de l'authenticité chez Josquin et les éditions de Petrucci: une investigation préliminaire". *Fontis artis musicae* 36 (1989): 108–115.

———. "Zusammenhänge zwischen den Motettem *Ave nobilissima creatura* und *Huc me sydereo* von Josquin des Prez". *Tijdschrift van der Vereniging voor Nederlandse Muziekgeschiedenis* 22 (1971): 67–73.

Ellis, S.R. "Citizenship and Immigration in Venice, 1305–1900". Ph.D. diss., University of Chicago, 1976.

Enschedé, Charles. *Typefounders in the Netherlands from the fifteenth to the nineteenth centuries* (Haarlem: Stichting Museum Enschedé, 1978)

Epp, Esther M. "Popular arrangements in the Petrucci chansonniers". Ph.D. diss., University of Toronto, 2000.

Ernesti, Johann Heinrich Gottfried. *Die Wol-eingerichtete Büchdrückerey*. Nürnberg: Endters Erben, 1733.

Essling, *Prince* Victor Masséna de l'. *Les livres à figures vénitiens de la fin du xvᵉ siècle et du commencement du xviᵉ*. Florence: Leclerc & Olschki, 1907–1914; rpt. London: Martino, 1994.

Eustachio Romano. *Musica Duorum. Rome 1521*, ed. Howard Mayer Brown and Edward E. Lowinsky. Monuments of Renaissance Music 6. Chicago: University of Chicago Press, 1975.

Expert, Henry, ed. *Les Maîtres musiciens de la Renaissance française*. Paris: Leduc, 1894–1908.

Expert, Henry, Jean de Valois and Aimé Agnel, eds. *Jean Mouton: Motets à 4 et 5 voix*. Maîtres anciens de la musique française 5. Paris: Heugel, 1975.

Fabiano, Andrea. *Le stampe musicali antiche del Fondo Torrefranca del Conservatorio Benedetto Marcello*. "Historiae Musicae Cultores Biblioteca" 65. Florence: Olschki, 1992.

Fabris, Dinko. "Una frottola intavolata per canto e liuto in une inedita versione manoscritta del primo cinquecento". *Bollettino della Società italiana del liuto* 4 (1992): 5–7.

———. "Le prime intavolature per liuto: tradizione manoscritta ed edizioni a stampa". Paper read at the conference "Venezia 1501: Petrucci e la stampa musicale", Venice, 12 October 2001.

Facchin, Francesco. *Frottole Libro Nono. Ottaviano Petrucci, Venezia 1508 (ma, 1509)*. Octaviani Petrutii Forosemproniensis Froctolae 3. Venice; Comitato per la Pubblicazione di Fonti della Cultura Musicale Veneta, and Padua: CLEUP, 1990.

Fahy, Conor. "Antonio Gardano e la stampa musicale rinascimentale: appunti su una pubblicazione recente". *La Bibliofilia* 94 (1992): 285–299.

———. "Ariosto, 'Orlando Furioso', Ferrara, Francesco Rosso, 1532: profilo di una edizione". In *Trasmissione dei testi a stampa nel periodo moderno: II. Il seminario internazionale, Roma—Viterbo, 27–29 giugno, 1985*, ed. Giovanni Crapulli: 123–146. Rome: Ateneo, 1987; rpt. in Fahy, *Saggi di bibliografia testuale*: 245–270. Medioevo e umanesimo 66. Padova: Antenore, 1988.

———. "Il concetto di 'esemplare ideale' ". *Trasmissione dei testi a stampa nel periodo moderno: I seminario internazionale, Roma, 23–26 marzo, 1983*, ed. Giovanni Crapulli: 49–60. Lessico intelletuale Europeo, xxxvi (Rome: Ateneo, 1985); rpt. in Fahy, *Saggi di bibliografia testuale*: 89–103. Medioevo e umanesimo 66. Padova: Antenore, 1988.

———. "Correzioni ed errori avvenuti durante la tiratura secondo uno stampatore del Cinquecento: contributo alla storia della tecnica tipografica in Italia". In Fahy, *Saggi di bibliografia testuale*: 155–168. Medioevo e umanesimo 66. Padova: Antenore, 1988.

———. "Descrizioni cinquecentesche della fabbricazione dei caratteri e del processo tipografico". *La Bibliofilìa* 88 (1986): 47–86.

Fallows, David. *A Catalogue of Polyphonic songs, 1415–1480*. Oxford: Oxford University Press, 1999.

———. "Fifteenth-century songs in Tongeren". In *Musicology and Archival Research. Musicologie et recherches en archives. Musicologie en Archiefonderzoek*, ed. Barbara Haggh, Frank Daelemans, and André Vanrie: 510–521. Archives et Bibliothèques de Belgique. Archief- en Bibliotheekwezen in Belgie 46. Brussels, Archives générales du Royaume, 1994.

———. "15th-century tablatures for plucked instruments: a summary, a revision and a suggestion". *The Lute Society Journal* 19 (1977): 7–33.

———. "French as a courtly language in fifteenth-century Italy: the musical evidence". *Renaissance Studies* 3 (1989): 429–441.

———. "Johannes Ockeghem: the changing image, the songs and a new source". *Early Music* 12 (1984): 218–230.

———. "Josquin and Milan". *Plainsong and Medieval Music* 5 (1996): 69–80.

———. "The Life of Johannes Regis, ca.1425 to 1496". *Revue belge de musicologie* 43 (1989): 143–172.

———. "Petrucci's *Canti* volumes: scope and repertory". *Basler Jahrbuch für historische Musikpraxis* 25 (2002): 39–52.

———. "Polyphonic song in the Florence of Lorenzo's youth, ossia: the provenance of the manuscript Berlin 78.C.28: Naples or Florence?". In *La musica a Firenze al tempo di Lorenzo il Magnifico*, ed. Piero Gargiulo: 47–61. Florence: Olschki, 1993.

———. "Prenez sur moy: Okeghem's tonal pun". *Plainsong and medieval music* 1 (1992): 63–75; rpt. in David Fallows, *Songs and Musicians in the fifteenth century*: 63–75. Aldershot: Variorum, 1996.

———. "Robert Morton's songs: a study of styles in the mid-fifteenth century". Ph.D diss., University of California at Berkeley, 1978.

———. "Robertus de Anglia and the Oporto song collection". In *Source materials and the interpretation of music: a memorial volume to Thurston Dart*, ed. Ian D. Bent: 99–128. London: Stainer & Bell, 1981.

Fallows, David, ed. *Bodleian Library. Manuscript Canon.Misc.213.* Late medieval and early Renaissance music in facsimile 1. Chicago: University of Chicago Press, 1995.

———. *The Songbook of Fridolin Sicher, around 1515: Sankt Gallen, Switzerland, Cod.Sang.461* [facsimile]. Peer: Alamire, 1996.

Fanelli, Jean Grundy. *Musica e libri sulla musica nella Biblioteca Marucelliana di Firenze pubblicati fino al 1800.* Lucca: LIM, 1999.

Fano, Fabio, ed. *Anonimi motetti.* Archivium musices metropolitanum Mediolanensis 9. Milan: Veneranda Fabbrica del Duomo di Milano, 1961.

Fatini, Giuseppe, ed. *Giuliano de'Medici, Duca di Nemours: Poesie.* Florence: Vallecchi, 1939.

Fava, Domenico. "Le conquiste tecniche di un grande tipografo del Quattrocento". *Gutenberg-Jahrbuch 1940:* 147–156.

———. *Primo congresso internazionale di bibliografia e bibliofilia: mostra bibliografico musicale: Bologna, Archiginnasio, Giugno 1929.* Bologna: Azzoguidi, 1929.

Febvre, Lucien Paul Victor, and Henri-Jean Martin. *L'Apparition du Livre.* Paris: Michel, 1958. Translated by D. Gerard as *The Coming of the book: the impact of printing 1450–1800.* London: Verso, 1984.

Federhofer, Hellmut. "Biographische Beiträge zu Erasmus Lapicida und Stephan Mahu". *Die Musikforschung* 5 (1952): 37–46.

———. "Musikdrucke von Ottaviano Petrucci in der Bibliothek des Franziskaner-klosters Güssing (Burgenland)". *Die Musikforschung* 16 (1963): 157–158.

Feicht, Hieronim, ed. *Muzyka staropolska. A selection of hitherto unpublished works of 12th–18th century.* Krakow: P.W.M., 1966.

Feininger, Laurence. "Eine neue Quelle zur Polyphonie des 15. Jahrhunderts". In *Festschrift Walter Senn zum 70. Geburtstag*, ed. Ewald Fässler: 53–63. Munich and Salzburg: Katzbichler, 1975.

Feininger, Laurence, ed. *Monumenta polyphoniae liturgicae*, Ser.1/i. Rome: Societas Universalis Sanctae Ceciliae, 1948.

Feld, Maurice D. "The early evolution of the authoritative text". *Harvard Library Bulletin* 26 (1978): 81–111.

Feldman, Martha. *City Culture and the madrigal at Venice.* Berkeley and Los Angeles: University of California Press, 1995.

Feldmann, Fritz. "Alte und neue Probleme um Cod.2016 des Musikalischen Instituts bei der Universität-Breslau". In *Festschrift Max Schneider zum achtzigsten Geburtstage*, ed. Walther Vetter: 49–66. Leipzig: VEB Deutscher Verlag für Musik, 1955.

———. *Der Codex Mf.2016 des Musikalischen Instituts bei der Universität Breslau.* Breslau: Priebatsch's Buchhandlung, 1932.

———. "Divergierende Überlieferungen in Isaacs 'Petrucci-Messen' als Beitrag zum Wort-Ton-Verhältnis um 1500". *Collectanea historiae musicae* 2 (1957): 203–225.

Fenlon, Iain. "Round Table IV: production and distribution of music in sixteenth- and seventeenth-century European society". *Acta musicologica* 59 (1987): 14–17.

———. *Music, print and culture in early sixteenth-century Italy*. The Panizzi Lectures, 199. London: The British Library, 1995.

Fenlon, Iain, and Patrizia Dalla Vecchia, eds. *Venezia 1501: Petrucci e la stampa musicale. Catalogo della mostra*. Venice: Edizioni della Laguna, 2001.

Fenlon, Iain, and James Haar. "Fonti e cronologia dei madrigali di Costanzo Festa". *Rivista italiana di musicologia* 13 (1978): 212–242.

———. *The Italian madrigal in the early sixteenth century: sources and interpretation*. Cambridge: Cambridge University Press, 1988.

Ferand, Ernst T. *Die Improvisation in der Musik*. Zurich: Rhein, 1938.

———. "Ein neuer Frottole-Fund". *Acta musicologica* 10 (1938): 132–141. Translated as "Two unknown frottole", *The Musical Quarterly* 28 (1941): 319–328.

Ferrarese, Francesca, and Cristina Gallo. *Il fondo musicale della Biblioteca capitolare del Duomo di Treviso*. Cataloghi di fondi musicali italiani 12. Rome: Torre d'Orfeo, 1990.

Ferrari-Barassi, Elena. "Alcune frottole 'petrucciane' fra Italia, Spagna e Germania". *Nuova rivista musicale italiana* 21 (1997): 47–70.

Festa, Costanzo. *Opera Omnia*, ed. Alexander Main and Albert Seay. Corpus mensurabilis musicae 25. s.l.: American Institute of Musicology, 1962–1978.

———. *Sacrae cantiones 3, 4, 5, 6 vocibus*, ed. Eduardo Dagnino. Monumenti polyphoniae Italicae 2. Rome: Pontifical Institute, 1936.

Fétis, François-Joseph. *Biographie universelle des musiciens et bibliographie générale de la musique*. Paris: Fournier, 1835. References are to the second edition, Paris: Firmin Didot Frères, 1860–1865; rpt. Brussels: Culture et Civilisation, 1972.

[Fétis, François-Joseph.] *Catalogue de la bibliothèque de F. J. Fétis, acquise par l'État belge*. Brussels: Muquardt, 1877. rpt. as Bibliotheca Musica Bononiensis, sezione I/vii. [Bologna: Forni, 1969].

Févin, Antoine. *Les oeuvres complètes de Antoine de Févin*. Henryville, PA: Institute of Medieval Music, 1980–1993.

———. *Sancta Trinitas*. London: Novello, 1973.

Févin, Robert. *Collected Works*, ed. Edward Clinkscale. Collected Works 13. Ottawa: Institute of Mediaeval Music, 1993.

Fiedler, Eric. *Die Messen des Gaspar Weerbeke (ca.1445–nach 1517)*. Tutzing: Schneider, 1997.

———. "A New mass by Gaspar van Weerbeke? Thoughts on comparative analysis". In *Studien zur Musikgeschichte. Ein Festschrift für Ludwig Finscher*, ed. Annegrit Laubenthal and Kara Kusan-Windweh: 72–87. Kassel: Bärenreiter, 1995.

Finck, Hermann. *Practica Musica* [facsimile]. Hildesheim: Olms, 1971.

Finlay, Robert. *Politics in Renaissance Venice*. London: Benn, 1980.

Finscher, Ludwig. *Loyset Compère (c.1450–1518): life and works*. Musicological Studies and Documents 12. Rome: American Institute of Musicology, 1966.

———. "Der Medici-Kodex—Geschichte und Edition". *Die Musikforschung* 30 (1977): 468–481.

———. "Eine wenig beachtete Quelle zu Johann Walters Passions-Turbae". *Die Musikforschung* 11 (1958): 189–195.

Fioravanti, Leonardo. *Del compendio de i secreti rationali libri cinque*. Venice: Valgrisi, 1564.

———. *Dello specchio di scientia universale libri tre*. Venice: Valgrisi, 1564.

Fischer, Kurt von, with Max Lütolf. *Handschriften mit mehrstimmigen Musik des 14., 15. und 16. Jahrhundert*. Répertoire international des sources musicales, Ser.B/IV, 3–4. Munich-Duisburg: Henle, 1972.

Fitch, Fabrice. *Johannes Ockeghem: masses and models*. Paris: Champion, 1997.

Fletcher, George. *New Aldine Studies*. San Francisco: Rosenthal, 1988.

Fletcher, John M. and James K. McConica. "A sixteenth-century inventory of the library of Corpus Christi College, Cambridge". *Transactions of the Cambridge Bibliographical Society* 3 (1959–1963): 187–199.

Florimo, Francesco. *Scuola musicale di Napoli e i suoi Conservatorii*. Naples: Morano, 1881–3; rpt. as Bibliotheca musica Bononiensis, iii, vol.9. Bologna: Forni, 1969.

Fogelmark, Staffan. *Flemish and related Panel-stamped bindings: evidence and principles*. New York: Bibliographical Society of America, 1990.

Folengo, Teofilo. *Macaronicum poema*. Venice: Costanti, 1540.

da Fonseca e Vasconcelles, Joaquim Antonio. *Primeira Parte do Index de Livraria de Musica do Rey Dom João IV*. Porto: Imprensa, 1874.

Forkel, Johann Nikolaus. *Allgemeine Geschichte der Musik in Denkmälern von der ältesten bis auf die neueste Zeit*. Leipzig: Schwickert, 1788–1801; rpt. Graz: Akademische Druck-u Verlagsanstalt, 1967.

Forney, Kristine Karen. "Orlando di Lasso's 'Opus 1': the making and marketing of a renaissance music book". *Revue belge de musicologie* 39–40 (1985–6): 33–60.

———. "Tielman Susato, sixteenth-century music printer: an archival and typographical investigation". Ph. D. diss., University of Kentucky, 1978.

Foss, Julius. "Det kgl. Cantori Stemme boger A.D.1541". *Årbog for Musik 1923* (1924): 24–41.

Fox, Bertha Mary. "A liturgical-repertorial study of renaissance polyphony in Bártfa Mus. Pr. 6 (a–d), National Széchényi Library, Budapest". Ph.D. diss., University of Illinois, 1977.

Francesco da Milano. *The Lute Music of Francesco Canova da Milano (1497–1543)*, ed. Arthur Ness. Harvard Publications in Music 3–4. Cambridge, MA: Harvard University Press, 1970.

———. *Opere complete per liuto*, ed. R. Chiesa. Milan: Suvini Zerboni, s.d.

Françon, Marcel. *Poèmes de transition (XVe–XVIe siècles): rondeaux du Ms. 402 de Lille*. Cambridge, MA: Harvard University Press, 1938.

Frankel, Stuart. "Phonology, verse metrics and music". Ph.D. diss., New York University, 1999.

Fulin, R. "Documenti per servire alla storia della tipografia veneziana". *Archivio veneto* 23 (1882): 84–212.

———. "Nuovi documenti per servire alla storia della tipografia veneziana". *Archivio veneto* 23 (1882): 390–405.

Fuller, Sarah. "Additional notes on the 15th-century chansonnier Bologna Q16". *Musica Disciplina*, xxiii (1969): 81–103

Fumagalli, G. *Lexicon typographicum Italicae: dictionnaire géographique d'Italie pour servir à l'histoire de l'imprimerie dans ce pays*. Florence: Olschki, 1905; rpt. Florence, Giuntina, 1966.

Fumagalli, G. and G. Belli. *Catalogo delle edizioni romane di Antonio Blado Asulano ed eredi possedute dalla Biblioteca nazionale centrale Vittorio Emanuele di Roma*. Rome: Ministero della pubblica Istruzioni, 1891.

Funke, Fritz. *Buchkunde: Ein Überblick über die Geschichte des Buches*. Munich: Saur, 1999.

Furbetta, Ornella. "L'arte della stampa nelle città di Pesaro e Urbino dal sec.xv al sec.xviii (con un'appendice sulla stampa in Piobbico)". *Atti e Memorie della R. Deputazione di Storia Patria per le Marche*, Ser. 7, 9 (1954): 113–183.

Furfaro, D. *La vita e l'opera di Leonardo Fioravanti*. Bologna: Azzoguidi, 1963.

Fusi, Daniele. "Le Frottole nell'edizione di Pietro Sambonetto (Siena 1515)". Tesi di Laurea, Università degli Studi di Siena, 1976–77.

Gabler, Hans Walter. "*Cupids Revenge* (Q1) and its compositors: Part 1. Composition and printing". *Studies in Bibliography* 24 (1971): 69–90.

Gallico, Claudio. *Un canzoniere musicale italiano del cinquecento. Bologna, Conservatorio di Musica 'G. B. Martini' MS. Q.21*. "Historiae Musicae Cultores" Biblioteca 13. Florence: Olschki, 1961.

———. "Un 'dialogo d'amore' di Niccolò da Correggio musicato da B. Tromboncino", *Studien zur Musikwissenswchaft* 25 (1962): 205–213.

————. "Dal laboratorio di Ottaviano Petrucci: immagine, trasmissione e cultura della musica". *Rivista italiana di musicologia* 17 (1982): 187–206.

————. "Il laboratorio di Ottaviano Petrucci a Venezia: musica e immagine grafica". In *Tempo di Giorgione*, ed. Ruggero Maschio: 78–83. Collana interpretazioni e documenti 5. Rome: Gangemi, 1994.

————. *Un Libro di poesie per musica dell'epoca d'Isabella d'Este*. Bollettino storico mantovano: quaderni 5. Mantua: s.n., 1961.

————. *Rimeria musicale popolare italiana nel Rinascimento*. Lucca: LIM, 1996.

Gallo, F. Alberto. "The Practice of *Cantus Planus Binatim* in Italy from the beginning of the 14th to the beginning of the 16th century". In *Le Polifonie primitive in Friuli e in Europa*, ed. Cesare Corsi and Pierluigi Petrobelli, 13–30. Miscellanea Musicologica 4. Rome: Torre d'Orfeo, 1989.

Gallo, F. Alberto, ed. *Il Codice musicale della Biblioteca Universitaria di Bologna* [facsimile]. Monumenta Lyrica Medii Aevi Italica: Ser.3. Mensurabilia, iii. Bologna: Forni, 1968.

Gallo, F. Alberto, and Giuseppe Vecchi, eds. *I più antichi monumenti sacri italiani* [facsimile]. Monumenta Lyrica Medii aevi, Italica. III Mensurabilia, i. Bologna: Forni, 1968.

Gallucci, Joseph J. "Festival music in Florence, *ca*.1480–*ca*.1520: Canti carnascialeschi, trionfi, and related forms". Ph.D. diss., Harvard University, 1966.

Gallucci, Joseph J., ed. *Florentine festival music, 1480–1520*. Recent researches in music of the renaissance 40. Madison, WI: A-R Editions, 1981.

Gamble, William. *Music engraving and printing*. London: Curwen, 1923; rpt. New York: Da Capo, 1971.

Gams, Pius Bonifacius. *Series Episcoporum ecclesiae catholicae*. Regensburg: Manz, 1873; rpt. Graz: Akademische Druck- und Verleganstalt, 1957.

Gandolfi, Riccardo. "Intorno al codice membranaceo di ballate e di canzoncine di autore diversi, con musica a due, tre, quattro voci, esistente nella biblioteca del R. Istituto Musicale di Firenze, N.2440". *Rivista musicale italiana* 18 (1911): 537–548.

Garbelotto, Antonio. "Codici musicali della biblioteca capitolare di Padova". *Rivista musicale italiana* 53 (1951): 289–314; 54 (1952): 218–230 and 289–315.

Gariboldi, Cesare. *Ricerche sull'arte tipografica in Ancona dal suo cominciamento tutto il secolo XVIII*. Ancona: Buon Pastore, 1890.

Garros, Madeleine. "Un exemplaire du 5ᵉ livre des *Frottole* de Petrucci à la Bibliothèque Sainte-Geneviève". *Revue de musicologie* 35 (1953): 172.

Garros, Madeleine and Simone Wallon. *Catalogue du fonds musical de la Bibliothèque Sainte-Geneviève de Paris*. Catalogus Musicus 4. Kassel: Bärenreiter, for the International Association of Music Librarians and the International Musicological Society, 1967.

Gaskell, Philip. *A new introduction to bibliography*. London: Oxford University Press, 1972; 2nd ed., 1995.

Gaskell, Philip, George Barber and Georgina Warrilow. "An annotated list of printers' manuals to 1850". *Journal of the Printing Historical Society* 4 (1968): 11–32.

Gaspari, Gaetano. *Catalogo della Biblioteca del Liceo Musicale di Bologna*. Bologna: dall'Acqua, 1890–1943; rpt. Bologna: Forni, 1961.

Geering, Arnold. *Die Organa und mehrstimmigen Conductus in den handscrhiften des deutschen Sprachgebietes vom 13. bis 16. Jahrhundert*. Publikationen der Schweizerischen Musikforschenden Gesellschaft, ser.2, i. Bern: Haupt, 1952.

————. *Die Vokalmusik in der Schweiz zu Zeit der Reformation*. Schweizerisches Jahrbuch für Musikwissenschaft 6 (1933).

Geering, Arnold and Hans Trümpy, eds. *Das Liederbuch des Johannes Heer von Glarus*. Schweizerische Musikdenkmäler 5. Basel: Bärenreiter, 1967.

Gehrenbeck, David. "Motetti de la Corona: a study of Ottaviano Petrucci's four last-known motet prints (Fossombrone, 1514–1519): with 44 transcriptions". Ph.D. diss., Union Theological Seminary, 1970.

Geldner, Ferdinand. *Inkunabelkunde*. Elemente des Buch- und Bibliothekswesens 5. Wiesbaden: Reichert, 1978.

Gentile, Luigi. *Nozze Campani-Mazzoni*. Florence, 1884.

Gerardy, Theo. "Datierung mit Hilfe des Papiers". In *Datierung und Filiation von Musik-handschriften der Josquin-Zeit*, ed. Ludwig Finscher: 217–228. Wolfenbütteler Forschungen 28 = Quellenstudien zur Musik der Renaissance 2. Wiesbaden: Harrassowitz, 1983.

Gerber, Rudolf, Ludwig Finscher and Wolfgang Dömling, eds. *Der Mensuralkodex des Nikolaus Apel (Ms. 1494 der Universitätsbibliothek Leipzig)*. Das erbe deutscher Musik 32–34. Kassel: Bärenreiter, 1956–1975.

Gerhardt, Carl. *Die Torgauer Walter-Handschriften: eine Studie zur Quellenkunde der Musikgeschichte der deutschen Reformationszeit*. Musikwissenschaftliche Arbeiten 4. Kassel: Bärenreiter, 1949.

Gérold, Théodore. *Le manuscrit de Bayeux*. Strasbourg: Faculté des Lettres de l'Université de Strasbourg, 1921.

Gerritsen, Johan. "Printing at Froben's: an eye-witness account". *Studies in Bibliography* 44 (1991): 144–63.

Gerulaitis, Leonardas. "A fifteenth-century artistic director of a printing firm: Bernard Maler". *Papers of the Bibliographical Society of America* 64 (1970): 324–32.

———. *Printing and Publishing in fifteenth-century Venice*. London: Mansell, 1976.

Gesamtkatalog der Wiegendrucke, i–viii. Leipzig, 1925–1940; rpt. Stuttgart, 1968; Neuarbeitung. Stuttgart, 1972–.

Gesner, Conrad. *Pandectarum*. Zurich: Froschauer, 1548.

Ghiselin, Johannes. *Collected Works*, ed. Clytus Gottwald. Corpus mensurabilis musicae 23. [Rome]: American Institute of Musicology. 1961–1968.

Ghinassi, G. "Fasi nell'elaborazione del 'Cortegiano' ". *Studi di filologia italiana* 25 (1967): 155–196.

Ghisi, Federico. "Poesie musicali italiane. Canzonette a ballo, strambotti, frottole, canti e trionfi carnascialeschi". *Note d'archivio* 16 (1939): 40–73.

Gialdroni, Teresa Maria, and Agostino Ziino. "Un Altro frammento petrucciano della messa 'Mente Tota' de Févin". *Fonti Musicali Italiae* 10 (2005), forthcoming.

———. "Ancora su Ottavio/Ottaviano Petrucci dal fondo notarile di Fossombrone". Forthcoming.

———. "New light on Ottaviano Petrucci's activity, 1520–38: an unknown print of the *Motteti dal fiore*". *Early Music* 29 (2001): 500–532.

Gianandrea, Antonio. "Di Ottaviano de'Petrucci da Fossombrone, inventore de'typi mobili metallici della musica nel secolo XV". *Il Bibliofilo* 2 (1881): 123–127 and 180–184.

Giazotto, Remo. *Musurgia nova*. Milan: Ricordi, 1959.

Gilbert, Felix. "Venice in the crisis of the League of Cambrai". In *Renaissance Venice*, ed. J.R. Hale: 274–292. London: Faber and Faber, 1973.

Giochi, Filippo M., and Alessandro Mordenti. *Annali della tipografia in Ancona, 1512–1799*. Sussidi eruditi 35. Rome: Edizioni di storia e letteratura, 1980.

Giorcelli, Giuseppe. "Documenti storici del Monferrato: XIX. Tipografi di Alessandria e di Valenza del secolo XV, e tipografi Monferrini dei secoli XV e XVI, che stamparono in Venezia". A *separatum* in I-Rn, paginated 27–84.

Giorgetti, A. "Lorenzo de'Medici capitano generale della repubblica fiorentina". *Archivio storico italiano*, Ser.4, 11 (1883): 194–215 and 310–320.

Giovio, Paolo. *Historiarum sui temporis*. Florence: Torrentinus, 1550.

Glahn, Hendrik. "Et Fransk Musikhåndskrift fra Begyndelsen af det 16. Århundrede". *Fund og Forskning* 5–6 (1955–1959): 90–109.

Glahn, Hendrik, ed. *Musik fra Christian IIIs tid*. Dania Sonans 4–5. Copenhagen: Egtved, 1978.

Glaister, Geoffrey. *Glossary of the Book*. London: Allen & Unwin, 1960. 2nd ed., revised as *Encyclopedia of the Book*. New Castle, DE: Oak Knoll, 1996.

Glareanus, Heinrich. *Dodecachordon*, translated Clement A. Miller. Musicological Studies and Documents 6. s.l.: American Institute of Musicology, 1965.

Glixon, Jonathan E. "*Far una bella procession*: Music and public ceremony at the Venetian *scuole grandi*". In *Altro Polo: essays on Italian music in the Cinquecento*, ed. Richard Charteris: 190–220. Sydney: Frederick May Foundation for Italian studies, Sydney University, 1990.

———. *Music at the Venetian* Scuole Grandi, *1440–1540*. Ph.D. diss., Princeton University, 1979.

———. "The Polyphonic Laude of Innocentius Dammonis". *The Journal of Musicology* 8 (1990): 19–53.

Goff, Frederick. "A few proof-sheets of the fifteenth century". *Gutenberg-Jahrbuch 1963*: 81–87

Göhler, Albert. *Verzeichnis der in der Frankfurter und Leipziger Messkatalogen der Jahe 1564 bis 1779 angezeigten Musikalien*. Leipzig: D.F. Kahnt, 1902; rpt. Hilversum: Knuf, 1965.

Goldschmidt, Ernst Philip. *Gothic and Renaisance Bookbindings*. London, 1928.

———. *The printed book of the Renaissance*. Cambridge: Cambridge University Press, 1950.

Göllner, Marie Louise. *Bayerische Staatsbibliothek: Katalog der Musikhandschriften, ii. Tabulaturen und Stimmbücher bis zur Mitte des 17. Jahrhunderts*. Kataloge bayerischer Musiksammlungen, v/2. Munich: Henle, 1979.

———. "*Praeter rerum seriem*: its history and sources". *Von Isaac bis Bach: Studien zur älteren deutschen Musikgeschichte: Festschrift Martin Just zum 60. Geburtstag*, ed. Frank Heidlberger, Wolfgang Osthoff, and Reinhard Wiesend: 41–51. Kassel: Bärenreiter. 1991.

Gombosi, Otto. *Jacob Obrecht: eine stilkritische Studie*. Leipzig: Breitkopf & Härtel, 1925.

———. "Die Musikalien der Pfarrkirche zu St. Aegidi in Bártfa". In *Festschrift für Johannes Wolf zu seinem sechzigsten Geburtstage*: 38–47. Berlin: Breslauer, 1929.

———. "Quellen aus dem 16.–17. Jahrhundert zur Geschichte der Musikpflege in Bartfeld (Bártfa) und Oberungarn". *Ungarische Jahrbuch* 12 (1932): 331–340.

Gombosi, Otto, ed. *Compositione di Meser Vincenzo Capirola. Lute-Book (circa 1517)*. Publications de la Société de musique d'autrefois, textes musicaux 1. Neuilly-sur-Seine: Société de Musique d'Autrefois, 1955.

Goovaerts, Alphonse. *Histoire et bibliographie de la typographie musicale dans les Pays-Bas*. Mémoires couronnés et autres mémoires publiées par l'Académie Royale des Sciences, des Lettres et des Beaux-Arts de Belgiques 29. Brussels: L'Académie Royale, 1880.

Gottardi, L. *La stampa musicale in Bologna dagli inizi e fino al 1700*. Diss., Università di Bologna, 1951.

Gottwald, Clytus. *Die Handschriften der Württembergischen Landesbibliothek Stuttgart: Codices musici I*. Wiesbaden: Harrassowitz, 1965.

———. *Johannes Ghiselin—Johannes Verbonnet*. Wiesbaden: Harrassowitz, 1962.

———. *Die Musikhandschriften der Staats- und Stadtbibliothek Augsburg*. Handschriftenkataloge der Staats- und Stadtbibliothek Augsburg 1. Wiesbaden: Harrassowitz, 1974.

———. *Die Musikhandschriften der Universitätsbibliothek München*. Wiesbaden: Harrassowitz, 1968.

———. "Eine neuentdeckte Quelle zur Musik der Reformationszeit". *Archiv für Musikwissenschaft* 19–20 (1962–1963): 114–123.

Graesse, Johann Georg Theodor. *Lehrbuch einer allgemeinen Literärgeschichte, iii/1: Das sechszehnte Jahrhundert*. Leipzig: Arnoldische Buchhandlung, 1852.

Gramigni, Silvia, and Annalisa Perissa. *Scuole di arti, mestieri e devozione a Venezia*. Venice: Arsenale Cooperativa, 1981.

Grendler, Paul. *The Roman Inquisition and the Venetian press, 1540–1605*. Princeton: Princeton University Press, 1977.

Grimaldi, Floriano. *La cappella musicale di Loreto nel Cinquecento: note d'archivio*. Ente Rassegna Musicali nuova serie di Loreto 1. Loreto: Ente Rassegna Musicali, 1981.

Gröber, Gustav. "Zu den Liederbüchern von Cortona". *Zeitschrift für romanische Philologie*, xi (1887): 371–394.

Guerzoni, Guido. "Ricadute occupazionali ed impatti economici della committenza artistica delle corti estensi tra Quattro e Cinquecento". *Economia e arte, secc.XIII–XVIII*, ed. Simonetta Cavaciocchi: 187–230. Florence: Le Monnier, 2002.

Guicciardini, Francesco. *Carteggi di Francesco Guicciardini*, ed. Roberto Palmarocchi and Pier Giorgio Ricci. Bologna: Zanichelli, 1938–1972.

———. *L'Historia d'Italia*. Florence: Torrentinus, 1561. Translated by Geffray Fenton, as *The Historie of Guicciardin*. London: Field, 1618.

Guidobaldi, Nicoletta. "Music publishing in sixteenth- and seventeenth-century Umbria". *Early Music History* 8 (1988): 1–36.

Guillo, Laurent. "Les motets de Layolle et les Psaumes de Piéton: deux nouvelles éditions lyonnaises du seizième siècle". *Fontes artis musicae* 32 (1984–1985): 186–191.

Gustavson, Royston. Hans Ott, Hieronymus Formschneider, and the *Novum et insigne opus musicum* (Nuremberg, 1536–1538)". Ph.D. diss., University of Melbourne, 1998.

Gutiérrez-Denhoff, Martella. "Untersuchungen zu Gestalt, Entstehung und Repertoire des Chansonniers Laborde". *Archiv für Musikwissenschaft* 41 (1984): 113–146.

———. *Der Wolfenbütteler Chansonnier: Untersuchungen zu Repertoire und Überlieferung*. Wolfenbütteler Forschungen 29. Wiesbaden: Harrassowitz, 1985.

Gutiérrez-Denhoff, Martella, ed. *Der Wolfenbütteler Chansonnier*. Musikalische Denkmäler 10. Mainz: Schott, 1988.

Haar, James. "The courtier as musician: Castiglione's view of the science and art of music". In *Castiglione: the ideal and the real in Renaissance culture*, ed. Robert W. Hanning and David Rosand: 165–189. New Haven: Yale University Press, 1983; rpt. in *The Science and art of Renaissance music*: 20–37. Princeton: Princeton University Press, 1998.

———. "The early madrigal: a re-appraisal of its sources and its character". *Music in medieval and early modern Europe: patronage, sources and texts*, ed. Iain Fenlon: 163–192. Cambridge: Cambridge University Press, 1981.

———. *Essays on Italian poetry and music in the Renaissance*. Berkeley and Los Angeles: University of California Press, 1986.

———. "Josquin in Rome: some evidence from the masses". *Papal music and musicians in late medieval and renaissance Rome*, ed. Richard Sherr: 213–223. Oxford: Clarendon, and Washington: Library of Congress, 1998.

———. "Lessons in theory from a sixteenth-century composer". In *Altro Polo: essays on Italian music in the Cinquecento*, ed. Richard Charteris: 51–81. Sydney: Frederick May Foundation for Italian Studies, Sydney University, 1990; rpt. in *The Science and art of Renaissance music*: 149–175. Princeton: Princeton University Press, 1998.

———. "The *Libraria* of Antonfrancesco Doni". *Musica Disciplina* 24 (1970): 101–123; rpt. in *The Science and art of Renaissance music*: 323–350. Princeton: Princeton University Press, 1998.

———. "The *Libro Primo* of Costanzo Festa". *Acta Musicologica* 52 (1980): 147–155.

———. "Madrigals from the last Florentine Republic". In *Essays presented to Myron P. Gilmore*, ed. Sergio Bertelli and Gloria Ramakus: ii, 383–403. Florence: La Nuova italia, 1978.

———. "Petrucci as Bookman", paper read at the conference "Venezia 1501: Petrucci e la stampa musicale", Venice, 11 October 2001.

———. "Petrucci's *Justiniane* revisited". *Journal of the American Musicological Society* 52 (1999): 1–38.

———. "Some remarks on the 'Missa La sol fa re mi' ". *Josquin des Pres: Proceedings of the International Josquin Festival-Conference held at the Julliard School at Lincoln Center in New York City, 21–25 June 1971*, ed. Edward E. Lowinsky with Bonnie J. Blackburn: 564–588. London: Oxford University Press, 1976.

Haar, James, ed. *Chanson and Madrigal, 1480–1530: studies in comparison and contrast*. Cambridge, MA: Harvard University Press, 1964.

Haas, Robert. "Die Musiksammlung der Nationalbibliothek in Wien. Ein Kapitel aus der Geschichte der musikalischen Denkmalpflege". *Jahrbuch der Musikbibliothek Peters für 1930* [vol.37] (1931): 48–62.

Haberkamp, Gertraut. *Die weltliche Vokalmusik in Spanien um 1500. Der* Cancionero musical de Colombina *von Sevilla und ausserspanische Handschriften*. Münchener Veräffentlichungen zur Musikgeschichte 12. Tutzing: Schneider, 1968.

Haberkamp, Gertraut, ed. *Die Musikhandschriften der Fürst Thurn und Taxis Hofbibliothek Regensburg. Thematischer Katalog*. Kataloge Bayerischer Musiksammlungen 6. Munich: Henle, 1981.

Haberkamp, Gertraut and August Scharnagl, eds. *Bischöfliche Zentralbibliothek Regensburg. Thematischer Katalog der Musikhandschriften. I: Sammlung Proske, Manuskripte des 16. und 17. Jahrhunderts aus den Signaturen A.R., B, C, An*. Kataloge Bayerischer Musiksammlungen, xiv/1. Munich: Henle, 1989.

Haberl, Franz Xavier. "Drucke von Ottaviano Petrucci auf der Bibliothek des Liceo filarmonico in Bologna: ein bibliographischer Beitrag zu Ant. Schmid's Ottaviano dei Petrucci (Wien 1845)". *Monatshefte für Musikgeschichte* 5 (1873): 49–57 and 92–99.

Haebler, Konrad. *Handbuch der Inkunabelkunde*. Leipzig: Hiersemann, 1925.

Haggh, Barbara. "Music, liturgy, and ceremony in Brussels, 1350–1500". Ph.D. diss., University of Illinois, 1988.

Hain, Ludwig. *Repertorium bibliographicum, in quo libri omnes ab arte typographica inventa usque ad annum md. typis expressi . . .* Stuttgart: Cotta, 1826–1838; rpt. Milan: Gorlich, 1948.

Hale, John Rigsby, ed. *Renaissance Venice*. London: Faber and Faber, 1973.

Hamm, Charles. "Interrelationships between manuscript and printed sources of polyphonic music in the early sixteenth century—an overview". *Datierung und Filiation von Musikhandschriften der Josquin-Zeit*, ed. Ludwig Finscher: 1–13. Wolfenbütteler Forschungen 26 = Quellenstudien zur Musik der Renaissance 2. Wiesbaden: Harrassowitz, 1983.

———. "The Manuscript San Pietro B 80". *Revue belge de musicologie* 14 (1960): 40–55.

Hamm, Charles, and Herbert Kellman, eds. *Census-Catalogue of manuscript sources of polyphonic music, 1400–1550*. Renaissance Manuscript Studies 1. s.l.: American Institute of Musicology; Neuhausen-Stuttgart: Hänssler, 1979–1988.

Hanen, Martha K. *The chansonnier El Escorial IV.a.24*. Musicological Studies 34. Henryville, PA: Institute of Medieval Music, 1983.

Hargraves, Geoffrey D. "Florentine script, Paduan script, and Roman Type". *Gutenberg Jahrbuch 1992*: 15–34.

Harris, Elizabeth. *The Common Press: being a record, description and delineation of the early eighteenth-century handpress in the Smithsonian Institute*. Boston: Godine, 1978.

Harris, Neil. "The Blind impressions of the *Hypnerotomachia Poliphili*, Venice: Aldus, 1499". Paper read at the International Gutenberg Conference, the 8th annual meeting of SHARP, Mainz, 3–8 July 2000.

Hawkins, *Sir* John. *A General history of the Science and Practice of Music*. London: for T. Payne and Son, 1776; rpt. New York: Dover, 1963; and Graz: Akademische Druck- und Verlagsanstalt, 1969.

Hayne van Ghizeghem. *Opera Omnia*, ed. Barton Hudson. Corpus mensurabilis musicae 74. s.l.: American Institute of Musicology, 1977.

Heartz, Daniel. "*Au pres de vous*—Claudin's chansons and the commerce of publisher's arrangements". *Journal of the American Musicological Society* 24 (1971): 193–225.

———. "A new Attaingnant book and the beginnings of French music printing". *Journal of the American Musicological Society* 14 (1961): 9–23.

———. *Pierre Attaingnant, royal printer of music: A historical study and bibliographical catalogue*. Berkeley and Los Angeles: University of California Press, 1969.

———. "Les Premières 'instructions' pour le luth (jusque vers 1550)". In *Le luth et sa musique*, ed. Jean Jacquot: 76–92. Colloques internationaux du Centre national de la recherche scientifique 511. Paris: Centre national de la recherche scientifique, 1976.

———. "Typography and format in early music printing: with particular reference to Attaingnant's first publications" *Notes* 23 (1966–1967): 702–706.

Heawood, Edward. "The position on the sheet of early watermarks". *The Library*, Ser.4, 9 (1929): 38–47.

————. *Watermarks. Mainly of the 17th and 18th Centuries.* Monumenta Chartæ Papyraceæ Historiam Illustrantia 1. Hilversum: Paper Publications Society, 1950, rpt. 1969.

Hefele, Carl Joseph von. *Histoire des Conciles d'après les documents originaux.* Paris: Letouzey, 1907–1952.

Heikamp, Dieter. "Zur Struktur der Messe 'L'omme armé super voces musicales' von Josquin Desprez". *Die Musikforschung* 19 (1966): 121–141.

Hellinga, Lotte. "Analytical bibliography and the study of early printed books: with a case-study of the Mainz Catholicon". *Gutenberg-Jahrbuch 1989*: 47–96

————. "The disseminations of a text in print: early editions of Poggio Bracciolini's 'Facetiae' ". In *Trasmissione dei testi a stampa nel periodo moderno: II. II seminario internazionale, Roma—Viterbo, 27–29 giugno, 1985*, ed. Giovanni Crapulli: 85–106. Rome: Ateneo. 1987.

————. "Notes on the order of setting a fifteenth-century book", *Quaerendo* 4 (1974): 64–69.

————. "Problems about technique and methods in a fifteenth-century printing house (Nicolaus Ketelaer and Gherardus de Leempt, Utrecht, 1473–1475)". In *Villes d'imprimerie et moulins à papier du XIVᵉ au XVIᵉ siècle: Aspects économiques et sociaux. Drukkerijen en papiermolens in Stad en Land van de 14de de tot de 16de eeuw: economische en sociale aspecten: Colloque international, Spa, 11–14.ix.1973. Actes: Handelingen.*, ed. Marinette Bruwier and Jean-Marie Duvosquel: 301–315. Collection Histoire pro-civitate, ser in 80 43. Brussels: Crédit Comunal de Belgique, 1976.

————. "Proof-reading in 1459: the Munich copy of Guillelmus Duranti, Rationale". In *Ars Impressoria . . . Festgabe für Severin Corsten*: 183–202. Munich: K.G. Saur, 1986.

————. "Slipped lines and fallen type in the Mainz Catholicon". *Gutenberg Jahrbuch 1992*: 35–40.

————. "Three notes on printers' copy: Strassburg, Oxford, Subiaco". *Transactions of the Cambridge Bibliographical Society* 9/ii (1987): 194–204.

Hellinga, Lotte, and John Goldfinch, eds. *Bibliography and the study of 15th-century civilisation.* London: British Library. 1987.

Hellinga, Wytze G. *Copy and Print in the Netherlands: an Atlas of historical bibliography.* Amsterdam: North-Holland Publishing Company, 1962.

Hergenroether, Joseph. *Leonis decimi pontificis maximi regesta.* Freiburg: Herder, 1884–1891.

Herman, Martin M. "Two volumes of Lamentation settings (Petrucci, 1506)". Ph.D. diss., Yale University, 1952.

Hermelink, Siegfried. "Ein Musikalienverzeichnis der Heidelberger Hofkapelle aus dem Jahre 1544". In *Ottheinrich: Gedenkschrift zur vierhundertjährigen Wiederkehr seiner Kurfürstenzeit in der Pfalz (1556–1559)*, ed. Georg Poensgen: 247–260. Ruperto-Carola: Sonderband. Heidelberg: s.n., 1956.

Hernon, Michael. "Perugia MS 431 (G20): a study of the secular Italian pieces". Ph.D. diss., George Peabody College for Teachers, 1972.

Heussner, Horst and Ingo Schultz. *Collectio musica: Musikbibliographie in Deutschland bis 1625.* Catalogus musicus 6. Kassel: Bärenreiter, for the International Association of Music Librarians and the International Musicological Society, 1973.

Hewitt, Helen. "A *chanson rustique* of the early Renaissance: *Bon temps*". *Aspects of medieval and renaissance music: a birthday offering to Gustave Reese*, ed. Jan LaRue et al.: 376–391. London: Oxford University Press, 1966.

————. "The chansons à forme libre in the Canti B of Petrucci". *Journal of the American Musicological Society* 3 (1950): 61–62.

Hewitt, Helen, ed. *Ottaviano Petrucci: Canti B.* Monuments of Renaissance Music 2. Chicago: University of Chicago Press, 1967.

————. *Harmonice Musices Odhecaton A.* The Mediaeval Academy of America Publications 42 = Studies and Documents 5. Cambridge, MA.: The Mediaeval Academy of America, 1942; rpt. New York: Da Capo, 1978.

Heyden, Sebald. *De arte canendi*, translated Clement A. Miller. Musicological Studies and Documents 26. s.l.: American Institute of Musicology, 1972.

————. *De arte canendi*. Monuments of Music and Music Literature in Facsimile, Ser.II: Music literature 139. New York: Broude, 1969.

Heyink, Rainer. *Der Gonzaga-Kodex Bologna Q19: Geschichte und Repertoire einer Musikhandschrift des 16. Jahrhunderts*. Beiträge zur Geschichte der Kirchenmusik 1. Paderborn: Schäningh, 1994.

Hierarchia Catholica Medii Aevi. Regensburg: Monasterii, 1901–1910.

Higgins, Paula. "Antoine Busnois and musical culture in late fifteenth-century France and Burgundy". Ph.D. diss., Princeton University, 1987.

————. "Tracing the career of late medieval composers: the case of Philippe Basiron of Bourges". *Acta Musicologica* 62 (1990): 1–28.

Higgins, Paula, intro. *Chansonnier Nivelle de la Chausée*. Geneva: Minkoff, 1984.

Hill, T. H. "Spelling and the bibliographer". *The Library*, Ser.5, 18 (1963): 1–28.

Hinman, Charlton. "Principles governing the use of variant spellings as evidence of alternate settings by two compositors". *The Library*, Ser.4, 20 (1940): 78–104.

————. *The printing and proof-reading of the First Folio of Shakespeare*. Oxford: Clarendon, 1963.

Hirsch, Rudolf. *Printing, selling and reading, 1450–1550*. Wiesbaden: Harrassowitz, 1967.

Hobson, Anthony. *Humanists and Bookbinders: the Origins and diffusion of humanistic bookbinding, 1459–1559, with a census of historiated plaquette and medallion bindings of the Renaissance*. Cambridge: Cambridge University Press, 1989.

Hofer, Philip. "Variant states of the first edition of Ludovico Arrighi Vicentino's *Operina*". In *Calligraphy and Palaeography: essays presented to Alfred Fairbank on his 70th birthday*, ed. A.S. Osley: 95–106. London: Faber and Faber, 1965.

Hoffmann-Erbrecht, Lothar. "Die Chorbücher der Stadtkirche zu Pirna". *Acta musicologica* 27 (1955): 121–137.

————. "Ein Frankfurter Messenkodex". *Archiv für Musikwissenschaft* 16 (1959): 328–334.

————. "Das *Opus musicum* des Jacob Praetorius von 1566". *Acta musicologica* 28 (1956): 96–121.

Hofmann-Brandt, Helma. "Eine neue Quelle zur mittelälterlichen Mehrstimmigkeit". In *Festschrift Bruno Stäblein zum 70. Geburtstag*, ed. Martin Ruhnke: 109–115. Kassel: Bärenreiter, 1967.

Holme, Randle. *The Academy of Armory*. Chester: Holme, 1688. A facsimile of the section on the Art of Printing and Typefounding was published in Menston by the Scolar Press, 1972.

Höweler, C.A., and F.H. Matter, *Fontes hymnodiae neerlandicae impressi 1539–1700: de melodie en van het Nederlandstalig Geestelijk Lied 1539–1700*. Bibliotheca Bibliographica Neerlandica 18. Nieuwkoop: de Graaf, 1985.

Hudson, Barton. "Antoine Brumel's *Nativitas unde gaudia*". *The Musical Quarterly* 59 (1973): 519–530.

————. "A Glimpse into a scribal workshop: Vienna, Österreichische Nationalbibliothek, MS. 11883. In *From Ciconia to Sweelinck: donum natalicium Willem Elders*, ed. Albert Clement and Eric Jas: 179–214. Chloe: Beihefte zum Daphnis 21. Amsterdam: Rodopi, 1994.

————. "Josquin and Brumel: the conflicting attributions". In *Proceedings of the International Josquin Symposium, Utrecht 1986*, ed. Willem Elders, with Frits de Haen: 67–92. Utrecht: Vereniging voor Nederlandse Muziekgeschiedenis, 1991.

————. "A neglected source of renaissance polyphony: Rome, Santa Maria Maggiore, JJ.III.4". *Acta musicologica* 48 (1976): 166–180.

————. "Two Ferrarese masses by Jacob Obrecht". *The Journal of Musicology* 4 (1985–1986): 276–302.

Hughes, Andrew. "New Italian and English sources of the fourteenth to sixteenth centuries". *Acta Musicologica* 39 (1967): 171–182.

Hughes-Hughes, A. *Catalogue of manuscript music in the British Museum*. London: Trustees of the British Museum, 1906–1909.

Huntington, Archer H. *Catalogue of the library of Ferdinand Columbus: reproduced in facsimile from the unique manuscript in the Columbine Library of Seville*. New York: Hispanic Society of America, 1905.

Huys, Bernard. *Catalogue des imprimés musicaux des XVe, XVIe et XVIIe siècles. Fonds général, Bibliothèque royale de Belgique*. Brussels: Bibliothèque royale de Belgique, 1965.

———. *De Gregoire le Grand à Stockhausen: douze siècles de notation musicale*. Brussels: Bibliothèque Albert Ier, 1966.

———. "An unknown Alamire-choirbook ('Occo Codex') recently acquired by the Royal Library of Belgium: a new source for the history of music in Amsterdam". *Tijdschrift van de Vereniging voor Nederlandse Muziekgeschiedenis* 24 (1974): 1–19.

Huys, Bernard, intro. *Occo Codex (Brussels, Royal Library Albert I, MS. IV.922)*. Facsimilia musica nederlandica 1. Buren: Knuf, 1979.

Index aureliensis: catalogus librorum sedecimo saeculo impressorum. Baden-Baden: Heitz, 1982–.

Insko, Wyatt, ed. *Krakowska Tabulatura Organowa: The Cracow Tablature (ca.1548)*. Dawna Muzyka Organowa. Lódz: Ludowy Instytut Muzyczny, 1992

Irigoin, Jean. "La datation par les filigranes du papier". In *Les matériaux du livre manuscrit*, ed. A. Gruys: 9–36. Codicologica 5. Leiden: Brill, 1980.

Isaac, Frank. *An index to the early printed books in the British Museum. Part II. MDI–MDXX. Section 2. Italy*. London: Trustees of the British Museum, 1938; rpt. London: Martino, 1999.

Isaac, Heinrich. *Choralis Constantinus*, ed. Edward Lerner. Facsimile series for scholars and musicians 14–16. Peer: Alamire, 1990–1994.

———. *Messe*, ed. Fabio Fano. Archivium musices metropolitanum mediolanense 10. Milan: Veneranda Fabbrica del Duomo di Milano, 1962.

———. *Messen*, ed. Martin Staehelin, from the papers of Herbert Birtner. Musikalische Denkmaler 7–8. Mainz: Schott, 1970–1973.

———. *Opera Omnia*, ed. Edward R. Lerner. Corpus mensurabilis musicae 65. Stuttgart: American Institute of Musicology; Hänssler, 1974–.

———. *Weltliche Werke*, ed. Johannes Wolf. Denkmäler der Tonkunst in Österreich 27. Vienna: Artaria; Leipzig: Breitkopf und Härtel, 1907.

Isaac, Marie-Thérèse, ed. *Ornementation typographique et bibliographie historique: actes du colloque de Mons (26–28 août 1987)*. Documenta et opuscula 8. Brussels: Emile van Balberghe, 1988.

Ivanoff, Vladimir. *Das Pesaro-Manuskript: ein Beitrag zur Frühgeschichte der Lautentabulatur*. Münchner Veröffentlichungen zur Musikgeschichte 45. Tutzing: Schneider, 1988.

Ivanoff, Vladimir, ed. *Eine Zentzale Quelle der frühen italienischen Lautenpraxis: Edition der Handschrift Pesaro, Biblioteca Oliveriana, Ms. 1144*. Münchner Editionen zur Musikgeschichte 7. Tutzing: Schneider, 1988.

Jachimecki, Zdislaw. "Eine polnische Orgeltabulatur aus dem Jahre 1548". *Zeitschrift für Musikwissenschaft*, ii (1920): 206–212

Jackson, Susan. "Berg and Neuber: music printers in sixteenth-century Nuremberg". Ph.D. diss., City University of New York, 1998.

Jammes, André. "Un chef-d'oeuvre méconnu d'Arrighi Vicentino". *Studia bibliographica in honorem Herman de la Fontaine Verwey*, ed. S. van der Woude (Amsterdam: Hertzberger, 1968): 296–316

Janssen, Frans A. "Some notes on setting by formes". *Quaerendo*, xvi (1986): 191–197

Jas, Eric. "Ockeghem as a model". In *Johannes Ockeghem: Actes du XLe Colloque international d'études humanistes*, ed. Philippe Vendrix: 757–785. Paris: Klincksieck, 1998.

———. "Some newly-discovered fragments of sixteenth-century polyphony". *Tijdschrift van de Vereniging voor Nederlandse Muziekgeschiedenis* 42 (1992): 69–89.

Jayne, Sears, and Francis R. Johnson, eds. *The Lumley Library: the catalogue of 1609*. British Museum Bicentenary Publications. London: Trustees of the British Museum, 1956.

Jeppesen, Knud. "Die drei Gafurius-Kodizes der Fabbricia del Duomo, Milano". *Acta musicologica* 3 (1931): 14–28.

————. "Über einige unbekannte Frottolenhandschriften". *Acta musicologica* 11 (1929): 81–114.

————. *La Frottola. I. Bemerkungen zur Bibliographie der ältesten weltlichen Notendrucks in Italien.* Acta Jutlandica 40/ii. Copenhagen: Hansen, 1968.

————. *La Frottola: II. Zur Bibliographie der handschriftlichen musikalischen Überlieferung des weltlichen italienischen Lieds um 1500.* Acta Jutlandica 41/i. Copenhagen: Hansen, 1969.

————. *La Frottola: III. Frottola und Volkslied: zur musikalischen Überlieferung des folkloristischen Guts in der Frottola.* Acta Jutlandica 42/i. Copenhagen: Hansen, 1970.

———— "The manuscript Florence, Biblioteca Nazionale Centrale, Banco Rari 230: an attempt at a diplomatic reconstruction". In *Aspects of Medieval and Renaissance Music: a birthday offering to Gustave Reese*, ed. Jan LaRue et al: 440–447. London: Oxford University Press, 1966.

————. "Népi dallamelemek Octavio Petrucci frottolakiadványaiban (1504–1514) / Das Volksliedgut in den Frottolenbüchern des Octavio Petrucci (1504–1514)". In *Emlékkänyv Kodály Zoltán hatvanadik születésnapjára / Mélanges offerts à Zoltán Kodály à l'occasion de son soixantième anniversaire*, ed. Béla Gunda: 265–274. Budapest: Kiadja a Magyar Néprajzi Pársaság, 1943.

————. "Die neuentdeckten Bücher der Lauden des Ottaviano dei Petrucci und andere musikalische Seltenheiten der Biblioteca Colombina zu Sevilla". *Zeitschrift für Musikwissenschaft* 12 (1929–1930): 73–89.

————. Review of Sartori's book on Petrucci, and Einsten's Antico edition. *Acta musicologica* 20 (1948): 78–85.

————. "An unknown pre-madrigalian music print in relation to other contemporary Italian sources (1520–1530)". In *Studies in musicology: essays in the history, style and bibliography of music in memory of Glen Haydon*, ed. James Pruett: 3–17. Chapel Hill: University of North Carolina Press, 1969.

Jeppesen, Knud, ed. *Italia Sacra Musica: Musiche corali italiane sconosciute della prima metà del cinquecento.* Copenhagen: Hansen, [1962].

————. *Die italienische Orgelmusik am Anfang des Cinquecento.* Copenhagen: Hansen, 1943, 1960.

————. *Der Kopenhagener Chansonnier.* Copenhagen: Levin & Munksgaard, 1927.

————. *Die mehrstimmige italienische Laude um 1500.* Leipzig: Breitkopf und Härtel, 1935.

Johns, Adrian. *The Nature of the book: print and knowledge in the making.* Chicago: University of Chicago Press, 1998.

Johnson, Alfred F. "Title Pages: their forms and development". In *Books and printing: a treasure for typophiles*, ed. Paul A. Bennett: 52–64. Cleveland: World Publishing, 1951.

Johnson, Alfred, and Victor Scholderer. *Short-title catalogue of books printed in Italy and of Italian books printed in other countries from 1465 to 1600 now in the British Museum.* London: Trustees of the British Museum, 1958.

Jonas, Luise. *Das Augsburger Liederbuch: die Musikhandschrift 2° 142a Codex der Staats- und Stadtbibliothek Augsburg: Edition und Kommentar.* Berliner Musikwissenschaftliche Arbeiten 21. Munich: Katzbichler, 1983.

Jones, George M. "The first chansonnier of the Biblioteca Riccardiana, Codex 2794". Ph.D. diss., New York University, 1972.

Jones, Lewis. "The Thibault Manuscript: an introduction". *Journal of the Lute Society* 22 (1982): 69–82; 23 (1983): 21–25.

Jones, P. J. "The end of Malatesta rule in Rimini". In *Italian Renaissance Studies*, ed. E. F. Jacob: 217–255. London: Faber and Faber, 1960.

Josquin des Pres. *The Collected works (New Josquin edition).* Utrecht: Vereniging der Nederlandse Muziekgeschiedenis, 1987–.

————. *Missa de beata Virgine*, ed. Peter Urquhart. Helsinki: Fazer, 1992.

————. *Missarum Liber Secundus* [facsimile]. Monumenta Musica Typographica Vetustiora 8. Bologna: Antiquae Musicae Italicae Studiosi, 1971.

————. *Werken van Josquin des Prés.* ed. Albert Smijers. Amsterdam: Alsbach, and Leipzig: Kistner & Siegel, 1921–1969.

Josquin des Pres e vari. *Messe, Magnificat, mottetto e inno*, ed. Amerigo Bortone. Archivium musices metropolitanum mediolanense 15. Milan: Veneranda Fabbrica del Duomo di Milano, 1969.

Judd, Cristle Collins. "Reading Aron reading Petrucci: the music examples of the *Trattato della natura et cognitione di tutti gli tuoni* (1525)". *Early Music History* 14 (1995): 121–152.

Just, Martin. "Heinrich Isaacs Motetten in italienischen Quellen". *Analecta musicologica* 1 (1963): 1–19.

———. *Der Mensuralkodex Mus.ms.40021 der Staatsbibliothek Preußischer Kulturbesitz Berlin: Untersuchungen zum Repertoire einer deutschen Quelle des 15. Jahrhunderts*. Würzburger musikhistorische Beiträge 1. Tutzing: Schneider, 1975.

———. "Zur Examinatio von Varianten". In *Datierung und Filiation von Musikhandschriften der Josquin–Zeit*, ed. Ludwig Finscher: 129–152. Quellenstudien zur Musik der Renaissance 2 = Wolfenbütteler Forschungen 26. Wiesbaden: Harrassowitz, 1983.

Juverini, Boris, Giuseppe Radole, and Sergio Puppis. *Le Frottole di Andrea Antico da Montona*. Trieste: Istituto Regionale per la Cultura Istriana, 1996.

Kabis, *Sister* Mary. "The works of Jean Richafort, renaissance composer". Ph.D. diss., New York University, 1957.

Kaltenbrunner, Ferdinand. *Die Vorgeschichtes der Gregorianischen Kalendarreform*. Vienna, 1876.

Kämper, Dietrich. "La Stangetta—eine Instrumentalkomposition Gaspars von Weerbecke?". In *Ars musica, musica scientia: Festschrift Heinrich Huschen*, ed. D. Altenburg: 277–288. Cologne: Bählau, 1970.

Kanazawa, Masakata. "Antonius Janue and revisions of his music". *Quadrivium* 12 (1971): 177–194.

———. "Two Vesper repertories from Verona, c.1500". *Rivista italiana di musicologia* 10 (1975): 155–179.

Kast, Paul. *Studien zu den Messen des Jean Mouton unter besonderer Berücksichtigung der Echtheitsfrage und der Chronologie*. Diss., Universität Frankfurt-am Main, 1955.

Kehrein, Joseph. *Lateinische Sequenzen des Mittelalters*. Mainz: Kupferberg, 1873; rpt. Hildesheim: Olms, 1969.

Kellman, Herbert. "Josquin and the courts of the Netherlands and France: the evidence of the sources". In *Josquin des Pres: Proceedings of the International Josquin Festival-Conference*, ed. Edward E. Lowinsky, Edward, with Bonnie J. Blackburn: 181–216. London: Oxford University Press, 1976.

———. "The origins of the Chigi codex: the date, provenance and original ownership of Rome, Biblioteca Vaticana, Chigiana C VIII 234". *Journal of the American Musicological Society* 11 (1958): 6–19.

Kellman, Herbert, ed. *The Treasury of Petrus Alamire: music and art in Flemish court manuscripts, 1500–1535*. Ghent: Ludion, 1999.

Kellman, Herbert, intro. *London, British Library, MS Royal 8 G.vii*. Renaissance Music in Facsimile 11. New York: Garland, 1987.

———. *Vatican City, Biblioteca Apostolica Vaticana, MS Chigi C VIII 234*. Renaissance Manuscripts in facsimile 11. New York: Garland, 1987.

Kemp, Walter H. "Some notes on music in Castiglione's *Il Libro del Cortegiano*". In *Cultural aspects of the Italian renaissance: essays in honour of Paul Oskar Kristeller*, ed. Cecil Clough: 354–369. Manchester: Manchester University Press, 1976.

Ker, Neil R. *Medieval Libraries of Great Britain. A List of Surviving Books*. Royal Historical Society Guides and Handbooks 3. 2nd ed., London: Royal Historical Society, 1964: with the *Supplement to the Second Edition*, ed. Andrew G. Watson. London: Royal Historical Society, 1987.

Kessels, Leon. "The Brussels/Tournai partbooks: structure, illumination and Flemish repertory". *Tijdschrift van de Vereniging voor nederlandse Muziekgeschiedenis* 37 (1987): 82–110.

Kiel, Jacobijn. "Terminus post Alamire? On some later scribes". In *The Burgundian-Habsburg court complex of Music mansuscripts (1500–1535 and the Workshop of Petrrus Alamire*, ed. Bruno Bouckaert and Eugeen Schreurs: 97–105. Yearbook of the Alamire Foundation 5. Leuven: Alamire, 2003.

King, Alec Hyatt. *Four Hundred Years of Music Printing*. London: British Museum, 1964.

———. "The significance of John Rastell in early music printing". *The Library*, Ser.5, 26 (1971): 197–214.

King, Margaret L. *Venetian Humanism in an age of patrician dominance*. Princeton: Princeton University Press, 1986.

Kingdon, Robert M. "The business activities of printers Henri and François Estienne". In *Aspects de la propagande religieuse*, ed. Henri Meylan: 258–275. Travaux d'Humanisme et Renaissance 28. Geneva: Droz, 1957.

Kinkeldey, Otto. "Music and music printing in incunabula". *Papers of the Bibliographical Society of America* 26 (1932): 89–118.

Kirnbauer, Martin. "A-Wn Mus.Hs.41950, Deutsche Lautentabulatur um 1525". Forthcoming.

———. "Petrucci and the fifteenth century: the lute duos". Paper read at the conference "Venezia 1501: Petrucci e la stampa musicale", Venice, 12 October 2001.

Kirsch, Dieter, and Lenz Meierott, eds. *Berliner Lautentabulaturen in Krakau. Beschreibender Katalog der handschriftlichen Tabulaturen für Laute und verwandte Instrumente in der Bibliotheka Jagiellońska Kraków aus dem Besitz der ehemaligen Preußischen Staatsbibliothek Berlin*. Schriften der Musikhochschule Würzburg 3. Mainz: Schott, 1992.

Kirsch, Winfried. "Andreas de Silva, ein Meister aus der ersten Hälfte des 16. Jahrhunderts". *Analecta musicologica* 2 (1965): 6–23.

———. "Josquin's motets in the German tradition". In *Josquin des Pres: Proceedings of the International Josquin Festival-Conference held at the Julliard School at Lincoln Center in New York City, 21–25 June 1971*, ed. Edward E. Lowinsky with Bonnie J. Blackburn: 261–279. London: Oxford University Press, 1976.

———. *Die Motetten des Andreas de Silva: Studien zur Geschichte der Motette im 16. Jahrhundert*. Tutzing: Schneider, 1974.

———. *Die Quellen der mehrstimmigen Magnificat- und Te Deum-Vertonung bus zur Mitte des 16. Jahrhunderts*. Tutzing: Schneider, 1966.

———. "Ein unbeachtetes Chorbuch von 1544 in Österreichische Nationalbibliothek, Wien". *Die Musikforschung* 14 (1961): 290–303.

Kirsop, Wallace. "Les habitudes de compositeurs: une technique d'analyse au service de l'édition critique et de l'histoire des idées". In *Trasmissione dei testi a stampa nel periodo moderno: I seminario internazionale, Roma, 23–26 marzo, 1983*, ed. Giovanni Crapulli: 17–47. Lessico intelletuale Europeo 36. Rome: Ateneo, 1985.

Kmetz, John. *Die Handschriften der Universitätsbibliothek Basel: Katalog der Musikhandschriften des 16. Jahrhunderts: Quellenkritische und historische Untersuchung*. Basel: Verlag der Universitätsbibliothek Basel, 1988.

Knighton, Tess. "A newly discovered keyboard source (Gonzalo de Baena's 'Arte nouamente inuentada pera aprender a tanger'; Lisbon 1540): a preliminary report". *Plainsong and Medieval Music* 5 (1996): 81–112.

———. "Petrucci in Spain". Paper read at the conference "Venezia 1501: Petrucci e la stampa musicale", Venice, 12 October 2001

Kock, Virginia. "Petrucci's *Motetti de la Corona, Libro Tertio*: an edition and commentary. Master's thesis, Tulane University, 1963.

Körte, Oswald. *Laute und Lautenmusik bis zur Mitte des 16. Jahrhunderts*. Publikationen der Internationale Musikgesellschaft: Beihefte 3. Leipzig: Breitkopf und Härtel, 1901.

Korth, Hans-Otto, and Jutta Lambrecht, eds. *Katalog der Musikabteilung. I.xiii: Die Signaturengruppe Mus.Ms. 40 000 ff. Erste Folge: Handschriften des 15.–19. Jahrhunderts in mensuraler und neuerer Notation: Katalog*. Munich: Henle, 1997.

Kos, Koraljka. "Bossinensis, Antico i instrumentalna glazba njihova vremena". In *Muzicke veceri u Donatu*: 37–53. Zagreb: Music Information Centre, 1983; rpt. in *Istra: Casopis za kultura* 30 (1993).

Kotterba, Karin, ed. *Die Orgeltabulatur des Leonhard Kleber*. Das erbe deutsche Musik 91–2. Frankfurt: Litolff, 1987.

Kottick, Edward L. "The music of the chansonnier Cordiforme: Paris, Bib. Nat. Rothschild 2973". Ph.D. diss., University of North Carolina, 1962.

Kozachek, Laura. "The repertory of the Specialnik Codex, Hradec Králové, Krajske Muzeum Knihovna, MS II A 7". Ph.D. diss., Harvard University, 1998.

Krautwurst, Franz. "Die Heilsbronner Chorbücher der Universitätsbibliothek Erlangen (Ms.473, 1–4)". *Jahrbuch für Fränkische Landesforschung* 25 (1965): 273–324; 27 (1967): 253–282.

Kreider, John Evan. *The printing of music, 1480–1680* [exhibition catalogue]. Vancouver: Alcuin Society, 1980.

———. "Works attributed in the sixteenth century to both Josquin des Prez and Pierre de la Rue". In *Proceedings of the International Josquin Symposium, Utrecht 1986*, ed. Willem Elders with Frits de Haen: 103–116. Utrecht: Vereniging voor Nederlandse Muziekgeschiedenis, 1991.

Kristeller, Paul. *Die italienischen Buchdrucker- und Verlegerzeichen bis 1525*. Strassburg: Heitz, 1893.

Kristeller, Paul Oskar. *Iter Italicum: a finding list of uncatalogued or incompletely catalogued humanistic manuscripts of the Renaissance in Italian and other libraries*. London: Warburg Institute, and Leiden: Brill, 1963–1995.

Krummel, Don W. *Bibliographical inventory to the early music in the Newberry Library, Chicago, Illinois*. Boston: G.K. Hall, 1977.

———. *Bibliotheca Bolduaniana: a renaissance music bibliography*. Detroit studies in music bibliography 22. Detroit: Music Information Coordinators, 1972.

———. "Citing the score: descriptive bibliography and printed music". *The Library*, Ser.6, 9 (1987): 329–346.

———. "Early German partbook type faces". *Gutenberg-Jahrbuch 1985*: 80–98.

———. *English Music Printing, 1553–1700*. London: Bibliographical Society, 1971.

———. "Music Publishing". *Music Printing and Publishing*, ed. D.W. Krummel and Stanley Sadie: 79–132. Grove Handbooks in Music. London: Macmillan, 1990.

———. "Musical functions and bibliographical forms". *The Library*, Ser.5, 32 (1976): 327–350.

———. "Oblong format in early music books". *The Library*, Ser.5, 26 (1971): 312–324.

Krummel, Don W., compiler. *Guide for dating early published music*. Kassel: Bärenreiter, 1974.

Kultzen, Brigitte. "Der Codex Escorial IV.a.24. Übertragung, Katalog, historische Einordnung einer Chansonsammlung aus der zweiten Hälfte des 15. Jahrhunderts". Diss., Universität Hamburg, 1956.

La Face Bianconi, Giuseppina. *Gli strambotti del codice estense Alpha.F.9.9*. Studi e testi per la storia della musica 8. Florence: Olschki, 1990.

La Rocca, G. "Storia dell'epistola di Baldassare Castiglione al re Enrico VII d'Inghilterra (il reperimento del testo ufficiale)". *Atti e memorie dell'Accademia Virgiliana di scienze, lettere ed arti in Mantova* 40 (1972).

La Rue, Pierre de. *Drei Missen: 1. Missa de Beata Virgine; 2. Missa de Virginibus; 3. Missa de Sancta Anna*, ed. René Bernard Lenaerts and Josef Robijns. Monumenta musicae Belgicae 8. Antwerp: Vereniging voor Muziekgeschiedenis te Antwerpen, 1960.

———. *Missa L'homme armé*, ed. Nigel Davison. Das Chorwerk 114. Wolfenbüttel: Mäseler, 1972.

———. *Opera Omnia*, ed. Nigel Davison, Evan Kreider and Herman Keahey. Corpus mensurabilis musicae 97. Neuhausen-Stuttgart: American Institute of Musicology; Hänssler, 1989–1992.

Labarre, Emile Joseph. *Dictionary-encyclopedia of paper and paper-making*. 2nd ed. Amsterdam: Swets & Zetlinger, 1952.

Labbei, Philip, and Gabriel Cossarti. *Sacrosancta Concilia ad regiam editionem exacta . . . Tomus decimusquartus ab anno M.DXII. ad annum M.DXLV.* Lyons: Societatis typographicae librorum ecclesiasticorum, 1672.

Lambrecht, Jutta. *Das "Heidelberger Kapellinventar" von 1544 (Codex Pal. Germ. 318): Edition und Kommentar.* Heidelberger Bibliotheksschriften 26. Heidelberg: Universitätsbibliothek, 1986.

Land, J. P. "De koorboeken van de St. Pieterskerk te Leiden". *Bouwsteenen, Jaarboek der Vereniging voor Nord Nederlandse Muziekgeschiedenis* 3 (1876–1881): 37–48.

Landucci, Luca. *Diario Fiorentino*, ed. I. del Badia. Florence: Sansoni, 1883.

————. *A Florentine Diary from 1450 to 1516 by Luca Landucci continued by an anonymous writer till 1542*, trans. Alice de Rosen Jervis. Freeport, NY: Books for Libraries Press, 1971.

Lane, Frederic C. "Rhythm and rapidity of turnover in Venetian Trade of the fifteenth century". *Venice and History: the collected papers of Frederic C. Lane*: 109–127. Baltimore: Johns Hopkins Press, 1966. Translated from "Ritmo e rapidità di giro d'affari nel commercio veneziano del quatrrocento". In *Studi in onore di Gino Luzzatto*, i, 254–273. Milan: Giuffre, 1949.

————. "Venetian Bankers, 1496–1533". *Journal of Political Economy* 45 (1937): 187–206; rpt. in *Venice and History: the collected papers of Frederic C. Lane*: 69–86. Baltimore: Johns Hopkins Press, 1966.

Larner, John. "Order and disorder in Romagna, 1450–1500". In *Violence and civil disorder in Italian cities, 1200–1500*, ed. Lauro Martines: 38–71. Contributions of the UCLA Center for Medieval and Renaissance Studies 5. Berkeley and Los Angeles: University of California Press, 1972.

Layer, Adolf. "Augsburger Musikdrucker der frühen Renaissancezeit". *Gutenberg-Jahrbuch 1965*: 124–139,

Layton, Evro. "Notes on some printers and publishers of 16th-century modern Greek books in Venice". *Thesaurismata* 18 (1981): 119–144.

Lazzari, Antonio. *Dizionario storico degli uomini illustri di Urbino.* Urbino: Colucci, 1796.

Leech-Wilkinson, Daniel. "Il Libro di appunti di un suonatore di tromba del quindicesimo secolo". *Rivista italiana di musicologia* 16 (1981): 16–39.

Leedy, Douglas, ed. *Chansons from Petrucci in original notation and in transcription.* Berkeley: Musica Sacra et Profana, c.1983.

Legg, J.W. *An agreement for bringing out the second Quignon Breviary.* London: Blades, East & Blades, 1916.

Leicht, P.S. "L'editore veneziano Michele Tramezino ed i suoi privilegi". In *Miscellanea di scritti di bibliografia ed erudizione in memoria di Luigi Ferrari*: 357–367. Florence: Olschki, 1957.

Lenaerts, René Bernard. *Het nederlandse polifonies lied in de 16ᵈᵉ eeuw.* Mechelen: Het Kompas, 1933.

Lenaerts, René-Bernard, ed. *Die Kunst der Niederländer.* Das Musikwerk. Cologne: Arno Volk, 1962.

Lenhart, John M. *Pre-Reformation printed books: a study in statistical and applied bibliography.* Franciscan Studies 14. New York: J.F. Wagner, 1935.

Leoni, Giovanni Battista. *Vita di Francesco Maria di Montefeltro della Rovere IIII duca d'Urbino.* Venice: Ciotti, 1605.

Lepschy, Anna Laura, John Took, and Denis E. Rhodes, eds. *Book production and letters in the western European Renaissance: essays in honour of Conor Fahy.* Publications of the Modern Humanities Research Association 12. London: Modern Humanities Research Association, 1986.

Lesure, François, intro. *Tablature de luth italienne: Cent dix pièces d'oeuvres vocales pour luth seul et accompagnement pour luth. Fac-Simile du Ms. de la Bibliothèque Nationale, Paris, Rés Vmd. Ms.27 ca.1505* [facsimile]. Geneva: Minkoff, 1981.

————. *Manuscrit italien de frottole (1502)* [facsimile]. Geneva: Minkoff, 1979.

Lesure, François and Genevieve Thibault. *Bibliographie des éditions d'Adrian Le Roy et Robert*

Ballard (1551–1598). Publications de la Société française de musicologie, Ser.2, 9. Paris: Société française de musicologie, 1955.

———. "Bibliographie des éditions d'Adrian Le Roy et Robert Ballard (1551–1598): supplément". *Revue de musicologie* 40 (1957): 166–172.

———. "Bibliographie des éditions musicales publiées par Nicolas du Chemin (1549–1576)". *Annales musicologiques* 1 (1953): 269–373; 4 (1956): 251–253.

Levitan, Joseph. "Ockeghem's clefless compositions". *Musical Quarterly* 23 (1937): 440–464.

Lewis, Mary. *Antonio Gardano, Venetian music printer 1538–1569: a descriptive bibliography and historical study*. New York: Garland, 1988–.

———. "Antonio Gardane's early connections with the Willaert circle". In *Music in medieval and early modern Europe: patronage, sources and texts*, ed. Iain Fenlon: 209–226. Cambridge: Cambridge University Press, 1981.

———. "Composer and printer in the sixteenth century: Gardane, Rore, and Zarlino". Paper read at the annual meeting of the American Musicological Society, Minneapolis, 19–22 October 1978.

———. "The printed music book in context: observations on some sixteenth-century editions". *Notes* 46 (1989–1990): 899–918.

———. "Twins, Cousins, and Heirs: relationships among editions of music printed in sixteenth-century Venice". In *Critica Musica: essays in honor of Paul Brainard*, ed. John Knowles: 193–224. Amsterdam: Gordon and Breach, 1996.

Lhéritier, Jean. *Opera Omnia*, ed. Leeman L. Perkins. Corpus mensurabilis musicae 48. s.l.: American Institute of Musicology, 1969.

Lichtenthal, Peter. *Dizionario e bibliografia della musica*. Milan: Fontana, 1826.

Lindmayr, Andrea. "Ockeghem's motets: style as an indicator of authorship: the case of *Ut heremia solus* reconsidered". In *Johannes Ockeghem: Actes du XLe Colloque international d'études humanistes, Tours, 3–8 février 1997*, ed. Philippe Vendrix: 499–520. Paris: Klincksieck, 1998.

———. "Ein Rätseltenor Ockeghems: des Rätsels Lösung". *Acta Musicologica* 60 (1988): 31–42.

Lippmann, Friedrich. "Musikhandschriften und -Drucke in der Bibliothek des Fürstenhauses Massimo, Rom. Katalog, I. Teil: Handschriften". *Analecta musicologica* 17 (1976): 254–295.

Litterick, Louise. "Attribution practice and Florence 2442". Paper read at the American Musicological Sessions of "Toronto 2000".

———. "The manuscript Royal 20.A.XVI of the British Library". Ph.D. diss., New York University, 1976.

———. "The revision of Ockeghem's 'Je n'ay dueil' ". *Le moyen français* 5 (1980): 29–38.

———. "Who wrote Ninot's chansons?". In *Papal music and musicians in late medieval and renaissance Rome*, ed. Richard Sherr: 240–270. Oxford: Clarendon, and Washington: Library of Congress, 1998.

Llorens, José Maria. *Capella Sixtinae Codices musicis notis instructi sive manu scripti praelo excussi*. Studi e Testi 202. Roma: Biblioteca Apostolica Vaticana, 1960.

———. "El codice Casanatense 2.856 identificado come el Cancionero de Isabella d'Este (Ferrara): esposa de Francesco Gonzaga (Mantua)". *Anuario Musical* 20 (1965): 161–178.

———. *Le opere musicale della Cappella Giulia: I. Manoscritti e edizioni fino al '700*. Studi e Testi 265. Vatican City: Biblioteca Apostolica Vaticana, 1971.

Loach, Donald. "Aegidius Tschudi's Songbook (St. Gall Ms 463): a humanistic document from the circle of Heinrich Glarean". Ph.D. diss., University of California at Berkeley, 1969.

Lockwood, Lewis. "Adrian Willaert and Cardinal Ippolito I d'Este: new light on Willaert's early career in Italy, 1515–1521". *Early Music History* 5 (1985): 85–112.

———. "Jean Mouton and Jean Michel: new evidence on French music and musicians in Italy, 1505–1520". *Journal of the American Musicological Society* 32 (1979): 191–246.

———. "Josquin at Ferrara: new documents and letters". In *Josquin des Pres: Proceedings of the International Josquin Festival-Conference held at the Julliard School at Lincoln Center in New York City, 21–25 June 1971*, ed. Edward E. Lowinsky, with Bonnie J. Blackburn: 103–136. London: Oxford University Press, 1976.

———. *Music in Renaissance Ferrara, 1400–1505: the creation of a musical center in the fifteenth century*. Cambridge, MA: Harvard University Press, 1984.

———. "Pietrobono and the instrumental tradition at Ferrara in the fifteenth century". *Rivista italiana di musicologia* 10 (1975): 115–133.

———. "A view of the early sixteenth-century parody mass". In *Twenty-fifth anniversary festschrift (1937–1962)*, ed. Albert Mell: 53–77. New York: Queen's College Department of Music, 1962.

———. "A Virtuoso singer at Ferrara and Rome: the case of Bidon". In *Papal music and musicians in late medieval and renaissance Rome*, ed. Richard Sherr: 224–239. Oxford: Clarendon, and Washington: Library of Congress, 1998.

Lodes, Birgit. "An anderem Ort, auf andere Art: Petruccis und Mewes' Obrecht-Drucke". *Basler Jahrbuch für historische Musikpraxis*, 25 (2002), 85.111.

Lodi, Pio. *Catalogo delle Opere musicali teoriche e pratiche . . . Città di Modena R. Biblioteca Estense*. Bollettino dell'Associazione dei Musicologi Italiani 8 (Parma, 1917); rpt. as Bibliotheca musica Bononiensis, ser 1, 2. Bologna: Forni, 1967.

Loge, Eckhard. *Eine Messen- und Motetten-handschrift des Kantors Matthias Krüger aus der Musikbibliothek Herzog Albrechts von Preussen*. Kassel: Bärenreiter, 1931.

Long, Michael. "Symbol and ritual in Josquin's *Missa Di dadi*". *Journal of the American Musicological Society* 42 (1989): 1–22.

Löpelmann, Martin, ed. *Die Liederhandschrift des Cardinals de Rohan (XV. Jahr.)*. Publikationen der Gesellschaft für romanische Literatur 44. Göttingen: Gesellschaft fur romanische Literatur, 1923.

Lovato, Antonio. *Catalogo del Fondo Musicale della Biblioteca Capitolare di Padova*. Edizioni Fondazione Levi, III.c.5. Venice: Fondazione Ugo e Olga Levi, 1998.

Lowinsky, Edward E.. "Conflicting views on conflicting signatures". *Journal of the American Musicological Society*, vii (1954): 181–204

———. *The Medici Codex of 1518: a choirbook of motets dedicated to Lorenzo de' Medici, Duke of Urbino*. Momuments of Renaissance Music 3–5. Chicago: University of Chicago Press, 1968.

———. "MS 1070 of the Royal College of Music in London". *Proceedings of the Royal Musical Association* 96 (1969–1970): 1–28.

———. "A music book for Anne Boleyn". In *Florilegium Historiale: essays presented to Wallace K. Ferguson*, ed. J. Rowe and W. Stockdale: 161–235. Toronto: University of Toronto Press, 1970.

———. "A newly discovered sixteenth-century motet manuscript at the Biblioteca Vallicelliana in Rome". *Journal of the American Musicological Society* 3 (1950): 173–232.

———. *Tonality and Atonality in Sixteenth-century music*. Berkeley and Los Angeles: University of California Press, 1962.

Lowry, Martin. *Nicholas Jenson and the rise of Venetian publishing in the Renaissance*. Oxford: Oxford University Press, 1991.

———. *The World of Aldus Manutius: business and scholarship in Renaissance Venice*. Oxford: Blackwell, 1979.

Luisi, Francesco. *Del cantar a libro . . . & sulla viola. La musica vocale nel Rinascimento: studi sulla musica vocale profana in Italia nei seoli XV e XVI*. Turin: RAI Radiotelevisione Italiana, 1977.

———. "Musica in commedia nel primo Cinquecento". In *Origini della Commedia nell'Europa del Cinquecento*, ed. Myriam Chiabò and Federico Doglio: 259–311. Rome: Ufficio Centrale per i Beni Librari e gli Istituti Culturali, 1994.

———. *Frottole di B. Tromboncino e M. Cara 'per cantar et sonar col lauto': saggio critico e scelta di transcrizioni*. Studi e testi 3. Rome: Torre d'Orfeo, 1987.

———. "Una sconosciuta fonte per la canzone vocale e proto-madrigalistica redatta intorno al 1530 (Venezia, Biblioteca del Conservatorio, Torr. Ms.B.32)". *Note d'Archivio per la storia musicale*, n.s., 4 (1986): 9–104.

———. *Il secondo libro di frottole di Andrea Antico*. Musica rinascimentale in Italia 3. Rome: Pro musica studium, 1976.

———. "Il 'Tentalora' ballo dei 'tempi passai': vecchie e nuove fonti". In *Musicologia Homana: Studies in honor of Warren and Ursula Kirkendale*, ed. Siegfried Gmeinwieser, David Hiley and Järg Riedlbauer: 75–113. Florence: Olschki, 1994.

Luisi, Francesco, ed. *Apografo miscellaneo Marciano: frottole canzoni e madrigali con alcuni alla pavana in villanesco (Edizione critica integrale dei Mss. Marc.It.Cl.IV.1795–1798)*. Edizioni Fondazione Levi, I.A.1, i. Venice: Fondazione Ugo e Olga Levi, 1979.

———. *Innocentius Dammonis: Laude libro primo, Venezia 1508* [facsimile]. Venice: Fondazione Ugo e Olga Levi, 2001.

———. *Laudario Giustinianeo: edizione comparate con note critiche del ritrovato laudario Ms.40 . . . 1*. Edizioni Fondazione Levi, IV.B.1. Venice: Fondazione Ugo e Olga Levi, 1983.

Luisi, Francesco, and Giovanni Zanovello, eds. *Frottole Libro Undecimo, Ottaviano Petrucci, Fossombrone 1514*. Octaviani Petrutii Forosemproniensis Froctolae 1. Venice: Comitato per la Pubblicazione di Fonti della Cultura Musicale Veneta, and Padua: CLEUP, 1997.

Lütteken, L. " 'Musicus et cantor diu in ecclesia Sancti Marci de Veneciis': note biografiche su Johannes de Quadris". *Rassegna veneta di studi musicali* 5–6 (1989–1990): 43–62.

Luzio, Alessandro. "Isabella d'Este nei primordi del papato di Leone X". *Archivio storico lombardo*, Ser.5, 33 (1906): 99–180 and 454–489.

Luzzatto, Gino. *Storia economica di Venezia dall'XI al XVI secolo*. Venice: Centro internazionale delle arte e del costume, 1961.

Maccarrone, Rosalia. "Il Libro XI di frottole edito da Ottaviano Petrucci (Fossombrone, 1514): trascrizione ed edizione critica". Tesi di Laurea, Università degli Studi di Padova, 1991.

MacCracken, Thomas G. "The manuscript Uppsala, Universitetsbiblioteket, Vokalmusik i Handskrift 76b". Ph.D. diss., University of Chicago, 1985.

MacCracken, Thomas G., intro. *Uppsala, Universitetsbiblioteket, Vokalmusik i handskrift 76b*. Renaissance Music in Facsimile 20. New York: Garland, 1986.

Macey, Patrick. "An inauthentic psalm motet attributed to Josquin". *Proceedings of the International Josquin Symposium*, ed. Willem Elders: 25–44. Utrecht: Vereniging voor Nederlandse Muziekgeschiedenis, 1991.

———. "Josquin as Classic: *Qui habitat, Memor esto*, and two imitations unmasked". *Journal of the Royal Musical Association* 118 (1993): 1–43.

———. "Josquin's 'Litle' Ave Maria: a misplaced motet for the *Vultum tuum* cycle?". *Tijdschrift van de Vereniging voor Nederlandse Muziekgeschiedenis* 39 (1989): 38–53.

———. "Josquin's *Misericordias domini* and Louis XI". *Early Music* 19 (1991): 163–177.

———. "Savonarola and the sixteenth-century motet". *Journal of the American Musicological Society* 36 (1983): 422–452.

———. "Some thoughts on Josquin's *Illibata dei virgo nutrix* and Galeazzo Maria Sforza". In *From Ciconia to Sweelink: donum natalicium Willem Elders*, ed. Albert Clement and Eric Jas: 111–124. Amsterdam: Rodopi, 1994.

Machiavelli, Nicolò. *Machiavelli: the chief works and others*, trans. A. Gilbert. Durham, NC: Duke University Press, 1965.

Maittaire, Michael. *Annales typographiques ad Ann. MDXXXV. Continuati . . . .* The Hague: Comitum, 1722.

Maldeghem, R.-J. van. *Trésor musical: collection authentique de musique sacrée et profane des anciens maîtres belges*. Brussels, 1865–1893.

Malfatti, B. "Ottaviano dei Petrucci da Fossombrone". *Gazzetta musicale di Milano* 8 (1850): issues for 6 and 27 October.

Mamini, Marcello. "Documenti quattrocenteschi di vita musicale alle Corti Feltresca e Malatestiana". *Studi urbinati*, n.s., 48 (1974): 115–128.

Manoussakas, Manoussos, and K. Staikos. *The Publishing Activity of the Greeks during the Italian Renaissance (1469–1523)*. Athens: Greek Ministry of Culture, 1987.

Mantuani, J. *Tabulae codicum manu scriptorum praeter graecos et orientales in biblioteca palatina vindobonensi asservatorum*. Vienna: Gerold, 1864–1912.

Manzoni, Giacomo. *Annali tipografici dei Soncino*. Bologna: Romagnoli, 1886–1885; rpt. Farnborough: Gregg, 1969.

———. "Francesco da Bologna, incisore di caratteri mobili metallici da stampa". *Studi di bibliografia analitica* 1 (1881).

Marciani, C. "Editori, tipografi, librai veneti nel Regno di Napoli nel Cinquecento". *Studi veneziani* 10 (1968): 457–554.

Marcon, Michela. "Il Libro VI di frottole edito da Ottaviano Petrucci (Venezia 1505 m.v.): trascrizione ed edizione critica". Tesi di Laurea, Università degli Studi di Padova, 1991.

Marcon, Susy, and Marino Zorzi, eds. *Aldo Manuzio e l'ambiente veneziano, 1494–1515*. Venice: il Cardo, 1994.

Mardersteig, G. "Aldo Manuzio e i caratteri di Francesco Griffo da Bologna". In *Studi di bibliografia e di storia in onore di Tammaro de Marinis*, ed. R. de Maio: iii, 105–147. [Verona]: Stamperia Valdonega, 1964.

Mariani, Franco. *Ottaviano Petrucci, inventore della stampa della musica a caratteri mobili: le vicende della cartiera di Carnello a Sora nel XVI secolo*. s.l.: s.n., 2001. This edition reprints two earlier titles by Mariani, firstly "Ottaviano Petrucci inventore della stampa della musica a caratteri mobili", in *Culutra e scuola* 125 (1993): pp. 144–155, on pp. 1–9 of the new edition; and *Le vicende della cartiera di Carnello a Sora nel XVI secolo* (Sora: s.n., 1996), on new pp. 11–32.

Marín Martinez, Tomás, José Manuel Ruiz Asençio and Klaus Wagner, eds. *Catálogo Concordado de la Biblioteca de Hernando Colón*. Madrid: Fundación MAPFRE América, Seville: Cabildo de la Catedral, 1993–. Two volumes have appeared to date.

Marix, Jeanne. "Harmonice Musices Odhecaton A: quelques précisions chronologiques". *Revue de musicologie* 16 (1935): 236–241.

Marix, Jeanne, ed. *Les musiciens de la cour de Bourgogne au XVe siècle (1420–1467)*. Paris: Editions Oiseau-Lyre, 1937.

Marker, Gary. *Publishing, printing, and the origins of intellectial life in Russia, 1700–1800*. Princeton: Princeton University Press, 1985.

Marshall, Robert G., ed. *Short-title catalogue of books printed in Italy and of books in Italian printed abroad, 1501–1600, held in selected north American libraries*. Boston: Hall, 1970.

Martinez-Gällner, Marie Louise. "Die Augsburger Bibliothek Herwart und ihre Lautentabulaturen". *Fontes artis musicae* 16 (1969): 29–48.

Martini, Giovanni Battista. *Carteggi inedito del P. Giambattista Martini coi più celebri musicisti del suo tempo*, ed. Federico Parisini. Bologna: Zanichelli, 1888; rpt. Bologna: Forni, 1969.

Martini, Johannes. *Magnificat e messe*, ed. Benevenuto Disertori. Archivium Musices metropolitanum mediolanese 12. Milan: Veneranda Fabbrica del Duomo di Milano, 1964.

———. *The Secular pieces*, ed. Edward G. Evans. Recent researches in the music of the Middle Ages and early Renaissance 1. Madison, WI: A. R. Editions, 1975.

Marx, Hans Joachim. "Neues zur Tabulatur-Handschrift St. Gallen Stiftsbibliothek, Cod.530". *Archiv für Musikwissenschaft* 37 (1980): 264–291.

Marx, Hans Joachim, ed. *Die Tabulaturen aus dem Besitz der Basler Humanisten Bonifacius Amerbach*. Tabulaturen des XVI. Jahrhunderts 1 = Schweizerische Musikdenkmäler 6. Basel: Bärenreiter, 1967.

Marx, Hans Joachim, with Thomas Warburton, eds. *St. Galler Orgelbuch: die Orgeltabulatur des Fridolin Sicher (St. Gallen, Codex 530)*. Schweizerische Musikdenkmäler 8. Winterthur: Amadeus, 1992.

Marzi, Demetrio. *La Questione della Riforma del Calendario nel Quinto Concilio Lateranense (1512–1517)*. Pubblicazioni del R. Istituto di Studi superiori pratici e di perfezionamento in Firenze. Sezione di filosofia e filologia 27. Florence: Carnesechi & figli, 1896.

Masetti-Zannini, Gian Ludovico. *Stampatori e librai a Roma nella seconda metà del Cinquecento: documenti inediti*. Rome: Palombi, 1980.

Massenkeil, Günther, ed. *Mehrstimmige Lamentationen aus der ersten Hälfte des 16. Jahrhunderts*. Musikalische Denkmäler 6. Mainz: Schott, 1965.

Massera, Giuseppe. *La "Mano musicale perfetta" di Francesco de Brugis dalle prefazioni ai Corali di L. A. Giunta*. "Historiae musicae cultores" Biblioteca 18. Florence: Olschki, 1963.

Maynard, Judson D. " 'Heir beginnis countering' ". *Journal of the American Musicological Society* 20 (1967): 182–196.

Mazzatinti, G. "Gubbio dal 1515 al 1522, da documenti inediti dell'Archivio comunale di Gubbio". *Bollettino della Società Umbria di Storia Patria* 1 (1895): 87–105.

McKenzie, David F. "Printers of the mind: some notes on bibliographical theories and printing-house practices". *Studies in Bibliography* 22 (1969): 1–75; rpt in *Making Meaning: 'Printers of the Mind' and other essays*: 13–85. Amherst: University of Massachusetts Press, 2003.

McKerrow, Ronald B. *An introduction to bibliography for literary students*. Oxford: Clarendon, 1927; rpt. New Castle, DE: Oak Knoll, 1994.

McMurtry, Douglas. *The Book: the story of printing and bookmaking*. 3rd ed., New York: Oxford University Press, 1943.

McMurtry, William. "The British Museum manuscript Additional 35087: a transcription of the French, Italian and Latin compositions with concordance and commentary". Ph.D. diss., North Texas State University, 1967.

McMurtry, William, intro. *Chansonnier of Hieronymus Lauweryn van Watervliet* [facsimile]. Peer: Alamire, 1989.

Meconi, Honey. "Another look at Absalon". *Tijdschrift van de Koninklijke Vereniging voor Nederlandse Musiekgeschedenis* 48 (1998): 3–29.

———. "Free from the crime of Venus: the biography of Pierre de la Rue". *Revista de Musicología* 16 (1983): 2673–2683.

———. "The Naming of things: Petrucci's mass prints and the commodification of music". Paper read at the conference "Venezia 1501: Petrucci e la stampa musicale", Venice, 12 October 2001.

———. "What is a music collection? Petrucci vs. the manuscripts". Paper read at the conference "Legacies: 500 years of printed music", University of North Texas, 27 October 2001.

Meconi, Honey, intro. *Basevi Codex. Florence, Biblioteca del Conservatorio, Ms.2439* [facsimile]. Peer: Alamire, 1990.

Meier, Bernhard. "Die Handschrift Porto 714 als Quelle zur Tonartenlehre des 15. Jahrhunderts". *Musica Disciplina* 7 (1953): 175–197.

Meissner, Ute. *Der Antwerpener Notendrucker Tylman Susato: eine bibliographische Studie zur niederländischen Chansonpublikationen in der ersten Hälfte des 16. Jahrhunderts*. Berliner Studien zur Musikwissenschaft 11. Berlin: Merseburger, 1967.

Melella, Patrizia. "Vita musicale e arte organaria a Santo Spirito in Sassia nel Cinquecento: note e documenti". In *La musica a Roma attraverso de fonti d'archivio: Atti del Convegno Internazionale, Roma 4–7 giugno 1992*, ed. Bianca Maria Antolini, Arnaldo Morelli and Vera Vita Spagnuolo: 507–519. Strumenti della ricerca musicale 2. Lucca: Libreria Musicale Italiana, 1994.

Melin, W.E. "The music of Johannes Tinctoris (c.1435–1511): a comparative study of history and practice". Ph.D. diss., Ohio State University, 1973.

Mercati, Giovanni. "Notizie varie di antica letteratura medica e di bibliografia: III. Su Francesco Calvo da Menaggio primo stampatore e Marco Fabio Calvo da Ravenna primo traduttore latino del corpo Ippocratico". *Studi e Testi* 31 (1917): 47–71.

Merritt, A. Tillman. "A chanson sequence by Févin". In *Essays on music in honor of Archibald Thompson Davison*: 91–99. Cambridge, MA: Department of Music, Harvard University, 1957.

Meyer, Christian. *Sources manuscrites en tablature: Luth et theorbe (c.1500–c.1800): Catalogue descriptif.* Three volumes to date: Collection d'études musicologiques 82, 87, 90. Baden-Baden: Koerner, 1991–.

―――. "Un répertoire protestant vers 1540: Bruxelles, Bibliothèque royale Albert 1er, Fétis 1782A A 1 L.P. (Suppl.Ms.). *Revue de Musicologie* 77 (1991): 81–87.

Meyer, Kathi. "The printing of music, 1473–1934". *The Dolphin* 2 (1935): 171–207.

Meyer-Baer, Kathi. *Liturgical music incunabula: a descriptive catalogue.* Bibliographical Society Publication [for 1954]. London: The Bibliographical Society, 1962.

Meyer, Kathi, and Paul Hirsch. *Katalog der Musikbibliothek Paul Hirsch.* Cambridge: Cambridge University Press, 1947.

Michelini Tocci, Luigi. "Il manoscritto di dedica della 'Epistola de vita et gestis Guidobaldi Urbini Ducis ad Henricum Angliae Regem' di Baldassare Castiglione". *Italia Medioevale e umanistica* 5 (1962): 273–282.

Miggiani, Maria Giovanna. " 'Il Petrarca imbrodolato': fortuna di testi petrarcheschi nel madrigale italiano del '500". Tesi di Laurea, Università di Venezia, 1985.

Miller, Beth L. "Antico, Andrea". *Music Printing and Publishing,* ed. D.W. Krummel and Stanley Sadie: 143–147. Grove Handbooks in Music. London: Macmillan, 1990.

Miller, Clement A. "The musical source of Brumel's *Missa Dringhs*". *Journal of the American Musicological Society* 21 (1968): 200–204.

Milsom, John. "The Nonsuch music library". *Sundry Sorts of Music Books: Essays on the British Library Collections, Presented to O. W. Neighbour on his 70th Birthday,* ed. Chris Banks, Arthur Searle and Malcolm Turner: 146–182. London: British Library, 1993.

―――. "Tallis, Byrd, and the 'Incorrected Copy': some cautionary notes for editors of early music printed from movable type". *Music and Letters* 77 (1996): 348–367.

Minamino, Hiroyuki. "A monkey business: Petrucci, Antico, and the frottola intabulation". *Journal of the Lute Society of America* 26–7 (1993–1994): 96–106.

Mischiati, Oscar. "Un'Antologia manoscritta in partitura del Secolo XVI: il MS. Bourdeney della Bibliothèque Nationale di Parigi". *Rivista italiana di musicologia* 10 (1975): 265–328.

―――. *Indici, cataloghi e avvisi degli editori e librai musicali italiani dal 1591 al 1798.* Florence: Olschki, 1984.

Moe, Lawrence H.. "Dance music in printed Italian lute tablatures from 1507 to 1611". Ph.D. diss., Harvard University, 1956.

Moerk, Alice Anne. "The Seville Chansonnier: an edition of Sevilla 5-I-43 and Paris, n.a.fr.4379 (part 1)". Ph.D. diss., West Virginia University, 1971.

Mohr, Peter. *Die Handschrift B 211–215 der Proske-Bibliothek zu Regensburg, mit kurzer Beschreibung der Handschriften B 216–219 und B 220–222.* Schriften des Landesinstituts für Musikforschung, Kiel 7. Kassel: Bärenreiter, 1955.

Molitor, Raphael. *Deutsche Choral-Wiegendrucke: ein Beitrag zur Geschichte des Chorals und des Notendrucks in Deutschland.* Regensburg: Pustet, 1904.

Moneti, Elena. "Un contratto editoriale Bolognese del 1489". *Studi e ricerche sulla Storia della stampa del quattrocento: ommagio dell'Italia a Giovanni Gutenberg nel V centenario della sua scoperta*: 211–216. Milan: Hoepli, 1942.

Mönkemeyer, Helmut, ed. *Hieronymus Formschneyder: Trium vocum carmina. Nürnberg, 1538.* Monumenta musicae ad usum practicum: eine Denkmalreihe für Freunde alter Musik 1–2. Celle: Moeck, 1985.

Morales, Cristóbal. *Opera Omnia,* ed. Higinio Anglés. Monumentos de la música española. Barcelona: Consejo superior de investigaciones cientificas: delegación de Roma, 1952–.

Moran, James. *Printing presses: history and development from the fifteenth century to modern times.* Berkeley and Los Angeles: University of California Press, 1973.

Moranti, Maria, and Luigi Moranti. "Librerie private in Urbino nei secoli XVI–XVII". *Atti e memorie della deputazione di storia patria per le Marche,* n.s., 83 (1978): 315–348.

Morawski, Jerzy, ed. *Musica Antiqua Polonica. Sredniowiecze.* Krakow: P.W.M., 1972.

Morell, Martin. "Georg Knoff: bibliophile and devotee of Italian music in late sixteenth-century Danzig". *Music in the German Renaissance: sources, styles, and contexts,* ed. John Kmetz: 103–126. Cambridge: Cambridge University Press, 1994.

Morelot, S. "Notice sur un manuscrit de musique ancienne de la Bibliothèque de Dijon". *Mémoires de la Commission des antiquités du Départment de la C™te d'Or* 4 (1856): 133–160.

Morison, Stanley. *A Tally of types.* 2nd ed., Cambridge: Cambridge University Press, 1973.

Mortimer, Ruth. *Harvard College Library Department of Printing and Graphic Arts: Catalogue of books and manuscripts. II: Italian 16th century books.* Cambridge, MA: Belknap Press, 1974.

Morton, Robert. *The collected works*, ed. Allan Atlas. Masters and monuments of the Renaissance 2. New York: Broude, 1981.

Mošin, V. *Anchor Watermarks.* Monumenta Chartæ Papyraceæ Historiam Illustrantia 13. Amsterdam: Paper Publications Society, 1973.

Mouser, Marilee J. "Petrucci and reception history: the influence of the Venetian motet prints, 1502–1508". Paper read at the conference "Legacies: 500 years of printed music", University of North Texas, 27 October 2001.

Mouton, Jean. *Missa "Alleluya" zu 4 Stimmen*, ed. Paul Kast. Das Chorwerk 70. Wolfenbüttel: Möseler, 1958.

———. *Fünf Motetten*, ed. Paul Kast. Das Chorwerk 76. Wolfenbüttel: Möseler, 1959.

———. *Opera Omnia*, ed. Andrew Minor. Corpus mensurabilis musicae 93. Rome: American Institute of Musicology. 1967–.

Moxon, Joseph. *Mechanick exercises on the whole art of printing*, ed. Herbert Davis and Harry Carter. London: Oxford University Press, 1958; 2nd ed., 1962, itself rpt. New York: Dover, 1978.

Munoz, Maria Trinidad. *Catalogo del Archivo del Monasterio Cisterciense de Santo Domingo de Silos, "El Antiguo", Toledo (1150–1900).* Ayegui: Ediciones Instituto de Historia Cisterciense, 1986–1990.

Munro, John. "The coinages of Renaissance Europe, ca.1500". In *Handbook of European History 1400–1600: late middle ages, Renaissance and Reformation*, ed. Thomas A. Brady, jr., Heiko A. Oberman, and James D. Tracy: 671–8. Leiden: Brill, 1994.

Murányi, Róbert Arpád. "Zwei unbekannte Druckschriften aus dem 16. Jahrhundert". *Studia musicologica* 27 (1985): 291–294.

Murphy, Richard. "Fantasia and Ricercar in the 16th century". Ph.D. diss., Yale University, 1954.

Nagel, Willibald. "Johann Heugel (ca.1500–1584/5)". *Sammelbände der International Musikgesellschaft* 7 (1905–1906): 80–110.

Naiditch, Paul G., ed. *A Catalogue of the Ahmanson-Murphy Aldine Collection at UCLA.* Los Angeles: Department of Special Collections, University Research Library, University of California, Los Angeles, 1989–1994.

Narducci, Enrico. *Catalogo di Manoscritti ora posseduti da D. Baldassare Boncompagni.* 2nd ed., notabilmente accresciuta: Rome: Tipografia delle Scienze, Matematice e Fisiche, 1892.

Nash, Ray, ed. *An account of calligraphy and printing in the sixteenth century, from Dialogues attributed to Christopher Plantin.* New York: Liturgical Arts Society, 1949.

Needham, Paul. "The Cambridge proof-sheets of Mentelin's Latin Bible". *Transactions of the Cambridge Bibliographical Society* 9 (1986–1990): 1–35.

———. "Concepts of Paper Study". In *Puzzles in Paper: concepts in historical watermarks*, ed. Daniel W. Mosser, Michael Saffle, and Ernest W. Sullivan: 1–36. New Castle, DE: Oak Knoll Press; and London: The British Library, 2000.

———. "Continental printed books sold in Oxford, c.1480–1483: two trade records". In *Incunabula: studies in fifteenth-century printed books presented to Lotte Hellinga*, ed. Martin Davies: 243–270. London: British Library, 1999.

———. "ISTC as a tool for analytical bibliography". In *Bibliography and the study of 15th-century civilisation*, ed. Lotte Hellinga and John Goldfinch: pp. 39–54. London: British Library. 1987.

Nef, Walter Robert. *Der St. Galler Organist Fridolin Sicher und seine Orgeltabulatur.* Schweizerisches Jahrbuch für Musikwissenschaft 7. Basel: Majer, 1938.

Ness, Arthur. "The Herwarth lute manuscripts at the Bavarian State Library". Ph.D. diss., New York University, 1983.

Neubacher, Jürgen. *Die Musikbibliothek des Hamburger Kantors und Musikdirectors Thomas Selle (1599–1663)*. Musicological Studies and Documents 52. Neuhausen: American Institute of Musicology and Hänssler, 1997.

Newton, Paul. "Florence, Biblioteca del Conservatorio di Musica Luigi Cherubini, manuscript Basevi 2439: critical edition and commentary". Ph.D. diss., North Texas State University, 1968.

Nielsen, Clare I. "Francesco Rampazetto, Venetian printer and a catalogue of his music editions". M.A. Thesis, Tufts University, 1987.

Ninot le Petit. *Collected works*, ed. Barton Hudson. Corpus mensurabilis musicae 87. s.l.: American Institute of Musicology, 1979.

Nitti, Francesco. *Leone X e la sua politica secondo documenti e carteggi inediti*. Florence: Barbéra, 1892.

Noakes, Susan. "The development of the book market in late Quattrocento Italy: printers' failures and the rôle of the middleman". *The Journal of Medieval and Renaissance Studies* 11 (1981): 23–55.

Noble, Jeremy. "Another *Regina Celi* attributed to Josquin". In *From Ciconia to Sweelinck: donum natalicum Willem Elders*, ed. Albert Clement and Eric Jas: 145–152. Amsterdam: Rodopi, 1994.

———. "The Limits of Petrucci's world" *Basler Jahrbuch für historische Musikpraxis*, 25 (2002): 9–12.

———. "Ottaviano Petrucci: his Josquin editions and some others". In *Essays presented to Myron P. Gilmore*, ed. Sergio Bertelli and Gloria Ramakus: ii, 433–445. Florence: La Nuova Italia, 1978.

Noble, Jeremy, and Gustave Reese. "Josquin Desprez". In *The New Grove Dictionary of music and musicians*, ed. Stanley Sadie: ix, 713–738. London: Macmillan, 1980; revised for the second edition with Patrick Macey and Jeffrey Dean, xiii, 220–266. London: Macmillan, 2003.

Noblitt, Thomas L. "Das Chorbuch des Nikolaus Leopold (München, Staatsbibliothek, Mus. Ms. 3154): Repertorium". *Archiv für Musikwissenschaft* 26 (1969): 169–208.

———. "Die Datierung der Handschrift Mus. ms. 3154 der Staatsbibliothek München". *Die Musikforschung* 27 (1974): 36–56.

———. "Manuscript Mus. 1/D/505 of the Sächsische Landesbibliothek Dresden". *Archiv für Musikwissenschaft* 30 (1973): 275–310.

———. "Manuscript Mus.1/D/506 of the Sächsische Landesbibliothek, Dresden (olim Annaberg, Bibliothek des St. Annenkirche, Ms. 1126)". *Musica disciplina* 28 (1974): 81–127.

———. "Obrecht's *Missa sine nomine* and its recently discovered model". *The Musical Quarterly* 68 (1982): 102–127.

———. "Problems of transmission in Obrecht's 'Missa Je ne demande' ". *The Musical Quarterly* 63 (1977): 211–223. Translated as "Problemi di trasmissione nella *Missa Je ne demande* di Obrecht". In *La critica del testo musicale: metodi e problemi della filologia musicale*, ed. Maria Caraci Vela: 129–140. Studi e testi musicali, n.s., 4. Lucca: Libreria Musicale Italiana, 1995.

———. "A reconstruction of Ms. Thomaskirche 51 of the Universitätsbibliothek Leipzig". *Tijdschrift van der Vereniging voor Nederlandse Muziekgeschiedenis* 31 (1981): 16–72.

———. "Textual criticism of selected works published by Petrucci". *Formen und Probleme der Überlieferung mehrstimmiger Musik im Zeitalter Josquins Desprez*, ed. Ludwig Finscher: 201–244. Wolfenbütteler Forschungen 6 = Quellenstudien zur Musik der Renaissance 1. Munich: Kraus International, 1981.

Noblitt, Thomas, ed. *Der Kodex des Magister Nicolaus Leopold, Staatsbibliothek München Mus.ms.3154*. Das erbe deutsche Musik 80. Kassel: Bärenreiter, 1987.

———. *Tricinia tum veterum tum recentiorum in arte musica symphonistarum, latina, germanica, brabantica et gallica, 1542*. Georg Rhau Musikdrucke aus den Jahren 1538 bis 1545 in praktischer Neuausgabe 9. Kassel: Bärenreiter, 1989.

Nordstrom, Lyle. "Ornamentation of Flemish Chansons as found in the Lute Duets of Francesco Spinacino". *Journal of the Lute Society of America* 2 (1969): 1–5.

Norton, Frederick John. *Italian printers, 1501–1520: an annotated list, with an introduction*. Cambridge Bibliographical Society monographs 3. Cambridge: Bowes and Bowes, 1958.

Norwich, John Julius. *A History of Venice*. New York: Knopf, 1982.

Nowacki, Edward. "The Latin Psalm-motet, 1500–1535". In *Renaissance Studien. Helmuth Osthoff zum 80. Geburtstag*, ed. Ludwig Finscher: 159–184. Frankfurter Beiträge zur Muskwissenschaft 11. Tutzing: Schneider, 1979.

Nowak, Leopold. "Die Musikhandschriften aus Fuggerschem besitz in der Österreichischen Nationalbibliothek". In *Die Österreichischen nationalbibliothek: Festschrift*, ed. Josef Blick: 505–515. Vienna: Bauer, 1948.

Nowak, Leopold, and Adolf Koczirz, eds. *Das deutsche Gesellschaftslied in Österreich von 1480 bis 1550*. Denkmäler der Tönkunst in Österreich 57. Vienna: Universal, 1930.

Nuttall, Derek, and M.R. Perkin, intro. *A Reprint of a part of Book III of The Academy of Armory by Randle Holme of the City of Chester, Gentleman Sewer in Extraordinary to His Majesty King Charles II: concerning the Art of Printing and Typefounding*. Menston: Scolar for private distribution to members of the Printing Historical Society, 1972.

Obrecht, Jacob. *Collected works*, general editor, Chris Maas. Utrecht: Vereniging voor nederlandse Muziekgeschenis, 1983–.

———. *Misse* [facsimile]. Cologne: Becker, s.d.

———. *Opera omnia. Editio altera*, ed. Albert Smijers and M. Van Crevel. Amsterdam: Alsbach, 1953–1964.

———. *Werken van Jacob Obrecht*, ed. Johannes Wolf. Amsterdam: Alsbach; and Leipzig: Breitkopf & Härtel, 1908–1921; rpt. Farnborough: Gregg, 1968.

O'Dette, Paul. "Quelques remarques sur l'exécution de la musique de danse de Dalza". In *Luth et sa Musique. II. Tours, 15–18 Septembre 1980*, ed. Jean-Michel Vaccaro: 183–191. Paris: Centre nationale de la recherche scientifique, 1984.

Offenbacher, E. "La bibliothèque de Willibald Pirckheimer". *La Bibliofilìa* 40 (1938): 241–263.

Ogg, Oscar, intro. *Three classics of Italian calligraphy: an unabridged reissue of the writing books of Arrighi, Tagliente, Palatino*. New York: Dover, 1953.

Olschki, Leo. "Una visita alla collezione del comm Lozzi". *La Bibliofilìa* 3 (1902).

Ongaro, Giulio. "The Library of a sixteenth-century music teacher". *The Journal of Musicology* 12 (1994): 357–375.

———. "Venetian printed anthologies of music in the 1560s and the role of the editor". In *The Dissemination of music: studies in the history of music publishing*, ed. Hans Lenneberg: 43–69. s.l.: Gordon and Breach, 1994.

Ordo divini Officii persolvendi sacrique peragendi pro ecclesia forosemproniensi . . . pro anno domini 1953. Urbania: Brumantesi, 1952.

Orf, Wolfgang. *Die Musikhandschriften Thomaskirche Mss. 49/50 und 51 in der Universitätsbibliothek Leipzig*. Quellenkataloge zur Musikgeschichte 13. Wilhelmshaven: Heinrichshofen, 1977.

Orlandi, Giovanni, ed. *Aldo Manuzio editore: dediche, prefazioni, note ai testi*. Milan: Il Polifilo, [1975].

Osley, Arthur S. *Scribes and Sources: handbook of the Chancery Hand in the sixteenth century. Texts from the Writing-masters*. Boston: Godine, 1980.

Osthoff, Helmuth. *Josquin Desprez*. Tutzing: Schneider, 1962, 1965.

———. *Theatergesang und darstellende Musik in der italienischen Renaissance*. Tutzing: Schneider, 1969.

Ottino, Giuseppe. *Di Bernardo Cennini e dell'arte della stampa in Firenze nei primi cento anni dall'invenzione di essa: sommario storico con documenti inediti*. Florence: Cellini, 1871.

———. *La stampa in Ancona*. Milan, 1878.

Owens, Jessie Ann. *Composers at work: the craft of musical composition 1450–1600*. New York: Oxford University Press, 1997.

———. "Stimmbuch", In *Die Musik in Geschichte und Gegenwart: Sachteil 8*, 1764–1775. Kassel: Bärenreiter, 1998.

Owens, Jessie Ann, intro. *Bologna, Civico Museo Bibliografico Musicale, MS.Q19 ("The Rusconi codex")*. Renaissance Music in Facsimile 1. New York: Garland, 1988.

———. *Kraków, Biblioteka Jagiellónska, Glogauer Liederbuch*. Renaissance Music in Facsimile 6. New York: Garland, 1986.

Owens, Jessie Ann, and Richard Agee. "La stampa della 'Musica nova' di Willaert". *Rivista italiana di musicologia* 24 (1989): 219–305.

Paisey, David L. "Blind printing in early continental books". In *Book Production and Letters in the Western European Renaissance: Essays in honour of Conor Fahy*, edite by Anna Laura Lepschy, John Took and Dennis Rhodes: 220–233. London: The Modern Humanities Research Association, 1986.

Palermo, Giangiacomo. "Sugli inizi dell'arte della stampa in Ancona (1512–1550)". *L'Archiginnasio* 32 (1937): 116–119.

Palomera, E.J. *Fray Diego Valadés o.f.m., evangelizador humanista de la Nueva España: su obra*. Mexico City: Editorial Jus, 1962.

Pannella, Liliana. "Le composizioni profane di una raccolta fiorentina del cinquecento". *Rivista italiana di musicologia* 3 (1968): 3–47.

Panzer, Georg Wolfgang. *Annales Typographici*. Nürnberg: Eberhard, 1793–1803.

Paris, Gaston, and Auguste Gevaert, eds. *Chansons du XVᵉ siècle publiées d'après le manuscrit de la Bibliothèque Nationale de Paris*. Paris: Firmin Didot, 1875.

Parisini, Andrea. "Uno studioso e polemista Calabrese nella Napoli musicale dell'Ottocento: Francesco Florimo". *Miscellanea Musicologica Calabrese* 2 = Ricerche Musicali A.M.Am Calabria 10 (1997): 109–129.

Partner, Peter. "The 'Budget' of the Roman church in the Renaissance period". In *Italian Renaissance Studies*, ed. E.F. Jacob: 256–278. London: Faber and Faber, 1960.

Paquini, Elisabetta. *Libri di musica a Firenze nel tre-quattrocento*. Studi e Testi per la storia della musica 12. Florence: Olschki, 2000.

Pastor, Ludwig. *Geschichte der Päpste*. Translated as *The History of the Popes from the close of the Middle Ages*, ed. R.F. Kerr. 3rd. ed., London, 1950.

Pastorello, Ester. *Tipografi, editori, librai a Venezia nel secolo XVI*. Biblioteca di bibliografia italiana 5. Florence: Olschki, 1924.

Patalas, A. *Catalogue of early music prints from the collections of the former Preußische Staatsbibliothek in Berlin, kept at the Jagiellonian Library in Cracow*. Kraków: Musica Iagellonica, 1999.

Pease, Edward J. "An edition of the Pixèrècourt manuscript". Ph.D. diss., Indiana University, 1960.

———. "A report on Codex Q16 of the Civico Museo Bibliografico Musicale". *Musica Disciplina* 20 (1966): 57–94.

Pedrell, Felipe. *Catàlech de la Biblioteca Musical de la Diputació de Barcelona*. Barcelona: Palau de la Diputació, 1909.

Perales de la Cal, Ramon, ed. *Cancionero de la Catedral de Segovia: facsimile*. Segovia: Caja de Ahorros y Monte de Piedad, 1977.

Perkins, Leeman L. "Notes bibliographiques au sujet de l'ancien fond musical de l'église de Saint Louis des Français à Rome". *Fontes artis musicae* 16 (1969): 57–71.

———. Review of Lowinsky, *Medici*. *The Musical Quarterly* 55 (1969): 255–269.

Perkins, Leeman L., and Howard Garey, eds. *The Mellon Chansonnier*. New Haven: Yale University Press, 1979.

Perz, Miroslaw. "Handschrift Nr. 1361 der Öffentlichen Städtischen Raczynski-Bibliothek in Poznan: als neue Quelle zur Geschichte der Polnischen Musik in der II. Hälfte des XV. Jahrhunderts". In *The Book of the first international musicological congress devoted to* the works of Frederick Chopin, Warszawa 16th–22nd February 1960: 588–592. Warsaw: Polish scientific publishers, 1963.

———. "The Lvov fragment: a sources for works by Dufay, Josquin, Petrus de Domarto, and Petrus de Grudencz in 15th-century Poland". *Tijdschrift van de Vereniging voor Nederlandse Muziekgeschiedenis* 36 (1986): 26–51.

Perz, Miroslaw, ed. *Sources of Polyphony up to c.1500*. Antiquitates Musicae in Polonia 13–14. Warsaw: PWM-Polish Scientific Publishers, 1973, 1976.

Petrarch. *Rime dispersi*, ed. A. Solerti. Florence: Sansoni, 1909.

Petrucci, Armando. *Writers and readers in medieval Italy: Studies in the history of written culture*, trans. Charles Radding. New Haven: Yale University Press, 1995.

Petrucci, Ottaviano. *Canti B numero cinquanta*. Monuments of Music and Music Literature in Facsimile, Ser.1, 23. New York: Broude, 1975.

———. *Canti C numero cento cinquanta*. Monuments of Music and Music Literature in Facsimile, Ser.1, 25. New York: Broude, 1978.

———. *Fragmenta Missarum* [facsimile]. Cologne: Becker, s.d.

———. *Harmonice Musices Odhecaton A*. Monuments of Music and Music Literature in Facsimile, Ser.1, 10. New York: Broude, 1973.

———. *Lamentationum Jeremie prophete liber primus* [facsimile]. Cologne: Becker, s.d.

———. *Lamentationum liber secundus* [facsimile]. Cologne: Becker, s.d.

———. *Missarum diversos* [sic] *auctoris liber primus* [facsimile]. Cologne: Becker, s.d.

———. *Missarum Liber Agricole, Ghiselin, de la Rue, Josquin* [facsimile]. Rome: Vivarelli & Gulla, 1973.

———. *Motetti A* [facsimile]. Cologne: Becker, s.d.

———. *Motetti C* [facsimile]. Cologne: Becker, s.d.

———. *Ottaviano Petrucci: Odhecaton (Venice, 1501)* [facsimile of the 1504 edition]. Milan: Bollettino Bibliografico Musicale, 1932.

Petrucci Nardelli, Franca. *La lettera e l'immagine: le iniziali "parlanti" nella tipografia italiana (secc.XVI–XVII)*. Florence, 1991.

Pettas, William. "The cost of printing a Florentine incunable". *La Bibliofilia* 75 (1973): 67–85.

———. *The Giunti of Florence: merchant publishers of the sixteenth century*. San Francisco: Bernard M. Rosenthal, 1980.

———. "An international Renaissance publishing family: the Giunti". *Library Quarterly* 44 (1974): 334–349.

Picker, Martin. "The Chanson albums of Marguerite of Austria". *Annales musicologiques* 6 (1958–1963): 145–285.

———. "A Florentine document of 1515 concerning music printing". *Quadrivium* 12 (1971): 283–290.

———. *Johannes Ockeghem and Jacob Obrecht: a guide to research*. Garland Composer resource manuals 13. New York: Garland, 1988.

———. "More 'Regret' chansons for Marguerite d'Autriche". *Le moyen français* 5 (1980): 81–101.

———. "The motet anthologies of Andrea Antico". In *A musical offering: essays in honor of Martin Bernstein*, ed. Edward Clinkscale and Claire Brook: 211–237. New York: Pendragon Press, 1977.

———. "The motet anthologies of Petrucci and Antico published between 1514 and 1521: a comparative study". In *Formen und Probleme der Überlieferung mehrstimmiger Musik im Zeitalter Josquins Desprez*, ed. Ludwig Finscher: 181–199. Wolfenbütteler Forschungen 6 = Quellenstudien zur Musik der Renaissance 1. Munich: Kraus International, 1981.

———. "A New Look at the 'little' chansonnier of Marguerite of Austria". *Jaarboek van het Vlaamse Centrum voor Oude Muziek* 3 (1987): 27–31.

———. "Newly discovered sources for *In minem sin*". *Journal of the American Musicological Society* 17 (1964): 134–143.

Picker, Martin, ed. *The Chanson albums of Marguerite of Austria: MSS 228 and 11239 of the*

Bibliothèque Royale de Belgique, Brussels. Berkeley and Los Angeles: University of California Press, 1965.

————. *Fors seulement: thirty compositions for three to five voices or instruments from the fifteenth and sixteenth centuries.* Recent Researches in music of the Middle Ages and early Renaissance 14. Madison, WI: A.R. Editions, 1981.

————. *The Motet books of Andrea Antico.* Monuments of Renaissance Music 8. Chicago: University of Chicago Press, 1987.

Picker, Martin, intro. *Album de Marguerite d'Autriche* [facsimile]. Peer: Alamire, 1986.

————. *Chansonnier of Marguerite of Austria. Brussel, Koninklijke Bibliotheek, MS.11239* [facsimile]. Peer: Alamire, 1988.

Picot, Émile. *Les Italiens en France au XVIe siècle.* Bordeaux: Gounouilhon, 1901–1918.

Pieri, Piero. *La crisi militare italiana nel Rinascimento nelle sue relazioni con la crisi politica ed economica.* Biblioteca di cultura storica 45. 2nd ed., Turin: Einaudi, 1952.

Pingue, Caterina. "Il VI libro di frottole edito da Ottaviano Petrucci". Tesi di laurea, Università degli Studi di Napoli, 1992.

Pipelare, Matthaeus. *Opera Omnia*, ed. Ronald Cross. Corpus mensurabilis musicae 34. s.l.: American Institute of Musicology, 1966–1967.

Pirro, André. *Histoire de la musique da le fin du XIVe siècle à la fin du XVIe.* Paris: Laurens, 1940.

————. "Leo X et la musique". In *Mélanges offerts à H. Hauvette* (Paris, 1934): 221–234; rpt. in *Mélanges André Pirro* (Geneva: Minkoff, 1977): 63–76. Translated as "Leo X and music", *Musical Quarterly* 21 (1935): 1–16.

Pirrotta, Nino. "Su alcuni testi italiani di composizioni polifoniche quattrocentesche". *Quadrivium* 14 (1973): 133–157.

————. "Before the madrigal". *The Journal of Musicology* 12 (1994): 237–252.

————. "Florence from barzelletta to madrigal". In *Musica Franca: essays in honor of Frank A. D'Accone*, ed. Irene Alm, Alyson McLamore and Colleen Reardon: 7–18. Stuyvesant, NY: Pendragon, 1996.

————. *Music and Culture in Italy from the Middle Ages to the Baroque.* Cambridge, MA: Harvard University Press, 1984.

————. "Two Anglo-Italian piecces in the manuscript Porto 714". In *Speculum muicae artis. Festgabe für Heinrich Husmann zum 60. Geburtstag am 16. Dezember 1968*, ed. Heinz Becker and Reinhard Gerlach: 253–261. Munich: Fink, 1970.

Pirrotta, Nino, and Elena Polovedo. *Music and Theatre from Poliziano to Monteverdi.* Cambridge: Cambridge University Press, 1982.

Pisano, Bernardo. *Collected Works*, ed. Frank D'Accone. Corpus mensurabilis musicae 32/i. s.l.: American Institute of Musicology, 1966.

Plamenac, Dragan. "Autour d'Ockeghem". *Revue musicale* 9 (1928): 26–37.

————. "*Excerpta Colombina*: items of musical interest in Fernando Colon's Regestrum". In *Miscelànea en homenaje a Monsenor Higinio Anglès*: ii, 663–687. Barcelona: Consejo superior de investigaciones cientificos, 1958–1961.

————. "Music libraries in Eastern Europe". *Notes* 19 (1961–1962): 411–420.

————. "A Postscript to 'The second chansonnier of the Biblioteca Riccardiana' ". *Annales musicologiques* 4 (1956): 261–265.

————. "The recently discovered complete copy of A. Antico's 'Frottole intabulate' (1517)". In *Aspects of medieval and renaissance music: a birthday offering to Gustave Reese.* ed. Jan LaRue *et al.*: 683–692. New York: Norton, 1966.

————. "A reconstruction of the French chansonnier in the Biblioteca Colombina, Seville". *The Musical Quarterly* 37 (1951): 501–542; 38 (1952): 85–117 and 245–277.

————. "The 'second' chansonnier of the Biblioteca Riccardiana (Codex 2356)". *Annales musicologiques* 2 (1954): 105–187.

————. "Toma Cechini, kapelnik stolnih crkava u Splitu i Hvaru u prvoj polovini XVII stoleca". *Rad Jugoslavenske akademije znanosti i umjetnosti* 262 (1938): 77–125.

Plamenac, Dragan, intro. *Dijon, Bibliothèque publique, manuscrit 517.* [facsimile]. Publications of mediaeval music manuscripts 12. Brooklyn: Institute of Mediaeval music, 1971.

————. *Facsimile reproduction of the manuscripts Sevilla 5-I-43 and Paris n.a.fr.4379 (Pt.1)*. Publications of mediaeval music manuscripts 8. Brooklyn: Institute of Mediaeval music, 1962.

Plantin, Christopher. *An Account of Calligraphy and Printing in the Sixteenth Century from dialogues attributed to Christophe Plantin, printed and published by him at Antwerp, 1567*, trans. Ray Nash. New York: Liturgical Arts Society, 1949.

Pogue, Samuel F. "Communication". *Journal of the American Musicological Society* 22 (1969): 139–141.

————. "The earliest music printing in France". *Huntington Library Quarterly* 50 (1987): 35–57.

————. *Jacques Moderne: Lyons music printer of the sixteenth century*. Travaux d'humanisme et Renaissance 101. Geneva: Droz, 1969.

————. "A sixteenth-century editor at work: Gardane and Moderne". *The Journal of Musicology* 1 (1982): 217–238.

Pollard, Alfred. *Last Words on the history of the title-page*. London, 1891.

Pollard, Graham, and Albert Ehrman. *The distribution of books by catalogue from the invention of printing to A.D. 1800, based on material in the Broxbourne Library*. Cambridge: for presentation to members of The Roxburghe Club, 1965.

Pompilio, Angelo. "Editori musicale a Napoli e in Italia nel Cinque-Seicento". In *Musica e cultura a Napoli dal XV al XIX secolo*, ed. Lorenzo Bianconi and R. Bossa: 79–102. Florence: Olschki, 1983.

————. "Strategie editoriale delle stamperie veneziane". In *Atti del XIV Congresso della Società Internazionale di Musicologia: Trasmissione e recensione delle forme di cultura musicale. Bologna 27 Agosto–1 Settembre 1987, Ferrara-Parma 30 Agosto 1987*, ed. Angelo Pompilio, Lorenzo Bianconi, Donatella Restani, and F. Alberto Gallo: i, 254–271. Turin: Edizioni di Torino, 1990.

Poole, H. Edmund. "Music Printing". *Music Printing and Publishing*, ed. D.W. Krummel and Stanley Sadie: 3–78. Grove Handbooks in Music. London: Macmillan, 1990.

Pope, Isabel, and Masakata Kanazawa, eds. *The Musical manuscript Montecassino 871: a Neapolitan repertory of sacred and secular music of the late fifteenth century*. London: Oxford University Press, 1978.

Potier, auctioneers. *Catalogue des livres rares en partie des XV et XVI siècles composant la Bibliothèque Musicale de M. Gaetano Gaspari*. Paris: Potier, 1862.

Potter, Jeremy H. "Nicolò Zoppino and the book-trade network of Perugia". *The Italian book, 1465–1800: studies presented to Dennis E. Rhodes on his 70th birthday*, ed. Denis V. Reidy: 135–159. London: The British Library, 1993.

Povey, K. "Variant formes in Elizabethan printing". *The Library*, Ser.5, 10 (1955): 41–48.

Preston, Alan. "Sacred polyphony in Renaissance Verona: a liturgical and stylistic study". Ph.D. diss., University of Illinois, 1969.

Prioris, Johannes. *Opera Omnia*, ed. T. Herman Keahey and Conrad Douglas. Corpus mensurabilis musicae 90. Neuhausen-Stuttgart: Hänssler, American Institute of Musicology, 1982.

Prizer, William. "La cappella di Francesco II Gonzaga e la musica sacra a Mantova nel primo ventennio del cinquecento". In *Mantova e i Gonzaga nella civiltà de Rinascimento: Atti del Convegno, Mantova 1974*: 267–276. Segrate: Edigraf, 1978.

————. "Cara, Marchetto". *The New Grove Dictionary of Music and Musicians*, ed. Stanley Sadie: iii, 764–766. London: Macmillan, 1980.

————. *Courtly pastimes: the frottole of Marchetto Cara*. Studies in musicology 33. Ann Arbor: UMI Research Press, 1980.

————. "Facciamo pure noi carnevale: non-Florentine carnival songs of the late fifteenth and early sixteenth centuries". In *Musica Franca: essays in honor of Frank A. D'Accone*, ed. Irene Alm, Alyson McLamore and Colleen Reardon: 173–211. Stuyvesant, NY: Pendragon, 1996.

————. "The frottola and the unwritten tradition". *Studi musicali* 15 (1986): 3–37.

————. "Isabella d'Este and Lucrezia Borgia as patrons of music: the frottola at Mantua and Ferrara". *Journal of the American Musicological Society* 38 (1985): 1–33,

————. "Laude di popolo, laude di corte: some thoughts on the style and function of the Renaissance lauda". In *La musica a Firenze al tempo di Lorenzo il Magnifico: congresso internazionale di studi*: 167–194. Florence: Olschki, 1993.

————. "Marchetto Cara and the north Italian frottola". Ph.D. diss., University of North Carolina at Chapel Hill, 1974.

————. "Paris, Bibliothèque Nationales, Rés.Vm⁷.676 and music at Mantua". In *Atti del XIV congresso della Società Internazionale di Musicologia, Bologna, 1997: trasmissione e recezione delle forme di cultura musicale*, ed. Angelo Pompilio, Lorenzo Bianconi, Donatella Restani, and F. Alberto Gallo: ii, 235–239. Turin, Edizioni di Torino, 1990.

————. "Secular music at Milan during the early cinquecento: Florence, Biblioteca del Conservatorio, MS Basevi 2441". *Musica Disciplina* 50 (1996): 9–57.

Proctor, Robert. *The Printing of Greek in the 15th century*. Illustrated Monographs of the Bibliographical Society 8. Oxford: Bibliographical Society, 1900.

Przywecka-Samecka, Maria. *Poczatki Drukarstwa Muzycznego w Europie Wiek XV*. Prace Wroclawskiego Towarzystwa Naukowego, Ser.A, 221. Wroclaw: Zaklad Narodowy im. Ossol'nskich, 1981.

Pullan, Brian. *Rich and poor in Renaissance Venice: the social institutions of a catholic state, to 1620*. Oxford: Blackwell, 1971.

Pulsiano, Phillip. "A checklist of books and articles containing reproductions of watermarks". *Essays in paper analysis*, ed. Stephen Spector: 115–153. Washington: Folger Shakespeare Library, 1986.

Puskás, Regula, comp. *Musikbibliothek Erwin R. Jacobi: Seltene Ausgaben und Manuskripte: Katalog*. 3rd ed., Zurich: Hug & Co., 1973.

Puttin, L. "Nuovi documenti sul prototipografo trevigiano Gerardo da Lisa". *Studi trevigiani* 1 (1984): 33–38.

Quadris, Johannes de. *Opera*, ed. Giulio Cattin. Antiquae musicae italicae: Monumenta veneta sacra 2. Bologna: Antiquae Musicae Italicae Studiosi, 1972.

Quaranta, Elena. *Oltre San Marco: Organizzazione e prassi della musica nelle chiese di Venezia nel Rinascimento*. Studi di Musica Veneta 26. Florence: Olschki, 1998.

Querol Gavaldá, Miguel, ed. *Cancionero musical de la Colombina*. Monumentos de la Mùsica Española 33. Barcelona: Consejo Superior de Investigaciones Científicas, Instituto Español de Musicología, 1971.

Quondam, Amadeo. "Nel giardino di Marcolini: un editore veneziano tra Aretino e Doni". *Giornale storico della letteratura italiana* 157 (1980): 75–116.

————. " 'Mercanzia d'onore', 'Mercanzia d'utile': produzione libraria e lavoro intelletuale a Venezia nel Cinquecento". In *Libri, editori e pubblico nell'Europa moderna*, ed. Armando Petrucci: 51–104. Bari: Laterza, 1977.

Radole, Giuseppe. *La Musica a Capodistria*. Trieste: Centro Studi Storic-Religiosi Friuli-Venezia Giulia, 1990.

————. *Musica e musicisti in Istria nel Cinque e Seicento*. Atti e Memorie della Società Istriana di Archeologia e Storia Patria 65 (= n.s., 13) (1965).

Raeli, Vito. "La collezione Corsini di antichi codici musicali e Girolamo Chiti". *Rivista musicale italiana* 25 (1918): 345–371; 26 (1919): 112–139; 27 (1920): 60–84.

Rahn, Douglas. "Melodic and textual types in French popular songs, ca.1500". Ph.D. diss., Columbia University, 1978.

Rasch, Rudolf, and Thiemo Wind. "The Music Library of Cornelis Schuyt". In *From Ciconia to Sweelinck: donum natalicium Willem Elders*, ed. Albert Clement and Eric Jas: 327–353. Chloe: Beihefte zum Daphnis 21. Amsterdam: Rodopi, 1994.

Rava, Carlos. *Arte dell'illustrazione nel libro italiano del Rinascimento*. Milan: Gärlich, 1945.

Raven, James. "Selling books across Europe, c.1450–1800: an overview". *Printing History* 34 (1993): 5–19.

Rawles, Stephen. "Description et classification des lettres ornées. Esquisse d'une méthodologie". *Ornementation typographique et bibliographie historique: actes du colloque de Mons (26–28 août 1987)*, ed. Marie-Thérèse Isaac: 27–40. Documenta et Opuscula 8. Brussels: Emile van Balberghe, 1988.

Raynaldus, O. *Annales ecclesiastici* 12–13. Lucca, 1754–55.

Reaney, Gilbert. "The manuscript Oxford, Bodleian Library, Canonici misc.213". *Musica Disciplina* 9 (1955): 73–104.

Redeker, Raimund. *Lateinische Widmungsvorreden zu Messen- und Motettendrucken der ersten Hälfte des 16. Jahrhunderts*. Schriften zur Musikwissenschaft aus Münster 6. Eisenach: Wagner, 1995.

Redmond, Mary. "A set of part-books for Giuliano de' Medici: Cortona, Biblioteca Comunale, Mss. 95–96 and Paris, Bibliothèque nationale, Nouvelle acquisition [française] 1817". Master's thesis, University of Illinois, 1970.

Rees, Owen. *Polyphony in Portugal, c.1530–c.1620: sources from the monastery of Santa Cruz, Coimbra*. Outstanding dissertations in music from British Universities. New York: Garland, 1995.

Reese, Gustave. "The first printed collection of part-music (the Odhecaton)". *The Musical Quarterly* 20 (1934): 39–76.

———. *Music in the Renaissance*. New York: Norton, 1954.

———. "Musical compositions in Renaissance intarsia". *Journal of the American Musicological Society* 10 (1957): 60–62.

Reese, Gustave, and Theodore Karp. "Monophony in a group of Renaissance chansonniers". *Journal of the American Musicological Society* 5 (1952): 4–15.

Regis, Johannes. *Opera Omnia*, ed. Cornelis Lindenburg. Corpus mensurabilis musicae 9. Rome: American Institute of Musicology, 1959.

Reich, Wolfgang, ed. *Selectae harmoniae de Passione Domini, 1538*. Georg Rhaus Musikdrucke aus den Jahren 1538 bis 1545 in praktischer Neuausgabe 10. Kassel: Bärenreiter, 1990.

Reidemeister, Peter. *Die Chanson-Handschrift 78 C 28 des Berliner Kupferstichkabinetts: Studien zur Form der Chanson im 15. Jahrhundert*. Munich: Katzbichler, 1973.

Reidy, Denis, ed. *The Italian book 1465–1800: Studies presented to Dennis E. Rhodes on his 70th Birthday*. London: The British Library, 1993.

Reisp, Branko, ed. *Catalogus librorum qui nundinis Labacensibus autumnalis in officina libraria Joannis Baptistae Mayr, venales prostant. Anno M. DC. LXXVIII* [facsimile]. Ljubljana: Mladinska Knjiga, 1966.

Renier, Rodolfo. "Un mazzetto di poesie musicali francesi". In *In memoria di Napoleone Caix e Ugo Angelo Canello. Miscellanea di filologia e linguistica*: 271–288. Florence: Le Monnier, 1886.

Renouard, Antoine Auguste. *Annales de l'imprimerie des Alde, ou histoire des trois Manuce et de leurs éditions*. 3rd ed., Paris: Renouard, 1834; rpt. as *Annali delle Edizioni Aldine. con Notizie sulla famiglia dei Giunta e repertorio delle loro Edizioni fino al 1550*. Bologna: Fiammenghi, 1954.

Répertoire international des sources musicales (RISM):
  Entries with an initial letter followed by a number are found in *Einzeldrucke vor 1800*, ed. Karl-Heinz Schlager. Répertoire international des sources musicales, Ser.A. Kassel: Bärenreiter, 1971–99.
  Entries with an initial year followed by a superscript number appear in *Recueils imprimés, XVIe–XVIIe siècles: liste chronologique*, ed. François Lesure. Répertoire international des sources musicales, Ser.B/I, i. Münich-Duisburg: Henle, 1960.
  There are also citations for Ser.B/IV, iii–iv (see Fischer) and v (see Bridgman); Ser.B/VII (see Boetticher); and Ser.B/VIII (see Ameln *et al.*).

Reynolds, Christopher. "The origins of San Pietro B 80 and the development of a Roman sacred repertory". *Early Music History* 1 (1981): 257–304.

————. *Papal Patronage and the music of St. Peter's 1380–1513*. Berkeley and Los Angeles: University of California Press, 1995.

Reynolds, Christopher, intro. *Vatican City, Biblioteca Apostolica Vaticana, San Pietro B 80*. Renaissance Music in Facsimile 23. New York: Garland, 1986.

Rhodes, Dennis E. "Antonio Zanchi of Bergamo, printer or publisher at Venice and Mantua". *Gutenberg-Jahrbuch 1956*: 141–144; rpt. in Dennis E. Rhodes, *Studies in early Italian printing*: 149–152. London: Pindar, 1982.

————. "Di alcuni prestiti e imitazioni tipografiche fra Roma a Perugia, 1515–1538". *La Bibliofilia* 71 (1969): 253–258.

————. "Further notes on the publisher Giacomo Mazzocchi", *Papers of the British School of Rome* 37 (1969 [1970]); rpt. in Dennis E. Rhodes, *Studies in early Italian printing*: 107–110. London: Pindar, 1982.

————. "On the use of the verb 'facere' in early colophons". *Studies in Bibliography* 26 (1973): 230–2; rpt. in Dennis E. Rhodes, *Studies in early Italian printing*: 49–51. London: Pindar, 1982.

————. *Silent Printers: anonymous printing at Venice in the Sixteenth Century*. The British Library Studies in the History of the Book. London: The British Library, 1995.

————. *Supplement* [to Johnson and Scholderer, *Short-title catalogue*]. London: British Library, 1986.

————. "Two new Italian printing centres of the sixteenth century". *The British Library Journal* 7 (1981): 172–176.

————. "An unknown library in Southern Italy in 1557". *Transactions of the Cambridge Bibliographical Society* 6 (1973); rpt. in Dennis E. Rhodes, *Studies in early European printing*: 221–231. (London: Pindar, 1983)

Richardson, Brian. *Print culture in Renaissance Italy: the editor and the vernacular text, 1470–1600*. Cambridge studies in publishing and printing history. Cambridge: Cambridge University Press, 1994.

Richter, Gunter. *Verlegerplakate des XVI. und XVII. Jahrhunderts bis zum Beginn des Dreissigjahrigen Krieges*. Wiesbaden: Pressler, 1965).

Riemann, Hugo. *Handbuch der Musikgeschichte*. Leipzig: Breitkopf & Härtel, 1901–1913.

————. "Der Mensural-Codex des Magister Nikolaus Apel von Königshofen (Codex MS 1494 der Leipziger-Universitätsbibliothek)". *Kirchenmusikalisches Jahrbuch* 12 (1897): 1–23.

————. "Notenschrift und Notendruck: bibliographisch-typographisch Studie". In *Festschrift zur 50 jährigen Jubelfeier des Bestehens der Firma C. G. Röder Leipzig*. Leipzig: Räder, 1896.

Rifkin, Joshua. "Motivik—Konstruktivismus—Humanismus: zu Josquins Motette *Huc me sydereo*. In *Die Motette: Beiträge zu ihrer Gattungsgeschichte*, ed. H. Schneider: 105–134. Neue Studien zur Musikwissenschaft. Mainz: Schott, 1991.

————. "A 'New' Renaissance manuscript". *Abstracts of papers read at the thirty-seventh annual meeting of the American Musicological Society, Philadelphia, American Musicological Society, 1971*, 2.

————. "Pietrequin Bonnel and Ms.2794 of the Biblioteca Riccardiana". *Journal of the American Musicological Society* 29 (1976): 284–296.

————. "Scribal concordances for some renaissance manuscripts in Florentine libraries". *Journal of the American Musicological Society* 26 (1973): 305–326.

Rigo, Paola. "Catalogo e tradizione degli scritti di Girolamo Donato". *Rendiconti dell'Accademia nazionale dei Lincei, Classe di Scienze morali, storiche e filologiche*, Ser.8, 31 (1976): 49–80.

Ringmann, Heribert. "Das Glogauer Liederbuch (um 1480)". *Zeitschrift für Musikwissenschaft* 15 (1932–1933): 49–60.

Ringmann, Heribert, and J. Klapper, eds. *Das Glogauer Liederbuch*. Das Erbe deutscher Musik 4, 8. Leipzig: Breitkopf und Härtel, 1936–7.

Ris-Paquot. *Dictionnaire Encyclopedique des Marques & monogrammes, chiffres, lettres initiales, signes figuratifs, etc., etc.*. Paris: 1874–1892; rpt. New York: Burt Franklin, s.d., as Bibliography and Reference Series 70.

Robijns, Jozef. "Eine Musikhandschrift des frühen 16. Jahrhunderts im Zeichen der Verehrung unserer Lieben Frau der Sieben Schmerzen (Brüssel, Kgl. Bibliothek, Hs.215–216)". *Kirchenmusikalisches Jahrbuch* 44 (1960): 28–43.

Robinson, John O. "Vienna, Austrian National Library, Manuscript 18810: a repertory study and manuscript inventory with concordances". *Royal Musical Association Research Chronicle* 19 (1983–1985): 68–84.

Rodocanachi, Emmanuel. *Histoire de Rome, Le Pontificat de Léon X, 1513–1521*. Paris: Hachette, 1931.

Roediger, Karl Erich. *Die geistlichen Musikhandschriften der Universitäts-Bibliothek Jena*. Jena: Frommann, 1935.

Rogers, D. "A Glimpse into Günther Zainer's workshop at Augsburg, c.1474". In *Buch und Text im 15. Jahrhundert*, ed. Lotte Hellinga and Helmer Härtel: 145–164. Wolfenbütteler Abhandlungen zur Renaissanceforschung 2. Hamburg: Hauswedell & Co., 1981.

———. "Johann Hamman at Venice: a survey of his career: with a note on the Sarum 'Horae' of 1494". In *Essays in honour of Victor Scholderer*, ed. Dennis Rhodes: 348–368. Mainz: Pressler, 1970.

Rokseth, Yvonne, ed. *Treize motets et un prélude pour orgue apres en 1531 chez Pierre Attaingnant*. Publications de la Société française de musicologie, Ser.1, 5. Paris: Droz, 1930.

Romani, Valentino. "Per un lessico della tipografia italiana del Cinquecento". *Nuovi Annali della Scuola Speciale per Archivisti e Bibliotecari, 1987*: 9–16.

Ronay, Christine L. "Sonnet settings in the Petrucci frottola books: an aspect of the return to literary standards (ca.1500–1520)". M.A. thesis, Harvard University, 1968.

Roncaglia, Gino. *La cappella musicale del Duomo di Modena*. "Historiae musicae cultores" Biblioteca 5. Florence: Olschki, 1957.

Ros-Fábregas, E. "The manuscript Barcelona, Biblioteca de Catalunya, M.454: study and edition in the context of the Iberian and Continental manuscript traditions". Ph.D. diss., City University of New York, 1992.

Rosaria Boccadifuoco, R. Maria, ed. *Per una Bibliografia musicale: testi, trattati, spartiti. Supplemento a Le Edizioni italiane del XVI secolo*. Rome: Istituto centrale per il catalogo unico delle Biblioteche Italiane e per le Informazione bibliografiche, 1999.

Roscoe, William. *Vita e pontificato di Leone X*. Milan, 1816.

Rosenfeld, Hellmut. "Bücherpreise, antiquariatspreis und einbandpreis im 16. und 17. Jahrhundert". *Gutenberg-Jahrbuch 1958*: 358–363.

Rosenthal, Albi. "A source survey: Early music books in the Sibley Library". In *Modern music librarianship: essays in honor of Ruth Watanabe*: 27–32. Stuyvesant: Pendrago, 1989.

Rossi, Adamo. "L'ultima parola sulla questione di Mᵒ Francesco de Bologna, intagliatore di lettere e tipografo". *Atti e Memorie della R. Deputazione di Storia Patria per le Provincie di Romagna*, Ser.3, 1 (1882–1883): 412–417.

Rossi, Franco. *La Fondazione Levi di Venezia: catalogo del fondo musicale*. Edizione Fondazione Levi: III.C.1. Venice: Fondazione Olga e Ugo Levi, 1986.

Rostirolla, Giancarlo. "La corrispondenza tra Martini e Girolamo Chiti: una fonte preziosa per la conoscenza del settecento musicale italiano". In *Padre Martini: musica e cultura nel settecento Europeo*, ed. Angelo Pompilio: 211–275. Quaderni della Rivista italiana di musicologia 12. Florence: Olschki, 1988.

Roth, Adalbert. "Zur Datierung der frühen Chorbücher der päpstlichen Kapelle". In *Datierung und Filiation von Musikhandschriften der Josquin-Zeit*, ed. Ludwig Finscher: 239–268. Wolfenbütteler Forschungen 26 = Quellenstudien zur Musik der Renaissance 2. Wiesbaden: Harrassowitz, 1983.

———. *Studien zum frühen Repertoire der päpstlichen Kapelle unter dem Pontifikat Sixtus IV (1471–1484): Die Chorbücher 15 und 51 des Fondo Cappella Sistina der Biblioteca Apostolica Vaticana*. Capellae Apostolicae Sixtinaeque collectanea acta monumenta 1. Vatican City: Biblioteca Apostolica Vaticana, 1991.

Rozzo, Ugo. "Biblioteche e libri proibiti nel Friuli del Cinquecento". *Atti dell'Accademia di Scienze Lettere e Arti di Udine* 85 (1993): 93–140.

Rubinstein, Nicolai. "Italian reactions to terrafirma expansion in the fifteenth century". *Renaissance Venice*, ed. John R. Hale: 197–217. London: Faber and Faber, 1973.

Rubsamen, Walter. "From frottola to madrigal: the changing pattern of secular Italian vocal music". In *Chanson and Madrigal, 1480–1530: studies in comparison and contrast*, ed. James Haar: 51–87. Cambridge, MA: Harvard University Press, 1964.

———. "The Justiniane or Veneziane of the fifteenth century". *Acta musicologica* 29 (1957): 172–185.

———. *Literary sources of secular music in Italy (ca 1500)*. University of California Publications in Music 1. Berkeley and Los Angeles: University of California Press, 1943.

———. "Music research in Italian libraries". *Notes* 6 (1948–1949): 220–233 and 543–569; 8 (1950–1951): 513

Rummonds, Richard-Gabriel. *Printing on the Iron Handpress*. New Castle, DE: Oak Knoll; London: British Library, 1998.

Ruysschaert, José. "Les différents colophons de l'*Antiquae urbis Romae cum regionibus simulachrum* de 1532". *Contributi alla storia del libro italiano: miscellanea in onore di Lamberto Donati*, ed. Roberto Ridolfi: 287–290. Biblioteca di bibliografia italiana 57. Florence: Olschki, 1969.

Sadie, Stanley, ed. *The New Grove Dictionary of music and musicians*. London: Macmillan, 1980: 2nd ed., 2001.

Sadoleto, Jacopo. *Epistolae Leonis X. Clementis VII. Pauli III. nomine scripte*. Rome: Generosus Salomonius, 1759.

Sampaio Ribeiro, Mário de. *Livraria de mùsica de el-rei D. João IV: estudo musical, histórico e bibliográfico*. Lisbon: Academia Portuguesa da História, 1967.

———. *Os manuscritos musicais n^as 6 e 12 da Biblioteca Geral da Universidade de Coimbra (Contribuiçao para um catálogo definitivo)*. Archegas para a História da Música em Portugal 5. Coimbra: Biblioteca Geral da Universidade de Coimbra, 1941.

Sander, Max. *Le livre à figures italien depuis 1467 jusqu'a 1530*. Milan: Hoepli, 1942–1943.

Sanuto, Mario. *I Diarii*, ed. Rinaldo Fulin *et al.*. Venice: Visentini, 1879–1903; rpt. Bologna: Forni, 1969–1970.

Sartori, Claudio. *Bibliografia della musica strumentale italiana stampata in Italia fino al 1700*. Biblioteca di bibliografia italiana 23 and 66. Florence: Olschki, 1952, 1968.

———. *Bibliografia delle opere musicali stampate da Ottaviano Petrucci*. Biblioteca di bibliografia italiana 18. Florence: Olschki, 1948: rpt. 2001.

———. *La Cappella musicale del Duomo di Milano: catalogo delle musiche dell'Archivio*. Milan: Veneranda Fabbrica del Duomo di Milano, 1957.

———. *Commemorazione di Ottaviano de' Petrucci, Conferenza tenuta a Fossombrone il 16. Ottobre 1966*. Fossombrone: Bartoloni & Aiudi, 1968.

———. *Dizionario degli editori musicali italiani (tipografi, incisori, librai-editori)*. Biblioteca di bibliografia italiana 32. Florence: Olschki, 1958.

———. "La famiglia degli editori Scotto". *Acta musicologica* 36 (1964): 19–30.

———. "A little known Petrucci publication: the second book of lute tablature by Francesco Bossinensis". *The Musical Quarterly* 34 (1948): 234–245.

———. "Nuove conclusione aggionte alla 'Bibliografia del Petrucci' ". *Collectanea historiae musicae* 1: 175–210. Biblioteca historiae musicae cultores 2. Florence: Olschki, 1953

———. "Precisazioni bibliografiche sulle opere di Girolamo Cavazzzoni". *Rivista musicale italiana* 44 (1940): 359–366.

———. "Il quarto codice di Gaffurio non è del tutto scomparso". *Biblioteca historiae musicae cultores* 2 = *Collectanea historiae musicae*, 1: 25–44. Florence: Olschki, 1953.

Scapecchi, Piero. "New light on the Ripoll edition of the *Expositio* of Donato Acciaioli". In *The Italian book, 1465–1800: studies presented to Dennis E. Rhodes on his 70th birthday*, ed. Denis V. Reidy: 31–33. London: British Library, 1993.

Schaal, Richard. "Die Musikbibliothek von Raimond Fugger". *Acta Musicologica* 29 (1957): 126–137.

———. *Das Inventar der Kantorei St. Anna in Augsburg: ein Beitrag zur protestantischen Musikpflege im 16. und beginnenden 17. Jahrhundert.* Catalogus Musicus 3. Kassel: Bärenreiter for the IAML and IMS, 1965.

Schavran, Henrietta. "The Manuscript Pavia, Biblioteca Universitaria, Codice Aldini 362: a study of song tradition in Italy circa 1440–1480". Ph.D.diss., New York University, 1978.

Schering, Arnold, ed. *Geschichte der Musik in Beispielen.* Leipzig: Breitkopf und Härtel, 1931; rpt. New York: Broude, [1950].

Scherliess, Volker. *Musikalische Noten auf Kunstwerken der italienischen Renaissance.* Hamburger Beiträge zur Musikwissenschaft 8. Hamburg: Wagner, 1972.

Schlagel, Stephanie. "Josquin des Prez and his motets: a case study in sixteenth-century reception history". Ph.D. diss., University of North Carolina at Chapel Hill, 1996.

Schmid, Anton. *Ottaviano dei Petrucci da Fossombrone, der erste Erfinder des Musiknotendruckes mit beweglichen Metalltypen und seine Nachfolger im sechzehnten Jahrhunderts.* Vienna: Rohrmann, 1845; rpt. Amsterdam: Grüner, 1968.

Schmidt, Henry Louis. "The first printed lute books: Francesco Spinacino's *Intabulatura de lauto, libro primo* and *libro secondo* (Venice: Petrucci, 1507)". Ph.D. diss., University of North Carolina at Chapel Hill, 1969.

Schmidt-Görg, J. "Vertrag einer römischen Musikdruckerei aus dem Jahre 1536". *Der Musikalienhandel* 7 (1956): 96–98.

Schmieder, Wolfgang, and Gisela Hartwieg. *Kataloge der Herzog-August-Bibliothek Wolfenbüttel. Die neue Reihe. XII. Musik. Ältere Drucke bis etwa 1750.* Frankfurt am Main: Klosterman, 1967.

Schneider, Matthias, intro. *Collection of German, French and instrumental pieces: Wien, Österreichische Nationalbibliothek MS 18 810* [facsimile]. Peer: Alamire, 1987.

Schneider, Max. "Eine unbekannte Lautentabulatur aus den Jahren 1537–1544". *Musikwissenschaftliche Beiträge. Festschrift für Johannes Wolf zu seinem sechzigsten Geburtstag,* ed. Walter Lott, Hellmut Osthoff and W. Wolffheim: 176–178. Berlin: Breslauer, 1929.

Schnoebelen, Anne. *Padre Martini's collection of letters in the Civico Museo Bibliografico Musicale in Bologna.* Annotated reference tools in music 2. New York: Pendragon, 1979.

Scholderer, Victor. "Citius quam asparagi coquuntur". *Gutenberg Jahrbuch 1931:* 107–108.

———. "A Fleming in Venetia: Gerardus de Lisa, printer, bookseller, schoolmaster, and musician". *The Library,* Ser.4, 10 (1930): 252–273; rpt. in *Fifty essays in fifteenth- and sixteenth-century bibliography,* ed. Dennis E. Rhodes: 113–125. Amsterdam: Hertzerberger, 1966.

———. "A further note on red printing in early books". *Gutenberg-Jahrbuch 1959:* 59–60; rpt. in *Fifty essays in fifteenth- and sixteenth-century bibliography,* ed. Dennis E. Rhodes: 267–268. Amsterdam: Hertzerberger, 1966.

———. *Greek printing types, 1465–1527.* London: The Trustees of the British Museum, 1927; rpt. Thessaloniki: Mastoridis, 1995.

———. "Printers and readers in Italy in the fifteenth century". *Proceedings of the British Academy* 35 (1949): 25–47.

———. "Printing at Ferrara in the fifteenth century". *Gutenberg-Jahrbuch, 1925:* 73–78; rpt. in *Fifty essays in fifteenth- and sixteenth-century bibliography,* ed. Dennis E. Rhodes: 91–95. Amsterdam: Hertzerberger, 1966.

———. "Red printing in early books". *Gutenberg-Jahrbuch 1958:* 105–107; rpt. in *Fifty essays in fifteenth- and sixteenth-century bibliography,* ed. Dennis E. Rhodes: 265–267. Amsterdam: Hertzerberger, 1966.

———. "The shape of early type". *Gutenberg-Jahrbuch 1927:* 24–25; rpt. in *Fifty essays in fifteenth- and sixteenth-century bibliography,* ed. Dennis E. Rhodes: 24–25. Amsterdam: Hertzerberger, 1966.

Schottenlohr, Karl. "Die Druckprivilegien des 16. Jahrhunderts". *Gutenberg-Jahrbuch 1933:* 89–110.

Schrade, Leo. "Ein Beitrag zur Geschichte der Tokkata". *Zeitschrift für Musikwissenschaft* 8 (1925–1926): 610–635.

Schreurs, Eugeen. "Mijn hert altijt heeft verlanghen as a model". Forthcoming.

———. "Newly-Discovered Fragments of a Late fifteenth-century songbook: an early source in score notation". In *Musicology and Archival Research. Musicologie et recherches en archives. Musicologie en Archiefonderzoek*, ed. Barbara Haggh, Frank Daelemans, and André Vanrie: 487–509. Archives et Bibliothèques de Belgique. Archief- en Bibliotheekwezen in Belgie 46. Brussels, Archives générales du Royaume, 1994.

Schreurs, Eugeen, ed. *Anthologie van muziekfragmenten uit de Lage Landen (Middeleuwen— Renaissance): polyfonie, monodie et leisteenfragmenten in facsimile. An Anthology of music fragments from the Low Countries (Middle Ages—Renaissance): polyphony, monophony and slate fragments in facsimile.* Peer: Alamire, 1995.

Schröder, Otto. "Das Eisenacher Cantorenbuch". *Zeitschrift für Musikwissenschaft* 14 (1931–1932): 173–178.

Schullian, Dorothy, and Curt Bühler. "A misprinted sheet in the 1479 'Mammotrectus super Bibliam' (Goff M.239)". *Papers of the Bibliographical Society of America* 61 (1967): 51–52.

Schwartz, Rudolf. "Zum Formenproblemen der Frottole Petruccis". In *Theodor Kroyer-Festschrift zum sechzigsten Geburtstage*, ed. Herman Zenk: 77–85. Regensburg: Bosse, 1933.

———. "Die Frottole im 15. Jahrhundert". *Vierteljahrschrift für Musikwissenschaft* 2 (1886): 427–466.

———. "Nochmals 'Die Frottole im 15. Jahrhundert' ". *Jahrbuch der Musikbibliothek Peters* 31 (1924): 47–60.

Schwartz, Rudolf, ed. *Ottaviano Petrucci: Frottole, Buch I und IV*. Publikationen älterer Musik 8. Leipzig: Breitkopf und Härtel, 1935.

Seay, Albert, ed. *Pierre Attaingnant: transcriptions of chansons for keyboard (1531)*. Corpus mensurabilis musicae 20. s.l.: American Institute of Musicology, 1961.

Self, Stephen, ed. *The si placet repertoire of 1480–1530*. Recent Researches in Music of the Renaissance 106. Madison: A-R Editions, 1996.

Selfridge-Field, Eleanor. "Vivaldi and Marcello: clues to provenance and chronology". In *Nuovi studi Vivaldiani: edizione e cronologia, critica delle opere*, ed. Antonio Fanna and Giovanni Morelli: 785–800. Florence: Olschki, 1988.

Selwyn, David. *The Library of Thomas Cranmer*. Oxford: Oxford University Press, 1996.

Senn, Walter. "Das Sammelwerk 'Quinquagena Carminum' aus der Offizin Peter Schöffers d.J.". *Acta Musicologica* 35 (1964): 183–185.

Sermisy, Claudin de. *Opera omnia*, ed. Gaston Allaire and Isabel Cazeaux. Corpus mensurabilis musicae 52. s.l.: American Institute of Musicology, 1970–1986.

Serra-Zanetti, A. *L'arte della stampa in Bologna nel primo ventennio del Cinquecento*. Biblioteca de "L'Archiginasio", n.s., 1. Bologna, 1959.

Serrai, Alfredo. *Storia della Bibliografia*, vol.4. Rome: Bulzoni, 1993.

Servolini, Alfredo. "Le edizioni fanesi di Girolamo Soncino". *Gutenberg-Jahrbuch 1957*: 110–115.

Servolini, Luigi. "L'arte tipografico in Urbino". *Gutenberg-Jahrbuch 1937*: 183–186.

———. "Eustachio Celebrino da Udine: intagliatore, calligrafo, poligrafo ed editore del sec.XVI". *Gutenberg-Jahrbuch 1944–1949*: 179–189.

Sevillano, J. "Catálogo musical del Archivio capitular de Tarazona". *Anuario musical* 16 (1961): 149–176.

Shakespeare, William. *Much Ado about Nothing*, ed. Charlton Hinman. Shakespeare Quarto Facsimiles 15. Oxford: Clarendon, 1971.

Sherr, Richard. "*Illibata Dei virgo nutrix* and Josquin's Roman style" *Journal of the Americna Musicological Society* 41 (1988): 434–64; rpt. as ch.VIII in *Music and Musicians in Renaissance Rome and other courts*. Aldershot: Ashgate, 1999.

———. "Josquin's Red Nose". In *Essays on Music and Culture in honor of Herbert Kellman*, ed. Barbara Haggh: 209–240. Paris: Minerve, 2001.

———. "Notes on two Roman manuscripts of the early sixteenth century". *The Musical Quarterly* 63 (1977): 48–73.

———. "The Papal Chapel ca.1492–1513 and its polyphonic sources". Ph.D. diss., Princeton University, 1975.

———. *Papal music manuscripts in the late fifteenth and early sixteenth centuries.* Renaissance music manuscripts 5. Neuhausen: Hänssler, 1996.

———. "The relationship between a Vatican copy of the Gloria of Josquin's Missa de Beata Virgine and Petrucci's print". *Atti del XIV congresso della Società Internazionale di Musicologia, Bologna, 1997: trasmissione e recezione delle forme di cultura musicale* (Turin, Edizioni di Torino, 1990): ii, 266–71; rpt. as ch.VII in *Music and Musicians in Renaissance Rome and other courts.* Aldershot: Ashgate, 1999.

———. "Speculations on repertory, performance practice, and ceremony in the Papal Chapel in the early sixteenth century". In *Collectanea II: Studien zur Geschichte der Päpstlichen Kapelle: Tagungsbericht Heidelberg 1989,* ed. Bernhard Janz: 103–123. Capellae Apostolicae Sixtinaeque Collectanea Acta Monumenta 4. Città del Vaticano: Biblioteca Apostolica Vaticana, 1994; rpt. as ch.XII in *Music and Musicians in Renaissance Rome and other courts.* Aldershot: Ashgate, 1999.

———. "Verdelot in Florence, Coppini in Rome, and the singer "La Fiore"". *Journal of the American Musicological Society* 37 (1984): 402–411; rpt. as ch.XIX in *Music and Musicians in Renaissance Rome and other courts.* Aldershot: Ashgate, 1999.

Sherr, Richard, ed. *Papal music and musicians in late medieval and renaissance Rome.* Oxford: Oxford University Press, 1998.

———. *The Sixteenth-Century motet: previously unpublished full scores of major works from the Renaissance in thirty volumes.* New York: Garland, 1991–.

i: *Selections from Motetti A numero trentatre (Venice, 1502).*

ii: *Selections from Motetti C (Venice, 1504).*

iii: *Selections from Motetti Libro quarto (Venice, 1505).*

iv: *Selections from Motetti de la Corona [Libro Primo] (Fossombrone, 1514).*

v: *Selections from Motetti de la Corona [Libro Secundo] (Fossombrone, 1519): Motetti de la Corona [Libro Tertio] (Fossombrone, 1519): Motetti de la Corona [Libro Quarto] (Fossombrone, 1519).*

Shine, Josephine. "The motets of Jean Mouton". Ph.D. diss., New York University, 1953.

Shipp, Clifford M. "A chansonnier of the Dukes of Lorraine: the Paris manuscript fonds français 1597". Ph.D. diss., North Texas State University, 1960.

Siegele, Ulrich. *Die Musiksammlung der Stadt Heilbronn: Katalog mit Beiträgen zur Geschichte der Sammlung und zur Quellenkunde des XVI. Jahrhunderts.* Veröffentlichungen des Archivs der Stadt Heilbronn 13. Heilbronn: Stadtarchiv, 1967.

Silbiger, Alexander. "An unknown early partbook of early sixteenth-century polyphony". *Studi musicali* 6 (1977): 43–67.

Silva, Andreas de. *Opera Omnia,* ed. Winfried Kirsch. Corpus mensurabilis musicae 49. s.l.: American Institute of Musicology, 1970–1971.

Simpson, Percy. *Proof-reading in the sixteenth, seventeenth and eighteenth centuries.* London: Oxford University Press, 1935.

Slavin, Denis. "On the origins of Escorial IV.a.24 (EscB)". *Studi musicali* 19 (1990): 260–303.

Slim, H. Colin. "Dosso Dossi's allegory at Florence about music". *Journal of the American Musicological Society* 43 (1990): 43–98.

———. "Gian and Gian Maria: some fifteenth-century namesakes", *The Musical Quarterly* 57 (1971): 562–574.

———. *A gift of madrigals and motets.* Chicago: University of Chicago Press, 1972.

———. "Keyboard music at Castell'Arquato by an early madrigalist". *Journal of the American Musicological Society* 15 (1962): 35–47.

———. "The keyboard ricercar and fantasia in Italy, *c.*1500–1550, with reference to parallel forms in European lute music of the same period". Ph.D. diss., Harvard University, 1960.

———. "The Music Library of the Augsburg Patrician, Hans Heinrich Herwart (1520–1583)". *Annales musicologiques* 7 (1964–1977): 67–109.

———. "Musical inscriptions in paintings by Caravaggio and his followers". In *Music and Context: essays for John M. Ward*, ed. Anne Dhu Shapiro: 241–263. Cambridge, MA: Department of Music, Harvard University, 1985.

———. "Musicians on Parnassus, *Studies in the Renaissance* 12 (1965): 134–163.

———. *The Prodigal Son at the whores': music, art and drama.* Distinguished Faculty Lecture 1. Irvine: University of California at Irvine, 1977.

———. "Spinacino, Francesco", *The New Grove*, 18, 832.

Smeijers, Fred. *Counterpunch: making type in the sixteenth century, designing typefaces now.* London: Hyphen Press, 1996.

Smijers, Albert. "Twee onbekende motetteksten van Jacob Obrecht". *Tijdschrift van de Vereniging voor nederlandse Muziekgeschiedenis* 16 (1940–1946): 129–134.

———. "Meerstemmige muziek van de Illustre Lieve Vrouwe Broederschap te 's-Hertogenbosch". *Tijdschrift van de Vereniging voor nederlandse Muziekgeschiedenis* 16 (1940–1946): 1–30.

———. "Vijftiende en zestiende eeuwste muziekhandschriften in Italië met werken van nederlandsche componisten". *Tidschrift van de Vereniging voor nederlandse Muziekgeschiedenis* 14 (1932–1935): 165–181.

Smijers, Albert, ed. *Van Ockeghem tot Sweelinck.* Amsterdam: Alsbach, 1949–1956.

Smith, Jeremy L. "The Hidden editions of Thomas East". *Notes* 53 (1996–1997): 1059–1091.

———. "Watermark evidence and the hidden editions of Thomas East". In *Puzzles in Paper: concepts in historical watermarks*, ed. Daniel W. Mosser, Michael Saffle, and Ernest W. Sullivan: 67–80. New Castle, DE: Oak Knoll Press; and London: The British Library, 2000.

Smith, Margaret M. *The TItle-Page: its early development, 1460–1510.* London: The British Library; and New Castle, DE: Oak Knoll Press, 2000.

Smith, William Liddell. "An Inventory of pre-1600 manuscripts, pertaining to music, in the Bundesstaatliche Studienbibliothek (Linz, Austria)". *Fontes artis musicae* 27 (1980): 162–171.

Smithers, Don. "A textual-musical inventory and concordance of Munich University Ms. 328–331". *Royal Musical Association Research Chronicle* 8 (1970): 34–89.

Snow, Robert J. "Petrucci: Intabulatura de lauto, libro primo [i.e. quarto] Joan Ambrosio Dalza". M.A. thesis, Indiana University, 1955.

———. "Toledo Cathedral MS *Reservado 23*". *The Journal of Musicology* 2 (1983): 246–277.

Sorbelli, Albano. " 'Il Mago che scolpi' i caratteri di Aldo Manuzio: Francesco Griffo da Bologna". *Gutenberg-Jahrbuch 1923*: 117–123.

———. *Storia della stampa in Bologna.* Bologna: Zanichelli, 1929.

Sotheby's auctioneers. *Music including important autographs by Beethoven and Wagner, London Friday 5 December 2003* [catalogue]. London: Sotheby's, 2003.

Southern, Eileen. "El Escorial, Monastery Library, Ms. IV.a.24". *Musica Disciplina* 23 (1969): 41–79.

Sparks, Edgar. *Cantus firmus in mass and motet, 1420–1520.* Berkeley and Los Angeles: University of California Press, 1963.

———. *The music of Noel Bauldeweyn.* American Musicological Society Studies and Documents 6. s.l.: American Musicological Society, 1972.

Sparrow, John. "Latin verse of the High Renaissance". In *Italian Renaissance Studies*, ed. E.F. Jacob: 354–409. London: Faber and Faber, 1960.

Spinacino, Francesco. *Intabulatura de Lauto Libro Primo (Venice: Petrucci 1507)* [facsimile]. Geneva: Minkoff 1978.

———. *Intabulatura de Lauto Libro Secondo (Venice: Petrucci 1507)* [facsimile]. Geneva: Minkoff 1978.

Springer, Hermann. "Zur Musiktypographie in der Inkunabelzeit". In *Beiträge zur Bücher-*

kunde und Philologie: August Wilmanns zum 25. März 1903 gewidmet: 173–180. Leipzig: Harrassowitz, 1903.

Staehelin, Martin. "Das Augsburger Fragment". *Augsburger Jahrbuch für Musikwissenschaft* 4 (1987): 7–63.

———. "Zum Egenolff-Diskantband der Bibliothèque nationale in Paris". *Archiv für Musikwissenschaft* 23 (1966): 93–109.

———. "Eine Florentiner Musik-Handschrift aus der Zeit um 1500 (Quellenkundliche Bemerkungen zur Frottola-Sammlung Ms. Egerton 3051 des British Museum und zum 'Wolffheim-Manuscskript' der Library of Congress)". *Schweizer Beiträge zur Musikwissenschaft*, Ser.3, 1 (1973): 55–81.

———. *Der Grüne Codex der Viadrina: eine wenig beachtete Quelle zur Musik des späten 15. und frühen 16. Jahrhunderts in Deutschland*. Akademie der Wissenschaften und der Literatur: Abhandlungen der Geistes- und Sozialwissenschaftlichen Klasse. Jahrgang 1970, No.10. Mainz: Verlag der Akademie der Wissenschaften und der Literatur, 1970.

———. *Die Messen Heinrich Isaacs*. Publikationen der schweizerischen musikforschenden Gesellschaft, Ser.2, 28. Bern: Haupt, 1977.

———. "Obrechtiana". *Tidschrift van de Vereniging voor Nederlandse Muziekgeschiedenis* 25 (1975): 1–37.

———. "Quellenkundliche Beitrag zum Werk von Johannes Ghiselin-Verbonnet". *Archiv für Musikwissenschaft* 24 (1967): 120–132.

———. "Zur Rezeption und Wirkungsgeschichte der Petrucci-Drucke". *Basler Jahrbuch für historische Musikpraxis* 25 (2002): 13–21.

———. "Zum Schicksal des alten Musikalien-Fonds von San Luigi dei Francesi in Rom". *Fontes artis musicae* 17 (1970): 120–127.

———. "Eine wenig beachtete Gruppe von Chorbüchern aus der erste Hälfte des 16. Jahrhunderts". *Report of the eleventh congress [of the I.M.S.] Copenhagen 1972*: ii, 664–668. Copenhagen: Hansen, 1974.

Stam, Edward. "Josquins Proportionskanon *Agnus Dei* und dessen piacentiner Überlieferung". *Tijdschrift van de Vereniging voor Nederlandse Muziekgeschiedenis* 26 (1976): 1–8.

Steele, John. "Antonio Barré: madrigalist, anthologist and publisher—some prelimiary findings". In *Altro Polo, Essays on Italian music in the Cinquecento*, ed. Richard Charteris: 82–112. Sydney: Frederick May Foundation for Italian Studies, University of Sydney, 1990.

Stenzl, Jurg. "Das Musikheft des Simon Zmutt von Sitten". *Schweizerische Beiträge zur Musikwissenschaft* 1 (1972): 115–132.

Steude, Wolfram. *Die Musik-Handschriften des 16. und 17. Jahrhunderts in der Sächsischen Landesbibliothek zu Dresden*. Quellenkataloge zur Musikgeschichte 6. Leipzig: VEB Deutscher Verlag für Musik, 1975.

Stevens, John, ed. *Music at the Court of Henry VIII*. Musica Britannica 28. London: Stainer and Bell, 1962.

Stevens, Kevin, and Paul Gehl. "The Eye of commerce: visual literacy among the makers of books in Italy". In *The Art Maket in Italy, 15th–17th Centuries: il Mercato dell'Arte in Italia, Secc. xv–xvii*, ed. Marcello Fantoni, Louisa Matthew and Sara Matthews-Grieco: 273–81. Ferrara: Panini, 2003.

Stevenson, Allan. "Chain-indentations in paper as evidence". *Studies in Bibliography* 6 (1954): 181–195.

———. "New uses of watermarks as bibliographical evidence". *Studies in Bibliography* 1 (1948–1949): 151–182.

———. "Paper as bibliographical evidence". *The Library*, Ser.5, 17 (1962): 197–212.

———. "Watermarks are twins". *Studies in Bibliography* 4 (1951–1952): 57–91.

Stevenson, Robert. "Josquin in the music of Spain and Portugal". In *Josquin des Pres: Proceedings of the International Josquin Festival-Conference held at the Julliard School at Lincoln Center in New York City, 21–25 June 1971*, ed. Edward E. Lowinsky with Bonnie J. Blackburn: 217–246. London: Oxford University Press, 1976.

————. *Renaissance and baroque musical sources in the Americas*. Washington: Organization of American States, 1970.

————. *Spanish music in the age of Columbus*. The Hague: Nijhoff, 1960.

————. "The Toledo manuscript polyphonic choirbooks and some other lost or little known Flemish sources". *Fontes artis musicae* 20 (1973): 87–107.

Steyn, Carol, ed. *The Medieval and Renaissance Manuscripts in the Grey Collection of the National Library of South Africa, Cape Town*. Analecta Cartusiana 180. Salzburg: Institut für Anglistik und Amerikanistik, 2002.

Strohm, Reinhard. "European politics and the distribution of music in the early fifteenth century". *Early Music History* 1 (1981): 305–323.

————. *Music in late medieval Bruges*. Oxford: Clarendon, 1985.

————. "Native and foreign polyphony in late medieval Austria". *Musica Disciplina* 28 (1984): 205–230.

————. *The rise of European music, 1380–1500*. Cambridge: Cambridge University Press, 1993.

————. "Ein Unbekanntes Chorbuch des 15. Jahrhunderts". *Die Musikforschung* 21 (1968): 40–42.

Struik, Dirk Jan. "Paulus van Middelburg, 1445–1533". *Medeelingen van het Nederlandsch historisch Instituut te Rome* 5 (1925): 79–118.

Sutherland, David A., ed. *The Lyons Contrapunctus (1528)*. Recent Researches in the Music of the Renaissance 21–22. Madison, WI: A-R Editions, 1976.

Tanselle, G. Thomas. "The Arrangement of descriptive bibliographies". *Studies in Bibliography* 37 (1984): 1–38.

————. "The bibliographical concepts of *Issue* and *State*". *Papers of the Bibliographical Society of America* 69 (1975): 17–66.

————. "The bibliographical description of paper". *Studies in Bibliography* 24 (1971): 27–67.

————. "The concept of *Ideal copy*". *Studies in Bibliography* 33 (1980): 18–53.

————. "The identification of type faces in bibliographical description". *Paper of the Bibliographical Society of America* 40 (1966): 185–202; rpt. in the *Journal of Typographic Research* 1 (1967): 427–447.

————. "Printing history and other history". *Studies in Bibliography* 48 (1995): 269–289.

————. "A sample bibliographical description, with commentary". *Studies in Bibliography* 40 (1987): 1–30.

————. "Title-page transcription and signature collation reconsidered". *Studies in bibliography* 38 (1985): 45–81.

————. "The use of type damage as evidence in bibliographical description". *The Library*, Ser.5, 23 (1968): 328–351. See also 24 (1969): 251.

Taricani, JoAnn. "A Renaissance Bibliophile as Musical Patron: the Evidence of the Herwart Sketchbooks". *Notes* 49 (1993): 1357–1389.

Taruskin, Richard. "Settling an old score: a note on contrafactum in Isaac's Lorenzo lament". *Current musicology* 21 (1976): 83–92.

Taruskin, Richard, ed. *D'ung aulter amer*. Ogni Sorte Editions, RS, 6. Miami: Grayson, 1983.

————. *Een vrolic wesen*. Ogni Sorte, RS, 2. Miami: Grayson, 1979.

————. *In mynen zin*. Ogni Sorte, RS, 8. Miami: Grayson, 1984.

————. *J'ay pris amours*. Ogni Sorte, RS, 5. Miami: Grayson, 1982.

————. *O venus bant*. Ogni Sorte, RS, 3. Miami: Grayson, 1979.

————. *T'Andernaken*. Ogni Sorte, RS, 7. Miami: Grayson, 1981.

Tebaldini, Giovanni. *L'archivio musicale della Capella Antoniana in Padova*. Padua: Libreria Antoniana, 1895.

Teramoto, Mariko. *Die Psalmmotettendrucke des Johannes Petrejus in Nürnberg (gedruckt 1538–1543)*. Frankfurter Beiträge für Musikwissenschaft 10. Tutzing: Schneider, 1983.

Teramoto, Mariko, and Armin Brinzing. *Katalog der Musikdrucke des Johannes Petreius in Nürnberg*. Catalogus Musicus 14. Kassel: Bärenreiter, 1993.

Thibault, Geneviève. "Les collections privées de livres et d'instruments de musique d'autrefois et d'aujourd'hui". In *Music Libraries and Instruments: papers read at the joint congress, Cambridge, 1959, of the International Association of Music Libraries and the Galpin Society*, ed. Unity Sherrington and Guy Oldham: 131–147. Hinrichsen's Music Books 11. London: Hinrichsen, 1961.

———. "Instrumental transcriptions of Josquin's French chansons". In *Josquin des Pres: Proceedings of the International Josquin Festival-Conference held at the Julliard School at Lincoln Center in New York City, 21–25 June 1971*, ed. Edward E. Lowinsky with Bonnie J. Blackburn: 454–474. London: Oxford University Press, 1976.

———. "Un manuscrit italien pour luth des premières années du XVIe siècle". In *Le luth et sa musique*, ed. Jean Jacquot: 43–76. Colloques internationaux du Centre national de la recherche scientifique 511. Paris: Centre national de la recherche scientifique, 1958/

———. "Notes et documents de la vogue de quelques livres français à Venise". *Humanisme et renaissance* 2 (1935): 61–65.

Thibault, Geneviève, and David Fallows, eds. *Chansonnier de Jean de Montchenu*. Publications de la Société française de musicologie, Ser.1, 23. Paris: Société française de musicologie, 1991.

Thomas, Elmer. "Two Petrucci prints of polyphonic Lamentations, 1506". Ph.D. diss., University of Illinois, 1970.

Thomas, Jennifer S. "The Sixteenth-Century motet: a comprehensive survey of the repertory, and case studies of the core texts, composers and repertory". Ph.D. diss., University of Cincinnati, 1999.

Thorpe, James. *Principles of textual criticism*. San Marino, CA: The Huntington Library, 1972.

Thürlings, Adolf. "Der Musikdruck mit beweglichen Metalltypen im 16. Jahrhundert und die Musikdrucke des Mathias Apiarius in Strassburg und Bern". *Vierteljahrschrift für Musikwissenschaft* 8 (1892): 389–418.

Tiersot, Julien. "Les livres de Petrucci". *Revue de musicologie* 7 (1926): 18–27.

Timpanaro, Sebastiano. *La genesi del metodo del Lachmann*. Bibliotechina del Saggiatore 28. Florence: Le Monnier, 1963.

Tinctoris, Johannes. *Opera Omnia*, ed. William Melin. Corpus mensurabilis musicae 18. s.l.: American Institute of Musicology, 1976.

———. *Opera Theoretica*, ed. Albert Seay. Corpus scriptorum de musica 22. s.l.: American Institute of Musicology, 1975.

Tirro, Frank. *Renaissance musical sources in the Archive of San Petronio in Bologna*. Renaissance Manuscript Studies 4. s.l.: American Institute of Musicology; and Neuhausen-Stuttgart: Hänssler, 1986.

Titcomb, Caldwell. "The Josquin acrostic re-examined". *Journal of the American Musicological Society* 16 (1963): 47–60.

Todd, William B. "Aldine anchors, initials and the 'counterfeit' Cicero". *Papers of the Bibliographical Society of America* 60 (1966): 413–417.

Toffetti, Marina. " 'Che detti Iacomo, et Georgio [. . .] siano obligati stampare': un inedito contratto fra la Veneranda Fabbrica del Duomo e i Rolla editori a Milano". *Le fonti musicali in Italia: Studi e ricerche* 7 (1993): 9–20.

Tonini, Luigi. "Sulle officine tipografiche riminesi". *Atti e memorie della R. Deputazione di storia patria per le provincie di Romagna* 4 (1866): 139.

Tonto, A. "I tipi della Stamperia del Popolo Romano (1561–1570)". *Gutenberg-Jahrbuch 1967*: 26–38.

Torchi, Luigi. "I monumenti dell'antica musica francese a Bologna". *Rivista musicale italiana* 13 (1906): 451–505 and 575–615.

Torchi, Luigi, ed. *L'Arte musicale in Italia*. Milan: Ricordi, 1897–1908; rpt. 1968.

Tordi, Domenico. "La stampa in Orvieto nei secoli XVI e XVII". *Bollettino della Regia Deputazione di Storia Patria per l'Umbria* 6 (1900): 183–230; 7 (1901): 247–283.

Torelli, P.P. "Sulle antiche memorie di Castel Durante". In G. Colucci, *Delle antichità Picene* 13. Fermo: Paccaroni, 1786–97; rpt. s.l., Maroni, 1988.

Torrefranco, Fausto. *Il segreto del Quattrocento*. Milan: Hoepli, 1939.

Torricelli, Francescomaria. *Antologia Oratoria poetica e storica dall'edito e dall'inedito*. Fossombrone: Farina, 1843–1846.

Traljič, S. M. "Prve kontramarke u talijanskom papiru prema materijalu iz naših archiva [The earliest countermarks in Italian papers preserved in our archives]". *Zbornik Historijskog Instituta Jugoslavenske Akademije* 2 (1959): 151–165.

Trend, John. "Musikschätze aus spanischen Bibliotheken". *Zeitschrift für Musikwissenschaft* 6 (1925–1926): 499–504.

Tromonin, K. *Tromonin's Watermark Album: a fascimile of the Moscow 1844 edition*. Hilversum: Paper Publications Society, 1965.

Trovato, Paolo. "Notes on standard language, grammar books and printing in Italy, 1470–1550". *Rivista Schifanoia* 2 (1991): 84–95.

———. "Per un Censimento dei manoscritti di tipografia in volgare (1470–1600)". In *Il libro di poesia dal copista al tipografo (Ferrara, 29–31 maggio 1987)*, ed. Marco Santagata and Amedeo Quondam: 43–81. Modena: Pannini, [1989].

Tschichold, Jan. "Non-arbitrary proportions of page and type area". In *Calligraphy and Palaeography: essays presented to Alfred Fairbank on his seventieth birthday*, ed. A.S. Osley. London: Faber and Faber, 1965.

Tucci, Ugo. "The psychology of the Venetian merchant in the sixteenth century". In *Renaissance Venice*, ed. John R. Hale: 346–378. London: Faber and Faber, 1973.

Turrini, Giuseppe. *L'Accademia Filarmonica di Verona dalla fondazione (maggio 1543) al 1600 e il suo patrimonio musicale antico*. Verona: La tipografia Veronese, 1941.

———. *Catalogo delle opere musicali: Città di Verona, Biblioteca della Soc. Accademia Filarmonica di Verona*. Bibliotheca musica Bononiensis, Sez.I, 18. Bologna: Forni, 1983.

———. "Il patrimonio musicale della Biblioteca Capitolare di Verona dal sec. XV al XIX". *Atti dell'Accademia d'Agricoltura, Scienze e Lettere di Verona*, ser.6, 11 (1953): 95–176.

Ugolini, Filippo. *Storia dei conti e duchi d'Urbino*, vol.2. Florence: Grazzini, Giannini & C., 1859.

Ulivoni, Paolo. "Stampatori e librai a Venezia nel Seicento". *Archivio Veneto*, ser.5, 109 (1977): 93–124.

Ullman, Berthold L. *The Origin and Development of Humanistic Script*. Storia e Letteratura, Raccolta di Studi e Testi 79. Rome: Edizioni di Storia e Letteratura, 1960.

Ullman, Berthold L, and Philip A Stadter. *The Public Library of Renaissance Florence: Niccolò Niccoli, Cosimo de'Medici and the Library of San Marco*. Medioevo e Umanesimo 10. Padua: Antenore, 1972.

Underwood, Kent. "The Renaissance lute in solo song and chamber ensemble: an examination of musical sources to ca.1530". Ph.D. diss., Stanford University, 1987.

Urkevich, Lisa A. "Anne Boleyn, a Music book, and the northern Renaissance courts: music manuscript 1070 of the Roual College of Music, London". Ph.D. diss., University of Maryland at College Part, 1997.

Vaccaro, Emerenziana. *Le marche dei tipografi ed editori italiani del secolo XVI nella Biblioteca Angelica di Roma*. Biblioteca di bibliografia italiana 98. Florence: Olschki, 1983.

Valentini, Ubaldo, and Giovanni Malusardi. *Incunaboli e Cinquecentine della Biblioteca Capitolare di Milano*. Archivio Ambrosiano 48. Milan: Nuove Edizioni Duomo, 1983.

Valetta. "L'Archivio musicale des S. Convento in Assisi". *La Gazzetta Musicale* 27 (1897).

Van Benthem, Jaap. "The Alamire fragments of the Plantin-Moretus Museum in Antwerp". In *Musicology and Archival Research. Musicologie et recherches en archives. Musicologie en Archiefonderzoek*, ed. Barbara Haggh, Frank Daelemans, and André Vanrie: 542–557. Archives et Bibliothèques de Belgique. Archief- en Bibliotheekwezen in Belgie 46 Brussels, Archives générales du Royaume, 1994.

———. "Einige wiederkannte Josquin-chansons im Codex 18746 der Österreichischen

Nationalbibliothek". *Tijdschrift van der Vereniging voor Nederlands Muziekgeschiedenis* 22 (1971): 18–42.

———. "*Fortuna in focus*: concerning 'conflicting' progressions in Josquin's *Fortuna dun gran tempo*". *Journal of the American Musicological Society* 30 (1980): 1–50.

———. "Josquin's three-part 'chansons rustiques': a critique of the readings in manuscripts and prints". In *Josquin des Pres: Proceedings of the International Josquin Festival-Conference held at the Julliard School at Lincoln Center in New York City, 21–25 June 1971*, ed. Edward E. Lowinsky with Bonnie J. Blackburn: 421–445. London: Oxford University Press, 1976.

———. " 'Kommst in der ersten Kreise!'. Josquin's *Missa L'ami baudichon*-ihre Original-gestalt und ihre Überlieferung in Petruccis *Missarum Josquin Liber Secundus*". *Basler Jahrbuch für historische Musikpraxis* 25 (2002): 71–83.

———. "Kompositorisches Verfahren im Josquins Proportionskanon *Agnus Dei*: Antwort an Edward Stam". *Tijdschrift van der Vereniging voor Nederlandse Muziekgeschiedenis* 26 (1976): 9–16.

———. "Motivik-Konstruktivismus-Humanismus: zu Josquins Motette *Huc me sydereo*". In *Die Motette: Beiträge zu ihrer Gattungsgeschichte*, ed. H. Schneider: 135–164. Neue Studies zur Musikwissenschaft. Mainz: Schott, 1991.

———. "Einige Musikintarsien des frühen 16.Jahrhunderts in Piacenza und Josquins Pro-portionskanon *Agnus Dei*". *Tijdschrift van de Vereniging voor Nederlandse Muziekgeschie-denis* 24 (1974): 97–111.

———. "Zur Struktur und Authentizität der Chansons à5 & 6 von Josquin des Prez". *Tidschrift van der Vereniging voor Nederlandse Muziekgeschiedenis* 20 (1970): 170–188.

———. "A Waif, a wedding and a worshipped child: Josquin's *Ut phebii radiis* and the Order of the Golden Fleece", *Tijdschrift van de Vereniging voor Nederlandse Muziekges-chiedenis* 37 (1987): 64–81.

———. "Was 'Une mousse de Biscaye' really appreciated by L'ami Baudichon", *Muziek en Wetenschap* 1 (1991): 175–194.

Van Campen, Adeline. "Conflicting attributions of *Credo Vilayge II* and *Credo Chascun me crie*". *Proceedings of the International Josquin Symposium, Utrecht 1986*, ed. Willem Elders, with Frits de Haen: 93–98. Utrecht: Vereniging voor Nederlandse Muziekgeschie-denis, 1991.

Van Crevel, Marcus. *Adrianus Petit Coclico. Leben und Beziehungen eines nach Deutschland emigrierten Josquinschülers*. The Hague: Nijhoff, 1940.

Van den Borren, Charles. "A proposito del Codicetto Vatic.lat.11953". *Note d'Archivio* 16 (1939): 17–18.

———. "Inventaire des manuscrits de musique polyphonique qui se trouvent en Bel-gique". *Acta musicologica* 5 (1933): 66–72, 120–127, 177–183; 6 (1934) 23–29, 65–73, 116–121.

Van den Borren, Charles, ed. *Polyphonia sacra: a continental miscellany of the fifteenth century*. London: Plainsong and Medieval Music Society, 1936.

Van der Straeten, Edmond. *La Musique aux Pays-Bas avant le XIXe siècle*. Brussels: Moc-quardt, 1867–1888; rpt. New York: Dover, s.d.

Van Duyse, Florimond. *Het eenstemmig Fransch en Nederlandsch wereldlijk lied in de Belgische gewesten ven de XIe eeuw tot heden*. Ghent, 1896.

———. "Oude Nederlandsche meerstemmige Liederboeken". *Tijdschrift van de Vereniging voor Noord-Nederlandse Muziekgeschiedenis* 3 (1888–1891): 125–175; 5 (1895–1897): 230–243.

Van Leijenhorst, C.G. "Paulus of Middelburg". *Contemporaries of Erasmus: a biographical register of the Renaissance and Reformation*, ed. Peter Bietenholz with Thomas Deutscher 3: 57–8. Toronto: University of Toronto Press, 1987.

Vanhulst, Henri. "Balthasar Bellère, marchand de musique a Douai (1603–1636)", *Revue de musicologie* 84 (1998): 175–198.

———. *Catalogue des Éditions de musique publiées à Louvain par Pierre Phalèse et ses fils, 1545–*

1578. Académie royale de Belgique: Mémoires de la classe des beaux-arts, Collection in-8o, Ser.2, 16. Brussels: Palais des Académies, 1990.

————. "Le contrat d'apprentissage conclu en 1562 entre Pierre Phalèse et Jean Laet". In *From Ciconia to Sweelinck. Donum natalicum Willem Elders*, ed. Albert Clement and Eric Jas: 255–259. Chloe, Beihefte zum Daphnis 21. Amsterdam: Rodopi, 1994.

————. "Plantin et le commerce international des éditions de musique polyphonique 1566–1578", *Revista de Musicolog'a* 16 (1993): 2630–2640.

Vaqueras, Bertrandus. *Opera Omnia*, ed. Richard Sherr. Corpus mensurabilis musicae 78. s.l.: American Institute of Musicology, 1978.

Väterlein, Christian, ed. *Das Glogauer Liederbuch*. Das erbe deutsche Musik 85–6. Kassel: Bärenreiter, 1981.

Vatielli, Francesco. "Una mostra bibliografica nella Biblioteca del Liceo Musicale di Bologna". *La Bibliofilia* 10 (1908): 193.

Vellekoop, Kees. "De Parce Domino-composities van Jacob Obrecht". *Medelingenblad van de Vereniging voor nederlandse Muziekgeschiedenis* 23 (1967): 44–50.

————. "Zusammenhänge zwischen Text und Zahl in der Kompositionsart Jacob Obrecht. Analyse der Motette 'Parce Domine' ". *Tijdschrift van de Vereniging voor nederlandse Muziekgeschiedenis* 20 (1966): 97–119.

Verdelot, Philippe. *Madrigals for four and five voices*, ed. Jessie Ann Owens. Sixteenth-century madrigal: previously unpublished full scores of major works from the Renaissance 28–30. New York: Garland, 1989.

Verdi, Adolfo. *Gli ultimi anni di Lorenzo de' Medici, duca d'Urbino (1515–1519)*. 2nd ed., Este, 1905).

Vernarecci, Augusto. *Fossombrone dai tempo antichissimi*. 2nd ed., Fossombrone: Monacelli, 1914; rpt. Bologna: Forni, 1969.

————. *Ottaviano de' Petrucci da Fossombrone, inventore dei tipi mobili metallici fusi della musica nel secolo XV*. 2nd ed., Bologna: Romagnoli, 1882; rpt. in 1884, and Bologna: Forni, 1971.

Vervliet, Hendrik D. L. "Une Instruction plantinienne à l'intention des correcteurs". *Gutenberg-Jahrbuch 1959*: 99–103.

Veyrin-Forrer, J. "Fabriquer un livre au XVIe siècle". In *Histoire de l'édition française*, ed. H.J. Martin, and R. Chartier. i: 279–301. Paris, 1982.

Villanis, L.A. "Alcuni codici manoscritti di musica del secolo XVI posseduti dalla Biblioteca Nazionale di Torino". In *Atti del Congresso internazionale di scienze storiche: Roma . . . 1–9 Aprile 1903*: 319–360. Rome: Tipografia della R. Accademia dei Lincei, 1905.

Vincenet, Johannes. *The Collected works of Johannes Vincenet (d. ca.1479)*, ed. Bertran Davis. Recent researches in the music of the middle ages and early renaissance 9–10. Madison, WI: A-R Editions, 1978.

Voet, Leon. *The Golden Compasses: a history and evaluation of the printing and publishing activities of the Officina Plantiniana at Antwerp*. Amsterdam: Van Gendt, 1969–1972.

Vogel, Emil. *Bibliothek der gedruckten weltlichen Vocalmusik Italiens aus den Jahren 1500–1700*. Berlin: Haack, 1892; rpt., ed. Alfred Einstein, Hildesheim: Olms, 1962.

————. "Der erste mit beweglichen Metalltypen hergestellte Notendruck". *Jahrbuch der Musikbibliothek Peters* 2 (1895): 47–60.

Vogel, Emil. Alfred Einstein, Claudio Sartori, and François Lesure. *Bibliografia della musica italiana vocale profana pubblicata dal 1500 al 1700*. Geneva: Minkoff, 1977.

Vollhardt, Reinhard. "Bibliographie der Musikwerke in der Ratschulbibliothek zu Zwickau". *Beilage der Monatshefte für Musikgeschichte* 35 (1893) and (1894): *passim*.

Wackernagel, Bettina. *Das Liederbuch des Dr. Hartmann Schedel* [facsimile]. Das Erbe deutsche Musik 84. Kassel: Bärenreiter, 1978.

Wagner, Klaus. "Aldo Manuzio e i prezzi dei suoi libri". *La Bibliofilia* 77 (1975): 77–82.

————. *Catalogo dei libri a stampa in lingua italiana della Biblioteca Colombina di Siviglia*. Modena and Ferrara: Panini, 1991.

Wallner, B.A. *Das Buxheimer Orgelbuch*. [facsimile]. Documenta Musicologica, Ser.2, 1. Kassel: Bärenreiter, 1955.

Warburton, Thomas. "Fridolin Sicher's 'Johannes Zela zons plus': a problem in identity". *Acta musicologica* 55 (1983): 74–89.

Warburton, Thomas, ed. *Keyboard intabulations of music by Josquin des Prez*. Recent researches in the music of the Renaissance 34. Madison, WI: A-R Editions, 1980.

Ward, John. "The Lute Books of Trinity College, Dublin: I. MS D.3.30/I: the so-called Dallis Lute Book". *The Lute Society Journal*, 9 (1967): 19–40.

Ward, Tom R. *The Polyphonic Office Hymn 1400–1520. A Descriptive Catalogue*. Stuttgart: Hänssler, American Institute of Musicology, 1980.

Wardrop, James. *The script of humanism: some aspects of Humanistic script, 1460–1560*. Oxford: Clarendon, 1963.

Waterschoot, Werner. "On ordering the *Poetische Werken* of Jan van der Noot". *Quaerendo* 1 (1971): 242–263.

Wathey, Andrew. "The peace of 1360–1369 and Anglo-French musical relations". *Early Music History* 9 (1990): 129–174.

Weaver, Robert L. *A Descriptive bibliographical catalog of the music printed by Hubert Waelrant and Jan de Laet*. Warren, MI: Harmonie Park, 1994.

——. *Waelrant and Laet: Music publishers in Antwerp's Golden Age*. Warren, MI: Harmonie Park, 1995.

Weckerlin, Jean Baptiste. *Bibliothèque du Conservatoire National de Musique et Déclamation: catalogue bibliographique*. Paris: Firmin-Didot et Cie., 1885.

Weerbeke, Gaspar van. *Messe e motetti*, ed. Gianpiero Tintori. Archivium musices metropolitanum mediolanense 11. Milan: Veneranda Fabbrica del Duomo di Milano, 1963.

Wegman, Rob C. *Born for the Muses: the life and masses of Jacob Obrecht*. Oxford Monographs on Music. London: Oxford University Press, 1994.

——. "Music and musicians at the Guild of Our Lady in Bergen op Zoom, c.1470–1510". *Early Music History* 9 (1990): 175–249.

Weiss, Susan Forscher. "Bologna Q18: some reflections on content and context". *Journal of the American Musicological Society* 41 (1988): 63–101.

——. "The Manuscript Bologna, Civico Museo Bibliografico Musicale, Codex Q18 (olim 143): a Bolognese instrumental collection of the early Cinquecento". Ph.D. diss., University of Maryland, 1985.

Welker, Lorenz. "Instrumentalspiel, instrumentaler Stil und die Instrumentalsätze bei Petrucci". *Basler Jahrbuch für historische Musikpraxis* 25 (2002): 113–26.

——. "Ottaviano Petrucci and the political-cultural elite of his time". Paper read at the conference "Venezia 1501: Petrucci e la stampa musicale", Venice, 10 October 2001.

Wendel, Carl. "Aus der Wiegenzeit des Notendrucks. Ein Bericht über die Geschichte und die Hauptereignisse der Noteninkunabel-Forschung". *Centralblatt für Bibliothekswesen* 19 (1902): 569–581.

Werner, Alajos. "A Szombathely püspöki könyvtár zenei ritkaságai [The musical rarities in the Bishop's library at Szombathely]". *Folia Sabariensia, Vasi Szemle* 4 (1934): 308–314; trans. as Werner, Luigi, "Una rarità musicale della Biblioteca Vescovile di Szombathely". *Note d'Archivio* 8 (1931).

Wesner, Amanda Z. "The chansons of Loyset Compère: authenticity and stylistic development". Ph.D. diss., Harvard University, 1992.

West, Martin L. *Textual criticism and editorial technique applicable to Greek and Latin texts*. Stuttgart: Teubner, 1973.

Wexler, Richard. "The complete works of Johannes Prioris". Ph.D. diss., New York University, 1974.

——. "Music and poetry in Renaissance Cognac". *Le moyen français* 5 (1979): 102–114.

——. "Newly identified works by Bartolomeo degli Organi in the MS Bologna Q 17". *Journal of the American Musicological Society* 23 (1970): 107–118.

Whisler, Bruce Allen. "Munich, Mus. Ms. 1516: a critical edition". Ph.D. diss., University of Rochester, 1974.

White, John R. "The tablature of Johannes of Lublin". *Musica Disciplina* 17 (1963): 137–162.

Willaert, Adrian. *Intavolatura de li Madrigali di Verdelotto.* [facsimile]. Archivum musicum: collana di testi rari 26. Florence: Studio per Edizioni Scelte, 1980.

———. *Opera Omnia*, ed. H. Zenck and Walter Gerstenberg. Corpus Mensurabilis Musicae 3. Rome: American Institute of Musicology, 1950–.

Wilson, Blake. *Music and merchants: the laudesi companies of republican Florence.* Oxford: Clarendon, 1992.

Winkler, Heinz-Jürgen. *Die Tenormotette von Johannes Regis in der Überlieferung des Chigi-Kodex.* Capellae Apostolicae Sixtinaeque Collectanea Acta Monumenta 5. Vatican City: Biblioteca Apostoloica Vaticana; and Tournhout: Brepols, 1999.

Winterfeld, Carl von. *Johannes Gabrieli und sein Zeitalter.* Berlin: Schlesinger, 1834; rpt. Hildesheim: Olms, 1965.

Wolf, Johannes. *Handbuch der Notationskunde.* Leipzig: Breitkopf und Härtel, 1913–1919.

Wolff, Arthur S. "The Chansonnier Biblioteca Casanatense 2856". Ph.D. diss., North Texas State University, 1970.

Wolffheim, Werner. *Versteigerung der Musikbibliothek des Herrn Dr. Werner Wolffheim.* Berlin: Breslauer & Liepmannsohn, 1928–1929.

Woodward, David. *Catalogue of watermarks in Italian printed maps, ca 1540–1600.* Chicago: Chicago University Press, 1996.

Yong, Kwee Him. "Sixteenth-century printed instrumental arrangements of works by Josquin des Pres". *Tijdschrift van de Vereniging voor Nederlandse Muziekgeschiedenis* 22 (1971): 43–66.

Youens, Laura Seale. "Music for the Lutheran Mass: Leipzig, Universitätsbibliothek, MS. Thomaskirche, 49/50". Ph.D. diss., Indiana University, 1978.

Zacconi, Lodovico. *Prattica di musica utile et necessaria.* Venice: Polo, 1592; rpt. Bologna: Forni, 1967.

Zanetti, Emilia, ed. *Cinque Secoli di stampa musicale in Europa.* Naples: Electa, 1985.

Zappella, Giuseppina. *Il Libro antico a stampa: struttura, tecniche, tipologi, evoluzione: parte prima.* I Manuale della Biblioteca 3/i. Milan: Editrice Bibliografica, 2001.

———. *Le marche dei tipografi e degli editori del Cinquecento: repertorio di figure, simboli e soggetti e dei relativi motti* (Milan: Bibliografica, 1986)

Zdekauer, Lodovico. *Fiera e marcato in italia sulla fine del medio evo.* Macerata, 1921.

Ziino, Agostino. "Appunti su una nuova fonte di musica polifonica intorno al 1500". *Nuova rivista musicale italiana* 10 (1976): 437–441.

Zonghi, A., and A. Zonghi. *Zonghi's watermarks.* Monumenta Chartæ Papyraceæ Historiam Illustrantia 3. Hilversum: Paper Publications Society, 1953.

Zorzi, Marino. "La circulazione del libro a Venezia nel Cinquecento: biblioteche private e pubbliche". *Ateneo Veneto* 178 (1990): 117–189.

Zupanovic, Lovro. "La musique Croate du XVIᵉ siècle". In *Musica Antiqua,* ii: 79–126. Bydgoszcz: Bydgoskie towarzystwo naukowe Filharmonia Pomorska im L. Paderewskiego, 1969.

Zupanovic, Lovro, ed. *Sedamnaest frottola [17 frottole].* Spomenici hrvatske glazbene proslosti 3. Zagreb: Drustvo hrvatskih Skladatelja, 1972.

INDEX OF LIBRARIES
HOLDING COPIES OF
PETRUCCI'S EDITIONS

(No.32); Isaac: *Misse* (1506) (No.31); Josquin: *Missarum I* (1516) (No.62); Josquin: *Missarum II* (1515) (No.59); Josquin: *Missarum III* (1514) (No.54); La Rue: *Misse* (1503) (No.11); Mouton: *Missarum I* (1515) (No.60); De Orto: *Misse* (1505) (No.20); Paulus: *Parabola* (1516) (No.63); Paulus: *Paulina* (1513) (No.52, 3 copies); *Lamentationum I* (1506) (No.27); *Lamentationum II* (1506) (No.28); *Missarum diversorum auctorum* (1508) (No.43); *Motetti B* (1503) (No.7); *I Motetti à5* (1508) (No.46); *Motetti C* (1504) (No.15, two copies); *Motetti de la Corona II* (1519) (No.64); *Motetti de la Corona III* (1519) (No.65); *Motetti de la Corona IV* (1519) (No.66)

GB-Lv (London, Victoria and Albert Museum, Library): Paulus: *Paulina* (1513) (No.52)

GB-Ob (Oxford, Bodleian Library): Paulus: *Paulina* (1513) (No.52, 3 copies); *Motetti IV* (1505) (No.21)

H-Bn (Budapest, Országos Széchényi Könyvtár): *Motetti A* [1505] (No.19); *Motetti B* (1503) (No.7)

H-SY (Szombathely, Püspöki Könyvtár): Josquin: *Missarum I* (1516) (No.62); Josquin: *Missarum II* (1515) (No.59); Josquin: *Missarum III* (1514) (No.54); Mouton: *Missarum I* (1515) (No.60); Paulus: *Paulina* (1513) (No.52)

HR-Ssf (Split, Samostan franjevaca konventualaca): *Motetti C* (1504) (No.15); *Motetti IV* (1505) (No.21)

I-Ac (Assisi, Biblioteca Comunale): Agricola: *Misse* (1504) (No.13); Ghiselin: *Misse* (1503) (No.9); Josquin: *Missarum I* (1516) (No.62); Josquin: *Missarum II* (1515) (No.59); Josquin: *Missarum III* (1514) (No.54); La Rue: *Misse* (1503) (No.11)

I-Bc (Bologna, Civico Museo Bibliografico Musicale G.B. Martini): Agricola: *Misse* (1504) (No.13); Brumel: *Misse* (1503) (No.8); Gaspar: *Misse* (1507) (No.32); Ghiselin: *Misse* (1503) (No.9); Isaac: *Misse* (1506) (No.31); Josquin: *Misse* (1502) (No.4); Josquin: *Missarum I* (1516) (No.62); Josquin: *Missarum II* (1505) (No.22); Josquin: *Missarum II* (1515) (No.59); Josquin: *Missarum III* (1514) (No.54); La Rue: *Misse* (1503)

(No.11); Obrecht: *Misse* (1503) (No.6); De Orto: *Misse* (1505) (No.20); *Canti B* (1502) (No.2); *Fragmenta Missarum* (1505) (No.24); *Lamentationum I* (1506) (No.27); *Lamentationum II* (1506) (No.28); *Missarum diversorum auctorum* (1508) (No.43); *Motetti A* (1502) (No.3); *Motetti B* (1503) (No.7); *Motetti C* (1504) (No.15); *Motetti de la Corona I* (1514) (No.55, 2 copies); *Motetti de la Corona II* (1519) (No.64); *Motetti de la Corona III* (1519) (No.65); *Motetti de la Corona IV* (1519) (No.66); *Odhecaton A* ([1501]/1503) (Nos.1 and 5)

I-BGc (Bergamo, Biblioteca Civica Angelo Mai): Févin: *Misse* (1515) (No.61); Josquin: *Missarum I* (1516) (No.62); Josquin: *Missarum II* (1515) (No.59); Josquin: *Missarum III* (1514) (No.54); Mouton: *Missarum I* (1515) (No.60); *Motetti de la Corona I* (1514) (No.55); *Motetti de la Corona II* (1519) (No.64); *Motetti de la Corona III* (1519) (No.65); *Motetti de la Corona IV* (1519) (No.66)

I-Fm (Florence, Biblioteca Marucelliana): Ghiselin: *Misse* (1503) (No.9); Agricola: *Misse* (1504) (No.13); Josquin: *Misse* (1502) (No.4); Josquin: *Missarum II* (1505) (No.22); Paulus: *Paulina* (1513) (No.52)

I-Fn (Florence, Biblioteca Nazionale Centrale): Castiglione: *Epistola* (1513) (No.53); *Motetti de la Corona I* (1514) (No.55); *Motetti de la Corona II* (1519) (No.64); *Motetti de la Corona III* (1519) (No.65); *Motetti de la Corona IV* (1519) (No.66)

I-FANas (Fano, Archivio di Stato): *Motetti del fiore* (1538) (No.69)

I-FBR (Fossombrone, Biblioteca Civica Passionei): Josquin: *Missarum I* (1516) (No.62); La Rue: *Misse* (1503) (No.11); Paulus: *Paulina* (1513) (No.52, 2 copies); *Motetti de la Corona IV* (1519) (No.66); [*Musica XII*] [c.1533] (No.68)

I-FPfanan (Frassinelle Polesine, private collection of Commendatore Fanan): *Motetti C* (1504) (No.15); *I Motetti à5* (1508) (No.46)

I-Mb (Milan, Biblioteca Nazionale Braidense): Bossinensis: *Libro II* (1511) (No.50)

I-Mc (Milan, Conservatorio di Musica Giuseppe Verdi, Biblioteca): Brumel: *Misse* (1503) (No.8); Gaspar: *Misse*

US-CA (Cambridge, Harvard University): Castiglione: *Epistola* (1513) (No.53); Josquin: *Misse* (1502) (No.4); Josquin: *Missarum III* (1514) (No.54); La Rue: *Misse* (1503) (No.11); Paulus: *Paulina* (1513) (No.52, 2 copies)

US-CIhc (Cincinnati, Hebrew Union College—Jewish Institute of Religion, Library): Paulus: *Paulina* (1513) (No.52)

US-DMu (Durham, Duke University Libraries): Paulus: *Paulina* (1513) (No.52)

US-Eu (Evanston, Northwestern University Libraries): Févin: *Misse* (1515) (No.61); Josquin: *Missarum III* (1514) (No.54)

US-Lu (Lawrence, University of Kansas Libraries): Paulus: *Paulina* (1513) (No.52)

US-MSu (Minneapolis, University of Minnesota, Library): Paulus: *Paulina* (1513) (No.52)

US-NH (New Haven, Yale University, Library): La Rue: *Misse* (1503) (No.11)

US-NYcu (New York, Columbia University, Library): Paulus: *Paulina* (1513) (No.52)

US-NYp (New York, New York Public Library): Paulus: *Paulina* (1513) (No.52); *Odhecaton A* (1503/1504) (Nos.5 and 14)

US-NYpm (New York, The Pierpont Morgan Library): Castiglione: *Epistola* (1513) (No.53)

US-NYts (New York, The Union Theological Seminary, Library): Paulus: *Paulina* (1513) (No.52);

US-PROu (Providence, Brown University libraries): Paulus: *Paulina* (1513) (No.52)

US-R (Rochester, Eastman School of Music, Sibley Music Library): Josquin: *Missarum I* (1516) (No.62, 2 copies); Josquin: *Missarum II* (1505) (No.22); Josquin: *Missarum II* (1515) (No.59); Josquin: *Missarum III* (1514) (No.54)

US-SLc (Saint Louis, Concordia Seminary Library): Paulus: *Paulina* (1513) (No.52)

US-SM (San Marino, Henry E. Huntington Library and Art Gallery): Paulus: *Paulina* (1513) (No.52)

US-Tm (Toledo, Toledo Museum of Art Library): *Motetti C* (1504) (No.15)

US-Wc (Washington, Library of Congress): Josquin: *Missarum I* (1516) (No.62); Mouton: *Missarum I* (1515) (No.60); Paulus: *Paulina* (1513) (No.52); *Odhecaton A* (1504) (No.14)

Private collection, sold at Sotheby's, London): Bossinensis: *Libro I* (1509) (No.49); Bossinensis: *Libro II* (1511) (No.50)

INDEX OF EDITIONS

This does not include any editions cited only in Tables 10-1 and 10-2: in addition, it omits those mentioned solely as sources with pieces also printed by Petrucci, and appearing in chapter 18. These can be traced through the list of such sources, in chapter 19.

Page references in boldface indicate the principal discussions of the Petrucci edition concerned.

GENERAL INDEX

The many references to technical features (such as examples of correction, of furniture taking ink, or of house practice; or evidence for the numbers of impressions or sorts for individual characters) which can be found in the detailed bibliographical descriptions (in chapter 20) are not indexed here. A few exceptions have been made, when more extensive discussion is attached to the description of an individual title; and for all cancels.

purchasers of music: 34, 230, 251, 260, 336–349, 353, 401, 403; character of: 7, 253; *see also* market for printed music

Qualile, Dominus: 348, 722
Quadris, Johannes de: 40, 292–3, 625–6; Works: *Cum autem venissem*: 899; *Incipit lamentatio ieremie*: 916; [Lamentations] *Caph. Non enim humilitavit* (*see* anonymous works); [Lamentations] *Heth. Cogitavit Dominus* (*see* anonymous works); *Popule meus*: 935; *Sepulto domino*: 944
Quaranta, Elena: 33

Rampazetto, Francesco: 400
Raphael Sanzio: 240
Rastell, John: 391
Ratdolt, Erhard: 205
Raulin: *Se suis trop ionnette*: 1067
Recanati: 33, 38, 285–6, 287, 288, 291, 341, 355, 357
Reese, Gustave: 426
Regis, Johann: 40, 273, 301; Works: *Ave Maria*: 891; *Ave Maria*: 891; *Clangat plebs / Sicut lilium*: 301, 898; *Credo Village*: 885; *Lux solemnis adest / Repleti sunt omnes*: 920; *Salve sponsa tui genitrix*: 942; *Sil vous playsist*: 1067
register: between impressions: 79, 138; of collation: 154, 155, 156, 254
Regius, Raphael: 82
Rein, Conrad: *Vulnerasti cor meum* (*see* anonymous works)
Reingot: *Fors seulement*: 1044
Renouard, August: 12
Reuchlin, Johann: 206
Reynolds, Christopher: 285
Rhodes, Dennis: 14, 340
Ribera, Antonio: *O bone Jesu* (*see* Compère)
Ricci, Dominico: 813
Ricci, Gioseffo: 104*n43*
Ricci, Luigi: 58, 67*n36*
ricercar: 295–296, 706, 717, 723
Richafort, Jean: 313; *Miseremini mei*: 922; *O genitrix gloriosa* (*see* Compère)
Rifkin, Joshua: 369
Rimini: 45, 51, 425
Rivo, Petro de: 729
Rochester, Sibley Music Library: 52
Rome: 45, 239–40, 291, 301, 304, 309, 334, 336, 358, 389; editions of the 1520s and 1530s published in: 384–390, 399, 404; Lateran Council at: 47–8, 210, 230–232, 235, 238, 305, 311, 365, 399, 728, 1150; privileges in: 95, 96, 97–101; S.

Giovanni Laterano: 342–3, 352, 813; S. Luigi dei Francese: 342–3, 510, 700, 771; S. Maria de Scala Urbii: 343, 734; Sack of: 63, 240, 389, 390, 400; Sistine Chapel: 52, 273, 342, 424; as source for Petrucci's music: 284, 287–8, 306, 308, 309, 313–4, 315
Rore, Cipriano: 799
Rosario Boccadifuoco, R. Maria: 418, 420
Rosenthal, Albi: 521, 706, 785
Rosselli, Petrus: *Missa Baysez moy*: 421
Rosseto Veronensis, Antonio: 282; *Che piu felice sorte*: 963
Rossi, Francesco: 96
Rossino Mantovano: 282; *A pe de la montagna*: 955; *Lirum bililirum*: 989; *Perche fai donna el gaton*: 1004; *Se ogni donna fusse*: 1017
Rosso Mantovano: *Da poi chel tuo bel viso*: 968
Rovagnate: 346, 560
Rufino da Padova: 385
Ruff, Simprecht: 426
Ruffo, Vicenzo: 95
Rusch, Adolf: 354
Rusconi: 71*n104*, 72*n105*,

saltarello: 296
Salzburg: 391
Sambonettus, Petrus: 5, 96, 331
San Leo: 347
Santini, Fortunato: 476
Santucius, Hieronymus de: 231, 735
Sanudo, Mario: 36, 44
Saraceno, Marino: 82
Sartori, Claudio: 3, 12–3, 26, 416–420, 772
Savoy, Charles of: 307
Savoy, Filiberta of: 54, 266, 307, 309
Savoy, Luisa of: 307
Schmid, Anton: 4, 10, 13, 23, 26, 47, 52, 59, 61, 349, 415–420, 424, 426, 606, 642, 700
Schneider, Hans: 687
Schnoebelen, Anne: 342, 539
Schöffer, Peter: 5, 354, 390–391
Schoenberg, Arnold: 7
Scholderer, Victor: 122, 363
Schuyt, Cornelis: 348–349
Scotto, Amadeo: 29, 31, 45, 85, 90, 92, 355; and Petrucci: 30, 32, 250, 268, 270–1, 274, 303, 318
Scotto, Girolamo: 4, 95, 136, 155, 206, 336, 348, 362, 392, 400–401, 404
Scotto, Ottaviano I: 29, 30–31, 82, 404; heirs of: 72*n105*